CONTENTS

The most sensational discovery charted this year has to be the confirmation, in February, that human remains found under a car park in Leicester were those of King Richard III. According to historical records, following his death at the Battle of Bosworth, the king's corpse was taken to the nearby city of Leicester where he was then buried in the grounds of the city's Grey Friars Priory. The correspondence between documentary and physical evidence strongly suggested this was indeed the body of Richard III, which was then confirmed by DNA analysis.

The brother of Edward IV, Richard was first named as Lord Protector, and it was Edward's eldest son, rather than Richard who was expected to succeed to the Crown. Fast-forward 530 years and the rules of succession to the throne remained pretty much unaltered from the days of Richard III. But all that was about to change! Under the Succession to the Crown Act, which received royal assent in April 2013, succession is no longer dependent on gender, meaning that the Duke and Duchess of Cambridge's first child could become monarch, regardless of whether it was a boy or girl. In the event, and after much anticipation in the media, HRH Prince George of Cambridge was born on 22 July 2013.

Other major historical events which occurred in 2013 included the resignation, in March, of Pope Benedict XVI, stating that his age meant that he lacked the necessary strength to properly fulfil the role, and becoming the first Pope to resign in 600 years. Shortly after Pope Benedict's announcement, former Prime Minister Margaret Thatcher died in early April. Conservative prime minister from 1979 to 1990 she was the first woman to hold the post. The funeral, with full military honours, took place at St Paul's Cathedral in London on 17 April and was attended by over 2,000 guests from around the world.

Despite the decision to drop 'almanack' from the title, *Whitaker's Concise* remains as it has always been, an invaluable historical record and the definitive guide to the forthcoming year. Please feel free to contact us with feedback and suggestions for next year's edition!

Ruth Northey
Executive Editor

THE YEAR 2014

CHRONOLOGICAL CYCLES AND ERAS

Dominical Letter	E
Epact	29
Golden Number (Lunar Cycle)	I
Julian Period	6727
Roman Indiction	7
Solar Cycle	7

	Beginning
Muslim year AH 1435*	4 Nov 2013
Japanese year Heisei 26	1 Jan
Roman year 2767 AUC	14 Jan
Regnal year 63	6 Feb
Chinese year of the Horse	31 Jan
Sikh new year	14 Mar
Hindu new year (Chaitra)	31 Mar
Indian (Saka) year 1936	22 Mar
Jewish year AM 5775*	25 Sep

* Year begins at sunset on the previous day

RELIGIOUS CALENDARS

CHRISTIAN

Epiphany	6 Jan
Presentation of Christ in the Temple	2 Feb
Ash Wednesday	5 Mar
The Annunciation	25 Mar
Palm Sunday	13 Apr
Maundy Thursday	17 Apr
Good Friday	18 Apr
Easter Day (western churches)	20 Apr
Easter Day (Eastern Orthodox)	20 Apr
Rogation Sunday	25 May
Ascension Day	29 May
Pentecost (Whit Sunday)	8 Jun
Trinity Sunday	15 Jun
Corpus Christi	19 Jun
All Saints' Day	1 Nov
Advent Sunday	30 Nov
Christmas Day	25 Dec

HINDU

Makar Sankranti	14 Jan
Vasant Panchami (Sarasvati Puja)	4 Feb
Shivaratri	28 Feb
Holi	17 Mar
Chaitra (Spring new year)	31 Mar
Ram Navami	8 Apr
Raksha-bandhan	10 Aug
Krishna Janmashtami	17 Aug
Ganesh Chaturthi, first day	29 Aug
Navaratri festival (Durga Puja), first day	25 Sep
Dussehra	4 Oct
Diwali (New Year festival of lights), first day	23 Oct

JEWISH

Purim	16 Mar
Pesach (Passover), first day	15 Apr
Shavuot (Feast of Weeks), first day	4 Jun
Rosh Hashanah (Jewish new year)	25 Sep
Yom Kippur (Day of Atonement)	4 Oct
Succot (Feast of Tabernacles), first day	9 Oct
Hanukkah, first day	17 Dec

MUSLIM

Al-Hijra (Muslim new year)	4 Nov 2013
Ashura	13 Nov 2013
Ramadan, first day	28 Jun
Eid-ul-Fitr	28 Jul
Hajj	2 Oct
Eid-ul-Adha	4 Oct

SIKH

Birthday of Guru Gobind Singh Ji	5 Jan
1 Chet (Sikh new year)	14 Mar
Hola Mohalla	17 Mar†
Baisakhi	13 Apr
Birthday of Guru Nanak Dev Ji	14 Apr†
Martyrdom of Guru Arjan Dev Ji	2 May
Martyrdom of Guru Tegh Bahadur Ji	24 Nov

† This festival is also currently celebrated according to the lunar calendar

CIVIL CALENDAR

Duchess of Cambridge's birthday	9 Jan
Countess of Wessex's birthday	20 Jan
Accession of the Queen	6 Feb
Duke of York's birthday	19 Feb
St David's Day	1 Mar
Earl of Wessex's birthday	10 Mar
Commonwealth Day	11 Mar
St Patrick's Day	17 Mar
Birthday of the Queen	21 Apr
St George's Day	23 Apr
Europe Day	9 May
Coronation Day	2 Jun
Duke of Edinburgh's birthday	10 Jun
The Queen's Official Birthday	14 Jun
Duke of Cambridge's birthday	21 Jun
Duchess of Cornwall's birthday	17 Jul
Princess Royal's birthday	15 Aug
Lord Mayor's Day	8 Nov
Remembrance Sunday	9 Nov
Prince of Wales' birthday	14 Nov
Wedding Day of the Queen	20 Nov
St Andrew's Day	30 Nov

LEGAL CALENDAR

LAW TERMS

Hilary Term	13 Jan to 16 Apr
Easter Term	29 Apr to 23 May
Trinity Term	3 Jun to 31 Jul
Michaelmas Term	1 Oct to 19 Dec

QUARTER DAYS	TERM DAYS
England, Wales and Northern Ireland	*Scotland*
Lady – 25 Mar	Candlemas – 28 Feb
Midsummer – 4 Jun	Whitsunday – 28 May
Michaelmas – 29 Sep	Lammas – 28 Aug
Christmas – 25 Dec	Martinmas – 28 Nov

2014

JANUARY					
Sunday		5	12	19	26
Monday		6	13	20	27
Tuesday		7	14	21	28
Wednesday	1	8	15	22	29
Thursday	2	9	16	23	30
Friday	3	10	17	24	31
Saturday	4	11	18	25	

FEBRUARY					
Sunday		2	9	16	23
Monday		3	10	17	24
Tuesday		4	11	18	25
Wednesday		5	12	19	26
Thursday		6	13	20	27
Friday		7	14	21	28
Saturday	1	8	15	22	

MARCH						
Sunday		2	9	16	23	30
Monday		3	10	17	24	31
Tuesday		4	11	18	25	
Wednesday		5	12	19	26	
Thursday		6	13	20	27	
Friday		7	14	21	28	
Saturday	1	8	15	22	29	

APRIL					
Sunday		6	13	20	27
Monday		7	14	21	28
Tuesday	1	8	15	22	29
Wednesday	2	9	16	23	30
Thursday	3	10	17	24	
Friday	4	11	18	25	
Saturday	5	12	19	26	

MAY					
Sunday		4	11	18	25
Monday		5	12	19	26
Tuesday		6	13	20	27
Wednesday		7	14	21	28
Thursday		8	15	22	29
Friday	2	9	16	23	30
Saturday	3	10	17	24	31

JUNE					
Sunday	1	8	15	22	29
Monday	2	9	16	23	30
Tuesday	3	10	17	24	
Wednesday	4	11	18	25	
Thursday	5	12	19	26	
Friday	6	13	20	27	
Saturday	7	14	21	28	

JULY					
Sunday		6	13	20	27
Monday		7	14	21	28
Tuesday	1	8	15	22	29
Wednesday	2	9	16	23	30
Thursday	3	10	17	24	31
Friday	4	11	18	25	
Saturday	5	12	19	26	

AUGUST						
Sunday		3	10	17	24	31
Monday		4	11	18	25	
Tuesday		5	12	19	26	
Wednesday		6	13	20	27	
Thursday		7	14	21	28	
Friday	1	8	15	22	29	
Saturday	2	9	16	23	30	

SEPTEMBER					
Sunday		7	14	21	28
Monday	1	8	15	22	29
Tuesday	2	9	16	23	30
Wednesday	3	10	17	24	
Thursday	4	11	18	25	
Friday	5	12	19	26	
Saturday	6	13	20	27	

OCTOBER					
Sunday		5	12	19	26
Monday		6	13	20	27
Tuesday		7	14	21	28
Wednesday	1	8	15	22	29
Thursday	2	9	16	23	30
Friday	3	10	17	24	31
Saturday	4	11	18	25	

NOVEMBER						
Sunday		2	9	16	23	30
Monday		3	10	17	24	
Tuesday		4	11	18	25	
Wednesday		5	12	19	26	
Thursday		6	13	20	27	
Friday		7	14	21	28	
Saturday	1	8	15	22	29	

DECEMBER					
Sunday		7	14	21	28
Monday	1	8	15	22	29
Tuesday	2	9	16	23	30
Wednesday	3	10	17	24	31
Thursday	4	11	18	25	
Friday	5	12	19	26	
Saturday	6	13	20	27	

PUBLIC HOLIDAYS	*England and Wales*	*Scotland*	*Northern Ireland*
New Year	1 January†	1, 2† January	1 January†
St Patrick's Day	—	—	17 March
*Good Friday	18 April	18 April	18 April
Easter Monday	21 April	—	21 April
Early May	5 May†	5 May	5 May†
Spring	26 May	26 May†	26 May
Battle of the Boyne	—	—	14 July‡
Summer	25 August	4 August	25 August
St Andrew's Day	—	1 December§	—
*Christmas	25, 26 December	25†, 26 December	25, 26 December

* In England, Wales and Northern Ireland, Christmas Day and Good Friday are common law holidays

† Subject to royal proclamation

‡ Subject to proclamation by the Secretary of State for Northern Ireland

§ The St Andrew's Day Holiday (Scotland) Bill was approved by parliament on 29 November 2006; it does not oblige employers to change their existing pattern of holidays but provides the legal framework in which the St Andrew's Day bank holiday could be substituted for an existing local holiday from another date in the year

Note: In the Channel Islands, Liberation Day is a bank and public holiday

2015

JANUARY						FEBRUARY					MARCH					
Sunday		4	11	18	25	*Sunday*	1	8	15	22	*Sunday*	1	8	15	22	29
Monday		5	12	19	26	*Monday*	2	9	16	23	*Monday*	2	9	16	23	30
Tuesday		6	13	20	27	*Tuesday*	3	10	17	24	*Tuesday*	3	10	17	24	31
Wednesday		7	14	21	28	*Wednesday*	4	11	18	25	*Wednesday*	4	11	18	25	
Thursday	1	8	15	22	29	*Thursday*	5	12	19	26	*Thursday*	5	12	19	26	
Friday	2	9	16	23	30	*Friday*	6	13	20	27	*Friday*	6	13	20	27	
Saturday	3	10	17	24	31	*Saturday*	7	14	21	28	*Saturday*	7	14	21	28	

APRIL					MAY						JUNE					
Sunday		5	12	19	26	*Sunday*	3	10	17	24	31	*Sunday*		7	14	21	28
Monday		6	13	20	27	*Monday*	4	11	18	25		*Monday*	1	8	15	22	29
Tuesday		7	14	21	28	*Tuesday*	5	12	19	26		*Tuesday*	2	9	16	23	30
Wednesday	1	8	15	22	29	*Wednesday*	6	13	20	27		*Wednesday*	3	10	17	24	
Thursday	2	9	16	23	30	*Thursday*	7	14	21	28		*Thursday*	4	11	18	25	
Friday	3	10	17	24		*Friday*	1	8	15	22	29	*Friday*	5	12	19	26	
Saturday	4	11	18	25		*Saturday*	2	9	16	23	30	*Saturday*	6	13	20	27	

JULY						AUGUST						SEPTEMBER					
Sunday		5	12	19	26	*Sunday*		2	9	16	23	30	*Sunday*		6	13	20	27
Monday		6	13	20	27	*Monday*		3	10	17	24	31	*Monday*		7	14	21	28
Tuesday		7	14	21	28	*Tuesday*		4	11	18	25		*Tuesday*	1	8	15	22	29
Wednesday	1	8	15	22	29	*Wednesday*		5	12	19	26		*Wednesday*	2	9	16	23	30
Thursday	2	9	16	23	30	*Thursday*		6	13	20	27		*Thursday*	3	10	17	24	
Friday	3	10	17	24	31	*Friday*		7	14	21	28		*Friday*	4	11	18	25	
Saturday	4	11	18	25		*Saturday*	1	8	15	22	29		*Saturday*	5	12	19	26	

OCTOBER						NOVEMBER					DECEMBER					
Sunday		4	11	18	25	*Sunday*	1	8	15	22	29	*Sunday*		6	13	20	27
Monday		5	12	19	26	*Monday*	2	9	16	23	30	*Monday*		7	14	21	28
Tuesday		6	13	20	27	*Tuesday*	3	10	17	24		*Tuesday*	1	8	15	22	29
Wednesday		7	14	21	28	*Wednesday*	4	11	18	25		*Wednesday*	2	9	16	23	30
Thursday	1	8	15	22	29	*Thursday*	5	12	19	26		*Thursday*	3	10	17	24	31
Friday	2	9	16	23	30	*Friday*	6	13	20	27		*Friday*	4	11	18	25	
Saturday	3	10	17	24	31	*Saturday*	7	14	21	28		*Saturday*	5	12	19	26	

PUBLIC HOLIDAYS	*England and Wales*	*Scotland*	*Northern Ireland*
New Year	1 January†	1, 2† January	1 January†
St Patrick's Day	—	—	17 March
*Good Friday	3 April	3 April	3 April
Easter Monday	6 April	—	6 April
Early May	4 May†	4 May	4 May†
Spring	25 May	25 May†	25 May
Battle of the Boyne	—	—	13 July‡
Summer	31 August	3 August	31 August
St Andrew's Day	—	30 Nov§	—
*Christmas	25, 28 December	25†, 28 December	25, 28 December

* In England, Wales and Northern Ireland, Christmas Day and Good Friday are common law holidays

† Subject to royal proclamation

‡ Subject to proclamation by the Secretary of State for Northern Ireland

§ The St Andrew's Day Holiday (Scotland) Bill was approved by parliament on 29 November 2006; it does not oblige employers to change their existing pattern of holidays but provides the legal framework in which the St Andrew's Day bank holiday could be substituted for an existing local holiday from another date in the year

Note: In the Channel Islands, Liberation Day is a bank and public holiday

FORTHCOMING EVENTS

* Provisional dates

JANUARY 2014

4–12	London Boat Show, Excel, London Docklands
9–1 Feb	London International Mime Festival
15–19	London Art Fair, Business Design Centre
16–2 Feb	Celtic Connections Music Festival, Glasgow
21–23	UK Open Dance Championships, Bournemouth International Centre
25–26	RSPB Big Garden Birdwatch

FEBRUARY

7–23	Leicester Comedy Festival
14–16	London Motorcycle Show, Excel, London Docklands
15–23	30th Jorvik Viking Festival, Jorvik Viking Centre, York
16	British Academy Film Awards, Royal Opera House, London
28–9 Mar	Bath Literature Festival

MARCH

6	World Book Day
6–9	Crufts Dog Show, NEC, Birmingham
8	International Women's Day
13–16	Affordable Art Fair, Battersea Park, London
14–23	National Science and Engineering Week
14–30	Ideal Home Show, Earls Court, London
19–25	BADA Antiques and Fine Art Fair, Duke of York Square, London
21	World Poetry Day
22–30	Oxford Literary Festival

APRIL

4–6	Ceramic Art London, Royal College of Art
8–10	London Book Fair, Earls Court, London
22	Earth Day

MAY

17–25 Aug	80th Glyndebourne Festival
20–24	RHS Chelsea Flower Show Centenary year, Royal Hospital, Chelsea
22–1 June	Hay Festival, Hay-on-Wye

JUNE

12–15	Affordable Art Fair, Hampstead, London
13–29	Aldeburgh Festival, Snape, Suffolk
14	Trooping the Colour, Horse Guards Parade, London
25–29	Glastonbury Festival of Contemporary Performing Arts, Somerset
25–5 July	New Designers Exhibition, Business Design Centre, London

JULY

2–13	Cheltenham Music Festival
8–13	RHS Hampton Court Palace Flower Show, Surrey
10–19	York Early Music Festival
11–27	Buxton Festival, Derbyshire
18–27	Edinburgh Jazz and Blues Festival
Mid-Jul–Mid-Sep	BBC Promenade Concerts, Royal Albert Hall, London
24–27	RHS Flower Show, Tatton Park, Cheshire
Mid-Jul	The Welsh Proms, St David's Hall, Cardiff
24–27	WOMAD Festival, Charlton Park, Wiltshire
26–2 Aug	Three Choirs Festival, Gloucester
31–3 Aug	50th Cambridge Folk Festival

AUGUST

1–23	Edinburgh Military Tattoo, Edinburgh Castle
1–9	National Eisteddfod of Wales, Carmarthenshire
*8–31	Edinburgh International Festival
*24–25	Notting Hill Carnival, London
25–29 Oct	Blackpool Illuminations, Blackpool Promenade

SEPTEMBER

6	Braemar Royal Highland Gathering, Aberdeenshire
8	International Literacy Day
*11–14	Heritage Open Days, England (nationwide)
Mid-Sep	RHS Wisley Flower Show, RHS Garden, Wisley
Mid-Sep	TUC Annual Congress
Sep–Oct	Labour Party Conference, Manchester
Sep–Oct	Conservative Party Conference, Birmingham

OCTOBER

4–8	Liberal Democrat Party Conference, Glasgow
16–19	Frieze Art Fair, Regent's Park, London
Mid-Oct	Booker Prize
Mid-Oct	BFI London Film Festival
Mid-Oct–Jan	Turner Prize Exhibition, Tate Britain, London

NOVEMBER

Early-Nov	London to Brighton Veteran Car Run
Mid-Nov	Classic Motor Show, NEC, Birmingham
8 Nov	Lord Mayor's Procession and Show, City of London
Mid-Nov	CBI Annual Conference

SPORTS EVENTS

JANUARY 2014
3–7 Cricket: Ashes Fifth Test, Sydney, Australia
12–19 Snooker: Masters, Alexandra Palace, London
13–26 Tennis: Australian Open, Melbourne, Australia
19–10 Feb Football: Africa Cup of Nations, South Africa

FEBRUARY
1–15 Rugby Union: Six Nations Championship
2 American Football: Superbowl XLVIII, New Jersey
7–9 Badminton: English National Championships, Milton Keynes
7–21 Athletics: XXII Olympic Winter Games, Sochi, Russia
10–16 Squash: British National Championships, Manchester

MARCH
2 Football: League Cup Final: Wembley Stadium, London
7–9 Athletics: World Indoor Championships, Gdansk/Sopot, Poland
16–6 Apr Cricket: ICC World Twenty20, Bangladesh

APRIL
5 Horse racing: Grand National, Aintree, Liverpool
6 Rowing: The Boat Race, Putney to Mortlake, London
10–13 Golf: Masters, Augusta, Georgia
13 Athletics: London Marathon
19–5 May Snooker: World Championship, Crucible Theatre, Sheffield

MAY
8–11 Equestrian: Badminton Horse Trials, Badminton
Early May Horse racing: Guineas Festival, Newmarket
14 Football: UEFA Europa League Final, Turin
14–18 Equestrian: Royal Windsor Horse Show, Home Park, Windsor
17 Football: FA Cup Final, Wembley Stadium, London
17 Football: Scottish Cup Final, Hampden Park, Glasgow
24 Rugby Union: Heineken Cup Final, Cardiff
24 Football: UEFA Champions League Final, Lisbon
24–7 Jun Motorcycling: TT Races, Isle of Man
20–8 Jun Tennis: French Open, Paris

JUNE
5–18 Football: FIFA World Cup, Brazil
7 Horse racing: The Derby, Epsom Downs
12–15 Golf: US Open, Pinehurst, North Carolina
16–21 Golf: British Amateur Golf Championship, Royal Portrush, Country Antrim
17–21 Horse racing: Royal Ascot
23–6 Jul Tennis: Wimbledon Championship, All England Lawn Tennis Club, London

JULY
2–6 Rowing: Henley Royal Regatta, Henley-on-Thames
5–27 Cycling: Tour de France
10–13 Golf: Women's British Open, Royal Brkdale
17–20 Golf: Open Championship, Royal Liverpool
23–3 Aug Athletics: XX Commonwealth Games, Glasgow
27–10 Aug Swimming: World Masters Championships, Montreal, Canada
Late Jul Horse racing: King George VI and Queen Elizabeth Diamond Stakes, Ascot

AUGUST
2–9 Sailing: Cowes Week, Isle of Wight
4–10 Golf: PGA Championship, Valhalla, Kentucky
16–28 Athletics: Summer Youth Olympic Games, Nanjing, China
23 Rugby League: Challenge Cup Final, Wembley Stadium, London
25–7 Sep Tennis: US Open, New York

SEPTEMBER
Early Sep Equestrian: Burghley Horse Trials, Stamford, Lincolnshire
Early Sep Horse racing: St Leger, Doncaster
Late Sep–Early Oct Horse racing: Cambridgeshire Meeting, Newmarket
Late Sep–Early Oct Athletics: Great North Run, Newcastle

OCTOBER
Early Oct Equestrian: Horse of the Year Show, NEC, Birmingham
Early–Mid-Oct Rugby League: Super League Final, Old Trafford, Manchester
Mid-Oct Horse racing: Champions Meeting, Newmarket

NOVEMBER
10–17 Tennis: ATP World Tour Finals, O2 Arena, London

CENTENARIES

2015

1515

22 Sep Anne of Cleves, fourth wife of Henry VIII, born

1715

1 Sep Louis XIV ('the Sun King'), King of France 1643–1715, died

23 Oct Peter II, Emperor of Russia 1727–30, born

1815

11 Jan Sir John Macdonald, first prime minister of Canada, born

15 Jan Emma, Lady Hamilton, mistress of Horatio Nelson, died

1 Apr Otto von Bismarck, first chancellor of the German Empire, born

24 Apr Anthony Trollope, novelist of the Victorian era, born

1915

11 Jan Lt.-Col. Robert Blair 'Paddy' Mayne, founding member of the Special Air Service (SAS), born

30 Jan John Profumo, CBE, Conservative minister at the centre of the Profumo Affair scandal, born

1 Feb Sir Stanley Matthews, footballer who won the first Ballon d'Or, born

4 Feb Sir Norman Wisdom, actor and comedian, born

11 Feb Sir Patrick Leigh Fermor, author and soldier awarded the Distinguished Service Order (DSO), born

21 Feb Ann Sheridan, American film actor, born

23 Feb Paul Tibbetts, Jr., American pilot of the *Enola Gay* aircraft, born

7 Apr Billie Holiday, American jazz singer and songwriter, born

10 Apr Harry Morgan, American actor who starred in *M*A*S*H*, born

22 Apr Second Battle of Ypres began

23 Apr Rupert Brooke, war poet, died

6 May Orson Welles, American actor and director, born

7 May RMS *Lusitania* torpedoed and sunk by a German U-boat

10 May Sir Denis Thatcher, husband of former prime minister Margaret Thatcher, born

20 May Moshe Dayan, Israeli defence minister and military chief-of-staff, born

9 Jun Les Paul, American guitarist and inventor of the solid-body electric guitar, born

10 Jun Saul Bellow, American Pulitzer and Nobel Prize winning author, born

29 Aug Ingrid Bergman, Swedish actor, born

15 Sep Helmut Schön, West German football manager whose team won the 1974 World Cup, born

12 Oct Edith Cavell, nurse and heroine of the First World War, died

17 Oct Arthur Miller, American playwright, born

23 Oct William Gilbert 'W. G.' Grace, England cricketer, died

24 Oct Bob Kane, American comic book artist who did the original drawings for *Batman*, born

25 Nov Gen. Augusto Pinochet, president of Chile 1974–90, born

12 Dec Frank Sinatra, American singer and film actor, born

19 Dec Édith Piaf, French singer, born

2014

1614

7 Apr Domenikos Theotokopoulos (El Greco), Cretan painter and sculptor, died

1714

1 Aug Anne, Queen of Great Britain and Ireland 1702–1714, died

1814

19 Jul Samuel Colt, American inventor of the revolver, born

10 Aug Henri Nestlé, German founder of food company Nestlé, born

6 Nov Adolphe Sax, Belgian inventor of the saxophone, born

9 Dec Joseph Bramah, inventor of the hydraulic press, died

1914

5 Jan George Reeves, American actor who starred as Superman, born

5 Feb William S. Burroughs, American novelist who wrote *Naked Lunch*, born

6 Feb Thurl Ravenscroft, American voice actor behind Kellogg's Tony the Tiger, born

20 Feb Peter Rogers, producer of 31 Carry On films, born

14 Mar Bill Owen, actor who played Compo in *Last of the Summer Wine*, born

2 Apr Sir Alec Guinness, actor, born

May Tenzing Norgay, Nepalese Sherpa, born

13 May Joe Louis, American former heavyweight boxing champion, born

28 Jun Franz Ferdinand, Archduke whose assassination instigated the First World War, died

28 Jun Sophie, Duchess of Hohenberg, assassinated wife of Franz Ferdinand, died

6 Jul Vince McMahon, American promoter who founded the World Wrestling Federation, born

10 Jul Joe Shuster, Canadian comic book artist, co-creator of *Superman*, born

4 Aug Britain declared war on Germany in response to the German invasion of Belgium

12 Sep Desmond Llewelyn, Welsh actor famous for playing Q in 17 James Bond films, born

14 Sep Clayton Moore, American actor who starred as *The Lone Ranger*, born

17 Oct Jerry Siegel, American co-creator of *Superman*, born

19 Oct First Battle of Ypres began

27 Oct Dylan Thomas, Welsh poet and writer, born

25 Nov Joe DiMaggio, American baseball player for the New York Yankees, born

THE UNITED KINGDOM

THE UK IN FIGURES

THE NATIONAL FLAG

THE ROYAL FAMILY

PRECEDENCE

THE PEERAGE

BARONETAGE AND KNIGHTAGE

THE PRIVY COUNCIL

PARLIAMENT

GOVERNMENT DEPARTMENTS AND PUBLIC BODIES

REGIONAL GOVERNMENT

EUROPEAN PARLIAMENT

LOCAL GOVERNMENT

LAW COURTS AND OFFICES

TRIBUNALS

POLICE

PRISONS

DEFENCE

EDUCATION

NATIONAL ACADEMIES

RESEARCH COUNCILS

HEALTH

SOCIAL WELFARE

WATER

ENERGY

TRANSPORT

RELIGION

COMMUNICATIONS

ENVIRONMENT

HERITAGE

BANKING AND FINANCE

TAXATION

LEGAL NOTES

THE MEDIA

TRADE AND PROFESSIONAL BODIES

TRADE UNIONS

CLUBS

THE UK IN FIGURES

The United Kingdom comprises Great Britain (England, Wales and Scotland) and Northern Ireland. The Isle of Man and the Channel Islands are Crown dependencies with their own legislative systems and are not part of the UK.

ABBREVIATIONS

ONS	Office for National Statistics
NISRA	Northern Ireland Statistics and Research Agency

All data is for the UK unless otherwise stated.

AREA OF THE UNITED KINGDOM

	Sq. km	*Sq. miles*
United Kingdom	243,122	93,870
England	130,280	50,301
Wales	20,733	8,005
Scotland	77,958	30,100
Northern Ireland	14,150	5,463

Source: ONS (Crown copyright)

POPULATION

The first official census of population in England, Wales and Scotland was taken in 1801 and a census has been taken every ten years since, except in 1941 when there was no census because of the Second World War. The last official census in the UK was taken on 27 March 2011 .

The first official census of population in Ireland was taken in 1841. However, all figures given below refer only to the area which is now Northern Ireland. Figures for Northern Ireland in 1921 and 1931 are estimates based on the censuses taken in 1926 and 1937 respectively.

Estimates of the population of England before 1801, calculated from the number of baptisms, burials and marriages, are:

1570	4,160,221	1670	5,773,646
1600	4,811,718	1700	6,045,008
1630	5,600,517	1750	6,517,035

Further details are available on the ONS website (W www.ons.gov.uk).

CENSUS RESULTS *Thousands*

	United Kingdom			England and Wales			Scotland			Northern Ireland		
	Total	*Male*	*Female*	*Total*	*Male*	*Female*	*Total*	*Male*	*Female*	*Total*	*Male*	*Female*
1801	—	—	—	8,893	4,255	4,638	1,608	739	869	—	—	—
1811	13,368	6,368	7,000	10,165	4,874	5,291	1,806	826	980	—	—	—
1821	15,472	7,498	7,974	12,000	5,850	6,150	2,092	983	1,109	—	—	—
1831	17,835	8,647	9,188	13,897	6,771	7,126	2,364	1,114	1,250	—	—	—
1841	20,183	9,819	10,364	15,914	7,778	8,137	2,620	1,242	1,378	1,649	800	849
1851	22,259	10,855	11,404	17,928	8,781	9,146	2,889	1,376	1,513	1,443	698	745
1861	24,525	11,894	12,631	20,066	9,776	10,290	3,062	1,450	1,612	1,396	668	728
1871	27,431	13,309	14,122	22,712	11,059	11,653	3,360	1,603	1,757	1,359	647	712
1881	31,015	15,060	15,955	25,974	12,640	13,335	3,736	1,799	1,936	1,305	621	684
1891	34,264	16,593	17,671	29,003	14,060	14,942	4,026	1,943	2,083	1,236	590	646
1901	38,237	18,492	19,745	32,528	15,729	16,799	4,472	2,174	2,298	1,237	590	647
1911	42,082	20,357	21,725	36,070	17,446	18,625	4,761	2,309	2,452	1,251	603	648
1921	44,027	21,033	22,994	37,887	18,075	19,811	4,882	2,348	2,535	1,258	610	648
1931	46,038	22,060	23,978	39,952	19,133	20,819	4,843	2,326	2,517	1,243	601	642
1951	50,225	24,118	26,107	43,758	21,016	22,742	5,096	2,434	2,662	1,371	668	703
1961	52,709	25,481	27,228	46,105	22,304	23,801	5,179	2,483	2,697	1,425	694	731
1971	55,515	26,952	28,562	48,750	23,683	25,067	5,229	2,515	2,714	1,536	755	781
1981	55,848	27,104	28,742	49,155	23,873	25,281	5,131	2,466	2,664	1,533*	750	783
1991	56,467	27,344	29,123	49,890	24,182	25,707	4,999	2,392	2,607	1,578	769	809
2001	58,789	28,581	30,208	52,042	25,327	26,715	5,062	2,432	2,630	1,685	821	864
2011	63,182	31,028	32,153	56,076	27,574	28,502	5,295	2,567	2,728	1,810	887	923

* Figure includes 44,500 non-enumerated persons

ISLANDS

	Isle of Man			Jersey			Guernsey		
	Total	*Male*	*Female*	*Total*	*Male*	*Female*	*Total*	*Male*	*Female*
1901	54,752	25,496	29,256	52,576	23,940	28,636	40,446	19,652	20,794
1921	60,284	27,329	32,955	49,701	22,438	27,263	38,315	18,246	20,069
1951	55,123	25,749	29,464	57,296	27,282	30,014	43,652	21,221	22,431
1971	56,289	26,461	29,828	72,532	35,423	37,109	51,458	24,792	26,666
1991	69,788	33,693	36,095	84,082	40,862	43,220	58,867	28,297	30,570
2001	76,315	37,372	38,943	87,186	42,485	44,701	59,807	29,138	30,669
2006	80,058	39,523	40,535	—	—	—	—	—	—
2011	84,497	41,971	42,526	97,857	48,296	49,561	62,915	31,025	31,890

Source: Guernsey Annual Publication Bulletin, Isle of Man Government, States of Jersey Statistics Unit

RESIDENT POPULATION

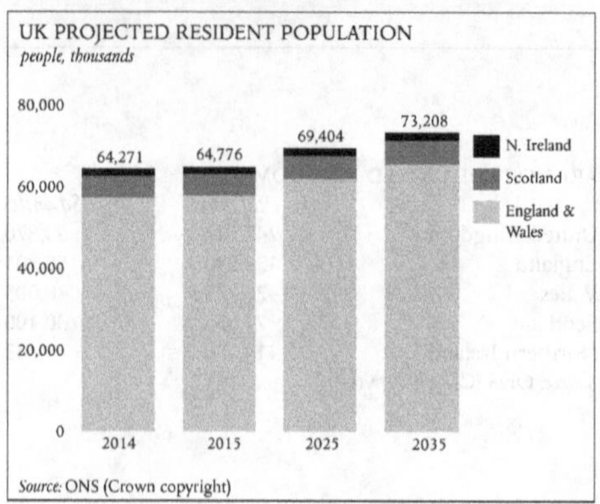

Source: ONS (Crown copyright)

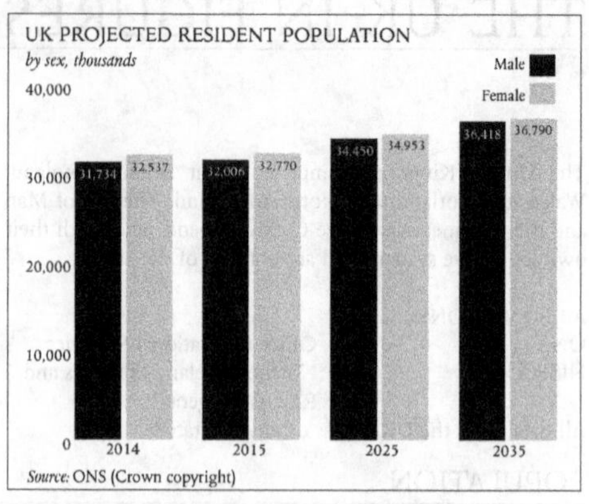

Source: ONS (Crown copyright)

BY AGE AND SEX (UK)
thousands

	Male	*Female*
0–9	3,802	3,629
10–19	3,920	3,746
20–29	4,309	4,295
30–39	4,142	4,178
40–49	4,576	4,691
50–59	3,814	3,895
60–69	3,333	3,494
70–79	2,067	2,402
80–89	939	1,477
90+	127	349

Source: ONS (Crown copyright)

BY ETHNIC GROUP (ENGLAND AND WALES)

The majority of the usual resident population, 48.2 million people (86 per cent), stated their ethnic group as White in the 2011 Census. White British was the largest within this group, with 45.1 million people (80.5 per cent).

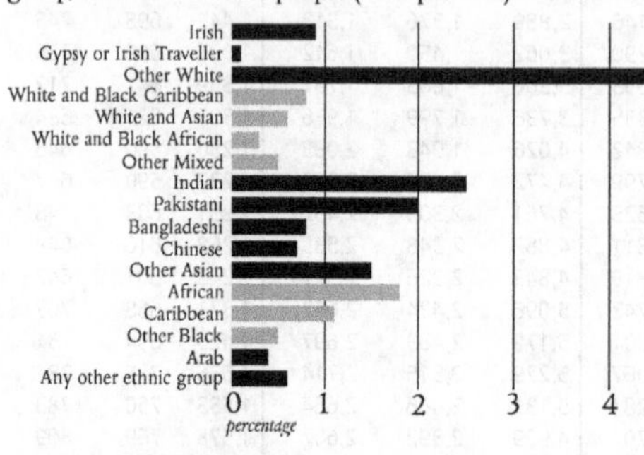

Source: ONS (Crown copyright)

IMMIGRATION

NI NUMBERS ALLOCATED TO ADULT OVERSEAS NATIONALS ENTERING THE UK (number, thousands)

Geographical Region	*2002–3*	*2011–12*
EU (incl. accession countries)	97.8	350.1
Europe – non-EU	14.7	12.8
Americas	26.3	27.7
Africa	66.0	40.7
Asia and Middle East	113.5	149.6
Australia and Oceania	27.1	19.5
Others and unknown	0.8	0.5
ALL NATIONALITIES	346.2	600.9

Source: ONS (Crown copyright)

BIRTHS

	Live births	*Birth rate**
United Kingdom	807,776	12.7
England and Wales	723,913	12.9
Scotland	58,590	11.1
Northern Ireland	25,273	14.0

* Live births per 1,000 population

Source: General Register Office for Scotland, NISRA, ONS (Crown copyright)

FERTILITY RATES

Total fertility rate is the average number of children which would be born to a woman if she experienced the age-specific fertility rates of the period in question throughout her child-bearing life span. The figures for the years 1960–2 are estimates.

	1960–2	*2000*	*2011*
United Kingdom	3.07	1.63	1.91
England and Wales	2.77	1.66	1.93
Scotland	2.98	1.48	1.73
Northern Ireland	3.47	1.75	2.06

Source: General Register Office for Scotland, NISRA, ONS (Crown copyright)

MATERNITY RATES FOR ENGLAND AND WALES 2011

	*All maternities**	*Singleton*	*All multiple†*	*Twins*	*Triplets*
All ages	716,040	704,535	11,505	11,330	172
<20	36,441	36,205	236	236	0
20–24	134,261	132,919	1,342	1,325	16
25–29	198,928	196,304	2,624	2,583	41
30–34	204,386	200,671	3,715	3,661	53
35–39	113,375	110,696	2,679	2,643	36
40–44	26,967	26,225	742	721	20
45+	1,682	1,515	167	161	6

* Includes stillbirths

† Total includes rates for twins, triplets, quads and above

Source: ONS (Crown copyright)

TOP TEN BABY NAMES (ENGLAND AND WALES)

	1904		2012	
	Girls	*Boys*	*Girls*	*Boys*
1	Mary	William	Amelia	Harry
2	Florence	John	Olivia	Oliver
3	Doris	George	Jessica	Jack
4	Edith	Thomas	Emily	Charlie
5	Dorothy	Arthur	Lily	Jacob
6	Annie	James	Ava	Thomas
7	Margaret	Charles	Mia	Alfie
8	Alice	Frederick	Isla	Riley
9	Elizabeth	Albert	Sophie	William
10	Elsie	Ernest	Isabella	James

Source: ONS (Crown copyright)

LIVE BIRTHS
by age of mother and registration type

Year	*under 20*	*20–29*	*30–39*	*40+*	*All ages*
Outside marriage/civil partnership					
1971	21,600	33,500	9,500	1,100	65,700
1981	26,400	43,100	35,200	900	81,000
1991	43,400	130,200	35,500	2,100	211,300
2001	39,500	124,900	68,500	5,100	238,100
2011	35,035	195,006	97,829	10,630	338,500
Within marriage/civil partnership					
1971	61,100	499,400	145,500	11,600	717,500
1981	30,100	367,200	150,200	6,000	553,500
1991	8,900	291,900	179,300	7,700	487,900
2001	4,600	143,800	196,900	11,100	356,500
2011	1,406	138,183	219,932	18,019	377,540

Source: ONS (Crown copyright)

LEGAL ABORTIONS

	2002	*2012*
England and Wales	175,932	185,122
Scotland	11,870	12,447

Source: Department of Health, NHS Scotland

DEATHS

INFANT MORTALITY RATE*	
United Kingdom	3.9
England and Wales	4.1
Scotland	4.0
Northern Ireland	3.6

* Deaths of infants under one year of age per 1,000 live births
Source: NISRA, ONS (Crown copyright), Scottish Government

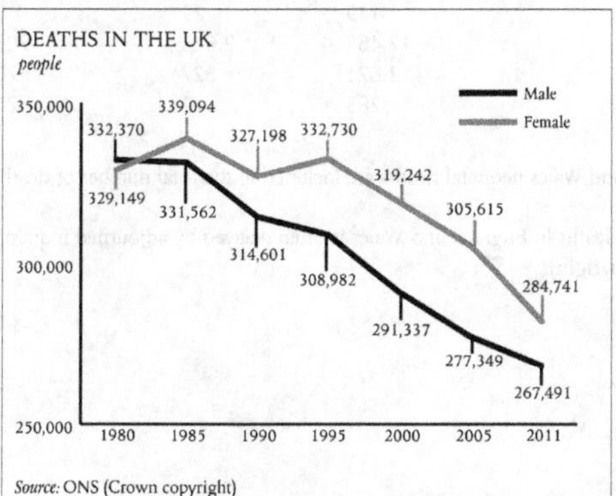

Source: ONS (Crown copyright)

MARRIAGE AND DIVORCE

	Marriages	*Divorces*
United Kingdom	*285,391	129,763
England and Wales	*247,890	117,558
Scotland	29,135	9,862
Northern Ireland	8,366	2,343

* Provisional figures
Source: General Register Office for Scotland, NISRA, ONS (Crown copyright)

HOUSEHOLDS

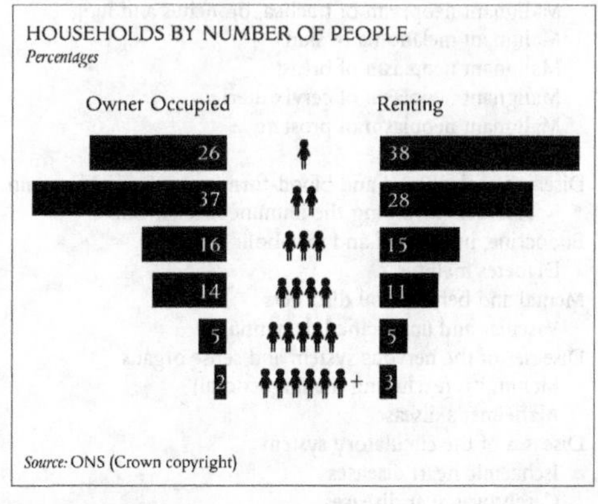

Source: ONS (Crown copyright)

EMPLOYMENT

MEDIAN FULL-TIME GROSS WEEKLY EARNINGS BY INDUSTRY, 2012

Industry	*Earnings*
Agriculture, forestry and fishing	£390.0
Mining and quarrying	£727.8
Manufacturing	£515.9
Electricity, gas, steam and air conditioning supply	£633.3
Water supply, sewerage and waste management	£521.5
Construction	£536.8
Wholesale and retail trade; motor repair	£397.3
Transportation and storage	£515.0
Accommodation and food services	£309.7
Information and communication	£677.4
Finance and insurance	£639.5
Real estate	£479.4
Professional, scientific and technical	£616.3
Administrative and support services	£402.5
Public administration and defence	£578.6
Education	£560.3
Human health and social work	£491.7
Arts, entertainment and recreation	£402.5
Other services	£440.8
ALL INDUSTRIES AND SERVICES	£506.0

DEATHS BY CAUSE, 2012

	England and Wales	*Scotland**	*N. Ireland**
Total deaths	499,331	53,661	14,204
Deaths from natural causes	481,869	50,986	13,419
Certain infectious and parasitic diseases	5,109	812	157
Intestinal infectious diseases	1,621	162	50
Respiratory and other tuberculosis	261	23	8
Meningococcal infection	64	4	4
Viral hepatitis	232	27	4
Human immunodeficiency virus (HIV)	209	16	2
Neoplasms	145,395	15,731	4,159
Malignant neoplasms	142,107	15,457	4,059
Malignant neoplasm of trachea, bronchus and lung	30,273	4,178	912
Malignant melanoma of skin	1,920	176	44
Malignant neoplasm of breast	10,373	1,041	342
Malignant neoplasm of cervix uteri	786	108	23
Malignant neoplasm of prostate	9,698	900	233
Leukaemia	4,355	388	123
Diseases of the blood and blood-forming organs and certain disorders involving the immune mechanism	943	87	33
Endocrine, nutritional and metabolic diseases	6,710	979	238
Diabetes mellitus	4,931	742	170
Mental and behavioural disorders	35,865	3,339	894
Vascular and unspecified dementia	34,998	2,994	841
Diseases of the nervous system and sense organs	21,173	2,055	671
Meningitis (excluding meningococcal)	120	10	2
Alzheimer's disease	8,859	917	335
Diseases of the circulatory system	141,362	15,913	3,951
Ischaemic heart diseases	64,164	7,636	1,966
Cerebrovascular diseases	35,846	4,594	1,094
Diseases of the respiratory system	70,708	6,791	1,923
Influenza	76	12	19
Pneumonia	26,055	1,948	737
Bronchitis, emphysema and other chronic obstructive pulmonary diseases	26,006	2,859	698
Asthma	1,126	80	33
Diseases of the digestive system	24,573	2,936	657
Gastric and duodenal ulcer	2,103	149	46
Diseases of the liver	7,462	1,095	215
Diseases of the skin and subcutaneous tissue	1,675	138	23
Diseases of the musculo-skeletal system and connective tissue	4,330	349	103
Osteoporosis	1,273	51	19
Diseases of the genitourinary system	9,762	1,082	331
Complications of pregnancy, childbirth and the puerperium	46	5	4
Certain conditions originating in the perinatal period†	205	134	57
Congenital malformations, deformations and chromosomal abnormalities†	1,149	151	72
Symptoms, signs and abnormal findings not classified elsewhere	10,723	481	145
Senility	9,120	268	106
Sudden infant death syndrome	149	29	5
Deaths from external causes	17,462	2,675	785
Suicide and intentional self-harm	3,671	527	220
Assault	‡283	72	27

* Figures for Scotland and Northern Ireland are for 2011

† Excludes neonatal deaths (those at age under 28 days): for England and Wales neonatal deaths are included in the total number of deaths but excluded from the cause figures

‡ This will not be a true figure as registration of homicide and assault deaths in England and Wales is often delayed by adjourned inquests

Source: General Register Office for Scotland, NISRA, ONS (Crown copyright)

THE NATIONAL FLAG

The national flag of the United Kingdom is the Union Flag, generally known as the Union Jack.

The Union Flag is a combination of the cross of St George, patron saint of England, the cross of St Andrew, patron saint of Scotland and the cross of St Patrick, patron saint of Ireland.

Cross of St George: cross Gules in a field Argent (red cross on a white ground)

Cross of St Andrew: saltire Argent in a field Azure (white diagonal cross on a blue ground)

Cross of St Patrick: saltire Gules in a field Argent (red diagonal cross on a white ground)

The Union Flag was first introduced in 1606 after the union of the kingdoms of England and Scotland under one sovereign. The cross of St Patrick was added in 1801 after the union of Great Britain and Ireland.

See also Flags of the World colour plates.

FLYING THE UNION FLAG

The correct orientation of the Union Flag when flying is with the broader diagonal band of white uppermost in the hoist (ie near the pole) and the narrower diagonal band of white uppermost in the fly (ie furthest from the pole).

The flying of the Union Flag on government buildings is decided by the Department for Culture, Media and Sport (DCMS) at the Queen's command. There is no formal definition of a government building but it is generally accepted to mean a building owned or used by the Crown and/or predominantly occupied or used by civil servants or the Armed Forces.

The Scottish or Welsh governments are responsible for drawing up their own flag-flying guidance for their buildings. In Northern Ireland, the flying of flags is constrained by The Flags Regulations (Northern Ireland) 2000 and the Police Emblems and Flag Regulations (Northern Ireland) 2002. Individuals, local authorities and other organisations may fly the Union Flag whenever they wish, subject to compliance with any local planning requirement.

FLAGS AT HALF-MAST

Flags are flown at half-mast (ie two-thirds up between the top and bottom of the flagstaff) on the following occasions:

- from the announcement of the death of the sovereign until the funeral
- the death or funeral of a member of the royal family*
- the funerals of foreign rulers*
- the funerals of prime ministers and ex-prime ministers of the UK*
- the funerals of first ministers and ex-first ministers of Scotland, Wales and Northern Ireland (unless otherwise commanded by the sovereign, this only applies to flags in their respective countries)*
- other occasions by special command from the Queen

* By special command from the Queen in each case

DAYS FOR FLYING FLAGS

On 25 March 2008 the DCMS announced that UK government departments in England, Scotland and Wales may fly the Union Flag on their buildings whenever they choose and not just on the designated days listed below. In addition, on the patron saints' days of Scotland and Wales, the appropriate national flag may be flown alongside the Union Flag on UK government buildings in the wider Whitehall area. When flying on designated days flags are hoisted from 8am to sunset.

Duchess of Cambridge's birthday	9 Jan
Countess of Wessex's birthday	20 Jan
Accession of the Queen	6 Feb
Duke of York's birthday	19 Feb
St David's Day (in Wales only)*	1 Mar
Earl of Wessex's birthday	10 Mar
Commonwealth Day (2014)	10 Mar
St Patrick's Day (in Northern Ireland only)†	17 Mar
The Queen's birthday	21 Apr
St George's Day (in England only)*	23 Apr
Europe Day†	9 May
Coronation Day	2 Jun
Duke of Edinburgh's birthday	10 Jun
The Queen's official birthday (2014)	14 Jun
Duke of Cambridge's birthday	21 Jun
Duchess of Cornwall's birthday	17 Jul
Princess Royal's birthday	15 Aug
Remembrance Day (2014)	9 Nov
Prince of Wales' birthday	14 Nov
Wedding Day of the Queen	20 Nov
St Andrew's Day (in Scotland only)*	30 Nov
Opening of parliament by the Queen‡	
Prorogation of parliament by the Queen‡	

* The appropriate national flag, or the European flag, may be flown in addition to the Union Flag (where there are two or more flagpoles), but not in a superior position

† Only the Union Flag should be flown

‡ Only in the Greater London area, whether or not the Queen performs the ceremony in person

THE ROYAL STANDARD

The Royal Standard comprises four quarterings – two for England (three lions passant), one for Scotland* (a lion rampant) and one for Ireland (a harp).

The Royal Standard is flown when the Queen is in residence at a royal palace, on transport being used by the Queen for official journeys and from Victoria Tower when the Queen attends parliament. It may also be flown on any building (excluding ecclesiastical buildings) during a visit by the Queen. If the Queen is to be present in a building, advice on flag flying can be obtained from the DCMS.

The Royal Standard is never flown at half-mast, even after the death of the sovereign, as the new monarch immediately succeeds to the throne.

* In Scotland a version with two Scottish quarterings is used

THE ROYAL FAMILY

THE SOVEREIGN

ELIZABETH II, by the Grace of God, of the United Kingdom of Great Britain and Northern Ireland and of her other Realms and Territories Queen, Head of the Commonwealth, Defender of the Faith

Her Majesty Elizabeth Alexandra Mary of Windsor, elder daughter of King George VI and of HM Queen Elizabeth the Queen Mother

Born 21 April 1926, at 17 Bruton Street, London W1

Ascended the throne 6 February 1952

Crowned 2 June 1953, at Westminster Abbey

Married 20 November 1947, in Westminster Abbey, HRH the Prince Philip, Duke of Edinburgh

Official residences Buckingham Palace, London SW1A 1AA; Windsor Castle, Berks; Palace of Holyroodhouse, Edinburgh

Private residences Sandringham, Norfolk; Balmoral Castle, Aberdeenshire

HUSBAND OF THE QUEEN

HRH THE PRINCE PHILIP, DUKE OF EDINBURGH, KG, KT, OM, GBE, Royal Victorian Chain, AC, QSO, PC, Ranger of Windsor Park

Born 10 June 1921, son of Prince and Princess Andrew of Greece and Denmark, naturalised a British subject 1947, created Duke of Edinburgh, Earl of Merioneth and Baron Greenwich 1947

CHILDREN OF THE QUEEN

HRH THE PRINCE OF WALES (Prince Charles Philip Arthur George), KG, KT, GCB, OM and Great Master of the Order of the Bath, AK, QSO, PC, ADC(P)

Born 14 November 1948, created Prince of Wales and Earl of Chester 1958, succeeded as Duke of Cornwall, Duke of Rothesay, Earl of Carrick and Baron Renfrew, Lord of the Isles and Great Steward of Scotland 1952

Married (1) 29 July 1981 Lady Diana Frances Spencer (Diana, Princess of Wales (1961–97), youngest daughter of the 8th Earl Spencer and the Hon. Mrs Shand Kydd), marriage dissolved 1996; (2) 9 April 2005 Mrs Camilla Rosemary Parker Bowles, now HRH the Duchess of Cornwall, GCVO (*born* 17 July 1947, daughter of Major Bruce Shand and the Hon. Mrs Rosalind Shand)

Residences Clarence House, London SW1A 1BA; Highgrove, Doughton, Tetbury, Glos GL8 8TN; Birkhall, Ballater, Aberdeenshire

Issue

1. HRH Duke of Cambridge (Prince William Arthur Philip Louis), KG, KT *born* 21 June 1982, *created* Duke of Cambridge, Earl of Strathearn and Baron Carrickfergus 2011 *married* 29 April 2011 Catherine Elizabeth Middleton, now HRH the Duchess of Cambridge (*born* 9 January 1982, elder daughter of Michael and Carole Middleton), and has issue, HRH Prince George of Cambridge (Prince George Alexander Louis), *born* 22 July 2013

Residence Kensington Palace, London W8 4PU; Amner Hall, Norfolk PE31 6RW

2. HRH Prince Henry of Wales (Prince Henry Charles Albert David), *born* 15 September 1984

Residence Nottingham Cottage, Kensington Palace, London W8 4PU

HRH THE PRINCESS ROYAL (Princess Anne Elizabeth Alice Louise), KG, KT, GCVO

Born 15 August 1950, declared the Princess Royal 1987

Married (1) 14 November 1973 Captain Mark Anthony Peter Phillips, CVO (*born* 22 September 1948); marriage dissolved 1992; (2) 12 December 1992 Vice-Adm. Sir Timothy James Hamilton Laurence, KCVO, CB, ADC (P) (*born* 1 March 1955)

Residence Gatcombe Park, Minchinhampton, Glos GL6 9AT

Issue

1. Peter Mark Andrew Phillips, *born* 15 November 1977, *married* 17 May 2008 Autumn Patricia Kelly, and has issue, Savannah Phillips, *born* 29 December 2010; Isla Elizabeth Phillips, *born* 29 March 2012

2. Zara Anne Elizabeth Tindall, MBE, *born* 15 May 1981, *married* 30 July 2011 Michael James Tindall, MBE

HRH THE DUKE OF YORK (Prince Andrew Albert Christian Edward), KG, GCVO, ADC(P)

Born 19 February 1960, created Duke of York, Earl of Inverness and Baron Killyleagh 1986

Married 23 July 1986 Sarah Margaret Ferguson, now Sarah, Duchess of York (*born* 15 October 1959, younger daughter of Major Ronald Ferguson and Mrs Hector Barrantes), marriage dissolved 1996

Residence Royal Lodge, Windsor Great Park, Berks

Issue

1. HRH Princess Beatrice of York (Princess Beatrice Elizabeth Mary), *born* 8 August 1988

2. HRH Princess Eugenie of York (Princess Eugenie Victoria Helena), *born* 23 March 1990

HRH THE EARL OF WESSEX (Prince Edward Antony Richard Louis), KG, GCVO, ADC(P)

Born 10 March 1964, created Earl of Wessex, Viscount Severn 1999

Married 19 June 1999 Sophie Helen Rhys-Jones, now HRH the Countess of Wessex, GCVO (*born* 20 January 1965, daughter of Mr and Mrs Christopher Rhys-Jones)

Residence Bagshot Park, Bagshot, Surrey GU19 5HS

Issue

1. Lady Louise Mountbatten-Windsor (Louise Alice Elizabeth Mary Mountbatten-Windsor), *born* 8 November 2003

2. Viscount Severn (James Alexander Philip Theo Mountbatten-Windsor), *born* 17 December 2007

NEPHEW AND NIECE OF THE QUEEN

Children of HRH the Princess Margaret, Countess of Snowdon and the Earl of Snowdon (*see* House of Windsor):

DAVID ALBERT CHARLES ARMSTRONG-JONES, VISCOUNT LINLEY, *born* 3 November 1961, *married* 8 October 1993 Hon. Serena Alleyne Stanhope, and has issue, Hon. Charles Patrick Inigo Armstrong-Jones, *born* 1 July 1999; Hon. Margarita Elizabeth Alleyne Armstrong-Jones, *born* 14 May 2002

LADY SARAH CHATTO (Sarah Frances Elizabeth), *born* 1 May 1964, *married* 14 July 1994 Daniel Chatto, and has issue, Samuel David Benedict Chatto, *born* 28 July 1996; Arthur Robert Nathaniel Chatto, *born* 5 February 1999

COUSINS OF THE QUEEN

Child of HRH the Duke of Gloucester and HRH Princess Alice, Duchess of Gloucester (*see* House of Windsor):
HRH THE DUKE OF GLOUCESTER (Prince Richard Alexander Walter George), KG, GCVO, Grand Prior of the Order of St John of Jerusalem
Born 26 August 1944
Married 8 July 1972 Birgitte Eva van Deurs, now HRH the Duchess of Gloucester, GCVO (*born* 20 June 1946, daughter of Asger Henriksen and Vivian van Deurs)
Residence Kensington Palace, London W8 4PU
Issue
1. Earl of Ulster (Alexander Patrick Gregers Richard), *born* 24 October 1974 *married* 22 June 2002 Dr Claire Alexandra Booth, and has issue, Lord Culloden (Xan Richard Anders), *born* 12 March 2007; Lady Cosima Windsor (Cosima Rose Alexandra), *born* 20 May 2010
2. Lady Davina Lewis (Davina Elizabeth Alice Benedikte), *born* 19 November 1977 *married* 31 July 2004 Gary Christie Lewis, and has issue, Senna Kowhai Lewis, *born* 22 June 2010; Tane Mahuta Lewis, *born* 25 May 2012
3. Lady Rose Gilman (Rose Victoria Birgitte Louise), *born* 1 March 1980 *married* 19 July 2008 George Edward Gilman, and has issue, Lyla Beatrix Christabel Gilman, *born* 30 May 2010; Rufus Gilman, *born* October/November 2012

Children of HRH the Duke of Kent and Princess Marina, Duchess of Kent (*see* House of Windsor):

HRH THE DUKE OF KENT (Prince Edward George Nicholas Paul Patrick), KG, GCMG, GCVO, ADC(P)
Born 9 October 1935
Married 8 June 1961 Katharine Lucy Mary Worsley, now HRH the Duchess of Kent, GCVO (*born* 22 February 1933, daughter of Sir William Worsley, Bt.)
Residence Wren House, Palace Green, London W8 4PY
Issue
1. Earl of St Andrews (George Philip Nicholas), *born* 26 June 1962, *married* 9 January 1988 Sylvana Tomaselli, and has issue, Lord Downpatrick (Edward Edmund Maximilian George), *born* 2 December 1988; Lady Marina-Charlotte Windsor (Marina-Charlotte Alexandra Katharine Helen), *born* 30 September 1992; Lady Amelia Windsor (Amelia Sophia Theodora Mary Margaret), *born* 24 August 1995
2. Lady Helen Taylor (Helen Marina Lucy), *born* 28 April 1964, *married* 18 July 1992 Timothy Verner Taylor, and has issue, Columbus George Donald Taylor, *born* 6 August 1994; Cassius Edward Taylor, *born* 26 December 1996; Eloise Olivia Katharine Taylor, *born* 3 March 2003; Estella Olga Elizabeth Taylor, *born* 21 December 2004
3. Lord Nicholas Windsor (Nicholas Charles Edward Jonathan), *born* 25 July 1970, *married* 4 November 2006 Princess Paola Doimi de Lupis Frankopan Subic Zrinski, and has issue, Albert Louis Philip Edward Windsor, *born* 22 September 2007; Leopold Ernest Augustus Guelph Windsor, *born* 8 September 2009

HRH PRINCESS ALEXANDRA, THE HON. LADY OGILVY (Princess Alexandra Helen Elizabeth Olga Christabel), KG, GCVO
Born 25 December 1936
Married 24 April 1963 the Rt. Hon. Sir Angus Ogilvy, KCVO (1928–2004), second son of 12th Earl of Airlie
Residence Thatched House Lodge, Richmond Park, Surrey TW10 5HP
Issue
1. James Robert Bruce Ogilvy, *born* 29 February 1964, *married* 30 July 1988 Julia Rawlinson, and has issue, Flora Alexandra Ogilvy, *born* 15 December 1994; Alexander Charles Ogilvy, *born* 12 November 1996
2. Marina Victoria Alexandra Ogilvy, *born* 31 July 1966, *married* 2 February 1990 Paul Julian Mowatt (marriage dissolved 1997), and has issue, Zenouska May Mowatt, *born* 26 May 1990; Christian Alexander Mowatt, *born* 4 June 1993

HRH PRINCE MICHAEL OF KENT (Prince Michael George Charles Franklin), GCVO
Born 4 July 1942
Married 30 June 1978 Baroness Marie-Christine Agnes Hedwig Ida von Reibnitz, now HRH Princess Michael of Kent (*born* 15 January 1945, daughter of Baron Gunther von Reibnitz)
Residence Kensington Palace, London W8 4PU
Issue
1. Lord Frederick Windsor (Frederick Michael George David Louis), *born* 6 April 1979, *married* 12 September 2009 Sophie Winkleman, and has issue, Maud Elizabeth Daphne Marina, *born* 15 August 2013
2. Lady Gabriella Windsor (Gabriella Marina Alexandra Ophelia), *born* 23 April 1981

ORDER OF SUCCESSION

1	HRH the Prince of Wales	21	Arthur Chatto
2	HRH the Duke of Cambridge	22	HRH the Duke of Gloucester
3	HRH Prince George of Cambridge	23	Earl of Ulster
4	HRH Prince Henry of Wales	24	Lord Culloden
5	HRH the Duke of York	25	Lady Cosima Windsor
6	HRH Princess Beatrice of York	26	Lady Davina Lewis
7	HRH Princess Eugenie of York	27	Senna Lewis
8	HRH the Earl of Wessex	28	Tane Lewis
9	Viscount Severn	29	Lady Rose Gilman
10	Lady Louise Mountbatten-Windsor	30	Lyla Gilman
11	HRH the Princess Royal	31	Rufus Gilman
12	Peter Phillips	32	HRH the Duke of Kent
13	Savannah Phillips	33	Earl of St Andrews
14	Isla Phillips	34	Lady Amelia Windsor
15	Zara Tindall	35	Albert Windsor
16	Viscount Linley	36	Leopold Windsor
17	Hon. Charles Armstrong-Jones	37	Lady Helen Taylor
18	Hon. Margarita Armstrong-Jones	38	Columbus Taylor
19	Lady Sarah Chatto	39	Cassius Taylor
20	Samuel Chatto	40	Eloise Taylor

Under the Succession to the Crown Act 2013 HRH Prince Michael of Kent and the Earl of St Andrews were restored to the succession and Tane Lewis became the first male not to precede his elder sister.

Lord Nicholas Windsor, Lord Downpatrick and Lady Marina-Charlotte Windsor renounced their rights to the throne on converting to Roman Catholicism in 2001, 2003 and 2008 respectively. Their children remain in succession provided that they are in communion with the Church of England.

ROYAL HOUSEHOLD

The PRIVATE SECRETARY is responsible for:

- informing and advising the Queen on constitutional, governmental and political matters in the UK, her other Realms and the wider Commonwealth, including communications with the prime minister and government departments
- organising the Queen's domestic and overseas official programme
- the Queen's speeches, messages, patronage, photographs, portraits and official presents
- communications in connection with the role of the royal family
- dealing with correspondence to the Queen from members of the public
- royal travel policy
- coordinating and initiating research to support engagements by members of the royal family

The COMMUNICATIONS AND PRESS SECRETARY is in charge of Buckingham Palace's press office and reports to the private secretary. The press secretary is responsible for:

- developing communications strategies to enhance the public understanding of the role of the monarchy
- briefing the British and international media on the role and duties of the Queen and issues relating to the royal family
- responding to media enquiries
- arranging media facilities in the UK and overseas to support royal functions and engagements
- the management of the royal website

The private secretary is keeper of the royal archives and is responsible for the care of the records of the sovereign and the royal household from previous reigns, preserved in the royal archives at Windsor. As keeper, it is the private secretary's responsibility to ensure the proper management of the records of the present reign with a view to their transfer to the archives as and when appropriate. The private secretary is an *ex officio* trustee of the Royal Collection Trust.

The KEEPER OF THE PRIVY PURSE AND TREASURER to the Queen is responsible for:

- the Sovereign Grant, which is the money paid from the government's Consolidated Fund to meet official expenditure relating to the Queen's duties as head of state and head of the Commonwealth and is provided by the government in return for the net surplus from the Crown Estate and other hereditary revenues (*see also* Royal Finances)
- through the director of personnel, the planning and management of personnel policy across the royal household, the administration of all its pension schemes and private estates employees, and the allocation of employee and pensioner housing
- information technology systems
- property services at occupied royal palaces in England, comprising Buckingham Palace, St James's Palace, Clarence House, Marlborough House Mews, the residential and office areas of Kensington Palace, Windsor Castle and buildings in the Home and Great Parks of Windsor and Hampton Court Mews and Paddocks
- internal audit services
- health and safety; insurance matters
- the privy purse, which is mainly financed by the net income of the Duchy of Lancaster, and meets both official and private expenditure incurred by the Queen
- liaison with other members of the royal family and their households on financial matters
- the Queen's private estates at Sandringham and Balmoral, the Queen's Racing Establishment and the Royal Studs and liaison with the Ascot Authority
- the Home Park at Windsor and liaison with the Crown Estate Commissioners concerning the Home Park and the Great Park at Windsor
- the Royal Philatelic Collection
- administrative aspects of the Military Knights of Windsor
- administration of the Royal Victorian Order, of which the keeper of the privy purse is secretary, Long and Faithful Service Medals, and the Queen's cups, medals and prizes, and policy on commemorative medals

The keeper of the privy purse is one of three royal trustees (in respect of his responsibilities for the Sovereign Grant) and is receiver-general of the Duchy of Lancaster and a member of the Duchy's Council.

The keeper of the privy purse is an *ex officio* trustee of the Historic Royal Palaces Trust and the Royal Collection Trust.

The DIRECTOR OF THE PROPERTY SECTION has day-to-day responsibility for the royal household's property section:

- fire and health and safety
- repairs and refurbishment of buildings and new building work
- utilities and telecommunications
- putting up stages, tents and other work in connection with ceremonial occasions, garden parties and other official functions

The property section is also responsible, on a sub-contract basis from the DCMS, for the maintenance of Marlborough House (which is occupied by the Commonwealth Secretariat).

The MASTER OF THE HOUSEHOLD is responsible for:

- delivering the majority of the official and private entertaining in the Queen's annual programme at residences in the UK, and on occasion overseas
- periodic support for entertaining by other members of the royal family
- furnishings and internal decorative refurbishment in conjunction with the director of the Royal Collection and Property Services
- housekeeping, catering and service provision for the royal household

The COMPTROLLER, LORD CHAMBERLAIN'S OFFICE is responsible for:

- the organisation of all ceremonial engagements, including state visits to the Queen in the UK, royal weddings and funerals, the state opening of parliament, Guards of Honour at Buckingham Palace, investitures, and the Garter and Thistle ceremonies
- garden parties at Buckingham Palace and the Palace of Holyroodhouse (except for catering and tents)
- the Crown Jewels, which are part of the Royal Collection, when they are in use on state occasions
- coordination of the arrangements for the Queen to be represented at funerals and memorial services and at the arrival and departure of visiting heads of state
- delivery of all official and approved travel operations
- advising on matters of precedence, style and titles, dress,

flying of flags, gun salutes, mourning and other ceremonial issues
- supervising the applications from tradesmen for Royal Warrants of Appointment
- advising on the commercial use of royal emblems and contemporary royal photographs
- the ecclesiastical household, the medical household, the body guards and certain ceremonial appointments such as Gentlemen Ushers and Pages of Honour
- the lords in waiting, who represent the Queen on various occasions and escort visiting heads of state during incoming state visits
- the Queen's bargemaster and watermen and the Queen's swans
- the Royal Almonry

The comptroller is also responsible for the Royal Mews, assisted by the CROWN EQUERRY, who has day-to-day responsibility for:

- the provision of carriage processions for the state opening of parliament, state visits, Trooping of the Colour, Royal Ascot, the Garter Ceremony, the Thistle Service, the presentation of credentials to the Queen by incoming foreign ambassadors and high commissioners, and other state and ceremonial occasions
- the provision of chauffeur-driven cars
- coordinating travel arrangements by road, air, rail or sea in respect of the royal household
- supervision and administration of the Royal Mews at Buckingham Palace, Windsor Castle, Hampton Court and the Palace of Holyroodhouse

The comptroller also has overall responsibility for the MARSHAL OF THE DIPLOMATIC CORPS, who is responsible for the relationship between the royal household and the Diplomatic Heads of Mission in London; and the SECRETARY OF THE CENTRAL CHANCERY OF THE ORDERS OF KNIGHTHOOD, who administers the Orders of Chivalry, makes arrangements for investitures and the distribution of insignia, and ensures the proper public notification of awards through *The London Gazette*.

The DIRECTOR OF THE ROYAL COLLECTION is responsible for:

- the administration and custodial control of the Royal Collection in all royal residences
- the care, display, conservation and restoration of items in the collection
- initiating and assisting research into the collection and publishing catalogues and books on the collection
- making the collection accessible to the public and educating and informing the public about the collection

The Royal Collection, which contains a large number of works of art, is held by the Queen as sovereign in trust for her successors and the nation and is not owned by her as an individual. The administration, conservation and presentation of the Royal Collection are funded by the Royal Collection Trust solely from income from visitors to Windsor Castle, Buckingham Palace and the Palace of Holyroodhouse. The Royal Collection Trust is chaired by the Prince of Wales. The Lord Chamberlain, the private secretary and the keeper of the privy purse are *ex officio* trustees and there are three external trustees appointed by the Queen.

The director of the Royal Collection is also at present the SURVEYOR OF THE QUEEN'S WORKS OF ART. The ROYAL LIBRARIAN is responsible for all books, manuscripts, coins and medals, insignia and works of art on paper including the watercolours, prints and drawings in the Print Room at Windsor Castle, and the SURVEYOR OF THE QUEEN'S PICTURES is responsible for pictures and miniatures.

Royal Collection Enterprises Limited is the trading subsidiary of the Royal Collection Trust. The company, whose chair is the Keeper of the Privy Purse, is responsible for:

- managing access by the public to Windsor Castle (including Frogmore House), Buckingham Palace (including the Royal Mews and the Queen's Gallery) and the Palace of Holyroodhouse (including the Queen's Gallery)
- running shops at each location
- managing the images and intellectual property rights of the Royal Collection

The director of the Royal Collection is also an *ex officio* trustee of the Historic Royal Palaces Trust.

PRIVATE SECRETARIES

THE QUEEN
Office: Buckingham Palace, London SW1A 1AA T 020-7930 4832
Private Secretary to the Queen, Rt. Hon. Sir Christopher Geidt, KCVO, OBE

PRINCE PHILIP, THE DUKE OF EDINBURGH
Office: Buckingham Palace, London SW1A 1AA T 020-7930 4832
Private Secretary, Brig. Archie Miller-Bakewell

THE PRINCE OF WALES AND THE DUCHESS OF CORNWALL
Office: Clarence House, London SW1A 1BA T 020-7930 4832
Principal Private Secretary, William Nye

THE DUKE AND DUCHESS OF CAMBRIDGE AND PRINCE HENRY OF WALES
Office: Clarence House, London SW1A 1BA
T 020-7930 4832
Principal Private Secretary, James Lowther-Pinkerton, LVO, MBE

THE DUKE OF YORK
Office: Buckingham Palace, London SW1A 1AA T 020-7024 4227
Private Secretary, Amanda Thirsk, LVO

THE EARL AND COUNTESS OF WESSEX
Office: Bagshot Park, Surrey GU19 5PL T 01276-707040
Private Secretary, Brig. John Smedley, LVO

THE PRINCESS ROYAL
Office: Buckingham Palace, London SW1A 1AA T 020-7024 4199
Private Secretary, Capt. N. P. Wright, CVO, RN

THE DUKE AND DUCHESS OF GLOUCESTER
Office: Kensington Palace, London W8 4PU T 020-7368 1000
Private Secretary, Alastair Todd

THE DUKE OF KENT
Office: York House, St James's Palace, London SW1A 1BQ
T 020-7930 4872
Private Secretary, Nicholas Marden

THE DUCHESS OF KENT
Office: Wren House, Palace Green, London W8 4PY
T 020-7937 2730
Personal Secretary, Chloe Hill

PRINCE AND PRINCESS MICHAEL OF KENT
Office: Kensington Palace, London W8 4PU
W www.princemichael.org.uk
Private Secretary, Nicholas Chance, LVO

PRINCESS ALEXANDRA, THE HON. LADY OGILVY
Office: Buckingham Palace, London SW1A 1AA T 020-7024 4270
Private Secretary, Diane Duke

SENIOR MANAGEMENT OF THE ROYAL HOUSEHOLD

Lord Chamberlain, Earl Peel, GCVO, PC
HEADS OF DEPARTMENT
Private Secretary to The Queen, Rt. Hon. Sir Christopher Geidt, KCVO, OBE
Keeper of the Privy Purse, Sir Alan Reid, GCVO
Master of the Household, Air Vice-Marshal Sir David Walker, KCVO, OBE
Comptroller, Lord Chamberlain's Office, Lt.-Col. Sir Andrew Ford, KCVO
Director of the Royal Collection, Jonathan Marsden, CVO
NON-EXECUTIVE MEMBERS
Private Secretary to the Duke of Edinburgh, Brig. Archie Miller-Bakewell
Private Secretary to the Prince of Wales and the Duchess of Cornwall, William Nye

ASTRONOMER ROYAL

The post of Astronomer Royal dates back to 1675, when astronomy had many practical applications in navigation. Today the post is largely honorary although the Astronomer Royal is expected to be available for consultation on scientific matters for as long as the holder remains a professional astronomer. The Astronomer Royal receives a stipend of £100 a year and is a member of the royal household.

Astronomer Royal, Lord Rees of Ludlow, OM, *apptd* 1995

MASTER OF THE QUEEN'S MUSIC

The office of Master of the Queen's Music is an honour conferred on a musician of great distinction. The office was first created in 1626, when the master was responsible for the court musicians. Since the reign of King George V, the position has had no fixed duties, although the Master may choose to produce compositions to mark royal or state occasions. The Master of the Queen's Music is paid an annual stipend of £15,000. In 2004 the length of appointment was changed from life tenure to a ten-year term.

Master of the Queen's Music, Sir Peter Maxwell Davies, *appt* 2004

POET LAUREATE

The post of Poet Laureate was officially established when John Dryden was appointed by royal warrant as Poet Laureate and Historiographer Royal in 1668. The post is attached to the royal household and was originally conferred on the holder for life; in 1999 the length of appointment was changed to a ten-year term. It is customary for the Poet Laureate to write verse to mark events of national importance. The postholder currently receives an honorarium of £5,750 a year.

The Poet Laureate, Carol Ann Duffy, *apptd* 2009

ROYAL FINANCES

Dating back to the late 17th century the Civil List was originally used by the sovereign to supplement hereditary revenues for paying the salaries of judges, ambassadors and other government officers as well as the expenses of the royal household. In 1760, on the accession of George III, it was decided that the Civil List would be provided by parliament to cover all relevant expenditure in return for the king surrendering the hereditary revenues of the Crown. At that time parliament undertook to pay the salaries of judges, ambassadors etc. In 1831 parliament agreed also to meet the costs of the royal palaces in return for a reduction in the Civil List.

Until 1 April 2012 the Civil List met the central staff costs and running expenses of the Queen's official household. Annual grants-in-aid provided for the maintenance of the occupied royal palaces (*see* Royal Household for a list of occupied palaces) and royal travel.

THE SOVEREIGN GRANT

Under the Sovereign Grant Act 2011, which came into force on 1 April 2012, the funding previously provided by the Civil List and the grants-in-aid was consolidated in the Sovereign Grant, which was set at £31m for 2012–13. It is provided by HM Treasury from public funds in exchange for the surrender by the Queen of the revenue of the Crown Estate.

Official expenditure met by the Sovereign Grant in 2012–13 amounted to £33.3m, an increase of £0.9m (2.6 per cent) compared with 2011–12. The excess of expenditure over the Sovereign Grant of £2.3m was drawn down from the Sovereign Grant reserve. From 2013–14 the Sovereign Grant will be calculated based on 15 per cent of the income account net surplus of the Crown Estate for the two financial years previous. The Crown Estate surplus for the financial year 2011–12 amounted to £240.2m, providing for a Sovereign Grant of £36.1m for 2013–14.

The legislative requirement is for Sovereign Grant accounts to be audited by the Comptroller and Auditor-General, scrutinised by the National Audit Office, and submitted to parliament annually. They are then subjected to the same audit scrutiny as for any other government department. The first annual report covering the new arrangements under the Sovereign Grant, for the year to 31 March 2013, was published in June 2013.

	2011–12	*2012–13*
Sovereign Grant*	£29,100,000	£31,000,000
Repayable to the Department for Transport	(£100,000)	—
Draw-down from the reserve	£5,400,000	£2,300,000
Net Funding Receipts	£34,400,000	£33,300,000
Net Expenditure	(£32,400,000)	(£33,300,000)

* Civil List and grants-in-aid for 2011–12

PARLIAMENTARY ANNUITIES

The Civil List Acts provided for other members of the royal family to receive parliamentary annuities from government funds to meet the expenses of carrying out their official duties. Since 1993 these annuities have been a statutory anomaly as the Queen reimbursed HM Treasury all the annuities except those paid to the late Queen Elizabeth the Queen Mother and the Duke of Edinburgh. The Sovereign Grant Act 2011 repeals all the parliamentary annuities paid to the royal family, with the exception of the Duke of Edinburgh. The Duke of Edinburgh's annuity (£359,000) is now paid directly from the Consolidated Fund.

THE PRIVY PURSE

The funds received by the privy purse pay for official expenses incurred by the Queen as head of state and for some of the Queen's private expenditure. The revenues of the Duchy of Lancaster are the principal source of income for the privy purse. The revenues of the Duchy were retained by George III in 1760 when the hereditary revenues were surrendered. The Duchy Council reports to the Chancellor of the Duchy of Lancaster, who is accountable directly to the sovereign rather than to parliament. However the chancellor does answer parliamentary questions on matters relating to the Duchy's responsibilities.

THE DUCHY OF LANCASTER, 1 Lancaster Place, London WC2E 7ED W www.duchyoflancaster.co.uk
Chancellor of the Duchy of Lancaster, Rt. Hon. Lord Hill of Oareford, CBE *apptd* 2013
Chair of the Council, Lord Shuttleworth, KCVO
Chief Executive and Clerk, Nathan Thompson
Receiver-General, Sir Alan Reid, GCVO
Attorney-General, Robert Miles, QC

PERSONAL INCOME

The Queen's personal income derives mostly from investments, and is used to meet private expenditure.

PRINCE OF WALES' FUNDING

The Duchy Estate was created in 1337 by Edward III for his son and heir Prince Edward (the Black Prince) who became the Duke of Cornwall. The Duchy's primary function is to provide an income from its assets for the Prince of Wales. Under a 1337 charter, confirmed by subsequent legislation, the Prince of Wales is not entitled to the proceeds or profit on the sale of Duchy assets but only to the annual income which is generated. The Duchy is responsible for the sustainable and commercial management of its properties, investment portfolio and around 53,154 hectares of land, based mostly in the south-west of England. The Prince of Wales has chosen to use a proportion of his income to meet the cost of his public and charitable work. The Duchy also funds the public, charitable and private activities of the Duchess of Cornwall, the Duke and Duchess of Cambridge and Prince Henry of Wales.

THE DUCHY OF CORNWALL, 10 Buckingham Gate, London SW1E 6LA T 020-7834 7346 W www.duchyofcornwall.org
Lord Warden of the Stannaries, Sir Nicholas Bacon, Bt., OBE
Receiver-General, James Leigh-Pemberton
Attorney-General, Jonathan Crow, QC
Secretary and Keeper of the Records, Alastair Martin

TAXATION

The sovereign is not legally liable to pay income tax or capital gains tax. In 1992 the Queen offered to pay income and capital gains tax on a voluntary basis from 6 April 1993, and the Prince of Wales offered to pay tax on a voluntary basis on his income from the Duchy of Cornwall (he was already taxed in all other respects).

The main provisions for the Queen and the Prince of Wales to pay tax, set out in a Memorandum of Understanding on Royal Taxation presented to parliament on 11 February 1993, are that the Queen will pay income tax and capital gains tax in respect of her private income and assets, and on the proportion of the income and capital gains of the Privy Purse used for private purposes. Inheritance tax will be paid on the Queen's assets, except for those which pass to the next sovereign, whether automatically or by gift or bequest. The Prince of Wales will pay income tax on income from the Duchy of Cornwall used for private purposes.

ROYAL SALUTES

ENGLAND

The basic royal salute is 21 rounds with an extra 20 rounds fired at Hyde Park because it is a royal park. At the Tower of London 62 rounds are fired on royal anniversaries (21 plus a further 20 because the Tower is a royal palace and a further 21 'for the City of London') and 41 on other occasions. When the Queen's official birthday coincides with the Duke of Edinburgh's birthday, 124 rounds are fired from the Tower (62 rounds for each birthday). Gun salutes occur on the following royal anniversaries:

- Accession Day
- The Queen's birthday
- Coronation Day
- Duke of Edinburgh's birthday
- The Queen's Official Birthday
- The Prince of Wales' birthday
- State opening of parliament

Gun salutes also occur when parliament is prorogued by the sovereign, on royal births and when a visiting head of state meets the sovereign in London, Windsor or Edinburgh.

In London, salutes are fired at Hyde Park and the Tower of London although on some occasions (state visits, state opening of parliament and the Queen's birthday parade) Green Park is used instead of Hyde Park. Other military saluting stations in England are at Colchester, Dover, Plymouth, Woolwich and York.

Constable of the Royal Palace and Fortress of London, Gen. Lord Dannatt, GCB, CBE, MC

Lieutenant of the Tower of London, Lt. Gen. Peter Pearson, CB, CBE

Master Gunner of St James's Park, Gen. Sir Timothy Granville-Chapman, GBE, KCB, ADC

Resident Governor and Keeper of the Jewel House, Col. Richard Harrold, OBE

Master Gunner within the Tower, HRH Prince Michael of Kent, GCVO

SCOTLAND

Royal salutes are authorised at Edinburgh Castle and Stirling Castle. A salute of 21 guns is fired on the following occasions:

- the anniversaries of the birth, accession and coronation of the sovereign
- the anniversary of the birth of the Duke of Edinburgh

A salute of 21 guns is fired in Edinburgh on the occasion of the opening of the general assembly of the Church of Scotland. A salute of 21 guns may also be fired in Edinburgh on the arrival of HM The Queen or a member of the royal family who is a Royal Highness on an official visit.

Military saluting stations are also situated at Cardiff Castle in Wales, Hillsborough Castle in Northern Ireland and in Gibraltar.

MILITARY RANKS AND TITLES

THE QUEEN

ARMY

Colonel-in-Chief

The Life Guards; The Blues and Royals (Royal Horse Guards and 1st Dragoons); The Royal Scots Dragoon Guards (Carabiniers and Greys); The Queen's Royal Lancers; Royal Tank Regiment; Corps of Royal Engineers; Grenadier Guards; Coldstream Guards; Scots Guards; Irish Guards; Welsh Guards; The Royal Regiment of Scotland; The Duke of Lancaster's Regiment (King's, Lancashire and Border); The Royal Welsh; Adjutant General's Corps; The Royal Mercian and Lancastrian Yeomanry; The Governor General's Horse Guards (of Canada); The King's Own Calgary Regiment (Royal Canadian Armoured Corps); Canadian Military Engineers Branch; Royal 22e Regiment (of Canada); Governor General's Foot Guards (of Canada); The Canadian Grenadier Guards; Le Régiment de la Chaudière (of Canada); 2nd Battalion Royal New Brunswick Regiment (North Shore); 48th Highlanders of Canada; The Argyll and Sutherland Highlanders of Canada (Princess Louise's); The Calgary Highlanders; Royal Australian Engineers; Royal Australian Infantry Corps; Royal Australian Army Ordnance Corps; Royal Australian Army Nursing Corps; The Corps of Royal New Zealand Engineers; Royal New Zealand Infantry Regiment; The Malawi Rifles; The Royal Malta Artillery

Affiliated Colonel-in-Chief

The Queen's Gurkha Engineers

Captain-General

Royal Regiment of Artillery; The Honourable Artillery Company; Combined Cadet Force; Royal Regiment of Canadian Artillery; Royal Regiment of Australian Artillery; Royal Regiment of New Zealand Artillery; Royal New Zealand Armoured Corps

Royal Colonel

The Argyll and Sutherland Highlanders, 5th Battalion The Royal Regiment of Scotland

Patron

Royal Army Chaplains' Department

ROYAL AIR FORCE

Air Commodore-in-Chief

Royal Auxiliary Air Force; Royal Air Force Regiment; Air Reserve of Canada; Royal Australian Air Force Reserve; Territorial Air Force (of New Zealand)

Commandant-in-Chief

RAF College, Cranwell

Royal Honorary Air Commodore

RAF Marham; 603 (City of Edinburgh) Squadron Royal Auxiliary Air Force

PRINCE PHILIP, DUKE OF EDINBURGH

ROYAL NAVY

Lord High Admiral of the United Kingdom

Admiral of the Fleet

Admiral of the Fleet, Royal Australian Navy

Admiral of the Fleet, Royal New Zealand Navy

Admiral, Royal Canadian Navy

Admiral, Royal Canadian Sea Cadets

ROYAL MARINES

Captain-General

ARMY

Field Marshal

Field Marshal, Australian Military Forces

Field Marshal, New Zealand Army

General, Royal Canadian Army

Colonel-in-Chief

The Queen's Royal Hussars (Queen's Own and Royal Irish); The Rifles; Corps of Royal Electrical and Mechanical Engineers; Intelligence Corps; Army Cadet Force Association; The Royal Canadian Regiment; The Royal Hamilton Light Infantry (Wentworth Regiment of Canada); The Cameron Highlanders of Ottawa; The Queen's Own Cameron Highlanders of Canada; The Seaforth Highlanders of Canada; The Royal Canadian Army Cadets; The Royal Australian Corps of Electrical and Mechanical Engineers; The Australian Army Cadet Corps

Colonel

Grenadier Guards

Royal Colonel

The Highlanders, 4th Battalion The Royal Regiment of Scotland

Honorary Colonel

City of Edinburgh University Officers' Training Corps; The Trinidad and Tobago Regiment

Member

Honourable Artillery Company

ROYAL AIR FORCE

Marshal of the Royal Air Force

Marshal of the Royal Australian Air Force

Marshal of the Royal New Zealand Air Force

General, Royal Canadian Air Force

Air Commodore-in-Chief

Air Training Corps; Royal Canadian Air Cadets

Honorary Air Commodore

RAF Northolt

THE PRINCE OF WALES

ROYAL NAVY

Admiral of the Fleet

Commodore-in-Chief

Royal Naval Command Plymouth

ARMY

Field Marshal

Colonel-in-Chief

The Royal Dragoon Guards; The Parachute Regiment; The Royal Gurkha Rifles; Army Air Corps; The Royal Canadian Dragoons; Lord Strathcona's Horse (Royal Canadians); The Royal Regiment of Canada; Royal Winnipeg Rifles; Royal Australian Armoured Corps; The Royal Pacific Islands Regiment; 1st The Queen's Dragoon Guards; The Black Watch (Royal Highland Regiment) of Canada; The Toronto Scottish Regiment (Queen Elizabeth The Queen Mother's Own); The Mercian Regiment

Royal Colonel

The Black Watch, 3rd Battalion The Royal Regiment of Scotland; 51st Highland, 7th Battalion The Royal Regiment of Scotland (Territorial Army)

Colonel

The Welsh Guards

Royal Honorary Colonel

The Queen's Own Yeomanry

ROYAL AIR FORCE

Marshal of the RAF

Honorary Air Commodore

RAF Valley

Air Commodore-in-Chief

Royal New Zealand Air Force

Colonel-in-Chief

Air Reserve Canada

THE DUCHESS OF CORNWALL

ROYAL NAVY
Commodore-in-Chief
Naval Medical Services; Royal Naval Chaplaincy Services
ARMY
Colonel-in-Chief
Queen's Own Rifles of Canada
Royal Colonel
4th Battalion The Rifles
ROYAL AIR FORCE
Honorary AIr Commodore
RAF Halton; RAF Leeming

THE DUKE OF CAMBRIDGE

ROYAL NAVY
Lieutenant
Commodore-in-Chief
Scotland Command; Submarines Command
ARMY
Colonel
Irish Guards
Captain
The Blues and Royals (Royal Horse Guards and 1st Dragoons)
ROYAL AIR FORCE
Flight Lieutenant
Honorary Air Commandant
RAF Coningsby

PRINCE HENRY OF WALES

ROYAL NAVY
Commodore-in-Chief
Small Ships and Diving Command
ARMY
Captain
The Blues and Royals (Royal Horse Guards and 1st Dragoons)
ROYAL AIR FORCE
Honorary Air Commandant
RAF Honington

THE DUKE OF YORK

ROYAL NAVY
Rear Admiral
Commodore-in-Chief
Fleet Air Arm
Admiral of the Marine Society and Sea Cadets
ARMY
Colonel-in-Chief
The Royal Irish Regiment (27th (Inniskilling), 83rd, 87th and The Ulster Defence Regiment); 9th/12th Royal Lancers (The Prince of Wales's); The Yorkshire Regiment; Small Arms School Corps; The Queen's York Rangers (First Americans); Royal New Zealand Army Logistics Regiment; The Royal Highland Fusiliers of Canada; The Princess Louise Fusiliers (Canada)
Royal Colonel
The Royal Highland Fusiliers, 2nd Battalion The Royal Regiment of Scotland
ROYAL AIR FORCE
Honorary Air Commodore
RAF Lossiemouth

THE EARL OF WESSEX

ROYAL NAVY
Commodore-in-Chief
Royal Fleet Auxiliary
Patron
Royal Fleet Auxiliary Association
ARMY
Colonel-in-Chief
Hastings and Prince Edward Regiment; Saskatchewan Dragoons; Prince Edward Island Regiment
Royal Colonel
2nd Battalion, The Rifles
Royal Honorary Colonel
Royal Wessex Yeomanry; The London Regiment
ROYAL AIR FORCE
Honorary Air Commodore
RAF Waddington

THE COUNTESS OF WESSEX

ARMY
Colonel-in-Chief
Queen Alexandra's Royal Army Nursing Corps; The Lincoln and Welland Regiment; South Alberta Light Horse Regiment
Royal Colonel
5th Battalion, The Rifles
Patron
Corps of Army Music; Queen Alexandra's Royal Army Nursing Corps Association
ROYAL AIR FORCE
Honorary Air Commodore
RAF Wittering
ROYAL NAVY
Sponsor
HMS *Daring*

THE PRINCESS ROYAL

ROYAL NAVY
Admiral (Chief Commandant for Women in the Royal Navy)
Commodore-in-Chief
HM Naval Base Portsmouth
ARMY
Colonel-in-Chief
The King's Royal Hussars; Royal Corps of Signals; Royal Logistic Corps; The Royal Army Veterinary Corps; 8th Canadian Hussars (Princess Louise's); Royal Newfoundland Regiment; Canadian Forces Communications and Electronics Branch; The Grey and Simcoe Foresters (Royal Canadian Armoured Corps); The Royal Regina Rifle Regiment; Canadian Forces Medical Branch; Royal Australian Corps of Signals; Royal Australian Corps of Transport; Royal New Zealand Corps of Signals; Royal New Zealand Nursing Corps
Affiliated Colonel-in-Chief
The Queen's Gurkha Signals; The Queen's Own Gurkha Transport Regiment
Royal Colonel
1st Battalion The Royal Regiment of Scotland; 52nd Lowland, 6th Battalion The Royal Regiment of Scotland
Colonel
The Blues and Royals (Royal Horse Guards and 1st Dragoons)
Honorary Colonel
University of London Officers' Training Corps
Commandant-in-Chief
First Aid Nursing Yeomanry (Princess Royal's Volunteer Corps)
ROYAL AIR FORCE
Honorary Air Commodore
RAF Brize Norton; University of London Air Squadron

THE DUKE OF GLOUCESTER

ARMY
Colonel-in-Chief
The Royal Anglian Regiment; Royal Army Medical Corps; Royal New Zealand Army Medical Corps

Deputy Colonel-in-Chief
The Royal Logistic Corps
Royal Colonel
6th Battalion, The Rifles
Honorary Royal Colonel
Royal Monmouthshire Royal Engineers (Militia)
ROYAL AIR FORCE
Honorary Air Marshal
Honorary Air Commodore
RAF Odiham; No. 501 (County of Gloucester) Squadron Royal Auxiliary Air Force

THE DUCHESS OF GLOUCESTER
ARMY
Colonel-in-Chief
Royal Army Dental Corps; Royal Australian Army Educational Corps; Royal New Zealand Army Educational Corps; Canadian Forces Dental Services; The Bermuda Regiment
Deputy Colonel-in-Chief
Adjutant-General's Corps
Royal Colonel
7th Battalion, The Rifles
Vice-Patron
Adjutant General's Corps Regimental Association
Patron
Royal Army Educational Corps Association; Army Families Federation

THE DUKE OF KENT
ARMY
Field Marshal
Colonel-in-Chief
The Royal Regiment of Fusiliers; Lorne Scots (Peel, Dufferin and Hamilton Regiment)
Deputy Colonel-in-Chief
The Royal Scots Dragoon Guards (Carabiniers and Greys)
Royal Colonel
1st Battalion The Rifles
Colonel
Scots Guards
ROYAL AIR FORCE
Honorary Air Chief Marshal
Honorary Air Commodore
RAF Leuchars

THE DUCHESS OF KENT
ARMY
Deputy Colonel-in-Chief
The Royal Dragoon Guards; Adjutant-General's Corps; The Royal Logistic Corps

PRINCE MICHAEL OF KENT
ROYAL NAVY
Honorary Rear Admiral of the Royal Naval Reserves
Commodore-in-Chief of the Maritime Reserves
ARMY
Colonel-in-Chief
Essex and Kent Scottish Regiment (Ontario)
Royal Honorary Colonel
Honourable Artillery Company
Senior Colonel
King's Royal Hussars
ROYAL AIR FORCE
Honorary Air Marshal
RAF Benson

PRINCESS ALEXANDRA, THE HON. LADY OGILVY
ROYAL NAVY
Patron
Queen Alexandra's Royal Naval Nursing Service
ARMY
Colonel-in-Chief
The Canadian Scottish Regiment (Princess Mary's)
Deputy Colonel-in-Chief
The Queen's Royal Lancers
Royal Colonel
3rd Battalion The Rifles
Royal Honorary Colonel
The Royal Yeomanry
ROYAL AIR FORCE
Patron and Air Chief Commandant
Princess Mary's RAF Nursing Service

KINGS AND QUEENS

ENGLISH KINGS AND QUEENS 927 TO 1603

HOUSES OF CERDIC AND DENMARK

Reign

927–939 **ÆTHELSTAN** Son of Edward the Elder, by Ecgwynn, and grandson of Alfred *acceded* to Wessex and Mercia *c.*924, established direct rule over Northumbria 927, effectively creating the Kingdom of England *reigned* 15 years

939–946 **EDMUND I** *born* 921, son of Edward the Elder, by Eadgifu *married* (1) Ælfgifu (2) Æthelflæd *killed* aged 25 *reigned* 6 years

946–955 **EADRED** Son of Edward the Elder, by Eadgifu *reigned* 9 years

955–959 **EADWIG** *born* before 943, son of Edmund and Ælfgifu *married* Ælfgifu *reigned* 3 years

959–975 **EDGAR I** *born* 943, son of Edmund and Ælfgifu *married* (1) Æthelflæd (2) Wulfthryth (3) Ælfthryth *died* aged 32 *reigned* 15 years

975–978 **EDWARD I (the Martyr)** *born c.*962, son of Edgar and Æthelflæd *assassinated* aged *c.*16 *reigned* 2 years

978–1016 **ÆTHELRED (the Unready)** *born* 968/9, son of Edgar and Ælfthryth *married* (1) Ælfgifu (2) Emma, daughter of Richard I, Count of Normandy, 1013–14 dispossessed of kingdom by Swegn Forkbeard (King of Denmark 987–1014) *died* aged *c.*47, *reigned* 38 years

1016 (Apr–Nov) **EDMUND II (Ironside)** *born* before 993, son of Æthelred and Ælfgifu *married* Ealdgyth died aged over 23 *reigned* 7 months

1016–1035 **CNUT (Canute)** *born c.*995, son of Swegn Forkbeard, King of Denmark, and Gunhild *married* (1) Ælfgifu (2) Emma, widow of Æthelred the Unready. Gained submission of West Saxons 1015, Northumbrians 1016, Mercia 1016, King of all England after Edmund's death, King of Denmark 1019–35, King of Norway 1028–35 *died* aged *c.*40 *reigned* 19 years

1035–1040 **HAROLD I (Harefoot)** *born* 1016/17, son of Cnut and Ælfgifu *married* Ælfgifu 1035 recognised as regent for himself and his brother Harthacnut; 1037 recognised as king *died* aged *c.*23 *reigned* 4 years

1040–1042 **HARTHACNUT (Harthacanute)** *born c.*1018, son of Cnut and Emma. Titular king of Denmark from 1028, acknowledged King of England 1035–7 with Harold I as regent; effective king after Harold's death *died* aged *c.*24 *reigned* 2 years

1042–1066 **EDWARD II (the Confessor)** *born* between 1002 and 1005, son of Æthelred the Unready and Emma *married* Eadgyth, daughter of Godwine, Earl of Wessex *died* aged over 60 *reigned* 23 years

1066 (Jan–Oct) **HAROLD II (Godwinesson)** *born c.*1020, son of Godwine, Earl of Wessex, and Gytha *married* (1) Eadgyth (2) Ealdgyth *killed* in battle aged *c.*46 *reigned* 10 months

THE HOUSE OF NORMANDY

1066–1087 **WILLIAM I (the Conqueror)** *born* 1027/8, son of Robert I, Duke of Normandy; obtained the Crown by conquest *married* Matilda, daughter of Baldwin, Count of Flanders *died* aged *c.*60, *reigned* 20 years

1087–1100 **WILLIAM II (Rufus)** *born* between 1056 and 1060, third son of William I; succeeded his father in England only *killed* aged *c.*40 *reigned* 12 years

1100–1135 **HENRY I (Beauclerk)** *born* 1068, fourth son of William I *married* (1) Edith or Matilda, daughter of Malcolm III of Scotland (2) Adela, daughter of Godfrey, Count of Louvain *died* aged 67 *reigned* 35 years

1135–1154 **STEPHEN** *born* not later than 1100, third son of Adela, daughter of William I, and Stephen, Count of Blois *married* Matilda, daughter of Eustace, Count of Boulogne. Feb–Nov 1141 held captive by adherents of Matilda, daughter of Henry I, who contested the Crown until 1153 *died* aged over 53 *reigned* 18 years

THE HOUSE OF ANJOU (PLANTAGENETS)

1154–1189 **HENRY II (Curtmantle)** *born* 1133, son of Matilda, daughter of Henry I, and Geoffrey, Count of Anjou *married* Eleanor, daughter of William, Duke of Aquitaine, and divorced queen of Louis VII of France *died* aged 56 *reigned* 34 years

1189–1199 **RICHARD I (Coeur de Lion)** *born* 1157, third son of Henry II *married* Berengaria, daughter of Sancho VI, King of Navarre *died* aged 42 *reigned* 9 years

1199–1216 **JOHN (Lackland)** *born* 1167, fifth son of Henry II *married* (1) Isabella or Avisa, daughter of William, Earl of Gloucester (divorced) (2) Isabella, daughter of Aymer, Count of Angoulême *died* aged 48 *reigned* 17 years

1216–1272 **HENRY III** *born* 1207, son of John and Isabella of Angoulême *married* Eleanor, daughter of Raymond, Count of Provence *died* aged 65 *reigned* 56 years

1272–1307 **EDWARD I (Longshanks)** *born* 1239, eldest son of Henry III *married* (1) Eleanor, daughter of Ferdinand III, King of Castile (2) Margaret, daughter of Philip III of France *died* aged 68 *reigned* 34 years

1307–1327 **EDWARD II** *born* 1284, eldest surviving son of Edward I and Eleanor *married* Isabella, daughter of Philip IV of France *deposed* Jan 1327 *killed* Sep 1327 aged 43 *reigned* 19 years

1327–1377 **EDWARD III** *born* 1312, eldest son of Edward II *married* Philippa, daughter of William, Count of Hainault *died* aged 64 *reigned* 50 years

1377–1399 **RICHARD II** *born* 1367, son of Edward (the Black Prince), eldest son of Edward III *married* (1) Anne, daughter of Emperor Charles IV (2) Isabelle, daughter of Charles VI of France *deposed* Sep 1399 *killed* Feb 1400 aged 33 *reigned* 22 years

THE HOUSE OF LANCASTER

1399–1413 **HENRY IV** *born* 1366, son of John of Gaunt, fourth son of Edward III, and Blanche, daughter of Henry, Duke of Lancaster *married* (1) Mary, daughter of Humphrey, Earl of Hereford (2) Joan, daughter of Charles, King of Navarre, and widow of John, Duke of Brittany *died* aged *c.*47 *reigned* 13 years

1413–1422 **HENRY V** *born* 1387, eldest surviving son of Henry IV and Mary *married* Catherine, daughter of Charles VI of France *died* aged 34 *reigned* 9 years

1422–1471 **HENRY VI** *born* 1421, son of Henry V *married* Margaret, daughter of René, Duke of Anjou and Count of Provence *deposed* Mar 1461 *restored* Oct 1470 *deposed* Apr 1471 *killed* May 1471 aged 49 *reigned* 39 years

THE HOUSE OF YORK

1461–1483 **EDWARD IV** *born* 1442, eldest son of Richard of York (grandson of Edmund, fifth son of Edward III; and son of Anne, great-granddaughter of Lionel, third son of Edward III) *married* Elizabeth Woodville, daughter of Richard, Lord Rivers, and widow of Sir John Grey *acceded* Mar 1461 *deposed* Oct 1470 *restored* Apr 1471 *died* aged 40 *reigned* 21 years

1483 (Apr–Jun) **EDWARD V** *born* 1470, eldest son of Edward IV *deposed* Jun 1483, *died* probably Jul–Sep 1483, aged 12 *reigned* 2 months

1483–1485 **RICHARD III** *born* 1452, fourth son of Richard of York *married* Anne Neville, daughter of Richard, Earl of Warwick, and widow of Edward, Prince of Wales, son of Henry VI *killed* in battle aged 32 *reigned* 2 years

THE HOUSE OF TUDOR

1485–1509 **HENRY VII** *born* 1457, son of Margaret Beaufort (great-granddaughter of John of Gaunt, fourth son of Edward III) and Edmund Tudor, Earl of Richmond *married* Elizabeth, daughter of Edward IV *died* aged 52 *reigned* 23 years

1509–1547 **HENRY VIII** *born* 1491, second son of Henry VII *married* (1) Catherine, daughter of Ferdinand II, King of Aragon, and widow of his elder brother Arthur (divorced) (2) Anne, daughter of Sir Thomas Boleyn (executed) (3) Jane, daughter of Sir John Seymour (died in childbirth) (4) Anne, daughter of John, Duke of Cleves (divorced) (5) Catherine Howard, niece of the Duke of Norfolk (executed) (6) Catherine, daughter of Sir Thomas Parr and widow of Lord Latimer *died* aged 55 *reigned* 37 years

1547–1553 **EDWARD VI** *born* 1537, son of Henry VIII and Jane Seymour *died* aged 15 *reigned* 6 years

1553 *(6/10–19 Jul) **JANE** *born* 1537, daughter of Frances (daughter of Mary Tudor, the younger daughter of Henry VII) and Henry Grey, Duke of Suffolk *married* Lord Guildford Dudley, son of the Duke of Northumberland *deposed* Jul 1553 *executed* Feb 1554 aged 16 *reigned* 13/9 days

1553–1558 **MARY I** *born* 1516, daughter of Henry VIII and Catherine of Aragon *married* Philip II of Spain *died* aged 42 *reigned* 5 years

1558–1603 **ELIZABETH I** *born* 1533, daughter of Henry VIII and Anne Boleyn *died* aged 69 *reigned* 44 years

* Depending on whether the date of her predecessor's death (6 July) or that of her official proclamation as Queen (10 July) is taken as the beginning of her reign

BRITISH KINGS AND QUEENS SINCE 1603

THE HOUSE OF STUART

Reign

1603–1625 **JAMES I (VI OF SCOTLAND)** *born* 1566, son of Mary, Queen of Scots (granddaughter of Margaret Tudor, elder daughter of Henry VII), and Henry Stewart, Lord Darnley *married* Anne, daughter of Frederick II of Denmark *died* aged 58 *reigned* 22 years

1625–1649 **CHARLES I** *born* 1600, second son of James I *married* Henrietta Maria, daughter of Henry IV of France *executed* 1649 aged 48 *reigned* 23 years

INTERREGNUM 1649–1660

1649–1653 Government by a council of state

1653–1658 Oliver Cromwell, Lord Protector

1658–1659 Richard Cromwell, Lord Protector

Reign

1660–1685 **CHARLES II** *born* 1630, eldest son of Charles I *married* Catherine, daughter of John IV of Portugal *died* aged 54 *reigned* 24 years

1685–1688 **JAMES II (VII OF SCOTLAND)** *born* 1633, second son of Charles I *married* (1) Lady Anne Hyde, daughter of Edward, Earl of Clarendon (2) Mary, daughter of Alphonso, Duke of Modena reign ended with flight from kingdom Dec 1688 *died* 1701 aged 67 *reigned* 3 years

INTERREGNUM

11 Dec 1688 to 12 Feb 1689

Reign

1689–1702 **WILLIAM III** *born* 1650, son of William II, Prince of Orange, and Mary Stuart, daughter of Charles I *married* Mary, elder daughter of James II *died* aged 51 *reigned* 13 years

and

1689–1694 **MARY II** *born* 1662, elder daughter of James II and Anne *died* aged 32 *reigned* 5 years

1702–1714 **ANNE** *born* 1665, younger daughter of James II and Anne *married* Prince George of Denmark, son of Frederick III of Denmark *died* aged 49 *reigned* 12 years

THE HOUSE OF HANOVER

1714–1727 **GEORGE I (Elector of Hanover)** *born* 1660, son of Sophia (daughter of Frederick, Elector Palatine, and Elizabeth Stuart, daughter of James I) and Ernest Augustus, Elector of Hanover *married* Sophia Dorothea, daughter of George William, Duke of Lüneburg-Celle *died* aged 67 *reigned* 12 years

1727–1760 **GEORGE II** *born* 1683, son of George I *married* Caroline, daughter of John Frederick, Margrave of Brandenburg-Anspach *died* aged 76 *reigned* 33 years

1760–1820 **GEORGE III** *born* 1738, son of Frederick, eldest son of George II *married* Charlotte, daughter of Charles Louis, Duke of Mecklenburg-Strelitz *died* aged 81 *reigned* 59 years

REGENCY 1811–1820
Prince of Wales regent owing to the insanity of George III

Reign

1820–1830 **GEORGE IV** *born* 1762, eldest son of George III *married* Caroline, daughter of Charles, Duke of Brunswick-Wolfenbüttel *died* aged 67 *reigned* 10 years

1830–1837 **WILLIAM IV** *born* 1765, third son of George III *married* Adelaide, daughter of George, Duke of Saxe-Meiningen *died* aged 71 *reigned* 7 years

1837–1901 **VICTORIA** *born* 1819, daughter of Edward, fourth son of George III *married* Prince Albert of Saxe-Coburg and Gotha *died* aged 81 *reigned* 63 years

THE HOUSE OF SAXE-COBURG AND GOTHA

1901–1910 **EDWARD VII** *born* 1841, eldest son of Victoria and Albert *married* Alexandra, daughter of Christian IX of Denmark *died* aged 68 *reigned* 9 years

THE HOUSE OF WINDSOR

1910–1936 **GEORGE V** *born* 1865, second son of Edward VII *married* Victoria Mary, daughter of Francis, Duke of Teck *died* aged 70 *reigned* 25 years

1936 (20 Jan–11 Dec) **EDWARD VIII** *born* 1894, eldest son of George V *married* (1937) Mrs Wallis Simpson *abdicated* 1936 *died* 1972 aged 77 *reigned* 10 months

1936–1952 **GEORGE VI** *born* 1895, second son of George V *married* Lady Elizabeth Bowes-Lyon, daughter of 14th Earl of Strathmore and Kinghorne *died* aged 56 *reigned* 15 years

1952– **ELIZABETH II** *born* 1926, elder daughter of George VI *married* Philip, son of Prince Andrew of Greece

KINGS AND QUEENS OF SCOTS 1016 TO 1603

Reign

1016–1034 **MALCOLM II** *born c.*954, son of Kenneth II *acceded* to Alba 1005, secured Lothian *c.*1016, obtained Strathclyde for his grandson Duncan *c.*1016, thus reigning over an area approximately the same as that governed by later rulers of Scotland *died* aged *c.*80 *reigned* 18 years

THE HOUSE OF ATHOLL

1034–1040 **DUNCAN I** son of Bethoc, daughter of Malcolm II, and Crinan, Mormaer of Atholl *married* a cousin of Siward, Earl of Northumbria *reigned* 5 years

1040–1057 **MACBETH** *born c.*1005, son of a daughter of Malcolm II and Finlaec, Mormaer of Moray *married* Gruoch, granddaughter of Kenneth III *killed* aged *c.*52 *reigned* 17 years

1057–1058 (Aug–Mar) **LULACH** *born c.*1032, son of Gillacomgan, Mormaer of Moray, and Gruoch (and stepson of Macbeth) *died* aged *c.*26 *reigned* 7 months

1058–1093 **MALCOLM III (Canmore)** *born c.*1031, elder son of Duncan I *married* (1) Ingibiorg (2) Margaret (St Margaret), granddaughter of Edmund II of England *killed* in battle aged *c.*62 *reigned* 35 years

1093–1097 **DONALD III BÁN** *born c.*1033, second son of Duncan I *deposed* May 1094 *restored* Nov 1094 *deposed* Oct 1097 *reigned* 3 years

1094 (May–Nov) **DUNCAN II** *born c.*1060, elder son of Malcolm III and Ingibiorg *married* Octreda of Dunbar *killed* aged *c.*34 *reigned* 6 months

1097–1107 **EDGAR** *born c.*1074, second son of Malcolm III and Margaret *died* aged *c.*32 *reigned* 9 years

1107–1124 **ALEXANDER I (the Fierce)** *born c.*1077, fifth son of Malcolm III and Margaret *married* Sybilla, illegitimate daughter of Henry I of England *died* aged *c.*47 *reigned* 17 years

1124–1153 **DAVID I (the Saint)** *born c.*1085, sixth son of Malcolm III and Margaret *married* Matilda, daughter of Waltheof, Earl of Huntingdon *died* aged *c.*68 *reigned* 29 years

1153–1165 **MALCOLM IV (the Maiden)** *born c.*1141, son of Henry, Earl of Huntingdon, second son of David I *died* aged *c.*24 *reigned* 12 years

1165–1214 **WILLIAM I (the Lion)** *born c.*1142, brother of Malcolm IV *married* Ermengarde, daughter of Richard, Viscount of Beaumont *died* aged *c.*72 *reigned* 49 years

1214–1249 **ALEXANDER II** *born* 1198, son of William I *married* (1) Joan, daughter of John, King of England (2) Marie, daughter of Ingelram de Coucy *died* aged 50 *reigned* 34 years

1249–1286 **ALEXANDER III** *born* 1241, son of Alexander II and Marie *married* (1) Margaret, daughter of Henry III of England (2) Yolande, daughter of the Count of Dreux *killed* accidentally aged 44 *reigned* 36 years

1286–1290 **MARGARET (the Maid of Norway)** *born* 1283, daughter of Margaret (daughter of Alexander III) and Eric II of Norway *died* aged 7 *reigned* 4 years

FIRST INTERREGNUM 1290–1292
Throne disputed by 13 competitors. Crown awarded to John Balliol by adjudication of Edward I of England

THE HOUSE OF BALLIOL

Reign

1292–1296 **JOHN (Balliol)** *born c.*1250, son of Dervorguilla, great-great-granddaughter of David I, and John de Balliol *married* Isabella, daughter of John, Earl of Surrey *abdicated* 1296 *died* 1313 aged *c.*63 *reigned* 3 years

SECOND INTERREGNUM 1296–1306
Edward I of England declared John Balliol to have forfeited the throne for contumacy in 1296 and took the government of Scotland into his own hands

THE HOUSE OF BRUCE

Reign

1306–1329 **ROBERT I (Bruce)** *born* 1274, son of Robert Bruce and Marjorie, Countess of Carrick, and great-grandson of the second daughter of David, Earl of Huntingdon, brother of William I *married* (1) Isabella, daughter of Donald, Earl of Mar (2) Elizabeth, daughter of Richard, Earl of Ulster *died* aged 54 *reigned* 23 years

1329–1371 **DAVID II** *born* 1324, son of Robert I and Elizabeth *married* (1) Joanna, daughter of Edward II of England (2) Margaret Drummond, widow of Sir John Logie (divorced) *died* aged 46 *reigned* 41 years
1332 (Sep–Dec) Edward Balliol, son of John Balliol
1333–1336 Edward Balliol

THE HOUSE OF STEWART

1371–1390 **ROBERT II (Stewart)** *born* 1316, son of Marjorie (daughter of Robert I) and Walter, High Steward of Scotland *married* (1) Elizabeth, daughter of Sir Robert Mure of Rowallan (2) Euphemia, daughter of Hugh, Earl of Ross *died* aged 74 *reigned* 19 years

1390–1406 **ROBERT III** *born c.*1337, son of Robert II and Elizabeth *married* Annabella, daughter of Sir John Drummond of Stobhall *died* aged *c.*69 *reigned* 16 years

1406–1437 **JAMES I** *born* 1394, son of Robert III *married* Joan Beaufort, daughter of John, Earl of Somerset *assassinated* aged 42 *reigned* 30 years

1437–1460 **JAMES II** *born* 1430, son of James I *married* Mary, daughter of Arnold, Duke of Gueldres *killed* accidentally aged 29 *reigned* 23 years

1460–1488 **JAMES III** *born* 1452, son of James II *married* Margaret, daughter of Christian I of Denmark *assassinated* aged 36 *reigned* 27 years

1488–1513 **JAMES IV** *born* 1473, son of James III *married* Margaret Tudor, daughter of Henry VII of England *killed* in battle aged 40 *reigned* 25 years

1513–1542 **JAMES V** *born* 1512, son of James IV *married* (1) Madeleine, daughter of Francis I of France (2) Mary of Lorraine, daughter of the Duc de Guise *died* aged 30 *reigned* 29 years

1542–1567 **MARY** *born* 1542, daughter of James V and Mary *married* (1) the Dauphin, afterwards Francis II of France (2) Henry Stewart, Lord Darnley (3) James Hepburn, Earl of Bothwell *abdicated* 1567, prisoner in England from 1568, *executed* 1587 *reigned* 24 years

1567–1625 **JAMES VI (and I of England)** *born* 1566, son of Mary, Queen of Scots, and Henry, Lord Darnley *acceded* 1567 to the Scottish throne *reigned* 58 years *succeeded* 1603 to the English throne, so joining the English and Scottish crowns in one person. The two kingdoms remained distinct until 1707 when the parliaments of the kingdoms became conjoined

WELSH SOVEREIGNS AND PRINCES

Wales was ruled by sovereign princes from the earliest times until the death of Llywelyn in 1282. The first English Prince of Wales was the son of Edward I, who was born in Caernarvon town on 25 April 1284. According to a discredited legend, he was presented to the Welsh chieftains as their prince, in fulfilment of a promise that they should have a prince who 'could not speak a word of English' and should be native born. This son, who afterwards became Edward II, was created 'Prince of Wales and Earl of Chester' at the Lincoln Parliament on 7 February 1301.

The title Prince of Wales is borne after individual conferment and is not inherited at birth, though some Princes have been declared and styled Prince of Wales but never formally so created (*s.*). The title was conferred on Prince Charles by the Queen on 26 July 1958. He was invested at Caernarvon on 1 July 1969.

INDEPENDENT PRINCES AD 844 TO 1282

844–878 Rhodri the Great
878–916 Anarawd, son of Rhodri
916–950 Hywel Dda, the Good
950–979 Iago ab Idwal (or Ieuaf)
979–985 Hywel ab Ieuaf, the Bad
985–986 Cadwallon, his brother
986–999 Maredudd ab Owain ap Hywel Dda
999–1005 Cynan ap Hywel ab Ieuaf
1005–1018 Aeddan ap Blegywryd
1018–1023 Llywelyn ap Seisyll
1023–1039 Iago ab Idwal ap Meurig
1039–1063 Gruffydd ap Llywelyn ap Seisyll
1063–1075 Bleddyn ap Cynfyn
1075–1081 Trahaern ap Caradog
1081–1137 Gruffydd ap Cynan ab Iago
1137–1170 Owain Gwynedd
1170–1194 Dafydd ab Owain Gwynedd
1194–1240 Llywelyn Fawr, the Great
1240–1246 Dafydd ap Llywelyn
1246–1282 Llywelyn ap Gruffydd ap Llywelyn

ENGLISH PRINCES SINCE 1301

1301 Edward (Edward II)
1343 Edward the Black Prince, son of Edward III
1376 Richard (Richard II), son of the Black Prince
1399 Henry of Monmouth (Henry V)
1454 Edward of Westminster, son of Henry VI
1471 Edward of Westminster (Edward V)
1483 Edward, son of Richard III (*d.* 1484)
1489 Arthur Tudor, son of Henry VII
1504 Henry Tudor (Henry VIII)
1610 Henry Stuart, son of James I (*d.* 1612)
1616 Charles Stuart (Charles I)
*c.*1638 (*s.*) Charles Stuart (Charles II)
1688 (*s.*) James Francis Edward Stuart (The Old Pretender), son of James II (*d.* 1766)
1714 George Augustus (George II)
1729 Frederick Lewis, son of George II (*d.* 1751)
1751 George William Frederick (George III)
1762 George Augustus Frederick (George IV)
1841 Albert Edward (Edward VII)
1901 George (George V)
1910 Edward (Edward VIII)
1958 Charles, son of Elizabeth II

PRINCESSES ROYAL

The style Princess Royal is conferred at the sovereign's discretion on his or her eldest daughter. It is an honorary title, held for life, and cannot be inherited or passed on. It was first conferred on Princess Mary, daughter of Charles I, in approximately 1642.

*c.*1642 Princess Mary (1631–60), daughter of Charles I
1727 Princess Anne (1709–59), daughter of George II
1766 Princess Charlotte (1766–1828), daughter of George III
1840 Princess Victoria (1840–1901), daughter of Victoria
1905 Princess Louise (1867–1931), daughter of Edward VII
1932 Princess Mary (1897–1965), daughter of George V
1987 Princess Anne (*b.* 1950), daughter of Elizabeth II

THE HOUSE OF WINDSOR

King George V assumed by royal proclamation (17 July 1917) for his House and family, as well as for all descendants in the male line of Queen Victoria who are subjects of these realms, the name of Windsor.

KING GEORGE V
(George Frederick Ernest Albert), second son of King Edward VII *born* 3 June 1865 *married* 6 July 1893 HSH Princess Victoria Mary Augusta Louise Olga Pauline Claudine Agnes of Teck (Queen Mary *born* 26 May 1867 *died* 24 March 1953) *succeeded* to the throne 6 May 1910 *died* 20 January 1936. *Issue*

1. HRH PRINCE EDWARD Albert Christian George Andrew Patrick David *born* 23 June 1894 *succeeded* to the throne as King Edward VIII, 20 January 1936 *abdicated* 11 December 1936 *created* Duke of Windsor 1937 *married* 3 June 1937 Mrs Wallis Simpson (Her Grace The Duchess of Windsor *born* 19 June 1896 *died* 24 April 1986) *died* 28 May 1972

2. HRH PRINCE ALBERT Frederick Arthur George *born* 14 December 1895 *created* Duke of York 1920 *married* 26 April 1923 Lady Elizabeth Bowes-Lyon, youngest daughter of the 14th Earl of Strathmore and Kinghorne (HM Queen Elizabeth the Queen Mother *born* 4 August 1900 *died* 30 March 2002) *succeeded* to the throne as King George VI, 11 December 1936 *died* 6 February 1952. *Issue*
- (1) HRH Princess Elizabeth Alexandra Mary *succeeded* to the throne as Queen Elizabeth II, 6 February 1952 (*see* Royal Family)
- (2) HRH Princess Margaret Rose (later HRH The Princess Margaret, Countess of Snowdon) *born* 21 August 1930 *married* 6 May 1960 Anthony Charles Robert Armstrong-Jones, GCVO *created* Earl of Snowdon 1961 (marriage dissolved 1978) *died* 9 February 2002, having had issue (*see* Royal Family)

3. HRH PRINCESS (Victoria Alexandra Alice) MARY *born* 25 April 1897 *created* Princess Royal 1932 *married* 28 February 1922 Viscount Lascelles, later the 6th Earl of Harewood (1882–1947) *died* 28 March 1965. *Issue*
- (1) George Henry Hubert Lascelles, 7th Earl of Harewood, KBE *born* 7 February 1923 *married* (1) 1949 Maria (Marion) Stein (marriage dissolved 1967) *died* 11 July 2011 *issue (a)* David Henry George, 8th Earl of Harewood *born* 1950 *(b)* James Edward *born* 1953 *(c)* (Robert) Jeremy Hugh *born* 1955 (2) 1967 Patricia Tuckwell *issue (d)* Mark Hubert *born* 1964
- (2) Gerald David Lascelles *born* 21 August 1924 *married* (1) 1952 Angela Dowding (marriage dissolved 1978) *died* 27 February 1998 *issue (a)* Henry Ulick *born* 1953 (2) 1978 Elizabeth Collingwood (Elizabeth Colvin) *issue (b)* Martin David *born* 1962

4. HRH PRINCE HENRY William Frederick Albert *born* 31 March 1900 *created* Duke of Gloucester, Earl of Ulster and Baron Culloden 1928 *married* 6 November 1935 Lady Alice Christabel Montagu-Douglas-Scott, daughter of the 7th Duke of Buccleuch and Queensberry (HRH Princess Alice, Duchess of Gloucester *born* 25 December 1901 *died* 29 October 2004) *died* 10 June 1974. *Issue*
- (1) HRH Prince William Henry Andrew Frederick *born* 18 December 1941 accidentally *killed* 28 August 1972
- (2) HRH Prince Richard Alexander Walter George (HRH The Duke of Gloucester, *see* Royal Family)

5. HRH PRINCE GEORGE Edward Alexander Edmund *born* 20 December 1902 *created* Duke of Kent, Earl of St Andrews and Baron Downpatrick 1934 *married* 29 November 1934 HRH Princess Marina of Greece and Denmark (*born* 30 November 1906 *died* 27 August 1968) *killed* on active service 25 August 1942. *Issue*
- (1) HRH Prince Edward George Nicholas Paul Patrick (HRH The Duke of Kent, *see* Royal Family)
- (2) HRH Princess Alexandra Helen Elizabeth Olga Christabel (HRH Princess Alexandra, the Hon. Lady Ogilvy, *see* Royal Family)
- (3) HRH Prince Michael George Charles Franklin (HRH Prince Michael of Kent, *see* Royal Family)

6. HRH PRINCE JOHN Charles Francis *born* 12 July 1905 *died* 18 January 1919

DESCENDANTS OF QUEEN VICTORIA

I. HRH Princess Victoria Adelaide Mary Louisa, Princess Royal (1840–1901) *m* Friedrich III (1831–88), later German Emperor

1. HIM Wilhelm II (1859–1941), later German Emperor *m* (1) Princess Augusta Victoria of Schleswig-Holstein-Sonderburg-Augustenburg (1858–1921) (2) Princess Hermine of Reuss (1887–1947). *Issue* Wilhelm (1882–1951); Eitel-Friedrich (1883–1942); Adalbert (1884–1948); August Wilhelm (1887–1949); Oskar (1888–1958); Joachim (1890–1920); Viktoria Luise (1892–1980)

2. Charlotte (1860–1919) *m* Bernhard, Duke of Saxe-Meiningen (1851–1928). *Issue* Feodora (1879–1945)

3. Heinrich (1862–1929) *m* Princess Irene of Hesse (*see* III.3). *Issue* Waldemar (1889–1945); Sigismund (1896–1978); Heinrich (1900–4)

4. Sigismund (1864–6)

5. Victoria (1866–1929) *m* (1) Prince Adolf of Schaumburg-Lippe (1859–1916) (2) Alexander Zubkov (1900–36)

6. Waldemar (1868–79)

7. Sophie (1870–1932) *m* Constantine I (1868–1923), later King of the Hellenes. *Issue* George II (1890–1947); Alexander I (1893–1920); Helena (1896–1982); Paul I (1901–64); Irene (1904–74); Katherine (1913–2007)

8. Margarethe (1872–1954) *m* Prince Friedrich Karl of Hesse (1868–1940). *Issue* Friedrich Wilhelm (1893–1916); Maximilian (1894–1914); Philipp (1896–1980); Wolfgang (1896–1989); Richard (1901–69); Christoph (1901–43)

II. HRH Prince Albert Edward (HM KING EDWARD VII) (1841–1910) *succeeded* 22 Jan 1901 *m* HRH Princess Alexandra of Denmark (1844–1925)

1. Albert Victor, Duke of Clarence and Avondale (1864–92)

2. George (HM KING GEORGE V) (1865–1936) (*see* House of Windsor)

3. Louise (1867–1931), later Princess Royal *m* 1st Duke of Fife (1849–1912). *Issue* Alexandra (1891–1959); Maud (1893–1945)

4. Victoria (1868–1935)

5. Maud (1869–1938) *m* Prince Carl of Denmark (1872–1957), later King Haakon VII of Norway. *Issue* Olav V (1903–91)

6. Alexander (6–7 Apr 1871)

III. HRH Princess Alice Maud Mary (1843–78) *m* Prince Ludwig (1837–92), later Grand Duke of Hesse

1. Victoria (1863–1950) *m* Prince Louis of Battenberg (1854–1921), later 1st Marquess of Milford Haven. *Issue* Alice (1885–1969); Louise (1889–1965); George (1892–1938); Louis (1900–79)

2. Elizabeth (1864–1918) *m* Grand Duke Sergius of Russia (1857–1905)

3. Irene (1866–1953) *m* Prince Heinrich of Prussia (*see* I.3)

4. Ernst Ludwig (1868–1937), Grand Duke of Hesse, *m* (1) Princess Victoria Melita of Saxe-Coburg (see IV.3) (2) Princess Eleonore of Solms-Hohensolms-Lich (1871–1937). *Issue* Elizabeth (1895–1903); George (1906–37); Ludwig (1908–68)

5. Frederick William (1870–3)

6. Alix (Tsaritsa of Russia) (1872–1918) *m* Nicholas II, Tsar of All the Russias (1868–1918). *Issue* Olga (1895–1918); Tatiana (1897–1918); Marie (1899–1918); Anastasia (1901–18); Alexis (1904–18)

7. Marie (1874–8)

IV. HRH Prince Alfred Ernest Albert, Duke of Edinburgh (1844–1900) *succeeded* as Duke of Saxe-Coburg and Gotha 1893 *m* Grand Duchess Marie Alexandrovna of Russia (1853–1920)

QUEEN VICTORIA (Alexandrina Victoria) (1819–1901) *succeeded* 20 Jun 1837 *m* (Francis) Albert Augustus Charles Emmanuel, Duke of Saxony, Prince of Saxe-Coburg and Gotha (HRH Albert, Prince Consort) (1819–61)

VI. HRH Princess Louise Caroline Alberta (1848–1939) *m* Marquess of Lorne (1845–1914), later 9th Duke of Argyll

VII. HRH Prince Arthur William Patrick Albert, Duke of Connaught (1850–1942) *m* Princess Louisa of Prussia (1860–1917)

1. Margaret (1882–1920) *m* Crown Prince Gustaf Adolf (1882–1973), later King of Sweden. *Issue* Gustaf Adolf (1906–47); Sigvard (1907–2002); Ingrid (1910–2000); Bertil (1912–97); Count Carl Bernadotte (1916–2012)

2. Arthur (1883–1938) *m* HH Duchess of Fife (1891–1959). *Issue* Alastair Arthur (1914–43)

3. (Victoria) Patricia (1886–1974) *m* Adm. Hon. Sir Alexander Ramsay (1881–1972). *Issue* Alexander (1919–2000)

VIII. HRH Prince Leopold George Duncan Albert, Duke of Albany (1853–84) *m* Princess Helena of Waldeck (1861–1922)

1. Alice (1883–1981) *m* Prince Alexander of Teck (1874–1957), later 1st Earl of Athlone. *Issue* May (1906–94); Rupert (1907–28); Maurice (Mar–Sep 1910)

2. Charles Edward (1884–1954), Duke of Albany until title suspended 1917, Duke of Saxe-Coburg-Gotha *m* Princess Victoria Adelheid of Schleswig-Holstein-Sonderburg-Glücksburg (1885–1970). *Issue* Johann Leopold (1906–72); Sibylla (1908–72); Dietmar Hubertus (1909–43); Caroline (1912–83); Friedrich Josias (1918–98)

IX. HRH Princess Beatrice Mary Victoria Feodore (1857–1944) *m* Prince Henry of Battenberg (1858–96)

1. Alexander, 1st Marquess of Carisbrooke (1886–1960) *m* Lady Irene Denison (1890–1956). *Issue* Iris (1920–82)

2. Victoria Eugénie (1887–1969) *m* Alfonso XIII, King of Spain (1886–1941). *Issue* Alfonso (1907–38); Jaime (1908–75); Beatriz (1909–2002); Maria (1911–96); Juan (1913–93); Gonzalo (1914–34)

3. Maj. Lord Leopold Mountbatten (1889–1922)

4. Maurice (1891–1914)

1. Alfred, Prince of Saxe-Coburg (1874–99)

2. Marie (1875–1938) *m* Ferdinand (1865–1927), later King of Roumania. *Issue* Carol II (1893–1953); Elisabeth (1894–1956); Marie (1900–61); Nicolas (1903–78); Ileana (1909–91); Mircea (1913–16)

3. Victoria Melita (1876–1936) *m* (1) Grand Duke Ernst Ludwig of Hesse (*see* III.4) (2) Grand Duke Kirill of Russia (1876–1938). *Issue* Marie (1907–51); Kira (1909–67); Vladimir (1917–92)

4. Alexandra (1878–1942) *m* Ernst, Prince of Hohenlohe Langenburg (1863–1950). *Issue* Gottfried (1897–1960); Maria (1899–1967); Alexandra (1901–63); Irma (1902–86)

5. Beatrice (1884–1966) *m* Alfonso of Orleans, Infante of Spain (1886–1975). *Issue* Alvaro (1910–97); Alonso (1912–36); Ataulfo (1913–74)

V. HRH Princess Helena Augusta Victoria (1846–1923) *m* Prince Christian of Schleswig-Holstein-Sonderburg-Augustenburg (1831–1917)

1. Christian Victor (1867–1900)

2. Albert (1869–1931), later Duke of Schleswig-Holstein

3. Helena (1870–1948)

4. Marie Louise (1872–1956), *m* Prince Aribert of Anhalt (1864–1933)

5. Harold (12–20 May 1876)

PRECEDENCE

ENGLAND AND WALES

The Sovereign
The Prince Philip, Duke of Edinburgh
The Prince of Wales
The Sovereign's younger sons
The Sovereign's grandsons
The Sovereign's cousins
Archbishop of Canterbury
Lord High Chancellor
Archbishop of York
The Prime Minister
Lord President of the Council
Speaker of the House of Commons
Speaker of the House of Lords
President of the Supreme Court
Lord Chief Justice of England and Wales
Lord Privy Seal
Ambassadors and High Commissioners
Lord Great Chamberlain
Earl Marshal
Lord Steward of the Household
Lord Chamberlain of the Household
Master of the Horse
Dukes, according to their patent of creation:
1. of England
2. of Scotland
3. of Great Britain
4. of Ireland
5. those created since the Union
Eldest sons of Dukes of the Blood Royal
Ministers, Envoys, and other important overseas visitors
Marquesses, according to their patent of creation:
1. of England
2. of Scotland
3. of Great Britain
4. of Ireland
5. those created since the Union
Dukes' eldest sons
Earls, according to their patent of creation:
1. of England
2. of Scotland
3. of Great Britain
4. of Ireland
5. those created since the Union
Younger sons of Dukes of Blood Royal
Marquesses' eldest sons
Dukes' younger sons
Viscounts, according to their patent of creation:
1. of England
2. of Scotland
3. of Great Britain
4. of Ireland
5. those created since the Union
Earls' eldest sons
Marquesses' younger sons
Bishop of London
Bishop of Durham
Bishop of Winchester
Other English Diocesan Bishops, according to seniority of consecration
Retired Church of England Diocesan Bishops, according to seniority of consecration
Suffragan Bishops, according to seniority of consecration
Secretaries of State, if of the degree of a Baron
Barons, according to their patent of creation:
1. of England
2. of Scotland (Lords of Parliament)
3. of Great Britain
4. of Ireland
5. those created since the Union, including Life Barons
Master of the Rolls
Deputy President of the Supreme Court
Justices of the Supreme Court, according to seniority of appointment
Treasurer of the Household
Comptroller of the Household
Vice-Chamberlain of the Household
Secretaries of State under the degree of Baron
Viscounts' eldest sons
Earls' younger sons
Barons' eldest sons
Knights of the Garter
Privy Counsellors
Chancellor of the Order of the Garter
Chancellor of the Exchequer
Chancellor of the Duchy of Lancaster
President of the Queen's Bench Division
President of the Family Division
Chancellor of the High Court
Lord Justices of Appeal, according to seniority of appointment
Judges of the High Court, according to seniority of appointment
Viscounts' younger sons
Barons' younger sons
Sons of Life Peers
Baronets, according to date of patent
Knights of the Thistle
Knights Grand Cross of the Bath
Knights Grand Cross of St Michael and St George
Knights Grand Cross of the Royal Victorian Order
Knights Grand Cross of the British Empire
Knights Commanders of the Bath
Knights Commanders of St Michael and St George
Knights Commanders of the Royal Victorian Order
Knights Commanders of the British Empire
Knights Bachelor
Circuit Judges, according to priority and order of their respective appointments
Master of the Court of Protection
Companions of the Bath
Companions of St Michael and St George
Commanders of the Royal Victorian Order
Commanders of the British Empire
Companions of the Distinguished Service Order
Lieutenants of the Royal Victorian Order
Officers of the British Empire
Companions of the Imperial Service Order
Eldest sons of younger sons of peers
Baronets' eldest sons
Eldest sons of knights, in the same order as their fathers
Members of the Royal Victorian Order
Members of the British Empire
Baronets' younger sons
Knights' younger sons, in the same order as their fathers
Esquires
Gentlemen

WOMEN

Women take the same rank as their husbands or as their brothers; but the daughter of a peer marrying a commoner retains her title as Lady or Honourable. Daughters of peers rank next immediately after the wives of their elder brothers, and before their younger brothers' wives. Daughters of peers marrying peers of a lower degree take the same order of precedence as that of their husbands; thus the daughter of a Duke marrying a Baron becomes of the rank of Baroness only, while her sisters married to commoners retain their rank and take precedence over the Baroness. Merely official rank on the husband's part does not give any similar precedence to the wife.

Peeresses in their own right take the same precedence as peers of the same rank, ie from their date of creation.

SCOTLAND

The Sovereign
The Prince Philip, Duke of Edinburgh
The Lord High Commissioner to the General Assembly of the Church of Scotland (while that assembly is sitting)
The Duke of Rothesay (eldest son of the Sovereign)
The Sovereign's younger sons
The Sovereign's grandsons
The Sovereign's nephews
Lord-Lieutenants
Lord Provosts, during their term of office*
Sheriffs Principal, during their term of office and within the bounds of their respective sheriffdoms
Lord Chancellor of Great Britain
Moderator of the General Assembly of the Church of Scotland
Keeper of the Great Seal of Scotland (the First Minister)
Presiding Officer
The Secretary of State for Scotland
Hereditary High Constable of Scotland
Hereditary Master of the Household in Scotland
Dukes, as in England
Eldest sons of Dukes of the Blood Royal
Marquesses, as in England
Dukes' eldest sons
Earls, as in England
Younger sons of Dukes of Blood Royal
Marquesses' eldest sons
Dukes' younger sons
Lord Justice General
Lord Clerk Register
Lord Advocate
The Advocate General
Lord Justice Clerk
Viscounts, as in England
Earls' eldest sons
Marquesses' younger sons
Lords of Parliament or Barons, as in England
Eldest sons of Viscounts
Earls' younger sons
Eldest sons of Lords of Parliament or Barons
Knights and Ladies of the Garter
Knights and Ladies of the Thistle
Privy Counsellors
Senators of the College of Justice (Lords of Session)
Viscounts' younger sons
Younger sons of Lords of Parliament or Barons
Baronets
Knights and Dames Grand Cross and Knights and Dames Grand Commanders of orders, as in England
Knights and Dames Commanders of orders, as in England
Solicitor-General for Scotland
Lord Lyon King of Arms
Sheriffs Principal, when not within own county
Knights Bachelor
Sheriffs
Companions of Orders, as in England
Commanders of the Royal Victorian Order
Commanders of the British Empire
Lieutenants of the Royal Victorian Order
Companions of the Distinguished Service Order
Officers of the British Empire
Companions of the Imperial Service Order
Eldest sons of younger sons of peers
Eldest sons of baronets
Eldest sons of knights, as in England
Members of the Royal Victorian Order
Members of the British Empire
Baronets' younger sons
Knights' younger sons
Queen's Counsel
Esquires
Gentlemen

* The Lord Provosts of Aberdeen, Dundee, Edinburgh and Glasgow are Lord-Lieutenants for these cities *ex officio* and take precedence as such

THE PEERAGE

ABBREVIATIONS AND SYMBOLS

S.	Scottish title	*c.p.*	civil partnership
I.	Irish title	*w.*	widower or widow
**	hereditary peer remaining in the House of Lords	M.	minor
°	there is no 'of' in the title	†	heir not ascertained at time of going to press
b.	born	F_	represents forename
s.	succeeded	S_	represents surname
m.	married	cr.	created
§	life peer disqualified from sitting in the House of Lords as a member of the judiciary	¶	life peer who has resigned permanently from the House of Lords

The rules which govern the creation and succession of peerages are extremely complicated. There are, technically, five separate peerages, the Peerage of England, of Scotland, of Ireland, of Great Britain, and of the United Kingdom. The Peerage of Great Britain dates from 1707 when an Act of Union combined the two kingdoms of England and Scotland and separate peerages were discontinued. The Peerage of the United Kingdom dates from 1801 when Great Britain and Ireland were combined under an Act of Union. Some Scottish peers have received additional peerages of Great Britain or of the UK since 1707, and some Irish peers additional peerages of the UK since 1801.

The Peerage of Ireland was not entirely discontinued from 1801 but holders of Irish peerages, whether pre-dating or created subsequent to the Union of 1801, were not entitled to sit in the House of Lords if they had no additional English, Scottish, Great Britain or UK peerage. However, they are eligible for election to the House of Commons and to vote in parliamentary elections. An Irish peer holding a peerage of a lower grade which enabled him to sit in the House of Lords was introduced there by the title which enabled him to sit, though for all other purposes he was known by his higher title.

In the Peerage of Scotland there is no rank of Baron; the equivalent rank is Lord of Parliament, abbreviated to 'Lord' (the female equivalent is 'Lady').

All peers of England, Scotland, Great Britain or the UK who are 21 years or over, and of British, Irish or Commonwealth nationality were entitled to sit in the House of Lords until the House of Lords Act 1999, when hereditary peers lost the right to sit. However, section two of the act provided an exception for 90 hereditary peers plus the holders of the office of Earl Marshal and Lord Great Chamberlain to remain as members of the House of Lords for their lifetime or pending further reform. Of the 90 hereditary peers, 75 were elected by the hereditary peers in their political party, or Crossbench grouping, and the remaining 15 by the whole house. Until 7 November 2002 any vacancy arising due to the death of one of the 90 excepted hereditary peers was filled by the runner-up to the original election. From 7 November 2002 any vacancy due to a death has been filled by holding a by-election. By-elections are conducted in accordance with arrangements made by the Clerk of the Parliaments and have to take place within three months of a vacancy occurring. If the vacancy is among the 75, only the excepted hereditary peers in the relevant party or Crossbench grouping are entitled to vote. If the vacancy is among the other 15, the whole house is entitled to vote.

In the list below, peers currently holding one of the 92 hereditary places in the House of Lords are indicated by **.

HEREDITARY WOMEN PEERS

Most hereditary peerages pass on death to the nearest male heir, but there are exceptions, and several are held by women.

A woman peer in her own right retains her title after marriage, and if her husband's rank is the superior she is designated by the two titles jointly, the inferior one second. Her hereditary claim still holds good in spite of any marriage whether higher or lower. No rank held by a woman can confer any title or even precedence upon her husband but the rank of a hereditary woman peer in her own right is inherited by her eldest son (or in some cases daughter).

After the Peerage Act 1963, hereditary women peers in their own right were entitled to sit in the House of Lords, subject to the same qualifications as men, until the House of Lords Act 1999.

LIFE PEERS

From 1876 to 2009 non-hereditary or life peerages were conferred on certain eminent judges to enable the judicial functions of the House of Lords to be carried out. These lords were known as Lords of Appeal in Ordinary or law lords. The judicial role of the House of Lords as the highest appeal court in the UK ended on 30 July 2009 and since 1 October 2009, under the Constitutional Reform Act 2005, any peer who holds a senior judicial office is disqualified from sitting in the House of Lords until they retire from that office. In the list of life peerages which follows, members of the judiciary who are currently disqualified from sitting and voting in the House of Lords until retirement, are marked by a '§'.

Under the Constitutional Reform and Governance Act 2010, five peers permanently resigned from the House of Lords. These are indicated in the following list by a '¶'.

Since 1958 life peerages have been conferred upon distinguished men and women from all walks of life, giving them seats in the House of Lords in the degree of Baron or Baroness. They are addressed in the same way as hereditary lords and barons, and their children have similar courtesy titles.

PEERAGES EXTINCT SINCE THE LAST EDITION

BARONY: Balfour of Inchrye (cr. 1945)

LIFE PEERAGES: Campbell of Alloway (cr. 1981); Chitnis (cr. 1977); Fraser of Carmyllie (cr. 1989); Gilbert (cr. 1997); King of West Bromwich (cr. 1999); Lofthouse of Pontefract (cr. 1997); McCarthy (cr. 1975); Northfield (cr. 1975); Rees-Mogg (cr. 1988); Thatcher (cr. 1992)

DISCLAIMER OF PEERAGES

The Peerage Act 1963 enables peers to disclaim their peerages for life. Peers alive in 1963 could disclaim within twelve months after the passing of the act (31 July 1963); a person subsequently succeeding to a peerage may disclaim within 12 months (one month if an MP) after the date of succession, or of reaching 21, if later. The disclaimer is irrevocable but does not affect the descent of the peerage after the disclaimant's death, and children of a disclaimed peer may, if they wish, retain their precedence and any courtesy titles and styles borne as children of a peer. The disclaimer permitted the disclaimant to sit in the House of Commons if elected as an MP. As the House of Lords Act 1999 removed hereditary peers from the House of Lords, they are now entitled to sit in the House of Commons without having to disclaim their titles.

The following peerages are currently disclaimed:

EARLDOM: Selkirk (1994)
VISCOUNTCY: Stansgate (1963)
BARONIES: Merthyr (1977); Reith (1972); Sanderson of Ayot (1971); Silkin (2002)
PEERS WHO ARE MINORS (ie under 21 years of age)
VISCOUNT: Selby (*b.* 1993)
BARONS: Glenconner (*b.* 1994); Hawke (*b.* 1995); Rodney (*b.* 1999)

FORMS OF ADDRESS

Forms of address are given under the style for each individual rank of the peerage. Both formal and social forms of address are given where usage differs; nowadays, the social form is generally preferred to the formal, which increasingly is used only for official documents and on very formal occasions.

ROLL OF THE PEERAGE

Crown Office, House of Lords, London SW1A 0PW

The Roll of the Peerage is kept at the Crown Office and maintained by the Registrar and Assistant Registrar of the Peerage in accordance with the terms of a 2004 royal warrant. The roll records the names of all living life peers and hereditary peers who have proved their succession to the satisfaction of the Lord Chancellor. The Roll of the Peerage is maintained in addition to the Clerk of the Parliaments' register of hereditary peers eligible to stand for election in House of Lords' by-elections.

A person whose name is not entered on the Roll of Peerage can not be addressed or mentioned by the title of a peer in any official document.

Registrar, Ian Denyer, MVO
Assistant Registrar, Grant Bavister

HEREDITARY PEERS

as at 31 August 2013

PEERS OF THE BLOOD ROYAL

Style, His Royal Highness the Duke of _/His Royal Highness the Earl of_/His Royal Highness the Lord_
Style of address (*formal*) May it please your Royal Highness; (*informal*) Sir

Created	*Title, order of succession, name, etc*	*Heir*
	Dukes	
1947	*Edinburgh (1st)*, HRH the Prince Philip, Duke of Edinburgh	The Prince of Wales *
1337	*Cornwall*, HRH the Prince of Wales, *s.* 1952	‡
1398 S.	*Rothesay*, HRH the Prince of Wales, *s.* 1952	‡
2011	*Cambridge (1st)*, HRH Prince William of Wales	HRH Prince George of Cambridge
1986	*York (1st)*, Prince Andrew, HRH the Duke of York	None
1928	*Gloucester (2nd)*, Prince Richard, HRH the Duke of Gloucester, *s.* 1974	Earl of Ulster
1934	*Kent (2nd)*, Prince Edward, HRH the Duke of Kent, *s.* 1942	Earl of St Andrews
	Earl	
1999	*Wessex (1st)*, Prince Edward, HRH the Earl of Wesex	Viscount Severn

* In June 1999 Buckingham Palace announced that the current Earl of Wessex will be granted the Dukedom of Edinburgh when the title reverts to the Crown. The title will only revert to the Crown on both the death of the current Duke of Edinburgh and the Prince of Wales' succession as king

‡ The title is held by the sovereign's eldest son from the moment of his birth or the sovereign's accession

DUKES

Coronet, Eight strawberry leaves

Style, His Grace the Duke of _
Envelope (formal), His Grace the Duke of _; *(social),* The Duke of _. *Letter (formal),* My Lord Duke; *(social),* Dear Duke.
Spoken (formal), Your Grace; *(social),* Duke
Wife's style, Her Grace the Duchess of _
Envelope (formal), Her Grace the Duchess of _; *(social),* The Duchess of _. *Letter (formal),* Dear Madam; *(social),* Dear Duchess. *Spoken,* Duchess
Eldest son's style, Takes his father's second title as a courtesy title (*see* Courtesy Titles)
Younger sons' style, 'Lord' before forename (F_) and surname (S_)
Envelope, Lord F_ S_. *Letter (formal),* My Lord; *(social),* Dear Lord F_. *Spoken (formal),* My Lord; *(social),* Lord F_
Daughters' style, 'Lady' before forename (F_) and surname (S_)
Envelope, Lady F_ S_. *Letter (formal),* Dear Madam; *(social),* Dear Lady F_. *Spoken,* Lady F_

Created		*Title, order of succession, name, etc*	*Heir*
1868 I.		*Abercorn (5th),* James Hamilton, KG, *b.* 1934, *s.* 1979, *m.*	Marquess of Hamilton, *b.* 1969
1701 S.		*Argyll (13th),* Torquhil Ian Campbell, *b.* 1968, *s.* 2001	Marquess of Lorne, *b.* 2004
1703 S.		*Atholl (12th),* Bruce George Ronald Murray, *b.* 1960, *s.* 2012, *m.*	Marquis of Tullibardine, *b.* 1985
1682		*Beaufort (11th),* David Robert Somerset, *b.* 1928, *s.* 1984, *m.*	Marquess of Worcester, *b.* 1952
1694		*Bedford (15th),* Andrew Ian Henry Russell, *b.* 1962, *s.* 2003, *m.*	Marquess of Tavistock, *b.* 2005
1663 S.		*Buccleuch (10th) and Queensberry (12th) (S. 1684),* Richard Walter John Montagu Douglas Scott, KBE, *b.* 1954, *s.* 2007, *m.*	Earl of Dalkeith, *b.* 1984
1694		*Devonshire (12th),* Peregrine Andrew Morny Cavendish, KCVO, CBE, *b.* 1944, *s.* 2004, *m.*	Earl of Burlington, *b.* 1969
1900		*Fife (3rd),* James George Alexander Bannerman Carnegie, *b.* 1929, *s.* 1959	Earl of Southesk, *b.* 1961
1675		*Grafton (12th),* Henry Oliver Charles FitzRoy, *b.* 1978, *s.* 2011, *m.*	Earl of Euston, *b.* 2012
1643 S.		*Hamilton (16th) and Brandon (13th) (1711),* Alexander Douglas Douglas-Hamilton, *b.* 1978, *s.* 2010 *Premier Peer of Scotland*	Marquess of Douglas and Clydesdale, *b.* 2012
1766 I.		*Leinster (9th),* Maurice FitzGerald, *b.* 1948, *s.* 2004, *m. Premier Duke, Marquess and Earl of Ireland*	Lord John F., *b.* 1952
1719		*Manchester (13th),* Alexander Charles David Drogo Montagu, *b.* 1962, *s.* 2002, *m.*	Lord Kimble W. D. M., *b.* 1964
1702		*Marlborough (11th),* John George Vanderbilt Henry Spencer-Churchill, *b.* 1926, *s.* 1972, *m.*	Marquess of Blandford, *b.* 1955
1707 S.	**	*Montrose (8th),* James Graham, *b.* 1935, *s.* 1992, *m.*	Marquis of Graham, *b.* 1973
1483	**	*Norfolk (18th),* Edward Wiliam Fitzalan-Howard, *b.* 1956, *s.* 2002, *m. Premier Duke and Earl Marshal*	Earl of Arundel and Surrey, *b.* 1987
1766		*Northumberland (12th),* Ralph George Algernon Percy, *b.* 1956, *s.* 1995, *m.*	Earl Percy, *b.* 1984
1675		*Richmond (10th) and Gordon (5th) (1876),* Charles Henry Gordon Lennox, *b.* 1929, *s.* 1989, *m.*	Earl of March and Kinrara, *b.* 1955
1707 S.		*Roxburghe (10th),* Guy David Innes-Ker, *b.* 1954, *s.* 1974, *m. Premier Baronet of Scotland*	Marquis of Bowmont and Cessford, *b.* 1981
1703		*Rutland (11th),* David Charles Robert Manners, *b.* 1959, *s.* 1999, *m.*	Marquess of Granby, *b.*1999
1684		*St Albans (14th),* Murray de Vere Beauclerk, *b.* 1939, *s.* 1988, *m.*	Earl of Burford, *b.* 1965
1547		*Somerset (19th),* John Michael Edward Seymour, *b.* 1952, *s.* 1984, *m.*	Lord Seymour, *b.* 1982
1833		*Sutherland (7th),* Francis Ronald Egerton, *b.* 1940, *s.* 2000, *m.*	Marquess of Stafford, *b.* 1975
1814		*Wellington (8th),* Arthur Valerian Wellesley, KG, LVO, OBE, MC, *b.* 1915, *s.* 1972, *w.*	Marquess of Douro, *b.* 1945
1874		*Westminster (6th),* Gerald Cavendish Grosvenor, KG, CB, CVO, OBE, TD, *b.* 1951, *s.* 1979, *m.*	Earl Grosvenor, *b.* 1991

MARQUESSES

Coronet, Four strawberry leaves alternating with four silver balls

Style, The Most Hon. the Marquess (of) _ . In Scotland the spelling 'Marquis' is preferred for pre-Union creations

Envelope (formal), The Most Hon. the Marquess of _; *(social),* The Marquess of _. *Letter (formal),* My Lord; *(social),* Dear Lord _. *Spoken (formal),* My Lord; *(social),* Lord _

Wife's style, The Most Hon. the Marchioness (of) _

Envelope (formal), The Most Hon. the Marchioness of _; *(social),* The Marchioness of _. *Letter (formal),* Madam; *(social),* Dear Lady _. *Spoken,* Lady _

Eldest son's style, Takes his father's second title as a courtesy title (*see* Courtesy Titles)

Younger sons' style, 'Lord' before forename and surname, as for Duke's younger sons

Daughters' style, 'Lady' before forename and surname, as for Duke's daughter

Created	*Title, order of succession, name, etc*	*Heir*
1916	*Aberdeen and Temair (7th),* Alexander George Gordon, *b.* 1955, *s.* 2002, *m.*	Earl of Haddo, *b.* 1983
1876	*Abergavenny (6th),* Christopher George Charles Nevill, *b.* 1955, *s.* 2000, *m.*	To Earldom only, David M. R. N., *b.* 1941
1821	*Ailesbury (8th),* Michael Sidney Cedric Brudenell-Bruce, *b.* 1926, *s.* 1974	Earl of Cardigan, *b.* 1952
1831	*Ailsa (8th),* Archibald Angus Charles Kennedy, *b.* 1956, *s.* 1994	Lord David T. K., *b.* 1958
1815	*Anglesey (8th),* Charles Alexander Vaughan Paget, *b.* 1950, *s.* 2013, *m.*	Earl of Uxbridge, *b.* 1986
1789	*Bath (7th),* Alexander George Thynn, *b.* 1932, *s.* 1992, *m.*	Viscount Weymouth, *b.* 1974
1826	*Bristol (8th),* Frederick William Augustus Hervey, *b.* 1979, *s.* 1999	Timothy H. H., *b.* 1960
1796	*Bute (7th),* John Colum Crichton-Stuart, *b.* 1958, *s.* 1993, *m.*	Earl of Dumfries, *b.* 1989
1812	° *Camden (6th),* David George Edward Henry Pratt, *b.* 1930, *s.* 1983	Earl of Brecknock, *b.* 1965
1815	** *Cholmondeley (7th),* David George Philip Cholmondeley, KCVO, *b.* 1960, *s.* 1990, *m. Lord Great Chamberlain*	Earl of Rocksavage, *b.* 2010
1816 I.	° *Conyngham (8th),* Henry Vivian Pierpoint Conyngham, *b.* 1951, *s.* 2009, *m.*	Earl of Mount Charles, *b.* 1975
1791 I.	*Donegall (8th),* Arthur Patrick Chichester, *b.* 1952, *s.* 2007, *m.*	Earl of Belfast, *b.* 1990
1789 I.	*Downshire (9th),* (Arthur Francis) Nicholas Wills Hill, *b.* 1959, *s.* 2003, *m.*	Earl of Hillsborough, *b.* 1996
1801 I.	*Ely (9th),* Charles John Tottenham, *b.* 1943, *s.* 2006, *m.*	Lord Timothy C. T., *b.* 1948
1801	*Exeter (8th),* (William) Michael Anthony Cecil, *b.* 1935, *s.* 1988, *m.*	Lord Burghley, *b.* 1970
1800 I.	*Headfort (7th),* Thomas Michael Ronald Christopher Taylour, *b.* 1959, *s.* 2005, *m.*	Earl of Bective, *b.* 1989
1793	*Hertford (9th),* Henry Jocelyn Seymour, *b.* 1958, *s.* 1997, *m.*	Earl of Yarmouth, *b.* 1993
1599 S.	*Huntly (13th),* Granville Charles Gomer Gordon, *b.* 1944, *s.* 1987, *m.* *Premier Marquess of Scotland*	Earl of Aboyne, *b.* 1973
1784	*Lansdowne (9th),* Charles Maurice Mercer Nairne Petty-Fitzmaurice, LVO *b.* 1941, *s.* 1999, *m.*	Earl of Kerry, *b.* 1970
1902	*Linlithgow (4th),* Adrian John Charles Hope, *b.* 1946, *s.* 1987, *m.*	Earl of Hopetoun, *b.* 1969
1816 I.	*Londonderry (10th),* Frederick Aubrey Vane-Tempest-Stewart, *b.* 1972, *s.* 2012	Lord Reginald A. V-T-S, *b.* 1977
1701 S.	*Lothian (13th) and Baron Kerr of Monteviot (life peerage, 2010),* Michael Andrew Foster Jude Kerr (Michael Ancram), PC, QC, *b.* 1945, *s.* 2004, *m.*	Lord Ralph W. F. J. K., *b.* 1957
1917	*Milford Haven (4th),* George Ivar Louis Mountbatten, *b.* 1961, *s.* 1970, *m.*	Earl of Medina, *b.* 1991
1838	*Normanby (5th),* Constantine Edmund Walter Phipps, *b.* 1954, *s.* 1994, *m.*	Earl of Mulgrave, *b.* 1994
1812	*Northampton (7th),* Spencer Douglas David Compton, *b.* 1946, *s.* 1978, *m.*	Earl Compton, *b.* 1973
1682 S.	*Queensberry (12th),* David Harrington Angus Douglas, *b.* 1929, *s.* 1954	Viscount Drumlanrig, *b.* 1967
1926	*Reading (4th),* Simon Charles Henry Rufus Isaacs, *b.* 1942, *s.* 1980, *m.*	Viscount Erleigh, *b.* 1986
1789	*Salisbury (7th) and Baron Gascoyne-Cecil (life peerage, 1999),* Robert Michael James Gascoyne-Cecil, KCVO, PC, *b.* 1946, *s.* 2003, *m.*	Viscount Cranborne, *b.* 1970
1800 I.	*Sligo (11th),* Jeremy Ulick Browne, *b.* 1939, *s.* 1991, *m.*	Sebastian U. B., *b.* 1964
1787	° *Townshend (8th),* Charles George Townshend, *b.* 1945, *s.* 2010, *m.*	Viscount Raynham, *b.* 1977
1694 S.	*Tweeddale (14th),* Charles David Montagu Hay, *b.* 1947, *s.* 2005	(Lord) Alistair J. M. H., *b.* 1955
1789 I.	*Waterford (8th),* John Hubert de la Poer Beresford, *b.* 1933, *s.* 1934, *m.*	Earl of Tyrone, *b.* 1958
1551	*Winchester (18th),* Nigel George Paulet, *b.* 1941, *s.* 1968, *m.* *Premier Marquess of England*	Earl of Wiltshire, *b.* 1969
1892	*Zetland (4th),* Lawrence Mark Dundas, *b.* 1937, *s.* 1989, *m.*	Earl of Ronaldshay, *b.* 1965

EARLS

Coronet, Eight silver balls on stalks alternating with eight gold strawberry leaves

Style, The Rt. Hon. the Earl (of) _
Envelope (formal), The Rt. Hon. the Earl (of) _; *(social)*, The Earl (of) _. *Letter (formal)*, My Lord; *(social)*, Dear Lord _. *Spoken (formal)*, My Lord; *(social)*, Lord _.
Wife's style, The Rt. Hon. the Countess (of) _
Envelope (formal), The Rt. Hon. the Countess (of) _; *(social)*, The Countess (of) _. *Letter (formal)*, Madam; *(social)*, Lady _. *Spoken (formal)*, Madam; *(social)*, Lady _.
Eldest son's style, Takes his father's second title as a courtesy title (*see* Courtesy Titles)
Younger sons' style, 'The Hon.' before forename and surname, as for Baron's children
Daughters' style, 'Lady' before forename and surname, as for Duke's daughter

Created		*Title, order of succession, name, etc*	*Heir*
1639 S.		*Airlie (13th)*, David George Coke Patrick Ogilvy, KT, GCVO, PC, Royal Victorian Chain, *b.* 1926, *s.* 1968, *m.*	Lord Ogilvy, *b.* 1958
1696		*Albemarle (10th)*, Rufus Arnold Alexis Keppel, *b.* 1965, *s.* 1979, *m.*	Viscount Bury, *b.* 2003
1952	°	*Alexander of Tunis (2nd)*, Shane William Desmond Alexander, *b.* 1935, *s.* 1969, *m.*	Hon. Brian J. A., *b.* 1939
1662 S.		*Annandale and Hartfell (11th)*, Patrick Andrew Wentworth Hope Johnstone, *b.* 1941, *s.* 1983, *m.* claim established 1985	Lord Johnstone, *b.* 1971
1789 I.	°	*Annesley (12th)*, Michael Robert Annesley, *b.* 1933, *s.* 2011, *m.*	Viscount Glerawly, *b.* 1957
1785 I.		*Antrim (9th)*, Alexander Randal Mark McDonnell, *b.* 1935, *s.* 1977, *m.*	Viscount Dunluce, *b.* 1967
1762 I.	**	*Arran (9th)*, Arthur Desmond Colquhoun Gore, *b.* 1938, *s.* 1983, *m.*	William H. G., *b.* 1950 (to the Earldom)
1955	° **	*Attlee (3rd)*, John Richard Attlee, *b.* 1956, *s.* 1991, *m.*	None
1714		*Aylesford (12th)*, Charles Heneage Finch-Knightley, *b.* 1947, *s.* 2008, *m.*	Lord Guernsey, *b.* 1985
1937	**	*Baldwin of Bewdley (4th)*, Edward Alfred Alexander Baldwin, *b.* 1938, *s.* 1976, *w.*	Viscount Corvedale, *b.* 1973
1922		*Balfour (5th)*, Roderick Francis Arthur Balfour, *b.* 1948, *s.* 2003, *m.*	Charles G. Y. B., *b.* 1951
1772	°	*Bathurst (9th)*, Allen Christopher Bertram Bathurst, *b.* 1961, *s.* 2011, *m.*	Lord Apsley, *b.* 1990
1919	°	*Beatty (3rd)*, David Beatty, *b.* 1946, *s.* 1972, *m.*	Viscount Borodale, *b.* 1973
1797 I.	°	*Belmore (8th)*, John Armar Lowry-Corry, *b.* 1951, *s.* 1960, *m.*	Viscount Corry, *b.* 1985
1739 I.		*Bessborough (12th)*, Myles Fitzhugh Longfield Ponsonby, *b.* 1941, *s.* 2002, *m.*	Viscount Duncannon, *b.* 1974
1815		*Bradford (7th)*, Richard Thomas Orlando Bridgeman, *b.* 1947, *s.* 1981, *m.*	Viscount Newport, *b.* 1980
1469 S.		*Buchan (17th)*, Malcolm Harry Erskine, *b.* 1930, *s.* 1984, *m.*	Lord Cardross, *b.* 1960
1746		*Buckinghamshire (10th)*, (George) Miles Hobart-Hampden, *b.* 1944, *s.* 1983, *m.*	Sir John V. Hobart, Bt., *b.* 1945
1800	°	*Cadogan (8th)*, Charles Gerald John Cadogan, KBE, *b.* 1937, *s.* 1997, *m.*	Viscount Chelsea, *b.* 1966
1878	°	*Cairns (6th)*, Simon Dallas Cairns, CVO, CBE, *b.* 1939, *s.* 1989, *m.*	Viscount Garmoyle, *b.* 1965
1455 S.	**	*Caithness (20th)*, Malcolm Ian Sinclair, PC, *b.* 1948, *s.* 1965, *w.*	Lord Berriedale, *b.* 1981
1800 I.		*Caledon (7th)*, Nicholas James Alexander, *b.* 1955, *s.* 1980, *m.*	Viscount Alexander, *b.* 1990
1661		*Carlisle (13th)*, George William Beaumont Howard, *b.* 1949, *s.* 1994	Hon. Philip C. W. H., *b.* 1963
1793		*Carnarvon (8th)*, George Reginald Oliver Molyneux Herbert, *b.* 1956, *s.* 2001, *m.*	Lord Porchester, *b.* 1992
1748 I.		*Carrick (11th)*, Arion Thomas Piers Hamilton Butler, *b.* 1975, *s.* 2008	Hon. Piers E. T. L. B., *b.* 1979
1800 I.	°	*Castle Stewart (8th)*, Arthur Patrick Avondale Stuart, *b.* 1928, *s.* 1961, *m.*	Viscount Stuart, *b.* 1953
1814	°**	*Cathcart (7th)*, Charles Alan Andrew Cathcart, *b.* 1952, *s.* 1999, *m.*	Lord Greenock, *b.* 1986
1647 I.		*Cavan*, The 12th Earl died in 1988.	†Roger C. Lambart, *b.* 1944
1827	°	*Cawdor (7th)*, Colin Robert Vaughan Campbell, *b.* 1962, *s.* 1993, *m.*	Viscount Emlyn, *b.* 1998
1801		*Chichester (9th)*, John Nicholas Pelham, *b.* 1944, *s.* 1944, *m.*	Richard A. H. P., *b.* 1952
1803 I.	**	*Clancarty (9th)*, Nicholas Power Richard Le Poer Trench, *b.* 1952, *s.* 1995, *m.*	None
1776 I.		*Clanwilliam (8th)*, Patrick James Meade, *b.* 1960, *s.* 2009, *m.*	Lord Gillford, *b.* 1998
1776		*Clarendon (8th)*, George Edward Laurence Villiers, *b.* 1976, *s.* 2009, *m.*	Lord Hyde, *b.* 2008
1620 I.		*Cork and Orrery (15th)*, John Richard Boyle, *b.* 1945, *s.* 2003, *m.*	Viscount Dungarvan, *b.* 1978
1850		*Cottenham (9th)*, Mark John Henry Pepys, *b.* 1983, *s.* 2000	Hon. Sam R. P., *b.* 1986
1762 I.	**	*Courtown (9th)*, James Patrick Montagu Burgoyne Winthrop Stopford, *b.* 1954, *s.* 1975, *m.*	Viscount Stopford, *b.* 1988
1697		*Coventry (13th)*, George William Coventry, *b.* 1939, *s.* 2004, *m.*	David D. S. C., *b.* 1973
1857	°	*Cowley (7th)*, Garret Graham Wellesley, *b.* 1934, *s.* 1975, *m.*	Viscount Dangan, *b.* 1965
1892		*Cranbrook (5th)*, Gathorne Gathorne-Hardy, *b.* 1933, *s.* 1978, *m.*	Lord Medway, *b.* 1968

1801	*Craven (9th),* Benjamin Robert Joseph Craven, *b.* 1989, *s.* 1990	Rupert J. E. C., *b.* 1926
1398 S.	*Crawford (29th) and Balcarres (12th) (S. 1651) and Baron Balniel (life peerage, 1974),* Robert Alexander Lindsay, KT, GCVO, PC, *b.* 1927, *s.* 1975, *m.* *Premier Earl on Union Roll*	Lord Balniel, *b.* 1958
1861	*Cromartie (5th),* John Ruaridh Blunt Grant Mackenzie, *b.* 1948, *s.* 1989, *m.*	Viscount Tarbat, *b.* 1987
1901	*Cromer (4th),* Evelyn Rowland Esmond Baring, *b.* 1946, *s.* 1991, *m.*	Viscount Errington, *b.* 1994
1633 S.	*Dalhousie (17th),* James Hubert Ramsay, *b.* 1948, *s.* 1999, *m., Lord Steward*	Lord Ramsay, *b.* 1981
1725 I.	*Darnley (11th),* Adam Ivo Stuart Bligh, *b.* 1941, *s.* 1980, *m.*	Lord Clifton, *b.* 1968
1711	*Dartmouth (10th),* William Legge, *b.* 1949, *s.* 1997, *m.*	Hon. Rupert L., *b.* 1951
1761	° *De La Warr (11th),* William Herbrand Sackville, *b.* 1948, *s.* 1988, *m.*	Lord Buckhurst, *b.* 1979
1622	*Denbigh (12th) and Desmond (11th) (I. 1622),* Alexander Stephen Rudolph Feilding, *b.* 1970, *s.* 1995, *m.*	Viscount Feilding, *b.* 2005
1485	*Derby (19th),* Edward Richard William Stanley, *b.* 1962, *s.* 1994, *m.*	Lord Stanley, *b.* 1998
1553	*Devon (18th),* Hugh Rupert Courtenay, *b.* 1942, *s.* 1998, *m.*	Lord Courtenay, *b.* 1975
1800 I.	*Donoughmore (8th),* Richard Michael John Hely-Hutchinson, *b.* 1927, *s.* 1981, *w.*	Viscount Suirdale, *b.* 1952
1661 I.	*Drogheda (12th),* Henry Dermot Ponsonby Moore, *b.* 1937, *s.* 1989, *m.*	Viscount Moore, *b.* 1983
1837	*Ducie (7th),* David Leslie Moreton, *b.* 1951, *s.* 1991, *m.*	Lord Moreton, *b.* 1981
1860	*Dudley (4th),* William Humble David Ward, *b.* 1920, *s.* 1969, *w.*	Viscount Ednam, *b.* 1947
1660 S.	** *Dundee (12th),* Alexander Henry Scrymgeour, *b.* 1949, *s.* 1983, *m.*	Lord Scrymgeour, *b.* 1982
1669 S.	*Dundonald (15th),* Iain Alexander Douglas Blair Cochrane, *b.* 1961, *s.* 1986, *m.*	Lord Cochrane, *b.* 1991
1686 S.	*Dunmore (12th),* Malcolm Kenneth Murray, *b.* 1946, *s.* 1995, *m.*	Hon. Geoffrey C. M., *b.*1949
1833	*Durham (7th),* Edward Richard Lambton, *b.* 1961, *s.* 2006, *m.*	Viscount Lambton, *b.* 1985
1643 S.	*Dysart (13th),* John Peter Grant of Rothiemurchus, *b.* 1946, *s.* 2011, *m.*	Lord Huntingtower, *b.* 1977
1837	*Effingham (7th),* David Mowbray Algernon Howard, *b.* 1939, *s.* 1996, *m.*	Lord Howard of Effingham, *b.* 1971
1507 S.	*Eglinton (18th) and Winton (9th) (S. 1600),* Archibald George Montgomerie, *b.* 1939, *s.* 1966, *m.*	Lord Montgomerie, *b.* 1966
1821	*Eldon (5th),* John Joseph Nicholas Scott, *b.* 1937, *s.* 1976, *m.*	Viscount Encombe, *b.* 1962
1633 S.	*Elgin (11th) and Kincardine (15th) (S. 1647),* Andrew Douglas Alexander Thomas Bruce, KT, *b.* 1924, *s.* 1968, *m.*	Lord Bruce, *b.* 1961
1789 I.	*Enniskillen (7th),* Andrew John Galbraith Cole, *b.* 1942, *s.* 1989, *m.*	Berkeley A. C., *b.* 1949
1789 I.	*Erne (6th),* Henry George Victor John Crichton, KCVO, *b.* 1937, *s.* 1940, *m.*	Viscount Crichton, *b.* 1971
1452 S.	** *Erroll (24th),* Merlin Sereld Victor Gilbert Hay, *b.* 1948, *s.* 1978, *m.* *Hereditary Lord High Constable and Knight Marischal of Scotland*	Lord Hay, *b.* 1984
1661	*Essex (11th),* Frederick Paul de Vere Capell, *b.* 1944, *s.* 2005	William J. C., *b.* 1952
1711	° *Ferrers (14th),* Robert William Saswalo Shirley, *b.* 1952, *s.* 2012, *m.*	Viscount Tamworth, *b.* 1984
1789	° *Fortescue (8th),* Charles Hugh Richard Fortescue, *b.* 1951, *s.* 1993, *m.*	John A. F. F., *b.* 1955
1841	*Gainsborough (6th),* Anthony Baptist Noel, *b.* 1950, *s.* 2009, *m.*	Viscount Campden, *b.* 1977
1623 S.	*Galloway (13th),* Randolph Keith Reginald Stewart, *b.* 1928, *s.* 1978, *w.*	Andrew C. S., *b.* 1949
1703 S.	** *Glasgow (10th),* Patrick Robin Archibald Boyle, *b.*1939, *s.* 1984, *m.*	Viscount of Kelburn, *b.* 1978
1806 I.	*Gosford (7th),* Charles David Nicholas Alexander John Sparrow Acheson, *b.* 1942, *s.* 1966, *m.*	Nicholas H. C. A., *b.* 1947
1945	*Gowrie (2nd),* Alexander Patrick Greysteil Hore-Ruthven, PC, *b.* 1939, *s.* 1955, *m.*	Viscount Ruthven of Canberra, *b.* 1964
1684 I.	*Granard (10th),* Peter Arthur Edward Hastings Forbes, *b.* 1957, *s.* 1992, *m.*	Viscount Forbes, *b.* 1981
1833	° *Granville (6th),* Granville George Fergus Leveson-Gower, *b.* 1959, *s.* 1996, *m.*	Lord Leveson, *b.* 1999
1806	° *Grey (6th),* Richard Fleming George Charles Grey, *b.* 1939, *s.* 1963, *m.*	Philip K. G., *b.* 1940
1752	*Guilford (10th),* Piers Edward Brownlow North, *b.* 1971, *s.* 1999, *m.*	Lord North, *b.* 2002
1619 S.	*Haddington (13th),* John George Baillie-Hamilton, *b.* 1941, *s.* 1986, *m.*	Lord Binning, *b.* 1985
1919	° *Haig (3rd),* Alexander Douglas Derrick Haig, *b.* 1961, *s.* 2009, *m.*	None
1944	*Halifax (3rd),* Charles Edward Peter Neil Wood, *b.* 1944, *s.* 1980, *m.*	Lord Irwin, *b.* 1977
1754	*Hardwicke (10th),* Joseph Philip Sebastian Yorke, *b.* 1971, *s.* 1974, *m.*	Viscount Royston, *b.* 2009
1812	*Harewood (8th),* David Henry George Lascelles, *b.* 1950, *s.* 2011, *m.*	Viscount Lascelles, *b.* 1978
1742	*Harrington (12th),* Charles Henry Leicester Stanhope, *b.* 1945, *s.* 2009, *m.*	Viscount Petersham, *b.* 1967
1809	*Harrowby (8th),* Dudley Adrian Conroy Ryder, *b.* 1951, *s.* 2007, *m.*	Viscount Sandon, *b.* 1981
1605 S.	** *Home (15th),* David Alexander Cospatrick Douglas-Home, CVO, CBE, *b.* 1943, *s.* 1995, *m.*	Lord Dunglass, *b.* 1987
1821	° ** *Howe (7th),* Frederick Richard Penn Curzon, PC, *b.* 1951, *s.* 1984, *m.*	Viscount Curzon, *b.* 1994
1529	*Huntingdon (16th),* William Edward Robin Hood Hastings Bass, LVO, *b.* 1948, *s.* 1990, *m.*	Hon. Simon A. R. H. H. B., *b.* 1950
1885	*Iddesleigh (5th),* John Stafford Northcote, *b.* 1957, *s.* 2004, *m.*	Viscount St Cyres, *b.* 1985
1756	*Ilchester (10th),* Robin Maurice Fox-Strangways, *b.* 1942, *s.* 2006, *m.*	Lord Stavordale, *b.* 1972
1929	*Inchcape (4th),* (Kenneth) Peter (Lyle) Mackay, *b.* 1943, *s.* 1994, *m.*	Viscount Glenapp, *b.* 1979
1919	*Iveagh (4th),* Arthur Edward Rory Guinness, *b.* 1969, *s.* 1992	Viscount Elveden, *b.* 2003
1925	° *Jellicoe (3rd),* Patrick John Bernard Jellicoe, *b.* 1950, *s.* 2007	Hon. Nicholas C. J., *b.* 1953
1697	*Jersey (10th),* George Francis William Child Villiers, *b.* 1976, *s.* 1998 *m.*	Hon. Jamie C. C. V., *b.* 1994

1822 I.	*Kilmorey (6th),* Sir Richard Francis Needham, PC, *b.* 1942, *s.* 1977, *m.* (Does not use title)	Viscount Newry and Mourne, *b.* 1966
1866	*Kimberley (5th),* John Armine Wodehouse, *b.* 1951, *s.* 2002, *m.*	Lord Wodehouse, *b.*1978
1768 I.	*Kingston (12th),* Robert Charles Henry King-Tenison, *b.* 1969, *s.* 2002, *m.*	Viscount Kingsborough, *b.* 2000
1633 S.	*Kinnoull (16th),* Charles William Harley Hay, *b.* 1962, *s.* 2013, *m.*	Robert P. H.-D.-H., *b.* 1941
1677 S.	*Kintore (14th),* James William Falconer Keith, *b.* 1976, *s.* 2004, *w.*	Lord Inverurie, *b.* 2010
1624 S.	*Lauderdale (18th),* Ian Maitland, *b.* 1937, *s.* 2008, *m.*	Viscount Maitland, *b.* 1965
1837	*Leicester (7th),* Edward Douglas Coke, *b.* 1936, *s.* 1994, *m.*	Viscount Coke, *b.* 1965
1641 S.	*Leven (15th) and Melville (14th) (S. 1690),* Alexander Ian Leslie Melville, *b.* 1984, *s.* 2012	Hon. Archibald R. L. M., *b.* 1957
1831	*Lichfield (6th),* Thomas William Robert Hugh Anson, *b.* 1978, *s.* 2005, *m.*	Viscount Anson, *b.* 2011
1803 I.	*Limerick (7th),* Edmund Christopher Pery, *b.* 1963, *s.* 2003, *m.*	Viscount Glentworth, *b.* 1991
1572	*Lincoln (19th),* Robert Edward Fiennes-Clinton, *b.* 1972, *s.* 2001	Hon. William J. Howson, *b.* 1980
1633 S.	** *Lindsay (16th),* James Randolph Lindesay-Bethune, *b.* 1955, *s.* 1989, *m.*	Viscount Garnock, *b.* 1990
1626	*Lindsey (14th) and Abingdon (9th) (1682),* Richard Henry Rupert Bertie, *b.* 1931, *s.* 1963, *m.*	Lord Norreys, *b.* 1958
1776 I.	*Lisburne (8th),* John David Malet Vaughan, *b.* 1918, *s.* 1965, *m.*	Viscount Vaughan, *b.* 1945
1822 I.	** *Listowel (6th),* Francis Michael Hare, *b.* 1964, *s.* 1997, *m.*	Hon. Timothy P. H., *b.* 1966
1905	** *Liverpool (5th),* Edward Peter Bertram Savile Foljambe, *b.* 1944, *s.* 1969, *m.*	Viscount Hawkesbury, *b.* 1972
1945	° *Lloyd George of Dwyfor (4th),* David Richard Owen Lloyd George, *b.* 1951, *s.* 2010, *m.*	Viscount Gwynedd, *b.* 1986
1785 I.	*Longford (8th),* Thomas Frank Dermot Pakenham, *b.* 1933, *s.* 2001, *m.*, (does not use title)	Edward M. P., *b.* 1970
1807	*Lonsdale (8th),* Hugh Clayton Lowther, *b.* 1949, *s.* 2006, *m.*	Hon. William J. L., *b.* 1957
1633 S.	*Loudoun (15th),* Simon Michael Abney-Hastings, *b.* 1974, *s.* 2012	Hon. Marcus W. A.-H., *b.* 1981
1838	*Lovelace (5th),* Peter Axel William Locke King, *b.* 1951, *s.* 1964, *m.*	None
1795 I.	*Lucan (7th),* Richard John Bingham, *b.* 1934, *s.* 1964, *m.* (missing since 8 November 1974)	Lord Bingham, *b.* 1967
1880	** *Lytton (5th),* John Peter Michael Scawen Lytton, *b.* 1950, *s.* 1985, *m.*	Viscount Knebworth, *b.* 1989
1721	*Macclesfield (9th),* Richard Timothy George Mansfield Parker, *b.* 1943, *s.* 1992, *m.*	Hon. J. David G. P., *b.* 1945
1800	*Malmesbury (7th),* James Carleton Harris, *b.* 1946, *s.* 2000, *m.*	Viscount FitzHarris, *b.* 1970
1776	*Mansfield and Mansfield (8th) (1792),* William David Mungo James Murray, *b.* 1930, *s.*1971, *m.*	Viscount Stormont, *b.* 1956
1565 S.	*Mar (14th) and Kellie (16th) (S. 1616) and Baron Erskine of Alloa Tower (life peerage, 2000),* James Thorne Erskine, *b.* 1949, *s.* 1994, *m.*	Hon. Alexander D. E., *b.* 1952
1785 I.	*Mayo (11th),* Charles Diarmuidh John Bourke, *b.* 1953, *s.* 2006, *m.*	Lord Naas, *b.* 1985
1627 I.	*Meath (15th),* John Anthony Brabazon, *b.* 1941, *s.* 1998, *m.*	Lord Ardee, *b.* 1977
1766 I.	*Mexborough (8th),* John Christopher George Savile, *b.* 1931, *s.* 1980, *m.*	Viscount Pollington, *b.* 1959
1813	*Minto (7th),* Gilbert Timothy George Lariston Elliot-Murray-Kynynmound, *b.* 1953, *s.*2005, *m.*	Viscount Melgund, *b.* 1984
1562 S.	*Moray (21st),* John Douglas Stuart, *b.* 1966, *s.* 2011, *m.*	Lord Doune, *b.* 2002
1815	*Morley (6th),* John St Aubyn Parker, KCVO, *b.* 1923, *s.*1962, *m.*	Viscount Boringdon, *b.* 1956
1458 S.	*Morton (22nd),* John Charles Sholto Douglas, *b.* 1927, *s.* 1976, *m.*	Lord Aberdour, *b.* 1952
1789	*Mount Edgcumbe (8th),* Robert Charles Edgcumbe, *b.* 1939, *s.* 1982	Piers V. E., *b.* 1946
1805	° *Nelson (10th),* Simon John Horatio Nelson, *b.* 1971, *s.* 2009, *m.*	Viscount Merton, *b.* 1994
1660 S.	*Newburgh (12th),* Don Filippo Giambattista Camillo Francesco Aldo Maria Rospigliosi, *b.* 1942, *s.* 1986, *m.*	Princess Donna Benedetta F. M. R., *b.* 1974
1827 I.	*Norbury (7th),* Richard James Graham-Toler, *b.* 1967, *s.* 2000	None
1806 I.	*Normanton (6th),* Shaun James Christian Welbore Ellis Agar, *b.* 1945, *s.* 1967, *w.*	Viscount Somerton, *b.* 1982
1647 S.	*Northesk (15th),* Patrick Charles Carnegy, *b.* 1940, *s.* 2010	Colin D. C., *b.* 1942
1801	*Onslow (8th),* Rupert Charles William Bullard Onslow, *b.* 1967, *s.* 2011, *m.*	Anthony E. E. O., *b.* 1955
1696 S.	*Orkney (9th),* (Oliver) Peter St John, *b.* 1938, *s.* 1998, *m.*	Viscount Kirkwall, *b.* 1969
1328 I.	*Ormonde and Ossory (I. 1527),* The 25th/18th Earl (7th Marquess) died in 1988	†Viscount Mountgarret *b.* 1961 (*see* that title)
1925	*Oxford and Asquith (3rd),* Raymond Benedict Bartholomew Michael Asquith, OBE, *b.* 1952, *s.* 2011, *m.*	Viscount Asquith, *b.* 1979
1929	° ** *Peel (3rd),* William James Robert Peel, GCVO, PC, *b.* 1947, *s.* 1969, *m.*, *Lord Chamberlain*	Viscount Clanfield, *b.* 1976
1551	*Pembroke (18th) and Montgomery (15th) (1605),* William Alexander Sidney Herbert, *b.* 1978, *s.* 2003, *m.*	Lord Herbert *b.* 2012
1605 S.	*Perth (18th),* John Eric Drummond, *b.* 1935, *s.* 2002, *m.*	Viscount Strathallan, *b.* 1965
1905	*Plymouth (3rd),* Other Robert Ivor Windsor-Clive, *b.* 1923, *s.* 1943, *m.*	Viscount Windsor, *b.* 1951
1785	*Portarlington (7th),* George Lionel Yuill Seymour Dawson-Damer, *b.* 1938, *s.* 1959, *m.*	Viscount Carlow, *b.* 1965
1689	*Portland (12th),* Count Timothy Charles Robert Noel Bentinck, *b.* 1953, *s.* 1997, *m.*	Viscount Woodstock, *b.* 1984
1743	*Portsmouth (10th),* Quentin Gerard Carew Wallop, *b.* 1954, *s.* 1984, *m.*	Viscount Lymington, *b.* 1981

1804	*Powis (8th),* John George Herbert, *b.* 1952, *s.* 1993, *m.*	Viscount Clive, *b.* 1979
1765	*Radnor (9th),* William Pleydell-Bouverie, *b.* 1955, *s.* 2008, *m.*	Viscount Folkestone, *b.* 1999
1831 I.	*Ranfurly (7th),* Gerald Françoys Needham Knox, *b.* 1929, *s.* 1988, *m.*	Viscount Northland, *b.* 1957
1771 I.	*Roden (10th),* Robert John Jocelyn, *b.* 1938, *s.* 1993, *m.*	Viscount Jocelyn, *b.* 1989
1801	*Romney (8th),* Julian Charles Marsham, *b.* 1948, *s.* 2004, *m.*	Viscount Marsham, *b.* 1977
1703 S.	*Rosebery (7th),* Neil Archibald Primrose, *b.* 1929, *s.* 1974, *m.*	Lord Dalmeny, *b.* 1967
1806 I.	*Rosse (7th),* William Brendan Parsons, *b.* 1936, *s.* 1979, *m.*	Lord Oxmantown, *b.* 1969
1801	** *Rosslyn (7th),* Peter St Clair-Erskine, QPM, *b.* 1958, *s.* 1977, *m.*	Lord Loughborough, *b.* 1986
1457 S.	*Rothes (22nd),* James Malcolm David Leslie, *b.* 1958, *s.* 2005, *m.*	Hon. Alexander J. L., *b.* 1962
1861	° *Russell (6th),* Nicholas Lyulph Russell, *b.* 1968, *s.* 2004	Hon. John F. R., *b.* 1971
1915	° *St Aldwyn (3rd),* Michael Henry Hicks Beach, *b.* 1950, *s.* 1992, *m.*	Hon. David S. H. B., *b.* 1955
1815	*St Germans (10th),* Peregrine Nicholas Eliot, *b.* 1941, *s.* 1988	Lord Eliot, *b.* 2004
1660	** *Sandwich (11th),* John Edward Hollister Montagu, *b.* 1943, *s.* 1995, *m.*	Viscount Hinchingbrooke, *b.* 1969
1690	*Scarbrough (13th),* Richard Osbert Lumley, *b.* 1973, *s.* 2004	Hon. Thomas H. L., *b.* 1980
1701 S.	*Seafield (13th),* Ian Derek Francis Ogilvie-Grant, *b.* 1939, *s.* 1969, *m.*	Viscount Reidhaven, *b.* 1963
1882	** *Selborne (4th),* John Roundell Palmer, GBE, *b.* 1940, *s.* 1971, *m.*	Viscount Wolmer, *b.* 1971
1646 S.	*Selkirk (11th),* Disclaimed for life 1994 (*see* Lord Selkirk of Douglas, Life Peers)	Master of Selkirk, *b.* 1978
1672	*Shaftesbury (12th),* Nicholas Edmund Anthony Ashley-Cooper, *b.* 1979, *s.* 2005, *m.*	Lord Ashley, *b.* 2011
1756 I.	*Shannon (10th),* Richard Henry John Boyle, *b.* 1960, *s.* 2013	Robert F. B., *b.* 1930
1442	** *Shrewsbury and Waterford (22nd) (I. 1446),* Charles Henry John Benedict Crofton Chetwynd Chetwynd-Talbot, *b.* 1952, *s.* 1980, *m. Premier Earl of England and Ireland*	Viscount Ingestre, *b.* 1978
1961	*Snowdon (1st) and Baron Armstrong-Jones (life peerage, 1999),* Antony Charles Robert Armstrong-Jones, GCVO, *b.* 1930, *m.*	Viscount Linley, *b.* 1961
1765	° *Spencer (9th),* Charles Edward Maurice Spencer, *b.* 1964, *s.* 1992, *m.*	Viscount Althorp, *b.* 1994
1703 S.	** *Stair (14th),* John David James Dalrymple, *b.* 1961, *s.* 1996, *m.*	Viscount Dalrymple, *b.* 2008
1984	*Stockton (2nd),* Alexander Daniel Alan Macmillan, *b.* 1943, *s.* 1986, *m.*	Viscount Macmillan of Ovenden, *b.* 1974
1821	*Stradbroke (6th),* Robert Keith Rous, *b.* 1937, *s.* 1983, *m.*	Viscount Dunwich, *b.* 1961
1847	*Strafford (8th),* Thomas Edmund Byng, *b.* 1936, *s.* 1984, *m.*	Viscount Enfield, *b.* 1964
1606 S.	*Strathmore and Kinghorne (18th) (S. 1677),* Michael Fergus Bowes Lyon, *b.* 1957, *s.* 1987, *m.*	Lord Glamis, *b.* 1986
1603	*Suffolk (21st) and Berkshire (14th) (1626),* Michael John James George Robert Howard, *b.* 1935, *s.* 1941, *m.*	Viscount Andover, *b.* 1974
1955	*Swinton (3rd),* Nicholas John Cunliffe-Lister, *b.* 1939, *s.* 2006, *m.*	Lord Masham *b.* 1970
1714	*Tankerville (10th),* Peter Grey Bennet, *b.* 1956, *s.* 1980	Adrian G. B., *b.* 1958
1822	° *Temple of Stowe (8th),* (Walter) Grenville Algernon Temple-Gore-Langton, *b.* 1924, *s.* 1988, *m.*	Lord Langton, *b.* 1955
1815	*Verulam (7th),* John Duncan Grimston, *b.* 1951, *s.* 1973, *m.*	Viscount Grimston, *b.* 1978
1729	° *Waldegrave (13th),* James Sherbrooke Waldegrave, *b.* 1940, *s.* 1995, *m.*	Viscount Chewton, *b.* 1986
1759	*Warwick (9th) and Brooke (9th) (1746),* Guy David Greville, *b.* 1957, *s.* 1996, *m.*	Lord Brooke, *b.* 1982
1633 S.	*Wemyss (13th) and March (9th) (S. 1697),* James Donald Charteris, *b.* 1948, *s.* 2008, *m.*	Lord Elcho, *b.* 1984
1621 I.	*Westmeath (13th),* William Anthony Nugent, *b.* 1928, *s.* 1971, *m.*	Sean C. W. N., *b.* 1965
1624	*Westmorland (16th),* Anthony David Francis Henry Fane, *b.* 1951, *s.* 1993, *m.*	Hon. Harry St C. F., *b.* 1953
1876	*Wharncliffe (5th),* Richard Alan Montagu Stuart Wortley, *b.* 1953, *s.* 1987, *m.*	Viscount Carlton, *b.* 1980
1801	*Wilton (8th),* Francis Egerton Grosvenor, *b.* 1934, *s.* 1999, *m.*	Viscount Grey de Wilton, *b.*1959
1628	*Winchilsea (17th) and Nottingham (12th) (1681),* Daniel James Hatfield Finch Hatton, *b.* 1967, *s.* 1999, *m.*	Viscount Maidstone, *b.* 1998
1766	° *Winterton (8th),* (Donald) David Turnour, *b.* 1943, *s.* 1991, *m.*	Robert C. T., *b.* 1950
1956	*Woolton (3rd),* Simon Frederick Marquis, *b.* 1958, *s.* 1969, *m.*	None
1837	*Yarborough (8th),* Charles John Pelham, *b.* 1963, *s.* 1991, *m.*	Lord Worsley, *b.* 1990

COUNTESSES IN THEIR OWN RIGHT

Style, The Rt. Hon. the Countess (of) _
Envelope (formal), The Rt. Hon. the Countess (of) _; *(social),* The Countess (of) _. *Letter (formal),* Madam; *(social),* Lady _. *Spoken (formal),* Madam; *(social),* Lady _.
Husband, Untitled
Children's style, As for children of an Earl

Created		*Title, order of succession, name, etc*	*Heir*
c.1115 S.	**	*Mar (31st),* Margaret of Mar, *b.* 1940, *s.* 1975, *m. Premier Earldom of Scotland*	Mistress of Mar, *b.* 1963
1947	°	*Mountbatten of Burma (2nd),* Patricia Edwina Victoria Knatchbull, CBE, *b.* 1924, *s.* 1979, *w.*	Lord Romsey, (*also* Lord Brabourne (8th) *see* that title)
c.1235 S.		*Sutherland (24th),* Elizabeth Millicent Sutherland, *b.* 1921, *s.* 1963, *w.*	Lord Strathnaver, *b.* 1947

VISCOUNTS

Coronet, Sixteen silver balls

Style, The Rt. Hon. the Viscount _
Envelope (formal), The Rt. Hon. the Viscount _; *(social),* The Viscount _. *Letter (formal),* My Lord; *(social),* Dear Lord _. *Spoken,* Lord _.
Wife's style, The Rt. Hon. the Viscountess _
Envelope (formal), The Rt. Hon. the Viscountess _; *(social),* The Viscountess _. *Letter (formal),* Madam; *(social),* Dear Lady _. *Spoken,* Lady _.
Children's style, 'The Hon.' before forename and surname, as for Baron's children
In Scotland, the heir apparent to a Viscount may be styled 'The Master of _ (title of peer)'

Created		*Title, order of succession, name, etc*	*Heir*
1945		*Addison (4th),* William Matthew Wand Addison, *b.* 1945, *s.* 1992, *m.*	Hon. Paul W. A., *b.* 1973
1946		*Alanbrooke (3rd),* Alan Victor Harold Brooke, *b.* 1932, *s.* 1972	None
1919	**	*Allenby (3rd),* Lt.-Col. Michael Jaffray Hynman Allenby, *b.* 1931, *s.* 1984, *m.*	Hon. Henry J. H. A., *b.* 1968
1911		*Allendale (4th),* Wentworth Peter Ismay Beaumont, *b.* 1948, *s.* 2002, *m.*	Hon. Wentworth A. I. B., *b.* 1979
1642 S.		*of Arbuthnott (17th),* John Keith Oxley Arbuthnott, *b.* 1950, *s.* 2012, *m.*	Master of Arbuthnott, *b.* 1977
1751 I.		*Ashbrook (11th),* Michael Llowarch Warburton Flower, *b.* 1935, *s.* 1995, *m.*	Hon. Rowland F. W. F., *b.* 1975
1917	**	*Astor (4th),* William Waldorf Astor, *b.* 1951, *s.* 1966, *m.*	Hon. William W. A., *b.* 1979
1781 I.		*Bangor (8th),* William Maxwell David Ward, *b.* 1948, *s.* 1993, *m.*	Hon. E. Nicholas W., *b.* 1953
1925		*Bearsted (5th),* Nicholas Alan Samuel, *b.* 1950, *s.* 1996, *m.*	Hon. Harry R. S., *b.* 1988
1963		*Blakenham (2nd),* Michael John Hare, *b.* 1938, *s.* 1982, *m.*	Hon. Caspar J. H., *b.* 1972
1935		*Bledisloe (4th),* Rupert Edward Ludlow Bathurst, *b.* 1964, *s.* 2009, *m.*	Hon. Benjamin B., *b.* 2004
1712		*Bolingbroke (9th) and St John (10th) (1716),* Nicholas Alexander Mowbray St John, *b.* 1974, *s.* 2011	Walter W. St J., *b.* 1921
1960		*Boyd of Merton (2nd),* Simon Donald Rupert Neville Lennox-Boyd, *b.* 1939, *s.* 1983, *m.*	Hon. Benjamin A. L.-B., *b.* 1964
1717 I.		*Boyne (11th),* Gustavus Michael Stucley Hamilton-Russell, *b.* 1965, *s.* 1995, *m.*	Hon. Gustavus A. E. H.-R., *b.* 1999
1929		*Brentford (4th),* Crispin William Joynson-Hicks, *b.* 1933, *s.* 1983, *m.*	Hon. Paul W. J.-H., *b.* 1971
1929	**	*Bridgeman (3rd),* Robin John Orlando Bridgeman, *b.* 1930, *s.* 1982, *m.*	Hon. Luke R. O. B., *b.* 1971
1868		*Bridport (4th) and 7th Duke, Bronte in Sicily, 1799,* Alexander Nelson Hood, *b.* 1948, *s.* 1969, *m.*	Hon. Peregrine A. N. H., *b.* 1974
1952	**	*Brookeborough (3rd),* Alan Henry Brooke, *b.* 1952, *s.* 1987, *m.*	Hon. Christopher A. B., *b.* 1954
1933		*Buckmaster (4th),* Adrian Charles Buckmaster, *b.* 1949, *s.* 2007, *m.*	Hon. Andrew N. B., *b.* 1980
1939		*Caldecote (3rd),* Piers James Hampden Inskip, *b.* 1947, *s.* 1999, *m.*	Hon. Thomas J. H. I., *b.* 1985
1941		*Camrose (4th),* Adrian Michael Berry, *b.* 1937, *s.* 2001, *m.*	Hon. Jonathan W. B., *b.* 1970
1954		*Chandos (3rd) and Baron Lyttelton of Aldershot (life peerage, 2000),* Thomas Orlando Lyttelton, *b.* 1953, *s.* 1980, *m.*	Hon. Oliver A. L., *b.* 1986

1665 I.	*Charlemont (15th),* John Dodd Caulfeild, *b.* 1966, *s.* 2001, *m.*	Hon. Shane A. C., *b.* 1996
1921	*Chelmsford (4th)* Frederic Corin Piers Thesiger, *b.* 1962, *s.* 1999, *m.*	Hon. Frederic T. *b.* 2006
1717 I.	*Chetwynd (10th),* Adam Richard John Casson Chetwynd, *b.* 1935, *s.* 1965, *m.*	Hon. Adam D. C., *b.* 1969
1911	*Chilston (4th),* Alastair George Akers-Douglas, *b.* 1946, *s.* 1982, *m.*	Hon. Oliver I. A.-D., *b.* 1973
1902	*Churchill (3rd) and 5th UK Baron Churchill (1815),* Victor George Spencer, *b.* 1934, *s.* 1973	To Barony only, Richard H. R. S., *b.* 1926
1718	*Cobham (12th),* Christopher Charles Lyttelton, *b.* 1947, *s.* 2006, *m.*	Hon. Oliver C. L., *b.* 1976
1902	** *Colville of Culross (5th),* Charles Mark Townshend Colville, *b.* 1959, *s.* 2010	Hon. Richmond J. I. C., *b.* 1961
1826	*Combermere (6th),* Thomas Robert Wellington Stapleton-Cotton, *b.* 1969, *s.* 2000	Hon. Laszlo M. W. S.-C., *b.* 2010
1917	*Cowdray (4th),* Michael Orlando Weetman Pearson, *b.* 1944, *s.* 1995, *m.*	Hon. Peregrine J. D. P., *b.* 1994
1927	** *Craigavon (3rd),* Janric Fraser Craig, *b.* 1944, *s.* 1974	None
1943	*Daventry (4th),* James Edward FitzRoy Newdegate, *b.* 1960, *s.* 2000, *m.*	Hon. Humphrey J. F. N., *b.* 1995
1937	*Davidson (3rd),* Malcolm William Mackenzie Davidson, *b.* 1934, *s.* 2012, *m.*	Hon. John N. A. D., *b.* 1971
1956	*De L'Isle (2nd),* Philip John Algernon Sidney, MBE, *b.* 1945, *s.* 1991, *m.*	Hon. Philip W. E. S., *b.* 1985
1776 I.	*De Vesci (7th),* Thomas Eustace Vesey, *b.* 1955, *s.* 1983, *m.*	Hon. Oliver I. V., *b.* 1991
1917	*Devonport (3rd),* Terence Kearley, *b.* 1944, *s.* 1973	Chester D. H. K., *b.* 1932
1964	*Dilhorne (2nd),* John Mervyn Manningham-Buller, *b.* 1932, *s.* 1980, *m.*	Hon. James E. M.-B., *b.* 1956
1622 I.	*Dillon (22nd),* Henry Benedict Charles Dillon, *b.* 1973, *s.* 1982	Hon. Richard A. L. D., *b.* 1948
1785 I.	*Doneraile (10th),* Richard Allen St Leger, *b.* 1946, *s.* 1983, *m.*	Hon. Nathaniel W. R. St J. St L., *b.* 1971
1680 I.	*Downe (12th),* Richard Henry Dawnay, *b.* 1967, *s.* 2002	Thomas P. D., *b.* 1978
1959	*Dunrossil (3rd),* Andrew William Reginald Morrison, *b.* 1953, *s.* 2000, *m.*	Hon. Callum A. B. M., *b.* 1994
1964	** *Eccles (2nd),* John Dawson Eccles, CBE, *b.* 1931, *s.* 1999, *m.*	Hon. William D. E., *b.* 1960
1897	*Esher (5th),* Christopher Lionel Baliol Brett, *b.* 1936, *s.* 2004, *m.*	Hon. Matthew C. A. B., *b.* 1963
1816	*Exmouth (10th),* Paul Edward Pellew, *b.* 1940, *s.* 1970, *m.*	Hon. Edward F. P., *b.* 1978
1620 S.	** *of Falkland (15th),* Lucius Edward William Plantagenet Cary, *b.* 1935, *s.* 1984, *m. Premier Scottish Viscount on the Roll*	Master of Falkland, *b.* 1963
1720	*Falmouth (9th),* George Hugh Boscawen, *b.* 1919, *s.* 1962, *w.*	Hon. Evelyn A. H. B., *b.* 1955
1720 I.	*Gage (8th),* (Henry) Nicolas Gage, *b.* 1934, *s.* 1993, *m.*	Hon. Henry W. G., *b.* 1975
1727 I.	*Galway (12th),* George Rupert Monckton-Arundell, *b.* 1922, *s.* 1980, *m.*	Hon. J. Philip M., *b.* 1952
1478 I.	*Gormanston (17th),* Jenico Nicholas Dudley Preston, *b.* 1939, *s.* 1940, *m. Premier Viscount of Ireland*	Hon. Jenico F. T. P., *b.* 1974
1816 I.	*Gort (9th),* Foley Robert Standish Prendergast Vereker, *b.* 1951, *s.* 1995, *m.*	Hon. Robert F. P. V., *b.* 1993
1900	** *Goschen (4th),* Giles John Harry Goschen, *b.* 1965, *s.* 1977, *m.*	Hon. Alexander J. E. G., *b.* 2001
1849	*Gough (5th),* Shane Hugh Maryon Gough, *b.* 1941, *s.* 1951	None
1929	*Hailsham (3rd),* Douglas Martin Hogg, PC, QC, *b.* 1945, *s.* 2001, *m.*	Hon. Quintin J. N. M. H., *b.* 1973
1891	*Hambleden (5th),* William Henry Bernard Smith, *b.* 1955, *s.* 2012, *m.*	Hon. Bernardo J. S., *b.* 1957
1884	*Hampden (7th),* Francis Anthony Brand, *b.* 1970, *s.* 2008, *m.*	Hon. Lucian A. B., *b.* 2005
1936	** *Hanworth (3rd),* David Stephen Geoffrey Pollock, *b.* 1946, *s.* 1996, *m.*	Harold W. C. P., *b.* 1988
1791 I.	*Harberton (11th),* Henry Robert Pomeroy, *b.* 1958, *s.* 2004, *m.*	Hon. Patrick C. P., b. 1995
1846	*Hardinge (7th),* Andrew Hartland Hardinge, *b.* 1960, *s.* 2004, *m.*	Hon. Thomas H. de M. H., *b.* 1993
1791 I.	*Hawarden (9th),* (Robert) Connan Wyndham Leslie Maude, *b.* 1961, *s.* 1991, *m.*	Hon. Varian J. C. E. M., *b.* 1997
1960	*Head (2nd),* Richard Antony Head, *b.* 1937, *s.* 1983, *m.*	Hon. Henry J. H., *b.* 1980
1550	*Hereford (19th),* Charles Robin De Bohun Devereux, *b.* 1975, *s.* 2004, *Premier Viscount of England*	Hon. Edward M. de B. D., *b.* 1977
1842	*Hill (9th),* Peter David Raymond Charles Clegg-Hill, *b.* 1945, *s.* 2003	Hon. Michael C. D. C.-H., *b.* 1988
1796	*Hood (8th),* Henry Lyttleton Alexander Hood, *b.* 1958, *s.* 1999, *m.*	Hon. Archibald L. S. H., *b.* 1993
1945	*Kemsley (3rd),* Richard Gomer Berry, *b.* 1951, *s.* 1999, *m.*	Hon. Luke G. B., *b.* 1998
1911	*Knollys (3rd),* David Francis Dudley Knollys, *b.* 1931, *s.* 1966, *m.*	Hon. Patrick N. M. K., *b.* 1962
1895	*Knutsford (6th),* Michael Holland-Hibbert, *b.* 1926, *s.* 1986, *m.*	Hon. Henry T. H.-H., *b.* 1959
1954	*Leathers (3rd),* Christopher Graeme Leathers, *b.* 1941, *s.* 1996, *m.*	Hon. James F. L., *b.* 1969
1781 I.	*Lifford (9th),* (Edward) James Wingfield Hewitt, *b.* 1949, *s.* 1987, *m.*	Hon. James T. W. H., *b.* 1979
1921	*Long (4th),* Richard Gerard Long, CBE, *b.* 1929, *s.* 1967, *m.*	Hon. James R. L., *b.* 1960
1957	*Mackintosh of Halifax (3rd),* (John) Clive Mackintosh, *b.* 1958, *s.* 1980, *m.*	Hon. Thomas H. G. M., *b.* 1985
1955	*Malvern (3rd),* Ashley Kevin Godfrey Huggins, *b.* 1949, *s.* 1978	Hon. M. James H., *b.* 1928
1945	*Marchwood (3rd),* David George Staveley Penny, *b.* 1936, *s.* 1979, *w.*	Hon. Peter G. W. P., *b.* 1965
1942	*Margesson (2nd),* Francis Vere Hampden Margesson, *b.* 1922, *s.* 1965, *m.*	Capt. Hon. Richard F. D. M., *b.* 1960
1660 I.	*Massereene (14th) and Ferrard (7th) (I. 1797),* John David Clotworthy Whyte-Melville Foster Skeffington, *b.* 1940, *s.* 1992, *m.*	Hon. Charles J. C. W.-M. F. S., *b.* 1973
1802	*Melville (10th),* Robert Henry Kirkpatrick Dundas, *b.* 1984, *s.* 2011	Hon. James D. B. D., *b.* 1986
1916	*Mersey (5th),* Edward John Hallam Bigham, *b.* 1966, *s.* 2006, *m.*	Hon. David E. H. B., *b.* 1938 (to Viscountcy); Mistress of Nairne, *b.* 2003 (to Lordship of Nairne)

Created	Title, order of succession, name, etc	Heir
1717 I.	*Midleton (12th),* Alan Henry Brodrick, *b.* 1949, *s.* 1988, *m.*	Hon. Ashley R. B., *b.* 1980
1962	*Mills (3rd),* Christopher Philip Roger Mills, *b.* 1956, *s.* 1988, *m.*	None
1716 I.	*Molesworth (12th),* Robert Bysse Kelham Molesworth, *b.* 1959, *s.* 1997	Hon. William J. C. M., *b.* 1960
1801 I.	*Monck (7th),* Charles Stanley Monck, *b.* 1953, *s.* 1982 (Does not use title)	Hon. George S. M., *b.* 1957
1957	*Monckton of Brenchley (3rd),* Christopher Walter Monckton, *b.* 1952, *s.* 2006, *m.*	Hon. Timothy D. R. M., *b.* 1955
1946	** *Montgomery of Alamein (2nd),* David Bernard Montgomery, CVO, CBE, *b.* 1928, *s.* 1976, *m.*	Hon. Henry D. M., *b.* 1954
1550 I.	*Mountgarret (18th),* Piers James Richard Butler, *b.* 1961, *s.* 2004	Hon. Edmund H. R. B., *b.* 1962
1952	*Norwich (2nd),* John Julius Cooper, CVO, *b.* 1929, *s.* 1954, *m.*	Hon. Jason C. D. B. C., *b.* 1959
1651 S.	*of Oxfuird (14th),* Ian Arthur Alexander Makgill, *b.* 1969, *s.* 2003	Master of Oxfuird, *b.* 2012
1873	*Portman (10th),* Christopher Edward Berkeley Portman, *b.* 1958, *s.* 1999, *m.*	Hon. Luke O. B. P., *b.* 1984
1743 I.	*Powerscourt (10th),* Mervyn Niall Wingfield, *b.* 1935, *s.* 1973, *m.*	Hon. Mervyn A. W., *b.* 1963
1900	** *Ridley (5th),* Matthew White Ridley, *b.* 1958, *s.* 2012, *m.*	Hon. Matthew W. R., *b.* 1993
1960	*Rochdale (2nd),* St John Durival Kemp, *b.* 1938, *s.* 1993, *m.*	Hon. Jonathan H. D. K., *b.* 1961
1919	*Rothermere (4th),* (Harold) Jonathan Esmond Vere Harmsworth, *b.* 1967, *s.* 1998, *m.*	Hon. Vere R. J. H. H., *b.* 1994
1937	*Runciman of Doxford (3rd),* Walter Garrison Runciman (Garry), CBE, *b.* 1934, *s.* 1989, *m.*	Hon. David W. R., *b.* 1967
1918	*St Davids (4th),* Rhodri Colwyn Philipps, *b.* 1966, *s.* 2009, *m.*	Hon. Roland A. J. E. P., *b.* 1970
1801	*St Vincent (8th),* Edward Robert James Jervis, *b.* 1951, *s.* 2006, *m.*	Hon. James R. A. J., *b.* 1982
1937	*Samuel (3rd),* David Herbert Samuel, OBE, PHD, *b.* 1922, *s.* 1978, *m.*	Hon. Dan J. S., *b.* 1925
1911	*Scarsdale (4th),* Peter Ghislain Nathaniel Curzon, *b.* 1949, *s.* 2000, *m.*	Hon. David J. N. C., *b.* 1958
1905 M.	*Selby (6th),* Christopher Rolf Thomas Gully, *b.* 1993, *s.* 2001	Hon. (James) Edward H. G. G., *b.* 1945
1805	*Sidmouth (8th),* Jeremy Francis Addington, *b.* 1947, *s.* 2005, *w.*	Hon. John A., *b.* 1990
1940	** *Simon (3rd),* Jan David Simon, *b.* 1940, *s.* 1993, *m.*	None
1960	** *Slim (2nd),* John Douglas Slim, OBE, *b.* 1927, *s.* 1970, *m.*	Hon. Mark W. R. S., *b.* 1960
1954	*Soulbury (4th),* Oliver Peter Ramsbotham, *b.* 1943, *s.* 2010, *m.*	Hon. Edward H. R., *b.* 1966
1776 I.	*Southwell (7th),* Pyers Anthony Joseph Southwell, *b.* 1930, *s.* 1960, *m.*	Hon. Richard A. P. S., *b.* 1956
1942	*Stansgate (2nd),* Anthony Neil Wedgwood Benn, *b.* 1925, *s.* 1960, *w.* Disclaimed for life 1963.	Stephen M. W. B., *b.* 1951
1959	*Stuart of Findhorn (3rd),* James Dominic Stuart, *b.* 1948, *s.* 1999, *m.*	Hon. Andrew M. S., *b.* 1957
1957	** *Tenby (3rd),* William Lloyd George, *b.* 1927, *s.* 1983, *m.*	Hon. Timothy H. G. L. G., *b.* 1962
1952	*Thurso (3rd),* John Archibald Sinclair, MP, *b.* 1953, *s.* 1995, *m.*	Hon. James A. R. S., *b.* 1984
1721	*Torrington (11th),* Timothy Howard St George Byng, *b.* 1943, *s.* 1961, *m.*	Colin H. C.-B., *b.* 1960
1936	** *Trenchard (3rd),* Hugh Trenchard, *b.* 1951, *s.* 1987, *m.*	Hon. Alexander T. T., *b.* 1978
1921	** *Ullswater (2nd),* Nicholas James Christopher Lowther, LVO, PC, *b.* 1942, *s.* 1949, *m.*	Hon. Benjamin J. L., *b.* 1975
1642 I.	** *Valentia (16th),* Frances William Dighton Annesley, *b.* 1959, *s.* 2005, *m.*	Hon. Peter J. A., *b.* 1967
1952	** *Waverley (3rd),* John Desmond Forbes Anderson, *b.* 1949, *s.* 1990	Hon. Forbes A. R. A., *b.* 1996
1938	*Weir (3rd),* William Kenneth James Weir, *b.* 1933, *s.* 1975, *m.*	Hon. James W. H. W., *b.* 1965
1918	*Wimborne (4th),* Ivor Mervyn Vigors Guest, *b.* 1968, *s.* 1993	Hon. Julien J. G., *b.* 1945
1923	** *Younger of Leckie (5th),* James Edward George Younger, *b.* 1955, *s.* 2003, *m.*	Hon. Alexander W. G. Y., *b.* 1993

BARONS/LORDS

Coronet, Six silver balls

Style, The Rt. Hon. the Lord _

Envelope (formal), The Rt. Hon. Lord _; *(social),* The Lord _. *Letter (formal),* My Lord; *(social),* Dear Lord _. *Spoken,* Lord _.

In the Peerage of Scotland there is no rank of Baron; the equivalent rank is Lord of Parliament and Scottish peers should always be styled 'Lord', never 'Baron'.

Wife's style, The Rt. Hon. the Lady _

Envelope (formal), The Rt. Hon. Lady _; *(social),* The Lady _. *Letter (formal),* My Lady; *(social),* Dear Lady _. *Spoken,* Lady _

Children's style, 'The Hon.' before forename (F_) and surname (S_)

Envelope, The Hon. F_ S_. *Letter,* Dear Mr/Miss/Mrs S_. *Spoken,* Mr/Miss/Mrs S_

In Scotland, the heir apparent to a Lord may be styled 'The Master of _ (title of peer)'

Created	Title, order of succession, name, etc	Heir
1911	*Aberconway (4th),* (Henry) Charles McLaren, *b.* 1948, *s.* 2003, *m.*	Hon. Charles S. M., *b.* 1984
1873	** *Aberdare (5th),* Alastair John Lyndhurst Bruce, *b.* 1947, *s.* 2005, *m.*	Hon. Hector M. N. B., *b.* 1974

1835	*Abinger (9th),* James Harry Scarlett, *b.* 1959, *s.* 2002, *m.*	Hon. Peter R. S., *b.* 1961
1869	*Acton (5th),* John Charles Ferdinand Harold Lyon-Dalberg-Acton, *b.* 1966, *s.* 2010, *m.*	Hon. John C. L.-D.-A., *b.* 1943
1887	** *Addington (6th),* Dominic Bryce Hubbard, *b.* 1963, *s.* 1982	Hon. Michael W. L. H., *b.* 1965
1896	*Aldenham (6th) and Hunsdon of Hunsdon (4th) (1923),* Vicary Tyser Gibbs, *b.* 1948, *s.* 1986, *m.*	Hon. Humphrey W. F. G., *b.* 1989
1962	*Aldington (2nd),* Charles Harold Stuart Low, *b.* 1948, *s.* 2000, *m.*	Hon. Philip T. A. L., *b.* 1990
1945	*Altrincham (3rd),* Anthony Ulick David Dundas Grigg, *b.* 1934, *s.* 2001, *m.*	Hon. (Edward) Sebastian G., *b.* 1965
1929	*Alvingham (2nd),* Maj.-Gen. Robert Guy Eardley Yerburgh, CBE, *b.* 1926, *s.* 1955, *m.*	Capt. Hon. Robert R. G. Y., *b.* 1956
1892	*Amherst of Hackney (5th),* Hugh William Amherst Cecil, *b.* 1968, *s.* 2009, *m.*	Hon. Jack W. A. C., *b.* 2001
1881	*Ampthill (5th),* David Whitney Erskine Russell, *b.* 1947, *s.* 2011	Hon. Anthony J. M. R., *b.* 1952
1947	*Amwell (3rd),* Keith Norman Montague, *b.* 1943, *s.* 1990, *m.*	Hon. Ian K. M., *b.* 1973
1863	*Annaly (6th),* Luke Richard White, *b.* 1954, *s.* 1990, *m.*	Hon. Luke H. W., *b.* 1990
1885	*Ashbourne (4th),* Edward Barry Greynville Gibson, *b.* 1933, *s.* 1983, *m.*	Hon Edward C. d'O. G., *b.* 1967
1835	*Ashburton (7th),* John Francis Harcourt Baring, KG, KCVO, *b.* 1928, *s.* 1991, *m.*	Hon. Mark F. R. B., *b.* 1958
1892	*Ashcombe (4th),* Henry Edward Cubitt, *b.* 1924, *s.* 1962, *m.*	Mark E. C., *b.* 1964
1911	** *Ashton of Hyde (4th),* Thomas Henry Ashton, *b.* 1958, *s.* 2008, *m.*	Hon. John E. A., *b.* 1966
1800 I.	*Ashtown (8th),* Roderick Nigel Godolphin Trench, *b.* 1944, *s.* 2010, *m.*	Hon. Timothy R. H. T., *b.* 1968
1956	** *Astor of Hever (3rd),* John Jacob Astor, *b.* 1946, *s.* 1984, *m.*	Hon. Charles G. J. A., *b.* 1990
1789 I.	*Auckland (10th) and Auckland (10th) (1793),* Robert Ian Burnard Eden, *b.* 1962, *s.* 1997, *m.*	Henry V. E., *b.* 1958
1313	*Audley,* Barony in abeyance between three co-heiresses since 1997	
1900	** *Avebury (4th),* Eric Reginald Lubbock, *b.* 1928, *s.* 1971, *m.*	Hon. Lyulph A. J. L., *b.* 1954
1718 I.	*Aylmer (14th),* (Anthony) Julian Aylmer, *b.* 1951, *s.* 2006, *m.*	Hon. Michael H. A., *b.* 1991
1929	*Baden-Powell (3rd),* Robert Crause Baden-Powell, *b.* 1936, *s.* 1962, *w.*	Hon. David M. B.-P., *b.* 1940
1780	*Bagot (10th),* (Charles Hugh) Shaun Bagot, *b.* 1944, *s.* 2001, *m.*	Richard C. V. B., *b.* 1941
1953	*Baillieu (3rd),* James William Latham Baillieu, *b.* 1950, *s.* 1973, *m.*	Hon. Robert L. B., *b.* 1979
1607 S.	*Balfour of Burleigh (8th),* Robert Bruce, *b.* 1927, *s.* 1967, *m.*	Hon. Victoria B., *b.* 1973
1924	*Banbury of Southam (3rd),* Charles William Banbury, *b.* 1953, *s.* 1981, *m.*	None
1698	*Barnard (11th),* Harry John Neville Vane, TD, *b.* 1923, *s.* 1964	Hon. Henry F. C. V., *b.* 1959
1887	*Basing (6th),* Stuart Anthony Whitfield Sclater-Booth, *b.* 1969, *s.* 2007, *m.*	Hon. Luke W. S.-B., *b.* 2000
1917	*Beaverbrook (3rd),* Maxwell William Humphrey Aitken, *b.* 1951, *s.* 1985, *m.*	Hon. Maxwell F. A., *b.* 1977
1647 S.	*Belhaven and Stenton (13th),* Robert Anthony Carmichael Hamilton, *b.* 1927, *s.* 1961, *m.*	Master of Belhaven, *b.* 1953
1848 I.	*Bellew (8th),* Bryan Edward Bellew, *b.* 1943, *s.* 2010, *m.*	Hon. Anthony R. B. B., *b.* 1972
1856	*Belper (5th),* Richard Henry Strutt, *b.* 1941, *s.* 1999, *m.*	Hon. Michael H. S., *b.* 1969
1421	*Berkeley (18th) and Gueterbock (life peerage, 2000),* Anthony Fitzhardinge Gueterbock, OBE, *b.* 1939, *s.* 1992, *m.*	Hon. Thomas F. G., *b.* 1969
1922	*Bethell (5th),* James Nicholas Bethell, *b.* 1967, *s.* 2007, *m.*	Hon. Jacob N. D. B., *b.* 2006
1938	*Bicester (3rd),* Angus Edward Vivian Smith, *b.* 1932, *s.* 1968	Hugh C. V. S., *b.* 1934
1903	*Biddulph (5th),* (Anthony) Nicholas Colin Maitland Biddulph, *b.* 1959, *s.* 1988, *m.*	Hon. Robert J. M. B., *b.* 1994
1938	*Birdwood (3rd),* Mark William Ogilvie Birdwood, *b.* 1938, *s.* 1962, *m.*	None
1958	*Birkett (2nd),* Michael Birkett, *b.* 1929, *s.* 1962, *w.*	Hon. Thomas B., *b.* 1982
1907	*Blyth (5th),* James Audley Ian Blyth, *b.* 1970, *s.* 2009, *m.*	Hon. Hugo A. J. B., *b.* 2006
1797	*Bolton (8th),* Harry Algar Nigel Orde-Powlett, *b.* 1954, *s.* 2001, *m.*	Hon. Thomas O.-P., *b.* 1979
1452 S.	*Borthwick (24th),* John Hugh Borthwick, *b.* 1940, *s.* 1996, *m.*	Hon. James H. A. B. of Glengelt, *b.* 1940
1922	** *Borwick (5th),* (Geoffrey Robert) James Borwick, *b.* 1955, *s.* 2007, *m.*	Hon. Edwin D. W. B., *b.* 1984
1761	*Boston (11th),* George William Eustace Boteler Irby, *b.* 1971, *s.* 2007, *m.*	Hon. Thomas W. G. B. I., *b.* 1999
1942	** *Brabazon of Tara (3rd),* Ivon Anthony Moore-Brabazon, PC, *b.* 1946, *s.* 1974, *m.*	Hon. Benjamin R. M.-B., *b.* 1983
1880	*Brabourne (8th),* Norton Louis Philip Knatchbull, *b.* 1947, *s.* 2005, *m.* (*also* Lord Romsey heir to Countess Mountbatten of Burma, *see* that title)	Hon. Nicholas L. C. N. K., *b.* 1981
1925	*Bradbury (3rd),* John Bradbury, *b.* 1940, *s.* 1994, *m.*	Hon. John B., *b.* 1973
1962	*Brain (2nd),* Christopher Langdon Brain, *b.* 1926, *s.* 1966, *m.*	Hon. Michael C. B., *b.* 1928
1938	*Brassey of Apethorpe (3rd),* David Henry Brassey, OBE, *b.* 1932, *s.* 1967, *m.*	Hon. Edward B., *b.* 1964
1788	*Braybrooke (10th),* Robin Henry Charles Neville, *b.* 1932, *s.* 1990, *m.*	Richard R. N., *b.* 1977
1957	** *Bridges (2nd),* Thomas Edward Bridges, GCMG, *b.* 1927, *s.* 1969, *m.*	Hon. Mark T. B., *b.* 1954
1945	*Broadbridge (4th),* Martin Hugh Broadbridge, *b.* 1929, *s.* 2000, *w.*	Hon. Richard J. M. B., *b.* 1959
1933	*Brocket (3rd),* Charles Ronald George Nall-Cain, *b.* 1952, *s.* 1967, *w.*	Hon. Alexander C. C. N.-C., *b.* 1984
1860	** *Brougham and Vaux (5th),* Michael John Brougham, CBE, *b.* 1938, *s.* 1967	Hon. Charles W. B., *b.* 1971
1776	*Brownlow (7th),* Edward John Peregrine Cust, *b.* 1936, *s.* 1978, *m.*	Hon. Peregrine E. Q. C., *b.* 1974

1942		*Bruntisfield (3rd),* Michael John Victor Warrender, *b.* 1949, *s.* 2007, *m.*	Hon. John M. P. C. W., *b.* 1996
1950		*Burden (4th),* Fraser William Elsworth Burden, *b.* 1964, *s.* 2000, *m.*	Hon. Ian S. B., *b.* 1967
1529		*Burgh (8th),* (Alexander) Gregory Disney Leith, *b.* 1958, *s.* 2001, *m.*	Hon. Alexander J. S. L., *b.* 1986
1903		*Burnham (7th),* Harry Frederick Alan Lawson, *b.* 1968, *s.* 2005	None
1897		*Burton (4th),* Evan Michael Ronald Baillie, *b.* 1949, *s.* 2013, *m.*	Hon. James E. B., *b.* 1975
1643		*Byron (13th),* Robert James Byron, *b.* 1950, *s.* 1989, *m.*	Hon. Charles R. G. B., *b.* 1990
1937		*Cadman (3rd),* John Anthony Cadman, *b.* 1938, *s.* 1966, *m.*	Hon. Nicholas A. J. C., *b.* 1977
1945		*Calverley (3rd),* Charles Rodney Muff, *b.* 1946, *s.* 1971, *m.*	Hon. Jonathan E. B., *b.* 1975
1383		*Camoys (7th),* (Ralph) Thomas Campion George Sherman Stonor, GCVO, PC, *b.* 1940, *s.* 1976, *m.*	Hon. R. William R. T. S., *b.* 1974
1715 I.		*Carbery (12th),* Michael Peter Evans-Freke, *b.* 1942, *s.* 2012, *m.*	Hon. Dominic R. C. E.-F., *b.* 1969
1834 I.		*Carew (7th) and Carew (7th) (1838),* Patrick Thomas Conolly-Carew, *b.* 1938, *s.* 1994, *m.*	Hon. William P. C.-C., *b.* 1973
1916		*Carnock (5th),* Adam Nicolson, *b.* 1957, *s.* 2008, *m.*	Hon. Thomas N., *b.* 1984
1796 I.		*Carrington (6th) and Carrington (6th) (1797) and Carington of Upton (life peerage, 1999),* Peter Alexander Rupert Carington, KG, GCMG, CH, MC, PC, *b.* 1919, *s.* 1938, *w.*	Hon. Rupert F. J. C., *b.* 1948
1812 I.		*Castlemaine (8th),* Roland Thomas John Handcock, MBE, *b.* 1943, *s.* 1973, *m.*	Hon. Ronan M. E. H., *b.* 1989
1936		*Catto (3rd),* Innes Gordon Catto, *b.* 1950, *s.* 2001, *m.*	Hon. Alexander G. C., *b.* 1952
1918		*Cawley (4th),* John Francis Cawley, *b.* 1946, *s.* 2001, *m.*	Hon. William R. H. C., *b.* 1981
1858		*Chesham (7th),* Charles Gray Compton Cavendish, *b.* 1974, *s.* 2009, *m.*	Hon. Oliver N. B. C., *b.* 2007
1945		*Chetwode (2nd),* Philip Chetwode, *b.* 1937, *s.* 1950, *m.*	Hon. Roger C., *b.* 1968
1945	**	*Chorley (2nd),* Roger Richard Edward Chorley, *b.* 1930, *s.* 1978, *m.*	Hon. Nicholas R. D. C., *b.* 1966
1858		*Churston (5th),* John Francis Yarde-Buller, *b.* 1934, *s.* 1991, *m.*	Hon. Benjamin F. A. Y.-B., *b.* 1974
1800 I.		*Clanmorris (8th),* Simon John Ward Bingham, *b.* 1937, *s.* 1988, *m.*	Robert D. de B. B., *b.* 1942
1672		*Clifford of Chudleigh (14th),* Thomas Hugh Clifford, *b.* 1948, *s.* 1988, *m.*	Hon. Alexander T. H. C., *b.* 1985
1299		*Clinton (22nd),* Gerard Nevile Mark Fane Trefusis, *b.* 1934, *s.* 1965, *m.*	Hon. Charles P. R. F. T., *b.* 1962
1955		*Clitheroe (2nd),* Ralph John Assheton, *b.* 1929, *s.* 1984, *m.*	Hon. Ralph C. A., *b.* 1962
1919		*Clwyd (4th),* (John) Murray Roberts, *b.* 1971, *s.* 2006	Hon. Jeremy T. R., *b.* 1973
1948		*Clydesmuir (3rd),* David Ronald Colville, *b.* 1949, *s.* 1996, *m.*	Hon. Richard C., *b.* 1980
1960	**	*Cobbold (2nd),* David Antony Fromanteel Lytton Cobbold, *b.* 1937, *s.* 1987, *m.*	Hon. Henry F. L. C., *b.* 1962
1919		*Cochrane of Cults (4th),* (Ralph Henry) Vere Cochrane, *b.* 1926, *s.* 1990, *m.*	Hon. Thomas H. V. C., *b.* 1957
1954		*Coleraine (2nd),* (James) Martin (Bonar) Law, *b.* 1931, *s.* 1980, *m.*	Hon. James P. B. L., *b.* 1975
1873		*Coleridge (5th),* William Duke Coleridge, *b.* 1937, *s.* 1984, *m.*	Hon. James D. C., *b.* 1967
1946		*Colgrain (4th),* Alastair Colin Leckie Campbell, *b.* 1951, *s.* 2008, *m.*	Hon. Thomas C. D. C., *b.* 1984
1917	**	*Colwyn (3rd),* (Ian) Anthony Hamilton-Smith, CBE, *b.* 1942, *s.* 1966, *m.*	Hon. Craig P. H.-S., *b.* 1968
1956		*Colyton (2nd),* Alisdair John Munro Hopkinson, *b.* 1958, *s.* 1996, *m.*	Hon. James P. M. H., *b.* 1983
1841		*Congleton (8th),* Christopher Patrick Parnell, *b.* 1930, *s.* 1967, *m.*	Hon. John P. C. P., *b.* 1959
1927		*Cornwallis (4th),* Fiennes Wykeham Jeremy Cornwallis, *b.* 1946, *s.* 2010, *m.*	Hon. Fiennes A. W. M. C., *b.* 1987
1874		*Cottesloe (5th),*John Tapling Fremantle, *b.* 1927, *s.* 1994, *m.*	Hon. Thomas F. H. F., *b.* 1966
1929		*Craigmyle (4th),* Thomas Columba Shaw, *b.* 1960, *s.* 1998, *m.*	Hon. Alexander F. S., *b.* 1988
1899		*Cranworth (3rd),* Philip Bertram Gurdon, *b.* 1940, *s.* 1964, *m.*	Hon. Sacha W. R. G., *b.* 1970
1959	**	*Crathorne (2nd),* Charles James Dugdale, KCVO, *b.* 1939, *s.* 1977, *w.*	Hon. Thomas A. J. D., *b.* 1977
1892		*Crawshaw (5th),* David Gerald Brooks, *b.* 1934, *s.* 1997, *m.*	Hon. John P. B., *b.* 1938
1940		*Croft (3rd),* Bernard William Henry Page Croft, *b.* 1949, *s.* 1997, *m.*	None
1797 I.		*Crofton (8th),* Edward Harry Piers Crofton, *b.* 1988, *s.* 2007	Hon. Charles M. G. C., *b.* 1988
1375		*Cromwell (7th),* Godfrey John Bewicke-Copley, *b.* 1960, *s.* 1982, *m.*	Hon. David G. B.-C., *b.* 1997
1947		*Crook (3rd),* Robert Douglas Edwin Crook, *b.* 1955, *s.* 2001, *m.*	Hon. Matthew R. C., *b.* 1990
1920		*Cullen of Ashbourne (3rd),* Edmund Willoughby Marsham Cokayne, *b.* 1916, *s.* 2000, *w.*	(Hon.) John O'B. M. C., *b.* 1920
1914		*Cunliffe (3rd),* Roger Cunliffe, *b.* 1932, *s.* 1963, *m.*	Hon. Henry C., *b.* 1962
1321		*Dacre (28th),* James Thomas Archibald Douglas-Home *b.* 1952, *s.* 2012, *w.*	Hon. Emily D.-H., *b.* 1983
1332		*Darcy de Knayth (19th),* Caspar David Ingrams, *b.* 1962, *s.* 2008, *m.*	Hon. Thomas R. I., *b.* 1999
1927		*Daresbury (4th),* Peter Gilbert Greenall, *b.* 1953, *s.* 1996, *m.*	Hon. Thomas E. G., *b.* 1984
1924		*Darling (3rd),* (Robert) Julian Henry Darling, *b.* 1944, *s.* 2003, *m.*	Hon. Robert J. C. D., *b.* 1972
1946		*Darwen (4th),* Paul Davies, *b.* 1962, *s.* 2011	Hon. Benjamin D., *b.* 1966
1932		*Davies (3rd),* David Davies, *b.* 1940, *s.* 1944, *m.*	Hon. David D. D., *b.* 1975
1812 I.		*Decies (7th),* Marcus Hugh Tristram de la Poer Beresford, *b.* 1948, *s.* 1992, *m.*	Hon. Robert M. D. de la P. B., *b.* 1988
1299		*de Clifford (27th),* John Edward Southwell Russell, *b.* 1928, *s.* 1982, *m.*	Miles E. S. R., *b.* 1966
1851		*De Freyne (8th),* Fulke Charles Arthur John French, *b.* 1957, *s.* 2009	Hon. Alexander J. C. F., *b.* 1988
1821		*Delamere (5th),* Hugh George Cholmondeley, *b.* 1934, *s.* 1979, *m.*	Hon. Thomas P. G. C., *b.* 1968
1838	**	*de Mauley (7th),* Rupert Charles Ponsonby, *b.* 1957, *s.* 2002, *m.*	Ashley G. P., *b.* 1959
1937	**	*Denham (2nd),* Bertram Stanley Mitford Bowyer, KBE, PC, *b.* 1927, *s.* 1948, *m.*	Hon. Richard G. G. B., *b.* 1959

1834	*Denman (6th),* Richard Thomas Stewart Denman, *b.* 1946, *s.* 2012, *m.*	Hon. Robert D., *b.* 1995
1887	*De Ramsey (4th),* John Ailwyn Fellowes, *b.* 1942, *s.* 1993, *m.*	Hon. Freddie J. F., *b.* 1978
1264	*de Ros (28th),* Peter Trevor Maxwell, *b.* 1958, *s.* 1983, *m. Premier Baron of England*	Hon. Finbar J. M., *b.* 1988
1881	*Derwent (5th),* Robin Evelyn Leo Vanden-Bempde-Johnstone, LVO, *b.* 1930, *s.* 1986, *m.*	Hon. Francis P. H. V.-B.-J., *b.* 1965
1831	*de Saumarez (7th),* Eric Douglas Saumarez, *b.* 1956, *s.* 1991, *m.*	Hon. Victor T. S., *b.* 1956
1910	*de Villiers (4th),* Alexander Charles de Villiers, *b.* 1940, *s.* 2001, *m.*	None
1930	*Dickinson (2nd),* Richard Clavering Hyett Dickinson, *b.* 1926, *s.* 1943, *m.*	Hon. Martin H. D., *b.* 1961
1620 I.	*Digby (12th) and Digby (5th) (1765),* Edward Henry Kenelm Digby, KCVO, *b.* 1924, *s.* 1964, *m.*	Hon. Henry N. K. D., *b.* 1954
1615	*Dormer (17th),* Geoffrey Henry Dormer, *b.* 1920, *s.* 1995, *m.*	Hon. William R. D., *b.* 1960
1943	*Dowding (3rd),* Piers Hugh Tremenheere Dowding, *b.* 1948, *s.* 1992	Hon. Mark D. J. D., *b.* 1949
1439	*Dudley (15th),* Jim Anthony Hill Wallace, *b.* 1930, *s.* 2002, *m.*	Hon. Jeremy W. G. W., *b.* 1964
1800 I.	*Dufferin and Clandeboye (11th),* John Francis Blackwood, *b.* 1944, *s.* 1991 (claim to the peerage not yet established), *m.*	Hon. Francis S. B., *b.* 1979
1929	*Dulverton (3rd),* (Gilbert) Michael Hamilton Wills, *b.* 1944, *s.* 1992, *m.*	Hon. Robert A. H. W., *b.* 1983
1800 I.	*Dunalley (7th),* Henry Francis Cornelius Prittie, *b.* 1948, *s.* 1992, *m.*	Hon. Joel H. P., *b.* 1981
1324 I.	*Dunboyne (30th),* Richard Pierce Theobald Butler, *b.* 1983, *s.* 2013	Michael J. B., *b.* 1944
1892	*Dunleath (6th),* Brian Henry Mulholland, *b.* 1950, *s.* 1997, *m.*	Hon. Andrew H. M., *b.* 1981
1439 I.	*Dunsany (21st),* Randal Plunkett, *b.* 1983, *s.* 2011	Hon. Oliver P., *b.* 1985
1780	*Dynevor (10th),* Hugo Griffith Uryan Rhys, *b.* 1966, *s.* 2008	Robert D. A. R., *b.* 1963
1963	*Egremont (2nd) and Leconfield (7th) (1859),* John Max Henry Scawen Wyndham, *b.* 1948, *s.* 1972, *m.*	Hon. George R. V. W., *b.* 1983
1643 S.	*Elibank (14th),* Alan D'Ardis Erskine-Murray, *b.* 1923, *s.* 1973, *w.*	Master of Elibank, *b.* 1964
1802	*Ellenborough (9th),* Rupert Edward Henry Law, *b.* 1955, *s.* 2013, *m.*	Hon. James R. T. L., *b.* 1983
1509 S.	*Elphinstone (19th) and Elphinstone (5th) (1885),* Alexander Mountstuart Elphinstone, *b.* 1980, *s.* 1994, *m.*	Master of Elphinstone, *b.* 2011
1934	** *Elton (2nd),* Rodney Elton, TD, *b.* 1930, *s.* 1973, *m.*	Hon. Edward P. E., *b.* 1966
1627 S.	*Fairfax of Cameron (14th),* Nicholas John Albert Fairfax, *b.* 1956, *s.* 1964, *m.*	Hon. Edward N. T. F., *b.* 1984
1961	*Fairhaven (3rd),* Ailwyn Henry George Broughton, *b.* 1936, *s.* 1973, *m.*	Maj. Hon. James H. A. B., *b.* 1963
1916	*Faringdon (3rd),* Charles Michael Henderson, KCVO, *b.* 1937, *s.* 1977, *m.*	Hon. James H. H., *b.* 1961
1756 I.	*Farnham (13th),* Simon Kenlis Maxwell, *b.* 1933, *s.* 2001, *m.*	Hon. Robin S. M., *b.* 1965
1856 I.	*Fermoy (6th),* Patrick Maurice Burke Roche, *b.* 1967, *s.* 1984, *m.*	Hon. E. Hugh B. R., *b.* 1972
1826	*Feversham (7th),* Jasper Orlando Slingsby Duncombe, *b.* 1968, *s.* 2009	Hon. Jake B. D., *b.* 1972
1798 I.	*ffrench (8th),* Robuck John Peter Charles Mario ffrench, *b.* 1956, *s.* 1986, *m.*	Hon. John C. M. J. F. ff., *b.* 1928
1909	*Fisher (4th),* Patrick Vavasseur Fisher, *b.* 1953, *s.* 2012, *m.*	Hon. John C. V. F., *b.* 1979
1295	*Fitzwalter (22nd),* Julian Brook Plumptre, *b.* 1952, *s.* 2004, *m.*	Hon. Edward B. P., *b.* 1989
1776	*Foley (9th),* Thomas Henry Foley, *b.* 1961, *s.* 2012	Rupert T. F., *b.* 1970
1445 S.	*Forbes (23rd),* Malcolm Nigel Forbes, *b.* 1946, *s.* 2013, *m. Premier Lord of Scotland*	Master of Forbes, *b.* 1970
1821	*Forester (9th),* Charles Richard George Weld-Forester, *b.* 1975, *s.* 2004, *m.*	Wolstan W. W.-F., *b.* 1941
1922	*Forres (4th),* Alastair Stephen Grant Williamson, *b.* 1946, *s.* 1978, *m.*	Hon. George A. M. W., *b.* 1972
1917	*Forteviot (4th),* John James Evelyn Dewar, *b.* 1938, *s.* 1993, *w.*	Hon. Alexander J. E. D., *b.* 1971
1951	** *Freyberg (3rd),* Valerian Bernard Freyberg, *b.* 1970, *s.* 1993	Hon. Joseph J. F., *b.* 2007
1917	*Gainford (4th),* George Pease, *b.* 1926, *s.* 2013, *m.*	Hon. Adrian C. P., *b.* 1960
1818 I.	*Garvagh (5th),* (Alexander Leopold Ivor) George Canning, *b.* 1920, *s.* 1956, *m.*	Hon. Spencer G. S. de R. C., *b.* 1953
1942	** *Geddes (3rd),* Euan Michael Ross Geddes, *b.* 1937, *s.* 1975, *m.*	Hon. James G. N. G., *b.* 1969
1876	*Gerard (5th),* Anthony Robert Hugo Gerard, *b.* 1949, *s.* 1992, *m.*	Hon. Rupert B. C. G., *b.* 1981
1824	*Gifford (6th),* Anthony Maurice Gifford, QC, *b.* 1940, *s.* 1961, *m.*	Hon. Thomas A. G., *b.* 1967
1917	*Gisborough (3rd),* Thomas Richard John Long Chaloner, *b.* 1927, *s.* 1951, *m.*	Hon. T. Peregrine L. C., *b.* 1961
1960	*Gladwyn (2nd),* Miles Alvery Gladwyn Jebb, *b.* 1930, *s.* 1996	None
1899	*Glanusk (5th),* Christopher Russell Bailey, *b.* 1942, *s.* 1997, *m.*	Hon. Charles H. B., *b.* 1976
1918	** *Glenarthur (4th),* Simon Mark Arthur, *b.* 1944, *s.* 1976, *m.*	Hon. Edward A. A., *b.* 1973
1911 M.	*Glenconner (4th),* Cody Charles Edward Tennant, *b.* 1994, *s.* 2010	Euan L. T., *b.* 1983
1964	*Glendevon (3rd),* Jonathan Charles Hope, *b.* 1952, *s.* 2009	None
1922	*Glendyne (4th),* John Nivison, *b.* 1960, *s.* 2008	None
1939	** *Glentoran (3rd),* (Thomas) Robin (Valerian) Dixon, CBE, *b.* 1935, *s.* 1995, *m.*	Hon. Daniel G. D., *b.* 1959
1909	*Gorell (5th),* John Picton Gorell Barnes, *b.* 1959, *s.* 2007, *m.*	Hon. Oliver G. B., *b.* 1993
1953	** *Grantchester (3rd),* Christopher John Suenson-Taylor, *b.* 1951, *s.* 1995, *m.*	Hon. Jesse D. S.-T., *b.* 1977
1782	*Grantley (8th),* Richard William Brinsley Norton, *b.* 1956, *s.* 1995	Hon. Francis J. H. N., *b.* 1960
1794 I.	*Graves (10th),* Timothy Evelyn Graves, *b.* 1960, *s.* 2002	None
1445 S.	*Gray (23rd),* Andrew Godfrey Diarmid Stuart Campbell-Gray, *b.* 1964, *s.* 2003, *m.*	Master of Gray, *b.* 1996
1950	*Greenhill (3rd),* Malcolm Greenhill, *b.* 1924, *s.* 1989	None

1927	** *Greenway (4th),* Ambrose Charles Drexel Greenway, *b.* 1941, *s.* 1975, *m.*	Hon. Nigel. P. G., *b.* 1944
1902	*Grenfell (3rd) and Grenfell of Kilvey (life peerage, 2000),* Julian Pascoe Francis St Leger Grenfell, *b.* 1935, *s.* 1976, *m.*	Richard A. St L. G., *b.* 1966
1944	*Gretton (4th),* John Lysander Gretton, *b.* 1975, *s.* 1989	Hon. John F. B. G., *b.* 2008
1397	*Grey of Codnor (6th),* Richard Henry Cornwall-Legh, *b.* 1936, *s.* 1996, *m.*	Hon. Richard S. C. C.-L., *b.* 1976
1955	*Gridley (3rd),* Richard David Arnold Gridley, *b.* 1956, *s.* 1996, *m.*	Peter A. C. G., *b.* 1940
1964	*Grimston of Westbury (3rd),* Robert John Sylvester Grimston, *b.* 1951, *s.* 2003, *m.*	Hon. Gerald C. W. G., *b.* 1953
1886	*Grimthorpe (5th),* Edward John Beckett, *b.* 1954, *s.* 2003, *m.*	Hon. Harry M. B., *b.* 1993
1945	*Hacking (3rd),* Douglas David Hacking, *b.* 1938, *s.* 1971, *m.*	Hon. Douglas F. H., *b.* 1968
1950	*Haden-Guest (5th),* Christopher Haden-Guest, *b.* 1948, *s.* 1996, *m.*	Hon. Nicholas H.-G., *b.* 1951
1886	*Hamilton of Dalzell (5th),* Gavin Goulburn Hamilton, *b.* 1968, *s.* 2006, *m.*	Hon. Francis A. J. G. H., *b.* 2009
1874	*Hampton (7th),* John Humphrey Arnott Pakington, *b.* 1964, *s.* 2003, *m.*	Hon. Charles R. C. P., *b.* 2005
1939	*Hankey (3rd),* Donald Robin Alers Hankey, *b.* 1938, *s.* 1996, *m.*	Hon. Alexander M. A. H., *b.* 1947
1958	*Harding of Petherton (2nd),* John Charles Harding, *b.* 1928, *s.* 1989, *w.*	Hon. William A. J. H., *b.* 1969
1910	*Hardinge of Penshurst (4th),* Julian Alexander Hardinge, *b.* 1945, *s.* 1997	Hon. Hugh F. H., *b.* 1948
1876	*Harlech (6th),* Francis David Ormsby-Gore, *b.* 1954, *s.* 1985, *m.*	Hon. Jasset D. C. O.-G., *b.* 1986
1939	*Harmsworth (3rd),* Thomas Harold Raymond Harmsworth, *b.* 1939, *s.* 1990, *m.*	Hon. Dominic M. E. H., *b.* 1973
1815	*Harris (8th),* Anthony Harris, *b.* 1942, *s.* 1996, *m.*	Rear-Adm. Michael G. T. H., *b.* 1941
1954	*Harvey of Tasburgh (3rd),* Charles John Giuseppe Harvey, *b.* 1951, *s.* 2010, *m.*	Hon. John H., *b.* 1993
1295	*Hastings (23rd),* Delaval Thomas Harold Astley, *b.* 1960, *s.* 2007, *m.*	Hon. Jacob A. A., *b.* 1991
1835	*Hatherton (8th),* Edward Charles Littleton, *b.* 1950, *s.* 1985, *m.*	Hon. Thomas E. L., *b.* 1977
1776 M.	*Hawke (12th),* William Martin Theodore Hawke, *b.* 1995, *s.* 2010	None
1927	*Hayter (4th),* George William Michael Chubb, *b.* 1943, *s.* 2003, *m.*	Hon. Thomas F. F. C., *b.* 1986
1945	*Hazlerigg (3rd),* Arthur Grey Hazlerigg, *b.* 1951, *s.* 2002, *m.*	Hon. Arthur W. G. H. *b.* 1987
1943	*Hemingford (3rd),* (Dennis) Nicholas Herbert, *b.* 1934, *s.* 1982, *m.*	Hon. Christopher D. C. H., *b.* 1973
1906	*Hemphill (6th),* Charles Andrew Martyn Martyn-Hemphill, *b.* 1954, *s.* 2012, *m.*	Hon. Richard P. L. M.-H., *b.* 1990
1799 I.	** *Henley (8th) and Northington (6th) (1885),* Oliver Michael Robert Eden, PC, *b.* 1953, *s.* 1977, *m.*	Hon. John W. O. E., *b.* 1988
1800 I.	*Henniker (9th) and Hartismere (6th) (1866),* Mark Ian Philip Chandos Henniker-Major, *b.* 1947, *s.* 2004, *m.*	Hon. Edward G. M. H.-M., *b.* 1985
1461	*Herbert (19th),* David John Seyfried Herbert, *b.* 1952, *s.* 2002, *m.*	Hon. Oliver R. S. H., *b.* 1976
1935	*Hesketh (3rd),* Thomas Alexander Fermor-Hesketh, KBE, PC, *b.* 1950, *s.* 1955, *m.*	Hon. Frederick H. F.-H., *b.* 1988
1828	*Heytesbury (7th),* James William Holmes à Court, *b.* 1967, *s.* 2004, *m.*	Peter M. H.. H. à. C., *b.* 1968
1886	*Hindlip (6th),* Charles Henry Allsopp, *b.* 1940, *s.* 1993, *m.*	Hon. Henry W. A., *b.* 1973
1950	*Hives (3rd),* Matthew Peter Hives, *b.* 1971, *s.* 1997	Hon. Michael B. H., *b.* 1926
1912	*Hollenden (4th),* Ian Hampden Hope-Morley, *b.* 1946, *s.* 1999, *m.*	Hon. Edward H.-M., *b.* 1981
1897	*Holm Patrick (4th),* Hans James David Hamilton, *b.* 1955, *s.* 1991, *m.*	Hon. Ion H. J. H., *b.* 1956
1797 I.	*Hotham (8th),* Henry Durand Hotham, *b.* 1940, *s.* 1967, *m.*	Hon. William B. H., *b.* 1972
1881	*Hothfield (6th),* Anthony Charles Sackville Tufton, *b.* 1939, *s.* 1991, *m.*	Hon. William S. T., *b.* 1977
1930	*Howard of Penrith (3rd),* Philip Esme Howard, *b.* 1945, *s.* 1999, *m.*	Hon. Thomas Philip H., *b.* 1974
1960	*Howick of Glendale (2nd),* Charles Evelyn Baring, *b.* 1937, *s.* 1973, *m.*	Hon. David E. C. B., *b.* 1975
1796 I.	*Huntingfield (7th),* Joshua Charles Vanneck, *b.* 1954, *s.* 1994, *w.*	Hon. Gerard C. A. V., *b.* 1985
1866	** *Hylton (5th),* Raymond Hervey Jolliffe, *b.* 1932, *s.* 1967, *m.*	Hon. William H. M. J., *b.* 1967
1933	*Iliffe (3rd),* Robert Peter Richard Iliffe, *b.* 1944, *s.* 1996, *m.*	Hon. Edward R. I., *b.* 1968
1543 I.	*Inchiquin (18th),* Conor Myles John O'Brien, *b.* 1943, *s.* 1982, *m.*	Conor J. A. O'B., *b.* 1952
1962	*Inchyra (3rd),* Christian James Charles Hoyer Millar, *b.* 1962, *s.* 2011, *m.*	Hon. Jake C. R. M., *b.* 1996
1964	** *Inglewood (2nd),* (William) Richard Fletcher-Vane, *b.* 1951, *s.* 1989, *m.*	Hon. Henry W. F. F.-V., *b.* 1990
1919	*Inverforth (4th),* Andrew Peter Weir, *b.* 1966, *s.* 1982	Hon. Benjamin A. W., *b.* 1997
1941	*Ironside (2nd),* Edmund Oslac Ironside, *b.* 1924, *s.* 1959, *m.*	Hon. Charles E. G. I., *b.* 1956
1952	*Jeffreys (3rd),* Christopher Henry Mark Jeffreys, *b.* 1957, *s.* 1986, *m.*	Hon. Arthur M. H. J., *b.* 1989
1906	*Joicey (5th),* James Michael Joicey, *b.* 1953, *s.* 1993, *m.*	Hon. William J. J., *b.* 1990
1937	*Kenilworth (4th),* (John) Randle Siddeley, *b.* 1954, *s.* 1981, *m.*	Hon. William R. J. S., *b.* 1992
1935	*Kennet (3rd),* William Aldus Thoby Young, *b.* 1957, *s.* 2009, *m.*	Hon. Archibald W. K. Y., *b.* 1992
1776 I.	*Kensington (8th) and Kensington (5th) (1886),* Hugh Ivor Edwardes, *b.* 1933, *s.* 1981, *m.*	Hon. W. Owen A. E., *b.* 1964
1951	*Kenswood (2nd),* John Michael Howard Whitfield, *b.* 1930, *s.* 1963, *m.*	Hon. Michael C. W., *b.* 1955
1788	*Kenyon (6th),* Lloyd Tyrell-Kenyon, *b.* 1947, *s.* 1993, *m.*	Hon. Lloyd N. T.-K., *b.* 1972
1947	*Kershaw (4th),* Edward John Kershaw, *b.* 1936, *s.* 1962, *m.*	Hon. John C. E. K., *b.* 1971
1943	*Keyes (3rd),* Charles William Packe Keyes, *b.* 1951, *s.* 2005, *m.*	Hon. (Leopold R.) J. K., *b.* 1956
1909	*Kilbracken (4th),* Christopher John Godley, *b.* 1945, *s.* 2006, *m.*	Hon. James J. G., *b.* 1972

1900	*Killanin (4th),* (George) Redmond Fitzpatrick Morris, *b.* 1947, *s.* 1999, *m.*	Hon. Luke M. G. M., *b.* 1975
1943	*Killearn (3rd),* Victor Miles George Aldous Lampson, *b.* 1941, *s.* 1996, *m.*	Hon. Miles H. M. L., *b.* 1977
1789 I.	*Kilmaine (8th),* John Francis Sandford Browne, *b.* 1983, *s.* 2013	Revd Aubrey R. C. B., *b.* 1931
1831	*Kilmarnock (8th),* Dr Robin Jordan Boyd, *b.* 1941, *s.* 2009, *m.*	Hon. Simon J. B., *b.* 1978
1941	*Kindersley (3rd),* Robert Hugh Molesworth Kindersley, *b.* 1929, *s.* 1976, *m.*	Hon. Rupert J. M. K., *b.* 1955
1223 I.	*Kingsale (36th),* Nevinson Mark de Courcy, *b.* 1958, *s.* 2005, *m., Premier Baron of Ireland*	Joseph K. C. de C., *b.* 1955
1902	*Kinross (5th),* Christopher Patrick Balfour, *b.* 1949, *s.* 1985, *m.*	Hon. Alan I. B., *b.* 1978
1951	*Kirkwood (3rd),* David Harvie Kirkwood, PHD, *b.* 1931, *s.* 1970, *m.*	Hon. James S. K., *b.* 1937
1800 I.	*Langford (9th),* Col. Geoffrey Alexander Rowley-Conwy, OBE, *b.* 1912, *s.* 1953, *m.*	Hon. Owain G. R.-C., *b.* 1958
1942	*Latham (2nd),* Dominic Charles Latham, *b.* 1954, *s.* 1970	Anthony M. L., *b.* 1954
1431	*Latymer (9th),* Crispin James Alan Nevill Money-Coutts, *b.* 1955, *s.* 2003, *m.*	Hon. Drummond W. T. M.-C., *b.* 1986
1869	*Lawrence (5th),* David John Downer Lawrence, *b.* 1937, *s.* 1968	None
1947	*Layton (3rd),* Geoffrey Michael Layton, *b.* 1947, *s.* 1989, *m.*	Jonathan F. L., *b.* 1942
1839	*Leigh (6th),* Christopher Dudley Piers Leigh, *b.* 1960, *s.* 2003, *m.*	Hon. Rupert D. L., *b.* 1994
1962	*Leighton of St Mellons (3rd),* Robert William Henry Leighton Seager, *b.* 1955, *s.* 1998	Hon. Simon J. L. S., *b.* 1957
1797	*Lilford (8th),* Mark Vernon Powys, *b.* 1975, *s.* 2005	Robert C. L. P., *b.* 1930
1945	*Lindsay of Birker (3rd),* James Francis Lindsay, *b.* 1945, *s.* 1994, *m.*	Alexander S. L., *b.* 1940
1758 I.	*Lisle (9th),* (John) Nicholas Geoffrey Lysaght, *b.* 1960, *s.* 2003	Hon. David J. L., *b.* 1963
1850	*Londesborough (9th),* Richard John Denison, *b.* 1959, *s.* 1968, *m.*	Hon. James F. D., *b.* 1990
1541 I.	*Louth (17th),* Jonathan Oliver Plunkett, *b.* 1952, *s.* 2013	Hon. Matthew O. P., *b.* 1982
1458 S.	*Lovat (16th) and Lovat (5th) (1837),* Simon Fraser, *b.* 1977, *s.* 1995	Hon. Jack F., *b.* 1984
1946	*Lucas of Chilworth (3rd),* Simon William Lucas, *b.* 1957, *s.* 2001, *m.*	Hon. John R. M. L., *b.* 1995
1663	** *Lucas (11th) and Dingwall (14th) (S. 1609),* Ralph Matthew Palmer, *b.* 1951, *s.* 1991	Hon. Lewis E. P., *b.* 1987
1929	** *Luke (3rd),* Arthur Charles St John Lawson-Johnston, *b.* 1933, *s.* 1996, *m.*	Hon. Ian J. St J. L.-J., *b.* 1963
1914	** *Lyell (3rd),* Charles Lyell, *b.* 1939, *s.* 1943	None
1859	*Lyveden (7th),* Jack Leslie Vernon, *b.* 1938, *s.* 1999, *m.*	Hon. Colin R. V., *b.* 1967
1959	*MacAndrew (3rd),* Christopher Anthony Colin MacAndrew, *b.* 1945, *s.* 1989, *m.*	Hon. Oliver C. J. M., *b.* 1983
1776 I.	*Macdonald (8th),* Godfrey James Macdonald of Macdonald, *b.* 1947, *s.* 1970, *m.*	Hon. Godfrey E. H. T. M., *b.* 1982
1937	*McGowan (4th),* Harry John Charles McGowan, *b.* 1971, *s.* 2003, *m.*	Hon. Dominic J. W. M., *b.* 1951
1922	*Maclay (3rd),* Joseph Paton Maclay, *b.* 1942, *s.* 1969, *m.*	Hon. Joseph P. M., *b.* 1977
1955	*McNair (3rd),* Duncan James McNair, *b.* 1947, *s.* 1989, *m.*	Hon. William S. A. M., *b.* 1958
1951	*Macpherson of Drumochter (3rd),* James Anthony Macpherson, *b.* 1979, *s.* 2008	Hon. Daniel T. M., *b.* 2013
1937	** *Mancroft (3rd),* Benjamin Lloyd Stormont Mancroft, *b.* 1957, *s.* 1987, *m.*	Hon. Arthur L. S. M., *b.* 1995
1807	*Manners (6th),* John Hugh Robert Manners, *b.* 1956, *s.* 2008	John A. D. M., *b.* 2011
1922	*Manton (4th),* Miles Ronald Marcus Watson, *b.* 1958, *s.* 2003, *m.*	Hon. Thomas N. C. D. W., *b.* 1985
1908	*Marchamley (4th),* William Francis Whiteley, *b.* 1968, *s.* 1994	None
1964	*Margadale (3rd),* Alastair John Morrison, *b.* 1958, *s.* 2003, *m.*	Hon. Declan J. M., *b.* 1993
1961	*Marks of Broughton (3rd),* Simon Richard Marks, *b.* 1950, *s.* 1998, *m.*	Hon. Michael M., *b.* 1989
1964	*Martonmere (2nd),* John Stephen Robinson, *b.* 1963, *s.* 1989	Hon. James I. R., *b.* 2003
1776 I.	*Massy (10th),* David Hamon Somerset Massy, *b.* 1947, *s.* 1995	Hon. John H. M., *b.* 1950
1935	*May (4th),* Jasper Bertram St John May, *b.* 1965, *s.* 2006	None
1928	*Melchett (4th),* Peter Robert Henry Mond, *b.* 1948, *s.* 1973	None
1925	*Merrivale (4th),* Derek John Philip Duke, *b.* 1948, *s.* 2007, *m.*	Hon. Thomas D., *b.* 1980
1911	*Merthyr (4th),* Trevor Oswin Lewis, CBE, *b.* 1935, *s.* 1977, *m.* Disclaimed for life 1977.	David T. L., *b.* 1977
1919	*Meston (3rd),* James Meston, QC, *b.* 1950, *s.* 1984, *m.*	Hon. Thomas J. D. M., *b.* 1977
1838	** *Methuen (7th),* Robert Alexander Holt Methuen, *b.* 1931, *s.* 1994, *m.*	James P. A. M.-C., *b.* 1952
1711	*Middleton (13th),* Michael Charles James Willoughby, *b.* 1948, *s.* 2011, *m.*	Hon. James W. M. W., *b.* 1976
1939	*Milford (4th),* Guy Wogan Philipps, *b.* 1961, *s.* 1999, *m.*	Hon. Archie S. P., *b.* 1997
1933	*Milne (3rd),* George Alexander Milne, *b.* 1941, *s.* 2005	Hon. Iain C. L. M., *b.* 1949
1951	*Milner of Leeds (3rd),* Richard James Milner, *b.* 1959, *s.* 2003, *m.*	None
1947	*Milverton (2nd), Revd* Fraser Arthur Richard Richards, *b.* 1930, *s.* 1978, *m.*	Hon. Michael H. R., *b.* 1936
1873	*Moncreiff (6th),* Rhoderick Harry Wellwood Moncreiff, *b.* 1954, *s.* 2002, *m.*	Hon. Harry J. W. M., *b.* 1986
1884	*Monk Bretton (3rd),* John Charles Dodson, *b.* 1924, *s.* 1933, *m.*	Hon. Christopher M. D., *b.* 1958
1885	*Monkswell (5th),* Gerard Collier, *b.* 1947, *s.* 1984, *m.*	Hon. James A. C., *b.* 1977
1728	*Monson (12th),* Nicholas John Monson, *b.* 1955, *s.* 2011, *m.*	Hon. Andrew A. J. M., *b.* 1959
1885	** *Montagu of Beaulieu (3rd),* Edward John Barrington Douglas-Scott-Montagu, *b.* 1926, *s.* 1929, *m.*	Hon. Ralph D.-S.-M., *b.* 1961
1839	*Monteagle of Brandon (6th),* Gerald Spring Rice, *b.* 1926, *s.* 1946, *m.*	Hon. Charles J. S. R., *b.* 1953

1943	** *Moran (2nd),* (Richard) John (McMoran) Wilson, KCMG, *b.* 1924, *s.* 1977, *m.*	Hon. James M. W., *b.* 1952
1918	*Morris (4th),* Thomas Anthony Salmon Morris, *b.* 1982, *s.* 2011	Hon. John M. M., *b.* 1983
1950	*Morris of Kenwood (3rd),* Jonathan David Morris, *b.* 1968, *s.* 2004, *m.*	Hon. Benjamin J. M., *b.* 1998
1831	*Mostyn (7th),* Gregory Philip Roger Lloyd-Mostyn, *b.* 1984, *s.* 2011	Roger Hugh L.-M., *b.* 1941
1933	*Mottistone (6th),* Christopher David Peter Seely, *b.* 1974, *s.* 2013	Hon. Richard W. A. S., *b.* 1988
1945	*Mountevans (3rd),* Edward Patrick Broke Evans, *b.* 1943, *s.* 1974, *m.*	Hon. Jeffrey de C. R. E., *b.* 1948
1283	*Mowbray (27th), Segrave (28th) (1295) and Stourton (24th) (1448),* Edward William Stephen Stourton, *b.* 1953, *s.* 2006, *m.*	Hon. James C. P. S., *b.* 1991
1932	*Moyne (3rd),* Jonathan Bryan Guinness, *b.* 1930, *s.* 1992, *m.*	Hon. Valentine G. B. G., *b.* 1959
1929	** *Moynihan (4th),* Colin Berkeley Moynihan, *b.* 1955, *s.* 1997, *m.*	Hon. Nicholas E. B. M., *b.* 1994
1781 I.	*Muskerry (9th),* Robert Fitzmaurice Deane, *b.* 1948, *s.* 1988, *m.*	Hon. Jonathan F. D., *b.* 1986
1627 S.	*Napier (15th) and Ettrick (6th) (1872),* Francis David Charles Napier, *b.* 1962, *s.* 2012, *m.*	Master of Napier, *b.* 1996
1868	*Napier of Magdala (6th),* Robert Alan Napier, *b.* 1940, *s.* 1987, *m.*	Hon. James R. N., *b.* 1966
1940	*Nathan (3rd),* Rupert Harry Bernard Nathan, *b.* 1957, *s.* 2007, *m.*	None
1960	*Nelson of Stafford (4th),* Alistair William Henry Nelson, *b.* 1973, *s.* 2006	Hon. James J. N., *b.* 1947
1959	*Netherthorpe (3rd),* James Frederick Turner, *b.* 1964, *s.* 1982, *m.*	Hon. Andrew J. E. T., *b.* 1993
1946	*Newall (2nd),* Francis Storer Eaton Newall, *b.* 1930, *s.* 1963, *m.*	Hon. Richard H. E. N., *b.* 1961
1776 I.	*Newborough (8th),* Robert Vaughan Wynn, *b.* 1949, *s.* 1998, *m.*	Antony C. V. W., *b.* 1949
1892	*Newton (5th),* Richard Thomas Legh, *b.* 1950, *s.* 1992, *m.*	Hon. Piers R. L., *b.* 1979
1930	*Noel-Buxton (3rd),* Martin Connal Noel-Buxton, *b.* 1940, *s.* 1980, *m.*	Hon. Charles C. N.-B., *b.* 1975
1957	*Norrie (2nd),* (George) Willoughby Moke Norrie, *b.* 1936, *s.* 1977, *m.*	Hon. Mark W. J. N., *b.* 1972
1884	** *Northbourne (5th),* Christopher George Walter James, *b.* 1926, *s.* 1982, *m.*	Hon. Charles W. H. J., *b.* 1960
1866	** *Northbrook (6th),* Francis Thomas Baring, *b.* 1954, *s.* 1990, *m.*	To the Baronetcy, Peter B. *b.* 1939
1878	*Norton (8th),* James Nigel Arden Adderley, *b.* 1947, *s.* 1993, *m.*	Hon. Edward J. A. A., *b.* 1982
1906	*Nunburnholme (6th),* Stephen Charles Wilson, *b.* 1973, *s.* 2000	Hon. David M. W., *b.* 1954
1950	*Ogmore (3rd),* Morgan Rees-Williams, *b.* 1937, *s.* 2004, *m.*	Hon. Tudor D. R.-W., *b.* 1991
1870	*O'Hagan (4th),* Charles Towneley Strachey, *b.* 1945, *s.* 1961	Hon. Richard T. S., *b.* 1950
1868	*O'Neill (4th),* Raymond Arthur Clanaboy O'Neill, KCVO, TD, *b.* 1933, *s.* 1944, *m.*	Hon. Shane S. C. O'N., *b.* 1965
1836 I.	*Oranmore and Browne (5th) and Mereworth (3rd) (1926),* Dominick Geoffrey Thomas Browne, *b.* 1929, *s.* 2002	Shaun D. B., *b.* 1964
1933	** *Palmer (4th),* Adrian Bailie Nottage Palmer, *b.* 1951, *s.* 1990, *m.*	Hon. Hugo B. R. P., *b.* 1980
1914	*Parmoor (5th),* Michael Leonard Seddon Cripps, *b.* 1942, *s.* 2008, *m.*	Hon. Henry W. A. C., *b.* 1976
1937	*Pender (3rd),* John Willoughby Denison-Pender, *b.* 1933, *s.* 1965, *m.*	Hon. Henry J. R. D.-P., *b.* 1968
1866	*Penrhyn (7th),* Simon Douglas-Pennant, *b.* 1938, *s.* 2003, *m.*	Hon. Edward S. D.-P., *b.* 1966
1603	*Petre (18th),* John Patrick Lionel Petre, *b.* 1942, *s.* 1989, *m.*	Hon. Dominic W. P., *b.* 1966
1918	*Phillimore (5th),* Francis Stephen Phillimore, *b.* 1944, *s.* 1994, *m.*	Hon. Tristan A. S. P., *b.* 1977
1945	*Piercy (3rd),* James William Piercy, *b.* 1946, *s.* 1981	Hon. Mark E. P. P., *b.* 1953
1827	*Plunket (8th),* Robin Rathmore Plunket, *b.* 1925, *s.* 1975, *m.*	Tyrone S. T. P., *b.* 1966
1831	*Poltimore (7th),* Mark Coplestone Bampfylde, *b.* 1957, *s.* 1978, *m.*	Hon. Henry A. W. B., *b.* 1985
1690 S.	*Polwarth (11th),* Andrew Walter Hepburne-Scott, *b.* 1947, *s.* 2005, *m.*	Master of Polwarth, *b.* 1973
1930	*Ponsonby of Shulbrede (4th) and Ponsonby of Roehampton (life peerage, 2000),* Frederick Matthew Thomas Ponsonby, *b.* 1958, *s.* 1990	Hon. Cameron J. J. P., *b.* 1995
1958	*Poole (2nd),* David Charles Poole, *b.* 1945, *s.* 1993, *m.*	Hon. Oliver J. P., *b.* 1972
1852	*Raglan (6th),* Geoffrey Somerset, *b.* 1932, *s.* 2010, *m.*	Iggy F. S., *b.* 2004
1932	*Rankeillour (5th),* Michael Richard Hope, *b.* 1940, *s.* 2005, *m.*	James F. H., *b.* 1968
1953	*Rathcavan (3rd),* Hugh Detmar Torrens O'Neill, *b.* 1939, *s.* 1994, *m.*	Hon. François H. N. O'N., *b.* 1984
1916	*Rathcreedan (3rd),* Christopher John Norton, *b.* 1949, *s.* 1990, *m.*	Hon. Adam G. N., *b.* 1952
1868 I.	*Rathdonnell (5th),* Thomas Benjamin McClintock-Bunbury, *b.* 1938, *s.* 1959, *m.*	Hon. William L. M.-B., *b.* 1966
1911	*Ravensdale (3rd),* Nicholas Mosley, MC, *b.* 1923, *s.* 1966, *m.*	Daniel N. M., *b.* 1982
1821	*Ravensworth (9th),* Thomas Arthur Hamish Liddell, *b.* 1954, *s.* 2004, *m.*	Hon. Henry A. T. L., *b.* 1987
1821	*Rayleigh (6th),* John Gerald Strutt, *b.* 1960, *s.* 1988, *m.*	Hon. John F. S., *b.* 1993
1937	** *Rea (3rd),* John Nicolas Rea, MD, *b.* 1928, *s.* 1981, *m.*	Hon. Matthew J. R., *b.* 1956
1628 S.	*Reay (15th),* Aeneas Simon Mackay, *b.* 1965, *s.* 2013, *m.*	Master of Reay, *b.* 2010
1902	*Redesdale (6th) and Mitford (life peerage 2000),* Rupert Bertram Mitford, *b.* 1967, *s.* 1991, *m.*	Hon. Bertram D. M., *b.* 2000
1940	*Reith (2nd),* Christopher John Reith, *b.* 1928, *s.* 1971, *m.* Disclaimed for life 1972.	Hon. James H. J. R., *b.* 1971
1928	*Remnant (3rd),* James Wogan Remnant, CVO, *b.* 1930, *s.* 1967, *m.*	Hon. Philip J. R., CBE, *b.* 1954
1806 I.	*Rendlesham (9th),* Charles William Brooke Thellusson, *b.* 1954, *s.* 1999, *m.*	Hon. Peter R. T., *b.* 1920
1933	*Rennell (4th),* James Roderick David Tremayne Rodd, *b.* 1978, *s.* 2006	None
1964	*Renwick (2nd),* Harry Andrew Renwick, *b.* 1935, *s.* 1973, *m.*	Hon. Robert J. R., *b.* 1966
1885	*Revelstoke (7th),* Alexander Rupert Baring, *b.* 1970, *s.* 2012	Hon. Thomas J. B., *b.* 1971
1905	*Ritchie of Dundee (6th),* Charles Rupert Rendall Ritchie, *b.* 1958, *s.* 2008, *m.*	Hon. Sebastian R., *b.* 2004

1935	*Riverdale (3rd),* Anthony Robert Balfour, *b.* 1960, *s.* 1998	Arthur M. B., *b.* 1938
1961	*Robertson of Oakridge (3rd),* William Brian Elworthy Robertson, *b.* 1975, *s.* 2009, *m.*	None
1938	*Roborough (3rd),* Henry Massey Lopes, *b.* 1940, *s.* 1992, *m.*	Hon. Massey J. H. L., *b.* 1969
1931	*Rochester (2nd),* Foster Charles Lowry Lamb, *b.* 1916, *s.* 1955, *w.*	Hon. David C. L., *b.* 1944
1934	*Rockley (4th),* Anthony Robert Cecil, *b.* 1961, *s.* 2011, *m.*	Hon. William E. C., *b.* 1996
1782 M.	*Rodney (11th),* John George Brydges Rodney, *b.* 1999, *s.* 2011	Nicholas S. H. R., *b.* 1947
1651 S.	*Rollo (14th) and Dunning (5th) (1869),* David Eric Howard Rollo, *b.* 1943, *s.* 1997, *m.*	Master of Rollo, *b.* 1972
1959	*Rootes (3rd),* Nicholas Geoffrey Rootes, *b.* 1951, *s.* 1992, *m.*	William B. R., *b.* 1944
1796 I.	*Rossmore (7th) and Rossmore (6th) (1838),* William Warner Westenra, *b.* 1931, *s.* 1958, *m.*	Hon. Benedict W. W., *b.* 1983
1939	** *Rotherwick (3rd),* (Herbert) Robin Cayzer, *b.* 1954, *s.* 1996, *m.*	Hon. H. Robin C., *b.* 1989
1885	*Rothschild (4th),* (Nathaniel Charles) Jacob Rothschild, OM, GBE, *b.* 1936, *s.* 1990, *m.*	Hon. Nathaniel P. V. J. R., *b.* 1971
1911	*Rowallan (4th),* John Polson Cameron Corbett, *b.* 1947, *s.* 1993	Hon. Jason W. P. C. C., *b.* 1972
1947	*Rugby (3rd),* Robert Charles Maffey, *b.* 1951, *s.* 1990, *m.*	Hon. Timothy J. H. M., *b.* 1975
1919	*Russell of Liverpool (3rd),* Simon Gordon Jared Russell, *b.* 1952, *s.* 1981, *m.*	Hon. Edward C. S. R., *b.* 1985
1876	*Sackville (7th),* Robert Bertrand Sackville-West, *b.* 1958, *s.* 2004, *m.*	Hon. Arthur S-W., *b.* 2000
1964	*St Helens (2nd),* Richard Francis Hughes-Young, *b.* 1945, *s.* 1980, *m.*	Hon. Henry T. H.-Y., *b.* 1986
1559	** *St John of Bletso (21st),* Anthony Tudor St John, *b.* 1957, *s.* 1978, *m.*	Hon. Oliver B. St J., *b.* 1995
1887	*St Levan (5th),* James Piers Southwell St Aubyn, *b.* 1950, *s.* 2013, *m.*	Hon. Hugh J. St. A., *b.* 1983
1885	*St Oswald (6th),* Charles Rowland Andrew Winn, *b.* 1959, *s.* 1999, *m.*	Hon. Rowland C. S. H. W., *b.* 1986
1960	*Sanderson of Ayot (2nd),* Alan Lindsay Sanderson, *b.* 1931, *s.* 1971, *m.* Disclaimed for life 1971.	Hon. Michael S., *b.* 1959
1945	*Sandford (3rd),* James John Mowbray Edmondson, *b.* 1949, *s.* 2009, *m.*	Hon. Devon J. E., *b.* 1986
1871	*Sandhurst (6th),* Guy Rees John Mansfield, QC, *b.* 1949, *s.* 2002, *m.*	Hon. Edward J. M., *b.* 1982
1888	*Savile (4th),* John Anthony Thornhill Lumley-Savile, *b.* 1947, *s.* 2008, *m.*	Hon. James G. A. L-S., *b.* 1975
1447	*Saye and Sele (21st),* Nathaniel Thomas Allen Fiennes, *b.* 1920, *s.* 1968, *m.*	Hon. Martin G. F., *b.* 1961
1826	*Seaford (6th),* Colin Humphrey Felton Ellis, *b.* 1946, *s.* 1999, *m.*	Hon. Benjamin F. T. E., *b.* 1976
1932	** *Selsdon (3rd),* Malcolm McEacharn Mitchell-Thomson, *b.* 1937, *s.* 1963, *m.*	Hon. Callum M. M. M.-T., *b.* 1969
1489 S.	*Sempill (21st),* James William Stuart Whitemore Sempill, *b.* 1949, *s.* 1995, *m.*	Master of Sempill, *b.* 1979
1916	*Shaughnessy (5th),* Charles George Patrick Shaughnessy, *b.* 1955, *s.* 2007, *m.*	David J. S., *b.* 1957
1946	*Shepherd (3rd),* Graham George Shepherd, *b.* 1949, *s.* 2001, *m.*	Hon. Patrick M. S., *b.* 1980
1964	*Sherfield (3rd),* Dwight William Makins, *b.* 1951, *s.* 2006, *m.*	None
1902	*Shuttleworth (5th),* Charles Geoffrey Nicholas Kay-Shuttleworth, KCVO, *b.* 1948, *s.* 1975, *m.*	Hon. Thomas E. K.-S., *b.* 1976
1950	*Silkin (3rd),* Christopher Lewis Silkin, *b.* 1947, *s.* 2001. Disclaimed for life 2002.	Rory L. S., *b.* 1954
1963	*Silsoe (3rd),* Simon Rupert Trustram Eve *b.* 1966, *s.* 2005	Hon. Peter N. T. E., *b.* 1930
1947	*Simon of Wythenshawe (3rd),* Matthew Simon, *b.* 1955, *s.* 2002	Martin S., *b.* 1944
1449 S.	*Sinclair (18th),* Matthew Murray Kennedy St Clair *b.* 1968, *s.* 2004, *m.*	Master of Sinclair, *b.* 2007
1957	*Sinclair of Cleeve (3rd),* John Lawrence Robert Sinclair, *b.* 1953, *s.* 1985	None
1919	*Sinha (6th),* Arup Kumar Sinha, *b.* 1966, *s.* 1999	Hon. Dilip K. S., *b.* 1967
1828	** *Skelmersdale (7th),* Roger Bootle-Wilbraham, *b.* 1945, *s.* 1973, *m.*	Hon. Andrew B.-W., *b.* 1977
1916	*Somerleyton (4th),* Hugh Francis Saville Crossley, *b.* 1971, *s.* 2012, *m.*	Hon. John de B. T. S. C., *b.* 2010
1784	*Somers (9th),* Philip Sebastian Somers Cocks, *b.* 1948, *s.* 1995	Alan B. C., *b.* 1930
1780	*Southampton (6th),* Charles James FitzRoy, *b.* 1928, *s.* 1989, *m.*	Hon. Edward C. F., *b.* 1955
1959	*Spens (4th),* Patrick Nathaniel George Spens, *b.* 1968, *s.* 2001, *m.*	Hon. Peter L. S., *b.* 2000
1640	*Stafford (15th),* Francis Melfort William Fitzherbert, *b.* 1954, *s.* 1986, *m.*	Hon. Benjamin J. B. F., *b.* 1983
1938	*Stamp (4th),* Trevor Charles Bosworth Stamp, MD, *b.* 1935, *s.* 1987, *m.*	Hon. Nicholas C. T. S., *b.* 1978
1839	*Stanley of Alderley (8th), Sheffield (8th) (I. 1738) and Eddisbury (7th) (1848),* Thomas Henry Oliver Stanley, *b.* 1927, *s.* 1971, *m.*	Hon. Richard O. S., *b.* 1956
1318	*Strabolgi (12th),* Andrew David Whitley Kenworthy, *b.* 1967, *s.* 2010, *m.*	Hon. Joel B. K., *b.* 2004
1954	*Strang (2nd),* Colin Strang, *b.* 1922, *s.* 1978, *m.*	None
1628	*Strange (17th),* Adam Humphrey Drummond of Megginch, *b.* 1953, *s.* 2005 *m.*	Hon. John A. H. D. of M. *b.* 1992
1955	*Strathalmond (3rd),* William Roberton Fraser, *b.* 1947, *s.* 1976, *m.*	Hon. William G. F., *b.* 1976
1936	*Strathcarron (3rd),* Ian David Patrick Macpherson, *b.* 1949, *s.* 2006, *m.*	Hon. Rory D. A. M., *b.* 1982
1955	** *Strathclyde (2nd),* Thomas Galloway Dunlop du Roy de Blicquy Galbraith, CH, PC, *b.* 1960, *s.* 1985, *m.*	Hon. Charles W. du R. de B. G., *b.* 1962
1900	*Strathcona and Mount Royal (4th),* Donald Euan Palmer Howard, *b.* 1923, *s.* 1959, *m.*	Hon. D. Alexander S. H., *b.* 1961
1836	*Stratheden (7th) and Campbell (7th) (1841),* David Anthony Campbell, *b.* 1963, *s.* 2011, *m.*	None
1884	*Strathspey (6th),* James Patrick Trevor Grant of Grant, *b.* 1943, *s.* 1992, *m.*	Hon. Michael P. F. G., *b.* 1953
1838	*Sudeley (7th),* Merlin Charles Sainthill Hanbury-Tracy, *b.* 1939, *s.* 1941	Nicholas E. J. H.-T., *b.* 1959

1786	*Suffield (12th),* Charles Anthony Assheton Harbord-Hamond, *b.* 1953, *s.* 2011, *m.*	Hon. John E. R. H.-H., *b.* 1956
1893	*Swansea (5th),* Richard Anthony Hussey Vivian, *b.* 1957, *s.* 2005, *m.*	Hon. James H. H. V., *b.* 1999
1907	*Swaythling (5th),* Charles Edgar Samuel Montagu, *b.* 1954, *s.* 1998, *m.*	Rupert A. S. M., *b.* 1965
1919	** *Swinfen (3rd),* Roger Mynors Swinfen Eady, *b.* 1938, *s.* 1977, *m.*	Hon. Charles R. P. S. E., *b.* 1971
1831 I.	*Talbot of Malahide (10th),* Reginald John Richard Arundell, *b.* 1931, *s.* 1987, *m.*	Hon. Richard J. T. A., *b.* 1957
1946	*Tedder (3rd),* Robin John Tedder, *b.* 1955, *s.* 1994, *m.*	Hon. Benjamin J. T., *b.* 1985
1884	*Tennyson (6th),* David Harold Alexander Tennyson, *b.* 1960, *s.* 2006	Alan J. D. T., *b.* 1965
1918	*Terrington (6th),* Christopher Richard James Woodhouse, MB, *b.* 1946, *s.* 2001, *m.*	Hon. Jack H. L. W., *b.* 1978
1940	*Teviot (2nd),* Charles John Kerr, *b.* 1934, *s.* 1968, *m.*	Hon. Charles R. K., *b.* 1971
1616	*Teynham (20th),* John Christopher Ingham Roper-Curzon, *b.* 1928, *s.* 1972, *m.*	Hon. David J. H. I. R.-C., *b.* 1965
1964	*Thomson of Fleet (3rd),* David Kenneth Roy Thomson, *b.* 1957, *s.* 2006, *m.*	Hon. Benjamin T., *b.* 2006
1792	*Thurlow (9th),* Roualeyn Robert Hovell-Thurlow-Cumming-Bruce, *b.* 1952, *s.* 2013, *m.*	Hon. Nicholas E. H.-T.-C.-B., *b.* 1986
1876	*Tollemache (5th),* Timothy John Edward Tollemache, *b.* 1939, *s.* 1975, *m.*	Hon. Edward J. H. T., *b.* 1976
1564 S.	*Torphichen (15th),* James Andrew Douglas Sandilands, *b.* 1946, *s.* 1975, *m.*	Robert P. S., *b.* 1950
1947	** *Trefgarne (2nd),* David Garro Trefgarne, PC, *b.* 1941, *s.* 1960, *m.*	Hon. George G. T., *b.* 1970
1921	*Trevethin (5th) and Oaksey (3rd) (1947),* Patrick John Tristram Lawrence, QC, *b.* 1960, *s.* 2012, *m.*	Hon. Oliver J. T. L., *b.* 1990
1880	*Trevor (5th),* Marke Charles Hill-Trevor, *b.* 1970, *s.* 1997, *m.*	Hon. Iain R. H.-T., *b.* 1971
1461 I.	*Trimlestown (21st),* Raymond Charles Barnewall, *b.* 1930, *s.* 1997	None
1940	*Tryon (3rd),* Anthony George Merrik Tryon, *b.* 1940, *s.* 1976	Hon. Charles G. B. T., *b.* 1976
1935	*Tweedsmuir (4th),* John William de l'Aigle (Toby) Buchan, *b.* 1950, *s.* 2008, *m.*	Hon. John A. G. B., *b.* 1986
1523	*Vaux of Harrowden (11th),* Anthony William Gilbey, *b.* 1940, *s.* 2002, *m.*	Hon. Richard H. G. G., *b.* 1965
1800 I.	*Ventry (8th),* Andrew Wesley Daubeny de Moleyns, *b.* 1943, *s.* 1987, *m.*	Hon. Francis W. D. de M., *b.* 1965
1762	*Vernon (11th),* Anthony William Vernon-Harcourt, *b.* 1939, *s.* 2000, *m.*	Hon. Simon A. V-H., *b.* 1969
1922	*Vestey (3rd),* Samuel George Armstrong Vestey, KCVO, *b.* 1941, *s.* 1954, *m.*	Hon. William G. V., *b.* 1983
1841	*Vivian (7th),* Charles Crespigny Hussey Vivian, *b.* 1966, *s.* 2004	Thomas C. B. V., *b.* 1971
1934	*Wakehurst (3rd),* (John) Christopher Loder, *b.* 1925, *s.* 1970, *m.*	Hon. Timothy W. L., *b.* 1958
1723	** *Walpole (10th) and Walpole of Wolterton (8th) (1756),* Robert Horatio Walpole, *b.* 1938, *s.* 1989, *m.*	Hon. Jonathan R. H. W., *b.* 1967
1780	*Walsingham (9th),* John de Grey, MC, *b.* 1925, *s.* 1965, *m.*	Hon. Robert de. G., *b.* 1969
1936	*Wardington (3rd),* William Simon Pease, *b.* 1925, *s.* 2005, *m.*	None
1792 I.	*Waterpark (7th),* Frederick Caryll Philip Cavendish, *b.* 1926, *s.* 1948, *m.*	Hon. Roderick A. C., *b.* 1959
1942	*Wedgwood (4th),* Piers Anthony Weymouth Wedgwood, *b.* 1954, *s.* 1970, *m.*	Antony J. W., *b.* 1944
1861	*Westbury (6th),* Richard Nicholas Bethell, MBE, *b.* 1950, *s.* 2001, *m.*	Hon. Alexander B., *b.* 1986
1944	*Westwood (3rd),* (William) Gavin Westwood, *b.* 1944, *s.* 1991, *m.*	Hon. W. Fergus W., *b.* 1972
1544/5	*Wharton (12th),* Myles Christopher David Robertson, *b.* 1964, *s.* 2000, *m.*	Hon. Megan Z. M., *b.* 2006
1935	*Wigram (2nd),* (George) Neville (Clive) Wigram, MC, *b.* 1915, *s.* 1960, *w.*	Maj. Hon. Andrew F. C. W., *b.* 1949
1491	** *Willoughby de Broke (21st),* Leopold David Verney, *b.* 1938, *s.* 1986, *m.*	Hon. Rupert G. V., *b.* 1966
1937	*Windlesham (4th),* James Rupert Hennessy, *b.* 1968, *s.* 2010, *m.*	Hon. George R. J. H., *b.* 2006
1951	*Wise (3rd),* Christopher John Clayton Wise, *b.* 1949, *s.* 2012	Martin H. W., *b.* 1950
1869	*Wolverton (8th),* Miles John Glyn, *b.* 1966, *s.* 2011	Jonathan C. G., *b.* 1990
1928	*Wraxall (3rd),* Eustace Hubert Beilby Gibbs, KCVO, CMG, *b.* 1929, *s.* 2001, *m.*	Hon. Anthony H. G., *b.* 1958
1915	*Wrenbury (3rd),* Revd John Burton Buckley, *b.* 1927, *s.* 1940, *m.*	Hon. William E. B., *b.* 1966
1838	*Wrottesley (6th),* Clifton Hugh Lancelot de Verdon Wrottesley, *b.* 1968, *s.* 1977, *m.*	Hon. Victor E. F. de V. W., *b.* 2004
1829	*Wynford (9th),* John Philip Robert Best, *b.* 1950, *s.* 2002, *m.*	Hon. Harry R. F. B., *b.* 1987
1308	*Zouche (18th),* James Assheton Frankland, *b.* 1943, *s.* 1965, *m.*	Hon. William T. A. F., *b.* 1984

BARONESSES/LADIES IN THEIR OWN RIGHT

Style, The Rt. Hon. the Lady _, *or* The Rt. Hon. the Baroness _, according to her preference. Either style may be used, except in the case of Scottish titles (indicated by S.), which are not baronies (*see* page 44) and whose holders are always addressed as Lady.

Envelope, may be addressed in same way as a Baron's wife or, if she prefers *(formal),* The Rt. Hon. the Baroness _; *(social),* The Baroness _. Otherwise as for a Baron's wife

Husband, Untitled

Children's style, As for children of a Baron

Created	*Title, order of succession, name, etc*	*Heir*
1664	*Arlington (11th),* Jennifer Jane Forwood, *b.* 1939, *s.* 1999, *w.* Title called out of abeyance 1999	Hon. Patrick J. D. F., *b.* 1967
1455	*Berners (16th),* Pamela Vivien Kirkham, *b.* 1929, *s.* 1995, *m.* Title called out of abeyance 1995	Hon. Rupert W. T. K., *b.* 1953
1529	*Braye (8th),* Mary Penelope Aubrey-Fletcher, *b.* 1941, *s.* 1985, *m.*	Two co-heirs
1283	*Fauconberg (9th) and Conyers (15th) (1509),* Diana Mary Miller, *b.* 1920, *s.* 2012, *w.*	Two co-heirs
1490 S.	*Herries of Terregles (14th),* Anne Elizabeth Fitzalan-Howard, *b.* 1938, *s.* 1975, *w.*	Lady Mary Mumford, *b.* 1940
1597	*Howard de Walden (10th),* Mary Hazel Caridwen Czernin, *b.* 1935, *s.* 2004, *m.* Title called out of abeyance 2004	Hon. Peter J. J. C. *b.* 1966
1602 S.	*Kinloss (13th),* Teresa Mary Nugent Freeman-Grenville, *b.* 1957, *s.* 2012	Hon. Hester J. A. H., *b.* 1960
1445 S.	** *Saltoun (20th),* Flora Marjory Fraser, *b.* 1930, *s.* 1979, *w.*	Hon. Katharine I. M. I. F., *b.* 1957
1313	*Willoughby de Eresby (27th),* (Nancy) Jane Marie Heathcote-Drummond-Willoughby, *b.* 1934, *s.* 1983	Two co-heirs

LIFE PEERS

Style, The Rt. Hon. the Lord _ /The Rt. Hon. the Lady _ , *or* The Rt. Hon. the Baroness _ , according to her preference
Envelope (formal), The Rt. Hon. Lord _/Lady_/ Baroness_; *(social),* The Lord _/Lady_/Baroness_
Letter (formal), My Lord/Lady; *(social),* Dear Lord/ Lady _. *Spoken,* Lord/Lady _
Wife's style, The Rt. Hon. the Lady _
Husband, Untitled
Children's style, 'The Hon.' before forename (F_) and surname (S_)
Envelope, The Hon. F_ S_. *Letter,* Dear Mr/Miss/Mrs S_. *Spoken,* Mr/Miss/Mrs S_

NEW LIFE PEERAGES

1 September 2012 to 31 August 2013:
Sir Charles Allen, CBE; Catherine Mary Bakewell, MBE; Richard Balfe; Sir Anthony Bamford; Michael Fitzhardinge Berkeley, CBE; Nicholas Bourne; Matthew Carrington; Paul Clive Deighton; Daniel Finkelstein, OBE; Annabel Goldie; Rosalind Grender, MBE; Sir William Haughey, OBE; Lady Hodgson, CBE; Christopher Holmes, MBE; John Horam; Christine Mary Humphreys; Jenny Jones; Alicia Kennedy; Sir Mervyn Allister King, GBE; Martha Lane Fox, CBE; Doreen Lawrence, OBE; Howard Leigh; Ian Paul Livingston; Zahida Manzoor, CBE; Jonathan Mendelsohn; John Alfred Stoddard Nash; Brian Paddick; James Palumbo; Jeremy Purvis; Dame Lucy Neville-Rolfe, CMG; Sir Stephen Sherbourne; Alison Suttie; Rumi Verjee, CBE; Michael Whitby; Rt. Revd and Rt. Hon. Rowan Douglas Williams, DPHIL; Susan Williams; Sir Ian Wrigglesworth

SYMBOLS
* Hereditary peer who has been granted a life peerage. For further details, please refer to the Hereditary Peers section. For example, life peer *Balniel* can be found under his hereditary title *Earl of Crawford and Balcarres*
§ Members of the Judiciary currently disqualified from sitting or voting in the House of Lords until they retire from that office. For further information *see* Law Courts and Offices
‡ Title not confirmed at time of going to press
¶ Peer who has permanently resigned from the House of Lords

CREATED UNDER THE APPELLATE JURISDICTION ACT 1876 (AS AMENDED)

BARONS
Created
2004 *Brown of Eaton-under-Heywood,* Simon Denis Brown, PC, *b.* 1937, *m.*
1991 *Browne-Wilkinson,* Nicolas Christopher Henry Browne-Wilkinson, PC, *b.* 1930, *m.*
2004 *Carswell,* Robert Douglas Carswell, PC, *b.* 1934, *m.*
2009 *Collins of Mapesbury,* Lawrence Antony Collins, PC, *b.* 1941
1986 *Goff of Chieveley,* Robert Lionel Archibald Goff, PC, *b.* 1926, *m.*
1985 *Griffiths,* (William) Hugh Griffiths, MC, PC, *b.* 1923, *m.*
1995 *Hoffmann,* Leonard Hubert Hoffmann, PC, *b.* 1934, *m.*
1997 *Hutton,* (James) Brian (Edward) Hutton, PC, *b.* 1931, *m.*
2009 §*Kerr of Tonaghmore,* Brian Francis Kerr, PC, *b.* 1948, *m.*
1993 *Lloyd of Berwick,* Anthony John Leslie Lloyd, PC, *b.* 1929, *m.*
2005 §*Mance,* Jonathan Hugh Mance, PC, *b.* 1943, *m.*
1998 *Millett,* Peter Julian Millett, PC, *b.* 1932, *m.*
1992 *Mustill,* Michael John Mustill, PC, *b.* 1931, *m.*
2007 *Neuberger of Abbotsbury,* David Edmond Neuberger, PC, *b.* 1948, *m.*
1994 *Nicholls of Birkenhead,* Donald James Nicholls, PC, *b.* 1933, *m.*
1999 *Phillips of Worth Matravers,* Nicholas Addison Phillips, KG, PC, *b.* 1938, *m.*
1997 *Saville of Newdigate,* Mark Oliver Saville, PC, *b.* 1936, *m.*
2000 *Scott of Foscote,* Richard Rashleigh Folliott Scott, PC, *b.* 1934, *m.*
1995 *Steyn,* Johan van Zyl Steyn, PC, *b.* 1932, *m.*
1982 *Templeman,* Sydney William Templeman, MBE, PC, *b.* 1920, *w.*
2003 *Walker of Gestingthorpe,* Robert Walker, PC, *b.* 1938, *m.*
1992 *Woolf,* Harry Kenneth Woolf, PC, *b.* 1933, *m.*

BARONESSES
2004 §*Hale of Richmond,* Brenda Marjorie Hale, DBE, PC, *b.* 1945, *m.*

CREATED UNDER THE LIFE PEERAGES ACT 1958

BARONS
Created
2001 *Adebowale,* Victor Olufemi Adebowale, CBE, *b.* 1962
2005 *Adonis,* Andrew Adonis, PC, *b.* 1963, *m.*
2011 *Ahmad of Wimbledon,* Tariq Mahmood Ahmad, *b.* 1968, *m.*
1998 *Ahmed,* Nazir Ahmed, *b.* 1957, *m.*
1996 *Alderdice,* John Thomas Alderdice, *b.* 1955, *m.*
2010 *Allan of Hallam,* Richard Beecroft Allan, *b.* 1966
2013 ‡*Allen,* Charles Allen, CBE, *b.* 1957
1998 *Alli,* Waheed Alli, *b.* 1964
2004 *Alliance,* David Alliance, CBE, *b.* 1932
1997 *Alton of Liverpool,* David Patrick Paul Alton, *b.* 1951, *m.*
2005 *Anderson of Swansea,* Donald Anderson, PC, *b.* 1939, *m.*
1992 *Archer of Weston-super-Mare,* Jeffrey Howard Archer, *b.* 1940, *m.*
1988 *Armstrong of Ilminster,* Robert Temple Armstrong, GCB, CVO, *b.* 1927, *m.*
1999 **Armstrong-Jones,* Earl of Snowdon, GCVO, *b.* 1930, *m.* (*see* Hereditary Peers)
2000 *Ashcroft,* Michael Anthony Ashcroft, KCMG, PC, *b.* 1946, *m.*
2001 *Ashdown of Norton-sub-Hamdon,* Jeremy John Durham (Paddy) Ashdown, GCMG, KBE, PC, *b.* 1941, *m.*
1993 *Attenborough,* Richard Samuel Attenborough, CBE, *b.* 1923, *m.*

1998 *Bach,* William Stephen Goulden Bach, *b.* 1946, *m.*
1997 ¶*Bagri,* Raj Kumar Bagri, CBE, *b.* 1930, *m.*
1997 *Baker of Dorking,* Kenneth Wilfred Baker, CH, PC, *b.* 1934, *m.*
2013 ‡*Balfe,* Richard Balfe, *b.* 1944, *m.*
2004 *Ballyedmond,* Dr Edward Haughey, OBE, *b.* 1944, *m.*
1974 **Balniel,* The Earl of Crawford and Balcarres, *b.* 1927, *m.* (*see* Hereditary Peers)
2013 ‡*Bamford,* Anthony Bamford *b.* 1945, *m.*
2010 *Bannside,* Revd Ian Richard Kyle Paisley, PC, *b.* 1926, *m.*
1992 *Barber of Tewkesbury,* Derek Coates Barber, *b.* 1918, *m.*
1983 *Barnett,* Joel Barnett, PC, *b.* 1923, *m.*
1997 *Bassam of Brighton,* (John) Steven Bassam, PC, *b.* 1953
2008 *Bates,* Michael Walton Bates, *b.* 1961
2010 *Beecham,* Jeremy Hugh Beecham, *b.* 1944, *m.*
1998 *Bell,* Timothy John Leigh Bell, *b.* 1941, *m.*
2013 *Berkeley of Knighton,* Michael Fitzhardinge Berkeley, CBE, *b.* 1948, *m.*
2001 *Best,* Richard Stuart Best, OBE, *b.* 1945, *m.*
2007 *Bew,* Prof. Paul Anthony Elliott Bew, *b.* 1950, *m.*
2001 *Bhatia,* Amirali Alibhai Bhatia, OBE, *b.* 1932, *m.*
2004 *Bhattacharyya,* Prof. (Sushantha) Kumar Bhattacharyya, CBE *b.* 1932, *m.*
2010 *Bichard,* Michael George Bichard, KCB, *b.* 1947
2006 *Bilimoria,* Karan Faridoon Bilimoria, CBE, *b.* 1961, *m.*
2005 *Bilston,* Dennis Turner, *b.* 1942, *m.*
2000 *Birt,* John Francis Hodgess Birt, *b.* 1944, *m.*
2010 *Black of Brentwood,* Guy Vaughan Black, *b.* 1964, *c. p.*
2001 *Black of Crossharbour,* Conrad Moffat Black, OC, PC (Canadian), *b.* 1944, *m.*
1997 *Blackwell,* Norman Roy Blackwell, *b.* 1952, *m.*
2010 *Blair of Boughton,* Ian Warwick Blair, QPM *b.* 1953, *m.*
2011 *Blencathra,* David John Maclean, PC, *b.* 1953
1995 *Blyth of Rowington,* James Blyth, *b.* 1940, *m.*
2010 *Boateng,* Paul Yaw Boateng, PC, *b.* 1951, *m.*
1996 *Borrie,* Gordon Johnson Borrie, QC, *b.* 1931, *w.*
2010 *Boswell of Aynho,* Timothy Eric Boswell, *b.* 1942, *m.*
2013 ‡*Bourne,* Nicholas Bourne, *b.* 1952
1996 *Bowness,* Peter Spencer Bowness, CBE, *b.* 1943, *m.*
2003 *Boyce,* Michael Boyce, KG, GCB, OBE, *b.* 1943, *m.*
2006 §*Boyd of Duncansby,* Colin David Boyd, PC, *b.* 1953, *m.*
2006 *Bradley,* Keith John Charles Bradley, PC, *b.* 1950, *m.*
1999 *Bradshaw,* William Peter Bradshaw, *b.* 1936, *m.*
1998 *Bragg,* Melvyn Bragg, *b.* 1939, *m.*
1987 *Bramall,* Edwin Noel Westby Bramall, KG, GCB, OBE, MC, *b.*1923, *m.*
2000 *Brennan,* Daniel Joseph Brennan, QC, *b.* 1942, *m.*
1976 *Briggs,* Asa Briggs, FBA, *b.* 1921, *m.*
2000 *Brittan of Spennithorne,* Leon Brittan, PC, QC, *b.* 1939, *m.*
2004 *Broers,* Prof. Alec (Nigel) Broers, *b.* 1938, *m.*
1997 *Brooke of Alverthorpe,* Clive Brooke, *b.* 1942, *m.*
2001 *Brooke of Sutton Mandeville,* Peter Leonard Brooke, CH, PC, *b.* 1934, *m.*
1998 *Brookman,* David Keith Brookman, *b.* 1937, *m.*
1979 *Brooks of Tremorfa,* John Edward Brooks, *b.* 1927, *m.*
2006 *Browne of Belmont,* Wallace Hamilton Browne, *b.* 1947
2010 *Browne of Ladyton,* Desmond Henry Browne, PC, *b.* 1952
2001 *Browne of Madingley,* Edmund John Phillip Browne, *b.* 1948

2006 *Burnett,* John Patrick Aubone Burnett, *b.* 1945, *m.*
1998 *Burns,* Terence Burns, GCB, *b.* 1944, *m.*
1998 *Butler of Brockwell,* (Frederick Edward) Robin Butler, KG, GCB, CVO, PC, *b.* 1938, *m.*
2004 *Cameron of Dillington,* Ewen (James Hanning) Cameron, *b.* 1949, *m.*
1984 *Cameron of Lochbroom,* Kenneth John Cameron, PC, *b.* 1931, *m.*
2001 *Campbell-Savours,* Dale Norman Campbell-Savours, *b.* 1943, *m.*
2002 *Carey of Clifton,* Rt. Revd George Leonard Carey, PC, *b.* 1935, *m.*
1999 **Carington of Upton,* Lord Carrington, GCMG, *b.* 1919, *m.* (*see* Hereditary Peers)
1999 *Carlile of Berriew,* Alexander Charles Carlile, QC, *b.* 1948, *m.*
2013 ‡*Carrington,* Matthew Carrington, *b.* 1947, *m.*
2008 *Carter of Barnes,* Stephen Andrew Carter, CBE, *b.* 1964, *m.*
2004 *Carter of Coles,* Patrick Robert Carter, *b.* 1946, *m.*
1990 *Cavendish of Furness,* (Richard) Hugh Cavendish, *b.* 1941, *m.*
1996 *Chadlington,* Peter Selwyn Gummer, *b.* 1942, *m.*
1964 *Chalfont,* (Alun) Arthur Gwynne Jones, OBE, MC, PC, *b.* 1919, *w.*
2005 *Chidgey,* David William George Chidgey, *b.* 1942, *m.*
1998 *Christopher,* Anthony Martin Grosvenor Christopher, CBE, *b.* 1925, *m.*
2001 *Clark of Windermere,* David George Clark, PC, PHD, *b.* 1939, *m.*
1998 *Clarke of Hampstead,* Anthony James Clarke, CBE, *b.* 1932, *m.*
2009 §*Clarke of Stone-Cum-Ebony,* Anthony Peter Clarke, PC, *b.* 1943, *m.*
1998 *Clement-Jones,* Timothy Francis Clement-Jones, CBE, *b.* 1949, *m.*
1990 *Clinton-Davis,* Stanley Clinton Clinton-Davis, PC, *b.* 1928, *m.*
2000 *Coe,* Sebastian Newbold Coe, KBE, CH, *b.* 1956, *m.*
2011 *Collins of Highbury,* Raymond Edward Harry Collins, *b.* 1954
2001 *Condon,* Paul Leslie Condon, QPM, *b.* 1947, *m.*
1997 *Cope of Berkeley,* John Ambrose Cope, PC, *b.* 1937, *m.*
2010 *Cormack,* Patrick Thomas Cormack, *b.* 1939, *m.*
2006 *Cotter,* Brian Joseph Michael Cotter, *b.* 1939, *m.*
1991 *Craig of Radley,* David Brownrigg Craig, GCB, OBE, *b.* 1929, *m.*
1987 *Crickhowell,* (Roger) Nicholas Edwards, PC, *b.* 1934, *m.*
2006 *Crisp,* (Edmund) Nigel (Ramsay) Crisp, KCB, *b.* 1952, *m.*
2003 *Cullen of Whitekirk,* William Douglas Cullen, KT, PC, *b.* 1935, *m.*
2005 *Cunningham of Felling,* John Anderson Cunningham, PC, *b.*1939, *m.*
1996 *Currie of Marylebone,* David Anthony Currie, *b.* 1946, *m.*
2011 *Curry of Kirkharle,* Donald Thomas Younger Curry, CBE, *b.* 1944, *m.*
2011 *Dannatt,* (Francis) Richard Dannatt, GCB, CBE, MC, *b.* 1950, *m.*
2007 *Darzi of Denham,* Ara Warkes Darzi, KBE, PC, *b.* 1960, *m.*
2006 *Davidson of Glen Clova,* Neil Forbes Davidson, QC, *b.* 1950, *m.*
2009 *Davies of Abersoch,* Evan Mervyn Davies, CBE, *b.* 1952, *m.*

1997 *Davies of Coity,* (David) Garfield Davies, CBE, *b.* 1935, *m.*
1997 *Davies of Oldham,* Bryan Davies, PC, *b.* 1939, *m.*
2010 *Davies of Stamford,* John Quentin Davies, *b.* 1944, *m.*
2006 *Dear,* Geoffrey (James) Dear, QPM, *b.* 1937, *m.*
2010 *Deben,* John Selwyn Gummer, PC, *b.* 1939, *m.*
2012 *Deighton,* Paul Clive Deighton, KBE, *b.* 1956, *m.*
1991 *Desai,* Prof. Meghnad Jagdishchandra Desai, PHD, *b.* 1940, *m.*
1997 *Dholakia,* Navnit Dholakia, OBE, PC, *b.* 1937, *m.*
1997 *Dixon,* Donald Dixon, PC, *b.* 1929, *m.*
1993 *Dixon-Smith,* Robert William Dixon-Smith, *b.* 1934, *m.*
2010 *Dobbs,* Michael John Dobbs, *b.* 1948, *m.*
1985 *Donoughue,* Bernard Donoughue, DPHIL, *b.* 1934
2004 *Drayson,* Paul Rudd Drayson, PC, *b.* 1960, *m.*
1994 *Dubs,* Alfred Dubs, *b.* 1932, *m.*
2004 *Dykes,* Hugh John Maxwell Dykes, *b.* 1939, *m.*
1995 *Eames,* Robert Henry Alexander Eames, OM, PHD, *b.* 1937, *m.*
1992 *Eatwell,* John Leonard Eatwell, PHD, *b.* 1945
1983 *Eden of Winton,* John Benedict Eden, PC, *b.* 1925, *m.*
2011 *Edmiston,* Robert Norman Edmiston, *b.* 1946, *m.*
1999 *Elder,* Thomas Murray Elder, *b.* 1950
1992 *Elis-Thomas,* Dafydd Elis Elis-Thomas, PC, *b.* 1946, *m.*
1981 *Elystan-Morgan,* Dafydd Elystan Elystan-Morgan, *b.* 1932, *w.*
2011 *Empey,* Reginald Norman Morgan Empey, OBE, *b.* 1947, *m.*
2000 **Erskine of Alloa Tower,* Earl of Mar and Kellie, *b.* 1949, *m.* (*see* Hereditary Peers)
1997 *Evans of Parkside,* John Evans, *b.* 1930, *m.*
2000 *Evans of Temple Guiting,* Matthew Evans, CBE, *b.* 1941, *m.*
1998 *Evans of Watford,* David Charles Evans, *b.* 1942, *m.*
1983 *Ezra,* Derek Ezra, MBE, *b.* 1919, *m.*
1997 *Falconer of Thoroton,* Charles Leslie Falconer, PC, QC, *b.* 1951, *m.*
1999 *Faulkner of Worcester,* Richard Oliver Faulkner, *b.* 1946, *m.*
2010 *Faulks,* Edward Peter Lawless Faulks, QC, *b.* 1950, *m.*
2001 *Fearn,* Ronald Cyril Fearn, OBE, *b.* 1931, *m.*
1996 *Feldman,* Basil Feldman, *b.* 1926, *m.*
2010 *Feldman of Elstree,* Andrew Simon Feldman, *b.* 1966, *m.*
1999 *Fellowes,* Robert Fellowes, GCB, GCVO, PC, *b.* 1941, *m.*
2011 *Fellowes of West Stafford,* Julian Alexander Fellowes, *b.* 1949, *m.*
1999 *Filkin,* David Geoffrey Nigel Filkin, CBE, *b.* 1944
2011 *Fink,* Stanley Fink, *b.* 1957, *m.*
2013 ‡*Finkelstein,* Daniel Finkelstein, OBE, *b.* 1962, *m.*
2011 *Flight,* Howard Emerson Flight, *b.* 1948, *m.*
1999 *Forsyth of Drumlean,* Michael Bruce Forsyth, PC, *b.* 1954, *m.*
2005 *Foster of Bishop Auckland,* Derek Foster, PC, *b.* 1937, *m.*
1999 ¶*Foster of Thames Bank,* Norman Robert Foster, OM, *b.* 1935, *m.*
2005 *Foulkes of Cumnock,* George Foulkes, PC, *b.* 1942, *m.*
2001 *Fowler,* (Peter) Norman Fowler, PC, *b.* 1938, *m.*
2011 *Framlingham,* Michael Nicholson Lord, *b.* 1938, *m.*
1997 *Freeman,* Roger Norman Freeman, PC, *b.* 1942, *m.*
2009 *Freud,* David Anthony Freud, *b.* 1950 *m.*
2010 *Gardiner of Kimble,* John Gardiner, *b.* 1956, *m.*
1997 *Garel-Jones,* (William Armand) Thomas Tristan Garel-Jones, PC, *b.* 1941, *m.*
1999 **Gascoyne-Cecil,* The Marquess of Salisbury, KVCO, PC, *b.* 1946, *m.* (*see* Hereditary Peers)
1999 *Gavron,* Robert Gavron, CBE, *b.* 1930, *m.*
2010 *German,* Michael James German, OBE, *b.* 1945, *m.*
2004 *Giddens,* Prof. Anthony Giddens, *b.* 1938, *m.*
2011 *Glasman,* Maurice Mark Glasman, *b.* 1961, *m.*
2011 *Glendonbrook,* Michael David Bishop, CBE, *b.* 1942
2011 *Gold,* David Laurence Gold, *b.* 1951, *m.*
1999 *Goldsmith,* Peter Henry Goldsmith, PC, QC, *b.* 1950, *m.*
1997 *Goodhart,* William Howard Goodhart, QC, *b.* 1933, *m.*
2005 *Goodlad,* Alastair Robertson Goodlad, KCMG, *b.* 1943, *m.*
1997 *Gordon of Strathblane,* James Stuart Gordon, CBE, *b.* 1936, *m.*
1999 *Grabiner,* Anthony Stephen Grabiner, QC, *b.* 1945, *m.*
2011 *Grade of Yarmouth,* Michael Ian Grade, CBE, *b.* 1943, *m.*
1983 *Graham of Edmonton,* (Thomas) Edward Graham, *b.* 1925, *m.*
2000 *Greaves,* Anthony Robert Greaves, *b.* 1942, *m.*
2010 *Green of Hurstpierpoint,* Stephen Keith Green, *b.* 1948, *m.*
2000 **Grenfell of Kilvey,* Lord Grenfell, *b.* 1935, *m.* (*see* Hereditary Peers)
2004 *Griffiths of Burry Port,* Revd Dr Leslie John Griffiths, *b.* 1942, *m.*
1991 *Griffiths of Fforestfach,* Brian Griffiths, *b.* 1941, *m.*
2001 *Grocott,* Bruce Joseph Grocott, PC, *b.* 1940, *m.*
2000 **Gueterbock,* Lord Berkeley, OBE, *b.* 1939, *m.* (*see* Hereditary Peers)
2000 *Guthrie of Craigiebank,* Charles Ronald Llewelyn Guthrie, GCB, LVO, OBE, *b.* 1938, *m.*
1995 *Habgood,* Rt. Revd John Stapylton Habgood, PC, PHD, *b.* 1927, *m.*
2010 *Hall of Birkenhead,* Anthony William Hall, CBE, *b.* 1951, *m.*
2007 *Hameed,* Dr Khalid Hameed, *b.* 1941, *m.*
2005 *Hamilton of Epsom,* Archibald Gavin Hamilton, PC, *b.* 1941, *m.*
2001 *Hannay of Chiswick,* David Hugh Alexander Hannay, GCMG, CH, *b.* 1935, *m.*
1998 *Hanningfield,* Paul Edward Winston White, *b.* 1940
1997 *Hardie,* Andrew Rutherford Hardie, QC, PC, *b.* 1946, *m.*
2006 *Harries of Pentregarth,* Rt. Revd Richard Douglas Harries, *b.* 1936, *m.*
1998 *Harris of Haringey,* (Jonathan) Toby Harris, *b.* 1953, *m.*
1996 *Harris of Peckham,* Philip Charles Harris, *b.* 1942, *m.*
1999 *Harrison,* Lyndon Henry Arthur Harrison, *b.* 1947, *m.*
2004 *Hart of Chilton,* Garry Richard Rushby Hart, *b.* 1940, *m.*
1993 *Haskel,* Simon Haskel, *b.* 1934, *m.*
1998 *Haskins,* Christopher Robin Haskins, *b.* 1937, *m.*
2005 *Hastings of Scarisbrick,* Michael John Hastings, CBE, *b.* 1958, *m.*
1997 *Hattersley,* Roy Sidney George Hattersley, PC, *b.* 1932
2013 ‡*Haughey,* William Haughey, OBE, *b.* 1956, *m.*
2004 *Haworth,* Alan Robert Haworth, *b.* 1948, *m.*
1992 *Hayhoe,* Bernard John (Barney) Hayhoe, PC, *b.* 1925, *m.*

1992 *Healey,* Denis Winston Healey, CH, MBE, PC, *b.* 1917, *w.*
2010 *Hennessy of Nympsfield,* Prof. Peter John Hennessy, *b.* 1947, *m.*
2001 *Heseltine,* Michael Ray Dibdin Heseltine, CH, PC, *b.* 1933, *m.*
1997 *Higgins,* Terence Langley Higgins, KBE, PC, *b.* 1928, *m.*
2010 *Hill of Oareford,* Jonathan Hopkin Hill, CBE, PC, *b.* 1960, *m.*
2000 *Hodgson of Astley Abbotts,* Robin Granville Hodgson, CBE, *b.* 1942, *m.*
1991 *Hollick,* Clive Richard Hollick, *b.* 1945, *m.*
2013 ‡*Holmes,* Christopher Holmes, MBE, *b.* 1971
1995 *Hope of Craighead,* (James Arthur) David Hope, KT, PC, *b.* 1938, *m.*
2005 *Hope of Thornes,* Rt. Revd David Michael Hope, KCVO, PC, *b.* 1940
2013 ‡*Horam,* John Horam, *b.* 1939, *m.*
2010 *Howard of Lympne,* Michael Howard, CH, PC, QC, *b.* 1941, *m.*
2004 *Howard of Rising,* Greville Patrick Charles Howard, *b.* 1941, *m.*
2005 *Howarth of Newport,* Alan Thomas Howarth, CBE, PC, *b.* 1944
1992 *Howe of Aberavon,* (Richard Edward) Geoffrey Howe, CH, PC, QC, *b.* 1926, *m.*
1997 *Howell of Guildford,* David Arthur Russell Howell, PC, *b.* 1936, *m.*
1978 *Howie of Troon,* William Howie, *b.* 1924, *w.*
1997 *Hoyle,* (Eric) Douglas Harvey Hoyle, *b.* 1930, *w.*
1997 *Hughes of Woodside,* Robert Hughes, *b.* 1932, *m.*
2000 *Hunt of Chesterton,* Julian Charles Roland Hunt, CBE, *b.* 1941, *m.*
1997 *Hunt of Kings Heath,* Philip Alexander Hunt, OBE, PC, *b.* 1949, *m.*
1997 *Hunt of Wirral,* David James Fletcher Hunt, MBE, PC, *b.* 1942, *m.*
1997 *Hurd of Westwell,* Douglas Richard Hurd, CH, CBE, PC, *b.* 1930, *w.*
2011 *Hussain,* Qurban Hussain, *b.* 1956, *m.*
1978 *Hutchinson of Lullington,* Jeremy Nicolas Hutchinson, QC, *b.* 1915, *w.*
2010 *Hutton of Furness,* John Matthew Patrick Hutton, PC, *b.* 1955, *m.*
1999 *Imbert,* Peter Michael Imbert, CVO, QPM, *b.* 1933, *m.*
1997 *Inge,* Peter Anthony Inge, KG, GCB, PC, *b.* 1935, *m.*
1987 *Irvine of Lairg,* Alexander Andrew Mackay Irvine, PC, QC, *b.* 1940, *m.*
1997 *Jacobs,* (David) Anthony Jacobs, *b.* 1931, *m.*
2006 *James of Blackheath,* David Noel James, CBE, *b.* 1937, *m.*
1997 *Janner of Braunstone,* Greville Ewan Janner, QC, *b.* 1928, *w.*
2007 *Janvrin,* Robin Berry Janvrin, GCB, GCVO, PC, *b.* 1946, *m.*
2006 *Jay of Ewelme,* Michael (Hastings) Jay, GCMG, *b.* 1946, *m.*
1987 *Jenkin of Roding,* (Charles) Patrick (Fleeming) Jenkin, PC, *b.* 1926, *m.*
2000 *Joffe,* Joel Goodman Joffe, CBE, *b.* 1932, *m.*
2001 *Jones,* (Stephen) Barry Jones, *b.* 1937, *m.*
2007 *Jones of Birmingham,* Digby Marritt Jones, *b.* 1955, *m.*
2005, *Jones of Cheltenham,* Nigel David Jones, *b.* 1948, *m.*
1997 *Jopling,* (Thomas) Michael Jopling, PC, *b.* 1930, *m.*
2000 *Jordan,* William Brian Jordan, CBE, *b.* 1936, *m.*
1991 *Judd,* Frank Ashcroft Judd, *b.* 1935, *m.*
2008 *Judge,* Igor Judge, PC, *b.* 1941, *m.*
2010 *Kakkar,* Prof. Ajay Kumar Kakkar, *b.* 1964
2004 *Kalms,* Harold Stanley Kalms, *b.* 1931, *m.*
2010 *Kennedy of Southwark,* Roy Francis Kennedy, *b.* 1962
2004 *Kerr of Kinlochard,* John (Olav) Kerr, GCMG, *b.* 1942, *m.*
2010 **Kerr of Monteviot,* Marquess of Lothian (Michael Ancram), PC, QC, *b.* 1945, *m.* (*see* Hereditary Peers)
2011 *Kestenbaum,* Jonathan Andrew Kestenbaum, *b.* 1959, *m.*
2001 *Kilclooney,* John David Taylor, PC (NI), *b.* 1937, *m.*
1996 *Kilpatrick of Kincraig,* Robert Kilpatrick, CBE, *b.* 1926, *m.*
1985 *Kimball,* Marcus Richard Kimball, *b.* 1928, *m.*
2001 *King of Bridgwater,* Thomas Jeremy King, CH, PC, *b.* 1933, *m.*
2013 *King of Lothbury,* Mervyn Allister King, GBE, *b.* 1948
1993 *Kingsdown,* Robert (Robin) Leigh-Pemberton, KG, PC, *b.* 1927, *m.*
2005 *Kinnock,* Neil Gordon Kinnock, PC, *b.* 1942, *m.*
1999 *Kirkham,* Graham Kirkham, *b.* 1944, *m.*
1975 *Kirkhill,* John Farquharson Smith, *b.* 1930, *m.*
2005 *Kirkwood of Kirkhope,* Archibald Johnstone Kirkwood, *b.* 1946, *m.*
2007 *Krebs,* Prof. John (Richard) Krebs, FRS, *b.* 1945, *m.*
2010 *Knight of Weymouth,* James Philip Knight, PC, *b.* 1965, *m.*
1987 *Knights,* Philip Douglas Knights, CBE, QPM, *b.* 1920, *m.*
2004 ¶*Laidlaw,* Irvine Alan Stewart Laidlaw, *b.* 1942, *m.*
1999 *Laird,* John Dunn Laird, *b.* 1944, *m.*
1998 *Laming,* (William) Herbert Laming, CBE, *b.* 1936, *m.*
1998 *Lamont of Lerwick,* Norman Stewart Hughson Lamont, PC, *b.* 1942, *m.*
1997 *Lang of Monkton,* Ian Bruce Lang, PC, *b.* 1940, *m.*
1992 *Lawson of Blaby,* Nigel Lawson, PC, *b.* 1932, *m.*
2000 *Layard,* Peter Richard Grenville Layard, *b.* 1934, *m.*
1999 *Lea of Crondall,* David Edward Lea, OBE, *b.* 1937
2006 *Leach of Fairford,* Charles Guy Rodney Leach, *b.* 1934, *m.*
2006 *Lee of Trafford,* John Robert Louis Lee, *b.* 1942, *m.*
2013 ‡*Leigh,* Howard Leigh, *b.* 1959, *m.*
2004 *Leitch,* Alexander Park Leitch, *b.* 1947, *m.*
1993 *Lester of Herne Hill,* Anthony Paul Lester, QC, *b.* 1936, *m.*
1997 *Levene of Portsoken,* Peter Keith Levene, KBE, *b.* 1941, *m.*
1997 *Levy,* Michael Abraham Levy, *b.* 1944, *m.*
1989 *Lewis of Newnham,* Jack Lewis, FRS, *b.* 1928, *m.*
2010 *Lexden,* Alistair Basil Cooke, OBE, *b.* 1945
2010 *Liddle,* Roger John Liddle, *b.* 1947, *m.*
2010 *Lingfield,* Robert George Alexander Balchin, *b.* 1942, *m.*
1999 *Lipsey,* David Lawrence Lipsey, *b.* 1948, *m.*
2013 *Livingston of Parkhead,* Ian Paul Livingston, *b.* 1964, *m.*
1997 *Lloyd-Webber,* Andrew Lloyd Webber, *b.* 1948, *m.*
2011 *Loomba,* Rajinder Paul Loomba, CBE, *b.* 1943, *m.*
2006 *Low of Dalston,* Prof. Colin Mackenzie Low, CBE, *b.* 1942, *m.*
2000 *Luce,* Richard Napier Luce, KG, GCVO, PC, *b.* 1936, *m.*
2000 **Lyttleton of Aldershot,* The Viscount Chandos, *b.* 1953, *m.* (*see* Hereditary Peers)

1984 ¶*McAlpine of West Green,* (Robert) Alistair McAlpine, *b.* 1942, *m.*
1988 *Macaulay of Bragar,* Donald Macaulay, QC, *b.* 1933, *m.*
2010 *McAvoy,* Thomas McLaughlin McAvoy, PC, *b.* 1943, *m.*
1976 *McCluskey,* John Herbert McCluskey, *b.* 1929, *m.*
1989 *McColl of Dulwich,* Ian McColl, CBE, FRCS, FRCSE, *b.* 1933, *m.*
2010 *McConnell of Glenscorrodale,* Dr Jack Wilson McConnell, PC, *b.* 1960, *m.*
2010 *Macdonald of River Glaven,* Kenneth Donald John Macdonald, QC, *b.* 1953, *m.*
1998 *Macdonald of Tradeston,* Angus John Macdonald, CBE, PC, *b.* 1940, *m.*
2010 *McFall of Alcluith,* John Francis McFall, PC, *b.* 1944, *m.*
1991 *Macfarlane of Bearsden,* Norman Somerville Macfarlane, KT, FRSE, *b.* 1926, *m.*
2001 *MacGregor of Pulham Market,* John Roddick Russell MacGregor, CBE, PC, *b.* 1937, *m.*
1979 *Mackay of Clashfern,* James Peter Hymers Mackay, KT, PC, FRSE, *b.* 1927, *m.*
1995 §*Mackay of Drumadoon,* Donald Sage Mackay, PC, *b.* 1946, *m.*
1999 *Mackenzie of Culkein,* Hector Uisdean MacKenzie, *b.* 1940
2004 *McKenzie of Luton,* William David McKenzie, *b.* 1946, *m.*
1998 *Mackenzie of Framwellgate,* Brian Mackenzie, OBE, *b.* 1943, *m.*
1974 *Mackie of Benshie,* George Yull Mackie, CBE, DSO, DFC, *b.* 1919, *m.*
1996 *MacLaurin of Knebworth,* Ian Charter MacLaurin, *b.* 1937, *m.*
2001 *Maclennan of Rogart,* Robert Adam Ross Maclennan, PC, *b.* 1936, *m.*
1995 *McNally,* Tom McNally, PC, *b.* 1943, *m.*
2011 *Magan of Castletown,* George Morgan Magan, *b.* 1945, *m.*
2001 *Maginnis of Drumglass,* Kenneth Wiggins Maginnis, *b.* 1938, *m.*
2007 *Malloch-Brown,* George Mark Malloch Brown, KCMG, PC, *b.* 1953, *m.*
2008 *Mandelson,* Peter Benjamin Mandelson, PC, *b.* 1953
2011 *Marks of Henley-on-Thames,* Jonathan Clive Marks, QC, *b.* 1952, *m.*
2006 *Marland,* Jonathan Peter Marland, *b.* 1956, *m.*
1991 *Marlesford,* Mark Shuldham Schreiber, *b.* 1931, *m.*
2009 *Martin of Springburn,* Michael Martin, PC, *b.* 1945, *m.*
1987 *Mason of Barnsley,* Roy Mason, PC, *b.* 1924, *m.*
2005 *Mawhinney,* Brian Stanley Mawhinney, PC, *b.* 1940, *m.*
2007 *Mawson,* Revd Andrew Mawson, OBE, *b.* 1954, *m.*
2004 *Maxton,* John Alston Maxton, *b.* 1936, *m.*
2001 *May of Oxford,* Robert McCredie May, OM, *b.* 1936, *m.*
1997 *Mayhew of Twysden,* Patrick Barnabas Burke Mayhew, PC, QC, *b.* 1929, *m.*
2013 ‡*Mendelsohn,* Jonathan Mendelsohn, *b.* 1966, *m.*
2000 *Mitchell,* Parry Andrew Mitchell, *b.* 1943, *m.*
2000 **Mitford,* Lord Redesdale, *b.* 1967, *m.* (*see* Hereditary Peers)
2008 *Mogg,* John (Frederick) Mogg, KCMG, *b.* 1943 *m.*
1997 *Molyneaux of Killead,* James Henry Molyneaux, KBE, PC, *b.* 1920
2010 *Monks,* John Stephen Monks, *b.* 1945, *m.*
2005 *Moonie,* Dr. Lewis George Moonie, *b.* 1947, *m.*
1992 *Moore of Lower Marsh,* John Edward Michael Moore, PC, *b.* 1937, *w.*
2000 *Morgan,* Kenneth Owen Morgan, *b.* 1934, *m.*
2001 *Morris of Aberavon,* John Morris, KG, PC, QC, *b.* 1931, *m.*
2006 *Morris of Handsworth,* William Manuel Morris, *b.* 1938, *m.*
2006 *Morrow,* Maurice George Morrow, *b.* 1948, *m.*
2001 *Moser,* Claus Adolf Moser, KCB, CBE, *b.* 1922, *m.*
2008 *Myners,* Paul Myners, CBE, *b.* 1948, *m.*
1997 *Naseby,* Michael Wolfgang Laurence Morris, PC, *b.* 1936, *m.*
2013 *Nash,* John Alfred Stoddard Nash, *b.* 1949
1997 *Neill of Bladen,* (Francis) Patrick Neill, QC, *b.* 1926, *m.*
1997 *Newby,* Richard Mark Newby, OBE, *b.* 1953, *m.*
1994 *Nickson,* David Wigley Nickson, KBE, FRSE, *b.* 1929, *m.*
2011 *Noon,* Gulam Kaderbhoy Noon, MBE, *b.* 1936, *m.*
1998 *Norton of Louth,* Philip Norton, *b.* 1951
2000 *Oakeshott of Seagrove Bay,* Matthew Alan Oakeshott, *b.* 1947, *m.*
2012 *O'Donnell,* Augustine Thomas (Gus) O'Donnell, GCB, *b.* 1952, *m.*
2005 *O'Neill of Clackmannan,* Martin John O'Neill, *b.* 1945, *m.*
2001 *Ouseley,* Herman George Ouseley, *b.* 1945, *m.*
1992 *Owen,* David Anthony Llewellyn Owen, CH, PC, *b.* 1938, *m.*
1999 *Oxburgh,* Ernest Ronald Oxburgh, KBE, FRS, PHD, *b.* 1934, *m.*
2013 ‡*Paddick,* Brian Paddick, *b.* 1958, *m.*
2011 *Palmer of Childs Hill,* Monroe Edward Palmer, OBE, *b.* 1938, *m.*
2013 ‡*Palumbo,* James Palumbo, *b.* 1953
1991 *Palumbo,* Peter Garth Palumbo, *b.* 1935, *m.*
2008 *Pannick,* David Philip Pannick, QC, *b.* 1956, *m.*
2000 *Parekh,* Bhikhu Chhotalal Parekh, *b.* 1935, *m.*
1992 *Parkinson,* Cecil Edward Parkinson, PC, *b.* 1931, *m.*
1999 *Patel,* Narendra Babubhai Patel, *b.* 1938
2000 *Patel of Blackburn,* Adam Hafejee Patel, *b.* 1940
2006 *Patel of Bradford,* Prof. Kamlesh Kumar Patel, OBE, *b.* 1960 *m.*
2005 *Patten of Barnes,* Christopher Francis Patten, CH, PC, *b.* 1944, *m.*
1997 *Patten,* John Haggitt Charles Patten, PC, *b.* 1945, *m.*
1996 *Paul,* Swraj Paul, PC, *b.* 1931, *m.*
1990 *Pearson of Rannoch,* Malcolm Everard MacLaren Pearson, *b.* 1942, *m.*
2001 *Pendry,* Thomas Pendry, PC, *b.* 1934, *m.*
1987 *Peston,* Maurice Harry Peston, *b.* 1931, *m.*
1998 *Phillips of Sudbury,* Andrew Wyndham Phillips, OBE, *b.* 1939, *m.*
1992 *Plant of Highfield,* Prof. Raymond Plant, PHD, *b.* 1945, *m.*
1987 *Plumb,* (Charles) Henry Plumb, *b.* 1925, *m.*
2000 **Ponsonby of Roehampton,* Lord Ponsonby of Shulbrede, *b.* 1958 (*see* Hereditary Peers)
2010 *Popat,* Dolar Amarshi Popat, *b.* 1953, *m.*
2000 *Powell of Bayswater,* Charles David Powell, KCMG, *b.* 1941
2010 *Prescott,* John Leslie Prescott, *b.* 1938, *m.*
1987 *Prior,* James Michael Leathes Prior, PC, *b.* 1927, *m.*
1982 *Prys-Davies,* Gwilym Prys Prys-Davies, *b.* 1923, *m.*
1997 *Puttnam,* David Terence Puttnam, CBE, *b.* 1941, *m.*
2013 ‡*Purvis,* Jeremy Purvis, *b.* 1974
1994 *Quirk,* Prof. (Charles) Randolph Quirk, CBE, FBA, *b.* 1920, *m.*

2001 *Radice,* Giles Heneage Radice, PC, *b.* 1936
2005 *Ramsbotham,* David John Ramsbotham, GCB, CBE, *b.* 1934, *m.*
2004 *Rana,* Dr Diljit Singh Rana, MBE, *b.* 1938, *m.*
1997 *Razzall,* (Edward) Timothy Razzall, CBE, *b.* 1943, *m.*
2005 *Rees of Ludlow,* Prof. Martin John Rees, OM, *b.* 1942, *m.*
2010 *Reid of Cardowan,* Dr John Reid, PC, *b.* 1947, *m.*
1991 *Renfrew of Kaimsthorn,* (Andrew) Colin Renfrew, FBA, *b.* 1937, *m.*
1999 *Rennard,* Christopher John Rennard, MBE, *b.* 1960
1997 *Renton of Mount Harry,* (Ronald) Timothy Renton, PC, *b.* 1932, *m.*
1997 *Renwick of Clifton,* Robin William Renwick, KCMG, *b.* 1937, *m.*
2010 *Ribeiro,* Bernard Francisco Ribeiro, CBE, *b.* 1944, *m.*
1990 *Richard,* Ivor Seward Richard, PC, QC, *b.* 1932, *m.*
2010 *Risby,* Richard John Grenville Spring, *b.* 1946, *m.*
1992 *Rix,* Brian Norman Roger Rix, CBE, *b.* 1924, *w.*
1997 *Roberts of Conwy,* (Ieuan) Wyn (Pritchard) Roberts, PC, *b.* 1930, *m.*
2004 *Roberts of Llandudno,* Revd John Roger Roberts, *b.* 1935, *m.*
1999 *Robertson of Port Ellen,* George Islay MacNeill Robertson, KT, GCMG, PC, *b.* 1946, *m.*
1992 *Rodgers of Quarry Bank,* William Thomas Rodgers, PC, *b.* 1928, *w.*
1999 *Rogan,* Dennis Robert David Rogan, *b.* 1942, *m.*
1996 *Rogers of Riverside,* Richard George Rogers, CH, RA, RIBA, *b.* 1933, *m.*
2001 *Rooker,* Jeffrey William Rooker, PC, *b.* 1941, *m.*
2000 *Roper,* John Francis Hodgess Roper, PC, *b.* 1935, *m.*
2004 *Rosser,* Richard Andrew Rosser, *b.* 1944, *m.*
2006 *Rowe-Beddoe,* David (Sydney) Rowe-Beddoe, *b.* 1937, *m.*
2004 *Rowlands,* Edward Rowlands, CBE, *b.* 1940, *m.*
1997 *Ryder of Wensum,* Richard Andrew Ryder, OBE, PC, *b.* 1949, *m.*
1996 *Saatchi,* Maurice Saatchi, *b.* 1946, *w.*
2009 *Sacks,* Chief Rabbi Dr Jonathan Henry Sacks, *b.* 1948, *m.*
1989 *Sainsbury of Preston Candover,* John Davan Sainsbury, KG, *b.* 1927, *m.*
1997 *Sainsbury of Turville,* David John Sainsbury, *b.* 1940, *m.*
1997 *Sandberg,* Michael Graham Ruddock Sandberg, CBE, *b.* 1927, *m.*
1985 *Sanderson of Bowden,* Charles Russell Sanderson, *b.* 1933, *m.*
2010 *Sassoon,* James Meyer Sassoon, *b.* 1955, *m.*
1998 *Sawyer,* Lawrence (Tom) Sawyer, *b.* 1943
1997 *Selkirk of Douglas,* James Alexander Douglas-Hamilton, PC, QC, *b.* 1942, *m.*
1996 *Sewel,* John Buttifant Sewel, CBE, *b.* 1946
2010 *Sharkey,* John Kevin Sharkey, *b.* 1947, *m.*
1999 *Sharman,* Colin Morven Sharman, OBE, *b.* 1943, *m.*
1994 *Shaw of Northstead,* Michael Norman Shaw, *b.* 1920, *m.*
2006 *Sheikh,* Mohamed Iltaf Sheikh, *b.* 1941, *m.*
2001 *Sheldon,* Robert Edward Sheldon, PC, *b.* 1923, *m.*
1994 *Sheppard of Didgemere,* Allan John George Sheppard, KCVO, *b.* 1932, *m.*
2013 ‡*Sherbourne,* Stephen Sherbourne, *b.* 1945
2010 *Shipley,* John Warren Shipley, OBE, *b.* 1946
2000 *Shutt of Greetland,* David Trevor Shutt, OBE, PC, *b.* 1942
1997 *Simon of Highbury,* David Alec Gwyn Simon, CBE, *b.* 1939, *m.*
1997 *Simpson of Dunkeld,* George Simpson, *b.* 1942, *m.*
2011 *Singh of Wimbledon,* Indarjit Singh, CBE, *b.* 1932, *m.*
1991 *Skidelsky,* Robert Jacob Alexander Skidelsky, DPHIL, *b.* 1939, *m.*
1997 *Smith of Clifton,* Trevor Arthur Smith, *b.* 1937, *m.*
2005 *Smith of Finsbury,* Christopher Robert Smith, PC, *b.* 1951
2008 *Smith of Kelvin,* Robert (Haldane) Smith, *b.* 1944, *m.*
1999 *Smith of Leigh,* Peter Richard Charles Smith, *b.* 1945, *m.*
2004 *Snape,* Peter Charles Snape, *b.* 1942
2005 *Soley,* Clive Stafford Soley, *b.* 1939
1990 *Soulsby of Swaffham Prior,* Ernest Jackson Lawson Soulsby, PHD, *b.* 1926, *m.*
2010 *Spicer,* (William) Michael Hardy Spicer, PC, *b.* 1943, *m.*
1997 *Steel of Aikwood,* David Martin Scott Steel, KT, KBE, PC, *b.* 1938, *m.*
2011 *Stephen,* Nicol Ross Stephen, *b.* 1960, *m.*
1991 *Sterling of Plaistow,* Jeffrey Maurice Sterling, GCVO, CBE, *b.* 1934, *m.*
2007 *Stern of Brentford,* Nicholas Herbert Stern, *b.* 1946, *m.*
2005 *Stevens of Kirkwhelpington,* John Arthur Stevens, QPM, *b.* 1942, *m.*
1987 *Stevens of Ludgate,* David Robert Stevens, *b.* 1936, *m.*
2010 *Stevenson of Balmacara,* Robert Wilfrid Stevenson, *b.* 1947, *m.*
1999 *Stevenson of Coddenham,* Henry Dennistoun Stevenson, CBE, *b.* 1945, *m.*
1992 *Stewartby,* (Bernard Harold) Ian (Halley) Stewart, RD, PC, FBA, FRSE, *b.* 1935, *m.*
2011 *Stirrup,* Graham Eric Stirrup, KG, GCB, AFC, *b.* 1949, *m.*
1983 *Stoddart of Swindon,* David Leonard Stoddart, *b.* 1926, *m.*
1997 *Stone of Blackheath,* Andrew Zelig Stone, *b.* 1942, *m.*
2011 *Stoneham of Droxford,* Benjamin Russell Mackintosh Stoneham 1940, *m.*
2011 *Storey,* Michael John Storey, CBE, *b.* 1949
2011 *Strasburger,* Paul Cline Strasburger, *b.* 1946
2009 *Sugar,* Alan Michael Sugar, *b.* 1947, *m.*
2001 *Sutherland of Houndwood,* Stewart Ross Sutherland, KT, *b.* 1941, *m.*
1971 *Tanlaw,* Simon Brooke Mackay, *b.* 1934, *m.*
1996 *Taverne,* Dick Taverne, QC, *b.* 1928, *m.*
1978 *Taylor of Blackburn,* Thomas Taylor, CBE, *b.* 1929, *m.*
2010 *Taylor of Goss Moor,* Matthew Owen John Taylor, *b.* 1963, *m.*
2006 *Taylor of Holbeach,* John Derek Taylor, CBE, *b.* 1943, *m.*
1996 *Taylor of Warwick,* John David Beckett Taylor, *b.* 1952, *m.*
1992 *Tebbit,* Norman Beresford Tebbit, CH, PC, *b.* 1931, *m.*
2001 *Temple-Morris,* Peter Temple-Morris, *b.* 1938, *m.*
2006 *Teverson,* Robin Teverson, *b.* 1952, *m.*
1996 *Thomas of Gresford,* Donald Martin Thomas, OBE, QC, *b.* 1937, *m.*
1997 *Thomas of Macclesfield,* Terence James Thomas, CBE, *b.* 1937, *m.*
1981 *Thomas of Swynnerton,* Hugh Swynnerton Thomas, *b.* 1931, *m.*
1990 *Tombs,* Francis Leonard Tombs, FENG, *b.* 1924, *w.*

1998 *Tomlinson,* John Edward Tomlinson, *b.* 1939
1994 *Tope,* Graham Norman Tope, CBE, *b.* 1943, *m.*
1981 *Tordoff,* Geoffrey Johnson Tordoff, *b.* 1928, *m.*
2010 *Touhig,* James Donnelly Touhig, PC, *b.* 1947, *m.*
2012 *Trees,* Alexander John Trees, PHD, *b.* 1946, *m.*
2004 *Triesman,* David Maxim Triesman, *b.* 1943
2006 *Trimble,* William David Trimble, PC, *b.* 1944, *m.*
2010 *True,* Nicholas Edward True, CBE, *b.* 1951, *m.*
2004 *Truscott,* Dr Peter Derek Truscott, *b.* 1959, *m.*
1993 *Tugendhat,* Christopher Samuel Tugendhat, *b.* 1937, *m.*
2004 *Tunnicliffe,* Denis Tunnicliffe, CBE, *b.* 1943, *m.*
2000 *Turnberg,* Leslie Arnold Turnberg, MD, *b.* 1934, *m.*
2005 *Turnbull,* Andrew Turnbull, KCB, CVO, *b.* 1945, *m.*
2005 *Turner of Ecchinswell,* (Jonathan) Adair Turner, *b.* 1955, *m.*
2005 *Tyler,* Paul Archer Tyler, CBE, *b.* 1941, *m.*
2004 *Vallance of Tummel,* Iain (David Thomas) Vallance, *b.* 1943, *m.*
1996 *Vincent of Coleshill,* Richard Frederick Vincent, GBE, KCB, DSO, *b.* 1931, *m.*
2013 ‡*Verjee,* Rumi Verjee, CBE, *b.* 1957
1985 *Vinson,* Nigel Vinson, LVO, *b.* 1931, *m.*
1990 *Waddington,* David Charles Waddington, GCVO, PC, QC, *b.* 1929, *m.*
1990 *Wade of Chorlton,* (William) Oulton Wade, *b.* 1932, *m.*
1992 *Wakeham,* John Wakeham, PC, *b.* 1932, *m.*
1999 *Waldegrave of North Hill,* William Arthur Waldegrave, PC, *b.* 1946, *m.*
2007 *Walker of Aldringham,* Michael John Dawson Walker, GCB, CMG, CBE, *b.* 1944, *m.*
1995 *Wallace of Saltaire,* William John Lawrence Wallace, PC, PHD, *b.* 1941, *m.*
2007 *Wallace of Tankerness,* James Robert Wallace, PC, QC, *b.* 1954, *m.*
1989 *Walton of Detchant,* John Nicholas Walton, TD, FRCP, *b.* 1922, *w.*
1998 *Warner,* Norman Reginald Warner, PC, *b.* 1940, *m.*
2011 *Wasserman,* Gordon Joshua Wasserman, *b.* 1938
1997 *Watson of Invergowrie,* Michael Goodall Watson, *b.* 1949, *m.*
1999 *Watson of Richmond,* Alan John Watson, CBE, *b.* 1941, *m.*
2010 *Wei,* Nathanael Ming-Yan Wei, *b.* 1977, *m.*
1976 *Weidenfeld,* (Arthur) George Weidenfeld, GBE, *b.* 1919, *m.*
2007 *West of Spithead,* Alan William John West, GCB, DSC, PC, *b.* 1948, *m.*
2013 ‡*Whitby,* Michael Whitby, *b.* 1948
1996 *Whitty,* John Lawrence (Larry) Whitty, PC, *b.* 1943, *m.*
2011 *Wigley,* Dafydd Wynne Wigley, PC, *b.* 1943, *m.*
2010 *Williams of Baglan,* Michael Charles Williams, *b.* 1949
1985 *Williams of Elvel,* Charles Cuthbert Powell Williams, CBE, PC, *b.* 1933, *m.*
2013 *Williams of Oystermouth,* Rt. Revd Rowan Douglas Williams, PC, DPHIL, *b.* 1950, *m.*
1999 *Williamson of Horton,* David (Francis) Williamson, GCMG, CB, PC, *b.* 1934, *m.*
2010 *Willis of Knaresborough,* George Philip Willis, *b.* 1941, *m.*
2010 *Wills,* Michael David Wills, PC, *b.* 1952, *m.*
2002 *Wilson of Dinton,* Richard Thomas James Wilson, GCB, *b.* 1942, *m.*
1992 *Wilson of Tillyorn,* David Clive Wilson, KT, GCMG, PHD, *b.* 1935, *m.*
1995 *Winston,* Robert Maurice Lipson Winston, FRCOG, *b.* 1940, *m.*
2010 *Wolfson of Aspley Guise,* Simon David Wolfson, *b.* 1967
1991 *Wolfson of Sunningdale,* David Wolfson, *b.* 1935, *m.*
2011 *Wood of Anfield,* Stewart Martin Wood, *b.* 1968, *m.*
1999 *Woolmer of Leeds,* Kenneth John Woolmer, *b.* 1940, *m.*
2013 ‡*Wrigglesworth,* Ian Wrigglesworth, *b.* 1939, *m.*
1994 *Wright of Richmond,* Patrick Richard Henry Wright, GCMG, *b.* 1931, *m.*
1984 *Young of Graffham,* David Ivor Young, PC, *b.* 1932, *m.*
2004 *Young of Norwood Green,* Anthony (Ian) Young, *b.* 1942, *m.*

BARONESSES

Created

2005 *Adams of Craigielea,* Katherine Patricia Irene Adams, *b.* 1947, *w.*
2007 *Afshar,* Prof. Haleh Afshar, OBE, *b.* 1944, *m.*
1997 *Amos,* Valerie Ann Amos, PC, *b.* 1954
2000 *Andrews,* Elizabeth Kay Andrews, OBE, *b.* 1943, *m.*
1996 *Anelay of St Johns,* Joyce Anne Anelay, DBE, PC, *b.* 1947, *m.*
2010 *Armstrong of Hill Top,* Hilary Jane Armstrong, PC, *b.* 1945, *m.*
1999 *Ashton of Upholland,* Catherine Margaret Ashton, PC, *b.* 1956, *m.*
2011 *Bakewell,* Joan Dawson Bakewell, DBE, *b.* 1933
2013 ‡*Bakewell,* Catherine Mary Bakewell, MBE
1999 *Barker,* Elizabeth Jean Barker, *b.* 1961
2010 *Benjamin,* Floella Karen Yunies Benjamin, OBE, *b.* 1949, *m.*
2011 *Berridge,* Elizabeth Rose Berridge, *b.* 1972
2000 *Billingham,* Angela Theodora Billingham, DPHIL, *b.* 1939, *w.*
1987 *Blackstone,* Tessa Ann Vosper Blackstone, PHD, *b.* 1942
1999 *Blood,* May Blood, MBE, *b.* 1938
2004 *Bonham-Carter of Yarnbury,* Jane Bonham Carter, *b.* 1957, *w.*
2000 *Boothroyd,* Betty Boothroyd, OM, PC, *b.* 1929
2005 *Bottomley of Nettlestone,* Virginia Hilda Brunette Maxwell Bottomley, PC, *b.* 1948, *m.*
2011 *Brinton,* Sarah Virginia Brinton, *b.* 1955, *m.*
2010 *Browning,* Angela Frances Browning, *b.* 1946, *m.*
1998 *Buscombe,* Peta Jane Buscombe, *b.* 1954, *m.*
2006 *Butler-Sloss,* (Ann) Elizabeth (Oldfield) Butler-Sloss, GBE, PC *b.* 1933, *m.*
1996 *Byford,* Hazel Byford, DBE, *b.* 1941, *m.*
2008 *Campbell of Loughborough,* Susan Catherine Campbell, CBE, *b.* 1948
2007 *Campbell of Surbiton,* Jane Susan Campbell, DBE, *b.* 1959, *m.*
1992 *Chalker of Wallasey,* Lynda Chalker, PC, *b.* 1942, *m.*
2005 *Clark of Calton,* Dr Lynda Margaret Clark, QC, *b.* 1949
2000 *Cohen of Pimlico,* Janet Cohen, *b.* 1940, *m.*
2005 *Corston,* Jean Ann Corston, PC, *b.* 1942, *w.*
2007 *Coussins,* Jean Coussins, *b.* 1950
1982 *Cox,* Caroline Anne Cox, *b.* 1937, *m.*
1998 *Crawley,* Christine Mary Crawley, *b.* 1950, *m.*
1990 *Cumberlege,* Julia Frances Cumberlege, CBE, *b.* 1943, *m.*
1993 *Dean of Thornton-le-Fylde,* Brenda Dean, PC, *b.* 1943, *m.*
2005 *Deech,* Ruth Lynn Deech, DBE, *b.* 1943, *m.*

2010 *Donaghy,* Rita Margaret Donaghy, CBE, *b.* 1944, *m.*
2010 *Doocey,* Elizabeth Deirdre Doocey, OBE, *b.* 1948, *m.*
2010 *Drake,* Jean Lesley Patricia Drake, CBE, *b.* 1948
2004 *D'Souza,* Dr Frances Gertrude Claire D'Souza, CMG, PC, *b.* 1944, *m.*
1990 ¶*Dunn,* Lydia Selina Dunn, DBE, *b.* 1940, *m.*
2010 *Eaton,* Ellen Margaret Eaton, DBE, *b.* 1942, *m.*
1990 *Eccles of Moulton,* Diana Catherine Eccles, *b.* 1933, *m.*
1997 *Emerton,* Audrey Caroline Emerton, DBE, *b.* 1935
1974 *Falkender,* Marcia Matilda Falkender, CBE, *b.* 1932
2004 *Falkner of Margravine,* Kishwer Falkner, *b.* 1955, *m.*
1994 *Farrington of Ribbleton,* Josephine Farrington, *b.* 1940, *m.*
2001 *Finlay of Llandaff,* Ilora Gillian Finlay, *b.* 1949, *m.*
1990 *Flather,* Shreela Flather, *b.* 1934, *m.*
1997 *Fookes,* Janet Evelyn Fookes, DBE, *b.* 1936
2006 *Ford,* Margaret Anne Ford, *b.* 1957, *m.*
2005 *Fritchie,* Irene Tordoff Fritchie, DBE, *b.* 1942, *m.*
1999 *Gale,* Anita Gale, *b.* 1940
2007 *Garden of Frognal,* Susan Elizabeth Garden, *b.* 1944, *m.*
1981 *Gardner of Parkes,* (Rachel) Trixie (Anne) Gardner, *b.* 1927, *w.*
2000 *Gibson of Market Rasen,* Anne Gibson, OBE, *b.* 1940, *m.*
2013 ‡*Goldie,* Annabel Goldie, *b.* 1950
2001 *Golding,* Llinos Golding, *b.* 1933, *m.*
1998 *Goudie,* Mary Teresa Goudie, *b.* 1946, *m.*
1993 *Gould of Potternewton,* Joyce Brenda Gould, *b.* 1932, *m.*
2001 *Greenfield,* Susan Adele Greenfield, CBE, *b.* 1950, *m.*
2000 *Greengross,* Sally Ralea Greengross, OBE, *b.* 1935, *m.*
2013 ‡*Grender,* Rosalind Grender, MBE
2010 *Grey-Thompson,* Tanni Carys Davina Grey-Thompson, DBE, *b.* 1969, *m.*
1991 *Hamwee,* Sally Rachel Hamwee, *b.* 1947
1999 *Hanham,* Joan Brownlow Hanham, CBE, *b.* 1939, *m.*
1999 *Harris of Richmond,* Angela Felicity Harris, *b.* 1944
1996 *Hayman,* Helene Valerie Hayman, GBE, PC, *b.* 1949, *m.*
2010 *Hayter of Kentish Town,* Dr Dianne Hayter, *b.* 1949, *m.*
2010 *Healy of Primrose Hill,* Anna Healy, *b.* 1955, *m.*
2004 *Henig,* Ruth Beatrice Henig, CBE, *b.* 1943, *m.*
2011 *Heyhoe Flint,* Rachel Heyhoe Flint, OBE, *b.* 1939, *m.*
1991 *Hilton of Eggardon,* Jennifer Hilton, QPM, *b.* 1936
2013 ‡*Hodgson,* Fiona Hodgson, CBE
1995 *Hogg,* Sarah Elizabeth Mary Hogg, *b.* 1946, *m.*
2010 *Hollins,* Prof. Sheila Clare Hollins, *b.* 1946, *m.*
1990 *Hollis of Heigham,* Patricia Lesley Hollis, PC, DPHIL, *b.* 1941, *m.*
1985 *Hooper,* Gloria Dorothy Hooper, CMG, *b.* 1939
2001 *Howarth of Breckland,* Valerie Georgina Howarth, OBE, *b.* 1940
2001 *Howe of Idlicote,* Elspeth Rosamond Morton Howe, CBE, *b.* 1932, *m.*
1999 *Howells of St Davids,* Rosalind Patricia-Anne Howells, *b.* 1931, *m.*
2010 *Hughes of Stretford,* Beverley Hughes, PC, *b.* 1950, *m.*
2013 ‡*Humphreys,* Christine Mary Humphreys
2010 *Hussein-Ece,* Meral Hussein Ece, OBE, *b.* 1953
1991 *James of Holland Park,* Phyllis Dorothy White (P. D. James), OBE, *b.* 1920, *w.*
1992 *Jay of Paddington,* Margaret Ann Jay, PC, *b.* 1939, *m.*
2011 *Jenkin of Kennington,* Anne Caroline Jenkin, *b.* 1955, *m.*
2010 *Jolly,* Judith Anne Jolly, *b.* 1951, *m.*
2013 ‡*Jones,* Jenny Jones, *b.* 1949
2006 *Jones of Whitchurch,* Margaret Beryl Jones, *b.* 1955
2013 ‡*Kennedy,* Alicia Kennedy, *b.* 1969, *m.*
1997 *Kennedy of the Shaws,* Helena Ann Kennedy, QC, *b.* 1950, *m.*
2012 *Kidron,* Beeban Tania Kidron, OBE, *b.* 1961 *m.*
2011 *King of Bow,* Oona Tamsyn King, *b.* 1967, *m.*
2006 *Kingsmill,* Denise Patricia Byrne Kingsmill, CBE, *b.* 1947, *m.*
2009 *Kinnock of Holyhead,* Glenys Elizabeth Kinnock, *b.* 1944, *m.*
1997 *Knight of Collingtree,* (Joan Christabel) Jill Knight, DBE, *b.* 1927, *w.*
2010 *Kramer,* Susan Veronica Kramer, *b.* 1950, *w.*
2013 *Lane-Fox of Soho,* Martha Lane Fox, CBE, *b.* 1973
2013 ‡*Lawrence,* Doreen Lawrence, OBE, *b.* 1952
2010 *Liddell of Coatdyke,* Helen Lawrie Liddell, PC, *b.* 1950, *m.*
1997 *Linklater of Butterstone,* Veronica Linklater, *b.* 1943, *m.*
2011 *Lister of Burtersett,* Margot Ruth Aline Lister, CBE, *b.* 1949, *m.*
1978 *Lockwood,* Betty Lockwood, *b.* 1924, *w.*
1997 *Ludford,* Sarah Ann Ludford, *b.*1951 disqualified as MEP
2004 *McDonagh,* Margaret Josephine McDonagh
1999 *McIntosh of Hudnall,* Genista Mary McIntosh, *b.* 1946
1997 *Maddock,* Diana Margaret Maddock, *b.* 1945, *m.*
1991 *Mallalieu,* Ann Mallalieu, QC, *b.* 1945, *m.*
2008 *Manningham-Buller,* Elizabeth (Lydia) Manningham-Buller, DCB, *b.* 1948, *m.*
2013 ‡*Manzoor,* Zahida Manzoor, CBE, *b.* 1958, *m.*
1970 *Masham of Ilton,* Susan Lilian Primrose Cunliffe-Lister, *b.* 1935, *w.*
1999 *Massey of Darwen,* Doreen Elizabeth Massey, *b.* 1938, *m.*
2006 *Meacher,* Molly Christine Meacher, *b.* 1940, *m.*
1998 *Miller of Chilthorne Domer,* Susan Elizabeth Miller, *b.* 1954
1993 *Miller of Hendon,* Doreen Miller, MBE, *b.* 1933, *m.*
2004 *Morgan of Drefelin,* Delyth Jane Morgan, *b.* 1961, *m.*
2011 *Morgan of Ely,* Mair Eluned Morgan, *b.* 1967, *m.*
2001 *Morgan of Huyton,* Sally Morgan, *b.* 1959, *m.*
2004 *Morris of Bolton,* Patricia Morris, OBE, *b.* 1953
2005 *Morris of Yardley,* Estelle Morris, PC, *b.* 1952
2004 *Murphy,* Elaine Murphy, *b.* 1947, *m.*
2004 *Neuberger,* Rabbi Julia (Babette Sarah) Neuberger, DBE, *b.* 1950, *m.*
2007 *Neville-Jones,* (Lilian) Pauline Neville-Jones, DCMG, PC, *b.* 1939
2013 ‡*Neville-Rolfe,* Lucy Jeanne Neville-Rolfe, DBE, CMG, *b.* 1953, *m.*
2010 *Newlove,* Helen Margaret Newlove, b. 1961, *w.*
1997 *Nicholson of Winterbourne,* Emma Harriet Nicholson, *b.* 1941, *m.*
1982 *Nicol,* Olive Mary Wendy Nicol, *b.* 1923, *m.*
2000 *Noakes,* Sheila Valerie Masters, DBE, *b.* 1949, *m.*
2000 *Northover,* Lindsay Patricia Granshaw, *b.* 1954
2010 *Nye,* Susan Nye, *b.* 1955, *m.*
1991 *O'Cathain,* Detta O'Cathain, OBE, *b.* 1938, *m.*
2009 *O'Loan,* Nuala Patricia, DBE, *b.* 1951, *m.*

1999 *O'Neill of Bengarve,* Onora Sylvia O'Neill, CBE, PHD, *b.* 1941
1989 *Oppenheim-Barnes,* Sally Oppenheim-Barnes, PC, *b.* 1930, *m.*
2006 *Paisley of St George's,* Eileen Emily Paisley, *b.* 1931, *m.*
2010 *Parminter,* Kathryn Jane Parminter, *b.* 1964, *m.*
1991 *Perry of Southwark,* Pauline Perry, *b.* 1931, *m.*
1997 *Pitkeathley,* Jill Elizabeth Pitkeathley, OBE, *b.* 1940
1981 *Platt of Writtle,* Beryl Catherine Platt, CBE, FENG, *b.* 1923, *m.*
1999 *Prashar,* Usha Kumari Prashar, CBE, PC, *b.* 1948, *m.*
2004 *Prosser,* Margaret Theresa Prosser, OBE, *b.* 1937
2006 *Quin,* Joyce Gwendoline Quin, PC *b.* 1944
1996 *Ramsay of Cartvale,* Margaret Mildred (Meta) Ramsay, *b.* 1936
2011 *Randerson,* Jennifer Elizabeth Randerson, *b.* 1948, *m.*
1994 *Rawlings,* Patricia Elizabeth Rawlings, *b.* 1939
1997 *Rendell of Babergh,* Ruth Barbara Rendell, CBE, *b.* 1930, *m.*
1998 *Richardson of Calow,* Kathleen Margaret Richardson, OBE, *b.* 1938, *m.*
2004 *Royall of Blaisdon,* Janet Anne Royall, PC, *b.* 1955, *m.*
1997 *Scotland of Asthal,* Patricia Janet Scotland, PC, QC, *b.* 1955, *m.*
2000 *Scott of Needham Market,* Rosalind Carol Scott, *b.* 1957
1991 *Seccombe,* Joan Anna Dalziel Seccombe, DBE, *b.* 1930, *m.*
2010 *Shackleton of Belgravia,* Fiona Sara Shackleton, LVO, *b.* 1956, *m.*
1998 *Sharp of Guildford,* Margaret Lucy Sharp, *b.* 1938, *m.*
1973 *Sharples,* Pamela Sharples, *b.* 1923, *m.*
2005 *Shephard of Northwold,* Gillian Patricia Shephard, PC, *b.* 1940, *m.*
2010 *Sherlock,* Maeve Christina Mary Sherlock, OBE, *b.* 1960
2010 *Smith of Basildon,* Angela Evans Smith, PC, *b.* 1959, *m.*
1995 *Smith of Gilmorehill,* Elizabeth Margaret Smith, *b.* 1940, *w.*
2010 *Stedman-Scott,* Deborah Stedman-Scott, OBE, *b.* 1955
1999 *Stern,* Vivien Helen Stern, CBE, *b.* 1941
2011 *Stowell of Beeston,* Tina Wendy Stowell, MBE, *b.* 1967
2013 ‡*Suttie,* Alison Suttie
1996 *Symons of Vernham Dean,* Elizabeth Conway Symons, PC, *b.* 1951
2005 *Taylor of Bolton,* Winifred Ann Taylor, PC *b.* 1947, *m.*
1994 *Thomas of Walliswood,* Susan Petronella Thomas, OBE, *b.* 1935, *m.*
2006 *Thomas of Winchester,* Celia Marjorie Thomas, MBE, *b.* 1945
1998 *Thornton,* (Dorothea) Glenys Thornton, *b.* 1952, *m.*
2005 *Tonge,* Dr. Jennifer Louise Tonge, *b.* 1941, *m.*
1980 *Trumpington,* Jean Alys Barker, DCVO, PC, *b.* 1922, *w.*
1985 *Turner of Camden,* Muriel Winifred Turner, *b.* 1927, *m.*
2011 *Tyler of Enfield,* Claire Tyler, *b.* 1957
1998 *Uddin,* Manzila Pola Uddin, *b.* 1959, *m.*
2007 *Vadera,* Shriti Vadera, PC, *b.* 1962
2005 *Valentine,* Josephine Clare Valentine, *b.* 1958, *m.*
2006 *Verma,* Sandip Verma, *b.* 1959, *m.*
2004 *Wall of New Barnet,* Margaret Mary Wall, *b.* 1941, *m.*
2000 *Walmsley,* Joan Margaret Walmsley, *b.* 1943
1985 *Warnock,* Helen Mary Warnock, DBE, *b.* 1924, *w.*
2007 *Warsi,* Sayeeda Hussain Warsi, PC, *b.* 1971
1999 *Warwick of Undercliffe,* Diana Mary Warwick, *b.* 1945, *m.*
2010 *Wheatcroft,* Patience Jane Wheatcroft, *b.* 1951, *m.*
2010 *Wheeler,* Margaret Eileen Joyce Wheeler, MBE, *b.* 1949
1999 *Whitaker,* Janet Alison Whitaker, *b.* 1936
1996 *Wilcox,* Judith Ann Wilcox, *b.* 1940, *w.*
1999 *Wilkins,* Rosalie Catherine Wilkins, *b.* 1946
2013 ‡*Williams,* Susan Williams, *b.* 1967, *m.*
1993 *Williams of Crosby,* Shirley Vivien Teresa Brittain Williams, PC, *b.* 1930, *w.*
2011 *Worthington,* Bryony Katherine Worthington, *b.* 1971, *m.*
2004 *Young of Hornsey,* Prof. Margaret Omolola Young, OBE, *b.* 1951, *m.*
1997 *Young of Old Scone,* Barbara Scott Young, *b.* 1948

LORDS SPIRITUAL

The Lords Spiritual are the Archbishops of Canterbury and York and 24 diocesan bishops of the Church of England. The Bishops of London, Durham and Winchester always have seats in the House of Lords; the other 21 seats are filled by the remaining diocesan bishops in order of seniority. The Bishop of Sodor and Man and the Bishop of Gibraltar are not eligible to sit in the House of Lords.

ARCHBISHOPS

Style, The Most Revd and Rt. Hon. the Lord Archbishop of _
Addressed as Archbishop *or* Your Grace

INTRODUCED TO HOUSE OF LORDS

2011 *Canterbury* (105th), Justin Portal Welby, *b.* 1956, *m., cons.* 2011, *elected* 2012

2005 *York* (97th), John Mugabi Tucker Sentamu, PC, PHD, *b.* 1949, *m., cons.* 1996, *elected* 2005, *trans.* 2005

BISHOPS

Style, The Rt. Revd the Lord Bishop of _
Addressed as My Lord
elected date of confirmation as diocesan bishop

INTRODUCED TO HOUSE OF LORDS
as at 31 August 2013

1996 *London* (132nd), Richard John Carew Chartres, KCVO, PC, *b.* 1947, *m., cons.* 1992, *elected* 1995

2013 *Durham* (73rd), vacant

2012 *Winchester* (97th), Timothy John Dakin, *b.* 1958, *m., cons.* 2012, *elected* 2012

2001 *Chester* (40th), Peter Robert Forster, PHD, *b.* 1950, *m., cons.* 1996, *elected* 1996

2003 *Newcastle* (11th), (John) Martin Wharton, *b.* 1944, *m., cons.* 1992, *elected* 1997

2003 *Leicester* (6th), Timothy John Stevens, *b.* 1946, *m.,* cons. 1995, *elected* 1999

2004 *Norwich* (71st), Graham Richard James, *b.* 1951, *m., cons.* 1993, *elected* 1999

2006 *Ripon and Leeds* (12th), John Richard Packer, *b.* 1946, *m., cons.* 1996, *elected* 2000

2009 *Wakefield* (12th), Stephen George Platten, *b.* 1947, *m., cons.* 2003, *elected* 2003

2009 *Bristol* (55th), Michael Arthur Hill, *b.* 1947, *m., cons.* 1998, *elected* 2003

2009 *Lichfield* (98th), Jonathan Michael Gledhill, *b.* 1949, *m., cons.* 1996, *elected* 2003

2009 *Gloucester* (40th), Michael Francis Perham, *b.* 1947, *m., cons.* 2004, *elected* 2004

2010 *Derby* (7th), Alastair Llewellyn John Redfern, *b.* 1948, *m., cons.* 1997, *elected* 2005

2010 *Birmingham* (9th), David Andrew Urquhart, *b.* 1952, *cons.* 2000, *elected* 2006

2011 *Oxford* (42nd), John Lawrence Pritchard, *b.* 1948, *m., cons.* 2002, *elected* 2007

2012 *Worcester* (113th), John Geoffrey Inge, PHD, *b.* 1955, *m., cons.* 2003, *elected* 2007

2013 *Coventry* (9th), Christopher John Cocksworth, PHD, *b.* 1959, *m., cons.* 2008, *elected* 2008

2013 *Truro* (15th), Timothy Martin Thornton, *b.* 1957, *m., cons.* 2001, *elected* 2008

2013 *Sheffield* (7th), Stephen John Lindsey Croft, *b.* 1957, *m., cons.* 2009, *elected* 2009

BISHOPS AWAITING SEATS, in order of seniority
as at 31 August 2013

St Albans (10th), Alan Gregory Clayton Smith, *b.* 1957, *cons.* 2001, *elected* 2009

Carlisle (66th), James William Scobie Newcome, *b.* 1953, *m., cons.* 2002, *elected* 2009

Southwell and Nottingham (11th), Paul Roger Butler, *b.* 1955, *m., cons.* 2004, *elected* 2009

Peterborough (38th), Donald Spargo Allister, *b.* 1952, *m., cons.* 2010, *elected* 2010

Portsmouth (9th), Christopher Richard James Foster, *b.* 1953, *m., cons.* 2001, *elected* 2010

Chelmsford (10th), Stephen Geoffrey Cottrell, *b.* 1958, *m., cons.* 2004, *elected* 2010

Rochester (107th), James Henry Langstaff, b. 1956, *m., cons.* 2004, *elected* 2010

Ely (69th), Stephen David Conway, *b.* 1957, *cons.* 2006, *elected* 2010

Southwark (10th), Christopher Thomas James Chessun, *b.* 1956, *cons.* 2005, *elected* 2011

Bradford (10th), Nicholas Baines, *b.* 1957, *m., cons.* 2011, *elected* 2011

Salisbury (78th), Nicholas Roderick Holtam, *b.* 1954, *m., cons.* 2011, *elected* 2011

Lincoln (71st), Christopher Lowson, *b.* 1953, *m., cons.* 2011, *elected* 2011

Chichester (103rd), Martin Clive Warner, PHD, *b.* 1958, *cons.* 2010, *elected* 2012

Blackburn (9th), Julian Tudor Henderson, *b.* 1954, *m., cons.* 2013, *elected* 2013

Manchester (12th), David Stuart Walker, *b.* 1957, *m., cons.* 2000, *elected* 2013

Bath and Wells (78th), vacant
Exeter (71st), vacant
Guildford (10th), vacant
Hereford (105th), vacant
Liverpool (8th), vacant
St Edmundsbury and Ipswich (11th), vacant

COURTESY TITLES

The heir apparent to a Duke, Marquess or Earl uses the highest of his father's other titles as a courtesy title. For example, the Marquess of Blandford is heir to the Dukedom of Marlborough, and Viscount Amberley to the Earldom of Russell. Titles of second heirs (when in use) are also given, and the courtesy title of the father of a second heir is indicated by * eg Earl of Mornington, eldest son of *Marquess of Douro.

The holder of a courtesy title is not styled 'the Most Hon.' or 'the Rt. Hon.', and in correspondence 'the' is omitted before the title. The heir apparent to a Scottish title may use the title 'Master'.

MARQUESSES
*Blandford – *Marlborough, D.*
Bowmont and Cessford – *Roxburghe, D.*
Douglas and Clydesdale – *Hamilton and Brandon, D.*
*Douro – *Wellington, D.*
Graham – *Montrose, D.*
Granby – *Rutland, D.*
*Hamilton – *Abercorn, D.*
Lorne – *Argyll, D.*
Stafford – *Sutherland, D.*
Tavistock – *Bedford, D.*
Tullibardine – *Atholl, D.*
*Worcester – *Beaufort, D.*

EARLS
*Aboyne – *Huntly, M.*
Arundel and Surrey – *Norfolk, D.*
Bective – *Headfort, M.*
Belfast – *Donegall, M.*
Brecknock – *Camden, M.*
*Burford – *St Albans, D.*
*Burlington – *Devonshire, D.*
*Cardigan – *Ailesbury, M.*
Compton – *Northampton, M.*
*Dalkeith – *Buccleuch, D.*
Dumfries – *Bute, M.*
Euston – *Grafton, D.*
Glamorgan – **Worcester, M.*
Grosvenor – *Westminster, D.*
*Haddo – *Aberdeen and Temair, M.*
Hillsborough – *Downshire, M.*
*Hopetoun – *Linlithgow, M.*
Kerry – *Lansdowne, M.*
*March and Kinrara – *Richmond, D.*
Medina – *Milford Haven, M.*
*Mount Charles – *Conyngham, M.*
Mornington – **Douro, M.*
Mulgrave – *Normanby, M.*
Percy – *Northumberland, D.*
Rocksavage – *Cholmondley, M.*
Ronaldshay – *Zetland, M.*
*St Andrews – *Kent, D.*
*Southesk – *Fife, D.*
Sunderland – **Blandford, M.*
*Tyrone – *Waterford, M.*
*Ulster – *Gloucester, D.*
Uxbridge – *Anglesey, M.*
*Wiltshire – *Winchester, M.*
Yarmouth – *Hertford, M.*

VISCOUNTS
Aithrie – **Hopetown, E.*
Alexander – *Caledon, E.*
Althorp – *Spencer, E.*
Andover – *Suffolk and Berkshire, E.*
Anson – *Lichfield, E.*
Asquith – *Oxford and Asquith, E.*
Boringdon – *Morley, E.*
Borodale – *Beatty, E.*
Brocas – *Jellicoe, E.*
Bury – *Albemarle, E.*
Campden – *Gainsborough, E.*
Carlow – *Portarlington, E.*
Carlton – *Wharncliffe, E.*
Chelsea – *Cadogan, E.*
Chewton – *Waldegrave, E.*
Clanfield – *Peel, E.*
Clive – *Powis, E.*
Coke – *Leicester, E.*
Corry – *Belmore, E.*
Corvedale – *Baldwin of Bewdley, E.*
Cranborne – *Salisbury, M.*
Crichton – *Erne, E.*
Curzon – *Howe, E.*
Dalrymple – *Stair, E.*
Dangan – *Cowley, E.*
Drumlanrig – *Queensberry, M.*
Duncannon – *Bessborough, E.*
Dungarvan – *Cork and Orrery, E.*
Dunluce – *Antrim, E.*
Dunwich – *Stradbroke, E.*
Ednam – *Dudley, E.*
Elveden – *Iveagh, E.*
Emlyn – *Cawdor, E*
Encombe – *Eldon, E.*
Enfield – *Strafford, E.*
Erleigh – *Reading, M.*
Errington – *Cromer, E.*
Feilding – *Denbigh and Desmond, E.*
FitzHarris – *Malmesbury, E.*
Folkestone – *Radnor, E.*
Forbes – *Granard, E.*
Formartine – **Haddo, E.*
Garmoyle – *Cairns, E.*
Garnock – *Lindsay, E.*
Glenapp – *Inchcape, E.*
Glentworth – *Limerick, E.*
Glerawly – *Annesley, E.*
Grey de Wilton – *Wilton, E.*
Grimstone – *Verulam, E.*
Gwynedd – *Lloyd George of Dwyfor, E.*
Hawkesbury – *Liverpool, E.*
Hinchingbrooke – *Sandwich, E.*
Ikerrin – *Carrick, E.*
Ingestre – *Shrewsbury, E.*
Jocelyn – *Roden, E.*
Kelburn – *Glasgow, E.*
Kingsborough – *Kingston, E.*
Kirkwall – *Orkney, E.*
Knebworth – *Lytton, E.*
Lambton – *Durham, E.*
Lascelles – *Harewood, E.*
Linley – *Snowdon, E.*
Lymington – *Portsmouth, E.*
Macmillan of Ovenden – *Stockton, E.*
Maidstone – *Winchilsea, E*
Maitland – *Lauderdale, E.*
Mandeville – *Manchester, D.*
Marsham – *Romney, E.*
Melgund – *Minto, E.*
Merton – *Nelson, E.*
Moore – *Drogheda, E.*
Newport – *Bradford, E.*
Northland – *Ranfurly, E*
Newry and Mourne – *Kilmorey, E.*
Petersham – *Harrington, E.*
Pollington – *Mexborough, E*
Raynham – *Townshend, M.*
Reidhaven – *Seafield, E.*
Royston – *Hardwicke, E.*
Ruthven of Canberra – *Gowrie, E.*
St Cyres – *Iddesleigh, E.*
Sandon – *Harrowby, E.*
Savernake – **Cardigan, E.*
Severn – *Wessex, E.*
Slane – **Mount Charles, E.*
Somerton – *Normanton, E.*
Stopford – *Courtown, E.*
Stormont – *Mansfield, E.*
Strabane – **Hamilton, M.*
Strathallan – *Perth, E.*
Stuart – *Castle Stewart, E.*
Suirdale – *Donoughmore, E.*
Tamworth – *Ferrers, E.*
Tarbat – *Cromartie, E.*
Vaughan – *Lisburne, E.*
Weymouth – *Bath, M.*
Windsor – *Plymouth, E.*
Wolmer – *Selborne, E.*
Woodstock – *Portland, E.*

BARONS (LORDS)
Aberdour – *Morton, E.*
Apsley – *Bathurst, E.*
Ardee – *Meath, E.*
Ashley – *Shaftesbury, E.*
Balniel – *Crawford and Balcarres, E.*
Berriedale – *Caithness, E.*
Bingham – *Lucan, E.*
Binning – *Haddington, E.*
Brooke – *Warwick, E.*
Bruce – *Elgin, E.*
Buckhurst – *De La Warr, E.*
Burghley – *Exeter, M.*
Cardross – *Buchan, E.*
Carnegie – **Southesk, E.*
Cavendish – **Burlington, E.*
Clifton – *Darnley, E.*
Cochrane – *Dundonald, E.*
Courtenay – *Devon, E.*
Culloden – **Ulster, E.*
Dalmeny – *Rosebery, E.*
Doune – *Moray, E.*
Downpatrick – **St Andrews, E.*
Dunglass – *Home, E.*
Elcho – *Wemyss and March, E.*
Eliot – *St Germans, E.*
Gillford – *Clanwilliam, E.*
Glamis – *Strathmore, E.*
Greenock – *Cathcart, E.*
Guernsey – *Aylesford, E.*
Hay – *Erroll, E.*
Herbert – *Pembroke and Montgomery, E.*
Howard of Effingham – *Effingham, E.*
Huntingtower – *Dysart, E.*
Hyde – *Clarendon, E.*
Inverurie – *Kintore, E.*
Irwin – *Halifax, E.*
Johnstone – *Annandale and Hartfell, E.*
Langton – *Temple of Stowe, E.*
Le Poer – **Tyrone, E.*
Leveson – *Granville, E*
Loughborough – *Rosslyn, E.*
Masham – *Swinton, E.*
Medway – *Cranbrook, E.*
Montgomerie – *Eglinton and Winton, E.*
Moreton – *Ducie, E.*
Naas – *Mayo, E.*
Norreys – *Lindsey and Abingdon, E.*
North – *Guilford, E.*
Ogilvy – *Airlie, E.*
Oxmantown – *Rosse, E.*
Porchester – *Carnarvon, E.*

Ramsay – *Dalhousie, E.*
Romsey – *Mountbatten of Burma, C.*
St. John – **Wiltshire, E.*
Scrymgeour – *Dundee, E.*
Settrington – **March and Kinrara, E.*
Seymour – *Somerset, D.*
Stanley – *Derby, E.*
Stavordale – *Ilchester, E.*
Strathavon – **Aboyne, E.*
Strathnaver – *Sutherland, C.*
Vere of Hanworth – **Burford, E.*
Wodehouse – *Kimberley, E.*
Worsley – *Yarborough, E.*

PEERS' SURNAMES

The following symbols indicate the rank of the peer holding each title:

C. Countess
D. Duke
E. Earl
M. Marquess
V. Viscount
* Life Peer

Where no designation is given, the title is that of a hereditary Baron or Baroness.

Abney-Hastings – *Loudoun, E.*
Acheson – *Gosford, E.*
Adams – *A. of Craigielea**
Adderley – *Norton*
Addington – *Sidmouth, V.*
Agar – *Normanton, E.*
Ahmad – *A. of Wimbledon**
Aitken – *Beaverbrook*
Akers-Douglas – *Chilston, V.*
Alexander – *A. of Tunis, E.*
Alexander – *Caledon, E.*
Allan – *A. of Hallam**
Allsopp – *Hindlip*
Alton – *A. of Liverpool**
Ancram – *Kerr of Monteviot**
Anderson – *A. of Swansea**
Anderson – *Waverley, V.*
Anelay – *A. of St Johns**
Annesley – *Valentia, V.*
Anson – *Lichfield, E.*
Archer – *A. of Weston-super-Mare**
Armstrong – *A. of Hill Top**
Armstrong – *A. of Ilminster**
Armstrong-Jones – *Snowdon, E.*
Arthur – *Glenarthur*
Arundell – *Talbot of Malahide*
Ashdown – *A. of Norton-sub-Hamdon**
Ashley-Cooper – *Shaftesbury, E.*
Ashton – *A. of Hyde*
Ashton – *A. of Upholland**
Asquith – *Oxford and Asquith, E.*
Assheton – *Clitheroe*
Astley – *Hastings*
Astor – *A. of Hever*
Aubrey-Fletcher – *Braye*
Bailey – *Glanusk*
Baillie – *Burton*
Baillie Hamilton – *Haddington, E.*
Baker – *B. of Dorking**
Balchin – *Lingfield**
Baldwin – *B. of Bewdley, E.*
Balfour – *Kinross*
Balfour – *Riverdale*
Bampfylde – *Poltimore*
Banbury – *B. of Southam*
Barber – *B. of Tewkesbury**
Baring – *Ashburton*
Baring – *Cromer, E.*
Baring – *Howick of Glendale*
Baring – *Northbrook*
Baring – *Revelstoke*
Barker – *Trumpington**
Barnes – *Gorell*
Barnewall – *Trimlestown*
Bassam – *B. of Brighton**
Bathurst – *Bledisloe, V.*
Beauclerk – *St Albans, D.*
Beaumont – *Allendale, V.*
Beckett – *Grimthorpe*
Benn – *Stansgate, V.*
Bennet – *Tankerville, E.*
Bentinck – *Portland, E.*
Beresford – *Decies*
Beresford – *Waterford, M.*
Berkeley – *B. of Knighton**
Berry – *Camrose, V.*
Berry – *Kemsley, V.*
Bertie – *Lindsey and Abingdon, E.*
Best – *Wynford*
Bethell – *Westbury*
Bewicke-Copley – *Cromwell*
Bigham – *Mersey, V.*
Bingham – *Clanmorris*
Bingham – *Lucan, E.*
Bishop – *Glendonbrook**
Black – *B. of Brentwood**
Black – *B. of Crossharbour**
Blair – *B. of Boughton**
Bligh – *Darnley, E.*
Blyth – *B. of Rowington**
Bonham Carter – *B.-C. of Yarnbury**
Bootle-Wilbraham – *Skelmersdale*
Boscawen – *Falmouth, V.*
Boswell – *B. of Aynho**
Bottomley – *B. of Nettlestone**
Bourke – *Mayo, E.*
Bowes Lyon – *Strathmore and Kinghorne, E.*
Bowyer – *Denham*
Boyd – *B. of Duncansby**
Boyd – *Kilmarnock*
Boyle – *Cork and Orrery, E.*
Boyle – *Glasgow, E.*
Boyle – *Shannon, E.*
Brabazon – *Meath, E.*
Brand – *Hampden, V.*
Brassey – *B. of Apethorpe*
Brett – *Esher, V.*
Bridgeman – *Bradford, E.*
Brittan – *B. of Spennithorne**
Brodrick – *Midleton, V.*
Brooke – *Alanbrooke, V.*
Brooke – *B. of Alverthorpe**
Brooke – *B. of Sutton Mandeville**
Brooke – *Brookeborough, V.*
Brooks – *B. of Tremorfa**
Brooks – *Crawshaw*
Brougham – *Brougham and Vaux*
Broughton – *Fairhaven*
Brown – *B. of Eaton-under-Heywood**
Browne – *B. of Belmont**
Browne – *B. of Ladyton**
Browne – *B. of Madingley**
Browne – *Kilmaine*
Browne – *Oranmore and Browne*
Browne – *Sligo, M.*
Bruce – *Aberdare*
Bruce – *Balfour of Burleigh*
Bruce – *Elgin and Kincardine, E.*
Brudenell-Bruce – *Ailesbury, M.*
Buchan – *Tweedsmuir*
Buckley – *Wrenbury*
Butler – *B. of Brockwell**
Butler – *Carrick, E.*
Butler – *Dunboyne*
Butler – *Mountgarret, V.*
Byng – *Strafford, E.*
Byng – *Torrington, V.*
Cameron – *C. of Dillington**
Cameron – *C. of Lochbroom**
Campbell – *Argyll, D.*
Campbell – *C. of Loughborough**
Campbell – *C. of Surbiton**
Campbell – *Cawdor, E.*
Campbell – *Colgrain*
Campbell – *Stratheden and Campbell*
Campbell-Gray – *Gray*
Canning – *Garvagh*
Capell – *Essex, E.*
Carey – *C. of Clifton**
Carington – *Carrington*
Carlile – *C. of Berriew**
Carnegie – *Fife, D.*
Carnegy – *Northesk, E.*
Carter – *C. of Barnes**
Carter – *C. of Coles**
Cary – *Falkland, V.*
Caulfeild – *Charlemont, V.*
Cavendish – *C. of Furness**
Cavendish – *Chesham*
Cavendish – *Devonshire, D.*
Cavendish – *Waterpark*
Cayzer – *Rotherwick*
Cecil – *Amherst of Hackney*
Cecil – *Exeter, M.*
Cecil – *Rockley*
Chalker – *C. of Wallasey**
Chaloner – *Gisborough*
Charteris – *Wemyss and March, E.*
Chetwynd-Talbot – *Shrewsbury and Waterford, E.*
Chichester – *Donegall, M.*
Child Villiers – *Jersey, E.*
Cholmondeley – *Delamere*
Chubb – *Hayter*
Clark – *C. of Calton**
Clarke – *C. of Hampstead**
Clarke – *C. of Stone-Cum-Ebony**
Clegg-Hill – *Hill, V.*
Clifford – *C. of Chudleigh*
Cochrane – *C. of Cults*
Cochrane – *Dundonald, E.*
Cocks – *Somers*
Cohen – *C. of Pimlico**
Cokayne – *Cullen of Ashbourne*
Coke – *Leicester, E.*
Cole – *Enniskillen, E.*
Collier – *Monkswell*
Collins – *C. of Highbury**
Collins – *C. of Mapesbury**
Colville – *Clydesmuir*
Colville – *C. of Culross, V.*
Compton – *Northampton, M.*
Conolly-Carew – *Carew*
Cooke – *Lexden**
Cooper – *Norwich, V*
Cope – *C. of Berkeley**
Corbett – *Rowallan*
Cornwall-Legh – *Grey of Codnor*
Courtenay – *Devon, E.*
Craig – *C. of Radley**
Craig – *Craigavon, V.*
Crichton – *Erne, E.*
Crichton-Stuart – *Bute, M.*
Cripps – *Parmoor*
Crossley – *Somerleyton*
Cubitt – *Ashcombe*
Cunliffe-Lister – *Masham of Ilton**
Cunliffe-Lister – *Swinton, E.*
Cunningham – *C. of Felling**
Currie – *C. of Marylebone**
Curry – *C. of Kirkharle**
Curzon – *Howe, E.*
Curzon – *Scarsdale, V.*
Cust – *Brownlow*

Czernin – *Howard de Walden*
Dalrymple – *Stair, E.*
Darzi – *D. of Denham**
Daubeny de Moleyns – *Ventry*
Davidson – *D. of Glen Clova**
Davies – *Darwen*
Davies – *D. of Abersoch**
Davies – *D. of Coity**
Davies – *D. of Oldham**
Davies – *D. of Stamford**
Dawnay – *Downe, V.*
Dawson-Damer – *Portarlington, E.*
Dean – *D. of Thornton-le-Fylde**
Deane – *Muskerry*
de Courcy – *Kingsale*
de Grey – *Walsingham*
Denison – *Londesborough*
Denison-Pender – *Pender*
Devereux – *Hereford, V.*
Dewar – *Forteviot*
Dixon – *Glentoran*
Dodson – *Monk Bretton*
Douglas – *Morton, E.*
Douglas – *Queensberry, M.*
Douglas-Hamilton – *Hamilton, D.*
Douglas-Hamilton – *Selkirk, E.*
Douglas-Hamilton – *Selkirk of Douglas**
Douglas-Home – *Dacre*
Douglas-Home – *Home, E.*
Douglas-Pennant – *Penrhyn*
Douglas-Scott-Montagu – *Montagu of Beaulieu*
Drummond – *Perth, E.*
Drummond of Megginch – *Strange*
Dugdale – *Crathorne*
Duke – *Merrivale*
Duncombe – *Feversham*
Dundas – *Melville, V.*
Dundas – *Zetland, M.*
Eady – *Swinfen*
Eccles – *E. of Moulton**
Ece – *Hussein-Ece**
Eden – *Auckland*
Eden – *E. of Winton**
Eden – *Henley*
Edgcumbe – *Mount Edgcumbe, E.*
Edmondson – *Sandford*
Edwardes – *Kensington*
Edwards – *Crickhowell**
Egerton – *Sutherland, D.*
Eliot – *St Germans, E.*
Elliot-Murray-Kynynmound – *Minto, E.*
Erskine – *Buchan, E.*
Erskine – *Mar and Kellie, E.*
Erskine-Murray – *Elibank*
Evans – *E. of Parkside**
Evans – *E. of Temple Guiting**
Evans – *E. of Watford**
Evans – *Mountevans*
Evans-Freke – *Carbery*
Eve – *Silsoe*
Fairfax – *F. of Cameron*
Falconer – *F. of Thoroton**
Falkner – *F. of Margravine**
Fane – *Westmorland, E.*
Farrington – *F. of Ribbleton**
Faulkner – *F. of Worcester**
Feilding – *Denbigh and Desmond, E.*
Feldman – *F. of Elstree**
Felton – *Seaford*
Fellowes – *De Ramsey*
Fellowes – *F. of West Stafford**
Fermor-Hesketh – *Hesketh*
Fiennes – *Saye and Sele*
Fiennes-Clinton – *Lincoln, E.*
Finch Hatton – *Winchilsea and Nottingham, E.*
Finch-Knightley – *Aylesford, E.*
Finlay – *F. of Llandaff**
Fitzalan-Howard – *Herries of Terregles*
Fitzalan-Howard – *Norfolk, D.*
FitzGerald – *Leinster, D.*
Fitzherbert – *Stafford*
FitzRoy – *Grafton, D.*
FitzRoy – *Southampton*
FitzRoy Newdegate – *Daventry, V.*
Fletcher-Vane – *Inglewood*
Flower – *Ashbrook, V.*
Foljambe – *Liverpool, E.*
Forbes – *Granard, E*
Forsyth – *F. of Drumlean**
Forwood – *Arlington*
Foster – *F. of Thames Bank**
Foulkes – *F. of Cumnock**
Fox-Strangways – *Ilchester, E.*
Frankland – *Zouche*
Fraser – *Lovat*
Fraser – *Saltoun*
Fraser – *Strathalmond*
Freeman-Grenville – *Kinloss*
Fremantle – *Cottesloe*
French – *De Freyne*
Galbraith – *Strathclyde*
Garden – *G. of Frognal**
Gardiner – *G. of Kimble**
Gardner – *G. of Parkes**
Gascoyne-Cecil – *Salisbury, M.*
Gathorne-Hardy – *Cranbrook, E.*
Gibbs – *Aldenham*
Gibbs – *Wraxall*
Gibson – *Ashbourne*
Gibson – *G. of Market Rasen**
Gilbey – *Vaux of Harrowden*
Glyn – *Wolverton*
Godley – *Kilbracken*
Goff – *G. of Chieveley**
Golding – *G. of Newcastle-under-Lyme**
Gordon – *Aberdeen, M.*
Gordon – *G. of Strathblane**
Gordon – *Huntly, M.*
Gordon Lennox – *Richmond, Gordon and Lennox D.*
Gore – *Arran, E.*
Gould – *G. of Potternewton**
Grade – *G. of Yarmouth**
Graham – *G. of Edmonton**
Graham – *Montrose, D.*
Graham-Toler – *Norbury, E.*
Granshaw – *Northover**
Grant of Grant – *Strathspey*
Grant of Rothiemurchus – *Dysart, E.*
Green – *G. of Hurstpierpoint**
Greenall – *Daresbury*
Greville – *Warwick and Brooke, E.*
Griffiths – *G. of Burry Port**
Griffiths – *G. of Fforestfach**
Grigg – *Altrincham*
Grimston – *G. of Westbury*
Grimston – *Verulam, E.*
Grosvenor – *Westminster, D.*
Grosvenor – *Wilton, E*
Guest – *Wimborne, V*
Gueterbock – *Berkeley*
Guinness – *Iveagh, E.*
Guinness – *Moyne*
Gully – *Selby, V.*
Gummer – *Chadlington**
Gummer – *Deben**
Gurdon – *Cranworth*
Guthrie – *G. of Craigiebank**
Gwynne Jones – *Chalfont**
Hale – *H. of Richmond**
Hall – *H. of Birkenhead**
Hamilton – *Abercorn, D.*
Hamilton – *Belhaven and Stenton*
Hamilton – *H. of Dalzell*
Hamilton – *H. of Epsom**
Hamilton – *Holm Patrick*
Hamilton-Russell – *Boyne, V.*
Hamilton-Smith – *Colwyn*
Hanbury-Tracy – *Sudeley*
Handcock – *Castlemaine*
Hannay – *H. of Chiswick**
Harbord-Hamond – *Suffield*
Harding – *H. of Petherton*
Hardinge – *H. of Penshurst*
Hare – *Blakenham, V.*
Hare – *Listowel, E.*
Harmsworth – *Rothermere, V.*
Harries – *H. of Pentregarth**
Harris – *H. of Haringey**
Harris – *H. of Peckham**
Harris – *H. of Richmond**
Harris – *Malmesbury, E.*
Hart – *H. of Chilton**
Harvey – *H. of Tasburgh*
Hastings – *H. of Scarisbrick**
Hastings Bass – *Huntingdon, E.*
Haughey – *Ballyedmond**
Hay – *Erroll, E.*
Hay – *Kinnoull, E.*
Hay – *Tweeddale, M.*
Hayter – *H. of Kentish Town**
Healy – *H. of Primrose Hill**
Heathcote-Drummond-Willoughby – *Willoughby de Eresby*
Hely-Hutchinson – *Donoughmore, E.*
Henderson – *Faringdon*
Hennessy – *H. of Nympsfield**
Hennessy – *Windlesham*
Henniker-Major – *Henniker*
Hepburne-Scott – *Polwarth*
Herbert – *Carnarvon, E.*
Herbert – *Hemingford*
Herbert – *Pembroke and Montgomery, E.*
Herbert – *Powis, E.*
Hervey – *Bristol, M.*
Hewitt – *Lifford, V.*
Hicks Beach – *St Aldwyn, E.*
Hill – *Downshire, M.*
Hill – *H. of Oareford**
Hill-Trevor – *Trevor*
Hilton – *H. of Eggardon**
Hobart-Hampden – *Buckinghamshire, E.*
Hodgson – *H. of Astley Abbotts**
Hogg – *Hailsham, V.*
Holland-Hibbert – *Knutsford, V.*
Hollis – *H. of Heigham**
Holmes à Court – *Heytesbury*
Hood – *Bridport, V.*
Hope – *Glendevon*
Hope – *H. of Craighead**
Hope – *H. of Thornes**
Hope – *Linlithgow, M.*
Hope – *Rankeillour*
Hope Johnstone – *Annandale and Hartfell, E.*
Hope-Morley – *Hollenden*
Hopkinson – *Colyton*
Hore Ruthven – *Gowrie, E.*
Hovell-Thurlow- Cumming-Bruce – *Thurlow*
Howard – *Carlisle, E.*
Howard – *Effingham, E.*
Howard – *H. of Lympne**
Howard – *H. of Penrith*
Howard – *H. of Rising**
Howard – *Strathcona and Mount Royal*
Howard – *Suffolk and Berkshire, E.*
Howarth – *H. of Breckland**
Howarth – *H. of Newport**
Howe – *H. of Aberavon**
Howe – *H. of Idlicote**
Howell – *H. of Guildford**
Howells – *H. of St. Davids**

Howie – *H. of Troon**
Hubbard – *Addington*
Huggins – *Malvern, V.*
Hughes – *H. of Stretford**
Hughes – *H. of Woodside**
Hughes-Young – *St Helens*
Hunt – *H. of Chesterton**
Hunt – *H. of Kings Heath**
Hunt – *H. of Wirral**
Hurd – *H. of Westwell**
Hutchinson – *H. of Lullington**
Hutton – *H. of Furness**
Ingrams – *Darcy de Knayth*
Innes-Ker – *Roxburghe, D.*
Inskip – *Caldecote, V.*
Irby – *Boston*
Irvine – *I. of Lairg**
Isaacs – *Reading, M.*
James – *J. of Blackheath**
James – *J. of Holland Park**
James – *Northbourne*
Janner – *J. of Braunstone**
Jay – *J. of Ewelme**
Jay – *J. of Paddington**
Jebb – *Gladwyn*
Jenkin – *J. of Kennington**
Jenkin – *J. of Roding**
Jervis – *St Vincent, V.*
Jocelyn – *Roden, E.*
Jolliffe – *Hylton*
Jones – *J. of Birmingham**
Jones – *J. of Cheltenham**
Jones – *J. of Whitchurch**
Joynson-Hicks – *Brentford, V.*
Kay-Shuttleworth – *Shuttleworth*
Kearley – *Devonport, V.*
Keith – *Kintore, E.*
Kemp – *Rochdale, V.*
Kennedy – *Ailsa, M*
Kennedy – *K. of Southwark**
Kennedy – *K. of the Shaws**
Kenworthy – *Strabolgi*
Keppel – *Albemarle, E.*
Kerr – *K. of Kinlochard**
Kerr – *K. of Tonaghmore**
Kerr – *Lothian, M.*
Kerr – *Teviot*
Kilpatrick – *K. of Kincraig**
King – *K. of Bow**
King – *K. of Lothbury**
King – *Lovelace, E.*
King-Tenison – *Kingston, E.*
Kinnock – *K. of Holyhead**
Kirkham – *Berners*
Kirkwood – *K. of Kirkhope**
Knatchbull – *Brabourne*
Knatchbull – *Mountbatten of Burma, C.*
Knight – *K. of Collingtree**
Knight – *K. of Weymouth**
Knox – *Ranfurly, E.*
Lamb – *Rochester*
Lambton – *Durham, E.*
Lamont – *L. of Lerwick**
Lampson – *Killearn*
Lane Fox – *L.-F. of Soho**
Lang – *L. of Monkton**
Lascelles – *Harewood, E.*
Law – *Coleraine*
Law – *Ellenborough*
Lawrence – *Trevethin and Oaksey*
Lawson – *Burnham*
Lawson – *L. of Blaby**
Lawson-Johnston – *Luke*
Lea – *L. of Crondall**
Leach – *L. of Fairford**
Lee – *L. of Trafford**
Legge – *Dartmouth, E.*
Legh – *Grey of Codnor*
Legh – *Newton*
Leigh-Pemberton – *Kingsdown**
Leith – *Burgh*
Lennox-Boyd – *Boyd of Merton, V.*
Le Poer Trench – *Clancarty, E.*
Leslie – *Rothes, E.*
Leslie Melville – *Leven and Melville, E.*
Lester – *L. of Herne Hill**
Levene – *L. of Portsoken**
Leveson-Gower – *Granville, E.*
Lewis – *L. of Newnham**
Lewis – *Merthyr*
Liddell – *L. of Coatdyke**
Liddell – *Ravensworth*
Lindesay-Bethune – *Lindsay, E.*
Lindsay – *Crawford and Balcarres, E.*
Lindsay – *L. of Birker*
Linklater – *L. of Butterstone**
Lister – *L. of Burtersett**
Littleton – *Hatherton*
Livingston – *L. of Parkhead**
Lloyd – *L. of Berwick**
Lloyd George – *Lloyd George of Dwyfor, E.*
Lloyd George – *Tenby, V.*
Lloyd-Mostyn – *Mostyn*
Loder – *Wakehurst*
Lopes – *Roborough*
Lord – *Framlingham**
Low – *Aldington*
Low – *L. of Dalston**
Lowry-Corry – *Belmore, E.*
Lowther – *Lonsdale, E.*
Lowther – *Ullswater, V.*
Lubbock – *Avebury*
Lucas – *L. of Chilworth*
Lumley – *Scarbrough, E.*
Lumley-Savile – *Savile*
Lyon-Dalberg-Acton – *Acton*
Lysaght – *Lisle*
Lyttelton – *Chandos, V.*
Lyttelton – *Cobham, V.*
Lytton Cobbold – *Cobbold*
McAlpine – *M. of West Green**
Macaulay – *M. of Bragar**
McClintock-Bunbury – *Rathdonnell*
McColl – *M. of Dulwich**
McConnell – *M. of Glenscorrodale**
MacDonald – *M. of River Glaven**
Macdonald – *M. of Tradeston**
McDonnell – *Antrim, E.*
McFall – *M. of Alcluith**
Macfarlane – *M. of Bearsden**
MacGregor – *M. of Pulham Market**
McIntosh – *M. of Hudnall**
Mackay – *Inchcape, E.*
Mackay – *M. of Clashfern**
Mackay – *M. of Drumadoon**
Mackay – *Reay*
Mackay – *Tanlaw**
Mackenzie – *Cromartie, E.*
MacKenzie – *M. of Culkein**
MacKenzie – *M. of Framwellgate**
McKenzie – *M. of Luton**
Mackie – *M. of Benshie**
Mackintosh – *M. of Halifax, V.*
McLaren – *Aberconway*
MacLaurin – *M. of Knebworth**
Maclean – *Blencathra**
MacLennan – *M. of Rogart**
Macmillan – *Stockton, E.*
Macpherson – *M. of Drumochter*
Macpherson – *Strathcarron*
Maffey – *Rugby*
Magan – *M. of Castletown**
Maginnis – *M. of Drumglass**
Maitland – *Lauderdale, E.*
Makgill – *Oxfuird, V.*
Makins – *Sherfield*
Manners – *Rutland, D.*
Manningham-Buller – *Dilhorne, V.*
Mansfield – *Sandhurst*
Marks – *M. of Broughton*
Marks – *M. of Henley-on-Thames**
Marquis – *Woolton, E.*
Marsham – *Romney, E.*
Martin – *M. of Springburn**
Martyn-Hemphill – *Hemphill*
Mason – *M. of Barnsley**
Massey – *M. of Darwen**
Masters – *Noakes**
Maude – *Hawarden, V.*
Maxwell – *de Ros*
Maxwell – *Farnham*
May – *M. of Oxford**
Mayhew – *M. of Twysden**
Meade – *Clanwilliam, E.*
Mercer Nairne Petty-Fitzmaurice – *Lansdowne, M.*
Millar – *Inchyra*
Miller – *M. of Chilthorne Domer**
Miller – *M. of Hendon**
Milner – *M. of Leeds*
Mitchell-Thomson – *Selsdon*
Mitford – *Redesdale*
Molyneaux – *M. of Killead**
Monckton – *M. of Brenchley, V.*
Monckton-Arundell – *Galway, V.*
Mond – *Melchett*
Money-Coutts – *Latymer*
Montagu – *Manchester, D.*
Montagu – *Sandwich, E.*
Montagu – *Swaythling*
Montagu Douglas Scott – *Buccleuch, D.*
Montagu Stuart Wortley – *Wharncliffe, E.*
Montague – *Amwell*
Montgomerie – *Eglinton and Winton, E.*
Montgomery – *M. of Alamein, V.*
Moore – *Drogheda, E.*
Moore – *M. of Lower Marsh**
Moore-Brabazon – *Brabazon of Tara*
Moreton – *Ducie, E*
Morgan – *M. of Drefelin**
Morgan – *M. of Ely**
Morgan – *M. of Huyton**
Morris – *Killanin*
Morris – *M. of Aberavon**
Morris – *M. of Bolton**
Morris – *M. of Handsworth**
Morris – *M. of Kenwood*
Morris – *M. of Yardley**
Morris – *Naseby**
Morrison – *Dunrossil, V.*
Morrison – *Margadale*
Mosley – *Ravensdale*
Mountbatten – *Milford Haven, M.*
Muff – *Calverley*
Mulholland – *Dunleath*
Murray – *Atholl, D.*
Murray – *Dunmore, E.*
Murray – *Mansfield and Mansfield, E.*
Nall-Cain – *Brocket*
Napier – *Napier and Ettrick*
Napier – *N. of Magdala*
Needham – *Kilmorey, E.*
Neill – *N. of Bladen**
Nelson – *N. of Stafford*
Neuberger – *N. of Abbotsbury**
Nevill – *Abergavenny, M.*
Neville – *Braybrooke*
Nicholls – *N. of Birkenhead**
Nicolson – *Carnock*
Nicholson – *N. of Winterbourne**
Nivison – *Glendyne*
Noel – *Gainsborough, E.*
North – *Guilford, E.*
Northcote – *Iddesleigh, E.*

Norton – *Grantley*
Norton – *N. of Louth**
Norton – *Rathcreedan*
Nugent – *Westmeath, E.*
Oakeshott – *O. of Seagrove Bay**
O'Brien – *Inchiquin*
Ogilvie-Grant – *Seafield, E.*
Ogilvy – *Airlie, E.*
O'Neill – *O'N. of Bengarve**
O'Neill – *O'N. of Clackmannan**
O'Neill – *Rathcavan*
Orde-Powlett – *Bolton*
Ormsby-Gore – *Harlech*
Paget – *Anglesey, M.*
Paisley – *Bannside**
Paisley – *P. of St George's**
Pakenham – *Longford, E.*
Pakington – *Hampton*
Palmer – *Lucas and Dingwall*
Palmer – *P. of Childs Hill**
Palmer – *Selborne, E.*
Parker – *Macclesfield, E.*
Parker – *Morley, E.*
Parnell – *Congleton*
Parsons – *Rosse, E.*
Patel – *P. of Blackburn**
Patel – *P. of Bradford**
Patten – *P. of Barnes**
Paulet – *Winchester, M.*
Pearson – *Cowdray, V.*
Pearson – *P. of Rannoch**
Pease – *Gainford*
Pease – *Wardington*
Pelham – *Chichester, E.*
Pelham – *Yarborough, E.*
Pellew – *Exmouth, V*
Penny – *Marchwood, V.*
Pepys – *Cottenham, E.*
Percy – *Northumberland, D.*
Perry – *P. of Southwark**
Pery – *Limerick, E.*
Philipps – *Milford*
Philipps – *St Davids, V.*
Phillips – *P. of Sudbury**
Phillips – *P. of Worth Matravers**
Phipps – *Normanby, M.*
Plant – *P. of Highfield**
Platt – *P. of Writtle**
Pleydell-Bouverie – *Radnor, E.*
Plumptre – *Fitzwalter*
Plunkett – *Dunsany*
Plunkett – *Louth*
Pollock – *Hanworth, V.*
Pomeroy – *Harberton, V.*
Ponsonby – *Bessborough, E.*
Ponsonby – *de Mauley*
Ponsonby – *P. of Shulbrede*
Powell – *P. of Bayswater**
Powys – *Lilford*
Pratt – *Camden, M.*
Preston – *Gormanston, V.*
Primrose – *Rosebery, E.*
Prittie – *Dunalley*
Ramsay – *Dalhousie, E.*
Ramsay – *R. of Cartvale**
Ramsbotham – *Soulbury, V.*
Rees – *R. of Ludlow**
Rees-Williams – *Ogmore*
Reid – *R. of Cardowan**
Rendell – *R. of Babergh**
Renfrew – *R. of Kaimsthorn**
Renton – *R. of Mount Harry**
Renwick – *R. of Clifton**
Rhys – *Dynevor*
Richards – *Milverton*
Richardson – *R. of Calow**
Ritchie – *R. of Dundee*
Roberts – *Clwyd*
Roberts – *R. of Conwy**
Roberts – *R. of Llandudno**
Robertson – *R. of Oakridge*
Robertson – *R. of Port Ellen**
Robertson – *Wharton*
Robinson – *Martonmere*
Roche – *Fermoy*
Rodd – *Rennell*
Rodgers – *R. of Quarry Bank**
Rogers – *R. of Riverside**
Roper-Curzon – *Teynham*
Rospigliosi – *Newburgh, E.*
Rous – *Stradbroke, E.*
Rowley-Conwy – *Langford*
Royall – *R. of Blaisdon**
Runciman – *R. of Doxford, V.*
Russell – *Ampthill*
Russell – *Bedford, D.*
Russell – *de Clifford*
Russell – *R. of Liverpool*
Ryder – *Harrowby, E.*
Ryder – *R. of Wensum**
Sackville – *De La Warr, E.*
Sackville-West – *Sackville*
Sainsbury – *S. of Preston Candover**
Sainsbury – *S. of Turville**
St Aubyn – *St Levan*
St Clair – *Sinclair*
St Clair-Erskine – *Rosslyn, E.*
St John – *Bolingbroke and St John, V.*
St John – *St John of Bletso*
St Leger – *Doneraile, V.*
Samuel – *Bearsted, V.*
Sanderson – *S. of Ayot*
Sanderson – *S. of Bowden**
Sandilands – *Torphichen*
Saumarez – *De Saumarez*
Savile – *Mexborough, E.*
Saville – *S. of Newdigate**
Scarlett – *Abinger*
Schreiber – *Marlesford**
Sclater-Booth – *Basing*
Scotland – *S. of Asthal**
Scott – *Eldon, E*
Scott – *S. of Foscote**
Scott – *S. of Needham Market**
Scrymgeour – *Dundee, E.*
Seager – *Leighton of St Mellons*
Seely – *Mottistone*
Seymour – *Hertford, M.*
Seymour – *Somerset, D.*
Shackleton – *S. of Belgravia**
Sharp – *S. of Guildford**
Shaw – *Craigmyle*
Shaw – *S. of Northstead**
Shephard – *S. of Northwold**
Sheppard – *S. of Didgemere**
Shirley – *Ferrers, E.*
Shutt – *S. of Greetland**
Siddeley – *Kenilworth*
Sidney – *De L'Isle, V.*
Simon – *S. of Highbury**
Simon – *S. of Wythenshawe*
Simpson – *S. of Dunkeld**
Sinclair – *Caithness, E.*
Sinclair – *S. of Cleeve*
Sinclair – *Thurso, V.*
Singh – *S. of Wimbledon**
Skeffington – *Massereene and Ferrard, V.*
Smith – *Bicester*
Smith – *Hambleden, V.*
Smith – *Kirkhill**
Smith – *S. of Basildon**
Smith – *S. of Clifton**
Smith – *S. of Finsbury**
Smith – *S. of Gilmorehill**
Smith – *S. of Kelvin**
Smith – *S. of Leigh**
Somerset – *Beaufort, D.*
Somerset – *Raglan*
Soulsby – *S. of Swaffham Prior**
Spencer – *Churchill, V.*
Spencer-Churchill – *Marlborough, D.*
Spring – *Risby**
Spring Rice – *Monteagle of Brandon*
Stanhope – *Harrington, E.*
Stanley – *Derby, E.*
Stanley – *S. of Alderley and Sheffield*
Stapleton-Cotton – *Combermere, V.*
Steel – *S. of Aikwood**
Sterling – *S. of Plaistow**
Stern – *S. of Brentford**
Stevens – *S. of Kirkwhelpington**
Stevens – *S. of Ludgate**
Stevenson – *S. of Balmacara**
Stevenson – *S. of Coddenham**
Stewart – *Galloway, E.*
Stewart – *Stewartby**
Stoddart – *S. of Swindon**
Stone – *S. of Blackheath**
Stoneham – *S. of Droxford**
Stonor – *Camoys*
Stopford – *Courtown, E.*
Stourton – *Mowbray, Segrave and S.*
Stowell – *S. of Beeston**
Strachey – *O'Hagan*
Strutt – *Belper*
Strutt – *Rayleigh*
Stuart – *Castle Stewart, E.*
Stuart – *Moray, E.*
Stuart – *S. of Findhorn, V.*
Suenson-Taylor – *Grantchester*
Sutherland – *S. of Houndwood**
Symons – *S. of Vernham Dean**
Taylor – *Kilclooney**
Taylor – *T. of Blackburn**
Taylor – *T. of Bolton**
Taylor – *T. of Goss Moor**
Taylor – *T. of Holbeach**
Taylor – *T. of Warwick**
Taylour – *Headfort, M.*
Temple-Gore-Langton – *Temple of Stowe, E*
Tennant – *Glenconner*
Thellusson – *Rendlesham*
Thesiger – *Chelmsford, V.*
Thomas – *T. of Gresford**
Thomas – *T. of Macclesfield**
Thomas – *T. of Swynnerton**
Thomas – *T. of Walliswood**
Thomas – *T. of Winchester**
Thomson – *T. of Fleet*
Thynn – *Bath, M.*
Tottenham – *Ely, M.*
Trefusis – *Clinton*
Trench – *Ashtown*
Tufton – *Hothfield*
Turner – *Bilston**
Turner – *Netherthorpe*
Turner – *T. of Camden**
Turner – *T. of Ecchinswell**
Turnour – *Winterton, E.*
Tyler – *T. of Enfield**
Tyrell-Kenyon – *Kenyon*
Vallance – *V. of Tummel*
Vanden-Bempde-Johnstone – *Derwent*
Vane – *Barnard*
Vane-Tempest-Stewart – *Londonderry, M.*
Vanneck – *Huntingfield*
Vaughan – *Lisburne, E.*
Vereker – *Gort, V.*
Verney – *Willoughby de Broke*
Vernon – *Lyveden*
Vesey – *De Vesci, V.*
Villiers – *Clarendon, E.*
Vincent – *V. of Coleshill**
Vivian – *Swansea*
Wade – *W. of Chorlton**
Waldegrave – *W. of North Hill**
Walker – *W. of Aldringham**
Walker – *W. of Gestingthorpe**
Wall – *W. of New Barnet**
Wallace – *Dudley*
Wallace – *W. of Saltaire**
Wallace – *W. of Tankerness**
Wallop – *Portsmouth, E.*
Walton – *W. of Detchant**
Ward – *Bangor, V.*
Ward – *Dudley, E.*
Warrender – *Bruntisfield*

ORDERS OF CHIVALRY

THE MOST NOBLE ORDER OF THE GARTER (1348)

KG
Ribbon, Blue
Motto, Honi soit qui mal y pense
(Shame on him who thinks evil of it)

The number of Knights and Ladies Companion is limited to 24

SOVEREIGN OF THE ORDER
The Queen

LADIES OF THE ORDER
HRH The Princess Royal, 1994
HRH Princess Alexandra, The Hon. Lady Ogilvy, 2003

ROYAL KNIGHTS
HRH The Prince Philip, Duke of Edinburgh, 1947
HRH The Prince of Wales, 1958
HRH The Duke of Kent, 1985
HRH The Duke of Gloucester, 1997
HRH The Duke of York, 2006
HRH The Earl of Wessex, 2006
HRH The Duke of Cambridge, 2008

EXTRA KNIGHTS COMPANION AND LADIES
Grand Duke Jean of Luxembourg, 1972
HM The Queen of Denmark, 1979
HM The King of Sweden, 1983
HM The King of Spain, 1988
HRH Princess Beatrix of the Netherlands, 1989
HIM The Emperor of Japan, 1998
HM The King of Norway, 2001

KNIGHTS AND LADIES COMPANION
Lord Carrington, 1985
Duke of Wellington, 1990
Lord Bramall, 1990
Lord Sainsbury of Preston Candover, 1992
Lord Ashburton, 1994
Lord Kingsdown, 1994
Sir Ninian Stephen, 1994
Sir Timothy Colman, 1996
Duke of Abercorn, 1999
Sir William Gladstone, 1999
Lord Inge, 2001
Sir Anthony Acland, 2001
Duke of Westminster, 2003
Lord Butler of Brockwell, 2003
Lord Morris of Aberavon, 2003
Lady Soames, 2005
Sir John Major, 2005
Lord Luce, 2008
Sir Thomas Dunne, 2008
Lord Phillips of Worth Matravers, 2011
Lord Boyce, 2011
Lord Stirrup, 2013

Prelate, Bishop of Winchester
Chancellor, Duke of Abercorn, KG
Register, Dean of Windsor
Garter King of Arms, Thomas Woodcock, CVO
Gentleman Usher of the Black Rod, Lt.-Gen. David Leakey, CMG, CBE
Secretary, Patric Dickinson, LVO

THE MOST ANCIENT AND MOST NOBLE ORDER OF THE THISTLE (REVIVED 1687)

KT
Ribbon, Green
Motto, Nemo me impune lacessit
(No one provokes me with impunity)

The number of Knights and Ladies of the Thistle is limited to 16

SOVEREIGN OF THE ORDER
The Queen

ROYAL KNIGHTS
HRH The Prince Philip, Duke of Edinburgh, 1952
HRH The Prince of Wales, Duke of Rothesay, 1977
HRH The Duke of Cambridge, Earl of Strathearn, 2012

ROYAL LADY OF THE ORDER
HRH The Princess Royal, 2000

KNIGHTS AND LADIES
Earl of Elgin and Kincardine, 1981
Earl of Airlie, 1985
Earl of Crawford and Balcarres, 1996
Lady Marion Fraser, 1996
Lord Macfarlane of Bearsden, 1996
Lord Mackay of Clashfern, 1997
Lord Wilson of Tillyorn, 2000
Lord Sutherland of Houndwood, 2002
Sir Eric Anderson, 2002
Lord Steel of Aikwood, 2004
Lord Robertson of Port Ellen, 2004
Lord Cullen of Whitekirk, 2007
Lord Hope of Craighead, 2009
Lord Patel, 2009

Chancellor, Earl of Airlie, KT, GCVO, PC
Dean, Very Revd Gilleasbuig Macmillan, CVO
Secretary and Lord Lyon King of Arms, David Sellar
Gentleman Usher of the Green Rod, Rear-Adm. Christopher Layman, CB, DSO, LVO
Assistant Secretary, Mrs C. Roads, LVO

THE MOST HONOURABLE ORDER OF THE BATH (1725)

GCB *Military* GCB *Civil*

GCB	Knight (or Dame) Grand Cross
KCB	Knight Commander
DCB	Dame Commander
CB	Companion

Ribbon, Crimson
Motto, Tria juncta in uno
(Three joined in one)

Remodelled 1815, and enlarged many times since. The order is divided into civil and military divisions. Women became eligible for the order from 1 January 1971.

THE SOVEREIGN

GREAT MASTER AND FIRST OR PRINCIPAL KNIGHT GRAND CROSS
HRH The Prince of Wales, KG, KT, GCB, OM

Dean of the Order, Dean of Westminster
Bath King of Arms, Adm. Lord Boyce, KG, GCB, OBE
Registrar and Secretary, Rear-Adm. Iain Henderson, CB, CBE
Genealogist, Thomas Woodcock, CVO
Gentleman Usher of the Scarlet Rod, Maj.-Gen. Charles Vyvyan, CB, CBE
Deputy Secretary, Secretary of the Central Chancery of the Orders of Knighthood
Chancery, Central Chancery of the Orders of Knighthood, St James's Palace, London SW1A 1BH

THE ORDER OF MERIT (1902)

OM *Military* OM *Civil*

OM
Ribbon, Blue and crimson

This order is designed as a special distinction for eminent men and women without conferring a knighthood upon them. The order is limited in numbers to 24, with the addition of foreign honorary members.

THE SOVEREIGN

HRH The Prince Philip, Duke of Edinburgh, 1968
Revd Prof. Owen Chadwick, KBE, 1983
Dr Frederick Sanger, 1986
Sir Michael Atiyah, 1992
Sir Aaron Klug, 1995
Lord Foster of Thames Bank, 1997
Sir Anthony Caro, 2000
Prof. Sir Roger Penrose, 2000
Sir Tom Stoppard, 2000
HRH The Prince of Wales, 2002
Lord May of Oxford, 2002
Lord Rothschild, 2002
Sir David Attenborough, 2005
Baroness Boothroyd, 2005
Sir Michael Howard, 2005
Sir Timothy Berners-Lee, KBE, 2007
Lord Eames, 2007
Lord Rees of Ludlow, 2007
Rt. Hon. Jean Chrétien, QC, 2009
Robert Neil MacGregor, 2010
Hon. John Howard, 2012
David Hockney, 2012

Honorary Member, Nelson Mandela, 1995

Secretary and Registrar, Lord Fellowes, GCB, GCVO, PC, QSO
Chancery, Central Chancery of the Orders of Knighthood, St James's Palace, London SW1A 1BH

THE MOST DISTINGUISHED ORDER OF ST MICHAEL AND ST GEORGE (1818)

GCMG KCMG

GCMG Knight (or Dame) Grand Cross
KCMG Knight Commander
DCMG Dame Commander
CMG Companion

Ribbon, Saxon blue, with scarlet centre
Motto, Auspicium melioris aevi *(Token of a better age)*

THE SOVEREIGN

GRAND MASTER
HRH The Duke of Kent, KG, GCMG, GCVO, ADC

Prelate, Rt. Revd David Urquhart
Chancellor, Lord Robertson of Port Ellen, KT, GCMG
Secretary, Permanent Under-Secretary of State at the Foreign and Commonwealth Office and Head of the Diplomatic Service
Registrar, Sir David Manning, GCMG, CVO
King of Arms, Sir Jeremy Greenstock, GCMG
Gentleman Usher of the Blue Rod, Sir Anthony Figgis, KCVO, CMG
Dean, Dean of St Paul's
Deputy Secretary, Secretary of the Central Chancery of the Orders of Knighthood
Hon. Genealogist, Timothy Duke
Chancery, Central Chancery of the Orders of Knighthood, St James's Palace, London SW1A 1BH

THE IMPERIAL ORDER OF THE CROWN OF INDIA (1877) FOR LADIES

CI

Badge, the royal cipher of Queen Victoria in jewels within an oval, surmounted by an heraldic crown and attached to a bow of light blue watered ribbon, edged white

The honour does not confer any rank or title upon the recipient

No conferments have been made since 1947

HM The Queen, 1947

THE ROYAL VICTORIAN ORDER (1896)

GCVO KCVO

GCVO Knight or Dame Grand Cross
KCVO Knight Commander
DCVO Dame Commander
CVO Commander
LVO Lieutenant
MVO Member

Ribbon, Blue, with red and white edges
Motto, Victoria

THE SOVEREIGN
GRAND MASTER
HRH The Princess Royal

Chancellor, Lord Chamberlain
Secretary, Keeper of the Privy Purse
Registrar, Secretary of the Central Chancery of the Orders of Knighthood
Chaplain, Chaplain of the Queen's Chapel of the Savoy
Hon. Genealogist, David White

THE MOST EXCELLENT ORDER OF THE BRITISH EMPIRE (1917)

GBE KBE

The order was divided into military and civil divisions in December 1918

GBE	Knight or Dame Grand Cross
KBE	Knight Commander
DBE	Dame Commander
CBE	Commander
OBE	Officer
MBE	Member

Ribbon, Rose pink edged with pearl grey with vertical pearl stripe in centre (military division); without vertical pearl stripe (civil division)
Motto, For God and the Empire

THE SOVEREIGN

GRAND MASTER
HRH The Prince Philip, Duke of Edinburgh, KG, KT, OM, GBE, PC

Prelate, Bishop of London
King of Arms, Adm. Sir Peter Abbott, GBE, KCB
Registrar, Secretary of the Central Chancery of the Orders of Knighthood
Secretary, Secretary of the Cabinet and Head of the Home Civil Service
Dean, Dean of St Paul's
Lady Usher of the Purple Rod, Dame Amelia Chilcott Fawcett, DBE
Chancery, Central Chancery of the Orders of Knighthood, St James's Palace, London SW1A 1BH

ORDER OF THE COMPANIONS OF HONOUR (1917)

CH

Ribbon, Carmine, with gold edges

This order consists of one class only and carries with it no title. The number of awards is limited to 65 (excluding honorary members).

Anthony, Rt. Hon. John, 1981
Attenborough, Sir David, 1995
Baker, Dame Janet, 1993
Baker of Dorking, Lord, 1992
Birtwistle, Sir Harrison, 2000
Brenner, Sydney, 1986
Brook, Peter, 1998
Brooke of Sutton Mandeville, Lord, 1992
Campbell, Rt. Hon. Sir Menzies, 2013
Carrington, Lord, 1983
Christie, Sir George, 2001
Coe, Lord, 2012
De Chastelain, Gen. John, 1999
Dench, Dame Judi, 2005
Fraser, Rt. Hon. Malcolm, 1977
Hannay of Chiswick, Lord, 2003
Hawking, Prof. Stephen, 1989
Healey, Lord, 1979
Heseltine, Lord, 1997
Higgs, Prof. Peter, 2012
Hockney, David, 1997
Hodgkin, Sir Howard, 2002
Howard, Sir Michael, 2002
Howard of Lympne, Lord, 2011
Howe of Aberavon, Lord, 1996
Hurd of Westwell, Lord, 1995
King of Bridgwater, Lord, 1992
Lessing, Doris, 1999
Lovelock, Prof. James, 2002
McKellen, Sir Ian Murray, 2008
McKenzie, Prof. Dan Peter, 2003
Major, Rt. Hon. Sir John, 1998
Owen, Lord, 1994
Patten of Barnes, Rt. Hon. Lord, 1997
Pawson, Prof. Anthony James, 2006
Riley, Bridget, 1998
Rogers of Riverside, Lord, 2008
Sanger, Dr. Frederick, 1981
Serota, Sir Nicholas, 2013
Somare, Rt. Hon. Sir Michael, 1978
Strathclyde, Rt. Hon. Lord, 2013
Tebbit, Lord, 1987
Young, Sir George, 2012

Honorary Members, Lee Kuan Yew, 1970; Prof. Amartya Sen, 2000; Bernard Haitink, 2002
Secretary and Registrar, Secretary of the Central Chancery of the Orders of Knighthood

THE DISTINGUISHED SERVICE ORDER (1886)

DSO

Ribbon, Red, with blue edges

Bestowed in recognition of especial services in action of commissioned officers in the Navy, Army and Royal Air Force and (since 1942) Mercantile Marine. The members are Companions only. A bar may be awarded for any additional act of service.

THE IMPERIAL SERVICE ORDER (1902)

ISO

Ribbon, Crimson, with blue centre

Appointment as companion of this order is open to members of the civil services whose eligibility is determined by the grade they hold. The order consists of the sovereign and companions to a number not exceeding 1,900, of whom 1,300 may belong to the home civil services and 600 to overseas civil services. The then prime minister announced in March 1993 that he would make no further recommendations for appointments to the order.

Secretary, Secretary of the Cabinet and Head of the Home Civil Service
Registrar, Secretary of the Central Chancery of the Orders of Knighthood

THE ROYAL VICTORIAN CHAIN (1902)

It confers no precedence on its holders

HM THE QUEEN

HM The King of Thailand, 1960
HM The Queen of Denmark, 1974
HM The King of Sweden, 1975
HRH Princess Beatrix of the Netherlands, 1982
Gen. Antonio Eanes, 1985
HM The King of Spain, 1986
Dr Richard von Weizsäcker, 1992
HM The King of Norway, 1994
Earl of Airlie, 1997
Rt. Revd and Rt. Hon. Lord Carey of Clifton, 2002
HRH Prince Philip, Duke of Edinburgh, 2007
HM The King of Saudi Arabia, 2007
HM The Sultan of Oman, 2010
Rt. Revd and Rt. Hon. Lord Williams of Oystermouth, 2012

BARONETAGE AND KNIGHTAGE

BARONETS

Style, 'Sir' before forename and surname, followed by 'Bt'.
Envelope, Sir F_ S_, Bt. *Letter (formal),* Dear Sir; *(social),* Dear Sir F_. *Spoken,* Sir F_
Wife's style, 'Lady' followed by surname
Envelope, Lady S_. *Letter (formal),* Dear Madam; *(social),* Dear Lady S_. *Spoken,* Lady S_
Style of Baronetess, 'Dame' before forename and surname, followed by 'Btss.' (*see also* Dames)

There are five different creations of baronetcies: Baronets of England (creations dating from 1611); Baronets of Ireland (creations dating from 1619); Baronets of Scotland or Nova Scotia (creations dating from 1625); Baronets of Great Britain (creations after the Act of Union 1707 which combined the kingdoms of England and Scotland); and Baronets of the United Kingdom (creations after the union of Great Britain and Ireland in 1801).

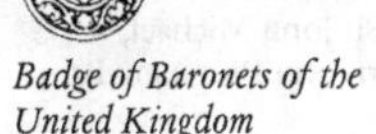

Badge of Baronets of the United Kingdom

Badge of Baronets of Nova Scotia

Badge of Ulster

The patent of creation limits the destination of a baronetcy, usually to male descendants of the first baronet, although special remainders allow the baronetcy to pass, if the male issue of sons fail, to the male issue of daughters of the first baronet. In the case of baronetcies of Scotland or Nova Scotia, a special remainder of 'heirs male and of tailzie' allows the baronetcy to descend to heirs general, including women. There are four existing Scottish baronets with such a remainder.

The Official Roll of the Baronetage is kept at the Crown Office and maintained by the Registrar and Assistant Registrar of the Baronetage. Anyone who considers that he or she is entitled to be entered on the roll may apply through the Crown Office to prove their succession. Every person succeeding to a baronetcy must exhibit proofs of succession to the Lord Chancellor. A person whose name is not entered on the official roll will not be addressed or mentioned by the title of baronet or baronetess in any official document, nor will he or she be accorded precedence as a baronet or baronetess.

BARONETCY EXTINCT SINCE THE LAST EDITION
Dupree (cr. 1921); Reid (cr. 1922); Williams (cr. 1909)

OFFICIAL ROLL OF THE BARONETAGE, Crown Office, House of Lords, London SW1A 0PW T 020-7219 2632
Registrar, Ian Denyer, MVO
Assistant Registrar, Grant Bavister

KNIGHTS

Style, 'Sir' before forename and surname, followed by appropriate post-nominal initials if a Knight Grand Cross, Knight Grand Commander or Knight Commander
Envelope, Sir F_ S_. *Letter (formal),* Dear Sir; *(social),* Dear Sir F_. *Spoken,* Sir F_
Wife's style, 'Lady' followed by surname
Envelope, Lady S_. *Letter (formal),* Dear Madam; *(social),* Dear Lady S_. *Spoken,* Lady S_

The prefix 'Sir' is not used by knights who are clerics of the Church of England, who do not receive the accolade. Their wives are entitled to precedence as the wife of a knight but not to the style of 'Lady'.

ORDERS OF KNIGHTHOOD
Knight Grand Cross, Knight Grand Commander, and Knight Commander are the higher classes of the Orders of Chivalry (*see* Orders of Chivalry). Honorary knighthoods of these orders may be conferred on men who are citizens of countries of which the Queen is not head of state. As a rule, the prefix 'Sir' is not used by honorary knights.

KNIGHTS BACHELOR

The Knights Bachelor do not constitute a royal order, but comprise the surviving representation of the ancient state orders of knighthood. The Register of Knights Bachelor, instituted by James I in the 17th century, lapsed, and in 1908 a voluntary association under the title of the Society of Knights (now the Imperial Society of Knights Bachelor) was formed with the primary objectives of continuing the various registers dating from 1257 and obtaining the uniform registration of every created Knight Bachelor. In 1926 a design for a badge to be worn by Knights Bachelor was approved and adopted; in 1974 a neck badge and miniature were added.

THE IMPERIAL SOCIETY OF KNIGHTS BACHELOR, 1 Throgmorton Avenue, London EC2N 2BY
Knight Principal, Sir Colin Berry
Prelate, Rt. Revd and Rt. Hon. Bishop of London
Registrar, Sir Gavyn Arthur
Hon. Treasurer, Sir Jeremy Elwes
Clerk to the Council, Col. Simon Doughty

LIST OF BARONETS AND KNIGHTS *as at 31 August 2013*

†	Not registered on the Official Roll of the Baronetage at the time of going to press
( )	The date of creation of the baronetcy is given in parentheses
I	Baronet of Ireland
NS	Baronet of Nova Scotia
S	Baronet of Scotland

A full entry in italic type indicates that the recipient of a knighthood died during the year in which the honour was conferred. The name is included for purposes of record. Peers are not included in this list.

Aaronson, Sir Michael John, Kt., CBE
Abbott, *Adm.* Sir Peter Charles, GBE, KCB
†Abdy, Sir Robert Etienne Eric, Bt. (1850)
Abed, *Dr* Sir Fazle Hasan, KCMG
Acher, Sir Gerald, Kt., CBE, LVO
Ackroyd, Sir Timothy Robert Whyte, Bt. (1956)
Acland, Sir Antony Arthur, KG, GCMG, GCVO
Acland, *Lt.-Col.* Sir (Christopher) Guy (Dyke), Bt. (1890), MVO
†Acland, Sir Dominic Dyke, Bt. (1678)
Adam, Sir Kenneth Hugo, Kt., OBE
Adams, Sir Geoffrey Doyne, KCMG
Adams, Sir William James, KCMG
Adsetts, Sir William Norman, Kt., OBE
Adye, Sir John Anthony, KCMG
Aga Khan IV, HH Prince Karim, KBE
Agnew, Sir Crispin Hamlyn, Bt. (S. 1629)
Agnew, Sir George Anthony, Bt. (1895)
Agnew, Sir Rudolph Ion Joseph, Kt.
†Agnew-Somerville, Sir James Lockett Charles, Bt. (1957)
Ah Koy, Sir James Michael, KBE
Aikens, *Rt. Hon.* Sir Richard John Pearson, Kt.
Ainslie, Sir Charles Benedict, Kt., CBE
†Ainsworth, Sir Anthony Thomas Hugh, Bt. (1917)
Aird, Sir (George) John, Bt. (1901)
Airy, *Maj.-Gen.* Sir Christopher John, KCVO, CBE
Aitchison, Sir Charles Walter de Lancey, Bt. (1938)
Ajegbo, Sir Keith Onyema, Kt., OBE
Akenhead, *Hon.* Sir Robert, Kt.
Akers-Jones, Sir David, KBE, CMG
Alberti, *Prof.* Sir Kurt George Matthew Mayer, Kt.
Albu, Sir George, Bt. (1912)
Alcock, *Air Chief Marshal* Sir (Robert James) Michael, GCB, KBE
Aldous, *Rt. Hon.* Sir William, Kt.
Aldridge, Sir Rodney Malcolm, Kt., OBE
Alexander, Sir Richard, Bt. (1945)
Alexander, Sir Douglas, Bt. (1921)
Allan, Sir Alexander Claud Stuart, KCB
Allen, *Prof.* Sir Geoffrey, Kt., PHD, FRS
Allen, Sir John Derek, Kt., CBE
Allen, Sir Mark John Spurgeon, Kt., CMG
Allen, *Hon.* Sir Peter Austin Philip Jermyn, Kt.
Allen, Sir Thomas Boaz, Kt., CBE
Allen, *Hon.* Sir William Clifford, KCMG
Allen, Sir William Guilford, Kt.
Alleyne, Sir George Allanmoore Ogarren, Kt.
Alleyne, *Revd* John Olpherts Campbell, Bt. (1769)
Allinson, Sir (Walter) Leonard, KCVO, CMG
Alliott, *Hon.* Sir John Downes, Kt.
Allison, *Air Chief Marshal* Sir John Shakespeare, KCB, CBE
Amet, *Hon.* Sir Arnold Karibone, Kt.
Amory, Sir Ian Heathcoat, Bt. (1874)
Anderson, *Dr* Sir James Iain Walker, Kt., CBE
Anderson, Sir John Anthony, KBE
Anderson, Sir Leith Reinsford Steven, Kt., CBE
Anderson, *Prof.* Sir Roy Malcolm, Kt.
Anderson, *Air Marshal* Sir Timothy Michael, KCB, DSO
Anderson, Sir (William) Eric Kinloch, KT.
Anderton, Sir (Cyril) James, Kt., CBE, QPM
Andrew, Sir Robert John, KCB
Andrews, Sir Derek Henry, KCB, CBE
Andrews, Sir Ian Charles Franklin, Kt., CBE, TD
Annesley, Sir Hugh Norman, Kt., QPM
Anson, *Vice-Adm.* Sir Edward Rosebery, KCB
Anson, Sir John, KCB
Anson, *Rear-Adm.* Sir Peter, Bt. (1831), CB
Anstruther, Sir Sebastian Paten Campbell, Bt. (S. 1694)
Anstruther-Gough-Calthorpe, Sir Euan Hamilton, Bt. (1929)
Antrobus, Sir Edward Philip, Bt. (1815)
Appleyard, Sir Leonard Vincent, KCMG
Appleyard, Sir Raymond Kenelm, KBE
Arbib, Sir Martyn, Kt.
Arbuthnot, Sir Keith Robert Charles, Bt. (1823)
Arbuthnot, Sir William Reierson, Bt. (1964)
Arbuthnott, *Prof.* Sir John Peebles, Kt., PHD, FRSE
†Archdale, Sir Nicholas Edward, Bt. (1928)
Arculus, Sir Ronald, KCMG, KCVO
Arculus, Sir Thomas David Guy, Kt.
Armitage, *Air Chief Marshal* Sir Michael John, KCB, CBE
Armitt, Sir John Alexander, Kt., CBE
Armour, *Prof.* Sir James, Kt., CBE
Armstrong, Sir Christopher John Edmund Stuart, Bt. (1841), MBE
Armstrong, Sir Patrick John, Kt., CBE
Armstrong, Sir Richard, Kt., CBE
Armytage, Sir John Martin, Bt. (1738)
Arnold, *Hon.* Sir Richard David, Kt.
Arnold, Sir Thomas Richard, Kt.
Arnott, Sir Alexander John Maxwell, Bt. (1896)
†Arthur, Sir Benjamin Nathan, Bt. (1841)
Arthur, Sir Gavyn Farr, Kt.
Arthur, *Lt.-Gen.* Sir (John) Norman Stewart, KCB, CVO
Arthur, Sir Michael Anthony, KCMG
Arulkumaran, *Prof.* Sir Sabaratnam, Kt.
Asbridge, Sir Jonathan Elliott, Kt.
Ash, *Prof.* Sir Eric Albert, Kt., CBE, FRS, FRENG
Ashburnham, Sir James Fleetwood, Bt. (1661)
Ashmore, *Admiral of the Fleet* Sir Edward Beckwith, GCB, DSC
Ashworth, *Dr* Sir John Michael, Kt.
Aske, Sir Robert John Bingham, Bt. (1922)
Askew, Sir Bryan, Kt.
Asquith, *Hon.* Sir Dominic Anthony Gerard, KCMG
Asscher, Prof. Sir (Adolf) William, Kt., MD, FRCP
Astill, *Hon.* Sir Michael John, Kt.
Astley-Cooper, Sir Alexander Paston, Bt. (1821)
Astwood, *Hon.* Sir James Rufus, KBE
Atcherley, Sir Harold Winter, Kt.
Atiyah, Sir Michael Francis, Kt., OM, PHD, FRS
Atkins, *Rt. Hon.* Sir Robert James, Kt.
Atkinson, *Prof.* Sir Anthony Barnes, Kt.
Atkinson, *Air Marshal* Sir David William, KBE
Atkinson, Sir Frederick John, KCB
Atkinson, Sir John Alexander, KCB, DFC
Atkinson, Sir Robert, Kt., DSC, FRENG
Atkinson, Sir William Samuel, Kt.
Atopare, Sir Sailas, GCMG
Attenborough, Sir David Frederick, Kt., OM, CH, CVO, CBE, FRS
Aubrey-Fletcher, Sir Henry Egerton, Bt. (1782)
Audland, Sir Christopher John, KCMG
Augier, *Prof.* Sir Fitzroy Richard, Kt.
Auld, *Rt. Hon.* Sir Robin Ernest, Kt.
Austin, Sir Anthony Leonard, Bt. (1894)
Austin, *Air Marshal* Sir Roger Mark, KCB, AFC
Austen-Smith, *Air Marshal* Sir Roy David, KBE, CB, CVO, DFC
Avei, Sir Moi, KBE
Ayckbourn, Sir Alan, Kt., CBE
Aykroyd, Sir James Alexander Frederic, Bt. (1929)

Aykroyd, Sir Henry Robert George, Bt. (1920)
Aylmer, Sir Richard John, Bt. (I. 1622)
Aylward, *Prof.* Sir Mansel, Kt., CB
Aynsley-Green, *Prof.* Sir Albert, Kt.

Bacha, Sir Bhinod, Kt., CMG
Backhouse, Sir Alfred James Stott, Bt. (1901)
Bacon, Sir Nicholas Hickman Ponsonby, Bt., OBE (1611 and 1627), *Premier Baronet of England*
Baddeley, Sir John Wolsey Beresford, Bt. (1922)
Badge, Sir Peter Gilmour Noto, Kt.
Baer, Sir Jack Mervyn Frank, Kt.
Bagge, Sir (John) Jeremy Picton, Bt. (1867)
Bagnall, *Air Chief Marshal* Sir Anthony, GBE, KCB
Bai, Sir Brown, KBE
Bailey, Sir Alan Marshall, KCB
Bailey, Sir Brian Harry, Kt., OBE
Bailey, Sir John Bilsland, KCB
†Bailey, Sir John Richard, Bt. (1919)
Bailhache, Sir Philip Martin, Kt.
Baillie, Sir Adrian Louis, Bt. (1823)
Bain, *Prof.* Sir George Sayers, Kt.
Baird, Sir Charles William Stuart, Bt. (1809)
†Baird, Sir James Andrew Gardiner, Bt. (S. 1695)
Baird, *Air Marshal* Sir John Alexander, KBE
Baird, *Vice-Adm.* Sir Thomas Henry Eustace, KCB
Bairsto, *Air Marshal* Sir Peter Edward, KBE, CB
Baker, Sir Bryan William, Kt.
Baker, *Prof.* Sir John Hamilton, Kt., QC
Baker, Sir John William, Kt., CBE
Baker, *Hon.* Sir Jonathan Leslie, Kt.
Baker, *Rt. Hon.* Sir (Thomas) Scott (Gillespie), Kt.
Balderstone, Sir James Schofield, Kt.
Baldry, Sir Antony Brian, Kt.
Baldwin, *Prof.* Sir Jack Edward, Kt., FRS
Ball, Sir Christopher John Elinger, Kt.
Ball, *Prof.* Sir John Macleod, Kt.
Ball, Sir Richard Bentley, Bt. (1911)
Ball, *Prof.* Sir Robert James, Kt., PHD
Ballantyne, *Dr* Sir Frederick Nathaniel, GCMG
Band, *Adm.* Sir Jonathon, GCB
Banham, Sir John Michael Middlecott, Kt.
Bannerman, Sir David Gordon, Bt. (S. 1682), OBE
Bannister, Sir Roger Gilbert, Kt., CBE, DM, FRCP
Barber, Sir Brendan, Kt.
Barber, Sir Michael Bayldon, Kt.
Barber, Sir (Thomas) David, Bt. (1960)
Barbour, *Very Revd* Robert Alexander Stewart, KCVO, MC
Barclay, Sir David Rowat, Kt.
Barclay, Sir Frederick Hugh, Kt.
Barclay, Sir Peter Maurice, Kt., CBE
†Barclay, Sir Robert Colraine, Bt. (S. 1668)
Barder, Sir Brian Leon, KCMG
Baring, Sir John Francis, Bt. (1911)
Barker, Sir Colin, Kt.
Barker, *Hon.* Sir (Richard) Ian, Kt.
Barling, *Hon.* Sir Gerald Edward, Kt.
Barlow, Sir Christopher Hilaro, Bt. (1803)
Barlow, Sir Frank, Kt., CBE
Barlow, Sir James Alan, Bt. (1902)
Barlow, Sir John Kemp, Bt. (1907)
Barnes, *The Most Revd* Brian James, KBE
Barnes, Sir (James) David (Francis), Kt., CBE
Barnett, *Hon.* Sir Michael Lancelot Patrick, Kt.
Barnewall, Sir Reginald Robert, Bt. (I. 1623)
Baron, Sir Thomas, Kt., CBE
†Barran, Sir John Ruthven, Bt. (1895)
Barrett, Sir Stephen Jeremy, KCMG
Barrett-Lennard, Sir Peter John, Bt. (1801)
Barrington, Sir Benjamin, Bt. (1831)
Barrington, Sir Nicholas John, KCMG, CVO
Barrington-Ward, *Rt. Revd* Simon, KCMG
Barron, Sir Donald James, Kt.
Barrons, *Gen.* Sir Richard, KCB, CBE, ADC
Barrow, Sir Anthony John Grenfell, Bt. (1835)
Barry, Sir (Lawrence) Edward (Anthony Tress), Bt. (1899)
Barter, Sir Peter Leslie Charles, Kt., OBE
Bartlett, Sir Andrew Alan, Bt. (1913)
Barttelot, *Col.* Sir Brian Walter de Stopham, Bt. (1875), OBE
Bates, Sir James Geoffrey, Bt. (1880)
Bates, Sir Richard Dawson Hoult, Bt. (1937)
Bateson, *Prof.* Sir Patrick, Kt.
Bather, Sir John Knollys, KCVO
Batho, Sir Peter Ghislain, Bt. (1928)
Bathurst, *Admiral of the Fleet* Sir (David) Benjamin, GCB
Batten, Sir John Charles, KCVO
Battersby, *Prof.* Sir Alan Rushton, Kt., FRS
Battishill, Sir Anthony Michael William, GCB
Baulcombe, *Prof.* Sir David Charles, Kt., FRS
Baxendell, Sir Peter Brian, Kt., CBE, FRENG
Bayly, *Prof.* Sir Christopher Alan, Kt.
Bayne, Sir Nicholas Peter, KCMG
Baynes, Sir Christopher Rory, Bt. (1801)
Bazalgette, Sir Peter Lytton, Kt.
Bazley, Sir Thomas John Sebastian, Bt. (1869)
Beach, *Gen.* Sir (William Gerald) Hugh, GBE, KCB, MC
Beache, *Hon.* Sir Vincent Ian, KCMG
Beale, *Lt.-Gen.* Sir Peter John, KBE, FRCP
Beamish, Sir Adrian John, KCMG
Bean, *Hon.* Sir David Michael, Kt.
Bear, Sir Michael David, Kt.
Beatson, *Rt. Hon.* Sir Jack, Kt.
Beavis, *Air Chief Marshal* Sir Michael Gordon, KCB, CBE, AFC
Beck, Sir Edgar Philip, Kt.
Beckett, Sir Richard Gervase, Bt. (1921), QC
Beckwith, Sir John Lionel, Kt., CBE
Beddington, *Prof.* Sir John Rex, Kt., CMG
Beecham, Sir Robert Adrian, Bt. (1914)
Beetham, *Marshal of the Royal Air Force* Sir Michael James, GCB, CBE, DFC, AFC
Beevor, Sir Thomas Agnew, Bt. (1784)
Beith, *Rt. Hon.* Sir Alan James, Kt.
Beldam, *Rt. Hon.* Sir (Alexander) Roy (Asplan), Kt.
Belgrave, *HE* Sir Elliott Fitzroy, GCMG
Belich, Sir James, Kt.
Bell, Sir David Charles Maurice, Kt.
Bell, Sir David Robert, KCB
Bell, *Prof.* Sir John Irving, Kt.
Bell, Sir John Lowthian, Bt. (1885)
Bell, *Prof.* Sir Peter Robert Frank, Kt.
Bell, *Hon.* Sir Rodger, Kt.
Bellamy, *Hon.* Sir Christopher William, Kt.
Bellingham, Sir Anthony Edward Norman, Bt. (1796)
Bender, Sir Brian Geoffrey, KCB
Benn, Sir (James) Jonathan, Bt. (1914)
Bennett, *Air Vice-Marshal* Sir Erik Peter, KBE, CB
Bennett, *Hon.* Sir Hugh Peter Derwyn, Kt.
Bennett, *Gen.* Sir Phillip Harvey, KBE, DSO
Bennett, Sir Ronald Wilfrid Murdoch, Bt. (1929)
Benson, Sir Christopher John, Kt.
Benyon, Sir William Richard, Kt.
Beresford, Sir (Alexander) Paul, Kt.
Beresford-Peirse, Sir Henry Njers de la Poer, Bt. (1814)
Berghuser, *Hon.* Sir Eric, Kt., MBE
Beringer, *Prof.* Sir John Evelyn, Kt., CBE
Berman, Sir Franklin Delow, KCMG
Berners-Lee, Sir Timothy John, OM, KBE, FRS
Bernard, Sir Dallas Edmund, Bt. (1954)
Bernstein, Sir Howard, Kt.
Berney, Sir Julian Reedham Stuart, Bt. (1620)
Berridge, *Prof.* Sir Michael John, Kt., FRS
Berriman, Sir David, Kt.
Berry, *Prof.* Sir Colin Leonard, Kt., FRCPATH
Berry, *Prof.* Sir Michael Victor, Kt., FRS
Berthoud, Sir Martin Seymour, KCVO, CMG
Berwick, *Prof.* Sir George Thomas, Kt., CBE
Best, Sir Richard Radford, KCVO, CBE
Best-Shaw, Sir John Michael Robert, Bt. (1665)
Bethel, Sir Baltron Benjamin, KCMG
Bethlehem, Sir Daniel, KCMG
Bett, Sir Michael, Kt., CBE
Bettison, Sir Norman George, Kt., QPM
Bevan, Sir James David, KCMG
Bevan, Sir Martyn Evan Evans, Bt. (1958)
Bevan, Sir Nicolas, Kt., CB

Bevan, Sir Timothy Hugh, Kt.
Beverley, *Lt.-Gen.* Sir Henry York La Roche, KCB, OBE, RM
Bibby, Sir Michael James, Bt. (1959)
Bickersteth, *Rt. Revd* John Monier, KCVO
Biddulph, Sir Ian D'Olier, Bt. (1664)
Bidwell, Sir Hugh Charles Philip, GBE
Biggam, Sir Robin Adair, Kt.
Bilas, Sir Angmai Simon, Kt., OBE
Bill, *Lt.-Gen.* Sir David Robert, KCB
Billière, *Gen.* Sir Peter Edgar de la Cour de la, KCB, KBE, DSO, MC
Bindman, Sir Geoffrey Lionel, Kt.
Bingham, *Hon.* Sir Eardley Max, Kt.
Birch, Sir John Allan, KCVO, CMG
Birch, Sir Roger, Kt., CBE, QPM
Bird, Sir Richard Geoffrey Chapman, Bt. (1922)
Birkett, Sir Peter, Kt.
Birkin, Sir John Christian William, Bt. (1905)
Birkin, Sir (John) Derek, Kt., TD
Birkmyre, Sir James, Bt. (1921)
Birrell, Sir James Drake, Kt.
Birt, Sir Michael, Kt.
Birtwistle, Sir Harrison, Kt., CH
Bischoff, Sir Winfried Franz Wilhelm, Kt.
Black, *Adm.* Sir (John) Jeremy, GBE, KCB, DSO
Black, Sir Robert David, Bt. (1922)
Blackburn, *Vice-Adm.* Sir David Anthony James, KCVO, CB
Blackburne, *Hon.* Sir William Anthony, Kt.
Blackett, Sir Hugh Francis, Bt. (1673)
Blackham, *Vice-Adm.* Sir Jeremy Joe, KCB
Blackman, Sir Frank Milton, KCVO, OBE
†Blair, Sir Patrick David Hunter, Bt. (1786)
Blair, *Hon.* Sir William James Lynton, Kt.
Blake, Sir Alfred Lapthorn, KCVO, MC
Blake, Sir Anthony Teilo Bruce, Bt. (I. 1622)
Blake, Sir Francis Michael, Bt. (1907)
Blake, *Hon.* Sir Nicholas John Gorrod, Kt.
Blake, Sir Peter Thomas, Kt., CBE
Blake, Sir Quentin Saxby, Kt., CBE
Blaker, Sir John, Bt. (1919)
Blakiston, Sir Ferguson Arthur James, Bt. (1763)
Blanch, Sir Malcolm, KCVO
Bland, Sir (Francis) Christopher (Buchan), Kt.
Bland, *Lt.-Col.* Sir Simon Claud Michael, KCVO
Blank, Sir Maurice Victor, Kt.
Blatherwick, Sir David Elliott Spiby, KCMG, OBE
Blelloch, Sir John Nial Henderson, KCB
Blennerhassett, Sir (Marmaduke) Adrian Francis William, Bt. (1809)
Blewitt, *Maj.* Sir Shane Gabriel Basil, GCVO
Blofeld, *Hon.* Sir John Christopher Calthorpe, Kt.
Blois, Sir Charles Nicholas Gervase, Bt. (1686)
Blom-Cooper, Sir Louis Jacques, Kt., QC
Blomefield, Sir Thomas Charles Peregrine, Bt. (1807)
Bloom, *Prof.* Sir Stephen Robert, Kt.
Bloomfield, Sir Kenneth Percy, KCB
Blundell, Sir Thomas Leon, Kt., FRS
†Blunden, Sir Hubert Chisholm, Bt. (I. 1766)
Blunt, Sir David Richard Reginald Harvey, Bt. (1720)
Blyth, Sir Charles (Chay), Kt., CBE, BEM
Boardman, *Prof.* Sir John, Kt., FSA, FBA
Bodey, *Hon.* Sir David Roderick Lessiter, Kt.
Bodmer, Sir Walter Fred, Kt., PHD, FRS
Body, Sir Richard Bernard Frank Stewart, Kt.
Bogle, Sir Nigel, Kt.
Bogan, Sir Nagora, KBE
Boileau, Sir Guy (Francis), Bt. (1838)
Boles, Sir Jeremy John Fortescue, Bt. (1922)
Bolt, *Air Marshal* Sir Richard Bruce, KBE, CB, DFC, AFC
Bona, Sir Kina, KBE
Bonallack, Sir Michael Francis, Kt., OBE
Bond, Sir John Reginald Hartnell, Kt.
Bond, *Prof.* Sir Michael Richard, Kt., FRCPSYCH, FRCPGLAS, FRCSE
Bone, *Prof.* Sir James Drummond, Kt., FRSE
Bone, Sir Roger Bridgland, KCMG
Bonfield, Sir Peter Leahy, Kt., CBE, FRENG
Bonham, Sir George Martin Antony, Bt. (1852)
Bonington, Sir Christian John Storey, Kt., CVO, CBE
Bonsall, Sir Arthur Wilfred, KCMG, CBE
Bonsor, Sir Nicholas Cosmo, Bt. (1925)
Boord, Sir Nicolas John Charles, Bt. (1896)
Boorman, *Lt.-Gen.* Sir Derek, KCB
Booth, Sir Clive, Kt.
Booth, Sir Douglas Allen, Bt. (1916)
Booth, Sir Gordon, KCMG, CVO
Boothby, Sir Brooke Charles, Bt. (1660)
Bore, Sir Albert, Kt.
Boreel, Sir Stephan Gerard, Bt. (1645)
Borthwick, Sir Anthony Thomas, Bt. (1908)
Borysiewicz, *Prof.* Sir Leszek Krzysztof, Kt.
Bosher, Sir Robin, Kt.
Bossom, *Hon.* Sir Clive, Bt. (1953)
Boswell, *Lt.-Gen.* Sir Alexander Crawford Simpson, KCB, CBE
Botham, Sir Ian Terence, Kt., OBE
Bottoms, *Prof.* Sir Anthony Edward, Kt.
Bottomley, Sir Peter James, Kt.
Boughey, Sir John George Fletcher, Bt. (1798)
Boulton, Sir Clifford John, GCB
†Boulton, Sir John Gibson, Bt. (1944)
Bouraga, Sir Phillip, KBE
Bourn, Sir John Bryant, KCB
Bowater, Sir Euan David Vansittart, Bt. (1939)
†Bowater, Sir Michael Patrick, Bt. (1914)
Bowden, Sir Andrew, Kt., MBE
Bowden, Sir Nicholas Richard, Bt. (1915)
Bowen, Sir Barry Manfield, KCMG
Bowen, Sir Geoffrey Fraser, Kt.
Bowen, Sir Mark Edward Mortimer, Bt. (1921)
Bowes Lyon, Sir Simon Alexander, KCVO
†Bowlby, Sir Richard Peregrine Longstaff, Bt. (1923)
Bowman, Sir Edwin Geoffrey, KCB
Bowman, Sir Jeffery Haverstock, Kt.
Bowman-Shaw, Sir (George) Neville, Kt.
Bowness, Sir Alan, Kt., CBE
Bowyer-Smyth, Sir Thomas Weyland, Bt. (1661)
Boyce, Sir Graham Hugh, KCMG
Boyce, Sir Robert Charles Leslie, Bt. (1952)
Boyd, Sir Alexander Walter, Bt. (1916)
Boyd, Sir John Dixon Iklé, KCMG
Boyd, Sir Michael, Kt.
Boyd, *Prof.* Sir Robert David Hugh, Kt.
Boyd-Carpenter, Sir (Marsom) Henry, KCVO
Boyd-Carpenter, *Lt.-Gen. Hon.* Sir Thomas Patrick John, KBE
Boyle, *Prof.* Sir Roger Michael, Kt., CBE
Boyle, Sir Stephen Gurney, Bt. (1904)
Brabham, Sir John Arthur, Kt., OBE
Bracewell-Smith, Sir Charles, Bt. (1947)
Bradbeer, Sir John Derek Richardson, Kt., OBE, TD
Bradfield, *Dr* Sir John Richard Grenfell, Kt., CBE
Bradford, Sir Edward Alexander Slade, Bt. (1902)
Bradshaw, *Lt-Gen.* Sir Adrian, KCB, OBE
Brady, *Prof.* Sir John Michael, Kt., FRS
Brailsford, Sir David John, Kt., CBE
Braithwaite, Sir Rodric Quentin, GCMG
Bramley, *Prof.* Sir Paul Anthony, Kt.
Branagh, Sir Kenneth Charles, Kt.
Branson, Sir Richard Charles Nicholas, Kt.
Braithwaite, *Rt. Hon.* Sir Nicholas Alexander, Kt., OBE
Bratza, *Hon.* Sir Nicolas Dušan, Kt.
Breckenridge, *Prof.* Sir Alasdair Muir, Kt., CBE
Brennan, *Hon.* Sir (Francis) Gerard, KBE
Brenton, Sir Anthony Russell, KCMG
Brewer, Sir David William, Kt., CMG
Brierley, Sir Ronald Alfred, Kt.
Briggs, *Rt. Hon.* Sir Michael Townley Featherstone, Kt.
Brighouse, *Prof.* Sir Timothy Robert Peter, Kt.
Bright, Sir Graham Frank James, Kt.

Bright, Sir Keith, Kt.
Brigstocke, *Adm.* Sir John Richard, KCB
Brinckman, Sir Theodore George Roderick, Bt. (1831)
†Brisco, Sir Campbell Howard, Bt. (1782)
Briscoe, Sir Brian Anthony, Kt.
Briscoe, Sir John Geoffrey James, Bt. (1910)
Brittan, Sir Samuel, Kt.
Britton, Sir Paul John James, Kt., CB
†Broadbent, Sir Andrew George, Bt. (1893)
Broadbent, Sir Richard John, KCB
Brocklebank, Sir Aubrey Thomas, Bt. (1885)
Brodie, Sir Benjamin David Ross, Bt. (1834)
Bromhead, Sir John Desmond Gonville, Bt. (1806)
Bromley, Sir Michael Roger, KBE
Bromley, Sir Rupert Charles, Bt. (1757)
Bromley-Davenport, Sir William Arthur, KCVO
Brook, *Prof.* Sir Richard John, Kt. OBE
Brooke, Sir Alistair Weston, Bt. (1919)
Brooke, Sir Francis George Windham, Bt. (1903)
Brooke, *Rt. Hon.* Sir Henry, Kt.
Brooke, Sir Richard Christopher, Bt. (1662)
Brooke, Sir Rodney George, Kt., CBE
Brooking, Sir Trevor David, Kt., CBE
Brooks, Sir Timothy Gerald Martin, KCVO
Brooksbank, Sir (Edward) Nicholas, Bt. (1919)
Broomfield, Sir Nigel Hugh Robert Allen, KCMG
†Broughton, Sir David Delves, Bt. (1661)
Broughton, Sir Martin Faulkner, Kt.
Broun, Sir Wayne Hercules, Bt. (S. 1686)
Brown, Sir (Austen) Patrick, KCB
Brown, *Adm.* Sir Brian Thomas, KCB, CBE
Brown, Sir David, Kt.
Brown, *Hon.* Sir Douglas Dunlop, Kt.
Brown, Sir George Francis Richmond, Bt. (1863)
Brown, Sir Mervyn, KCMG, OBE
Brown, Sir Peter Randolph, Kt.
Brown, *Rt. Hon.* Sir Stephen, GBE
Brown, Sir Stephen David Reid, KCVO
Browne, Sir Nicholas Walker, KBE, CMG
Brownrigg, Sir Nicholas (Gawen), Bt. (1816)
Browse, *Prof.* Sir Norman Leslie, Kt., MD, FRCS
Bruce, Sir (Francis) Michael Ian, Bt. (S. 1628)
Bruce, *Rt. Hon.* Sir Malcolm Gray Bruce, Kt.
Bruce-Clifton, Sir Hervey Hamish Peter, Bt. (1804)
Bruce-Gardner, Sir Robert Henry, Bt. (1945)
Brunner, Sir Hugo Laurence Joseph, KCVO
Brunner, Sir John Henry Kilian, Bt. (1895)
Brunton, Sir Gordon Charles, Kt.
†Brunton, Sir James Lauder, Bt. (1908)
Bryant, *Air Chief Marshal* Sir Simon, KCB, CBE, ADC
Bubb, Sir Stephen John Limrick, Kt.
Buchan-Hepburn, Sir John Alastair Trant Kidd, Bt. (1815)
Buchanan, Sir Andrew George, Bt. (1878), KCVO
Buchanan, *Dr* Sir John Gordon St Clair, Kt.
Buchanan, Sir Robert Wilson (Robin), Kt.
Buchanan-Jardine, Sir John Christopher Rupert, Bt. (1885)
Buckland, Sir Ross, Kt.
Buckley, *Dr* Sir George William, Kt.
Buckley, Sir Michael Sidney, Kt.
Buckley, *Lt.-Cdr.* Sir (Peter) Richard, KCVO
Buckley, *Hon.* Sir Roger John, Kt.
Bucknall, *Lt-Gen.* Sir James Jeffrey Corfield, KCB
Buckworth-Herne-Soame, Sir Charles John, Bt. (1697)
Budd, Sir Alan Peter, GBE, Kt.
Budd, Sir Colin Richard, KCMG
Bull, Sir George Jeffrey, Kt.
Bull, Sir Simeon George, Bt. (1922)
Bullock, Sir Stephen Michael, Kt.
Bultin, Sir Bato, Kt., MBE
Bunbury, Sir Michael William, Bt. (1681), KCVO
Bunyard, Sir Robert Sidney, Kt., CBE, QPM
Burbidge, Sir Peter Dudley, Bt. (1916)
Burden, Sir Anthony Thomas, Kt., QPM
Burdett, Sir Savile Aylmer, Bt. (1665)
Burgen, Sir Arnold Stanley Vincent, Kt., FRS
Burgess, *Gen.* Sir Edward Arthur, KCB, OBE
Burgess, Sir (Joseph) Stuart, Kt., CBE, PHD, FRSC
Burgess, *Prof.* Sir Robert George, Kt.
Burke, Sir James Stanley Gilbert, Bt. (I. 1797)
Burke, Sir (Thomas) Kerry, Kt.
Burn, *Prof.* Sir John, Kt.
Burnell-Nugent, *Vice-Adm.* Sir James Michael, KCB, CBE, ADC
Burnett, Sir Charles David, Bt., (1913)
Burnett, *Hon.* Sir Ian Duncan, Kt.
Burnett, Sir Walter John, Kt.
Burney, Sir Nigel Dennistoun, Bt. (1921)
Burns, *Dr* Sir Henry, Kt.
Burns, Sir (Robert) Andrew, KCMG
Burnton, *Rt. Hon.* Sir Stanley Jeffrey, Kt.
Burrell, Sir Charles Raymond, Bt. (1774)
Burridge, *Air Chief Marshal* Sir Brian Kevin, KCB, CBE, ADC
Burston, Sir Samuel Gerald Wood, Kt., OBE
Burt, Sir Peter Alexander, Kt.
Burton, Sir Carlisle Archibald, Kt., OBE
Burton, *Lt.-Gen.* Sir Edmund Fortescue Gerard, KBE
Burton, Sir Graham Stuart, KCMG
Burton, *Hon.* Sir Michael John, Kt.
Burton, Sir Michael St Edmund, KCVO, CMG
Butler, *Hon.* Sir Arlington Griffith, KCMG
Butler, *Dr* Sir David Edgeworth, Kt., CBE
Butler, Sir Michael Dacres, GCMG
Butler, Sir Percy James, Kt., CBE
†Butler, Sir Reginald Richard Michael, Bt. (1922)
Butler, Sir Richard Pierce, Bt. (1628)
Butterfield, *Hon.* Sir Alexander Neil Logie, Kt.
Butterfill, Sir John Valentine, Kt.
Buxton, Sir Jocelyn Charles Roden, Bt. (1840)
Buxton, *Rt. Hon.* Sir Richard Joseph, Kt.
Buzzard, Sir Anthony Farquhar, Bt. (1929)
Byatt, Sir Ian Charles Rayner, Kt.
Byford, Sir Lawrence, Kt., CBE, QPM
Byron, *Rt. Hon.* Sir Charles Michael Dennis, Kt.

†Cable-Alexander, Sir Patrick Desmond William, Bt. (1809)
Cadbury, Sir (George) Adrian (Hayhurst), Kt.
Cadbury, Sir (Nicholas) Dominic, Kt.
Cadogan, *Prof.* Sir John Ivan George, Kt., CBE, FRS, FRSE
Cahn, Sir Albert Jonas, Bt. (1934)
Cahn, Sir Andrew Thomas, KCMG
Caine, Sir Michael (Maurice Micklewhite), Kt., CBE
Caines, Sir John, KCB
Cairns, *Very Revd* John Ballantyne, KCVO
Caldwell, Sir Edward George, KCB
Callaghan, Sir William Henry, Kt.
Callan, Sir Ivan Roy, KCVO, CMG
Callman, *His Hon.* Sir Clive Vernon, Kt.
Calman, *Prof.* Sir Kenneth Charles, KCB, MD, FRCP, FRCS, FRSE
Calne, *Prof.* Sir Roy Yorke, Kt., FRS
Calvert-Smith, Sir David, Kt., QC
Cameron, Sir Hugh Roy Graham, Kt., QPM
Campbell, *Prof.* Sir Colin Murray, Kt.
Campbell, Sir Ian Tofts, Kt., CBE, VRD
Campbell, Sir Ilay Mark, Bt. (1808)
Campbell, Sir James Alexander Moffat Bain, Bt. (S. 1668)
Campbell, Sir Lachlan Philip Kemeys, Bt. (1815)
Campbell, Sir Roderick Duncan Hamilton, Bt. (1831)
Campbell, Sir Robin Auchinbreck, Bt. (S. 1628)
Campbell, *Rt. Hon.* Sir Walter Menzies, Kt., CH, CBE, QC
Campbell, *Rt. Hon.* Sir William Anthony, Kt.
Campbell-Orde, Sir John Alexander, Bt. (1790)
Cannadine, *Prof.* Sir David Nicholas, Kt.

†Carden, Sir Christopher Robert, Bt. (1887)
†Carden, Sir John Craven, Bt. (I. 1787)
Carew, Sir Rivers Verain, Bt. (1661)
Carey, Sir de Vic Graham, Kt.
Carleton-Smith, *Maj.-Gen.* Sir Michael Edward, Kt., CBE
Carlisle, Sir James Beethoven, GCMG
Carlisle, Sir John Michael, Kt.
Carlisle, Sir Kenneth Melville, Kt.
Carnegie, Sir Roderick Howard, Kt.
Carnwath, *Rt. Hon.* Sir Robert John Anderson, Kt., CVO
Caro, Sir Anthony Alfred, Kt., OM, CBE
Carr, Sir (Albert) Raymond (Maillard), Kt.
Carr, *Very Revd Dr* Arthur Wesley, KCVO
Carr, Sir Peter Derek, Kt., CBE
Carr, Sir Roger Martyn, Kt.
Carr-Ellison, *Col.* Sir Ralph Harry, KCVO, TD
Carrick, *Hon.* Sir John Leslie, KCMG
Carrick, Sir Roger John, KCMG, LVO
Carruthers, Sir Ian James, Kt., OBE
Carsberg, *Prof.* Sir Bryan Victor, Kt.
Carter, Sir David Anthony, Kt.
Carter, *Prof.* Sir David Craig, Kt., FRCSE, FRCSGLAS, FRCPE
Carter, Sir John Alexander, Kt.
Carter, Sir John Gordon Thomas, Kt.
Carter, Sir Philip David, Kt., CBE
Cartledge, Sir Bryan George, KCMG
Caruna, *Hon.* Sir Peter Richard, KCMG, QC
†Cary, Sir Nicholas Robert Hugh, Bt. (1955)
Cash, Sir Andrew John, Kt., OBE
Cass, Sir Geoffrey Arthur, Kt.
Cassel, Sir Timothy Felix Harold, Bt. (1920)
Cassels, Sir John Seton, Kt., CB
Cassels, *Adm.* Sir Simon Alastair Cassillis, KCB, CBE
Cassidi, *Adm.* Sir (Arthur) Desmond, GCB
Castell, Sir William Martin, Kt.
Castledine, *Prof.* Sir George, Kt.
Catherwood, Sir (Henry) Frederick (Ross), Kt.
Catto, *Prof.* Sir Graeme Robertson Dawson, Kt.
Cave, Sir John Charles, Bt. (1896)
Cave-Browne-Cave, Sir John Robert Charles, Bt. (1641)
Cayley, Sir Digby William David, Bt. (1661)
Cazalet, *Hon.* Sir Edward Stephen, Kt.
Cazalet, Sir Peter Grenville, Kt.
Cecil, *Rear-Adm.* Sir (Oswald) Nigel Amherst, KBE, CB
Chadwick, *Rt. Hon.* Sir John Murray, Kt.
Chadwick, Sir Joshua Kenneth Burton, Bt. (1935)
Chadwick, *Revd Prof.* (William) Owen, OM, KBE, FBA
Chadwyck-Healey, Sir Charles Edward, Bt. (1919)
Chakrabarti, Sir Sumantra, KCB
Chalmers, Sir Iain Geoffrey, Kt.
Chalmers, Sir Neil Robert, Kt.
Chalstrey, Sir (Leonard) John, Kt., MD, FRCS
Chan, *Rt. Hon.* Sir Julius, GCMG, KBE
Chan, Sir Thomas Kok, Kt., OBE
Chance, Sir (George) Jeremy ffolliott, Bt. (1900)
Chandler, Sir Colin Michael, Kt.
Chantler, *Prof.* Sir Cyril, Kt., MD, FRCP
Chaplin, Sir Malcolm Hilbery, Kt., CBE
Chapman, Sir David Robert Macgowan, Bt. (1958)
Chapman, Sir Frank, Kt.
Chapman, Sir George Alan, Kt.
Chapman, Sir Sidney Brookes, Kt., MP
Chapple, *Field Marshal* Sir John Lyon, GCB, CBE
Charles, *Hon.* Sir Arthur William Hessin, Kt.
Charlton, Sir Robert (Bobby), Kt., CBE
Charnley, Sir (William) John, Kt., CB, FRENG
Chartres, *Rt. Revd and Rt. Hon.* Richard John Carew, KCVO
Chataway, *Rt. Hon.* Sir Christopher, Kt.
†Chaytor, Sir Bruce Gordon, Bt. (1831)
Checketts, *Sqn. Ldr.* Sir David John, KCVO
Checkland, Sir Michael, Kt.
Cheshire, *Air Chief Marshal* Sir John Anthony, KBE, CB
Chessells, Sir Arthur David (Tim), Kt.
†Chetwynd, Sir Peter James Talbot, Bt. (1795)
Cheyne, Sir Patrick John Lister, Bt. (1908)
Chichester, Sir James Henry Edward, Bt. (1641)
Chichester-Clark, Sir Robin, Kt.
Chilcot, *Rt. Hon.* Sir John Anthony, GCB
Child, Sir (Coles John) Jeremy, Bt. (1919)
Chilwell, *Hon.* Sir Muir Fitzherbert, Kt.
Chinn, Sir Trevor Edwin, Kt., CVO
†Chinubhai, Sir Prashat, Bt. (1913)
Chipperfield, *Prof.* Sir David Alan, Kt., CBE
Chipperfield, Sir Geoffrey Howes, KCB
Chisholm, Sir John Alexander Raymond, Kt., FRENG
Chitty, Sir Thomas Willes, Bt. (1924)
Cholmeley, Sir Hugh John Frederick Sebastian, Bt. (1806)
Chow, Sir Chung Kong, Kt.
Chow, Sir Henry Francis, Kt., OBE
Christie, Sir George William Langham, Kt., CH
Christopher, Sir Duncan Robin Carmichael, KBE, CMG
Chung, Sir Sze-yuen, GBE, FRENG
Clark, Sir Francis Drake, Bt. (1886)
Clark, Sir John Arnold, Kt.
Clark, Sir Jonathan George, Bt. (1917)
Clark, Sir Terence Joseph, KBE, CMG, CVO
Clarke, Sir (Charles Mansfield) Tobias, Bt. (1831)
Clarke, *Hon.* Sir Christopher Simon Courtenay Stephenson, Kt.
Clarke, *Hon.* Sir David Clive, Kt.
Clarke, Sir Jonathan Dennis, Kt.
Clarke, Sir Paul Robert Virgo, KCVO
Clarke, Sir Robert Cyril, Kt.
†Clarke, Sir Rupert Grant Alexander, Bt. (1882)
Clay, Sir Edward, KCMG
Clay, Sir Richard Henry, Bt. (1841)
Clayton, Sir David Robert, Bt. (1732)
Cleaver, Sir Anthony Brian, Kt.
Clementi, Sir David Cecil, Kt.
Clerk, Sir Robert Maxwell, Bt. (1679), OBE
Clerke, Sir Francis Ludlow Longueville, Bt. (1660)
Clifford, Sir Roger Joseph, Bt. (1887)
Clifford, Sir Timothy Peter Plint, Kt.
Coates, Sir Anthony Robert Milnes, Bt. (1911)
Coates, Sir David Frederick Charlton, Bt. (1921)
Coats, Sir Alastair Francis Stuart, Bt. (1905)
Cochrane, Sir (Henry) Marc (Sursock), Bt. (1903)
Cockburn, Sir John Elliot, Bt. (S. 1671)
Cockburn-Campbell, Sir Alexander Thomas, Bt. (1821)
Cockell, Sir Merrick, Kt.
Cockshaw, Sir Alan, Kt., FRENG
Codrington, Sir Christopher George Wayne, Bt. (1876)
†Codrington, Sir Giles Peter, Bt. (1721)
Coghill, Sir Patrick Kendal Farley, Bt. (1778)
Coghlin, *Rt. Hon.* Sir Patrick, Kt.
Cohen, Sir Ivor Harold, Kt., CBE, TD
Cohen, *Prof.* Sir Philip, Kt., PHD, FRS
Cohen, Sir Ronald, Kt.
Cole, Sir (Robert) William, Kt.
Coleman, Sir Robert John, KCMG
Coleridge, *Hon.* Sir Paul James Duke, Kt.
Coles, Sir (Arthur) John, GCMG
Colfox, Sir (William) John, Bt. (1939)
Collett, Sir Ian Seymour, Bt. (1934)
Collins, Sir Alan Stanley, KCVO, CMG
Collins, *Hon.* Sir Andrew David, Kt.
Collins, Sir Bryan Thomas Alfred, Kt., OBE, QFSM
Collins, Sir John Alexander, Kt
Collins, Sir Kenneth Darlingston, Kt.
Collins, *Prof.* Sir Rory Edwards, Kt.
Collyear, Sir John Gowen, Kt.
Colman, *Hon.* Sir Anthony David, Kt.
Colman, Sir Michael Jeremiah, Bt. (1907)
Colman, Sir Timothy, KG
†Colquhoun of Luss, Sir Malcolm Rory, Bt. (1786)
Colt, Sir Edward William Dutton, Bt. (1694)
Colthurst, Sir Charles St John, Bt. (1744)
Conant, Sir John Ernest Michael, Bt. (1954)
Conner, *Rt. Revd* Sir David John, KCVO
Connery, Sir Sean, Kt.

Connor, Sir William Joseph, Kt.
Conran, Sir Terence Orby, Kt.
Cons, *Hon.* Sir Derek, Kt.
Constantinou, Sir Theophilus George, Kt., CBE
Conway, *Prof.* Sir Gordon Richard, KCMG, FRS
Cook, Sir Christopher Wymondham Rayner Herbert, Bt. (1886)
Cook, *Prof.* Sir Peter Frederic Chester, Kt.
Cooke, *Col.* Sir David William Perceval, Bt. (1661)
Cooke, Sir Howard Felix Hanlan, GCMG, GCVO
Cooke, *Hon.* Sir Jeremy Lionel, Kt.
Cooke, *Prof.* Sir Ronald Urwick, Kt.
Cooksey, Sir David James Scott, GBE
Cooper, *Gen.* Sir George Leslie Conroy, GCB, MC
Cooper, Sir Richard Adrian, Bt. (1905)
Cooper, Sir Robert Francis, KCMG, MVO
Cooper, *Maj.-Gen.* Sir Simon Christie, GCVO
Cooper, Sir William Daniel Charles, Bt. (1863)
Coote, Sir Christopher John, Bt. (I. 1621), *Premier Baronet of Ireland*
Copisarow, Sir Alcon Charles, Kt.
Corbett, *Maj.-Gen.* Sir Robert John Swan, KCVO, CB
Cordy-Simpson, *Lt.-Gen.* Sir Roderick Alexander, KBE, CB
Corfield, Sir Kenneth George, Kt., FRENG
Corness, Sir Colin Ross, Kt.
Cornforth, Sir John Warcup, Kt., CBE, DPHIL, FRS
Corry, Sir James Michael, Bt. (1885)
Cortazzi, Sir (Henry Arthur) Hugh, GCMG
Cory, Sir (Clinton Charles) Donald, Bt. (1919)
Cory-Wright, Sir Richard Michael, Bt. (1903)
Cossons, Sir Neil, Kt., OBE
Cotter, Sir Patrick Laurence Delaval, Bt. (I. 1763)
Cotterell, Sir John Henry Geers, Bt. (1805)
†Cotts, Sir Richard Crichton Mitchell, Bt. (1921)
Coulson, *Hon.* Sir Peter David William, Kt.
Couper, Sir James George, Bt. (1841)
Courtenay, Sir Thomas Daniel, Kt.
Cousins, *Air Chief Marshal* Sir David, KCB, AFC
Coville, *Air Marshal* Sir Christopher Charles Cotton, KCB
Cowan, *Gen.* Sir Samuel, KCB, CBE
Coward, *Lt-Gen.* Sir Gary Robert, KBE, CB, OBE
Coward, *Vice-Adm.* Sir John Francis, KCB, DSO
Cowper-Coles, Sir Sherard Louis, KCMG, LVO
Cox, Sir Alan George, Kt., CBE
Cox, *Prof.* Sir David Roxbee, Kt.
Cox, Sir George Edwin, Kt.
Craft, *Prof.* Sir Alan William, Kt.
Cragnolini, Sir Luciano, Kt.
Craig, Sir (Albert) James (Macqueen), GCMG
Craig-Cooper, Sir (Frederick Howard) Michael, Kt., CBE, TD
Crane, *Prof.* Sir Peter Robert, Kt.
Cranston, *Hon.* Sir Ross Frederick, Kt.
Craufurd, Sir Robert James, Bt. (1781)
Craven, Sir John Anthony, Kt.
Craven, Sir Philip Lee, Kt., MBE
Crawford, *Prof.* Sir Frederick William, Kt., FRENG
Crawford, Sir Robert William Kenneth, Kt. CBE
Crawley-Boevey, Sir Thomas Michael Blake, Bt. (1784)
Crew, Sir (Michael) Edward, Kt., QPM
Crewe, *Prof.* Sir Ivor Martin, Kt.
Cresswell, *Hon.* Sir Peter John, Kt.
Crisp, Sir John Charles, Bt. (1913)
Critchett, Sir Charles George Montague, Bt. (1908)
Crittin, *Hon.* Sir John Luke, KBE
Croft, Sir Owen Glendower, Bt. (1671)
Croft, Sir Thomas Stephen Hutton, Bt. (1818)
†Crofton, Sir Hugh Denis, Bt. (1801)
†Crofton, Sir Julian Malby, Bt. (1838)
Crombie, Sir Alexander, Kt.
Crompton, Sir Dan, Kt., CBE, QPM
Cropper, Sir James Anthony, KCVO
Crossley, Sir Sloan Nicholas, Bt. (1909)
Crowe, Sir Brian Lee, KCMG
Cruickshank, Sir Donald Gordon, Kt.
Cruthers, Sir James Winter, Kt.
Cubbon, Sir Brian Crossland, GCB
Cubie, *Dr* Sir Andrew, Kt., CBE
Cubitt, Sir Hugh Guy, Kt., CBE
Cubitt, *Maj.-Gen.* Sir William George, KCVO, CBE
Cullen, Sir (Edward) John, Kt., FRENG
Culme-Seymour, Sir Michael Patrick, Bt. (1809)
Culpin, Sir Robert Paul, Kt.
Cummins, Sir Michael John Austin, Kt.
Cunliffe, *Prof.* Sir Barrington, Kt., CBE
Cunliffe, Sir David Ellis, Bt. (1759)
Cunliffe, Sir Jonathan Stephen, Kt., CB
Cunliffe-Owen, Sir Hugo Dudley, Bt. (1920)
Cunningham, *Lt.-Gen.* Sir Hugh Patrick, KBE
Cunningham, Sir Roger Keith, Kt., CBE
Cunningham, Sir Thomas Anthony, Kt.
Cunynghame, Sir Andrew David Francis, Bt. (S. 1702)
†Currie, Sir Donald Scott, Bt. (1847)
Curtain, Sir Michael, KBE
Curtis, Sir Barry John, Kt.
Curtis, *Hon.* Sir Richard Herbert, Kt.
Curtis, Sir William Peter, Bt. (1802)
Curtiss, *Air Marshal* Sir John Bagot, KCB, KBE
Curwen, Sir Christopher Keith, KCMG
Cuschieri, *Prof.* Sir Alfred, Kt.

Dain, Sir David John Michael, KCVO
Dales, Sir Richard Nigel, KCVO
Dalrymple-Hay, Sir Malcolm John Robert, Bt. (1798)
†Dalrymple-White, Sir Jan Hew, Bt. (1926)
Dalton, *Vice-Adm.* Sir Geoffrey Thomas James Oliver, GCB
Dalton, Sir Richard John, KCMG
Dalton, *Air Chief Marshal* Sir Stephen Gary George, GCB
Dalyell, Sir Tam (Thomas), Bt. (NS 1685)
Dancer, Sir Eric, KCVO, CBE
Daniel, Sir John Sagar, Kt., DSC
†Darell, Sir Guy Jeffrey Adair, Bt. (1795), MC
Darrington, Sir Michael John, Kt.
Darroch, Sir Nigel Kim, KCMG
Dasgupta, *Prof.* Sir Partha Sarathi, Kt.
Dashwood, *Prof.* Sir (Arthur) Alan, KCMG, CBE, QC
Dashwood, Sir Edward John Francis, Bt. (1707), *Premier Baronet of Great Britain*
†Dashwood, Sir Frederick George Mahon, Bt. (1684)
Daunt, Sir Timothy Lewis Achilles, KCMG
Davenport-Handley, Sir David John, Kt., OBE
David, Sir Jean Marc, Kt., CBE, QC
David, *His Hon.* Sir Robin (Robert) Daniel George, Kt.
Davies, Sir Alan Seymour, Kt.
Davies, Sir (Charles) Noel, Kt.
Davies, *Prof.* Sir David Evan Naughton, Kt., CBE, FRS, FRENG
Davies, *Hon.* Sir (David Herbert) Mervyn, Kt., MC, TD
Davies, Sir David John, Kt.
Davies, Sir Frank John, Kt., CBE
Davies, *Prof.* Sir Graeme John, Kt., FRENG
Davies, Sir John Howard, Kt.
Davies, Sir John Michael, KCB
Davies, Sir Peter Maxwell, Kt., CBE
Davies, Sir Rhys Everson, Kt., QC
Davis, Sir Andrew Frank, Kt., CBE
Davis, Sir Crispin Henry Lamert, Kt.
Davis, Sir John Gilbert, Bt. (1946)
Davis, *Rt. Hon.* Sir Nigel Anthony Lambert, Kt.
Davis, Sir Peter John, Kt.
Davis-Goff, Sir Robert (William), Bt. (1905)
Davison, *Rt. Hon.* Sir Ronald Keith, GBE, CMG
†Davson, Sir George Trenchard Simon, Bt. (1927)
Dawanincura, Sir John Norbert, Kt., OBE
Dawbarn, Sir Simon Yelverton, KCVO, CMG
Dawson, *Hon.* Sir Daryl Michael, KBE, CB
Dawson, Sir Nicholas Antony Trevor, Bt. (1920)
Dawtry, Sir Alan (Graham), Kt., CBE, TD
Day, Sir Derek Malcolm, KCMG
Day, *Air Chief Marshal* Sir John Romney, KCB, OBE, ADC
Day, Sir (Judson) Graham, Kt.
Day, Sir Michael John, Kt., OBE
Day, Sir Simon James, Kt.
Deane, *Hon.* Sir William Patrick, KBE
Dearlove, Sir Richard Billing, KCMG, OBE

†Debenham, Sir Thomas Adam, Bt. (1931)
de Deney, Sir Geoffrey Ivor, KCVO
Deeny, *Hon.* Sir Donnell Justin Patrick, Kt.
De Halpert, *Rear-Adm.* Sir Jeremy Michael, KCVO, CB
de Hoghton, Sir (Richard) Bernard (Cuthbert), Bt. (1611)
De la Bère, Sir Cameron, Bt. (1953)
de la Rue, Sir Andrew George Ilay, Bt. (1898)
De Silva, *Rt. Hon.* Sir (George) Desmond Lorenz, Kt., QC
Dellow, Sir John Albert, Kt., CBE
Delves, *Lt.-Gen.* Sir Cedric Norman George, KBE
Denholm, Sir John Ferguson (Ian), Kt., CBE
Denison-Smith, *Lt.-Gen.* Sir Anthony Arthur, KBE
Denny, Sir Anthony Coningham de Waltham, Bt. (I. 1782)
Denny, Sir Charles Alistair Maurice, Bt. (1913)
Derbyshire, Sir Andrew George, Kt.
de Trafford, Sir John Humphrey, Bt. (1841)
Deverell, *Gen.* Sir John Freegard, KCB, OBE
De Ville, Sir Harold Godfrey Oscar, Kt., CBE
Devitt, Sir James Hugh Thomas, Bt. (1916)
de Waal, Sir (Constant Henrik) Henry, KCB, QC
Dewey, Sir Anthony Hugh, Bt. (1917)
De Witt, Sir Ronald Wayne, Kt.
Diamond, *Prof.* Sir Ian David, Kt., FRSE
Dick-Lauder, Sir Piers Robert, Bt. (S. 1690)
Dilke, Revd Charles John Wentworth, Bt. (1862)
Dilnot, Sir Andrew William, Kt., CBE
Dillon, Sir Andrew Patrick, Kt., CBE
Dillwyn-Venables-Llewelyn, Sir John Michael, Bt. (1890)
Dixon, Sir Jeremy, Kt.
Dixon, Sir Jonathan Mark, Bt. (1919)
Dixon, Sir Peter John Bellett, Kt.
Djanogly, Sir Harry Ari Simon, Kt., CBE
Dobson, *Vice-Adm.* Sir David Stuart, KBE
Dodds, Sir Ralph Jordan, Bt. (1964)
Dollery, Sir Colin Terence, Kt.
Don-Wauchope, Sir Roger (Hamilton), Bt. (S. 1667)
Donald, Sir Alan Ewen, KCMG
Donald, *Air Marshal* Sir John George, KBE
Donaldson, *Prof.* Sir Liam Joseph, Kt.
Donaldson, *Prof.* Sir Simon Kirwan, Kt.
Donne, Sir John Christopher, Kt.
Donnelly, Sir Joseph Brian, KBE, CMG
Dorey, Sir Graham Martyn, Kt.
Dorman, Sir Philip Henry Keppel, Bt. (1923)
Doughty, Sir William Roland, Kt.
Douglas, *Prof.* Sir Neil James, Kt.
Douglas, *Hon.* Sir Roger Owen, Kt.
Dowell, Sir Anthony James, Kt., CBE
Dowling, Sir Robert, Kt.
Downey, Sir Gordon Stanley, KCB
Downs, Sir Diarmuid, Kt., CBE, FRENG
Downward, *Maj.-Gen.* Sir Peter Aldcroft, KCVO, CB, DSO, DFC
Dowson, Sir Philip Manning, Kt., CBE
Doyle, Sir Reginald Derek Henry, Kt., CBE
D'Oyly, Sir Hadley Gregory Bt. (1663)
Drake, *Hon.* Sir (Frederick) Maurice, Kt., DFC
Drewry, *Lt.-Gen.* Sir Christopher Francis, KCB, CBE
Drinkwater, Sir John Muir, Kt., QC
Drury, Sir (Victor William) Michael, Kt., OBE
Dryden, Sir John Stephen Gyles, Bt. (1733 and 1795)
du Cann, *Rt. Hon.* Sir Edward Dillon Lott, KBE
Duckworth, Sir James Edward Dyce, Bt. (1909)
du Cros, Sir Claude Philip Arthur Mallet, Bt. (1916)
Dudley-Williams, Sir Alastair Edgcumbe James, Bt. (1964)
Duff, *Prof.* Sir Gordon William, Kt.
Duff-Gordon, Sir Andrew Cosmo Lewis, Bt. (1813)
Duffell, *Lt.-Gen.* Sir Peter Royson, KCB, CBE, MC
Duffy, Sir (Albert) (Edward) Patrick, Kt., PHD
Dugdale, Sir William Stratford, Bt. (1936), CBE, MC
Duggin, Sir Thomas Joseph, Kt.
Dunbar, Sir Archibald Ranulph, Bt. (S. 1700)
Dunbar, Sir Robert Drummond Cospatrick, Bt. (S. 1698)
Dunbar, Sir James Michael, Bt. (S. 1694)
Dunbar of Hempriggs, Sir Richard Francis, Bt. (S. 1706)
Dunbar-Nasmith, *Prof.* Sir James Duncan, Kt., CBE
Duncan, Sir James Blair, Kt.
Dunlop, Sir Thomas, Bt. (1916)
Dunn, *Rt. Hon.* Sir Robin Horace Walford, Kt., MC
Dunne, Sir Martin, KCVO
Dunne, Sir Thomas Raymond, KG, KCVO
Dunning, Sir Simon William Patrick, Bt. (1930)
Dunnington-Jefferson, Sir Mervyn Stewart, Bt. (1958)
Dunstone, Sir Charles William, Kt.
Dunt, *Vice-Adm.* Sir John Hugh, KCB
Duntze, Sir Daniel Evans, Bt. (1774)
Dupre, Sir Tumun, Kt., MBE
Durand, Sir Edward Alan Christopher David Percy, Bt. (1892)
Durant, Sir (Robert) Anthony (Bevis), Kt.
Durie, Sir David Robert Campbell, KCMG
Durrant, Sir William Alexander Estridge, Bt. (1784)
Duthie, *Prof.* Sir Herbert Livingston, Kt.
Duthie, Sir Robert Grieve (Robin), Kt., CBE
Dutton, *Lt-Gen.* Sir James Benjamin, KCB, CBE
Dwyer, Sir Joseph Anthony, Kt.
Dyke, Sir David William Hart, Bt. (1677)
Dymock, *Vice-Adm.* Sir Anthony Knox, KBE, CB
Dyson, Sir James, Kt., CBE
Dyson, *Rt. Hon.* Sir John Anthony, Kt.

Eady, *Hon.* Sir David, Kt.
Eardley-Wilmot, Sir Michael John Assheton, Bt. (1821)
Earle, Sir (Hardman) George (Algernon), Bt. (1869)
Eaton, *Adm.* Sir Kenneth John, GBE, KCB
Eberle, *Adm.* Sir James Henry Fuller, GCB
Ebrahim, Sir (Mahomed) Currimbhoy, Bt. (1910)
Eddington, Sir Roderick Ian, Kt.
Eder, *Hon.* Sir Henry Bernard, Kt.
Edge, *Capt.* Sir (Philip) Malcolm, KCVO
†Edge, Sir William, Bt. (1937)
Edmonstone, Sir Archibald Bruce Charles, Bt. (1774)
Edward, *Rt. Hon.* Sir David Alexander Ogilvy, KCMG
Edwardes, Sir Michael Owen, Kt.
Edwards, Sir Christopher John Churchill, Bt. (1866)
Edwards, *Prof.* Sir Christopher Richard Watkin, Kt.
Edwards, Sir Llewellyn Roy, Kt.
Edwards, Sir Robert Paul, Kt.
Edwards, *Prof.* Sir Samuel Frederick, Kt., FRS
†Edwards-Moss, Sir David John, Bt. (1868)
Edwards-Stuart, *Hon.* Sir Antony James Cobham, Kt.
Egan, Sir John Leopold, Kt.
Ehrman, Sir William Geoffrey, KCMG
Eichelbaum, *Rt. Hon.* Sir Thomas, GBE
Elder, Sir Mark Philip, Kt., CBE
Eldon, Sir Stewart Graham, KCMG, OBE
Elias, *Rt. Hon.* Sir Patrick, Kt.
Eliott of Stobs, Sir Charles Joseph Alexander, Bt. (S. 1666)
Elliot, Sir Gerald Henry, Kt.
Elliott, Sir Clive Christopher Hugh, Bt. (1917)
Elliott, Sir David Murray, KCMG, CB
Elliott, *Prof.* Sir John Huxtable, Kt., FBA
Elliott, *Prof.* Sir Roger James, Kt., FRS
Ellis, Sir Herbert Douglas, Kt., OBE
Ellis, Sir Vernon James, Kt.
Ellwood, Sir Peter Brian, Kt., CBE
Elphinstone, Sir John, Bt. (S. 1701)
Elphinstone, Sir John Howard Main, Bt. (1816)
Elton, Sir Arnold, Kt., CBE
Elton, Sir Charles Abraham Grierson, Bt. (1717)
Elton, Sir Leslie, Kt.
Elvidge, Sir John, KCB
Elwes, *Dr* Sir Henry William, KCVO

Elwes, Sir Jeremy Vernon, Kt., CBE
Elwood, Sir Brian George Conway, Kt., CBE
Elworthy, *Air Cdre. Hon.* Sir Timothy Charles, KCVO, CBE
Enderby, *Prof.* Sir John Edwin, Kt. CBE, FRS
Engle, Sir George Lawrence Jose, KCB, QC
English, Sir Terence Alexander Hawthorne, KBE, FRCS
Ennals, Sir Paul Martin, Kt., CBE
Epstein, *Prof.* Sir (Michael) Anthony, Kt., CBE, FRS
Errington, *Col.* Sir Geoffrey Frederick, Bt. (1963), OBE
Erskine, Sir (Thomas) Peter Neil, Bt. (1821)
Erskine-Hill, Sir Alexander Rodger, Bt. (1945)
Esmonde, Sir Thomas Francis Grattan, Bt. (I. 1629)
Esplen, Sir John Graham, Bt. (1921)
Esquivel, *Rt. Hon.* Sir Manuel, KCMG
Essenhigh, *Adm.* Sir Nigel Richard, GCB
Etherington, Sir Stuart James, Kt.
Etherton, *Rt. Hon.* Sir Terence Michael Elkan Barnet, Kt.
Evans, Sir Anthony Adney, Bt. (1920)
Evans, *Rt. Hon.* Sir Anthony Howell Meurig, Kt., RD
Evans, *Prof.* Sir Christopher Thomas, Kt., OBE
Evans, *Air Chief Marshal* Sir David George, GCB, CBE
Evans, *Hon.* Sir David Roderick, Kt.
Evans, Sir Harold Matthew, Kt.
Evans, *Prof.* Sir John Grimley, Kt., FRCP
Evans, Sir John Stanley, Kt., QPM
Evans, Sir Jonathan, KCB
Evans, *Prof.* Sir Martin John, Kt., FRS
Evans, Sir Richard Harry, Kt., CBE
Evans, *Prof.* Sir Richard John, Kt.
Evans, Sir Robert, Kt., CBE, FRENG
Evans-Lombe, *Hon.* Sir Edward Christopher, Kt.
†Evans-Tipping, Sir David Gwynne, Bt. (1913)
Eveleigh, *Rt. Hon.* Sir Edward Walter, Kt., ERD
Everard, Sir Henry Peter Charles, Bt. (1911)
Every, Sir Henry John Michael, Bt. (1641)
Ewart, Sir William Michael, Bt. (1887)
Eyre, Sir Reginald Edwin, Kt.
Eyre, Sir Richard Charles Hastings, Kt., CBE
Fagge, Sir John Christopher Frederick, Bt. (1660)
Fahy, Sir Peter, Kt., QPM
Fairbairn, Sir (James) Brooke, Bt. (1869)
Fairlie-Cuninghame, Sir Robert Henry, Bt. (S. 1630)
Fairweather, Sir Patrick Stanislaus, KCMG
Faldo, Sir Nicholas Alexander, Kt., MBE
†Falkiner, Sir Benjamin Simon Patrick, Bt. (I. 1778)
Fall, Sir Brian James Proetel, GCVO, KCMG
Falle, Sir Samuel, KCMG, KCVO, DSC
Fang, *Prof.* Sir Harry, Kt., CBE
Fareed, Sir Djamil Sheik, Kt.
Farmer, Sir Thomas, Kt., CVO, CBE
Farquhar, Sir Michael Fitzroy Henry, Bt. (1796)
Farquharson, Sir Angus Durie Miller, KCVO, OBE
Farrell, Sir Terence, Kt., CBE
Farrer, Sir (Charles) Matthew, GCVO
Farrington, Sir Henry William, Bt. (1818)
Fat, Sir (Maxime) Edouard (Lim Man) Lim, Kt.
Faulkner, Sir (James) Dennis (Compton), Kt., CBE, VRD
Fay, Sir (Humphrey) Michael Gerard, Kt.
Fayrer, Sir John Lang Macpherson, Bt. (1896)
Feachem, *Prof.* Sir Richard George Andrew, KBE
Fean, Sir Thomas Vincent, KCVO
Feilden, Sir Henry Rudyard, Bt. (1846)
Feldmann, *Prof.* Sir Marc, Kt.
Fell, Sir David, KCB
Fender, Sir Brian Edward Frederick, Kt., CMG, PHD
Fenn, Sir Nicholas Maxted, GCMG
Fenwick, Sir Leonard Raymond, Kt., CBE
Fergus, Sir Howard Archibald, KBE
Ferguson, Sir Alexander Chapman, Kt., CBE
Ferguson-Davie, Sir Michael, Bt. (1847)
Fergusson of Kilkerran, Sir Charles, Bt. (S. 1703)
Fergusson, Sir Ewan Alastair John, GCMG, GCVO
Fersht, *Prof.* Sir Alan Roy, Kt., FRS
Ferris, *Hon.* Sir Francis Mursell, Kt., TD
ffolkes, Sir Robert Francis Alexander, Bt. (1774), OBE
Field, Sir Malcolm David, Kt.
Field, *Hon.* Sir Richard Alan, Kt.
Fielding, Sir Leslie, KCMG
Fields, Sir Allan Clifford, KCMG
Fieldsend, *Hon.* Sir John Charles Rowell, KBE
Fiennes, Sir Ranulph Twisleton-Wykeham, Bt. (1916), OBE
Figg, Sir Leonard Clifford William, KCMG
Figgis, Sir Anthony St John Howard, KCVO, CMG
Finch, Sir Robert Gerard, Kt.
Finlay, Sir David Ronald James Bell, Bt. (1964)
Finlayson, Sir Garet Orlando, KCMG, OBE
Finney, Sir Thomas, Kt., OBE
†Fison, Sir Charles William, Bt. (1905)
†Fitzgerald, *Revd* Daniel Patrick, Bt. (1903)
FitzGerald, Sir Adrian James Andrew, Bt. (1880)
FitzHerbert, Sir Richard Ranulph, Bt. (1784)
Fitzpatrick, *Air Marshal* Sir John Bernard, KBE, CB
Flanagan, Sir Ronald, GBE
Flanagan, Sir Maurice, KBE
Flaux, *Hon.* Sir Julian Martin, Kt.
Floud, *Prof.* Sir Roderick Castle, Kt.
Floyd, *Rt. Hon.* Sir Christopher David, Kt.
Floyd, Sir Giles Henry Charles, Bt. (1816)
Foley, *Lt.-Gen.* Sir John Paul, KCB, OBE, MC
Follett, *Prof.* Sir Brian Keith, Kt., FRS
Forbes, Sir James Thomas Stewart, Bt. (1823)
Forbes, *Adm.* Sir Ian Andrew, KCB, CBE
Forbes, *Vice-Adm.* Sir John Morrison, KCB
Forbes, *Hon.* Sir Thayne John, Kt.
†Forbes Adam, Revd Stephen Timothy Beilby, Bt. (1917)
Forbes-Leith, Sir George Ian David, Bt. (1923)
Forbes of Craigievar, Sir Andrew Iain Ochoncar, Bt. (S. 1630)
Ford, *Lt-Col.* Sir Andrew Charles, KCVO
Ford, Sir Andrew Russell, Bt. (1929)
Ford, Sir David Robert, KBE, LVO
Ford, Sir John Archibald, KCMG, MC
Ford, *Gen.* Sir Robert Cyril, GCB, CBE
Forestier-Walker, Sir Michael Leolin, Bt. (1835)
Forrest, *Prof.* Sir (Andrew) Patrick (McEwen), Kt.
Forsyth-Johnson, Sir Bruce Joseph, Kt., CBE (Bruce Forsyth)
Forte, Hon. Sir Rocco John Vincent, Kt.
Forwood, Sir Peter Noel, Bt. (1895)
Foskett, *Hon.* Sir David Robert, Kt.
Foster, Sir Andrew William, Kt.
Foster, *Prof.* Sir Christopher David, Kt.
†Foster, Sir Saxby Gregory, Bt. (1930)
Foulkes, Sir Arthur Alexander, GCMG
Fountain, *Hon.* Sir Cyril Stanley Smith, Kt.
Fowke, Sir David Frederick Gustavus, Bt. (1814)
Fowler, Sir (Edward) Michael Coulson, Kt.
Fox, Sir Christopher, Kt., QPM
Fox, Sir Paul Leonard, Kt., CBE
France, Sir Christopher Walter, GCB
Francis, Sir Horace William Alexander, Kt., CBE, FRENG
Frank, Sir Robert Andrew, Bt. (1920)
Franklin, Sir Michael David Milroy, KCB, CMG
Fraser, Sir Charles Annand, KCVO
Fraser, Sir Iain Michael Duncan, Bt. (1943)
Fraser, Sir James Murdo, KBE
Fraser, Sir Simon James, KCMG
Fraser, Sir William Kerr, GCB
Frayling, *Prof.* Sir Christopher John, Kt.
Frederick, Sir Christopher St John, Bt. (1723)
Freedman, *Rt. Hon. Prof.* Sir Lawrence David, KCMG, CBE

Freeland, Sir John Redvers, KCMG
Freeman, Sir James Robin, Bt. (1945)
French, *Air Marshal* Sir Joseph Charles, KCB, CBE
Frere, *Vice-Adm.* Sir Richard Tobias, KCB
Fretwell, Sir (Major) John (Emsley), GCMG
Friend *Prof.* Sir Richard Henry, Kt.
Froggatt, Sir Peter, Kt.
Fry, Sir Graham Holbrook, KCMG
Fry, Sir Peter Derek, Kt.
Fry, *Lt.-Gen.* Sir Robert Allan, KCB, CBE
Fry, *Dr* Sir Roger Gordon, Kt., OBE
Fulford, *Rt. Hon.* Sir Adrian Bruce, Kt.
Fuller, Sir James Henry Fleetwood, Bt. (1910)
Fulton, *Lt.-Gen.* Sir Robert Henry Gervase, KBE
Furness, Sir Stephen Roberts, Bt. (1913)

Gage, *Rt. Hon.* Sir William Marcus, Kt., QC
Gains, Sir John Christopher, Kt.
Gainsford, Sir Ian Derek, Kt.
Gale, Sir Roger James, Kt.
Galsworthy, Sir Anthony Charles, KCMG
Galway, Sir James, Kt., OBE
Gamble, Sir David Hugh Norman, Bt. (1897)
Gambon, Sir Michael John, Kt., CBE
Gammell, Sir William Benjamin Bowring, Kt.
Gardiner, Sir John Eliot, Kt., CBE
Gardner, *Prof.* Sir Richard Lavenham, Kt.
Gardner, Sir Roy Alan, Kt.
Garland, *Hon.* Sir Patrick Neville, Kt.
Garland, *Hon.* Sir Ransley Victor, KBE
Garland, *Dr* Sir Trevor, KBE
Garner, Sir Anthony Stuart, Kt.
Garnett, *Adm.* Sir Ian David Graham, KCB
Garnier, Sir Edward Henry, Kt., QC
Garnier, *Rear-Adm.* Sir John, KCVO, CBE
Garrard, Sir David Eardley, Kt.
Garrett, Sir Anthony Peter, Kt., CBE
Garrick, Sir Ronald, Kt., CBE, FRENG
Garthwaite, Sir (William) Mark (Charles), Bt. (1919)
Gaskell, Sir Richard Kennedy Harvey, Kt.
Gass, Sir Simon Lawrance, KCMG, CVO
Geidt, *Rt. Hon.* Sir Christopher, KCVO, OBE
Geim, *Prof.* Sir Andre Konstantin, Kt.
Geno, Sir Makena Viora, KBE
Gent, Sir Christopher Charles, Kt.
George, Sir Arthur Thomas, Kt.
George, *Prof.* Sir Charles Frederick, Kt., MD, FRCP
George, Sir Richard William, Kt., CVO
Gerken, *Vice-Adm.* Sir Robert William Frank, KCB, CBE
Gershon, Sir Peter Oliver, Kt., CBE
Gethin, Sir Richard Joseph St Lawrence, Bt. (I. 1665)
Gibbings, Sir Peter Walter, Kt.
Gibbons, Sir (John) David, KBE
Gibbons, Sir William Edward Doran, Bt. (1752)
Gibbs, *Hon.* Sir Richard John Hedley, Kt.
Gibbs, Sir Roger Geoffrey, Kt.
†Gibson, *Revd* Christopher Herbert, Bt. (1931)
Gibson, Sir Ian, Kt., CBE
Gibson, Sir Kenneth Archibald, Kt.
Gibson, *Rt. Hon.* Sir Peter Leslie, Kt.
Gibson-Craig-Carmichael, Sir David Peter William, Bt. (S. 1702 and 1831)
Gieve, Sir Edward John Watson, KCB
Giffard, Sir (Charles) Sydney (Rycroft), KCMG
Gilbart-Denham, *Lt.-Col.* Sir Seymour Vivian, KCVO
Gilbert, *Air Chief Marshal* Sir Joseph Alfred, KCB, CBE
Gilbert, *Rt. Hon.* Sir Martin John, Kt., CBE
†Gilbey, Sir Walter Gavin, Bt. (1893)
Gill, Sir Anthony Keith, Kt.
Gill, Sir Arthur Benjamin Norman, Kt., CBE
Gill, Sir Robin Denys, KCVO
Gillam, Sir Patrick John, Kt.
Gillen, *Hon.* Sir John de Winter, Kt.
Gillett, Sir Nicholas Danvers Penrose, Bt. (1959)
Gillinson, Sir Clive Daniel, Kt., CBE
Gilmore, *Prof.* Sir Ian Thomas, Kt.
Gilmour, *Hon.* Sir David Robert, Bt. (1926)
Gilmour, Sir John Nicholas, Bt. (1897)
Gina, Sir Lloyd Maepeza, KBE
Giordano, Sir Richard Vincent, KBE
Girolami, Sir Paul, Kt.
Girvan, *Rt. Hon.* Sir (Frederick) Paul, Kt.
Gladstone, Sir (Erskine) William, Bt. (1846), KG
Glean, Sir Carlyle Arnold, GCMG
Glidewell, *Rt. Hon.* Sir Iain Derek Laing, Kt.
Globe, *Hon.* Sir Henry Brian, Kt.
Glover, Sir Victor Joseph Patrick, Kt.
Glyn, Sir Richard Lindsay, Bt. (1759 and 1800)
Gobbo, Sir James Augustine, Kt., AC
Goldberg, *Prof.* Sir David Paul Brandes, Kt.
Goldring, *Rt. Hon.* Sir John Bernard, Kt.
Gomersall, Sir Stephen John, KCMG
Gonsalves-Sabola, *Hon.* Sir Joaquim Claudino, Kt
Gooch, Sir Miles Peter, Bt. (1866)
Gooch, Sir Arthur Brian Sherlock Heywood, Bt. (1746)
Good, Sir John James Griffen, Kt. CBE
Goodall, Sir (Arthur) David Saunders, GCMG
Goodall, *Air Marshal* Sir Roderick Harvey, KBE, CB, AFC
Goode, Prof. Sir Royston Miles, Kt., CBE, QC
Goodenough, Sir Anthony Michael, KCMG
Goodenough, Sir William McLernon, Bt. (1943)
Goodhart, Sir Philip Carter, Kt.
Goodhart, Sir Robert Anthony Gordon, Bt. (1911)
Goodison, Sir Nicholas Proctor, Kt.
Goodman, Sir Patrick Ledger, Kt., CBE
Goodson, Sir Mark Weston Lassam, Bt. (1922)
Goodwin, Sir Frederick, KBE
Goodwin, Sir Matthew Dean, Kt., CBE
Goody, *Prof.* Sir John Rankine, Kt.
Goold, Sir George William, Bt. (1801)
Gordon, Sir Donald, Kt.
Gordon, Sir Gerald Henry, Kt., CBE, QC
Gordon, Sir Robert James, Bt. (S. 1706)
Gordon-Cumming, Sir Alexander Penrose, Bt. (1804)
Gore, Sir Hugh Frederick Corbet, Bt. (I. 1622)
Gore-Booth, Sir Josslyn Henry Robert, Bt. (I. 1760)
Goring, Sir William Burton Nigel, Bt. (1678)
Gorman, Sir John Reginald, Kt., CVO, CBE, MC
Goschen, Sir (Edward) Alexander, Bt. (1916)
Gosling, Sir (Frederick) Donald, KCVO
Goswell, Sir Brian Lawrence, Kt.
Goulden, Sir (Peter) John, GCMG
Goulding, Sir (William) Lingard Walter, Bt. (1904)
Gourlay, Sir Simon Alexander, Kt.
Gowans, Sir James Learmonth, Kt., CBE, FRCP, FRS
Gowers, *Prof.* Sir William Timothy, Kt.
Gozney, Sir Richard Hugh Turton, KCMG
Graaff, Sir David de Villiers, Bt. (1911)
Grabham, Sir Anthony Henry, Kt.
Graham, Sir Alexander Michael, GBE
Graham, Sir James Bellingham, Bt. (1662)
Graham, Sir James Fergus Surtees, Bt. (1783)
Graham, Sir James Thompson, Kt., CMG
Graham, Sir John Alexander Noble, Bt. (1906), GCMG
Graham, Sir John Alistair, Kt.
Graham, Sir John Moodie, Bt. (1964)
Graham, Sir Peter, KCB, QC
Graham, *Lt.-Gen.* Sir Peter Walter, KCB, CBE
†Graham, Sir Ralph Stuart, Bt. (1629)
Graham-Moon, Sir Peter Wilfred Giles, Bt. (1855)
Graham-Smith, *Prof.* Sir Francis, Kt.
Grange, Sir Kenneth Henry, Kt., CBE
Grant, Sir Archibald, Bt. (S. 1705)
Grant, Sir Clifford, Kt.
Grant, Sir Ian David, Kt., CBE
Grant, Sir (John) Anthony, Kt.
Grant, Sir John Douglas Kelso, KCMG
Grant, *Prof.* Sir Malcolm John, Kt., CBE
Grant, Sir Patrick Alexander Benedict, Bt. (S. 1688)

Grant, Sir Paul Joseph Patrick, Kt.
Grant, *Lt.-Gen.* Sir Scott Carnegie, KCB
Grant-Suttie, Sir James Edward, Bt. (S. 1702)
Granville-Chapman, *Gen.* Sir Timothy John, GBE, KCB, ADC
Grattan-Bellew, Sir Henry Charles, Bt. (1838)
Gray, *Hon.* Sir Charles Anthony St John, Kt.
Gray, Sir Charles Ireland, Kt., CBE
Gray, *Prof.* Sir Denis John Pereira, Kt., OBE, FRCGP
Gray, *Dr.* Sir John Armstrong Muir, Kt., CBE
Gray, Sir Robert McDowall (Robin), Kt.
Gray, Sir William Hume, Bt. (1917)
Graydon, *Air Chief Marshal* Sir Michael James, GCB, CBE
Grayson, Sir Jeremy Brian Vincent Harrington, Bt. (1922)
Green, Sir Allan David, KCB, QC
Green, Sir Andrew Fleming, KCMG
Green, Sir Edward Patrick Lycett, Bt. (1886)
Green, Sir Gregory David, KCMG
Green, *Hon.* Sir Guy Stephen Montague, KBE
Green, *Prof.* Sir Malcolm, Kt.
Green, Sir Owen Whitley, Kt.
Green, Sir Philip Green, Kt.
Green-Price, Sir Robert John, Bt. (1874)
Greenaway, Sir John Michael Burdick, Bt. (1933)
Greenbury, Sir Richard, Kt.
Greener, Sir Anthony Armitage, Kt.
Greengross, Sir Alan David, Kt.
Greenstock, Sir Jeremy Quentin, GCMG
Greenwell, Sir Edward Bernard, Bt. (1906)
Greenwood, *Prof.* Sir Brian Mellor, Kt., CBE
Greenwood, *Prof.* Sir Christopher John, Kt., CMG
Gregory, *Prof.* Sir Michael John, Kt., CBE
Gregson, Sir Peter John, Kt.
Gregson, Sir Peter Lewis, GCB
Grey, Sir Anthony Dysart, Bt. (1814)
†Grey-Egerton, Sir William de Malpas, Bt. (1617)
Grierson, Sir Ronald Hugh, Kt.
Griffiths, Sir Eldon Wylie, Kt.
Grigson, *Hon.* Sir Geoffrey Douglas, Kt.
Grimshaw, Sir Nicholas Thomas, Kt., CBE
Grimwade, Sir Andrew Sheppard, Kt., CBE
Grose, *Vice-Adm.* Sir Alan, KBE
Gross, *Rt. Hon.* Sir Peter Henry, Kt.
Grossart, Sir Angus McFarlane McLeod, Kt., CBE
Grotrian, Sir Philip Christian Brent, Bt. (1934)
Ground, Sir Richard William, Kt., OBE, QC
Grove, Sir Charles Gerald, Bt. (1874)
Grundy, Sir Mark, Kt.
Guinness, Sir Howard Christian Sheldon, Kt., VRD
Guinness, Sir John Ralph Sidney, Kt., CB
Guinness, Sir Kenelm Edward Lee, Bt. (1867)
Guise, Sir Christopher James, Bt. (1783)
Gull, Sir Rupert William Cameron, Bt. (1872)
Gumbs, Sir Emile Rudolph, Kt.
Gunn, Sir Robert Norman, Kt.
Gunning, Sir Charles Theodore, Bt. (1778)
Gunston, Sir John Wellesley, Bt. (1938)
Gurdon, *Prof.* Sir John Bertrand, Kt., DPHIL, FRS
Guthrie, Sir Malcolm Connop, Bt. (1936)

Haddacks, *Vice-Adm.* Sir Paul Kenneth, KCB
Haddon-Cave, *Hon.* Sir Charles Anthony, Kt.
Hadlee, Sir Richard John, Kt., MBE
Hagart-Alexander, Sir Claud, Bt. (1886)
Hague, *Prof.* Sir Douglas Chalmers, Kt., CBE
Haines, *Prof.* Sir Andrew Paul, Kt.
Haji-Ioannou, Sir Stelios, Kt.
Halberg, Sir Murray Gordon, Kt., MBE
Hall, *Dr* Sir Andrew James, Kt.
Hall, *Prof.* Sir David Michael Baldock, Kt.
Hall, Sir Ernest, Kt., OBE
Hall, Sir Geoffrey, Kt.
Hall, Sir Graham Joseph, Kt.
Hall, Sir Iain Robert, Kt.
Hall, Sir (Frederick) John (Frank), Bt. (1923)
Hall, Sir John, Kt.
Hall, Sir John Bernard, Bt. (1919)
Hall, Sir John Douglas Hoste, Bt. (S. 1687)
Hall, HE *Prof.* Sir Kenneth Octavius, GCMG
Hall, Sir Peter Edward, KBE, CMG
Hall, *Prof.* Sir Peter Geoffrey, Kt., FBA
Hall, Sir Peter Reginald Frederick, Kt., CBE
Hall, *Revd* Wesley Winfield, Kt.
Hall, Sir William Joseph, KCVO
Halpern, Sir Ralph Mark, Kt.
Halsey, *Revd* John Walter Brooke, Bt. (1920)
Halstead, Sir Ronald, Kt., CBE
Hamblen, *Hon.* Sir Nicholas Archibald, Kt.
†Hambling, Sir Herbert Peter Hugh, Bt. (1924)
Hamilton, Sir Andrew Caradoc, Bt. (S. 1646)
Hamilton, Sir Nigel, KCB
Hamilton-Dalrymple, *Maj.* Sir Hew Fleetwood, Bt. (S. 1698), GCVO
Hamilton-Spencer-Smith, Sir John, Bt. (1804)
Hammick, Sir Stephen George, Bt. (1834)
Hammond, Sir Anthony Hilgrove, KCB, QC
Hampel, Sir Ronald Claus, Kt.
Hampson, Sir Stuart, Kt.
Hampton, Sir (Leslie) Geoffrey, Kt.
Hampton, Sir Philip Roy, Kt.
Hanbury-Tenison, Sir Richard, KCVO
Hancock, Sir David John Stowell, KCB
Hanham, Sir William John Edward, Bt. (1667)
Hankes-Drielsma, Sir Claude Dunbar, KCVO
Hanley, *Rt. Hon.* Sir Jeremy James, KCMG
Hanmer, Sir Wyndham Richard Guy, Bt. (1774)
Hannam, Sir John Gordon, Kt.
Hanson, Sir (Charles) Rupert (Patrick), Bt. (1918)
Hanson, Sir John Gilbert, KCMG, CBE
Harcourt-Smith, *Air Chief Marshal* Sir David, GBE, KCB, DFC
Hardie Boys, *Rt. Hon.* Sir Michael, GCMG
Harding, Sir George William, KCMG, CVO
Harding, *Marshal of the Royal Air Force* Sir Peter Robin, GCB
Hardy, Sir David William, Kt.
Hardy, Sir James Gilbert, Kt., OBE
Hardy, Sir Richard Charles Chandos, Bt. (1876)
Hare, Sir David, Kt., FRSL
Hare, Sir Nicholas Patrick, Bt. (1818)
Haren, *Dr* Sir Patrick Hugh, Kt.
Harford, Sir Mark John, Bt. (1934)
Harington, Sir Nicholas John, Bt. (1611)
Harkness, *Very Revd* James, KCVO, CB, OBE
Harley, *Gen.* Sir Alexander George Hamilton, KBE, CB
Harman, *Hon.* Sir Jeremiah LeRoy, Kt.
Harman, Sir John Andrew, Kt.
Harmsworth, Sir Hildebrand Harold, Bt. (1922)
Harper, *Air Marshal* Sir Christopher Nigel, KBE
Harper, Sir Ewan William, Kt. CBE
Harper, *Prof.* Sir Peter Stanley, Kt., CBE
Harris, Sir Christopher John Ashford, Bt. (1932)
Harris, *Prof.* Sir Henry, Kt., FRCP, FRCPATH, FRS
Harris, *Air Marshal* Sir John Hulme, KCB, CBE
Harris, *Prof.* Sir Martin Best, Kt., CBE
Harris, Sir Michael Frank, Kt.
Harris, Sir (Theodore) Wilson, Kt.
Harris, Sir Thomas George, KBE, CMG,
Harrison, *Prof.* Sir Brian Howard, Kt.
Harrison, Sir David, Kt., CBE, FRENG
Harrison, *Hon.* Sir Michael Guy Vicat, Kt.
Harrison, Sir Michael James Harwood, Bt. (1961)
Harrison, Sir (Robert) Colin, Bt. (1922)
Harrison, Sir Terence, Kt., FRENG
Harrop, Sir Peter John, KCB
Hart, *Hon.* Sir Anthony Ronald, Kt.
Hart, Sir Graham Allan, KCB
Hartwell, Sir (Francis) Anthony Charles Peter, Bt. (1805)

Harvey, Sir Charles Richard Musgrave, Bt. (1933)
Harvey, Sir Nicholas Barton, Kt.
Harvie, Sir John Smith, Kt., CBE
Harvie-Watt, Sir James, Bt. (1945)
Harwood, Sir Ronald, Kt., CBE
Haselhurst, *Rt. Hon.* Sir Alan Gordon Barraclough, Kt.
Haskard, Sir Cosmo Dugal Patrick Thomas, KCMG, MBE
Hastie, *Cdre* Sir Robert Cameron, KCVO, CBE, RD
Hastings, Sir Max Macdonald, Kt.
Hastings, *Dr* Sir William George, Kt., CBE
Hatter, Sir Maurice, Kt.
Havelock-Allan, Sir (Anthony) Mark David, Bt. (1858)
Hawkes, Sir John Garry, Kt., CBE
Hawkhead, Sir Anthony Gerard, Kt., CBE
Hawkins, Sir Richard Caesar, Bt. (1778)
†Hawley, Sir Henry Nicholas, Bt. (1795)
Hawley, Sir James Appleton, KCVO, TD
Haworth, Sir Philip, Bt. (1911)
Hay, Sir David Russell, Kt., CBE, FRCP, MD
Hay, Sir John Erroll Audley, Bt. (S. 1663)
†Hay, Sir Ronald Frederick Hamilton, Bt. (S. 1703)
Hayes, Sir Brian, Kt., CBE, QPM
Hayes, Sir Brian David, GCB
Hayman-Joyce, *Lt.-Gen.* Sir Robert John, KCB, CBE
Hayter, Sir Paul David Grenville, KCB, LVO
Hayward, Sir Jack Arnold, Kt., OBE
Head, Sir Richard Douglas Somerville, Bt. (1838)
Heap, Sir Peter William, KCMG
Heap, *Prof.* Sir Robert Brian, Kt., CBE, FRS
Hearne, Sir Graham James, Kt., CBE
Heathcote, *Brig.* Sir Gilbert Simon, Bt. (1733), CBE
†Heathcote, Sir Timothy Gilbert, Bt. (1733)
Heatley, Sir Peter, Kt., CBE
Hedley, *Hon.* Sir Mark, Kt.
Hegarty, Sir John Kevin, Kt.
Heiser, Sir Terence Michael, GCB
Heller, Sir Michael Aron, Kt.
Henderson, Sir Denys Hartley, Kt.
Henderson, *Hon.* Sir Launcelot Dinadan James, Kt.
Henderson, *Maj.* Sir Richard Yates, KCVO
Hendry, *Prof.* Sir David Forbes, Kt.
Hendy, Sir Peter Gerard, Kt., CBE
Hennessy, Sir James Patrick Ivan, KBE, CMG
†Henniker, Sir Adrian Chandos, Bt. (1813)
Henniker-Heaton, Sir Yvo Robert, Bt. (1912)
Henriques, *Hon.* Sir Richard Henry Quixano, Kt.
†Henry, Sir Patrick Denis, Bt. (1923)
Henshaw, Sir David George, Kt.
Hepple, *Prof.* Sir Bob Alexander, Kt.
Herbecq, Sir John Edward, KCB
Herbert, *Adm.* Sir Peter Geoffrey Marshall, KCB, OBE
Heron, Sir Conrad Frederick, KCB, OBE
Heron, Sir Michael Gilbert, Kt.
Heron-Maxwell, Sir Nigel Mellor, Bt. (S. 1683)
Hervey, Sir Roger Blaise Ramsay, KCVO, CMG
Hervey-Bathurst, Sir Frederick William John, Bt. (1818)
Heseltine, *Rt. Hon.* Sir William Frederick Payne, GCB, GCVO
Hewetson, Sir Christopher Raynor, Kt., TD
Hewett, Sir Richard Mark John, Bt. (1813)
Hewitt, Sir (Cyrus) Lenox (Simson), Kt., OBE
Hewitt, Sir Nicholas Charles Joseph, Bt. (1921)
Heygate, Sir Richard John Gage, Bt. (1831)
Heywood, Sir Jeremy John, KCB, CVO
Heywood, Sir Peter, Bt. (1838)
Hickinbottom, *Hon.* Sir Gary Robert, Kt.
Hickman, Sir (Richard) Glenn, Bt. (1903)
Hicks, Sir Robert, Kt.
Hidden, *Hon.* Sir Anthony Brian, Kt.
Hielscher, Sir Leo Arthur, Kt.
Higgins, Sir David Hartmann, Kt.
Higgins, *Rt. Hon.* Sir Malachy Joseph, Kt.
Hildyard, *Hon.* Sir Robert Henry Thoroton, Kt.
Hill, Sir Arthur Alfred, Kt., CBE
Hill, Sir Brian John, Kt.
Hill, *Prof.* Sir Geoffrey William, Kt.
Hill, Sir James Frederick, Bt. (1917)
Hill, Sir John Alfred Rowley, Bt. (I. 1779)
Hill, *Vice-Adm.* Sir Robert Charles Finch, KBE, FRENG
Hill-Norton, *Vice-Adm. Hon.* Sir Nicholas John, KCB
Hill-Wood, Sir Samuel Thomas, Bt. (1921)
Hillhouse, Sir (Robert) Russell, KCB
Hills, Sir Graham John, Kt.
Hills, Sir John Robert, Kt., CBE
Hilly, Sir Francis Billy, KCMG
Hine, *Air Chief Marshal* Sir Patrick Bardon, GCB, GBE
Hintze, Sir Michael, Kt.
Hirsch, *Prof.* Sir Peter Bernhard, Kt., PHD, FRS
Hirst, Sir Michael William, Kt.
Hoare, *Prof.* Sir Charles Anthony Richard, Kt., FRS
Hoare, Sir David John, Bt. (1786)
Hoare, Sir Charles James, Bt. (I. 1784)
Hobart, Sir John Vere, Bt. (1914)
Hobbs, *Maj.-Gen.* Sir Michael Frederick, KCVO, CBE
Hobday, Sir Gordon Ivan, Kt.
Hobhouse, Sir Charles John Spinney, Bt. (1812)
Hobson, Sir Ronald, KCVO
†Hodge, Sir Andrew Rowland, Bt. (1921)
Hodge, Sir James William, KCVO, CMG
Hodgkin, Sir (Gordon) Howard (Eliot), Kt., CH, CBE
Hodgkinson, Sir Michael Stewart, Kt.
Hodgson, Sir Maurice Arthur Eric, Kt., FRENG
Hodson, Sir Michael Robin Adderley, Bt. (I. 1789)
Hogan-Howe, Sir Bernard, Kt., QPM
Hogg, Sir Christopher Anthony, Kt.
Hogg, Sir Piers Michael James, Bt. (1846)
Holcroft, Sir Charles Anthony Culcheth, Bt. (1921)
Holden, Sir Paul, Bt. (1893)
Holden, Sir John David, Bt. (1919)
Holden-Brown, Sir Derrick, Kt.
Holder, Sir John Henry, Bt. (1898)
Holderness, Sir Martin William, Bt. (1920)
Holdgate, Sir Martin Wyatt, Kt., CB, PHD
Holland, *Hon.* Sir Alan Douglas, Kt.
Holland, *Hon.* Sir Christopher John, Kt.
Holland, Sir Geoffrey, KCB
Holland, Sir John Anthony, Kt.
Holliday, *Prof.* Sir Frederick George Thomas, Kt., CBE, FRSE
Hollom, Sir Jasper Quintus, KBE
Holm, Sir Ian (Holm Cuthbert), Kt., CBE
Holman, *Hon.* Sir (Edward) James, Kt.
Holman, *Prof.* Sir John Stranger, Kt.
Holmes, Sir John Eaton, GCVO, KBE, CMG
Holroyd, *Air Marshal* Sir Frank Martyn, KBE, CB
Holroyd, Sir Michael De Courcy Fraser, Kt., CBE
Holroyde, *Hon.* Sir Timothy Victor, Kt.
Holt, *Prof.* Sir James Clarke, Kt.
Home, Sir William Dundas, Bt. (S. 1671)
Honywood, Sir Filmer Courtenay William, Bt. (1660)
†Hood, Sir John Joseph Harold, Bt. (1922)
Hookway, Sir Harry Thurston, Kt.
Hooper, *Rt. Hon.* Sir Anthony, Kt.
Hope, Sir Colin Frederick Newton, Kt.
Hope, Sir Alexander Archibald Douglas, Bt. (S. 1628)
Hope-Dunbar, Sir David, Bt. (S. 1664)
Hopkin, *Prof.* Sir Deian Rhys, Kt.
Hopkin, Sir Royston Oliver, KCMG
Hopkins, Sir Anthony Philip, Kt., CBE
Hopkins, Sir Michael John, Kt., CBE, RA, RIBA
Hopwood, *Prof.* Sir David Alan, Kt., FRS
Hordern, *Rt. Hon.* Sir Peter Maudslay, Kt.
Horlick, *Vice-Adm.* Sir Edwin John, KBE, FRENG
Horlick, Sir James Cunliffe William, Bt. (1914)
Horlock, *Prof.* Sir John Harold, Kt., FRS, FRENG
Horn-Smith, Sir Julian Michael, Kt.

Hornby, Sir Derek Peter, Kt.
Horne, Sir Alan Gray Antony, Bt. (1929)
Horne, *Dr* Sir Alistair Allan, Kt. CBE
Horner, *Hon.* Sir Thomas Mark, Kt.
Horsbrugh-Porter, Sir Andrew Alexander Marshall, Bt. (1902)
Horsfall, Sir Edward John Wright, Bt. (1909)
Hort, Sir Andrew Edwin Fenton, Bt. (1767)
Hosker, Sir Gerald Albery, KCB, QC
Hoskins, *Prof.* Sir Brian John, Kt. CBE, FRS
†Hoskyns, Sir Edwyn Wren, Bt. (1676)
Hoskyns, Sir John Austin Hungerford Leigh, Kt.
Hotung, Sir Joseph Edward, Kt.
Houghton, *Gen.* Sir John Nicholas Reynolds, GCB, CBE
Houghton, Sir John Theodore, Kt., CBE, FRS
Houghton, Sir Stephen Geoffrey, Kt., CBE
Houldsworth, Sir Richard Thomas Reginald, Bt. (1887)
Hourston, Sir Gordon Minto, Kt.
Housden, Sir Peter James, KCB
House, Sir Stephen, Kt., QPM
Houssemayne du Boulay, Sir Roger William, KCVO, CMG
Houstoun-Boswall, Sir (Thomas) Alford, Bt. (1836)
Howard, Sir David Howarth Seymour, Bt. (1955)
Howard, *Prof.* Sir Michael Eliot, Kt., OM, CH, CBE, MC
Howard-Lawson, Sir John Philip, Bt. (1841)
Howarth, Sir (James) Gerald Douglas, Kt.
Howells, Sir Eric Waldo Benjamin, Kt., CBE
Howes, Sir Christopher Kingston, KCVO, CB
Howlett, *Gen.* Sir Geoffrey Hugh Whitby, KBE, MC
Hoy, Sir Christopher Andrew, Kt., MBE
Hugh-Jones, Sir Wynn Normington, Kt., LVO
Hughes, *Rt. Hon.* Sir Anthony Philip Gilson, Kt.
Hughes, Sir Thomas Collingwood, Bt. (1773)
Hughes, Sir Trevor Poulton, KCB
Hughes-Hallett, Sir Thomas Michael Sydney, Kt.
Hughes-Morgan, Sir (Ian) Parry David, Bt. (1925)
Hull, *Prof.* Sir David, Kt.
Hulse, Sir Edward Jeremy Westrow, Bt. (1739)
Hum, Sir Christopher Owen, KCMG
Humphreys, *Prof.* Sir Colin John, Kt., CBE
Hunt, Sir John Leonard, Kt.
Hunt, *Adm.* Sir Nicholas John Streynsham, GCB, LVO
Hunt, *Dr* Sir Richard Timothy, Kt.
Hunt-Davis, *Brig.* Sir Miles Garth, GCVO, CBE
Hunter, Sir Alistair John, KCMG
Hunter, *Prof.* Sir Laurence Colvin, Kt., CBE, FRSE
Hunter, *Dr* Sir Philip John, Kt., CBE
Hunter, Sir Thomas Blane, Kt.
Huntington-Whiteley, Sir Hugo Baldwin, Bt. (1918)
Hurn, Sir (Francis) Roger, Kt.
Hurst, Sir Geoffrey Charles, Kt., MBE
Husbands, Sir Clifford Straugh, GCMG
Hutchison, *Rt. Hon.* Sir Michael, Kt.
Hutchison, Sir Peter Craft, Bt. (1956), CBE
Hutchison, Sir Robert, Bt. (1939)
Hutt, Sir Dexter Walter, Kt.
Huxtable, *Gen.* Sir Charles Richard, KCB, CBE
Hytner, Sir Nicholas, Kt.
Iacobescu, Sir George, Kt., CBE
Ibbotson, *Vice-Adm.* Sir Richard Jeffrey, KBE, CB, DSC
Ibbs, Sir (John) Robin, KBE
Imbert-Terry, Sir Michael Edward Stanley, Bt. (1917)
Imray, Sir Colin Henry, KBE, CMG
Ingham, Sir Bernard, Kt.
Ingilby, Sir Thomas Colvin William, Bt. (1866)
Inglis, Sir Brian Scott, Kt.
Inglis of Glencorse, Sir Roderick John, Bt. (S. 1703)
Ingram, Sir James Herbert Charles, Bt. (1893)
Ingram, Sir John Henderson, Kt., CBE
Inkin, Sir Geoffrey David, Kt., OBE
Innes, Sir Alastair Charles Deverell, Bt. (NS 1686)
Innes of Edingight, Sir Malcolm Rognvald, KCVO
Innes, Sir Peter Alexander Berowald, Bt. (S. 1628)
Insall, Sir Donald William, Kt., CBE
Irvine, Sir Donald Hamilton, Kt., CBE, MD, FRCGP
Irving, *Prof.* Sir Miles Horsfall, Kt., MD, FRCS, FRCSE
Irwin, *Lt.-Gen.* Sir Alistair Stuart Hastings, KCB, CBE
Irwin, *Hon.* Sir Stephen John, Kt.
Isaacs, Sir Jeremy Israel, Kt.
Isham, Sir Norman Murray Crawford, Bt. (1627), OBE
Italeli, *HE* Sir Iakoba Taeia, GCMG
Ive, Sir Jonathan Paul, KBE
Ivory, Sir Brian Gammell, Kt., CBE
Jack, Sir Malcolm Roy, KCB
Jack, *Hon.* Sir Raymond Evan, Kt.
Jackling, Sir Roger Tustin, KCB, CBE
Jackson, Sir Barry Trevor, Kt.
Jackson, Sir Kenneth Joseph, Kt.
Jackson, *Gen.* Sir Michael David, GCB, CBE
Jackson, Sir Michael Roland, Bt. (1902)
†Jackson, Sir Neil Keith, Bt. (1815)
Jackson, Sir Nicholas Fane St George, Bt. (1913)
Jackson, *Hon.* Sir Peter Arthur Brian, Kt.
Jackson, *Rt. Hon.* Sir Rupert Matthew, Kt.
Jackson, Sir (William) Roland Cedric, Bt. (1869)
Jacob, *Rt. Hon.* Sir Robert Raphael Hayim (Robin), Kt.
Jacobi, Sir Derek George, Kt., CBE
Jacobs, Sir Cecil Albert, Kt., CBE
Jacobs, *Rt. Hon.* Sir Francis Geoffrey, KCMG, QC
Jacobs, *Hon.* Sir Kenneth Sydney, KBE
Jacomb, Sir Martin Wakefield, Kt.
Jaffray, Sir William Otho, Bt. (1892)
Jagger, Sir Michael Philip, Kt.
James, Sir Cynlais Morgan, KCMG
James, Sir Jeffrey Russell, KBE
James, Sir John Nigel Courtenay, KCVO, CBE
Jardine of Applegirth, Sir William Murray, Bt. (S. 1672)
Jardine, Sir Andrew Colin Douglas, Bt. (1916)
Jarman, *Prof.* Sir Brian, Kt., OBE
Jarratt, Sir Alexander Anthony, Kt., CB
Jawara, *Hon.* Sir Dawda Kairaba, Kt.
Jay, Sir Antony Rupert, Kt., CVO
Jeewoolall, Sir Ramesh, Kt.
Jeffrey, Sir William Alexander, KCB
Jeffreys, *Prof.* Sir Alec John, Kt., FRS
Jeffries, *Hon.* Sir John Francis, Kt.
Jehangir, Sir Cowasji, Bt. (1908)
†Jejeebhoy, Sir Jehangir, Bt. (1857)
Jenkins, Sir Brian Garton, GBE
Jenkins, Sir Elgar Spencer, Kt., OBE
Jenkins, Sir James Christopher, KCB, QC
Jenkins, Sir John, KCMG, LVO
Jenkins, Sir Michael Nicholas Howard, Kt., OBE
Jenkins, Sir Paul Christopher, KCB
Jenkins, Sir Simon, Kt.
Jenkinson, Sir John Banks, Bt. (1661)
Jenks, Sir (Richard) Peter, Bt. (1932)
Jenner, *Air Marshal* Sir Timothy Ivo, KCB
Jennings, Sir John Southwood, Kt., CBE, FRSE
Jennings, Sir Peter Neville Wake, Kt., CVO
†Jephcott, Sir David Welbourn, Bt. (1962)
Jessel, Sir Charles John, Bt. (1883)
Jewkes, Sir Gordon Wesley, KCMG
Job, Sir Peter James Denton, Kt.
John, Sir David Glyndwr, KCMG
John, Sir Elton Hercules (Reginald Kenneth Dwight), Kt., CBE
Johns, *Vice-Adm.* Sir Adrian James, KCB, CBE, ADC
Johns, *Air Chief Marshal* Sir Richard Edward, GCB, KCVO, CBE
Johnson, Sir Colpoys Guy, Bt. (1755)
Johnson, *Gen.* Sir Garry Dene, KCB, OBE, MC
Johnson, Sir John Rodney, KCMG
†Johnson, Sir Patrick Eliot, Bt. (1818)
Johnson, *Hon.* Sir Robert Lionel, Kt.
Johnson-Ferguson, Sir Ian Edward, Bt. (1906)
Johnston, *Lt.-Gen.* Sir Maurice Robert, KCB, CVO, OBE
Johnston, Sir Thomas Alexander, Bt. (S. 1626)
Johnston, Sir William Ian Ridley, Kt., CBE, QPM
Johnstone, Sir Geoffrey Adams Dinwiddie, KCMG

Johnstone, Sir (George) Richard Douglas, Bt. (S.1700)
Johnstone, Sir (John) Raymond, Kt., CBE
Jolliffe, Sir Anthony Stuart, GBE
Jolly, Sir Arthur Richard, KCMG
Jonas, Sir John Peter, Kt., CBE
Jones, Sir Alan Jeffrey, Kt.
Jones, Sir David Charles, Kt., CBE
Jones, Sir Harry George, Kt., CBE
Jones, Sir John Francis, Kt.
Jones, Sir Kenneth Lloyd, Kt., QPM
Jones, Sir Lyndon, Kt.
Jones, Sir Mark Ellis Powell, Kt.
Jones, Sir (Owen) Trevor, Kt.
Jones, Sir Richard Anthony Lloyd, KCB
Jones, Sir Robert Edward, Kt.
Jones, Sir Roger Spencer, Kt., OBE
Jones, Sir Simon Warley Frederick Benton, Bt. (1919)
†Joseph, *Hon.* Sir James Samuel, Bt. (1943)
Jowell, *Prof.* Sir Jeffrey Lionel, KCMG, QC
Jowitt, *Hon.* Sir Edwin Frank, Kt.
Judge, Sir Paul Rupert, Kt.
Jugnauth, *Rt. Hon.* Sir Anerood, KCMG
Jungius, *Vice-Adm.* Sir James George, KBE

Kaberry, *Hon.* Sir Christopher Donald, Bt. (1960)
Kabui, Sir Frank Utu Ofagioro, GCMG, OBE
Kadoorie, *Hon.* Sir Michael David, Kt.
Kakaraya, Sir Pato, KBE
Kamit, Sir Leonard Wilson, Kt., CBE
Kao, *Prof.* Sir Charles Kuen, KBE
Kapoor, Sir Anish Mikhail, Kt., CBE
Kaputin, Sir John Rumet, KBE, CMG
Kaufman, *Rt. Hon.* Sir Gerald Bernard, Kt.
Kavali, Sir Thomas, Kt., OBE
Kay, *Rt. Hon.* Sir Maurice Ralph, Kt.
Kaye, Sir Paul Henry Gordon, Bt. (1923)
Keane, Sir John Charles, Bt. (1801)
Kearney, *Hon.* Sir William John Francis, Kt., CBE
Keegan, *Dr* Sir Donal Arthur John, KCVO, OBE
Keene, *Rt. Hon.* Sir David Wolfe, Kt.
Keith, *Hon.* Sir Brian Richard, Kt.
Keith, *Rt. Hon.* Sir Kenneth, KBE
†Kellett, Sir Stanley Charles, Bt. (1801)
Kelly, Sir Christopher William, KCB
Kelly, Sir David Robert Corbett, Kt., CBE
Kemakeza, Sir Allan, Kt.
Kemball, *Air Marshal* Sir (Richard) John, KCB, CBE
Kemp-Welch, Sir John, Kt.
Kenilorea, *Rt. Hon.* Sir Peter, KBE
Kennaway, Sir John Lawrence, Bt. (1791)
Kennedy, Sir Francis, KCMG, CBE
†Kennedy, Sir George Matthew Rae, Bt. (1836)
Kennedy, *Hon.* Sir Ian Alexander, Kt.
Kennedy, *Prof.* Sir Ian McColl, Kt.
Kennedy, *Rt. Hon.* Sir Paul Joseph Morrow, Kt.
Kennedy, *Air Chief Marshal* Sir Thomas Lawrie, GCB, AFC
Kenny, Sir Anthony John Patrick, Kt., DPHIL, DLITT, FBA
Kenny, *Gen.* Sir Brian Leslie Graham, GCB, CBE
Kentridge, Sir Sydney Woolf, KCMG, QC
Kenyon, Sir Nicholas Roger, Kt., CBE
Keogh, *Prof.* Sir Bruce Edward, KBE
Kerr, *Adm.* Sir John Beverley, GCB
Kerr, Sir Ronald James, Kt., CB
Kershaw, *Prof.* Sir Ian, Kt.
Kerslake, Sir Robert Walker, Kt.
Keswick, Sir Henry Neville Lindley, Kt.
Keswick, Sir John Chippendale Lindley, Kt.
Kevau, *Prof.* Sir Isi Henao, Kt., CBE
Khaw, *Prof.* Sir Peng Tee, Kt.
Kikau, *Ratu* Sir Jone Latianara, KBE
†Kimber, Sir Rupert Edward Watkin, Bt. (1904)
King, *Prof.* Sir David Anthony, Kt., FRS
King, Sir John Christopher, Bt. (1888)
King, *Hon.* Sir Timothy Roger Alan, Kt.
King, Sir Wayne Alexander, Bt. (1815)
Kingman, *Prof.* Sir John Frank Charles, Kt., FRS
Kingsley, Sir Ben, Kt.
Kinloch, Sir David, Bt. (S. 1686)
Kinloch, Sir David Oliphant, Bt. (1873)
Kipalan, Sir Albert, Kt.
Kirch, Sir David Roderick, KBE
Kirkpatrick, Sir Ivone Elliott, Bt. (S. 1685)
Kirkwood, *Hon.* Sir Andrew Tristram Hammett, Kt.
Kiszely, *Lt.-Gen.* Sir John Panton, KCB, MC
Kitchin, *Rt. Hon.* Sir David James Tyson, Kt.
Kitson, *Gen.* Sir Frank Edward, GBE, KCB, MC
Kitson, Sir Timothy Peter Geoffrey, Kt.
Kleinwort, Sir Richard Drake, Bt. (1909)
Klug, Sir Aaron, Kt., OM
Knight, Sir Harold Murray, KBE, DSc
Knight, Sir Kenneth John, Kt., CBE, QFSM
Knight, *Air Chief Marshal* Sir Michael William Patrick, KCB, AFC
Knight, *Prof.* Sir Peter, Kt.
Knill, Sir Thomas John Pugin Bartholomew, Bt. (1893)
Knowles, Sir Charles Francis, Bt. (1765)
Knowles, Sir Durward Randolph, Kt., OBE
Knowles, Sir Nigel Graham, Kt.
Knox, Sir David Laidlaw, Kt.
Knox, *Hon.* Sir John Leonard, Kt.
Knox-Johnston, Sir William Robert Patrick (Sir Robin), Kt., CBE, RD
Kohn, *Dr* Sir Ralph, Kt.
Koraea, Sir Thomas, Kt.
Kornberg, *Prof.* Sir Hans Leo, Kt., DSc, SCD, PHD, FRS
Korowi, Sir Wiwa, GCMG
Kroto, *Prof.* Sir Harold Walter, Kt., FRS
Kulukundis, Sir Elias George (Eddie), Kt., OBE
Kwok-Po Li, *Dr* Sir David, Kt., OBE

Lachmann, *Prof.* Sir Peter Julius, Kt.
Lacon, Sir Edmund Vere, Bt. (1818)
Lacy, Sir Patrick Brian Finucane, Bt. (1921)
Laing, Sir (John) Martin (Kirby), Kt., CBE
Laird, Sir Gavin Harry, Kt., CBE
†Lake, Sir Edward, Bt. (1711)
Lakin, Sir Michael, Bt. (1909)
Lamb, Sir Albert Thomas, KBE, CMG, DFC
Lamb, *Lt.-Gen.* Sir Graeme Cameron Maxwell, KBE, CMG, DSO
Lambert, Sir John Henry, KCVO, CMG
Lambert, *Vice-Adm.* Sir Paul, KCB
†Lambert, Sir Peter John Biddulph, Bt. (1711)
Lambert, Sir Richard Peter, Kt.
Lampl, Sir Peter, Kt., OBE
Lamport, Sir Stephen Mark Jeffrey, KCVO
Landale, Sir David William Neil, KCVO
Landau, Sir Dennis Marcus, Kt.
Lander, Sir Stephen James, KCB
Lane, Prof. Sir David Philip, Kt.
Langham, Sir John Stephen, Bt. (1660)
Langlands, Sir Robert Alan, Kt.
Langley, *Hon.* Sir Gordon Julian Hugh, Kt.
Langrishe, Sir James Hercules, Bt. (I. 1777)
Langstaff, *Hon.* Sir Brian Frederick James, Kt.
Lankester, Sir Timothy Patrick, KCB
Lapli, Sir John Ini, GCMG
Lapthorne, Sir Richard Douglas, Kt., CBE
Large, Sir Andrew McLeod Brooks, Kt.
Latasi, *Rt. Hon.* Sir Kamuta, KCMG, OBE
Latham, *Rt. Hon.* Sir David Nicholas Ramsey, Kt.
Latham, Sir Michael Anthony, Kt.
Latham, Sir Richard Thomas Paul, Bt. (1919)
Latimer, Sir Graham Stanley, KBE
Latour-Adrien, *Hon.* Sir Maurice, Kt.
Laughton, Sir Anthony Seymour, Kt.
Laurence, *Vice-Adm.* Sir Timothy James Hamilton, KCVO, CB, ADC
Laurie, Sir Robert Bayley Emilius, Bt. (1834)
Lauterpacht, Sir Elihu, Kt., CBE, QC
Lauti, *Rt. Hon.* Sir Toaripi, GCMG
Lawler, Sir Peter James, Kt., OBE
Lawrence, Sir Clive Wyndham, Bt. (1906)
Lawrence, Sir Edmund Wickham, GCMG, OBE
Lawrence, Sir Henry Peter, Bt. (1858)
Lawrence, Sir Ivan John, Kt., QC
Lawrence, Sir William Fettiplace, Bt. (1867)
Lawrence-Jones, Sir Christopher, Bt. (1831)

Laws, *Rt. Hon.* Sir John Grant McKenzie, Kt.
Laws, Sir Stephen Charles, KCB
Lawson, Sir Charles John Patrick, Bt. (1900)
Lawson, *Gen.* Sir Richard George, KCB, DSO, OBE
Lawson-Tancred, Sir Andrew Peter, Bt. (1662)
Lawton, *Prof.* Sir John Hartley, Kt., CBE, FRS
Layard, *Adm.* Sir Michael Henry Gordon, KCB, CBE
Lea, *Vice-Adm.* Sir John Stuart Crosbie, KBE
Lea, Sir Thomas William, Bt. (1892)
Leahy, Sir Daniel Joseph, Kt.
Leahy, Sir John Henry Gladstone, KCMG
Leahy, Sir Terence Patrick, Kt.
Learmont, *Gen.* Sir John Hartley, KCB, CBE
Leaver, Sir Christopher, GBE
Le Cheminant, *Air Chief Marshal* Sir Peter de Lacey, GBE, KCB, DFC
Lechler, *Prof.* Sir Robert Ian, Kt.
†Lechmere, Sir Nicholas Anthony Hungerford, Bt. (1818)
Lee, Sir Christopher Frank Carandini, Kt., CBE
†Leeds, Sir John Charles Hildyard, Bt. (1812)
Lees, Sir David Bryan, Kt.
Lees, Sir Thomas Edward, Bt. (1897)
Lees, Sir Thomas Harcourt Ivor, Bt. (1804)
Lees, Sir (William) Antony Clare, Bt. (1937)
Leese, Sir Richard Charles, Kt., CBE
Leeson, *Air Marshal* Sir Kevin James, KCB, CBE
le Fleming, Sir David Kelland, Bt. (1705)
Legard, Sir Charles Thomas, Bt. (1660)
Legg, Sir Thomas Stuart, KCB, QC
Leggatt, *Rt. Hon.* Sir Andrew Peter, Kt.
Leggatt, *Hon.* George Andrew Midsomer, Kt.
Leggatt, Sir Hugh Frank John, Kt.
Leggett, *Prof.* Sir Anthony James, KBE
Leigh, Sir Edward Julian Egerton, Kt.
Leigh, Sir Geoffrey Norman, Kt.
Leigh, *Dr* Sir Michael, KCMG
Leigh, Sir Richard Henry, Bt. (1918)
Leighton, Sir John Mark Nicholas, Kt.
Leighton, Sir Michael John Bryan, Bt. (1693)
Leith-Buchanan, Sir Gordon Kelly McNicol, Bt. (1775)
Le Marchant, Sir Francis Arthur, Bt. (1841)
Lennox-Boyd, The Hon. Sir Mark Alexander, Kt.
Leon, Sir John Ronald, Bt. (1911)
Lepping, Sir George Geria Dennis, GCMG, MBE
Le Quesne, Sir (John) Godfray, Kt., QC
Leslie, Sir John Norman Ide, Bt. (1876)
Lester, Sir James Theodore, Kt.
Lethbridge, Sir Thomas Periam Hector Noel, Bt. (1804)
Lever, Sir Jeremy Frederick, KCMG, QC
Lever, Sir Paul, KCMG
Lever, Sir (Tresham) Christopher Arthur Lindsay, Bt. (1911)
Leveson, *Rt. Hon.* Sir Brian Henry, Kt.
Levi, Sir Wasangula Noel, Kt., CBE
Levinge, Sir Richard George Robin, Bt. (I. 1704)
Lewinton, Sir Christopher, Kt.
Lewis, Sir David Thomas Rowell, Kt.
Lewis, Sir John Anthony, Kt., OBE
Lewis, Sir Lawrence Vernon Harcourt, KCMG, GCM
Lewis, Sir Leigh Warren, KCB
Lewis, Sir Terence Murray, Kt., OBE, GM, QPM
Lewison, *Rt. Hon.* Sir Kim Martin Jordan, Kt.
Ley, Sir Ian Francis, Bt. (1905)
Li, Sir Ka-Shing, KBE
Lickiss, Sir Michael Gillam, Kt.
Liddington, Sir Bruce, Kt.
Lightman, *Hon.* Sir Gavin Anthony, Kt.
Lighton, Sir Thomas Hamilton, Bt. (I. 1791)
Likierman, *Prof.* Sir John Andrew, Kt.
Lilleyman, *Prof.* Sir John Stuart, Kt.
Linacre, Sir (John) Gordon (Seymour), Kt., CBE, AFC, DFM
Lindblom, *Hon.* Sir Keith John, Kt.
Lindop, Sir Norman, Kt.
Lindsay, *Hon.* Sir John Edmund Frederic, Kt.
†Lindsay, Sir James Martin Evelyn, Bt. (1962)
†Lindsay-Hogg, Sir Michael Edward, Bt. (1905)
Lipton, Sir Stuart Anthony, Kt.
Lipworth, Sir (Maurice) Sydney, Kt.
Lister-Kaye, Sir John Phillip Lister, Bt. (1812)
Lithgow, Sir William James, Bt. (1925)
Llewellyn, Sir Roderic Victor, Bt. (1922)
Llewellyn-Smith, *Prof.* Sir Christopher Hubert, Kt.
Lloyd, *Prof.* Sir Geoffrey Ernest Richard, Kt., FBA
Lloyd, Sir Nicholas Markley, Kt.
Lloyd, *Rt. Hon.* Sir Peter Robert Cable, Kt.
Lloyd, Sir Richard Ernest Butler, Bt. (1960)
Lloyd, *Rt. Hon.* Sir Timothy Andrew Wigram, Kt.
Lloyd-Edwards, *Capt.* Sir Norman, KCVO, RD
Lloyd Jones, *Rt. Hon.* Sir David, Kt.
Loader, Air Marshal Sir Clive Robert, KCB, OBE
Lobban, Sir Iain Robert, KCMG, CB
Lobo, Sir Rogerio Hyndman, Kt., CBE
Lockett, Sir Michael Vernon, KCVO
Lockhead, Sir Moir, Kt., OBE
Loder, Sir Edmund Jeune, Bt. (1887)
Logan, Sir David Brian Carleton, KCMG
Longmore, *Rt. Hon.* Sir Andrew Centlivres, Kt.
Lorimer, Sir (Thomas) Desmond, Kt.
Los, *Hon.* Sir Kubulan, Kt., CBE
Loughran, Sir Gerald Finbar, KCB
Lourdenadin, Sir Ninian Mogan, KBE, KCMG
Lovelock, Sir Douglas Arthur, KCB
Lovill, Sir John Roger, Kt., CBE
Lowa, *Rt. Revd* Sir Samson, KBE
Lowe, *Air Chief Marshal* Sir Douglas Charles, GCB, DFC, AFC
Lowe, Sir Frank Budge, Kt.
Lowe, Sir Thomas William Gordon, Bt. (1918)
Lowson, Sir Ian Patrick, Bt. (1951)
Lowther, *Col.* Sir Charles Douglas, Bt. (1824)
Loyd, Sir Julian St John, KCVO
Lu, Sir Tseng Chi, Kt.
Lucas, *Prof.* Sir Colin Renshaw, Kt.
Lucas, Sir Thomas Edward, Bt. (1887)
Lucas-Tooth, Sir (Hugh) John, Bt. (1920)
Lumsden, Sir David James, Kt.
Lushington, Sir John Richard Castleman, Bt. (1791)
Lyall Grant, Sir Mark Justin, KCMG
Lyle, Sir Gavin Archibald, Bt. (1929)
Lynch-Blosse, *Capt.* Sir Richard Hely, Bt. (1622)
Lynch-Robinson, Sir Dominick Christopher, Bt. (1920)
Lyne, *Rt. Hon.* Sir Roderic Michael John, KBE, CMG
Lyons, Sir John, Kt.
Lyons, Sir Michael Thomas, Kt.

McAllister, Sir Ian Gerald, Kt., CBE
McAlpine, Sir William Hepburn, Bt. (1918)
McCaffrey, Sir Thomas Daniel, Kt.
McCamley, Sir Graham Edward, KBE
McCarthy, Sir Callum, Kt.
McCartney, *Rt. Hon.* Sir Ian, Kt.
McCartney, Sir (James) Paul, Kt., MBE
Macartney, Sir John Ralph, Bt. (I. 1799)
McClement, *Vice-Admiral* Sir Timothy Pentreath, KCB, OBE
McClintock, Sir Eric Paul, Kt.
McCloskey, *Hon.* Sir John Bernard, Kt.
McColl, Sir Colin Hugh Verel, KCMG
McColl, *Gen.* Sir John Chalmers, KCB, CBE, DSO
McCollum, *Rt. Hon.* Sir William, Kt.
McCombe, *Rt. Hon.* Sir Richard George Bramwell, Kt.
McConnell, Sir Robert Shean, Bt. (1900)
MacCormac, Sir Richard Cornelius, Kt., CBE
†McCowan, Sir David William, Bt. (1934)
MacCulloch, *Prof.* Sir Diarmaid Ninian John, Kt.
McCulloch, *Rt. Revd* Nigel Simeon, KCVO
McCullough, *Hon.* Sir (Iain) Charles (Robert), Kt.
MacDermott, *Rt. Hon.* Sir John Clarke, Kt.
Macdonald, Sir Alasdair Uist, Kt., CBE
Macdonald, Sir Kenneth Carmichael, KCB
McDonald, *Prof.* Sir James, Kt.
McDonald, Sir Trevor, Kt., OBE
Macdonald of Sleat, Sir Ian Godfrey Bosville, Bt. (S. 1625)
McDowell, Sir Eric Wallace, Kt., CBE

MacDuff, *Hon.* Sir Alistair Geoffrey, Kt.
Mace, *Lt.-Gen.* Sir John Airth, KBE, CB
McEwen, Sir John Roderick Hugh, Bt. (1953)
McFarland, Sir John Talbot, Bt. (1914)
MacFarlane, *Prof.* Sir Alistair George James, Kt., CBE, FRS
McFarlane, *Rt. Hon.* Sir Andrew Ewart, Kt.
Macfarlane, Sir (David) Neil, Kt.
McGeechan, Sir Ian Robert, Kt., OBE
McGrath, Sir Brian Henry, GCVO
Macgregor, Sir Ian Grant, Bt. (1828)
McGregor, Sir James David, Kt., OBE
MacGregor of MacGregor, Sir Malcolm Gregor Charles, Bt. (1795)
McGrigor, Sir James Angus Rhoderick Neil, Bt. (1831)
McIntosh, Sir Neil William David, Kt., CBE
McIntosh, Sir Ronald Robert Duncan, KCB
McIntyre, Sir Donald Conroy, Kt., CBE
McIntyre, Sir Meredith Alister, Kt.
Mackay, *Hon.* Sir Colin Crichton, Kt.
MacKay, *Prof.* Sir Donald Iain, Kt.
MacKay, Sir Francis Henry, Kt.
McKay, Sir Neil Stuart, Kt., CB
McKay, Sir William Robert, KCB
Mackay-Dick, *Maj.-Gen.* Sir Iain Charles, KCVO, MBE
Mackechnie, Sir Alistair John, Kt.
McKellen, Sir Ian Murray, Kt., CH, CBE
Mackenzie, Sir (James William) Guy, Bt. (1890)
Mackenzie, *Gen.* Sir Jeremy John George, GCB, OBE
†Mackenzie, Sir Peter Douglas, Bt. (S. 1673)
†Mackenzie, Sir Roderick McQuhae, Bt. (S. 1703)
Mackeson, Sir Rupert Henry, Bt. (1954)
McKillop, Sir Thomas Fulton Wilson, Kt.
McKinnon, *Rt. Hon.* Sir Donald Charles, GCVO
McKinnon, Sir James, Kt.
McKinnon, *Hon.* Sir Stuart Neil, Kt.
Mackintosh, Sir Cameron Anthony, Kt.
Mackworth, Sir Digby (John), Bt. (1776)
McLaughlin, Sir Richard, Kt.
Maclean of Dunconnell, Sir Charles Edward, Bt. (1957)
Maclean, *Hon.* Sir Lachlan Hector Charles, Bt., CVO (NS 1631)
Maclean, Sir Murdo, Kt.
†McLeod, Sir James Roderick Charles, Bt. (1925)
MacLeod, Sir (John) Maxwell Norman, Bt. (1924)
Macleod, Sir (Nathaniel William) Hamish, KBE
McLintock, Sir Michael William, Bt. (1934)
Maclure, Sir John Robert Spencer, Bt. (1898)
McMahon, Sir Brian Patrick, Bt. (1817)
McMahon, Sir Christopher William, Kt.
McMaster, Sir Brian John, Kt., CBE
McMichael, *Prof.* Sir Andrew James, Kt., FRS
MacMillan, *Lt.-Gen.* Sir John Richard Alexander, KCB, CBE
McMullin, *Rt. Hon.* Sir Duncan Wallace, Kt.
McMurtry, Sir David, Kt., CBE
Macnaghten, Sir Malcolm Francis, Bt. (1836)
McNair-Wilson, Sir Patrick Michael Ernest David, Kt.
McNamara, *Air Chief Marshal* Sir Neville Patrick, KBE
Macnaughton, *Prof.* Sir Malcolm Campbell, Kt.
McNee, Sir David Blackstock, Kt., QPM
McNulty, Sir (Robert William) Roy, Kt., CBE
MacPhail, Sir Bruce Dugald, Kt.
MacPherson, Sir Nicholas, KCB
Macpherson, Sir Ronald Thomas Steward (Tommy), CBE, MC, TD
Macpherson of Cluny, *Hon.* Sir William Alan, Kt., TD
McQuarrie, Sir Albert, Kt.
MacRae, Sir (Alastair) Christopher (Donald Summerhayes), KCMG
Macready, Sir Nevil John Wilfrid, Bt. (1923), CBE
MacSween, *Prof.* Sir Roderick Norman McIver, Kt.
Mactaggart, Sir John Auld, Bt. (1938)
McVicar, Sir David, Kt.
McWilliam, Sir Michael Douglas, KCMG
McWilliams, Sir Francis, GBE
Madden, Sir David Christopher Andrew, KCMG
Madden, Sir Charles Jonathan, Bt. (1919)
Maddison, *Hon.* Sir David George, Kt.
Madejski, Sir John Robert, Kt., OBE
Madel, Sir (William) David, Kt.
Magee, Sir Ian Bernard Vaughan, Kt., CB
Magnus, Sir Laurence Henry Philip, Bt. (1917)
Maguire, *Hon.* Sir Paul Richard, Kt.
Mahon, Sir William Walter, Bt. (1819), LVO
Maiden, Sir Colin James, Kt., DPHIL
Maini, *Prof.* Sir Ravinder Nath, Kt.
Maino, Sir Charles, KBE
†Maitland, Sir Charles Alexander, Bt. (1818)
Major, *Rt. Hon.* Sir John, KG, CH
Malbon, *Vice-Adm.* Sir Fabian Michael, KBE
†Malcolm, Sir Alexander Elton, Bt. (S. 1665), OBE
Males, *Hon.* Sir Stephen Martin, Kt.
Malet, Sir Harry Douglas St Lo, Bt. (1791)
Mallaby, Sir Christopher Leslie George, GCMG, GCVO
Mallick, *Prof.* Sir Netar Prakash, Kt.
Mallinson, Sir William James, Bt. (1935)
Malpas, Sir Robert, Kt., CBE
Mancham, Sir James Richard Marie, KBE
Mander, Sir (Charles) Nicholas, Bt. (1911)
Manduell, Sir John, Kt., CBE
Mann, *Hon.* Sir George Anthony, Kt.
Mann, Sir Rupert Edward, Bt. (1905)
Manning, Sir David Geoffrey, GCMG, CVO
Mano, Sir Koitaga, Kt., MBE
Mans, *Lt-Gen.* Sir Mark Francis Noel, KCB, CBE
Mansel, Sir Philip, Bt. (1622)
Mansfield, *Prof.* Sir Peter, Kt.
Manuella, Sir Tulaga, GCMG, MBE
Manzie, Sir (Andrew) Gordon, KCB
Mara, Sir Nambuga, KBE
Margetson, Sir John William Denys, KCMG
Margetts, Sir Robert John, Kt., CBE
Markesinis, *Prof.* Sir Basil Spyridonos, Kt. QC
Markham, *Prof.* Sir Alexander Fred, Kt.
Markham, Sir (Arthur) David, Bt. (1911)
Marling, Sir Charles William Somerset, Bt. (1882)
Marmot, Prof. Sir Michael Gideon, Kt.
Marr, Sir Leslie Lynn, Bt. (1919)
Marriner, Sir Neville, Kt., CBE
†Marsden, Sir Tadgh Orlando Denton, Bt. (1924)
Marsh, *Prof.* Sir John Stanley, Kt., CBE
Marshall, Sir Michael John, Kt., CBE
Marshall, *Prof.* Sir (Oshley) Roy, Kt., CBE
Marshall, Sir Peter Harold Reginald, KCMG
Marshall, *Prof. Emeritus* Sir Woodville Kemble, Kt.
Martin, Sir Clive Haydon, Kt., OBE
Martin, Sir George Henry, Kt., CBE
Martin, Sir Gregory Michael Gerard, Kt.
Martin, *Prof.* Sir Laurence Woodward, Kt.
Martin, Sir (Robert) Bruce, Kt., QC
Marychurch, Sir Peter Harvey, KCMG
Masefield, Sir Charles Beech Gordon, Kt.
Mason, *Hon.* Sir Anthony Frank, KBE
Mason, Sir (Basil) John, Kt., CB, DSC, FRS
Mason, *Prof.* Sir David Kean, Kt., CBE
Mason, Sir John Peter, Kt., CBE
Mason, Sir Peter James, KBE
Mason, *Prof.* Sir Ronald, KCB, FRS
Massey, *Vice-Adm.* Sir Alan, KCB, CBE, ADC
Massie, Sir Herbert William, Kt., CBE
Matane, HE Sir Paulias Nguna, GCMG, OBE
Matheson of Matheson, Sir Fergus John, Bt. (1882)
Mathews, *Vice-Adm.* Sir Andrew David Hugh, KCB
Mathewson, Sir George Ross, Kt., CBE, PHD, FRSE
Matthews, Sir Terence Hedley, Kt., OBE
Maud, *Hon.* Sir Humphrey John Hamilton, KCMG
Maughan, Sir Deryck, Kt.
Mawer, Sir Philip John Courtney, Kt.
Maxwell, Sir Michael Eustace George, Bt. (S. 1681)

Maxwell Macdonald (formerly Stirling-Maxwell), Sir John Ronald, Bt. (NS 1682)
Maxwell-Scott, Sir Dominic James, Bt. (1642)
May, *Rt. Hon.* Sir Anthony Tristram Kenneth, Kt.
Mayfield, Sir Andrew Charles, Kt.
Mayhew-Sanders, Sir John Reynolds, Kt.
Meadow, *Prof.* Sir (Samuel) Roy, Kt., FRCP, FRCPE
Meale, Sir Joseph Alan, Kt.
Medlycott, Sir Mervyn Tregonwell, Bt. (1808)
Meeran, *His Hon.* Sir Goolam Hoosen Kader, Kt.
Meldrum, Sir Graham, Kt., CBE, QFSM
Melhuish, Sir Michael Ramsay, KBE, CMG
Mellars, *Prof.* Sir Paul Anthony, Kt., FBA
Mellon, Sir James, KCMG
Melmoth, Sir Graham John, Kt.
Melville, *Prof.* Sir David, Kt., CBE
Merifield, Sir Anthony James, KCVO, CB
Metcalf, *Prof.* Sir David Harry, Kt., CBE
†Meyer, Sir (Anthony) Ashley Frank, Bt. (1910)
Meyer, Sir Christopher John Rome, KCMG
†Meyrick, Sir Timothy Thomas Charlton, Bt. (1880)
Miakwe, *Hon.* Sir Akepa, KBE
Michael, Sir Duncan, Kt.
Michael, *Dr* Sir Jonathan, Kt.
Michael, Sir Peter Colin, Kt., CBE
Michels, Sir David Michael Charles, Kt.
Middleton, Sir John Maxwell, Kt.
Middleton, Sir Peter Edward, GCB
Miers, Sir (Henry) David Alastair Capel, KBE, CMG
Milbank, Sir Anthony Frederick, Bt. (1882)
Milborne-Swinnerton-Pilkington, Sir Thomas Henry, Bt. (S. 1635)
Milburn, Sir Anthony Rupert, Bt. (1905)
Miles, Sir Peter Tremayne, KCVO
†Miles, Sir Philip John, Bt. (1859)
Millais, Sir Geoffrey Richard Everett, Bt. (1885)
Millar, *Prof.* Sir Fergus Graham Burtholme, Kt.
Miller, Sir Albert Joel, KCMG, LVO, MBE, QPM, CPM
Miller, Sir Donald John, Kt., FRSE, FRENG
Miller, *Air Marshal* Sir Graham Anthony, KBE
†Miller, Sir Anthony Thomas, Bt. (1705)
Miller, Sir Hilary Duppa (Hal), Kt.
Miller, Sir Jonathan Wolfe, Kt., CBE
Miller, Sir Peter North, Kt.
Miller, Sir Robin Robert William, Kt.
Miller, Sir Ronald Andrew Baird, Kt., CBE
Miller of Glenlee, Sir Stephen William Macdonald, Bt. (1788)
Mills, Sir Ian, Kt.
Mills, Sir Jonathan Edward Harland (John), Kt., FRSE
Mills, Sir Keith Edward, GBE, Kt.
Mills, Sir Peter Frederick Leighton, Bt. (1921)
Milman, Sir David Patrick, Bt. (1800)
Milne, Sir John Drummond, Kt.
Milne-Watson, Sir Andrew Michael, Bt. (1937)
Milner, Sir Timothy William Lycett, Bt. (1717)
Mirrlees, *Prof.* Sir James Alexander, Kt., FBA
Mitchell, Sir David Bower, Kt.
Mitchell, *Rt. Hon.* Sir James FitzAllen, KCMG
Mitchell, *Very Revd* Patrick Reynolds, KCVO
Mitchell, *Hon.* Sir Stephen George, Kt.
Mitting, *Hon.* Sir John Edward, Kt.
Moate, Sir Roger Denis, Kt.
Moberly, Sir Patrick Hamilton, KCMG
Moffat, Sir Brian Scott, Kt., OBE
Moffat, *Lt.-Gen.* Sir (William) Cameron, KBE
Moir, Sir Christopher Ernest, Bt. (1916)
Molesworth-St Aubyn, Sir William, Bt. (1689)
Molony, Sir Thomas Desmond, Bt. (1925)
Moncada, *Prof.* Sir Salvador, Kt.
Montagu, Sir Nicholas Lionel John, KCB
Montagu-Pollock, Sir Giles Hampden, Bt. (1872)
Montague, Sir Adrian Alastair, Kt., CBE
Montgomery, Sir (Basil Henry) David, Bt. (1801), CVO
Montgomery, *Vice-Adm.* Sir Charles Percival Ross, KBE, ADC
Montgomery-Cuninghame, Sir John Christopher Foggo, Bt. (NS 1672)
Moody-Stuart, Sir Mark, KCMG
Moollan, Sir Abdool Hamid Adam, Kt.
†Moon, Sir Roger, Bt. (1887)
Moor, *Hon.* Sir Philip Drury, Kt.
Moorcroft, Sir William, KBE
Moore, *Most Revd* Desmond Charles, KBE
Moore, Sir Francis Thomas, Kt.
Moore, Sir John Michael, KCVO, CB, DSC
Moore, *Vice Adm.* Sir Michael Antony Claës, KBE, LVO
Moore, *Prof.* Sir Norman Winfrid, Bt. (1919)
Moore, Sir Patrick William Eisdell, Kt., OBE
Moore, Sir Roger George, KBE
Moore, Sir William Roger Clotworthy, Bt. (1932), TD
Moore-Bick, *Rt. Hon.* Sir Martin James, Kt.
Moores, Sir Peter, Kt., CBE
Morauta, Sir Mekere, KCMG
Mordaunt, Sir Richard Nigel Charles, Bt. (1611)
Morgan, *Vice-Adm.* Sir Charles Christopher, KBE
Morgan, *Rt. Hon.* Sir (Charles) Declan, Kt.
Morgan, Sir Graham, Kt.
Morgan, *Hon.* Sir Paul Hyacinth, Kt.
Morison, *Hon.* Sir Thomas Richard Atkin, Kt.
Moritz, Sir Michael Jonathan, KBE
Morland, *Hon.* Sir Michael, Kt.
Morland, Sir Robert Kenelm, Kt.
Morpeth, Sir Douglas Spottiswoode, Kt., TD
†Morris, Sir Allan Lindsay, Bt. (1806)
Morris, *Air Marshal* Sir Arnold Alec, KBE, CB
Morris, Sir Derek James, Kt.
Morris, Sir Keith Elliot Hedley, KBE, CMG
Morris, *Prof.* Sir Peter John, Kt.
Morris, Sir Trefor Alfred, Kt., CBE, QPM
Morris, *Very Revd* William James, KCVO
Morrison, Sir (Alexander) Fraser, Kt., CBE
Morrison, Sir Kenneth Duncan, Kt., CBE
Morrison-Bell, Sir William Hollin Dayrell, Bt. (1905)
Morrison-Low, Sir Richard Walter, Bt. (1908)
Morritt, *Rt. Hon.* Sir (Robert) Andrew, Kt., CVO
Morse, Sir Christopher Jeremy, KCMG
Moses, *Rt. Hon.* Sir Alan George, Kt.
Moses, *Very Revd* Dr John Henry, KCVO
Moss, Sir David Joseph, KCVO, CMG
Moss, Sir Stephen Alan, Kt.
Moss, Sir Stirling Craufurd, Kt., OBE
Mostyn, *Hon.* Sir Nicholas Anthony Joseph Ghislain, Kt.
Mostyn, Sir William Basil John, Bt. (1670)
Motion, Sir Andrew, Kt.
Mott, Sir John Harmer, Bt. (1930)
Mottram, Sir Richard Clive, GCB
†Mount, Sir (William Robert) Ferdinand, Bt. (1921)
Mountain, Sir Edward Brian Stanford, Bt. (1922)
Mowbray, Sir John Robert, Bt. (1880)
Moylan, *Hon.* Sir Andrew John Gregory, Kt.
Moynihan, *Dr* Sir Daniel, Kt.
†Muir, Sir Richard James Kay, Bt. (1892)
Muir-Mackenzie, Sir Alexander Alwyne Henry Charles Brinton, Bt. (1805)
Mulcahy, Sir Geoffrey John, Kt.
Mummery, *Rt. Hon.* Sir John Frank, Kt.
Munby, *Rt. Hon.* Sir James Lawrence, Kt.
Munro, Sir Alan Gordon, KCMG
†Munro, Sir Ian Kenneth, Bt. (S. 1634)
Munro, Sir Alasdair Thomas Ian, Bt. (1825)
Muria, *Hon.* Sir Gilbert John Baptist, Kt.
Murray, Sir David Edward, Kt.
Murray, *Rt. Hon.* Sir Donald Bruce, Kt.
Murray, Sir Nigel Andrew Digby, Bt. (S. 1628)

Murray, Sir Patrick Ian Keith, Bt. (S. 1673)
Murray, Sir Robert Sydney, Kt., CBE
Murray, Sir Robin MacGregor, Kt.
†Murray, Sir Rowland William, Bt. S. 1630)
Musgrave, Sir Christopher John Shane, Bt. (1782)
Musgrave, Sir Christopher Patrick Charles, Bt. (1611)
Myers, Sir Philip Alan, Kt., OBE, QPM
Myers, *Prof.* Sir Rupert Horace, KBE
Mynors, Sir Richard Baskerville, Bt. (1964)

Naipaul, Sir Vidiadhar Surajprasad, Kt.
Nairn, Sir Michael, Bt. (1904)
Naish, Sir (Charles) David, Kt.
Nalau, Sir Jerry Kasip, KBE
Nall, Sir Edward William Joseph Bt. (1954)
Namaliu, *Rt. Hon.* Sir Rabbie Langanai, KCMG
Napier, Sir Charles Joseph, Bt. (1867)
Napier, Sir John Archibald Lennox, Bt. (S. 1627)
Narey, Sir Martin James, Kt.
Naylor, Sir Robert, Kt.
Naylor-Leyland, Sir Philip Vyvyan, Bt. (1895)
Neal, Sir Eric James, Kt., CVO
Neale, Sir Gerrard Anthony, Kt.
Neave, Sir Paul Arundell, Bt. (1795)
Neill, *Rt. Hon.* Sir Brian Thomas, Kt.
Neill, Sir (James) Hugh, KCVO, CBE, TD
†Nelson, Sir Jamie Charles Vernon Hope, Bt. (1912)
Nelson, *Hon.* Sir Robert Franklyn, Kt.
Neubert, Sir Michael John, Kt.
New, *Maj.-Gen.* Sir Laurence Anthony Wallis, Kt., CB, CBE
Newall, Sir Paul Henry, Kt., TD
Newbigging, Sir David Kennedy, Kt., OBE
Newby, *Prof.* Sir Howard Joseph, Kt., CBE
Newey, *Hon.* Sir Guy Richard, Kt.
Newington, Sir Michael John, KCMG
Newman, Sir Francis Hugh Cecil, Bt. (1912)
Newman, Sir Geoffrey Robert, Bt. (1836)
Newman, *Hon.* Sir George Michael, Kt.
Newman, Sir Kenneth Leslie, GBE, QPM
Newman, *Vice-Adm.* Sir Roy Thomas, KCB
Newman Taylor, *Prof.* Sir Anthony John, Kt., CBE
Newsam, Sir Peter Anthony, Kt.
Newson-Smith, Sir Peter Frank Graham, Bt. (1944)
Newton, *Revd* George Peter Howgill, Bt. (1900)
Newton, Sir John Garnar, Bt. (1924)
Newton, *Lt-Gen.* Sir Paul Raymond, KBE
Nice, Sir Geoffrey, Kt., QC
Nicol, *Hon.* Sir Andrew George Lindsay, Kt.
Nichol, Sir Duncan Kirkbride, Kt., CBE
Nicholas, Sir David, Kt., CBE
Nicholas, Sir John William, KCVO, CMG
Nicholls, Sir Nigel Hamilton, KCVO, CBE
Nichols, Sir Richard Everard, Kt.
Nicholson, Sir Bryan Hubert, GBE, Kt.
Nicholson, Sir Charles Christian, Bt. (1912)
Nicholson, Sir David, KCB, CBE
Nicholson, *Rt. Hon.* Sir Michael, Kt.
Nicholson, Sir Paul Douglas, KCVO, Kt.
Nicholson, Sir Robin Buchanan, Kt., PHD, FRS, FRENG
Nicoll, Sir William, KCMG
Nightingale, Sir Charles Manners Gamaliel, Bt. (1628)
Nixon, Sir Simon Michael Christopher, Bt. (1906)
Noble, Sir David Brunel, Bt. (1902)
Noble, Sir Timothy Peter, Bt. (1923)
Nombri, Sir Joseph Karl, Kt., ISO, BEM
Norman, Sir Mark Annesley, Bt. (1915)
Norman, Sir Ronald, Kt., OBE
Norman, Sir Torquil Patrick Alexander, Kt., CBE
Normington, Sir David John, GCB
Norrington, Sir Roger Arthur Carver, Kt., CBE
Norris, *Hon.* Sir Alastair Hubert, Kt.
Norriss, Air Marshal Sir Peter Coulson, KBE, CB, AFC
North, Sir Peter Machin, Kt., CBE, QC, DCL, FBA
North, Sir Thomas Lindsay, Kt.
North, Sir (William) Jonathan (Frederick), Bt. (1920)
Norton, *Maj.-Gen.* Sir George Pemberton Ross, KCVO, CBE
Norton-Griffiths, Sir John, Bt. (1922)
Nossal, Sir Gustav Joseph Victor, Kt., CBE
Nott, *Rt. Hon.* Sir John William Frederic, KCB
Nourse, *Rt. Hon.* Sir Martin Charles, Kt.
Novoselov, *Prof.* Sir Konstantin, Kt.
†Nugent, Sir Christopher George Ridley, Bt. (1806)
Nugent, Sir Nicholas Myles John, Bt. (I. 1795)
Nugent, Sir (Walter) Richard Middleton, Bt. (1831)
Nunn, Sir Trevor Robert, Kt., CBE
Nunneley, Sir Charles Kenneth Roylance, Kt.
Nursaw, Sir James, KCB, QC
Nurse, Sir Paul Maxime, Kt.
Nuttall, Sir Harry, Bt. (1922)
Nutting, Sir John Grenfell, Bt. (1903), QC

Oakeley, Sir John Digby Atholl, Bt. (1790)
Oakes, Sir Christopher, Bt. (1939)
†Oakshott, Hon. Sir Michael Arthur John, Bt. (1959)
Oates, Sir Thomas, Kt., CMG, OBE
O'Brien, Sir Frederick William Fitzgerald, Kt.
O'Brien, Sir Robert Stephen, Kt., CBE
O'Brien, Sir Timothy John, Bt. (1849)
O'Brien, Sir William, Kt.
O'Brien, *Adm.* Sir William Donough, KCB, DSC
O'Connell, Sir Bernard, Kt.
O'Connell, Sir Maurice James Donagh MacCarthy, Bt. (1869)
O'Connor, Sir Denis Francis, Kt., CBE, QPM
Odell, Sir Stanley John, Kt.
Odgers, Sir Graeme David William, Kt.
O'Donnell, Sir Christopher John, Kt.
O'Donoghue, *Lt.-Gen.* Sir Kevin, KCB, CBE
O'Dowd, Sir David Joseph, Kt., CBE, QPM
Ogden, *Dr* Sir Peter James, Kt.
Ogden, Sir Robert, Kt., CBE
Ogilvy, Sir Francis Gilbert Arthur, Bt. (S. 1626)
Ogilvy-Wedderburn, Sir Andrew John Alexander, Bt. (1803)
Ogio, *HE* Sir Michael, GCMG, CBE
Ognall, *Hon.* Sir Harry Henry, Kt.
Ohlson, Sir Brian Eric Christopher, Bt. (1920)
Oldham, *Dr* Sir John, Kt., OBE
Oliver, Sir James Michael Yorrick, Kt.
Oliver, Sir Stephen John Lindsay, Kt., QC
O'Loghlen, Sir Colman Michael, Bt. (1838)
Olver, Sir Richard Lake, Kt.
Omand, Sir David Bruce, GCB
O'Nions, Prof. Sir Robert Keith, Kt., FRS, PHD
Ondaatje, Sir Christopher, Kt., CBE
Onslow, Sir Richard Paul Atherton, Bt. (1797)
Oppenheimer, Sir Michael Bernard Grenville, Bt. (1921)
Oppenshaw, Sir Charles Peter Lawford, Kt., QC
O'Rahilly, *Prof.* Sir Stephen Patrick, Kt., FRS
Orde, Sir Hugh Stephen Roden, Kt., OBE, QPM
O'Regan, *Dr* Sir Stephen Gerard (Tipene), Kt.
O'Reilly, Sir Anthony John Francis, Kt.
O'Reilly, *Prof.* Sir John James, Kt.
Orr, Sir John, Kt., OBE
Orr-Ewing, Sir (Alistair) Simon, Bt. (1963)
Orr-Ewing, Sir Archibald Donald, Bt. (1886)
Osborn, Sir John Holbrook, Kt.
Osborn, Sir Richard Henry Danvers, Bt. (1662)
Osborne, Sir Peter George, Bt. (I. 1629)
O'Shea, *Prof.* Sir Timothy Michael Martin, Kt.
Osmotherly, Sir Edward Benjamin Crofton, Kt., CB
O'Sullevan, Sir Peter John, Kt., CBE
Oswald, Sir (William Richard) Michael, KCVO
Otton, Sir Geoffrey John, KCB
Otton, *Rt. Hon.* Sir Philip Howard, Kt.
Oulton, Sir Antony Derek Maxwell, GCB, QC

Ouseley, *Hon.* Sir Brian Walter, Kt.
Outram, Sir Alan James, Bt. (1858)
Owen, Sir Geoffrey, Kt.
Owen, *Hon.* Sir Robert Michael, Kt.
Owen-Jones, Sir Lindsay Harwood, KBE

Packer, Sir Richard John, KCB
Paget, Sir Julian Tolver, Bt. (1871), CVO
Paget, Sir Richard Herbert, Bt. (1886)
Paice, *Rt. Hon.* Sir James Edward Thornton, Kt.
Paine, Sir Christopher Hammon, Kt., FRCP, FRCR
Pakenham, *Hon.* Sir Michael Aiden, KBE, CMG
Palin, *Air Chief Marshal* Sir Roger Hewlett, KCB, OBE
Palmer, Sir Albert Rocky, Kt.
Palmer, Sir (Charles) Mark, Bt. (1886)
Palmer, Sir Geoffrey Christopher John, Bt. (1660)
Palmer, *Rt. Hon.* Sir Geoffrey Winston Russell, KCMG
Palmer, Sir John Edward Somerset, Bt. (1791)
Palmer, *Maj.-Gen.* Sir (Joseph) Michael, KCVO
Palmer, Sir Reginald Oswald, GCMG, MBE
Panter, Sir Howard Hugh, Kt.
Pappano, Sir Antonio, Kt.
Parbo, Sir Arvi Hillar, Kt.
Park, *Hon.* Sir Andrew Edward Wilson, Kt.
Parker, Sir Alan William, Kt., CBE
Parker, Sir Eric Wilson, Kt.
Parker, Sir (Thomas) John, GBE
Parker, *Rt. Hon.* Sir Jonathan Frederic, Kt.
Parker, *Hon.* Sir Kenneth Blades, Kt.
Parker, *Maj.* Sir Michael John, KCVO, CBE
Parker, *Gen.* Sir Nicholas Ralph, KCB, CBE
Parker, Sir Richard (William) Hyde, Bt. (1681)
Parker, Sir (Thomas) John, Kt.
Parker, Sir William Peter Brian, Bt. (1844)
Parkes, Sir Edward Walter, Kt., FRENG
Parkinson, Sir Michael, Kt., CBE
Parry, *Prof.* Sir Eldryd Hugh Owen, KCMG, OBE
Parry, Sir Emyr Jones, GCMG
Parry-Evans, *Air Chief Marshal* Sir David, GCB, CBE
Parsons, Sir John Christopher, KCVO
Parsons, Sir Richard Edmund (Clement Fownes), KCMG
Partridge, Sir Michael John Anthony, KCB
Partridge, Sir Nicholas Wyndham, Kt., OBE
Pascoe, *Gen.* Sir Robert Alan, KCB, MBE
Pasley, Sir Robert Killigrew Sabine, Bt. (1794)
Paston-Bedingfeld, Sir Henry Edgar, Bt. (1661)
Paterson, Sir Dennis Craig, Kt.
Patey, Sir William Charters, KCMG
Patten, *Rt. Hon.* Sir Nicholas John, Kt.
Pattie, *Rt. Hon.* Sir Geoffrey Edwin, Kt.
Pattison, *Prof.* Sir John Ridley, Kt., DM, FRCPATH
Pattullo, Sir (David) Bruce, Kt., CBE
Pauncefort-Duncombe, Sir David Philip Henry, Bt. (1859)
Payne, *Prof.* Sir David Neil, Kt., CBE, FRS
Peace, Sir John Wilfrid, Kt.
Peach, Sir Leonard Harry, Kt.
Peach, *Air Chief Marshal* Sir Stuart William, KCB, CBE
Peacock, *Prof.* Sir Alan Turner, Kt., DSc
Pearce, Sir (Daniel Norton) Idris, Kt., CBE, TD
Pearse, Sir Brian Gerald, Kt.
Pearson, Sir Francis Nicholas Fraser, Bt. (1964)
Pearson, Sir Keith, Kt.
Pearson, *Gen.* Sir Thomas Cecil Hook, KCB, CBE, DSO
Peart, *Prof.* Sir William Stanley, Kt., MD, FRS
Pease, Sir Joseph Gurney, Bt. (1882)
Pease, Sir Richard Thorn, Bt. (1920)
Peat, Sir Gerrard Charles, KCVO
Peat, Sir Michael Charles Gerrard, GCVO
Peckham, *Prof.* Sir Michael John, Kt.,
Peek, Sir Richard Grenville, Bt. (1874)
Peirse, *Air Vice-Marshal* Sir Richard Charles Fairfax, KCVO, CB
Pelgen, Sir Harry Friedrich, Kt., MBE
Pelham, *Dr* Sir Hugh Reginald Brentnall, Kt., FRS
Pelly, Sir Richard John, Bt. (1840)
Pendry, *Prof.* Sir John Brian, Kt., FRS
Penrose, *Prof.* Sir Roger, Kt., OM, FRS
Penry-Davey, *Hon.* Sir David Herbert, Kt.
Pepper, *Dr.* Sir David Edwin, KCMG
Pepper, *Prof.* Sir Michael, Kt.
Pepys, *Prof.* Sir Mark Brian, Kt.
Perowne, *Vice-Adm.* Sir James Francis, KBE
Perring, Sir John Raymond, Bt. (1963)
Perris, Sir David (Arthur), Kt., MBE
Perry, Sir David Howard, KCB
Perry, Sir Michael Sydney, GBE
Pervez, Sir Mohammed Anwar, Kt., OBE
Peters, *Prof.* Sir David Keith, Kt., FRCP
Petit, Sir Dinshaw Manockjee, Bt. (1890)
†Peto, Sir Francis Michael Morton, Bt. (1855)
Peto, Sir Henry Christopher Morton Bampfylde, Bt. (1927)
Peto, *Prof.* Sir Richard, Kt., FRS
Petrie, Sir Peter Charles, Bt. (1918), CMG
Pettigrew, Sir Russell Hilton, Kt.
†Philipson-Stow, Sir (Robert) Matthew, Bt. (1907)
Phillips, Sir (Gerald) Hayden, GCB
Phillips, Sir John David, Kt., QPM
Phillips, Sir Jonathan, KCB
Phillips, Sir Peter John, Kt., OBE
Phillips, Sir Robin Francis, Bt. (1912)
Phillips, Sir Tom Richard Vaughan, KCMG
Pickard, Sir (John) Michael, Kt.
Pickthorn, Sir James Francis Mann, Bt. (1959)
Pidgeon, Sir John Allan Stewart, Kt.
†Piers, Sir James Desmond, Bt. (I. 1661)
Piggott-Brown, Sir William Brian, Bt. (1903)
Pigot, Sir George Hugh, Bt. (1764)
Pigott, *Lt.-Gen.* Sir Anthony David, KCB, CBE
Pigott, Sir Berkeley Henry Sebastian, Bt. (1808)
Pike, *Lt.-Gen.* Sir Hew William Royston, KCB, DSO, MBE
Pike, Sir Michael Edmund, KCVO, CMG
Pile, Sir Anthony John Devereux, Bt. (1900)
Pill, *Rt Hon.* Sir Malcolm Thomas, Kt.
Pilling, Sir Joseph Grant, KCB
Pinsent, Sir Christopher Roy, Bt. (1938)
Pinsent, Sir Matthew Clive, Kt., CBE
Pissarides, *Prof.* Sir Christopher Antoniou, Kt., FBA
Pitcher, Sir Desmond Henry, Kt.
Pitchers, *Hon.* Sir Christopher (John), Kt.
Pitchford, *Rt. Hon.* Sir Christopher John, Kt.
Pitoi, Sir Sere, Kt., CBE
Pitt, Sir Michael Edward, Kt.
Plastow, Sir David Arnold Stuart, Kt.
Platt, Sir Martin Philip, Bt. (1959)
Pledger, *Air Chief Marshal* Sir Malcolm David, KCB, OBE, AFC
Plender, *Hon.* Sir Richard Owen, Kt.
Plumbly, Sir Derek John, KCMG
Pohai, Sir Timothy, Kt., MBE
Pole, Sir John Chandos, Bt. (1791)
Pole, Sir (John) Richard (Walter Reginald) Carew, Bt. (1628)
Polkinghorne, *Revd Canon* John Charlton, KBE, FRS
Pollard, Sir Charles, Kt.
†Pollen, Sir Richard John Hungerford, Bt. (1795)
Pollock, Sir George Frederick, Bt. (1866)
Pomeroy, Sir Brian Walter, Kt., CBE
Ponder, *Prof.* Sir Bruce Anthony John, Kt.
†Ponsonby, Sir Charles Ashley, Bt. (1956)
Poore, Sir Roger Ricardo, Bt. (1795)
Popplewell, *Hon.* Sir Andrew John, Kt.
Popplewell, *Hon.* Sir Oliver Bury, Kt.
†Porritt, Sir Jonathon Espie, Bt. (1963), CBE
Portal, Sir Jonathan Francis, Bt. (1901)
Porter, *Prof.* Sir Keith Macdonald, Kt.
Porter, *Rt. Hon.* Sir Robert Wilson, Kt., PC (NI)
Potter, *Rt. Hon.* Sir Mark Howard, Kt.
Pound, Sir John David, Bt. (1905)
Povey, Sir Keith, Kt., QPM
Powell, Sir John Christopher, Kt.
Powell, Sir Nicholas Folliott Douglas, Bt. (1897)
Power, Sir Alastair John Cecil, Bt. (1924)

Pownall, Sir Michael Graham, KCB
Prance, *Prof.* Sir Ghillean Tolmie, Kt., FRS
Pratchett, Sir Terence David John, Kt., OBE
Prendergast, Sir (Walter) Kieran, KCVO, CMG
Prescott, Sir Mark, Bt. (1938)
Preston, Sir Philip Charles Henry Hulton, Bt. (1815)
Prevost, Sir Christopher Gerald, Bt. (1805)
Price, Sir David Ernest Campbell, Kt.
Price, Sir Francis Caradoc Rose, Bt. (1815)
Price, Sir Frank Leslie, Kt.
Prideaux, Sir Humphrey Povah Treverbian, Kt., OBE
Priestly, Sir Julian Gordon, KCMG
†Primrose, Sir John Ure, Bt. (1903)
Pringle, *Hon.* Sir John Kenneth, Kt.
†Pringle, Sir Simon Robert, Bt. (S. 1683)
†Prichard-Jones, Sir David John Walter, Bt. (1910)
Proby, Sir William Henry, Bt. (1952)
Proctor-Beauchamp, Sir Christopher Radstock, Bt. (1745)
Prosser, Sir David John, Kt.
Prosser, Sir Ian Maurice Gray, Kt.
Pryke, Sir Christopher Dudley, Bt. (1926)
Puapua, *Rt. Hon.* Sir Tomasi, GCMG, KBE
Pulford, *Air Marshal* Sir Andrew Douglas, KCB, CBE
Purves, Sir William, Kt., CBE, DSO
Purvis, *Vice-Adm.* Sir Neville, KCB

Quan, Sir Henry (Francis), KBE
Quilter, Sir Anthony Raymond Leopold Cuthbert, Bt. (1897)

Radcliffe, Sir Sebastian Everard, Bt. (1813)
Radda, *Prof.* Sir George Karoly, Kt., CBE, FRS
Rae, Sir William, Kt., QPM
Raeburn, Sir Michael Edward Norman, Bt. (1923)
Rake, Sir Michael Derek Vaughan, Kt.
Ralli, Sir David Charles, Bt. (1912)
Ramakrishnan, *Dr* Sir Venkatraman, Kt.
Ramdanee, Sir Mookteswar Baboolall Kailash, Kt.
Ramphal, Sir Shridath Surendranath, GCMG
Ramphul, Sir Baalkhristna, Kt.
Ramphul, Sir Indurduth, Kt.
Ramsay, Sir Alexander William Burnett, Bt. (1806)
Ramsay, Sir Allan John (Hepple), KBE, CMG
Ramsay-Fairfax-Lucy, Sir Edmund John William Hugh, Bt. (1836)
Ramsden, Sir John Charles Josslyn, Bt. (1689)
Ramsey, *Dr* Sir Frank Cuthbert, KCMG
Ramsey, *Hon.* Sir Vivian Arthur, Kt.
Rankin, Sir Ian Niall, Bt. (1898)
Rasch, Sir Simon Anthony Carne, Bt. (1903)
Rashleigh, Sir Richard Harry, Bt. (1831)
Ratford, Sir David John Edward, KCMG, CVO
Rattee, *Hon.* Sir Donald Keith, Kt.
Rattle, Sir Simon Dennis, Kt., CBE
Rawlins, *Hon.* Sir Hugh Anthony, Kt.
Rawlins, *Prof.* Sir Michael David, Kt., FRCP, FRCPED
Rawlinson, Sir Anthony Henry John, Bt. (1891)
Rea, *Prof.* Sir Desmond, Kt., OBE
Read, *Air Marshal* Sir Charles Frederick, KBE, CB, DFC, AFC
Read, *Prof.* Sir David John, Kt.
Read, Sir John Emms, Kt.
†Reade, Sir Kenneth Ray, Bt. (1661)
Reardon-Smith, Sir (William) Antony (John), Bt. (1920)
Reddaway, Sir David Norman, KCMG, MBE
Redgrave, Sir Steven Geoffrey, Kt., CBE
Redmayne, Sir Giles Martin, Bt. (1964)
Redmond, Sir Anthony Gerard, Kt.
Redwood, Sir Peter Boverton, Bt. (1911)
Reed, *Prof.* Sir Alec Edward, Kt., CBE
Reedie, Sir Craig Collins, Kt., CBE
Rees, Sir David Allan, Kt., PHD, DSC, FRS
Rees, Sir Richard Ellis Meuric, Kt., CBE
Reeve, Sir Anthony, KCMG, KCVO
Reffell, *Adm.* Sir Derek Roy, KCB
Reich, Sir Erich Arieh, Kt.
Reid, Sir Alexander James, Bt. (1897)
Reid, Sir David Edward, Kt.
Reid, *Rt. Hon.* Sir George, Kt.
Reid, Sir (Philip) Alan, GCVO
Reid, Sir Robert Paul, Kt.
Reid, Sir William Kennedy, KCB
Reiher, Sir Frederick Bernard Carl, KCMG, KBE
Reilly, *Lt.-Gen.* Sir Jeremy Calcott, KCB, DSO
Renals, Sir Stanley, Bt. (1895)
Renouf, Sir Clement William Bailey, Kt.
Renshaw, Sir John David Bine, Bt. (1903)
Renwick, Sir Richard Eustace, Bt. (1921)
Reporter, Sir Shapoor Ardeshirji, KBE
Reynolds, Sir David James, Bt. (1923)
Reynolds, Sir Peter William John, Kt., CBE
Rhodes, Sir John Christopher Douglas, Bt. (1919)
Rice, *Prof.* Sir Charles Duncan, Kt.
Rice, *Maj.-Gen.* Sir Desmond Hind Garrett, KCVO, CBE
Rice, Sir Timothy Miles Bindon, Kt.
Richard, Sir Cliff, Kt., OBE
Richards, Sir Brian Mansel, Kt., CBE, PHD
Richards, *Hon.* Sir David Anthony Stewart, Kt.
Richards, Sir David Gerald, Kt.
Richards, *Gen.* Sir David, Julian, GCB, CBE, DSO
Richards, Sir Francis Neville, KCMG, CVO
Richards, *Prof.* Sir Michael Adrian, Kt., CBE
Richards, Sir Rex Edward, Kt., DSC, FRS
Richards, *Rt. Hon.* Sir Stephen Price, Kt.
Richardson, Sir Anthony Lewis, Bt. (1924)
Richardson, *Rt. Hon.* Sir Ivor Lloyd Morgan, Kt.
Richardson, Sir John Patrick, KBE
Richardson, *Lt.-Gen.* Sir Robert Francis, KCB, CVO, CBE
Richardson, Sir Thomas Legh, KCMG
Richardson-Bunbury, Sir (Richard David) Michael, Bt. (I. 1787)
Richmond, Sir David Frank, KBE, CMG
Richmond, *Prof.* Sir Mark Henry, Kt., FRS
Ricketts, Sir Peter Forbes, GCMG
Ricketts, Sir Stephen Tristram, Bt. (1828)
Ricks, *Prof.* Sir Christopher Bruce, Kt.
†Riddell, Sir Walter John, Bt. (S. 1628)
Ridgway, *Lt.-Gen.* Sir Andrew Peter, KBE, CB
Ridley, Sir Adam (Nicholas), Kt.
Ridley, Sir Michael Kershaw, KCVO
Rifkind, *Rt. Hon.* Sir Malcolm Leslie, KCMG
Rigby, Sir Anthony John, Bt. (1929)
Rigby, Sir Peter, Kt.
Rimer, *Rt. Hon.* Sir Colin Percy Farquharson, Kt.
Ripley, Sir William Hugh, Bt. (1880)
Ritako, Sir Thomas Baha, Kt., MBE
Ritblat, Sir John Henry, Kt.
Ritchie, *Prof.* Sir Lewis Duthie, Kt., OBE
†Rivett-Carnac, Sir Jonathan James, Bt. (1836)
Rix, *Rt. Hon.* Sir Bernard Anthony, Kt.
Robb, Sir John Weddell, Kt.
Roberts, Sir Derek Harry, Kt., CBE, FRS, FRENG
Roberts, *Prof.* Sir Edward Adam, KCMG
Roberts, Sir Gilbert Howland Rookehurst, Bt. (1809)
Roberts, Sir Hugh Ashley, GCVO
Roberts, Sir Ivor Anthony, KCMG
Roberts, *Dr* Sir Richard John, Kt.
Roberts, *Maj.-Gen.* Sir Sebastian John Lechmere, KCVO, OBE
Roberts, Sir Samuel, Bt. (1919)
†Roberts-Buchanan, Sir James Elton Denby, Bt. (1909)
Robertson, Sir Simon Manwaring, Kt.
Robins, Sir Ralph Harry, Kt., FRENG
Robinson, Sir Anthony, Kt.
Robinson, Sir Bruce, KCB
†Robinson, Sir Christopher Philipse, Bt. (1854)
Robinson, Sir Gerrard Jude, Kt.
Robinson, Sir Ian, Kt.
Robinson, Sir John James Michael Laud, Bt. (1660)
Robinson, *Dr* Sir Kenneth, Kt.
†Robinson, Sir Peter Frank, Bt. (1908)
Robson, Sir John Adam, KCMG
Robson, Sir Stephen Arthur, Kt., CB
Roch, *Rt. Hon.* Sir John Ormond, Kt.
Roche, Sir David O'Grady, Bt. (1838)

Roche, Sir Henry John, Kt.
Rodgers, Sir (Andrew) Piers (Wingate Aikin-Sneath), Bt. (1964)
Rodley, *Prof.* Sir Nigel, KBE
Rogers, *Air Chief Marshal* Sir John Robson, KCB, CBE
Rogers, Sir Peter, Kt.
Rogers, Sir Robert James, KCB
Rollo, *Lt.-Gen.* Sir William Raoul, KCB, CBE
Ropner, Sir John Bruce Woollacott, Bt. (1952)
Ropner, Sir Robert Clinton, Bt. (1904)
Rose, Sir Arthur James, Kt., CBE
Rose, *Rt. Hon.* Sir Christopher Dudley Roger, Kt.
Rose, Sir Clive Martin, GCMG
Rose, Sir David Lancaster, Bt. (1874)
Rose, *Gen.* Sir (Hugh) Michael, KCB, CBE, DSO, QGM
Rose, Sir John Edward Victor, Kt.
Rose, Sir Julian Day, Bt. (1872 and 1909)
Rose, Sir Stuart Alan Ransom, Kt.
Rosenthal, Sir Norman Leon, Kt.
Ross, *Maj.* Sir Andrew Charles Paterson, Bt. (1960)
Ross, *Lt.-Gen.* Sir Robert Jeremy, KCB, OBE
Ross, *Lt.-Col.* Sir Walter Hugh Malcolm, GCVO, OBE
Ross, Sir Walter Robert Alexander, KCVO
Rossi, Sir Hugh Alexis Louis, Kt.
Roth, *Hon.* Sir Peter Marcel, Kt.
Rothschild, Sir Evelyn Robert Adrian de, Kt.
Rove, *Revd* Ikan, KBE
Rowe, *Rear-Adm.* Sir Patrick Barton, KCVO, CBE
Rowe-Ham, Sir David Kenneth, GBE
Rowland, Sir (John) David, Kt.
Rowland, Sir Geoffrey Robert, Kt.
Rowlands, Sir David, KCB
Rowley, Sir Richard Charles, Bt. (1836)
Rowling, Sir John Reginald, Kt.
Rowlinson, *Prof.* Sir John Shipley, Kt., FRS
Royce, *Hon.* Sir Roger John, Kt.
Royden, Sir Christopher John, Bt. (1905)
Rubin *Prof.* Sir Peter Charles, Kt.
Rudd, Sir (Anthony) Nigel (Russell), Kt.
Ruddock, Sir Paul, Kt.
Rudge, Sir Alan Walter, Kt., CBE, FRS
Rugge-Price, Sir James Keith Peter, Bt. (1804)
Ruggles-Brise, Sir Timothy Edward, Bt. (1935)
Rumbold, Sir Henry John Sebastian, Bt. (1779)
Rusby, *Vice-Adm.* Sir Cameron, KCB, LVO
Rushdie, Sir (Ahmed) Salman, Kt.
†Russell, Sir (Arthur) Mervyn, Bt. (1812)
Russell, Sir Charles Dominic, Bt. (1916)
Russell, Sir George, Kt., CBE
Russell, Sir Muir, KCB
Russell, Sir Robert, Kt.
Rutter, *Prof.* Sir Michael Llewellyn, Kt., CBE, MD, FRS
Ryan, Sir Derek Gerald, Bt. (1919)
Rycroft, Sir Richard John, Bt. (1784)
Ryder, *Rt. Hon.* Sir Ernest Nigel, Kt., TD
Sacranie, Sir Iqbal Abdul Karim Mussa, Kt., OBE
Sainsbury, *Rt. Hon.* Sir Timothy Alan Davan, Kt.
St Clair-Ford, Sir Robin Sam, Bt. (1793)
St George, Sir John Avenel Bligh, Bt. (I. 1766)
St John-Mildmay, Sir Walter John Hugh, Bt. (1772)
St Omer, *Hon. Dr* Sir Dunstan Gerbert Raphael, KCMG
Sainty, Sir John Christopher, KCB
Sakora, *Hon.* Sir Bernard Berekia, KBE
Sales, *Hon.* Sir Philip James, Kt.
Salisbury, Sir Robert William, Kt.
Salt, Sir Patrick MacDonnell, Bt. (1869)
Salt, Sir (Thomas) Michael John, Bt. (1899)
Salusbury-Trelawny, Sir John William Richard, Bt. (1628)
Salz, Sir Anthony Michael Vaughan, Kt.
Sampson, Sir Colin, Kt., CBE, QPM
Samuel, Sir John Michael Glen, Bt. (1898)
Samuelson, Sir James Francis, Bt. (1884)
Samuelson, Sir Sydney Wylie, Kt., CBE
Samworth, Sir David Chetwode, Kt., CBE
Sanders, Sir Robert Tait, KBE, CMG
Sanders, Sir Ronald Michael, KCMG
Sanderson, Sir Frank Linton, Bt. (1920)
Sands, Sir Roger Blakemore, KCB
Sants, Sir Hector William Hepburn, Kt.
Sarei, Sir Alexis Holyweek, Kt., CBE
Sargent, Sir William Desmond, Kt., CBE
Satchwell, Sir Kevin Joseph, Kt.
Saunders, Sir Bruce Joshua, KBE
Saunders, *Hon.* Sir John Henry Boulton, Kt.
Savill, *Prof.* Sir John Stewart, Kt.
Savory, Sir Michael Berry, Kt.
Sawers, Sir Robert John, KCMG
Saxby, *Prof.* Sir Robin Keith, Kt.
Scarlett, Sir John McLeod, KCMG, OBE
Scheele, Sir Nicholas Vernon, KCMG
Schiemann, *Rt. Hon.* Sir Konrad Hermann Theodor, Kt.
Scholar, Sir Michael Charles, KCB
Scholey, Sir David Gerald, Kt., CBE
Scholey, Sir Robert, Kt., CBE, FRENG
Schubert, Sir Sydney, Kt.
Scipio, Sir Hudson Rupert, Kt.
Scott, Sir Anthony Percy, Bt. (1913)
Scott, Sir David Richard Alexander, Kt., CBE
Scott, *Prof.* Sir George Peter, Kt.
Scott, Sir James Jervoise, Bt. (1962)
Scott, Sir John Hamilton, KCVO
Scott, Sir Kenneth Bertram Adam, KCVO, CMG
Scott, Sir Oliver Christopher Anderson, Bt. (1909)
Scott, *Prof.* Sir Philip John, KBE
Scott, Sir Ridley, Kt.
Scott, Sir Robert David Hillyer, Kt.
Scott, Sir Walter John, Bt. (1907)
Scott-Lee, Sir Paul Joseph, Kt., QPM
Seale, Sir Clarence David, Kt.
Seale, Sir John Henry, Bt. (1838)
Sebastian, Sir Cuthbert Montraville, GCMG, OBE
†Sebright, Sir Rufus Hugo Giles, Bt. (1626)
Seccombe, Sir (William) Vernon Stephen, Kt.
Seconde, Sir Reginald Louis, KCMG, CVO
Sedley, *Rt. Hon.* Sir Stephen John, Kt.
Seely, Sir Nigel Edward, Bt. (1896)
Seeto, Sir Ling James, Kt., MBE
Seeyave, Sir Rene Sow Choung, Kt., CBE
Semple, Sir John Laughlin, KCB
Sergeant, Sir Patrick, Kt.
Serota, Sir Nicholas Andrew, Kt., CH
†Seton, Sir Charles Wallace, Bt. (S. 1683)
Seton, Sir Iain Bruce, Bt. (S. 1663)
Severne, *Air Vice-Marshal* Sir John de Milt, KCVO, OBE, AFC
Shadbolt, *Prof.* Sir Nigel Richard, Kt.
Shaffer, Sir Peter Levin, Kt., CBE
Shakerley, Sir Nicholas Simon Adam, Bt. (1838)
Shakespeare, Sir Thomas William, Bt. (1942)
Sharp, Sir Adrian, Bt. (1922)
Sharp, Sir Leslie, Kt., QPM
Sharp, Sir Sheridan Christopher Robin, Bt. (1920)
Sharples, Sir James, Kt., QPM
Shaw, Sir Charles De Vere, Bt. (1821)
Shaw, *Prof.* Sir John Calman, Kt., CBE
Shaw, Sir Neil McGowan, Kt.
Shaw, Sir Run Run, Kt., CBE
Shaw-Stewart, Sir Ludovic Houston, Bt. (S. 1667)
Shebbeare, Sir Thomas Andrew, KCVO
Sheehy, Sir Patrick, Kt.
Sheffield, Sir Reginald Adrian Berkeley, Bt. (1755)
Shehadie, Sir Nicholas Michael, Kt., OBE
Sheil, *Rt. Hon.* Sir John, Kt.
Sheinwald, Sir Nigel Elton, GCMG
Shelley, Sir John Richard, Bt. (1611)
Shepherd, Sir Colin Ryley, Kt.
Shepherd, Sir John Alan, KCVO, CMG
Shepherd, Sir Richard Charles Scrimgeour, Kt.
Sher, Sir Antony, KBE
Sherston-Baker, Sir Robert George Humphrey, Bt. (1796)
Shiffner, Sir Henry David, Bt. (1818)
Silber, *Hon.* Sir Stephen Robert, Kt.
Shinwell, Sir (Maurice) Adrian, Kt.
Shirreff, *Gen.* Sir Alexander Richard David, KCB, CBE
Shock, Sir Maurice, Kt.
Shortridge, Sir Jon Deacon, KCB

†Shuckburgh, Sir James Rupert Charles, Bt. (1660)
Sieff, *Hon.* Sir David, Kt.
Silber, *Rt. Hon.* Sir Stephen Robert, Kt.
Simeon, Sir Richard Edmund Barrington, Bt. (1815)
Simmonds, *Rt. Hon. Dr* Sir Kennedy Alphonse, KCMG
Simmons, *Air Marshal* Sir Michael George, KCB, AFC
Simmons, Sir Stanley Clifford, Kt.
Simms, Sir Neville Ian, Kt., FRENG
Simon, *Hon.* Sir Peregrine Charles Hugh, Kt.
Simonet, Sir Louis Marcel Pierre, Kt., CBE
Simpson, Sir Peter Austin, Kt., OBE
Simpson, *Dr* Sir Peter Jeffery, Kt.
Sims, Sir Roger Edward, Kt.
Sinclair, Sir Clive Marles, Kt.
Sinclair, Sir Robert John, Kt.
Sinclair, Sir William Robert Francis, Bt. (S.1704)
Sinclair-Lockhart, Sir Simon John Edward Francis, Bt. (S. 1636)
Sinden, Sir Donald Alfred, Kt., CBE
Singer, *Hon.* Sir Jan Peter, Kt.
Singh, *His Hon.* Sir Mota, Kt., QC
Singh, Sir Pritpal, Kt.
Singh, *Hon.* Sir Rabinder, Kt.
Singleton, Sir Roger, Kt., CBE
Sione, Sir Tomu Malaefone, GCMG, OBE
Sissons, *Prof.* Sir (John Gerald) Patrick, Kt.
†Sitwell, Sir George Reresby Sacheverell, Bt. (1808)
Skeggs, Sir Clifford George, Kt.
Skehel, Sir John James, Kt., FRS
Skingsley, *Air Chief Marshal* Sir Anthony Gerald, GBE, KCB
Skinner, Sir (Thomas) Keith (Hewitt), Bt. (1912)
Skipwith, Sir Patrick Alexander d'Estoteville, Bt. (1622)
Slack, Sir William Willatt, KCVO, FRCS
Slade, Sir Benjamin Julian Alfred, Bt. (1831)
Slade, *Rt. Hon.* Sir Christopher John, Kt.
Slaney, *Prof.* Sir Geoffrey, KBE
Slater, *Adm.* Sir John (Jock) Cunningham Kirkwood, GCB, LVO
Sleight, Sir Richard, Bt. (1920)
Smiley, *Lt.-Col.* Sir John Philip, Bt. (1903)
Smith, *Prof.* Sir Adrian Frederick Melhuish, Kt., FRS
Smith, *Hon.* Sir Andrew Charles, Kt.
Smith, Sir Andrew Thomas, Bt. (1897)
Smith, *Prof.* Sir David Cecil, Kt., FRS
Smith, Sir David Iser, KCVO
Smith, Sir Dudley (Gordon), Kt.
Smith, *Prof.* Sir Eric Brian, Kt., PHD
Smith, Sir John Alfred, Kt., QPM
Smith, Sir Joseph William Grenville, Kt.
Smith, Sir Kevin, Kt., CBE
Smith, Sir Martin Gregory, Kt.
Smith, Sir Michael John Llewellyn, KCVO, CMG
Smith, Sir (Norman) Brian, Kt., CBE, PHD
Smith, Sir Paul Brierley, Kt., CBE
Smith, *Hon.* Sir Peter (Winston), Kt.
Smith, Sir Robert Courtney, Kt., CBE
Smith, Sir Robert Hill, Bt. (1945)
Smith, *Gen.* Sir Rupert Anthony, KCB, DSO, OBE, QGM
Smith, Sir Steven Murray, Kt.
Smith-Dodsworth, Sir David John, Bt. (1784)
Smith-Gordon, Sir (Lionel) Eldred (Peter), Bt. (1838)
†Smith-Marriott, Sir Peter Francis, Bt. (1774)
Smurfit, *Dr.* Sir Michael William Joseph, KBE
Smyth, Sir Timothy John, Bt. (1956)
Snowden, *Prof.* Sir Christopher Maxwell, Kt.
Snyder, Sir Michael John, Kt.
Soar, *Adm.* Sir Trevor Alan, KCB, OBE
Sobers, Sir Garfield St Auburn, Kt.
Solomon, Sir Harry, Kt.
Somare, *Rt. Hon.* Sir Michael Thomas, GCMG, CH
Somerville, *Brig.* Sir John Nicholas, Kt., CBE
Songo, Sir Bernard Paul, Kt., CMG, OBE
Sorrell, Sir John William, Kt., CBE
Sorrell, Sir Martin Stuart, Kt.
Soulsby, Sir Peter Alfred, Kt.
Soutar, *Air Marshal* Sir Charles John Williamson, KBE
Souter, Sir Brian, Kt.
Southby, Sir John Richard Bilbe, Bt. (1937)
Southern, *Prof.* Sir Edwin Mellor, Kt.
Southgate, Sir Colin Grieve, Kt.
Southgate, Sir William David, Kt.
Southward, *Dr* Sir Nigel Ralph, KCVO
Sowrey, *Air Marshal* Sir Frederick Beresford, KCB, CBE, AFC
Sparrow, Sir John, Kt.
Spearman, Sir Alexander Young Richard Mainwaring, Bt. (1840)
Speed, Sir (Herbert) Keith, Kt., RD
Speelman, Sir Cornelis Jacob, Bt. (1686)
Spencer, Sir Derek Harold, Kt., QC
Spencer, *Vice-Adm.* Sir Peter, KCB
Spencer, *Hon.* Sir Robin Godfrey, Kt.
Spencer-Nairn, Sir Robert Arnold, Bt. (1933)
Spicer, Sir James Wilton, Kt.
Spicer, Sir Nicholas Adrian Albert, Bt. (1906)
Spiers, Sir Donald Maurice, Kt., CB, TD
Spooner, Sir James Douglas, Kt.
Spring, Sir Dryden Thomas, Kt.
Spurling, Sir John Damian, KCVO, OBE
Squire, *Air Chief Marshal* Sir Peter Ted, GCB, DFC, AFC, ADC
Stadlen, *Hon.* Sir Nicholas Felix, Kt.
Stagg, Sir Charles Richard Vernon, KCMG
Staite, Sir Richard John, Kt., OBE
†Stamer, Sir Peter Tomlinson, Bt. (1809)
Stanhope, *Adm.* Sir Mark, GCB, OBE, ADC
Stanier, Sir Beville Douglas, Bt. (1917)
Stanley, *Rt. Hon.* Sir John Paul, Kt., MP
Staples, Sir Richard Molesworth, Bt. (I. 1628)
Starkey, Sir John Philip, Bt. (1935)
Staughton, *Rt. Hon.* Sir Christopher Stephen Thomas Jonathan Thayer, Kt.
Stear, *Air Chief Marshal* Sir Michael James Douglas, KCB, CBE
Steel, *Hon.* Sir David William, Kt.
Steer, Sir Alan William, Kt.
Stephen, *Rt. Hon.* Sir Ninian Martin, KG, GCMG, GCVO, KBE
Stephens, Sir (Edwin) Barrie, Kt.
Stephens, Sir Jonathan Andrew de Sievrac, KCB
Stephens, Sir William Benjamin Synge, Kt.
Stephenson, Sir Henry Upton, Bt. (1936)
Stephenson, Sir Paul Robert, Kt., QPM
Sterling, Sir Michael John Howard, Kt.
Sternberg, Sir Sigmund, Kt.
Stevens, Sir Jocelyn Edward Greville, Kt., CVO
Stevenson, Sir Hugh Alexander, Kt.
Stevenson, Sir Simpson, Kt.
Stewart, Sir Alan d'Arcy, Bt. (I. 1623)
Stewart, Sir Brian John, Kt., CBE
Stewart, Sir David James Henderson, Bt. (1957)
Stewart, Sir David John Christopher, Bt. (1803)
Stewart, Sir James Moray, KCB
Stewart, Sir (John) Simon (Watson), Bt. (1920)
Stewart, Sir John Young, Kt., OBE
Stewart, Sir Patrick, Kt., OBE
Stewart, *Lt.-Col.* Sir Robert Christie, KCVO, CBE, TD
Stewart, Sir Robin Alastair, Bt. (1960)
Stewart, *Prof.* Sir William Duncan Paterson, Kt., FRS, FRSE
Stewart-Clark, Sir John, Bt. (1918)
Stewart-Richardson, Sir Simon Alaisdair, Bt. (S. 1630)
Stibbon, *Gen.* Sir John James, KCB, OBE
Stilgoe, Sir Richard Henry Simpson, Kt., OBE
Stirling, Sir Alexander John Dickson, KBE, CMG
Stirling, Sir Angus Duncan Aeneas, Kt.
Stirling-Hamilton, Sir Malcolm William Bruce, Bt. (S. 1673)
Stirling of Garden, *Col.* Sir James, KCVO, CBE, TD
Stockdale, Sir Thomas Minshull, Bt. (1960)
Stoddart, *Prof.* Sir James Fraser, Kt.
Stone, Sir Christopher, Kt.
Stonhouse, *Revd* Michael Philip, Bt. (1628 and 1670)
Stonor, *Air Marshal* Sir Thomas Henry, KCB
Stoppard, Sir Thomas, Kt., OM, CBE
Storey, *Hon.* Sir Richard, Bt., CBE (1960)
Stothard, Sir Peter Michael, Kt.
Stott, Sir Adrian George Ellingham, Bt. (1920)
Stoute, Sir Michael Ronald, Kt.
Stowe, Sir Kenneth Ronald, GCB, CVO

Stracey, Sir John Simon, Bt. (1818)
Strachan, Sir Curtis Victor, Kt., CVO
Strachan, Sir Hew Francis Anthony, Kt.
Strachey, Sir Charles, Bt. (1801)
Straker, Sir Louis Hilton, KCMG
Strang Steel, Sir (Fiennes) Michael, Bt. (1938), CBE
Stratton, *Prof.* Sir Michael Rudolf, Kt., FRS
Street, *Hon.* Sir Laurence Whistler, KCMG
Streeton, Sir Terence George, KBE, CMG
Strickland-Constable, Sir Frederic, Bt. (1641)
Stringer, Sir Donald Edgar, Kt., CBE
Stringer, Sir Howard, Kt.
Strong, Sir Roy Colin, Kt., PHD, FSA
Stronge, Sir James Anselan Maxwell, Bt. (1803)
Stuart, Sir James Keith, Kt.
Stuart, Sir Kenneth Lamonte, Kt.
†Stuart, Sir Phillip Luttrell, Bt. (1660)
†Stuart-Forbes, Sir William Daniel, Bt. (S. 1626)
Stuart-Menteth, Sir Charles Greaves, Bt. (1838)
Stuart-Paul, *Air Marshal* Sir Ronald Ian, KBE
Stuart-Smith, *Hon.* Sir Jeremy Hugh, Kt.
Stuart-Smith, *Rt. Hon.* Sir Murray, KCMG, Kt.
Stubbs, Sir William Hamilton, Kt., PHD
Stucley, *Lt.* Sir Hugh George Coplestone Bampfylde, Bt. (1859)
Studd, Sir Edward Fairfax, Bt. (1929)
Studholme, Sir Henry William, Bt. (1956)
Stunell, *Rt. Hon.* Sir Robert Andrew, Kt., OBE
Sturridge, Sir Nicholas Anthony, KCVO
Stuttard, Sir John Boothman, Kt.
†Style, Sir William Frederick, Bt. (1627)
Sullivan, *Rt. Hon.* Sir Jeremy Mirth, Kt.
Sullivan, Sir Richard Arthur, Bt. (1804)
Sulston, Sir John Edward, Kt.
Sunderland, Sir John Michael, Kt.
Supperstone, *Hon.* Sir Michael Alan, Kt.
Sutherland, Sir John Brewer, Bt. (1921)
Sutherland, Sir William George MacKenzie, Kt.
Sutton, *Air Marshal* Sir John Matthias Dobson, KCB
Sutton, Sir Richard Lexington, Bt. (1772)
Swaffield, Sir James Chesebrough, Kt., CBE, RD
Swan, Sir Conrad Marshall John Fisher, KCVO, PHD
Swan, Sir John William David, KBE
Swann, Sir Michael Christopher, Bt. (1906), TD
Sweeney, Sir George, Kt.
Sweeney, *Hon.* Sir Nigel Hamilton, Kt.
Sweeting, *Prof.* Sir Martin Nicholas, Kt., OBE, FRS
Swinburn, *Lt.-Gen.* Sir Richard Hull, KCB
Swinnerton-Dyer, *Prof.* Sir (Henry) Peter (Francis), Bt. (1678), KBE, FRS
Swinton, *Maj.-Gen.* Sir John, KCVO, OBE
Swire, Sir Adrian Christopher, Kt.
Swire, Sir John Anthony, Kt., CBE
Sykes, Sir David Michael, Bt. (1921)
Sykes, Sir Francis John Badcock, Bt. (1781)
Sykes, Sir Hugh Ridley, Kt.
Sykes, *Prof.* Sir (Malcolm) Keith, Kt.
Sykes, Sir Richard, Kt.
Sykes, Sir Tatton Christopher Mark, Bt. (1783)
Symons, *Vice-Adm.* Sir Patrick Jeremy, KBE
Synge, Sir Robert Carson, Bt. (1801)
Tang, Sir David Wing-cheung, KBE
Tanner, Sir David Whitlock, Kt., CBE
Tapsell, *Rt. Hon.* Sir Peter Hannay Bailey, Kt.
Tapps-Gervis-Meyrick, Sir George Christopher Cadafael, Bt. (1791)
†Tate, Sir Edward Nicolas, Bt. (1898)
Taureka, *Dr* Sir Reubeh, KBE
Tauvasa, Sir Joseph James, KBE
Tavare, Sir John, Kt., CBE
Tavener, *Prof.* Sir John Kenneth, Kt.
Taylor, Sir (Arthur) Godfrey, Kt.
Taylor, Sir Cyril Julian Hebden, GBE
Taylor, Sir Edward Macmillan (Teddy), Kt.
Taylor, Sir Hugh Henderson, KCB
Taylor, *Rt. Revd* John Bernard, KCVO
Taylor, *Dr* Sir John Michael, Kt., OBE
Taylor, *Prof.* Sir Martin John, Kt., FRS
Taylor, Sir Nicholas Richard Stuart, Bt. (1917)
Taylor, *Prof.* Sir William, Kt., CBE
Taylor, Sir William George, Kt.
Teagle, *Vice-Adm.* Sir Somerford Francis, KBE
Teare, *Hon.* Sir Nigel John Martin, Kt.
Teasdale, *Prof.* Sir Graham Michael, Kt.
Tebbit, Sir Kevin Reginald, KCB, CMG
Temple, *Prof.* Sir John Graham, Kt.
Temple, Sir Richard Carnac Chartier, Bt. (1876)
Temu, *Hon. Dr* Sir Puka, KBE, CMG
Tennyson-D'Eyncourt, Sir Mark Gervais, Bt. (1930)
Terry, *Air Marshal* Sir Colin George, KBE, CB
Terry, *Air Chief Marshal* Sir Peter David George, GCB, AFC
Thatcher, Sir Mark, Bt. (1990)
Thomas, Sir David John Godfrey, Bt. (1694)
Thomas, Sir Derek Morison David, KCMG
Thomas, *Prof.* Sir Eric Jackson, Kt.
Thomas, Sir Gilbert Stanley, Kt., OBE
Thomas, Sir Jeremy Cashel, KCMG
Thomas, Sir (John) Alan, Kt.
Thomas, *Prof.* Sir John Meurig, Kt., FRS
Thomas, Sir Keith Vivian, Kt.
Thomas, *Dr* Sir Leton Felix, KCMG, CBE
Thomas, Sir Philip Lloyd, KCVO, CMG
Thomas, Sir Quentin Jeremy, Kt., CB
Thomas, *Rt. Hon.* Sir Roger John Laugharne, Kt.
Thomas, *Rt. Hon.* Sir Swinton Barclay, Kt.
Thomas, Sir William Michael, Bt. (1919)
Thomas, Sir (William) Michael (Marsh), Bt. (1918)
Thompson, Sir Christopher Peile, Bt. (1890)
Thompson, Sir Clive Malcolm, Kt.
Thompson, Sir David Albert, KCMG
Thompson, Sir Gilbert Williamson, Kt., OBE
Thompson, *Prof.* Sir Michael Warwick, Kt., DSc
Thompson, Sir Nicholas Annesley, Bt. (1963)
Thompson, Sir Nigel Cooper, KCMG, CBE
Thompson, Sir Paul Anthony, Bt. (1963)
Thompson, Sir Peter Anthony, Kt.
Thompson, *Dr* Sir Richard Paul Hepworth, KCVO
Thompson, Sir Thomas d'Eyncourt John, Bt. (1806)
Thomson, Sir (Frederick Douglas) David, Bt. (1929)
Thomson, Sir John Adam, GCMG
Thomson, Sir Mark Wilfrid Home, Bt. (1925)
Thomson, Sir Thomas James, Kt., CBE, FRCP
Thorne, Sir Neil Gordon, Kt., OBE, TD
Thornton, *Air Marshal* Sir Barry Michael, KCB
Thornton, Sir (George) Malcolm, Kt.
Thornton, Sir Richard Eustace, KCVO, OBE
†Thorold, Sir (Anthony) Oliver, Bt. (1642)
Thorpe, *Rt. Hon.* Sir Mathew Alexander, Kt.
Thurecht, Sir Ramon Richard, Kt., OBE
Thwaites, Sir Bryan, Kt., PHD
Tickell, Sir Crispin Charles Cervantes, GCMG, KCVO
Tidmarsh, Sir James Napier, KCVO, MBE
Tilt, Sir Robin Richard, Kt.
Tiltman, Sir John Hessell, KCVO
Timmins, *Col.* Sir John Bradford, KCVO, OBE, TD
Tims, Sir Michael David, KCVO
Tindle, Sir Ray Stanley, Kt., CBE
Tirvengadum, Sir Harry Krishnan, Kt.
Tjoeng, Sir James Neng, KBE
Tod, *Vice-Adm.* Sir Jonathan James Richard, KCB, CBE
Todd, *Prof.* Sir David, Kt., CBE
Todd, Sir Ian Pelham, KBE, FRCS
Toka, Sir Mahuru Dadi, Kt., MBE
Tollemache, Sir Lyonel Humphry John, Bt. (1793)
Tomkys, Sir (William) Roger, KCMG
Tomlinson, *Prof.* Sir Bernard Evans, Kt., CBE
Tomlinson, Sir John Rowland, Kt., CBE
Tomlinson, Sir Michael John, Kt., CBE

Tomlinson, *Rt. Hon.* Sir Stephen Miles, Kt.
Tooke, *Prof.* Sir John Edward, Kt.
Tooley, Sir John, Kt.
ToRobert, Sir Henry Thomas, KBE
Torpy, *Air Chief Marshal* Sir Glenn Lester, GCB, CBE, DSO
Torry, Sir Peter James, GCVO, KCMG
Touche, Sir Anthony George, Bt. (1920)
Touche, Sir Rodney Gordon, Bt. (1962)
Toulson, *Rt. Hon.* Sir Roger Grenfell, Kt.
Tovadek, Sir Martin, Kt. CMG
Tovey, Sir Brian John Maynard, KCMG
ToVue, Sir Ronald, Kt., OBE
Towneley, Sir Simon Peter Edmund Cosmo William, KCVO
Townsend, Sir Cyril David, Kt.
Traill, Sir Alan Towers, GBE
Trainor, *Prof.* Sir Richard Hughes, KBE
Treacher, *Adm.* Sir John Devereux, KCB
Treacy, *Rt. Hon.* Sir Colman Maurice, Kt.
Treacy, *Hon.* Sir (James Mary) Seamus, Kt.
Treitel, *Prof.* Sir Guenter Heinz, Kt., FBA, QC
Trescowthick, Sir Donald Henry, KBE
†Trevelyan, Sir Andrew John, Bt. (1662 and 1874)
Trezise, Sir Kenneth Bruce, Kt., OBE
Trippier, Sir David Austin, Kt., RD
†Tritton, Sir Jeremy Ernest, Bt. (1905)
Trollope, Sir Anthony Simon, Bt. (1642)
Trotman-Dickenson, Sir Aubrey Fiennes, Kt.
Trotter, Sir Neville Guthrie, Kt.
Troubridge, Sir Thomas Richard, Bt. (1799)
Trousdell, *Lt.-Gen.* Sir Philip Charles Cornwallis, KBE, CB
Truscott, Sir Ralph Eric Nicholson, Bt. (1909)
Tsang, Sir Donald Yam-keun, KBE
Tuck, Sir Bruce Adolph Reginald, Bt. (1910)
Tucker, *Hon.* Sir Richard Howard, Kt.
Tuckey, *Rt. Hon.* Sir Simon Lane, Kt.
Tugendhat, *Hon.* Sir Michael George, Kt.
Tuite, Sir Christopher Hugh, Bt. (1622), PHD
Tuivaga, Sir Timoci Uluiburotu, Kt.
Tully, Sir William Mark, KBE
Tupper, Sir Charles Hibbert, Bt. (1888)
Turbott, Sir Ian Graham, Kt., CMG, CVO
Turing, Sir John Dermot, Bt. (S. 1638)
Turner, Sir Colin William Carstairs, Kt., CBE, DFC
Turner, *Hon.* Sir Michael John, Kt.
Turnquest, Sir Orville Alton, GCMG, QC
Tusa, Sir John, Kt.
Tweedie, *Prof.* Sir David Philip, Kt.
Tyree, Sir (Alfred) William, Kt., OBE
Tyrwhitt, Sir Reginald Thomas Newman, Bt. (1919)

Udny-Lister, Sir Edward Julian, Kt.
Underhill, *Rt. Hon.* Sir Nicholas Edward, Kt.
Underwood, *Prof.* Sir James Cressee Elphinstone, Kt.
Unwin, Sir (James) Brian, KCB
Ure, Sir John Burns, KCMG, LVO
Urquhart, Sir Brian Edward, KCMG, MBE
Urwick, Sir Alan Bedford, KCVO, CMG
Usher, Sir Andrew John, Bt. (1899)
Utting, Sir William Benjamin, Kt., CB

Vardy, Sir Peter, Kt.
Varney, Sir David Robert, Kt.
Vasquez, Sir Alfred Joseph, Kt., CBE, QC
Vassar-Smith, Sir John Rathbone, Bt. (1917)
Vavasour, Sir Eric Michael Joseph Marmaduke, Bt. (1828)
Veness, Sir David, Kt., CBE, QPM
Venner, Sir Kenneth Dwight Vincent, KBE
Vereker, Sir John Michael Medlicott, KCB
†Verney, Sir John Sebastian, Bt. (1946)
Verney, *Hon.* Sir Lawrence John, Kt., TD
Verney, Sir Edmund Ralph, Bt. (1818)
Vernon, Sir James William, Bt. (1914)
Vernon, Sir (William) Michael, Kt.
Vestey, Sir Paul Edmund, Bt. (1921)
Vickers, *Prof.* Sir Brian William, Kt.
Vickers, Sir John Stuart, Kt.
Vickers, *Lt.-Gen.* Sir Richard Maurice Hilton, KCB, CVO, OBE
Vickers, Sir Roger Henry, KCVO
Viggers, *Lt-Gen.* Sir Frederick Richard, KCB, CMG, MBE
Viggers, Sir Peter John, Kt.
Vincent, Sir William Percy Maxwell, Bt. (1936)
Vineall, Sir Anthony John Patrick, Kt.
Vos, *Hon.* Sir Geoffrey Michael, Kt.
†Vyvyan, Sir Ralph Ferrers Alexander, Bt. (1645)

Wade-Gery, Sir Robert Lucian, KCMG, KCVO
Waena, Sir Nathaniel Rahumaea, GCMG
Waine, *Rt. Revd* John, KCVO
Waite, *Rt. Hon.* Sir John Douglas, Kt.
Waka, Sir Lucas Joseph, Kt., OBE
Wake, Sir Hereward, Bt. (1621), MC
Wakefield, Sir (Edward) Humphry (Tyrell), Bt. (1962)
Wakefield, Sir Norman Edward, Kt.
Wakeford, Sir Geoffrey Michael Montgomery, Kt., OBE
Wakeham, *Prof.* Sir William Arnot, Kt.
†Wakeley, Sir Nicholas Jeremy, Bt. (1952)
Wald, *Prof.* Sir Nicholas John, Kt.
Wales, Sir Robert Andrew, Kt.
Waley-Cohen, Sir Stephen Harry, Bt. (1961)
Walford, Sir Christopher Rupert, Kt.
Walker, *Gen.* Sir Antony Kenneth Frederick, KCB
Walker, Sir Christopher Robert Baldwin, Bt. (1856)
Walker, Sir David Alan, Kt.
Walker, Air Vice-Marshal Sir David Allan, KCVO, OBE
Walker, Sir Harold Berners, KCMG
Walker, Sir John Ernest, Kt., DPHIL, FRS
Walker, *Air Marshal* Sir John Robert, KCB, CBE, AFC
Walker, Sir Miles Rawstron, Kt., CBE
Walker, Sir Patrick Jeremy, KCB
Walker, *Hon.* Sir Paul James, Kt.
Walker, Sir Rodney Myerscough, Kt.
Walker, Sir Roy Edward, Bt. (1906)
Walker, *Hon.* Sir Timothy Edward, Kt.
Walker, Sir Victor Stewart Heron, Bt. (1868)
Walker-Okeover, Sir Andrew Peter Monro, Bt. (1886)
Walker-Smith, *Hon.* Sir John Jonah, Bt. (1960)
Wall, Sir (John) Stephen, GCMG, LVO
Wall, *Rt. Hon.* Sir Nicholas Peter Rathbone, Kt.
Wall, *Gen.* Sir Peter Anthony, GCB, CBE, ADC
Wallace, *Lt.-Gen.* Sir Christopher Brooke Quentin, KBE
Wallace, *Prof.* Sir David James, Kt., CBE, FRS
Waller, *Rt. Hon.* Sir (George) Mark, Kt.
Waller, Sir John Michael, Bt. (I. 1780)
Wallis, Sir Peter Gordon, KCVO
Wallis, Sir Timothy William, Kt.
Walmsley, *Vice-Adm.* Sir Robert, KCB
Walport, *Dr* Sir Mark Jeremy, Kt.
†Walsham, Sir Gerald Percy Robert, Bt. (1831)
Walters, Sir Dennis Murray, Kt., MBE
Walters, Sir Frederick Donald, Kt.
Walters, Sir Peter Ingram, Kt.
Wamiri, Sir Akapite, KBE
Ward, *Rt. Hon.* Sir Alan Hylton, Kt.
Ward, Sir Austin, Kt., QC
Ward, *Hon.* Sir (Frederik) Gordon (Roy), Kt., OBE
Ward, *Prof.* Sir John MacQueen, Kt., CBE
Ward, Sir Joseph James Laffey, Bt. (1911)
Ward, Sir Timothy James, Kt.
Wardale, Sir Geoffrey Charles, KCB
Wardlaw, Sir Henry Justin, Bt. (NS. 1631)
Waring, Sir (Alfred) Holburt, Bt. (1935)
Warmington, Sir Rupert Marshall, Bt. (1908)
Warner, Sir Philip Courtenay Thomas, Bt. (1910)
Warner, Sir Gerald Chierici, KCMG
Warren, Sir David Alexander, KCMG
Warren, Sir (Frederick) Miles, KBE
Warren, Sir Kenneth Robin, Kt.
Warren, Sir Nicholas Roger, Kt.
Wass, Sir Douglas William Gretton, GCB
Waterlow, Sir Christopher Rupert, Bt. (1873)
Waterlow, Sir (James) Gerard, Bt. (1930)
Waters, *Gen.* Sir (Charles) John, GCB, CBE
Waters, Sir (Thomas) Neil (Morris), Kt.
Waterworth, Sir Alan William, KCVO

Wates, Sir Christopher Stephen, Kt.
Watson, *Prof.* Sir David John, Kt., PHD
Watson, Sir Graham Robert, Kt.
Watson, Sir (James) Andrew, Bt. (1866)
Watson, *Prof.* Sir Robert Tony, Kt., CMG
Watson, Sir Ronald Matthew, Kt., CBE
Watson, Sir Simon Conran Hamilton, Bt. (1895)
Watt, *Gen.* Sir Charles Redmond, KCB, KCVO, CBE, ADC
Watts, Sir John Augustus Fitzroy, KCMG, CBE
Watts, Sir Philip Beverley, KCMG
Weatherall, *Prof.* Sir David John, Kt., FRS
Weatherall, *Vice-Adm.* Sir James Lamb, KCVO, KBE
Weatherup, *Hon.* Sir Ronald Eccles, Kt.
Webb, *Prof.* Sir Adrian Leonard, Kt.
Webb-Carter, *Maj.-Gen.* Sir Evelyn John, KCVO, OBE
Webster, *Vice-Adm.* Sir John Morrison, KCB
Wedgwood, Sir Ralph Nicholas, Bt. (1942)
Weekes, Sir Everton DeCourcey, KCMG, OBE
Weinberg, Sir Mark Aubrey, Kt.
Weir, *Hon.* Sir Reginald George, Kt.
Weir, Sir Roderick Bignell, Kt.
Welby, Sir (Richard) Bruno Gregory, Bt. (1801)
Welch, Sir John Reader, Bt. (1957)
Weldon, Sir Anthony William, Bt. (I. 1723)
Wellend, *Prof.* Sir Mark Edward, Kt.
†Wells, Sir Christopher Charles, Bt. (1944)
Wells, Sir John Julius, Kt.
Wells, Sir William Henry Weston, Kt., FRICS
Wesker, Sir Arnold, Kt.
Wessely, *Prof.* Sir Simon Charles, Kt.
Westbrook, Sir Neil Gowanloch, Kt., CBE
Westmacott, Sir Peter John, KCMG
Weston, Sir Michael Charles Swift, KCMG, CVO
Weston, Sir (Philip) John, KCMG
Whalen, Sir Geoffrey Henry, Kt., CBE
Wheeler, Sir Harry Anthony, Kt., OBE
Wheeler, *Rt. Hon.* Sir John Daniel, Kt.
Wheeler, Sir John Frederick, Bt. (1920)
Wheeler, *Gen.* Sir Roger Neil, GCB, CBE
Wheeler-Booth, Sir Michael Addison John, KCB
Wheler, Sir Trevor Woodford, Bt. (1660)
Whitaker, Sir John James Ingham (Jack), Bt. (1936)
Whitbread, Sir Samuel Charles, KCVO
Whitchurch, Sir Graeme Ian, Kt., OBE
White, *Prof.* Sir Christopher John, Kt., CVO
White, Sir Christopher Robert Meadows, Bt. (1937)
White, Sir David (David Jason), Kt., OBE
White, Sir David Harry, Kt.
White, Sir George Stanley James, Bt. (1904)
White, *Adm.* Sir Hugo Moresby, GCB, CBE
White, Sir John Woolmer, Bt. (1922)
White, Sir Nicholas Peter Archibald, Bt. (1802)
White, Sir Willard Wentworth, Kt., CBE
White-Spunner, *Lt.-Gen.* Sir Barnabas William Benjamin, KCB, CBE
Whitehead, Sir John Stainton, GCMG, CVO
Whitehead, Sir Philip Henry Rathbone, Bt. (1889)
Whiteley, *Gen.* Sir Peter John Frederick, GCB, OBE, RM
Whitfield, Sir William, Kt., CBE
Whitmore, Sir Clive Anthony, GCB, CVO
Whitmore, Sir John Henry Douglas, Bt. (1954)
Whitson, Sir Keith Roderick, Kt.
Wickerson, Sir John Michael, Kt.
Wicks, Sir Nigel Leonard, GCB, CVO, CBE
†Wigan, Sir Michael Iain, Bt. (1898)
Wiggin, Sir Alfred William (Jerry), Kt., TD
†Wiggin, Sir Richard Edward John, Bt. (1892)
Wiggins, Sir Bradley Marc, Kt., CBE
Wigram, Sir John Woolmore, Bt. (1805)
Wilbraham, Sir Richard Baker, Bt. (1776)
Wild, Sir John Ralston, Kt., CBE
Wiles, *Prof.* Sir Andrew John, KBE
Wilkes, *Gen.* Sir Michael John, KCB, CBE
Wilkie, *Hon.* Sir Alan Fraser, Kt.
Wilkinson, Sir (David) Graham (Brook) Bt. (1941)
Wilkinson, *Prof.* Sir Denys Haigh, Kt., FRS
Willcocks, Sir David Valentine, Kt., CBE, MC
Willcocks, *Lt.-Gen.* Sir Michael Alan, KCB, CVO
Williams, Sir (Arthur) Gareth Ludovic Emrys Rhys, Bt. (1918)
Williams, Sir Charles Othniel, Kt.
Williams, Sir Daniel Charles, GCMG, QC
Williams, Sir David Reeve, Kt., CBE
Williams, *Hon.* Sir Denys Ambrose, KCMG
Williams, Sir Donald Mark, Bt. (1866)
Williams, *Prof.* Sir (Edward) Dillwyn, Kt., FRCP
Williams, Sir Francis Owen Garbett, Kt., CBE
Williams, *Hon.* Sir (John) Griffith, Kt.
Williams, Sir (Lawrence) Hugh, Bt. (1798)
Williams, Sir Nicholas Stephen, Kt.
Williams, Sir Paul Michael, Kt., OBE
Williams, Sir Peter Michael, Kt.
Williams, Sir (Robert) Philip Nathaniel, Bt. (1915)
Williams, Sir Robin Philip, Bt. (1953)
Williams, *Prof.* Sir Roger, Kt.
Williams, Sir (William) Maxwell (Harries), Kt.
Williams, *Hon.* Sir Wyn Lewis, Kt.
Williams-Bulkeley, Sir Richard Thomas, Bt. (1661)
Williams-Wynn, Sir David Watkin, Bt. (1688)
Williamson, Sir George Malcolm, Kt.
Williamson, *Marshal of the Royal Air Force* Sir Keith Alec, GCB, AFC
Williamson, Sir Robert Brian, Kt., CBE
Willink, Sir Edward Daniel, Bt. (1957)
Wills, Sir David James Vernon, Bt. (1923)
Wills, Sir David Seton, Bt. (1904)
Wilmot, Sir David, Kt., QPM
Wilmot, Sir Henry Robert, Bt. (1759)
Wilmut, *Prof.* Sir Ian, Kt., OBE
Wilsey, *Gen.* Sir John Finlay Willasey, GCB, CBE
Wilshaw, Sir Michael, Kt.
Wilson, *Prof.* Sir Alan Geoffrey, Kt.
Wilson, *Vice-Adm.* Sir Barry Nigel, KCB
Wilson, Sir David, Bt. (1920)
Wilson, Sir David Mackenzie, Kt.
Wilson, Sir James William Douglas, Bt. (1906)
Wilson, *Brig.* Sir Mathew John Anthony, Bt. (1874), OBE, MC
Wilson, *Rt. Hon.* Sir Nicholas Allan Roy, Kt.
Wilson, *Prof.* Sir Robert James Timothy, Kt.
Wilson, Sir Robert Peter, KCMG
Wilson, *Air Chief Marshal* Sir (Ronald) Andrew (Fellowes), KCB, AFC
Wingate, *Capt.* Sir Miles Buckley, KCVO
Winkley, Sir David Ross, Kt.
Winnington, Sir Anthony Edward, Bt. (1755)
Winship, Sir Peter James Joseph, Kt., CBE
Winter, *Dr* Sir Gregory Winter, Kt., CBE
Winterton, Sir Nicholas Raymond, Kt.
Wiseman, Sir John William, Bt. (1628)
Witty, Sir Andrew, Kt.
Wolfendale, *Prof.* Sir Arnold Whittaker, Kt., FRS
Wolseley, Sir Charles Garnet Richard Mark, Bt. (1628)
†Wolseley, Sir James Douglas, Bt. (I. 1745)
†Wombwell, Sir George Philip Frederick, Bt. (1778)
Womersley, Sir Peter John Walter, Bt. (1945)
Woo, Sir Leo Joseph, Kt., MBE
Woo, Sir Po-Shing, Kt.
Wood, Sir Andrew Marley, GCMG
Wood, Sir Anthony John Page, Bt. (1837)
Wood, Sir Ian Clark, Kt., CBE
Wood, *Hon.* Sir John Kember, Kt., MC
Wood, Sir Martin Francis, Kt., OBE
Wood, Sir Michael Charles, KCMG
Wood, *Hon.* Sir Roderic Lionel James, Kt.
Woodard, *Rear Adm.* Sir Robert Nathaniel, KCVO
Woodhead, *Vice-Adm.* Sir (Anthony) Peter, KCB

Woodhead, Sir Christopher Anthony, Kt.
Woodhouse, *Rt. Hon.* Sir (Arthur) Owen, KBE, DSC
Woods, *Prof.* Sir Kent Linton, Kt.
Woods, Sir Robert Kynnersley, Kt., CBE
Woodward, Sir Clive Ronald, Kt., OBE
Woodward, Sir Thomas Jones (Tom Jones), Kt., OBE
Wootton, Sir David Hugh, Kt.
Worsley, Sir William Ralph, Bt. (1838)
Worsthorne, Sir Peregrine Gerard, Kt.
Wratten, *Air Chief Marshal* Sir William John, GBE, CB, AFC
Wraxall, Sir Charles Frederick Lascelles, Bt. (1813)
Wrey, Sir George Richard Bourchier, Bt. (1628)
Wright, Sir Allan Frederick, KBE
Wright, Sir David John, GCMG, LVO
Wright, *Hon.* Sir (John) Michael, Kt.
Wright, *Prof.* Sir Nicholas Alcwyn, Kt.
Wright, Sir Peter Robert, Kt., CBE
Wright, *Air Marshal* Sir Robert Alfred, KBE, AFC
Wright, Sir Stephen John Leadbetter, KCMG
Wrightson, Sir Charles Mark Garmondsway, Bt. (1900)
Wrigley, *Prof.* Sir Edward Anthony (Sir Tony), Kt., PHD, PBA
Wrixon-Becher, Sir John William Michael, Bt. (1831)
Wroughton, Sir Philip Lavallin, KCVO
Wu, Sir Gordon Ying Sheung, KCMG
Wynne, Sir Graham Robert, Kt., CBE

Yacoub, *Prof.* Sir Magdi Habib, Kt., FRCS
Yaki, Sir Roy, KBE
Yang, *Hon.* Sir Ti Liang, Kt.
Yardley, Sir David Charles Miller, Kt., LLD
Yarrow, Sir Eric Grant, Bt. (1916), MBE
Yassaie, *Dr* Sir Hossein, Kt.
Yocklunn, Sir John (Soong Chung), KCVO
Yoo Foo, Sir (François) Henri, Kt.
Young, Sir Brian Walter Mark, Kt.
Young, Sir Colville Norbert, GCMG, MBE
Young, Sir Dennis Charles, KCMG
Young, *Rt. Hon.* Sir George Samuel Knatchbull, Bt. (1813), CH
Young, Sir Jimmy Leslie Ronald, Kt., CBE
Young, Sir John Kenyon Roe, Bt. (1821)
Young, Sir John Robertson, GCMG
Young, Sir Leslie Clarence, Kt., CBE
Young, Sir Nicholas Charles, Kt.
Young, Sir Robin Urquhart, KCB
Young, Sir Roger William, Kt.
Young, Sir Stephen Stewart Templeton, Bt. (1945)
Young, Sir William Neil, Bt. (1769)
Younger, *Capt.* Sir John David Bingham, KCVO
Younger, Sir Julian William Richard, Bt. (1911)
Yuwi, Sir Matiabe, KBE

Zambellas, *Adm.* Sir George Michael, KCB, DSC
Zeeman, *Prof.* Sir (Erik) Christopher, Kt., FRS
Zissman, Sir Bernard Philip, Kt.
Zochonis, Sir John Basil, Kt.
Zunz, Sir Gerhard Jacob (Jack), Kt., FRENG
Zurenuoc, Sir Manasupe Zure, Kt., OBE
Zurenuoc, Sir Zibang, KBE

THE ORDER OF ST JOHN

THE MOST VENERABLE ORDER OF THE HOSPITAL OF ST JOHN OF JERUSALEM (1888)

GCStJ	Bailiff/Dame Grand Cross
KStJ	Knight of Justice/Grace
DStJ	Dame of Justice/Grace
CStJ	Commander
OStJ	Officer
SBStJ	Serving Brother
SSStJ	Serving Sister

Motto, Pro Fide, Pro Utilitate Hominum
(For the faith and in the service of humanity)

The Order of St John, founded in the early 12th century in Jerusalem, was a religious order with a particular duty to care for the sick. In Britain the order was dissolved by Henry VIII in 1540 but the British branch was revived in the early 19th century. The branch was not accepted by the Grand Magistracy of the Order in Rome but its search for a role in the tradition of the hospitallers led to the founding of the St John Ambulance Association in 1877 and later the St John Ambulance Brigade; in 1882 the St John Ophthalmic Hospital was founded in Jerusalem. A royal charter was granted in 1888 establishing the Order of St John as a British Order of Chivalry with the sovereign as its head.

Since October 1999 the whole order worldwide has been governed by a Grand Council which includes a representative from each of the eight priories (England, Scotland, Wales, South Africa, New Zealand, Canada, Australia and the USA). In addition there are also five commanderies in Northern Ireland, Jersey, Guernsey, the Isle of Man and Western Australia. There are also branches in about 30 other Commonwealth countries. Apart from St John Ambulance, the Order is also responsible for the Jerusalem Eye Hospital. Admission to the order is usually conferred in recognition of service to either one of these institutions. Membership does not confer any rank, style, title or precedence on a recipient.

SOVEREIGN HEAD OF THE ORDER
HM The Queen

GRAND PRIOR
HRH The Duke of Gloucester, KG, GCVO

Lord Prior, Prof. Anthony Mellows, OBE, TD
Prelate, Rt. Revd John Nicholls
Deputy Lord Prior, vacant
Sub Prior, Stuart Shilson, LVO
Secretary General, Vice-Adm. Sir Paul Lambert, KCB
Headquarters, 3 Charterhouse Mews, London EC1M 6BB
T 020-7251 3292 W www.orderofstjohn.org

DAMES

Style, 'Dame' before forename and surname, followed by appropriate post-nominal initials. Where such an award is made to a lady already in possession of a higher title, the appropriate initials follow her name
Envelope, Dame F_ S_, followed by appropriate post-nominal letters. *Letter (formal),* Dear Madam; *(social),* Dear Dame F_. *Spoken,* Dame F_
Husband, Untitled

Dame Grand Cross and Dame Commander are the higher classes for women of the Order of the Bath, the Order of St Michael and St George, the Royal Victorian Order, and the Order of the British Empire. Dames Grand Cross rank after the wives of Baronets and before the wives of Knights Grand Cross. Dames Commanders rank after the wives of Knights Grand Cross and before the wives of Knights Commanders.

Honorary Dames Commanders may be conferred on women who are citizens of countries of which the Queen is not head of state.

LIST OF DAMES *As at 31 August 2013*

Women peers in their own right and life peers are not included in this list. Female members of the royal family are not included in this list; details of the orders they hold can be found within the Royal Family section.

If a dame has a double barrelled or hyphenated surname, she is listed under the first element of the name.

Abaijah, Dame Josephine, DBE
Abramsky, Dame Jennifer Gita, DBE
Airlie, The Countess of, DCVO
Alexander, Dame Helen Anne, DBE
Allen, *Prof.* Dame Ingrid Victoria, DBE
Andrews, Dame Julie, DBE
Angiolini, *Rt. Hon.* Dame Elish, DBE, QC
Anglesey, Shirley Marchioness of, DBE
Anson, Lady (Elizabeth Audrey), DBE
Anstee, Dame Margaret Joan, DCMG
Archer, *Dr* Dame Mary Doreen, DBE
Arden, *Rt. Hon.* Dame Mary Howarth (Mrs Mance), DBE
Asplin, *Hon.* Dame Sarah Jane (Mrs Sherwin), DBE
Atkins, Dame Eileen, DBE
Bacon, Dame Patricia Anne, DBE
Baker, Dame Janet Abbott (Mrs Shelley), CH, DBE
Barbour, Dame Margaret (Mrs Ash), DBE
Baron, *Hon.* Dame Florence Jacqueline, DBE
Barrow, Dame Jocelyn Anita (Mrs Downer), DBE
Barstow, Dame Josephine Clare (Mrs Anderson), DBE
Bassey, Dame Shirley, DBE
Beasley, *Prof.* Dame Christine Joan, DBE
Beaurepaire, Dame Beryl Edith, DBE
Beckett, *Rt. Hon.* Dame Margaret Mary, DBE
Beer, *Prof.* Dame Gillian Patricia Kempster, DBE, FBA
Begg, Dame Anne, DBE
Beral, *Prof.* Dame Valerie, DBE
Bertschinger, *Dr* Dame Claire, DBE
Bevan, Dame Yasmin, DBE
Bewley, Dame Beulah Rosemary, DBE
Bibby, Dame Enid, DBE
Black, *Prof.* Dame Carol Mary, DBE
Black, *Rt. Hon.* Dame Jill Margaret, DBE
Blackadder, Dame Elizabeth Violet, DBE
Blaize, Dame Venetia Ursula, DBE
Blaxland, Dame Helen Frances, DBE
Blume, Dame Hilary Sharon Braverman, DBE
Booth, *Hon.* Dame Margaret Myfanwy Wood, DBE
Bourne, Dame Susan Mary (Mrs Bourne), DBE
Bowtell, Dame Ann Elizabeth, DCB
Braddock, *Dr* Dame Christine, DBE
Brain, Dame Margaret Anne (Mrs Wheeler), DBE
Breakwell, *Prof.* Dame Glynis Marie, DBE
Brennan, Dame Maureen, DBE
Brennan, Dame Ursula, DCB
Brewer, *Dr* Dame Nicola Mary, DCMG
Bridges, Dame Mary Patricia, DBE
Brindley, Dame Lynne Janie, DBE
Brittan, Dame Diana (Lady Brittan of Spennithorne), DBE
Browne, Lady Moyra Blanche Madeleine, DBE
Buckland, Dame Yvonne Helen Elaine, DBE
Burnell, *Prof.* Dame Susan Jocelyn Bell, DBE
Burslem, Dame Alexandra Vivien, DBE
Byatt, Dame Antonia Susan, DBE, FRSL
Caldicott, Dame Fiona, DBE, FRCP, FRCPSYCH
Cameron, *Prof.* Dame Averil Millicent, DBE
Campbell-Preston, Dame Frances Olivia, DCVO
Carnall, Dame Ruth, DBE
Cartwright, Dame Silvia Rose, DBE
Clark, *Prof.* Dame Jill MacLeod, DBE
Clark, *Prof.* Dame (Margaret) June, DBE, PHD
Cleverdon, Dame Julia Charity, DCVO, CBE
Coates, Dame Sally, DBE
Collarbone, Dame Patricia, DBE
Contreras, *Prof.* Dame Marcela, DBE
Corsar, *Hon.* Dame Mary Drummond, DBE
Coward, Dame Pamela Sarah, DBE
Cowley, *Prof.* Dame Sarah Ann, DBE
Cox, *Hon.* Dame Laura Mary, DBE
Cramp, *Prof.* Dame Rosemary Jean, DBE
Cullum, *Prof.* Dame Nicola Anne, DBE
Dacon, Dame Monica Jessie, DBE, CMG
Davies, *Prof.* Dame Kay Elizabeth, DBE
Davies, *Hon.* Dame Nicola Velfor, DBE
Davies, *Prof.* Dame Sally Claire, DBE
Davies, Dame Wendy Patricia, DBE
Davis, Dame Karlene Cecile, DBE
Dawson, *Prof.* Dame Sandra Jane Noble, DBE
Dell, Dame Miriam Patricia, DBE
Dench, Dame Judith Olivia (Mrs Williams), CH, DBE
Descartes, Dame Marie Selipha Sesenne, DBE, BEM
Devonshire, The Duchess of, DCVO
Digby, Lady, DBE
Dobbs, *Hon.* Dame Linda Penelope, DBE
Docherty, Dame Jacqueline, DBE
Donald, *Prof.* Dame Athene Margaret, DBE, FRS
Dowling, *Prof.* Dame Ann Patricia, DBE
Duffield, Dame Vivien Louise, DBE
Dumont, Dame Ivy Leona, DCMG
Dunnell, Dame Karen, DCB
Dyche, Dame Rachael Mary, DBE
Elcoat, Dame Catherine Elizabeth, DBE
Ellis, Dame Diana Margaret (Mrs Ellis), DBE
Ellison, Dame Jill, DBE
Elton, Dame Susan Richenda (Lady Elton), DCVO
Engel, Dame Pauline Frances (Sister Pauline Engel), DBE
Esteve-Coll, Dame Elizabeth Anne Loosemore, DBE
Evans, Dame Anne Elizabeth Jane, DBE
Evans, Dame Madeline Glynne Dervel, DBE, CMG
Fagan, Dame (Florence) Mary, DCVO

Farnham, Dame Marion (Lady Farnham), DCVO
Fawcett, Dame Amelia Chilcott, DBE
Fenner, Dame Peggy Edith, DBE
Fielding, Dame Pauline, DBE
Finch, *Prof.* Dame Janet Valerie, DBE
Fisher, Dame Jacqueline, DBE
Forgan, Dame Elizabeth Anne Lucy, DBE
Fradd, Dame Elizabeth, DBE
Fraser, Lady Antonia, DBE
Fraser, Dame Dorothy Rita, DBE
Fry, Dame Margaret Louise, DBE
Furse, Dame Clara Hedwig Frances, DBE
Gallagher, Dame Monica Josephine, DBE
Gaymer, Dame Janet Marion, DBE, QC
Ghosh, Dame Helen Frances, DCB
Gibb, Dame Moira Margaret, DBE
Glen-Haig, Dame Mary Alison, DBE
Glenn, *Prof.* Dame Hazel Gillian, DBE
Glennie, *Dr* Dame Evelyn Elizabeth Ann, DBE
Gloster, *Rt. Hon.* Dame Elisabeth (Lady Popplewell), DBE
Glover, Dame Audrey Frances, DBE, CMG
Goad, Dame Sarah Jane Frances, DCVO
Goodall, *Dr* Dame (Valerie) Jane, DBE
Goodfellow, *Prof.* Dame Julia Mary, DBE
Gordon, Dame Minita Elmira, GCMG, GCVO
Gordon, *Hon.* Dame Pamela Felicity, DBE
Gow, Dame Jane Elizabeth (Mrs Whiteley), DBE
Grafton, The Duchess of, GCVO
Grant, Dame Mavis, DBE
Green, Dame Pauline, DBE
Grey, Dame Beryl Elizabeth (Mrs Svenson), DBE
Griffiths, Dame Anne, DCVO
Grimthorpe, The Lady, DCVO
Guilfoyle, Dame Margaret Georgina Constance, DBE
Guthardt, *Revd Dr* Dame Phyllis Myra, DBE
Hadid, Dame Zaha, DBE
Hakin, *Dr* Dame Barbara Ann, DBE
Hall, *Prof.* Dame Wendy, DBE
Hallett, *Rt. Hon.* Dame Heather Carol, DBE
Hallett, Dame Nancy Karen, DBE
Harbison, Dame Joan Irene, DBE
Harper, Dame Elizabeth Margaret Way, DBE
Harris, Lady Pauline, DBE
Hassan, Dame Anna Patricia Lucy, DBE
Hay, Dame Barbara Logan, DCMG, MBE
Henderson, Dame Fiona Douglas, DCVO
Hercus, *Hon.* Dame (Margaret) Ann, DCMG
Higgins, *Prof.* Dame Joan Margaret, DBE
Higgins, *Prof.* Dame Julia Stretton, DBE, FRS
Higgins, *Prof.* Dame Rosalyn, DBE, QC
Hill, *Air Cdre* Dame Felicity Barbara, DBE
Hill, *Prof.* Dame Judith Eileen, DBE
Hine, Dame Deirdre Joan, DBE, FRCP
Hodgson, Dame Patricia Anne, DBE
Hogg, *Hon.* Dame Mary Claire (Mrs Koops), DBE
Holborow, Lady Mary Christina, DCVO
Hollows, Dame Sharon, DBE
Holmes, Dame Kelly, DBE
Holroyd, Lady Margaret (Margaret Drabble), DBE
Holt, Dame Denise Mary, DCMG
Hoodless, Dame Elisabeth Anne, DBE
Hufton, *Prof.* Dame Olwen, DBE
Humphrey, *Prof.* Dame Caroline, DBE
Husband, *Prof.* Dame Janet Elizabeth Siarey, DBE
Hussey, Dame Susan Katharine (Lady Hussey of North Bradley), GCVO
Hutton, Dame Deirdre Mary, DBE
Hyde, Dame Helen, DBE
Imison, Dame Tamsyn, DBE
Ion, *Dr* Dame Susan Elizabeth, DBE
Isaacs, Dame Albertha Madeline, DBE
James, Dame Naomi Christine (Mrs Haythorne), DBE
Jenkins, Dame (Mary) Jennifer (Lady Jenkins of Hillhead), DBE
John, Dame Susan, DBE
Johnson, *Prof.* Dame Anne Mandall, DBE
Jonas, Dame Judith Mayhew
Jones, Dame Gwyneth (Mrs Haberfeld-Jones), DBE
Jordan, *Prof.* Dame Carole, DBE
Joseph, Dame Monica Theresa, DBE
Jowell, *Rt. Hon.* Dame Tessa Jane, DBE
Julius, *Dr* Dame DeAnne Shirley, DCMG, CBE
Karika, Dame Pauline Margaret Rakera George (Mrs Taripo), DBE
Keeble, *Dr* Dame Reena, DBE
Keegan, Dame Elizabeth Mary, DBE
Keegan, Dame Geraldine Mary Marcella, DBE
Kekedo, Dame Rosalina Violet, DBE
Kelleher, Dame Joan, DBE
Kellett-Bowman, Dame (Mary) Elaine, DBE
Kelly, Dame Barbara Mary, DBE
Kelly, Dame Lorna May Boreland, DBE
Kershaw, Dame Janet Elizabeth Murray (Dame Betty), DBE
Kettlewell, *Comdt.* Dame Marion Mildred, DBE
Kidu, Lady, DBE
King, *Hon.* Dame Eleanor Warwick, DBE
King, *Prof.* Dame Julia Elizabeth, DBE
Kinnair, Dame Donna, DBE
Kirby, Dame Carolyn Emma, DBE
Kirby, Dame Georgina Kamiria, DBE
Kramer, *Prof.* Dame Leonie Judith, DBE
La Grenade, *HE.* Dame Cécile Ellen Fleurette, GCMG, OBE
Laine, Dame Cleo (Clementine) Dinah (Lady Dankworth), DBE
Lake-Tack, *HE* Dame Louise Agnetha, GCMG
Lamb, Dame Dawn Ruth, DBE
Lang, *Hon.* Dame Beverley Ann Macnaughton, DBE
Lavender, *Prof.* Dame Tina, DBE
Leather, Dame Susan Catherine, DBE
Lee, *Prof.* Dame Hermione, DBE
Leslie, Dame Alison Mariot, DCMG
Leslie, Dame Ann Elizabeth Mary, DBE
Lewis, Dame Edna Leofrida (Lady Lewis), DBE
Lively, Dame Penelope Margaret, DBE
Lott, Dame Felicity Ann Emwhyla (Mrs Woolf), DBE
Louisy, Dame (Calliopa) Pearlette, GCMG
Lynn, Dame Vera (Mrs Lewis), DBE
MacArthur, Dame Ellen Patricia, DBE
Macdonald, Dame Mary Beaton, DBE
McDonald, Dame Mavis, DCB
MacIntyre, *Prof.* Dame Sarah Jane, DBE
Macmillan of Ovenden, Katharine, Viscountess, DBE
Macur, *Rt. Hon.* Dame Julia Wendy, DBE
McVittie, Dame Joan Christine, DBE
Mayhew, Dame Judith, DBE
Major, Dame Malvina Lorraine (Mrs Fleming), DBE
Major, Dame Norma Christina Elizabeth, DBE
Marsden, *Dr* Dame Rosalind Mary, DCMG
Marsh, Dame Mary Elizabeth, DBE
Mason, Dame Monica Margaret, DBE
Mellor, Dame Julie Thérèse Mellor, DBE
Metge, *Dr* Dame (Alice) Joan, DBE
Middleton, Dame Elaine Madoline, DCMG, MBE
Mirren, Dame Helen, DBE
Monroe, *Prof.* Dame Barbara, DBE
Moore, Dame Julie, DBE
Moores, Dame Yvonne, DBE
Morgan, *Dr* Dame Gillian Margaret, DBE
Morris, Dame Sylvia Ann, DBE

Morrison, *Hon.* Dame Mary Anne, GCVO
Muirhead, Dame Lorna Elizabeth Fox, DBE
Muldoon, Lady Thea Dale, DBE, QSO
Mullally, *Revd* Dame Sarah Elisabeth, DBE
Mumford, Lady Mary Katharine, DCVO
Murray, Dame Jennifer Susan, DBE
Nelson, *Prof.* Dame Janet Laughland, DBE
Neville, Dame Elizabeth, DBE, QPM
Newell, Dame Priscilla Jane, DBE
Ogilvie, Dame Bridget Margaret, DBE, PHD, DSc
Oliver, Dame Gillian Frances, DBE
Ollerenshaw, Dame Kathleen Mary, DBE, DPHIL
Owers, Dame Anne Elizabeth (Mrs Cook), DBE
Oxenbury, Dame Shirley Ann, DBE
Palmer, Dame Felicity Joan, DBE
Paraskeva, *Rt. Hon.* Dame Janet, DBE
Park, Dame Merle Florence (Mrs Bloch), DBE
Parker, *Hon.* Dame Judith Mary Frances, DBE
Partridge, *Prof.* Dame Linda, DBE
Patel, Dame Indira, DBE
Paterson, Dame Vicki, DBE
Pauffley, *Hon.* Dame Anna Evelyn Hamilton, DBE
Penhaligon, Dame Annette (Mrs Egerton), DBE
Pereira, *Hon.* Dame Janice Mesadis, DBE
Perkins, Dame Mary Lesley, DBE
Peters, Dame Mary Elizabeth, DBE
Pindling, Lady (Marguerite M.), DCMG
Platt, Dame Denise, DBE
Plowright, Dame Joan Ann, DBE
Polak, *Prof.* Dame Julia Margaret, DBE
Poole, Dame Avril Anne Barker, DBE
Porter, Dame Shirley (Lady Porter), DBE
Powell, Dame Sally Ann Vickers, DBE
Pringle, Dame Anne Fyfe, DCMG
Proudman, *Hon.* Dame Sonia Rosemary Susan, DBE
Pugh, *Dr* Dame Gillian Mary, DBE
Quinn, Dame Sheila Margaret Imelda, DBE
Rafferty, *Rt. Hon.* Dame Anne Judith, DBE
Rawson, *Prof.* Dame Jessica Mary, DBE
Rebuck, Dame Gail Ruth, DBE
Rees, *Prof.* Dame Judith Anne, DBE
Rees, *Prof.* Dame Lesley Howard, DBE
Reeves, Dame Helen May, DBE
Rego, Dame Paula Figueiroa, DBE
Reynolds, Dame Fiona Claire, DBE
Richard, Dame Alison (Fettes), DBE
Richardson, Dame Mary, DBE
Rigg, Dame Diana, DBE
Rimington, Dame Stella, DCB
Ritterman, Dame Janet, DBE
Roberts, Dame Jane Elisabeth, DBE
Roberts, *Hon.* Dame Priscilla Jane Stephanie (Lady Roberts), DCVO
Robins, Dame Ruth Laura, DBE
Robinson, *Prof.* Dame Carol Vivien, DBE
Robottom, Dame Marlene, DBE
Roe, Dame Marion Audrey, DBE
Roe, Dame Raigh Edith, DBE
Ronson, Dame Gail, DBE
Ross-Wawrzynski, Dame Dana (Mrs Ross-Wawrzynski), DBE
Rothwell, *Prof.* Dame Nancy Jane, DBE
Ruddock, *Rt. Hon.* Dame Joan Mary, DBE
Runciman of Doxford, The Viscountess, DBE
Russell, *Dr* Dame Philippa Margaret, DBE
Sackler, Dame Theresa, DBE
Salas, Dame Margaret Laurence, DBE
Salmond, *Prof.* Dame Mary Anne, DBE
Savill, Dame Rosalind Joy, DBE
Sawyer, *Rt. Hon.* Dame Joan Augusta, DBE
Scardino, Dame Marjorie, DBE
Scott, Dame Catherine Margaret (Mrs Denton), DBE
Seward, Dame Margaret Helen Elizabeth, DBE
Sharp, *Hon.* Dame Victoria Madeleine, DBE
Shedrick, *Dr* Dame Daphne Marjorie, DBE
Shirley, Dame Stephanie, DBE
Shovelton, Dame Helena, DBE
Sibley, Dame Antoinette (Mrs Corbett), DBE
Silver, *Dr* Dame Ruth Muldoon, DBE
Slade, *Hon.* Dame Elizabeth Ann, DBE
Smith, Dame Dela, DBE
Smith, *Rt. Hon.* Dame Janet Hilary (Mrs Mathieson), DBE
Smith, *Hon.* Dame Jennifer Meredith, DBE
Smith, Dame Margaret Natalie (Maggie) (Mrs Cross), DBE
Soames, Lady (Mary), KG, DBE
Somers, Dame Phyllis (Mrs Somers), DBE
Southgate, *Prof.* Dame Lesley Jill, DBE
Spencer, Dame Rosemary Jane, DCMG
Steel, *Hon.* Dame (Anne) Heather (Mrs Beattie), DBE
Stocking, Dame Barbara Mary, DBE
Storey, Dame Sarah Joanne, DBE
Strachan, Dame Valerie Patricia Marie, DCB
Strathern, *Prof.* Dame Anne Marilyn, DBE
Street, Dame Susan Ruth, DCB
Stringer, *Prof.* Dame Joan Kathleen, DBE
Sutherland, Dame Veronica Evelyn, DBE, CMG
Suzman, Dame Janet, DBE
Swift, *Hon.* Dame Caroline Jane (Mrs Openshaw), DBE, QC
Symmonds, Dame Olga Patricia, DBE
Tanner, *Dr* Dame Mary Elizabeth, DBE
Taylor, Dame Meg, DBE
Te Kanawa, Dame Kiri Janette, DBE
Theis, *Hon.* Dame Lucy Morgan, DBE
Thirlwall, *Hon.* Dame Kathryn Mary, DBE
Thomas, *Prof.* Dame Jean Olwen, DBE
Thomas, Dame Maureen Elizabeth (Lady Thomas), DBE
Thornton, *Prof.* Dame Janet Maureen, DBE
Tickell, Dame Clare Oriana, DBE
Tinson, Dame Sue, DBE
Tizard, Dame Catherine Anne, GCMG, GCVO, DBE
Tokiel, Dame Rosa, DBE
Trotter, Dame Janet Olive, DBE
Turner-Warwick, Dame Margaret Elizabeth Harvey, DBE, FRCP, FRCPED
Twelftree, Dame Marcia, DBE
Uchida, Dame Mitsuko, DBE
Uprichard, Dame Mary Elizabeth, DBE
Varley, Dame Joan Fleetwood, DBE
Wagner, Dame Gillian Mary Millicent (Lady Wagner), DBE
Wall, Dame (Alice) Anne, (Mrs Michael Wall), DCVO
Wallace, *Prof.* Dame Helen Sarah, DBE, CMG
Wallis, Dame Sheila Ann, DBE
Walter, Dame Harriet Mary, DBE
Warburton, Dame Anne Marion, DCVO, CMG
Waterhouse, Dr Dame Rachel Elizabeth, DBE
Waterman, *Dr* Dame Fanny, DBE
Watkinson, Dame Angela Eileen, DBE
Webb, *Prof.* Dame Patricia, DBE
Weir, Dame Gillian Constance (Mrs Phelps), DBE
Weller, Dame Rita, DBE
Weston, Dame Margaret Kate, DBE
Westwood, Dame Vivienne Isabel, DBE
Williams, Dame Josephine, DBE
Wilson, Dame Jacqueline, DBE
Wilson-Barnett, *Prof.* Dame Jenifer, DBE
Winstone, Dame Dorothy Gertrude, DBE, CMG
Wolfson de Botton, Dame Janet (Mrs Wolfson de Botton), DBE
Wong Yick-ming, Dame Rosanna, DBE
Zaffar, Dame Naila, DBE

DECORATIONS AND MEDALS

PRINCIPAL DECORATIONS AND MEDALS
IN ORDER OF WEAR

VICTORIA CROSS (VC), 1856 (*see* below)
GEORGE CROSS (GC), 1940 (*see* below)

BRITISH ORDERS OF KNIGHTHOOD (*see also* Orders of Chivalry)
Order of the Garter
Order of the Thistle
Order of St Patrick
Order of the Bath
Order of Merit
Order of the Star of India
Order of St Michael and George
Order of the Indian Empire
Order of the Crown of India
Royal Victorian Order (Classes I, II and III)
Order of the British Empire (Classes I, II and III)
Order of the Companions of Honour
Distinguished Service Order
Royal Victorian Order (Class IV)
Order of the British Empire (Class IV)
Imperial Service Order
Royal Victorian Order (Class V)
Order of the British Empire (Class V)

BARONET'S BADGE

KNIGHT BACHELOR'S BADGE

INDIAN ORDER OF MERIT (MILITARY)

DECORATIONS
Conspicuous Gallantry Cross (CGC), 1995
Royal Red Cross Class I (RRC), 1883
Distinguished Service Cross (DSC), 1914
Military Cross (MC), December 1914
Distinguished Flying Cross (DFC), 1918
Air Force Cross (AFC), 1918
Royal Red Cross Class II (ARRC)
Order of British India
Kaisar-i-Hind Medal
Order of St John

MEDALS FOR GALLANTRY AND DISTINGUISHED CONDUCT
Union of South Africa Queen's Medal for Bravery, in Gold
Distinguished Conduct Medal (DCM), 1854
Conspicuous Gallantry Medal (CGM), 1874
Conspicuous Gallantry Medal (Flying)
George Medal (GM), 1940
Queen's Police Medal for Gallantry
Queen's Fire Service Medal for Gallantry
Royal West African Frontier Force Distinguished Conduct Medal
King's African Rifles Distinguished Conduct Medal
Indian Distinguished Service Medal
Union of South Africa Queen's Medal for Bravery, in Silver
Distinguished Service Medal (DSM), 1914
Military Medal (MM), 1916
Distinguished Flying Medal (DFM), 1918
Air Force Medal (AFM)
Constabulary Medal (Ireland)
Medal for Saving Life at Sea (Sea Gallantry Medal)
Indian Order of Merit (Civil)
Indian Police Medal for Gallantry
Ceylon Police Medal for Gallantry
Sierra Leone Police Medal for Gallantry
Sierra Leone Fire Brigades Medal for Gallantry
Overseas Territories Police Medal for Gallantry
Queen's Gallantry Medal (QGM), 1974
Royal Victorian Medal (RVM), Gold, Silver and Bronze
British Empire Medal (BEM)
Canada Medal
Queen's Police Medal for Distinguished Service (QPM)
Queen's Fire Service Medal for Distinguished Service (QFSM)
Queen's Volunteer Reserves Medal
Queen's Medal for Chiefs

CAMPAIGN MEDALS AND STARS
Including authorised United Nations, European Community/Union and North Atlantic Treaty Organisation medals (in order of date of campaign for which awarded)

Iraq Reconstruction Service Medal
Civilian Service Medal (Afghanistan)

POLAR MEDALS (in order of date)

IMPERIAL SERVICE MEDAL

POLICE MEDALS FOR VALUABLE SERVICE
Indian Police Medal for Meritorious Service
Ceylon Police Medal for Merit
Sierra Leone Police Medal for Meritorious Service
Sierra Leone Fire Brigades Medal for Meritorious Service
Overseas Territories Police Medal for Meritorious Service

BADGE OF HONOUR

JUBILEE, CORONATION AND DURBAR MEDALS
Queen Victoria, King Edward VII, King George V, King George VI, Queen Elizabeth II, Visit Commemoration and Long and Faithful Service Medals

EFFICIENCY AND LONG SERVICE DECORATIONS AND MEDALS
Medal for Meritorious Service
Accumulated Campaign Service Medal
Medal for Long Service and Good Conduct (Military)
Naval Long Service and Good Conduct Medal
Medal for Meritorious Service (Royal Navy 1918–28)
Indian Long Service and Good Conduct Medal
Indian Meritorious Service Medal
Royal Marines Meritorious Service Medal (1849–1947)
Royal Air Force Meritorious Service Medal (1918–1928)
Royal Air Force Long Service and Good Conduct Medal
Medal for Long Service and Good Conduct (Ulster Defence Regiment)
Indian Long Service and Good Conduct Medal
Royal West African Frontier Force Long Service and Good Conduct Medal
Royal Sierra Leone Military Forces Long Service and Good Conduct Medal

King's African Rifles Long Service and Good Conduct Medal
Indian Meritorious Service Medal
Police Long Service and Good Conduct Medal
Fire Brigade Long Service and Good Conduct Medal
African Police Medal for Meritorious Service
Royal Canadian Mounted Police Long Service Medal
Ceylon Police Long Service Medal
Ceylon Fire Services Long Service Medal
Sierra Leone Police Long Service Medal
Overseas Territories Police Long Service Medal
Sierra Leone Fire Brigades Long Service Medal
Mauritius Police Long Service and Good Conduct Medal
Mauritius Fire Services Long Service and Good Conduct Medal
Mauritius Prisons Service Long Service and Good Conduct Medal
Overseas Territories Fire Brigades Long Service Medal
Overseas Territories Prison Service Medal
Hong Kong Disciplined Services Medal
Army Emergency Reserve Decoration (ERD)
Volunteer Officers' Decoration (VD)
Volunteer Long Service Medal
Volunteer Officers' Decoration (for India and the Colonies)
Volunteer Long Service Medal (for India and the Colonies)
Colonial Auxiliary Forces Officers' Decoration
Colonial Auxiliary Forces Long Service Medal
Medal for Good Shooting (Naval)
Militia Long Service Medal
Imperial Yeomanry Long Service Medal
Territorial Decoration (TD), 1908
Ceylon Armed Services Long Service Medal
Efficiency Decoration (ED)
Territorial Efficiency Medal
Efficiency Medal
Special Reserve Long Service and Good Conduct Medal
Decoration for Officers of the Royal Navy Reserve (RD), 1910
Decoration for Officers of the Royal Naval Volunteer Reserve (VRD)
Royal Naval Reserve Long Service and Good Conduct Medal
Royal Naval Volunteer Reserve Long Service and Good Conduct Medal
Royal Naval Auxiliary Sick Berth Reserve Long Service and Good Conduct Medal
Royal Fleet Reserve Long Service and Good Conduct Medal
Royal Naval Wireless Auxiliary Reserve Long Service and Good Conduct Medal
Royal Naval Auxiliary Service Medal
Air Efficiency Award (AE), 1942
Volunteer Reserves Service Medal
Ulster Defence Regiment Medal
Northern Ireland Home Service Medal
Queen's Medal (for Champion Shots of the RN and RM)
Queen's Medal (for Champion Shots of the New Zealand Naval Forces)
Queen's Medal (for Champion Shots in the Military Forces)
Queen's Medal (for Champion Shots of the Air Forces)
Cadet Forces Medal, 1950
HM Coastguard Long Service and Good Conduct Medal
Special Constabulary Long Service Medal
Canadian Forces Decoration
Royal Observer Corps Medal
Civil Defence Long Service Medal
Ambulance Service (Emergency Duties) Long Service and Good Conduct Medal
Royal Fleet Auxiliary Service Medal
Prison Services (Operational Duties) Long Service and Good Conduct Medal
Rhodesia Medal
Royal Ulster Constabulary Service Medal
Northern Ireland Prison Service Medal
Union of South Africa Commemoration Medal
Indian Independence Medal
Pakistan Medal
Ceylon Armed Services Inauguration Medal
Ceylon Police Independence Medal (1948)
Sierra Leone Independence Medal
Jamaica Independence Medal
Uganda Independence Medal
Malawi Independence Medal
Fiji Independence Medal
Papua New Guinea Independence Medal
Solomon Islands Independence Medal
Service Medal of the Order of St John
Badge of the Order of the League of Mercy
Voluntary Medical Service Medal (1932)
Women's Royal Voluntary Service Medal
South African Medal for War Services
Overseas Territories Special Constabulary Medal

HONORARY MEMBERSHIP OF COMMONWEALTH ORDERS

OTHER COMMONWEALTH MEMBERS' ORDERS, DECORATIONS AND MEDALS

FOREIGN ORDERS

FOREIGN DECORATIONS

FOREIGN MEDALS

THE VICTORIA CROSS (1856)

FOR CONSPICUOUS BRAVERY

VC

Ribbon, Crimson, for all Services (until 1918 it was blue for the Royal Navy)

Instituted on 29 January 1856, the Victoria Cross was awarded retrospectively to 1854, the first being held by Lt. C. D. Lucas, RN, for bravery in the Baltic Sea on 21 June 1854 (gazetted 24 February 1857). The first 62 crosses were presented by Queen Victoria in Hyde Park, London, on 26 June 1857.

The Victoria Cross is worn before all other decorations, on the left breast, and consists of a cross-pattée of bronze, 3.8cm in diameter, with the royal crown surmounted by a lion in the centre, and beneath there is the inscription *For Valour*. Holders of the VC currently receive a tax-free annuity of £1,500, irrespective of need or other conditions. In 1911, the right to receive the cross was extended to Indian soldiers, and in 1920 to matrons, sisters and nurses, the staff of the nursing services and other services pertaining to hospitals and nursing, and to civilians of either sex regularly or temporarily under the orders, direction or supervision of the naval, military, or air forces of the crown.

SURVIVING RECIPIENTS OF THE VICTORIA CROSS
as at 31 August 2013

Apiata, *Cpl.* B. H., VC (New Zealand Special Air Service) 2004 *Afghanistan*

Beharry, *LSgt.* J. G., VC (Princess of Wales's Royal Regiment) 2005 *Iraq*

Cruickshank, *Flt. Lt.* J. A., VC (RAFVR)
1944 *World War*
Donaldson, *Cpl.* M. G. S., VC (Australian Special Air Service)
2008 *Afghanistan*
Payne, *WO* K., VC, DSC (USA) (Australian Army Training Team)
1969 *Vietnam*
Rambahadur Limbu, *Capt.,* VC, MVO (10th Princess Mary's Gurkha Rifles)
1965 *Sarawak*
Roberts-Smith, *Cpl.* B., VC (Australian Special Air Service)
2010 *Afghanistan*
Speakman, *Sgt.* W., VC (Black Watch, attached KOSB)
1951 *Korea*

THE GEORGE CROSS (1940)

FOR GALLANTRY

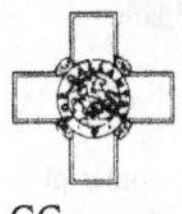

GC

Ribbon, Dark blue, threaded through a bar adorned with laurel leaves
Instituted 24 September 1940 (with amendments, 3 November 1942)

The George Cross is worn before all other decorations (except the VC) on the left breast (when worn by a woman it may be worn on the left shoulder from a ribbon of the same width and colour fashioned into a bow). It consists of a plain silver cross with four equal limbs, the cross having in the centre a circular medallion bearing a design showing St George and the Dragon. The inscription *For Gallantry* appears round the medallion and in the angle of each limb of the cross is the royal cypher 'G VI' forming a circle concentric with the medallion. The reverse is plain and bears the name of the recipient and the date of the award. The cross is suspended by a ring from a bar adorned with laurel leaves on dark blue ribbon 3.8cm wide.

The cross is intended primarily for civilians; awards to the fighting services are confined to actions for which purely military honours are not normally granted. It is awarded only for acts of the greatest heroism or of the most conspicuous courage in circumstances of extreme danger. From 1 April 1965, holders of the cross have received a tax-free annuity, which is currently £1,500. The cross has twice been awarded collectively rather than to an individual: to Malta (1942) and the Royal Ulster Constabulary (1999).

In October 1971 all surviving holders of the Albert Medal and the Edward Medal exchanged those decorations for the George Cross.

SURVIVING RECIPIENTS OF THE GEORGE CROSS
as at 31 August 2013

If the recipient originally received the Albert Medal (AM) or the Edward Medal (EM), this is indicated by the initials in parentheses.

Archer, *Col.* B. S. T., GC, OBE, ERD, 1941
Bamford, J., GC, 1952
Beaton, J., GC, CVO, 1974
Butson, *Lt.-Col.* A. R. C., GC, CD, MD (AM), 1948
Croucher, *Lance Cpl.* M., GC, 2008
Finney, C., GC, 2003
Flintoff, H. H., GC (EM), 1944
Gledhill, A. J., GC, 1967
Gregson, J. S., GC (AM), 1943
Hughes, *WO2* K. S., GC, 2010
Johnson, *WO1 (SSM)* B., GC, 1990
Kinne, D. G., GC, 1954
Lowe, A. R., GC (AM), 1949
Norton, *Maj.* P. A., GC, 2006
Pratt, M. K., GC, 1978
Purves, Mrs M., GC (AM), 1949
Raweng, Awang anak, GC, 1951
Stevens, H. W., GC, 1958
Walker, C., GC, 1972
Wooding, E. A., GC (AM), 1945

THE ELIZABETH CROSS (2009)

EC

Instituted 1 July 2009

The Elizabeth Cross consists of a silver cross with a laurel wreath passing between the arms, which bear the floral symbols of England (rose), Scotland (thistle), Ireland (shamrock) and Wales (daffodil). The centre of the cross bears the royal cypher and the reverse is inscribed with the name of the person for whom it is in honour. The cross is accompanied by a memorial scroll and a miniature.

The cross was created to commemorate UK armed forces personnel who have died on operations or as a result of an act of terrorism. It may be granted to and worn by the next of kin of any eligible personnel who died from 1 January 1948 to date. It offers the wearer no precedence. Those that are eligible include the next of kin of personnel who died while serving on a medal earning operation, as a result of an act of terrorism, or on a non-medal earning operation where death was caused by the inherent high risk of the task.

The Elizabeth Cross is not intended as a posthumous medal for the fallen but as an emblem of national recognition of the loss and sacrifice made by the personnel and their families.

CHIEFS OF CLANS IN SCOTLAND

Only chiefs of whole Names or Clans are included, except certain special instances (marked *) who, though not chiefs of a whole Name, were or are for some reason (eg the Macdonald forfeiture) independent. Under decision (*Campbell-Gray*, 1950) that a bearer of a 'double or triple-barrelled' surname cannot be held chief of a part of such, several others cannot be included in the list at present.

THE ROYAL HOUSE: HM The Queen

AGNEW: Sir Crispin Agnew of Lochnaw, Bt., QC
ANSTRUTHER: Tobias Anstruther of Anstruther and Balcaskie
ARBUTHNOTT: Viscount of Arbuthnott
BANNERMAN: Sir David Bannerman of Elsick, Bt.
BARCLAY: Peter C. Barclay of Towie Barclay and of that Ilk
BORTHWICK: Lord Borthwick
BOYLE: Earl of Glasgow
BRODIE: Alexander Brodie of Brodie
BROUN OF COLSTOUN: Sir Wayne Broun of Colstoun, Bt.
BRUCE: Earl of Elgin and Kincardine, KT
BUCHAN: David Buchan of Auchmacoy
BURNETT: J. C. A. Burnett of Leys
CAMERON: Donald Cameron of Lochiel
CAMPBELL: Duke of Argyll
CARMICHAEL: Richard Carmichael of Carmichael
CARNEGIE: Duke of Fife
CATHCART: Earl Cathcart
CHARTERIS: Earl of Wemyss and March
CLAN CHATTAN: K. Mackintosh of Clan Chattan
CHISHOLM: Hamish Chisholm of Chisholm *(The Chisholm)*
COCHRANE: Earl of Dundonald
COLQUHOUN: Sir Malcolm Rory Colquhoun of Luss, Bt.
CRANSTOUN: David Cranstoun of that Ilk
CUMMING: Sir Alastair Cumming of Altyre, Bt.
DARROCH: Capt. Duncan Darroch of Gourock
DEWAR: Michael Dewar of that Ilk and Vogrie
DRUMMOND: Earl of Perth
DUNBAR: Sir James Dunbar of Mochrum, Bt.
DUNDAS: David Dundas of Dundas
DURIE: Andrew Durie of Durie, CBE
ELIOTT: Mrs Margaret Eliott of Redheugh
ERSKINE: Earl of Mar and Kellie
FARQUHARSON: Capt. A. Farquharson of Invercauld, MC
FERGUSSON: Sir Charles Fergusson of Kilkerran, Bt.
FORBES: Lord Forbes
FORSYTH: Alistair Forsyth of that Ilk
FRASER: Lady Saltoun
*FRASER (OF LOVAT): Lord Lovat
GAYRE: R. Gayre of Gayre and Nigg
GORDON: Marquess of Huntly
GRAHAM: Duke of Montrose
GRANT: Lord Strathspey
GUTHRIE: Alexander Guthrie of Guthrie
HAIG: Earl Haig
HALDANE: Martin Haldane of Gleneagles
HANNAY: David Hannay of Kirkdale and of that Ilk
HAY: Earl of Erroll
HENDERSON: Alistair Henderson of Fordell
HUNTER: Pauline Hunter of Hunterston
IRVINE OF DRUM: David Irvine of Drum
JARDINE: Sir William Jardine of Applegirth, Bt.
JOHNSTONE: Earl of Annandale and Hartfell
KEITH: Earl of Kintore
KENNEDY: Marquess of Ailsa
KERR: Marquess of Lothian, PC
KINCAID: Madam Arabella Kincaid of Kincaid
LAMONT: Revd Peter Lamont of that Ilk
LEASK: Jonathan Leask of that Ilk
LENNOX: Edward Lennox of that Ilk
LESLIE: Earl of Rothes
LINDSAY: Earl of Crawford and Balcarres, KT, GCVO, PC
LIVINGSTONE (or MACLEA): Niall Livingstone of the Bachuil
LOCKHART: Angus Lockhart of the Lee
LUMSDEN: Gillem Lumsden of that Ilk and Blanerne
MACALESTER: William St J. McAlester of Loup and Kennox
MACARTHUR; John MacArthur of that Ilk
MCBAIN: J. H. McBain of McBain
MACDONALD: Lord Macdonald *(The Macdonald of Macdonald)*
*MACDONALD OF CLANRANALD: Ranald Macdonald of Clanranald
*MACDONALD OF KEPPOCH: Ranald MacDonald of Keppoch
*MACDONALD OF SLEAT (CLAN HUSTEAIN): Sir Ian Macdonald of Sleat, Bt.
*MACDONELL OF GLENGARRY: Ranald MacDonell of Glengarry
MACDOUGALL: Morag MacDougall of MacDougall
MACDOWALL: Fergus Macdowall of Garthland
MACGREGOR: Sir Malcolm MacGregor of MacGregor, Bt.
MACINTYRE: Donald MacIntyre of Glenoe
MACKAY: Lord Reay
MACKENZIE: Earl of Cromartie
MACKINNON: Anne Mackinnon of Mackinnon
MACKINTOSH: John Mackintosh of Mackintosh *(The Mackintosh of Mackintosh)*
MACLACHLAN: Euan MacLachlan of MacLachlan
MACLAREN: Donald MacLaren of MacLaren and Achleskine
MACLEAN: Hon. Sir Lachlan Maclean of Duart, Bt., CVO
MACLENNAN: Ruaraidh MacLennan of MacLennan
MACLEOD: Hugh MacLeod of MacLeod
MACMILLAN: George MacMillan of MacMillan
MACNAB: J. W. A. Macnab of Macnab *(The Macnab)*
MACNAGHTEN: Sir Malcolm Macnaghten of Macnaghten and Dundarave, Bt.
MACNEACAIL: John Macneacail of Macneacail and Scorrybreac
MACNEIL OF BARRA: Rory Macneil of Barra *(The Macneil of Barra)*
MACPHERSON: Hon. Sir William Macpherson of Cluny, TD
MACTAVISH: Steven MacTavish of Dunardry
MACTHOMAS: Andrew MacThomas of Finegand
MAITLAND: Earl of Lauderdale
MAKGILL: Viscount of Oxfuird
MALCOLM (MACCALLUM): Robin N. L. Malcolm of Poltalloch
MAR: Countess of Mar
MARJORIBANKS: Andrew Marjoribanks of that Ilk
MATHESON: Maj. Sir Fergus Matheson of Matheson, Bt.
MENZIES: David Menzies of Menzies
MOFFAT: Madam Moffat of that Ilk
MONCREIFFE: Hon. Peregrine Moncreiffe of that Ilk
MONTGOMERIE: Earl of Eglinton and Winton
MORRISON: Dr John Ruairidh Morrison of Ruchdi
MUNRO: Hector Munro of Foulis
MURRAY: Duke of Atholl
NESBITT (or NISBET): Mark Nesbitt of that Ilk
OGILVY: Earl of Airlie, KT, GCVO, PC
OLIPHANT: Richard Oliphant of that Ilk
RAMSAY: Earl of Dalhousie
RIDDELL: Sir Walter Riddell of Riddell, Bt.
ROBERTSON: Alexander Robertson of Struan *(Struan-Robertson)*
ROLLO: Lord Rollo
ROSE: David Rose of Kilravock
ROSS: David Ross of that Ilk and Balnagowan
RUTHVEN: Earl of Gowrie, PC
SCOTT: Duke of Buccleuch and Queensberry, KBE
SCRYMGEOUR: Earl of Dundee
SEMPILL: Lord Sempill
SHAW: John Shaw of Tordarroch
SINCLAIR: Earl of Caithness
SKENE: Danus Skene of Skene
STIRLING: Fraser Stirling of Cader
STRANGE: Maj. Timothy Strange of Balcaskie
SUTHERLAND: Countess of Sutherland
SWINTON: John Swinton of that Ilk
TROTTER: Alexander Trotter of Mortonhall, CVO
URQUHART: Wilkins F. Urquhart of Urquhart
WALLACE: Ian Wallace of that Ilk
WEDDERBURN: Master of Dundee
WEMYSS: Michael Wemyss of that Ilk

THE PRIVY COUNCIL

The sovereign in council, or Privy Council, was the chief source of executive power until the system of cabinet government developed in the 18th century. Now the Privy Council's main functions are to advise the sovereign and to exercise its own statutory responsibilities independent of the sovereign in council.

Membership of the Privy Council is automatic upon appointment to certain government and judicial positions in the UK, eg cabinet ministers must be Privy Counsellors and are sworn in on first assuming office. Membership is also accorded by the Queen to eminent people in the UK and independent countries of the Commonwealth of which she is Queen, on the recommendation of the prime minister. Membership of the council is retained for life, except for very occasional removals.

The administrative functions of the Privy Council are carried out by the Privy Council Office under the direction of the president of the council, who is always a member of the cabinet. (*See also* Parliament)

President of the Council, Rt. Hon. Nick Clegg
Clerk of the Council, Richard Tilbrook

Style The Right (or Rt.) Hon._
*Envelope, The Right (or Rt.) Hon. F_ S_*
*Letter, Dear Mr/Miss/Mrs S_*
*Spoken, Mr/Miss/Mrs S_*

It is incorrect to use the letters PC after the name in conjunction with the prefix The Rt. Hon., unless the Privy Counsellor is a peer below the rank of Marquess and so is styled The Rt. Hon. because of his/her rank.

MEMBERS *as at August 2013*

HRH The Duke of Edinburgh, 1951
HRH The Prince of Wales, 1977

Abernethy, *Hon.* Lord (Alastair Cameron), 2005
Adonis, Lord, 2009
Aikens, Sir Richard, 2008
Ainsworth, Robert, 2005
Airlie, Earl of, 1984
Aldous, Sir William, 1995
Alebua, Ezekiel, 1988
Alexander, Douglas, 2005
Alexander, Danny, 2010
Amos, Baroness, 2003
Anderson of Swansea, Lord, 2000
Anelay of St Johns, Baroness, 2009
Angiolini, Dame Elish, 2006
Anthony, Douglas, 1971
Arbuthnot, James, 1998
Arden, Dame Mary, 2000
Armstrong of Hill Top, Baroness, 1999
Arthur, *Hon.* Owen, 1995
Ashdown of Norton-sub-Hamdon, Lord, 1989
Ashcroft, Lord, 2012
Ashton of Upholland, Baroness, 2006
Atkins, Sir Robert, 1995
Auld, Sir Robin, 1995
Baker, Sir Thomas, 2002
Baker of Dorking, Lord, 1984
Balls, Ed, 2007
Bannside, Lord, 2005
Barker, Gregory, 2012
Barnett, Lord, 1975
Barron, Kevin, 2001
Bassam of Brighton, Lord, 2009
Battle, John, 2002
Beatson, Sir Jack, 2013
Beckett, Dame Margaret, 1993
Beith, Sir Alan, 1992
Beldam, Sir Roy, 1989
Benn, Anthony, 1964
Benn, Hilary, 2003
Bercow, John, 2009
Birch, William, 1992
Black, Dame Jill, 2011
Blackstone, Baroness, 2001
Blair, Anthony, 1994
Blanchard, Peter, 1998
Blears, Hazel, 2005
Blencathra, Lord, 1995
Blunkett, David, 1997
Boateng, Lord, 1999
Bolger, James, 1991
Bonomy, *Hon.* Lord (Iain Bonomy), 2010
Boothroyd, Baroness, 1992
Boscawen, *Hon.* Robert, 1992
Bottomley of Nettlestone, Baroness, 1992
Boyd of Duncansby, Lord, 2000
Brabazon of Tara, Lord, 2013
Bracadale, *Hon.* Lord (Alistair Campbell), 2013
Bradley, Lord, 2001
Bradshaw, Ben, 2009
Brake, Thomas, 2011
Brathwaite, Sir Nicholas, 1991
Briggs, Sir Michael, 2013
Brittan of Spennithorne, Lord, 1981
Brodie, *Hon.* Lord (Philip Brodie), 2013
Brooke, Sir Henry, 1996
Brooke of Sutton Mandeville, Lord, 1988
Brown, Gordon, 1996
Brown, Nicholas, 1997
Brown, Sir Stephen, 1983
Brown of Eaton-under-Heywood, Lord, 1992
Browne of Ladyton, Lord, 2005
Browne-Wilkinson, Lord, 1983
Bruce, Sir Malcolm, 2006
Burnham, Andy, 2007
Burns, Simon, 2011
Burnton, Sir Stanley, 2008
Burstow, Paul, 2012
Butler of Brockwell, Lord, 2004
Butler-Sloss, Baroness, 1988
Buxton, Sir Richard, 1997
Byers, Stephen, 1998
Byrne, Liam, 2008
Byron, Sir Dennis, 2004
Cable, Vincent, 2010
Caborn, Richard, 1999
Caithness, Earl of, 1990
Cameron, David, 2005
Cameron of Lochbroom, Lord, 1984
Camoys, Lord, 1997
Campbell, Sir Walter Menzies, 1999
Campbell, Sir William, 1999
Canterbury, Archbishop of, 2013
Carey of Clifton, Lord, 1991
Carloway, *Hon.* Lord (Colin Sutherland), 2008
Carmichael, Alistair, 2010
Carnwath of Notting Hill, *Hon.* Lord (Sir Robert Carnwath), 2002
Carrington, Lord, 1959
Carswell, Lord, 1993
Chadwick, Sir John, 1997
Chalfont, Lord, 1964
Chalker of Wallasey, Baroness, 1987
Chan, Sir Julius, 1981
Chataway, Sir Christopher, 1970
Chilcot, Sir John, 2004
Christie, Perry, 2004
Clark, Greg, 2010
Clark, Helen, 1990
Clark of Windermere, Lord, 1997
Clarke, Charles, 2001
Clarke, Kenneth, 1984
Clarke, *Hon.* Lord (Matthew Clarke), 2008
Clarke, Thomas, 1997
Clarke of Stone-Cum-Ebony, Lord, 1998
Clegg, Nicholas, 2008
Clinton-Davis, Lord, 1998
Clwyd, Ann, 2004
Coghlin, Sir Patrick, 2009
Collins of Mapesbury, Lord, 2007
Cooper, Yvette, 2007
Cope of Berkeley, Lord, 1988
Corston, Baroness, 2003
Cosgrove, *Hon.* Lady (Hazel Cosgrove), 2003

Coulsfield, *Hon.* Lord (John Coulsfield), 2000
Crawford and Balcarres, Earl of, 1972
Creech, *Hon.* Wyatt, 1999
Crickhowell, Lord, 1979
Cullen of Whitekirk, Lord, 1997
Cunningham of Felling, Lord, 1993
Curry, David, 1996
Darling, Alistair, 1997
Darzi of Denham, Lord, 2009
Davey, Edward, 2012
Davies, Denzil, 1978
Davies, Ronald, 1997
Davies of Oldham, Lord, 2006
Davis, David, 1997
Davis, Sir Nigel, 2011
Davis, Terence, 1999
Davison, Sir Ronald, 1978
de la Bastide, Michael, 2004
de Silva, Sir Desmond, 2011
Dean of Thornton-le-Fylde, Baroness, 1998
Deben, Lord, 1985
Denham, John, 2000
Denham, Lord, 1981
Dholakia, Lord, 2010
Dixon, Lord, 1996
Dobson, Frank, 1997
Dodds, Nigel, 2010
Donaldson, Jeffrey, 2007
Dorrell, Stephen, 1994
Dorrian, *Hon.* Lady (Leona Dorrian), 2013
Douglas, *Dr* Denzil, 2011
Drayson, Lord, 2008
D'Souza, Baroness, 2009
du Cann, Sir Edward, 1964
Duncan, Alan, 2010
Duncan Smith, Iain, 2001
Dunn, Sir Robin, 1980
Dyson, Sir John, 2001
Eassie, *Hon.* Lord (Ronald Mackay), 2006
East, Paul, 1998
Eden of Winton, Lord, 1972
Edward, Sir David, 2005
Eggar, Timothy, 1995
Eichelbaum, Sir Thomas, 1989
Elias, Sir Patrick, 2009
Elias, *Hon.* Dame, Sian, 1999
Elis-Thomas, Lord, 2004
Emslie, *Hon.* Lord (George Emslie), 2011
Esquivel, Manuel, 1986
Etherton, Sir Terence, 2008
Evans, Sir Anthony, 1992
Eveleigh, Sir Edward, 1977
Falconer of Thoroton, Lord, 2003
Fallon, Michael, 2012
Fellowes, Lord, 1990
Fergusson, Alexander, 2010
Field, Frank, 1997
Flint, Caroline, 2008
Floyd, Sir Christopher, 2013
Forsyth of Drumlean, Lord, 1995
Foster, Donald, 2010
Foster of Bishop Auckland, Lord, 1993
Foulkes of Cumnock, Lord, 2002
Fowler, Lord, 1979
Fox, Liam, 2010
Francois, Mark, 2010
Fraser, Malcolm, 1976
Freedman, Sir Lawrence, 2009
Freeman, John, 1966
Freeman, Lord, 1993
Fulford, Sir Adrian, 2013
Gage, Sir William, 2004
Garel-Jones, Lord, 1992
Gault, Thomas, 1992
Geidt, Sir Christopher, 2007
George, Bruce, 2000
Gibson, Sir Peter, 1993
Gilbert, Sir Martin, 2009
Gill, *Hon.* Lord (Brian Gill), 2002
Gillan, Cheryl, 2010
Girvan, Sir (Frederick) Paul, 2007
Glidewell, Sir Iain, 1985
Gloster, Dame Elizabeth, 2013
Goff of Chieveley, Lord, 1982
Goggins, Paul, 2009
Goldring, Sir John, 2008
Goldsmith, Lord, 2002
Goodlad, Lord, 1992
Gove, Michael, 2010
Gowrie, Earl of, 1984
Graham, Sir Douglas, 1998
Graham of Edmonton, Lord, 1998
Grayling, Chris, 2010
Green, Damian, 2012
Greening, Justine, 2011
Grieve, Dominic, 2010
Griffiths, Lord, 1980
Grocott, Lord, 2002
Gross, Sir Peter, 2011
Habgood, *Rt. Revd*, Lord, 1983
Hague, William, 1995
Hailsham, Viscount, 1992
Hain, Peter, 2001
Hale of Richmond, Baroness, 1999
Hallett, Dame Heather, 2005
Hamilton, *Hon.* Lord (Arthur Hamilton), 2002
Hamilton of Epsom, Lord, 1991
Hammond, Philip, 2010
Hanley, Sir Jeremy, 1994
Hanson, David, 2007
Hardie, Lord, 1997
Hardie Boys, Sir Michael, 1989
Harman, Harriet, 1997
Haselhurst, Sir Alan, 1999
Hattersley, Lord, 1975
Hayes, John, 2013
Hayhoe, Lord, 1985
Hayman, Baroness, 2000
Healey, John, 2008
Healey, Lord, 1964
Heathcoat-Amory, David, 1996
Henley, Lord, 2013
Henry, John, 1996
Herbert, Nick, 2010
Heseltine, Lord, 1979
Heseltine, Sir William, 1986
Hesketh, Lord, 1991
Hewitt, Patricia, 2001
Higgins, Lord, 1979
Higgins, Sir Malachy, 2007
Hill, Keith, 2003
Hill of Oareford, Lord, 2013
Hodge, *Hon.* Lord (Patrick Hodge), 2013
Hodge, Margaret, 2003
Hoffmann, Lord, 1992
Hollis of Heigham, Baroness, 1999
Hoon, Geoffrey, 1999
Hooper, Sir Anthony, 2004
Hope of Craighead, Lord, 1989
Hope of Thornes, Lord, 1991
Hordern, Sir Peter, 1993
Howard of Lympne, Lord, 1990
Howarth, George, 2005
Howarth of Newport, Lord, 2000
Howe, Earl, 2013
Howe of Aberavon, Lord, 1972
Howell of Guildford, Lord, 1979
Howells, Kim, 2009
Hoyle, Lindsay, 2013
Hughes, Sir Anthony, 2006
Hughes, Simon, 2010
Hughes of Stretford, Baroness, 2004
Hunt, Jeremy, 2010
Hunt, Jonathon, 1989
Hunt of Kings Heath, Lord, 2009
Hunt of Wirral, Lord, 1990
Hurd of Westwell, Lord, 1982
Hutchison, Sir Michael, 1995
Hutton, Lord, 1988
Hutton of Furness, Lord, 2001
Inge, Lord, 2004
Ingraham, Hubert, 1993
Ingram, Adam, 1999
Irvine of Lairg, Lord, 1997
Jack, Michael, 1997
Jackson, Sir Rupert, 2008
Jacob, Sir Robert, 2004
Jacobs, Francis, 2005
Janvrin, Lord, 1998
Jay of Paddington, Baroness, 1998
Jenkin of Roding, Lord, 1973
Johnson, Alan, 2003
Jones, Carwyn, 2010
Jones, David, 2012
Jones, Lord, 1999
Jopling, Lord, 1979
Jowell, Dame Tessa, 1998
Judge, Lord, 1996
Jugnauth, Sir Anerood, 1987
Kaufman, Sir Gerald, 1978
Kay, Sir Maurice, 2004
Keene, Sir David, 2000
Keith, Sir Kenneth, 1998
Kelly, Ruth, 2004
Kenilorea, Sir Peter, 1979
Kennedy, Charles, 1999
Kennedy, Jane, 2003
Kennedy, Sir Paul, 1992
Kerr of Tonaghmore, Lord, 2004
Khan, Sadiq, 2009
King of Bridgwater, Lord, 1979
Kingarth, *Hon.* Lord (Derek Emslie), 2006
Kingsdown, Lord, 1987
Kinnock, Lord, 1983
Kirkwood, *Hon.* Lord (Ian Kirkwood), 2000
Kitchin, Sir David, 2011
Knight, Gregory, 1995

Knight of Weymouth, Lord, 2008
Lammy, David, 2008
Lamont of Lerwick, Lord, 1986
Lang of Monkton, Lord, 1990
Lansley, Andrew, 2010
Latasi, Sir Kamuta, 1996
Latham, Sir David, 2000
Lauti, Sir Toaripi, 1979
Laws, David, 2010
Laws, Sir John, 1999
Lawson of Blaby, Lord, 1981
Leggatt, Sir Andrew, 1990
Letwin, Oliver, 2002
Leveson, Sir Brian, 2006
Lewison, Sir Kim, 2011
Liddell of Coatdyke, Baroness, 1998
Lidington, David, 2010
Lilley, Peter, 1990
Lloyd of Berwick, Lord, 1984
Lloyd, Sir Peter, 1994
Lloyd, Sir Timothy, 2005
Lloyd Jones, Sir David, 2012
Llwyd, Elfyn, 2011
London, Bishop of, 1995
Longmore, Sir Andrew, 2001
Lothian, Marquess of, 1996
Luce, Lord, 1986
Lyne, Sir Roderic, 2009
McAvoy, Lord, 2003
McCartney, Sir Ian, 1999
McCollum, Sir Liam, 1997
McCombe, Sir Richard, 2012
McConnell of Glenscorrodale, Lord, 2001
MacDermott, Sir John, 1987
Macdonald of Tradeston, Lord, 1999
McFadden, Patrick, 2008
McFall of Alcluith, Lord, 2004
McFarlane, Sir Andrew, 2011
MacGregor of Pulham Market, Lord, 1985
McGuire, Anne, 2008
Mackay, Andrew, 1998
McKay, Sir Ian, 1992
Mackay of Clashfern, Lord, 1979
Mackay of Drumadoon, Lord, 1996
McKinnon, Sir Donald, 1992
Maclean, *Hon.* Lord (Ranald MacLean), 2001
McLeish, Henry, 2000
Maclennan of Rogart, Lord, 1997
McLoughlin, Patrick, 2005
McMullin, Sir Duncan, 1980
McNally, Lord, 2005
McNulty, Anthony, 2007
MacShane, Denis, 2005
Major, Sir John, 1987
Malloch-Brown, Lord, 2007
Mance, Lord, 1999
Mandelson, Lord, 1998
Marnoch, *Hon.* Lord (Michael Marnoch), 2001
Martin of Springburn, Lord, 2000
Marwick, Tricia, 2012
Mason of Barnsley, Lord, 1968
Mates, Michael, 2004
Maude, *Hon.* Francis, 1992
Mawhinney, Lord, 1994
May, Sir Anthony, 1998
May, Theresa, 2003
Mayhew of Twysden, Lord, 1986
Meacher, Michael, 1997
Mellor, David, 1990
Menzies, *Hon.* Lord (Duncan Menzies), 2012
Michael, Alun, 1998
Milburn, Alan, 1998
Miliband, David, 2005
Miliband, Ed, 2007
Miller, Maria, 2012
Millett, Lord, 1994
Mitchell, Andrew, 2010
Mitchell, Sir James, 1985
Mitchell, Dr Keith, 2004
Molyneaux of Killead, Lord, 1983
Moore, Michael, 1990
Moore, Michael, 2010
Moore of Lower Marsh, Lord, 1986
Moore-Bick, Sir Martin, 2005
Morgan, Sir Declan, 2009
Morgan, Rhodri, 2000
Morris of Aberavon, Lord, 1970
Morris of Yardley, Baroness, 1999
Morritt, Sir Robert, 1994
Moses, Sir Alan, 2005
Moyle, Roland, 1978
Mulholland, Frank, 2011
Mummery, Sir John, 1996
Munby, Sir James, 2009
Mundell, David, 2010
Murphy, James, 2008
Murphy, Paul, 1999
Murray, *Hon.* Lord (Ronald Murray), 1974
Murray, Sir Donald, 1989
Musa, Wilbert, 2005
Mustill, Lord, 1985
Namaliu, Sir Rabbie, 1989
Naseby, Lord, 1994
Needham, Sir Richard, 1994
Neill, Sir Brian, 1985
Neuberger of Abbotsbury, Lord, 2004
Neville-Jones, Baroness, 2010
Nicholls of Birkenhead, Lord, 1995
Nicholson, Sir Michael, 1995
Nimmo Smith, *Hon.* Lord (William Nimmo Smith), 2005
Nott, Sir John, 1979
Nourse, Sir Martin, 1985
O'Brien, Mike, 2009
O'Brien, Stephen, 2013
O'Donnell, Turlough, 1979
Oppenheim-Barnes, Baroness, 1979
Osborne, George, 2010
Osborne, *Hon.* Lord (Kenneth Osborne), 2001
Otton, Sir Philip, 1995
Owen, Lord, 1976
Paeniu, Bikenibeu, 1991
Paice, Sir James, 2010
Palmer, Sir Geoffrey, 1986
Paraskeva, Dame Janet, 2010
Parker, Sir Jonathan, 2000
Parkinson, Lord, 1981
Paterson, Owen, 2010
Paton, *Hon.* Lady (Ann Paton), 2007
Patten, Lord, 1990
Patten, Sir Nicholas, 2009
Patten of Barnes, Lord, 1989
Patterson, Percival, 1993
Pattie, Sir Geoffrey, 1987
Paul, Lord, 2009
Peel, Earl, 2006
Pendry, Lord, 2000
Penrose, *Hon.* Lord (George Penrose), 2000
Peters, Winston, 1998
Philip, *Hon.* Lord (Alexander Philip), 2005
Phillips of Worth Matravers, Lord, 1995
Pickles, Eric, 2010
Pill, Sir Malcolm, 1995
Pitchford, Sir Christopher, 2010
Portillo, Michael, 1992
Potter, Sir Mark, 1996
Prashar, Baroness, 2009
Primarolo, Dawn, 2002
Prior, Lord, 1970
Prosser, *Hon.* Lord (William Prosser), 2000
Puapua, Sir Tomasi, 1982
Purnell, James, 2007
Quin, Baroness, 1998
Radice, Lord, 1999
Rafferty, Dame Anne, 2011
Ramsden, James, 1963
Randall, John, 2010
Raynsford, Nick, 2001
Redwood, John, 1993
Reed, *Hon.* Lord (Robert Reed), 2008
Reid, Sir George, 2004
Reid of Cardowan, Lord, 1998
Renton of Mount Harry, Lord, 1989
Richard, Lord, 1993
Richards, Sir Stephen, 2005
Richardson, Sir Ivor, 1978
Riddell, Peter, 2010
Rifkind, Sir Malcolm, 1986
Rimer, Sir Colin, 2007
Rix, Sir Bernard, 2000
Robathan, Andrew, 2010
Roberts of Conwy, Lord, 1991
Robertson, Hugh, 2012
Robertson of Port Ellen, Lord, 1997
Robinson, Peter, 2007
Roch, Sir John, 1993
Rodgers of Quarry Bank, Lord, 1975
Rooker, Lord, 1999
Roper, Lord, 2005
Rose, Sir Christopher, 1992
Ross, *Hon.* Lord (Donald MacArthur), 1985
Royall of Blaisdon, Baroness, 2008
Ruddock, Dame Joan, 2010
Ryan, Joan, 2007
Ryder, Sir Ernest, 2013
Ryder of Wensum, Lord, 1990
Sainsbury, Sir Timothy, 1992
Salisbury, Marquess of, 1994
Salmond, Alex, 2007
Sandiford, Erskine, 1989
Saville of Newdigate, Lord, 1994
Sawyer, Dame Joan, 2004
Schiemann, Sir Konrad, 1995
Scotland of Asthal, Baroness, 2001
Scott of Foscote, Lord, 1991

Seaga, Edward, 1981
Sedley, Sir Stephen, 1999
Selkirk of Douglas, Lord, 1996
Shapps, Grant, 2010
Sheldon, Lord, 1977
Shephard of Northwold, Baroness, 1992
Sheil, Sir John, 2005
Shipley, Jennifer, 1998
Short, Clare, 1997
Shutt of Greetland, Lord, 2009
Simmonds, Kennedy Sir, 1984
Sinclair, Ian, 1977
Slade, Sir Christopher, 1982
Smith, Andrew, 1997
Smith, Dame Janet, 2002
Smith, *Hon.* Lady (Anne Smith), 2013
Smith, Jacqueline, 2003
Smith of Basildon, Baroness, 2009
Smith of Finsbury, Lord, 1997
Soames, *Hon.* (Arthur) Nicholas, 2011
Somare, Sir Michael, 1977
Spellar, John, 2001
Spelman, Caroline, 2010
Spicer, Lord, 2013
Stanley, Sir John, 1984
Staughton, Sir Christopher, 1988
Steel of Aikwood, Lord, 1977
Stephen, Sir Ninian, 1979
Stewartby, Lord, 1989
Steyn, Lord, 1992
Strang, Gavin, 1997
Strathclyde, Lord, 1995
Straw, Jack, 1997
Stuart-Smith, Sir Murray, 1988
Stunnell, Sir Andrew, 2012
Sullivan, Sir Jeremy, 2009
Sumption, *Hon.* Lord (Jonathan Sumption), 2011
Sutherland, *Hon.* Lord (Ranald Sutherland), 2000
Swayne, Desmond, 2011
Swire, Hugo, 2010
Symons of Vernham Dean, Baroness, 2001
Tapsell, Sir Peter, 2011
Taylor of Bolton, Baroness, 1997
Tebbit, Lord, 1981
Templeman, Lord, 1978
Thomas, Edmund, 1996
Thomas, Sir Roger, 2003
Thomas, Sir Swinton, 1994
Thorpe, Jeremy, 1967
Thorpe, Sir Matthew, 1995
Timms, Stephen, 2006
Tipping, Andrew, 1998
Tizard, Robert, 1986
Tomlinson, Sir Stephen, 2011
Touhig, Lord, 2006
Toulson, Sir Roger, 2007
Treacy, Sir Colman, 2012
Trefgarne, Lord, 1989
Trimble, Lord, 1997
Trumpington, Baroness, 1992
Tuckey, Sir Simon, 1998
Ullswater, Viscount, 1994
Underhill, Sir Nicholas, 2013
Upton, Simon, 1999
Vadera, Baroness, 2009
Vaz, Keith, 2006
Villiers, Theresa, 2010
Waddington, Lord, 1987
Waite, Sir John, 1993
Wakeham, Lord, 1983
Waldegrave of North Hill, Lord, 1990
Walker of Gestingthorpe, Lord, 1997
Wall, Sir Nicholas, 2004
Wallace of Saltaire, Lord, 2012
Wallace of Tankerness, Lord, 2000
Waller, Sir Mark, 1996
Ward, Sir Alan, 1995
Warner, Lord, 2006
Warsi, Baroness, 2010
West of Spithead, Lord, 2010
Wheatley, *Hon.* Lord (John Wheatley), 2007
Wheeler, Sir John, 1993
Whitty, Lord, 2005
Widdecombe, Ann, 1997
Wigley, Dafydd, 1997
Willetts, David, 2010
Williams, Alan, 1977
Williams of Crosby, Baroness, 1974
Williams of Elvel, Lord, 2013
Williams of Oystermouth, Lord, 2002
Williamson of Horton, Lord, 2007
Wills, Lord, 2008
Wilson, Brian, 2003
Wilson, Sir Nicholas, 2005
Winterton, Rosie, 2006
Wingti, Paias, 1987
Withers, Reginald, 1977
Woodhouse, Sir Owen, 1974
Woodward, Shaun, 2007
Woolf, Lord, 1986
York, Archbishop of, 2005
Young, Sir George, 1993
Young of Graffham, Lord, 1984
Zacca, Edward, 1992

PRIVY COUNCIL OF NORTHERN IRELAND

The Privy Council of Northern Ireland had responsibilities in Northern Ireland similar to those of the Privy Council in Great Britain until the Northern Ireland Act 1974. Membership of the Privy Council of Northern Ireland is retained for life. Since the Northern Ireland Constitution Act 1973 no further appointments have been made. The postnominal initials PC (NI) are used to differentiate its members from those of the Privy Council.

MEMBERS *as at August 2013*
Bailie, Robin, 1971
Bleakley, David, 1971
Dobson, John, 1969
Kilclooney, Lord, 1970
Porter, Sir Robert, 1969

PARLIAMENT

The UK constitution is not contained in any single document but has evolved over time, formed by statute, common law and convention. A constitutional monarchy, the UK is governed by ministers of the crown in the name of the sovereign, who is head both of the state and of the government.

The organs of government are the legislature (parliament), the executive and the judiciary. The executive comprises HM government (the cabinet and other ministers), government departments and local authorities (*see* Government Departments, Public Bodies and Local Government). The judiciary (*see* Law Courts and Offices) pronounces on the law, both written and unwritten, interprets statutes and is responsible for the enforcement of the law; the judiciary is independent of both the legislature and the executive.

THE MONARCHY

The sovereign personifies the state and is, in law, an integral part of the legislature, head of the executive, head of the judiciary, commander-in-chief of all armed forces of the crown and supreme governor of the Church of England. In the Channel Islands and the Isle of Man, which are crown dependencies, the sovereign is represented by a lieutenant-governor. In the member states of the Commonwealth of which the sovereign is head of state, her representative is a governor-general; in UK overseas territories the sovereign is usually represented by a governor, who is responsible to the British government.

Although in practice the powers of the monarchy are now very limited, and restricted mainly to the advisory and ceremonial, there are important acts of government which require the participation of the sovereign. These include summoning, proroguing and dissolving parliament, giving royal assent to bills passed by parliament, appointing important office-holders, eg government ministers, judges, bishops and governors, conferring peerages, knighthoods and other honours, and granting pardon to a person wrongly convicted of a crime. The sovereign appoints the prime minister; by convention this office is held by the leader of the political party which enjoys, or can secure, a majority of votes in the House of Commons. In international affairs the sovereign, as head of state, has the power to declare war and make peace, to recognise foreign states and governments, to conclude treaties and to annex or cede territory. However, as the sovereign entrusts executive power to ministers of the crown and acts on the advice of her ministers, which she cannot ignore, royal prerogative powers are in practice exercised by ministers, who are responsible to parliament.

Ministerial responsibility does not diminish the sovereign's importance to the smooth working of government. She holds meetings of the Privy Council (*see* below), gives audiences to her ministers and other officials at home and overseas, receives accounts of cabinet decisions, reads dispatches and signs state papers; she must be informed and consulted on every aspect of national life; and she must show complete impartiality.

COUNSELLORS OF STATE

If the sovereign travels abroad for more than a few days or suffers from a temporary illness, it is necessary to appoint members of the royal family, known as counsellors of state, under letters patent to carry out the chief functions of the monarch, including the holding of Privy Councils and giving royal assent to acts passed by parliament. The normal procedure is to appoint three or four members of the royal family among those members remaining in the UK, provided they are over 21. There are currently five counsellors of state.

In the event of the sovereign on accession being under the age of 18 years, or by infirmity of mind or body, rendered incapable of performing the royal functions, provision is made for a regency.

THE PRIVY COUNCIL

The sovereign in council, or Privy Council, was the chief source of executive power until the system of cabinet government developed. Its main function today is to advise the sovereign on the approval of various statutory functions and acts of the royal prerogative. These powers are exercised through orders in council and royal proclamations, approved by the Queen at meetings of the Privy Council. The council is also able to exercise a number of statutory duties without approval from the sovereign, including powers of supervision over the registering bodies for the medical and allied professions. These duties are exercised through orders of council.

Although appointment as a privy counsellor is for life, only those who are currently government ministers are involved in the day-to-day business of the council. A full council is summoned only on the death of the sovereign or when the sovereign announces his or her intention to marry. (For a full list of privy counsellors, *see* the Privy Council section.)

There are a number of advisory Privy Council committees whose meetings the sovereign does not attend. Some are prerogative committees, such as those dealing with legislative matters submitted by the legislatures of the Channel Islands and the Isle of Man or with applications for charters of incorporation; and some are provided for by statute, eg those for the universities of Oxford and Cambridge and some Scottish universities.

Administrative work is carried out by the Privy Council Office under the direction of the Lord President of the Council, a cabinet minister.

JUDICIAL COMMITTEE OF THE PRIVY COUNCIL

Supreme Court Building, Parliament Square, London SW1P 3BD
T 020-7960 1500 W www.jcpc.gov.uk

The Judicial Committee of the Privy Council is the court of final appeal from courts of the UK dependencies, courts of independent Commonwealth countries which have retained the right of appeal and courts of the Channel Islands and the Isle of Man. It also hears very occasional appeals from a number of ancient and ecclesiastical courts.

The committee is composed of privy counsellors who hold, or have held, high judicial office. Only three or five judges hear each case, and these are usually justices of the supreme court.

PARLIAMENT

Parliament is the supreme law-making authority and can legislate for the UK as a whole or for any parts of it separately (the Channel Islands and the Isle of Man are crown dependencies and not part of the UK). The main functions of parliament are to pass laws, to enable the government to raise taxes and to scrutinise government policy and administration, particularly proposals for expenditure. International treaties and agreements are customarily presented to parliament before ratification.

Parliament can trace its roots to two characteristics of Anglo-Saxon rule: the *witan* (a meeting of the king, nobles and advisors) and the *moot* (county meetings where local matters were discussed). However, it was the parliament that Simon de Montfort called in 1265 that is accepted as the forerunner to modern parliament, as it included non-noble representatives from counties, cities and towns alongside the nobility. The nucleus of early parliaments at the beginning of the 14th century were the officers of the king's household and the king's judges, joined by such ecclesiastical and lay magnates as the king might summon to form a prototype 'House of Lords', and occasionally by the knights of the shires, burgesses and proctors of the lower clergy. By the end of Edward III's reign a 'House of Commons' was beginning to appear; the first known Speaker was elected in 1377.

Parliamentary procedure is based on custom and precedent, partly formulated in the standing orders of both houses of parliament. Each house has the right to control its own internal proceedings and to commit for contempt. The system of debate in the two houses is similar; when a motion has been moved, the Speaker proposes the question as the subject of a debate. Members speak from wherever they have been sitting. Questions are decided by a vote on a simple majority. Draft legislation is introduced, in either house, as a bill. Bills can be introduced by a government minister or a private member, but in practice the majority of bills which become law are introduced by the government. To become law, a bill must be passed by each house (for parliamentary stages, *see* Parliamentary Information) and then sent to the sovereign for the royal assent, after which it becomes an act of parliament.

Proceedings of both houses are public, except on extremely rare occasions. The minutes (called *Votes and Proceedings in the Commons,* and *Minutes of Proceedings in the Lords*) and the speeches (*The Official Report of Parliamentary Debates,* Hansard) are published daily. Proceedings are also recorded for transmission on radio and television and stored in the Parliamentary Recording Unit before transfer to the National Sound Archive. Television cameras have been allowed into the House of Lords since 1985 and into the House of Commons since 1989; committee meetings may also be televised.

The Fixed Term Parliament Act 2011 fixed the duration of a parliament at five years in normal circumstances, the term being reckoned from the date given on the writs for the new parliament. The term of a parliament has been prolonged by legislation in such rare circumstances as the two World Wars (31 January 1911 to 25 November 1918; 26 November 1935 to 15 June 1945). The life of a parliament is divided into sessions, usually of one year in length, beginning and ending most often in May.

DEVOLUTION

The Scottish parliament and the National Assembly for Wales have legislative power over all devolved matters, ie matters not reserved to Westminster or otherwise outside its powers. The Northern Ireland Assembly has legislative authority in the fields previously administered by the Northern Ireland departments. The assembly was suspended in October 2002 and dissolved in April 2003, before being reinstated on 8 May 2007. For further information, *see* Regional Government.

THE HOUSE OF LORDS

London SW1A 0PW
T 020-7219 3000 **Information Office** 020-7219 3107
E hlinfo@parliament.uk W www.parliament.uk

The House of Lords is the second chamber, or 'Upper House', of the UK's bicameral parliament. Until the beginning of the 20th century, the House of Lords had considerable power, being able to veto any bill submitted to it by the House of Commons. Since 1911, however, it has no powers over money bills and its power of veto over public legislation has been reduced to the power to delay bills for up to one session of parliament (usually one year). Today the main functions of the House of Lords are to contribute to the legislative process, to act as a check on the government, and to provide a forum of expertise. Its judicial role as final court of appeal ended in 2009 as a result of the establishment of a new UK Supreme Court (*see* Law Courts and Offices section).

The House of Lords has a number of select committees. Some relate to the internal affairs of the house – such as its management and administration – while others carry out important investigative work on matters of public interest. The main areas of work are: Europe, science, the economy, the constitution and communications. House of Lords' investigative committees look at broad issues and do not mirror government departments as the select committees in the House of Commons do.

On 12 June 2003 the government announced reforms of the judicial function and the role of the Lord Chancellor as a judge and presiding officer of the House of Lords. In 2006 the position of Lord Chancellor was significantly altered by the Constitutional Reform Act 2005. The office holder is no longer the presiding officer of the House of Lords nor head of the judiciary in England and Wales, but remains a cabinet minister (the Lord Chancellor and Secretary of State for Justice), and is currently a member of the House of Commons. The function of the presiding officer of the House of Lords was devolved to the newly created post of the Speaker of the House of Lords, commonly known as Lord Speaker. The Rt. Hon. Baroness Hayman was elected as the first Lord Speaker by the house on 4 July 2006.

Members of the House of Lords comprise mainly life peers created under the Life Peerages Act 1958, along with 92 hereditary peers under the House of Lords Act 1999 and Lords of Appeal in Ordinary, ie law lords, under the Appellate Jurisdiction Act 1876*. The Archbishops of Canterbury and York, the Bishops of London, Durham and Winchester, and the 21 senior diocesan bishops of the Church of England are also members.

The House of Lords Act provides for 90 hereditary peers to remain in the House of Lords until further reform of the House has been carried out. Of these, 75 (42 Conservative, 28 crossbench, three Liberal Democrat and two Labour) are elected by hereditary peers in their political party or crossbench grouping. Elections for each of the party groups and the crossbenches were held in October and November 1999. In addition, 15 office holders were elected by the whole house. Two hereditary peers with royal duties, the Earl Marshal and the Lord Great Chamberlain, have also remained members. Since November 2002, by-elections have been held to fill vacancies left by deaths of hereditary peers; the by-elections take place under the Alternative Vote System and must occur within three months of the death of the hereditary peer (*see also* The Peerage).

Peers are disqualified from sitting in the house if they are:

- aliens, ie any peer who is not a British citizen, a Commonwealth citizen (under the British Nationality Act 1981) or a citizen of the Republic of Ireland
- under the age of 21

- undischarged bankrupts or, in Scotland, those whose estate is sequestered
- holders of a disqualifying judicial office
- members of the European Parliament
- convicted of treason

Bishops retire at the age of 70 and cease to be members of the house at that time.

Members who do not wish to attend sittings of the House of Lords may apply for leave of absence for the duration of a parliament, or retire permanently.

Members of the House of Lords, who are not paid a salary, may claim a flat-rate daily attendance allowance of £300 (for peers that attend for a full sitting day) or £150 (for those peers that attend for less than a full sitting day), or may choose to make no claim for each sitting day they attend the house.

* Although the office of Lord of Appeal in Ordinary no longer exists, retired law lords remain in the House of Lords as life peers. Law lords who became justices of the UK Supreme Court are not permitted to sit or vote in the House of Lords until they retire.

COMPOSITION *as at 10 September 2013*

Archbishops and bishops	23
Life peers under the Appellate Jurisdiction Act 1876 and the Life Peerages Act 1958	641
Peers under the House of Lords Act 1999	89
Total	753

STATE OF THE PARTIES *as at 10 September 2013*†

Conservative	208
Labour	216
Liberal Democrat	89
Crossbench	183
Archbishops and bishops	23
Other	34
Total	753

† Excluding 44 peers on leave of absence, eight disqualified as senior members of the judiciary and one disqualified as an MEP

HOUSE OF LORDS PAY BANDS FOR SENIOR STAFF

Senior staff are placed in the following pay bands according to their level of responsibility and taking account of other factors such as experience and marketability.

Judicial group 4	£172,753
Senior band 3	£101,500–£145,629
Senior band 2	£82,900–£135,970
Senior band 1A	£67,600–£113,202
Senior band 1	£58,200–£100,374
Band A1	£56,723–£72,788
Band A2	£47,164–£60,221

OFFICERS AND OFFICIALS

The house is presided over by the Lord Speaker, whose powers differ from those of the Speaker of the House of Commons. The Lord Speaker has no power to rule on matters of order because the House of Lords is self-regulating. The maintenance of the rules of debate is the responsibility of all the members who are present.

A panel of deputy speakers is appointed by Royal Commission. The first deputy speaker is the Chair of Committees, a salaried officer of the house appointed at the beginning of each session. He or she chairs a number of 'domestic' committees relating to the internal affairs of the house. The first deputy speaker is assisted by a panel of deputy chairs, headed by the salaried Principal Deputy Chair of Committees, who is also chair of the European Union Committee of the house.

The Clerk of the Parliaments is the accounting officer and the chief permanent official responsible for the administration of the house. The Gentleman Usher of the Black Rod is responsible for security and other services and also has royal duties as secretary to the Lord Great Chamberlain.

Lord Speaker (£101,038), Rt. Hon. Baroness D'Souza, CMG
Chair of Committees (£84,524), Lord Sewel, CBE
Principal Deputy Chair of Committees (£79,076), Lord Boswell of Aynho
Clerk of the Parliaments (Judicial Group 4), D. R. Beamish
Clerk Assistant (Senior Band 3), E. C. Ollard
Reading Clerk and Clerk of the Overseas Office (Senior Band 2), Dr R. H. Walters
Clerk of Committees (Senior Band 2), Dr F. P. Tudor
Director of Facilities (Senior Band 2), C. V. Woodall
Finance Director (Senior Band 1A), A. Makower
Director of Human Resources (Senior Band 1A), T. V. Mohan
Registrar of Members' Interests (Senior Band 2A), B. P. Keith
Director of Information Services and Librarian (Senior Band 2), Dr E. Hallam Smith
Clerk of Legislation (Senior Band 1A), S. P. Burton
Principal Clerk of Select Committees (Senior Band 1A), J. Vaughan
Editor of the Official Report (Senior Band 1), J. S. Vice
Director of Parliamentary Archives (Senior Band 1), A. Brown
Deputy Finance Director and Head of Finance (Senior Band 1), J. P. Smith
Director of Public Information (Band A1), B. Hiscock
Counsel to the Chair of Committees (Senior Band 2), P. Milledge; M. Thomas
Legal Adviser to the Human Rights Committee (Senior Band 2), M. Hunt
Change Manager (Senior Band 1), Mrs M. E. Ollard
Clerk of the European Union Committee (Senior Band 1A), J. Vaughan
Clerks of Select Committees (Senior Band 1), C. Johnson; D. Sagar
Gentleman Usher of the Black Rod and Serjeant-at-Arms (Senior Band 2), Lt.-Gen. David Leakey, CMG, CBE
Yeoman Usher of the Black Rod and Deputy Serjeant-at-Arms (Band A2), N. Baverstock

LORD GREAT CHAMBERLAIN'S OFFICE

Lord Great Chamberlain, Marquess of Cholmondeley, KCVO
Secretary to the Lord Great Chamberlain, Lt.-Gen. David Leakey, CMG, CBE

SELECT COMMITTEES

The main House of Lords select committees, as at June 2013, are as follows:

Administration and Works Committee – Chair, Lord Sewel, CBE; *Clerk,* Sarah Jones
Communications Committee – Chair, Lord Inglewood; *Clerk,* Anna Murphy
Constitution Committee – Chair, Rt. Hon. Baroness Jay of Paddington; *Clerk,* Nicolas Besly
Delegated Powers and Regulatory Reform – Chair, Baroness Thomas of Winchester; *Clerk,* Christine Salmon Percival
Economic Affairs – Chair, Rt. Hon. Lord MacGregor of Pulham Market; *Clerk,* Bill Sinton
European Union – Chair, Lord Boswell of Aynho; *Clerk,* Jake Vaughan

European Union – Sub-committees:
A (Economic and Financial Affairs) – Chair, Lord Harrison; *Clerk,* Stuart Stoner
B (Internal Market, Infrastructure and Employment) – Chair, Baroness O'Cathain, OBE; *Clerk,* Nicole Mason
C (External Affairs) – Chair, Lord Tugendhat; *Clerk,* Kathryn Colvin
D (Agriculture, Fisheries, Environment and Energy) – Chair, Baroness Scott of Needham Market; *Clerk,* Aaron Speer
E (Justice, Institutions and Consumer Protection) – Chair, Rt. Hon. Baroness Corston; *Clerk,* Elisa Rubio
F (Home Affairs, Health and Education) – Chair, Lord Hannay of Chiswick, GCMG, CH; *Clerk,* Michael Torrance
House Committee – Chair, Rt. Hon. Baroness D'Souza, CMG; *Clerk,* James Whittle
Inquiries Act 2005 Committee – Chair, Rt. Hon. Lord Shutt of Greetland; *Clerk,* Michael Collon
Liaison Committee – Chair, Lord Sewel, CBE; *Clerk,* Philippa Tudor
Lords' Conduct Sub-committee – Chair, Baroness Manningham-Buller, DCB; *Clerk,* Nick Besly
Mental Capacity Act Committee – Chair, Rt. Hon. Lord Hardie; *Clerk,* Judith Brooke
National Security Strategy Joint Commitee – Chair, Rt. Hon. Dame Margaret Beckett, DBE, MP; *Clerks,* Philippa Helme *(Commons)*; Chris Clarke *(Lords)*
Olympic and Paralympic Legacy Committee – Chair, Lord Harris of Harringey; *Clerk,* Duncan Sagar
Privileges and Conduct – Chair, Lord Sewel; *Clerk,* Christopher Johnson
Refreshment Committee – Chair, Lord Sewel, CBE; *Clerk,* Sarah Jones
Science and Technology – Chair, Lord Krebs; *Clerk,* Chris Atkinson
Science and Technology Sub-Committee I – Chair, Lord Willis of Knaresborough; *Clerk,* Elisa Rubio
Secondary Legislation Scrutiny Committee – Chair, Rt. Hon. Lord Goodlad, KCMG; *Clerk,* Christine Salmon Percival
Selection Committee – Chair, Lord Sewel, CBE; *Clerk,* vacant
Soft Powers and the UK's Influence Committee – Chair, Rt. Hon. Lord Howell of Guildford; *Clerk,* Susannah Street
Draft Voting Eligibility (Prisoners) Bill Joint Committee – Chair, Nick Gibb, MP; *Clerks,* Sêan Woodward *(Commons)*; Stephanie Johnson *(Lords)*
Human Rights Joint Committee – Chair, Dr Hywel Francis, MP; *Clerks,* Mike Hennessy *(Commons)*; Mark Davies *(Lords)*
Security Joint Committee – Chair, Rt. Hon. John Randall, MP; *Clerks,* Philippa Helme *(Commons)*; James Whittle *(Lords)*
Statutory Instruments Joint Committee – Chair, George Mudie, MP; *Clerks,* Sarah Petit *(Commons)*; Jane White *(Lords)*

THE HOUSE OF COMMONS

London SW1A 0AA
T 020-7219 3000 **W** www.parliament.uk

HOUSE OF COMMONS INFORMATION OFFICE
14 Tothill Street, London SW1H 9NB
T 020-7219 4272 **E** hcinfo@parliament.uk

The members of the House of Commons are elected by universal adult suffrage. For electoral purposes, the UK is divided into constituencies, each of which returns one member to the House of Commons, the member being the candidate who obtains the largest number of votes cast in the constituency. To ensure equitable representation, the four Boundary Commissions keep constituency boundaries under review and recommend any redistribution of seats which may seem necessary because of population movements etc. At the 2010 general election the number of seats increased from 646 to 650. Of the present 650 seats, there are 533 for England, 40 for Wales, 59 for Scotland and 18 for Northern Ireland.

NUMBER OF SEATS IN THE HOUSE OF COMMONS BY COUNTRY

	2005	*2010*
England	529	533
Wales	40	40
Scotland	59	59
Northern Ireland	18	18
Total	646	650

ELECTIONS

Elections are by secret ballot, each elector casting one vote; voting is not compulsory. (For entitlement to vote in parliamentary elections, *see* Legal Notes.) When a seat becomes vacant between general elections, a by-election is held.

British subjects and citizens of the Irish Republic can stand for election as MPs provided they are 18 or over and not subject to disqualification. Those disqualified from sitting in the house include:

- undischarged bankrupts
- people sentenced to more than one year's imprisonment
- members of the House of Lords (but hereditary peers not sitting in the Lords are eligible)
- holders of certain offices listed in the House of Commons Disqualification Act 1975, eg members of the judiciary, civil service, regular armed forces, police forces, some local government officers and some members of public corporations and government commissions

A candidate does not require any party backing but his or her nomination for election must be supported by the signatures of ten people registered in the constituency. A candidate must also deposit £500 with the returning officer, which is forfeit if the candidate does not receive more than 5 per cent of the votes cast. All election expenses at a general election, except the candidate's personal expenses, are subject to a statutory limit of £7,150, plus five pence for each elector in a borough constituency or seven pence for each elector in a county constituency.

See pages 128–173 for an alphabetical list of MPs and results of the general election in 2010.

STATE OF THE PARTIES *as at 6 June 2013**

Party	*Seats*
Conservative	303
Labour	255
Liberal Democrats	56
Democratic Unionist Party	8
Scottish National Party	6
Sinn Fein (have not taken their seats)	5
Plaid Cymru	3
Social Democratic & Labour Party	3
Alliance	1
Green	1
Respect	1
Independent	4
The Speaker and three Deputy Speakers	4
Total	650

* Working majority of 77; 303 Conservative and 56 Liberal Democrat MPs less 282 of all other parties (excluding the speaker, deputy speakers and Sinn Fein)

BUSINESS

The week's business of the house is outlined each Thursday by the leader of the house, after consultation between the chief government whip and the chief opposition whip. A quarter to a third of the time will be taken up by the government's legislative programme and the rest by other business. As a rule, bills likely to raise political controversy are introduced in the Commons before going on to the Lords, and the Commons claims exclusive control in respect of national taxation and expenditure. Bills such as the finance bill, which imposes taxation, and the consolidated fund bills, which authorise expenditure, must begin in the Commons. A bill of which the financial provisions are subsidiary may begin in the Lords, and the Commons may waive its rights in regard to Lords' amendments affecting finance.

The Commons has a public register of MPs' financial and certain other interests; this is published annually as a House of Commons paper. Members must also disclose any relevant financial interest or benefit in a matter before the house when taking part in a debate, in certain other proceedings of the house, or in consultations with other MPs, with ministers or with civil servants.

MEMBERS' PAY AND ALLOWANCES

Since 1911 members of the House of Commons have received salary payments; facilities for free travel were introduced in 1924. Salary rates for the last 30 years are as follows:

1984 Jan	£16,106	1999 Apr	£47,008
1985 Jan	16,904	2000 Apr	48,371
1986 Jan	17,702	2001 Apr	49,822
1987 Jan	18,500	2002 Apr	55,118
1988 Jan	22,548	2003 Apr	56,358
1989 Jan	24,107	2004 Apr	57,485
1990 Jan	26,701	2005 Apr	59,095
1991 Jan	28,970	2006 Apr	59,686
1992 Jan	30,854	2007 Apr	61,181
1993 Jan	30,854	2008 Apr	63,291
1994 Jan	31,687	2009 Apr	64,766
1995 Jan	33,189	2010 Apr	65,738
1996 Jan	34,085	2011 Apr	65,738
1996 Jul	43,000	2012 Apr	65,738
1997 Apr	43,860	2013 Apr	66,396
1998 Apr	45,066	2014 Apr	67,060

The Independent Parliamentary Standards Authority (IPSA) was established under the Parliamentary Standards Act 2009 and is responsible for the independent regulation and administration of the MPs' Scheme of Business Costs and Expenses, as well as for paying the salaries of MPs and their staff members. Since May 2011, the IPSA has also been responsible for determining MPs' pay and setting the level of any increase to their salary.

For 2013–14, the office costs expenditure budget is £25,350 for London area MPs and £22,750 for non-London area MPs. The maximum annual staff budget for London area MPs is £144,000 and £137,200 for non-London area MPs.

Since 1972 MPs have been able to claim reimbursement for the additional cost of staying overnight away from their main residence while on parliamentary business. This is not payable to London area MPs and those MPs who reside in 'grace and favour' accommodation. Accommodation expenses for MPs claiming rental payments is capped at £20,000 per year; for MPs who own their own homes, mortgage interest and associated expenses up to £8,850 are payable.

For ministerial salaries *see* Government Departments.

MEMBERS' PENSIONS

Pension arrangements for MPs were first introduced in 1964. Under the Parliamentary Contributory Pension Fund (PCPF), MPs receive a pension on retirement based upon their salary in their final year, and upon their number of years' service as an MP. Members may pay a contribution rate of 7.75, 9.75 or 13.75 per cent and build up a pension of 1.6, 2 or 2.5 per cent of salary for each year of service. Pensions are normally payable upon retirement at age 65; the pension payable is subject to a maximum of 66.6 per cent of salary, inclusive of pensions from employment or self-employment prior to becoming an MP. There are provisions in place for: early retirement for those MPs who cease to serve between the ages of 55 and 65; MPs of any age who retire due to ill health; and pensions for widows/widowers of MPs. All pensions are index-linked. There is also an Exchequer contribution; currently 20.2 per cent of an MP's salary.

The House of Commons Members' Fund provides for annual or lump sum grants to ex-MPs, their widows or widowers, and children of those who either ceased to serve as an MP prior to the PCPF being established or who are experiencing hardship. Members contribute £24 a year and the Exchequer £215,000 a year to the fund.

HOUSE OF COMMONS PAY BANDS FOR SENIOR STAFF

Senior Staff are placed in the following Senior Civil Service pay bands. These pay bands apply to the most senior staff in departments and agencies.

Pay Band 1	£58,200–£93,380
Pay Band 1A	£67,600–£105,560
Pay Band 2	£82,900–£124,845
Pay Band 3	£101,500–£139,829

OFFICERS AND OFFICIALS

The House of Commons is presided over by the Speaker, who has considerable powers to maintain order. A deputy speaker, called the Chairman of Ways and Means, and two deputy chairs may preside over sittings of the House of Commons; they are elected by the house, and, like the Speaker, neither speak nor vote other than in their official capacity.

The staff of the house are employed by a commission chaired by the Speaker. The heads of the six House of Commons departments are permanent officers of the house, not MPs. The Clerk of the House is the principal adviser to the Speaker on the privileges and procedures of the house, the conduct of the business of the house, and committees. The Serjeant-at-Arms is responsible for security and ceremonial functions of the house.

Speaker (£142,162)*, Rt. Hon. John Bercow, MP
Chairman of Ways and Means (£107,108),
Rt. Hon. Lindsay Hoyle, MP
First Deputy Chairman of Ways and Means (£102,098),
Nigel Evans, MP
Second Deputy Chairman of Ways and Means (£102,098),
Rt. Hon. Dawn Primarolo, MP
Parliamentary Commissioner for Standards, Kathryn Hudson

* Salaries in parentheses are the maximum available. The Speaker and Deputies have opted not to take the statutory increases awarded to them each year as office holders.

OFFICES OF THE SPEAKER AND CHAIRMAN OF WAYS AND MEANS

Speaker's Secretary, Peter Barratt
Chaplain to the Speaker, Revd Rose Hudson-Wilkin

Secretary to the Chairman of Ways and Means, Sara Howe
Clerk of the House of Commons and Chief Executive, Sir Robert Rogers, KCB

OFFICE OF THE CHIEF EXECUTIVE
Head of Office, Matthew Hamlyn
Director of Internal Audit, Paul Dillon-Robinson

DEPARTMENT OF CHAMBER AND COMMITTEE SERVICES

Director-General and Clerk Assistant, David Natzler
Principal Clerks
Table Office, Paul Evans
Journals, Liam Laurence Smyth
Overseas Office, Crispin Poyser
Director of Departmental Services, Tom Goldsmith

VOTE OFFICE
Deliverer of the Vote, Catherine Fogarty
Deputy Deliverers of the Vote, Owen Sweeney *(Parliamentary)*; Tom McVeagh *(Production)*

COMMITTEE DIRECTORATE
Clerk of Committees, Andrew Kennon
Principal Clerk and Deputy Head of Committee Office, Philippa Helme
Clerk of Domestic Committees/Secretary to the Commission, Robert Twigger
Select Committees, Paul Evans; Mark Hutton; Christopher Stanton
Head of Scrutiny Unit, Jessica Mulley

LEGISLATION DIRECTORATE
Clerk of Legislation, Jacqy Sharpe
Principal Clerks
Bills, Simon Patrick
National Parliament Office (Brussels), Edward Beale
Ways and Means Office, Sara Howe

OFFICIAL REPORT DIRECTORATE
Editor, Lorraine Sutherland
Deputy Editor, Alex Newton
Director of Broadcasting, John Angeli

SERJEANT-AT-ARMS DIRECTORATE
Serjeant-at-Arms, Lawrence Ward
Deputy Serjeant-at-Arms, Richard Latham
Assistant Serjeant-at-Arms, Lesley Scott

OFFICE OF SPEAKER'S COUNSEL
Speaker's Counsel and Head of Legal Services Office, Michael Carpenter
Counsel for European Legislation, Paul Hardy
Assistant Counsel for European Legislation, Joanne Dee
Counsel for Domestic Legislation, Peter Davis
Deputy Counsel for Domestic Legislation, Peter Brooksbank; Peter Davies; Daniel Greenberg
Principal Assistant Counsel, Helen Emes
Legal Assistants, Klara Banaszak

DEPARTMENT OF FACILITIES

Director-General, John Borley
Director of Business Management, Della Herd
Parliamentary Director of Estates, Mel Barlex
Director of Accommodation Services, James Robertson
Director of Facilities Finance, Philip Collins
Executive Officer, Katherine Gray
Director of Catering Services, Richard Tapner-Evans
Operations Manager, Robert Gibbs
Executive Chef, Mark Hill

DEPARTMENT OF FINANCE

Director of Finance, Myfanwy Barrett
Director of Financial Management, Chris Ridley
Director of Commercial Services, Veronica Daly
Head of Pensions and Payroll, Lucy Tindal

DEPARTMENT OF HUMAN RESOURCES AND CHANGE

Director-General of HR and Change, Andrew J. Walker
Director of Business Management and Delivery, Janet Rissen
Director of Change, Selven Naicker
Head of Occupational Safety, Health and Wellbeing Service, Dr Marianne McDougall

DEPARTMENT OF INFORMATION SERVICES

Director-General and Librarian, John Pullinger
Directors, John Benger *(Service Delivery)*; Prof. David Cope *(Parliamentary Office of Science and Technology)*; Adam Mellows-Facer *(Research)*; Aileen Walker *(Public Engagement)*; Steve Wise *(Information Management)*; Edward Wood *(Public Information)*
Head of Media and Communications Service, Lee Bridges
Head of Public Information and Outreach, Claire Cowan
Visitor Services, Deborah Newman

PARLIAMENTARY INFORMATION AND COMMUNICATION TECHNOLOGY (ICT)

Director of Parliamentary ICT, Joan Miller
Director of Technology Directorate, Steve O'Connor
Director of Operations and Members Services, Matthew Taylor
Director of Resources, Fergus Reid
Director of Programmes and Projects, Rebecca Elton
Director of Network Programme, Innis Montgomery

SELECT COMMITTEES

The more significant committees, as at April 2013, are:

DEPARTMENTAL COMMITTEES
Business, Innovation and Skills – Chair, Adrian Bailey, MP; *Clerk,* James Davies
Communities and Local Government – Chair, Clive Betts, MP; *Clerk,* Glen McKee
Culture, Media and Sport – Chair, John Whittingdale, MP; *Clerk,* Elizabeth Flood
Defence – Chair, Rt. Hon. James Arbuthnot, MP; *Clerk,* Alda Barry
Education – Chair, Graham Stuart, MP; *Clerk,* Dr Lynn Gardner
Energy and Climate Change – Chair, Tim Yeo, MP; *Clerk,* Sarah Hartwell-Naguib
Environment, Food and Rural Affairs – Chair, Anne McIntosh, MP; *Clerk,* David Weir
Foreign Affairs – Chair, Richard Ottaway, MP; *Clerk,* Kenneth Fox
Health – Chair, Rt. Hon. Stephen Dorell, MP; *Clerk,* David Lloyd
Home Affairs – Chair, Rt. Hon. Keith Vaz, MP; *Clerk,* Tom Healey
International Development – Chair, Rt. Hon. Sir Malcolm Bruce, MP; *Clerk,* Dr David Harrison
Justice – Chair, Rt. Hon. Sir Alan Beith, MP; *Clerk,* Nick Walker
Northern Ireland Affairs – Chair, Laurence Robertson, MP; *Clerk,* Mike Clark
Scottish Affairs – Chair, Ian Davidson, MP; *Clerk,* Eliot Wilson
Transport – Chair, Louise Ellman, MP; *Clerk,* Dr Mark Egan
Treasury – Chair, Andrew Tyrie, MP; *Clerk,* Chris Stanton

Welsh Affairs – Chair, David T. C. Davies, MP; *Clerk,* Markek Kubala
Work and Pensions – Chair, Dame Anne Begg, MP; *Clerk,* Carol Oxborough

NON-DEPARTMENTAL COMMITTEES
Environmental Audit – Chair, Joan Walley, MP; *Clerk,* Simon Fiander
Political and Constitutional Reform – Chair, Graham Allen, MP; *Clerk,* Joanna Dodd
Procedure – Chair, Charles Walker, MP; *Clerk,* Huw Yardley
Public Accounts – Chair, Rt. Hon. Margaret Hodge, MP; *Clerk,* Adrian Jenner
Public Administration – Chair, Bernard Jenkin, MP; *Clerks,* Emily Commander; Catherine Tyack
Science and Technology – Chair, Andrew Miller, MP; *Clerk,* Dr Stephen McGinness

NATIONAL AUDIT OFFICE
157–197 Buckingham Palace Road, London SW1W 9SP
T 020-7798 7000
E enquiries@nao.gsi.gov.uk W www.nao.org.uk

The National Audit Office came into existence under the National Audit Act 1983 to replace and continue the work of the former Exchequer and Audit Department. The act reinforced the office's total financial and operational independence from the government and brought its head, the Comptroller and Auditor-General, into a closer relationship with parliament as an officer of the House of Commons.

The National Audit Office provides independent information, advice and assurance to parliament and the public about all aspects of the financial operations of government departments and many other bodies receiving public funds. It does this by examining and certifying the accounts of these organisations. It also regularly publishes reports to parliament on the results of its value for money investigations of the economy (the efficiency and effectiveness with which public resources have been used). The National Audit Office is also the auditor by agreement of the accounts of certain international and other organisations. In addition, the office authorises the issue of public funds to government departments.
Comptroller and Auditor-General, Amyas Morse
Assistant Auditors-General, Gabrielle Cohen; Ed Humpherson; Lynda McMullan; Martin Sinclair
Chief Operating Officer, Michael Whitehouse

PARLIAMENTARY INFORMATION

The following is a short glossary of aspects of the work of parliament. Unless otherwise stated, references are to House of Commons procedures.

BILL – Proposed legislation is termed a bill. The stages of a public bill (for private bills, *see* below) in the House of Commons are as follows:

First reading: This stage introduces the legislation to the house and, for government bills, merely constitutes an order to have the bill printed.

Second reading: The debate on the principles of the bill.

Committee stage: The detailed examination of a bill, clause by clause. In most cases this takes place in a public bill committee, or the whole house may act as a committee. Public bill committees may take evidence before embarking on detailed scrutiny of the bill. Very rarely, a bill may be examined by a select committee.

Report stage: Detailed review of a bill as amended in committee, on the floor of the house, and an opportunity to make further changes.

Third reading: Final debate on the full bill in the Commons.

Public bills go through the same stages in the House of Lords, but with important differences: the committee stage is taken in committee of the whole house or in a grand committee, in which any peer may participate. There are no time limits, all amendments are debated, and further amendments can be made at third reading.

A bill may start in either house, and has to pass through both houses to become law. Both houses have to agree the final text of a bill, so that amendments made by the second house are then considered in the originating house, and if not agreed, sent back or themselves amended, until agreement is reached.

CHILTERN HUNDREDS – A nominal office of profit under the crown, the acceptance of which requires an MP to vacate his/her seat. The Manor of Northstead is similar. These are the only means by which an MP may resign.

CONSOLIDATED FUND BILL – A bill to authorise the issue of money to maintain government services. The bill is dealt with without debate.

EARLY DAY MOTION – A motion put on the notice paper by an MP without, in general, the real prospect of its being debated. Such motions are expressions of back-bench opinion.

FATHER OF THE HOUSE – The MP whose continuous service in the House of Commons is the longest. The present Father of the House is Sir Peter Tapsell, MP.

GRAND COMMITTEES – There are three grand committees in the House of Commons, one each for Northern Ireland, Scotland and Wales; they consider matters relating specifically to that country. In the House of Lords, bills may be sent to a grand committee instead of a committee of the whole house (*see also* Bill).

HOURS OF MEETING – The House of Commons normally meets on Mondays and Tuesdays at 2.30pm, Wednesdays at 11.30am, Thursdays at 10.30am and some Fridays at 9.30am. (*See also* Westminster Hall Sittings, below.) The House of Lords normally meets at 2.30pm Mondays and Tuesdays, 3pm on Wednesdays and at 11am on Thursdays. The House of Lords occasionally sits on Fridays at 10am.

LEADER OF THE OPPOSITION – In 1937 the office of leader of the opposition was recognised and a salary was assigned to the post. In 2013–14 this is £128,836 (including a parliamentary salary of £66,396). The present leader of the opposition is the Rt. Hon. Ed Miliband, MP.

THE LORD CHANCELLOR – The office of Lord High Chancellor of Great Britain was significantly altered by the Constitutional Reform Act 2005. Previously, the Lord Chancellor was (*ex officio*) the Speaker of the House of Lords, and took part in debates and voted in divisions in the House of Lords. The Department for Constitutional Affairs was created in 2003 and became the Ministry of Justice in 2007, incorporating most of the responsibilities of the Lord Chancellor's department. The role of Speaker has been transferred to the post of Lord Speaker. The Constitutional Reform Act 2005 also brought to an end the Lord Chancellor's role as head of the judiciary. A Judicial Appointments Commission was created in April 2006, and a supreme court (separate from the House of Lords) was established in 2009.

THE LORD GREAT CHAMBERLAIN – The Lord Great Chamberlain is a Great Officer of State, the office being hereditary since the grant of Henry I to the family of De Vere, Earls of Oxford. It is now a joint hereditary office rotating on the death of the sovereign between the Cholmondeley, Carington and Ancaster families.

The Lord Great Chamberlain, currently the Marquess of Cholmondeley, is responsible for the royal apartments in the Palace of Westminster, the Royal Gallery, the administration of the Chapel of St Mary Undercroft and, in conjunction with the Lord Speaker and the Speaker of the House of Commons, Westminster Hall. The Lord Great Chamberlain has the right to perform specific services at a coronation and has particular responsibility for the internal administrative arrangements within the House of Lords for state openings of parliament.

THE LORD SPEAKER – The first Lord Speaker of the House of Lords, the Rt. Hon. Baroness Hayman, took up office on 4 July 2006. Unlike in the case of the Lord Chancellor, the Lord Speaker is independent of the government and elected by members of the House of Lords rather than appointed by the prime minister. Although the Lord Speaker's primary role is to preside over proceedings in the House of Lords, she does not have the same powers as the Speaker of the House of Commons. For example, the Lord Speaker is not responsible for maintaining order during debates, as this is the responsibility of the house as a whole. The Lord Speaker sits in the Lords on one of the woolsacks, which are couches covered in red cloth and stuffed with wool.

OPPOSITION DAY – A day on which the topic for debate is chosen by the opposition. There are 20 such days in a normal session. On 17 days, subjects are chosen by the leader of the opposition; on the remaining three days by the leader of the next largest opposition party.

PARLIAMENT ACTS 1911 AND 1949 – Under these acts, bills may become law without the consent of the Lords, though the House of Lords has the power to delay a public bill for a parliamentary session.

PRIME MINISTER'S QUESTIONS – The prime minister answers questions from 12 to 12.30pm on Wednesdays.

PRIVATE BILL – A bill promoted by a body or an individual to give powers additional to, or in conflict with, the general law, and to which a special procedure applies to enable people affected to object.

PRIVATE MEMBER'S BILL – A public bill promoted by an MP or peer who is not a member of the government.

PRIVATE NOTICE QUESTION – A question adjudged of urgent importance on submission to the Speaker (in the Lords, the Lord Speaker), answered at the end of oral questions.

PRIVILEGE – The House of Commons has rights and immunities to protect it from obstruction in carrying out its duties. These are known as parliamentary privilege and enable Members of Parliament to debate freely. The most important privilege is that of freedom of speech. MPs cannot be prosecuted for sedition or sued for libel or slander over anything said during proceedings in the house. This enables them to raise in the house questions affecting the public good which might be difficult to raise outside owing to the possibility of legal action against them. The House of Lords has similar privileges.

QUESTION TIME – Oral questions are answered by ministers in the Commons from 2.30 to 3.30pm on Mondays and Tuesdays, 11.30am to 12.30pm on Wednesdays, and 10.30 to 11.30am on Thursdays. Questions are also taken at the start of the Lords sittings, with a daily limit of four oral questions.

ROYAL ASSENT – The royal assent is signified by letters patent to such bills and measures as have passed both Houses of Parliament (or bills which have been passed under the Parliament Acts 1911 and 1949). The sovereign has not given royal assent in person since 1854. On occasion, for instance in the prorogation of parliament, royal assent may be pronounced to the two houses by Lords Commissioners. More usually royal assent is notified to each house sitting separately in accordance with the Royal Assent Act 1967. The old French formulae for royal assent are then endorsed on the acts by the Clerk of the Parliaments.

The power to withhold assent resides with the sovereign but has not been exercised in the UK since 1707.

SELECT COMMITTEES – Consisting usually of 10 to 15 members of all parties, select committees are a means used by both houses in order to investigate certain matters.

Most select committees in the House of Commons are tied to departments: each committee investigates subjects within a government department's remit. There are other select committees dealing with matters such as public accounts (ie the spending by the government of money voted by parliament) and European legislation, and also committees advising on procedures and domestic administration of the house. Major select committees usually take evidence in public; their evidence and reports are published on the parliament website and in hard copy by The Stationery Office (TSO). House of Commons select committees are reconstituted after a general election.

In the House of Lords, select committees do not mirror government departments but cover broader issues. There is a select committee on the European Union (EU), which has six sub-committees dealing with specific areas of EU policy, a select committee on science and technology, a select committee on economic affairs and also one on the constitution. There is also a select committee on delegated powers and regulatory reform and one on privileges and conduct. In addition, *ad hoc* select committees have been set up from time to time to investigate specific subjects. There are also joint committees of the two houses, eg the committees on statutory instruments and on human rights.

THE SPEAKER – The Speaker of the House of Commons is the spokesperson and chair of the Chamber. He or she is elected by the house at the beginning of each parliament or when the previous Speaker retires or dies. The Speaker neither speaks in debates nor votes in divisions except when the voting is equal.

VACANT SEATS – When a vacancy occurs in the House of Commons during a session of parliament, the writ for the by-election is moved by a whip of the party to which the member whose seat has been vacated belonged. If the house is in recess, the Speaker can issue a warrant for a writ, should two members certify to him that a seat is vacant.

WESTMINSTER HALL SITTINGS – Following a report by the Modernisation of the House of Commons Select Committee, the Commons decided in May 1999 to set up a second debating forum. It is known as 'Westminster Hall' and sittings are in the Grand Committee Room on Tuesdays from 9.30 to 11.30am, Wednesdays from 9.30 to 11.30am and from 2 to 5pm, and Thursdays from 2.30 to 5.30pm. Sittings are open to the public at the times indicated.

WHIPS – In order to secure the attendance of members of a particular party in parliament, particularly on the occasion of an important vote, whips (originally known as 'whippers-in') are appointed. The written appeal or circular letter issued by them is also known as a 'whip', its urgency being denoted by the number of times it is underlined. Failure to respond to a three-line whip is tantamount in the Commons to secession (at any rate temporarily) from the party. Whips are provided with office accommodation in both houses, and government and some opposition whips receive salaries from public funds.

PARLIAMENTARY ARCHIVES

Houses of Parliament, London SW1A 0PW
T 020-7219 3074 **E** archives@parliament.uk
W www.parliament.uk/archives

Since 1497, the records of parliament have been kept within the Palace of Westminster. They are in the custody of the Clerk of Parliaments. In 1946 the House of Lords Record

Office, which became the Parliamentary Archives in 2006, was established to supervise their preservation and their availability to the public. Some 3 million documents are preserved, including acts of parliament from 1497, journals of the House of Lords from 1510, minutes and committee proceedings from 1610, and papers laid before parliament from 1531. Among the records are the Petition of Right, the death warrant of Charles I, the Declaration of Breda, and the Bill of Rights. Records are made available through a public search room.

Director of the Parliamentary Archives, Dr Caroline Shenton

GOVERNMENT OFFICE

The government is the body of ministers responsible for the administration of national affairs, determining policy and introducing into parliament any legislation necessary to give effect to government policy. The majority of ministers are members of the House of Commons but members of the House of Lords, or of neither house, may also hold ministerial responsibility. The prime minister is, by current convention, always a member of the House of Commons.

THE PRIME MINISTER

The office of prime minister, which had been in existence for nearly 200 years, was officially recognised in 1905 and its holder was granted a place in the table of precedence. The prime minister, by tradition also First Lord of the Treasury and Minister for the Civil Service, is appointed by the sovereign and is usually the leader of the party which enjoys, or can secure, a majority in the House of Commons. Other ministers are appointed by the sovereign on the recommendation of the prime minister, who also allocates functions among ministers and has the power to dismiss ministers from their posts.

The prime minister informs the sovereign on state and political matters, advises on the dissolution of parliament, and makes recommendations for important crown appointments, ie the award of honours, etc.

As the chair of cabinet meetings and leader of a political party, the prime minister is responsible for translating party policy into government activity. As leader of the government, the prime minister is responsible to parliament and to the electorate for the policies and their implementation.

The prime minister also represents the nation in international affairs, eg summit conferences.

THE CABINET

The cabinet developed during the 18th century as an inner committee of the Privy Council, which was the chief source of executive power until that time. The cabinet is composed of about 20 ministers chosen by the prime minister, usually the heads of government departments (generally known as secretaries of state unless they have a special title, eg Chancellor of the Exchequer), the leaders of the two houses of parliament, and the holders of various traditional offices.

The cabinet's functions are the final determination of policy, control of government and coordination of government departments. The exercise of its functions is dependent upon the incumbent party's (or parties') majority support in the House of Commons. Cabinet meetings are held in private, taking place once or twice a week during parliamentary sittings and less often during a recess. Proceedings are confidential, the members being bound by their oath as privy counsellors not to disclose information about the proceedings.

The convention of collective responsibility means that the cabinet acts unanimously even when cabinet ministers do not all agree on a subject. The policies of departmental ministers must be consistent with the policies of the government as a whole, and once the government's policy has been decided, each minister is expected to support it or resign.

The convention of ministerial responsibility holds a minister, as the political head of his or her department, accountable to parliament for the department's work. Departmental ministers usually decide all matters within their responsibility, although on matters of political importance they normally consult their colleagues collectively. A decision by a departmental minister is binding on the government as a whole.

POLITICAL PARTIES

Before the reign of William and Mary the principal officers of state were chosen by and were responsible to the sovereign alone, and not to parliament or the nation at large. Such officers acted sometimes in concert with one another but more often independently, and the fall of one did not, of necessity, involve that of others, although all were liable to be dismissed at any moment.

In 1693 the Earl of Sunderland recommended to William III the advisability of selecting a ministry from the political party which enjoyed a majority in the House of Commons, and the first united ministry was drawn in 1696 from the Whigs, to which party the king owed his throne. This group became known as the 'junto' and was regarded with suspicion as a novelty in the political life of the nation, being a small section meeting in secret apart from the main body of ministers. It may be regarded as the forerunner of the cabinet and in the course of time it led to the establishment of the principle of joint responsibility of ministers, so that internal disagreement caused a change of personnel or resignation of the whole body of ministers.

The accession of George I, who was unfamiliar with the English language, led to a disinclination on the part of the sovereign to preside at meetings of his ministers and caused the emergence of a prime minister, a position first acquired by Robert Walpole in 1721 and retained by him without interruption for 20 years and 326 days. The office of prime minister was formally recognised in 1905 when it was established by royal warrant.

DEVELOPMENT OF PARTIES

In 1828 the Whigs became known as Liberals, a name originally given by opponents to imply laxity of principles, but gradually accepted by the party to indicate its claim to be pioneers and champions of political reform and progressive legislation. In 1861 a Liberal Registration Association was founded and Liberal Associations became widespread. In 1877 a National Liberal Federation was formed, with its headquarters in London. The Liberal Party was in power for long periods during the second half of the 19th century and for several years during the first quarter of the 20th century, but after a split in the party in 1931, the numbers elected remained small. In 1988 a majority of the Liberals agreed on a merger with the Social Democratic Party under the title Social and Liberal Democrats; since 1989 they have been known as the Liberal Democrats. A minority continue separately as the Liberal Party.

Soon after the change from Whig to Liberal, the Tory Party became known as Conservative, a name believed to have been invented by John Wilson Croker in 1830 and to have been generally adopted around the time of the passing of the Reform Act of 1832 – to indicate that the preservation of national institutions was the leading principle of the party. After the Home Rule crisis of 1886 the dissentient Liberals entered into a compact with the Conservatives, under which the latter undertook not to contest their seats, but a separate Liberal Unionist organisation was maintained until 1912, when it was united with the Conservatives.

Labour candidates for parliament made their first appearance at the general election of 1892, when there were 27 standing as Labour or Liberal-Labour. In 1900 the Labour Representation Committee (LRC) was set up in order to establish a distinct Labour group in parliament, with its own whips, its own policy, and a readiness to cooperate with any party which might be engaged in promoting legislation in the direct interests of labour. In 1906 the LRC became known as the Labour Party.

The Green Party was founded in 1973 and campaigns for social and environmental justice. The party began as 'People', was renamed the Ecology Party, and became the Green Party in 1985.

The Respect Party was founded in 2004 as a left-wing alternative to the three major political parties. It has a broad socialist agenda, opposing war and privatisation.

Plaid Cymru was founded in 1926 to provide an independent political voice for Wales and to campaign for self-government in Wales.

The Scottish National Party (SNP) was founded in 1934 to campaign for independence for Scotland.

The Social Democratic and Labour Party (SDLP) was founded in 1970, emerging from the civil rights movement of the 1960s, with the aim of promoting reform, reconciliation and partnership across the sectarian divide in Northern Ireland, and of opposing violence from any quarter.

The Democratic Unionist Party (DUP) was founded in 1971 to resist moves by the Ulster Unionist Party which were considered a threat to the Union. Its aim is to maintain Northern Ireland as an integral part of the UK.

The Alliance Party of Northern Ireland was formed in 1970 as a non-sectarian unionist party.

Sinn Fein first emerged in the 1900s as a federation of nationalist clubs. It is a left-wing republican and labour party that seeks to end British governance in Ireland and achieve a 32-county republic.

GOVERNMENT AND OPPOSITION

The government is formed by the party which wins the largest number of seats in the House of Commons at a general election, or which has the support of a majority of members in the House of Commons. By tradition, the leader of the majority party is asked by the sovereign to form a government, while the largest minority party becomes the official opposition with its own leader and a shadow cabinet. Leaders of the government and opposition sit on the front benches of the Commons with their supporters (the back-benchers) sitting behind them.

FINANCIAL SUPPORT

Financial support for opposition parties in the House of Commons was introduced in 1975 and is commonly known as Short Money, after Edward Short, the leader of the house at that time, who introduced the scheme. Short Money is only payable to those parties that have more than one sitting MP or 150,000 votes in total, and is only intended to provide assistance for parliamentary duties. Short Money allocations for 2013–14 are:

DUP	£161,883
Green	£64,292
Labour	£6,509,319
Plaid Cymru	£77,763
SDLP	£68,677
SNP	£182,386
*Sinn Fein	£112,258

* The sum paid to Sinn Fein and any other party that may choose not to take their seats in the House of Commons is calculated on the same basis as Short Money, but is known as Representative Money

A specific allocation for the leader of the opposition's office was introduced in April 1999 and has been set at £757,097 for the year 2013–14.

Financial support for opposition parties in the House of Lords was introduced in 1996 and is commonly known as Cranborne Money, after former leader of the house, Viscount Cranborne. In 2013–14 the Labour Party's Cranborne Money allocation is £555,748, while the Convenor of Crossbench Peers' allocation is £71,770.

The following list of political parties are those with at least one MP or sitting member of the House of Lords in the present parliament.

ALLIANCE PARTY OF NORTHERN IRELAND

88 University Street, Belfast BT7 1HE
T 028-9032 4274 E alliance@allianceparty.org
W www.allianceparty.org
Party Leader, David Ford
Deputy Party Leader, Naomi Long, MP
President, Billy Webb
Chair, Andrew Muir
Hon. Treasurers, Mervyn Jones; Dan McGuinness

CONSERVATIVE PARTY

Conservative Campaign Headquarters, 30 Millbank, London SW1P 4DP
T 020-7222 9000 W www.conservatives.com
Parliamentary Party Leader, Rt. Hon. David Cameron, MP
Leader in the Lords and Chancellor of the Duchy of Lancaster, Rt. Hon. Lord Hill of Oareford, CBE
Leader in the Commons and Lord Privy Seal, Rt. Hon. Andrew Lansley, CBE, MP
Chairs, Lord Feldman of Elstree; Rt. Hon. Grant Shapps, MP
Party Treasurers, Michael Farmer; James Lupton, CBE

GREEN PARTY

Development House, 56–64 Leonard Street, London, EC2A 4LT
T 020-7549 0310 E office@greenparty.org.uk
W www.greenparty.org.uk
Party Leader, Natalie Bennett
Deputy Leader, Adrian Ramsay
Chair of Party Executive, Tim Dawes
Finance Coordinator, Michael Coffey

LABOUR PARTY

1 Brewer's Green, London SW1H 0RH
T 0845-092 2299 W www.labour.org.uk
General Secretary, Iain McNicol
General Secretary, Welsh Labour, Dave Hagendyk
General Secretary, Scottish Labour Party, Ian Price

SHADOW CABINET *as at June 2013*

Leader of the Opposition, Rt. Hon. Ed Miliband, MP
Deputy Leader, Party Chair and Secretary of State for Culture, Media and Sport, Rt. Hon. Harriet Harman, QC, MP
Chancellor of the Exchequer, Rt. Hon. Ed Balls, MP
Secretary of State for Foreign and Commonwealth Affairs, Rt. Hon. Douglas Alexander, MP
Secretary of State for the Home Department and Minister for Women and Equalities, Rt. Hon Yvette Cooper, MP
Secretary of State for Business, Innovation and Skills, Chuka Umunna, MP
Minister for the Cabinet Office, Jon Trickett, MP
Secretary of State for Communities and Local Government, Rt. Hon. Hilary Benn, MP
Secretary of State for Defence, Rt. Hon. Jim Murphy, MP
Secretary of State for Education, Stephen Twigg, MP

Secretary of State for Energy and Climate Change, Rt. Hon. Caroline Flint, MP
Secretary of State for Environment, Food and Rural Affairs, Mary Creagh, MP
Secretary of State for Health, Rt. Hon. Andy Burnham, MP
Secretary of State for International Development, Ivan Lewis, MP
Lord Chancellor and Secretary of State for Justice, Rt. Hon. Sadiq Khan, MP
Secretary of State for Northern Ireland, Vernon Coaker, MP
Secretary of State for Scotland, Margaret Curran, MP
Secretary of State for Transport, Maria Eagle, MP
Chief Secretary to the Treasury, Rachel Reeves, MP
Secretary of State for Wales, Owen Smith, MP
Secretary of State for Work and Pensions, Rt. Hon. Liam Byrne, MP
Deputy Chair and Campaign Coordinator, Tom Watson, MP
Leader of the House of Commons, Angela Eagle, MP
Leader of the House of Lords, Rt. Hon. Baroness Royall of Blaisdon
Policy Review Coordinator, Jon Cruddas, MP
**Attorney-General,* Emily Thornberry, MP
**Minister for Care and Older People,* Liz Kendall, MP
**Minister without Portfolio,* Michael Dugher, MP
**Minister without Portfolio,* Lord Wood of Anfield
* Attends shadow cabinet meetings but is not a cabinet member

LABOUR WHIPS
Commons Chief Whip, Rt. Hon. Rosie Winterton, MP
Lords Chief Whip, Rt. Hon. Lord Bassam of Brighton

LIBERAL DEMOCRATS

8–10 Great George Street, London SW1P 3AE
T 020-7222 7999 E info@libdems.org.uk W www.libdems.org.uk
Parliamentary Party Leader, Rt. Hon. Nick Clegg, MP
Deputy Party Leader, Rt. Hon. Simon Hughes, MP
Leader in the Lords, Rt. Hon. Lord McNally
Deputy Leader in the Commons, David Heath, MP
President, Tim Farron, MP
Chief Executive, Tim Gordon
Hon. Treasurer, Sir Ian Wrigglesworth

NORTHERN IRELAND DEMOCRATIC UNIONIST PARTY

91 Dundela Avenue, Belfast BT4 3BU
T 028-9047 1155
E info@mydup.com W www.mydup.com
Parliamentary Party Leader, Rt. Hon. Peter Robinson, MLA
Deputy Leader, Rt. Hon Nigel Dodds, OBE, MP, MLA
Chair, Lord Morrow, MLA
Treasurer, Gregory Campbell, MP, MLA

PLAID CYMRU – THE PARTY OF WALES

Ty Gwynfor, Anson Court, Atlantic Wharf, Caerdydd CF10 4AL
T 029-2047 2272 E post@plaidcymru.org
W www.partyofwales.org
Party Leader, Leanne Wood, AM
Party President, Jill Evans, MEP
Parliamentary Group Leader, Rt. Hon. Elfyn Llwyd, MP
Chief Executive, Rhuanedd Richards

RESPECT PARTY

PO Box 167, Manchester M19 0AH
T 07794-192670 E info@respectparty.org
W www.respectparty.org
Party Leader, vacant
Chair, Abjol Miah
National Secretary, Chris Chilvers

SCOTTISH NATIONAL PARTY

Gordon Lamb House, 3 Jackson's Entry, Edinburgh EH8 8PJ
T 0800-633 5432 E info@snp.org W www.snp.org
Westminster Parliamentary Party Leader, Angus Robertson, MP
Westminster Parliamentary Party Chief Whip, Stewart Hosie, MP
Scottish Parliamentary Party Leader and Leader of the SNP, Rt. Hon. Alex Salmond, MSP
Scottish Parliamentary Party Chief Whip, Brian Adam, MSP
Party President, Ian Hudghton, MEP
National Treasurer, Colin Beattie, MSP
Chief Executive, Peter Murrell

SINN FEIN

53 Falls Road, Belfast BT12 4PD
T 028-9034 7350 E admin@sinnfein.ie W www.sinnfein.ie
Party President, Gerry Adams
Vice-President, Mary Lou McDonald
Chair, Declan Kearney

SOCIAL DEMOCRATIC AND LABOUR PARTY

121 Ormeau Road, Belfast BT7 1SH
T 028-9024 7700 E info@sdlp.ie W www.sdlp.ie
Parliamentary Party Leader, Dr Alisdair McDonnell, MP, MLA
Deputy Leader, Dolores Kelly, MLA
Party Whip, Pat Ramsey, MLA
Chair, Joe Byrne, MLA
Treasurer, Peter McEvoy
General Secretary, Gerry Cosgrove

ULSTER UNIONIST PARTY

Strandtown Hall, 2–4 Belmont Road, Belfast BT4 2AN
T 028-9047 4630
E uup@uup.org W www.uup.org
Party Leader, Mike Nesbitt, MLA
Party Chairman, Lord Empey of Shandon, OBE
Hon. Treasurer, Cllr Mark Cosgrove
Vice-Chair, Roy McCune

UK INDEPENDENCE PARTY

PO Box 408, Newton Abbot, Devon TQ12 9BG
T 0800-587 6587
E mail@ukip.org W www.ukip.org
Party Leader, Nigel Farage, MEP
Chair, Steve Crowther
Chief Executive, Will Gilpin
Treasurer, Stuart Wheeler

MEMBERS OF PARLIAMENT *as at 3 June 2013*

* Denotes new MP at the 2010 General Election
† Previously MP in another seat
‡ Previously MP for another party
§ Elected via a by-election after the 2010 General Election
¶ Currently suspended from the parliamentary Labour Party

Abbott, Diane (*b.* 1953) *Lab., Hackney North & Stoke Newington,* Maj. 14,461
***Abrahams**, Deborah (*b.* 1960) *Lab., Oldham East & Saddleworth,* Maj. 3,558
***Adams**, Nigel (*b.* 1966) *C., Selby & Ainsty,* Maj. 12,265
Afriyie, Adam (*b.* 1965) *C., Windsor,* Maj. 19,054
Ainsworth, Rt. Hon. Robert (*b.* 1952) *Lab., Coventry North East,* Maj. 11,775
***Aldous**, Peter (*b.* 1961) *C., Waveney,* Maj. 769
Alexander, Rt. Hon. Danny (*b.* 1972) *LD, Inverness, Nairn, Badenoch & Strathspey,* Maj. 8,765
†**Alexander**, Rt. Hon. Douglas (*b.* 1967) *Lab., Paisley & Renfrewshire South,* Maj. 16,614
***Alexander**, Heidi (*b.* 1975) *Lab., Lewisham East,* Maj. 6,216
***Ali**, Rushanara (*b.* 1975) *Lab., Bethnal Green & Bow,* Maj. 11,574
Allen, Graham (*b.* 1953) *Lab., Nottingham North,* Maj. 8,138
†**Amess**, David (*b.* 1952) *C., Southend West,* Maj. 7,270
Anderson, David (*b.* 1953) *Lab., Blaydon,* Maj. 9,117
***Andrew**, Stuart (*b.* 1971) *C., Pudsey,* Maj. 1,659
†**Arbuthnot**, Rt. Hon. James (*b.* 1952) *C., Hampshire North East,* Maj. 18,597
§**Ashworth**, Jon (*b.* 1978) *Lab., Leicester South,* Maj. 12,078
Austin, Ian (*b.* 1965) *Lab., Dudley North,* Maj. 649
Bacon, Richard (*b.* 1962) *C., Norfolk South,* Maj. 10,940
Bailey, Adrian (*b.* 1945) *Lab. (Co-op), West Bromwich West,* Maj. 5,651
Bain, William (*b.* 1972) *Lab., Glasgow North East,* Maj. 15,942
Baker, Norman (*b.* 1957) *LD, Lewes,* Maj. 7,647
***Baker**, Steven (*b.* 1971) *C., Wycombe,* Maj. 9,560
Baldry, Rt. Hon. Sir Tony (*b.* 1950) *C., Banbury,* Maj. 18,227
***Baldwin**, Harriett (*b.* 1960) *C., West Worcestershire,* Maj. 6,804
†**Balls**, Rt. Hon. Ed (*b.* 1967) *Lab. (Co-op), Morley & Outwood,* Maj. 1,101
Banks, Gordon (*b.* 1955) *Lab., Ochil & Perthshire South,* Maj. 5,187
***Barclay**, Stephen (*b.* 1972) *C., Cambridgeshire North East,* Maj. 16,425
Barker, Rt. Hon. Gregory (*b.* 1966) *C., Bexhill & Battle,* Maj. 12,880
†**Baron**, John (*b.* 1959) *C., Basildon & Billericay,* Maj. 12,398
Barron, Rt. Hon. Kevin (*b.* 1946) *Lab., Rother Valley,* Maj. 5,866
***Barwell**, Gavin (*b.* 1972) *C., Croydon Central,* Maj. 2,969
†**Bayley**, Hugh (*b.* 1952) *Lab., York Central,* Maj. 6,451
***Bebb**, Guto (*b.* 1968) *C., Aberconwy,* Maj. 3,398
†**Beckett**, Rt. Hon. Dame Margaret (*b.* 1943) *Lab., Derby South,* Maj. 6,122
Begg, Dame Anne (*b.* 1955) *Lab., Aberdeen South,* Maj. 3,506
Beith, Rt. Hon. Sir Alan (*b.* 1943) *LD, Berwick-upon-Tweed,* Maj. 2,690
Bellingham, Henry (*b.* 1955) *C., Norfolk North West,* Maj. 14,810
Benn, Rt. Hon. Hilary (*b.* 1953) *Lab., Leeds Central,* Maj. 10,645
Benton, Joe (*b.* 1933) *Lab., Bootle,* Maj. 21,181
Benyon, Richard (*b.* 1960) *C., Newbury,* Maj. 12,248
Bercow, Rt. Hon. John (*b.* 1963) *The Speaker, Buckingham,* Maj. 12,529
†**Beresford**, Sir Paul (*b.* 1946) *C., Mole Valley,* Maj. 15,653
***Berger**, Luciana (*b.* 1981) *Lab. (Co-op), Liverpool, Wavertree,* Maj. 7,167
***Berry**, Jake (*b.* 1978) *C., Rossendale & Darwen,* Maj. 4,493
†**Betts**, Clive (*b.* 1950) *Lab., Sheffield South East,* Maj. 10,505
***Bingham**, Andrew (*b.* 1962) *C., High Peak,* Maj. 4,677
Binley, Brian (*b.* 1942) *C., Northampton South,* Maj. 6,004
***Birtwistle**, Gordon (*b.* 1943) *LD, Burnley,* Maj. 1,818
***Blackman**, Bob (*b.* 1956) *C., Harrow East,* Maj. 3,403
Blackman-Woods, Dr Roberta (*b.* 1957) *Lab., Durham, City of,* Maj. 3,067
***Blackwood**, Nicola (*b.* 1979) *C., Oxford West & Abingdon,* Maj. 176
†**Blears**, Rt. Hon. Hazel (*b.* 1956) *Lab., Salford & Eccles,* Maj. 5,725
***Blenkinsop**, Tom (*b.* 1980) *Lab., Middlesbrough South & East Cleveland,* Maj. 1,677
***Blomfield**, Paul (*b.* 1953) *Lab., Sheffield Central,* Maj. 165
†**Blunkett**, Rt. Hon. David (*b.* 1947) *Lab., Sheffield, Brightside & Hillsborough,* Maj. 13,632
Blunt, Crispin (*b.* 1960) *C., Reigate,* Maj. 13,591
***Boles**, Nick (*b.* 1965) *C., Grantham & Stamford,* Maj. 14,826
Bone, Peter (*b.* 1952) *C., Wellingborough,* Maj. 11,787
†**Bottomley**, Sir Peter (*b.* 1944) *C., Worthing West,* Maj. 11,729
***Bradley**, Karen (*b.* 1970) *C., Staffordshire Moorlands,* Maj. 6,689
Bradshaw, Rt. Hon. Ben (*b.* 1960) *Lab., Exeter,* Maj. 2,721
Brady, Graham (*b.* 1967) *C., Altrincham & Sale West,* Maj. 11,595
Brake, Rt. Hon. Tom (*b.* 1962) *LD, Carshalton & Wallington,* Maj. 5,260
***Bray**, Angie (*b.* 1953) *C., Ealing Central & Acton,* Maj. 3,716
Brazier, Julian (*b.* 1953) *C., Canterbury,* Maj. 6,048
Brennan, Kevin (*b.* 1959) *Lab., Cardiff West,* Maj. 4,750
***Bridgen**, Andrew (*b.* 1964) *C., Leicestershire North West,* Maj. 7,511
***Brine**, Steve (*b.* 1974) *C., Winchester,* Maj. 3,048
†**Brokenshire**, James (*b.* 1968) *C., Old Bexley & Sidcup,* Maj. 15,857
Brooke, Annette (*b.* 1947) *LD, Dorset Mid & Poole North,* Maj. 269
†**Brown**, Rt. Hon. Gordon (*b.* 1951) *Lab., Kirkcaldy & Cowdenbeath,* Maj. 23,009
Brown, Lyn (*b.* 1960) *Lab., West Ham,* Maj. 22,534
†**Brown**, Rt. Hon. Nicholas (*b.* 1950) *Lab., Newcastle upon Tyne East,* Maj. 4,453
†**Brown**, Russell (*b.* 1951) *Lab., Dumfries & Galloway,* Maj. 7,449
†**Browne**, Jeremy (*b.* 1970) *LD, Taunton Deane,* Maj. 3,993
***Bruce**, Fiona (*b.* 1957) *C., Congleton,* Maj. 7,063
Bruce, Rt. Hon. Sir Malcolm (*b.* 1944) *LD, Gordon,* Maj. 6,748
Bryant, Chris (*b.* 1962) *Lab., Rhondda,* Maj. 11,553
†**Buck**, Karen (*b.* 1958) *Lab., Westminster North,* Maj. 2,126
***Buckland**, Robert (*b.* 1968) *C., Swindon South,* Maj. 3,544
Burden, Richard (*b.* 1954) *Lab., Birmingham Northfield,* Maj. 2,782
***Burley**, Aidan (*b.* 1979) *C., Cannock Chase,* Maj. 3,195
Burnham, Rt. Hon. Andy (*b.* 1970) *Lab., Leigh,* Maj. 15,011
***Burns**, Conor (*b.* 1972) *C., Bournemouth West,* Maj. 5,583

†**Burns**, Rt. Hon. Simon (*b.* 1952) *C., Chelmsford,* Maj. 5,110
Burrowes, David (*b.* 1969) *C., Enfield Southgate,* Maj. 7,626
Burstow, Rt. Hon. Paul (*b.* 1962) *LD, Sutton & Cheam,* Maj. 1,608
†**Burt**, Alistair (*b.* 1955) *C., Bedfordshire North East,* Maj. 18,942
Burt, Lorely (*b.* 1957) *LD, Solihull,* Maj. 175
***Byles**, Daniel (*b.* 1974) *C., Warwickshire North,* Maj. 54
Byrne, Rt. Hon. Liam (*b.* 1970) *Lab., Birmingham Hodge Hill,* Maj. 10,302
Cable, Rt. Hon. Dr Vincent (*b.* 1943) *LD, Twickenham,* Maj. 12,140
***Cairns**, Alun (*b.* 1970) *C., Vale of Glamorgan,* Maj. 4,307
Cameron, Rt. Hon. David (*b.* 1966) *C., Witney,* Maj. 22,740
Campbell, Alan (*b.* 1957) *Lab., Tynemouth,* Maj. 5,739
Campbell, Gregory (*b.* 1953) *DUP, Londonderry East,* Maj. 5,355
Campbell, Rt. Hon. Sir Menzies (*b.* 1941) *LD, Fife North East,* Maj. 9,048
Campbell, Ronnie (*b.* 1943) *Lab., Blyth Valley,* Maj. 6,668
Carmichael, Rt. Hon. Alistair (*b.* 1965) *LD, Orkney & Shetland,* Maj. 9,928
***Carmichael**, Neil (*b.* 1961) *C., Stroud,* Maj. 1,299
†**Carswell**, Douglas (*b.* 1971) *C., Clacton,* Maj. 12,068
†**Cash**, Bill (*b.* 1940) *C., Stone,* Maj. 13,292
Caton, Martin (*b.* 1951) *Lab., Gower,* Maj. 2,683
§**Champion**, Sarah (*b.* 1969) *Lab., Rotherham,* Maj. 5,318
***Chapman**, Jenny (*b.* 1973) *Lab., Darlington,* Maj. 3,388
***Chishti**, Rehman (*b.* 1978) *C., Gillingham & Rainham,* Maj. 8,680
†**Chope**, Christopher (*b.* 1947) *C., Christchurch,* Maj. 15,410
Clappison, James (*b.* 1956) *C., Hertsmere,* Maj. 17,605
Clark, Rt. Hon. Greg (*b.* 1967) *C., Tunbridge Wells,* Maj. 15,576
Clark, Katy (*b.* 1967) *Lab., Ayrshire North & Arran,* Maj. 9,895
Clarke, Rt. Hon. Kenneth (*b.* 1940) *C., Rushcliffe,* Maj. 15,811
†**Clarke**, Rt. Hon. Thomas (*b.* 1941) *Lab., Coatbridge, Chryston & Bellshill,* Maj. 20,714
Clegg, Rt. Hon. Nick (*b.* 1967) *LD, Sheffield, Hallam,* Maj. 15,284
†**Clifton-Brown**, Geoffrey (*b.* 1953) *C., The Cotswolds,* Maj. 12,864
Clwyd, Rt. Hon. Ann (*b.* 1937) *Lab., Cynon Valley,* Maj. 9,617
Coaker, Vernon (*b.* 1953) *Lab., Gedling,* Maj. 1,859
Coffey, Ann (*b.* 1946) *Lab., Stockport,* Maj. 6,784
***Coffey**, Thérèse (*b.* 1971) *C., Suffolk Coastal,* Maj. 9,128
***Collins**, Damian (*b.* 1974) *C., Folkestone & Hythe,* Maj. 10,122
***Colvile**, Oliver (*b.* 1959) *C., Plymouth, Sutton & Devonport,* Maj. 1,149
†**Connarty**, Michael (*b.* 1947) *Lab., Linlithgow & Falkirk East,* Maj. 12,553
Cooper, Rosie (*b.* 1950) *Lab., Lancashire West,* Maj. 4,343
†**Cooper**, Rt. Hon. Yvette (*b.* 1969) *Lab., Pontefract & Castleford,* Maj. 10,979
Corbyn, Jeremy (*b.* 1949) *Lab., Islington North,* Maj. 12,401
Cox, Geoffrey (*b.* 1960) *C., Devon West & Torridge,* Maj. 2,957
Crabb, Stephen (*b.* 1973) *C., Preseli Pembrokeshire,* Maj. 4,605
Crausby, David (*b.* 1946) *Lab., Bolton North East,* Maj. 4,084
Creagh, Mary (*b.* 1967) *Lab., Wakefield,* Maj. 1,613
***Creasy**, Stella (*b.* 1977) *Lab. (Co-op), Walthamstow,* Maj. 9,478
***Crockart**, Mike (*b.* 1966) *LD, Edinburgh West,* Maj. 3,803
***Crouch**, Tracey (*b.* 1975) *C., Chatham & Aylesford,* Maj. 6,069
†**Cruddas**, Jonathan (*b.* 1965) *Lab., Dagenham & Rainham,* Maj. 2,630
†**Cryer**, John (*b.* 1964) *Lab., Leyton & Wanstead,* Maj. 6,416
***Cunningham**, Alex (*b.* 1955) *Lab., Stockton North,* Maj. 6,676
†**Cunningham**, Jim (*b.* 1941) *Lab., Coventry South,* Maj. 3,845
Cunningham, Sir Tony (*b.* 1952) *Lab., Workington,* Maj. 4,575
***Curran**, Margaret (*b.* 1958) *Lab., Glasgow East,* Maj. 11,840
***Dakin**, Nic (*b.* 1955) *Lab., Scunthorpe,* Maj. 2,549
***Danczuk**, Simon (*b.* 1966) *Lab., Rochdale,* Maj. 889
†**Darling**, Rt. Hon. Alistair (*b.* 1953) *Lab., Edinburgh South West,* Maj. 8,447
Davey, Rt. Hon. Edward (*b.* 1965) *LD, Kingston & Surbiton,* Maj. 7,560
David, Wayne (*b.* 1957) *Lab., Caerphilly,* Maj. 10,775
†**Davidson**, Ian (*b.* 1950) *Lab. (Co-op), Glasgow South West,* Maj. 14,671
Davies, David (*b.* 1970) *C., Monmouth,* Maj. 10,425
†**Davies**, Geraint (*b.* 1960) *Lab. (Co-op), Swansea West,* Maj. 504
***Davies**, Glyn (*b.* 1944) *C., Montgomeryshire,* Maj. 1,184
Davies, Philip (*b.* 1972) *C., Shipley,* Maj. 9,944
†**Davis**, Rt. Hon. David (*b.* 1948) *C., Haltemprice & Howden,* Maj. 11,602
***de Bois**, Nick (*b.* 1959) *C., Enfield North,* Maj. 1,692
***De Piero**, Gloria (*b.* 1972) *Lab., Ashfield,* Maj. 192
Denham, Rt. Hon. John (*b.* 1953) *Lab., Southampton Itchen,* Maj. 192
***Dinenage**, Caroline (*b.* 1971) *C., Gosport,* Maj. 14,413
Djanogly, Jonathan (*b.* 1965) *C., Huntingdon,* Maj. 10,819
Dobbin, Jim (*b.* 1941) *Lab. (Co-op), Heywood & Middleton,* Maj. 5,971
†**Dobson**, Rt. Hon. Frank (*b.* 1940) *Lab., Holborn & St Pancras,* Maj. 9,942
***Docherty**, Thomas (*b.* 1975) *Lab., Dunfermline & Fife West,* Maj. 5,470
Dodds, Rt. Hon. Nigel (*b.* 1958) *DUP, Belfast North,* Maj. 2,224
Doherty, Pat (*b.* 1945) *SF, Tyrone West,* Maj. 10,685
‡**Donaldson**, Rt. Hon. Jeffrey (*b.* 1962) *DUP, Lagan Valley,* Maj. 10,486
†**Donohoe**, Brian (*b.* 1948) *Lab., Ayrshire Central,* Maj. 12,007
Doran, Frank (*b.* 1949) *Lab., Aberdeen North,* Maj. 8,361
Dorrell, Rt. Hon. Stephen (*b.* 1952) *C., Charnwood,* Maj. 15,029
Dorries, Nadine (*b.* 1958) *C., Bedfordshire Mid,* Maj. 15,152
§**Doughty**, Stephen (*b.* 1980) *Lab. (Co-op), Cardiff South and Penarth,* Maj. 5,334
†**Dowd**, Jim (*b.* 1951) *Lab., Lewisham West & Penge,* Maj. 5,828
***Doyle**, Gemma (*b.* 1981) *Lab. (Co-op), Dunbartonshire West,* Maj. 17,408
***Doyle-Price**, Jackie (*b.* 1969) *C., Thurrock,* Maj. 92
***Drax**, Richard (*b.* 1958) *C., Dorset South,* Maj. 7,443
***Dromey**, Jack (*b.* 1948) *Lab., Birmingham Erdington,* Maj. 3,277
Duddridge, James (*b.* 1971) *C., Rochford & Southend East,* Maj. 11,050
***Dugher**, Michael (*b.* 1975) *Lab., Barnsley East,* Maj. 11,090

Duncan, Rt. Hon. Alan (*b.* 1957) *C., Rutland & Melton,* Maj. 14,000
†**Duncan Smith**, Rt. Hon. Iain (*b.* 1954) *C., Chingford & Woodford Green,* Maj. 12,963
Dunne, Philip (*b.* 1958) *C., Ludlow,* Maj. 9,749
Durkan, Mark (*b.* 1960) *SDLP, Foyle,* Maj. 4,824
Eagle, Angela (*b.* 1961) *Lab., Wallasey,* Maj. 8,507
†**Eagle**, Maria (*b.* 1961) *Lab., Garston & Halewood,* Maj. 16,877
*__Edwards__, Jonathan (*b.* 1976) *PC, Carmarthen East & Dinefwr,* Maj. 3,481
Efford, Clive (*b.* 1958) *Lab., Eltham,* Maj. 1,663
*__Elliott__, Julie (*b.* 1963) *Lab., Sunderland Central,* Maj. 6,725
*__Ellis__, Michael (*b.* 1967) *C., Northampton North,* Maj. 1,936
*__Ellison__, Jane (*b.*1964) *C., Battersea,* Maj. 5,977
Ellman, Louise (*b.* 1945) *Lab. (Co-op), Liverpool Riverside,* Maj. 14,173
Ellwood, Tobias (*b.* 1966) *C., Bournemouth East,* Maj. 7,728
*__Elphicke__, Charlie (*b.* 1971) *C., Dover,* Maj. 5,274
Engel, Natascha (*b.* 1967) *Lab., Derbyshire North East,* Maj. 2,445
*__Esterson__, Bill (*b.* 1966) *Lab., Sefton Central,* Maj. 3,862
*__Eustice__, George (*b.* 1971) *C., Camborne & Redruth,* Maj. 66
*__Evans__, Chris (*b.* 1976) *Lab. (Co-op), Islwyn,* Maj. 12,215
*__Evans__, Graham (*b.* 1963) *C., Weaver Vale,* Maj. 991
†**Evans**, Jonathan (*b.* 1950) *C., Cardiff North,* Maj. 194
Evans, Nigel (*b.* 1957) *C., Deputy Speaker, Ribble Valley,* Maj. 14,769
†**Evennett**, David (*b.* 1949) *C., Bexleyheath & Crayford,* Maj. 10,344
†**Fabricant**, Michael (*b.* 1950) *C., Lichfield,* Maj. 17,683
†**Fallon**, Rt. Hon. Michael (*b.* 1952) *C., Sevenoaks,* Maj. 17,515
Farrelly, Paul (*b.* 1962) *Lab., Newcastle-under-Lyme,* Maj. 1,552
Farron, Tim (*b.* 1970) *LD, Westmorland & Lonsdale,* Maj. 12,264
Featherstone, Lynne (*b.* 1951) *LD, Hornsey & Wood Green,* Maj. 6,875
Field, Rt. Hon. Frank (*b.* 1942) *Lab., Birkenhead,* Maj. 15,195
Field, Mark (*b.* 1934) *C., Cities of London & Westminster,* Maj. 11,076
†**Fitzpatrick**, Jim (*b.* 1952) *Lab., Poplar & Limehouse,* Maj. 6,030
Flello, Robert (*b.* 1966) *Lab., Stoke-on-Trent South,* Maj. 4,130
Flint, Rt. Hon. Caroline (*b.* 1961) *Lab., Don Valley,* Maj. 3,595
Flynn, Paul (*b.* 1935) *Lab., Newport West,* Maj. 3,544
Foster, Rt. Hon. Don (*b.* 1947) *LD, Bath,* Maj. 11,883
*__Fovargue__, Yvonne (*b.* 1956) *Lab., Makerfield,* Maj. 12,490
†**Fox**, Rt. Hon. Dr Liam (*b.* 1961) *C., North Somerset,* Maj. 7,862
Francis, Dr Hywel (*b.* 1946) *Lab., Aberavon,* Maj. 11,039
†**Francois**, Rt. Hon. Mark (*b.* 1965) *C., Rayleigh & Wickford,* Maj. 22,338
*__Freeman__, George (*b.* 1967) *C., Norfolk Mid,* Maj. 13,856
*__Freer__, Mike (*b.* 1960) *C., Finchley & Golders Green,* Maj. 5,809
*__Fullbrook__, Lorraine (*b.* 1959) *C., Ribble South,* Maj. 5,554
*__Fuller__, Richard (*b.* 1962) *C., Bedford,* Maj. 1,353
Gale, Sir Roger (*b.* 1943) *C., Thanet North,* Maj. 13,528
†‡§**Galloway**, George (*b.* 1954) *Respect, Bradford West,* Maj. 10,140
Gapes, Mike (*b.* 1952) *Lab. (Co-op), Ilford South,* Maj. 11,297
Gardiner, Barry (*b.* 1957) *Lab., Brent North,* Maj. 8,028
Garnier, Sir Edward (*b.* 1952) *C., Harborough,* Maj. 9,877
*__Garnier__, Mark (*b.* 1963) *C., Wyre Forest,* Maj. 2,643
Gauke, David (*b.* 1971) *C., Hertfordshire South West,* Maj. 14,920
George, Andrew (*b.* 1958) *LD, St Ives,* Maj. 1,719
Gibb, Nick (*b.* 1960) *C., Bognor Regis & Littlehampton,* Maj. 13,063
*__Gilbert__, Stephen (*b.* 1976) *LD, St Austell & Newquay,* Maj. 1,312
Gildernew, Michelle (*b.* 1970) *SF, Fermanagh & South Tyrone,* Maj. 4
Gillan, Rt. Hon. Cheryl (*b.* 1952) *C., Chesham & Amersham,* Maj. 16,710
*__Gilmore__, Sheila (*b.* 1950) *Lab., Edinburgh East,* Maj. 9,181
*__Glass__, Pat (*b.* 1956) *Lab., Durham North West,* Maj. 7,612
*__Glen__, John (*b.* 1974) *C., Salisbury,* Maj. 5,966
*__Glindon__, Mary (*b.* 1957) *Lab., Tyneside North,* Maj. 12,884
†**Godsiff**, Roger (*b.* 1946) *Lab., Birmingham Hall Green,* Maj. 3,799
Goggins, Rt. Hon. Paul (*b.* 1953) *Lab., Wythenshawe & Sale East,* Maj. 7,575
*__Goldsmith__, Zac (*b.* 1975) *C., Richmond Park,* Maj. 4,091
Goodman, Helen (*b.* 1958) *Lab., Bishop Auckland,* Maj. 5,218
Goodwill, Robert (*b.* 1956) *C., Scarborough & Whitby,* Maj. 8,130
Gove, Rt. Hon. Michael (*b.* 1967) *C., Surrey Heath,* Maj. 17,289
*__Graham__, Richard (*b.* 1958) *C., Gloucester,* Maj. 2,420
*__Grant__, Helen (*b.* 1961) *C., Maidstone & The Weald,* Maj. 5,889
Gray, James (*b.* 1954) *C., Wiltshire North,* Maj. 7,483
Grayling, Rt. Hon. Chris (*b.* 1962) *C., Epsom & Ewell,* Maj. 16,134
*__Greatrex__, Tom (*b.* 1974) *Lab. (Co-op), Rutherglen & Hamilton West,* Maj. 21,002
Green, Rt. Hon. Damian (*b.* 1956) *C., Ashford,* Maj. 17,297
*__Green__, Kate (*b.* 1960) *Lab., Stretford & Urmston,* Maj. 8,935
Greening, Rt. Hon. Justine (*b.* 1969) *C., Putney,* Maj. 10,053
*__Greenwood__, Lilian (*b.* 1966) *Lab., Nottingham South,* Maj. 1,772
Grieve, Rt. Hon. Dominic (*b.* 1956) *C., Beaconsfield,* Maj. 21,782
Griffith, Nia (*b.* 1956) *Lab., Llanelli,* Maj. 4,701
*__Griffiths__, Andrew (*b.* 1970) *C., Burton,* Maj. 6,304
*__Gummer__, Ben (*b.* 1978) *C., Ipswich,* Maj. 2,079
Gwynne, Andrew (*b.* 1974) *Lab., Denton & Reddish,* Maj. 9,831
*__Gyimah__, Sam (*b.* 1976) *C., Surrey East,* Maj. 16,874
Hague, Rt. Hon. William (*b.* 1961) *C., Richmond (Yorks),* Maj. 23,336
Hain, Rt. Hon. Peter (*b.* 1950) *Lab., Neath,* Maj. 9,775
*__Halfon__, Robert (*b.* 1969) *C., Harlow,* Maj. 4,925
*__Hames__, Duncan (*b.* 1977) *LD, Chippenham,* Maj. 2,470
Hamilton, David (*b.* 1950) *Lab., Midlothian,* Maj. 4,545
Hamilton, Fabian (*b.* 1955) *Lab., Leeds North East,* Maj. 10,349
Hammond, Rt. Hon. Philip (*b.* 1955) *C., Runnymede & Weybridge,* Maj. 16,509
Hammond, Stephen (*b.* 1962) *C., Wimbledon,* Maj. 11,408
*__Hancock__, Matthew (*b.* 1978) *C., Suffolk West,* Maj. 13,050
‡**Hancock**, Mike (*b.* 1946) *Ind., Portsmouth South,* Maj. 5,200
†**Hands**, Greg (*b.* 1965) *C., Chelsea & Fulham,* Maj. 16,722
Hanson, Rt. Hon. David (*b.* 1957) *Lab., Delyn,* Maj. 2,272
Harman, Rt. Hon. Harriet (*b.* 1950) *Lab., Camberwell & Peckham,* Maj. 17,187
Harper, Mark (*b.* 1970) *C., Forest of Dean,* Maj. 11,064

*__Harrington__, Richard (*b.* 1957) *C., Watford,* Maj. 1,425
*__Harris__, Rebecca (*b.* 1967) *C., Castle Point,* Maj. 7,632
†**Harris**, Tom (*b.* 1964) *Lab., Glasgow South,* Maj. 12,658
*__Hart__, Simon (*b.* 1963) *C., Carmarthen West & Pembrokeshire South,* Maj. 3,423
Harvey, Sir Nick (*b.* 1961) *LD, Devon North,* Maj. 5,821
†**Haselhurst**, Rt. Hon. Sir Alan (*b.* 1937) *C., Saffron Walden,* Maj. 15,242
Havard, Dai (*b.* 1949) *Lab., Merthyr Tydfil & Rhymney,* Maj. 4,056
Hayes, John (*b.* 1958) *C., South Holland & The Deepings,* Maj. 21,880
†**Heald**, Oliver (*b.* 1954) *C., Hertfordshire North East,* Maj. 15,194
†**Healey**, Rt. Hon. John (*b.* 1960) *Lab., Wentworth & Dearne,* Maj. 13,920
Heath, David (*b.* 1954) *LD, Somerton & Frome,* Maj. 1,817
*__Heaton-Harris__, Chris (*b.* 1967) *C., Daventry,* Maj. 19,188
Hemming, John (*b.* 1960) *LD, Birmingham Yardley,* Maj. 3,002
*__Henderson__, Gordon (*b.* 1948) *C., Sittingbourne & Sheppey,* Maj. 12,383
Hendrick, Mark (*b.* 1958) *Lab. (Co-op), Preston,* Maj. 7,733
†**Hendry**, Charles (*b.* 1959) *C., Wealden,* Maj. 17,179
Hepburn, Stephen (*b.* 1959) *Lab., Jarrow,* Maj. 12,908
Herbert, Rt. Hon. Nick (*b.* 1963) *C., Arundel & South Downs,* Maj. 16,691
‡**Hermon**, Lady (Sylvia) (*b.* 1956) *Ind., Down North,* Maj. 14,364
Heyes, David (*b.* 1946) *Lab., Ashton-under-Lyne,* Maj. 9,094
Hillier, Meg (*b.* 1969) *Lab. (Co-op), Hackney South & Shoreditch,* Maj. 14,288
*__Hilling__, Julie (*b.* 1955) *Lab., Bolton West,* Maj. 92
*__Hinds__, Damian (*b.* 1969) *C., Hampshire East,* Maj. 13,497
Hoban, Mark (*b.* 1964) *C., Fareham,* Maj. 17,092
Hodge, Rt. Hon. Margaret (*b.* 1944) *Lab., Barking,* Maj. 16,555
†**Hodgson**, Sharon (*b.* 1966) *Lab., Washington & Sunderland West,* Maj. 11,458
Hoey, Kate (*b.* 1946) *Lab., Vauxhall,* Maj. 10,651
*__Hollingbery__, George (*b.* 1963) *C., Meon Valley,* Maj. 12,125
Hollobone, Philip (*b.* 1964) *C., Kettering,* Maj. 9,094
Holloway, Adam (*b.* 1965) *C., Gravesham,* Maj. 9,312
†**Hood**, Jim (*b.* 1948) *Lab., Lanark & Hamilton East,* Maj. 13,478
Hopkins, Kelvin (*b.* 1941) *Lab., Luton North,* Maj. 7,520
*__Hopkins__, Kris (*b.* 1963) *C., Keighley,* Maj. 2,940
Horwood, Martin (*b.* 1962) *LD, Cheltenham,* Maj. 4,920
Hosie, Stewart (*b.* 1963) *SNP, Dundee East,* Maj. 1,821
†**Howarth**, Rt. Hon. George (*b.* 1949) *Lab., Knowsley,* Maj. 25,690
†**Howarth**, Sir Gerald (*b.* 1947) *C., Aldershot,* Maj. 5,586
Howell, John (*b.* 1955) *C., Henley,* Maj. 16,588
Hoyle, Rt. Hon. Lindsay (*b.* 1957) *Lab., Deputy Speaker, Chorley,* Maj. 2,593
†**Hughes**, Rt. Hon. Simon (*b.* 1951) *LD, Bermondsey & Old Southwark,* Maj. 8,530
Hunt, Rt. Hon. Jeremy (*b.* 1966) *C., Surrey South West,* Maj. 16,318
*__Hunt__, Tristram (*b.* 1974) *Lab., Stoke-on-Trent Central,* Maj. 5,566
Hunter, Mark (*b.* 1957) *LD, Cheadle,* Maj. 3,272
*__Huppert__, Julian (*b.* 1978) *LD, Cambridge,* Maj. 6,792
Hurd, Nick (*b.* 1962) *C., Ruislip, Northwood & Pinner,* Maj. 19,060
Irranca-Davies, Huw (*b.* 1963) *Lab., Ogmore,* Maj. 13,246
†**Jackson**, Glenda (*b.* 1936) *Lab., Hampstead & Kilburn,* Maj. 42
Jackson, Stewart (*b.* 1965) *C., Peterborough,* Maj. 4,861
*__James__, Margot (*b.* 1957) *C., Stourbridge,* Maj. 5,164
James, Siân (*b.* 1959) *Lab., Swansea East,* Maj. 10,838
*__Jamieson__, Cathy (*b.* 1956) *Lab. (Co-op), Kilmarnock & Loudoun,* Maj. 12,378
§**Jarvis**, Dan (*b.* 1972) *Lab., Barnsley Central,* Maj. 11,771
*__Javid__, Sajid (*b.* 1969) *C., Bromsgrove,* Maj. 11,308
†**Jenkin**, Bernard (*b.* 1959) *C., Harwich & Essex North,* Maj. 11,447
Johnson, Rt. Hon. Alan (*b.* 1950) *Lab., Hull West & Hessle,* Maj. 5,740
Johnson, Diana (*b.* 1966) *Lab., Hull North,* Maj. 641
*__Johnson__, Gareth (*b.* 1969) *C., Dartford,* Maj. 10,628
*__Johnson__, Jo (*b.* 1971) *C., Orpington,* Maj. 17,200
*__Jones__, Andrew (*b.* 1963) *C., Harrogate & Knaresborough,* Maj. 1,039
Jones, Rt. Hon. David (*b.* 1952) *C., Clwyd West,* Maj. 6,419
*__Jones__, Graham (*b.* 1966) *Lab., Hyndburn,* Maj. 3,090
Jones, Helen (*b.* 1954) *Lab., Warrington North,* Maj. 6,771
Jones, Kevan (*b.* 1964) *Lab., Durham North,* Maj. 12,076
*__Jones__, Marcus (*b.* 1974) *C., Nuneaton,* Maj. 2,069
*__Jones__, Susan (*b.* 1968) *Lab., Clwyd South,* Maj. 2,834
†**Jowell**, Rt. Hon. Dame Tessa (*b.* 1947) *Lab., Dulwich & West Norwood,* Maj. 9,365
†¶ Joyce, Eric (*b.* 1960) *Ind., Falkirk,* Maj. 7,843
†**Kaufman**, Rt. Hon. Sir Gerald (*b.* 1930) *Lab., Manchester, Gorton,* Maj. 6,703
Kawczynski, Daniel (*b.* 1972) *C., Shrewsbury & Atcham,* Maj. 7,944
†**Keeley**, Barbara (*b.* 1952) *Lab., Worsley & Eccles South,* Maj. 4,337
*__Kelly__, Chris (*b.* 1978) *C., Dudley South,* Maj. 3,856
*__Kendall__, Liz (*b.* 1971) *Lab., Leicester West,* Maj. 4,017
†‡**Kennedy**, Rt. Hon. Charles (*b.* 1959) *LD, Ross, Skye & Lochaber,* Maj. 13,070
Khan, Rt. Hon. Sadiq (*b.* 1970) *Lab., Tooting,* Maj. 2,524
*__Kirby__, Simon (*b.* 1964) *C., Brighton Kemptown,* Maj. 1,328
†**Knight**, Rt. Hon. Greg (*b.* 1949) *C., Yorkshire East,* Maj. 13,486
*__Kwarteng__, Kwasi (*b.* 1975) *C., Spelthorne,* Maj. 10,019
Laing, Eleanor (*b.* 1958) *C., Epping Forest,* Maj. 15,131
Lamb, Norman (*b.* 1957) *LD, Norfolk North,* Maj. 11,626
Lammy, Rt. Hon. David (*b.* 1972) *Lab., Tottenham,* Maj. 16,931
†**Lancaster**, Mark (*b.* 1970) *C., Milton Keynes North,* Maj. 8,961
Lansley, Rt. Hon. Andrew (*b.* 1956) *C., Cambridgeshire South,* Maj. 7,838
*__Latham__, Pauline (*b.* 1948) *C., Derbyshire Mid,* Maj. 11,292
*__Lavery__, Ian (*b.* 1962) *Lab., Wansbeck,* Maj. 7,031
Laws, Rt. Hon. David (*b.* 1965) *LD, Yeovil,* Maj. 13,036
Lazarowicz, Mark (*b.* 1953) *Lab. (Co-op), Edinburgh North & Leith,* Maj. 1,724
*__Leadsom__, Andrea (*b.* 1963) *C., Northamptonshire South,* Maj. 20,478
*__Lee__, Jessica (*b.* 1976) *C., Erewash,* Maj. 2,501
*__Lee__, Phillip (*b.* 1970) *C., Bracknell,* Maj. 15,074
Leech, John (*b.* 1971) *LD, Manchester Withington,* Maj. 1,850
*__Lefroy__, Jeremy (*b.* 1959) *C., Stafford,* Maj. 5,460
†**Leigh**, Edward (*b.* 1950) *C., Gainsborough,* Maj. 10,559
*__Leslie__, Charlotte (*b.* 1978) *C., Bristol North West,* Maj. 3,274
†**Leslie**, Chris (*b.* 1972) *Lab. (Co-op), Nottingham East,* Maj. 6,969
Letwin, Rt. Hon. Oliver (*b.* 1956) *C., Dorset West,* Maj. 3,923
§**Lewell-Buck**, Emma (*b.* 1978) *Lab., South Shields,* Maj. 6,505

***Lewis**, Brandon (*b.* 1971) *C., Great Yarmouth,* Maj. 4,276
Lewis, Ivan (*b.* 1967) *Lab., Bury South,* Maj. 3,292
Lewis, Dr Julian (*b.* 1951) *C., New Forest East,* Maj. 11,307
†**Liddell-Grainger**, Ian (*b.* 1959) *C., Bridgwater & Somerset West,* Maj. 9,249
Lidington, Rt. Hon. David (*b.* 1956) *C., Aylesbury,* Maj. 12,618
†**Lilley**, Rt. Hon. Peter (*b.* 1943) *C., Hitchin & Harpenden,* Maj. 15,271
***Lloyd**, Stephen (*b.* 1957) *LD, Eastbourne,* Maj. 3,435
†**Llwyd**, Rt. Hon. Elfyn (*b.* 1951) *PC, Dwyfor Meirionnydd,* Maj. 6,367
***Long**, Naomi (*b.* 1971) *All., Belfast East,* Maj. 1,533
***Lopresti**, Jack (*b.* 1969) *C., Filton & Bradley Stoke,* Maj. 6,914
***Lord**, Jonathan (*b.* 1962) *C., Woking,* Maj. 6,807
Loughton, Tim (*b.* 1962) *C., Worthing East & Shoreham,* Maj. 11,105
Love, Andy (*b.* 1949) *Lab. (Co-op), Edmonton,* Maj. 9,613
***Lucas**, Caroline (*b.* 1960) *Green, Brighton Pavilion,* Maj. 1,252
Lucas, Ian (*b.* 1960) *Lab., Wrexham,* Maj. 3,658
†**Luff**, Peter (*b.* 1955) *C., Worcestershire Mid,* Maj. 15,864
***Lumley**, Karen (*b.* 1964) *C., Redditch,* Maj. 5,821
†**McCabe**, Steve (*b.* 1955) *Lab., Birmingham Selly Oak,* Maj. 3,482
***McCann**, Michael (*b.* 1964) *Lab., East Kilbride, Strathaven & Lesmahagow,* Maj. 14,503
McCarthy, Kerry (*b.* 1965) *Lab., Bristol East,* Maj. 3,722
***McCartney**, Jason (*b.* 1968) *C., Colne Valley,* Maj. 4,837
***McCartney**, Karl (*b.* 1968) *C., Lincoln,* Maj. 1,058
***McClymont**, Gregg (*b.* 1976) *Lab., Cumbernauld, Kilsyth & Kirkintilloch East,* Maj. 13,755
†**McCrea**, Revd Dr William (*b.* 1948) *DUP, Antrim South,* Maj. 1,183
McDonagh, Siobhain (*b.* 1960) *Lab., Mitcham & Morden,* Maj. 13,666
§**McDonald**, Andy (*b.* 1958) *Lab., Middlesbrough,* Maj. 8,211
McDonnell, Dr Alasdair (*b.* 1949) *SDLP, Belfast South,* Maj. 5,926
McDonnell, John (*b.* 1951) *Lab., Hayes & Harlington,* Maj. 10,824
McFadden, Rt. Hon. Pat (*b.* 1965) *Lab., Wolverhampton South East,* Maj. 6,593
***McGovern**, Alison (*b.* 1980) *Lab., Wirral South,* Maj. 531
McGovern, James (*b.* 1956) *Lab., Dundee West,* Maj. 7,278
McGuire, Rt. Hon. Anne (*b.* 1949) *Lab., Stirling,* Maj. 8,354
†**McIntosh**, Anne (*b.* 1954) *C., Thirsk and Malton,* Maj. 11,281
†**McKechin**, Ann (*b.* 1961) *Lab., Glasgow North,* Maj. 3,898
§**McKenzie**, Iain (*b.* 1959) *Lab., Inverclyde,* Maj. 5,838
***McKinnell**, Catherine (*b.* 1976) *Lab., Newcastle upon Tyne North,* Maj. 3,414
***MacLeod**, Mary (*b.* 1969) *C., Brentford & Isleworth,* Maj. 1,958
†**McLoughlin**, Rt. Hon. Patrick (*b.* 1957) *C., Derbyshire Dales,* Maj. 13,866
MacNeil, Angus (*b.* 1970) *SNP, Na h-Eileanan an Iar,* Maj. 1,885
***McPartland**, Stephen (*b.* 1976) *C., Stevenage,* Maj. 3,578
Mactaggart, Fiona (*b.* 1953) *Lab., Slough,* Maj. 5,523
***McVey**, Esther (*b.* 1967) *C., Wirral West,* Maj. 2,436
Mahmood, Khalid (*b.* 1961) *Lab., Birmingham Perry Barr,* Maj. 11,908
***Mahmood**, Shabana (*b.* 1980) *Lab., Birmingham Ladywood,* Maj. 10,105
Main, Anne (*b.* 1957) *C., St Albans,* Maj. 2,305
§**Malhotra**, Seema (*b.* 1972) *Lab. (Co-op), Feltham & Heston,* Maj. 6,203
Mann, John (*b.* 1960) *Lab., Bassetlaw,* Maj. 8,215
Marsden, Gordon (*b.* 1953) *Lab., Blackpool South,* Maj. 1,852
§**Maskey**, Paul (*b.* 1967) *SF, Belfast West,* Maj. 13,123
†**Maude**, Rt. Hon. Francis (*b.* 1953) *C., Horsham,* Maj. 11,460
May, Rt. Hon. Theresa (*b.* 1956) *C., Maidenhead,* Maj. 16,769
***Maynard**, Paul (*b.* 1975) *C., Blackpool North & Cleveleys,* Maj. 2,150
†**Meacher**, Rt. Hon. Michael (*b.* 1939) *Lab., Oldham West & Royton,* Maj. 9,352
Meale, Sir Alan (*b.* 1949) *Lab., Mansfield,* Maj. 6,012
***Mearns**, Ian (*b.* 1957) *Lab., Gateshead,* Maj. 12,549
***Menzies**, Mark (*b.* 1971) *C., Fylde,* Maj. 13,185
Mercer, Patrick (*b.* 1956) *Ind., Newark,* Maj. 16,152
***Metcalfe**, Stephen (*b.* 1966) *C., Basildon South & Thurrock East,* Maj. 5,772
Miliband, Rt. Hon. Ed (*b.* 1969) *Lab., Doncaster North,* Maj. 10,909
Miller, Andrew (*b.* 1949) *Lab., Ellesmere Port & Neston,* Maj. 4,331
Miller, Rt. Hon. Maria (*b.* 1964) *C., Basingstoke,* Maj. 13,176
***Mills**, Nigel (*b.* 1974) *C., Amber Valley,* Maj. 536
Milton, Anne (*b.* 1955) *C., Guildford,* Maj. 7,782
†**Mitchell**, Rt. Hon. Andrew (*b.* 1956) *C., Sutton Coldfield,* Maj. 17,005
†**Mitchell**, Austin (*b.* 1934) *Lab., Great Grimsby,* Maj. 714
§**Molloy**, Francie (*b.* 1950) *SF, Mid Ulster,* Maj. 4,681
Moon, Madeleine (*b.* 1950) *Lab., Bridgend,* Maj. 2,263
†**Moore**, Rt. Hon. Michael (*b.* 1965) *LD, Berwickshire, Roxburgh & Selkirk,* Maj. 5,675
***Mordaunt**, Penny (*b.* 1973) *C., Portsmouth North,* Maj. 7,289
Morden, Jessica (*b.* 1968) *Lab., Newport East,* Maj. 1,650
***Morgan**, Nicky (*b.* 1972) *C., Loughborough,* Maj. 3,744
***Morrice**, Graeme (*b.* 1959) *Lab., Livingston,* Maj. 10,791
***Morris**, Anne Marie (*b.* 1957) *C., Newton Abbot,* Maj. 523
***Morris**, David (*b.* 1966) *C., Morecambe & Lunesdale,* Maj. 866
***Morris**, Grahame (*b.* 1961) *Lab., Easington,* Maj. 14,982
***Morris**, James (*b.* 1967) *C., Halesowen & Rowley Regis,* Maj. 2,023
***Mosley**, Stephen (*b.* 1972) *C., Chester, City of,* Maj. 2,583
***Mowat**, David (*b.* 1957) *C., Warrington South,* Maj. 1,553
Mudie, George (*b.* 1945) *Lab., Leeds East,* Maj. 10,293
Mulholland, Greg (*b.* 1970) *LD, Leeds North West,* Maj. 9,103
Mundell, Rt. Hon. David (*b.* 1962) *C., Dumfriesshire, Clydesdale & Tweeddale,* Maj. 4,194
Munn, Meg (*b.* 1959) *Lab. (Co-op), Sheffield Heeley,* Maj. 5,807
***Munt**, Tessa (*b.* 1959) *LD, Wells,* Maj. 800
Murphy, Conor (*b.* 1963) *SF, Newry & Armagh,* Maj. 8,331
†**Murphy**, Rt. Hon. Jim (*b.* 1967) *Lab., Renfrewshire East,* Maj. 10,420
Murphy, Rt. Hon. Paul (*b.* 1948) *Lab., Torfaen,* Maj. 9,306
***Murray**, Ian (*b.* 1976) *Lab., Edinburgh South,* Maj. 316
***Murray**, Sheryll (*b.* 1956) *C., Cornwall South East,* Maj. 3,220
†**Murrison**, Dr Andrew (*b.* 1961) *C., Wiltshire South West,* Maj. 10,367
***Nandy**, Lisa (*b.* 1979) *Lab., Wigan,* Maj. 10,487
***Nash**, Pamela (*b.* 1984) *Lab., Airdrie & Shotts,* Maj. 12,408
Neill, Robert (*b.* 1952) *C., Bromley & Chislehurst,* Maj. 13,900
Newmark, Brooks (*b.* 1958) *C., Braintree,* Maj. 16,121
***Newton**, Sarah (*b.* 1962) *C., Truro & Falmouth,* Maj. 435

*__Nokes__, Caroline (*b.* 1972) *C., Romsey & Southampton North,* Maj. 4,156
*__Norman__, Jesse (*b.* 1962) *C., Hereford & Herefordshire South,* Maj. 2,481
*__Nuttall__, David (*b.* 1962) *C., Bury North,* Maj. 2,243
O'Brien, Stephen (*b.* 1957) *C., Eddisbury,* Maj. 13,255
*__O'Donnell__, Fiona (*b.* 1960) *Lab., East Lothian,* Maj. 12,258
*__Offord__, Matthew (*b.* 1969) *C., Hendon,* Maj. 106
*__Ollerenshaw__, Eric (*b.* 1950) *C., Lancaster & Fleetwood,* Maj. 333
*__Onwurah__, Chi (*b.* 1965) *Lab., Newcastle upon Tyne Central,* Maj. 7,464
*__Opperman__, Guy (*b.* 1965) *C., Hexham,* Maj. 5,788
Osborne, Rt. Hon. George (*b.* 1971) *C., Tatton,* Maj. 14,487
†**Osborne**, Sandra (*b.* 1956) *Lab., Ayr, Carrick & Cumnock,* Maj. 9,911
†**Ottaway**, Richard (*b.* 1945) *C., Croydon South,* Maj. 15,818
Owen, Albert (*b.* 1960) *Lab., Ynys Mon,* Maj. 2,461
Paice, Rt. Hon. Sir James (*b.* 1949) *C., Cambridgeshire South East,* Maj. 5,946
*__Paisley Jr__, Ian (*b.* 1966) *DUP, Antrim North,* Maj. 12,558
*__Parish__, Neil (*b.* 1956) *C., Tiverton & Honiton,* Maj. 9,320
*__Patel__, Priti (*b.* 1972) *C., Witham,* Maj. 15,196
Paterson, Rt. Hon. Owen (*b.* 1956) *C., Shropshire North,* Maj. 15,828
*__Pawsey__, Mark (*b.* 1957) *C., Rugby,* Maj. 6,000
*__Pearce__, Teresa (*b.* 1955) *Lab., Erith & Thamesmead,* Maj. 5,703
Penning, Mike (*b.* 1957) *C., Hemel Hempstead,* Maj. 13,406
Penrose, John (*b.* 1964) *C., Weston-Super-Mare,* Maj. 2,691
*__Percy__, Andrew (*b.* 1977) *C., Brigg & Goole,* Maj. 5,147
*__Perkins__, Toby (*b.* 1970) *Lab., Chesterfield,* Maj. 549
*__Perry__, Claire (*b.* 1964) *C., Devizes,* Maj. 13,005
*__Phillips__, Stephen (*b.* 1970) *C., Sleaford & Hykeham North,* Maj. 19,905
*__Phillipson__, Bridget (*b.* 1983) *Lab., Houghton & Sunderland South,* Maj. 10,990
Pickles, Rt. Hon. Eric (*b.* 1952) *C., Brentwood & Ongar,* Maj. 16,920
*__Pincher__, Christopher (*b.* 1969) *C., Tamworth,* Maj. 6,090
*__Poulter__, Daniel (*b.* 1978) *C., Suffolk Central & Ipswich North,* Maj. 13,786
Pound, Stephen (*b.* 1948) *Lab., Ealing North,* Maj. 9,301
§**Powell**, Lucy (*b.* 1974) *Lab., Manchester Central,* Maj. 9,936
Primarolo, Rt. Hon. Dawn (*b.* 1954) *Lab., Bristol South,* Maj. 4,734
Prisk, Mark (*b.* 1962) *C., Hertford & Stortford,* Maj. 15,437
Pritchard, Mark (*b.* 1966) *C., The Wrekin,* Maj. 9,450
Pugh, Dr John (*b.* 1948) *LD, Southport,* Maj. 6,024
*__Qureshi__, Yasmin (*b.* 1963) *Lab., Bolton South East,* Maj. 8,634
*__Raab__, Dominic (*b.* 1974) *C., Esher & Walton,* Maj. 18,593
†**Randall**, Rt. Hon. John (*b.* 1955) *C., Uxbridge & Ruislip South,* Maj. 11,216
†**Raynsford**, Rt. Hon. Nick (*b.* 1945) *Lab., Greenwich & Woolwich,* Maj. 10,153
*__Reckless__, Mark (*b.* 1970) *C., Rochester & Strood,* Maj. 9,953
Redwood, Rt. Hon. John (*b.* 1951) *C., Wokingham,* Maj. 13,492
Reed, Jamie (*b.* 1973) *Lab., Copeland,* Maj. 3,833
§**Reed**, Steve (*b.* 1963) *Lab., Croydon North,* Maj. 11,761
*__Rees-Mogg__, Jacob (*b.* 1969) *C., Somerset North East,* Maj. 4,914
*__Reevell__, Simon (*b.* 1966) *C., Dewsbury,* Maj. 1,526
*__Reeves__, Rachel (*b.* 1979) *Lab., Leeds West,* Maj. 7,016
Reid, Alan (*b.* 1954) *LD, Argyll & Bute,* Maj. 3,431
*__Reynolds__, Emma (*b.* 1977) *Lab., Wolverhampton North East,* Maj. 2,484
*__Reynolds__, Jonathan (*b.* 1980) *Lab. (Co-op), Stalybridge & Hyde,* Maj. 2,744
†**Rifkind**, Rt. Hon. Sir Malcolm (*b.* 1946) *C., Kensington,* Maj. 8,616
Riordan, Linda (*b.* 1953) *Lab. (Co-op), Halifax,* Maj. 1,472
*__Ritchie__, Margaret (*b.* 1958) *SDLP, South Down,* Maj. 8,412
†**Robathan**, Rt. Hon. Andrew (*b.* 1951) *C., Leicestershire South,* Maj. 15,524
Robertson, Angus (*b.* 1969) *SNP, Moray,* Maj. 5,590
Robertson, Rt. Hon. Hugh (*b.* 1962) *C., Faversham & Kent Mid,* Maj. 17,088
†**Robertson**, John (*b.* 1952) *Lab., Glasgow North West,* Maj. 13,611
Robertson, Laurence (*b.* 1958) *C., Tewkesbury,* Maj. 6,310
Robinson, Geoffrey (*b.* 1938) *Lab., Coventry North West,* Maj. 6,288
Rogerson, Dan (*b.* 1975) *LD, Cornwall North,* Maj. 2,981
Rosindell, Andrew (*b.* 1966) *C., Romford,* Maj. 16,954
*__Rotheram__, Steve (*b.* 1961) *Lab., Liverpool Walton,* Maj. 19,818
Roy, Frank (*b.* 1958) *Lab., Motherwell & Wishaw,* Maj. 16,806
Roy, Lindsay (*b.* 1949) *Lab., Glenrothes,* Maj. 16,455
Ruane, Chris (*b.* 1958) *Lab., Vale of Clwyd,* Maj. 2,509
*__Rudd__, Amber (*b.* 1963) *C., Hastings & Rye,* Maj. 1,993
Ruddock, Rt. Hon. Dame Joan (*b.* 1943) *Lab., Lewisham Deptford,* Maj. 12,499
Ruffley, David (*b.* 1962) *C., Bury St Edmunds,* Maj. 12,380
Russell, Sir Bob (*b.* 1946) *LD, Colchester,* Maj. 6,982
*__Rutley__, David (*b.* 1961) *C., Macclesfield,* Maj. 11,959
Sanders, Adrian (*b.* 1959) *LD, Torbay,* Maj. 4,078
*__Sandys__, Laura (*b.* 1964) *C., Thanet South,* Maj. 7,617
*__Sarwar__, Anas (*b.* 1983) *Lab., Glasgow Central,* Maj. 10,551
§**Sawford**, Andy (*b.* 1976) *Lab. (Co-op), Corby,* Maj. 7,791
Scott, Lee (*b.* 1956) *C., Ilford North,* Maj. 5,404
†**Seabeck**, Alison (*b.* 1954) *Lab., Plymouth Moor View,* Maj. 1,588
Selous, Andrew (*b.* 1962) *C., Bedfordshire South West,* Maj. 16,649
*__Shannon__, Jim (*b.* 1955) *DUP, Strangford,* Maj. 5,876
Shapps, Rt. Hon. Grant (*b.* 1968) *C., Welwyn Hatfield,* Maj. 7,423
*__Sharma__, Alok (*b.* 1967) *C., Reading West,* Maj. 6,004
Sharma, Virendra (*b.* 1947) *Lab., Ealing Southall,* Maj. 9,291
†**Sheerman**, Barry (*b.* 1940) *Lab. (Co-op), Huddersfield,* Maj. 4,472
*__Shelbrooke__, Alec (*b.* 1976) *C., Elmet & Rothwell,* Maj. 4,521
Shepherd, Sir Richard (*b.* 1942) *C., Aldridge-Brownhills,* Maj. 15,256
†**Sheridan**, Jim (*b.* 1952) *Lab., Paisley & Renfrewshire North,* Maj. 15,280
*__Shuker__, Gavin (*b.* 1981) *Lab. (Co-op), Luton South,* Maj. 2,329
Simmonds, Mark (*b.* 1964) *C., Boston & Skegness,* Maj. 12,426
Simpson, David (*b.* 1959) *DUP, Upper Bann,* Maj. 3,361
†**Simpson**, Keith (*b.* 1949) *C., Broadland,* Maj. 7,292
*__Skidmore__, Chris (*b.* 1981) *C., Kingswood,* Maj. 2,445
Skinner, Dennis (*b.* 1932) *Lab., Bolsover,* Maj. 11,182
†**Slaughter**, Andrew (*b.* 1960) *Lab., Hammersmith,* Maj. 3,549
Smith, Rt. Hon. Andrew (*b.* 1951) *Lab., Oxford East,* Maj. 4,581
†**Smith**, Angela C. (*b.* 1961) *Lab., Penistone & Stocksbridge,* Maj. 3,049
Smith, Chloe (*b.* 1982) *C., Norwich North,* Maj. 3,901
*__Smith__, Henry (*b.* 1969) *C., Crawley,* Maj. 5,928
*__Smith__, Julian (*b.* 1971) *C., Skipton & Ripon,* Maj. 9,950
*__Smith__, Nick (*b.* 1960) *Lab., Blaenau Gwent,* Maj. 10,516

*__Smith__, Owen (*b.* 1970) *Lab., Pontypridd,* Maj. 2,785
Smith, Sir Robert (*b.* 1958) *LD, Aberdeenshire West & Kincardine,* Maj. 6,684
†**Soames**, Rt. Hon. Nicholas (*b.* 1948) *C., Sussex Mid,* Maj. 7,402
*__Soubry__, Anna (*b.* 1956) *C., Broxtowe,* Maj. 389
†**Spellar**, Rt. Hon. John (*b.* 1947) *Lab., Warley,* Maj. 10,756
Spelman, Rt. Hon. Caroline (*b.* 1958) *C., Meriden,* Maj. 16,253
*__Spencer__, Mark (*b.* 1970) *C., Sherwood,* Maj. 214
Stanley, Rt. Hon. Sir John (*b.* 1942) *C., Tonbridge & Malling,* Maj. 18,178
*__Stephenson__, Andrew (*b.* 1981) *C., Pendle,* Maj. 3,585
*__Stevenson__, John (*b.* 1963) *C., Carlisle,* Maj. 853
*__Stewart__, Bob (*b.* 1949) *C., Beckenham,* Maj. 17,784
*__Stewart__, Iain (*b.* 1972) *C., Milton Keynes South,* Maj. 5,201
*__Stewart__, Rory (*b.* 1973) *C., Penrith & The Border,* Maj. 11,241
Straw, Rt. Hon. Jack (*b.* 1946) *Lab., Blackburn,* Maj. 9,856
†**Streeter**, Gary (*b.* 1955) *C., Devon South West,* Maj. 15,874
*__Stride__, Mel (*b.* 1961) *C., Devon Central,* Maj. 9,230
†**Stringer**, Graham (*b.* 1950) *Lab., Blackley & Broughton,* Maj. 12,303
Stuart, Gisela (*b.* 1955) *Lab., Birmingham, Edgbaston,* Maj. 1,274
Stuart, Graham (*b.* 1962) *C., Beverley & Holderness,* Maj. 12,987
Stunell, Rt. Hon. Andrew (*b.* 1942) *LD, Hazel Grove,* Maj. 6,371
*__Sturdy__, Julian (*b.* 1971) *C., York Outer,* Maj. 3,688
Sutcliffe, Gerry (*b.* 1953) *Lab., Bradford South,* Maj. 4,622
*__Swales__, Ian (*b.* 1953) *LD, Redcar,* Maj. 5,214
Swayne, Rt. Hon. Desmond (*b.* 1956) *C., New Forest West,* Maj. 16,896
Swinson, Jo (*b.* 1980) *LD, Dunbartonshire East,* Maj. 2,184
Swire, Rt. Hon. Hugo (*b.* 1959) *C., Devon East,* Maj. 9,114
Syms, Robert (*b.* 1956) *C., Poole,* Maj. 7,541
Tami, Mark (*b.* 1963) *Lab., Alyn & Deeside,* Maj. 2,919
†**Tapsell**, Rt. Hon. Sir Peter (*b.* 1930) *C., Louth & Horncastle,* Maj. 13,871
†**Teather**, Sarah (*b.* 1974) *LD, Brent Central,* Maj. 1,345
Thomas, Gareth (*b.* 1967) *Lab. (Co-op), Harrow West,* Maj. 3,143
Thornberry, Emily (*b.* 1960) *Lab., Islington South & Finsbury,* Maj. 3,569
§**Thornton**, Mike (*b.* 1952) *LD, Eastleigh,* Maj. 1,771
Thurso, John (*b.* 1953) *LD, Caithness, Sutherland & Easter Ross,* Maj. 4,826
Timms, Rt. Hon. Stephen (*b.* 1955) *Lab., East Ham,* Maj. 27,826
Timpson, Edward (*b.* 1973) *C., Crewe & Nantwich,* Maj. 6,046
*__Tomlinson__, Justin (*b.* 1976) *C., Swindon North,* Maj. 7,060
Tredinnick, David (*b.* 1950) *C., Bosworth,* Maj. 5,032
Trickett, Jon (*b.* 1950) *Lab., Hemsworth,* Maj. 9,844
*__Truss__, Elizabeth (*b.* 1975) *C., Norfolk South West,* Maj. 13,140
Turner, Andrew (*b.* 1953) *C., Isle of Wight,* Maj. 10,527
*__Turner__, Karl (*b.* 1971) *Lab., Hull East,* Maj. 8,597
Twigg, Derek (*b.* 1959) *Lab., Halton,* Maj. 15,504
†**Twigg**, Stephen (*b.* 1966) *Lab. (Co-op), Liverpool Derby West,* Maj. 18,467
Tyrie, Andrew (*b.* 1957) *C., Chichester,* Maj. 15,877
*__Umunna__, Chuka (*b.* 1978) *Lab., Streatham,* Maj. 3,259
*__Uppal__, Paul (*b.* 1967) *C., Wolverhampton South West,* Maj. 691
Vaizey, Ed (*b.* 1969) *C., Wantage,* Maj. 13,547
Vara, Shailesh (*b.* 1960) *C., Cambridgeshire North West,* Maj. 16,677
Vaz, Rt. Hon. Keith (*b.* 1956) *Lab., Leicester East,* Maj. 14,082
*__Vaz__, Valerie (*b.* 1954) *Lab., Walsall South,* Maj. 1,755
*__Vickers__, Martin (*b.* 1950) *C., Cleethorpes,* Maj. 4,298
Villiers, Rt. Hon. Theresa (*b.* 1968) *C., Chipping Barnet,* Maj. 11,927
Walker, Charles (*b.* 1967) *C., Broxbourne,* Maj. 18,804
*__Walker__, Robin (*b.* 1978) *C., Worcester,* Maj. 2,982
†**Wallace**, Ben (*b.* 1970) *C., Wyre & Preston North,* Maj. 15,844
Walley, Joan (*b.* 1949) *Lab., Stoke-on-Trent North,* Maj. 8,235
Walter, Robert (*b.* 1948) *C., Dorset North,* Maj. 7,625
*__Ward__, David (*b.* 1953) *Ind., Bradford East,* Maj. 365
†**Watkinson**, Dame Angela (*b.* 1941) *C., Hornchurch & Upminster,* Maj. 16,371
Watson, Tom (*b.* 1967) *Lab., West Bromwich East,* Maj. 6,696
Watts, Dave (*b.* 1951) *Lab., St Helens North,* Maj. 13,101
*__Weatherley__, Mike (*b.* 1957) *C., Hove,* Maj. 1,868
†**Webb**, Prof. Steve (*b.* 1965) *LD, Thornbury & Yate,* Maj. 7,116
Weir, Mike (*b.* 1957) *SNP, Angus,* Maj. 3,282
*__Wharton__, James (*b.* 1984) *C., Stockton South,* Maj. 332
*__Wheeler__, Heather (*b.* 1959) *C., Derbyshire South,* Maj. 7,128
*__White__, Chris (*b.* 1967) *C., Warwick & Leamington,* Maj. 3,513
*__Whiteford__, Eilidh (*b.* 1969) *SNP, Banff & Buchan,* Maj. 4,027
Whitehead, Dr Alan (*b.* 1950) *Lab., Southampton, Test,* Maj. 2,413
*__Whittaker__, Craig (*b.* 1962) *C., Calder Valley,* Maj. 6,431
†**Whittingdale**, John (*b.* 1959) *C., Maldon,* Maj. 19,407
†**Wiggin**, Bill (*b.* 1966) *C., Herefordshire North,* Maj. 9,887
Willetts, Rt. Hon. David (*b.* 1956) *C., Havant,* Maj. 12,160
†**Williams**, Hywel (*b.* 1953) *PC, Arfon,* Maj. 1,455
Williams, Mark (*b.* 1966) *LD, Ceredigion,* Maj. 8,324
Williams, Roger (*b.* 1948) *LD, Brecon & Radnorshire,* Maj. 3,747
Williams, Stephen (*b.* 1966) *LD, Bristol West,* Maj. 11,366
*__Williamson__, Chris (*b.* 1956) *Lab., Derby North,* Maj. 613
*__Williamson__, Gavin (*b.* 1976) *C., Staffordshire South,* Maj. 16,590
Willott, Jenny (*b.* 1974) *LD, Cardiff Central,* Maj. 4,576
Wilson, Phil (*b.* 1959) *Lab., Sedgefield,* Maj. 8,696
Wilson, Rob (*b.* 1965) *C., Reading East,* Maj. 7,605
Wilson, Sammy (*b.* 1953) *DUP, Antrim East,* Maj. 6,770
†**Winnick**, David (*b.* 1933) *Lab., Walsall North,* Maj. 990
Winterton, Rt. Hon. Rosie (*b.* 1958) *Lab., Doncaster Central,* Maj. 6,229
†**Wishart**, Peter (*b.* 1962) *SNP, Perth & Perthshire North,* Maj. 4,379
*__Wollaston__, Sarah (*b.* 1962) *C., Totnes,* Maj. 4,927
Wood, Mike (*b.* 1946) *Lab., Batley & Spen,* Maj. 4,406
*__Woodcock__, John (*b.* 1978) *Lab. (Co-op), Barrow & Furness,* Maj. 5,208
†‡**Woodward**, Rt. Hon. Shaun (*b.* 1958) *Lab., St Helens South & Whiston,* Maj. 14,122
Wright, David (*b.* 1967) *Lab., Telford,* Maj. 981
Wright, Iain (*b.* 1972) *Lab., Hartlepool,* Maj. 5,509
†**Wright**, Jeremy (*b.* 1972) *C., Kenilworth & Southam,* Maj. 12,552
*__Wright__, Simon (*b.* 1979) *LD, Norwich South,* Maj. 310
Yeo, Tim (*b.* 1945) *C., Suffolk South,* Maj. 8,689
†**Young**, Rt. Hon. Sir George (*b.* 1941) *C., Hampshire North West,* Maj. 18,583
*__Zahawi__, Nadhim (*b.* 1967) *C., Stratford-on-Avon,* Maj. 11,346

GENERAL ELECTION RESULTS

The results of voting in each parliamentary division at the general election of 6 May 2010 are given below.

BOUNDARY CHANGES

The constituency boundaries were redrawn for the 2010 election in England, Wales and Northern Ireland. As a result of the review the number of constituencies increased from 646 to 650, with four new seats in England. Only 138 constituencies had no boundary changes, 59 of them in Scotland.

For the majority of constituencies where a boundary change has taken place, it is not appropriate to make a direct comparison between the results of 2005 and 2010. The seat of Hammersmith, for example, comprises 60 per cent of the old Hammersmith and Fulham constituency and 40 per cent of the old Ealing and Shepherds Bush constituency; it cannot therefore be described as a simple hold for the Labour party. The term 'notional' used here refers to a theoretical set of results, published by Professors Rallings and Thrasher of Plymouth University, which estimates the way each new constituency might have voted in the 2005 general election.

KEY

* New MP
† Previously MP in another seat
‡ Previously MP for another party
§ Notional result; *see* explanation of boundary changes
¶ By-election held after 2010 general election
E. Electorate T. Turnout

Abbreviations

AD	Apolitical Democrats
Alliance	Alliance
Animals	Animals Count
Anti-War	Fight for an Anti-War Government
APP	Animal Protection Party
Battersea	Putting the People of Battersea First
BB	A Better Britain for All
BB&C	Beer, Baccy and Crumpet
BCP	Basingstoke Common Man
Bean	New Millennium Bean
Beer	Reduce Tax on Beer Party
Best	The Best of a Bad Bunch
BIB	Bushra Irfan of Blackburn
BIC	Bromsgrove Independent Conservative
Blaenau Voice	Blaenau Gwent People's Voice
Blue	Blue Environment Party
BNP	British National Party
BP Elvis	Bus-Pass Elvis Party
C.	Conservative
Ch. M.	Christian Movement for Great Britain
Ch. P.	Christian Party
Christian	Christian
CIP	Campaign for Independent Politicians
City Ind.	City Independent
Clause 28	Clause 28, Children's Protection Christian Democrats
CLR	Cannabis Law Reform
CME	Church of the Millitant Elvis
CNBPG	Community Need Before Private Greed
Comm.	Communist Party
Comm. Brit.	Communist Party of Britain
Comm. Lge	Communist League
Cornish D.	Cornish Democrats
CPA	Christian People's Alliance
CSP	Common Sense Party
CUP	Communities United Party
Currency	Virtue Currency Cognitive Appraisal Party
D. Nat.	Democratic Nationalist
DDP	Direct Democracy Party
Deficit	Cut the Deficit Party
Dem. 2015	Democracy 2015
Dem. Lab.	Democratic Labour Party
DUP	Democratic Unionist Party
Elvis	Elvis Loves Pets
Eng. Dem.	English Democrats
Eng. Ind.	English Independence Party
F and R	For Freedom and Responsibility
FDP	Fancy Dress Party
Good	The Common Good
Green	Green
Green Belt	Independent Save Our Green Belt
Green Soc.	Alliance for Green Socialism
Humanity	Humanity
Impact	Impact Party
Ind.	Independent
Ind. CCF	New Independent Conservative Chelsea and Fulham
Ind. CHC	Independent Community and Health Concern
Ind. EACPS	Independent Ealing Action Communities Public Services
Ind. Fed.	Independents Federation UK
Ind. People	Independent People Together
Ind. Rantzen	Independent Rantzen
Ind. Voice	Independent Voice for Halifax
Integrity	Integrity UK
ISP	Independent Socialist Party
IZB	Islam Zinda Baad Platform
J & AC	Justice & Anti-Corruption Party
Jacobite	Scottish Jacobite Party
Joy	The Joy of Talk
JP	Justice Party
King George	Save King George Hospital
Lab.	Labour
Lab. (Co-op)	Labour and Co-operative
Land	Land is Power
LD	Liberal Democrat
Leave EU	Independent Leave the EU Alliance
Lib.	Liberal
Libertarian	Libertarian Party
Lincs. Ind.	Lincolnshire Independents
LLPBPP	Local Liberals People Before Politics Party
Loony	Monster Raving Loony Party
LPBP	London People Before Profit
LTT	Lawfulness Trustworthiness and Transparency
Macc. Ind.	The Macclesfield Independent
Magna Carta	The Magna Carta Party
Mansfield Ind.	Mansfield Independent Forum
Meb. Ker.	Mebyon Kernow
Med. Ind.	Medway Independent
Mid. England	Middle England Party
MP Expense	A Vote Against MP Expense Abuse
MRP	Money Reform Party
Nat. Dem.	National Democrat
ND	No Description
New Party	The New Party
NF	National Front
NFP	Nationwide Reform Party
NHA	National Health Action
Nine11	Nine Eleven Was An Inside Job
No Vote	No Candidate Deserves My Vote
Nobody	Nobody Party
NSPS	Northampton – Save Our Public Services
Parenting	Equal Parenting Alliance
PBP	People Before Profit
PC	Plaid Cymru
Peace	Peace Party
PDP	People's Democratic Party
Pirate	Pirate Party UK
PNDP	People's National Democratic Party
Poetry	The True English (Poetry) Party
PP Essex	Peoples Party Essex
PPN-V	Peace Party Non-Violence Justice Environment
R and E	Citizens for Undead Rights and Equality
RA	Solihull and Meridien Residents' Association
RAL	Residents' Association of London
Reform	Reform 2000
Respect	Respect the Unity Coalition
RP	The Restoration Party
RRG	Radical Reform Group
SACL	Scotland Against Crooked Lawyers
Save QM	Independents to Save Queen Mary's Hospital

Science	The Science Party
SDLP	Social Democratic and Labour Party
SEP	Socialist Equality Party
SF	Sinn Fein
SMA	Scrap Members Allowances
Snouts	Get Snouts Out The Trough
SNP	Scottish National Party
Soc.	Socialist Party
Soc. Alt.	Socialist Alternative Party
Soc. Dem.	Social Democratic Party
Soc. Lab.	Socialist Labour Party
South	All the South Party
Speaker	The Speaker
SSP	Scottish Socialist Party
Staffs Ind.	Staffordshire Independent Group
Tendring	Tendring First
TOC	Tamsin Omond to the Commons
Trust	Trust
TUSC	Trade Unionist and Socialist Coalition
TUV	Traditional Unionist Voice
UCUNF	Ulster Conservatives and Unionists – New Force
UK Integrity	Independents Federation UK – Honest Integrity Democracy
UKIP	UK Independence Party
UPP	United People's Party
UPS	Unity for Peace and Socialism
Voice	United Voice
Wessex Reg.	Wessex Regionalist
Workers Lib.	Alliance for Workers Liberty
WP	Workers' Party
WR	Wessex Regionalists
WRP	Workers' Revolutionary Party
You	You Party
Youth	Youth Party
YP	Go Mad and Vote For Yourself Party
YPP	Young People's Party
YRDPL	Your Right to Democracy Party Limited

PARLIAMENTARY CONSTITUENCIES AS AT 6 MAY 2010 GENERAL ELECTION

UK Turnout
E. 45,533,536 T. 29,643,522 (65.1%)

ENGLAND

§ALDERSHOT
E. 71,469 T. 45,384 (63.50%) C. hold
Gerald Howarth, C. 21,203
Adrian Collett, LD 15,617
Jonathan Slater, Lab. 5,489
Robert Snare, UKIP 2,041
Gary Crowd, Eng. Ind. 803
Juliana Brimicombe, Ch. P. 231
C. majority 5,586 (12.31%)
Notional 1.41% swing C. to LD
(2005: C. majority 6,345 (15.12%))

§ALDRIDGE-BROWNHILLS
E. 59,355 T. 38,634 (65.09%) C. hold
Richard Shepherd, C. 22,913
Ashiq Hussain, Lab. 7,647
Ian Jenkins, LD 6,833
Karl Macnaughton, Green 847
Sue Gray, Ch. P. 394
C. majority 15,266 (39.51%)
Notional 12.01% swing Lab. to C.
(2005: C. majority 5,732 (15.49%))

§ALTRINCHAM & SALE WEST
E. 71,254 T. 49,393 (69.32%) C. hold
Graham Brady, C. 24,176
Jane Brophy, LD 12,581
Tom Ross, Lab. 11,073
Kenneth Bullman, UKIP 1,563
C. majority 11,595 (23.47%)
Notional 0.83% swing C. to LD
(2005: C. majority 7,618 (17.57%))

§AMBER VALLEY
E. 70,171 T. 45,958 (65.49%) C. gain
*Nigel Mills, C. 17,746
Judy Mallaber, Lab. 17,210
Tom Snowdon, LD 6,636
Michael Clarke, BNP 3,195
Sue Ransome, UKIP 906
Sam Thing, Loony 265
C. majority 536 (1.17%)
Notional 6.85% swing Lab. to C.
(2005: Lab. majority 5,512 (12.53%))

§ARUNDEL & SOUTH DOWNS
E. 77,564 T. 55,982 (72.18%) C. hold
Nick Herbert, C. 32,333
Derek Deedman, LD 15,642
Tim Lunnon, Lab. 4,835
Stuart Bower, UKIP 3,172
C. majority 16,691 (29.81%)
Notional 3.00% swing LD to C.
(2005: C. majority 12,291 (23.81%))

§ASHFIELD
E. 77,379 T. 48,196 (62.29%) Lab. hold
*Gloria De Piero, Lab. 16,239
Jason Zadrozny, LD 16,047
Garry Hickton, C. 10,698
Edward Holmes, BNP 2,781
Tony Ellis, Eng. Dem. 1,102
Terry Coleman, UKIP 933
Eddie Smith, Ind. 396
Lab. majority 192 (0.40%)
Notional 17.23% swing Lab. to LD
(2005: Lab. majority 10,370 (24.28%))

§ASHFORD
E. 81,269 T. 55,185 (67.90%) C. hold
Damian Green, C. 29,878
Chris Took, LD 12,581
Chris Clark, Lab. 9,204
Jeffrey Elenor, UKIP 2,508
Steve Campkin, Green 1,014
C. majority 17,297 (31.34%)
Notional 2.25% swing C. to LD
(2005: C. majority 12,268 (25.02%))

§ASHTON UNDER LYNE
E. 67,564 T. 38,432 (56.88%) Lab. hold
David Heyes, Lab. 18,604
Seema Kennedy, C. 9,510
Paul Larkin, LD 5,703
David Lomas, BNP 2,929
Angela McManus, UKIP 1,686
Lab. majority 9,094 (23.66%)
Notional 7.34% swing Lab. to C.
(2005: Lab. majority 13,199 (38.33%))

§AYLESBURY
E. 77,934 T. 53,162 (68.21%) C. hold
David Lidington, C. 27,736
Steven Lambert, LD 15,118
Kathryn White, Lab. 6,695
Chris Adams, UKIP 3,613
C. majority 12,618 (23.73%)
Notional 2.12% swing LD to C.
(2005: C. majority 9,314 (19.49%))

§BANBURY
E. 86,986 T. 56,241 (64.66%) C. hold
Tony Baldry, C. 29,703
David Rundle, LD 11,476
Les Sibley, Lab. 10,773
Dr David Fairweather, UKIP 2,806
Alastair White, Green 959
Roseanne Edwards, Ind. 524
C. majority 18,227 (32.41%)
Notional 1.51% swing LD to C.
(2005: C. majority 10,090 (18.79%))

§BARKING
E. 73,864 T. 45,343 (61.39%) Lab. hold
Margaret Hodge, Lab. 24,628
Simon Marcus, C. 8,073
Nick Griffin, BNP 6,620
Dominic Carman, LD 3,719
Frank Maloney, UKIP 1,300
George Hargreaves, Ch. P. 482
Jayne Forbes, Green 317
Crucial Chris Dowling, Loony 82
Thomas Darwood, Ind. 77
Dapo Sijuwola, RP 45
Lab. majority 16,555 (36.51%)
Notional 1.73% swing C. to Lab.
(2005: Lab. majority 12,183 (33.04%))

§¶BARNSLEY CENTRAL
E. 65,543 T. 37,001 (56.45%) Lab. hold
Eric Illsley, Lab. 17,487
Christopher Wiggin, LD 6,394
Piers Tempest, C. 6,388
Ian Sutton, BNP 3,307
David Silver, UKIP 1,727
Donald Wood, Ind. 732
Tony Devoy, Ind. 610
Terry Robinson, Soc. Lab. 356
Lab. majority 11,093 (29.98%)
Notional 4.17% swing Lab. to LD
(2005: Lab. majority 11,839 (38.32%))

§BARNSLEY EAST
E. 68,435 T. 38,386 (56.09%) Lab. hold
*Michael Dugher, Lab. 18,059
John Brown, LD 6,969
James Hockney, C. 6,329
Colin Porter, BNP 3,301
Tony Watson, UKIP 1,731
Kevin Hogan, Ind. 712
Eddie Devoy, Ind. 684
Ken Capstick, Soc. Lab. 601
Lab. majority 11,090 (28.89%)
Notional 14.02% swing Lab. to LD
(2005: Lab. majority 18,298 (56.94%))

§BARROW & FURNESS
E. 68,758 T. 44,124 (64.17%) Lab. Co-op hold
*John Woodcock, Lab. Co-op 21,226
John Gough, C. 16,018
Barry Rabone, LD 4,424
John Smith, UKIP 841
Mike Ashburner, BNP 840
Christopher Loynes, Green 530
Brian Greaves, Ind. 245
Lab. Co-op majority 5,208 (11.80%)
Notional 0.37% swing Lab. to C.
(2005: Lab. Co-op majority 4,843 (12.54%))

§BASILDON & BILLERICAY
E. 65,482 T. 41,569 (63.48%) C. hold
John Baron, C. 21,922
Allan Davies, Lab. 9,584
Mike Hibbs, LD 6,538
Irene Bateman, BNP 1,934
Alan Broad, UKIP 1,591
C. majority 12,338 (29.68%)
Notional 9.23% swing Lab. to C.
(2005: C. majority 4,559 (11.22%))

§BASILDON SOUTH & THURROCK EAST
E. 71,815 T. 44,735 (62.29%) C. gain
*Stephen Metcalfe, C. 19,624
Angela Smith, Lab. Co-op 13,852
Geoff Williams, LD 5,977
Kerry Smith, UKIP 2,639
Chris Roberts, BNP 2,518
None Of The Above X, ND 125
C. majority 5,772 (12.90%)
Notional 7.52% swing Lab. to C.
(2005: Lab. majority 905 (2.14%))

§BASINGSTOKE
E. 75,470 T. 50,654 (67.12%) C. hold
Maria Miller, C. 25,590
John Shaw, LD 12,414
Funda Pepperell, Lab. 10,327
Stella Howell, UKIP 2,076
Steve Saul, BCP 247
C. majority 13,176 (26.01%)
Notional 4.55% swing LD to C.
(2005: C. majority 2,651 (6.27%))

§BASSETLAW
E. 76,542 T. 49,577 (64.77%) Lab. hold
John Mann, Lab. 25,018
Keith Girling, C. 16,803
David Dobbie, LD 5,570
Andrea Hamilton, UKIP 1,779
Grahame Whithurst, Ind. 407
Lab. majority 8,215 (16.57%)
Notional 0.67% swing Lab. to C.
(2005: Lab. majority 8,256 (17.92%))

§BATH
E. 65,603 T. 47,086 (71.77%) LD hold
Don Foster, LD 26,651
Fabian Richter, C. 14,768
Hattie Ajderian, Lab. 3,251
Eric Lucas, Green 1,120
Ernie Warrender, UKIP 890
Steve Hewett, Ch. P. 250
ANON, ND 69
Sean Geddis, Ind. 56
Robert Craig, South 31
LD majority 11,883 (25.24%)
Notional 5.84% swing C. to LD
(2005: LD majority 5,624 (13.56%))

§BATLEY & SPEN
E. 76,732 T. 51,109 (66.61%) Lab. hold
Mike Wood, Lab. 21,565
Janice Small, C. 17,159
Neil Bentley, LD 8,095
David Exley, BNP 3,685
Matt Blakeley, Green 605
Lab. majority 4,406 (8.62%)
Notional 2.46% swing Lab. to C.
(2005: Lab. majority 6,060 (13.54%))

§BATTERSEA
E. 74,300 T. 48,792 (65.67%) C. gain
*Jane Ellison, C. 23,103
Martin Linton, Lab. 17,126
Layla Moran, LD 7,176
Guy Evans, Green 559
Christopher MacDonald, UKIP 505
Hugh Salmon, Battersea 168
Tom Fox, Ind. 155
C. majority 5,977 (12.25%)
Notional 6.53% swing Lab. to C.
(2005: Lab. majority 332 (0.81%))

§BEACONSFIELD
E. 74,982 T. 52,490 (70.00%) C. hold
Dominic Grieve, C. 32,053
John Edwards, LD 10,271
Jeremy Miles, Lab. 6,135
Delphine Gray-Fisk, UKIP 2,597
Jem Bailey, Green 768
Andrew Cowen, MP Expense 475
Quentin Baron, Ind. 191
C. majority 21,782 (41.50%)
Notional 4.70% swing LD to C.
(2005: C. majority 14,794 (32.09%))

§BECKENHAM
E. 66,219 T. 47,686 (72.01%) C. hold
*Bob Stewart, C. 27,597
Steve Jenkins, LD 9,813
Damien Egan, Lab. 6,893
Owen Brolly, UKIP 1,551
Roger Tonks, BNP 1,001
Ann Garrett, Green 608
Dan Eastgate, Eng. Dem. 223
C. majority 17,784 (37.29%)
Notional 3.15% swing C. to LD
(2005: C. majority 16,913 (40.40%))

§BEDFORD
E. 68,491 T. 45,102 (65.85%) C. gain
*Richard Fuller, C. 17,546
Patrick Hall, Lab. 16,193
Henry Vann, LD 8,957
Mark Adkin, UKIP 1,136
William Dewick, BNP 757
Ben Foley, Green 393
Samrat Bhandari, Ind. 120
C. majority 1,353 (3.00%)
Notional 5.52% swing Lab. to C.
(2005: Lab. majority 3,413 (8.04%))

§BEDFORDSHIRE MID
E. 76,023 T. 54,897 (72.21%) C. hold
Nadine Dorries, C. 28,815
Linda Jack, LD 13,663
David Reeves, Lab. 8,108
Bill Hall, UKIP 2,826
Malcolm Bailey, Green 773
John Cooper, Eng. Dem. 712
C. majority 15,152 (27.60%)
Notional 2.26% swing LD to C.
(2005: C. majority 11,593 (23.08%))

§BEDFORDSHIRE NORTH EAST
E. 78,060 T. 55,552 (71.17%) C. hold
Alistair Burt, C. 30,989
Mike Pitt, LD 12,047
Edward Brown, Lab. 8,957
Brian Capell, UKIP 2,294
Ian Seeby, BNP 1,265
C. majority 18,942 (34.10%)
Notional 2.55% swing LD to C.
(2005: C. majority 12,128 (24.59%))

BEDFORDSHIRE SOUTH WEST
E. 76,559 T. 50,774 (66.32%) C. hold
Andrew Selous, C. 26,815
Rod Cantrill, LD 10,166
Jennifer Bone, Lab. 9,948
Martin Newman, UKIP 2,142
Mark Tolman, BNP 1,703
C. majority 16,649 (32.79%)
0.69% swing LD to C.
(2005: C. majority 8,277 (18.07%))

§BERMONDSEY & OLD SOUTHWARK
E. 77,623 T. 44,651 (57.52%) LD hold
Simon Hughes, LD 21,590
Val Shawcross, Lab. 13,060
Loanna Morrison, C. 7,638
Stephen Tyler, BNP 1,370
Tom Chance, Green 718
Alan Kirkby, Ind. 155
Steve Freeman, ND 120
LD majority 8,530 (19.10%)
Notional 1.55% swing Lab. to LD
(2005: LD majority 5,769 (16.00%))

§BERWICK-UPON-TWEED
E. 57,403 T. 38,439 (66.96%) LD hold
Sir Alan Beith, LD 16,806
Anne-Marie Trevelyan, C. 14,116
Alan Strickland, Lab. 5,061
Michael Weatheritt, UKIP 1,243
Peter Mailer, BNP 1,213
LD majority 2,690 (7.00%)
Notional 8.29% swing LD to C.
(2005: LD majority 8,585 (23.58%))

§BETHNAL GREEN & BOW
E. 81,243 T. 50,728 (62.44%) Lab. gain
*Rushanara Ali, Lab. 21,784
Ajmal Masroor, LD 10,210
Abjol Miah, Respect 8,532
Zakir Khan, C. 7,071
Jeffrey Marshall, BNP 1,405
Farid Bakht, Green 856
Patrick Brooks, Ind. 277
Alexander Van Terheyden, Pirate 213
Hasib Hikmat, Voice 209
Haji Choudhury, Ind. 100
Ahmed Malik, Ind. 71
Lab. majority 11,574 (22.82%)
Notional 14.11% swing Respect to Lab.
(2005: Respect majority 804 (2.10%))

§BEVERLEY & HOLDERNESS
E. 79,611 T. 53,199 (66.82%) C. hold
Graham Stuart, C. 25,063
Craig Dobson, LD 12,076
Ian Saunders, Lab. 11,224
Neil Whitelam, BNP 2,080
Andrew Horsfield, UKIP 1,845
Bill Rigby, Green 686
Ron Hughes, Ind. 225
C. majority 12,987 (24.41%)
Notional 1.58% swing LD to C.
(2005: C. majority 3,097 (6.23%))

§BEXHILL & BATTLE
E. 79,208 T. 54,587 (68.92%) C. hold
Greg Barker, C. 28,147
Mary Varrall, LD 15,267
James Royston, Lab. 6,524
Stuart Wheeler, Trust 2,699
Neil Jackson, BNP 1,950
C. majority 12,880 (23.60%)
Notional 3.96% swing C. to LD
(2005: C. majority 15,893 (31.52%))

§BEXLEYHEATH & CRAYFORD
E. 64,985 T. 43,182 (66.45%) C. hold
David Evennett, C. 21,794
Howard Dawber, Lab. 11,450
Karelia Scott, LD 5,502
Stephen James, BNP 2,042
John Dunford, UKIP 1,557
John Griffiths, Eng. Dem. 466
Adrian Ross, Green 371
C. majority 10,344 (23.95%)
Notional 5.81% swing Lab. to C.
(2005: C. majority 5,167 (12.33%))

§BIRKENHEAD
E. 62,773 T. 35,323 (56.27%) Lab. hold
Frank Field, Lab. 22,082
Andrew Gilbert, C. 6,687
Stuart Kelly, LD 6,554
Lab. majority 15,395 (43.58%)
Notional 2.34% swing Lab. to C.
(2005: Lab. majority 14,638 (46.21%))

§BIRMINGHAM EDGBASTON
E. 68,573 T. 41,571 (60.62%) Lab. hold
Gisela Stuart, Lab. 16,894
Deirdre Alden, C. 15,620
Roger Harmer, LD 6,387
Trevor Lloyd, BNP 1,196
Greville Warwick, UKIP 732
Phil Simpson, Green 469
Harry Takhar, Impact 146
Charith Fernando, Ch. P. 127
Lab. majority 1,274 (3.06%)
Notional 0.47% swing Lab. to C.
(2005: Lab. majority 1,555 (4.01%))

§BIRMINGHAM ERDINGTON
E. 66,405 T. 35,546 (53.53%) Lab. hold
*Jack Dromey, Lab. 14,869
Robert Alden, C. 11,592
Ann Holtom, LD 5,742
Kevin McHugh, BNP 1,815
Maria Foy, UKIP 842
Tony Tomkins, Ind. 240
Terry Williams, NF 229
Timothy Gray, Ch. P. 217
Lab. majority 3,277 (9.22%)
Notional 10.43% swing Lab. to C.
(2005: Lab. majority 9,677 (30.07%))

§BIRMINGHAM HALL GREEN
E. 76,580 T. 48,727 (63.63%) Lab. hold
Roger Godsiff, Lab. 16,039
Salma Yaqoob, Respect 12,240
Jerry Evans, LD 11,988
Jo Barker, C. 7,320
Alan Blumenthal, UKIP 950
Andrew Gardner, Ind. 190
Lab. majority 3,799 (7.80%)
Notional 11.07% swing Lab. to Respect
(2005: Lab. majority 6,649 (15.90%))

§BIRMINGHAM HODGE HILL
E. 75,040 T. 42,472 (56.60%) Lab. hold
Liam Byrne, Lab. 22,077
Tariq Khan, LD 11,775
Shailesh Parekh, C. 4,936
Richard Lumby, BNP 2,333
Waheed Rafiq, UKIP 714
Peter Johnson, Soc. Dem. 637
Lab. majority 10,302 (24.26%)
Notional 3.61% swing LD to Lab.
(2005: Lab. majority 7,063 (17.05%))

§BIRMINGHAM LADYWOOD
E. 73,646 T. 35,833 (48.66%) Lab. hold
*Shabana Mahmood, Lab. 19,950
Ayoub Khan, LD 9,845
Nusrat Ghani, C. 4,277
Christopher Booth, UKIP 902
Peter Beck, Green 859
Lab. majority 10,105 (28.20%)
Notional 2.49% swing LD to Lab.
(2005: Lab. majority 6,804 (23.23%))

§BIRMINGHAM NORTHFIELD
E. 71,338 T. 41,814 (58.61%) Lab. hold
Richard Burden, Lab. 16,841
Keely Huxtable, C. 14,059
Mike Dixon, LD 6,550
Les Orton, BNP 2,290
John Borthwick, UKIP 1,363
Susan Pearce, Green 406
Dick Rodgers, Good 305
Lab. majority 2,782 (6.65%)
Notional 6.64% swing Lab. to C.
(2005: Lab. majority 7,879 (19.93%))

§BIRMINGHAM PERRY BARR
E. 71,304 T. 42,045 (58.97%) Lab. hold
Khalid Mahmood, Lab. 21,142
Karen Hamilton, LD 9,234
William Norton, C. 8,960
Melvin Ward, UKIP 1,675
John Tyrrell, Soc. Lab. 527
Deborah Hey-Smith, Ch. P. 507
Lab. majority 11,908 (28.32%)
Notional 4.05% swing LD to Lab.
(2005: Lab. majority 7,825 (20.22%))

§BIRMINGHAM SELLY OAK
E. 74,805 T. 46,563 (62.25%) Lab. hold
Steve McCabe, Lab. 17,950
Nigel Dawkins, C. 14,468
David Radcliffe, LD 10,371
Lynette Orton, BNP 1,820
Jeffrey Burgess, UKIP 1,131
James Burn, Green 664
Samuel Leeds, Ch. P. 159
Lab. majority 3,482 (7.48%)
Notional 4.83% swing Lab. to C.
(2005: Lab. majority 7,564 (17.14%))

§BIRMINGHAM YARDLEY
E. 72,321 T. 40,850 (56.48%) LD hold
John Hemming, LD 16,162
Lynnette Kelly, Lab. 13,160
Meirion Jenkins, C. 7,836
Tanya Lumby, BNP 2,153
Graham Duffen, UKIP 1,190
Paul Morris, NF 349
LD majority 3,002 (7.35%)
Notional 0.02% swing Lab. to LD
(2005: LD majority 2,864 (7.30%))

§BISHOP AUCKLAND
E. 68,370 T. 41,136 (60.17%) Lab. hold
Helen Goodman, Lab. 16,023
Barbara Harrison, C. 10,805
Mark Wilkes, LD 9,189
Adam Walker, BNP 2,036
Sam Zair, LLPBPP 1,964
Dave Brothers, UKIP 1,119
Lab. majority 5,218 (12.68%)
Notional 7.20% swing Lab. to C.
(2005: Lab. majority 10,047 (26.35%))

§BLACKBURN
E. 72,331 T. 45,499 (62.90%) Lab. hold
Jack Straw, Lab. 21,751
Michael Law-Riding, C. 11,895
Paul English, LD 6,918
Robin Evans, BNP 2,158
Bushra Irfanullah, BIB 1,424
Bobby Anwar, UKIP 942
Grace Astley, Ind. 238
Janis Sharp, Ind. 173
Lab. majority 9,856 (21.66%)
Notional 1.11% swing C. to Lab.
(2005: Lab. majority 8,048 (19.45%))

§BLACKLEY & BROUGHTON
E. 69,489 T. 34,204 (49.22%) Lab. hold
Graham Stringer, Lab. 18,563
James Edsberg, C. 6,260
William Hobhouse, LD 4,861
Derek Adams, BNP 2,469
Kay Phillips, Respect 996
Bob Willescroft, UKIP 894
Shafiq-Uz Zaman, Ch. P. 161
Lab. majority 12,303 (35.97%)
Notional 6.74% swing Lab. to C.
(2005: Lab. majority 13,060 (43.35%))

§BLACKPOOL NORTH & CLEVELEYS
E. 65,888 T. 40,591 (61.61%) C. gain
*Paul Maynard, C. 16,964
Penny Martin, Lab. 14,814
Bill Greene, LD 5,400
Roy Hopwood, UKIP 1,659
James Clayton, BNP 1,556
Tony Davies, Loony 198
C. majority 2,150 (5.30%)
Notional 6.89% swing Lab. to C.
(2005: Lab. majority 3,241 (8.48%))

§BLACKPOOL SOUTH
E. 63,025 T. 35,191 (55.84%) Lab. hold
Gordon Marsden, Lab. 14,448
Ron Bell, C. 12,597
Doreen Holt, LD 5,082
Roy Goodwin, BNP 1,482
Hamish Howitt, UKIP 1,352
Si Thu Tun, Integrity 230
Lab. majority 1,851 (5.26%)
Notional 6.21% swing Lab. to C.
(2005: Lab. majority 5,911 (17.67%))

§BLAYDON
E. 67,808 T. 44,913 (66.24%) Lab. hold
Dave Anderson, Lab. 22,297
Neil Bradbury, LD 13,180
Glenn Hall, C. 7,159
Keith McFarlane, BNP 2,277
Lab. majority 9,117 (20.30%)
Notional 3.28% swing LD to Lab.
(2005: Lab. majority 5,748 (13.75%))

BLYTH VALLEY
E. 64,263 T. 38,566 (60.01%) Lab. hold
Ronnie Campbell, Lab. 17,156
Jeffrey Reid, LD 10,488
Barry Flux, C. 6,412
Steve Fairbairn, BNP 1,699
James Condon, UKIP 1,665
Barry Elliott, Ind. 819
Allan White, Eng. Dem. 327
Lab. majority 6,668 (17.29%)
3.27% swing Lab. to LD
(2005: Lab. majority 8,527 (23.84%))

§BOGNOR REGIS & LITTLEHAMPTON
E. 70,812 T. 46,852 (66.16%) C. hold
Nick Gibb, C. 24,087
Simon McDougall, LD 11,024
Michael Jones, Lab. 6,580
Douglas Denny, UKIP 3,036
Andrew Moffat, BNP 1,890
Melissa Briggs, Ind. 235
C. majority 13,063 (27.88%)
Notional 2.31% swing LD to C.
(2005: C. majority 8,617 (20.15%))

§BOLSOVER
E. 72,766 T. 43,988 (60.45%) Lab. hold
Dennis Skinner, Lab. 21,994
Lee Rowley, C. 10,812
Denise Hawksworth, LD 6,821
Martin Radford, BNP 2,640
Ray Calladine, UKIP 1,721
Lab. majority 11,182 (25.42%)
Notional 11.23% swing Lab. to C.
(2005: Lab. majority 19,260 (47.68%))

§BOLTON NORTH EAST
E. 67,281 T. 43,277 (64.32%) Lab. hold
David Crausby, Lab. 19,870
Deborah Dunleavy, C. 15,786
Paul Ankers, LD 5,624
Neil Johnson, UKIP 1,815
Norma Armston, You 182
Lab. majority 4,084 (9.44%)
Notional 1.27% swing Lab. to C.
(2005: Lab. majority 4,527 (11.99%))

§BOLTON SOUTH EAST
E. 69,928 T. 39,604 (56.64%) Lab. hold
*Yasmin Qureshi, Lab. 18,782
Andy Morgan, C. 10,148
Donal O'Hanlon, LD 6,289
Sheila Spink, BNP 2,012
Ian Sidaway, UKIP 1,564
Alan Johnson, Green 614
Navaid Syed, CPA 195
Lab. majority 8,634 (21.80%)
Notional 5.61% swing Lab. to C.
(2005: Lab. majority 11,483 (33.03%))

§BOLTON WEST
E. 71,250 T. 47,576 (66.77%) Lab. hold
*Julie Hilling, Lab. 18,327
Susan Williams, C. 18,235
Jackie Pearcey, LD 8,177
Harry Lamb, UKIP 1,901
Rachel Mann, Green 545
Jimmy Jones, Ind. 254
Doug Bagnall, You 137
Lab. majority 92 (0.19%)
Notional 5.88% swing Lab. to C.
(2005: Lab. majority 5,041 (11.95%))

§BOOTLE
E. 71,426 T. 41,277 (57.79%) Lab. hold
Joe Benton, Lab. 27,426
James Murray, LD 6,245
Sohail Qureshi, C. 3,678
Paul Nuttall, UKIP 2,514
Charles Stewart, BNP 942
Pete Glover, TUSC 472
Lab. majority 21,181 (51.31%)
Notional 1.59% swing Lab. to LD
(2005: Lab. majority 20,125 (54.48%))

§BOSTON & SKEGNESS
E. 70,529 T. 43,125 (61.15%) C. hold
Mark Simmonds, C. 21,325
Paul Kenny, Lab. 8,899
Philip Smith, LD 6,371
Christopher Pain, UKIP 4,081
David Owens, BNP 2,278
Peter Wilson, Ind. 171
C. majority 12,426 (28.81%)
Notional 7.00% swing Lab. to C.
(2005: C. majority 6,391 (14.81%))

§BOSWORTH
E. 77,296 T. 54,274 (70.22%) C. hold
David Tredinnick, C. 23,132
Michael Mullaney, LD 18,100
Rory Palmer, Lab. 8,674
John Ryde, BNP 2,458
Dutch Veldhuizen, UKIP 1,098
James Lampitt, Eng. Dem. 615
Michael Brooks, Science 197
C. majority 5,032 (9.27%)
Notional 5.87% swing C. to LD
(2005: C. majority 5,335 (10.72%))

§BOURNEMOUTH EAST
E. 71,125 T. 44,024 (61.90%) C. hold
Tobias Ellwood, C. 21,320
Lisa Northover, LD 13,592
David Stokes, Lab. 5,836
David Hughes, UKIP 3,027
Steven Humphrey, Ind. 249
C. majority 7,728 (17.55%)
Notional 1.76% swing LD to C.
(2005: C. majority 5,874 (14.04%))

§BOURNEMOUTH WEST
E. 71,753 T. 41,659 (58.06%) C. hold
*Conor Burns, C. 18,808
Alasdair Murray, LD 13,225
Sharon Carr-Brown, Lab. 6,171
Philip Glover, UKIP 2,999
Harvey Taylor, Ind. 456
C. majority 5,583 (13.40%)
Notional 2.92% swing LD to C.
(2005: C. majority 2,766 (7.55%))

§BRACKNELL
E. 76,885 T. 52,140 (67.82%) C. hold
*Phillip Lee, C. 27,327
Ray Earwicker, LD 11,623
John Piasecki, Lab. 8,755
Murray Barter, UKIP 2,297
Mark Burke, BNP 1,253
David Young, Green 825
Dan Haycocks, SMA 60
C. majority 15,704 (30.12%)
Notional 0.97% swing C. to LD
(2005: C. majority 10,037 (21.96%))

§BRADFORD EAST
E. 65,116 T. 40,457 (62.13%) LD gain
*David Ward, LD 13,637
Terry Rooney, Lab. 13,272
Mohammed Riaz, C. 10,860
Neville Poynton, BNP 1,854
Raja Hussain, Ind. 375
Peter Shields, Ind. 237
Gerry Robinson, NF 222
LD majority 365 (0.90%)
Notional 7.57% swing Lab. to LD
(2005: Lab. majority 5,227 (14.24%))

§BRADFORD SOUTH
E. 63,580 T. 37,995 (59.76%) Lab. hold
Gerry Sutcliffe, Lab. 15,682
Matt Palmer, C. 11,060
Alun Griffiths, LD 6,948
Sharon Sutton, BNP 2,651
Jamie Illingworth, UKIP 1,339
James Lewthwaite, D. Nat. 315
Lab. majority 4,622 (12.16%)
Notional 5.91% swing Lab. to C.
(2005: Lab. majority 8,444 (23.99%))

§¶BRADFORD WEST
E. 62,519 T. 40,576 (64.90%) Lab. hold
Marsha Singh, Lab. 18,401
Zahid Iqbal, C. 12,638
David Hall-Matthews, LD 4,732
Jenny Sampson, BNP 1,370
Arshad Ali, Respect 1,245
David Ford, Green 940
Jason Smith, UKIP 812
Neil Craig, D. Nat. 438
Lab. majority 5,763 (14.20%)
Notional 2.93% swing C. to Lab.
(2005: Lab. majority 3,050 (8.34%))

§BRAINTREE
E. 71,162 T. 49,203 (69.14%) C. hold
Brooks Newmark, C. 25,901
Bill Edwards, Lab. 9,780
Steve Jarvis, LD 9,247
Michael Ford, UKIP 2,477
Paul Hooks, BNP 1,080
Daisy Blench, Green 718
C. majority 16,121 (32.76%)
Notional 6.74% swing Lab. to C.
(2005: C. majority 8,658 (19.28%))

§BRENT CENTRAL
E. 74,076 T. 45,324 (61.19%) LD gain
Sarah Teather, LD 20,026
Dawn Butler, Lab. 18,681
Sachin Rajput, C. 5,068
Shahar Ali, Green 668
Errol Williams, Ch. P. 488
Abdi Duale, Respect 230
Dean McCastree, Ind. 163
LD majority 1,345 (2.97%)
Notional 10.99% swing Lab. to LD
(2005: Lab. majority 7,469 (19.02%))

§BRENT NORTH
E. 83,896 T. 52,298 (62.34%) Lab. hold
Barry Gardiner, Lab. 24,514
Harshadbhai Patel, C. 16,486
James Allie, LD 8,879
Atiq Malik, Ind. 734
Martin Francis, Green 725
Sunita Webb, UKIP 380
Jannen Vamadeva, Ind. 333
Arvind Tailor, Eng. Dem. 247
Lab. majority 8,028 (15.35%)
Notional 2.35% swing Lab. to C.
(2005: Lab. majority 8,830 (20.04%))

§BRENTFORD & ISLEWORTH
E. 83,546 T. 53,765 (64.35%) C. gain
*Mary Macleod, C. 20,022
Ann Keen, Lab. 18,064
Andrew Dakers, LD 12,718
Jason Hargreaves, UKIP 863
John Hunt, Green 787
Paul Winnet, BNP 704
David Cunningham, Eng. Dem. 230
Aamir Bhatti, Ch. P. 210
Evangeline Pillai, CPA 99
Teresa Vanneck-Surplice, Ind. 68
C. majority 1,958 (3.64%)
Notional 5.96% swing Lab. to C.
(2005: Lab. majority 3,633 (8.29%))

§BRENTWOOD & ONGAR
E. 73,224 T. 50,592 (69.09%) C. hold
Eric Pickles, C. 28,793
David Kendall, LD 11,872
Heidi Benzing, Lab. 4,992
Michael McGough, UKIP 2,037
Paul Morris, BNP 1,447
Jess Barnecutt, Green 584
Robin Tilbrook, Eng. Dem. 491
James Sapwell, Ind. 263
Danny Attfield, ND 113
C. majority 16,921 (33.45%)
Notional 3.12% swing LD to C.
(2005: C. majority 12,522 (27.21%))

§BRIDGWATER & SOMERSET WEST
E. 76,560 T. 54,493 (71.18%) C. hold
Ian Liddell-Grainger, C. 24,675
Theo Butt Philip, LD 15,426
Kathryn Pearce, Lab. 9,332
Peter Hollings, UKIP 2,604
Donna Treanor, BNP 1,282
Charles Graham, Green 859
Bob Cudlipp, Ind. 315
C. majority 9,249 (16.97%)
Notional 2.88% swing C. to LD
(2005: C. majority 10,081 (19.77%))

§BRIGG & GOOLE
E. 67,345 T. 43,874 (65.15%) C. gain
*Andrew Percy, C. 19,680
Ian Cawsey, Lab. 14,533
Richard Nixon, LD 6,414
Nigel Wright, UKIP 1,749
Stephen Ward, BNP 1,498
C. majority 5,147 (11.73%)
Notional 9.79% swing Lab. to C.
(2005: Lab. majority 3,217 (7.84%))

§BRIGHTON KEMPTOWN
E. 66,017 T. 42,705 (64.69%) C. gain
*Simon Kirby, C. 16,217
Simon Burgess, Lab. Co-op 14,889
Juliet Williams, LD 7,691
Ben Duncan, Green 2,330
James Chamberlain-Webber, UKIP 1,384
Dave Hill, TUSC 194
C. majority 1,328 (3.11%)
Notional 3.97% swing Lab. to C.
(2005: Lab. majority 1,853 (4.83%))

§BRIGHTON PAVILION
E. 74,004 T. 51,834 (70.04%) Green gain
*Dr Caroline Lucas, Green 16,238
Nancy Platts, Lab. 14,986
Charlotte Vere, C. 12,275
Bernadette Millam, LD 7,159
Nigel Carter, UKIP 948
Ian Fyvie, Soc. Lab. 148
Soraya Kara, R and E 61
Leo Atreides, ND 19
Green majority 1,252 (2.42%)
Notional 8.45% swing Lab. to Green
(2005: Lab. majority 5,867 (13.11%))

§BRISTOL EAST
E. 69,448 T. 45,017 (64.82%) Lab. hold
Kerry McCarthy, Lab. 16,471
Adeela Shafi, C. 12,749
Mike Popham, LD 10,993
Brian Jenkins, BNP 1,960
Philip Collins, UKIP 1,510
Glenn Vowles, Green 803
Stephen Wright, Eng. Dem. 347
Rae Lynch, TUSC 184
Lab. majority 3,722 (8.27%)
Notional 4.54% swing Lab. to C.
(2005: Lab. majority 7,335 (17.35%))

§BRISTOL NORTH WEST
E. 73,469 T. 50,336 (68.51%) C. gain
*Charlotte Leslie, C. 19,115
Paul Harrod, LD 15,841
Sam Townend, Lab. 13,059
Robert Upton, UKIP 1,175
Ray Carr, Eng. Dem. 635
Alex Dunn, Green 511
C. majority 3,274 (6.50%)
Notional 8.86% swing Lab. to C.
(2005: Lab. majority 2,781 (5.69%))

§BRISTOL SOUTH
E. 78,579 T. 48,377 (61.56%) Lab. hold
Dawn Primarolo, Lab. 18,600
Mark Wright, LD 13,866
Mark Lloyd Davies, C. 11,086
Colin Chidsey, BNP 1,739
Colin McNamee, UKIP 1,264
Charlie Bolton, Green 1,216
Craig Clarke, Eng. Dem. 400
Tom Baldwin, TUSC 206
Lab. majority 4,734 (9.79%)
Notional 7.53% swing Lab. to LD
(2005: Lab. majority 10,928 (24.86%))

§BRISTOL WEST
E. 82,728 T. 55,347 (66.90%) LD hold
Stephen Williams, LD 26,593
Paul Smith, Lab. 15,227
Nick Yarker, C. 10,169
Ricky Knight, Green 2,090
Chris Lees, UKIP 655
Danny Kushlick, Ind. 343
Jon Baker, Eng. Dem. 270
LD majority 11,366 (20.54%)
Notional 9.00% swing Lab. to LD
(2005: LD majority 1,147 (2.55%))

§BROADLAND
E. 73,168 T. 52,676 (71.99%) C. hold
Keith Simpson, C. 24,338
Daniel Roper, LD 17,046
Allyson Barron, Lab. 7,287
Stuart Agnew, UKIP 2,382
Edith Crowther, BNP 871
Susan Curran, Green 752
C. majority 7,292 (13.84%)
Notional 0.06% swing C. to LD
(2005: C. majority 6,573 (13.97%))

§BROMLEY & CHISLEHURST
E. 65,427 T. 44,037 (67.31%) C. hold
Bob Neill, C. 23,569
Sam Webber, LD 9,669
Chris Kirby, Lab. 7,295
Emmett Jenner, UKIP 1,451
Rowena Savage, BNP 1,070
Roisin Robertson, Green 607
Jon Cheeseman, Eng. Dem. 376
C. majority 13,900 (31.56%)
Notional 5.13% swing LD to C.
(2005: C. majority 8,236 (20.57%))

BROMSGROVE
E. 73,086 T. 51,630 (70.64%) C. hold
*Sajid Javid, C. 22,558
Sam Burden, Lab. 11,250
Philip Ling, LD 10,124
Steven Morson, UKIP 2,950
Adrian Kriss, BIC 2,182
Elizabeth Wainwright, BNP 1,923
Mark France, Ind. 336
Ken Wheatley, Ind. 307
C. majority 11,308 (21.90%)
0.41% swing Lab. to C.
(2005: C. majority 10,080 (21.08%))

BROXBOURNE
E. 71,391 T. 45,658 (63.95%) C. hold
Charles Walker, C. 26,844
Michael Watson, Lab. 8,040
Allan Witherick, LD 6,107
Steve McCole, BNP 2,159
Martin Harvey, UKIP 1,890
Debbie LeMay, Eng. Dem. 618
C. majority 18,804 (41.18%)
6.43% swing Lab. to C.
(2005: C. majority 11,509 (28.33%))

§BROXTOWE
E. 72,042 T. 52,727 (73.19%) C. gain
*Anna Soubry, C. 20,585
Nick Palmer, Lab. 20,196
David Watts, LD 8,907
Mike Shore, BNP 1,422
Chris Cobb, UKIP 1,194
David Mitchell, Green 423
C. majority 389 (0.74%)
Notional 2.59% swing Lab. to C.
(2005: Lab. majority 2,139 (4.44%))

§BUCKINGHAM
E. 74,996 T. 48,335 (64.45%)
Speaker hold
‡John Bercow, Speaker 22,860
John Stevens, Ind. 10,331
Nigel Farage, UKIP 8,401
Patrick Phillips, Ind. 2,394
Debbie Martin, Ind. 1,270
Lynne Mozar, BNP 980
Colin Dale, Loony 856
Geoff Howard, Ind. 435
David Hews, Ch. P. 369
Anthony Watts, Ind. 332
Simon Strutt, Deficit 107
Speaker majority 12,529 (25.92%)
(2005: C. majority 18,716 (37.83%))

BURNLEY
E. 66,616 T. 41,845 (62.82%) LD gain
*Gordon Birtwistle, LD 14,932
Julie Cooper, Lab. 13,114
Richard Ali, C. 6,950
Sharon Wilkinson, BNP 3,747
Andrew Brown, Ind. 1,876
John Wignall, UKIP 929
Andrew Hennessey, Ind. 297
LD majority 1,818 (4.34%)
9.58% swing Lab. to LD
(2005: Lab. majority 5,778 (14.82%))

§BURTON
E. 74,874 T. 49,823 (66.54%) C. gain
*Andrew Griffiths, C. 22,188
Ruth Smeeth, Lab. 15,884
Michael Rodgers, LD 7,891
Alan Hewitt, BNP 2,409
Philip Lancaster, UKIP 1,451
C. majority 6,304 (12.65%)
Notional 8.73% swing Lab. to C.
(2005: Lab. majority 2,132 (4.81%))

§BURY NORTH
E. 66,759 T. 44,961 (67.35%) C. gain
*David Nuttall, C. 18,070
Maryam Khan, Lab. 15,827
Richard Baum, LD 7,645
John Maude, BNP 1,825
Stephen Evans, UKIP 1,282
Bill Brison, Ind. 181
Graeme Lambert, Pirate 131
C. majority 2,243 (4.99%)
Notional 5.02% swing Lab. to C.
(2005: Lab. majority 2,059 (5.05%))

§BURY ST EDMUNDS
E. 84,727 T. 58,718 (69.30%) C. hold
David Ruffley, C. 27,899
David Chappell, LD 15,519
Kevin Hind, Lab. 9,776
John Howlett, UKIP 3,003
Mark Ereira-Guyer, Green 2,521
C. majority 12,380 (21.08%)
Notional 2.76% swing C. to LD
(2005: C. majority 10,080 (19.03%))

§BURY SOUTH
E. 73,544 T. 48,267 (65.63%) Lab. hold
Ivan Lewis, Lab. 19,508
Michelle Wiseman, C. 16,216
Vic D'Albert, LD 8,796
Jean Purdy, BNP 1,743
Paul Chadwick, UKIP 1,017
Valerie Morris, Eng. Dem. 494
George Heron, Green 493
Lab. majority 3,292 (6.82%)
Notional 8.01% swing Lab. to C.
(2005: Lab. majority 9,779 (22.84%))

§CALDER VALLEY
E. 76,903 T. 51,780 (67.33%) C. gain
*Craig Whittaker, C. 20,397
Steph Booth, Lab. 13,966
Hilary Myers, LD 13,037
John Gregory, BNP 1,823
Greg Burrows, UKIP 1,173
Kate Sweeny, Green 858
Tim Cole, Ind. 194
Barry Greenwood, Ind. 175
Paul Rogan, Eng. Dem. 157
C. majority 6,431 (12.42%)
Notional 7.58% swing Lab. to C.
(2005: Lab. majority 1,303 (2.73%))

§CAMBERWELL & PECKHAM
E. 78,618 T. 46,659 (59.35%) Lab. hold
Harriet Harman, Lab. 27,619
Columba Blango, LD 10,432
Andy Stranack, C. 6,080
Jenny Jones, Green 1,361
Yohara Robby Munilla, Eng. Dem. 435
Joshua Ogunleye, WRP 211
Margaret Sharkey, Soc. Lab. 184
Decima Francis, Ind. 93
Steven Robbins, Ind. 87
Patricia Knox, ND 82
Jill Mountford, Workers Lib 75
Lab. majority 17,187 (36.84%)
Notional 3.00% swing Lab. to LD
(2005: Lab. majority 16,608 (42.83%))

§CAMBORNE & REDRUTH
E. 63,968 T. 42,493 (66.43%) C. gain
*George Eustice, C. 15,969
Julia Goldsworthy, LD 15,903
Jude Robinson, Lab. 6,945
Derek Elliott, UKIP 2,152
Loveday Jenkin, Meb. Ker. 775
Euan McPhee, Green 581
Robert Hawkins, Soc. Lab. 168
C. majority 66 (0.16%)
Notional 5.21% swing LD to C.
(2005: LD majority 2,733 (7.08%))

§CAMBRIDGE
E. 77,081 T. 50,130 (65.04%) LD hold
*Julian Huppert, LD 19,621
Nick Hillman, C. 12,829
Daniel Zeichner, Lab. 12,174
Tony Juniper, Green 3,804
Peter Burkinshaw, UKIP 1,195
Martin Booth, TUSC 362
Holborn Old, Ind. 145
LD majority 6,792 (13.55%)
Notional 6.98% swing LD to C.
(2005: LD majority 5,834 (12.27%))

§CAMBRIDGESHIRE NORTH EAST
E. 73,224 T. 52,264 (71.38%) C. hold
*Stephen Barclay, C. 26,862
Lorna Spenceley, LD 10,437
Peter Roberts, Lab. 9,274
Robin Talbot, UKIP 2,991
Susan Clapp, BNP 1,747
Debra Jordan, Ind. 566
Graham Murphy, Eng. Dem. 387
C. majority 16,425 (31.43%)
Notional 0.79% swing LD to C.
(2005: C. majority 7,726 (16.30%))

§CAMBRIDGESHIRE NORTH WEST
E. 88,857 T. 58,283 (65.59%) C. hold
Shailesh Vara, C. 29,425
Kevin Wilkins, LD 12,748
Chris York, Lab. 9,877
Robert Brown, UKIP 4,826
Stephen Goldspink, Eng. Dem. 1,407
C. majority 16,677 (28.61%)
Notional 2.64% swing LD to C.
(2005: C. majority 10,925 (20.62%))

§CAMBRIDGESHIRE SOUTH
E. 78,995 T. 59,056 (74.76%) C. hold
Andrew Lansley, C. 27,995
Sebastian Kindersley, LD 20,157
Tariq Sadiq, Lab. 6,024
Robin Page, Ind. 1,968
Helene Davies-Green, UKIP 1,873
Simon Saggers, Green 1,039
C. majority 7,838 (13.27%)
Notional 2.46% swing C. to LD
(2005: C. majority 9,634 (18.20%))

§CAMBRIDGESHIRE SOUTH EAST
E. 83,068 T. 57,602 (69.34%) C. hold
Jim Paice, C. 27,629
Jonathan Chatfield, LD 21,683
John Cowan, Lab. 4,380
Andy Monk, UKIP 2,138
Simon Sedgwick-Jell, Green 766
Geoffrey Woollard, Ind. 517
Daniel Bell, CPA 489
C. majority 5,946 (10.32%)
Notional 2.67% swing C. to LD
(2005: C. majority 8,110 (15.66%))

§CANNOCK CHASE
E. 74,509 T. 45,559 (61.15%) C. gain
*Aidan Burley, C. 18,271
Susan Woodward, Lab. 15,076
Jon Hunt, LD 7,732
Terence Majorowicz, BNP 2,168
Malcolm McKenzie, UKIP 1,580
Ron Turville, Ind. 380
Royston Jenkins, Snouts 259
Mike Walters, Ind. 93
C. majority 3,195 (7.01%)
Notional 14.01% swing Lab. to C.
(2005: Lab. majority 8,726 (21.00%))

§CANTERBURY
E. 76,808 T. 49,209 (64.07%) C. hold
Julian Brazier, C. 22,050
Guy Voizey, LD 16,002
Jean Samuel, Lab. 7,940
Howard Farmer, UKIP 1,907
Geoff Meaden, Green 1,137
Anne Belsey, MRP 173
C. majority 6,048 (12.29%)
Notional 5.36% swing C. to LD
(2005: C. majority 7,579 (16.37%))

§CARLISLE
E. 65,263 T. 42,200 (64.66%) C. gain
*John Stevenson, C. 16,589
Michael Boaden, Lab. 15,736
Neil Hughes, LD 6,567
Paul Stafford, BNP 1,086
Michael Owen, UKIP 969
John Reardon, Green 614
John Metcalfe, TUSC 376
Peter Howe, ND 263
C. majority 853 (2.02%)
Notional 7.74% swing Lab. to C.
(2005: Lab. majority 5,085 (13.46%))

§CARSHALTON & WALLINGTON
E. 66,520 T. 45,918 (69.03%) LD hold
Tom Brake, LD 22,180
Dr Ken Andrew, C. 16,920
Shafi Khan, Lab. 4,015
Frank Day, UKIP 1,348
Charlotte Lewis, BNP 1,100
George Dow, Green 355
LD majority 5,260 (11.46%)
Notional 4.26% swing C. to LD
(2005: LD majority 1,225 (2.93%))

CASTLE POINT
E. 67,284 T. 45,026 (66.92%) C. gain
*Rebecca Harris, C. 19,806
Bob Spink, Green Belt 12,174
Julian Ware-Lane, Lab. 6,609
Brendan D'Cruz, LD 4,232
Philip Howell, BNP 2,205
C. majority 7,632 (16.95%)
(2005: C. majority 8,201 (17.91%))

§CHARNWOOD
E. 74,473 T. 53,542 (71.89%) C. hold
Stephen Dorrell, C. 26,560
Robin Webber-Jones, LD 11,531
Eric Goodyer, Lab. 10,536
Cathy Duffy, BNP 3,116
Miles Storier, UKIP 1,799
C. majority 15,029 (28.07%)
Notional 0.10% swing C. to LD
(2005: C. majority 8,613 (18.05%))

§CHATHAM & AYLESFORD
E. 71,122 T. 43,807 (61.59%) C. gain
*Tracey Crouch, C. 20,230
Jonathan Shaw, Lab. 14,161
John McClintock, LD 5,832
Colin McCarthy-Stewart, BNP 1,365
Steve Newton, UKIP 1,314
Sean Varnham, Eng. Dem. 400
Dave Arthur, Green 396
Maureen Smith, Ch. P. 109
C. majority 6,069 (13.85%)
Notional 11.05% swing Lab. to C.
(2005: Lab. majority 3,289 (8.25%))

§CHEADLE
E. 72,458 T. 52,512 (72.47%) LD hold
Mark Hunter, LD 24,717
Ben Jeffreys, C. 21,445
Martin Miller, Lab. 4,920
Tony Moore, UKIP 1,430
LD majority 3,272 (6.23%)
Notional 0.59% swing LD to C.
(2005: LD majority 3,672 (7.41%))

§CHELMSFORD
E. 77,529 T. 54,593 (70.42%) C. hold
Simon Burns, C. 25,207
Stephen Robinson, LD 20,097
Peter Dixon, Lab. 5,980
Ken Wedon, UKIP 1,527
Mike Bateman, BNP 899
Angela Thomson, Green 476
Claire Breed, Eng. Dem. 254
Ben Sherman, Beer 153
C. majority 5,110 (9.36%)
Notional 0.08% swing LD to C.
(2005: C. majority 4,358 (9.20%))

§CHELSEA & FULHAM
E. 66,295 T. 39,856 (60.12%) C. hold
Greg Hands, C. 24,093
Alexander Hilton, Lab. 7,371
Dirk Hazell, LD 6,473
Julia Stephenson, Green 671
Timothy Gittos, UKIP 478
Brian McDonald, BNP 388
Roland Courtenay, Ind. CCF 196
George Roseman, Eng. Dem. 169
Godfrey Spickernell, Blue 17
C. majority 16,722 (41.96%)
Notional 6.08% swing Lab. to C.
(2005: C. majority 10,253 (29.79%))

§CHELTENHAM
E. 78,998 T. 52,786 (66.82%) LD hold
Martin Horwood, LD 26,659
Mark Coote, C. 21,739
James Green, Lab. 2,703
Peter Bowman, UKIP 1,192
Dancing Ken Hanks, Loony 493
LD majority 4,920 (9.32%)
Notional 4.33% swing C. to LD
(2005: LD majority 316 (0.66%))

§CHESHAM & AMERSHAM
E. 70,333 T. 52,444 (74.57%) C. hold
Cheryl Gillan, C. 31,658
Tim Starkey, LD 14,948
Anthony Gajadharsingh, Lab. 2,942
Alan Stevens, UKIP 2,129
Nick Wilkins, Green 767
C. majority 16,710 (31.86%)
Notional 2.28% swing LD to C.
(2005: C. majority 12,974 (27.31%))

§CHESTER, CITY OF
E. 68,874 T. 46,790 (67.94%) C. gain
*Stephen Mosley, C. 18,995
Christine Russell, Lab. 16,412
Elizabeth Jewkes, LD 8,930
Allan Weddell, UKIP 1,225
Ed Abrams, Eng. Dem. 594
Tom Barker, Green 535
John Whittingham, Ind. 99
C. majority 2,583 (5.52%)
Notional 3.86% swing Lab. to C.
(2005: Lab. majority 973 (2.20%))

§CHESTERFIELD
E. 71,878 T. 45,839 (63.77%) Lab. gain
*Toby Perkins, Lab. 17,891
Paul Holmes, LD 17,342
Carolyn Abbott, C. 7,214
David Phillips, UKIP 1,432
Ian Jerram, Eng. Dem. 1,213
Duncan Kerr, Green 600
John Noneoftheabove Daramy, Ind. 147
Lab. majority 549 (1.20%)
Notional 3.78% swing LD to Lab.
(2005: LD majority 2,733 (6.36%))

§CHICHESTER
E. 81,462 T. 56,787 (69.71%) C. hold
Andrew Tyrie, C. 31,427
Martin Lury, LD 15,550
Simon Holland, Lab. 5,937
Andrew Moncrieff, UKIP 3,873
C. majority 15,877 (27.96%)
Notional 3.82% swing LD to C.
(2005: C. majority 10,457 (20.32%))

CHINGFORD & WOODFORD GREEN
E. 64,831 T. 43,106 (66.49%) C. hold
Iain Duncan Smith, C. 22,743
Cath Arakelian, Lab. 9,780
Geoffrey Seeff, LD 7,242
Julian Leppert, BNP 1,288
Nick Jones, UKIP 1,133
Lucy Craig, Green 650
None of The Above, Ind. 202
Barry White, Ind. 68
C. majority 12,963 (30.07%)
1.27% swing Lab. to C.
(2005: C. majority 10,641 (27.53%))

§CHIPPENHAM
E. 72,105 T. 52,385 (72.65%) LD hold
*Duncan Hames, LD 23,970
Wilfred Emmanuel-Jones, C. 21,500
Greg Lovell, Lab. 3,620
Julia Reid, UKIP 1,783
Michael Simpkins, BNP 641
Samantha Fletcher, Green 446
John Maguire, Eng. Dem. 307
Richard Sexton, Ch. P. 118
LD majority 2,470 (4.72%)
Notional 0.01% swing C. to LD
(2005: LD majority 2,183 (4.70%))

§CHIPPING BARNET
E. 77,798 T. 50,608 (65.05%) C. hold
Theresa Villiers, C. 24,700
Damien Welfare, Lab. 12,773
Stephen Barber, LD 10,202
James Fluss, UKIP 1,442
Kate Tansley, Green 1,021
Philip Clayton, Ind. 470
C. majority 11,927 (23.57%)
Notional 5.77% swing Lab. to C.
(2005: C. majority 5,457 (12.02%))

§CHORLEY
E. 70,950 T. 49,774 (70.15%) Lab. hold
Lindsay Hoyle, Lab. 21,515
Alan Cullens, C. 18,922
Stephen Fenn, LD 6,957
Nick Hogan, UKIP 2,021
Chris Curtis, Ind. 359
Lab. majority 2,593 (5.21%)
Notional 5.60% swing Lab. to C.
(2005: Lab. majority 7,285 (16.41%))

§CHRISTCHURCH
E. 68,861 T. 49,416 (71.76%) C. hold
Christopher Chope, C. 27,888
Martyn Hurll, LD 12,478
Robert Deeks, Lab. 4,849
David Williams, UKIP 4,201
C. majority 15,410 (31.18%)
Notional 0.05% swing C. to LD
(2005: C. majority 14,640 (31.28%))

§CITIES OF LONDON & WESTMINSTER
E. 66,489 T. 36,931 (55.54%) C. hold
Mark Field, C. 19,264
David Rowntree, Lab. 8,188
Naomi Smith, LD 7,574
Dr Derek Chase, Green 778
Paul Weston, UKIP 664
Frank Roseman, Eng. Dem. 191
Dennis Delderfield, Ind. 98
Jack Nunn, Pirate 90
Mad Cap'n Tom, Ind. 84
C. majority 11,076 (29.99%)
Notional 3.51% swing Lab. to C.
(2005: C. majority 7,352 (22.96%))

§CLACTON
E. 67,194 T. 43,123 (64.18%) C. hold
Douglas Carswell, C. 22,867
Ivan Henderson, Lab. 10,799
Michael Green, LD 5,577
Jim Taylor, BNP 1,975
Terry Allen, Tendring 1,078
Chris Southall, Green 535
Christopher Humphrey, Ind. 292
C. majority 12,068 (27.99%)
Notional 9.74% swing Lab. to C.
(2005: C. majority 3,629 (8.50%))

CLEETHORPES
E. 70,214 T. 44,966 (64.04%) C. gain
*Martin Vickers, C. 18,939
Shona McIsaac, Lab. 14,641
Malcolm Morland, LD 8,192
Stephen Harness, UKIP 3,194
C. majority 4,298 (9.56%)
7.81% swing Lab. to C.
(2005: Lab. majority 2,642 (6.06%))

§COLCHESTER
E. 74,062 T. 46,139 (62.30%) LD hold
Bob Russell, LD 22,151
Will Quince, C. 15,169
Jordan Newell, Lab. 5,680
John Pitts, UKIP 1,350
Sidney Chaney, BNP 705
Peter Lynn, Green 694
Eddie Bone, Eng. Dem. 335
Garryck Noble, PP Essex 35
Paul Shaw, ND 20
LD majority 6,982 (15.13%)
Notional 0.24% swing LD to C.
(2005: LD majority 6,388 (15.60%))

§COLNE VALLEY
E. 80,062 T. 55,296 (69.07%) C. gain
*Jason McCartney, C. 20,440
Nicola Turner, LD 15,603
Debbie Abrahams, Lab. 14,589
Barry Fowler, BNP 1,893
Melanie Roberts, UKIP 1,163
Chas Ball, Green 867
Dr Jackie Grunsell, TUSC 741
C. majority 4,837 (8.75%)
Notional 6.55% swing Lab. to C.
(2005: Lab. majority 1,267 (2.51%))

CONGLETON
E. 73,692 T. 50,780 (68.91%) C. hold
*Fiona Bruce, C. 23,250
Peter Hirst, LD 16,187
David Bryant, Lab. 8,747
Lee Slaughter, UKIP 2,147
Paul Edwards, Ind. 276
Paul Rothwell, ND 94
Adam Parton, Ind. 79
C. majority 7,063 (13.91%)
2.30% swing C. to LD
(2005: C. majority 8,246 (17.66%))

§COPELAND
E. 63,291 T. 42,787 (67.60%) Lab. hold
Jamie Reed, Lab. 19,699
Christopher Whiteside, C. 15,866
Frank Hollowell, LD 4,365
Clive Jefferson, BNP 1,474
Ted Caley-Knowles, UKIP 994
Jill Perry, Green 389
Lab. majority 3,833 (8.96%)
Notional 2.14% swing Lab. to C.
(2005: Lab. majority 5,157 (13.24%))

¶CORBY
E. 78,305 T. 54,236 (69.26%) C. gain
*Louise Bagshawe, C. 22,886
Phil Hope, Lab. 20,991
Portia Wilson, LD 7,834
Roy Davies, BNP 2,525
C. majority 1,895 (3.49%)
3.31% swing Lab. to C.
(2005: Lab. (Co-op) majority 1,517 (3.13%))

§CORNWALL NORTH
E. 68,662 T. 46,844 (68.22%) LD hold
Dan Rogerson, LD 22,512
Sian Flynn, C. 19,531
Miriel O'Connor, UKIP 2,300
Janet Hulme, Lab. 1,971
Joanie Willett, Meb. Ker. 530
LD majority 2,981 (6.36%)
Notional 0.25% swing LD to C.
(2005: LD majority 2,892 (6.87%))

§CORNWALL SOUTH EAST
E. 72,237 T. 49,617 (68.69%) C. gain
*Sheryll Murray, C. 22,390
Karen Gillard, LD 19,170
Michael Sparling, Lab. 3,507
Stephanie McWilliam, UKIP 3,083
Roger Creagh-Osborne, Green 826
Roger Holmes, Meb. Ker. 641
C. majority 3,220 (6.49%)
Notional 9.13% swing LD to C.
(2005: LD majority 5,485 (11.77%))

§COTSWOLDS, THE
E. 76,728 T. 54,832 (71.46%) C. hold
Geoffrey Clifton-Brown, C. 29,075
Mike Collins, LD 16,211
Mark Dempsey, Lab. 5,886
Adrian Blake, UKIP 2,292
Kevin Lister, Green 940
Alex Steel, Ind. 428
C. majority 12,864 (23.46%)
Notional 1.08% swing LD to C.
(2005: C. majority 10,742 (21.29%))

§COVENTRY NORTH EAST
E. 73,035 T. 43,383 (59.40%) Lab. hold
Bob Ainsworth, Lab. 21,384
Hazel Noonan, C. 9,609
Russell Field, LD 7,210
Tom Gower, BNP 1,863
Dave Nellist, Soc. Alt. 1,592
Chris Forbes, UKIP 1,291
Ron Lebar, Ch. M. 434
Lab. majority 11,775 (27.14%)
Notional 5.47% swing Lab. to C.
(2005: Lab. majority 14,621 (38.08%))

§COVENTRY NORTH WEST
E. 72,871 T. 46,560 (63.89%) Lab. hold
Geoffrey Robinson, Lab. 19,936
Gary Ridley, C. 13,648
Vincent McKee, LD 8,344
Edward Sheppard, BNP 1,666
Mark Nattrass, UKIP 1,295
John Clarke, Ind. 640
Justin Wood, Green 497
Nikki Downes, Soc. Alt. 370
William Sidhu, Ch. M. 164
Lab. majority 6,288 (13.51%)
Notional 3.92% swing Lab. to C.
(2005: Lab. majority 8,934 (21.35%))

§COVENTRY SOUTH
E. 73,652 T. 45,924 (62.35%) Lab. hold
Jim Cunningham, Lab. 19,197
Kevin Foster, C. 15,352
Brian Patton, LD 8,278
Mark Taylor, UKIP 1,767
Judy Griffiths, Soc. Alt. 691
Stephen Gray, Green 639
Lab. majority 3,845 (8.37%)
Notional 3.41% swing Lab. to C.
(2005: Lab. majority 6,237 (15.18%))

CRAWLEY
E. 72,781 T. 47,504 (65.27%) C. gain
*Henry Smith, C. 21,264
Chris Oxlade, Lab. 15,336
John Vincent, LD 6,844
Richard Trower, BNP 1,672
Chris French, UKIP 1,382
Phil Smith, Green 598
Arshad Khan, JP 265
Andrew Hubner, Ind. 143
C. majority 5,928 (12.48%)
6.28% swing Lab. to C.
(2005: Lab. majority 37 (0.09%))

§CREWE & NANTWICH
E. 77,460 T. 51,084 (65.95%) C. hold
Edward Timpson, C. 23,420
David Williams, Lab. 17,374
Roy Wood, LD 7,656
James Clutton, UKIP 1,414
Phil Williams, BNP 1,043
Mike Parsons, Ind. 177
C. majority 6,046 (11.84%)
Notional 13.67% swing Lab. to C.
(2005: Lab. majority 6,999 (15.50%))

§CROYDON CENTRAL
E. 78,880 T. 49,757 (63.08%) C. gain
*Gavin Barwell, C. 19,657
Gerry Ryan, Lab. (Co-op) 16,688
Peter Lambell, LD 6,553
Andrew Pelling, Ind. 3,239
Cliff Le May, BNP 1,448
Ralph Atkinson, UKIP 997
Bernice Golberg, Green 581
James Gitau, Ch. P. 264
John Cartwright, Loony 192
Michael Castle, Ind. 138
C. majority 2,969 (5.97%)
Notional 3.34% swing Lab. to C.
(2005: Lab. majority 328 (0.72%))

§¶CROYDON NORTH
E. 85,212 T. 51,678 (60.65%) Lab. hold
Malcolm Wicks, Lab. 28,949
Jason Hadden, C. 12,466
Gerry Jerome, LD 7,226
Shasha Khan, Green 1,017
Jonathan Serter, UKIP 891
Novlette Williams, Ch. P. 586
Mohommad Shaikh, Respect 272
Ben Stevenson, Comm. 160
Mohamed Seyed, Ind. 111
Lab. majority 16,483 (31.90%)
Notional 0.27% swing C. to Lab.
(2005: Lab. majority 14,185 (31.37%))

§CROYDON SOUTH
E. 81,301 T. 56,322 (69.28%) C. hold
Richard Ottaway, C. 28,684
Simon Rix, LD 12,866
Jane Avis, Lab. 11,287
Jeffrey Bolter, UKIP 2,504
Gordon Ross, Green 981
C. majority 15,818 (28.08%)
Notional 1.75% swing C. to LD
(2005: C. majority 14,228 (27.95%))

§DAGENHAM & RAINHAM
E. 69,764 T. 44,232 (63.40%) Lab. hold
Jon Cruddas, Lab. 17,813
Simon Jones, C. 15,183
Michael Barnbrook, BNP 4,952
Joseph Bourke, LD 3,806
Craig Litwin, UKIP 1,569
Gordon Kennedy, Ind. 308
Paula Watson, Ch. P. 305
Debbie Rosaman, Green 296
Lab. majority 2,630 (5.95%)
Notional 4.87% swing Lab. to C.
(2005: Lab. majority 6,372 (15.69%))

§DARLINGTON
E. 69,352 T. 42,896 (61.85%) Lab. hold
*Jenny Chapman, Lab. 16,891
Edward Legard, C. 13,503
Mike Barker, LD 10,046
Amanda Foster, BNP 1,262
Charlotte Bull, UKIP 1,194
Lab. majority 3,388 (7.90%)
Notional 9.14% swing Lab. to C.
(2005: Lab. majority 10,417 (26.18%))

§DARTFORD
E. 76,271 T. 50,080 (65.66%) C. gain
*Gareth Johnson, C. 24,428
John Adams, Lab. 13,800
James Willis, LD 7,361
Gary Rogers, Eng. Dem. 2,178
Richard Palmer, UKIP 1,842
Stephane Tindame, Ind. 264
John Crockford, FDP 207
C. majority 10,628 (21.22%)
Notional 11.56% swing Lab. to C.
(2005: Lab. majority 860 (1.90%))

§DAVENTRY
E. 71,451 T. 51,774 (72.46%) C. hold
*Chris Heaton-Harris, C. 29,252
Christopher McGlynn, LD 10,064
Paul Corazzo, Lab. 8,168
Jim Broomfield, UKIP 2,333
Alan Bennett-Spencer, Eng. Dem. 1,187
Steve Whiffen, Green 770
C. majority 19,188 (37.06%)
Notional 0.71% swing C. to LD
(2005: C. majority 11,776 (25.15%))

§DENTON & REDDISH
E. 64,765 T. 37,635 (58.11%) Lab. hold
Andrew Gwynne, Lab. 19,191
Julie Searle, C. 9,360
Stephen Broadhurst, LD 6,727
William Robinson, UKIP 2,060
Jeff Dennis, Ind. 297
Lab. majority 9,831 (26.12%)
Notional 6.25% swing Lab. to C.
(2005: Lab. majority 13,128 (38.62%))

§DERBY NORTH
E. 71,484 T. 45,080 (63.06%) Lab. hold
*Chris Williamson, Lab. 14,896
Stephen Mold, C. 14,283
Lucy Care, LD 12,638
Peter Cheeseman, BNP 2,000
Elizabeth Ransome, UKIP 829
David Gale, Ind. 264
David Geraghty, Pirate 170
Lab. majority 613 (1.36%)
Notional 7.39% swing Lab. to C.
(2005: Lab. majority 5,691 (14.58%))

§DERBY SOUTH
E. 71,012 T. 41,188 (58.00%) Lab. hold
Margaret Beckett, Lab. 17,851
Jack Perschke, C. 11,729
David Batey, LD 8,430
Stephen Fowke, UKIP 1,821
Alan Graves, Ind. 1,357
Lab. majority 6,122 (14.86%)
Notional 9.26% swing Lab. to C.
(2005: Lab. majority 11,655 (28.99%))

§DERBYSHIRE DALES
E. 63,367 T. 46,780 (73.82%) C. hold
Patrick McLoughlin, C. 24,378
Joe Naitta, LD 10,512
Colin Swindell, Lab. 9,061
Ian Guiver, UKIP 1,779
Josh Stockell, Green 772
Nick The Flying Brick Delves, Loony 228
Amila Y'mech, Humanity 50
C. majority 13,866 (29.64%)
Notional 3.74% swing LD to C.
(2005: C. majority 8,810 (20.82%))

§DERBYSHIRE MID
E. 66,297 T. 47,342 (71.41%) C. hold
*Pauline Latham, C. 22,877
Hardyal Dhindsa, Lab. 11,585
Sally McIntosh, LD 9,711
Lewis Allsebrook, BNP 1,698
Anthony Kay, UKIP 1,252
RU Seerius, Loony 219
C. majority 11,292 (23.85%)
Notional 5.66% swing Lab. to C.
(2005: C. majority 5,329 (12.54%))

§DERBYSHIRE NORTH EAST
E. 71,422 T. 47,034 (65.85%) Lab. hold
Natascha Engel, Lab. 17,948
Huw Merriman, C. 15,503
Richard Bull, LD 10,947
James Bush, UKIP 2,636
Lab. majority 2,445 (5.20%)
Notional 8.56% swing Lab. to C.
(2005: Lab. majority 9,564 (22.31%))

§DERBYSHIRE SOUTH
E. 70,610 T. 50,419 (71.40%) C. gain
*Heather Wheeler, C. 22,935
Michael Edwards, Lab. 15,807
Alexis Diouf, LD 8,012
Peter Jarvis, BNP 2,193
Charles Swabey, UKIP 1,206
Paul Liversuch, Soc. Lab. 266
C. majority 7,128 (14.14%)
Notional 9.80% swing Lab. to C.
(2005: Lab. majority 2,436 (5.45%))

§DEVIZES
E. 67,374 T. 46,340 (68.78%) C. hold
*Claire Perry, C. 25,519
Fiona Hornby, LD 12,514
Jurab Ali, Lab. 4,711
Patricia Bryant, UKIP 2,076
Mark Fletcher, Green 813
Martin Houlden, Ind. 566
Nic Coombe, Libertarian 141
C. majority 13,005 (28.06%)
Notional 0.33% swing C. to LD
(2005: C. majority 12,259 (28.63%))

§DEVON CENTRAL
E. 71,204 T. 53,873 (75.66%) C. hold
*Mel Stride, C. 27,737
Philip Hutty, LD 18,507
Moira Macdonald, Lab. 3,715
Bob Edwards, UKIP 2,870
Colin Mathews, Green 1,044
C. majority 9,230 (17.13%)
Notional 6.07% swing LD to C.
(2005: C. majority 2,338 (4.99%))

§DEVON EAST
E. 73,109 T. 53,092 (72.62%) C. hold
Hugo Swire, C. 25,662
Paull Robathan, LD 16,548
Gareth Manson, Lab. 5,721
Mike Amor, UKIP 4,346
Sharon Pavey, Green 815
C. majority 9,114 (17.17%)
Notional 1.03% swing C. to LD
(2005: C. majority 9,168 (19.23%))

§DEVON NORTH
E. 74,508 T. 51,321 (68.88%) LD hold
Nick Harvey, LD 24,305
Philip Milton, C. 18,484
Stephen Crowther, UKIP 3,720
Mark Cann, Lab. 2,671
L'Anne Knight, Green 697
Gary Marshall, BNP 614
Rodney Cann, Ind. 588
Nigel Vidler, Eng. Dem. 146
Gerrard Sables, Comm. Brit. 96
LD majority 5,821 (11.34%)
Notional 0.32% swing C. to LD
(2005: LD majority 5,276 (10.71%))

§DEVON SOUTH WEST
E. 70,059 T. 49,860 (71.17%) C. hold
Gary Streeter, C. 27,908
Anna Pascoe, LD 12,034
Luke Pollard, Lab. 6,193
Hugh Williams, UKIP 3,084
Vaughan Brean, Green 641
C. majority 15,874 (31.84%)
Notional 5.64% swing LD to C.
(2005: C. majority 9,442 (20.12%))

§DEVON WEST & TORRIDGE
E. 76,574 T. 55,257 (72.16%) C. hold
Geoffrey Cox, C. 25,230
Adam Symons, LD 22,273
Robin Julian, UKIP 3,021
Darren Jones, Lab. 2,917
Cathrine Simmons, Green 1,050
Nick Baker, BNP 766
C. majority 2,957 (5.35%)
Notional 0.01% swing C. to LD
(2005: C. majority 2,732 (5.37%))

§DEWSBURY
E. 78,901 T. 54,008 (68.45%) C. gain
*Simon Reevell, C. 18,898
Shahid Malik, Lab. 17,372
Andrew Hutchinson, LD 9,150
Khizar Iqbal, Ind. 3,813
Roger Roberts, BNP 3,265
Adrian Cruden, Green 849
Michael Felse, Eng. Dem. 661
C. majority 1,526 (2.83%)
Notional 5.85% swing Lab. to C.
(2005: Lab. majority 3,999 (8.88%))

§DON VALLEY
E. 73,214 T. 43,430 (59.32%) Lab. hold
Caroline Flint, Lab. 16,472
Matthew Stephens, C. 12,877
Edward Simpson, LD 7,422
Erwin Toseland, BNP 2,112
William Shaw, UKIP 1,904
Bernie Aston, Eng. Dem. 1,756
Martin Williams, Ind. 887
Lab. majority 3,595 (8.28%)
Notional 10.64% swing Lab. to C.
(2005: Lab. majority 11,333 (29.56%))

§DONCASTER CENTRAL
E. 75,207 T. 41,745 (55.51%) Lab. hold
Rosie Winterton, Lab. 16,569
Gareth Davies, C. 10,340
Patrick Wilson, LD 8,795
Lawrence Parramore, Eng. Dem. 1,816
John Bettney, BNP 1,762
Michael Andrews, UKIP 1,421
Scott Pickles, Ind. 970
Derek Williams, R and E 72
Lab. majority 6,229 (14.92%)
Notional 8.72% swing Lab. to C.
(2005: Lab. majority 10,325 (27.33%))

§DONCASTER NORTH
E. 72,381 T. 41,483 (57.31%) Lab. hold
Ed Miliband, Lab. 19,637
Sophie Brodie, C. 8,728
Edward Sanderson, LD 6,174
Pamela Chambers, BNP 2,818
Wayne Crawshaw, Eng. Dem. 2,148
Liz Andrews, UKIP 1,797
Bill Rawcliffe, TUSC
Lab. majority 10,909 (26.30%)
Notional 2.77% swing Lab. to C.
(2005: Lab. majority 12,027 (31.85%))

§DORSET MID & POOLE NORTH
E. 72,647 T. 46,788 (64.40%) LD hold
Annette Brooke, LD 21,100
Nick King, C. 20,831
Darren Brown, Lab. 2,748
Dave Evans, UKIP 2,109
LD majority 269 (0.57%)
Notional 6.27% swing LD to C.
(2005: LD majority 5,931 (13.12%))

§DORSET NORTH
E. 73,698 T. 54,141 (73.46%) C. hold
Bob Walter, C. 27,640
Emily Gasson, LD 20,015
Mike Bunney, Lab. 2,910
Jeremy Nieboer, UKIP 2,812
Anna Hayball, Green 546
Roger Monksummers, Loony 218
C. majority 7,625 (14.08%)
Notional 2.75% swing LD to C.
(2005: C. majority 4,200 (8.58%))

DORSET SOUTH
E. 73,838 T. 50,310 (68.14%) C. gain
*Richard Drax, C. 22,667
Jim Knight, Lab. 15,224
Ros Kayes, LD 9,557
Mike Hobson, UKIP 2,034
Brian Heatley, Green 595
Andy Kirkwood, YP 233
C. majority 7,443 (14.79%)
9.26% swing Lab. to C.
(2005: Lab. majority 1,812 (3.73%))

DORSET WEST
E. 76,869 T. 57,337 (74.59%) C. hold
Oliver Letwin, C. 27,287
Sue Farrant, LD 23,364
Dr Steve Bick, Lab. 3,815
Oliver Chisholm, UKIP 2,196
Susan Greene, Green 675
C. majority 3,923 (6.84%)
1.11% swing LD to C.
(2005: C. majority 2,461 (4.62%))

§DOVER
E. 71,832 T. 50,385 (70.14%) C. gain
*Charlie Elphicke, C. 22,174
Gwyn Prosser, Lab. 16,900
John Brigden, LD 7,962
Victor Matcham, UKIP 1,747
Dennis Whiting, BNP 1,104
Michael Walters, Eng. Dem. 216
David Clark, CPA 200
George Lee-Delisle, Ind. 82
C. majority 5,274 (10.47%)
Notional 10.43% swing Lab. to C.
(2005: Lab. majority 5,005 (10.40%))

§DUDLEY NORTH
E. 60,838 T. 38,602 (63.45%) Lab. hold
Ian Austin, Lab. 14,923
Graeme Brown, C. 14,274
Mike Beckett, LD 4,066
Malcolm Davis, UKIP 3,267
Ken Griffiths, BNP 1,899
Kevin Inman, NF 173
Lab. majority 649 (1.68%)
Notional 4.73% swing Lab. to C.
(2005: Lab. majority 4,106 (11.14%))

§DUDLEY SOUTH
E. 60,572 T. 38,165 (63.01%) C. gain
*Chris Kelly, C. 16,450
Rachel Harris, Lab. 12,594
Jonathan Bramall, LD 5,989
Philip Rowe, UKIP 3,132
C. majority 3,856 (10.10%)
Notional 9.51% swing Lab. to C.
(2005: Lab. majority 3,222 (8.91%))

§DULWICH & WEST NORWOOD
E. 72,817 T. 48,214 (66.21%) Lab. hold
Tessa Jowell, Lab. 22,461
Jonathan Mitchell, LD 13,096
Kemi Adegoke, C. 10,684
Shane Collins, Green 1,266
Elizabeth Jones, UKIP 707
Lab. majority 9,365 (19.42%)
Notional 0.84% swing Lab. to LD
(2005: Lab. majority 7,853 (19.75%))

DURHAM, CITY OF
E. 68,832 T. 46,252 (67.20%) Lab. hold
Roberta Blackman-Woods, Lab. 20,496
Carol Woods, LD 17,429
Nick Varley, C. 6,146
Ralph Musgrave, BNP 1,153
Nigel Coghill-Marshall, UKIP 856
Jonathan Collings, Ind. 172
Lab. majority 3,067 (6.63%)
0.37% swing Lab. to LD
(2005: Lab. majority 3,274 (7.38%))

§DURHAM NORTH
E. 67,548 T. 40,967 (60.65%) Lab. hold
Kevan Jones, Lab. 20,698
David Skelton, C. 8,622
Ian Lindley, LD 8,617
Pete Molloy, BNP 1,686
Bruce Reid, UKIP 1,344
Lab. majority 12,076 (29.48%)
Notional 8.93% swing Lab. to C.
(2005: Lab. majority 16,781 (44.94%))

§DURHAM NORTH WEST
E. 70,618 T. 43,815 (62.05%) Lab. hold
*Pat Glass, Lab. 18,539
Owen Temple, LD 10,927
Michelle Tempest, C. 8,766
Watts Stelling, Ind. 2,472
Michael Stewart, BNP 1,852
Andrew McDonald, UKIP 1,259
Lab. majority 7,612 (17.37%)
Notional 8.33% swing Lab. to LD
(2005: Lab. majority 13,443 (34.03%))

§EALING CENTRAL & ACTON
E. 63,489 T. 47,200 (74.34%) C. gain
*Angie Bray, C. 17,944
Bassam Mahfouz, Lab. 14,228
Jon Ball, LD 13,041
Julie Carter, UKIP 765
Sarah Edwards, Green 737
Suzanne Fernandes, Ch. P. 295
Sam Akaki, Ind. EACPS 190
C. majority 3,716 (7.87%)
Notional 5.02% swing Lab. to C.
(2005: Lab. majority 839 (2.16%))

§EALING NORTH
E. 67,902 T. 47,678 (70.22%) Lab. hold
Stephen Pound, Lab. 24,023
Ian Gibb, C. 14,722
Chris Lucas, LD 6,283
Dave Furness, BNP 1,045
Ian De Wulverton, UKIP 685
Christopher Warleigh-Lack, Green 505
Petar Ljubisic, Ch. P. 415
Lab. majority 9,301 (19.51%)
Notional 0.45% swing C. to Lab.
(2005: Lab. majority 8,126 (18.61%))

§EALING SOUTHALL
E. 60,379 T. 42,756 (70.81%) Lab. hold
Virendra Sharma, Lab. 22,024
Gurcharan Singh, C. 12,733
Nigel Bakhai, LD 6,383
Suneil Basu, Green 705
Mehboob Anil, Ch. P. 503
Sati Chaggar, Eng. Dem. 408
Lab. majority 9,291 (21.73%)
Notional 8.30% swing Lab. to C.
(2005: Lab. majority 13,140 (38.33%))

§EASINGTON
E. 63,873 T. 34,914 (54.66%) Lab. hold
*Grahame Morris, Lab. 20,579
Tara Saville, LD 5,597
Richard Harrison, C. 4,790
Cheryl Dunn, BNP 2,317
Martyn Aiken, UKIP 1,631
Lab. majority 14,982 (42.91%)
Notional 7.74% swing Lab. to LD
(2005: Lab. majority 18,874 (58.39%))

§EAST HAM
E. 90,675 T. 50,373 (55.55%) Lab. hold
Stephen Timms, Lab. 35,471
Paul Shea, C. 7,645
Chris Brice, LD 5,849
Barry O'Connor, Eng. Dem. 822
Judy Maciejowska, Green 586
Lab. majority 27,826 (55.24%)
Notional 7.71% swing C. to Lab.
(2005: Lab. majority 13,649 (33.08%))

§EASTBOURNE
E. 77,840 T. 52,124 (66.96%) LD gain
*Stephen Lloyd, LD 24,658
Nigel Waterson, C. 21,223
Dave Brinson, Lab. 2,497
Stephen Shing, Ind. 1,327
Roger Needham, UKIP 1,305
Colin Poulter, BNP 939
Michael Baldry, Ind. 101
Keith Gell, Ind. 74
LD majority 3,435 (6.59%)
Notional 4.00% swing C. to LD
(2005: C. majority 672 (1.41%))

§¶EASTLEIGH
E. 77,435 T. 53,650 (69.28%) LD hold
Chris Huhne, LD 24,966
Maria Hutchings, C. 21,102
Leo Barraclough, Lab. 5,153
Ray Finch, UKIP 1,933
Tony Stephen Pewsey, Eng. Dem. 249
Dave Stone, Ind. 154
Keith Low, Nat. Dem. 93
LD majority 3,864 (7.20%)
Notional 3.04% swing C. to LD
(2005: LD majority 534 (1.12%))

§EDDISBURY
E. 65,306 T. 45,414 (69.54%) C. hold
Stephen O'Brien, C. 23,472
Robert Thompson, LD 10,217
Pat Merrick, Lab. 9,794
Charles Dodman, UKIP 1,931
C. majority 13,255 (29.19%)
Notional 0.13% swing LD to C.
(2005: C. majority 6,408 (14.83%))

§EDMONTON
E. 63,902 T. 40,377 (63.19%)
Lab. (Co-op) hold
Andy Love, Lab. (Co-op) 21,665
Andrew Charalambous, C. 12,052
Iarla Kilbane-Dawe, LD 4,252
Roy Freshwater, UKIP 1,036
Jack Johnson, Green 516
Erol Basarik, Reform 379
Clive Morrison, Ch. P. 350
David Mclean, Ind. 127
Lab. (Co-op) majority 9,613 (23.81%)
Notional 2.26% swing Lab. (Co-op) to C.
(2005: Lab. (Co-op) majority 10,312 (28.33%))

§ELLESMERE PORT & NESTON
E. 63,097 T. 44,233 (70.10%) Lab. hold
Andrew Miller, Lab. 19,750
Stuart Penketh, C. 15,419
Denise Aspinall, LD 6,663
Henry Crocker, UKIP 1,619
Jonathan Starkey, Ind. 782
Lab. majority 4,331 (9.79%)
Notional 3.10% swing Lab. to C.
(2005: Lab. majority 6,713 (15.99%))

§ELMET & ROTHWELL
E. 77,724 T. 55,789 (71.78%) C. gain
*Alec Shelbrooke, C. 23,778
James Lewis, Lab. 19,257
Stewart Golton, LD 9,109
Sam Clayton, BNP 1,802
Darren Oddy, UKIP 1,593
Christopher Nolan, Ind. 250
C. majority 4,521 (8.10%)
Notional 9.77% swing Lab. to C.
(2005: Lab. majority 6,078 (11.43%))

§ELTHAM
E. 62,590 T. 41,964 (67.05%) Lab. hold
Clive Efford, Lab. 17,416
David Gold, C. 15,753
Steven Toole, LD 5,299
Roberta Woods, BNP 1,745
Ray Adams, UKIP 1,011
Arthur Hayles, Green 419
Mike Tibby, Eng. Dem. 217
Andrew Graham, Ind. 104
Lab. majority 1,663 (3.96%)
Notional 1.82% swing Lab. to C.
(2005: Lab. majority 2,904 (7.60%))

§ENFIELD NORTH
E. 66,258 T. 44,453 (67.09%) C. hold
*Nick de Bois, C. 18,804
Joan Ryan, Lab. 17,112
Paul Smith, LD 5,403
Tony Avery, BNP 1,228
Madge Jones, UKIP 938
Bill Linton, Green 489
Anthony Williams, Ch. P. 161
Raquel Weald, Eng. Dem. 131
Anna Athow, WRP 96
Gonul Daniels, Ind. 91
C. majority 1,692 (3.81%)
Notional 0.73% swing Lab. to C.
(2005: C. majority 937 (2.35%))

§ENFIELD SOUTHGATE
E. 64,138 T. 44,352 (69.15%) C. hold
David Burrowes, C. 21,928
Bambos Charalambous, Lab. 14,302
Johar Khan, LD 6,124
Peter Krakowiak, Green 632
Bob Brock, UKIP 505
Dr Asit Mukhopadhyay, Ind. 391
Samad Billoo, Respect 174
Ben Weald, Eng. Dem. 173
Mal Malakounides, ND 88
Jeremy Sturgess, BB 35
C. majority 7,626 (17.19%)
Notional 7.24% swing Lab. to C.
(2005: C. majority 1,127 (2.72%))

§EPPING FOREST
E. 72,198 T. 46,584 (64.52%) C. hold
Eleanor Laing, C. 25,148
Ann Haigh, LD 10,017
Katie Curtis, Lab. 6,641
Pat Richardson, BNP 1,982
Andrew Smith, UKIP 1,852
Simon Pepper, Green 659
Kim Sawyer, Eng. Dem. 285
C. majority 15,131 (32.48%)
Notional 1.08% swing C. to LD
(2005: C. majority 13,473 (31.33%))

§EPSOM & EWELL
E. 78,104 T. 54,955 (70.36%) C. hold
Chris Grayling, C. 30,868
Jonathan Lees, LD 14,734
Craig Montgomery, Lab. 6,538
Elizabeth Wallace, UKIP 2,549
Peter Ticher, RRG 266
C. majority 16,134 (29.36%)
Notional 2.05% swing C. to LD
(2005: C. majority 16,342 (33.47%))

§EREWASH
E. 69,654 T. 47,642 (68.40%) C. gain
*Jessica Lee, C. 18,805
Cheryl Pidgeon, Lab. 16,304
Martin Garnett, LD 8,343
Mark Bailey, BNP 2,337
Jodie Sutton, UKIP 855
Lee Fletcher, Green 534
Luke Wilkins, Ind. 464
C. majority 2,501 (5.25%)
Notional 10.45% swing Lab. to C.
(2005: Lab. majority 6,782 (15.66%))

§ERITH & THAMESMEAD
E. 69,918 T. 42,476 (60.75%) Lab. hold
*Teresa Pearce, Lab. 19,068
Colin Bloom, C. 13,365
Alexander Cunliffe, LD 5,116
Kevin Saunders, BNP 2,184
Pamela Perrin, UKIP 1,139
Laurence Williams, Eng. Dem. 465
Abbey Akinoshun, ND 438
Sid Cordle, CPA 379
Marek Powley, Green 322
Lab. majority 5,703 (13.43%)
Notional 6.34% swing Lab. to C.
(2005: Lab. majority 9,870 (26.11%))

ESHER & WALTON
E. 75,338 T. 54,543 (72.40%) C. hold
*Dominic Raab, C. 32,134
Lionel Blackman, LD 13,541
Francis Eldergill, Lab. 5,829
Bernard Collignon, UKIP 1,783
Tony Popham, Ind. 378
Chinners Chinnery, Loony 341
Mike Kearsley, Eng. Dem. 307
Andy Lear, Best 230
C. majority 18,593 (34.09%)
8.97% swing LD to C.
(2005: C. majority 7,727 (16.14%))

§EXETER
E. 77,157 T. 52,247 (67.72%) Lab. hold
Ben Bradshaw, Lab. 19,942
Hannah Foster, C. 17,221
Graham Oakes, LD 10,581
Keith Crawford, UKIP 1,930
Chris Gale, Lib. 1,108
Paula Black, Green 792
Robert Farmer, BNP 673
Lab. majority 2,721 (5.21%)
Notional 6.03% swing Lab. to C.
(2005: Lab. majority 8,559 (17.27%))

FAREHAM
E. 75,878 T. 54,345 (71.62%) C. hold
Mark Hoban, C. 30,037
Alex Bentley, LD 12,945
James Carr, Lab. 7,719
Steve Richards, UKIP 2,235
Peter Doggett, Green 791
Joe Jenkins, Eng. Dem. 618
C. majority 17,092 (31.45%)
1.73% swing LD to C.
(2005: C. majority 11,702 (24.09%))

§FAVERSHAM & KENT MID
E. 68,858 T. 46,712 (67.84%) C. hold
Hugh Robertson, C. 26,250
David Naghi, LD 9,162
Ash Rehal, Lab. 7,748
Sarah Larkins, UKIP 1,722
Tim Valentine, Green 890
Graham Kemp, NF 542
Hairy Knorm Davidson, Loony 398
C. majority 17,088 (36.58%)
Notional 1.62% swing LD to C.
(2005: C. majority 8,927 (21.00%))

§¶FELTHAM & HESTON
E. 81,058 T. 48,526 (59.87%)
Lab. (Co-op) hold
Alan Keen, Lab. (Co-op) 21,174
Mark Bowen, C. 16,516
Munira Wilson, LD 6,669
John Donnelly, BNP 1,714
Jerry Shadbolt, UKIP 992
Elizabeth Anstis, Green 530
Dharmendra Tripathi, Ind. 505
Asa Khaira, Ind. 180
Roger Williams, Ind. 168
Matthew Linley, WRP 78
Lab. (Co-op) majority 4,658 (9.60%)
Notional 4.83% swing Lab. (Co-op) to C.
(2005: Lab. (Co-op) majority 7,598 (19.25%))

§FILTON & BRADLEY STOKE
E. 69,003 T. 48,301 (70.00%) C. hold
*Jack Lopresti, C. 19,686
Ian Boulton, Lab. 12,772
Peter Tyzack, LD 12,197
John Knight, UKIP 1,506
David Scott, BNP 1,328
Jon Lucas, Green 441
Ruth Johnson, Ch. P. 199
Vote Zero None of the Above, ND 172
C. majority 6,914 (14.31%)
Notional 6.37% swing Lab. to C.
(2005: C. majority 653 (1.58%))

§FINCHLEY & GOLDERS GREEN
E. 77,198 T. 47,157 (61.09%) C. hold
*Mike Freer, C. 21,688
Alison Moore, Lab. 15,879
Laura Edge, LD 8,036
Susan Cummins, UKIP 817
Donald Lyven, Green 737
C. majority 5,809 (12.32%)
Notional 5.81% swing Lab. to C.
(2005: C. majority 294 (0.70%))

§FOLKESTONE & HYTHE
E. 78,003 T. 52,800 (67.69%) C. hold
*Damian Collins, C. 26,109
Lynne Beaumont, LD 15,987
Donald Worsley, Lab. 5,719
Frank McKenna, UKIP 2,439
Harry Williams, BNP 1,662
Penny Kemp, Green 637
David Plumstead, Ind. 247
C. majority 10,122 (19.17%)
Notional 2.58% swing C. to LD
(2005: C. majority 12,446 (24.33%))

FOREST OF DEAN
E. 68,419 T. 48,763 (71.27%) C. hold
Mark Harper, C. 22,853
Bruce Hogan, Lab. 11,789
Chris Coleman, LD 10,676
Tim Congdon, UKIP 2,522
James Greenwood, Green 923
C. majority 11,064 (22.69%)
9.19% swing Lab. to C.
(2005: C. majority 2,049 (4.30%))

§FYLDE
E. 65,917 T. 43,690 (66.28%) C. hold
*Mark Menzies, C. 22,826
Bill Winlow, LD 9,641
Liam Robinson, Lab. 8,624
Martin Bleeker, UKIP 1,945
Philip Mitchell, Green 654
C. majority 13,185 (30.18%)
Notional 4.15% swing C. to LD
(2005: C. majority 11,117 (28.67%))

§GAINSBOROUGH
E. 72,144 T. 49,251 (68.27%) C. hold
Edward Leigh, C. 24,266
Pat O'Connor, LD 13,707
Jamie McMahon, Lab. 7,701
Steve Pearson, UKIP 2,065
Malcolm Porter, BNP 1,512
C. majority 10,559 (21.44%)
Notional 1.80% swing LD to C.
(2005: C. majority 7,895 (17.73%))

§GARSTON & HALEWOOD
E. 71,312 T. 42,825 (60.05%) Lab. hold
Maria Eagle, Lab. 25,493
Paula Keaveney, LD 8,616
Richard Downey, C. 6,908
Tony Hammond, UKIP 1,540
Diana Raby, Respect 268
Lab. majority 16,877 (39.41%)
Notional 5.74% swing LD to Lab.
(2005: Lab. majority 10,814 (27.92%))

§GATESHEAD
E. 66,492 T. 38,257 (57.54%) Lab. hold
*Ian Mearns, Lab. 20,712
Frank Hindle, LD 8,163
Hazel Anderson, C. 5,716
Kevin Scott, BNP 1,787
John Tennant, UKIP 1,103
Andy Redfern, Green 379
Elaine Brunskill, TUSC 266
David Walton, Ch. P. 131
Lab. majority 12,549 (32.80%)
Notional 3.94% swing Lab. to LD
(2005: Lab. majority 14,245 (40.68%))

§GEDLING
E. 70,590 T. 48,190 (68.27%) Lab. hold
Vernon Coaker, Lab. 19,821
Bruce Laughton, C. 17,962
Julia Bateman, LD 7,350
Stephen Adcock, BNP 1,598
Dave Marshall, UKIP 1,459
Lab. majority 1,859 (3.86%)
Notional 2.89% swing Lab. to C.
(2005: Lab. majority 4,335 (9.63%))

§GILLINGHAM & RAINHAM
E. 70,865 T. 46,786 (66.02%) C. gain
*Rehman Chishti, C. 21,624
Paul Clark, Lab. 12,944
Andrew Stamp, LD 8,484
Robert Oakley, UKIP 1,515
Brian Ravenscroft, BNP 1,149
Dean Lacey, Eng. Dem. 464
Trish Marchant, Green 356
Gordon Bryan, ND 141
George Meegan, Med. Ind. 109
C. majority 8,680 (18.55%)
Notional 9.29% swing Lab. to C.
(2005: Lab. majority 15 (0.03%))

§GLOUCESTER
E. 79,322 T. 50,764 (64.00%) C. gain
*Richard Graham, C. 20,267
Parmjit Dhanda, Lab. 17,847
Jeremy Hilton, LD 9,767
Mike Smith, UKIP 1,808
Alan Platt, Eng. Dem. 564
Bryan Meloy, Green 511
C. majority 2,420 (4.77%)
Notional 8.86% swing Lab. to C.
(2005: Lab. majority 6,063 (12.95%))

GOSPORT
E. 72,720 T. 46,939 (64.55%) C. hold
*Caroline Dinenage, C. 24,300
Rob Hylands, LD 9,887
Graham Giles, Lab. 7,944
Andrew Rice, UKIP 1,496
Barry Bennett, BNP 1,004
Bob Shaw, Eng. Dem. 622
Andrea Smith, Green 573
David Smith, Ind. 493
Charles Read, Ind. 331
Brian Hart, Ind. 289
C. majority 14,413 (30.71%)
1.27% swing LD to C.
(2005: C. majority 5,730 (13.32%))

§GRANTHAM & STAMFORD
E. 78,000 T. 52,799 (67.69%) C. hold
*Nicholas Boles, C. 26,552
Harrish Bisnauthsing, LD 11,726
Mark Bartlett, Lab. 9,503
Christopher Robinson, BNP 2,485
Tony Wells, UKIP 1,604
Mark Horn, Lincs Ind. 929
C. majority 14,826 (28.08%)
Notional 1.18% swing C. to LD
(2005: C. majority 7,308 (15.77%))

GRAVESHAM
E. 70,195 T. 47,303 (67.39%) C. hold
Adam Holloway, C. 22,956
Kathryn Smith, Lab. (Co-op) 13,644
Anna Arrowsmith, LD 6,293
Geoffrey Clark, UKIP 2,265
Steven Uncles, Eng. Dem. 1,005
Richard Crawford, Green 675
Alice Dartnell, Ind. 465
C. majority 9,312 (19.69%)
9.12% swing Lab. (Co-op) to C.
(2005: C. majority 654 (1.45%))

GREAT GRIMSBY
E. 61,229 T. 32,954 (53.82%) Lab. hold
Austin Mitchell, Lab. 10,777
Victoria Ayling, C. 10,063
Andrew de Freitas, LD 7,388
Henry Hudson, UKIP 2,043
Steve Fyfe, BNP 1,517
Ernie Brown, Ind. 835
Adrian Howe, PNDP 331
Lab. majority 714 (2.17%)
10.53% swing Lab. to C.
(2005: Lab. majority 7,654 (23.22%))

GREAT YARMOUTH
E. 70,315 T. 43,057 (61.23%) C. gain
*Brandon Lewis, C. 18,571
Tony Wright, Lab. 14,295
Simon Partridge, LD 6,188
Alan Baugh, UKIP 2,066
Bosco Tann, BNP 1,421
Laura Biggart, Green 416
Margaret McMahon-Morris, LTT 100
C. majority 4,276 (9.93%)
8.66% swing Lab. to C.
(2005: Lab. majority 3,055 (7.38%))

§GREENWICH & WOOLWICH
E. 65,489 T. 41,188 (62.89%) Lab. hold
Nick Raynsford, Lab. 20,262
Spencer Drury, C. 10,109
Joseph Lee, LD 7,498
Lawrence Rustem, BNP 1,151
Andy Hewett, Green 1,054
Edward Adeleye, Ch. P. 443
Topo Wresniwiro, Eng. Dem. 339
Onay Kasab, TUSC 267
Dr Tammy Alingham, Ind. 65
Lab. majority 10,153 (24.65%)
Notional 5.12% swing Lab. to C.
(2005: Lab. majority 11,638 (32.77%))

§GUILDFORD
E. 77,082 T. 55,567 (72.09%) C. hold
Anne Milton, C. 29,618
Sue Doughty, LD 21,836
Tim Shand, Lab. 2,812
Mazhar Manzoor, UKIP 1,021
John Morris, PPN-V 280
C. majority 7,782 (14.00%)
Notional 6.91% swing LD to C.
(2005: C. majority 89 (0.17%))

§HACKNEY NORTH & STOKE NEWINGTON
E. 73,874 T. 46,488 (62.93%) Lab. hold
Diane Abbott, Lab. 25,553
Keith Angus, LD 11,092
Darren Caplan, C. 6,759
Matt Sellwood, Green 2,133
Maxine Hargreaves, Ch. P. 299
Suzanne Moore, ND 285
Knigel Knapp, Loony 182
Paul Shaer, Ind. 96
Alessandra Williams, Ind. 61
Dr Jack Pope-De-Locksley, Magna Carta 28
Lab. majority 14,461 (31.11%)
Notional 2.61% swing LD to Lab.
(2005: Lab. majority 8,002 (25.88%))

§HACKNEY SOUTH & SHOREDITCH
E. 72,816 T. 42,858 (58.86%) Lab. hold
Meg Hillier, Lab. 23,888
Dave Raval, LD 9,600
Simon Nayyar, C. 5,800
Polly Lane, Green 1,493
Michael King, UKIP 651
Ben Rae, Lib. 539
John Williams, Ch. P. 434
Nusret Sen, DDP 202
Paul Davies, Comm. Lge 110
Denny De La Haye, Ind. 95
Jane Tuckett, Ind. 26
Michael Spinks, Ind. 20
Lab. majority 14,288 (33.34%)
Notional 0.99% swing LD to Lab.
(2005: Lab. majority 9,629 (31.37%))

§HALESOWEN & ROWLEY REGIS
E. 63,693 T. 43,979 (69.05%) C. gain
*James Morris, C. 18,115
Sue Hayman, Lab. 16,092
Philip Tibbets, LD 6,515
Derek Baddeley, UKIP 2,824
Derek Thompson, Ind. 433
C. majority 2,023 (4.60%)
Notional 7.13% swing Lab. to C.
(2005: Lab. majority 4,010 (9.66%))

§HALIFAX
E. 70,380 T. 43,555 (61.89%) Lab. hold
Linda Riordan, Lab. 16,278
Philip Allott, C. 14,806
Elisabeth Wilson, LD 8,335
Tom Bates, BNP 2,760
Diane Park, Ind. Voice 722
Jay Sangha, UKIP 654
Lab. majority 1,472 (3.38%)
Notional 2.69% swing Lab. to C.
(2005: Lab. majority 3,481 (8.75%))

§HALTEMPRICE & HOWDEN
E. 70,403 T. 48,737 (69.23%) C. hold
David Davis, C. 24,486
Jon Neal, LD 12,884
Danny Marten, Lab. 7,630
James Cornell, BNP 1,583
Joanne Robinson, Eng. Dem. 1,485
Shan Oakes, Green 669
C. majority 11,602 (23.81%)
Notional 6.64% swing LD to C.
(2005: C. majority 5,080 (10.52%))

§HALTON
E. 68,884 T. 41,338 (60.01%) Lab. hold
Derek Twigg, Lab. 23,843
Ben Jones, C. 8,339
Frank Harasiwka, LD 5,718
Andrew Taylor, BNP 1,563
John Moore, UKIP 1,228
Jim Craig, Green 647
Lab. majority 15,504 (37.51%)
Notional 2.87% swing Lab. to C.
(2005: Lab. majority 16,060 (43.25%))

§HAMMERSMITH
E. 72,348 T. 47,452 (65.59%) Lab. hold
Andy Slaughter, Lab. 20,810
Shaun Bailey, C. 17,261
Merlene Emerson, LD 7,567
Rollo Miles, Green 696
Vanessa Crichton, UKIP 551
Lawrence Searle, BNP 432
Stephen Brennan, Ind. 135
Lab. majority 3,549 (7.48%)
Notional 0.48% swing Lab. to C.
(2005: Lab. majority 3,673 (8.44%))

§HAMPSHIRE EAST
E. 72,250 T. 51,317 (71.03%) C. hold
*Damian Hinds, C. 29,137
Adam Carew, LD 15,640
Jane Edbrooke, Lab. 4,043
Hugh McGuinness, UKIP 1,477
Matt Williams, Eng. Dem. 710
Don Jerrard, J & AC 310
C. majority 13,497 (26.30%)
Notional 6.61% swing LD to C.
(2005: C. majority 5,968 (13.09%))

§HAMPSHIRE NORTH EAST
E. 72,196 T. 52,939 (73.33%) C. hold
James Arbuthnot, C. 32,075
Denzil Coulson, LD 13,478
Barry Jones, Lab. 5,173
Ruth Duffin, UKIP 2,213
C. majority 18,597 (35.13%)
Notional 4.52% swing LD to C.
(2005: C. majority 11,189 (26.09%))

§HAMPSHIRE NORTH WEST
E. 76,040 T. 53,292 (70.08%) C. hold
Sir George Young, C. 31,072
Thomas McCann, LD 12,489
Sarah Evans, Lab. 6,980
Stan Oram, UKIP 2,751
C. majority 18,583 (34.87%)
Notional 4.67% swing LD to C.
(2005: C. majority 12,683 (25.53%))

§HAMPSTEAD & KILBURN
E. 79,713 T. 52,822 (66.27%) Lab. hold
Glenda Jackson, Lab. 17,332
Chris Philp, C. 17,290
Edward Fordham, LD 16,491
Bea Campbell, Green 759
Magnus Nielsen, UKIP 408
Victoria Moore, BNP 328
Tamsin Omond, TOC 123
Gene Alcantara, Ind. 91
Lab. majority 42 (0.08%)
Notional 6.65% swing Lab. to C.
(2005: Lab. majority 474 (1.14%))

§HARBOROUGH
E. 77,917 T. 54,945 (70.52%) C. hold
Edward Garnier, C. 26,894
Zuffar Haq, LD 17,097
Kevin McKeever, Lab. 6,981
Geoff Dickens, BNP 1,715
Marrietta King, UKIP 1,462
David Ball, Eng. Dem. 568
Jeff Stephenson, Ind. 228
C. majority 9,797 (17.83%)
Notional 4.73% swing LD to C.
(2005: C. majority 4,047 (8.38%))

§HARLOW
E. 67,439 T. 43,878 (65.06%) C. gain
*Robert Halfon, C. 19,691
Bill Rammell, Lab. 14,766
David White, LD 5,990
Eddy Butler, BNP 1,739
John Croft, UKIP 1,591
Oluyemi Adeeko, Ch. P. 101
C. majority 4,925 (11.22%)
Notional 5.90% swing Lab. to C.
(2005: Lab. majority 230 (0.58%))

§HARROGATE & KNARESBOROUGH
E. 75,269 T. 53,134 (70.59%) C. gain
*Andrew Jones, C. 24,305
Claire Kelley, LD 23,266
Kevin McNerney, Lab. 3,413
Steven Gill, BNP 1,094
John Upex, UKIP 1,056
C. majority 1,039 (1.96%)
Notional 9.09% swing LD to C.
(2005: LD majority 7,980 (16.22%))

§HARROW EAST
E. 68,554 T. 48,006 (70.03%) C. gain
*Bob Blackman, C. 21,435
Tony McNulty, Lab. 18,032
Nahid Boethe, LD 6,850
Abhijit Pandya, UKIP 896
Madeleine Atkins, Green 793
C. majority 3,403 (7.09%)
Notional 6.99% swing Lab. to C.
(2005: Lab. majority 2,934 (6.89%))

§HARROW WEST
E. 71,510 T. 46,116 (64.49%) Lab. (Co-op) hold
Gareth Thomas, Lab. (Co-op) 20,111
Dr Rachel Joyce, C. 16,968
Christopher Noyce, LD 7,458
Herbert Crossman, UKIP 954
Rowan Langley, Green 625
Lab. (Co-op) majority 3,143 (6.82%)
Notional 5.72% swing Lab. (Co-op) to C.
(2005: Lab. (Co-op) majority 7,742 (18.26%))

HARTLEPOOL
E. 68,923 T. 38,242 (55.49%) Lab. hold
Iain Wright, Lab. 16,267
Alan Wright, C. 10,758
Reg Clark, LD 6,533
Stephen Allison, UKIP 2,682
Ronnie Bage, BNP 2,002
Lab. majority 5,509 (14.41%)
12.82% swing Lab. to C.
(2005: Lab. majority 7,478 (21.10%))

§HARWICH & ESSEX NORTH
E. 70,743 T. 49,000 (69.26%) C. hold
Bernard Jenkin, C. 23,001
James Raven, LD 11,554
Darren Barrenger, Lab. 9,774
Simon Anselmi, UKIP 2,527
Stephen Robey, BNP 1,065
Chris Fox, Green 909
Peter Thompson Bates, Ind. 170
C. majority 11,447 (23.36%)
Notional 0.00% swing C. to LD
(2005: C. majority 5,583 (11.73%))

§HASTINGS & RYE
E. 78,000 T. 49,814 (63.86%) C. gain
*Amber Rudd, C. 20,468
Michael Foster, Lab. 18,475
Nicholas Perry, LD 7,825
Anthony Smith, UKIP 1,397
Nicholas Prince, BNP 1,310
Rodney Bridger, Eng. Dem. 339
C. majority 1,993 (4.00%)
Notional 3.27% swing Lab. to C.
(2005: Lab. majority 1,156 (2.54%))

§HAVANT
E. 69,712 T. 43,903 (62.98%) C. hold
David Willetts, C. 22,433
Alex Payton, LD 10,273
Robert Smith, Lab. 7,777
Gary Kerrin, UKIP 2,611
Fungus Addams, Eng. Dem. 809
C. majority 12,160 (27.70%)
Notional 1.79% swing LD to C.
(2005: C. majority 6,395 (15.58%))

§HAYES & HARLINGTON
E. 70,233 T. 42,637 (60.71%) Lab. hold
John McDonnell, Lab. 23,377
Scott Seaman-Digby, C. 12,553
Satnam Kaur Khalsa, LD 3,726
Chris Forster, BNP 1,520
Andrew Cripps, NF 566
Cliff Dixon, Eng. Dem. 464
Jessica Lee, Green 348
Aneel Shahzad, Ch. P. 83
Lab. majority 10,824 (25.39%)
Notional 1.65% swing Lab. to C.
(2005: Lab. majority 10,594 (28.68%))

§HAZEL GROVE
E. 63,074 T. 41,981 (66.56%) LD hold
Andrew Stunell, LD 20,485
Annesley Abercorn, C. 14,114
Richard Scorer, Lab. 5,234
John Whittaker, UKIP 2,148
LD majority 6,371 (15.18%)
Notional 2.37% swing LD to C.
(2005: LD majority 7,694 (19.92%))

§HEMEL HEMPSTEAD
E. 72,754 T. 49,471 (68.00%) C. hold
Mike Penning, C. 24,721
Dr Richard Grayson, LD 11,315
Ayfer Orhan, Lab. 10,295
Janet Price, BNP 1,615
David Alexander, UKIP 1,254
Mick Young, Ind. 271
C. majority 13,406 (27.10%)
Notional 1.94% swing LD to C.
(2005: C. majority 168 (0.36%))

§HEMSWORTH
E. 72,552 T. 43,840 (60.43%) Lab. hold
Jon Trickett, Lab. 20,506
Ann Myatt, C. 10,662
Alan Belmore, LD 5,667
Ian Womersley, Ind. 3,946
Ian Kitchen, BNP 3,059
Lab. majority 9,844 (22.45%)
Notional 7.03% swing Lab. to C.
(2005: Lab. majority 14,026 (36.51%))

§HENDON
E. 78,923 T. 46,374 (58.76%) C. gain
*Matthew Offord, C. 19,635
Andrew Dismore, Lab. 19,529
Matthew Harris, LD 5,734
Robin Lambert, UKIP 958
Andrew Newby, Green 518
C. majority 106 (0.23%)
Notional 4.14% swing Lab. to C.
(2005: Lab. majority 3,231 (8.06%))

§HENLEY
E. 75,005 T. 53,520 (71.36%) C. hold
John Howell, C. 30,054
Andrew Crick, LD 13,466
Richard McKenzie, Lab. 5,835
Laurence Hughes, UKIP 1,817
Mark Stevenson, Green 1,328
John Bews, BNP 1,020
C. majority 16,588 (30.99%)
Notional 1.93% swing LD to C.
(2005: C. majority 13,366 (27.13%))

§HEREFORD & HEREFORDSHIRE SOUTH
E. 71,435 T. 48,381 (67.73%) C. gain
*Jesse Norman, C. 22,366
Sarah Carr, LD 19,885
Philippa Roberts, Lab. 3,506
Valentine Smith, UKIP 1,638
John Oliver, BNP 986
C. majority 2,481 (5.13%)
Notional 3.76% swing LD to C.
(2005: LD majority 1,089 (2.39%))

§HEREFORDSHIRE NORTH
E. 66,525 T. 47,568 (71.50%) C. hold
Bill Wiggin, C. 24,631
Lucy Hurds, LD 14,744
Neil Sabharwal, Lab. 3,373
Jonathan Oakton, UKIP 2,701
Felicity Norman, Green 1,533
John King, Ind. 586
C. majority 9,887 (20.78%)
Notional 3.82% swing C. to LD
(2005: C. majority 12,688 (28.43%))

§HERTFORD & STORTFORD
E. 78,459 T. 55,377 (70.58%) C. hold
Mark Prisk, C. 29,810
Andrew Lewin, LD 14,373
Steve Terry, Lab. 7,620
David Sodey, UKIP 1,716
Roy Harris, BNP 1,297
Loucas Xenophontos, Ind. 325
Martin Adams, Ind. 236
C. majority 15,437 (27.88%)
Notional 1.95% swing C. to LD
(2005: C. majority 12,756 (25.95%))

§HERTFORDSHIRE NORTH EAST
E. 72,200 T. 50,425 (69.84%) C. hold
Oliver Heald, C. 26,995
Hugh Annand, LD 11,801
David Kirkman, Lab. 8,291
Adrianne Smyth, UKIP 2,075
Rosemary Bland, Green 875
Richard Campbell, Ind. 209
David Ralph, YRDPL 143
Philip Reichardt, Ind. 36
C. majority 15,194 (30.13%)
Notional 1.19% swing LD to C.
(2005: C. majority 9,510 (19.75%))

§HERTFORDSHIRE SOUTH WEST
E. 78,248 T. 56,750 (72.53%) C. hold
David Gauke, C. 30,773
Christopher Townsend, LD 15,853
Harry Mann, Lab. 6,526
Mark Benson, UKIP 1,450
Deirdre Gates, BNP 1,302
James Hannaway, Ind. 846
C. majority 14,920 (26.29%)
Notional 4.66% swing LD to C.
(2005: C. majority 8,640 (16.97%))

HERTSMERE
E. 73,062 T. 47,270 (64.70%) C. hold
James Clappison, C. 26,476
Sam Russell, Lab. 8,871
Anthony Rowlands, LD 8,210
David Rutter, UKIP 1,712
Daniel Seabrook, BNP 1,397
Arjuna Krishna-Das, Green 604
C. majority 17,605 (37.24%)
5.59% swing Lab. to C.
(2005: C. majority 11,093 (26.06%))

§HEXHAM
E. 61,375 T. 43,483 (70.85%) C. hold
*Guy Opperman, C. 18,795
Andrew Duffield, LD 13,007
Antoine Tinnion, Lab. 8,253
Steve Ford, Ind. 1,974
Quentin Hawkins, BNP 1,205
Colin Moss, Ind. 249
C. majority 5,788 (13.31%)
Notional 1.70% swing C. to LD
(2005: C. majority 4,957 (12.03%))

§HEYWOOD & MIDDLETON
E. 80,171 T. 46,125 (57.53%) Lab. hold
Jim Dobbin, Lab. 18,499
Michael Holly, C. 12,528
Wera Hobhouse, LD 10,474
Peter Greenwood, BNP 3,239
Victoria Cecil, UKIP 1,215
Chrissy Lee, Ind. 170
Lab. majority 5,971 (12.95%)
Notional 6.82% swing Lab. to C.
(2005: Lab. majority 11,034 (26.58%))

§HIGH PEAK
E. 71,973 T. 50,337 (69.94%) C. gain
*Andrew Bingham, C. 20,587
Caitlin Bisknell, Lab. 15,910
Alistair Stevens, LD 10,993
Sylvia Hall, UKIP 1,690
Peter Allen, Green 922
Lance Dowson, Ind. 161
Tony Alves, ND 74
C. majority 4,677 (9.29%)
Notional 6.54% swing Lab. to C.
(2005: Lab. majority 1,750 (3.80%))

§HITCHIN & HARPENDEN
E. 73,851 T. 54,707 (74.08%) C. hold
Peter Lilley, C. 29,869
Nigel Quinton, LD 14,598
Oliver de Botton, Lab. 7,413
Graham Wilkinson, UKIP 1,663
Richard Wise, Green 807
Margaret Henderson, Ind. 109
Simon Byron, R and E 108
Eric Hannah, YRDPL 90
Peter Rigby, Ind. 50
C. majority 15,271 (27.91%)
Notional 2.50% swing LD to C.
(2005: C. majority 11,064 (22.90%))

§HOLBORN & ST PANCRAS
E. 86,863 T. 54,649 (62.91%) Lab. hold
Frank Dobson, Lab. 25,198
Jo Shaw, LD 15,256
George Lee, C. 11,134
Natalie Bennett, Green 1,480
Robert Carlyle, BNP 779
Max Spencer, UKIP 587
John Chapman, Ind. 96
Mikel Susperregi, Eng. Dem. 75
Iain Meek, Ind. 44
Lab. majority 9,942 (18.19%)
Notional 0.38% swing Lab. to LD
(2005: Lab. majority 8,348 (18.95%))

§HORNCHURCH & UPMINSTER
E. 78,487 T. 53,390 (68.02%) C. hold
Angela Watkinson, C. 27,469
Kath McGuirk, Lab. 11,098
Karen Chilvers, LD 7,426
William Whelpley, BNP 3,421
Lawrence Webb, UKIP 2,848
Melanie Collins, Green 542
David Durant, Ind. 305
Johnson Olukotun, Ch. P. 281
C. majority 16,371 (30.66%)
Notional 7.14% swing Lab. to C.
(2005: C. majority 8,058 (16.38%))

HORNSEY & WOOD GREEN
E. 79,916 T. 55,042 (68.87%) LD hold
Lynne Featherstone, LD 25,595
Karen Jennings, Lab. 18,720
Richard Merrin, C. 9,174
Pete McAskie, Green 1,261
Stephane De Roche, Ind. 201
Rohen Kapur, Ind. 91
LD majority 6,875 (12.49%)
3.72% swing Lab. to LD
(2005: LD majority 2,395 (5.06%))

§HORSHAM
E. 76,835 T. 55,841 (72.68%) C. hold
Francis Maude, C. 29,447
Godfrey Newman, LD 17,987
Andrew Skudder, Lab. 4,189
Harry Aldridge, UKIP 2,839
Nick Fitter, Green 570
Steve Lyon, Ch. P. 469
Jim Duggan, PPN-V 253
Derek Kissach, Ind. 87
C. majority 11,460 (20.52%)
Notional 0.57% swing C. to LD
(2005: C. majority 10,780 (21.66%))

§HOUGHTON & SUNDERLAND SOUTH
E. 68,729 T. 38,021 (55.32%) Lab. hold
*Bridget Phillipson, Lab. 19,137
Robert Oliver, C. 8,147
Chris Boyle, LD 5,292
Colin Wakefield, Ind. 2,462
Karen Allen, BNP 1,961
Richard Elvin, UKIP 1,022
Lab. majority 10,990 (28.91%)
Notional 8.44% swing Lab. to C.
(2005: Lab. majority 16,986 (45.78%))

§HOVE
E. 71,708 T. 49,819 (69.47%) C. gain
*Mike Weatherley, C. 18,294
Celia Barlow, Lab. 16,426
Paul Elgood, LD 11,240
Ian Davey, Green 2,568
Paul Perrin, UKIP 1,206
Brian Ralfe, Ind. 85
C. majority 1,868 (3.75%)
Notional 2.37% swing Lab. to C.
(2005: Lab. majority 448 (1.00%))

§HUDDERSFIELD
E. 66,316 T. 40,524 (61.11%) Lab. hold
Barry Sheerman, Lab. 15,725
Karen Tweed, C. 11,253
James Blanchard, LD 10,023
Andrew Cooper, Green 1,641
Rachel Firth, BNP 1,563
Paul Cooney, TUSC 319
Lab. majority 4,472 (11.04%)
Notional 7.14% swing Lab. to C.
(2005: Lab. majority 7,883 (22.29%))

§HULL EAST
E. 67,530 T. 34,184 (50.62%) Lab. hold
*Karl Turner, Lab. 16,387
Jeremy Wilcock, LD 7,790
Christine Mackay, C. 5,667
Mike Hookem, UKIP 2,745
Joe Uttley, NF 880
Mike Burton, Eng. Dem. 715
Lab. majority 8,597 (25.15%)
Notional 5.35% swing Lab. to LD
(2005: Lab. majority 11,740 (35.84%))

§HULL NORTH
E. 64,082 T. 33,291 (51.95%) Lab. hold
Diana Johnson, Lab. 13,044
Denis Healy, LD 12,403
Victoria Aitken, C. 4,365
John Mainprize, BNP 1,443
Paul Barlow, UKIP 1,358
Martin Deane, Green 478
Michael Cassidy, Eng. Dem. 200
Lab. majority 641 (1.93%)
Notional 12.18% swing Lab. to LD
(2005: Lab. majority 7,384 (26.29%))

§HULL WEST & HESSLE
E. 69,017 T. 31,505 (45.65%) Lab. hold
Alan Johnson, Lab. 13,378
Mike Ross, LD 7,636
Gary Shores, C. 6,361
Ken Hordon, UKIP 1,688
Edward Scott, BNP 1,416
Peter Mawer, Eng. Dem. 876
Keith Gibson, TUSC 150
Lab. majority 5,742 (18.23%)
Notional 7.92% swing Lab. to LD
(2005: Lab. majority 9,430 (34.06%))

§HUNTINGDON
E. 83,557 T. 54,266 (64.94%) C. hold
Jonathan Djanogly, C. 26,516
Martin Land, LD 15,697
Anthea Cox, Lab. 5,982
Ian Curtis, UKIP 3,258
Jonathan Salt, Ind. 1,432
John Clare, Green 652
Lord Toby Jug, Loony 548
Carrie Holliman, APP 181
C. majority 10,819 (19.94%)
Notional 2.08% swing C. to LD
(2005: C. majority 11,652 (24.10%))

§HYNDBURN
E. 67,221 T. 42,672 (63.48%) Lab. hold
*Graham Jones, Lab. 17,531
Karen Buckley, C. 14,441
Andrew Rankine, LD 5,033
David Shapcott, BNP 2,137
Granville Barker, UKIP 1,481
The Revd Kevin Logan, CPA 795
Kerry Gormley, Green 463
Christopher Reid, Eng. Dem. 413
Craig Hall, Ind. 378
Lab. majority 3,090 (7.24%)
Notional 3.28% swing Lab. to C.
(2005: Lab. majority 5,528 (13.80%))

§ILFORD NORTH
E. 71,995 T. 47,018 (65.31%) C. hold
Lee Scott, C. 21,506
Sonia Klein, Lab. 16,102
Alex Berhanu, LD 5,966
Danny Warville, BNP 1,545
Henri van der Stighelen, UKIP 871
Caroline Allen, Green 572
The Revd Robert Hampson, CPA 456
C. majority 5,404 (11.49%)
Notional 3.68% swing Lab. to C.
(2005: C. majority 1,735 (4.14%))

ILFORD SOUTH
E. 75,246 T. 51,191 (68.03%)
Lab. (Co-op) hold
Mike Gapes, Lab. (Co-op) 25,301
Toby Boutle, C. 14,014
Anood Al-Samerai, LD 8,679
Wilson Chowdhry, Green 1,319
Terry Murray, UKIP 1,132
John Jestico, King George 746
Lab. (Co-op) majority 11,287 (22.05%)
0.22% swing C. to Lab. (Co-op)
(2005: Lab. (Co-op) majority 9,228 (21.61%))

§IPSWICH
E. 78,371 T. 46,941 (59.90%) C. gain
*Benedict Gummer, C. 18,371
Chris Mole, Lab. 16,292
Mark Dyson, LD 8,556
Chris Streatfield, UKIP 1,365
Dennis Boater, BNP 1,270
Tim Glover, Green 775
Kim Christofi, Ch. P. 149
Peter Turtill, Ind. 93
Sally Wainman, Ind. 70
C. majority 2,079 (4.43%)
Notional 8.12% swing Lab. to C.
(2005: Lab. majority 5,235 (11.81%))

ISLE OF WIGHT
E. 109,966 T. 70,264 (63.90%) C. hold
Andrew Turner, C. 32,810
Jill Wareham, LD 22,283
Mark Chiverton, Lab. 8,169
Mike Tarrant, UKIP 2,435
Geoff Clynch, BNP 1,457
Ian Dunsire, Eng. Dem. 1,233
Bob Keats, Green 931
Paul Martin, Mid. England 616
Pete Harris, Ind. 175
Paul Randle-Jolliffe, Ind. 89
Edward Corby, Ind. 66
C. majority 10,527 (14.98%)
2.22% swing C. to LD
(2005: C. majority 12,978 (19.42%))

ISLINGTON NORTH
E. 68,120 T. 44,554 (65.41%) Lab. hold
Jeremy Corbyn, Lab. 24,276
Rhodri Jamieson-Ball, LD 11,875
Adrian Berrill-Cox, C. 6,339
Emma Dixon, Green 1,348
Dominic Lennon, UKIP 716
Lab. majority 12,401 (27.83%)
3.25% swing LD to Lab.
(2005: Lab. majority 6,716 (21.32%))

ISLINGTON SOUTH & FINSBURY
E. 67,649 T. 43,555 (64.38%) Lab. hold
Emily Thornberry, Lab. 18,407
Bridget Fox, LD 14,838
Antonia Cox, C. 8,449
James Humphreys, Green 710
Rose-Marie McDonald, UKIP 701
John Dodds, Eng. Dem. 301
Richard Deboo, Animals 149
Lab. majority 3,569 (8.19%)
3.32% swing LD to Lab.
(2005: Lab. majority 484 (1.56%))

§JARROW
E. 64,350 T. 38,784 (60.27%) Lab. hold
Stephen Hepburn, Lab. 20,910
Jeffrey Milburn, C. 8,002
Tom Appleby, LD 7,163
Andy Swaddle, BNP 2,709
Lab. majority 12,908 (33.28%)
Notional 6.38% swing Lab. to C.
(2005: Lab. majority 12,749 (36.35%))

KEIGHLEY
E. 65,893 T. 47,692 (72.38%) C. gain
*Kris Hopkins, C. 20,003
Jane Thomas, Lab. 17,063
Nader Fekri, LD 7,059
Andrew Brons, BNP 1,962
Paul Latham, UKIP 1,470
Steven Smith, NF 135
C. majority 2,940 (6.16%)
8.32% swing Lab. to C.
(2005: Lab. majority 4,852 (10.48%))

§KENILWORTH & SOUTHAM
E. 59,630 T. 48,431 (81.22%) C. hold
Jeremy Wright, C. 25,945
Nigel Rock, LD 13,393
Nicholas Milton, Lab. 6,949
John Moore, UKIP 1,214
James Harrison, Green 568
Joe Rukin, Ind. 362
C. majority 12,552 (25.92%)
Notional 1.20% swing C. to LD
(2005: C. majority 10,956 (24.80%))

§KENSINGTON
E. 65,961 T. 35,150 (53.29%) C. hold
Sir Malcolm Rifkind, C. 17,595
Sam Gurney, Lab. 8,979
Robin Meltzer, LD 6,872
Lady Caroline Pearson, UKIP 754
Zahra-Melan Ebrahimi-Fardouee, Green 753
Eddie Adams, Green Soc. 197
C. majority 8,616 (24.51%)
Notional 5.19% swing Lab. to C.
(2005: C. majority 4,540 (14.13%))

§KETTERING
E. 68,837 T. 47,328 (68.75%) C. hold
Philip Hollobone, C. 23,247
Phil Sawford, Lab. 14,153
Chris Nelson, LD 7,498
Clive Skinner, BNP 1,366
Derek Hilling, Eng. Dem. 952
Dave Bishop, BP Elvis 112
C. majority 9,094 (19.21%)
Notional 9.41% swing Lab. to C.
(2005: C. majority 176 (0.39%))

§KINGSTON & SURBITON
E. 81,116 T. 57,111 (70.41%) LD hold
Edward Davey, LD 28,428
Helen Whately, C. 20,868
Max Freedman, Lab. 5,337
Jonathan Greensted, UKIP 1,450
Chris Walker, Green 555
Monkey the Drummer, Loony 247
Anthony May, CPA 226
LD majority 7,560 (13.24%)
Notional 2.43% swing LD to C.
(2005: LD majority 9,084 (18.11%))

§KINGSWOOD
E. 66,361 T. 47,906 (72.19%) C. gain
*Chris Skidmore, C. 19,362
Roger Berry, Lab. 16,917
Sally Fitzharris, LD 8,072
Neil Dowdney, UKIP 1,528
Michael Carey, BNP 1,311
Nick Foster, Green 383
Michael Blundell, Eng. Dem. 333
C. majority 2,445 (5.10%)
Notional 9.43% swing Lab. to C.
(2005: Lab. majority 6,145 (13.76%))

§KNOWSLEY
E. 79,561 T. 44,658 (56.13%) Lab. hold
George Howarth, Lab. 31,650
Flo Clucas, LD 5,964
David Dunne, C. 4,004
Steven Greenhalgh, BNP 1,895
Anthony Rundle, UKIP 1,145
Lab. majority 25,686 (57.52%)
Notional 0.25% swing Lab. to LD
(2005: Lab. majority 24,333 (58.02%))

LANCASHIRE WEST
E. 75,975 T. 48,473 (63.80%) Lab. hold
Rosie Cooper, Lab. 21,883
Adrian Owens, C. 17,540
John Gibson, LD 6,573
Damon Noone, UKIP 1,775
Peter Cranie, Green 485
David Braid, Clause 28 217
Lab. majority 4,343 (8.96%)
2.57% swing Lab. to C.
(2005: Lab. majority 6,084 (14.10%))

§LANCASTER & FLEETWOOD
E. 69,908 T. 42,701 (61.08%) C. gain
*Eric Ollerenshaw, C. 15,404
Clive Grunshaw, Lab. 15,071
Stuart Langhorn, LD 8,167
Gina Dowding, Green 1,888
Fred McGlade, UKIP 1,020
Debra Kent, BNP 938
Keith Riley, Ind. 213
C. majority 333 (0.78%)
Notional 4.80% swing Lab. to C.
(2005: Lab. majority 3,428 (8.82%))

§LEEDS CENTRAL
E. 64,698 T. 37,394 (57.80%) Lab. hold
Hilary Benn, Lab. 18,434
Michael Taylor, LD 7,789
Alan Lamb, C. 7,541
Kevin Meeson, BNP 3,066
Dave Procter, Ind. 409
We Beat The Scum One-Nil, ND 155
Lab. majority 10,645 (28.47%)
Notional 4.76% swing Lab. to LD
(2005: Lab. majority 12,916 (37.98%))

§LEEDS EAST
E. 65,067 T. 37,813 (58.11%) Lab. hold
George Mudie, Lab. 19,056
Barry Anderson, C. 8,763
Andrew Tear, LD 6,618
Trevor Brown, BNP 2,947
Michael Davies, Green Soc. 429
Lab. majority 10,293 (27.22%)
Notional 5.49% swing Lab. to C.
(2005: Lab. majority 13,689 (38.21%))

§LEEDS NORTH EAST
E. 67,899 T. 47,535 (70.01%) Lab. hold
Fabian Hamilton, Lab. 20,287
Matthew Lobley, C. 15,742
Aqila Choudhry, LD 9,310
Warren Hendon, UKIP 842
Tom Redmond, BNP 758
Celia Foote, Green Soc. 596
Lab. majority 4,545 (9.56%)
Notional 2.97% swing Lab. to C.
(2005: Lab. majority 6,762 (15.51%))

§LEEDS NORTH WEST
E. 65,399 T. 43,483 (66.49%) LD hold
Greg Mulholland, LD 20,653
Julia Mulligan, C. 11,550
Judith Blake, Lab. 9,132
Geoffrey Bulmer, BNP 766
Mark Thackray, UKIP 600
Martin Hemingway, Green 508
Alan Procter, Eng. Dem. 153
Trevor Bavage, Green Soc. 121
LD majority 9,103 (20.93%)
Notional 5.44% swing C. to LD
(2005: LD majority 2,064 (4.96%))

§LEEDS WEST
E. 67,453 T. 38,752 (57.45%) Lab. hold
*Rachel Reeves, Lab. 16,389
Ruth Coleman, LD 9,373
Joe Marjoram, C. 7,641
Joanna Beverley, BNP 2,377
David Blackburn, Green 1,832
Jeff Miles, UKIP 1,140
Lab. majority 7,016 (18.10%)
Notional 10.36% swing Lab. to LD
(2005: Lab. majority 13,699 (38.83%))

§LEICESTER EAST
E. 72,986 T. 47,995 (65.76%) Lab. hold
Keith Vaz, Lab. 25,804
Jane Hunt, C. 11,722
Ali Asghar, LD 6,817
Colin Gilmore, BNP 1,700
Mo Taylor, Green 733
Felicity Ransome, UKIP 725
Avtar Sadiq, UPS 494
Lab. majority 14,082 (29.34%)
Notional 4.77% swing Lab. to C.
(2005: Lab. majority 16,400 (38.89%))

§¶LEICESTER SOUTH
E. 77,175 T. 47,124 (61.06%) Lab. hold
Sir Peter Soulsby, Lab. 21,479
Parmjit Singh Gill, LD 12,671
Ross Grant, C. 10,066
Adrian Waudby, BNP 1,418
Dave Dixey, Green 770
Christopher Lucas, UKIP 720
Lab. majority 8,808 (18.69%)
Notional 4.96% swing LD to Lab.
(2005: Lab. majority 3,727 (8.78%))

§LEICESTER WEST
E. 64,900 T. 35,819 (55.19%) Lab. hold
*Elizabeth Kendall, Lab. 13,745
Celia Harvey, C. 9,728
Peter Coley, LD 8,107
Gary Reynolds, BNP 2,158
Stephen Ingall, UKIP 883
Geoff Forse, Green 639
Steven Huggins, Ind. 181
Steve Score, TUSC 157
Shaun Dyer, Pirate 113
David Bowley, Ind. 108
Lab. majority 4,017 (11.21%)
Notional 7.60% swing Lab. to C.
(2005: Lab. majority 8,539 (26.42%))

LEICESTERSHIRE NORTH WEST
E. 71,219 T. 51,952 (72.95%) C. gain
*Andrew Bridgen, C. 23,147
Ross Willmott, Lab. (Co-op) 15,636
Paul Reynolds, LD 8,639
Ian Meller, BNP 3,396
Martin Green, UKIP 1,134
C. majority 7,511 (14.46%)
11.98% swing Lab. (Co-op) to C.
(2005: Lab. (Co-op) majority 4,477 (9.50%))

§LEICESTERSHIRE SOUTH
E. 76,639 T. 54,577 (71.21%) C. hold
Andrew Robathan, C. 27,000
Aladdin Ayesh, LD 11,476
Sally Gimson, Lab. 11,392
Paul Preston, BNP 2,721
John Williams, UKIP 1,988
C. majority 15,524 (28.44%)
Notional 1.03% swing LD to C.
(2005: C. majority 7,704 (15.77%))

§LEIGH
E. 76,350 T. 44,332 (58.06%) Lab. hold
Andy Burnham, Lab. 21,295
Shazia Awan, C. 9,284
Chris Blackburn, LD 8,049
Gary Chadwick, BNP 2,724
Mary Lavelle, UKIP 1,535
Norman Bradbury, Ind. 988
Terry Dainty, Ind. 320
Ryan Hessell, Ch. P. 137
Lab. majority 12,011 (27.09%)
Notional 7.17% swing Lab. to C.
(2005: Lab. majority 15,098 (38.73%))

§LEWES
E. 68,708 T. 50,088 (72.90%) LD hold
Norman Baker, LD 26,048
Jason Sugarman, C. 18,401
Hratche Koundarjian, Lab. 2,508
Peter Charlton, UKIP 1,728
Susan Murray, Green 729
David Lloyd, BNP 594
Ondrej Soucek, Ind. 80
LD majority 7,647 (15.27%)
Notional 0.81% swing LD to C.
(2005: LD majority 7,889 (16.89%))

§LEWISHAM DEPTFORD
E. 67,058 T. 41,220 (61.47%) Lab. hold
Joan Ruddock, Lab. 22,132
Tam Langley, LD 9,633
Gemma Townsend, C. 5,551
Darren Johnson, Green 2,772
Ian Page, Soc. Alt. 645
Malcolm Martin, CPA 487
Lab. majority 12,499 (30.32%)
Notional 3.56% swing Lab. to LD
(2005: Lab. majority 13,012 (37.43%))

§LEWISHAM EAST
E. 65,926 T. 41,719 (63.28%) Lab. hold
*Heidi Alexander, Lab. 17,966
Pete Pattisson, LD 11,750
Jonathan Clamp, C. 9,850
Roderick Reed, UKIP 771
Priscilla Cotterell, Green 624
James Rose, Eng. Dem. 426
George Hallam, CNBPG 332
Lab. majority 6,216 (14.90%)
Notional 6.41% swing Lab. to LD
(2005: Lab. majority 8,758 (23.31%))

§LEWISHAM WEST & PENGE
E. 69,022 T. 45,028 (65.24%) Lab. hold
Jim Dowd, Lab. 18,501
Alex Feakes, LD 12,673
Chris Phillips, C. 11,489
Peter Staveley, UKIP 1,117
Romayne Phoenix, Green 931
Stephen Hammond, CPA 317
Lab. majority 5,828 (12.94%)
Notional 3.10% swing Lab. to LD
(2005: Lab. majority 7,779 (19.15%))

§LEYTON & WANSTEAD
E. 63,541 T. 40,159 (63.20%) Lab. hold
*John Cryer, Lab. 17,511
Farooq Qureshi, LD 11,095
Ed Northover, C. 8,928
Graham Wood, UKIP 1,080
Ashley Gunstock, Green 562
Jim Clift, BNP 561
Sonika Bhatti, Ch. P. 342
Martin Levin, Ind. Fed. 80
Lab. majority 6,416 (15.98%)
Notional 2.57% swing Lab. to LD
(2005: Lab. majority 7,253 (21.11%))

§LICHFIELD
E. 72,586 T. 51,563 (71.04%) C. hold
Michael Fabricant, C. 28,048
Ian Jackson, LD 10,365
Steve Hyden, Lab. 10,230
Karen Maunder, UKIP 2,920
C. majority 17,683 (34.29%)
Notional 0.74% swing LD to C.
(2005: C. majority 7,791 (16.49%))

§LINCOLN
E. 73,540 T. 45,721 (62.17%) C. gain
*Karl McCartney, C. 17,163
Gillian Merron, Lab. 16,105
Reg Shore, LD 9,256
Robert West, BNP 1,367
Nick Smith, UKIP 1,004
Ernest Coleman, Eng. Dem. 604
Gary Walker, Ind. 222
C. majority 1,058 (2.31%)
Notional 5.89% swing Lab. to C.
(2005: Lab. majority 3,806 (9.47%))

§LIVERPOOL RIVERSIDE
E. 74,539 T. 38,801 (52.05%) Lab. hold
Louise Ellman, Lab. 22,998
Richard Marbrow, LD 8,825
Kegang Wu, C. 4,243
Tom Crone, Green 1,355
Peter Stafford, BNP 706
Pat Gaskell, UKIP 674
Lab. majority 14,173 (36.53%)
Notional 0.30% swing LD to Lab.
(2005: Lab. majority 11,731 (35.93%))

§LIVERPOOL WALTON
E. 62,612 T. 34,335 (54.84%) Lab. hold
*Steve Rotheram, Lab. 24,709
Patrick Moloney, LD 4,891
Adam Marsden, C. 2,241
Peter Stafford, BNP 1,104
Joe Nugent, UKIP 898
John Manwell, CPA 297
Daren Ireland, TUSC 195
Lab. majority 19,818 (57.72%)
Notional 1.47% swing LD to Lab.
(2005: Lab. majority 17,611 (54.77%))

§LIVERPOOL WAVERTREE
E. 62,518 T. 37,914 (60.64%)
Lab. (Co-op) hold
*Luciana Berger, Lab. (Co-op) 20,132
Colin Eldridge, LD 12,965
Andrew Garnett, C. 2,830
Neil Miney, UKIP 890
Rebecca Lawson, Green 598
Kim Singleton, Soc. Lab. 200
Steven McEllenborough, BNP 150
Frank Dunne, Ind. 149
Lab. (Co-op) majority 7,167 (18.90%)
Notional 5.00% swing LD to Lab. (Co-op)
(2005: Lab. (Co-op) majority 2,911 (8.91%))

§LIVERPOOL WEST DERBY
E. 63,082 T. 35,784 (56.73%)
Lab. (Co-op) hold
*Stephen Twigg, Lab. (Co-op) 22,953
Paul Twigger, LD 4,486
Stephen Radford, Lib 3,327
Pamela Hall, C. 3,311
Hilary Jones, UKIP 1,093
Kai Andersen, Soc. Lab. 614
Lab. (Co-op) majority 18,467 (51.61%)
Notional 3.16% swing LD to Lab. (Co-op)
(2005: Lab. (Co-op) majority 13,874 (45.29%))

§LOUGHBOROUGH
E. 77,502 T. 52,838 (68.18%) C. gain
*Nicky Morgan, C. 21,971
Andy Reed, Lab. (Co-op) 18,227
Mike Willis, LD 9,675
Kevan Stafford, BNP 2,040
John Foden, UKIP 925
C. majority 3,744 (7.09%)
Notional 5.48% swing Lab. (Co-op) to C.
(2005: Lab. (Co-op) majority 1,816 (3.88%))

§LOUTH & HORNCASTLE
E. 77,650 T. 50,494 (65.03%) C. hold
Sir Peter Tapsell, C. 25,065
Fiona Martin, LD 11,194
Patrick Mountain, Lab. 8,760
Julia Green, BNP 2,199
Pat Nurse, UKIP 2,183
Daniel Simpson, Lincs Ind. 576
Colin Mair, Eng. Dem. 517
C. majority 13,871 (27.47%)
Notional 0.80% swing LD to C.
(2005: C. majority 9,813 (21.08%))

LUDLOW
E. 66,631 T. 48,732 (73.14%) C. hold
Philip Dunne, C. 25,720
Heather Kidd, LD 15,971
Anthony Hunt, Lab. 3,272
Christopher Gill, UKIP 2,127
Christina Evans, BNP 1,016
Jacqui Morrish, Green 447
Alan Powell, Loony 179
C. majority 9,749 (20.01%)
7.82% swing LD to C.
(2005: C. majority 2,027 (4.36%))

§LUTON NORTH
E. 65,062 T. 43,018 (66.12%) Lab. hold
Kelvin Hopkins, Lab. 21,192
Jeremy Brier, C. 13,672
Rabi Martins, LD 4,784
Colin Brown, UKIP 1,564
Shelley Rose, BNP 1,316
Simon Hall, Green 490
Lab. majority 7,520 (17.48%)
Notional 0.55% swing C. to Lab.
(2005: Lab. majority 6,439 (16.39%))

§LUTON SOUTH
E. 59,962 T. 42,216 (70.40%)
Lab. (Co-op) hold
*Gavin Shuker, Lab. (Co-op) 14,725
Nigel Huddleston, C. 12,396
Qurban Hussain, LD 9,567
Esther Rantzen, Ind. Rantzen 1,872
Tony Blakey, BNP 1,299
Charles Lawman, UKIP 975
Stephen Rhodes, Ind. 463
Marc Scheimann, Green 366
Joe Hall, Ind. 264
Faruk Choudhury, Ind. 130
Stephen Lathwell, Ind. 84
Frank Sweeney, WRP 75
Lab. (Co-op) majority 2,329 (5.52%)
Notional 4.59% swing Lab. (Co-op) to C.
(2005: Lab. (Co-op) majority 5,698 (14.71%))

§MACCLESFIELD
E. 73,417 T. 50,059 (68.18%) C. hold
*David Rutley, C. 23,503
Roger Barlow, LD 11,544
Adrian Heald, Lab. 10,164
Brendan Murphy, Macc. Ind. 2,590
Jacqueline Smith, UKIP 1,418
John Knight, Green 840
C. majority 11,959 (23.89%)
Notional 3.11% swing C. to LD
(2005: C. majority 9,464 (20.66%))

§MAIDENHEAD
E. 72,844 T. 53,720 (73.75%) C. hold
Theresa May, C. 31,937
Tony Hill, LD 15,168
Pat McDonald, Lab. 3,795
Kenneth Wight, UKIP 1,243
Tim Rait, BNP 825
Peter Forbes, Green 482
Peter Prior, F and R 270
C. majority 16,769 (31.22%)
Notional 7.82% swing LD to C.
(2005: C. majority 7,650 (15.58%))

§MAIDSTONE & THE WEALD
E. 71,041 T. 48,928 (68.87%) C. hold
*Helen Grant, C. 23,491
Peter Carroll, LD 17,602
Rav Seeruthun, Lab. 4,769
Gareth Kendall, UKIP 1,637
Stuart Jeffery, Green 655
Gary Butler, NF 643
Heidi Simmonds, Ch. P. 131
C. majority 5,889 (12.04%)
Notional 8.48% swing C. to LD
(2005: C. majority 12,922 (28.99%))

§MAKERFIELD
E. 73,641 T. 43,771 (59.44%) Lab. hold
*Yvonne Fovargue, Lab. 20,700
Itrat Ali, C. 8,210
David Crowther, LD 7,082
Bob Brierley, Ind. 3,424
Ken Haslam, BNP 3,229
John Mather, Ind. 1,126
Lab. majority 12,490 (28.53%)
Notional 9.98% swing Lab. to C.
(2005: Lab. majority 17,903 (48.49%))

§MALDON
E. 68,861 T. 47,895 (69.55%) C. hold
John Whittingdale, C. 28,661
Elfreda Tealby-Watson, LD 9,254
Swatantra Nandanwar, Lab. 6,070
Jesse Pryke, UKIP 2,446
Len Blaine, BNP 1,464
C. majority 19,407 (40.52%)
Notional 0.40% swing C. to LD
(2005: C. majority 13,631 (32.13%))

§¶MANCHESTER CENTRAL
E. 90,110 T. 39,927 (44.31%) Lab. hold
Tony Lloyd, Lab. 21,059
Marc Ramsbottom, LD 10,620
Suhail Rahuja, C. 4,704
Tony Trebilcock, BNP 1,636
Gayle O'Donovan, Green 915
Nicola Weatherill, UKIP 607
Ron Sinclair, Soc. Lab. 153
John Cartwright, Ind. 120
Jonty Leff, WRP 59
Robert Skelton, SEP 54
Lab. majority 10,439 (26.15%)
Notional 6.11% swing Lab. to LD
(2005: Lab. majority 11,636 (38.36%))

§MANCHESTER GORTON
E. 75,933 T. 38,325 (50.47%) Lab. hold
Gerald Kaufman, Lab. 19,211
Qassim Afzal, LD 12,508
Caroline Healy, C. 4,224
Justine Hall, Green 1,048
Karen Reissman, TUSC 507
Mohammed Zulfikar, Respect 337
Peter Harrison, Ch. P. 254
Tim Dobson, Pirate 236
Lab. majority 6,703 (17.49%)
Notional 1.06% swing Lab. to LD
(2005: Lab. majority 6,355 (19.61%))

§MANCHESTER WITHINGTON
E. 74,371 T. 45,031 (60.55%) LD hold
John Leech, LD 20,110
Lucy Powell, Lab. 18,216
Christopher Green, C. 5,005
Brian Candeland, Green 798
Bob Gutfreund-Walmsley, UKIP 698
Yasmin Zalzala, Ind. 147
Marcus Farmer, Ind. 57
LD majority 1,894 (4.21%)
Notional 1.41% swing Lab. to LD
(2005: LD majority 531 (1.39%))

§MANSFIELD
E. 80,069 T. 48,395 (60.44%) Lab. hold
Joseph Meale, Lab. 18,753
Tracy Critchlow, C. 12,741
Michael Wyatt, LD 7,469
Andre Camilleri, Mansfield Ind. 4,339
David Hamilton, UKIP 2,985
Rachel Hill, BNP 2,108
Lab. majority 6,012 (12.42%)
Notional 9.49% swing Lab. to C.
(2005: Lab. majority 13,776 (31.39%))

§MEON VALLEY
E. 70,488 T. 51,238 (72.69%) C. hold
*George Hollingbery, C. 28,818
Liz Leffman, LD 16,693
Howard Linsley, Lab. 3,266
Steve Harris, UKIP 1,490
Pat Harris, Eng. Dem. 582
Sarah Coats, APP 255
Graeme Quar, Ind. 134
C. majority 12,125 (23.66%)
Notional 9.38% swing LD to C.
(2005: C. majority 2,378 (4.91%))

§MERIDEN
E. 83,826 T. 52,162 (62.23%) C. hold
Caroline Spelman, C. 26,956
Ed Williams, Lab. 10,703
Simon Slater, LD 9,278
Frank O'Brien, BNP 2,511
Barry Allcock, UKIP 1,378
Elly Stanton, Green 678
Nikki Sinclaire, RA 658
C. majority 16,253 (31.16%)
Notional 7.90% swing Lab. to C.
(2005: C. majority 7,412 (15.37%))

§¶MIDDLESBROUGH
E. 65,148 T. 33,455 (51.35%) Lab. hold
Sir Stuart Bell, Lab. 15,351
Chris Foote-Wood, LD 6,662
John Walsh, C. 6,283
Joan McTigue, Ind. 1,969
Michael Ferguson, BNP 1,954
Robert Parker, UKIP 1,236
Lab. majority 8,689 (25.97%)
Notional 6.45% swing Lab. to LD
(2005: Lab. majority 12,476 (38.87%))

§MIDDLESBROUGH SOUTH & CLEVELAND EAST
E. 72,664 T. 46,214 (63.60%) Lab. hold
*Tom Blenkinsop, Lab. 18,138
Paul Bristow, C. 16,461
Nick Emmerson, LD 7,340
Stuart Lightwing, UKIP 1,881
Shaun Gatley, BNP 1,576
Mike Allen, Ind. 818
Lab. majority 1,677 (3.63%)
Notional 7.44% swing Lab. to C.
(2005: Lab. majority 8,096 (18.51%))

§MILTON KEYNES NORTH
E. 85,841 T. 53,888 (62.78%) C. gain
Mark Lancaster, C. 23,419
Andrew Pakes, Lab. 14,458
Jill Hope, LD 11,894
Michael Phillips, UKIP 1,772
Richard Hamilton, BNP 1,154
Alan Francis, Green 733
Revd John Lennon, CPA 206
Matt Bananamatt Fensome, Loony 157
Anant Vyas, Ind. 95
C. majority 8,961 (16.63%)
Notional 9.17% swing Lab. to C.
(2005: Lab. majority 848 (1.71%))

§MILTON KEYNES SOUTH
E. 90,487 T. 55,333 (61.15%) C. gain
*Iain Stewart, C. 23,034
Phyllis Starkey, Lab. 17,833
Peter Jones, LD 9,787
Philip Pinto, UKIP 2,074
Matthew Tait, BNP 1,502
Katrina Deacon, Green 774
Suzanne Nti, CPA 245
Jonathan Worth, NFP 84
C. majority 5,201 (9.40%)
Notional 6.22% swing Lab. to C.
(2005: Lab. majority 1,497 (3.04%))

§MITCHAM & MORDEN
E. 65,939 T. 43,797 (66.42%) Lab. hold
Siobhain McDonagh, Lab. 24,722
Melanie Hampton, C. 11,056
Diana Coman, LD 5,202
Tony Martin, BNP 1,386
Andrew Mills, UKIP 857
Smarajit Roy, Green 381
Rathy Alagaratnam, Ind. 155
Ernest Redgrave, Ind. 38
Lab. majority 13,666 (31.20%)
Notional 0.44% swing Lab. to C.
(2005: Lab. majority 12,739 (32.08%))

MOLE VALLEY
E. 72,612 T. 54,324 (74.81%) C. hold
Sir Paul Beresford, C. 31,263
Alice Humphreys, LD 15,610
James Dove, Lab. 3,804
Leigh Jones, UKIP 2,752
Rob Sedgwick, Green 895
C. majority 15,653 (28.81%)
2.27% swing LD to C.
(2005: C. majority 11,997 (24.28%))

§MORECAMBE & LUNESDALE
E. 69,965 T. 43,616 (62.34%) C. gain
*David Morris, C. 18,035
Geraldine Smith, Lab. 17,169
Leslie Jones, LD 5,971
Mark Knight, UKIP 1,843
Chris Coates, Green 598
C. majority 866 (1.99%)
Notional 6.86% swing Lab. to C.
(2005: Lab. majority 4,849 (11.74%))

§MORLEY & OUTWOOD
E. 74,200 T. 48,856 (65.84%)
Lab. (Co-op) hold
Ed Balls, Lab. (Co-op) 18,365
Antony Calvert, C. 17,264
James Monaghan, LD 8,186
Chris Beverley, BNP 3,535
David Daniel, UKIP 1,506
Lab. (Co-op) majority 1,101 (2.25%)
Notional 9.35% swing Lab. (Co-op) to C.
(2005: Lab. (Co-op) majority 8,669 (20.95%))

§NEW FOREST EAST
E. 72,858 T. 50,036 (68.68%) C. hold
Julian Lewis, C. 26,443
Terry Scriven, LD 15,136
Peter Sopowski, Lab. 4,915
Peter Day, UKIP 2,518
Beverley Golden, Green 1,024
C. majority 11,307 (22.60%)
Notional 3.20% swing LD to C.
(2005: C. majority 7,653 (16.21%))

§NEW FOREST WEST
E. 68,332 T. 47,572 (69.62%) C. hold
Desmond Swayne, C. 27,980
Mike Plummer, LD 11,084
Janice Hurne, Lab. 4,666
Martin Lyon, UKIP 2,783
Janet Richards, Green 1,059
C. majority 16,896 (35.52%)
Notional 0.60% swing C. to LD
(2005: C. majority 16,183 (36.71%))

§NEWARK
E. 71,785 T. 51,228 (71.36%) C. hold
Patrick Mercer, C. 27,590
Dr Ian Campbell, Lab. 11,438
Pauline Jenkins, LD 10,246
Tom Irvine, UKIP 1,954
C. majority 16,152 (31.53%)
Notional 4.68% swing Lab. to C.
(2005: C. majority 10,077 (22.17%))

§NEWBURY
E. 83,411 T. 58,589 (70.24%) C. hold
Richard Benyon, C. 33,057
David Rendel, LD 20,809
Hannah Cooper, Lab. 2,505
David Black, UKIP 1,475
Adrian Hollister, Green 490
Brian Burgess, Ind. 158
David Yates, AD 95
C. majority 12,248 (20.90%)
Notional 7.24% swing LD to C.
(2005: C. majority 3,452 (6.42%))

NEWCASTLE-UNDER-LYME
E. 69,433 T. 43,191 (62.21%) Lab. hold
Paul Farrelly, Lab. 16,393
Robert Jenrick, C. 14,841
Nigel Jones, LD 8,466
David Nixon, UKIP 3,491
Lab. majority 1,552 (3.59%)
8.39% swing Lab. to C.
(2005: Lab. majority 8,108 (20.38%))

§NEWCASTLE UPON TYNE CENTRAL
E. 60,507 T. 34,157 (56.45%) Lab. hold
*Chinyelu Onwurah, Lab. 15,694
Gareth Kane, LD 8,228
Nick Holder, C. 6,611
Ken Booth, BNP 2,302
Martin Davies, UKIP 754
John Pearson, Green 568
Lab. majority 7,466 (21.86%)
Notional 0.60% swing Lab. to LD
(2005: Lab. majority 7,509 (23.07%))

§NEWCASTLE UPON TYNE EAST
E. 64,487 T. 37,840 (58.68%) Lab. hold
Nicholas Brown, Lab. 17,043
Wendy Taylor, LD 12,590
Dominic Llewellyn, C. 6,068
Alan Spence, BNP 1,342
Andrew Gray, Green 620
Martin Levy, Comm. 177
Lab. majority 4,453 (11.77%)
Notional 4.60% swing Lab. to LD
(2005: Lab. majority 6,987 (20.97%))

§NEWCASTLE UPON TYNE NORTH
E. 67,110 T. 43,946 (65.48%) Lab. hold
*Catherine McKinnell, Lab. 17,950
Ronald Beadle, LD 14,536
Stephen Parkinson, C. 7,966
Terry Gibson, BNP 1,890
Ian Proud, UKIP 1,285
Anna Heyman, Green 319
Lab. majority 3,414 (7.77%)
Notional 4.54% swing Lab. to LD
(2005: Lab. majority 6,878 (16.84%))

§NEWTON ABBOT
E. 69,343 T. 48,283 (69.63%) C. gain
*Anne-Marie Morris, C. 20,774
Richard Younger-Ross, LD 20,251
Patrick Canavan, Lab. 3,387
Jackie Hooper, UKIP 3,088
Corinne Lindsey, Green 701
Keith Sharp, Ind. 82
C. majority 523 (1.08%)
Notional 5.79% swing LD to C.
(2005: LD majority 4,830 (10.50%))

§NORFOLK MID
E. 74,260 T. 50,765 (68.36%) C. hold
*George Freeman, C. 25,123
David Newman, LD 11,267
Elizabeth Hughes, Lab. 8,857
Toby Coke, UKIP 2,800
Tim Birt, Green 1,457
Christine Kelly, BNP 1,261
C. majority 13,856 (27.29%)
Notional 0.02% swing C. to LD
(2005: C. majority 7,793 (16.29%))

§NORFOLK NORTH
E. 67,841 T. 49,661 (73.20%) LD hold
Norman Lamb, LD 27,554
Trevor Ivory, C. 15,928
Phil Harris, Lab. 2,896
Michael Baker, UKIP 2,680
Andrew Boswell, Green 508
Simon Mann, Ind. 95
LD majority 11,626 (23.41%)
Notional 3.06% swing C. to LD
(2005: LD majority 8,575 (17.28%))

§NORFOLK NORTH WEST
E. 73,207 T. 47,800 (65.29%) C. hold
Henry Bellingham, C. 25,916
William Summers, LD 11,106
Manish Sood, Lab. 6,353
John Gray, UKIP 1,841
David Fleming, BNP 1,839
Michael de Whalley, Green 745
C. majority 14,810 (30.98%)
Notional 2.09% swing C. to LD
(2005: C. majority 8,417 (18.34%))

§NORFOLK SOUTH
E. 76,165 T. 54,993 (72.20%) C. hold
Richard Bacon, C. 27,133
Jacky Howe, LD 16,193
Mick Castle, Lab. 7,252
Evan Heasley, UKIP 2,329
Helen Mitchell, BNP 1,086
Jo Willcott, Green 1,000
C. majority 10,940 (19.89%)
Notional 3.25% swing LD to C.
(2005: C. majority 6,719 (13.39%))

§NORFOLK SOUTH WEST
E. 74,298 T. 49,150 (66.15%) C. hold
*Elizabeth Truss, C. 23,753
Stephen Gordon, LD 10,613
Peter Smith, Lab. 9,119
Kay Hipsey, UKIP 3,061
Dennis Pearce, BNP 1,774
Lori Allen, Green 830
C. majority 13,140 (26.73%)
Notional 0.48% swing LD to C.
(2005: C. majority 6,817 (15.00%))

§NORMANTON, PONTEFRACT & CASTLEFORD
E. 82,239 T. 46,239 (56.23%) Lab. hold
Yvette Cooper, Lab. 22,293
Nick Pickles, C. 11,314
Chris Rush, LD 7,585
Graham Thewlis-Hardy, BNP 3,864
Gareth Allen, Ind. 1,183
Lab. majority 10,979 (23.74%)
Notional 12.49% swing Lab. to C.
(2005: Lab. majority 20,608 (48.73%))

§NORTHAMPTON NORTH
E. 64,230 T. 40,271 (62.70%) C. gain
*Michael Ellis, C. 13,735
Sally Keeble, Lab. 11,799
Andrew Simpson, LD 11,250
Ray Beasley, BNP 1,316
Jim Macarthur, UKIP 1,238
Tony Lochmuller, Green 443
Eamonn Fitzpatrick, Ind. 334
Timothy Webb, Ch. P. 98
Malcolm Mildren, Ind. 58
C. majority 1,936 (4.81%)
Notional 6.90% swing Lab. to C.
(2005: Lab. majority 3,340 (9.00%))

§NORTHAMPTON SOUTH
E. 66,923 T. 38,978 (58.24%) C. gain
*Brian Binley, C. 15,917
Clyde Loakes, Lab. 9,913
Paul Varnsverry, LD 7,579
Tony Clarke, Ind. 2,242
Derek Clark, UKIP 1,897
Kevin Sills, Eng. Dem. 618
Julie Hawkins, Green 363
Dave Green, NSPS 325
Kevin Willsher, Ind. 65
Liam Costello, SMA 59
C. majority 6,004 (15.40%)
Notional 9.59% swing Lab. to C.
(2005: Lab. majority 1,445 (3.78%))

§NORTHAMPTONSHIRE SOUTH
E. 82,032 T. 59,890 (73.01%) C. hold
*Andrea Leadsom, C. 33,081
Scott Collins, LD 12,603
Matthew May, Lab. 10,380
Barry Mahoney, UKIP 2,406
Tony Tappy, Eng. Dem. 735
Marcus Rock, Green 685
C. majority 20,478 (34.19%)
Notional 0.12% swing C. to LD
(2005: C. majority 11,356 (22.85%))

§NORWICH NORTH
E. 65,258 T. 42,573 (65.24%) C. gain
Chloe Smith, C. 17,280
John Cook, Lab. 13,379
John Stephen, LD 7,783
Glenn Tingle, UKIP 1,878
Jessica Goldfinch, Green 1,245
Thomas Richardson, BNP 747
Bill Holden, Ind. 143
Andrew Holland, Ch. P. 118
C. majority 3,901 (9.16%)
Notional 12.88% swing Lab. to C.
(2005: Lab. majority 6,769 (16.60%))

§NORWICH SOUTH
E. 73,649 T. 47,551 (64.56%) LD gain
*Simon Wright, LD 13,960
Charles Clarke, Lab. 13,650
Antony Little, C. 10,902
Adrian Ramsay, Green 7,095
Steve Emmens, UKIP 1,145
Leonard Heather, BNP 697
Gabriel Polley, WRP 102
LD majority 310 (0.65%)
Notional 4.03% swing Lab. to LD
(2005: Lab. majority 3,023 (7.40%))

§NOTTINGHAM EAST
E. 58,707 T. 33,112 (56.40%) Lab. (Co-op) hold
*Christopher Leslie, Lab. (Co-op) 15,022
Sam Boote, LD 8,053
Ewan Lamont, C. 7,846
Pat Wolfe, UKIP 1,138
Benjamin Hoare, Green 928
Parvaiz Sardar, Ch. P. 125
Lab. (Co-op) majority 6,969 (21.05%)
Notional 1.89% swing Lab. (Co-op) to LD
(2005: Lab. (Co-op) majority 7,083 (24.22%))

§NOTTINGHAM NORTH
E. 63,240 T. 34,285 (54.21%) Lab. hold
Graham Allen, Lab. 16,646
Martin Curtis, C. 8,508
Tim Ball, LD 5,849
Bob Brindley, BNP 1,944
Irenea Marriott, UKIP 1,338
Lab. majority 8,138 (23.74%)
Notional 8.65% swing Lab. to C.
(2005: Lab. majority 12,870 (41.04%))

§NOTTINGHAM SOUTH
E. 67,441 T. 40,789 (60.48%) Lab. hold
*Lilian Greenwood, Lab. 15,209
Rowena Holland, C. 13,437
Tony Sutton, LD 9,406
Tony Woodward, BNP 1,140
Ken Browne, UKIP 967
Matthew Butcher, Green 630
Lab. majority 1,772 (4.34%)
Notional 7.43% swing Lab. to C.
(2005: Lab. majority 6,665 (19.20%))

§NUNEATON
E. 67,837 T. 44,646 (65.81%) C. gain
*Marcus Jones, C. 18,536
Jayne Innes, Lab. 16,467
Christina Jebb, LD 6,846
Martyn Findley, BNP 2,797
C. majority 2,069 (4.63%)
Notional 7.19% swing Lab. to C.
(2005: Lab. majority 3,894 (9.74%))

§OLD BEXLEY & SIDCUP
E. 65,665 T. 45,492 (69.28%) C. hold
James Brokenshire, C. 24,625
Rick Everitt, Lab. 8,768
Duncan Borrowman, LD 6,996
John Brooks, BNP 2,132
David Coburn, UKIP 1,532
Elaine Cheeseman, Eng. Dem. 520
John Hemming-Clark, Save QM 393
Jonathan Rooks, Green 371
Napoleon Dynamite, Loony 155
C. majority 15,857 (34.86%)
Notional 6.43% swing Lab. to C.
(2005: C. majority 9,309 (22.00%))

§¶OLDHAM EAST & SADDLEWORTH
E. 72,765 T. 44,520 (61.18%) Lab. hold
Phil Woolas, Lab. 14,186
Elwyn Watkins, LD 14,083
Kashif Ali, C. 11,773
Alwyn Stott, BNP 2,546
David Bentley, UKIP 1,720
Gulzar Nazir, Ch. P. 212
Lab. majority 103 (0.23%)
Notional 5.08% swing Lab. to LD
(2005: Lab. majority 4,245 (10.39%))

§OLDHAM WEST & ROYTON
E. 72,651 T. 42,910 (59.06%) Lab. hold
Michael Meacher, Lab. 19,503
Kamran Ghafoor, C. 10,151
Mark Alcock, LD 8,193
David Joines, BNP 3,049
Helen Roberts, UKIP 1,387
Shahid Miah, Respect 627
Lab. majority 9,352 (21.79%)
Notional 2.74% swing Lab. to C.
(2005: Lab. majority 10,454 (27.13%))

§ORPINGTON
E. 67,732 T. 48,911 (72.21%) C. hold
*Joseph Johnson, C. 29,200
David McBride, LD 12,000
Stephen Morgan, Lab. 4,400
Mick Greenhough, UKIP 1,360
Tess Culnane, BNP 1,241
Tamara Galloway, Green 511
Chriss Snape, Eng. Dem. 199
C. majority 17,200 (35.17%)
Notional 12.19% swing LD to C.
(2005: C. majority 5,221 (10.79%))

§OXFORD EAST
E. 81,886 T. 51,651 (63.08%) Lab. hold
Andrew Smith, Lab. 21,938
Steve Goddard, LD 17,357
Edward Argar, C. 9,727
Sushila Dhall, Green 1,238
Julia Gasper, UKIP 1,202
David O'Sullivan, SEP 116
Roger Crawford, Parenting 73
Lab. majority 4,581 (8.87%)
Notional 4.07% swing LD to Lab.
(2005: Lab. majority 332 (0.73%))

§OXFORD WEST & ABINGDON
E. 86,458 T. 56,480 (65.33%) C. gain
*Nicola Blackwood, C. 23,906
Evan Harris, LD 23,730
Richard Stevens, Lab. 5,999
Paul Williams, UKIP 1,518
Chris Goodall, Green 1,184
Keith Mann, APP 143
C. majority 176 (0.31%)
Notional 6.87% swing LD to C.
(2005: LD majority 6,816 (13.43%))

PENDLE
E. 66,417 T. 45,045 (67.82%) C. gain
*Andrew Stephenson, C. 17,512
Gordon Prentice, Lab. 13,927
Afzal Anwar, LD 9,095
James Jackman, BNP 2,894
Graham Cannon, UKIP 1,476
Richard Masih, Ch. P. 141
C. majority 3,585 (7.96%)
6.63% swing Lab. to C.
(2005: Lab. majority 2,180 (5.30%))

§PENISTONE & STOCKSBRIDGE
E. 68,501 T. 46,516 (67.91%) Lab. hold
Angela Smith, Lab. 17,565
Spencer Pitfield, C. 14,516
Ian Cuthbertson, LD 9,800
Paul James, BNP 2,207
Grant French, UKIP 1,936
Paul McEnhill, Eng. Dem. 492
Lab. majority 3,049 (6.55%)
Notional 7.45% swing Lab. to C.
(2005: Lab. majority 8,617 (20.43%))

§PENRITH & THE BORDER
E. 64,548 T. 45,087 (69.85%) C. hold
*Rory Stewart, C. 24,071
Peter Thornton, LD 12,830
Barbara Cannon, Lab. 5,834
John Stanyer, UKIP 1,259
Chris Davidson, BNP 1,093
C. majority 11,241 (24.93%)
Notional 0.32% swing C. to LD
(2005: C. majority 10,795 (25.58%))

§PETERBOROUGH
E. 70,316 T. 44,927 (63.89%) C. hold
Stewart Jackson, C. 18,133
Ed Murphy, Lab. 13,272
Nick Sandford, LD 8,816
Frances Fox, UKIP 3,007
Rob King, Eng. Dem. 770
Fiona Radic, Green 523
John Swallow, Ind. 406
C. majority 4,861 (10.82%)
Notional 0.94% swing Lab. to C.
(2005: C. majority 4,005 (8.93%))

§PLYMOUTH MOOR VIEW
E. 67,261 T. 41,526 (61.74%) Lab. hold
Alison Seabeck, Lab. 15,433
Matthew Groves, C. 13,845
Stuart Bonar, LD 7,016
Bill Wakeham, UKIP 3,188
Roy Cook, BNP 1,438
Wendy Miller, Green 398
David Marchesi, Soc. Lab. 208
Lab. majority 1,588 (3.82%)
Notional 7.77% swing Lab. to C.
(2005: Lab. majority 7,740 (19.37%))

§PLYMOUTH SUTTON & DEVONPORT
E. 71,035 T. 43,894 (61.79%) C. gain
*Oliver Colville, C. 15,050
Linda Gilroy, Lab. (Co-op) 13,901
Judy Evans, LD 10,829
Andrew Leigh, UKIP 2,854
Tony Brown, Green 904
Brian Gerrish, Ind. 233
Robert Hawkins, Soc. Lab. 123
C. majority 1,149 (2.62%)
Notional 6.86% swing Lab. (Co-op) to C.
(2005: Lab. (Co-op) majority 4,472 (11.11%))

§POOLE
E. 64,661 T. 47,436 (73.36%) C. hold
Robert Syms, C. 22,532
Philip Eades, LD 14,991
Jason Sanderson, Lab. 6,041
Nick Wellstead, UKIP 2,507
David Holmes, BNP 1,188
Ian Northover, Ind. 177
C. majority 7,541 (15.90%)
Notional 0.79% swing LD to C.
(2005: C. majority 6,035 (14.32%))

§POPLAR & LIMEHOUSE
E. 74,956 T. 46,700 (62.30%) Lab. hold
Jim Fitzpatrick, Lab. 18,679
Tim Archer, C. 12,649
George Galloway, Respect 8,160
Jonathan Fryer, LD 5,209
Wayne Lochner, UKIP 565
Andrew Osborne, Eng. Dem. 470
Chris Smith, Green 449
Kabir Mahmud, Ind. 293
Mohammed Hoque, Ind. 167
Jim Thornton, Ind. 59
Lab. majority 6,030 (12.91%)
Notional 1.04% swing C. to Lab.
(2005: Lab. majority 3,823 (10.84%))

§PORTSMOUTH NORTH
E. 70,329 T. 44,118 (62.73%) C. gain
*Penny Mordaunt, C. 19,533
Sarah McCarthy-Fry, Lab. (Co-op) 12,244
Darren Sanders, LD 8,874
Mike Fitzgerald, UKIP 1,812
David Knight, Eng. Dem. 1,040
Iain Maclennan, Green 461
Mick Tosh, TUSC 154
C. majority 7,289 (16.52%)
Notional 8.64% swing Lab. (Co-op) to C.
(2005: Lab. (Co-op) majority 315 (0.77%))

§PORTSMOUTH SOUTH
E. 70,242 T. 41,264 (58.75%) LD hold
Mike Hancock, LD 18,921
Flick Drummond, C. 13,721
John Ferrett, Lab. 5,640
Christopher Martin, UKIP 876
Geoff Crompton, BNP 873
Tim Dawes, Green 716
Ian DuCane, Eng. Dem. 400
Les Cummings, J & AC 117
LD majority 5,200 (12.60%)
Notional 2.30% swing C. to LD
(2005: LD majority 2,955 (8.00%))

§PRESTON
E. 62,460 T. 32,505 (52.04%) Lab. (Co-op) hold
Mark Hendrick, Lab. (Co-op) 15,668
Mark Jewell, LD 7,935
Nerissa Warner-O'Neill, C. 7,060
Richard Muirhead, UKIP 1,462
George Ambroze, Ch. P. 272
Krishna Tayya, Ind. 108
Lab. (Co-op) majority 7,733 (23.79%)
Notional 2.50% swing Lab. (Co-op) to LD
(2005: Lab. (Co-op) majority 8,338 (27.67%))

§PUDSEY
E. 69,257 T. 49,083 (70.87%) C. gain
*Stuart Andrew, C. 18,874
Jamie Hanley, Lab. 17,215
Jamie Matthews, LD 10,224
Ian Gibson, BNP 1,549
David Dews, UKIP 1,221
C. majority 1,659 (3.38%)
Notional 7.56% swing Lab. to C.
(2005: Lab. majority 5,204 (11.74%))

§PUTNEY
E. 63,370 T. 40,785 (64.36%) C. hold
Justine Greening, C. 21,223
Stuart King, Lab. 11,170
James Sandbach, LD 6,907
Bruce Mackenzie, Green 591
Peter Darby, BNP 459
Hugo Wareham, UKIP 435
C. majority 10,053 (24.65%)
Notional 9.92% swing Lab. to C.
(2005: C. majority 1,723 (4.80%))

§RAYLEIGH & WICKFORD
E. 75,905 T. 52,343 (68.96%) C. hold
Mark Francois, C. 30,257
Susan Gaszczak, LD 7,919
Michael Le-Surf, Lab. 7,577
John Hayter, Eng. Dem. 2,219
Tino Callaghan, UKIP 2,211
Anthony Evennett, BNP 2,160
C. majority 22,338 (42.68%)
Notional 2.13% swing LD to C.
(2005: C. majority 12,983 (27.37%))

§READING EAST
E. 74,922 T. 49,985 (66.72%) C. hold
Rob Wilson, C. 21,269
Gareth Epps, LD 13,664
Anneliese Dodds, Lab. 12,729
Adrian Pitfield, UKIP 1,086
Rob White, Green 1,069
Joan Lloyd, Ind. 111
Michael Turberville, Ind. 57
C. majority 7,605 (15.21%)
Notional 1.97% swing LD to C.
(2005: C. majority 739 (1.71%))

§READING WEST
E. 72,118 T. 47,530 (65.91%) C. gain
*Alok Sharma, C. 20,523
Naz Sarkar, Lab. 14,519
Daisy Benson, LD 9,546
Bruce Hay, UKIP 1,508
Howard Thomas, CSP 852
Adrian Windisch, Green 582
C. majority 6,004 (12.63%)
Notional 12.05% swing Lab. to C.
(2005: Lab. majority 4,931 (11.47%))

REDCAR
E. 67,125 T. 41,963 (62.51%) LD gain
*Ian Swales, LD 18,955
Vera Baird, Lab. 13,741
Steve Mastin, C. 5,790
Martin Bulmer, UKIP 1,875
Kevin Broughton, BNP 1,475
Hannah Walter, TUSC 127
LD majority 5,214 (12.43%)
21.80% swing Lab. to LD
(2005: Lab. majority 12,116 (31.18%))

§REDDITCH
E. 68,550 T. 44,018 (64.21%) C. gain
*Karen Lumley, C. 19,138
Jacqui Smith, Lab. 13,317
Nicholas Lane, LD 7,750
Anne Davis, UKIP 1,497
Andy Ingram, BNP 1,394
Kevin White, Green 393
Vincent Schittone, Eng. Dem. 255
Scott Beverley, Ch. P. 101
Paul Swansborough, Ind. 100
Derek Fletcher, Nobody 73
C. majority 5,821 (13.22%)
Notional 9.21% swing Lab. to C.
(2005: Lab. majority 2,163 (5.20%))

§REIGATE
E. 71,604 T. 49,978 (69.80%) C. hold
Crispin Blunt, C. 26,688
Jane Kulka, LD 13,097
Robert Hull, Lab. 5,672
Joe Fox, UKIP 2,089
Keith Brown, BNP 1,345
Jonathan Essex, Green 1,087
C. majority 13,591 (27.19%)
Notional 0.89% swing LD to C.
(2005: C. majority 11,093 (25.41%))

§RIBBLE VALLEY
E. 78,068 T. 52,287 (66.98%) C. hold
Nigel Evans, C. 26,298
Paul Foster, Lab. 11,529
Allan Knox, LD 10,732
Stephen Rush, UKIP 3,496
Tony Johnson, ND 232
C. majority 14,769 (28.25%)
Notional 6.58% swing Lab. to C.
(2005: C. majority 6,953 (15.09%))

§RICHMOND (YORKS)
E. 79,478 T. 53,412 (67.20%) C. hold
William Hague, C. 33,541
Lawrence Meredith, LD 10,205
Eileen Driver, Lab. 8,150
Leslie Rowe, Green 1,516
C. majority 23,336 (43.69%)
Notional 0.64% swing LD to C.
(2005: C. majority 19,450 (38.73%))

§RICHMOND PARK
E. 77,060 T. 59,268 (76.91%) C. gain
*Zac Goldsmith, C. 29,461
Susan Kramer, LD 25,370
Eleanor Tunnicliffe, Lab. 2,979
Peter Dul, UKIP 669
James Page, Green 572
Susan May, CPA 133
Charles Hill, Ind. 84
C. majority 4,091 (6.90%)
Notional 7.00% swing LD to C.
(2005: LD majority 3,613 (7.09%))

§ROCHDALE
E. 78,952 T. 45,907 (58.15%) Lab. hold
*Simon Danczuk, Lab. 16,699
Paul Rowen, LD 15,810
Mudasir Dean, C. 8,305
Chris Jackson, NF 2,236
Colin Denby, UKIP 1,999
Mohammed Salim, IZB 545
John Whitehead, Ind. 313
Lab. majority 889 (1.94%)
Notional 0.79% swing LD to Lab.
(2005: Lab. majority 149 (0.35%))

§ROCHESTER & STROOD
E. 73,882 T. 47,971 (64.93%) C. hold
*Mark Reckless, C. 23,604
Teresa Murray, Lab. 13,651
Geoffrey Juby, LD 7,800
Ron Sands, Eng. Dem. 2,182
Simon Marchant, Green 734
C. majority 9,953 (20.75%)
Notional 9.81% swing Lab. to C.
(2005: C. majority 503 (1.14%))

§ROCHFORD & SOUTHEND EAST
E. 71,080 T. 41,631 (58.57%) C. hold
James Duddridge, C. 19,509
Kevin Bonavia, Lab. 8,459
Graham Longley, LD 8,084
James Moyies, UKIP 2,405
Geoff Strobridge, BNP 1,856
Andrew Vaughan, Green 707
Anthony Chytry, Ind. 611
C. majority 11,050 (26.54%)
Notional 6.37% swing Lab. to C.
(2005: C. majority 5,307 (13.80%))

§ROMFORD
E. 71,193 T. 46,481 (65.29%) C. hold
Andrew Rosindell, C. 26,031
Rachel Voller, Lab. 9,077
Helen Duffett, LD 5,572
Robert Bailey, BNP 2,438
Gerard Batten, UKIP 2,050
Dr Peter Thorogood, Eng. Dem. 603
Gary Haines, Green 447
Philip Hyde, Ind. 151
David Sturman, Ind. 112
C. majority 16,954 (36.48%)
Notional 3.94% swing Lab. to C.
(2005: C. majority 12,120 (28.59%))

§ROMSEY & SOUTHAMPTON NORTH
E. 66,901 T. 48,939 (73.15%) C. gain
*Caroline Nokes, C. 24,345
Sandra Gidley, LD 20,189
Aktar Beg, Lab. 3,116
John Meropoulos, UKIP 1,289
C. majority 4,156 (8.49%)
Notional 4.48% swing LD to C.
(2005: LD majority 204 (0.46%))

§ROSSENDALE & DARWEN
E. 73,003 T. 47,128 (64.56%) C. gain
*Jake Berry, C. 19,691
Janet Anderson, Lab. 15,198
Robert Sheffield, LD 8,541
David Duthie, UKIP 1,617
Kevin Bryan, NF 1,062
Michael Johnson, Eng. Dem. 663
Tony Melia, Impact 243
Mike Sivieri, Ind. 113
C. majority 4,493 (9.53%)
Notional 8.94% swing Lab. to C.
(2005: Lab. majority 3,696 (8.35%))

§ROTHER VALLEY
E. 72,841 T. 46,758 (64.19%) Lab. hold
Kevin Barron, Lab. 19,147
Lynda Donaldson, C. 13,281
Wesley Paxton, LD 8,111
Will Blair, BNP 3,606
Tina Dowdall, UKIP 2,613
Lab. majority 5,866 (12.55%)
Notional 7.96% swing Lab. to C.
(2005: Lab. majority 11,558 (28.47%))

§¶ROTHERHAM
E. 63,565 T. 37,506 (59.00%) Lab. hold
Denis MacShane, Lab. 16,741
Jackie Whiteley, C. 6,279
Rebecca Taylor, LD 5,994
Marlene Guest, BNP 3,906
Peter Thirlwall, Ind. 2,366
Caven Vines, UKIP 2,220
Lab. majority 10,462 (27.89%)
Notional 8.27% swing Lab. to C.
(2005: Lab. majority 13,865 (41.33%))

§RUGBY
E. 68,914 T. 47,468 (68.88%) C. gain
*Mark Pawsey, C. 20,901
Andy King, Lab. 14,901
Jerry Roodhouse, LD 9,434
Mark Badrick, BNP 1,375
Roy Sandison, Green 451
Barry Milford, UKIP 406
C. majority 6,000 (12.64%)
Notional 8.92% swing Lab. to C.
(2005: Lab. majority 2,397 (5.20%))

§RUISLIP, NORTHWOOD & PINNER
E. 70,873 T. 50,205 (70.84%) C. hold
Nick Hurd, C. 28,866
Anita McDonald, Lab. 9,806
Thomas Papworth, LD 8,345
Jason Pontey, UKIP 1,351
Ian Edward, NF 899
Graham Lee, Green 740
Ruby Akhtar, Ch. P. 198
C. majority 19,060 (37.96%)
Notional 3.63% swing Lab. to C.
(2005: C. majority 13,274 (30.71%))

RUNNYMEDE & WEYBRIDGE
E. 72,566 T. 48,150 (66.35%) C. hold
Philip Hammond, C. 26,915
Andrew Falconer, LD 10,406
Paul Greenwood, Lab. 6,446
Toby Micklethwait, UKIP 3,146
Jenny Gould, Green 696
David Sammons, Ind. 541
C. majority 16,509 (34.29%)
0.38% swing LD to C.
(2005: C. majority 12,349 (28.37%))

§RUSHCLIFFE
E. 72,955 T. 53,687 (73.59%) C. hold
Kenneth Clarke, C. 27,470
Karrar Khan, LD 11,659
Andrew Clayworth, Lab. 11,128
Matthew Faithfull, UKIP 2,179
Richard Mallender, Green 1,251
C. majority 15,811 (29.45%)
Notional 0.63% swing C. to LD
(2005: C. majority 9,932 (20.60%))

§RUTLAND & MELTON
E. 77,185 T. 55,220 (71.54%) C. hold
Alan Duncan, C. 28,228
Grahame Hudson, LD 14,228
John Morgan, Lab. 7,893
Peter Baker, UKIP 2,526
Keith Addison, BNP 1,757
Leigh Higgins, Ind. 588
C. majority 14,000 (25.35%)
Notional 3.65% swing C. to LD
(2005: C. majority 12,998 (26.29%))

§SAFFRON WALDEN
E. 76,035 T. 54,369 (71.51%) C. hold
Sir Alan Haselhurst, C. 30,155
Peter Wilcock, LD 14,913
Barbara Light, Lab. 5,288
Roger Lord, UKIP 2,228
Christine Mitchell, BNP 1,050
Reza Hossain, Green 735
C. majority 15,242 (28.03%)
Notional 3.39% swing LD to C.
(2005: C. majority 10,483 (21.25%))

§ST ALBANS
E. 70,058 T. 52,835 (75.42%) C. hold
Anne Main, C. 21,533
Sandy Walkington, LD 19,228
Roma Mills, Lab. 9,288
John Stocker, UKIP 2,028
Jack Easton, Green 758
C. majority 2,305 (4.36%)
Notional 3.74% swing C. to LD
(2005: C. majority 1,334 (2.94%))

§ST AUSTELL & NEWQUAY
E. 76,346 T. 47,238 (61.87%) LD hold
*Stephen Gilbert, LD 20,189
Caroline Righton, C. 18,877
Lee Jameson, Lab. 3,386
Dick Cole, Meb. Ker. 2,007
Clive Medway, UKIP 1,757
James Fitton, BNP 1,022
LD majority 1,312 (2.78%)
Notional 4.83% swing LD to C.
(2005: LD majority 5,723 (12.44%))

§ST HELENS NORTH
E. 74,985 T. 44,556 (59.42%) Lab. hold
Dave Watts, Lab. 23,041
Paul Greenall, C. 9,940
John Beirne, LD 8,992
Gary Robinson, UKIP 2,100
Stephen Whatham, Soc. Lab. 483
Lab. majority 13,101 (29.40%)
Notional 4.55% swing Lab. to C.
(2005: Lab. majority 15,265 (36.49%))

§ST HELENS SOUTH & WHISTON
E. 77,975 T. 46,081 (59.10%) Lab. hold
Shaun Woodward, Lab. 24,364
Brian Spencer, LD 10,242
Val Allen, C. 8,209
James Winstanley, BNP 2,040
John Sumner, UKIP 1,226
Lab. majority 14,122 (30.65%)
Notional 1.94% swing LD to Lab.
(2005: Lab. majority 10,987 (26.76%))

§ST IVES
E. 66,930 T. 45,921 (68.61%) LD hold
Andrew George, LD 19,619
Derek Thomas, C. 17,900
Philippa Latimer, Lab. 3,751
Mick Faulkner, UKIP 2,560
Tim Andrewes, Green 1,308
Jonathan Rogers, Cornish D. 396
Simon Reed, Meb. Ker. 387
LD majority 1,719 (3.74%)
Notional 10.39% swing LD to C.
(2005: LD majority 10,711 (24.52%))

§SALFORD & ECCLES
E. 75,482 T. 41,533 (55.02%) Lab. hold
Hazel Blears, Lab. 16,655
Norman Owen, LD 10,930
Matthew Sephton, C. 8,497
Tina Wingfield, BNP 2,632
Duran O'Dwyer, UKIP 1,084
David Henry, TUSC 730
Stephen Morris, Eng. Dem. 621
Richard Carvath, Ind. 384
Lab. majority 5,725 (13.78%)
Notional 9.43% swing Lab. to LD
(2005: Lab. majority 10,707 (32.64%))

§SALISBURY
E. 67,429 T. 48,481 (71.90%) C. hold
*John Glen, C. 23,859
Nick Radford, LD 17,893
Tom Gann, Lab. 3,690
Frances Howard, UKIP 1,392
Sean Witheridge, BNP 765
Nick Startin, Green 506
King Arthur, Ind. 257
John Holme, Ind. 119
C. majority 5,966 (12.31%)
Notional 3.60% swing C. to LD
(2005: C. majority 8,860 (19.50%))

SCARBOROUGH & WHITBY
E. 75,443 T. 49,282 (65.32%) C. hold
Robert Goodwill, C. 21,108
Annajoy David, Lab. 12,978
Tania Exley-Moore, LD 11,093
Michael James, UKIP 1,484
Trisha Scott, BNP 1,445
Dilys Cluer, Green 734
Peter Popple, Ind. 329
Juliet Boddington, Green Soc. 111
C. majority 8,130 (16.50%)
6.92% swing Lab. to C.
(2005: C. majority 1,245 (2.65%))

§SCUNTHORPE
E. 63,089 T. 37,034 (58.70%) Lab. hold
*Nic Dakin, Lab. 14,640
Caroline Johnson, C. 12,091
Neil Poole, LD 6,774
Jane Collins, UKIP 1,686
Douglas Ward, BNP 1,447
Natalie Hurst, Green 396
Lab. majority 2,549 (6.88%)
Notional 9.18% swing Lab. to C.
(2005: Lab. majority 8,638 (25.24%))

§SEDGEFIELD
E. 64,727 T. 40,222 (62.14%) Lab. hold
Phil Wilson, Lab. 18,141
Neil Mahapatra, C. 9,445
Alan Thompson, LD 8,033
Mark Walker, BNP 2,075
Brian Gregory, UKIP 1,479
Paul Gittins, Ind. 1,049
Lab. majority 8,696 (21.62%)
Notional 11.60% swing Lab. to C.
(2005: Lab. majority 18,198 (44.82%))

§SEFTON CENTRAL
E. 67,512 T. 48,463 (71.78%) Lab. hold
*Bill Esterson, Lab. 20,307
Debi Jones, C. 16,445
Richard Clein, LD 9,656
Peter Harper, UKIP 2,055
Lab. majority 3,862 (7.97%)
Notional 2.03% swing Lab. to C.
(2005: Lab. majority 4,950 (12.02%))

§SELBY & AINSTY
E. 72,789 T. 51,728 (71.07%) C. hold
*Nigel Adams, C. 25,562
Jan Marshall, Lab. 13,297
Tom Holvey, LD 9,180
Darren Haley, UKIP 1,635
Duncan Lorriman, BNP 1,377
Graham Michael, Eng. Dem. 677
C. majority 12,265 (23.71%)
Notional 9.70% swing Lab. to C.
(2005: C. majority 2,060 (4.31%))

§SEVENOAKS
E. 69,591 T. 49,408 (71.00%) C. hold
Michael Fallon, C. 28,076
Alan Bullion, LD 10,561
Gareth Siddorn, Lab. 6,541
Chris Heath, UKIP 1,782
Paul Golding, BNP 1,384
Louise Uncles, Eng. Dem. 806
Mark Ellis, Ind. 258
C. majority 17,515 (35.45%)
Notional 3.13% swing LD to C.
(2005: C. majority 13,060 (29.19%))

§SHEFFIELD BRIGHTSIDE & HILLSBOROUGH
E. 68,186 T. 38,914 (57.07%) Lab. hold
David Blunkett, Lab. 21,400
Jonathan Harston, LD 7,768
John Sharp, C. 4,468
John Sheldon, BNP 3,026
Pat Sullivan, UKIP 1,596
Maxine Bowler, TUSC 656
Lab. majority 13,632 (35.03%)
Notional 10.77% swing Lab. to LD
(2005: Lab. majority 18,801 (56.58%))

§SHEFFIELD CENTRAL
E. 69,519 T. 41,468 (59.65%) Lab. hold
*Paul Blomfield, Lab. 17,138
Paul Scriven, LD 16,973
Andrew Lee, C. 4,206
Jillian Creasy, Green 1,556
Tracey Smith, BNP 903
Jeffrey Shaw, UKIP 652
Rod Rodgers, Ind. 40
Lab. majority 165 (0.40%)
Notional 7.36% swing Lab. to LD
(2005: Lab. majority 5,025 (15.12%))

§SHEFFIELD HALLAM
E. 69,378 T. 51,135 (73.70%) LD hold
Nick Clegg, LD 27,324
Nicola Bates, C. 12,040
Jack Scott, Lab. 8,228
Nigel James, UKIP 1,195
Steve Barnard, Green 919
David Wildgoose, Eng. Dem. 586
Martin Fitzpatrick, Ind. 429
Ray Green, Ch. P. 250
Mark Adshead, Loony 164
LD majority 15,284 (29.89%)
Notional 6.86% swing C. to LD
(2005: LD majority 7,416 (16.17%))

§SHEFFIELD HEELEY
E. 65,869 T. 40,871 (62.05%) Lab. hold
Meg Munn, Lab. 17,409
Simon Clement-Jones, LD 11,602
Anne Crampton, C. 7,081
John Beatson, BNP 2,260
Charlotte Arnott, UKIP 1,530
Gareth Roberts, Green 989
Lab. majority 5,807 (14.21%)
Notional 9.23% swing Lab. to LD
(2005: Lab. majority 12,340 (32.67%))

§SHEFFIELD SOUTH EAST
E. 67,284 T. 41,408 (61.54%) Lab. hold
Clive Betts, Lab. 20,169
Gail Smith, LD 9,664
Nigel Bonson, C. 7,202
Christopher Hartigan, BNP 2,345
Jonathan Arnott, UKIP 1,889
Steven Andrew, Comm. Brit. 139
Lab. majority 10,505 (25.37%)
Notional 9.00% swing Lab. to LD
(2005: Lab. majority 15,843 (43.36%))

§SHERWOOD
E. 71,043 T. 48,954 (68.91%) C. gain
*Mark Spencer, C. 19,211
Emilie Oldknow, Lab. 18,997
Kevin Moore, LD 7,283
James North, BNP 1,754
Margot Parker, UKIP 1,490
Russ Swan, Ind. 219
C. majority 214 (0.44%)
Notional 8.17% swing Lab. to C.
(2005: Lab. majority 6,869 (15.90%))

§SHIPLEY
E. 67,689 T. 49,427 (73.02%) C. hold
Philip Davies, C. 24,002
Susan Hinchcliffe, Lab. 14,058
John Harris, LD 9,890
Kevin Warnes, Green 1,477
C. majority 9,944 (20.12%)
Notional 9.58% swing Lab. to C.
(2005: C. majority 450 (0.97%))

SHREWSBURY & ATCHAM
E. 75,438 T. 53,045 (70.32%) C. hold
Daniel Kawczynski, C. 23,313
Charles West, LD 15,369
Jon Tandy, Lab. 10,915
Peter Lewis, UKIP 1,627
James Whittall, BNP 1,168
Alan Whittaker, Green 565
James Gollings, Impact 88
C. majority 7,944 (14.98%)
0.06% swing LD to C.
(2005: C. majority 1,808 (3.59%))

SHROPSHIRE NORTH
E. 78,926 T. 51,869 (65.72%) C. hold
Owen Paterson, C. 26,692
Ian Croll, LD 10,864
Ian McLaughlan, Lab. 9,406
Sandra List, UKIP 2,432
Phil Reddall, BNP 1,667
Steve Boulding, Green 808
C. majority 15,828 (30.52%)
0.33% swing LD to C.
(2005: C. majority 11,020 (23.69%))

§SITTINGBOURNE & SHEPPEY
E. 75,354 T. 48,578 (64.47%) C. hold
*Gordon Henderson, C. 24,313
Angela Harrison, Lab. 11,930
Keith Nevols, LD 7,943
Ian Davison, UKIP 2,610
Lawrence Tames, BNP 1,305
Mad Mike Young, Loony 319
David Cassidy, Ind. 158
C. majority 12,383 (25.49%)
Notional 12.72% swing Lab. to C.
(2005: C. majority 22 (0.05%))

§SKIPTON & RIPON
E. 77,381 T. 54,724 (70.72%) C. hold
*Julian Smith, C. 27,685
Helen Flynn, LD 17,735
Claire Hazelgrove, Lab. 5,498
Rodney Mills, UKIP 1,909
Bernard Allen, BNP 1,403
Roger Bell, Ind. 315
Dylan Gilligan, Youth 95
Robert Leakey, Currency 84
C. majority 9,950 (18.18%)
Notional 2.63% swing C. to LD
(2005: C. majority 11,596 (23.43%))

§SLEAFORD & NORTH HYKEHAM
E. 85,550 T. 59,530 (69.59%) C. hold
*Stephen Phillips, C. 30,719
David Harding-Price, LD 10,814
James Normington, Lab. 10,051
Marianne Overton, Lincs Ind. 3,806
Rodger Doughty, UKIP 2,163
Mike Clayton, BNP 1,977
C. majority 19,905 (33.44%)
Notional 0.46% swing LD to C.
(2005: C. majority 12,687 (24.15%))

§SLOUGH
E. 77,068 T. 47,742 (61.95%) Lab. hold
Fiona Mactaggart, Lab. 21,884
Diana Coad, C. 16,361
Chris Tucker, LD 6,943
Peter Mason-Apps, UKIP 1,517
Miriam Kennet, Green 542
Sunil Chaudhary, Ch. P. 495
Lab. majority 5,523 (11.57%)
Notional 4.14% swing Lab. to C.
(2005: Lab. majority 7,924 (19.86%))

§SOLIHULL
E. 77,863 T. 55,129 (70.80%) LD gain
Lorely Burt, LD 23,635
Maggie Throup, C. 23,460
Sarah-Jayne Merrill, Lab. 4,891
Andrew Terry, BNP 1,624
John Ison, UKIP 1,200
Neill Watts, RA 319
LD majority 175 (0.32%)
Notional 0.28% swing C. to LD
(2005: C. majority 124 (0.25%))

§SOMERSET NORTH
E. 77,304 T. 57,941 (74.95%) C. hold
Dr Liam Fox, C. 28,549
Brian Mathew, LD 20,687
Steven Parry-Hearn, Lab. 6,448
Susan Taylor, UKIP 2,257
C. majority 7,862 (13.57%)
Notional 0.98% swing LD to C.
(2005: C. majority 6,007 (11.61%))

§SOMERSET NORTH EAST
E. 67,412 T. 51,203 (75.96%) C. hold
*Jacob Rees-Mogg, C. 21,130
Dan Norris, Lab. 16,216
Gail Coleshill, LD 11,433
Peter Sandell, UKIP 1,754
Michael Jay, Green 670
C. majority 4,914 (9.60%)
Notional 4.57% swing Lab. to C.
(2005: C. majority 212 (0.46%))

§SOMERTON & FROME
E. 81,548 T. 60,612 (74.33%) LD hold
David Heath, LD 28,793
Annunziata Rees-Mogg, C. 26,976
David Oakensen, Lab. 2,675
Barry Harding, UKIP 1,932
Niall Warry, Leave EU 236
LD majority 1,817 (3.00%)
Notional 0.94% swing C. to LD
(2005: LD majority 595 (1.12%))

§SOUTH HOLLAND & THE DEEPINGS
E. 76,243 T. 50,188 (65.83%) C. hold
John Hayes, C. 29,639
Jennifer Conroy, LD 7,759
Gareth Gould, Lab. 7,024
Richard Fairman, UKIP 3,246
Roy Harban, BNP 1,796
Ashley Baxter, Green 724
C. majority 21,880 (43.60%)
Notional 0.27% swing C. to LD
(2005: C. majority 15,127 (32.48%))

§SOUTH RIBBLE
E. 75,822 T. 51,458 (67.87%) C. gain
*Lorraine Fullbrook, C. 23,396
David Borrow, Lab. 17,842
Peter Fisher, LD 7,271
David Duxbury, UKIP 1,895
Rosalind Gauci, BNP 1,054
C. majority 5,554 (10.79%)
Notional 8.11% swing Lab. to C.
(2005: Lab. majority 2,528 (5.42%))

§¶SOUTH SHIELDS
E. 63,294 T. 36,518 (57.70%) Lab. hold
David Miliband, Lab. 18,995
Karen Allen, C. 7,886
Stephen Psallidas, LD 5,189
Donna Watson, BNP 2,382
Shirley Ford, Green 762
Siamak Kaikavoosi, Ind. 729
Victor Thompson, Ind. 316
Sam Navabi, Ind. 168
Roger Nettleship, Anti-War 91
Lab. majority 11,109 (30.42%)
Notional 6.36% swing Lab. to C.
(2005: Lab. majority 13,368 (41.61%))

§SOUTHAMPTON ITCHEN
E. 74,532 T. 44,412 (59.59%) Lab. hold
John Denham, Lab. 16,326
Royston Smith, C. 16,134
David Goodall, LD 9,256
Alan Kebbell, UKIP 1,928
John Spottiswoode, Green 600
Tim Cutter, TUSC 168
Lab. majority 192 (0.43%)
Notional 10.28% swing Lab. to C.
(2005: Lab. majority 8,479 (21.00%))

§SOUTHAMPTON TEST
E. 71,931 T. 44,187 (61.43%) Lab. hold
Alan Whitehead, Lab. 17,001
Jeremy Moulton, C. 14,588
David Callaghan, LD 9,865
Pearline Hingston, UKIP 1,726
Chris Bluemel, Green 881
Charles Sanderson, Ind. 126
Lab. majority 2,413 (5.46%)
Notional 6.86% swing Lab. to C.
(2005: Lab. majority 7,817 (19.17%))

§SOUTHEND WEST
E. 66,527 T. 43,606 (65.55%) C. hold
David Amess, C. 20,086
Peter Welch, LD 12,816
Thomas Flynn, Lab. 5,850
Garry Cockrill, UKIP 1,714
Tony Gladwin, BNP 1,333
Barry Bolton, Green 644
Dr Vel, Ind. 617
Terry Phillips, Eng. Dem. 546
C. majority 7,270 (16.67%)
Notional 2.77% swing C. to LD
(2005: C. majority 9,008 (22.20%))

SOUTHPORT
E. 67,202 T. 43,757 (65.11%) LD hold
John Pugh, LD 21,707
Brenda Porter, C. 15,683
Jim Conalty, Lab. 4,116
Terry Durrance, UKIP 2,251
LD majority 6,024 (13.77%)
2.23% swing C. to LD
(2005: LD majority 3,838 (9.32%))

SPELTHORNE
E. 70,479 T. 47,304 (67.12%) C. hold
*Kwasi Kwarteng, C. 22,261
Mark Chapman, LD 12,242
Adam Tyler-Moore, Lab. 7,789
Christopher Browne, UKIP 4,009
Ian Swinglehurst, Ind. 314
Rod Littlewood, Best 244
Paul Couchman, TUSC 176
John Gore, CIP 167
Grahame Leon-Smith, Ind. Fed. 102
C. majority 10,019 (21.18%)
6.11% swing C. to LD
(2005: C. majority 9,936 (23.20%))

§STAFFORD
E. 70,587 T. 50,239 (71.17%) C. gain
*Jeremy Lefroy, C. 22,047
David Kidney, Lab. 16,587
Barry Stamp, LD 8,211
Roy Goode, UKIP 1,727
Roland Hynd, BNP 1,103
Mike Shone, Green 564
C. majority 5,460 (10.87%)
Notional 7.44% swing Lab. to C.
(2005: Lab. majority 1,852 (4.01%))

§STAFFORDSHIRE MOORLANDS
E. 62,071 T. 43,815 (70.59%) C. hold
*Karen Bradley, C. 19,793
Charlotte Atkins, Lab. 13,104
Henry Jebb, LD 7,338
Steve Povey, UKIP 3,580
C. majority 6,689 (15.27%)
Notional 5.71% swing Lab. to C.
(2005: C. majority 1,618 (3.86%))

§STAFFORDSHIRE SOUTH
E. 73,390 T. 50,440 (68.73%) C. hold
*Gavin Williamson, C. 26,834
Kevin McElduff, Lab. 10,244
Sarah Fellows, LD 8,427
Mike Nattrass, UKIP 2,753
David Bradnock, BNP 1,928
Andrew Morris, Ind. 254
C. majority 16,590 (32.89%)
Notional 1.12% swing Lab. to C.
(2005: C. majority 8,346 (30.65%))

§STALYBRIDGE & HYDE
E. 69,037 T. 40,879 (59.21%) Lab. hold
*Jonathan Reynolds, Lab. 16,189
Rob Adlard, C. 13,445
John Potter, LD 6,965
Anthony Jones, BNP 2,259
John Cooke, UKIP 1,342
Ruth Bergan, Green 679
Lab. majority 2,744 (6.71%)
Notional 8.47% swing Lab. to C.
(2005: Lab. majority 8,455 (23.64%))

§STEVENAGE
E. 68,937 T. 44,651 (64.77%) C. gain
*Stephen McPartland, C. 18,491
Sharon Taylor, Lab. (Co-op) 14,913
Julia Davies, LD 7,432
Marion Mason, UKIP 2,004
Andrew Green, BNP 1,007
Charles Vickers, Eng. Dem. 366
Stephen Phillips, No Vote 327
David Cox, Ind. 80
Andrew Ralph, YRDPL 31
C. majority 3,578 (8.01%)
Notional 8.03% swing Lab. (Co-op) to C.
(2005: Lab. (Co-op) majority 3,288 (8.05%))

§STOCKPORT
E. 63,525 T. 39,128 (61.59%) Lab. hold
Ann Coffey, Lab. 16,697
Stephen Holland, C. 9,913
Stuart Bodsworth, LD 9,778
Duncan Warner, BNP 1,201
Mike Kelly, UKIP 862
Peter Barber, Green 677
Lab. majority 6,784 (17.34%)
Notional 5.74% swing Lab. to C.
(2005: Lab. majority 9,982 (28.82%))

§STOCKTON NORTH
E. 67,363 T. 39,498 (58.63%) Lab. hold
*Alex Cunningham, Lab. 16,923
Ian Galletley, C. 10,247
Philip Latham, LD 6,342
James Macpherson, BNP 1,724
Frank Cook, Ind. 1,577
Gordon Parkin, UKIP 1,556
Ian Saul, Eng. Dem. 1,129
Lab. majority 6,676 (16.90%)
Notional 8.35% swing Lab. to C.
(2005: Lab. majority 12,742 (33.60%))

§STOCKTON SOUTH
E. 74,552 T. 50,284 (67.45%) C. gain
*James Wharton, C. 19,577
Dari Taylor, Lab. 19,245
Jacquie Bell, LD 7,600
Neil Sinclair, BNP 1,553
Peter Braney, UKIP 1,471
Yvonne Hossack, Ind. 536
Ted Strike, Ch. P. 302
C. majority 332 (0.66%)
Notional 7.05% swing Lab. to C.
(2005: Lab. majority 5,834 (13.44%))

§STOKE-ON-TRENT CENTRAL
E. 60,995 T. 32,470 (53.23%) Lab. hold
*Tristram Hunt, Lab. 12,605
John Redfern, LD 7,039
Norsheen Bhatti, C. 6,833
Simon Darby, BNP 2,502
Carol Lovatt, UKIP 1,402
Paul Breeze, Ind. 959
Gary Elsby, Ind. 399
Brian Ward, City Ind. 303
Alby Walker, Ind. 295
Matthew Wright, TUSC 133
Lab. majority 5,566 (17.14%)
Notional 8.33% swing Lab. to LD
(2005: Lab. majority 9,717 (33.80%))

§STOKE-ON-TRENT NORTH
E. 72,052 T. 40,196 (55.79%) Lab. hold
Joan Walley, Lab. 17,815
Andy Large, C. 9,580
John Fisher, LD 7,120
Melanie Baddeley, BNP 3,196
Geoffrey Locke, UKIP 2,485
Lab. majority 8,235 (20.49%)
Notional 8.77% swing Lab. to C.
(2005: Lab. majority 13,666 (38.03%))

§STOKE-ON-TRENT SOUTH
E. 68,031 T. 39,852 (58.58%) Lab. hold
Rob Flello, Lab. 15,446
James Rushton, C. 11,316
Zulfiqar Ali, LD 6,323
Michael Coleman, BNP 3,762
Mark Barlow, UKIP 1,363
Terry Follows, Staffs Ind. 1,208
Mark Breeze, Ind. 434
Lab. majority 4,130 (10.36%)
Notional 6.15% swing Lab. to C.
(2005: Lab. majority 8,324 (22.67%))

§STONE
E. 66,979 T. 47,229 (70.51%) C. hold
Bill Cash, C. 23,890
Christine Tinker, LD 10,598
Jo Lewis, Lab. 9,770
Andrew Illsley, UKIP 2,481
Damon Hoppe, Green 490
C. majority 13,292 (28.14%)
Notional 0.81% swing C. to LD
(2005: C. majority 8,191 (18.72%))

§STOURBRIDGE
E. 69,637 T. 47,234 (67.83%) C. gain
*Margot James, C. 20,153
Lynda Waltho, Lab. 14,989
Christopher Bramall, LD 7,733
Maddy Westrop, UKIP 2,103
Robert Weale, BNP 1,696
Will Duckworth, Green 394
Alun Nicholas, Ind. 166
C. majority 5,164 (10.93%)
Notional 6.93% swing Lab. to C.
(2005: Lab. majority 1,280 (2.92%))

§STRATFORD-ON-AVON
E. 69,516 T. 50,542 (72.71%) C. hold
*Nadhim Zahawi, C. 26,052
Martin Turner, LD 14,706
Robert Johnston, Lab. 4,809
Brett Parsons, UKIP 1,846
George Jones, BNP 1,097
Neil Basnett, Ind. 1,032
Karen Varga, Green 527
Fred Bishop, Eng. Dem. 473
C. majority 11,346 (22.45%)
Notional 0.72% swing C. to LD
(2005: C. majority 10,928 (23.90%))

§STREATHAM
E. 74,531 T. 46,837 (62.84%) Lab. hold
*Chuka Umunna, Lab. 20,037
Chris Nicholson, LD 16,778
Rahoul Bhansali, C. 8,578
Rebecca Findlay, Green 861
Geoffrey Macharia, Ch. P. 237
Janus Polenceus, Eng. Dem. 229
Paul Lepper, WRP 117
Lab. majority 3,259 (6.96%)
Notional 5.25% swing Lab. to LD
(2005: Lab. majority 6,584 (17.47%))

§STRETFORD & URMSTON
E. 70,091 T. 44,910 (64.07%) Lab. hold
*Kate Green, Lab. 21,821
Alex Williams, C. 12,886
Steve Cooke, LD 7,601
David Owen, UKIP 1,508
Margaret Westbrook, Green 916
Samuel Jacob, Ch. P. 178
Lab. majority 8,935 (19.90%)
Notional 0.69% swing Lab. to C.
(2005: Lab. majority 8,310 (21.28%))

§STROUD
E. 78,305 T. 57,973 (74.03%) C. gain
*Neil Carmichael, C. 23,679
David Drew, Lab. (Co-op) 22,380
Dennis Andrewartha, LD 8,955
Martin Whiteside, Green 1,542
Steve Parker, UKIP 1,301
Alan Lomas, Ind. 116
C. majority 1,299 (2.24%)
Notional 2.05% swing Lab. (Co-op) to C.
(2005: Lab. (Co-op) majority 996 (1.85%))

§SUFFOLK CENTRAL & IPSWICH NORTH
E. 75,848 T. 53,420 (70.43%) C. hold
*Daniel Poulter, C. 27,125
Andrew Aalders-Dunthorne, LD 13,339
Bhavna Joshi, Lab. 8,636
Roy Philpot, UKIP 2,361
Andrew Stringer, Green 1,452
Mark Trevitt, Ind. 389
Richard Vass, New Party 118
C. majority 13,786 (25.81%)
Notional 0.76% swing LD to C.
(2005: C. majority 7,786 (16.07%))

§SUFFOLK COASTAL
E. 76,687 T. 54,893 (71.58%) C. hold
*Therese Coffey, C. 25,475
Daisy Cooper, LD 16,347
Adam Leeder, Lab. 8,812
Prof. Stephen Bush, UKIP 3,156
Rachel Fulcher, Green 1,103
C. majority 9,128 (16.63%)
Notional 2.91% swing C. to LD
(2005: C. majority 9,674 (18.43%))

§SUFFOLK SOUTH
E. 72,498 T. 51,416 (70.92%) C. hold
Tim Yeo, C. 24,550
Nigel Bennett, LD 15,861
Emma Bishton, Lab. 7,368
David Campbell Bannerman, UKIP 3,637
C. majority 8,689 (16.90%)
Notional 1.63% swing LD to C.
(2005: C. majority 6,664 (13.64%))

§SUFFOLK WEST
E. 74,413 T. 48,089 (64.62%) C. hold
*Matthew Hancock, C. 24,312
Belinda Brooks-Gordon, LD 11,262
Ohid Ahmed, Lab. 7,089
Ian Smith, UKIP 3,085
Ramon Johns, BNP 1,428
Andrew Appleby, Ind. 540
Colin Young, CPA 373
C. majority 13,050 (27.14%)
Notional 2.28% swing C. to LD
(2005: C. majority 8,735 (19.92%))

§SUNDERLAND CENTRAL
E. 74,485 T. 42,463 (57.01%) Lab. hold
*Julie Elliott, Lab. 19,495
Lee Martin, C. 12,770
Paul Dixon, LD 7,191
John McCaffrey, BNP 1,913
Pauline Featonby-Warren, UKIP 1,094
Lab. majority 6,725 (15.84%)
Notional 4.85% swing Lab. to C.
(2005: Lab. majority 9,464 (25.53%))

SURREY EAST
E. 76,855 T. 54,640 (71.09%) C. hold
*Sam Gyimah, C. 31,007
David Lee, LD 14,133
Mathew Rodda, Lab. 4,925
Helena Windsor, UKIP 3,770
Martin Hogbin, Loony 422
Sandy Pratt, Ind. 383
C. majority 16,874 (30.88%)
0.72% swing C. to LD
(2005: C. majority 15,921 (32.32%))

SURREY HEATH
E. 77,690 T. 54,347 (69.95%) C. hold
Michael Gove, C. 31,326
Alan Hilliar, LD 14,037
Matthew Willey, Lab. 5,552
Mark Stroud, UKIP 3,432
C. majority 17,289 (31.81%)
4.58% swing LD to C.
(2005: C. majority 10,845 (22.66%))

§SURREY SOUTH WEST
E. 77,980 T. 57,259 (73.43%) C. hold
Jeremy Hunt, C. 33,605
Mike Simpson, LD 17,287
Richard Mollet, Lab. 3,419
Roger Meekins, UKIP 1,486
Cherry Allan, Green 690
Helen Hamilton, BNP 644
Luke Leighton, Pirate 94
Arthur Price, Ind. 34
C. majority 16,318 (28.50%)
Notional 8.63% swing LD to C.
(2005: C. majority 5,969 (11.23%))

§SUSSEX MID
E. 77,182 T. 55,855 (72.37%) C. hold
Nicholas Soames, C. 28,329
Serena Tierney, LD 20,927
David Boot, Lab. 3,689
Marc Montgomery, UKIP 1,423
Paul Brown, Green 645
Stuart Minihane, BNP 583
Baron Von Thunderclap, Loony 259
C. majority 7,402 (13.25%)
Notional 0.32% swing LD to C.
(2005: C. majority 6,462 (12.62%))

§SUTTON & CHEAM
E. 66,658 T. 48,508 (72.77%) LD hold
Paul Burstow, LD 22,156
Philippa Stroud, C. 20,548
Kathy Allen, Lab. 3,376
John Clarke, BNP 1,014
David Pickles, UKIP 950
Peter Hickson, Green 246
John Dodds, Eng. Dem. 106
Matthew Connolly, CPA 52
Martin Cullip, Libertarian 41
Dr Brian Hammond, UK Integrity 19
LD majority 1,608 (3.31%)
Notional 1.45% swing LD to C.
(2005: LD majority 2,689 (6.22%))

§SUTTON COLDFIELD
E. 74,489 T. 50,589 (67.91%) C. hold
Andrew Mitchell, C. 27,303
Robert Pocock, Lab. 10,298
Richard Brighton, LD 9,117
Robert Grierson, BNP 1,749
Edward Siddall-Jones, UKIP 1,587
Joe Rooney, Green 535
C. majority 17,005 (33.61%)
Notional 3.44% swing Lab. to C.
(2005: C. majority 12,318 (26.72%))

§SWINDON NORTH
E. 78,391 T. 50,295 (64.16%) C. gain
*Justin Tomlinson, C. 22,408
Victor Agarwal, Lab. 15,348
Jane Lock, LD 8,668
Stephen Halden, UKIP 1,842
Reginald Bates, BNP 1,542
Bill Hughes, Green 487
C. majority 7,060 (14.04%)
Notional 10.14% swing Lab. to C.
(2005: Lab. majority 2,675 (6.25%))

§SWINDON SOUTH
E. 72,622 T. 47,119 (64.88%) C. gain
*Robert Buckland, C. 19,687
Anne Snelgrove, Lab. 16,143
Damon Hooton, LD 8,305
Robin Tingey, UKIP 2,029
Jenni Miles, Green 619
Alastair Kirk, Ch. P. 176
Karsten Evans, Ind. 160
C. majority 3,544 (7.52%)
Notional 5.51% swing Lab. to C.
(2005: Lab. majority 1,493 (3.50%))

TAMWORTH
E. 72,693 T. 46,390 (63.82%) C. gain
*Christopher Pincher, C. 21,238
Brian Jenkins, Lab. 15,148
Jenny Pinkett, LD 7,516
Paul Smith, UKIP 2,253
Charlene Detheridge, Ch. P. 235
C. majority 6,090 (13.13%)
9.50% swing Lab. to C.
(2005: Lab. majority 2,569 (5.87%))

§TATTON
E. 65,689 T. 45,231 (68.86%) C. hold
George Osborne, C. 24,687
David Lomax, LD 10,200
Richard Jackson, Lab. 7,803
Sarah Flannery, Ind. 2,243
Michael Gibson, Poetry 298
C. majority 14,487 (32.03%)
Notional 1.17% swing LD to C.
(2005: C. majority 11,537 (27.73%))

§TAUNTON DEANE
E. 82,537 T. 58,150 (70.45%) LD hold
Jeremy Browne, LD 28,531
Mark Formosa, C. 24,538
Martin Jevon, Lab. 2,967
Tony McIntyre, UKIP 2,114
LD majority 3,993 (6.87%)
Notional 1.78% swing C. to LD
(2005: LD majority 1,868 (3.30%))

§TELFORD
E. 65,061 T. 41,310 (63.49%) Lab. hold
David Wright, Lab. 15,974
Tom Biggins, C. 14,996
Phil Bennion, LD 6,399
Denis Allen, UKIP 2,428
Phil Spencer, BNP 1,513
Lab. majority 978 (2.37%)
Notional 6.32% swing Lab. to C.
(2005: Lab. majority 5,651 (15.01%))

§TEWKESBURY
E. 76,655 T. 53,961 (70.39%) C. hold
Laurence Robertson, C. 25,472
Alistair Cameron, LD 19,162
Stuart Emmerson, Lab. 6,253
Brian Jones, UKIP 2,230
Matthew Sidford, Green 525
George Ridgeon, Loony 319
C. majority 6,310 (11.69%)
Notional 4.04% swing C. to LD
(2005: C. majority 9,130 (19.78%))

§THANET NORTH
E. 69,432 T. 43,343 (62.43%) C. hold
Roger Gale, C. 22,826
Michael Britton, Lab. 9,298
Laura Murphy, LD 8,400
Rosamund Parker, UKIP 2,819
C. majority 13,528 (31.21%)
Notional 7.94% swing Lab. to C.
(2005: C. majority 6,118 (15.33%))

§THANET SOUTH
E. 71,596 T. 45,933 (64.16%) C. hold
*Laura Sandys, C. 22,043
Dr Stephen Ladyman, Lab. 14,426
Peter Bucklitsch, LD 6,935
Trevor Shonk, UKIP 2,529
C. majority 7,617 (16.58%)
Notional 7.41% swing Lab. to C.
(2005: C. majority 810 (1.76%))

§THIRSK & MALTON
E. 76,231 T. 38,142 (50.03%) C. hold
Anne McIntosh, C. 20,167
Howard Keal, LD 8,886
Jonathan Roberts, Lab. 5,169
Toby Horton, UKIP 2,502
John Clark, Lib. 1,418
C. majority 11,281 (29.58%)
Notional 1.75% swing C. to LD
(2005: C. majority 14,117 (28.50%))

§THORNBURY & YATE
E. 64,092 T. 48,226 (75.24%) LD hold
Steve Webb, LD 25,032
Matthew Riddle, C. 17,916
Roxanne Egan, Lab. 3,385
Jenny Knight, UKIP 1,709
Thomas Beacham, Ind. Fed. 126
Anthony Clements, ND 58
LD majority 7,116 (14.76%)
Notional 4.35% swing LD to C.
(2005: LD majority 11,060 (23.45%))

§THURROCK
E. 92,390 T. 45,821 (49.60%) C. gain
*Jackie Doyle-Price, C. 16,869
Carl Morris, Lab. 16,777
Carys Davis, LD 4,901
Emma Colgate, BNP 3,618
Clive Broad, UKIP 3,390
Arinola Araba, Ch. P. 266
C. majority 92 (0.20%)
Notional 6.61% swing Lab. to C.
(2005: Lab. majority 5,358 (13.02%))

§TIVERTON & HONITON
E. 76,810 T. 54,894 (71.47%) C. hold
*Neil Parish, C. 27,614
Jon Underwood, LD 18,294
Vernon Whitlock, Lab. 4,907
Daryl Stanbury, UKIP 3,277
Cathy Connor, Green 802
C. majority 9,320 (16.98%)
Notional 0.28% swing C. to LD
(2005: C. majority 9,007 (17.55%))

TONBRIDGE & MALLING
E. 71,790 T. 51,314 (71.48%) C. hold
Sir John Stanley, C. 29,723
Elizabeth Simpson, LD 11,545
Daniel Griffiths, Lab. 6,476
David Waller, UKIP 1,911
Steve Dawe, Green 764
Mike Easter, NF 505
Lisa Rogers, Eng. Dem. 390
C. majority 18,178 (35.43%)
1.02% swing LD to C.
(2005: C. majority 13,352 (28.99%))

§TOOTING
E. 73,836 T. 50,655 (68.60%) Lab. hold
Sadiq Khan, Lab. 22,038
Mark Clarke, C. 19,514
Nasser Butt, LD 7,509
Strachan McDonald, UKIP 624
Roy Vickery, Green 609
Susan John-Richards, Ind. 190
Shereen Paul, Ch. P. 171
Lab. majority 2,524 (4.98%)
Notional 3.60% swing Lab. to C.
(2005: Lab. majority 5,169 (12.17%))

§TORBAY
E. 76,151 T. 49,210 (64.62%) LD hold
Adrian Sanders, LD 23,126
Marcus Wood, C. 19,048
David Pedrick-Friend, Lab. 3,231
Julien Parrott, UKIP 2,628
Ann Conway, BNP 709
Sam Moss, Green 468
LD majority 4,078 (8.29%)
Notional 1.14% swing C. to LD
(2005: LD majority 2,727 (6.01%))

§TOTNES
E. 67,937 T. 47,843 (70.42%) C. hold
*Dr Sarah Wollaston, C. 21,940
Julian Brazil, LD 17,013
Carole Whitty, Lab. 3,538
Jeff Beer, UKIP 2,890
Lydia Somerville, Green 1,181
Mike Turner, BNP 624
Simon Drew, Ind. 390
Dr Stephen Hopwood, Ind. 267
C. majority 4,927 (10.30%)
Notional 2.27% swing LD to C.
(2005: C. majority 2,693 (5.76%))

TOTTENHAM
E. 69,933 T. 40,687 (58.18%) Lab. hold
David Lammy, Lab. 24,128
David Schmitz, LD 7,197
Sean Sullivan, C. 6,064
Jenny Sutton, TUSC 1,057
Anne Gray, Green 980
Winston McKenzie, UKIP 466
Neville Watson, Ind. People 265
Abimbola Kadara, Ch. P. 262
Sheik Thompson, Ind. 143
Errol Carr, Ind. 125
Lab. majority 16,931 (41.61%)
0.22% swing LD to Lab.
(2005: Lab. majority 13,034 (41.16%))

§TRURO & FALMOUTH
E. 70,598 T. 48,768 (69.08%) C. gain
*Sarah Newton, C. 20,349
Terrye Teverson, LD 19,914
Charlotte Mackenzie, Lab. 4,697
Harry Blakeley, UKIP 1,911
Loic Rich, Meb. Ker. 1,039
Ian Wright, Green 858
C. majority 435 (0.89%)
Notional 5.07% swing LD to C.
(2005: LD majority 3,931 (9.25%))

§TUNBRIDGE WELLS
E. 72,042 T. 50,320 (69.85%) C. hold
Greg Clark, C. 28,302
David Hallas, LD 12,726
Gary Heather, Lab. 5,448
Victor Webb, UKIP 2,054
Hazel Dawe, Green 914
Andrew McBride, BNP 704
Farel Bradbury, Ind. 172
C. majority 15,576 (30.95%)
Notional 2.79% swing LD to C.
(2005: C. majority 11,572 (25.38%))

TWICKENHAM
E. 79,861 T. 59,721 (74.78%) LD hold
Vince Cable, LD 32,483
Deborah Thomas, C. 20,343
Brian Tomlinson, Lab. 4,583
Brian Gilbert, UKIP 868
Steve Roest, Green 674
Chris Hurst, BNP 654
Harry Cole, R and E 76
Paul Armstrong, Magna Carta 40
LD majority 12,140 (20.33%)
0.52% swing C. to LD
(2005: LD majority 9,965 (19.28%))

§TYNEMOUTH
E. 75,680 T. 52,668 (69.59%) Lab. hold
Alan Campbell, Lab. 23,860
Wendy Morton, C. 18,121
John Appleby, LD 7,845
Dorothy Brooke, BNP 1,404
Natasha Payne, UKIP 900
Julia Erskine, Green 538
Lab. majority 5,739 (10.90%)
Notional 0.38% swing Lab. to C.
(2005: Lab. majority 5,490 (11.65%))

§TYNESIDE NORTH
E. 77,690 T. 46,405 (59.73%) Lab. hold
*Mary Glindon, Lab. 23,505
David Ord, LD 10,621
Gagan Mohindra, C. 8,514
John Burrows, BNP 1,860
Claudia Blake, UKIP 1,306
Bob Batten, NF 599
Lab. majority 12,884 (27.76%)
Notional 4.81% swing Lab. to LD
(2005: Lab. majority 14,929 (37.38%))

§UXBRIDGE & RUISLIP SOUTH
E. 71,168 T. 45,076 (63.34%) C. hold
John Randall, C. 21,758
Sidharath Garg, Lab. 10,542
Michael Cox, LD 8,995
Dianne Neal, BNP 1,396
Mark Wadsworth, UKIP 1,234
Mike Harling, Green 477
Roger Cooper, Eng. Dem. 403
Francis Mcallister, NF 271
C. majority 11,216 (24.88%)
Notional 3.44% swing Lab. to C.
(2005: C. majority 7,178 (18.01%))

§VAUXHALL
E. 74,811 T. 43,191 (57.73%) Lab. hold
Kate Hoey, Lab. 21,498
Caroline Pidgeon, LD 10,847
Glyn Chambers, C. 9,301
Joseph Healy, Green 708
Jose Navarro, Eng. Dem. 289
Lana Martin, Ch. P. 200
Daniel Lambert, Soc. 143
Jeremy Drinkall, WP 109
James Kapetanos, APP 96
Lab. majority 10,651 (24.66%)
Notional 0.06% swing LD to Lab.
(2005: Lab. majority 8,503 (24.54%))

§WAKEFIELD
E. 70,834 T. 44,444 (62.74%) Lab. hold
Mary Creagh, Lab. 17,454
Alex Story, C. 15,841
David Smith, LD 7,256
Ian Senior, BNP 2,581
Miriam Hawkins, Green 873
Mark Harrop, Ind. 439
Lab. majority 1,613 (3.63%)
Notional 6.94% swing Lab. to C.
(2005: Lab. majority 7,349 (17.50%))

§WALLASEY
E. 65,915 T. 41,654 (63.19%) Lab. hold
Angela Eagle, Lab. 21,578
Leah Fraser, C. 13,071
Steve Pitt, LD 5,693
Derek Snowden, UKIP 1,205
Emmanuel Mwaba, Ind. 107
Lab. majority 8,507 (20.42%)
Notional 1.78% swing Lab. to C.
(2005: Lab. majority 9,130 (23.98%))

§WALSALL NORTH
E. 65,183 T. 36,187 (55.52%) Lab. hold
David Winnick, Lab. 13,385
Helyn Clack, C. 12,395
Nadia Fazal, LD 4,754
Christopher Woodall, BNP 2,930
Elizabeth Hazell, UKIP 1,737
Peter Smith, Dem. Lab. 842
Babar Shakir, Ch. P. 144
Lab. majority 990 (2.74%)
Notional 9.03% swing Lab. to C.
(2005: Lab. majority 6,901 (20.79%))

§WALSALL SOUTH
E. 64,830 T. 40,882 (63.06%) Lab. hold
*Valerie Vaz, Lab. 16,211
Richard Hunt, C. 14,456
Dr Murli Sinha, LD 5,880
Derek Bennett, UKIP 3,449
Gulzaman Khan, Ch. P. 482
Mohammed Mulia, ND 404
Lab. majority 1,755 (4.29%)
Notional 8.24% swing Lab. to C.
(2005: Lab. majority 7,910 (20.77%))

WALTHAMSTOW
E. 64,625 T. 40,994 (63.43%) Lab. hold
*Stella Creasy, Lab. 21,252
Farid Ahmed, LD 11,774
Andy Hemsted, C. 5,734
Judith Chisholm-Benli, UKIP 823
Daniel Perrett, Green 767
Nancy Taaffe, TUSC 279
Ashar Mall, Ch. P. 248
Paul Warburton, Ind. 117
Lab. majority 9,478 (23.12%)
0.04% swing Lab. to LD
(2005: Lab. majority 7,993 (23.21%))

WANSBECK
E. 63,045 T. 38,273 (60.71%) Lab. hold
*Ian Lavery, Lab. 17,548
Simon Reed, LD 10,517
Campbell Storey, C. 6,714
Stephen Finlay, BNP 1,418
Linda Lee-Stokoe, UKIP 974
Nic Best, Green 601
Malcolm Reid, Ind. 359
Michael Flynn, Ch. P. 142
Lab. majority 7,031 (18.37%)
5.19% swing Lab. to LD
(2005: Lab. majority 10,581 (28.75%))

§WANTAGE
E. 80,456 T. 56,341 (70.03%) C. hold
Ed Vaizey, C. 29,284
Alan Armitage, LD 15,737
Steven Mitchell, Lab. 7,855
Jacqueline Jones, UKIP 2,421
Adam Twine, Green 1,044
C. majority 13,547 (24.04%)
Notional 4.30% swing LD to C.
(2005: C. majority 8,039 (15.44%))

§WARLEY
E. 63,106 T. 38,270 (60.64%) Lab. hold
John Spellar, Lab. 20,240
Jasbir Parmar, C. 9,484
Edward Keating, LD 5,929
Nigel Harvey, UKIP 2,617
Lab. majority 10,756 (28.11%)
Notional 1.94% swing Lab. to C.
(2005: Lab. majority 11,206 (31.99%))

§WARRINGTON NORTH
E. 71,601 T. 44,211 (61.75%) Lab. hold
Helen Jones, Lab. 20,135
Paul Campbell, C. 13,364
David Eccles, LD 9,196
Albert Scott, Ind. 1,516
Lab. majority 6,771 (15.32%)
Notional 6.61% swing Lab. to C.
(2005: Lab. majority 11,382 (28.53%))

§WARRINGTON SOUTH
E. 80,506 T. 54,874 (68.16%) C. gain
*David Mowat, C. 19,641
Nick Bent, Lab. 18,088
Jo Crotty, LD 15,094
James Ashington, UKIP 1,624
Steph Davies, Green 427
C. majority 1,553 (2.83%)
Notional 6.00% swing Lab. to C.
(2005: Lab. majority 4,337 (9.17%))

§WARWICK & LEAMINGTON
E. 58,030 T. 49,032 (84.49%) C. gain
*Chris White, C. 20,876
James Plaskitt, Lab. 17,363
Alan Beddow, LD 8,977
Christopher Lenton, UKIP 926
Ian Davison, Green 693
Jim Cullinane, Ind. 197
C. majority 3,513 (7.16%)
Notional 8.76% swing Lab. to C.
(2005: Lab. majority 4,393 (10.35%))

§WARWICKSHIRE NORTH
E. 70,143 T. 47,265 (67.38%) C. gain
*Dan Byles, C. 18,993
Mike O'Brien, Lab. 18,939
Stephen Martin, LD 5,481
Jason Holmes, BNP 2,106
Steven Fowler, UKIP 1,335
David Lane, Eng. Dem. 411
C. majority 54 (0.11%)
Notional 7.69% swing Lab. to C.
(2005: Lab. majority 6,684 (15.27%))

§WASHINGTON & SUNDERLAND WEST
E. 68,910 T. 37,334 (54.18%) Lab. hold
Sharon Hodgson, Lab. 19,615
Ian Cuthbert, C. 8,157
Peter Andras, LD 6,382
Ian McDonald, BNP 1,913
Linda Hudson, UKIP 1,267
Lab. majority 11,458 (30.69%)
Notional 11.56% swing Lab. to C.
(2005: Lab. majority 17,060 (52.56%))

§WATFORD
E. 80,798 T. 55,208 (68.33%) C. gain
*Richard Harrington, C. 19,291
Sal Brinton, LD 17,866
Claire Ward, Lab. 14,750
Andrew Emerson, BNP 1,217
Graham Eardley, UKIP 1,199
Ian Brandon, Green 885
C. majority 1,425 (2.58%)
Notional 6.08% swing Lab. to C.
(2005: Lab. majority 1,151 (2.33%))

§WAVENEY
E. 78,532 T. 51,141 (65.12%) C. gain
*Peter Aldous, C. 20,571
Bob Blizzard, Lab. 19,802
Alan Dean, LD 6,811
Jack Tyler, UKIP 2,684
Graham Elliott, Green 1,167
Louis Barfe, Ind. 106
C. majority 769 (1.50%)
Notional 6.75% swing Lab. to C.
(2005: Lab. majority 5,950 (12.00%))

§WEALDEN
E. 76,537 T. 54,969 (71.82%) C. hold
Charles Hendry, C. 31,090
Chris Bowers, LD 13,911
Lorna Blackmore, Lab. 5,266
Dan Docker, UKIP 3,319
David Jonas, Green 1,383
C. majority 17,179 (31.25%)
Notional 2.79% swing LD to C.
(2005: C. majority 12,812 (25.66%))

§WEAVER VALE
E. 66,538 T. 43,990 (66.11%) C. gain
*Graham Evans, C. 16,953
John Stockton, Lab. 15,962
Peter Hampson, LD 8,196
Colin Marsh, BNP 1,063
Paul Remfry, UKIP 1,018
Howard Thorp, Green 338
Mike Cooksley, Ind. 270
Tom Reynolds, Ind. 133
Will Charlton, Ind. 57
C. majority 991 (2.25%)
Notional 8.14% swing Lab. to C.
(2005: Lab. majority 5,277 (14.03%))

§WELLINGBOROUGH
E. 76,857 T. 51,661 (67.22%) C. hold
Peter Bone, C. 24,918
Jayne Buckland, Lab. 13,131
Kevin Barron, LD 8,848
Adrian Haynes, UKIP 1,636
Rob Walker, BNP 1,596
Terry Spencer, Eng. Dem. 530
Jonathan Hornett, Green 480
Paul Crofts, TUSC 249
Gary Donaldson, Ind. 240
Marcus Lavin, Ind. 33
C. majority 11,787 (22.82%)
Notional 10.78% swing Lab. to C.
(2005: C. majority 610 (1.25%))

WELLS
E. 79,432 T. 55,864 (70.33%) LD gain
*Tessa Munt, LD 24,560
David Heathcoat-Amory, C. 23,760
Andy Merryfield, Lab. 4,198
Jake Baynes, UKIP 1,711
Richard Boyce, BNP 1,004
Chris Briton, Green 631
LD majority 800 (1.43%)
3.59% swing C. to LD
(2005: C. majority 3,040 (5.74%))

WELWYN HATFIELD
E. 72,058 T. 48,972 (67.96%) C. hold
Grant Shapps, C. 27,894
Mike Hobday, Lab. 10,471
Paul Zukowskyj, LD 8,010
David Platt, UKIP 1,643
Jill Weston, Green 796
Nigel Parker, Ind. 158
C. majority 17,423 (35.58%)
11.14% swing Lab. to C.
(2005: C. majority 5,946 (13.30%))

§WENTWORTH & DEARNE
E. 72,586 T. 42,106 (58.01%) Lab. hold
John Healey, Lab. 21,316
Michelle Donelan, C. 7,396
Nick Love, LD 6,787
John Wilkinson, UKIP 3,418
George Baldwin, BNP 3,189
Lab. majority 13,920 (33.06%)
Notional 7.49% swing Lab. to C.
(2005: Lab. majority 17,551 (45.55%))

§WEST BROMWICH EAST
E. 62,824 T. 37,950 (60.41%) Lab. hold
Tom Watson, Lab. 17,657
Alistair Thompson, C. 10,961
Ian Garrett, LD 4,993
Terry Lewin, BNP 2,205
Mark Cowles, Eng. Dem. 1,150
Steve Grey, UKIP 984
Lab. majority 6,696 (17.64%)
Notional 7.68% swing Lab. to C.
(2005: Lab. majority 11,947 (33.00%))

§WEST BROMWICH WEST
E. 65,013 T. 36,171 (55.64%) Lab. hold
Adrian Bailey, Lab. 16,263
Andrew Hardie, C. 10,612
Sadie Smith, LD 4,336
Russ Green, BNP 3,394
Mac Ford, UKIP 1,566
Lab. majority 5,651 (15.62%)
Notional 7.64% swing Lab. to C.
(2005: Lab. majority 9,821 (30.90%))

§WEST HAM
E. 85,313 T. 46,951 (55.03%) Lab. hold
Lyn Brown, Lab. 29,422
Virginia Morris, C. 6,888
Martin Pierce, LD 5,392
Stan Gain, CPA 1,327
Kamran Malik, Ind. 1,245
Michael Davidson, NF 1,089
Kim Gandy, UKIP 766
Jane Lithgow, Green 645
Grace Agbogun-Toko, Ind. 177
Lab. majority 22,534 (47.99%)
Notional 4.16% swing C. to Lab.
(2005: Lab. majority 12,274 (31.76%))

§WESTMINSTER NORTH
E. 66,739 T. 39,598 (59.33%) Lab. hold
Karen Buck, Lab. 17,377
Joanne Cash, C. 15,251
Mark Blackburn, LD 5,513
Tristan Smith, Green 478
Stephen Curry, BNP 334
Jasna Badzak, UKIP 315
Dr Ali Bahaijoub, Ind. 101
Edward Roseman, Eng. Dem. 99
Gabriela Fajardo, Ch. P. 98
Abby Dharamsey, Ind. 32
Lab. majority 2,126 (5.37%)
Notional 0.61% swing Lab. to C.
(2005: Lab. majority 2,120 (6.59%))

§WESTMORLAND & LONSDALE
E. 67,881 T. 51,487 (75.85%) LD hold
Tim Farron, LD 30,896
Gareth McKeever, C. 18,632
Jonathan Todd, Lab. 1,158
John Mander, UKIP 801
LD majority 12,264 (23.82%)
Notional 11.06% swing C. to LD
(2005: LD majority 806 (1.70%))

§WESTON-SUPER-MARE
E. 78,487 T. 52,716 (67.17%) C. hold
John Penrose, C. 23,356
Mike Bell, LD 20,665
David Bradley, Lab. 5,772
Paul Spencer, UKIP 1,406
Peryn Parsons, BNP 1,098
John Peverelle, Eng. Dem. 275
Steve Satch, Ind. 144
C. majority 2,691 (5.10%)
Notional 0.42% swing LD to C.
(2005: C. majority 2,088 (4.26%))

§WIGAN
E. 75,564 T. 44,140 (58.41%) Lab. hold
*Lisa Nandy, Lab. 21,404
Michael Winstanley, C. 10,917
Mark Clayton, LD 6,797
Alan Freeman, UKIP 2,516
Charles Mather, BNP 2,506
Lab. majority 10,487 (23.76%)
Notional 7.69% swing Lab. to C.
(2005: Lab. majority 15,501 (39.15%))

§WILTSHIRE NORTH
E. 66,313 T. 48,699 (73.44%) C. hold
James Gray, C. 25,114
Mike Evemy, LD 17,631
Jason Hughes, Lab. 3,239
Charles Bennett, UKIP 1,908
Phil Chamberlain, Green 599
Philip Allnatt, Ind. 208
C. majority 7,483 (15.37%)
Notional 0.01% swing LD to C.
(2005: C. majority 6,888 (15.34%))

§WILTSHIRE SOUTH WEST
E. 71,645 T. 49,018 (68.42%) C. hold
Andrew Murrison, C. 25,321
Trevor Carbin, LD 14,954
Rebecca Rennison, Lab. 5,613
Michael Cuthbert-Murray, UKIP 2,684
Crispin Black, Ind. 446
C. majority 10,367 (21.15%)
Notional 1.15% swing LD to C.
(2005: C. majority 8,568 (18.85%))

§WIMBLEDON
E. 65,723 T. 47,395 (72.11%) C. hold
Stephen Hammond, C. 23,257
Shas Sheehan, LD 11,849
Andrew Judge, Lab. 10,550
Mark McAleer, UKIP 914
Rajeev Thacker, Green 590
David Martin, Ch. P. 235
C. majority 11,408 (24.07%)
Notional 0.42% swing LD to C.
(2005: C. majority 2,480 (5.69%))

§WINCHESTER
E. 73,806 T. 55,955 (75.81%) C. gain
*Steve Brine, C. 27,155
Martin Tod, LD 24,107
Patrick Davies, Lab. 3,051
Jocelyn Penn-Bull, UKIP 1,139
Mark Lancaster, Eng. Dem. 503
C. majority 3,048 (5.45%)
Notional 9.09% swing LD to C.
(2005: LD majority 6,524 (12.74%))

§WINDSOR
E. 69,511 T. 49,588 (71.34%) C. hold
Adam Afriyie, C. 30,172
Julian Tisi, LD 11,118
Amanjit Jhund, Lab. 4,910
John-Paul Rye, UKIP 1,612
Peter Phillips, BNP 950
Derek Wall, Green 628
Peter Hooper, Ind. 198
C. majority 19,054 (38.42%)
Notional 8.05% swing LD to C.
(2005: C. majority 9,605 (22.32%))

§WIRRAL SOUTH
E. 56,099 T. 39,906 (71.13%) Lab. hold
*Alison McGovern, Lab. 16,276
Jeff Clarke, C. 15,745
Jamie Saddler, LD 6,611
David Scott, UKIP 1,274
Lab. majority 531 (1.33%)
Notional 3.98% swing Lab. to C.
(2005: Lab. majority 3,538 (9.30%))

§WIRRAL WEST
E. 55,050 T. 39,372 (71.52%) C. hold
*Esther McVey, C. 16,726
Phillip Davies, Lab. 14,290
Peter Reisdorf, LD 6,630
Philip Griffiths, UKIP 899
David Kirwan, Ind. 506
David James, CSP 321
C. majority 2,436 (6.19%)
Notional 2.34% swing Lab. to C.
(2005: C. majority 569 (1.51%))

§WITHAM
E. 66,750 T. 46,835 (70.16%) C. hold
*Priti Patel, C. 24,448
Margaret Phelps, LD 9,252
John Spademan, Lab. 8,656
David Hodges, UKIP 3,060
James Abbott, Green 1,419
C. majority 15,196 (32.45%)
Notional 1.06% swing C. to LD
(2005: C. majority 7,241 (17.29%))

§WITNEY
E. 78,766 T. 57,769 (73.34%) C. hold
David Cameron, C. 33,973
Dawn Barnes, LD 11,233
Joe Goldberg, Lab. 7,511
Stuart Macdonald, Green 2,385
Nikolai Tolstoy, UKIP 2,001
Howling Hope, Loony 234
Paul Wesson, Ind. 166
Johnnie Cook, Ind. 151
Colin Bex, Wessex Reg. 62
Aaron Barschak, Ind. 53
C. majority 22,740 (39.36%)
Notional 6.29% swing LD to C.
(2005: C. majority 13,874 (26.78%))

WOKING
E. 73,838 T. 52,786 (71.49%) C. hold
*Jonathan Lord, C. 26,551
Rosie Sharpley, LD 19,744
Tom Miller, Lab. 4,246
Rob Burberry, UKIP 1,997
Julie Roxburgh, PPN-V 204
Ruth Temple, Magna Carta 44
C. majority 6,807 (12.90%)
0.73% swing C. to LD
(2005: C. majority 6,612 (14.36%))

§WOKINGHAM
E. 76,219 T. 54,528 (71.54%) C. hold
John Redwood, C. 28,754
Prue Bray, LD 15,262
George Davidson, Lab. 5,516
Mark Ashwell, Ind. 2,340
Ann Zebedee, UKIP 1,664
Marjory Bisset, Green 567
Top Cat Owen, Loony 329
Robin Smith, Ind. 96
C. majority 13,492 (24.74%)
Notional 4.65% swing LD to C.
(2005: C. majority 7,257 (15.44%))

§WOLVERHAMPTON NORTH EAST
E. 59,324 T. 34,894 (58.82%) Lab. hold
*Emma Reynolds, Lab. 14,448
Julie Rook, C. 11,964
Colin Ross, LD 4,711
Simon Patten, BNP 2,296
Paul Valdmanis, UKIP 1,138
Shangara Bhatoe, Soc. Lab. 337
Lab. majority 2,484 (7.12%)
Notional 9.00% swing Lab. to C.
(2005: Lab. majority 8,628 (25.12%))

§WOLVERHAMPTON SOUTH EAST
E. 60,450 T. 34,707 (57.41%) Lab. hold
Pat McFadden, Lab. 16,505
Ken Wood, C. 9,912
Richard Whitehouse, LD 5,277
Gordon Fanthom, UKIP 2,675
Sudhir Handa, Ind. 338
Lab. majority 6,593 (19.00%)
Notional 8.79% swing Lab. to C.
(2005: Lab. majority 12,309 (36.58%))

§WOLVERHAMPTON SOUTH WEST
E. 59,160 T. 40,160 (67.88%) C. gain
*Paul Uppal, C. 16,344
Rob Marris, Lab. 15,653
Robin Lawrence, LD 6,430
Amanda Mobberley, UKIP 1,487
Raymond Barry, Parenting 246
C. majority 691 (1.72%)
Notional 3.52% swing Lab. to C.
(2005: Lab. majority 2,114 (5.31%))

WORCESTER
E. 72,831 T. 48,974 (67.24%) C. gain
*Robin Walker, C. 19,358
Michael Foster, Lab. 16,376
Jackie Alderson, LD 9,525
Jack Bennett, UKIP 1,360
Spencer Lee Kirby, BNP 1,219
Louis Stephen, Green 735
Andrew Robinson, Pirate 173
Peter Nielsen, Ind. 129
Andrew Christian-Brookes, Ind. 99
C. majority 2,982 (6.09%)
6.43% swing Lab. to C.
(2005: Lab. majority 3,144 (6.78%))

§WORCESTERSHIRE MID
E. 72,171 T. 50,931 (70.57%) C. hold
Peter Luff, C. 27,770
Margaret Rowley, LD 11,906
Robin Lunn, Lab. 7,613
John White, UKIP 3,049
Gordon Matthews, Green 593
C. majority 15,864 (31.15%)
Notional 0.04% swing LD to C.
(2005: C. majority 12,906 (27.33%))

§WORCESTERSHIRE WEST
E. 73,270 T. 54,093 (73.83%) C. hold
*Harriett Baldwin, C. 27,213
Richard Burt, LD 20,459
Penelope Barber, Lab. 3,661
Caroline Bovey, UKIP 2,119
Malcolm Victory, Green 641
C. majority 6,754 (12.49%)
Notional 3.23% swing LD to C.
(2005: C. majority 3,053 (6.03%))

§WORKINGTON
E. 59,607 T. 39,259 (65.86%) Lab. hold
Tony Cunningham, Lab. 17,865
Judith Pattinson, C. 13,290
Stan Collins, LD 5,318
Martin Wingfield, BNP 1,496
Stephen Lee, UKIP 876
Rob Logan, Eng. Dem. 414
Lab. majority 4,575 (11.65%)
Notional 5.66% swing Lab. to C.
(2005: Lab. majority 8,226 (22.97%))

§WORSLEY & ECCLES SOUTH
E. 72,473 T. 41,701 (57.54%) Lab. hold
Barbara Keeley, Lab. 17,892
Iain Lindley, C. 13,555
Richard Gadsden, LD 6,883
Andrew Townsend, UKIP 2,037
Paul Whitelegg, Eng. Dem. 1,334
Lab. majority 4,337 (10.40%)
Notional 7.61% swing Lab. to C.
(2005: Lab. majority 10,001 (25.62%))

§WORTHING EAST & SHOREHAM
E. 74,001 T. 48,397 (65.40%) C. hold
Tim Loughton, C. 23,458
James Doyle, LD 12,353
Emily Benn, Lab. 8,087
Mike Glennon, UKIP 2,984
Susan Board, Green 1,126
Clive Maltby, Eng. Dem. 389
C. majority 11,105 (22.95%)
Notional 1.70% swing LD to C.
(2005: C. majority 8,180 (18.37%))

§WORTHING WEST
E. 75,945 T. 49,123 (64.68%) C. hold
Peter Bottomley, C. 25,416
Hazel Thorpe, LD 13,687
Ian Ross, Lab. 5,800
John Wallace, UKIP 2,924
David Aherne, Green 996
Stuart Dearsley, Christian 300
C. majority 11,729 (23.88%)
Notional 1.50% swing LD to C.
(2005: C. majority 9,383 (20.89%))

§WREKIN, THE
E. 65,544 T. 45,968 (70.13%) C. hold
Mark Pritchard, C. 21,922
Paul Kalinauckas, Lab. (Co-op) 12,472
Ali Cameron-Daw, LD 8,019
Malcolm Hurst, UKIP 2,050
Susan Harwood, BNP 1,505
C. majority 9,450 (20.56%)
Notional 8.85% swing Lab. (Co-op) to C.
(2005: C. majority 1,187 (2.85%))

§WYCOMBE
E. 74,502 T. 48,151 (64.63%) C. hold
*Steven Baker, C. 23,423
Steve Guy, LD 13,863
Andrew Lomas, Lab. 8,326
John Wiseman, UKIP 2,123
Madassar Khokar, Ind. 228
David Fitton, Ind. 188
C. majority 9,560 (19.85%)
Notional 4.83% swing C. to LD
(2005: C. majority 7,597 (17.29%))

§WYRE & PRESTON NORTH
E. 71,201 T. 51,308 (72.06%) C. hold
*Ben Wallace, C. 26,877
Danny Gallagher, LD 11,033
Cat Smith, Lab. 10,932
Nigel Cecil, UKIP 2,466
C. majority 15,844 (30.88%)
Notional 3.86% swing C. to LD
(2005: C. majority 12,082 (27.51%))

§WYRE FOREST
E. 76,711 T. 50,899 (66.35%) C. gain
*Mark Garnier, C. 18,793
Dr Richard Taylor, Ind. CHC 16,150
Nigel Knowles, Lab. 7,298
Neville Farmer, LD 6,040
Michael Wrench, UKIP 1,498
Gordon Howells, BNP 1,120
C. majority 2,643 (5.19%)
Notional 7.35% swing Ind. CHC to C.
(2005: Ind. CHC majority 4,613 (9.51%))

WYTHENSHAWE & SALE EAST
E. 79,923 T. 40,751 (50.99%) Lab. hold
Paul Goggins, Lab. 17,987
Janet Clowes, C. 10,412
Martin Eakins, LD 9,107
Bernard Todd, BNP 1,572
Chris Cassidy, UKIP 1,405
Lynn Worthington, TUSC 268
Lab. majority 7,575 (18.59%)
5.67% swing Lab. to C.
(2005: Lab. majority 10,827 (29.92%))

§YEOVIL
E. 82,314 T. 57,160 (69.44%) LD hold
David Laws, LD 31,843
Kevin Davis, C. 18,807
Lee Skevington, Lab. 2,991
Nigel Pearson, UKIP 2,357
Robert Baehr, BNP 1,162
LD majority 13,036 (22.81%)
Notional 2.74% swing C. to LD
(2005: LD majority 8,779 (17.33%))

§YORK CENTRAL
E. 74,908 T. 46,483 (62.05%) Lab. hold
Hugh Bayley, Lab. 18,573
Susan Wade Weeks, C. 12,122
Christian Vassie, LD 11,694
Andy Chase, Green 1,669
Jeff Kelly, BNP 1,171
Paul Abbott, UKIP 1,100
Eddie Vee, Loony 154
Lab. majority 6,451 (13.88%)
Notional 6.02% swing Lab. to C.
(2005: Lab. majority 10,344 (25.92%))

§YORK OUTER
E. 74,965 T. 53,300 (71.10%) C. gain
*Julian Sturdy, C. 22,912
Madeleine Kirk, LD 19,224
James Alexander, Lab. 9,108
Judith Morris, UKIP 1,100
Cathy Smurthwaite, BNP 956
C. majority 3,688 (6.92%)
Notional 3.68% swing LD to C.
(2005: LD majority 203 (0.44%))

§YORKSHIRE EAST
E. 80,342 T. 51,254 (63.79%) C. hold
Greg Knight, C. 24,328
Robert Adamson, LD 10,842
Paul Rounding, Lab. 10,401
Chris Daniels, UKIP 2,142
Gary Pudsey, BNP 1,865
Ray Allerston, Soc. Dem. 914
Michael Jackson, Green 762
C. majority 13,486 (26.31%)
Notional 0.06% swing C. to LD
(2005: C. majority 6,284 (13.31%))

WALES

ABERAVON
E. 50,789 T. 30,958 (60.95%) Lab. hold
Hywel Francis, Lab. 16,073
Keith Davies, LD 5,034
Caroline Jones, C. 4,411
Paul Nicholls-Jones, PC 2,198
Kevin Edwards, BNP 1,276
Andrew Tutton, Ind. 919
Captain Beany, Bean 558
Joe Callan, UKIP 489
Lab. majority 11,039 (35.66%)
5.32% swing Lab. to LD
(2005: Lab. majority 13,937 (46.30%))

§ABERCONWY
E. 44,593 T. 29,966 (67.20%) C. gain
*Guto Bebb, C. 10,734
Ronald Hughes, Lab. 7,336
Mike Priestley, LD 5,786
Phil Edwards, PC 5,341
Mike Wieteska, UKIP 632
Louise Wynne-Jones, Ch. P. 137
C. majority 3,398 (11.34%)
Notional 7.63% swing Lab. to C.
(2005: Lab. majority 1,070 (3.93%))

ALYN & DEESIDE
E. 60,931 T. 39,923 (65.52%) Lab. hold
Mark Tami, Lab. 15,804
Will Gallagher, C. 12,885
Paul Brighton, LD 7,308
Maurice Jones, PC 1,549
John Walker, BNP 1,368
James Howson, UKIP 1,009
Lab. majority 2,919 (7.31%)
8.15% swing Lab. to C.
(2005: Lab. majority 8,378 (23.60%))

§ARFON
E. 41,198 T. 26,078 (63.30%) PC gain
Hywel Williams, PC 9,383
Alan Pugh, Lab. 7,928
Robin Millar, C. 4,416
Sarah Green, LD 3,666
Elwyn Williams, UKIP 685
PC majority 1,455 (5.58%)
Notional 3.70% swing Lab. to PC
(2005: Lab. majority 456 (1.82%))

BLAENAU GWENT
E. 52,438 T. 32,395 (61.78%) Lab. gain
*Nick Smith, Lab. 16,974
Dai Davies, Blaenau Voice 6,458
Matt Smith, LD 3,285
Liz Stevenson, C. 2,265
Rhodri Davies, PC 1,333
Anthony King, BNP 1,211
Mike Kocan, UKIP 488
Alyson O'Connell, Soc. Lab. 381
Lab. majority 10,516 (32.46%)
29.2% swing Blaenau Voice to Lab.
(2005: Ind. Law majority 9,121 (25.87%))(2006: Ind. Davies majority 2,484 (9.14%))

BRECON & RADNORSHIRE
E. 53,589 T. 38,845 (72.49%) LD hold
Roger Williams, LD 17,929
Suzy Davies, C. 14,182
Christopher Lloyd, Lab. 4,096
Janet Davies, PC 989
Clive Easton, UKIP 876
Dorienne Robinson, Green 341
Jeffrey Green, Ch. P. 222
Lord Offa, Loony 210
LD majority 3,747 (9.65%)
0.27% swing LD to C.
(2005: LD majority 3,905 (10.18%))

§BRIDGEND
E. 58,700 T. 38,347 (65.33%) Lab. hold
Madeleine Moon, Lab. 13,931
Helen Baker, C. 11,668
Wayne Morgan, LD 8,658
Nick Thomas, PC 2,269
Brian Urch, BNP 1,020
David Fulton, UKIP 801
Lab. majority 2,263 (5.90%)
Notional 5.98% swing Lab. to C.
(2005: Lab. majority 6,089 (17.87%))

§CAERPHILLY
E. 62,134 T. 38,992 (62.75%) Lab. hold
Wayne David, Lab. 17,377
Maria Caulfield, C. 6,622
Lindsay Whittle, PC 6,460
Kay David, LD 5,988
Laurence Reid, BNP 1,635
Tony Jenkins, UKIP 910
Lab. majority 10,755 (27.58%)
Notional 6.57% swing Lab. to C.
(2005: Lab. majority 13,517 (37.32%))

CARDIFF CENTRAL
E. 61,162 T. 36,151 (59.11%) LD hold
Jenny Willott, LD 14,976
Jenny Rathbone, Lab. 10,400
Karen Robson, C. 7,799
Chris Williams, PC 1,246
Susan Davies, UKIP 765
Sam Coates, Green 575
Ross Saunders, TUSC 162
Mark Beech, Loony 142
Alun Mathias, Ind. 86
LD majority 4,576 (12.66%)
1.41% swing LD to Lab.
(2005: LD majority 5,593 (15.48%))

CARDIFF NORTH
E. 65,553 T. 47,630 (72.66%) C. gain
*Jonathan Evans, C. 17,860
Julie Morgan, Lab. 17,666
John Dixon, LD 8,724
Llywelyn Rhys, PC 1,588
Lawrence Gwynn, UKIP 1,130
Christopher von Ruhland, Green 362
Derek Thomson, Ch. P. 300
C. majority 194 (0.41%)
1.47% swing Lab. to C.
(2005: Lab. majority 1,146 (2.53%))

§¶CARDIFF SOUTH & PENARTH
E. 73,704 T. 44,370 (60.20%) Lab. (Co-op) hold
Alun Michael, Lab. (Co-op) 17,263
Simon Hoare, C. 12,553
Dominic Hannigan, LD 9,875
Farida Aslam, PC 1,851
Simon Zeigler, UKIP 1,145
George Burke, Ind. 648
Matt Townsend, Green 554
Clive Bate, Ch. P. 285
Robert Griffiths, Comm 196
Lab. (Co-op) majority 4,710 (10.62%)
Notional 6.03% swing Lab. (Co-op) to C.
(2005: Lab. (Co-op) majority 8,955 (22.68%))

§CARDIFF WEST
E. 62,787 T. 40,957 (65.23%) Lab. hold
Kevin Brennan, Lab. 16,893
Angela Jones-Evans, C. 12,143
Rachael Hitchinson, LD 7,186
Mohammed Sarul Islam, PC 2,868
Mike Henessey, UKIP 1,117
Jake Griffiths, Green 750
Lab. majority 4,750 (11.60%)
Notional 5.33% swing Lab. to C.
(2005: Lab. majority 8,361 (22.25%))

§CARMARTHEN EAST & DINEFWR
E. 52,385 T. 38,011 (72.56%) PC hold
*Jonathan Edwards, PC 13,546
Christine Gwyther, Lab. 10,065
Andrew Morgan, C. 8,506
Bill Powell, LD 4,609
John Atkinson, UKIP 1,285
PC majority 3,481 (9.16%)
Notional 4.19% swing PC to Lab.
(2005: PC majority 6,551 (17.54%))

§CARMARTHEN WEST & PEMBROKESHIRE SOUTH
E. 57,519 T. 40,507 (70.42%) C. gain
*Simon Hart, C. 16,649
Nick Ainger, Lab. 13,226
John Gossage, LD 4,890
John Dixon, PC 4,232
Ray Clarke, UKIP 1,146
Henry Langen, Ind. 364
C. majority 3,423 (8.45%)
Notional 6.88% swing Lab. to C.
(2005: Lab. majority 2,043 (5.32%))

§CEREDIGION
E. 59,043 T. 38,258 (64.80%) LD hold
Mark Williams, LD 19,139
Penri James, PC 10,815
Luke Evetts, C. 4,421
Richard Boudier, Lab. 2,210
Elwyn Williams, UKIP 977
Leila Kiersch, Green 696
LD majority 8,324 (21.76%)
Notional 10.57% swing PC to LD
(2005: LD majority 218 (0.61%))

§CLWYD SOUTH
E. 53,748 T. 34,681 (64.53%) Lab. hold
*Susan Elan Jones, Lab. 13,311
John Bell, C. 10,477
Bruce Roberts, LD 5,965
Janet Ryder, PC 3,009
Sarah Hynes, BNP 1,100
Nick Powell, UKIP 819
Lab. majority 2,834 (8.17%)
Notional 5.83% swing Lab. to C.
(2005: Lab. majority 6,220 (19.84%))

§CLWYD WEST
E. 57,913 T. 38,111 (65.81%) C. hold
David Jones, C. 15,833
Donna Hutton, Lab. 9,414
Llyr Huws Gruffydd, PC 5,864
Michele Jones, LD 5,801
Warwick Nicholson, UKIP 864
Revd Dr David Griffiths, Ch. P. 239
Joe Blakesley, Ind. 96
C. majority 6,419 (16.84%)
Notional 8.35% swing Lab. to C.
(2005: C. majority 51 (0.14%))

§CYNON VALLEY
E. 50,656 T. 29,876 (58.98%) Lab. hold
Ann Clwyd, Lab. 15,681
Dafydd Trystan Davies, PC 6,064
Lee Thacker, LD 4,120
Juliette Ash, C. 3,010
Frank Hughes, UKIP 1,001
Lab. majority 9,617 (32.19%)
Notional 8.65% swing Lab. to PC
(2005: Lab. majority 14,390 (49.48%))

DELYN
E. 53,470 T. 36,984 (69.17%) Lab. hold
David Hanson, Lab. 15,083
Antoinette Sandbach, C. 12,811
Bill Brereton, LD 5,747
Peter Ryder, PC 1,844
Jennifer Matthys, BNP 844
Andrew Haigh, UKIP 655
Lab. majority 2,272 (6.14%)
6.70% swing Lab. to C.
(2005: Lab. majority 6,644 (19.54%))

§DWYFOR MEIRIONNYDD
E. 45,354 T. 28,906 (63.73%) PC hold
Elfyn Llwyd, PC 12,814
Simon Baynes, C. 6,447
Alwyn Humphreys, Lab. 4,021
Steve Churchman, LD 3,538
Louise Hughes, Ind. 1,310
Frank Wykes, UKIP 776
PC majority 6,367 (22.03%)
Notional 7.28% swing PC to C.
(2005: PC majority 8,706 (29.02%))

§GOWER
E. 61,696 T. 41,671 (67.54%) Lab. hold
Martin Caton, Lab. 16,016
Byron Davies, C. 13,333
Mike Day, LD 7,947
Darren Price, PC 2,760
Adrian Jones, BNP 963
Gordon Triggs, UKIP 652
Lab. majority 2,683 (6.44%)
Notional 5.26% swing Lab. to C.
(2005: Lab. majority 6,703 (16.95%))

§ISLWYN
E. 54,826 T. 34,690 (63.27%)
Lab. (Co-op) hold
*Christopher Evans, Lab. (Co-op) 17,069
Daniel Thomas, C. 4,854
Steffan Lewis, PC 4,518
Asghar Ali, LD 3,597
Dave Rees, Ind. 1,495
John Voisey, BNP 1,320
Jason Crew, UKIP 936
Paul Taylor, Ind. 901
Lab. (Co-op) majority 12,215 (35.21%)
Notional 9.05% swing Lab. (Co-op) to C.
(2005: Lab. (Co-op) majority 17,582 (51.91%))

LLANELLI
E. 55,637 T. 37,461 (67.33%) Lab. hold
Nia Griffith, Lab. 15,916
Myfanwy Davies, PC 11,215
Christopher Salmon, C. 5,381
Myrddin Edwards, LD 3,902
Andrew Marshall, UKIP 1,047
Lab. majority 4,701 (12.55%)
3.96% swing Lab. to PC
(2005: Lab. majority 7,234 (20.47%))

MERTHYR TYDFIL & RHYMNEY
E. 54,715 T. 32,076 (58.62%) Lab. hold
Dai Havard, Lab. 14,007
Amy Kitcher, LD 9,951
Maria Hill, C. 2,412
Clive Tovey, Ind. 1,845
Glyndwr Cennydd Jones, PC 1,621
Richard Barnes, BNP 1,173
Adam Brown, UKIP 872
Alan Cowdell, Soc. Lab. 195
Lab. majority 4,056 (12.64%)
16.92% swing Lab. to LD
(2005: Lab. majority 13,934 (46.48%))

MONMOUTH
E. 62,768 T. 46,519 (74.11%) C. hold
David Davies, C. 22,466
Hamish Sandison, Lab. 12,041
Martin Blakebrough, LD 9,026
Jonathan Clark, PC 1,273
Derek Rowe, UKIP 1,126
Steve Millson, Green 587
C. majority 10,425 (22.41%)
6.25% swing Lab. to C.
(2005: C. majority 4,527 (9.92%))

§MONTGOMERYSHIRE
E. 48,730 T. 33,813 (69.39%) C. gain
*Glyn Davies, C. 13,976
Lembit Opik, LD 12,792
Heledd Fychan, PC 2,802
Nick Colbourne, Lab. 2,407
David Rowlands, UKIP 1,128
Milton Ellis, NF 384
Bruce Lawson, Ind. 324
C. majority 1,184 (3.50%)
Notional 13.15% swing LD to C.
(2005: LD majority 7,048 (22.80%))

§NEATH
E. 57,186 T. 37,122 (64.91%) Lab. hold
Peter Hain, Lab. 17,172
Alun Llewelyn, PC 7,397
Frank Little, LD 5,535
Emmeline Owens, C. 4,847
Michael Green, BNP 1,342
James Bevan, UKIP 829
Lab. majority 9,775 (26.33%)
Notional 4.58% swing Lab. to PC
(2005: Lab. majority 12,710 (35.49%))

NEWPORT EAST
E. 54,437 T. 34,448 (63.28%) Lab. hold
Jessica Morden, Lab. 12,744
Ed Townsend, LD 11,094
Dawn Parry, C. 7,918
Keith Jones, BNP 1,168
Fiona Cross, PC 724
David Rowlands, UKIP 677
Liz Screen, Soc. Lab. 123
Lab. majority 1,650 (4.79%)
8.35% swing Lab. to LD
(2005: Lab. majority 6,838 (21.49%))

NEWPORT WEST
E. 62,111 T. 39,720 (63.95%) Lab. hold
Paul Flynn, Lab. 16,389
Matthew Williams, C. 12,845
Veronica German, LD 6,587
Timothy Windsor, BNP 1,183
Hugh Moelwyn Hughes, UKIP 1,144
Jeff Rees, PC 1,122
Pippa Bartolotti, Green 450
Lab. majority 3,544 (8.92%)
3.18% swing Lab. to C.
(2005: Lab. majority 5,458 (15.27%))

§OGMORE
E. 55,527 T. 34,650 (62.40%) Lab. hold
Huw Irranca-Davies, Lab. 18,644
Emma Moore, C. 5,398
Jackie Radford, LD 5,260
Danny Clark, PC 3,326
Kay Thomas, BNP 1,242
Carolyn Passey, UKIP 780
Lab. majority 13,246 (38.23%)
Notional 4.28% swing Lab. to C.
(2005: Lab. majority 14,839 (46.29%))

§PONTYPRIDD
E. 58,219 T. 36,671 (62.99%) Lab. hold
*Owen Smith, Lab. 14,220
Michael Powell, LD 11,435
Lee Gonzalez, C. 5,932
Ioan Bellin, PC 2,673
David Bevan, UKIP 1,229
Simon Parsons, Soc. Lab. 456
Donald Watson, Ch. P. 365
John Matthews, Green 361
Lab. majority 2,785 (7.59%)
Notional 13.31% swing Lab. to LD
(2005: Lab. majority 11,694 (34.21%))

§PRESELI PEMBROKESHIRE
E. 57,419 T. 39,602 (68.97%) C. hold
Stephen Crabb, C. 16,944
Mari Rees, Lab. 12,339
Nick Tregoning, LD 5,759
Henry Jones-Davies, PC 3,654
Richard Lawson, UKIP 906
C. majority 4,605 (11.63%)
Notional 5.05% swing Lab. to C.
(2005: C. majority 601 (1.53%))

RHONDDA
E. 51,554 T. 31,072 (60.27%) Lab. hold
Chris Bryant, Lab. 17,183
Geraint Davies, PC 5,630
Paul Wasley, LD 3,309
Philip Howe, Ind. 2,599
Juliet Henderson, C. 1,993
Taffy John, UKIP 358
Lab. majority 11,553 (37.18%)
7.48% swing Lab. to PC
(2005: Lab. majority 16,242 (52.14%))

SWANSEA EAST
E. 59,823 T. 32,676 (54.62%) Lab. hold
Sian James, Lab. 16,819
Robert Speht, LD 5,981
Christian Holliday, C. 4,823
Dic Jones, PC 2,181
Clive Bennett, BNP 1,715
David Rogers, UKIP 839
Tony Young, Green 318
Lab. majority 10,838 (33.17%)
1.66% swing Lab. to LD
(2005: Lab. majority 11,249 (36.48%))

SWANSEA WEST
E. 61,334 T. 35,593 (58.03%) Lab. hold
*Geraint Davies, Lab. 12,335
Peter May, LD 11,831
Rene Kinzett, C. 7,407
Harri Roberts, PC 1,437
Alan Bateman, BNP 910
Tim Jenkins, UKIP 716
Keith Ross, Green 404
Ian McCloy, Ind. 374
Rob Williams, TUSC 179
Lab. majority 504 (1.42%)
5.74% swing Lab. to LD
(2005: Lab. majority 4,269 (12.90%))

TORFAEN
E. 61,178 T. 37,640 (61.53%) Lab. hold
Paul Murphy, Lab. 16,847
Jonathan Burns, C. 7,541
David Morgan, LD 6,264
Rhys ab Elis, PC 2,005
Jennifer Noble, BNP 1,657
Fred Wildgust, Ind. 1,419
Gareth Dunn, UKIP 862
Richard Turner-Thomas, Ind. 607
Owen Clarke, Green 438
Lab. majority 9,306 (24.72%)
8.19% swing Lab. to C.
(2005: Lab. majority 14,791 (41.11%))

§VALE OF CLWYD
E. 55,781 T. 35,534 (63.70%) Lab. hold
Chris Ruane, Lab. 15,017
Matt Wright, C. 12,508
Paul Penlington, LD 4,472
Caryl Wyn Jones, PC 2,068
Ian Si'Ree, BNP 827
Tom Turner, UKIP 515
Mike Butler, Green Soc. 127
Lab. majority 2,509 (7.06%)
Notional 3.56% swing Lab. to C.
(2005: Lab. majority 4,629 (14.18%))

§VALE OF GLAMORGAN
E. 70,262 T. 48,667 (69.27%) C. gain
*Alun Cairns, C. 20,341
Alana Davies, Lab. 16,034
Eluned Parrott, LD 7,403
Ian Johnson, PC 2,667
Kevin Mahoney, UKIP 1,529
Rhodri Thomas, Green 457
John Harrold, Ch. P. 236
C. majority 4,307 (8.85%)
Notional 6.11% swing Lab. to C.
(2005: Lab. majority 1,574 (3.37%))

WREXHAM
E. 50,872 T. 32,976 (64.82%) Lab. hold
Ian Lucas, Lab. 12,161
Tom Rippeth, LD 8,503
Gareth Hughes, C. 8,375
Arfon Jones, PC 2,029
Melvin Roberts, BNP 1,134
John Humberstone, UKIP 774
Lab. majority 3,658 (11.09%)
5.67% swing Lab. to LD
(2005: Lab. majority 6,819 (22.44%))

YNYS MON
E. 50,075 T. 34,444 (68.78%) Lab. hold
Albert Owen, Lab. 11,490
Dylan Rees, PC 9,029
Anthony Ridge-Newman, C. 7,744
Matt Wood, LD 2,592
Peter Rogers, Ind. 2,225
Elaine Gill, UKIP 1,201
The Rev David Owen, Ch. P. 163
Lab. majority 2,461 (7.14%)
1.82% swing PC to Lab.
(2005: Lab. majority 1,242 (3.50%))

SCOTLAND

ABERDEEN NORTH
E. 64,808 T. 37,701 (58.17%) Lab. hold
Frank Doran, Lab. 16,746
Joanna Strathdee, SNP 8,385
Kristian Chapman, LD 7,001
Stewart Whyte, C. 4,666
Roy Jones, BNP 635
Ewan Robertson, SSP 268
Lab. majority 8,361 (22.18%)
1.00% swing SNP to Lab.
(2005: Lab. majority 6,795 (18.55%))

ABERDEEN SOUTH
E. 64,031 T. 43,034 (67.21%) Lab. hold
Anne Begg, Lab. 15,722
John Sleigh, LD 12,216
Amanda Harvie, C. 8,914
Mark McDonald, SNP 5,102
Susan Ross, BNP 529
Rhonda Reekie, Green 413
Robert Green, SACL 138
Lab. majority 3,506 (8.15%)
2.45% swing LD to Lab.
(2005: Lab. majority 1,348 (3.24%))

ABERDEENSHIRE WEST & KINCARDINE
E. 66,110 T. 45,195 (68.36%) LD hold
Sir Robert Smith, LD 17,362
Alex Johnstone, C. 13,678
Dennis Robertson, SNP 7,086
Greg Williams, Lab. 6,159
Gary Raikes, BNP 513
Anthony Atkinson, UKIP 397
LD majority 3,684 (8.15%)
4.89% swing LD to C.
(2005: LD majority 7,471 (17.94%))

AIRDRIE & SHOTTS
E. 62,364 T. 35,849 (57.48%) Lab. hold
*Pamela Nash, Lab. 20,849
Sophia Coyle, SNP 8,441
Ruth Whitfield, C. 3,133
John Love, LD 2,898
John McGeechan, Ind. 528
Lab. majority 12,408 (34.61%)
3.93% swing Lab. to SNP
(2005: Lab. majority 14,084 (42.48%))

ANGUS
E. 62,863 T. 37,960 (60.39%) SNP hold
Mike Weir, SNP 15,020
Alberto Costa, C. 11,738
Kevin Hutchens, Lab. 6,535
Sanjay Samani, LD 4,090
Martin Gray, UKIP 577
SNP majority 3,282 (8.65%)
2.22% swing C. to SNP
(2005: SNP majority 1,601 (4.20%))

ARGYLL & BUTE
E. 67,165 T. 45,207 (67.31%) LD hold
Alan Reid, LD 14,292
Gary Mulvaney, C. 10,861
David Graham, Lab. 10,274
Michael MacKenzie, SNP 8,563
Elaine Morrison, Green 789
George Doyle, Ind. 272
John Black, Jacobite 156
LD majority 3,431 (7.59%)
2.72% swing LD to C.
(2005: LD majority 5,636 (13.04%))

AYR, CARRICK & CUMNOCK
E. 73,320 T. 45,893 (62.59%) Lab. hold
Sandra Osborne, Lab. 21,632
William Grant, C. 11,721
Charles Brodie, SNP 8,276
James Taylor, LD 4,264
Lab. majority 9,911 (21.60%)
0.30% swing Lab. to C.
(2005: Lab. majority 9,997 (22.19%))

AYRSHIRE CENTRAL
E. 68,352 T. 43,915 (64.25%) Lab. hold
Brian Donohoe, Lab. 20,950
Maurice Golden, C. 8,943
John Mullen, SNP 8,364
Andrew Chamberlain, LD 5,236
James McDaid, Soc. Lab. 422
Lab. majority 12,007 (27.34%)
1.51% swing C. to Lab.
(2005: Lab. majority 10,423 (24.31%))

AYRSHIRE NORTH & ARRAN
E. 74,953 T. 46,116 (61.53%) Lab. hold
Katy Clark, Lab. 21,860
Patricia Gibson, SNP 11,965
Philip Lardner, C. 7,212
Gillian Cole-Hamilton, LD 4,630
Louise McDaid, Soc. Lab. 449
Lab. majority 9,895 (21.46%)
2.26% swing Lab. to SNP
(2005: Lab. majority 11,296 (25.55%))

BANFF & BUCHAN
E. 64,300 T. 38,466 (59.82%) SNP hold
*Eilidh Whiteford, SNP 15,868
Jimmy Buchan, C. 11,841
Glen Reynolds, Lab. 5,382
Galen Milne, LD 4,365
Richard Payne, BNP 1,010
SNP majority 4,027 (10.47%)
10.67% swing SNP to C.
(2005: SNP majority 11,837 (31.81%))

BERWICKSHIRE, ROXBURGH & SELKIRK
E. 73,826 T. 49,014 (66.39%) LD hold
Michael Moore, LD 22,230
John Lamont, C. 16,555
Ian Miller, Lab. 5,003
Paul Wheelhouse, SNP 4,497
Sherry Fowler, UKIP 595
Chris Black, Jacobite 134
LD majority 5,675 (11.58%)
0.71% swing LD to C.
(2005: LD majority 5,901 (13.00%))

CAITHNESS, SUTHERLAND & EASTER ROSS
E. 47,257 T. 28,768 (60.88%) LD hold
John Thurso, LD 11,907
John Mackay, Lab. 7,081
Jean Urquhart, SNP 5,516
Alastair Graham, C. 3,744
Gordon Campbell, Ind. 520
LD majority 4,826 (16.78%)
6.38% swing LD to Lab.
(2005: LD majority 8,168 (29.53%))

COATBRIDGE, CHRYSTON & BELLSHILL
E. 70,067 T. 41,635 (59.42%) Lab. hold
Tom Clarke, Lab. 27,728
Frances McGlinchey, SNP 7,014
Kenneth Elder, LD 3,519
Fiona Houston, C. 3,374
Lab. majority 20,714 (49.75%)
0.58% swing Lab. to SNP
(2005: Lab. majority 19,519 (50.90%))

CUMBERNAULD, KILSYTH & KIRKINTILLOCH EAST
E. 64,037 T. 41,150 (64.26%) Lab. hold
*Gregg McClymont, Lab. 23,549
Julie Hepburn, SNP 9,794
Rod Ackland, LD 3,924
Stephanie Fraser, C. 3,407
William O'Neill, SSP 476
Lab. majority 13,755 (33.43%)
1.92% swing SNP to Lab.
(2005: Lab. majority 11,562 (29.58%))

DUMFRIES & GALLOWAY
E. 74,581 T. 52,173 (69.95%) Lab. hold
Russell Brown, Lab. 23,950
Peter Duncan, C. 16,501
Andrew Wood, SNP 6,419
Richard Brodie, LD 4,608
William Wright, UKIP 695
Lab. majority 7,449 (14.28%)
4.27% swing C. to Lab.
(2005: Lab. majority 2,922 (5.74%))

DUMFRIESSHIRE, CLYDESDALE & TWEEDDALE
E. 66,627 T. 45,892 (68.88%) C. hold
David Mundell, C. 17,457
Claudia Beamish, Lab. 13,263
Catriona Bhatia, LD 9,080
Aileen Orr, SNP 4,945
Steven McKeane, UKIP 637
Alis Ballance, Green 510
C. majority 4,194 (9.14%)
2.62% swing Lab. to C.
(2005: C. majority 1,738 (3.90%))

DUNBARTONSHIRE EAST
E. 63,795 T. 47,948 (75.16%) LD hold
Jo Swinson, LD 18,551
Mary Galbraith, Lab. 16,367
Mark Nolan, C. 7,431
Iain White, SNP 5,054
James Beeley, UKIP 545
LD majority 2,184 (4.55%)
2.07% swing LD to Lab.
(2005: LD majority 4,061 (8.69%))

DUNBARTONSHIRE WEST
E. 66,085 T. 42,266 (63.96%) Lab. (Co-op) hold
*Gemma Doyle, Lab. (Co-op) 25,905
Graeme McCormick, SNP 8,497
Helen Watt, LD 3,434
Martyn McIntyre, C. 3,242
Mitch Sorbie, UKIP 683
Katharine McGavigan, Soc. Lab. 505
Lab. (Co-op) majority 17,408 (41.19%)
5.50% swing SNP to Lab. (Co-op)
(2005: Lab. (Co-op) majority 12,553 (30.18%))

DUNDEE EAST
E. 65,471 T. 40,568 (61.96%) SNP hold
Stewart Hosie, SNP 15,350
Katrina Murray, Lab. 13,529
Chris Bustin, C. 6,177
Clive Sneddon, LD 4,285
Shiona Baird, Green 542
Mike Arthur, UKIP 431
Angela Gorrie, SSP 254
SNP majority 1,821 (4.49%)
1.76% swing Lab. to SNP
(2005: SNP majority 383 (0.97%))

DUNDEE WEST
E. 63,013 T. 37,126 (58.92%) Lab. hold
Jim McGovern, Lab. 17,994
Jim Barrie, SNP 10,716
John Barnett, LD 4,233
Colin Stewart, C. 3,461
Andy McBride, Ind. 365
Jim McFarlane, TUSC 357
Lab. majority 7,278 (19.60%)
2.52% swing SNP to Lab.
(2005: Lab. majority 5,379 (14.56%))

DUNFERMLINE & FIFE WEST
E. 73,769 T. 48,947 (66.35%) Lab. gain
*Thomas Docherty, Lab. 22,639
Willie Rennie, LD 17,169
Joe McCall, SNP 5,201
Belinda Hacking, C. 3,305
Otto Inglis, UKIP 633
Lab. majority 5,470 (11.18%)
8.05% swing Lab. to LD
(2005: Lab. majority 11,562 (27.27%))(2006: LD majority 1,800 (5.21%))

EAST KILBRIDE, STRATHAVEN & LESMAHAGOW
E. 76,534 T. 50,946 (66.57%) Lab. hold
*Michael McCann, Lab. 26,241
John McKenna, SNP 11,738
Graham Simpson, C. 6,613
John Loughton, LD 5,052
Kirsten Robb, Green 1,003
John Houston, Ind. 299
Lab. majority 14,503 (28.47%)
1.19% swing Lab. to SNP
(2005: Lab. majority 14,723 (30.84%))

EAST LOTHIAN
E. 73,438 T. 49,161 (66.94%) Lab. hold
*Fiona O'Donnell, Lab. 21,919
Michael Veitch, C. 9,661
Stuart Ritchie, LD 8,288
Andrew Sharp, SNP 7,883
James Mackenzie, Green 862
Jon Lloyd, UKIP 548
Lab. majority 12,258 (24.93%)
0.28% swing Lab. to C.
(2005: Lab. majority 7,620 (16.65%))

EDINBURGH EAST
E. 60,941 T. 39,865 (65.42%) Lab. hold
*Sheila Gilmore, Lab. 17,314
George Kerevan, SNP 8,133
Beverley Hope, LD 7,751
Martin Donald, C. 4,358
Robin Harper, Green 2,035
Gary Clark, TUSC 274
Lab. majority 9,181 (23.03%)
0.01% swing SNP to Lab.
(2005: Lab. majority 6,202 (15.62%))

EDINBURGH NORTH & LEITH
E. 69,204 T. 47,356 (68.43%) Lab. (Co-op) hold
Mark Lazarowicz, Lab. (Co-op) 17,740
Kevin Lang, LD 16,016
Iain McGill, C. 7,079
Calum Cashley, SNP 4,568
Kate Joester, Green 1,062
John Hein, Lib. 389
Willie Black, TUSC 233
David Jacobsen, Soc. Lab. 141
Cameron MacIntyre, Ind. 128
Lab. Co-op majority 1,724 (3.64%)
0.70% swing Lab. (Co-op) to LD
(2005: Lab. (Co-op) majority 2,153 (5.05%))

EDINBURGH SOUTH
E. 59,354 T. 43,801 (73.80%) Lab. hold
*Ian Murray, Lab. 15,215
Fred Mackintosh, LD 14,899
Neil Hudson, C. 9,452
Sandy Howat, SNP 3,354
Steve Burgess, Green 881
Lab. majority 316 (0.72%)
0.11% swing Lab. to LD
(2005: Lab. majority 405 (0.95%))

EDINBURGH SOUTH WEST
E. 66,359 T. 45,462 (68.51%) Lab. hold
Alistair Darling, Lab. 19,473
Jason Rust, C. 11,026
Tim McKay, LD 8,194
Kaukab Stewart, SNP 5,530
Clare Cooney, Green 872
Colin Fox, SSP 319
Caroline Bellamy, Comm. Lge 48
Lab. majority 8,447 (18.58%)
1.05% swing C. to Lab.
(2005: Lab. majority 7,242 (16.49%))

EDINBURGH WEST
E. 65,161 T. 46,447 (71.28%) LD hold
*Michael Crockart, LD 16,684
Cameron Day, Lab. 12,881
Stewart Geddes, C. 10,767
Sheena Cleland, SNP 6,115
LD majority 3,803 (8.19%)
11.35% swing LD to Lab.
(2005: LD majority 13,600 (30.05%))

FALKIRK
E. 81,869 T. 50,777 (62.02%) Lab. hold
Eric Joyce, Lab. 23,207
John McNally, SNP 15,364
Katie Mackie, C. 5,698
Kieran Leach, LD 5,225
Brian Goldie, UKIP 1,283
Lab. majority 7,843 (15.45%)
7.00% swing Lab. to SNP
(2005: Lab. majority 13,475 (29.45%))

FIFE NORTH EAST
E. 62,969 T. 40,064 (63.62%) LD hold
Sir Menzies Campbell, LD 17,763
Miles Briggs, C. 8,715
Mark Hood, Lab. 6,869
Rod Campbell, SNP 5,685
Mike Scott-Hayward, UKIP 1,032
LD majority 9,048 (22.58%)
5.01% swing LD to C.
(2005: LD majority 12,571 (32.60%))

GLASGOW CENTRAL
E. 60,062 T. 30,580 (50.91%) Lab. hold
*Anas Sarwar, Lab. 15,908
Osama Saeed, SNP 5,357
Chris Young, LD 5,010
John Bradley, C. 2,158
Alastair Whitelaw, Green 800
Ian Holt, BNP 616
James Nesbitt, SSP 357
Ramsay Urquhart, UKIP 246
Finlay Archibald, Pirate 128
Lab. majority 10,551 (34.50%)
0.54% swing SNP to Lab.
(2005: Lab. majority 8,531 (30.43%))

GLASGOW EAST
E. 61,516 T. 32,164 (52.29%) Lab. gain
*Margaret Curran, Lab. 19,797
John Mason, SNP 7,957
Kevin Ward, LD 1,617
Hamira Khan, C. 1,453
Joseph Finnie, BNP 677
Frances Curran, SSP 454
Arthur Thackeray, UKIP 209
Lab. majority 11,840 (36.81%)
3.42% swing Lab. to SNP
(2005: Lab. majority 13,507 (43.66%))(2008: SNP majority 365 (1.39%))

GLASGOW NORTH
E. 51,416 T. 29,613 (57.59%) Lab. hold
Ann McKechin, Lab. 13,181
Katy Gordon, LD 9,283
Patrick Grady, SNP 3,530
Erin Boyle, C. 2,089
Martin Bartos, Green 947
Thomas Main, BNP 296
Angela McCormick, TUSC 287
Lab. majority 3,898 (13.16%)
0.60% swing LD to Lab.
(2005: Lab. majority 3,338 (11.96%))

GLASGOW NORTH EAST
E. 59,859 T. 29,409 (49.13%) Lab. hold
Willie Bain, Lab. 20,100
Billy McAllister, SNP 4,158
Eileen Baxendale, LD 2,262
Ruth Davidson, C. 1,569
Walter Hamilton, BNP 798
Graham Campbell, TUSC 187
Kevin McVey, SSP 179
Jim Berrington, Soc. Lab. 156
Lab. majority 15,942 (54.21%)
9.3% swing SNP to Lab.
(2005: Speaker majority 10,134 (35.66%))(2009: Lab. majority 8,111 (39.38%))

GLASGOW NORTH WEST
E. 60,968 T. 35,582 (58.36%) Lab. hold
John Robertson, Lab. 19,233
Natalie McKee, LD 5,622
Mags Park, SNP 5,430
Richard Sullivan, C. 3,537
Moira Crawford, Green 882
Scott Mclean, BNP 699
Marc Livingstone, Comm. 179
Lab. majority 13,611 (38.25%)
4.31% swing LD to Lab.
(2005: Lab. majority 10,093 (29.63%))

GLASGOW SOUTH
E. 65,029 T. 40,094 (61.66%) Lab. hold
Tom Harris, Lab. 20,736
Malcolm Fleming, SNP 8,078
Shabnum Mustapha, LD 4,739
Davena Rankin, C. 4,592
Marie Campbell, Green 961
Mike Coyle, BNP 637
Brian Smith, TUSC 351
Lab. majority 12,658 (31.57%)
1.51% swing Lab. to SNP
(2005: Lab. majority 10,832 (28.19%))

GLASGOW SOUTH WEST
E. 58,182 T. 31,781 (54.62%) Lab. (Co-op) hold
Ian Davidson, Lab. (Co-op) 19,863
Chris Stephens, SNP 5,192
Isabel Nelson, LD 2,870
Maya Henderson Forrest, C. 2,084
Tommy Sheridan, TUSC 931
David Orr, BNP 841
Lab. (Co-op) majority 14,671 (46.16%)
0.65% swing SNP to Lab. (Co-op)
(2005: Lab. (Co-op) majority 13,896 (44.86%))

GLENROTHES
E. 67,893 T. 40,501 (59.65%) Lab. hold
Lindsay Roy, Lab. 25,247
David Alexander, SNP 8,799
Harry Wills, LD 3,108
Sheila Low, C. 2,922
Kris Seunarine, UKIP 425
Lab. majority 16,448 (40.61%)
6.04% swing SNP to Lab.
(2005: Lab. majority 10,664 (28.54%))(2008: Lab. majority 6,737 (18.61%))

GORDON
E. 73,420 T. 48,775 (66.43%) LD hold
Malcolm Bruce, LD 17,575
Richard Thomson, SNP 10,827
Barney Crockett, Lab. 9,811
Ross Thomson, C. 9,111
Sue Edwards, Green 752
Elise Jones, BNP 699
LD majority 6,748 (13.83%)
7.61% swing LD to SNP
(2005: LD majority 11,026 (24.81%))

¶INVERCLYDE
E. 59,209 T. 37,502 (63.34%) Lab. hold
David Cairns, Lab. 20,993
Innes Nelson, SNP 6,567
Simon Hutton, LD 5,007
David Wilson, C. 4,502
Peter Campbell, UKIP 433
Lab. majority 14,426 (38.47%)
3.64% swing SNP to Lab.
(2005: Lab. majority 11,259 (31.19%))

INVERNESS, NAIRN, BADENOCH & STRATHSPEY
E. 72,528 T. 47,086 (64.92%) LD hold
Danny Alexander, LD 19,172
Mike Robb, Lab. 10,407
John Finnie, SNP 8,803
Jim Ferguson, C. 6,278
Dr Donald Boyd, Ch. P. 835
Donnie MacLeod, Green 789
Ross Durance, UKIP 574
George MacDonald, TUSC 135
Kit Fraser, Joy 93
LD majority 8,765 (18.61%)
4.62% swing Lab. to LD
(2005: LD majority 4,148 (9.37%))

KILMARNOCK & LOUDOUN
E. 74,131 T. 46,553 (62.80%) Lab. (Co-op) hold
*Cathy Jamieson, Lab. (Co-op) 24,460
George Leslie, SNP 12,082
Janette McAlpine, C. 6,592
Sebastian Tombs, LD 3,419
Lab. (Co-op) majority 12,378 (26.59%)
3.49% swing SNP to Lab. (Co-op)
(2005: Lab. (Co-op) majority 8,703 (19.61%))

KIRKCALDY & COWDENBEATH
E. 73,665 T. 45,802 (62.18%) Lab. hold
Gordon Brown, Lab. 29,559
Douglas Chapman, SNP 6,550
John Mainland, LD 4,269
Lindsay Paterson, C. 4,258
Peter Adams, UKIP 760
Susan Archibald, Ind. 184
Donald MacLaren of MacLaren, Ind. 165
Derek Jackson, Land 57
Lab. majority 23,009 (50.24%)
3.33% swing SNP to Lab.
(2005: Lab. majority 18,216 (43.58%))

LANARK & HAMILTON EAST
E. 74,773 T. 46,554 (62.26%) Lab. hold
Jim Hood, Lab. 23,258
Clare Adamson, SNP 9,780
Colin McGavigan, C. 6,981
Douglas Herbison, LD 5,249
Duncan McFarlane, Ind. 670
Rob Sale, UKIP 616
Lab. majority 13,478 (28.95%)
0.34% swing SNP to Lab.
(2005: Lab. majority 11,947 (27.41%))

LINLITHGOW & FALKIRK EAST
E. 80,907 T. 51,450 (63.59%) Lab. hold
Michael Connarty, Lab. 25,634
Tam Smith, SNP 13,081
Stephen Glenn, LD 6,589
Andrea Stephenson, C. 6,146
Lab. majority 12,553 (24.40%)
0.13% swing SNP to Lab.
(2005: Lab. majority 11,202 (24.15%))

LIVINGSTON
E. 75,924 T. 47,907 (63.10%) Lab. hold
*Graeme Morrice, Lab. 23,215
Lis Bardell, SNP 12,424
Charles Dundas, LD 5,316
Alison Adamson-Ross, C. 5,158
David Orr, BNP 960
Alistair Forrest, UKIP 443
Ally Hendry, SSP 242
Jim Slavin, Ind. 149
Lab. majority 10,791 (22.52%)
3.51% swing Lab. to SNP
(2005: Lab. majority 13,097 (29.54%);
2005 by-election: Lab. majority 2,680
(9.09%))

MIDLOTHIAN
E. 61,387 T. 39,242 (63.93%) Lab. hold
David Hamilton, Lab. 18,449
Colin Beattie, SNP 8,100
Ross Laird, LD 6,711
James Callander, C. 4,661
Ian Baxter, Green 595
Gordon Norrie, UKIP 364
George McCleery, Ind. 196
Willie Duncan, TUSC 166
Lab. majority 10,349 (26.37%)
1.07% swing Lab. to SNP
(2005: Lab. majority 7,265 (19.27%))

MORAY
E. 65,925 T. 41,004 (62.20%) SNP hold
Angus Robertson, SNP 16,273
Douglas Ross, C. 10,683
Kieron Green, Lab. 7,007
James Paterson, LD 5,956
Donald Gatt, UKIP 1,085
SNP majority 5,590 (13.63%)
0.50% swing SNP to C.
(2005: SNP majority 5,676 (14.63%))

MOTHERWELL & WISHAW
E. 66,918 T. 39,123 (58.46%) Lab. hold
Frank Roy, Lab. 23,910
Marion Fellows, SNP 7,104
Stuart Douglas, LD 3,840
Patsy Gilroy, C. 3,660
Ray Gunnion, TUSC 609
Lab. majority 16,806 (42.96%)
0.97% swing SNP to Lab.
(2005: Lab. majority 15,222 (41.02%))

NA H-EILEANAN AN IAR
E. 22,266 T. 14,717 (66.10%) SNP hold
Angus MacNeil, SNP 6,723
Donald John MacSween, Lab. 4,838
Murdo Murray, Ind. 1,412
Jean Davis, LD 1,097
Sheena Norquay, C. 647
SNP majority 1,885 (12.81%)
1.20% swing Lab. to SNP
(2005: SNP majority 1,441 (10.41%))

OCHIL & PERTHSHIRE SOUTH
E. 75,115 T. 50,469 (67.19%) Lab. hold
Gordon Banks, Lab. 19,131
Annabelle Ewing, SNP 13,944
Gerald Michaluk, C. 10,342
Graeme Littlejohn, LD 5,754
David Bushby, UKIP 689
Hilary Charles, Green 609
Lab. majority 5,187 (10.28%)
4.40% swing SNP to Lab.
(2005: Lab. majority 688 (1.47%))

ORKNEY & SHETLAND
E. 33,085 T. 19,346 (58.47%) LD hold
Alistair Carmichael, LD 11,989
Mark Cooper, Lab. 2,061
John Mowat, SNP 2,042
Frank Nairn, C. 2,032
Robert Smith, UKIP 1,222
LD majority 9,928 (51.32%)
6.98% swing Lab. to LD
(2005: LD majority 6,627 (37.35%))

PAISLEY & RENFREWSHIRE NORTH
E. 63,704 T. 43,707 (68.61%) Lab. hold
Jim Sheridan, Lab. 23,613
Mags MacLaren, SNP 8,333
Alistair Campbell, C. 6,381
Ruaraidh Dobson, LD 4,597
Gary Pearson, Ind. 550
Chris Rollo, SSP 233
Lab. majority 15,280 (34.96%)
4.03% swing SNP to Lab.
(2005: Lab. majority 11,001 (26.91%))

PAISLEY & RENFREWSHIRE SOUTH
E. 61,197 T. 39,998 (65.36%) Lab. hold
Douglas Alexander, Lab. 23,842
Andy Doig, SNP 7,228
Gordon McCaskill, C. 3,979
Ashay Ghai, LD 3,812
Paul Mack, Ind. 513
Jimmy Kerr, SSP 375
William Hendry, Ind. 249
Lab. majority 16,614 (41.54%)
3.27% swing SNP to Lab.
(2005: Lab. majority 13,232 (34.95%))

PERTH & PERTHSHIRE NORTH
E. 72,141 T. 48,268 (66.91%) SNP hold
Pete Wishart, SNP 19,118
Peter Lyburn, C. 14,739
Jamie Glackin, Lab. 7,923
Peter Barrett, LD 5,954
Douglas Taylor, Trust 534
SNP majority 4,379 (9.07%)
2.88% swing C. to SNP
(2005: SNP majority 1,521 (3.31%))

RENFREWSHIRE EAST
E. 66,249 T. 51,181 (77.26%) Lab. hold
Jim Murphy, Lab. 25,987
Richard Cook, C. 15,567
Gordon Macdonald, LD 4,720
Gordon Archer, SNP 4,535
Donald MacKay, UKIP 372
Lab. majority 10,420 (20.36%)
3.16% swing C. to Lab.
(2005: Lab. majority 6,657 (14.04%))

ROSS, SKYE & LOCHABER
E. 51,836 T. 34,838 (67.21%) LD hold
Charles Kennedy, LD 18,335
John McKendrick, Lab. 5,265
Alasdair Stephen, SNP 5,263
Donald Cameron, C. 4,260
Eleanor Scott, Green 777
Philip Anderson, UKIP 659
Ronnie Campbell, Ind. 279
LD majority 13,070 (37.52%)
3.14% swing LD to Lab.
(2005: LD majority 14,249 (43.79%))

RUTHERGLEN & HAMILTON WEST
E. 76,408 T. 46,981 (61.49%)
Lab. (Co-op) hold
*Tom Greatrex, Lab. (Co-op) 28,566
Graeme Horne, SNP 7,564
Ian Robertson, LD 5,636
Malcolm Macaskill, C. 4,540
Janice Murdoch, UKIP 675
Lab. (Co-op) majority 21,002 (44.70%)
1.51% swing SNP to Lab. (Co-op)
(2005: Lab. (Co-op) majority 16,112
(37.24%))

STIRLING
E. 66,080 T. 46,791 (70.81%) Lab. hold
Anne McGuire, Lab. 19,558
Bob Dalrymple, C. 11,204
Alison Lindsay, SNP 8,091
Graham Reed, LD 6,797
Mark Ruskell, Green 746
Paul Henke, UKIP 395
Lab. majority 8,354 (17.85%)
3.47% swing C. to Lab.
(2005: Lab. majority 4,767 (10.91%))

NORTHERN IRELAND

§ANTRIM EAST
E. 60,204 T. 30,502 (50.66%) DUP hold

Sammy Wilson, DUP	13,993
Rodney McCune, UCUNF	7,223
Gerry Lynch, Alliance	3,377
Oliver McMullan, SF	2,064
Justin McCamphill, SDLP	2,019
Samuel Morrison, TUV	1,826

DUP majority 6,770 (22.20%)
Notional 0.2% swing UCUNF to DUP
(2005: DUP majority 6,996 (21.76%))

§ANTRIM NORTH
E. 73,338 T. 42,397 (57.81%) DUP hold

*Ian Paisley Junior, DUP	19,672
Jim Allister, TUV	7,114
Daithi McKay, SF	5,265
Irwin Armstrong, UCUNF	4,634
Declan O'Loan, SDLP	3,738
Jayne Dunlop, Alliance	1,368
Lyle Cubitt, ND	606

DUP majority 12,558 (29.62%)
(2005: DUP majority 18,486 (41.80%))

§ANTRIM SOUTH
E. 63,054 T. 34,009 (53.94%) DUP hold

Revd William McCrea, DUP	11,536
Sir Reg Empey, UCUNF	10,353
Mitchel McLaughlin, SF	4,729
Michelle Byrne, SDLP	2,955
Alan Lawther, Alliance	2,607
Melwyn Lucas, TUV	1,829

DUP majority 1,183 (3.48%)
Notional 3.6% swing DUP to UCUNF
(2005: DUP majority 3,778 (10.74%))

§BELFAST EAST
E. 59,007 T. 34,488 (58.45%) Alliance gain

*Naomi Long, Alliance	12,839
Peter Robinson, DUP	11,306
Trevor Ringland, UCUNF	7,305
David Vance, TUV	1,856
Niall Donnelly, SF	817
Mary Muldoon, SDLP	365

Alliance majority 1,533 (4.45%)
Notional 22.87% swing DUP to Alliance
(2005: DUP majority 7,900 (22.87%))

§BELFAST NORTH
E. 65,504 T. 36,993 (56.47%) DUP hold

Nigel Dodds, DUP	14,812
Gerry Kelly, SF	12,588
Alban Maginness, SDLP	4,544
Fred Cobain, UCUNF	2,837
William Webb, Alliance	1,809
Martin McAuley, Ind.	403

DUP majority 2,224 (6.01%)
Notional 5.00% swing DUP to SF
(2005: DUP majority 5,832 (16.02%))

§BELFAST SOUTH
E. 59,524 T. 34,186 (57.43%) SDLP hold

Dr Alasdair McDonnell, SDLP	14,026
Jimmy Spratt, DUP	8,100
Paula Bradshaw, UCUNF	5,910
Anna Lo, Alliance	5,114
Adam McGibbon, Green	1,036

SDLP majority 5,926 (17.33%)
Notional 8.41% swing DUP to SDLP
(2005: SDLP majority 188 (0.52%))

§¶BELFAST WEST
E. 59,522 T. 32,133 (53.99%) SF hold

Gerry Adams, SF	22,840
Alex Attwood, SDLP	5,261
William Humphrey, DUP	2,436
Bill Manwaring, UCUNF	1,000
Maire Hendron, Alliance	596

SF majority 17,579 (54.71%)
Notional 1.07% swing SDLP to SF
(2005: SF majority 19,527 (52.57%))

DOWN NORTH
E. 60,698 T. 33,481 (55.16%) Ind. gain

Lady Sylvia Hermon, Ind.	21,181
Ian Parsley, UCUNF	6,817
Stephen Farry, Alliance	1,876
Mary Kilpatrick, TUV	1,634
Steven Agnew, Green	1,043
Liam Logan, SDLP	680
Vincent Parker, SF	250

Ind. majority 14,364 (42.90%)
(2005: UUP majority 4,944 (15.31%))

§DOWN SOUTH
E. 70,784 T. 42,589 (60.17%) SDLP hold

*Margaret Ritchie, SDLP	20,648
Caitriona Ruane, SF	12,236
Jim Wells, DUP	3,645
John McCallister, UCUNF	3,093
Ivor McConnell, TUV	1,506
Cadogan Enright, Green	901
David Griffin, Alliance	560

SDLP majority 8,412 (19.75%)
Notional 0.06% swing SDLP to SF
(2005: SDLP majority 8,801 (19.87%))

FERMANAGH & SOUTH TYRONE
E. 67,908 T. 46,803 (68.92%) SF hold

Michelle Gildernew, SF	21,304
Rodney Connor, Ind.	21,300
Fearghal McKinney, SDLP	3,574
Vasundhara Kamble, Alliance	437
John Stevenson, Ind.	188

SF majority 4 (0.01%)
(2005: SF majority 4,582 (9.39%))

§FOYLE
E. 65,843 T. 37,889 (57.54%) SDLP hold

Mark Durkan, SDLP	16,922
Martina Anderson, SF	12,098
Maurice Devenney, DUP	4,489
Eammon McCann, PBP	2,936
David Harding, UCUNF	1,221
Keith McGrellis, Alliance	223

SDLP majority 4,824 (12.73%)
Notional 0.17% swing SDLP to SF
(2005: SDLP majority 5,570 (13.08%))

§LAGAN VALLEY
E. 65,257 T. 36,540 (55.99%) DUP hold

Jeffrey Donaldson, DUP	18,199
Daphne Trimble, UCUNF	7,713
Trevor Lunn, Alliance	4,174
Keith Harbinson, TUV	3,154
Brian Heading, SDLP	1,835
Paul Butler, SF	1,465

DUP majority 10,486 (28.70%)
Notional 3.3% swing DUP to UCUNF
(2005: DUP majority 13,493 (35.33%))

§LONDONDERRY EAST
E. 63,220 T. 34,950 (55.28%) DUP hold

Gregory Campbell, DUP	12,097
Cathal O hOisin, SF	6,742
Lesley Macaulay, UCUNF	6,218
Thomas Conway, SDLP	5,399
William Ross, TUV	2,572
Bernard Fitzpatrick, Alliance	1,922

DUP majority 5,355 (15.32%)
Notional 4.13% swing DUP to SF
(2005: DUP majority 8,192 (21.26%))

NEWRY & ARMAGH
E. 74,308 T. 44,906 (60.43%) SF hold

Conor Murphy, SF	18,857
Dominic Bradley, SDLP	10,526
Danny Kennedy, UCUNF	8,558
William Irwin, DUP	5,764
William Frazer, Ind.	656
Andrew Muir, Alliance	545

SF majority 8,331 (18.55%)
1.19% swing SDLP to SF
(2005: SF majority 8,195 (16.16%))

§STRANGFORD
E. 60,539 T. 32,505 (53.69%) DUP hold

*Jim Shannon, DUP	14,926
Mike Nesbitt, UCUNF	9,050
Deborah Girvan, Alliance	2,828
Claire Hanna, SDLP	2,164
Terry Williams, TUV	1,814
Michael Coogan, SF	1,161
Barbara Haig, Green	562

DUP majority 5,876 (18.08%)
Notional 7.6% swing DUP to UCUNF
(2005: DUP majority 10,934 (33.32%))

TYRONE WEST
E. 61,148 T. 37,275 (60.96%) SF hold

Pat Doherty, SF	18,050
Thomas Buchanan, DUP	7,365
Ross Hussey, UCUNF	5,281
Joe Byrne, SDLP	5,212
Michael Bower, Alliance	859
Ciaran McClean, Ind.	508

SF majority 10,685 (28.67%)
3.79% swing DUP to SF
(2005: SF majority 5,005 (11.51%))

¶ULSTER MID
E. 64,594 T. 40,842 (63.23%) SF hold

Martin McGuinness, SF	21,239
Ian McCrea, DUP	5,876
Tony Quinn, SDLP	5,826
Sandra Overend, UCUNF	4,509
Walter Millar, TUV	2,995
Ian Butler, Alliance	397

SF majority 15,363 (37.62%)
6.73% swing DUP to SF
(2005: SF majority 10,976 (24.16%))

UPPER BANN
E. 74,732 T. 41,383 (55.38%) DUP hold

David Simpson, DUP	14,000
Harry Hamilton, UCUNF	10,639
John O'Dowd, SF	10,237
Dolores Kelly, SDLP	5,276
Brendan Heading, Alliance	1,231

DUP majority 3,361 (8.12%)
Notional 1.9% swing DUP to UCUNF
(2005: DUP majority 5,298 (11.93%))

BY-ELECTIONS 2010–13

For a list of party abbreviations *see* General Election results:

BARNSLEY CENTRAL
3 March 2011
E. 65,471 T. 24,219 (36.99%) Lab. hold
Dan Jarvis, Lab. 14,724
Jane Collins, UKIP 2,953
James Hockney, C. 1,999
Enis Dalton, BNP 1,463
Tony Devoy, Ind. 1,266
Dominic Carman, LD 1,012
Kevin Riddiough, Eng. Dem. 544
Howling 'Laud' Hope, Loony 198
Michael Val Davies, Ind. 60
Lab. maj. 11,771 (48.60%)
13.3% swing LD to Lab.
(2010: Lab. maj. 11,093 (29.98%))

BELFAST WEST
9 June 2011
E. 61,441 T. 22,951 (37.35%) SF hold
Paul Maskey, SF 16,211
Alex Atwood, SDLP 3,088
Gerry Carroll, PBP 1,751
Brian Kingston, DUP 1,393
Bill Manwaring, UUP 386
Aaron McIntyre, Alliance 122
SF maj. 13,123 (50.6%)
1.2% swing SDLP to SF
(2010: SF maj. 17,579 (54.71%))

BRADFORD WEST
29 March 2012
E. 64,613 T. 32,814 (50.79%) Respect gain
George Galloway, Respect 18,341
Imran Hussain, Lab. 8,201
Jackie Whiteley, C. 2,746
Jeanette Sunderland, LD 1,505
Sonja McNally, UKIP 1,085
Dawud Islam, Green 481
Neil Craig, D. Nat 344
Howling 'Laud' Hope, Loony 111
Respect maj. 10,140 (30.90%)
36.6% swing Lab. to Respect
(2010: Lab. maj. 5,763 (14.20%))

CARDIFF SOUTH AND PENARTH
15 November 2012
E. 75,764 T. 19,436 (25.65%) Lab. hold
Stephen Doughty, Lab. 9,193
Craig Williams, C. 3,859
Bablin Molik, LD 2,103
Luke Nichols, PC 1,854
Simon Zeigler, UKIP 1,179
Anthony Slaughter, Green 800
Andrew Jordan, Soc. Lab. 235
Robert Griffiths, Comm. 213
Lab. maj. 5,334 (27.44%)
8.4% swing C. to Lab.
(2010: Lab. maj. 4,710 (10.62%))

CORBY
15 November 2012
E. 79,878 T. 35,665 (44.65%) Lab. gain
Andy Sawford, Lab. 17,267
Christine Emmett, C. 9,476
Margot Parker, UKIP 5,108
Jill Hope, LD 1,770
Gordon Riddell, BNP 614
David Wickham, Eng. Dem. 432
Jonathan Hornett, Green 378
Ian Gillman, Ind. 212
Peter Reynolds, CLR 137
David Bishop, CME 99
Mr Mozzarella, Ind. 73
Rohen Kapur, Young 39
Adam Lotun, Dem. 2015. 35
Christopher Scotton, UPP 25
Lab.maj. 7,791 (21.84%)
12.7% swing C. to Lab.
(2010: C. maj. 1,895 (3.49%))

CROYDON NORTH
29 November 2012
E. 93,036 T. 24,568 (26.41%) Lab. hold
Steve Reed, Lab. 15,898
Andrew Stranack, C. 4,137
Winston McKenzie, UKIP 1,400
Marisha Ray, LD 860
Shasha Khan, Green 855
Lee Jasper, Respect 707
Stephen Hammond, CPA 192
Richard Edmonds, NF 161
Ben Stevenson, Comm. 119
John Cartwright, Loony 110
Simon Lane, Nine11 66
Robin Smith, Young 63
Lab. maj. 11,761 (47.87%)
8.0% swing C. to Lab.
(2010: Lab. maj. 16,483 (31.90%))

EASTLEIGH
28 February 2013
E. 79,004 T. 41,616 (52.68%) LD hold
Mike Thornton, LD 13,342
Diane James, UKIP 11,571
Maria Hutchings, C. 10,559
John O'Farrell, Lab. 4,088
Danny Stupple, Ind. 768
Iain Maclennan, NHA 392
Ray Hall, BB&C 235
Kevin Milburn, CPA 163
Howling 'Laud' Hope, Loony 136
Jim Duggan, Peace 128
David Bishop, Elvis 72
Mike Walters, Eng. Dem. 70
Daz Procter, TUSC 62
Colin Bex, WR 30
LD maj. 1,771 (4.26%)
19.3% swing LD to UKIP
(2010: LD maj. 3,864 (7.20%))

FELTHAM AND HESTON
15 December 2011
E. 80,813 T. 23,224 (28.74%) Lab. hold
Seema Malhotra, Lab. 12,639
Mark Bowen, C. 6,436
Roger Crouch, LD 1,364
Andrew Charalambous, UKIP 1,276
Dave Furness, BNP 540
Daniel Goldsmith, Green 426
Roger Cooper, Eng. Dem. 322
George Hallam, PBPA 128
David Bishop, BP Elvis 93
Lab. maj. 6,203 (26.71%)
8.6% swing C. to Lab.
(2010: Lab. maj. 4,658 (9.60%))

INVERCLYDE
30 June 2011
E. 61,856 T. 28,097 (45.42%) Lab. hold
Iain McKenzie, Lab. 15,118
Anne McLaughlin, SNP 9,280
David Wilson, C. 2,784
Sophie Bridger, LD 627
Mitch Sorbie, UKIP 288
Lab. maj. 5,838 (20.78%)
8.9% swing Lab. to SNP
(2010: Lab. maj. 14,426 (38.47%))

LEICESTER SOUTH
5 May 2011
E. 77,880 T. 34,180 (43.89%) Lab. hold
Jon Ashworth, Lab. 19,771
Zuffar Haq, LD 7,693
Jane Hunt, C. 5,169
Adhijit Pandya, UKIP 994
Howling 'Laud' Hope, Loony 553
Lab. maj. 12,078 (35.34%)
8.4% swing LD to Lab.
(2010: Lab. maj. 8,808 (18.69%))

MANCHESTER CENTRAL
15 November 2012
E. 91,692 T. 16,648 (18.16%) Lab. hold
Lucy Powell, Lab. 11,507
Marc Ramsbottom, LD 1,571
Matthew Sephton, C. 754
Christopher Cassidy, UKIP 749
Tom Dylan, Green 652
Eddy O'Sullivan, BNP 492
Loz Kaye, Pirate 308
Alex Davidson, TUSC 220
Catherine Higgins, Respect 182
Howling 'Laud' Hope, Loony 78
Lee Holmes, PDP 71
Peter Clifford, Comm. Lge 64
Lab. maj. 9,936 (59.68%)
16.8% swing LD to Lab.
(2010: Lab. maj. 10,439 (26.15%))

MIDDLESBROUGH
29 November 2012
E. 65,095 T. 16,866 (25.91%) Lab. hold
Andy McDonald, Lab. 10,201
Richard Elvin, UKIP 1,990
George Selmer, LD 1,672
Ben Houchen, C. 1,063
Imdad Hussain, Peace 1,060
Peter Foreman, BNP 328
John Malcolm, TUSC 277
Mark Helsehurst, ND 275
Lab. maj. 8,211 (47.7%)
3.3% swing UKIP to Lab.
(2010: Lab. maj. 8,689 (26.0%))

MID ULSTER
7 March 2013
E. 67,192 T. 37,208 (55.38%) SF hold
Francie Molloy, SF 17,462
Nigel Lutton, Ind. 12,781
Patsy McGlone, SDLP 6,478
Eric Bullick, Alliance 487
SF maj. 4,681 (12.58%)
3.4% swing SF to Ind.
(2010: SF maj. 15,363 (37.62%))

OLDHAM EAST & SADDLEWORTH
13 January 2011
E. 72,788 T. 34,786 (47.79%) Lab. hold
Debbie Abrahams, Lab. 14,718
Elwyn Watkins, LD 11,160
Kashif Ali, C. 4,481
Paul Nuttall, UKIP 2,029
Derek Adams, BNP 1,560
Peter Allen, Green 530
The Flying Brick, Loony 145
Stephen Saul, Pirate 96
David Bishop, BP Elvis 67
Lab. maj. 3,558 (10.23%)
5.0% swing LD to Lab.
(2010: Lab. maj. 103 (0.23%))

ROTHERHAM
29 November 2012

E. 63,420 T. 21,450 (33.82%)	Lab. hold
Sarah Champion, Lab.	9,966
Jane Collins, UKIP	4,648
Marlene Guest, BNP	1,804
Yvonne Ridley, Respect	1,778
Simon Wilson, C.	1,157
David Wildgoose, Eng. Dem.	703
Simon Copley, Ind.	582
Michael Beckett, LD	451
Ralph Dyson, TUSC	281
Paul Dickson, Ind.	51
Clint Bristow, ND	29

Lab. maj. 5,318 (24.79%)
7.0% swing Lab. to UKIP
(2010: Lab. maj. 10,462 (27.9%))

SOUTH SHIELDS
2 May 2013

E. 62,979 T. 24,736 (39.28%)	Lab. hold
Emma Lewell-Buck, Lab.	12,493
Richard Elvin, UKIP	5,988
Karen Allen, C.	2,857
Ahmed Khan, Ind.	1,331
Phil Brown, ISP	750
Lady Dorothy Brookes, UKIP	711
Hugh Annand, LD	352
Howling 'Laud' Hope, Loony	197
Thomas Darwood, Ind.	57

Lab. maj. 6,505 (26.30%)
4.1% swing Lab. to C.
(2010: Lab. maj. 11,109 (30.42%))

THE GOVERNMENT

A coalition government formed of the Conservative Party and Liberal Democrat Party (since 12 May 2010)

as at 10 September 2013

* Liberal Democrats

THE CABINET

Prime Minister, First Lord of the Treasury and Minister for the Civil Service
Rt. Hon. David Cameron, MP
Deputy Prime Minister, Lord President of the Council (with special responsibility for political and constitutional reform)
*Rt. Hon. Nick Clegg, MP
Chancellor of the Exchequer
Rt. Hon. George Osborne, MP
First Secretary of State, Secretary of State for Foreign and Commonwealth Affairs
Rt. Hon. William Hague, MP
Secretary of State for the Home Department
Rt. Hon. Theresa May, MP
Secretary of State for Business, Innovation and Skills and President of the Board of Trade
*Rt. Hon. Dr Vincent Cable, MP
Secretary of State for Communities and Local Government
Rt. Hon. Eric Pickles, MP
Secretary of State for Culture, Media and Sport and Minister for Women and Equalities
Rt. Hon. Maria Miller, MP
Secretary of State for Defence
Rt. Hon. Philip Hammond, MP
Secretary of State for Education
Rt. Hon. Michael Gove, MP
Secretary of State for Energy and Climate Change
*Rt. Hon. Ed Davey, MP
Secretary of State for Environment, Food and Rural Affairs
Rt. Hon. Owen Paterson, MP
Secretary of State for Health
Rt. Hon. Jeremy Hunt, MP
Secretary of State for International Development
Rt. Hon. Justine Greening, MP
Secretary of State for Justice and Lord Chancellor
Rt. Hon. Chris Grayling, MP
Secretary of State for Northern Ireland
Rt. Hon. Theresa Villiers, MP
Secretary of State for Scotland
*Rt. Hon. Michael Moore, MP
Secretary of State for Transport
Rt. Hon. Patrick McLoughlin, MP
Secretary of State for Wales
Rt. Hon. David Jones, MP
Secretary of State for Work and Pensions
Rt. Hon. Iain Duncan Smith, MP
Chief Secretary to the Treasury
*Rt. Hon. Danny Alexander, MP
Leader of the House of Lords and Chancellor of the Duchy of Lancaster
Rt. Hon. Lord Hill of Oareford, CBE

ALSO ATTENDING CABINET MEETINGS

Attorney-General
†Rt. Hon. Dominic Grieve, QC, MP
Leader of the House of Commons and Lord Privy Seal
Rt. Hon. Andrew Lansley, CBE, MP
Minister for the Cabinet Office and Paymaster General
Rt. Hon. Francis Maude, MP
Minister for Government Policy
Rt. Hon. Oliver Letwin, MP
‡*Minister of State for the Cabinet Office and Minister of State for Schools*
Rt. Hon. David Laws, MP
Minister of State for Universities and Science
Rt. Hon. David Willetts, MP
Minister without Portfolio (Minister of State)
Rt. Hon. Kenneth Clarke, QC, MP
Parliamentary Secretary to the Treasury and Chief Whip
Rt. Hon. Sir George Young, CH, MP
§*Senior Minister of State at the Foreign and Commonwealth Office and Minister of State for Faith and Communities*
Rt. Hon. Baroness Warsi

† only attends cabinet meetings when ministerial responsibilities are on the agenda
‡ position held jointly with the Department for Education
§ position held jointly with CLG

LAW OFFICERS

Attorney-General
Rt. Hon. Dominic Grieve, QC, MP
Solicitor-General
Oliver Heald, QC, MP
Advocate-General for Scotland
*Rt. Hon. Lord Wallace of Tankerness, QC

MINISTERS OF STATE

Business, Innovation and Skills
†Rt. Hon. Michael Fallon, MP
†Lord Livingston of Parkhead
*Rt. Hon. David Willetts, MP
Cabinet Office
*‡Rt. Hon. David Laws, MP
Rt. Hon. Oliver Letwin, MP
Communities and Local Government
Mark Prisk, MP
†Rt. Hon. Baroness Warsi
Culture, Media and Sport
Rt. Hon. Hugh Robertson, MP
Defence
Rt. Hon. Mark Francois, MP
Rt. Hon. Andrew Robathan, MP
Education
*§Rt. Hon. David Laws, MP
Energy and Climate Change
Rt. Hon. Gregory Barker, MP
Rt. Hon Michael Fallon, MP
Environment, Food and Rural Affairs
*David Heath, CBE, MP
Foreign and Commonwealth Office
¶Lord Livingston of Parkhead
Rt. Hon. David Lidington, MP
Rt. Hon. Hugo Swire, MP
**Rt. Hon. Baroness Warsi
Health
*Norman Lamb, MP

Home Office
*Jeremy Browne, MP
††Rt. Hon. Damian Green, MP
Mark Harper, MP
International Development
Rt. Hon. Alan Duncan, MP
Justice
‡‡Rt. Hon. Damian Green, MP
*Rt. Hon. Lord McNally
Northern Ireland Office
Mike Penning, MP
Transport
Rt. Hon. Simon Burns, MP
Work and Pensions
Mark Hoban, MP
*Steve Webb, MP

† position held jointly with the Foreign and Commonwealth Office
‡ position held jointly with the Department for Education
§ position held jointly with Cabinet Office
¶ position held jointly with BIS
** position held jointly with CLG
†† position held jointly with Ministry of Justice
‡‡ position held jointly with the Home Office

UNDER-SECRETARIES OF STATE

Business, Innovation and Skills
†Matthew Hancock, MP
Viscount Younger of Leckie
*Jo Swinson, MP
Communities and Local Government
Nick Boles, MP
*Rt. Hon. Don Foster, MP
Baroness Hanham, CBE
Brandon Lewis, MP
Culture, Media and Sport
‡Helen Grant, MP
*Jo Swinson, MP
Hon. Ed Vaizey, MP
Defence
Lord Astor of Hever
Philip Dunne, MP
Dr Andrew Murrison, MP
Education
§Matthew Hancock, MP
Lord Nash
Edward Timpson, MP
Elizabeth Truss, MP
Energy and Climate Change
Baroness Verma
Environment, Food and Rural Affairs
Richard Benyon, MP
Lord de Mauley
Foreign and Commonwealth Office
Alistair Burt, MP
Mark Simmonds, MP
Health
Rt. Hon. Earl Howe
Dr Daniel Poulter, MP
Anna Soubry, MP
Home Office
James Brokenshire, MP
Lord Taylor of Holbeach, CBE
International Development
*Lynne Featherstone, MP
Justice
¶Helen Grant, MP
Jeremy Wright, MP
Scotland Office
Rt. Hon. David Mundell, MP
Transport
*Norman Baker, MP
Stephen Hammond, MP
Wales Office
**Stephen Crabb, MP
*Baroness Randerson
Work and Pensions
Lord Freud
Esther McVey, MP

† position held jointly with the Depatment for Education
‡ position held jointly with the Ministry of Justice
§ position held jointly with BIS
¶ position held jointly with DCMS
** alongside role as Lord Commissioner of HM Treasury (Whip)

OTHER MINISTERS

Cabinet Office
Nick Hurd, MP *(Parliamentary Secretary)*
Chloe Smith, MP *(Parliamentary Secretary)*
John Hayes, MP
Rt. Hon. Grant Shapps
Office of the Leader of the House of Commons
*Rt. Hon. Tom Brake, MP *(Parliamentary Secretary and Deputy Leader of the Commons)*
Treasury
Rt. Hon. Greg Clark, MP *(Financial Secretary)*
David Gauke, MP *(Exchequer Secretary)*
Sajid Javid, MP *(Economic Secretary)*
Lord Deighton, KBE *(Commercial Secretary)*

GOVERNMENT WHIPS

HOUSE OF LORDS

Lords Chief Whip and Captain of the Honourable Corps of Gentlemen-at-Arms
Rt. Hon. Baroness Anelay of St Johns, DBE
Deputy Chief Whip and Captain of the Queen's Bodyguard of the Yeomen of the Guard
Lord Newby, OBE
Lords-in-Waiting
Earl Attlee
Lord Ahmad of Wimbledon
Lord Gardiner of Kimble
Lord Popat
*Rt. Hon. Lord Wallace of Saltaire
Baronesses-in-Waiting
*Baroness Garden of Frognal
*Baroness Northover
Baroness Stowell of Beeston, MBE

HOUSE OF COMMONS

Chief Whip and Parliamentary Secretary to the Treasury
Rt. Hon. Sir George Young, CH, MP
Deputy Chief Whip and Treasurer of HM Household
Rt. Hon. John Randall, MP
Deputy Chief Whip and Comptroller of HM Household
*Rt. Hon. Alistair Carmichael, MP
Government Whip and Vice-Chamberlain of HM Household
Rt. Hon. Greg Knight, MP
Lords Commissioners of HM Treasury (Whips)
†Stephen Crabb, MP; David Evennett, MP; Robert Goodwill, MP; Mark Lancaster,MP; Anne Milton, MP; Rt. Hon. Desmond Swayne, MP
Assistant Whips
Karen Bradley, MP; Greg Hands, MP; *Mark Hunter, MP; Jo Johnson, MP; Nicky Morgan, MP; Robert Syms, MP; *Jenny Willott, MP

† alongside role as Under-Secretary of State at the Wales Office

GOVERNMENT DEPARTMENTS

THE CIVIL SERVICE

Under the Next Steps programme, launched in 1988, many semi-autonomous executive agencies were established to carry out much of the work of the civil service. Executive agencies operate within a framework set by the responsible minister which specifies policies, objectives and available resources. All executive agencies are set annual performance targets by their minister. Each agency has a chief executive, who is responsible for the day-to-day operations of the agency and who is accountable to the minister for the use of resources and for meeting the agency's targets. The minister accounts to parliament for the work of the agency. Nearly 75 per cent of civil servants now work in executive agencies. In the first quarter of 2013 there were 408,910 permanent civil servants.

The Senior Civil Service was created in 1996 and comprises around 4,000 staff from permanent secretary to the former grade 5 level, including all agency chief executives. All government departments and executive agencies are now responsible for their own pay and grading systems for civil servants outside the Senior Civil Service.

SALARIES 2013–14

MINISTERIAL SALARIES *from 1 April 2013*

Ministers who are members of the House of Commons receive a parliamentary salary of £66,396 in addition to their ministerial salary.

Prime minister	£76,762
Cabinet minister (Commons)	£68,827
Cabinet minister (Lords)	£101,038
Minister of state (Commons)	£33,002
Minister of state (Lords)	£78,891
Parliamentary under-secretary (Commons)	£23,697
Parliamentary under-secretary (Lords)	£68,710

SPECIAL ADVISERS' SALARIES *from 1 April 2013*

Special advisers to government ministers are paid out of public funds; their salaries are negotiated individually, but are usually in the range of £40,352 to £106,864.

CIVIL SERVICE SALARIES *from 1 April 2013*

Senior Civil Servants	
Permanent secretary	£141,800–£277,300
Band 3	£103,000–£208,100
Band 2	£84,000–£162,500
Band 1A	£67,600–£128,900
Band 1	£60,000–£117,800

Staff are placed in pay bands according to their level of responsibility and taking account of other factors such as experience and marketability. Movement within and between bands is based on performance. Following the delegation of responsibility for pay and grading to government departments and agencies from 1 April 1996, it is no longer possible to show service-wide pay rates for staff outside the Senior Civil Service.

GOVERNMENT DEPARTMENTS

For more information on government departments, *see* W www.gov.uk/government/publications/government-ministers-and-responsibilities

ATTORNEY-GENERAL'S OFFICE

Attorney-General's Office, 20 Victoria Street, London SW1H 0NF
T 020-7271 2492
E correspondence@attorneygeneral.gsi.gov.uk
W www.gov.uk/government/organisations/attorney-generals-office

The law officers of the crown for England and Wales are the Attorney-General and the Solicitor-General. The Attorney-General, assisted by the Solicitor-General, is the chief legal adviser to the government and is also ultimately responsible for all crown litigation. He has overall responsibility for the work of the Law Officers' Departments (the Treasury Solicitor's Department, the Crown Prosecution Service – incorporating the Revenue and Customs Prosecutions Office and the Serious Fraud Office, and HM Crown Prosecution Service Inspectorate). The Attorney-General also oversees the armed forces' prosecuting authority and the government legal service. He has a specific statutory duty to superintend the discharge of their duties by the Director of Public Prosecutions (who heads the Crown Prosecution Service) and the Director of the Serious Fraud Office. The Attorney-General has specific responsibilities for the enforcement of the criminal law and also performs certain public interest functions, eg protecting charities and appealing unduly lenient sentences. He also deals with questions of law arising in bills and with issues of legal policy.

Following the devolution of power to the Northern Ireland Assembly on 12 April 2010, the assembly now appoints the Attorney General for Northern Ireland. The Attorney General for England and Wales holds the office of Advocate General for Northern Ireland, with significantly reduced responsibilities in Northern Ireland.

Attorney-General, Rt. Hon. Dominic Grieve, QC, MP
Parliamentary Private Secretary, Jessica Lee, MP
Solicitor-General, Oliver Heald, QC, MP
Director-General, Rowena Collins Rice

DEPARTMENT FOR BUSINESS, INNOVATION AND SKILLS

1 Victoria Street, London SW1H 0ET
T 020-7215 5000 W www.bis.gov.uk

The Department for Business, Innovation and Skills (BIS) was established in June 2009 by merging the Department for Business, Enterprise and Regulatory Reform and the Department for Innovation, Universities and Skills. Its purpose is to connect people to opportunity and prosperity right across the country and help businesses succeed. The department and its partner bodies provide expertise across a wide range of areas including skills development, investment in new business ideas and technologies, regulation, consumer rights, building Britain's research base and higher education.

Secretary of State for Business, Innovation and Skills and President of the Board of Trade, Rt. Hon. Dr Vince Cable, MP
Principal Private Secretary, Hannah Wiskin
Senior Private Secretary, Emily Hamblin

Special Advisers, Emily Walch; Giles Wilkes
Minister of State, Rt. Hon. David Willetts, MP *(Universities and Science)*
Senior Private Secretary, Benedict Collins
Special Adviser, Nick Hillman
Minister of State, Lord Livingston of Parkhead *(Trade and Investment)**
Senior Private Secretary, Simon Clode
Minister of State, Rt. Hon. Michael Fallon, MP *(Business and Enterprise)*†
Private Secretary, Phillip Carr
Parliamentary Under-Secretary of State, Jo Swinson, MP *(Employment Relations and Consumer Affairs)*‡
Private Secretary, Emily Cloke
Parliamentary Under-Secretary of State, Viscount Younger of Leckie *(Business, Innovation and Skills)*
Private Secretary, Victoria Miles-Keay
Parliamentary Under-Secretary of State, Matthew Hancock, MP *(Skills)*§
Private Secretary, Athith Shetty
Permanent Secretary, Martin Donnelly
Senior Private Secretary, Samantha Baker
Head of Parliamentary Unit, Ian Webster

* Jointly with the Foreign and Commonwealth Office
† Jointly with the Department for Energy and Climate Change
‡ Jointly with the Department for Culture, Media and Sport
§ Jointly with the Department of Education

DEPARTMENTAL BOARD
Chair, Rt. Hon. Dr Vince Cable, MP *(Secretary of State)*
Members, Nick Baird *(Chief Executive, UK Trade and Investment)*; Martin Donnelly *(Permanent Secretary)*; Rt. Hon. Michael Fallon, MP; Bernadette Kelly *(Business and Enterprise)*; Lord Livingston of Parkhead; Philippa Lloyd *(People and Strategy)*; Howard Orme *(Finance and Commercial)*; Sir John O'Reilly *(Knowledge and Innovation)*; Mark Russell *(Chief Executive, Shareholder Executive)*; Rachel Sandby-Thomas, CB *(Enterprise and Skills)*; Jo Swinson, MP; Rt. Hon. David Willetts, MP
Non-Executive Members, Alan Aubrey; Dale Murray; Dalton Philips; Prof. Wendy Purcell; Sir Andrew Witty

BETTER REGULATION EXECUTIVE
1 Victoria Street, London SW1 0ET
T 020-7215 5000 E betterregulation@bis.gsi.gov.uk
W www.gov.uk/government/policy-teams/better-regulation-executive

The Better Regulation Executive (BRE) is part of BIS. It leads on delivering the coalition's commitment to reduce the overall burden of regulation on business over the lifetime of the current parliament in order to increase growth and create jobs. Each government department is responsible for delivering its part of this agenda within a framework maintained by BRE.

BRE is managing a series of reviews, announced in the Budget of March 2012, through which poor practice in the enforcement of regulation will be challenged.
Non-Executive Chair, Lord Curry of Kirkharle
Chief Executive, Graham Turnock

SHAREHOLDER EXECUTIVE
1 Victoria Street, London SW1H 0ET
T 020-7215 6689
W www.shareholderexecutive.gov.uk

The Shareholder Executive was set up in September 2003 to work with other departments in government to improve the government's capabilities and performance as a shareholder, and to offer corporate finance expertise and advice across government. Its goal is to create a climate of ownership that, while challenging, is genuinely supportive and provides the framework for the 28 businesses under its remit to be successful. In addition, the Shareholder Executive's Government Property Unit is responsible for maximising value from the state's property portfolio.
Chair, Patrick O'Sullivan
Chief Executive, Mark Russell

CABINET OFFICE
70 Whitehall, London SW1A 2AS
T 020-7276 1234; Switchboard 020-7276 3000
W www.gov.uk/government/organisations/cabinet-office

The Cabinet Office, alongside the Treasury, sits at the centre of the government, with an overarching purpose of making government work better. It supports the prime minister and the cabinet, helping to ensure effective development, coordination and implementation of policy and operations across all government departments. The Cabinet Office also leads work to ensure that the Civil Service provides the most effective and efficient support to the government to meet its objectives. The department is headed by the Minister for the Cabinet Office.
Prime Minister, First Lord of the Treasury and Minister for the Civil Service, Rt. Hon. David Cameron, MP
Principal Private Secretary, Chris Martin
Deputy Prime Minister, Rt. Hon. Nick Clegg, MP
Principal Private Secretary, Lucy Smith
Minister for the Cabinet Office and Paymaster General, Rt. Hon. Francis Maude, MP
Principal Private Secretary, Daniel Gieve
Private Secretaries, Victoria James; William Newton; Joanna Shayer
Minister for Government Policy, Rt. Hon. Oliver Letwin, MP
Private Secretary, Guy Horsington
Minister for Civil Society, Nick Hurd, MP
Private Secretary, Lara Bogie
Minister of State, Rt. Hon. David Laws, MP*
Private Secretary, Nick Donlevy
Minister for Political and Constitutional Reform, Chloe Smith, MP
Private Secretary, Joanne Elizabeth Jessop
Minister without Portfolio, Rt. Hon. Kenneth Clarke, QC, MP
Private Secretary, Owain Robertson
Minister without Portfolio, Rt. Hon. Grant Shapps, MP
Private Secretary, Christopher Maxsted
Minister without Portfolio, John Hayes, MP
Private Secretary, Kellie Hurst
Parliamentary Secretary, Jo Johnson, MP
Cabinet Secretary, Sir Jeremy Heywood, KCB, CVO
Principal Private Secretary, Rachel Hopcroft
Private Secretaries, Scott Bailey; Mark Doran, Becky Wyse
Head of the Civil Service, Sir Bob Kerslake
Principal Private Secretary, Rachel Hopcroft
Private Secretaries, Scott Bailey; Mark Doran, Becky Wyse
Permanent Secretary and First Parliamentary Counsel, Richard Heaton
Private Secretary (CO), Hannah Boardman
Private Secretary (OPC), John Healey

MANAGEMENT BOARD
Chair, Rt. Hon. Francis Maude, MP
Board Members, Melanie Dawes *(Director-General, Economic and Domestic Affairs Secretariat)*; Sue Gray *(Director General, Propriety and Ethics Team, and Director of Private*

* Position held jointly with the Department for Education

Offices Group); Richard Heaton (*Permanent Secretary and First Parliamentary Counsel*); Sir Jeremy Heywood, KCB, CVO (*Cabinet Secretary*); Nick Hurd, MP (*Minister for Civil Society*); Bruce Mann (*Finance Director and Board Secretary*)

Non-Executive Directors, Lord Browne of Madingley; Dame Barbara Stocking; Ian Davis; Rona Fairhead

HONOURS AND APPOINTMENTS SECRETARIAT
Room G-39, Horse Guards Road, London SW1A 2HQ
T 020-7276 2777
Head, Richard Tilbrook

GOVERNMENT POLICY

PRIME MINISTER'S OFFICE
10 Downing Street, London SW1A 2AA
T 020-7930 4433
W www.number-10.gov.uk
Prime Minister, Rt. Hon. David Cameron, MP
Parliamentary Private Secretary, Sam Gyimah, MP
Principal Private Secretary, Chris Martin
Private Secretaries, Emma Boggis; John Casson; Gus Jaspert; Claire Lombardelli
Speech Writer to the Prime Minister, Tim Kiddell
Chief Operating Officer, Helen Lederer
Director of Communications, Craig Oliver
Prime Minister's Official Spokesman, Steve Field
Head of News and Deputy Spokesperson, Vickie Sheriff
Chief of Staff (Political), Ed Llewellyn
Deputy Chief of Staff (Political), Catherine Fall
Political Press Secretary to the Prime Minister, Gabby Bertin

POLICY AND IMPLEMENTATION UNIT
Head of Policy Unit, Paul Kirby
Head of Implementation Unit, Kris Murrin
Head of Analytics Team, Ivan Collister

DEPUTY PRIME MINISTER'S OFFICE
Principal Private Secretary to the Deputy Prime Minister, Lucy Smith
Parliamentary Private Secretary to the Deputy Prime Minister, Duncan Hames, MP
Head of Communications andOfficial Spokesman to the Deputy Prime Minister, James Sorene
Deputy Prime Minister's Chief of Staff, Jonny Oates
Deputy Prime Minister's Special Adviser for Economic Affairs, Chris Saunders
Head of the Deputy Prime Minister's Office, Philip Rycroft

CONSTITUTION GROUP
Director, Ciaran Martin

ECONOMIC AND DOMESTIC AFFAIRS
Director-General, Melanie Dawes
Head of Implementation Unit, Open Public Services and Regulatory Reform, Will Cavendish

EUROPEAN AND GLOBAL ISSUES
Head, Ivan Rogers

GOVERNMENT IN PARLIAMENT
Head, Richard Heaton

PRIVATE OFFICES GROUP
Director-General, Propriety and Ethics, Sue Gray

NATIONAL SECURITY

Comprises the National Security Secretariat (consisting of the Civil Contingencies Secretariat; Office of Cyber Security and Information Assurance; Intelligence and Security; and the Foreign and Defence Policy Secretariat) and the Joint Intelligence Organisation

NATIONAL SECURITY SECRETARIAT
National Security Adviser, Sir Kim Darroch, KCMG
Deputy Security Advisers, Julian Miller, CB; Olly Robbins
Head of Civil Contigencies Secretariat, Christina Scott
Head of Office of Cyber Security and Information Assurance, James Quinault
Head of Intelligence and Security Secretariat, Dominic Wilson
Head of Foreign and Defence Policy Secretariat, Liane Saunders

JOINT INTELLIGENCE ORGANISATION
Chair, Joint Intelligence Committee, Jon Day
Head of the Joint Intelligence Organisation, Paul Rimmer

EFFICIENCY AND REFORM GROUP

Chief Procurement Officer, Bill Crothers
Deputy Chief Procurement Officer, Sally Collier
Executive Directors, Mike Bracken (*Head of Government Digital Service*); Katharine Davidson (*Strategy Team*); William Jordan (*Executive Director*); John McCready (*Head of Government Property Unit*); Liam Maxwell (*Chief Information Officer*) David Shields (*Managing Director Government Procurement Service*)

CIVIL SERVICE REFORM
Head, Katherine Kerswell

GOVERNMENT SERVICES

Head of Government HR, Chris Last

CABINET OFFICE CORPRATE ERVICES

Head of HR, Melanie Steel
Head of Government and Internal Communications, Alex Aiken
Head of Finance, Estates and Information Communications and Technology, Bruce Mann, CB
Chief Economist, Liz McKeown

OFFICE FOR CIVIL SOCIETY
The Office for Civil Society takes a key role in delivering the government's Big Society agenda.
Executive Directors, Paul Maltby; Helen Stephenson

INDEPENDENT OFFICES

CIVIL SERVICE COMMISSION
1 Horse Guards Road, London SW1A 2HQ
T 020-7271 0831
W http://civilservicecommission.independent.gov.uk

The Civil Service Commission regulates the requirement that selection for appointment to the Civil Service must be on merit on the basis of fair and open competition; the commission publishes its recruitment principles and audit departments and agencies' performance against these. Commissioners personally chair competitions for the most senior jobs in the civil service. In addition, the commission hears complaints from civil servants under the Civil Service Code.

The commission was established as a statutory body in November 2010 under the provisions of the Constitutional Reform and Governance Act 2010.

First Commissioner, Sir David Normington, GCB
Commissioners, Jonathan Baume; Kathryn Bishop; Adele Biss; Peter Blausten; Christine Farnish; Andrew Flanagan; Dame Moira Gibb, DBE; Wanda Goldwag; Eliza Hermann; Angela Sarkis

THE COMMISSIONER FOR PUBLIC APPOINTMENTS
G/8, 1 Horse Guards Road, London SW1A 2HQ
T 020-7271 0831 E publicappointments@csc.gsi.gov.uk
W http://publicappointmentscommissioner.independent.gov.uk

The Commissioner for Public Appointments is responsible for monitoring, regulating and reporting on ministerial appointments to public bodies. The commissioner can investigate complaints about the way in which appointments were made.

Commissioner for Public Appointments, Sir David Normington, GCB
Principal Policy Adviser, Terry Willows

OFFICE OF THE PARLIAMENTARY COUNSEL
1 Horse Guards Road, London SW1A 2HQ
T 02-7276 6586 E goodlaw@cabinet-office.gsi.gov.ukk
W www.gov.uk/government/organisations/office-of-the-parliamentary-counsel

The Office of the Parliamentary Counsel is a group of government lawyers who specialise in drafting government bills; advising departments on the rules and procedures of Parliament; reviewing orders and regulations which amend Acts of Parliament; and assisting the government on a range of legal and constitutional issues.

First Parliamentary Counsel, Richard Heaton, CB
Chief Executive, Jim Barron, CBE

DEPARTMENT FOR COMMUNITIES AND LOCAL GOVERNMENT

Eland House, Bressenden Place, London SW1E 5DU
T 0303-444 0000
W www.gov.uk/government/organisations/department-for-communities-and-local-government

The Department for Communities and Local Government was formed in May 2006 with a remit to promote community cohesion and prevent extremism, and was given responsibility for housing, urban regeneration and planning. It unites the communities and civil renewal functions previously undertaken by the Home Office, with responsibility for regeneration, neighbourhood renewal and local government (previously held by the Office of the Deputy Prime Minister, which was abolished following a cabinet reshuffle in May 2006). The department ensures that the Fire and Rescue services have the resources they need to reduce the number of deaths from fire, promote fire prevention activity and respond swiftly to national emergencies. The department also has responsibility for equality policy on race and faith (functions that were previously split between several government departments).

Secretary of State for Communities and Local Government, Rt. Hon. Eric Pickles, MP
Principal Private Secretary, David Hill
Parliamentary Private Secretary, John Glen, MP
Special Advisers, Jess Cunniffe; Zoe Thorogood; Sheridan Westlake
Minister of State, Rt. Hon. Baroness Warsi* *(Faith and Communities)*
Private Secretary, Gillie Severin
Minister of State, Mark Prisk, MP *(Housing)*
Private Secretary, Mark Livesey
Minister of State, Nick Boles, MP *(Planning)*
Private Secretary, Fakruz Zaman
Parliamentary Under-Secretary of State, Rt. Hon. Don Foster, OBE, MP *(Integration, Localism, Decentralisation and Community Rights and Building Regulations)*
Private Secretary, Kerr McKendrick
Parliamentary Under-Secretary of State, Brandon Lewis, MP *(Fire and Resilience, Thames Gateway)*
Private Secretary, Ruth Long
Parliamentary Under-Secretary of State, Baroness Hanham, CBE *(Productivity, Transparency, European Regional Development Fund)*
Private Secretary, Kerida Allaway
Permanent Secretary, Sir Bob Kerslake
Principal Private Secretary, Leigh Bura
Private Secretary, Lucy Rigler
Chief Scientific Adviser, Prof. Jeremy Watson

* Also holds position of Senior Minister of State at the Foreign and Commonwealth Office

MANAGEMENT BOARD
Chair, Rt. Hon. Eric Pickles, MP
Members, Andrew Campbell; Louise Casey, CB; Helen Edwards, CBE; Sue Higgins; Sir Bob Kerslake *(Permanent Secretary);* Peter Schofield
Non-Executive Members, Diana Brightmore-Armour; Stephen Hay; Nick Markham; Sara Weller *(Lead)*

DEPARTMENT FOR CULTURE, MEDIA AND SPORT

2–4 Cockspur Street, London SW1Y 5DH
T 020-7211 6000 E enquiries@culture.gov.uk
W www.culture.gov.uk

The Department for Culture, Media and Sport (DCMS) was established in July 1997 and aims to improve the quality of life for all those in the UK through cultural and sporting activities while championing the tourism, creative and leisure industries. It is responsible for government policy relating to the arts, sport, the National Lottery, tourism, libraries, museums and galleries, broadcasting, creative industries – including film and the music industry – press freedom and regulation, licensing, gambling, the historic environment, telecommunications and online and media ownership and mergers.

The department is also responsible for 47 public bodies that help deliver the department's strategic aims and objectives, the listing of historic buildings and scheduling of ancient monuments, the export licensing of cultural goods, and the management of the Government Art Collection and the Royal Parks (its sole executive agency). It has the responsibility for humanitarian assistance in the event of a disaster, as well as for the organisation of the annual Remembrance Day ceremony at the Cenotaph. In September 2012, the Government Equalities Office became part of DCMS, having previously been part of the Home Office.

Secretary of State for Culture, Media and Sport and Minister for Women and Equalities, Rt. Hon. Maria Miller, MP
Principal Private Secretary, vacant
Special Advisers, Jo Hindley; Nick King
Parliamentary Private Secretary, Mary McLeod, MP
Minister of State, Rt. Hon. Hugh Robertson, MP *(Tourism and Heritage)*
Private Secretary, Alana Curtis
Parliamentary Under-Secretary of State, Ed Vaizey, MP *(Culture, Communications and Creative Industries)*
Private Secretary, Hanna Johnson
Parliamentary Under-Secretary of State, Helen Grant, MP* *(Women and Equalities)*
Private Secretary, Cecile Ogwudire
Parliamentary Under-Secretary of State, Jo Swinson, MP† *(Women and Equalities)*
Prvate Secretary, Natalie Davis
Permanent Secretary, Sue Owen

* Position held jointly with the Ministry of Justice
† Position held jointly with the Department for Business, Innovation and Skills

MANAGEMENT BOARD
Chair, Sue Owen
Members, David Brooker *(Sport and Olympic Legacy);* Rachel Clark *(Government Equalities Office);* Samantha Foley *(Finance and Commercial; Lottery and Gambling);* Rita French; Helen McNamara *(Media; Strategy; Change);* Clare Pillman *(Culture and Heritage; People);* Jon Zeff *(Broadband; Digital Economy; Departmental Communications)*
Non-Executive Members, Ajay Chowdhury; Dr Tracy Long; Ruby McGregor-Smith, CBE; David Verey

GOVERNMENT EQUALITIES OFFICE (GEO)
100 Parliament Street, London SW1A 2BQ **T** 020-7211 6000
E enquiries@culture.gsi.gov.uk

The GEO is responsible for the government's overall strategy on equality. Its work includes leading the development of a more integrated approach on equality across government with the aim of improving equality and reducing discrimination and disadvantage for all. The office is also responsible for leading policy on gender equality, sexual orientation and transgender equality matters.
Minister for Women and Equality, Rt. Hon. Maria Miller, MP
Parliamentary Under-Secretary of State (Women and Growth; Women on Boards; Lesbian, Gay, Bisexual, and Transgender strategy, Public Sector Equality Duty, Body Confidence), Jo Swinson, MP
Parliamentary Under-Secretary of State (Same-sex Marriage; Equality and Human Rights Commission; Equality Legislation; Violence against Women and Girls), Helen Grant, MP

MINISTRY OF DEFENCE
see Defence chapter

DEPARTMENT FOR EDUCATION
Sanctuary Buildings, Great Smith Street, London SW1P 3BT
T 0870-001 2345 **Public Enquiries** 0370-000 2288
W www.gov.uk/government/organisations/department-for-education

The Department for Education (DfE) was established in May 2010 in place of the Department for Children, Schools and Families (DCSF), in order to refocus the department on its core purpose of supporting teaching and learning. The department is responsible for education and children's services, while the Department for Business, Innovation and Skills is responsible for higher education.

The department's objectives include the expansion of the academies programme, to allow schools to apply to become independent of their local authority, and the introduction of the free schools programme, to allow any suitable proposers, such as parents, businesses or charities, to set up their own school.
Secretary of State for Education, Rt. Hon. Michael Gove, MP
Principal Private Secretary, Pamela Dow
Deputy Principal Private Secretary, Elin Jones
Senior Private Secretary, Louise Evans
Private Secretaries, Elizabeth Kelly; Victoria Woodcock
Special Advisers, Henry Cook; Dominic Cummings; Henry de Zoete
Parliamentary Private Secretary, Simon Wright, MP
Minister of State, Rt. Hon. David Laws, MP *(Schools)**
Senior Private Secretary, Lydia Mulholland
Parliamentary Private Secretaries, Gavin Barwell, MP; Simon Wright, MP
Parliamentary Under-Secretary of State, Edward Timpson, MP *(Children and Families)*
Private Secretary, Rafi Addlestone
Parliamentary Private Secretaries, Gavin Barwell, MP; Simon Wright, MP
Parliamentary Under-Secretary of State, Matthew Hancock, MP *(Further Education, Skills and Lifelong Learning)*†
Senior Private Secretary, Athith Shetty
Parliamentary Under-Secretary of State, Lord Nash *(Schools)*
Private Secretary, Bonnie Wang
Parliamentary Under-Secretary of State, Elizabeth Truss, MP *(Early Years' Education)*
Private Secretary, Matthew Edwards
Parliamentary Clerk, Eligio Cerval-Pena
Spokesperson in the House of Lords, Lord Nash
Permanent Secretary, Chris Wormald
Private Secretaries, Hannah Lewis; Kris Nursiah

* Position held jointly with the Cabinet Office
† Position held jointly with the Department for Business, Innovation and Skills

MANAGEMENT BOARD
Chair, Chris Wormald *(Permanent Secretary)*
Members, Shona Dunn; Janette Durbin; Tom Jeffery; Simon Judge; Andrew McCully; Hilary Spencer
Non-Executive Members, Theodore Agnew; Sue John; Paul Marshall; David Meller

DEPARTMENT OF ENERGY AND CLIMATE CHANGE
3 Whitehall Place, London SW1A 2AW
T 0300-060 4000 **E** correspondence@decc.gsi.gov.uk
W www.gov.uk/government/organisations/department-of-energy-climate-change

The Department of Energy and Climate Change (DECC) was formed in 2008 to bring together energy policy, previously the responsibility of BERR (now the Department for Business, Innovation and Skills), and climate change mitigation policy, previously the responsibility of the Department for Environment, Food and Rural Affairs. DECC works to make sure that the UK has secure, clean, affordable energy supplies and promote international action to mitigate climate change.
Secretary of State for the Department of Energy and Climate Change, Rt. Hon. Ed Davey, MP
Private Secretary, Ross Gribbin
Parliamentary Private Secretary, Stephen Gilbert, MP
Minister of State, Rt. Hon. Gregory Barker, MP
Private Secretary, Anjoum Noorani
Parliamentary Private Secretary, Laura Sandys, MP
Minister of State, Rt. Hon. Michael Falon, MP
Private Secretary, Jessica Ayers
Parliamentary Private Secretary, Theresa Coffey, MP
Parliamentary Under-Secretary of State, Baroness Verma of Leicester
Private Secretary, Stephen Burke

EXECUTIVE COMMITTEE
Permanent Secretary, Stephen Lovegrove
Private Secretary, Grace Carey
Members, Steven Fries *(Chief Economist)* Vanessa Howlison *(Director, Finance and Information);* Prof. David Mackay *(Chief Scientific Adviser);* Vanessa Nicholls *(Acting Chief Operating Officer);* Alison Rumsey *(HR Director);* Stephen Speed *(Acting Director General, International Climate Change and Energy Efficiency Group);* Simon Virley *(Director General, Energy Markets and Infrastructure)*

DEPARTMENT FOR ENVIRONMENT, FOOD AND RURAL AFFAIRS

Nobel House, 17 Smith Square, London SW1P 3JR
T 020-7238 3000 **Helpline** 0845-933 5577
E helpline@defra.gsi.gov.uk
W www.gov.uk/government/organisations/department-for-environment-food-rural-affairs

The Department for Environment, Food and Rural Affairs (DEFRA) is responsible for government policy on the environment, rural matters and farming and food production. In association with the agriculture departments of the Scottish government, the National Assembly for Wales and the Northern Ireland Office, the department is responsible for negotiations in the EU on the common agricultural and fisheries policies, and for single European market questions relating to its responsibilities. Its remit includes international agricultural and food trade policy.

The department's five strategic priorities are climate change adaptation; sustainable consumption and production; the protection of natural resources and the countryside; sustainable rural communities; and sustainable farming and food, including animal health and welfare. DEFRA is also the lead government department for emergencies in animal and plant diseases, flooding, food and water supply, dealing with the consequences of a chemical, biological, radiological or nuclear incident, and other threats to the environment.

Secretary of State for Environment, Food and Rural Affairs, Rt. Hon. Owen Paterson, MP
Principal Private Secretary, Dr Jeremy Marlow
Senior Private Secretary, Mike Barrett
Private Secretaries, Jamie Brothwell; Sarah Cundy; Adam Stevens; Emma Southard
Minister of State, David Heath, CBE, MP *(Agriculture and Food)*
Senior Private Secretary, Jackie Clayton
Private Secretaries, Jaspreet Bassi; Grace Duffy; Denise Lawes; Suzie Pinkett
Parliamentary Private Secretary, vacant
Parliamentary Under-Secretary of State, Richard Benyon, MP *(Natural Environment and Fisheries)*
Senior Private Secretary, Simon Stannard
Private Secretaries, David How; Lucy Johnson; Sally Viner
Parliamentary Under-Secretary of State, Lord de Mauley *(Environmental Regulation, Sustainable Development, Waste and Recycling)*
Senior Private Secretary, Tonima Saha
Private Secretaries, Thomas Etheridge; Kathryn Holdsworth; Gladstone Pereira
Permanent Secretary, Ms Bronwyn Hill
Senior Private Secretary, David Read
Private Secretaries, Lisa Austin; Stratos Ttofis

SUPERVISORY BOARD
Chair, Ms Bronwyn Hill *(Permanent Secretary)*
Members, Prof Ian Boyd *(Chief Scientific Adviser);* Catherine Doran; Iain Ferguson; Sir Tony Hawkhead; Paul Rew; Tom Taylor *(Finance);* Ian Trenholm *(Chief Operating Officer);* Peter Unwin *(Policy Delivery);* Katrina Williams *(Strategy, Evidence and Customers)*

FOREIGN AND COMMONWEALTH OFFICE

King Charles Street, London SW1A 2AH
T 020-7008 1500 W www.gov.uk/government/organisations/foreign-commonwealth-office

The Foreign and Commonwealth Office (FCO) provides the means of communication between the British government and other governments – and international governmental organisations – on all matters falling within the field of international relations. The FCO operates in nearly 270 places across the world through a network of embassies and consulates, which help to protect and promote national interests. FCO diplomats are skilled in understanding and influencing what is happening abroad, supporting British citizens who are travelling and living overseas, helping to manage migration into Britain, promoting British trade and other interests abroad and encouraging foreign investment in the UK.

Secretary of State for Foreign and Commonwealth Affairs, Rt. Hon. William Hague, MP
Principal Private Secretary, Thomas Drew
Special Advisers, Chloe Dalton; Denzil Davidson; Arminka Helic; Naweed Khan
Parliamentary Private Secretary, Keith Simpson, MP
Senior Minister of State, Rt. Hon. Baroness Warsi*
Private Secretary (acting), Nick Heath
Minister of State, Rt. Hon. David Lidington, MP
Private Secretary, Olaf Henricson-Bell
Minister of State, Rt. Hon. Hugo Swire, MP
Private Secretary, Rachel Lloyd
Minister of State, Lord Livingston of Parkhead†
Private Secretary, Nick Whittingham
Parliamentary Under-Secretary of State, Mark Simmonds, MP
Private Secretary, Ben Wastnage
Parliamentary Under-Secretary of State, Alistair Burt, MP
Private Secretary, Catherine Allum
Permanent Under-Secretary of State and Head of HM Diplomatic Service, Sir Simon Fraser, KCMG
Private Secretary, Tamsin Heath
Special Representatives, Sir Andrew Burns *(Post-Holocaust Issues);* Simon Gass *(Afghanistan and Pakistan);* Robin Gwynn *(Sudan and South Sudan);* Rear-Adm. Neil Morisetti *(Climate Change);* Rt. Hon. Stephen O'Brien *(Sahel)*

* Position held jointly with the Department for Communities and Local Government

† Position held jointly with the Department for Business, Innovation and Skills

BOARD
Chair, Sir Simon Fraser, CMG
Members, Nick Baird *(Chief Executive, UK Trade and Investment);* Simon Gass *(Political);* Prof. Robin Grimes *(FCO Chief Scientific Advisor);* Robert Hannigan, KCMG *(Defence and Intelligence);* Matthew Rycroft *(Chief Operating Officer);* Barbara Woodward *(Economic and Consular)*
Non-Executive Members, Julia Bond; Sir Richard Lambert; Rudy Markham; Heather Rabbatts, CBE

DEPARTMENT OF HEALTH

Richmond House, 79 Whitehall, London SW1A 2NS
T 020-7210 4850
W https://www.gov.uk/government/organisations/department-of-health

The Department of Health leads, shapes and funds health and care in England, making sure people have the support, care and treatment they need and that this is delivered in a compassionate, respectful and dignified manner.

The department leads across health and care by creating national policies and legislation to meet current and future challenges. It provides funding, assures the delivery and continuity of services and accounts to parliament in a way that represents the best interests of the patient, public and taxpayer.

Secretary of State for Health, Rt. Hon. Jeremy Hunt, MP
Principal Private Secretary, Kristen McLeod
Private Secretary, Rebecca Besalel
Minister of State, Norman Lamb, MP *(Care Services, Mental Health, Disability)*
Private Secretary, Diane Kirby
Parliamentary Under-Secretary of State, Daniel Poulter, MP *(Health Services)*
Private Secretary, Aurelia Valota
Parliamentary Under-Secretary, Earl Howe *(Quality)*
Private Secretary, Dr Stephen Jones
Parliamentary Under-Secretary of State, Anna Soubry, MP *(Public Health, Devolved Matters)*
Private Secretary, Louise Norton-Smith
Parliamentary Clerk, Tim Elms

DEPARTMENTAL BOARD
Chair, Rt. Hon. Jeremy Hunt, MP
Members, Prof. Dame Sally Davies, DBE *(Chief Medical Officer)*; Richard Douglas, CB *(Principal Accounting Officer, Strategy, Finance and NHS)*; Earl Howe; Norman Lamb, MP; Una O'Brien *(Permanent Secretary)*; Daniel Poulter, MP; Jon Rouse *(Social Care, Local Government and Care Partnerships)*; Anna Soubry, MP
Non-Executive Members, Catherine Bell; David Heymann; Chris Pilling; Peter Sands; Mike Wheeler

SOLICITOR'S OFFICE*
Solicitor, Gill Aitken
Director of DWP / Department of Health Legal Services, Isabel Letwin, CBE

* Also the solicitor's office for the Department for Work and Pensions

SPECIAL HEALTH AUTHORITIES
Health Education England
W http://hee.nhs.uk
Health Research Authority
W www.hra.nhs.uk/
NHS Blood and Transplant
W www.nhsbt.nhs.uk
NHS Business Services Authority
W www.nhsbsa.nhs.uk
NHS Litigation Authority
W www.nhsla.com
NHS Trust Development Authority
W www.ntda.nhs.uk

HOME OFFICE

2 Marsham Street, London SW1P 4DF
T 020-7035 4848 E public.enquiries@homeoffice.gsi.gov.uk
W www.gov.uk/government/organisations/home-office

The Home Office deals with those internal affairs in England and Wales which have not been assigned to other government departments. The Secretary of State for the Home Department is the link between the Queen and the public, and exercises certain powers on her behalf, including that of the royal pardon.

The Home Office aims to build a safe, just and tolerant society and to maintain and enhance public security and protection; to support and mobilise communities so that they are able to shape policy and improvement for their locality, overcome nuisance and anti-social behaviour, maintain and enhance social cohesion and enjoy their homes and public spaces peacefully; to deliver departmental policies and responsibilities fairly, effectively and efficiently; and to make the best use of resources. These objectives reflect the priorities of the government and the home secretary in areas of crime, citizenship and communities, namely to reduce crime and the fear of crime through visible, responsive and accountable policing; to reduce organised and international crime; to combat terrorism and other threats to national security; to ensure the effective delivery of justice; to reduce re-offending and protect the public; to reduce the availability and abuse of dangerous drugs; to regulate entry to, and settlement in, the UK in the interests of sustainable growth and social inclusion; and to support strong, active communities in which people of all races and backgrounds are valued and participate on equal terms.

The Home Office delivers these aims through the immigration services, its agencies and non-departmental public bodies, and by working with partners in private, public and voluntary sectors, individuals and communities. The home secretary is also the link between the UK government and the governments of the Channel Islands and the Isle of Man.

Secretary of State for the Home Department, Rt. Hon. Theresa May, MP
Principal Private Secretary, David Oliver
Assistant Private Secretary, Frances Smith
Special Advisers, Fiona Cunningham; Nick Timothy
Minister of State (Immigration), Mark Harper, MP
Private Secretary, Benjamin Brown
Minister of State (Policing and Criminal Justice), Damian Green, MP*
Private Secretary, Yasmin Brooks
Minister of State, Jeremy Browne, MP
Private Secretary, Ewan Mackenzie
Parliamentary Under-Secretary of State (Crime and Security), James Brokenshire, MP
Private Secretary, Katherine Richardson
Parliamentary Under-Secretary of State (Criminal Information), Lord Taylor of Holbeach, CBE,
Private Secretary, Benedict Collins
Permanent Secretary, Mark Sedwill
Private Secretary, Jenny Stewart

* Position held jointly with Ministry of Justice

MANAGEMENT BOARD
Chair, Mark Sedwill
Members, Mike Anderson *(Safeguarding, Immigration and International Group)*; Philip Augar; Charles Farr *(Office for Security and Counter Terrorism)*; Sarah Rapson *(Identity and Passport Service)*; Helen Kilpatrick *(Financial and Commercial)*; Stephen Rimmer *(Crime and Policing Group)*; Kevin White, CB *(Human Resources)*; Rob Whiteman *(UK Border Agency)*; Simon Wren *(Communications)*

DEPARTMENT FOR INTERNATIONAL DEVELOPMENT

22 Whitehall, London SW1A 2EG
T 020-7023 1353
Abercrombie House, Eaglesham Road, East Kilbride, Glasgow G75 8EA T 01355-844000 **Public Enquiries** 0845-300 4100
E enquiry@dfid.gov.uk
W www.gov.uk/government/organisations/department-for-international-development

The Department for International Development (DFID) is responsible for promoting sustainable development and reducing poverty. The central focus of the government's policy, based on the 1997, 2000, 2006 and 2009 white papers on international development, is a commitment to the internationally agreed Millennium Development Goals, to be achieved by 2015. These seek to eradicate extreme poverty and hunger; achieve universal primary education; promote gender equality and empower women; reduce child mortality; improve maternal health; combat HIV/AIDS, malaria and other diseases; improve sanitation and access to clean water; ensure environmental sustainability; and encourage a global partnership for development.

DFID's assistance is concentrated in the poorest countries of sub-Saharan Africa and Asia, but also contributes to poverty reduction and sustainable development in middle-income countries, including those in Latin America and Eastern Europe. It also responds to overseas emergencies. The department works in partnership with governments of developing countries, charities, non-governmental organisations and businesses. It also works with multilateral institutions, including the World Bank, United Nations agencies and the European Commission. The department has headquarters in London and East Kilbride, offices in many developing countries, and staff based in British embassies and high commissions around the world.

Secretary of State for International Development, Rt. Hon. Justine Greening, MP
Principal Private Secretary, Vel Gnanendran
Parliamentary Private Secretary, Julian Smith
Special Advisers, Victoria Crawford; Guy Levin
Parliamentary Clerk, Rob Foot
Minister of State, Rt. Hon. Alan Duncan, MP
Private Secretary, Jonny Hall
Parliamentary Private Secretary, Ben Gummer, MP
Parliamentary Under-Secretary of State, Lynne Featherstone, MP
Private Secretary, Emily Travis
House of Lords Spokesperson, Baroness Northover
Whips, John Randall *(Commons)*; Lord Ahmad *(Lords)*
Permanent Secretary, Mark Lowcock
Principal Private Secretary, Sarah Metcalf

MANAGEMENT BOARD

Chair, Mark Lowcock
Members, Mark Bowman *(Humanitarian, Security and Conflict)*; Richard Calvert *(Finance and Corporate Performance)*; Nick Dyer *(acting Policy and Global Programmes)*; Joy Hutcheon *(Country Programmes)*
Non-Executive Members, Vivienne Cox; Richard Keys; Tim Robinson; Eric Salama

CDC GROUP

123 Victoria Street, London SW1E 6DE
T 020-7963 4700 E enquiries@cdcgroup.com
W www.cdcgroup.com

Founded in 1948, CDC is a government-owned Development Finance Institution that invests in the creation and growth of viable private businesses in the poorest countries in order to contribute to economic growth and reduce poverty. In 2012 CDC invested £397m across Africa and South Asia. CDC is a public limited company with the Department for International Development as its 100 per cent shareholder.

Chair, Richard Gillingwater, CBE
Chief Executive, Diana Noble

MINISTRY OF JUSTICE

102 Petty France, London SW1P 9AJ
T 020-3334 3555 E general.queries@justice.gsi.gov.uk
W www.justice.gov.uk

The Ministry of Justice (MoJ) was established in May 2007. MoJ is headed by the Lord Chancellor and Secretary of State for Justice who is responsible for improvements to the justice system so that it better serves the public. He is also responsible for some areas of constitutional policy (those not covered by the Deputy Prime Minister).

The MoJ has seven key priorities, as set out in the departmental business plan published on 26 June 2013. These are to promote UK growth; reform the rehabiliation system; protect the public and punish offenders as part of a more effective and cost-efficient custodial system; to transform youth custody; to transform courts and tribunals and the criminal justice system; to transform legal aid; and to advance civil liberties and reform the law.

The Lord Chancellor and Secretary of State for Justice is the government minister responsible to parliament for the judiciary, the court system and prisons and probation. The Lord Chief Justice has been the head of the judiciary since 2006.

MoJ incorporates the National Offender Management Service, which includes HM Prison Service and the National Probation Service; Her Majesty's Courts and Tribunals Service; and the Legal Aid Agency.

MoJ has several associated departments, non-departmental public bodies and executive agencies, including the National Archives and the Office of the Public Guardian.

Lord Chancellor and Secretary of State for Justice, Rt. Hon. Chris Grayling, MP
Principal Private Secretary, James Crawforth
Special Advisers, Amy Fisher; Will Gallagher
Parliamentary Private Secretary, Lee Scott, MP
Minister of State and Deputy Leader of the House of Lords, Rt. Hon. Lord McNally
Private Secretary, Chris Beal
Minister of State, Rt. Hon. Damian Green, MP*
Private Secretary, Yasmin Brooks
Parliamentary Under-Secretary of State, Helen Grant, MP†
Private Secretary, Victoria Mayo
Parliamentary Under-Secretary of State, Jeremy Wright, MP
Private Secretary, Chloe Burton
Permanent Secretary, Dame Ursula Brennan, DCB
Private Secretary, Gita Sisupalan
Parliamentary Clerk, Ann Nixon

* Position held jointly with Home Office
† Position held jointly with the Department for Culture, Media and Sport

DEPARTMENTAL BOARD

Chair, Rt. Hon. Chris Grayling, MP *(Lord Chancellor and Secretary of State for Justice)*
Members, Ann Beasley *(Director-General, Finance)*; Ursula Brennan *(Permanent Secretary)*; Matthew Coats *(Director-General, Legal Aid Agency & Corporate Services Group)* Helen Grant, MP; Rt. Hon. Damian Green, MP; Peter Handcock *(Chief Executive, HM Courts & Tribunals Service)*; Catherine Lee *(Acting Director-General, Law & Access to Justice Group)*; Rt. Hon. Lord McNally; Antonia Romeo *(Director-General, Criminal Justice)*; Michael Spurr *(Chief Executive, National Offender Management Service)*; Jeremy Wright, MP
Non-Executive Members, Tim Breedon; Bill Griffiths; Dame Sue Street, DCB

NORTHERN IRELAND OFFICE

1 Horse Guards Road, London SW1A 2HQ
Stormont House, Stormont Estate, Belfast BT4 3SH
T 028-9052 0700
W www.gov.uk/government/organisations/northern-ireland-office

The Northern Ireland Office was established in 1972, when the Northern Ireland (Temporary Provisions) Act transferred the legislative and executive powers of the Northern Ireland parliament and government to the UK parliament and a secretary of state. Under the terms of the 1998 Good Friday Agreement, power was devolved to the Northern Ireland

Assembly in 1999. The assembly took on responsibility for the relevant areas of work previously undertaken by the departments of the Northern Ireland Office, covering agriculture and rural development, the environment, regional development, social development, education, higher education, training and employment, enterprise, trade and investment, culture, arts and leisure, health, social services, public safety and finance and personnel. In October 2002 the Northern Ireland Assembly was suspended and Northern Ireland returned to direct rule, but despite repeated setbacks, devolution was restored on 8 May 2007. For further details, *see* Regional Government section.

The Northern Ireland Office is currently responsible for overseeing the devolution settlement, in addition to handling security issues, international issues affecting Northern Ireland and matters relating to its political and constitutional future. In April 2010 the office transferred responsibility for policing and criminal justice to the Northern Ireland Assembly and Executive.

Secretary of State for Northern Ireland, Rt. Hon. Theresa Villiers, MP
Minister of State, Mike Penning, MP
Director General, Julian King, CMG, CVO

OFFICE OF THE ADVOCATE-GENERAL FOR SCOTLAND

Dover House, Whitehall, London SW1A 2AU
T 020-7270 6770
Office of the Solicitor to the Advocate-General, Victoria Quay, Leith, Edinburgh EH6 6QQ
T 0131-244 1635 E privateoffice@advocategeneral.gsi.gov.uk
W www.gov.uk/government/organisations/office-of-the-advocate-general-for-scotland

The Advocate-General for Scotland is one of the three law officers of the crown, alongside the Attorney-General and the Solicitor-General for England and Wales. He is the legal adviser to the UK government on Scottish law and is supported by staff in the Office of the Advocate-General for Scotland. The office is divided into the Legal Secretariat, based mainly in London, and the Office of the Solicitor to the Advocate-General, based in Edinburgh.

The post was created as a consequence of the constitutional changes set out in the Scotland Act 1998, which created a devolved Scottish parliament. The Lord Advocate and the Solicitor-General for Scotland then became part of the Scottish government and the Advocate-General took over their previous role as legal adviser to the UK government on Scots law. *See also* Regional Government section and Ministry of Justice.

Advocate-General for Scotland, Rt. Hon. Lord Wallace of Tankerness, QC
Private Secretary, Lucy Proctor

OFFICE OF THE LEADER OF THE HOUSE OF COMMONS

1 Horse Guards Road, London SW1A 2HQ
T 020-7276 1005 E leader@commonsleader.x.gsi.gov.uk
W www.gov.uk/government/organisations/the-office-of-the-leader-of-the-house-of-commons

The Office of the Leader of the House of Commons is responsible for the arrangement of government business in the House of Commons and for planning and supervising the government's legislative programme. The Leader of the House of Commons upholds the rights and privileges of the house and acts as a spokesperson for the government as a whole.

The leader reports regularly to the cabinet on parliamentary business and the legislative programme. In his capacity as leader of the house, he is a member of the House of Commons Commission. He also chairs the cabinet committee on the legislative programme. As Lord Privy Seal, he is chair of the board of trustees of the Chevening Estate.

The Deputy Leader of the House of Commons supports the leader in handling the government's business in the house. He is responsible for monitoring MPs' and peers' correspondence.

Leader of the House of Commons and Lord Privy Seal, Rt. Hon. Andrew Lansley, CBE, MP
Head of Office, Mike Winter
Deputy Head of Office, Christine Hill
Assistant Private Secretaries, Niall Clarke-Petty *(Parliamentary Business);* Mark Fernandes *(Parliamentary Reform)*
Deputy Leader of the House of Commons, Rt. Hon. Tom Brake, MP
Private Secretary (acting), Lagle Heinla

PRIVY COUNCIL OFFICE

2 Carlton Gardens, London SW1Y 5AA
T 020-7747 5310 E pcosecretariat@pco.x.gsi.gov.uk
W http://privycouncil.independent.gov.uk

The primary function of the office is to act as the secretariat to the Privy Council. It is responsible for the arrangements leading to the making of all royal proclamations and orders in council; for certain formalities connected with ministerial changes; for considering applications for the granting (or amendment) of royal charters; for the scrutiny and approval of by-laws and statutes of chartered institutions and of the governing instruments of universities and colleges; and for the appointment of high sheriffs and Privy Council appointments to governing bodies. Under the relevant acts, the office is responsible for the approval of certain regulations and rules made by the regulatory bodies of the medical and certain allied professions.

The Lord President of the Council is the ministerial head of the office and presides at meetings of the Privy Council. The Clerk of the Council is the administrative head of the Privy Council office.

Lord President of the Council and Deputy Prime Minister, Rt. Hon. Nick Clegg, MP
Clerk of the Council, Richard Tilbrook
Head of Secretariat and Deputy Clerk, Ceri King
Deputy Clerk, Christopher Berry

SCOTLAND OFFICE

Dover House, Whitehall, London SW1A 2AU
T 020-7270 6754
1 Melville Crescent, Edinburgh EH3 7HW
T 0131-244 9010
E sofsscotland@scotlandoffice.gsi.gov.uk
W www.gov.uk/government/organisations/scotland-office

The Scotland Office is the department of the Secretary of State for Scotland which represents Scottish interests within the UK government in matters reserved to the UK parliament. The Secretary of State for Scotland maintains the stability of the devolution settlement for Scotland; delivers secondary legislation under the Scotland Act 1998; is responsible for the conduct and funding of the Scottish parliament elections; manages the Scottish vote provision and authorises the monthly payment of funds from the UK consolidated fund to the Scottish consolidated fund; and publishes regular information on the state of the Scottish economy.

Matters reserved to the UK parliament include the constitution, foreign affairs, defence, international development, the civil service, financial and economic matters, national security, immigration and nationality, misuse of drugs, trade and industry, various aspects of energy regulation (eg coal, electricity, oil, gas and nuclear energy), various aspects of transport, social security, employment, abortion, genetics, surrogacy, medicines, broadcasting and equal opportunities. Devolved matters include health and social work, education and training, local government and housing, justice and police, agriculture, forestry, fisheries, the environment, tourism, sports, heritage, economic development and internal transport. *See also* Regional Government section and Ministry of Justice.

Secretary of State for Scotland, Rt. Hon. Michael Moore, MP
Principal Private Secretary, Colin Faulkner
Parliamentary Under-Secretary of State, Rt. Hon. David Mundell, MP
Private Secretary, Jennifer Manton
Advocate-General and Spokesperson in the House of Lords, Rt. Hon. Lord Wallace of Tankerness, QC
Private Secretary, Lucy Proctor

DEPARTMENT FOR TRANSPORT

Great Minster House, 33 Horseferry Road, London SW1P 4DR
T 0300-330 3000
W www.gov.uk/government/organisations/department-for-transport

The Department for Transport (DfT) is tasked with ensuring that Britain has an efficient transport network that is an engine for sustainable economic growth. Its main responsibilities include aviation, public transport, freight, regional and local transport, social inclusion, railways, roads and road safety, science and research, shipping and vehicles and sustainable travel. Among its current projects is the delivery of a new high-speed rail network, alongside reforming the existing railways and looking at new strategies for roads and aviation.

Secretary of State for Transport, Rt. Hon. Patrick McLoughlin, MP
Principal Private Secretary, Phil West
Minister of State, Rt. Hon. Simon Burns, MP
Private Secretary, Rosa Estevez
Parliamentary Under-Secretary of State, Norman Baker, MP
Private Secretary, Alex Philpott
Parliamentary Under-Secretary of State, Stephen Hammond, MP
Private Secretary, Tom Newman-Taylor
Permanent Secretary, Philip Rutnam
Private Secretary, Natalie Golding

MANAGEMENT BOARD

Chair, Rt. Hon Patrick McLoughlin, MP *(Secretary of State)*
Members, Norman Baker, MP; Rt. Hon Simon Burns, MP; Lucy Chadwick *(International, Security and Environment);* Steve Gooding *(Roads, Traffic and Local);* Claire Moriarty *(Rail);* Jonathan Moor *(Resources and Strategy);* David Prout *(High Speed 2);* Philip Rutnam *(Permanent Secretary)*
Non-Executive Members, Richard Brown; Alan Cook, Sally Davis; John Kirkland; Sam Laidlaw; Mary Reilly; Ed Smith

HM TREASURY

1 Horse Guards Road, London SW1A 2HQ
T 020-7270 4558 E public.enquiries@hm-treasury.gov.uk
W www.gov.uk/government/organisations/hm-treasury

HM Treasury is the country's economics and finance ministry, and is responsible for formulating and implementing the government's financial and economic policy. It aims to raise the rate of sustainable growth, boost prosperity, and provide the conditions necessary for universal economic and employment opportunities. The Office of the Lord High Treasurer has been continuously in commission for over 200 years. The Lord High Commissioners of HM Treasury are the First Lord of the Treasury (who is also the prime minister), the Chancellor of the Exchequer and five junior lords. This board of commissioners is assisted at present by the chief secretary, the parliamentary secretary (who is also the government chief whip in the House of Commons), the financial secretary, the economic secretary, the exchequer secretary and the commercial secretary. The prime minister as first lord is not primarily concerned with the day-to-day aspects of Treasury business; neither are the parliamentary secretary and the junior lords as government whips. Treasury business is managed by the Chancellor of the Exchequer and the other Treasury ministers, assisted by the permanent secretary.

The chief secretary is responsible for public expenditure, including spending reviews and strategic planning; in-year control; public-sector pay and pensions; Annually Managed Expenditure and welfare reform; efficiency in public services; procurement and capital investment. He also has responsibility for the Treasury's interest in devolution.

The financial secretary has responsibility for financial services policy including banking and financial services reform and regulation; financial stability; city competitiveness; wholesale and retail markets in the UK, Europe and internationally; and the Financial Services Authority. His other responsibilities include banking support; bank lending; UK Financial Investments; Equitable Life; and personal savings and pensions policy. He also provides support to the chancellor on EU and wider international finance issues.

The exchequer secretary is a title only used occasionally, normally when the post of paymaster-general is allocated to a minister outside of the Treasury (as it is at present; Francis Maude, MP was appointed paymaster-general and minister of the Cabinet Office in May 2010). The exchequer secretary's responsibilities include strategic oversight of the UK tax system; corporate and small business taxation, with input from the commercial secretary; departmental minister for HM Revenue and Customs and the Valuation Office Agency; and lead minister on European and international tax issues.

The economic secretary's responsibilities include environmental issues such as taxation of transport, international climate change and energy; North Sea oil taxation; tax credits and child poverty; assisting the chief secretary on welfare reform; charities and the voluntary sector; excise duties and gambling; stamp duty land tax; EU Budget; the Royal Mint; and departmental minister for HM Treasury Group.

The role of commercial secretary was created in 2010. Responsibilities include enterprise and productivity; corporate finance; assisting the financial secretary on financial services, banking policy promoting the government's financial services policies and the competitiveness of the UK; asset freezing and financial crime; foreign exchange reserves and debt management policy; National Savings and Investments; and the Debt Management Office. The commercial secretary is also the treasury spokesperson in the House of Lords.

Prime Minister and First Lord of the Treasury, Rt. Hon. David Cameron, MP
Chancellor of the Exchequer, Rt. Hon. George Osborne, MP
Principal Private Secretary, Clare Lombardelli
Private Secretary, Melanie Pitt
Special Advisers to the Chancellor of the Exchequer, Ramesh Chhabra; Poppy Mitchell-Rose
Chief Economic Adviser, Dave Ramsden
Council of Economic Advisers, Rupert Harrison; Torsten Henricson-Bell *(Chair);* Eleanor Shawcross

Chief Secretary to the Treasury, Rt. Hon. Danny Alexander, MP
Special Advisers to the Chief Secretary, John Foster; Will de Peyer
Private Secretary, Will Garton
Financial Secretary to the Treasury, Rt. Hon Greg Clark, MP
Private Secretary, Sam Mackay
Exchequer Secretary to the Treasury, David Gauke, MP
Private Secretary, Oliver Haydon
Economic Secretary to the Treasury, Sajid Javid, MP
Private Secretary, Miranda Claremont
Commercial Secretary to the Treasury, Lord Deighton
Private Secretary, Emily Marsh
Permanent Secretary to the Treasury, Sir Nicholas Macpherson
Private Secretary and Speechwriter, Juliet Palfrey
Lords Commissioners of HM Treasury (Whips), Stephen Crabb, MP; David Evennett, MP; Robert Goodwill, MP; Mark Lancaster, MP; Anne Milton, MP; Rt. Hon. Desmond Swayne, MP
Assistant Whips, Karen Bradley, MP; Greg Hands, MP; Mark Hunter, MP; Jo Johnson, MP; Nicky Morgan, MP; Robert Syms, MP; Jenny Willott, MP

MANAGEMENT BOARD
Chair, Sir Nicholas Macpherson *(Permanent Secretary)*
Executive Members, Kirstin Baker *(Finance and Commercial);* James Bowler *(Strategy, Planning and Budget);* Alison Cottrell *(Corporate Services);* Michael Ellam *(International and EU);* Lindsey Fussell *(Public Services);* Julian Kelly *(Finance and Commercial);* John Kingman *(Second Permanent Secretary);* Indra Morris *(Tax and Welfare);* Dave Ramsden *(Chief Economic Adviser);* Charles Roxburgh *(Financial Services);* Tom Scholar *(Second Permanent Secretary)* Sharon White *(Public Spending)*
Non-Executive Members, Dame Amelia Fawcett; Baroness Sarah Hogg; Dame Deirdre Hutton; Michael O'Higgins

ROYAL MINT LTD
PO Box 500, Llantrisant, Pontyclun CF72 8YT
T 01443-222111
W www.royalmint.com

From 1975 the Royal Mint operated as a trading fund and was established as an executive agency in 1990. Since 2010 it has operated as Royal Mint Ltd, a company 100 per cent owned by HM Treasury, with an exclusive contract to supply all coinage for the UK.

The Royal Mint actively competes in world markets for a share of the available circulating coin business and about half of the coins and blanks it produces annually are exported. It is the leading export mint, accounting for around 15 per cent of the world market. The Royal Mint also manufactures special proof and uncirculated quality coins in gold, silver and other metals; military and civil decorations and medals; commemorative and prize medals; and royal and official seals.
Master of the Mint, Chancellor of the Exchequer *(ex officio)*
Chair, Peter Warry
Chief Executive, Adam Lawrence

WALES OFFICE

Gwydyr House, Whitehall, London SW1A 2NP
T 029-2092 4220
E correspondence@walesoffice.gsi.gov.uk
W www.gov.uk/government/organisations/wales-office

The Wales Office was established in 1999 when most of the powers of the Welsh Office were handed over to the National Assembly for Wales. It is the department of the Secretary of State for Wales, who is the key government figure liaising with the devolved government in Wales and who represents Welsh interests in the cabinet and parliament. The secretary of state has the right to attend and speak at sessions of the National Assembly (and must consult the assembly on the government's legislative programme). *See also* Regional Government section and Ministry of Justice.
Secretary of State for Wales, Rt. Hon. David Jones, MP
Principal Private Secretary, Stephen Hillcoat
Parliamentary Under-Secretary of State, Stephen Crabb, MP
Parliamentary Under-Secretary of State, Baroness Randerson
Director of Office, Glynne Jones

DEPARTMENT FOR WORK AND PENSIONS

Caxton House, Tothill Street, London SW1H 9NA
T 020-7340 4000 E enquiries@dwp.gsi.gov.uk
W www.gov.uk/government/organisations/department-fo-work-pensions

The Department for Work and Pensions was formed in June 2001 from parts of the former Department of Social Security, the Department for Education and Employment and the Employment Service. The department helps unemployed people of working age into work, helps employers to fill their vacancies and provides financial support to people unable to help themselves, through back-to-work programmes. The department also administers the child support system, social security benefits and the social fund. In addition, the department has reciprocal social security arrangements with other countries.
Secretary of State for Work and Pensions, Rt. Hon. Iain Duncan Smith, MP
Principal Private Secretary, Paul McComb
Private Secretaries, Kate Davies; Rupert Gill
Minister of State (Employment), Mark Hoban, MP
Private Secretary, Pippa Knott
Assistant Private Secretaries, Andrew Hobson; Carmen Pardavila; Phillip Platts
Minister of State (Pensions and Child Maintenance), Steve Webb, MP
Private Secretary, Michael Dynan-Oakley
Assistant Private Secretaries, Karis Fiorrucci; Liz Wenzerul; Joe Stacey
Parliamentary Under-Secretary (Disabled People), Esther McVey, MP
Private Secretary, Mark Swindells
Assistant Private Secretaries, Fiona Dickson; Fiona Fairbarn; Ellie Tack
Parliamentary Under-Secretary of State (Welfare Reform), Lord Freud
Private Secretary, Jessica Yuille
Assistant Private Secretaries, Alice Golding; Martin King; Caroline Nicholls

EXECUTIVE TEAM
Permanent Secretary and Head of Department, Robert Devereux
Directors-General, Gill Aitken *(Professional Services);* Mike Driver *(Finance);* Chris Last *(Human Resources);* Andy Nelson *(IT and Chief Information Officer);* Sue Owen *(Strategy);* Noel Shanahan *(Operations)*

EXECUTIVE AGENCIES

Executive agencies are well-defined business units that carry out services with a clear focus on delivering specific outputs within a framework of accountability to ministers. They can be set up or disbanded without legislation, and they are organisationally independent from the department they are answerable to. In the following list the agencies are shown in the accounts of their sponsor departments. Legally they act on behalf of the relevant secretary of state. Their chief executives also perform the role of accounting officers, which means they are responsible for the money spent by their organisations. Staff employed by agencies are civil servants.

ATTORNEY-GENERAL'S OFFICE

TREASURY SOLICITOR'S DEPARTMENT

1 Kemble Street, London WC2B 4TS
T 020-7210 3000
E thetreasurysolicitor@tsol.gsi.gov.uk
W www.tsol.gov.uk

The Treasury Solicitor's Department, which became an executive agency in 1996, provides legal services for many government departments and other publicly funded bodies, and is answerable to the Attorney-General. Those departments and bodies without their own lawyers are provided with legal advice and litigation services. The Treasury Solicitor is also the Queen's Proctor, and is responsible for collecting ownerless goods *(bona vacantia)* on behalf of the crown.

HM Procurator-General and Treasury Solicitor (Permanent Secretary), Sir Paul Jenkins, KCB
Deputy Treasury Solicitor, Peter Fish
Heads of Divisions, Daniel Denman *(European Division);* Zane Denton *(Bona Vacantia Division);* Susanna McGibbon *(Litigation Group)*

DEPARTMENT FOR BUSINESS, INNOVATION AND SKILLS

COMPANIES HOUSE

Crown Way, Cardiff CF14 3UZ
T 0303-123 4500
E enquiries@companies-house.gov.uk
W www.companies-house.gov.uk

Companies House incorporates and dissolves companies, examines and stores company information delivered under the Companies Act and related legislation; and makes this information available to the public.

Registrar of Companies for England and Wales and Chief Executive, Tim Moss
Registrar of Companies for Scotland, Dorothy Blair
Registrar of Companies for Northern Ireland, Helen Shilliday

THE INSOLVENCY SERVICE

4 Abbey Orchard Street, London SW1P 2HT
Insolvency Enquiry Line 0845-602 9848
E Insolvency.EnquiryLine@insolvency.gsi.gov.uk
W www.bis.gov.uk/insolvency

The role of the service includes administration and investigation of the affairs of bankrupts, individuals subject to debt relief orders, partnerships and companies in compulsory liquidation; dealing with the disqualification of directors in all corporate failures; authorising and regulating the insolvency profession; providing banking and investment services for bankruptcy and liquidation estate funds; assessing and paying statutory entitlement to redundancy payments when an employer cannot, or will not, pay its employees; and advising ministers on insolvency, redundancy and related issues. The service has around 2,100 staff, operating from 35 locations across Great Britain.

Inspector-General and Chief Executive, Dr Richard Judge
Deputy Chief Executive, Graham Horne

INTELLECTUAL PROPERTY OFFICE

Concept House, Cardiff Road, Newport NP10 8QQ
T 0300-300 2000 E information@ipo.gov.uk
W www.ipo.gov.uk

The Intellectual Property Office (an operating name of the Patent Office) was set up in 1852 to act as the UK's sole office for the granting of patents. It was established as an executive agency in 1990 and became a trading fund in 1991. The office is responsible for the granting of intellectual property (IP) rights which include patents, trade marks, designs and copyright.

Comptroller-General and Chief Executive, John Alty

LAND REGISTRY

Trafalgar House, 1 Bedford Park, Croydon CR0 2AQ
T 0844-892 1111 E customersupport@landregistry.gsi.gov.uk
W www.landregistry.gov.uk

An executive agency and trading fund of BIS, Land Registry maintains the Land Register – the definitive source of information for more than 23 million property titles in England and Wales. The Land Register has been open to public inspection since 1990.

Chief Land Registrar and Chief Executive, Ed Lester

MET OFFICE

FitzRoy Road, Exeter, Devon EX1 3PB
T 0870-900 0100 E enquiries@metoffice.gov.uk
W www.metoffice.gov.uk

The Met Office is the UK's National Weather Service, operating as an executive agency of BIS, having transferred from the MoD in July 2011. It is a world leader in providing weather and climate services, and employs more than 1,800 people at 60 locations throughout the world.

Chief Executive, John Hirst

NATIONAL MEASUREMENT OFFICE

Stanton Avenue, Teddington, Middx TW11 0JZ
T 020-8943 7272 E info@nmo.gov.uk
W www.bis.gov.uk/nmo

The National Measurement Office (NMO) was created in April 2009, merging the functions of the National Weights and Measures Laboratory and the National Measurement System. NMO is responsible for all aspects of the national measurement system and provides a legal metrology infrastructure necessary to facilitate fair competition, support innovation, promote international trade and protect consumers, health and the environment.

Chief Executive, Peter Mason

ORDNANCE SURVEY

Adanac Drive, Southampton SO16 0AS
T 0845-605 0505
E customerservices@ordnancesurvey.co.uk
W www.ordnancesurvey.co.uk

Ordnance Survey is the national mapping agency for Great Britain. It is a government department and executive agency operating as a trading fund since 1999.

Director-General and Chief Executive, Dr Vanessa Lawrence, CB

SKILLS FUNDING AGENCY

Cheylesmore House, Quinton Road, Coventry CV1 2WT
T 0845-377 5000 E info@skillsfundingagency.bis.gov.uk
W www.skillsfundingagency.bis.gov.uk

The Skills Funding Agency was established in April 2010 as one of two successor organisations of the Learning and Skills

Council. It is a partner organisation of the Department of Business, Innovation and Skills. Its job is to fund and promote adult further education (FE) and skills training in England, including traineeships and apprenticeships. The agency delivers £4.1bn of skills training through contracts with over 1,000 colleges, private training organisations and employers.
Chief Executive, Kim Thorneywork

UK SPACE AGENCY
Polaris House, North Star Avenue, Swindon, Wiltshire SN2 1SZ
T 020-7215 5000 E info@ukspaceagency.bis.gsi.gov.uk
W www.bis.gov.uk/ukspaceagency

The UK Space Agency was established on 23 March 2010 and became an executive agency on 1 April 2011. It was created to provide a single voice for UK space ambitions, and is responsible for all strategic decisions on the UK civil space programme. Responsibilities of the UK Space Agency include coordinating UK civil space activity; supporting academic research; nurturing the UK space industry; raising the profile of UK space activities at home and abroad; working to increase understanding of space science and its practical benefits; and inspiring the next generation of UK scientists and engineers.
Chief Executive, Dr David Parker

CABINET OFFICE

GOVERNMENT PROCUREMENT SERVICE
Floor 9, The Capital Building, Old Hall Street, Liverpool L3 9PP
T 0345-410 2222 E info@gps.gsi.gov.uk
W http://gps.cabinetoffice.gov.uk

The Government Procurement Service is an executive agency of the Cabinet Office, providing a professional procurement service to central government and the UK public sector including local government, health, education, devolved administrations, emergency services, defence and not-for-profit organisations.
Chief Procurement Officer, Bill Crothers
Managing Director, Sally Collier

DEPARTMENT FOR COMMUNITIES AND LOCAL GOVERNMENT

PLANNING INSPECTORATE
Room 3/13, Temple Quay House, 2 The Square, Temple Quay, Bristol BS1 6PN
T 0303-444 5000
E enquiries@pins.gsi.gov.uk
W www.gov.uk/government/organisations/planning-inspectorate; www.planningportal.gov.uk/planning/planninginspectorate
Crown Buildings, Cathays Park, Cardiff CF10 3NQ
T 029-2082 3866 E wales@pins.gsi.gov.uk
W http://planninginspectorate.wales.gov.uk

The main work of the inspectorate consists of national infrastructure planning under the Planning Act 2008 as amended by the Localism Act 2011, the processing of planning and enforcement appeals, and holding examinations into development plan documents. It also deals with listed building consent appeals; advertisement appeals; rights of way cases; cases arising from the Environmental Protection and Water acts, the Transport and Works Act 1992 and other highways legislation; and reporting on planning applications called in for decision by the Department for Communities and Local Government and the Welsh government.
Chief Executive, Sir Michael Pitt

THE QUEEN ELIZABETH II CONFERENCE CENTRE
Broad Sanctuary, London SW1P 3EE
T 020-7222 4000
E info@qeiicc.co.uk W www.qeiicc.co.uk

The centre provides secure conference facilities for national and international government and private sector use.
Chief Executive, Mark Taylor

DEPARTMENT FOR CULTURE, MEDIA AND SPORT

THE ROYAL PARKS
The Old Police House, Hyde Park, London W2 2UH
T 0300-061 2001 E hq@royalparks.gsi.gov.uk
W www.royalparks.org.uk

Royal Parks is responsible for maintaining and developing over 2,000 hectares (5,000 acres) of urban parkland contained within the eight royal parks in London: Bushy Park (with the Longford river); Green Park; Greenwich Park; Hyde Park; Kensington Gardens; Regent's Park (with Primrose Hill); Richmond Park and St James's Park.
Chief Executive, Linda Lennon, CBE

DEPARTMENT FOR EDUCATION

THE EDUCATION FUNDING AGENCY
Sanctuary Buildings, 20 Great Smith Street, London SW1P 3BT
T 0370-000 2288
W www.gov.uk/government/organisations/education-funding-agency

Formed on 1 April 2012, the Education Funding Agency (EFA) is the DFE's delivery agency for funding and compliance. It provides revenue and capital funding for education for learners aged between 3 and 19 years, or aged between 3 and 25 years for those with learning difficulties and disabilities. The EFA also supports the delivery of building and maintenance programmes for schools, academies, free schools and sixth-form colleges.
Chief Executive, Peter Lauener

NATIONAL COLLEGE FOR TEACHING AND LEADERSHIP
Triumph Road, Nottingham NG8 1DH
T 0845-609 0009 E enquiries@nationalcollege.org.uk
W www.nationalcollege.org.uk

On 1 April 2013 the National College merged with the Teaching Agency to become the National College for Teaching and Leadership. The new executive agency has two key aims: improving the quality of the workforce; and helping schools to help each other to improve. It is also the awarding body for Qualified Teacher Status (QTS).
Chief Executive, Charlie Taylor

STANDARDS AND TESTING AGENCY
53–55 Butts Road, Earlsdon Park, Coventry CV1 3BH
T 0370-000 2288 E assessments@education.gov.uk
W www.gov.uk/government/organisations/standards-and-testing-agency

The Standards and Testing Agency (STA) opened on 1 October 2011 and is responsible for the development and delivery of all statutory assessments from early years to the end of Key Stage 3.
Chief Executive, Ian Todd

DEPARTMENT FOR ENVIRONMENT, FOOD AND RURAL AFFAIRS

ANIMAL HEALTH AND VETERINARY LABORATORIES AGENCY

Woodham Lane, New Haw, Addlestone, Surrey KT15 3NB
T 01932-341 111 E AH.corporate_centre@ahvla.gsi.gov.uk
W www.gov.uk/government/organisations/animal-health-and-veterinary-laboratories-agency

The Animal Health and Veterinary Laboratories Agency (AHVLA) is an executive agency of DEFRA. It was formed on 1 April 2011 following the merger of Animal Health and the Veterinary Laboratories Agency.

The agency is responsible, on behalf of DEFRA, the Welsh government and the Scottish government for protecting the health and welfare of farmed animals, including playing a key role in the prevention, detection and management of exotic and endemic diseases in animals. It is also responsible for delivering research and laboratory services for animal and public health and for advising policy departments regarding the veterinary evidence base for policy development.

The AHVLA's services include a wide range of core functions covering veterinary research, disease surveillance, specialised testing and an emergency response capability. This includes protecting the welfare of farmed animals; the eradication of endemic disease; import and export certification; animal by-product regulation; and preparedness for managing exotic animal diseases.

The AHVLA is also reponsible for licensing the trade in endangered species for conservation purposes; for ensuring that eggs are correctly labelled and that marketing regulations are being complied with.
Chief Executive, Chris Hadkiss

CENTRE FOR ENVIRONMENT, FISHERIES AND AQUACULTURE SCIENCE (CEFAS)

Pakefield Road, Lowestoft, Suffolk NR33 0HT
T 01502-562244 W www.cefas.defra.gov.uk

Established in April 1997, the agency provides research and consultancy services in fisheries science and management, aquaculture, fish health and hygiene, environmental impact assessment, and environmental quality assessment.
Chief Executive (acting), Mike Waldock

FOOD AND ENVIRONMENT RESEARCH AGENCY

Sand Hutton, York YO41 1LZ
T 01904-462000 E info@fera.gsi.gov.uk
W www.defra.gov.uk/fera

The Food and Environment Research Agency was formed on 1 April 2009 from the merger of the Central Science Laboratory, the Government Decontamination Service, and DEFRA's Plant Health division and Plant Varieties office. The agency's purpose is to support and develop a sustainable food chain, a healthy natural environment, and to protect the community from biological and chemical risks. It does this by providing evidence, analysis and professional advice to the government, international organisations and the private sector. The agency brings together expertise in multi-disciplinary science to rapidly diagnose threats, evaluate risk and inform policy in food and environmental areas; and in responding to and recovering from unforeseen or emergency situations.
Chief Executive, Adrian Belton

RURAL PAYMENTS AGENCY

PO Box 69, Reading RG1 3YD
T 0845-603 7777
E enquiries@rpa.gsi.gov.uk W www.rpa.defra.gov.uk

The RPA was established in 2001. It is the single paying agency responsible for Common Agricultural Policy (CAP) schemes in England and for certain other schemes throughout the UK; it is also responsible for operating cattle tracing services across Great Britain, conducting inspections of farms, processing plants and fresh produce markets in England, and managing the Rural Land Register.
Chief Executive, Mark Grimshaw

VETERINARY MEDICINES DIRECTORATE

Woodham Lane, New Haw, Addlestone, Surrey KT15 3LS
T 01932-336911 E postmaster@vmd.defra.gsi.gov.uk
W www.vmd.defra.gov.uk

The Veterinary Medicines Directorate is responsible for all aspects of the authorisation and control of veterinary medicines, including post-authorisation surveillance of residues in animals and animal products. It is also responsible for the development and enforcement of legislation concerning veterinary medicines and the provision of policy advice to ministers.
Chief Executive, Prof. Pete Borriello

FOREIGN AND COMMONWEALTH OFFICE

FCO SERVICES

Hanslope Park, Milton Keynes MK19 7BH
T 01908-515 789 E fcoservices.customercontactcentre@fco.gov.uk
W www.gov.uk/government/organisations/fco-services

FCO Services was established as an executive agency in April 2006 and became a trading fund in April 2008. It operates as the service delivery arm of the FCO, keeping their people, assets and information across the globe safe and secure from the threats they face. FCO Services also works with other government departments to deliver a range of security services supporting the efficiency and reform agenda.
Chief Executive, Chris Moxey

WILTON PARK CONFERENCE CENTRE

Wiston House, Steyning, W. Sussex BN44 3DZ
T 01903-815020 E admin@wiltonpark.org.uk
W www.wiltonpark.org.uk

Wilton Park organises international affairs conferences and is hired out to government departments and commercial users.
Chair, Iain Ferguson
Chief Executive, Richard Burge

DEPARTMENT OF HEALTH

MEDICINES AND HEALTHCARE PRODUCTS REGULATORY AGENCY (MHRA)

151 Buckingham Palace Road, London SW1W 9SS
E info@mhra.gsi.gov.uk W www.mhra.gov.uk

The MHRA is responsible for regulating all medicines and medical devices in the UK by ensuring they work and are acceptably safe.

The MHRA also includes the National Institute for Biological Standards and Control (NIBSC) and the Clinical Practice Research Datalink (CPRD).
Chair, Sir Gordon Duff
Chief Executive, Dr Ian Hudson

HOME OFFICE

HM PASSPORT SERVICE

4th Floor, Peel Building, 2 Marsham Street, London SW1P 4DF
Passport Advice Line 0300-222 0000
General Register Office 0300-123 1837
W www.gov.uk/government/organisations/hm-passport-office

HM Passport Service (formerly known as the Identity and Passport Service) is an executive agency of the Home Office established in April 2006. The agency incorporates the UK Passport Service and the General Register Office. The UK Passport Service issues, renews and amends passports for UK nationals both at home and abroad. The General Register Office is responsible for overseeing the system of civil registration in England and Wales, which involves administering the marriage laws; securing an effective system for the registration of births, adoptions, civil partnerships, marriages and deaths; maintaining an archive of births, civil partnerships, marriages and deaths; maintaining the adopted children's register, adoption contact register and other registers; and supplying certificates from the registers and the archives for research or family history purposes.
Chief Executive (acting), Paul Pugh

NATIONAL FRAUD AUTHORITY

Third Floor, Fry Building, 2 Marsham Street, London SW1P 4DF
T 020-7035 3431 **E** NFAcontact@nfa.gsi.gov.uk
W www.gov.uk/government/organisations/national-fraud-authority

The National Fraud Authority (NFA) was established on 1 October 2008 to increase protection for the UK economy from the harm caused by fraud. It works with private, public and third sector organisations to initiate, coordinate and communicate counter-fraud activity across the economy. The authority's priorities include improving information sharing between the private and public sectors in order to prevent and detect more fraud; to increase and improve the reporting of fraud through the Action Fraud reporting centre, and to harness the information collected to achieve better prevention and enforcement of fraud; to improve the level of support and advice given to fraud victims; and to improve public and business awareness of fraud.
Chief Executive, Stephen Harrison
Director of Engagement, Peter Wilson
Director of Knowledge, Edward Nkune

MINISTRY OF JUSTICE

HER MAJESTY'S COURTS AND TRIBUNALS SERVICE

see Law Courts and Offices

LEGAL AID AGENCY

102 Petty France, London SW1H 9AJ
T 0300-200 2020 **E** legal.queries@legalaid.gsi.gov.uk
W www.justice.gov.uk

The Legal Aid Agency provides civil and criminal legal aid and advice in England and Wales. Formed on 1 April 2013 as part of the Legal Aid, Sentencing and Punishment of Offenders Act 2012, the agency replaces the Legal Services Commission, a non-departmental public body of the MoJ.
Chief Executive, Matthew Coats

NATIONAL ARCHIVES

Kew, Richmond, Surrey TW9 4DU
T 020-8876 3444 **W** www.nationalarchives.gov.uk

The National Archives is a non-ministerial government department and an executive agency of the Ministry of Justice. It incorporates the Public Record Office, Historical Manuscripts Commission, Office of Public Sector Information and Her Majesty's Stationery Office. As the official archive of the UK government, it preserves, protects and makes accessible the historical collection of official records.

The National Archives also manages digital information including the UK government web archive which contains over one billion digital documents, and devises solutions for keeping government records readable now and in the future.

The organisation administers the UK's public records system under the Public Records Acts of 1958 and 1967. The records it holds span 1,000 years – from the Domesday Book to the latest government papers to be released – and fill more than 167km (104 miles) of shelving.
Chief Executive and Keeper, Oliver Morley

NATIONAL OFFENDER MANAGEMENT SERVICE

see The Prison Service

OFFICE OF THE PUBLIC GUARDIAN

PO Box 16185, Birmingham B2 2WH
T 0300-456 0300 **E** customerservices@publicguardian.gsi.gov.uk

The Office of the Public Guardian (OPG) supports and protects those who lack the mental capacity to make decisions for themselves. It supports the Public Guardian in the registration of Enduring Powers of Attorney (EPA) and Lasting Powers of Attorney (LPA), and the supervision of deputies appointed by the Court of Protection. The OPG also has responsibility for mental capacity policy, and provides guidance to public, legal and health professionals. The office's responsibility extends across England and Wales.
Chief Executive and Public Guardian, Alan Eccles

DEPARTMENT FOR TRANSPORT

DRIVER AND VEHICLE LICENSING AGENCY (DVLA)

Longview Road, Swansea SA6 7JL
T 0300-790 6801
W www.gov.uk/government/organisations/driver-and-vehicle-licensing-agency

The DVLA was established as an executive agency in 1990. It became a trading fund in 2004, but relinquished this status on 1 April 2011. The DVLA is responsible for registering and licensing drivers and vehicles, and for collection and enforcement of vehicle excise duty (£6bn in 2012–13). The DVLA also maintains records of all those who are entitled to drive various types of vehicle (currently over 44 million people), all vehicles entitled to travel on public roads (currently almost 37 million), and drivers' endorsements, disqualifications and medical conditions.
Chief Executive (acting), Malcolm Dawson, OBE

DRIVING STANDARDS AGENCY

The Axis Building, 112 Upper Parliament Street, Nottingham NG1 6LP
T 0115-936 6666 **E** customer.services@dsa.gsi.gov.uk
W www.gov.uk/government/organisations/driving-standards-agency

The Driving Standards Agency (DSA) is responsible for carrying out theory and practical driving tests for car drivers, motorcyclists, bus and lorry drivers, and for maintaining the statutory register of approved driving instructors and the voluntary register of large goods vehicle instructors and fleet driver trainers. It also supervises Compulsory Basic Training (CBT) for learner motorcyclists. There are two area offices, which manage over 400 practical driving test centres across

Britain and 140 theory test centres. The DSA will merge with the Vehicle & Operator Services Agency (VOSA) to become a single agency in April 2014.
Chief Executive, Alastair Peoples

GOVERNMENT CAR SERVICE
46 Ponton Road, London SW8 5AX
T 020-7944 3889 W www.dft.gov.uk/gcs

The agency provides secure transport to various government departments and offices.
Chief Executive, Marian Duncan

HIGHWAYS AGENCY
Federated House, London Road, Dorking RH4 1SZ
T 0300-123 5000
E ha_info@highways.gsi.gov.uk W www.highways.gov.uk

The Highways Agency is responsible for operating, maintaining and improving England's 7,000km (4,300 miles) of motorways and trunk roads – known as the strategic road network – on behalf of the Secretary of State for Transport.

The Chief Secretary to the Treasury announced on 27 June 2013 that the Highways Agency would become a publicly owned corporation, although no timetable has been set for this transition.
Chief Executive, Graham Dalton

MARITIME AND COASTGUARD AGENCY
Spring Place, 105 Commercial Road, Southampton SO15 1EG
T 023-8032 9100
W www.gov.uk/government/organisations/maritime-and-coastguard-agency

The agency's aims are to prevent loss of life, continuously improve maritime safety and protect the marine environment.
Chief Executive, Sir Alan Massey
Chief Coastguard (acting), Peter Dymond, OBE

VEHICLE CERTIFICATION AGENCY
1 Eastgate Office Centre, Eastgate Road, Bristol BS5 6XX
T 0300-330 5797 E enquiries@vca.gov.uk
W www.gov.uk/government/organisations/vehicle-certification-agency

The agency is the UK authority responsible for ensuring that new road vehicles, agricultural tractors, off-road vehicles and vehicle parts have been designed and constructed to meet internationally agreed standards of safety and environmental protection.
Chief Executive, Paul Markwick

VEHICLE AND OPERATOR SERVICES AGENCY
Berkeley House, Croydon Street, Bristol BS5 0DA
T 0300-123 9000 E enquiries@vosa.gov.uk W www.gov.uk/vosa

The Vehicle and Operator Services Agency (VOSA) was formed in April 2003 from the merger of the Vehicle Inspectorate and the Traffic Area Network. The agency works with the independent traffic commissioners to improve road safety and the environment; safeguard fair competition by promoting and enforcing compliance with commercial operator licensing requirements; process applications for licences to operate lorries and buses; register bus services; operate and administer testing schemes for all vehicles, including the supervision of the MOT testing scheme; enforce the law on vehicles to ensure that they comply with legal standards and regulations; enforce drivers' hours and licensing requirements; provide training and advice for commercial operators; investigate vehicle defects and recalls; and provide support to the police by examining vehicles involved in accidents for contributory defects.

VOSA and the Driving Standards Agency will merge to form a single agency in April 2014.
Chief Executive, Alastair Peoples

HM TREASURY

NATIONAL SAVINGS AND INVESTMENTS
Glasgow G58 1SB
T 0500-007 007 W www.nsandi.com

NS&I (National Savings and Investments) came into being in 1861 when the Palmerston government set up the Post Office Savings Bank, a savings scheme which aimed to encourage ordinary wage earners 'to provide for themselves against adversity and ill health'. NS&I was established as a government department in 1969. It became an executive agency of the Chancellor of the Exchequer in 1996 and is responsible for the design, marketing and administration of savings and investment products for personal savers and investors. It has over 26 million customers and almost £100bn invested. *See also* Banking and Finance, National Savings.
Chief Executive, Jane Platt

UK DEBT MANAGEMENT OFFICE
Eastcheap Court, 11 Philpot Lane, London EC3M 8UD
T 020-7862 6500 W www.dmo.gov.uk

The UK Debt Management Office (DMO) was launched as an executive agency of HM Treasury in April 1998. The Chancellor of the Exchequer determines the policy and financial framework within which the DMO operates, but delegates operational decisions on debt and cash management and the day-to-day running of the office to the chief executive. The DMO's remit is to carry out the government's debt management policy of minimising financing costs over the long term, and to minimise the cost of offsetting the government's net cash flows over time, while operating at a level of risk approved by ministers in both cases. The DMO is also responsible for providing loans to local authorities through the Public Works Loan Board, for managing the assets of certain public-sector bodies through the Commissioners for the Reduction of the National Debt.
Chief Executive, Robert Stheeman

NON-MINISTERIAL GOVERNMENT DEPARTMENTS

Non-ministerial government departments are part of central government but are not headed by a minister and are not funded by a sponsor department. They are created to implement specific legislation, but do not have the ability to change it. Departments may have links to a minister, but the minister is not responsible for the department's overall performance. Staff employed by non-ministerial departments are civil servants.

CHARITY COMMISSION

PO Box 1227, Liverpool L69 3UG
T 0845-300 0218 W www.charitycommission.gov.uk

The Charity Commission is established by law as the independent regulator and registrar of charities in England and Wales. Its aim is to provide the best possible regulation of these charities in order to ensure their legal compliance and increase their efficiency, accountability and effectiveness, as well as to encourage public trust and confidence in them. The commission maintains a register of over 160,000

charities. It is accountable to both parliament and the First-tier Tribunal (Charity), and the chamber of the Upper Tribunal or high court for decisions made in exercising the commission's legal powers. The Charity Commission has offices in London, Liverpool, Taunton and Newport.
Chair, William Shawcross, CVO
Chief Executive, Sam Younger, CBE, FRSA

CROWN ESTATE

16 New Burlington Place, London W1S 2HX
T 020-7851 5000 E enquiries@thecrownestate.co.uk
W www.thecrownestate.co.uk

The Crown Estate is part of the hereditary possessions of the sovereign 'in right of the crown', managed under the provisions of the Crown Estate Act 1961. It had a capital value of £8.6bn in 2012, and includes substantial blocks of urban property, primarily in London, almost 140,000 hectares (345,000 acres) of rural land, over half of the foreshore, and the sea bed out to the 12 nautical mile territorial limit throughout the UK. The Crown Estate has a duty to maintain and enhance the capital value of estate and the income obtained from it. Under the terms of the act, the estate pays its revenue surplus to the Treasury every year.
Chair and First Commissioner, Sir Stuart Hampson
Chief Executive and Second Commissioner, Alison Nimmo, CBE, FRICS

CROWN PROSECUTION SERVICE

Rose Court, 2 Southwark Bridge Road, London SE1 9HS
T 020-3357 0000 E enquiries@cps.gsi.gov.uk
W www.cps.gov.uk

The Crown Prosecution Service (CPS) is the independent body responsible for prosecuting people in England and Wales. The CPS was established as a result of the Prosecution of Offences Act 1985. It works closely with the police to advise on lines of inquiry and to decide on appropriate charges and other disposals in all but minor cases. *See also* Law Courts and Offices.

The Revenue and Customs Prosecutions Office, which prosecutes major drug trafficking and tax fraud cases in the UK, was incorporated into the CPS on 1 January 2010.
Director of Public Prosecutions, Alison Saunders, CB
Chief Executive, Peter Lewis, CB

FOOD STANDARDS AGENCY

Aviation House, 125 Kingsway, London WC2B 6NH
T 020-7276 8829
E helpline@foodstandards.gsi.gov.uk
W www.food.gov.uk

Established in April 2000, the FSA is a UK-wide non-ministerial government body responsible for food safety and hygiene. The agency has the general function of developing policy in these areas and provides information and advice to the government, other public bodies and consumers. The FSA also works with local authorities to enforce food safety regulations and has staff working in UK meat plants to check that the requirements of the regulations are being met.
Chair (acting), Tim Bennett
Chief Executive, Catherine Brown

FOOD STANDARDS AGENCY NORTHERN IRELAND, 10A–C Clarendon Road, Belfast BT1 3BG T 028-9041 7700 E infofsani@foodstandards.gsi.gov.uk
FOOD STANDARDS AGENCY SCOTLAND, 6th Floor, St Magnus House, 25 Guild Street, Aberdeen AB11 6NJ T 01224-285100 E scotland@foodstandards.gsi.gov.uk
FOOD STANDARDS AGENCY WALES, 11th Floor, South Gate House, Wood Street, Cardiff CF10 1EW T 029-2067 8999 E wales@foodstandards.gsi.gov.uk

FORESTRY COMMISSION

Silvan House, 231 Corstorphine Road, Edinburgh EH12 7AT
T 0131-334 0303 E enquiries@forestry.gsi.gov.uk
W www.forestry.gov.uk

The Forestry Commission is the government department responsible for forestry policy in England and Scotland. It is divided into Forestry Commission England and Forestry Commission Scotland, which report to forestry ministers (the Secretary of State for Environment, Food & Rural Affairs in the UK government, and to ministers in the Scottish government), to whom it is responsible for advice on and implementation of forestry policy. It has an agency, Forest Research, which carries out scientific research and technical development relevant to forestry. The public forests are managed through two additional executive agencies, known as Forest Enterprise England and Forest Enterprise Scotland.

On 1 April 2013 the functions of its Welsh division, Forestry Commission Wales, were subsumed into Natural Resources Wales, a new body established by the Welsh government to regulate and manage natural resources in Wales.

The commission's principal objectives are to protect and expand England's and Scotland's forests and woodlands; enhance the economic value of forest resources; conserve and improve the biodiversity, landscape and cultural heritage of forests and woodlands; develop opportunities for woodland recreation; and increase public understanding of, and community participation in, forestry. It does this by managing public forests in its care to implement these objectives; by supporting other woodland owners with grants, regulation, advice and tree felling licences; and, through its Forest Research agency, by carrying out scientific research and technical development in support of these objectives.
Chair (acting), Sir Harry Studholme
Director-General, Deputy Chair and Director, England, Ian Gambles
Forestry Commissioner Scotland, Dr Bob McIntosh

FORESTRY COMMISSION ENGLAND, 620 Bristol Business Park, Coldharbour Lane, Bristol BS16 1EJ T 0117-906 6000
FORESTRY COMMISSION SCOTLAND, Silvan House, 231 Corstorphine Road, Edinburgh EH12 7AT T 0845-367 3787

GOVERNMENT ACTUARY'S DEPARTMENT

Finlaison House, 15–17 Furnival Street, London EC4A 1AB
T 020-7211 2601
Room T18, 44 Drumsheugh Gardens, Edinburgh EH3 7SW
T 0131-467 1077
E enquiries@gad.gov.uk W www.gad.gov.uk

The Government Actuary's Department was established in 1919 and provides actuarial advice to UK government departments, government agencies, local government bodies, private sector employers, pension scheme trustees and overseas governments. The actuaries provide valuations and advice for public-service pensions and social security schemes, and advise the government on occupational pension schemes and private-sector pensions policy. They also provide advice on investment risk management stategies, project and enterprise risk, demographic studies and healthcare financing.
Government Actuary, Trevor Llanwarne, CB
Deputy Government Actuary, George Russell

Chief Actuaries (London), Sandra Bell; Ian Boonin; Tracey Cutler; Adrian Hale; Stephen Humphrey; Aidan Smith; Sue Vivian
Chief Actuary (Scotland), Ken Kneller

HM REVENUE AND CUSTOMS (HMRC)

100 Parliament Street, London SW1A 2BQ
Income Tax Enquiries 0300-200 3300
National Insurance Enquiries 0300-200 3500
VAT Enquiries 0300-200 3700
W www.hmrc.gov.uk

HMRC was formed following the integration of the Inland Revenue and HM Customs and Excise, which was made formal by parliament in April 2005. It collects and administers direct taxes (capital gains tax, corporation tax, income tax, inheritance tax and national insurance contributions) and indirect taxes (excise duties, insurance premium tax, petroleum revenue tax, stamp duty, stamp duty land tax, stamp duty reserve tax and value-added tax). HMRC also pays and administers child benefit, tax credits and the Child Trust Fund, in addition to being responsible for environmental taxes, national minimum wage enforcement,recovery of student loans, the climate change levy and landfill tax. HMRC also administers the Government Banking Service.
Chair, Ian Barlow
Chief Executive and Permanent Secretary, Lin Homer
Tax Assurance Commissioner and Second Permanent Secretary, Edward Troup

VALUATION OFFICE AGENCY

Wingate House, 93–107 Shaftesbury Avenue, London W1D 5BU
T 020-7734 9825 E customerservices@voa.gsi.gov.uk
W www.voa.gov.uk

Established in 1991, the Valuation Office is an executive agency of HM Revenue and Customs. It is responsible for compiling and maintaining the business rating and council tax valuation lists for England and Wales; valuing property throughout Great Britain for the purposes of taxes administered by HMRC; providing statutory and non-statutory property valuation services in England, Wales and Scotland; and giving policy advice to ministers on property valuation matters. In April 2009 the VOA assumed responsibility for the functions of The Rent Service, which provided a rental valuation service to local authorities in England, and fair rent determinations for landlords and tenants.
Chief Executive, Penny Ciniewicz

OFFICE OF FAIR TRADING (OFT)

Fleetbank House, 2–6 Salisbury Square, London EC4Y 8JX
T 020-7211 8000
E enquiries@oft.gsi.gov.uk W www.oft.gov.uk

The OFT is a non-ministerial government department established by statute in 1973, and it is the UK's consumer and competition authority. It encourages businesses to comply with competition and consumer law and to improve their trading practices through self-regulation. It acts decisively to stop serious or flagrant offenders, studies markets and recommends action where required, and empowers consumers with the knowledge and skills to make informed choices.

The operations of the Competition Commission and the Office of Fair Trading will merge in April 2014 to form the Competition and Markets Authority (CMA), subject to legislation.
Chair, Philip Collins
Chief Executive Officer, Clive Maxwell

OFFICE OF GAS AND ELECTRICITY MARKETS (OFGEM)

9 Millbank, London SW1P 3GE
T 020-7901 7295 E consumeraffairs@ofgem.gov.uk
W www.ofgem.gov.uk

OFGEM is the regulator for Britain's gas and electricity industries. Its role is to protect and advance the interests of consumers by promoting competition where possible, and through regulation only where necessary. OFGEM operates under the direction and governance of the Gas and Electricity Markets Authority, which makes all major decisions and sets policy priorities for OFGEM. OFGEM's powers are provided for under the Gas Act 1986 and the Electricity Act 1989, as amended by the Utilities Act 2000. It also has enforcement powers under the Competition Act 1998 and the Enterprise Act 2002.
Chair, Lord Mogg, KCMG
Chief Executive (acting), Andrew Wright

OFFICE OF QUALIFICATIONS AND EXAMINATIONS REGULATION (OFQUAL)

OFQUAL, Spring Place, Coventry Business Park, Herald Avenue, Coventry CV5 6UB
T 0300-303 3346 E info@ofqual.gov.uk
W www.ofqual.gov.uk

OFQUAL became the independent regulator of qualifications, examinations and assessments on 1 April 2010. It is responsible for maintaining standards, improving confidence and distributing information about qualifications and examinations, as well as regulating general and vocational qualifications in England and vocational qualifications in Northern Ireland.
Chief Executive, Glenys Stacey

OFFICE OF RAIL REGULATION

1 Kemble Street, London WC2B 4AN
T 020-7282 2000 E contact.cct@orr.gsi.gov.uk
W www.rail-reg.gov.uk

The Office of the Rail Regulator was set up under the Railways Act 1993. It became the ORR in July 2004, under the provisions of the Railways and Transport Safety Act 2003. On 1 April 2006, in addition to its role as economic regulator, the ORR became the health and safety regulator for the rail industry. This transfer of responsibility from the Health and Safety Executive was given effect under the Railways Act 2005. The board and chair are appointed by the Secretary of State for Transport. The ORR's key roles are to ensure that Network Rail, the owner and operator of the national railway infrastructure (the track and signalling), manages the network efficiently and in a way that meets the needs of its users; to encourage continuous improvement in health and safety performance while securing compliance with relevant health and safety law, including taking enforcement action as necessary; and to develop policy and enhance relevant railway health and safety legislation. It is also responsible for licensing operators of railway assets, setting the terms for access by operators to the network and other railway facilities, and enforcing competition law in the rail sector.
Chair, Anna Walker
Chief Executive, Richard Price

OFFICE FOR STANDARDS IN EDUCATION, CHILDREN'S SERVICES AND SKILLS (OFSTED)

Piccadilly Gate, Store Street, Manchester M1 2WD
T 0300-123 1231 E enquiries@ofsted.gov.uk
W www.ofsted.gov.uk

Ofsted was established under the Education (Schools Act) 1992 and was relaunched on 1 April 2007 with a wider remit, bringing together four formerly separate inspectorates. It works to raise standards in services through the inspection and regulation of care for children and young people, and inspects education and training for children of all ages. *See also* Education.
HM Chief Inspector, Sir Michael Wilshaw
Chair, Baroness Morgan of Huyton

SECURITY AND INTELLIGENCE SERVICES

GOVERNMENT COMMUNICATIONS HEADQUARTERS (GCHQ)

Hubble Road, Cheltenham GL51 0EX
T 01242-221491
W www.gchq.gov.uk

GCHQ produces signals intelligence in support of national security and the UK's economic wellbeing, and in the prevention or detection of serious crime. Additionally, GCHQ's Information Security arm, CESG, is the national technical authority for information assurance, and provides advice and assistance to government departments, the armed forces and other national infrastructure bodies on the security of their communications and information systems. GCHQ was placed on a statutory footing by the Intelligence Services Act 1994 and is headed by a director who is directly accountable to the foreign secretary.
Director, Sir Iain Lobban, KCMG, CB

SECRET INTELLIGENCE SERVICE (MI6)

PO Box 1300, London SE1 1BD
W www.sis.gov.uk

Established in 1909 as the Foreign Section of the Secret Service Bureau, the Secret Intelligence Service produces secret intelligence in support of the government's security, defence, foreign and economic policies. It was placed on a statutory footing by the Intelligence Services Act 1994 and is headed by a chief, known as 'C', who is directly accountable to the foreign secretary.
Chief, Sir John Sawers

SECURITY SERVICE (MI5)

PO Box 3255, London SW1P 1AE
T 020-7930 9000
W www.mi5.gov.uk

The Security Service is responsible for security intelligence work against covertly organised threats to the UK. It is organised into seven branches, each with dedicated areas of responsibility, which include countering terrorism, espionage and the proliferation of weapons of mass destruction. The Security Service also provides security advice to a wide range of organisations to help reduce vulnerability to threats from individuals, groups or countries hostile to UK interests. The home secretary has parliamentary accountability for the Security Service. There is a network of regional offices around the UK plus a Northern Ireland headquarters.
Director-General, Andrew Parker

SERIOUS FRAUD OFFICE

2–4 Cockspur Street, London SW1Y 5BS
T 020-7239 7272 E public.enquiries@sfo.gsi.gov.uk
W www.sfo.gov.uk

The Serious Fraud Office is an independent government department that investigates and prosecutes serious or complex fraud and corruption. It is part of the UK criminal justice system with jurisdiction over England, Wales and Northern Ireland but not Scotland, the Isle of Man or the Channel Islands. The office is headed by a director who is accountable to the Attorney-General.
Director, David Green, CB, QC

UK STATISTICS AUTHORITY

1 Drummond Gate, London SW1V 2QQ
T 0845-604 1857 E authority.enquiries@statistics.gsi.gov.uk
W www.statisticsauthority.gov.uk

The UK Statistics Authority was established on 1 April 2008 by the Statistics and Registration Service Act 2007 as an independent body operating at arm's length from government, reporting to the UK parliament and the devolved legislatures. Its overall objective is to promote and safeguard the production and publication of official statistics and ensure their quality and comprehensiveness. The authority's main functions are the oversight of the Office for National Statistics (ONS); monitoring and reporting on all UK official statistics, which includes around 30 central government departments and the devolved administrations; and the production of a code of practice for statistics and the assessment of official statistics against the code.

BOARD
Chair, Sir Andrew Dilnot, CBE
Board Members, Richard Alldritt *(Head of Assessment);* Dr Colette Bowe; Partha Dasgupta; Carolyn Fairbairn; Dame Moira Gibb, DBE; Prof. David Hand; Dr David Levy; Jil Matheson *(National Statistician);* Prof. David Rhind, CBE, FRS, FBA *(Deputy Chair, Official Statistics);* Prof. Sir Adrian Smith, FRS *(Deputy Chair, ONS);* Glen Watson *(Director-General, ONS)*

OFFICE FOR NATIONAL STATISTICS (ONS)

Cardiff Road, Newport NP10 8XG
T 0845-601 3034 E info@statistics.gov.uk
W www.ons.gov.uk

The ONS was created in 1996 by the merger of the Central Statistical Office and the Office of Population Censuses and Surveys. On 1 April 2008 it became the executive office of the UK Statistics Authority. As part of these changes, the office's responsibility for the General Register Office transferred to the Identity and Passport Service of the Home Office.

The ONS is responsible for preparing, interpreting and publishing key statistics on the government, economy and society of the UK. Its key responsibilities include designing, managing and running the Census and providing statistics on health and other demographic matters in England and Wales; the production of the UK National Accounts and other economic indicators; the organisation of population censuses in England and Wales and surveys for government departments and public bodies.
National Statistician, Jil Matheson
Director-General, Glen Watson

UK EXPORT FINANCE (ECGD)

1 Horse Guards Road, London SW1A 2HQ
T 020-7271 8010 E customer.service@ukef.gsi.gov.uk
W www.gov.uk/uk-export-finance

UK Export Finance (the operating name of the Exports Credits Guarantee Department) is the UK export credit agency and was established in 1919. A separate government department reporting to the Secretary of State for Business, Innovation and Skills, it has more than 90 years' experience of working closely with exporters, project sponsors, banks and buyers to help UK exporters and overseas investors. UK Export Finance provides support principally in the form of guarantees to banks making loans to buyers of UK goods and services and insurance for UK exporters against risk of non-payment.

Chief Executive, David Godfrey
Non-Executive Chair, Guy Beringer, QC

UK TRADE AND INVESTMENT

1 Victoria Street, London SW1H 0ET
T 020-7215 5000 W www.ukti.gov.uk

UK Trade and Investment is a government organisation that helps UK-based companies succeed in international markets. It assists overseas companies to bring high quality investment to the UK economy.

Chief Executive, Nick Baird

WATER SERVICES REGULATION AUTHORITY (OFWAT)

Centre City Tower, 7 Hill Street, Birmingham B5 4UA
T 0121-644 7500 E mailbox@ofwat.gsi.gov.uk
W www.ofwat.gov.uk

OFWAT is the independent economic regulator of the water and sewerage companies in England and Wales. It is responsible for ensuring that the water industry in England and Wales provides customers with a good quality service at a fair price. This is done by keeping bills for consumers as low as possible; monitoring and comparing the services that companies provide; scrutinising the companies' costs and investment; and encouraging competition where this benefits consumers.

Chair, Jonson Cox
Chief Executive, Regina Finn

PUBLIC BODIES

The following section is a listing of public bodies and other civil service organisations: it is not a complete list of these organisations.

Whereas executive agencies are either part of a government department or are one in their own right (*see* Government Departments section), public bodies carry out their functions to a greater or lesser extent at arm's length from central government. Ministers are ultimately responsible to parliament for the activities of the public bodies sponsored by their department and in almost all cases (except where there is separate statutory provision) ministers make the appointments to their boards. Departments are responsible for funding and ensuring good governance of their public bodies.

The term 'public body' is a general one which includes public corporations, such as the BBC; NHS bodies; and non-departmental public bodies (NDPBs).

In October 2010, the government announced proposals to drastically reform public bodies or 'quangos' (quasi-autonomous non-governmental organisations, another term for NDPBs). In total, 901 bodies were reviewed – 679 NDPBs and 222 other statutory bodies. Consequently, the government introduced the Public Bodies Bill, which received royal assent on 14 December 2011 and became the Public Bodies Act 2011, allowing the government to abolish, merge or transfer the functions of the public bodies listed in the appropriate schedules to the Act.

ADJUDICATOR'S OFFICE

PO Box 10280, Nottingham NG2 9PF
T 0300-057 1111 W www.adjudicatorsoffice.gov.uk

The Adjudicator's Office investigates complaints from individuals and businesses about the way that HM Revenue and Customs, the Valuation Office Agency and the Insolvency Service have handled a person's affairs. The Adjudicator's Office will only consider a complaint after the respective organisation's internal complaints procedure has been exhausted.

The Adjudicator, Judy Clements, OBE

ADVISORY, CONCILIATION AND ARBITRATION SERVICE (ACAS)

22nd Floor, Euston Tower, 286 Euston Road, London NW1 3JJ
Helpline 0845-747 4747 W www.acas.org.uk

The Advisory, Conciliation and Arbitration Service was set up under the Employment Protection Act 1975 (the provisions now being found in the Trade Union and Labour Relations (Consolidation) Act 1992).

ACAS is largely funded by the Department for Business, Innovation and Skills. A council sets its strategic direction, policies and priorities, and ensures that the agreed strategic objectives and targets are met. It consists of a chair and 11 employer, trade union and independent members, appointed by the Secretary of State for Business, Innovation and Skills.

ACAS aims to improve organisations and working life through better employment relations, to provide up-to-date information, independent advice and high-quality training, and to work with employers and employees to solve problems and improve performance.

ACAS has regional offices, in Birmingham, Bristol, Bury St Edmonds, Cardiff, Fleet, Glasgow, Leeds, Liverpool, Manchester, Newcastle upon Tyne and Nottingham. The head office is in London.

Chair, Ed Sweeney
Chief Executive, Anne Sharp

ADVISORY COUNCIL ON NATIONAL RECORDS AND ARCHIVES

The National Archives, Kew, Surrey TW9 4DU
T 020-8392 5377
W www.nationalarchives.gov.uk/advisorycouncil

The Advisory Council on National Records and Archives advises the Lord Chancellor on issues relating to public records that are over 30 years old including public access to them. The council meets four times a year, and its main task is to consider requests for the extended closure of public records; it also reaches decisions regarding government departments that want to keep records.

The Forum on Historical Manuscripts and Academic Research, a sub-committee of the Advisory Council, provides advice to the Lord Chancellor on matters relating to historical manuscripts, records and archives, other than public records.

Chair, Lord Dyson, PC *(Master of the Rolls)*

AGRICULTURE AND HORTICULTURE DEVELOPMENT BOARD

Stoneleigh Park, Kenilworth, Warwickshire CV8 2TL
T 02476-692051 E info@ahdb.org.uk W www.ahdb.org.uk

The Agriculture and Horticulture Development Board (AHDB) is funded by the agriculture and horticulture industries through statutory levies, with the duty to improve efficiency and competitiveness within six sectors: pig meat in England; milk in Great Britain; beef and lamb in England; commercial horticulture in Great Britain; cereals and oilseeds in the UK; and potatoes in Great Britain. The AHDB represents about 75 per cent of total UK agricultural output. Levies raised from the six sectors are ring-fenced to ensure that they can only be used to the benefit of the sectors from which they were raised.

Chair, John Godfrey, CBE
Independent members, Lorraine Clinton; Tim Kelly; Will Lifford
Sector members, Tim Bennett *(milk)*; Neil Bragg *(horticulture)*; John Cross *(beef and lamb)*; Stewart Houston *(pig meat)*; David Piccaver *(potatoes)*; Jonathan Tipples *(cereals and oilseeds)*
Chief Executive, Tom Taylor

ARCHITECTURE AND DESIGN SCOTLAND

Bakehouse Close, 146 Canongate, Edinburgh EH8 8DD
T 0131-556 6699 E info@ads.org.uk
W www.ads.org.uk

Architecture and Design Scotland (A+DS) was established in 2005 by the Scottish government as the national champion for good architecture, urban design and planning in the built environment; it works with a wide range of organisations at national, regional and local levels.

Chair, Karen Anderson
Chief Executive, Jim MacDonald

ARMED FORCES' PAY REVIEW BODY

6th Floor, Victoria House, Southampton Row, London WC1B 4AD
T 020-7271 0469 W www.ome.uk.com

The Armed Forces' Pay Review Body was appointed in 1971. It advises the prime minister and the Secretary of State for Defence on the pay and allowances of members of naval, military and air forces of the Crown.

Chair, John Steele
Members, Mary Carter; Prof. Peter Dolton; Very Revd. Dr Graham Forbes, CBE; Vice-Adm. Sir Richard Ibbotson, CB, KBE; Paul Kernaghan, CBE, QPM; Judy McKnight, CBE; John Steele

ARTS COUNCIL ENGLAND

14 Great Peter Street, London SW1P 3NQ
T 0845-300 6200 E enquiries@artscouncil.org.uk
W www.artscouncil.org.uk

Arts Council England is the national development agency for the arts in England. Using public money from government and the National Lottery, it supports a range of artistic activities, including theatre, music, literature, dance, photography, digital art, carnival and crafts. Between 2010 and 2015, Arts Council England is investing £1.9bn of public money from the government and around £1.1bn from the National Lottery.

The governing body, the national council, comprises 14 members, who are appointed by the Secretary of State for Culture, Media and Sport usually for a term of four years. There are also five councils, responsible for the agreement of area strategies, plans and priorities for action within the national framework.

National Council Chair, Sir Peter Bazalgette
National Council Members, Prof. Jon Cook; Joe Docherty; Sheila Healy; Sir Nicholas Kenyon; Keith Khan; Peter Phillips; Alistair Spalding, CBE; Rosemary Squire, OBE; Veronica Wadley
Chief Executive, Alan Davey

ARTS COUNCIL OF NORTHERN IRELAND

77 Malone Road, Belfast BT9 6AQ
T 028-9038 5200 E info@artscouncil-ni.org
W www.artscouncil-ni.org

The Arts Council of Northern Ireland is the prime distributor of government funds in support of the arts in Northern Ireland. It is funded by the Department of Culture, Arts and Leisure and from National Lottery funds.

Chair, Bob Collins
Members, David Alderdice; Anna Carragher; Damien Coyle *(Vice-Chair)*; Eibhlinn Ni Dhochartaigh; Noelle McAlinden; Katherine McCloskey; Prof. Ian Montgomery; Paul Mullan; Prof. Paul Seawright; Conor Shields; Brian Sore; Nisha Tandon; Janine Walker
Chief Executive, Roisin McDonough

ARTS COUNCIL OF WALES

Bute Place, Cardiff CF10 5AL
T 0845-873 4900 E info@artscouncilofwales.org.uk
W www.artswales.org.uk

The Arts Council of Wales was established in 1994 by royal charter and is the development body for the arts in Wales. It funds arts organisations with funding from the Welsh government and is the distributor of National Lottery funds to the arts in Wales. Grant-in-aid allocated by the Welsh government for 2013–14 totalled £34.25m.

Chair, Prof. Dai Smith
Members, Emma Evans; John Geraint; Michael Griffiths; Melanie Hawthorne; Dr Lesley Hodgson; Margaret Jervis, MBE; Andrew Miller; Osi Rhys Osmond; Richard Turner; Alan Watkin; Prof. Gerwyn Wiliams; John Carey Williams; Dr Kate Woodward; Marian Wyn Jones
Chief Executive, Nick Capaldi

AUDIT SCOTLAND

110 George Street, Edinburgh EH2 4LH
T 0845-146 1010 E info@auditscotland.gov.uk
W www.audit-scotland.gov.uk

Audit Scotland was set up in 2000 to provide services to the Accounts Commission and the Auditor-General for Scotland. Together they help to ensure that public-sector bodies in Scotland are held accountable for the proper, efficient and effective use of public funds.

Audit Scotland's work covers about 200 bodies including local authorities; health boards; further education colleges; Scottish Water; the Scottish government; government agencies such as the Prison Service and non-departmental public bodies such as the Scottish Police Authority and the Scottish Fire and Rescue Service.

Audit Scotland carries out financial and regularity audits to ensure that public-sector bodies adhere to the highest standards of financial management and governance. It also performs audits to ensure that these bodies achieve the best value for money. All of Audit Scotland's work in connection with local authorities is carried out for the Accounts Commission; its other work is undertaken for the Auditor-General.

Auditor-General, Caroline Gardner
Chair of the Accounts Commission, John Baillie

BANK OF ENGLAND

Threadneedle Street, London EC2R 8AH
T 020-7601 4444 E enquiries@bankofengland.co.uk
W www.bankofengland.co.uk

The Bank of England was incorporated in 1694 under royal charter. It was nationalised in 1946 under the Bank of England Act of that year which gave HM Treasury statutory powers over the bank. It is the banker of the government and it manages the issue of banknotes. Since 1998 it has been operationally independent and its Monetary Policy Committee has been responsible for setting short-term interest rates to meet the government's inflation target. Its responsibility for banking supervision was transferred to the Financial Services Authority in the same year. As the central reserve bank of the country, the Bank of England keeps the accounts of British banks, and of most overseas central banks; the larger banks and building societies are required to maintain with it a proportion of their cash resources. The bank's core purposes are monetary stability and financial stability. The Banking Act 2009 increased the responsibilities of the bank, including giving it a new financial stability objective and creating a special resolution regime for dealing with failing banks.

In 2013, through the Prudential Regulation Authority (PRA), the bank became responsible for the prudential regulation and supervision of banks, building societies, credit unions, insurers and major investment firms.

Governor, Mark Carney
Deputy Governors, Andrew Bailey; Charles Bean; Paul Tucker
Court of Directors, The Governor; the Deputy Governors; Sir Roger Carr; Michael Cohrs; Bradley Fried; Tim Frost; Sir David Lees; Dave Prentis; Lady Susan Rice; John Stewart
Monetary Policy Committee, The Governor; Charles Bean; Dr Ben Broadbent; Spencer Dale; Paul Fisher; Ian McCafferty; Prof. David Miles; Paul Tucker; Dr Martin Weale

Financial Policy Committee, The Governor; the Deputy Governors; Dame Clara Furse; Andy Haldane; Donald Kohn; Richard Sharp; Martin Taylor; Martin Wheatley
Chief Legal Adviser, Graham Nicholson
Chief Cashier and Executive Director, Banking Services, Chris Salmon
The Auditor, Stephen Brown

BIG LOTTERY FUND

1 Plough Place, London EC4A 1DE
T 020-7211 1800 **Advice Line** 0845-410 2030
E general.enquiries@biglotteryfund.org.uk
W www.biglotteryfund.org.uk

The Big Lottery Fund was launched in 2004, merging the New Opportunities Fund and the Lottery Charities Board (Community Fund). The fund is responsible for giving out 40 per cent of all funds raised for good causes by the National Lottery, amounting to around £600m a year. The money is distributed to charitable, benevolent and philanthropic organisations in the voluntary and community sectors, as well as health, education and environmental projects.

Chair, Peter Ainsworth
Vice-Chair, Anna Southall
Regional Chairs, Nat Sloane *(England)*; Frank Hewitt *(Northern Ireland)*; Maureen McGinn *(Scotland)*; Sir Adrian Webb *(Wales)*
Chief Executive, Dawn Austwick

BOUNDARY COMMISSIONS

ENGLAND
Room 3/21, 1 Horse Guards Road, London SW1A 2HQ
T 020-7276 1102 E information@bcommengland.gsi.gov.uk
W www.independent.gov.uk/boundarycommissionforengland
Deputy Chair, Hon. Mr Justice Sales

WALES
Hastings House, Fitzalan Court, Cardiff CF24 0BL
T 029-2046 4819 E bcomm.wales@wales.gsi.gov.uk
W www.bcomm-wales.gov.uk
Deputy Chair, Hon. Mr Wyn Williams

SCOTLAND
Thistle House, 91 Haymarket Terrace, Edinburgh EH12 5HD
T 0131-538 7510 E bcs@scottishboundaries.gov.uk
W www.bcomm-scotland.gov.uk
Deputy Chair, Hon. Lord Woolman

NORTHERN IRELAND
Forestview, Purdy's Lane, Belfast BT8 7AR
T 028-9069 4800 E bcni@belfast.org.uk
W www.boundarycommission.org.uk
Deputy Chair, Hon. Mr Justice McCloskey

The commissions, established in 1944, are constituted under the Parliamentary Constituencies Act 1986 (as amended). The Speaker of the House of Commons is the *ex officio* chair of all four commissions in the UK.

Following the passing of the Parliamentary Voting System and Constituencies Act 2011, the number of Westminster constituencies will be reduced from 650 to 600. The act also required each of the four commissions to review the parliamentary constituencies in their part of the UK every five years. All four of the boundary commissions commenced their sixth reviews of UK Parliament Constituencies in March 2011. However, on 29 January 2013, parliament amended the legislation governing the sixth review, so the commissions are no longer required to complete their respective reviews. The revised legislation requires that the next reviews of UK parliament constituencies are undertaken using the electoral register from 1 September 2015; these reviews must be submitted during September 2018.

BRITISH BROADCASTING CORPORATION (BBC)

Television Centre, Wood Lane, London W12 7RJ
T 020-8743 8000 W www.bbc.co.uk

The BBC was incorporated under royal charter in 1926 as the successor to the British Broadcasting Company Ltd. The BBC's current charter, which came into force on 1 January 2007 and extends to 31 December 2016, recognises the BBC's editorial independence and sets out its public purposes. The BBC Trust was formed under the new charter and replaces the Board of Governors; it sets the strategic direction of the BBC and has a duty to represent the interests of licence fee payers. The chair, vice-chair and other trustees are appointed by the Queen-in-Council. The BBC is financed by television licence revenue and by grant-in-aid from parliament for the World Service (radio). *See also* Broadcasting.

BBC TRUST MEMBERS
Chair, Lord Patten, CH, PC
Vice-Chair, Dr Diane Coyle, OBE
National Trustees, Alison Hastings *(England);* Aideen McGinley, OBE *(Northern Ireland);* Bill Matthews *(Scotland);* Elan Closs Stephens *(Wales)*
Trustees, Sonita Alleyne, OBE; Richard Ayre; Anthony Fry; David Liddiment; Suzanna Taverne; Lord Williams of Baglan

EXECUTIVE BOARD
Director-General and Chair, Tony Hall
Directors, Lucy Adams *(HR, BBC Academy and Internal Communications);* Helen Boaden *(Radio);* Anne Bulford, OBE *(Operations and Finance);* Danny Cohen *(Television);* Tim Davie *(Audio and Music);* James Harding *(News and Current Affairs);* James Purnell *(Strategy & Digital)*
Non-Executive Directors, Simon Burke; Sally Davis; Brian McBride; Dame Fiona Reynolds, DBE

STATION CONTROLLERS
BBC1, Charlotte Moore
BBC2, Janice Hadlow
BBC3, Zai Bennett
BBC News Channel, Sam Taylor
BBC Parliament, Peter Knowles
BBC Northern Ireland, Peter Johnston
BBC Scotland, Ken MacQuarrie
BBC Wales, Rhodri Talfan-Davies
CBBC, Damian Kavanagh
CBeebies, Cheryl Taylor
Radio 1 and 1Xtra, Ben Cooper
Radio 2, 6 Music and Asian Network, Bob Shennan
Radio 3, Roger Wright
Radio 4, Gwyneth Williams
Radio 5 Live and 5 Live Sports Extra, Jonathan Wall

BRITISH COUNCIL

Bridgewater House, 58 Whitworth Street, Manchester M1 6BB
T 0161-957 7755 E general.enquiries@britishcouncil.org
W www.britishcouncil.org

The British Council was established in 1934, incorporated by royal charter in 1940 and granted a supplemental charter in 1993. It is an independent, non-political organisation

which promotes Britain abroad and is the UK's international organisation for educational and cultural relations. The British Council is represented in over 200 towns and cities in over 100 countries.
Chair, Vernon Ellis
Chief Executive, Martin Davidson, CMG

BRITISH FILM INSTITUTE

21 Stephen Street, London W1T 1LN
T 020-7255 1444 W www.bfi.org.uk

The BFI, established in 1933, offers opportunities for people throughout the UK to experience, learn and discover more about the world of film and moving image culture. It incorporates the BFI National Archive, the BFI Reuben Library, BFI Southbank, BFI Distribution, the annual BFI London Film Festival as well as the BFI London Lesbian and Gay Film Festival, and the BFI IMAX cinema. It also publishes the monthly *Sight and Sound* magazine and provides advice and support for regional cinemas and film festivals across the UK.

Following the closure of the UK Film Council in April 2011, the BFI became the lead body for film in the UK, in charge of allocating lottery money for the development and production of new British films.
Chair, Greg Dyke
Chief Executive, Amanda Nevill

BRITISH LIBRARY

96 Euston Road, London NW1 2DB
T 0843-208 1144 E customer-services@bl.uk
W www.bl.uk

The British Library was established in 1973. It is the UK's national library and occupies a key position in the library and information network. It aims to serve scholarship, research, industry, commerce and all other major users of information. Its services are based on a collection of over 150 million separate items, including books, journals, manuscripts, maps, stamps, music, patents, newspapers and sound recordings in all written and spoken languages. The library is now based at three sites: London (St Pancras and Colindale) and Boston Spa, W. Yorks. The library's sponsoring department is the Department for Culture, Media and Sport.

Access to the reading rooms at St Pancras is limited to holders of a British Library reader's pass; information about eligibility is available from the reader admissions office. The exhibition galleries and public areas are open to all, free of charge.

BRITISH LIBRARY BOARD
Chair, Rt. Hon. Baroness Blackstone
Members, Dawn Airey; David Barclay; Dr Robert Black, CBE, FRSA, FRSE; Prof. Sir Kenneth Calman; Rt. Hon. Lord Fellowes, GCB, GCVO; Prof. Dame Wendy Hall, CBE; Roly Keating; Dr Mike Lynch, OBE; Prof. Kate McLuskie; Dr Stephen Page; Patrick Plant; Maggie Semple, OBE

EXECUTIVE
Chief Executive, Roly Keating
Director, Collections, Caroline Brazier
Director, Audiences, Frances Brindle
Chief Operating Officer, Phil Spence
Chief Digital Officer, Richard Boulderstone
Chief Financial Officer, Steve Morris

BRITISH LIBRARY NEWSPAPERS

Colindale Avenue, London NW9 5HE
T 020-7412 7353

BRITISH LIBRARY, BOSTON SPA

Boston Spa, Wetherby, W. Yorks LS23 7BQ
T 01937-546070

BRITISH MUSEUM

Great Russell Street, London WC1B 3DG
T 020-7323 8000 E information@britishmuseum.org
W www.britishmuseum.org

The British Museum houses the national collection of antiquities, ethnography, coins and paper money, medals, prints and drawings. The British Museum may be said to date from 1753, when parliament approved the holding of a public lottery to raise funds for the purchase of the collections of Sir Hans Sloane and the Harleian manuscripts, and for their proper housing and maintenance. The building (Montagu House) was opened in 1759. The existing buildings were erected between 1823 and the present day, and the original collection has increased to its current dimensions by gifts and purchases. Total government grant-in-aid for 2013–14 is £43.9m.
Chair, Niall Fitzgerald, KBE
Trustees, Karen Armstrong; Prof. Sir Christopher Bayly; Hon. Nigel Boardman; Cheryl Carolus; Dame Liz Forgan, DBE; Prof. Clive Gamble; Anthony Gormley, OBE; Penny Hughes, CBE; Sir George Iacobescu, CBE; James Lupton, CBE; John Micklethwait; Sir Paul Nurse, PRS; Gavin Patterson; Prof. Amartya Sen; Sir Martin Sorrell; Ahdaf Soueif; Lord Stern of Brentford, FBA; Lord Turner of Ecchinswell; Baroness Wheatcroft of Blackheath

OFFICERS
Director, Neil MacGregor, OM, FSA
Deputy Director, Joanna Mackle

KEEPERS
Keeper of Africa, Oceania and the Americas, Lissant Bolton
Keeper of Ancient Egypt and Sudan, Neal Spencer
Keeper of Asia, Jan Stuart
Keeper of Coins and Medals, Philip Attwood
Keeper of Greece and Rome, J. Lesley Fitton
Keeper of the Middle East, John Curtis
Keeper of Prehistory and Europe and Head of Portable Antiquities and Treasure, Roger Bland
Keeper of Prints and Drawings, Hugo Chapman
Keeper of Conservation and Scientific Research, David Saunders

BRITISH PHARMACOPOEIA COMMISSION

151 Buckingham Palace Road, London SW1W 9SZ
T 020-3080 6561 E bpcom@mhra.gsi.gov.uk
W www.pharmacopoeia.com

The British Pharmacopoeia Commission sets standards for medicinal products used in human and veterinary medicines and is responsible for publication of the *British Pharmacopoeia* (a publicly available statement of the standard that a product must meet throughout its shelf-life), the *British Pharmacopoeia (Veterinary)* and the *British Approved Names.* It has 17 members, including two lay members, who are appointed by the Department of Health.
Chair, vacant
Vice-Chair, Mr V'lain Fenton-May
Secretary and Scientific Director, Dr S. Atkinson

CARE QUALITY COMMISSION

Finsbury Tower, 103–105 Bunhill Row, London EC1Y 8TG
T 0300-061 6161 E enquiries@cqc.org.uk W www.cqc.org.uk

The Care Quality Commission (CQC) is the independent regulator of health and adult social care services in England, including care provided by the NHS, local authorities, private companies and voluntary organisations. It is also in CQC's remit to protect the interests of people whose rights are restricted under the Mental Health Act.

Chair, David Prior
Board Members, Louis Appleby; Anna Bradley; Camilla Cavendish; Paul Corrigan; Dr Jennifer Dixon; John Harwood; Steve Hitchens; Michael Mire; Kay Sheldon
Chief Executive, David Behan

CENTRAL ARBITRATION COMMITTEE

22nd Floor, Euston Tower, 286 Euston Road, London NW1 3JJ
T 020-7904 2300 E enquiries@cac.gov.uk W www.cac.gov.uk

The Central Arbitration Committee (CAC) is a permanent independent body with statutory powers whose main function is to adjudicate on applications relating to the statutory recognition and de-recognition of trade unions for collective bargaining purposes, where such recognition or de-recognition cannot be agreed voluntarily. In addition, the CAC has a statutory role in determining disputes between trade unions and employers over the disclosure of information for collective bargaining purposes, and in resolving applications and complaints under the information and consultation regulations, and performs a similar role in relation to the legislation on the European Works Council, European companies, European cooperative societies and cross-border mergers. The CAC and its predecessors have also provided voluntary arbitration in collective disputes, but this role has not been used for some years.

Chair, Sir Michael Burton
Chief Executive, Simon Gouldstone

CERTIFICATION OFFICE FOR TRADE UNIONS AND EMPLOYERS' ASSOCIATIONS

Euston Tower, 286 Euston Road, London NW1 3JJ
T 020-7210 3734 E info@certoffice.org
W www.certoffice.org

The Certification Office is an independent statutory authority. The Certification Officer is appointed by the Secretary of State for Business, Innovation and Skills and is responsible for maintaining a list of trade unions and employers' associations; ensuring compliance with statutory requirements and keeping available for public inspection annual returns from trade unions and employers' associations; determining complaints concerning trade union elections, certain ballots and certain breaches of trade union rules; ensuring observance of statutory requirements governing mergers between trade unions and employers' associations; overseeing the political funds and finances of trade unions and employers' associations; and for certifying the independence of trade unions.

The Certification Officer, David Cockburn

CHURCH COMMISSIONERS

Church House, Great Smith Street, London SW1P 3AZ
T 020-7898 1000 E commissioners.enquiry@churchofengland.org
W www.churchofengland.org/about-us/structure/churchcommissioners

The Church Commissioners were established in 1948 by the amalgamation of Queen Anne's Bounty (established 1704) and the Ecclesiastical Commissioners (established 1836). They are responsible for the management of some of the Church of England's assets, the income from which is predominantly used to help pay for the stipend and pension of the clergy and to support the church's work throughout the country. The commissioners own UK and global company shares, over 43,000ha (106,000 acres) of agricultural land, a residential estate in central London, and commercial property across Great Britain, plus an interest in overseas property via managed funds. They also carry out administrative duties in connection with pastoral reorganisation and closed churches.

The 33 commissioners are: the Archbishops of Canterbury and of York; eleven people elected by the General Synod, comprising four bishops, three clergy and four lay persons; three Church Estates Commissioners; two cathedral deans; nine people appointed by the crown and the archbishops; six holders of state office, comprising the Prime Minister, the Lord Chancellor, the Lord President of the Council, the Secretary of State for Culture, Media and Sport, the Speaker of the House of Commons and the Lord Speaker.

CHURCH ESTATES COMMISSIONERS
First, A. Whittam Smith, CBE
Second, Sir Tony Baldry, MP
Third, Andrew Mackie

OFFICERS
Chief Executive, Secretary, Andrew Brown
Official Solicitor, Stephen Slack

COAL AUTHORITY

200 Lichfield Lane, Mansfield, Notts NG18 4RG
T 01623-637000 E thecoalauthority@coal.gov.uk
W http://coal.decc.gov.uk

The Coal Authority was established under the Coal Industry Act 1994 to manage certain functions previously undertaken by British Coal, including ownership of unworked coal. It is responsible for licensing coal mining operations and for providing information on coal reserves and past and future coal mining. It settles subsidence damage claims which are not the responsibility of licensed coal mining operators. It deals with the management and disposal of property, and with surface hazards such as abandoned coal mine entries and mine water discharges.

Chair, Stephen Dingle
Chief Executive, Philip Lawrence

COMMITTEE ON STANDARDS IN PUBLIC LIFE

1 Horseguards Road, London SW1A 2HQ
T 020-7271 2948 E public@standards.gsi.gov.uk
W www.public-standards.org.uk

The Committee on Standards in Public Life was set up in October 1994. It is formed of 10 people appointed by the prime minister, comprising the chair, three political members nominated by the leaders of the three main political parties and six independent members. The committee's remit is to examine concerns about standards of conduct of all holders of public office, including arrangements relating to financial and commercial activities, and to make recommendations as to any changes in present arrangements which might be required to ensure the highest standards of propriety in public life. It is also charged with reviewing issues in relation to the funding of political parties. The committee does not investigate individual allegations of misconduct.

Chair, Lord Paul Bew
Members, Rt. Hon. Dame Margaret Beckett, DBE, MP; Oliver Heald, MP; Patricia Moberly; Sir Derek Morris; Dame Denise Platt, DBE; David Prince, CBE; Sheila Drew Smith, OBE; Richard Thomas, CBE

COMMONWEALTH WAR GRAVES COMMISSION

2 Marlow Road, Maidenhead, Berks SL6 7DX
T 01628-634221 E casualty.enq@cwgc.org
W www.cwgc.org

The Commonwealth War Graves Commission (formerly Imperial War Graves Commission) was founded by royal charter in 1917. It is responsible for the commemoration of around 1.7 million members of the forces of the Commonwealth who lost their lives in the two world wars. More than one million graves are maintained in 23,274 burial grounds throughout the world. Over three-quarters of a million men and women who have no known grave or who were cremated are commemorated by name on memorials built by the commission.

The funds of the commission are derived from the six participating governments, ie the UK, Canada, Australia, New Zealand, South Africa and India.

President, HRH The Duke of Kent, KG, GCMG, GCVO, ADC
Chair, Secretary of State for Defence (UK)
Vice-Chair, Air Chief Marshal Sir Joe French, KCB, CBE
Members, High Commissioners in London for Australia, Canada, India, New Zealand and South Africa; Edward Chaplin, CMG, OBE; Robert Fox, MBE; Kevan Jones, MP; Hon. Ros Kelly; Vice-Adm. Sir Tim Laurence, KCVO, CB; Keith Simpson, MP; Prof. Sir Hew Strachan, FRSE
Director-General and Secretary to the Commission, Alan Pateman-Jones
Director of Legal Services, Gillian Stedman

COMPETITION COMMISSION

Victoria House, Southampton Row, London WC1B 4AD
T 020-7271 0100 E info@cc.gsi.gov.uk
W www.competition-commission.org.uk

The commission was established in 1948 as the Monopolies and Restrictive Practices Commission (later the Monopolies and Mergers Commission); it became the Competition Commission in April 1999 under the Competition Act 1998. The commission conducts in-depth inquiries into mergers, markets and the regulation of major industries. Every inquiry the commission undertakes is in response to a reference made to it by another authority, usually the Office of Fair Trading. The commission has no power to conduct inquiries on its own initiative. The Enterprise Act 2002 introduced a new regime for the assessment of mergers and markets in the UK – in most related investigations the commission is responsible for making decisions on the competition questions and for making and implementing decisions on appropriate remedies.

The operations of the Competition Commission and the Office of Fair Trading will merge in 2014 to form the Competition and Markets Authority (CMA), subject to legislation.

Chair, Roger Witcomb
Deputy Chairs, Martin Cave, OBE; Simon Polito; Alasdair Smith
Council Members, Pamela Boys, CB; Grey Denham; Dame Janet Paraskeva; Lesley Watkins
Chief Executive, Secretary and Accounting Officer, David Saunders

COMPETITION SERVICE

Victoria House, Bloomsbury Place, London WC1A 2EB
T 020-7979 7979 E info@catribunal.org.uk
W www.catribunal.org.uk

The Competition Service is the financial corporate body by which the Competition Appeal Tribunal is administered and through which it receives funding for the performance of its judicial functions.

Registrar, Charles Dhanowa, OBE, QC

CONSUMER COUNCIL FOR WATER

Victoria Square House, Victoria Square, Birmingham B2 4AJ
T 0121-345 1000 E enquiries@ccwater.org.uk
W www.ccwater.org.uk

The Consumer Council for Water was established in 2005 under the Water Act 2003 to represent consumers' interests in respect of price, service and value for money from their water and sewerage services, and to investigate complaints from customers about their water company. There are four regional committees in England and one in Wales.

Chair, Dame Yvonne Buckland, DBE

CORPORATION OF TRINITY HOUSE

Trinity House, Tower Hill, London EC3N 4DH
T 020-7481 6900 E enquiries@thls.org
W www.trinityhouse.co.uk

The Corporation of Trinity House is the General Lighthouse Authority for England, Wales and the Channel Islands, and was granted its first charter by Henry VIII in 1514. Its remit is to assist the safe passage of a variety of vessels through some of the busiest sea-lanes in the world; it does this by deploying and maintaining approximately 600 aids to navigation, ranging from lighthouses to a satellite navigation service. The corporation also has certain statutory jurisdiction over aids to navigation maintained by local harbour authorities and is responsible for marking or dispersing wrecks dangerous to navigation, except those occurring within port limits or wrecks of HM ships.

The statutory duties of Trinity House are funded by the General Lighthouse Fund, which is provided from light dues levied on ships calling at ports of the UK and the Republic of Ireland. The corporation is a deep-sea pilotage authority, authorised by the Secretary of State for Transport to license deep-sea pilots. In addition Trinity House is a charitable organisation that maintains a number of retirement homes for mariners and their dependants, funds a four-year training scheme for those seeking a career in the merchant navy, and also dispenses grants to a wide range of maritime charities. The charity work is wholly funded by its own activities.

The corporation is controlled by a board of Elder Brethren; a separate board controls the Lighthouse Service. The Elder Brethren also act as nautical assessors in marine cases in the Admiralty Division of the High Court.

ELDER BRETHREN
Master, HRH The Princess Royal, KG, KT, GCVO
Deputy Master, Capt. Ian McNaught
Wardens, Simon Sherrard *(Nether)*; Cdre David Squire, CBE, FNI, FCMI *(Rental)*
Elder Brethren, HRH The Duke of Edinburgh, KG, KT, OM, GBE; HRH The Prince of Wales, KG, KT, GCB; HRH The Duke of York, KG, GCVO, ADC; Capt. Roger Barker; Adm. Lord Boyce, KG, GCB, OBE; Lord Browne of Madingley; Capt. John Burton-Hall, RD; Lord Carrington, KG, GCMG, CH, PC; Viscount Cobham; Capt. Sir Malcolm Edge, KCVO; Capt. Ian Gibb; Capt. Duncan Glass, OBE; Capt. Stephen Gobbi; Lord Greenway; Rear-Adm. Sir Jeremy de Halpert, KCVO, CB; Capt. Nigel Hope, RD; Lord Mackay of Clashfern, KT, PC; Sir John Major, KG, CH; Capt. Peter Mason, CBE; Cdre. Peter Melson, CVO, CBE, RN; Capt. David Orr; Capt. Nigel Palmer, OBE; Sir John Parker, FRENG; Douglas Potter;

Capt. Nigel Pryke; Capt. Derek Richards, RD, RNR; Lord Robertson of Port Ellen, KT, GCMG, PC; Rear-Adm. Sir Patrick Rowe, KCVO, CBE; Cdre. Jim Scorer; Simon Sherrard; Adm. Sir Jock Slater, GCB, LVO; Rear-Adm. David Snelson, CB, FNI; Cdre. David Squire, CBE, RFA; Rear-Adm. Lord Sterling of Plaistow, GCVO, CBE, RNR; Capt. Colin Stewart, LVO; Sir Adrian Swire, AE; Capt. Sir Miles Wingate, KCVO; Capt. Thomas Woodfield, OBE; Capt. Richard Woodman

OFFICERS
Secretary, Cdr Graham Hockley
Director of Finance, Jerry Wedge
Director of Navigation, Capt. Roger Barker
Director of Operations, Cdre. Jim Scorer

CREATIVE SCOTLAND

Waverley Gate, 2–4 Waterloo Place, Edinburgh EH1 3EG
T 0330-333 2000 E enquiries@creativescotland.com
W www.creativescotland.com

Creative Scotland is the organisation tasked with leading the development of the arts, creative and screen industries across Scotland. It was created in 2010 as an amalgamation of the Scottish Arts Council and Scottish Screen, and it encourages and sustains the arts through investment in the form of grants, bursaries, loans and equity. It aims to invest in talent; artistic production; audiences, access and participation; and the cultural economy. The budget for 2012–13 was £52m.
Chair, Sir Sandy Crombie
Board, Peter Cabrelli; Gwilym Gibbons; Steve Grimmond; Prof. Robin MacPherson; Barclay Price; Dr Gary West; Ruth Wishart
Chief Executive, Janet Archer

CRIMINAL CASES REVIEW COMMISSION

5 Philip's Place, Birmingham B3 2PW
T 0121-233 1473 E info@ccrc.gov.uk
W www.ccrc.gov.uk

The Criminal Cases Review Commission is the independent body set up under the Criminal Appeal Act 1995. It is a non-departmental public body reporting to parliament via the Lord Chancellor and Secretary of State for Justice. It is responsible for investigating possible miscarriages of justice in England, Wales and Northern Ireland, and deciding whether or not to refer cases back to an appeal court. Members of the commission are appointed in accordance with the Commissioner for Public Appointments' code of practice.
Chair, Richard Foster, CBE
Members, Penelope Barrett; Jim England; Angela Flower; Julie Goulding; Celia Hughes; Alistair R. MacGregor, QC; Paul Mageean; Ian Nichol; Ewen Smith; Ranjit Sondhi
Chief Executive, Karen Kneller

CRIMINAL INJURIES COMPENSATION AUTHORITY (CICA)

Tay House, 300 Bath Street, Glasgow G2 4LN
Helpline: 0300-003 3601
W www.justice.gov.uk/about/criminal-injuries-compensation-authority

CICA is the government body responsible for administering the Criminal Injuries Compensation Scheme in England, Scotland and Wales (separate arrangements apply in Northern Ireland). CICA deals with every aspect of applications for compensation under the 1996, 2001 and 2008 Criminal Injuries Compensation Schemes and can make awards of between £1,000 and £500,000. Appeals against decisions made by CICA can be put to the First-tier Tribunal (Criminal Injuries Compensation) (*see* Tribunals).
Chief Executive, Carole Oatway

CROFTING COMMISSION

Great Glen House, Leachkin Road, Inverness IV3 8NW
T 01463-663450 E info@croftingscotland.gov.uk
W www.croftingscotland.gov.uk

The Crofting Commission was established on 1 April 2012, taking over the regulation of crofting from the Crofters Commission. The aim of the Crofting Commission is to regulate crofting, to promote the occupancy of crofts, active land use, and shared management of the land by crofters, as a means of sustaining and enhancing rural communities in Scotland.
Chief Executive, Catriona Maclean

DISCLOSURE AND BARRING SERVICE

PO Box 110, Liverpool L69 3EF
T 0870-909 0811 E customerservices@dbs.gsi.gov.uk
W https://www.gov.uk/government/organisations/disclosure-and-barring-service

The Disclosure and Barring Service (DBS) is an executive non-departmental public body of the Home Office. It helps employers make safer recruitment decisions and prevent unsuitable people from working with vulnerable groups, including children. It was formed on 1 December 2012 and replaces the Criminal Records Bureau (CRB) and Independent Safeguarding Authority (ISA). The DBS is responsible for the children's barred list and adults' barred list for England, Wales and Northern Ireland.
Chair, Bill Griffiths
Chief Executive, Adriènne Kelbie

ENGLISH HERITAGE (HISTORIC BUILDINGS AND MONUMENTS COMMISSION FOR ENGLAND)

1 Waterhouse Square, 138–142 Holborn, London EC1N 2ST
T 020-7973 3000 W www.english-heritage.org.uk

English Heritage was established under the National Heritage Act 1983. On 1 April 1999 it merged with the Royal Commission on the Historical Monuments of England to become the new lead body for England's historic environment. It is sponsored by the Department for Culture, Media and Sport and its duties are to carry out and sponsor archaeological, architectural and scientific surveys and research designed to increase the understanding of England's past and its changing condition; to identify buildings, monuments and landscapes for protection while also offering expert advice, skills and grants to conserve these sites; to encourage town planners to make imaginative re-use of historic buildings to aid regeneration of the centres of cities, towns and villages; to manage and curate selected sites; and to curate and make publicly accessible the English Heritage Archive (formerly known as the National Monuments Record), whose records of over one million historic sites and buildings, and extensive collections of photographs, maps, drawings and reports, constitute the central database and archive of England's historic environment.
Chair, Baroness Andrews, OBE
Commissioners, Lynda Addison, OBE; Prof. Sir Barry Cunliffe, CBE; Peter Draper; David Fursdon; Prof. Ronald Hutton; Jane Kennedy; Vice-Adm. Sir Tim Laurence, KCVO, CB, ADC; Martin Moore; Graham Morrison; John Walker, CBE; Baroness Young of Hornsey, OBE
Chief Executive, Dr Simon Thurley

ENVIRONMENT AGENCY

National Customer Contact Centre, PO Box 544, Rotherham S60 1BY
T 0370-850 6506 E enquiries@environment-agency.gov.uk,
Incident Hotline 0800-807060
W www.environment-agency.gov.uk

Established in 1996 under the Environment Act 1995, the Environment Agency is a non-departmental public body sponsored by the Department for Environment, Food and Rural Affairs. On 1 April 2013, Natural Resources Wales took over the Environment Agency's responsibilities in Wales. Around 70 per cent of the agency's funding is from the government, with the rest raised from various charging schemes. The agency is responsible for pollution prevention and control in England and for the management and use of water resources, including flood defences, fisheries and navigation. Its remit also includes: scrutinising potentially hazardous business operations; helping businesses to use resources more efficiently; taking action against those who do not take environmental responsibilities seriously; looking after wildlife; working with farmers; helping people get the most out of their environment; and improving the quality of inner city areas and parks by restoring rivers and lakes.

The Environment Agency has head offices in London and Bristol, and six regional offices. Its total grant-in-aid for 2013–14 is £662m.

Chair, Rt. Hon. Lord Smith of Finsbury
Board Members, Peter Ainsworth; Karen Burrows; Dr Clive Elphick; Emma Howard Boyd; Richard Leafe; Robert Light; Richard McDonald; John Varley; Jeremy Walker
Chief Executive, Paul Leinster, CBE

EQUALITY AND HUMAN RIGHTS COMMISSION

Arndale House, The Arndale Centre, Manchester M4 3AQ
T 0161-829 8100 E info@equalityhumanrights.com
W www.equalityhumanrights.com

The Equality and Human Rights Commission (EHRC) is a statutory body, established under the Equality Act 2006 and launched in October 2007. It inherited the responsibilities of the Commission for Racial Equality, the Disability Rights Commission and the Equal Opportunities Commission. The EHRC's purpose is to reduce inequality, eliminate discrimination, strengthen relations between people, and promote and protect human rights. It enforces equality legislation on age, disability and health, gender, race, religion and belief, sexual orientation or transgender status, and encourages compliance with the Human Rights Act 1998 throughout England, Wales and Scotland.

Chair, Baroness O'Neill of Bengarve, CBE, PHD, FBA
Deputy Chair, Caroline Waters, OBE
Commissioners, Sarah Anderson, CBE; Evelyn Asante-Mensah, OBE; Ann Beynon, OBE; Laura Carstensen; Chris Holmes, MBE; Kaliani Lyle; Prof. Sarwan Singh; Sarah Veale, CBE
Chief Executive, Mark Hammond

EQUALITY COMMISSION FOR NORTHERN IRELAND

Equality House, 7–9 Shaftesbury Square, Belfast BT2 7DP
T 028-9050 0600 **Textphone** 028-9050 0589
E information@equalityni.org W www.equalityni.org

The Equality Commission was set up in 1999 under the Northern Ireland Act 1998 and is responsible for promoting equality, keeping the relevant legislation under review, eliminating discrimination on the grounds of race, disability, sexual orientation, gender (including marital and civil partner status, gender reassignment, pregnancy and maternity), age, religion and political opinion and for overseeing the statutory duties on public authorities to promote equality of opportunity and good relations.

Chief Commissioner, Dr Michael Wardlow
Deputy Chief Commissioner, Jane Morrice
Chief Executive, Evelyn Collins, CBE, FRSA

GAMBLING COMMISSION

Victoria Square House, Victoria Square, Birmingham B2 4BP
T 0121-230 6666
E info@gamblingcommission.gov.uk
W www.gamblingcommission.gov.uk

The Gambling Commission was established under the Gambling Act 2005, and took over the role previously occupied by the Gaming Board for Great Britain in regulating and licensing all commercial gambling – apart from spread betting and the National Lottery – ie casinos, bingo, betting, remote gambling, gaming machines and lotteries. It also advises local and central government on related issues, and is responsible for the protection of children and the vulnerable from being exploited or harmed by gambling. The commission is sponsored by the Department for Culture, Media and Sport, with its work funded by licence fees paid by the gambling industry.

Chair, Philip Graf
Chief Executive, Jenny Williams

HEALTH AND SAFETY EXECUTIVE

Redgrave Court, Merton Road, Bootle, Merseyside L20 7HS
Incident Centre 0845-300 9923 W www.hse.gov.uk

The Health and Safety Commission (HSC) and the Health and Safety Executive (HSE) merged on 1 April 2008 to form a single national regulatory body – the HSE – responsible for promoting the cause of better health and safety at work. The HSE is sponsored by the Department for Work and Pensions.

HSE regulates all industrial and commercial sectors except operations in the air and at sea. This includes agriculture, construction, manufacturing, services, transport, mines, offshore oil and gas, quarries and major hazard sites in chemicals and petrochemicals.

HSE is responsible for developing and enforcing health and safety law; providing guidance and advice; commissioning research; conducting inspections and accident and ill-health investigations; developing standards; and licensing or approving some work activities such as asbestos removal. The HSE's nuclear directorate merged with a number of other bodies on 1 April 2011 to form the Office for Nuclear Regulation, an agency of the HSE.

Chair, Judith Hackitt, CBE
Board Members, Nick Baldwin; Jonathan Baume; George Brechin; Isobel Garner; David Gartside; Paul Kenny; John C. Morgan; Frances Outram; Prof. Richard Taylor; Sarah Veale, CBE
Chief Executive, Geoffrey Podger, CB

HER MAJESTY'S OFFICERS OF ARMS

COLLEGE OF ARMS (HERALDS' COLLEGE)
130 Queen Victoria Street, London EC4V 4BT
T 020-7248 2762 E enquiries@college-of-arms.gov.uk
W www.college-of-arms.gov.uk

The Sovereign's Officers of Arms (Kings, Heralds and Pursuivants of Arms) were first incorporated by Richard III in 1484. The powers vested by the crown in the Earl Marshal (the Duke of Norfolk) with regard to state ceremonial are largely exercised through the college. The college is also the official repository of the arms and pedigrees of English, Welsh, Northern Irish and Commonwealth (except Canadian) families and their descendants, and its records include official copies of the records of the Ulster King of Arms, the originals of which remain in Dublin. The 13 officers of the college specialise in genealogical and heraldic work for their respective clients.

Arms have long been, and still are, granted by letters patent from the Kings of Arms. A right to arms can only be established by the registration in the official records of the College of Arms of a pedigree showing direct male line descent from an ancestor already appearing therein as being entitled to arms, or by making application through the College of Arms for a grant of arms. Grants are made to corporations as well as to individuals.

Earl Marshal, Duke of Norfolk

KINGS OF ARMS

Garter, T. Woodcock, CVO, FSA
Clarenceux, P. L. Dickinson, LVO
Norroy and Ulster, Sir Henry Paston-Bedingfeld, Bt.

HERALDS

Chester, T. H. S. Duke
Lancaster, R. J. B. Noel
Windsor (and Registrar), W. G. Hunt, TD
Somerset, D. V. White
Richmond (and Earl Marshal's Secretary), C. E. A. Cheesman, FSA
York, M. P. D. O'Donoghue

PURSUIVANT

Portcullis, Hon. C. J. Fletcher-Vane

COURT OF THE LORD LYON

HM New Register House, Edinburgh EH1 3YT
T 0131-556 7255 W www.lyon-court.com

Her Majesty's Officers of Arms in Scotland perform ceremonial duties and in addition may be consulted by members of the public on heraldic and genealogical matters in a professional capacity.

KING OF ARMS

Lord Lyon King of Arms, David Sellar, FSA SCOT, FRHISTS

HERALDS

Rothesay, Sir Crispin Agnew of Lochnaw, Bt., QC
Snawdoun, Mrs C. G. W. Roads, LVO, FSA, FSA SCOT
Marchmont, The Hon. Adam Bruce, WS

PURSUIVANTS

Ormond, Mark D. Dennis
Dingwall, Mrs Derek Holton
Unicorn, John Malden

EXTRAORDINARY OFFICERS

Orkney Herald Extraordinary, Sir Malcolm Innes of Edingight, KCVO, WS
Angus Herald Extraordinary, R. O. Blair, CVO, WS
Islay Herald Extraordinary, Alastair Campbell of Airds
Ross Herald Extraordinary, C. J. Burnett, FSA SCOT

HERALD PAINTER

Herald Painter, Mrs Derek Holton

HIGHLANDS AND ISLANDS ENTERPRISE

Cowan House, Inverness Retail and Business Park, Inverness IV2 7GF
T 01463-234171 E info@hient.co.uk W www.hie.co.uk

Highlands and Islands Enterprise (HIE) was set up under the Enterprise and New Towns (Scotland) Act 1991. Its role is to deliver community and economic development in line with the Scottish government economic strategy. It focuses on helping high-growth businesses, improving regional competitiveness and strengthening communities. HIE's budget for 2013–14 is £75.9m.

Chair, Prof. Lorne Crerar
Chief Executive, Alex Paterson

HISTORIC ROYAL PALACES

Apartment 39A, Hampton Court Palace, Surrey KT8 9AU
T 0844-482 7777 E operators@hrp.org.uk W www.hrp.org.uk

Historic Royal Palaces was established in 1998 as a royal charter body with charitable status and is contracted by the Secretary of State for Culture, Media and Sport to manage the palaces on his behalf. The palaces – the Tower of London, Hampton Court Palace, the Banqueting House, Kensington Palace and Kew Palace – are owned by the Queen on behalf of the nation.

The organisation is governed by a board comprising a chair and 11 non-executive trustees. The chief executive is accountable to the board of trustees and ultimately to parliament. Historic Royal Palaces receives no funding from the government or the Crown.

TRUSTEES

Chair, Charles Mackay, CBE
Appointed by the Queen, Val Gooding, CBE; Sir Trevor McDonald, OBE; Jonathan Marsden, CVO, FSA; Sir Alan Reid, GCVO *(Deputy Chair)*
Appointed by the Secretary of State, Sophie Andreae, DSG, FSA; Dawn Austwick, OBE; Ian Barlow; Liz Cleaver; Malcolm Reading; Louise Wilson, FRSA
Ex officio, Gen. Lord Dannatt, GCB, CBE, MC *(Constable of the Tower of London)*

OFFICER

Chief Executive, Michael Day

HOMES AND COMMUNITIES AGENCY

Maple House, 149 Tottenham Court Road, London W1T 7BN
T 0300-1234 500 E mail@homesandcommunities.co.uk
W www.homesandcommunities.co.uk

The Homes and Communities Agency (HCA) is the national housing regeneration agency for England. With a capital investment budget of around £4bn for 2012–15, the HCA contributes to economic growth by delivering high-quality affordable housing. The HCA also provides investment to improve existing social housing as well as identifying and regenerating surplus public-sector land.

Chair, Robert Napier, CBE
Chief Executive, Andy Rose

HUMAN TISSUE AUTHORITY (HTA)

2nd Floor, 151 Buckingham Palace Road, London SW1W 9SZ
T 020-7269 1900 E enquiries@hta.gov.uk
W www.hta.gov.uk

The Human Tissue Authority (HTA) was established on 1 April 2005 under the Human Tissue Act 2004, and is sponsored and part-funded by the Department of Health. It regulates organisations that remove, store and use tissue for research, medical treatment, post-mortem examination,

teaching and display in public. The HTA also gives approval for organ and bone marrow donations from living people. Under the EU tissues and cells directives, the HTA is one of the two designated competent authorities for the UK responsible for regulating tissues and cells. The HTA is also the sole competent authority for the UK under the EU organ donation directive.
Chair, Baroness Warwick of Undercliffe
Chief Executive, Alan Clamp

IMPERIAL WAR MUSEUMS (IWM)

Lambeth Road, London SE1 6HZ
T 020-7416 5000 E mail@iwm.org.uk
W www.iwm.org.uk

IWM is the world's leading authority on conflict and its impact, focusing on Britain, its former empire and the Commonwealth, from the First World War to the present. IWM aims to enrich people's understanding of the causes, course and consequences of war and conflict.

IWM comprises the organisation's flagship, IWM London; IWM North in Trafford, Manchester; IWM Duxford in Cambridgeshire; the Churchill War Rooms in Whitehall; and HMS *Belfast* in the Pool of London.

The total grant-in-aid (including grants for special projects) for 2013–14 is £20.28m.

OFFICERS
Chair, Sir Francis Richards, KCMG, CVO
Trustees, Lord Ashcroft, KCMG; Lord Black of Brentwood; Prof. Sir Miles Irving, FRCS; Lt.-Gen. Sir John Kiszely, KCB, MC; Tom McKane; Bronwen Maddox; Dame Judith Mayhew Jonas, DBE; Air Chief Marshal Sir Stuart Peach, KCB, CBE, FRAES; Sir John Scarlett, KCMG, OBE; Prof. Sir Hew Strachan, FRSE; Jonathan Watkins; Adm. Lord West of Spithead, GCB, DSC; Sir Nick Williams; HE Hon. Mike Rann; HE Gordon Campbell; HE Dr Jaimini Bhagwati; HE Rt. Hon. Dr Lockwood Smith; HE Wajid Shamsul Hasan; HE Dr Zola Skweyiya; HE Dr Chris Nonis
Director-General, Diane Lees
Directors, Richard Ashton *(IWM Duxford);* Jon Card *(Secretary, Business and Governance);* Sue Coleman *(Marketing and Development);* Graham Boxer *(IWM North);* Samantha Heywood *(Learning and Interpretation)*; Phil Reed *(Churchill War Rooms and HMS Belfast);* Alan Stoneman *(Corporate Services);* Mark Whitmore *(Collections and Research)*

INDUSTRIAL INJURIES ADVISORY COUNCIL

Second Floor, Caxton House, Tothill Street, London SW1H 9NA
T 020-7449 5618 E iiac@dwp.gsi.gov.uk
W http://iiac.independent.gov.uk

The Industrial Injuries Advisory Council was established under the National Insurance (Industrial Injuries) Act 1946, which came into effect on 5 July 1948. Statutory provisions governing its work are set out in the Social Security Administration Act 1992 and corresponding Northern Ireland legislation. The council currently consists of 17 independent members appointed by the Secretary of State for Work and Pensions, and has three roles: to advise on the prescription of diseases; to consider and advise on draft regulations and proposals concerning the industrial injuries disablement benefit scheme referred to it by the Secretary of State for Work and Pensions or the Department for Social Development in Northern Ireland; and to advise on any other matter concerning the scheme or its administration.
Chair, Prof. Keith Palmer

INFORMATION COMMISSIONER'S OFFICE

Wycliffe House, Water Lane, Wilmslow, Cheshire SK9 5AF
T 0303-123 1113 W www.ico.gov.uk

The Information Commissioner's Office (ICO) oversees and enforces the Freedom of Information Act 2000 and the Data Protection Act 1998, with the objective of promoting public access to official information and protecting personal information.

The Data Protection Act 1998 sets out rules for the processing of personal information and applies to records held on computers and some paper files. The Freedom of Information Act 2000 is designed to help end the culture of unnecessary secrecy and open up the inner workings of the public sector to citizens and businesses.

The ICO also enforces and oversees the privacy and electronic communications regulations 2003 and the environmental regulations 2004. It also has limited responsibilities under the INSPIRE regulations 2009.

The Information Commissioner reports annually to parliament on the performance of his/her functions under the acts and has obligations to assess breaches of the acts. As of April 2010, the ICO has been able to fine organisations up to £500,000 for serious breaches of the Data Protection Act.
Information Commissioner, Christopher Graham

JOINT NATURE CONSERVATION COMMITTEE

Monkstone House, City Road, Peterborough PE1 1JY
T 01733-562626 E communications@jncc.gov.uk
W www.jncc.defra.gov.uk

The committee was established under the Environmental Protection Act 1990 and was reconstituted by the Natural Environment and Rural Communities Act 2006. It advises the government and devolved administrations on UK and international nature conservation issues. Its work contributes to maintaining and enriching biological diversity, conserving geological features and sustaining natural systems.
Chair, Dr Peter Bridgewater
Deputy Chair, Judith Webb, MBE

LAW COMMISSION

Steel House, 11 Tothill Street, London SW1H 9LJ
T 020-3334 0200 E chief.executive@lawcommission.gsi.gov.uk
W www.lawcom.gov.uk

The Law Commission was set up under the Law Commissions Act 1965 to make proposals to the government for the examination of the law in England and Wales and for its revision where it is unsuited for modern requirements, obscure or otherwise unsatisfactory. It recommends to the lord chancellor programmes for the examination of different branches of the law and suggests whether the examination should be carried out by the commission itself or by some other body. The commission is also responsible for the preparation of Consolidation and Statute Law (Repeals) Bills.
Chair, Hon. Mr Justice Lloyd Jones
Commissioners, E. J. Cooke; David Hertzell; Prof. David Ormerod; Frances Patterson, QC
Chief Executive, Elaine Lorimer

NATIONAL ARMY MUSEUM

Royal Hospital Road, London SW3 4HT
T 020-7730 0717 E info@nam.ac.uk
W www.nam.ac.uk

The National Army Museum explores the impact of the British Army on the story of Britain, Europe and the world. It was established by royal charter in 1960 and moved to its current site in Chelsea in 1970. The museum houses a wide array of artefacts, paintings, photographs, uniforms and equipment.

Chair, General Sir Jack Deverell, KCB, OBE
Council Members, Keith Baldwin; Mihir Bose; Patrick Bradley; Brig. Douglas Erskine Crum; Lord Hamilton of Epsom; Prof. William Philpott; Maj.-Gen. C. Vyvyan, CB, CBE; Lt.-Gen Sir Barney White-Spunner, KCB, CBE; Deborah Younger
Director, Janice Murray, FRSA

NATIONAL GALLERIES OF SCOTLAND

73 Belford Road, Edinburgh EH4 3DS
T 0131-624 6200 E enquiries@nationalgalleries.org
W www.nationalgalleries.org

The National Galleries of Scotland comprise three galleries in Edinburgh: the National Gallery of Scotland, the Scottish National Portrait Gallery and the Scottish National Gallery of Modern Art. There are also partner galleries at Paxton House, Berwickshire, and Duff House, Banffshire.

TRUSTEES
Chair, Ben Thomson
Trustees, Tricia Bey; Richard Burns; Prof. Ian Howard; James Knox; Lesley Knox; Ray Macfarlane; Alasdair Morton; Catherine Muirden; Nicky Wilson

OFFICERS
Director-General, Sir John Leighton
Directors, Christopher Baker *(Scottish National Portrait Gallery);* Nicola Catterall *(Chief Operating Officer);* Michael Clarke, CBE *(National Gallery of Scotland);* Dr Simon Groom *(Scottish National Gallery of Modern Art and Dean Gallery);* Jacqueline Ridge *(Keeper of Conservation)*

NATIONAL GALLERY

Trafalgar Square, London WC2N 5DN
T 020-7747 2885 E information@ng-london.org.uk
W www.nationalgallery.org.uk

The National Gallery, which houses a permanent collection of western European painting from the 13th to the 20th century, was founded in 1824, following a parliamentary grant of £60,000 for the purchase and exhibition of the Angerstein collection of pictures. The present site was first occupied in 1838; an extension to the north of the building with a public entrance in Orange Street was opened in 1975; the Sainsbury Wing was opened in 1991; and the Getty Entrance opened off Trafalgar Square at the east end of the main building in 2004. Total government grant-in-aid for 2013–14 is £25.52m.

BOARD OF TRUSTEES
Chair, M. Getty
Trustees, L. Batchelor; G. Dalal; Prof. D. Dalwood; Prof. D. Ekserdjian; Lady Heseltine; M. Hintze; Prof. A. Hurlbert; J. Nelson; H. Rothschild; C. Sebag-Montefiore; M. Shah; J. Singer; C. Thomson

OFFICERS
Director, Dr N. Penny
Director of Public Engagement and Deputy Director, Dr S. Foister
Director of Finance and Operations, vacant
Director of Collections, Dr A. Roy

NATIONAL HERITAGE MEMORIAL FUND

7 Holbein Place, London SW1W 8NR
T 020-7591 6000 E enquire@hlf.org.uk
W www.nhmf.org.uk

The National Heritage Memorial Fund was set up under the National Heritage Act 1980 in memory of people who have given their lives for the United Kingdom. The fund provides grants to organisations based in the UK, mainly so that they can buy items of outstanding interest and of importance to the national heritage. These must either be at risk or have a memorial character. The fund is administered by a chair and 14 trustees who are appointed by the prime minister.

The National Heritage Memorial Fund receives an annual grant from the Department for Culture, Media and Sport. Under the National Lottery etc Act 1993, the trustees of the fund became responsible for the distribution of funds for both the National Heritage Memorial Fund and the Heritage Lottery Fund.

Chair, Dame Jenny Abramsky, CBE
Chief Executive, Carole Souter, CBE

NATIONAL LIBRARY OF SCOTLAND

George IV Bridge, Edinburgh EH1 1EW
T 0131-623 3700 E enquiries@nls.uk W www.nls.uk

The library, which was founded as the Advocates' Library in 1682, became the National Library of Scotland (NLS) in 1925. Funded by the Scottish government, it contains about 15 million printed items: two million maps, 25,000 newspaper and magazine titles and 100,000 manuscripts, including the John Murray Archive. The library receives around 320,000 new items every year and has material in 490 languages. It has an unrivalled Scottish collection as well as online catalogues and digital resources which can be accessed through the NLS website. Material can be consulted in the reading rooms, which are open to anyone with a valid library card.

The National Library of Scotland Act 2012 modernised the make-up and responsibilities of the board of trustees. At present there are nine, one of whom is nominated by the Faculty of Advocates. All of them are appointed by the Scottish ministers.

Chair, James Boyle
Trustees, Andrea Batchelor; Prof. Graham Caie, FRSA, FEA, FRSE; A. Lorraine Fannin, OBE; Jonathan Lake, QC; Charles Lovatt; Moira Methven; Dr Richard Parsons; Dr Willis Pickard
National Librarian and Chief Executive, Martyn Wade
Heads of Department, John Coll *(Access);* Graeme Forbes *(Ingest);* Murat Guven *(Resources);* Susan McKenzie *(Fnance);* Alexandra Miller *(Communications and Enterprise);* Robin Smith *(Collections and Interpretation)*

NATIONAL LIBRARY OF WALES/LLYFRGELL GENEDLAETHOL CYMRU

Aberystwyth, Ceredigion, Wales SY23 3BU
T 01970-632800 W www.llgc.org.uk

The National Library of Wales was founded by royal charter in 1907, and is funded by the Welsh government. It contains about five million printed books, 40,000 manuscripts, four million deeds and documents, numerous maps, prints and drawings, and a sound and moving image collection. It specialises in manuscripts and books relating to Wales and the Celtic peoples. It is the repository for pre-1858 Welsh probate records, manorial records and tithe documents, and certain legal records. Admission is by reader's ticket to the reading rooms but entry to the exhibition programme is free.

Total grant-in-aid from the Welsh government for 2013–14 is £12.2m.

Trustees, Lord Aberdare; David Barker; Tricia Carter; Roy Evans; John Gittins; Sir Deian Hopkin *(President);* Colin John *(Treasurer);* Wyn Penri Jones; Enid Morgan; Roy Roberts; David Hugh Thomas; Michael Trickey; Gareth Haulfryn Williams; Huw Williams

Librarian and Chief Executive, Andrew Green

Heads of Departments, R. Arwel Jones *(Public Services);* Avril Jones *(Collection Services);* David Michael *(Corporate Services)*

NATIONAL LOTTERY COMMISSION

4th Floor, Victoria Square House, Victoria Square, Birmingham B2 4BP
T 0121-230 6750 E info@natlotcomm.gov.uk
W www.natlotcomm.gov.uk

The National Lottery Commission replaced the Office of the National Lottery (OFLOT) in 1999 under the National Lottery Act 1998. The commission is responsible for the granting, varying and enforcing of licences to run the National Lottery. Its duties are to ensure that the National Lottery is run with all due propriety, that the interests of players are protected and, subject to these two objectives, that returns to the good causes are maximised. The commission does not have a role in the distribution of funds to good causes: this is undertaken by 16 distributors.

The Department for Culture, Media and Sport sponsors the the National Lottery Commission, which in turn regulates Camelot, the lottery operator. Camelot, was granted a third licence to run the lottery from 1 February 2009 for ten years.

Following the Public Bodies Order 2013, the functions of the National Lottery Commission will be subsumed by the Gambling Commission in late 2013.

Chair, Dr Anne Wright, CBE

Commissioners, Mary Chapman; Robert Foster; James Froomberg; Mark Harris *(Chief Executive);* Deep Sagar; Sarah Thane, CBE

NATIONAL MUSEUM OF THE ROYAL NAVY

HM Naval Base (PP66), Portsmouth PO1 3NH
T 023-9272 7574
W www.nmrn.org.uk

The National Museum of the Royal Navy comprises five museums: HMS *Victory,* the National Museum of the Royal Navy Portsmouth, the Fleet Air Arm Museum, the Royal Navy Submarine Museum and the Royal Marines Museum. The Fleet Air Museum is located at RNAS Yeovilton, Somerset, while the other four are situated in Portsmouth and Gosport.

Chair, Adm. Sir Jonathon Band, GCB

Trustees, John Brookes, OBE; Prof. John Craven; Sir Robert Crawford, CBE; Neil Davidson, FCA; Lieut.-Gen. Sir Robert Fulton, KBE; Rear-Adm. Terry Loughran, CB; Vice-Adm. Sir Tim McClement, KCB, OBE; Kim Marshall; Tim Schadla-Hall; Dr Caroline Williams

Director-General, Prof. Dominic Tweddle

NATIONAL MUSEUM WALES/AMGUEDDFA CYMRU

Cathays Park, Cardiff CF10 3NP
T 029-2039 7951
W www.museumwales.ac.uk

Amgueddfa Cymru – National Museum Wales aims to provide a complete illustration of the geology, mineralogy, zoology, botany, ethnography, archaeology, art, history and special industries of Wales. It comprises National Museum Cardiff; St Fagans: National History Museum; Big Pit: National Coal Museum, Blaenafon; the National Roman Legion Museum, Caerleon; the National Slate Museum, Llanberis; the National Wool Museum, Dre-fach Felindre; the National Waterfront Museum, Swansea; and the National Collections Centre, Nantgarw. Total funding from the Welsh government for 2013–14 is £26.1m.

Trustees, Elisabeth Elias *(President)*; Prof. Tony Atkins; Carole-Anne Davies; Dr Haydn Edwards; Miriam Hazel Griffiths; Dr Glenda Jones; Emeritus Prof. Richard G. Wyn Jones, FLSW; Christina Macaulay; J. Peter W. Morgan, FCA *(Treasurer)*; Prof. Jonathan Osmond; Prof. Robert Pickard; Victoria Mary Provis; Dr Keshav Singhal; David Beresford Vokes; Gareth Williams

Director-General, David Anderson

NATIONAL MUSEUMS LIVERPOOL

127 Dale Street, Liverpool L2 2JH
T 0151-207 0001 W www.liverpoolmuseums.org.uk

National Museums Liverpool is a group of museums and collections including the World Museum, the Merseyside Maritime Museum (also home to the Border Force National Museum, known as 'Seized! The Border and Customs Uncovered'), the Lady Lever Art Gallery, the Walker Art Gallery, Sudley House, the International Slavery Museum and the Museum of Liverpool. Total government grant-in-aid for 2013–14 is £21.3m.

Chair, Prof. Phil Redmond, CBE

Trustees, Prof. John Ashton, CBE; Carmel Booth; Laura Carstensen; Sir Robert Crawford, CBE; Clive Elphick; Joe Goodwin; Nisha Katona; Norma Kurland; Andrew McCluskey; Tony McGuirk, CBE; Philip Price; Neil Scales, OBE; Deborah Shackleton, CBE; Dr Nicola Thorp

Director, Dr David Fleming, OBE

Director of Art Galleries, Sandra Penketh

Director, World Museum Liverpool, Steve Judd

Director, Museum of Liverpool, Janet Dugdale

Head of International Slavery Museum, Dr Richard Benjamin

NATIONAL MUSEUMS NORTHERN IRELAND

Cultra, Holywood, Northern Ireland BT18 0EU
T 0845-608 0000 E info@nmni.com
W www.nmni.com

Across four unique sites National Museums Northern Ireland cares for and presents inspirational collections reflecting the creativity, innovation, history, culture and people of Northern Ireland and beyond.

Together the Ulster Museum, Ulster Folk and Transport Museum, Ulster American Folk Park and Armagh County Museum offer a unique opportunity to experience the heritage and way of life of Northern Ireland.

Chair, Dan Harvey, OBE

Trustees, Neil Bodger; Pat Carvill, CB; Dr Richard Browne McMinn; David Moore; Anne Peoples; Dr Brian Scott; Tom Shaw, CBE; Dr Alastair Walker

Director and Chief Executive, Tim Cooke

NATIONAL MUSEUMS SCOTLAND

Chambers Street, Edinburgh EH1 1JF
T 0300-123 6789 E info@nms.ac.uk W www.nms.ac.uk

National Museums Scotland provides advice, expertise and support to the museums community across Scotland, and undertakes fieldwork that often involves collaboration at local, national and international levels. National Museums

Scotland comprises the National Museum of Scotland, the National War Museum, the National Museum of Rural Life, the National Museum of Flight, the National Museum of Costume and the National Museums Collection Centre. Its collections represent more than two centuries of collecting and include Scottish and classical archaeology, decorative and applied arts, world cultures and social history and science, technology and the natural world.

Up to 15 trustees can be appointed by the Minister for Culture and External Affairs for a term of four years, and may serve a second term.

Chair, Bruce Minto
Trustees, Prof. Chris Breward; Dr Isabel Bruce, OBE, FRSSA; Gordon Drummond; Chris Fletcher; Dr Anna Gregor, CBE, FRCR, FRCP; Andrew Holmes; Michael Kirwan, FCA; Miller McLean, FCIBS, FIB; Prof. Malcolm McLeod, CBE, FRSE; Prof. Stuart Monro, OBE, FGS, FRSE; Prof. Walter Nimmo, FRCA, FRCP, FRSE; James Troughton, RIBA; Sir John Ward, CBE, FRSE, FRSA; Iain Watt, FCIBS
Director, Dr Gordon Rintoul

NATIONAL PORTRAIT GALLERY

St Martin's Place, London WC2H 0HE
T 020-7306 0055 W www.npg.org.uk

The National Portrait Gallery was formed after a grant was made in 1856 to form a gallery of the portraits of the most eminent persons in British history. Today the gallery collects portraits of those who have made, or are making, a significant contribution to British history and culture. The collection includes works across all media, from painting and sculpture to photography and digital portraits. The present building was opened in 1896 and the Ondaatje Wing (including the Balcony Gallery, Tudor Gallery, IT Gallery, lecture theatre and roof-top restaurant) opened in May 2000. There are three regional partnerships displaying portraits at Montacute House, Beningbrough Hall and Bodelwyddan Castle. Total government grant-in-aid for 2013–14 is £7.04m.

BOARD OF TRUSTEES
Chair, Sir William Proby, Bt., CBE
Trustees, Dr Brian Allen; Allegra Berman; Prof. Dame Carol Black, DBE; Sir Nicholas Blake, QC; Dr Rosalind P. Blakesley; Dr Augustus Casely-Hayford; Kim Evans, OBE; Rt. Hon. Nick Clegg, MP; Rt. Hon. Lord Janvrin, GCB, GCVO, QSO; Christopher Le Brun, PRA; Mary McCartney; David Ross; Stephan Shakespeare; Marina Warner, CBE, FBA
Director, Sandy Nairne

NATURAL ENGLAND

Foundry House, 3 Millsands, Riverside Exchange, Sheffield S3 8NH
T 0845-600 3078 E enquiries@naturalengland.org.uk
W www.naturalengland.org.uk

Natural England is the government's advisor on the natural environment, providing practical advice, grounded in science, on how best to safeguard England's natural wealth for the benefit of everyone.

The organisation's remit is to ensure that the natural environment is conserved, enhanced and managed for the benefit of present and future generations, thereby contributing to sustainable development. Its priorities are to reconnect people with nature; protect natural assets; and maximise the opportunities offered by a greener economy.

Natural England works with farmers and land managers; business and industry; planners and developers; national and local government; charities and conservationists; interest groups and local communities to help them improve their local environment.

Chief Executive, Dave Webster

NATURAL HISTORY MUSEUM

Cromwell Road, London SW7 5BD
T 020-7942 5000 W www.nhm.ac.uk

The Natural History Museum originates from the natural history departments of the British Museum, which grew extensively during the 19th century; in 1860 it was agreed that the natural history collections should be separated from the British Museum's collections of books, manuscripts and antiquities. Part of the site of the 1862 International Exhibition in South Kensington was acquired for the new museum, and the museum opened to the public in 1881. In 1963 the Natural History Museum became completely independent with its own board of trustees. The Natural History Museum at Tring, bequeathed by the second Lord Rothschild, has formed part of the museum since 1937. The Geological Museum merged with the Natural History Museum in 1985. In September 2009 the Natural History Museum opened the Darwin Centre, which contains public galleries, a high-tech interactive area known as the Attenborough Studio, scientific research facilities and storage for 28 million zoological specimens, 17 million entomology specimens and three million botanical specimens. Total government grant-in-aid for 2013–14 is £44.3m

Chair, Oliver Stocken
Trustees, Daniel Alexander, QC; Prof. Sir Roy Anderson, FRS, FMEDSCI; Prof. Sir John Beddington, CMG, FRS; Louise Charlton; Prof. David Drewry; Prof. Christopher Gilligan; Prof. Alex Halliday, FRS; Prof. Sir John Holman; Dr Derek Langslow, CBE; Sir David Omand, GCB; Dr Kim Winser, OBE
Museum Director, Dr Michael Dixon
Directors, Neil Greenwood *(Finance and Corporate Services);* Dr Justin Morris *(Public Engagement);* Prof. Ian Owens *(Science)*

NATURAL RESOURCES WALES

Ty Cambria, 29 Newport Road, Cardiff CF24 0TP
T 0300-065 3000 E enquiries@naturalresourceswales.gov.uk
W www.naturalresourceswales.gov.uk

Natural Resources Wales is the principal adviser to the Welsh government on the environment. It became operational on 1 April 2013 following a merger of the Countryside Council for Wales, Environment Agency Wales and the Forestry Commission Wales. It is responsible for ensuring that the natural resources of Wales are sustainably maintained, enhanced and used; now and in the future.

Chair, Prof. Peter Matthews, FRSC, FCIWEM, FIWO
Board Members, Dr Mike Brooker; Dr Ruth Hall; Dr Madeleine Havard; Revd Hywel Davies; Harry Legge-Bourke; Andy Middleton; Morgan Parry; Dr Emyr Roberts *(Chief Executive);* Nigel Reader, CBE; Prof. Lynda Warren; Sir Paul Williams, OBE

NHS PAY REVIEW BODY

6th Floor, Victoria House, Southampton Row, London WC1B 4AD
T 020-7271 0490 W www.ome.uk.com

The NHS Pay Review Body (NHSPRB) makes recommendations to the prime minister, Secretary of State for Health and ministers in Scotland, Wales and Northern Ireland on the remuneration of all paid staff under agenda for change and employed in the NHS. The review body was established in 1983 for nurses and allied health professionals. Its remit has since expanded to cover over 1.8 million staff; ie almost all staff in the NHS, with the exception of dentists, doctors and very senior managers.

Chair, Jerry Cope

Members, Prof. David Blackaby; Dame Denise Holt; Joan Ingram; Graham Jagger; Colin Kennedy; Janet Rubin; Prof. Anna Vignoles

NORTHERN IRELAND HUMAN RIGHTS COMMISSION

Temple Court, 39 North Street, Belfast BT1 1NA
T 028-9024 3987 E information@nihrc.org W www.nihrc.org

The Northern Ireland Human Rights Commission is a non-departmental public body, established by the Northern Ireland Act 1998 and set up in March 1999. Its purpose is to protect and promote human rights in Northern Ireland. Its main functions include reviewing the law and practice relating to human rights, advising government and the Northern Ireland Assembly, and promoting an awareness of human rights. It can also investigate human rights violations and take cases to court. The members of the commission are appointed by the Secretary of State for Northern Ireland.

Chief Commissioner, Prof. Michael O'Flaherty

Commissioners, Christine Collins; John Corey; Milton Kerr, QPM; Grainia Long; Alan McBride; Marion Reynolds; Paul Yam

Director, Virginia McVea

NORTHERN LIGHTHOUSE BOARD

84 George Street, Edinburgh EH2 3DA
T 0131-473 3100 E enquiries@nlb.org.uk
W www.nlb.org.uk

The Northern Lighthouse Board is the general lighthouse authority for Scotland and the Isle of Man and owes its origin to an act of parliament passed in 1786. At present there are 19 commissioners who operate under the Merchant Shipping Act 1995.

The commissioners control 208 lighthouses, many lighted and unlighted buoys, a DGPS (differential global positioning system) station and an ELORAN (long-range navigation) system. *See also* Transport.

Chair, Capt. H. Michael Close

Commissioners, Lord Advocate; Solicitor-General for Scotland; Lord Provosts of Edinburgh, Glasgow and Aberdeen; Convener of Highland Council; Convener of Argyll and Bute Council; Sheriffs-Principal of North Strathclyde, Tayside, Central and Fife, Grampian, Highlands and Islands, South Strathclyde, Dumfries and Galloway, Lothians and Borders and Glasgow and Strathkelvin; Capt. Alastair Beveridge; Capt. Michael Brew; Graham Crerar; Alistair MacKenzie; John Ross, CBE

Chief Executive, Roger Lockwood, CB

NUCLEAR DECOMMISSIONING AUTHORITY

Herdus House, Westlakes Science and Technology Park, Moor Row, Cumbria CA24 3HU
T 01925-802001 E enquiries@nda.gov.uk W www.nda.gov.uk

The Nuclear Decommissioning Authority (NDA) was created under the Energy Act 2004. It is a strategic authority that owns 19 sites and associated civil nuclear liabilities and assets of the public sector, previously under the control of the UK Energy Authority and British Nuclear Fuels. The NDA's responsibilities include decommissioning and cleaning up civil nuclear facilities; ensuring the safe management of waste products, both radiocative and non-radioactive; implementing government policy on the long-term management of nuclear waste; and developing UK-wide low-level waste strategy plans.

Total planned expenditure for 2013–14 is £3.2bn, with total grant-in-aid standing at £2.3bn. The remaining £0.9bn will come from commercial operations.

Chair, Stephen Henwood

Chief Executive, John Clarke

OFFICE FOR BUDGET RESPONSIBILITY

20 Victoria Street, London SW1H 0NF
T 020-7271 2520 E obrenquiries@obr.gsi.gov.uk
W http://budgetresponsibility.independent.gov.uk

The Office for Budget Responsibility (OBR) was created in 2010 to provide independent and authoritative analysis of the UK's public finances. It has four main roles: producing forecasts for the economy and public finances; judging progress towards the government's fiscal targets; assessing the long-term sustainability of the public finances; and scrutinising HM Treasury's costing of tax and welfare spending measures.

Chair, Robert Chote

Committee Members, Steve Nickell, CBE; Graham Parker, CBE

OFFICE OF COMMUNICATIONS (OFCOM)

Riverside House, 2A Southwark Bridge Road, London SE1 9HA
T 0300-123 3000 W www.ofcom.org.uk

OFCOM was established in 2003 under the Office of Communications Act 2002 as the independent regulator and competition authority for the UK communications industries with responsibility for television, radio, telecommunications and wireless communications services.

Following the passing of the Postal Services Act 2011, OFCOM has assumed regulatory responsibility for postal services from Postcomm, the Postal Services Commission.

Chair, Colette Bowe

Deputy Chair, Dame Patricia Hodgson, DBE

Board Members, Jill Ainscough; Lord Blackwell; Dame Lynne Brindley, DBE; Tim Gardam; Stuart McIntosh; Mike McTighe

Chief Executive, Ed Richards

OFFICE OF TAX SIMPLIFICATION

HM Treasury, 1 Horse Guards Road, London SW1A 2HQ
E ots@ots.gsi.gov.uk
W www.gov.uk/government/organisations/office-of-tax-simplification

The chancellor and exchequer secretary to HM Treasury launched the Office of Tax Simplification (OTS) on 20 July 2010 to provide the government with independent advice on simplifying the UK tax system.

The Office has been established as an independent office of HM Treasury for the life of the current parliament and draws together expertise from across the tax and legal professions, the business community and other interested parties.

Chair, Rt. Hon. Michael Jack

Tax Director, John Whiting

OFFICE OF MANPOWER ECONOMICS (OME)

6th Floor, Victoria House, Southampton Row, London WC1B 4AD
T 020-7271 0497 W www.ome.uk.com

The Office of Manpower Economics (OME) was established in 1971. It is an independent non-statutory organisation which is responsible for servicing independent review bodies that advise on the pay of various public sector groups, the Police Negotiating Board and the Police Advisory Board for England and Wales. The OME is also responsible for servicing *ad hoc* bodies of inquiry and for undertaking research into pay and associated matters as requested by the government.

The OME has been allocated a total of £2.5m by the Department for Business, Innovation and Skills for 2013–14.

OME Director, Geoff Dart

Directors, Jenny Eastabrook *(Armed Forces' and School Teachers' Secretariats);* Margaret McEvoy *(Doctors' and Dentists' and NHS Pay Review Body Secretariats, Research and Analysis Group);* Keith Masson *(Senior Salaries', Prison Service and Police Board Secretariats)*

PARADES COMMISSION

Windsor House, 9–15 Bedford Street, Belfast BT2 7EL
T 028-9089 5900 E info@paradescommissionni.org
W www.paradescommission.org

The Parades Commission was set up under the Public Processions (Northern Ireland) Act 1998. Its function is to encourage and facilitate local accommodation of contentious parades; where this is not possible, the commission is empowered to make legal determinations about such parades, which may include imposing conditions on aspects of the notified parade (such as restrictions on routes/areas and exclusion of certain groups with a record of bad behaviour).

The chair and members are appointed by the Secretary of State for Northern Ireland; the membership must, as far as is practicable, be representative of the community in Northern Ireland.

Chair, Peter Osborne

Members, Douglas Bain, CBE; Delia Close; Revd Brian Kennaway; Frances Nolan, MBE; George Patterson; Robin Percival

PAROLE BOARD FOR ENGLAND AND WALES

Grenadier House, 99–105 Horseferry Road, London SW1P 2DX
T 0300-047 4600 W www.justice.gov.uk/about/parole-board

The Parole Board was established under the Criminal Justice Act 1967 and became an independent executive non-departmental public body under the Criminal Justice and Public Order Act 1994. It is the body that protects the public by making risk assessments about prisoners to decide who may safely be released into the community and who must remain in, or be returned to, custody. Board decisions are taken at two main types of panels of up to three members: 'paper panels' for the majority of cases, or oral hearings for decisions concerning prisoners serving life or indeterminate sentences for public protection.

Chair, Rt. Hon. Sir David Calvert-Smith

Chief Executive, Claire Bassett

PAROLE BOARD FOR SCOTLAND

Saughton House, Broomhouse Drive, Edinburgh EH11 3XD
T 0131-244 8373
E paroleboardforscotlandexecutive@scotland.gsi.gov.uk
W www.scottishparoleboard.gov.uk

The board directs and advises the Scottish ministers on the release of prisoners on licence, and related matters.

Chair, John Watt

Vice-Chair, Ms H. Baillie

PENSION PROTECTION FUND (PPF)

Knollys House, 17 Addiscombe Road, Croydon CR0 6SR
T 0845-600 2541 E information@ppf.gsi.gov.uk
W www.pensionprotectionfund.org.uk

The PPF became operational in 2005. It was established to pay compensation to members of eligible defined-benefit pension schemes where a qualifying insolvency event in relation to the employer occurs and where there is a lack of sufficient assets in the pension scheme. The PPF also administers the Financial Assistance Scheme, which helps members whose schemes wound-up before 2005. It is also responsible for the Fraud Compensation Fund (which provides compensation to occupational pension schemes that suffer a loss that can be attributed to dishonesty). The chair and board of the PPF are appointed by, and accountable to, the Secretary of State for Work and Pensions, and are responsible for paying compensation, calculating annual levies (which help fund the PPF), and setting and overseeing investment strategy.

Chair, Lady Barbara Judge

Chief Executive, Alan Rubenstein

PENSIONS REGULATOR

Napier House, Trafalgar Place, Brighton BN1 4DW
T 0845-600 0707 E customersupport@tpr.gov.uk
W www.thepensionsregulator.gov.uk

The Pensions Regulator was established in 2005 as the regulator of work-based pension schemes in the UK, replacing the Occupational Pensions Regulatory Authority (OPRA). It aims to protect the benefits of occupational and personal pension scheme members by working with trustees, employers, pension providers and advisors. The regulator's work focuses on encouraging better management and administration of schemes, ensuring that final salary schemes have a sensible funding plan, and encouraging money purchase schemes to provide members with the information that they need to make informed choices about their pension fund. The Pensions Act 2004 and the Pensions Act 2008 gave the regulator a range of powers which can be used to protect scheme members, but a strong emphasis is placed on educating and enabling those responsible for managing pension schemes, and powers are used only where necessary. The regulator offers three free online resources to help trustees, employers, professionals and advisors understand their role, duties and obligations.

Chair, Michael O'Higgins

Chief Executive, Bill Galvin

POLICE ADVISORY BOARD FOR ENGLAND AND WALES

6th Floor, Victoria House, Southampton Row, London WC1B 4AD
T 020-7271 0472 W www.ome.uk.com

The Police Advisory Board for England and Wales was established in 1965 and provides advice to the home secretary on general questions affecting the police in England and Wales. It also considers draft regulations which the secretary of state proposes to make with respect to matters other than hours of duty, leave, pay and allowances or the issue, use and return of police clothing, personal equipment and other effects.

Independent Chair, John Randall

Independent Deputy Chair, Prof. Gillian Morris

POLICE NEGOTIATING BOARD (PNB)

6th Floor, Victoria House, Southampton Row, London WC1B 4AD
T 020-7271 0472 W www.ome.uk.com

The PNB was established in 1980 to negotiate pay; allowances; hours of duty; the issue, use and return of police clothing, personal equipment and accoutrements; leave; and pensions of UK police officers, and to make recommendations on these matters to the home secretary, the Northern Ireland secretary and Scottish ministers.
Independent Chair, John Randall
Independent Deputy Chair, Prof. Gillian Morris

PRISON SERVICE PAY REVIEW BODY

6th Floor, Victoria House, Southampton Row, London WC1B 4AD
T 020-7215 8369 W www.ome.uk.com

The Prison Service Pay Review Body was set up in 2001. It makes independent recommendations on the pay of prison governors, operational managers, prison officers and related grades for the Prison Service in England and Wales and for the Northern Ireland Prison Service.
Chair, Dr Peter Knight, CBE
Members, Prof. John Beath; Karen Heaton; Ann Jarvis; Esmond Lindop; Peter Maddison; Jan Parkinson

REVIEW BODY ON DOCTORS' AND DENTISTS' REMUNERATION

6th Floor, Victoria House, Southampton Row, London WC1B 4AD
T 020-7271 0486 W www.ome.uk.com

The Review Body on Doctors' and Dentists' Remuneration was set up in 1971. It advises the prime minister, first ministers in Scotland, Wales and Northern Ireland, and the ministers for Health, in England, Scotland, Wales and Northern Ireland on the remuneration of doctors and dentists taking any part in the National Health Service.
Chair, Prof. Paul Curnan
Members, Lucinda Bolton; Mark Butler; John Glennie, OBE; Alan Henry; Prof. Kevin Lee; Prof. Steve Thompson; Nigel Turner

ROYAL AIR FORCE MUSEUM

Grahame Park Way, London NW9 5LL
T 020-8205 2266 E london@rafmuseum.org
W www.rafmuseum.org.uk

The museum has two sites, one at the former airfield at Hendon and the second at Cosford, in the West Midlands, both of which illustrate the development of aviation from before the Wright brothers to the present-day RAF. The museum's collection across both sites consists of over 170 aircraft, as well as artefacts, aviation memorabilia, fine art and photographs.
Chair, Air Chief Marshal Sir John Day, KCB, OBE
Trustees, Viscount Chelsea; Brendan Connor; Gerry Grimstone; Richard Holman, FCA; Rt. Hon. Lord Hutton of Furness; John Michaelson; Jane Middleton, FCCA, FRAES; Tom O' Leary; Andrew Reid; Michael Schindler; Robin Southwell; Alan Spence; Air Chief Marshal Sir Glenn Torpy, GCB, CBE, DSO; Malcolm White, OBE, FRAES
Director-General, Air Vice-Marshal Peter Dye, OBE

ROYAL BOTANIC GARDEN EDINBURGH

20A Inverleith Row, Edinburgh EH3 5LR
T 0131-552 7171 W www.rbge.org.uk

The Royal Botanic Garden Edinburgh (RBGE) originated as the Physic Garden, established in 1670 beside the Palace of Holyroodhouse. The garden moved to its present 28-hectare site at Inverleith, Edinburgh, in 1821. There are also three regional gardens: Benmore Botanic Garden, near Dunoon, Argyll; Logan Botanic Garden, near Stranraer, Wigtownshire; and Dawyck Botanic Garden, near Stobo, Peeblesshire. Since 1986 RBGE has been administered by a board of trustees established under the National Heritage (Scotland) Act 1985. It receives an annual grant from the Scottish government's Rural and Environmental Research and Analysis Directorate.

The RBGE is an international centre for scientific research on plant diversity and for horticulture education and conservation. It has an extensive library, a herbarium with almost three million preserved plant specimens, and over 15,000 species in the living collections.
Chair, Sir Muir Russell, KCB, FRSE
Trustees, Patricia Henton, FRSE; Angela McNaught; Tim Rollinson, CBE; Prof. Janet Sprent, OBE, FRSE; Dr Ian Sword, CBE, FRSE
Regius Keeper and Queen's Botanist in Scotland, Prof. Stephen Blackmore, CBE, FRSE

ROYAL BOTANIC GARDENS, KEW

Kew Gardens, Richmond, Surrey TW9 3AB
T 020-8332 5655
Wakehurst, Ardingly, W. Sussex RH17 6TN
T 01444-894066
E info@kew.org W www.kew.org

Kew Gardens was originally laid out as a private garden for the now demolished White House for George III's mother, Princess Augusta, in 1759. The gardens were much enlarged in the 19th century, notably by the inclusion of the grounds of the former Richmond Lodge. In 1965 Kew acquired the gardens at Wakehurst on a long lease from the National Trust. Under the National Heritage Act 1983 a board of trustees was set up to administer the gardens, which in 1984 became an independent body supported by grant-in-aid from the Department for Environment, Food and Rural Affairs.

The functions of RBG, Kew are to carry out research into plant sciences, to disseminate knowledge about plants and to provide the public with the opportunity to gain knowledge and enjoyment from the gardens' collections. There are extensive national reference collections of living and preserved plants and a comprehensive library and archive. The main emphasis is on plant conservation and biodiversity; Wakehurst houses the Millennium Seed Bank Partnership, which is the largest *ex situ* conservation project in the world – its aim is to save seed from 25 per cent of the earth's wild plant species by 2020.
Chair, Marcus Agius
Trustees, Prof. Michael Crawley; Prof. Jonathan Drori, CBE; Tessa Green; Dr Geoffrey Hawtin; Timothy Hornsby, CBE; Sir Henry Keswick; Mr George Loudon; Prof. Malcolm Press; Prof. Nicola Spence; Ms Jennifer Ullman; Sir Ferrers Vyvyan
Director, Richard Deverell

ROYAL COMMISSION ON THE ANCIENT AND HISTORICAL MONUMENTS OF SCOTLAND

John Sinclair House, 16 Bernard Terrace, Edinburgh EH8 9NX
T 0131-662 1456 E info@rcahms.gov.uk
W www.rcahms.gov.uk

The Royal Commission on the Ancient and Historical Monuments of Scotland (RCAHMS) was established by a royal warrant in 1908, which was revised in 1992, and is appointed to provide for the collecting, recording and interpretation of information on the architectural, industrial, archaeological and maritime heritage of Scotland, to give a picture of the human influence on Scotland's places from the earliest times to the present day. It is funded by the Scottish government. More than 15 million items, including photographs, maps, drawings and documents, are available through the search room, and online databases provide access to over 600,000 images and information on 300,000 buildings and sites. RCAHMS also holds Scotland's national collection of historical aerial photography as well as The Aerial Reconnaissance Archives (TARA) of international wartime photography.

Chair, Prof. John Hume, OBE, FSA SCOT

Commissioners, Dr Kate Byrne, FRSA; Tom Dawson, FSA SCOT; Mark Hopton, FSA SCOT; Dr Jeremy Huggett, FSA, FSA SCOT; Prof. John Hunter, OBE, FSA, FSA SCOT; Paul Jardine; Dr Gordon Masterton, OBE, FICE, FIES; Jude Quartson-Mochrie; Elspeth Reid

Chief Executive, Diana Murray, FSA, FSA SCOT

ROYAL COMMISSION ON THE ANCIENT AND HISTORICAL MONUMENTS OF WALES

Crown Building, Plas Crug, Aberystwyth SY23 1NJ
T 01970-621200 E nmr.wales@rcahmw.gov.uk
W www.rcahmw.gov.uk

The Royal Commission on the Ancient and Historical Monuments of Wales, established in 1908, is the investigation body and national archive for the historic environment of Wales. It has the lead role in ensuring that Wales's archaeological, built and maritime heritage is authoritatively recorded, and seeks to promote the understanding and appreciation of this heritage nationally and internationally. The commission is funded by the Welsh government.

Chair, Dr Eurwyn Wiliam, FSA

Vice-Chair, Henry Owen-John, FSA

Commissioners, Mrs Anne S. Eastham, FSA; Ms Catherine S. Hardman; Jonathan Hudson; Thomas O. S. Lloyd, OBE, FSA; Dr Mark Redknap, FSA; Prof. Christopher Williams, FRHISTS

ROYAL MAIL GROUP

100 Victoria Embankment, London EC4Y 0HQ
T 08457 740 740 W www.royalmailgroup.com

The conveyance of public correspondence began in 1635 and the mail service was made a parliamentary responsibility with the setting up of a Post Office in 1657. The Post Office ceased to be a government department in 1969 when responsibility for the running of the postal, telecommunications, giro and remittance services was transferred to a public authority of the same name.

The Postal Services Act 2000 turned the Post Office into a wholly owned public limited company establishing a regulatory regime under the Postal Service Commission. The Post Office Group changed its name to Consignia plc in March 2001 when its new corporate structure took effect; in November 2002 the name was changed to Royal Mail Group plc. Following the passing of the Postal Services Act 2011, Royal Mail is now open to private ownership. A buyer will be able to own up to 90 per cent of the shares in the company, with Royal Mail staff offered the remaining 10 per cent.

The chair, chief executive and members of the board are appointed by the Secretary of State for Business, Innovation and Skills but responsibility for the running of Royal Mail Group as a whole rests with the board in its corporate capacity.

BOARD

Chair, Donald Brydon, CBE

Members, John Allan; Jan Babiak; Moya Greene *(Chief Executive);* Mark Higson *(Managing Director, Operations and Modernisation);* Nick Horler; Cath Keers; Matthew Lester *(Chief Finance Officer);* John Millidge *(Company Secretary);* Paul Murray; Orna Ni-Chionna; Les Owen

ROYAL MUSEUMS GREENWICH

National Maritime Museum, Greenwich, London SE10 9NF
T 020-8858 4422 W www.rmg.co.uk

Royal Museums Greenwich comprises the National Maritime Museum, the Queen's House and the Royal Observatory Greenwich. It also works in collaboration with the Cutty Sark Trust. The National Maritime Museum provides information on the maritime history of Great Britain and is the largest institution of its kind in the world, with over two million items in its collections related to seafaring, navigation and astronomy. Originally the home of Charles I's Queen, Henrietta Maria, the Queen's House was designed by Inigo Jones and built between 1616–18, although it was structurally altered between 1629–35. It now contains a fine-art collection. The Royal Observatory, Greenwich is the home of Greenwich Mean Time and the prime meridian of the world. It also contains London's only planetarium, Harrison's timekeepers and the UK's largest refracting telescope.

Director, Kevin Fewster, FRSA

Chair, Lord Sterling of Plaistow, GCVO, CBE

Trustees, Eleanor Boddington; Sir Robert Crawford, CBE; Prof. Geoffrey Crossick; Linda Hutchinson; Dr Christopher Lintott; David Moorhouse, CBE; Dr David Quarmby, CBE

SCHOOL TEACHERS' REVIEW BODY

6th Floor, Victoria House, Southampton Row, London WC1B 4AD
T 020-7271 0474 W www.ome.uk.com

The School Teachers' Review Body was set up under the School Teachers' Pay and Conditions Act 1991. It is required to examine and report on such matters relating to the statutory conditions of employment of school teachers in England and Wales as may be referred to it by the education secretary.

Chair, Dame Patricia Hodgson, DBE

Members, Peter Batley; Jonathan Crossley-Holland; Debbie Meech; Stella Pantelides; Jill Pullen; Dr Patricia Rice

SCIENCE MUSEUM

Exhibition Road, London SW7 2DD
T 0870-870 4868 E feedback@sciencemuseum.org.uk
W www.sciencemuseum.org.uk

The Science Museum, part of the Science Museum Group (SMG), houses the national collections of science, technology, industry and medicine. The museum began as the science collection of the South Kensington Museum and first opened in 1857. In 1883 it acquired the collections of the Patent Museum and in 1909 the science collections were transferred to the new Science Museum, leaving the art collections with the Victoria and Albert Museum. The Wellcome Wing was opened in July 2000.

The SMG also incorporates the National Railway Museum, York; the National Media Museum, Bradford; Locomotion: the National Railway Museum at Shildon; and the Museum of Science and Industry, Manchester.

Total government grant-in-aid for 2013–14 was £43.67m.

Chair, Dr Douglas Gurr

Trustees, Lady Chisholm; Howard Covington; Prof. Dame Athene Donald, DBE, FRS; Andreas Goss; Lord Grade of Yarmouth, CBE; Lord Faulkner of Worcester; Peter Fell; Prof. Ludmilla Jordanova; Simon Linnett; Prof. Averil Macdonald; Sir Howard Newby, CBE; Dr Gill Samuels, CBE; James Smith; Janet Street-Porter; Christopher Swinson, OBE

Director of SMG, Ian Blatchford
Director of Science Museum, Ian Blatchford
Director of Museum of Science & Industry, Jean Franczyk
Director of National Media Museum, Jo Quinton-Tulloch
Director of National Railway Museum, Paul Kirkman

SCOTTISH CRIMINAL CASES REVIEW COMMISSION

5th Floor, Portland House, 17 Renfield Street, Glasgow G2 5AH
T 0141-270 7030 E info@sccrc.org.uk W www.sccrc.org.uk

The commission is a non-departmental public body, funded by the Scottish Government Criminal Justice Directorate, and established by Act of Parliament in April 1999. It assumed the role previously performed by the Secretary of State for Scotland to consider alleged miscarriages of justice in Scotland and refer cases meeting the relevant criteria to the high court for determination. Members are appointed by the Queen on the recommendation of the first minister; senior executive staff are appointed by the commission.

Chair, Jean Couper, CBE
Members, Gerrard Bann; Prof. Brian Caddy; Stewart Campbell; Peter Ferguson, QC; Prof. George Irving, CBE; Gerard McClay; Frances McMenamin, QC
Chief Executive, Gerard Sinclair

SCOTTISH ENTERPRISE

Atrium Court, 50 Waterloo Street, Glasgow G2 6HQ
T 0845-607 8787 E enquiries@scotent.co.uk
W www.scottish-enterprise.com

Scottish Enterprise was established in 1991 and its purpose is to stimulate the sustainable growth of Scotland's economy. It is mainly funded by the Scottish government and is responsible to the Scottish ministers. Working in partnership with the private and public sectors, Scottish Enterprise will invest £336m in 2013–14 to further the development of Scotland's economy by helping ambitious and innovative businesses grow and become more successful. Scottish Enterprise is particularly interested in supporting companies that provide renewable energy, encourage trade overseas, increase innovation, and those that will help Scotland become a low-carbon economy. Its grant-in-aid allocation (capital and resource allocation) for 2013–14 is £264.5m.

Chair, Crawford Gillies
Chief Executive, Dr Lena C. Wilson

SCOTTISH ENVIRONMENT PROTECTION AGENCY (SEPA)

Erskine Court, Castle Business Park, Stirling FK9 4TR
T 01786-457700 Hotline 0800-807060
E info@sepa.org.uk W www.sepa.org.uk

SEPA was established in 1996 and is the public body responsible for environmental protection in Scotland. It regulates potential pollution to land, air and water; the storage, transport and disposal of controlled waste; and the safekeeping and disposal of radioactive materials. It does this within a complex legislative framework of acts of parliament, EU directives and regulations, granting licences to operations of industrial processes and waste disposal. SEPA also operates Floodline (T 0845-988 1188), a public service providing information on the possible risk of flooding 24 hours a day, 365 days a year.

Chair, David Sigsworth
Chief Executive, James Curran
Directors, Calum MacDonald *(Operations);* David Pirie *(Science and Strategy)*

SCOTTISH LAW COMMISSION

140 Causewayside, Edinburgh EH9 1PR
T 0131-668 2131 E info@scotlawcom.gsi.gov.uk
W www.scotlawcom.gov.uk

The Scottish Law Commission, established in 1965, keeps the law in Scotland under review and makes proposals for its development and reform. It is responsible to the Scottish ministers through the Scottish government law and courts directorate.

Chair (part-time), Lady Clark of Calton
Chief Executive, M. McMillan
Commissioners, Ms L. Dunlop, QC; P. Layden, QC, TD; Prof. H. MacQueen; Dr A. Steven

SCOTTISH LEGAL AID BOARD

44 Drumsheugh Gardens, Edinburgh EH3 7SW
T 0131-226 7061 Helpline 0845-122 8686
E general@slab.org.uk W www.slab.org.uk

The Scottish Legal Aid Board was set up under the Legal Aid (Scotland) Act 1986 to manage legal aid in Scotland. It reports to the Scottish government. Board members are appointed by Scottish ministers.

Chair, Iain Robertson, CBE
Members, Les Campbell; Rani Dhir; Alastair Kinroy, QC; Ray MacFarlane; Vincent McGovern; Bill McQueen, CBE; Ros Micklem; Derek Ogg, QC; Sheriff Ray Small
Chief Executive, Lindsay Montgomery, CBE

SCOTTISH NATURAL HERITAGE (SNH)

Great Glen House, Leachkin Road, Inverness IV3 8NW
T 01463-725000 E enquiries@snh.gov.uk
W www.snh.org.uk

SNH was established in 1992 under the Natural Heritage (Scotland) Act 1991. It is the government's adviser on all aspects of nature and landscape across Scotland and its role is to help the public understand, value and enjoy Scotland's nature, as well as to support those people and organisations that manage it.

Chair, Andrew Thin
Chief Executive, Ian Jardine
Directors, Andrew Bachell *(Operations);* Susan Davies *(Policy and Advice);* Joe Moore *(Corporate Services)*

SEAFISH

18 Logie Mill, Logie Green Road, Edinburgh EH7 4HS
T 0131-558 3331 E seafish@seafish.co.uk
W www.seafish.org

Established under the Fisheries Act 1981, Seafish works with all sectors of the UK seafood industry to satisfy consumers, raise standards, improve efficiency and secure a sustainable and profitable future. Services range from research and development, economic consulting, market research and training and accreditation through to legislative advice for the seafood industry. It is sponsored by the four UK fisheries departments, which appoint the board, and is funded by a levy on seafood.

Chair, Elaine Hayes
Chief Executive, Dr Paul Williams

SENIOR SALARIES REVIEW BODY

6th Floor, Victoria House, Southampton Row, London WC1B 4AD
T 020-7271 0494 W www.ome.uk.com

The Senior Salaries Review Body (formerly the Top Salaries Review Body) was set up in 1971 to advise the prime minister on the remuneration of the judiciary, senior civil servants, senior officers of the armed forces and very senior managers in the NHS. In 1993 its remit was extended to cover the pay, pensions and allowances of MPs, ministers and others whose pay is determined by the Ministerial and Other Salaries Act 1975, and also the allowances of peers. If asked, it advises on the pay of officers and members of the devolved parliament and assemblies.

Chair, Bill Cockburn, CBE, TD

Members, Prof. Richard Disney; Margaret Edwards; Martin Fish; Dame Hazel Genn; Prof. David Metcalf, CBE; Bruce Warman

STUDENT LOANS COMPANY LTD

100 Bothwell Street, Glasgow G2 7JD
T 0141-306 2000 W www.slc.co.uk

The Student Loans Company (SLC) is owned by the Department for Business, Innovation and Skills and the Secretary of State for Scotland. It processes and administers financial assistance, in the form of grants and loans, for undergraduates who have secured a place at university or college. The SLC also provides loans for tuition fees, which are paid directly to the university or college.

Chair, Ed Smith
Chief Executive, Mick Laverty

TATE

W www.tate.org.uk

TATE BRITAIN
Millbank, London SW1P 4RG
T 020-7887 8888 E visiting.britain&modern@tate.org.uk

TATE MODERN
Bankside, London SE1 9TG
T 020-7887 8888 E visiting.britain&modern@tate.org.uk

TATE LIVERPOOL
Albert Dock, Liverpool L3 4BB
T 0151-702 7400 E visiting.liverpool@tate.org.uk

TATE ST IVES
Porthmeor Beach, St Ives, Cornwall TR26 1TG
T 01736-796226 E visiting.stives@tate.org.uk

Tate comprises four art galleries: Tate Britain and Tate Modern in London, Tate Liverpool and Tate St Ives.

Tate Britain, which opened in 1897, displays the national collection of British art from 1500 to the present day – with special attention and dedicated space given to Blake, Turner and Constable.

Opened in May 2000, Tate Modern displays the Tate collection of international modern art dating from 1900 to the present day. It includes works by Dalí, Picasso, Matisse and Warhol as well as many contemporary works. It is housed in the former Bankside Power Station in London, which was redesigned by the Swiss architects Herzog and de Meuron.

Tate Liverpool opened in 1988 and houses mainly 20th-century art and Tate St Ives, which features work by artists from and working in St Ives and includes the Barbara Hepworth Museum and Sculpture Garden, opened in 1993.

BOARD OF TRUSTEES
Chair, Lord Browne of Madingley
Trustees, Tomma Abts; Lionel Barber; Tom Bloxham, MBE; Prof. David Ekserdjian; Mala Gaonkar; Maja Hoffman; Lisa Milroy; Elisabeth Murdoch; Franck Petitgas; Monisha Shah; Gareth Thomas; Wolfgang Tillmans

OFFICERS
Director, Tate, Sir Nicholas Serota, CH
Directors, Dr Penelope Curtis *(Tate Britain);* Chris Dercon *(Tate Modern);* Caroline Collier *(Tate National);* Andrea Nixon *(Tate Liverpool);* Mark Osterfield *(Tate St Ives)*

TOURISM BODIES

Visit Britain, Visit Scotland, Visit Wales and the Northern Ireland Tourist Board are responsible for developing and marketing the tourist industry in their respective regions. Visit Wales is not listed here as it is part of the Welsh government, within the Department for Heritage, and not a public body.

VISIT BRITAIN
Sanctuary Buildings, 20 Great Smith Street, London SW1P 3BT
T 020-7578 1000 E industry.relations@visitbritain.org
W www.visitbritain.org
Chair, Christopher Rodrigues, CBE
Chief Executive, Sandie Dawe, MBE

VISIT SCOTLAND
Ocean Point One, 94 Ocean Drive, Edinburgh EH6 6JH
T 0131-472 2222
E info@visitscotland.com W www.visitscotland.com
Chair, Dr Mike Cantlay
Chief Executive, Malcolm Roughead, OBE

NORTHERN IRELAND TOURIST BOARD
St Anne's Court, 59 North Street, Belfast BT1 1NB
T 028-9023 1221
E info@nitb.com W www.discovernorthernireland.com
Chair, Howard Hastings
Chief Executive, Alan Clarke

TRANSPORT FOR LONDON (TFL)

Windsor House, 42–50 Victoria Street, London SW1H 0TL
E enquire@tfl.gov.uk W www.tfl.gov.uk

TfL was created in July 2000 and is the integrated body responsible for the capital's transport system. Its role is to implement the Mayor of London's transport strategy and manage the transport services across London for which the mayor has responsibility. These services include London's buses, London Underground, London Overground, the Docklands Light Railway (DLR), Tramlink, London River Services and Victoria Coach Station. TfL also runs the Emirates Air Line and the London Transport Museum.

TfL is responsible for managing the Congestion Charging scheme and for maintaining 360 miles (580km) of main roads and all of London's 6,000 traffic lights. It also regulates the city's taxis and private hire vehicles. TfL runs Barclays Cycle Hire and the Dial-a-ride scheme, a door-to-door service for disabled people unable to use buses, trams or the London Underground.

Chair, Boris Johnson
Members, Peter Anderson; Sir John Armitt, CBE; Sir Brendan Barber; Richard Barnes; Charles Belcher; Roger Burnley; Brian Cooke; Isabel Dedring; Baroness Grey-Thompson, DBE; Angela Knight; Michael Liebreich; Eva Lindholm; Daniel Moylan; Bob Oddy; Keith Williams; Steve Wright, MBE
Commissioner, Sir Peter Hendy, CBE

UK ATOMIC ENERGY AUTHORITY

Culham Science Centre, Abingdon, Oxfordshire OX14 3DB
T 01235-466647 W www.uk-atomic-energy.org.uk/ www.ccfe.ac.uk

The UK Atomic Energy Authority (UKAEA) was established by the Atomic Energy Authority Act 1954 and took over

responsibility for the research and development of the civil nuclear power programme. The UKAEA reports to the Department for Business, Innovation and Skills and is responsible for managing UK fusion research including operating the Joint European Torus (JET) on behalf of the European Fusion Development Agency (EFDA) at its site in Culham, Oxfordshire. In October 2009, as part of the government's Operation Efficiency Programme, the authority sold its commercial arm, UKAEA Limited; as a result, the UKAEA no longer provides nuclear decommissioning services.
Chair, Prof. Roger Cashmore
Chief Executive, Prof. Steven Cowley

UK SPORT

40 Bernard Street, London WC1N 1ST
T 020-7211 5100 E info@uksport.gov.uk W www.uksport.gov.uk

UK Sport was established by royal charter in 1997 and is accountable to parliament through the Department for Culture, Media and Sport. Its mission is to lead sport in the UK to world-class success. This means working with partner organisations to deliver medals at the Olympic and Paralympic Games and organising, bidding for and staging major sporting events in the UK; increasing the UK's sporting activity and influence overseas; and promoting sporting conduct, ethics and diversity in society. UK Sport is funded by a mix of grant-in-aid and National Lottery income. For 2013–14 projected grant-in-aid and National Lottery funding will amount to approximately £125m.
Chair, Rod Carr, CBE
Chief Executive, Liz Nicholl, OBE

VICTORIA AND ALBERT MUSEUM

Cromwell Road, London SW7 2RL
T 020-7942 2000 W www.vam.ac.uk

The Victoria and Albert Museum (V&A) is the national museum of fine and applied art and design. It descends directly from the Museum of Manufactures, which opened in Marlborough House in 1852 after the Great Exhibition of 1851. The museum was moved in 1857 to become part of the South Kensington Museum. It was renamed the Victoria and Albert Museum in 1899. It also houses the National Art Library and Print Room.

The museum administers the V&A Museum of Childhood at Bethnal Green, which opened in 1872; the building is the most important surviving example of the type of glass and iron construction used by Joseph Paxton for the Great Exhibition. Total government grant-in-aid for 2013–14 is £39.4m.
Chair, Sir Paul Ruddock
Trustees, Joao Baptista; Nicholas Coleridge, CBE; Mark Damazer, CBE; Edwin Davies, CBE; Prof. Margot Finn; Andrew Hochhauser, QC; Stephen McGuckin; Michelle Ogundehin; Dame Theresa Sackler; Samir Shah, OBE; Sir John Sorrell; Bob Stefanowski; Dr Paul Thompson; Harold Tillman, CBE; Edmund de Waal, OBE; Prof. Evelyn Welch
Director, Prof. Martin Roth

WALLACE COLLECTION

Hertford House, Manchester Square, London W1U 3BN
T 020-7563 9500 E collections@wallacecollection.org
W www.wallacecollection.org

The Wallace Collection was bequeathed to the nation by the widow of Sir Richard Wallace, in 1897, and Hertford House was subsequently acquired by the government. The collection contains works by Titian and Rembrandt, and includes porcelain, furniture and an array of arms and armour.
Chair, Sir John Ritblat
Trustees, Prof. Jasper Conran, OBE; Prof. Frances Corner, OBE; Duke of Devonshire, KCVO, CBE; Richard Dorment; Jennifer Eady, QC; Rupert Hambro; Jagdip Jagpal; Denise Lewis; Jessica Pulay; Sir Hugh Roberts, GCVO, FSA; Kate de Rothschild Agius; Dr Ashok Roy; Adrian Sassoon; TImothy Schrofer
Director, Dr Christoph Vogtherr

REGIONAL GOVERNMENT

LONDON

GREATER LONDON AUTHORITY (GLA)

City Hall, The Queen's Walk, London SE1 2AA
T 020-7983 4000 E mayor@london.gov.uk
W www.london.gov.uk

On 7 May 1998 London voted in favour of the formation of the Greater London Authority (GLA). The first elections to the GLA took place on 4 May 2000 and the new authority took over its responsibilities on 3 July 2000. In July 2002 the GLA moved to one of London's most spectacular buildings, newly built on a brownfield site on the south bank of the Thames, adjacent to Tower Bridge. The fourth and most recent election to the GLA took place on 3 May 2012.

The structure and objectives of the GLA stem from its main areas of responsibility: transport, policing, fire and emergency planning, economic development, planning, culture and health. There are four functional bodies which form part of the wider GLA group and report to the GLA: the Mayor's Office for Policing and Crime (MOPAC), Transport for London (TfL), the London Fire and Emergency Planning Authority (LFEPA) and the London Legacy Development Corporation, established in 2012.

The GLA consists of a directly elected mayor, the Mayor of London, and a separately elected assembly, the London Assembly. The mayor has the key role of decision making, with the assembly performing the tasks of regulating and scrutinising these decisions, and investigating issues of importance to Londoners. In addition, the GLA has around 600 permanent staff to support the activities of the mayor and the assembly, which are overseen by a head of paid service. The mayor may appoint two political advisers and not more than ten other members of staff, though he does not necessarily exercise this power, but he does not appoint the chief executive, the monitoring officer or the chief finance officer. These must be appointed jointly by the assembly and the mayor.

Every aspect of the assembly and its activities must be open to public scrutiny and therefore accountable. The assembly holds the mayor to account through scrutiny of his strategies, decisions and actions. Mayor's Question Time, conducted on ten occasions a year at City Hall, is carried out by direct questioning at assembly meetings and by conducting detailed investigations in committee.

People's Question Time and Talk London give Londoners the chance to question the mayor and the assembly about plans, priorities and policies for London. People's Question Time is held twice a year, and Talk London is held four times a year in venues across London.

The role of the mayor can be broken down into a number of key areas:

- to represent and promote London at home and abroad and speak up for Londoners
- to devise strategies and plans to tackle London-wide issues, such as crime, transport, housing, planning, economic development and regeneration, environment, public services, society and culture, sport and health; and to set budgets for TfL, MOPAC, LFEPA and the London Legacy Development Corporation
- the mayor is chair of TfL, and is responsible for the Metropolitan Police's priorities and performance

The role of the assembly can be broken down into a number of key areas:

- to hold the mayor to account by examining his decisions and actions
- to have the power to amend the mayor's budget by a majority of two-thirds
- to have the power to summon the mayor, senior staff of the GLA and functional bodies
- to investigate issues of London-wide significance and make proposals to appropriate stakeholders
- to examine the work of MOPAC and to review the police and crime plan for London through the newly formed Police and Crime Committee

Mayor, Boris Johnson
Deputy Mayors, Victoria Borwick *(Statutory Deputy Mayor);* Richard Blakeway *(Housing, Land and Property);* Isabel Dedring *(Transport);* Stephen Greenhalgh *(Policing and Crime)*; Sir Edward Lister *(Policy and Planning, and Chief of Staff);* Kit Malthouse *(Business and Enterprise);* Munira Mirza *(Education and Culture)*
Chair of the London Assembly, Darren Johnson
Deputy Chair of the Assembly, Roger Evans

ELECTIONS AND VOTING SYSTEMS

The assembly is elected every four years at the same time as the mayor, and consists of 25 members. There is one member from each of the 14 GLA constituencies topped up with 11 London-wide members who are either representatives of political parties or individuals standing as independent candidates. The last election was on 3 May 2012.

Two distinct voting systems are used to appoint the existing mayor and the assembly. The mayor is elected using the supplementary vote system (SVS). With SVS, electors have two votes: one to give a first choice for mayor and one to give a second choice; they cannot vote twice for the same candidate. If one candidate gets more than half of all the first-choice votes, he or she becomes mayor. If no candidate gets more than half of the first-choice votes, the two candidates with the most first-choice votes remain in the election and all the other candidates drop out. The second-choice votes on the ballot papers for the candidates who have dropped out are then counted. Where these second-choice votes are for the two remaining candidates they are added to the first-choice votes these candidates already have. The candidate with the most first- and second-choice votes combined becomes the Mayor of London.

The assembly is appointed using the additional member system (AMS). Under AMS, electors have two votes. The first vote is for a constituency candidate. The second vote is for a party list or individual candidate contesting the London-wide assembly seats. The 14 constituency members are elected under the first-past-the-post system, the same system used in general and local elections. Electors vote for one candidate and the candidate with the most votes wins. The additional members are drawn from party lists or are independent candidates who stand as London members; they are chosen using a form of proportional representation.

The Greater London Returning Officer (GLRO) is the independent official responsible for running the election in London. He is supported in this by returning officers in each of the 14 London constituencies.

GLRO, John Bennett

TRANSPORT FOR LONDON (TFL)

TfL is the integrated body responsible for London's transport system. Its role is to implement the mayor's transport strategy for London and manage transport services across the capital for which the mayor has responsibility. TfL is directed by a management board whose members are chosen for their understanding of transport matters and are appointed by the mayor, who chairs the board. TfL's role is:

- to manage the London Underground, buses, Croydon Tramlink, London Overground and the Docklands Light Railway (DLR)
- to manage a 580km network of main roads and all 6,000 of London's traffic lights
- to regulate taxis and minicabs
- to run the London River Services, Victoria Coach Station and London Transport Museum
- to help to coordinate the Dial-a-Ride, Capital Call and Taxicard schemes for door-to-door services for transport users with mobility problems

The London Borough Councils maintain the role of highway and traffic authorities for 95 per cent of London's roads. A £5 congestion charge for motorists driving into central London between the hours of 7am and 6.30pm, Monday to Friday (excluding public holidays) was introduced on 17 February 2003, and was subsequently raised to £8 on 4 July 2005. On 19 February 2007, the charge zone roughly doubled in size after a westward expansion and the charging hours were shortened, to finish at 6pm. On 4 January 2011, the westward expansion was removed from the charging zone and the charge was increased to £10; an automated payment system was also introduced.

TfL introduced a low emission zone (LEZ) for London on 4 February 2008 which is in constant operation. Following tougher emissions standards introduced on 3 January 2012 there is a daily charge for polluting vehicles entering the zone (which covers most of Greater London) that do not meet Euro 3 or Euro 4 emissions standards. With the exception of minibuses, vehicles over three-and-a-half tonnes such as lorries, buses and coaches, face a daily charge of £200. Vehicles up to three-and-a-half tonnes and minibuses (with more than eight passenger seats) up to five tonnes pay a daily charge of £100. For further information *see* W www.tfl.gov.uk/lez

Since 2 January 2009, Londoners over pensionable age (or over 60 if born before 1950) and those with eligible disabilities are entitled to free travel on the capital's transport network at any time. War veterans who are receiving ongoing payments under the war pensions scheme, or those receiving guaranteed income payments under the armed forces compensation scheme can travel free at any time on bus, underground, DLR, tram and London Overground services and at certain times on National Rail services.

In the summer of 2010, the London cycle hire scheme launched with 6,000 new bicycles for hire from 400 docking stations across eight boroughs, the City and the Royal parks. The scheme has been expanded and there are now around 8,300 bicycles available from 15,000 docking stations across London. As at December 2012, 18 million bicycles had been hired since the scheme began.

Commissioner of Transport for London, Peter Hendy, CBE

MAYOR'S OFFICE FOR POLICING AND CRIME (MOPAC)

The Mayor's Office for Policing and Crime (MOPAC) was set up in response to the Police Reform and Social Responsibility Act 2011, replacing the Metropolitan Police Authority. MOPAC is headed by the mayor, or the appointed statutory deputy mayor for policing and crime. Operational responsibility of MOPAC remains under the responsibility of the Metropolitan Police Commissioner. The major areas of focus of MOPAC are:

- operational policing and crime reduction including counter terrorism
- ensuring the Metropolitan Police effectively reduce gang crime and violence in London and coordinating support for communities and local organisations to prevent gang activities
- criminal justice, including preventing reoffending, reducing crime and decreasing demand within the criminal justice system in addition to reducing alcohol and drug abuse.

The Police and Crime Committee, consisting of nine elected members of the London Assembly, scrutinises the work of MOPAC and meet regularly to hold to account the Deputy Mayor for Policing and Crime.

Deputy Mayor for Policing and Crime, Stephen Greenhalgh

LONDON FIRE AND EMERGENCY PLANNING AUTHORITY (LFEPA)

In July 2000 the London Fire and Civil Defence Authority became the London Fire and Emergency Planning Authority. It consists of 17 members, eight drawn from the assembly, seven from the London boroughs and two mayoral appointees. The role of the LFEPA is:

- to set the strategy for the provision of fire services
- to ensure that the fire brigade can meet all the normal requirements efficiently
- to ensure that effective arrangements are made for the fire brigade to receive emergency calls and deal with them promptly
- to ensure members of the fire brigade are properly trained and equipped
- to ensure that information useful to the development of the fire brigades is gathered
- to ensure arrangements for advice and guidance on fire protection are made

Chair, James Cleverly

LONDON LEGACY DEVELOPMENT CORPORATION

Following the London 2012 Olympic Games, the London Legacy Development Corporation was made responsible for the long-term planning, development, management and maintenance of the Queen Elizabeth Olympic Park (formerly the Olympic Park) and its facilities. The organisation is tasked with transforming the area into a thriving neighbourhood.

Chair, Boris Johnson

SALARIES *as at July 2013*	
Mayor	£143,911
Deputy Mayors	
Victoria Borwick	£96,092
Richard Blakeway	£127,784
Isabel Dedring	£127,784
Stephen Greenhalgh	£127,784
Sir Edward Lister	£139,000
Kit Malthouse	£127,784
Munira Mirza	£127,784
Chair of the Assembly	£64,103
Assembly Members	£53,439

LONDON ASSEMBLY COMMITTEES

Chair, Audit Panel, John Biggs
Chair, Budget and Performance Committee, John Biggs
Chair, Budget Monitoring Sub-Committee, John Biggs
Chair, Confirmation Hearings Committee, various
Chair, Economy Committee, Stephen Knight
Chair, Environment Committee, Murad Qureshi

Chair, GLA Oversight Committee, Len Duvall
Chair, Health Committee, Onkar Sahota
Chair, Housing Committee, Darren Johnson
Chair, Planning Committee, Nicky Gavron
Chair, Police and Crime Committee, Joanne McCartney
Chair, Regeneration Committee, Gareth Bacon
Chair, Taser Working Group, Joanne McCartney
Chair, Transport Committee, Valerie Shawcross

LONDON ASSEMBLY MEMBERS

as at 3 May 2012

Arbour, Tony, *C., South West,* Maj. 19,262
Arnold, Jennette, *Lab. North East,* Maj. 66,188
Bacon, Gareth, *C., London List*
Biggs, John, *Lab., City and East,* Maj. 82,744
Boff, Andrew, *C., London List*
Borwick, Victoria, *C., London List*
Cleverly, James, *C., Bexley and Bromley,* Maj. 47,768
Copley, Tom, *Lab. London List*
Dismore, Andrew, *Lab., Barnet and Camden,* Maj. 21,299
Duvall, Len, *Lab., Greenwich and Lewisham,* Maj. 38,037
Evans, Roger, *C., Havering and Redbridge,* Maj. 3,899
Gavron, Nicky, *Lab., London List*
Johnson, Darren, *Green, London List*
Jones, Jenny, *Green, London List*
Knight, Stephen, *LD, London List*
Malthouse, Kit, *C., West Central,* Maj. 29,131
McCartney, Joanne, *Lab., Enfield and Haringey,* Maj. 36,741
O'Connell, Steve, *C., Croydon and Sutton,* Maj. 9,418
Pidgeon, Caroline, *LD, London List*
Qureshi, Murad, *Lab., London List*
Sahota, Onkar, *Lab., Ealing and Hillingdon,* Maj. 3,110
Shah, Navin, *Lab., Brent and Harrow,* Maj. 29,796
Shawcross, Valerie, *Lab., Lambeth and Southwark,* Maj. 52,702
Tracey, Richard, *C., Merton and Wandsworth,* Maj. 9,981
Twycross, Fiona, *Lab., London List*

STATE OF THE PARTIES *as at 3 May 2012*

Party	*Seats*
Conservative (C.)	9
Labour (Lab.)	12
Liberal Democrats (LD)	2
Green	2

MAYORAL ELECTION RESULTS

as at 3 May 2012

Electorate 5,910,460 Turnout 38%

Change in turnout from 2008: -7.33%
Good votes: 1st choice 2,208,475 (98.21%); 2nd choice 1,763,009 (79.83%)
Rejected votes: 1st choice 40,210 (1.79%); 2nd choice 445,466 (20.17%)

First	*Party*	*Votes*	*%*
Boris Johnson	C.	971,931	44.01
Ken Livingstone	Lab.	889,918	40.30
Jenny Jones	Green	98,913	4.48
Brian Paddick	LD	91,774	4.16
Siobhan Benita	Ind.	83,914	3.80
Lawrence Webb	UKIP	43,274	1.96
Carlos Cortiglia	BNP	28,751	1.30

Second	*Party*	*Votes*	*%*
Brian Paddick	LD	363,692	20.63
Jenny Jones	Green	363,193	20.60
Ken Livingstone	Lab.	335,398	19.02
Boris Johnson	C.	253,709	14.39
Siobhan Benita	Ind.	212,412	12.05
Lawrence Webb	UKIP	161,252	9.15
Carlos Cortiglia	BNP	73,353	4.16

LONDON ASSEMBLY ELECTION RESULTS

as at 3 May 2012

E. Electorate T. Turnout
See General Election Results for a list of party abbreviations

CONSTITUENCIES
E. 5,910,460 T. 38%

BARNET AND CAMDEN
E. 446,248 T. 38%

Andrew Dismore, Lab.	74,677
Brian Coleman, C.	53,378
Audrey Poppy, Green	17,904
Chris Richards, LD	13,800
Michael Corby, UKIP	7,331

Lab. majority 21,299

BEXLEY AND BROMLEY
E. 447,465 T. 38.1%

James Cleverly, C.	88,482
Josie Channer, Lab.	40,714
Sam Webber, LD,	11,396
David Cobum, UKIP	10,771
Jonathan Rooks, Green	9,209
Donna Treanor, BNP	7,563

C. majority 47,768

BRENT AND HARROW
E. 389,737 T. 38%

Navin Shah, Lab.	70,400
Sachin Rajput, C.	40,604
Charlotte Henry, LD	15,690
Shahrar Ali, Green	10,546
Mick McGough, UKIP	7,830

Lab. majority 29,796

CITY AND EAST
E. 500,427 T. 34.8%

John Biggs, Lab.	107,667
John Moss, C.	24,923
Chris Smith, Green	10,891
Richard Macmillan, LD	7,351
Paul Borg, BNP	7,031
Kamran Malik, CUP	6,774
Steven Woolfe, UKIP	5,243
Paul Davies, Comm. Lge	1,108

Lab. majority 82,744

CROYDON AND SUTTON
E. 436,451 T. 35.7%

Stephen O'Connell, C.	60,152
Louisa Woodley, Lab.	50,734
Abigail Lock, LD	21,889
Winston McKenzie, UKIP	10,757
Gordon Ross, Green	10,287

C. majority 9,418

EALING AND HILLINGDON
E. 439,143 T. 37.9%

Onkar Sahota, Lab.	65,584
Richard Barnes, C.	62,474
Michael Cox, LD	11,805
Mike Harling, Green	10,877
Helen Knight, UKIP	6,750
Dave Furness, BNP	4,284
Ian Edward, NF	2,035

Lab. majority 3,110

ENFIELD AND HARINGEY
E. 383,623 T. 38.3%

Joanne McCartney, Lab.	74,034
Andy Hemsted, C.	37,293
Dawn Barnes, LD	13,601
Peter Krakowiak, Green	12,278
Peter Staveley, UKIP	4,298
Marie Nicholas, BNP	3,081

Lab. majority 36,741

GREENWICH AND LEWISHAM
E. 359,742 T. 37.2%

Len Duvall, Lab.	65,366
Alex Wilson, C.	27,329
Roger Sedgley, Green	12,427
John Russell, LD	9,393
Barbara Raymond, PBP	6,873
Paul Oakley, UKIP	4,997
Roberta Woods, BNP	3,551
Tess Culnane, NF	1,816

Lab. majority 38,037

HAVERING AND REDBRIDGE
E. 389,814 T. 36.9%

Roger Evans, C.	53,285
Mandy Richards, Lab.	49,386
Lawrence Webb, UKIP	9,471
Melvin Brown, RAL	8,239
Farrukh Islam, LD	6,435
Robert Taylor, BNP	5,234
Haroon Saad, Green	5,207
Mark Twiddy, Eng. Dem.	2,573
Richard Edmonds, NF	1,936

C. majority 3,899

LAMBETH AND SOUTHWARK
E. 422,981 T. 37.8%

Valerie Shawcross, Lab.	83,239
Michael Mitchell, C.	30,537
Rob Blackie, LD	18,359
Jonathan Bartley, Green	18,144
James Fluss, UKIP	4,395
Daniel Lambert, Soc.	2,938

Lab. majority 52,702

MERTON AND WANDSWORTH
E. 376,365 T. 40.9%

Richard Tracey, C.	65,197
Leonie Cooper, Lab.	55,216
Lisa Smart, LD	11,904
Roy Vickery, Green	11,307
Mazhar Manzoor, UKIP	3,717
Thamilini Kulendran, Ind.	2,424
James Martin, Soc.	1,343

C. majority 9,981

NORTH EAST
E. 499,418 T. 39.1%

Jennette Arnold, Lab.	101,902
Naomi Newstead, C.	35,714
Caroline Allen, Green	29,677
Farooq Qureshi, LD	13,237
Paul Wiffen, UKIP	6,623
Ijaz Hayat, Ind.	4,842

Lab. majority 66,188

SOUTH WEST
E. 437,945 T. 40.2%

Tony Arbour, C.	69,151
Lisa Homan, Lab.	49,889
Munira Wilson, LD	28,947
Daniel Goldsmith, Green	17,070
Jeff Bolter, UKIP	8,505

C. majority 19,262

WEST CENTRAL
E. 381,101 T. 39.2%

Kit Malthouse, C.	73,761
Todd Foreman, Lab.	44,630
Susanna Rustin, Green	12,799
Layla Moran, LD	10,035
Elizabeth Jones, UKIP	5,161

C. majority 29,131

LONDON-WIDE MEMBERS

Conservative	*Labour Party*
Gareth Bacon	Tom Copley
Andrew Boff	Nicky Gavron
Victoria Borwick	Murad Qureshi
	Fiona Twycross
Green Party	*Liberal Democrat*
Darren Johnson	Stephen Knight
Jenny Jones	Caroline Pidgeon

WALES

WELSH GOVERNMENT

Cathays Park, Cardiff CF10 3NQ
T 0845-010 3300 W http://wales.gov.uk

The Welsh government is the devolved government of Wales. It is accountable to the National Assembly for Wales, the Welsh legislature which represents the interests of the people of Wales, and makes laws for Wales. The Welsh government and the National Assembly for Wales were established as separate institutions under the Government of Wales Act 2006.

The Welsh government comprises the first minister, who is usually the leader of the largest party in the National Assembly for Wales; up to 14 ministers and deputy ministers; and a counsel general (the chief legal adviser).

Following the referendum on 3 March 2011 on granting further law-making powers to the National Assembly, the Welsh government's functions now include the ability to propose bills to the National Assembly on subjects within 20 set areas of policy. Subject to limitations prescribed by the Government of Wales Act 2006, acts of the National Assembly may make any provision that could be made by act of parliament. The 20 areas of responsibility devolved to the National Assembly for Wales (and within which Welsh ministers exercise executive functions) are: agriculture, fisheries, forestry and rural development; ancient monuments and historic buildings; culture; economic development; education and training; environment; fire and rescue services and promotion of fire safety; food; health and health services; highways and transport; housing; local government; the National Assembly for Wales; public administration; social welfare; sport and recreation; tourism; town and county planning; water and flood defence; and the Welsh language.

First Minister of Wales, Rt. Hon. Carwyn Jones, AM
Minister for Communities and Tackling Poverty, Huw Lewis, AM
Minister for Culture and Sport, John Griffiths, AM
Minister for Economy, Science and Transport, Edwina Hart, MBE, AM
Minister for Education and Skills, Leighton Andrews, AM
Minister for Finance and Leader of the House, Jane Hutt, AM
Minister for Health and Social Services, Mark Drakeford, AM
Minister for Housing and Regeneration, Carl Sargeant, AM
Minister for Local Government and Government Business, Lesley Griffiths, AM
Minister for Natural Resources and Food, Alun Davies, AM
Deputy Minister for Children and Social Services, Gwenda Thomas, AM
Deputy Minister for Skills and Technology, Jeff Cuthbert, AM
Counsel General of Wales, Theodore Huckle, QC
Chief Whip, Janice Gregory, AM

MANAGEMENT BOARD
Permanent Secretary, Derek Jones
Director-General, Strategic Planning, Finance and Performance, Michael Hearty
Director-General, Economy, Science and Transport, James Price
Director-General, Education and Skills, Owen Evans
Director-General, Health, Social Services and Children and Chief Executive of NHS Wales, David Sissling
Director-General, Local Government and Communities, Dr June Milligan

Director-General, People, Places and Corporate Services, Bernard Galton
Director-General, Sustainable Futures, Gareth Jones (acting)
Non-Executive Directors, Elan Closs Stephens; James Turner; Adrian Webb

DEPARTMENTS
Department for Education and Skills
Department for Health, Social Services and Children
Department for Economy, Science and Transport
Department for Strategic Planning, Finance and Performance
Local Government and Communities
People, Places and Corporate Services
Permanent Secretary's Division (Office of the First Minister; Legal Services Department; European and External Affairs Division; Constitutional Affairs and Inter-governmental Relations Division)
Sustainable Futures

ASSEMBLY COMMITTEES
Children and Young People
Communities, Equality and Local Government
Constitutional and Legislative Affairs
Enterprise and Business
Environment and Sustainability
Finance
Health and Social Care
Petitions
Public Accounts
Scrutiny of the First Minister
Standards of Conduct

ASSEMBLY COMMISSION
The Assembly Commission was created under the Government of Wales Act 2006 to ensure that the assembly is provided with the property, staff and services required for it to carry out its functions. The commission also sets the National Assembly's strategic aims, objectives, standards and values. The Assembly Commission consists of the presiding officer, plus four other assembly members, one nominated by each of the four party groups. The five commissioners are accountable to the National Assembly.
Presiding Officer, Rosemary Butler, AM
Commissioners, Peter Black, Angela Burns, Rhodri Glyn Thomas, Sandy Mewies
Chief Executive and Clerk of the Assembly, Claire Clancy

NATIONAL ASSEMBLY FOR WALES

Cardiff Bay, Cardiff CF99 1NA
T 0845-010 5500 W www.assemblywales.org

In July 1997 the government announced plans to establish a National Assembly for Wales. In a referendum in September 1997 about 50 per cent of the electorate voted, of whom 50.3 per cent voted in favour of a national assembly. Elections are held every four years and the first election took place on 6 May 1999. The fourth election took place on 5 May 2011.

National Assembly members are elected using the additional member system. Voters are given two votes: one for a constituency member and one for a regional member. The constituency members are elected under the first-past-the-post system, also used to elect constituency members to the London Assembly. Four regional members in each of the five constituencies are then chosen from party lists or independent candidates using a form of proportional representation.

Until 2007 the National Assembly for Wales was a corporate body comprising both the executive and legislative branches of government. It had no primary law-making powers and only had responsibility for exercising and implementing ministerial functions which had previously been vested in the Secretary of State for Wales.

The Government of Wales Act 2006 introduced a radical change to the functions and status of the National Assembly for Wales. With effect from 25 May 2007 the act formally separated the National Assembly for Wales (the legislature – made up of 60 elected assembly members) and the Welsh government (the executive – comprising the first minister, Welsh ministers, deputy Welsh ministers and the counsel general). It also made changes to the electoral process: candidates are no longer permitted to stand as both constituency and regional members. The act enabled the National Assembly for Wales to formulate its own legislation (assembly measures) on the 20 devolved areas for which it has responsibility (*see* Welsh government); the assembly was given legislative competence (the legal authority to pass measures) on a case-by-case basis by the UK parliament.

The act also included a mechanism that would allow for full transfer of legislative powers relating to all devolved matters to the National Assembly, provided that the people of Wales voted for such a proposal in a referendum. In a referendum held on 3 March 2011, 63.5 per cent voted in favour of giving the National Assembly full legislative powers for all devolved matters. The National Assembly for Wales can now pass legislation (assembly acts) on the 20 devolved areas for which it has responsibility. An assembly act has the same powers as an act of the UK parliament and may be proposed by the Welsh government, assembly committees, an assembly member or the assembly commission.

The National Assembly for Wales also scrutinises and monitors the Welsh government. It meets in plenary in the Senedd debating chamber. The 60 assembly members examine and approve assembly bills and approve certain items of subordinate legislation; approve the Welsh government and assembly commission's budget; hold Welsh ministers to account; and analyse and debate their decisions and policies.
Presiding Officer, Rosemary Butler AM

SALARIES *2012–13*

First Minister*	£80,870
Minister/Presiding Officer*	£41,949
Deputy Minister/Deputy Presiding Officer*	£26,385
Assembly Members (AM)†	£53,852

* Also receives the assembly member salary
† Reduced by two-thirds if the member is already an MP or an MEP

MEMBERS OF THE NATIONAL ASSEMBLY FOR WALES

as at 1 July 2012
Andrews, Leighton, *Lab., Rhondda,* Maj. 6,739
Antoniw, Mick, *Lab., Pontypridd,* Maj. 7,694
Asghar, Mohammad, *C., South Wales East region*
Black, Peter, *LD, South Wales West region*
Burns, Angela, *C., Carmarthen West and South Pembrokeshire,* Maj. 1,504
Butler, Rosemary, *Lab., Newport W.,* Maj. 4,220
Chapman, Christine, *Lab., Cynon Valley,* Maj. 6,515
Cuthbert, Jeff, *Lab., Caerphilly,* Maj. 4,924
Davies, Alun, *Lab., Blaenau Gwent,*Maj. 9,120
Davies, Andrew R. T., *C., South Wales Central region*
Davies, Byron, *C., South Wales West region*
Davies, Jocelyn, *PC, South Wales East region*
Davies, Keith, *Lab., Llanelli,* Maj. 80
Davies, Paul, *C., Preseli Pembrokeshire,* Maj. 2,175
Davies, Suzy, *C., South Wales West region*

Drakeford, Mark, *Lab., Cardiff West,* Maj. 5,901
Elis-Thomas, Lord, *PC, Dwyfor Meirionnydd,* Maj. 5,417
Evans, Rebecca, *Lab., Mid and West Wales region*
Finch-Saunders, Janet, *C., Aberconwy,* Maj. 1,567
George, Russell, *C., Montgomeryshire,* Maj. 2,324
Gething, Vaughan, *Lab., Cardiff South and Penarth,* Maj. 6,259
Graham, William, *C., South Wales East region*
Gregory, Janice, *Lab., Ogmore,* Maj. 9,576
Griffiths, John, *Lab., Newport East,* Maj. 5,388
Griffiths, Lesley, *Lab., Wrexham,* Maj. 3,337
Hart, Edwina, *Lab., Gower,* Maj. 4,864
Hedges, Mike, *Lab., Swansea East,* Maj. 8,281
Hutt, Jane, *Lab., Vale of Glamorgan,* Maj. 3,775
Huws Gruffydd, Llyr, *PC, North Wales region*
Isherwood, Mark, *C., North Wales region*
James, Julie, *Lab., Swansea West,* Maj. 4,654
Jenkins, Bethan, *PC, South Wales West region*
Jones, Alun Ffred, *PC, Arfon,* Maj. 5,394
Jones, Ann, *Lab., Vale of Clwyd,* Maj. 4,011
Jones, Carwyn, *Lab., Bridgend,* Maj. 6,775
Jones, Elin, *PC, Ceredigion,* Maj. 1,777
Lewis, Huw, *Lab., Merthyr Tydfil and Rhymney,* Maj. 7,051
Melding, David, *C., South Wales Central region*
Mewies, Sandra, *Lab., Delyn,* Maj. 2,881
Millar, Darren, *C., Clwyd West,* Maj. 4,248
Morgan, Julie, *Lab., Cardiff North,* Maj. 1,782
Neagle, Lynne, *Lab., Torfaen,* Maj. 6,088
Parrott, Eluned, *LD, South Wales Central region*
Powell, William, *LD, Mid and West Wales region*
Price, Gwyn, *Lab., Islwyn,* Maj. 7,589
Ramsay, Nicholas, *C., Monmouth,* Maj. 6,117
Rathbone, Jenny, *Lab., Cardiff Central,* Maj. 38
Rees, David, *Lab., Aberavon,* Maj. 9,311
Roberts, Aled, *LD, North Wales region*
Sandbach, Antoinette, *C., North Wales region*
Sargeant, Carl, *Lab., Alyn and Deeside,* Maj. 5,581
Skates, Ken, *Lab., Clwyd South,* Maj. 2,659
Thomas, Gwenda, *Lab., Neath,* Maj. 6,390
Thomas, Rhodri Glyn, *PC, Carmarthen East and Dinefwr,* Maj. 4,148
Thomas, Simon, *PC, Mid and West Wales region*
Watson, Joyce, *Lab., Mid and West Wales region*
Whittle, Lindsay, *PC, South Wales East region*
Williams, Kirsty, *LD, Brecon and Radnorshire,* Maj. 2,757
Wood, Leanne, *PC, South Wales Central region*
Wyn Jones, Ieuan, *PC, Ynys Mon,* Maj. 2,937

STATE OF THE PARTIES
as at 1 July 2013

	Constituency AMs	*Regional AMs*	*AM total*
Labour (Lab.)	28*	2	30
Conservative (C.)	6	8†	14
Plaid Cymru (PC)	5	6	11
Liberal Democrats (LD)	1	4	5
Total	40	20	60

* Includes the Presiding Officer
† Includes the Deputy Presiding Officer

NATIONAL ASSEMBLY ELECTION RESULTS
as at 5 May 2011

E. Electorate T. Turnout
See General Election Results for a list of party abbreviations

CONSTITUENCIES
E. 2,289,555 T. 41.5%

ABERAVON (S. WALES WEST)
E. 50,754 T. 18,879 (37.20%)

David Rees, Lab.	12,104
Paul Nicholls-Jones, PC	2,793
Tamojen Morgan, C.	2,704
Helen Ceri Clarke, LD	1,278

Lab. majority 9,311 (49.32%)
8.65% swing PC to Lab.

ABERCONWY (WALES N.)
E. 44,978 T. 20,288 (45.11%)

Janet Finch-Saunders, C.	6,888
Iwan Huws, PC	5,321
Eifion Wyn Williams, Lab.	5,206
Mike Priestley, LD	2,873

C. majority 1,567 (7.72%)
7.95% swing PC to C.

ALYN AND DEESIDE (WALES N.)
E. 61,751 T. 22,769 (36.87%)

Carl Sargeant, Lab.	11,978
John Bell, C.	6,397
Pete Williams, LD	1,725
Shane Brennan, PC	1,710
Michael Whitby, BNP	959

Lab. majority 5,581 (24.51%)
4.29% swing C. to Lab.

ARFON (WALES N.)
E. 41,093 T. 17,664 (42.99%)

Alun Ffred Jones, PC	10,024
Christina Rees, Lab.	4,630
Aled Davies, C.	2,209
Rhys Jones, LD	801

PC majority 5,394 (30.54%)
2.45% swing Lab. to PC

BLAENAU GWENT (S. WALES EAST)
E. 53,230 T. 20,211 (37.97%)

Alun Davies, Lab.	12,926
Jayne Sullivan, Ind.	3,806
Darren Jones, PC	1,098
Bob Hayward, C.	1,066
Brian Urch, BNP	948
Martin Blakeborough, LD	367

Lab. majority 9,120 (45.12%)
33.95% swing Ind. to Lab.

BRECON AND RADNORSHIRE (WALES MID AND W.)
E. 53,546 T. 28,348 (52.94%)

Kirsty Williams, LD	12,201
Chris Davies, C.	9,444
Christopher Lloyd, Lab.	4,797
Gary Price, PC	1,906

LD majority 2,757 (9.73%)
4.45% swing LD to C.

BRIDGEND (S. WALES WEST)
E. 59,104 T. 24,035 (40.67%)

Carwyn Jones, Lab.	13,499
Alex Williams, C.	6,724
Tim Thomas, PC	2,076
Briony Davies, LD	1,736

Lab. majority 6,775 (28.19%)
8.89% swing C. to Lab.

CAERPHILLY (S. WALES EAST)
E. 62,049 T. 25,570 (41.21%)

Jeff Cuthbert, Lab.	12,521
Ron Davies, PC	7,597
Owen Meredith, C.	3,368
Kay David, LD	1,062
Anthony King, BNP	1,022

Lab. majority 4,924 (19.26%)
5.25% swing PC to Lab.

CARDIFF CENTRAL (S. WALES CENTRAL)
E. 64,347 T. 23,628 (36.72%)

Jenny Rathbone, Lab.	8,954
Nigel Howells, LD	8,916
Matt Smith, C.	3,559
Chris Williams, PC	1,690
Mathab Khan, Ind.	509

Lab. majority 38 (0.16%)
14.74% swing LD to Lab.

CARDIFF NORTH
(S. WALES CENTRAL)
E. 66,934 T. 34,431 (51.44%)

Julie Morgan, Lab.	16,384
Jonathan Morgan, C.	14,602
Ben Foday, PC	1,850
Matt Smith, LD	1,595

Lab. majority 1,782 (5.18%)
9.77% swing C. to Lab.

CARDIFF SOUTH AND PENARTH
(S. WALES CENTRAL)
E. 75,038 T. 27,479 (36.62%)

Vaughan Gething, Lab.	13,814
Ben Gray, C.	7,555
Liz Musa, PC	3,324
Sian Cliff, LD	2,786

Lab. majority 6,259 (22.78%)
6.24% swing C. to Lab.

CARDIFF WEST (S. WALES CENTRAL)
E. 64,219 T. 27,726 (43.17%)

Mark Drakeford, Lab.	13,067
Craig Williams, C.	7,167
Neil McEvoy, PC	5,551
David Morgan, LD	1,942

Lab. majority 5,901 (21.28%)
3.77% C. to Lab.

CARMARTHEN EAST AND DINEFWR
(WALES MID AND W.)
E. 54,243 T. 27,828 (51.30%)

Rhodri Glyn Thomas, PC	12,501
Anthony Jones, Lab.	8,353
Henrietta Hensher, C.	5,635
Will Griffiths, LD	1,339

PC majority 4,148 (14.91%)
7.01% swing PC to Lab.

CARMARTHEN WEST AND
SOUTH PEMBROKESHIRE
(WALES MID AND W.)
E. 58,435 T. 28,156 (48.18%)

Angela Burns, C.	10,095
Christine Gwyther, Lab.	8,591
Nerys Evans, PC	8,373
Selwyn Runnett, LD	1,097

C. majority 1,504 (5.34%)
2.50% swing Lab. to C.

CEREDIGION (WALES MID AND W.)
E. 56,983 T. 29,076 (51.03%)

Elin Jones, PC	12,020
Liz Evans, LD	10,243
Luke Evetts, C.	2,755
Richard Boudier, Lab.	2,544
Chris Simpson, Green	1,514

PC majority 1,777 (6.11%)
3.51% swing PC to LD

CLWYD SOUTH (WALES N.)
E. 54,499 T. 19,498 (37.59%)

Ken Skates, Lab.	8,500
Paul Rogers, C.	5,841
Mabon ap Gwynfor, PC	3,719
Bruce Roberts, LD	1,977

Lab. majority 2,659 (13.27%)
3.77% swing C. to Lab.

CLWYD WEST (WALES N.)
E. 57,980 T. 25,153 (43.38%)

Darren Millar, C.	10,890
Crispin Jones, Lab.	6,642
Eifion Lloyd Jones, PC	5,775
Brian Cossey, LD	1,846

C. majority 4,248 (16.89%)
5.40% swing Lab. to C.

CYNON VALLEY (S. WALES CENTRAL)
E. 52,133 T. 18,760 (35.98%)

Christine Chapman, Lab.	11,626
Dafydd Trystan Davies, PC	5,111
Dan Saxton, C.	1,531
Ian Walton, LD	492

Lab. majority 6,515 (34.73%)
2.96% swing PC to Lab.

DELYN (WALES N.)
E. 53,996 T. 23,194 (42.96%)

Sandy Mewies, Lab.	10,695
Matt Wright, C.	7,814
Carrie Harper, PC	2,918
Michele Jones, LD	1,767

Lab. majority 2,881 (12.42%)
5.03% swing C. to Lab.

DWYFOR MEIRONNYDD
(WALES MID AND W.)
E. 44,669 T. 20,743 (46.44%)

Dafydd Elis-Thomas, PC	9,656
Simon Baynes, C.	4,239
Louise Hughes, Llais Gwynedd	3,225
Martyn Stuart Singleton, Lab.	2,623
Steven William Churchman, LD	1,000

PC majority 5,417 (26.11%)
6.99% swing PC to C.

GOWER (S. WALES WEST)
E. 61,909 T. 26,773 (43.25%)

Edwina Hart, Lab.	12,866
Caroline Jones, C.	8,002
Darren Price, PC	3,249
Peter May, LD	2,656

Lab. majority 4,864 (18.17%)
6.92% swing C. to Lab.

ISLWYN (S. WALES EAST)
E. 54,893 T. 20,908 (38.09%)

Gwyn Price, Lab.	12,116
Steffan Lewis, PC	4,527
David Chipp, C.	2,497
Peter Whalley, BNP	1,115
Tom Sullivan, LD	653

Lab. majority 7,589 (36.30%)
10.09% swing PC to Lab.

LLANELLI (WALES MID AND W.)
E. 58,838 T. 26,070 (44.31%)

Keith Davies, Lab.	10,359
Helen Mary Jones, PC	10,279
Andrew Morgan, C.	2,880
Sian Caiach, Putting Llanelli First	2,004
Cheryl Philpott, LD	548

Lab. majority 80 (0.31%)
7.19% swing PC to Lab.

MERTHYR TYDFIL AND RHYMNEY
(S. WALES EAST)
E. 55,031 T. 19,320 (35.11%)

Huw Lewis, Lab.	10,483
Tony Rogers, Ind.	3,432
Amy Kitcher, LD	2,480
Noel Turner, PC	1,701
Chris O'Brien, C.	1,224

Lab. majority 7,051 (36.50%)
0.14% swing Ind. to Lab.

MONMOUTH (S. WALES EAST)
E. 64,857 T. 30,001 (46.26%)

Nick Ramsay, C.	15,087
Mark Whitcutt, Lab.	8,970
Janet Ellard, LD	2,937
Fiona Cross, PC	2,263
Steve Uncles, Eng. Dem.	744

C. majority 6,117 (20.39%)
4.13% swing C. to Lab.

MONTGOMERYSHIRE
(WALES MID AND W.)
E. 48,675 T. 22,933 (47.11%)

Russell George, C.	10,026
Wyn Williams, LD	7,702
Nick Colbourne, Lab.	2,609
David Senior, PC	2,596

C. majority 2,324 (10.13%)
9.50% swing LD to C.

NEATH (S. WALES WEST)
E. 57,533 T. 23,849 (41.45%)

Gwenda Thomas, Lab.	12,736
Alun Llewelyn, PC	6,346
Alex Powell, C.	2,780
Michael Green, BNP	1,004
Mathew McCarthy, LD	983

Lab. majority 6,390 (26.79%)
9.54% swing PC to Lab.

NEWPORT EAST (S. WALES EAST)
E. 55,120 T. 19,460 (35.30%)

John Griffiths, Lab.	9,888
Nick Webb, C.	4,500
Ed Townsend, LD	3,703
Chris Paul, PC	1,369

Lab. majority 5,388 (27.69%)
9.11% swing C. to Lab.

NEWPORT WEST (S. WALES EAST)
E. 63,180 T. 23,014 (36.43%)
Rosemary Butler, Lab. 12,011
David Williams, C. 7,791
Lyndon Binding, PC 1,626
Liz Newton, LD 1,586
Lab. majority 4,220 (18.34%)
6.21% swing C. to Lab.

OGMORE (S. WALES WEST)
E. 55,442 T. 20,264 (36.55%)
Janice Gregory, Lab. 12,955
Danny Clark, PC 3,379
Martyn Hughes, C. 2,945
Gerald Francis, LD 985
Lab. majority 9,576 (47.26%)
6.28% swing PC to Lab.

PONTYPRIDD (S. WALES CENTRAL)
E. 60,028 T. 23,333 (38.87%)
Mick Antoniw, Lab. 11,864
Michael Powell, LD 4,170
Joel James, C. 3,659
Ioan Bellin, PC 3,139
Ken Owen, ND 501
Lab. majority 7,694 (32.97%)
9.28% swing LD to Lab.

PRESELI PEMBROKESHIRE
(WALES MID AND W.)
E. 57,758 T. 27,218 (47.12%)
Paul Davies, C. 11,541
Terry Mills (Lab.) 9,366
Rhys Sinnett, PC 4,226
Rob Kilmister, LD 2,085
C. majority 2,175 (7.99%)
1.58% swing C. to Lab.

RHONDDA (S. WALES CENTRAL)
E. 52,532 T. 20,027 (38.12%)
Leighton Andrews, Lab. 12,650
Sarah Evans-Fear, PC 5,911
James Jeffreys, C. 969
George Summers, LD 497
Lab. majority 6,739 (33.65%)
2.77% swing PC to Lab.

SWANSEA EAST (S. WALES WEST)
E. 60,246 T. 18,910 (58.36%)
Mike Hedges, Lab. 11,035
Daniel Boucher, C. 2,754
Dic Jones, PC 2,346
Sam Samuel, LD. 1,673
Joanne Shannon, BNP 1,102
Lab. majority 8,281 (43.79%)
6.05% swing C. to Lab.

SWANSEA WEST (S. WALES WEST)
E. 62,345 T. 21,805 (34.97%)
Julie James, Lab. 9,885
Steve Jenkins, C. 5,231
Rob Speht, LD 3,654
Carl Harris, PC 3,035
Lab. majority 4,654 (21.34%)
4.09% swing C. to Lab.

TORFAEN (S. WALES EAST)
E. 61,126 T. 22,328 (36.53%)
Lynne Neagle, Lab. 10,318
Elizabeth Haynes, Ind. 4,230
Natasha Asghar, C. 3,306
Jeff Rees, PC 2,716
Susan Harwood, BNP 906
Will Griffiths, LD 852
Lab. majority 6,088 (27.27%)
0.52% swing Lab. to Ind.

VALE OF CLWYD (WALES N.)
E. 56,232 T. 23,056 (41.00%)
Ann Jones, Lab. 11,691
Ian Gunning, C. 7,680
Alun Lloyd Jones, PC 2,597
Heather Prydderch, LD 1,088
Lab. majority 4,011 (17.40%)
8.49% swing C. to Lab.

VALE OF GLAMORGAN
(S. WALES CENTRAL)
E. 71,602 T. 33,254 (46.80%)
Jane Hutt, Lab. 15,746
Angela Jones-Evans, C. 11,971
Ian Johnson, PC 4,024
Damian Chick, LD 1,513
Lab. majority 3,775 (11.35%)
5.55% swing C. to Lab.

WREXHAM (WALES N.)
E. 53,516 T. 18,687 (34.92%)
Lesley Griffiths, Lab. 8,368
John Marek, C. 5,031
Bill Brereton 2,692
Marc Jones, PC 2,596
Lab. majority 3,337 (17.86%)
3.15% swing C. to Lab.

YNYS MON (WALES N.)
E. 49,431 T. 24,067 (48.69%)
Ieuan Wyn Jones, PC 9,969
Paul Williams, C. 7,032
Joe Lock, Lab. 6,307
Rhys Taylor, LD 759
PC majority 2,937 (12.20%)
7.27% swing PC to C.

REGIONS
E. 2,289,555 T. 41.4%

MID AND WEST WALES
E. 433,147 T. 210,352 (48.56%)

PC	56,384	(26.7%)
C.	52,905	(25.1%)
Lab.	47,348	(22.5%)
LD	26,847	(12.7%)
UKIP	9,211	(4.4%)
Green	8,660	(4.1%)
Soc. Lab.	3,951	(1.9%)
BNP	2,821	(1.3%)
Welsh Christian Party	1,630	(0.8%)
Comm. Brit.	595	(0.3%)

PC majority 3,479 (1.65%)
3.25% swing PC to C. (2007 PC majority 17,652)

ADDITIONAL MEMBERS
Rebecca Evans, *Lab.*
Simon Thomas, *PC*
William Powell, *LD*
Joyce Watson, *Lab.*

NORTH WALES
E. 473,296 T. 194,798 (41.16%)

Lab.	62,677	(32.2%)
C.	52,201	(26.8%)
PC	41,701	(21.4%)
LD	11,507	(5.9%)
UKIP	9,608	(4.9%)
Soc. Lab.	4,895	(2.5%)
BNP	4,785	(2.5%)
Green	4,406	(2.3%)
Welsh Christian Party	1,401	(0.7%)
Ind.	1,094	(0.6%)
Comm. Brit.	523	(0.3%)

Lab. majority 10,476 (5.38%)
5.05% swing PC to Lab. (2007 Lab. majority 1,273)

ADDITIONAL MEMBERS
Mark Isherwood, *C.*
Antoinette Sandbach, *C.*
Aled Roberts, *LD*
Llyr Huws Griffiths, *PC*

SOUTH WALES CENTRAL
E. 506,293 T. 208,333 (41.15%)

Lab.	85,445	(41.0%)
C.	45,751	(22.0%)
PC	28,606	(13.7%)
LD	16,514	(7.9%)
Green	10,774	(5.2%)
UKIP	8,292	(4.0%)
Soc. Lab.	4,690	(2.3%)
BNP	3,805	(1.8%)
Welsh Christian Party	1,873	(0.9%)
Loony	1,237	(0.6%)
TUSC	830	(0.4%)
Comm. Brit.	516	(0.2%)

Lab. majority 39,694 (19.05%)
6.55% swing LD to C. (2007 Lab. majority 25,652)

ADDITIONAL MEMBERS
David Melding, *C.* Leanne Wood, *PC*
Andrew Davies, *C.* John Dixon, *LD*

SOUTH WALES EAST
E. 469,486 T. 181,024 (38.56%)

Lab.	82,699	(45.7%)
C.	35,459	(19.6%)
PC	21,851	(12.1%)
LD	10,798	(6.0%)
UKIP	9,526	(5.3%)
BNP	6,485	(3.6%)
Green	4,857	(2.7%)
Soc. Lab.	4,427	(2.4%)
Welsh Christian Party	2,441	(1.3%)
Eng. Dem.	1,904	(1.1%)
Comm. Brit.	578	(0.3%)

Lab. majority 47,240 (26.10%)
5.95% swing LD to Lab. (2007 Lab. majority 30,063)

ADDITIONAL MEMBERS
William Graham, *C.* Jocelyn Davies, *PC*
Mohammad Asghar, *C.* Lindsay Whittle, *PC*

SOUTH WALES WEST
E. 407,333 T. 154,381 (37.90%)

Lab.	71,766	(46.5%)
Con.	27,457	(17.8%)
PC	21,258	(13.8%)
LD	10,683	(6.9%)
UKIP	6,619	(4.3%)
Soc. Lab.	5,057	(3.3%)
BNP	4,714	(3.1%)
Green	3,952	(2.6%)
Welsh Christian Party	1,602	(1.0%)
TUSC	809	(0.5%)
Comm. Brit.	464	(0.3%)

Lab. majority 44,309 (28.70%)
8.10% swing LD to Lab. (2007 Lab. majority 29,528)

ADDITIONAL MEMBERS
Suzy Davies, *C.* Peter Black, *LD*
Byron Davies, *C.* Bethan Jenkins, *PC*

SCOTLAND

SCOTTISH GOVERNMENT

St Andrew's House, Regent Road, Edinburgh EH1 3DG
T 0845-774 1741 **Enquiry Line** 0131-556 840
E ceu@scotland.gsi.gov.uk **W** www.scotland.gov.uk

The devolved government for Scotland is responsible for most of the issues of day-to-day concern to the people of Scotland, including health, education, justice, rural affairs and transport.

The Scottish government was known as the Scottish executive when it was established in 1999, following the first elections to the Scottish parliament. The current administration was formed after elections in May 2007.

The government is led by a first minister who is nominated by the parliament and in turn appoints the other Scottish ministers who make up the cabinet.

Civil servants in Scotland are accountable to Scottish ministers, who are themselves accountable to the Scottish parliament.

CABINET
First Minister, Rt. Hon. Alex Salmond, MSP
Deputy First Minister and Cabinet Secretary for Health, Wellbeing and Cities Strategy, Alex Neil, MSP
Deputy First Minister and Cabinet Secretary for Infrastructure, Investments and Cities, Nicola Sturgeon, MSP
Cabinet Secretary for Culture and External Affairs, Fiona Hyslop, MSP
Cabinet Secretary for Education and Lifelong Learning, Michael Russell, MSP
Cabinet Secretary for Finance, Employment and Sustainable Growth, John Swinney, MSP
Cabinet Secretary for Justice, Kenny MacAskill, MSP
Cabinet Secretary for Rural Affairs and the Environment, Richard Lochhead, MSP
Minister for Children and Young People, Aileen Campbell, MSP
Minister for Commonwealth Games and Sport, Shona Robison, MSP
Minister for Community Safety and Legal Affairs (with responsibility for tackling sectarianism), Roseanna Cunningham, MSP
Minister for Energy, Enterprise and Tourism, Fergus Ewing, MSP
Minister for Environment and Climate Change, Paul Wheelhouse, MSP
Minister for External Affairs and International Development, Humza Yousaf, MSP
Minister for Housing and Welfare, Margaret Burgess, MSP
Minister for Learning, Science and Scotland's Languages (with responsibility for Gaelic and Scots), Alasdair Allan, MSP
Minister for Local Government and Planning, Derek Mackay, MSP
Minister for Parliamentary Business, Joe Fitzpatrick, MSP
Minister for Public Health, Michael Matheson, MSP
Minister for Transport and Veteran Affairs, Keith Brown, MSP
Minister for Youth Employment, Angela Constance, MSP

LAW OFFICERS
Lord Advocate, Frank Mulholland, QC
Solicitor-General for Scotland, Lesley Thomson

STRATEGIC BOARD
Permanent Secretary, Sir Peter Housden, KCB
Director-General, Enterprise, Environment and Digital, Graeme Dickson
Director-General, Finance, Alyson Stafford
Director-General, Governance and Communities, Paul Gray
Director-General, Health and Social Care, Derek Feeley
Director-General, Learning and Justice, Leslie Evans
Director-General, Strategy and External Affairs, Ken Thomson

NON-DEPARTMENTAL AGENCIES

HISTORIC SCOTLAND
Longmore House, Salisbury Place, Edinburgh EH9 1SH
T 0131-668 8600 W www.historic-scotland.gov.uk
Chief Executive (acting), Ian Walford

NATIONAL RECORDS OF SCOTLAND
HM General Register House, 2 Princes Street, Edinburgh EH1 3YY
T 0131-535 1314 E enquiries@nas.gov.uk
W www.nas.gov.uk
Keeper of the Records of Scotland, Tim Ellis

GOVERNMENT DEPARTMENTS

DIRECTOR-GENERAL ENTERPRISE, ENVIRONMENT AND DIGITAL
St Andrew's House, Edinburgh EH1 3DG
Directorates: Agriculture, Food and Rural Affairs; Business; Chief Scientific Adviser for Rural Affairs and the Environment; Digital; DG Coordination – Enterprise, Environment and Digital; Energy and Climate Change; Environment and Forestry; Marine Scotland
Director-General, Graeme Dickson

EXECUTIVE AGENCIES
Accountant in Bankruptcy
Drinking Water Quality Regulator
James Hutton Institute
Moredun Research Institute
Scottish Agricultural College
Transport Scotland
Waterwatch

DIRECTOR-GENERAL FINANCE
Victoria Quay, Edinburgh EH6 6QQ
Directorates: Finance Directorate; Scottish Procurement and Commercial Directorate
Director-General, Alyson Stafford

EXECUTIVE AGENCIES
Audit Scotland
Scottish Public Pensions Agency

DIRECTOR-GENERAL GOVERNANCE AND COMMUNITIES
Saughton House, Broomhouse Drive, Edinburgh, EH11 3XD
Directorates: Housing, Regeneration and Welfare; HR and Organisational Development; ISIS (Information Services and Information Systems); Legal Services (Solicitor to the Scottish Government); Local Government and Communities; Inspectorate of Prosecution in Scotland; Office of the Scottish Parliament Counsel
Director-General, Paul Gray

EXECUTIVE AGENCY
Scottish Housing Regulator

DIRECTOR-GENERAL HEALTH AND SOCIAL CARE
St Andrew's House, Regent Road, Edinburgh EH1 3DG
Directorates: Coordination – Health and Social Care; Chief Medical Officer – Public Health and Sport; Chief Nursing Officer, Patients, Public and Health Professions; Children and Families; Commonwealth Games and Sport; Health and Healthcare Improvement; Health and Social Care Integration; Health Finance and Information; Health Workforce and Performance
Director-General Health and Social Care and Chief Executive, Derek Feeley

EXECUTIVE AGENCIES
Disclosure Scotland
Scottish Children's Reporters Administration

DIRECTOR-GENERAL LEARNING AND JUSTICE
St Andrew's House, Edinburgh EH1 3DG
Directorates: Coordination – Learning and Justice; Education Analytical Services; Employability, Skills and Lifelong Learning; Justice; Learning; Office of the Chief Scientific Adviser; Safer Communities
Director-General, Leslie Evans

EXECUTIVE AGENCIES
Education Scotland
HM Chief Inspector of Prosecution in Scotland
HM Inspectorate of Constabulary
HM Inspectorate of Prisons
Justices of the Peace Advisory Committee
Scottish Prison Service
Student Awards Agency for Scotland
Visiting Committees for Scottish Penal Establishments

DIRECTOR-GENERAL STRATEGY AND EXTERNAL AFFAIRS
Directorates: Cabinet Directorate; Communications; International and Constitution; Strategy and Performance

EXECUTIVE AGENCY
Historic Scotland

NON-DEPARTMENTAL OFFICES

AUDIT SCOTLAND
110 George Street, Edinburgh EH2 4LH
T 0845-146 1010 E info@audit-scotland.gov.uk
W www.audit-scotland.gov.uk
Auditor-General, Caroline Gardner
Accounts Commission Chair, Prof. John Baillie

CROWN OFFICE AND PROCURATOR FISCAL SERVICE
25 Chambers Street, Edinburgh EH1 1LA
T 0131-226 2626
Chief Executive and Crown Agent, Catherine Dyer

OFFICE OF THE PERMANENT SECRETARY
St Andrew's House, Regent Road, Edinburgh EH1 3DG
T 0131-556 8400
Permanent Secretary, Sir Peter Housden, KCB

SCOTTISH PARLIAMENT

Edinburgh EH99 1SP
T 0131-348 5000 Textphone 0800-092 7100
E sp.info@scottish.parliament.uk
W www.scottish.parliament.uk

In July 1997 the government announced plans to establish a Scottish parliament. In a referendum on 11 September 1997 about 60 per cent of the electorate voted. Of those who voted, 74.3 per cent voted in favour of the parliament and 63.5 per cent voted in support of granting the Parliament tax-raising powers. Elections are held every four years. The first elections were held on 6 May 1999, when around 59 per cent of the electorate voted. The first meeting was held on 12 May 1999 and the Scottish parliament was officially opened on 1 July 1999 at the Assembly Hall, Edinburgh. A new building to house parliament was opened, in the presence of the Queen, at Holyrood on 9 October 2004. On 5 May 2011 the fourth elections to the Scottish parliament took place.

The Scottish parliament has 129 members (including the presiding officer), comprising 73 constituency members and 56 additional regional members, mainly from party lists. It can introduce primary legislation and has the power to raise or lower the basic rate of income tax by up to three pence in the pound. Members of the Scottish parliament are elected using the additional member system, the same system used to elect London Assembly and Welsh Assembly members.

The areas for which the Scottish parliament is responsible include: education; health; law; environment; economic development; local government; housing; police; fire services; planning; financial assistance to industry; tourism; heritage and the arts; agriculture; social work; sports, public registers and records; forestry; food standards; and some transport.

SALARIES *as at 1 May 2013*	
First Minister*	£84,160
Cabinet Secretaries*	£43,660
Lord Advocate*	£57,038
Solicitor-General for Scotland*	£41,246
Ministers*	£27,348
MSPs†	£58,097
Presiding Officer*	£43,660
Deputy Presiding Officer*	£27,348

* In addition to the MSP salary
† Reduced by two-thirds if the member is already an MP or an MEP

MEMBERS OF THE SCOTTISH PARLIAMENT

as at 1 July 2013

Adam, George, *SNP, Paisley,* Maj. 248
Adamson, Clare, *SNP, Central Scotland region*
Allan, Alasdair, *SNP, Na h-Eileanan an Iar,* Maj. 4,772
Allard, Christian, *SNP, North East Scotland region*
Baillie, Jackie, *Lab., Dumbarton,* Maj. 1,639
Baker, Claire, *Lab., Mid Scotland and Fife region*
Baker, Richard, *Lab., North East Scotland region*
Baxter, Jayne, *Lab., Mid Scotland and Fife region*
Beamish, Claudia, *Lab., South Scotland region*
Beattie, Colin, *SNP, Midlothian North and Musselburgh,* Maj. 2,996
Biagi, Marco, *SNP, Edinburgh Central,* Maj. 237
Bibby, Neil, *Lab., West Scotland region*
Boyack, Sarah, *Lab., Lothian region*
Brodie, Chic, *SNP, South Scotland region*
Brown, Gavin, *C., Lothian region*
Brown, Keith, *SNP, Clackmannanshire and Dunblane,* Maj. 3,609
Burgess, Margaret, *SNP, Cunninghame South,* Maj. 2,348
Campbell, Aileen, *SNP, Clydesdale,* Maj. 4,216
Campbell, Roderick, *SNP, North East Fife,* Maj. 2,592
Carlaw, Jackson, *C., West Scotland region*
Chisholm, Malcolm, *Lab., Edinburgh Northern and Leith,* Maj. 595
Coffey, Willie, *SNP, Kilmarnock and Irvine Valley,* Maj. 5,993
Constance, Angela, *SNP, Almond Valley,* Maj. 5,542
Crawford, Bruce, *SNP, Stirling,* Maj. 5,671
Cunningham, Roseanna, *SNP, Perthshire South and Kinross-shire,* Maj. 7,166
Davidson, Ruth, *C., Glasgow region*
Dey, Graeme, *SNP, Angus South,* Maj. 10,583
Don, Nigel, *SNP, Angus North and Mearns,* Maj. 7,286
Doris, Bob, *SNP, Glasgow region*
Dornan, James, *SNP, Glasgow Cathcart,* Maj. 1,592
Dugdale, Kezia, *Lab., Lothian region*
Eadie, Helen, *Lab., Cowdenbeath,* Maj. 1,247
Eadie, Jim, *SNP, Edinburgh Southern,* Maj. 693
Ewing, Annabelle, *SNP, Mid Scotland and Fife region*
Ewing, Fergus, *SNP, Inverness and Nairn,* Maj. 9,745
Fabiani, Linda, *SNP, East Kilbride,* Maj. 1,949
Fee, Mary, *Lab., West Scotland region*
Ferguson, Patricia, *Lab., Glasgow Maryhill and Springburn,* Maj. 1,252
Fergusson, Alex, *C., Galloway and West Dumfries,* Maj. 862
Findlay, Neil, *Lab., Lothian region*
Finnie, John, *Ind., Highlands and Islands region*
FitzPatrick, Joe, *SNP, Dundee City West,* Maj. 6,405
Fraser, Murdo, *C., Mid Scotland and Fife region*
Gibson, Kenneth, *SNP, Cunninghame North,* Maj. 6,117
Gibson, Rob, *SNP, Caithness, Sutherland and Ross,* Maj. 7,458
Goldie, Annabel, *C., West Scotland region*
Grahame, Christine, *SNP, Midlothian South, Tweeddale and Lauderdale,* Maj. 4,924
Grant, Rhoda, *Lab., Highlands and Islands region*
Gray, Iain, *Lab., East Lothian,* Maj. 151
Griffin, Mark, *Lab., Central Scotland region*
Harvie, Patrick, *Green, Glasgow region*
Henry, Hugh, *Lab., Renfrewshire South,* Maj. 2,577
Hepburn, Jamie, *SNP, Cumbernauld and Kilsyth,* Maj. 3,459
Hume, Jim, *LD, South Scotland region*
Hyslop, Fiona, *SNP, Linlithgow,* Maj. 4,091
Ingram, Adam, *SNP, Carrick, Cumnock and Doon Valley,* Maj. 2,581
Johnstone, Alex, *C., North East Scotland region*
Johnstone, Alison, *Green, Lothian region*
Keir, Colin, *SNP, Edinburgh West,* Maj. 2,689
Kelly, James, *Lab., Rutherglen,* Maj. 1,779
Kidd, Bill, *SNP, Glasgow Anniesland,* Maj. 7
Lamont, Johann, *Lab., Glasgow Pollok,* Maj. 623
Lamont, John, *C., Ettrick, Roxburgh and Berwickshire,* Maj. 5,334
Lochhead, Richard, *SNP, Moray,* Maj. 10,944
Lyle, Richard, *SNP, Central Scotland region*
McAlpine, Joan, *SNP, South Scotland region*
McArthur, Liam, *LD, Orkney,* Maj. 860
MacAskill, Kenny, *SNP, Edinburgh Eastern,* Maj. 2,233
McCulloch, Margaret, *Lab., Central Scotland region*
MacDonald, Angus, *SNP, Falkirk East,* Maj. 3,535
MacDonald, Gordon, *SNP, Edinburgh Pentlands,* Maj. 1,758
Macdonald, Lewis, *Lab., North East Scotland region*
MacDonald, Margo, *Ind., Lothian region*
***McDonald**, Mark, *SNP, Aberdeen Donside,* Maj. 2,025

* Mark McDonald won the Aberdeen Donside by-election following the death of the SNP MSP Brian Adam in April 2013.

McDougall, Margaret, *Lab., West Scotland region*
McGrigor, Jamie, *C., Highlands and Islands region*
McInnes, Alison, *LD, North East Scotland region*
Macintosh, Ken, *Lab., Eastwood,* Maj. 2,012
Mackay, Derek, *SNP Renfrewshire North and West,* Maj. 1,564
McKelvie, Christina, *SNP, Hamilton, Larkhall and Stonehouse,* Maj. 2,213
MacKenzie, Mike, *SNP, Highlands and Islands region*
McLeod, Aileen, *SNP, South Scotland region*
McLeod, Fiona, *SNP, Strathkelvin and Bearsden,* Maj. 1,802
McLetchie, David, *C., Lothian region*
McMahon, Michael, *Lab., Uddingston and Bellshill,* Maj. 714
McMahon, Siobhan, *Lab., Central Scotland region*
McMillan, Stuart, *SNP, West Scotland region*
McNeil, Duncan, *Lab., Greenock and Inverclyde,* Maj. 511
McTaggart, Anne, *Lab., Glasgow region*
Malik, Hanzala, *Lab., Glasgow region*
Marra, Jenny, *Lab., North East Scotland region*
Martin, Paul, *Lab., Glasgow Provan,* Maj. 2,079
Marwick, Tricia, *SNP, Mid Fife and Glenrothes,* Maj. 4,188
Mason, John, *SNP, Glasgow Shettleston,* Maj. 586
Matheson, Michael, *SNP, Falkirk West,* Maj. 5,745
Maxwell, Stewart, *SNP, West Scotland region*
Milne, Nanette, *C., North East Scotland region*
Mitchell, Margaret, *C., Central Scotland region*
Murray, Elaine, *Lab., Dumfriesshire,* Maj. 3,156
Neil, Alex, *SNP, Airdrie and Shotts,* Maj. 2,001
Paterson, Gil, *SNP, Clydebank and Milngavie,* Maj. 714
Pearson, Graeme, *Lab, South Scotland region*
Pentland, John, *Lab., Motherwell and Wishaw,* Maj. 587
Rennie, Willie, *LD, Mid Scotland and Fife region*
Robertson, Dennis, *SNP, Aberdeenshire West,* Maj. 4,112
Robison, Shona, *SNP, Dundee City East,* Maj. 10,679
Russell, Michael, *SNP, Argyll and Bute,* Maj. 8,543
Salmond, Alex, *SNP, Aberdeenshire East,* Maj. 15,295
Scanlon, Mary, *C., Highlands and Islands region*
Scott, John, *C., Ayr,* Maj. 1,113
Scott, Tavish, *LD, Shetland Islands,* Maj. 1,617
Simpson, Richard, *Lab., Mid Scotland and Fife region*
Smith, Drew, *Lab., Glasgow region*
Smith, Elaine, *Lab., Coatbridge and Chryston,* Maj. 2,741
Smith, Liz, *C., Mid Scotland and Fife region*
Stevenson, Stewart, *SNP, Banffshire and Buchan Coast,* Maj. 12,220
Stewart, David, *Lab., Highlands and Islands region*
Stewart, Kevin, *SNP, Aberdeen Central,* Maj. 617
Sturgeon, Nicola, *SNP, Glasgow Southside,* Maj. 4,349
Swinney, John, *SNP, Perthshire North,* Maj. 10,353
Thompson, Dave, *SNP, Skye, Lochaber and Badenoch* Maj. 4,995
Torrance, David, *SNP, Kirkcaldy,* Maj. 182
Urquhart, Jean, *Ind., Highlands and Islands region*
Walker, Bill, *Ind., Dunfermline,* Maj. 590
Watt, Maureen, *SNP, Aberdeen South and North Kincardine,* Maj. 6,323
Wheelhouse, Paul, *SNP, South Scotland region*
White, Sandra, *SNP, Glasgow Kelvin,* Maj. 882
Wilson, John, *SNP, Central Scotland region*
Yousaf, Humza, *SNP, Glasgow region*

STATE OF THE PARTIES
as at 1 July 2013

	Constituency MSPs	*Regional MSPs*	*Total*
Scottish National Party (SNP)	51	14	65
Scottish Labour Party (Lab.)	15	22	37
Scottish Conservative and Unionist Party (C.)	3	12	15
Scottish Liberal Democrats (LD)	2	3	5
Scottish Green Party (Green)	0	2	2
Independent (Ind.)	1	3	4
‡Presiding Officer	1	0	1
Total	73	56	129

‡The presiding officer was elected as a constituency member for the SNP but has no party allegiance while in post

The Presiding Officer, Tricia Marwick, MSP
Deputy Presiding Officers, John Scott, MSP *(C.)*; Elaine Smith, MSP *(Lab.)*

SCOTTISH PARLIAMENT ELECTION RESULTS

as at 5 May 2011
E. Electorate T. Turnout
See General Election Results for a list of party abbreviations

CONSTITUENCIES
E. 3,985,161 T. 50.4%

ABERDEEN CENTRAL
(Scotland North East Region)
E. 57,396 T. 25,149 (43.82%)

Kevin Stewart, SNP	10,058
Lewis Macdonald, Lab.	9,441
Sandy Wallace, C.	3,100
Sheila Thomson, LD	2,349
Mike Phillips, NF	201

SNP majority 617 (2.45%)
0.54% swing Lab. to SNP

ABERDEEN DONSIDE
(Scotland North East Region)
E. 56,145 T. 26,761 (47.66%)

Brian Adam, SNP	14,790
Barney Crockett, Lab.	7,615
Ross Thomson, C.	2,166
Millie McLeod, LD.	1,606
David Henderson, Ind.	371
Christopher Willett, NF	213

SNP majority 7,175 (26.81%)
6.87% swing Lab. to SNP

ABERDEEN SOUTH AND KINCARDINE NORTH
(Scotland North East Region)
E. 54,338 T. 28,697 (52.81%)

Maureen Watt, SNP	11,947
Greg Williams, Lab.	5,624
John Sleigh, LD	4,994
Stewart Whyte, C.	4,058

SNP majority 6,323 (22.03%)
15.77% swing LD to SNP

ABERDEENSHIRE EAST
(Scotland North East Region)
E. 57,591 T. 30,286 (52.59%)
Alex Salmond, SNP 19,533
Alison McInnes, LD 4,238
Geordie Burnett Stuart, C. 4,211
Peter Smyth, Lab. 2,304
SNP majority 15,295 (50.5%)
19.53% swing LD to SNP

ABERDEENSHIRE WEST
(Scotland North East Region)
E. 53,779 T. 28,636 (53.25%)
Dennis Robertson, SNP 12,186
Mike Rumbles, LD 8,074
Nanette Milne, C. 6,027
Jean Morrison, Lab. 2,349
SNP majority 4,112 (14.36%)
13.45% swing LD to SNP

AIRDRIE AND SHOTTS
(Scotland Central Region)
E. 51, 336 T. 23,894 (46.54%)
Alex Neil, SNP 11,984
Karen Whitefield, Lab. 9,983
Robert Crozier, C. 1,396
John Love, LD 531
SNP majority 2,001 (8.37%)
5.50% swing Lab. to SNP

ALMOND VALLEY
(Lothian Region)
E. 59,896 T. 30,737 (51.32%)
Angela Constance, SNP 16,704
Lawrence Fitzpatrick, Lab. 11,162
Andrew Hardie, C. 1,886
Emma Sykes, LD 656
Neil McIvor, NF 329
SNP majority 5,542 (18.03%)
9.01% swing Lab. to SNP

ANGUS NORTH AND MEARNS
(Scotland North East Region)
E. 52,124 T. 24,920 (47.81%)
Nigel Don, SNP 13,660
Alex Johnstone, C. 6,374
Kevin Hutchens, Lab. 3,160
Sanjay Samani, LD 1,726
SNP majority 7,286 (29.24%)
4.15% swing C. to SNP

ANGUS SOUTH
(Scotland North East Region)
E. 54,922 T. 27,643 (50.33%)
Graeme Dey, SNP 16,164
Hughie Campbell
Adamson, C. 5,581
William Campbell, Lab. 3,703
David Fairweather, AIR 1,321
Clive Sneddon, LD 874
SNP majority 10,583 (38.28%)
9.31% swing C. to SNP

ARGYLL AND BUTE
(Highlands and Islands Region)
E. 49,028 T. 26,476 (54.00%)
Michael Russell, SNP 13,390
Jamie McGrigor, C. 4,847
Mick Rice, Lab. 4,041
Alison Hay, LD 3,220
George Doyle, Ind. 542
George White, Lib. 436
SNP majority 8,543 (32.27%)
8.52% swing C. to SNP

AYR
(Scotland South Region)
E. 61,563 T. 33,373 (54.21%)
John Scott, C. 12,997
Chic Brodie, SNP 11,884
Gordon McKenzie, Lab. 7,779
Eileen Taylor, LD 713
C. majority 1,113 (3.34%)
5.16% swing C. to SNP

BANFFSHIRE AND BUCHAN COAST
(Scotland North East Region)
E. 53,698 T. 25,004 (46.56%)
Stewart Stevenson, SNP 16,812
Michael Watt, C. 4,592
Alan Duffill, Lab. 2,642
Galen Milne, LD 958
SNP majority 12,220 (48.87%)
3.48% swing C. to SNP

CAITHNESS, SUTHERLAND AND ROSS
(Highlands and Islands Region)
E. 55,116 T. 28,600 (51.89%)
Rob Gibson, SNP 13,843
Robbie Rowantree, LD 6,385
John MacKay, Lab. 5,438
Edward Mountain, C. 2,934
SNP majority 7,458 (26.08%)
17.32% swing LD to SNP

CARRICK, CUMNOCK AND
DOON VALLEY
(Scotland South Region)
E. 59,368 T. 28,703 (48.35%)
Adam Ingram, SNP 13,250
Richard Leonard, Lab. 10,669
Peter Kennerley, C. 4,160
Andrew Chamberlain, LD 624
SNP majority 2,581 (8.99%)
11.77% swing Lab. to SNP

CLACKMANNANSHIRE & DUNBLANE
(Mid Scotland and Fife Region)
E. 49,415 T. 27,416 (55.48%)
Keith Brown, SNP 13,253
Richard Simpson, Lab. 9,644
Callum Campbell, C. 3,501
Tim Brett, LD 1,018
SNP majority 3,609 (13.16%)
5.20% swing Lab. to SNP

CLYDEBANK AND MILNGAVIE
(Scotland West Region)
E. 53,018 T. 28,369 (53.51%)
Gils Paterson, SNP 12,278
Des McNulty, Lab. 11,564
Alice Struthers, C. 2,758
John Duncan, LD 1,769
SD majority 714 (2.52%)
6.56% swing Lab. to SNP

CLYDESDALE
(Scotland South Region)
E. 56,828 T. 29,937 (52.68%)
Aileen Campbell, SNP 14,931
Karen Gillon, Lab. 10,715
Colin McGavigan, C. 4,291
SNP majority 4,216 (14.08%)
8.89% swing Lab. to SNP

COATBRIDGE AND CHRYSTON
(Scotland Central Region)
E. 51,206 T. 23,279 (45.46%)
Elaine Smith, Lab. 12,161
John Wilson, SNP 9,420
Jason Lingiah, C. 1,317
Rod Ackland, LD 381
Lab. majority 2,741 (11.77%)
3.28% swing Lab. to SNP

COWDENBEATH
(Mid Scotland and Fife Region)
E. 54,284 T. 25,670 (47.29%)
Helen Eadie, Lab. 11,926
Ian Chisholm, SNP 10,679
Belinda Don, C. 1,792
Keith Legg, LD 997
Mike Heenan, Land Party 276
Lab. majority 1,247 (4.86%)
4.85% swing Lab. to SNP

CUMBERNAULD AND KILSYTH
(Scotland Central Region)
E. 48,006 T. 25,254 (52.61%)
Jamie Hepburn, SNP 13,595
Cathie Craigie, Lab. 10,136
James Boswell, C. 1,156
Martin Oliver, LD 367
SNP majority 3,459 (13.7%)
10.79% Lab. to SNP

CUNNINGHAME NORTH
(Scotland West Region)
E. 56,548 T. 29,536 (52.23%)
Kenneth Gibson, SNP 15,539
Allan Wilson, Lab. 9,422
Maurice Golden, C. 4,032
Mallika Punukollu, LD 543
SNP majority 6,117 (20.71%)
10.29% swing Lab. to SNP

CUNNINGHAME SOUTH
(Scotland South Region)
E. 50,926 T. 22,056 (43.31%)
Margaret Burgess, SNP 10,993
Irene Oldfather, Lab. 8,645
Alistair Haw, C. 1,871
Ruby Kirkwood, LD 547
SNP majority 2,348 (10.65%)
9.93% swing Lab. to SNP

DUMBARTON
(Scotland West Region)
E. 53,470 T. 28,508 (53.32%)
Jackie Baillie, Lab. 12,562
Iain Robertson, SNP 10,923
Graham Smith, C. 3,395
Helen Watt, LD 858
George Rice, Ind. 770
Lab. majority 1,639 (5.75%)
0.24% swing SNP to Lab.

DUMFRIESSHIRE
(Scotland South Region)
E. 59,716 T. 31,895 (53.41%)
Elaine Murray, Lab. 12,624
Gill Dykes, C. 9,468
Aileen Orr, SNP 8,384
Richard Brodie, LD 1,419
Lab. majority 3,156 (9.89%)
5.99% swing C. to Lab.

DUNDEE EAST
(Scotland North East Region)
E. 54,404 T. 25,753 (47.34%)
Shona Robison, SNP 16,541
Mohammed Asif, Lab. 5,862
Brian Docherty, C. 2,550
Allan Petrie, LD 800
SNP majority 10,679 (41.47%)
12.47% swing Lab. to SNP

DUNDEE WEST
(Scotland North East Region)
E. 53,841 T. 24,461 (45.43%)
Joe Fitzpatrick, SNP 14,089
Richard McCready, Lab. 7,684
Colin Stewart, C. 1,625
Alison Burns, LD 1,063
SNP majority 6,405 (26.18%)
8.88% swing Lab. to SNP

DUNFERMLINE
(Scotland Mid and Fife Region)
E. 55,479 T. 29,299 (52.81%)
Bill Walker, SNP 11,010
Alex Rowley, Lab. 10,420
Jim Tolson, LD 5,776
James Reekie, C. 2,093
SNP majority 599 (2.01%)
13.41% swing LD to SNP

EAST KILBRIDE
(Scotland Central Region)
E. 58,251 T. 29,911 (51.35%)
Linda Fabiani, SNP 14,359
Andy Kerr, Lab. 12,410
Graham Simpson, C. 2,260
Douglas Herbison, LD 468
John Houston, Ind. 414
SNP majority 1,949 (6.52%)
6.64% swing Lab. to SNP

EAST LOTHIAN
(Scotland South Region)
E. 56,333 T. 32,177 (57.12%)
Iain Gray, Lab. 12,536
David Berry, SNP 12,385
Derek Brownlee, C. 5,344
Ettie Spencer, LD 1,912
Lab. majority 151 (0.47%)
3.12% swing Lab to SNP

EASTWOOD
(Scotland West Region)
E. 50,476 T. 31,924 (63.25%)
Ken Macintosh, Lab. 12,662
Jackson Carlaw, C. 10,650
Stewart Maxwell, SNP 7,777
Gordon Cochrane, LD 835
Lab. majority 2,012 (6.3%)
8.74% swing C. to Lab.

EDINBURGH CENTRAL
(Lothian Region)
E. 53,606 T. 29,014 (54.12%)
Marco Biagi, SNP 9,480
Sarah Boyack, Lab. 9,243
Alex Cole-Hamilton, LD 5,937
Iain McGill, C. 4,354
SNP majority 237 (0.82%)
10.16% swing Lab. to SNP

EDINBURGH EASTERN
(Lothian Region)
E. 55,773 T. 30,728 (55.09%)
Kenny MacAskill, SNP 14,552
Ewan Aitken, Lab. 12,319
Cameron Buchanan, C. 2,630
Martin Veart, LD 1,227
SNP majority 2,233 (7.27%)
4.53% swing Lab. to SNP

EDINBURGH NORTHERN AND LEITH
(Lothian Region)
E. 59,138 T. 30,885 (52.23%)
Malcolm Chisholm, Lab. 12,858
Shirley-Anne Somerville, SNP 12,263
Sheila Low, C. 2,928
Don Farthing, LD 2,836
Lab. majority 595 (1.93%)
2.66% swing Lab. to SNP

EDINBURGH PENTLANDS
(Lothian Region)
E. 52,620 T. 30,049 (57.11%)
Gordon MacDonald, SNP 11,197
David McLetchie, C. 9,439
Ricky Henderson, Lab. 7,993
Simon Clark, LD 1,420
SNP majority 1,758 (5.85%)
7.42% swing C. to SNP

EDINBURGH SOUTHERN
(Lothian Region)
E. 54,868 T. 33,796 (61.60%)
Jim Eadie, SNP 9,947
Paul Godzik, Lab. 9,254
Mike Pringle, LD 8,297
Gavin Brown, C. 6,298
SNP majority 693 (2.05%)
12.06% swing LD to SNP

EDINBURGH WESTERN
(Lothian Region)
E. 56,338 T. 33,452 (59.38%)
Colin Keir, SNP 11,965
Margaret Smith, LD 9,276
Lesley Hinds, Lab. 7,164
Gordon Lindhurst, C. 5,047
SNP majority 2,689 (8.04%)
12.60% swing LD to SNP

ETTRICK, ROXBURGH AND BERWICKSHIRE
(Scotland South Region)
E. 54,327 T. 28,816 (53.04%)
John Lamont, C. 12,933
Paul Wheelhouse, SNP 7,599
Euan Robson, LD 4,990
Rab Stewart, Lab. 2,986
Jesse Rae, Ind. 308
C. majority 5,334 (18.51%)
1.39% swing C. to SNP

FALKIRK EAST
(Scotland Central Region)
E. 56,408 T. 28,168 (49.94%)
Angus MacDonald, SNP 14,302
Cathy Peattie, Lab. 10,767
Lynn Munro, C. 2,372
Ross Laird, LD 727
SNP majority 3,535 (12.55%)
9.33% swing Lab. to SNP

FALKIRK WEST
(Scotland Central Region)
E. 55,739 T. 28,199 (50.59%)
Michael Matheson, SNP 15,607
Dennis Goldie, Lab. 9,862
Allan Finnie, C. 2,086
Callum Chomczuk, LD 644
SNP majority 5,745 (20.37%)
8.91% swing Lab. to SNP

FIFE MID AND GLENROTHES
(Scotland Mid and Fife Region)
E. 53,701 T. 26,313 (49.0%)
Tricia Marwick, SNP 13,761
Claire Baker, Lab. 9,573
Allan Smith, C. 1,676
Jim Parker, ASPP 673
Callum Leslie, LD 630
SNP majority 4,188 (15.92%)
3.43% swing Lab. to SNP

FIFE NORTH EAST
(Scotland Mid and Fife Region)
E. 58,858 T. 29,676 (50.42%)
Roderick Campbell, SNP 11,029
Iain Smith, LD 8,437
Miles Briggs, C. 5,618
Colin Davidson, Lab. 3,613
Mike Scott-Hayward, UKIP 979
SNP majority 2,592 (8.73%)
15.02% swing LD to SNP

GALLOWAY AND WEST DUMFRIES
(Scotland South Region)
E. 56,611 T. 29,997 (52.99%)
Alex Fergusson, C. 11,071
Aileen McLeod, SNP 10,209
Willie Scobie, Lab. 7,954
Joe Rosiejak, LD 763
C. majority 862 (2.87%)
2.40% swing C. to SNP

GLASGOW ANNIESLAND
(Glasgow Region)
E. 55,411 T. 23,918 (43.16%)
Bill Kidd, SNP 10,329
Bill Butler, Lab. 10,322
Matthew Smith, C. 2,011
Paul McGarry, LD 1,000
Marc Livingstone, Comm. Brit. 256
SNP majority 7 (0.03%)
10.09% swing Lab. to SNP

GLASGOW CATHCART
(Glasgow Region)
E. 58,525 T. 26,222 (44.8%)
James Dornan, SNP 11,918
Charlie Gordon, Lab. 10,326
Richard Sullivan, C. 2,410
Eileen Baxendale, LD 1,118
John McKee, Ind. 450
SNP majority 1,592 (6.07%)
6.53% swing Lab. to SNP

GLASGOW KELVIN
(Glasgow Region)
E. 61,893 T. 24,548 (39.66%)
Sandra White, SNP 10,640
Pauline McNeil, Lab. 9,758
Natalie McKee, LD 1,900
Ruth Davidson, C. 1,845
Tom Muirhead, Ind. 405
SNP majority 882 (3.59%)
4.03% swing Lab. to SNP

GLASGOW MARYHILL AND SPRINGBURN
(Glasgow Region)
E. 56,622 T. 20,531 (36.26%)
Patricia Ferguson, Lab. 9,884
Bob Doris, SNP 8,592
Stephanie Murray, C. 1,222
Sophie Bridger, LD 833
Lab. majority 1,292 (6.29%)
5.43% swing Lab. to SNP

GLASGOW POLLOK
(Glasgow Region)
E. 58,429 T. 22,915 (39.22%)
Johann Lamont, Lab. 10,875
Chris Stephens, SNP 10,252
Andrew Morrison, C. 1,298
Isabel Nelson, LD 490
Lab. majority 623 (2.72%)
8.53% swing Lab. to SNP

GLASGOW PROVAN
(Glasgow Region)
E. 55,118 T. 19,185 (34.81%)
Paul Martin, Lab. 10,037
Anne McLaughlin, SNP 7,958
Majid Hussain, C. 777
Michael O'Donnell, LD 413
Lab. majority 2,079 (10.84%)
8.68% swing Lab. to SNP

GLASGOW SHETTLESTON
(Glasgow Region)
E. 55,874 T. 21,204 (37.95%)
John Mason, SNP 10,128
Frank McAveety, Lab. 9,542
David Wilson, C. 1,163
Ruaraidh Dobson, LD 371
SNP majority 586 (2.76%)
12.61% swing Lab. to SNP

GLASGOW SOUTHSIDE
(Glasgow Region)
E. 52,325 T. 22,608 (43.21%)
Nicola Sturgeon, SNP 12,306
Stephen Curran, Lab. 7,957
David Meikle, C. 1,733
Kenneth Elder, LD 612
SNP majority 4,349 (19.24%)
9.68% swing Lab. to SNP

GREENOCK AND INVERCLYDE
(Scotland West Region)
E. 56,989 T. 28,298 (49.50%)
Duncan McNeil, Lab. 12,387
Stuart McMillan, SNP 11,876
Graeme Brooks, C. 2,011
Ross Finnie, LD 1,934
Lab. majority 511 (1.81%)
6.90% swing Lab. to SNP

HAMILTON, LARKHALL AND STONEHOUSE
(Scotland Central Region)
E. 56,123 T. 25,354 (45.18%)
Christina McKelvie, SNP 12,202
Tom McCabe, Lab. 9,989
Margaret Mitchell, C. 2,547
Ewan Hoyle, LD 616
SNP majority 2,213 (8.73%)
10.99% swing Lab. to SNP

INVERNESS & NAIRN
(Highlands and Islands Region)
E. 62,168 T. 32,731 (52.65%)
Fergus Ewing, SNP 16,870
David Stewart, Lab. 7,125
Mary Scanlon, C. 3,797
Christine Jardine, LD 3,763
Donald Boyd, Christian Party 646
Ross Durance, UKIP 530
SNP majority 9,745 (29.77%)
4.85% swing Lab. to SNP

KILMARNOCK AND IRVINE VALLEY
(Scotland Central Region)
E. 63,257 T. 31,858 (50.36%)
Willie Coffey, SNP 16,964
Matt McLaughlin, Lab. 10,971
Grant Fergusson, C. 3,309
Robbie Simpson, LD 614
SNP majority 5,993 (18.81%)
7.40% swing Lab. to SNP

KIRKCALDY
(Scotland Mid and Fife Region)
E. 60,079 T. 27,803 (46.28%)
David Torrance, SNP 12,579
Marilyn Livingstone, Lab. 12,397
Ian McFarlane, C. 2,007
John Mainland, LD 820
SNP majority 182 (0.65%)
6.19% swing Lab. to SNP

LINLITHGOW
(Lothian Region)
E. 65,025 T. 34,182 (52.57%)
Fiona Hyslop, SNP 17,027
Mary Mulligan, Lab. 12,936
Christopher Donnelly, C. 2,646
Jennifer Lang, LD 1,015
Mike Coyle, NF 558
SNP majority 4,091 (11.97%)
6.42% swing Lab. to SNP

MIDLOTHIAN NORTH AND MUSSELBURGH
(Lothian Region)
E. 58,246 T. 29,818 (51.19%)
Colin Beattie, SNP 14,079
Bernard Harkins, Lab. 11,083
Scott Douglas, C. 2,541
Ian Younger, LD 1,254
Alan Hay, Ind. 861
SNP majority 2,996 (10.05%)
7.61% swing Lab. to SNP

MIDLOTHIAN SOUTH, TWEEDDALE AND LAUDERDALE
(Lothian Region)
E. 57,781 T. 31,841 (55.11%)
Christine Grahame, SNP 13,855
Jeremy Purvis, LD 8,931
Ian Miller, Lab. 5,312
Peter Duncan, C. 3,743
SNP majority 4,924 (15.46%)
5.87% swing LD to SNP

MORAY
(Highlands and Islands Region)
E. 56,215 T. 28,596 (50.87%)
Richard Lochhead, SNP 16,817
Douglas Ross, C. 5,873
Kieron Green, Lab. 3,580
Jamie Paterson, LD 1,327
Donald Gatt, UKIP 999
SNP majority 10,944 (38.27%)
6.19% swing C. to SNP

MOTHERWELL AND WISHAW
(Scotland Central Region)
E. 53,610 T. 24,451 (45.61%)
John Pentland, Lab. 10,713
Clare Adamson, SNP 10,126
Bob Burgess, C. 1,753
John Swinburne, ASPP 945
Tom Selfridge, Christian Party 547
Beverley Hope, LD 367
Lab. majority 587 (2.4%)
10.20% swing Lab. to SNP

NA H-EILEANAN AN IAR
(Highlands and Islands Region)
E. 21,834 T. 13,011 (59.59%)
Alasdair Allan, SNP 8,496
Donald Crichton, Lab. 3,724
Charlie McGrigor, C. 563
Peter Morrison, LD 228
SNP majority 4,772 (36.68%)
15.82% swing Lab. to SNP

ORKNEY
(Highlands and Islands Region)
E. 16,393 T. 8,152 (49.73%)
Liam McArthur, LD 2,912
James Stockan, Ind. 2,052
George Adam, SNP 2,044
Jamie Halcro Johnston, C. 686
William Sharkey, Lab. 458
LD majority 860 (10.55%)
17.70% swing LD to Ind.

PAISLEY
(Scotland West Region)
E. 52,066 T. 25,590 (49.15%)
George Adam, SNP 10,913
Evan Williams, Lab. 10,665
Malcolm MacAskill, C. 2,229
Eileen McCartin, LD 1,783
SNP majority 248 (0.97%)
7.80% swing Lab. to SNP

PERTHSHIRE NORTH
(Scotland and Mid Fife Region)
E. 53,412 T. 29,953 (56.08%)
John Swinney, SNP 18,219
Murdo Fraser, C. 7,866
Pete Cheema, Lab. 2,672
Victor Clements, LD 1,196
SNP majority 10,353 (34.56%)
6.53% swing C. to SNP

PERTHSHIRE SOUTH AND KINROSS-SHIRE
(Scotland and Mid Fife Region)
E. 58,093 T. 31,216 (53.73%)
Roseanna Cunningham, SNP 16,073
Liz Smith, C. 8,907
Tricia Duncan, Lab. 3,980
Willie Robertson, LD 2,256
SNP majority 7,166 (22.96%)
9.25% swing C. to SNP

RENFREWSHIRE NORTH AND WEST
(Scotland West Region)
E. 49,060 T. 27,495 (56.04%)
Derek Mackay, SNP 11,510
Stuart Clark, Lab. 9,946
Annabel Goldie, C. 5,489
Andrew Page, LD 550
SNP majority 1,564 (5.69%)
8.42% swing Lab. to SNP

RENFREWSHIRE SOUTH
(Scotland West Region)
E. 50,221 T. 26,908 (53.58%)
Hugh Henry, Lab. 12,933
Andrew Doig, SNP 10,356
Alistair Campbell, C. 2,917
Gordon Anderson, LD 702
Lab. majority 2,577 (9.58%)
5.41% swing Lab. to SNP

RUTHERGLEN
(Glasgow Region)
E. 57,777 T. 27,122 (46.94%)
James Kelly, Lab. 12,489
Jim McGuigan, SNP 10,710
Martyn McIntyre, C. 2,096
Lisa Strachan, LD 1,174
Caroline Johnstone, Ind. 633
Lab. majority 1,779 (6.56%)
7.43% swing Lab. to SNP

SHETLAND ISLANDS
(Highlands and Islands Region)
E. 17,505 T. 9,391 (53.65%)
Tavish Scott, LD 4,462
Billy Fox, Ind. 2,845
Jean Urquhart, SNP 1,134
Jamie Kerr, Lab. 620
Sandy Cross, C. 330
LD majority 1,617 (17.22%)
5.5% swing LD to Ind.

SKYE, LOCHABER AND BADENOCH
(Highlands and Islands Region)
E. 57,024 T. 31,915 (55.97%)
Dave Thompson, SNP 14,737
Alan MacRae, LD 9,742
Linda Stewart, Lab. 4,112
Kerensa Carr, C. 2,834
Ronnie Campbell, Ind. 490
SNP majority 4,995 (15.65%)
12.97% swing LD to SNP

STIRLING
(Scotland and Mid Fife Region)
E. 51,458 T. 30,406 (59.09%)
Bruce Crawford, SNP 14,859
John Hendry, Lab. 9,188
Neil Benny, C. 4,610
Graham Reed, LD 1,296
Jack Black, Ind. 454
SNP majority 5,671 (18.65%)
9.93% swing Lab. to SNP

STRATHKELVIN AND BEARSDEN
(Scotland West Region)
E. 59,323 T. 33,752 (56.90%)
Fiona McLeod, SNP 14,258
David Whitton, Lab. 12,456
Jean Turner, Ind. 6,742
Stephanie Fraser, C. 4,438
Gordon Macdonald, LD 2,600
SNP majority 1,802 (5.34%)
7.69% swing Lab. to SNP

UDDINGSTON AND BELLSHILL
(Central Scotland Region)
E. 55,584 T. 24,995 (44.97%)
Michael McMahon, Lab. 11,531
Richard Lyle, SNP 10,817
Mark Brown, C. 2,117
Fraser Macgregor, LD 530
Lab majority 714 (2.86%)
9.04% swing Lab. to SNP

REGIONS
E. 3,985,161 T. 50.4%

GLASGOW
E. 514,393 T. 208,712 (40.57%)

SNP	83,109	(39.8%)
Lab.	73,031	(35.0%)
C.	12,749	(6.1%)
Green	12,454	(6.0%)
Respect	6,972	(3.3%)
LD	5,312	(2.5%)
ASPP	3,750	(1.8%)
BNP	2,424	(1.2%)
Socialist Labour	2,276	(1.1%)
Christian Party	1,501	(0.7%)
Scottish Unionist Party	1,447	(0.7%)
SSP	1,362	(0.7%)
UKIP	1,123	(0.5%)
Pirate	581	(0.3%)
Ind. Johnstone	338	(0.2%)
SHP	283	(0.1%)

Lab. majority 10,078 (4.83%)
8.04% swing Lab. to SNP (2007 Lab. majority 23,006)

ADDITIONAL MEMBERS
Humza Yousaf, *SNP*
Bob Doris, *SNP*
Hanzala Malik, *Lab.*
Drew Smith, *Lab.*
Anne McTaggert, *Lab.*
Ruth Davidson, *C.*
Patrick Harvie, *Green*

HIGHLANDS AND ISLANDS
E. 337,588 T. 179,010 (53.03%)

SNP	85,082	(47.5%)
Lab.	25,884	(14.5%)
C.	21,729	(12.1%)
LD	20,843	(11.6%)
Green	9,076	(5.1%)
Christian Party	3,541	(2%)
UKIP	3,372	(1.9%)
ASPP	2,770	(1.5%)
Ban Bankers Bonuses	1,764	(1%)
Lib.	1,696	(0.9%)
Soc. Lab.	1,406	(0.8%)
BNP	1,134	(0.6%)
SSP	509	(0.3%)
Solidarity	204	(0.1%)

SNP majority 59,198 (33.07%)
8.16% swing Lab. to SNP (2007 SNP majority 26,978)

ADDITIONAL MEMBERS
John Finnie, *SNP*
Jean Urquhart, *SNP*
Mike MacKenzie, *SNP*
Rhoda Grant, *Lab.*
David Stewart, *Lab.*
Jamie McGrigor, *C.*
Mary Scanlon, *C.*

LOTHIAN
E. 515,978 T. 283,203 (54.89%)

SNP	110,953	(39.2%)
Lab.	70,544	(24.9%)
C.	33,019	(11.7%)
Green	21,505	(7.6%)
Ind. MacDonald	18,732	(6.6%)
LD	15,588	(5.5%)
ASPP	3,218	(1.1%)
BNP	1,978	(0.7%)
UKIP	1,822	(0.6%)
Soc. Lab.	1,681	(0.6%)
SSP	1,183	(0.4%)
Christian Party	914	(0.3%)
Lib.	697	(0.2%)
CPA	553	(0.2%)
Solidarity	327	(0.1%)
Ind. Hogg	294	(0.1%)
Ind. O'Neill	134	(0.1%)
Ind. Brown	61	(0.1%)

SNP majority 40,409 (14.27%)
7.0% swing Lab. to SNP (2007 SNP majority 524)

ADDITIONAL MEMBERS
Sarah Boyack, *Lab.*
Kezia Dugdale, *Lab.*
Neil Findlay, *Lab.*
David McLetchie, *C.*
Gavin Brown, *C.*
Alison Johnstone, *Green*
Margo MacDonald, *Ind.*

SCOTLAND CENTRAL
E. 497,737 T. 233,560 (46.92%)

SNP	108,261	(46.4%)
Lab.	82,459	(35.3%)
C.	14,870	(6.4%)
ASPP	5,793	(2.5%)
Green	5,634	(2.4%)
LD	3,318	(1.4%)
Christian Party	3,173	(1.4%)
Soci. Lab.	2,483	(1.1%)
BNP	2,214	(0.9%)
Scottish Unionist Party	1,555	(0.7%)
UKIP	1,263	(0.5%)
Ind. O'Donnell	821	(0.4%)
SSP	820	(0.4%)
Solidarity	559	(0.2%)
SHP	337	(0.1%)

Lab. majority 25,802 (11.05%)
10.08% swing Lab. to SNP (2007 Lab. majority 23,386)

ADDITIONAL MEMBERS
Richard Lyle, *SNP*
John Wilson, *SNP*
Clare Adamson, *SNP*
Siobhan McMahon, *Lab.*
Mark Griffin, *Lab.*
Margaret McCulloch, *Lab.*
Margaret Mitchell, *C.*

SCOTLAND MID AND FIFE
E. 503,559 T. 258,163 (51.27%)

SNP	116,691	(45.2%)
Lab.	64,623	(25.0%)
C.	36,458	(14.1%)
LD	15,103	(5.9%)
Green	10,914	(4.2%)
ASPP	4,113	(1.6%)
UKIP	2,838	(1.1%)
Soc. Lab.	1,771	(0.7%)
BNP	1,726	(0.7%)
Ind. Rodger	1,466	(0.6%)
SSP	834	(0.3%)
Christian Party	786	(0.3%)
CPA	638	(0.2%)
Solidarity	202	(0.1%)

SNP majority 52,068 (10.9%)
7.43% swing Lab. to SNP (2007 Lab. majority 18,168)

ADDITIONAL MEMBERS
Annabelle Ewing, *SNP*
John Park, *Lab.*
Claire Baker, *Lab.*
Richard Simpson, *Lab.*
Murdo Fraser, *C.*
Liz Smith, *C.*
Willie Rennie, *LD*

SCOTLAND NORTH EAST
E. 550,162 T. 267,045 (48.54%)

SNP	140,749	(52.7%)
Lab.	43,893	(16.4%)
C.	37,681	(14.1%)
LD	18,178	(6.8%)
Green	10,407	(3.9%)
ASPP	4,420	(1.7%)
UKIP	2,477	(0.9%)
Christian Party	2,159	(0.8%)
BNP	1,925	(0.7%)
Soc. Lab.	1,459	(0.5%)
Ind. Cox	758	(0.3%)
NF	640	(0.2%)
AIR	471	(0.2%)
Solidarity	286	(0.1%)
Ind. Henderson	237	(0.1%)
Ind. McBride	190	(0.1%)

SNP majority 96,856 (36.27%)
7.68% swing Lab. to SNP (2007 SNP majority 53,140)

ADDITIONAL MEMBERS
Mark McDonald, *SNP*
Richard Baker, *Lab.*
Jenny Marra, *Lab.*
Lewis McDonald, *Lab.*
Alex Johnstone, *C.*
Nanette Milne, *C.*
Alison McInnes, *LD*

SCOTLAND SOUTH
E. 529,682 T. 278,987 (52.67%)

SNP	114,270	(41.0%)
Lab.	70,595	(25.3%)
C.	54,352	(19.5%)
LD	15,096	(5.4%)
Green	8,656	(3.1%)
ASPP	4,418	(1.6%)
UKIP	3,243	(1.2%)
Soc. Lab.	2,906	(1.0%)
BNP	2,017	(0.7%)
Christian Party	1,924	(0.7%)
Solidarity	813	(0.3%)
SSP	697	(0.2%)

SNP majority 43,675 (15.66%)
7.95% swing Lab. to SNP (2007 Lab. majority 2,709)

ADDITIONAL MEMBERS
Joan McAlpine, *SNP*
Aileen McLeod, *SNP*
Paul Wheelhouse, *SNP*
Chic Brodie, *SNP*
Claudia Beamish, *Lab.*
Graeme Pearson, *Lab.*
Jim Hume, *LD*

SCOTLAND WEST
E. 536,062 T. 282,371 (52.68%)

SNP	117,306	(41.5%)
Lab.	92,530	(32.8%)
C.	35,995	(12.7%)
LD	9,148	(3.2%)
Green	8,414	(3.0%)
ASPP	4,771	(1.7%)
Soc. Lab.	2,865	(1.0%)
Christian Party	2,468	(0.9%)
BNP	2,162	(0.8%)
UKIP	2,000	(0.7%)
SSP	1,752	(0.6%)
Ban Bankers Bonuses	1,204	(0.4%)
Pirate	850	(0.3%)
Ind. Vassie	460	(0.2%)
Solidarity	446	(0.2%)

SNP majority 24,776 (8.77%)
7.4% swing Lab. to SNP (2007 Lab. majority 15,772)

ADDITIONAL MEMBERS
Stewart Maxwell, *SNP*
Stuart McMillan, *SNP*
Mary Fee, *Lab.*
Neil Bibby, *Lab.*
Margaret McDougall, *Lab.*
Annabel Goldie, *C.*
Jackson Carlaw, *C.*

NORTHERN IRELAND

NORTHERN IRELAND EXECUTIVE

Stormont Castle, Stormont, Belfast BT4 3TT
T 028-9052 8400
W www.northernireland.gov.uk

The first minister and deputy first minister head the executive committee of ministers and, acting jointly, determine the total number of ministers in the executive. First and deputy first ministers are elected by Northern Ireland assembly members through a formula of parallel consent that requires a majority of designated unionists, a majority of designated nationalists and a majority of the whole assembly to vote in favour. The parties elected to the assembly select ministerial portfolios in proportion to party strengths using the d'Hondt nominating procedure.

The executive committee includes five DUP ministers, four SF ministers, two Alliance members, one Social Democratic and Labour Party minister and one Ulster Unionist minister alongside the first minister Peter Robinson, MLA of the DUP and the deputy first minister, Martin McGuinness, MLA, of SF.

EXECUTIVE COMMITTEE

First Minister, Rt. Hon. Peter Robinson, MLA
Deputy First Minister, Martin McGuinness, MLA
Junior Ministers, Jennifer McCann, MLA; Jonathan Bell, MLA
Minister for Agriculture and Rural Development, Michelle O'Neill, MLA
Minister for Culture, Arts and Leisure, Caral ni Chuilin, MLA
Minister for Education, John O'Dowd, MLA
Minister for Employment and Learning, Dr Stephen Farry, MLA
Minister for Enterprise, Trade and Investment, Arlene Foster, MLA
Minister for Environment, Alex Attwood, MLA
Minister for Finance and Personnel, Sammy Wilson, MP, MLA
Minister for Health, Social Services and Public Safety, Edwin Poots, MLA
Minister for Justice, David Ford, MLA
Minister for Regional Development, Danny Kennedy, MLA
Minister for Social Development, Nelson McCausland, MLA

OFFICE OF THE FIRST MINISTER AND DEPUTY FIRST MINISTER

Stormont Castle, Stormont, Belfast BT4 3TT
T 028-9052 8400 W www.ofmdfmni.gov.uk

DEPARTMENT OF AGRICULTURE AND RURAL DEVELOPMENT

Dundonald House, Upper Newtownards Road, Belfast BT4 3SB
T 028-9052 0100 W www.dardni.gov.uk

EXECUTIVE AGENCIES
Forest Service
Rivers Agency

DEPARTMENT OF CULTURE, ARTS AND LEISURE

Causeway Exchange, 1–7 Bedford Street, Belfast BT1 7FB
T 028-9025 8825 W www.dcalni.gov.uk

DEPARTMENT OF EDUCATION

Rathgael House, Balloo Road, Bangor, Co. Down BT19 7PR
T 028-9127 9279 W www.deni.gov.uk

DEPARTMENT FOR EMPLOYMENT AND LEARNING

Adelaide House, 39–49 Adelaide Street, Belfast BT2 8FD
T 028-9025 7777 W www.delni.gov.uk

DEPARTMENT OF ENTERPRISE, TRADE AND INVESTMENT

Netherleigh, Massey Avenue, Belfast BT4 2JP T 028-9052 9900
W www.detini.gov.uk

EXECUTIVE AGENCIES
General Consumer Council for Northern Ireland
Health and Safety Executive
Invest Northern Ireland
Northern Ireland Tourist Board

DEPARTMENT OF THE ENVIRONMENT

Clarence Court, 10–18 Adelaide Street, Belfast BT2 8GB
T 028-9054 0540 W www.doeni.gov.uk

EXECUTIVE AGENCIES
Driver and Vehicle Agency (Northern Ireland)
NI Environment Agency

DEPARTMENT OF FINANCE AND PERSONNEL

Rathgael House, Balloo Road, Bangor BT19 7NA T 028-9185 8111
W www.dfpni.gov.uk

EXECUTIVE AGENCIES
Northern Ireland Statistics and Research Agency (Incorporates Land Registers of Northern Ireland and Ordnance Survey of Northern Ireland)

DEPARTMENT OF HEALTH, SOCIAL SERVICES AND PUBLIC SAFETY

Castle Buildings, Stormont, Belfast BT4 3SJ T 028-9052 0500
W www.dhsspsni.gov.uk

DEPARTMENT FOR REGIONAL DEVELOPMENT

Clarence Court, 10–18 Adelaide Street, Belfast BT2 8GB
T 028-9054 0540 W www.drdni.gov.uk

DEPARTMENT FOR SOCIAL DEVELOPMENT

Lighthouse Building, 1 Cromac Place, Gasworks Business Park, Ormeau Road, Belfast BT7 2JB T 028-9082 9000
W www.dsdni.gov.uk

EXECUTIVE AGENCIES
Charity Commission for Northern Ireland
ILEX Urban Regeneration Company
Northern Ireland Housing Executive
Social Security Agency

DEPARTMENT OF JUSTICE

Block B, Castle Buildings, Stormont Estate, Belfast BT4 3SG
T 028-9076 3000 W www.dojni.gov.uk

EXECUTIVE AGENCIES
Forensic Science Agency
Northern Ireland Courts and Tribunals Service
Northern Ireland Prison Service
Youth Justice Agency

NORTHERN IRELAND AUDIT OFFICE

106 University Street, Belfast BT7 1EU
T 028-9025 1000 E info@niauditoffice.gov.uk
W www.niauditoffice.gov.uk
Comptroller and Auditor-General, Kieran Donnelly

NORTHERN IRELAND AUTHORITY FOR UTILITY REGULATION

Queens House, 14 Queen Street, Belfast BT1 6ED
T 028-9031 1575 E info@uregni.gov.uk W www.uregni.gov.uk
Chair, Dr Bill Emery

NORTHERN IRELAND ASSEMBLY

Parliament Buildings, Stormont, Belfast BT4 3XX
T 028-9052 1137 E info@niassembly.gov.uk
W www.niassembly.gov.uk

The Northern Ireland Assembly was established as a result of the Belfast Agreement (also known as the Good Friday Agreement) in April 1998. The agreement was endorsed through a referendum held in May 1998 and subsequently given legal force through the Northern Ireland Act 1998.

The Northern Ireland Assembly has full legislative and executive authority for all matters that are the responsibility of the government's Northern Ireland departments – known as transferred matters. Excepted and reserved matters are defined in schedules 2 and 3 of the Northern Ireland Act 1998 and remain the responsibility of UK parliament.

The first assembly election occurred on 25 June 1998 and the 108 members elected met for the first time on 1 July 1998. Members of the Northern Ireland Assembly are elected by the single transferable vote system from 18 constituencies – six per constituency. Under the single transferable vote system every voter has a single vote that can be transferred from one candidate to another. Voters number their candidates in order of preference. Where candidates reach their quota of votes and are elected, surplus votes are transferred to other candidates according to the next preference on each voter's ballot slip. The candidate in each round with the fewest votes is eliminated and their surplus votes are redistributed according to the voter's next preference. The process is repeated until the required number of members are elected.

On 29 November 1999 the assembly appointed ten ministers as well as the chairs and deputy chairs for the ten statutory departmental committees. Devolution of powers to the Northern Ireland Assembly occurred on 2 December 1999, following several delays concerned with Sinn Fein's inclusion in the executive while Irish Republican Army (IRA) weapons were yet to be decommissioned.

Since the devolution of powers, the assembly has been suspended by the Secretary of State for Northern Ireland on four occasions. The first was between 11 February and 30 May 2000, with two 24-hour suspensions on 10 August and 22 September 2001 – all owing to a lack of progress in decommissioning. The final suspension took place on 14 October 2002 after unionists walked out of the executive following a police raid on Sinn Fein's office investigating alleged intelligence gathering.

The assembly was formally dissolved in April 2003 in anticipation of an election, which eventually took place on 26 November 2003. The results of the election changed the balance of power between the political parties, with an increase in the number of seats held by the Democratic Unionist Party (DUP) and Sinn Fein (SF), so that they became the largest parties. The assembly was restored to a state of suspension following the November election while political parties engaged in a review of the Belfast Agreement aimed at fully restoring the devolved institutions.

In July 2005 the leadership of the IRA formally ordered an end to its armed campaign; it authorised a representative to engage with the Independent International Commission on Decommissioning in order to verifiably put the arms beyond use. On 26 September 2005 General John de Chastelain, the chair of the commission, along with two independent church witnesses confirmed that the IRA's entire arsenal of weapons had been decommissioned.

Following the passing of the Northern Ireland Act 2006 the secretary of state created a non-legislative fixed-term assembly, whose membership consisted of the 108 members elected in the 2003 election. It first met on 15 May 2006 with the remit of making preparations for the restoration of devolved government; its discussions informed the next round of talks called by the British and Irish governments held at St Andrews. The St Andrews agreement of 13 October 2006 led to the establishment of the transitional assembly.

The Northern Ireland (St Andrews Agreement) Act 2006 set out a timetable to restore devolution, and also set the date for the third election to the assembly as 7 March 2007. The DUP and SF again had the largest number of Members of the Legislative Assembly (MLAs) elected, and although the initial restoration deadline of 26 March was missed, the leaders of the DUP and SF (Revd Dr Ian Paisley, MP, MLA and Gerry Adams, MLA, respectively) took part in a historic meeting and made a joint commitment to establish an executive committee in the assembly to which devolved powers were restored on 8 May 2007. After completing a full four-year mandate, new assembly elections took place on 5 May 2011 to elect the 108 members of the legislative assembly.

SALARIES	*2013–14*	*2014–15*
First Minister/Deputy First Minister	£120,000	£120,000
Minister	£86,000	£86,000
MLA	£48,000	£48,000

NORTHERN IRELAND ASSEMBLY MEMBERS

* New Member of the Legislative Assembly (MLA)
† Previously MLA for another party
as at 1 July 2012

Agnew, Steven, *Green, North Down*
Allister, Jim, *TUV, North Antrim*
Anderson, Sydney, *DUP, Upper Bann*
Attwood, Alex, *SDLP, Belfast West*
Beggs, Roy, *UUP, East Antrim*
Bell, Jonathan, *DUP, Strangford*
Boylan, Cathal, *SF, Newry and Armagh*
Boyle, Michaela, *SF, West Tyrone*
Bradley, Dominic, *SDLP, Newry and Armagh*
Bradley, Paula, *DUP, Belfast North*
Brady, Mickey, *SF, Newry and Armagh*
Brown, Pam, *DUP, South Antrim*
Buchanan, Thomas, *DUP, West Tyrone*
Byrne, Joe, *SDLP, West Tyrone*
Campbell, Gregory, *DUP, East Londonderry*
Clarke, Trevor, *DUP, South Antrim*
Cochrane, Judith, *Alliance, Belfast East*
Copeland, Michael, *UUP, Belfast East*
Craig, Jonathan, *DUP, Lagan Valley*
Cree, Leslie, *UUP, North Down*
Dallat, John, *SDLP, East Londonderry*
Dickson, Stewart, *Alliance, East Antrim*
Dobson, Jo-Anne, *UUP, Upper Bann*
Douglas, Sammy, *DUP, Belfast East*
Dunne, Gordon, *DUP, North Down*
Durkan, Mark, *SDLP, Foyle*
Easton, Alex, *DUP, North Down*
Eastwood, Colum, *SDLP, Foyle*
Elliot, Tom, *UUP, Fermanagh and South Tyrone*
Farry, Stephen, *Alliance, North Down*
***Fearon**, Megan, *SF, Newry and Armagh*
Flanagan, Phil, *SF, Fermanagh and South Tyrone*
Ford, David, *Alliance, South Antrim*
Foster, Arlene, *DUP, Fermanagh and South Tyrone*
Frew, Paul, *DUP, North Antrim*
Gardiner, Samuel, *UUP, Upper Bann*

Girvan, Paul, *DUP, South Antrim*
Givan, Paul, *DUP, Lagan Valley*
Hale, Brenda, *DUP, Lagan Valley*
Hamilton, Simon, *DUP, Strangford*
Hay, William, *DUP, Foyle*
Hazzard, Chris, *SF, South Down*
Hilditch, David, *DUP, East Antrim*
Humphrey, William, *DUP, Belfast North*
Hussey, Ross, *UUP, West Tyrone*
Irwin, William, *DUP, Newry and Armagh*
Kelly, Dolores, *SDLP, Upper Bann*
Kelly, Gerry, *SF, Belfast North*
Kennedy, Danny, *UUP, Newry and Armagh*
Kinahan, Danny, *UUP, South Antrim*
Lo, Anna, *Alliance, Belfast South*
Lunn, Trevor, *Alliance, Lagan Valley*
Lynch, Sean, *SF, Fermanagh and South Tyrone*
Lyttle, Chris, *Alliance, Belfast East*
Maginness, Alban, *SDLP, Belfast North*
Maskey, Alex, *SF, Belfast South*
***McAleer**, Declan, *SF, West Tyrone*
†**McCallister**, John, *NI21, South Down*
McCann, Fra, *SF, Belfast West*
McCann, Jennifer, *SF, Belfast West*
McCarthy, Kieran, *Alliance, Strangford*
McCartney, Raymond, *SF, Foyle*
McCausland, Nelson, *DUP, Belfast North*
McClarty, David, *Ind., East Londonderry*
***McCorley**, Rosaleen, *SF, Belfast West*
†**McCrea**, Basil, *NI21, Lagan Valley*
McCrea, Ian, *DUP, Mid Ulster*
McDevitt, Conall, *SDLP, Belfast South*
McDonnell, Dr Alasdair, *SDLP, Belfast South*
McElduff, Barry, *SF, West Tyrone*
***McGahan**, Bronwyn, *SF, Fermanagh and South Tyrone*
McGimpsey, Michael, *UUP, Belfast South*
McGlone, Patsy, *SDLP, Mid Ulster*
McGuinness, Martin, *SF, Mid Ulster*
McIlveen, David, *DUP, North Antrim*
McIlveen, Michelle, *DUP, Strangford*
McKay, Daithi, *SF, North Antrim*
McKevitt, Karen, *SDLP, South Down*
McLaughlin, Maeve, *SF, Foyle*
McLaughlin, Mitchel, *SF, South Antrim*
McMullan, Oliver, *SF, East Antrim*
†**McNarry**, David, *UKIP, Strangford*
McQuillan, Adrian, *DUP, East Londonderry*
***Milne**, Ian, *SF, Mid Ulster*
Morrow, Lord, *DUP, Fermanagh and South Tyrone*
Moutray, Stephen, *DUP, Upper Bann*
Nesbitt, Mike, *UUP, Strangford*
Newton, Robin, *DUP, Belfast East*
Ni Chuilin, Caral, *SF, Belfast North*
O'Dowd, John, *SF, Upper Bann*
O'Neill, Michelle, *SF, Mid Ulster*
O hOisin, Cathal, *SF, East Londonderry*
Overend, Sandra, *UUP, Mid Ulster*
Poots, Edwin, *DUP, Lagan Valley*
Ramsey, Pat, *SDLP, Foyle*
Ramsey, Sue, *SF, Belfast West*
Robinson, George, *DUP, East Londonderry*
Robinson, Peter, *DUP, Belfast East*
Rodgers, Sean, *SDLP, South Down*
Ross, Alastair, *DUP, East Antrim*
Ruane, Caitriona, *SF, South Down*
Sheehan, Pat, *SF, Belfast West*
Spratt, Jimmy, *DUP, Belfast South*
Storey, Mervyn, *DUP, North Antrim*
Swann, Robin, *UUP, North Antrim*
Weir, Peter, *DUP, North Down*
Wells, Jim, *DUP, South Down*
Wilson, Sammy, *DUP, East Antrim*

STATE OF THE PARTIES *as at 1 July 2013*

Party	*Seats*
Democratic Unionist Party (DUP)	38
Sinn Fein (SF)	29
Social Democratic and Labour Party (SDLP)	14
Ulster Unionist Party (UUP)	13
Alliance Party (Alliance)	8
NI21	2
Green Party	1
Independent (Ind.)	1
Traditional Unionist Voice (TUV)	1
UK Independence Party (UKIP)	1
Total	108

NORTHERN IRELAND ASSEMBLY ELECTION RESULTS

as at 5 May 2011
E. 1,210,009 T. 55.64%

E. Electorate T. Turnout
First = first-preference votes
Final = final total for that candidate, after all necessary transfers of lower-preference votes
R. = round
* = eliminated last
See General Election Results for a list of party abbreviations

ANTRIM EAST
E. 61,617 T. 29,430 (47.76%)

	First	*Final*	*Elected (R.)*
Sammy Wilson, DUP	7,181	7,181	First (1)
David Hilditch, DUP	3,288	4,219	Second (2)
Roy Beggs, UUP	3,042	4,194	Fifth (9)
Stewart Dickson, Alliance	2,889	4,777	Fourth (9)
Oliver McMullan, SF	2,369	3,389	Sixth (10)
*Rodney McCune, UUP	1,851	2,890	
Gerardine Mulvenna, Alliance	1,620		
Alastair Ross, DUP	1,608	4,267	Third (6)
Ruth Wilson, TUV	1,346		
Justin McCamphill, SDLP	1,333		
Gordon Lyons, DUP	1,321		
Daniel Donnelly, Green	664		
Steven Moore, BNP	511		

ANTRIM NORTH
E. 74,760 T. 40,983 (54.82%)

	First	*Final*	*Elected (R.)*
Paul Frew, DUP	6,581	6,581	First (1)
Daithi McKay, SF	6,152	6,152	Second (1)
Mervyn Storey, DUP	6,083	6,083	Third (1)
Jim Allister, TUV	4,061	5,430	Sixth (9)
*Declan O'Loan, SDLP	3,682	4,816	
David McIlveen, DUP	3,275	6,594	Fourth (8)
Evelyne Robinson, DUP	3,256		
Robin Swann, UUP	2,518	5,557	Fifth (9)
Bill Kennedy, UUP	2,189		
Jayne Dunlop, Alliance	1,848		
Audrey Patterson, TUV	668		

ANTRIM SOUTH
E. 65,231 T. 32,652 (50.06%)

	First	*Final*	*Elected (R.)*
Paul Girvan, DUP	4,844	4,844	First (1)
Mitchel McLaughlin, SF	4,662	4,662	Second (1)
Trevor Clarke, UUP	4,607	4,607	Third (1)
David Ford, Alliance	4,554	4,660	Fourth (2)
Danny Kinahan, UUP	3,445	5,585	Fifth (3)
*Thomas Burns, SDLP	3,406	3,591	
Pam Lewis, DUP	2,866	4,668	Sixth (4)
Adrian Cochrane-Watson, UUP	2,285		
Mel Lucas, TUV	1,091		
Stephen Parkes, BNP	404		

BELFAST EAST
E. 61,263 T. 32,828 (53.59%)

	First	*Final*	*Elected (R.)*
Peter Robinson, DUP	9,149	9,149	First (1)
Judith Cochrane, Alliance	4,329	4,755	Third (7)
Chris Lyttle, Alliance	4,183	4,696	Fourth (9)
Sammy Douglas, DUP	2,668	4,783	Fifth (11)
Robin Newton, DUP	2,436	4,801	Second (2)
Michael Copeland, UUP	2,194	3,723	Sixth (11)
*Dawn Purvis, Ind.	1,702	2,789	
Brian Ervine, PUP	1,493		
Niall O'Donnghaile, SF	1,030		
Philip Robinson, UUP	943		
Harry Toan, TUV	712		
Martin Gregg, Green	572		
Ann Cooper, BNP	337		
Magdalena Wolska, SDLP	250		
Tommy Black, SP	201		
Kevin McNally, WP	102		
Stephen Stewart, Ind.	46		

BELFAST NORTH
E. 68,119 T. 34,280 (50.32%)

	First	*Final*	*Elected (R.)*
Gerry Kelly, SF	6,674	6,674	First (1)
Nelson McCausland, DUP	5,200	5,200	Second (1)
Alban Maginness, SDLP	4,025	5,004	Fourth (6)
William Humphrey, DUP	3,724	4,332	Fifth (7)
Paula Bradley, DUP	3,488	4,065	Sixth (7)
Caral Ni Chuilin, SF	2,999	4,868	Third (6)
*Fred Cobain, UUP	2,758	3,623	
Billy Webb, Alliance	2,096		
Raymond McCord, Ind.	1,176		
JJ Magee, SF	998		
John Lavery, WP	332		

BELFAST SOUTH
E. 62,484 T. 32,752 (52.42%)

	First	*Final*	*Elected (R.)*
Anna Lo, Alliance	6,390	6,390	First (1)
Dr Alasdair McDonnell, SDLP	4,527	4,916	Second (2)
Jimmy Spratt, DUP	4,045	4,281	Sixth (5)
Alex Maskey, SF	4,038	4,452	Fourth (5)
*Ruth Patterson, DUP	3,800	4,163	
Connall McDevitt, SDLP	3,191	4,445	Fifth (5)
Michael McGimpsey, UUP	2,988	4,622	Third (5)
Mark Finlay, UUP	1,394		
Claire Bailey, Green	889		
Brian Faloon, PBP	414		
Paddy Meehan, SP	234		
Nico Torregrosa, UKIP	234		
Paddy Lynn, WP	135		
Charles Smyth, Pro-Capitalism	29		

BELFAST WEST
E. 61,520 T. 35,618 (57.89%)

	First	*Final*	*Elected (R.)*
Paul Maskey, SF	5,343	5,343	First (1)
Jennifer McCann, SF	5,239	5,239	Second (1)
Fra McCann, SF	4,481	5,167	Third (10)
Sue Ramsey, SF	4,116	4,823	Fifth (11)
Alex Attwood, SDLP	3,765	5,152	Fourth (10)
Pat Sheehan, SF	3,723	4,327	Sixth (11)
*Brian Kingston, DUP	2,587	3,867	
Gerry Carroll, PBP	1,661		
Bill Manwaring, UUP	1,471		
Colin Keenan, SDLP	802		
John Lowry, WP	586		
Pat Lawlor, SP	384		
Dan McGuinness, Alliance	365		
Brian Pelan, Ind.	122		

DOWN NORTH
E. 62,170 T. 28,528 (45.89%)

	First	*Final*	*Elected (R.)*
Alex Easton, DUP	5,175	5,175	First (1)
Gordon Dunne, DUP	3,741	4,121	Second (2)
Peter Weir, DUP	3,496	4,101	Third (2)
Stephen Farry, Alliance	3,131	4,078	Fourth (10)
Steven Agnew, Green	2,207	3,229	Sixth (11)
*Anne Wilson, Alliance	2,100	3,130	
Alan McFarland, Ind.	1,879		
Alan Chambers, Ind.	1,765		
Leslie Cree, UUP	1,585	4,015	Fifth (10)
Colin Breen, UUP	1,343		
Liam Logan, SDLP	768		
Fred McGlade, UKIP	615		
Conor Keenan, SF	293		

DOWN SOUTH
E. 73,240 T. 42,551 (58.10%)

	First	*Final*	*Elected (R.)*
Margaret Ritchie, SDLP	8,506	8,506	First (1)
Catriona Ruane, SF	5,955	6,192	Second (2)
Jim Wells, DUP	5,200	6,543	Third (5)
John McCallister, UUP	4,409	6,240	Fourth (6)
Willie Clarke, SF	3,882	6,777	Fifth (7)
Karen McKevitt, SDLP	3,758	5,347	Sixth (9)
Naomi Bailie, SF	3,050		
*Eamonn O'Neill, SDLP	2,663	4,883	
Henry Reilly, UKIP	2,332		
Cadogan Enright, Green	1,107		
David Griffin, Alliance	864		

FERMANAGH AND SOUTH TYRONE
E. 70,985 T. 48,949 (68.96%)

	First	*Final*	*Elected (R.)*
Michelle Gildernew, SF	9,110	9,110	First (1)
Tom Elliott, UUP	6,896	6,896	Second (1)
Arlene Foster, DUP	6,876	6,876	Third (3)
Sean Lynch, SF	5,146	6,476	Fifth (6)
Phil Flanagan, SF	5,082	6,137	Sixth (6)
Maurice Morrow, DUP	4,844	7,229	Fourth (5)
*Tommy Gallagher, SDLP	4,606	6,075	
Kenny Donaldson, UUP	2,366		
Alex Elliott, TUV	1,231		
Pat Cox, Ind.	997		
Hannah Su, Alliance	845		

FOYLE
E. 68,663 T. 39,686 (57.80%)

	First	Final	Elected (R.)
William Hay, DUP	7,154	7,154	First (1)
Martina Anderson, SF	6,950	6,950	Second (1)
Mark Durkan, SDLP	4,970	5,794	Third (4)
Raymond McCartney, SF	3,638	6,245	Fourth (7)
Pat Ramsey, SDLP	3,138	4,876	Sixth (7)
*Eamonn McCann (PBP)	3,120	3,916	
Colum Eastwood, SDLP	2,967	5,563	Fifth (7)
Pol Callaghan, SDLP	2,624		
Paul Fleming, SF	2,612		
Paul McFadden, Ind.	1,280		
Keith McGrellis, Alliance	334		
Terry Doherty, Ind.	60		

LAGAN VALLEY
E. 67,532 T. 35,842 (53.07%)

	First	Final	Elected (R.)
Edwin Poots, DUP	7,329	7,329	First (1)
Basil McCrea, UUP	5,771	5,771	Second (1)
Trevor Lunn, Alliance	4,389	5,120	Fourth (6)
Paul Givan, DUP	4,352	5,518	Fifth (7)
Jonathan Craig, DUP	4,263	5,081	Third (5)
Brenda Hale, DUP	2,910	4,791	Sixth (7)
*Pat Catney, SDLP	2,165	3,406	
Mark Hill, UUP	1,482		
Mary-Kate Quinn, SF	1,203		
Lyle Rea, TUV	1,031		
Conor Quinn, Green	592		

LONDONDERRY EAST
E. 65,226 T. 35,303 (54.12%)

	First	Final	Elected (R.)
Gregory Campbell, DUP	6,319	6,319	First (1)
Cathal O hOisin, SF	4,681	4,962	Third (6)
George Robinson, DUP	3,855	4,823	Fourth (7)
David McClarty (Ind.)	3,003	4,405	Fifth (7)
John Dallat, SDLP	2,967	5,207	Second (6)
Bernadette Archibald, SF	2,639		
Adrian McQuillan, DUP	2,633	3,782	Sixth (7)
Thomas Conway	2,222		
Barney Fitzpatrick, Alliance	1,905		
Boyd Douglas, TUV	1,568		
Lesley Macaulay, UUP	1,472		
*David Harding, UUP	1,458	3,460	

NEWRY AND ARMAGH
E. 77,544 T. 47,562 (61.34%)

	First	Final	Elected (R.)
Conor Murphy, SF	9,127	9,127	First (1)
Danny Kennedy, UUP	8,718	8,718	Second (1)
Dominic Bradley, SDLP	7,123	7,123	Third (1)
Cathal Boylan, SF	6,614	8,092	Fourth (2)
William Irwin, DUP	6,101	7,502	Fifth (3)
*Thomas O'Hanlon, SDLP	3,825	5,014	
Mickey Brady, SF	3,254	5,625	Sixth (6)
Barrie Halliday, TUV	830		
David Murphy, Alliance	734		
Robert Woods, UKIP	98		
James Malone, ND	90		

STRANGFORD
E. 62,178 T. 30,186 (48.55%)

	First	Final	Elected (R.)
Michelle McIlveen, DUP	4,573	4,573	First (1)
Kieran McCarthy, Alliance	4,284	4,284	Second (1)
Jonathan Bell, DUP	4,265	4,265	Third (1)
Simon Hamilton, DUP	3,456	5,745	Fourth (5)
Mike Nesbitt, UUP	3,273	4,072	Fifth (6)
David McNarry, UUP	2,733	3,767	Sixth (6)
*Joe Boyle, SDLP	2,525	3,308	
Billy Walker, DUP	2,175		
Mickey Coogan, SF	902		
Terry Williams, TUV	841		
Cecil Andrews, UKIP	601		

TYRONE WEST
E. 62,970 T. 40,323 (64.04%)

	First	Final	Elected (R.)
Barry McElduff, SF	6,008	6,008	First (1)
Pat Doherty, SF	5,630	5,630	Second (1)
Michaela Boyle, SF	5,053	7,792	Third (4)
Tom Buchanan, DUP	5,027	5,162	Fifth (5)
Ross Hussey, UUP	4,072	4,398	Sixth (5)
*Allan Bresland, DUP	4,059	4,124	
Joe Byrne, SDLP	3,353	5,321	Fourth (5)
Declan McAleer, SF	3,008		
Paddy McGowan, Ind.	1,145		
Eugene McMenamin, Ind.	1,096		
Eric Bullick, Ind.	852		

ULSTER MID
E.66,602 T. 43,522 (65.35%)

	First	Final	Elected (R.)
Martin McGuinness, SF	8,957	8,957	First (1)
Ian McCrea, DUP	7,127	7,127	Second (1)
Michelle O'Neill, SF	5,178	5,735	Sixth (7)
Patsy McGlone, SDLP	5,065	6,110	Third (5)
Sandra Overend, UUP	4,409	7,130	Fourth (6)
Francie Molloy, SF	4,263	5,191	Fifth (7)
*Ian Milne, SF	2,635	4,412	
Walter Millar, TUV	2,075		
Austin Kelly, SDLP	1,214		
Hugh McCloy, Ind.	933		
Michael McDonald, Alliance	398		
Harry Hutchinson, PBP	243		
Gary McCann, Ind.	241		

UPPER BANN
E. 77,905 T. 43,113 (55.34%)

	First	Final	Elected (R.)
John O'Dowd, SF	6,649	6,649	First (1)
Sydney Anderson, DUP	5,584	6,163	Second (5)
Stephen Moutray, DUP	5,645	6,085	Third (5)
*Johnny McGibbon, SF	4,879	5,438	
Dolores Kelly, SDLP	4,846	5,787	Sixth (7)
Sam Gardiner, UUP	3,676	6,012	Fourth (7)
Colin McCusker, UUP	3,402		
Joanne Dobson, UUP	3,348	5,827	Fifth (7)
Harry Hamilton, Alliance	1,979		
David Vance, TUV	1,026		
Sheila McQuaid, Alliance	786		
Barbara Trotter, UKIP	272		

EUROPEAN PARLIAMENT

European parliament elections take place at five-yearly intervals; the first direct elections to the parliament were held in 1979. In mainland Britain, members of the European parliament (MEPs) were elected in all constituencies on a first-past-the-post basis until 1999, when a regional system of proportional representation was introduced; in Northern Ireland three MEPs have been elected by the single transferable vote system of proportional representation since 1979. Under the terms of the Lisbon Treaty, the UK gained an extra seat in December 2011, taking the total to 73. This seat was added to the West Midlands region and filled by the highest-ranked losing candidate standing for the region in the 2009 European parliament elections.

At the 2009 European parliament elections all UK MEPs were elected under a 'closed-list' regional system of proportional representation, with England being divided into nine regions (residents of Gibraltar vote in the South West region) and Scotland, Wales and Northern Ireland each constituting a single region each. Parties submitted a list of candidates for each region in their own order of preference. Votes were cast for a party or an independent candidate, and the first seat in each region was allocated to the party or candidate with the highest number of votes. The rest of the seats in each region were then allocated broadly in proportion to each party's share of the vote. Each region returned the following number of members: East Midlands, 5; Eastern, 7; London, 8; North East, 3; North West, 8; South East, 10; South West, 6; West Midlands, 6; Yorkshire and the Humber, 6; Wales, 4; Northern Ireland, 3; Scotland, 6.

If a vacancy occurs due to the resignation or death of an MEP, it is filled by the next available person on that party's list. If an independent MEP resigns or dies, a by-election is held. Where an MEP leaves the party on whose list he/she was elected, there is no requirement to resign the post of MEP.

British subjects and nationals of member states of the European Union are eligible for election to the European parliament provided they are aged 18 or over and not subject to disqualification. Since 1994, eligible citizens have had the right to vote in elections to the European parliament in the UK as long as they are entered on the electoral register.

MEPs previously received a salary set at the level of the national parliamentary salary of their country. In July 2009 an MEP statute introduced a uniform salary for all MEPs, set at a rate of 38.5 per cent of the basic salary of a European court of justice judge. In 2013 this approximated an annual salary of €95,482 (£80,600).

The next elections to the European parliament will take place in 2014. For further information visit the UK's European parliament website (W www.europarl.org.uk).

UK MEMBERS *as at July 2013*

* Denotes membership of the last European parliament
† Previously sat as a member of the Conservative party
‡ Previously sat as a member of UKIP
§ Previously sat as a member of UCUNF

Agnew, John (*b.* 1949), *UKIP, Eastern*
Anderson, Martina (*b.* 1962), *SF, Northern Ireland*
‡Andreasen, Marta (*b.* 1954), *C., South East*
***Ashworth**, Richard (*b.* 1947), *C., South East*
***Atkins**, Rt. Hon. Sir Robert (*b.* 1946), *C., North West*
***Batten**, Gerard (*b.* 1954), *UKIP, London*
Bearder, Catherine (*b.* 1949), *LD, South East*
Bennion, Phil (*b.* 1954), *LD, West Midlands*
***Bloom**, Godfrey (*b.* 1949), *UKIP, Yorkshire and the Humber*
***Bowles**, Sharon (*b.* 1953), *LD, South East*
***Bradbourn**, Philip, OBE (*b.* 1951), *C., West Midlands*
Brons, Andrew (*b.* 1947), *BNP, Yorkshire and the Humber*
Bufton, John (*b.* 1962), *UKIP, Wales*
***Callanan**, Martin (*b.* 1961), *C., North East*
‡Campbell Bannerman, David (*b.* 1960), *C., Eastern*
***Cashman**, Michael (*b.* 1950), *Lab., West Midlands*
***Chichester**, Giles (*b.* 1946), *C., South West*
***Clark**, Derek Rowland (*b.* 1933), *UKIP, East Midlands*
***Colman**, Trevor (*b.* 1941), *UKIP, South West*
Dartmouth, Earl of (*b.* 1949), *UKIP, South West*
***Davies**, Chris (*b.* 1954), *LD, North West*
***Deva**, Nirj (*b.* 1948), *C., South East*
Dodds, Diane (*b.* 1958), *DUP, Northern Ireland*
***Duff**, Andrew (*b.* 1950), *LD, Eastern*
***Elles**, James (*b.* 1949), *C., South East*
***Evans**, Jill (*b.* 1959), *PC, Wales*
***Farage**, Nigel (*b.* 1964), *UKIP, South East*
Ford, Vicky (*b.* 1967), *C., Eastern*
Foster, Jacqueline (*b.* 1947), *C., North West*
Fox, Ashley (*b.* 1969), *C., South West*
Girling, Julie (*b.* 1956), *C., South West*
Griffin, Nick (*b.* 1959), *BNP, North West*
***Hall**, Fiona (*b.* 1955), *LD, North East*
***Hannan**, Daniel (*b.* 1971), *C., South East*
***Harbour**, Malcolm (*b.* 1947), *C., West Midlands*
***†Helmer**, Roger (*b.* 1944), *UKIP, East Midlands*
***Honeyball**, Mary (*b.* 1952), *Lab., London*
***Howitt**, Richard (*b.* 1961), *Lab., Eastern*
***Hudghton**, Ian (*b.* 1951), *SNP, Scotland*
***Hughes**, Stephen (*b.* 1952), *Lab., North East*
***Kamall**, Dr Syed (*b.* 1967), *C., London*
***Karim**, Sajjad (*b.* 1970), *C., North West*
***Kirkhope**, Timothy (*b.* 1945), *C., Yorkshire and the Humber*
***Lambert**, Jean (*b.* 1950), *Green, London*
***Ludford**, Baroness (*b.* 1951), *LD, London*
Lyon, George (*b.* 1956), *LD, Scotland*
***McAvan**, Linda (*b.* 1962), *Lab., Yorkshire and the Humber*
***McCarthy**, Arlene (*b.* 1960), *Lab., North West*
McClarkin, Emma (*b.* 1978), *C., East Midlands*
McIntyre, Anthea (*b.* 1954), *C., West Midlands*
***†McMillan-Scott**, Edward (*b.* 1949), *LD, Yorkshire and the Humber*
***Martin**, David (*b.* 1954), *Lab., Scotland*
***Moraes**, Claude (*b.* 1965), *Lab., London*
***Nattrass**, Mike (*b.* 1945), *UKIP, West Midlands*
***Newton Dunn**, Bill (*b.* 1941), *LD, East Midlands*
***§Nicholson**, Jim (*b.* 1945), *UUP, Northern Ireland*
Nuttall, Paul (*b.* 1976), *UKIP, North West*
***Simpson**, Brian (*b.* 1953), *Lab., North West*
‡Sinclaire, Nikki (*b.* 1968), *Ind., West Midlands*
***Skinner**, Peter (*b.* 1959), *Lab., South East*
***Smith**, Alyn (*b.* 1973), *SNP, Scotland*
***Stevenson**, Struan (*b.* 1948), *C., Scotland*
***Stihler**, Catherine (*b.* 1973), *Lab., Scotland*
***Sturdy**, Robert (*b.* 1944), *C., Eastern*
Swinburne, Dr Kay (*b.* 1967), *C., Wales*
***Tannock**, Dr Charles (*b.* 1957), *C., London*
Taylor, Keith (*b.* 1953), *Green, South East*
Taylor, Rebecca (*b.* 1975), *LD, Yorkshire and the Humber*

***Van Orden**, Geoffrey (*b.* 1945), *C., Eastern*
Vaughan, Derek (*b.* 1961), *Lab., Wales*
***Watson**, Sir Graham (*b.* 1956), *LD, South West*
***Willmott**, Glenis (*b.* 1951), *Lab., East Midlands*
Yannakoudakis, Marina (*b.* 1956), *C., London*

STATE OF THE PARTIES *as at April 2013*

Party	*Seats*
Conservative (C.)	27
Labour (Lab.)	13
UK Independence Party (UKIP)	11
Liberal Democrats (LD)	11
British National Party (BNP)	2
Green Party (Green)	2
Scottish National Party (SNP)	2
Others*	5
Total	73

* The Democratic Unionist Party (DUP), Plaid Cymru (PC), the Ulster Unionist Party (UUP) and Sinn Fein (SF) have one seat each; additionally there is one independent MEP (Ind.)

UK REGIONS *as at 4 June 2009 election*

Abbreviations

AC	Animals Count
ChP	Christian Party
JT	Jury Team
Libertas	Libertas
No2EU	No2EU Yes to Democracy
Peace	Peace Party
Pensioners	Pensioners Party
Roman	Roman Party
SGB	Socialist Party of Great Britain
SLP	Socialist Labour Party
SSP	Scottish Socialist Party
TUV	Traditional Unionist Voice
UCUNF	Ulster Conservatives and Unionists – New Force
UKF	United Kingdom First
YD	Wai D (Your Decision)
Yes2EU	YES2EUROPE

For other abbreviations, *see* UK General Election Results.

E. 44,173,690 T. 34.48%

EASTERN

(Bedfordshire, Cambridgeshire, Essex, Hertfordshire, Luton, Norfolk, Peterborough, Southend-on-Sea, Suffolk, Thurrock)

E. 4,252,669	T. 38.0%
C.	500,331 (31.2%)
UKIP	313,921 (19.6%)
LD	221,235 (13.8%)
Lab.	167,833 (10.5%)
Green	141,016 (8.8%)
BNP	97,013 (6.1%)
UKF	38,185 (2.4%)
Eng. Dem.	32,211 (2.0%)
CPA	24,646 (1.5%)
No2EU	13,939 (0.9%)
SLP	13,599 (0.8%)
AC	13,201 (0.8%)
Libertas	9,940 (0.6%)
Ind.	9,916 (0.6%)
JT	6,354 (0.4%)
C. majority	186,410

(June 2004, C. maj. 169,366)

MEMBERS ELECTED
1. *G. Van Orden, *C.* 2. D. Campbell Bannerman, *UKIP* 3. *R. Sturdy, *C.* 4. *A. Duff, *LD* 5. *R. Howitt, *Lab.* 6. V. Ford, *C.* 7. J. Agnew, *UKIP*

EAST MIDLANDS

(Derby, Derbyshire, Leicester, Leicestershire, Lincolnshire, Northamptonshire, Nottingham, Nottinghamshire, Rutland)

E. 3,312,944	T. 37.51%
C.	370,275 (30.2%)
Lab.	206,945 (16.9%)
UKIP	201,984 (16.4%)
LD	151,428 (12.3%)
BNP	106,319 (8.7%)
Green	83,939 (6.8%)
Eng. Dem.	28,498 (2.3%)
UKF	20,561 (1.7%)
CPA	17,907 (1.5%)
SLP	13,590 (1.1%)
No2EU	11,375 (0.9%)
Libertas	7,882 (0.6%)
JT	7,362 (0.6%)
C. majority	204,243

(June 2004, C. maj. 4,864)

MEMBERS ELECTED
1. *R. Helmer, *C.* 2.*G. Willmott, *Lab.* 3. *D. Clark, *UKIP* 4. E. McClarkin, *C.* 5. *W. Newton Dunn, *LD*

LONDON

E. 5,257,624	T. 33.53%
C.	479,037 (27.4%)
Lab.	372,590 (21.3%)
LD	240,156 (13.7%)
Green	190,589 (10.9%)
UKIP	188,440 (10.8%)
BNP	86,420 (4.9%)
CPA	51,336 (2.9%)
Ind.	50,014 (2.9%)
Eng. Dem.	24,477 (1.4%)
No2EU	17,758 (1.0%)
SLP	15,306 (0.9%)
Libertas	8,444 (0.5%)
JT	7,284 (0.4%)
Ind, SC	4,918 (0.3%)
SGB	4,050 (0.2%)
Yes2EU	3,384 (0.2%)
Ind.	3,248 (0.2%)
Ind.	1,972 (0.1%)
Ind.	1,603 (0.1%)
C. majority	106,447

(June 2004, C. maj. 38,357)

MEMBERS ELECTED
1. *C. Tannock, *C.* 2. *C. Moraes, *Lab.* 3. *Baroness Ludford, *LD* 4. *S. Kamall, *C.* 5. *J. Lambert, *Green* 6. *G. Batten, *UKIP* 7. *M. Honeyball, *Lab.* 8. M. Yannakoudakis, *C.*

NORTH EAST

(Co. Durham, Darlington, Hartlepool, Middlesbrough, Northumberland, Redcar and Cleveland, Stockton-on-Tees, Tyne and Wear)

E. 1,939,709	T. 30.50%
Lab.	147,338 (25.0%)
C.	116,911 (19.8%)
LD	103,644 (17.6%)
UKIP	90,700 (15.4%)
BNP	52,700 (8.9%)
Green	34,081 (5.8%)
Eng. Dem.	13,007 (2.2%)
SLP	10,238 (1.7%)
No2EU	8,066 (1.4%)
CPA	7,263 (1.2%)
Libertas	3,010 (0.5%)
JT	2,904 (0.5%)
Lab. majority	30,427

(June 2004, Lab. maj. 121,088)

MEMBERS ELECTED
1. *S. Hughes, *Lab.* 2. *M. Callanan, *C.* 3. *Ms F. Hall, *LD*

NORTHERN IRELAND

(Northern Ireland forms a three-member seat with a single transferable vote system)

E. 1,141,979	T. 42.81%
	1st Pref. Votes
Bairbre de Brún, *SF*	126,184 (26.0%)
Diane Dodds, *DUP*	88,346 (18.2%)
Jim Nicholson, *UCUNF*	82,893 (17.1%)
Alban Maginness, *SDLP*	78,489 (16.2%)
Jim Allister, *TUV*	66,197 (13.7%)
Ian James Parsley, *Alliance*	26,699 (5.5%)
Steven Agnew, *Green*	15,764 (3.3%)

MEMBERS ELECTED
1. *B. de Brún, *SF* 2. *J. Nicholson, *UCUNF* 3. D. Dodds, *DUP*

NORTH WEST

(Blackburn-with-Darwen, Blackpool, Cheshire, Cumbria, Greater Manchester, Halton, Lancashire, Merseyside, Warrington)

E. 1,651,825	T. 31.90%
C.	423,174 (25.6%)
Lab.	336,831 (20.4%)
UKIP	261,740 (15.8%)
LD	235,639 (14.3%)
BNP	132,094 (8.0%)
Green	127,133 (7.7%)
Eng. Dem.	40,027 (2.4%)
SLP	26,224 (1.6%)
CPA	25,999 (1.6%)
No2EU	23,580 (1.4%)
JT	8,783 (0.5%)
Libertas	6,980 (0.4%)
Ind.	3,621 (0.2%)
C. majority	86,343

(June 2004, Lab. maj. 66,942)

MEMBERS ELECTED
1. *Sir R. Atkins, *C.* 2. A. McCarthy, *Lab.* 3. P. Nuttall, *UKIP* 4. *C. Davies, *LD* 5. *S. Karim, *C.* 6. *B. Simpson, *Lab.* 7. J. Foster, *C.* 8. N. Griffin, *BNP*

SCOTLAND

E. 3,873,163	T. 28.60%
SNP	321,007 (29.1%)
Lab.	229,853 (20.8%)
C.	185,794 (16.8%)
LD	127,038 (11.5%)
Green	80,442 (7.3%)
UKIP	57,788 (5.2%)
BNP	27,174 (2.5%)
SLP	22,135 (2.0%)
CPA	16,738 (1.5%)
SSP	10,404 (0.9%)
Ind.	10,189 (0.9%)
No2EU	9,693 (0.9%)
JT	6,257 (0.6%)
SNP majority	91,154

(June 2004, Lab. maj. 79,360)

MEMBERS ELECTED
1. *I. Hudghton, *SNP* 2. *D. Martin, *Lab.* 3. *S. Stevenson, *C.* 4. *A. Smith, *SNP* 5. G. Lyon, *LD* 6. *C. Stihler, *Lab.*

SOUTH EAST

(Bracknell Forest, Brighton and Hove, Buckinghamshire, East Sussex, Hampshire, Isle of Wight, Kent, Medway, Milton Keynes, Newbury, Oxfordshire, Portsmouth, Reading, Slough, Southampton, Surrey, West Sussex, Windsor and Maidenhead, Wokingham)

E. 6,231,875	T. 38.19%
C.	812,288 (34.8%)
UKIP	440,002 (18.8%)
LD	330,340 (14.1%)
Green	271,506 (11.6%)
Lab.	192,592 (8.2%)
BNP	101,769 (4.4%)
Eng. Dem.	52,526 (2.2%)
CPA	35,712 (1.5%)
No2EU	21,455 (0.9%)
Libertas	16,767 (0.7%)
SLP	15,484 (0.7%)
UKF	15,261 (0.7%)
JT	14,172 (0.6%)
Peace Party	9,534 (0.4%)
Roman Party	5,450 (0.2%)
C. majority	372,286

(June 2004, C. maj. 345,259)

MEMBERS ELECTED
1. *D. Hannan, *C.* 2. *N. Farage, *UKIP* 3. *R. Ashworth, *C.* 4. *S. Bowles, *LD* 5. *Dr C. Lucas, *Green* 6. *N. Deva, *C.* 7. M. Andreasen, *UKIP* 8. *J. Elles, *C.* 9. *P. Skinner, *Lab.* 10. C. Bearder, *LD*

SOUTH WEST

(Bath and North East Somerset, Bournemouth, Bristol, Cornwall, Devon, Dorset, Gloucestershire, North Somerset, Plymouth, Poole, Somerset, South Gloucestershire, Swindon, Torbay, Wiltshire, Isles of Scilly, Gibraltar)

E. 3,998,479	T. 39.04%
C.	468,472 (30.2%)
UKIP	341,845 (22.1%)
LD	266,253 (17.2%)
Green	144,179 (9.3%)
Labour	118,716 (7.7%)
BNP	60,889 (3.9%)
Pensioners	37,785 (2.4%)
Eng. Dem.	25,313 (1.6%)
CPA	21,329 (1.4%)
Meb. Ker.	14,922 (1.0%)
SLP	10,033 (0.6%)
No2EU	9,741 (0.6%)
Ind.	8,971 (0.6%)
Libertas	7,292 (0.5%)
FPFT	7,151 (0.5%)
JT	5,758 (0.4%)
YD	789 (0.1%)
C. majority	126,627

(June 2004, C. maj. 130,587)

MEMBERS ELECTED
1. *G. Chichester, *C.* 2. T. Colman, *UKIP* 3. *G. Watson, *LD* 4. J. McCulloch Girling, *C.* 5. W. Dartmouth, *UKIP* 6. A. Fox, *C.*

WALES

E. 2,251,968	T. 30.50%
C.	145,193 (21.2%)
Lab.	138,852 (20.3%)
PC	126,702 (18.5%)
UKIP	87,585 (12.8%)
LD	73,082 (10.7%)
Green	38,160 (5.6%)
BNP	37,114 (5.4%)
ChP	13,037 (1.9%)
SLP	12,402 (1.8%)
No2EU	8,600 (1.3%)
JT	3,793 (0.6%)
C. majority	6,341

(June 2004, Lab. maj. 120,039)

MEMBERS ELECTED
1. K. Swinburne, *C.* 2. D. Vaughan. *Lab.* 3. *J. Evans, *PC* 4. J. Bufton, *UKIP*

WEST MIDLANDS

(Herefordshire, Shropshire, Staffordshire, Stoke-on-Trent, Telford and Wrekin, Warwickshire, West Midlands Metropolitan area, Worcestershire)

E. 4,056,370	T. 35.07%
C.	396,487 (28.1%)
UKIP	300,471 (21.3%)
Lab.	240,201 (17.0%)
LD	170,246 (12.0%)
BNP	121,967 (8.6%)
Green	88,244 (6.2%)
Eng. Dem.	32,455 (2.3%)
CPA	18,784 (1.3%)
SLP	14,724 (1.0%)
No2EU	13,415 (0.9%)
JT	8,721 (0.6%)
Libertas	6,961 (0.5%)
C. majority	96,016

(June 2004, C. maj. 56,324)

MEMBERS ELECTED
1. *P. Bradbourn, *C.* 2. *M. Nattrass, *UKIP* 3. *M. Cashman, *Lab.* 4. *M. Harbour, *C.* 5. *L. Lynne, *LD* 6. N. Sinclaire, *UKIP*

YORKSHIRE AND THE HUMBER

(East Riding of Yorkshire, Kingston-upon-Hull, North East Lincolnshire, North Lincolnshire, North Yorkshire, South Yorkshire, West Yorkshire, York)

E. 3,792,415	T. 32.51%
C.	299,802 (24.5%)
Lab.	230,009 (18.8%)
UKIP	213,750 (17.4%)
LD	161,552 (13.2%)
BNP	120,139 (9.8%)
Green	104,456 (8.5%)
Eng. Dem.	31,287 (2.6%)
SLP	19,380 (1.6%)
CPA	16,742 (1.4%)
No2EU	15,614 (1.3%)
JT	7,181 (0.6%)
Libertas	6,268 (0.5%)
C. majority	69,793

(June 1999, Lab. maj. 25,844)

MEMBERS ELECTED
1. *E. McMillan-Scott, *C.* 2. *L. McAvan, *Lab.* 3. *G. Bloom, *UKIP* 4. *D. Wallis, *LD* 5. *T. Kirkhope, *C.* 6. A. Brons, *BNP*

LOCAL GOVERNMENT

Major changes in local government were introduced in England and Wales in 1974 and in Scotland in 1975 by the Local Government Act 1972 and the Local Government (Scotland) Act 1973. Further significant alterations were made in England by the Local Government Acts of 1985, 1992 and 2000.

The structure in England was based on two tiers of local authorities (county councils and district councils) in the non-metropolitan areas; and a single tier of metropolitan councils in the six metropolitan areas of England and London borough councils in London.

Following reviews of the structure of local government in England by the Local Government Commission (now the Boundary Commission for England), 46 unitary (all-purpose) authorities were created between April 1995 and April 1998 to cover certain areas in the non-metropolitan counties. The remaining county areas continue to have two tiers of local authorities. The county and district councils in the Isle of Wight were replaced by a single unitary authority on 1 April 1995; the former counties of Avon, Cleveland, Humberside and Berkshire were replaced by unitary authorities; and Hereford and Worcester was replaced by a new county council for Worcestershire (with district councils) and a unitary authority for Herefordshire. On 1 April 2009 the county areas of Cornwall, Durham, Northumberland, Shropshire and Wiltshire were given unitary status and two new unitary authorities were created for Bedfordshire (Bedford and Central Bedfordshire) and Cheshire (Cheshire East and Cheshire West & Chester) replacing the two-tier county/district system in these areas.

The Local Government (Wales) Act 1994 and the Local Government etc (Scotland) Act 1994 abolished the two-tier structure in Wales and Scotland with effect from 1 April 1996, replacing it with a single tier of unitary authorities.

In Northern Ireland a reform programme is currently underway to reduce the number of local authorities from 26 to 11. Legislation to finalise the boundaries of the new 11 local government district authorities was approved by the Northern Ireland Assembly on 12 June 2012; the process is expected to be completed by April 2015.

ELECTIONS

Local elections are normally held on the first Thursday in May. Generally, all citizens of the UK, the Republic of Ireland, Commonwealth and other European Union citizens who are 18 years or over and resident on the qualifying date in the area for which the election is being held, are entitled to vote at local government elections. A register of electors is prepared and published annually by local electoral registration officers.

A returning officer has the overall responsibility for an election. Voting takes place at polling stations, arranged by the local authority and under the supervision of a presiding officer specially appointed for the purpose. Candidates, who are subject to various statutory qualifications and disqualifications designed to ensure that they are suitable to hold office, must be nominated by electors for the electoral area concerned.

In England, the Local Government Boundary Commission for England is responsible for carrying out periodic reviews of electoral arrangements, to consider whether the boundaries of wards or divisions within a local authority need to be altered to take account of changes in electorate; structural reviews, to consider whether a single, unitary authority should be established in an area instead of an existing two-tier system; and administrative boundary reviews of district or county authorities.

The Local Democracy and Boundary Commission for Wales, the Local Government Boundary Commission for Scotland and the local government boundary commissioner for Northern Ireland (appointed when required by the Boundary Commission for Northern Ireland) are responsible for reviewing the electoral arrangements and boundaries of local authorities within their respective regions.

The Local Government Act 2000 provided for the secretary of state to change the frequency and phasing of elections in England and Wales.

LOCAL GOVERNMENT BOUNDARY COMMISSION FOR ENGLAND, Layden House, 76–86 Turnmill Street, London EC1M 5LG **T** 020-7664 8534 **E** reviews@lgbce.org.uk **W** www.lgbce.org.uk

LOCAL DEMOCRACY AND BOUNDARY COMMISSION FOR WALES, Ground Floor, Hastings House, Fitzalan Court, Cardiff CF24 0BL **T** 029-2046 4819 **E** ldbc.wales@wales.gsi.gov.uk **W** www.lgbc-wales.gov.uk

LOCAL GOVERNMENT BOUNDARY COMMISSION FOR SCOTLAND, Thistle House, 91 Haymarket Terrace, Edinburgh EH12 5HD **T** 0131-538 7510 **E** lgbcs@scottishboundaries.gov.uk **W** www.lgbc-scotland.gov.uk

BOUNDARY COMMISSION FOR NORTHERN IRELAND, Forestview, Purdy's Lane, Belfast BT8 7AR **T** 028-9069 4800 **E** bcni@belfast.org.uk **W** www.boundarycommission.org.uk

INTERNAL ORGANISATION

The council as a whole is the final decision-making body within any authority. Councils are free to a great extent to make their own internal organisational arrangements. The Local Government Act, given royal assent on 28 July 2000, allows councils to adopt one of three broad categories of constitution which include a separate executive:

- A directly elected mayor with a cabinet selected by that mayor
- A cabinet, either elected by the council or appointed by its leader
- A directly elected mayor and council manager

Normally, questions of policy are settled by the full council, while the administration of the various services is the responsibility of committees of councillors. Day-to-day decisions are delegated to the council's officers, who act within the policies laid down by the councillors.

FINANCE

Local government in England, Wales and Scotland is financed from four sources: council tax, non-domestic rates, government grants and income from fees and charges for services.

COUNCIL TAX

Council tax is a local tax levied by each local council. Liability for the council tax bill usually falls on the owner-occupier or tenant of a dwelling which is their sole or main residence. Council tax bills may be reduced because of the personal circumstances of people resident in a property, and there are discounts in the case of dwellings occupied by fewer than two adults.

In England, unitary and metropolitan authorities are responsible for collecting their own council tax from which the police authorities claim their share. In areas where there are two tiers of local authority, each county, district and police authority sets its own council tax rate; the district authorities collect the combined council tax and the county councils and police authorities claim their share from the district councils' collection funds. In Wales, each unitary authority and each police authority sets its own council tax rate. The unitary authorities collect the combined council tax and the police authorities claim their share from the funds. In Scotland, each local authority sets its own rate of council tax.

The tax relates to the value of the dwelling. In England and Scotland each dwelling is placed in one of eight valuation bands, ranging from A to H, based on the property's estimated market value as at 1 April 1991. In Wales there are nine bands, ranging from A to I, based on the estimated market value of property as at 1 April 2003.

The valuation bands and ranges of values in England, Wales and Scotland are:

England

A	Up to £40,000	E	£88,001–£120,000
B	£40,001–£52,000	F	£120,001–£160,000
C	£52,001–£68,000	G	£160,001–£320,000
D	£68,001–£88,000	H	Over £320,001

Wales

A	Up to £44,000	F	£162,001–£223,000
B	£44,001–£65,000	G	£223,001–£324,000
C	£65,001–£91,000	H	£324,001–£424,000
D	£91,001–£123,000	I	Over £424,001
E	£123,001–£162,000		

Scotland

A	Up to £27,000	E	£58,001–£80,000
B	£27,001–£35,000	F	£80,001–£106,000
C	£35,001–£45,000	G	£106,001–£212,000
D	£45,001–£58,000	H	Over £212,001

The council tax within a local area varies between the different bands according to proportions laid down by law. The charge attributable to each band as a proportion of the Band D charge set by the council is approximately:

A	67%	F	144%
B	78%	G	167%
C	89%	H	200%
D	100%	I	233%*
E	122%		

* Wales only

The average Band D council tax bill for each authority area is given in the tables starting on p. 261. There may be variations from the given figure within each district council area because of different parish or community precepts being levied.

NON-DOMESTIC RATES

Non-domestic (business) rates are collected by billing authorities; these are the district councils in those areas of England with two tiers of local government and are unitary authorities in other parts of England, in Wales and in Scotland. In respect of England and Wales, the Local Government Finance Act 1988 provides for liability for rates to be assessed on the basis of a poundage (multiplier) tax on the rateable value of property (hereditaments). Separate multipliers are set by the Department for Communities and Local Government (CLG) in England, the Welsh government and the Scottish government. Rates are collected by the billing authority for the area where a property is located. Rate income collected by billing authorities is paid into a national non-domestic rating (NNDR) pool and redistributed to individual authorities on the basis of the adult population figure as prescribed by CLG, the Welsh government or the Scottish government. The rates pools are maintained separately in England, Wales and Scotland. Actual payment of rates in certain cases is subject to transitional arrangements, to phase in the larger increases and reductions in rates resulting from the effects of the latest revaluation.

Rateable values for the 2010 rating lists came into effect on 1 April 2010. They are derived from the rental value of property as at 1 April 2003 and determined on certain statutory assumptions by the Valuation Office Agency in England and Wales, and by local area assessors in Scotland. New property which is added to the list, and significant changes to existing property, necessitate amendments to the rateable value on the same basis. Rating lists (valuation rolls in Scotland) remain in force until the next general revaluation, which usually take place every five years to reflect changes in the property market. The next revaluations for England, Wales and Scotland are scheduled for 2017 and in 2015 for Northern Ireland.

Certain types of property are exempt from rates, eg agricultural land and buildings, certain businesses and some places of public religious worship. Charities and other non-profit-making organisations may receive full or partial relief. Empty commercial property in England and Wales is exempt from business rates for the first three months that the property is vacant (six months for an industrial property), after which full business rates are normally payable. In Scotland an empty commercial property is exempt from business rates for the first three months and entitled to a 50 per cent discount thereafter, except for some types of premises, such as factories, which are entirely exempt.

COMPLAINTS

ENGLAND

In England the Local Government Ombudsman investigates complaints of injustice arising from maladministration by local authorities and certain other bodies. The Local Government Ombudsman will not usually consider a complaint unless the local authority concerned has had an opportunity to investigate and reply to a complainant.

Under the Local Government Act 2000, First-tier Tribunal (Local Government Standards in England) decides references and appeals regarding the conduct of members of local authorities (*see* Tribunals).

LOCAL GOVERNMENT OMBUDSMAN, PO Box 4771, Coventry CV4 0EH **T** 0300-061 0614 **E** advice@lgo.org.uk **W** www.lgo.org.uk

Ombudsmen, Jane Martin, Anne Seex

WALES

The office of Public Services Ombudsman for Wales came into force on 1 April 2006, incorporating the functions of the Local Government Ombudsman for Wales.

PUBLIC SERVICES OMBUDSMAN FOR WALES, 1 Ffordd yr Hen Gae, Pencoed CF35 5LJ T 0300-790 0203
E ask@ombudsman-wales.org.uk
W www.ombudsman-wales.org.uk
Ombudsman, Peter Tyndall

SCOTLAND

The Scottish Public Services Ombudsman is responsible for complaints regarding the maladministration of local government in Scotland.

SCOTTISH PUBLIC SERVICES OMBUDSMAN, 4 Melville Street, Edinburgh EH3 7NS T 0800-377 7330
W www.spso.org.uk
Ombudsman, Jim Martin

NORTHERN IRELAND

The Northern Ireland Commissioner for Complaints fulfils a similar function in Northern Ireland, investigating complaints about local authorities and certain public bodies. Complaints are made to the relevant local authority in the first instance but may also be made directly to the commissioner.

NORTHERN IRELAND COMMISSIONER FOR COMPLAINTS, Freepost BEL 1478, Belfast BT1 6BR
T 0800-343424 E ombudsman@ni-ombudsman.org.uk
W www.ni-ombudsman.org.uk
Northern Ireland Commissioner for Complaints, Tom Frawley, CBE

THE QUEEN'S REPRESENTATIVES

The lord-lieutenant of a county is the permanent local representative of the Crown in that county. The appointment of lord-lieutenants is now regulated by the Lieutenancies Act 1997. They are appointed by the sovereign on the recommendation of the prime minister. The retirement age is 75. The office of lord-lieutenant dates from 1551, and its holder was originally responsible for maintaining order and for local defence in the county. The duties of the post include attending on royalty during official visits to the county, performing certain duties in connection with the armed forces (and in particular the reserve forces), and making presentations of honours and awards on behalf of the Crown. In England, Wales and Northern Ireland, the lord-lieutenant usually also holds the office of *Custos Rotulorum.* As such, he or she acts as head of the county's commission of the peace (which recommends the appointment of magistrates).

The office of sheriff (from the Old English *shire-reeve*) of a county was created in the tenth century. The sheriff was the special nominee of the sovereign, and the office reached the peak of its influence under the Norman kings. The Provisions of Oxford (1258) laid down a yearly tenure of office. Since the mid-16th century the office has been purely civil, with military duties taken over by the lord-lieutenant of the county. The sheriff (commonly known as 'high sheriff') attends on royalty during official visits to the county, acts as the returning officer during parliamentary elections in county constituencies, attends the opening ceremony when a high court judge goes on circuit, executes high court writs, and appoints under-sheriffs to act as deputies. The appointments and duties of the sheriffs in England and Wales are laid down by the Sheriffs Act 1887.

The serving high sheriff submits a list of names of possible future sheriffs to a tribunal, which chooses three names to put to the sovereign. The tribunal nominates the high sheriff annually on 12 November and the sovereign picks the name of the sheriff to succeed in the following year. The term of office runs from 25 March to the following 24 March (the civil and legal year before 1752). No person may be chosen twice in three years if there is any other suitable person in the county.

CIVIC DIGNITIES

District councils in England and local councils in Wales may petition for a royal charter granting borough or 'city' status to the council.

In England and Wales the chair of a borough or county borough council may be called a mayor, and the chair of a city council may be called a lord mayor (if lord mayoralty has been conferred on that city). Parish councils in England and community councils in Wales may call themselves 'town councils', in which case their chair is the town mayor.

In Scotland the chair of a local council may be known as a convenor; a provost is the mayoral equivalent. The chair of the councils for the cities of Aberdeen, Dundee, Edinburgh and Glasgow are lord provosts.

ENGLAND

There are 27 counties, divided into 201 districts, 55 unitary authorities (plus the Isles of Scilly) and 36 metropolitan boroughs.

The populations of most of the unitary authorities are in the range of 100,000 to 300,000. The district councils have populations broadly in the range of 60,000 to 100,000; some, however, have larger populations, because of the need to avoid dividing large towns, and some in mainly rural areas have smaller populations.

The main conurbations outside Greater London – Tyne and Wear, West Midlands, Merseyside, Greater Manchester, West Yorkshire and South Yorkshire – are divided into 36 metropolitan boroughs, most of which have a population of over 200,000.

There are also around 9,500 town and parish councils.

ELECTIONS

For districts, counties and for around 8,700 parishes, there are elected councils, consisting of directly elected councillors. The councillors elect one of their number as chair annually.

In general, councils can have whole council elections, elections by thirds or elections by halves. However all metropolitan authorities must hold elections by thirds. The electoral cycle of any new unitary authority is specified in the appropriate statutory order under which it is established.

FUNCTIONS

In areas with a two-tier system of local governance, functions are divided between the district and county authorities, with those functions affecting the larger area or population generally being the responsibility of the county council. A few functions continue to be exercised over the larger area by joint bodies, made up of councillors from each authority within the area.

Generally the allocation of functions is as follows:

County councils: education; strategic planning; traffic, transport and highways; fire service; consumer protection; refuse disposal; smallholdings; social care; libraries

District councils: local planning; housing; highways (maintenance of certain urban roads and off-street car parks); building regulations; environmental health; refuse collection; cemeteries and crematoria; collection of council tax and non-domestic rates

Unitary and metropolitan councils: their functions are all those listed above, except that the fire service is exercised by a joint body

Concurrently by county and district councils: recreation (parks, playing fields, swimming pools); museums; encouragement of the arts, tourism and industry

PARISH COUNCILS
Parish or town councils are the most local tier of government in England. There are currently around 10,000 parishes in England, of which around 9,500 have councils served by approximately 100,000 councillors. Since 15 February 2008 local councils have been able to create new parish councils without seeking approval from the government. Around 80 per cent of parish councils represent populations of less than 2,500; parishes with no parish council can be grouped with neighbouring parishes under a common parish council. A parish council comprises at least five members, the number being fixed by the district council. Elections are held every four years, at the time of the election of the district councillor for the ward including the parish. Full parish councils must be formed for those parishes with more than 999 electors – below this number, parish meetings comprising the electors of the parish must be held at least twice a year.

Parish council functions include: allotments; encouragement of arts and crafts; community halls, recreational facilities (eg open spaces, swimming pools), cemeteries and crematoria; and many minor functions. They must also be given an opportunity to comment on planning applications. They may, like county and district councils, spend limited sums for the general benefit of the parish. They levy a precept on the district councils for their funds. Parish precepts for 2013–14 totalled £368m, a decrease of 4.1 per cent on 2012–13.

FINANCE
Local government revenue expenditure is budgeted to be £102.2bn in 2013–14; of this £23.4bn is to be raised through council tax, £10.8bn from the business rate retention scheme and £67bn from government grants. The remainder will be drawn down from local authority reserves.

Since April 2013 local authorities, except police authorities, retain a share of business rates and keep the growth on that share (the 'rate retention scheme'). Revenue support grant is paid to local authorities to enable all authorities in the same class to broadly set the same council tax; in 2013–14 revenue support grant totals £15.2bn. In addition central government pays specific grants in support of revenue expenditure on particular services. Police authorities will receive all of their funding through police grant from 2013–14 onwards (£7.6bn in 2013–14).

In England, the average council tax per dwelling for 2013–14 is £1,045. The average council tax bill for a Band D dwelling (occupied by two adults, including parish precepts) for 2013–14 is £1,456, an increase of 0.8 per cent from 2012–13. The average Band D council tax is £1,510 in shire districts, £1,421 in metropolitan areas, £1,486 in unitary authority areas and £1,302 in London. Since 2006–7 the London figure has included a levy to fund the 2012 Olympic Games, which equates to a £20 a year increase on a Band D council tax. This levy is expected to continue until 2016.

The non-domestic rating multiplier for England for 2013–14 is 47.1p (46.2p for small businesses). The City of London is able to set a different multiplier from the rest of England; for 2013–14 this is 47.5p (46.6p for small businesses).

Under the Local Government and Housing Act 1989, local authorities have four main ways of paying for capital expenditure: borrowing and other forms of extended credit; capital grants from central government towards some types of capital expenditure; 'usable' capital receipts from the sale of land, houses and other assets; and revenue.

The amount of capital expenditure which a local authority can finance by borrowing (or other forms of credit) is effectively limited by the credit approvals issued to it by central government. Most credit approvals can be used for any kind of local authority capital expenditure; these are known as basic credit approvals. Others (supplementary credit approvals) can be used only for the kind of expenditure specified in the approval, and so are often given to fund particular projects or services.

Local authorities can use all capital receipts from the sale of property or assets for capital spending, except in the case of sales of council houses. Generally, the 'usable' part of a local authority's capital receipts consists of 25 per cent of receipts from the sale of council houses and 50 per cent of other housing assets such as shops or vacant land. The balance has to be set aside as provision for repaying debt and meeting other credit liabilities.

EXPENDITURE
Local authority budgeted revenue expenditure for 2013–14 is:

Service	*£ million*
*Education	38,793
Highways and transport	5,129
Social care	21,286
†Public Health	2,699
Housing (excluding HRA)	2,122
Cultural, environment and planning	9,345
Police	11,166
Fire and rescue	2,174
Central services	3,679
Mandatory rent allowances	14,642
Mandatory rent rebates	536
Rent rebates granted to HRA tenants	4,296
Other services	229
Less appropriations from accumulated absences account	(6)
Net current expenditure	117,091
Capital financing	4,441
‡Capital expenditure charged to revenue account	3,316
Council tax benefit	–
Discretionary non-domestic rate relief	39
Bad debt provision	48
Flood defence payments to Environment Agency	31
Private Finance Initiative schemes	90
Carbon Reduction Commitment	37
Less adjustments permitted by regulation	(14)
Less interest receipts	(417)
Less specific grants outside AEF	(22,229)
Less Business Rates Supplement	(250)
Less Community Infrastructure Levy	(18)
REVENUE EXPENDITURE	102,165

HRA = Housing Revenue Account
AEF = aggregate external finance
* Education expenditure is not comparable to previous years due to a number of schools becoming centrally funded Academies
† Under the Health and Social Care Act 2012 public health duties transferred to local authorities in 2013–14
‡ This figure includes the Transport for London grant funding for Crossrail

LONDON

The Greater London Council was abolished in 1986 and London was divided into 32 borough councils, which have a status similar to the metropolitan borough councils in the rest of England, and the City of London Corporation.

In March 1998 the government announced proposals for a Greater London Authority (GLA) covering the area of the 32 London boroughs and the City of London, which would comprise a directly elected mayor and a 25-member assembly. A referendum was held in London on 7 May 1998 and 72 per cent of electors voted in favour of the GLA. A London mayor was elected on 4 May 2000 and the authority assumed its responsibilities on 3 July 2000 (*see also* Regional Government).

LONDON BOROUGH COUNCILS

The London boroughs have whole council elections every four years, in the year immediately following the county council election year. The most recent elections took place on 6 May 2010.

The borough councils have responsibility for the following functions: building regulations, cemeteries and crematoria, consumer protection, education, youth employment, environmental health, electoral registration, food, drugs, housing, leisure services, libraries, local planning, local roads, museums, parking, recreation (parks, playing fields, swimming pools), refuse collection and street cleaning, social services, town planning and traffic management.

CITY OF LONDON CORPORATION

The City of London Corporation is the local authority for the City of London. Its legal definition is the 'Mayor and Commonalty and Citizens of the City of London'. It is governed by the court of common council, which consists of the lord mayor, 25 other aldermen and 100 common councilmen. The lord mayor and two sheriffs are nominated annually by the City guilds (the livery companies) and elected by the court of aldermen. Aldermen and councilmen are elected from the 25 wards into which the City is divided; councilmen must stand for re-election annually. The council is a legislative assembly, and there are no political parties.

The corporation has the same functions as the London borough councils. In addition, it runs the City of London Police; is the health authority for the Port of London; has health control of animal imports throughout Greater London, including at Heathrow airport; owns and manages public open spaces throughout Greater London; runs the central criminal court; and runs Billingsgate, Smithfield and Spitalfields markets.

THE CITY GUILDS (LIVERY COMPANIES)

The livery companies of the City of London grew out of early medieval religious fraternities and began to emerge as trade and craft guilds, retaining their religious aspect, in the 12th century. From the early 14th century, only members of the trade and craft guilds could call themselves citizens of the City of London. The guilds began to be called livery companies, because of the distinctive livery worn by the most prosperous guild members on ceremonial occasions, in the late 15th century.

By the early 19th century the power of the companies within their trades had begun to wane, but those wearing the livery of a company continued to play an important role in the government of the City of London. Liverymen still have the right to nominate the lord mayor and sheriffs, and most members of the court of common council are liverymen.

WALES

The Local Government (Wales) Act 1994 abolished the two-tier structure of eight county and 37 district councils which had existed since 1974, and replaced it, from 1 April 1996, with 22 unitary authorities. The new authorities were elected in May 1995. Each unitary authority inherited all the functions of the previous county and district councils, except fire services (which are provided by three combined fire authorities, composed of representatives from the unitary authorities) and national parks (which are the responsibility of three independent national park authorities).

COMMUNITY COUNCILS

In Wales community councils are the equivalent of parishes in England. Unlike England, where many areas are not in any parish, communities have been established for the whole of Wales, approximately 865 communities in all. Community meetings may be convened as and when desired.

Community or town councils exist in around 740 of the communities and further councils may be established at the request of a community meeting. Community councils have broadly the same range of powers as English parish councils. Community councillors are elected for a term of four years.

ELECTIONS

Elections take place every four years; the last elections took place in May 2012.

FINANCE

Total budgeted revenue expenditure for 2013–14 is £8bn, an increase of 2 per cent on 2012–13. Total budget requirement, which excludes expenditure financed by specific and special government grants and any use of reserves, is £6.2bn. This comprises revenue support grant of £3.5bn, support from the national non-domestic rate pool of £1bn, police grant of £240m and £1.4bn to be raised through council tax. The non-domestic rating multiplier for Wales for 2013–14 is 46.4p. The average Band D council tax levied in Wales for 2013–14 is £1,226, comprising unitary authorities £1,000, police and crime commissioners £199 and community councils £27.

EXPENDITURE

Local authority budgeted net expenditure for 2013–14 is:

Service	*£ million*
Education	2,639.8
Social services	1,564.7
Council fund housing, including housing benefit	1,098.2
Local environmental services	420.1
Roads and transport	307.1
Libraries, culture, heritage, sport and recreation	263.1
Planning, economic and community development	124.8
Council tax collection	33.7
Debt financing	333.8
Central administrative and other revenue expenditure	307.1
Police	697.8
Fire	149.3
National parks	17.3
Gross revenue expenditure	7,956.8
Less specific and special government grants	(1,932.0)
Net revenue expenditure	6,024.8
Less appropriations from reserves	(66.2)
Council tax reduction scheme	244.0
BUDGET REQUIREMENT	6,202.6

SCOTLAND

The Local Government etc (Scotland) Act 1994 abolished the two-tier structure of nine regional and 53 district councils which had existed since 1975 and replaced it, from 1 April 1996, with 29 unitary authorities on the mainland; the three islands councils remained. The new authorities were elected in April 1995.

In July 1999 the Scottish parliament assumed responsibility for legislation on local government.

ELECTIONS

The unitary authorities consist of directly elected councillors. The Scottish Local Government (Elections) Act 2002 moved elections from a three-year to a four-year cycle, but to avoid the local authority elections coinciding with the Scottish parliament elections in May 2011, the last local authority elections took place in May 2012.

FUNCTIONS

The functions of the councils and islands councils are: education; social work; strategic planning; the provision of infrastructure such as roads; consumer protection; flood prevention; coast protection; valuation and rating; the police and fire services; civil defence; electoral registration; public transport; registration of births, deaths and marriages; housing; leisure and recreation; development and building control; environmental health; licensing; allotments; public conveniences; and the administration of district courts.

COMMUNITY COUNCILS

Scottish community councils differ from those in England and Wales. Their purpose as defined in statute is to ascertain and express the views of the communities they represent, and to take in the interests of their communities such action as appears to be expedient or practicable. Around 1,200 community councils have been established under schemes drawn up by local authorities in Scotland.

FINANCE

Budgeted total revenue support for 2013–14 is £9.7bn, comprising £7.2bn general resource grant, non-domestic rate income of £2.4bn and ring-fenced grants of £98.9m. As a consequence of the creation of the Scottish Police Services Authority and the Scottish Fire and Rescue Service on 1 April 2013, police and fire services are no longer funded through the local government settlement. The non-domestic rate multiplier or poundage for 2013–14 is 46.2p. Larger businesses in 2013–14 (rateable value in excess of £35,000) pay a poundage supplement of 0.9p, which contributes towards the cost of the small business bonus scheme. All non-domestic properties with a rateable value of £18,000 or less may be eligible for non-domestic rates relief of up to 100 per cent. The average Band D council tax for 2013–14 is £1,149.

EXPENDITURE

Local authority budgeted net expenditure for 2013–14 is:

Service	*£ million*
Education	4,565.5
Cultural and related services	590.2
Social work services	2,960.4
Roads and transport	457.9
Environmental services	671.9
Planning and development services	276.5
Other	2,087.3
TOTAL	11,609.7

NORTHERN IRELAND

Currently, Northern Ireland has a system of 26 single-tier district councils. A reform programme is underway to reduce the number of district councils from 26 to 11; the process is expected to be completed by April 2015.

ELECTIONS

Council members are elected for periods of four years at a time on the principle of proportional representation. The last elections took place in May 2011.

FUNCTIONS

The district councils have three main roles. These are:

Executive: responsibility for a wide range of local services including building regulations; community services; consumer protection; cultural facilities; environmental health; miscellaneous licensing and registration provisions, including dog control; litter prevention; recreational and social facilities; refuse collection and disposal; street cleaning; and tourist development

Representative: nominating representatives to sit as members of the various statutory bodies responsible for the administration of regional services such as drainage, education, fire, health and personal social services, housing, and libraries

Consultative: acting as the medium through which the views of local people are expressed on the operation in their area of other regional services – notably conservation (including water supply and sewerage services), planning and roads – provided by those departments of central government which have an obligation, statutory or otherwise, to consult the district councils about proposals affecting their areas

FINANCE

Government in Northern Ireland is part-funded by a system of rates, which supplement the Northern Ireland budget from the UK government. The ratepayer receives a combined tax bill consisting of the regional rate, set by the Northern Ireland executive, and the district rate, which is set by each district council. The regional and district rates are both collected by the Land and Property Services Agency (formerly the Rate Collection Agency). The product of the district rates is paid over to each council while the product of the regional rate supports expenditure by the departments of the executive and assembly.

Since April 2007 domestic rates bills have been based on the capital value of a property, rather than the rental value. The capital value is defined as the price the property might reasonably be expected to realise had it been sold on the open market on 1 January 2005. Non-domestic rates bills are based on 2001 rental values.

Rate bills are calculated by multiplying the property's net annual rental value (in the case of non-domestic property), or capital value (in the case of domestic property), by the regional and district rate poundages respectively.

For 2013–14 the overall average domestic poundage is 0.7227p compared to 0.7047p in 2012–13. The overall average non-domestic rate poundage in 2013–14 is 60.49p compared to 56.88p in 2012–13.

POLITICAL COMPOSITION OF LOCAL COUNCILS

as at May 2013

Abbreviations

All.	Alliance
BNP	British National Party
C.	Conservative
DUP	Democratic Unionist Party
Green	Green
Ind.	Independent
Ind. Un.	Independent Unionist
Lab.	Labour
LD	Liberal Democrat
Lib.	Liberal
O.	Other
PC	Plaid Cymru
R	Residents Associations/Ratepayers
SD	Social Democrat
SDLP	Social Democratic and Labour Party
SF	Sinn Fein
SNP	Scottish National Party
Soc.	Socialist
UKIP	UK Independence Party
UUP	Ulster Unionist Party
v.	Vacant

Total number of seats is given in parentheses after council name.

ENGLAND

COUNTY COUNCILS

Buckinghamshire (49)	C. 36; UKIP 6; LD 5; Ind. 1; Lab. 1
Cambridgeshire (69)	C. 32; LD 14; UKIP 12; Lab. 7; Ind. 4
Cumbria (84)	Lab. 35; C. 26; LD 16; Ind. 7
Derbyshire (64)	Lab. 43; C. 18; LD 3
Devon (62)	C. 38; LD 9; Lab. 7; UKIP 4; Ind. 3; Green 1
Dorset (45)	C. 27; LD 12; Lab. 5; UKIP. 1
East Sussex (49)	C. 20; LD 10; Lab. 7; UKIP 7; Ind. 3; O. 2
Essex (75)	C. 42; Lab. 9; LD 9 UKIP 9; Ind. 4; Green 2
Gloucestershire (53)	C. 23; LD 14; Lab. 9; UKIP 3; Ind. 2; O. 1
Hampshire (78)	C. 45; LD 17; UKIP 10; Lab. 4; O. 1
Hertfordshire (77)	C. 46; LD 16; Lab. 15
Kent (84)	C. 45; Lab. 13; UKIP 17; LD 7; Green 1; R 1
Lancashire (84)	Lab. 39; C 35; LD 6; Ind. 3; Green 1
Leicestershire (55)	C. 30; LD 13; Lab. 10; UKIP 2
Lincolnshire (77)	C. 36; UKIP 16; Lab. 12; Ind. 3; LD 3; O. 7
Norfolk (84)	C. 40; UKIP 15; Lab. 14; LD 10; Green 4; Ind. 1
North Yorkshire (72)	C. 45; LD 8; Ind. 7; Lab. 7; UKIP 2; O. 1
Northamptonshire (57)	C. 36; Lab. 11; LD 6; UKIP 3; Ind. 1
Nottinghamshire (67)	Lab. 34; C. 21; LD 8; O. 2; Ind. 1
Oxfordshire (63)	C. 31; Lab. 15; LD 11; Ind. 4; Green 2
Somerset (55)	C. 29; LD 18; Lab. 3; UKIP 3; Ind. 2
Staffordshire (62)	C. 34; Lab. 24; Ind. 2; UKIP 2
Suffolk (75)	C. 39; Lab. 15; UKIP 9; LD 7; Ind. 3; Green 2
Surrey (81)	C. 58; LD. 9; O. 5; R 3; UKIP 3; Green 1; Ind. 1; Lab. 1
Warwickshire (62)	C. 26; Lab. 22; LD 9; Ind. 3; Green 2
West Sussex (71)	C. 46; UKIP 10; LD 8; Lab. 6; Ind. 1
Worcestershire (57)	C. 30; Lab. 12; O. 4; LD 3; UKIP 3; Green 2; Ind. 2; Lib. 1

DISTRICT COUNCILS

Adur (29)	C. 24; Ind. 2; Lab. 1; LD 1; UKIP 1
Allerdale (56)	Lab. 26; Ind. 14; C. 12; O. 2; UKIP 1; v. 1
Amber Valley (45)	C. 24; Lab. 20; v. 1
Arun (56)	C. 45; LD 5; Ind. 3; Lab. 3
Ashfield (33)	Lab. 24; Ind. 5; LD 4
Ashford (43)	C. 30; Lab. 5; O. 4; Ind. 2; LD 2
Aylesbury Vale (59)	C. 36; LD 17; Ind. 2; Lab. 2; UKIP 2
Babergh (43)	C. 18; LD 12; Ind. 9; Lab. 3; O. 1
Barrow-in-Furness (36)	Lab. 29; C. 7
Basildon (42)	C. 23; Lab. 12; Ind. 3; LD 2; UKIP 1; v. 1
Basingstoke and Deane (60)	C. 30; LD 14; Lab. 11; Ind. 4; UKIP 1
Bassetlaw (48)	Lab. 34; C. 11; Ind. 3
Blaby (39)	C. 28; Lab. 5; LD 5; v. 1
Bolsover (37)	Lab. 32; Ind. 2; R 2; v. 1
Boston (32)	C. 17; Ind. 10; Lab. 3; O. 2
Braintree (60)	C. 45; Lab. 10; Green 2; Ind. 1; O. 1; v. 1
Breckland (54)	C. 47; Lab. 4; Ind. 2; O. 1
Brentwood (37)	C. 21; LD 9; O. 4; Lab. 2; Ind. 1
Broadland (47)	C. 33; LD 13; Lab. 1; v. 1
Bromsgrove (39)	C. 27; Lab. 10; R 2
Broxbourne (30)	C. 27; Lab. 3
Broxtowe (44)	C. 18; Lab. 17; LD 9
Burnley (45)	Lab. 26; LD 14; C. 5
Cambridge (42)	LD 21; Lab. 19; O. 6; C. 1; Ind. 1
Cannock Chase (41)	Lab. 24; C. 12; LD 5
Canterbury (50)	C. 36; LD 10; Lab. 3; Ind. 1
Carlisle (52)	Lab. 28; C. 20; LD 2; Ind. 2
Castle Point (41)	C. 25; Ind. 16
Charnwood (52)	C. 34; Lab. 14; LD 1; BNP 1; Ind. 1; O. 1
Chelmsford (57)	C. 40; LD 16; O. 1
Cheltenham (40)	LD 24; C. 12; O. 4
Cherwell (50)	C. 41; Lab. 5; LD 3; Ind. 1
Chesterfield (48)	Lab. 34; LD 12; Ind. 2
Chichester (48)	C. 36; LD 8; Ind. 3; O. 1
Chiltern (40)	C. 31; LD 5; Ind. 2; Lab. 1; UKIP 1
Chorley (47)	Lab. 24; C. 20; Ind. 3
Christchurch (24)	C. 22; Ind. 2
Colchester (60)	LD 26; C. 23; Lab. 8; Ind. 3
Copeland (51)	Lab. 34; C. 15; Ind. 2
Corby (29)	Lab. 22; C. 4; LD 3
Cotswolds (44)	C. 27; LD 12; Ind. 5
Craven (30)	C. 16; Ind. 8; LD 4
Crawley (37)	C. 21; Lab. 16

Dacorum (51)	C. 43; LD 7; Lab. 1
Dartford (44)	C. 31; Lab. 9; R 4
Daventry (36)	C. 29; Lab. 6; LD 1
Derbyshire Dales (39)	C. 29; Lab. 5; LD 4; Ind. 1
Dover (45)	C. 26; Lab. 19
East Cambridgeshire (39)	C. 25; LD 9; Ind. 5
East Devon (59)	C. 42; LD 10; Ind. 4; O. 3
East Dorset (36)	C. 30; LD 6
East Hampshire (44)	C. 39; LD 5
East Hertfordshire (50)	C. 45; Ind. 3; LD 2
East Lindsey (60)	C. 30; Ind. 15; Lab. 10; LD 4; UKIP 1
East Northamptonshire (40)	C. 34; Ind. 3; Lab. 2; v. 1
East Staffordshire (39)	C. 21; Lab. 16; Ind. 1; LD 1
Eastbourne (27)	LD 15; C. 12
Eastleigh (44)	LD 40; C. 4
Eden (38)	C. 15; LD 10; Ind. 9; O. 4
Elmbridge (60)	C. 32; R 20; LD 6; O. 2
Epping Forest (58)	C. 38; R 12; LD 4; Ind. 2; Lab. 1; UKIP 1
Epsom and Ewell (38)	R 26; LD 6; C. 3; Lab. 3
Erewash (51)	C. 26; Lab. 25
Exeter (40)	Lab. 24; C. 11; LD 5
Fareham (31)	C. 22; LD 6; UKIP 2; Ind. 1
Fenland (40)	C. 34; O. 4; Ind. 3
Forest Heath (27)	C. 23; LD 2; Ind. 1; Lab. 1
Forest of Dean (48)	C. 18; Lab. 17; Ind. 9; O. 2; LD 1; UKIP 1
Fylde (51)	C. 28; Ind. 17; LD 3; O. 3
Gedling (50)	Lab. 31; C. 15; LD 4
Gloucester (36)	C. 18; Lab. 9; LD 9
Gosport (34)	C. 24; Lab. 5; LD 5
Gravesham (44)	Lab. 27; C. 17
Great Yarmouth (39)	Lab. 20; C. 19
Guildford (48)	C. 34; LD 12; Lab. 2
Hambleton (44)	C. 39; Ind. 3; LD 2
Harborough (37)	C. 27; LD 9; Ind. 1
Harlow (33)	Lab. 20; C. 12; Ind. 1
Harrogate (54)	C. 31; LD 19; Ind. 2; O. 2
Hart (35)	C. 16; LD 10; O. 7; Ind. 2
Hastings (32)	Lab. 23; C. 9
Havant (38)	C. 34; Lab. 3; LD 1
Hertsmere (39)	C. 34; Lab. 5
High Peak (43)	Lab. 21; C. 13; LD 3; Ind. 3; O. 3
Hinckley and Bosworth (34)	LD 19; C. 14; Lab. 1
Horsham (44)	C. 33; LD 8; Ind. 2; UKIP 1
Huntingdonshire (52)	C. 37; LD 6; O. 5; Ind. 3; Lab. 1
Hyndburn (35)	Lab. 23; C. 9; Ind. 3
Ipswich (48)	Lab. 33; C. 12; LD 3
Kettering (36)	C. 25; Lab. 9; Ind. 1; UKIP 1
King's Lynn and West Norfolk (62)	C. 42; Lab. 12; Ind. 4; LD 2; O. 1; v. 1
Lancaster (60)	Lab. 24; C. 15; Ind. 13; Green 8
Lewes (41)	C. 20; LD 18; UKIP 2; Ind. 1
Lichfield (56)	C. 46; Lab. 10
Lincoln City (33)	Lab. 24; C. 8; Ind. 1
Maidstone (55)	C. 30; LD 19; Ind. 5; Lab. 1
Maldon (31)	C. 27; Ind. 3; Lab. 1
Malvern Hills (38)	C. 20; LD 8; Ind. 6; Green 3; UKIP 1
Mansfield (36)	Lab. 23; Ind. 11; O. 2
Melton (28)	C. 18; Lab. 5; Ind. 4
Mendip (47)	C. 31; LD 13; Ind. 2; Lab. 1
Mid Devon (42)	C. 24; Ind. 10; LD 6; Lib. 1; O. 1
Mid Suffolk (40)	C. 21; LD 6; Ind. 5; Green 4; O. 2; Lab. 1; UKIP 1
Mid Sussex (54)	C. 46; LD 6; Ind. 1; Lab. 1
Mole Valley (41)	LD 18; C. 15; Ind. 7; SD 1
New Forest (60)	C. 52; LD 6; UKIP 2
Newark and Sherwood (46)	C. 22; Lab. 15; Ind. 4; LD 3; O. 2
Newcastle-under-Lyme (60)	Lab. 34; C. 15; LD 10; Ind. 1
North Devon (43)	C. 18; LD 14; Ind. 11
North Dorset (33)	C. 22; LD 7; Ind. 4
North East Derbyshire (53)	Lab. 34; C. 17; Ind. 2
North Hertfordshire (49)	C. 33; Lab. 11; LD 5
North Kesteven (43)	C. 26; O. 11; Ind. 3; LD 3
North Norfolk (48)	C. 27; LD 18; Ind. 2; UKIP 1
North Warwickshire (35)	Lab. 18; C. 16; Ind. 1
North West Leicestershire (38)	C. 20; Lab. 16; Ind. 1; LD 1
Northampton (45)	C. 26; Lab. 15; LD 4
Norwich (39)	Lab. 21; Green 15; LD 3
Nuneaton and Bedworth (34)	Lab. 24; C. 6; Ind. 3; Green 1
Oadby and Wigston (26)	LD 22; C. 2; O. 2
Oxford (48)	Lab. 29; LD 13; Green 5; Ind. 1
Pendle (49)	C. 18; Lab. 18; LD 12; BNP 1
Preston (57)	Lab. 31; C. 19; LD 5; Ind. 2
Purbeck (24)	C. 13; LD 10; Ind. 1
Redditch (29)	Lab. 15; C. 13; Ind. 1
Reigate and Banstead (51)	C. 37; R 7; Green 3; Ind. 2; LD 2
Ribble Valley (40)	C. 34; LD 5; Ind. 1
Richmondshire (34)	Ind. 18; C. 13; LD 2; UKIP 1
Rochford (39)	C. 31; LD 4; Green 2; R 2
Rossendale (36)	Lab. 24; C. 9; Ind. 1; LD 1; O. 1
Rother (38)	C. 25; LD 5; Ind. 4; Lab. 2; O. 2
Rugby (48)	C. 25; Lab. 10; LD 6; Ind. 1
Runnymede (42)	C. 34; R 6; Ind. 1; UKIP 1
Rushcliffe (50)	C. 36; LD 6; Lab. 5; Green 2; Ind. 1
Rushmoor (39)	C. 25; Lab. 11; UKIP 2; Ind. 1
Ryedale (30)	C. 18; Lib. 5; Ind. 3; LD 3; O. 1
St Albans (58)	C. 29; LD 19; Lab. 8; Green 1; Ind. 1
St Edmundsbury (45)	C. 36; Ind. 5; Lab. 3; Green 1
Scarborough (50)	C. 23; Ind. 9; Lab. 7; O. 4; LD 2; UKIP 2; v. 2; Green 1
Sedgemoor (48)	C. 31; Lab. 13; Ind. 2; LD 2
Selby (41)	C. 29; Lab. 10; Ind. 2
Sevenoaks (54)	C. 47; Lab. 5; LD 2
Shepway (46)	C. 42; O. 2; Ind. 1; LD 1
South Bucks (40)	C. 37; LD 1; Ind. 1; O. 1
South Cambridgeshire (57)	C. 34; LD 16; Ind. 6; Lab. 1
South Derbyshire (36)	C. 19; Lab. 17
South Hams (40)	C. 30; LD 4; Green 3; Ind. 2; Lab. 1
South Holland (37)	C. 25; Ind. 12
South Kesteven (58)	C. 38; Ind. 13; Lab. 7
South Lakeland (51)	LD 34; C. 14; Lab. 3
South Norfolk (46)	C. 36; LD 8; Ind. 2
South Northamptonshire (42)	C. 32; Ind. 6; LD 3; Lab. 1
South Oxfordshire (48)	C. 32; Ind. 4; Lab. 4; LD 4; R 2; O. 2; UKIP 1
South Ribble (55)	C. 32; Lab. 21; LD 2
South Somerset (60)	LD 31; C. 25; Ind. 4
South Staffordshire (49)	C. 41; Ind. 6; Lab. 2
Spelthorne (39)	C. 26; Ind. 8; LD 5
Stafford (59)	C. 35; Lab. 18; Ind. 3; O. 2; Green 1

Staffordshire Moorlands (56)	C. 34; Ind. 10; Lab. 8; LD 4
Stevenage (39)	Lab. 31; C. 6; LD 2
Stratford-on-Avon (53)	C. 30; LD 14; Ind. 6; O. 3; Lab. 1
Stroud (51)	C. 21; Lab. 17; Green 6; LD 6; O. 1
Suffolk Coastal (55)	C. 44; LD 5; Lab. 4; Ind. 2
Surrey Heath (40)	C. 35; Ind. 2; Lab. 2; LD 1
Swale (47)	C. 31; Lab. 13; Ind. 2; O. 1
Tamworth (30)	C. 17; Lab. 12; Ind. 1
Tandridge (42)	C. 34; LD 6; Ind. 2
Taunton Deane (56)	C. 27; LD 23; Ind. 3; Lab. 3
Teignbridge (46)	C. 25; LD 12; Ind. 9
Tendring (60)	C. 33; Ind. 9; Lab. 9; O. 7; LD 2
Test Valley (48)	C. 36; LD 12
Tewkesbury (38)	C. 23; LD 11; Ind. 2; O. 2
Thanet (56)	Lab. 26; C. 23; Ind. 3; O. 2; UKIP 2
Three Rivers (48)	LD 28; C. 13; Lab. 6; Ind. 1
Tonbridge and Malling (53)	C. 48; LD 4; Lab. 1
Torridge (36)	C. 16; Ind. 10; LD 5; O. 5; Green 1; Lab. 1
Tunbridge Wells (48)	C. 37; LD 5; Ind. 2; Lab. 2; UKIP 2
Uttlesford (44)	C. 33; LD 7; Ind. 3; v. 1
Vale of White Horse (51)	C. 28; LD 21; Ind. 1; Lab. 1
Warwick (46)	C. 25; LD 9; Lab. 8; Ind. 4
Watford (37)	LD 25; Lab. 8; Green 3; Ind. 1
Waveney (48)	C. 24; Lab. 22; Green 1; Ind. 1
Waverley (57)	C. 54; UKIP 3
Wealden (55)	C. 47; O. 4; LD 3; Ind. 1
Wellingborough (36)	C. 28; Lab. 8
Welwyn and Hatfield (48)	C. 34; Lab. 11; LD 2; Ind. 1
West Devon (31)	C. 16; Ind. 11; LD 3; O. 1
West Dorset (48)	C. 32; LD 11; Ind. 5
West Lancashire (54)	C. 28; Lab. 26
West Lindsey (37)	C. 21; LD 10; Ind. 2; Lab. 2; O. 2
West Oxfordshire (49)	C. 39; Lab. 4; LD 4; Ind. 2
West Somerset (28)	C. 19; Ind. 7; Lab. 2
Weymouth and Portland (36)	C. 13; Lab. 12; LD 8; Ind. 3
Winchester (57)	C. 29; LD 25; Lab. 2; Ind. 1
Woking (36)	C. 21; LD 15
Worcester (35)	C. 17; Lab. 15; LD 2; Green 1
Worthing (37)	C. 24; LD 12; Ind. 1
Wychavon (45)	C. 37; LD 5; Ind. 2; Lab. 1
Wycombe (60)	C. 41; LD 9; Lab. 6; Ind. 2; O. 1; UKIP 1
Wyre (55)	C. 40; Lab. 15
Wyre Forest (42)	C. 19; Ind. 8 Lab. 8; LD 7

LONDON BOROUGH COUNCILS

Barking and Dagenham (51)	Lab. 49; C. 1; Ind. 1
Barnet (63)	C. 37; Lab. 22; LD 3; Ind. 1
Bexley (63)	C. 52; Lab. 11
Brent (63)	Lab. 41; LD 16; C. 6
Bromley (60)	C. 53; LD 4; Lab. 3
Camden (54)	Lab. 30; LD 13; C. 10; Green 1
Croydon (70)	C. 37; Lab. 33
Ealing (69)	Lab. 40; C. 23; LD 5; UKIP 1
Enfield (63)	Lab. 36; C. 26; Ind. 1
Greenwich (51)	Lab. 40; C. 11
Hackney (57)	Lab. 49; C. 5; LD 3
Hammersmith and Fulham (46)	C. 31; Lab. 15
Haringey (57)	Lab. 34; LD 21; Ind. 2
Harrow (63)	C. 25; Lab. 25; O. 8; Ind. 3; LD 1; UKIP 1
Havering (54)	C. 32; R 12; Lab. 5; Ind. 4; UKIP 1
Hillingdon (65)	C. 47; Lab. 18
Hounslow (60)	Lab. 35; C. 20; UKIP 4; Ind. 1
Islington (48)	Lab. 36; LD 11; Ind. 1
Kensington and Chelsea (54)	C. 42; Lab. 8; LD 3; Ind. 1
Kingston upon Thames (48)	LD 25; C. 21; Ind. 1; v. 1
Lambeth (63)	Lab. 43; LD 15; C. 4; Ind. 1
Lewisham (55)	Lab. 43; LD 10; C. 1; Green 1
Merton (60)	Lab. 27; C. 21; O. 5; R 3; LD 2; Ind. 1; v. 1
Newham (60)	Lab. 60
Redbridge (63)	C. 29; Lab. 21; LD 7; O. 4; Ind. 2
Richmond upon Thames (54)	C. 29; LD 24; Ind. 1
Southwark (63)	Lab. 34; LD 25; C. 3; Ind. 1
Sutton (54)	LD 42; C. 11; Lab. 1
Tower Hamlets (51)	Lab. 27; Ind. 14; C. 7; O. 2; LD 1
Waltham Forest (60)	Lab. 36; C. 18; LD 6
Wandsworth (60)	C. 47; Lab.13
Westminster (60)	C. 48; Lab. 12

METROPOLITAN BOROUGHS

Barnsley (63)	Lab. 52; Ind. 6; C. 5
Birmingham (120)	Lab. 77; C. 28; LD 15
Bolton (60)	Lab. 41; C. 16; LD 3
Bradford (90)	Lab. 44; C. 23; LD 8; Ind. 6; O. 6; Green 3
Bury (51)	Lab. 36; C. 13; LD 2
Calderdale (51)	Lab. 21; C. 17; LD 11; Ind. 2
Coventry (54)	Lab. 43; C. 11
Doncaster (64)	Lab. 50; C. 8; LD 3; Ind. 2; v. 1
Dudley (72)	Lab. 41; C. 28; Ind. 2; Green 1
Gateshead (66)	Lab. 55; LD 11
Kirklees (69)	Lab. 33; C. 18; LD 10; Green 5; Ind. 3
Knowsley (63)	Lab. 63
Leeds (99)	Lab. 63; C. 19; LD 10; Ind. 5; Green 2
Liverpool (90)	Lab. 75; LD 9; Lib. 3; Green 2; Ind. 1
Manchester (96)	Lab. 86; LD 9; Ind. 1
Newcastle-upon-Tyne (78)	Lab. 51; LD 26; Ind.1
North Tyneside (60)	Lab. 43; C. 12; LD 5
Oldham (60)	Lab. 44; LD 14; C. 2
Rochdale (60)	Lab. 43; C. 12; LD 5
Rotherham (63)	Lab. 57; C. 4; Ind. 1; UKIP 1
St Helens (48)	Lab. 40; LD 5; C. 3
Salford (60)	Lab. 52; C. 8
Sandwell (72)	Lab. 67; C. 2; Ind. 1; O. 1
Sefton (66)	Lab. 36; LD 20; C. 8; Ind. 2
Sheffield (84)	Lab. 60; LD 22; Green 2
Solihull (51)	C. 28; LD 10; Green 6; Lab. 6; Ind. 1
South Tyneside (54)	Lab. 49; UKIP 3; C. 1; Ind. 1
Stockport (63)	LD 29; Lab. 21; C. 10; Ind. 3
Sunderland (75)	Lab. 64; C. 8; Ind. 3
Tameside (57)	Lab. 52; C. 5
Trafford (63)	C. 34; Lab. 25; LD 4
Wakefield (63)	Lab. 52; C. 11
Walsall (60)	Lab. 28; C. 23; LD 5; Ind. 2; O. 1; v. 1
Wigan (75)	Lab. 63; Ind. 7; O. 3; LD 2
Wirral (66)	Lab. 37; C. 22; LD 3; Ind. 1
Wolverhampton (60)	Lab. 44; C. 13; LD 2; O. 1

UNITARY COUNCILS

Bath and North East Somerset (65)	LD 29; C. 26; Ind. 5; Lab. 5
Bedford (40)	C. 12; Lab. 12; LD 12; Ind. 4
Blackburn with Darwen (64)	Lab. 45; C. 14; LD 5
Blackpool (42)	Lab. 28; C. 13; LD 1
Bournemouth (54)	C. 46; Ind. 3; Lab. 3; LD 2
Bracknell Forest (42)	C. 38; Ind. 2; Lab. 2
Brighton and Hove (54)	Green 22; C. 18; Lab. 13; Ind. 1
Bristol (70)	Lab. 28; LD 23; C. 14; Green 4; Ind. 1
Central Bedfordshire (59)	C. 48; Ind. 5; LD 4; Lab. 1; O. 1
Cheshire East (82)	C. 51; Lab. 16; Ind. 11; LD 4
Cheshire West and Chester (75)	C. 42; Lab. 32; LD 1
Cornwall (123)	Ind. 38; LD 36; C. 30; Lab. 8; UKIP 6; O. 4; Green 1
Darlington (53)	Lab. 33; C. 15; LD 5
Derby (51)	Lab. 28; C. 14; LD 9
Durham (126)	Lab. 94; Ind. 19; LD 9; C. 4
East Riding of Yorkshire (67)	C. 53; Lab. 6; Ind. 4; LD 3; SD 1
Halton (56)	Lab. 50; LD 4; C. 2
Hartlepool (32)	Lab. 18; Ind. 6; O. 5; C. 3
Herefordshire (58)	C. 30; Ind. 14; O. 9; LD 3; Green 1; Lab. 1
*Isles of Scilly (21)	Ind. 21
Isle of Wight (40)	Ind. 20; C. 15; Lab. 2; UKIP 2; LD 1
Kingston-upon-Hull (59)	Lab. 41; LD 16; C. 2
Leicester (54)	Lab. 52; C. 1; LD 1
Luton (48)	Lab. 36; LD 8; C. 4
Medway (55)	C. 35; Lab. 17; LD 3
Middlesbrough (49)	Lab. 30; Ind. 8; O. 5; C. 4; LD 1; Green 1
Milton Keynes (51)	C. 20; Lab. 15; LD 15; UKIP 1
North East Lincolnshire (42)	Lab. 25; C. 11; LD 4; UKIP 2
North Lincolnshire (43)	C. 23; Lab. 20
North Somerset (61)	C. 41; Ind. 9; LD 6; Lab. 5
Northumberland (67)	Lab. 32; C. 21; LD 9; Ind. 3; O. 2
Nottingham (55)	Lab. 49; C. 4; Ind. 1; v. 1
Peterborough (57)	C. 32; Lab. 11; Ind. 10; LD 4
Plymouth (57)	Lab. 32; C. 24; LD 1
Poole (42)	C. 20; LD 18; O. 4
Portsmouth (42)	LD 25; C. 12; Lab. 5
Reading (46)	Lab. 26; C. 12; LD 4; Green 3; Ind. 1
Redcar and Cleveland (59)	Lab. 28; LD 13; O. 8; C. 6; Ind. 3
Rutland (26)	C. 17; Ind. 7; LD 2
Shropshire (74)	C. 48; LD 12; Lab. 9; Ind. 5
Slough (41)	Lab. 35; C. 5; LD 1
South Gloucestershire (70)	C. 33; LD 21; Lab. 15; UKIP 1
Southampton (48)	Lab. 28; C. 16; LD 2; O. 2
Southend-on-Sea (51)	C. 26; Ind. 9; LD 9; Lab. 6; O. 1
Stockton-on-Tees (56)	Lab. 27; O. 13; C. 12; LD 4
Stoke-on-Trent (44)	Lab. 32; Ind. 9; C. 2; O. 1
Swindon (57)	C. 29; Lab. 23; LD 4; Ind. 1
Telford and Wrekin (54)	Lab. 33; C. 17; LD 4
Thurrock (49)	Lab. 25; C. 21; Ind. 2; UKIP 1
Torbay (37)	C. 21; LD 10; O. 5; Lab. 1
Warrington (57)	Lab. 41; LD 12; C. 4
West Berkshire (52)	C. 39; LD 13
Wiltshire (98)	C. 59; LD 26; Ind. 8; Lab. 4; UKIP 1
Windsor and Maidenhead (57)	C. 47; Ind. 6; LD 2; UKIP 2
Wokingham (54)	C. 43; LD 8; Ind. 3
York (47)	Lab. 25; C. 9; LD 9; Green 2; Ind. 2

* Thirteen councillors are elected by the residents of the isle of St Mary's and two councillors each are elected by the residents of the four other islands (Bryher, St Agnes, St Martins and Tresco)

WALES

Blaenau Gwent (42)	Lab. 33; Ind. 9
Bridgend (54)	Lab. 39; Ind. 6; O. 4; LD 3; C. 1; PC 1
Caerphilly (73)	Lab. 50; PC 19; Ind. 3; v. 1
Cardiff (75)	Lab. 46; LD 15; C. 7; Ind. 3; O. 2; PC 2
Carmarthenshire (74)	PC 28; Ind. 22; Lab. 22; O. 2
Ceredigion (42)	PC 19; Ind. 12; LD 7; O. 4
Conwy (59)	Ind. 18; C. 13; PC 12; Lab. 10; LD 5; v. 1
Denbighshire (47)	Lab. 18; Ind. 13; C. 8; PC 8
Flintshire (70)	Lab. 30; Ind. 22; C. 8; LD 7; O. 2; v. 1
Gwynedd (75)	PC 37; Ind. 18; O. 14; Lab. 4; LD 2
Merthyr Tydfil (33)	Lab. 24; Ind. 7; O. 1; UKIP 1
Monmouthshire (43)	C. 19; Lab. 11; Ind. 10; LD 3
Neath Port Talbot (64)	Lab. 51; PC 8; Ind. 3; SD 1; O. 1
Newport (50)	Lab. 37; C. 10; Ind. 2; LD 1
Pembrokeshire (60)	Ind. 32; O. 12; Lab. 7; PC 5; C. 3; LD 1
Powys (73)	O. 48; C. 10; LD 9; Lab. 6
Rhondda Cynon Taff (75)	Lab. 60; PC 9; Ind. 4; C. 1; LD 1
Swansea (72)	Lab. 49; LD 12; Ind. 7; C. 4
Torfaen (44)	Lab. 30; Ind. 8; C. 4; PC 2
Vale of Glamorgan (47)	Lab. 21; C. 11; PC 7; O. 4; Ind. 3; UKIP 1
Wrexham (52)	Lab. 23; Ind. 19; C. 5; LD 4; PC 1
Ynys Mon (Isle of Anglesey) (30)	Ind. 13; PC 12; Lab. 3; LD 1; O. 1

SCOTLAND

Aberdeen (43)	Lab. 17; SNP 15; LD 5; C. 3; Ind. 3
Aberdeenshire (68)	SNP 27; C. 14; LD 13; Ind. 11; Lab. 2; Green 1
Angus (29)	SNP 14; Ind. 9; C. 4; LD 1; Lab. 1
Argyll and Bute (36)	Ind. 15; SNP 11; LD 4; C. 3; O. 3
Clackmannanshire (18)	Lab. 8; SNP 8; C. 1; Ind. 1
Dumfries and Galloway (47)	C. 15; Lab. 14; SNP 10; Ind. 5; O. 3
Dundee (29)	SNP 16; Lab. 10; C. 1; Ind. 1; LD 1
East Ayrshire (32)	SNP 15; Lab. 14; C. 2; Ind. 1
East Dunbartonshire (24)	Lab. 9; SNP 8; LD 3; C. 2; Ind. 2
East Lothian (23)	Lab. 10; SNP 8; C. 3; Ind. 1; O. 1
East Renfrewshire (20)	Lab. 8; C. 6; SNP 4; Ind. 2
Edinburgh (58)	Lab. 21; SNP 17; C. 11; Green 6; LD 3
Eilean Siar (Western Isles) (31)	Ind. 22; SNP 6; Lab. 3
Falkirk (32)	Lab. 14; SNP 13; Ind. 3; C. 2
Fife (78)	Lab. 35; SNP 26; LD 10; Ind. 4; C. 3
Glasgow (79)	Lab. 44; SNP 27; Green 5; C. 1; LD 1; O. 1

Highland (80)	Ind. 35; SNP 21; LD 14; Lab. 8; O. 2
Inverclyde (20)	Lab. 10; SNP 6; LD 2; C. 1; Ind. 1
Midlothian (18)	Lab. 8; SNP 8; Green 1; Ind. 1
Moray (26)	Ind. 11; SNP 9; C. 3; Lab. 3
North Ayrshire (30)	SNP 12; Lab. 11; Ind. 6; C. 1
North Lanarkshire (70)	Lab. 41; SNP 25; Ind. 3; O. 1
Orkney Islands (21)	Ind. 18; O. 3
Perth and Kinross (41)	SNP 18; C. 10; LD 5; Lab. 4; Ind. 4
Renfrewshire (40)	Lab. 22; SNP 15; C. 1; Ind. 1; LD 1
Scottish Borders (34)	C. 10; SNP 9; Ind. 7; LD 6; O. 2
Shetland Islands (22)	Ind. 22
South Ayrshire (30)	C. 9; Lab. 9; SNP 9; Ind. 3
South Lanarkshire (67)	Lab. 34; SNP 27; C. 3; Ind. 2; LD 1
Stirling (22)	SNP 9; Lab. 8; C. 4; Green 1
West Dunbartonshire (22)	Lab. 12; SNP 6; Ind. 3; O. 1
West Lothian (33)	Lab. 16; SNP 15; C. 1; Ind. 1

NORTHERN IRELAND

Antrim (19)	DUP 5; UUP 5; SF 4; SDLP 3; All. 2
Ards (23)	DUP 11; UUP 6; All. 4; Ind. 1; SDLP 1
Armagh City (22)	SF 6; UUP 6; SDLP 5; DUP 4; Ind. 1
Ballymena (24)	DUP 12; UUP 4; SDLP 2; SF 2; O. 2; All. 1; Ind. 1
Ballymoney (16)	DUP 9; Ind. 2; SF 2; SDLP 1; UUP 1; O. 1
Banbridge (17)	UUP 7; DUP 5; SDLP 2; SF 2; All. 1
Belfast (51)	DUP 16; SF 16; SDLP 8; All. 6; UUP 3; O. 2
Carrickfergus (17)	DUP 8; UUP 4; All. 3; Ind. 2
Castlereagh (23)	DUP 11; All. 6; UUP 3; SDLP 2; Green 1
Coleraine (22)	DUP 8; UUP 6; SDLP 3; All. 2; Ind. 2; SF 1
Cookstown (16)	SF 6; SDLP 4; DUP 3; UUP 3
Craigavon (26)	DUP 9; SF 8; UUP 6; SDLP 2; All. 1
Derry City (30)	SDLP 14; SF 10; DUP 5; UUP 1
Down (23)	SDLP 9; SF 5; DUP 3; UUP 3; All. 1; Green 1; Ind. 1
Dungannon and South Tyrone (22)	SF 8; DUP 6; UUP 4; SDLP 3; Ind. 1
Fermanagh (23)	SF 9; UUP 6; DUP 4; SDLP 3; Ind. 1
Larne (15)	DUP 4; All. 3; UUP 3; Ind. 2; SDLP 1; SF 1; O. 1
Limavady (15)	SF 6; SDLP 3; DUP 3; UUP 2; O. 1
Lisburn (30)	DUP 15; SF 4; UUP 4; All. 3; SDLP 3; Ind. 1
Magherafelt (16)	SF 9; DUP 3; SDLP 2; UUP 2
Moyle (15)	SF 4; Ind. 3; UUP 3; DUP 2; SDLP 2; O. 1
Newry and Mourne (30)	SF 14; SDLP 9; UUP 3; Ind. 2; DUP 1; UKIP 1
Newtownabbey (25)	DUP 12; UUP 5; All. 5; SF 2; SDLP
North Down (25)	DUP 12; All. 5; UUP 4; Ind. 3; Green 1
Omagh (21)	SF 10; DUP 3; SDLP 3; UUP 3; Ind. 2
Strabane (16)	SF 8; DUP 4; Ind. 2; SDLP 1; UUP 1

ENGLAND

The region of England lies between 55° 46′ and 49° 57′ 30″ N. latitude (from a few miles north of the mouth of the Tweed to the Lizard), and between 1° 46′ E. and 5° 43′ W. longitude (from Lowestoft to Land's End). England is bounded on the north by the Cheviot Hills; on the south by the English Channel; on the east by the Straits of Dover (Pas de Calais) and the North Sea; and on the west by the Atlantic Ocean, Wales and the Irish Sea. It has a total area of 130,432 sq. km (50,360 sq. miles): land 130,279 sq. km (50,301 sq. miles); inland water 153 sq. km (59 sq. miles).

POPULATION

The population at the 2011 census was 53,012,456 (men 26,069,148; women 26,943,308). The average density of the population in 2011 was 406 persons per sq. km (1,053 per sq. mile).

FLAG

The flag of England is the cross of St George, a red cross on a white field (cross gules in a field argent). The cross of St George, the patron saint of England, has been used since the 13th century.

RELIEF

There is a marked division between the upland and lowland areas of England. In the extreme north the Cheviot Hills (highest point, the Cheviot, 815m/2,674ft) form a natural boundary with Scotland. Running south from the Cheviots, though divided from them by the Tyne Gap, is the Pennine range (highest point, Cross Fell, 893m/2,930ft), the main orological feature of the country. The Pennines culminate in the Peak District of Derbyshire (Kinder Scout, 636m/2,088ft). West of the Pennines are the Cumbrian mountains, which include Scafell Pike (978m/3,210ft), the highest peak in England, and to the east are the Yorkshire Moors, their highest point being Urra Moor (454m/1,490ft).

In the west, the foothills of the Welsh mountains extend into the bordering English counties of Shropshire (the Wrekin, 407m/1,334ft; Long Mynd, 516m/1,694ft) and Hereford and Worcester (the Malvern Hills – Worcestershire Beacon, 425m/1,394ft). Extensive areas of highland and moorland are also to be found in the south-western peninsula formed by Somerset, Devon and Cornwall, principally Exmoor (Dunkery Beacon, 519m/1,704ft), Dartmoor (High Willhays, 621m/2,038ft) and Bodmin Moor (Brown Willy, 420m/1,377ft). Ranges of low, undulating hills run across the south of the country, including the Cotswolds in the Midlands and south-west, the Chilterns to the north of London, and the North (Kent) and South (Sussex) Downs of the south-east coastal areas.

The lowlands of England lie in the Vale of York, East Anglia and the area around the Wash. The lowest-lying are the Cambridgeshire Fens in the valleys of the Great Ouse and the river Nene, which are below sea-level in places. Since the 17th century extensive drainage has brought much of the Fens under cultivation. The North Sea coast between the Thames and the Humber, low-lying and formed of sand and shingle for the most part, is subject to erosion and defences against further incursion have been built along many stretches.

HYDROGRAPHY

The Severn is the longest river in Great Britain, rising in the north-eastern slopes of Plynlimon (Wales) and entering England in Shropshire, with a total length of 354km (220 miles) from its source to its outflow into the Bristol Channel, where it receives the Bristol Avon on the east and the Wye on the west; its other tributaries are the Vyrnwy, Tern, Stour, Teme and Upper (or Warwickshire) Avon. The Severn is tidal below Gloucester, and a high bore or tidal wave sometimes reverses the flow as high as Tewkesbury (21.75km/13.5 miles above Gloucester). The scenery of the greater part of the river is very picturesque, and the Severn is a noted salmon river, with some of its tributaries being famous for trout. Navigation is assisted by the Gloucester and Berkeley Ship Canal (26km/16.25 miles), which admits vessels of 350 tons to Gloucester. The Severn Tunnel was begun in 1873 and completed in 1886 at a cost of £2m and after many difficulties caused by flooding. It is 7km (4 miles 628 yards) in length (of which 3.67km/2.25 miles are under the river). The Severn road bridge between Haysgate, Gwent, and Almondsbury, Glos, with a centre span of 988m (3,240ft), was opened in 1966.

The longest river wholly in England is the Thames, with a total length of 346km (215 miles) from its source in the Cotswold hills to the Nore, and is navigable by ocean-going ships to London Bridge. The Thames is tidal to Teddington (111km/69 miles from its mouth) and forms county boundaries almost throughout its course; on its banks are situated London, Windsor Castle, Eton College and Oxford University. Of the remaining English rivers, those flowing into the North Sea are the Tyne, Wear, Tees, Ouse and Trent from the Pennine Range, the Great Ouse (257km/160 miles), which rises in Northamptonshire, and the Orwell and Stour from the hills of East Anglia. Flowing into the English Channel are the Sussex Ouse from the Weald, the Itchen from the Hampshire Hills, and the Axe, Teign, Dart, Tamar and Exe from the Devonian hills. Flowing into the Irish Sea are the Mersey, Ribble and Eden from the western slopes of the Pennines and the Derwent from the Cumbrian mountains.

The English Lakes, notable for their picturesque scenery and poetic associations, lie in Cumbria's Lake District; the largest are Windermere (14.7 sq. km/5.7 sq. miles), Ullswater (8.8 sq. km/3.4 sq. miles) and Derwent Water (5.3 sq. km/2.0 sq. miles).

ISLANDS

The Isle of Wight is separated from Hampshire by the Solent. The capital, Newport, stands at the head of the estuary of the Medina, and Cowes (at the mouth) is the chief port. Other centres are Ryde, Sandown, Shanklin, Ventnor, Freshwater, Yarmouth, Totland Bay, Seaview and Bembridge.

Lundy (the name is derived from the Old Norse for 'puffin island'), 18km (11 miles) north-west of Hartland Point, Devon, is around 5km (3 miles) long and almost 1km (half a mile) wide on average, with a total area of around 452 hectares (1,116 acres), and a population of 27. It became the property of the National Trust in 1969 and is now principally a bird sanctuary and the UK's first marine conservation zone.

The Isles of Scilly comprise around 140 islands and skerries (total area, 10 sq. km/6 sq. miles) situated 45 km (28 miles) south-west of Land's End in Cornwall. Only five are inhabited: St Mary's, St Agnes, Bryher, Tresco and St Martin's. The population at the 2011 census was 2,200. The entire group has been designated an Area of Outstanding Natural Beauty because of its unique flora and fauna. Tourism and the winter/spring flower trade for the home market form the basis of the economy of the islands. The island group is a recognised rural development area.

EARLY HISTORY

Archaeological evidence suggests that England has been inhabited since at least the Palaeolithic period, though the extent of the various Palaeolithic cultures was dependent upon the degree of glaciation. The succeeding Neolithic and Bronze Age cultures have left abundant remains throughout the country; the best-known of these are the henges and stone circles of Stonehenge (ten miles north of Salisbury, Wilts) and Avebury (Wilts), both of which are believed to have been of religious significance. In the latter part of the Bronze Age the Goidels, a people of the Celtic race, invaded the country and brought with them Celtic civilisation and dialects; as a result place names in England bear witness to the spread of the invasion across the whole region.

THE ROMAN CONQUEST

The Roman conquest of Gaul (57–50 BC) brought Britain into close contact with Roman civilisation, but although Julius Caesar raided the south of Britain in 55 and 54 BC, conquest was not undertaken until nearly 100 years later. In AD 43 the Emperor Claudius dispatched Aulus Plautius, with a well-equipped force of 40,000, and himself followed with reinforcements in the same year. Success was delayed by the resistance of Caratacus (Caractacus), the British leader from AD 48–51, who was finally captured and sent to Rome, and by a great revolt in AD 61 led by Boudicca (Boadicea), Queen of the Iceni, but the south of Britain was secured by AD 70, and Wales and the area north to the Tyne by about AD 80.

In AD 122, the Emperor Hadrian visited Britain and built a continuous rampart, since known as Hadrian's Wall, from Wallsend to Bowness (Tyne to Solway). The work was entrusted by the Emperor Hadrian to Aulus Platorius Nepos, legate of Britain from AD 122 to 126, and it was intended to form the northern frontier of the Roman Empire.

The Romans administered Britain as a province under a governor, with a well-defined system of local government, each Roman municipality ruling itself and its surrounding territory, while London was the centre of the road system and the seat of the financial officials of the Province of Britain. Colchester, Lincoln, York, Gloucester and St Albans stand on the sites of five Roman municipalities, and Wroxeter, Caerleon, Chester, Lincoln and York were at various times the sites of legionary fortresses. Well-preserved Roman towns have been uncovered at or near Silchester *(Calleva Atrebatum)*, ten miles south of Reading, Wroxeter *(Viroconium Cornoviorum)*, near Shrewsbury, and St Albans *(Verulamium)* in Hertfordshire.

Four main groups of roads radiated from London, and a fifth (the Fosse) ran obliquely from Lincoln through Leicester, Cirencester and Bath to Exeter. Of the four groups radiating from London, one ran south-east to Canterbury and the coast of Kent, a second to Silchester and thence to parts of western Britain and south Wales, a third (later known as Watling Street) ran through St Albans to Chester, with various branches, and the fourth reached Colchester, Lincoln, York and the eastern counties.

In the fourth century Britain was subjected to raids along the east coast by Saxon pirates, which led to the establishment of a system of coastal defences from the Wash to Southampton Water, with forts at Brancaster, Burgh Castle (Yarmouth), Walton (Felixstowe), Bradwell, Reculver, Richborough, Dover, Lympne, Pevensey and Porchester (Portsmouth). The Irish (Scoti) and Picts in the north were also becoming more aggressive and from around AD 350 incursions became more frequent and more formidable. As the Roman Empire came increasingly under attack towards the end of the fourth century, many troops were removed from Britain for service in other parts of the empire. The island was eventually cut off from Rome by the Teutonic conquest of Gaul, and with the withdrawal of the last Roman garrison early in the fifth century, the Romano-British were left to themselves.

SAXON SETTLEMENT

According to legend, the British King Vortigern called in the Saxons to defend his lands against the Picts. The Saxon chieftains Hengist and Horsa landed at Ebbsfleet, Kent, and established themselves in the Isle of Thanet, but the events during the one-and-a-half centuries between the final break with Rome and the re-establishment of Christianity are unclear. However, it would appear that over the course of this period the raids turned into large-scale settlement by invaders traditionally known as Angles (England north of the Wash and East Anglia), Saxons (Essex and southern England) and Jutes (Kent and the Weald), which pushed the Romano-British into the mountainous areas of the north and west. Celtic culture outside Wales and Cornwall survives only in topographical names. Various kingdoms established at this time attempted to claim overlordship of the whole country, hegemony finally being achieved by Wessex (with the capital at Winchester) in the ninth century. This century also saw the beginning of raids by the Vikings (Danes), which were resisted by Alfred the Great (871–899), who fixed a limit on the advance of Danish settlement by the Treaty of Wedmore (878), giving them the area north and east of Watling Street on the condition that they adopt Christianity.

In the tenth century the kings of Wessex recovered the whole of England from the Danes, but subsequent rulers were unable to resist a second wave of invaders. England paid tribute *(Danegeld)* for many years, and was invaded in 1013 by the Danes and ruled by Danish kings (including Cnut) from 1016 until 1042, when Edward the Confessor was recalled from exile in Normandy. On Edward's death in 1066 Harold Godwinson (brother-in-law of Edward and son of Earl Godwin of Wessex) was chosen to be King of England. After defeating (at Stamford Bridge, Yorkshire, 25 September 1066) an invading army under Harald Hadraada, King of Norway (aided by the outlawed Earl Tostig of Northumbria, Harold's brother), Harold was himself defeated at the Battle of Hastings on 14 October 1066, and the Norman conquest secured the throne of England for Duke William of Normandy, a cousin of Edward the Confessor.

CHRISTIANITY

Christianity reached the Roman province of Britain from Gaul in the third century (or possibly earlier). Alban, traditionally Britain's first martyr, was put to death as a Christian during the persecution of Diocletian (22 June 303) at his native town *Verulamium*, and the Bishops of *Londinium, Eboracum* (York), and *Lindum* (Lincoln) attended the Council of Arles in 314. However, the Anglo-Saxon invasions submerged the Christian religion in England until the sixth century: conversion was undertaken in the north from 563 by Celtic missionaries from Ireland led by St Columba, and in the south by a mission sent from Rome in 597 which was led by St Augustine, who became the first archbishop of Canterbury. England appears to have been converted again by the end of the seventh century and followed, after the Council of Whitby in 663, the practices of the Roman Church, which brought the kingdom into the mainstream of European thought and culture.

PRINCIPAL CITIES

There are 51 cities in England and space constraints prevent us from including profiles of them all. Below is a selection of England's principal cities with the date on which city status was conferred in parenthesis. Other cities are Bradford (pre-1900), Chelmsford (2012), Chichester (pre-1900), Coventry (pre-1900), Derby (1977), Ely (pre-1900), Exeter (pre-1900), Gloucester (pre-1900), Hereford (pre-1900), Kingston-upon-Hull (pre-1900), Lancaster (1937), Lichfield (pre-1900), London (pre-1900), Peterborough (pre-1900), Plymouth (1928), Portsmouth (1926), Preston (2002), Ripon (pre-1900), Salford (1926), Stoke-on-Trent (1925), Sunderland (1992), Truro (pre-1900), Wakefield (pre-1900), Wells (pre-1900), Westminster (pre-1900), Wolverhampton (2000) and Worcester (pre-1900).

Certain cities have also been granted a lord mayoralty – this grant confers no additional powers or functions and is purely honorific. Cities with lord mayors are Birmingham, Bradford, Bristol, Canterbury, Chester, Coventry, Exeter, Kingston-upon-Hull, Leeds, Leicester, Liverpool, London, Manchester, Newcastle-upon-Tyne, Norwich, Nottingham, Oxford, Plymouth, Portsmouth, Sheffield, Stoke-on-Trent, Westminster and York.

BATH (PRE-1900)

Bath stands on the River Avon between the Cotswold Hills to the north and the Mendips to the south. In the early 18th century, Bath became England's premier spa town where the rich and celebrated members of fashionable society gathered to 'take the waters' and enjoy the town's theatres and concert rooms. During this period the architect John Wood laid the foundations for a new Georgian city to be built using the honey-coloured stone for which Bath is famous today.

Contemporary Bath is a thriving tourist destination and remains a leading cultural, religious and historical centre with many art galleries and historic sites including the Pump Room (1790); the Royal Crescent (1767); the Circus (1754); the 18th-century Assembly Rooms (housing the Museum of Costume); Pulteney Bridge (1771); the Guildhall and the Abbey, now over 500 years old, which is built on the site of a Saxon monastery. In 2006 the Bath Thermae Spa was completed and the hot springs re-opened to the public for the first time since 1978.

BIRMINGHAM (PRE-1900)

Birmingham is Britain's second largest city, with a population of over one million. The generally accepted derivation of 'Birmingham' is the *ham* (dwelling-place) of the *ing* (family) of *Beorma,* presumed to have been Saxon. During the Industrial Revolution the town grew into a major manufacturing centre and in 1889 was granted city status.

Recent developments include Millennium Point, which houses Thinktank, the Birmingham science museum, and Brindleyplace, a development of shops, offices and leisure facilities on a former industrial site clustered around canals. In 2003 the Bullring shopping centre was officially opened as part of the city's urban regeneration programme.

The principal buildings are the Town Hall (1834–50), the Council House (1879), Victoria Law Courts (1891), the University of Birmingham (1906–9), the 13th-century Church of St Martin-in-the-Bull-Ring (rebuilt 1873), the cathedral (formerly St Philip's Church) (1711), the Roman Catholic cathedral of St Chad (1839–41), the Assay Office (1773), the Rotunda (1964) and the National Exhibition Centre (1976). There is also the Birmingham Museum and Art Gallery which was founded in 1885 and is home to a collection of Pre-Raphaelite paintings.

BRIGHTON AND HOVE (2000)

Brighton and Hove is situated on the south coast of England, around 96 km (60 miles) south of London. Originally a fishing village called Brighthelmstone, it was transformed into a fashionable seaside resort in the 18th century when Dr Richard Russell popularised the benefits of his 'sea-water cure'; as one of the closest beaches to London, Brighton began to attract wealthy visitors. One of these was the Prince Regent (the future King George IV), who first visited in 1783 and became so fond of the city that in 1807 he bought the former farmhouse he had been renting, and gradually turned it into Brighton's most recognisable building, the Royal Pavilion. The Pavilion is renowned for its Indo-Saracenic exterior, featuring minarets and an enormous central dome designed by John Nash, combined with the lavish chinoiserie of Frederick Crace's and Robert Jones' interiors.

Brighton and Hove's Regency heritage can also be seen in the numerous elegant squares and crescents designed by Amon Wilds and Augustin Busby that dominate the seafront.

BRISTOL (PRE-1900)

Bristol was a royal borough before the Norman conquest. The earliest form of the name is *Bricgstow.*

The principal buildings include the 12th-century Cathedral with Norman chapter house and gateway; the 14th-century Church of St Mary Redcliffe; Wesley's Chapel, Broadmead; the Merchant Venturers' Almshouses; the Council House (1956); the Guildhall; the Exchange (erected from the designs of John Wood in 1743); Cabot Tower; the University and Clifton College. The Roman Catholic cathedral at Clifton was opened in 1973.

The Clifton Suspension Bridge, with a span of 214m (702ft) over the Avon, was projected by Isambard Kingdom Brunel in 1836 but was not completed until 1864. Brunel's SS *Great Britain,* the first ocean-going propeller-driven ship, now forms a museum at the Western Dockyard, from where she was originally launched in 1843. The docks themselves have been extensively restored and redeveloped; the 19th-century two-storey former tea warehouse is now the Arnolfini centre for contemporary arts, and an 18th-century sail loft houses the Architecture Centre. On Princes Wharf 1950s transit sheds have been renovated and converted into the museum of Bristol, M Shed, which opened in June 2011.

CAMBRIDGE (1951)

Cambridge, a settlement far older than its ancient university, lies on the River Cam (or Granta). The city is a county town and regional headquarters. Its industries include technology research and development, and biotechnology. Among its open spaces are Jesus Green, Sheep's Green, Coe Fen, Parker's Piece, Christ's Pieces, the University Botanic Garden, and the 'Backs' – lawns and gardens through which the Cam winds behind the principal line of college buildings. Historical sites east of the Cam include King's Parade, Great St Mary's Church, Gibbs' Senate House and King's College Chapel.

University and college buildings provide the outstanding features of Cambridge's architecture but several churches (especially St Benet's, the oldest building in the city, and Holy Sepulchre or the Round Church) are also notable. The Guildhall (1937) stands on a site, of which at least part has held municipal buildings since 1224.

CANTERBURY (PRE-1900)

Canterbury, seat of the Archbishop of Canterbury, the primate of the Church of England, dates back to prehistoric times. It was the Roman *Durovernum Cantiacorum* and the

Saxon *Cant-wara-byrig* (stronghold of the men of Kent). It was here in 597 that St Augustine began the conversion of the English to Christianity, when Ethelbert, King of Kent, was baptised.

Of the Benedictine St Augustine's Abbey, burial place of the Jutish Kings of Kent, only ruins remain. According to Bede, St Martin's Church, on the eastern outskirts of the city was the place of worship of Queen Bertha, the Christian wife of King Ethelbert, before the advent of St Augustine.

In 1170 the rivalry of Church and State culminated in the murder in Canterbury Cathedral, by Henry II's knights, of Archbishop Thomas Becket. His shrine became a great centre of pilgrimage, as described in Chaucer's *Canterbury Tales.* After the Reformation pilgrimages ceased, but the prosperity of the city was strengthened by an influx of Huguenot refugees, who introduced weaving. The poet and playwright Christopher Marlowe was born and raised in Canterbury and the city is home to the 1,200-seat Marlowe Theatre, which re-opened to the public in October 2011, following an extensive £25m re-build.

The cathedral, its architecture ranging from the 11th to the 15th centuries, is famous worldwide. Visitors are attracted particularly to the Martyrdom, the Black Prince's Tomb and the Warriors' Chapel.

The medieval city walls are built on Roman foundations and the 14th-century West Gate is one of the finest buildings of its kind in the country.

CHESTER (PRE-1900)

Chester is situated on the River Dee. Its recorded history dates from the first century when the Romans founded the fortress of *Deva.* The city's name is derived from the Latin *castra* (a camp or encampment). During the Middle Ages, Chester was the principal port of north-west England but declined with the silting of the Dee estuary and competition from Liverpool. The city was also an important military centre, notably during Edward I's Welsh campaigns and the Elizabethan Irish campaigns. During the Civil War, Chester supported the King and was besieged from 1643 to 1646. Chester's first charter was granted *c.*1175 and the city was incorporated in 1506. The office of sheriff is the earliest created in the country (1120s), and in 1992 the mayor was granted the title of Lord Mayor, who also enjoys the title 'Admiral of the Dee'.

The city's architectural features include the city walls (an almost complete two-mile circuit), the unique 13th-century Rows (covered galleries above the street-level shops), the Victorian Gothic Town Hall (1869), the castle (rebuilt 1788 and 1822) and numerous half-timbered buildings. The cathedral was a Benedictine abbey until the Dissolution of the Monasteries. Remaining monastic buildings include the chapter house, refectory and cloisters and there is a modern free-standing bell tower. The Norman church of St John the Baptist was a cathedral church in the early Middle Ages.

DURHAM (PRE-1900)

The city of Durham's prominent Norman cathedral and castle are set high on a wooded peninsula overlooking the River Wear. The cathedral was founded as a shrine for the body of St Cuthbert in 995. The present building dates from 1093 and among its many treasures is the tomb of the Venerable Bede (673–735). Durham's prince bishops had unique powers up to 1836, being lay rulers as well as religious leaders. As a palatinate, Durham could have its own army, nobility, coinage and courts. The castle was the main seat of the prince bishops for nearly 800 years; it is now used as a college by the University of Durham. The university, founded in the early 19th century on the initiative of Bishop William Van Mildert, is England's third oldest.

Among other buildings of interest is the Guildhall in the Market Place which dates from the 14th century. Annual events include Durham's regatta in June (claimed to be the oldest rowing event in Britain) and the annual Gala (formerly Durham Miners' Gala) in July.

LEEDS (PRE-1900)

Leeds, situated in the lower Aire Valley, was first incorporated by Charles I in 1626. The earliest forms of the name are *Loidis* or *Ledes,* the origins of which are obscure.

The principal buildings are the Civic Hall (1933), the Town Hall (1858), the Municipal Buildings and Art Gallery (1884) with the Henry Moore Gallery (1982), the Corn Exchange (1863) and the University. The parish church (St Peter's) was rebuilt in 1841; the 17th-century St John's Church has a fine interior with a famous English Renaissance screen; the last remaining 18th-century church in the city is Holy Trinity in Boar Lane (1727). Kirkstall Abbey (about three miles from the centre of the city), founded by Henry de Lacy in 1152, is one of the most complete examples of a Cistercian house now remaining. Temple Newsam, birthplace of Lord Darnley and largely rebuilt by Sir Arthur Ingram *c.*1620, was acquired by the council in 1922. Adel Church, about five miles from the centre of the city, is a fine Norman structure. The Royal Armouries Museum forms part of a group of museums that house the national collection of antique arms and armour.

LEICESTER (1919)

Leicester is situated in central England. The city was an important Roman settlement and also one of the five Viking boroughs of Danelaw. In 1485 Richard III was buried in Leicester following his death at the nearby Battle of Bosworth. In 1589 Queen Elizabeth I granted a charter to the city and the ancient title was confirmed by letters patent in 1919.

The textile industry was responsible for Leicester's early expansion and the city still maintains a strong manufacturing base. Cotton mills and factories are now undergoing extensive regeneration and are being converted into offices, apartments, bars and restaurants. The principal buildings include the two universities (the University of Leicester and De Montfort University), as well as the Town Hall, the 13th-century Guildhall, De Montfort Hall, Leicester Cathedral, the Jewry Wall (the UK's highest standing Roman wall), St Nicholas Church and St Mary de Castro church. The motte and Great Hall of Leicester can be seen from the castle gardens, situated next to the River Soar.

LINCOLN (PRE-1900)

Situated 64km (40 miles) inland on the River Witham, Lincoln derives its name from a contraction of *Lindum Colonia,* the settlement founded in AD 48 by the Romans to command the crossing of Ermine Street and Fosse Way. Sections of the third-century Roman city wall can be seen, including an extant gateway (Newport Arch), and excavations have discovered traces of a sewerage system unique in Britain. The Romans also drained the surrounding fenland and created a canal system, laying the foundations of Lincoln's agricultural prosperity and also the city's importance in the medieval wool trade as a port and staple town.

As one of the five boroughs of Danelaw, Lincoln was an important trading centre in the ninth and tenth centuries and prosperity from the wool trade lasted until the 14th century. This wealth enabled local merchants to build parish churches, of which three survive, and there are also remains of a 12th-century Jewish community. However, the removal of the staple to Boston in 1369 heralded a decline, from which the city only recovered fully in the 19th century, when improved fen drainage made Lincoln agriculturally important. Improved canal and rail links led to industrial development, mainly in the manufacture of machinery and engineering products.

The castle was built shortly after the Norman Conquest and is unusual in having two mounds; on one motte stands a keep (Lucy's Tower) added in the 12th century. It currently houses one of the four surviving copies of the Magna Carta. The cathedral was begun *c.*1073 but was mostly destroyed by fire and earthquake in the 12th century. Rebuilding was begun by St Hugh and completed over a century later. Other notable architectural features are the 12th-century High Bridge, the oldest in Britain still to carry buildings, and the Guildhall, situated above the 15th-century Stonebow gateway.

LIVERPOOL (PRE-1900)

Liverpool, on the north bank of the river Mersey, 5km (3 miles) from the Irish Sea, is the United Kingdom's foremost port for Atlantic trade. Tunnels link Liverpool with Birkenhead and Wallasey.

There are 2,100 acres of dockland on both sides of the river and the Gladstone and Royal Seaforth Docks can accommodate tanker-sized vessels. Liverpool Free Port was opened in 1984.

Liverpool was created a free borough in 1207 and a city in 1880. From the early 18th century it expanded rapidly with the growth of industrialisation and the transatlantic slave trade. Surviving buildings from this period include the Bluecoat Chambers (1717, formerly the Bluecoat School), the Town Hall (1754, rebuilt to the original design 1795), and buildings in Rodney Street, Canning Street and the suburbs. Notable from the 19th and 20th centuries are the Anglican cathedral, built from the designs of Sir Giles Gilbert Scott, the Catholic Metropolitan Cathedral (designed by Sir Frederick Gibberd, consecrated 1967) and St George's Hall (1842), regarded as one of the finest modern examples of classical architecture. The refurbished Albert Dock (designed by Jesse Hartley) contains the Merseyside Maritime Museum, the International Slavery Museum and the Tate Liverpool art gallery.

MANCHESTER (PRE-1900)

Manchester (the *Mamucium* of the Romans, who occupied it in AD 79) is a commercial and industrial centre connected with the sea by the Manchester Ship Canal, opened in 1894, 57km (35.5 miles) long, and accommodating ships up to 15,000 tons.

The principal buildings are the Town Hall, erected in 1877 from the designs of Alfred Waterhouse, with a large extension of 1938; the Royal Exchange (1869, enlarged 1921); the Central Library (1934); Heaton Hall; the 17th-century Chetham Library; the Rylands Library (1900), which includes the Althorp collection; the university precinct; the 15th-century cathedral (formerly the parish church); the Manchester Central conference and exhibition centre and the Bridgewater Hall (1996) concert venue. Manchester is the home of the Hallé Orchestra, the Royal Northern College of Music, the Royal Exchange Theatre and numerous public art galleries.

The town received its first charter of incorporation in 1838 and was created a city in 1853.

NEWCASTLE UPON TYNE (PRE-1900)

Newcastle upon Tyne, on the north bank of the River Tyne, is 13km (8 miles) from the North Sea. A cathedral and university city, it is the administrative, commercial and cultural centre for north-east England and the principal port.

The principal buildings include the Castle Keep (12th century), Black Gate (13th century), Blackfriars (13th century), West Walls (13th century), St Nicholas's Cathedral (15th century, fine lantern tower), St Andrew's Church (12th–14th century), St John's (14th–15th century), All Saints (1786 by Stephenson), St Mary's Roman Catholic Cathedral (1844), Trinity House (17th century), Sandhill (16th-century houses), Guildhall (Georgian), Grey Street (1834–9), Central Station (1846–50), Laing Art Gallery (1904), University of Newcastle Physics Building (1962) and Medical Building (1985), Civic Centre (1963) and the Central Library (1969). Open spaces include the Town Moor (927 acres) and Jesmond Dene. Numerous bridges span the Tyne at Newcastle, including the Tyne Bridge (1928) and the tilting Millennium Bridge (2001) – which links the city with Gateshead to the south.

The city's name is derived from the 'new castle' (1080) erected as a defence against the Scots. In 1400 it was made a county, and in 1882 a city.

NORWICH (PRE-1900)

Norwich grew from an early Anglo-Saxon settlement near the confluence of the rivers Yare and Wensum, and now serves as the provincial capital for the predominantly agricultural region of East Anglia. The name is thought to relate to the most northerly of a group of Anglo-Saxon villages or *wics*. The city's first known charter was granted in 1158 by Henry II.

Norwich serves its surrounding area as a market town and commercial centre, with banking and insurance prominent among the city's businesses. From the 14th century until the Industrial Revolution, Norwich was the regional centre of the woollen industry, but now the biggest single industry is financial services and principal trades are engineering, printing, shoemaking, the production of chemicals and clothing, food processing and technology. Norwich is accessible to seagoing vessels by means of the River Yare, entered at Great Yarmouth, 32km (20 miles) to the east.

Among many historic buildings are the cathedral (completed in the 12th century and surmounted by a 15th-century spire 96m (315ft) in height); the keep of the Norman castle (now a museum and art gallery); the 15th-century flint-walled Guildhall; some thirty medieval parish churches; St Andrew's and Blackfriars' Halls; the Tudor houses preserved in Elm Hill and the Georgian Assembly House. The University of East Anglia is on the city's western boundary.

NOTTINGHAM (PRE-1900)

Nottingham stands on the River Trent. *Snotingaham* or *Notingeham,* literally the homestead of the people of Snot, is the Anglo-Saxon name for the Celtic settlement of *Tigguocobauc,* or the house of caves. In 878, Nottingham became one of the five boroughs of Danelaw. William the Conqueror ordered the construction of Nottingham Castle, while the town itself developed rapidly under Norman rule. Its laws and rights were later formally recognised by Henry II's charter in 1155. The castle became a favoured residence of King John. In 1642 King Charles I raised his personal standard at Nottingham Castle at the start of the Civil War.

Architecturally, Nottingham has a wealth of notable buildings, particularly those designed in the Victorian era by T. C. Hine and Watson Fothergill. The city council owns the castle, of Norman origin but restored in 1878, Wollaton Hall (1580–8), Newstead Abbey (once home of Lord Byron), the Guildhall (1888) and Council House (1929). St Mary's, St Peter's and St Nicholas' churches are of interest, as is the Roman Catholic cathedral (Pugin, 1842–4). Nottingham was granted city status in 1897.

OXFORD (PRE-1900)

Oxford is a university city, an important industrial centre and a market town.

Oxford is known for its architecture, its oldest specimens being the reputedly Saxon tower of St Michael's Church, the remains of the Norman castle and city walls, and the Norman church at Iffley. It also has many Gothic buildings, such as the Divinity Schools, the Old Library at Merton College, William of Wykeham's New College, Magdalen and Christ Church colleges and many other college buildings. Later centuries are represented by the Laudian quadrangle at St John's College, the Renaissance Sheldonian Theatre by Wren, Trinity College Chapel, All Saints Church, Hawksmoor's mock-Gothic at All Souls College, and the 18th-century Queen's College. In addition to individual buildings, High Street and Radcliffe Square both form interesting architectural compositions. Most of the colleges have gardens, those of Magdalen, New College, St John's and Worcester being the largest.

The Oxford University Museum of Natural History, renowned for its spectacular neo-gothic architecture, houses the university's scientific collections of zoological, entomological and geological specimens and is attached to the neighbouring Pitt Rivers Museum which houses ethnographic and archaeological objects from around the world. The Ashmolean is the city's museum of art and archaeology and Modern Art Oxford hosts a programme of contemporary art exhibitions.

ST ALBANS (PRE-1900)

The origins of St Albans, situated on the River Ver, stem from the Roman town of *Verulamium*. Named after the first Christian martyr in Britain, who was executed there, St Albans has developed around the Norman abbey and cathedral church (consecrated 1115), built partly of materials from the old Roman city. The museums house Iron Age and Roman artefacts and the Roman theatre, unique in Britain, has a stage as opposed to an amphitheatre. Archaeological excavations in the city centre have revealed evidence of pre-Roman, Saxon and medieval occupation.

The town's significance grew to the extent that it was a signatory and venue for the drafting of the Magna Carta. It was also the scene of riots during the Peasants' Revolt, the French King John was imprisoned there after the Battle of Poitiers, and heavy fighting took place there during the Wars of the Roses.

Previously controlled by the Abbot, the town achieved a charter in 1553 and city status in 1877. The street market, first established in 1553, is still an important feature of the city, as are many hotels and inns, surviving from the days when St Albans was an important coach stop.

SALISBURY (PRE-1900)

The history of Salisbury centres around the cathedral and cathedral close. The city evolved from an Iron Age camp a mile to the north of its current position which was strengthened by the Romans and called *Serviodunum*. The Normans built a castle and cathedral on the site and renamed it Sarum. In 1220 Bishop Richard Poore and the architect Elias de Derham decided to build a new Gothic style cathedral. The cathedral was completed 38 years later and a community known as New Sarum, now called Salisbury, grew around it. Originally the cathedral had a squat tower; the 123m (404ft) spire that makes the cathedral the tallest medieval structure in the world was added *c.*1315. A walled close with houses for the clergy was built around the cathedral; the Medieval Hall still stands today, alongside buildings dating from the 13th to the 20th century, including some designed by Sir Christopher Wren.

A prosperous wool and cloth trade allowed Salisbury to flourish until the 17th century. When the wool trade declined new crafts were established including cutlery, leather and basket work, saddlery, lacemaking, joinery and malting. By 1750 it had become an important road junction and coaching centre and in the Victorian era the railways enabled a new age of expansion and prosperity.

SHEFFIELD (PRE-1900)

Sheffield is situated at the junction of the Sheaf, Porter, Rivelin and Loxley valleys with the River Don and was created a city in 1893.

The parish church of St Peter and St Paul, founded in the 12th century, became the cathedral church of the Diocese of Sheffield in 1914. The Roman Catholic Cathedral Church of St Marie (founded 1847) was created a cathedral for the new diocese of Hallam in 1980. Parts of the present building date from *c.*1435. The principal buildings are the Town Hall (1897), the Cutlers' Hall (1832), City Hall (1932), Graves Art Gallery (1934), Mappin Art Gallery, the Crucible Theatre and the restored Lyceum theatre, which dates from 1897 and was reopened in 1990. Three major sporting and entertainment venues were opened between 1990 and 1991: Sheffield Arena, Don Valley Stadium and Pond's Forge. The Millennium Galleries opened in 2001.

SOUTHAMPTON (1964)

Southampton is a major seaport on the south coast of England, situated between the mouths of the Test and Itchen rivers. Southampton's natural deep-water harbour has made the area an important settlement since the Romans built the first port (known as *Clausentum*) in the first century, and Southampton's port has witnessed several important departures, including those of King Henry V in 1415 for the Battle of Agincourt, RMS *Titanic* in 1912, and the *Mayflower* in 1620.

The city's strategic importance, not only as a seaport but also as a centre for aircraft production, meant that it was heavily bombed during the Second World War; however, many historically significant structures remain, including the Wool House, dating from 1417 and now used as the Maritime Museum; parts of the Norman city walls which are among the most complete in the UK; the Bargate, which was originally the main gateway into the city; God's House Tower, now the Museum of Archaeology; St Michael's, the city's oldest church; and the Tudor Merchants Hall.

WINCHESTER (PRE-1900)

Winchester, the ancient capital of England, is situated on the River Itchen. The city is rich in architecture of all types, especially notable is the cathedral. Built in 1079–93 the cathedral exhibits examples of Norman, early English and Perpendicular styles and is the burial place of author Jane Austen. Winchester College, founded in 1382, is one of the country's most famous public schools, and the original building (1393) remains largely unaltered. St Cross Hospital, another great medieval foundation, lies one mile south of the city. The almshouses were founded in 1136 by Bishop Henry de Blois, and Cardinal Henry Beaufort added a new almshouse of 'Noble Poverty' in 1446. The chapel and dwellings are of great architectural interest, and visitors may still receive the 'Wayfarer's Dole' of bread and ale.

Excavations have done much to clarify the origins and development of Winchester. Part of the forum and several of the streets from the Roman town have been discovered. Excavations in the Cathedral Close have uncovered the entire site of the Anglo-Saxon cathedral (known as the Old Minster) and parts of the New Minster which was built by Alfred's son, Edward the Elder, and is the burial place of the

Alfredian dynasty. The original burial place of St Swithun, before his remains were translated to a site in the present cathedral, was also uncovered.

Excavations in other parts of the city have thrown much light on Norman Winchester, notably on the site of the Royal Castle (adjacent to which the new Law Courts have been built) and in the grounds of Wolvesey Castle, where the great house built by Bishops Giffard and Henry de Blois in the 12th century has been uncovered. The Great Hall, built by Henry III between 1222 and 1236, survives and houses the Arthurian Round Table.

YORK (PRE-1900)

The city of York is an archiepiscopal seat. Its recorded history dates from AD 71, when the Roman Ninth Legion established a base under Petilius Cerealis that would later become the fortress of *Eburacum*, or *Eboracum*. In Anglo-Saxon times the city was the royal and ecclesiastical centre of Northumbria, and after capture by a Viking army in AD 866 it became the capital of the Viking kingdom of Jorvik. By the 14th century the city had become a great mercantile centre, mainly because of its control of the wool trade, and was used as the chief base against the Scots. Under the Tudors its fortunes declined, although Henry VIII made it the headquarters of the Council of the North. Excavations on many sites, including Coppergate, have greatly expanded knowledge of Roman, Viking and medieval urban life.

The city is rich in examples of architecture of all periods. The earliest church was built in AD 627 and, from the 12th to 15th centuries, the present Minster was built in a succession of styles. Other examples within the city are the medieval city walls and gateways, churches and guildhalls. Domestic architecture includes the Georgian mansions of The Mount, Micklegate and Bootham.

LORD-LIEUTENANTS AND HIGH SHERIFFS

Area	*Lord-Lieutenant*	*High Sheriff (2013–14)*
Bedfordshire	Helen Nellis	Deborah Inskip
Berkshire	Hon. Mary Bayliss	Prof. Suzanna Rose
Bristol	Mary Prior, MBE	Dr Shaheen Chaudhry
Buckinghamshire	Sir Henry Aubrey-Fletcher	Sir Stuart Hampson
Cambridgeshire	Hugh Duberly, CBE	Hon. Aubrey Buxton
Cheshire	David Briggs, MBE	Martin Beaumont
Cornwall	Col. Edward Bolitho, OBE	James Kitson
Cumbria	Claire Hensman	Diana Matthews
Derbyshire	William Tucker	Derek Mapp
Devon	Eric Dancer, CBE	John Lee, OBE
Dorset	Valerie Pitt-Rivers	Catriona Payne
Durham	Susan Snowdon	Peter Bell
East Riding of Yorkshire	Hon. Susan Cunliffe-Lister	Stephen Larard
East Sussex	Peter Field	Graham Peters
Essex	Lord Petre	Julia Abel Smith
Gloucestershire	Dame Janet Trotter, DBE	Hon. Hugh Tollemache
Greater London	Sir David Brewer, CMG	David Jones
Greater Manchester	Warren Smith	Paul Griffiths
Hampshire	Dame Mary Fagan, DCVO	Rupert Younger
Herefordshire	Countess of Darnley	Robert Dyke Tabor
Hertfordshire	Countess of Verulam	Viscountess Trenchard
Isle of Wight	Maj.-Gen. Martin White, CB, CBE	Mary Case
Kent	Viscount De L'Isle, MBE	Lord Colgrain
Lancashire	Lord Shuttleworth, KCVO	Letitia Dean
Leicestershire	Lady Gretton	Sally Bowie
Lincolnshire	Anthony Worth	Toby Dennis
Merseyside	Dame Lorna Fox Muirhead, DBE	Robert Meadows
Norfolk	Richard Jewson	Countess of Leicester
North Yorkshire	Lord Crathorne, KCVO	Revd Rachel Benson
Northamptonshire	Lady Juliet Townsend, LVO	James Shepherd-Cross
Northumberland	Duchess of Northumberland	Peter Loyd
Nottinghamshire	Sir John Peace	Nicola Weston
Oxfordshire	Tim Stevenson, OBE	Prof. Graham Upton
Rutland	Dr Laurence Howard, OBE	Patricia Rutland
Shropshire	A. Heber-Percy	Diana Flint
Somerset	Lady Gass	Maureen Whitmore
South Yorkshire	David Moody	Lady Sykes
Staffordshire	Ian Dudson, CBE	Susan Inge-Innes-Lillingston
Suffolk	Lord Tollemache	Sir Edward Greenwell Bt.
Surrey	Dame Sarah Goad, DCVO	Dr Helen Bowcock
Tyne and Wear	N. Sherlock, OBE	George Scott
Warwickshire	Timothy Cox	Keith Sach
West Midlands	Paul Sabapathy, CBE	Dr Christine Braddock, CBE
West Sussex	Susan Pyper	David Burgess, MBE
West Yorkshire	Dr Ingrid Roscoe	Virginia Lloyd
Wiltshire	Sarah Troughton	William Wyldbore-Smith
Worcestershire	Lt.-Col. Patrick Holcroft, LVO, OBE	Nicholas Wentworth-Stanley

COUNTY COUNCILS

Council & Administrative Headquarters	*Telephone*	*Population**	*Council Tax†*	*Chief Executive‡*
Buckinghamshire, Aylesbury	01296-395000	505,283	£1,078	Chris Williams
Cambridgeshire, Cambridge	0345-045 5200	621,210	£1,100	Mark Lloyd
Cumbria, Carlisle	01228-606060	499,858	£1,162	Diane Wood *(acting)*
Derbyshire, Matlock	01629-580000	769,686	£1,077	Ian Stephenson
Devon, Exeter	0845-155 1015	746,399	£1,116	Phil Norrey
Dorset, Dorchester	01305-221000	412,905	£1,168	Debbie Ward
East Sussex, Lewes	0345-608 0190	526,671	£1,158	Becky Shaw
Essex, Chelmsford	0845-7430 430	1,393,587	£1,087	Joanna Killian
Gloucestershire, Gloucester	01452-425000	596,984	£1,091	Peter Bungard
Hampshire, Winchester	01962-841841	1,317,788	£1,038	Andrew Smith
Hertfordshire, Hertford	01992-555555	1,116,062	£1,119	John Wood
Kent, Maidstone	0845-824 7247	1,463,740	£1,048	David Cockburn
Lancashire, Preston	0845-053 0000	1,171,339	£1,086	Phil Halsall
Leicestershire, Leicester	0116-232 3232	650,489	£1,063	John Sinnott
Lincolnshire, Lincoln	01522-552222	713,653	£1,066	Tony McArdle
Norfolk, Norwich	0344-800 8020	857,888	£1,145	Anne Gibson *(acting)*
North Yorkshire, Northallerton	01609-780780	598,376	£1,057	Richard Flinton
Northamptonshire, Northampton	0300-126 1000	691,952	£1,028	Paul Blantern
Nottinghamshire, Nottingham	0115-982 3823	785,802	£1,193	Mick Burrows
Oxfordshire, Oxford	01865-792422	653,798	£1,185	Joanna Simons
Somerset, Taunton	0845-345 9166	529,972	£1,027	Sheila Wheeler
Staffordshire, Stafford	0300-111 8000	848,489	£1,027	Nick Bell
Suffolk, Ipswich	0845-606 6067	728,163	£1,127	Deborah Cadman
Surrey, Kingston upon Thames	0845-600 9009	1,132,390	£1,173	David McNulty
Warwickshire, Warwick	01926-410410	545,474	£1,155	Jim Graham
West Sussex, Chichester	01243-777100	806,892	£1,162	Kieran Stigant
Worcestershire, Worcester	01905-763763	566,169	£1,039	Trish Haines

* *Source:* ONS – Census 2011 (Crown copyright)

† Average 2013–14 Band D council tax in the county area exclusive of precepts for fire and police authorities. County councils claim their share of the combined council tax from the collection funds of the district authorities into whose area they fall. Average Band D council tax bills for the billing authority are given on the following pages

‡ Or equivalent postholder

LONDON BOROUGH COUNCILS

Council	*Telephone*	*Population**	*Council Tax†*	*Chief Executive‡*
Barking and Dagenham	020-8592 4500	185,911	£1,319	Graham Farrant
Barnet	020-8359 2000	356,386	£1,416	Andrew Travers *(acting)*
Bexley	020-8303 7777	231,997	£1,432	Will Tuckley
Brent	020-8937 1234	311,215	£1,362	Christine Gilbert *(acting)*
Bromley	020-8464 3333	309,392	£1,313	Doug Patterson
Camden	020-7974 4444	220,338	£1,325	Mike Cooke
CITY OF LONDON CORPORATION	020-7606 3030	7,375	£943	John Barradell, OBE
Croydon	020-8726 6000	363,378	£1,474	Nathan Elbery
Ealing	020-8825 5000	338,449	£1,363	Martin Smith
Enfield	020-8379 1000	312,466	£1,403	Rob Leak
Greenwich	020-8854 8888	254,557	£1,284	Mary Ney
Hackney	020-8356 5000	246,270	£1,301	Tim Shields
Hammersmith and Fulham	020-8748 3020	182,493	£1,061	Derek Myers
Haringey	020-8489 0000	254,926	£1,487	Nick Walkley
Harrow	020-8863 5611	239,056	£1,513	Michael Lockwood
Havering	01708-434343	237,232	£1,498	Cheryl Coppell
Hillingdon	01895-250111	273,936	£1,416	Fran Beasley
Hounslow	020-8583 2000	253,957	£1,388	Mary Harpley
Islington	020-7527 2000	206,125	£1,265	Lesley Seary
Kensington and Chelsea	020-7361 3000	158,649	£1,086	Derek Myers
Kingston upon Thames	020-8547 5757	160,060	£1,683	Bruce McDonald
Lambeth	020-7926 1000	303,086	£1,228	Derrick Anderson, CBE
Lewisham	020-8314 6000	275,885	£1,363	Barry Quirk, CBE
Merton	020-8543 2222	199,693	£1,410	Ged Curran
Newham	020-8430 2000	307,984	£1,249	Kim Bromley-Derry
Redbridge	020-8554 5000	278,970	£1,399	Roger Hampson
Richmond upon Thames	020-8891 1411	186,990	£1,590	Gillian Norton
Southwark	020-7525 5000	288,283	£1,215	Eleanor Kelly
Sutton	020-8770 5000	190,146	£1,444	Niall Bolger
Tower Hamlets	020-7364 5000	254,096	£1,189	Stephen Halsey
Waltham Forest	020-8496 3000	258,249	£1,455	Martin Esom
Wandsworth	020-8871 6000	306,995	£692	Paul Martin
WESTMINSTER	020-7641 6000	219,396	£681	Mike More

DISTRICT COUNCILS

District Council	*Telephone*	*Population**	*Council Tax†*	*Chief Executive‡*
Adur	01903-239999	61,182	£1,593	Peter Latham
Allerdale	01900-702702	96,422	£1,569	Harry Dyke
Amber Valley	01773-570222	122,309	£1,505	Sylvia Delahay & Julian Townsend
Arun	01903-737500	149,518	£1,522	Nigel Lynn
Ashfield	01623-450000	119,497	£1,606	Philip Marshall
Ashford	01233-331111	117,956	£1,427	John Bunnett
Aylesbury Vale	01296-585858	174,137	£1,501	Andrew Grant
Babergh	01473-822801	87,740	£1,511	Charlie Adan
Barrow-in-Furness	01229-876300	69,087	£1,584	Phil Huck
Basildon	01268-533333	174,497	£1,554	Bala Mahendran
Basingstoke and Deane	01256-844844	167,799	£1,373	Tony Curtis
Bassetlaw	01909-533533	112,863	£1,611	Neil Taylor *(acting)*
Blaby	0116-275 0555	93,915	£1,508	Sandra Whiles
Bolsover	01246-240000	75,866	£1,580	Wesley Lumley
Boston	01205-314200	64,637	£1,442	Richard Harbord
Braintree	01376-552525	147,084	£1,489	Nicola Beach
Breckland	01362-656870	130,491	£1,485	Trevor Holden *(acting)*
Brentwood	01277-312500	73,601	£1,474	Alison Crowe
Broadland	01603-431133	124,646	£1,523	Phil Kirby
Bromsgrove	01527-881288	93,637	£1,509	Kevin Dicks
Broxbourne	01992-785555	93,609	£1,380	Jeff Stack *(acting)*
Broxtowe	0115-917 7777	109,487	£1,617	Ruth Hyde, OBE
Burnley	01282-425011	87,059	£1,567	Steve Rumbelow
CAMBRIDGE	01223-457000	123,867	£1,512	Antoinette Jackson
Cannock Chase	01543-462621	97,462	£1,495	Stephen Brown
CANTERBURY	01227-862000	151,145	£1,452	Colin Carmichael
CARLISLE	01228-817000	107,524	£1,573	Jason Gooding
Castle Point	01268-882200	88,011	£1,537	David Marchant
Charnwood	01509-263151	166,100	£1,471	Geoff Parker
CHELMSFORD	01245-606606	168,310	£1,498	Steve Packham
Cheltenham	01242-262626	115,732	£1,486	Andrew North
Cherwell	01295-252535	141,868	£1,547	Sue Smith
Chesterfield	01246-345345	103,788	£1,468	Huw Bowen
Chichester	01243-785166	113,794	£1,483	Diane Shepherd
Chiltern	01494-729000	92,635	£1,512	Alan Goodrum
Chorley	01257-515151	107,155	£1,496	Gary Hall
Christchurch	01202-495000	47,752	£1,596	David McIntosh
Colchester	01206-282222	173,074	£1,490	Adrian Pritchard
Copeland	0845-054 8600	70,603	£1,573	Paul Walker
Corby	01536-464000	61,225	£1,403	Norman Stronach *(acting)*
Cotswold	01285-623000	82,881	£1,490	David Neudegg
Craven	01756-700600	55,409	£1,529	Paul Shevlin
Crawley	01293-438000	106,597	£1,488	Lee Harris
Dacorum	01442-228000	144,847	£1,452	Daniel Zammit
Dartford	01322-343434	97,365	£1,452	Graham Harris
Daventry	01327-871100	77,843	£1,415	Ian Vincent
Derbyshire Dales	01629-761100	71,116	£1,545	Dorcas Bunton
Dover	01304-821199	111,674	£1,484	Nadeem Aziz
East Cambridgeshire	01353-665555	83,818	£1,542	John Hill
East Devon	01395-516551	132,457	£1,514	Mark Williams
East Dorset	01202-886201	87,166	£1,653	David McIntosh
East Hampshire	01730-266551	115,608	£1,450	Sandy Hopkins
East Hertfordshire	01279-655261	137,687	£1,486	George Robertson
East Lindsey	01507-601111	136,401	£1,407	Stuart Davy
East Northamptonshire	01832-742000	86,765	£1,428	David Oliver
East Staffordshire	01283-508000	113,583	£1,486	Andy O'Brien
Eastbourne	01323-410000	99,412	£1,603	Robert Cottrill
Eastleigh	023-8068 8000	125,199	£1,439	Bernie Topham
Eden	01768-817817	52,564	£1,568	Robin Hooper
Elmbridge	01372-474474	130,875	£1,584	Robert Moran
Epping Forest	01992-564000	124,659	£1,503	Glen Chipp
Epsom and Ewell	01372-732000	75,102	£1,551	Frances Rutter
Erewash	0115-907 2244	112,081	£1,485	Jeremy Jaroszek
EXETER	01392-277888	117,773	£1,485	Karime Hassan
Fareham	01329-236100	111,581	£1,391	Peter Grimwood
Fenland	01354-654321	95,262	£1,617	Paul Medd
Forest Heath	01638-719000	59,748	£1,510	Ian Gallin
Forest of Dean	01594-810000	81,961	£1,516	Sue Pangbourne
Fylde	01253-658658	75,757	£1,516	Allan Oldfield

District Council	*Telephone*	*Population**	*Council Tax†*	*Chief Executive‡*
Gedling	0115-901 3901	113,543	£1,599	John Robinson
GLOUCESTER	01452-522232	121,688	£1,480	Julian Wain
Gosport	023-9258 4242	82,622	£1,453	Ian Lycett
Gravesham	01474-337000	101,720	£1,439	David Hughes
Great Yarmouth	01493-856100	97,277	£1,502	Jane Ratcliffe
Guildford	01483-505050	137,183	£1,550	David Hill
Hambleton	0845-121 1555	89,140	£1,448	Phillip Morton
Harborough	01858-828282	85,382	£1,498	Anna Graves
Harlow	01279-446655	81,944	£1,550	Malcolm Morley
Harrogate	01423-500600	157,869	£1,554	Wallace Sampson
Hart	01252-622122	91,033	£1,462	Geoff Bonner
Hastings	01424 451066	90,254	£1,614	Neil Dart
Havant	023-9247 4174	120,684	£1,443	Sandy Hopkins
Hertsmere	020-8207 2277	100,031	£1,447	Donald Graham
High Peak	0845-129 7777	90,892	£1,504	Simon Baker
Hinckley and Bosworth	01455-238141	105,078	£1,449	Steve Atkinson
Horsham	01403-215100	131,301	£1,482	Tom Crowley
Huntingdonshire	01480-388388	169,508	£1,558	Jo Lancaster
Hyndburn	01254-388111	80,734	£1,534	David Welsby
Ipswich	01473-432000	133,384	£1,609	Russell Williams
Kettering	01536-410333	93,475	£1,432	David Cook, MBE
King's Lynn and West Norfolk	01553-616200	147,451	£1,504	Ray Harding
LANCASTER	01524-582000	138,375	£1,512	Mark Cullinan
Lewes	01273-471600	97,502	£1,645	Jenny Rowlands
Lichfield	01543-308000	100,654	£1,460	Diane Tilley
LINCOLN	01522-881188	93,541	£1,497	Andrew Taylor
Maidstone	01622-602000	155,143	£1,505	Alison Broom
Maldon	01621-854477	61,629	£1,510	Fiona Marshall
Malvern Hills	01684-862151	74,631	£1,482	Chris Bocock
Mansfield	01623-463463	104,466	£1,620	Ruth Marlow
Melton	01664-502502	50,376	£1,500	Lynn Aisbett
Mendip	01749-648999	109,279	£1,485	Stuart Brown
Mid Devon	01884-255255	77,750	£1,577	Kevin Finan
Mid Suffolk	01449-720711	96,731	£1,503	Charlie Adan
Mid Sussex	01444-458166	139,860	£1,508	Kathryn Hall
Mole Valley	01306-885001	85,375	£1,539	Yvonne Rees
New Forest	023-8028 5000	176,462	£1,472	David Yates
Newark and Sherwood	01636-650000	114,817	£1,657	Andrew Muter
Newcastle-under-Lyme	01782-717717	123,871	£1,458	John Sellgren
North Devon	01271-327711	93,667	£1,567	Mike Mansell
North Dorset	01258-454111	68,583	£1,605	Liz Goodall
North East Derbyshire	01246-231111	99,023	£1,579	Wes Lumley
North Hertfordshire	01462-474000	127,114	£1,486	David Scholes
North Kesteven	01529-414155	107,766	£1,463	Ian Fytche
North Norfolk	01263-513811	101,499	£1,525	Sheila Oxtoby
North Warwickshire	01827-715341	62,014	£1,590	Jeremy Hutchinson
North West Leicestershire	01530-454545	93,468	£1,516	Christine Fisher
Northampton	01604-837837	212,069	£1,448	David Kennedy
NORWICH	0344-980 3333	132,512	£1,576	Laura McGillivray
Nuneaton and Bedworth	024-7637 6376	125,252	£1,540	Alan Franks
Oadby and Wigston	0116-288 8961	56,170	£1,498	Mark Hall
OXFORD	01865-249811	151,906	£1,614	Peter Sloman
Pendle	01282-661661	89,452	£1,557	Stephen Barnes
PRESTON	01772-906900	140,202	£1,582	Lorraine Norris
Purbeck	01929-556561	44,973	£1,643	Steve Mackenzie
Redditch	01527-534123	84,214	£1,501	Kevin Dicks
Reigate and Banstead	01737-276000	137,835	£1,583	John Jory
Ribble Valley	01200-425111	57,132	£1,460	Marshal Scott
Richmondshire	01748-829100	51,965	£1,549	Tony Clark
Rochford	01702-546366	83,287	£1,539	Paul Warren
Rossendale	01706-217777	67,982	£1,559	Helen Lockwood
Rother	01424-787999	90,588	£1,593	Malcolm Johnston & Anthony Leonard
Rugby	01788-533533	100,075	£1,524	Ian David & Andrew Gabbitas
Runnymede	01932-838383	80,510	£1,522	Paul Turrell
Rushcliffe	0115-981 9911	111,129	£1,612	Allen Graham
Rushmoor	01252-398398	93,807	£1,435	Andrew Lloyd
Ryedale	01653-600666	51,751	£1,536	Janet Waggott
ST ALBANS	01727-866100	140,664	£1,473	James Blake
St Edmundsbury	01284-763233	111,008	£1,512	Ian Gallin
Scarborough	01723-232323	108,793	£1,555	Jim Dillon
Sedgemoor	0845-408 2540	114,588	£1,456	Kerry Rickards

District Council	*Telephone*	*Population**	*Council Tax†*	*Chief Executive‡*
Selby	01757-705101	83,449	£1,538	Martin Connor
Sevenoaks	01732-227000	114,893	£1,513	Dr Pav Ramewal
Shepway	01303-853000	107,969	£1,547	Alistair Stewart
South Bucks	01895-837200	66,867	£1,494	Alan Goodrum
South Cambridgeshire	0345-045 0500	148,755	£1,536	Jean Hunter
South Derbyshire	01283-221000	94,611	£1,482	Frank McArdle
South Hams	01803-861234	83,140	£1,541	Richard Sheard
South Holland	01775-761161	88,270	£1,442	Trevor Holden
South Kesteven	01476-406080	133,788	£1,426	Beverly Agass
South Lakeland	01539-733333	103,658	£1,572	Lawrence Conway
South Norfolk	01508-533633	124,012	£1,541	Sandra Dinneen
South Northamptonshire	01327-322322	85,189	£1,460	Sue Smith
South Oxfordshire	01491-823000	134,257	£1,533	David Buckle
South Ribble	01772-421491	109,057	£1,518	Mike Nuttall
South Somerset	01935-462462	161,243	£1,491	Mark Williams
South Staffordshire	01902-696000	108,131	£1,417	Steve Winterflood
Spelthorne	01784-451499	95,598	£1,556	Roberto Tambini
Stafford	01785-619000	130,869	£1,439	Ian Thompson
Staffordshire Moorlands	01538-483483	97,106	£1,456	Simon Baker
Stevenage	01438-242242	83,957	£1,455	Nick Parry
Stratford-on-Avon	01789-267575	120,485	£1,516	Paul Lankester
Stroud	01453-766321	112,779	£1,546	David Hagg
Suffolk Coastal	01394-383789	124,298	£1,498	Stephen Baker
Surrey Heath	01276-707100	86,144	£1,587	Karen Whelan
Swale	01795-417330	135,835	£1,547	Abdool Kara
Tamworth	01827-709709	76,813	£1,425	Tony Goodwin
Tandridge	01883-722000	82,998	£1,592	Louise Round
Taunton Deane	01823-356356	110,187	£1,420	Penny James
Teignbridge	01626-361101	124,220	£1,554	Nicola Bulbeck
Tendring	01255-686868	138,048	£1,473	Ian Davidson
Test Valley	01264-368000	116,398	£1,408	Roger Tetstall
Tewkesbury	01684-295010	81,943	£1,443	Michael Dawson
Thanet	01843-577000	134,186	£1,486	Dr Sue McGonigal
Three Rivers	01923-776611	87,317	£1,461	Dr Steven Halls
Tonbridge and Malling	01732-844522	120,805	£1,479	Julie Beilby
Torridge	01237-428700	63,839	£1,545	Jenny Wallace
Tunbridge Wells	01892-526121	115,049	£1,451	William Benson
Uttlesford	01799-510510	79,443	£1,514	John Mitchell
Vale of White Horse	01235-520202	120,988	£1,520	David Buckle
Warwick	01926-450000	137,648	£1,506	Chris Elliott
Watford	01923-226400	90,301	£1,516	Manny Lewis
Waveney	01502-562111	115,254	£1,457	Stephen Baker
Waverley	01483-523333	121,572	£1,589	Mary Orton
Wealden	01323-443322	148,915	£1,635	Charles Lant
Wellingborough	01933-229777	75,356	£1,370	John Campbell
Welwyn & Hatfield	01707-357000	110,535	£1,501	Michel Saminaden
West Devon	01822-813600	53,553	£1,611	Richard Sheard
West Dorset	01305-251010	99,264	£1,615	David Clarke
West Lancashire	01695-577177	110,685	£1,500	Gill Rowe & Kim Webber
West Lindsey	01427-676676	89,250	£1,498	Manjeet Gill
West Oxfordshire	01993-861000	104,779	£1,491	David Neudegg
West Somerset	01643-703704	34,675	£1,468	Adrian Dyer
Weymouth and Portland	01305-838000	65,167	£1,692	David Clarke
WINCHESTER	01962-840222	116,595	£1,443	Simon Eden
Woking	01483-755855	99,198	£1,589	Ray Morgan, OBE
WORCESTER	01905-723471	98,768	£1,457	Duncan Sharkey
Worthing	01903-239999	104,640	£1,516	Peter Latham
Wychavon	01386-565000	116,944	£1,441	Jack Hegarty
Wycombe	01494-461000	171,644	£1,461	Karen Satterford
Wyre	01253-891000	107,749	£1,494	Garry Payne
Wyre Forest	01562-732928	97,975	£1,504	Ian Miller

METROPOLITAN BOROUGH COUNCILS

Metropolitan Borough Council	*Telephone*	*Population**	*Council Tax†*	*Chief Executive‡*
Barnsley	01226-770770	231,221	£1,415	Diana Terris
BIRMINGHAM	0121-303 9944	1,073,045	£1,269	Stephen Hughes
Bolton	01204-333333	276,786	£1,464	Sean Harriss
BRADFORD	01274-432001	522,452	£1,318	Tony Reeves
Bury	0161-253 5000	185,060	£1,511	Mike Kelly
Calderdale	01422-357257	203,826	£1,452	Merran McRae
COVENTRY	0500-834 3333	318,960	£1,479	Martin Reeves
Doncaster	01302-734444	302,402	£1,332	Johanna Miller
Dudley	0300-555 2345	312,925	£1,281	John Polychronakis
Gateshead	0191-433 3000	200,214	£1,603	Jane Robinson
Kirklees	01484-221000	422,458	£1,440	Adrian Lythgo
Knowsley	0151-489 6000	145,893	£1,497	Sheena Ramsey
LEEDS	0113-222 4444	751,485	£1,324	Tom Riordan
LIVERPOOL	0151-233 3000	466,415	£1,553	Ged Fitzgerald
MANCHESTER	0161-234 5000	503,127	£1,379	Sir Howard Bernstein
NEWCASTLE UPON TYNE	0191-232 8520	280,177	£1,515	Pat Ritchie
North Tyneside	0191-643 5991	200,801	£1,488	Graham Haywood
Oldham	0161-911 3000	224,897	£1,604	Charlie Parker
Rochdale	01706-647474	211,699	£1,537	Jim Taylor
Rotherham	01709-382121	257,280	£1,470	Martin Kimber
St Helens	01744-676789	175,308	£1,395	Carole Hudson, CBE
SALFORD	0161-794 4711	233,933	£1,533	Barbara Spicer
Sandwell	0121-569 2200	308,063	£1,331	Jan Britton
Sefton	0151-922 4040	273,790	£1,500	Margaret Carney
SHEFFIELD	0114-273 4567	552,698	£1,493	John Mothersole
Solihull	0121-704 6000	206,674	£1,345	Mark Rogers
South Tyneside	0191-427 1717	148,127	£1,451	Martin Swales
Stockport	0161-480 4949	283,275	£1,604	Eamonn Boylan
SUNDERLAND	0191-520 5555	275,506	£1,346	Dave Smith
Tameside	0161-342 8355	219,324	£1,417	Steven Pleasant
Trafford	0161-912 2000	226,578	£1,313	Theresa Grant
WAKEFIELD	0845-8506 506	325,837	£1,341	Joanne Roney, OBE
Walsall	01922-650000	269,323	£1,566	Paul Sheehan
Wigan	01942-244991	317,849	£1,403	Donna Hall
Wirral	0151-606 2000	319,783	£1,501	Graham Burgess
WOLVERHAMPTON	01902-556556	249,470	£1,472	Simon Warren

UNITARY COUNCILS

Unitary Council	*Telephone*	*Population**	*Council Tax†*	*Chief Executive‡*
Bath and North East Somerset	01225-477000	176,016	£1,468	Dr Jo Farrar
Bedford	01234-267422	157,479	£1,571	Philip Simpkins
Blackburn with Darwen	01254-585585	147,489	£1,488	Harry Catherall
Blackpool	01253-477477	142,065	£1,523	Neil Jack
Bournemouth	01202-451451	183,491	£1,499	Tony Williams
Bracknell Forest	01344-352000	113,205	£1,376	Timothy Wheadon
BRIGHTON AND HOVE	01273-290000	273,369	£1,508	Penny Thompson, CBE
BRISTOL	0117-922 2000	428,234	£1,597	Nicola Yates
Central Bedfordshire	0300-300 8000	254,381	£1,652	Richard Carr
Cheshire East	0300-123 5500	370,127	£1,470	Mike Suarez
Cheshire West and Chester	0300-123 8123	329,608	£1,518	Steve Robinson
Cornwall	0300-123 4100	532,273	£1,477	Paul Masters
Darlington	01325-380651	105,564	£1,465	Ada Burns
DERBY	01332-293111	248,752	£1,379	Adam Wilkinson
DURHAM	0300-123 7070	513,242	£1,608	George Garlick
East Riding of Yorkshire	01482-887700	334,179	£1,510	Nigel Pearson
Halton	0151-907 8300	125,746	£1,382	David Parr
Hartlepool	01429-266522	92,028	£1,686	Dave Stubbs
Herefordshire	01432-260000	183,477	£1,519	Alastair Neill
Isle of Wight	01983-821000	138,265	£1,475	Dave Burbage
Isles of Scilly§	01720-422537	2,203	£1,193	Barry Keel *(acting)*
KINGSTON-UPON-HULL	01482-609100	256,406	£1,369	Darryl Stephenson
LEICESTER	0116-254 9922	329,839	£1,484	Sir Peter Soulsby
Luton	01582-546000	203,201	£1,446	Trevor Holden
Medway	01634-333333	263,925	£1,355	Neil Davies
Middlesbrough	01642-245432	138,412	£1,597	Gill Rollings
Milton Keynes	01908-691691	248,821	£1,417	David Hill
North East Lincolnshire	01472-313131	159,616	£1,511	Tony Hunter
North Lincolnshire	01724-296296	167,446	£1,562	Simon Driver
North Somerset	01934-888888	202,566	£1,447	Graham Turner
Northumberland	01670-533000	316,028	£1,513	Steve Stewart
NOTTINGHAM	0115-915 5555	305,680	£1,644	Ian Curryer
PETERBOROUGH	01733-747474	183,631	£1,378	Gillian Beasley
PLYMOUTH	01752-668000	256,384	£1,508	Tracey Lee
Poole	01202-633633	147,645	£1,458	John McBride
PORTSMOUTH	023-9282 2251	205,056	£1,384	David Williams
Reading	0118-9373737	155,698	£1,531	Ian Wardle
Redcar and Cleveland	0164-277 4774	135,177	£1,644	Amanda Skelton
Rutland	01572-722577	37,369	£1,701	Helen Briggs
Shropshire	0345-678 9000	306,129	£1,488	Clive Wright
Slough	01753-475111	140,205	£1,399	Ruth Bagley, OBE
South Gloucestershire	01454-868686	262,767	£1,539	Amanda Deeks
SOUTHAMPTON	023-8022 3855	236,882	£1,475	Dawn Baxendale *(acting)*
Southend-on-Sea	01702-215000	173,658	£1,351	Robert Tinlin
Stockton-on-Tees	01642-393939	191,610	£1,565	Neil Schneider
STOKE-ON-TRENT	01782-234567	249,008	£1,429	John van de Laarschot
Swindon	01793-445500	209,156	£1,395	Gavin Jones
Telford and Wrekin	01952-380000	166,641	£1,477	Richard Partington
Thurrock	01375-652652	157,705	£1,333	Graham Farrant
Torbay	01803-201201	130,959	£1,503	Caroline Taylor *(acting)*
Warrington	01925-444400	202,228	£1,402	Steven Broomhead *(acting)*
West Berkshire	01635-42400	153,822	£1,538	Nick Carter
Wiltshire	0300-456 0100	470,981	£1,517	C. Brand, C. Godfrey & M. Rae
Windsor and Maidenhead	01628-683800	144,560	£1,182	Mike McGaughrin
Wokingham	0118-974 6000	154,380	£1,494	Andy Couldrick
YORK	01904-551550	198,051	£1,420	Kersten England

* *Source:* ONS – Census 2011 (Crown copyright)

† Average Band D council tax bill for 2013–14

‡ Or equivalent postholder

§ Under the Isles of Scilly Clause the council has additional functions to other unitary authorities

Councils in CAPITAL LETTERS have city status

MAP OF COUNCILS IN ENGLAND

LONDON

THE CITY OF LONDON CORPORATION

The City of London is the historic centre at the heart of London known as 'the square mile' around which the vast metropolis has grown over the centuries. The City's residential population was 7,400 at the 2011 census and in addition, around a third of a million people work in the City. The civic government is carried on by the City of London Corporation through the court of Common Council.

The City is an international financial and business centre, generating about £30bn a year for the British economy. It includes the head offices of the principal banks, insurance companies and mercantile houses, in addition to buildings ranging from the historic Roman Wall and the 15th-century Guildhall, to the massive splendour of St Paul's Cathedral and the architectural beauty of Wren's spires.

The City of London was described by Tacitus in AD 62 as 'a busy emporium for trade and traders'. Under the Romans it became an important administration centre and hub of the road system. Little is known of London in Saxon times, when it formed part of the kingdom of the East Saxons. In 886 Alfred recovered London from the Danes and reconstituted it a burgh under his son-in-law. In 1066 the citizens submitted to William the Conqueror who in 1067 granted them a charter, which is still preserved, establishing them in the rights and privileges they had hitherto enjoyed.

THE MAYORALTY

The mayoralty was probably established about 1189, the first mayor being Henry Fitz Ailwyn who filled the office for 23 years and was succeeded by Fitz Alan (1212–14). A new charter was granted by King John in 1215, directing the mayor to be chosen annually, which has been done ever since, though in early times the same individual often held the office more than once. A familiar instance is that of 'Whittington, thrice Lord Mayor of London' (in reality four times: 1397, 1398, 1406 and 1419); and many modern cases have occurred. The earliest instance of the phrase 'lord mayor' in English is in 1414. It was used more generally in the latter part of the 15th century and became invariable from 1535 onwards. At Michaelmas the liverymen in Common Hall choose two aldermen who have served the office of sheriff for presentation to the Court of Aldermen, and one is chosen to be lord mayor for the following mayoral year.

LORD MAYOR'S DAY

The lord mayor of London was previously elected on the feast of St Simon and St Jude (28 October), and from the time of Edward I, at least, was presented to the King or to the Barons of the Exchequer on the following day, unless that day was a Sunday. The day of election was altered to 16 October in 1346, and after some further changes was fixed for Michaelmas Day in 1546, but the ceremonies of admittance and swearing-in of the lord mayor continued to take place on 28 and 29 October respectively until 1751. In 1752, at the reform of the calendar, the lord mayor was continued in office until 8 November, the 'new style' equivalent of 28 October. The lord mayor is now presented to the lord chief justice at the royal courts of justice on the second Saturday in November to make the final declaration of office, having been sworn in at Guildhall on the preceding day. The procession to the royal courts of justice is popularly known as the Lord Mayor's Show.

REPRESENTATIVES

Aldermen are mentioned in the 11th century and their office is of Saxon origin. They were elected annually between 1377 and 1394, when an act of parliament of Richard II directed them to be chosen for life. Aldermen now serve a six-year term of office before submitting themselves for re-election.

The Common Council was, at an early date, substituted for a popular assembly called the *Folkmote.* At first only two representatives were sent from each ward, but now each of the City's 25 wards is represented by an alderman and at least two Common Councilmen (the number depending on the size of the ward). Common Councilmen are elected every four years.

OFFICERS

Sheriffs were Saxon officers; their predecessors were the *wic-reeves* and *portreeves* of London and Middlesex. At first they were officers of the Crown, and were named by the Barons of the Exchequer; but Henry I (in 1132) gave the citizens permission to choose their own sheriffs, and the annual election of sheriffs became fully operative under King John's charter of 1199. The citizens lost this privilege, as far as the election of the sheriff of Middlesex was concerned, by the Local Government Act 1888; but the liverymen continue to choose two sheriffs of the City of London, who are appointed on Midsummer Day and take office at Michaelmas.

The office of chamberlain is an ancient one, the first contemporary record of which is 1237. The town clerk (or common clerk) is first mentioned in 1274.

ACTIVITIES

The work of the City of London Corporation is assigned to a number of committees which present reports to the Court of Common Council. These committees are: Administration of the Sir William Coxen Trust Fund; Audit and Risk Management; Barbican Centre; Barbican Residential; Board of Governors of the City of London Freeman's School, the City of London School, the City of London School for Girls, the Guildhall School of Music and Drama and the Museum of London; Christ's Hospital; City Bridge Trust; Community and Children's Services; Court of Aldermen; Court of Common Council; Culture, Heritage and Libraries; Epping Forest and Commons; Establishment; Finance; Freedom Applications; Gresham (city side); Guildhall Improvement; Hampstead Heath, Highgate Wood and Queen's Park; Investment; Livery; Markets; Open Spaces, City Gardens and West Ham Park; Planning and Transportation; Police; Policy and Resources; Port Health and Environmental Services and Standards Committees.

The City's estate, in the possession of which the City of London Corporation differs from other municipalities, is managed by the City Lands and Bridge House Estates Committee, the chairmanship of which carries with it the title of chief commoner.

The Honourable the Irish Society, which manages the City Corporation's estates in Ulster, consists of a governor and five other aldermen, the recorder, and 19 common councilmen, of whom one is elected deputy governor.

THE LORD MAYOR 2013–14
The Rt. Hon. the Lord Mayor, Fiona Woolf*
Private Secretary, William Chapman
* Provisional at time of going to press

THE SHERIFFS 2013–14
Alderman Sir Paul Judge *(Tower)*; Robert Waddingham

OFFICERS, ETC
Town Clerk, John Barradell
Chamberlain, Chris Bilsland
Chief Commoner (2013), George Gillon
Clerk, The Honourable the Irish Society, C. Fisher

THE ALDERMEN
with office held and date of appointment to that office

Name and Ward	*Common Councilman*	*Alderman*	*Sheriff*	*Lord Mayor*
Sir David Howard, Bt., *Cornhill*	1972	1986	1997	2000
Sir Robert Finch, *Coleman Street*	–	1992	1999	2003
Sir David Lewis, *Broad Street*	–	2001	2006	2007
Ian Luder, *Castle Baynard*	1998	2005	2007	2008
Nicholas Anstee, *Aldersgate*	1987	1996	2003	2009
Sir Michael Bear, *Portsoken*	2003	2005	2007	2010
Sir David Wootton, *Langbourn*	2002	2005	2009	2011
Roger Gifford, *Cordwainer*	–	2004	2008	2012

All the above have passed the Civic Chair

Dr Andrew Parmley, *Vintry*	1992	2001	–	
Benjamin R. Hall, *Farringdon Wn.*	1995	2002	–	
Alison Gowman, *Dowgate*	1991	2002	–	
Gordon Haines, *Queenhithe*	–	2004	–	
Alan Yarrow, *Bridge & Bridge Wt.*	–	2007	–	
Jeffrey Evans, *Cheap*	–	2007	–	
Sir Paul Judge, *Tower*	–	2007	–	
Fiona Woolf, CBE, *Candlewick*	–	2007	2010	
David Graves, *Cripplegate*	–	2008	–	
John Garbutt, *Walbrook*	–	2009	–	
Neil Redcliffe, *Bishopsgate*	–	2009	–	
Peter Hewitt, *Aldgate*	–	2012	–	
Charles Bowman, *Lime Street*	–	2013	–	
Timothy Hailes, *Bassishaw*	–	2013	–	
Julian Malins, QC, *Farringdon Wt.*	–	2013	–	
Matthew Richardson, *Billingsgate*	–	2012	–	
William Russell, *Bread Street*	–	2013	–	

THE COMMON COUNCIL
Deputy: each common councilman so described serves as deputy to the alderman of her/his ward.

Abrahams, G. C. (2000)	*Farringdon Wt.*
Absalom, J. D. (1994)	*Farringdon Wt.*
Ayers, *Deputy* K. E., MBE (1996)	*Bassishaw*
Anderson, R. K. (2013)	*Aldersgate*
Bain-Stewart, A. (2005)	*Farringdon Wn.*
Barker, *Deputy* J. A., OBE (1981)	*Cripplegate Wn.*
Barrow, *Deputy* D. (2007)	*Aldgate*
Bennett, *Deputy* J. A. (2005)	*Broad Street*
Boden, C. P. (2013)	*Castle Baynard*
Boleat, M. J. (2002)	*Cordwainer*
Bradshaw, D. J. (1991)	*Cripplegate Wn.*
Brewster, J. W., OBE (2011)	Bishopsgate
Cassidy, *Deputy* M. J., CBE (1989)	*Coleman Street*
Catt, R. M. (2004)	*Castle Baynard*
Chadwick, R. A. H. (1994)	*Tower*
Challis, N. K. (2005)	*Castle Baynard*
Chapman, J. D. (2006)	*Langbourn*
Colthurst, H. N. A. (2013)	*Lime Street*
Cotgrove, D. (1991)	*Lime Street*
Cressey, N. (2009)	*Portsoken*
Currie, *Deputy* Miss S. E. M., OBE (1985)	*Cripplegate Wt.*
Davies, P. S. (2009)	*Broad Street*
Day, M. J. (2005)	*Bishopsgate*
Deane, A. J. (2011)	*Farringdon Wt.*
Dostalova, K. (2013)	*Farringdon Wn.*
Dove, W. H., MBE (1993)	*Bishopsgate*
Duckworth, S. D. (2000)	*Bishopsgate*
Dudley, Revd Dr M. R. (2002)	*Aldersgate*
Duffield, R. W. (2004)	*Farringdon Wn.*
Dunphy, P. G. (2009)	*Cornhill*
Eskenzi, *Deputy* A. N., CBE (1970)	*Farringdon Wn.*
Eve, *Deputy* R. A. (1980)	*Cheap*
Everett, K. M. (1984)	*Candlewick*
Farr, M. C. (1998)	*Walbrook*
Fernandes, S. A. (2009)	*Coleman Street*
Fletcher, J. W. (2011)	*Portsoken*
Fraser, S. J. (1993)	*Coleman Street*
Fraser, *Deputy* W. B., OBE (1981)	*Vintry*
Fredericks, M. B. (2008)	*Tower*
Frew, L. (2013)	*Walbrook*
Gani, I. S. (2013)	*Portsoken*
Gillon, G. M. F. (1995)	*Cordwainer*
Ginsburg, *Deputy* S. (1990)	*Bishopsgate*
Graves, A. C. (1985)	*Bishopsgate*
Haines, *Deputy* Revd S. D. (2005)	*Cornhill*
Harris, B. N. (2004)	*Bridge*
Haywood, C. M. (2013)	*Broad Street*
Hoffman, T. D. D. (2002)	*Vintry*
Holmes, A. (2013)	*Farringdon Wn.*
Howard, R. P. (2011)	*Lime Street*
Hudson, M. (2007)	*Castle Baynard*
Hyde, W. (2011)	*Bishopsgate*
Ingham Clark, J. (2013)	*Billingsgate*
James, Clare (2008)	*Farringdon Wn.*
Jones, G. P., QC (2013)	*Farringdon Wt.*
Jones, *Deputy* H. L. M. (2004)	*Portsoken*
King, *Deputy* A. J. N. (1999)	*Queenhithe*
Knowles, *Deputy* S. K., MBE (1984)	*Candlewick*
Lawrence, *Deputy* G. A. (2002)	*Farringdon Wt.*
Leck, P. (1998)	*Aldersgate*
Littlechild, V. (2009)	*Cripplegate Wn.*
Llewelyn-Davies, A. (2009)	*Billingsgate*
Lodge, O. A. W., TD (2009)	*Bread Street*
Lord, *Deputy* C. E., OBE (2009)	*Farringdon Wt.*
Lumley, J. S. P. (2013)	*Aldersgate*

McGuinness, *Deputy* C. S. (1997) *Castle Baynard*
McMurtie, A. S. (2013) *Coleman Street*
Malins, *Deputy* J. H., QC (1981) *Farringdon Wt.*
Martinelli, P. J. (2009) *Farringdon Wt.*
Mayhew, J. P. (1996) *Aldersgate*
Mead, *Deputy* Mrs W. (1997) *Farringdon Wt.*
Merrett, R. A. (2009) *Bassishaw*
Mooney, B. D. F. (1998) *Queenhithe*
Moore, G. W. (2009) *Cripplegate Wn.*
Morris, H. F. (2008) *Aldgate*
Moys, Mrs S. D. (2001) *Aldgate*
Nash, *Deputy* Mrs J. C., OBE (1983) *Aldersgate*
Newman, Mrs B. P., CBE (1989) *Aldersgate*
Owen-Ward, *Deputy* J. R., MBE (1983) *Bridge*
Page, M. (2002) *Farringdon Wn.*
Patel, D. (2013) *Aldgate*
Pembroke, Mrs A. M. F. (1978) *Cheap*
Pleasance, J. L. (2013) *Langbourn*
Pollard, J. H. G. (2002) *Dowgate*
Price, E. C. L. (2013) *Farringdon Wt.*
Priest, H. J. S. (2009) *Castle Baynard*
Pulman, *Deputy* G. A. G. (1983) *Tower*
Punter, C. (1993) *Cripplegate Wn.*
Regan, *Deputy* R. D. (1998) *Farringdon Wn.*
Regis, D. (2009) *Portsoken*
Richardson, A. F. M. (2013) *Farringdon Wt.*
Richardson, M. C. (2009) *Coleman Street*
Rogula, E. (2008) *Lime Street*
Rounding, V. (2011) *Farringdon Wn.*
Scott, J. G. S. (1999) *Broad Street*
Seaton, I. (2009) *Bassishaw*
Shilson, *Deputy*, G. R. E., DPHIL (2009) *Bread Street*
Simons, J. L. (2004) *Castle Baynard*
Sleigh, T. (2013) *Bishopsgate*
Smith, G. M. (2013) *Farringdon Wn.*
Snyder, *Deputy* Sir Michael (1986) *Cordwainer*
Starling, Mrs A. J. (2006) *Cripplegate Wt.*
Streeter, P. T. (2013) *Bishopsgate*
Thompson, D. J. (2004) *Aldgate*
Thomson, *Deputy* J. M. D. (2013) *Walbrook*
Tomlinson, J. (2004) *Cripplegate Wt.*
Tumbridge, J. R. (2009) *Tower*
Welbank, *Deputy* M. (2005) *Billingsgate*
Wheatley, M. R. P. H. D. (2013) *Dowgate*
Woodhouse, P. (2013) *Langbourn*

THE CITY GUILDS (LIVERY COMPANIES)

The constitution of the livery companies has been unchanged for centuries. There are three ranks of membership: freemen, liverymen and assistants. A person can become a freeman by patrimony (through a parent having been a freeman); by servitude (through having served an apprenticeship to a freeman); or by redemption (by purchase).

Election to the livery is the prerogative of the company, who can elect any of its freemen as liverymen. Assistants are usually elected from the livery and form a Court of Assistants which is the governing body of the company. The master (in some companies called the prime warden) is elected annually from the assistants.

The register for 2013–14 lists 25,225 liverymen of the guilds entitled to vote at elections at Common Hall.

The order of precedence, omitting extinct companies, is given in parentheses after the name of each company in the list below. In certain companies the election of master or prime warden for the year does not take place until the autumn. In such cases the master or prime warden for 2012–13, rather than 2013–14, is given.

THE TWELVE GREAT COMPANIES

In order of civic precedence

MERCERS *(1). Hall,* Mercers' Hall, Ironmonger Lane, London EC2V 8HE *Livery,* 237. *Clerk,* Menna McGregor *Master,* Simon Wathen

GROCERS *(2). Hall,* Grocers' Hall, Princes Street, London EC2R 8AD *Livery,* 338. *Clerk,* Brig. Robert Pridham, OBE *Master,* Henry Colthurst

DRAPERS *(3). Hall,* Drapers' Hall, Throgmorton Avenue, London EC2N 2DQ *Livery,* 310. *Clerk,* Col. Richard Winstanley, OBE *Master,* Adm. Lord Boyce, KG, GCB, OBE

FISHMONGERS *(4). Hall,* Fishmongers' Hall, London Bridge, London EC4R 9EL *Livery,* 388. *Clerk,* Maj.-Gen. Colin Boag, CB, CBE *Prime Warden,* Andrew Morgan

GOLDSMITHS *(5). Hall,* Goldsmiths' Hall, Foster Lane, London EC2V 6BN *Livery,* 313. *Clerk,* Rear-Adm. Richard Melly *Prime Warden,* R. D. Agutter

MERCHANT TAYLORS *(6/7). Hall,* Merchant Taylors' Hall, 30 Threadneedle Street, London EC2R 8JB *Livery,* 330. *Clerk,* Rear-Adm. Nicholas Harris, CB, MBE *Master,* J. A. J. Price

SKINNERS *(6/7). Hall,* Skinners' Hall, 8 Dowgate Hill, London EC4R 2SP *Livery,* 400. *Clerk,* Maj.-Gen. Brian Plummer, CBE *Master,* Dudley Buchanan

HABERDASHERS *(8). Hall,* Haberdashers' Hall, 18 West Smithfield, London EC1A 9HQ *Livery,* 314. *Clerk,* Cdre Philip Thicknesse, RN *Master,* J. E. N. Bates

SALTERS *(9). Hall,* Salters' Hall, 4 Fore Street, London EC2Y 5DE *Livery,* 175. *Clerk,* Capt. David Morris, RN *Master,* Mark Callingham

IRONMONGERS *(10). Hall,* Ironmongers' Hall, 1 Shaftesbury Place, London EC2Y 8AA *Livery,* 98. *Clerk,* Col. Hamon Massey *Master,* R. J. Patteson-Knight

VINTNERS *(11). Hall,* Vintners' Hall, Upper Thames Street, London EC4V 3BG *Livery,* 352. *Clerk,* Brig. Jonathan Bourne-May *Master,* Anthony Sykes

CLOTHWORKERS *(12). Hall,* Clothworkers' Hall, Dunster Court, Mincing Lane, London EC3R 7AH *Livery,* 200. *Clerk,* Andrew Blessley *Master,* Christopher McLean May

OTHER CITY GUILDS

In alphabetical order

ACTUARIES *(91).* Cheapside House, 138 Cheapside, London EC2V 6BW *Livery,* 234. *Clerk,* David Johnson *Master,* Charles Cowling

AIR PILOTS AND AIR NAVIGATORS *(81). Hall,* Cobham House, 9 Warwick Court, Gray's Inn, London WC1R 5DJ *Livery,* 600. *Clerk,* Paul Tacon *Grand Master,* HRH the Duke of York, KG, GCVO, ADC(P) *Master,* Tudor Owen

APOTHECARIES *(58). Hall,* Apothecaries' Hall, 14 Black Friars Lane, London EC4V 6EJ *Livery,* 1,250. *Clerk,* A. Wallington-Smith *Master,* Dr P. J. H. Tooley

ARBITRATORS *(93).* 13 Hall Gardens, Colney Heath, St Albans, Herts AL4 0QF *Livery,* 108. *Clerk,* Gaye Duffy *Master,* Dr Derek Ross

ARMOURERS AND BRASIERS *(22). Hall,* Armourers' Hall, 81 Coleman Street, London EC2R 5BJ *Livery,* 128. *Clerk,* Cdre Christopher Waite, RN *Master,* Jonathan Stopford Haw

BAKERS *(19). Hall,* Bakers' Hall, 9 Harp Lane, London EC3R 6DP *Livery,* 350. *Clerk,* Cdre M. W. Westwood, RN *Master,* David Bentley

BARBERS *(17). Hall,* Barber-Surgeons' Hall, Monkwell Square, Wood Street, London EC2Y 5BL *Livery,* 220. *Clerk,* Col. Peter Durrant, MBE *Master,* Lord Ribeiro, CBE, FRCS

BASKETMAKERS *(52).* 79 Barnfield Wood Road, Beckenham BR3 6ST *Livery,* 300. *Clerk,* Julie Fox *Prime Warden,* Graham Aslet

BLACKSMITHS *(40)*. 9 Little Trinity Lane, London EC4V 2AD *Livery,* 235. *Clerk,* Christopher Jeal *Prime Warden,* Adrian Oliver

BOWYERS *(38)*. 46 The Haydens, Tonbridge, Kent TN9 1NS, *Livery,* 88. *Clerk,* Richard Sawyer *Master,* Michael Wren

BREWERS *(14)*. *Hall,* Brewers' Hall, Aldermanbury Square, London EC2V 7HR *Livery,* 190. *Clerk,* David Ross, CBE *Master,* Stephen Goodyear

BRODERERS *(48)*. Ember House, 35–37 Creek Road, East Molesey, Surrey KT8 9BE *Livery,* 126. *Clerk,* Peter J. C. Crouch *Master,* Peter Lumley

BUILDERS MERCHANTS *(88)*. 4 College Hill, London EC4R 2RB *Livery,* 187. *Clerk,* T. Statham *Master,* David McIntosh

BUTCHERS *(24)*. *Hall,* Butchers' Hall, 87 Bartholomew Close, London EC1A 7EB *Livery,* 633. *Clerk,* Cdre Anthony Morrow, CVO *Master,* Ian Kelly

CARMEN *(77)*. Five Kings House, 1 Queen Street Place, London EC4R 1QS *Livery,* 500. *Clerk,* Walter Gill *Master,* Cdr R. M. H. Bawtree, OBE, RN

CARPENTERS *(26)*. *Hall,* Carpenters' Hall, 1 Throgmorton Avenue, London EC2N 2JJ *Livery,* 208. *Clerk,* Brig. Tim Gregson, MBE *Master,* Martin Mosley

CHARTERED ACCOUNTANTS *(86)*. Larksfield, Kent Hatch Road, Crockham Hill, Edenbridge, Kent TN8 6SX *Livery,* 339. *Clerk,* Peter Dickinson *Master,* W. M. T. Fowle, CBE

CHARTERED ARCHITECTS *(98)*. 164 Stockbridge Road, Winchester SO22 6RW *Livery,* 165. *Clerk,* Ian Head *Master,* Jackie Howes

CHARTERED SECRETARIES AND ADMINISTRATORS *(87)*. 3rd Floor, Saddlers' House, 40 Gutter Lane, London EC2V 6BR *Livery,* 270. *Clerk,* Hugo Summerson, FRICS *Master,* Mr Zbigniew Lis

CHARTERED SURVEYORS *(85)*. 75 Meadway Drive, Horsell, Woking, Surrey GU21 4TF *Livery,* 365. *Clerk,* Amanda Jackson *Master,* Elizabeth Edwards

CLOCKMAKERS *(61)*. Salters' Hall, 4 Fore Street, London EC2Y 5DE *Livery,* 289. *Clerk,* Lt.-Col. O. P. Bartrum, MBE *Master,* Prof. Paul Jarrett, FRCS

COACHMAKERS AND COACH-HARNESS MAKERS *(72)*. 48 Aldernay Street,London SW1V 4EX *Livery,* 500. *Clerk,* Cdr Mark Leaning, RN *Master,* Hon. Michael Callaghan

CONSTRUCTORS *(99)*. 5 Delft Close, Locks Heath, Southampton SO31 7TQ *Livery,* 134. *Clerk,* Kim Tyrrell *Master,* Alan Longhurst

COOKS *(35)*. 18 Solent Drive, Warsash, Southampton SO31 9HB *Livery,* 75. *Clerk,* Vice-Adm. P. J. Wilkinson, CB, CVO *Master,* B. F. W. Baughan

COOPERS *(36)*. *Hall,* Coopers' Hall, 13 Devonshire Square, London EC2M 4TH *Livery,* 260. *Clerk,* Lt.-Col. Adrian Carroll *Master,* M. A. Zuckerman

CORDWAINERS *(27)*. Clothworkers' Hall, Dunster Court, Mincing Lane, London EC3R 7AH *Livery,* 181. *Clerk,* John Miller *Master,* Glenn Shaw

CURRIERS *(29)*. 4 Little Orchard Place, Esher, Surrey KT10 9PP *Livery,* 100. *Clerk,* Capt. Simon Bevan, RN *Master,* Graham Stow, CBE

CUTLERS *(18)*. *Hall,* Cutlers' Hall, Warwick Lane, London EC4M 7BR *Livery,* 100. *Clerk,* Rupert Meacher *Master,* Christopher Robinson

DISTILLERS *(69)*. 1 The Sanctuary, Westminster, London SW1P 3JT *Livery,* 260. *Clerk,* Edward Macey-Dare *Master,* David Raines

DYERS *(13)*. *Hall,* Dyers' Hall, 10 Dowgate Hill, London EC4R 2ST *Livery,* 136. *Clerk,* J. R. Vaizey *Prime Warden,* J. M. Holme

ENGINEERS *(94)*. Wax Chandlers' Hall, 6 Gresham Street, London EC2V 7AD *Livery,* 330. *Clerk,* Tony Willenbruch *Master,* Air Vice-Marshal Graham Skinner, CBE

ENVIRONMENTAL CLEANERS *(97)*. 10 Seaton Close, Lynclen Gate, Putney SW15 3TJ *Livery,* 185. *Clerk,* Keith Lambert *Master,* Maureen Marden

FAN MAKERS *(76)*. Skinners' Hall, 8 Dowgate Hill, London EC4R 2SP *Livery,* 202. *Clerk,* Martin Davies *Master,* Douglas Clasby

FARMERS *(80)*. *Hall,* The Farmers' and Fletchers' Hall, 3 Cloth Street, London EC1A 7LD *Livery,* 330. *Clerk,* Col. David King, OBE *Master,* Baroness Byford

FARRIERS *(55)*. 19 Queen Street, Chipperfield, Kings Langley, Herts WD4 9BT *Livery,* 351. *Clerk,* Charlotte Clifford *Master,* Simon Fleet

FELTMAKERS *(63)*. Post Cottage,Greywell, Hook, Hants RG29 1DA *Livery,* 180. *Clerk,* Maj. J. T. H. Coombs *Master,* Simon Bartley

FIREFIGHTERS *(108)*. The Insurance Hall, 20 Aldermanbury, London EC2V 7HY *Livery,* 103. *Clerk,* Sir Martin Bonham, Bt. *Master,* Beryl Jeffery

FLETCHERS *(39)*. *Hall,* The Farmers' and Fletchers' Hall, 3 Cloth Street, London EC1A 7LD *Livery,* 143. *Clerk,* Kate Pink *Master,* Mrs Lesley Agutter

FOUNDERS *(33)*. *Hall,* Founders' Hall, 1 Cloth Fair, London EC1A 7JQ *Livery,* 175. *Clerk,* J. P. Knight *Master,* A. J. Gillett

FRAMEWORK KNITTERS *(64)*. The Grange, Kimcote, Lutterworth LE17 5RU *Livery,* 200. *Clerk,* Capt. Shaun Mackaness *Master,* Stephen Woolfe

FRUITERERS *(45)*. Chapelstones, 84 High Street, Codford St Mary, Warminster BA12 0ND *Livery,* 283. *Clerk,* Lt.-Col. L. French *Master,* Prof. J. F. Price

FUELLERS *(95)*. 26 Merrick Square, London SE1 4JB *Livery,* 141. *Clerk,* Sir Anthony Reardon Smith, Bt. *Master,* Dennis Woods

FURNITURE MAKERS *(83)*. *Hall,* Furniture Makers' Hall, 12 Austin Friars, London EC2N 2HE *Livery,* 205. *Clerk,* Jonny Westbrooke *Master,* Jonathan Hindle

GARDENERS *(66)*. 25 Luke Street, London EC2A 4AR *Livery,* 298. *Clerk,* Maj. Jeremy Herrtage *Master,* HRH Earl of Wessex

GIRDLERS *(23)*. *Hall,* Girdlers' Hall, Basinghall Avenue, London EC2V 5DD *Livery,* 80. *Clerk,* Brig. Ian Rees *Master,* Neil Seaton

GLASS SELLERS *(71)*. North Farm House, High Road, Loughton IG10 4JJ *Livery,* 230. *Clerk,* Vincent Emms *Master,* Alderman Dr Andrew Parmley

GLAZIERS AND PAINTERS OF GLASS *(53)*. *Hall,* Glaziers' Hall, 9 Montague Close, London SE1 9DD *Livery,* 292. *Clerk,* Cdr Andrew Gordon-Lennox *Master,* John Dallimore

GLOVERS *(62)*. Seniors Farmhouse, Semley, Shaftesbury, Dorset SP7 9AX *Livery,* 250. *Clerk,* T. D. Butler *Master,* Alison J. Gowman

GOLD AND SILVER WYRE DRAWERS *(74)*. 9A Prince of Wales Mansions, Prince of Wales Drive, London SW11 4BG *Livery,* 280. *Clerk,* Cdr. R. House *Master,* R. J. d'O. Hope

GUNMAKERS *(73)*. The Proof House, 48–50 Commercial Road, London E1 1LP *Livery,* 350. *Clerk,* John Allen *Master,* S. R. de C. Grant-Rennick

HACKNEY CARRIAGE DRIVERS *(104)*. 25 The Grove, Parkfield, Latimer, Bucks HP5 1UE *Livery,* 97. *Clerk,* Mary Whitworth *Master,* G. Woodhouse

HORNERS *(54)*. PO Box 145, Hill House, 210 Upper Richmond Road, London SW15 6NP *Livery,* 225. *Clerk,* Jonathan Charles Mead *Master,* Keith Pinker

INFORMATION TECHNOLOGISTS *(100)*. *Hall,* Information Technologists' Hall, 39A Bartholomew Close, London EC1A 7JN *Livery,* 349. *Clerk,* Mike Jenkins *Master,* Michael Webster

INNHOLDERS *(32). Hall,* Innholders' Hall, 30 College Street, London EC4R 2RH *Livery,* 149. *Clerk,* Dougal Bulger *Master,* A. J. Brighton

INSURERS *(92).* The Hall, 20 Aldermanbury, London EC2V 7HY *Livery,* 387. *Clerk,* Mrs S. Clark *Master,* B. Masojada

INTERNATIONAL BANKERS *(106).* 12 Austin Friars, London EC2N 2HE *Livery,* 212. *Clerk,* Nicholas Westgarth *Master,* Jane Platt, CBE

JOINERS AND CEILERS *(41).* 75 Meadway Drive, Horsell, Woking, Surrey GU21 4TF *Livery,* 115. *Clerk,* Amanda Jackson *Master,* Anthony Bown

LAUNDERERS *(89). Hall,* Launderers' Hall, 9 Montague Close, London Bridge, London SE1 9DD *Livery,* 215. *Clerk,* Terry Winter *Master,* Ivan Kerry

LEATHERSELLERS *(15).* 21 Garlick Hill, London EC4V 2AU *Livery,* 150. *Clerk,* Brig. David Santa-Olalla *Master,* Martin Pebody

LIGHTMONGERS *(96).* 1 Manor House Garden, High Street, Wanstead, London E11 2RU *Livery,* 168. *Clerk,* Phillip Hyde *Master,* John Harding

LORINERS *(57).* 30 Elm Park, Royal Wootton Bassett, Wiltshire SN4 7TA *Livery,* 400. *Clerk,* Honor Page *Master,* D. S. Frost, CBE

MAKERS OF PLAYING CARDS *(75).* 256 St David's Square, London E14 3WE *Livery,* 147. *Clerk,* David Barrett *Master,* Revd Canon N. Nicholson

MANAGEMENT CONSULTANTS *(105).* Skinners' Hall, 8 Dowgate Hill, London EC4R 2SP *Livery,* 177. *Clerk,* Leslie Johnson *Master,* Geoff Llewellyn

MARKETORS *(90).* Plaisterers' Hall, 1 London Wall, London EC2Y 5JU *Livery,* 250. *Clerk,* D. John Hammond *Master,* Sally Muggeridge, FCIM

MASONS *(30).* 22 Cannon Hill, Southgate, London N14 6LG *Livery,* 163. *Clerk,* Heather Rowell *Master,* John Burton, MBE

MASTER MARINERS *(78). Hall,* HQS Wellington, Temple Stairs, Victoria Embankment, London WC2R 2PN *Livery,* 160. *Clerk,* Cdre Angus Menzies, RN *Master,* Capt. John Hughes

MUSICIANS *(50).* 6th Floor, 2 London Wall Building, London EC2M 5PP *Livery,* 417. *Clerk,* Hugh Lloyd *Master,* Sir Anthony Cleaver

NEEDLEMAKERS *(65).* PO Box 3682, Windsor, Berkshire SL4 3WR *Livery,* 200. *Clerk,* Philip Grant *Master,* Sue Kent

PAINTER-STAINERS *(28). Hall,* Painters' Hall, 9 Little Trinity Lane, London EC4V 2AD *Livery,* 310. *Clerk,* C. J. Twyman *Master,* H. S. Evans

PATTENMAKERS *(70).* 3 The High Street, Sutton Valence, Kent ME17 3AG *Livery,* 200. *Clerk,* Col. R. Murfin, TD *Master,* S. J. Goodman

PAVIORS *(56).* Pavior's House, Charter House, Charterhouse Square, London, EC1M 6AN*Livery,* 283. *Clerk,* John Freestone *Master,* John Dance

PEWTERERS *(16). Hall,* Pewterers' Hall, Oat Lane, London EC2V 7DE *Livery,* 141. *Clerk,* Capt. Paddy Watson, RN *Master,* Michael Johnson

PLAISTERERS *(46). Hall,* Plaisterers' Hall, 1 London Wall, London EC2Y 5JU *Livery,* 236. *Clerk,* Nigel Bamping *Master,* D. Bradshaw

PLUMBERS *(31).* Wax Chandlers' Hall, 6 Gresham Street, London EC2V 7AD *Livery,* 360. *Clerk,* Air Cdre Paul Nash, OBE *Master,* Nick Gale

POULTERS *(34).* 57 Cullum Welch House, Golden Lane Estate, London EC17 0SH *Livery,* 204. *Clerk,* Vernon Ashford *Master,* Harvey Peebles

SADDLERS *(25). Hall,* Saddlers' Hall, 40 Gutter Lane, London EC2V 6BR *Livery,* 75. *Clerk,* Col. N. Lithgow, CBE *Master,* Mrs P. Jameson

SCIENTIFIC INSTRUMENT MAKERS *(84).* 9 Montague Close, London SE1 9DD *Livery,* 185. *Clerk,* Neville Watson *Master,* D. W. Kent

SCRIVENERS *(44).* HQS Wellington, Temple Stairs, Victoria Embankment, London WC2R 2PN *Livery,* 183. *Clerk,* Giles Cole *Master,* John Tunesi of Liongam

SECURITY PROFESSIONALS *(108).* 34 Tye Green, Glemsford, Suffolk CO10 7RG *Livery,* 150. *Clerk,* Tricia Boswell *Master,* Gp Capt. Brian Hughes

SHIPWRIGHTS *(59).* Ironmongers Hall, Shaftesbury Place, London EC2Y 8AA *Livery,* 450. *Clerk,* Lt.-Col. Andy Milne, RM *Prime Warden,* Simon Robinson, CBE *Grand Master,* HRH the Prince of Wales, KG, KT, GCB

SOLICITORS *(79).* 4 College Hill, London EC4R 2RB *Livery,* 350. *Clerk,* Neil Cameron *Master,* David McIntosh

SPECTACLE MAKERS *(60).* Apothecaries' Hall, Black Friars Lane, London EC4V 6EL *Livery,* 390. *Clerk,* Lt.-Col. John Salmon, OBE *Master,* C. E. Hunt

STATIONERS AND NEWSPAPER MAKERS *(47). Hall,* Stationers' Hall, Ave Maria Lane, London EC4M 7DD *Livery,* 520. *Clerk,* William Alden, MBE *Master,* Tom Hempenstall

TALLOW CHANDLERS *(21). Hall,* Tallow Chandlers' Hall, 4 Dowgate Hill, London EC4R 2SH *Livery,* 180. *Clerk,* Brig. D. Homer, MBE *Master,* Ian Robertson

TAX ADVISERS *(107).* 191 West End Road, Ruislip, Middx HA4 6LD *Freemen,* 143. *Clerk,* Paul Herbage *Master,* John Dewhurst

TIN PLATE WORKERS (ALIAS WIRE WORKERS) *(67).* PO Box 71002, London W4 9FH *Livery,* 220. *Clerk,* Piers Baker *Master,* Colin Hayfield

TOBACCO PIPE MAKERS AND TOBACCO BLENDERS *(82).* 23 Florence Road, Sanderstead, Surrey CR2 0PQ *Livery,* 132. *Clerk,* Paul D. Bethel *Master,* John Nokes

TURNERS *(51).* Skinner's Hall, 8 Dowgate Hill, London EC4R 2SP *Livery,* 186. *Clerk,* Alex Robertson *Master,* Rhidian Jones

TYLERS AND BRICKLAYERS *(37).* 3 Farmers' Way, Seer Green, Bucks HP9 2YY *Livery,* 155. *Clerk,* John Brooks *Master,* David Cole-Adams

UPHOLDERS *(49).* E clerk@upholders.co.uk, *Livery,* 171. *Clerk,* Susan Nevard *Master,* Nick Meyer

WATER CONSERVATORS *(102).* The Lark, 2 Bell Lane, Worlington, Bury St Edmunds, Suffolk IP28 8SE *Livery,* 210. *Clerk,* Ralph Riley *Master,* Ivor Richards, OBE

WAX CHANDLERS *(20). Hall,* Wax Chandlers' Hall, 6 Gresham Street, London EC2V 7AD *Livery,* 120. *Clerk,* Georgina Brown *Master,* Lt.-Col. John Chambers

WEAVERS *(42).* Saddlers' House, Gutter Lane, London EC2V 6BR *Livery,* 125. *Clerk,* John Snowdon *Upper Bailiff,* Jolyon Tibbitts

WHEELWRIGHTS *(68).* 16 Gordon Avenue, Twickenham TW1 1NQ *Livery,* 220. *Clerk,* Bridget Hynard *Master,* Stephen Kirk

WOOLMEN *(43).* The Old Post Office, 56 Lower Way, Great Brickhill, Bucks MK17 9AG *Livery,* 150. *Clerk,* Gillian Wilson *Master,* Bill Clark

WORLD TRADERS *(101).* 13 Hall Gardens, Colney Heath, St. Albans, Herts AL4 0QF *Livery,* 240. *Clerk,* Mrs Gaye Duffy *Master,* Dr Heather McLaughlin

PARISH CLERKS *(No Livery*).* Acreholt, 33 Medstead Road, Beech, Alton, Hants GU34 4AD *Members,* 91. *Clerk,* Alana Coombes *Master,* Prof. Jonathan Rawlings

WATERMEN AND LIGHTERMEN *(No Livery*). Hall,* Watermen's Hall, 16–18 St Mary-at-Hill, London EC3R 8EF *Craft Owning Freemen,* 387. *Clerk,* Colin Middlemiss *Master,* Robert Prentice

* Parish Clerks and Watermen and Lightermen have requested to remain with no livery

WALES

Cymru

The principality of Wales (Cymru) occupies the extreme west of the central southern portion of the island of Great Britain, with a total area of 20,778 sq. km (8,022 sq. miles): land 20,733 sq. km (8,005 sq. miles); inland water 45 sq. km (17 sq. miles). It is bordered in the north by the Irish Sea, in the south by the Bristol Channel, in the east by the English counties of Cheshire West and Chester, Shropshire, Herefordshire and Gloucestershire, and in the west by St George's Channel.

Across the Menai Straits is Ynys Mon (Isle of Anglesey) (715 sq. km/276 sq. miles), communication with which is facilitated by the Menai Suspension Bridge (305m/1,000ft long) built by Telford in 1826, and by the Britannia Bridge (351m/1,151ft), a two-tier road and rail truss arch design, rebuilt in 1972 after a fire destroyed the original tubular railway bridge built by Stephenson in 1850. Holyhead harbour, on Holy Isle (north-west of Anglesey), provides ferry services to Dublin (113km/70 miles).

POPULATION

The population at the 2011 census was 3,063,456 (men 1,504,228; women 1,559,228). The average density of population in 2011 was 147 persons per sq. km (382 per sq. mile).

RELIEF

Wales is a country of extensive tracts of high plateau and shorter stretches of mountain ranges deeply dissected by river valleys. Lower-lying ground is largely confined to the coastal belt and the lower parts of the valleys. The highest mountains are those of Snowdonia in the north-west (Snowdon, 1,085m/3,559ft and Aran Fawddwy, 906m/2,971ft). Snowdonia is also home to Cader Idris (Pen y Gadair, 892m/2,928ft). Other high peaks are to be found in the Cambrian range (Plynlimon, 752m/2,467ft), and the Black Mountains, Brecon Beacons and Black Forest ranges in the south-east (Pen y Fan, 886m/2,906ft; Waun Fâch, 811m/2,660ft; Carmarthen Van, 802m/2,630ft).

HYDROGRAPHY

The principal river in Wales is the Severn, which flows from the slopes of Plynlimon to the English border. The Wye (209km/130 miles) also rises in the slopes of Plynlimon. The Usk (90km/56 miles) flows into the Bristol Channel through Gwent. The Dee (113km/70 miles) rises in Bala Lake and flows through the Vale of Llangollen, where an aqueduct (built by Telford in 1805) carries the Pontcysyllte branch of the Shropshire Union Canal across the valley. The estuary of the Dee is the navigable portion, it is 23km (14 miles) in length and about 8km (5 miles) in breadth. The Towy (109km/68 miles), Teifi (80km/50 miles), Taff (64km/40 miles), Dovey (48km/30 miles), Taf (40km/25 miles) and Conway (39km/24 miles) are wholly Welsh rivers.

The largest natural lake is Bala (Llyn Tegid) in Gwynedd, nearly 7km (4 miles) long and 1.6km (1 mile) wide. Lake Vyrnwy is an artificial reservoir, about the size of Bala, it forms the water supply of Liverpool; Birmingham's water is supplied from reservoirs in the Elan and Claerwen valleys.

WELSH LANGUAGE

According to the 2011 census results, the percentage of people aged three years and over who are able to speak Welsh is:

Blaenau Gwent	7.8	Neath Port Talbot	15.3
Bridgend	9.7	Newport	9.3
Caerphilly	11.2	Pembrokeshire	19.2
Cardiff	11.1	Powys	18.6
Carmarthenshire	43.9	Rhondda Cynon Taf	12.3
Ceredigion	47.3	Swansea	11.4
Conwy	27.4	Torfaen	9.8
Denbighshire	24.6	Vale of Glamorgan	10.8
Flintshire	13.2	Wrexham	12.9
Gwynedd	65.4	Ynys Mon (Isle of Anglesey)	57.2
Merthyr Tydfil	8.9		
Monmouthshire	9.9	*Total in Wales*	19.0

FLAG

The flag of Wales, the Red Dragon *(Y Ddraig Goch)*, is a red dragon on a field divided white over green (per fess argent and vert a dragon passant gules). The flag was augmented in 1953 by a royal badge on a shield encircled with a riband bearing the words *Ddraig Goch Ddyry Cychwyn* and imperially crowned, but this augmented flag is rarely used.

EARLY HISTORY

The earliest inhabitants of whom there is any record appear to have been subdued or exterminated by the Goidels (a people of Celtic race) in the Bronze Age. A further invasion of Celtic Brythons and Belgae followed in the ensuing Iron Age. The Roman conquest of southern Britain and Wales was for some time successfully opposed by Caratacus (Caractacus or Caradog), chieftain of the Catuvellauni and son of Cunobelinus (Cymbeline). South-east Wales was subjugated and the legionary fortress at Caerleon-on-Usk established by around AD 75–7; the conquest of Wales was completed by Agricola around AD 78. Communications were opened up by the construction of military roads from Chester to Caerleon-on-Usk and Caerwent, and from Chester to Conwy (and thence to Carmarthen and Neath). Christianity was introduced in the fourth century, during the Roman occupation.

ANGLO-SAXON ATTACKS

The Anglo-Saxon invaders of southern Britain drove the Celts into the mountain stronghold of Wales, and into Strathclyde (Cumberland and south-west Scotland) and Cornwall, giving them the name of *Waelisc* (Welsh), meaning 'foreign'. The West Saxons' victory of Deorham (AD 577) isolated Wales from Cornwall and the battle of Chester (AD 613) cut off communication with Strathclyde and northern Britain. In the eighth century the boundaries of the Welsh were further restricted by the annexations of Offa, King of Mercia, and counter-attacks were largely prevented by the construction of an artificial boundary from the Dee to the Wye (Offa's Dyke).

In the ninth century Rhodri Mawr (844–878) united the country and successfully resisted further incursions of the Saxons by land and raids of Norse and Danish pirates by sea, but at his death his three provinces of Gwynedd (north), Powys (central) and Deheubarth (south) were divided among his three sons, Anarawd, Mervyn and Cadell. Cadell's son Hywel Dda ruled a large part of Wales and codified its laws but the provinces were not united again until the rule of Llewelyn ap Seisyllt (husband of the heiress of Gwynedd) from 1018 to 1023.

THE NORMAN CONQUEST

After the Norman conquest of England, William I created palatine counties along the Welsh frontier, and the Norman barons began to make encroachments into Welsh territory. The Welsh princes recovered many of their losses during the civil wars of Stephen's reign (1135–54), and in the early 13th century Owen Gruffydd, prince of Gwynedd, was the dominant figure in Wales. Under Llywelyn ap Iorwerth (1194–1240) the Welsh united in powerful resistance to English incursions and Llywelyn's privileges and *de facto* independence were recognised in the Magna Carta. His grandson, Llywelyn ap Gruffydd, was the last native prince; he was killed in 1282 during hostilities between the Welsh and English, allowing Edward I of England to establish his authority over the country. On 7 February 1301, Edward of Caernarvon, son of Edward I, was created Prince of Wales, a title subsequently borne by the eldest son of the sovereign.

Strong Welsh national feeling continued, expressed in the early 15th century in the rising led by Owain Glyndwr, but the situation was altered by the accession to the English throne in 1485 of Henry VII of the Welsh House of Tudor. Wales was politically annexed by England under the Act of Union of 1535, which extended English laws to the principality and gave it parliamentary representation for the first time.

EISTEDDFOD

The Welsh are a distinct nation, with a language and literature of their own; the national bardic festival (Eisteddfod), instituted by Prince Rhys ap Griffith in 1176, is still held annually.

PRINCIPAL CITIES

There are six cities in Wales (with date city status conferred): Bangor (pre-1900), Cardiff (1905), Newport (2002), St Asaph (2012), St David's (1994) and Swansea (1969).

Cardiff and Swansea have also been granted Lord Mayoralities.

CARDIFF

Cardiff *(Caerdydd)*, at the mouth of the rivers Taff, Rhymney and Ely, is the capital city of Wales and at the 2001 census had a population of 305,353. The city has changed dramatically in recent years following the regeneration of Cardiff Bay and construction of a barrage, which has created a permanent freshwater lake and waterfront for the city. As the capital city, Cardiff is home to the National Assembly for Wales and is a major administrative, retail, business and cultural centre.

The city is home to many fine buildings including the City Hall, Cardiff Castle, Llandaff Cathedral, the National Museum of Wales, university buildings, law courts and the Temple of Peace and Health. The Millennium Stadium opened in 1999 and has hosted high-profile events since 2001.

SWANSEA

Swansea *(Abertawe)* is a seaport with a population of 223,293 at the 2001 census. The Gower peninsula was brought within the city boundary under local government reform in 1974.

The principal buildings are the Norman Castle (rebuilt *c.*1330), the Royal Institution of South Wales, founded in 1835 (including library), the University of Wales Swansea at Singleton and the Guildhall, containing Frank Brangwyn's British Empire panels. The Dylan Thomas Centre, formerly the old Guildhall, was restored in 1995. More recent buildings include the County Hall, the Maritime Quarter Marina, the Wales National Pool and the National Waterfront Museum.

Swansea was chartered by the Earl of Warwick (1158–84), and further charters were granted by King John, Henry III, Edward II, Edward III and James II, Oliver Cromwell and the Marcher Lord William de Breos. It was formally invested with city status in 1969 by HRH The Prince of Wales.

LORD-LIEUTENANTS AND HIGH SHERIFFS

Area	*Lord-Lieutenant*	*High Sheriff (2013–14)*
Clwyd	Henry Fetherstonhaugh, OBE	Celia Jenkins
Dyfed	Hon. Robin Lewis, OBE	John Davies
Gwent	S. Boyle	Murray MacFarlane
Gwynedd	His Hon. Huw Daniel	Marian Wyn Jones
Mid Glamorgan	Kate Thomas, CVO	Rory McLaggan
Powys	Hon. Mrs E. Legge-Bourke, LVO	Bernard Harris, MBE
South Glamorgan	Dr Peter Beck, MD, FRCP	Morfudd Meredith
West Glamorgan	D. Byron Lewis	Gaynor Richards, MBE

LOCAL COUNCILS

Council	*Administrative Headquarters*	*Telephone*	*Population**	*Council Tax†*	*Chief Executive*
Blaenau Gwent	Ebbw Vale	01495-311556	69,814	£1,526	David Waggett
Bridgend	Bridgend	01656-643643	139,178	£1,347	Darren Mepham
Caerphilly	Hengoed	01443-815588	178,806	£1,128	Sandra Aspinall *(interim)*
CARDIFF	Cardiff	029-2087 2087	346,090	£1,120	Christine Salter *(interim)*
Carmarthenshire	Carmarthen	01267-234567	183,777	£1,254	Mark James
Ceredigion	Aberaeron	01545-570881	75,922	£1,205	Bronwen Morgan
Conwy	Conwy	01492-574000	115,228	£1,176	Iwan Davies
Denbighshire	Ruthin	01824-706000	93,734	£1,336	Dr Mohammed Mehmet
Flintshire	Mold	01352-752121	152,506	£1,221	Colin Everett
Gwynedd	Caernarfon	01766-771000	121,874	£1,323	Harry Thomas
Merthyr Tydfil	Merthyr Tydfil	01685-725000	58,802	£1,428	Gareth Chapman
Monmouthshire	Cwmbran	01633-644644	91,323	£1,236	Paul Matthews
Neath Port Talbot	Port Talbot	01639-686868	139,812	£1,476	Steven Phillips
NEWPORT	Newport	01633-656656	145,736	£1,057	Will Godfrey
Pembrokeshire	Haverfordwest	01437-764551	122,439	£974	Bryn Parry-Jones
Powys	Llandrindod Wells	01597-827460	132,976	£1,203	Jeremy Patterson
Rhondda Cynon Taff	Tonypandy	01443-424000	234,410	£1,398	Keith Griffiths
SWANSEA	Swansea	01792-636000	239,023	£1,220	Jack Straw
Torfaen	Pontypool	01495-762200	91,075	£1,246	Alison Ward
Vale of Glamorgan	Barry	01446-700111	126,336	£1,206	vacant
Wrexham	Wrexham	01978-292000	134,844	£1,201	Dr Helen Paterson
Ynys Mon (Isle of Anglesey)	Ynys Mon	01248-750057	69,751	£1,194	Richard Parry Jones

* *Source:* ONS – Census 2011 (Crown copyright)
† Average Band D council tax bill 2013–14
Councils in CAPITAL LETTERS have city status

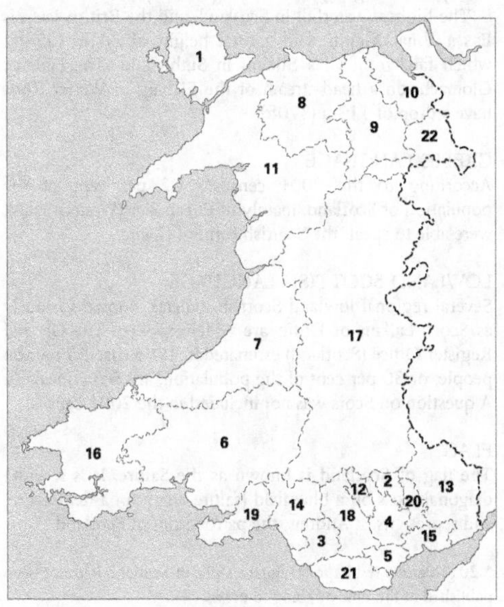

Key	*Council*	*Key*	*Council*
1	Anglesey (Ynys Mon)	12	Merthyr Tydfil
2	Blaenau Gwent	13	Monmouthshire
3	Bridgend	14	Neath Port Talbot
4	Caerphilly	15	Newport
5	Cardiff	16	Pembrokeshire
6	Carmarthenshire	17	Powys
7	Ceredigion	18	Rhondda Cynon Taff
8	Conwy	19	Swansea
9	Denbighshire	20	Torfaen
10	Flintshire	21	Vale of Glamorgan
11	Gwynedd	22	Wrexham

SCOTLAND

Scotland occupies the northern portion of the main island of Great Britain and includes the Inner and Outer Hebrides, Orkney, Shetland and many other islands. It lies between 60° 51′ 30″ and 54° 38′ N. latitude and between 1° 45′ 32″ and 6° 14′ W. longitude, with England to the southeast, the North Channel and the Irish Sea to the southwest, the Atlantic Ocean on the north and west, and the North Sea on the east.

The greatest length of the mainland (Cape Wrath to the Mull of Galloway) is 441km (274 miles), and the greatest breadth (Buchan Ness to Applecross) is 248km (154 miles). The customary measurement of the island of Great Britain is from the site of John o' Groats house, near Duncansby Head, Caithness, to Land's End, Cornwall, a total distance of 970km (603 miles) in a straight line and approximately 1,448km (900 miles) by road.

The total area of Scotland is 78,807 sq. km (30,427 sq. miles): land 77,907 sq. km (30,080 sq. miles), inland water 900 sq. km (347 sq. miles).

POPULATION

The population at the 2011 census was 5,295,403 (men 2,567,444; women 2,727,959). The average density of the population in 2011 was 67 persons per sq. km (174 per sq. mile).

RELIEF

There are three natural orographic divisions of Scotland. The southern uplands have their highest points in Merrick (843m/2,766ft), Rhinns of Kells (814m/2,669ft) and Cairnsmuir of Carsphairn (797m/2,614ft), in the west; and the Tweedsmuir Hills in the east (Broad Law 840m/2,756ft; Dollar Law 817m/2,682ft; Hartfell 808m/2,651ft).

The central lowlands, formed by the valleys of the Clyde, Forth and Tay, divide the southern uplands from the Highlands, which extend from close to the extreme north of the mainland to the central lowlands, and are divided into a northern and a southern system by the Great Glen.

The Grampian Mountains, the southern Highland system, include in the west Ben Nevis (1,343m/4,406ft), the highest point in the British Isles, and in the east the Cairngorm Mountains (Ben Macdui 1,309m/4,296ft; Braeriach 1,295m/4,248ft; Cairn Gorm 1,245m/4,084ft). The North West Highlands area contains the mountains of Wester and Easter Ross (Carn Eige 1,183m/3,880ft; Sgurr na Lapaich 1,151m/3,775ft).

Created, like the central lowlands, by a major geological fault, the Great Glen (97km/60 miles long) runs between Inverness and Fort William, and contains Loch Ness, Loch Oich and Loch Lochy. These are linked to each other and to the north-east and south-west coasts of Scotland by the Caledonian Canal, providing a navigable passage between the Moray Firth and the Inner Hebrides.

HYDROGRAPHY

The western coast is fragmented by peninsulas and islands, and indented by fjords (sea-lochs), the longest of which is Loch Fyne (68km/42 miles long) in Argyll. Although the east coast tends to be less fractured and lower, there are several great drowned inlets (firths), including the Firth of Forth, Firth of Tay and the Moray Firth, as well as the Firth of Clyde in the west.

The lochs are the principal hydrographic feature. The largest in Scotland and in Britain is Loch Lomond (70 sq. km/27 sq. miles), in the Grampian valleys and the longest and deepest is Loch Ness (39km/24 miles long and 244m/800ft deep), in the Great Glen.

The longest river is the Tay (188km/117 miles), noted for its salmon. It flows into the North Sea, with Dundee on the estuary, which is spanned by the Tay Bridge (3,136m/ 10,289ft) opened in 1887 and the Tay Road Bridge (2,245m/7,365ft) opened in 1966. Other noted salmon rivers are the Dee (145km/90 miles) which flows into the North Sea at Aberdeen, and the Spey (177km/110 miles), the swiftest flowing river in the British Isles, which flows into Moray Firth. The Tweed, which gave its name to the woollen cloth produced along its banks, marks in the lower stretches of its 154km (96 mile) course the border between Scotland and England.

The most important river commercially is the Clyde (171km/106 miles), formed by the junction of the Daer and Portrail water, which flows through the city of Glasgow to the Firth of Clyde. During its course it passes over the picturesque Falls of Clyde, Bonnington Linn (9m/30ft), Corra Linn (26m/84ft), Dundaff Linn (3m/10ft) and Stonebyres Linn (24m/80ft), above and below Lanark. The Forth (106km/66 miles), upon which stands Edinburgh, the capital, is spanned by the Forth Railway Bridge (1890), which is 1,625m (5,330ft) long, and the Forth Road Bridge (1964), which has a total length of 1,876m (6,156ft) (over water) and a single span of 914m (3,000ft).

The highest waterfall in Scotland, and the British Isles, is Eas a'Chùal Aluinn with a total height of 201m (658ft), which falls from Glas Bheinn in Sutherland. The Falls of Glomach, on a head-stream of the Elchaig in Wester Ross, have a drop of 113m (370ft).

GAELIC LANGUAGE

According to the 2001 census*, 1.2 per cent of the population of Scotland, mainly in Eilean Siar (Western Isles), were able to speak the Scottish form of Gaelic.

LOWLAND SCOTTISH LANGUAGE

Several regional lowland Scottish dialects, known variously as Scots, Lallans or Doric, are widely spoken. The General Register Office (Scotland) estimated in 1996 that 1.5 million people, or 30 per cent of the population, are Scots speakers. A question on Scots was not included in the 2001 census.

FLAG

The flag of Scotland is known as the Saltire. It is a white diagonal cross on a blue field (saltire argent in a field azure) and represents St Andrew, the patron saint of Scotland.

* 2011 census results for language skills in Scotland had not been published at the time of going to press

THE SCOTTISH ISLANDS*

ORKNEY

The Orkney Islands (total area 972 sq. km/376 sq. miles) lie about 10km (six miles) north of the mainland, separated from it by the Pentland Firth. Of the 90 islands and islets (holms and skerries) in the group, about one-third are inhabited.

* With the exception of the total populations of Orkney and Shetland, 2011 census results for the Scottish Islands had not been published at the time of going to press

The total population at the 2011 census was 21,349; the 2001 populations of the islands shown here include those of smaller islands forming part of the same council district.

Mainland, 15,339	Rousay, 267
Burray, 357	Sanday, 478
Eday, 121	Shapinsay, 300
Flotta, 81	South Ronaldsay, 854
Hoy, 392	Stronsay, 358
North Ronaldsay, 70	Westray, 563
Papa Westray, 65	

The islands are rich in prehistoric and Scandinavian remains, the most notable being the Stone Age village of Skara Brae, the burial chamber of Maes Howe, the many brochs (towers) and the 12th-century St Magnus Cathedral. Scapa Flow, between the Mainland and Hoy, was the war station of the British Grand Fleet from 1914 to 1919 and the scene of the scuttling of the surrendered German High Seas Fleet (21 June 1919).

Most of the islands are low-lying and fertile, and farming (principally beef cattle) is the main industry. Flotta, to the south of Scapa Flow, is the site of the oil terminal for the Piper, Claymore and Tartan fields in the North Sea.

The capital is Kirkwall (population 6,206) situated on Mainland.

SHETLAND

The Shetland Islands have a total area of 1,427 sq. km (551 sq. miles) and a population at the 2011 census of 23,167. They lie about 80km (50 miles) north of the Orkneys, with Fair Isle about half way between the two groups. Out Stack, off Muckle Flugga, 1.6km (one mile) north of Unst, is the most northerly part of the British Isles (60° 51′ 30″ N. lat.).

There are over 100 islands, of which 16 are inhabited. Populations at the 2001 census were:

Mainland, 17,575	Muckle Roe, 104
Bressay, 384	Trondra, 133
East Burra, 66	Unst, 720
Fair Isle, 69	West Burra, 784
Fetlar, 86	Whalsay, 1,034
Housay, 76	Yell, 957

Shetland's many archaeological sites include Jarlshof, Mousa and Clickhimin, and its long connection with Scandinavia has resulted in a strong Norse influence on its place names and dialect.

Industries include fishing, knitwear and farming. In addition to the fishing fleet there are fish processing factories, and the traditional handknitting of Fair Isle and Unst is now supplemented with machine-knitted garments. Farming is mainly crofting, with sheep being raised on the moorland and hills of the islands. Latterly the islands have become a centre of the North Sea oil industry, with pipelines from the Brent and Ninian fields running to the terminal at Sullom Voe, the largest of its kind in Europe.

The capital is Lerwick (population 6,830) situated on Mainland. Lerwick is the main centre for supply services for offshore oil exploration and development.

THE HEBRIDES

Until the late 13th century the Hebrides included other Scottish islands in the Firth of Clyde, the peninsula of Kintyre (Argyll), the Isle of Man, and the (Irish) Isle of Rathlin. The origin of the name is probably the Greek *Eboudai,* latinised as *Hebudes* by Pliny, and corrupted to its present form. The Norwegian name *Sudreyjar* (Southern Islands) was latinised as *Sodorenses,* a name that survives in the Anglican bishopric of Sodor and Man.

There are over 500 islands and islets, of which about 100 are inhabited, though mountainous terrain and extensive peat bogs mean that only a fraction of the total area is under cultivation. Stone, Bronze and Iron Age settlement has left many remains, including those at Callanish on Lewis, and Norse colonisation influenced language, customs and place names. Occupations include farming (mostly crofting and stock-raising), fishing and the manufacture of tweeds and other woollens. Tourism is also an important part of the economy.

The Inner Hebrides lie off the west coast of Scotland and are relatively close to the mainland. The largest and best-known is Skye (area 1,665 sq. km/643 sq. miles; pop. 9,251; chief town, Portree), which contains the Cuillin Hills (Sgurr Alasdair 993m/3,257ft), Bla Bheinn (928m/3,046ft), the Storr (719m/2,358ft) and the Red Hills (Beinn na Caillich 732m/2,403ft). Other islands in the Highland council area include Raasay (pop. 194), Rum, Eigg (pop. 131) and Muck.

Further south the Inner Hebridean islands include Arran (pop. 5,058) containing Goat Fell (874m/2,868ft); Coll and Tiree (pop. 934); Colonsay and Oronsay (pop. 113); Easdale (pop. 58); Gigha (pop. 110); Islay (area 608 sq. km/235 sq. miles; pop. 3,457); Jura (area 414 sq. km/160 sq. miles; pop. 188) with a range of hills culminating in the Paps of Jura (Beinn-an-Oir, 785m/2,576ft, and Beinn Chaolais, 755m/2,477ft); Lismore (pop. 146); Luing (pop. 220); and Mull (area 950 sq. km/367 sq. miles; pop. 2,696; chief town Tobermory) containing Ben More (967m/3,171ft).

The Outer Hebrides, separated from the mainland by the Minch, now form the Eilean Siar (Western Isles) council area (area 2,897 sq. km/1,119 sq. miles; pop. 26,502). The main islands are Lewis with Harris (area 1,994 sq. km/770 sq. miles, pop. 19,918), whose chief town, Stornoway, is the administrative headquarters; North Uist (pop. 1,320); South Uist (pop. 1,818); Benbecula (pop. 1,249) and Barra (pop. 1,078). Other inhabited islands include Bernera (233), Berneray (136), Eriskay (133), Grimsay (201), Scalpay (322) and Vatersay (94).

EARLY HISTORY

There is evidence of human settlement in Scotland dating from the third millennium BC, the earliest settlers being Mesolithic hunters and fishermen. Early in the second millennium BC, Neolithic farmers began to cultivate crops and rear livestock; their settlements were on the west coast and in the north, and included Skara Brae and Maeshowe (Orkney). Settlement by the early Bronze Age 'Beaker Folk', so-called from the shape of their drinking vessels, in eastern Scotland dates from about 1800 BC. Further settlement is believed to have occurred from 700 BC onwards, as tribes were displaced from further south by new incursions from the Continent and the Roman invasions from AD 43.

Julius Agricola, the Roman governor of Britain AD 77–84, extended the Roman conquests in Britain by advancing into Caledonia, culminating with a victory at Mons Graupius, probably in AD 84; he was recalled to Rome shortly afterwards and his forward policy was not pursued. Hadrian's Wall, mostly completed by AD 30, marked the northern frontier of the Roman empire except for the period between about AD 144 and 190 when the frontier moved north to the Forth-Clyde isthmus and a turf wall, the Antonine Wall, was manned.

After the Roman withdrawal from Britain, there were centuries of warfare between the Picts, Scots, Britons, Angles and Vikings. The Picts, generally accepted to be descended from the indigenous Iron Age people of northern Scotland, occupied the area north of the Forth. The Scots, a Gaelic-speaking people of northern Ireland, colonised the area of

Argyll and Bute (the kingdom of Dalriada) in the fifth century AD and then expanded eastwards and northwards. The Britons, speaking a Brythonic Celtic language, colonised Scotland from the south from the first century BC; they lost control of south-eastern Scotland (incorporated into the kingdom of Northumbria) to the Angles in the early seventh century but retained Strathclyde (south-western Scotland and Cumbria). Viking raids from the late eighth century were followed by Norse settlement in the western and northern isles, Argyll, Caithness and Sutherland from the mid-ninth century onwards.

UNIFICATION

The union of the areas which now comprise Scotland began in AD 843 when Kenneth mac Alpin, king of the Scots from *c.*834, also became king of the Picts, joining the two lands to form the kingdom of Alba (comprising Scotland north of a line between the Forth and Clyde rivers). Lothian, the eastern part of the area between the Forth and the Tweed, seems to have been leased to Kenneth II of Alba (reigned 971–995) by Edgar of England *c.*973, and Scottish possession was confirmed by Malcolm II's victory over a Northumbrian army at Carham *c.*1016. At about this time Malcolm II (reigned 1005–34) placed his grandson Duncan on the throne of the British kingdom of Strathclyde, bringing under Scots rule virtually all of what is now Scotland.

The Norse possessions were incorporated into the kingdom of Scotland from the 12th century onwards. An uprising in the mid-12th century drove the Norse from most of mainland Argyll. The Hebrides were ceded to Scotland by the Treaty of Perth in 1266 after a Norwegian expedition in 1263 failed to maintain Norse authority over the islands. Orkney and Shetland fell to Scotland in 1468–9 as a pledge for the unpaid dowry of Margaret of Denmark, wife of James III, although Danish claims of suzerainty were relinquished only with the marriage of Anne of Denmark to James VI in 1590.

From the 11th century, there were frequent wars between Scotland and England over territory and the extent of England's political influence. The failure of the Scottish royal line with the death of Margaret of Norway in 1290 led to disputes over the throne which were resolved by the adjudication of Edward I of England. He awarded the throne to John Balliol in 1292 but Balliol's refusal to be a puppet king led to war. Balliol surrendered to Edward I in 1296 and Edward attempted to rule Scotland himself. Resistance to Scotland's loss of independence was led by William Wallace, who defeated the English at Stirling Bridge (1297), and Robert Bruce, crowned in 1306, who held most of Scotland by 1311 and routed Edward II's army at Bannockburn (1314). England recognised the independence of Scotland in the Treaty of Northampton in 1328. Subsequent clashes include the disastrous battle of Flodden (1513) in which James IV and many of his nobles fell.

THE UNION

In 1603 James VI of Scotland succeeded Elizabeth I on the throne of England (his mother, Mary Queen of Scots, was the great-granddaughter of Henry VII), his successors reigning as sovereigns of Great Britain. Political union of the two countries did not occur until 1707.

THE JACOBITE REVOLTS

After the abdication (by flight) in 1688 of James VII and II, the crown devolved upon William III (grandson of Charles I) and Mary II (elder daughter of James VII and II). In 1689 Graham of Claverhouse roused the Highlands on behalf of James VII and II, but died after a military success at Killiecrankie.

After the death of Anne (younger daughter of James VII and II), the throne devolved upon George I (great-grandson of James VI and I). In 1715, armed risings on behalf of James Stuart (the Old Pretender, son of James VII and II) led to the indecisive battle of Sheriffmuir, and the Jacobite movement died down until 1745, when Charles Stuart (the Young Pretender) defeated the Royalist troops at Prestonpans and advanced to Derby (1746). From Derby, the adherents of 'James VIII and III' (the title claimed for his father by Charles Stuart) fell back on the defensive and were finally crushed at Culloden (16 April 1746) by an army led by by the Duke of Cumberland, son of George II.

PRINCIPAL CITIES

ABERDEEN

Aberdeen, 209km (130 miles) north-east of Edinburgh, received its charter as a Royal Burgh in 1124. Scotland's third largest city, Aberdeen lies between two rivers, the Dee and the Don, facing the North Sea; the city has a strong maritime history and is today a major centre for offshore oil exploration and production. It is also an ancient university town and distinguished research centre. Other industries include engineering, food processing, textiles, paper manufacturing and chemicals.

Places of interest include King's College, St Machar's Cathedral, Brig o' Balgownie, Duthie Park and Winter Gardens, Hazlehead Park, the Kirk of St Nicholas, Mercat Cross, Marischal College and Marischal Museum, Provost Skene's House, Aberdeen Art Gallery, Gordon Highlanders Museum, Satrosphere Science Centre, and Aberdeen Maritime Museum.

DUNDEE

The Royal Burgh of Dundee is situated on the north bank of the Tay estuary. The city's port and dock installations are important to the offshore oil industry and the airport also provides servicing facilities. Principal industries include textiles, biotechnology and digital media, lasers, printing, tyre manufacture, food processing, engineering and tourism.

The unique City Churches – three churches under one roof, together with the 15th-century St Mary's Tower – are the most prominent architectural feature. Dundee is home to two historic ships: the Dundee-built RRS *Discovery* which took Capt. Scott to the Antarctic lies alongside Discovery Quay, and the frigate *Unicorn,* the only British-built wooden warship still afloat, is moored in Victoria Dock. Places of interest include Mills Public Observatory, the Tay road and rail bridges, Dundee Contemporary Arts centre, McManus Galleries, Claypotts Castle, Broughty Castle, Verdant Works (textile heritage centre) and the Sensation Science Centre.

EDINBURGH

Edinburgh is the capital city and seat of government in Scotland. The new Scottish parliament building designed by Enric Miralles was completed in 2004 and is open to visitors. The city is built on a group of hills and both the Old and New Towns are inscribed on the UNESCO World Cultural and Natural Heritage List for their cultural significance.

Other places of interest include the castle, which houses the Stone of Scone and also includes St Margaret's Chapel, the oldest building in Edinburgh, and near it, the Scottish National War Memorial; the Palace of Holyroodhouse, the Queen's official residence in Scotland; Parliament House, the present seat of the judicature; Princes Street; three universities (Edinburgh, Heriot-Watt, Napier); St Giles' Cathedral; St Mary's (Scottish Episcopal) Cathedral (Sir George Gilbert Scott); the General Register House (Robert

Adam); the National and Signet libraries; the National Gallery of Scotland; the Royal Scottish Academy; the Scottish National Portrait Gallery and the Edinburgh International Conference Centre.

GLASGOW

Glasgow, a Royal Burgh, is Scotland's largest city and its principal commercial and industrial centre. The city occupies the north and south banks of the Clyde, formerly one of the chief commercial estuaries in the world. The main industries include engineering, electronics, finance, chemicals and printing. The city is also a key tourist and conference destination.

The chief buildings are the 13th-century Gothic cathedral, the university (Sir George Gilbert Scott), the City Chambers, the Royal Concert Hall, St Mungo Museum of Religious Life and Art, Pollok House, the School of Art (Charles Rennie Mackintosh), Kelvingrove Art Gallery and Museum, the Gallery of Modern Art, the Riverside Museum: Scotland's Museum of Transport and Travel (Zaha Hadid), the Burrell Collection museum and the Mitchell Library. The city is home to the Royal Scottish National Orchestra, Scottish Opera, Scottish Ballet and BBC Scotland and Scottish Television (STV).

INVERNESS

Inverness was granted city status in 2000. The city's name is derived from the Gaelic for 'the mouth of the Ness', referring to the river on which it lies. Inverness is recorded as being at the junction of the old trade routes since AD 565. Today the city is the main administrative centre for the north of Scotland and is the capital of the Highlands. Tourism is one of the city's main industries.

Among the city's most notable buildings is Abertarff House, built in 1593 and the oldest secular building remaining in Inverness. Balnain House, built as a town house in 1726, is a fine example of early Georgian architecture. The Old High Church, on St Michael's Mount, is the original parish church of Inverness and is built on the site of the earliest Christian church in the city. Parts of the church date back to the 14th century.

Stirling was granted city status in 2002 and Perth in 2012. Aberdeen, Dundee, Edinburgh and Glasgow have also been granted Lord Mayoralty/Lord Provostship.

LORD-LIEUTENANTS

Title	*Name*
Aberdeen City*	Lord Provost Peter Stephen
Aberdeenshire	James Ingleby
Angus	Mrs G. Osborne
Argyll and Bute	Patrick Stewart, MBE
Ayrshire and Arran	John Duncan, QPM
Banffshire	Clare Russell
Berwickshire	Maj. A. Trotter
Caithness	Miss M. Dunnett
Clackmannanshire	Rt. Hon. George Reid
Dumfries	Jean Tulloch
Dunbartonshire	Rear-Adm. Michael Gregory, OBE
Dundee City*	Lord Provost John Letford
East Lothian	W. Garth Morrison, CBE
Edinburgh City*	Rt. Hon. Lord Provost George Grubb
Eilean Siar (Western Isles)	A. Matheson, OBE
Fife	Mrs C. Dean
Glasgow City*	Rt. Hon. Lord Provost Robert Winter
Inverness	Donald Angus Cameron of Lochiel
Kincardineshire	Carol Kinghorn
Lanarkshire	Mushtaq Ahmad, OBE
Midlothian	Patrick Prenter, CBE
Moray	Grenville Shaw Johnston, OBE, TD
Nairn	Ewen Brodie of Lethan
Orkney	Dr Anthony Trickett, MBE
Perth and Kinross	Brig. Melville Jameson, CBE
Renfrewshire	Guy Clark
Ross and Cromarty	Janet Bowen
Roxburgh, Ettrick and Lauderdale	Hon. Capt. Gerald Maitland-Carew
Shetland	Robert Hunter
Stirling and Falkirk	Marjory McLachlan
Sutherland	Dr Monica Maitland Main
The Stewartry of Kirkcudbright	Lt.-Col. Sir Malcolm Walter Hugh Ross, GCVO, OBE
Tweeddale	Capt. Sir David Younger, KCVO
West Lothian	Mrs I. Brydie, MBE
Wigtown	Marion Brewis

* The Lord Provosts of the four cities of Aberdeen, Dundee, Edinburgh and Glasgow are Lord-Lieutenants *ex officio* for those districts

LOCAL COUNCILS

Council	*Administrative Headquarters*	*Telephone*	*Population**	*Council Tax†*	*Chief Executive*
ABERDEEN	Aberdeen	0845-608 0910	222,793	£1,230	Valerie Watts
Aberdeenshire	Aberdeen	0845-608 1207	252,973	£1,141	Colin Mackenzie
Angus	Forfar	0845-277 7778	115,978	£1,072	Richard Stiff
Argyll and Bute	Lochgilphead	01546-602127	88,166	£1,178	Sally Loudon
Clackmannanshire	Alloa	01259-450000	51,442	£1,148	Elaine McPherson
Dumfries and Galloway	Dumfries	01387-260000	151,324	£1,049	Gavin Stevenson
DUNDEE	Dundee	01382-434000	147,268	£1,211	David Dorward
East Ayrshire	Kilmarnock	01563-576000	122,767	£1,189	Fiona Lees
East Dunbartonshire	Kirkintilloch	0845-045 4510	105,026	£1,142	Gerry Cornes
East Lothian	Haddington	01620-827827	99,717	£1,118	Angela Leitch
East Renfrewshire	Giffnock	0141-577 3000	90,574	£1,126	Lorraine McMillan
EDINBURGH	Edinburgh	0131-200 2000	476,626	£1,169	Sue Bruce
Eilean Siar (Western Isles)	Stornoway	01851-703773	27,684	£1,024	Malcolm Burr
Falkirk	Falkirk	01324-506070	155,990	£1,070	Mary Pitcaithly, OBE
Fife	Glenrothes	0845-155 0000	365,198	£1,118	Steve Grimmond
GLASGOW	Glasgow	0141-287 2000	593,245	£1,213	George Black
Highland	Inverness	01463-702000	232,132	£1,163	Steve Barron
Inverclyde	Greenock	01475-717171	81,485	£1,198	John Mundell
Midlothian	Dalkeith	0131-270 7500	83,187	£1,210	Kenneth Lawrie
Moray	Elgin	01343-543451	93,295	£1,135	Roddy Burns
North Ayrshire	Irvine	01294-310000	138,146	£1,152	Elma Murray
North Lanarkshire	Motherwell	01698-302222	337,727	£1,098	Gavin Whitefield
Orkney	Kirkwall	01856-873535	21,349	£1,037	Alistair Buchan
Perth and Kinross	Perth	01738-475000	146,652	£1,158	Bernadette Malone
Renfrewshire	Paisley	0300-300 0300	174,908	£1,165	David Martin
Scottish Borders	Melrose	01835-824000	113,870	£1,084	Tracey Logan
Shetland	Lerwick	01595-693535	23,167	£1,053	Mark Boden
South Ayrshire	Ayr	0300-123 0900	112,799	£1,154	Aileen Howat
South Lanarkshire	Hamilton	01698-454444	313,830	£1,101	Lindsay Freeland
STIRLING	Stirling	0845-277 7000	90,247	£1,197	Bob Jack
West Dunbartonshire	Dumbarton	01389-737000	90,720	£1,163	Joyce White
West Lothian	Livingston	01506-280000	175,118	£1,128	Graham Hope

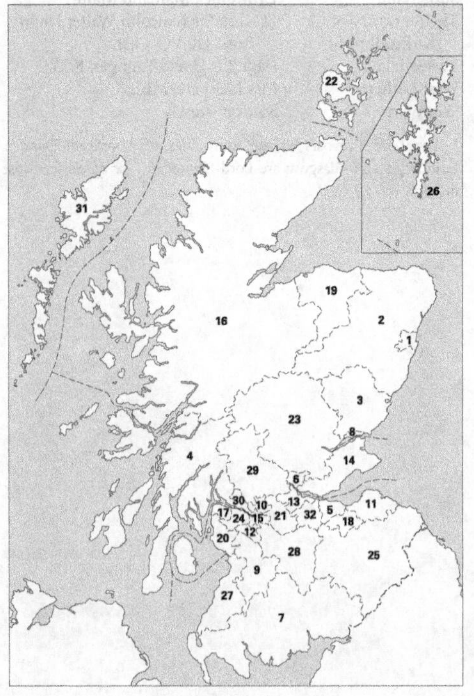

Key	*Council*	*Key*	*Council*
1	Aberdeen City	18	Midlothian
2	Aberdeenshire	19	Moray
3	Angus	20	North Ayrshire
4	Argyll and Bute	21	North Lanarkshire
5	City of Edinburgh	22	Orkney
6	Clackmannanshire	23	Perth and Kinross
7	Dumfries and Galloway	24	Renfrewshire
8	Dundee City	25	Scottish Borders
9	East Ayrshire	26	Shetland
10	East Dunbartonshire	27	South Ayrshire
11	East Lothian	28	South Lanarkshire
12	East Renfrewshire	29	Stirling
13	Falkirk	30	West Dunbartonshire
14	Fife	31	Western Isles (Eilean Siar)
15	Glasgow City	32	West Lothian
16	Highland		
17	Inverclyde		

* *Source:* ONS – Census 2011 (Crown copyright)
† Average Band D council tax bill 2013–14
Councils in CAPITAL LETTERS have city status

NORTHERN IRELAND

Northern Ireland has a total area of 14,149 sq. km (5,463 sq. miles): land, 13,576 sq. km (5,242 sq. miles); inland water, 573 sq. km (221 sq. miles).

The population of Northern Ireland at the 2011 census was 1,810,863 (men 887,323; women 923,540). The average density of population in 2011 was 128 persons per sq. km (331 per sq. mile).

FLAG
The official national flag of Northern Ireland is the Union Flag.

PRINCIPAL CITIES

In addition to Belfast and Londonderry, three other places in Northern Ireland have been granted city status: Armagh (1994), Lisburn (2002) and Newry (2002).

BELFAST

Belfast, the administrative centre of Northern Ireland, is situated at the mouth of the River Lagan at its entrance to Belfast Lough. The city grew to be a great industrial centre, owing to its easy access by sea to Scottish coal and iron.

The principal buildings are of a relatively young age and include the parliament buildings at Stormont, the City Hall, Waterfront Hall, the Law Courts, the Public Library and the Museum and Art Gallery. In March 2012, a new museum, Titanic Belfast, opened on the banks of the Lagan River – the site where RMS *Titanic* was built and launched. The £97m museum forms the centrepiece of a £7bn regeneration project that is turning the 185-acre waterfront into a new mixed-use maritime quarter.

Belfast received its first charter of incorporation in 1613 and was created a city in 1888; the title of lord mayor was conferred in 1892.

LONDONDERRY

Londonderry (originally Derry) is situated on the River Foyle, and has important associations with the City of London. The Irish Society was created by the City of London in 1610, and under its royal charter of 1613 it fortified the city and was for a long time closely associated with its administration. Because of this connection the city was incorporated in 1613 under the new name of Londonderry.

The city is famous for the great siege of 1688–9, when for 105 days the town held out against the forces of James II. The city walls are still intact and form a circuit of 1.6 km (one mile) around the old city.

Interesting buildings are the Protestant cathedral of St Columb's (1633) and the Guildhall, reconstructed in 1912 and containing a number of beautiful stained glass windows, many of which were presented by the livery companies of London.

CONSTITUTIONAL HISTORY

Northern Ireland is subject to the same fundamental constitutional provisions which apply to the rest of the UK. It had its own parliament and government from 1921 to 1972, but after increasing civil unrest the Northern Ireland (Temporary Provisions) Act 1972 transferred the legislative and executive powers of the Northern Ireland parliament and government to the UK parliament and a secretary of state. The Northern Ireland Constitution Act 1973 provided for devolution in Northern Ireland through an assembly and executive, but a power-sharing executive formed by the Northern Ireland political parties in January 1974 collapsed in May 1974. Following the collapse of the power-sharing executive Northern Ireland returned to direct rule governance under the provisions of the Northern Ireland Act 1974, placing the Northern Ireland department under the direction and control of the Northern Ireland secretary.

In December 1993 the British and Irish governments published the Joint Declaration complementing their political talks, and making clear that any settlement would need to be founded on principles of democracy and consent.

On 12 January 1998 the British and Irish governments issued a joint document, *Propositions on Heads of Agreement,* proposing the establishment of various new cross-border bodies; further proposals were presented on 27 January. A draft peace settlement was issued by the talks' chairman, US Senator George Mitchell, on 6 April 1998 but was rejected by the Unionists the following day. On 10 April agreement was reached between the British and Irish governments and the eight Northern Ireland political parties still involved in the talks (the Good Friday Agreement). The agreement provided for an elected Northern Ireland Assembly, a North/South Ministerial Council, and a British-Irish Council comprising representatives of the British, Irish, Channel Islands and Isle of Man governments and members of the new assemblies for Scotland, Wales and Northern Ireland. Further points included the abandonment of the Republic of Ireland's constitutional claim to Northern Ireland; the decommissioning of weapons; the release of paramilitary prisoners and changes in policing.

The agreement was ratified in referendums held in Northern Ireland and the Republic of Ireland on 22 May 1998. In the UK, the Northern Ireland Act received royal assent in November 1998.

On 28 April 2003 the secretary of state again assumed responsibility for the direction of the Northern Ireland departments on the dissolution of the Northern Ireland Assembly, following its initial suspension from midnight on 14 October 2002. In 2006, following the passing of the Northern Ireland Act, the secretary of state created a non-legislative fixed-term assembly which would cease to operate either when the political parties agreed to restore devolution, or on 24 November 2006 (whichever occurred first). In October 2006 a timetable to restore devolution was drawn up (St Andrews Agreement) and a transitional Northern Ireland Assembly was formed on 24 November. The transitional assembly was dissolved in January 2007 in preparation for elections to be held on 7 March; following the elections a power-sharing executive was formed and the new 108-member Northern Ireland Assembly became operational on 8 May 2007.

See also Regional Government.

LORD-LIEUTENANTS AND HIGH SHERIFFS

County	*Lord-Lieutenant*	*High Sheriff (2013)*
Antrim	Joan Christie	Mervyn Rankin
Armagh	The Earl of Caledon	James Magowan
Belfast City	Dame Mary Peters, DBE	Brian Kingston
Down	David Lindsay	Ivan Cunningham
Fermanagh	Viscount Brookeborough	Roisin McManus
Londonderry	Denis Desmond, CBE	Philip Gilliland
Londonderry City	Dr Sir Donal Keegan, KCVO, OBE	James Kerr
Tyrone	Robert Scott, OBE	William Baxter, QPM

LOCAL COUNCILS

Council	*County Area*	*Map Key*	*Telephone*	*Population**	*Chief Executive*
Antrim	Down	1	028-9446 3113	53,428	David McCammick
Ards	Down	2	028-9182 4000	78,078	Ashley Boreland
ARMAGH	Armagh	3	028-3752 9600	59,340	John Briggs
Ballymena	Antrim	4	028-2566 0300	64,044	Anne Donaghy
Ballymoney	Antrim	5	028-2766 0200	31,224	John Dempsey
Banbridge	Down	6	028-4066 0600	48,339	Liam Hannaway
BELFAST	Antrim & Down	7	028-9032 0202	280,962	Peter McNaney
Carrickfergus	Antrim	8	028-9335 8000	39,114	Sheila McClelland
Castlereagh	Down	9	028-9049 4500	67,242	Stephen Reid
Coleraine	Londonderry	10	028-7034 7034	59,067	Roger Wilson
Cookstown	Tyrone	11	028-8676 2205	37,013	Adrian McCreesh *(acting)*
Craigavon	Armagh	12	028-3831 2400	93,023	Dr Theresa Donaldson
DERRY	Londonderry	13	028-7136 5151	107,877	Sharon O'Connor
Down	Down	14	028-4461 0800	69,731	John Dumigan
Dungannon & South Tyrone	Tyrone	15	028-8772 0300	57,852	Alan Burke *(acting)*
Fermanagh	Fermanagh	16	028-6632 5050	61,805	Brendan Hegarty
Larne	Antrim	17	028-2827 2313	32,180	Geraldine McGahey
Limavady	Londonderry	18	028-7772 2226	33,536	Liam Flanigan
LISBURN	Antrim	19	028-9250 9250	120,165	Norman Davidson
Magherafelt	Londonderry	20	028-7939 7979	45,038	John McLaughlin
Moyle	Antrim	21	028-2076 2225	17,050	Richard Lewis
NEWRY & Mourne	Down & Armagh	22	028-3031 3031	99,480	Thomas McCall
Newtownabbey	Antrim	23	028-9034 0000	85,139	Jacqui Dixon
North Down	Down	24	028-9127 0371	78,937	Trevor Polley
Omagh	Tyrone	25	028 8224 5321	51,356	Daniel McSorley
Strabane	Tyrone	26	028-7138 2204	39,843	Daniel McSorley *(interim)*

* *Source:* ONS – Census 2011 (Crown copyright)
Councils in CAPITAL LETTERS have city status

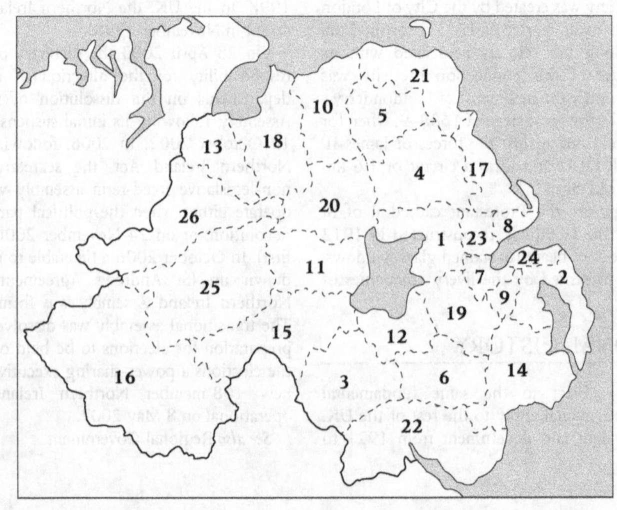

THE ISLE OF MAN

Ellan Vannin

The Isle of Man is an island situated in the Irish Sea, at latitude 54° 3′–54° 25′ N. and longitude 4° 18′–4° 47′ W., nearly equidistant from England, Scotland and Ireland. Although the early inhabitants were of Celtic origin, the Isle of Man was part of the Norwegian Kingdom of the Hebrides until 1266, when this was ceded to Scotland. Subsequently granted to the Stanleys (Earls of Derby) in the 15th century and later to the Dukes of Atholl, it was brought under the administration of the Crown in 1765. The island forms the bishopric of Sodor and Man.

The total land area is 572 sq. km (221 sq. miles). The 2011 census showed a resident population of 84,497 (men, 41,971; women, 42,526). The main language in use is English. Around 1,660 people are able to speak the Manx Gaelic language.

CAPITAL – ΨDouglas; population, 27,938 (2011). ΨCastletown (3,097) is the ancient capital; the other towns are ΨPeel (5,093) and ΨRamsey (7,821)

FLAG – A red flag charged with three conjoined armoured legs in white and gold

NATIONAL DAY – 5 July (Tynwald Day)

GOVERNMENT

The Isle of Man is a self-governing Crown dependency, with its own parliamentary, legal and administrative system. The British government is responsible for international relations and defence. Under the UK Act of Accession, Protocol 3, the island's relationship with the European Union is limited to trade alone and does not extend to financial aid. The Lieutenant-Governor is the Queen's personal representative on the island.

The legislature, Tynwald, is the oldest parliament in the world in continuous existence. It has two branches: the Legislative Council and the House of Keys. The council consists of the President of Tynwald, the Bishop of Sodor and Man, the Attorney-General (who does not have a vote) and eight members elected by the House of Keys. The House of Keys has 24 members, elected by universal adult suffrage. The branches sit separately to consider legislation and sit together, as Tynwald Court, for most other parliamentary purposes.

The presiding officer of Tynwald Court is the President of Tynwald, elected by the members, who also presides over sittings of the Legislative Council. The presiding officer of the House of Keys is the Speaker, who is elected by members of the house.

The principal members of the Manx government are the chief minister and nine departmental ministers, who comprise the Council of Ministers.

Lieutenant-Governor, HE Adam Wood
President of Tynwald, Hon. Clare Christian
Speaker, House of Keys, Hon. Steve Rodan, SHK
The First Deemster and Clerk of the Rolls, His Hon. David Doyle
Clerk of Tynwald, Secretary to the House of Keys and Counsel to the Speaker, Roger Phillips
Clerk of the Legislative Council and Deputy Clerk of Tynwald, Jonathan King
Attorney-General, Stephen Harding
Chief Minister, Hon. Allan Bell, MHK
Chief Secretary, Will Greenhow

ECONOMY

Most of the income generated in the island is earned in the services sector with financial and professional services accounting for just over half of the national income. Tourism and manufacturing are also major generators of income while the island's other traditional industries of agriculture and fishing now play a smaller role in the economy. Under the terms of protocol 3, the island has tariff-free access to EU markets for its goods.

In April 2013 the island's unemployment rate was 2.5 per cent and inflation (RPI) was 3.3 per cent.

FINANCE

The budget for 2013–14 provides for net revenue expenditure of £547.9m. The principal sources of government revenue are taxes on income and expenditure. Income tax is payable at a rate of 10 per cent on the first £10,500 of taxable income for single resident individuals and 20 per cent on the balance, after personal allowances of £9,300. These bands are doubled for married couples. The rate of income tax for trading companies is zero per cent except for income from banking and land and property, which is taxed at 10 per cent. By agreement with the British government, the island keeps most of its rates of indirect taxation (VAT and duties) the same as those in the UK. However, VAT on tourist accommodation, property, repairs and renovations is charged at 5 per cent. A reciprocal agreement on national insurance benefits and pensions exists between the governments of the Isle of Man and the UK. Taxes are also charged on property (rates), but these are comparatively low.

The major government expenditure items are social care, health and education, which account for 66 per cent of the government budget. The island makes an annual contribution to the UK for defence and other external services.

The island has a special relationship with the European Union and neither contributes money to nor receives funds from the EU budget.

Ψ = sea port

THE CHANNEL ISLANDS

The Channel Islands, situated off the north-west coast of France (at a distance of 16km (10 miles) at their closest point), are the only portions of the Dukedom of Normandy still belonging to the Crown, to which they have been attached since the Norman Conquest of 1066. They were the only British territory to come under German occupation during the Second World War, following invasion on 30 June and 1 July 1940. Guernsey and Jersey were relieved by British forces on 9 May 1945, Sark on 10 May 1945 and Alderney on 16 May 1945; 9 May (Liberation Day) is now observed as a bank and public holiday in Guernsey and Jersey.

The islands consist of Jersey (11,630ha/28,717 acres), Guernsey (6,340ha/15,654 acres), and the dependencies of Guernsey: Alderney (795ha/1,962 acres), Brecqhou (30ha/74 acres), Great Sark (419ha/1,035 acres), Little Sark (97ha/239 acres), Herm (130ha/320 acres), Jethou (18ha/44 acres) and Lihou (15ha/38 acres) – a total of 19,474ha/48,083 acres, or 195 sq. km/75 sq. miles.

The 2011 census (taken in March) showed the population of Jersey as 97,857. Guernsey did not complete the same census, but the most recent official records for Guernsey and Alderney estimated the populations at 63,085 and 1,903 respectively. Sark's population is estimated to be around 600. The official language is English but French is often used for ceremonial purposes. In country districts of Jersey and Guernsey and throughout Sark a Norman-French *patois* is also in use, though to a lesser extent.

GOVERNMENT

The islands are Crown dependencies with their own legislative assemblies (the States in Jersey and Alderney, the States of Deliberation in Guernsey and the Chief Pleas in Sark), systems of local administration and law, and their own courts. *Projets de Loi* (Acts) passed by the States require the sanction of the Queen-in-council. The UK government is responsible for defence and international relations, although the islands are increasingly entering into agreements with other countries in their own right. The Channel Islands are not part of the European Union but, under protocol 3 of the UK's Treaty of Accession, have trading rights with the free movement of goods within the EU. A common customs tariff, levies and agricultural and import measures apply to trade between the islands and non-member countries

In both Jersey and Guernsey bailiwicks the Lieutenant-Governor and Commander-in-Chief, who is appointed by the Crown, is the personal representative of the Queen and the channel of communication between the Crown (via the Privy Council) and the islands' governments.

The head of government in both Jersey and Guernsey is the Chief Minister. Jersey has a ministerial system of government; the executive comprises the Council of Ministers and consists of a chief minister and nine other ministers. The ministers are assisted by up to 12 assistant ministers. Members of the States who are not in the executive are able to sit on a number of scrutiny panels and the Public Accounts Committee to examine the policy of the executive and hold ministers to account. Guernsey is administered by a number of departments and committees. There are ten States departments with mandated responsibilities, each department is constituted of a minister and four members of the States. Each of the ministers has a seat on the Policy Council which is presided over by the Chief Minister. The States of Deliberation, the island's parliamentary assembly, is the overarching executive. There are also five parliamentary committees, each led by a chair, responsible for scrutinising policy, finance and legislation, parliamentary procedural matters and public sector pay negotiations. Alderney has a legislature comprising a President and ten members elected by universal suffrage. Sark has a directly elected legislature of 28 members *(conseillers)* who serve on a number of committees.

Justice is administered by the royal courts of Jersey and Guernsey, each consisting of the bailiff and 12 elected jurats. The bailiffs of Jersey and Guernsey, appointed by the Crown, are presidents of the royal courts of their respective islands.

Each bailiwick constitutes a deanery under the jurisdiction of the Bishop of Winchester.

ECONOMY

A mild climate and good soil have led to the development of intensive systems of agriculture and horticulture, which form a significant part of the economy. Equally important are earnings from tourism and banking and finance: the low rates of income and corporation tax and the absence of death duties make the islands an important offshore financial centre. The financial services sector contributes over 50 per cent of GDP in Jersey and around 40 per cent in Guernsey. In addition, there is no VAT or equivalent tax in Guernsey and only small goods and services tax in Jersey (5 per cent since 1 June 2011). The Channel Islands stock exchange is located in Guernsey, which also has a thriving e-gaming sector.

Principal exports are agricultural produce and flowers; imports are chiefly machinery, manufactured goods, food, fuel and chemicals. Trade with the UK is regarded as internal.

British currency is legal tender in the Channel Islands but each bailiwick issues its own coins and notes (*see* Currency section). They also issue their own postage stamps; UK stamps are not valid.

JERSEY

Lieutenant-Governor and Commander-in-Chief of Jersey, HE Gen. Sir John McColl, KCB, CBE, DSO, *apptd* 2011
Secretary and ADC, Lt.-Col. A. Woodrow, LVO, OBE, MC
Bailiff of Jersey, Sir Michael Birt
Deputy Bailiff, W. Bailhache
Attorney-General, Timothy Le Cocq, QC
Receiver-General, David Pett
Solicitor-General, Howard Sharp, QC
Greffier of the States, M. de la Haye
States Treasurer, L. Rowley
Chief Minister, Senator I. Gorst

FINANCE

	2011	*2012*
Revenue income	£793,016,000	£862,364,000
Revenue expenditure	£828,620,000	£792,338,000
Capital expenditure	£73,405,000	£36,844,000

CHIEF TOWN – ΨSt Helier, on the south coast
FLAG – A white field charged with a red saltire cross, and the arms of Jersey in the upper centre

GUERNSEY AND DEPENDENCIES

Lieutenant-Governor and Commander-in-Chief of the Bailiwick of Guernsey and its Dependencies, HE Air Marshal Peter Walker, CB, CBE, *apptd* 2011
Presiding Officer of the Royal Court and of the States of Deliberation, Bailiff Richard Collas
Deputy Presiding Officer of the Royal Court and States of Deliberation, Richard McMahon, QC
HM Procureur and Receiver-General (Attorney-General), Howard Roberts, QC
HM Comptroller (Solicitor-General), Megan Pullum, QC

GUERNSEY
Chief Minister, Deputy Peter Harwood
Chief Executive, Mike Brown

FINANCE	2011	2012
Revenue income	£346,341,000	£362,343,000
Revenue expenditure	£332,858,000	£341,712,000
Capital expenditure	£16,681,000	£16,361,000

CHIEF TOWNS – ΨSt Peter Port, on the east coast of Guernsey; St Anne on Alderney
FLAG – White, bearing a red cross of St George, with a gold cross of Normandy overall in the centre

ALDERNEY
President of the States, Stuart Trought
Chief Executive, Roy Burke
Greffier, Sarah Kelly

SARK
Sark was the last European territory to abolish feudal parliamentary representation. Elections for a democratic legislative assembly took place in December 2008, with the *conseillers* taking their seats in the newly constituted Chief Pleas in January 2009.
Seigneur of Sark, John Beaumont, OBE
Seneschal, Lt.-Col. R Guille, MBE
Greffier, Trevor Hamon

OTHER DEPENDENCIES
Herm and Lihou are owned by the States of Guernsey; Herm is leased, Lihou is uninhabited. Jethou is leased by the Crown to the States of Guernsey and is sub-let by the States. Brecqhou is within the legislative and judicial territory of Sark.

Ψ = seaport

LAW COURTS AND OFFICES

SUPREME COURT OF THE UNITED KINGDOM

The Supreme Court of the United Kingdom is the highest domestic judicial authority; it replaced the appellate committee of the House of Lords (the house functioning in its judicial capacity) on 1 October 2009. It is the final court of appeal for cases heard in Great Britain and Northern Ireland (except for criminal cases from Scotland). Cases concerning the interpretation and application of European Union law, including preliminary rulings requested by British courts and tribunals, which are decided by the Court of Justice of the European Union (CJEU) (*see* European Union), and the supreme court can make a reference to the CJEU in appropriate cases. Additionally, in giving effect to rights contained in the European Convention on Human Rights, the supreme court must take account of any decision of the European Court of Human Rights.

The supreme court also assumed jurisdiction in relation to devolution matters under the Scotland Act 1998 (now partly superseded by the Scotland Act 2012), the Northern Ireland Act 1988 and the Government of Wales Act 2006; these powers were transferred from the Judicial Committee of the Privy Council. Ten of the 12 Lords of Appeal in Ordinary from the House of Lords transferred to the 12-member supreme court when it came into operation (at the same time one law lord retired and another was appointed Master of the Rolls). All new justices of the supreme court are now appointed by an independent selection commission, and are not members of the House of Lords.

President of the Supreme Court (£216,307), Rt. Hon. Lord Neuberger of Abbotsbury, *born* 1948, *apptd* 2012
Deputy President of the Supreme Court (£208,926), Rt. Hon. Lady Hale of Richmond, *born* 1945, *apptd* 2013

JUSTICES OF THE SUPREME COURT *as at September 2013* (each £208,926)
Style, The Rt. Hon. Lord/Lady–

Rt. Hon. Lord Mance, *born* 1943, *apptd* 2005
Rt. Hon. Lord Kerr of Tonaghmore, *born* 1948, *apptd* 2009
Rt. Hon. Lord Clarke of Stone-cum-Ebony, *born* 1943, *apptd* 2009
Rt. Hon. Lord Wilson of Culworth (Sir Nicholas Wilson), *born* 1945, *apptd* 2011
Rt. Hon. Lord Sumption (Jonathan Sumption), *born* 1948, *apptd* 2012
Rt. Hon. Lord Reed (Robert Reed), *born* 1956, *apptd* 2012
Rt. Hon. Lord Carnwath of Notting Hill, CVO (Sir Robert Carnwath), *born* 1945, *apptd* 2012
Rt. Hon. Lord Hughes of Ombersley (Sir Antony Hughes), *born* 1948, *apptd* 2013
Rt. Hon. Lord Toulson (Sir Roger Toulson), *born* 1946, *apptd* 2013
Rt. Hon. Lord Hodge, *born* 1953, *apptd* 2013

UNITED KINGDOM SUPREME COURT
Parliament Square, London SW1P 3BD T 020-7960 1900
Chief Executive, Jenny Rowe

JUDICATURE OF ENGLAND AND WALES

The legal system in England and Wales is divided into criminal law and civil law. Criminal law is concerned with acts harmful to the community and the rules laid down by the state for the benefit of citizens, whereas civil law governs the relationships and transactions between individuals. Administrative law is a kind of civil law usually concerning the interaction of individuals and the state, and most cases are heard in tribunals specific to the subject (*see* Tribunals section). Scotland and Northern Ireland possess legal systems that differ from the system in England and Wales in law, judicial procedure and court structure, but retain the distinction between criminal and civil law.

Under the provisions of the Criminal Appeal Act 1995, a commission was set up to direct and supervise investigations into possible miscarriages of justice and to refer cases to the appeal courts on the grounds of conviction and sentence; these functions were formerly the responsibility of the home secretary.

SENIOR COURTS OF ENGLAND AND WALES

The senior courts of England and Wales (until September 2009 known as the supreme court of judicature of England and Wales) comprise the high court, the crown court and the court of appeal. The President of the Courts of England and Wales, a new title given to the Lord Chief Justice under the Constitutional Reform Act 2005, is the head of the judiciary.

The high court was created in 1875 and combined many previously separate courts. Sittings are held at the royal courts of justice in London or at around 120 district registries outside the capital. It is the superior civil court and is split into three divisions – the chancery division, the Queen's bench division and the family division – each of which is further divided. The chancery division is headed by the Chancellor of the High Court and is concerned mainly with equity, trusts, tax and bankruptcy, while also including two specialist courts, the patents court and the companies court. The Queen's bench division (QBD) is the largest of the three divisions, and is headed by its own president. It deals with common law (ie tort, contract, debt and personal injuries), some tax law, eg VAT tribunal appeals, and encompasses the admiralty court and the commercial court. The QBD also administers the technology and construction court. The family division was created in 1970 and is headed by its own president, who is also Head of Family Justice, and hears cases concerning divorce, access to and custody of children, and other family matters. The divisional court of the high court sits in the family and chancery divisions, and hears appeals from the magistrates' courts and county courts.

The crown court was set up in 1972 and sits at 77 centres throughout England and Wales. It deals with more serious (indictable) criminal offences, which are triable before a judge and jury, including treason, murder, rape, kidnapping, armed robbery and Official Secrets Act offences. It also handles cases transferred from the magistrates' courts where the magistrate decides his or her own power of sentence is inadequate, or where someone appeals against a magistrate's decision, or in a case that is triable 'either way' where the accused has chosen a jury trial. The crown court centres are divided into three tiers: high court judges, circuit judges and sometimes recorders (part-time circuit judges), sit in first-tier centres, hearing the most serious criminal offences (eg murder, treason, rape, manslaughter) and some civil high court cases. The second-tier centres are presided over by high court judges, circuit judges or recorders and also deal with

HIERARCHY OF ENGLISH AND WELSH COURTS

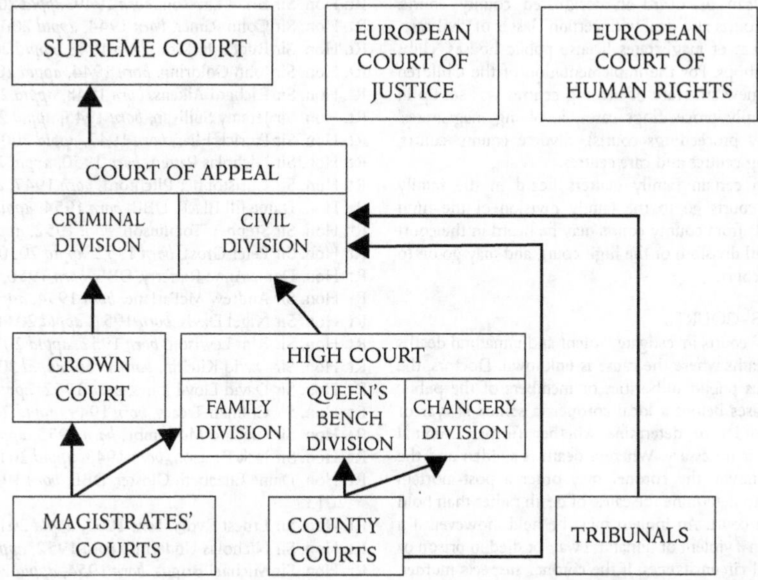

the most serious criminal cases. Third-tier courts deal with the remaining criminal offences, with circuit judges or recorders presiding.

The court of appeal hears appeals against both fact and law, and was last restructured in 1966 when it replaced the court of criminal appeal. It is split into the civil division (which hears appeals from the high court, tribunals and in certain cases, the county courts) and the criminal division (which hears appeals from the crown court). Cases are heard by Lords Justices of Appeal and high court judges if deemed suitable for reconsideration.

The Constitutional Reform Act 2005 instigated several key changes to the judiciary in England and Wales. These included the establishment of the independent supreme court, which opened in October 2009; the reform of the post of Lord Chancellor, transferring its judicial functions to the President of the Courts of England and Wales; a duty on government ministers to uphold the independence of the judiciary by barring them from trying to influence judicial decisions through any special access to judges; the formation of a fully transparent and independent Judicial Appointments Commission that is responsible for selecting candidates to recommend for judicial appointment to the Lord Chancellor and Secretary of State for Justice; and the creation of the post of Judicial Appointments and Conduct Ombudsman.

CRIMINAL CASES

In criminal matters the decision to prosecute (in the majority of cases) rests with the Crown Prosecution Service (CPS), which is the independent prosecuting body in England and Wales. The CPS is headed by the director of public prosecutions, who works under the superintendence of the Attorney-General. Certain categories of offence continue to require the Attorney-General's consent for prosecution.

Most minor criminal cases (summary offences) are dealt with in magistrates' courts, usually by a bench of three unpaid lay magistrates (justices of the peace) sitting without a jury and assisted on points of law and procedure by a legally trained clerk. There were 26,966 justices of the peace as at 1 April 2011. In some courts a full-time, salaried and legally qualified district judge (magistrates' court) – formerly known as a stipendiary judge – presides alone. There were 137 district judges (magistrates' courts) as at 1 April 2011. Magistrates' courts oversee the completion of 95 per cent of all criminal cases. Magistrates' courts also house some family proceedings courts (which deal with relationship breakdown and childcare cases) and youth courts. Cases of medium seriousness (known as 'offences triable either way') where the defendant pleads not guilty can be heard in the crown court for a trial by jury, if the defendant so chooses. Preliminary proceedings in a serious case to decide whether there is evidence to justify committal for trial in the crown court are dealt with in the magistrates' courts.

The 77 centres that the crown court sits in are divided into seven regions. There are 673 circuit judges and 1,221 recorders (part-time circuit judges); they must sit a minimum of 15 days per year and are usually subject to a maximum of 30. A jury is present in all trials that are contested.

Appeals from magistrates' courts against sentence or conviction are made to the crown court, and appeals upon a point of law are made to the high court, which may ultimately be appealed to the supreme court. Appeals from the crown court, either against sentence or conviction, are made to the court of appeal (criminal division). Again, these appeals may be brought to the supreme court if a point of law is contested, and if the house considers it is of sufficient importance.

CIVIL CASES

Most minor civil cases – including contract, tort (especially personal injuries), property, divorce and other family matters, bankruptcy etc – are dealt with by the county courts, of which there are 216 (*see* W www.justice.gov.uk for further details). Cases are heard by circuit judges, recorders or district judges. For cases involving small claims (with certain exceptions, where the amount claimed is £5,000 or less) there are informal and simplified procedures designed to enable parties to present their cases themselves without recourse to lawyers. Where there are financial limits on county court jurisdiction, claims that exceed those limits may be tried in the county courts with the consent of the parties, subject to the court's agreement, or in certain circumstances on transfer from the high court. Outside London, bankruptcy proceedings can be heard in designated county courts. Magistrates' courts also deal with certain classes of civil case, and committees of magistrates license public houses, clubs and betting shops. For the implementation of the Children Act 1989, a new structure of hearing centres was set up in 1991 for family proceedings cases, involving magistrates' courts (family proceedings courts), divorce county courts, family hearing centres and care centres.

Appeals in certain family matters heard in the family proceedings courts go to the family division of the high court. Appeals from county courts may be heard in the court of appeal (civil division) or the high court, and may go on to the supreme court.

CORONERS' COURTS

The coroners' courts investigate violent and unnatural deaths or sudden deaths where the cause is unknown. Doctors, the police, various public authorities or members of the public may bring cases before a local coroner (a senior lawyer or doctor), in order to determine whether further criminal investigation is necessary. Where a death is sudden and the cause is unknown, the coroner may order a post-mortem examination to determine the cause of death rather than hold an inquest in court. An inquest must be held, however, if a person died in a violent or unnatural way, or died in prison or other unusual circumstances. If the coroner suspects murder, manslaughter or infanticide, he or she must summon a jury.

SENIOR JUDICIARY OF ENGLAND AND WALES

Lord Chief Justice of England and Wales and Head of Criminal Justice (£242,243), Rt. Hon. Lord Thomas, *born* 1947, *apptd* 2013
Master of the Rolls and Head of Civil Justice (£216,307), Rt. Hon. Lord Dyson, *born* 1943, *apptd* 2012
President of the Queen's Bench Division (£208,926), Sir (Roger) John Thomas, *born* 1947, *apptd* 2011
President of the Family Division and Head of Family Justice (£208,926), Rt. Hon. Sir James Munby, *born* 1948, *apptd* 2013
Chancellor of the High Court (£208,926), Rt. Hon. Sir Terence Etherton, *born* 1951, *apptd* 2013

SENIOR COURTS OF ENGLAND AND WALES

COURT OF APPEAL

Presiding Judge, Criminal Division, Lord Chief Justice of England and Wales
Presiding Judge, Civil Division, Master of the Rolls
Vice-President, Civil Division (£198,674), Rt. Hon. Sir Maurice Kay, *born* 1942, *apptd* 2010
Vice-President, Criminal Division (£198,674), vacant

LORD JUSTICES OF APPEAL *as at June 2013* (each £198,674)
Style, The Rt. Hon. Lord/Lady Justice [surname]

Rt. Hon. Sir Mathew Thorpe, *born* 1938, *apptd* 1995
Rt. Hon. Sir John Mummery, *born* 1938, *apptd* 1996
Rt. Hon. Sir John Laws, *born* 1945, *apptd* 1999
Rt. Hon. Dame Mary Arden, DBE, *born* 1947, *apptd* 2000
Rt. Hon. Sir Andrew Longmore, *born* 1944, *apptd* 2001
Rt. Hon. Sir Maurice Kay, *born* 1942, *apptd* 2004
Rt. Hon. Sir Timothy Lloyd, *born* 1946, *apptd* 2005
Rt. Hon. Sir Martin Moore-Bick, *born* 1948, *apptd* 2005
Rt. Hon. Sir Alan Moses, *born* 1945, *apptd* 2005
Rt. Hon. Sir Stephen Richards, *born* 1950, *apptd* 2005
Rt. Hon. Dame Heather Hallett, DBE, *born* 1949, *apptd* 2005
Rt. Hon. Sir Anthony Hughes, *born* 1948, *apptd* 2006
Rt. Hon. Sir Brian Leveson, *born* 1949, *apptd* 2006
Rt. Hon. Sir Colin Rimer, *born* 1944, *apptd* 2007
Rt. Hon. Sir Rupert Jackson, *born* 1948, *apptd* 2008
Rt. Hon. Sir John Goldring, *born* 1944, *apptd* 2008
Rt. Hon. Sir Richard Aikens, *born* 1948, *apptd* 2008
Rt. Hon. Sir Jeremy Sullivan, *born* 1945, *apptd* 2009
Rt. Hon. Sir Patrick Elias, *born* 1947, *apptd* 2009
Rt. Hon. Sir Nicholas Patten, *born* 1950, *apptd* 2009
Rt. Hon. Sir Christopher Pitchford, *born* 1947, *apptd* 2010
Rt. Hon. Dame Jill Black, DBE, *born* 1954, *apptd* 2010
Rt. Hon. Sir Stephen Tomlinson, *born* 1952, *apptd* 2010
Rt. Hon. Sir Peter Gross, *born* 1952, *apptd* 2010
Rt. Hon. Dame Anne Rafferty, DBE, *born* 1950, *apptd* 2011
Rt. Hon. Sir Andrew McFarlane, *born* 1954, *apptd* 2011
Rt. Hon. Sir Nigel Davis, *born* 1951, *apptd* 2011
Rt. Hon. Sir Kim Lewison, *born* 1952, *apptd* 2011
Rt. Hon. Sir David Kitchin, *born* 1955, *apptd* 2011
Rt. Hon. Sir David Lloyd Jones, *born* 1952, *apptd* 2012
Rt. Hon. Sir Colman Treacy, *born* 1949, *apptd* 2012
Rt. Hon. Sir Richard McCombe, *born* 1952, *apptd* 2012
Rt. Hon. Sir Jack Beatson, *born* 1948, *apptd* 2013
Rt. Hon. Dame Elizabeth Gloster, DBE, *born* 1949, *apptd* 2013
Rt. Hon. Sir Ernest Ryder, *born* 1957, *apptd* 2013
Rt. Hon. Sir Nicholas Underhill, *born* 1952, *apptd* 2013
Rt. Hon. Sir Michael Briggs, *born* 1954, *apptd* 2013
Rt. Hon. Sir Christopher Floyd, *born* 1951, *apptd* 2013
Rt. Hon. Dame Victoria Sharp, DBE, *born* 1956, *apptd* 2013
Rt. Hon. Sir Adrian Fulford, *born* 1953, *apptd* 2013
Rt. Hon. Dame Julia Macur, *born* 1957, *apptd* 2013
Rt. Hon. Sir Geoffrey Vos, *born* 1955, *apptd* 2013
Rt. Hon. Sir Christopher Clarke, *born* 1947, *apptd* 2013
Ex Officio Judges, Lord Chief Justice of England and Wales; Master of the Rolls; President of the Queen's Bench Division; President of the Family Division; and Chancellor of the High Court

COURTS-MARTIAL APPEAL COURT

Judges, Lord Chief Justice of England and Wales; Master of the Rolls; Lord Justices of Appeal; and Judges of the High Court of Justice

HIGH COURT

CHANCERY DIVISION

Chancellor of the High Court (£208,926), Rt. Hon. Sir Terence Etherton, *born* 1951, *apptd* 2013
Private Secretary, Elaine Harbert
Legal Secretary, Vannina Ettori
Clerk, Amanda Collins

JUDGES *as at June 2013* (each £174,481)
Style, The Hon. Mr/Mrs Justice [surname]

Hon. Sir Peter Smith, *born* 1952, *apptd* 2002
Hon. Sir David Richards, *born* 1951, *apptd* 2003
Hon. Sir George Mann, *born* 1951, *apptd* 2004
Hon. Sir Nicholas Warren, *born* 1949, *apptd* 2005
Hon. Sir Michael Briggs, *born* 1954, *apptd* 2006
Hon. Sir Launcelot Henderson, *born* 1951, *apptd* 2007
Hon. Sir Paul Morgan, *born* 1952, *apptd* 2007
Hon. Sir Alastair Norris, *born* 1950, *apptd* 2007
Hon. Sir Gerald Barling, *born* 1949, *apptd* 2007
Hon. Sir Philip Sales, *born* 1962, *apptd* 2008
Hon. Dame Sonia Proudman, DBE, *born* 1949, *apptd* 2008
Hon. Sir Richard Arnold, *born* 1961, *apptd* 2008
Hon. Sir Peter Roth, *born* 1952, *apptd* 2009
Hon. Sir Guy Newey, *born* 1959, *apptd* 2010
Hon. Sir Robert Hildyard, *born* 1952, *apptd* 2011
Hon. Dame Sarah Asplin, DBE, *born* 1959, *apptd* 2012

Hon. Sir Colin Birss, *born* 1964, *apptd* 2013
Hon. Dame Vivien Rose, DBE, *born* 1960, *apptd* 2013
Hon. Sir Christopher Nugee, *born* 1959, *apptd* 2013

The Chancery Division also includes three specialist courts: the Companies Court, the Patents Court and the Bankruptcy Court.

QUEEN'S BENCH DIVISION

President (£208,926), Rt. Hon. Sir (Roger) John Thomas, *born* 1947, *apptd* 2011
Vice-President (£198,674), Rt. Hon. Dame Heather Hallett, DBE, *born* 1949, *apptd* 2011
Secretary and Clerk, Jean Curtin

JUDGES *as at June 2013* (each £174,481)
Style, The Hon. Mr/Mrs Justice [surname]

Hon. Sir Andrew Collins, *born* 1942, *apptd* 1994
Hon. Sir Michael Burton, *born* 1946, *apptd* 1998
Hon. Sir Stephen Silber, *born* 1944, *apptd* 1999
Hon. Sir Richard Henriques, *born* 1943, *apptd* 2000
Hon. Sir Andrew Smith, *born* 1947, *apptd* 2000
Hon. Sir Duncan Ouseley, *born* 1950, *apptd* 2000
Hon. Sir Robert Owen, *born* 1944, *apptd* 2001
Hon. Sir Colin Mackay, *born* 1943, *apptd* 2001
Hon. Sir John Mitting, *born* 1947, *apptd* 2001
Hon. Sir Brian Keith, *born* 1944, *apptd* 2001
Hon. Sir Jeremy Cooke, *born* 1949, *apptd* 2001
Hon. Sir Richard Field, *born* 1947, *apptd* 2002
Hon. Sir Peregrine Simon, *born* 1950, *apptd* 2002
Hon. Sir (Roger) John Royce, *born* 1944, *apptd* 2002
Hon. Dame Laura Cox, DBE, *born* 1951, *apptd* 2002
Hon. Sir Michael Tugendhat, *born* 1944, *apptd* 2003
Hon. Sir Paul Walker, *born* 1954, *apptd* 2004
Hon. Sir Christopher Clarke, *born* 1947, *apptd* 2005
Hon. Sir Charles Openshaw, *born* 1947, *apptd* 2005
Hon. Dame Caroline Swift, DBE, *born* 1955, *apptd* 2005
Hon. Sir Brian Langstaff, *born* 1948, *apptd* 2005
Hon. Sir Vivian Ramsey, *born* 1950, *apptd* 2005
Hon. Sir Stephen Irwin, *born* 1953, *apptd* 2006
Hon. Sir Nigel Teare, *born* 1952, *apptd* 2006
Hon. Sir Griffith Williams, *born* 1944, *apptd* 2007
Hon. Sir Wyn Williams, *born* 1951, *apptd* 2007
Hon. Sir Timothy King, *born* 1949, *apptd* 2007
Hon. Sir John Saunders, *born* 1949, *apptd* 2007
Hon. Sir Julian Flaux, *born* 1955, *apptd* 2007
Hon. Sir David Foskett, *born* 1949, *apptd* 2007
Hon. Sir Robert Akenhead, *born* 1949, *apptd* 2007
Hon. Sir Nicholas Blake, *born* 1949, *apptd* 2007
Hon. Sir Ross Cranston, *born* 1948, *apptd* 2007
Hon. Sir Peter Coulson, *born* 1958, *apptd* 2008
Hon. Sir William Blair, *born* 1950, *apptd* 2008
Hon. Sir Alistair MacDuff, *born* 1945, *apptd* 2008
Hon. Sir Ian Burnett, *born* 1958, *apptd* 2008
Hon. Sir Nigel Sweeney, *born* 1954, *apptd* 2008
Hon. Dame Elizabeth Slade, DBE, *born* 1949, *apptd* 2008
Hon. Sir Nicholas Hamblen, *born* 1957, *apptd* 2008
Hon. Sir Gary Hickinbottom, *born* 1955, *apptd* 2009
Hon. Sir Timothy Holroyde, *born* 1955, *apptd* 2009
Hon. Dame Victoria Sharp, DBE, *born* 1956, *apptd* 2009
Hon. Sir Andrew Nicol, *born* 1951, *apptd* 2009
Hon. Sir Kenneth Parker, *born* 1945, *apptd* 2009
Hon. Sir Antony Edwards-Stuart, *born* 1946, *apptd* 2009
Hon. Dame Nicola Davies, DBE, *born* 1953, *apptd* 2010
Hon. Dame Kathryn Thirlwall, DBE, *born* 1957, *apptd* 2010
Hon. Sir Michael Supperstone, *born* 1950, *apptd* 2010
Hon. Sir Robin Spencer, *born* 1955, *apptd* 2010
Hon. Sir Keith Lindblom, *born* 1956, *apptd* 2010
Hon. Sir Henry Bernard Eder, *born* 1952, *apptd* 2011
Hon. Sir Henry Globe, *born* 1949, *apptd* 2011
Hon. Sir Andrew Popplewell, *born* 1959, *apptd* 2011
Hon. Sir Rabinder Singh, *born* 1964, *apptd* 2011
Hon. Dame Beverley Lang, DBE, *born* 1955, *apptd* 2011
Hon. Sir Charles Haddon-Cave, *born* 1956, *apptd* 2011
Hon. Sir Stephen Males, *born* 1955, *apptd* 2012
Hon. Sir Jeremy Stuart-Smith, *born* 1955, *apptd* 2012
Hon. Sir George Leggatt, *born* 1957, *apptd* 2012
Hon. Sir Mark Turner, *born* 1959, *apptd* 2013
Hon. Sir Jeremy Baker, *born* 1958, *apptd* 2013
Hon. Sir Stephen Stewart, *born* 1953, *apptd* 2013
Hon. Sir Robert Jay, QC, *born* 1959, *apptd* 2013
Hon. Sir James Dingemans, *born* 1964, *apptd* 2013
Hon. Sir Clive Lewis, *born* 1960, *apptd* 2013
Hon. Dame Sue Carr, DBE, *born* 1964, *apptd* 2013
Hon. Sir Andrew Gilbart, *born* 1950, *apptd* 2013
Hon. Dame Frances Patterson, *born* 1955, *apptd* 2013
Hon. Sir Stephen Phillips, *born* 1961, *apptd* 2013
Hon. Dame Geraldine Andrews, *born* 1959, *apptd* 2013

The Queen's Bench Division also includes the Divisional Court, the Admiralty Court, Commercial Court and Technology and Construction Court.

FAMILY DIVISION

President (£208,926), Rt. Hon. Sir James Munby, *born* 1948, *apptd* 2013
Secretary, Mrs Sarah Leung
Clerk, George Pitchley

JUDGES *as at June 2013* (each £174,481)
Style, The Hon. Mr/Mrs Justice [surname]

Hon. Sir Edward Holman, *born* 1947, *apptd* 1995
Hon. Dame Mary Hogg, DBE, *born* 1947, *apptd* 1995
Hon. Sir Arthur Charles, *born* 1948, *apptd* 1998
Hon. Sir David Bodey, *born* 1947, *apptd* 1999
Hon. Sir Paul Coleridge, *born* 1949, *apptd* 2000
Hon. Sir Mark Hedley, *born* 1946, *apptd* 2002
Hon. Dame Anna Pauffley, DBE, *born* 1956, *apptd* 2003
Hon. Sir Roderic Wood, *born* 1951, *apptd* 2004
Hon. Dame Florence Baron, DBE, *born* 1952, *apptd* 2004
Hon. Sir Andrew Moylan, *born* 1953, *apptd* 2007
Hon. Dame Eleanor King, DBE, *born* 1957, *apptd* 2008
Hon. Dame Judith Parker, DBE, *born* 1950, *apptd* 2008
Hon. Sir Jonathan Baker, *born* 1955, *apptd* 2009
Hon. Sir Nicholas Mostyn, *born* 1957, *apptd* 2010
Hon. Sir Peter Arthur Jackson, *born* 1955, *apptd* 2010
Hon. Dame Lucy Theis, *born* 1960, *apptd* 2010
Hon. Sir Philip Moor, *born* 1959, *apptd* 2011
Hon. Sir Stephen Cobb, *born* 1960, *apptd* 2013
Hon. Sir Michael Keehan, *born* 1960, *apptd* 2013
Hon. Sir Anthony Hayden, *born* 1961, *apptd* 2013

DEPARTMENTS AND OFFICES OF THE SENIOR COURTS OF ENGLAND AND WALES

Royal Courts of Justice, London WC2A 2LL
T 020-7947 6000

ADMINISTRATIVE COURT OFFICE

T 020-7947 6655
Judge in charge of the Administrative Court (£174,481), Hon. Sir Duncan Ouseley
Master of the Crown Office, and Queen's Coroner and Attorney (£103,950), M. Egan, QC
Deputy Master of the Crown Office, Mrs L. G. Knapman
Court Manager, Miss A. Lee

ADMIRALTY, COMMERCIAL AND LONDON MERCANTILE COURT
Ground Floor, 7 Rolls Building, Fetter Lane, London EC4A 1NL
T 020-7947 6112
Registrar (£103,950), J. Kay, QC
Admiralty Marshal, M. Parker
Admiralty Court Manager, W. Lusty
Judge in charge of Commercial Court (£174,481), Hon. Sir Jeremy Cooke
Commercial Court Senior Lists Officer, J. Kelly

BANKRUPTCY AND COMPANIES COURT REGISTRY
7 Rolls Building, Fetter Lane, London EC4A 1NL T 020-7947 6294
Chief Registrar (£129,579), S. Baister
Bankruptcy Registrars (£103,950), S. Barber; C. Derrett; C. Jones; D. Shafer
Court Manager, T. Pollen

CENTRAL OFFICE OF THE QUEEN'S BENCH DIVISION
Senior Master and Queen's Remembrancer (£129,579), S. D. Whitaker
Masters of the Queen's Bench Division (£103,950), J. D. Cooke; R. Eastman; B. J. F. Fontaine; J. K. Kay, QC; H. J. Leslie; V. McCloud; R. R. Roberts; B. Yoxall
Court Manager, Miss A. Lee

CHANCERY CHAMBERS
T 020-7947 6148
Chief Master (£129,579), J. Winegarten
Masters of the Senior Courts (£103,950), T. J. Bowles; N. W. Bragge; M. Marsh; N. S. Price; P. R. Teverson
Court Manager, T. Pollen

COSTS OFFICE
T 020-7947 6423
Senior Costs Judge (£129,579), P. T. Hurst
Masters of the Senior Courts (£103,950), C. D. N. Campbell; A. Gordon-Saker; P. Haworth; C. Leonard; J. E. O'Hare; J. Simons; C. C. Wright
Court Manager, T. Pollen

COURT OF APPEAL CIVIL DIVISION
T 020-7947 6915
Deputy Registrars, Marie Bancroft-Rimer, Sally Meacher
Court Manager, Miss K. Langan

COURT OF APPEAL CRIMINAL DIVISION
T 020-7947 6011
Registrar (£103,950), M. Egan, QC
Deputy Registrar, Mrs L. G. Knapman
Court Manager, Miss C. Brownbill

COURT OF PROTECTION
Royal Courts of Justice, Strand, London WC2A 2LL
T 0300-456 4600
Senior Judge (£129,579), D. Lush
Court Manager, J. Matthews

ELECTION PETITIONS OFFICE
Room E13, Royal Courts of Justice, Strand, London WC2A 2LL
T 020-7947 6877

The office accepts petitions and deals with all matters relating to the questioning of parliamentary, European Parliament, local government and parish elections, and with applications for relief under the 'representation of the people' legislation.
Prescribed Officer, The Senior Master and Senior Remembrancer (£129,579), S. D. Whitaker
Chief Clerk, Geraint Evans

EXAMINERS OF THE COURT
Empowered to take examination of witnesses in all divisions of the High Court.
Examiners, His Hon. M. W. M. Chism; A. G. Dyer; A. W. Hughes; Mrs G. M. Keene; R. M. Planterose

PRINCIPAL REGISTRY (FAMILY DIVISION)
First Avenue House, 42–49 High Holborn, London WC1V 6NP
T 020-7947 6000
Senior District Judge (£129,579), P. Waller
District Judges (£103,950), Mrs A. Aitken; M. C. Berry; Ms S. M. Bowman; Ms H. C. Bradley; Ms P. Cushing; Mrs L. Gordon-Saker; R. Harper; Ms H. MacGregor; K. Malik; Ms C. Reid; Ms L. D. Roberts; R. Robinson; Ms S. Walker; K. J. White

TECHNOLOGY AND CONSTRUCTION COURT (TCC)
Ground Floor, 7 Rolls Building, Fetter Lane, London EC4A 1NL
T 020-7947 6022
Judge in charge of the TCC (£174,481), Hon. Sir Robert Akenhead
Court Manager, W. Lusty
List Officer, S. Gibbon

COURT FUNDS OFFICE
Glasgow G58 1AB T 0845-223 8500

The Court Funds Office (CFO) provides a banking and administration service for the civil courts throughout England and Wales, including the High Court.
Head of CFO, Eddie Bloomfield

OFFICIAL SOLICITOR AND PUBLIC TRUSTEE
81 Chancery Lane, London WC2A 1DD
T 020-7911 7127

The Official Solicitor and the Public Trustee are independent statutory office holders. Their office (OSPT) is an arms-length body of the Ministry of Justice that exists to support their work.The Official Solicitor provides access to the justice system to those who are vulnerable by virtue of minority or lack of mental capacity. The Public Trustee acts as executor or administrator of estates and as the appointed trustee of settlements, providing an effective executor and trustee service of last resort.
Official Solicitor to the Senior Courts, Alistair Pitblado
Public Trustee, Eddie Bloomfield

PROBATE SERVICE
London Probate Department
PRFD, 7th Floor, First Avenue House, 42–49 High Holborn, London WC1V 6NP T 020-7947 6939
Probate Manager, Ms T. Constantinou

DISTRICT PROBATE REGISTRARS/MANAGERS
Birmingham District Registrar, Miss P. Walbeoff
Brighton District Probate Manager, M. Hussain
Bristol District Registrar, Mrs B. Phillips
Cardiff District (Wales) Registrar, Mrs F. Herdman
Ipswich District Registrar, Miss H. Whitby
Leeds District Probate Manager, Mrs S. Holding
Liverpool District Probate Manager, Mrs D. Shone
Manchester District Registrar, K. Murphy
Newcastle District Registrar, Mrs M. C. Riley
Oxford District Registrar, Mrs F. Herdman
Winchester District Registrar, A. Butler

JUDGE ADVOCATES GENERAL
The Judge Advocate General is the judicial head of the Service justice system, and the leader of the judges who

preside over trials in the court martial and other Service courts. The defendants are service personnel from the Royal Navy, the army and the Royal Air Force, and civilians accompanying them overseas.

JUDGE ADVOCATE GENERAL OF THE FORCES
9th Floor, Thomas More Building, Royal Courts of Justice, Strand, London WC2A 2LL
T 020-7218 8095
Judge Advocate General (£139,933), His Hon. Judge Blackett
Vice Judge Advocate General (£121,993), Michael Hunter
Assistant Judge Advocates General (£103,950)*, J. P. Camp; M. R. Elsom; R. D. Hill; A. M. Large; A. J. B. McGrigor; E. Peters
Style, Judge [surname]

* Salary includes £2,000 London salary lead and a London allowance of £2,000

HIGH COURT AND CROWN COURT CENTRES

First-tier centres deal with both civil and criminal cases and are served by high court and circuit judges. Second-tier centres deal with criminal cases only and are served by high court and circuit judges. Third-tier centres deal with criminal cases only and are served only by circuit judges.

LONDON REGION
First-tier – None
Second-tier – Central Criminal Court
Third-tier – Blackfriars, Croydon, Harrow, Inner London, Isleworth, Kingston upon Thames, Snaresbrook, Southwark, Wood Green, Woolwich
Delivery Director, Sheila Proudlock, 3rd Floor, Rose Court, 2 Southwark Bridge, London SE1 9HS
Heads of Departments, Martin John *(Civil, Family and Tribunals);* Dave Weston *(Crime London)*

The high court (first-tier) in Greater London sits at the Royal Courts of Justice.

MIDLANDS REGION
First-tier – Birmingham, Lincoln, Nottingham, Stafford, Warwick
Second-tier – Leicester, Northampton, Shrewsbury, Worcester, Wolverhampton
Third-tier – Coventry, Derby, Hereford, Stoke on Trent
Delivery Director, Lucy Garrod, PO Box 11772, 6th Floor, Temple Court, Bull Street, Birmingham B4 6WF

NORTH-EAST REGION
First-tier – Leeds, Newcastle upon Tyne, Sheffield, Teesside
Second-tier – Bradford, York
Third-tier – Doncaster, Durham, Kingston upon Hull, Great Grimsby
Delivery Director, Mark Swales, 11th Floor, Pinnacle, Albion Street, Leeds LS1 5AA T 0113-251 1204
Head of Crime (interim), Graham Goldsmith

NORTH-WEST REGION
First-tier – Carlisle, Chester, Liverpool, Manchester (Crown Square), Preston
Third-tier – Barrow in Furness, Bolton, Burnley, Knutsford, Lancaster, Manchester (Minshull Street), Warrington
Delivery Director, Gill Hague, PO Box 4237, Manchester Civil Justice Centre, 1 Bridge Street West, Manchester M60 1TE T 0161-240 5000
Heads of Departments, Lorraine Edgar *(Regional Support Unit);* Paul McGladrigan *(Crime);* Simon Vowles *(Civil, Family and Tribunals)*

SOUTH-EAST REGION
First-tier – Cambridge, Chelmsford, Lewes, Norwich, Oxford
Second-tier – Guildford, Ipswich, Luton, Maidstone, Reading, St Albans
Third-tier – Aylesbury, Basildon, Canterbury, Chichester, Croydon, King's Lynn, Peterborough, Southend
Delivery Director, Chris Jennings, 5th Floor, Fox Court, 14 Gray's Inn Road, London WC1X 8HN T 020-3206 0627
Cluster Managers, Philip Densham *(Thames Valley);* Dr Jim Doherty *(Kent);* Yvonne Mckenna-Young *(Cambridgeshire and Essex);* Dave Manning *(Surrey and Sussex);* Ian Miller *(Norfolk and Suffolk);* Mark Stewart *(Bedfordshire and Hertfordshire)*

SOUTH-WEST REGION
First-tier – Bristol, Exeter, Truro, Winchester
Second-tier – Dorchester & Weymouth, Gloucester, Plymouth
Third-tier – Barnstaple, Bournemouth, Newport (IoW), Portsmouth, Salisbury, Southampton, Swindon, Taunton
Delivery Director, Sandra Aston, PO Box 484, Queensway House, Weston-super-Mare, N. Somerset BS23 7BJ T 01934 528668

WALES REGION
First-tier – Caernarfon, Cardiff, Merthyr Tydfil, Mold, Swansea
Second-tier – Carmarthen, Newport, Welshpool
Third-tier – Dolgellau, Haverfordwest
Delivery Director, Luigi Strinati, Wales Support Unit, Fitzalan Place, Cardiff CF24 0RZ T 029-2067 8311

CIRCUIT JUDGES

Circuit judges are barristers of at least seven years' standing or recorders of at least five years' standing. Circuit judges serve in the county courts and the crown court.
Style, His/Her Hon. Judge [surname]
Senior Presiding Judge, Rt. Hon. Lord Justice Gross
Senior Circuit Judges, each £139,933
Circuit Judges at the Central Criminal Court, London (Old Bailey Judges), each £139,933
Circuit Judges, each £129,579

MIDLAND CIRCUIT
Presiding Judges, Hon. Mr Justice Flaux (until 31 Dec. 2013) Hon. Mr Justice Haddon-Cave (from 1 Jan. 2014); Hon. Mrs Justice Thirlwall

NORTH-EASTERN CIRCUIT
Presiding Judges, Hon. Mr Justice Coulson; Hon. Mr Justice Globe

NORTHERN CIRCUIT
Presiding Judges, Hon. Mr Justice Holroyde; Hon. Mr Justice Turner

SOUTH-EASTERN CIRCUIT
Presiding Judges, Hon. Mr Justice Nicol; Hon. Mr Justice Singh; Hon. Mr Justice Spencer; Hon. Mr Justice Sweeney

WALES CIRCUIT
Presiding Judges, Hon. Mrs Justice Davies Hon. Mr Justice Griffith Williams (from 1 Jan. 2014); Hon. Mr Justice Wyn Williams

WESTERN CIRCUIT
Presiding Judges, Hon. Mr Justice Burnett; Hon. Mr Justice Sharp; Hon. Mr Justice Teare

DISTRICT JUDGES

District judges, formerly known as registrars of the court, are solicitors of at least seven years' standing and serve in county courts.

District Judges, each £103,950

DISTRICT JUDGES (MAGISTRATES' COURTS)

District judges (magistrates' courts), formerly known as stipendiary magistrates, serve in magistrates courts where they hear criminal cases, youth cases and some civil proceedings. Some may be authorised to handle extradition proceedings and terrorist cases. District judges (magistrates' courts) must be barristers or solicitors of at least seven years' standing and must have served as deputy district judges for a minimum of two years or 30 days' sittings.

District Judges (Magistrates' Courts), each £103,950

OFFICE OF THE CHIEF MAGISTRATE
181 Marylebone Road, London NW1 5BR
T 020-3126 3106

The Chief Magistrate (senior district judge) is responsible for hearing many of the sensitive or complex cases – extradition and special jurisdiction cases in particular – in the magistrates' courts. The Chief Magistrate also supports and guides district judges (magistrates' court), and liaises with the senior judiciary and presiding judges on matters pertaining to magistrates' courts.

The Office of the Chief Magistrate provides administrative support to both the Chief Magistrate and to all the district judges sitting at magistrates' courts in England and Wales.

Chief Magistrate, Howard Riddle
Deputy Chief Magistrate, Emma Arbuthnot

CROWN PROSECUTION SERVICE

Rose Court, 2 Southwark Bridge Road, London SE1 9HS
T 020-3357 0000 E enquiries@cps.gsi.gov.uk W www.cps.gov.uk

The Crown Prosecution Service (CPS) is responsible for prosecuting cases investigated by the police in England and Wales, with the exception of cases conducted by the Serious Fraud Office and certain minor offences.

The CPS is headed by the director of public prosecutions (DPP), who works under the superintendence of the attorney-general. The service is divided into 13 areas across England and Wales, with each area led by a chief crown prosecutor.

Director of Public Prosecutions, Alison Saunders
Chief Executive, Peter Lewis, CB
Chief Operating Officer, Jim Brisbane
Principal Legal Adviser, Alison Levitt, QC
Directors, Nick Hunt *(Strategy and Policy);* Helen Kershaw *(Private Office);* Joanne Millington *(Communication);* Dale Simon *(Public Accountability and Inclusion);* Paul Staff *(Business Information Systems and Finance);* Mark Summerfield *(Human Resources)*

CPS AREAS

EAST MIDLANDS, 2 King Edward Court, King Edward Street, Nottingham NG1 1EL T 0115-852 3300
Chief Crown Prosecutor, Steve Chappell

EASTERN, County House, 100 New London Road, Chelmsford, Essex CM2 0RG T 01245-455800
Chief Crown Prosecutor, Grace Ononiwu

LONDON, 5th Floor, Rose Court, 2 Southwark Bridge, London SE1 9HS T 020-3357 0000
Chief Crown Prosecutor, Alison Saunders, CB

MERSEY–CHESHIRE, 7th Floor, Royal Liver Building, Pier Head, Liverpool L3 1HN T 0151-239 6400
Chief Crown Prosecutor, Claire Lindley

NORTH EAST, St Ann's Quay, 112 Quayside, Newcastle Upon Tyne, NE1 3BD T 0191-260 4200
Chief Crown Prosecutor, Wendy Williams

NORTH WEST, 1st Floor, Stocklund House, Castle Street, Carlisle CA3 8SY T 01228-882900
Chief Crown Prosecutor, Nazir Afzal, OBE

SOUTH EAST, 29 Union Street, Maidstone, Kent ME14 1PT T 01622-356300
Chief Crown Prosecutor, Roger Coe-Salazar

SOUTH WEST, 5th Floor, Kite Wing, Temple Quay House, 2 The Square, Bristol BS1 6PN T 0117-930 2800
Chief Crown Prosecutor, Barry Hughes

THAMES AND CHILTERN, Eaton Court, 112 Oxford Road, Reading, Berks RG1 7LL T 0118-951 3600
Chief Crown Prosecutor, Baljit Ubhey, OBE

WALES, 20th Floor, Capital Tower, Greyfriars Road, Cardiff CF10 3PL T 029-2080 3800
Chief Crown Prosecutor, Ed Beltrami

WESSEX, 3rd Floor, Black Horse House, 8–10 Leigh Road, Eastleigh, Hants SO50 9FH T 02380-673 800
Chief Crown Prosecutor (acting), Kate Brown

WEST MIDLANDS, Colmore Gate, 2 Colmore Row, Birmingham B3 2QA T 0121-262 1300
Chief Crown Prosecutor, Harry Ireland

YORKSHIRE AND HUMBERSIDE, 27 Park Place, Leeds LS1 2SZ T 0113-290 2700
Chief Crown Prosecutor, Martin Goldman

HER MAJESTY'S COURTS AND TRIBUNALS SERVICE

1st Floor, 102 Petty France, London SW1H 9AJ
W www.justice.gov.uk

Her Majesty's Courts Service and the Tribunals Service merged on 1 April 2011 to form HM Courts and Tribunals Service. It is an agency of the Ministry of Justice, operating as a partnership between the Lord Chancellor, the Lord Chief Justice and the Senior President of Tribunals. It is responsible for administering the criminal, civil and family courts and tribunals in England and Wales and non-devolved tribunals in Scotland and Northern Ireland.

Chief Executive, Peter Handcock, CBE

JUDICIAL APPOINTMENTS COMMISSION

Steel House, 11 Tothill Street, London SW1H 9LJ
T 020-3334 0123 E jaas@jac.gsi.gov.uk
W www.judicialappointments.gov.uk

The Judicial Appointments Commission was established as an independent non-departmental public body in April 2006 by the Constitutional Reform Act 2005. Its role is to select judicial office holders independently of government (a responsibility previously held by the Lord Chancellor) for courts and tribunals in England and Wales, and for some tribunals whose jurisdiction extends to Scotland or Northern Ireland. It has a statutory duty to encourage diversity in the range of persons available for selection and is sponsored by the Ministry of Justice and accountable to parliament through the Lord Chancellor. It is made up of 15 commissioners, including a chair.

Chair, Christopher Stephens
Commissioners, Hon. Sir David Bean; District Judge Birchall; Rt. Hon. Dame Jill Black, DBE; Martin Forde, QC; Prof. Noel Lloyd, CBE; Judge Alison McKenna; Alexandra Marks; Stella Pantelides; Lt.-Gen. Sir Andrew Ridgway, KBE, CB; Ranjit Sondhi, CBE; Dame Valerie Strachan, DCB; Hon. Judge Deborah Taylor; John Thornhill FRSA; Hon. Sir Alan Wilkie
Chief Executive, Nigel Reeder

DIRECTORATE OF JUDICIAL OFFICES

The Judicial Office was established in April 2006 to support the judiciary in discharging its responsibilities under the Constitutional Reform Act 2005. It is led by a chief executive, who reports to the Lord Chief Justice rather than to ministers, and its work is directed by the judiciary rather than by the administration of the day. The Judicial Office incorporates the Judicial College, sponsorship of the Family and Civil Justice Councils, the Office for Judicial Complaints and Office of the Chief Coroner.

CHIEF EXECUTIVE'S OFFICE
T 020-7947 7598
Chief Executive Officer, Jillian Kay
Personal Secretary, Maxine Fidler

JUDICIAL COMMITTEE OF THE PRIVY COUNCIL

The Judicial Committee of the Privy Council is the final court of appeal for the United Kingdom overseas territories (*see* UK Overseas Territories section), crown dependencies and those independent Commonwealth countries which have retained this avenue of appeal and the sovereign base areas of Akrotiri and Dhekelia in Cyprus. The committee also hears appeals against pastoral schemes under the Pastoral Measure 1983, and deals with appeals from veterinary disciplinary bodies.

Until October 2009, the Judicial Committee of the Privy Council was the final arbiter in disputes as to the legal competence of matters done or proposed by the devolved legislative and executive authorities in Scotland, Wales and Northern Ireland. This is now the responsibility of the UK Supreme Court.

In 2012–13 the Judicial Committee heard a total of 36 appeals and dealt with 51 petitions for special leave to appeal.

The members of the Judicial Committee are the justices of the supreme court, and Privy Counsellors who hold or have held high judicial office in the United Kingdom or in certain designated courts of Commonwealth countries from which appeals are taken to committee.

JUDICIAL COMMITTEE OF THE PRIVY COUNCIL
Parliament Square, London SW1A 2AJ T 020-7960 1500
Registrar of the Privy Council, Louise di Mambro
Chief Clerk, Jackie Lindsay

SCOTTISH JUDICATURE

Scotland has a legal system separate from, and differing greatly from, the English legal system in enacted law, judicial procedure and the structure of courts.

In Scotland the system of public prosecution is headed by the Lord Advocate and is independent of the police, who have no say in the decision to prosecute. The Lord Advocate, discharging his functions through the Crown Office in Edinburgh, is responsible for prosecutions in the high court, sheriff courts and justice of the peace courts. Prosecutions in the high court are prepared by the Crown Office and conducted in court by one of the law officers, by an advocate-depute, or by a solicitor advocate. In the inferior courts the decision to prosecute is made and prosecution is preferred by procurators fiscal, who are lawyers and full-time civil servants subject to the directions of the Crown Office. A permanent legally qualified civil servant, known as the crown agent, is responsible for the running of the Crown Office and the organisation of the Procurator Fiscal Service, of which he or she is the head.

Scotland is divided into six sheriffdoms, each with a full-time sheriff principal. The sheriffdoms are further divided into sheriff court districts, each of which has a legally qualified resident sheriff or sheriffs, who are the judges of the court.

In criminal cases sheriffs principal and sheriffs have the same powers; sitting with a jury of 15 members, they may try more serious cases on indictment, or, sitting alone, may try lesser cases under summary procedure. Minor summary offences are dealt with in justice of the peace courts, which replaced district courts formerly operated by local authorities, and presided over by lay justices of the peace (of whom some 500 regularly sit in court) and, in Glasgow only, by stipendiary magistrates. Juvenile offenders (children under 16) may be brought before an informal children's hearing comprising three local lay people. The superior criminal court is the high court of justiciary which is both a trial and an appeal court. Cases on indictment are tried by a high court judge, sitting with a jury of 15, in Edinburgh and on circuit in other towns. Appeals from the lower courts against conviction or sentence are also heard by the high court, which sits as an appeal court only in Edinburgh. There is no further appeal to the UK supreme court in criminal cases.

In civil cases the jurisdiction of the sheriff court extends to most kinds of action. Appeals against decisions of the sheriff may be made to the sheriff principal and thence to the court of session, or direct to the court of session, which sits only in Edinburgh. The court of session is divided into the inner and the outer house. The outer house is a court of first instance in which cases are heard by judges sitting singly, sometimes with a jury of 12. The inner house, itself subdivided into two divisions of equal status, is mainly an appeal court. Appeals may be made to the inner house from the outer house as well as from the sheriff court. An appeal may be made from the inner house to the UK supreme court.

The judges of the court of session are the same as those of the high court of justiciary, with the Lord President of the court of session also holding the office of Lord Justice General in the high court. Senators of the College of Justice are Lords Commissioners of Justiciary as well as judges of the court of session. On appointment, a senator takes a judicial title, which is retained for life. Although styled The Hon./Rt. Hon. Lord, the senator is not a peer, although some judges are peers in their own right.

The office of coroner does not exist in Scotland. The local procurator fiscal inquires privately into sudden or suspicious deaths and may report findings to the crown agent. In some cases a fatal accident inquiry may be held before the sheriff.

COURT OF SESSION AND HIGH COURT OF JUSTICIARY

The Lord President and Lord Justice General (£216,307), Rt. Hon. Lord Gill, *born* 1942, *apptd* 2012
Private Secretary, P. Gilmour

INNER HOUSE
Lords of Session (each £198,674)

FIRST DIVISION
The Lord President

Rt. Hon Lord Eassie (Ronald Mackay), *born* 1945, *apptd* 2006
Rt. Hon. Lord Menzies (Duncan Menzies), *born* 1953, *apptd* 2012
Rt. Hon Lady Smith (Anne Smith), *born* 1955, *apptd* 2012
Rt. Hon. Lord Brodie (Philip Brodie), *born* 1950, *apptd* 2012

SECOND DIVISION
Lord Justice Clerk (£208,926), Rt. Hon. Lord Carloway, *born* 1954, *apptd* 2012
Rt. Hon. Lady Paton (Ann Paton), *born* 1952, *apptd* 2007
Rt. Hon. Lady Dorrian (Leona Dorrian), *born* 1957, *apptd* 2012
Rt. Hon. Lord Bracadale (Alistair Campbell), *born* 1949, *apptd* 2013
Hon. Lord Drummond Young (James Drummond Young), *born* 1950, *apptd* 2001

OUTER HOUSE
Lords of Session (each £174,481)
Hon. Lord Glennie (Angus Glennie), *born* 1950, *apptd* 2005
Hon. Lord Kinclaven (Alexander F. Wylie), *born* 1951, *apptd* 2005
Hon. Lord Turnbull (Alan Turnbull), *born* 1958, *apptd* 2006
Rt. Hon. Lady Clark of Calton (Lynda Clark), *born* 1949, *apptd* 2006
Hon. Lord Brailsford (Sidney Brailsford), *born* 1954, *apptd* 2006
Hon. Lord Uist (Roderick Macdonald), *born* 1951, *apptd* 2006
Hon. Lord Malcolm (Colin M. Campbell), *born* 1953, *apptd* 2007
Hon. Lord Matthews (Hugh Matthews), *born* 1953, *apptd* 2007
Hon. Lord Woolman (Stephen Woolman), *born* 1953, *apptd* 2008
Hon. Lord Pentland (Paul Cullen), *born* 1957, *apptd* 2008
Hon. Lord Bannatyne (Iain Peebles), *born* 1954, *apptd* 2008
Hon. Lady Stacey (Valerie E. Stacey), *born* 1954, *apptd* 2009
Hon. Lord Tyre (Colin Tyre), *born* 1956, *apptd* 2010
Hon. Lord Doherty (Raymond Doherty), *born* 1958, *apptd* 2010
Hon. Lord Stewart (Angus Stewart), *born* 1946, *apptd* 2010
Rt. Hon. Lord Boyd of Duncansby (Colin Boyd), *born* 1953, *apptd* 2012
Hon. Lord Jones (Michael Jones), *born* 1948, *apptd* 2012
Hon. Lord Burns (David Burns), *born* 1952, *apptd* 2012
Hon. Lady Scott (Margaret Scott), *born* 1960, *apptd* 2012
Hon. Lady Wise (Morag Wise), *born* 1963, *apptd* 2013
Hon. Lord Armstrong (Iain Armstrong), *born* 1956, *apptd* 2013

COURT OF SESSION AND HIGH COURT OF JUSTICIARY
Parliament House, Parliament Square, Edinburgh EH1 1RQ
T 0131-225 2595
Principal Clerk of Session and Justiciary, G. Marwick
Deputy Principal Clerk of Session and Principal Extractor, G. Prentice
Deputy Principal Clerk of Justiciary, J. Moyes
Officer in Charge of Offices of Court, Y. Anderson
Officer in Charge of Justiciary Office, vacant
Keeper of the Rolls, G. Combe
Division Clerks, D. Cullen; E. Dickson; R. Jenkins
Appeal Clerks, D. Cullen; A. Mackay; C Reid
Clerking Service Managers, A. McArdle; L. MacLachlan; D. MacLeod
Depute Clerks of Session and Justiciary, N. Boyle; R. Broome; G. Burton; Z. Conway; L. Curran; T. Fiddes; C. Fyffe; A. Galloway; A. Hutchison; T. Kell; K. Kier; A. Lynch; G. McLeod; L. McNamara; N. Marchant; I. Martin; R. Martin; M. Megarrell; D. Morrison; R. Newlands; K. O'Hare; C. Richardson; C. Scott; G. Scott; L. Sexto; C. Stark; K. Todd; C. Truby; P. Weir

JUDICIAL APPOINTMENTS BOARD FOR SCOTLAND
38–39 Drumsheugh Gardens, Edinburgh EH3 7SW
T 0131-528 5101

The board's remit is to provide the first minister with the names of candidates recommended for appointment to the posts of senator of the college of justice, chair of the Scottish Land Court, sheriff principal, sheriff and part-time sheriff.
Chair, Sir Muir Russell, KCB, FRSE

JUDICIAL OFFICE FOR SCOTLAND
Parliament House, Edinburgh EH1 1RQ
T 0131-240 6677 W www.scotland-judiciary.org.uk

The Judicial Office for Scotland came into being on 1 April 2010 as part of the changes introduced by the Judiciary and Courts (Scotland) Act 2008. It provides support for the Lord President in his role as head of the Scottish judiciary with responsibility for the training, welfare, deployment and conduct of judges and the efficient disposal of business in the courts.
Executive Director, Steve Humphreys

SCOTTISH COURT SERVICE
Saughton House, Broomhouse Drive, Edinburgh EH11 3XD
T 0131-444 3300 W www.scotcourts.gov.uk

The Scottish Court Service is responsible for the provision of staff, buildings and technology to support Scotland's courts, the independent judiciary, the courts' Rules Councils and the Office of the Public Guardian. On 1 April 2010 it was established by the Judiciary and Courts (Scotland) Act 2008 as an independent body, governed by a corporate board and chaired by the Lord President.
Chief Executive, Eric McQueen

SCOTTISH GOVERNMENT JUSTICE DIRECTORATE
Legal System Division, Room 2W, St Andrew's House, Edinburgh EH1 3DG
T 0131-244 2698

The Justice Directorate is responsible for the appointment of judges and sheriffs to meet the needs of the business of the supreme and sheriffs court in Scotland. It is also responsible for providing resources for the efficient administration of certain specialist courts and tribunals.
Deputy Director, Jan Marshall

SCOTTISH LAND COURT
126 George Street, Edinburgh EH2 4HH
T 0131-271 4360

The court deals with disputes relating to agricultural and crofting land in Scotland.
Chair (£139,933), Hon. Lord McGhie (James McGhie), QC
Deputy Chair, R. J. Macleod
Members, D. J. Houston; A. Macdonald *(part-time)*; J. A. Smith *(part-time)*
Principal Clerk, Barbara Brown

SHERIFF COURT OF CHANCERY
27 Chambers Street, Edinburgh EH1 1LB
T 0131-225 2525

The court deals with service of heirs and completion of title in relation to heritable property.
Sheriff of Chancery, M. Stephen

SHERIFF COURTS
The majority of cases in Scotland are handled by one of the 49 sheriff courts. Criminal cases are heard by a sheriff and a jury (solemn procedure) but can be heard by a sheriff

alone (summary procedure). Civil cases are heard by a single sheriff.

Scotland is split into six sheriffdoms, each headed by a sheriff principal.

SALARIES
Sheriff Principal, £139,933
Sheriff, £129,579

SHERIFFDOMS
GLASGOW AND STRATHKELVIN
Sheriff Principal, C. A. L. Scott
GRAMPIAN, HIGHLAND AND ISLANDS
Sheriff Principal, D. Pyle
LOTHIAN AND BORDERS
Sheriff Principal, M. M. Stephen
NORTH STRATHCLYDE
Sheriff Principal, B. A. Kerr, QC
SOUTH STRATHCLYDE, DUMFRIES AND GALLOWAY
Sheriff Principal, B. A. Lockhart
TAYSIDE, CENTRAL AND FIFE
Sheriff Principal, R. A. Dunlop, QC

JUSTICE OF THE PEACE COURTS

Justice of the peace courts replaced district courts and are a unique feature of Scotland's judicial system. Justices of the peace are lay magistrates who either sit alone, or in a bench of three, and deal with summary crimes such as speeding and careless driving. In court, justices have access to solicitors, who fulfill the role of legal advisers or clerks of court.

A justice of the peace court can be presided over by a stipendiary magistrate – a legally qualified solicitor or advocate who sits alone. They deal with more serious summary business similar to sheriffs, such as drink driving and assault. All sheriffs principal have powers to appoint stipendiary magistrates, but at present they have only been appointed in the justice of the peace court in the Sheriffdom of Glasgow and Strathkelvin.

CROWN OFFICE AND PROCURATOR FISCAL SERVICE

CROWN OFFICE
25 Chambers Street, Edinburgh EH1 1LA
T 0844-561 1020 W www.crownoffice.gov.uk
Chief Executive and Crown Agent, Catherine Dyer

PROCURATORS FISCAL

SALARY: £75,000–£162,500

NORTH FEDERATION
Area Procurator Fiscal, Liam Murphy
EAST FEDERATION
Area Procurator Fiscal, John Logue
WEST FEDERATION
Area Procurator Fiscal, John Dunn
NATIONAL FEDERATION
Director of Serious Casework, David Harvie

COURT OF THE LORD LYON

HM New Register House, Edinburgh EH1 3YT
T 0131-556 7255 W www.lyon-court.com

The Court of the Lord Lyon is the Scottish Court of Chivalry (including the genealogical jurisdiction of the *Ri-Sennachie* of Scotland's Celtic kings). The Lord Lyon King of Arms has jurisdiction, subject to appeal to the Court of Session and the House of Lords, in questions of heraldry and the right to bear arms. The court also administers the Public Register of All Arms and Bearings and the Public Register of All Genealogies in Scotland. Pedigrees are established by decrees of Lyon Court and by letters patent. As Royal Commissioner in Armory, the Lord Lyon grants patents of arms to virtuous and well-deserving Scots and to petitioners (personal or corporate) in the Queen's overseas realms of Scottish connection, and also issues birthbrieves. For information on Her Majesty's Officers of Arms in Scotland, *see* the Court of the Lord Lyon in the Public Bodies section.

Lord Lyon King of Arms, David Sellar, FSA SCOT, FRHISTS
Lyon Clerk and Keeper of the Records, Mrs C. G. W. Roads, LVO, FSA SCOT, FSA
Procurator Fiscal, Alexander M. S. Green
Macer, Roderick Macpherson

NORTHERN IRELAND JUDICATURE

In Northern Ireland the legal system and the structure of courts closely resemble those of England and Wales; there are, however, often differences in enacted law.

The court of judicature of Northern Ireland comprises the court of appeal, the high court of justice and the crown court. The practice and procedure of these courts is similar to that in England. The superior civil court is the high court of justice, from which an appeal lies to the Northern Ireland court of appeal; the UK supreme court is the final civil appeal court.

The crown court, served by high court and county court judges, deals with criminal trials on indictment. Cases are heard before a judge and, except those certified by the Director of Public Prosecutions under the Justice and Security Act 2007, a jury. Appeals from the crown court against conviction or sentence are heard by the Northern Ireland court of appeal; the UK supreme court is the final court of appeal.

The decision to prosecute in criminal cases in Northern Ireland rests with the Director of Public Prosecutions.

Minor criminal offences are dealt with in magistrates' courts by a legally qualified district judge (magistrates' courts) and, where an offender is under the age of 18, by youth courts each consisting of a district judge (magistrates' courts) and two lay magistrates (at least one of whom must be a woman). As at June 2013 there were 195 justices of the peace in Northern Ireland. Appeals from magistrates' courts are heard by the county court, or by the court of appeal on a point of law or an issue as to jurisdiction.

Magistrates' courts in Northern Ireland can deal with certain classes of civil case but most minor civil cases are dealt with in county courts. Judgments of all civil courts are enforceable through a centralised procedure administered by the Enforcement of Judgments Office.

COURT OF JUDICATURE

The Royal Courts of Justice, Belfast BT1 3JF
T 028-9023 5111
Lord Chief Justice of Northern Ireland (£216,307), Rt. Hon. Sir Declan Morgan, *born* 1952, *apptd* 2009
Principal Private Secretary, Laurene McAlpine

LORDS JUSTICES OF APPEAL (£198,674)
Style, The Rt. Hon. Lord Justice [surname]

Rt. Hon. Sir Malachy Higgins, *born* 1944, *apptd* 2007
Rt. Hon. Sir Paul Girvan, *born* 1948, *apptd* 2007
Rt. Hon. Sir Patrick Coghlin, *born* 1945, *apptd* 2008

HIGH COURT JUDGES (£174,481)
Style, The Hon. Mr Justice [surname]

Hon. Sir John Gillen, *born* 1947, *apptd* 1999
Hon. Sir Ronald Weatherup, *born* 1947, *apptd* 2001

Hon. Sir Reginald Weir, *born* 1947, *apptd* 2003
Hon. Sir Donnell Deeny, *born* 1950, *apptd* 2004
Hon. Sir Seamus Treacy, *born* 1956, *apptd* 2007
Hon. Sir William Benjamin Stephens, *born* 1954, *apptd* 2007
Hon. Sir Bernard McCloskey, *born* 1956, *apptd* 2008
Hon. Sir Paul Maguire, *born* 1952, *apptd* 2012
Hon. Sir Mark Horner, *born* 1956, *apptd* 2012
*Hon. Sir Thomas Burgess, *born* 1943, *apptd* 2012
Hon. Sir John O'Hara, *born* 1956, *apptd* 2013

* Temporary appointment

MASTERS OF THE HIGH COURT (£103,950)
Master, Queen's Bench and Appeals, C. J. McCorry
Master, Office of Care and Protection, H. Wells
Master, Chancery and Probate, R. A. Ellison
Master, Matrimonial, C. W. G. Redpath
Master, Queen's Bench and Matrimonial, E. Bell
Master, Taxing Office, J. Baillie
Master, Bankruptcy, F. Kelly

OFFICIAL SOLICITOR
Official Solicitor to the Court of Judicature, Miss B. M. Donnelly

COUNTY COURTS

JUDGES (£129,579†)
Style, His/Her Hon. Judge [surname]

Judge Babington; Judge Devlin; Judge Finnegan, QC; Judge Fowler, QC; Judge Grant; Judge Kerr, QC; Judge Kinney; Judge Loughran; Judge Lynch, QC; Judge McFarland; Judge McReynolds; Judge Marrinan; Judge Miller, QC; Judge Philpott, QC; Judge Sherrard; Judge Smyth, QC; Judge Smyth

† County court judges are paid £139,933 so long as they are required to carry out significantly different work from their counterparts elsewhere in the UK

RECORDERS
Belfast (£139,933), Judge McFarland
Londonderry (£138,548), Judge Babington

DISTRICT JUDGES (£103,950)
Only barristers and solicitors with ten years' standing are eligible to become district judges. There are four district judges in Northern Ireland.

MAGISTRATES' COURTS

DISTRICT JUDGES (MAGISTRATES' COURTS) (£103,950)
There are 21 district judges (magistrates' courts) in Northern Ireland.

NORTHERN IRELAND COURTS AND TRIBUNALS SERVICE

23–27 Oxford Street, Belfast BT1 3LA
T 028-9032 8594 W www.courtsni.gov.uk
Chief Executive, J. Durkin

CROWN SOLICITOR'S OFFICE

Royal Courts of Justice, Chichester Street, Belfast BT1 3JE
T 028-9054 2555
Crown Solicitor, J. Conn

PUBLIC PROSECUTION SERVICE

93 Chichester Street, Belfast BT1 3JR
T 028-9054 2444 W www.ppsni.gov.uk
Director of Public Prosecutions, Barra McGrory, QC

TRIBUNALS

Information on all the tribunals listed here, with the exception of the independent tribunals and the tribunals based in Scotland, Wales and Northern Ireland, can be found on the Ministry of Justice website (W www.justice.gov.uk).

HM COURTS AND TRIBUNALS SERVICE

5th Floor, 102 Petty France, London SW1H 9AJ
T 0845-600 0877 W www.justice.gov.uk

HM Courts Service and the Tribunals Service merged on 1 April 2011 to form HM Courts and Tribunals Service, an integrated agency providing support for the administration of justice in courts and tribunals. It is an agency within the Ministry of Justice, operating as a partnership between the Lord Chancellor, the Lord Chief Justice and the Senior President of Tribunals. It is responsible for the administration of the criminal, civil and family courts and tribunals in England and Wales and non-devolved tribunals in Scotland and Northern Ireland. The agency's work is overseen by a board headed by an independent chair working with non-executive, executive and judicial members.

A two-tier tribunal system, comprising the First-tier Tribunal and Upper Tribunal, was established on 3 November 2008 as a result of radical reform under the Tribunals, Courts and Enforcement Act 2007. Both of these tiers are split into a number of separate chambers. These chambers group together individual tribunals (also known as 'jurisdictions') which deal with similar work or require similar skills. Cases start in the First-tier Tribunal and there is a right of appeal to the Upper Tribunal. Some tribunals transferred to the new two-tier system immediately, with more transferring between 2009 and 2011. The exception is employment tribunals, which remain outside this structure. The Act also allowed legally qualified tribunal chairs and adjudicators to swear the judicial oath and become judges.

Senior President, Rt. Hon. Sir Jeremy Sullivan
Chief Executive, Peter Handcock, CBE

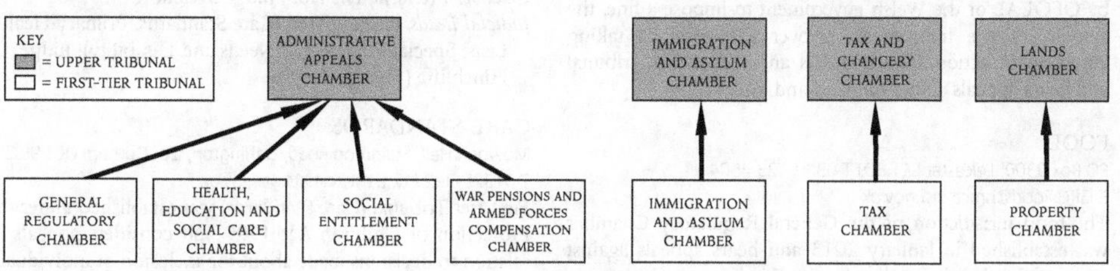

FIRST-TIER TRIBUNAL

The main function of the First-tier Tribunal is to hear appeals by citizens against decisions of the government. In most cases appeals are heard by a panel made up of one judge and two specialists in their relevant field, known as 'members'. Both judges and members are appointed through the Independent Judicial Appointments Commission. Most of the tribunals administered by central government are part of the First-tier Tribunal, which is split into seven separate chambers.

GENERAL REGULATORY CHAMBER

Chamber President, Judge Warren
Judicial Leads, Judge Brodrick (Transport); Judge Hunter, QC (Immigration Services); Judge Alison McKenna (Charity); Judge Warren (Claims Management Services, Community Right to Bid, Environment, Examination Board, Food, Gambling, Information Rights, Professional Regulation); His Hon. Judge Wulwik (Consumer Credit, Estate Agents)

CHARITY

PO Box 9300, Leicester LE1 8DJ
T 0300-123 4504 E charitytribunal@hmcts.gsi.gov.uk

Under the Charities Act 2006 (only applicable to England and Wales), First-tier Tribunal (Charity) hears appeals against the decisions of the Charity Commission, applications for the review of decisions made by the Charity Commission and considers references from the Attorney-General or the Charity Commission on points of law. The tribunal currently only has jurisdiction in respect of Charity Commission decisions, which fall within their remit, made on or after 18 March 2008.

CLAIMS MANAGEMENT SERVICES

PO Box 9300, Leicester LE1 8DJ
T 0300-123 4504 E cmst@tribunals.gsi.gov.uk

Under the Compensation Act 2006, Claims Management Services hears appeals pertaining to decisions made by the claims regulator in relation to personal injury; criminal injuries compensation; employment matters; housing disrepair; financial products and services; and industrial injury disablement benefits.

COMMUNITY RIGHT TO BID

PO Box 9300, Leicester LE1 8DJ
E grc.communityrights@hmcts.gsi.gov.uk

The Community Right to Bid jurisdiction of the General Regulatory Chamber was established in January 2013 and currently hears appeals against review decisions made by local authorities under the Localism Act 2011.

CONSUMER CREDIT

PO Box 9300, Leicester LE1 8DJ T 0300-123 4504
E grc.consumercredit@hmcts.gsi.gov.uk

Under the Consumer Credit Act 1974 and the amended Consumer Credit Act 2006, First-tier Tribunal (Consumer Credit) hears appeals against licensing decisions made by the Office of Fair Trading. The tribunal also hears appeals relating to the implementation of requirements or a civil penalty on licensees under the 1974 Act; and the refusal to register, cancellation of registration, or imposition of a penalty under the Money Laundering Regulations 2007.

ENVIRONMENT

PO Box 9300, Leicester LE1 8DJ T 0300-123 4503
E grc.environment@hmcts.gsi.gov.uk

First-tier Tribunal (Environment) was created to decide appeals regarding civil sanctions made by environmental regulators. Established in April 2010, the jurisdiction of the tribunal extends to England and Wales.

ESTATE AGENTS
PO Box 9300, Leicester LE1 8DJ T 0300-123 4504
E grc.estateagents@hmcts.gsi.gov.uk
First-tier Tribunal (Estate Agents) hears appeals, under the Estate Agents Act 1979, against decisions made by the Office of Fair Trading pertaining to orders prohibiting a person from being employed as an estate agent when that person has been, for example, convicted of fraud or another offence involving dishonesty. The tribunal also hears appeals relating to decisions refusing to revoke or vary a prohibition order or warning order, as well as appeals regarding the issuing of a warning order when a person has not fulfilled their obligations under the Act.

EXAMINATION BOARD
PO Box 9300, Leicester LE1 8DJ T 0300-123 4504
E grc.examboard@hmcts.gsi.gov.uk
Regulated awarding organisations can appeal to the Examination Board tribunal if they disagree with a decision by OFQUAL or the Welsh government to impose a fine, the amount of the fine, or to recover the costs of taking enforcement action. The board is an independent tribunal and hears appeals across England and Wales.

FOOD
PO Box 9300, Leicester LE1 8DJ T 0300-123 4504
E GRC.Food@hmcts.gsi.gov.uk
The food jurisdiction of the General Regulatory Chamber was established in January 2013 and hears appeals against some of the decisions taken by the Food Standards Agency, Department for Environment, Food and Rural Affairs and local authority trading standards departments. It also deals with appeals against decisions under the Fish Labelling (England) Regulations and decisions under EU Council Regulation (EC) No 1099/2009 on the protection of animals at the time of killing.

GAMBLING
PO Box 9300, Leicester LE1 8DJ
T 0300-123 4504 E grc.gambling@hmcts.gsi.gov.uk
First-tier Tribunal (Gambling) hears and decides appeals against decisions made by the Gambling Commission. The cases heard by the tribunal involve the provision and withdrawal of both operating and personal management licenses.

IMMIGRATION SERVICES
7th Floor, Victory House, 30–34 Kingsway, London WC2B 6EX
T 020-3077 5860 E imset@hmcts.gsi.gov.uk
First-tier Tribunal (Immigration Services) is an independent judicial body established in 2000. It hears appeals against decisions made by the Office of the Immigration Services Commissioner and considers disciplinary charges brought against immigration advisors by the Commissioner. The tribunal can sit anywhere in the UK.

INFORMATION RIGHTS
PO Box 9300, Leicester LE1 8DJ T 0300-123 4504
E informationtribunal@hmcts.gsi.gov.uk
Formerly known as the Information Tribunal, First-tier Tribunal (Information Rights) determines appeals against notices issued by the Information Commissioner and sits at venues across the UK.

When a minister of the crown issues a certificate on the grounds of national security, the appeal must be transferred to the Administrative Appeals Chamber of the Upper Tribunal upon receipt by First-tier Tribunal (Information Rights).

PROFESSIONAL REGULATION
PO Box 9300, Leicester LE1 8DJ T 0300-123 4504
E grc.professionalregulation@hmcts.gsi.gov.uk
The professional regulation jurisdiction, which replaced the Alternative Business Structures jurisdiction in 2013, was created to deal with appeals made against decisions of professional regulatory bodies. Currently it hears appeals made by the Council for Licensed Conveyancers under the Legal Services Act 2007.

TRANSPORT
7th Floor, Victory House, 30–34 Kingsway, London WC2B 6EX
T 020-3077 5860 E transport@hmcts.gsi.gov.uk
First-tier Tribunal (Transport) hears appeals against decisions of the Registrar of Approved Driving Instructors, hears and decides appeals for London service permits against decisions made by Transport for London and is able to resolve disputes over postal charges under the Postal Services Act 2000.

HEALTH, EDUCATION AND SOCIAL CARE CHAMBER

Chamber President, His Hon. Judge Sycamore
Judicial Leads, Judge Aitken (Care Standards, Primary Health Lists, Special Educational Needs and Disability); Judge Hinchliffe (Mental Health)

CARE STANDARDS
Mowden Hall, Staindrop Road, Darlington, Co. Durham DL3 9BG
T 01325-392712 E cst@hmcts.gsi.gov.uk
First-tier Tribunal (Care Standards) was established under the Protection of Children Act 1999 and considers appeals in relation to decisions made about the inclusion of individuals' names on the list of those considered unsuitable to work with children or vulnerable adults, restrictions from teaching and employment in schools/further education institutions, and the registration of independent schools. It also deals with general registration decisions made about care homes, children's homes, childcare providers, nurses' agencies, social workers, residential family centres, independent hospitals and fostering agencies.

MENTAL HEALTH
Secretariat: PO Box 8793, 5th Floor, Leicester LE1 8BN
T 0300-123 2201 E mhrtenquiries@hmcts.gsi.gov.uk
The First-tier Tribunal (Mental Health) hears applications and references for people detained under the Mental Health Act 1983 (as amended by the Mental Health Act 2007). There are separate mental health tribunals for Wales and Scotland.

PRIMARY HEALTH LISTS
Mowden Hall, Staindrop Road, Darlington, Co. Durham DL3 9BG
T 01325-391130
First-tier Tribunal (Primary Health Lists) took over the role of the Family Health Services Appeal Authority on 18 January 2010. The tribunal is independent of the Department of Health and considers appeals against the decisions of primary care trusts (PCTs), including appeals by GPs, dentists, pharmacists and opticians regarding action taken against them.

SPECIAL EDUCATIONAL NEEDS AND DISABILITY
Mowden Hall, Staindrop Road, Darlington, Co. Durham DL3 9BG
T 01325-392760 E sendistqueries@hmcts.gsi.gov.uk
First-tier Tribunal (Special Educational Needs and Disability) considers parents' appeals against the decisions of local authorities about children's special educational needs if

parents cannot reach agreement with the local authority. It also considers claims of disability discrimination in schools.

IMMIGRATION AND ASYLUM CHAMBER

Chamber President, Judge Clements
PO Box 6987, Loughborough LE11 2XZ
T 0300-123 1711 E customer.service@hmcts.gsi.gov.uk
The Immigration and Asylum Chamber replaced the Asylum and Immigration Tribunal in February 2010. It is an independent tribunal dealing with appeals against decisions made by the UK Border Agency, such as refusing a person asylum or leave to remain in the UK.

PROPERTY CHAMBER

Chamber President, Judge McGrath
PO Box 9300, Leicester LE1 8DJ T 0300-123 4504
E customer.service@hmcts.gsi.gov.uk
Formed on 1 July 2013, the Property Chamber has jurisdiction in England and Wales and incorporates the functions of the rent assessment committees (which sit as residential property tribunals, leasehold valuation tribunals, rent tribunals and rent assessment committees), the agricultural land tribunals and the Adjudicator to HM Land Registry. The Chamber is organised into three main jurisdictions: residential property, land registration and agricultural land.

SOCIAL ENTITLEMENT CHAMBER

Chamber President, His Hon. Judge Martin
Judicial Leads, His Hon. Judge Martin (Social Security and Child Support); Sehba Storey (Asylum Support); Anthony Summers (Criminal Injuries Compensation)

ASYLUM SUPPORT

2nd Floor, Anchorage House, 2 Clove Crescent, London E14 2BE
T 020-7538 6171
First-tier Tribunal (Asylum Support) deals with appeals against decisions made by the Home Office. The Home Office decides whether asylum seekers, failed asylum seekers and/or their dependants are entitled to support and accommodation on the grounds of destitution, as provided by section 4 and part IV of the Immigration and Asylum Act 1999. The tribunal can only consider appeals against a refusal or termination of support. It can, if appropriate, require the Secretary of State for the Home Department to reconsider the original decision, substitute the original decision with the tribunal's own decision or dismiss the appeal.

CRIMINAL INJURIES COMPENSATION

Head Office, Wellington House, 134–136 Wellington Street, Glasgow G2 2XL T 0141-354 8555
Judicial Review Enquiries, 5th Floor, Field House, 15–25 Breams Buildings, London EC4A 1DZ
E cic.enquiries@hmcts.gsi.gov.uk
First-tier Tribunal (Criminal Injuries Compensation) determines appeals against review decisions made by the Criminal Injuries Compensation Authority on applications for compensation made by victims of violent crime. It only considers appeals on claims made on or after 1 April 1996 under the Criminal Injuries Compensation Scheme.

SOCIAL SECURITY AND CHILD SUPPORT

Administrative Support Centre, PO Box 14620, Birmingham B16 6FR T 0845-408 3500
First-tier Tribunal (Social Security and Child Support) arranges and hears appeals on a range of decisions made by the Department for Work and Pensions, HM Revenue and Customs, and local authorities. Appeals considered include those concerned with income support, jobseeker's allowance, child support, tax credits, retirement pensions, housing benefit, council tax benefit, disability living allowance, vaccine damage and compensation recovery.

The tribunal also contains an executive agency responsible for the administration of appeals, headed by the chief executive of HM Courts and Tribunals Service.

TAX CHAMBER

Chamber President, Judge Bishopp

MP EXPENSES

3rd Floor, Temple Court, 35 Bull Street, Birmingham B4 6EQ
T 0845-223 8080 E taxappeals@tribunals.gsi.gov.uk
First-tier Tribunal (MP Expenses) hears appeals against certain decisions made by the Compliance Officer, an independent office holder appointed by the Independent Parliamentary Standards Authority, the organisation responsible for determining and paying MP expenses. Appeals can be made by current or former MPs under the Parliamentary Standards Act 2009. The jurisdiction is UK-wide.

TAX

3rd Floor, Temple Court, 35 Bull Street, Birmingham B4 6EQ
T 0845-223 8080 E taxappeals@tribunals.gsi.gov.uk
First-tier Tribunal (Tax) hears most appeals against decisions of HM Revenue and Customs in relation to income tax, corporation tax, capital gains tax, inheritance tax, national insurance contributions and VAT or duties. Appeals can be made by individuals or organisations, single taxpayers or large multinational companies. The jurisdiction is UK-wide.

WAR PENSIONS AND ARMED FORCES COMPENSATION CHAMBER

Chamber President, Judge Stubbs
5th Floor, Fox Court, 14 Gray's Inn Road, London WC1X 8HN
T 020-3206 0701 E armedforces.chamber@hmcts.gsi.gov.uk
The War Pensions and Armed Forces Compensation Chamber of the First-tier Tribunal is the successor to the Pensions Appeal Tribunal which has existed in different forms since the War Pensions Act 1919. The tribunal hears appeals brought by ex-servicemen and women against decisions of the Secretary of State for Defence under the war pensions legislation for injuries sustained before 5 April 2005, and under the armed forces compensation scheme for injuries after that date. Under the war pensions legislation, the tribunal decides on entitlement to a war pension, the degree of disablement and entitlement to certain allowances (eg for mobility needs). Under the armed forces compensation scheme, the tribunal decides both the entitlement to an award and the tariff level of the award. The tribunal's jurisdiction covers England and Wales.

UPPER TRIBUNAL

Comprising four separate chambers, the Upper Tribunal deals mostly with appeals from, and enforcement of, decisions taken by the First-tier Tribunal, but it also handles some cases that do not go through the First-tier Tribunal. Additionally, it has assumed some of the supervisory powers of the courts to deal with the actions of tribunals, government departments and some other public authorities. All the decision-makers of the Upper Tribunal are judges or expert members sitting in a panel chaired by a judge, and are specialists in the areas of law they handle. Over time their decisions are expected to build comprehensive case law for each area covered by the tribunals.

ADMINISTRATIVE APPEALS CHAMBER

Chamber President, Hon. Sir Arthur Charles
5th Floor, 7 Rolls Buildings, Fetter Lane, London EC4A 1NL
T 020-7071 5662 E adminappeals@hmcts.gsi.gov.uk

The Administrative Appeals Chamber considers appeals against most of the decisions of the following First-tier chambers: Social Entitlement; Health, Education and Social Care; General Regulatory; and War Pensions and Armed Forces Compensation. It also considers appeals against decisions of the Independent Safeguarding Authority (England and Wales), Traffic Commissioners (England, Wales and Scotland) and appeals from decisions of a number of independent tribunals in Northern Ireland, Scotland and Wales. Its judges also decide Forfeiture Act references (England, Wales and Scotland).

For England and Wales, the Administrative Appeals Chamber considers applications for judicial review of the First-tier Tribunal in certain cases.

IMMIGRATION AND ASYLUM CHAMBER

Chamber President, Hon. Sir Nicholas Blake
PO Box 6987, Leicester LE1 6ZX
T 0845-600 0877 E customer.service@hmcts.gsi.gov.uk

The Immigration and Asylum Chamber was created on 15 February 2010. It hears appeals against decisions made by the Immigration and Asylum Chamber in the First-tier Tribunal in matters of immigration, asylum and nationality.

LANDS CHAMBER

Chamber President, Hon. Sir Keith Lindblom
45 Bedford Square, London WC1B 3AS
T 020-7612 9710 E lands@hmcts.gsi.gov.uk

The Lands Chamber determines questions relating to the valuation of land, rating appeals from valuation tribunals, appeals from leasehold valuation tribunals and residential property tribunals, applications to discharge or modify restrictions on the use of land, and compulsory purchase compensation. The tribunal may also arbitrate under a reference by consent.

TAX AND CHANCERY CHAMBER

Chamber President, Hon. Sir Nicholas Warren
45 Bedford Square, London WC1B 3DN
T 020-7612 9700 E financeandtaxappeals@hmcts.gsi.gov.uk

The Tax and Chancery Chamber decides applications for permission to appeal and appeals on point of law from decisions of the First-tier Tribunal in tax or charity cases. The jurisdiction of the former Financial Services and Markets tribunal transferred to the chamber in April 2010. As a result the chamber hears appeals against decisions issued by the Financial Conduct Authority (FCA) and from the Pensions Regulator. The chamber has jurisdiction throughout the UK in tax cases and references against decisions of the FCA; for charity cases its jurisdiction extends to England and Wales. In references against decisions of the Pensions Regulator it has jurisdiction in England, Wales and Scotland.

SPECIAL IMMIGRATION APPEALS COMMISSION

15–25 Bream's Buildings, London EC4A 1DZ
T 0300-123 1711 E siac.poacoffice@hmcts.gsi.gov.uk
W www.siac.hmcts.gov.uk

The commission was set up under the Special Immigration Appeals Commission Act 1997. It remains separate from the First-tier and Upper Tribunal structure but is part of HM Courts and Tribunals Service. Its main function is to consider appeals against orders for deportations in cases which involve, in the main, considerations of national security or the public interest. The commission also hears appeals against decisions to deprive persons of citizenship status.

Chair, Hon. Sir Stephen Irwin

EMPLOYMENT TRIBUNALS

ENGLAND AND WALES

Public Enquiry Line: 0845-795 9775

Employment Tribunals for England and Wales sit in 12 regions. The tribunals deal with matters of employment law, redundancy, dismissal, contract disputes, sexual, racial and disability discrimination and related areas of dispute which may arise in the workplace. A public register of judgments is held at 100 Southgate Street, Bury St Edmunds, Suffolk IP33 2AQ.

President, David John Latham

SCOTLAND

Central Office, Eagle Building, 215 Bothwell Street, Glasgow G2 7TS T 0141-204 0730

Tribunals in Scotland have the same remit as those in England and Wales. Employment judges are appointed by the Lord President of the Court of Session and lay members by the Lord Chancellor. A public register of judgments made in employment tribunals in Scotland is held at the Glasgow office.

President, Shona Simon

EMPLOYMENT APPEAL TRIBUNAL

London Office, 2nd Floor, Fleetbank House, 2–6 Salisbury Square, London EC4Y 8JX T 020-7273 1041
E londoneat@hmcts.gsi.gov.uk
Edinburgh Office, 52 Melville Street, Edinburgh EH3 7HF
T 0131-225 3963 E edinburgheat@hmcts.gsi.gov.uk

The Employment Appeal Tribunal hears appeals (on points of law only) arising from decisions made by employment tribunals. Hearings are conducted by a judge, either alone or accompanied by two lay members who have practical experience in employment relations.

President, Hon. Sir Brian Langstaff
Registrar, Pauline Donleavy

SCOTTISH TRIBUNALS SERVICE

First Floor, Bothwell House, Hamilton Business Park, Caird Park, Hamilton ML3 0QA T 0800-345 7060 W www.scotland.gov.uk
Chief Executive (acting), Martin McKenna

The Scottish Tribunals Service currently provides administrative support for the following Scottish tribunals:

THE ADDITIONAL SUPPORT NEEDS TRIBUNAL FOR SCOTLAND, Europa Building, 450 Argyle Street, Glasgow G2 8LH T 0845-120 2906
E asntsinquiries@scotland.gsi.gov.uk
W www.asntscotland.gov.uk
President, Dr Joe Morrow

HOMEOWNER HOUSING PANEL, Europa Building, 450 Argyle Street, Glasgow G2 8LH T 0141-242 0175
E hohpadmin@scotland.gsi.gov.uk
W www.hohp.scotland.gov.uk
President, Aileen Devanny

THE LANDS TRIBUNAL FOR SCOTLAND, George House, 126 George Street, Edinburgh EH2 4HH T 0131-271 4350
E mailbox@lands-tribunal-scotland.org.uk
W www.lands-tribunal-scotland.org.uk
President, Hon. Lord McGhie, QC

THE MENTAL HEALTH TRIBUNAL FOR SCOTLAND, Bothwell House, First Floor, Hamilton Business Park, Caird Park, Hamilton ML3 0QA T 0800-345 7060
E mhts@scotland.gsi.gov.uk W www.mhtscotland.gov.uk
President, Dr Joe Morrow

THE PENSIONS APPEAL TRIBUNAL SCOTLAND, George House, 126 George Street, Edinburgh EH2 4HH T 0131-271 4340 E info@patscotland.org.uk W www.patscotland.org.uk
President, Colin N. McEachran, QC

THE PRIVATE RENTED HOUSING PANEL, Europa Building, 450 Argyle Street, Glasgow G2 8LH T 0141-242 0142 E prhpadmin@scotland.gsi.gov.uk W www.prhpscotland.gov.uk
President, Aileen Devanny

THE SCOTTISH CHARITY APPEALS PANEL, 2 W, St Andrew's House, Regent Road, Edinburgh EH1 3DG T 0131-244 3311 E scap@scotland.gsi.gov.uk W www.scap.gov.uk
Chairs, Saria Akhter; Aileen Devanny; Joseph Hughes; Gary McIlravey; John Walker; William Wood

NORTHERN IRELAND COURTS AND TRIBUNALS SERVICE

Laganside House, 23–27 Oxford Street, Belfast BT1 3LA
T 028-9032 8594 W www.courtsni.gov.uk
Lord Chief Justice of Northern Ireland, Rt. Hon. Sir Declan Morgan

The Northern Ireland Courts and Tribunals Service currently provides administrative support for the following Northern Ireland tribunals:

THE APPEALS SERVICE, Cleaver House, 3 Donegall Square North, Belfast BT1 5GA T 028-9051 8518 E appeals.service.belfast@dsdni.gov.uk
President of the Appeal Tribunals, Conall Maclynn

THE CARE TRIBUNAL, 3rd Floor, Bedford House, 16–22 Bedford Street, Belfast BT2 7FD T 028-9072 4893 E caretribunal@courtsni.gov.uk
Chairs, W. Harry Black; Diane Drennan

THE CHARITY TRIBUNAL, 3rd Floor, Bedford House, 16–22 Bedford Street, Belfast BT2 7FD T 028-9072 4892 E tribunalsunit@courts.ni.gov.uk
President, Damien McMahon

CRIMINAL INJURIES COMPENSATION APPEALS PANEL NORTHERN IRELAND, 3rd Floor, Bedford House, 16–22 Bedford Street, Belfast BT2 7FD T 028-9041 2204 E cicapnicustomer@courtsni.gov.uk
Chair, John Duffy

LANDS TRIBUNAL, Royal Courts of Justice, 2nd Floor, Chichester Street, Belfast BT1 3JJ T 028-9032 7703 E lands.tribunal@dfpni.gov.uk
President, Rt. Hon. Sir Patrick Coghlin

MENTAL HEALTH REVIEW TRIBUNAL 3rd Floor, Bedford House, 16–22 Bedford Street, Belfast BT2 7FD T 028-9072 4843 E mhrt@courtsni.gov.uk
Chair, Fraser Elliott, QC

NORTHERN IRELAND HEALTH AND SAFETY TRIBUNAL, 3rd Floor, Bedford House, 16–22 Bedford Street, Belfast BT2 7FD T 028-9072 4892 E tribunalsunit@courtsni.gov.uk
Chairs, James Leonard; Damien McMahon; Petra Shiels

NORTHERN IRELAND TRAFFIC PENALTY TRIBUNAL, 3rd Floor, Bedford House, 16–22 Bedford Street, Belfast BT2 7FD T 028-9072 8732 E tribunalsunit@courtsni.gov.uk
Adjudicators, Michael Bready; Maura Hutchinson; Peter King; Robin Steer

NORTHERN IRELAND VALUATION TRIBUNAL, 3rd Floor, Bedford House, 16–22 Bedford Street, Belfast BT2 7FD T 028-9072 4887 E tribunalsunit@courtsni.gov.uk
President, James Leonard

OFFICE OF SOCIAL SECURITY COMMISSIONERS AND CHILD SUPPORT COMMISSIONERS, 3rd Floor, Bedford House, 16–22 Bedford Street, Belfast BT2 7FD T 028-9072 4883 E socialsecuritycommissioners@courtsni.gov.uk
Chief Commissioner, Dr Kenneth Mullan

PAROLE COMMISSIONERS FOR NORTHERN IRELAND, Linum Chambers, 9th Floor, 2 Bedford Square, Bedford Street, Belfast BT2 7ES T 028-9054 5900 E info@parolecomni.org.uk W www.parolecomni.org.uk
Chief Commissioner, Ms Christine Glenn

PENSIONS APPEAL COMMISSIONERS, 3rd Floor, Bedford House, 16–22 Bedford Street, Belfast BT2 7FD T 028-9072 4884 E pensionsappealcommissioners@courtsni.gov.uk
Chief Commissioner, Dr Kenneth Mullan

PENSIONS APPEAL TRIBUNALS, 3rd Floor, Bedford House, 16–22 Bedford Street, Belfast BT2 7FD T 028-9072 4886 E pensions@courtsni.gsi.gov.uk
President, Dr Kenneth Mullan

RENT ASSESSMENT PANEL, Cleaver House, 3 Donegall Square North, Belfast BT1 5GA T 028-9051 8518 E appeals.service.belfast@dsdni.gov.uk

SPECIAL EDUCATIONAL NEEDS AND DISABILITY TRIBUNAL, 3rd Floor, Bedford House, 16–22 Bedford Street, Belfast BT2 7FD T 028-9072 4887 E sendtribunal@courtsni.gov.uk
President, Damian G. McCormick

INDEPENDENT TRIBUNALS

The following represents a selection of tribunals not administered by HM Courts and Tribunals Service.

CIVIL AVIATION AUTHORITY

CAA House, 45–59 Kingsway, London WC2B 6TE
T 020-7453 6172 E legal@caa.co.uk
W www.caa.co.uk

The Civil Aviation Authority (CAA) does not have a separate tribunal department as such, but for certain purposes the CAA must conform to tribunal requirements, for example, to deal with appeals against the refusal or revocation of aviation licences and certificates issued by the CAA, and the allocation of routes outside of the EU to airlines.

The chair and four non-executive members who may sit on panels for tribunal purposes are appointed by the Secretary of State for Transport.

Chair, Dame Deirdre Hutton, DBE

COMPETITION APPEAL TRIBUNAL

Victoria House, Bloomsbury Place, London WC1A 2EB
T 020-7979 7979 E info@catribunal.org.uk
W www.catribunal.org.uk

The Competition Appeal Tribunal (CAT) is a specialist tribunal established to hear certain cases in the sphere of UK competition and economic regulatory law. It hears appeals against decisions of the Office of Fair Trading (OFT) and the sectoral regulators, and also certain decisions of the Secretary of State for Business, Innovation and Skills and the Competition Commission. The CAT also has jurisdiction to award damages in respect of infringements of EU or UK competition law and to hear appeals against decisions of OFCOM in telecommunications matters.

President, Hon. Sir Gerald Barling

COPYRIGHT TRIBUNAL

4 Abbey Orchard Street, London SW1P 2JJ
T 020-7034 2836 E copyright.tribunal@ipo.gov.uk
W www.ipo.gov.uk/copy/tribunal

The Copyright Tribunal resolves disputes over the terms and conditions of licences offered by, or licensing schemes operated by, collective management organisations in the

copyright and related rights area. Its decisions are appealable to the high court on points of law only.
Chair, Hon. Sir Colin Birss

INDUSTRIAL TRIBUNALS AND THE FAIR EMPLOYMENT TRIBUNAL (NORTHERN IRELAND)
Killymeal House, 2 Cromac Quay, Ormeau Road, Belfast BT7 2JD
T 028-9032 7666 E mail@employmenttribunalsni.org
W www.employmenttribunalsni.co.uk
The industrial tribunal system in Northern Ireland was set up in 1965 and has a similar remit to the employment tribunals in the rest of the UK. There is also a Fair Employment Tribunal, which hears and determines individual cases of alleged religious or political discrimination in employment. Employers can appeal to the Fair Employment Tribunal if they consider the directions of the Equality Commission to be unreasonable, inappropriate or unnecessary, and the Equality Commission can make application to the tribunal for the enforcement of undertakings or directions with which an employer has not complied.
President, Eileen McBride

INVESTIGATORY POWERS TRIBUNAL
PO Box 33220, London SW1H 9ZQ
T 020-7035 3711 E info@ipt-uk.com W www.ipt-uk.com
The Investigatory Powers Tribunal replaced the Interception of Communications Tribunal, the Intelligence Services Tribunal, the Security Services Tribunal and the complaints function of the commissioner appointed under the Police Act 1997.

The Regulation of Investigatory Powers Act 2000 (RIPA) provides for a tribunal made up of senior members of the legal profession, independent of the government and appointed by the Queen, to consider all complaints against the intelligence services and those against public authorities in respect of powers covered by RIPA; and to consider proceedings brought under section 7 of the Human Rights Act 1998 against the intelligence services and law enforcement agencies in respect of these powers.
President, vacant

NATIONAL HEALTH SERVICE TRIBUNAL (SCOTLAND)
Anderson Strathern LLP, Lomond House, 9 George Square, Glasgow G2 1DY
T 0141-242 6060 E nhstribunal@nhs.net
The Scottish National Health Service Tribunal considers representations that the continued inclusion of a family health service practitioner (eg a doctor, dentist, optometrist or pharmacist) on a health board's list would be prejudicial to the efficiency of the service concerned, by virtue either of fraudulent practices or unsatisfactory personal or professional conduct. If this is established, the tribunal has the power to disqualify practitioners from working in the NHS family health services.
Chair, J. Michael D. Graham

SOLICITORS' DISCIPLINARY TRIBUNAL
3rd Floor, Gate House, 1 Farringdon Street, London EC4M 7LG
T 020-7329 4808 E enquiries@solicitorsdt.com
W www.solicitorstribunal.org.uk
The Solicitors' Disciplinary Tribunal is an independent statutory body whose members are appointed by the Master of the Rolls. The tribunal adjudicates upon alleged breaches of the rules and regulations applicable to solicitors and their firms, including the Solicitors' Code of Conduct 2007. It also decides applications by former solicitors for restoration to the Roll.
President, Andrew Spooner

SOLICITORS' DISCIPLINE TRIBUNAL (SCOTTISH)
Unit 3.5, The Granary Business Centre, Coal Road, Cupar, Fife KY15 5YQ
T 01334-659088 W www.ssdt.org.uk
The Scottish Solicitors' Discipline Tribunal is an independent statutory body with a panel of 21 members, 11 of whom are solicitors appointed by the Lord President of the Court of Session. Its principal function is to consider complaints of misconduct against solicitors in Scotland.
Chair, A. Cockburn

TRAFFIC PENALTY TRIBUNAL
Barlow House, Minshull Street, Manchester M1 3DZ
T 0161-242 5252 E info@trafficpenaltytribunal.gov.uk
W www.trafficpenaltytribunal.gov.uk
The Traffic Penalty Tribunal considers appeals from motorists against penalty charge notices issued by Civil Enforcement Authorities in England (outside London) and Wales under the Traffic Management Act 2004, and considers appeals against bus lane contraventions in England (outside London) under the Bus Lane Contraventions Regulations 2005. Parking adjudicators are appointed with the express consent of the Lord Chancellor and must be lawyers of five years' standing.
Head of Service, Louise Hutchinson

VALUATION TRIBUNAL SERVICE
2nd Floor, Black Lion House, 45 Whitechapel Road, London E1 1DU
T 0300-123 2035 W www.valuationtribunal.gov.uk
The Valuation Tribunal Service (VTS) was created as a corporate body by the Local Government Act 2003, and is responsible for providing or arranging the services required for the operation of the Valuation Tribunal for England. The VTS board consists of a chair and members appointed by the secretary of state. The VTS is sponsored by the Department for Communities and Local Government.
Chair, Anne Galbraith, CBE

VALUATION TRIBUNAL FOR ENGLAND
President's Office, 2nd Floor, Black Lion House, 45 Whitechapel Road, London E1 1DU
T 020-7246 3900 W www.valuationtribunal.gov.uk
The Valuation Tribunal for England (VTE) came into being on 1 October 2009, replacing 56 valuation tribunals in England. Provision for the VTE was made in the Local Government and Public Involvement in Health Act 2007. The VTE hears appeals concerning council tax and non-domestic (business) rates, as well as a small number of appeals against drainage boards' assessments of drainage rates. A separate panel is constituted for each hearing, and consists of a chair and two other members.
President, Prof. Graham Zellick CBE, QC

VALUATION TRIBUNAL SERVICE FOR WALES
Government Buildings, Block A (L1), Sarn Mynach, Llandudno Junction LL31 9RZ
T 0300-062 5350 E VTWaleseast@vtw.gsi.gov.uk
W www.valuation-tribunals-wales.org.uk
The Valuation Tribunal for Wales (VTW) was established by the Valuation Tribunal for Wales Regulations 2010, and hears and determines appeals concerning council tax, non-domestic rating and drainage rates in Wales. The governing council, comprising the president, four regional representatives and one member who is appointed by the Welsh government, performs the management functions on behalf of the tribunal.
Chief Executive, Andrew Shipsides

OMBUDSMAN SERVICES

The following section is a listing of selected ombudsman services. Ombudsmen are a free, independent and impartial means of resolving certain disputes outside of the courts. These disputes are, in the majority of cases, concerned with whether something has been badly or unfairly handled (for example owing to delay, neglect, inefficiency or failure to follow proper procedures). Most ombudsman schemes are established by statute; they cover various public and private bodies and generally examine matters only after the relevant body has been given a reasonable opportunity to deal with the complaint.

After conducting an investigation an ombudsman will usually issue a written report, which normally suggests a resolution to the dispute and often includes recommendations concerning the improvement of procedures.

OMBUDSMAN ASSOCIATION

PO Box 308, Twickenham TW1 9BE
T 020-8894 9272 **E** secretary@ombudsmanassociation.org
W www.ombudsmanassociation.org

The Ombudsman Association was established in 1994 and exists to provide information to the government, public bodies, and the public about ombudsmen and other complaint-handling services. An ombudsman scheme must meet four criteria in order to attain full Ombudsman Association membership: independence from the organisations the ombudsman has the power to investigate, fairness, effectiveness and public accountability. Complaint Handler membership is open to complaint-handling bodies that do not meet these criteria in full. Ombudsmen schemes from the UK, Ireland, British crown dependencies and overseas territories may apply to the Ombudsman Association for membership.
Secretary, Ian Pattison

The following is a selection of organisations that are members of the Ombudsman Association.

FINANCIAL OMBUDSMAN SERVICE

South Quay Plaza, 183 Marsh Wall, London E14 9SR
T 020-7964 1000 **E** complaint.info@financial-ombudsman.org.uk
W www.financial-ombudsman.org.uk

The Financial Ombudsman Service settles individual disputes between businesses providing financial services and their customers. The service answers around a million enquiries every year and deals with over 250,000 disputes. The service examines complaints about most financial matters, including banking, insurance, mortgages, pensions, savings, loans and credit cards. *See also* Banking and Finance.
Chief Ombudsman and Chief Executive, Natalie Ceeney, CBE

HOUSING OMBUDSMAN SERVICE

81 Aldwych, London WC2B 4HN
T 0300-111 3000 **E** info@housing-ombudsman.org.uk
W www.housing-ombudsman.org.uk

The Housing Ombudsman Service, established in 1997, deals with complaints and disputes involving tenants and housing associations and social landlords, certain private-sector landlords and managing agents. The ombudsman has a statutory jurisdiction over all registered social landlords in England. Private and other landlords can join the service on a voluntary basis. On 1 April 2013 a new Housing Ombudsman Service was launched with an extended jurisdiction covering all housing associations and local authorities.
Ombudsman, Dr Mike Biles

INDEPENDENT POLICE COMPLAINTS COMMISSION (IPCC)

PO Box 473, Sale M33 0BW
T 0300-020 0096 **E** enquiries@ipcc.gsi.gov.uk
W www.ipcc.gov.uk

The IPCC succeeded the Police Complaints Authority in 2004. It was established under the Police Reform Act 2002. The IPCC is responsible for carrying out independent investigations into serious incidents or allegations of misconduct by those serving with the police in England and Wales. It has the power to initiate, undertake and oversee investigations and is also responsible for the way in which complaints are handled by local police forces. The IPCC's further responsibilities relate to serious complaints and conduct matters concerning staff at HM Revenue and Customs and the UK Border Agency. Following the establishment of the Mayor's Office for Policing and Crime (MOPAC) in 2012, the IPCC is accountable for deciding whether to investigate allegations of criminal offence against MOPAC or his deputy. The most recent responsibility assigned to the IPCC relates to the new police and complaints commissioners for each force in England and Wales, and whether investigations should be made regarding any allegations that they or their deputy have committed a criminal offence.
Chair, Dame Anne Owers
Deputy Chair, Deborah Glass, OBE
Chief Executive, Jane Furniss

LEGAL OMBUDSMAN

PO Box 6806, Wolverhampton WV1 9WJ
T 0300-555 0333 **E** enquiries@legalombudsman.org.uk
W www.legalombudsman.org.uk

The Legal Ombudsman was set up by the Office for Legal Complaints under the Legal Services Act 2007 and is the single body for all consumer legal complaints in England and Wales. It replaced the Office of the Legal Services Ombudsman in 2010. The Legal Ombudsman aims to resolve disputes between individuals and authorised legal practitioners, including barristers, law cost draftsmen, legal executives, licensed conveyancers, notaries, patent attorneys, probate practitioners, registered European lawyers, solicitors and trade mark attorneys.
Chief Ombudsman, Adam Sampson

LOCAL GOVERNMENT OMBUDSMAN

Advice Team, PO Box 4771, Coventry CV4 0EH
T 0300-061 0614 **W** www.lgo.org.uk

The Local Government Ombudsman deals with complaints about councils and some other authorities and organisations, including education admission appeal panels and adult social care providers.

There are two ombudsmen in England, each with responsibility for different regions; they aim to provide satisfactory redress for complainants and better administration for the authorities. The ombudsmen investigate complaints about most council matters, including housing, planning, education, social care, housing benefit, transport and highways, environment and waste, and council tax. *See also* Local Government.
Local Government Ombudsmen, Jane Martin; Anne Seex

NORTHERN IRELAND OMBUDSMAN

Progressive House, 33 Wellington Place, Belfast BT1 6HN
T 028-9023 3821 E ombudsman@ni-ombudsman.org.uk
W www.ni-ombudsman.org.uk

The ombudsman (also known as the Assembly Ombudsman for Northern Ireland and the Northern Ireland Commissioner for Complaints) is appointed under legislation with powers to investigate complaints by people claiming to have sustained injustice arising from action taken by a Northern Ireland government department, or any other public body within his remit. The ombudsman can investigate all local councils, education and library boards, health and social services boards and trusts, as well as all government departments and their agencies. As commissioner for complaints, the ombudsman can investigate complaints about doctors, dentists, pharmacists, optometrists and other healthcare professionals.
Ombudsman, Dr Tom Frawley, CBE
Deputy Ombudsman, Marie Anderson

OFFICE OF THE PENSIONS OMBUDSMAN

11 Belgrave Road, London SW1V 1RB
T 020-7630 2200 E enquiries@pensions-ombudsman.org.uk
W www.pensions-ombudsman.org.uk

The Pensions Ombudsman is appointed by the Secretary of State for Work and Pensions, under the Pension Schemes Act 1993 as amended by the Pensions Act 1995. He investigates and decides complaints and disputes about the way that personal and occupational pension schemes are run. As the Ombudsman for the Board of the Pension Protection Fund, he can deal with disputes about the decisions made by the board or the actions of their staff. He also deals with appeals against decisions made by the scheme manager under the Financial Assistance Scheme.
Pensions Ombudsman, Tony King
Deputy Pensions Ombudsman, Jane Irvine

OMBUDSMAN SERVICES

Brew House, Wilderspool Park, Greenalls Avenue, Warrington WA4 6HL
W www.ombudsman-services.org

Ombudsman Services provides independent dispute resolution for the communications, copyright licensing, energy and property sectors.

Ombudsman Services: Communications investigates complaints from consumers about companies which provide communication services to the public.

Ombudsman Services: Copyright Licensing helps to resolve complaints about bodies that either own or administer, on behalf of third parties, the licensing of copyright materials.

Ombudsman Services: Energy helps to resolve complaints from consumers about energy (gas and electricity companies). This service is also responsible for handling investigations concerning the government's Green Deal policy, which launched in January 2013, and offers long-term loans towards energy-saving home improvements.

Ombudsman Services: Property investigates complaints from consumers about chartered surveying companies, surveyors, estate agents and other property professionals.
Chair, Dame Janet Finch
Chief Ombudsman, Lewis Shand Smith

OMBUDSMAN SERVICES: COMMUNICATIONS

PO Box 730, Warrington WA4 6WU
T 0330-440 1614

OMBUDSMAN SERVICES: COPYRIGHT LICENSING

PO Box 1124, Warrington WA4 9GH
T 0330-440 1601

OMBUDSMAN SERVICES: ENERGY

PO Box 966, Warrington WA4 9DF
T 0330-440 1624

OMBUDSMAN SERVICES: PROPERTY

PO Box 1021, Warrington WA4 9FE
T 0330-440 1634

PARLIAMENTARY AND HEALTH SERVICE OMBUDSMAN

Millbank Tower, Millbank, London SW1P 4QP
T 0345-015 4033 E phso.enquiries@ombudsman.org.uk
W www.ombudsman.org.uk

The Parliamentary Ombudsman (also known as the Parliamentary Commissioner for Administration) is independent of government and is an officer of parliament. She is responsible for investigating complaints referred to her by MPs from members of the public who claim to have sustained injustice in consequence of maladministration by or on behalf of government departments and certain non-departmental public bodies in the UK. Certain types of action by government departments or bodies are excluded from investigation.

The Health Service Ombudsman is responsible for investigating complaints about services funded by the National Health Service in England that have not been dealt with by the service providers to the satisfaction of the complainant. This includes complaints about doctors, dentists, pharmacists and opticians. Complaints can be referred directly by the member of the public who claims to have sustained injustice or hardship in consequence of the failure in a service provided by a relevant organisation.

The parliamentary and the health offices are traditionally held by the same person.
Parliamentary Ombudsman and Health Service Ombudsman, Dame Julie Mellor, DBE
Chief Operating Officer, Helen Hughes

PROPERTY OMBUDSMAN

Milford House, 43–55 Milford Street, Salisbury, Wiltshire SP1 2BP
T 01722-333306 E admin@tpos.co.uk
W www.tpos.co.uk

The Property Ombudsman (TPO) scheme was established in 1998 and provides a free, impartial and independent service for dealing with unresolved disputes between registered firms and buyers, sellers, tenants and landlords of property in the UK.

The ombudsman's role is to consider complaints against the registered firms' obligation to act in accordance with the TPO Codes of Practice and to propose a full and final resolution to the dispute. Consumers are not bound by the ombudsman's decision, however, registered firms are.

With over 11,000 estate agent offices and 10,000 lettings offices registered, TPO is the primary dispute resolution service for the property industry.
Ombudsman, Christopher Hamer

PUBLIC SERVICES OMBUDSMAN FOR WALES

1 Ffordd yr Hen Gae, Pencoed CF35 5LJ
T 0300-790 0203
W www.ombudsman-wales.org.uk

The office of Public Services Ombudsman for Wales was established, with effect from 1 April 2006, by the Public Services Ombudsman (Wales) Act 2005. The ombudsman, who is appointed by the Queen, investigates complaints of injustice caused by maladministration or service failure by the Assembly Commission (and public bodies sponsored by the assembly); Welsh government; National Health Service bodies, including GPs, family health service providers and hospitals; registered social landlords; local authorities, including community councils; fire and rescue authorities; police authorities; national park authorities; and countryside and environmental organisations. Free leaflets explaining the process of making a complaint are available from the ombudsman's office.
Ombudsman, Peter Tyndall

REMOVALS INDUSTRY OMBUDSMAN SCHEME

PO Box 841, Chesham, Bucks HP5 9BB
T 01525-850054 E ombudsman@removalsombudsman.co.uk
W www.removalsombudsman.org.uk

The Removals Industry Ombudsman Scheme was established to resolve disputes between removal companies that are members of the scheme and their clients, both domestic and commercial. The ombudsman investigates complaints such as breaches of contract, unprofessional conduct, delays, or breaches in the code of practice.
Ombudsman, Lynne Stone

SCOTTISH PUBLIC SERVICES OMBUDSMAN

Freepost EH641, Edinburgh EH3 0BR
T 0800-377 7330 E www.spso.org.uk/contact-us
W www.spso.org.uk

The Scottish Public Services Ombudsman (SPSO) was established in 2002. The SPSO is the final stage for complaints about public services in Scotland. Its service is free and independent. SPSO investigates complaints about the Scottish government, its agencies and departments; colleges and universities; councils; housing associations; NHS Scotland; prisons; some water and sewerage service providers; and most other Scottish public bodies. The Ombudsman looks at complaints regarding poor service or administrative failure and can only look at those that have been through the formal complaints process of the organisation concerned.
Scottish Public Services Ombudsman, Jim Martin

WATERWAYS OMBUDSMAN

PO Box 854, Altrincham WA15 5JS
T 0161-980 4858 E enquiries@waterways-ombudsman.org
W www.waterways-ombudsman.org

From July 2012, the Waterways Ombudsman investigates complaints about the Canal and River Trust and its subsidiaries.
Ombudsman, Andrew Walker

THE POLICE SERVICE

There are 45 police forces in the United Kingdom: 43 in England and Wales, including the Metropolitan Police and the City of London Police, Police Scotland and the Police Service of Northern Ireland. The Isle of Man, Jersey and Guernsey have their own forces responsible for policing in their respective islands and bailiwicks. The National Crime Agency, operational from December 2013, is responsible for preventing organised crime and strengthening UK borders.

Since 1964, police authorities – separate independent bodies for each police force – were responsible for the supervision of local policing in England and Wales. Following the government's white paper *Policing in the 21st Century* it was concluded that, in order to make the police more accountable, police authorities should be replaced with a directly elected commissioner for each force, supported by a police and crime panel. In November 2012, following the enactment of the Police Reform and Social Responsibility Act 2011, elections to install police and crime commissioners (PCCs) were held in 41 police force areas across England and Wales. The PCCs are responsible for appointing the chief constable of their force, establishing local priorities and setting out budgets. The PCCs are not in place to run their local force but rather to hold them to account. The Mayor of London acts as the PCC for the Metropolitan Police supported by the Mayor's Office for Policing and Crime (MOPAC), which replaced the Metropolitan Police Authority in January 2012. The City of London Corporation acts as the police authority for the City of London Police.

In England the police and crime panels are made up of representatives from each local authority in a police force area. In Wales they are independent public bodies, established and maintained by the secretary of state, rather than local authority committees.

Under the Police and Fire Reform (Scotland) Act 2012, Police Scotland was established on 1 April 2013, merging the eight separate territorial police forces, the Scottish Crime and Drug Enforcement Agency and the Association of Chief Police Officers in Scotland. Responsible for policing the whole of Scotland, Police Scotland is the second largest force in the UK after the Metropolitan Police. The service is led by a chief constable who is supported by a team of four deputy constables, assistant chief constables and three directors. The Scottish Police Authority, established in October 2012, is responsible for maintaining policing, promoting policing principles, the continuous improvement of policing and holds the Chief Constable to account. In Northern Ireland, the Northern Ireland Policing Board, an independent public body consisting of 19 political and independent members, fulfils a similar role.

Police forces in England, Scotland and Wales are financed by central and local government grants and a precept on the council tax. The Police Service of Northern Ireland is wholly funded by central government.

The home secretary, the Scottish government and the Northern Ireland Minister of Justice are responsible for the organisation, administration and operation of the police service. They regulate police ranks, discipline, hours of duty and pay and allowances. All police forces are subject to inspection by HM Inspectorate of Constabulary, which reports to the home secretary and the Northern Ireland Minister of Justice. Police forces in Scotland are inspected by HM Inspectorate of Constabulary for Scotland which operates independently of the Scottish government.

COMPLAINTS

The Independent Police Complaints Commission (IPCC) was established under the Police Reform Act 2002. The IPCC is responsible for carrying out independent investigations into serious incidents or allegations of misconduct by those serving with the police in England and Wales. It has the power to initiate, undertake and oversee investigations and is also responsible for the way in which complaints are handled by local police forces. The IPCC's further responsibilities relate to serious complaints and conduct matters relating to staff at HM Revenue and Customs, and the UK Border Agency. Following the establishment of MOPAC in 2012, the IPCC is also responsible for deciding whether any allegations that MOPAC or its deputy has committed a criminal offence should be investigated. The most recent responsibility assigned to the IPCC is to decide whether investigations should be made regarding any allegations of criminal offence against the PCCs or their deputies.

If a complaint is relatively minor, the police force will attempt to resolve it internally and an official investigation might not be required. In more serious cases the IPCC or police force may refer the case to the Crown Prosecution Service, which will decide whether to bring criminal charges against the officer(s) involved. An officer who is dismissed, required to resign or reduced in rank, whether as a result of a complaint or not, can appeal to a police appeals tribunal established by the relevant police authority.

Following the Police and Fire Reform (Scotland) Act 2012 which brought together Scotland's eight police services into the single Police Service of Scotland, the remit of the Police Complaints Commissioner for Scotland (PCCS) was expanded to include investigations into the most serious incidents concerning the police. In relation to the change, the PCCS was renamed the Police Investigations and Review Commissioner (PIRC).

The Police Ombudsman for Northern Ireland provides an independent police complaints system for Northern Ireland, dealing with all stages of the complaints procedure. Complaints that cannot be resolved informally are investigated and the ombudsman recommends a suitable course of action to the Chief Constable of the Police Service of Northern Ireland or the Northern Ireland Policing Board based on the investigation's findings. The ombudsman may recommend that a police officer be prosecuted, but the decision to prosecute a police officer rests with the Director of Public Prosecutions.

INDEPENDENT POLICE COMPLAINTS COMMISSION, PO Box 473, Sale M33 0BW **T** 0300-020 0096
E enquiries@ipcc.gsi.gov.uk **W** www.ipcc.gov.uk

POLICE INVESTIGATIONS AND REVIEW COMMISSIONER, Hamilton House, Hamilton Business Park, Hamilton ML3 0QA **T** 0808-178 5577
E enquiries@pirc.gsi.gov.uk **W** www.pirc.scotland.gov.uk
Police Investigations and Review Commissioner, John McNeill

POLICE OMBUDSMAN FOR NORTHERN IRELAND, New Cathedral Buildings, 11 Church Street, Belfast BT1 1PG
T 028-9082 8600 **E** info@policeombudsman.org
W www.policeombudsman.org
Police Ombudsman, Dr Michael Maguire

POLICE SERVICES

COLLEGE OF POLICING

Leamington Road, Ryton-on-Dunsmore, Coventry CV8 3EN
T 0800-496 3322 **E** contactus@college.pnn.police.uk
W www.college.police.uk

The College of Policing was established in December 2012 as the first professional body set up for policing. It works on behalf of the public to raise professional standards in policing and to assist forces to reduce crime and protect the public. It engages with the public through the Police and Crime Commissioners to ensure that it is responsive to the issues of greatest concern.

The government has designated the college as a centre for reviewing and testing practices and interventions to identify which are effective in reducing crime. It makes this information accessible for all in policing, particularly frontline practitioners. The college also supports continuous professional development and sets national standards for promotion and progression.

Chief Executive, Alex Marshall, QPM
Chair, Shirley Pearce, CBE

NATIONAL CRIME AGENCY

The National Crime Agency (NCA) is an operational crime fighting agency introduced under the Crime and Courts Act 2013 and will be fully operational by December 2013. The NCA's remit is to fight organised crime, strengthen UK borders, tackle fraud and cyber crime and protect children and young people. The agency will take on the work of the Serious Organised Crime Agency and the Child Exploitation and Online Protection Centre, and will also incorporate functions previously carried out by the National Policing Improvement Agency.

Director-General, Keith Bristow, QPM

NATIONAL DOMESTIC EXTREMISM UNIT

PO Box 61701, London SW1H 0XN **T** 020-3276 1616

The role of the National Domestic Extremism Unit (NDEU) is to support all police forces to help reduce the criminal threat from domestic extremism in the UK. The primary responsibilities of the NDEU are to provide intelligence on domestic extremism and strategic public order issues in the UK. The NDEU provides tactical advice to the police service alongside information and guidance to the UK government in order to promote a single and coordinated police response.

National Coordinator for Domestic Extremism, Anton Setchell

UK MISSING PERSONS BUREAU

Foxley Hall, Bramshill, Hook, Hampshire RG27 0JW
T 0845-000 5481 **E** missingpersonsbureau@soca.mn.police.uk
W www.missingpersons.police.uk

The UK Missing Persons Bureau acts as the centre for the exchange of information connected with the search for missing persons nationally and internationally alongside the police and other related organisations. The unit focuses on cross-matching missing persons with unidentified persons or bodies by maintaining records, including a dental index of ante-mortem chartings of long-term missing persons and post-mortem chartings from unidentified bodies.

Information is supplied and collected for all persons who have been missing in the UK for over 72 hours (or fewer where police deem appropriate), foreign nationals reported missing in the UK, UK nationals reported missing abroad and all unidentified bodies and persons found within the UK.

SPECIALIST FORCES

BRITISH TRANSPORT POLICE

25 Camden Road, London NW1 9LN **T** 0800-405040
W www.btp.police.uk
Strength (June 2013), 2,909

British Transport Police is the national police force for the railways in England, Wales and Scotland, including the London Underground system, Docklands Light Railway, Glasgow Subway, Midland Metro tram system, Sunderland Metro, Croydon Tramlink and Emirates AirLine. The chief constable reports to the British Transport Police Authority. The members of the authority are appointed by the transport secretary and include representatives from the rail industry as well as independent members. Officers are paid the same salary as those in other police forces.

Chief Constable, Andrew Trotter, OBE, QPM
Deputy Chief Constable, Paul Crowther

CIVIL NUCLEAR CONSTABULARY

Building F6, Culham Science Centre, Abingdon,
Oxfordshire OX14 3DB **T** 01235-466606 **W** www.cnc.police.uk
*Strength (June 2013), c.*1,000

The Civil Nuclear Constabulary (CNC) operates under the strategic direction of the Department of Energy and Climate Change. The CNC is a specialised armed force that protects civil nuclear sites and nuclear materials. The constabulary is responsible for policing UK civil nuclear industry facilities and for escorting nuclear material between establishments within the UK and worldwide.

Chief Constable, Michael Griffiths, CBE
Deputy Chief Constable, John Sampson

MINISTRY OF DEFENCE POLICE

Ministry of Defence Police and Guarding Agency, Wethersfield,
Braintree, Essex CM7 4AZ **T** 01371-854000 **W** www.mod.police.uk
*Strength (June 2013), c.*2,600

Part of the Ministry of Defence Police and Guarding Agency, the Ministry of Defence Police is a statutory civil police force with particular responsibility for the security and policing of the MoD environment. It contributes to the physical protection of property and personnel within its jurisdiction and provides a comprehensive police service to the MoD as a whole.

Chief Constable, Alfred Hitchcock
Deputy Chief Constable, G. McAuley

THE SPECIAL CONSTABULARY

Darby House, 162 Bletchingley Road, Merstham, Surrey RH1 3DN
W www.policespecials.com
*Strength (June 2013), c.*20,000

The Special Constabulary is a force of trained volunteers who support and work with their local police force, usually for a minimum of four hours a week (the Metropolitan Police Special Constabulary usually asks for a minimum commitment of eight hours a week). Special constables are thoroughly grounded in the basic aspects of police work, such as self-defence, powers of arrest, common crimes and preparing evidence for court, before they can begin to carry out any police duties. Once they have completed their training, they have the same powers as a regular officer and wear a similar uniform.

POLICE FORCES

The telephone number for each local police force in England, Wales and Scotland is T 101

Force	Strength†	Chief Constable	Police and Crime Commissioner
ENGLAND*			
Avon and Somerset	2,940	Nick Gargan	Sue Mountstevens
Bedfordshire	1,147	Alfred Hitchcock, QPM	Olly Martins
Cambridgeshire	1,306	Simon Parr	Sir Graham Bright
Cheshire	1,908	David Whatton, QPM	John Dwyer
Cleveland	1,459	Jacqui Cheer, QPM	Barry Coppinger
Cumbria	1,127	Bernard Lawson, QPM	Richard Rhodes
Derbyshire	1,982	Mick Creedon, QPM	Alan Charles
Devon and Cornwall	3,212	Shaun Sawyer	Tony Hogg
Dorset	1,316	Debbie Simpson	Martyn Underhill
Durham	1,372	Mike Barton	Ron Hogg
Essex	3,408	Stephen Kavanagh	Nick Alston
Gloucestershire	1,199	Suzette Davenport	Martin Surl
Greater Manchester	7,282	Sir Peter Fahy, QPM	Tony Lloyd
Hampshire	3,361	Andy Marsh	Simon Hayes
Hertfordshire	1,948	Andy Bliss, QPM	David Lloyd
Humberside	1,865	Justine Curran	Matthew Grove
Kent	3,374	Ian Learmonth, QPM	Ann Barnes
Lancashire	3,178	Steve Finnigan, CBE, QPM	Clive Grunshaw
Leicestershire	2,008	Simon Cole	Sir Clive Loader
Lincolnshire	1,138	Neil Rhodes	Alan Hardwick
Merseyside	4,033	Jon Murphy, QPM	Jane Kennedy
Norfolk	1,516	Phil Gormley, QPM	Stephen Bett
North Yorkshire	1,444	Tim Madgwick	Julia Mulligan
Northamptonshire	1,276	Adrian Lee	Adam Simmonds
Northumbria	3,810	Sue Sim	Vera Baird
Nottinghamshire	2,119	Chris Eyre	Paddy Tipping
South Yorkshire	2,803	David Crompton, QPM	Shaun Wright
Staffordshire	1,795	Mike Cunningham, QPM	Matthew Ellis
Suffolk	1,166	Simon Ash, QPM	Tim Passmore
Surrey	1,941	Lynne Owens, QPM	Kevin Hurley
Sussex	2,731	Martin Richards, QPM	Katy Bourne
Thames Valley	4,197	Sara Thornton, CBE, QPM	Anthony Stansfeld
Warwickshire	779	Andy Parker, QPM	Ron Ball
West Mercia	2,146	David Shaw	Bill Longmore
West Midlands	7,872	Chris Sims, QPM	Bob Jones
West Yorkshire	5,435	Mark Gilmore, QPM	Mark Burns-Williamson
Wiltshire	1,057	Patrick Geenty	Angus Macpherson
WALES			
Dyfed-Powys	1,141	Jackie Roberts, QPM	Christopher Salmon
Gwent	1,412	Carmel Napier, QPM	Ian Johnston
North Wales	1,464	Mark Polin, QPM	Winston Roddick
South Wales	2,876	Peter Vaughan, QPM	Alun Michael
POLICE SCOTLAND	17,436	Stephen House, QPM	–
POLICE SERVICE OF NORTHERN IRELAND	7,033	Matt Baggott, CBE, QPM	0845-600 8000
ISLANDS			
Isle of Man	236	Gary Roberts	01624-631212
States of Jersey	237	Mike Bowron, QPM	01534-612612
Guernsey	153	Patrick Rice	01481-725111

* For the City of London Police and the Metropolitan Police Service *see* London Forces

† Size of force as at February 2013

Source: R. Hazell & Co, Sweet & Maxwell *Police and Constabulary Almanac 2013*

LONDON FORCES

CITY OF LONDON POLICE

37 Wood Street, London EC2P 2NQ T 020-7601 2222
W www.cityoflondon.police.uk
Strength (February 2013), 791

The City of London has one of the most important financial centres in the world and the force has particular expertise in fraud investigation. The force concentrates on three main priorities: economic crime, counter terrorism and community policing. It has a wholly elected police authority, the police committee of the City of London Corporation, which appoints the commissioner.
Commissioner, Adrian Leppard, QPM
Assistant Commissioner, Ian Dyson
Commander, Wayne Chance

METROPOLITAN POLICE SERVICE

New Scotland Yard, Broadway, London SW1H 0BG T 101
W www.met.police.uk
Strength (February 2013), 31,124
Commissioner, Sir Bernard Hogan-Howe, QPM
Deputy Commissioner, Craig Mackey, QPM

The Metropolitan Police Service is divided into three main areas for operational purposes:
TERRITORIAL POLICING
Most of the day-to-day policing of London is carried out by 32 borough operational command units operating within the same boundaries as the London borough councils.
Assistant Commissioner, Simon Byrne
SPECIALIST CRIME AND OPERATIONS (SC&O)
SC&O provides two main services: protecting and reducing the harm caused by serious crime and criminal networks and providing specialist policing services across London. SC&O enables the Metropolitan Police Service to respond quickly to life threatening incidents, provide a range of specialist training to detectives, and conduct forensic examinations of crime scenes in the capital.
Assistant Commissioner, Mark Rowley, QPM
SPECIALIST OPERATIONS
Specialist Operations is divided into three commands:

- *Counter Terrorism Command* is responsible for the prevention and disruption of terrorist activity, domestic extremism and related offences both within London and nationally, providing an explosives disposal and chemical, biological, radiological and nuclear capability within London, assisting the security services in fulfilling their roles and providing a single point of contact for international partners in counter-terrorism matters.
- *Protection Command* is responsible for the protection and security of high-profile persons; key public figures, including the royal family and the prime minister and others. It is also responsible for protecting royal residences and embassies, providing residential protection for visiting heads of state, heads of government and foreign ministers and advising the diplomatic community on security.
- *Security Command* works in conjunction with authorities at the Houses of Parliament to provide security for peers, MPs, employees and visitors to the palace of Westminster. It is also responsible for policing Heathrow and London City airports.

Assistant Commissioner, Cressida Dick, QPM

RATES OF PAY

London weighting of £2,277 per annum is awarded to all police officers working in London irrespective of their ranks and in addition to the salaries listed below (as at August 2013):

Chief Constables of Greater Manchester, Strathclyde and West Midlands*	£178,431–£181,455
Chief Constable*	£127,017–£169,359
Deputy Chief Constable*	£108,873–£139,119
Assistant Chief Constable and Commanders*	£90,726–£105,849
Chief Superintendent	£74,394–£78,636
Superintendent Range 2†	£71,331–£75,909
Superintendent	£62,298–£72,585
Chief Inspector‡§	£51,789 (£53,853)–£53,919 (£55,980)
Inspector‡§	£46,788 (£48,840)–£50,751 (£52,818)
Sergeant‡	£36,519–£41,040
Constable‡	£19,000–£36,519
Metropolitan Police	
Commissioner	£260,088
Deputy Commissioner	£214,722
City of London Police	
Commissioner	£160,902
Assistant Commissioner	£132,714
Police Service of Northern Ireland	
Chief Constable	£193,548
Deputy Chief Constable	£157,257

* Chief Officers may receive a bonus of at least 5 per cent of pensionable pay if their performance is deemed exceptional
† For Superintendents who were not given the rank of Chief Superintendent on its re-introduction on 1 January 2002
‡ Officers who have been on the highest available salary for one year have access to a competence-related payment of £1,212 a year
§ London salary in parentheses

STAFF ASSOCIATIONS

Police officers are not permitted to join a trade union or to take strike action. All ranks have their own staff associations.
CHIEF POLICE OFFICERS' STAFF ASSOCIATION, 10 Victoria Street, London SW1H 0NN T 020-7084 8950
Chair, Craig Mackey, QPM

ENGLAND AND WALES

POLICE FEDERATION OF ENGLAND AND WALES, Federation House, Highbury Drive, Leatherhead, Surrey KT22 7UY T 01372-352000 W www.polfed.org
Chair, Steve Williams
General Secretary, Ian Rennie
POLICE SUPERINTENDENTS' ASSOCIATION OF ENGLAND AND WALES, 67A Reading Road, Pangbourne, Reading RG8 7JD T 0118-984 4005 W www.policesupers.com
President, Chief Supt. Irene Curtis
National Secretary, Chief Supt. Graham Cassidy (until March 2014), Chief Supt. Tim Jackson (from March 2014)

SCOTLAND

ASSOCIATION OF SCOTTISH POLICE SUPERINTENDENTS, Milngavie Police Station, 99 Main Street, East Dunbartonshire G62 6JH T 0141-532 4022 W www.scottishpolicesupers.org.uk
General Secretary, Carol Forfar
SCOTTISH POLICE FEDERATION, 5 Woodside Place, Glasgow G3 7QF T 0141-331 2436 W www.spf.org.uk
Chair, Brian Docherty
General Secretary, Calum Steele

NORTHERN IRELAND

POLICE FEDERATION FOR NORTHERN IRELAND, 77–79 Garnerville Road, Belfast BT4 2NX T 028-9076 4200 W www.policefed-ni.org.uk
Chair, Terry Spence, QPM
Secretary, Stevie McCann
SUPERINTENDENTS' ASSOCIATION OF NORTHERN IRELAND, PSNI College, Garnerville Road, Belfast BT4 2NX T 028-9092 2201 W www.policesuperintendentsni.org
President, Chief Supt. Nigel Grimshaw
Hon. Secretary, Supt. Jonathan Kearney

THE PRISON SERVICE

The prison services in the UK are the responsibility of the Secretary of State for Justice, the Scottish Secretary for Justice and the Minister of Justice in Northern Ireland. The chief executive (director-general in Northern Ireland), officers of the National Offender Management Service (NOMS), the Scottish Prison Service (SPS) and the Northern Ireland Prison Service are responsible for the day-to-day running of the system.

There are 126 prison establishments in England and Wales, 16 in Scotland and three in Northern Ireland. Convicted prisoners are classified according to their assessed security risk and are housed in establishments appropriate to that level of security. There are no open prisons in Northern Ireland. Female prisoners are housed in women's establishments or in separate wings of mixed prisons. Remand prisoners are, where possible, housed separately from convicted prisoners. Offenders under the age of 21 are usually detained in a Young Offender Institution, which may be a separate establishment or part of a prison. Appellant and failed asylum seekers are held in Immigration Removal Centres, or in separate units of other prisons.

Fourteen prisons are now run by the private sector in England and Wales, and in England, Wales and Scotland all escort services have been contracted out to private companies. In Scotland, two prisons (Kilmarnock and Addiewell) were built and financed by the private sector and are being operated by private contractors.

There are independent prison inspectorates in England, Wales and Scotland which report annually on conditions and the treatment of prisoners. The Chief Inspector of Criminal Justice in Northern Ireland and HM Inspectorate of Prisons for England and Wales perform an inspectorate role for prisons in Northern Ireland. Every prison establishment also has an independent monitoring board made up of local volunteers.

Any prisoner whose complaint is not satisfied by the internal complaints procedures may complain to the prisons and probation ombudsman for England and Wales, the Scottish public services ombudsman or the prisoner ombudsman for Northern Ireland. The prisons and probation inspectors, the prisons ombudsman and the independent monitoring boards report to the home secretary and to the Minister of Justice in Northern Ireland.

PRISON STATISTICS

The projected 'high scenario' prison population for 2018 in England and Wales is 90,900; the 'low scenario' is 80,300.

PRISON POPULATION (UK) *as at June 2013*

	Remand	*Sentenced*	*Other*
ENGLAND AND WALES	10,986	71,233	1,623
Male	10,382	68,000	1,607
Female	604	3,233	16
SCOTLAND*	1,162	5,898	–
Male	1,084	5,577	–
Female	78	321	–
N. IRELAND	450	1,399	0
Male	436	1,358	0
Female	14	41	0
UK TOTAL	12,598	78,530	1,623

* Figures from August 2013

Sources: MoJ; Scottish Prison Service; NI Prison Service

PRISON CAPACITY (ENGLAND AND WALES) *as at August 2013*

Male prisoners	80,438
Female prisoners	3,907
Total	84,345
Useable operational capacity	87,794
Under home detention curfew supervision	2,475

Source: MoJ – *Offender Management Statistics*

SENTENCED PRISON POPULATION BY SEX AND OFFENCE (ENGLAND AND WALES) *as at 30 June 2013*

	Male	*Female*
Violence against the person	18,606	907
Sexual offences	10,498	77
Burglary	6,885	199
Robbery	8,592	323
Theft, handling	4,057	469
Fraud and forgery	1,192	159
Drugs offences	9,748	473
Motoring offences	706	22
Other offences	7,165	541
Offence not recorded	437	43
*Total**	67,886	3,213

* Figures do not include civil (non-criminal) prisoners or fine defaulters

Source: MoJ – *Offender Management Statistics*

SENTENCED POPULATION BY LENGTH OF SENTENCE (ENGLAND AND WALES) *as at 30 June 2013*

	Adults	*Young offenders*
Less than 12 months	5,996	864
12 months to less than 4 years	16,763	2,795
4 years to less than life	24,977	1,405
Indeterminate	12,960	226
*Total**	60,696	5,290

* Figures do not include civil (non-criminal) prisoners or fine defaulters

Source: MoJ – *Offender Management Statistics*

AVERAGE DAILY POPULATION BY TYPE OF CUSTODY 2012–13 (SCOTLAND)

Remand: sub total	1,437
Persons under sentence: sub total	6,577
Under 4 years	3,723
4 years and over	2,820
Total	8,014

Source: SPS – *Annual Report and Accounts 2012–13*

SUICIDES IN PRISON IN 2012 (ENGLAND AND WALES)

Male	59
Female	1
Total	60

Source: MoJ

THE PRISON SERVICES

NATIONAL OFFENDER MANAGEMENT SERVICE

T 0300-047 6325 E public.enquiries@noms.gsi.gov.uk
W www.justice.gov.uk

HM Prison Service became part of the National Offender Management Service (NOMS) on 1 April 2008 as part of the reorganisation of the Ministry of Justice (MoJ).

SALARIES *as at April 2013*

Senior manager A	£64,765–£82,892
Senior manager B	£60,980–£80,458
Senior manager C	£56,920–£72,458
Senior manager D	£45,700–£61,038
Manager E	£33,335–£46,024
Manager F	£29,685–£39,041
Manager G	£25,105–£32,140

THE NOMS BOARD

Chief Executive, Michael Spurr
Director of Commissioning and Commercial, Ian Blakeman
Director of Probation and Contracted Services, Colin Allars
Director of National Operational Services, Digby Griffith
Director of Public Sector Prisons, Phil Copple
Director of Human Resources, Carol Carpenter
Director of Information and Communications Technology, Martin Bellamy
Director of Finance and Analysis, Andrew Emmett

DEPUTY DIRECTORS OF CUSTODY

Andrew Cross *(East Midlands);* Adrian Smith *(East of England);* Michelle Jarman-Howe *(Kent and Sussex);* Nick Pascoe *(London);* Alan Tallentire *(North-East);* Alan Scott *(North-West);* Claudia Sturt *(South-Central);* Ferdie Parker *(South-West);* Ian Mullholland *(Wales);* Luke Serjeant *(West Midlands);* Amy Rice *(Yorkshire and Humberside)*; Richard Vince *(High Security)*

OPERATING COSTS OF NOMS 2012–13

Staff costs	£2,316,401,000
Other operating costs	£2,121,551,000
Operating income	(£394,412,000)
Net operating costs (before tax)	£4,043,540,000
Net operating costs (after tax)	£4,044,273,000

Source: NOMS – *Annual Report 2012–13*

SCOTTISH PRISON SERVICE (SPS)

Calton House, 5 Redheughs Rigg, Edinburgh EH12 9HW
T 0131-244 8747 E gaolinfo@sps.pnn.gov.uk
W www.sps.gov.uk

SALARIES 2013–14

Senior managers in the Scottish Prison Service, including governors and deputy governors of prisons, are paid across three pay bands depending on the size of the establishment:

Band I	£54,930–£68,433
Band H	£43,601–£56,704
Band G	£34,333–£47,149

SPS BOARD

Chief Executive, Colin McConnell
Directors, Willie Pretswell *(Finance);* Catherine Topley *(Human Resources);* Dan Gunn *(Operations);* Jane Richardson *(Partnerships and Commissioning)*
Non-Executive Directors, Allan Burns; Harry McGuigan; Jane Martin; Susan Matheson; William Morton; Zoe Van Zwanenberg

OPERATING COSTS OF SPS 2012–13

Total income	(£7,493,000)
Total expenditure	£349,094,000
Staff costs	£144,221,000
Running costs	£176,593,000
Other current expenditure	£28,290,000
Operating cost	£341,601,000
Interest payable and similar charges	£11,455,000
Net operating cost	£353,056,000

Source: SPS – *Annual Report and Accounts 2012–13*

NORTHERN IRELAND PRISON SERVICE

Dundonald House, Upper Newtownards Road, Belfast BT4 3SU
T 028-9052 5065 E info@niprisonservice.gov.uk
W www.dojni.gov.uk

SALARIES 2013–14

Governor 1	£74,747–£80,550
Governor 2	£67,983–£72,183
Governor 3	£58,824–£62,766
Governor 4	£51,156–£55,407
Governor 5	£44,934–£50,396

SENIOR STAFF

Director-General, Sue McAllister
Directors, Ronnie Armour *(Human Resources and Organisational Development);* Joanne McBurney *(Human Resources and Organisational Development);* Mark Adam *(Corporate Change Manager)*

OPERATING COSTS OF NORTHERN IRELAND PRISON SERVICE 2012–13

Staff costs	£84,531,000
Net running costs	£30,311,000
Depreciation and Amortisation	£11,829,000
Operating expenditure	£126,671
Net operating costs for the year	£173,660

Source: NI Prison Service – *Annual Report and Accounts 2012–13*

PRISON ESTABLISHMENTS

ENGLAND AND WALES *as at June 2013*

Prison	*Address*	*Prisoners*	*Governor/Director*
ALTCOURSE (private prison)	Liverpool L9 7WU	999	Bob McColm
ASHFIELD (private prison)	Bristol BS16 9QJ	400	Ray Duckworth
*‡ASKHAM GRANGE	York YO23 3FT	93	Diane Pellew
‡AYLESBURY	Bucks HP20 1EH	408	Kevin Leggett
BEDFORD	Bedford MK40 1HG	460	Ian Blakeman
BELMARSH	London SE28 0EB	771	Phil Wragg
BIRMINGHAM	Birmingham B18 4AS	1,385	Peter Small
BLANTYRE HOUSE	Kent TN17 2NH	118	James Bourke
BLUNDESTON	Suffolk NR32 5BG	506	David Bamford

Prison	*Address*	*Prisoners*	*Governor/Director*
†‡BRINSFORD	Wolverhampton WV10 7PY	485	Carl Hardwick
‡BRISTOL	Bristol BS7 8PS	612	Andrea Albutt
‡BRIXTON	London SW2 5XF	749	Edmond Tullett
*BRONZEFIELD (private prison)	Middlesex TW15 3JZ	443	Charlotte Pattison-Rideout
BUCKLEY HALL	Lancs OL12 9DP	434	Susan Kennedy
BULLINGDON	Oxon OX25 1PZ	1,067	Andy Lattimore
BURE	Norfolk NR10 5GB	522	Sue Doolan
†CARDIFF	Cardiff CF24 0UG	791	Richard Booty
CHANNINGS WOOD	Devon TQ12 6DW	718	Gavin O'Malley
‡CHELMSFORD	Essex CM2 6LQ	529	Rob Davis
COLDINGLEY	Surrey GU24 9EX	507	Glenn Knight
‡COOKHAM WOOD	Kent ME1 3LU	113	Emily Thomas
DARTMOOR	Devon PL20 6RR	654	Terry Witton
‡DEERBOLT	Co. Durham DL12 9BG	428	Gabrielle Lee
‡DONCASTER (private prison)	Doncaster DN5 8UX	1,116	John Biggin
†DORCHESTER	Dorset DT1 1JD	255	Carole Draper
DOVEGATE (private prison)	Staffs ST14 8XR	1,011	Craig Thomson
§DOVER	Kent CT17 9DR	291	Sara Pennington
*DOWNVIEW	Surrey SM2 5PD	288	Jonathan French
*‡DRAKE HALL	Staffs ST21 6LQ	283	Paul Newton
DURHAM	Durham DH1 3HU	866	Tim Allen *(acting)*
*‡EAST SUTTON PARK	Kent ME17 3DF	93	James Bourke
*‡EASTWOOD PARK	Glos GL12 8DB	290	Simon Beecroft
ELMLEY	Kent ME12 4DZ	1,241	Paul Woods
ERLESTOKE	Wilts SN10 5TU	487	Andy Rogers
EVERTHORPE	E. Yorks HU15 1RB	663	Ed Cornmell
†‡EXETER	Devon EX4 4EX	523	Jeannine Hendrick
FEATHERSTONE	Wolverhampton WV10 7PU	680	Deborah Butler
†‡FELTHAM	Middx TW13 4ND	600	Glenn Knight
FORD	W. Sussex BN18 0BX	511	Sharon Williams
‡FOREST BANK (private prison)	Manchester M27 8FB	1,310	Trevor Shortt
*FOSTON HALL	Derby DE65 5DN	291	Ken Kan
FRANKLAND	Durham DH1 5YD	782	Dave Thompson
FULL SUTTON	York YO41 1PS	586	Paul Foweather
GARTH	Preston PR26 8NE	779	Terry Williams
GARTREE	Leics LE16 7RP	703	Ian Telfer
†‡GLEN PARVA	Leicester LE18 4TN	635	Michael Wood
GRENDON/SPRING HILL	Bucks HP18 0TL	546	Jamie Bennett
‡GUYS MARSH	Dorset SP7 0AH	565	Duncan Burles
§HASLAR	Hampshire PO12 2AW	169	Paul Millett
HAVERIGG	Cumbria LA18 4NA	637	Tony Corcoran
HEWELL	Worcs B97 6QS	1,170	Stephanie Roberts-Bibby
HIGH DOWN	Surrey SM2 5PJ	1,090	Ian Bickers
HIGHPOINT	Suffolk CB8 9YG	1,296	Damian Evans
†‡HINDLEY	Lancs WN2 5TH	174	Peter Francis
‡HOLLESLEY BAY	Suffolk IP12 3JW	416	Declan Moore
*‡HOLLOWAY	London N7 0NU	416	Julia Killick
HOLME HOUSE	Stockton-on-Tees TS18 2QU	1,098	Jenny Mooney
‡HULL	Hull HU9 5LS	727	Norman Griffin
‡HUNTERCOMBE	Oxon RG9 5SB	422	Nigel Atkinson
ISIS	Thamesmead SE28 0NZ	564	Grahame Hawkings
ISLE OF WIGHT	Isle of Wight PO30 5RS	1,130	Andy Lattimore
KENNET	Merseyside L31 1HX	290	Steve Valentine
KIRKHAM	Lancs PR4 2RN	611	Graham Beck
KIRKLEVINGTON GRANGE	Cleveland TS15 9PA	269	Steve Robson
†‡LANCASTER FARMS	Lancaster LA1 3QZ	494	Derek Harrison
LEEDS	Leeds LS12 2TJ	1,166	Carolyn Lund *(acting)*
LEICESTER	Leicester LE2 7AJ	325	Ali Dodds
‡LEWES	E. Sussex BN7 1EA	596	Nigel Foote
LEYHILL	Glos GL12 8BT	512	Chantel King
LINCOLN	Lincoln LN2 4BD	605	Ian Thomas
LINDHOLME	Doncaster DN7 6EE	900	Marian Mahoney
LITTLEHEY	Cambs PE28 0SR	1,089	David Taylor
LIVERPOOL	Liverpool L9 3DF	1,144	John Illingsworth
LONG LARTIN	Worcs WR11 8TZ	611	Simon Cartwright
*‡LOW NEWTON	Durham DH1 5YA	260	Alan Richer
LOWDHAM GRANGE (private prison)	Notts NG14 7DA	884	Brian Anderson
MAIDSTONE	Kent ME14 1UZ	545	Dave Atkinson
MANCHESTER	Manchester M60 9AH	1,111	Hannah Lane *(acting)*
‡MOORLAND/HATFIELD	Doncaster DN7 6BW	1,246	Marian Mahoney
§MORTON HALL	Lincoln LN6 9PT	372	Karen Head
THE MOUNT	Herts HP3 0NZ	758	Steven Bradford
*‡NEW HALL	W. Yorks WF4 4XX	373	Diane Pellew
NORTH SEA CAMP	Lincs PE22 0QX	414	Graham Batchford
‡NORTHALLERTON	N. Yorks DL6 1NW	231	Chris Dyer
‡NORTHUMBERLAND	Northumberland NE65 9XF	1,316	Matt Spencer
‡NORWICH	Norfolk NR1 4LU	696	Will Styles

Prison	*Address*	*Prisoners*	*Governor/Director*
NOTTINGHAM	Notts NG5 3AG	1,039	James Shanley
OAKWOOD	W. Midlands WV10 7QD	1,587	John McLaughlin
ONLEY	Warks CV23 8AP	678	Dave Harding
†‡PARC (private prison)	Bridgend CF35 6AP	1,302	Janet Wallsgrove
‡PENTONVILLE	London N7 8TT	1,332	Gary Monaghon
*†PETERBOROUGH (private prison)	Peterborough PE3 7PD	469	Nick Leader
‡PORTLAND	Dorset DT5 1DL	521	Russ Trent
PRESTON	Lancs PR1 5AB	646	Paul Holland
RANBY	Notts DN22 8EU	1,044	Neil Richards
†‡READING	Berks RG1 3HY	215	Darren Hughes
RISLEY	Cheshire WA3 6BP	1,092	Jerry Spencer
‡ROCHESTER	Kent ME1 3QS	653	Andy Hudson
RYE HILL (private prison)	Warks CV23 8SZ	620	Dave Thompson, OBE
*SEND	Surrey GU23 7LJ	267	Karen Elgar
STAFFORD	Stafford ST16 3AW	723	Bridie Oakes-Richards
STANDFORD HILL	Kent ME12 4AA	461	Sarah Coccia
STOCKEN	Leics LE15 7RD	831	Michael Wood
‡STOKE HEATH	Shropshire TF9 2JL	741	John Huntington
*‡STYAL	Cheshire SK9 4HR	439	John Hewitson
SUDBURY	Derbys DE6 5HW	576	Stephen Ruddy
SWALESIDE	Kent ME12 4AX	1,101	Sarah Coccia
†‡SWANSEA	Swansea SA1 3SR	404	Lauren Watson
‡SWINFEN HALL	Staffs WS14 9QS	628	Teresa Clarke
THAMESIDE	London SE28 0FJ	854	Guy Baulf
‡THORN CROSS	Cheshire WA4 4RL	294	Mahala McGuffie
USK/PRESCOED	Monmouthshire NP15 1XP	493	Steve Cross
VERNE	Dorset DT5 1EQ	600	James Lucas
WAKEFIELD	W. Yorks WF2 9AG	742	Susan Howard
WANDSWORTH	London SW18 3HS	1,228	Kenny Brown
‡WARREN HILL	Suffolk IP12 3JW	112	Bev Bevan
WAYLAND	Norfolk IP25 6RL	1,000	Steve Rodford, OBE
WEALSTUN	W. Yorks LS23 7AZ	816	Andrew Dickinson
‡WERRINGTON	Stoke-on-Trent ST9 0DX	117	Babafemi Dada
‡WETHERBY	W. Yorks LS22 5ED	223	Sara Snell
WHATTON	Nottingham NG13 9FQ	834	Lynn Saunders
WHITEMOOR	Cambs PE15 0PR	455	Paul Cawkwell
WINCHESTER	Winchester SO22 5DF	686	David Rogers
WOLDS (private prison)	E. Yorks HU15 2JZ	347	Cathy James
WOODHILL	Bucks MK4 4DA	744	Nigel Smith
WORMWOOD SCRUBS	London W12 0AE	1,184	Phil Taylor, OBE
WYMOTT	Preston PR26 8LW	1,113	Terry Williams

SCOTLAND *as at April 2013*

ABERDEEN	Aberdeen AB11 8FN	179	Audrey Mooney
ADDIEWELL(private prison)	West Lothian EH55 8QA	767	Audrey Park
†BARLINNIE	Glasgow G33 2QX	1,207	Derek McGill
*†‡CORNTON VALE	Stirling FK9 5NU	251	Kate Donegan
†DUMFRIES	Dumfries DG2 9AX	193	Rhona Hotchkiss
†EDINBURGH	Edinburgh EH11 3LN	898	Teresa Medhurst
GLENOCHIL	Tullibody FK10 3AD	650	Nigel Ironside
GRAMPIAN	Aberdeenshire AB42 2YY	–	Jim Farish
†‡GREENOCK	Greenock PA16 9AH	246	Jim Kerr
*†INVERNESS	Inverness IV2 3HH	131	Caroline Johnston
†‡KILMARNOCK (private prison)	Kilmarnock KA1 5AA	577	Sandy McEwan
LOW MOSS	Glasgow G64 2PZ	668	Michael Stoney
OPEN ESTATE	Angus DD8 3QY	236	Fraser Munro
†PERTH	Perth PH2 8AT	656	Mike Inglis
PETERHEAD	Aberdeenshire AB42 2YY	123	Audrey Mooney, OBE
†‡POLMONT	Falkirk FK2 0AB	668	Sue Brookes
SHOTTS	Lanarkshire ML7 4LE	534	Ian Whitehead

NORTHERN IRELAND *as at April 2013*

*†‡HYDEBANK WOOD	Belfast BT8 8NA	226	Paul Norbury
†§MAGHABERRY	Co. Antrim BT28 2NF	1,059	Pat Maguire
MAGILLIGAN	Co. Londonderry BT49 0LR	564	Alan Longwell

PRISON ESTABLISHMENTS KEY

* Women's establishment or establishment with units for women
† Remand Centre or establishment with units for remand prisoners
‡ Young Offender Institution or establishment with units for young offenders
§ Immigration Removal Centre or establishment with units for immigration detainees

DEFENCE

The armed forces of the UK comprise the Royal Navy, the Army and the Royal Air Force (RAF). The Queen is Commander-in-Chief of all the armed forces. The Secretary of State for Defence is responsible for the formulation and content of defence policy and for providing the means by which it is conducted. The formal legal basis for the conduct of defence in the UK rests on a range of powers vested by statute and letters patent in the Defence Council, chaired by the Secretary of State for Defence. Beneath the ministers lies the top management of the Ministry of Defence (MoD), headed jointly by the Permanent Secretary and the Chief of Defence Staff. The Permanent Secretary is the government's principal civilian adviser on defence and has the primary responsibility for policy, finance, management and administration. The Permanent Secretary is also personally accountable to parliament for the expenditure of all public money allocated to defence purposes. The Chief of the Defence Staff is the professional head of the armed forces in the UK and the principal military adviser to the secretary of state and the government.

The Defence Board is the executive of the Defence Council. Chaired by the Permanent Secretary, it acts as the main executive board of the Ministry of Defence, providing senior level leadership and strategic management of defence.

The Central Staff, headed by the Vice-Chief of the Defence Staff and the Second Permanent Under-Secretary of State, is the policy core of the department. Defence Equipment and Support, headed by the Chief of Defence Materiel, is responsible for purchasing defence equipment and providing logistical support to the armed forces.

A permanent Joint Headquarters for the conduct of joint operations was set up at Northwood in 1996. The Joint Headquarters connects the policy and strategic functions of the MoD head office with the conduct of operations and is intended to strengthen the policy/executive division.

The UK pursues its defence and security policies through its membership of NATO (to which most of its armed forces are committed), the European Union, the Organisation for Security and Cooperation in Europe and the UN (*see* International Organisations section).

STRENGTH OF THE REGULAR ARMED FORCES

	Royal Navy	*Army*	*RAF*	*All Services*
1975 strength	76,200	167,100	95,000	338,300
2000 strength	42,850	110,050	54,720	207,620
2005 strength	39,940	109,290	51,870	201,100
2006 strength	39,390	107,730	48,730	195,850
2007 strength	38,850	106,340	45,480	190,670
2008 strength	38,560	104,980	43,370	186,910
2009 strength	38,340	106,700	43,560	188,600
2010 strength	38,730	108,920	44,050	191,700
2011 strength	37,660	106,240	42,460	186,360
2012 strength	35,540	104,250	40,000	179,790
2013 strength	33,960	99,730	37,030	170,710

Source: Defence Analytical Services and Advice (DASA) *National Statistics* (Crown copyright)

SERVICE PERSONNEL BY RANK AND GENDER

	Males	*Females*
Officers	25,390	3,670
Other Ranks	128,710	12,940

Source: DASA *National Statistics* (Crown copyright)

UK regular forces include trained and untrained personnel and nursing services, but exclude Gurkhas, full-time reserve service personnel, mobilised reservists and naval activated reservists. As at 1 April 2013 these groups provisionally numbered:

All Gurkhas	3,510
Full-time reserve service	2,440
Mobilised reservists	
Army	1,170
RAF	60
Naval activated reservists	50

Source: DASA *National Statistics* (Crown copyright)

CIVILIAN PERSONNEL

1993 level	159,600
2000 level	121,300
2001 level	118,200
2002 level	110,100
2003 level	107,600
2004 level	108,990
2005 level	107,680
2006 level	102,970
2007 level	95,790
2008 level	88,690
2009 level	86,620
2010 level	85,850
2011 level	83,060
2012 level	70,940
2013 level	65,400

Source: DASA *National Statistics* (Crown copyright)

UK REGULAR FORCES: DEATHS

In 2012 there were a total of 129 deaths among the UK regular armed forces, of which 19 were serving in the Royal Navy and Royal Marines, 95 in the Army and 15 in the RAF. The largest single cause of death was as a result of hostile action (killed in action and died of wounds), which accounted for 40 deaths (31 per cent of the total) in 2012. Land transport accidents accounted for 15 deaths (12 per cent) and other accidents accounted for a further 26 deaths (20 per cent). Suicides and open verdicts accounted for seven deaths or 5 per cent of the total.

NUMBER OF DEATHS AND MORTALITY RATES

	2008	*2009*	*2010*	*2011*	*2012*
Total number	137	205	187	132	129
Royal Navy	40	23	30	19	19
Army	79	158	136	98	95
RAF	18	24	21	15	15
Mortality rates per thousand					
Tri-service rate	0.74	1.07	0.97	0.70	0.71
Navy	1.10	0.58	0.78	0.52	0.53
Army	0.73	1.33	1.16	0.90	0.89
RAF	0.37	0.55	0.50	0.32	0.43

Source: DASA *National Statistics* (Crown copyright)

NUCLEAR FORCES
The Vanguard Class SSBN (ship submersible ballistic nuclear) provides the UK's strategic nuclear deterrent. Each Vanguard Class submarine is capable of carrying 16 Trident D5 missiles equipped with nuclear warheads.

There is a ballistic missile early warning system station at RAF Fylingdales in North Yorkshire.

ARMS CONTROL
The 1990 Conventional Armed Forces in Europe (CFE) Treaty, which commits all NATO and former Warsaw Pact members to limiting their holdings of five major classes of conventional weapons, has been adapted to reflect the changed geo-strategic environment and negotiations continue for its implementation. The Open Skies Treaty, which the UK signed in 1992 and entered into force in 2002, allows for the overflight of states parties by other states parties using unarmed observation aircraft.

The UN Convention on Certain Conventional Weapons (as amended 2001), which bans or restricts the use of specific types of weapons that are considered to cause unnecessary or unjustifiable suffering to combatants, or to affect civilians indiscriminately, was ratified by the UK in 1995. In 1968 the UK signed and ratified the Nuclear Non-Proliferation Treaty, which came into force in 1970 and was indefinitely and unconditionally extended in 1995. In 1996 the UK signed the Comprehensive Nuclear Test Ban Treaty and ratified it in 1998. The UK is a party to the 1972 Biological and Toxin Weapons Convention, which provides for a worldwide ban on biological weapons, and the 1993 Chemical Weapons Convention, which came into force in 1997 and provides for a verifiable worldwide ban on chemical weapons.

DEFENCE BUDGET DEPARTMENTAL EXPENDITURE LIMITS
£ billion

	Resource budget	*Capital budget*	*Total DEL*
2012–13 (outturn)	27.1	7.4	34.5
2013–14 (forecast)	26.5	9.8	36.3
2014–15 (forecast)	24.5	9.0	33.5

Source: HM Treasury – *Budget 2013* (Crown copyright)

MINISTRY OF DEFENCE

Main Building, Whitehall, London SW1A 2HB
T 020-7218 9000
W www.gov.uk/government/organisations/ministry-of-defence

Secretary of State for Defence, Rt. Hon. Philip Hammond, MP
Private Secretary, Emma Davies
Special Advisers, Hayden Allen, Graham Hook
Minister of State, Rt. Hon. Andrew Robathan, MP *(Armed Forces)*
Private Secretary, Gareth Martin
Minister of State, Rt. Hon. Mark Francois, MP *(Defence Personnel, Welfare and Veterans)*
Private Secretary, Charles Seeley
Parliamentary Under-Secretary of State, Dr Andrew Murrison, MP *(International Security Strategy)*
Private Secretary, Anna Platt
Parliamentary Under-Secretary of State, Philip Dunne, MP *(Defence Equipment, Support and Technology)*
Private Secretary, Tom Burden
Parliamentary Under-Secretary of State and Lords Spokesman, Lord Astor of Hever
Private Secretary, Alan Lawson

CHIEFS OF STAFF
Chief of the Defence Staff, Gen. Sir Nicholas Houghton, GCB, CBE, ADC
Vice Chief of the Defence Staff, Air Chief Marshal Sir Stuart Peach, KCB, CBE, ADC
Chief of the Naval Staff and First Sea Lord, Adm. Sir George Zambellas, KCB, DSC, ADC
Commander Operations, Rear-Adm. Matt Parr
Chief of the General Staff, Gen. Sir Peter Wall, GCB, CBE, ADC
Assistant Chief of the General Staff, Maj.-Gen. David Cullen, OBE
Chief of the Air Staff, Air Chief Marshal Sir Andrew Pulford, KCB, CBE, ADC
Assistant Chief of the Air Staff, Air Vice-Marshal Edward Stringer, CBE

SENIOR OFFICIALS
Permanent Under-Secretary of State, Jon Thompson
Second Permanent Under-Secretary of State, Jon Day
Chief of Defence Materiel, Bernard Gray
Chief Scientific Adviser, Prof. Vernon Gibson, FRS
Director-General Finance, David Williams

THE DEFENCE COUNCIL
The Defence Council is the senior committee of the MoD, and was established by royal prerogative under letters patent in April 1964. The letters patent confer on the Defence Council the command over all of the armed forces and charge the council with such matters relating to the administration of the armed forces as the Secretary of State for Defence should direct them to execute. It consists of the Secretary of State for Defence, the Minister of State for the Armed Forces, the Minister of State for Defence Personnel, Welfare and Veterans, the Parliamentary Under-Secretary of State and Minister for Defence Equipment, Support and Technology, the Parliamentary Under-Secretary of State and Minister for International Security Strategy, the Parliamentary Under-Secretary of State and Lords Spokesman on Defence, the Chief of the Defence Staff, the Permanent Under-Secretary of State of the MoD, the Chief of the Naval Staff and First Sea Lord, the Chief of the General Staff, the Chief of the Air Staff, the Vice-Chief of the Defence Staff, the Commander Joint Forces Command, the Chief of Defence Materiel, the Chief Scientific Adviser and the Director-General Finance.

CENTRAL STAFF
Vice-Chief of the Defence Staff, Air Chief Marshal Sir Stuart Peach, KCB, CBE, ADC

JOINT FORCES COMMAND
Commander Joint Forces Command, Gen. Sir Richard Barrons, KCB, CBE, ADC
Chief of Joint Operations, Lt.-Gen. David Capewell, OBE
Chief of Staff (Operations), Maj.-Gen. James Bashall, CBE
Chief of Staff HQ, Maj.-Gen. P. Jones, CBE

FLEET COMMAND
First Sea Lord, Adm. Sir George Zambellas, KCB, DSC, ADC
Fleet Commander and Deputy Chief of Naval Staff, Vice-Adm. P. Jones, CB

NAVAL HOME COMMAND
Second Sea Lord and Chief of Naval Personnel and Training, and Chief Naval Logistics Officer, Vice-Adm. David Steel, CBE
Naval Secretary and Chief of Staff (Personnel), Rear-Admiral (Simon) Jonathan Woodcock, OBE

LAND FORCES
Commander Land Forces, Lt.-Gen. Sir Adrian Bradshaw, KCB, OBE
Chief of Staff Land Forces, Maj.-Gen. Tyrone Urch, CBE

AIR COMMAND
Deputy Commander Operations, Air Marshal Greg Bagwell, CB, CBE
Deputy Commander Capability and Air Member for Personnel and Capability, Air Marshal Barry North, OBE

DEFENCE EQUIPMENT AND SUPPORT
Chief of Defence Materiel, Bernard Gray
Chief of Materiel (Fleet), Vice-Adm. Sir Andrew Mathews, KCB
Chief of Materiel (Land), Lt.-Gen. Christopher Deverell, MBE
Chief of Materiel (Air), Air Marshal Simon Bollom, CB

EXECUTIVE AGENCIES

DEFENCE SCIENCE AND TECHNOLOGY LABORATORY
Porton Down, Salisbury, Wiltshire SP4 0JQ T 01980-613000
E centralenquiries@dstl.gov.uk
W www.gov.uk/government/organisations/defence-science-and-technology-laboratory
Chief Executive, Jonathan Lyle

DEFENCE SUPPORT GROUP
Building 203, Monxton Road, Andover, Hampshire SP11 8HT
T 01264-383295 E info@dsg.mod.uk W www.dsg.mod.uk
Chief Executive, Archie Hughes

UK HYDROGRAPHIC OFFICE
Admiralty Way, Taunton, Somerset TA1 2DN T 01823-337900
E customerservices@ukho.gov.uk W www.ukho.gov.uk
Chief Executive, Ian Moncrieff, CBE

ARMED FORCES TRAINING AND RECRUITMENT

Flag Officer Sea Training (FOST) is responsible for all Royal Navy and Royal Fleet Auxiliary training. FOST's International Defence Training provides the focal point for all aspects of naval training. Training is divided into five streams: Naval Core Training (responsible for new entry, command, leadership and management training); Royal Marine; Submarine; Surface and Aviation.

The Army Recruiting and Training Division (ARTD) is responsible for the four key areas of army training: soldier initial training, at the School of Infantry or at one of the army's four other facilities; officer initial training at the Royal Military Academy Sandhurst; trade training at one of the army's specialist facilities; and resettlement training for those about to leave the army. Trade training facilities include: the Armour Centre; the Defence College of Logistics and Personnel Administration; the Royal School of Artillery; the Royal School of Military Engineering and the Army Aviation Centre.

The Royal Air Force No. 22 (Training) Group exists to recruit RAF personnel and provide trained specialist personnel to the armed forces as a whole, such as providing the army air corps with trained helicopter pilots. The group is split into eight areas: RAF College Cranwell and Inspectorate of Recruiting; the Directorate of Flying Training (DFT); the Directorate of Joint Technical Training (DJTT); the Air Cadet Organisation (ACO); Core Headquarters; the Defence College of Aeronautical Engineering (DCAE); the Defence College of Communications and Information Systems (DCCIS) and the Defence College of Electro-Mechanical Engineering (DCEME).

USEFUL WEBSITES
W www.royalnavy.mod.uk
W www.army.mod.uk
W www.raf.mod.uk

THE ROYAL NAVY

In Order of Seniority

LORD HIGH ADMIRAL OF THE UNITED KINGDOM
HRH The Prince Philip, Duke of Edinburgh, KG, KT, OM, GBE, AC, QSO, PC, *apptd* 2011

ADMIRALS OF THE FLEET
HRH The Prince Philip, Duke of Edinburgh, KG, KT, OM, GBE, AC, QSO, PC, *apptd* 1953
Sir Edward Ashmore, GCB, DSC, *apptd* 1977
Sir Benjamin Bathurst, GCB, *apptd* 1995
HRH The Prince of Wales, KG, KT, GCB, OM, AK, QSO, PC, ADC, *apptd* 2012

ADMIRALS
(Former Chiefs or Vice Chiefs of Defence Staff and First Sea Lords who remain on the active list)
Slater, Sir Jock, GCB, LVO, *apptd* 1991
Boyce, Lord, KG, GCB, OBE, *apptd* 1995
Abbott, Sir Peter, GBE, KCB, *apptd* 1995
Essenhigh, Sir Nigel, GCB, *apptd* 1998
West of Spithead, Lord, GCB, DSC, PC, *apptd* 2000
Band, Sir Jonathon, GCB, *apptd* 2002
Stanhope, Sir Mark, GCB, OBE, *apptd* 2004

ADMIRALS
HRH The Princess Royal, KG, KT, GCVO, QSO *(Chief Commandant for Women in the Royal Navy)*
Zambellas, Sir George, KCB, DSC, ADC *(First Sea Lord and Chief of Naval Staff)*

VICE-ADMIRALS
Mathews, Sir Andrew, KCB *(Chief of Materiel (Fleet) and Chief of Fleet Support to the Navy Board)*
Johnstone-Burt, (Charles) Anthony, CB, OBE *(Chief of Staff to the Supreme Allied Commander Transformation)*
Jones, Philip, CB *(Fleet Commander, Deputy Chief of Naval Staff and Chief Naval Warfare Officer)*
Richards, Alan, CB *(Chief of Defence Intelligence)*
Steel, David, CBE *(Second Sea Lord, Chief of Naval Personnel and Training and Chief Naval Logistics Officer)*
Hudson, Peter, CBE *(Cdr Maritime Command)*
Corder, Ian, CB *(UK Military Representative to NATO and the EU)*

REAR-ADMIRALS
HRH The Duke of York, KG, GCVO, ADC
Lister, Simon, CB, OBE *(Director Submarines and Chief Naval Engineering Officer)*
Williams, Bruce, CBE *(Deputy Director-General EU Military Staff)*
Potts, Duncan *(Assistant Chief of Naval Staff (Capability), Rear-Adm. Surface Ships (Head of Fighting Arm) and Controller of the Navy))*
Harding, Russell, OBE *(Assistant Chief of Naval Staff (Aviation and Carriers) and Rear-Adm. Fleet Air Arm (Head of Fighting Arm))*
Johnstone, Clive, CBE *(Assistant Chief of Naval Staff (Policy))*
Hockley, Christopher *(Flag Officer Scotland, Northern England and Northern Ireland, Flag Officer Reserves and Flag Officer Regional Forces)*
Gower, John, OBE *(Assistant Chief of Defence Staff (Nuclear & Chemical, Biological))*
Parr, Matthew *(Cdr (Operations) and Rear-Adm. Submarines (Head of Fighting Arm))*
Fraser, Timothy *(Senior British Military Adviser Central Command)*
Parker, Henry *(Director Maritime Capability and Transformation)*
Brunton, Steven *(Director Ship Acquisition and Deputy Director Ships)*
Jess, Ian *(Assistant Chief of Naval Staff (Support))*
Beverstock, Mark *(Chief Strategic Systems Executive)*
Morse, James *(Commandant Joint Service Command and Staff College)*
Woodcock, (Simon) Jonathan, OBE *(Naval Secretary and Assistant Chief of Naval Staff (Personnel))*
Lowe, Timothy *(Deputy Cdr Strike Force NATO)*
Williams, Simon *(Defence Services Secretary and Assistant Chief of Defence Staff (Personnel and Training))*
Karsten, Thomas *(National Hydrographer and Deputy Chief Executive (Hydrography))*
Tarrant, R. *(Cdr UK Maritime Forces)*
Bennett, Paul *(Director Concepts and Doctrine, Development, Concepts and Doctrine Centre)*
Key, Benjamin *(Flag Officer Sea Training)*
Ancona, Simon *(Assistant Chief of Defence Staff (Military Strategy))*

MEDICAL
McArthur, Calum, QHP *(Surgeon Rear-Adm., Cdr Joint Medical Command, Chief Naval Medical Officer and Medical Director-General (Naval))*

ROYAL MARINES

CAPTAIN-GENERAL
HRH The Prince Philip, Duke of Edinburgh, KG, KT, OM, GBE, AC, QSO, PC

LIEUTENANT-GENERAL
Capewell, David, OBE *(Chief of Joint Operations)*
Messenger, Gordon, DSO, OBE *(Deputy Cdr Land Command, Izmir)*

MAJOR-GENERALS
Howes, (F. H. R.) Buster, CB, OBE *(Head of the British Defence Staff, USA and Defence Attaché)*
Hook, David, CBE *(Response Force Task Group Study)*
Chicken, (Simon) Timothy, OBE *(Senior Directing Staff (Navy), Royal College of Defence Studies)*
Davis, Edward, CBE *(Cdr UK Amphibious Forces and Commandant-General Royal Marines)*

The Royal Marines were formed in 1664 and are part of the Naval Service. Their primary purpose is to conduct amphibious and land warfare. The principal operational units are:

- Three Commando Brigade, an amphibious all-arms brigade trained to operate in arduous environments (a core element of the UK's Joint Rapid Reaction Force). The commando units, 40 Commando, 42 Commando and 45 Commando each have a strength of around 700 and are based in Taunton, Plymouth and Arbroath, respectively. 43 Commando Fleet Protection Group is over 500 strong and is based at HM Naval Base Clyde on the west coast of Scotland.
- 1 Assault Group, which has its headquarters located in Devonport, Plymouth is responsible for ten landing craft training squadron at Poole, Dorset and 11 amphibious trials and training squadron at Instow, Devon

The Royal Marines also provide detachments for warships and land-based naval parties as required.

ROYAL MARINES RESERVES (RMR)
The Royal Marines Reserve is a commando-trained volunteer force with the principal role, when mobilised, of supporting the Royal Marines. The RMR consists of approximately 600 trained ranks who are distributed between the five RMR centres in the UK. Approximately 10 per cent of the RMR are working with the regular corps on long-term attachments within all of the Royal Marines regular units.

OTHER PARTS OF THE NAVAL SERVICE

FLEET AIR ARM
The Fleet Air Arm (FAA) provides the Royal Navy with a multi-role aviation combat capability able to operate autonomously at short notice worldwide in all environments, over the sea and land. The FAA numbers some 6,200 people, which comprises 11.5 per cent of the total Royal Naval strength. It operates some 200 combat aircraft and more than 50 support/training aircraft.

ROYAL FLEET AUXILIARY SERVICE (RFA)
The Royal Fleet Auxiliary Service is a civilian-manned flotilla of 13 ships owned by the MoD. Its primary role is to supply the Royal Navy and host nations while at sea with fuel, ammunition, food and spares, enabling them to maintain operations away from their home ports. It also provides amphibious support and secure sea transport for military units and their equipment. The ships routinely support and embark Royal Naval Air Squadrons.

ROYAL NAVAL RESERVE (RNR)
The Royal Naval Reserve is an integral part of the Naval Service. It is a part-time force of 2,300 trained men and women who are deployed with the Royal Navy in times of tension, humanitarian crisis or conflict.

The Royal Naval Reserve has 22 units throughout the UK; 19 of these provide initial training while three other specialist units provide intelligence and aviation training. Basic training is provided at HMS *Raleigh,* Torpoint in Cornwall for ratings and at the Britannia Royal Naval College, Dartmouth in Devon for officers; both these and most other RNR courses are of two weeks' duration or less.

QUEEN ALEXANDRA'S ROYAL NAVAL NURSING SERVICE
The first nursing sisters were appointed to naval hospitals in 1884 and the Queen Alexandra's Royal Naval Nursing Service (QARNNS) gained its current title in 1902. Nursing ratings were introduced in 1960 and men were integrated into the service in 1982; QARNNS recruits qualified nurses as both officers and ratings, and student nurse training can be undertaken in the service.

Patron, HRH Princess Alexandra, the Hon. Lady Ogilvy, KG, GCVO

Director of Naval Nursing Services and Matron-in-Chief, Capt. Inga Kennedy, QHNS, QARNNS

HM FLEET

as at November 2013

Submarines	
Vanguard Class	Vanguard, Vengeance, Victorious, Vigilant
Trafalgar Class	Talent, Tireless, Torbay, Trenchant, Triumph
Astute Class	Astute, Ambush
Landing Platform Helicopter	Ocean, Illustrious*
Landing Platform Dock	Albion, Bulwark
Destroyers	
Type 45	Daring, Dauntless, Diamond, Dragon, Defender
Frigates	
Type 23	Argyll, Iron Duke, Kent, Lancaster, Monmouth, Montrose, Northumberland, Portland, Richmond, St Albans, Somerset, Sutherland, Westminster
Mine Warfare Vessels	
Hunt Class	Atherstone, Brocklesby, Cattistock, Chiddingfold, Hurworth, Ledbury, Middleton, Quorn
Sandown Class	Bangor, Blyth, Grimsby, Pembroke, Penzance, Ramsey, Shoreham
Patrol Vessels	
Archer Class P2000 Training Boats	Archer, Biter, Blazer, Charger, Dasher, Example, Exploit, Explorer, Express, Puncher, Pursuer, Raider, Ranger, Smiter, Tracker, Trumpeter
Gibraltar Squadron 16m Fast Patrol Boats	Sabre, Scimitar
River Class	Mersey, Severn, Tyne, Clyde
Survey Vessels	
Ice Patrol Ships	Endurance†, Protector
Ocean Survey Vessel	Scott
Coastal Survey Vessel	Gleaner
Multi-Role Survey Vessels	Echo, Enterprise

* HMS *Illustrious* was formerly an aircraft carrier but is now operating in the Landing Platform Helicopter role

† HMS *Endurance* is currently non-operational

ROYAL FLEET AUXILIARY

Landing Ship Dock (Auxiliary)	RFA Cardigan Bay, RFA Mounts Bay, RFA Lyme Bay
Wave Class	RFA Wave Knight, RFA Wave Ruler
Rover Class	RFA Black Rover, RFA Gold Rover
Leaf Class	RFA Orangeleaf
Fort Class	RFA Fort Austin, RFA Fort Rosalie, RFA Fort Victoria
Forward Repair Ship	RFA Diligence
Joint Casualty Treatment Ship/Maritime Afloat Training Capability	RFA Argus

THE ARMY

In Order of Seniority

THE QUEEN

FIELD MARSHALS
HRH The Prince Philip, Duke of Edinburgh, KG, KT, OM, GBE, AC, QSO, PC, *apptd* 1953
Lord Bramall, KG, GCB, OBE, MC, *apptd* 1982
Lord Vincent of Coleshill, GBE, KCB, DSO, *apptd* 1991

Sir John Chapple, GCB, CBE, *apptd* 1992
HRH The Duke of Kent, KG, GCMG, GCVO, ADC, *apptd* 1993
Lord Inge, KG, GCB *apptd* 1994
HRH The Prince of Wales, KG, KT, GCB, OM, AK, QSO, PC, ADC *apptd* 2012
Lord Guthrie of Craigiebank, GCB, LVO, OBE, *apptd* 2012

FORMER CHIEFS OF STAFF
Gen. Sir Roger Wheeler, GCB, CBE, *apptd* 1997
Gen. Lord Walker of Aldringham, GCB, CMG, CBE, *apptd* 2000
Gen. Sir Mike Jackson, GCB, CBE, DSO, *apptd* 2003
Gen. Sir Timothy Granville-Chapman, GBE, KCB, *apptd* 2005
Gen. Lord Dannatt, GCB, CBE, MC, *apptd* 2006

GENERALS
Richards, Sir David, GCB, CBE, DSO, ADC *(Chief of the Defence Staff)*
Houghton, Sir Nick, GCB, CBE, ADC *(Vice Chief of the Defence Staff)*
Wall, Sir Peter, GCB, CBE, ADC *(Chief of the General Staff)*
Shirreff, Sir Richard, KCB, CBE *(Deputy Supreme Allied Cdr Europe)*
Barrons, Sir Richard, KCB, CBE, ADC *(Cdr Joint Force Command)*

LIEUTENANT-GENERALS
Mayall, S., CB *(Defence Senior Adviser to the Middle East)*
Bucknall, Sir James, KCB, CBE *(Cdr Allied Rapid Reaction Corps)*
Carter, N., CBE, DSO *(Deputy Cdr International Security Assistance Force and UK National Contingent Cdr – Afghanistan)*
Bradshaw, Sir Adrian, KCB, OBE *(Cdr Land Forces)*
Page, J., CB, OBE *(Cdr Force Development and Training)*
Deverell, C., MBE *(Chief of Materiel (Land) and Quartermaster General)*
Berragan, G., CB *(Adjutant-General)*
Everard, J., CBE *(Deputy Chief of Defence Staff (Military Strategy and Operations))*
Gregory, A., CB *(Chief of Defence Personnel)*
Lorimer, J., DSO *(pending assignment)*

MAJOR-GENERALS
Brealey, B., CB *(Director-General Capability)*
Inshaw, T. *(Director Information Systems and Services)*
Boag, C., CB, CBE *(GOC Support Command)*
Caplin, N., CB *(Senior Directing Staff (Army) Royal College of Defence Studies)*
Gordon, J., CB, CBE *(Senior British Loan Service Officer, Oman)*
Poffley, M., OBE *(Assistant Chief of Defence Staff (Capability and Force Design))*
Foster, A., CMG, MBE *(Deputy Force Cdr UN Stabilisation Mission, D. R. Congo (MONUSCO))*
Evans, T., CBE, DSO *(Commandant Royal Military Academy, Sandhurst)*
Jones, P., CBE *(Chief of Staff HQ, Joint Forces Command)*
Porter, S., CBE *(Supreme Allied Cdr Transformation Representative Europe)*
Beckett, T., CBE *(Chief of Staff HQ International Security Assistance Force Joint Command)*
Conway, M. *(Director-General Army Legal Services)*
Copeland, I., CB *(Director Joint Support Chain)*
Davis, R., CBE *(Director-General Army Recruiting and Training)*
Jaques, P., CBE *(Director-General Logistics, Support and Equipment)*
Burley, S., CB, MBE *(Military Secretary)*
Bashall, J., CBE *(Chief of Staff (Operations), Permanent Joint HQ, UK)*
Wilks, C., CBE *(Director Land Equipment)*
Pope, N., CBE *(Director Land Capability Transformation and Master General of the Ordnance)*
Norton, Sir George, KCVO, CBE *(Deputy Cdr NATO Rapid Deployment Corps, Naples)*
Woodhouse, Revd J., QHC, CF *(Chaplain-General)*
Ashmore, N., OBE *(Head Strategic Asset Management and Programme Team)*
Storrie, A., CBE *(Assistant Chief of Defence Staff (Military Strategy))*
Cullen, D., OBE *(Assistant Chief of the General Staff)*
Rowan, J., OBE, QHS *(Assistant Chief of Defence Staff (Health))*
Radford, T., DSO, OBE *(GOC Theatre Troops)*
Eeles, N. *(GOC Scotland)*
Riddell-Webster, M., CBE, DSO *(Director Defence College of Management and Technology)*
Carleton-Smith, M., CBE *(Director Special Forces)*
Free, J., CBE *(Chief of Staff, HQ Allied Rapid Reaction Corps)*
Nugee, R., CBE *(Director-General Personnel)*
Abraham, K. *(Director-General Army Reform)*
Weighill, R., CBE *(Deputy Chief of Staff (Plans) Joint Force Command, Naples)*
Henderson, J. *(GOC – British Forces, Germany)*
Carmichael, E., MBE, QHDS *(Director-General Army Medical Services)*
Munro, R., TD *(Deputy Cdr Land Forces (Reserves))*
Chiswell, J., CBE, MC *(GOC 1st (UK) Armoured Division)*
Fox, P., CBE *(Director Customer Design)*
Smyth-Osbourne, E., CBE *(Deputy Chief of Staff Outreach)*
Urch, T., CBE *(Chief of Staff Land Forces)*
Cripwell, R. *(Cdr British Forces Cyprus)*
Sanders, P., CBE, DSO *(Assistant Chief of Defence Staff (Operations))*
Crackett, J., TD *(Assistant Chief of Defence Staff (Reserves and Cadets))*
Cowan, J., CBE, DSO *(GOC 3rd (UK) Division)*

CONSTITUTION OF THE ARMY

The army consists of the Regular Army, the Regular Reserve and the Territorial Army (TA). It is commanded by the Chief of the General Staff, who is the professional Head of Service and Chair of the Executive Committee of the Army Board, which provides overall strategic policy and direction to the Commander-in-Chief Land Forces. There are four subordinate commands that report to the Commander-in-Chief Land Forces: the Field Army; Personnel and Support Command, headed by the Adjutant-General; Force Development and Training Command and the Joint Helicopter Command. The army is divided into functional arms and services, subdivided into regiments and corps (listed below in order of precedence). During 2008, as part of the Future Army Structure (FAS) reform programme, the infantry was re-structured into large multi-battalion regiments, which involved amalgamations and changes in title for some regiments.

Members of the public can write for general information to Headquarters Adjutant-General Secretariat, Trenchard Lines, Upavon, Wiltshire SN9 6BE. All enquiries with regard to records of serving personnel (Regular and Territorial Army) should be directed to The Army Personnel Centre Help Desk, Kentigern House, 65 Brown Street, Glasgow G2 8EX T 0845-600 9663. Enquirers should note that the Army is governed in the release of personal information by various acts of parliament.

ORDER OF PRECEDENCE OF CORPS AND REGIMENTS OF THE BRITISH ARMY

ARMS

HOUSEHOLD CAVALRY
The Life Guards
The Blues and Royals (Royal Horse Guards and 1st Dragoons)

ROYAL HORSE ARTILLERY
(when on parade, the Royal Horse Artillery take precedence over the Household Cavalry)

ROYAL ARMOURED CORPS
1st the Queen's Dragoon Guards
The Royal Scots Dragoon Guards (Carabiniers and Greys)
The Royal Dragoon Guards
The Queen's Royal Hussars (The Queen's Own and Royal Irish)
9th/12th Royal Lancers (Prince of Wales')
The King's Royal Hussars
The Light Dragoons
The Queen's Royal Lancers
1st Royal Tank Regiment
2nd Royal Tank Regiment

ROYAL REGIMENT OF ARTILLERY
(with the exception of the Royal Horse Artillery (*see* above))

CORPS OF ROYAL ENGINEERS
ROYAL CORPS OF SIGNALS
REGIMENTS OF FOOT GUARDS
Grenadier Guards
Coldstream Guards
Scots Guards
Irish Guards
Welsh Guards

REGIMENTS OF INFANTRY
The Royal Regiment of Scotland
The Princess of Wales' Royal Regiment (Queen and Royal Hampshire's)
The Duke of Lancaster's Regiment (King's, Lancashire and Border)
The Royal Regiment of Fusiliers
The Royal Anglian Regiment
The Rifles
The Yorkshire Regiment
The Mercian Regiment
The Royal Welsh
The Royal Irish Regiment
The Parachute Regiment
The Royal Gurkha Rifles

SPECIAL AIR SERVICE
ARMY AIR CORPS

SERVICES

ROYAL ARMY CHAPLAINS' DEPARTMENT
THE ROYAL LOGISTIC CORPS
ROYAL ARMY MEDICAL CORPS
CORPS OF ROYAL ELECTRICAL AND MECHANICAL ENGINEERS
ADJUTANT-GENERAL'S CORPS
ROYAL ARMY VETERINARY CORPS
SMALL ARMS SCHOOL CORPS
ROYAL ARMY DENTAL CORPS
INTELLIGENCE CORPS
ARMY PHYSICAL TRAINING CORPS
QUEEN ALEXANDRA'S ROYAL ARMY NURSING CORPS
CORPS OF ARMY MUSIC
THE ROYAL MONMOUTHSHIRE ROYAL ENGINEERS (MILITIA) (TA)
THE HONOURABLE ARTILLERY COMPANY (TA)
REST OF THE TERRITORIAL ARMY (TA)

ARMY EQUIPMENT

Tanks	325
Challenger 2	325
Reconnaissance vehicles	738
Fuchs	11
Jackal	400
Scimitar	327
Armoured Infantry Fighting Vehicle	526
Warrior	526
Armoured Personnel Carrier	2,059+
AFV432	646
Bulldog	380
Mastiff	277
Ridgeback	118
Saxon (Northern Ireland only)	109
Spartan	394
Warthog	115
Wolfhound	20+
Light Forces Vehicle (Panther)	401
Artillery pieces	670
Anti-tank missile†	800+
Aircraft	8*
Defender	4
King Air	4
Helicopters	298
Apache	66
Gazelle	133
Lynx	99
Unmanned aerial vehicle	450
Surface-to-air missile	338+
Land radar	157
Amphibious craft	6
Logistics and support vehicles	5

* Includes 3 King Air and 1 Defender on order
† 2009 figure

THE TERRITORIAL ARMY (TA)

The Territorial Army is part of the UK's reserve land forces and provides support to the regular army at home and overseas. The TA is divided into three types of unit: national, regional, and sponsored. TA soldiers serving in regional units complete a minimum of 27 days training a year, comprising some evenings, weekends and an annual two-week camp. National units normally specialise in a specific role or trade, such as logistics, IT, communications or medical services. Members of national units have a lower level of training commitment and complete 19 days training a year.

Sponsored reserves are individuals who will serve, as members of the workforce of a company contracted to the MoD, in a military capacity and have agreed to accept a reserve liability to be called up for active service in a crisis. The TA's total strength is around 35,000.

QUEEN ALEXANDRA'S ROYAL ARMY NURSING CORPS

The Queen Alexandra's Royal Army Nursing Corps (QARANC) was founded in 1902 as Queen Alexandra's Imperial Military Nursing Service and gained its present title in 1949. The QARANC has trained nurses for the register since 1950 and also trains and employs health care assistants to Level 2 NVQ, with the option to train to Level 3. The corps recruits qualified nurses as officers and other ranks and in 1992 male nurses already serving in the army were transferred to the QARANC.

Colonel-in-Chief, HRH The Countess of Wessex, GCVO
Colonels Commandant, Col. Rosemary Kennedy, TD; Col. Sue Bush

THE ROYAL AIR FORCE

In Order of Seniority

THE QUEEN

MARSHAL OF THE ROYAL AIR FORCE
HRH The Prince Philip, Duke of Edinburgh, KG, KT, OM, GBE, AC, QSO, PC, *apptd* 1953
HRH The Prince of Wales, KG, KT, GCB, OM, AK, QSO, PC, ADC, *apptd* 2012

FORMER CHIEFS OF THE AIR STAFF

MARSHALS OF THE ROYAL AIR FORCE
Sir Michael Beetham, GCB, CBE, DFC, AFC, *apptd* 1982
Sir Keith Williamson, GCB, AFC, *apptd* 1985
Lord Craig of Radley, GCB, OBE, *apptd* 1988

AIR CHIEF MARSHALS
Sir Michael Graydon, GCB, CBE, *apptd* 1991
Sir Richard Johns, GCB, KCVO, OBE, *apptd* 1994
Sir Peter Squire, GCB, DFC, AFC *apptd* 1999
Lord Stirrup, KG, GCB, AFC, *apptd* 2003
Sir Glenn Torpy, GCB, CBE, DSO *apptd* 2006
Sir Stephen Dalton, GCB, *apptd* 2009

AIR RANK LIST

AIR CHIEF MARSHALS
Peach, Sir Stuart, KCB, CBE, ADC *(Vice Chief of the Defence Staff)*
Pulford, Sir Andrew, KCB, CBE, ADC *(Chief of the Air Staff)*

AIR MARSHALS
Harper, Sir Christopher, KBE, *(Director-General International Military Staff)*
Garwood, R., CB, CBE, DFC *(Director-General of the Military Aviation Authority)*
Hillier, S., CBE, DFC *(Deputy Chief of the Defence Staff (Military Capability))*
Bollom, S., CB *(Chief of Materiel (Air) and Air Member for Materiel)*
Bagwell, G., CB, CBE *(Deputy Cdr Operations and Air Member for Operations)*
Stacey, G., CB, MBE *(Deputy Cdr Joint Force Command, Brunssum)*
North, B., OBE *(Deputy Cdr Capability and Air Member for Personnel and Capability)*

AIR VICE-MARSHALS
Wiles, M., CB, CBE, *(Chief of Staff Personnel and Air Secretary)*
Dixon, C., CB, OBE *(Cdr Joint Helicopter Command)*
Evans, C., QHP *(Surgeon-General HQ Joint Medical Command)*
Lloyd, M., CB *(Air Officer Commanding, No. 22 Group and Chief of Staff Training)*
Irvine, L. *(Director RAF Legal Services)*
Young, J., CB, OBE *(Director Technical, Defence Equipment and Support)*
Pentland, R., CB, QHC *(Chaplain Chief and Director-General Chaplaincy Services (RAF))*
Green, M., CBE *(Director UAE Strategic Partnership)*
Osborn, P., CBE *(Director Capability Joint Forces Command)*
Howard, G. *(Assistant Chief of the Defence Staff Logistics Operations)*
Atha, S., DSO *(Air Officer Commanding No. 1 Group)*
Morrison, I., CBE *(Director-General, Saudi Armed Forces Project)*
Paterson, R., OBE *(Chief Executive, Service Personnel and Veterans Agency)*
Judson, R. *(Director Joint Warfare, Joint Forces Command)*
Mozumder, A., QHP *(Cdr Defence Primary Healthcare, HQ Surgeon-General)*
Rigby, J., CBE *(Director Cyber, Intelligence and Information Integration)*
Clark, M. *(Director Technical in the Military Aviation Authority)*
Farnell, G., OBE *(Director Combat (Air), Defence Equipment and Support)*
Atherton, P., OBE *(Director Operations, Military Aviation Authority)*
Brecht, M. *(Chief of Staff Capability, Air Command)*
Ewen, P. *(Director Air Support, Defence Equipment and Support)*
Reynolds, S., CBE, DFC *(Air Officer Commanding No. 2 Group and Chief of Staff (Operations))*
Stringer, E., CBE *(Assistant Chief of the Air Staff)*
Bishop, T., OBE *(Chief of Staff Support and Executive Officer (Air))*

CONSTITUTION OF THE RAF

The RAF consists of a single command, Air Command, based at RAF High Wycombe. RAF Air Command was formed on 1 April 2007 from the amalgamation of Strike Command and Personnel and Training Command.

Air Command consists of three groups, each organised around specific operational duties. No. 1 Group is the coordinating organisation for the tactical fast-jet forces responsible for attack, offensive support and air defence operations. No. 2 Group provides air combat support including air transport and air to air refuelling; intelligence surveillance; targeting and reconnaissance; and force protection. No. 22 (Training) Group recruits personnel and provides trained specialist personnel to the RAF, as well as to the Royal Navy and the Army (*see also* Armed Forces Training and Recruitment).

RAF EQUIPMENT

AIRCRAFT	
BAe 125	6
BAe 146	2
Dominie	9
Firefly	38
Globemaster	7
Hawk	145
Hercules	43
Islander	2
Nimrod	14
Sentinel	5
Sentry	6
Shadow	4
Super King Air (leased)	7
Tornado	105
Tristar	9
Tucano	95
Tutor	101
Typhoon	72
VC10	16

HELICOPTERS	
Chinook	41
Griffin	16
Merlin	28
Puma	34
Sea King	25
Squirrel	31

ROYAL AUXILIARY AIR FORCE

The Auxiliary Air Force was formed in 1924 to train an elite corps of civilians to serve their country in flying squadrons in their spare time. In 1947 the force was awarded the prefix 'royal' in recognition of its distinguished war service and the Sovereign's Colour for the Royal Auxiliary Air Force (RAuxAF) was presented in 1989. The RAuxAF continues to recruit civilians who undertake military training in their spare time to support the Royal Air Force in times of emergency or war.

Air Commodore-in-Chief, HM The Queen
Honorary Inspector-General (Air Vice-Marshal) Royal Auxiliary Air Force, Lord Beaverbrook
Inspector Royal Auxiliary Air Force, Gp Capt. Gary Bunkell, QVRM, AE, ADC

PRINCESS MARY'S ROYAL AIR FORCE NURSING SERVICE

The Princess Mary's Royal Air Force Nursing Service (PMRAFNS) was formed on 1 June 1918 as the Royal Air Force Nursing Service. In June 1923, His Majesty King George V gave his royal assent for the Royal Air Force Nursing Service to be known as the Princess Mary's Royal Air Force Nursing Service. Men were integrated into the PMRAFNS in 1980.

Patron and Air Chief Commandant, HRH Princess Alexandra, The Hon. Lady Ogilvy, KG, GCVO
Director of Nursing Services and Matron-in-Chief, Gp Capt. Jacqueline Gross

SERVICE SALARIES

The following rates of pay apply from 1 April 2013 and are rounded to the nearest pound.

The pay rates shown are for army personnel. The rates also apply to personnel of equivalent rank and pay band in the other services (*see* below for table of relative ranks).

Rank	*Annual salary*
SECOND LIEUTENANT	£24,971
LIEUTENANT	
On appointment	£30,014
After 1 year in rank	£30,807
After 2 years in rank	£31,596
After 3 years in rank	£32,381
After 4 years in rank	£33,175
CAPTAIN	
On appointment	£38,463
After 1 year in rank	£39,493
After 2 years in rank	£40,536
After 3 years in rank	£41,583
After 4 years in rank	£42,617
After 5 years in rank	£43,660
After 6 years in rank	£44,694
After 7 years in rank	£45,222
After 8 years in rank	£45,741
MAJOR	
On appointment	£48,450
After 1 year in rank	£49,646
After 2 years in rank	£50,834
After 3 years in rank	£52,039
After 4 years in rank	£53,231
After 5 years in rank	£54,436
After 6 years in rank	£55,632
After 7 years in rank	£56,824
After 8 years in rank	£58,025
LIEUTENANT-COLONEL	
On appointment	£67,999
After 1 year in rank	£68,900
After 2 years in rank	£69,793
After 3 years in rank	£70,687
After 4 years in rank	£71,580
After 5 years in rank	£75,691
After 6 years in rank	£76,700
After 7 years in rank	£77,718
After 8 years in rank	£78,737
COLONEL	
On appointment	£82,381
After 1 year in rank	£83,402
After 2 years in rank	£84,427
After 3 years in rank	£85,448
After 4 years in rank	£86,469
After 5 years in rank	£87,490
After 6 years in rank	£88,511
After 7 years in rank	£89,535
After 8 years in rank	£90,560
BRIGADIER	
On appointment	£98,172
After 1 year in rank	£99,165
After 2 years in rank	£100,157
After 3 years in rank	£101,145
After 4 years in rank	£102,145

PAY SYSTEM FOR SENIOR MILITARY OFFICERS

Pay rates effective from 1 April 2013 for all military officers of 2* rank and above (excluding medical and dental officers). All pay rates are rounded to the nearest pound.

Rank	
MAJOR-GENERAL (2*)	*Annual salary*
Scale 1	£109,369
Scale 2	£111,506
Scale 3	£113,687
Scale 4	£115,911
Scale 5	£118,179
Scale 6	£120,492
LIEUTENANT-GENERAL (3*)	
Scale 1	£127,253
Scale 2	£133,491
Scale 3	£140,041
Scale 4	£145,542
Scale 5	£149,834
Scale 6	£154,254
GENERAL (4*)	
Scale 1	£166,937
Scale 2	£171,110
Scale 3	£175,389
Scale 4	£179,773
Scale 5	£183,369
Scale 6	£187,036

Field Marshal – appointments to this rank will not usually be made in peacetime. The salary for holders of the rank is equivalent to the salary of a 5-star General, a salary created only in times of war. In peacetime, the equivalent rank to Field Marshal is the Chief of the Defence Staff. From 1 April 2013, the annual salary range for the Chief of the Defence Staff is £240,504–£255,225.

OFFICERS COMMISSIONED FROM THE SENIOR RANKS

Rank	*Annual salary*
Level 15	£51,411
Level 14	£51,075
Level 13	£50,722
Level 12	£50,037
Level 11	£49,355
Level 10	£48,665
Level 9	£47,980
Level 8	£47,295
Level 7*	£46,439
Level 6	£45,911
Level 5	£45,375
Level 4†	£44,316
Level 3	£43,789
Level 2	£43,249
Level 1‡	£42,193

* Officers commissioned from the ranks with more than 15 years' service enter on level 7

† Officers commissioned from the ranks with between 12 and 15 years' service enter on level 4

‡ Officers commissioned from the ranks with less than 12 years' service enter on level 1

SOLDIERS' SALARIES

Under the Pay 2000 scheme, personnel are paid in either a high or low band in accordance with how their trade has been allocated to those bands at each rank. Pay is based on trade and rank, not on individual appointment, or in response to temporary changes in role.

Rates of pay effective from 1 April 2013 (rounded to the nearest pound) are:

Rank	*Lower band*	*Higher band*
PRIVATE		
Level 1	£17,767	£17,767
Level 2	£18,245	£19,113
Level 3	£18,723	£21,049
Level 4	£20,318	£22,088
LANCE CORPORAL (levels 5–7 also applicable to Privates)		
Level 5	£21,386	£24,422
Level 6	£21,751	£25,610
Level 7	£22,682	£26,786
Level 8	£23,720	£27,991
Level 9	£24,580	£29,357
CORPORAL		
Level 1	£26,786	£27,991
Level 2	£27,991	£29,357
Level 3	£29,357	£30,795
Level 4	£29,582	£31,513
Level 5	£29,814	£32,274
Level 6	£29,051	£32,942
Level 7	£30,271	£33,661

Rank	*Lower band*	*Higher band*
SERGEANT		
Level 1	£30,446	£33,229
Level 2	£31,243	£34,089
Level 3	£32,028	£34,953
Level 4	£32,352	£35,393
Level 5	£33,196	£36,083
Level 6	£34,342	£36,772
Level 7	£34,604	£37,462
STAFF SERGEANT		
Level 1	£33,702	£37,487
Level 2	£34,143	£38,393
Level 3	£35,252	£39,310
Level 4	£36,079	£40,220
WARRANT OFFICER II (levels 5–7 also applicable to Staff Sergeants)		
Level 5	£36,569	£41,134
Level 6	£38,222	£42,044
Level 7	£38,808	£42,650
Level 8	£39,310	£43,257
Level 9	£40,200	£43,876
WARRANT OFFICER I		
Level 1	£39,157	£42,688
Level 2	£39,917	£43,527
Level 3	£40,723	£44,275
Level 4	£41,529	£45,089
Level 5	£42,339	£45,895
Level 6	£43,527	£46,713
Level 7	£44,757	£47,428

RELATIVE RANK – ARMED FORCES

Royal Navy	*Army*	*Royal Air Force*
1 Admiral of the Fleet	1 Field Marshal	1 Marshal of the RAF
2 Admiral (Adm.)	2 General (Gen.)	2 Air Chief Marshal
3 Vice-Admiral (Vice-Adm.)	3 Lieutenant-General (Lt.-Gen.)	3 Air Marshal
4 Rear-Admiral (Rear-Adm.)	4 Major-General (Maj.-Gen.)	4 Air Vice-Marshal
5 Commodore (Cdre)	5 Brigadier (Brig.)	5 Air Commodore (Air Cdre)
6 Captain (Capt.)	6 Colonel (Col.)	6 Group Captain (Gp Capt.)
7 Commander (Cdr)	7 Lieutenant-Colonel (Lt.-Col.)	7 Wing Commander (Wg Cdr)
8 Lieutenant-Commander (Lt.-Cdr)	8 Major (Maj.)	8 Squadron Leader (Sqn Ldr)
9 Lieutenant (Lt.)	9 Captain (Capt.)	9 Flight Lieutenant (Flt Lt)
10 Sub-Lieutenant (Sub-Lt.)	10 Lieutenant (Lt.)	10 Flying Officer (FO)
11 Midshipman	11 Second Lieutenant (2nd Lt.)	11 Pilot Officer (PO)

SERVICE RETIRED PAY *on compulsory retirement*

Those who leave the services having served at least five years, but not long enough to qualify for the appropriate immediate pension, now qualify for a preserved pension and terminal grant, both of which are payable at age 60. The tax-free resettlement grants shown below are payable on release to those who qualify for a preserved pension and who have completed nine years' service from age 21 (officers) or 12 years from age 18 (other ranks).

The annual rates for army personnel are given. The rates also apply to personnel of equivalent rank in the other services, including the nursing services.

OFFICERS

Applicable to officers who give full pay service on the active list on or after 30 April 2013. Pensionable earnings for senior officers (*) is defined as the total amount of basic pay received during the year ending on the day prior to retirement, or the amount of basic pay received during any 12-month period within 3 years prior to retirement, whichever is the higher. Figures for senior officers are percentage rates of pensionable earnings on final salary arrangements on or after 30 April 2013.

No. of years reckonable service	*Capt. and below*	*Major*	*Lt.-Col.*	*Colonel*	*Brigadier*	*Major-General**	*Lieutenant-General**	*General**
16	£12,738	£15,171	£19,891	£24,062	£28,545	—	—	—
17	£13,325	£15,891	£20,908	£25,165	£29,658	—	—	—
18	£13,912	£16,612	£21,924	£26,268	£30,770	—	—	—
19	£14,499	£17,333	£22,941	£27,372	£31,883	—	—	—
20	£15,086	£18,053	£23,957	£28,475	£32,996	—	—	—
21	£15,673	£18,774	£24,973	£29,578	£34,109	—	—	—
22	£16,260	£19,495	£25,990	£30,682	£35,222	—	—	—
23	£16,848	£20,215	£27,006	£31,785	£36,335	—	—	—
24	£17,435	£20,936	£28,023	£32,888	£37,447	38.5%	—	—
25	£18,022	£21,656	£29,039	£33,992	£38,560	39.7%	—	—
26	£18,609	£22,377	£30,056	£35,095	£39,673	40.8%	—	—
27	£19,196	£23,098	£31,072	£35,198	£40,786	42.0%	42.0%	—
28	£19,783	£23,818	£32,089	£37,302	£41,899	43.1%	43.1%	—
29	£20,370	£24,539	£33,105	£38,405	£43,012	44.3%	44.3%	—
30	£20,957	£25,260	£34,122	£39,508	£44,125	45.4%	45.4%	45.4%
31	£21,544	£25,980	£35,138	£40,612	£45,237	46.6%	46.6%	46.6%
32	£22,131	£26,701	£36,155	£41,715	£46,350	47.7%	47.7%	47.7%
33	£22,719	£27,422	£37,171	£42,818	£47,463	48.9%	48.9%	48.9%
34	£23,306	£28,142	£38,188	£43,922	£48,576	50.0%	50.0%	50.0%

WARRANT OFFICERS, NCOS AND PRIVATES

(Applicable to soldiers who give full pay service on or after 30 April 2013)

No. of years reckonable service	*Below Corporal*	*Corporal*	*Sergeant*	*Staff Sergeant*	*Warrant Officer Level II*	*Warrant Officer Level I*
22	£7,538	£9,724	£10,661	£12,144	£12,965	£13,787
23	£7,801	£10,064	£11,033	£12,568	£13,418	£14,268
24	£8,064	£10,403	£11,405	£12,992	£13,870	£14,749
25	£8,328	£10,742	£11,777	£13,416	£14,323	£15,230
26	£8,591	£11,082	£12,150	£13,840	£14,775	£15,711
27	£8,854	£11,421	£12,522	£14,264	£15,228	£16,193
28	£9,117	£11,761	£12,894	£14,687	£15,381	£16,674
29	£9,380	£12,100	£13,266	£15,111	£16,133	£17,155
30	£9,643	£12,439	£13,638	£15,535	£16,586	£17,636
31	£9,906	£12,779	£14,010	£15,959	£17,038	£18,117
32	£10,169	£13,118	£14,382	£16,383	£17,491	£18,599
33	£10,433	£13,458	£14,754	£16,807	£17,943	£19,080
34	£10,696	£13,797	£15,127	£17,231	£18,396	£19,561
35	£10,959	£14,137	£15,499	£17,655	£18,848	£20,042
36	£11,222	£14,476	£15,871	£18,079	£19,301	£20,524
37	£11,485	£14,815	£16,243	£18,502	£19,754	£21,005

GRANTS AND GRATUITIES

Terminal grants are in each case three times the rate of retired pay or pension. There are special rates of retired pay for certain other ranks not shown above. Lower rates are payable in cases of voluntary retirement.

A gratuity of £4,330 is payable for officers with short service commissions for each year completed. Resettlement grants are £14,898 for officers and £10,182 for other ranks.

EDUCATION

THE UK EDUCATION SYSTEM

The structure of the education system in the UK is a devolved matter with each of the countries of the UK having separate systems under separate governments. There are differences between the school systems in terms of the curriculum, examinations and final qualifications and, at university level, in terms of the nature of some degrees and in the matter of tuition fees. The systems in England, Wales and Northern Ireland are similar and have more in common with one another than the Scottish system, which differs significantly.

Education in England is overseen by the Department for Education (DfE) and the Department for Business, Innovation and Skills (BIS).

In Wales, responsibility for education lies with the Department for Education and Skills (DfES) within the Welsh government. Ministers in the Scottish government are responsible for education in Scotland, led by the directorates of Learning and Lifelong Learning, while in Northern Ireland responsibility lies with the Department of Education (DENI) and the Department for Employment and Learning (DELNI) within the Northern Ireland government.

DEPARTMENT FOR EDUCATION T 0370-000 2288
W www.gov.uk/government/organisations/department-for-education

DEPARTMENT FOR BUSINESS, INNOVATION AND SKILLS T 020-7215 5000
W www.gov.uk/government/organisations/department-for-business-innovation-skills

DEPARTMENT FOR EDUCATION AND SKILLS (DFES)
T 0300-060 3300; 0845-010 3300
W www.learning.wales.gov.uk

SCOTTISH GOVERNMENT – EDUCATION
T 08457-741741; 0131-556 8400
W www.scotland.gov.uk/Topics/Education

DEPARTMENT OF EDUCATION (NI) T 028-9127 9279
W www.deni.gov.uk

DEPARTMENT FOR EMPLOYMENT AND LEARNING (NI) T 028-9025 7777 W www.delni.gov.uk

RECENT DEVELOPMENTS

All parts of the UK saw changes in education policy this year, many of them concerning school curricula and qualifications. Major changes made or announced include:

ENGLAND

- A new national curriculum for all school subjects and key stages, with new programmes of study and attainment targets
- From 2015, GCSEs will cease to be modular courses. Instead full exams will be taken in the summer at the end of two years of study (though November re-sits will be allowed in English language and maths). Controlled assessments (coursework done under exam conditions) will be scrapped and exams will be essay-based. The pass mark will be higher and the qualifications will be graded from 8 to 1, rather than A* to G. Teaching under the new specifications for English literature and history began in September 2013 and changes to the nine core GCSE subjects should be ready for teaching from 2015
- From September 2013, students will no longer be able to sit A-level exams in January in either year of A-level studies. A-levels will still be examined unit by unit, but all exams will be taken in the summer. Revised qualifications are expected to be ready for first teaching in 2015. Later, all A-level assessment will move to the end of the two-year courses and AS-levels will become stand-alone qualifications rather than contributing to A-levels
- Though teachers' pay in England, as in Wales, will increase by 1 per cent in 2013, from 2014 annual pay increments based on length of service will no longer be awarded. As of September 2014, schools will be free to decide on the pay progression of individual teachers, based on appraisal of their performance. Pay scales will still be available, but for reference only
- Further education colleges in England will be able to enrol 14 to 16-year-olds who wish to study vocational qualifications from September 2013 and establish their own '14 to 16 centres'. A new sector-led Further Education Guild is proposed to ensure teaching standards. Traineeships, including work placements, flexible training and studying English and maths were introduced in August 2013.

WALES

- Published a new strategy for education, *Improving Schools,* for those aged 3 to 16. The strategy aims to improve literacy and numeracy (national literacy and numeracy have already been introduced and another numerical reasoning test is due in May 2014); reduce the impact of deprivation on educational outcomes; and see 65 per cent of children achieve GCSE Level 2 in English/Welsh and mathematics by 2015
- Announced its attention to retain unreformed GCSEs and A-levels alongside a revised Welsh Baccalaureate (WB). From September 2013, the WB qualification will be graded for learners starting Advanced level and a revised model is planned for first teaching in September 2015. New GCSEs in English language and Welsh first language, as well as two new GCSEs covering numeracy and mathematical techniques will be created for September 2015, while Essential Skills and Wider Key Skills qualifications (for use post-16), addressing concerns about content and assessment, will be trialled during 2014

SCOTLAND

Scotland sees the first year of new National qualifications as part of its Curriculum for Excellence strategy. The Scottish government also announced £1.25bn towards building 67 new schools by March 2018 and £3m over the next three years to support higher quality learning for teachers overseen by a new National Implementation Board. A new bill aims to make access to university fairer.

NORTHERN IRELAND

Northern Ireland also rejected changes to A-levels and is consulting on the way schools are funded to tackle education disadvantage. Its revised curriculum began in earnest in September 2013 and *Learning to Learn – A Framework for Early Years Education and Learning* will extend the Foundation Stage to include a non-compulsory pre-school year as well as the first two years of primary school.

STATE SCHOOL SYSTEM

PRE-SCHOOL

Pre-school education for children from 3 to 5 years of age is not compulsory. Parents may take as little or as much of their entitlement as they choose, although a free place is available for every 3- and 4-year-old whose parents want one. All 3- and 4-year-olds in England are entitled to 15 hours a week of free early education over 38 weeks of the year until they reach compulsory school age (the term following their fifth birthday). Disadvantaged 2-year-olds are now also entitled to 15 hours-a-week of free early education. This is delivered flexibly over a minimum of two days each week during normal term times. Free places are funded by local authorities and are delivered by a range of providers in the maintained and non-maintained sectors – nursery schools; nursery classes in primary schools; private schools; private day nurseries; voluntary playgroups; pre-schools; and registered childminders. In order to receive funding, providers must be working towards the early learning goals and other features of the Early Years Foundation Stage curriculum, must be inspected on a regular basis by Ofsted and must meet any conditions set by the local authority.

In Wales, every child is entitled to receive free Foundation Phase education for a minimum of two hours a day from the term following their third birthday.

In Scotland, councils have a duty to provide a pre-school education for all 3- and 4-year-olds whose parents request one. Following new legislation, education authorities must offer each child 475 hours of free pre-school education a year (less for children who start pre-school later in the year), although they may provide more if they choose.

In Northern Ireland, the Department of Education aims to provide a funded place for all 3- and 4-year-old children in their final pre-school year. All places offer 2.5 hours a day, five days a week for at least 38 weeks a year.

PRIMARY AND SECONDARY SCHOOLS

By law, full-time education starts at the age of five for children in England, Scotland and Wales and at the age of four in Northern Ireland. In practice, most children in the UK start school before their fifth birthday: in England all children will be entitled to a primary school place from the September after their fourth birthday.

Children in England are required to stay in education or training until the end of the academic year in which they turn 17 (from 2013) or 18 (from 2015). In all other parts of the UK, compulsory schooling ends at age 16, but children born between certain dates may leave school before their 16th birthday. Most young people stay in some form of education until 17 or 18.

Primary education consists mainly of infant schools for children aged 5 to 7, junior schools for those aged 7 to 11, and combined infant and junior schools for both age groups. First schools in some parts of England cater for ages 5 to 10 as the first stage of a three-tier system of first (lower), middle and secondary (upper) schools. Scotland has only primary schools with no infant/junior division.

Children usually leave primary school and move on to secondary school at the age of 11 (or 12 in Scotland). In the few areas of England that have a three-tier system of schools, middle schools cater for children after they leave first schools for three to four years between the ages of 8 and 14, depending on the local authority.

Secondary schools cater for children aged 11 to 16 and, if they have a sixth form, for those who choose to stay on to the age of 17 or 18. From the age of 16, students may move instead to further education colleges or work-based training.

Most UK secondary schools are co-educational. The largest secondary schools have more than 1,500 pupils and around 60 per cent of secondary pupils in the UK are in schools that take more than 1,000 pupils.

Most state-maintained secondary schools in England, Wales and Scotland are comprehensive schools, which admit pupils without reference to ability. In England there remain some areas with grammar schools, catering for pupils aged 11 to 18, which select pupils on the basis of high academic ability. Over half of state secondary schools in England (52 per cent in June 2013) are now academies: academies are funded directly by the state rather than being maintained by local authorities. Northern Ireland still has 68 grammar schools; the 11-plus has been officially discontinued but schools, or consortia of schools, use their own unregulated entry tests.

More than 90 per cent of pupils in the UK attend publicly funded schools and receive free education. The rest attend privately funded 'independent' schools, which charge fees, or are educated at home.

The bulk of the UK government's expenditure on school education is through local authorities (Education and Library Boards in Northern Ireland), who pass on state funding to schools and other educational institutions.

SPECIAL EDUCATION

Schools and local authorities in England and Wales, Education and Library Boards (ELBs) in Northern Ireland and education authorities in Scotland are required to identify and secure provision for children with special educational needs and to involve parents in decisions. The majority of children with special educational needs are educated in ordinary mainstream schools, sometimes with supplementary help from outside specialists. Parents of children with special educational needs (referred to as additional support needs in Scotland) have a right of appeal to independent tribunals if their wishes are not met.

Special educational needs provision may be made in maintained special schools, special units attached to mainstream schools or in mainstream classes themselves, all funded by local authorities. There are also non-maintained special schools run by voluntary bodies, mainly charities, who may receive grants from central government for capital expenditure and equipment but whose other costs are met primarily from the fees charged to local authorities for pupils placed in the schools. Some independent schools also provide education wholly or mainly for children with special educational needs.

ADDITIONAL SUPPORT NEEDS TRIBUNALS FOR SCOTLAND T 0845-120 2906 W www.asntscotland.gov.uk

FIRST-TIER TRIBUNAL (SPECIAL EDUCATIONAL NEEDS AND DISABILITY) T 01325-392760 W www.justice.gov.uk/tribunals/send

SPECIAL EDUCATIONAL NEEDS TRIBUNAL FOR WALES T 01597-829800 W sentw.gov.uk

HOME EDUCATION

In England and Wales parents have the right to educate their children at home and do not have to be qualified teachers to do so. Home-educated children do not have to follow the National Curriculum or take national tests nor do they need a fixed timetable, formal lessons or to observe school hours, days or terms. However, by law parents must ensure that the home education provided is full-time and suitable for the child's age, ability and aptitude and, if appropriate, for any special educational needs. Parents have no legal obligation to notify the local authority that a child is being educated at home, but if they take a child out of school, they must notify the school in writing and the school must report this to the local authority. Local authorities can make informal enquiries of parents to establish that a suitable education is being provided. For children in special schools, parents must seek the consent of the local authority before taking steps to educate them at home.

In Northern Ireland, ELBs monitor the quality of home provision and provide general guidance on appropriate materials and exam types through regular home visits.

The home schooling law in Scotland is similar to that of England. One difference, however, is that if parents wish to take a child out of school they must have permission from the local education authority.

HOME EDUCATION ADVISORY SERVICE
T 01707-371854 W www.heas.org.uk

HOME EDUCATION IN NORTHERN IRELAND
W www.hedni.org

SCHOOLHOUSE HOME EDUCATION ASSOCIATION (SCOTLAND) T 01307-463120 W www.schoolhouse.org.uk

FURTHER EDUCATION

In the UK, further education (FE) is generally understood as post-secondary education, ie any education undertaken after an individual leaves school that is below higher education level. FE therefore embraces a wide range of general and vocational study undertaken by people of all ages from 16 upwards, full-time or part-time, who may be self-funded, employer-funded or state-funded.

FE in the UK is often undertaken at further education colleges, although some takes place on employers' premises. Many of these colleges offer some courses at higher education level; some FE colleges teach certain subjects to 14- to 16-year-olds under collaborative arrangements with schools. Colleges' income comes from public funding, student fees and work for and with employers.

HIGHER EDUCATION

Higher education (HE) in the UK describes courses of study, provided in universities, specialist colleges of higher education and in some FE colleges, where the level of instruction is above that of A-level or equivalent exams.

All UK universities and colleges that provide HE are autonomous bodies with their own internal systems of governance. They are not owned by the state. However, most receive a portion of their income from state funds distributed by the separate HE funding councils for England, Scotland and Wales, and the Department for Employment and Learning in Northern Ireland. The rest of their income comes from a number of sources including fees from home and overseas students, government funding for research, endowments and work with or for business.

EXPENDITURE

UK-MANAGED EXPENDITURE ON EDUCATION
(Real terms adjusted to 2011–12 price levels) *£bn*

2003–4	75.8	2008–9	90.9
2004–5	78.7	2009–10	94.3
2005–6	82.8	2011–12	88.2
2006–7	84.2	2011–12	88.2
2007–8	88.5	2012–13 (est)	87.3

Source: Public Expenditure Statistical Analyses (PESA) 2013

SCHOOLS

ENGLAND AND WALES

In England and Wales, publicly funded schools are referred to as 'state schools'. The four main categories of state school – community, foundation, voluntary-aided and voluntary-controlled – are maintained by local authorities, which have a duty to ensure there is a suitable place for every school-age child resident in their area. Each school has a governing body, made up of volunteers elected or appointed by parents, staff, the community and the local authority, which is responsible for strategic management, ensuring accountability, monitoring school performance, setting budgets and appointing the headteacher and senior staff. The headteacher is responsible for the school's day-to-day management and operations and for decisions requiring professional teaching expertise.

In *Community schools,* which are non-denominational, local authorities are the employers of the staff, own the land and buildings and set the admissions criteria.

In *Foundation schools,* the governing body employs the staff and sets the admissions criteria. The land and buildings are usually owned by the governing body or a charitable foundation. A foundation school may have a religious character, although most do not. A *trust school* is a distinct type of foundation school that forms a charitable trust with an outside partner – for example, a business, a university, an educational charity or simply another school – that shares the school's aspirations. The decision to become a trust school is taken by the governing body while taking account of parents' views. Community schools can take on foundation status and set up a trust in a single process.

Most *voluntary-aided schools* are religious schools founded by Christian denominations or other faiths. As with foundation schools, the governing body employs the staff and sets the admissions criteria, which may include priority for members of the faith or denomination. The school buildings and land are normally owned and provided by a charitable foundation, often a religious organisation, which appoints a majority of the school's governors and makes a small contribution to major building costs.

Voluntary-controlled schools are similar to voluntary-aided schools in that they often have a particular religious ethos, commonly Church of England, and the school land and buildings are normally owned by a charity. However, as with community schools, the local authority employs the school's staff, sets the admissions criteria and bears all the costs.

Among the local authority-maintained schools are some with particular characteristics:

- *Community and foundation special schools* cater for children with specific special educational needs, which may include physical disabilities or learning difficulties
- *Grammar schools* are secondary schools catering for pupils aged 11 to 18 that select all of their pupils based on academic ability. In England there are 164 grammar schools, concentrated in certain local authority areas. Wales has none
- *Maintained boarding schools* are state-funded and offer free tuition but charge fees for board and lodging

In Wales, Welsh-medium primary and secondary schools were first established in the 1950s and 1960s, originally in response to the wishes of Welsh-speaking parents who wanted their children to be educated through the medium of the Welsh language. Now, many children who are not from Welsh-speaking homes also attend Welsh-medium and bilingual schools throughout Wales. There are 461 Welsh-medium primary schools, where the main or sole medium of instruction is in the Welsh language, and 55 Welsh-medium secondary schools, where more than half of foundation subjects (other than English and Welsh) and religious education are taught wholly or partly in Welsh.

England now has increasing numbers of *Academies.* Those set-up before the Academies Act 2010 were sponsored by business, faith or voluntary groups who contributed to funding their land and buildings, while the government covered the running costs at a level comparable to other local schools. The Academies Act 2010 streamlined the process of becoming an academy, enabled high-performing schools to convert without a sponsor and allowed primary and special schools to become academies. All academies now receive funding from central government at the level they would have received if still maintained by their local authority, with extra funding only to cover those services the local authority no longer provides. Academies have greater freedoms over how they use their budgets, set staff pay and conditions and deliver the curriculum. As at July 2013 there were 3,049 academies, of which 1,279 were primaries.

SCOTLAND

Most schools in Scotland, known as 'publicly funded' schools, are state-funded and charge no fees. Funding is met from resources raised by the Scottish local authorities and from an annual grant from the Scottish government. Scotland does not have school governing bodies like the rest of the UK: local authorities retain greater responsibility for the management and performance of publicly funded schools. Headteachers manage at least 80 per cent of a school's budget, covering staffing, furnishings, repairs, supplies, services and energy costs. Expenditure on new buildings, modernisation projects and equipment is financed by the local authority within the limits set by the Scottish government.

Scotland has approaching 400 state-funded *faith schools*, the majority of which are Catholic. It has no grammar schools.

Integrated community schools form part of the Scottish government's strategy to promote social inclusion and to raise educational standards. They encourage closer and better joint working among education, health and social work agencies and professionals, greater pupil and parental involvement in schools, and improved support and service provision for vulnerable children and young people.

Scotland has a number of *grant-aided schools* that are independent of local authorities but supported financially by the Scottish government. These schools are managed by boards and most of them provide education for children and young people with special educational needs.

NORTHERN IRELAND

Most schools in Northern Ireland are maintained by the state and generally charge no fees, though fees may be charged in preparatory departments of some grammar schools. There are different types of state-funded schools, each under the control of management committees, which also employ the teachers.

Controlled schools (nursery, primary, special, secondary and grammar schools) are managed by Northern Ireland's five ELBs through boards of governors which consist of teachers, parents, members of the ELB and transferor representatives (mainly from the Protestant churches).

Catholic maintained schools (nursery, primary, special and secondary) are under the management of boards of governors that consist of teachers, parents and members nominated by the employing authority, the Council for Catholic Maintained Schools (CCMS).

Other maintained schools (primary, special and secondary) are, in the main, Irish-medium schools that provide education in an Irish-speaking environment. The Department of Education has a duty to encourage and facilitate the development of Irish-medium education. Northern Ireland has 23 standalone Irish-medium schools, most of them primary schools, and ten Irish-medium units attached to English-medium host schools.

Voluntary schools are mainly grammar schools, which select most pupils according to academic ability. They are managed by boards of governors consisting of teachers, parents and, in most cases, representatives from the Department of Education and the ELB.

Integrated schools (primary and secondary) educate pupils from both the Protestant and Catholic communities as well as those of other faiths and no faith; each school is managed by a board of governors. There are at present 62 integrated schools maintained by the state, 24 of which are controlled schools.

From 2013 all pupils are guaranteed access to a much wider range of courses, with a minimum of 24 courses at Key Stage 4, and 27 at post-16. At least one-third of the courses on offer will be academic and another third will be vocational. Schools are working with other schools, FE colleges and other providers to offer the wider range of courses.

INDEPENDENT SCHOOLS

Around 7 per cent of the UK's schoolchildren are educated by privately funded 'independent' schools that charge fees and set their own admissions policies. Independent schools are required to meet certain minimum standards but need not teach the National Curriculum. *See also* Independent Schools.

UK SCHOOLS BY CATEGORY (2011–12)

	England	*Wales*
Maintained nursery schools	423	22
*Maintained primary and secondary schools	20,086	1,633
Community	–	1,367
Voluntary-aided	–	160
Voluntary-controlled	–	93
Foundation	–	13
Pupil referral units	403	38
Maintained special schools	967	43
†Non-maintained special schools	75	–
†Academies	1,540	–
Independent schools	2,420	66
Total	25,911	1,802

* Breakdown not available for England (DfE) for 2011–12
† Includes City Technology Colleges and free schools; excludes voluntary and private pre-school education centres
‡ Figure includes two hospital schools
Source: DfE; Welsh government

Scotland	
Publicly funded schools	2,597
Primary	2,080
Secondary	368
Special	149
Independent schools	102
Total	2,699

Source: Scottish government

Northern Ireland	
State-maintained nursery schools	97
State-maintained primary and secondary schools	1,070
Controlled	481
Voluntary	51
Catholic maintained	463
Other maintained	28
Integrated	62
Special schools	40
Independent schools	15
Total	1,222

Source: DENI

INSPECTION

ENGLAND

The Office for Standards in Education, Children's Services and Skills (Ofsted) is the main body responsible for inspecting education in English schools. As well as inspecting all publicly funded and some independent schools, Ofsted inspects a range of other services in England, including childcare, children's homes, pupil referral units, local authority children's services, further education, initial teacher training and publicly funded adult skills training.

Ofsted is an independent, non-ministerial government department that reports directly to parliament, headed by Her Majesty's Chief Inspector (HMCI). Ofsted is required to promote improvement in the public services that it inspects; ensure that these services focus on the interests of their users – children, parents, learners and employers; and see that these services are efficient, effective and promote value for money. The inspection regime changed in 2012 to focus on four areas: achievement, teaching, leadership and behaviour.

Ofsted publishes the findings of its inspection reports, its recommendations and statistical information on its website.

OFFICE FOR STANDARDS IN EDUCATION, CHILDREN'S SERVICES AND SKILLS T 0300-123 1231 W www.ofsted.gov.uk

WALES

Estyn is the office of Her Majesty's Inspectorate for Education and Training in Wales. It is independent of, but funded by, the Welsh government and is led by Her Majesty's Chief Inspector of Education and Training in Wales.

Estyn's role is to inspect quality and standards in education and training in Wales, including in primary, secondary, special and independent schools, and pupil referral units, publicly funded nursery schools and settings, further education, adult community-based and work-based learning, local authorities and teacher education and training.

Estyn also provides advice on quality and standards in education and training to the Welsh government and others and its remit includes making public good practice based on inspection evidence. Estyn publishes the findings of its inspection reports, its recommendations and statistical information on its website.

HER MAJESTY'S INSPECTORATE FOR EDUCATION AND TRAINING IN WALES T 029-2044 6446 W www.estyn.gov.uk

SCOTLAND

HM Inspectorate of Education (HMIE) merged with Learning and Teaching Scotland in July 2011 to become Education Scotland, an executive agency of the Scottish government. Education Scotland operates independently and impartially while being directly accountable to Scottish ministers for the standards of its work. The agency's core business is inspection and review. It is responsible for delivering measurable year-on-year improvements, with maximum efficiency, by promoting excellence, building on strengths, and identifying and addressing under-performance.

Inspection reports and reviews, recommendations, examples of good practice and statistical information are published on Education Scotland's website.

EDUCATION SCOTLAND T 0141 282 5000 W www.educationscotland.gov.uk

NORTHERN IRELAND

The Education and Training Inspectorate (ETINI) provides inspection services for the Department of Education and Employment and Learning Northern Ireland.

ETINI carries out inspections of all schools, pre-school services, special education, further education colleges, initial teacher training, training organisations, and curriculum advisory and support services. Since September 2013 regional colleges of further education have received four weeks' notification of inspection, while all other organisations have received two weeks' notification of inspection.

The inspectorate's role is to improve services and it provides evidence-based advice to ministers in order to assist in the formulation of policies. It publishes the findings of its inspection reports, its recommendations and statistical information on its website.

EDUCATION AND TRAINING INSPECTORATE T 028-9127 9726 W www.etini.gov.uk

THE NATIONAL CURRICULUM

ENGLAND

The National Curriculum, first introduced in 1988, is mandatory in all state schools for children from age 5 onwards.

Until age 5, or the end of Reception Year in primary school, children are in the Early Years Foundation Stage (EYFS), which has its own learning and development requirements for children in nursery and primary schools. Changes to the EYFS came into effect in September 2012. These included simplifying the statutory assessment of children's development at age five; reducing the number of early learning goals from 69 to 17; stronger emphasis on the prime areas (communication and language, physical development and personal, social and emotional development); and, for parents, a new progress check at age two on their child's development.

Following the EYFS, the National Curriculum is organised into 'Key Stages', and sets out the core subjects that must be taught and the standards or attainment targets for each subject at each Key Stage.

- Key Stage 1 covers Years 1 and 2 of primary school, for children aged 5–7
- Key Stage 2 covers Years 3 to 6 of primary school, for children aged 7–11
- Key Stage 3 covers Years 7 to 9 of secondary school, for children aged 11–14
- Key Stage 4 covers Years 10 and 11 of secondary school, for children aged 14–16

Within the framework of the National Curriculum, schools may plan and organise teaching and learning in the way that best meets the needs of their pupils, but maintained schools are expected to follow the programmes of study associated with particular subjects. The programmes of study describe the subject knowledge, skills and understanding that pupils are expected to develop during each Key Stage.

In July 2013 (*see* Recent Developments) the government published updated versions of the National Curriculum framework. These set out the subjects to be compulsory at each Key Stage and the programmes of study for the majority of subjects (all subjects at Key Stages 1 to 3 plus citizenship, computing and PE at Key Stage 4). A formal consultation on the National Curriculum for Key Stage 4 English, mathematics and science will follow in autumn 2013 in line with the reform of GCSEs in these subjects.

KEY STAGES 1 AND 2 COMPULSORY SUBJECTS	
English	Design and technology
Mathematics	Geography
Science	History
Art and design	Music
Computing	Physical education

Foreign languages will be compulsory in Key Stage 2, but not Key Stage 1: schools can choose from French, German, Italian, Mandarin, Spanish, Latin or Ancient Greek.

In Key Stage 3, compulsory subjects include those listed above for Key Stage 2 (though the language taught should be a modern foreign language) plus citizenship.

Pupils in Key Stage 4 study a mix of compulsory and optional subjects in preparation for national examinations such as GCSEs. Pupils at this key stage also have to undertake careers education and work-related learning. In addition, schools must offer at least one subject from each of four 'entitlement' areas: arts (art and design, music, dance, drama and media arts); design and technology; humanities (history and geography); and modern foreign languages. To meet the entitlement requirements, schools must ensure that courses in these areas lead to approved qualifications, and allow pupils to take courses in all four areas if they wish to do so.

KEY STAGE 4 COMPULSORY SUBJECTS	
English	Citizenship
Mathematics	Physical education
Science	

Schools must teach religious education (RE) at all key stages, although parents have the right to withdraw children for all or part of the RE curriculum. Secondary schools must provide sex and relationship education.

Statutory assessment must be undertaken for all pupils in publicly funded schools in the relevant years. It first takes place towards the end of the Early Years Foundation Stage, when children's level of development is compared to and recorded against a Foundation Stage Profile. Pupils receive a phonics screening check at the end of the first year in Key Stage 1, repeated the following year if necessary. Teacher assessments in English, mathematics and science take place at the end of Key Stage 1 (Year 2) and Key Stage 2 (Year 6); at the end of Key Stage 3 (Year 9) teachers assess progress in all subjects being studied. National tests in English and mathematics take place in Year 6. At Key Stage 4, national examinations are the main form of assessment.

The assessment process for English at the end of Key Stage 2 now involves three elements. Reading comprehension is assessed by an external national test. Written comprehension is subject only to teacher assessment. Grammar, punctuation and spelling are assessed by a new external test introduced in May 2013.

Each year the DfE publishes on its website achievement and attainment tables, showing performance measures for every school and local authority. The tables for primary schools are based mainly on the results of the tests taken by children at the end of Key Stage 2 when they are usually aged 11; since 2010 the tables also include teacher assessment results. The tables for secondary schools and for attainment post-16 rely mainly on the results of national examinations. All tables include indicators of the progress that pupils have made since their last assessment.

DEPARTMENT FOR EDUCATION T 0370-000 2288
W www.education.gov.uk

WALES

Wales introduced a Foundation Phase curriculum for 3- to 7-year-olds from September 2008. The emphasis is on learning-by-doing and children's skills and knowledge are planned across seven areas of learning. They are:

- Personal and social development, well-being and cultural diversity
- Language, literacy and communication skills
- Mathematical development
- Welsh language development
- Knowledge and understanding of the world
- Physical development
- Creative development

Full details of the Foundation Phase can be found in *Framework for Children's Learning for 3- to 7-year-olds in Wales,* available on the Welsh government website (*see* below).

The National Curriculum exists for 7- to 16-year-olds. Originally it was broadly similar to that of England, with distinctive characteristics for Wales reflected in the programmes of study. From September 2008 a revised school curriculum was implemented, consisting of the National Curriculum subjects together with non-statutory frameworks for personal and social education, the world of work, religious education and skills.

The National Curriculum in Wales includes the following subjects:

- *Key Stage 2* – English, Welsh, mathematics, science, design and technology, ICT, history, geography, art and design, music, and physical education
- *Key Stage 3* – as Key Stage 2, plus a modern foreign language
- *Key Stage 4* – English, Welsh, mathematics, science and physical education

Welsh is compulsory for pupils at all key stages, either as a first or as a second language. In 2010, 16.5 per cent of pupils were taught Welsh as a first language. In April 2012, the Minister for Education and Skills approved the implementation of an action plan to raise standards and attainment in Welsh second language education. A comprehensive review of the strategy is due in 2015.

Statutory testing at the end of Key Stage 2 was removed for pupils in Wales from 2004–5. Only statutory teacher assessment remains. It is also done at the end of Key Stage 1 (in future, the Foundation Phase) and Key Stage 3, and is being strengthened by moderation and accreditation arrangements.

The new National Literacy and Numeracy Framework (LNF), outlining the skills 5- to 14-year-olds are expected to acquire, became statutory from September 2013. For literacy, this means children should become accomplished in reading for information, writing for information and expressing themselves fluently and grammatically in speech. In numeracy, children are expected to develop numerical reasoning and use number skills, measuring skills and data skills.

New national reading and numeracy for pupils in years 2 to 9 took place for the first time in Wales in May 2013 (*see* Recent Developments). The tests are designed to give teachers a clearer insight into a learner's development and progress in order to allow them to intervene at an earlier stage if learners are falling behind.

The reading test includes a statutory 'core' test, and a set of optional test materials to help teachers to further investigate learners' strengths and areas where they need to develop.

The numeracy test is split into two papers: numerical procedures and numerical reasoning. The procedural paper consists of a set of questions designed to assess the basic, essential numeracy skills such as addition, multiplication and division.

The numerical reasoning paper is to follow in May 2014. This will assess learners' ability to use the most effective procedure or set of procedures to find the solution to numeracy problems they are likely to encounter in their everyday lives.

Learners in Welsh medium schools will take a reading test in Welsh only in years 2 and 3, but in both English and Welsh from year 4 onwards. Schools will have the option to use both tests in year 3. Learners will take the numeracy test in either English or Welsh.

THE WELSH GOVERNMENT – EDUCATION AND SKILLS W http://wales.gov.uk/topics/educationandskills/schoolshome/curriculuminwales/arevisedcurriculumforwales
W www.learning.wales.gov.uk W www.wales.gov.uk

SCOTLAND

The curriculum in Scotland is not prescribed by statute but is the responsibility of education authorities and individual schools. However, schools and authorities are expected to follow the Scottish government's guidance on management and delivery of the curriculum.

Advice and guidance are provided by the Scottish government primarily through Education Scotland.

Scotland is pursuing its biggest education reform for a generation by introducing a new curriculum – Curriculum for Excellence – which aims to provide more autonomy for teachers, greater choice and opportunity for pupils and a single coherent curriculum for all children and young people aged 3 to 18.

The purpose of Curriculum for Excellence is encapsulated in 'the four capacities': to enable each child or young person to be a successful learner, a confident individual, a responsible citizen and an effective contributor. It focuses on providing a broad curriculum that develops skills for learning, skills for life and skills for work, with a sustained focus on literacy and numeracy. The period of education from pre-school through to the end of secondary stage 3, when pupils reach age 14, has the particular purpose of providing each young person in Scotland with this broad general education.

Curriculum for Excellence sets out 'experiences and outcomes', which describe broad areas of learning and what is to be achieved within them. They are:

- Expressive arts (including art and design, dance, drama, music)
- Health and wellbeing (including physical education, food and health, relationships and sexual health and mental, physical and social wellbeing)
- Languages
- Mathematics
- Religious and moral education
- Sciences
- Social studies (including history, geography, society and economy)
- Technologies (including business, computing, food and textiles, craft, design, engineering and graphics)

The experiences and outcomes are written at five levels with progression to examinations and qualifications during the senior phase, which covers secondary stages 4 to 6 when students are generally aged 14 to 17. The framework is designed to be flexible so that pupils can progress at their own pace.

Level	*Stage*
Early	The pre-school years and primary 1 (ages 3–5), or later for some
First	To the end of primary 4 (age 8), but earlier or later for some
Second	To the end of primary 7 (age 11), but earlier or later for some
Third and Fourth	Secondary 1 to secondary 3 (ages 12–14), but earlier for some. The fourth level experiences and outcomes are intended to provide possibilities for choice and young people's programmes will not include all of the fourth level outcomes
Senior phase	Secondary 4 to secondary 6 (ages 15–18), and college or other means of study

Under the new curriculum, assessment of students' progress and achievements from ages 3 to 15 is carried out by teachers who are required to base their assessment judgments on a range of evidence rather than single assessment instruments such as tests. Teachers have access to an online National Assessment Resource (NAR), which provides a range of assessment material and national exemplars across the curriculum areas.

In the senior phase, young people aged 16 to 18, including those studying outside school, build up a portfolio of national qualifications, awarded by the Scottish Qualifications Authority (SQA).

Provision is made for teaching in Gaelic in many parts of Scotland and the number of pupils, from nursery to secondary, in Gaelic-medium education is growing.

EDUCATION SCOTLAND T 0141-282 5000
W www.educationscotland.gov.uk

SCOTTISH QUALIFICATIONS AUTHORITY
T 0845-279 1000 W www.sqa.org.uk

NORTHERN IRELAND

Since September 2007 Northern Ireland has been phasing in a revised statutory curriculum that places greater emphasis than before on developing skills and preparing young people for life and work. The new curriculum has now been in place across Years 1 to 12 since September 2009.

The revised curriculum includes a new Foundation Stage to cover years one and two of primary school. This is to allow a more appropriate learning style for the youngest pupils and to ease the transition from pre-school. Key Stage 1 now covers primary years 3 and 4, until children are 8, and Key Stage 2 covers primary years 5, 6 and 7, until children are 11. At post-primary, Key Stage 3 covers Years 8, 9 and 10 and Key Stage 4 Years 11 and 12.

The revised primary curriculum is made up of RE and the following areas of learning:

- Language and literacy
- Mathematics and numeracy
- The arts
- The world around us
- Personal development and mutual understanding
- Physical education

The revised post-primary curriculum includes a new area of learning for life and work, made up of employability, personal development, local and global citizenship and home economics (at Key Stage 3). In addition, it is made up of RE and the following areas of learning:

- Language and literacy
- Mathematics and numeracy
- Modern languages
- The arts
- Environment and society
- Physical education
- Science and technology

At Key Stage 4, the statutory requirements have been significantly reduced to learning for life and work, physical education, RE and developing skills and capabilities. The aim is to provide greater choice and flexibility for pupils and allow them access to a wider range of academic and vocational courses provided under the revised curriculum's 'Entitlement Framework' (EF).

From September 2013, schools are required to provide pupils with access to at least 18 courses at Key Stage 4 and 21 courses at post-16. This will increase to 24 and 27 courses respectively by September 2015. At least one third of the courses must be 'general' with one third 'applied'. The remaining third is at the discretion of each school. Individual pupils decide on the number and mix of courses they wish to follow.

RE is a compulsory part of the Northern Ireland curriculum, although parents have the right to withdraw their children from part or all of RE or collective worship. Schools have to provide RE in accordance with a core syllabus drawn up by the province's four main churches (Church of Ireland, Presbyterian, Methodist and Roman Catholic) and specified by the Department of Education.

Revised assessment and reporting arrangements have been introduced to support the revised curriculum. The focus from Foundation to Key Stage 3 is on 'Assessment for Learning'. This programme includes classroom-based teacher assessment, computer-based assessment of literacy and numeracy and pupils deciding on their strengths and weaknesses and how they might progress to achieve their potential. Assessment information is given to parents in an annual report. Pupils at Key Stage 4 and beyond continue to be assessed through public examinations.

The Council for the Curriculum, Examinations and Assessment (CCEA), a non-departmental public body reporting to the Department of Education in Northern Ireland, is unique in the UK in combining the functions of a curriculum advisory body, an awarding body and a qualifications regulatory body. It advises the government on what should be taught in Northern Ireland's schools and colleges, ensures that the qualifications and examinations offered by awarding bodies in Northern Ireland are of an appropriate quality and standard and, as the leading awarding body itself, offers a range of qualifications including GCSEs, A-levels and AS-levels.

The CCEA hosts a dedicated curriculum website covering all aspects of the revised curriculum, assessment and reporting.

COUNCIL FOR THE CURRICULUM, EXAMINATIONS AND ASSESSMENT T 028-9026 1200 W www.ccea.org.uk

NORTHERN IRELAND CURRICULUM T 028-9028 1200 W www.nicurriculum.org.uk

QUALIFICATIONS

ENGLAND, WALES AND NORTHERN IRELAND

There is a very wide range of public examinations and qualifications available, accredited by the Office of Qualifications and Examinations Regulation (OFQUAL) in England, the Department for Education and Skills (DfES) in Wales, and the Council for the Curriculum, Examinations and Assessment (CCEA) in Northern Ireland. Up-to-date information on all accredited qualifications and awarding bodies is available online at the Register of Regulated Qualifications website.

There are four main frameworks that group all accredited qualifications that place similar demands on individuals as learners into the same levels (from entry level to level 8). Entry level, for example, covers basic knowledge and skills in English, maths and ICT not geared towards specific occupations, while level 3 includes qualifications such as A-levels which are appropriate for those wishing to go to university, and level 7 covers Master's degrees and vocational qualifications appropriate for senior professionals and managers.

Young people aged 14 to 19 in schools or (post-16) colleges or apprenticeships may gain academic qualifications such as GCSEs, AS-levels and A-levels; qualifications linked to particular career fields, like diplomas, vocational qualifications such as BTECs and NVQs; and functional key or basic skills qualifications. The frameworks in England, Wales and Northern Ireland are:

- National Qualifications Framework (NQF)
- Qualifications and Credit Framework (QCF) in England and Northern Ireland
- Credit and Qualifications Framework for Wales (CQFW)
- Framework for Higher Education Qualifications (FHEQ)

NQF AND QCF QUALIFICATIONS

Courses in these frameworks are entry level up to level 8. QCF courses are vocational and use a credit system so that learners can study units at their own pace and build these up into qualifications over time.

NQF and QCF qualifications include: English for Speakers of Other Languages (ESOL); Skills for Life; GCSEs and A-levels; International Baccalaureate; BTEC courses; Foundation Learning; National Vocational Qualifications (NVQs); Cambridge Nationals; Higher National Certificates (HNC); and Higher National Diplomas (HND).

FRAMEWORK FOR HIGHER EDUCATION QUALIFICATIONS (FHEQ)

This framework starts at level 4 and goes up to level 8 and includes the following qualifications: Certificate of Higher Education; Diploma of Higher Education; Bachelor's degrees; Master's degrees; and Doctoral degrees.

COUNCIL FOR THE CURRICULUM, EXAMINATIONS AND ASSESSMENT (NORTHERN IRELAND)
T 028-9026 1200 W www.ccea.org.uk

DEPARTMENT FOR EDUCATION AND SKILLS (DfES)
T 0300-0603300; 0845-010 3300
W http://wales.gov.uk/topics/educationandskills

REGISTER OF REGULATED QUALIFICATIONS
T 0300-303 3346 W http://register.ofqual.gov.uk

OFFICE OF QUALIFICATIONS AND EXAMINATIONS REGULATION (OFQUAL) T 0300-303 3344
W www.ofqual.gov.uk

GCSE

The vast majority of pupils in their last year of compulsory schooling in England, Wales and Northern Ireland take at least one General Certificate of Secondary Education (GCSE) exam, though GCSEs may be taken at any age. GCSEs assess the performance of pupils on a subject-specific basis and are mostly taken after a two-year course. They are available in more than 50 subjects, most of them academic subjects, though some, known as vocational or applied GCSEs, involve the study of a particular area of employment and the development of work-related skills. Some subjects are also offered as short-course qualifications, equivalent to half a standard GCSE, or as double awards, equivalent to two GCSEs.

GCSEs have traditionally been assessed by exams at the end of the course and by coursework completed by students during the course. GCSE certificates are awarded on an eight-point scale from A* to G. In most subjects two different papers, foundation and higher, are provided for different ranges of ability with grades A*–D available from the higher tier and C–G available from the foundation tier.

Major changes to GCSEs are planned in England (*see* Recent Developments). From 2015, GCSEs will move from modules and coursework to just exams at the end of the two-year course, the pass mark will be higher and the qualifications will be graded 8 to 1, rather than A* to G. There will no longer be controlled assessments (coursework done under exam conditions) and final exams will be essay-based. Changes will initially be for nine core GCSE subjects: English language, English literature, mathematics, chemistry, biology, physics, science (double award), geography and history; which should be ready for teaching from September 2015. First teaching of new specifications for English literature and history began in Spetember 2013.

The intention is that reformed qualifications in English literature and language, mathematics, the sciences, history and geography will be ready for first teaching in September 2015. Other subjects will be introduced from 2016.

All GCSE specifications, assessments and grading procedures are monitored by OFQUAL, DfES and the CCEA.

Since September 2010 the government has allowed state schools to offer pupils International GCSE (iGCSE) exams in key subjects including English, mathematics, science and ICT. The iGCSEs do not include coursework and are viewed by some experts as more rigorous than traditional GCSEs.

GCE A-LEVEL AND AS-LEVEL

GCE (General Certificate of Education) advanced levels (A-levels) are the qualifications that the majority of young people in England, Wales and Northern Ireland use to gain entry to university.

A-levels are subject-based qualifications mostly taken by UK students aged 16 to 19 over a two-year course in school sixth forms or at college, but they can be taken at any age. They are available in more than 45, mostly academic, subjects, though there are some A-levels in vocational areas, often termed 'applied A-levels'.

An A-level qualification consists of advanced subsidiary (AS) and A2 units. The AS is a standalone qualification and is worth half a full A-level qualification. It normally consists of two units, assessed at the standard expected for a learner half way through an A-level course, that together contribute 50 per cent towards the full A-level.

The A2 is the second half of a full A-level qualification. It normally consists of two units, assessed at the standard expected for a learner at the end of a full A-level course, that together are worth 50 per cent of the full A-level qualification. Most units are assessed by examination but some are by internal assessment. Each unit is graded A–E. Revised A-level specifications were introduced in September 2008, with a new A* grade awarded from 2010 to reward exceptional candidates.

An extended project was introduced in September 2008 as a separate qualification. It is a single piece of work on a topic of the student's own choosing that requires a high degree of planning, preparation, research and autonomous working. Awards are graded A–E and the extended project is accredited as half an A-level.

Since September 2013 students in England can no longer sit A-level exams in January in either their first or second year of A-level studies. A-levels will still be examined unit by unit, but all exams will be taken in the summer exam period.

OFQUAL is working on reforming the way A-levels are assessed so that all assessment takes place at the end of the course, rather than at the end of each year of A-level study, and on a standalone AS qualification that is 'decoupled' from, or no longer contributes to, a full A-level qualification. It is also reviewing curriculum content of current A-levels in: mathematics and further mathematics; English (language, literature, language and literature); physics; chemistry; biology; history; geography; psychology; art and design; sociology; business studies; economics; and computing.

For the subjects listed above where little or no change is needed, OFQUAL expects awarding organisations to start revising qualifications in line with the new assessment structure in autumn 2013. The intention is for these qualifications to be available to schools and colleges in autumn 2014 and to be ready for first teaching in September 2015.

For the subjects listed above where more significant change is required, universities will consider the subject content requirements before further consultation. New A-level qualifications in these subjects will be developed for first teaching from September 2016.

INTERNATIONAL BACCALAUREATE

The International Baccalaureate (IB) offers three educational programmes for students aged 3 to 19.

Some 201 schools and colleges in the UK, both state and independent, now offer the IB diploma programme for students aged 16 to 19. Based around detailed academic study of a wide range of subjects, including languages, the arts, science, maths, history and geography, this leads to a single qualification recognised by UK universities.

The IB diploma is made up of a compulsory 'core' plus six separate subjects where individuals have some choice over what they study. The compulsory core contains three elements: theory of knowledge; creativity, action and service; and a 4,000-word extended essay.

The diploma normally takes two years to complete and most of the assessment is done through externally marked examinations. Candidates are awarded points for each part of the programme, up to a maximum of 45. A candidate must score 24 points or more to achieve a full diploma.

Successfully completing the diploma earns points on the 'UCAS tariff', the UK system for allocating points to qualifications used for entry to higher education. An IB diploma total of 24 points is worth 260 UCAS points – the same as a B and two C grades at A-level. The maximum of 45 points earns 720 UCAS points – equivalent to six A-levels at grade A.

WELSH BACCALAUREATE

The Welsh Baccalaureate Qualification (WBQ), available for 14- to 19-year-olds in Wales, combines a compulsory core, which incorporates personal development skills, with options from existing academic and vocational qualifications, such as A-levels, GCSEs and NVQs, to make one broader award. The WBQ can be studied in English or Welsh, or a combination of the two. Candidates who meet the requirements of the compulsory core and options relevant to each level of the qualification are awarded the Welsh Baccalaureate Foundation, Intermediate or Advanced Diploma as appropriate.

WJEC (Welsh Joint Education Committee), which administers the WBQ, has also developed two new WBQs at level 1 and level 2 suitable for delivery over one year and with a particular focus on employability. These are currently only available as a pilot in some colleges or work-based learning providers.

DIPLOMAS

Diplomas were a qualification combining practical experience with academic learning for 14 to 19-year-olds brought in by the former Labour government and developed in partnership with employers. Changes in government policy mean the 'umbrella' qualification has been phased out and is no longer offered as of 2013.

BTECS, OCR NATIONALS AND OTHER VOCATIONAL QUALIFICATIONS

Vocational qualifications can range from general qualifications where a person learns skills relevant to a variety of jobs, to specialist qualifications designed for a particular sector. They are available from several awarding bodies, such as City & Guilds, Edexcel and OCR, and can be taken at many different levels.

BTEC qualifications and OCR Nationals are particular types of work-related qualifications, available in a wide range of subjects, including: art and design, business, health and social care, information technology, media, public services, science and sport. The qualifications offer a mix of theory and practice, can include work experience and can take the form of (or be part of) a technical certificate, one of the key components of an Apprenticeship. They can be studied full-time at college or school, or part-time at college. BTEC qualifications are available at various levels on the National Qualifications Framework (NQF), including Higher National

Certificates and Diplomas (HNCs and HNDs), at higher education level; OCR Nationals are achieved at levels 1 to 3.

Learners complete a range of assignments, case studies and practical activities, as well as a portfolio of evidence that shows what work has been completed. Assessment is usually done by the teacher or trainer, sometimes externally. BTEC and OCR Nationals are graded as pass, merit or distinction. BTEC and OCR Nationals at level 3 can qualify the learner for university entry.

All vocational and work-related qualifications fit into the Qualifications and Credit Framework (QCF). QCF qualifications are made up of units that can be studied at each individual's own pace and built up to full qualifications over time. Every qualification and unit on the QCF has a credit value, showing how long it takes to complete. One credit is equivalent to ten hours. When an individual takes QCF units or qualifications, their learning is 'banked' and stored on their personal learner record, showing what they have completed and how they can progress further.

There are more than 2,500 new vocational qualifications on the QCF, available in a broad range of subjects from a wide range of learning providers and some employers. Available in England, Northern Ireland and Wales, they are also recognised in Scotland.

NVQS

A National Vocational Qualification (NVQ) is a 'competence-based' qualification that is recognised by employers. Individuals learn practical, work-related tasks designed to help them develop the skills and knowledge to do a particular job effectively. NVQs can be taken in school, at college or by people already in work. There are more than 1,300 different NVQs available from the vast majority of business sectors. NVQs exist at levels 1 to 5 on the NQF and as new vocational qualifications on the QCF, though some will continue to be called NVQs. An NVQ qualification at level 2 or 3 can also be taken as part of an apprenticeship.

FUNCTIONAL SKILLS

Functional skills are a new set of qualifications launched across England during 2010, available for all learners aged 14 and above. They test the practical skills in English, mathematics and ICT that allow people to work confidently, effectively and independently in life. These skills are an integral part of the secondary school curriculum and of other qualifications and apprenticeships. Stand-alone functional skills qualifications are also available. These skills are assessed mainly by a set of practical tasks completed within a given time limit, though new ways of assessment such as electronic and online methods are being considered. Functional skills replace previous skills for life qualifications and the three main key skills qualifications in England. In Wales these new qualifications are known as 'essential skills'.

APPRENTICESHIPS

An apprenticeship combines on-the-job training with nationally recognised qualifications, allowing individuals to gain skills and qualifications while working and earning a wage. More than 200 different types of apprenticeships are available, offering over 1,200 job roles; they take between one and four years to complete. There are three levels available:

- Intermediate Level Apprenticeships – at level 2 on the National Qualifications Framework (NQF), they are equivalent to five good GCSE passes
- Advanced Level Apprenticeships – at level 3 on the NQF, they are equivalent to two A-level passes
- Higher Apprenticeships – lead to qualifications at NVQ Level 4 or, in some cases, a foundation degree

In England, the National Apprenticeship Service (NAS), launched in 2009, has responsibility for the delivery of apprenticeships including the provision of an online vacancy matching system. In 2011–12, some 520,600 young people started apprenticeships in England. The Welsh government and the Department for Employment and Learning (DEL) are responsible for the apprenticeship programmes in Wales and Northern Ireland respectively.

NATIONAL APPRENTICESHIP SERVICE (NAS)
T 02476-826482 W www.apprenticeships.org.uk

SCOTLAND

Scotland has its own system of public examinations and qualifications. The Scottish Qualifications Authority (SQA) is Scotland's national body for qualifications, responsible for developing, accrediting, assessing and certificating all Scottish qualifications apart from university degrees and some professional body qualifications.

There are qualifications at all levels of attainment. Almost all school candidates gain SQA qualifications in the fourth year of secondary school and most obtain further qualifications in the fifth or sixth year or in further education colleges. Increasingly, people also take them in the workplace.

SQA, with partners such as Universities Scotland, has introduced the Scottish Credit and Qualifications Framework (SCQF) as a way of comparing and understanding Scottish qualifications. It includes qualifications across academic and vocational sectors and compares them by giving a level and credit points. There are 12 levels in the SCQF, level 1 being the least difficult and level 12 the most difficult. The number of SCQF credit points shows how much learning has to be done to achieve the qualification. For instance, one SCQF credit point equals about 10 hours of learning including assessment.

The main national qualifications available include:

- Standard Grades which are taken over the third and fourth years at secondary school. Students often choose to study seven or eight subjects, among which Mathematics and English are compulsory. There are three levels of study at Standard Grade: Foundation, General and Credit. Students usually sit exams at two levels – either Foundation/General or General/Credit – to ensure they have the best chance of achieving as high a grade as possible.
- National Units are the building blocks of National Courses, but they are also recognised qualifications in their own right and are designed to take approximately 40 hours of teaching time to complete.
- National Courses usually comprise three National Units and an externally marked assessment. National Courses are available at a number of levels including Access 1, Access 2, Access 3, Intermediate 1, Intermediate 2, Higher and Advanced Higher.
- Skills for Work courses encourage school pupils to become familiar with the world of work. They involve a strong element of learning through involvement in practical and vocational activities and develop knowledge, skills and experience that are related to employment. They are available at a number of levels and are frequently delivered in partnership between schools and colleges.
- Wider Achievement qualifications provide young people with the opportunity to have learning and skills formally recognised, whether developed in or outside the classroom. Available at a number of levels in subjects including Employability, Leadership and Enterprise, these qualifications help schools deliver skills for learning, life and work.
- Scottish Baccalaureates consist of a coherent group of Higher and Advanced Higher qualifications and, uniquely,

an interdisciplinary project of candidates' own choosing which is marked at Advanced Higher level in one of four broad topics – languages, science, expressive arts or social studies. Aimed at high-achieving candidates in their sixth year, the Scottish Baccalaureate is designed to encourage personalised, in-depth study and interdisciplinary learning in the later stages of secondary school.

As part of the Curriculum for Excellence programme (*see* above) SQA has developed new National qualifications that became available in schools from August 2013, replacing Standard Grade, Intermediate and Access qualifications at all levels. New Higher and Advanced Higher qualifications will be available from August 2014 and August 2015 respectively:

SCQF Level	*New national qualifications*	*Replaces*
1 and 2	National 1 and 2	Access 1 and Access 2
3	National 3	Access 3 Standard Grade (Foundation Level)
4	National 4	Standard Grade (General Level) Intermediate 1
5	National 5	Standard Grade (Credit Level) Intermediate 2
6	Higher (new)	Higher
7	Advanced Higher (new)	Advanced Higher

All new qualifications will run concurrently with existing qualifications until 2015/16.

SQA has also developed five new Awards – in modern languages, personal achievement, personal development, religion and wellbeing – that cover work from across different subject areas, and are shorter than traditional courses and recognise success across different levels of difficulty. These started in August 2012 and are marked and assessed by schools and colleges rather than by external assessment or exams. New Awards in Cycling and Scottish Studies began in August 2013.

SQA QUALIFICATIONS

HIGHER NATIONAL CERTIFICATES AND HIGHER NATIONAL DIPLOMAS

Higher National Certificates and Higher National Diplomas (HNCs and HNDs) are offered by colleges, some universities and many other training providers – including employers. Both HNCs and HNDs are comprised of Higher National Units and cover a wide range of subject areas. Many HNDs allow the holder entry to the second or third year of a degree course. HNCs are available at SCQF level 7, HNDs at level 8.

SCOTTISH VOCATIONAL QUALIFICATIONS

Scottish Vocational Qualifications (SVQs) are based on national standards drawn up by people from industry, commerce and education. Possession of an SVQ demonstrates ability to perform in a job to agreed national standards. Primarily delivered to candidates in full-time employment, SVQs are available at SCQF levels 4 to 12.

PROFESSIONAL DEVELOPMENT AWARDS

Professional Development Awards (PDAs) are designed to develop and deliver high level skills in a sharp, flexible and focused way. They are for people already in work who wish to extend or broaden their skills. Candidates often take a PDA after completing a degree or vocational qualification. PDAs are available at SCQF levels 6 to 12.

THE SCOTTISH QUALIFICATIONS AUTHORITY (SQA)
T 0845-279 1000 W www.sqa.org.uk
SCOTTISH CREDIT AND QUALIFICATIONS FRAMEWORK (SCQF) T 0845-270 7371
W www.scqf.org.uk

FURTHER EDUCATION AND LIFELONG LEARNING

ENGLAND

The further education (FE) system in England provides a wide range of education and training opportunities for young people and adults. From the age of 16, young people who wish to remain in education, but not in a school setting, can undertake further education (including skills training) in an FE college. There are two main types of college in the FE sector: sixth form colleges and general further education (GFE) colleges. Some FE colleges focus on a particular area, such as art and design or agriculture and horticulture. Each institution decides its own range of subjects and courses. Students at FE colleges can study for a wide and growing range of academic and/or work-related qualifications, from entry level to higher education level.

Though the Department for Business, Innovation and Skills is responsible for the FE sector and for funding FE for adults (19 or over), the Department for Education funds all education and training for 16- to 18-year-olds.

The proportion of 16- to 18-year-olds in education or training has risen steadily over recent years. But those in full-time education fell from 68.6 per cent in 2011 to 67.2 per cent in 2012, mainly due to fewer 18-year-olds going to higher education institutions. By the time that England's education-leaving age rises to 18 in 2015, 100 per cent should be in education or training. It is assumed that most of the additional students will go into FE or work-based training rather than staying on at school.

The 'September Guarantee', introduced in 2007, offers a place in post-16 education or training to all 16- and 17-year-olds who want one. In 2012, 92.4 per cent of 16- and 17-year-olds received an offer of a place. A new Education Funding Agency (EFA) was established in April 2012 as an executive agency of the Department for Education (DfE). It is responsible for education funding for 16- to 19-year-olds as well as academies.

The FE sector in England, as in other parts of the UK, also provides a range of opportunities for adults.

The Skills Funding Agency (SFA), part of the Department for Business, Innovation and Skills, is presently responsible for funding and regulating education and training for adults. It will invest government funding of £4.09bn in FE and skills training places in 2013–14.

In November 2010, the government announced a new strategy for FE, including more adult apprenticeships (provision for 200,000 adults by 2014–15); fully funded training for 19- to 24-year-olds undertaking their first full level 2 (GCSE equivalent) or first level 3 qualification when they do not already have one; and fully funded basic skills for people who left school without basic skills in reading, writing and mathematics. 'Train to Gain', the programme that funded trainees sponsored by employers, was replaced in July 2011 by a programme focused on helping small employers to train low-skilled staff. This was followed in December 2011 by a plan to reform FE that focuses on students and in April 2012 by the creation of a National Careers Service.

In April 2013, the government announced plans to make vocational qualifications more 'rigorous' (removing up to 2,550 qualifications), to make the skills system more 'responsive' and to create new traineeships (*see* Recent Developments).

From 2014, Tech-levels will take as long to complete as A-Levels and will need to be endorsed by either a professional association or by five employers registered with Companies House. These qualifications will focus on hands-on practical training, leading to recognised occupations for example in engineering, computing, accounting or hospitality.

Applied General Qualifications will take the same time to complete as AS-levels and will focus on broader study of a technical area, not directly linked to an occupation. These qualifications will need backing from three universities to count in performance tables.

A Tech-level along with a core maths qualification, for example AS-level maths, and an extended project will amount to an over-arching Technical Baccalaureate.

There are currently 19 employer-led, funded and designed centres of training excellence called National Skills Academies in various stages of development. Each academy operates in a key sector of the economy, and operates in partnership with colleges, schools and independent training providers to offer specialist training within their sector.

Among the many voluntary bodies providing adult education, the Workers' Educational Association (WEA) is the UK's largest, operating throughout England and Scotland. It provides part-time courses to adults in response to local need in community centres, village halls, schools, pubs or workplaces. Similar but separate WEA organisations operate in Wales and Northern Ireland.

The National Institute of Adult Continuing Education (NIACE), a charitable non-governmental organisation, promotes lifelong learning opportunities for adults in England and Wales.

NATIONAL INSTITUTE OF ADULT CONTINUING EDUCATION (NIACE) T 0116-204 4200
W www.niace.org.uk

THE SKILLS FUNDING AGENCY T 0845-377 5000
W www.skillsfundingagency.bis.gov.uk

WORKERS' EDUCATIONAL ASSOCIATION (WEA)
T 020-7426 3450 W www.wea.org.uk

WALES

In Wales, the aims and makeup of the FE system are similar to those outlined for England. The Welsh government funds a wide range of learning programmes for young people through colleges, local authorities and private organisations. The Welsh government has set out plans to improve learning opportunities for all post-16 learners in the shortest possible time, to increase the engagement of disadvantaged young people in the learning process, and to transform the learning network to increase learner choice, reduce duplication of provision and encourage higher-quality learning and teaching in all post-16 provision. One goal is to ensure that, by 2015, 95 per cent of young people will be ready for high-skilled employment or higher education by the age of 25.

In Wales, responsibility for adult and continuing education lies with the Department for Education and Skills (DfES) within the Welsh government. Wales operates a range of programmes to support skills development, including subsidised work-based training courses for employees and the Workforce Development Programme, where employers can use the free services of experienced skills advisers to develop staff training plans.

COLEG HARLECH WEA T 01248-353254
W www.harlech.ac.uk/en/

NIACE DYSGU CYMRU T 029-2037 0900
W www.niacedc.org.uk

WEA SOUTH WALES T 029-2023 5277
W www.swales.wea.org.uk

SCOTLAND

Scotland's 41 FE colleges (known simply as colleges) are at the forefront of lifelong learning, education, training and skills in Scotland. Colleges cater for the needs of learners both in and out of employment at all stages in their lives from middle secondary school and earlier to retirement. Colleges' courses span much of the range of learning needs, from specialised vocational education and training through to general educational programmes. The level of provision ranges from essential life skills and provision for students with learning difficulties to HNCs and HNDs. Some colleges, notably those in the Highlands and Islands, also deliver degrees and postgraduate qualifications.

The Scottish Funding Council (SFC) is the statutory body responsible for funding teaching and learning provision, research and other activities in Scotland's colleges. Overall strategic direction for the sector is provided by the Lifelong Learning Directorate of the Scottish government, which provides annual guidance to the SFC and liaises closely with bodies such as Scotland's Colleges, the Scottish Qualifications Authority and the FE colleges themselves to ensure that its policies remain relevant and practical.

The Scottish government takes responsibility for community learning and development in Scotland while Skills Development Scotland, a non-departmental public body, is charged with improving Scotland's skills performance by linking skills supply and demand and helping people and organisations to learn, develop and make use of these skills to greater effect. ILA Scotland is a Scottish government scheme delivered by Skills Development Scotland that provides funding for training to individuals over the age of 16 with an income of less than £22,000 a year.

ILA SCOTLAND T 0808-100 1090 W www.ilascotland.org.uk

SCOTLAND'S COLLEGES T 01786-892000
W www.scotlandscolleges.ac.uk

SCOTTISH FUNDING COUNCIL T 0131-313 6500
W www.sfc.ac.uk

SKILLS DEVELOPMENT SCOTLAND T 0141-285 6000
W www.skillsdevelopmentscotland.co.uk

NORTHERN IRELAND

FE in Northern Ireland is provided through six multi-campus colleges. Most secondary schools also provide a sixth form where students can choose to attend for two additional years to complete their AS-levels and A-levels.

Colleges Northern Ireland (CNI) acts as the representative body for the six FE colleges which, like their counterparts in the rest of the UK, are independent corporate bodies where management responsibility lies with each individual college's governing body. The range of courses that they offer spans essential skills, a wide choice of vocational and academic programmes and higher education programmes. The majority of full-time enrolments in the six colleges are in the 16 to 19 age group, while most part-time students are over 19.

The Department for Employment and Learning (DELNI) is responsible for the policy, strategic development and financing of the statutory FE sector and for lifelong learning, and also provides support to a small number of non-statutory FE providers. The Educational Guidance Service for Adults (EGSA), an independent, not-for-profit organisation, has a network of local offices based across Northern Ireland which provide services to adult learners, learning advisers, providers, employers and others interested in improving access to learning for adults.

COLLEGES NORTHERN IRELAND (CNI) T 028-9068 2296
W www.anic.ac.uk

THE EDUCATIONAL GUIDANCE SERVICE FOR ADULTS T 028-9024 4274 W www.egsa.org.uk

WEA NORTHERN IRELAND T 028-9032 9718
W www.wea-ni.com

FINANCIAL SUPPORT

The *Education Maintenance Allowance* (EMA) in England, a scheme that paid 16- to 19-year-olds from low income families a weekly allowance to continue in education, was replaced by a bursary scheme for full-time 16- to 19-year-old students facing financial hardship from September 2011. Those in care, leaving care, on income support or on certain disability benefits will be guaranteed a bursary of £1,200 a year. There is also the possibility of help with transport costs for some students.

There are similar EMA schemes in Scotland, Wales and Northern Ireland, but with slightly different eligibility conditions. Students must apply to the EMA scheme for the part of the UK where they intend to study. In Northern Ireland 16- to 19-year-old students, who meet the relevant criteria, and live in a household that has an annual income of £20,500 or less a year (£22,500 if there is more than one young person in the household who qualifies for child benefit) automatically get £30 a week in 2013–14.

Colleges and learning providers award learner support funds directly to new students aged 19 and over.

Care to Learn is available in England to help young parents under the age of 20 who are caring for their own child or children with the costs of childcare and travel while they are in some form of publicly funded learning (below higher education level). The scheme is not income assessed and pays up to £160 a week (£175 in London) to cover costs.

Dance and Drama Awards (DaDA) are state-funded scholarships for students over the age of 16 enrolled at one of 19 private dance and drama schools in England, who are taking specified courses at National Certificate or National Diploma level. Awards, based on household income, cover some of students' tuition fees and up to £5,185 maintenance in 2013–14.

Young people studying away from home because their chosen course is not available locally may qualify for the *Residential Support Scheme*.

Information and advice on funding support and applications are available from the Learner Support helpline (T 0800-121 8989) or on the GOV.UK website (*see* below).

Discretionary Support Funds (DSF) are available in colleges and school sixth forms to help students who have trouble meeting the costs of participating in further education.

In Wales, students aged 19 or over on FE courses may be eligible for the *Assembly Learning Grant for Further Education* (ALG (FE)). This is a means-tested payment of up to £1,500 for full-time students and up to £750 for those studying part-time. *Discretionary Financial Contingency Funds* are also available to all students in Wales suffering hardship and are administered by the institutions themselves.

In Scotland, FE students can apply to their college for discretionary support in the form of *Further Education Bursaries*. These can include allowances for maintenance, travel, study, childcare and additional support needs. *Individual Learning Accounts* provide up to £200 for those with incomes of less than £22,000.

In Northern Ireland, FE students may be eligible for *Further Education Awards*, non-refundable assistance administered on behalf of the five Education and Library Boards by the Western Education and Library Board.

UK FE students over 18 whose costs are not fully met from the grants described above may also be eligible for *Professional and Career Development Loans*. These loans – also available to HE students – cover up to 80 per cent of course fees (up to 100 per cent for those unemployed for three months); other course costs, such as books, travel and childcare; and living expenses, such as rent, food and clothing (for those who are unemployed or working fewer than 30 hours a week). The loans, of between £300 and £10,000, are available from participating high street banks – currently Barclays and the Co-operative. The Skills Funding Agency (SFA) pays the interest on the loan while the student is studying and for one month afterwards. Once students complete their courses, they must pay interest at the rate fixed when they took out the loan, which will be competitive with other commercially available 'unsecured' personal loans.

CAREERS SCOTLAND
W www.careers-scotland.org.uk/Education/Funding/Funding.asp

GOV.UK W www.gov.uk/further-education-courses/financial-help

STUDENT FINANCE WALES T 0845-602 8845
W www.studentfinancewales.co.uk

WESTERN EDUCATION AND LIBRARY BOARD
T 028-8241 1411 W www.welbni.org

HIGHER EDUCATION

Publicly funded higher education (HE) in the UK is provided in more than 300 universities, higher education colleges and other specialist HE institutions, and a significant number of FE colleges offering higher education courses.

The Higher Education Funding Council for England (HEFCE) funds teaching and research in 128 English higher education institutions (HEIs) and 187 FE colleges.

The Higher Education Funding Council for Wales (HEFCW) distributes funding for HE in Wales through Wales's 10 HEIs and some FE colleges.

The Scottish Funding Council (SFC) – which is also responsible for FE in Scotland – is the national, strategic body responsible for funding HE teaching and research in Scotland's 19 HEIs and 41 colleges.

In Northern Ireland, HE is provided by two universities, the Open University (OU) and two university colleges, six regional institutes of further and higher education and the OU, which operates UK-wide. Unlike other parts of the UK, Northern Ireland has no higher education funding council; the Department for Employment and Learning fulfils that role.

All UK universities and a number of HE colleges award their own degrees and other HE qualifications. HE providers who do not have their own degree-awarding powers offer degrees under 'validation arrangements' with other institutions that do have those powers. The OU, for example, runs a validation service which enables a number of other institutions to award OU degrees, after the OU has assured itself that the academic standards of their courses are as high as the OU's own standards.

Each HE institution is responsible for the standards of the awards it makes and the quality of the education it provides to its students, and each has its own internal quality assurance procedures. External quality assurance for HE institutions throughout the UK is provided by the Quality Assurance Agency for Higher Education (QAA).

The QAA is independent of government, funded by subscriptions from all publicly funded UK universities and colleges of HE. Its main role is to safeguard the standards of HE qualifications. It does this by defining standards for HE through a framework known as the academic infrastructure. QAA also carries out reviews of the quality of UK HE institutions via a system known as 'institutional audits'. QAA also advises government on a range of HE quality issues, including applications for the grant of degree-awarding powers. It publishes reports on its review activities on its website.

DEPARTMENT FOR EMPLOYMENT AND LEARNING
T 028-9025 7777 W www.delni.gov.uk

HIGHER EDUCATION FUNDING COUNCIL FOR ENGLAND T 0117-931 7317 W www.hefce.ac.uk

HIGHER EDUCATION FUNDING COUNCIL FOR WALES T 029-2076 1861 W www.hefcw.ac.uk

SCOTTISH FUNDING COUNCIL T 0131-313 6500
W www.sfc.ac.uk

THE QUALITY ASSURANCE AGENCY FOR HIGHER EDUCATION T 01452-557000 W www.qaa.ac.uk
See also Universities for information on the Research Assessment Exercise (being replaced from 2014 by the Research Excellence Framework) and listings of universities in the UK.

STUDENTS APPLYING TO UNIVERSITY

	2012	*2013*	*Difference*
Total applicants	618,247	637,456	3.1%
Total choices	2,636,963	2,712,358	2.9%

Source: UCAS

STUDENTS IN HIGHER EDUCATION (2011–12)*

	Full-time	*Part-time*	*Total*
HE students	–	–	2,496,645
Postgraduate students	309,425	259,080	568,505
Undergraduate students	1,411,975	516,165	1,928,140

*Includes UK, EU and non-EU students
Source: Higher Education Statistics Agency (HESA) 2012

UK HIGHER EDUCATION QUALIFICATIONS AWARDED (2011–12)

	Full-time	*Part-time*
First degrees	350,800	40,185
Other undergraduate qualifications	63,930	68,200
Postgraduate Certificate in Education (PGCE)	18,980	1,300
Other postgraduate qualifications	14,890	34,645
Total higher degrees including doctorates	149,950	44,330

Source: HESA 2012

COURSES

HE institutions in the UK mainly offer courses leading to the following qualifications. These qualifications go from levels 4 to 8 on England's National Qualifications Framework, levels 7 to 12 on Scotland's Credit and Qualifications Framework. Individual HEIs may not offer all of these.

Certificates of Higher Education (CertHE), awarded after one year's full-time study (or equivalent). If available to students on longer courses, they certify that students have reached a minimum standard in their first year.

Diplomas of Higher Education (DipHE) *and other Higher Diplomas,* awarded after two to three years' full-time study (or equivalent). They certify that a student has achieved a minimum standard in first- and second-year courses and, in the case of nursing, third-year courses. They can often be used for entry to the third year of a related degree course.

Foundation degrees, awarded after two years of full-time study (or equivalent). These degrees combine academic study with work-based learning, and have been designed jointly by universities, colleges and employers with a particular area of work in mind. They are usually accepted as a basis for entry to the third year of a related degree course.

Bachelor's degrees, also referred to as *first degrees.* There are different titles; Bachelor of Arts (BA) and Bachelor of Science (BSc) being the most common. In England, Wales and Northern Ireland most Bachelor's degree courses are typically 'with Honours' and awarded after three years of full-time study, although in some subjects the courses last longer. In Scotland, where young people often leave school and go to university a year younger, HE institutions typically offer Ordinary Bachelor's degrees after three years' study and Bachelor's degrees with Honours after four years. Honours degrees are graded as first, upper-second (2:1), lower second (2:2), or third. HEIs in England, Wales and Northern Ireland may allow students who fail the first year of an Honours degree by a small margin to transfer to an Ordinary degree course, if they have one. Ordinary degrees may also be awarded to Honours degree students who do not finish an Honours degree course but complete enough of it to earn a pass.

Postgraduate or *Higher degrees.* Graduates may go on to take *Master's degrees,* which involve one or two years' work and can be taught or research-based. They may also take one-year postgraduate diplomas and certificates, often linked to a specific profession, such as the *Postgraduate Certificate in Education* (PGCE) required to become a state school teacher. A *doctorate,* leading to a qualification such as a Doctor of Philosophy – a PHD or DPHIL – usually involves at least three years of full-time research.

The framework for HE qualifications in England, Wales and Northern Ireland (FHEQ) and the framework for qualifications of HE institutions in Scotland, can both be found on the QAA website (W www.qaa.ac.uk/academicinfrastructure/FHEQ/SCQF/), which describes the achievement represented by HE qualifications.

ADMISSIONS

When preparing to apply to a university or other HE college, individuals can compare facts and figures on institutions and courses using the government's Unistats website. This includes details of students' views from the annual National Student Survey.

For the vast majority of full-time undergraduate courses, individuals need to apply online through UCAS, the organisation responsible for managing applications to HE courses in the UK. More than half a million people wanting to study at a university or college each year use this UCAS service, which has useful online tools to help students find the right course.

UCAS also provides two specialist applications services used by more than 50,000 people each year: the Conservatoires UK Admissions Service (CUKAS), for those applying to UK music conservatoires, and the Graduate Teacher Training Registry (GTTR), for postgraduate applications for initial teacher training courses in England and Wales and some in Scotland. Details of initial teacher training courses in Scotland can also be obtained from Universities Scotland and from Teach in Scotland, the website created by the Scottish government to promote teaching.

Each university or college sets its own entry requirements. These can be in terms of particular exam grades or total points on the 'UCAS tariff' (UCAS's system for allocating points to different qualifications on a common basis), or be non-academic, like having a health check. HEIs will make 'firm offers' to candidates who have already gained the qualifications they present for entry, and 'conditional offers' to those who have yet to take their exams or obtain their results. Conditional offers often require a minimum level of achievement in a specified subject, for example '300 points to include grade A at A-level Chemistry'. If candidates' achievements are lower than specified in their conditional offers, the university or college may not accept them; then, if they still wish to go into HE, they need to find another institution through the UCAS 'clearing' process.

The OU conducts its own admissions. It is the UK's only university dedicated to distance learning and the UK's largest for part-time HE. Because it is designed to be 'open' to all, no qualifications are needed for entry to the majority of its courses.

Individuals can search over 58,000 UK postgraduate courses and research opportunities on UK graduate careers website Prospects. The application process for postgraduate places can vary between institutions. Most universities and colleges accept direct applications and many accept applications through UKPASS, a free, centralised online service run by UCAS that allows individuals to submit up to ten different applications, track their progress and attach supporting material, such as references.

UNISTATS W http://unistats.direct.gov.uk
UCAS T 0871-468 0468 W www.ucas.com
UNIVERSITIES SCOTLAND T 0131-226 1111
W www.universities-scotland.ac.uk
TEACH IN SCOTLAND T 0845-345 4745
W www.teachinginscotland.com
PROSPECTS T 0161-277 5200 W www.prospects.ac.uk
UKPASS T 0871-334 4447 W http://ukpass.ac.uk

TUITION FEES AND STUDENT SUPPORT

TUITION FEES

HE institutions in England, Wales and Northern Ireland are allowed to charge variable tuition fees for full-time HE courses. Although students from outside the EU can be charged the full cost of their courses, the amount that HEIs may charge students from the UK and other EU countries was capped from 2006 at £3,000 a year plus inflationary increases. From September 2012, universities have been able to charge up to £9,000 a year in tuition fees. The exact fee depends on the course studied and the institution attended. Full-time students do not have to pay their fees before or during their course, as tuition fee loans are available to cover the full cost; these do not have to be repaid until the student is working (*see* below).

In recent years, Scottish HE institutions have charged flat rate fees, set by the Scottish government, to undergraduate students classed as being ordinarily resident in England, Wales or Northern Ireland; though, as explained above, they can get repayable tuition fee loans to cover the cost. Since 2012 universities can set their own fees, up to £9,000 a year, for undergraduates starting courses. On average, Scottish universities have opted to charge £6,841. However, undergraduate students classed as being ordinarily resident in Scotland or another EU country do not have to pay tuition fees at Scottish HE institutions. All tuition fees are paid on their behalf by the Scottish government through the Student Awards Agency for Scotland (SAAS); students must apply for this funding every year.

STUDENT LOANS, GRANTS AND BURSARIES

ENGLAND

All students starting a full-time HE course in 2013–14 can apply through Student Finance England for financial support. Two student loans are available from the government: a *tuition fee loan* of up to £9,000 for 2013–14; and a *maintenance loan* (for students aged under 60) to help with living expenses of up to £5,500 for those living away from home (£7,675 if studying away from home in London) and £4,375 for those living with their parents during term time, or £6,535 if living and studying abroad for at least one term.

The tuition fee loan is not affected by household income and is paid directly to the relevant HE institution. A proportion (currently 65 per cent) of the maximum maintenance loan is available irrespective of household income while the rest depends on an income assessment. Student Finance England usually pays the money into the student's own bank account in three instalments, one at the start of each term.

Repayment of both loans does not start until the April after the student has left university or college and is earning more than £21,000 a year. At this point the individual's employer will take 9 per cent of any salary above the £21,000 threshold through the Pay As You Earn (PAYE) system. The self-employed make repayments through their tax returns. Someone earning £20,000 a year, the average starting salary for graduates entering full-time employment, will have to pay back £8.65 a week. Student loans accrue interest from the date they are paid out, up until they are repaid in full. Generally, the interest rate for student loans is set in September each year. The latest rate can be found online (W www.studentloanrepayment.co.uk/interest).

Students can also apply for a *maintenance grant* towards living expenses which does not have to be repaid. The maximum grant available for 2013–14 is £3,354 for the academic year. This is available to full-time HE students with a household income of £25,000 or under. Those with a household income of £42,611 or under receive a partial grant. The exact amount paid depends upon income. Students eligible for help through the maintenance grant receive some of it instead of the maintenance loan. The amount they are eligible for through the maintenance loan is reduced by £1 for every £1 of maintenance grant that they are entitled to (up to a maximum of £1,354). This means that students from lower income households generally have less to repay when they finish studying and start work.

Certain groups of students who claim means-tested state benefits can get the *special support grant,* also worth up to £3,354, instead of the maintenance grant. Likely recipients include single parents and students with certain disabilities. If a student receives the special support grant, it does not affect the amount of maintenance loan that he or she receives.

Bursaries are an additional source of help available from universities and colleges. They do not have to be repaid.

Students can use the student finance calculator on the Student Finance England website to work out what financial support they may get.

Part-time Higher Education Students in England are entitled to tuition fee loans (which replaced grants) of up to £6,750 in 2013–14. Following government changes to student finance, the maximum universities and colleges can charge part-time students in tuition fees is £6,750. Part-time students who earn over £21,000 a year have to start paying back their loans after four years even if their course has not finished.

Details are available on the Student Finance England website.

If the student's chosen HE institution runs the *additional fee support scheme,* it could provide extra financial help if the student is on a low income and in certain other circumstances. Help may also be available through the institution's *access to learning fund,* for students in financial difficulty.

STUDENT FINANCE ENGLAND T 0845-300 5090
W www.sfengland.slc.co.uk

WALES

Welsh students starting a full-time HE course in 2013–14 can apply through Student Finance Wales for the forms of financial support described below.

A similar system of tuition fee and maintenance loans and grants operates in Wales as in England but Welsh students can also receive a substantial tuition fee grant. Maximum maintenance loans are: up to £5,150 for students living away from home (£7,215 if studying away from home in London) and £3,987 for those living with their parents during term time. From September 2013, eligible Welsh students can access a non means-tested tuition fee loan of up to £3,575 and grant of up to £5,425 to cover the exact amount that the institution charges for a course.

Welsh-domiciled students may apply for an *assembly learning grant* (ALG) of up to £5,161 to help meet general living costs. This is paid in three instalments, one at the start of each term, like the student maintenance loan. The amount that a student gets depends on household income. The maximum ALG is available to those with a household income of £18,370 or under. Those with an income of £50,020 or under receive a partial grant. The amount of maintenance loan a student can receive is reduced by 50p for every £1 of ALG they receive up to a maximum of £2,575.

Students needing extra help may also be entitled to receive adult dependants' grant (ADG), childcare grant (CCG), parents' learning allowance (PLA) and disabled students' allowance (DSA).

Students can use the student finance calculator on the Student Finance Wales website to work out what financial support they may be entitled to.

Welsh HE institutions also hold financial contingency funds to provide discretionary assistance to students experiencing financial difficulties.

Part-time Undergraduate Higher Education Students studying at least 50 per cent of an equivalent full-time course are entitled to receive a *fee grant* of up to £1,025, depending on their household income (partial fee grant is available for those with household incomes up to £25,435). Students needing extra help may also be entitled to receive adult dependants' grant (ADG), childcare grant (CCG), parents' learning allowance (PLA) and disabled students' allowance (DSA). Part-time students can also apply for a course-related grant worth up to £1,155 (partial course grant is available for those with household incomes up to £28,180). The Welsh government is due to introduce part-time fee loans from 2014/15.

STUDENT FINANCE WALES T 0845-602 8845
W www.studentfinancewales.co.uk

SCOTLAND

All students starting a full-time HE course in 2013–14 can apply through the Student Awards Agency for Scotland for financial support. Living cost support is mainly provided through a *student loan*, the majority of which is income-assessed. The maximum loan for 2013–14 is £6,500.

The *young students' bursary* (YSB) is available to young students from low-income backgrounds and is non-repayable. Eligible students receive this bursary instead of part of the student loan, thus reducing their level of repayable debt. In 2013–14 the maximum annual support provided through YSB is £1,750 if household income is £17,000 or less a year.

The *independent students' bursary* (ISB) similarly replaces part of the loan and reduces repayable debt for low-income students classed as 'independent' of parental support. The maximum paid is £750 a year to those whose household income is £17,000 or less a year.

Travel expenses are included within the student loan. There are also *supplementary grants* available to certain categories of students such as lone parents (£2,640) and those with dependants (£1,305). Extra help is also available to those who have a disability, learning difficulty or mental health problem.

STUDENT AWARDS AGENCY FOR SCOTLAND
T 0300-555 0505
W www.saas.gov.uk/student_support/index.htm

NORTHERN IRELAND

All students starting a full-time HE course in 2013–14 can apply through Student Finance Northern Ireland for financial support. The arrangements for both full-time and part-time students are similar to those for England. The main difference is that the income-assessed *maintenance grant* (or *special support grant* for students on certain income-assessed benefits) for new full-time students studying at UK universities and colleges is worth up to £3,475 while eligible continuing students can apply for a minimum institutional bursary of £347. Loans for living costs of £3,750 for study in Northern Ireland, £4,840 elsewhere in the UK (£6,780 in London) and £4,840 in the Republic of Ireland are available.

STUDENT FINANCE NORTHERN IRELAND
T 0845-600 0662 W www.studentfinanceni.co.uk

DISABLED STUDENTS' ALLOWANCES

Disabled Students' Allowances (DSAs) are grants available throughout the UK to help meet the extra course costs that students can face as a direct result of a disability, ongoing health condition, mental health condition or specific learning difficulty. They help disabled people to study in HE on an equal basis with other students. They are paid on top of the standard student finance package and do not have to be repaid. The amount that an individual gets depends on the type of extra help needed, not on household income. This amounts to £5,161 for specialist equipment for the entire course, non-medical helper allowance of £20,520 a year and a general allowance of £1,724 a year. Eligible individuals should apply as early as possible to their relevant UK awarding authority.

POSTGRADUATE AWARDS

In general, postgraduate students do not qualify for mandatory support like student loans. An exception to this is students taking a Postgraduate Certificate in Education (PGCE), who can qualify for the finance package usually available only to undergraduates.

There is heavy competition for any postgraduate funding available. Individuals can search for postgraduate awards and scholarships on two websites: Hot Courses and Prospects. They can also search for grants available from educational trusts, often reserved for students from poorer backgrounds or for those who have achieved academic excellence, on the Educational Grants Advisory Service (EGAS) website. Otherwise they need to fund their own fees and living expenses.

Postgraduates from Scotland can get £3,400 towards tuition fees but no support for living costs. In Northern Ireland, the Department for Employment and Learning and the Education and Library Boards provide postgraduate funding for certain courses. Postgraduate students with an impairment, health condition or learning difficulty can apply for disabled students' allowances (*see* above) for both taught courses and research places. For both full-time and part-time postgraduate students there is a single allowance of up to £10,260 a year.

DEPARTMENT FOR EMPLOYMENT AND LEARNING (DELNI) T 028-9025 7777 W www.delni.gov.uk

EDUCATIONAL GRANTS ADVISORY SERVICE (EGAS) T 020-7254 6251 W www.family-action.org.uk

HOT COURSES W www.scholarship-search.org.uk

PROSPECTS W www.prospects.ac.uk

STUDENT AWARDS AGENCY FOR SCOTLAND (SAAS) T 0300-555 0505 W www.student-support-saas.gov.uk

TEACHER TRAINING

See Professional Education.

EMPLOYEES AND SALARIES

EMPLOYEES

QUALIFIED TEACHERS IN MAINTAINED SCHOOLS (NOVEMBER 2011)
Full-time equivalent, thousands

	England	*Wales*	*Scotland*	*NI*	*UK*
Nursery and primary schools	199.9	13.5	24.2	8.0	245.6
Secondary schools	204.9*	12.7	23.9	9.5	251.0
Special schools	14.5	0.7	2.0	0.8	18.0
Education elsewhere†	7.8	–	–	–	7.8
Total	427.1	26.9	50.1	18.3	522.4

* Includes academies and city technology colleges in England
† Figure includes pupil referral units and is a separate statistic for England only

SUPPORT STAFF IN MAINTAINED SCHOOLS, ENGLAND AND WALES (2011–12)
Full-time equivalent, thousands

	England	*Wales*
Total support staff	370.1*	22.3
Teaching assistants	232.3	–
Other support staff	137.8*	–

* Includes academies and city technology colleges in England

ACADEMIC STAFF IN UK HIGHER EDUCATION INSTITUTIONS (2011–12)

	Full-time	*Part-time*	*Total*
Professors	15,955	2,505	18,465
Non-professors	101,890	61,035	162,925
Teaching only	8,620	37,205	45,825
Teaching and research	75,015	18,945	93,960
Research only	33,655	7,190	40,845
Neither teaching or research	560	195	755

Source: HESA 2013

SALARIES

State school teachers in England and Wales are employed by local authorities or the governing bodies of their schools, but their conditions and, currently, pay are set nationally.

There are teaching and learning responsibility payments for specific posts, special needs work and recruitment and retention factors which may be awarded at the discretion of the school governing body or the local authority. Schemes for 'Excellent Teachers' and 'Advanced Skills Teachers' came to an end in August 2013. Headteachers and other school leaders are paid on a separate leadership pay spine. All teachers are eligible for membership of the Teachers' Pension Scheme.

Academies are free to set their own salaries. In 2012, the average pay of full-time regular qualified classroom teachers in maintained secondary schools was £36,100 compared with £35,200 in secondary academies and £32,200 in maintained nursery and primary schools, compared with £31,100 in primary academies.

All teachers in England and Wales received a 1 per cent pay rise in September 2013, after the government accepted recommendations made by the School Teachers Review Body. From September 2013 every school will need to have revised its pay and appraisal policies, setting out how pay progression will, in future, be linked to a teacher's performance.

After completing initial teacher training (ITT) and achieving qualified teacher status (QTS), newly qualified teachers (NQTs) in maintained schools can expect to start on a salary of £21,588 a year in England and Wales (or £27,000 in inner London). As at September 2013 the pay ranges for teachers in England and Wales are:

Main pay range (including NQTs)	
London fringe	£22,626–£32,588
Outer London	£25,117–£35,116
Inner London	£27,000–£36,387
Rest of England and Wales	£21,588–£31,552
Upper pay range	
London fringe	£35,218–£37,795
Outer London	£37,599–£40,433
Inner London	£41,497–£45,000
Rest of England and Wales	£34,181–£36,756

Pay structures for teachers in Scotland were agreed up until April 2011 when pay was frozen until 31 March 2013. At the time of going to press, pay negotiations were still ongoing. Teachers are paid on a seven-point scale where the entry point is for newly qualified teachers undertaking their probationary year. There is no equivalent in Scotland of the upper pay spine operated in England and Wales. Experienced, ambitious teachers who reach the top of the main pay scale are eligible to become chartered teachers and earn more on a separate pay spine. However, to do so they must study for further professional qualifications. Headteachers and deputies have a separate pay spine as do 'principals' or heads of department. Additional allowances are payable to teachers under a range of circumstances, such as working in distant islands and remote schools.

As at September 2013, salary scales for teachers in Scotland remain at 2011 levels:

Headteacher/deputy headteacher	£42,288–£82,542
Principal teacher	£37,284–£48,120
Chartered teacher	£35,253–£41,925
Main grade	£21,438–£34,200

Teachers in Northern Ireland have broadly similar payscales to teachers in England and Wales, although there is neither an Advanced Skills Teacher grade nor an Excellent Teacher scheme. Classroom teachers who take on teaching and learning responsibilities outside their normal classroom duties may be awarded one of five teaching allowances.

Salary scales for teachers in Northern Ireland have been frozen since 2011, except for those earning £21,000 or less, who receive an increase of at least £250 a year. As at September 2013, salary scales in Northern Ireland are:

Principal (headteacher)	£42,379–£105,379
Classroom teacher (upper pay scale)	£34,181–£36,756
Classroom teacher (main pay scale)	£21,588–£31,552
Associate teachers	£13,734
Teaching allowances	£1,847–£11,911

Since 2007, most academic staff in HE across the UK are paid on a single national pay scale as a result of a national framework agreement negotiated by the HE unions and HE institutions. Staff are paid according to rates on a 51-point national pay spine and academic and academic-related staff are graded according to a national grading structure. In 2012–13 the pay spine ranged from £13,486 to £56,467. As HE institutions are autonomous employers, precise job grades and salaries may vary but the following table outlines salaries that typically tally with certain job roles in HE.

Principal lecturer	£45,941–£53,233
Senior lecturer	£36,298–£44,607
Lecturer	£30,424–£35,244
Junior researcher	£24,049–£29,541

UNIVERSITIES

The following is a list of universities, which are those institutions that have been granted degree awarding powers by either a royal charter or an act of parliament, or have been permitted to use the word 'university' (or 'university college') by the Privy Council. There are other recognised bodies in the UK with degree awarding powers, as well as institutions offering courses leading to a degree from a recognised body. Further information is available at W www.bis.gov.uk

Student figures represent the number of undergraduate and postgraduate students based on information available at May 2013.

For information on tuition fees and student loans, *see* Education, Higher Education.

RESEARCH ASSESSMENT EXERCISE

The research assessment exercise (RAE) gives a rating to each university department or specialist college put forward for evaluation, based on the quality of its research. It enables the higher education funding bodies to distribute public funds for research selectively on the basis of quality. Institutions conducting the best research receive a larger proportion of the available grant so that the infrastructure for the top level of research in the UK is protected and developed. The table below shows the top five universities or specialist colleges for each discipline based on the mean average ranking of the overall quality of their research. The research excellence framework (REF) is the new system for assessing the quality of research in UK higher education institutions. It will replace the RAE and will be completed in 2014.

Subject	*Universities or university colleges*
Anthropology	LSE (1), SOAS (1), Cambridge (3), Roehampton (4), UCL (5)
Archaeology	Durham (1), Reading (2), Cambridge (3), Oxford (3), Liverpool (5)
Biological sciences	Institute of Cancer Research (1), Manchester (2), Oxford (2), Sheffield (2), Dundee (5), RHUL (5)
Business and management	London Business School (1), Imperial (2), Cambridge (3), Cardiff (4), Bath (5), King's (5), Lancaster (5), LSE (5), Oxford (5), Warwick (5)
Chemistry	Cambridge (1), Nottingham (2), Oxford (3), Bristol (4), Edinburgh (4), St Andrews (4)
Classics	Cambridge (1), Oxford (2), UCL (3), Durham (4), King's (4), Warwick (4)
Communication and media studies	Westminster (1), East Anglia (2), Goldsmiths (3), LSE (3), Cardiff (5)
Computer science	Cambridge (1), Edinburgh (2), Imperial (2), Southampton (2), Manchester (5), Oxford (5), UCL (5)
Dentistry	Manchester (1), Queen Mary (2), King's (3), Sheffield (4), Bristol (5), Cardiff (5)
Drama and performing arts	Queen Mary (1), St Andrews (1), Manchester (3), Warwick (4), Bristol (5), King's (5)
Economics	LSE (1), UCL (2), Essex (3), Oxford (3), Warwick (3)
Engineering (electronic)	Leeds (1), Bangor (2), Manchester (2), Surrey (2), Imperial (5)
Engineering (general)	Cambridge (1), Oxford (2), Leeds (3), Nottingham (3), Imperial (5), Swansea (5)
English	York (1), Edinburgh (2), Manchester (2), Queen Mary (2), Exeter (5), Nottingham (5), Oxford (5)
French	Oxford (1), King's (2), Warwick (2), Aberdeen (4), Cambridge (4), St Andrews (4)
Geography	Bristol (1), Cambridge (1), Durham (1), Oxford (1), Queen Mary (1)
German, Dutch and Scandinavian	Oxford (1), Cambridge (2), Durham (2), King's (2), Leeds (2), RHUL (2), St Andrews (2)
History	Imperial (1), Essex (2), Kent (2), Liverpool (2), Oxford (2), Warwick (2)
Law	LSE (1), UCL (2), Oxford (3), Durham (4), Nottingham (4)
Mathematics (applied)	Cambridge (1), Oxford (1), Bristol (3), Bath (4), Portsmouth (4), St Andrews (4)
Mathematics (pure)	Imperial (1), Warwick (2), Oxford (3), Cambridge (4), Bristol (5), Edinburgh (5), Heriot-Watt (5)
Music	RHUL (1), Birmingham (2), Manchester (2), Cambridge (4), King's (4), Sheffield (4), Southampton (4)
Philosophy	UCL (1), St Andrews (1), King's (3), Reading (3), Sheffield (3)
Physics	Lancaster (1), Bath (2), Cambridge (2), Nottingham (2), St Andrews (2)
Politics	Essex (1), Sheffield (1), Aberystwyth (3), Oxford (4), LSE (5)
Psychology	Cambridge (1), Oxford (2), Birmingham (3), UCL (4), Birkbeck (5), Cardiff (5)
Sociology	Essex (1), Goldsmiths (1), Manchester (1), York (1), Lancaster (5)
Sports-related subjects	Birmingham (1), Loughborough (1), Bristol (3), Liverpool John Moores (4), Stirling (5)
Theology and religious studies	Durham (1), Aberdeen (2), Cambridge (3), Oxford (3), UCL (3)

UG= undergraduate PG= postgraduate

UNIVERSITY OF ABERDEEN (1495)

King's College, Aberdeen AB24 3FX T 01224-272000
W www.abdn.ac.uk
Fee: £9,000 *Students:* 11,955 UG; 3,560 PG
Chancellor, HRH the Duchess of Rothesay
Vice-Chancellor, Prof. Ian Diamond
University Secretary, Steve Cannon

UNIVERSITY OF ABERTAY DUNDEE (1994)

Bell Street, Dundee DD1 1HG T 01382-308000
W www.abertay.ac.uk
Fee: £7,000 *Students:* 4,402 UG; 416 PG
Chancellor, Lord Cullen of Whitekirk, KT, PC, FRSE
Vice-Chancellor, Prof. Nigel Seaton, FRENG
Registrar, Dr Colin Fraser, PHD

ANGLIA RUSKIN UNIVERSITY (1992)

Chelmsford Campus, Bishop Hall Lane, Chelmsford, Essex CM1 1SQ T 0845-271 3333 W www.anglia.ac.uk
Fee: £9,000 *Students:* 24,000 UG; 7,000 PG

Chancellor, Lord Ashcroft, KCMG
Vice-Chancellor, Prof. Michael Thorne, FRS, PHD
Secretary and Clerk, Stephen Bennett

UNIVERSITY OF THE ARTS LONDON (Formerly The London Institute (1986), University of the Arts London was formed in 2004)
272 High Holborn, London WC1V 7EY T 020-7514 6000
W www.arts.ac.uk
Fee: £9,000 *Students:* 13,925 UG; 3,375 PG
Chancellor, Kwame Kwei-Armah
Rector, Nigel Carrington
Secretary and Registrar, Stephen Marshall

COLLEGES
CAMBERWELL COLLEGE OF ARTS (1898)
Peckham Road, London SE5 8UF T 020-7514 6302
W www.camberwell.arts.ac.uk
Head of College, Prof. Chris Wainwright
CENTRAL SAINT MARTINS COLLEGE OF ART & DESIGN (1854)
Granary Building, 1 Granary Square, London N1C 4AA
T 020-7514 7000 W www.csm.arts.ac.uk
Head of College, Jeremy Till
CHELSEA COLLEGE OF ART & DESIGN (1895)
Millbank, London SW1P 4JU T 020-7514 7751
W www.chelsea.arts.ac.uk
Head of College, Prof. Chris Wainwright
LONDON COLLEGE OF COMMUNICATION (1894)
Elephant & Castle, London SE1 6SB T 020-7514 6569
W www.lcc.arts.ac.uk
Head of College, Natalie Brett
LONDON COLLEGE OF FASHION (1963)
20 John Princes Street, London W1G 0BJ T 020-7514 7344
W www.fashion.arts.ac.uk
Head of College, Prof. Frances Corner
WIMBLEDON COLLEGE OF ART (1930)
Merton Hall Road, London SW19 3QA T 020-7514 9641
W www.wimbledon.arts.ac.uk
Head of College, Chris Wainwright

ASTON UNIVERSITY (1966)
Aston Triangle, Birmingham B4 7ET T 0121-204 3000
W www.aston.ac.uk
Fee: £9,000 *Students:* 7,930 UG; 2,275 PG
Chancellor, Sir John Sunderland
Vice-Chancellor, Prof. Dame Julia King, DBE, FRENG, FRSA
Registrar, John Walter

UNIVERSITY OF BATH (1966)
Bath BA2 7AY T 01225-388388 W www.bath.ac.uk
Fee: £9,000 *Students:* 10,690 UG; 4,759 PG
Chancellor, Lord Tugendhat
Vice-Chancellor, Prof. Dame Glynis Breakwell, DBE, FRSA
University Secretary, Mark Humphriss

BATH SPA UNIVERSITY (2005)
Newton Park, Newton St Loe, Bath BA2 9BN T 01225-875875
W www.bathspa.ac.uk
Fee: £9,000 *Students:* 5,715 UG; 2,835 PG
Vice-Chancellor, Prof. Christina Slade
Academic Registrar, Christopher Ellicott

UNIVERSITY OF BEDFORDSHIRE (1993)
University Square, Luton LU1 3JU T 01234-400400
W www.beds.ac.uk
Fee: £9,000 *Students:* 15,410 UG; 6,865 PG
Chancellor, Baroness Howells of St Davids, OBE
Vice-Chancellor, Bill Rammell
Registrar, Alice Hynes

UNIVERSITY OF BIRMINGHAM (1900)
Edgbaston, Birmingham B15 2TT T 0121-414 3344
W www.birmingham.ac.uk
Fee: £9,000 *Students:* 19,195 UG; 11,875 PG
Chancellor, Sir Dominic Cadbury (ret. 31 Dec 2013)
Vice-Chancellor and Principal, Prof. David Eastwood
Registrar and Secretary, Lee Sanders

BIRMINGHAM CITY UNIVERSITY (1992)
City North Campus, Birmingham B42 2SU T 0121-331 5000
W www.bcu.ac.uk
Fee: £9,000 *Students:* 19,525 UG; 3,645 PG
Chancellor, Lord Mayor of Birmingham, John Lines
Vice-Chancellor, Prof. Cliff Allan
University Secretary, Ms Christine Abbott

UNIVERSITY OF BOLTON (2005)
Deane Road, Bolton BL3 5AB T 01204-900600
W www.bolton.ac.uk
Fee: £8,400 *Students:* 6,088 UG; 1,611 PG
Chancellor, Rt. Hon. Baroness Morris of Bolton, OBE, DPHIL, LLD
Vice-Chancellor, Dr George Holmes, PHD
Registrar and Secretary, Sue Duncan

BOURNEMOUTH UNIVERSITY (1992)
Fern Barrow, Poole, Dorset BH12 5BB T 01202-524111
W www.bournemouth.ac.uk
Fee: £9,000 *Students:* 14,682 UG; 2,001 PG
Chancellor, Rt. Hon. Lord Phillips of Worth Matravers, PC, QC
Vice-Chancellor, Prof. John Vinney
Clerk, Noel Richardson

UNIVERSITY OF BRADFORD (1966)
Bradford, W. Yorks BD7 1DP T 0800-073 1225
W www.bradford.ac.uk
Fee: £9,000 *Students:* 10,569 UG; 4,048 PG
Chancellor, Imran Khan
Vice-Chancellor and Principal, Prof. Brian Cantor, CBE
University Secretary, Adrian Pearce

UNIVERSITY OF BRIGHTON (1992)
Mithras House, Lewes Road, Brighton BN2 4AT T 01273-600900
W www.bton.ac.uk
Fee: £9,000 *Students:* 16,948 UG; 4,249 PG
Chairman, Lord Mogg, KCMG
Vice-Chancellor, Prof. Julian Crampton
Registrar, Carol Burns

UNIVERSITY OF BRISTOL (1909)
Senate House, Tyndall Avenue, Bristol BS8 1TH T 0117-928 9000
W www.bris.ac.uk
Fee: £9,000 *Students:* 13,435 UG; 5,710 PG
Chancellor, Rt. Hon. Baroness Hale of Richmond, DBE, PC
Vice-Chancellor, Prof. Eric Thomas
Registrar, Robin Geller

BRUNEL UNIVERSITY (1966)
Uxbridge, Middx UB8 3PH T 01895-274000 W www.brunel.ac.uk
Fee: £9,000 *Students:* 9,888 UG; 3,552 PG
Chancellor, Sir Richard Sykes
Vice-Chancellor, Prof. Julia Buckingham
Registrar, Sue Gemmill

UNIVERSITY OF BUCKINGHAM (1983)
Buckingham MK18 1EG T 01280-814080
W www.buckingham.ac.uk
Fee: £5,980 *Students:* 1,083 UG; 470 PG

Chancellor, Lord Tanlaw
Vice-Chancellor, Prof. Terence Kealey, DPHIL
Registrar, Anne Miller

BUCKINGHAMSHIRE NEW UNIVERSITY (2007)
High Wycombe Campus, Queen Alexandra Road, High Wycombe HP11 2JZ T 0800-0565 660 W www.bucks.ac.uk
Fee: £8,000 *Students:* 7,745 UG; 785 PG
Vice-Chancellor, Prof. Ruth Farwell
Director of Academic Quality, Ellie Smith

UNIVERSITY OF CAMBRIDGE (1209)
The Old Schools, Trinity Lane, Cambridge CB2 1TN
T 01223-337733 W www.cam.ac.uk
Fee: £9,000 *Students:* 11,925 UG; 6,470 PG
Chancellor, Lord Sainsbury of Turville, FRS (King's)
Vice-Chancellor, Prof. Sir Leszek Borysiewicz, FRS (Wolfson)
High Steward, Lord Watson of Richmond, CBE (Jesus)
Deputy High Steward, Mrs A. Lonsdale, CBE (Murray Edwards)
Commissary, Lord Mackay of Clashfern, KT, PC, FRSE (Trinity)
Pro-Vice-Chancellors, Dr J. C. Barnes (Murray Edwards); Prof. L. F. Gladden, CBE, FRS (Trinity); Prof. J. M. Rallison (Trinity); Prof. J. K. M. Sanders, FRS (Selwyn); Prof. S. J. Young, FRENG (Emmanuel)
Proctors, Revd Dr J. M. Holmes (Queens'); R. K. Taplin, MBE (Downing)
Orator, Dr R. J. E. Thompson (Selwyn)
Registrar, Dr J. W. Nicholls (Emmanuel)
Librarian, Mrs A. E. Jarvis (Wolfson)
Director of the Fitzwilliam Museum, T. Knox (Gonville and Caius)
Academic Secretary, G. P. Allen (Wolfson)
Director of Finance, A. M. Reid (Wolfson)
Executive Director of Development, Ms A. Traub
Esquire Bedells, Mrs N. Hardy (Jesus); Ms S. V. Scarlett (Lucy Cavendish)
University Advocate, Dr R. E. Thornton (Emmanuel)

COLLEGES AND HALLS *with dates of foundation*
CHRIST'S (1505)
Master, Prof. F. P. Kelly, CBE, FRS
CHURCHILL (1960)
Master, Prof. Sir David Wallace, CBE, FRS
CLARE (1326)
Master, Prof. A. J. Badger
CLARE HALL (1966)
President, Prof. D. J. Ibbetson, FBA
CORPUS CHRISTI (1352)
Master, Mr S. Laing
DARWIN (1964)
Master, C. M. R. Fowler
DOWNING (1800)
Master, Prof. G. R. Grimmett
EMMANUEL (1584)
Master, Dame Fiona Reynolds, DBE
FITZWILLIAM (1966)
Master, Mrs N. M. Padfield
GIRTON (1869)
Mistress, Prof. S. J. Smith, FBA
GONVILLE AND CAIUS (1348)
Master, Prof. Sir Alan Fersht, FRS
HOMERTON (1824)
Principal, Prof. G. Ward
HUGHES HALL (1885)
President, Mrs S. L. Squire
JESUS (1496)
Master, Prof. I. H. White
KING'S (1441)
Provost, Prof. M. R. E. Proctor, FRS
LUCY CAVENDISH (1965)
President, Prof. J. M. Todd, OBE
MAGDALENE (1542)
Master, Rt. Revd Lord Williams of Oystermouth, PC, DPHIL, FRSL, FBA
MURRAY EDWARDS (1954)
President, Dame Barbara Stocking, DBE
NEWNHAM (1871)
Principal, Prof. Dame Carol Black, DBE, FRCP
PEMBROKE (1347)
Master, Sir Richard Dearlove, KCMG, OBE
PETERHOUSE (1284)
Master, Prof. A. K. Dixon, FRCP
QUEENS' (1448)
President, Prof. Lord Eatwell
ROBINSON (1977)
Warden, Prof. A. D. Yates
ST CATHARINE'S (1473)
Master, Prof. Dame Jean Thomas, DBE, FRS
ST EDMUND'S (1896)
Master, Prof. J. P. Luzio, FRCPATH
ST JOHN'S (1511)
Master, Prof. C. M. Dobson, FRS
SELWYN (1882)
Master, Prof. R. J. Bowring
SIDNEY SUSSEX (1596)
Master, Prof. R. V. Penty
TRINITY (1546)
Master, Sir Gregory Winter, CBE, FRS
TRINITY HALL (1350)
Master, Prof. M. J. Daunton, FBA
WOLFSON (1965)
President, Prof. Sir Richard Evans, FBA

CANTERBURY CHRIST CHURCH UNIVERSITY (2005)
North Holmes Road, Canterbury CT1 1QU T 01227-767700 W www.canterbury.ac.uk
Fee: £8,500 *Students:* 17,948 UG; 3,960 PG
Chancellor, Rt. Revd and Rt. Hon. Justin Welby
Vice-Chancellor (acting), Andrew Ironside
Academic Registrar, Lorri Curri

CARDIFF METROPOLITAN UNIVERSITY (2011)
Western Avenue, Cardiff CF5 2YB T 029-2041 6138 W www.cardiffmet.ac.uk
Fee: £9,000 *Students:* 8,410 UG; 4,600 PG
Vice-Chancellor and Principal, Prof. Anthony Chapman

CARDIFF UNIVERSITY (1883)
Cardiff CF10 3XQ T 029-2087 4000 W www.cardiff.ac.uk
Fee: £9,000 *Students:* 20,611 UG; 7,133 PG
Chancellor, Prof. Sir Martin Evans, FRS
Vice-Chancellor, Prof. Colin Riordan
Chief Operating Officer, Hugh Jones

UNIVERSITY OF CENTRAL LANCASHIRE (1992)
Preston PR1 2HE T 01772-201201 W www.uclan.ac.uk
Fee: £9,000 *Students:* 27,010 UG; 4,520 PG
Chancellor, Sir Richard Evans, CBE
Vice-Chancellor, Prof. Malcolm McVicar

UNIVERSITY OF CHESTER (2005)
Parkgate Road, Chester CH1 4BJ T 01244-511000 W www.chester.ac.uk
Fee: £9,000 *Students:* 17,800 UG; 4,800 PG
Chancellor, Duke of Westminster, KG, CB, CVO

Vice-Chancellor, Canon Prof. Tim Wheeler
Registrar, Jonathan Moores

UNIVERSITY OF CHICHESTER (2005)
College Lane, Chichester PO19 6PE T 01243-816000
W www.chi.ac.uk
Fee: £8,500 *Students:* 4,730 UG; 910 PG
Vice-Chancellor, Prof. Clive Behagg, PHD
Secretary, Isabel Cherrett

CITY UNIVERSITY LONDON (1966)
Northampton Square, London EC1V 0HB T 020-7040 5060
W www.city.ac.uk
Fee: £9,000 *Students:* 10,130 UG; 9,210 PG
Chancellor, Roger Gifford
Vice-Chancellor, Prof. Paul Curran
Secretary, Frank Toop

COVENTRY UNIVERSITY (1992)
Priory Street, Coventry CV1 5FB T 024-7688 7688
W www.coventry.ac.uk
Fee: £9,000 *Students:* 20,000 UG; 1,000 PG
Chancellor, Sir John Egan
Vice-Chancellor, Prof. Madeleine Atkins, CBE
Registrar, Kate Quantrell

CRANFIELD UNIVERSITY (1969)
Cranfield, Bedfordshire MK43 0AL T 01234-750111
W www.cranfield.ac.uk
Students: 2,000 PG (postgraduate only)
Chancellor, Baroness Young of Old Scone
Vice-Chancellor, Prof. Sir Peter Gregson
Registrar, Prof. William Stephens

UNIVERSITY FOR THE CREATIVE ARTS (2008)
Falkner Road, Farnham, Surrey GU9 7DS T 01252-722441
W www.ucreative.ac.uk
Fee: £8,500 *Students:* 5,460 UG; 295 PG
Chancellor, Zandra Rhodes, CBE
Vice-Chancellor, Dr Simon Ofield-Kerr
University Secretary, Marion Wilks

UNIVERSITY OF CUMBRIA (2007)
Fusehill Street, Carlisle CA1 2HH T 01228-616234
W www.cumbria.ac.uk
Fee: £9,000 *Students:* 8,935 UG; 1,775 PG
Chancellor, Most Revd and Rt. Hon. Dr John Sentamu, Archbishop of York
Vice-Chancellor, Prof. Peter Strike
Registrar and Secretary, Neil Harris

DE MONTFORT UNIVERSITY (1992)
The Gateway, Leicester LE1 9BH T 0845-945 4647
W www.dmu.ac.uk
Fee: £9,000 *Students:* 17,950 UG; 3,840 PG
Chancellor, Lord Waheed Alli
Vice-Chancellor, Prof. Dominic Shellard
Head of Academic Services, Jon Lees

UNIVERSITY OF DERBY (1992)
Kedleston Road, Derby DE22 1GB T 01332-590500
W www.derby.ac.uk
Fee: £9,000 *Students:* 15,540 UG; 2,955 PG
Chancellor, Duke of Devonshire, KCVO, CBE
Vice-Chancellor, Prof. John Coyne
Registrar, June Hughes

UNIVERSITY OF DUNDEE (1967)
Nethergate, Dundee DD1 4HN T 01382-383000
W www.dundee.ac.uk
Fee: £9,000 *Students:* 10,945 UG; 5,555 PG
Chancellor, Lord Patel, KT, FRSE
Vice-Chancellor and Principal, Prof. Pete Downes, OBE, FRSE
University Secretary, Dr Jim McGeorge

DURHAM UNIVERSITY (1832)
The Palatine Centre, Stockton Road, Durham DH1 3LE
T 0191-334 2000 W www.dur.ac.uk
Fee: £9,000 *Students:* 12,087 UG; 4,576 PG
Chancellor, Sir Thomas Allen, CBE
Vice-Chancellor, Prof. Christopher Higgins, FRSE, FMEDSCI
Acting Registrar and Treasurer, Paulina Lubacz

COLLEGES
COLLINGWOOD (1972)
Principal, Prof. J. Elliott
GREY
Master, Prof. T. Allen
HATFIELD (1846)
Master, Prof. T. P. Burt
JOHN SNOW (2001)
Principal, Prof. Carolyn Summerbell
JOSEPHINE BUTLER (2006)
Principal, A. Simpson
ST AIDAN'S
Principal, Dr Susan F. Frenk
ST CHAD'S (1904)
Principal, Revd Dr J. P. M. Cassidy
ST CUTHBERT'S SOCIETY (1888)
Principal, Prof. Elizabeth Archibald
ST HILD AND ST BEDE (1975)
Principal, Prof. Chris Hutchison
ST JOHN'S (1909)
Principal, Revd Dr D. Wilkinson
ST MARY'S
Principal, Prof. S. Hackett
STEPHENSON (2001)
Principal, Prof. John Ashworth
TREVELYAN (1966)
Principal, Prof. H. M. Evans
UNIVERSITY (1832)
Master, Prof. D. Held
USTINOV
Principal, Prof. Maggie O'Neill
VAN MILDERT (1965)
Master, Prof. D. Harper

UNIVERSITY OF EAST ANGLIA (1963)
Norwich Research Park, Norwich NR4 7TJ
T 01603-456161 W www.uea.ac.uk
Fee: £9,000 *Students:* 12,905 UG; 4,705 PG
Chancellor, Rose Tremain, CBE
Vice-Chancellor, Prof. Edward Acton
Registrar and Secretary, Brian Summers

UNIVERSITY OF EAST LONDON (1898)
University Way, London E16 2RD T 020-8223 3000
W www.uel.ac.uk
Fee: £9,000 *Students:* 17,070 UG; 6,155 PG
Acting Vice-Chancellor, Prof. John Joughin
Acting Deputy Vice-Chancellor, Dusty Amroliwala

EDGE HILL UNIVERSITY (2006)
St Helens Road, Ormskirk, Lancs L39 4QP T 01695-575171
W www.edgehill.ac.uk
Fee: £9,000 *Students:* 14,607 UG; 7,745 PG
Chancellor, Prof. Tanya Byron
Vice-Chancellor, Dr John Cater
Registrar, Ian Jones

UNIVERSITY OF EDINBURGH (1583)
Old College, South Bridge, Edinburgh EH8 9YL **T** 0131-650 1000
W www.ed.ac.uk
Fee: £9,000 *Students:* 18,970 UG; 8,705 PG
Chancellor, HRH the Princess Royal, KG, KT, GCVO
Vice-Chancellor and Principal, Prof. Sir Timothy O'Shea, FRSE
University Secretary, Sarah Smith

EDINBURGH NAPIER UNIVERSITY (1992)
Sighthill Campus, Edinburgh EH11 4BN **T** 0845-260 6040
W www.napier.ac.uk
Fee: £6,630 *Students:* 11,375 UG; 2,685 PG
Chancellor, Tim Waterstone
Vice-Chancellor, Prof. Dame Joan Stringer, DBE
Secretary, Dr Gerry Webber

UNIVERSITY OF ESSEX (1965)
Wivenhoe Park, Colchester CO4 3SQ **T** 01206-873333
W www.essex.ac.uk
Fee: £9,000 *Students:* 8,861 UG; 3,462 PG
Chancellor, Lord Phillips of Sudbury, OBE
Vice-Chancellor, Prof. Anthony Forster, DPHIL
Registrar, Bryn Morris

UNIVERSITY OF EXETER (1955)
Stocker Road, Exeter EX4 4PY **T** 01392-661000
W www.exeter.ac.uk
Fee: £9,000 *Students:* 14,179 UG; 3,835 PG
Chancellor, Baroness Floella Benjamin, OBE
Vice-Chancellor and Chief Executive, Prof. Sir Steve Smith, PHD
Chief Operating Officer, Dr Claire Baines

UNIVERSITY OF GLASGOW (1451)
University Avenue, Glasgow G12 8QQ **T** 0141-330 2000
W www.gla.ac.uk
Fee: £9,000 *Students:* 17,238 UG; 6,036 PG
Chancellor, Prof. Sir Kenneth Calman, KCB, MD, FRCS
Vice-Chancellor, Prof. Anton Muscatelli, FRSE
Secretary of Court, David Newall

GLASGOW CALEDONIAN UNIVERSITY (1993)
City Campus, Cowcaddens Road, Glasgow G4 0BA
T 0141-331 3000 **W** www.gcu.ac.uk
Fee: £7,000 *Students:* 12,228 UG; 2,173 PG
Chancellor, Prof. Muhammad Yunus
Vice-Chancellor, Prof. Pamela Gillies, CBE
Head of Student Administration Services, Stephen Lopez

UNIVERSITY OF GLOUCESTERSHIRE (2001)
The Park, Cheltenham GL50 2RH **T** 0844-801 0001
W www.glos.ac.uk
Fee: £8,250 *Students:* 6,900 UG; 1,894 PG
Chancellor, Baroness Fritchie
Vice-Chancellor, Stephen Marston
Company Secretary, Julie Thackray

UNIVERSITY OF GREENWICH (1992)
Old Royal Naval College, Park Row, Greenwich, London SE10 9LS
T 020-8331 8000 **W** www.gre.ac.uk
Fee: £9,000 *Students:* 21,040 UG; 5,400 PG
Chancellor, Lord Hart of Chilton
Vice-Chancellor, Prof. David Maguire
Secretary, Linda Cording

HERIOT-WATT UNIVERSITY (1966)
Edinburgh EH14 4AS **T** 0131-449 5111 **W** www.hw.ac.uk
Fee: £9,000 *Students:* 6,615 UG; 4,255 PG
Chancellor, Dr Robert Buchan
Vice-Chancellor and Principal, Prof. Steve Chapman, FRSE
Secretary, Ann Marie Dalton

UNIVERSITY OF HERTFORDSHIRE (1992)
College Lane, Hatfield, Herts AL10 9AB **T** 01707-284000
W www.herts.ac.uk
Fee: £9,000 *Students:* 18,340 UG; 4,010 PG
Chancellor, Marquess of Salisbury
Vice-Chancellor, Prof. Quintin McKellar, CBE
Registrar, Philip Waters

UNIVERSITY OF HUDDERSFIELD (1992)
Queensgate, Huddersfield HD1 3DH **T** 01484-422288
W www.hud.ac.uk
Fee: £7,950 *Students:* 16,276 UG; 4,997 PG
Chancellor, Prof. Sir Patrick Stewart, OBE
Vice-Chancellor, Prof. Bob Cryan, PHD, DSc
University Secretary, Tony Mears

UNIVERSITY OF HULL (1927)
Cottingham Road, Hull HU6 7RX **T** 01482-346311
W www.hull.ac.uk
Fee: £9,000 *Students:* 15,102 UG; 2,467 PG
Chancellor, Baroness Bottomley of Nettlestone, PC
Vice-Chancellor, Prof. Calie Pistorius, PHD
Registrar, Jeannette Strachan

IMPERIAL COLLEGE LONDON (1907)
South Kensington, London SW7 2AZ **T** 020-7589 5111
W www.imperial.ac.uk
Fee: £9,000 *Students:* 9,050 UG; 6,950 PG
Rector, Sir Keith O'Nions, FRS
Deputy Rector, Prof. Stephen Richardson
Academic Registrar, Nigel Wheatley

KEELE UNIVERSITY (1962)
Keele, Staffs ST5 5BG **T** 01782-732000 **W** www.keele.ac.uk
Fee: £9,000 *Students:* 7,702 UG; 2,459 PG
Chancellor, Jonathon Porritt, CBE
Vice-Chancellor, Prof. Nick Foskett, PHD
Director of Planning and Academic Administration, Dr Simone Clarke

UNIVERSITY OF KENT (1965)
Canterbury, Kent CT2 7NZ **T** 01227-764000 **W** www.kent.ac.uk
Fee: £9,000 *Students:* 15,925 UG; 2,955 PG
Chancellor, Sir Robert Worcester, KBE
Vice-Chancellor, Prof. Dame Julia Goodfellow, DBE, CBE, PHD
Academic Registrar, Jon Pink

KINGSTON UNIVERSITY (1992)
River House, 53–57 High Street, Kingston upon Thames, Surrey KT1 1LQ **T** 020-8417 9000 **W** www.kingston.ac.uk
Fee: £9,000 *Students:* 20,535 UG; 5,520 PG
Chancellor, Bonnie Greer, OBE
Vice-Chancellor, Prof. Julius Weinberg
Academic Registrar, Marie Sheehan

UNIVERSITY OF LANCASTER (1964)
Bailrigg, Lancaster LA1 4YW **T** 01524-65201 **W** www.lancs.ac.uk
Fee: £9,000 *Students:* 9,235 UG; 3,845 PG
Chancellor, Sir Christian Bonington, CBE
Vice-Chancellor, Prof. Mark E. Smith
University Secretary, Fiona Aiken

UNIVERSITY OF LEEDS (1904)
Leeds LS2 9JT **T** 0113-243 1751 **W** www.leeds.ac.uk
Fee: £9,000 *Students:* 23,803 UG; 7,001 PG
Chancellor, Lord Bragg, PC, LLD, DLITT, DCL
Vice-Chancellor, Sir Alan Langlands
Registrar, J. Roger Gair

LEEDS METROPOLITAN UNIVERSITY (1992)
City Campus, Leeds LS1 3HE T 0113-812 0000
W www.leedsmet.ac.uk
Fee: £8,500 *Students:* 23,745 UG; 4,240 PG
Chancellor, Sir Bob Murray, CBE
Vice-Chancellor, Prof. Susan Price
Secretary and Registrar, Jenny Share

LEEDS TRINTY UNIVERSITY (1966)
Brownberrie Lane, Leeds LS18 5HD T 0113-283 7100
W www.leedstrinity.ac.uk
Fee: £9,000 *Students:* 2,670 UG; 645 PG
Chancellor, Gabby Logan
Vice-Chancellor, Prof. Margaret House
Secretary, vacant

UNIVERSITY OF LEICESTER (1957)
University Road, Leicester LE1 7RH T 0116-252 2522
W www.le.ac.uk
Fee: £9,000 *Students:* 11,095 UG; 5,960 PG
Chancellor, Lord Grocott
Vice-Chancellor, Prof. Sir Robert Burgess, PHD
Registrar, Dave Hall

UNIVERSITY OF LINCOLN (1992)
Brayford Pool, Lincoln LN6 7TS T 01522-882000
W www.lincoln.ac.uk
Fee: £9,000 *Students:* 10,021 UG; 1,323 PG
Chancellor, Lord Adebowale, CBE
Vice-Chancellor, Prof. Mary Stuart
Registrar, Chris Spendlove

UNIVERSITY OF LIVERPOOL (1903)
Liverpool, Merseyside L69 7ZX T 0151-794 2000
W www.liv.ac.uk
Fee: £9,000 *Students:* 15,507 UG; 3,298 PG
Chancellor, Prof. Sir David King, CH, PC, FRCP
Vice-Chancellor, Prof. Sir Howard Newby, FRSA
Chief Operating Officer, Patrick Hackett

LIVERPOOL HOPE UNIVERSITY (2005)
Hope Park, Liverpool L16 9JD T 0151-291 3000
W www.hope.ac.uk
Fee: £9,000 *Students:* 5,760 UG; 1,985 PG
Chancellor, Baroness Cox, FRCN
Vice-Chancellor and Rector, Prof. Gerald Pillay, FRSA
University Secretary, Graham Donelan

LIVERPOOL JOHN MOORES UNIVERSITY (1992)
Kingsway House, 2nd Floor, Hatton Garden, Liverpool L3 2AJ
T 0151-231 2121 W www.ljmu.ac.uk
Fee: £9,000 *Students:* 20,430 UG; 4,025 PG
Chancellor, Rt. Hon. Sir Brian Leveson
Vice-Chancellor, Prof. Nigel Weatherill, FRENG, DSc
Secretary, Denise Tipping

UNIVERSITY OF LONDON (1836)
Senate House, Malet Street, London WC1E 7HU T 020-7862 8000
W www.london.ac.uk
Fee: £9,000
Chancellor, HRH the Princess Royal, KG, KT, GCVO
Vice-Chancellor, Prof. Sir Adrian Smith
Chair of the Board of Trustees, Dame Jenny Abramsky
University Secretary, Chris Cobb

COLLEGES

BIRKBECK COLLEGE
Malet Street, London WC1E 7HX
Students: 13,445 UG; 6,140 PG
President, Baroness Bakewell, DBE
Master, Prof. David Latchman

CENTRAL SCHOOL OF SPEECH AND DRAMA
Eton Avenue, London NW3 3HY
Students: 615 UG; 375 PG
President, Michael Grandage, CBE
Principal, Prof. Gavin Henderson, CBE

COURTAULD INSTITUTE OF ART
Somerset House, Strand, London WC2R 0RN
Students: 155 UG; 285 PG
Director, Prof. Deborah Swallow

GOLDSMITHS COLLEGE
New Cross, London SE14 6NW
Students, 5,210 UG; 3,255 PG
Warden, Pat Loughrey

HEYTHROP COLLEGE
Kensington Square, London W8 5HN
Students: 570 UG; 470 PG
Principal, Michael Holman, SJ

INSTITUTE OF CANCER RESEARCH
123 Old Brompton Road, London SW7 3RP
Students: 290 PG (postgraduate only)
Chief Executive, Prof. Alan Ashworth

INSTITUTE OF EDUCATION
20 Bedford Way, London WC1H 0AL
Students: 485 UG; 5,770 PG
Director, Prof. Chris Husbands

KING'S COLLEGE LONDON (includes Guy's, King's and St Thomas's Schools of Medicine, Dentistry and Biomedical Sciences)
Strand, London WC2R 2LS
Students: 15,755 UG; 10,705 PG
Principal, Prof. Sir Richard Trainor, KBE

LONDON BUSINESS SCHOOL
Regent's Park, London NW1 4SA
Students: 2,080 PG (postgraduate only)
Dean, Prof. Sir Andrew Likierman

LONDON SCHOOL OF ECONOMICS AND POLITICAL SCIENCE
Houghton Street, London WC2A 2AE
Students: 4,010 UG; 5,790 PG
Director, Prof. Craig Calhoun

LONDON SCHOOL OF HYGIENE AND TROPICAL MEDICINE
Keppel Street, London WC1E 7HT
Students: 1,250 PG (postgraduate only)
Director, Prof. Peter Piot

QUEEN MARY (incorporating St Bartholomew's and the London School of Medicine and Dentistry)
Mile End Road, London E1 4NS
Students: 11,200 UG; 3,660 PG
Principal, Prof. Simon Gaskell

ROYAL ACADEMY OF MUSIC
Marylebone Road, London NW1 5HT
Students: 335 UG; 410 PG
Principal, Prof. Jonathan Freeman-Attwood

ROYAL HOLLOWAY
Egham Hill, Egham, Surrey TW20 0EX
Students: 7,355 UG; 2,510 PG
Principal, Prof. Paul Layzell

ROYAL VETERINARY COLLEGE
Royal College Street, London NW1 0TU
Students: 1,575 UG; 545 PG
Principal, Prof. Stuart Reid

ST GEORGE'S
Cranmer Terrace, London SW17 0RE
Students: 4,410 UG; 705 PG
Principal, Prof. Peter Kopelman

SCHOOL OF ORIENTAL AND AFRICAN STUDIES
Thornhaugh Street, Russell Square, London WC1H 0XG
Students: 2,970 UG; 2,430 PG
Director, Prof. Paul Webley

UNIVERSITY COLLEGE LONDON (including UCL Medical School and School of Pharmacy)
Gower Street, London WC1E 6BT
Students: 13,495 UG; 12,030 PG
Provost and President, Prof. Malcolm Grant, CBE

INSTITUTES

INSTITUTE OF ADVANCED LEGAL STUDIES
Charles Clore House, 17 Russell Square, London WC1B 5DR
Dean and Chief Executive, Prof. Roger Kain, CBE, FBA

INSTITUTE OF CLASSICAL STUDIES
Senate House, Malet Street, London WC1E 7HU
Director, Prof. John North

INSTITUTE OF COMMONWEALTH STUDIES
Senate House, Malet Street, London WC1E 7HU
Director, Prof. Philip Murphy

INSTITUTE OF ENGLISH STUDIES
Senate House, Malet Street, London WC1E 7HU
Director, Prof. Warwick Gould, FRSL

INSTITUTE OF GERMANIC AND ROMANCE STUDIES
Senate House, Malet Street, London WC1E 7HU
Director, Prof. Bill Marshall

INSTITUTE OF HISTORICAL RESEARCH
Senate House, Malet Street, London WC1E 7HU
Director, Prof. Miles Taylor

INSTITUTE OF MUSICAL RESEARCH
Senate House, Malet Street, London WC1E 7HU
Director, Dr Paul Archbold

INSTITUTE OF PHILOSOPHY
Senate House, Malet Street, London WC1E 7HU
Director, Prof. Barry Smith

INSTITUTE FOR THE STUDY OF THE AMERICAS
Senate House, Malet Street, London WC1E 7HU
Director, Prof. Linda Newson

SCHOOL OF ADVANCED STUDY
Senate House, Malet Street, London WC1E 7HU
Dean and Chief Executive, Prof. Roger Kain, CBE, FBA

UNIVERSITY OF LONDON INSTITUTE IN PARIS
9–11 rue de Constantine, 75340 Paris Cedex 07, France
Dean, Prof. Andrew Hussey, OBE

UNIVERSITY MARINE BIOLOGICAL STATION
Millport, Isle of Cumbrae KA28 0EG
Acting Director, Dr Fiona Hannah

WARBURG INSTITUTE
Woburn Square, London WC1H 0AB
Director, Prof. Peter Mack

LONDON METROPOLITAN UNIVERSITY (2002)
166–220 Holloway Road, London N7 8DB T 020-7423 0000
W www.londonmet.ac.uk
Fee: £9,000 *Students:* 17,705 UG; 5,575 PG
Patron, HRH the Duke of York, KG, GCVO, ADC(P)
Vice-Chancellor, Prof. Malcolm Gillies
University Secretary, Alison Wells

LONDON SOUTH BANK UNIVERSITY (1992)
103 Borough Road, London SE1 0AA T 020-7815 7815
W www.lsbu.ac.uk
Fee: £8,450 *Students:* 18,276 UG; 5,074 PG
Chancellor, Richard Farleigh
Vice-Chancellor, Martin Earwicker
Academic Registrar, Andrew Fischer

LOUGHBOROUGH UNIVERSITY (1966)
Ashby Road, Loughborough, Leics LE11 3TU T 01509-263171
W www.lboro.ac.uk
Fee: £9,000 *Students:* 11,467 UG; 3,984 PG
Chancellor, Sir Nigel Rudd, CBE, FRSE, PHD
Vice-Chancellor and President, Prof. Robert Allison
Chief Operating Officer, Andrew Burgess

UNIVERSITY OF MANCHESTER (2004)
Oxford Road, Manchester M13 9PL T 0161-306 6000
W www.manchester.ac.uk
Fee: £9,000 *Students:* 27,996 UG; 11,957 PG
Chancellor, Tom Bloxham, MBE
Vice-Chancellor, Prof. Dame Nancy Rothwell, FRS
Registrar, Will Spinks

MANCHESTER METROPOLITAN UNIVERSITY (1992)
All Saints, Manchester M15 6BH T 0161-247 2000
W www.mmu.ac.uk
Fee: £9,000 *Students:* 28,005 UG; 6,425 PG
Chancellor, Dianne Thompson, CBE, FRSA
Vice-Chancellor, Prof. John Brooks, DSc
Registrar, Gwyn Arnold

MIDDLESEX UNIVERSITY (1992)
Hendon Campus, The Burroughs, London NW4 4BT
T 020-8411 5555 W www.mdx.ac.uk
Fee: £9,000 *Students:* 18,365 UG; 5,175 PG
Chancellor, Lord Sheppard of Didgemere, KCVO
Vice-Chancellor, Prof. Michael Driscoll

NEWCASTLE UNIVERSITY (1963)
Newcastle upon Tyne NE1 7RU T 0191-222 6000 W www.ncl.ac.uk
Fee: £9,000 *Students:* 15,778 UG; 5,600 PG
Chancellor, Prof. Sir Liam Donaldson
Vice-Chancellor, Prof. Chris Brink, FRS, DPHIL
Registrar, Dr John Hogan

UNIVERSITY OF NORTHAMPTON (2005)
Park Campus, Boughton Green Road, Northampton NN2 7AL
T 01604-735500 W www.northampton.ac.uk
Fee: £8,750 *Students:* 9,561 UG; 750 PG
Chancellor, Baroness Falkner of Margravine
Vice-Chancellor, Prof. Nick Petford, PHD, DSc
Interim Director of Academic Services, Philip Henry

NORTHUMBRIA UNIVERSITY AT NEWCASTLE (1992)
Ellison Building, Ellison Place, Newcastle upon Tyne NE1 8ST
T 0191-232 6002 W www.northumbria.ac.uk
Fee: £9,000 *Students:* 28,780 UG; 5,758 PG
Chancellor, Lord Stevens of Kirkwhelpington, QPM
Vice-Chancellor, Prof. Andrew Wathey, FRSA, DPHIL
Director of Academic Services, Prof. Jane Core

UNIVERSITY OF NOTTINGHAM (1948)
University Park, Nottingham NG7 2RD T 0115-951 5151
W www.nottingham.ac.uk
Fee: £9,000 *Students:* 32,803 UG; 9,166 PG
Chancellor, Sir Andrew Witty
Vice-Chancellor, Prof. David Greenaway
Registrar, Dr Paul Greatrix

NOTTINGHAM TRENT UNIVERSITY (1992)
Burton Street, Nottingham NG1 4BU T 0115-941 8418
W www.ntu.ac.uk
Fee: £8,750 *Students:* 22,426 UG; 8,750 PG
Chancellor, Sir Michael Parkinson, CBE
Vice-Chancellor, Prof. Neil Gorman, PHD
Registrar, David Samson

OPEN UNIVERSITY (1969)
Walton Hall, Milton Keynes MK7 6AA T 01908-274066
W www.open.ac.uk
Fee: £6,000 *Students:* 188,920 UG; 12,350 PG
Chancellor, Lord Puttnam, CBE
Vice-Chancellor, Martin Bean
University Secretary, Fraser Woodburn

UNIVERSITY OF OXFORD (*c.*12th century)
University Offices, Wellington Square, Oxford OX1 2JD
T 01865-270000 W www.ox.ac.uk
Fee: £9,000 *Students:* 11,832 UG; 9,857 PG
Chancellor, Lord Patten of Barnes, CH, PC (Balliol, St Antony's)
Vice-Chancellor, Prof. Andrew Hamilton, FRS (Harris Manchester, Kellogg, Wolfson)
Pro-Vice-Chancellors, Dr S. J. Goss (Wadham); Prof. W. James (Brasenose); Dr S. L. Mapstone (St Hilda's); Prof. J. N. P. Rawlins (Wolfson); Prof. I. A. Walmsley (St. Hugh's)
Registrar, Prof. E. G. McKendrick (Lady Margaret Hall)
Deputy Registrar, M. D. Sibly (St Anne's)
Public Orator, R. H. A. Jenkyns (Lady Margaret Hall)
Director of University Library Services and Bodley's Librarian, Dr S. E. Thomas (Balliol)
Director of the Ashmolean Museum, Prof. C. Brown (Worcester)
Keeper of Archives, S. Bailey (Linacre)
Director of Estates, P. Goffin
Director of Finance, G. F. B. Kerr (Keble)

COLLEGES AND HALLS *with dates of foundation*
ALL SOULS (1438)
Warden, Prof. Sir John Vickers, FBA
BALLIOL (1263)
Master, Prof. Sir Drummond Bone, FRSE
BLACKFRIARS (1221)
Regent, Very Revd Dr Simon Gaine
BRASENOSE (1509)
Principal, Prof. Alan K. Bowman, FBA, FSA
CAMPION HALL (1896)
Master, Revd Brendan Callaghan
CHRIST CHURCH (1546)
Dean, Very Revd Dr Christopher A. Lewis
CORPUS CHRISTI (1517)
President, Prof. Richard Carwardine, FBA
EXETER (1314)
Rector, Ms Frances Cairncross, CBE, FRSE
GREEN TEMPLETON (2008)
Principal, Prof. Sir David Watson
HARRIS MANCHESTER (1889)
Principal, Revd Dr Ralph Waller, FRSE
HERTFORD (1740)
Principal, Will Hutton
JESUS (1571)
Principal, Lord Krebs, FRS, FMEDSCI
KEBLE (1870)
Warden, Sir Jonathan Phillips, KCB
KELLOGG (1990)
President, Prof. Jonathan M. Michie
LADY MARGARET HALL (1878)
Principal, Dr Frances Lannon
LINACRE (1962)
Principal, Dr Nick Brown
LINCOLN (1427)
Rector, Prof. Henry Woudhuysen, FBA
MAGDALEN (1458)
President, Prof. David Clary, FRS
MANSFIELD (1886)
Principal, Baroness Helena Kennedy, QC
MERTON (1264)
Warden, Prof. Sir Martin Taylor, FRS
NEW COLLEGE (1379)
Warden, Prof. Sir Curtis Price, KBE
NUFFIELD (1958)
Warden, Andrew Dilnot, CBE
ORIEL (1326)
Provost, Moira Wallace, CBE
PEMBROKE (1624)
Master, Dame Lynne Brindley, DBE
QUEEN'S (1341)
Provost, Prof. Paul Madden, FRS, FRSE
REGENT'S PARK (1810)
Principal, Revd Dr Robert Ellis
ST ANNE'S (1878)
Principal, Tim Gardam
ST ANTONY'S (1953)
Warden, Prof. Margaret MacMillan
ST BENET'S HALL (1897)
Master, Prof. Werner Jeanrond
ST CATHERINE'S (1963)
Master, Prof. Roger Ainsworth
ST CROSS (1965)
Master, Sir Mark Jones, FRSE
ST EDMUND HALL (*c.*1278)
Principal, Prof. Keith Gull, CBE, FRS, FMEDSCI
ST HILDA'S (1893)
Principal, Sheila Forbes, CBE
ST HUGH'S (1886)
Principal, Dame Elish Angiolini, DBE, QC
ST JOHN'S (1555)
President, Prof. Margaret J. Snowling, FBA, FMEDSCI
ST PETER'S (1929)
Principal, Mark Damazer, CBE
ST STEPHEN'S HOUSE (1876)
Principal, Revd Dr Robin Ward
SOMERVILLE (1879)
Principal, Dr Alice Prochaska
TRINITY (1554)
President, Sir Ivor Roberts, KCMG
UNIVERSITY (1249)
Master, Sir Ivor Crewe
WADHAM (1610)
Warden, Lord Macdonald of River Glaven, QC
WOLFSON (1981)
President, Prof. Dame Hermione Lee, DBE, FBA, FRSL
WORCESTER (1714)
Provost, Prof. Jonathan Bate
WYCLIFFE HALL (1877)
Acting Principal, Revd Simon Vibert

OXFORD BROOKES UNIVERSITY (1992)
Gipsy Lane, Oxford OX3 0BP T 01865-741111
W www.brookes.ac.uk
Fee: £9,000 *Students:* 14,165 UG; 4,260 PG
Chancellor, Shami Chakrabarti, CBE
Vice-Chancellor, Prof. Janet Beer
Registrar, Paul Large

UNIVERSITY OF PLYMOUTH (1992)
Drake Circus, Plymouth PL4 8AA T 01752-600600
W www.plymouth.ac.uk
Fee: £9,000 *Students:* 24,384 UG; 3,225 PG
Vice-Chancellor and Chief Executive, Prof. Wendy Purcell
University Secretary, Jane Hopkinson

UNIVERSITY OF PORTSMOUTH (1992)
University House, Winston Churchill Avenue,
Portsmouth PO1 2UP T 023-9284 8484
W www.port.ac.uk
Fee: £9,000 *Students:* 22,700 UG; 4,000 PG
Chancellor, Sandi Toksvig
Vice-Chancellor, Prof. Graham Galbraith, PHD
Secretary, Sally Hartley

QUEEN MARGARET UNIVERSITY (2007)
Musselburgh, Edinburgh EH21 6UU T 0131-474 0000
W www.qmu.ac.uk
Fee: £6,750 *Students:* 3,485 UG; 1,765 PG
Chancellor, Sir Tom Farmer, CVO, CBE

Vice-Chancellor, Prof. Petra Wend, FRSA
Secretary, Irene Hynd

QUEEN'S UNIVERSITY BELFAST (1908)
University Road, Belfast BT7 1NN T 028-9024 5133
W www.qub.ac.uk
Fee: £9,000 *Students:* 17,886 UG; 5,121 PG
Chancellor, HE Kamalesh Sharma
Vice-Chancellor, Prof. Sir Peter Gregson, FRENG, MRIA
Registrar, James O'Kane

UNIVERSITY OF READING (1926)
Whiteknights, PO Box 217, Reading RG6 6AH T 0118-987 5123
W www.reading.ac.uk
Fee: £9,000 *Students:* 8,940 UG; 4,570 PG
Chancellor, Sir John Madejski, OBE
Vice-Chancellor, Sir David Bell, KCB
University Secretary, Keith Hodgson

ROBERT GORDON UNIVERSITY (1992)
Schoolhill, Aberdeen AB10 1FR T 01224-262000
W www.rgu.ac.uk
Fee: £9,663 *Students:* 15,753 UG; 6,064 PG
Chancellor, Sir Ian Wood, CBE
Vice-Chancellor, Prof. Ferdinand von Prondzynski
Academic Registrar, Hilary Douglas

ROEHAMPTON UNIVERSITY (2004)
Erasmus House, Roehampton Lane, London SW15 5PU
T 020-8392 3000 W www.roehampton.ac.uk
Fee: £8,500 *Students:* 6,179 UG; 969 PG
Chancellor, John Simpson, CBE
Vice-Chancellor, Prof. Paul O'Prey
Registrar, Laurence Benson

ROYAL COLLEGE OF ART (1967)
Kensington Gore, London SW7 2EU T 020-7590 4444
W www.rca.ac.uk
Fee: £9,000 *Students:* 1,250 PG (postgraduate only)
Provost, Sir James Dyson
Rector, Dr Paul Thompson
Academic Registrar, Corinne Smith

ROYAL COLLEGE OF MUSIC (1882)
Prince Consort Road, London SW7 2BS T 020-7591 4300
W www.rcm.ac.uk
Fee: £9,000 *Students:* 385 UG; 335 PG
President, HRH the Prince of Wales, KG, KT, GCB
Director, Prof. Colin Lawson, DMUS, FRCM
Deputy Director, Kevin Porter

UNIVERSITY OF ST ANDREWS (1413)
St Andrews, Fife KY16 9AJ T 01334-476161
W www.st-andrews.ac.uk
Fee: £9,000 *Students:* 7,795 UG; 2,055 PG
Chancellor, Sir Menzies Campbell, CBE, QC
Vice-Chancellor and Principal, Prof. Louise Richardson, FRSE
Academic Registrar, Ester Ruskuc

UNIVERSITY OF SALFORD (1967)
The Crescent, Salford, Greater Manchester M5 4WT
T 0161-295 5000 W www.salford.ac.uk
Fee: £9,000 *Students:* 15,109 UG; 4,119 PG
Chancellor, Dr Irene Khan
Vice-Chancellor, Prof. Martin Hall

UNIVERSITY OF SHEFFIELD (1905)
Western Bank, Sheffield S10 2TN T 0114-222 2000
W www.sheffield.ac.uk
Fee: £9,000 *Students:* 17,720 UG; 7,047 PG
Chancellor, Sir Peter Middleton, GCB
Vice-Chancellor, Prof. Sir Keith Burnett, CBE, DPHIL, FRS
Registrar and Secretary, Dr Philip Harvey

SHEFFIELD HALLAM UNIVERSITY (1992)
City Campus, Howard Street, Sheffield S1 1WB T 0114-225 5555
W www.shu.ac.uk
Fee: £9,000 *Students:* 26,819 UG; 6,430 PG
Chancellor, Prof. Lord Winston, DSc, FRCOG, FRCP
Vice-Chancellor, Prof. Philip Jones, LLB, LLM
Secretary & Registrar, Elizabeth Winders

UNIVERSITY OF SOUTH WALES (1992)
Pontypridd CF37 1DL T 0845-5767 778 W www.southwales.ac.uk
Fee: £9,000 *Students:* 25,175 UG; 5,250 PG
Chancellor, Lord Morris of Aberavon, KG, PC, QC
Vice-Chancellor, Julie Lydon
Registrar, William Callaway

UNIVERSITY OF SOUTHAMPTON (1952)
Building 37, Highfield, Southampton SO17 1BJ T 023-8059 5000
W www.soton.ac.uk
Fee: £9,000 *Students:* 16,500 UG; 6,850 PG
Chancellor, Dame Helen Alexander, DBE
Vice-Chancellor, Prof. Don Nutbeam
Registrar, Tessa Harrison

SOUTHAMPTON SOLENT UNIVERSITY (2005)
East Park Terrace, Southampton SO14 0YN T 023-8031 9000
W www.solent.ac.uk
Fee: £7,800 *Students:* 11,865 UG; 665 PG
Chancellor, Adm. Lord West of Spithead, GCB, DSC, PC
Vice-Chancellor, Prof. Van Gore

STAFFORDSHIRE UNIVERSITY (1992)
College Road, Stoke-on-Trent, Staffs ST4 2DE T 01782-294000
W www.staffs.ac.uk
Fee: £8,490 *Students:* 18,245 UG; 3,515 PG
Chancellor, vacant
Vice-Chancellor and Chief Executive, Prof. Michael Gunn
University Secretary, Ken Sproston

UNIVERSITY OF STIRLING (1967)
Stirling FK9 4LA T 01786-473171 W www.stir.ac.uk
Fee: £6,750 *Students:* 8,223 UG; 3,650 PG
Chancellor, Dr James Naughtie, OBE
Vice-Chancellor, Prof. Gerry McCormac, FRSE
University Secretary, Jocelyn Prudence

UNIVERSITY OF STRATHCLYDE (1964)
16 Richmond Street, Glasgow G1 1XQ T 0141-552 4400
W www.strath.ac.uk
Fee: £9,000 *Students:* 15,400 UG; 9,130 PG
Chancellor, Lord Smith of Kelvin
Vice-Chancellor, Prof. Sir Jim McDonald, FRENG, FRSE
Chief Operating Officer, Hugh Hall

UNIVERSITY OF SUNDERLAND (1992)
Edinburgh Building, Chester Road, Sunderland SR1 3SD
T 0191-515 2000 W www.sunderland.ac.uk
Fee: £8,500 *Students:* 14,620 UG; 2,760 PG
Chancellor, Steve Cram, MBE
Vice-Chancellor and Chief Executive, Prof. Peter Fidler

UNIVERSITY OF SURREY (1966)
Guildford, Surrey GU2 7XH T 01483-300800 W www.surrey.ac.uk
Fee: £9,000 *Students:* 10,695 UG; 4,360 PG
Chancellor, HRH the Duke of Kent, KG, GCMG, GCVO
Vice-Chancellor, Prof. Sir Christopher Snowden, FRS, FRENG
Registrar, Dr David Ashton

UNIVERSITY OF SUSSEX (1961)
Sussex House, Brighton BN1 9RH T 01273-606755
W www.sussex.ac.uk
Fee: £9,000 *Students:* 9,120 UG; 4,388 PG
Chancellor, Sanjeev Bhaskar, OBE
Vice-Chancellor, Prof. Michael Farthing, DSc, MD, FRCP
Academic Registrar, John Duffy

SWANSEA METROPOLITAN UNIVERSITY (2008)
Mount Pleasant, SA1 6ED T 01792-481000 W www.smu.ac.uk
Fee: £7,500 *Students:* 4,650 UG; 1,205 PG
Vice-Chancellor, Prof. Medwin Hughes

UNIVERSITY OF TEESSIDE (1992)
Middlesbrough, Tees Valley TS1 3BA T 01642-218121
W www.tees.ac.uk
Fee: £8,450 *Students:* 25,797 UG; 2,983 PG
Chancellor, Prof. Graham Henderson, CBE
Vice-Chancellor, Lord Sawyer
University Secretary, Morgan McClintock

UNIVERSITY OF ULSTER (1984)
Cromore Road, Coleraine, Co. Londonderry BT52 1SA
T 028-7012 3456 W www.ulster.ac.uk
Fee: £6,000 *Students:* 20,740 UG; 5,820 PG
Chancellor, James Nesbitt
Vice-Chancellor, Prof. Richard Barnett
Administrative Manager, Norma Cameron

UNIVERSITY OF WALES (1893)
King Edward VII Avenue, Cathays Park, Cardiff CF10 3NS
T 029-2037 6999 W www.wales.ac.uk
Fee: £9,000
Chancellor, HRH the Prince of Wales, KG, KT, GCB
Vice-Chancellor, Prof. Medwin Hughes

ACCREDITED INSTITUTIONS

ABERYSTWYTH UNIVERSITY
Penglais, Ceredigion SY23 3FL
T 01970-623111
Students: 9,910 UG; 1,795 PG
Vice-Chancellor, Prof. April McMahon, FRSE, FBA

BANGOR UNIVERSITY
Gwynedd LL57 2DG
T 01248-351151
Students: 8,435 UG; 2,820 PG
Vice-Chancellor, Prof. John Hughes

GLYNDWR UNIVERSITY
Mold Road, Wrexham LL11 2AW
T 01978-290666
Students: 8,120 UG; 1,415 PG
Vice-Chancellor, Prof. Michael Scott

SWANSEA UNIVERSITY
Singleton Park SA2 8PP
T 01792-205678
Students: 12,355 UG; 2,415 PG
Vice-Chancellor, Prof. Richard B. Davies

UNIVERSITY OF WALES, TRINITY SAINT DAVID
Carmarthen SA31 3EP
T 01267-676767
Students: 5,140 UG; 995 PG
Vice-Chancellor, Prof. Medwin Hughes

UNIVERSITY OF WARWICK (1965)
Coventry CV4 7AL T 024-7652 3523 W www.warwick.ac.uk
Fee: £9,000 *Students:* 17,025 UG; 10,420 PG
Chancellor, Sir Richard Lambert
Vice-Chancellor, Prof. Nigel Thrift, FBA, PHD, DSc
Registrar, Ken Sloan

UNIVERSITY OF WEST LONDON (1992)
St Mary's Road, Ealing, London W5 5RF T 020-8579 5000
W www.uwl.ac.uk
Fee: £8,200 *Students:* 10,995 UG; 1,405 PG
Chancellor, Laurence Geller
Vice-Chancellor, Prof. Peter John
University Secretary, Maureen Skinner

UNIVERSITY OF WESTMINSTER (1992)
309 Regent Street, London W1B 2HW T 020-7911 5000
W www.westminster.ac.uk
Fee: £9,000 *Students:* 16,665 UG; 4,840 PG
Chancellor, Lord Paul, PC
Vice-Chancellor and Rector, Prof. Geoffrey Petts
Registrar and Secretary, Carole Mainstone

UNIVERSITY OF THE WEST OF ENGLAND (1992)
Frenchay Campus, Coldharbour Lane, Bristol BS16 1QY
T 0117-965 6261 W www.uwe.ac.uk
Fee: £9,000 *Students:* 24,405 UG; 5,985 PG
Chancellor, Sir Ian Carruthers, OBE
Vice-Chancellor, Prof. Steve West
Academic Registrar, Andrea Cheshire

UNIVERSITY OF THE WEST OF SCOTLAND (1992)
Paisley PA1 2BE T 0141-848 3000 W www.uws.ac.uk
Fee: £7,250 *Students:* 13,613 UG; 1,570 PG
Chancellor, Dame Elish Angiolini, DBE, QC
Vice-Chancellor and Principal, Prof. Craig Mahoney
Registrar and Secretary, Donna McMillan

UNIVERSITY OF WINCHESTER (2005)
Winchester SO22 4NR T 01962-841515 W www.winchester.ac.uk
Fee: £8,500 *Students:* 5,400 UG; 930 PG
Chancellor, Dame Mary Fagan, DCVO
Vice-Chancellor, Prof. Joy Carter
Director of Student Recruitment and Marketing, Dr Karen Pendlebury

UNIVERSITY OF WOLVERHAMPTON (1988)
Wulfruna Street, Wolverhampton WV1 1LY T 01902-321000
W www.wlv.ac.uk
Fee: £8,650 *Students:* 18,179 UG; 4,474 PG
Chancellor, Lord Paul, PC
Vice-Chancellor, Prof. Geoff Layer, OBE, FRSA
Registrar, Helen Lloyd Wildman

UNIVERSITY OF WORCESTER (2005)
Henwick Grove, Worcester WR2 6AJ T 01905-855000
W www.worcester.ac.uk
Fee: £8,650 *Students:* 9,141 UG; 1,694 PG
Chancellor, HRH the Duke of Gloucester, KG, GCVO
Vice-Chancellor, Prof. David Green
Registrar, John Ryan

UNIVERSITY OF YORK (1963)
Heslington, York YO10 5DD T 01904-320000 W www.york.ac.uk
Fee: £9,000 *Students:* 11,352 UG; 3,382 PG
Chancellor, Greg Dyke
Vice-Chancellor, Prof. Brian Cantor, CBE, FRENG
Registrar, Dr David Duncan

YORK ST JOHN UNIVERSITY (2006)
Lord Mayor's Walk, York YO31 7EX T 01904-624624
W www.yorksj.ac.uk
Fee: £9,000 *Students:* 3,844 UG; 1,150 PG
Vice-Chancellor, Prof. David Fleming
Registrar, Alison Kennell

PROFESSIONAL EDUCATION

The organisations selected below provide specialist training, conduct examinations or are responsible for maintaining a register of those with professional qualifications in their sector, thereby controlling entry into a profession.

EU RECOGNITION

It is possible for those with professional qualifications obtained in the UK to have these recognised in other European countries. Further information can be obtained from:

UK NCP, Oriel House, Oriel Road, Cheltenham GL50 1XP
T 0871-330 7033 W www.ecctis.co.uk

ACCOUNTANCY

Salary range for chartered accountants:

Certified £15,000–£25,000 (starting) rising to £25,000–£45,000+ (qualified), £40,000–£100,000+ at senior levels
Management £29,000 (starting), £58,000 (average), £45,000–£120,000+ at senior levels
Public finance £18,00–£30,000 (starting), £32,000–£65,000 (qualified), £80,000+ at senior levels

Most chartered accountancy trainees are graduates, although some contracts are available to school-leavers. The undergraduate degree is followed by a three-year training contract with an approved employer culminating in professional exams provided by the Institute of Chartered Accountants in England and Wales (ICAEW), the Institute of Chartered Accountants of Scotland (ICAS) or the Institute of Chartered Accountants in Ireland (ICAI). Success in the examination and membership of one of the institutes allows the use of the designation 'chartered accountant' and the letters ACA or CA.

The Association of Chartered Certified Accountants (ACCA) is the global body for professional accountants. The ACCA aims to offer business-relevant qualifications to students in a range of business sectors and countries seeking a career in accountancy, finance and management. The ACCA Qualification consists of up to 14 examinations, practical experiences and a professional ethics module. Chartered certified accountants can use the designatory letters ACCA.

Chartered management accountants focus on accounting for businesses, and most do not work in accountancy practices but in industry, commerce, not-for-profit and public-sector organisations. Graduates who have not studied a business or accounting undergraduate degree must gain the Chartered Institute of Management Accountants (CIMA) Certificate in Business Accounting before studying for the CIMA Professional Qualification, which requires three years of practical experience, nine examinations and a pass in the Institute's Test of Professional Competence in Management Accounting (TOPCIMA). In May 2011, CIMA and the American Institute of Certified Public Accountants agreed on the creation of a new professional designation, the Chartered Global Management Accountant (CGMA), which will represent a worldwide standard of professional excellence in management accounting.

The Chartered Institute of Public Finance and Accountancy (CIPFA) is the professional body for people working in public finance. Chartered public finance accountants usually work for public bodies, but they can also work in the private sector. To gain chartered public finance accountant status (CPFA), trainees must complete a professional qualification in public sector accountancy. In addition, CIPFA also offers a postgraduate diploma for those already working in leadership positions.

ASSOCIATION OF CHARTERED CERTIFIED ACCOUNTANTS (ACCA), 29 Lincoln's Inn Fields, London WC2A 3EE T 020-7059 5000 E info@accaglobal.com W www.accaglobal.com
Chief Executive, Helen Brand

CHARTERED INSTITUTE OF MANAGEMENT ACCOUNTANTS (CIMA), 26 Chapter Street, London SW1P 4NP T 020-8849 2251 E cima.contact@cimaglobal.com W www.cimaglobal.com
Chief Executive, Charles Tilley

CHARTERED INSTITUTE OF PUBLIC FINANCE AND ACCOUNTANCY (CIPFA), 3 Robert Street, London WC2N 6RL T 020-7543 5600 E corporate@cipfa.org.uk W www.cipfa.org.uk
Chief Executive, Steve Freer

INSTITUTE OF CHARTERED ACCOUNTANTS IN ENGLAND AND WALES (ICAEW), Chartered Accountants' Hall, Moorgate Place, London EC2R 6EA T 020-7920 8100 E generalenquiries@icaew.com W www.icaew.com
Chief Executive, Michael Izza

INSTITUTE OF CHARTERED ACCOUNTANTS IN IRELAND (ICAI), 47–49 Pearse Street, Dublin T 0353-1637 7200 W www.charteredaccountants.ie
Chief Executive, Pat Costello

INSTITUTE OF CHARTERED ACCOUNTANTS OF SCOTLAND (ICAS), CA House, 21 Haymarket Yards, Edinburgh EH12 5BH T 0131-347 0100 E enquiries@icas.org.uk W www.icas.org.uk
Chief Executive, Anton Colella

ACTUARIAL SCIENCE

Salary range: £25,000–£35,000 for graduate trainees; £40,000–£55,000 after qualification; £60,000–£100,000+ for senior roles

Actuaries apply financial and statistical theories to solve business problems. These problems usually involve analysing future financial events in order to assess investment risks. To qualify, graduate trainees must complete 15 exams and three years worth of actuarial work-based training; most graduate trainees take between three and six years to qualify. Students can become Associate members of the Institute and Faculty of Actuaries (IFoA) and gain the right to describe themselves as an actuary and to use the letters AIA or AFA. Members of the profession who wish to continue their studies to an advanced level, or who specialise in a particular actuarial field, may take further specialist exams to qualify as a Fellow and bear the designations FIA or FFA.

The IFoA is the UK's chartered professional body dedicated to educating, developing and regulating actuaries based both in the UK and internationally. The IFoA represent and regulate their members and oversee their education at all stages of qualification and development throughout their careers.

The Financial Reporting Council (FRC) is the unified independent regulator for corporate reporting, auditing, actuarial practice, corporate governance and the professionalism of accountants and actuaries. The FRC's Board for Actuarial Standards sets and maintains technical actuarial standards independently of the profession, while the Professional Oversight Board of the FRC oversees the regulation of the accountancy and actuarial professions by their respective professional bodies. The Accountancy and Actuarial Discipline Board operates an investigation and discipline scheme in relation to members of the profession who raise issues affecting UK public interest.

FINANCIAL REPORTING COUNCIL (FRC), 5th Floor, Aldwych House, 71–91 Aldwych, London WC2B 4HN
T 020-7492 2300 E enquiries@frc.org.uk W www.frc.org.uk
Chief Executive, Stephen Haddrill

INSTITUTE AND FACULTY OF ACTUARIES, Staple Inn Hall, High Holborn, London WC1V 7QJ T 020-7632 2100
W www.actuaries.org.uk
Chief Executive, Derek Cribb

ARCHITECTURE

Salary range: £15,000–£26,000 during training; newly registered £26,000–£35,000; project architect and senior roles £35,000–£80,000+

It takes a minimum of seven years to become an architect, involving three stages: a three-year first degree, a two-year second degree or diploma and two years of professional experience followed by the successful completion of a professional practice examination.

The Architects Registration Board (ARB) is the independent regulator for the profession. It was set up by an act of parliament in 1997 and is responsible for maintaining the register of UK architects, prescribing qualifications that lead to registration as an architect, investigating complaints about the conduct and competence of architects, and ensuring that only those who are registered with ARB offer their services as an architect. It is only following registration with ARB that an architect can apply for chartered membership of the Royal Institute of British Architects (RIBA). RIBA, the UK body for architecture and the architectural profession, received its royal charter in 1837 and validates courses at over 40 schools of architecture in the UK; it also validates overseas courses. RIBA provides support and guidance for its members in the form of training, technical services and events and sets standards for the education of architects.

The Chartered Institute of Architectural Technologists is the international qualifying body for Chartered Architectural Technologists (MCIAT) and Architectural Technicians (TCIAT).

ARCHITECTS REGISTRATION BOARD (ARB) 8 Weymouth Street, London W1W 5BU T 020-7580 5861
E info@arb.org.uk W www.arb.org.uk
Registrar and Chief Executive, Alison Carr

CHARTERED INSTITUTE OF ARCHITECTURAL TECHNOLOGISTS 397 City Road, London EC1V 1NH
T 020-7278 2206 E info@ciat.org.uk W www.ciat.org.uk
Chief Executive, Francesca Berriman

ROYAL INCORPORATION OF ARCHITECTS IN SCOTLAND 15 Rutland Square, Edinburgh EH1 2BE
T 0131-229 7545 E info@rias.org.uk W www.rias.org.uk
Secretary, Neil Baxter

ROYAL INSTITUTE OF BRITISH ARCHITECTS (RIBA) 66 Portland Place, London W1B 1AD T 020-7580 5533
E info@riba.org W www.architecture.com
Chief Executive, Harry Rich

ENGINEERING

Salary range:
Civil/structural £23,000–£28,000 (graduate); £40,000–£80,000+ with experience (chartered status, in senior posts)
Chemical £28,000 average (graduate); £50,000 average–£70,000+ (chartered)
Electrical £20,000–£25,000 (graduate); £28,000–£38,000 with experience; £40,000–£50,000 (chartered)

The Engineering Council holds the national registers of Engineering Technicians (EngTech), Incorporated Engineers (IEng), Chartered Engineers (CEng) and Information and Communication Technology Technicians (ICT*Tech*). It also sets and maintains the internationally recognised standards of competence and ethics that govern the award and retention of these titles.

To apply for the EngTeach, IEng, CEng or ICT*Tech* titles, an individual must be a member of one of the 36 engineering institutions and societies (listed below) currently licensed by the Engineering Council to assess candidates. Applicants must demonstrate that they possess a range of technical and personal competences and are committed to keeping these up-to-date.

ENGINEERING COUNCIL, 246 High Holborn, London WC1V 7EX T 020-3206 0500 E info@engc.org.uk
W www.engc.org.uk
Chief Executive, Jon Prichard

LICENSED MEMBERS

BCS – The Chartered Institute for IT W www.bcs.org
British Institute of Non-Destructive Testing W www.bindt.org
Chartered Institute of Plumbing and Heating Engineering W www.ciphe.org.uk
Chartered Institution of Building Services Engineers W www.cibse.org
Chartered Institution of Highways and Transportation W www.ciht.org.uk
Chartered Institution of Water and Environmental Management W www.ciwem.org.uk
Energy Institute W www.energyinst.org.uk
Institute of Acoustics W www.ioa.org.uk
Institute of Cast Metals Engineers W www.icme.org.uk
Institute of Healthcare Engineering and Estate Management W www.iheem.org.uk
Institute of Highway Engineers W www.theihe.org
Institute of Marine Engineering, Science and Technology W www.imarest.org
Institute of Materials, Minerals and Mining W www.iom3.org
Institute of Measurement and Control W www.instmc.org.uk
Institute of Physics W www.iop.org
Institute of Physics and Engineering in Medicine W www.ipem.ac.uk
Institute of Water W www.instituteofwater.org.uk
Institution of Agricultural Engineers W www.iagre.org
Institution of Chemical Engineers W www.icheme.org
Institution of Civil Engineers W www.ice.org.uk
Institution of Diesel and Gas Turbine Engineers W www.idgte.org
Institution of Engineering Designers W www.ied.org.uk
Institution of Engineering and Technology W www.theiet.org
Institution of Fire Engineers W www.ife.org.uk
Institution of Gas Engineers and Managers W www.igem.org.uk
Institution of Lighting Professionals W www.theilp.org.uk
Institution of Mechanical Engineers W www.imeche.org
Institution of Railway Signal Engineers W www.irse.org
Institution of Royal Engineers W www.instre.org
Institution of Structural Engineers W www.istructe.org
Nuclear Institute W www.nuclearinst.com
Royal Aeronautical Society W www.aerosociety.com

Royal Institution of Naval Architects W www.rina.org.uk
Society of Environmental Engineers W www.environmental.org.uk
Society of Operations Engineers W www.soe.org.uk
Welding Institute W www.twiprofessional.com

HEALTHCARE

CHIROPRACTIC

Salary range: £20,000–£40,000 starting salary; with own practice £50,000–£70,000

Chiropractors diagnose and treat conditions caused by problems with joints, ligaments, tendons and nerves of the body. The General Chiropractic Council (GCC) is the independent statutory regulatory body for chiropractors and its role and remit is defined in the Chiropractors Act 1994. The GCC sets the criteria for the recognition of chiropractic degrees and for standards of proficiency and conduct. Details of the institutions offering degree programmes are available on the GCC website (*see* below). It is illegal for anyone in the UK to use the title 'chiropractor' unless registered with the GCC.

The British Chiropractic Association, Scottish Chiropractic Association, Mctimoney Chiropractic Association and United Chiropractic Association are the representative bodies for the profession and are sources of further information.

BRITISH CHIROPRACTIC ASSOCIATION, 59 Castle Street, Reading RG1 7SN T 0118-950 5950
E enquiries@chiropractic-uk.co.uk
W www.chiropractic-uk.co.uk
Executive Director, Sue Wakefield

GENERAL CHIROPRACTIC COUNCIL (GCC), 44 Wicklow Street, London WC1X 9HL T 020-7713 5155
E enquiries@gcc-uk.org W www.gcc-uk.org
Chief Executive and Registrar, David Howell, CB, OBE, MBE

SCOTTISH CHIROPRACTIC ASSOCIATION, 1 Chisholm Avenue, Bishopton, Renfrewshire PA7 5JH T 0141-404 0260
E admin@sca-chiropractic.org W www.sca-chiropractic.org
Administrator, Morag Cairns

DENTISTRY

Salary range: see Health: Employees and Salaries

The General Dental Council (GDC) is the organisation that regulates dental professionals in the UK. All dentists, dental hygienists, dental therapists, clinical dental technicians, dental nurses and orthodontic therapists must be registered with the GDC to work in the UK.

There are various different routes to qualify for registration as a dentist, including holding a degree from a UK university, completing the GDC's qualifying examination or holding a relevant European Economic Area or overseas diploma. The GDC's purpose is to protect the public through the regulation of UK dental professionals. It keeps up-to-date registers of dental professionals, works to set standards of dental practice, behaviour and education, and helps to protect patients by hearing complaints and taking action against professionals where necessary.

Founded in 1880, the British Dental Association (BDA) is the professional association and trade union for dentists in the UK. The majority of its members are in general practice.

BRITISH DENTAL ASSOCIATION (BDA), 64 Wimpole Street, London W1G 8YS T 020-7935 0875
E enquiries@bda.org W www.bda.org
Chief Executive, Peter Ward

GENERAL DENTAL COUNCIL (GDC), 37 Wimpole Street, London W1G 8DQ T 020-7887 3800 E information@gdc-uk.org
W www.gdc-uk.org
Chief Executive, Evlynne Gilvarry

MEDICINE

Salary range: see Health: Employees and Salaries

The General Medical Council (GMC) regulates medical education and training in the UK. This covers undergraduate study (usually five years), the two-year foundation programme taken by doctors directly after graduation and all subsequent postgraduate study, including specialty and GP training.

All doctors must be registered with the GMC, which is responsible for protecting the public. It does this by setting standards for professional practice, overseeing medical education, keeping a register of qualified doctors and taking action where a doctor's fitness to practise is in doubt. Doctors are eligible for full registration upon successful completion of the first year of training after graduation.

Following the foundation programme, many doctors undertake specialist training (provided by the colleges and faculties listed below) to become either a consultant or a GP. Once specialist training has been completed, doctors are awarded the Certificate of Completion of Training (CCT) and are eligible to be placed on either the GMC's specialist register or its GP register.

GENERAL MEDICAL COUNCIL (GMC), 350 Euston Road, London NW1 3JN T 0161-923 6602 E gmc@gmc-uk.org
W www.gmc-uk.org
Chief Executive, Niall Dickson

SOCIETY OF APOTHECARIES OF LONDON, Black Friars Lane, London EC4V 6EJ T 020-7236 1189
E clerk@apothecaries.org W www.apothecaries.org
Master, Dr Rodney Taylor

SPECIALIST TRAINING COLLEGES AND FACULTIES

College of Emergency Medicine W www.collemergencymed.ac.uk
Faculty of Pharmaceutical Medicine W www.fpm.org.uk
Faculty of Public Health W www.fph.org.uk
Royal College of Anaesthetists W www.rcoa.ac.uk
Royal College of General Practitioners W www.rcgp.org.uk
Royal College of Obstetricians and Gynaecologists W www.rcog.org.uk
Royal College of Opthalmologists W www.rcophth.ac.uk
Royal College of Paediatrics and Child Health W www.rcpch.ac.uk
Royal College of Pathologists W www.rcpath.org
Royal College of Physicians, London W www.rcplondon.ac.uk
Royal College of Physicians and Surgeons of Glasgow W www.rcpsg.ac.uk
Royal College of Physicians of Edinburgh W www.rcpe.ac.uk
Royal College of Psychiatrists W www.rcpsych.ac.uk
Royal College of Radiologists W www.rcr.ac.uk
Royal College of Surgeons of Edinburgh W www.rcsed.ac.uk
Royal College of Surgeons of England W www.rcseng.ac.uk

MEDICINE, SUPPLEMENTARY PROFESSIONS

The standard of professional education for arts therapists, biomedical scientists, chiropodists and podiatrists, clinical scientists, dietitians, hearing aid dispensers, occupational therapists, operating department practitioners, orthoptists, paramedics, physiotherapists, practitioner psychologists, prosthetists and orthotists, radiographers, social workers in England and speech and language therapists is regulated by the Health and Care Professions Council (HCPC), which only registers those practitioners who meet certain standards of training, professional skills, behaviour and health. Each profession regulated by the HCPC has at least one professional title that is protected by law.

HEALTH AND CARE PROFESSIONS COUNCIL (HCPC), Park House, 184 Kennington Park Road, London SE11 4BU
T 0845-300 6184 E registration@hcpc-uk.org
W www.hcpc-uk.org
Chief Executive and Registrar, Marc Seale

ART, DRAMA AND MUSIC THERAPIES
Salary range: £25,500–£47,000

An art, drama or music therapist encourages people to express their feelings and emotions through art, such as painting and drawing, drama or music. A postgraduate qualification in the relevant therapy is required. Details of accredited training programmes in the UK can be obtained from the following organisations:

BRITISH ASSOCIATION FOR MUSIC THERAPY, 24–27 White Lion Street, London N1 9PD T 020-7837 6100 E info@bamt.org W www.bamt.org
Chair, Donald Wetherick

BRITISH ASSOCIATION OF ART THERAPISTS, 24–27 White Lion Street, London N1 9PD T 020-7686 4216 E info@baat.org W www.baat.org
Chief Executive, Val Huet

BRITISH ASSOCIATION OF DRAMA THERAPISTS, Waverley, Battledown Approach, Cheltenham, Gloucestershire GL52 6RE T 0124-2235 5155 E info@badth.org.uk W www.badth.org.uk
Chair, Dr Bruce Howard Bayley

BIOMEDICAL SCIENCES
Salary range: £21,000–£34,000; £30,000–£40,000 with experience

The Institute of Biomedical Science (IBMS) is the professional body for biomedical scientists in the UK. Biomedical scientists carry out investigations on tissue and body fluid samples to diagnose disease and monitor the progress of a patient's treatment. The IBMS sets quality standards for the profession through training, education, assessments, examinations and continuous professional development.

INSTITUTE OF BIOMEDICAL SCIENCE (IBMS), 12 Coldbath Square, London EC1R 5HL T 020-7713 0214 E mail@ibms.org W www.ibms.org
Chief Executive, Jill Rodney

CHIROPODY AND PODIATRY
Salary range: £21,000–£40,000

Chiropodists and podiatrists assess, diagnose and treat problems of the lower leg and foot. The Society of Chiropodists and Podiatrists is the professional body and trade union for the profession. Qualifications granted and degrees recognised by the society are approved by the HCPC. HCPC registration is required in order to use the titles chiropodist and podiatrist.

SOCIETY OF CHIROPODISTS AND PODIATRISTS, 1 Fellmonger's Path, Tower Bridge Road, London SE1 3LY T 020-7234 8620 W www.scpod.org
Chief Executive, Joanna Brown

CLINICAL SCIENCE
Salary range: £25,000–£95,000+

Clinical scientists conduct tests in laboratories in order to diagnose and manage disease. The Association of Clinical Scientists is responsible for setting the criteria for competence of applicants to the HCPC's register and to present a Certificate of Attainment to candidates following a successful assessment. This certificate will allow direct registration with the HCPC.

ASSOCIATION OF CLINICAL SCIENTISTS, c/o Association for Clinical Biochemistry, 130–132 Tooley Street, London SE1 2TU T 020-7940 8960 E info@assclinsci.org W www.assclinsci.org
Chair, Prof. Richard Lerski

DIETETICS
Salary range: £21,000–£40,000

Dietitians advise patients on how to improve their health and counter specific health problems through diet. The British Dietetic Association, established in 1936, is the professional association for dietitians. Full membership is open to UK-registered dietitians, who must also be registered with the HCPC.

BRITISH DIETETIC ASSOCIATION, 5th Floor, Charles House, 148–149 Great Charles Street Queensway, Birmingham B3 3HT T 0121-200 8080 E info@bda.uk.com W www.bda.uk.com
Chief Executive, Andy Burman

OCCUPATIONAL THERAPY
Salary range: £21,000–£40,000

Occupational therapists work with people who have physical, mental and/or social problems, either from birth or as a result of accident, illness or ageing, and aim to make them as independent as possible. The professional qualification and eligibility for registration may be obtained upon successful completion of a validated course in any of the educational institutions approved by the College of Occupational Therapists, which is the professional body for occupational therapy in the UK. The courses are normally degree-level courses based in higher education institutions.

COLLEGE OF OCCUPATIONAL THERAPISTS, 106–114 Borough High Street, London SE1 1LB T 020-7357 6480 W www.cot.org.uk
Chief Executive, Julia Scott

MENTAL HEALTH
Salary range:
Clinical psychologist £25,000, rising to £45,000–£80,000+ at senior levels
Counsellor £19,000–£26,000, rising to £30,000–£40,000 with experience
Educational psychologist £21,000, rising to £34,000 (chartered) and up to £63,000 at senior levels
Psychotherapist £21,000–£27,500 (starting), rising to £45,000 with experience

Psychologists and counsellors are mental health professionals who can work in a range of settings including prisons, schools and hospitals as well as businesses. The British Psychological Society (BPS) is the representative body for psychology and psychologists in the UK. The BPS is responsible for the development, promotion and application of psychology for the public good. The Association of Educational Psychologists (AEP) represents the interests of educational psychologists. The British Association for Counselling and Psychotherapy (BACP) sets educational standards and provides professional support to counsellors, pyschotherapists and others working in counselling, pyschotherapy or counselling-related roles. The BPS website provides more information on the different specialisations that may be pursued by psychologists.

ASSOCIATION OF EDUCATIONAL PSYCHOLOGISTS (AEP), 4 The Riverside Centre, Frankland Lane, Durham DH1 5TA T 0191-384 9512 E enquiries@aep.org.uk W www.aep.org.uk
General Secretary, Kate Fallon

BRITISH ASSOCIATION FOR COUNSELLING AND PSYCHOTHERAPY (BACP), BACP House, 15 St John's Business Park, Lutterworth, Leicestershire LE17 4HB T 01455-883300 E bacp@bacp.co.uk W www.bacp.co.uk
President, Dr Michael Shooter, CBE

BRITISH PSYCHOLOGICAL SOCIETY (BPS),
St Andrews House, 48 Princess Road East, Leicester LE1 7DR
T 0116-254 9568 E enquiries@bps.org.uk W www.bps.org.uk
President, Peter Banister

ORTHOPTICS
Salary range: £21,000 (graduate), rising to £30,000–£80,000 in senior posts

Orthoptists undertake the diagnosis and treatment of all types of squint and other anomalies of binocular vision, working in close collaboration with ophthalmologists. The all-graduate workforce comes from two universities: the University of Liverpool and the University of Sheffield.
BRITISH AND IRISH ORTHOPTIC SOCIETY,
62 Wilson Street, London EC2R 2BU T 01353-665541
E membership@orthoptics.org.uk W www.orthoptics.org.uk
Chair, Lesley-Anne Baxter

PARAMEDICAL SERVICES
Salary range: £21,000–£34,000

Paramedics deal with accidents and emergencies, assessing patients and carrying out any specialist treatment and care needed in the first instance. The body that represents ambulance professionals is the College of Paramedics.
COLLEGE OF PARAMEDICS, The Exchange, Express Park, Bristol Road, Bridgwater TA6 4RR T 01278-420014
E help@collegeofparamedics.co.uk
W www.collegeofparamedics.co.uk
Chief Executive, Dave Hodge

PHYSIOTHERAPY
Salary range: £21,000–£40,000

Physiotherapists are concerned with movement and function and deal with problems arising from injury, illness and ageing. Full-time three- or four-year degree courses are available at around 35 higher education institutions in the UK. Information about courses leading to state registration is available from the Chartered Society of Physiotherapy.
CHARTERED SOCIETY OF PHYSIOTHERAPY,
14 Bedford Row, London WC1R 4ED T 020-7306 6666
W www.csp.org.uk
Chief Executive, Phil Gray

PROSTHETICS AND ORTHOTICS
Salary range: £21,000 on qualification, up to £67,000 as a consultant

Prosthetists provide artificial limbs, while orthotists provide devices to support or control a part of the body. It is necessary to obtain an honours degree to become a prosthetist or orthotist. Training is centred at the University of Salford and the University of Strathclyde.
BRITISH ASSOCIATION OF PROSTHETISTS AND ORTHOTISTS, Sir James Clark Building, Abbey Mill Business Centre, Paisley PA1 1TJ T 0141-561 7217
E enquiries@bapo.com W www.bapo.com
Chair, Stephen Mottram

RADIOGRAPHY
Salary range: £21,000–£40,000, rising to £67,000 in senior posts

In order to practise both diagnostic and therapeutic radiography in the UK, it is necessary to have successfully completed a course of education and training recognised by the HCPC. Such courses are offered by universities throughout the UK and lead to the award of a degree in radiography. Further information is available from the Society and College of Radiographers, the trade and professional body which represents the whole of the radiographic workforce in the UK.
SOCIETY AND COLLEGE OF RADIOGRAPHERS,
207 Providence Square, Mill Street, London SE1 2EW
T 020-7740 7200 W www.sor.org
Chief Executive, Richard Evans

SPEECH AND LANGUAGE THERAPY
Salary range: £21,000–£40,000

Speech and language therapists (SLTs) work with people with communication, swallowing, eating and drinking problems. The Royal College of Speech and Language Therapists is the professional body for speech and language therapists and support workers. Alongside the HCPC, it accredits education and training courses leading to qualification.
ROYAL COLLEGE OF SPEECH AND LANGUAGE THERAPISTS, 2 White Hart Yard, London SE1 1NX
T 020-7378 1200 E info@rcslt.org W www.rcslt.org
Chief Executive, Kamini Gadhok, MBE

NURSING
Salary range: see Health: Employees and Salaries

In order to practise in the UK, all nurses and midwives must be registered with the Nursing and Midwifery Council (NMC). The NMC is a statutory regulatory body that establishes and maintains standards of education, training, conduct and performance for nursing and midwifery. Courses leading to registration are currently at a minimum of diploma in higher education, with some offered at degree level. All are a minimum of three years if undertaken full-time. The NMC approves programmes run jointly by higher education institutions with their healthcare service partners who offer clinical placements. The nursing part of the register has four fields of practice: adult, children's, learning disability and mental health nursing. During the first year of a nursing course, the common foundation programme, students are taught across all four fields of practice. In addition, those studying to become adult nurses gain experience of nursing in relation to medicine, surgery, maternity care and nursing in the home. The NMC also sets standards for programmes leading to registration as a midwife and a range of post-registration courses including specialist practice programmes, nurse prescribing and those for teachers of nursing and midwifery. The NMC has a part of the register for specialist community public health nurses and approves programmes for health visitors, occupational health nurses and school nurses.

The Royal College of Nursing is the largest professional union for nursing in the UK, representing qualified nurses, healthcare assistants and nursing students in the NHS and the independent sector.
NURSING AND MIDWIFERY COUNCIL (NMC), 23 Portland Place, London W1B 1PZ T 020-7637 7181
E communications@nmc-uk.org W www.nmc-uk.org
Chief Executive and Registrar (acting), Jackie Smith
ROYAL COLLEGE OF NURSING, 20 Cavendish Square, London W1G 0RN T 020-7409 3333 W www.rcn.org.uk
Chief Executive and General Secretary, Dr Peter Carter

OPTOMETRY AND DISPENSING OPTICS
Salary range:
Optometrist £19,000–£53,000, up to £80,000 for consultant posts
Dispensing Optician £14,000–£35,000

There are various routes to qualification as a dispensing optician. Qualification takes three years in total, and can be completed by combining a distance learning course or day release while working as a trainee under the supervision of a qualified and registered optician. Alternatively, students can do a two-year full-time course followed by one year of supervised practice with a qualified and registered optician. Training must be done at a training establishment approved by the regulatory body – the General Optical Council (GOC). There are six training establishments which are approved by the GOC: ABDO (Association of British Dispensing Opticians) College, Anglia Ruskin University, Bradford College, City University, City and Islington College and Glasgow Caledonian University. All routes are concluded by professional qualifying examinations, successful completion of which leads to registration with the GOC, which is compulsory for all practising dispensing opticians. After two years post-qualifying experience and completing training to fit contact lenses, students have the option to take a career progression course at the University of Bradford that allows them to graduate with a degree in optometry in one calendar year.

Optometrists must obtain an undergraduate optometry degree from one of the nine institutions approved by the GOC (Anglia Ruskin University, Aston University, the University of Bradford, Cardiff University, City University, Glasgow Caledonian University, the University of Manchester, Plymouth University or the University of Ulster). Following graduation, trainees must complete a year of supervised salaried training with a registered optometrist after which they must pass a series of assessments set by the College of Optometrists. As with dispensing opticians, optometrists must be registered with the GOC in order to practise.

Continuing Education and Training (CET) is a statutory requirement for all registrered dispensing opticians and optometrists to retain GOC registration.

ASSOCIATION OF BRITISH DISPENSING OPTICIANS (ABDO), Godmersham Park, Godmersham, Canterbury, Kent CT4 7DT T 020-7298 5100 E general@abdolondon.org.uk W www.abdo.org.uk
General Secretary, Sir Anthony Garrett, CBE

COLLEGE OF OPTOMETRISTS, 42 Craven Street, London WC2N 5NG T 020-7839 6000
W www.college-optometrists.org
Chief Executive, Bryony Pawinska

GENERAL OPTICAL COUNCIL (GOC), 41 Harley Street, London W1G 8DJ T 020-7580 3898 E goc@optical.org
W www.optical.org
Chief Executive, Samantha Peters

OSTEOPATHY

Salary Range: £20,000–£100,000+

Osteopathy is a system of diagnosis and treatment for a wide range of conditions. It works with the structure and function of the body, and is based on the principle that the well-being of an individual depends on the skeleton, muscles, ligaments and connective tissues functioning smoothly together. The General Osteopathic Council (GOsC) regulates the practice of osteopathy in the UK and maintains a register of those entitled to practise. It is a criminal offence for anyone to describe themselves as an osteopath unless they are registered with the GOsC.

To gain entry to the register, applicants must hold a recognised qualification from an osteopathic education institute accredited by the GOsC; this involves a four- to five-year honours degree programme combined with clinical training.

GENERAL OSTEOPATHIC COUNCIL (GOsC), Osteopathy House, 176 Tower Bridge Road, London SE1 3LU
T 020-7357 6655 E info@osteopathy.org.uk
W www.osteopathy.org.uk
Chief Executive and Registrar, Tim Walker

PHARMACY

Salary range: £21,000–£68,000+

Pharmacists are involved in the preparation and use of medicines, from the discovery of their active ingredients to their use by patients. Pharmacists also monitor the effects of medicines, both for patient care and for research purposes.

The General Pharmaceutical Council (GPhC) is the independent regulatory body for pharmacists in England, Scotland and Wales, having taken over the regulating function of the Royal Pharmaceutical Society in 2010. The GPhC maintains the register of pharmacists, pharmacy technicians and pharmacy premises; it also sets national standards for training, ethics, proficiency and continuing professional development. The Pharmaceutical Society of Northern Ireland (PSNI) performs the same role in Northern Ireland. In order to register, students must complete a four-year degree in pharmacy that is accredited by either the GPhC or the PSNI followed by one year of pre-registration training at an approved pharmacy, and must then pass an entrance examination.

GENERAL PHARMACEUTICAL COUNCIL (GPhC), 129 Lambeth Road, London SE1 7BT T 020-3365 3400
W www.pharmacyregulation.org
Chief Executive and Registrar, Duncan Rudkin

PHARMACEUTICAL SOCIETY OF NORTHERN IRELAND (PSNI), 73 University Street, Belfast BT7 1HL
T 028-9032 6927 W www.psni.org.uk
Chief Executive, Trevor Patterson

ROYAL PHARMACEUTICAL SOCIETY, 1 Lambeth High Street, London SE1 7JN T 020-7572 2737
E support@rpharms.com W www.rpharms.com
Chief Executive, Helen Gordon

INFORMATION MANAGEMENT

Salary range: Archivist £21,000–£30,000 (starting); £30,000–£55,000+ in senior posts
Information Officer £17,000–£25,000 (starting); £26,000–£50,000+ in senior posts
Librarian £19,000–£23,000 (newly qualified); £24,000–£32,000 (chartered); £55,000+ in senior posts

The Chartered Institute of Library and Information Professionals (CILIP) is the leading professional body for librarians, information specialists and knowledge managers. The Archives and Records Association is the professional body for archivists and record managers. The Association of Special Libraries and Information Bureau (ASLIB) is a member association for people who manage information and knowledge in organisations across all sectors. ASLIB provides its members with access to leading publications in information and knowledge management, networking opportunities and professional development.

ARCHIVES AND RECORDS ASSOCIATION, Prioryfield House, 20 Canon Street, Taunton, Somerset TA1 1SW
T 01823-327030 E ara@archives.org.uk
W www.archives.org.uk
Chief Executive, John Chambers

ASLIB, Howard House, Wagon Lane, Bingley, W. Yorks BD16 1WA T 01274-777700 E dheath@aslib.com
W www.aslib.com
Director, Rebecca Marsh

CHARTERED INSTITUTE OF LIBRARY AND INFORMATION PROFESSIONALS (CILIP), 7 Ridgmount Street, London WC1E 7AE T 020-7255 0500 E info@cilip.org.uk W www.cilip.org.uk
Chief Executive, Annie Mauger

JOURNALISM

Salary range: starting salaries £12,000 (trainee)–£15,000; £24,500 (average) for established journalists, rising to £50,000–£85,000 for senior journalists/editors

The National Council for the Training of Journalists (NCTJ) accredits 70 courses for journalists run by 42 education providers; it also provides professional support to journalists.

The Broadcast Journalism Training Council (BJTC) is an association of the UK' s main broadcast journalism employers and accredits courses in broadcast journalism.

BROADCAST JOURNALISM TRAINING COUNCIL (BJTC), 18 Miller's Close, Rippingale Nr. Bourne, Lincolnshire PE10 0TH T 0845-600 8789 E sec@bjtc.org.uk W www.bjtc.org.uk
Secretary, Martyn Hurd

NATIONAL COUNCIL FOR THE TRAINING OF JOURNALISTS (NCTJ), The New Granary, Station Road, Newport, Saffron Walden, Essex CB11 3PL T 01799-544014 E info@nctj.com W www.nctj.com
Chief Executive, Joanne Butcher

LAW

There are three types of practising lawyers: barristers, notaries and solicitors. Solicitors tend to work as a group in firms, and can be approached directly by individuals. They advise on a variety of legal issues and must decide the most appropriate course of action, if any. Notaries have all the powers of a solicitor other than the conduct of litigation. Most of them are primarily concerned with the preparation and authentication of documents for use abroad. Barristers are usually self-employed. If a solicitor believes that a barrister is required, he or she will instruct one on behalf of the client; the client will not have contact with the barrister without the solicitor being present.

When specialist expertise is needed, barristers give opinions on complex matters of law, and when clients require representation in the higher courts (crown courts, the high court, the court of appeal and the supreme court), barristers provide a specialist advocacy service. However, solicitors – who represent their clients in the lower courts such as magistrates' courts and county courts – can also apply for advocacy rights in the higher courts instead of briefing a barrister.

THE BAR

Salary range: £10,000–£200,000+

The governing body of the Bar of England and Wales is the General Council of the Bar, also known as the Bar Council. Since January 2006, the regulatory functions of the Bar Council (including regulating the education and training requirements for those wishing to enter the profession) have been undertaken by the Bar Standards Board.

In the first (or 'academic') stage of training, aspiring barristers must obtain a law degree of a good standard (at least second class). Alternatively, those with a non-law degree (at least second class) may complete a one-year full-time or two-year part-time Common Professional Examination (CPE) or Graduate Diploma in Law (GDL).

The second (vocational) stage is the completion of the Bar Professional Training Course (BPTC), which is available at nine validated institutions in the UK and must be applied for around one year in advance (W www.barprofessionaltraining.org.uk). All barristers must join one of the four Inns of Court prior to commencing the BPTC.

Students are 'called to the Bar' by their Inn after completion of the vocational stage, but cannot practise as a barrister until completion of the third stage, which is called 'pupillage'. Call to the Bar does not entitle a person to practise as a barrister – successful completion of pupillage is now a prerequisite. Pupillage lasts for two six-month periods: the 'non-practising six' and the 'practising six'. The former consists of shadowing an experienced barrister, while the latter involves appearing in court as a barrister.

Admission to the Bar of Northern Ireland is controlled by the General Council of the Bar of Northern Ireland; admission as an Advocate to the Scottish Bar is through the Faculty of Advocates.

FACULTY OF ADVOCATES, Parliament House, Edinburgh EH1 1RF T 0131-226 5071 W www.advocates.org.uk
Dean, Richard Keen, QC

GENERAL COUNCIL OF THE BAR (THE BAR COUNCIL), 289–293 High Holborn, London WC1V 7HZ T 020-7242 0082 E contactus@barcouncil.org.uk W www.barcouncil.org.uk
Chief Executive, Stephen Crowne

BAR STANDARDS BOARD address as above E contactus@barstandardsboard.org.uk W www.barstandardsboard.org.uk
Chair of the Bar Council, Peter Lodder, QC
Director, Bar Standards Board, Dr Vanessa Davies

GENERAL COUNCIL OF THE BAR OF NORTHERN IRELAND, The Bar Library, 91 Chichester Street, Belfast BT1 3JQ W www.barlibrary.com
Chief Executive, Brendan Garland

THE INNS OF COURT

HONOURABLE SOCIETY OF GRAY' S INN, 8 South Square, London WC1R 5ET T 020-7458 7800 W www.graysinn.org.uk
Under-Treasurer, Brig. Anthony Faith, CBE

HONOURABLE SOCIETY OF LINCOLN' S INN, Treasury Office, Lincoln's Inn, London WC2A 3TL T 020-7405 1393 E mail@lincolnsinn.org.uk W www.lincolnsinn.org.uk
Under-Treasurer, Mary Kerr

HONOURABLE SOCIETY OF THE INNER TEMPLE, Inner Temple, London EC4Y 7HL T 020-7797 8250 W www.innertemple.org.uk
Treasurer, Simon Thorley

HONOURABLE SOCIETY OF THE MIDDLE TEMPLE, Middle Temple Lane, London EC4Y 9AT T 020-7427 4800 E members@middletemple.org.uk W www.middletemple.org.uk
Chief Executive, Catherine Quinn

NOTARIES PUBLIC

Notaries are qualified lawyers with a postgraduate diploma in notarial practice. Once a potential notary has passed the postgraduate diploma, they can petition the Court of Faculties for a 'faculty'. After the faculty is granted, the notary is able to practise; however, for the first two years this must be under the supervision of an experienced notary. The admission and regulation of notaries in England and Wales is a statutory function of the Faculty Office. This jurisdiction was confirmed by the Courts and Legal Services Act 1990. The Notaries Society of England and Wales is the representative body for practising notaries.

THE FACULTY OFFICE, 1 The Sanctuary, Westminster, London SW1P 3JT T 020-7222 5381
E faculty.office@1thesanctuary.com
W www.facultyoffice.org.uk
Registrars, Peter Beesley; Howard Dellar

THE NOTARIES SOCIETY OF ENGLAND AND WALES, PO Box 226, Melton, Woodbridge IP12 1WX T 01394-380436
E admin@thenotariessociety.org.uk
W www.thenotariessociety.org.uk
Secretary, Christopher Vaughan

SOLICITORS

Salary range: £16,000–£19,000 (trainee); £25,000–£75,000 after qualification; £100,000+ (associate or partner)

Graduates from any discipline can train to be a solicitor; however, if the undergraduate degree is not in law, a one-year conversion course – either the Common Professional Examination (CPE) or the Graduate Diploma in Law (GDL) – must be completed. The next stage, and the beginning of the vocational phase, is the Legal Practice Course (LPC), which takes one year and is obligatory for both law and non-law graduates. The LPC provides professional instruction for prospective solicitors and can be completed on a full-time or part-time basis. Trainee solicitors then enter the final stage, which is a paid period of supervised work that lasts two years for full-time contracts. The employer that provides the training contract must be authorised by the Solicitors Regulation Authority (SRA) (the regulatory body of the Law Society of England and Wales), the Law Society of Scotland or the Law Society of Northern Ireland. The SRA also monitors the training contract to ensure that it provides the trainee with the expertise to qualify as a solicitor.

Conveyancers are specialist property lawyers, dealing with the legal processes involved in transferring buildings, land and associated finances from one owner to another. This was the sole responsibility of solicitors until 1987 but under current legislation it is now possible for others to train as conveyancers.

COUNCIL FOR LICENSED CONVEYANCERS (CLC), 16 Glebe Road, Chelmsford, Essex CM1 1QG T 01245-349599
E clc@clc-uk.org W www.clc-uk.org
Chief Executive, Sheila Kumar

THE LAW SOCIETY OF ENGLAND AND WALES, The Law Society's Hall, 113 Chancery Lane, London WC2A 1PL
T 020-7242 1222 W www.lawsociety.org.uk
Chief Executive, Des Hudson

LAW SOCIETY OF NORTHERN IRELAND, 96 Victoria Street, Belfast BT1 3GN T 028-9023 1614
W www.lawsoc-ni.org
Chief Executive, Alan Hunter

LAW SOCIETY OF SCOTLAND, 26 Drumsheugh Gardens, Edinburgh EH3 7YR T 0131-226 7411
E lawscot@lawscot.org.uk W www.lawscot.org.uk
Chief Executive, Lorna Jack

SOLICITORS REGULATION AUTHORITY (SRA), The Cube, 199 Wharfside Street, Birmingham B1 1RN
T 0870-606 2555 W www.sra.org.uk
Chief Executive, Antony Townsend

SOCIAL WORK

Salary range: £24,000–£30,000 (starting), rising to £42,000 as an experienced manager; £57,000+ at senior levels

Social workers tend to specialise in either adult or children's services. The HCPC obtained regulatory responsibility from the General Social Care Council in August 2012 and is responsible for setting standards of conduct and practice for social care workers and their employers; regulating the workforce and social work education and training. A degree or postgraduate qualification is needed in order to become a social worker. For more information *see* Social Welfare.

HEALTH AND CARE PROFESSIONS COUNCIL (HCPC), Park House, 184 Kennington Park Road, London SE11 4BU
T 0845-300 6184 E registration@hcpc-uk.org
W www.hcpc-uk.org
Chief Executive and Registrar, Marc Seale

SURVEYING

Salary range: £18,000–£26,000 (starting); £35,000–£50,000+ (senior); £70,000+ (partner)

The Royal Institution of Chartered Surveyors (RICS) is the professional body that represents and regulates property professionals including land surveyors, valuers, auctioneers, quantity surveyors and project managers. Entry to the institution, following completion of a RICS-accredited degree, is through completion of the Assessment of Professional Competence (APC), which involves a period of practical training concluded by a final assessment of competence. Entry as a technical surveyor requires completion of the Assessment of Technical Competence (ATC), which mirrors the format of the APC. The different levels of RICS membership are MRICS (member) or FRICS (fellow) for chartered surveyors, and AssocRICS for associate members.

Relevant courses can also be accredited by the Chartered Institute of Building (CIOB), which represents managers working in a range of construction disciplines. The CIOB offers four levels of membership to those who satisfy its requirements: FCIOB (fellow), MCIOB (member), ICIOB (incorporated) and ACIOB (associate).

CHARTERED INSTITUTE OF BUILDING (CIOB), Englemere, King's Ride, Ascot SL5 7TB T 01344-630700
E reception@ciob.org.uk W www.ciob.org.uk
Chief Executive, Chris Blythe

ROYAL INSTITUTION OF CHARTERED SURVEYORS (RICS), RICS HQ, Parliament Square, London SW1P 3AD
T 024-7686 8555 E contactrics@rics.org W www.rics.org
Chief Executive, Sean Tompkins

TEACHING

Salary range: £21,000–£64,000; headteacher £42,000–£112,000 (for more detailed information *see* Education: Employees and Salaries)

The General Teaching Councils (GTCs) for Northern Ireland, Scotland and Wales maintain registers of qualified teachers in their respective countries, and registration is a legal requirement in order to teach in local authority schools. On 1 April 2013, the Teaching Agency merged with the National College to form the National College for Teaching and Leadership (NCTL), an executive agency of the Department for Education, which became the awarding body for Qualified Teacher Status (QTS). The Graduate Teacher Training Registry (GTTR) processes applications for entry to postgraduate teaching courses in England, Wales and Scotland. All new entrants to the UK teaching profession must have QTS, which requires completing an initial teacher training (ITT) period. In order to gain QTS, individuals must be graduates.

Teachers in Further Education (FE) need not have QTS, though new entrants to FE are required to work towards a specified FE qualification recognised by the Learning and Skills Improvement Service. Similarly, academic staff in Higher Education require no formal teaching qualification, but are expected to obtain a qualification that meets standards set by the Higher Education Academy.

Details of routes to gaining QTS and funding for ITT are available in England from the NCTL, in Wales from the Teacher Training & Education Recruitment Forum Wales, in Scotland from Teach in Scotland and in Northern Ireland from the Department of Education.

The College of Teachers, under the terms of its royal charter, provides professional qualifications and membership to teachers and those involved in education in the UK and overseas.

COLLEGE OF TEACHERS, Institute of Education, 20 Bedford Way, London WC1H 0AL T 020-7911 5536 W www.collegeofteachers.ac.uk
Chief Executive and Registrar, Matthew Martin

DEPARTMENT OF EDUCATION NORTHERN IRELAND, Rathgael House, Balloo Road, Bangor BT19 7PR T 028-9127 9279 E mail@deni.gov.uk W www.deni.gov.uk
Permanent Secretary, Paul Sweeney

GENERAL TEACHING COUNCIL FOR NORTHERN IRELAND, 3rd Floor, Albany House, 73–75 Great Victoria Street, Belfast BT2 7AF T 028-9033 3390 E info@gtcni.org.uk W www.gtcni.org.uk
Chair, Ivan Arbuthnot

GENERAL TEACHING COUNCIL FOR SCOTLAND, Clerwood House, 96 Clermiston Road, Edinburgh EH12 6UT T 0131-314 6000 E gtcs@gtcs.org.uk W www.gtcs.org.uk
Chief Executive, Anthony Finn

GENERAL TEACHING COUNCIL FOR WALES, 9th Floor, Eastgate House, 35–43 Newport Road, Cardiff CF24 0AB T 029-2046 0099 E information@gtcw.org.uk W www.gtcw.org.uk
Chair, Angela Jardine

GRADUATE TEACHER TRAINING REGISTRY (GTTR), Rosehill, New Barn Lane, Cheltenham GL52 3LZ T 0871-468 0469 E enquiries@gttr.ac.uk W www.gttr.ac.uk
Chief Executive, Mary Curnock Cook, OBE

HIGHER EDUCATION ACADEMY, Innovation Way, York Science Park, Heslington, York YO10 5BR T 01904-717500 E enquiries@heacademy.ac.uk W www.heacademy.ac.uk
Chief Executive, Craig Mahoney

LEARNING AND SKILLS IMPROVEMENT SERVICE, Friars House, Manor House Drive, Coventry CV1 2TE T 024-7662 7900 E enquiries@lsis.org.uk W www.lsis.org.uk
Chief Executive, Rob Wye

NATIONAL COLLEGE FOR TEACHING AND LEADERSHIP, 53–55 Butts Road, Earlsdon Park, Coventry CV1 3BH T 0800-389 2500 E teacher.enquiry@education.gsi.gov.uk W www.education.gov.uk
Chief Executive, Charlie Taylor

VETERINARY MEDICINE

Salary range: £30,000–£53,000+

The regulatory body for veterinary surgeons in the UK is the Royal College of Veterinary Surgeons (RCVS), which keeps the register of those entitled to practise veterinary medicine as well as the register and list of qualified veterinary nurses. Holders of recognised degrees from any of the seven UK university veterinary schools or from certain EU or overseas universities are entitled to be registered, and holders of certain other degrees may take a statutory membership examination. The UK's veterinary schools are located at the University of Bristol, the University of Cambridge, the University of Edinburgh, the University of Glasgow, the University of Liverpool, the University of Nottingham and the Royal Veterinary College in London; all veterinary degrees last for five years except that offered at Cambridge, which lasts for six.

The British Veterinary Association is the professional body representing veterinary surgeons. The British Veterinary Nursing Association is the professional body representing veterinary nurses.

BRITISH VETERINARY ASSOCIATION, 7 Mansfield Street, London W1G 9NQ T 020-7636 6541 E bvahq@bva.co.uk W www.bva.co.uk
Secretary General, Henrietta Alderman

BRITISH VETERINARY NURSING ASSOCIATION, 82 Greenway Business Centre, Harlow Business Park, Harlow CM19 5QE T 01279-408644 E bvna@bvna.co.uk W www.bvna.org.uk
Honorary Secretary, Fiona Andrew

ROYAL COLLEGE OF VETERINARY SURGEONS (RCVS), Belgravia House, 62–64 Horseferry Road, London SW1P 2AF T 020-7222 2001 E info@rcvs.org.uk W www.rcvs.org.uk
Registrar, Nick Stace

INDEPENDENT SCHOOLS

Independent schools (non-maintained mainstream schools) charge fees and are owned and managed under special trusts, with profits being used for the benefit of the schools concerned. In 2011–12 there were 2,502 non-maintained mainstream schools in the UK, educating over 622,000 pupils, or around 6.4 per cent of the total school-age population. The approximate number of pupils at non-maintained mainstream schools in 2011–12 was:

UK	622,800
England	581,800
Wales	8,900
Scotland	31,400
Northern Ireland	700

The Independent Schools Council (ISC), formed in 1974, acts on behalf of the eight independent schools' associations which constitute it. These associations are:

Association of Governing Bodies of Independent Schools (AGBIS)
Council of British International Schools (COBIS)
Girls' Schools Association (GSA)
Headmasters' & Headmistresses' Conference (HMC)
Independent Association of Prep Schools (IAPS)
Independent Schools Association (ISA)
Independent Schools' Bursars Association (ISBA)
The Society of Heads

In 2012–13 there were 508,601 pupils being educated in 1,223 schools in membership of associations within the Independent Schools Council (ISC). Most schools not in membership of an ISC association are likely to be privately owned. The Independent Schools Inspectorate (ISI) was demerged from ISC with effect from 1 January 2008 and is legally and operationally independent of ISC. ISI works as an accredited inspectorate of schools in membership of the ISC associations under a framework agreed with the Department for Education (DfE). A school must pass an ISI accreditation inspection to qualify for membership of an association within ISC.

In 2012 at GCSE 60 per cent of all exams taken by candidates in ISC associations' member schools achieved either an A* or A grade (compared to the national average of 22.4 per cent), and at A-level 18 per cent of entries were awarded an A* grade (national average, 7.9 per cent). In 2012–13 a total of 166,643 (33.7 per cent) pupils at schools in ISC associations received help with their fees, mainly in the form of bursaries and scholarships from the schools. ISC schools provided more than £620m of assistance with fees.

INDEPENDENT SCHOOLS COUNCIL
St Vincent House, 30 Orange Street, London WC2H 7HH
T 020-7766 7070 W www.isc.co.uk

The list of schools below was compiled from the Independent Schools Yearbook 2012–13 (ed. Judy Mott, published by A&C Black) which includes schools whose heads are members of one of the ISC's five Heads' Associations. Further details are available online (W www.isyb.co.uk).

The fees shown below represent the upper limit payable for the year 2012–13.

School	*Web Address*	*Termly Fees* Day	Board	*Head*
ENGLAND				
Abbey Gate College, Cheshire	www.abbeygatecollege.co.uk	£3,468	–	Mrs L. Horner
The Abbey School, Berks	www.theabbey.co.uk	£4,430	–	Mrs B. Stanley
Abbots Bromley School, Staffs	www.abbotsbromley.net	£4,970	£8,325	Mrs J. Dowling
Abbot's Hill School, Herts	www.abbotshill.herts.sch.uk	£5,055	–	Mrs E. Thomas
Abbotsholme School, Derbys	www.abbotsholme.co.uk	£6,350	£9,320	S. Fairclough
Abingdon School, Oxon	www.abingdon.org.uk	£5,047	£10,350	Miss O. Lusk
Ackworth School, W. Yorks	www.ackworthschool.com	£4,034	£7,199	Mrs K. Bell
AKS, Lancs	www.arnoldkeqms.com	£2,986	–	J. Keefe
Aldenham School, Herts	www.aldenham.com	£6,323	£9,210	J. Fowler
Alderley Edge School for Girls, Cheshire	www.aesg.co.uk	£3,167	–	Mrs S. Goff
Alleyn's School, London SE22	www.alleyns.org.uk	£5,085	–	Dr G.Savage
Ampleforth College, N. Yorks	www.college.ampleforth.org.uk	£6,370	£9,747	Revd C. Everitt
Ardingly College, W. Sussex	www.ardingly.com	£7,105	£9,400	P. Green
Ashford School, Kent	www.ashfordschool.co.uk	£4,999	£9,801	M. Buchanan
Ashville College, N. Yorks	www.ashville.co.uk	£3,923	£7,680	D. Lauder
Austin Friars St Monica's Senior School, Cumbria	www.austinfriars.cumbria.sch.uk	£3,875	–	M. Harris
Bablake School, W. Midlands	www.bablake.com	£3,147	–	J. Watson
Badminton School, Bristol	www.badmintonschool.co.uk	£5,480	£10,280	Mrs R. Tear
Bancroft's School, Essex	www.bancrofts.org	£4,528	–	Mrs M. Ireland
Barnard Castle School, Durham	www.barnardcastleschool.org.uk	£3,843	£6,900	A. Stevens
Bearwood College, Berks	www.bearwoodcollege.co.uk	£5,700	£9,780	S. Aiano
Bedales School, Hants	www.bedales.org.uk	£5,545	£10,310	K. Budge
Bede's Senior School, E. Sussex	www.bedes.org	£5,670	£9,395	Dr R. Maloney
Bedford Girls' School, Beds	www.bedfordgirlsschool.co.uk	£3,686	–	Miss J. MacKenzie

Bedford Modern School, Beds	www.bedmod.co.uk	£3,700	–	M. Hall
Bedford School, Beds	www.bedfordschool.org.uk	£5,409	£9,017	J. Moule
Bedstone College, Shrops	www.bedstone.org	£4,230	£7,670	D. Gajadharsingh
Beechwood Sacred Heart School, Kent	www.beechwood.org.uk	£5,050	£8,380	A. Lennon
Benenden School, Kent	www.benenden.kent.sch.uk	–	£10,470	Mrs C. Oulton
Berkhamsted School, Herts	www.berkhamstedschool.org	£5,820	£9,272	M. Steed
Bethany School, Kent	www.bethanyschool.org.uk	£5,166	£8,221	M. Healy
Birkdale School, S. Yorks	www.birkdaleschool.org.uk	£3,684	–	Dr P. Owen
Birkenhead School, Merseyside	www.birkenheadschool.co.uk	£3,330	–	D. Clark
Bishop's Stortford College, Herts	www.bishops-stortford-college.herts.sch.uk	£5,189	£7,480	J. Gladwin
Blackheath High School, London SE3	www.blackheathhighschool.gdst.net	£4,264	–	Mrs E. Laws
Bloxham School, Oxon	www.bloxhamschool.com	£5,250	£9,615	M. Allbrook
Blundell's School, Devon	www.blundells.org	£6,065	£9,400	Mrs N. Huggett
Bolton School Boys' Division, Lancs	www.boltonschool.org/seniorboys	£3,389	–	P. Britton
Bolton School Girls' Division, Lancs	www.boltonschool.org/seniorgirls	£3,389	–	Miss S. Hincks
Bootham School, N. Yorks	www.boothamschool.com	£5,225	£8,800	J. Taylor
Bournemouth Collegiate School, Dorset	www.bournemouthcollegiateschool.co.uk	£4,200	£7,560	S. Duckitt
Box Hill School, Surrey	www.boxhillschool.com	£5,350	£9,230	M. Eagers
Bradfield College, Berks	www.bradfieldcollege.org.uk	£8,236	£10,295	S. Henderson
Bradford Grammar School, W. Yorks	www.bradfordgrammar.com	–	£10,989	K. Riley
Bredon School, Glos	www.bredonschool.org	£5,470	£8,580	J. Hewitt
Brentwood School, Essex	www.brentwoodschool.co.uk	£4,937	£8,863	D. Davies
Brighton College, E. Sussex	www.brightoncollege.net	£6,535	£11,500	R. Cairns
Brighton & Hove High School, E. Sussex	www.bhhs.gdst.net	£3,735	–	Ms J. Smith
Brigidine School Windsor, Berks	www.brigidine.org.uk	£4,350	–	M. Hockley
Bristol Grammar School, Bristol	www.bristolgrammarschool.co.uk	£4,100	–	R. MacKinnon
Bromley High School, Kent	www.bromleyhigh.gdst.net	£4,452	–	Ms L. Simpson
Bromsgrove School, Worcs	www.bromsgrove-school.co.uk	£4,500	£8,645	C. Edwards
Bruton School for Girls, Somerset	www.brutonschool.co.uk	£4,540	£8,200	Mrs N. Botterill
Bryanston School, Dorset	www.bryanston.co.uk	£8,507	£10,375	Ms S. Thomas
Burgess Hill School for Girls, W. Sussex	www.burgesshill-school.com	£4,750	£8,400	Mrs A. Aughwane
Bury Grammar School Boys, Lancs	www.bgsboys.co.uk	£3,028	–	R. Marshall
Bury Grammar School Girls, Lancs	www.bgsg.bury.sch.uk	£3,028	–	Mrs R. Georghiou
Canford School, Dorset	www.canford.com	£7,425	£9,500	J. Lever
Caterham School, Surrey	www.caterhamschool.co.uk	£5,010	£9,348	J Thomas
Central Newcastle High School, Tyne and Wear	www.newcastlehigh.gdst.net	£3,583	–	Mrs H. French
Channing School, London N6	www.channing.co.uk	£4,890	–	Mrs B. Elliott
Charterhouse, Surrey	www.charterhouse.org.uk	£7,603	£10,560	Revd J. Witheridge
Cheadle Hulme School, Cheshire	www.cheadlehulmeschool.co.uk	£3,253	–	Miss L. Pearson
Cheltenham College, Glos	www.cheltenhamcollege.org	£7,986	£10,557	Dr A. Peterken
The Cheltenham Ladies' College, Glos	www.cheltladiescollege.org	£7,487	£11,048	Ms E. Jardine-Young
Chetham's School of Music, Greater Manchester	www.chethams.com	sliding scale	–	Mrs C. Moreland
Chigwell School, Essex	www.chigwell-school.org	£4,935	£7,920	M. Punt
Christ's Hospital, W. Sussex	www.christs-hospital.org.uk	£5,835	£9,000	J. Franklin
Churcher's College, Hants	www.churcherscollege.com	£3,985	–	S. Williams
City of London Freemen's School, Surrey	www.clfs.surrey.sch.uk	£4,938	£7,863	P. MacDonald
City of London School, London EC4	www.clsb.org.uk	£4,601	–	D. Levin
City of London School for Girls, London EC2	www.clsg.org.uk	£4,509	–	Miss D. Vernon
Claremont Fan Court School, Surrey	www.claremont-school.co.uk	£4,730	–	J. Insall-Reid
Clayesmore School, Dorset	www.clayesmore.com	£7,266	£9,931	M. Cooke
Clifton College, Bristol	www.cliftoncollegeuk.com	£6,995	£10,250	M. Moore
Clifton High School, Bristol	www.cliftonhigh.bristol.sch.uk	£3,950	£7,100	Dr A. Neill
Cobham Hall, Kent	www.cobhamhall.com	£6,158	£9,263	P. Mitchell
Cokethorpe School, Oxon	www.cokethorpe.org.uk	£5,150	–	D. Ettinger
Colfe's School, London SE12	www.colfes.com	£4,545	–	R. Russell
Colston's School, Bristol	www.colstons.bristol.sch.uk	£3,745	–	P. Fraser
Combe Bank School, Kent	www.combebankschool.co.uk	£4,970	–	Mrs E. Abbotts
Concord College, Shrops	www.concordcollegeuk.com	£3,980	£9,533	N. Hawkins
Cranford House School, Oxon	www.cranfordhouse.net	£4,650	–	Mrs C. Hamilton

Cranleigh School, Surrey	www.cranleigh.org	£8,335	£10,230	G. Waller
Croydon High School, Surrey	www.croydonhigh.gdst.net	£4,413	–	Mrs D. Leonard
Culford School, Suffolk	www.culford.co.uk	£5,500	£8,820	J. Johnson-Munday
Dame Allan's Boys' School, Tyne and Wear	www.dameallans.co.uk	£3,439	–	Dr J. Hind
Dame Allan's Girls' School, Tyne and Wear	www.dameallans.co.uk	£3,439	–	Dr J. Hind
Dauntsey's School, Wilts	www.dauntseys.org	£5,350	£9,020	M. Lascelles
Dean Close School, Glos	www.deanclose.org.uk	£7,060	£9,960	J. Lancashire
Denstone College, Staffs	www.denstonecollege.org	£4,183	£7,284	D. Derbyshire
Derby Grammar School, Derbys	www.derbygrammar.co.uk	£3,665	–	R. Paine
Derby High School, Derbys	www.derbyhigh.derby.sch.uk	£3,540	–	Mrs D. Gould
Dodderhill School, Worcs	www.dodderhill.co.uk	£3,185	–	Mrs C. Mawston
Dover College, Kent	www.dovercollege.org.uk	£4,450	£8,800	G. Holden
d'Overbroeck's College, Oxon	www.doverbroecks.com	£6,420	£9,705	S. Cohen
Downe House, Berks	www.downehouse.net	£7,455	10,300	Mrs E. McKendrick
Dulwich College, London SE21	www.dulwich.org.uk	£5,237	£10,827	Dr J. Spence
Dunottar School, Surrey	www.dunottarschool.com	£4,375	–	Mrs N. Matthews
Durham High School for Girls, Durham	www.dhsfg.org.uk	£3,440	–	Mrs L. Renwick
Durham School, Durham	www.durhamschool.co.uk	£5,075	£7,699	E. George
Eastbourne College, E. Sussex	www.eastbourne-college.co.uk	£6,340	£9,625	S. Davies
Edgbaston High School, W. Midlands	www.edgbastonhigh.co.uk	£3,335	–	Dr R. Weeks
Ellesmere College, Shrops	www.ellesmere.com	£5,325	£8,985	B. Wignall
Eltham College, London SE9	www.eltham-college.org.uk	£4,502	–	P. Henderson
Emanuel School, London SW11	www.emanuel.org.uk	£5,031	–	M. Hanley-Browne
Epsom College, Surrey	www.epsomcollege.org.uk	£6,885	£10,074	J. Piggott
Eton College, Berks	www.etoncollege.com	–	£10,689	A. Little
Ewell Castle School, Surrey	www.ewellcastle.co.uk	£4,230	–	A. Tibble
Exeter School, Devon	www.exeterschool.org.uk	£3,480	–	R. Griffin
Farlington School, W. Sussex	www.farlingtonschool.net	£5,130	£8,415	Miss L. Higson
Farnborough Hill, Hants	www.farnborough-hill.org.uk	£3,870	–	Mrs S. Buckle
Farringtons School, Kent	www.farringtons.org.uk	£4,040	£7,760	Mrs C. James
Felsted School, Essex	www.felsted.org	£6,570	£8,795	Dr M. Walker
Forest School, London E17	www.forest.org.uk	£4,834	–	Mrs S. Kerr-Dineen
Framlingham College, Suffolk	www.framlinghamcollege.co.uk	£5,558	£8,647	P. Taylor
Francis Holland School, London NW1	www.francisholland.org.uk	£5,000	£5,000	Mrs V. Durham
Francis Holland School, London SW1	www.francisholland.org.uk	£5,100	–	Mrs L. Elphinstone
Frensham Heights, Surrey	www.frenshamheights.org	£5,770	£8,545	A. Fisher
Friends' School, Essex	www.friends.org.uk	£5,140	£8,240	G. Wigley
Fulneck School, W. Yorks	www.fulneckschool.co.uk	£3,670	£6,900	Mrs D. Newman
Gateways School, W. Yorks	www.gatewayschool.co.uk	£3,650	–	Dr T. Johnson
Giggleswick School, N. Yorks	www.giggleswick.org.uk	£6,365	£9,295	G. Boult
The Godolphin and Latymer School, London W6	www.godolphinandlatymer.com	£5,545	–	Mrs R. Mercer
The Godolphin School, Wilts	www.godolphin.org	£5,973	£8,645	Mrs S. Price
The Grange School, Cheshire	www.grange.org.uk	£3,285	–	C. Jeffery
Greenacre School for Girls, Surrey	www.greenacre.surrey.sch.uk	£4,262	–	Mrs L. Redding
Gresham's School, Norfolk	www.greshams.com	£7,240	£9,440	P. John
Guildford High School, Surrey	www.guildfordhigh.surrey.sch.uk	£4,567	–	Mrs F. Boulton
The Haberdashers' Aske's Boys' School, Herts	www.habsboys.org.uk	£5,085	–	P. Hamilton
Haberdashers' Aske's School for Girls, Herts	www.habsgirls.org.uk	£4,222	–	Miss B. O'Connor
Haileybury, Herts	www.haileybury.com	£7,095	£9,447	J. Davies
Halliford School, Middx	www.hallifordschool.co.uk	£4,000	–	P. Cottam
Hampshire Collegiate School, Hants	www.hampshirecs.org.uk	£4,571	£7,565	H. MacDonald
Hampton School, Middx	www.hamptonschool.org.uk	£5,085	–	B. Martin
Harrogate Ladies' College, N. Yorks	www.hlc.org.uk	£4,650	£8,120	Mrs R. Wilkinson
Harrow School, Middx	www.harrowschool.org.uk	–	£10,720	J. Hawkins
Headington School, Oxon	www.headington.org	£4,656	£9,014	Mrs C. Jordan
Heathfield School, Berks	www.heathfieldschool.net	–	£9,997	Mrs J. Heywood
Heathfield School, Middx	www.heathfield.gdst.net	£4,462	–	Mrs A. Stevens
Hereford Cathedral School, Herefordshire	www.herefordcs.com	£3,967	–	P. Smith
Hethersett Old Hall School, Norfolk	www.hohs.co.uk	£4,150	£7,725	S. Crump

Highgate School, London N6	www.highgateschool.org.uk	£5,605	–	A. Pettitt
Hill House School, S. Yorks	www.hillhouse.doncaster.sch.uk	£3,370	–	D. Holland
Hollygirt School, Notts	www.hollygirt.co.uk	£3,245	–	Mrs P. Hutley
Hull Collegiate School, E. Yorks	www.hullcollegiateschool.co.uk	£3,364	–	R. Haworth
Hurstpierpoint College, W. Sussex	www.hppc.co.uk	£6,595	£9,810	T. Manly
Hymers College, E. Yorks	www.hymerscollege.co.uk	£3,057	–	D. Elstone
Immanuel College, Herts	www.immanuelcollege.co.uk	£4,622	–	C. Dormer
Ipswich High School, Suffolk	www.ipswichhighschool.co.uk	£3,691	–	Ms E. Purves
Ipswich School, Suffolk	www.ipswich.suffolk.sch.uk	£4,084	£7,559	N. Weaver
James Allen's Girls' School (JAGS), London SE22	www.jags.org.uk	£4,701	–	Mrs M. Gibbs
The John Lyon School, Middx	www.johnlyon.org	£4,820	–	Miss K. Haynes
Kelly College, Devon	www.kellycollege.com	£4,995	£8,755	Dr G. Hawley
Kent College, Kent	www.kentcollege.com	£5,273	£9,499	Dr D. Lamper
Kent College Pembury, Kent	www.kent-college.co.uk	£5,552	£8,950	Mrs S. Huang
Kimbolton School, Cambs	www.kimbolton.cambs.sch.uk	£4,340	£7,185	J. Belbin
King Edward VI High School for Girls, W. Midlands	www.kehs.org.uk	£3,540	–	Miss S. Evans
King Edward VI School, Hants	www.kes.hants.sch.uk	£4,045	–	A. Thould
King Edward's School, Somerset	www.kesbath.com	£3,905	–	M. Boden
King Edward's School, W. Midlands	www.kes.org.uk	£3,642	–	J. Claughton
King Edward's School, Surrey	www.kesw.org	£6,330	£9,050	J. Attwater
King Henry VIII School, W. Midlands	www.khviii.com	£3,147	–	J. Slack
King William's College, Isle of Man	www.kwc.im	£6,332	£9,221	M. Humphreys
Kingham Hill School, Oxon	www.kingham-hill.oxon.sch.uk	£5,300	£8,780	Revd N. Seward
King's College School, London SW19	www.kcs.org.uk	£6,070	–	A. Halls
King's College, Somerset	www.kings-taunton.co.uk	£6,150	£9,150	R. Biggs
King's High School, Warwicks	www.kingshighwarwick.co.uk	£3,360	–	Mrs E. Surber
King's School, Somerset	www.kingsbruton.com	£6,474	£9,045	I. Wilmshurst
The King's School, Kent	www.kings-school.co.uk	£7,765	£10,380	P. Roberts
The King's School, Cheshire	www.kingschester.co.uk	£3,686	–	C. Ramsey
King's Ely, Cambs	www.kingsely.org	£5,778	£8,364	Mrs S. Freestone
The King's School, Glos	www.thekingsschool.co.uk	£5,500	–	A. Macnaughton
The King's School, Cheshire	www.kingsmac.co.uk	£3,390	–	Dr S. Hyde
King's Rochester, Kent	www.kings-rochester.co.uk	£5,400	£8,760	J. Walker
The King's School, Worcs	www.ksw.org.uk	£3,790	–	T. Keyes
Kingsley School, Devon	www.kingsleyschoolbideford.co.uk	£3,990	£7,620	A. Waters
The Kingsley School, Warwicks	www.thekingsleyschool.com	£3,599	–	Ms H. Owens
Kingston Grammar School, Surrey	www.kgs.org.uk	£5,155	–	Mrs S. Fletcher
Kingswood School, Somerset	www.kingswood.bath.sch.uk	£4,059	£8,747	S. Morris
Kirkham Grammar School, Lancs	www.kirkhamgrammar.co.uk	£3,129	£5,929	D. Walker
The Lady Eleanor Holles School, Middx	www.lehs.org.uk	£5,150	–	Mrs G. Low
Lancing College, W. Sussex	www.lancingcollege.co.uk	£6,999	£9,996	J. Gillespie
Langley School, Norfolk	www.langleyschool.co.uk	£3,985	£8,100	D. Findlay
Latymer Upper School, London W6	www.latymer-upper.org	£5,235	–	D. Goodhew
Lavant House, W. Sussex	www.lavanthouse.org.uk	£4,515	£7,105	Mrs K. Bartholomew
The Grammar School at Leeds, W. Yorks	www.gsal.org.uk	£3,760	–	M. Gibbons
Leicester Grammar School, Leics	www.leicestergrammar.org.uk	£3,620	–	C. King
Leicester High School for Girls, Leics	www.leicesterhigh.co.uk	£3,375	–	Mrs J. Burns
Leighton Park School, Berks	www.leightonpark.com	£6,184	£9,438	N. Williams
Leweston School, Dorset	www.leweston.co.uk	£5,560	£8,605	A. Aylward
The Leys School, Cambs	www.theleys.net	£5,980	£8,990	M. Slater
Lichfield Cathedral School, Staffs	www.lichfieldcathedralschool.com	£4,330	£5,690	D. Corran
Lincoln Minster School, Lincs	www.lincolnminsterschool.co.uk	£3,936	£7,613	C. Rickart
Longridge Towers School, Northumberland	www.lts.org.uk	£3,744	£7,628	T. Manning
Lord Wandsworth College, Hants	www.lordwandsworth.org	£6,400	£9,030	F. Livingstone
Loughborough Grammar School, Leics	www.lesgrammar.org	£3,471	£6,452	P. Fisher
Loughborough High School, Leics	www.leshigh.org	£3,266	–	Mrs G. Byrom
Luckley-Oakfield School, Berks	www.luckley.wokingham.sch.uk	£4,649	£8,137	Mrs J. Tudor
LVS Ascot (The Licensed Victuallers' School), Berks	www.lvs.ascot.sch.uk	£4,725	£8,300	Mrs C. Cunniffe
Magdalen College School, Oxon	www.mcsoxford.org	£4,644	–	Dr T. Hands

Malvern College, Worcs	www.malverncollege.org.uk	£7,035	£10,984	A. Clark
Malvern St James, Worcs	www.malvernstjames.co.uk	£5,215	£11,025	Mrs P. Woodhouse
The Manchester Grammar School, Greater Manchester	www.mgs.org	£3,515	–	Dr C. Ray
Manchester High School for Girls, Greater Manchester	www.manchesterhigh.co.uk	£3,300	–	Mrs A. Hewitt
Manor House School, Surrey	www.manorhouseschool.org	£4,580	–	Miss Z. Axton
The Marist Senior School, Berks	www.themaristschools.com	£3,745	–	K. McCloskey
Marlborough College, Wilts	www.marlboroughcollege.org	£8,880	£10,450	J. Leigh
Marymount International School, Surrey	www.marymountlondon.com	£6,493	£10,923	Ms S. Gallagher
The Maynard School, Devon	www.maynard.co.uk	£3,664	–	Ms B. Hughes
Merchant Taylors' Boys' School, Merseyside	www.merchanttaylors.com	£3,272	–	D. Cook
Merchant Taylors' Girls' School, Merseyside	www.merchanttaylors.com	£3,272	–	Mrs L. Robinson
Merchant Taylors' School, Middx	www.mtsn.org.uk	£6,664	–	S. Wright
Mill Hill School, London NW7	www.millhill.org.uk	£5,747	£9,080	Dr D. Luckett
Millfield, Somerset	www.millfieldschool.com	£7,025	£10,420	C. Considine
Milton Abbey School, Dorset	www.miltonabbey.co.uk	£7,575	£10,075	G. Doodes
Moira House Girls School, E. Sussex	www.moirahouse.co.uk	£4,885	£8,850	Mrs L. Watson
Monkton Combe School, Somerset	www.monktoncombeschool.com	£5,950	£9,400	R. Backhouse
More House School, London SW1	www.morehouse.org.uk	£5,100	–	R. Carlysle
Moreton Hall, Shrops	www.moretonhall.org	£7,740	£9,390	J. Forster
Mount St Mary's College, Derbys	www.msmcollege.com	£3,816	£8,125	L. McKell
The Mount School, London NW7	www.mountschool.com	£3,970	–	Ms C. Cozens
The Mount School, N. Yorks	www.mountschoolyork.co.uk	£5,145	£7,995	Ms J. Lodrick
New Hall School, Essex	www.newhallschool.co.uk	£5,294	£8,181	Mrs K. Jeffrey
Newcastle School for Boys, Tyne and Wear	www.newcastleschool.co.uk	£3,620	–	D. Tickner
Newcastle-under-Lyme School, Staffs	www.nuls.org.uk	£3,328	–	N. Rugg
The Newcastle upon Tyne Church High School, Tyne and Wear	www.churchhigh.com	£3,799	–	Mrs J. Gatenby
North Cestrian Grammar School, Cheshire	www.ncgs.co.uk	£2,877	–	D. Vanstone
North London Collegiate School, Middx	www.nlcs.org.uk	£5,180	–	Mrs B. McCabe
Northampton High School, Northants	www.northamptonhigh.gdst.net	£3,955	–	Mrs S. Dixon
Northwood College, Middx	www.northwoodcollege.co.uk	£4,600	–	Miss J. Pain
Norwich High School, Norfolk	www.norwichhigh.gdst.net	£3,677	–	J. Morrow
Norwich School, Norfolk	www.norwich-school.org.uk	£4,220	–	S. Griffiths
Notre Dame Senior School, Surrey	www.notredame.co.uk	£4,515	–	D. Plummer
Notting Hill and Ealing High School, London W13	www.nhehs.gdst.net	£4,668	–	Ms L. Hunt
Nottingham Girls' High School, Notts	www.nottinghamgirlshigh.gdst.net	£3,555	–	Mrs S. Gorham
Nottingham High School, Notts	www.nottinghamhigh.co.uk	£3,869	–	K. Fear
Oakham School, Rutland	www.oakham.rutland.sch.uk	£5,875	£9,785	N. Lashbrook
Ockbrook School, Derbys	www.ockbrooksch.co.uk	£3,440	£6,530	Mrs A. Steele
Oldham Hulme Grammar Schools, Lancs	www.ohgs.co.uk	£3,060	–	Dr P. Neeson
The Oratory School, Oxon	www.oratory.co.uk	£6,855	£9,465	C. Dytor
Oswestry School, Shrops	www.oswestryschool.org.uk	£4,380	£7,795	D. Robb
Oundle School, Northants	www.oundleschool.org.uk	£6,345	£9,890	C. Bush
Our Lady of Sion School, W. Sussex	www.sionschool.org.uk	£3,465	–	M. Scullion
Our Lady's Abingdon Senior School, Oxon	www.olab.org.uk	£3,944	–	S. Oliver
Oxford High School, Oxon	www.oxfordhigh.gdst.net	£3,867	–	Mrs J. Carlisle
Padworth College, Berks	www.padworth.com	£4,175	£8,700	Mrs L. Melhuish
Palmers Green High School, London N21	www.pghs.co.uk	£4,115	–	Mrs C. Edmundson
Pangbourne College, Berks	www.pangbournecollege.com	£6,790	£9,600	T. C Garnier
The Perse Upper School, Cambs	www.perse.co.uk	£4,681	–	E. Elliott
The Peterborough School, Cambs	www.thepeterboroughschool.co.uk	£4,165	£7,754	A. Meadows
Pipers Corner School, Bucks	www.piperscorner.co.uk	£4,670	£7,695	Mrs H. Ness-Gifford
Pitsford School, Northants	www.pitsfordschool.com	£4,064	–	N. Toone
Plymouth College, Devon	www.plymouthcollege.com	£4,450	£8,495	Dr S. Wormleighton

Pocklington School, E. Yorks	www.pocklingtonschool.com	£3,990	£7,208	M. Ronan
Polam Hall School, Durham	www.polamhall.com	£3,990	£7,660	J. Moreland
Portland Place School, London W1	www.portland-place.co.uk	£5,475	–	T. Cook
The Portsmouth Grammar School, Hants	www.pgs.org.uk	£4,222	–	J. Priory
Portsmouth High School, Hants	www.portsmouthhigh.co.uk	£3,710	–	Mrs J. Prescott
Princess Helena College, Herts	www.princesshelenacollege.co.uk	£5,740	£8,285	Mrs J. Duncan
Princethorpe College, Warwicks	www.princethorpe.co.uk	£3,241	–	E. Hester
Prior Park College, Somerset	www.thepriorfoundation.com	£4,701	£8,478	J. Murphy-O'Connor
Prior's Field, Surrey	www.priorsfieldschool.com	£5,145	£8,295	Mrs J. Roseblade
The Purcell School, Herts	www.purcell-school.org	£8,259	£10,562	D. Thomas
Putney High School, London SW15	www.putneyhigh.gdst.net	£4,692	–	Dr D. Lodge
Queen Anne's School, Berks	www.qas.org.uk	£6,305	£9,290	Mrs J. Harrington
Queen Elizabeth Grammar School, W. Yorks	www.wgsf.org.uk	£3,450	–	D. Craig
Queen Elizabeth's Grammar School, Lancs	www.qegsblackburn.com	£3,426	–	S. Corns
Queen Elizabeth's Hospital (QEH), Bristol	www.qehbristol.co.uk	£3,922	–	S. Holliday
Queen Margaret's School, N. Yorks	www.queenmargarets.com	£5,700	£8,996	Dr P. Silverwood
Queen Mary's School, N. Yorks	www.queenmarys.org	£4,805	£6,340	Mrs S. Lewis-Beckett
Queen's College, London, London W1	www.qcl.org.uk	£5,125	–	Dr F. Ramsey
Queen's College, Somerset	www.queenscollege.org.uk	£5,100	£8,230	C. Alcock
Queen's Gate School, London SW7	www.queensgate.org.uk	£5,300	–	Mrs R. Kamaryc
The Queen's School, Cheshire	www.queens.cheshire.sch.uk	£3,665	–	Mrs E. Clark
Queenswood, Herts	www.queenswood.org	£7,590	£9,990	Mrs P. Edgar
Radley College, Oxon	www.radley.org.uk	–	£10,300	A. McPhail
Ratcliffe College, Leics	www.ratcliffe-college.co.uk	£4,646	£7,239	G. Lloyd
The Read School, N. Yorks	www.readschool.co.uk	£3,215	£6,930	J. Sweetman
Reading Blue Coat School, Berks	www.rbcs.org.uk	£4,490	–	M. Windsor
The Red Maids' School, Bristol	www.redmaids.co.uk	£3,700	–	Mrs I. Tobias
Redland High School for Girls, Bristol	www.redlandhigh.com	£3,550	–	Mrs C. Bateson
Reed's School, Surrey	www.reeds.surrey.sch.uk	£6,790	£8,982	D. Jarrett
Reigate Grammar School, Surrey	www.reigategrammar.org	£4,984	–	S. Fenton
Rendcomb College, Glos	www.rendcombcollege.org.uk	£6,335	£8,690	R. Martin
Repton School, Derbys	www.repton.org.uk	£7,242	£9,760	R. Holroyd
Rishworth School, W. Yorks	www.rishworth-school.co.uk	£3,690	£7,805	A. Gloag
Roedean School, E. Sussex	www.roedean.co.uk	£6,050	£10,450	Mrs F. King
Rossall School, Lancs	www.rossallschool.org.uk	£3,900	£9,960	Dr S. Winkley
The Royal Grammar School, Surrey	www.rgs-guildford.co.uk	£4,690	–	Dr J. Cox
Royal Grammar School, Tyne and Wear	www.rgs.newcastle.sch.uk	£3,432	–	Dr B. Trafford
RGS Worcester, Worcs	www.rgsw.org.uk	£3,336	–	A. Rattue
The Royal High School Bath, Somerset	www.royalhighbath.gdst.net	£3,710	£7,510	Mrs R. Dougall
The Royal Hospital School, Suffolk	www.royalhospitalschool.org	£4,332	£7,999	J. Lockwood
The Royal Masonic School for Girls, Herts	www.royalmasonic.herts.sch.uk	£4,850	£8,040	Mrs D. Rose
Royal Russell School, Surrey	www.royalrussell.co.uk	£4,905	£9,700	C. Hutchinson
The Royal Wolverhampton School, W. Midlands	www.theroyalschool.co.uk	£4,085	£8,755	M. Heywood
Rugby School, Warwicks	www.rugbyschool.net	£6,300	£10,033	P. Derham
Ryde School with Upper Chine, Isle of Wight	www.rydeschool.org.uk	£3,625	£7,480	Dr N. England
Rye St Antony, Oxon	www.ryestantony.co.uk	£4,260	£6,930	Miss A. Jones
St Albans High School for Girls, Herts	www.stahs.org.uk	£4,310	–	Mrs R. Martin
St Albans School, Herts	www.st-albans.herts.sch.uk	£4,911	–	A. Grant
St Andrew's School, Beds	www.standrewsschoolbedford.com	£3,632	–	S. Skehan
Saint Augustine's Priory School, London W5	www.saintaugustinespriory.org.uk	£3,920	–	Mrs S. Raffray
St Bede's College, Greater Manchester	www.stbedescollege.co.uk	£3,060	–	D. Kearney
St Bees School, Cumbria	www.st-bees-school.org	£5,148	£8,674	J. Davies
St Benedict's School, London W5	www.stbenedicts.org.uk	£4,240	–	C. Cleugh
St Catherine's School, Surrey	www.stcatherines.info	£5,220	£8,590	Mrs A. Phillips

St Catherine's School, Middx	www.stcatherineschool.co.uk	£3,820	–	Sister P. Thomas
St Christopher School, Herts	www.stchris.co.uk	£5,165	£9,140	R. Palmer
St Columba's College, Herts	www.stcolumbascollege.org	£3,948	–	D. Buxton
St Dominic's High School for Girls, Staffs	www.stdominicsschool.co.uk	£3,875	–	H. Trump
St Dominic's Priory School, Staffs	www.stdominicspriory.co.uk	£3,321	–	Mrs M. Adamson
St Dunstan's College, London SE6	www.stdunstans.org.uk	£4,687	–	Mrs J. Davies
St Edmund's College, Herts	www.stedmundscollege.org	£4,985	£8,330	P. Durn
St Edmund's School, Kent	www.stedmunds.org.uk	£5,857	£9,114	Mrs L. Moelwyn-Hughes
St Edward's, Oxford, Oxon	www.stedwards.oxon.sch.uk	£8,227	£10,283	S. Jones
St Edward's School, Glos	www.stedwards.co.uk	£4,377	–	Mrs P. Clayfield
Saint Felix School, Suffolk	www.stfelix.co.uk	£4,550	£7,950	S. Letman
St Francis' College, Herts	www.st-francis.herts.sch.uk	£4,100	£8,065	Mrs D. MacGinty
St Gabriel's, Berks	www.stgabriels.co.uk	£4,575	–	A. Jones
St George's College, Surrey	www.stgeorgesweybridge.com	£5,120	–	J. Peake
St George's School, W. Midlands	www.sgse.co.uk	£3,255	–	Sir Robert Dowling
St George's, Ascot, Berks	www.stgeorges-ascot.org.uk	£6,325	£9,725	Mrs R. Owens
St Helen & St Katharine, Oxon	www.shsk.org.uk	£4,140	–	Miss R. Edbrooke
St Helen's School, Middx	www.sthn.co.uk	£4,610	–	Dr M. Short
St James Senior Boys' School, Surrey	www.stjamesboys.co.uk	£4,550	–	D. Boddy
St James Senior Girls' School, London W14	www.stjamesgirls.co.uk	£4,685	–	Mrs L. Hyde
St John's College, Hants	www.stjohnscollege.co.uk	£3,255	£7,035	G. Best
St John's School, Surrey	www.stjohnsleatherhead.co.uk	£6,755	–	M. Collier
St Joseph's College, Suffolk	www.stjos.co.uk	£4,240	£8,710	C. Lumb
St Joseph's College, Berks	www.sjcr.org.uk	£3,775	–	A. Colpus
St Lawrence College, Kent	www.slcuk.com	£5,294	£9,188	A. Spencer
St Leonards-Mayfield School, E. Sussex	www.mayfieldgirls.org	£5,875	£9,270	Miss A. Beary
St Margaret's School, Herts	www.stmargaretsbushey.org.uk	£4,640	£8,590	Mrs L. Crighton
St Margaret's School, London NW3	www.st-margarets.co.uk	£3,698	–	M. Webster
St Martha's, Herts	www.st-marthas.co.uk	£3,720	–	J. Sheridan
Saint Martin's, W. Midlands	www.saintmartins-school.com	£3,600	–	Mrs J. Carwithen
St Mary's School Ascot, Berks	www.st-marys-ascot.co.uk	£7,170	£10,080	Mrs M. Breen
St Mary's Calne, Wilts	www.stmaryscalne.org	£7,667	£10,500	Dr F. Kirk
St Mary's School, Cambs	www.stmaryscambridge.co.uk	£4,355	£9,380	Miss C. Avery
St Mary's School, Essex	www.stmaryscolchester.org.uk	£3,500	–	Mrs H. Vipond
St Mary's College, Merseyside	www.stmarys.ac	£3,116	–	M. Kennedy
St Mary's School, Bucks	www.stmarysschool.co.uk	£4,496	–	Mrs J. Ross
St Mary's School, Dorset	www.st-marys-shaftesbury.co.uk	£5,723	£8,327	R. James
St Nicholas' School, Hants	www.st-nicholas.hants.sch.uk	£3,915	–	Mrs A. Whatmough
St Paul's Girls' School, London W6	www.spgs.org	£6,720	–	Ms C. Farr
St Paul's School, London SW13	www.stpaulsschool.org.uk	£6,558	£9,822	Prof. M. Bailey
St Peter's School York, N. Yorks	www.st-peters.york.sch.uk	£4,972	£8,005	L. Winkley
St Swithun's School, Hants	www.stswithuns.com	£5,605	£9,070	Ms J. Gandee
St Teresa's Effingham, Surrey	www.st-teresas.com	£4,910	£8,425	M. Farmer
Scarborough College, N. Yorks	www.scarboroughcollege.co.uk	£3,967	£6,507	Mrs I. Nixon
Seaford College, W. Sussex	www.seaford.org	£5,630	£8,900	T. Mullins
Sedbergh School, Cumbria	www.sedberghschool.org	£6,930	£9,405	A. Fleck
Sevenoaks School, Kent	www.sevenoaksschool.org	£6,990	£10,707	Mrs C. Ricks
Shebbear College, Devon	www.shebbearcollege.co.uk	£3,650	£6,995	S. Weale
Sheffield High School, S. Yorks	www.sheffieldhighschool.org.uk	£3,502	–	Mrs V. Dunsford
Sherborne Girls, Dorset	www.sherborne.com	£7,070	£9,735	Mrs J. Dwyer
Sherborne School, Dorset	www.sherborne.org	£8,175	£10,100	C. Davis
Shiplake College, Oxon	www.shiplake.org.uk	£5,970	£8,850	A. Davies
Shrewsbury High School, Shrops	www.shrewsburyhigh.gdst.net	£3,694	–	M. Getty
Shrewsbury School, Shrops	www.shrewsbury.org.uk	£6,860	£9,795	M. Turner
Sibford School, Oxon	www.sibford.oxon.sch.uk	£4,003	£7,777	M. Goodwin
Sidcot School, Somerset	www.sidcot.org.uk	£4,900	£8,800	I. Kilpatrick
Silcoates School, W. Yorks	www.silcoates.org.uk	£3,992	–	D. Wideman
Solihull School, W. Midlands	www.solsch.org.uk	£3,530	–	D. Lloyd
South Hampstead High School, London NW3	www.shhs.gdst.net	£4,560	–	Miss H. Pike
Stafford Grammar School, Staffs	www.staffordgrammar.co.uk	£3,510	–	M. Darley
Stamford High School, Lincs	www.ses.lincs.sch.uk	£4,208	£7,676	S. Roberts
Stamford School, Lincs	www.ses.lincs.sch.uk	£4,208	£7,676	S. Roberts
Stanbridge Earls School, Hants	www.stanbridgeearls.co.uk	£6,884	£9,091	Mrs M. McMurray

The Stephen Perse Foundation, Cambs	www.stephenperse.com	£4,890	–	Miss P. Kelleher
Stockport Grammar School, Cheshire	www.stockportgrammar.co.uk	£3,237	–	A. Chicken
Stonar School, Wilts	www.stonarschool.com	£4,655	£8,320	T. Nutt
Stonyhurst College, Lancs	www.stonyhurst.ac.uk	£5,305	£9,481	A. Johnson
Stover School, Devon	www.stover.co.uk	£3,690	£7,553	Mrs S. Bradley
Stowe School, Bucks	www.stowe.co.uk	£7,230	£9,965	Dr A. Wallersteiner
Streatham & Clapham High School, London SW16	www.schs.gdst.net	£4,540	–	Dr M. Sachania
Sunderland High School, Tyne and Wear	www.sunderlandhigh.co.uk	£2,951	–	Dr A. Slater
Surbiton High School, Surrey	www.surbitonhigh.com	£4,456	–	Ms E. Haydon
Sutton High School, Surrey	www.suttonhigh.gdst.net	£4,493	–	Mrs K. Crouch
Sutton Valence School, Kent	www.svs.org.uk	£6,005	£9,150	B. Grindlay
Sydenham High School, London SE26	www.sydenhamhighschool.gdst.net	£4,455	–	Mrs K. Pullen
Talbot Heath, Dorset	www.talbotheath.org	£3,715	£6,581	Mrs A. Holloway
Taunton School, Somerset	www.tauntonschool.co.uk	£5,320	£8,920	Dr J. Newton
Teesside High School, Cleveland	www.teessidehigh.co.uk	£3,985	–	Ms D. Duncan
Tettenhall College, W. Midlands	www.tettenhallcollege.co.uk	£4,384	£8,179	M. Long
Thetford Grammar School, Norfolk	www.thetgram.norfolk.sch.uk	£3,657	–	G. Price
Thornton College, Bucks	www.thorntoncollege.com	£3,789	£6,210	Miss A. Williams
Tonbridge School, Kent	www.tonbridge-school.co.uk	£8,206	£10,941	T. Haynes
Tormead School, Surrey	www.tormeadschool.org.uk	£4,210	–	Mrs C. Foord
Trent College, Notts	www.trentcollege.net	£4,850	£8,335	Mrs G. Dixon
Tring Park School for the Performing Arts, Herts	www.tringpark.com	£6,700	£10,030	S. Anderson
Trinity School, Surrey	www.trinity-school.org	£4,352	–	M. Bishop
Trinity School, Devon	www.trinityschool.co.uk	£3,550	£7,750	T. Waters
Truro High School for Girls, Cornwall	www.trurohigh.co.uk	£3,630	£6,901	Mrs C. Pascoe
Truro School, Cornwall	www.truroschool.com	£3,950	£7,335	A. Gordon-Brown
Tudor Hall, Oxon	www.tudorhallschool.com	£5,954	£9,345	Miss W. Griffiths
University College School, London NW3	www.ucs.org.uk	£5,525	–	K. Durham
Uppingham School, Rutland	www.uppingham.co.uk	£7,100	£10,143	R. Harman
Wakefield Girls' High School, W. Yorks	www.wgsf.org.uk	£3,450	–	Mrs G. Wallwork
Walthamstow Hall, Kent	www.walthamstow-hall.co.uk	£5,260	–	Mrs J. Milner
Warminster School, Wilts	www.warminsterschool.org.uk	£4,450	£8,200	M. Priestley
Warwick School, Warwicks	www.warwickschool.org	£3,539	£7,553	E. Halse
Wellingborough School, Northants	www.wellingboroughschool.org	£4,198	–	G. Bowe
Wellington College, Berks	www.wellingtoncollege.org.uk	£7,870	£10,500	Dr A. Seldon
Wellington School, Somerset	www.wellington-school.org.uk	£4,170	£8,013	M. Reader
Wells Cathedral School, Somerset	www.wellscathedralschool.org	£5,069	£8,514	Mrs E. Cairncross
West Buckland School, Devon	www.westbuckland.devon.sch.uk	£4,075	£7,630	J. Vick
Westfield School, Tyne and Wear	www.westfield.newcastle.sch.uk	£3,688	–	Mrs M. Farndale
Westholme School, Lancs	www.westholmeschool.com	£3,068	–	Mrs L. Croston
Westminster School, London SW1	www.westminster.org.uk	£7,846	£10,450	Dr M. Spurr
Westonbirt, Glos	www.westonbirt.gloucs.sch.uk	£6,755	£10,240	Mrs N. Dangerfield
Whitgift School, Surrey	www.whitgift.co.uk	£5,097	–	Dr C. Barnett
Wimbledon High School, London SW19	www.wimbledonhigh.gdst.net	£4,668	–	Mrs H. Hanbury
Winchester College, Hants	www.winchestercollege.org	–	£10,900	R. Townsend
Windermere School, Cumbria	www.windermereschool.co.uk	£4,890	£8,755	I. Lavender
Wisbech Grammar School, Cambs	www.wisbechgrammar.com	£3,645	–	N. Hammond
Withington Girls' School, Greater Manchester	www.withington.manchester.sch.uk	£3,320	–	Mrs S. Marks
Woldingham School, Surrey	www.woldinghamschool.co.uk	£6,205	£9,920	Mrs J. Triffitt
Wolverhampton Grammar School, W. Midlands	www.wgs.org.uk	£3,888	–	J. Darby
Woodbridge School, Suffolk	www.woodbridge.suffolk.sch.uk	£4,675	£8,493	S. Cole
Woodhouse Grove School, W. Yorks	www.woodhousegrove.co.uk	£3,640	£7,400	D. Humphreys
Worksop College, Notts	www.wsnl.co.uk	£5,170	£8,040	G. Horgan
Worth School, W. Sussex	www.worthschool.co.uk	£6,745	£9,283	G. Carminati
Wrekin College, Shrops	www.wrekincollege.com	£5,235	£8,635	R. Pleming
Wychwood School, Oxon	www.wychwoodschool.org	£4,100	£6,600	Mrs A. Johnson
Wycliffe College, Glos	www.wycliffe.co.uk	£5,710	£9,515	Mrs M. Burnet Ward
Wycombe Abbey School, Bucks	www.wycombeabbey.com	–	£10,650	Mrs C. Hall

Wykeham House School, Hants	www.wykehamhouse.com	£3,650	–	Mrs L. Clarke
Yarm School, Stockton-on-Tees	www.yarmschool.org	£3,652	–	D. Dunn
The Yehudi Menuhin School, Surrey	www.yehudimenuhinschool.co.uk	sliding scale	–	Dr R. Hillier

WALES

Christ College, Brecon	www.christcollegebrecon.com	£5,160	£7,970	Mrs E. Taylor
Haberdashers' Monmouth School for Girls, Monmouth	www.habs-monmouth.org	£4,047	£7,704	Mrs H. Davy
Monmouth School, Monmouth	www.habs-monmouth.org	£4,372	£7,704	Dr S. Connors
Rougemont School, Newport	www.rougemontschool.co.uk	£3,664	–	Dr J. Tribbick
Ruthin School, Ruthin	www.ruthinschool.co.uk	£3,916	£7,500	T. Belfield
Rydal Penrhos School, Colwyn Bay	www.rydal-penrhos.com	£4,685	£9,340	P. Lee-Browne

SCOTLAND

Dollar Academy, Dollar	www.dollaracademy.org.uk	£3,435	£4,404	D. Knapman
The High School of Dundee, Dundee	www.highschoolofdundee.org.uk	£3,434	–	Dr J. Halliday
The Edinburgh Academy, Edinburgh	www.edinburghacademy.org.uk	£3,853	–	M. Longmore
Fettes College, Edinburgh	www.fettes.com	£7,025	£9,370	M. Spens
George Heriot's School, Edinburgh	www.george-heriots.com	–	£9,950	A. Hector
The Glasgow Academy, Glasgow	www.theglasgowacademy.org.uk	£3,490	–	P. Brodie
The High School of Glasgow, Glasgow	www.glasgowhigh.com	£3,412	–	C. Mair
Glenalmond College, Perth	www.glenalmondcollege.co.uk	£6,390	£9,370	G. Woods
Hutchesons' Grammar School, Glasgow	www.hutchesons.org	£3,386	–	Dr K. Greig
Kelvinside Academy, Glasgow	www.kelvinsideacademy.org.uk	£3,484	–	R. Karling
Kilgraston, Bridge of Earn	www.kilgraston.com	£4,830	£8,235	F. Thompson
Lomond School, Helensburgh	www.lomondschool.com	£3,270	£6,995	S. Mills
Loretto School, Musselburgh	www.loretto.com	£6,290	£9,250	Ms E. Logan
The Mary Erskine School, Edinburgh	www.esms.edin.sch.uk	£3,122	£6,264	J. Gray
Merchiston Castle School, Edinburgh	www.merchiston.co.uk	£6,515	£8,885	A. Hunter
Morrison's Academy, Crieff	www.morrisonsacademy.org	£3,444	–	G. Pengelley
Robert Gordon's College, Aberdeen	www.rgc.aberdeen.sch.uk	£3,568	–	H. Ouston
St Aloysius' College, Glasgow	www.staloysius.org	£3,120	–	J. Stoer
St Columba's School, Kilmacolm	www.st-columbas.org	£3,260	–	D. Girdwood
St Leonards School, St Andrews	www.stleonards-fife.org	£3,796	£9,038	Dr M. Carslaw
St Margaret's School for Girls, Aberdeen	www.st-margaret.aberdeen.sch.uk	£3,476	–	Dr Julie Land
Stewart's Melville College, Edinburgh	www.esms.edin.sch.uk	£3,122	£6,264	J. Gray
Strathallan School, Perth	www.strathallan.co.uk	£6,163	£9,083	B. Thompson

NORTHERN IRELAND

Bangor Grammar School, Bangor	www.bangorgrammarschool.org.uk	–		S. Connolly
Belfast Royal Academy, Belfast	www.belfastroyalacademy.com	£140	–	J. Dickson
Campbell College, Belfast	www.campbellcollege.co.uk	£2,244	–	R. Robinson
Coleraine Academical Institution, Coleraine	www.coleraineai.com	£140	–	Dr D. Carruthers
Foyle College, Londonderry	www.foylenet.org	£135	–	W. Magill
Methodist College, Belfast	www.methody.org	£140	–	J. Naismith
The Royal Belfast Academical Institution, Belfast	www.rbai.org.uk	£795	–	Miss J. Williamson
The Royal School Dungannon, Dungannon	www.royaldungannon.com	£135	–	D. Burnett

CHANNEL ISLANDS

Elizabeth College, Guernsey	www.elizabethcollege.gg	£2,853	–	G. Hartley
The Ladies' College, Guernsey	www.ladiescollege.com	£2,280	–	Ms J. Riches
Victoria College, Jersey	www.victoriacollege.je	£1,476	–	A. Watkins

NATIONAL ACADEMIES OF SCHOLARSHIP

The national academies are self-governing bodies whose members are elected as a result of achievement and distinction in the academy's field. Within their discipline, the academies provide advice, support education and exceptional scholars, stimulate debate, promote UK research worldwide and collaborate with international counterparts.

Three of the national academies – the Royal Society, the British Academy and the Royal Academy of Engineering – receive grant-in-aid funding from the Department for Business, Innovation and Skills (BIS). The Academy for Medical Sciences receives core funding from the Department of Health, and the Royal Society of Edinburgh is aided by funds provided by the Scottish government. In addition to government funding, the national academies generate additional income from donations, membership contributions, trading and investments.

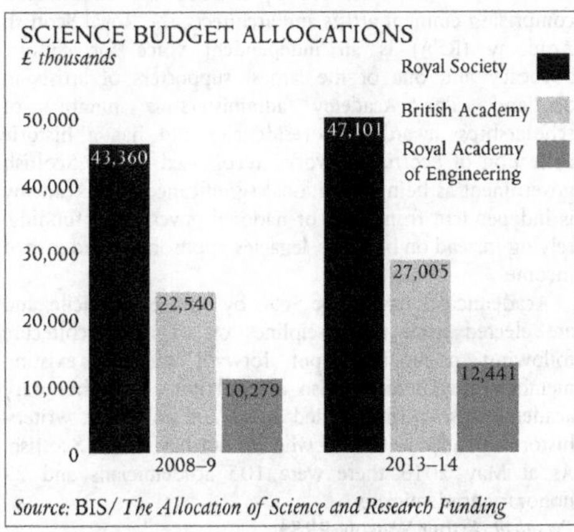

Source: BIS/ *The Allocation of Science and Research Funding*

ACADEMY OF MEDICAL SCIENCES (1998)

41 Portland Place, London W1B 1QH
T 020-3176 2150 W www.acmedsci.ac.uk

Founded in 1998, the Academy of Medical Sciences is the independent body in the UK representing the diversity of medical science. The Academy seeks to improve health through research, as well as to promote medical science and its translation into benefits for society.

The academy is self-governing and receives funding from a variety of sources including the fellowship, charitable donations, government and industry.

Fellows are elected from a broad range of medical sciences: biomedical, clinical and population based. The academy includes in its remit veterinary medicine, dentistry, nursing, medical law, economics, sociology and ethics. Elections are from nominations put forward by existing fellows.

As at April 2013 there were 1,095 fellows and 35 honorary fellows.
President, Prof. Sir John Tooke, PMEDSCI
Executive Director, Dr Helen Munn

BRITISH ACADEMY (1902)

10–11 Carlton House Terrace, London SW1Y 5AH
T 020-7969 5200 W www.britac.ac.uk

The British Academy is an independent, self-governing learned society for the promotion of the humanities and social sciences. It was founded in 1901 and granted a royal charter in 1902. The British Academy supports advanced academic research and is a channel for the government's support of research in those disciplines.

The fellows are scholars who have attained distinction in one of the branches of study that the academy exists to promote. Candidates must be nominated by existing fellows. As at April 2013, there are 936 fellows, 21 honorary fellows and 305 corresponding fellows overseas.
President, Prof. Sir Adam Roberts, KCMG
Chief Executive, Dr Robin Jackson

ROYAL ACADEMY OF ENGINEERING (1976)

3 Carlton House Terrace, London SW1Y 5DG
T 020-7766 0600 W www.raeng.org.uk

The Royal Academy of Engineering was established as the Fellowship of Engineering in 1976. It was granted a royal charter in 1983 and its present title in 1992. It is an independent, self-governing body whose object is the pursuit, encouragement and maintenance of excellence in the whole field of engineering, in order to promote the advancement of science, art and practice of engineering for the benefit of the public.

Election to the fellowship is by invitation only, from nominations supported by the body of fellows. As at May 2013 there were 1,352 fellows, including 45 honorary fellows and 101 international fellows. The Duke of Edinburgh is the senior fellow and the Princess Royal and the Duke of Kent are both royal fellows.
President, Sir John Parker, FRENG
Chief Executive, Philip Greenish, CBE

ROYAL SOCIETY (1660)

6–9 Carlton House Terrace, London SW1Y 5AG
T 020-7451 2500 W www.royalsociety.org

The Royal Society is an independent academy promoting the natural and applied sciences. Founded in 1660 and granted a royal charter in 1662, the society has three roles: as the UK academy of science, as a learned society and as a funding agency. It is an independent, self-governing body under a royal charter, promoting and advancing all fields of physical and biological sciences, of mathematics and engineering, medical and agricultural sciences and their application.

Fellows are elected for their contributions to science, both in fundamental research resulting in greater understanding, and also in leading and directing scientific and technological progress in industry and research establishments. Each year up to 44 new fellows, who must be citizens or residents of the Commonwealth or Ireland, and up to eight foreign members may be elected. In addition one honorary fellow may also be elected annually from those not eligible for election as fellows or foreign members. As at May 2013, there were 1,562 fellows and 177 foreign members covering

all scientific disciplines. The Queen is the patron of the Royal Society, and there are also six royal fellows.
President, Sir Paul Nurse, PRS
Executive Director, Dr Julie Maxton

ROYAL SOCIETY OF EDINBURGH (1783)

22–26 George Street, Edinburgh EH2 2PQ
T 0131-240 5000 W www.royalsoced.org.uk

The Royal Society of Edinburgh (RSE) is an educational charity and Scotland's national academy. An independent body with charitable status, its multidisciplinary membership represents a knowledge resource for the people of Scotland. Granted its royal charter in 1783 for the 'advancement of learning and useful knowledge', the society organises conferences, debates and lectures; conducts independent inquiries; facilitates international collaboration and showcases the country's research and development capabilities; provides educational activities for primary and secondary school students; and awards prizes and medals. The society also awards over £2m annually to Scotland's top researchers and entrepreneurs working in Scotland.

As at May 2013 there were 1,569 fellows, comprising 1,441 fellows, 64 honorary fellows and 64 corresponding fellows overseas.
President, Sir John Arbuthnott, PHD, FRCPATH, FRSE
General Secretary, Prof. Alice Brown, CBE, FRSE

PRIVATELY FUNDED ARTS ACADEMIES

The Royal Academy and the Royal Scottish Academy support the visual arts community in the UK, hold educational events and promote interest in the arts. They are entirely privately funded through contributions by 'friends' (regular donors who receive benefits such as free entry, previews and magazines), bequests, corporate donations and exhibitions.

ROYAL ACADEMY OF ARTS (1768)

Burlington House, Piccadilly, London W1J 0BD
T 020-7300 8000 W www.royalacademy.org.uk

Founded by George III in 1768, the Royal Academy of Arts is an independent, self-governing society devoted to the encouragement and promotion of the fine arts.

Membership of the academy is limited to 80 academicians, all of whom are either painters, engravers, printmakers, draughtsmen, sculptors or architects. There must always be at least 14 sculptors, 12 architects and 8 printmakers among the academicians. Candidates must be professionally active in the UK and are nominated and elected by the existing academicians. The members are known as royal academicians (RAs) and are responsible for both the governance and direction of the academy. When RAs reach the age of 75, they become senior academicians and can no longer serve as officers or on the committees.

The title of honorary academician is awarded to a small number of distinguished artists who are not UK citizens; as at May 2013, there were 22 honorary academicians. Unlike the RAs, they do not take part in the governance of the academy and are unable to vote.
President, Christopher Le Brun, PRA
Secretary & Chief Executive, Dr Charles Saumarez Smith, CBE

ROYAL SCOTTISH ACADEMY (1838)

The Mound, Edinburgh EH2 2EL
T 0131-225 6671 W www.royalscottishacademy.org

Founded in 1826 and led by a body of academicians comprising eminent artists and architects, the Royal Scottish Academy (RSA) is an independent voice for cultural advocacy and one of the largest supporters of artists in Scotland. The Academy administers a number of scholarships, awards and residencies and has a historic collection of Scottish artworks, recognised by the Scottish government as being of national significance. The Academy is independent from local or national government funding, relying instead on bequests, legacies, sponsorship and earned income.

Academicians have to be Scots by birth or domicile, and are elected from the disciplines of art and architecure following nominations put forward by the existing membership. There are also a small number of honorary academicians – distinguished artists and architects, writers, historians and musicians – who do not have to be Scottish. As at May 2013 there were 105 academicians and 29 honorary academicians.
President, Arthur Watson, PRSA
Secretary, Marion Smith, RSA

RESEARCH COUNCILS

The government funds basic and applied civil science research, mostly through seven research councils, which are established under royal charter and supported by the Department for Business, Innovation and Skills (BIS). Research Councils UK is the strategic partnership of these seven councils* (for further information *see* W www.rcuk.ac.uk). The councils support research and training in universities and other higher education and research facilities.

The science budget, administered by BIS, is the main source of public sector funding for research councils, with further public funds provided through the Large Facilities Capital Fund and the Higher Education Innovation Fund. Additional funds may also be provided by other government departments, devolved administrations, the European Commission and other international bodies. The councils also receive income for research specifically commissioned by government departments and the private sector, and income from charitable sources.

GOVERNMENT SCIENCE BUDGET
£ thousand

	2012–13	*2013–14*
Arts and Humanities Research Council	98,535	98,522
Biotechnology and Biological Sciences Research Council	397,071	391,271
Economic and Social Research Council	167,335	166,186
Engineering and Physical Sciences Research Council	794,150	781,150
Medical Research Council	624,092	639,645
Natural Environment Research Council	352,929	356,929
Science and Technology Facilities Council*	519,398	516,627
Large Facilities Capital Fund	61,307	47,769
Higher Education Innovation Fund†	150,000	150,000

* Includes cross-council facilities and international subscriptions budgets, which are managed by STFC on behalf of all research councils

† Includes £37m from the Higher Education Funding Council for England (HEFCE)

Source: BIS – *The Allocation of Science and Research Funding 2011/12–2014/15*

ARTS AND HUMANITIES RESEARCH COUNCIL*

Polaris House, North Star Avenue, Swindon SN2 1FL
T 01793-416000 W www.ahrc.ac.uk

The AHRC is the successor organisation to the Arts and Humanities Research Board and was incorporated by royal charter and established in April 2005. It provides funding for postgraduate training and research in the arts and humanities; in any one year, the AHRC makes approximately 700 research awards and around 2,000 postgraduate scholarships. Awards are made after a rigorous peer review system, which ensures the quality of applications.
Chair, Prof. Sir Alan Wilson, FBA, FRS
Chief Executive, Prof. Rick Rylance, FRSA

BIOTECHNOLOGY AND BIOLOGICAL SCIENCES RESEARCH COUNCIL*

Polaris House, North Star Avenue, Swindon SN2 1UH
T 01793-413200 W www.bbsrc.ac.uk

Established by royal charter in 1994, the BBSRC is the UK funding agency for research in the non-clinical life sciences. It funds research into how all living organisms function and behave, benefiting the agriculture, food, health, pharmaceutical and chemical sectors. To deliver its mission, the BBSRC supports research and training in universities and research centres throughout the UK, including providing strategic research grants to the institutes listed below.
Chair, Prof. Sir Tom Blundell
Chief Executive, Prof. D. Kell

INSTITUTES

BABRAHAM INSTITUTE, Babraham Hall, Babraham, Cambridge CB22 3AT T 01223-496000
Director, Prof. M. Wakelam

GENOME ANALYSIS CENTRE, Norwich Research Park, Colney, Norwich NR4 7UH T 01603-450861
Director, Dr J. Rogers

INSTITUTE FOR BIOLOGICAL, ENVIRONMENTAL AND RURAL SCIENCES (ABERYSTWYTH UNIVERSITY), Penglais, Aberystwyth, Ceredigion SY23 3DA T 01970-622316
Director, Prof. W. Powell

INSTITUTE OF FOOD RESEARCH, Norwich Research Park, Colney Lane, Norwich NR4 7UA T 01603-255000
Director, Prof. D. Boxer

JOHN INNES CENTRE, Norwich Research Park, Colney, Norwich NR4 7UH T 01603-450000
Director, Prof. D. Sanders

PIRBRIGHT INSTITUTE, Pirbright Laboratory, Ash Road, Pirbright, Surrey GU24 0NF T 01483-232441
Director, Prof. J. Fazakerley

ROSLIN INSTITUTE (UNIVERSITY OF EDINBURGH), Roslin Biocentre, Roslin, Midlothian EH25 9PS T 0131-651 9100
Director, Prof. D. Hume

ROTHAMSTED RESEARCH, Rothamsted, Harpenden, Herts AL5 2JQ T 01582-763133
Director, Prof. M. Moloney

ECONOMIC AND SOCIAL RESEARCH COUNCIL*

Polaris House, North Star Avenue, Swindon SN2 1UJ
T 01793-413000 E comms@esrc.ac.uk
W www.esrc.ac.uk

The purpose of the ESRC is to promote and support research and postgraduate training in the social sciences. It also provides advice, disseminates knowledge and promotes public understanding in these areas. The ESRC provides core funding to the centres listed below. Further information can be obtained on the ESRC website, including details of centres it funds in collaboration with other research councils.
Chair, Dr Alan Gillespie, CBE
Chief Executive, Prof. Paul Boyle

RESEARCH CENTRES

CENTRE FOR CLIMATE CHANGE, ECONOMICS AND POLICY, LSE, Houghton Street, London WC2A 2AE
T 020-7107 5433
Directors, Prof. Judith Rees; Prof. Andy Gouldson

CENTRE FOR COMPETITION POLICY, University of East Anglia, Norwich NR4 7TJ T 01603-593715
Director, Prof. Morten Hviid

CENTRE FOR COMPETITIVE ADVANTAGE IN THE GLOBAL ECONOMY, Department of Economics, University of Warwick, Coventry, Warks CV4 7AL T 02476-151176
Director, Prof. Nick Crafts

CENTRE FOR CORPUS APPROACHES TO SOCIAL SCIENCE (CASS), FASS Building, Lancaster University, Lancaster, Lancashire LA1 4YW E CASS@lancs.ac.uk
Director, Prof. Tony McEnery

CENTRE FOR ECONOMIC PERFORMANCE, London School of Economics and Political Science, Houghton Street, London WC2A 2AE T 020-7955 7673
Director, Prof. John Van Reenen

CENTRE FOR LONGITUDINAL STUDIES, Institute of Education, 20 Bedford Way, London WC1H 0AL T 020-7612 6875
Director, Prof. Jane Elliott

CENTRE FOR MACROECONOMICS, LSE, Houghton Street, London WC2A 2AE T 0203-486 2818
Director, Prof. Wouter Den Haan

CENTRE FOR MARKET AND PUBLIC ORGANISATION, University of Bristol, 2 Priory Road, Bristol BS8 1TX T 0117-331 0799
Director, Prof. Simon Burgess

CENTRE FOR RESEARCH ON SOCIO-CULTURAL CHANGE, University of Manchester, 178 Waterloo Place, Oxford Road, Manchester M13 9PL T 0161-275 8985
Directors, Prof. Fiona Devine; Prof. Marie Gillespie; Prof. Penny Harvey; Prof. John Law; Prof. Sophie Watson; Prof. Karel Williams

CENTRE FOR TIME USE RESEARCH, Departments of Sociology and Economics, University of Oxford, Manor Road Building, Manor Road, Oxford OX1 3UQ T 01865-286171
Director, Prof. Jonathan Gershuny

CENTRE FOR TRANSLATIONAL RESEARCH IN PUBLIC HEALTH, Fuse, Institute of Health & Society, Newcastle University, Baddiley-Clark Building, Richardson Road, Newcastle upon Tyne NE2 4AX T 0191-222 8751
Director, Prof. Martin White

CENTRE OF EXCELLENCE FOR PUBLIC HEALTH RESEARCH (NORTHERN IRELAND), School of Medicine, Dentistry and Biomedical Sciences, Room 01012, Institute of Clinical Science B, Royal Victoria Hospital, Grosvenor Road, Belfast BT12 6BJ T 028-9063 5051
Director, Prof. Frank Kee

CENTRE OF MICROECONOMIC ANALYSIS OF PUBLIC POLICY, Institute for Fiscal Studies, 7 Ridgmount Street, London WC1E 7AE T 020-7291 4800
Director, Prof. Richard Blundell

CENTRE ON DYNAMICS OF ETHNICITY, University of Manchester, Oxford Road, Manchester M13 9PL E censusbriefings@ethnicity.ac.uk
Director, Prof. James Nazroo

CENTRE ON MICRO-SOCIAL CHANGE, University of Essex, Colchester, Essex CO4 3SQ T 01206-872957
Director, Prof. Mike Brewer

CENTRE ON MIGRATION, POLICY AND SOCIETY, University of Oxford, 58 Banbury Road, Oxford OX2 6QS T 01865-274711
Director, Prof. Michael Keith

CENTRE ON SKILLS, KNOWLEDGE AND ORGANISATIONAL PERFORMANCES, Department of Education, University of Oxford, 15 Norham Gardens, Oxford OX2 6PY T 01865-611030
Director, Prof. Ken Mayhew

DEAFNESS, COGNITION AND LANGUAGE RESEARCH CENTRE, 49 Gordon Square, London WC1H 0PD T 020-7679 8679
Director, Prof. Bencie Woll

NATIONAL CENTRE FOR RESEARCH METHODS, Social Sciences, Room 4139, Murray Building, University of Southampton, Southampton SO17 1BJ T 0238-059 4539
Director, Prof. Patrick Sturgis

SYSTEMIC RISK CENTRE, LSE, Houghton Street, London WC2A 2AE T 01793 442 524
Directors, Dr Jon Danielsson; Dr Jean-Pierre Zigrand

THIRD SECTOR RESEARCH CENTRE, Park House, 40 Edgbaston Park Road, University of Birmingham, Birmingham B15 2RT T 0121-414 3086
Director, Prof. Peter Alcock

UK ENERGY RESEARCH CENTRE, 58 Princes Gate, Exhibition Road, London SW7 2PG T 020-7594 1574
Executive Director, Prof. John Loughead, OBE, FRENG

ENGINEERING AND PHYSICAL SCIENCES RESEARCH COUNCIL*

Polaris House, North Star Avenue, Swindon SN2 1ET
T 01793-444000 W www.epsrc.ac.uk

Formed in 1994 by royal charter, the EPSRC is the UK government's main agency for funding research and training in engineering and the physical sciences in universities and other organisations throughout the UK. It also provides advice, disseminates knowledge and promotes public understanding in these areas.

Chair, Paul Golby, FRENG
Chief Executive, Prof. David Delpy, FMEDSCI, FRENG, FRS

MEDICAL RESEARCH COUNCIL*

2nd Floor, David Phillips Building, Polaris House, North Star Avenue, Swindon, Wiltshire SN2 1FL T 01793-416200 W www.mrc.ac.uk

The MRC is a publicly funded organisation dedicated to improving human health. The MRC supports research across the entire spectrum of medical sciences, in universities, hospitals, centres and institutes.

Chair, Donald Brydon, CBE
Chief Executive, Prof. Sir John Savill
Chair, Infections and Immunity Board, Prof. Doreen Cantrell
Chair, Molecular and Cellular Medicine Board, Prof. Stephen Hill
Chair, Neurosciences and Mental Health Board, Prof. Hugh Perry
Chair, Population and Systems Medicine Board, Prof. David Lomas

MRC UNITS, CENTRES AND INSTITUTES

Anatomical Neuropharmacology Unit W mrcanu.pharm.ox.ac.uk
Asthma UK Centre in Allergic Mechanisms of Asthma W www.asthma-allergy.ac.uk
Centre for Behavioural and Clinical Neuroscience Institute (BCNI) W www.psychol.cam.ac.uk
Biostatistics Unit W www.mrc-bsu.cam.ac.uk
Centre for Brain Ageing and Vitality W www.ncl.ac.uk/cbav
Cancer Cell Unit W www.mrc-ccu.cam.ac.uk
Cancer Research UK/BHF Clinical Trial Service Unit & Epidemiological Studies Unit (CTSU) W www.ctsu.ox.ac.uk
Cancer Research UK Gray Institute for Radiation Oncology and Biology, University of Oxford W www.rob.ox.ac.uk
Centre for Causal Analyses in Translational Epidemiology W www.bristol.ac.uk/caite
Cell Biology Unit W www.ucl.ac.uk/lmcb
Clinical Sciences Centre (CSC) W www.csc.mrc.ac.uk
Clinical Trials Unit W www.ctu.mrc.ac.uk
Cognition and Brain Sciences Unit W www.mrc-cbu.cam.ac.uk

Centre for Cognitive Ageing and Cognitive Epidemiology W www.ccace.ed.ac.uk
The Crucible Centre W www.ucl.ac.uk/crucible
Centre for Developmental and Biomedical Genetics W cdbg.shef.ac.uk
Centre for Developmental Neurobiology at King's College London W www.kcl.ac.uk/depsta/biomedical/mrc
Centre for Drug Safety Science W www.liv.ac.uk/drug-safety/
Centre for Environment and Health W www.environment-health.ac.uk
Centre of Epidemiology for Child Health W www.ucl.ac.uk/ich/research-ich/mrc-cech
Epidemiology Unit W www.mrc-epid.cam.ac.uk
Functional Genomics Unit W www.mrcfgu.ox.ac.uk
Centre in Genome Damage and Stability W www.sussex.ac.uk/gdsc
Centre for Genomics and Global Health W www.cggh.ox.ac.uk
Institute of Hearing Research W www.ihr.mrc.ac.uk
Institute of Hearing Research (Glasgow) T 0141-211 4695
Human Genetics Unit W www.hgu.mrc.ac.uk
Human Immunology Unit W www.imm.ox.ac.uk
Human Nutrition Research W www.mrc-hnr.cam.ac.uk
Centre for Immune Regulation W www.mrcbcir.bham.ac.uk
Centre for Inflammation Research W www.cir.ed.ac.uk
International Nutrition Group W www.ing.mrc.ac.uk
Laboratory of Molecular Biology (LMB) W www2.mrc-lmb.cam.ac.uk
Lifecourse Epidemiology Unit W www.mrc.soton.ac.uk
Unit for Lifelong Health and Ageing W www.nshd.mrc.ac.uk
Mammalian Genetics Unit W www.har.mrc.ac.uk
Centre for Medical Molecular Virology W www.ucl.ac.uk/infection-immunity/mrc_ucl-centre
Metabolic Diseases Unit, W www.mrc-cord.org
Mitochondrial Biology Unit W www.mrc-mbu.cam.ac.uk
Centre for Molecular Bacteriology and Infection, W www3.imperial.ac.uk/cmbi
Molecular Haemotology Unit T 01865-222398
National Institute for Medical Research (NIMR) including the MRC Biomedical NMR Centre W www.nimr.mrc.ac.uk; www.nmrcentre.mrc.ac.uk
Centre for Neuromuscular Diseases W www.cnmd.ac.uk
Centre for Neuropsychiatric Genetics and Genomics W http://medicine.cardiff.ac.uk/cngg/
Centre for Obesity and Related Metabolic Diseases W www.mrc-cord.org
Centre for Outbreak Analysis and Modelling W www1.imperial.ac.uk
Prion Unit W www.prion.ucl.ac.uk
Protein Phosphorylation Unit W www.ppu.mrc.ac.uk
Centre for Regenerative Medicine W www.crm.ed.ac.uk
Centre for Reproductive Health (CRH) W www.crh.ed.ac.uk
Research Complex at Harwell (RCaH) W www.rc-harwell.ac.uk
Scottish Collaboration for Public Health Research and Policy W www.scphrp.ac.uk
Social and Public Health Sciences Unit W www.sphsu.mrc.ac.uk
Social, Genetic and Developmental Psychiatry Research Centre W www.kcl.ac.uk/iop/depts/mrc/index.aspx
Centre for Stem Cell Biology and Regenerative Medicine W www.stemcells.cam.ac.uk
Centre for Synaptic Plasticity W www.bris.ac.uk/synaptic/
Toxicology Unit W www.tox.mrc.ac.uk
Centre for Transplantation W http://transplantation.kcl.ac.uk/sections/site/about-us
Centre for Virus Research W www.cvr.ac.uk
Weatherall Institute of Molecular Medicine (WIMM) W www.imm.ox.ac.uk/wimm-research
MRC (UK), the Gambia W www.mrc.gm
UVRI Uganda Research Unit on AIDS W www.mrcuganda.org

NATIONAL PHYSICAL LABORATORY

Hampton Road, Teddington, Middx TW11 0LW
T 020-8977 3222 W www.npl.co.uk

The National Physical Laboratory (NPL) was established in 1900 and is the UK's national measurement institute. It develops, maintains and disseminates national measurement standards for physical quantities such as mass, length, time, temperature, voltage and force. It also conducts underpinning research on engineering materials and information technology, and disseminates good measurement practice.
Managing Director, B. Bowsher

ASSOCIATION OF INDEPENDENT RESEARCH AND TECHNOLOGY ORGANISATIONS LIMITED (AIRTO)
T 020-8943 6600 E enquiries@airto.co.uk W www.airto.co.uk

(AIRTO) is a membership body, based at and run by the NPL, for organisations operating in the UK's research and technology sector. Members' activities span a wide range of disciplines from life sciences to engineering. Their work includes basic research, development and design of innovative products or processes, instrumentation testing and certification, and technology and management consultancy. AIRTO publishes a directory to help clients identify the organisations that might be able to assist them. For a full list of members, *see* AIRTO's website.
President, Prof. Richard Brook, OBE, FRENG

NATURAL ENVIRONMENT RESEARCH COUNCIL*

Polaris House, North Star Avenue, Swindon SN2 1EU
T 01793-411500 W www.nerc.ac.uk

The NERC funds and carries out impartial scientific research in the sciences relating to the natural environment. Its work covers the full range of atmospheric, earth, biological, terrestrial and aquatic sciences, from the depths of the oceans to the upper atmosphere. Its mission is to gather and apply knowledge, create understanding and predict the behaviour of the natural environment and its resources.
Chair, Edmund Wallis
Chief Executive, Prof. Duncan Wingham

RESEARCH CENTRES

BRITISH ANTARCTIC SURVEY, High Cross, Madingley Road, Cambridge CB3 0ET T 01223-221400
Director, Prof. Alan Rodger

BRITISH GEOLOGICAL SURVEY, Kingsley Dunham Centre, Keyworth, Nottingham NG12 5GG T 0115-936 3100
Executive Director, Prof. John Ludden

CENTRE FOR ECOLOGY AND HYDROLOGY, Maclean Building, Benson Lane, Crowmarsh Gifford, Wallingford OX10 8BB T 01491-838800
Director, Prof. Mark J. Bailey

NATIONAL CENTRE FOR ATMOSPHERIC SCIENCE, NCAS Headquarters, School of Earth and Environment, University of Leeds, Leeds LS2 9JT T 0113-343 6408
Director, Prof. Stephen Mobbs

NATIONAL CENTRE FOR EARTH OBSERVATION, Department of Meteorology, University of Reading, Earley Gate Building 58, Reading RG6 6BB T 0118-378 6728
Director, Prof. Alan O'Neill

NATIONAL OCEANOGRAPHY CENTRE, University of Southampton Waterfront Campus, European Way, Southampton SO14 3ZH T 023-8059 6666
Director, Prof. Ed Hill, OBE

SCIENCE AND TECHNOLOGY FACILITIES COUNCIL*

Polaris House, North Star Avenue, Swindon SN2 1SZ
T 01793-442000 W www.stfc.ac.uk

Formed by royal charter on 1 April 2007, through the merger of the Council for the Central Laboratory of the Research Councils and the Particle Physics and Astronomy Research Council, the STFC is a non-departmental public body reporting to BIS.

The STFC invests in large national and international research facilities, while delivering science, technology and expertise for the UK. The council is involved in research projects including the Diamond Light Source Synchrotron and the Large Hadron Collider, and develops new areas of science and technology. The EPSRC has transferred its responsibility for nuclear physics to the STFC.

Chair, Prof. Michael Sterling, FRENG
Chief Executive, Prof. John Womersley

RESEARCH CENTRES

CHILBOLTON OBSERVATORY, Chilbolton, Stockbridge, Hampshire SO20 6BJ T 01264-860391

DARESBURY LABORATORY, Daresbury Science and Innovation Campus, Warrington WA4 4AD T 01925-603000

RUTHERFORD APPLETON LABORATORY, Harwell Science and Innovation Campus, Didcot OX11 0QX T 01235-445000

UK ASTRONOMY TECHNOLOGY CENTRE, Royal Observatory, Edinburgh, Blackford Hill, Edinburgh EH9 3HJ T 0131-668 8100

HEALTH

NATIONAL HEALTH SERVICE

The National Health Service (NHS) came into being on 5 July 1948 under the National Health Service Act 1946, covering England and Wales and, under separate legislation, Scotland and Northern Ireland. The NHS is now administered by the Secretary of State for Health (in England), the Welsh government, the Scottish government and the Northern Ireland Executive.

The function of the NHS is to provide a comprehensive health service designed to secure improvement in the physical and mental health of the people and to prevent, diagnose and treat illness. It was founded on the principle that treatment should be provided according to clinical need rather than ability to pay, and should be free at the point of delivery.

Hospital, mental, dental, nursing, ophthalmic and ambulance services and facilities for the care of expectant and nursing mothers and young children are provided by the NHS to meet all reasonable requirements. Rehabilitation services such as occupational therapy, physiotherapy, speech therapy and surgical and medical appliances are supplied where appropriate. Specialists and consultants who work in NHS hospitals can also engage in private practice, including the treatment of their private patients in NHS hospitals.

STRUCTURE

The structure of the NHS remained relatively stable for the first 30 years of its existence. In 1974, a three-tier management structure comprising regional health authorities, area health authorities and district management teams was introduced in England, and the NHS became responsible for community health services. In 1979, area health authorities were abolished and district management teams were replaced by district health authorities.

The National Health Service and Community Care Act 1990 provided for more streamlined regional health authorities and district health authorities, and for the establishment of family health services authorities (FHSAs) and NHS trusts. The concept of the 'internal market' was introduced into health care, whereby care was provided through NHS contracts where health authorities or boards and GP fundholders (the purchasers) were responsible for buying health care from hospitals, non-fundholding GPs, community services and ambulance services (the providers). The Act also paved the way for the community care reforms, which were introduced in April 1993, and changed the way care is administered for older people, the mentally ill, the physically disabled and people with learning disabilities.

ENGLAND

Under the Health and Social Care Act 2012, which gained royal assent in March 2012, the NHS in England is undergoing a complete operational and budgetary restructure at a cost of approximately £1.4bn. The full implementation of all the changes will not be complete for some time. During the transition period, all vital NHS services in England will continue as normal.

Hospitals will be extensively affected by the overhaul, with the cap on income from private hospital patients rising from 1.5 per cent to 49 per cent. All hospitals will become foundation trusts, competing for treatment contracts from clinical commissioning groups (CCGs).

On 1 April 2013 the new commissioning board, NHS England, took on full statutory responsibilities; at the same time, strategic health authorities (SHAs) and primary care trusts (PCTs) which, alongside the Department of Health, had been responsible for NHS planning and delivery, were abolished. NHS England is an executive non-departmental public body of the Department of Health with a remit to:

- provide national leadership to improve the quality of care
- oversee the operation of clinical commissioning groups
- allocate resources to clinical commissioning groups
- commission primary care and specialist services

The secretary of state has ultimate responsibility for the provision of a comprehensive health service in England and for ensuring the system works to its optimum capacity to meet the needs of its patients. The Department of Health is responsible for strategic leadership of the health and social care systems, but will cease to be the headquarters of the NHS, nor will it directly manage any NHS organisations.

NHS ENGLAND, PO Box 16738, Redditch B97 9PT
T 0300-311 2233 W www.england.nhs.uk
Chief Executive, Sir David Nicholson

CLINICAL COMMISSIONING GROUPS (CCGS)

On 1 April 2013, PCTs, which controlled 80 per cent of the NHS budget and commissioned most NHS services, were abolished. They were replaced with CCGs which took on many of the functions of the PCTs in addition to some functions previously assumed by the Department of Health. All GP practices now belong to a CCG which also includes other health professionals, such as nurses. CCGs commission most services, including:

- mental health and learning disability services
- planned hospital care
- rehabilitative care
- urgent and emergency care (including out-of-hours)
- most community health services

CCGs can commission any service provider that meets NHS standards and costs. These can be NHS hospitals, social enterprises, charities, or private-sector providers. At the end of March 2013, there were 211 CCGs.

HEALTH AND WELLBEING BOARDS

Every upper-tier local authority will establish a health and wellbeing board to act as a forum for local commissioners across the NHS, social care, public health and other services. The boards are intended to:

- encourage integrated commissioning of health and social care services
- increase democratic input into strategic decisions about health and wellbeing services
- strengthen working relationships between health and social care

PUBLIC HEALTH ENGLAND (PHE)

This new organisation provides national leadership and expert services to support public health and also works with local government and the NHS to respond to emergencies. PHE's responsibilities are to:

- coordinate a national public health service
- support the public to make healthier choices
- provide leadership to the public health delivery system
- support the development of the public health workforce

REGULATION

Since the restructuring of the NHS in England began in April 2013, some elements of the regulation system have changed. Responsibility for the regulation of particular aspects of care is shared across a number of different bodies, including the Care Quality Commission (CQC), Monitor, and individual professional regulatory bodies, such as the General Medical Council, Nursing and Midwifery Council, General Dental Council and the Health and Care Professions Council.

CARE QUALITY COMMISSION (CQC)

The CQC regulates all health and social care services in England, including those provided by the NHS, local authorities, private companies or voluntary organisations. In addition it protects the interests of people detained under the Mental Health Act. The CQC ensures that all essential standards of quality and safety are met where care is provided, from hospitals to private care homes. By law all NHS providers (such as hospitals and ambulance services) must register with the CQC to show they are protecting people from the risk of infection. The CQC possesses a range of legal powers and duties and will take action if providers do not meet essential standards of quality or safety.

MONITOR

Monitor is the sector regulator for health services in England. Their job is to protect and promote the interests of patients. Monitor's aim is to promote competition, regulate prices and ensure the continuity of services for NHS foundation trusts. Under the new structure, most NHS providers need to be registered with both the CQC and Monitor to be able to legally provide services.

HEALTHWATCH

Healthwatch is a new organisation established following the restructuring of the NHS, which functions at a national and local level as an independent consumer body, gathering and representing the views of the public about health and social care services in England.

CARE QUALITY COMMISSION, Finsbury Tower, 103–105 Bunhill Row, London EC1Y 8TG T 03000-616161 W www.cqc.org.uk
Chief Executive, David Behan

MONITOR, Wellington House, 133–155 Waterloo Road, London SE1 8UG T 020-3747 0000 W www.monitor-nhsft.gov.uk
Chief Executive, Dr David Bennett

HEALTHWATCH, Citygate, Gallowgate, Newcastle upon Tyne NE1 4PA T 03000-683000 W www.healthwatch.co.uk
Chief Executive, Dr Katherine Rake, OBE

AUTHORITIES AND TRUSTS

Overseen by the NHS Trust Development Authority all NHS trusts are expected to become foundation trusts by 2014.

ACUTE TRUSTS

Hospitals in England are managed by acute trusts. There are 160 acute trusts, of which 99 have foundation trust status. Acute trusts ensure hospitals provide high-quality healthcare and spend money efficiently. They employ a large sector of the NHS workforce, including doctors, nurses, pharmacists, midwives, and health visitors. Acute trusts also employ those in supplementary medical professions, such as physiotherapists, radiographers and podiatrists, in addition to many other non-medical staff.

AMBULANCE TRUSTS

There are 12 ambulance services (four foundation trusts) in England, providing emergency services to healthcare.

CLINICAL SENATES AND STRATEGIC CLINICAL NETWORKS

Clinical senates are advisory groups of experts from across health and social care. There are 12 senates covering England comprising clinical leaders from across the healthcare system, in addition to members from social care and public health.

There are 12 strategic clinical networks across England, comprising groups of clinical experts covering a particular disease, patient or professional group. They offer advice to CCGs and NHS England.

Neither organisation is a statutory body, and although they comment on CCG plans to NHS England, they are unable to veto them.

FOUNDATION TRUSTS

NHS foundation trusts are independent legal entities with unique governance arrangements. Each NHS foundation trust has a duty to consult and involve a board of governors in the strategic planning of its organisation. They have financial freedoms and can raise capital from both the public and private sectors within borrowing limits determined by projected cash flows and based on affordability. They are overseen by Monitor.

MENTAL HEALTH TRUSTS

There are 58 mental health trusts in England, 41 of which have reached foundation trust status. They provide health and social care services for people with mental health problems.

NHS TRUST DEVELOPMENT AUTHORITY (TDA)

Following the abolition of SHAs in 2013, the TDA became responsible for overseeing the performance, management and governance of NHS trusts, including clinical quality, and managing their progress towards foundation trust status.

SPECIAL HEALTH AUTHORITIES

Special health authorities are health authorities that have a nationwide remit, such as:

- The National Blood and Transplant Authority
- NHS Business Services Authority
- NHS Litigation Authority

WALES

The NHS Wales was reorganised according to Welsh Assembly commitments laid out in the *One Wales* strategy which came into effect in October 2009. There are now seven local health boards (LHBs) that are responsible for delivering all health care services within a geographical area, rather than the trust and local health board system that existed previously. Community health councils (CHCs) are statutory lay bodies that represent the public for the health service in their region. The number of CHCs is being reduced to seven, contiguous with the LHBs. These seven CHCs are to be underpinned by 23 area associations.

NHS TRUSTS

There are three NHS trusts in Wales. The Welsh Ambulance Services NHS Trust is for emergency services; the Velindre NHS Trust offers specialist services in cancer care; while Public Health Wales serves as a unified public health organisation for Wales.

LOCAL HEALTH BOARDS

The websites of the seven LHBs, and contact details for community health councils and NHS trusts, are available in the *NHS Wales Directory* on the NHS Wales website (W www.wales.nhs.uk).

ABERTAWE BRO MORGANNWG UNIVERSITY HEALTH BOARD, One Talbot Gateway, Baglan Energy Park, Baglan, Port Talbot SA12 7BR T 01656-752752
Chief Executive, Paul Roberts

ANEURIN BEVAN HEALTH BOARD, St Cadoc's Hospital, Lodge Road, Caerleon, Newport NP18 3XQ T 01633-436700
Chief Executive, Dr Andrew Goodall

BETSI CADWALADR UNIVERSITY HEALTH BOARD, Ysbyty Gwynedd, Penrhosgarnedd, Bangor, Gwynedd LL57 2PW T 01248-384384
Chief Executive, Mary Burrows

CARDIFF AND VALE UNIVERSITY HEALTH BOARD, Whitchurch Hospital, Park Road, Whitchurch, Cardiff CF14 7XB T 029-2074 7747
Chief Executive, Adam Cairns

CWM TAF HEALTH BOARD, Ynysmeurig House, Navigation Park, Abercynon, Rhondda Cynon Taff CF45 4SN T 01443-744800
Chief Executive, Allison Williams

HYWEL DDA HEALTH BOARD, Merlin's Court, Winch Lane, Haverfordwest, Pembrokeshire SA61 1SB T 01437-771220
Chief Executive, Trevor Purt

POWYS TEACHING HEALTH BOARD, Mansion House, Bronllys, Brecon, Powys LD3 0LS T 01874-771661
Chief Executive, Andrew Cottom

SCOTLAND

The Scottish government Health Directorate is responsible both for NHS Scotland and for the development and implementation of health and community care policy. The chief executive of NHS Scotland leads the central management of the NHS, is accountable to ministers for the efficiency and performance of the service and heads the Health Department which oversees the work of the 14 regional health boards. These boards provide strategic management for the entire local NHS system and are responsible for ensuring that services are delivered effectively and efficiently.

In addition to the 14 regional health boards there are a further seven special boards and one public health body, which provide national services, such as the Scottish ambulance service and NHS Health Scotland. The new health body, Healthcare Improvement Scotland, was formed on 1 April 2011 by the Public Services Reform Act 2010 to improve the quality of Scottish healthcare.

REGIONAL HEALTH BOARDS

AYRSHIRE AND ARRAN, Eglinton House, Ailsa Hospital, Dalmellington Road, Ayr KA6 6AB T 0800-169 1441 W www.nhsaaa.net
Chief Executive, John Burns

BORDERS, Newstead, Melrose TD6 9DA T 01896-826000 W www.nhsborders.org.uk
Chief Executive, Calum Campbell

DUMFRIES AND GALLOWAY, Ryan North, Crichton Hall, Dumfries DG1 4TG T 01387-272705 W www.nhsdg.scot.nhs.uk
Chief Executive, Jeff Ace

FIFE, Hayfield House, Hayfield Road, Kirkcaldy, Fife KY2 5AH T 01592-643355 W www.nhsfife.org
Chief Executive, John Wilson

FORTH VALLEY, Carseview House, Castle Business Park, Stirling FK9 4SW T 01786-463031 W www.nhsforthvalley.com
Chief Executive, Prof. Fiona MacKenzie

GRAMPIAN, Summerfield House, 2 Eday Road, Aberdeen AB15 6RE T 0845-456 6000 W www.nhsgrampian.org
Chief Executive, Richard Carey

GREATER GLASGOW AND CLYDE, J B Russell House, Gartnavel Royal Hospital Campus, 1055 Great Western Road, Glasgow G12 0XH T 0141-201 4444 W www.nhsgg.org.uk
Chief Executive, Robert Calderwood

HIGHLAND, Assynt House, Beechwood Park, Inverness IV2 3BW T 01463-717123 W www.nhshighland.scot.nhs.uk
Chief Executive, Elaine Mead

LANARKSHIRE, Kirklands, Fallside Road, Bothwell G71 8BB T 0845-313 0130 W www.nhslanarkshire.org.uk
Chief Executive, Ian Ross

LOTHIAN, Waverley Gate, 2–4 Waterloo Place, Edinburgh EH1 3EG T 0131-536 9000 W www.nhslothian.scot.nhs.uk
Chief Executive, Tim Davison

ORKNEY, Balfour Hospital, New Scapa Road, Kirkwall, Orkney KW15 1BH T 01856-888000 W www.ohb.scot.nhs.uk
Chief Executive, Cathie Cowan

SHETLAND, Brevik House, South Road, Lerwick ZE1 0TG T 01595-743060 W www.shb.scot.nhs.uk
Chief Executive, Ralph Roberts

TAYSIDE, Level 10, Ninewells Hospital, Dundee DD1 9SY T 01382-660111 W www.nhstayside.scot.nhs.uk
Chief Executive, Gerry Marr

WESTERN ISLES, 37 South Beach Street, Stornoway, Isle of Lewis HS1 2BB T 01851-702997 W www.wihb.scot.nhs.uk
Chief Executive, Gordon Jamieson

NORTHERN IRELAND

On 1 April 2009 the four health and social services boards in Northern Ireland were replaced by a single health and social care board for the whole of Northern Ireland. The new board together with its local commissioning groups (whose boundaries are subject to review pending the outcome of local government reform) are responsible for improving the health and social wellbeing of people in the area for which they are responsible, planning and commissioning services, and coordinating the delivery of services in a cost-effective manner.

HEALTH AND SOCIAL CARE BOARD, 12–22 Linenhall Street, Belfast BT2 8BS T 028-9032 1313 W www.hscboard.hscni.net
Chief Executive, John Compton

FINANCE

The NHS is still funded mainly through general taxation, although in recent years more reliance has been placed on the NHS element of national insurance contributions, patient charges and other sources of income.

The budgeted departmental expenditure limit for the NHS in England was set at £111.3bn for 2013–14. Expenditure for the NHS in Wales, Scotland and Northern Ireland is set by the devolved governments.

EMPLOYEES AND SALARIES

NHS HEALTH SERVICE STAFF 2013 (ENGLAND)
Full-time equivalent

All hospital, community and dental staff	1,184,396
Consultants	40,737
Registrars	38,277
Qualified nursing and midwifery staff	348,643
General practitioners*	35,871
Qualified scientific, therapeutic and technical staff	154,242

* Figure is from Sep 2012; all other data is from April 2013
Source: Health and Social Care Information Centre

SALARIES
Many general practitioners (GPs) are self-employed and hold contracts, either on their own or as part of a Clinical Commissioning Group (CCG). The profit of GPs varies according to the services they provide for their patients and the way they choose to provide these services. Salaried GPs who are part of a CCG earn between £54,319 to £81,969 dependent on, among other factors, length of service and experience. Most NHS dentists are self-employed contractors. A contract for dentists was introduced on 1 April 2006 which provides dentists with an annual income in return for carrying out an agreed amount, or units, of work. A salaried dentist employed by the NHS, who works mainly with community dental services earn between £38,095 and £81,480.

BASIC SALARIES FOR HOSPITAL MEDICAL AND DENTAL STAFF* *from 1 April 2013*

Consultant (2003 contract)	£75,249–£101,451
Consultant (pre-2003 contract)	£62,477–£80,988
Specialist registrar	£31,301–£47,175
Speciality registrar (full)	£30,002–£47,175
Speciality registrar (fixed term)	£30,002–£39,693
Senior house officer	£28,076–£39,092
House officer	£22,636–£25,461

* These figures do not include merit awards, discretionary points or banding supplements

NURSES
From 1 December 2004 the *Agenda for Change* pay system was introduced throughout the UK for all NHS staff with the exception of medical and dental staff, doctors in public health medicine and the community health service. Nurses' salaries are incorporated in the *Agenda for Change* nine pay band structure, which provides additional payments for flexible working such as providing out-of-hours services, working weekends and nights and being 'on-call'. There is also additional payments for those staff who work in 'high-cost' areas such as London.

SALARIES FOR NURSES AND MIDWIVES
from 1 April 2013

Nurse/Midwife consultant	£39,239–£67,805
Modern matron	£39,239–£67,805
Nurse advanced/team manager	£30,764–£40,558
Midwife higher level	£30,764–£40,558
Nurse specialist/team leader	£25,783–£34,530
Hospital/community midwife	£25,783–£34,530
Registered nurse/entry level midwife	£21,388–£27,901

HEALTH SERVICES

PRIMARY CARE

Primary care comprises the services provided by general practitioners, community health centres, pharmacies, dental practices and opticians. Primary nursing care includes the work carried out by practice nurses, community nurses, community midwives and health visitors.

PRIMARY MEDICAL SERVICES
In England, primary medical services (PMS) are provided by around 40,200 GPs, working in around 8,090 GP practices, with 55.7 million registered patients..

In Wales, responsibility for primary medical services rests with local health boards (LHBs), in Scotland with the 14 regional health boards and in Northern Ireland with the health and social care board.

Any vocationally trained doctor may provide general or personal medical services. GPs may also have private fee-paying patients, but not if that patient is already an NHS patient on that doctor's patient list.

A person who is ordinarily resident in the UK is eligible to register with a GP (or PMS provider) for free primary care treatment. Should a patient have difficulty in registering with a doctor, he or she should contact the local CCG for help. When a person is away from home he/she can still access primary care treatment from a GP if they ask to be treated as a temporary resident. In an emergency any doctor in the service will give treatment and advice.

GPs or CCGs are responsible for the care of their patients 24 hours a day, seven days a week, but can fulfil the terms of their contract by delegating or transferring responsibility for out-of-hours care to an accredited provider.

In addition, NHS walk-in centres throughout England are usually open seven days a week, from early in the morning until late in the evening. They are nurse-led and provide treatment for minor illnesses and injuries, health information and self-help advice.

HEALTH COSTS
Some people are exempt from, or entitled to help with, health costs such as prescription charges, ophthalmic and dental costs, and in some cases help towards travel costs to and from hospital.

The following list is intended as a general guide to those who may be entitled to help, or who are exempt from some of the charges relating to the above:

- children under 16 and young people in full-time education who are under 19
- people aged 60 or over
- pregnant women and women who have had a baby in the last 12 months and have a valid maternity exemption certificate (MatEx)
- people, or their partners, who are in receipt of income support, income-based jobseeker's allowance and/or income-based employment and support allowance
- people in receipt of the pension credit
- diagnosed glaucoma patients, people who have been advised by an ophthalmologist that they are at risk of glaucoma and people aged 40 or over who have an immediate family member who is a diagnosed glaucoma patient
- NHS in-patients
- NHS out-patients for all prescribed contraceptives, medication given at a hospital, NHS walk-in centre, personally administered by a GP or supplied at a hospital or primary care trust clinic for the treatment of tuberculosis or a sexually transmissable infection
- out-patients of the NHS Hospital Dental Service
- people registered blind or partially sighted
- people who need complex lenses
- war pensioners whose treatment/prescription is for their accepted disablement and who have a valid exemption certificate
- people who are entitled to, or named on, a valid NHS tax credit exemption or HC2 certificate
- people who have a medical exemption (MedEx) certificate, including those with cancer or diabetes

People in other circumstances may also be eligible for help; *see* booklet HC12 (England) and HCS2 (Scotland) for further information.

WALES
On 1 April 2007 all prescription charges (including those for medical supports and appliances and wigs) for people living in Wales were abolished. The above guide still applies for NHS dental and optical charges although all people aged under 25 living in Wales are also entitled to free dental examinations.

SCOTLAND
On 1 April 2011 all prescription charges in Scotland were abolished. Those entitled to free prescriptions in Scotland

include patients registered with a Scottish GP and receiving a prescription from a Scottish pharmacy, and Scottish patients who have an English GP and an entitlement card.

NORTHERN IRELAND

On 1 April 2010 all prescription charges in Northern Ireland were abolished. All prescriptions dispensed in Northern Ireland are free, even for patients visiting from England, Wales or Scotland.

PHARMACEUTICAL SERVICES

Patients may obtain medicines and appliances under the NHS from any pharmacy whose owner has entered into arrangements with the CCG to provide this service. There are also some suppliers who only provide special appliances. In rural areas, where access to a pharmacy may be difficult, patients may be able to obtain medicines, etc, from a dispensing doctor.

In England, a charge of £7.85 is payable for each item supplied (except for contraceptives for which there is no charge), unless the patient is exempt and the declaration on the back of the prescription form is completed. Prescription prepayment certificates (£29.10 valid for three months, £104.00 valid for a year) may be purchased by those patients not entitled to exemption who require frequent prescriptions.

DENTAL SERVICES

Dentists, like doctors, may take part in the NHS and also have private patients. Dentists are responsible to the local health provider in whose areas they provide services. Patients may go to any dentist who is taking part in the NHS and is willing to accept them. On 1 April 2006 the charging system for NHS dentistry in England and Wales was changed. There is now a three-tier payment system based on the individual course of treatment required.

NHS DENTAL CHARGES
from 1 April 2013

	England/Wales
Band 1* – Examination, diagnosis, preventive care (eg x-rays, scale and polish)	£18.00/£12.70
Band 2 – Band 1 + basic additional treatment (eg fillings and extractions)	£49.00/£41.10
Band 3 – Bands 1 and 2 + all other treatment (eg crowns, dentures and bridges)	£214.00/£177.00

* Urgent and out-of-hours treatment is also charged at this payment tier

The cost of individual treatment plans should be known prior to treatment and some dental practices may require payment in advance. There is no charge for writing a prescription or removing stitches and only one charge is payable for each course of treatment even if more than one visit to the dentist is required. If additional treatment is required within two months of visiting the dentist and this is covered by the course of treatment most recently paid for (eg payment was made for the second tier of treatment but an additional filling is required) then this will be provided free of charge.

SCOTLAND AND NORTHERN IRELAND

Scotland and Northern Ireland have yet to simplify their charging systems. NHS dental patients pay 80 per cent of the cost of the individual items of treatment provided up to a maximum of £384. Patients in Scotland are entitled to free basic and extensive examinations.

GENERAL OPHTHALMIC SERVICES

General ophthalmic services are administered by local health providers. Testing of sight may be carried out by any ophthalmic medical practitioner or ophthalmic optician (optometrist). The optician must give the prescription to the patient, who can take this to any supplier of glasses to have them dispensed. Only registered opticians can supply glasses to children and to people registered as blind or partially sighted.

Free eyesight tests and help towards the cost are available to people in certain circumstances. Help is also available for the purchase of glasses or contact lenses (*see* Health Costs section). In Scotland eye examinations, which include a sight test, are free to all. Help is also available for the purchase of glasses or contact lenses to those entitled to help with health costs in the same way it is available to those in England and Wales.

CHILD HEALTH SERVICES

Pre-school services at GP surgeries or child health clinics provide regular monitoring of children's physical, mental and emotional health and development and advise parents on their children's health and welfare.

NHS DIRECT AND NHS 24

NHS Direct is a website and 24-hour nurse-led advice telephone service for England and Wales. It provides medical advice as well as directing people to the appropriate part of the NHS for treatment if necessary (T 111 W www.nhsdirect.nhs.uk or W www.nhsdirect.wales.nhs.uk in Wales).

NHS 24 provides an equivalent service for Scotland (T 0845-424 2424 W www.nhs24.com).

SECONDARY CARE AND OTHER SERVICES

HOSPITALS

NHS hospitals provide acute and specialist care services, treating conditions which normally cannot be dealt with by primary care specialists, and provide for medical emergencies.

NUMBER OF BEDS 2012–13

	Average daily	
	available beds	*occupation of beds*
England	138,239	121,067
Wales*	11,807	10,060
Scotland*	16,503	13,565
Northern Ireland	6,287	5,259

* Figures are for 2011–12

Sources: Department of Health; Welsh government, ISD Scotland, NI Direct

HOSPITAL CHARGES

Acute or foundation trusts can provide hospital accommodation in single rooms or small wards, if not required for patients who need privacy for medical reasons. The patient is still an NHS patient, but there may be a charge for these additional facilities. Acute or foundation trusts can charge for certain patient services that are considered to be additional treatments over and above the normal hospital service provision. There is no blanket policy to cover this and each case is considered in the light of the patient's clinical need. However, if an item or service is considered to be an integral part of a patient's treatment by their clinician, then a charge should not be made.

In some NHS hospitals, accommodation and services are available for the treatment of private patients where it does not interfere with care for NHS patients. Income generated by treating private patients is then put back into local NHS services. Private patients undertake to pay the full costs of medical treatment, accommodation, medication and other related services. Charges for private patients are set locally.

WAITING LISTS

England

In July 2004 a target of an 18-week maximum wait, from start time (ie seeing a GP) to treatment, was introduced. For April 2013, 303,491 referral to treatment (RTT) patients started admitted treatment and 830,792 started non-admitted treatment. Of the admitted patients, 91.6 per cent were treated within 18 weeks, and for non-admitted patients 97.2 per cent were treated within 18 weeks. The *Revision to the Operating Framework for the NHS in England 2010/11*, published in June 2010, abolished the performance management of the 18-week waiting time target although referral-to-treatment data will continue to be published.

Wales

In Wales the main target is for referral to treatment to take no longer than 26 weeks. In April 2013, 84 per cent of 83,156 patients were treated within 26 weeks and 96.4 per cent were treated within 36 weeks of the date the referral letter was received in the hospital. There are also operational standards for maximum waiting times for first out-patient appointments and in-patient or day-case treatment but these are not set targets. The standards are 14 weeks for in-patient or day case treatment, and ten weeks for a first out-patient appointment.

Scotland

An 18-week referral to treatment target, due to be delivered from December 2011, was set out in the publication *Better Health, Better Care*. In March 2013, 90.6 per cent of patients on an 18 week referral to treatment pathway were reported as being seen within 18 weeks, a decrease from 91.5 per cent in March 2012.

Northern Ireland

From March 2013 the aim was for at least 60 per cent of patients to wait no longer than nine weeks for a first out-patient appointment, with no patient waiting longer than 18 weeks. The total number of people waiting for a first out-patient appointment at the end of March 2013 was 99,774; of these, 19,764 had been waiting over nine weeks, a decrease from 28,278 at the end of March 2012. The number of people waiting for in-patient treatment at the end of March 2013 was 47,689 – of these, 31.2 per cent had been waiting for more than 13 weeks.

AMBULANCE SERVICE

The NHS provides emergency ambulance services free of charge via the 999 emergency telephone service. Air ambulances, provided through local charities and partially funded by the NHS, are used throughout the UK. They assist with cases where access may be difficult or heavy traffic could hinder road progress. Non-emergency ambulance services are provided free to patients who are deemed to require them on medical grounds.

Since 1 April 2001 all services have had a system of call prioritisation. The prioritisation procedures require all emergency calls to be classified as either immediately life threatening (category A) or other emergency (category B). Services are expected to reach 75 per cent of category A calls within eight minutes and 95 per cent of category B calls within 19 minutes.

BLOOD AND TRANSPLANT SERVICES

There are four national bodies which coordinate the blood donor programme and transplant and related services in the UK. Donors give blood at local centres on a voluntary basis.

NHS BLOOD AND TRANSPLANT, Oak House, Reeds Crescent, Watford, Herts WD24 4QN T 0300-123 2323 W www.nhsbt.nhs.uk

WELSH BLOOD SERVICE, Ely Valley Road, Talbot Green, Pontyclun CF72 9WB T 01443-622000 W www.welsh-blood.org.uk

SCOTTISH NATIONAL BLOOD TRANSFUSION SERVICE, 21 Ellen's Glen Road, Edinburgh EH17 7QT T 0131-536 5700 W www.scotblood.co.uk

NORTHERN IRELAND BLOOD TRANSFUSION SERVICE, Lisburn Road, Belfast BT9 7TS T 028-9032 1414 W www.nibts.org

HOSPICES

Hospice or palliative care may be available for patients with life-threatening illnesses. It may be provided at the patient's home or in a voluntary or NHS hospice or in hospital, and is intended to ensure the best possible quality of life for the patient during their illness, and to provide help and support to both the patient and the patient's family. The National Council for Palliative Care coordinates NHS and voluntary services in England, Wales and Northern Ireland; the Scottish Partnership for Palliative Care performs the same function in Scotland.

NATIONAL COUNCIL FOR PALLIATIVE CARE, The Fitzpatrick Building, 188–194 York Way, London N7 9AS T 020-7697 1520 W www.ncpc.org.uk

SCOTTISH PARTNERSHIP FOR PALLIATIVE CARE, 1A Cambridge Street, Edinburgh EH1 2DY T 0131-229 0538 W www.palliativecarescotland.org.uk

COMPLAINTS

Patient advice and liaison services (PALS) have been established for every NHS and PCT in England. PALS can give advice on local complaints procedure, or resolve concerns informally. If the case is not resolved locally or the complainant is not satisfied with the way a local NHS body or practice has dealt with their complaint, they may approach the Parliamentary and Health Service Ombudsman in England, the Scottish Public Services Ombudsman, Public Services Ombudsman for Wales or the Northern Ireland Commissioner for Complaints.

HEALTH ADVICE AND MEDICAL TREATMENT ABROAD

IMMUNISATION

Country-by-country guidance is set out on the website W www.fitfortravel.nhs.uk. Health care professionals can obtain information about immunisation recommendations from the Department of Health publication *Health Information for Overseas Travel* (the 'Yellow Book').

RECIPROCAL ARRANGEMENTS

The European Health Insurance Card (EHIC) allows UK residents access to state-provided health care that may become necessary while temporarily travelling in all European Economic Area countries and Switzerland either free or at a reduced cost. A card is free, valid for up to five years and should be obtained before travelling. Applications can be made by telephone (T 0845-606 2030), online (W www.ehic.org.uk) or by post (a form is available from the post office).

The UK also has bilateral agreements with several other countries, including Australia and New Zealand, for the free provision of urgent medical treatment.

European Economic Area nationals visiting the UK and visitors from other countries with which the UK has bilateral health care agreements are entitled to receive emergency health care on the NHS on the same terms as it is available to UK residents.

SOCIAL WELFARE

SOCIAL SERVICES

The Secretary of State for Health (in England), the Welsh government, the Scottish government and the Secretary of State for Northern Ireland are responsible, under the Local Authority Social Services Act 1970, for the provision of social services for older people, disabled people, families and children, and those with mental disorders. Personal social services are administered by local authorities according to policies, with standards set by central and devolved government. Each authority has a director and a committee responsible for the social services functions placed upon them. Local authorities provide, enable and commission care after assessing the needs of their population. The private and voluntary sectors also play an important role in the delivery of social services, and an estimated 6 million people in the UK provide substantial regular care for a member of their family.

The Care Quality Commission (CQC) was established in April 2009, bringing together the independent regulation of health, mental health and adult social care. Prior to 1 April 2009 this work was carried out by three separate organisations: the Healthcare Commission, the Mental Health Act Commission and the Commission for Social Care Inspection. The CQC is responsible for the registration of health and social care providers, the monitoring and inspection of all health and adult social care, issuing fines, public warnings or closures if standards are not met and for undertaking regular performance reviews. Since April 2007 the Office for Standards in Education, Children's Services and Skills (Ofsted) has been responsible for inspecting and regulating all care services for children and young people in England. Both Ofsted and CQC collate information on local care services and make this information available to the public.

The Care and Social Services Inspectorate Wales (CSSIW), an operationally independent part of the Welsh government, is reponsible for the regulation and inspection of all social care services in Wales. A new unified body, the Care Inspectorate, was established on 1 April 2011, replacing the Scottish Commission for the Regulation of Care (the Care Commission) and is now the independent care services regulator for Scotland.

The Department of Health, Social Services and Public Safety is responsible for social care services in Northern Ireland.

CARE QUALITY COMMISSION (CQC), Citygate, Gallowgate, Newcastle upon Tyne NE1 4PA T 0300-061 6161 W www.cqc.org.uk

OFFICE FOR STANDARDS IN EDUCATION, CHILDREN'S SERVICES AND SKILLS (Ofsted), Piccadilly Gate, Store Street, Manchester M1 2WD T 0300-123 1231 E enquiries@ofsted.gov.uk W www.ofsted.gov.uk

CARE AND SOCIAL SERVICES INSPECTORATE WALES (CSSIW), Welsh Government, Rhydcar Business Park, Merthyr Tydfil CF48 1UZ T 0300-062 8800 E cssiw@wales.gsi.gov.uk W www.cssiw.org.uk

CARE INSPECTORATE, Compass House, 11 Riverside Drive, Dundee DD1 4NY T 0845-600 9527 E enquiries@careinspectorate.com W www.scswis.com

DEPARTMENT OF HEALTH, SOCIAL SERVICES AND PUBLIC SAFETY, Castle Buildings, Stormont, Belfast BT4 3SJ T 028-9052 0500 E webmaster@dhsspsni.gov.uk W www.dhsspsni.gov.uk

STAFF

Total Social Services Staff (England, full-time)	150,700
Community	52,600
Residential	33,500
Other	30,600
Domiciliary	19,100
Day	14,800

Source: Department of Health

OLDER PEOPLE

Services for older people are designed to enable them to remain living in their own homes for as long as possible. Local authority services include advice, domestic help, meals in the home, alterations to the home to aid mobility, emergency alarm systems, day and/or night attendants, laundry services and the provision of day centres and recreational facilities. Charges may be made for these services. Respite care may also be provided in order to allow carers temporary relief from their responsibilities.

Local authorities and the private sector also provide 'sheltered housing' for older people, sometimes with resident wardens.

If an older person is admitted to a residential home, charges are made according to a means test; if the person cannot afford to pay, the costs are met by the local authority.

DISABLED PEOPLE

Services for disabled people are designed to enable them to remain living in their own homes wherever possible. Local authority services include advice, adaptations to the home, meals in the home, help with personal care, occupational therapy, educational facilities and recreational facilities. Respite care may also be provided in order to allow carers temporary relief from their responsibilities.

Special housing may be available for disabled people who can live independently, and residential accommodation for those who cannot.

FAMILIES AND CHILDREN

Local authorities are required to provide services aimed at safeguarding the welfare of children in need and, wherever possible, allowing them to be brought up by their families. Services include advice, counselling, help in the home and the provision of family centres. Many authorities also provide short-term refuge accommodation for women and children.

DAY CARE

In allocating day care places to children, local authorities give priority to children with special needs, whether in terms of their health, learning abilities or social needs. Since September 2001 Ofsted has been responsible for the regulation and registration of all early years childcare and education provision in England (previously the responsibility of the local authorities). All day care and childminding services that care for children under eight years of age for more than two hours a day must register with Ofsted and are inspected at least every two years. As at 31 March 2013 there were 95,987 registered childcare providers in England.

CHILD PROTECTION

Children considered to be at risk of physical injury, neglect or sexual abuse are placed on the local authority's child protection register. Local authority social services staff, schools, health visitors and other agencies work together to prevent and detect cases of abuse. As at 31 March 2012, there was a total of 50,573 children on child protection registers or subject to a child protection plan in the UK. In England, there were 42,850 children on child protection registers, of these, 18,220 were at risk of neglect, 4,690 of physical abuse, 2,220 of sexual abuse and 12,330 of emotional abuse. At 31 March 2011 there were 2,890 children on child protection registers in Wales, 2,706 in Scotland and 2,127 in Northern Ireland.

LOCAL AUTHORITY CARE

Local authorities are required to provide accommodation for children who have no parents or guardians or whose parents or guardians are unable or unwilling to care for them. A family proceedings court may also issue a care order where a child is being neglected or abused, or is not attending school; the court must be satisfied that this would positively contribute to the well-being of the child.

The welfare of children in local authority care must be properly safeguarded. Children may be placed with foster families, who receive payments to cover the expenses of caring for the child or children, or in residential care.

Children's homes may be run by the local authority or by the private or voluntary sectors; all homes are subject to inspection procedures. As at 31 March 2012, 67,050 children in the UK were in the care of local authorities, of these, 50,260 were in foster placements and 5,930 were in children's homes, hostels or secure units.

ADOPTION

Local authorities are required to provide an adoption service, either directly or via approved voluntary societies. In 2011–12, there were 2,680 children aged under 18 entered in the adopted children register in the UK.

PEOPLE WITH LEARNING DISABILITIES

Services for people with learning disabilities are designed to enable them to remain living in the community wherever possible. Local authority services include short-term care, support in the home, the provision of day care centres, and help with other activities outside the home. Residential care is provided for the severely or profoundly disabled.

MENTALLY ILL PEOPLE

Under the care programme approach, mentally ill people should be assessed by specialist services and receive a care plan, and a key worker should be appointed for each patient. Regular reviews of the person's progress should be conducted. Local authorities provide help and advice to mentally ill people and their families, and places in day centres and social centres. Social workers can apply for a mentally disturbed person to be compulsorily detained in hospital. Where appropriate, mentally ill people are provided with accommodation in special hospitals, local authority accommodation, or at homes run by private or voluntary organisations. Patients who have been discharged from hospitals may be placed on a supervision register.

NATIONAL INSURANCE

The National Insurance (NI) scheme operates under the Social Security Contributions and Benefits Act 1992 and the Social Security Administration Act 1992, and orders and regulations made thereunder. The scheme is financed by contributions payable by earners, employers and others (*see* below). Money collected under the scheme is used to finance the National Insurance Fund (from which contributory benefits are paid) and to contribute to the cost of the National Health Service.

NATIONAL INSURANCE FUND

Estimated receipts, payments and statement of balances of the National Insurance Fund for 2013–14:

Receipts	*£ million*
Net national insurance contributions	83,236
Compensation from the Consolidated Fund for statutory sick, maternity, paternity and adoption pay recoveries	2,511
Income from investments	117
State scheme premiums	37
Other receipts	47
TOTAL RECEIPTS	85,947
Payments	*£ million*
Benefits	
At present rates	86,615
Increase due to proposed rate changes	2,055
Personal and stakeholder pensions contracted-out rebates	41
Age-related rebates for contracted-out money purchase schemes	6
Administration costs	1,180
Redundancy fund payments	450
Transfer to Northern Ireland	305
Other payments	158
TOTAL PAYMENTS	90,810
Balances	*£ million*
Opening balance	31,844
Excess of receipts over payments	(4,862)
BALANCE AT END OF YEAR	26,982

CONTRIBUTIONS

There are six classes of National Insurance contributions (NICs):

Class 1	paid by employees and their employers
Class 1A	paid by employers who provide employees with certain benefits in kind for private use, such as company cars
Class 1B	paid by employers who enter into a pay as you earn (PAYE) settlement agreement (PSA) with HM Revenue and Customs
Class 2	paid by self-employed people
Class 3	voluntary contributions paid to protect entitlement to the state pension for those who do not pay enough NI contributions in another class
Class 4	paid by the self-employed on their taxable profits over a set limit. These are normally paid by self-employed people in addition to class 2 contributions. Class 4 contributions do not count towards benefits.

The lower and upper earnings limits and the percentage rates referred to below apply from April 2013 to April 2014.

CLASS 1

Class 1 contributions are paid where a person:

- is an employed earner (employee), office holder (eg company director) or employed under a contract of service in Great Britain or Northern Ireland
- is 16 or over and under state pension age
- earns at or above the earnings threshold of £149 per week (including overtime pay, bonus, commission, etc, without deduction of superannuation contributions)

Class 1 contributions are made up of primary and secondary contributions. Primary contributions are those paid by the employee and these are deducted from earnings by the employer. Since 6 April 2001 the employee's and employer's earnings thresholds have been the same and are referred to as the earnings threshold. Primary contributions are not paid on earnings below the earnings threshold of £149.00 per week. However, between the lower earnings limit of £109.00 per week and the earnings threshold of £149.00 per week, NI contributions are treated as having been paid to protect the benefit entitlement position of lower earners. Contributions are payable at the rate of 12 per cent on earnings between the earnings threshold and the upper earnings limit of £797.00 per week (10.6 per cent for contracted-out employment). Above the upper earnings limit 2 per cent is payable.

Some married women or widows pay a reduced rate of 5.85 per cent on earnings between the earnings threshold and upper earnings limits and 2 per cent above this. It is no longer possible to elect to pay the reduced rate but those who had reduced liability before 12 May 1977 may retain it for as long as certain conditions are met.

Secondary contributions are paid by employers of employed earners at the rate of 13.8 per cent on all earnings above the earnings threshold of £149.00 per week. There is no upper earnings limit for employers' contributions. Employers operating contracted-out salary related schemes pay reduced contributions of 10.4 per cent. The contracted-out rate applies only to that portion of earnings between the earnings threshold and the upper earnings limit. Employers' contributions below and above those respective limits are assessed at the appropriate not contracted-out rate.

CLASS 2

Class 2 contributions are paid where a person is self-employed and is 16 or over and under state pension age. Contributions are paid at a flat rate of £2.70 per week regardless of the amount earned. However, those with earnings of less than £5,725 a year can apply for small earnings exception. Those granted exemption from class 2 contributions may pay class 2 or class 3 contributions voluntarily. Self-employed earners (whether or not they pay class 2 contributions) may also be liable to pay class 4 contributions based on profits. There are special rules for those who are concurrently employed and self-employed.

Married women and widows can no longer choose not to pay class 2 contributions but those who elected not to pay class 2 contributions before 12 May 1977 may retain the right for as long as certain conditions are met.

Class 2 contributions are collected by the national insurance contributions department of HM Revenue and Customs (HMRC), by direct debit or quarterly bills.

CLASS 3

Class 3 contributions are voluntary flat-rate contributions of £13.55 per week payable by persons over the age of 16 who would otherwise be unable to qualify for retirement pension and certain other benefits because they have an insufficient record of class 1 or class 2 contributions. This may include those who are not working, those not liable for class 1 or class 2 contributions, or those excepted from class 2 contributions. Married women and widows who on or before 11 May 1977 elected not to pay class 1 (full rate) or class 2 contributions cannot pay class 3 contributions while they retain this right. Class 3 contributions are collected by HMRC by quarterly bills or direct debit.

CLASS 4

Self-employed people whose profits and gains are over £7,755 a year pay class 4 contributions in addition to class 2 contributions. This applies to self-employed earners over 16 and under the state pension age. Class 4 contributions are calculated at 9 per cent of annual profits or gains between £7,755 and £41,450 and 2 per cent above. Class 4 contributions are assessed and collected by HMRC. It is possible, in some circumstances, to apply for exceptions from liability to pay class 4 contributions or to have the amount of contribution reduced.

PENSIONS

Many people will qualify for a state pension; however, there are further pension choices available, such as workplace, personal and stakeholder pensions. There are also other non-pension savings and investment options. The following section provides background information on existing pension schemes.

Flat Rate State Pension

The government has proposed that the new flat rate (single-tier) pension will be introduced from April 2016 (W www.gov.uk/changes-state-pension).

Current pensioners and everyone reaching state pension age before the introduction of the single-tier pension will continue to receive their state pension in line with existing rules.

STATE PENSION SCHEME

The state pension scheme consists of:

- basic state pension
- additional state pension

People may be able to get both or either when they reach state pension age and meet the qualifying conditions.

The state pension does not have to be claimed at state pension age, people can delay claiming it to earn extra weekly state pension or a lump sum payment.

Basic State Pension

The amount of basic state pension paid is dependent on the number of 'qualifying years' a person has established during their working life. In 2013–14, the full basic state pension is £110.15 a week (*see also* Benefits, State Pension: Categories A and B).

Working Life

The working life is from the start of the tax year (6 April) in which a person reaches 16 to the end of the tax year (5 April) before the one in which they reach state pension age (*see* State Pension Age).

Qualifying Years

A 'qualifying year' is a tax year in which a person has sufficient earnings upon which they have paid, are treated as having paid, or have been credited with national insurance (NI) contributions (*see* National Insurance Credits section).

Since 6 April 2010, a person who has 30 qualifying years will be entitled to a full basic state pension. Someone with less than 30 qualifying years will be entitled to a proportion of the full basic state pension based on the number of qualifying years they have. Just one qualifying year, achieved through paid or credited contributions, will give entitlement to the basic state pension worth one-thirtieth of the full basic state pension.

Until 6 April 2010, women normally needed 39 qualifying years for a full basic state pension (£110.15 in 2013–14) and men normally needed 44 qualifying years. A reduced-rate basic state pension was payable if the number of qualifying years was less than 90 per cent of the working life, but to receive any basic state pension at all, a person must have had enough qualifying years, normally 10 or 11, to receive a basic state pension of at least 25 per cent of the full rate.

National Insurance Credits
Those in receipt of carer's allowance, working tax credit (with a disability element), jobseeker's allowance, incapacity benefit, employment support allowance, unemployability supplement, statutory sick pay, statutory maternity pay or statutory adoption pay may have class 1 NI contributions credited to them each week. People may also get credits if they are unemployed and looking for work or too sick to work, even if they have not paid enough contributions to receive benefit. Since April 2010, spouses and civil partners of members of HM forces may get credits if they are on an accompanied assignment outside the UK. Persons undertaking certain training courses or jury service or who have been wrongly imprisoned for a conviction which is quashed on appeal may also get class 1 NI credits for each week they fulfil certain conditions. Class 1 credits may also be available to men approaching state pension age. Until 5 April 2010, these credits were awarded for the tax years in which they reached age 60 and continued until age 64, if they were not liable to pay contributions and were not absent from the UK for more than six months in any tax year. Since 6 April 2010 these credits are being phased out in line with the increase in women's state pension age. Class 1 NI credits count toward all future contributory benefits. A class 3 NI credit for basic state pension and bereavement benefit purposes is awarded, where required, for each week the working tax credit (without a disability element) has been received or child benefit, for a child under 12, has been received. Class 3 credits may also be awarded, on application, to approved foster carers and people caring for at least 20 hours a week. Since 6 April 2011, class 3 credits have been available to adults under state pension age who care for a family member under 12. Before 6 April 2010 class 3 credits were automatically awarded to young people in the tax years of their 16th, 17th and 18th birthdays if they did not work or earn enough to pay NI contributions. Since 6 April 2010 these credits are no longer awarded.

State Pension Age
State pension age is currently 65 for men and between 60 and 65 for women. However, this will increase to 66 in 2020. Further information can be obtained from the online state pension calculator (W www.gov.uk/calculate-state-pension).

Using the NI Contribution Record of Another Person to Claim a State Pension
Married people or civil partners whose own NI record is incomplete may get a lower-rate basic state pension calculated using their partner's NI contribution record. This can be up to £66.00 a week in April 2013–14. Married men and civil partners may only be able to qualify if their wife or civil partner was born on or after 6 April 1950. A state pension may also be payable to widows, widowers, surviving civil partners, and people who are divorced or whose civil partnership has been dissolved, based on their late or ex-spouse's/civil partner's NI contributions.

Non-contributory State Pensions
A non-contributory state pension may be payable to those aged 80 or over who live in England, Scotland or Wales, and have done so for a total of ten years or more for any continuous period in the 20 years after their 60th birthday, if they are not entitled to another category of state pension, or are entitled to one below the rate of £66.00 a week in 2013–14 (*see also* Benefits, State Pension for people aged 80 and over).

Graduated Retirement Benefit
Graduated Retirement Benefit (GRB) is based on the amount of graduated NI contributions paid into the GRB scheme between April 1961 and April 1975 (*see also* Benefits, Graduated Retirement Benefit).

Home Responsibilities Protection
From 6 April 1978 until 5 April 2010, it was possible for people who had low income or were unable to work because they cared for children or a sick or disabled person at home to reduce the number of qualifying years required for basic state pension. This was called home responsibilities protection (HRP); the number of years for which HRP was given was deducted from the number of qualifying years needed. HRP could, in some cases, also qualify the recipient for additional state pension. From April 2003 to April 2010 HRP was also available to approved foster carers.

From 6 April 2010, HRP was replaced by weekly credits for parents and carers. A class 3 national insurance credit is given, where eligible, towards basic state pension and bereavement benefits for spouses and civil partners. An earnings factor credit towards additional state pension is also awarded. Any years of HRP accrued before 6 April 2010 have been converted into qualifying years of credits for people reaching state pension age after that date, up to a maximum of 22 years for basic state pension purposes.

Additional State Pension
The amount of additional state pension paid depends on the amount of earnings a person has, or is treated as having, between the lower and upper earnings limits (from April 2009, the upper accruals point replaced the upper earnings limit for additional pension) for each complete tax year between 6 April 1978 (when the scheme started) and the tax year before they reach state pension age. The right to additional state pension does not depend on the person's right to basic state pension.

From 1978 to 2002, additional state pension was called the State Earnings-Related Pension Scheme (SERPS). SERPS covered all earnings by employees from 6 April 1978 to 5 April 1997 on which standard rate class 1 NI contributions had been paid, and earnings between 6 April 1997 and 5 April 2002 if the standard rate class 1 NI contributions had been contracted-in.

In 2002, SERPS was reformed through the state second pension, by improving the pension available to low and moderate earners and extending access to certain carers and people with long-term illness or disability. If earnings on which class 1 NI contributions have been paid or can be treated as paid are above the annual NI lower earnings limit (£5,668 for 2013–14) but below the statutory low earnings threshold (£15,000 for 2013–14), the state second pension regards this as earnings of £15,000 and it is treated as equivalent. Certain carers and people with long-term illness and disability will be considered as having earned at the low earnings threshold for each complete tax year since 2002–3 even if they do not work at all, or earn less than the annual NI lower earnings limit.

The amount of additional state pension paid also depends on when a person reaches state pension age; changes phased in from 6 April 1999 mean that pensions are calculated differently from that date.

Inheritance
Men or women widowed before 6 October 2002 can inherit all of their late spouse's SERPS pension. From 6 October 2002, the maximum percentage of SERPS pension that a person can inherit from a late spouse or civil partner depends on their late spouse or civil partner's date of birth:

Maximum SERPS entitlement	*d.o.b (men)*	*d.o.b (women)*
100%	5/10/37 or earlier	5/10/42 or earlier
90%	6/10/37 to 5/10/39	6/10/42 to 5/10/44
80%	6/10/39 to 5/10/41	6/10/44 to 5/10/46
70%	6/10/41 to 5/10/43	6/10/46 to 5/10/48
60%	6/10/43 to 5/10/45	6/10/48 to 5/7/50
50%	6/10/45 or later	6/7/50 or later

The maximum state second pension a person can inherit from a late spouse or civil partner is 50 per cent. If a person is bereaved before they have reached their state pension age, inherited SERPS or state second pension can be paid as part of widowed parents allowance (in the case of a person who has dependent children) or otherwise only from state pension age.

State Pension Statements
The Department for Work and Pensions provide state pension statements. These statements give an estimate of the amount of state pension an individual may get based on their current National Insurance contribution record. The statement also explains how this estimate may change with further qualifying years. There is also an online state pension calculator which informs the user of their state pension age, an estimate of their basic state pension and how they are affected by changes to the state pension (W www.gov.uk/calculate-state-pension).

CONTRACTED-OUT PENSIONS

'Contracting-out' means leaving the additional state pension and joining a workplace, company or occupational pension scheme to build up benefits into an alternative pension scheme.

Contracting-Out with an Occupational Pension Scheme
An occupational pension scheme is an arrangement some employers set up to give the people who work for them a pension when they retire. The government is gradually introducing a requirement for all employers to provide their workers with a workplace pension. All employers will be included by 2018.

Providing that a company pension scheme meets certain conditions, it can be used to contract employees out of the additional state pension. Employees who join a scheme that is contracted-out will automatically be contracted-out of the additional state pension.

Employers providing such contracted-out schemes pay a lower rate of National Insurance contributions for those employees who join their schemes, and employees themselves also pay reduced-rate contributions.

Contracted-Out Salary-Related (COSR) Scheme
- these schemes (also known as contracted-out defined benefit (DB) or final salary schemes) provide a pension related to earnings and the length of pensionable service
- any notional additional state pension built up from 6 April 1978 to 5 April 1997 will be reduced by the amount of guaranteed minimum pension (GMP) accrued during that period (the contracted-out deduction). GMP is payable at 65 for men and 60 for women
- since 6 April 1997 these schemes no longer provide a GMP. Instead, as a condition of contracting-out they have to ensure that the benefits provided are at least as good as a prescribed standard (known as the Reference Scheme Test)
- when someone contracts-out of the additional state pension through these schemes, both the scheme member and the employer pay a reduced rate of NI contributions (known as the contracted-out rebate) to compensate for the additional state pension given up

Changes to contracted-out pensions from 2012
The rules for contracting-out of the additional state pension changed from 6 April 2012. The changes means contracting-out will not be possible through:
- a money purchase (defined contribution) occupational pension scheme
- a personal pension or stakeholder pension

From that date, employees have not been able to contract-out of the state second pension on a money purchase basis. Anyone contracted-out through this basis from that date was automatically contracted back into the additional state pension. However, those rights built up before the abolition date will be used to provide pension benefits. These changes have not affected contracting-out via a salary-related occupational pension scheme. However, the introduction of the single tier pension scheme will close and contracting out on a DB basis will end.

STAKEHOLDER PENSION SCHEMES

Introduced in 2001, stakeholder pensions are available to everyone but are principally for moderate earners who do not have access to a good value company pension scheme. Stakeholder pensions must meet a number of minimum standards to make sure they are flexible, portable and annual management charges are capped. The minimum contribution is £20.

As with personal pensions it is possible to invest up to £3,600 (including tax relief) into stakeholder pensions each year without evidence of earnings. Contributions can be made on someone else's behalf, for example a non-working partner.

AUTOMATIC ENROLMENT INTO WORKPLACE PENSIONS

Beginning in October 2012, employers will automatically enrol workers into a workplace pension. This applies to people who are not already in a workplace pension scheme and who:
- earn over £9,440 per annum
- are aged 22 or over
- are under state pension age
- work in the UK

Employees who meet the above requirements are entitled to opt out of the scheme if they wish to. If an employee remains in the scheme, they, together with their employer, will pay into it every month. The government will also contribute through tax relief. Further information is available at W www.gov.uk/workplace-pensions

COMPLAINTS

The Pensions Advisory Service provides information and guidance to members of the public, on state, company, personal and stakeholder schemes. They also help any member of the public who has a problem, complaint or dispute with their occupational or personal pensions.

There are two bodies for pension complaints. The Financial Ombudsman Service deals with complaints which predominantly concern the sale and/or marketing of occupational, stakeholder and personal pensions. The Pensions Ombudsman deals with complaints which predominantly concern the management (after sale or marketing) of occupational, stakeholder and personal pensions.

The Pensions Regulator is the UK regulator for work-based pension schemes; it concentrates its resources on schemes where there is the greatest risk to the security of members' benefits, promotes good administration practice for all work-based schemes and works with trustees, employers and professional advisers to put things right when necessary.

WAR PENSIONS AND THE ARMED FORCES COMPENSATION SCHEME

The Service Personnel and Veterans Agency (SPVA) is part of the Ministry of Defence. SPVA was formed on 1 April 2007 from the former Armed Forces Personnel Administration Agency and the Veterans Agency to provide services to both serving personnel and veterans.

SPVA is responsible for the administration of the war pensions scheme and the armed forces compensation scheme (AFCS) to members of the armed forces in respect of disablement or death due to service. There is also a scheme for civilians and civil defence workers in respect of the Second World War, and other schemes for groups such as merchant seamen and Polish armed forces who served under British command during the Second World War. The agency is also responsible for the administration of the armed forces pension scheme (AFPS), which provides occupational pensions for ex-service personnel *(see* Defence).

THE WAR PENSIONS SCHEME

War disablement pension is awarded for the disabling effects of any injury, wound or disease which was the result of, or was aggravated by, service in the armed forces prior to 6 April 2005. Claims are only considered once the person has left the armed forces. The amount of pension paid depends on the severity of disablement, which is assessed by comparing the health of the claimant with that of a healthy person of the same age and sex. The person's earning capacity or occupation are not taken into account in this assessment. A pension is awarded if the person has a disablement of 20 per cent or more and a lump sum is usually payable to those with a disablement of less than 20 per cent. No award is made for noise-induced sensorineural hearing loss where the assessment of disablement is less than 20 per cent.

A pension is payable to war widows, widowers and surviving civil partners where the spouse's or civil partner's death was due to, or hastened by, service in the armed forces prior to 6 April 2005 or where the spouse or civil partner was in receipt of a war disablement pension constant attendance allowance (or would have been if not in hospital) at the time of death. A pension is also payable to widows, widowers or surviving civil partners if the spouse or civil partner was receiving the war disablement pension at the 80 per cent rate or higher in conjunction with unemployability supplement at the time of death. War widows, widowers and surviving civil partners receive a standard rank-related rate, but a lower weekly rate is payable to war widows, widowers and surviving civil partners of personnel of the rank of Major or below who are under the age of 40, without children and capable of maintaining themselves. This is increased to the standard rate at age 40. Allowances are paid for children (in addition to child benefit) and adult dependants. An age allowance is automatically given when the widow, widower or surviving civil partner reaches 65 and increased at ages 70 and 80.

Pensioners living overseas receive the same pension rates as those living in the UK. All war disablement pensions and allowances and pensions for war widows, widowers and surviving civil partners are tax-free in the UK; this does not always apply in overseas countries due to different tax laws.

SUPPLEMENTARY ALLOWANCES

A number of supplementary allowances may be awarded to a war pensioner and are intended to meet various needs. The principal supplementary allowances are unemployability supplement, allowance for lowered standard of occupation and constant attendance allowance. Others include exceptionally severe disablement allowance, severe disablement occupational allowance, treatment allowance, mobility supplement, comforts allowance, clothing allowance, age allowance and widow/widower/surviving civil partner's age allowance. Rent and children's allowances are also available with pensions for war widows, widowers and surviving civil partners.

ARMED FORCES COMPENSATION SCHEME

The armed forces compensation scheme (AFCS) became effective on 6 April 2005 and covers all regular (including Gurkhas) and reserve personnel whose injury, ill health or death is caused by service on or after 6 April 2005. Ex-members of the armed forces who served prior to this date or who are in receipt of any pension under the war pensions scheme will continue to receive their pension and any associated benefits in the normal way.

The AFCS provides compensation where service in the armed forces is the only or main cause of injury, illness or death. Under the terms of the scheme a lump sum is payable to service or ex-service personnel based on a 15-level tariff, graduated according to the seriousness of the injury. A guaranteed income payment (GIP), payable for life, is payable to those who could be expected to experience a serious loss of earning capability. A survivors GIP (SGIP) will also be paid to surviving spouses, civil partners and unmarried partners who meet certain criteria. GIP and SGIP are calculated by multiplying the pensionable pay of the service person by a factor that depends on the age at the person's last birthday. The younger the person, the higher the factor, because there are more years to normal retirement age.

DEPARTMENT FOR WORK AND PENSIONS BENEFITS

Most benefits are paid in addition to those in receipt of payments under the AFCS and the war pensions scheme, but may be affected by any supplementary allowances in payment with war pensions. Any state pension for which a war widow, widower or surviving civil partner qualifies for on their own NI contribution record can be paid in addition to monies received under the war pensions scheme.

CLAIMS AND QUESTIONS

Further information on the war pensions scheme, the AFCS and the nearest Veterans' Welfare Office can be obtained from the Service Personnel and Veterans Agency by telephone (T 0800-169 2277, if calling from the UK or, if living overseas, T (+44) (125) 386-6043).

SERVICE PERSONNEL AND VETERANS AGENCY,
Norcross Lane, Thornton-Cleveleys FY5 3WP
E veterans.help@spva.gsi.gov.uk W www.veterans-uk.info

TAX CREDITS

Tax credits are administered by HM Revenue and Customs (HMRC). They are based on an individual's or couple's household income and current circumstances. Adjustments can be made during the year to reflect changes in income and/or circumstances. Further information regarding the qualifying conditions for tax credits, how to claim and the rates payable is available online on the HMRC website (W www.hmrc.gov.uk/taxcredits).

WORKING TAX CREDIT

Working tax credit is a payment from the government to support people on low incomes. It may be claimed by:

- those aged 25 or over who work at least 30 hours a week
- those aged 16 or over who work at least 16 hours a week, who are responsible for a child or young person, or have a disability that puts them at a disadvantage of getting a job

- those aged 60 or over, who work at least 16 hours a week
- couples who are responsible for a child or young person, who work at least 24 hours per week between them with one partner working at least 16 hours a week

The amount received depends on the circumstances and number of hours worked a week.

WORKING TAX CREDIT FOR INDIVIDUALS WITHOUT CHILDREN 2013–14

The amounts shown are for a selection of incomes and statuses.

Annual Income/Status	*Tax Credit per annum*
£5,200*	
Single	–
Couple	–
Single adult with a disability	£4,780
£9,500	
Single	£1,455
Couple	£3,425
Single adult with a disability	£3,520
£10,000	
Single	£1,250
Couple	£3,220
Single adult with a disability	£3,315
£12,000	
Single	£430
Couple	£2,400
Single adult with a disability	£2,495
£16,000	
Single	–
Couple	£760
Single adult with a disability	£855

* An annual income of £5,100 represents the 2013–14 income of an adult (21 and over) working 16 hours a week at the national minimum wage: six months at the 2012–13 rate of £6.19 a hour and six months at the rate of £6.31 a hour (national minimum wage from October 2013)

CHILDCARE

In families with children where a lone parent works at least 16 hours a week or couples who work at least 24 hours per week between them with one partner working at least 16 hours a week or where one partner works at least 16 hours a week and the other is disabled, an in-patient in hospital, or in prison, the family is entitled to the childcare element of working tax credit. Depending on circumstances this payment can contribute up to £122.50 of childcare costs for one child and up to £210 a week for two or more children. Families can only claim if they use an approved or registered childcare provider.

CHILD TAX CREDIT

Child tax credit combines all income-related support for children and is paid direct to the main carer. The credit is made up of a main 'family' payment with additional payments for each extra child in the household, for children with a disability and an extra payment for children who are severely disabled. Child tax credit is available to households where:

- there is at least one dependant under 16
- there is at least one dependant between 16 and 20 who is in relevant education or training or is registered for work, education or training with an approved body

BENEFITS

The following is intended as a general guide to the benefits system. Conditions of entitlement and benefit rates change annually and all prospective claimants should check exact entitlements and rates of benefit directly with their local Jobcentre Plus office, pension centre or online (W www.gov.uk). Leaflets relating to the various benefits and contribution conditions for different benefits are available from local Jobcentre Plus offices.

UNIVERSAL CREDIT

From 29 April 2013, Universal Credit began to gradually be introduced in certain areas of the country. Universal Credit is a single new payment for those looking for work or on a low income. Universal Credit will eventually replace:

- Income-based jobseekers allowance
- Income-related employment support allowance
- Income support
- Child tax credit
- Working tax credit
- Housing benefit

For more information go to W www.gov.uk/universalcredit

CONTRIBUTORY BENEFITS

Entitlement to contributory benefits depends on national insurance contribution conditions being satisfied either by the claimant or by someone on the claimant's behalf (depending on the kind of benefit). The class or classes of national insurance contribution relevant to each benefit are:

Jobseeker's allowance (contribution-based)	Class 1
Incapacity benefit	Class 1 or 2
Employment and Support Allowance (contributory)	Class 1 or 2
Widow's benefit and bereavement benefit	Class 1, 2 or 3
State pensions, categories A and B	Class 1, 2 or 3

The system of contribution conditions relates to yearly levels of earnings on which national insurance (NI) contributions have been paid.

JOBSEEKER'S ALLOWANCE

Jobseeker's allowance (JSA) replaced unemployment benefit and income support for unemployed people under state pension age from 7 October 1996. There are two routes of entitlement. Contribution-based JSA is paid at a personal rate (ie additional benefit for dependants is not paid) to those who have made sufficient NI contributions in two particular tax years. Savings and partner's earnings are not taken into account and payment can be made for up to six months. Rates of JSA correspond to income support rates.

Claims are made through Jobcentre Plus. A person wishing to claim JSA must generally be unemployed or working on average less than 16 hours a week, capable of work and available for any work which he or she can reasonably be expected to do, usually for at least 40 hours a week. The claimant must agree and sign a 'jobseeker's agreement', which will set out his or her plans to find work, and must actively seek work. If the claimant refuses work or training the benefit may be sanctioned for between one and 26 weeks.

A person will be sanctioned from JSA for up to 26 weeks if he or she has left a job voluntarily without just cause or through misconduct. In these circumstances, it may be possible to receive hardship payments, particularly where the claimant or the claimant's family is vulnerable, eg if sick or pregnant, or with children or caring responsibilities.

Weekly Rates from April 2013	
Person aged 16–24	£56.80
Person aged 25 to state pension age*	£71.70

* Since October 2003 people aged between 60 and state pension age can choose to claim pension credits instead of JSA

INCAPACITY BENEFIT

Since 31 January 2011 people can no longer make claims for incapacity benefit. Those seeking incapacity benefit should now claim employment and support allowance (ESA) instead. Those claiming incapacity benefit prior to 31 January 2011 will continue to receive it for as long as they qualify, although it is intended that remaining recipients of incapacity benefit will be moved to employment and support allowance by 2014. There are three rates of incapacity benefit:

- short-term lower rate for the first 28 weeks of sickness
- short-term higher rate from weeks 29 to 52
- long-term rate from week 53 onwards

The terminally ill and those entitled to the highest rate care component of disability living allowance are paid the long-term rate after 28 weeks. Incapacity benefit is taxable after 28 weeks.

An age addition payment may be available where incapacity for work commenced before the age of 45. Increases are also available for adult dependants caring for children.

The 'personal capability' assessment is the main test for incapacity benefit claims. Claimants are assessed on their ability to carry out a range of work-related activities and may also be required to attend a medical examination. Incapacity benefit claimants (excluding people who are severely disabled and those who are terminally ill) are invited back for work-focused interviews at intervals of not longer than three years. The interviews do not include medical tests, but if the claimant is due for a medical test around the same time, their local office will aim to schedule both together.

Weekly Rates from April 2013

Short-term incapacity benefit lower rate	
Person under state pension age	£76.45
Person over state pension age	£97.25
Short-term incapacity benefit higher rate	
Person under state pension age	£90.50
Person over state pension age	£101.35
Long-term incapacity benefit	
Person under state pension age	£101.35
Person over state pension age	–

EMPLOYMENT AND SUPPORT ALLOWANCE

From 27 October 2008, employment and support allowance (ESA) replaced incapacity benefit and income support paid on the grounds of incapacity or disability. The benefit consists of two strands, contribution-based benefit and income-related benefit, so that people no longer need to make two claims for benefit in order to gain their full entitlement. Contributory ESA is available to those who have limited capability for work but cannot get statutory sick pay from their employer. Those over pensionable age are not entitled to ESA. Apart from those who qualify under the special provisions for people incapacitated in youth, entitlement to contributory ESA is based on a person's NI contribution record. In order to qualify for contributory ESA, two contribution conditions, based on the last three years before the tax year in which benefit is claimed, must be satisfied. The amount of contributory ESA payable may be reduced where the person receives more than a specified amount of occupational or personal pension. Contributory ESA is paid only in respect of the person claiming the benefit – there are no additional amounts for dependants.

At the outset, new claimants are paid a basic allowance (the same rate as jobseeker's allowance) for 13 weeks while their medical condition is assessed and a work capability assessment is conducted. Following the completion of the assessment phase those claimants capable of engaging in work-related activities will receive a work-related activity component on top of the basic rate. The work-related activity component can be subject to sanctions if the claimant does not engage in the conditionality requirements without good reason. The maximum sanction is equal to the value of the work-related activity component of the benefit.

Those with the most severe health conditions or disabilities will receive the support component, which is more than the work-related activity component. Claimants in receipt of the support component are not required to engage in work-related activities, although they can volunteer to do so or undertake permitted work if their condition allows.

Weekly Rates from April 2013

ESA plus work-related activity component	up to £100.15
ESA plus support component	up to £106.50

BEREAVEMENT BENEFITS

Bereavement benefits replaced widow's benefit on 9 April 2001. Those claiming widow's benefit before this date will continue to receive it under the old scheme for as long as they qualify. The new system provides bereavement benefits for widows, widowers and, from 5 December 2005, surviving civil partners (providing that their deceased spouse or civil partner paid NI contributions). The new system offers benefits in three forms:

- *Bereavement payment* – may be received by a man or woman who is under the state pension age at the time of their spouse or civil partner's death, or whose husband, wife or civil partner was not entitled to a category A retirement pension when he or she died. It is a single tax-free lump sum of £2,000 payable immediately on widowhood or loss of a civil partner
- *Widowed parent's allowance* – a taxable benefit payable to the surviving partner if he or she is entitled or treated as entitled to child benefit, or to a widow if she is expecting her husband's baby at the time of his death
- *Bereavement allowance* – a taxable weekly benefit paid for 52 weeks after the spouse or civil partner's death. If aged over 55 and under state pension age the full allowance is payable, if aged between 45 and 54 a percentage of the full rate is paid. A widow, widower or surviving civil partner may receive this allowance if his or her widowed parent's allowance ends before 52 weeks

It is not possible to receive widowed parent's allowance and bereavement allowance at the same time. Bereavement benefits and widow's benefit, in any form, cease upon remarriage or a new civil partnership or are suspended during a period of cohabitation as partners without being legally married or in a civil partnership.

Weekly Rates from April 2013

Bereavement payment (lump sum)	£2,000
Widowed parent's allowance (or widowed mother's allowance)	£108.30
Bereavement allowance (or widow's pension), full entitlement (aged 55 and over at time of spouse's or civil partner's death)	£108.30

Amount of bereavement allowance (or widow's pension) by age of widow/widower or surviving civil partner at spouse's or civil partner's death:

aged 54	£100.72
aged 53	£93.14
aged 52	£85.56
aged 51	£77.98
aged 50	£70.40
aged 49	£62.81

aged 48	£55.23
aged 47	£47.65
aged 46	£40.07
aged 45	£32.49

STATE PENSION: CATEGORIES A AND B

Category A pension is payable for life to men and women who reach state pension age, who satisfy the contributions conditions and who claim for it. Category B pension may be payable to married women, married men and civil partners who are not entitled to a basic state pension on their own NI contributions or whose own basic state pension entitlement is less than £64.40 a week in 2012–13. It is based on their wife's, husband's or civil partner's NI contributions and is payable when both members of the couple have reached state pension age. Married men and civil partners may only be able to qualify for a category B pension if their wife or civil partner was born on or after 6 April 1950. Category B pension is also payable to widows, widowers and surviving civil partners who are bereaved before state pension age if they were previously entitled to widowed parent's allowance or bereavement allowance based on their late spouse's or civil partner's NI contributions. If they were receiving widowed parent's allowance on reaching state pension age, they could qualify for a category B pension payable at the same rate as their widowed parent's allowance comprising a basic pension, plus, if applicable, the appropriate share of their late spouse's or late civil partner's additional state pension. If their widowed parent's allowance had stopped before they reached state pension age, or they had been getting bereavement allowance at any time before state pension age, their category B pension will consist of inheritable additional state pension only. No basic state pension is included, although they may qualify for a basic state pension or have their own basic state pension improved by substituting their late spouse's or late civil partner's NI records for their own.

Widows who are bereaved when over state pension age can qualify for a category B pension regardless of the age of their husband when he died. This is payable at the same rate as the basic state pension the widow's late husband was entitled to (or would have been entitled to) at the time of his death. It can also be paid to widowers and civil partners who are bereaved when over state pension age if their wife or civil partner had reached state pension age when they died. Widowers and surviving civil partners who reached state pension age on or after 6 April 2010 and bereaved when over state pension age can qualify for a category B pension regardless of the age of their wife or civil partner when they died.

Where a person is entitled to both a category A and category B pension then they can be combined to give a composite pension, but this cannot be more than the full rate pension. Where a person is entitled to more than one category A or category B pension then only one can be paid. In such cases the person can choose which to get; if no choice is made, the most favourable one is paid.

A person may defer claiming their pension beyond state pension age. In doing so they may earn increments which will increase the weekly amount paid by 1 per cent per five weeks of deferral (equivalent to 10.4 per cent/year) when they claim their state pension. If a person delays claiming for at least 12 months they are given the option of a one-off taxable lump sum, instead of a pension increase, based on the weekly pension deferred, plus interest of at least 2 per cent above the Bank of England base rate. Historically, if a married man deferred his category A pension, his wife could not claim a category B pension on his contributions but could earn increments on her state pension during this time. Since 6 April 2010, a category B pension has been treated independently of the spouse's or partner's pension. It is possible to take a category B pension even if the spouse or partner has deferred theirs.

It is no longer possible to claim an increase on a state pension for another adult (known as adult dependency increase). Those who received the increase before April 2010 can keep receiving it until the conditions are no longer met or until 5 April 2020, whichever is first.

Provision for children is made through child tax credits. An age addition of 25p a week is payable with a state pension if a pensioner is aged 80 or over.

Since 1989 pensioners have been allowed to have unlimited earnings without affecting their state pension. *See also* Pensions.

Weekly Rates from April 2013

Category A or B pension for a single person	£110.15
Based on husband's/wife's/civil partner's NI contributions	£66.00

GRADUATED RETIREMENT BENEFIT

Graduated retirement benefit (GRB) is based on the amount of graduated NI contributions paid into the GRB scheme between April 1961 and April 1975; however, it is still paid in addition to any state pension to those who made the relevant contributions. A person will receive graduated retirement benefit based on their own contributions, even if not entitled to a basic state pension. Widows, widowers and surviving civil partners may inherit half of their deceased spouse's or civil partner's entitlement, but none that the deceased spouse or civil partner may have been eligible for from a former spouse or civil partner. If a person defers making a claim beyond state pension age, they may earn an increase or a one-off lump sum payment in respect of their deferred graduated retirement benefit; calculated in the same way as for category A or B state pension.

NON-CONTRIBUTORY BENEFITS

These benefits are paid from general taxation and are not dependent on NI contributions.

JOBSEEKER'S ALLOWANCE (INCOME-BASED)

Those who do not qualify for contribution-based jobseeker's allowance (JSA), those who have exhausted their entitlement to contribution-based JSA or those for whom contribution-based JSA provides insufficient income may qualify for income-based JSA. The amount paid depends on age, whether they are single or a couple, number of dependants and amount of income and savings. Income-based JSA comprises three parts:

- a personal allowance for the jobseeker and his/her partner*
- premiums for people with special needs
- amounts for housing costs

* Since April 2003, child dependants have been provided for through the child tax credit system

The rules of entitlement are the same as for contribution-based JSA.

If one person in a couple was born after 28 October 1957 and neither person in the couple has responsibility for a child or children, then the couple will have to make a joint claim for JSA if they wish to receive income-based JSA.

Weekly Rates from April 2013

Person aged 16–24	£56.80
Person aged 25 to state pension age	£71.70
Couple with one or both under 18*	£56.80
Couple aged 18 to state pension age	£112.55
Lone parent aged under 18	£56.80
Lone parent aged 18 to state pension age	£71.70

* depending on circumstances

MATERNITY ALLOWANCE

Maternity allowance (MA) is a benefit available for pregnant women who cannot get statutory maternity pay (SMP) from their employer or have been employed/self-employed during or close to their pregnancy. In order to qualify for payment, a woman must have been employed and/or self-employed for at least 26 weeks in the 66-week period up to and including the week before the baby is due (test period). These weeks do not have to be in a row and any part weeks worked will count towards the 26 weeks. She must also have an average weekly earning of at least £30 (maternity allowance threshold) over any 13 weeks of the woman's choice within the test period.

Self-employed women who pay class 2 NI contributions or who hold a small earnings exception certificate are deemed to have enough earnings to qualify for MA.

A woman can choose to start receiving MA from the 11th week before the week in which the baby is due (if she stops work before then) up to the day following the day of birth. The exact date MA starts will depend on when the woman stops work to have her baby or if the baby is born before she stops work. However, where the woman is absent from work wholly or partly due to her pregnancy in the four weeks before the week the baby is due to be born, MA will start the day following the first day of absence from work. MA is paid for a maximum of 39 weeks.

The woman may be entitled to get extra payments for her husband, civil partner or someone else who looks after her children.

Weekly Rate from April 2013

Standard rate	£136.78 or 90 per cent of the woman's average weekly earnings if less than £136.78

CHILD BENEFIT

Child benefit is payable for virtually all children aged under 16 and for those aged 16 and 17 if they are in relevant education or training or are registered for work, education or training with an approved body.

Weekly Rates at April 2013

Eldest/only child	£20.30
Each subsequent child	£13.40

GUARDIAN'S ALLOWANCE

Guardian's allowance is payable to a person who is bringing up a child or young person because the child's parents have died, or in some circumstances, where only one parent has died. To receive the allowance the person must be in receipt of child benefit for the child or young person, although they do not have to be the child's legal guardian.

Weekly Rate (in addition to child benefit) from April 2013

Each child	£15.90

CARER'S ALLOWANCE

Carer's allowance (CA) is a benefit payable to people who spend at least 35 hours a week caring for a severely disabled person. To qualify for CA a person must be caring for someone in receipt of one of the following benefits:

- attendance allowance
- disability living allowance care component at the middle or highest rate
- constant attendance allowance, paid at not less than the normal maximum rate with an industrial injuries disablement payment or basic (full-day) rate, under the industrial injuries or war pension schemes.

Weekly Rate from April 2013

Carer's allowance	£59.75

SEVERE DISABLEMENT ALLOWANCE

Since April 2001 severe disablement allowance (SDA) has not been available to new claimants. Those claiming SDA before that date will continue to receive it for as long as they qualify.

Weekly Rates from April 2013

Basic rate	£71.80
Age related addition*:	
Higher rate	£10.70
Middle rate	£6.00
Lower rate	£6.00

* The age addition applies to the age when incapacity began

ATTENDANCE ALLOWANCE

This may be payable to people aged 65 or over who need help with personal care because they are physically or mentally disabled, and who have needed help for a period of at least six months. Attendance allowance has two rates: the lower rate is for day or night care, and the higher rate is for day and night care. People not expected to live for more than six months because of a progressive disease can receive the highest rate of attendance allowance straight away.

Weekly Rates from April 2013

Higher rate	£79.15
Lower rate	£53.00

DISABILITY LIVING ALLOWANCE

This may be payable to people aged under 65 who have had personal care and/or mobility needs because of an illness or disability for a period of at least three months and are likely to have those needs for a further six months or more. The allowance has two components: the care component, which has three rates, and the mobility component, which has two rates. The rates depend on the care and mobility needs of the claimant. People not expected to live for more than six months because of a progressive disease will automatically receive the highest rate of the care component.

Weekly Rates from April 2013

Care component	
Higher rate	£79.15
Middle rate	£53.00
Lowest rate	£21.00
Mobility component	
Higher rate	£55.25
Lower rate	£21.00

STATE PENSION FOR PEOPLE AGED 80 AND OVER

A state pension, also referred to as category D pension, is provided for people aged 80 and over if they are not entitled to another category of pension or are entitled to a state pension that is less than £66.00 a week. The person must also live in Great Britain and have done so for a period of ten years or more in any continuous 20-year period since their 60th birthday.

Weekly Rate from April 2013

Single person	£66.00
Age addition	£0.25

INCOME SUPPORT

Broadly speaking income support is a benefit for those between age 16 and the age they can receive pension credit, whose income is below a certain level, who work on average less than 16 hours a week and who are:

- bringing up children alone
- registered sick or disabled
- a student who is also a lone parent or disabled
- caring for someone who is sick or elderly

Income support is not payable if the claimant, or claimant and partner, have capital or savings in excess of £16,000 – and deductions are made for capital and savings in excess of £6,000. For people permanently in residential care and nursing homes deductions apply for capital in excess of £10,000.

Sums payable depend on fixed allowances laid down by law for people in different circumstances. If both partners are eligible for income support, either may claim it for the couple. People receiving income support may be able to receive housing benefit, help with mortgage or home loan interest and help with healthcare. They may also be eligible for help with exceptional expenses from the Social Fund. Special rates may apply to some people living in residential care or nursing homes.

INCOME SUPPORT PREMIUMS

Income support premiums are extra weekly payments for those with additional needs. People qualifying for more than one premium will normally only receive the highest single premium for which they qualify. However, family premium, disabled child premium, severe disability premium and carer premium are payable in addition to other premiums.

Child tax credit replaced premiums for people with children for all new income support claims from 6 April 2004. People with children who were already in receipt of income support in April 2004 and have not claimed child tax credit may qualify for:

- the family premium if they have at least one child
- the disabled child premium if they have a child who receives disability living allowance or is registered blind
- the enhanced disability child premium if they have a child in receipt of the higher rate disability living allowance care component

Carers may qualify for:

- the carer premium if they or their partner are in receipt of carer's allowance

Long-term sick or disabled people may qualify for:

- the disability premium if they or their partner are receiving certain benefits because they are disabled or cannot work; are registered blind; or if the claimant has been incapable of work or receiving statutory sick pay for at least 364 days (196 days if the person is terminally ill), including periods of incapacity separated by eight weeks or less
- the severe disability premium if the person lives alone and receives the middle or higher rate of disability living allowance care component and no one receives carer's allowance for caring for that person
- the enhanced disability premium if the person is in receipt of the higher rate disability living allowance care component

People with a partner aged over 60 may qualify for:

- the pensioner premium

WEEKLY RATES OF INCOME SUPPORT
from April 2013

Single person	
aged 16–24	£56.80
aged 25+	£71.70
aged under 18 and a single parent	£56.80
aged 18+ and a single parent	£71.70
Couples	
Both under 18	£56.80
Both under 18, in certain circumstances	£85.80
One under 18, one aged 18–24	£56.80
One under 18, one aged 25+	£71.70
Both aged 18+	£112.55
Premiums	
Carer premium	£33.30
Severe disability premium	£59.50
Enhanced disability premium	
Single person	£15.15
Couples	£21.75
Pensioner premium (couple)	£109.50

PENSION CREDIT

Pension credit was introduced on 6 October 2003 and replaced income support for those aged 60 and over. Between April 2010 and April 2020 the pension credit qualifying age is increasing from 60 to 65 alongside the increase in women's state pension age.

There are two elements to pension credit:

THE GUARANTEE CREDIT

The guarantee credit guarantees a minimum income of £145.40 for single people and £222.05 for couples, with additional elements for people who have:

- eligible housing costs
- severe disabilities
- caring responsibilities

Income from state pension, private pensions, earnings, working tax credit and certain benefits are taken into account when calculating the pension credit. For savings and capital in excess of £10,000, £1 for every £500 or part of £500 held is taken into account as income when working out entitlement to pension credit.

People receiving the guarantee credit element of pension credit will be able to receive housing benefit, council tax benefit and help with healthcare costs.

Weekly Rates from April 2013

Additional amount for severe disability	
Single person	£59.50
Couple (one qualifies)	£59.50
Couple (both qualify)	£119.00
Additional amount for carers	£33.30

THE SAVINGS CREDIT

Single people aged 65 or over (and couples where one member is 65 or over) may be entitled to a savings credit which provides additional support for pensioners who have made modest provision towards their retirement. The savings credit is calculated by taking into account any qualifying income above the savings credit threshold. For 2013–14 the threshold is £115.30 for single people and £183.90 for couples. The maximum savings credit is £18.06 per week (£22.89 a week for couples).

Income that qualifies towards the savings credit includes state pensions, earnings, second pensions and income taken into account from capital above £10,000.

Some people will be entitled to the guarantee credit, some to the savings credit and some to both.

Where only the savings credit is in payment, people need to claim standard housing benefit or council tax benefit. Although local authorities take any savings credit into account in the housing benefit or council tax benefit assessment, for people aged 65 and over housing benefit or council tax benefit is enhanced to ensure that gains in pension credit are not depleted.

HOUSING BENEFIT

Housing benefit is designed to help people with rent (including rent for accommodation in guesthouses, lodgings or hostels). It does not cover mortgage payments. The amount of benefit paid depends on:

- the income of the claimant, and partner if there is one, including earned income, unearned income (any other income including some other benefits) and savings
- number of dependants
- certain extra needs of the claimant, partner or any dependants
- number and gross income of people sharing the home who are not dependent on the claimant
- how much rent is paid

Housing benefit is not payable if the claimant, or claimant and partner, have savings in excess of £16,000. The amount of benefit is affected if savings held exceed £6,000 (£10,000 for people living in residential care and nursing homes). Housing benefit is not paid for meals, fuel or certain service charges that may be included in the rent. Deductions are also made for most non-dependants who live in the same accommodation as the claimant (and their partner). If the claimant is living with a partner or civil partner there can only be one claim.

The maximum amount of benefit (which is not necessarily the same as the amount of rent paid) may be paid where the claimant is in receipt of income support, income-based jobseeker's allowance, the guarantee element of pension credit or where the claimant's income is less than the amount allowed for their needs. Any income over that allowed for their needs will mean that their benefit is reduced.

LOCAL HOUSING ALLOWANCE

Local housing allowance (LHA), which was rolled out nationally from 7 April 2008, is a way of calculating the rent element of housing benefit based on the area in which a person lives and household size. It affects people in the deregulated private rented sector who make a new claim for housing benefit or existing recipients who move address. LHA ensures that tenants in similar circumstances in the same area receive the same amount of financial support for their housing costs. It does not affect the way a person's income or capital is taken into account. LHA is paid to the tenant rather than the landlord in most circumstances. A weekly limit on payments is now in place so LHA does not exceed:

- £250 for a one bedroom property
- £290 for a two bedroom property
- £340 for a three bedroom property
- £400 for a four bedroom property

COUNCIL TAX REDUCTION

From April 2013, council tax benefit was replaced by council tax reduction. Nearly all the rules that apply to housing benefit apply to council tax reduction, which helps people on low incomes to pay council tax bills. The amount payable depends on how much council tax is paid and who lives with the claimant. The benefit may be available to those receiving income support, income-based jobseeker's allowance, the guarantee element of pension credit or to those whose income is less than that allowed for their needs. Any income over that allowed for their needs will mean that they will receive less help with their council tax reduction. Deductions are made for non-dependants.

A full council tax bill is based on at least two adults living in a home. Residents are able to get a 25 per cent reduction on their bill if they count as an adult for council tax and live on their own. If the property is the resident's main home and there is no-one who counts as an adult, the bill is reduced by 50 per cent.

THE SOCIAL FUND

REGULATED PAYMENTS

Sure Start Maternity Grant

Sure start maternity grant (SSMG) is a one-off payment of £500 to help people on low incomes pay for essential items for new babies that are expected, born, adopted, the subject of a parental order (following a surrogate birth) or, in certain circumstances, the subject of a residency order. SSMG can be claimed any time from within 11 weeks of the expected birth and up to three months after the birth, adoption or date of parental or residency order. Those eligible are people in receipt of income support, income-based jobseeker's allowance, pension credit, child tax credit at a rate higher than the family element or working tax credit where a disability or severe disability element is in payment. Since 11 April 2011, new rules have been applied for babies due, born or adopted on this date. These are that SSMG is only available if there are no other children under 16 in the family or in the case of a dependent child's new baby, SSMG is only available if the dependent is under the age of 20 and has no other children.

Funeral Payments

Payable to help cover the necessary cost of burial or cremation, a new burial plot with an exclusive right of burial (where burial is chosen), certain other expenses, and up to £700 for any other funeral expenses, such as the funeral director's fees, the coffin or flowers. Those eligible are people receiving income support, income-based jobseeker's allowance, pension credit, child tax credit at a higher rate than the family element, working tax credit where a disability or severe disability element is in payment, council tax benefit or housing benefit who have good reason for taking responsibility for the funeral expenses. These payments are recoverable from any estate of the deceased.

Cold Weather Payments

A payment of £25.00 per seven day period between 1 November and 31 March when the average temperature is recorded at or forecast to be 0°C or below over seven consecutive days in the qualifying person's area. Payments are made to people on pension credit or child tax credit with a disability element, those on income support whose benefit includes a pensioner or disability premium, and those on income-based jobseeker's allowance or employment and support allowance who have a child who is disabled or under the age of five. Payments are made automatically and do not have to be repaid.

Winter Fuel Payments

For 2013–14 the winter fuel payment is set at £200 for households with someone aged 60–79 and £300 for households with someone aged 80 or over. The rate paid is based on the person's age and circumstances in the 'qualifying week' between 16 and 22 September 2013. The majority of eligible people are paid automatically before Christmas, although a few need to claim. Payments do not have to be repaid.

Christmas Bonus

The Christmas bonus is a one-off tax-free £10 payment made before Christmas to those people in receipt of a qualifying benefit in the qualifying week.

DISCRETIONARY PAYMENTS

Community Care Grants

These are intended to help people in receipt of income support, income-based jobseeker's allowance or employment and support allowance, pension credit, or payments on account of such benefits (or those likely to receive these benefits within the next six weeks because they are leaving residential or institutional accommodation) to live as independently as possible in the community; ease exceptional pressures on families; care for a prisoner or young offender released on temporary licence; help people set up home as part of a resettlement programme and/or assist with certain travelling expenses. They do not have to be repaid.

Budgeting Loans

These are interest-free loans to people who have been receiving income support, income-based jobseeker's allowance or employment and support allowance, pension credit or payments on account of such benefits for at least 26 weeks, for intermittent expenses that may be difficult to budget for. The smallest amount available to borrow is £100.

Crisis Loans

These are interest-free loans to anyone aged 16 or over, whether receiving benefits or not, who is without resources in an emergency or due to a disaster, where there is no other means of preventing serious damage or serious risk to their or their family members' health or safety.

SAVINGS

Savings over £500 (£1,000 for people aged 60 or over) are taken into account for community care grants and savings of £1,000 (£2,000 for people aged 60 or over) are taken into account for budgeting loans. All savings are taken into account for crisis loans. Savings are not taken into account for sure start maternity grant, funeral payments, cold weather payments, winter fuel payments or the Christmas bonus.

INDUSTRIAL INJURIES AND DISABLEMENT BENEFITS

The Industrial Injuries Scheme, administered under the Social Security Contributions and Benefits Act 1992, provides a range of benefits designed to compensate for disablement resulting from an industrial accident (ie an accident arising out of and in the course of an earner's employment) or from a prescribed disease due to the nature of a person's employment. Those who are self-employed are not covered by this scheme.

INDUSTRIAL INJURIES DISABLEMENT BENEFIT

A person may be able to claim industrial injuries disablement benefit if they are ill or disabled due to an accident or incident that happened at work or in connection with work in England, Scotland or Wales. The amount of benefit awarded depends on the person's age and the degree of disability as assessed by a doctor.

The benefit is payable whether the person works or not and those who are incapable of work are entitled to draw other benefits, such as statutory sick pay or incapacity benefit, in addition to industrial injuries disablement benefit. It may also be possible to claim the following allowances:

- reduced earnings allowance for those who are unable to return to their regular work or work of the same standard and who had their accident (or whose disease started) before 1 October 1990. At state pension age this is converted to retirement allowance
- constant attendance allowance for those with a disablement of 100 per cent who need constant care. There are four rates of allowance depending on how much care the person needs
- exceptionally severe disablement allowance can be claimed in addition to constant care attendance allowance at one of the higher rates for those who need constant care permanently

Weekly Rates of Benefit from April 2013

Degree of disablement	*Aged 18+ or with dependants*
100 per cent	£161.60
90	£145.44
80	£129.28
70	£113.12
60	£96.96
50	£80.80
40	£64.64
30	£48.48
20	£32.32
Unemployability supplement	£99.90
Reduced earnings allowance (maximum)	£64.64
Retirement allowance (maximum)	£16.16
Constant attendance allowance (normal maximum rate)	£64.70
Exceptionally severe disablement allowance	£64.70

OTHER BENEFITS

People who are disabled because of an accident or disease that was the result of work that they did before 5 July 1948 are not entitled to industrial injuries disablement benefit. They may, however, be entitled to payment under the Workmen's Compensation Scheme or the Pneumoconiosis, Byssinosis and Miscellaneous Diseases Benefit Scheme. People who suffer from certain industrial diseases caused by dust, or their dependants, can make a claim for an additional payment under the Pneumoconiosis Act 1979 if they are unable to get damages from the employer who caused or contributed to the disease.

Diffuse Mesothelioma Payment

Since 1 October 2008 any person suffering from the asbestos-related disease, diffuse mesothelioma, who is unable to make a claim under the Pneumoconiosis Act 1979, have not received payment in respect of the disease from an employer, via a civil claim or elsewhere, and are not entitled to compensation from a MoD scheme, can claim a one-off lump sum payment. The scheme covers people whose exposure to asbestos occurred in the UK and was not as a result of their work as an employee (ie they lived near a factory using asbestos). The amount paid depends on the age of the person when the disease was diagnosed, or the date of the claim if the diagnosis date is not known. The current rate is £83,330 for those aged 37 and under to £12,945 for persons aged 77 and over. From 1 October 2009 claims must be received within 12 months of the date of diagnosis. If the sufferer has died, their dependants may be able to claim, but must do so within 12 months of the date of death.

CLAIMS AND QUESTIONS

Entitlement to benefit and regulated Social Fund payments is determined by a decision maker on behalf of the Secretary of State for the Department for Work and Pensions. A claimant who is dissatisfied with that decision can ask for an explanation. He or she can dispute the decision by applying to have it revised or, in particular circumstances, superseded. The claimant can go to the Social Security and Child Support Tribunal where the case will be heard by an independent tribunal. There is a further right of appeal to a social security commissioner against the tribunal's decision but this is on a point of law only and leave to appeal must first be obtained.

Decisions on claims and applications for housing benefit and council tax benefit are made by local authorities. The explanation, dispute and appeals process is the same as for other benefits.

All decisions on applications to the discretionary Social Fund are made by Jobcentre Plus Social Fund decision makers. Applicants can ask for a review of the decision within 28 days of the date on the decision letter. The Social Fund review officer will review the case and there is a further right of review by an independent Social Fund inspector.

EMPLOYER PAYMENTS

STATUTORY MATERNITY PAY

Employers pay statutory maternity pay (SMP) to pregnant women who have been employed by them full or part-time continuously for at least 26 weeks into the 15th week before the week the baby is due, and whose earnings on average at least equal the lower earnings limit applied to NI contributions (£109 a week if the end of the qualifying week is in the 2013–14 tax year). SMP can be paid for a maximum period of up to 39 weeks. If the qualifying conditions are met women will receive a payment of 90 per cent of their average earnings for the first six weeks, followed by 33 weeks at £136.78 or 90 per cent of the woman's average weekly earnings if this is less than £136.78. SMP can be paid, at the earliest, 11 weeks before the week in which the baby is due, up to the day following the birth. Women can decide when they wish their maternity leave and pay to start and can work until the baby is born. However, where the woman is absent from work wholly or partly due to her pregnancy in the four weeks before the week the baby is due to be born, SMP will start the day following the first day of absence from work.

Employers are reimbursed for 92 per cent of the SMP they pay. Small employers with annual gross NI payments of £45,000 or less recover 103 per cent of the SMP paid out.

STATUTORY PATERNITY PAY

Ordinary Statutory Paternity Pay

Employers pay ordinary statutory paternity pay (OSPP) to employees who are taking leave when a child is born or placed for adoption. To qualify the employee must:

- have responsibility for the child's upbringing
- be the biological father of the child (or the child's adopter), or the spouse/civil partner/partner of the mother or adopter
- have been employed by the same employer for at least 26 weeks ending with the 15th week before the baby is due (or the week in which the adopter is notified of having been matched with a child)
- continue working for the employer up to the child's birth (or placement for adoption)
- be earning an average of at least £109 a week (before tax)

Employees who meet these conditions receive payment of £136.78 or 90 per cent of the employee's average weekly earnings if this is less than £136.78. The employee can choose to be paid for one or two consecutive weeks. The earliest the OSPP period can begin is the date of the child's birth or placement for adoption. The OSPP period must be completed within eight weeks of that date. OSPP is not payable for any week in which the employee works. Employers are reimbursed in the same way as for statutory maternity pay.

ADDITIONAL PATERNITY LEAVE AND PAY

Regulations introduced on 6 April 2010 give parents greater flexibility in how they use their maternity and paternity provisions. For births from 3 April 2011, additional paternity leave (APL) entitles eligible fathers to take up to 19 weeks' additional paternity leave, allowing for up to a total of one year's leave to be shared between the couple. APL entitlement requires the mother to have returned to work; it must also be taken between 20 weeks and one year after the child is born. APL may be paid if taken during the mother's statutory maternity pay period or maternity allowance period.

The APL entitlement will also apply to husbands, partners or civil partners who are not the child's father but expect to have the main responsibility (apart from the mother) for the child's upbringing.

The current rate of additional statutory paternity pay is £136.78 a week or 90 per cent of the emplyee's average weekly earnings if this is less than £136.78.

STATUTORY ADOPTION PAY

Employers pay statutory adoption pay (SAP) to employees taking adoption leave from their employers. To qualify for SAP the employee must:

- be newly matched with a child by an adoption agency
- have been employed by the same employer for at least 26 weeks ending the week in which they have been notified of being matched with a child
- be earning an average of at least £109 a week (before tax)

Employees who meet these conditions receive payment of £136.78 or 90 per cent of their average weekly earnings if this is less than £136.78 for up to 39 weeks. The earliest SAP can be paid from is two weeks before the expected date of placement; the latest it can start is the date of the child's placement. Where a couple adopt a child, only one of them may receive SAP, the other may be able to receive statutory paternity pay if they meet the eligibility criteria. Employers are reimbursed in the same way as for statutory maternity pay.

The additional paternity leave entitlement (*see* above) will also apply to adoptions where adoptive parents are notified of a match on or after 3 April 2011.

STATUTORY SICK PAY

Employers pay statutory sick pay (SSP) for up to a maximum of 28 weeks to any employee incapable of work for four or more consecutive days. Employees must have done some work under their contract of service and have average weekly earnings of at least £109 from April 2013. SSP is a daily payment and is usually paid for the days that an employee would normally work, these days are known as qualifying days. SSP is not paid for the first three qualifying days in a period of sickness. SSP is paid at £86.70 per week and is subject to PAYE and NI contributions. Employees who cannot obtain SSP may be able to claim incapacity benefit. Employers may be able to recover some SSP costs.

THE WATER INDUSTRY

In the UK, the water industry provides services to over 54 million consumers each day and has an annual turnover of around £10bn. It supplies around 17 billion litres of water a day to domestic and commercial customers and collects and treats more than 16 billion litres of wastewater a day. It also manages assets that include around 1,400 water treatment and 9,350 wastewater treatment works, 550 impounding reservoirs, over 6,500 service reservoirs/water towers and 800,000km of water mains and sewers.

Water services in England and Wales are provided by private companies. In Scotland and Northern Ireland there are single authorities, Scottish Water and Northern Ireland Water, that are publicly owned companies answerable to their respective governments. In drinking water quality tests carried out in 2012 by the Drinking Water Inspectorate, the water industry in England and Wales achieved 99.96 per cent compliance with the standards required by the EU Drinking Water Directive; Scotland achieved 99.84 per cent and Northern Ireland 99.83 per cent.

Water UK is the industry association that represents all UK water and wastewater service suppliers at national and European level and is funded directly by its members, who are the service suppliers for England, Scotland, Wales and Northern Ireland; every member has a seat on the Water UK Council.

WATER UK, 1 Queen Anne's Gate, London SW1H 9BT
T 020-7344 1844 W www.water.org.uk
Chief Executive, Pamela Taylor

ENGLAND AND WALES

In England and Wales, the Secretary of State for Environment, Food and Rural Affairs and the Welsh government have overall responsibility for water policy and oversee environmental standards for the water industry.

The statutory consumer representative body for water services is the Consumer Council for Water.

CONSUMER COUNCIL FOR WATER, 1st Floor, Victoria Square House, Victoria Square, Birmingham B2 4AJ
T 0121-345 1000 W www.ccwater.org.uk

REGULATORY BODIES

The Water Services Regulation Authority (OFWAT) was established in 1989 when the water and sewerage industry in England and Wales was privatised. Its statutory role and duties are laid out under the Water Industry Act 1991 and it is the independent economic regulator of the water and sewerage companies in England and Wales. OFWAT's main duties are to ensure that the companies can finance and carry out their statutory functions and to protect the interests of water customers. OFWAT is a non-ministerial government department headed by a board following a change in legislation introduced by the Water Act 2003.

Under the Competition Act 1998, from 1 March 2000 the Competition Appeal Tribunal has heard appeals against the regulator's decisions regarding anti-competitive agreements and abuse of a dominant position in the marketplace. The Water Act 2003 placed a new duty on OFWAT to contribute to the achievement of sustainable development.

The Environment Agency has statutory duties and powers in relation to water resources, pollution control, flood defence, fisheries, recreation, conservation and navigation in England and Wales. It is also responsible for issuing permits, licences, consents and registrations such as industrial licences to extract water and fishing licences.

The Drinking Water Inspectorate (DWI) is the drinking water quality regulator for England and Wales, responsible for assessing the quality of the drinking water supplied by the water companies and investigating any incidents affecting drinking water quality, initiating prosecution where necessary. The DWI science and strategy group provides scientific advice on drinking water policy issues to DEFRA and the Welsh government.

OFWAT, Centre City Tower, 7 Hill Street, Birmingham B5 4UA
T 0121-644 7500 E mailbox@ofwat.gsi.gov.uk
W www.ofwat.gov.uk
Chair, Jonson Cox
Chief Executive, Regina Finn

METHODS OF CHARGING

In England and Wales, most domestic customers still pay for domestic water supply and sewerage services through charges based on the rateable value of their property. OFWAT estimates that the proportion of household customers in England and Wales to have metered supplies will increase from 41.5 per cent in 2011–12 to around 50 per cent in 2014–15. Nearly all non-household customers are charged according to consumption.

Under the Water Industry Act 1999, water companies can continue basing their charges on the old rateable value of the property. Domestic customers can continue paying on an unmeasured basis unless they choose to pay according to consumption. After having a meter installed (which is free of charge), a customer can revert to unmeasured charging within 12 months. However, water companies may charge by meter for new homes, or homes where there is a high discretionary use of water. Domestic, school and hospital customers cannot be disconnected for non-payment.

Price limits for the period 2010–15 were set by OFWAT in November 2009.

On average, household water and sewerage bills for 2013–14 will increase by an average of 3.5 per cent (£13). This takes into account a rate of inflation of 3 per cent, resulting in an average household bill of £388. Average household water bills in 2013–14 range from £96 for Portsmouth Water to £249 for Wessex Water; the overall average is £186. The average household sewerage bill costs £224, ranging from £147 for Thames Water up to £319 for South West Water.

SCOTLAND

In 2002 the three existing water authorities in Scotland (East of Scotland Water, North of Scotland Water and West of Scotland Water) merged to form Scottish Water. Scottish Water, which serves around 2.4 million households and provides 1.3 billion litres of water per day while removing 840 million litres of waste water, is a public sector company, structured and managed like a private company, but remains answerable to the Scottish parliament. Scottish Water is regulated by the Water Industry Commission for Scotland

AVERAGE HOUSEHOLD BILLS 2013–14*
£

	Water			*Sewerage*		
	Unmetred	*Metred*	*Overall*	*Unmetred*	*Metred*	*Overall*
WATER AND SEWERAGE COMPANIES						
Anglian	252	174	194	291	223	240
Dwr Cymru	210	131	181	293	190	253
Northumbrian	177	132	164	209	163	195
Severn Trent	185	164	177	169	139	158
South West	347	194	230	514	267	319
Southern	165	155	158	319	275	291
Thames	217	187	207	153	138	147
United Utilities	208	167	193	224	195	213
Wessex	300	210	249	260	200	229
Yorkshire	192	137	167	229	166	201
WATER ONLY COMPANIES						
Bristol	213	163	191	–	–	–
Cambridge	152	119	130	–	–	–
Cholderton	220	154	204	–	–	–
Dee Valley	177	128	150	–	–	–
†Essex and Suffolk	263	187	221	–	–	–
Portsmouth	98	88	96	–	–	–
Sembcorp Bournemouth	179	141	154	–	–	–
South East	255	169	201	–	–	–
South Staffordshire	146	140	144	–	–	–
Sutton & East Surrey	209	156	186	–	–	–
‡Veolia Central†	191	151	174	–	–	–
‡Veolia East	211	158	171	–	–	–
‡Veolia Southeast	235	200	203	–	–	–

* Including 3 per cent rate of inflation
† A subsidiary of Northumbrian
‡ In 2012 the three Veolia companies merged as Affinity Water
Source: OFWAT

(established under the Water Services (Scotland) Act 2005), the Scottish Environment Protection Agency (SEPA) and the Drinking Water Quality Regulator for Scotland. The Water Industry Commissioner is responsible for regulating all aspects of economic and customer service performance, including water and sewerage charges. SEPA, created under the Environment Act 1995, is responsible for environmental issues, including controlling pollution and promoting the cleanliness of Scotland's rivers, lochs and coastal waters. The Public Services Reform (Scotland) Act 2010 transferred the complaints handling function of Waterwatch Scotland regarding Scottish Water, to the Scottish Public Services Ombudsman. Consumer Focus Scotland replaced Waterwatch Scotland in 2011 in representing the views and interests of Scottish Water customers and is a statutory consultee for matters relating to the Scottish water industry.

METHODS OF CHARGING

Scottish Water sets charges for domestic and non-domestic water and sewerage provision through charges schemes which are regulated by the Water Industry Commission for Scotland. In February 2004 the harmonisation of all household charges across the country was completed following the merger of the separate authorities under Scottish Water. In November 2009 the Water Industry Commission for Scotland published *The Strategic Review of Charges 2010–2015,* stating that annual price rises would be kept at 5 per cent below the rate of inflation during this five-year period. For the year 2013–14, the combined service charge, covering the water supply and waste water collection, rose by 2.8 per cent, which represented the first increase in four years. The average household bill for 2013–14 therefore increased to around £334.

CONSUMER FOCUS SCOTLAND, Royal Exchange House, 100 Queen Street, Glasgow G1 3DN T 0141-226 5261 W www.consumerfocus.org.uk/scotland

SCOTTISH ENVIRONMENT PROTECTION AGENCY, Erskine Court, Castle Business Park, Stirling FK9 4TR T 01786-457700 W www.sepa.org.uk

SCOTTISH WATER, Castle House, 6 Castle Drive, Dunfermline KY11 8GG T 0845-601 8855 W www.scottishwater.co.uk
Chief Executive, Douglas Millican

WATER INDUSTRY COMMISSION FOR SCOTLAND, First Floor, Moray House, Forthside Way, Stirling FK8 1QZ T 01786-430200 W www.watercommission.co.uk

NORTHERN IRELAND

Formerly an executive agency of the Department for Regional Development, Northern Ireland Water is a government-owned company but with substantial independence from government. Northern Ireland Water was set up as a result of government reform of water and sewerage services in April 2007. It is responsible for policy and coordination with regard to the supply, distribution and cleanliness of water, and the provision and maintenance of sewerage services. The Northern Ireland Authority for Utility Regulation (known as the Utility Regulator) is responsible for regulating the water services provided by Northern Ireland Water. The Drinking Water Inspectorate, a unit in the Northern Ireland Environment Agency (NIEA), regulates drinking water quality. Another NIEA unit, the Water Management Unit, has responsibility for the protection of the aquatic environment. The Consumer Council for Northern Ireland is the consumer representative body for water services.

METHODS OF CHARGING

The water and sewerage used by domestic customers in Northern Ireland is currently paid for by the Department for Regional Development (DRD), a system which will continue during 2013–2014. In March 2010, the Northern Ireland Assembly passed the Water and Sewerage Services (Amendment) Act (Northern Ireland) 2010, which ensured that Northern Ireland Water would continue to receive DRD subsidy until at least 2014. Non-domestic customers in Northern Ireland became subject to water and sewerage charges and trade effluent charges where applicable in April 2008.

CONSUMER COUNCIL FOR NORTHERN IRELAND, 116 Holywood Road, Belfast BT4 1NY T 0800-121 6022 W www.consumercouncil.org.uk

NORTHERN IRELAND AUTHORITY FOR UTILITY REGULATION, Queens House, 14 Queen Street, Belfast BT1 6ED T 028-9031 1575 W www.uregni.gov.uk

NORTHERN IRELAND WATER, PO Box 1026, Belfast BT1 9DJ T 0845-744 0088 W www.niwater.com
Chief Executive, Trevor Haslett

WATER SERVICE COMPANIES

(not a member of Water UK; † associate member of Water UK)*

AFFINITY WATER, Tamblin Way, Hatfield, Herts AL10 9EZ T 01707-268111 W www.affinitywater.co.uk

*ALBION WATER LTD, 71 Clarence Road, Teddington, Middx TW11 0BN T 020-8977 3055 W www.albionwater.co.uk

ANGLIAN WATER SERVICES LTD, Anglian House, Ambury Road, Huntingdon PE29 3NZ T 01480-323 000 W www.anglianwater.co.uk

BRISTOL WATER PLC, PO Box 218, Bridgwater Road, Bristol BS99 7AU T 0117-966 5881 W www.bristolwater.co.uk

CAMBRIDGE WATER PLC, 90 Fulbourn Road, Cambridge CB1 9JN T 01223-706050 W www.cambridge-water.co.uk

†CHOLDERTON & DISTRICT WATER COMPANY LTD, Estate Office, Cholderton, Salisbury, Wiltshire SP4 0DR T 01980-629203 W www.choldertonwater.co.uk

DEE VALLEY WATER PLC, Packsaddle, Wrexham Road, Rhostyllen, Wrexham LL14 4EH T 01978-846946 W www.deevalleywater.co.uk

DWR CYMRU (WELSH WATER), Pentwyn Road, Nelson, Treharris, Mid Glamorgan CF46 6LY T 01443-452300 W www.dwrcymru.co.uk

ESSEX & SUFFOLK WATER PLC (subsidiary of Northumbrian Water Ltd), Customer Centre, PO Box 292, Durham DH1 9TX T 0845-782 0111 W www.eswater.co.uk

NORTHUMBRIAN WATER LTD, Abbey Road, Pity Me, Durham DH1 5FJ T 0870-608 4820 W www.nwl.co.uk

PORTSMOUTH WATER PLC, PO Box 8, West Street, Havant, Hants PO9 1LG T 023-9249 9888 W www.portsmouthwater.co.uk

SEMBCORP BOURNEMOUTH WATER LTD, George Jessel House, Francis Avenue, Bournemouth, Dorset BH11 8NX T 01202-591111 W www.sembcorpbw.co.uk

SEVERN TRENT WATER LTD, 2 St Johns Street, Coventry CV1 2LZ T 024-7771 5000 W www.stwater.co.uk

SOUTH EAST WATER LTD, Rocfort Road, Snodland, Kent ME6 5AH T 0333-000 0001 W www.southeastwater.co.uk

SOUTH STAFFORDSHIRE WATER PLC, Green Lane, Walsall WS2 7PD T 0845-607 0456 W www.south-staffs-water.co.uk

SOUTH WEST WATER LTD, Peninsula House, Rydon Lane, Exeter EX2 7HR T 01392-443020 W www.southwestwater.co.uk

SOUTHERN WATER SERVICES LTD, Southern House, Yeoman Road, Worthing, Sussex BN13 3NX T 01903-264444 W www.southernwater.co.uk

SUTTON AND EAST SURREY WATER PLC, London Road, Redhill, Surrey RH1 1LJ T 01737-772000 W www.waterplc.com

THAMES WATER UTILITIES LTD, PO Box 286, Swindon SN38 2RA T 0845-920 0800 W www.thameswater.co.uk

UNITED UTILITIES WATER PLC, Haweswater House, Lingley Mere Business Park, Great Sankey, Warrington WA5 3LP T 0845-746 2200 W www.unitedutilities.com

WESSEX WATER SERVICES LTD, Claverton Down, Bath BA2 7WW T 01225-526000 W www.wessexwater.co.uk

YORKSHIRE WATER SERVICES LTD, Western House, Western Way, Bradford BD6 2LZ T 01274-691111 W www.yorkshirewater.com

ISLAND WATER AUTHORITIES

(not members of Water UK)

COUNCIL OF THE ISLES OF SCILLY, Town Hall, St Mary's, Isles of Scilly TR21 0LW T 01720-424000 W www.scilly.gov.uk

GUERNSEY WATER, PO Box 30, Brickfield House, St Andrew, Guernsey GY1 3AS T 01481-239500 W www.water.gg

ISLE OF MAN WATER AND SEWERAGE AUTHORITY, Tromode Road, Douglas, Isle of Man IM2 5PA T 01624-695949 W www.gov.im/water

JERSEY WATER, PO Box 69, Mulcaster House, Westmount Road, St Helier, Jersey JE4 9PN T 01534-707301 W www.jerseywater.je

ENERGY

The main primary sources of energy in Britain are coal, oil, natural gas, renewables and nuclear power. The main secondary sources (ie sources derived from the primary sources) are electricity, coke and smokeless fuels and petroleum products. The UK was a net importer of fuels in the 1970s, however as a result of growth in oil and gas production from the North Sea, the UK became a net exporter of energy for most of the 1980s. Output decreased in the late 1980s following the Piper Alpha disaster until the mid 1990s, after which the UK again became a net exporter. Since 2004, the UK reverted back to become a net importer of energy and has since continued to be so. In value terms, on an Overseas Trade Statistics (OTS) basis, the total fuel deficit for 2012 was £22bn. The Department of Energy and Climate Change (DECC) is responsible for promoting energy efficiency.

INDIGENOUS PRODUCTION OF PRIMARY FUELS
Million tonnes of oil equivalent

	2011	*2012*
Primary oils	56.9	48.8
Natural gas	45.3	38.9
Primary electricity	17.5	17.4
Coal	11.6	10.6
Bioenergy and waste	5.8	6.4
Total	136.8	122.1

Source: DECC

INLAND ENERGY CONSUMPTION BY PRIMARY FUEL
Million tonnes of oil equivalent, seasonally adjusted

	2011	*2012*
Natural gas	77.3	73.1
Petroleum	67.1	65.9
Coal	32.4	41.1
Nuclear electricity	15.6	15.2
Bioenergy and waste	7.3	7.8
Wind and hydro electricity	1.8	2.2
Net Imports	0.5	1.0
Total	202.1	206.3

Source: DECC

TRADE IN FUELS AND RELATED MATERIALS (2012)

	Quantity, million tonnes of oil equivalent	*Value £m*
Imports	170.7	62,733
Crude oil	61.6	30,353
Petroleum products	32.4	18,494
*Natural gas	47.1	10,034
Coal and other solid fuel	28.5	3,178
Electricity	1.2	674
Exports	86.8	40,707
Crude oil	36.6	16,810
Petroleum products	37.0	20,433
*Natural gas	12.4	3,036
Coal and other solid fuel	0.7	325
Electricity	0.2	102

* Estimate
Source: HMRC/DECC, ONS

OIL

Until the 1960s Britain imported almost all its oil supplies. In 1969 oil was discovered in the Arbroath field in the North Sea. The first oilfield to be brought into production was Argyll in 1975, and since the mid-1970s Britain has been a major producer of crude oil.

To date, the UK has produced around 3.5 billion tonnes of oil. It is estimated that there are around 800 million tonnes remaining to be produced. Licences for exploration and production are granted to companies by the DECC. At the end of 2004, 565 seaward production licences and 101 onshore petroleum exploration and development licenses had been awarded. At the end of 2012, there were a total of 339 offshore oil and gas fields in production. To date, the UK has produced around 27 billion barrels of oil. An estimated 3 to 8 billion barrels remain to be produced. Total UK oil production peaked in 1999 and is now declining. At around a third of the 1999 level, production stood at 44.6 million tonnes in 2012. Profits from oil production are subject to a special tax regime with different taxes applying depending on the date of approval of each field.

DRILLING ACTIVITY (2012)
by number of wells started

	Offshore	*Onshore*
Exploration	22	4
Appraisal	31	0
Development	122	13

Source: DECC

INDIGENOUS PRODUCTION AND REFINERY RECEIPTS
Thousand tonnes

	2011	*2012*
Indigenous production	51,972	44,561
Crude oil	48,571	42,052
*NGLs	3,401	2,508
Refinery receipts	79,746	74,380

* Natural Gas Liquids: condensates and petroleum gases derived at onshore treatment plants
Source: DECC

DELIVERIES OF PETROLEUM PRODUCTS FOR INLAND CONSUMPTION BY ENERGY USE
Thousand tonnes

	2011	*2012*
Transport	47,573	47,039
Industry	3,947	3,857
Domestic	2,401	2,433
Other	1,253	1,166
Total	55,174	54,495

Source: DECC

COAL

Mines were in private ownership until 1947 when they were nationalised and came under the management of the National Coal Board, later the British Coal Corporation. The corporation held a near monopoly on coal production until 1994 when the industry was restructured. Under the Coal Industry Act 1994, the Coal Authority was established to take over ownership of coal reserves and to issue licences to private mining companies. The Coal Authority is also responsible for the physical legacy of mining, eg subsidence damage claims that are not the responsibility of licensees, and for holding and making available all existing records. It also publishes current data on the coal industry on its website (W www.coal.decc.gov.uk).

The mines owned by the British Coal Corporation were sold as five separate businesses in 1994 and coal production is now undertaken entirely in the private sector. Coal output was around 50 million tonnes a year in 1994 but has since declined to around 16.1 million tonnes. As at 31 March 2013 there were four large and seven small underground mines as well as 34 surface mines in production or development in the UK.

The main consumer of coal in the UK is the electricity supply industry. Coal still supplies over a third of the UK's electricity needs but as indigenous production has declined, imports have continued to make up the shortfall and now represent around 70 per cent of UK coal supply, 40 per cent of which is currently supplied from Russia.

UK government policy is to meet the long-term challenges posed by climate change while continuing to ensure secure, clean and affordable energy. Coal's availability, flexibility and reliability compared to other sources mean that it is expected to continue to play an important role in the future generating mix, but its carbon emissions will need to be managed through the introduction of abatement technologies including carbon capture and storage (CCS).

CCS attempts to mitigate the effects of global warming by capturing the carbon dioxide emissions from power stations that burn fossil fuels, preventing the gas from being released into the atmosphere, and storing it in underground geological formations. CCS is still in its infancy and only through its successful demonstration and development will it be possible for coal to remain a part of a low-carbon UK energy mix. The government is committed to public sector investment in CCS technology on four power stations and has made it clear that there can be no new coal power stations in England and Wales without CCS on a defined amount of capacity. As part of a wider package of reforms to the electricity market, the government will also be introducing an Emissions Performance Standard, which will limit the emissions from new fossil fuel power stations.

COAL PRODUCTION AND FOREIGN TRADE
Thousand tonnes

	2011	*2012*
Surface mining	11,315	10,894
Deep-mined	7,312	6,153
Imports	32,527	44,815
Exports	(491)	(488)
**Total supply*	51,500	64,327
TOTAL	51,591	64,206

* Includes an estimate for slurry and stock change
Source: DECC

INLAND COAL USE
Thousand tonnes

	2011	*2012*
Fuel producers		
Electricity generators	41,850	54,906
Coke manufacture	5,398	5,079
Blast furnaces	995	987
Heat generation	562	592
*Other conversion industries	335	325
Final consumption		
Industry	1,682	1,602
Transport	15	16
Domestic	716	674
Public administration	26	12
Commercial	5	5
Agriculture	1	1
Miscellaneous	7	6

* Mainly recycled products
Source: DECC

GAS

From the late 18th century gas in Britain was produced from coal. In the 1960s town gas began to be produced from oil-based feedstocks using imported oil. In 1965 gas was discovered in the North Sea in the West Sole field, which became the first gasfield in production in 1967, and from the late 1960s natural gas began to replace town gas. From October 1998 Britain was connected to the continental European gas system via a pipeline from Bacton, Norfolk to Zeebrugge, Belgium. Gas is transported through 278,000km of mains pipeline including 7,600km of high-pressure gas pipelines owned and operated in the UK by National Grid Gas plc.

The gas industry in Britain was nationalised in 1949 and operated as the Gas Council. The Gas Council was replaced by the British Gas Corporation in 1972 and the industry became more centralised. The British Gas Corporation was privatised in 1986 as British Gas plc. In 1993 the Monopolies and Mergers Commission found that British Gas's integrated business in Great Britain as a gas trader and the owner of the gas transportation system could operate against the public interest. In February 1997, British Gas demerged its trading arm to become two separate companies, BG plc and Centrica plc. BG Group, as the company is now known, is an international natural gas company whose principal business is finding and developing gas reserves and building gas markets. Its core operations are located in the UK, South America, Egypt, Trinidad and Tobago, Kazakhstan and India. Centrica runs the trading and services operations under the British Gas brand name in Great Britain. In October 2000 BG demerged its pipeline business, Transco, which became part of Lattice Group, finally merging with the National Grid Group in 2002 to become National Grid Transco plc.

In July 2005 National Grid Transco plc changed its name to National Grid plc and Transco plc became National Grid Gas plc. In the same year National Grid Gas also completed the sale of four of its eight gas distribution networks. The distribution networks transport gas at lower pressures, which eventually supply the consumers such as domestic customers. The Scotland and south-east of England networks were sold to Scotia Gas Networks. The Wales and south-west network was sold to Wales & West Utilities and the network in the north-east to Northern Gas Networks. This was the biggest change in the corporate structure of gas infrastructure since privatisation in 1986.

Competition was gradually introduced into the industrial gas market from 1986. Supply of gas to the domestic market was opened to companies other than British Gas, starting in April 1996 with a pilot project in the West Country and Wales, with the rest of the UK following soon after.

Declines in UK indigenous gas production and increasing demand led to the UK becoming a net importer of gas once more in 2004. With the depletion of the UK Continental Shelf reserves, UK gas production has seen growing rates of decline. In 2012, UK gas production was 14 per cent lower than in 2011 and 64 per cent lower than the record level seen in 2000. As part of the Energy Act 2008, the government planned to strengthen regulation of the offshore gas supply infrastructure, to allow private sector investment to help maintain UK energy supplies.

BG GROUP PLC, Thames Valley Park, Reading RG6 1PT
T 0118-935 3222 W www.bg-group.com
Chair, Andrew Gould
Chief Executive, Chris Finlayson

CENTRICA PLC, Millstream, Maidenhead Road, Windsor, Berkshire SL4 5GD T 01753-494000 W www.centrica.com
Chair, Sir Roger Carr
Chief Executive, Sam Laidlaw

NATIONAL GRID PLC, Lakeside House, The Lakes, Northampton NN4 7HD T 0845-605 6677
W www.nationalgrid.com
Chair, Sir Peter Gershon, CBE
Chief Executive, Steve Holliday

UK GAS CONSUMPTION BY INDUSTRY
GWh

	2011	*2012*
Domestic	293,400	339,080
Industry	113,564	110,723
Public administration	45,295	48,005
Commercial	34,609	37,045
Agriculture	1,778	1,536
Miscellaneous	10,247	11,048
Total gas consumption	504,842	553,386

Source: DECC

ELECTRICITY

The first power station in Britain generating electricity for public supply began operating in 1882. In the 1930s a national transmission grid was developed and it was reconstructed and extended in the 1950s and 1960s. Power stations were operated by the Central Electricity Generating Board.

Under the Electricity Act 1989, 12 regional electricity companies, responsible for the distribution of electricity from the national grid to consumers, were formed from the former area electricity boards in England and Wales. Four companies were formed from the Central Electricity Generating Board: three generating companies (National Power plc, Nuclear Electric plc and Powergen plc) and the National Grid Company plc, which owned and operated the transmission system in England and Wales. National Power and Powergen were floated on the stock market in 1991.

National Power was demerged in October 2000 to form two separate companies: International Power plc and Innogy plc, which manages the bulk of National Power's UK assets. Nuclear Electric was split into two parts in 1996.

The National Grid Company was floated on the stock market in 1995 and formed a new holding company, National Grid Group. National Grid Group completed a merger with Lattice in 2002 to form National Grid Transco, a public limited company (*see* Gas).

Following privatisation, generators and suppliers in England and Wales traded via the Electricity Pool. A competitive wholesale trading market known as NETA (New Electricity Trading Arrangements) replaced the Electricity Pool in March 2001, and was extended to include Scotland via the British Electricity Transmissions and Trading Arrangements (BETTA) in 2005. As part of BETTA, National Grid became the system operator for all transmission. The introduction of competition into the domestic electricity market was completed in May 1999. Since competition was introduced, over 19 million of Britain's 28 million electricity customers have switched their supplier.

In Scotland, three new companies were formed under the Electricity Act 1989: Scottish Power plc and Scottish Hydro-Electric plc, which were responsible for generation, transmission, distribution and supply; and Scottish Nuclear Ltd. Scottish Power and Scottish Hydro-Electric were floated on the stock market in 1991. Scottish Hydro-Electric merged with Southern Electric in 1998 to become Scottish and Southern Energy plc. Scottish Nuclear was incorporated into British Energy in 1996. BETTA opened the Scottish market to the same competition that had applied in England and Wales.

In Northern Ireland, Northern Ireland Electricity plc (NIE) was set up in 1993 under a 1991 Order in Council. In 1993 it was floated on the stock market and in 1998 it became part of the Viridian Group and was responsible for distribution and supply until NIE was sold to ESB Independent Energy in December 2010. In June 2010, Airtricity became the first new electricity supplier since the Northern Ireland electricity market was opened to competition in 2007.

On 12 July 2011, the government published *Planning Our Electric Future: a White Paper for Secure, Affordable and Low-carbon Electricity* in response to the challenges set by increasing electricity demands. It has been agreed that over £110bn in investment is needed to update the grid and build new power stations.

On 30 September 2003 the Electricity Association, the industry's main trade association, was replaced with three separate trade bodies: the Association of Electricity Producers; the Energy Networks Association; and the Energy Retail Association. In April 2012, following a merger between the Association of Electricity Producers, the Energy Retail Association and the UK Business Council for Sustainable Energy, Energy UK – the new trade association for the gas and electricity sector – was established.

ENERGY NETWORKS ASSOCIATION, 6th floor, Dean Bradley House, 52 Horseferry Road, London SW1P 2AF
T 020-7706 5100 W www.energynetworks.org
Chief Executive, David Smith

ENERGY UK, Charles House, 5–11 Regent Street, London SW1Y 4LR T 020-7930 9390 W www.energy-uk.org.uk
Chief Executive, Angela Knight

ELECTRICITY PRODUCTION, SUPPLY AND CONSUMPTION
GWh

	2011	*2012*
Electricity produced		
Nuclear	68,980	70,405
Hydro	5,690	5,284
Wind, wave and solar photovoltaics	15,755	20,775
Coal	108,571	143,181
Oil	3,117	3,065
Gas	146,520	100,073
Renewables	13,200	15,198
Other	2,715	2,887
Total	364,548	360,869
Electricity supplied		
Production	364,548	360,869
*Other sources	2,906	2,966
Imports	8,689	13,791
Exports	(2,467)	(1,746)
Total	373,676	375,880
Electricity consumed		
Industry	102,348	97,820
Transport	4,083	4,089
Other	211,442	215,666
Domestic	111,603	114,698
Public administration	18,396	18,891
Commercial	77,495	78,206
Agriculture	3,948	3,871
Total	317,873	317,575

* Pumped storage production
Source: DECC

GAS AND ELECTRICITY SUPPLIERS

With the gas and electricity markets open, most suppliers offer their customers both services. The majority of gas/electricity companies have become part of larger multi-utility companies, often operating internationally.

As part of measures to reduce the UK's carbon output, the government has outlined plans to introduce 'smart meters' to all UK homes. Smart meters perform the traditional meter function of measuring energy consumption, in addition to more advanced functions such as allowing energy suppliers to communicate directly with their customers and removing the need for meter readings and bill estimates. The meters also allow domestic customers to have direct access to energy consumption information.

The following list comprises a selection of suppliers offering gas and electricity. Organisations in italics are subsidiaries of the companies listed in capital letters directly above.

ENGLAND, SCOTLAND AND WALES

CENTRICA PLC, Millstream, Maidenhead Road, Windsor, Berkshire SL4 5GD T 01753-494000 W www.centrica.com

British Gas, PO Box 4805, Worthing BN11 9QW T 0800-048 0202 W www.britishgas.co.uk

EDF ENERGY, Osprey House, Osprey Road, Exeter, EX2 7WN T 0800-056 7777 W www.edfenergy.com

E.ON, 6th Floor, 100 Pall Mall, London SW1Y 5NQ T 024-7618 3843 W www.eon-uk.com

NORTHERN POWERGRID, Houghton le Spring DH4 7LA T 0845-070 7172 W www.northernpowergrid.com

NPOWER, PO Box 93, Peterlee SR8 2XX T 0800-073 3000 W www.npower.com

SCOTTISHPOWER, PO Box 8729, Bellshill ML4 3YD T 0845-270 0700 W www.scottishpower.com

SSE PLC, Inveralmond House, 200 Dunkeld Road, Perth PH1 3AQ T 0800-980 8831 W www.sse.co.uk

Scottish Hydro, T 0800-980 8754 W www.hydro.co.uk

Southern Electric, T 0800-980 8476 W www.southern-electric.co.uk

SWALEC, T 0800-980 9041 W www.swalec.co.uk

NORTHERN IRELAND

AIRTRICITY (a member of Scottish and Southern Energy), Red Oak South, South County Business Park, Leopardstown, Dublin 18 T 1850-812220 W www.airtricity.com

ELECTRIC IRELAND, Forsyth House, Cromac Square, Belfast BT2 8LA T 0845-600 5335 W www.electricireland.ie

VIRIDIAN GROUP LTD, Greenwood House, 64 Newforge Lane, Belfast BT9 5NF T 028-9066 8416 W www.viridiangroup.co.uk

Energia, 3rd Floor, Mill House, Ashtowngate, Navan Road, Dublin 15 T 1850-363744 W www.energia.ie

REGULATION OF THE GAS AND ELECTRICITY INDUSTRIES

The Office of the Gas and Electricity Markets (OFGEM) regulates the gas and electricity industries in Great Britain. It was formed in 1999 by the merger of the Office of Gas Supply and the Office of Electricity Regulation. OFGEM's overriding aim is to protect and promote the interests of all gas and electricity customers by promoting competition and regulating monopolies. It is governed by an authority and its powers are provided for under the Gas Act 1986, the Electricity Act 1989, the Competition Act 1998, the Utilities Act 2000 and the Enterprise Act 2002. Energywatch was the independent gas and electricity watchdog, set up in November 2000 through the Utility Act to protect and promote the interests of gas and electricity consumers. In October 2008 Energywatch merged with Postwatch and the National Consumer Council to form a new advocacy body, Consumer Focus. In October 2010, the government announced that Consumer Focus would be abolished and some of its functions would transfer to Citizens Advice, Citizens Advice Scotland and the Consumer Council for Northern Ireland. This transfer began in April 2013 with full responsibility to be transferred to the Citizens Advice service in 2014.

CITIZENS ADVICE, Myddleton House, 115–123 Pentonville Road, London N1 9LZ T 020-7833 2181 W www.citizensadvice.org.uk

CITIZENS ADVICE SCOTLAND, 1st Floor, Spectrum House, 2 Powderhall Road, Edinburgh EH7 4GB T 0131-550 1000 W www.cas.org.uk

CONSUMER COUNCIL FOR NORTHERN IRELAND, 116 Holywood Road, Belfast BT4 1NY T 028-9067 2488 W www.consumercouncil.org.uk

THE OFFICE OF THE GAS AND ELECTRCITY MARKETS (OFGEM), 9 Millbank, London SW1 3GE T 020-7901 7000 W www.ofgem.gov.uk

NUCLEAR POWER

Nuclear reactors began to supply electricity to the national grid in 1956. Nuclear power is currently generated in the UK at nine sites: one magnox reactor (Wylfa 1, expected shutdown in September 2014) following the closure of Oldbury nuclear power station in February 2012, seven advanced gas-cooled reactors (AGR) and one pressurised water reactor (PWR), Sizewell 'B' in Suffolk. The AGRs and PWR are owned by a private company, British Energy, while the magnox reactor is state-owned by the Nuclear

Decommissioning Authority. The first of a series of new-generation plants is expected to come on-line around 2018; all but one of the current sites (Sizewell 'B') will be shut down by 2035.

In April 2005 the responsibility for the decommissioning of civil nuclear reactors and other nuclear facilities used in research and development was handed to the Nuclear Decommissioning Authority (NDA). The NDA is a non-departmental public body, funded mainly by the DECC. Until April 2007, UK Nirex was responsible for the disposal of intermediate and some low-level nuclear waste. After this date Nirex was integrated into the NDA and renamed the Radioactive Waste Management directorate.

There are currently 22 magnox reactors owned by the NDA which are in various stages of decommissioning, including the world's first commercial power station at Calder Hall on the Sellafield site in Cumbria. The decommissioning of these sites is scheduled for completion within the next 15 to 20 years. In the case of the Dounreay research facility in Scotland, controls on access to contaminated land are expected to remain in place until around 2300.

In 2012 electricity supplied from nuclear sources accounted for 19.5 per cent of the total electricity supply. The 2008 Energy bill paved the way for the construction of up to ten new nuclear power stations by 2020. A number of factors have led to government backing for nuclear power: domestic gas supplies are running low; oil and gas prices are high; carbon emissions must be cut to comply with EU legislation and meet global climate change targets; and a number of coal-fired power stations that fail to meet clean air requirements are due to be closed.

Nuclear power has its advantages: reactors emit virtually no carbon dioxide and uranium prices remain relatively steady. However, the advantages of low emissions are countered by the high costs of construction and difficulties in disposing of nuclear waste. Currently, the only method is to store it securely until it has slowly decayed to safe levels. Public distrust persists despite the advances in safety technology.

SAFETY AND REGULATION

The Office for Nuclear Regulation (OCR), an agency of the Health and Safety Executive is the nuclear industry's regulator. Operations at all UK nuclear power stations are governed by a site licence which is issued under the Nuclear Installations Act. The OCR monitors compliance and has the jurisdiction to close down a reactor if the terms of the licence are breached. The DECC is responsible for security at all the UK's nuclear power stations, which are policed by the Civil Nuclear Constabulary, a specialised armed force created in April 2005. In 2009 Magnox Electric Ltd was found guilty of breaking the Radioactive Substances Act 2003: it had left a radioactive leak on a holding tank at Bradwell power station, Essex, unchecked for 14 years.

RENEWABLE SOURCES

Renewable sources of energy principally include biofuels, hydro, wind and solar. Renewable sources produced over 10.0 million tonnes of oil equivalent for primary energy usage in 2012; of this, about 7.5 million tonnes was used to generate electricity, 1.5 million tonnes to generate heat and 1.0 million tonnes was used as transport fuels. In 2012, the UK generated 11.3 per cent of its total electricity production from renewable sources, up by 1.9 per cent from 2011.

The government's principal mechanism for developing renewable energy sources is the Renewables Obligation (RO), which aims to increase the contribution of electricity from renewables in the UK. There are separate RO schemes for England and Wales, Scotland and Northern Ireland. For both England and Wales and Scotland, the RO is set so that 9.7 per cent of licensed electricity sales should be from renewable sources eligible for the RO by 2009/10, and 15.4 per cent should be eligible by 2015/16. For Northern Ireland, these figures are 3.5 per cent and 6.3 per cent. In 2012, renewable sources accounted for 10.6 per cent of sales on an RO basis, an increase of 1.2 per cent from 2011.

A renewables obligation has been in place in England and Wales since April 2002 to give incentives to generators to supply progressively higher levels of renewable energy over time. These measures included exempting renewable energy sources from the climate change levy, capital grants, enhanced research funding and regional planning to meet renewables targets.

In addition to the RO, in April 2010, the government launched a Feed-in Tariff (FIT) scheme in Great Britain to encourage the uptake of small-scale low carbon electricity generation technologies, principally renewables such as solar photovoltaics, wind and hydro-electricity.

The government approved an EU-wide agreement in March 2007 to generate 20 per cent of energy production from renewable sources by 2020. It has since negotiated down the national share in this target to 15 per cent of energy production by 2020. In July 2009 the government published a Renewable Energy Strategy in order to meet this target. Other impediments to the expansion of renewable energy production include planning restrictions, rising raw material prices, and the possible redirection of funds to develop CCS technology and nuclear energy sources. For further information on renewable energy *see* The Environment.

RENEWABLE ENERGY UTILISATION

By source, 2012

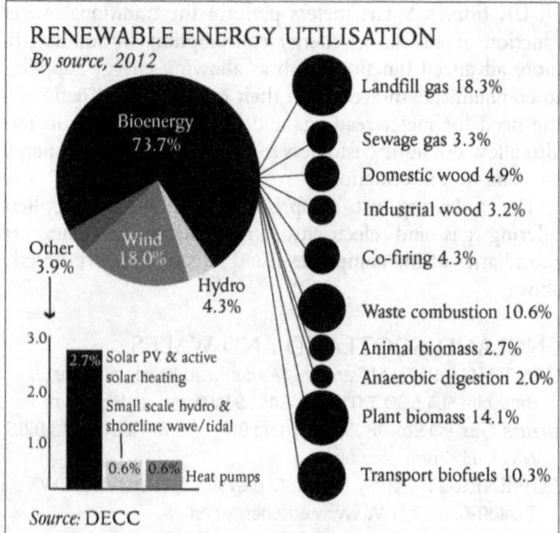

Source: DECC

TRANSPORT

CIVIL AVIATION

Since the privatisation of British Airways in 1987, UK airlines have been operated entirely by the private sector. In 2012, total capacity of British airlines amounted to 50 billion tonne-km, of which 41 billion tonne-km was on scheduled services. UK airlines carried around 134 million passengers; 114 million on scheduled services and 20 million on charter flights. Passenger traffic through UK airports increased by 0.6 per cent in 2012. Traffic at the six main London area airports (Gatwick, Heathrow, London City, Luton, Southend and Stansted) increased by 1 per cent over 2012 and other UK regional airports saw a increase of 0.1 per cent.

Leading British airlines include British Airways, EasyJet, Monarch, Thomas Cook Airlines, Thomson Airways and Virgin Atlantic. Irish airline Ryanair also operates frequent flights from the UK.

There are around 140 licensed civil aerodromes in Britain, with Heathrow and Gatwick handling the highest volume of passengers.

The Civil Aviation Authority (CAA), an independent statutory body, is responsible for the regulation of UK airlines. This includes economic and airspace regulation, air safety, consumer protection and environmental research and consultancy. All commercial airline companies must be granted an air operator's certificate, which is issued by the CAA to operators meeting the required safety standards. The CAA issues airport safety licences, which must be obtained by any airport used for public transport and training flights. All British-registered aircraft must be granted an airworthiness certificate, and the CAA issues professional licences to pilots, flight crew, ground engineers and air traffic controllers. The CAA also manages the Air Travel Organiser's Licence (ATOL), the UK's principal travel protection scheme. The CAA's costs are met entirely from charges on those whom it regulates; there is no direct government funding of the CAA's work.

The Transport Act 2000 separated the CAA from its subsidiary, National Air Traffic Services (NATS), which provides air traffic control services to aircraft flying in UK airspace and over the eastern part of the North Atlantic. NATS is a public private partnership (PPP) between the Airline Group (a consortium of UK airlines), which holds 42 per cent of the shares; NATS staff, who hold 5 per cent; BAA, which holds 4 per cent, and the government, which holds 49 per cent and a golden share. In 2012–13 NATS handled a total of 2,126,000 flights, a decrease of 1.9 per cent on 2011–12 figures.

AIR PASSENGERS 2012

All UK Airports: Total	220,928,971
Aberdeen	3,330,126
Barra (HIAL)	11,415
Belfast City	2,246,202
Belfast International	4,313,685
Benbecula (HIAL)	31,364
Birmingham	8,922,539
Blackpool	235,238
Bournemouth	695,545
Bristol	5,921,530
Cambridge	2,130
Campbeltown (HIAL)	9,144
Cardiff	1,028,123
City of Derry (Eglinton)	398,209
Doncaster Sheffield	693,661
Dundee	54,655
Durham Tees Valley	166,251
East Midlands	4,076,178
Edinburgh	9,195,061
Exeter	701,743
Gatwick	34,235,982
Glasgow	7,157,859
Gloucestershire	15,292
Heathrow	70,037,417
Humberside	234,142
Inverness (HIAL)	604,098
Islay (HIAL)	21,609
Isle of Man	697,123
Isles of Scilly (St Mary's)	97,012
Isles of Scilly (Tresco)	25,563
Kent International	8,595
Kirkwall (HIAL)	140,683
Lands End (St Just)	33,108
Leeds Bradford	2,990,517
Lerwick (Tingwall)	5,041
Liverpool	4,463,257
London City	3,016,664
Luton	9,617,697
Lydd	445
Manchester	19,736,502
Newcastle	4,366,196
Newquay	166,609
Norwich	396,676
Oxford (Kidlington)	7,223
Penzance Heliport	61,747
Prestwick	1,067,933
Scatsta	304,480
Shoreham	480
Southampton	1,694,120
Southend	617,027
Stansted	17,472,669
Stornoway (HIAL)	119,411
Sumburgh (HIAL)	150,567
Tiree (HIAL)	7,545
Wick (HIAL)	24,976
Channel Islands Airports: Total	2,423,244
Alderney	64,165
Guernsey	890,746
Jersey	1,468,333

HIAL = Highlands and Islands Airports Ltd
Source: Civil Aviation Authority

CAA, CAA House, 45–59 Kingsway, London WC2B 6TE
T 020-7379 7311 W www.caa.co.uk

Heathrow Airport	T 0844-335 1801
Gatwick Airport	T 0844-892 0322
Manchester Airport	T 0871-271 0711
Stansted Airport	T 0844-335 1803

BRITISH AIRLINES

BRITISH AIRWAYS, PO Box 365, Waterside, Harmondsworth UB7 0GB T 0844-493 0787 W www.britishairways.com

EASYJET, Hangar 89, London Luton Airport LU2 9PF T 0843-104 5000 W www.easyjet.com

MONARCH, Prospect House, Prospect Way, London Luton Airport LU2 9NU T 0871-940 5040 W www.monarch.co.uk
THOMAS COOK AIRLINES, 2–4 Godwin Street, Bradford, W. Yorks BD1 2ST T 0127-438 4119 W www.thomascook.com
THOMSON AIRWAYS, Wigmore House, Wigmore Place, Wigmore Lane, Luton, Beds LU2 9TN T 0871-231 4787 W www.thomson.co.uk
VIRGIN ATLANTIC, The Office, Manor Royal, Crawley, W. Sussex RH10 9NU T 0844-811 0000 W www.virgin-atlantic.com

RAILWAYS

The railway network in Britain was developed by private companies in the 19th century. In 1948 the main railway companies were nationalised and were run by a public authority, the British Transport Commission. The commission was replaced by the British Railways Board in 1963, operating as British Rail. On 1 April 1994, responsibility for managing the track and railway infrastructure passed to a newly formed company, Railtrack plc. In October 2001 Railtrack was put into administration under the Railways Act 1993. In October 2002 Railtrack was taken out of administration and replaced by the not-for-profit company Network Rail. The British Railways Board continued as operator of all train services until 1996–7, when they were sold or franchised to the private sector.

The Strategic Rail Authority (SRA) was created to provide strategic leadership to the rail industry and formally came into being on 1 February 2001 following the passing of the Transport Act 2000. In January 2002 it published its first strategic plan, setting out the strategic priorities for Britain's railways over the next ten years. In addition to its coordinating role, the SRA was responsible for allocating government funding to the railways and awarding and monitoring the franchises for operating rail services.

On 15 July 2004 the transport secretary announced a new structure for the rail industry in the white paper *The Future of Rail*. These proposals were implemented under the Railways Act 2005, which abolished the SRA, passing most of its functions to the Department for Transport; established the Rail Passengers Council as a single national body, dissolving the regional committees; and gave devolved governments in Scotland and Wales more say in decisions at a local level. In addition, responsibility for railway safety regulation was transferred to the Office of Rail Regulation from the Health and Safety Executive.

OFFICE OF RAIL REGULATION

The Office of Rail Regulation (ORR) was established on 5 July 2004 by the Railways and Transport Safety Act 2003, replacing the Office of the Rail Regulator. As the railway industry's economic and safety regulator, the ORR's principal function is to regulate Network Rail's stewardship of the national network. The ORR also licenses operators of railway assets, approves agreements for access by operators to track, stations and light maintenance depots, and enforces domestic competition law. The ORR is led by a board appointed by the Secretary of State for Transport and chaired by Anna Walker.

SERVICES

For privatisation, under the Railways Act 1993, domestic passenger services were divided into 25 train operating units, which were franchised to private sector operators via a competitive tendering process. The train operators formed the Association of Train Operating Companies (ATOC) to act as the official voice of the passenger rail industry and provide its members with a range of services enabling them to comply with conditions imposed on them through their franchise agreements and operating licences.

As at July 2013 there were 23 passenger train operating companies: Arriva Trains Wales, c2c, Chiltern Railways, CrossCountry, East Coast, East Midlands Trains, Eurostar, First Capital Connect, First Great Western, First Hull Trains, First TransPennine Express, Grand Central, Greater Anglia, Heathrow Express, London Midland, London Overground, Merseyrail, Northern Rail, ScotRail, South West Trains, Southeastern, Southern and Virgin Trains.

Network Rail publishes a national timetable which contains details of rail services operated over the UK network and sea ferry services which provide connections with Ireland, the Isle of Man, the Isle of Wight, the Channel Islands and some European destinations.

The national rail enquiries service offers information about train times and fares for any part of the country, Transport for London (TfL) provides London-specific travel information for all modes of travel and Eurostar provides information for international channel tunnel rail services:

NATIONAL RAIL ENQUIRIES
T 0845-748 4950 W www.nationalrail.co.uk
TRANSPORT FOR LONDON
T 0843-222 1234 W www.tfl.gov.uk
EUROSTAR
T 08432-186186 W www.eurostar.com

PASSENGER FOCUS AND LONDON TRAVELWATCH

Passenger Focus is the operating name of the Passengers' Council, a single national consumer body for rail, which is funded by the Department for Transport but whose independence is guaranteed by an act of parliament. Under the Passengers' Council (non-railway functions) Order of February 2010, Passenger Focus also represents bus passengers in England, outside London. Included in this remit are local bus services and scheduled domestic coach journeys.

Established in July 2000, London TravelWatch is the operating name of the official watchdog organisation representing the interests of transport users in and around the capital. Officially known as the London Transport Users' Committee, it is sponsored and funded by the London Assembly and is independent of the transport operators. London TravelWatch represents users of buses, the Underground, river and rail services in and around London, including Eurostar and Heathrow Express, Croydon Tramlink and the Docklands Light Railway. The interests of pedestrians, cyclists and motorists are also represented, as are those of taxi users.

FREIGHT

On privatisation in 1996, British Rail's bulk freight operations were sold to North and South Railways – subsequently called English, Welsh and Scottish Railways (EWS). In 2007, EWS was bought by Deutsche Bahn and in January 2009 was re-named DB Schenker. The other major companies in the rail freight sector are: Colas Rail, Direct Rail Services, Freightliner and GB Railfreight (GBRf). In 2011–12 freight moved by rail amounted to 21.05 billion tonne-kilometres, a 9.4 per cent increase from 2010–11.

NETWORK RAIL

Network Rail is responsible for the tracks, bridges, tunnels, level crossings, viaducts and 18 main stations that form Britain's rail network. In addition to providing the timetables for the passenger and freight operators, Network Rail is also responsible for all the signalling and electrical control equipment needed to operate the rail network and for monitoring and reporting performance across the industry.

Network Rail is a private company run as a commercial business; it is directly accountable to its members and regulated by the ORR. The members have similar rights to those of shareholders in a public company except they do not receive dividends or share capital and thereby have no financial or economic interest in Network Rail. All of Network Rail's profits are reinvested into maintaining and upgrading the rail infrastructure.

ASSOCIATION OF TRAIN OPERATING COMPANIES, 3rd Floor, 40 Bernard Street, London WC1N 1BY T 020-7841 8000 W www.atoc.org

LONDON TRAVELWATCH, Dexter House, 2 Royal Mint Court, London EC3N 4QN T 020-3176 2999 W www.londontravelwatch.org.uk

NETWORK RAIL, Kings Place, 90 York Way, London N1 9AG T 020-7557 8000 W www.networkrail.co.uk

OFFICE OF RAIL REGULATION, 1 Kemble Street, London WC2B 4AN T 020-7282 2000 W www.rail-reg.gov.uk

PASSENGER FOCUS, Freepost RTEH-XAGE-BYKZ, PO Box 5594, Southend-on-Sea SS1 9PZ T 0300-123 2350 W www.passengerfocus.org.uk

RAIL SAFETY

On 1 April 2006 responsibility for health and safety policy and enforcement on the railways transferred from the Health and Safety Executive to the Office of Rail Regulation (ORR).

In 2012–13 a total of 55 passengers, railway staff and other members of the public were fatally injured in all rail incidents (excluding suicides), compared with 65 in 2011–12.

ACCIDENTS ON RAILWAYS

	2011–12	*2012–13*
Rail incident fatalities	65	55
Passengers	5	4
Railway employees	1	2
Public	59	49
Rail incident major injuries	430	457
Passengers	261	299
Railway employees	129	114
Public	40	44

SUICIDES AND ATTEMPTED SUICIDES 2012–13

Fatalities	238
Major Injuries	35

Source: RSSB – *Annual Safety Performance Report 2012–13*

OTHER RAIL SYSTEMS

Responsibility for the London Underground passed from the government to the Mayor and Transport for London on 15 July 2003, with a public-private partnership already in place. Plans for a public-private partnership for London Underground were pushed through by the government in February 2002 despite opposition from the Mayor of London and a range of transport organisations. Under the PPP, long-term contracts with private companies were estimated to enable around £16bn to be invested in renewing and upgrading the London Underground's infrastructure over 15 years. In July 2007, Metronet, which was responsible for two of three PPP contracts, went into administration; TfL took over both contracts. Responsibility for stations, trains, operations, signalling and safety remains in the public sector. In 2012–13 there were 1,215 million passenger journeys on the London Underground.

In addition to Glasgow Subway, which is classified as an underground system (12.7 million passenger journeys in 2012–13), Britain has eight other light rail and tram systems: Blackpool Tramway, Croydon Tramlink, Docklands Light Railway (DLR), Manchester Metrolink, Midland Metro, Nottingham Express Transit (NET), Sheffield Supertram and Tyne and Wear Metro.

In 2012–13 there were 222 million passenger light rail and tram journeys in Great Britain; an increase of 9 per cent on 2011–12 figures.

THE CHANNEL TUNNEL

The earliest recorded scheme for a submarine transport connection between Britain and France was in 1802. Tunnelling began simultaneously on both sides of the Channel three times: in 1881, in the early 1970s, and on 1 December 1987, when construction workers bored the first of the three tunnels which form the Channel Tunnel. Engineers 'holed through' the first tunnel (the service tunnel) on 1 December 1990 and tunnelling was completed in June 1991. The tunnel was officially inaugurated by the Queen and President Mitterrand of France on 6 May 1994.

The submarine link comprises two rail tunnels, each carrying trains in one direction, which measure 7.6m (24.93ft) in diameter. Between them lies a smaller service tunnel, measuring 4.8m (15.75ft) in diameter. The service tunnel is linked to the rail tunnels by 130 cross-passages for maintenance and safety purposes. The tunnels are 50km (31 miles) long, 38km (24 miles) of which is under the seabed at an average depth of 40m (132ft). The rail terminals are situated at Folkestone and Calais, and the tunnels go underground at Shakespeare Cliff, Dover and Sangatte, west of Calais.

RAIL LINKS

The British Channel Tunnel Rail Link route runs from Folkestone to St Pancras station, London, with intermediate stations at Ashford and Ebbsfleet in Kent.

Construction of the rail link was financed by the private sector with a substantial government contribution. A private sector consortium, London and Continental Railways Ltd (LCR), comprising Union Railways and the UK operator of Eurostar, owns the rail link and was responsible for its design and construction. The rail link was constructed in two phases: phase one, from the Channel Tunnel to Fawkham Junction, Kent, began in October 1998 and opened to fare-paying passengers on 28 September 2003; phase two, from Southfleet Junction to St Pancras, was completed in November 2007.

There are direct services from the UK to Calais, Disneyland Paris, Lille and Paris in France and Brussels in Belgium. There are also direct services to Avignon in the south of France between July and September and during the winter months (December to April) to the French Alps. High-speed trains also run from Lille to the south of France.

Eurostar, the high-speed passenger train service, connects London with Paris in 2 hours 15 minutes, Brussels in 1 hour 51 minutes and Lille in 1 hour 20 minutes. There are Eurostar terminals at London St Pancras, Ashford and Ebbsfleet in Kent, Paris Gare Du Nord and Lille in France, and Brussels-South in Belgium.

ROADS

HIGHWAY AUTHORITIES

The powers and responsibilities of highway authorities in England and Wales are set out in the Highways Act 1980; for Scotland there is separate legislation.

Responsibility for motorways and other trunk roads in Great Britain rests in England with the Secretary of State for

Transport, in Scotland with the Scottish government, and in Wales with the Welsh government. The highway authority for non-trunk roads in England, Wales and Scotland is, in general, the local authority in whose area the roads lie. With the establishment of the Greater London Authority in July 2000, Transport for London became the highway authority for roads in London.

In Northern Ireland the Department for Regional Development is the statutory road authority responsible for public roads and their maintenance and construction; the Roads Service executive agency carries out these functions on behalf of the department.

FINANCE

In England all aspects of trunk road and motorway funding are provided directly by the government to the Highways Agency, which operates, maintains and improves a network of motorways and trunk roads around 6,920km (4,300 miles) long, on behalf of the secretary of state. Since 2001 the length of the network that the Highways Agency is responsible for has been decreasing owing to a policy of de-trunking, which transfers responsibility for non-core roads to local authorities. For the financial year 2013–14 the Highways Agency's total budget, excluding depreciation, is £2,781m: £749m for maintenance, £926m for major schemes and the remainder for traffic management, technology improvements, other programmes and administration costs.

Government support for local authority capital expenditure on roads and other transport infrastructure is provided through grant and credit approvals as part of the Local Transport Plan (LTP). Local authorities bid for resources on the basis of a five-year programme built around delivering integrated transport strategies. As well as covering the structural maintenance of local roads and the construction of major new road schemes, LTP funding also includes smaller-scale safety and traffic management measures with associated improvements for public transport, cyclists and pedestrians.

For the financial year 2013–14, total allocated LTP funding amounted to £1,070m: £750m for maintenance and £320m for integrated transport measures.

Total expenditure by the Welsh government in 2012–13 to improve and maintain the motorway and trunk road network in Wales was £126.2m, a further £13.9m was allocated under the transport grant scheme (now closed to new schemes) and £27.8m was allocated for the delivery of regional transport plans, under which expenditure on local road schemes is determined. Total budgeted expenditure for the motorway and trunk road network in 2013–14 is £114.1m, with a further £16.0m allocated to regional transport plans.

Since 1 July 1999 all decisions on Scottish transport expenditure have been devolved to the Scottish government. Total expenditure on motorways and trunk roads in Scotland during 2012–13 was £762.5m (including depreciation and other annually managed expenditure charges). Planned expenditure for 2013–14 is £711.8m.

In Northern Ireland total expenditure by the Roads Service on all roads in 2012–13 was £129.4m, with £59.9m spent on trunk roads and motorways. Planned expenditure for 2013–14 is £132.7m, with £97.7m allocated for trunk roads and motorways.

The Transport Act 2000 gave English and Welsh local authorities (outside London) powers to introduce road-user charging or workplace parking levy schemes. The act requires that the net revenue raised is used to improve local transport services and facilities for at least ten years. The aim is to reduce congestion and encourage greater use of alternative modes of transport. Schemes developed by local authorities require government approval. The UK's first toll road, the M6 Toll, opened in December 2003 and runs for 43.5km (27 miles) around Birmingham from junction 3a to junction 11a on the M6.

Charging schemes in London are allowed under the 1999 Greater London Authority Act. The Central London Congestion Charge Scheme began on 17 February 2003 *(see also* Regional Government).

ROAD LENGTHS 2012
Miles

	England	*Wales*	*Scotland*	*Great Britain*
Major Roads	20,069	2,586	6,389	29,044
Motorways	1,878	88	282	2,248
Minor Roads	165,491	18,364	30,227	214,082
Total	187,438	21,038	36,898	245,374

Source: Department for Transport

FREIGHT TRANSPORT BY ROAD (GREAT BRITAIN) 2010

GOODS MOVED

By mode of working (billion tonne kilometres)	
All modes	138.9
Own account	50.0
Public haulage	88.9
By gross weight of vehicle (billion tonne kilometres)	
All vehicles	138.9
3.5–25 tonnes	12.8
Over 25 tonnes	126.0

GOODS LIFTED

By mode of working (million tonnes)	
All modes	1,489
Own account	689
Public haulage	800
By gross weight of vehicle (million tonnes)	
All vehicles	1,489
3.5–25 tonnes	197
Over 25 tonnes	1,292

Source: Department for Transport

ROAD TRAFFIC BY TYPE OF VEHICLE (GREAT BRITAIN) 2011

	Million vehicle km
All motor vehicles	488,900
Cars and taxis	387,400
Light goods vehicles	66,600
Heavy goods vehicles	25,600
Buses and coaches	4,700
Motorcycles	4,600
Pedal cycles	4,900

Source: Department for Transport

BUSES

The majority of bus services outside London are provided on a commercial basis by private operators. Local authorities have powers to subsidise services where needs are not being met by a commercial service.

Since April 2008 people aged 60 and over and disabled people who qualify under the categories listed in the Transport Act 2000 have been able to travel for free on any local bus across England between 9.30am and 11pm Monday to Friday and all day on weekends and bank holidays. Local authorities recompense operators for the reduced fare revenue. A similar scheme operates in Wales and within London, although there is no time restriction. In Scotland, people aged 60 and over and disabled people have been able to travel for free on any local or long-distance bus since April 2006.

In London, Transport for London (TfL) has overall responsibility for setting routes, service standards and fares for the bus network. Almost all routes are competitively tendered to commercial operators.

In Northern Ireland, passenger transport services are provided by Ulsterbus and Metro (formerly Citybus), two wholly owned subsidiaries of the Northern Ireland Transport Holding Company. Along with Northern Ireland Railways, Ulsterbus and Metro operate under the brand name of Translink and are publicly owned. Ulsterbus is responsible for virtually all bus services in Northern Ireland except Belfast city services, which are operated by Metro. People living in Northern Ireland aged 65 and over can travel on buses and trains for free once they have obtained a Senior SmartPass from Translink.

LOCAL BUS PASSENGER JOURNEYS 2011–12

	No. of journeys (millions)
England	4,678
London	2,324
Scotland	439
Wales	116
Total	5,233

Source: Department for Transport

TAXIS AND PRIVATE HIRE VEHICLES

A taxi is a public transport vehicle with fewer than nine passenger seats, which is licensed to 'ply for hire'. This distinguishes taxis from private hire vehicles (PHVs) which must be booked in advance through an operator. In London, taxis and private hire vehicles are licensed by the Public Carriage Office (PCO), part of TfL. Outside London, local authorities are responsible for the licensing of taxis and private hire vehicles operational in their respective administrative areas. At the end of March 2013 there were 78,000 licensed taxis and 152,600 PHVs in England and Wales, of these 73,000 taxis and 148,600 PHVs were in England with around 31 per cent of both taxis and PHVs based in London.

ROAD SAFETY

In May 2011, the government published *The Strategic Framework for Road Safety* which identified key indicators at national and local level intended to monitor the progress towards improving safety and decreasing the number of fatalities and seriously injured casualities on Great Britain's roads.

The key findings from the Department for Transport's 2012 annual road casuality report found that the number of people killed in road accidents reported to the police had decreased by 8 per cent, from 1,901 in 2011 to 1,754 in 2012; the lowest figure since national records began in 1926. The total number of reported casualities in Great Britain (slight injuries, serious injuries and fatalities) decreased by 4 per cent, from 203,950 in 2011 to 195,723 in 2012. Total reported child casualities (0–15 years) continued to decrease, by 11 per cent in 2012 to 17,251, with the number of children killed or seriously injured also decreasing by 6 per cent to 2,272 in 2012.

ROAD ACCIDENT CASUALTIES 2012

	Killed	*Serious*	*Slight*	*Total*
Average for 2005–9	2,816	27,225	216,010	246,050
England	1,491	20,139	152,953	174,583
Wales	93	941	7,531	8,565
Scotland	170	1,959	10,446	12,575
Great Britain	1,754	23,039	170,930	195,723

Source: Department for Transport

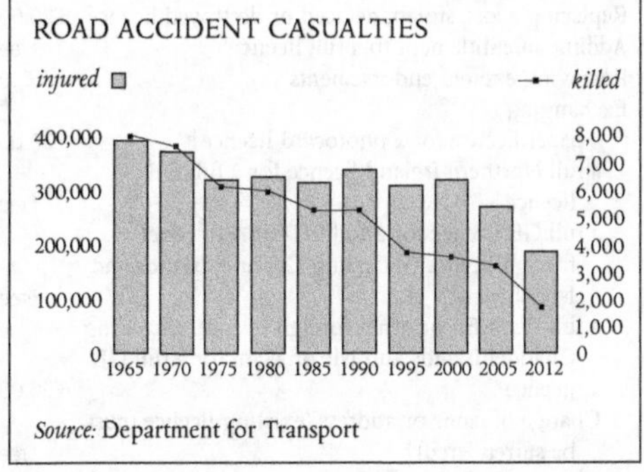

Source: Department for Transport

DRIVING LICENCES

It is necessary to hold a valid full licence in order to drive unaccompanied on public roads in the UK. Learner drivers must obtain a provisional driving licence before starting to learn to drive and must then pass theory and practical tests to obtain a full driving licence.

There are separate tests for driving motorcycles, cars, passenger-carrying vehicles (PCVs) and large goods vehicles (LGVs). Drivers must hold full car entitlement before they can apply for PCV or LGV entitlements.

The Driver and Vehicle Licensing Agency (DVLA) ceased the issue of paper licences in March 2000, but those currently in circulation will remain valid until they expire or the details on them change. The photocard driving licence was introduced to comply with the second EC directive on driving licences. This requires a photograph of the driver to be included on all UK licences issued from July 2001.

To apply for a first photocard driving licence, individuals are required to complete the form *Application for a Driving Licence* (D1).

The minimum age for driving motor cars, light goods vehicles up to 3.5 tonnes and motorcycles is 17 (moped, 16). Since June 1997, drivers who collect six or more penalty points within two years of qualifying lose their licence and are required to take another test. Forms and leaflets are available from post offices and online (W www.gov.uk/dvlaforms or W www.gov.uk/government/organisations/driver-and-vehicle-licensing-agency).

The DVLA is responsible for issuing driving licences, registering and licensing vehicles, and collecting excise duty in Great Britain. Driver and Vehicle Licensing Northern Ireland (DVLNI), part of the Driver and Vehicle Agency (DVA), has similar responsibilities in Northern Ireland.

DRIVING LICENCE FEES
As at August 2013

Provisional licence	
Car, motorcycle or moped	£50.00
Bus or lorry	Free
After disqualification until passing re-test	Free
Changing a provisional licence to a full licence	Free

Renewal	
Renewing the photo on the licence (must be renewed every 10 years)	£20.00
At age 70 and over	Free
For medical reasons	Free
Bus or lorry entitlement	Free
After disqualification	£65.00
After disqualification for some drink driving offences*	£90.00
After revocation (under the New Drivers Act)	£50.00
Replacing a lost, stolen, defaced or destroyed licence	£20.00
Adding an entitlement to a full licence	Free
Removing expired endorsements	£20
Exchanging	
a paper licence for a photocard licence†	£20.00
a full Northern Ireland licence for a full GB licence	Free
a full GB licence for a full EU/EEA or other foreign licence (including Channel Islands and Isle of Man)‡	Free
a full EU/EEA or other foreign licence (including Channel Islands and Isle of Man) for a full GB licence	£50.00
Change of name or address (existing licence must be surrendered)†	Free

* For an alcohol-related offence where the DVLA need to arrange medical enquiries

† If a paper licence is exchanged for a photocard at the same time as name or address details are changed there is no charge

‡ If a GB licence was held previously

DRIVING TESTS

The Driving Standards Agency (DSA) is responsible for carrying out driving tests and approving driving instructors in Great Britain. Driver and Vehicle Testing, part of the Driver and Vehicle Agency, is responsible for testing drivers and vehicles in Northern Ireland.

DRIVING TESTS TAKEN AND PASSED
April 2012–March 2013

	Number Taken	Percentage Passed
Practical Test		
Car	1,485,360	47.1
Motorcycle Module 1	70,323	70.5
Motorcycle Module 2	68,994	68.9
LGV/PCV/Car and Trailer*	72,534	53.0
Driver CPC†	13,036	85.8
Theory Test		
Car	1,365,324	58.9
Motorcycle	80,365	74.3
LGV/PCV		
Multiple choice	36,868	76.9
Hazard perception	35,936	80.9
Driver CPC†	24,834	50.9

LGV = Large goods vehicle; PCV = Passenger-carrying vehicle

* There is no theory test for Car and Trailer

† Driver Certificate of Professional Competence – legal requirement for all professional bus, coach and lorry drivers

Source: DSA

The theory and practical driving tests can be booked with a postal application, online (W www.gov.uk/book-practical-driving-test) or by phone (T 0300-200 1122).

DRIVING TEST FEES (WEEKDAY/EVENING* AND WEEKEND)
As at August 2013

Theory tests	
Car and motorcycle	£31.00
Bus and lorry	
Multiple choice	£35.00
Hazard perception	£15.00
Driver CPC	£30.00
Practical tests	
Car	£62.00/£75.00
Tractor and other specialist vehicles	£62.00/£75.00
Motorcycle	
Module 1 (off-road)	£15.50/£15.50
Module 2 (on-road)	£75.00/£88.50
Lorry and bus	£115.00/£141.00
Driver CPC	£55.00/£63.00
Car and trailer	£115.00/£141.00
Extended tests for disqualified drivers	
Car	£124.00/£150.00
Motorcycle	
Module 1 (on-road)	£150.00/£177.00

* After 4.30pm

VEHICLE LICENCES

Registration and first licensing of vehicles is through local offices of the DVLA in Swansea. Local facilities for relicensing are available at any post office which deals with vehicle licensing. Applicants will need to take their vehicle registration document (V5C) or, if this is not available, the applicant must complete form V62. Forms are available at post offices and online (W www.gov.uk/dvlaforms)

MOTOR VEHICLES LICENSED (GREAT BRITAIN)
As at 31 March 2013

	Thousands
All cars	28,842
Light goods vehicles	3,298
Motorcycles	1,199
Heavy goods vehicles	458
Buses and coaches	166
Other vehicles*	672
Total	34,635

* Includes rear diggers, lift trucks, rollers, ambulances, Hackney Carriages, three-wheelers and agricultural vehicles

Source: Department for Transport

VEHICLE EXCISE DUTY

Details of the present duties chargeable on motor vehicles are available at post offices and online (W www.gov.uk/government/publications/rates-of-vehicle-tax-v149). The Vehicle Excise and Registration Act 1994 provides *inter alia* that any vehicle kept on a public road but not used on roads is chargeable to excise duty as if it were in use. All non-commercial vehicles constructed before 1 January 1973 are exempt from vehicle excise duty. Any vehicle licensed on or after 31 January 1998, not in use and not kept on public roads must be registered as SORN (Statutory Off Road Notification) to be exempted from vehicle excise duty. From 1 January 2004 the registered keeper of a vehicle remains responsible for taxing a vehicle or making a SORN declaration until that liability is formally transferred to a new keeper.

RATES OF DUTY *from APRIL 2013*
Cars registered on or after 1 March 2001 and first-year rates*

Band	CO_2 Emissions (g/km)	Petrol and Diesel Car 6 months	Petrol and Diesel Car 12 months	Alternative Fuel Car 6 months	Alternative Fuel Car 12 months
A	Up to 100	–	£0.00	–	£0.00
B	101–110	–	£20.00	–	£10.00
C	111–120	–	£30.00	–	£20.00
D	121–130	£57.75	£105.00	£52.25	£95.00
E	131–140	£68.75	£125.00	£63.25	£115.00
F	141–150	£77.00	£140.00	£71.50	£130.00
G	151–165	£96.25	£175.00	£90.75	£165.00
H	166–175	£101	£200.00 (£285.00)	£104.50	£190.00 (£275.00)
I	176–185	£121	£220.00 (£335.00)	£115.50	£210.00 (£325.00)
J	186–200	£143	£260.00 (£475.00)	£137.50	£250.00 (£465.00)
K†	201–225	£154	£280.00 (£620.00)	£148.50	£270.00 (£610.00)
L	226–255	£261.25	£475.00 (£840.00)	£255.75	£465.00 (£830.00)
M	255+	£269.50	£490.00 (£1,065.00)	£264.00	£480.00 (£1,055.00)

* First-year rates (figures in parentheses) are payable for some vehicles' first tax disc taken out at first registration
† Includes cars that have a CO_2 emission figure over 225g/km but were registered before 23 March 2006

RATES OF DUTY *from April 2013*

	6 months	12 months
Cars registered before 1 March 2001		
Under 1,549cc	£77.00	£140.00
Over 1,549cc	£123.75	£225.00
Light goods vehicles registered on or after 1 March 2001		
	£121.00	£220.00
Euro 4 light goods vehicles registered between 1 March 2003 and 31 December 2006	£77.00	£140.00
Euro 5 light goods vehicles registered between 1 January 2009 and 31 December 2010	£77.00	£140.00
Motorcycles (with or without sidecar)		
Not over 150cc	–	£17.00
151–400cc	–	£37.00
401–600cc	£31.35	£57.00
600cc+	£42.90	£78.00
Tricycles		
Not over 150cc	–	£17.00
All others	£42.90	£78.00

MOT TESTING

Cars, motorcycles, motor caravans, light goods and dual-purpose vehicles more than three years old must be covered by a current MOT test certificate. However, some vehicles (ie minibuses, ambulances and taxis) may require a certificate at one year old. All certificates must be renewed annually. The MOT testing scheme is administered by the Vehicle and Operator Services Agency (VOSA) on behalf of the Secretary of State for Transport.

A fee is payable to MOT testing stations, which must be authorised to carry out tests. The current maximum fees are:

For cars, private hire and public service vehicles, motor caravans, dual purpose vehicles, ambulances and taxis (all up to eight passenger seats)	£54.85
For motorcycles	£29.65
For motorcycles with sidecar	£37.80
For three-wheeled vehicles (up to 450kg unladen weight)	£37.80
*Private passenger vehicles and ambulances with:	
9–12 passenger seats	£57.30 (£64.00)
13–16 passenger seats	£59.55 (£80.50)
16+ passenger seats	£80.65 (£124.50)
Goods vehicles (3,000–3,500kg)	£58.60

* Figures in parentheses include seatbelt installation check

SHIPPING AND PORTS

Sea trade has always played a central role in Britain's economy. By the 17th century Britain had built up a substantial merchant fleet and by the early 20th century it dominated the world shipping industry. Until the late 1990s the size and tonnage of the UK-registered trading fleet had been steadily declining. By the end of 2011 the number of ships in the UK-flagged merchant fleet had increased by 70 per cent while gross tonnage had more than quadrupled since 1999. The UK-flagged merchant fleet now constitutes 1.2 per cent of the world merchant fleet in terms of vessels and 1.7 per cent in terms of gross tonnage.

Freight is carried by liner and bulk services, almost all scheduled liner services being containerised. About 95 per cent by weight of Britain's overseas trade is carried by sea; this amounts to 75 per cent of its total value. Passengers and vehicles are carried by roll-on, roll-off ferries, hovercraft, hydrofoils and high-speed catamarans. There were around 42 million ferry passengers in 2012*, of whom 20 million travelled internationally.

Lloyd's of London provides the most comprehensive shipping intelligence service in the world. *Lloyd's Shipping Index*, published daily, lists some 25,000 ocean-going vessels and gives the latest known report of each.

PORTS

There are more than 650 ports in Great Britain for which statutory harbour powers have been granted. Of these about 120 are commercially significant ports. In 2012* the largest ports in terms of freight tonnage were Grimsby and Immingham (60 million tonnes), London (44 million tonnes), Milford Haven (40 million tonnes), Southampton (38 million tonnes), Tees and Hartlepool (34 million tonnes),

Liverpool (33 million tonnes), Felixstowe (26 million tonnes), Forth (25 million tonnes) and Dover (23 million tonnes). Belfast (15 million tonnes) is the principal freight port in Northern Ireland.

Broadly speaking, ports are owned and operated by private companies, local authorities or trusts. The largest operator is Associated British Ports which owns 21 ports. Provisional port traffic results show that 501 million tonnes were handled by UK ports in 2012, a decrease of 3.5 per cent on the previous year's figure of 519 million tonnes.

* Provisional figures

MARINE SAFETY

The Maritime and Coastguard Agency (MCA) is an executive agency of the Department for Transport responsible for implementing the government's maritime safety policy in the UK and works to prevent the loss of life on the coast and at sea.

HM Coastguard maintains a 24-hour search and rescue response and coordination capability for the whole of the UK coast and the internationally agreed search and rescue region. HM Coastguard is responsible for mobilising and organising resources in response to people in distress at sea, or at risk of injury or death on the UK's cliffs or shoreline.

The MCA also inspects and surveys ships to ensure that they are meeting UK and international safety rules, provides certification to seafarers, registers vessels and responds to pollution from shipping and offshore installations.

Locations hazardous to shipping in coastal waters are marked by lighthouses and other lights and buoys. The lighthouse authorities are the Corporation of Trinity House (for England, Wales and the Channel Islands), the Northern Lighthouse Board (for Scotland and the Isle of Man), and the Commissioners of Irish Lights (for Northern Ireland and the Republic of Ireland). Trinity House maintains 66 lighthouses, 10 light vessels/floats, nearly 500 buoys, 19 beacons, 48 radar beacons and seven DGPS (Differential Global Positioning System) stations*. The Northern Lighthouse Board maintains 206 lighthouses, 163 buoys, 29 beacons, 29 radar beacons, 30 AIS (automatic identification system) stations, four DGPS stations and one LORAN (long-range navigation) station; and Irish Lights looks after 74 lighthouses, 124 buoys, 33 beacons, 22 radar beacons, three DGPS stations, one LANBY (large automatic navigational buoy) with AIS in operation on ten lighthouses.

Harbour authorities are responsible for pilotage within their harbour areas; and the Ports Act 1991 provides for the transfer of lights and buoys to harbour authorities where these are used mainly for local navigation.

* DGPS is a satellite-based navigation system

UK-OWNED TRADING VESSELS

500 gross tons and over, as at end 2011

Type of vessel	*No.*	*Gross tonnage*
Tankers	139	5,536,000
Fully cellular container	114	6,125,000
Dry bulk carriers	74	3,378,000
Ro-Ro (passenger and cargo)	106	1,761,000
Passenger	34	1,586,000
Other general cargo	116	664,000
Specialised carriers	28	1,376,000
All vessels	611	20,426,000

Source: Department for Transport

UK SEA PASSENGER* MOVEMENTS 2011

Type of journey	*No. of passenger movements*
International	
Ro-Ro Passengers on short sea routes	21,149,000
Passengers on cruises beginning or ending at UK ports*	1,618,000
Passengers on long sea journeys	57,000
Total	22,824,000

* Passengers are included at both departure and arrival if their journeys begin and end at a UK seaport

Source: Department for Transport

UK SHIPPING FORECAST AREAS

Weather bulletins for shipping are broadcast daily on BBC Radio 4 at 00h 48m, 05h 20m, 12h 01m and 17h 54m. All transmissions are broadcast on long wave at 1515m (198kHz) and the 00h 48m and 05h 20m transmissions are also broadcast on FM. The bulletins consist of a gale warning summary, general synopsis, sea-area forecasts and coastal station reports. In addition, gale warnings are broadcast at the first available programme break after receipt. If this does not coincide with a news bulletin, the warning is repeated after the next news bulletin. Shipping forecasts and gale warnings are also available on the Met Office and BBC Weather websites.

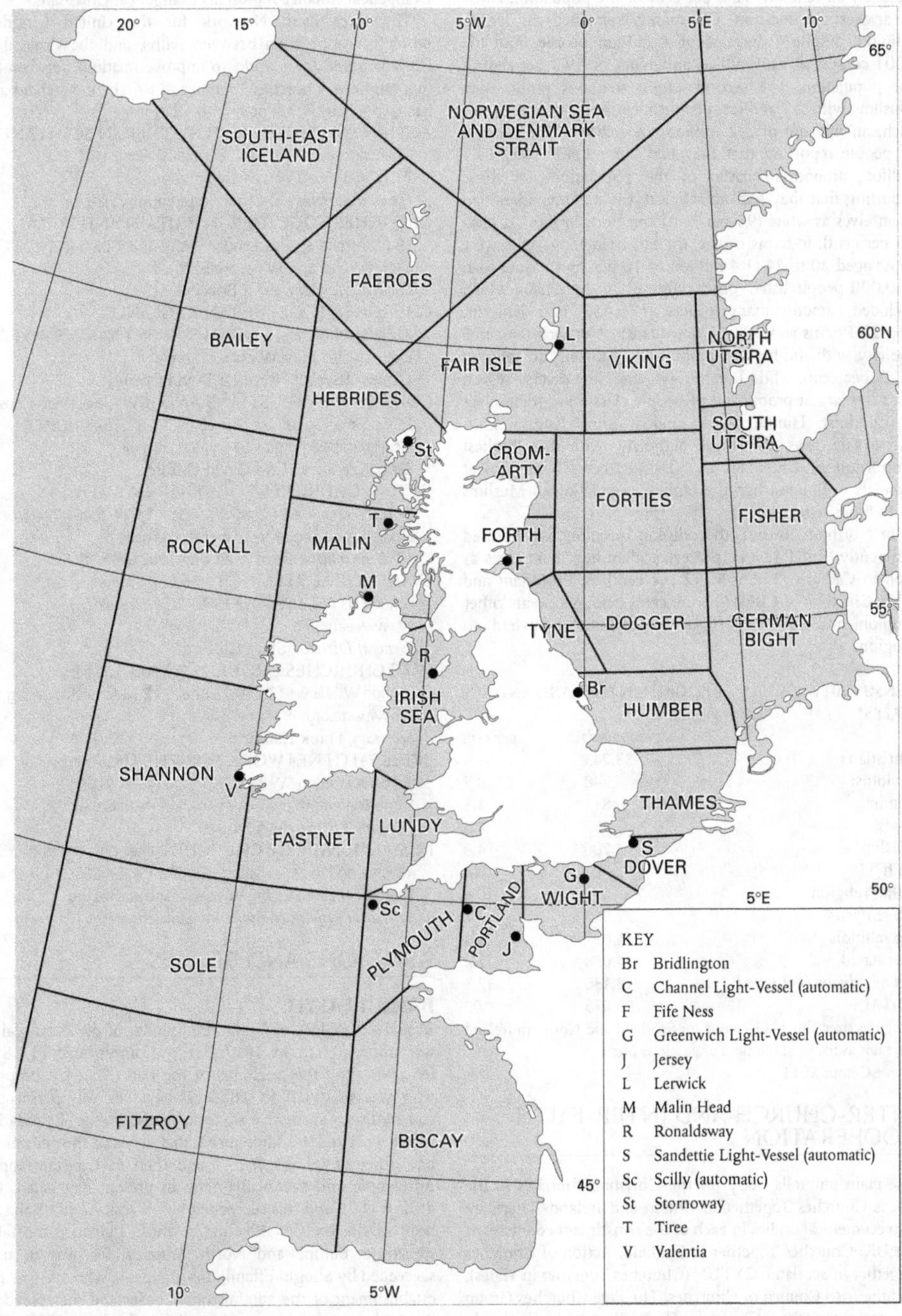

RELIGION IN THE UK

The 2011 census in England and Wales included a voluntary question on religion; 92.8 per cent of the population chose to answer the question. Christianity remained the largest religion, despite a decrease of 4 million people from the 2001 census, to 33.2 million adherents, or 59.3 per cent of the population. The second largest religious group were Muslims with 2.7 million people identifying themselves as such, an increase of 1.2 million since 2001. The number of people reporting that they had 'no religion' was 14.1 million, around a quarter of the population. Of those reporting that they had no religion, the majority identified themselves as white (93 per cent) and born in the UK (also 93 per cent); in terms of age, the largest demographic were those aged 20 to 24 (1.4 million or 10 per cent). More than 240,000 people listed 'other religion' on the census, which included, among many others, 176,632 Jedi Knights, 56,620 Pagans and 39,061 Spiritualists. Norwich remained the city with the highest proportion reporting no religion (42.5 per cent), while London was the most diverse region with the largest proportion of people classifying themselves as Buddhist, Hindu, Jewish and Muslim. Knowsley, in Merseyside, was the local authority with the highest proportion of Christians at 80.9 per cent, while Tower Hamlets in London had the highest population of Muslims at 34.5 per cent.

In Northern Ireland, the religion question was phrased differently; 738,033 (41 per cent) identified themselves as Roman Catholic, 752,555 (42 per cent) as 'Protestant and other Christian', 14,859 (0.8 per cent) belonged to an 'other religion' and 183,164 (10 per cent) stated they had no religion.

CENSUS 2011 RESULTS – RELIGION IN ENGLAND AND WALES*

	thousands	*per cent*
Christian	33,243	59.3
Buddhist	248	0.4
Hindu	817	1.5
Jewish	263	0.5
Muslim	2,706	4.8
Sikh	423	0.8
Other religion	241	0.4
All religions	37,941	67.7
No religion	14,097	25.1
Not stated	4,038	7.2
All no religion/not stated	18,135	32.3
TOTAL	56,076	100

* Figures from the 2011 census for Scotland and Northern Ireland were not available at the time of going to press

Source: Census 2011

INTER-CHURCH AND INTER-FAITH COOPERATION

The main umbrella body for the Christian churches in the UK is Churches Together in Britain and Ireland. There are also ecumenical bodies in each of the constituent countries of the UK: Churches Together in England, Action of Churches Together in Scotland, CYTUN (Churches Together in Wales), and the Irish Council of Churches. The Free Churches Group (formerly the Free Churches Council), which is closely associated with Churches Together in England, represents most of the free churches in England and Wales, and the Evangelical Alliance represents evangelical Christians.

The Inter Faith Network for the United Kingdom promotes cooperation between faiths, and the Council of Christians and Jews works to improve relations between the two religions. Churches Together in Britain and Ireland also has a commission on inter-faith relations.

ACTION OF CHURCHES TOGETHER IN SCOTLAND, Inglewood House, Alloa, Clackmannanshire FK10 2HU
T 01259-216980 W www.acts-scotland.org
General Secretary, Brother Stephen Smyth

CHURCHES TOGETHER IN BRITAIN AND IRELAND, 39 Eccleston Square, London SW1V 1BX T 0845-680 6851
E info@ctbi.org.uk W www.ctbi.org.uk
General Secretary, Revd Bob Fyffe

CHURCHES TOGETHER IN ENGLAND, 27 Tavistock Square, London WC1H 9HH T 020-7529 8131
E office@cte.org.uk W www.cte.org.uk
General Secretary, Revd Dr David Cornick

COUNCIL OF CHRISTIANS AND JEWS, Godliman House, 21 Godliman Street, London EC4V 5BD T 020-7015 5160
E cjrelations@ccj.org.uk W www.ccj.org.uk
Chief Executive, Revd David Gifford

CYTUN (CHURCHES TOGETHER IN WALES), 58 Richmond Road, Cardiff CF24 3UR T 029-2046 4204
E post@cytun.org.uk W www.cytun.org.uk
Chief Executive, Revd Aled Edwards, OBE

EVANGELICAL ALLIANCE, 176 Copenhagen Street, London N1 0ST T 020-7520 3830 E info@eauk.org
W www.eauk.org
General Director, Steve Clifford

FREE CHURCHES GROUP, 27 Tavistock Square, London WC1H 9HH T 020-7529 8131 E freechurch@cte.org.uk
W www.cte.org.uk
Secretary, Frank Kantor

INTERFAITH NETWORK FOR THE UK, 2 Grosvenor Gardens, London SW1W 0DH T 020-7730 0410
E ifnet@interfaith.org.uk W www.interfaith.org.uk
Director, Dr Harriet Crabtree

IRISH COUNCIL OF CHURCHES, Inter-Church Centre, 48 Elmwood Avenue, Belfast BT9 6AZ T 028-9066 3145
E info@irishchurches.org W www.irishchurches.org
Executive Officer, Mervyn McCullagh

RELIGIONS AND BELIEFS

BAHA'I FAITH

Baha'u'llah ('Glory of God'), the founder of the Baha'i faith, was born in Iran in 1817. He was imprisoned in 1852 for advocating the teachings of the Bab ('Gate'), a prophet who was martyred in 1850. Baha'u'llah was persecuted and sent into successive stages of exile, first to Baghdad – where in 1863 he announced that he was the 'promised one' foretold by the Bab – and then to Constantinople, Adrianople and eventually Acre, in present day Israel. He died in 1892 and was succeeded by his son, Abdu'l-Baha, as head of the Baha'i faith, under whose guidance the faith spread to Europe and North America. He was in turn succeeded by Shoghi Effendi, his grandson, who oversaw the establishment of the administrative order and the spread of the faith around the world until his death in 1957. The Universal House of Justice, an elected international governing council, was formed in 1963 in accordance with Baha'u'llah's teachings.

The Baha'i faith espouses the oneness of humanity and of religion and teaches that there is only one God, whose will has been revealed to mankind by a series of messengers, such as Zoroaster, Abraham, Moses, Buddha, Krishna, Christ, Muhammad, the Bab and Baha'u'llah, who were seen as the founders of separate religions, but whose common purpose was to bring God's message to mankind. The Baha'i faith attributes the differences in teachings between religions to humanity's changing needs. Baha'i teachings include that all races and both sexes are equal and deserving of equal opportunities and treatment, that education is a fundamental right and that extremes of wealth and poverty should be eliminated. In addition, the faith exhorts mankind to establish a world federal system to promote peace and unity.

In an effort to translate these principles into action, Baha'is have initiated an educational process across the world that seeks to raise the capacity of people of all ages and from all backgrounds to contribute towards the betterment of society. There is no clergy; each local community elects a local spiritual assembly to tend to its administrative needs. A national spiritual assembly is elected annually by locally elected delegates, and every five years the national spiritual assemblies meet together to elect the Universal House of Justice, the supreme international governing body of the Baha'i Faith. Worldwide there are over 13,000 local spiritual assemblies and around 6 million members.

BAHA'I COMMUNITY OF THE UK, 27 Rutland Gate, London SW7 1PD T 020-7584 2566 E nsa@bahai.org.uk W www.bahai.org.uk

Director, Office of Public Affairs, Dr Kishan Manocha

BUDDHISM

Buddhism originated in what is now the Bihar area of northern India in the teachings of Siddhartha Gautama, who became the *Buddha* ('Enlightened One'). In the Thai or Suriyakati calendar the beginning of the Buddhist era is dated from the death of Buddha; the year 2014 is therefore 2557 by the Thai Buddhist reckoning.

Fundamental to Buddhism is the concept of rebirth, whereby each life carries with it the consequences of the conduct of earlier lives (known as the law of *karma)* and this cycle of death and rebirth is broken only when the state of *nirvana* has been reached. Buddhism steers a middle path between belief in personal continuity and the belief that death results in total extinction.

While doctrine does not have a pivotal position in Buddhism, a statement of four 'Noble Truths' is common to all its schools and varieties. These are: suffering is inescapable in even the most fortunate of existences; craving is the root cause of suffering; abandonment of the selfish mindset is the way to end suffering; and bodily and mental discipline, accompanied by the cultivation of wisdom and compassion, provides the spiritual path ('Noble Eightfold Path') to accomplish this. Buddhists deny the idea of a creator and prefer to emphasise the practical aspects of moral and spiritual development.

The schools of Buddhism can be broadly divided into three: *Theravada,* the generally monastic-led tradition practised in Sri Lanka and South-East Asia; *Mahayana,* the philosophical and popular traditions of the Far East; and *Esoteric,* the Tantric-derived traditions found in Tibet and Mongolia and, to a lesser extent, China and Japan. The extensive Theravada scriptures are contained in the *Pali Canon,* which dates in its written form from the first century BC. Mahayana and Esoteric schools have Sanskrit-derived translations of these plus many more additional scriptures as well as exegetical material.

In the East the new and full moons and the lunar quarter days were (and to a certain extent, still are) significant in determining the religious calendar. Most private homes contain a shrine where offerings, worship and other spiritual practices (such as meditation, chanting or mantra recitation) take place on a daily basis. Buddhist festivals vary according to local traditions within the different schools and there is little uniformity – even in commemorating the birth, enlightenment and death of the Buddha.

There is no governing authority for Buddhism in the UK. Communities representing all schools of Buddhism operate independently. The Buddhist Society was established in 1924; it runs courses, lectures and meditation groups, and publishes books about Buddhism. The Network of Buddhist Organisations was founded in 1993 to promote fellowship and dialogue between Buddhist organisations and to facilitate cooperation in matters of common interest.

There are estimated to be at least 375 million Buddhists worldwide. Of the 248,000 Buddhists in England and Wales (according to the 2011 census), 72,000 are white British (the majority are converts), 49,000 Chinese, 93,000 'other Asian' and 36,000 are 'other ethnic'.

THE BUDDHIST SOCIETY, 58 Eccleston Square, London SW1V 1PH T 020-7834 5858 E info@thebuddhistsociety.org W www.thebuddhistsociety.org

LONDON BUDDHIST CENTRE, 51 Roman Road, London E2 0HU T 0845-458 4716 E info@lbc.org.uk W www.lbc.org.uk

THE NETWORK OF BUDDHIST ORGANISATIONS, PO Box 4147, Maidenhead SL60 1DN T 0845-345 8978 E secretary@nbo.org.uk W www.nbo.org.uk

THE OFFICE OF TIBET, Tibet House, 1 Culworth Street, London NW8 7AF T 020-7722 5378 E samdup@tibet.com W www.tibet.com

Representative of HH the Dalai Lama, Thubten Samdup

SOKA GAKKAI INTERNATIONAL (UK), Taplow Court Grand Cultural Centre, Cliveden Road, Taplow, Berkshire SL6 0ER T 01628-773163 W www.sgi-uk.org

CHRISTIANITY

Christianity is a monotheistic faith based on the person and teachings of Jesus Christ, and all Christian denominations claim his authority. Central to its teaching is the concept of God and his son Jesus Christ, who was crucified and resurrected in order to enable mankind to attain salvation.

The Jewish scriptures predicted the coming of a *Messiah,* an 'anointed one', who would bring salvation. To Christians, Jesus of Nazareth, a Jewish rabbi (teacher) who was born in Palestine, was the promised Messiah. Jesus' birth, teachings, crucifixion and subsequent resurrection are recorded in the *Gospels,* which, together with other scriptures that summarise Christian belief, form the *New Testament.* This, together with the Hebrew scriptures – entitled the *Old Testament* by Christians – makes up the Bible, the sacred texts of Christianity.

Christians believe that sin distanced mankind from God, and that Jesus was the son of God, sent to redeem mankind from sin by his death. In addition, many believe that Jesus will return again at some future date, triumph over evil and establish a kingdom on earth, thus inaugurating a new age. The Gospel assures Christians that those who believe in Jesus and obey his teachings will be forgiven their sins and will be resurrected from the dead.

The Apostles were Jesus' first converts and are recognised by Christians as the founders of the Christian community. Early Christianity spread rapidly throughout the eastern provinces of the Roman Empire but was subjected to great persecution until AD 313, when Emperor Constantine's Edict of Toleration confirmed its right to exist.

Christianity was established as the religion of the Roman Empire in AD 381.

Between AD 325 and 787 there were seven Oecumenical Councils at which bishops from the entire Christian world assembled to resolve various doctrinal disputes. The estrangement between East and West began after Constantine moved the centre of the Roman Empire from Rome to Constantinople, and it grew after the division of the Roman Empire into eastern and western halves. Linguistic and cultural differences between Greek East and Latin West served to encourage separate ecclesiastical developments which became pronounced in the tenth and early 11th centuries. Administration of the church was divided between five ancient patriarchates: Rome and all the West, Constantinople (the imperial city – the 'New Rome'), Jerusalem and all of Palestine, Antioch and all the East, and Alexandria and all of Africa. Of these, only Rome was in the Latin West and after the schism in 1054, Rome developed a structure of authority centralised on the Papacy, while the Orthodox East maintained the style of localised administration. Papal authority over the doctrine and jurisdiction of the church in Western Europe was unrivalled after the split with the Eastern Orthodox Church until the Protestant Reformation in the 16th century.

Christian practices vary widely between different Christian churches, but prayer, charity and giving (for the maintenance of the church buildings, for the work of the church, and to those in need) are common to all. In addition, certain days of observance, ie the *Sabbath, Easter* and *Christmas,* are celebrated by most Christians. The Orthodox, Roman Catholic and Anglican churches celebrate many more days of observance, based on saints and significant events in the life of Jesus. The belief in sacraments, physical signs believed to have been ordained by Jesus Christ to symbolise and convey spiritual gifts, varies greatly between Christian denominations; *baptism* and the *Eucharist* are practised by most Christians. Baptism, symbolising repentance and faith in Jesus, is an act marking entry into the Christian community; the Eucharist, the ritual re-enactment of the Last Supper, Jesus' final meal with his disciples, is also practised by most denominations. Other sacraments, such as anointing the sick, the laying on of hands to symbolise the passing on of the office of priesthood or to heal the sick, and speaking in tongues, where it is believed that the person is possessed by the Holy Spirit, are less common. In denominations where infant baptism is practised, confirmation (where the person confirms the commitments made on their behalf in infancy) is common. Matrimony and the ordination of priests are also widely believed to be sacraments. Many Protestants regard only baptism and the Eucharist to be sacraments; the Quakers and the Salvation Army reject the use of sacraments.

See Churches for contact details of the Church of England, the Roman Catholic Church and other Christian churches in the UK.

HINDUISM

Hinduism has no historical founder but had become highly developed in India by *c.*2500 BC. Its adherents originally called themselves Aryans; Muslim invaders first called the Aryans 'Hindus' (derived from 'Sindhu', the name of the river Indus) in the eighth century.

Most Hindus hold that *satya* (truthfulness), honesty, sincerity and devotion to God are essential for good living. They believe in one supreme spirit *(Brahman),* and in the transmigration of *atman* (the soul). Most Hindus accept the doctrine of *karma* (consequences of actions), the concept of *samsara* (successive lives) and the possibility of all atmans achieving *moksha* (liberation from samsara) through *jnana* (knowledge), *yoga* (meditation), *karma* (work or action) and *bhakti* (devotion).

Most Hindus offer worship to *murtis* (images of deities) representing different incarnations or aspects of Brahman, and follow their *dharma* (religious and social duty) according to the traditions of their *varna* (social class), *ashrama* (stage in life), *jaiti* (caste) and *kula* (family).

Hinduism's sacred texts are divided into *shruti* ('that which is heard'), including the *Vedas,* and *smriti* ('that which is remembered'), including the *Ramayana,* the *Mahabharata,* the *Puranas* (ancient myths), and the sacred law books. Most Hindus recognise the authority of the *Vedas,* the oldest holy books, and accept the philosophical teachings of the *Upanishads,* the *Vedanta Sutras* and the *Bhagavad-Gita.*

Hindus believe Brahman to be omniscient, omnipotent, limitless and all-pervading. Brahman is usually worshipped in its deity form. Brahma, Vishnu and Shiva are the most important deities or aspects of Brahman worshipped by Hindus; their respective consorts are Saraswati, Lakshmi and Durga or Parvati, also known as Shakti. There are believed to have been ten *avatars* (incarnations) of Vishnu, of whom the most important are Rama and Krishna. Other popular gods are Ganesha, Hanuman and Subrahmanyam. All Hindu gods are seen as aspects of the supreme spirit (Brahman), not as competing deities.

Orthodox Hindus revere all gods and goddesses equally, but there are many denominations, including the Hare-Krishna movement (ISKCon), the Arya Samaj and the Swaminarayan Hindu mission, in which worship is concentrated on one deity. The *guru* (spiritual teacher) is seen as the source of spiritual guidance.

Hinduism does not have a centrally trained and ordained priesthood. The pronouncements of the *shankaracharyas* (heads of monasteries) of Shringeri, Puri, Dwarka and Badrinath are heeded by the orthodox but may be ignored by the various sects.

The commonest form of worship is *puja,* in which water, flowers, food, fruit, incense and light are offered to the deity. Puja may be done either in a home shrine or a *mandir* (temple). Many British Hindus celebrate *samskars* (purification rites), to name a baby, for the sacred thread (an initiation ceremony), marriage and cremation.

The largest communities of Hindus in Britain are in Leicester, London, Birmingham and Bradford, and developed as a result of immigration from India, eastern Africa and Sri Lanka.

There are an estimated 800 million Hindus worldwide; there are around 817,000 adherents, according to the 2011 census in England and Wales, and around 135 temples in the UK.

ARYA SAMAJ LONDON, 69 Argyle Road, London W13 0LY
T 020-8991 1732 E aryasamajlondon@yahoo.co.uk
Vice-President, Amrit Lal Bhardwaj

BHARATIYA VIDYA BHAVAN, Institute of Indian Art and Culture, 4A Castletown Road, London W14 9HE
T 020-7381 3086/4608 E info@bhavan.net W www.bhavan.net
Executive Director, Dr M. N. Nandakumara

INTERNATIONAL SOCIETY FOR KRISHNA CONSCIOUSNESS (ISKCON), Bhaktivedanta Manor, Dharam Marg, Hilfield Lane, Aldenham, Watford, Herts WD25 8EZ T 01923-851000 E info@krishnatemple.com
W www.krishnatemple.com
Temple President, Sruti Dharma Das

NATIONAL COUNCIL OF HINDU TEMPLES (UK), 1 Hans Close, Stoke, Coventry CV2 4WA T 0780-505 4776
E info@nchtuk.org W www.nchtuk.org
General Secretary, Dr Raj Pandit Sharma

SWAMINARAYAN HINDU MISSION (SHRI SWAMINARAYAN MANDIR), 105–119 Brentfield Road, London NW10 8LD T 020-8965 2651 E info@mandir.org W www.mandir.org

HUMANISM

Humanism traces its roots back to ancient times, with Chinese, Greek, Indian and Roman philosophers expressing Humanist ideas some 2,500 years ago. Confucius, the Chinese philosopher who lived *c.*500 BC, believed that religious observances should be replaced with moral values as the basis of social and political order and that 'the true way' is based on reason and humanity. He also stressed the importance of benevolence and respect for others, and believed that the individual situation should be considered rather than the global application of traditional rules.

Humanists believe that there is no God or other supernatural being, that humans have only one life (Humanists do not believe in an afterlife or reincarnation) and that humans can live ethical and fulfilling lives without religious beliefs through a moral code derived from a shared history, personal experience and thought. There are no sacred Humanist texts. Particular emphasis is placed on science as the only reliable source of knowledge of the universe. Many Humanists recognise a need for ceremonies to mark important occasions in life and the British Humanist Association has a network of celebrants who are trained and accredited to conduct baby namings, weddings and funerals. The British Humanist Association's campaigns for a secular society (a society based on freedom of religious or non-religious belief with no privileges for any particular set of beliefs) are based on equality and human rights. The association also campaigns for inclusive schools that meet the needs of all parents and pupils, regardless of their religious or non-religious beliefs. According to figures from the 2011 census, there are just over 15,000 Humanists in England and Wales.

BRITISH HUMANIST ASSOCIATION, 39 Moreland Street, London EC1V 8BB T 020-7324 3060 E info@humanism.org.uk W www.humanism.org.uk
Chief Executive, Andrew Copson

ISLAM

Islam (which means 'peace arising from submission to the will of Allah' in Arabic) is a monotheistic religion which was taught in Arabia by the Prophet Muhammad, who was born in Mecca (Al-Makkah) in 570 AD. Islam spread to Egypt, north Africa, Spain and the borders of China in the century following the Prophet's death, and is now the predominant religion in Indonesia, the near and Middle East, northern and parts of western Africa, Pakistan, Bangladesh, Malaysia and some of the former Soviet republics. There are also large Muslim communities in other countries.

For Muslims (adherents of Islam), there is one God *(Allah)*, who holds absolute power. Muslims believe that Allah's commands were revealed to mankind through the prophets, who include Abraham, Moses and Jesus, but that Allah's message was gradually corrupted until revealed finally and in perfect form to Muhammad through the angel *Jibril* (Gabriel) over a period of 23 years. This last, incorruptible message is said to have been recorded in the *Qur'an* (Koran), which contains 114 divisions called *surahs,* each made up of *ayahs* of various lengths, and is held to be the essence of all previous scriptures. The *Ahadith* are the records of the Prophet Muhammad's deeds and sayings (the *Sunnah*) as practised and recounted by his immediate followers. A culture and a system of law and theology gradually developed to form a distinctive Islamic civilisation. Islam makes no distinction between sacred and worldly affairs and provides rules for every aspect of human life. The *Shariah* is the sacred law of Islam based primarily upon prescriptions derived from the *Qur'an* and the *Sunnah* of the Prophet.

The 'five pillars of Islam' are *shahadah* (a declaration of faith in the oneness and supremacy of Allah and the messengership of Muhammad); *salat* (formal prayer, to be performed five times a day facing the *Ka'bah* (the most sacred shrine in the holy city of Mecca)); *zakat* (welfare due, paid annually on all savings at the rate of 2.5 per cent); *sawm* (fasting during the month of Ramadan from dawn until sunset); and *hajj* (pilgrimage to Mecca made once in a lifetime if the believer is financially and physically able). Some Muslims would add *jihad* as the sixth pillar (striving for the cause of good and resistance to evil).

Two main groups developed among Muslims. *Sunni* Muslims accept the legitimacy of Muhammad's first four *caliphs* (successors as head of the Muslim community) and of the authority of the Muslim community as a whole. About 90 per cent of Muslims are Sunni Muslims.

Shi'ites recognise only Muhammad's son-in-law Ali as his rightful successor and the *Imams* (descendants of Ali, not to be confused with *imams,* who are prayer leaders or religious teachers) as the principal legitimate religious authority. The largest group within Shi'ism is *Twelver Shi'ism,* which has been the official school of law and theology in Iran since the 16th century; other subsects include the *Ismailis,* the *Druze* and the *Alawis,* the latter two differing considerably from the main body of Muslims. The *Ibadis* of Oman are neither Sunni nor Shia, deriving from the strictly observant *Khariji* (Seceders). There is no organised priesthood, but learned men such as imams, *ulama,* and *ayatollahs* are accorded great respect. The *Sufis* are the mystics of Islam. Mosques are centres for worship and teaching and also for social and welfare activities.

Islam was first recorded in western Europe in the eighth century AD when 800 years of Muslim rule began in Spain. Later, Islam spread to eastern Europe. More recently, Muslims came to Europe from Africa, the Middle East and Asia in the late 19th century. Both the Sunni and Shia traditions are represented in Britain, but the majority of Muslims in Britain adhere to Sunni Islam. Efforts to establish a representative national body for Muslims in Britain resulted in the founding, in 1997, of the Muslim Council of Britain. In addition, there are many other Muslim organisations in the UK. There are around 1.6 billion Muslims worldwide, with around 2.7 million adherents in England and Wales and about 1,500 mosques in the UK.

IMAMS AND MOSQUES COUNCIL, 20–22 Creffield Road, London W5 3RP T 020-8992 6636 E msraza@muslimcollege.ac.uk
Director, Moulana M. S. Raza

ISLAMIC CULTURAL CENTRE – THE LONDON CENTRAL MOSQUE, 146 Park Road, London NW8 7RG T 020-7725 2213 E info@iccuk.org W www.iccuk.org
Director, Dr Ahmad Al-Dubayan

MUSLIM WORLD LEAGUE LONDON, 46 Goodge Street, London W1T 4LU T 020-7636 7568
Director, Dr Ahmad Makhoodom

JAINISM

Jainism traces its history to Vardhamana Jnatriputra, known as *Tirthankara Mahavira* ('the Great Hero') whose traditional dates were 599–527 BC. Jains believe he was the last of the current era in a series of 24 *Jinas* (those who overcome all passions and desires) or *Tirthankaras* (those who show a way across the ocean of life) stretching back to remote antiquity. Born to a noble family in north-eastern India (presently the state of Bihar), he renounced the world for the life of a wandering ascetic and after 12 years of austerity and meditation he attained enlightenment. He then preached his message until, at the age of 72, he left the mortal world and achieved total liberation *(moksha)* from the cycle of death and rebirth.

Jains declare that the Hindu rituals of transferring merit are not acceptable as each living being is responsible for its own actions. They recognise some of the minor deities of the Hindu pantheon, but the supreme objects of worship are the Tirthankaras. The pious Jain does not ask favours from the Tirthankaras, but seeks to emulate their example in his or her own life.

Jains believe that the universe is eternal and self-subsisting, that there is no omnipotent creator God ruling it and the destiny of the individual is in his or her own hands. *Karma,* the fruit of past actions, is believed to determine the place of every living being and rebirth may be in the heavens, on earth as a human, an animal or other lower being, or in the hells. The ultimate goal of existence for Jains is *moksha,* a state of perfect knowledge and tranquillity for each individual soul, which can be achieved only by gaining enlightenment.

The Jainist path to liberation is defined by the three jewels: *Samyak Darshan* (right perception), *Samyak Jnana* (right knowledge) and *Samyak Charitra* (right conduct). Of the five fundamental precepts of the Jains, *Ahimsa* (non-injury to any form of being, in any mode: thought, speech or action) is the first and foremost, and was popularised by Gandhi as *Ahimsa paramo dharma* (non-violence is the supreme religion).

The largest population of Jains can be found in India but there are approximately 30,000 Jains in Britain, with sizeable communities in North America, East Africa, Australia and smaller groups in many other countries.

INSTITUTE OF JAINOLOGY, Unit 18, Silicon Business Centre, 28 Wadsworth Road, Perivale, Greenford, Middx UB6 7JZ T 020-8997 2300 E secretary@jainology.org W www.jainology.org
Deputy Chair, Dr Harshad Sanghrajka

JUDAISM

Judaism is the oldest monotheistic faith. The primary text of Judaism is the Hebrew bible or *Tanakh,* which records how the descendants of Abraham were led by Moses out of their slavery in Egypt to Mount Sinai where God's law *(Torah)* was revealed to them as the chosen people. The *Talmud,* which consists of commentaries on the *Mishnah* (the first text of rabbinical Judaism), is also held to be authoritative, and may be divided into two main categories: the *halakah* (dealing with legal and ritual matters) and the *aggadah* (dealing with theological and ethical matters not directly concerned with the regulation of conduct). The *midrash* comprises rabbinic writings containing biblical interpretations in the spirit of the aggadah. The halakah has become a source of division: orthodox Jews regard Jewish law as derived from God and therefore unalterable; progressive Jews seek to interpret it in the light of contemporary considerations; and conservative Jews aim to maintain most of the traditional rituals but to allow changes in accordance with tradition. Reconstructionist Judaism, a 20th-century movement, regards Judaism as a culture rather than a theological system and accepts all forms of Jewish practice.

The family is the basic unit of Jewish ritual, with the synagogue playing an important role as the centre for public worship and religious study. A synagogue is led by a group of laymen who are elected to office. The Rabbi is primarily a teacher and spiritual guide. The *Sabbath* is the central religious observance. Most British Jews are descendants of either the *Ashkenazim* of central and eastern Europe or the *Sephardim* of Spain, Portugal and the Middle East.

The Chief Rabbi of the United Hebrew Congregations of the Commonwealth is appointed by a Chief Rabbinate Conference, and is the rabbinical authority of the mainstream Orthodox sector of the Ashkenazi Jewish community, the largest body of which is the United Synagogue. His formal ecclesiastical authority is not recognised by the Reform Synagogues of Great Britain (the largest progressive group), the Union of Liberal and Progressive Synagogues, the Spanish and Portuguese Jews' Congregation or the Assembly of Masorti Synagogues. He is, however, generally recognised both outside the Jewish community and within it as the public religious representative of the totality of British Jewry. The Chief Rabbi is President of the London *Beth Din* (Court of Judgment), a rabbinic court. The *Dayanim* (Judges) adjudicate in disputes or on matters of Jewish law and tradition; they also oversee dietary law administration, marriage, divorce and issues of personal status.

The Board of Deputies of British Jews, established in 1760, is the representative body of British Jewry. The basis of representation is through the election of deputies by synagogues and communal organisations. It protects and promotes the interests of British Jewry, acts as the central voice of the community and seeks to counter anti-Jewish discrimination and anti-Semitic activities.

There are approximately 13.5 million Jews worldwide; in the UK there are an estimated 263,000 adherents and over 400 synagogues.

OFFICE OF THE CHIEF RABBI, 305 Ballards Lane, London N12 8GB T 020-8343 6301 E info@chiefrabbi.org W www.chiefrabbi.org
Chief Rabbi, Ephraim Mirvis

BETH DIN (COURT OF THE CHIEF RABBI), 305 Ballards Lane, London N12 8GB T 020-8343 6270 E info@bethdin.org.uk W www.theus.org.uk
Registrar, David Frei
Dayanim, Yonason Abraham; Menachem Gelley *(Senior Dayan);* Ivan Binstock; Shmuel Simons

ASSEMBLY OF MASORTI SYNAGOGUES, Alexander House, 3 Shakespeare Road, London N3 1XE T 020-8349 6650 E enquiries@masorti.org.uk W www.masorti.org.uk
Executive Director, Michael Gluckman

BOARD OF DEPUTIES OF BRITISH JEWS, 6 Bloomsbury Square, London WC1A 2LP T 020-7543 5400 E info@bod.org.uk W www.bod.org.uk
Chief Executive, vacant

FEDERATION OF SYNAGOGUES, 65 Watford Way, London NW4 3AQ T 020-8202 2263 E info@federationofsynagogues.com W www.federationofsynagogues.com
President, Alan Finlay
Chief Executive, Dr Eli Kienwald

LIBERAL JUDAISM, The Montagu Centre, 21 Maple Street, London W1T 4BE T 020-7580 1663 W www.liberaljudaism.org
Chief Executive, Rabbi Danny Rich

THE MOVEMENT FOR REFORM JUDAISM, The Sternberg Centre for Judaism, 80 East End Road, London N3 2SY T 020-8349 5640 E admin@reformjudaism.org.uk W www.reformjudaism.org.uk
Chief Executive, Ben Rich

SPANISH AND PORTUGUESE JEWS' CONGREGATION, 2 Ashworth Road, London W9 1JY T 020-7289 2573 E howardmiller@spsyn.org.uk W www.sandp.org.uk
Chief Executive, Howard Miller

UNION OF ORTHODOX HEBREW CONGREGATIONS, 140 Stamford Hill, London N16 6QT T 020-8802 6226
Executive Coordinator, Chanoch Kesselman
Secretary, Chayim Schneck

UNITED SYNAGOGUE HEAD OFFICE, Adler House, 735 High Road, London N12 0US T 020-8343 8989 E info@theus.org.uk W www.theus.org.uk
Chief Executive, Jeremy Jacobs

PAGANISM

Paganism draws on the ideas of the Celtic people of pre-Roman Europe and is closely linked to Druidism. The first historical record of Druidry comes from classical Greek and Roman writers of the third century BC, who noted the existence of Druids among a people called the Keltoi who inhabited central and southern Europe. The word druid may derive from the Indo-European 'dreo-vid', meaning 'one who knows the truth'. In practice it was probably understood to mean something like 'wise-one' or 'philosopher-priest'.

Paganism is a pantheistic nature-worshipping religion which incorporates beliefs and ritual practices from ancient times. Pagans place much emphasis on the natural world and the ongoing cycle of life and death is central to their beliefs. Most Pagans believe that they are part of nature and not separate from, or superior to it, and seek to live in a way that minimises harm to the natural environment (the word Pagan derives from the Latin *Paganus,* meaning 'rural'). Paganism strongly emphasises the equality of the sexes, with women playing a prominent role in the modern Pagan movement and goddess worship featuring in most ceremonies. Paganism cannot be defined by any principal beliefs because it is shaped by each individual's experiences.

The Pagan Federation was founded in 1971 to provide information on Paganism, campaigns on issues which affect Paganism and provides support to members of the Pagan community. Within the UK the Pagan Federation is divided into 13 districts each with a district manager, regional and local coordinators. Local meetings are called 'moots' and take place in private homes, pubs or coffee bars. The Pagan Federation publishes a quarterly journal, *Pagan Dawn,* formerly *The Wiccan* (founded in 1968). The federation also publishes other material, arranges members-only and public events and maintains personal contact by letter with individual members and the wider Pagan community. Regional gatherings and conferences are held throughout the year.

THE PAGAN FEDERATION, BM Box 7097, London WC1N 3XX **E** secretary@paganfed.org
W www.paganfed.org
President, Mike Stygal

SIKHISM

The Sikh religion dates from the birth of Guru Nanak in the Punjab in 1469. 'Guru' means teacher but in Sikh tradition has come to represent the divine presence of God giving inner spiritual guidance. Nanak's role as the human vessel of the divine guru was passed on to nine successors, the last of whom (Guru Gobind Singh) died in 1708. The immortal guru is now held to reside in the sacred scripture, *Guru Granth Sahib,* and so to be present in all Sikh gatherings.

Guru Nanak taught that there is one God and that different religions are like different roads leading to the same destination. He condemned religious conflict, ritualism and caste prejudices. The fifth Guru, Guru Arjan Dev, largely compiled the Sikh Holy scripture, a collection of hymns *(gurbani)* known as the *Adi Granth.* It includes the writings of the first five gurus and the ninth guru, and selected writings of Hindu and Muslim saints whose views are in accord with the gurus' teachings. Guru Arjan Dev also built the Golden Temple at Amritsar, the centre of Sikhism. The tenth guru, Guru Gobind Singh, passed on the guruship to the sacred scripture, Guru Granth Sahib, and founded the *Khalsa,* an order intended to fight against tyranny and injustice. Male initiates to the order added 'Singh' to their given names and women added 'Kaur'. Guru Gobind Singh also made the wearing of five symbols obligatory: *kaccha* (a special undergarment), *kara* (a steel bangle), *kirpan* (a small sword), *kesh* (long unshorn hair, and consequently the wearing of a turban) and *kangha* (a comb). These practices are still compulsory for those Sikhs who are initiated into the Khalsa (the *Amritdharis*). Those who do not seek initiation are known as *Sehajdharis.*

There are no professional priests in Sikhism; anyone with a reasonable proficiency in the Punjabi language can conduct a service. Worship can be offered individually or communally, and in a private house or a *gurdwara* (temple). Sikhs are forbidden to eat meat prepared by ritual slaughter; they are also asked to abstain from smoking, alcohol and other intoxicants. Such abstention is compulsory for the Amritdharis.

There are about 24 million Sikhs worldwide and, according to the 2011 census, there are 423,000 adherents in England and Wales. Every gurdwara manages its own affairs; there is no central body in the UK. The Sikh Missionary Society provides an information service.

SIKH MISSIONARY SOCIETY UK, 10 Featherstone Road, Southall, Middx UB2 5AA **T** 020-8574 1902
E info@sikhmissionarysociety.org
W www.sikhmissionarysociety.org
Hon. General Secretary, Teja Singh Mangat

ZOROASTRIANISM

Zoroastrians are followers of the Iranian prophet Spitaman Zarathushtra (or Zoroaster in its hellenised form) who lived *c.*1200–1500 BC. Zoroastrians were persecuted in Iran following the Arab invasion of Persia in the seventh century AD and a group (who are known as Parsis) migrated to India in the ninth century AD to avoid harassment and persecution. Zarathushtra's words are recorded in 17 hymns called the *Gathas,* which, together with other scriptures, form the *Avesta.*

Zoroastrianism teaches that there is one God, *Ahura Mazda* ('Wise Lord'), and that all creation stems ultimately from God; the Gathas teach that human beings have free will, are responsible for their own actions and can choose between good and evil. It is believed that choosing *Asha* (truth or righteousness), with the aid of *Vohu Manah* (good mind), leads to happiness for the individual and society, whereas choosing evil leads to unhappiness and conflict. The *Gathas* also encourage hard work, good deeds and charitable acts. Zoroastrians believe that after death the immortal soul is judged by God, and is then sent to paradise or hell, where it will stay until the end of time to be resurrected for the final judgment.

In Zoroastrian places of worship, an urn containing fire is the central feature; the fire symbolises purity, light and truth and is a visible symbol of the *Fravashi* or *Farohar* (spirit), the presence of Ahura Mazda in every human being. Zoroastrians respect nature and much importance is attached to cultivating land and protecting air, earth and water.

The Zoroastrian Trust Funds of Europe is the main body for Zoroastrians in the UK. Founded in 1861 as the Religious Funds of the Zoroastrians of Europe, it disseminates information on the Zoroastrian faith, provides a place of worship and maintains separate burial grounds for Zoroastrians. It also holds religious and social functions and provides assistance to Zoroastrians as considered necessary, including the provision of loans and grants to students of Zoroastrianism, and participates in inter-faith educational activities.

There are approximately 145,000 Zoroastrians worldwide, of which around 4,000 reside in England and Wales, mainly in London and the South East.

ZOROASTRIAN TRUST FUNDS OF EUROPE, Zoroastrian Centre, 440 Alexandra Avenue, Harrow, Middx HA2 9TL
T 020-8866 0765 **E** secretary@ztfe.com **W** www.ztfe.com
President, Malcolm Deboo

CHURCHES

There are two established (ie state) churches in the UK: the Church of England and the Church of Scotland. There are no established churches in Wales or Northern Ireland, though the Church in Wales, the Scottish Episcopal Church and the Church of Ireland are members of the Anglican Communion.

CHURCH OF ENGLAND

The Church of England is divided into the two provinces of Canterbury and York, each under an archbishop. The two provinces are subdivided into 44 dioceses.

Legislative provision for the Church of England is made by the General Synod, established in 1970. It also discusses and expresses opinion on any other matter of religious or public interest. The General Synod has 467 members in total, divided between three houses: the House of Bishops, the House of Clergy and the House of Laity. It is presided over jointly by the Archbishops of Canterbury and York and normally meets twice a year. The synod has the power, delegated by parliament, to frame statute law (known as a 'measure') on any matter concerning the Church of England. A measure must be laid before both houses of parliament, who may accept or reject it but cannot amend it. Once accepted the measure is submitted for royal assent and then has the full force of law. In addition to the General Synod, there are synods at diocesan level. The entire General Synod is re-elected once every five years. The ninth General Synod was inaugurated by the Queen on 23 November 2010.

The Archbishops' Council was established in January 1999. Its creation was the result of changes to the Church of England's national structure proposed in 1995 and subsequently approved by the synod and parliament. The council's purpose, set out in the National Institutions Measure 1998, is 'to coordinate, promote and further the work and mission of the Church of England'. It reports to the General Synod. The Archbishops' Council comprises the Archbishops of Canterbury and York, *ex officio,* the prolocutors elected by the convocations of Canterbury and York, the chair and vice-chair of the House of Laity, two bishops, two clergy and two lay persons elected by their respective houses of the General Synod, the Church Estates Commissioner, and up to six persons appointed jointly by the two archbishops.

There are also a number of national boards, councils and other bodies working on matters such as social responsibility, mission, Christian unity and education, which report to the General Synod through the Archbishops' Council.

GENERAL SYNOD OF THE CHURCH OF ENGLAND/ ARCHBISHOPS' COUNCIL, Church House, Great Smith Street, London SW1P 3NZ T 020-7898 1000
Secretary-General, William Fittall

THE ORDINATION OF WOMEN

The canon making it possible for women to be ordained to the priesthood was promulgated in the General Synod in February 1994 and the first 32 women priests were ordained on 12 March 1994.

PORVOO DECLARATION

The Porvoo Declaration was approved by the General Synod of the Church of England in July 1995. Churches that approve the declaration regard baptised members of each other's churches as members of their own, and allow free interchange of episcopally ordained ministers within the rules of each church.

MEMBERSHIP AND MINISTRY

In 2011, 139,700 people were baptised, 51,880 people were married in parish churches, the Church of England had an electoral roll membership of 1.2 million, and each week over 1.1 million people attended services. As at December 2012 there were over 15,900 churches and places of worship; 350 dignitaries (including bishops, archdeacons and cathedral clergy); 7,080 full-time parochial stipendiary clergy; 240 full-time non-parochial stipendiary clergy; 3,110 self-supporting ministers; 1,520 chaplains and other ministries; 250 lay workers and Church Army evangelists; 6,540 licensed readers and 2,750 readers with permission to officiate and active emeriti; and approximately 5,700 active retired ordained clergy.

	Full-time Equivalent Diocesan Clergy 2012		*Electoral Roll Membership*
	Male	*Female*	*2011*
Bath and Wells	147	57	35,300
Birmingham	115	50	16,900
Blackburn	150	23	33,000
Bradford	71	22	11,100
Bristol	88	21	15,900
Canterbury	107	28	20,100
Carlisle	99	27	20,400
Chelmsford	267	93	46,600
Chester	176	61	46,300
Chichester	262	25	52,600
Coventry	102	22	17,400
Derby	105	46	17,900
Durham	134	36	23,100
Ely	83	50	19,200
Europe	–	–	11,100
Exeter	175	40	30,600
Gloucester	95	35	24,000
Guildford	140	41	30,100
Hereford	57	35	17,100
Leicester	98	43	17,200
Lichfield	246	58	44,500
Lincoln	114	36	25,600
Liverpool	150	57	28,700
London	452	84	77,300
Manchester	162	67	33,400
Newcastle	90	30	16,300
Norwich	148	40	18,600
Oxford	297	100	56,400
Peterborough	103	37	19,300
Portsmouth	77	25	16,900
Ripon and Leeds	81	41	16,300
Rochester	161	46	30,100
St Albans	171	76	38,700
St Edmundsbury and Ipswich	96	43	22,800
Salisbury	143	51	40,800
Sheffield	109	41	18,000
Sodor and Man	14	3	2,600
Southwark	265	84	49,900
Southwell and Nottingham	94	46	19,400

	Full-time Equivalent Diocesan Clergy 2012		Electoral Roll Membership
	Male	Female	2011
Truro	76	24	15,400
Wakefield	101	37	18,700
Winchester	139	34	38,000
Worcester	87	28	18,400
York	166	38	33,900
*Total**	6,011	1,873	1,206,000

* Figures are rounded to the nearest 10 and may not add up as a result.

STIPENDS*

	2013–14	2014–15
Archbishop of Canterbury	£74,780	£76,280
Archbishop of York	£64,090	£65,370
Bishop of London	£58,740	£59,920
Other diocesan bishops	£40,600	£41,410
Suffragan bishops	£33,120	£33,780
Assistant bishops (full-time)	£32,060	£32,700
Deans	£33,120	£33,780
Archdeacons (recommended)	£32,360	£33,010
Residentiary canons	£25,630†	£26,140†
Incumbents and clergy of similar status	£23,740†	£24,210†

* For those appointed on or after 1 April 2004; transitional arrangements are in place for those appointed prior to this date
† Adjusted regionally to reflect variations in the cost of living

CANTERBURY

105TH ARCHBISHOP AND PRIMATE OF ALL ENGLAND
Most Revd and Rt. Hon. Justin Welby, *cons.* 2011, *apptd* 2013; Lambeth Palace, London SE1 7JU
Signs Justin Cantuar:

BISHOPS SUFFRAGAN
Dover, Rt. Revd Trevor Willmott, *cons.* 2002, *apptd* 2009; Upway, St Martin's Hill, Canterbury, Kent CT1 1PR
Ebbsfleet, vacant
Richborough, Rt. Revd Norman Banks, *cons.* 2011, *apptd* 2011; The Vicarage, Walsingham, Norfolk NR22 6BL

DEAN
Very Revd Robert Willis, *apptd* 2001

Organist, D. Flood, FRCO, *apptd* 1988

ARCHDEACONS
Ashford, Ven. Philip Down, *apptd* 2011
Canterbury, Ven. Sheila Watson, *apptd* 2007
Maidstone, Ven. Stephen Taylor, *apptd* 2011

Vicar-General of Province and Diocese, Chancellor Sheila Cameron, QC
Commissary-General, Morag Ellis, QC
Joint Registrars of the Province, Canon John Rees; Stephen Slack
Diocesan Registrar and Legal Adviser, Owen Carew Jones
Diocesan Secretary, Julian Hills, Diocesan House, Lady Wootton's Green, Canterbury CT1 1NQ T 01227-459401

YORK

97TH ARCHBISHOP AND PRIMATE OF ENGLAND
Most Revd and Rt. Hon. Dr John Sentamu, *cons.* 1996, *trans.* 2005; Bishopthorpe, York YO23 2GE
Signs Sentamu Ebor:

BISHOPS SUFFRAGAN
Hull, Rt. Revd Richard Frith, *cons.* 1998, *apptd* 1998; Hullen House, Woodfield Lane, Hessle, Hull HU13 0ES
Selby, Rt. Revd Martin Wallace, *cons.* 2003, *apptd* 2003; Bishop's House, Barton le Street, Malton, York YO17 6PL
Whitby, vacant

PRINCIPAL EPISCOPAL VISITOR
Beverley, Rt. Revd Glyn Webster, *cons.* 2013, *apptd* 2013; Holy Trinity Rectory, Micklegate, York YO1 6LE

DEAN
Very Revd Vivienne Faull, *apptd* 2012

Director of Music, Robert Sharpe, *apptd* 2008

ARCHDEACONS
Cleveland, Ven. Paul Ferguson, *apptd* 2001
East Riding, Ven. David Butterfield, *apptd* 2006
York, Ven. Sarah Bullock, *apptd* 2013

Chancellor of the Diocese, His Hon. Judge Collier, QC, *apptd* 2006
Registrar and Legal Secretary, Lionel Lennox
Diocesan Secretary, Peter Warry, Diocesan House, Aviator Court, Clifton Moor, York YO30 4WJ T 01904-699500

LONDON *(CANTERBURY)*

132ND BISHOP
Rt. Revd and Rt. Hon. Richard Chartres, KCVO, *cons.* 1992, *apptd* 1995; The Old Deanery, Dean's Court, London EC4V 5AA
Signs Richard Londin:

AREA BISHOPS
Edmonton, Rt. Revd Peter Wheatley, *cons.* 1999, *apptd* 1999; 27 Thurlow Road, London NW3 5PP
Kensington, Rt. Revd Paul Williams, *cons.* 2009, *apptd* 2008; Dial House, Riverside, Twickenham, Middlesex TW1 3DT
Stepney, Rt. Revd Adrian Newman, *cons.* 2011, *apptd* 2011; 63 Coburn Road, London E3 2DB
Willesden, Rt. Revd Peter Broadbent, *cons.* 2001, *apptd* 2001; 173 Willesden Lane, London NW6 7YN

BISHOP SUFFRAGAN
Fulham, Rt. Revd Jonathan Baker, *cons.* 2011, *apptd* 2013; The Old Deanery, Dean's Court, London EC4V 5AA

DEAN OF ST PAUL'S
Rt. Revd Dr David Ison, PHD, *apptd* 2012

Director of Music, Andrew Carwood, *apptd* 2007

ARCHDEACONS
Charing Cross, Ven. Dr William Jacob, *apptd* 1996
Hackney, Ven. Rachel Treweek, *apptd* 2011
Hampstead, Ven. Luke Miller, *apptd* 2010
London, Ven. David Meara, *apptd* 2009
Middlesex, Ven. Stephan Welch, *apptd* 2006
Northolt, Ven. Duncan Green, *apptd* 2013

Chancellor, Nigel Seed, QC, *apptd* 2002
Registrar and Legal Secretary, Paul Morris
Diocesan Secretary, Andrew Brookes, London Diocesan House, 36 Causton Street, London SW1P 4AU T 020-7932 1100

DURHAM *(YORK)*

73RD BISHOP
vacant

BISHOP SUFFRAGAN
Jarrow, Rt. Revd Mark Bryant, *cons.* 2007, *apptd* 2007; Bishop's House, 25 Ivy Lane, Low Fell, Gateshead NE9 6QD

DEAN
Very Revd Michael Sadgrove, *apptd* 2003

Organist, James Lancelot, FRCO, *apptd* 1985

ARCHDEACONS
Auckland, Ven. Nicholas Barker, *apptd* 2007
Durham, Ven. Ian Jagger, *apptd* 2006
Sunderland, Ven. Stuart Bain, *apptd* 2002

Chancellor, His Hon. Judge Bursell, QC, *apptd* 1989
Registrar and Legal Secretary, Hilary Monckton-Milnes
Diocesan Secretary, vacant, Diocesan Office, Auckland Castle, Bishop Auckland DL14 7QJ T 01388-660010

WINCHESTER *(CANTERBURY)*

97TH BISHOP
Rt. Revd Tim Dakin, *cons.* 2012, *apptd* 2011; Wolvesey, Winchester SO23 9ND
Signs Tim Winton:

BISHOPS SUFFRAGAN
Basingstoke, Rt. Revd Peter Hancock, *cons.* 2010, *apptd* 2010; Bishop's Lodge, Colden Lane, Old Alresford, Hants SO24 9DY
Southampton, Rt. Revd Jonathan Frost, *cons.* 2010, *apptd* 2010; Bishop's House, St Mary's Church Close, Wessex Lane, Southampton SO18 2ST

DEANS
Dean of Winchester, Very Revd James Atwell, *apptd* 2005
Dean of Jersey (A Peculiar), Very Revd Robert Key, *apptd* 2005
Dean of Guernsey (A Peculiar), Very Revd Paul Mellor, *apptd* 2003
Director of Music, Andrew Lumsden, *apptd* 2002

ARCHDEACONS
Bournemouth, Ven. Dr Peter Rouch, *apptd* 2011
Winchester, Ven. Michael Harley, *apptd* 2009

Chancellor, His Hon. Judge Clark, QC, *apptd* 1993
Registrar and Legal Secretary, Andrew Johnson
Diocesan Secretary, Andrew Robinson, Old Alresford Place, Alresford, Hants SO24 9DH T 01962-737300

BATH AND WELLS *(CANTERBURY)*

79TH BISHOP
vacant

BISHOP SUFFRAGAN
Taunton, Rt. Revd Peter Maurice, *cons.* 2006, *apptd* 2006; The Palace, Wells BA5 2PD

DEAN
Very Revd John Clarke, *apptd* 2004

Organist, Matthew Owens, *apptd* 2005

ARCHDEACONS
Bath, Ven. Andrew Piggott, *apptd* 2005
Taunton, Ven. John Reed, *apptd* 1999
Wells, Ven. Nicola Sullivan, *apptd* 2006

Chancellor, Timothy Briden, *apptd* 1993
Registrar and Legal Secretary, Tim Berry
Diocesan Secretary, Nick Denison, The Old Deanery, St Andrew's Street, Wells, Somerset BA5 2UG T 01749-670777

BIRMINGHAM *(CANTERBURY)*

8TH BISHOP
Rt. Revd David Urquhart, *cons.* 2000, *apptd* 2006; Bishop's Croft, Old Church Road, Harborne, Birmingham B17 0BG
Signs David Birmingham:

BISHOP SUFFRAGAN
Aston, Rt. Revd Andrew Watson, *cons.* 2008, *apptd* 2008; 1 Colmore Row, Birmingham B3 2BJ

DEAN
Very Revd Catherine Ogle, *apptd* 2010

Director of Music, Marcus Huxley, FRCO, *apptd* 1986

ARCHDEACONS
Aston, Ven. Dr Brian Russell, *apptd* 2005
Birmingham, Ven. Hayward Osborne, *apptd* 2001

Chancellor, Mark Powell, QC, *apptd* 2012
Registrar and Legal Secretary, Hugh Carslake
Diocesan Secretary, Andrew Halstead, 1 Colmore Row, Birmingham B3 2BJ T 0121-426 0400

BLACKBURN *(YORK)*

9TH BISHOP
Rt. Revd Julian Henderson, *cons.* 2013, *apptd* 2013; Bishop's House, Ribchester Road, Blackburn BB1 9EF
Signs Julian Blackburn

BISHOPS SUFFRAGAN
Burnley, Rt. Revd John Goddard, *cons.* 2000, *apptd* 2000; Church House, Cathedral Close, Blackburn BB1 5AA
Lancaster, Rt. Revd Geoffrey Pearson, *cons.* 2006, *apptd* 2006; The Vicarage, Whinney Brow Lane, Shireshead, Forton, Preston PR3 0AE

DEAN
Very Revd Christopher Armstrong, *apptd* 2001

Organist and Director of Music, Samuel Holden

ARCHDEACON
Blackburn, Ven. John Hawley, *apptd* 2002
Lancaster, Ven. Michael Everitt, *apptd* 2011

Chancellor, His Hon. Judge Bullimore, *apptd* 1990
Registrar and Legal Secretary, Stephen Crossley
Diocesan Secretary, Graeme Pollard, Diocesan Office, Cathedral Close, Blackburn BB1 5AA T 01254-503070

BRADFORD *(YORK)*

10TH BISHOP
Rt. Revd Nicholas Baines, *cons.* 2003, *apptd* 2010; Bishopscroft, Ashwell Road, Heaton, Bradford BD9 4AU
Signs Nicholas Bradford:

DEAN
Jerry Lepine, *apptd* 2013

Director of Music, Alex Woodrow, *apptd* 2012

ARCHDEACONS
Bradford, Ven. David Lee, *apptd* 2004
Craven, Ven. Paul Slater, *apptd* 2005

Chancellor, His Hon. Judge Walford, *apptd* 1999
Registrar and Legal Secretary, Peter Foskett
Diocesan Secretary, Debbie Child, Kadugli House, Elmsley Street, Steeton, Keighley BD20 6SE T 01535-650555

BRISTOL *(CANTERBURY)*
55TH BISHOP
Rt. Revd Michael Hill, *cons.* 1998, *apptd* 2003; 58A High Street, Winterbourne, Bristol BS36 1JQ
Signs Michael Bristol:

BISHOP SUFFRAGAN
Swindon, Rt. Revd Dr Lee Rayfield, *cons.* 2005, *apptd* 2005; Mark House, Field Rise, Swindon, Wiltshire SN1 4HP

DEAN
Very Revd David Hoyle, *apptd* 2010
Organist and Director of Music, Mark Lee, *apptd* 1998

ARCHDEACONS
Bristol, vacant
Malmesbury, Ven. Christine Froude, *apptd* 2011

Chancellor, The Worshipful Revd Justin Gau
Registrar and Legal Secretary, Tim Berry
Diocesan Secretary, Lesley Farrall, First Floor, Hillside House, 1500 Parkway North, Stoke Gifford, Bristol BS34 8YU

CARLISLE *(YORK)*
67TH BISHOP
Rt. Revd James Newcome, *cons.* 2002, *apptd* 2009; Bishop's House, Ambleside Road, Keswick CA12 4DD
Signs James Carliol

BISHOP SUFFRAGAN
Penrith, Rt. Revd Robert Freeman, *cons.* 2011, *apptd* 2011; Holm Croft, Castle Road, Kendal, Cumbria LA9 7AU

DEAN
Very Revd Mark Boyling, *apptd* 2004
Organist, Jeremy Suter, FRCO, *apptd* 1991

ARCHDEACONS
Carlisle, Ven. Kevin Roberts, *apptd* 2009
West Cumberland, Ven. Dr Richard Pratt, *apptd* 2009
Westmorland and Furness, Ven. Penny Driver, *apptd* 2012

Chancellor, Geoffrey Tattersall, QC, *apptd* 2003
Registrar and Legal Secretary, Jane Lowdon
Diocesan Secretary, Derek Hurton, Church House, West Walls, Carlisle CA3 8UE T 01228-522573

CHELMSFORD *(CANTERBURY)*
10TH BISHOP
Rt. Revd Stephen Cottrell, *cons.* 2004, *apptd* 2010; Bishopscourt, Main Road, Margaretting, Ingatestone, Essex CM4 0HD
Signs Stephen Chelmsford

BISHOPS SUFFRAGAN
Barking, Rt. Revd David Hawkins, *cons.* 2002, *apptd* 2002; Barking Lodge, Verulam Avenue, London E17 8ES
Bradwell, Rt. Revd John Wraw, *cons.* 2012, *apptd* 2012; Bishop's House, Orsett Road, Horndon-on-the-Hill, Stanford-le-Hope, Essex SS17 8NS
Colchester, Rt. Revd Christopher Morgan, *cons.* 2001, *apptd* 2001; 1 Fitzwalter Road, Colchester, Essex CO3 3SS

DEAN
Very Revd Peter S. M. Judd, *apptd* 1997
Director of Music, James Davey, *apptd* 2012

ARCHDEACONS
Chelmsford, Ven. David Lowman, *apptd* 2013
Colchester, Ven. Annette Cooper, *apptd* 2004
Harlow, Ven. Martin Webster, *apptd* 2009
Southend, Ven. David Lowman, *apptd* 2001
West Ham, Ven. Elwin Cockett, *apptd* 2007

Chancellor, George Pulman, QC, *apptd* 2001
Registrar and Legal Secretary, Aiden Hargreaves-Smith
Chief Executive, John Ball, 53 New Street, Chelmsford, Essex CM1 1AT T 01245-294400

CHESTER *(YORK)*
40TH BISHOP
Rt. Revd Peter Forster, PHD, *cons.* 1996, *apptd* 1996; Bishop's House, Abbey Square, Chester CH1 2JD
Signs Peter Cestr:

BISHOPS SUFFRAGAN
Birkenhead, Rt. Revd Keith Sinclair, *cons.* 2007, *apptd* 2007; Bishop's Lodge, 67 Bidston Road, Prenton CH43 6TR
Stockport, Rt. Revd Robert Atwell, *cons.* 2008, *apptd* 2008; Bishop's Lodge, Back Lane, Dunham Town, Altrincham WA14 4SG

DEAN
Very Revd Dr Gordon McPhate, *apptd* 2002
Organist and Director of Music, Philip Rushforth, FRCO, *apptd* 2008

ARCHDEACONS
Chester, Ven. Dr Michael Gilbertson, *apptd* 2010
Macclesfield, Ven. Ian Bishop, *apptd* 2011

Chancellor, His Hon. Judge Turner, QC, *apptd* 1998
Registrar and Legal Secretary, Helen McFall
Diocesan Secretary, George Colville, Church House, Lower Lane, Aldford, Chester CH3 6HP T 01244-681973

CHICHESTER *(CANTERBURY)*
103RD BISHOP
Rt. Revd Dr Martin Warner, *cons.* 2010, *apptd* 2012; The Palace, Chichester PO19 1PY
Signs Martin Cicestr:

BISHOPS SUFFRAGAN
Horsham, Rt. Revd Mark Sowerby, *cons.* 2009, *apptd* 2009; 21 Guildford Road, Horsham, W. Sussex RH12 1LU
Lewes, vacant

DEAN
Very Revd Nicholas Frayling, *apptd* 2002
Organist, Sarah Baldock, *apptd* 2007

ARCHDEACONS
Chichester, Ven. Douglas McKittrick, *apptd* 2002
Horsham, Ven. Roger Combes, *apptd* 2003
Lewes and Hastings, Ven. Philip Jones, *apptd* 2005

Chancellor, Prof. Mark Hill
Registrar and Legal Secretary, Matthew Chinery
Diocesan Secretary, Angela Sibson, OBE, Diocesan Church House, 211 New Church Road, Hove, E. Sussex BN3 4ED T 01273-421021

COVENTRY *(CANTERBURY)*
9TH BISHOP
Rt. Revd Dr Christopher Cocksworth, *cons.* 2008, *apptd* 2008; The Bishop's House, 23 Davenport Road, Coventry CV5 6PW
Signs Christopher Coventry

BISHOP SUFFRAGAN
Warwick, Rt. Revd John Stroyan, *cons.* 2005, *apptd* 2005; Warwick House, 139 Kenilworth Road, Coventry CV4 7AP

DEAN
Very Revd John Whitcombe, *apptd* 2013

Director of Music, Mr Kerry Beaumont, *apptd* 2006

ARCHDEACONS
Coventry, Ven. John Green, CB, *apptd* 2013
Warwick, Ven. Morris Rodham, *apptd* 2010

Chancellor, Stephen Eyre, *apptd* 2009
Registrar and Legal Secretary, Mary Allanson
Diocesan Secretary, Simon Lloyd, Cathedral & Diocesan Offices, 1 Hilltop, Coventry CV1 5AB T 024-7652 1200

DERBY *(CANTERBURY)*
7TH BISHOP
Rt. Revd Dr Alastair Redfern, *cons.* 1997, *apptd* 2005; The Bishop's House, 6 King Street, Duffield, Belper, Derbyshire DE56 4EU
Signs Alastair Derby

BISHOP SUFFRAGAN
Repton, Rt. Revd Humphrey Southern, *cons.* 2007, *apptd* 2007; Repton House, Lea, Matlock, Derbyshire DE4 5JP

DEAN
Very Revd Dr John Davies, *apptd* 2010

Organist, Peter Gould, *apptd* 1982

ARCHDEACONS
Chesterfield, Ven. Christine Wilson, *apptd* 2010
Derby, Ven. Dr Christopher Cunliffe, *apptd* 2006

Chancellor, His Hon. Judge Bullimore, *apptd* 1981
Registrar and Legal Secretary, Mrs Nadine Waldron
Diocesan Secretary, vacant, Derby Church House, Full Street, Derby DE1 3DR T 01332-388650

ELY *(CANTERBURY)*
69TH BISHOP
Rt. Revd Stephen Conway, *cons.* 2006, *apptd* 2011; The Bishop's House, Ely CB7 4DW
Signs Stephen Ely

BISHOP SUFFRAGAN
Huntingdon, Rt. Revd David Thomson, DPHIL, *cons.* 2008, *apptd* 2008; 14 Lynn Road, Ely, Cambs CB6 1DA

DEAN
Very Revd Mark Bonney, *apptd* 2012

Director of Music, Paul Trepte, FRCO, *apptd* 1991

ARCHDEACONS
Cambridge, Ven. John Beer, *apptd* 2004
Huntingdon and Wisbech, Ven. Hugh McCurdy, *apptd* 2005

Chancellor, His Hon. Judge Leonard, QC
Registrar, Howard Dellar
Diocesan Secretary, Graham Shorter, Bishop Woodford House, Barton Road, Ely, Cambs CB7 4DX T 01353-652700

EXETER *(CANTERBURY)*
71ST BISHOP
vacant

BISHOPS SUFFRAGAN
Crediton, Rt. Revd Nick McKinnel, *cons.* 2012, *apptd* 2012; 32 The Avenue, Tiverton, Devon EX16 4HW
Plymouth, Rt. Revd John Ford, *cons.* 2006, *apptd* 2005; 31 Riverside Walk, Tamerton Foliot, Plymouth PL5 4AQ

DEAN
Very Revd Jonathan Draper, *apptd* 2012

Director of Music, Andrew Millington, *apptd* 1999

ARCHDEACONS
Barnstaple, Ven. David Gunn-Johnson, *apptd* 2003
Exeter, Ven. Christopher Futcher, *apptd* 2012
Plymouth, Ven. Ian Chandler, *apptd* 2010
Totnes, Ven. John Rawlings, *apptd* 2006

Chancellor, Hon. Sir Andrew McFarlane
Registrar and Legal Secretary, M. Follett
Diocesan Secretary, Mark Beedell, The Old Deanery, The Cloisters, Exeter EX1 1HS T 01392-272686

GIBRALTAR IN EUROPE *(CANTERBURY)*
4TH BISHOP
vacant

BISHOP SUFFRAGAN
In Europe, Rt. Revd David Hamid, *cons.* 2002, *apptd* 2002; 14 Tufton Street, London SW1P 3QZ

Dean, Cathedral Church of the Holy Trinity, Gibraltar, Very Revd Dr John Paddock

Chancellor, Pro-Cathedral of St Paul, Valletta, Malta, Canon Simon Godfrey
Chancellor, Pro-Cathedral of the Holy Trinity, Brussels, Belgium, Canon Dr Robert Innes

ARCHDEACONS
Eastern, Ven. Patrick Curran
North-West Europe, Canon Meurig Williams *(acting)*
France, Revd Ian Naylor *(acting)*
Gibraltar, Ven. David Sutch
Italy, Ven. Jonathan Boardman
Scandinavia and Germany, Ven. Jonathan Lloyd
Switzerland, Ven. Peter Potter

Chancellor, Mark Hill
Registrar and Legal Secretary, Aiden Hargreaves-Smith
Diocesan Secretary, Adrian Mumford, 14 Tufton Street, London SW1P 3QZ T 020-7898 1155

GLOUCESTER *(CANTERBURY)*
40TH BISHOP
Rt. Revd Michael Perham, *cons.* 2004, *apptd* 2004; 2 College Green, Gloucester GL1 2LR
Signs Michael Gloucestr

BISHOP SUFFRAGAN
Tewkesbury, vacant

DEAN
Very Revd Stephen Lake, *apptd* 2011

Director of Music, Adrian Partington, *apptd* 2007

ARCHDEACONS
Cheltenham, Ven. Robert Springett, *apptd* 2010
Gloucester, Ven. Jackie Searle, *apptd* 2012

Chancellor and Vicar-General, June Rodgers, *apptd* 1990
Registrar and Legal Secretary, Jos Moule

Diocesan Secretary, Ben Preece Smith, Church House, College Green, Gloucester GL1 2LY T 01452-410022

GUILDFORD *(CANTERBURY)*

10TH BISHOP
vacant

BISHOP SUFFRAGAN
Dorking, Rt. Revd Ian Brackley, *cons.* 1996, *apptd* 1995; Dayspring, 13 Pilgrims Way, Guildford GU4 8AD

DEAN
vacant

Organist, Katherine Dienes-Williams, *apptd* 2007

ARCHDEACONS
Dorking, vacant
Surrey, Ven. Stuart Beake, *apptd* 2005

Chancellor, Andrew Jordan
Registrar and Legal Secretary, Peter Beesley
Diocesan Secretary, Stephen Marriott, Diocesan House, Quarry Street, Guildford GU1 3XG T 01483-790300

HEREFORD *(CANTERBURY)*

105TH BISHOP
vacant

BISHOP SUFFRAGAN
Ludlow, Rt. Revd Alistair Magowan, *cons.* 2009, *apptd* 2009; Bishop's House, Corvedale Road, Craven Arms, Shropshire SY7 9BT

DEAN
Very Revd Michael Tavinor, *apptd* 2002

Organist and Director of Music, Geraint Bowen, FRCO, *apptd* 2001

ARCHDEACONS
Hereford, Ven. Paddy Benson, *apptd* 2011
Ludlow, Rt. Revd Alistair Magowan, *apptd* 2009

Chancellor, His Hon. Judge Kaye, QC
Registrars and Legal Secretaries, Peter Beesley; Howard Dellar
Diocesan Secretary, John Clark, The Palace, Hereford HR4 9BL T 01432-373300

LEICESTER *(CANTERBURY)*

6TH BISHOP
Rt. Revd Timothy Stevens, *cons.* 1995, *apptd* 1999; Bishop's Lodge, 10 Springfield Road, Leicester LE2 3BD
Signs Timothy Leicester

ASSISTANT BISHOP
Rt. Revd Christopher Boyle, *cons.* 2000, *apptd* 2009; St Martins House, 7 Peacock Lane, Leicester LE1 5PZ

DEAN
Very Revd David Monteith, *apptd* 2013

Director of Music, Dr Christopher Johns

ARCHDEACONS
Leicester, Ven. Timothy Stratford, *apptd* 2012
Loughborough, Ven. David Newman, *apptd* 2009

Chancellor, Mark Blackett-Ord
Registrar and Legal Secretary, Revd Trevor Kirkman
Diocesan Secretary, Jonathan Kerry, St Martin's House, 7 Peacock Lane, Leicester LE1 5PZ T 0116-261 5200

LICHFIELD *(CANTERBURY)*

98TH BISHOP
Rt. Revd Jonathan Gledhill, *cons.* 1996, *apptd* 2003; Bishop's House, 22 The Close, Lichfield WS13 7LG
Signs Jonathan Lichfield

BISHOPS SUFFRAGAN
Shrewsbury, Rt. Revd Mark Rylands, *cons.* 2009, *apptd* 2009; Athlone House, 66 London Road, Shrewsbury SY2 6PG
Stafford, Rt. Revd Geoffrey Annas, *cons.* 2010, *apptd* 2010; Ash Garth, Broughton Crescent, Barlaston, Stoke-on-Trent ST12 9DD
Wolverhampton, Rt. Revd Clive Gregory, *cons.* 2007, *apptd* 2007; 61 Richmond Road, Wolverhampton WV3 9JH

DEAN
Very Revd Adrian Dorber, *apptd* 2005

Directors of Music, Ben and Cathy Lamb, *apptd* 2010
Organist, Martyn Rawles, *apptd* 2010

ARCHDEACONS
Lichfield, Ven. Simon Baker, *apptd* 2013
Salop, Ven. Paul Thomas, *apptd* 2011
Stoke-on-Trent, vacant
Walsall, Ven. Christopher Sims, *apptd* 2009

Chancellor, Stephen Eyre, *apptd* 2012
Registrar and Legal Secretary, N. Blackie
Diocesan Secretary, Julie Jones, St Mary's House, The Close, Lichfield, Staffs WS13 7LD T 01543-306030

LINCOLN *(CANTERBURY)*

72ND BISHOP
Rt. Revd Christopher Lowson, *cons.* 2011, *apptd* 2011; Bishop's Office, The Old Palace, Minster Yard, Lincoln LN2 1PU
Signs Christopher Lincoln

BISHOPS SUFFRAGAN
Grantham, Rt. Revd Dr Timothy Ellis, *cons.* 2006, *apptd* 2006; Saxonwell Vicarage, Church Street, Long Bennington, Newark NG23 5ES
Grimsby, vacant

DEAN
Very Revd Philip Buckler, *apptd* 2007

Director of Music, A. Prentice, *apptd* 2003

ARCHDEACONS
Lincoln, Ven. Timothy Barker, *apptd* 2009
Stow and Lindsey, Ven. Jane Sinclair, *apptd* 2007

Chancellor, His Hon. Judge Bishop, QC, *apptd* 2007
Registrar and Legal Secretary, Caroline Mockford, *apptd* 2008
Diocesan Secretary (interim), Revd Canon Richard Bowett, Edward King House, Minster Yard, Lincoln LN2 1PU T 01522-504050

LIVERPOOL *(YORK)*

8TH BISHOP
vacant

BISHOP SUFFRAGAN
Warrington, Rt. Revd Richard Blackburn, *cons.* 2009, *apptd* 2009; 34 Central Avenue, Eccleston Park, Liverpool L34 2QP

DEAN
Very Revd Pete Wilcox, *apptd* 2012

Director of Music, David Poulter, *apptd* 2008

ARCHDEACONS
Liverpool, Ven. Richard Panter, *apptd* 2002
Warrington, Ven. Peter Bradley, *apptd* 2001

Chancellor, Hon. Sir Mark Hedley
Registrar and Legal Secretary, Howard Dellar
Diocesan Secretary, Mike Eastwood, St James House, 20 St James Street, Liverpool L1 7BY T 0151-709 9722

MANCHESTER *(YORK)*

12TH BISHOP
Rt. Revd David Walker, *cons.* 2000, *apptd* 2013; Bishopscourt, Bury New Road, Manchester M7 4LE
Signs David Manchester

BISHOPS SUFFRAGAN
Bolton, Rt. Revd Christopher Edmondson, *cons.* 2008, *apptd* 2008; Bishop's Lodge, Walkden Road, Worsley, Manchester M28 2WH
Middleton, Rt. Revd Mark Davies, *cons.* 2008, *apptd* 2008; The Hollies, Manchester Road, Rochdale OL11 3QY

DEAN
Revd Rogers Govender, *apptd* 2006

Organist, Christopher Stokes, *apptd* 1992

ARCHDEACONS
Bolton, Ven. David Bailey, *apptd* 2008
Manchester, Ven. Mark Ashcroft, *apptd* 2009
Rochdale, Ven. Cherry Vann, *apptd* 2008
Salford, Ven. David Sharples, *apptd* 2009

Chancellor, Geoffrey Tattersall, QC
Registrar and Legal Secretary, Jane Monks
Diocesan Secretary, Martin Miller, Diocesan Church House, 90 Deansgate, Manchester M3 2GH T 0161-828 1400

NEWCASTLE *(YORK)*

11TH BISHOP
Rt. Revd J. Martin Wharton, CBE, *cons.* 1992, *apptd* 1997; Bishop's House, 29 Moor Road South, Gosforth, Newcastle upon Tyne NE3 1PA
Signs Martin Newcastle

ASSISTANT BISHOP
Rt. Revd Frank White, *cons.* 2002, *apptd* 2010

DEAN
Very Revd Christopher C. Dalliston, *apptd* 2003

Director of Music, Michael Stoddart, *apptd* 2009

ARCHDEACONS
Lindisfarne, Ven. Dr Peter Robinson, *apptd* 2008
Northumberland, Ven. Geoffrey Miller, *apptd* 2004

Chancellor, Euan Duff, *apptd* 2013
Registrar and Legal Secretary, Jane Lowdon
Diocesan Secretary, Shane Waddle, Church House, St John's Terrace, North Shields NE29 6HS T 0191-270 4100

NORWICH *(CANTERBURY)*

71ST BISHOP
Rt. Revd Graham R. James, *cons.* 1993, *apptd* 2000; Bishop's House, Norwich NR3 1SB
Signs Graham Norvic:

BISHOPS SUFFRAGAN
Lynn, Rt. Revd Jonathan Meyrick, *cons.* 2011, *apptd* 2011; The Old Vicarage, Castle Acre, King's Lynn PE32 2AA
Thetford, Rt. Revd Alan Winton, PHD, *cons.* 2009, *apptd* 2009; The Red House, 53 Norwich Road, Stoke Holy Cross, Norwich NR14 8AB

DEAN
Very Revd Graham Smith, *apptd* 2004

Master of Music, Ashley Grote, *apptd* 2012

ARCHDEACONS
Lynn, Ven. John Ashe, *apptd* 2009
Norfolk, Ven. Steven Betts, *apptd* 2012
Norwich, Ven. Jan McFarlane, *apptd* 2008

Chancellor, Ruth Arlow, *apptd* 2012
Registrar and Legal Secretary, Stuart Jones
Diocesan Secretary, Richard Butler, Diocesan House, 109 Dereham Road, Easton, Norwich, Norfolk NR9 5ES T 01603-880853

OXFORD *(CANTERBURY)*

42ND BISHOP
Rt. Revd John Pritchard, *cons.* 2002, *apptd* 2007; Diocesan Church House, North Hinksey Lane, Oxford OX2 0NB
Signs John Oxon:

AREA BISHOPS
Buckingham, Rt. Revd Dr Alan Wilson, *cons.* 2003, *apptd* 2003; Sheridan, Grimms Hill, Great Missenden, Bucks HP16 9BD
Dorchester, Rt. Revd Colin Fletcher, *cons.* 2000, *apptd* 2000; Arran House, Sandy Lane, Yarnton, Oxon OX5 1PB
Reading, Rt. Revd Andrew Proud, *cons.* 2011, *apptd* 2011; Bishop's House, Tidmarsh Lane, Tidmarsh, Reading RG8 8HA

DEAN OF CHRIST CHURCH
Very Revd Dr Christopher Lewis, *apptd* 2003

Organist, Dr Stephen Darlington, FRCO, *apptd* 1985

ARCHDEACONS
Berkshire, Ven. Norman Russell, *apptd* 1998
Buckingham, Ven. Karen Gorham, *apptd* 2007
Oxford, Ven. Martin Gorick, *apptd* 2013

Chancellor, Revd Dr Rupert Bursell, *apptd* 2001
Registrar and Legal Secretary, Revd Canon John Rees
Diocesan Secretary, Rosemary Pearce, Diocesan Church House, North Hinksey, Oxford OX2 0NB T 01865-208202

PETERBOROUGH *(CANTERBURY)*

38TH BISHOP
Rt. Revd Donald Allister, *cons.* 2010, *apptd* 2009; Bishop's Lodging, The Palace, Peterborough PE1 1YA
Signs Donald Petriburg:

BISHOP SUFFRAGAN
Brixworth, Rt. Revd John Holbrook, *cons.* 2011, *apptd* 2011; Orchard Acre, 11 North Street, Mears Ashby, Northants NN6 0DW

DEAN
Very Revd Charles Taylor, *apptd* 2007

Director of Music, Robert Quinney, *apptd* 2013

ARCHDEACONS
Northampton, Ven. Christine Allsopp, *apptd* 2005
Oakham, Ven. Gordon Steele, *apptd* 2012

Chancellor, David Pittaway, QC, *apptd* 2005
Registrar and Legal Secretary, Revd Raymond Hemingray
Diocesan Secretary, Andrew Roberts, Diocesan Office, The Palace, Peterborough PE1 1YB T 01733-887000

PORTSMOUTH *(CANTERBURY)*

9TH BISHOP
Rt. Revd Christopher Foster, *cons.* 2010, *apptd* 2010; Bishopsgrove, 26 Osborn Road, Fareham, Hants PO16 7DQ
Signs Christopher Portsmouth

DEAN
Very Revd David Brindley, *apptd* 2002

Organist, David Price, *apptd* 1996

ARCHDEACONS
Isle of Wight, Ven. Peter Sutton, *apptd* 2012
Portsdown, Ven. Joanne Grenfell, *apptd* 2013
The Meon, Ven. Gavin Collins, *apptd* 2011

Chancellor, C. Clark, QC
Registrar and Legal Secretary, Hilary Tyler
Diocesan Secretary, Wendy Kennedy, Diocesan Offices, 1st Floor, Peninsular House, Wharf Road, Portsmouth PO2 8HB T 023-9289 9664

RIPON AND LEEDS *(YORK)*

12TH BISHOP
Rt. Revd John Packer, *cons.* 1996, *apptd* 2000; Hollin House, Weetwood Avenue LS16 5NG
Signs John Ripon and Leeds

BISHOP SUFFRAGAN
Knaresborough, Rt. Revd James Bell, *cons.* 2004, *apptd* 2004; Thistledown, Main Street, Exelby, Bedale DL8 2HD

DEAN
Revd Keith Jukes, *apptd* 2007

Director of Music, Andrew Bryden, *apptd* 2003

ARCHDEACONS
Leeds, Ven. Paul Hooper, *apptd* 2012
Richmond (acting), Revd Nicholas Henshall

Chancellor, His Hon. Judge Simon Grenfell, *apptd* 1992
Registrars and Legal Secretaries, Nicola Harding; Christopher Tunnard
Diocesan Secretary, Dr Sue Proctor, Diocesan Office, St Mary's Street, Leeds LS9 7DP T 0113-200 0540

ROCHESTER *(CANTERBURY)*

107TH BISHOP
Rt. Revd James Langstaff, *cons.* 2004, *apptd* 2010; Bishopscourt, 24 St Margaret's Street, Rochester ME1 1TS
Signs James Roffen:

BISHOP SUFFRAGAN
Tonbridge, Rt. Revd Dr Brian C. Castle, *cons.* 2002, *apptd* 2002; Bishop's Lodge, 48 St Botolph's Road, Sevenoaks TN13 3AG

DEAN
Very Revd Dr Mark Beach, *apptd* 2012

Director of Music, Scott Farrell, *apptd* 2008

ARCHDEACONS
Bromley & Bexley, Ven. Dr Paul Wright, *apptd* 2003
Rochester, Ven. Simon Burton-Jones, *apptd* 2010
Tonbridge, Ven. Clive Mansell, *apptd* 2002

Chancellor, John Gallagher, *apptd* 2006
Registrar and Legal Secretary, Owen Carew-Jones
Diocesan Secretary (acting), Geoff Marsh, St Nicholas Church, Boley Hill, Rochester ME1 1SL T 01634-560000

ST ALBANS *(CANTERBURY)*

10TH BISHOP
Rt. Revd Dr Alan Smith, *cons.* 2001, *apptd* 2009, *trans.* 2009; Abbey Gate House, St Albans AL3 4HD
Signs Alan St Albans

BISHOPS SUFFRAGAN
Bedford, Rt. Revd Richard Atkinson, OBE, *cons.* 2012, *apptd* 2012; Bishop's Lodge, Bedford Road, Cardington, Bedford MK44 3SS
Hertford, Rt. Revd Paul Bayes, *cons.* 2010, *apptd* 2010; Bishopswood, 3 Stobarts Close, Knebworth, Herts SG3 6ND

DEAN
Very Revd Dr Jeffrey John, *apptd* 2004

Organist, Andrew Lucas, *apptd* 1998

ARCHDEACONS
Bedford, Ven. Paul Hughes, *apptd* 2004
Hertford, Ven. Trevor Jones, *apptd* 1997
St Albans, Ven. Jonathan Smith, *apptd* 2008

Chancellor, Roger Kaye, *apptd* 2002
Registrar and Legal Secretary, Lee Coley
Diocesan Secretary, Susan Pope, Holywell Lodge, 41 Holywell Hill, St Albans AL1 1HE T 01727-854532

ST EDMUNDSBURY AND IPSWICH *(CANTERBURY)*

10TH BISHOP
Rt. Revd Nigel Stock, *cons.* 2000, *apptd* 2007; Bishop's House, 4 Park Road, Ipswich IP1 3ST
Signs Nigel St Edmun and Ipswich

BISHOP SUFFRAGAN
Dunwich, vacant

DEAN
Very Revd Frances Ward, *apptd* 2010

Director of Music, James Thomas, *apptd* 1997

ARCHDEACONS
Sudbury, Ven. Dr David Jenkins, *apptd* 2010
Suffolk, Ven. Ian Morgan, *apptd* 2012
Chancellor, David Etherington, QC
Registrar and Legal Secretary, James Hall
Diocesan Secretary, Nicholas Edgell, Diocesan Office, St Nicholas Centre, 4 Cutler Street, Ipswich IP1 1UQ T 01473-298500

SALISBURY *(CANTERBURY)*

78TH BISHOP
Rt. Revd Nicholas Holtam, *cons.* 2011, *apptd* 2011; South Canonry, 71 The Close, Salisbury SP1 2ER
Signs Nicholas Sarum

BISHOPS SUFFRAGAN
Ramsbury, Rt. Revd Edward Condry, DPHIL, *cons.* 2012, *apptd* 2012; Bishop's Office, Southbroom House, London Road, Devizes SN10 1LT
Sherborne, Rt. Revd Graham Kings, PHD, *cons.* 2009, *apptd* 2009; Sherborne Area Office, St Nicholas' Church Centre, Wareham Road, Corfe Mullen BH21 3LE

DEAN
Very Revd June Osborne, *apptd* 2004

Organist, David Halls, *apptd* 2005

ARCHDEACONS
Dorset, Ven. Stephen Waine, *apptd* 2010
Sarum, Ven. Alan Jeans, *apptd* 2003
Sherborne, Ven. Paul Taylor, *apptd* 2004
Wilts, Ven. Ruth Worsley, *apptd* 2012

Chancellor, His Hon. Judge Wiggs, *apptd* 1997
Registrar and Legal Secretary, Andrew Johnson
Diocesan Secretary, Lucinda Herklots, Church House, Crane Street, Salisbury SP1 2QB T 01722-411922

SHEFFIELD *(YORK)*
7TH BISHOP
Rt. Revd Steven Croft, PHD, *cons.* 2009, *apptd* 2008; Bishopscroft, Snaithing Lane, Sheffield S10 3LG
Signs Steven Sheffield

BISHOP SUFFRAGAN
Doncaster, Rt. Revd Peter Burrows, *cons.* 2012, *apptd* 2011; Doncaster House, Church Lane, Fishlake, Doncaster DN7 5JW

DEAN
Very Revd Peter Bradley, *apptd* 2003

Master of Music, Neil Taylor, *apptd* 1997

ARCHDEACONS
Doncaster, Ven. Steve Wilcockson, *apptd* 2012
Sheffield and Rotherham, Ven. Martyn Snow, *apptd* 2010

Chancellor, Prof. David McClean, *apptd* 1992
Registrar and Legal Secretary, Andrew Vidler
Diocesan Secretary, Malcolm Fair, Church House, 95–99 Effingham Street, Rotherham S65 1BL T 01709-309100

SODOR AND MAN *(YORK)*
81ST BISHOP
Rt. Revd Robert Paterson, *cons.* 2008, *apptd* 2008; The Bishop's House, The Falls, Tromode Road, Douglas, Isle of Man IM4 4PZ
Signs Robert Sodor as Mannin

ARCHDEACON OF MAN
Ven. Andrew Brown, *apptd* 2011
Vicar-General and Chancellor, Clare Faulds
Registrar, Kenneth Gumbley
Diocesan Secretary, Laura Stuart, Keeil Cottage, Clarum Road, Ballaragh, Lonan, Isle of Man IM4 7PL T 01624-861618

SOUTHWARK *(CANTERBURY)*
10TH BISHOP
Rt. Revd Christopher Chessun, *cons.* 2005, *apptd* 2011; Trinity House, 4 Chapel Court, Borough High Street, London SE1 1HW
Signs Christopher Southwark

AREA BISHOPS
Croydon, Rt. Revd Jonathan Clark, *cons.* 2012, *apptd* 2012; St Matthew's House, 100 George Street, London CR0 1PE
Kingston upon Thames, Rt. Revd Dr Richard Cheetham, *cons.* 2002, *apptd* 2002, 620 Kingston Road, Raynes Park, London SW20 8DN
Woolwich, Rt. Revd Dr Michael Ipgrave, OBE, *cons.* 2012, *apptd* 2012; Trinity House, 4 Chapel Court, Borough High Street, London SE1 1HW

DEAN
Very Revd Andrew Nunn, *apptd* 2011

Organist, Peter Wright, FRCO, *apptd* 1989

ARCHDEACONS
Croydon, Ven. Christopher Skilton, *apptd* 2013
Lambeth, Ven. Simon Gates, *apptd* 2013
Lewisham & Greenwich, Ven. Alastair Cutting, *apptd* 2013
Reigate, Ven. Daniel Kajumba, *apptd* 2001
Southwark, Ven. Dr Jane Steen, *apptd* 2013
Wandsworth, Ven. Stephen Roberts, *apptd* 2005

Chancellor, Philip Petchey
Registrar and Legal Secretary, Paul Morris
Diocesan Secretary, Simon Parton, Trinity House, 4 Chapel Court, Borough High Street, London SE1 1HW T 020-7939 9400

SOUTHWELL AND NOTTINGHAM *(YORK)*
11TH BISHOP
Rt. Revd Paul Butler, *cons.* 2004, *apptd* 2009; Bishop's Manor, Southwell NG25 0JR
Signs Paul Southwell and Nottingham

BISHOP SUFFRAGAN
Sherwood, Rt. Revd Anthony Porter, *cons.* 2006, *apptd* 2006; Jubilee House, Westgate, Southwell NG25 0JH

DEAN
Very Revd John Guille, *apptd* 2007

Organist, Paul Hale, *apptd* 1989

ARCHDEACONS
Newark, Ven. David Picken, *apptd* 2012
Nottingham, Ven. Peter Hill, *apptd* 2007

Chancellor, Linda Box, *apptd* 2005
Registrar and Legal Secretary, Amanda Redgate
Chief Executive, Nigel Spraggins, Jubilee House, Westgate, Southwell, Notts NG25 0JH T 01636-814331

TRURO *(CANTERBURY)*
15TH BISHOP
Rt. Revd Tim Thornton, *cons.* 2001, *apptd* 2008; Lis Escop, Truro TR3 6QQ
Signs Tim Truro

BISHOP SUFFRAGAN
St Germans, Rt. Revd Christopher Goldsmith, DPHIL, *cons.* 2013, *apptd* 2013; Vounder, Tresillian, Truro TR2 4BW

DEAN
Very Revd Roger Bush, *apptd* 2012

Organist and Director of Music, Chris Gray, *apptd* 2008

ARCHDEACONS
Bodmin, Ven. Audrey Elkington, *apptd* 2011
Cornwall, Ven. Bill Stuart-White, *apptd* 2012

Chancellor, Timothy Briden, *apptd* 1998
Registrar and Legal Secretary, Martin Follett
Diocesan Secretary, Esther Pollard, Diocesan House, Kenwyn, Truro TR1 1JQ T 01872-274351

WAKEFIELD *(YORK)*
12TH BISHOP
Rt. Revd Stephen Platten, *cons.* 2003, *apptd* 2003; Bishop's Lodge, Woodthorpe Lane, Wakefield WF2 6JL
Signs Stephen Wakefield

BISHOP SUFFRAGAN
Pontefract, Rt. Revd Tony Robinson, *cons.* 2003, *apptd* 2002; Pontefract House, Manygates Lane, Sandal, Wakefield WF2 7DR

DEAN
Very Revd Jonathan Greener, *apptd* 2007

Director of Music, Thomas Moore, *apptd* 2010

ARCHDEACONS
Halifax, Ven. Anne Dawtry, *apptd* 2011
Pontefract, Ven. Peter Townley, *apptd* 2008

Chancellor, His Hon. Judge Downes, *apptd* 2006
Registrars and Legal Secretaries, Julian Gill; Julia Wilding
Diocesan Secretary, Ashley Ellis, Church House, 1 South Parade, Wakefield WF1 1LP T 01924-371802

WORCESTER *(CANTERBURY)*

113TH BISHOP
Rt. Revd Dr John Inge, *cons.* 2003, *apptd* 2007; The Bishop's Office, The Old Palace, Deansway, Worcester WR1 2JE
Signs John Wigorn

SUFFRAGAN BISHOP
Dudley, vacant

DEAN
Very Revd Peter Atkinson, *apptd* 2006

Organist, Dr Peter Nardone, *apptd* 2012

ARCHDEACONS
Dudley, Ven. Fred Trethewey, *apptd* 2001
Worcester, Ven. Roger Morris, *apptd* 2008
Chancellor, Charles Mynors, *apptd* 1999
Registrar and Legal Secretary, Michael Huskinson
Diocesan Secretary, Robert Higham, The Old Palace, Deansway, Worcester WR1 2JE T 01905-20537

ROYAL PECULIARS

WESTMINSTER
The Collegiate Church of St Peter
Dean, Very Revd Dr John Hall
Sub Dean, Revd Canon Dr Robert Reiss
Archdeacon, Ven. Dr Jane Hedges
Chapter Clerk, Receiver-General and Registrar, Sir Stephen Lamport, KCVO, Chapter Office, 20 Dean's Yard, London SW1P 3PA
Organist, James O'Donnell, *apptd* 1999
Legal Secretary, Christopher Vyse, *apptd* 2000

WINDSOR
The Queen's Free Chapel of St George within Her Castle of Windsor
Dean, Rt. Revd David Conner, KCVO, *apptd* 1998
Chapter Clerk, Charlotte Manley, LVO, OBE, *apptd* 2003; Chapter Office, The Cloisters, Windsor Castle, Windsor, Berks SL4 1NJ
Director of Music, James Vivian, *apptd* 2013

OTHER ANGLICAN CHURCHES

THE CHURCH IN WALES

The Anglican Church was the established church in Wales from the 16th century until 1920, when the estrangement of the majority of Welsh people from Anglicanism resulted in disestablishment. Since then the Church in Wales has been an autonomous province consisting of six sees. The bishops are elected by an electoral college comprising elected lay and clerical members, who also elect one of the diocesan bishops as Archbishop of Wales.

The legislative body of the Church in Wales is the Governing Body, which has 144 members divided between the three orders of bishops, clergy and laity. Its president is the Archbishop of Wales and it meets twice annually. Its decisions are binding upon all members of the church. The church's property and finances are the responsibility of the Representative Body. There are 56,396 members of the Church in Wales, with 487 stipendiary clergy and 899 parishes.

THE REPRESENTATIVE BODY OF THE CHURCH IN WALES, 39 Cathedral Road, Cardiff CF11 9XF T 029-2034 8200 *Secretary,* John Shirley
12TH ARCHBISHOP OF WALES, Most Revd Dr Barry Morgan (Bishop of Llandaff), *elected* 2003
Signs Barry Cambrensis

BISHOPS
Bangor (81st), Rt. Revd Andrew John, *b.* 1964, *cons.* 2008, *elected* 2008; Ty'r Esgob, Upper Garth Road, Bangor, Gwynedd LL57 2SS *Signs* Andrew Bangor. *Stipendiary clergy,* 49
Llandaff (102nd), Most Revd Dr Barry Morgan (*also* Archbishop of Wales), *b.* 1947, *cons.* 1993, *trans.* 1999; Llys Esgob, The Cathedral Green, Llandaff, Cardiff CF5 2YE *Signs* Barry Cambrensis. *Stipendiary clergy,* 115
Monmouth (10th), Rt. Revd Richard Pain, *b.* 1956, *cons.* 2013, *elected* 2013; Bishopstown, Stow Hill, Newport NP20 4EA *Signs* Richard Monmouth. *Stipendiary clergy,* 87
St Asaph (76th), Rt. Revd Gregory Cameron, *b.* 1959, *cons.* 2009, *elected* 2009; Esgobty, Upper Denbigh Road, St Asaph, Denbighshire LL17 0TW *Signs* Gregory Llanelwy. *Stipendiary clergy,* 109
St David's (128th), Rt. Revd (John) Wyn Evans, *b.* 1946, *cons.* 2008, *elected* 2008; Llys Esgob, Abergwili, Carmarthen SA31 2JG *Signs* Wyn St Davids. *Stipendiary clergy,* 98
Swansea and Brecon (9th), Rt. Revd John Davies, *b.* 1953, *cons.* 2008, *elected* 2008; Ely Tower, Castle Square, Brecon, Powys LD3 9DJ *Signs* John Swansea & Brecon. *Stipendiary clergy,* 71

The stipend for a diocesan bishop of the Church in Wales is £40,935 a year for 2013–14.

SCOTTISH EPISCOPAL CHURCH

The Scottish Episcopal Church was founded after the Act of Settlement (1690) established the presbyterian nature of the Church of Scotland. The Scottish Episcopal Church is a member of the worldwide Anglican Communion. The governing authority is the General Synod, an elected body of 140 members (70 from the clergy and 70 from the laity) which meets once a year. The bishop who convenes and presides at meetings of the General Synod is called the 'primus' and is elected by his fellow bishops.

There are 34,916 members of the Scottish Episcopal Church, seven bishops, 524 serving clergy and 323 churches and places of worship.

THE GENERAL SYNOD OF THE SCOTTISH EPISCOPAL CHURCH, 21 Grosvenor Crescent, Edinburgh EH12 5EE T 0131-225 6357 W www.scotland.anglican.org
Secretary-General, John Stuart
PRIMUS OF THE SCOTTISH EPISCOPAL CHURCH, Most Revd David Chillingworth (Bishop of St Andrews, Dunkeld and Dunblane), *elected* 2009

BISHOPS
Aberdeen and Orkney, Rt. Revd Dr Bob Gillies, *b.* 1951, *cons.* 2007, *elected* 2007. *Clergy,* 50
Argyll and the Isles, Rt. Revd Kevin Pearson, *b.* 1954, *cons.* 2011, *elected* 2010. *Clergy,* 27
Brechin, Rt. Revd Dr Nigel Peyton, *b.* 1951, *cons.* 2011, *elected* 2011. *Clergy,* 35

Edinburgh, Rt. Revd Dr John Armes, *b.* 1955, *cons.* 2012, *elected* 2012. *Clergy,* 170
Glasgow and Galloway, Rt. Revd Dr Gregor Duncan, *b.* 1950, *cons.* 2010, *elected* 2010. *Clergy,* 113
Moray, Ross and Caithness, Rt. Revd Mark Strange, *b.* 1961, *cons.* 2007, *elected* 2007. *Clergy,* 56
St Andrews, Dunkeld and Dunblane, Most Revd David Chillingworth, *b.* 1951, *cons.* 2005, *elected* 2005. *Clergy,* 89

The minimum stipend of a diocesan bishop of the Scottish Episcopal Church for 2013 is £35,610 (ie 1.5 times the standard clergy stipend of £23,740).

CHURCH OF IRELAND

The Anglican Church was the established church in Ireland from the 16th century but never secured the allegiance of the majority and was disestablished in 1871. The Church of Ireland is divided into the provinces of Armagh and Dublin, each under an archbishop. The provinces are subdivided into 12 dioceses.

The legislative body is the General Synod, which has 660 members in total, divided between the House of Bishops (12 members) and the House of Representatives (216 clergy and 432 laity). The Archbishop of Armagh is elected by the House of Bishops; other episcopal elections are made by an electoral college.

There are 383,186 members of the Church of Ireland, 248,821 in Northern Ireland and 134,365 in the Republic of Ireland. There are two archbishops, ten bishops and 476 stipendiary clergy.

CENTRAL OFFICE, Church of Ireland House, Church Avenue, Rathmines, Dublin 6 T (+353) (1) 497 8422
Chief Officer and Secretary of the Representative Church Body, Adrian Clements

PROVINCE OF ARMAGH

Archbishop of Armagh, Primate of all Ireland and Metropolitan, Most Revd Richard Clarke, PHD, *b.* 1949, *cons.* 1996, *trans.* 2012. *Clergy,* 49

BISHOPS

Clogher, Rt. Revd John McDowell, *b.* 1956, *cons.* 2011, *apptd* 2011. *Clergy,* 31
Connor, Rt. Revd Alan Abernethy, *b.* 1957, *cons.* 2007, *apptd* 2007. *Clergy,* 96
Derry and Raphoe, Rt. Revd Kenneth Good, *b.* 1952, *cons.* 2002, *apptd* 2002. *Clergy,* 53
Down and Dromore, Rt. Revd Harold Miller, *b.* 1950, *cons.* 1997, *apptd* 1997. *Clergy,* 91
Kilmore, Elphin and Ardagh, Rt. Revd Ferran Glenfield, *b.* 1954, *cons.* 2013, *apptd* 2013. *Clergy,* 20
Tuam, Killala and Achonry, Rt. Revd Patrick Rooke, *b.* 1955, *cons.* 2011, *apptd* 2011. *Clergy,* 11

PROVINCE OF DUBLIN

Archbishop of Dublin, Bishop of Glendalough, Primate of Ireland and Metropolitan, Most Revd Michael Jackson, PHD, DPHIL, *b.* 1956, *apptd* 2011. *Clergy,* 82

BISHOPS

Cashel and Ossory, Rt. Revd Michael Burrows, *b.* 1961, *cons.* 2006, *apptd* 2006. *Clergy,* 42
Cork, Cloyne and Ross, Rt. Revd Paul Colton, PHD, *b.* 1960, *cons.* 1999, *apptd* 1999. *Clergy,* 34
Limerick and Killaloe, Rt. Revd Trevor W4lliams, *b.* 1948, *cons.* 2008, *apptd* 2008. *Clergy,* 19
Meath and Kildare, vacant. *Clergy,* 18

OVERSEAS

PRIMATES

Primate and Presiding Bishop of Aotearoa, New Zealand and Polynesia, Most Revd William Turei
Primate of Australia, Most Revd Phillip Aspinall
Primate of Brazil, Most Revd Maurício Araújo de Andrade
Archbishop of the Province of Burundi, Most Revd Bernard Ntahoturi
Archbishop and Primate of Canada, Most Revd Frederick Hiltz
Archbishop of the Province of Central Africa, Most Revd Albert Chama
Primate of the Central Region of America, Most Revd Armando Soria
Archbishop of the Province of Congo, Most Revd Henry Isingoma
Primate of the Province of Hong Kong Sheng Kung Hui, Most Revd Dr Paul Kwong
Archbishop of the Province of the Indian Ocean, Most Revd Ian Ernest
Primate of Japan (Nippon Sei Ko Kai), Most Revd Nathaniel Uematsu
President-Bishop of Jerusalem and the Middle East, Most Revd Dr Mouneer Anis
Archbishop of the Province of Kenya, Most Revd Eliud Wabukala
Archbishop of the Province of Korea, Most Revd Paul Kim
Archbishop of the Province of Melanesia, Most Revd David Vunagi
Archbishop of Mexico, Most Revd Carlos Touche-Porter
Archbishop of the Province of Myanmar (Burma), Most Revd Stephen Oo
Archbishop of the Province of Nigeria, Most Revd Nicholas Okoh
Archbishop of Papua New Guinea, vacant
Prime Bishop of the Philippines, Most Revd Edward Malecdan
Archbishop of the Province of Rwanda, Most Revd Onesphore Rwaje
Primate of the Province of South East Asia, Most Revd Bolly Lapok
Metropolitan of the Province of Southern Africa, Most Revd Thabo Makgoba
Presiding Bishop of the Southern Cone of America, Most Revd Hector Muñoz
Archbishop of the Province of the Sudan, Most Revd Daniel Yak
Archbishop of the Province of Tanzania, Most Revd Jacob Chimeledya
Archbishop of the Province of Uganda, Most Revd Stanley Ntagali
Presiding Bishop and Primate of the USA, Most Revd Katharine Schori
Archbishop of the Province of West Africa, Most Revd Dr Solomon Johnson
Archbishop of the Province of the West Indies, Most Revd Dr John Holder

OTHER CHURCHES AND EXTRA-PROVINCIAL DIOCESES

Anglican Church of Bermuda, extra-provincial to Canterbury
Bishop, Rt. Revd Nicholas Dill
Church of Ceylon, extra-provincial to Canterbury
Bishop of Colombo, Rt. Revd Dhiloraj Canagasabey
Bishop of Kurunagala, Rt. Revd Greg Francis
Episcopal Church of Cuba, Rt. Revd Griselda Del Carpio
Falkland Islands, extra-provincial to Canterbury
Bishop, Rt. Revd Stephen Venner (Bishop to the Forces)

Lusitanian Church (Portuguese Episcopal Church), extra-provincial to Canterbury
Bishop, Rt. Revd Jose Cabral
Reformed Episcopal Church of Spain, extra-provincial to Canterbury
Bishop, Rt. Revd Carlos López-Lozano

MODERATION OF CHURCHES IN FULL COMMUNION WITH THE ANGLICAN COMMUNION
Church of Bangladesh, Most Revd Paul Sarkar
Church of North India, Most Revd Philip Marandih
Church of South India, Most Revd Gnanasigamony Devakadasham
Church of Pakistan, Most Revd Samuel Azariah

CHURCH OF SCOTLAND

The Church of Scotland is the national church of Scotland. The church is reformed in doctrine, and presbyterian in constitution; ie based on a hierarchy of courts of ministers and elders and, since 1990, of members of a diaconate. At local level the Kirk Session consists of the parish minister and ruling elders. At district level the presbyteries, of which there are 44 in Britain, consist of all the ministers in the district, one ruling elder from each congregation, and those members of the diaconate who qualify for membership. The General Assembly is the supreme authority, and is presided over by a Moderator chosen annually by the Assembly. The sovereign, if not present in person, is represented by a Lord High Commissioner who is appointed each year by the Crown.

The Church of Scotland has around 400,000 members and 800 parish ministers. The majority of parishes are in Scotland, but there are also churches in England, Europe and overseas.

Lord High Commissioner (2013–14), Rt. Hon. Lord Selkirk of Douglas, QC
Moderator of the General Assembly (2013–14), Rt. Revd Lorna Hood
Principal Clerk, Revd John Chalmers
Depute Clerk, Revd Dr George Whyte
Procurator, Laura Dunlop, QC
Law Agent and Solicitor of the Church, Janette Wilson
Parliamentary Officer, Chloe Clemmons
General Treasurer, Iain Grimmond
Secretary, Church and Society Council, Revd Ewan Aitken
CHURCH OFFICE, 121 George Street, Edinburgh EH2 4YN
T 0131-225 5722

PRESBYTERIES AND CLERKS
Aberdeen, Revd George Cowie; Revd John Ferguson
Abernethy, Catherine Buchan
Angus, Revd Mike Goss
Annandale and Eskdale, Revd Bryan Haston
Ardrossan, Revd Alan Saunderson
Argyll, Ian MacLagan
Ayr, Revd Kenneth Elliott
Buchan, George Berstan
Caithness, Revd Ronald Johnstone
Dumbarton, Revd David Clark
Dumfries and Kirkcudbright, Revd William Hogg
Dundee, Revd James Wilson
Dunfermline, Revd Elizabeth Kenny
Dunkeld and Meigle, Revd John Russell
Duns, Helen Longmuir
Edinburgh, Revd Dr George Whyte
England, Revd Alistair Cumming
Europe, Revd John Cowie
Falkirk, Revd Robert Allan
Glasgow, Very Revd William Hewitt
Gordon, Revd Euan Glen
Greenock and Paisley, Revd Dr Peter McEnhill
Hamilton, Revd Shaw Paterson
Inverness, Revd Reginald Campbell
Irvine and Kilmarnock, Steuart Dey
Jedburgh, Revd W. Frank Campbell
Kincardine and Deeside, Revd Hugh Conkey
Kirkcaldy, Revd Rosemary Frew
Lanark, Revd Helen Jamieson
Lewis, Revd Thomas Sinclair
Lochaber, Ella Gill
Lochcarron-Skye, Revd Allan Macarthur
Lothian, John McCulloch
Melrose and Peebles, Revd Victoria Linford
Moray, Revd Hugh Smith
Orkney, Revd James Wishart
Perth, Revd Alan Reid
Ross, Ronald Gunstone
St Andrews, Revd James Redpath
Shetland, Revd Charles Greig
Stirling, Revd Alex Millar
Sutherland, Mary Stobo
Uist, Wilson McKinlay
West Lothian, Revd Duncan Shaw
Wigtown and Stranraer, vacant

The stipends for ministers in the Church of Scotland in 2013 range from £25,253–£31,035, depending on length of service.

ROMAN CATHOLIC CHURCH

The Roman Catholic Church is a worldwide Christian church acknowledging as its head the Bishop of Rome, known as the Pope (father). Despite its widespread usage, 'Pope' is actually an unofficial term. The *Annuario Pontificio,* (Pontifical Yearbook) lists eight official titles: Bishop of Rome, Vicar of Jesus Christ, Successor of the Prince of the Apostles, Supreme Pontiff of the Universal Church, Primate of Italy, Archbishop and Metropolitan of the Roman Province, Sovereign of the State of the Vatican City and Servant of the Servants of God.

The Pope leads a communion of followers of Christ, who believe they continue His presence in the world as servants of faith, hope and love to all society. The Pope is held to be the successor of St Peter and thus invested with the power which was entrusted to St Peter by Jesus Christ. A direct line of succession is therefore claimed from the earliest Christian communities. With the fall of the Roman Empire the Pope also became an important political leader. His territory is now limited to the 0.44 sq. km (0.17 sq. miles) of the Vatican City State, created to provide some independence to the Pope from Italy and other nations. The episcopal jurisdiction of the Roman Catholic Church is called the Holy See.

The Pope exercises spiritual authority over the church with the advice and assistance of the Sacred College of Cardinals, the supreme council of the church. The number of cardinals was fixed at 70 by Pope Sixtus V in 1586 but has increased steadily since the pontificate of John XXIII. On 28 February 2013, the date of Pope Benedict XVI's resignation, there were 207 cardinals.

Following the death or resignation of the Pope, the members of the College of Cardinals under the age of 80 are called to the Vatican to elect a successor. They are known as cardinal electors and form an assembly called the conclave. The conclave, which comprised 115 cardinal electors when it convened in March 2013, conducts a secret ballot in complete seclusion to elect the next Pope. A two-thirds majority is necessary before the vote can be accepted as final. When a cardinal receives the necessary number of votes, the Dean of the Sacred College formally asks him if he will accept election and the name by which he wishes to be known. On his acceptance of the office of Supreme Pontiff, the conclave is dissolved and the first Cardinal Deacon announces the election to the assembled crowd in St Peter's Square.

The Pope has full legislative, judicial and administrative power over the whole Roman Catholic Church. He is aided in his administration by the curia, which is made up of a number of departments. The Secretariat of State is the central office for carrying out the Pope's instructions and is presided over by the Cardinal Secretary of State. It maintains relations with the departments of the curia, with the episcopate, with the representatives of the Holy See in various countries, governments and private persons. The congregations and pontifical councils are the Pope's ministries and include departments such as the Congregation for the Doctrine of Faith, whose field of competence concerns faith and morals; the Congregation for the Clergy and the Congregation for the Evangelisation of Peoples, the Pontifical Council for the Family and the Pontifical Council for the Promotion of Christian Unity.

The Holy See, composed of the Pope and those who help him in his mission for the church, is recognised by the Conventions of Vienna as an international moral body. Apostolic nuncios are the Pope's diplomatic representatives; in countries where no formal diplomatic relations exist between the Holy See and that country, the papal representative is known as an apostolic delegate.

According to the 2013 Pontifical Yearbook the number of Roman Catholics worldwide was 1.214 billion in 2011; the number of bishops was 5,143 and there were 413,318 priests.

SUPREME PONTIFF

His Holiness Pope Francis (Jorge Mario Bergoglio), *born* Buenos Aires, Argentina, 17 December 1936; *ordained priest* 13 December 1969; *appointed Archbishop* (of Buenos Aires), 28 February 1998; *created Cardinal* 21 February 2001; *assumed pontificate* 13 March 2013

PONTIFF EMERITUS

His Holiness Pope Benedict XVI (Joseph Ratzinger), *born* Bavaria, Germany, 16 April 1927; *ordained priest* 29 June 1951; *appointed Archbishop* (of Munich), 24 March 1977; *created Cardinal* 27 June 1977; *assumed pontificate* 19 April 2005; *resigned pontificate* 28 February 2013

SECRETARIAT OF STATE

Secretary of State, Most Revd Pietro Parolin
First Section (General Affairs), Most Revd Giovanni Angelo Becciu (Titular Archbishop of Roselle)
Second Section (Relations with Other States), Most Revd Dominique Mamberti (Titular Archbishop of Sagona)

BISHOPS' CONFERENCE

The Catholic Bishops' Conference of England and Wales is the permanent assembly of Catholic Bishops and Ordinaries in the two member countries. The membership of the Conference comprises the Archbishops, Bishops and Auxiliary Bishops of the 22 Dioceses within England and Wales, the Bishop of the Forces (Military Ordinariate), the Eparch of the Ukrainian Catholic Eparchy of the Holy Family of London (Great Britain), the Ordinary of the Personal Ordinariate of Our Lady of Walsingham, and the Apostolic Prefect of the Falkland Islands. The Conference is headed by a president and vice-president. There are six departments, each with an episcopal chair: Education and Formation, Christian Life and Worship, Christian Responsibility and Citizenship, Dialogue and Unity, Evangelisation and Catechesis, and International Affairs.

The Bishops' Conference Standing Committee is made up of two directly elected bishops in addition to the Metropolitan Archbishops and chairs from each of the above departments. The committee has general responsibility for continuity of policy between the plenary sessions of the conference, preparing the conference agenda and implementing its decisions.

The administration of the Bishops' Conference is funded by a levy on each diocese, according to income. A general secretariat in London coordinates and supervises the Bishops' Conference administration activities. There are also other agencies and consultative bodies affiliated to the conference.

The Bishops' Conference of Scotland is the permanently constituted assembly of the bishops of Scotland. The conference is headed by the president (Most Revd Philip Tartaglia, Archbishop of Glasgow). The conference establishes various agencies which perform advisory functions in relation to the conference. The more important of these agencies are called commissions; each one is headed by a bishop president who, with the other members of the commissions, are appointed by the conference.

The Irish Catholic Bishops' Conference (also known as the Irish Episcopal Conference) has as its president Cardinal Seán Brady of Armagh. Its membership comprises all the archbishops and bishops of Ireland. It appoints various commissions and agencies to assist with the work of the Catholic Church in Ireland.

The Catholic Church in the UK has over 900,000 mass attendees, 5,500 priests and 4,550 churches.

Bishops' Conferences secretariats:

ENGLAND AND WALES, 39 Eccleston Square, London SW1V 1BX T 020-7630 8220 E secretariat@cbcew.org.uk W www.catholicchurch.org.uk
General Secretary, Mgr Marcus Stock

SCOTLAND, 64 Aitken Street, Airdrie ML6 6LT T 01236-764061 W www.bpsconfscot.com
General Secretary, Mgr Hugh Bradley

IRELAND, Columba Centre, Maynooth, County Kildare T (+353) (1) 505 3000 E info@catholicbishops.ie W www.catholicbishops.ie
Secretary, Most Revd Kieran O'Reilly (Bishop of Killaloe)
Executive Secretary, Revd Gearoid Dullea

GREAT BRITAIN

APOSTOLIC NUNCIO TO GREAT BRITAIN

Most Revd Antonio Mennini, 54 Parkside, London SW19 5NE T 020-8944 7189

ENGLAND AND WALES

THE MOST REVD ARCHBISHOPS

Westminster, Vincent Nichols, *cons.* 1992, *apptd* 2009
Archbishop Emeritus, Cardinal Cormac Murphy-O'Connor, *cons.* 1977, *elevated* 2001 *Auxiliaries,* Alan Hopes, *cons.* 2003; John Arnold, *cons.* 2006; John Sherrington, *cons* 2011. *Clergy,* 318. *Archbishop's House,* Ambrosden Avenue, London SW1P 1QJ T 020-7798 9033

Birmingham, Bernard Longley, *cons.* 2003, *apptd* 2009
Auxiliaries, William Kenney, *cons.* 1987; Philip Pargeter (retd), *cons.* 1990; David McGough, *cons.* 2005. *Clergy,* 430. *Archbishop's House,* 8 Shadwell Street, Birmingham B4 6EY T 0121-236 9090

Cardiff, George Stack, *cons.* 2001, *apptd* 2011. *Clergy,* 47. *Archbishop's House,* 41–43 Cathedral Road, Cardiff CF11 9HD T 029-2022 0411

Liverpool, vacant *Auxiliary,* Thomas Williams, *cons.* 2003. *Clergy,* 419. *Liverpool Archdiocesan Centre for Evangelisation,* Croxteth Drive, Sefton Park, Liverpool L17 1AA T 0151-522 1000

Southwark, Peter Smith, *cons.* 1995, *apptd* 2010 *Auxiliaries,* John Hine, *cons.* 2001; Patrick Lynch, *cons.* 2006; Paul Hendricks, *cons.* 2006. *Clergy,* 433. *Archbishop's House,* 150 St George's Road, London SE1 6HX T 020-7928 2495

THE RT. REVD BISHOPS

Arundel and Brighton, Kieran Conry, *cons.* 2001, *apptd* 2001. *Clergy,* 96. *Bishop's House,* The Upper Drive, Hove, E. Sussex BN3 6NB T 01273-506387

Brentwood, Thomas McMahon, *cons.* 1980, *apptd* 1980. *Clergy,* 170. *Bishop's Office,* Cathedral House, Ingrave Road, Brentwood, Essex CM15 8AT T 01277-232266

Clifton, Declan Lang, *cons.* 2001, *apptd* 2001. *Clergy,* 153. *Bishop's House,* St Ambrose, North Road, Leigh Woods, Bristol BS8 3PW T 0117-973 3072

East Anglia, Alan Hopes, *cons.* 2003, *apptd* 2013. *Clergy,* 129. *Diocesan Curia,* The White House, 21 Upgate, Poringland, Norwich NR14 7SH T 01508-492202

Hallam, John Rawsthorne, *cons.* 1981, *apptd* 1997. *Clergy,* 71. *Bishop's House,* 75 Norfolk Road, Sheffield S2 2SZ T 0114-278 7988

Hexham and Newcastle, Seamus Cunningham, *cons.* 2009, *apptd* 2009. *Clergy,* 164. *Bishop's House,* East Denton Hall, 800 West Road, Newcastle upon Tyne NE5 2BJ T 0191-228 0003

Lancaster, Michael Campbell, *cons.* 2008, *apptd* 2009. *Clergy,* 97. *Bishop's Office,* The Pastoral Centre, Balmoral Road, Lancaster LA1 3BT T 01524-596050

Leeds, vacant. *Clergy,* 193. *Diocesan Curia,* Hinsley Hall, 62 Headingley Lane, Leeds LS6 2BX T 0113-261 8022

Menevia (Wales), Thomas Burns, *cons.* 2002, *apptd* 2008. *Clergy,* 60. *Diocesan Curia,* 27 Convent Street, Swansea SA1 2BX T 01792-644017

Middlesbrough, Terence Drainey, *cons.* 2008, *apptd* 2007. *Clergy,* 83. *Diocesan Curia,* 50A The Avenue, Linthorpe, Middlesbrough TS5 6QT T 01642-850505

Northampton, Peter Doyle, *cons.* 2005, *apptd* 2005. *Clergy,* 116. *Bishop's House,* Marriott Street, Northampton NN2 6AW T 01604-715635

Nottingham, Malcolm McMahon, *cons.* 2000, *apptd* 2000. *Clergy,* 166. *Bishop's House,* 27 Cavendish Road East, The Park, Nottingham NG7 1BB T 0115-947 4786

Plymouth, Christopher Budd, *cons.* 1986, *apptd* 1985. *Clergy,* 75. *Bishop's House,* 31 Wyndham Street West, Plymouth PL1 5RZ T 01752-224414

Portsmouth, Philip Egan, *cons.* 2012, *apptd* 2012. *Clergy,* 274. *Bishop's House,* Bishop Crispian Way, Portsmouth, Hants PO1 3HG T 023-9282 0894

Salford, Terence Brain, *cons.* 1991, *apptd* 1997. *Clergy,* 244. *Diocesan Curia,* Wardley Hall, Worsley, Manchester M28 2ND T 0161-794 2825

Shrewsbury, Mark Davies, *cons.* 2010, *apptd* 2010. *Clergy* 119. *Diocesan Curia,* 2 Park Road South, Prenton, Wirral CH43 4UX T 0151-652 9855

Wrexham (Wales), Peter Brignall, *cons.* 2012, *apptd* 2012. *Clergy,* 19. *Bishop's House,* Sontley Road, Wrexham LL13 7EW T 01978-262726

SCOTLAND

THE MOST REVD ARCHBISHOPS

St Andrews and Edinburgh, Leo Cushley, *cons.* 1985, *elevated* 2013. *Apostolic Administrator,* Most Revd Philip Tartaglia (Archbishop of Glasgow), *apptd* 2013. *Archbishop Emeritus,* HE Cardinal Keith Patrick O'Brien, *cons.* 1985, *elevated* 2003. *Clergy,* 91. *Diocesan Office,* 100 Strathearn Road, Edinburgh EH9 1BB T 0131-623 8900

Glasgow, Philip Tartaglia, *cons.* 2005, *elevated* 2012. *Clergy,* 206. *Diocesan Curia,* 196 Clyde Street, Glasgow G1 4JY T 0141-226 5898

THE RT. REVD BISHOPS

Aberdeen, Hugh Gilbert, *cons.* 2011, *apptd* 2011. *Clergy,* 47. *Bishop's House,* 3 Queen's Cross, Aberdeen AB15 4XU T 01224-319154

Argyll and the Isles, Joseph Toal, *cons.* 2008, *apptd* 2008. *Clergy,* 32. *Bishop's House,* Esplanade, Oban, Argyll PA34 5AB T 01631-567436

Dunkeld, vacant. *Clergy,* 43. *Diocesan Curia,* 24–28 Lawside Road, Dundee DD3 6XY T 01382-225453

Galloway, John Cunningham, *cons.* 2004, *apptd* 2004. *Clergy,* 19. *Diocesan Office,* 8 Corsehill Road, Ayr KA7 2ST T 01292-266750

Motherwell, Joseph Devine, *cons.* 1977, *apptd* 1983. *Clergy,* 123. *Diocesan Curia,* Coursington Road, Motherwell ML1 1PP T 01698-269114

Paisley, vacant. *Clergy,* 75. *Diocesan Curia,* Cathedral Precincts, Incle Street, Paisley PA1 1HR T 0141-847 6131

BISHOPRIC OF THE FORCES

Rt. Revd Richard Moth, *cons.* 2009, *apptd* 2009. *Administration,* RC Bishopric of the Forces, Wellington House, St Omer Barracks, Thornhill Road, Aldershot, Hants GU11 2BG T 01252-348234

IRELAND

There is one hierarchy for the whole of Ireland. Several of the dioceses have territory partly in the Republic of Ireland and partly in Northern Ireland.

APOSTOLIC NUNCIO TO IRELAND

Most Revd Charles John Brown (Titular Archbishop of Aquileia), 183 Navan Road, Dublin 7 T (+353) (1) 838 0577

THE MOST REVD ARCHBISHOPS

Armagh, Cardinal Sean Brady (*also* Primate of all Ireland), *cons.* 1995, *apptd* 1996, *created Cardinal* 2007. *Coadjutor Archbishop,* Most Revd Eamon Martin, *cons.* 2013. *Clergy,* 156. *Bishop's Residence,* Ara Coeli, Cathedral Road, Armagh BT61 7QY T 028-3752 2045

Cashel and Emly, Dermot Clifford, *cons.* 1986, *apptd* 1988. *Clergy,* 83. *Archbishop's House,* Thurles, Co. Tipperary T (+353) (504) 21512

Dublin, Diarmuid Martin, *cons.* 1999, *apptd Coadjutor Archbishop* 2003, *succeeded as Archbishop* 2004. *Archbishop Emeritus,* HE Cardinal Desmond Connell, *cons.* 1988, *elevated* 2001. *Auxiliaries,* Raymond Field, *cons.* 1997; Eamonn Walsh, *cons.* 1990. *Clergy,* 529. *Archbishop's House,* Drumcondra, Dublin 9 T (+353) (1) 837 9253

Tuam, Dr Michael Neary, *cons.* 1992, *apptd* 1995. *Clergy,* 110. *Archbishop's House,* Tuam, Co. Galway T (+353) (93) 24166

THE MOST REVD BISHOPS

Achonry, Brendan Kelly, *cons.* 2008, *apptd* 2007. *Clergy,* 53. *Bishop's House,* Edmondstown, Ballaghaderreen, Co. Roscommon T (+353) (94) 986 0021

Ardagh and Clonmacnois, Colm O'Reilly, *cons.* 1983, *apptd* 1983. *Clergy,* 61. *Diocesan Office,* St Michael's, Ballinalee Road, Longford, Co. Longford T (+353) (43) 46432

Clogher, Liam MacDaid, *cons.* 2010, *apptd* 2010. *Clergy,* 74. *Bishop's House,* Monaghan T (+353) (47) 81019

Clonfert, John Kirby, *cons.* 1988, *apptd* 1988. *Clergy,* 37. *Bishop's House,* Coorheen, Loughrea, Co. Galway T (+353) (91) 841560

Cloyne, William Crean, *cons.* 2013, *apptd* 2013. *Clergy,* 126. *Diocesan Office,* Cobh, Co. Cork T (+353) (21) 481 1430

Cork and Ross, John Buckley, *cons.* 1984, *apptd* 1998. *Clergy,* 133. *Diocesan Office,* Cork and Ross Offices, Redemption Road, Cork T (+353) (21) 430 1717

Derry, vacant. *Clergy,* 108. *Bishop's House,* St Eugene's Cathedral, Derry BT48 9YG T 028-7126 2302

Down and Connor, Noel Treanor, *cons.* 2008, *apptd* 2008. *Auxiliaries,* Anthony Farquhar, *cons.* 1983; Donal McKeown, *cons.* 2001. *Clergy,* 209. *Bishop's Residence,* Lisbreen, 73 Somerton Road, Belfast, Co. Antrim BT15 4DE T 028-9077 6185

Dromore, John McAreavey, *cons.* 1999, *apptd* 1999. *Clergy,* 33. *Bishop's House,* 44 Armagh Road, Newry, Co. Down BT35 6PN T 028-3026 2444

Elphin, Christopher Jones, *cons.* 1994, *apptd* 1994. *Clergy,* 66. *Bishop's House,* St Mary's, Sligo T (+353) (71) 916 2670

Ferns, Denis Brennan, *cons.* 2006, *apptd* 2006. *Clergy,* 88. *Bishop's House,* Summerhill, Wexford T (+353) (53) 912 2177

Galway, Kilmacduagh and Kilfenora, Martin Drennan, *cons.* 1997, *apptd* 2005. *Clergy,* 57. *Diocesan Office,* The Cathedral, Galway T (+353) (91) 563566

Kerry, William Murphy, *cons.* 1995, *apptd* 1995. *Clergy,* 88. *Bishop's House,* Killarney, Co. Kerry T (+353) (64) 663 1168

Kildare and Leighlin, Denis Nulty, *cons.* 2013, *apptd* 2013. *Clergy,* 72. *Bishop's House,* Carlow T (+353) (59) 917 6725

Killala, John Fleming, *cons.* 2002, *apptd* 2002. *Clergy,* 49. *Bishop's House,* Ballina, Co. Mayo T (+353) (96) 21518

Killaloe, Dr Kieran O'Reilly, *cons.* 2010, *apptd* 2010. *Clergy,* 97. *Diocesan Office,* Westbourne, Ennis, Co. Clare T (+353) (65) 682 8638

Kilmore, Leo O'Reilly, *cons.* 1997, *apptd* 1998. *Clergy,* 67. *Bishop's House,* Cullies, Co. Cavan T (+353) (49) 433 1496

Limerick, Brendan Leahy, *cons.* 2013, *apptd* 2013. *Clergy,* 109. *Diocesan Office,* Social Service Centre, Henry Street, Limerick T (+353) (61) 315856

Meath, Michael Smith, *cons.* 1984, *apptd* 1990. *Clergy,* 131. *Bishop's House,* Dublin Road, Mullingar, Co. Westmeath T (+353) (44) 934 8841

Ossory, Seamus Freeman, *cons.* 2007, *apptd* 2007. *Clergy,* 81. *Diocesan Office,* James's Street, Kilkenny T (+353) (56) 776 2448

Raphoe, Dr Philip Boyce, *cons.* 1995, *apptd* 1995. *Clergy,* 80. *Bishop's House,* Ard Adhamhnáin, Letterkenny, Co. Donegal T (+353) (74) 912 1208

Waterford and Lismore, William Lee, *cons.* 1993, *apptd* 1993. *Clergy,* 114. *Bishop's House,* John's Hill, Waterford T (+353) (51) 874463

OTHER CHURCHES IN THE UK

ASSOCIATED PRESBYTERIAN CHURCHES OF SCOTLAND

The Associated Presbyterian Churches came into being in 1989 as a result of a division within the Free Presbyterian Church of Scotland. The Associated Presbyterian Churches is reformed and evangelistic in nature and emphasises the importance of doctrine based primarily on the Bible and secondly on the Westminster Confession of Faith. There are an estimated 500 members, 9 ministers and 12 congregations in Scotland. There are also congregations in Canada.

ASSOCIATED PRESBYTERIAN CHURCHES OF SCOTLAND, APC Manse, Polvinster Road, Oban PA34 5TN T 01631-567076 W www.apchurches.org
Moderator of Presbytery, Hugh McKenzie
Clerk of Presbytery, Revd Archibald McPhail

BAPTIST CHURCH

Baptists trace their origins to John Smyth, who in 1609 in Amsterdam reinstituted the baptism of conscious believers as the basis of the fellowship of a gathered church. Members of Smyth's church established the first Baptist church in England in 1612. They came to be known as 'General' Baptists and their theology was Arminian, whereas a later group of Calvinists who adopted the baptism of believers came to be known as 'Particular' Baptists. The two sections of the Baptists were united into one body, the Baptist Union of Great Britain and Ireland, in 1891. In 1988 the title was changed to the Baptist Union of Great Britain.

Baptists emphasise the complete autonomy of the local church, although individual churches are linked in various kinds of associations. There are international bodies (such as the Baptist World Alliance) and national bodies, but some Baptist churches belong to neither. However, in Great Britain the majority of churches and associations belong to the Baptist Union of Great Britain. There are also Baptist Unions in Wales, Scotland and Ireland, which are much smaller than the Baptist Union of Great Britain, and there is some overlap of membership.

There are currently around 135,000 members, 2,500 ministers and 2,084 churches associated with the Baptist Union of Great Britain. The Baptist Union of Great Britain is one of the founder members of the European Baptist Federation (1948) and the Baptist World Alliance (1905); the latter represents 42 million members worldwide.

In the Baptist Union of Wales (Undeb Bedyddwyr Cymru) there are 12,423 members, 99 pastors and 406 churches, including those in England.

In the Baptist Union of Scotland there are 11,700 members, 163 pastors and 167 churches.

BAPTIST UNION OF GREAT BRITAIN, Baptist House, PO Box 44, 129 Broadway, Didcot, Oxon OX11 8RT T 01235-517700 E info@baptist.org.uk W www.baptist.org.uk
President (2013–14), Revd Ernie Whalley
General Secretary, Revd Lynn Green

BAPTIST UNION OF WALES, Y Llwyfan, College Road, Carmarthen SA31 3EQ T 01267-245660 E peter@bedyddwyrcymru.co.uk W www.buw.org.uk
President of the English Assembly (2013–14), Clive Sheridan
President of the Welsh Assembly (2013–14), Revd Eirian Wyn
General Secretary of the Baptist Union of Wales, Revd Peter Thomas

BAPTIST UNION OF SCOTLAND, 48 Speirs Wharf, Glasgow G4 9TH T 0141-423 6169 E admin@scottishbaptist.org.uk
General Director, Revd A. Donaldson

THE BRETHREN

The Brethren was founded in Dublin in 1827–8, basing itself on the structures and practices of the early church and rejecting denominationalism and clericalism. Many groups sprang up; the group at Plymouth became the best known, resulting in its designation by others as the 'Plymouth Brethren'. Early worship had a prescribed form but quickly assumed an unstructured, non-liturgical format.

There are services devoted to worship, usually involving the breaking of bread, and separate preaching meetings. There is no salaried ministry.

A theological dispute led in 1848 to schism between the Open Brethren and the Closed or Exclusive Brethren, each branch later suffering further divisions.

Open Brethren churches are run by appointed elders and are completely independent, but freely cooperate with each other. Exclusive Brethren churches believe in a universal fellowship between congregations. They do not have appointed elders, but use respected members of their congregation to perform certain administrative functions.

The Brethren are established throughout the UK, Ireland, Europe, India, Africa and Australasia. In the UK there are over 70,000 members, 1,250 assembly halls and over 200 full-time Bible teachers, evangelists and administrators. There are a number of publishing houses that publish Brethren-related literature. Chapter Two is the main supplier of such literature in the UK; it also has a Brethren history archive which is available for use by appointment.

CHAPTER TWO, Conduit Mews, London SE18 7AP
T 020-8316 5389 E info@chaptertwobooks.org.uk
W www.chaptertwobooks.org.uk

CONGREGATIONAL FEDERATION

The Congregational Federation was founded by members of Congregational churches in England and Wales who did not join the United Reformed Church in 1972. There are also churches in Scotland and France affiliated to the federation. The federation exists to encourage congregations of believers to worship in free assembly, but it has no authority over them and emphasises their right to independence and self-governance.

The federation has 7,737 members, 185 accredited ministers and 272 churches in England, Wales and Scotland.

CONGREGATIONAL FEDERATION, 6 Castle Gate, Nottingham NG1 7AS T 0115-911 1460
E admin@congregational.org.uk W www.congregational.org.uk
President of the Federation (2013–14), Margaret Morris
General Secretary, Revd M. Heaney

FELLOWSHIP OF INDEPENDENT EVANGELICAL CHURCHES

The Fellowship of Independent Evangelical Churches (FIEC) was founded by Revd E. J. Poole-Connor (1872–1962) in 1922. In 1923 the fellowship published its first register of non-denominational pastors, evangelists and congregations who had accepted the doctrinal basis for the fellowship.

Members of the fellowship have two primary convictions: firstly to defend the evangelical faith, and secondly that evangelicalism is the bond that unites the fellowship, rather than forms of worship or church government.

The FIEC exists to promote the welfare of non-denominational Bible churches and to give expression to the fundamental doctrines of evangelical Christianity. It supports individual churches by gathering and disseminating information and resources and advising churches on current theological, moral, social and practical issues.

More than 500 churches throughout the UK are linked through the fellowship.

FELLOWSHIP OF INDEPENDENT EVANGELICAL CHURCHES, 39 The Point, Market Harborough, Leics LE16 7QU T 01858-434540 E admin@fiec.org.uk
W www.fiec.org.uk
National Director, John Stevens

FREE CHURCH OF ENGLAND

The Free Church of England, otherwise called the Reformed Episcopal Church, is an independent church, constituted according to the historic faith, tradition and practice of the Church of England. Its roots lie in the 18th century, but it started to grow significantly from the 1840s onwards, as clergy and congregations joined it from the established church in protest against the Oxford Movement. The historic episcopate was conferred on the English church in 1876 through bishops of the Reformed Episcopal Church (which had broken away from the Protestant Episcopal Church in the USA in 1873). A branch of the Reformed Episcopal Church was founded in the UK and this merged with the Free Church of England in 1927 to create the present church.

Worship is according to the *Book of Common Prayer* and some modern liturgy is permissable. Only men are ordained to the orders of deacon, presbyter and bishop.

The Free Church of England has 23 ministers, 17 congregations and around 900 members, now mainly confined to England with one congregation in St Petersburg, Russia.

THE FREE CHURCH OF ENGLAND, 329 Wolverhampton Road West, Bentley, Walsall WV13 2RL T 01902-607335
W www.fcofe.org.uk
Bishop Primus, Rt. Revd Dr John Fenwick
General Secretary, Rt. Revd Paul Hunt

FREE CHURCH OF SCOTLAND

The Free Church of Scotland was formed in 1843 when over 400 ministers withdrew from the Church of Scotland as a result of interference in the internal affairs of the church by the civil authorities. In 1900, all but 26 ministers joined with others to form the United Free Church (most of which rejoined the Church of Scotland in 1929). In 1904 the remaining 26 ministers were recognised by the House of Lords as continuing the Free Church of Scotland.

The church maintains strict adherence to the Westminster Confession of Faith (1648) and accepts the Bible as the sole rule of faith and conduct. Its general assembly meets annually. It also has links with reformed churches overseas. The Free Church of Scotland has about 12,000 members, 90 ministers and 100 congregations.

FREE CHURCH OF SCOTLAND, 15 North Bank Street, The Mound, Edinburgh EH1 2LS T 0131-226 5286
E offices@freechurchofscotland.org.uk W www.freechurch.org
Chief Administrative Officer, Rod Morrison

FREE PRESBYTERIAN CHURCH OF SCOTLAND

The Free Presbyterian Church of Scotland was formed in 1893 by two ministers of the Free Church of Scotland who refused to accept a Declaratory Act passed by the Free Church General Assembly in 1892. The Free Presbyterian Church of Scotland is Calvinistic in doctrine and emphasises observance of the Sabbath. It adheres strictly to the Westminster Confession of Faith (1648).

The church has about 1,000 members in Scotland and about 4,000 in overseas congregations. It has 17 ministers and 40 churches in the UK.

FREE PRESBYTERIAN MANSE, Laide, Ross-shire, IV22 2NB
E outreach@fpchurch.org.uk W www.fpchurch.org.uk
Moderator (2013–14), Neil M. Ross
Clerk of the Synod, Revd John MacLeod

HOLY APOSTOLIC CATHOLIC ASSYRIAN CHURCH OF THE EAST

The Holy Apostolic Catholic Assyrian Church of the East traces its beginnings to the middle of the first century. It spread from Upper Mesopotamia throughout the territories of the Persian Empire. The Assyrian Church of the East became theologically separated from the rest of the Christian community following the Council of Ephesus in 431. The church is headed by the Catholicos Patriarch and is episcopal in government. The liturgical language is Syriac (Aramaic). The Assyrian Church of the East and the Roman Catholic Church agreed a common Christological declaration in 1994, and a process of dialogue between the Assyrian Church of the East and the Chaldean Catholic Church, which is in communion with Rome but shares the Syriac liturgy, was instituted in 1996.

The church has about 400,000 members in the Middle East, India, Russia, Europe, North America and Australasia. In Great Britain there is one parish, which is situated in

London. The church in Great Britain forms part of the Diocese of Europe under HG Mar Odisho Oraham.

HOLY APOSTOLIC CATHOLIC ASSYRIAN CHURCH OF THE EAST, St Mary's Church, Westminster Road, Hanwell, London W7 3TU T 020-8567 1814

INDEPENDENT METHODIST CHURCHES

The Independent Methodist Churches were formed in 1805 and remained independent when the Methodist Church in Great Britain was formed in 1932. They are mainly concentrated in the industrial areas of the north of England.

The churches are Methodist in doctrine but their organisation is congregational. All the churches are members of the Independent Methodist Connexion of Churches. The controlling body of the Connexion is the Annual Meeting, to which churches send delegates. The Connexional President is elected every two years. Between annual meetings the affairs of the Connexion are handled by the Connexional Committee and departmental committees. Ministers are appointed by the churches and trained through the Connexion. The ministry is open to both men and women and is unpaid.

There are 1,600 members, 82 ministers and 78 churches in Great Britain.

INDEPENDENT METHODIST RESOURCE CENTRE, The Resource Centre, Fleet Street, Wigan WN5 0DS T 01942-223526 E resourcecentre@imcgb.org.uk W www.imcgb.org.uk

President, Eric Southwick

General Secretary, Brian Rowney

LUTHERAN CHURCH

Lutheranism is based on the teachings of Martin Luther, the German leader of the Protestant Reformation. The authority of the scriptures is held to be supreme over church tradition. The teachings of Lutheranism are explained in detail in 16th-century confessional writings, particularly the Augsburg Confession. Lutheranism is one of the largest Protestant denominations and it is particularly strong in northern Europe and the USA. Some Lutheran churches are episcopal, while others have a synodal form of organisation; unity is based on doctrine rather than structure. Most Lutheran churches are members of the Lutheran World Federation, based in Geneva.

Lutheran services in Great Britain are held in 15 languages to serve members of different nationalities. Services usually follow ancient liturgies. English-language congregations are members either of the Lutheran Church in Great Britain or of the Evangelical Lutheran Church of England. The Lutheran Church in Great Britain and other Lutheran churches in Britain are members of the Lutheran Council of Great Britain, which represents them and coordinates their common work.

There are around 70 million Lutherans worldwide, with around 180,000 members in Great Britain.

THE LUTHERAN COUNCIL OF GREAT BRITAIN, 30 Thanet Street, London WC1H 9QH T 020-7554 9753 E enquiries@lutheran.org.uk W www.lutheran.org.uk

Chair, Revd Torbjorn Holt

METHODIST CHURCH

The Methodist movement started in England in 1729 when the Revd John Wesley, an Anglican priest, and his brother Charles met with others in Oxford and resolved to conduct their lives by 'rule and method'. In 1739 the Wesleys began evangelistic preaching and the first Methodist chapel was founded in Bristol in the same year. In 1744 the first annual conference was held, at which the Articles of Religion were drawn up. Doctrinal emphases included repentance, faith, the assurance of salvation, social concern and the priesthood of all believers. After John Wesley's death in 1791 the Methodists withdrew from the established church to form the Methodist Church. Methodists gradually drifted into many groups, but in 1932 the Wesleyan Methodist Church, the United Methodist Church and the Primitive Methodist Church united to form the Methodist Church of Great Britain.

The governing body of the Methodist Church is the Conference. The Conference meets annually in June or July and consists of two parts: the ministerial and representative sessions. The Methodist Church is structured as a 'Connexion' of churches, circuits and districts. The local churches in a defined area form a circuit, and a number of these circuits make up each of the 31 districts. There are around 80 million Methodists worldwide. In Great Britain there are nearly 230,000 members, 3,680 presbyters, 171 Deacons and 5,023 churches.

THE METHODIST CHURCH OF GREAT BRITAIN, Methodist Church House, 25 Marylebone Road, London NW1 5JR T 020-7486 5502 E helpdesk@methodistchurch.org.uk W www.methodist.org.uk

President of the Conference (2013–14), Revd Ruth Gee

General Secretary and Secretary of the Conference, Revd Dr Martyn Atkins

THE METHODIST CHURCH IN IRELAND

The Methodist Church in Ireland is autonomous but has close links with British Methodism. It has a community roll of 50,879 members, 126 ministers, 313 lay preachers and 215 churches.

METHODIST CHURCH IN IRELAND, 1 Fountainville Avenue, Belfast BT9 6AN T 028-9032 4554 E secretary@irishmethodist.org W www.irishmethodist.org

President (2013–14), Revd Dr Heather M. E. Morris

Secretary, Donald P. Ker

ORTHODOX CHURCHES

EASTERN ORTHODOX CHURCH

The Eastern (or Byzantine) Orthodox Church is a communion of self-governing Christian churches that recognises the honorary primacy of the Ecumenical Patriarch of Constantinople.

The position of Orthodox Christians is that the faith was fully defined during the period of the Oecumenical Councils. In doctrine it is strongly trinitarian, and stresses the mystery and importance of the sacraments. It is episcopal in government. The structure of the Orthodox Christian year differs from that of western churches.

Orthodox Christians throughout the world are estimated to number about 300 million; there are around 300,000 in the UK.

GREEK ORTHODOX CHURCH (PATRIARCHATE OF ANTIOCH)

The church is led by John X, Patriarch of Antioch, who was enthroned in February 2013. The UK forms part of the Archdiocese of Europe. There are 15 parishes in the UK and the Republic of Ireland, including St George's Cathedral in London, and 23 clergy.

ANTIOCHIAN ORTHODOX DEANERY OF THE UK AND IRELAND, 29 Willis Road, Cale Green, Stockport, Cheshire SK3 8HQ T 0161-476 4847 E orthodox@.clara.net W www.antiochian-orthodox.co.uk

Dean, Archpriest Fr. Gregory Hallam

GREEK ORTHODOX CHURCH (PATRIARCHATE OF CONSTANTINOPLE)

The presence of Greek Orthodox Christians in Britain dates back at least to 1677 when Archbishop Joseph Geogirenes of Samos fled from Turkish persecution and came to London.

The present Greek cathedral in Moscow Road, Bayswater, was opened for public worship in 1879, and the Diocese of Thyateira and Great Britain was established in 1922. There are now 115 parishes and other communities (including two monasteries) in the UK, served by four bishops, 119 clergy, nine cathedrals and 104 parishes.

THE PATRIARCHATE OF CONSTANTINOPLE IN GREAT BRITAIN, Archdiocese of Thyateira and Great Britain, Thyateira House, 5 Craven Hill, London W2 3EN
T 020-7723 4787 E mail@thyateira.org.uk
W www.thyateira.org.uk
Archbishop, Gregorios of Thyateira and Great Britain

THE RUSSIAN ORTHODOX CHURCH (PATRIARCHATE OF MOSCOW) AND THE RUSSIAN ORTHODOX CHURCH OUTSIDE RUSSIA

The records of Russian Orthodox Church activities in Britain date from the visit to England of Tsar Peter I in the early 18th century. Clergy were sent from Russia to serve the chapel established to minister to the staff of the Imperial Russian Embassy in London.

In 2007, after an 80-year division, the Russian Orthodox Church Outside Russia agreed to become an autonomous part of the Russian Orthodox Church, Patriarchate of Moscow. The reunification agreement was signed by Patriarch Alexy II, 15th Patriarch of Moscow and All Russia and Metropolitan Laurus, leader of the Russian Orthodox Church Outside Russia on 17 May at a ceremony at Christ the Saviour Cathedral in Moscow. Patriarch Alexy II died on 5 December 2008. Metropolitan Kirill of Smolensk and Kaliningrad was enthroned as the 16th Patriarch of Moscow and All Russia on 1 February 2009, having been elected by a secret ballot of clergy on 27 January 2009.

The diocese of Sourozh is the diocese of the Russian Orthodox Church in Great Britain and Ireland and is led by Archbishop Elisey of Sourozh.

DIOCESE OF SOUROZH, Diocesan Office, Cathedral of the Dormition, 67 Ennismore Gardens, London SW7 1NH
T 020-7584 0096 W www.sourozh.org
Diocesan Hierarch, Archbishop Elisey (Ganaba) of Sourozh

SERBIAN ORTHODOX CHURCH (PATRIARCHATE OF SERBIA)

There are seven parishes in Great Britain and around 4,000 members. Great Britain is part of the Diocese of Great Britain and Scandinavia, which is led by Bishop Dositej. The church can be contacted via the church of St Sava in London.

SERBIAN ORTHODOX CHURCH IN GREAT BRITAIN, Church of Saint Sava, 89 Lancaster Road, London W11 1QQ
T 020-7727 8367 E crkva@spclondon.org
W www.spclondon.org
Archpriest, Very Revd Radomir Acimovic

OTHER NATIONALITIES

The Patriarchates of Romania and Bulgaria (Diocese of Western Europe) have memberships estimated at 20,000 and 2,000 respectively, while the Georgian Orthodox Church has around 500 members. The Belarusian (membership estimated at 2,400) and Latvian (membership of around 100) Orthodox churches are part of the Patriarchate of Constantinople.

ORIENTAL ORTHODOX CHURCHES

The term 'Oriental Orthodox Churches' is now generally used to describe a group of six ancient eastern churches (Armenian, Coptic, Eritrean, Ethiopian, Indian (Malankara) and Syrian) which rejected the Christological definition of the Council of Chalcedon (AD 451). There are around 50 million members worldwide of the Oriental Orthodox Churches and over 20,000 in the UK.

ARMENIAN ORTHODOX CHURCH (CATHOLICOSATE OF ETCHMIADZIN)

The Armenian Orthodox Church is led by HH Karekin II, Catholicos of All Armenians. The Rt. Revd Dr Vahan Hovhanessian is the Primate of the Armenian Church of the UK and Ireland and President of the Armenian Community and Church Council.

ARMENIAN CHURCH OF GREAT BRITAIN, The Armenian Vicarage, Iverna Gardens, London W8 6TP
T 020-7937 0152 E information@armenianchurch.org.uk
W www.armenianchurch.co.uk
Primate, Rt. Revd Bishop Dr Vahan Hovhanessian

COPTIC ORTHODOX CHURCH

The Coptic Orthodox Church is headed by Pope Tawadros II, who was appointed in November 2012, following the death of Pope Shenouda III in March 2012. There are three dioceses in the UK: the Midlands (led by HG Bishop Missael); Ireland, Scotland and north-east England (led by HG Bishop Antony); and churches directly under the Patriarch of Alexandria.

CATHEDRAL OF ST GEORGE AT THE COPTIC ORTHODOX CHURCH CENTRE, Shephalbury Manor, Broadhall Way, Stevenage, Herts SG2 8NP T 01438-745232
E admin@copticcentre.com W www.copticcentre.com
Bishop, HG Bishop Angaelos

BRITISH ORTHODOX CHURCH

The British Orthodox Church is canonically part of the Coptic Orthodox Patriarchate of Alexandria. As it ministers to British people, all of its services are in English.

THE BRITISH ORTHODOX CHURCH, 10 Heathwood Gardens, Charlton, London SE7 8EP T 020-8854 3090
E info@britishorthodox.org W www.britishorthodox.org
Metropolitan, Abba Seraphim

ERITREAN ORTHODOX TEWAHEDO CHURCH

The Eritrean Orthodox Church was granted independence in 1994 by Pope Shenouda III, following the declaration of Eritrea's independence from Ethiopia in 1993. In 2006, the Eritrean government removed the third patriarch, Abune Antonios, from office and imprisoned him; the government replaced him with Abune Dioskoros in 2007, although the Oriental Orthodox Churches continue to recognise Antonios as the rightful patriarch.

ERITREAN DIOCESE OFFICE (UK), 27 Hillrise Mansions, Warltersville Road, London N19 3PU T 0161-312 9422
E info@eritreanorthodoxchurch.org
W www.eritreanorthodoxchurch.org
Diocesan Bishop, HG Abune Makarios

INDIAN ORTHODOX CHURCH

The Indian Orthodox Church, also known as the Malankara Orthodox Church, traces its origins to the first century. The mother church of all the parishes in the UK and the Republic of Ireland is St Gregorios Church in London.

INDIAN ORTHODOX CHURCH, St Gregorios Indian Orthodox Church, Cranfield Road, Brockley, London SE4 1UF
T 020-8691 9456 E vicar@indian-orthodox.co.uk
W www.indian-orthodox.co.uk
Diocesan Metropolitan, HG Dr Mathews Mar Thimothios
Vicar, Revd Fr Thomas P. John

SYRIAN ORTHODOX CHURCH

The Syrian (Syriac) Orthodox Church of Antioch is an Oriental Orthodox Church based in the Eastern Mediterranean. The Patriarchate Vicariate in the UK is represented by HE Archbishop Mor Athanasius Toma Dawood.

SYRIAN ORTHODOX CHURCH IN THE UK, St Thomas Cathedral, 7–11 Armstrong Road, London W3 7JL
T 020-8654 7531 E enquiry-uk@syrianorthodoxchurch.net
W www.syrianorthodoxchurch.net
Archbishop, HE Mor Athanasius Toma Dawood

COUNCIL OF ORIENTAL ORTHODOX CHURCHES IN THE UK AND IRELAND, 264 Upper Fant Road, Maidstone, Kent ME16 8BX E fatherpeter@britishorthodox.org
W www.orientalcounciluk.org

The Council of Oriental Orthodox Churches was established to make known and advance the spiritual, ecclesiastical and charitable activities of the member churches.

Secretary, Fr Peter Farrington

PENTECOSTAL CHURCHES

Pentecostalism is inspired by the descent of the Holy Spirit upon the apostles at Pentecost. The movement began in Los Angeles, USA, in 1906 and is characterised by baptism with the Holy Spirit, divine healing, speaking in tongues (glossolalia) and a literal interpretation of the scriptures.

The Pentecostal movement in Britain dates from 1907. Initially, groups of Pentecostalists were led by laymen and did not organise formally. However, in 1915 the Elim Foursquare Gospel Alliance (more commonly called the Elim Pentecostal Church) was founded in Ireland by George Jeffreys and currently has about 550 churches, 68,500 adherents and 650 accredited ministers. In 1924 about 70 independent assemblies formed a fellowship called Assemblies of God in Great Britain and Ireland, which now incorporates 572 churches, around 75,000 adherents and 1,015 ministers.

The Apostolic Church grew out of the 1904–5 Christian revivals in South Wales and was established in 1916. The Apostolic Church has 100 churches, 7,183 adherents and 117 ministers in the UK. The New Testament Church of God was established in England in 1953 and has over 125 congregations, nearly 30,000 members and over 300 ministers across England and Wales.

In recent years many aspects of Pentecostalism have been adopted by the growing charismatic movement within the Roman Catholic, Protestant and Eastern Orthodox churches. There are about 105 million Pentecostalists worldwide, with over 350,000 adherents in the UK.

THE APOSTOLIC CHURCH, PO Box 51298, London SE11 9AJ T 020-7587 1802 E info@apostolic-church.org
National Leader, Emmanuel Mbakwe

ASSEMBLIES OF GOD INCORPORATED, National Ministry Centre, Mattersey, Doncaster DN10 5HD T 017-7781 7663
E info@aog.org.uk W www.aog.org.uk
National Leader, John Partington

THE ELIM PENTECOSTAL CHURCH, Elim International Centre, De Walden Road, West Malvern, Worcestershire WR14 4DF T 0845-302 6750 E info@elimhq.net
W www.elim.org.uk
General Superintendent, Revd John Glass

THE NEW TESTAMENT CHURCH OF GOD, 3 Cheyne Walk, Northampton NN1 5PT T 01604-824222
W www.ntcg.org.uk
Administrative Bishop, Eric Brown

PRESBYTERIAN CHURCH IN IRELAND

Irish Presbyterianism traces its origins back to the Plantation of Ulster in 1606, when English and Scottish Protestants began to settle on the land confiscated from the Irish chieftains. The first presbytery was established in Ulster in 1642 by chaplains of a Scottish army that had been sent to crush a Catholic rebellion in 1641.

The Presbyterian Church in Ireland is reformed in doctrine and belongs to the World Alliance of Reformed Churches. Structurally, the 545 congregations are grouped in 19 presbyteries under the General Assembly. This body meets annually and is presided over by a moderator who is elected for one year. The ongoing work of the church is undertaken by 12 boards under which there are specialist committees.

There are over 240,000 members of Irish presbyterian churches in Ireland and Northern Ireland.

THE PRESBYTERIAN CHURCH IN IRELAND, Assembly Buildings, 2–10 Fisherwick Place, Belfast BT1 6DW
T 028-9032 2284 E info@presbyterianireland.org
W www.presbyterianireland.org
Moderator (2013–14), Rt. Revd Dr Robert Lyle Craig
Clerk of Assembly and General Secretary, Revd Dr Donald Watts

PRESBYTERIAN CHURCH OF WALES

The Presbyterian Church of Wales or Calvinistic Methodist Church of Wales is Calvinistic in doctrine and presbyterian in constitution. It was formed in 1811 when Welsh Calvinists severed the relationship with the established church by ordaining their own ministers. It secured its own confession of faith in 1823 and a Constitutional Deed in 1826, and since 1864 the General Assembly has met annually, presided over by a moderator elected for a year. The doctrine and constitutional structure of the Presbyterian Church of Wales was confirmed by act of parliament in 1931–2.

The Church has 25,000 members, 58 ministers and 653 congregations.

THE PRESBYTERIAN CHURCH OF WALES, Tabernacle Chapel, 81 Merthyr Road, Whitchurch, Cardiff CF14 1DD
T 029-2062 7465 E swyddfa.office@ebcpcw.org.uk
W www.ebcpcw.org.uk
Moderator (2013–14), Revd Trefor Lewis
General Secretary, Revd Meirian Morris

RELIGIOUS SOCIETY OF FRIENDS (QUAKERS)

Quakerism is a religious denomination which was founded in the 17th century by George Fox and others in an attempt to revive what they saw as the original 'primitive Christianity'. The movement, at first called Friends of the Truth, started in the Midlands, Yorkshire and north-west England, but there are now Quakers all over the UK and in 36 countries around the world. The colony of Pennsylvania, founded by William Penn, was originally a Quaker settlement.

Quakers place an emphasis on the experience of God in daily life rather than on sacraments or religious occasions. There is no church calendar. Worship is largely silent and there are no appointed ministers; the responsibility for conducting a meeting is shared equally among those present. Religious tolerance and social reform have always been important to Quakers, together with a commitment to peace and non-violence in resolving disputes.

There are more than 23,000 'friends' or Quakers in Great Britain. There are around 475 places where Quaker meetings are held, many of them Quaker-owned Friends Meeting Houses. The Britain Yearly Meeting is the name given to the central organisation of Quakers in Britain.

THE RELIGIOUS SOCIETY OF FRIENDS (QUAKERS) IN BRITAIN, Friends House, 173–177 Euston Road, London NW1 2BJ T 020-7663 1000 E enquiries@quaker.org.uk
W www.quaker.org.uk
Recording Clerk, Paul Parker

SALVATION ARMY

The Salvation Army is an international Christian organisation working in 126 countries worldwide. As a church and registered charity, The Salvation Army is funded through donations from its members, the general public and, where appropriate, government grants.

The Salvation Army was founded by Methodists William and Catherine Booth, in the East End of London in 1865, and now has over 800 local church and community centres, more than 70 residential support centres for homeless people, 18 care homes for older people and six substance-misuse centres. It also runs a clothing recycling programme, charity shops, a prison-visiting service and a family-tracing service. In 1878 it adopted a quasi-military command structure intended to inspire and regulate its endeavours and to reflect its view that the church was engaged in spiritual warfare.

UK TERRITORIAL HEADQUARTERS, 101 Newington Causeway, London SE1 6BN T 020-7367 4500
E info@salvationarmy.org.uk W www.salvationarmy.org.uk
UK Territorial Commander, Commissioner Clive Adams

SEVENTH-DAY ADVENTIST CHURCH

The Seventh-day Adventist Church is a worldwide Christian church marked by its observance of Saturday as the Sabbath and by its emphasis on the imminent second coming of Jesus Christ. Adventists summarise their faith in '28 fundamental beliefs'.

The church grew out of the Millerite movement in the USA during the mid-19th century and was formally established in 1863. The church has an ethnically and culturally diverse worldwide membership of over 17 million, with a presence in 209 countries. In the UK and Ireland there are approximately 34,000 members worshipping in 301 churches and companies.

BRITISH UNION CONFERENCE OF SEVENTH-DAY ADVENTISTS, Stanborough Park, Watford WD25 9JZ
T 01923-672251 E info@adventist.org.uk
W www.adventist.org.uk
President, Pastor Ian Sweeney

THE (SWEDENBORGIAN) NEW CHURCH

The New Church is based on the teachings of the 18th-century Swedish scientist and theologian Emanuel Swedenborg (1688–1772), who believed that Jesus Christ appeared to him and instructed him to reveal the spiritual meaning of the Bible. He claimed to have visions of the spiritual world, including heaven and hell, and conversations with angels and spirits. He published several theological works, including descriptions of the spiritual world and a Bible commentary.

Swedenborgians believe that the second coming of Jesus Christ is taking place, being not an actual physical reappearance of Christ, but rather his return in spirit. It is also believed that concurrent with our life on earth is life in a parallel spiritual world, of which we are usually unconscious until death. There are around 30,000 Swedenborgians worldwide, with around 8,500 members, 19 churches and 13 ministers in the UK.

THE GENERAL CONFERENCE OF THE NEW CHURCH, Swedenborg House, 20 Bloomsbury Way, London WC1A 2TH T 01827-712370
E enquiries@generalconference.org.uk
W www.generalconference.org.uk
Company Secretary, Zoë Brooks

UNDEB YR ANNIBYNWYR CYMRAEG

Undeb Yr Annibynwyr Cymraeg (the Union of Welsh Independents) was formed in 1872 and is a voluntary association of Welsh Congregational churches and personal members. It is mainly Welsh-speaking. Congregationalism in Wales dates back to 1639 when the first Welsh Congregational church was opened in Gwent.

Member churches are traditionally congregationalist in organisation and Calvinistic in doctrine, although a wide range of interpretations are permitted. Each church has complete independence in the governance and administration of its affairs.

The Union has around 24,000 members, 80 ministers and 440 member churches.

UNDEB YR ANNIBYNWYR CYMRAEG, 5 Axis Court, Riverside Business Park, Swansea Vale, Swansea SA7 0AJ
T 01792-795888 E undeb@annibynwyr.org
W www.annibynwyr.org
President of the Union (2012–14), Revd J. Ronald Williams
General Secretary, Revd Dr Geraint Tudur

UNITED REFORMED CHURCH

The United Reformed Church (URC) was first formed by the union of most of the Congregational churches in England and Wales with the Presbyterian Church of England in 1972. It is Calvinistic in doctrine, and its followers form independent self-governing congregations bound under God by covenant, a principle laid down in the writings of Robert Browne (1550–1633). From the late 16th century the movement was driven underground by persecution, but the cause was defended at the Westminster Assembly in 1643 and the Savoy Declaration of 1658 laid down its principles. Congregational churches formed county associations for mutual support and in 1832 these associations merged to form the Congregational Union of England and Wales.

In the 1960s there was close cooperation locally and nationally between congregational and presbyterian churches. This led to union negotiations and a Scheme of Union, supported by an act of parliament in 1972. In 1981 a further unification took place, with the Reformed Association of Churches of Christ becoming part of the URC. In 2000 a third union took place, with the Congregational Union of Scotland. At its basis the URC reflects local church initiative and responsibility with a conciliar pattern of oversight.

The URC is divided into 13 synods, each with a synod moderator. There are around 1,500 churches which serve over 60,000 adults and around 45,000 children and young people. There are around 615 ministers in active service.

The General Assembly is the central body, and comprises around 400 representatives, mainly appointed by the synods, of which half are lay persons and half are ministers. Since 2010 the General Assembly has met biennially to elect two moderators (one lay and one ordained), who then become the public representatives of the URC.

UNITED REFORMED CHURCH, 86 Tavistock Place, London WC1H 9RT T 020-7916 2020 E urc@urc.org.uk
W www.urc.org.uk
Moderators of the General Assembly (2012–14), Revd Dr Michael Jagessar; John Ellis
General Secretary, Revd Roberta Rominger

WESLEYAN REFORM UNION

The Wesleyan Reform Union was founded by Methodists who left or were expelled from Wesleyan Methodism in 1849 following a period of internal conflict. Its doctrine is conservative evangelical and its organisation is congregational, each church having complete independence in the government and administration of its affairs. The union has around 1,540 members, 20 ministers and 96 churches.

THE WESLEYAN REFORM UNION, Wesleyan Reform Church House, 123 Queen Street, Sheffield S1 2DU
T 0114-272 1938 E gen.sec@thewru.co.uk
W www.thewru.com
President (2013–14), Michael Alderson
General Secretary, Revd Colin Braithwaite

NON-TRINITARIAN CHURCHES

CHRISTADELPHIAN

Christadelphians believe that the Bible is the word of God and that it reveals both God's dealings with mankind in the past and his plans for the future. These plans centre on the work of Jesus Christ, who it is believed will return to Earth to establish God's kingdom. The Christadelphian group was founded in the USA in the 1850s by the Englishman, Dr John Thomas.

THE CHRISTADELPHIAN MAGAZINE AND PUBLISHING ASSOCIATION LTD, 404 Shaftmoor Lane, Hall Green, Birmingham B28 8SZ T 0121-777 6328
E enquiries@thechristadelphian.com
W www.thechristadelphian.com

CHURCH OF CHRIST, SCIENTIST

The Church of Christ, Scientist was founded by Mary Baker Eddy in the USA in 1879 to 'reinstate primitive Christianity and its lost element of healing'. Christian Science teaches the need for spiritual regeneration and salvation from sin, but it is best known for its reliance on prayer alone in the healing of sickness. Adherents believe that such healing is the result of divine laws, or divine science, and is in direct line with that practised by Jesus Christ (revered, not as God, but as the son of God) and by the early Christian church.

The denomination consists of The First Church of Christ, Scientist, in Boston, Massachusetts, USA ('The Mother Church') and its branch churches in almost 80 countries worldwide. The Bible and Mary Baker Eddy's book, *Science and Health with Key to the Scriptures,* are used for daily spiritual guidance and healing by all members and are read at services. There are no clergy; those engaged in full-time healing are called Christian Science practitioners, of whom there are around 1,500 worldwide. The church also publishes *The Christian Science Monitor.*

No membership figures are available, since Mary Baker Eddy felt that numbers are no measure of spiritual vitality and ruled that such statistics should not be published. There are almost 2,000 branch churches worldwide, including over 100 in the UK.

CHRISTIAN SCIENCE COMMITTEE ON PUBLICATION, 90 Long Acre, London WC2E 9RZ
T 020-8150 0245 E londoncs@csps.com
W www.christianscience.co.uk
District Manager for the UK and Ireland, Tony Lobl

CHURCH OF JESUS CHRIST OF LATTER-DAY SAINTS

The Church of Jesus Christ of Latter-day Saints (often referred to as the 'Mormon church') was founded in New York State, USA, in 1830, and came to Britain in 1837. The oldest continuous congregation of the church is in Preston, Lancashire.

Mormons are Christians who claim to belong to the 'restored church' of Jesus Christ. They believe that true Christianity died when the last original apostle died, but that it was given back to the world by God and Jesus Christ through Joseph Smith, the church's founder and first president. They accept and use the Bible as scripture, but believe in continuing revelation from God; Mormons also use additional scriptures, including *The Book of Mormon: Another Testament of Jesus Christ.* The importance of the family is central to the church's beliefs and practices. Church members set aside Monday evenings as family home evenings when Christian family values are taught. Polygamy was formally discontinued in 1890.

The church has no paid ministry: local congregations are headed by a leader chosen from among their number. The world governing body, based in Utah, USA, is led by a president, believed to be the chosen prophet, and his two counsellors. There are 14.8 million members worldwide, with nearly 190,000 adherents and 332 congregations in the UK.

THE CHURCH OF JESUS CHRIST OF LATTER-DAY SAINTS, British Headquarters, 751 Warwick Road, Solihull, W. Midlands B91 3DQ T 0121-712 1200 W www.lds.org.uk

JEHOVAH'S WITNESSES

The movement now known as Jehovah's Witnesses grew from a Bible study group formed by Charles Taze Russell in 1872 in Pennsylvania, USA. In 1896 it adopted the name of the Watch Tower Bible and Tract Society, and in 1931 its members became known as Jehovah's Witnesses.

Jehovah's (God's) Witnesses believe in the Bible as the word of God, and consider it to be inspired and historically accurate. They take the scriptures literally, except where there are obvious indications that they are figurative or symbolic, and reject the doctrine of the Trinity. Witnesses also believe that all those approved of by Jehovah will have eternal life on a cleansed and beautified earth; only 144,000 will go to heaven to rule with Jesus Christ. They believe that the second coming of Christ began in 1914, that his thousand-year reign over the earth is imminent, and that armageddon (a final battle in which evil will be defeated) will precede Christ's rule of peace. Jehovah's Witnesses refuse to take part in military service and do not accept blood transfusions.

The eight-member world governing body is based in New York, USA. There is no paid ministry, but each congregation has elders assigned to look after various duties and every Witness takes part in the public ministry in their neighbourhood. At the last count, in 2012, there were 7.78 million Jehovah's Witnesses worldwide, with 135,654 Witnesses in Great Britain organised into 1,544 congregations.

BRITISH HEADQUARTERS, The Ridgeway, London NW7 1RN T 020-8906 2211 E opi.gb@jw.org W www.jw.org

UNITARIAN AND FREE CHRISTIAN CHURCHES

Unitarianism has its historical roots in the Judaeo-Christian tradition but rejects the deity of Christ and the doctrine of the Trinity. It allows the individual to embrace insights from all of the world's faiths and philosophies, as there is no fixed creed. It is accepted that beliefs may evolve in the light of personal experience.

Unitarian communities first became established in Poland and Transylvania in the 16th century. The first avowedly Unitarian place of worship in the British Isles opened in London in 1774. The General Assembly of Unitarian and Free Christian Churches came into existence in 1928 as the result of the amalgamation of two earlier organisations.

There are around 5,000 Unitarians in Great Britain and around 80 Unitarian ministers. Nearly 200 self-governing congregations and fellowship groups, including a small number overseas, are members of the General Assembly.

GENERAL ASSEMBLY OF UNITARIAN AND FREE CHRISTIAN CHURCHES, Essex Hall, 1–6 Essex Street, London WC2R 3HY T 020-7240 2384 E info@unitarian.org.uk
W www.unitarian.org.uk
President (2013–14), Revd Bill Darlinson
Vice-President (2013–14), Marion Baker

COMMUNICATIONS

POSTAL SERVICES

Royal Mail is the government-owned postal service of the United Kingdom. Royal Mail Group Ltd, which is owned by Royal Mail Holdings plc, operates Parcelforce Worldwide, General Logistics Systems (GLS), the Post Office Ltd and Royal Mail. On 1 April 2012, the Post Office Ltd became a direct subsidary of Royal Mail Holdings plc and a sister company to Royal Mail Group Ltd in a commercial agreement.

Each working day Royal Mail delivers over 59 million items to 29 million addresses across the UK. Following the passing of the Postal Services Act 2011, the Office of Communications (OFCOM) assumed regulatory responsibility for postal services from the Postal Services Commission (Postcomm) on 1 October 2011. OFCOM's primary responsibility is to secure the provision of a universal postal service with regard to its financial sustainability. Royal Mail was designated as the universal service provider and charged with providing this service at a uniform price throughout the UK.

Citizens Advice is responsible for consumer advocacy.

ROYAL MAIL GROUP LTD, 100 Victoria Embankment, London EC4Y 0HQ T 08457-740740 W www.royalmailgroup.com

CITIZENS ADVICE, Myddleton House, 115–123 Pentonville Road, London N1 9LZ T 020-7833 2181 W www.citizensadvice.org.uk

OFCOM, Riverside House, 2A Southwark Bridge Road, London SE1 9HA T 0300-123 3000 W www.ofcom.org.uk

PRICING IN PROPORTION

Since August 2006 Royal Mail has priced mail according to its size as well as its weight. The system is intended to reflect the fact that larger, bulkier items cost more to handle than smaller, lighter ones. There are four basic categories of correspondence:

LETTER: *Length* up to 240mm, *width* up to 165mm, *thickness* up to 5mm, *weight* up to 100g; eg most cards, postcards and bills

LARGE LETTER: *Length* up to 353mm, *width* up to 250mm, *thickness* up to 25mm, *weight* up to 750g; eg most A4 documents and magazines

SMALL PARCEL: *Length* up to 450mm, *width* up to 350mm, *thickness* up to 80mm, *weight* up to 2kg, eg books, clothes and gifts

MEDIUM PARCEL: *Length* up to 610mm, *width* up to 460mm, *thickness* up to 460mm, *weight* up to 20kg; eg gifts, shoes, heavy or bulky items

Rolled and cylinder shaped parcels, eg posters and prints, which measure up to 450mm in length and 80mm in diameter and which do not exceed 2kg can be sent as small parcels. Items with dimensions larger than those listed above are classified as large parcels and can only be sent via Parcelforce Worldwide, where items can measure up to 150cm in length, with a combined length and width of less than 300cm, and must weigh no more than 30kg.

INLAND POSTAL SERVICES

Following are details of a number of popular postal services along with prices correct as at April 2013. For a full list of prices *see* W www.royalmail.com

FIRST AND SECOND CLASS

Format	*Maximum weight*	*First class*	*Second class**
Letter/postcard*	100g	£0.60	£0.50
Large letter	100g	£0.90	£0.69
	250g	£1.20	£1.10
	500g	£1.60	£1.40
	750g	£2.30	£1.90
Small parcel	1,000g	£3.00	£2.60
	2,000g	£6.85	£5.60
Medium parcel	1,000g	£5.65	£5.20
	2,000g	£8.90	£8.00
	5,000g	£15.10	£13.35
	10,000g	£21.25	£19.65
	20,000g	£32.40	£27.70

* First class post is normally delivered on the following working day and second class within three working days

LARGE PARCEL RATES*

Maximum weight	*Lowest tariff*
2kg	£9.97
5kg	£10.77
10kg	£13.27
15kg	£18.72
20kg	£23.07
25kg	£32.07
30kg	£35.42

* Up to 150cm long, with a combined length and width of less than 300cm. The rate listed is for delivery within two working days

OVERSEAS POSTAL SERVICES

For charging purposes Royal Mail divides the world into four zones: UK, Europe, World Zone 1 and World Zone 2. A complete listing can be found at W www.royalmail.com/international-zones

Europe: Albania, Andorra, Armenia, Austria, Azerbaijan, Azores, Balearic Islands, Belarus, Belgium, Bosnia and Hercegovina, Bulgaria, Canary Islands, Corsica, Croatia, Cyprus, Czech Rep., Denmark, Estonia, Finland, France, Georgia, Germany, Gibraltar, Greece, Greenland, Hungary, Iceland, Ireland, Italy, Kazakhstan, Kosovo, Kyrgyzstan, Latvia, Liechtenstein, Lithuania, Luxembourg, Macedonia, Madeira, Malta, Moldova, Monaco, Montenegro, Netherlands, Norway, Poland, Portugal, Romania, Russia, San Marino, Serbia, Slovakia, Slovenia, Spain, Sweden, Switzerland, Tajikistan, Turkey, Turkmenistan, Ukraine, Uzbekistan

World Zone 1: N. America, S. America, Africa, the Middle East, the Far East and S. E. Asia

World Zone 2: Australia, British Indian Ocean Territory, Fiji, French Polynesia, Kiribati, Laos, Macau, Nauru, New Caledonia, New Zealand, Palau, Papua New Guinea, Pitcairn Islands, Singapore, Solomon Islands, Tonga, Tuvalu, Samoa

OVERSEAS SURFACE MAIL RATES

Maximum weight	*Standard tariff*
*Letters up to 100g**	
20g	£0.78
60g	£1.33
100g	£1.88

* Can only be sent by Surface Mail to destinations outside of Europe

Small parcels up to 100g	£2.60
Letters, small parcels and printed papers over 100g	£3.25

plus an additional £1.60, or part thereof, up to 2,000g*

* Up to 5,000g for printed papers

AIRMAIL RATES

Maximum weight	*Standard tariff*
EUROPE	
Letters up to 100g	
20g	£0.88
40g	£1.28
60g	£1.68
80g	£2.03
100g	£2.38
Small parcels up to 100g	
100g	£3.00
Letters, small parcels and printed papers over 100g	
250g	£3.50
1,250g	£9.30
plus an additional £1.45, or part thereof, up to 2,000g*	
WORLD ZONE 1	
Letters up to 100g	
10g	£0.88
20g	£1.28
40g	£1.88
60g	£2.48
80g	£3.08
100g	£3.50
Small parcels up to 100g	
100g	£3.50
Letters, small parcels and printed papers over 100g	
250g	£4.50
plus an additional £2.70, or part thereof, up to 2,000g*	
WORLD ZONE 2	
Letters up to 100g	
10g	£0.88
20g	£1.28
40g	£1.88
60g	£2.48
80g	£3.08
100g	£3.50
Small parcels up to 100g	
100g	£3.50
Letters, small parcels and printed papers over 100g	
250g	£4.70
plus an additional £2.85, or part thereof, up to 2,000g*	

* Up to 5,000g for printed papers

SPECIAL DELIVERY SERVICES

INTERNATIONAL SIGNED FOR AND AIRSURE

International Signed For provides a signature on delivery, tracking in the UK (when sending by Airmail) and in some overseas destinations, and compensation for loss or damage. The price for the service in addition to Airmail is £5.30 including additional compensation of £7.90. Airsure offers end-to-end tracking and online confirmation of delivery, which includes a standard compensation cover of £50. The price, in addition to Airmail, is £5.00 within the EU with added compensation of £7.60, or £5.40 for delivery to the rest of the world, with compensation of £8.00.

SAME DAY

A courier service which provides same day delivery of urgent items in most places in the UK. With collection within the hour of booking, satellite tracking, delivery confirmation and compensation up to £20,000, the service is charged for on a loaded mile basis T 0845-850 5522

SIGNED FOR

A service which offers proof of delivery including a signature from the receiver and compensation cover up to £50. The first class service is delivered the next working day and prices vary from £1.70 to £33.50 depending on the size and weight of the item. The second class service allows two to three working days for delivery with a charge of £1.60 to £28.80.

SPECIAL DELIVERY GUARANTEED

A guaranteed next working day delivery service by 9am or 1pm with a refund option guaranteed for late delivery. With many options available, Royal Mail offers a full list of prices online W www.royalmail.com/personal/uk-delivery/special-delivery

OTHER SERVICES

KEEPSAFE

Mail is held for up to two months while the addressee is away, and is delivered when the addressee returns. Prices start at £12.40 for 17 days up to £41.00 for 66 days.

PASSPORT APPLICATIONS

Many post offices process passport applications. To find your nearest post office offering this service and for further information *see* W www.postoffice.co.uk

POST OFFICE BOX

A Post Office (PO) Box provides a short and memorable alternative address. Mail is held at a local delivery office until the addressee is ready to collect it, or delivered to a street address for an extra fee. Prices start at £138.60 for six months or £244.20 for a year.

POSTCODE FINDER

Customers can search an online database to find UK postcodes and addresses. For more information *see* Royal Mail's postcode finder W www.royalmail.com/postcode-finder

REDELIVERY

Customers can request a redelivery of an item for up to 18 days if it was unable to be delivered. A 48-hour notice period is required for redelivery or the item can be held at the recipient's local Post Office branch for a fee of £1.50 upon collection in addition to proof of identity and the original 'Something for you' card.

REDIRECTION

Customers may arrange the redirection of their mail via post, at the Post Office or online, subject to verification of their identity. The service is available for 0–3 months, 3–6 months or 6–12 months at varying prices depending on the location of delivery. A full price list is available at W www.royalmail.com/personal/receiving-mail/redirection

TRACK AND TRACE

An online service for customers to track the progress of items sent using special delivery. It is accessible from W www.royalmail.com and W www.postoffice.co.uk/track-trace

CONTACTS

Parcelforce Worldwide
T 08448-004466 W www.parcelforce.com
Post Office enquiries T 08457-223344 W www.postoffice.co.uk
Postcode enquiry line T 0906-302 1222/08457-111222

TELECOMMUNICATIONS

Mobile network technology has improved dramatically since the launch in 1985 of the first-generation global system for mobile communications (GSM), which offered little or no data capability. In 1992 Vodafone launched a new GSM network, usually referred to as 2G or second generation, which used digital encoding and allowed voice and low-speed data communications. This technology was extended, via the enhanced data transfer rate of 2.5G, to 3G – a family of mobile standards that provide high bandwidth support to applications such as voice- and video-calling, high-speed data transfer, television streaming and full internet access. Most recently, a 4G superfast mobile spectrum was rolled out, which delivers speeds of up to 100 megabits per second (Mbps), allowing for faster download speeds on a range of devices.

FOURTH GENERATION (4G) AND WI-FI

In March 2011 OFCOM announced plans for the auction of additional spectrum (the airwaves on which all communications rely) to provide the necessary capacity for 4G technology in the UK. OFCOM originally aimed to begin the auction in early 2012, but following a consultation regarding the proposals in 2011, the auction did not take place until February 2013. The spectrum was auctioned in two bands – 800 MHz and 2.6 GHz – which lie within the 'sweetspot', the frequency in greatest demand. This combination of low and high frequencies provides the potential to cope with high demand of 4G services. The auction raised £2.34bn for HM Treasury, less than the £3.5bn that was forecast by the Office for Budget Responsibility, and considerably less than the 3G auction in 2000 which raised £22bn. The winning bidders for the distribution of 4G mobile broadband were Everything Everywhere (EE), Hutchison 3G UK, Niche Spectrum Ventures (a BT subsidiary), Telefonica (O2) and Vodafone.

4G coverage is expected to cover 98 per cent of the UK population indoors and above that when outdoors. The speeds offered by 4G are approximately five to ten times faster than 3G networks which allows for higher quality and faster streaming of media such as TV and films. The UK population in more rural areas that was often outside 3G coverage should also be able to access mobile broadband through the 4G spectrum.

EE was the first operator to launch 4G in late 2012 and by April 2013 the service was available in ten cities where the broadband speed was doubled to more than 20Mbps. The 4G service is currently available in 50 towns and cities across the UK.

The use of Wi-Fi (wireless networking) experienced minimal expansion in 2012 as the UK was displaced as the country with the highest location of public Wi-Fi locations by South Korea. In the fourth quarter of 2012, the UK had 182,345 recognised hotspots, almost 50,000 more locations than in the USA. Following the 2012 Olympic Games in London, there is Wi-Fi access throughout 120 London Underground stations, available for a fee in ticket halls and on escalators and platforms.

FIXED-LINE SERVICES

2011 once again saw a decline in the number of fixed lines in the UK to 33.2 million connections from 33.4 million connections in 2010. This followed a trend which had begun in 2002 when fixed-line telephone connections started to decrease. There has been a particularly high rate of decline in business customers, indicating a trend towards the use of mobile phones, emails and voice over internet protocol (VoIP) services such as Skype. BT's share of fixed-call minutes also continued to decline, standing at 35.9 per cent in 2011, a decrease from 33.4 per cent in 2010.

As the average cost of a residential fixed broadband connection fell in 2011 to £15.73, the average headline speed increased by 4.0Mbps to 16.8Mbps, as users invested in higher speed packages, including 'superfast' services with a headline speed of up to 30Mbps or more. In the 12 months to May 2012, the proportion of superfast fixed broadband connections increased from 2 to 8 per cent.

MOBILE COMMUNICATIONS

Mobile retail revenue increased by 1 per cent in 2011; the first increase for three years. This small increase was predominantly due to a 17.7 per cent increase in data revenues. Messaging revenues decreased by 2.6 per cent and voice revenues by 0.9 per cent. This trend follows the increasing number of smartphones being used for communication, with social media platforms, often pre-installed, serving as popular mediums of keeping in touch while on the move. The total number of mobile connections increased again in 2011, by 0.5 per cent to 81.6 million, which, taking into account an increase in population, resulted in there being 129.8 active mobile connections for every 100 people.

In 2011 it was estimated that 32.6 million subscribers accessed the internet using their mobile phones, an increase of nearly 10 million since 2010. This increase was driven largely by the uptake of smartphones by subscribers, with 3 per cent of UK households now using a smartphone as their only means of home internet access. Smartphone ownership has also resulted in subscribers using their device to provide mobile connectivity for their computers, an activity known as tethering. This is done to utilise the larger computer screen to improve viewing quality in addition to eliminating the need to purchase a separate mobile broadband package for a home PC. OFCOM estimates that 12.6 per cent of smartphone owners use tethering.

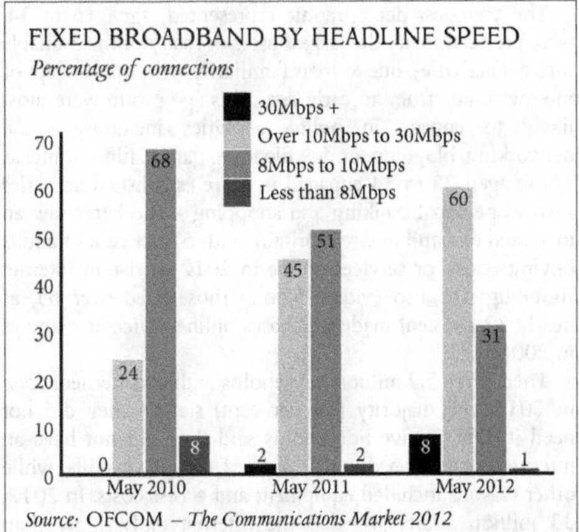

Source: OFCOM – *The Communications Market 2012*

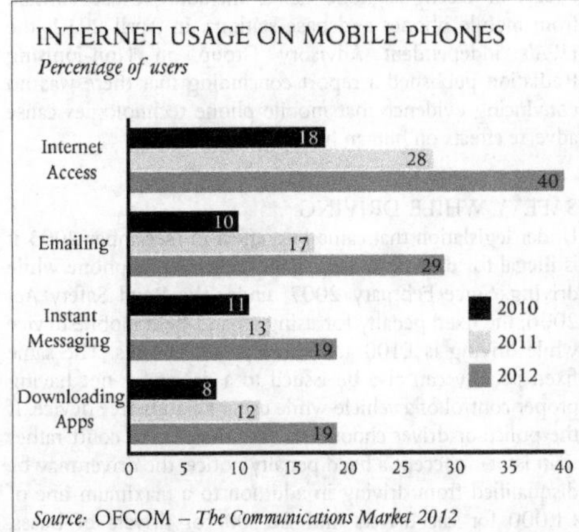

Source: OFCOM – *The Communications Market 2012*

MOBILE INTERNET USAGE
In the year to March 2012 internet browsing on mobile phones increased from 28 to 40 per cent and emailing from 17 to 29 per cent. Instant messaging also increased in popularity, with 19 per cent of mobile users stating they used services such as Whatsapp and BlackBerry Messenger to communicate, the same percentage as those who used mobile internet to download apps to their devices.

HEALTH
In 1999 the Independent Expert Group on Mobile Phones (IEGMP) was established to examine the possible effects on health of mobile phones, base stations and transmitters. The main findings of the IEGMP's report *Mobile Phones and Health,* published in May 2000, were:

- exposure to radio frequency radiation below guideline levels did not cause adverse health effects to the general population
- the use of mobile phones by drivers of any vehicle can increase the chance of accidents
- the widespread use of mobile phones by children for non-essential calls should be discouraged because if there are unrecognised adverse health effects children may be more vulnerable
- there is no general risk to the health of people living near to base stations on the basis that exposures are expected to be much lower than guidelines set by the International Commission on Non-Ionising Radiation Protection

The government set up the Mobile Telecommunications Health and Research (MTHR) programme in 2001 to undertake independent research into the possible health risks from mobile telephone technology. The MTHR programme published its report in September 2007 concluding that, in the short term, neither mobile phones nor base stations have been found to be associated with any biological or adverse health effects. An international cohort study into the possible long-term health effects of mobile phone use was launched by the MTHR in April 2010. The study is known as COSMOS and aims to follow the health of 250,000 mobile phone users from five countries over 20 to 30 years. The full 2007 report and details of COSMOS can be found on the MTHR website (W www.mthr.org.uk).

A national measurement programme, to ensure that emissions from mobile phone base stations do not exceed the ICNIRP guideline levels, is overseen by OFCOM and annual audits of these levels can be found on the sitefinder part of its website. The Health Protection Agency (HPA), part of Public Health England from 1 April 2013, is responsible for providing information and advice in relation to the health effects of electromagnetic fields, including those emitted from mobile phones and base stations. In April 2012, the HPA's independent Advisory Group on Non-ionising Radiation published a report concluding that there was no convincing evidence that mobile phone technologies cause adverse effects on human health.

SAFETY WHILE DRIVING
Under legislation that came into effect in December 2003 it is illegal for drivers to use a hand-held mobile phone while driving. Since February 2007, under the Road Safety Act 2006, the fixed penalty for using a hand-held mobile device while driving is £100 and three penalty points. The same fixed penalty can also be issued to a driver for not having proper control of a vehicle while using a hands-free device. If the police or driver chooses to take the case to court rather than issue or accept a fixed penalty notice, the driver may be disqualified from driving in addition to a maximum fine of £1,000 for car drivers and £2,500 for drivers of buses, coaches or heavy goods vehicles. The only exceptions for using a mobile phone while driving are to call the emergency services, or when the driver is safely parked.

REGULATION

Under the Communications Act 2003, OFCOM is the independent regulator and competition authority for the UK communications industries, with responsibilities across television, radio, telecommunications and wireless communications services. Competition in the communications market is also regulated by the Office of Fair Trading, although OFCOM takes the lead in competition investigations in the UK market. The Competition Appeal Tribunal hears appeals against OFCOM's decisions, and price-related appeals are referred to the Competition Commission.

OFCOM, Riverside House, 2A Southwark Bridge Road, London SE1 9HA T 020-7981 3040 W www.ofcom.org.uk

INTERNET

INTERNET TRENDS

In 2012, 21 million households in Great Britain had internet access. This represented 80 per cent of households, up from 77 per cent in 2011. Of the households with internet access, 93 per cent used a fixed broadband connection, of which 30 per cent used a cable or fibre optic connection.

There was rapid growth in the use of tablet computers to access the internet, with 21 per cent of adults using a tablet to access the internet outside of the home or workplace in 2012, although 34 per cent of people still used a laptop to access the internet 'on the go'.

Over a two-year period between 2010–12, the number of adults who used a mobile phone to access the internet increased from 24 per cent to 51 per cent, with 80 per cent of those aged 16 to 34 reporting that they used their mobile phone to access the internet in 2012. The dramatic increase in these figures is predominantly due to the ownership of smartphones with enhanced technology to facilitate easier internet access.

In 2012, almost half of all adults used social networking sites such as Facebook and Twitter with 87 per cent of those aged 16 to 24 using these media platforms as a form of internet communication. For this age range, social networking replaced sending emails as the most popular internet activity; the first time email use had not been identified as the most performed internet activity since comparable records began.

The youngest demographic represented, aged 16 to 24, were proportionally the largest users of many of the available internet activities, due to their familiarity with the concept of internet usage from an early age. This age group were most likely to engage in online activities including social networking, blogging, or downloading games, films or music. Those aged 25 to 34 engaged in more established activities such as personal banking and shopping – the latter saw an increased demand in Great Britain, with 67 per cent of adults buying goods or services online in 2012. A rise in internet shopping was also evident among those aged over 65, as nearly 32 per cent made purchases online, twice as many as in 2008.

There were 5.2 million households with no internet access in 2012, the majority (54 per cent) stating they did not need it. One in five households said they did not have an internet connection due to a lack of computer skills, while other reasons included equipment and access costs. In 2012, 33 million adults accessed the internet daily, more than double the figure that did so in 2006.

TOP 10 BROADBAND SUBSCRIBERS BY COUNTRY

Country (2011 position)	*2012*
1. China (all territories) (1)	167,014,744
2. USA (2)	94,000,180
3. Japan (3)	37,292,400
4. Germany (4)	29,555,500
5. Russia (10)	22,830,900
6. France (5)	22,632,200
7. United Kingdom (6)	21,269,300
8. South Korea (7)	18,103,946
9. Brazil (9)	17,867,925
10. India (12)	13,991,600

Sources: Office for National Statistics – *Internet Access – Households and Individuals, 2012* (Crown Copyright); www.point-topic.com

GLOSSARY OF TERMS

The following is a list of selected internet terms. It is by no means exhaustive but is intended to cover those that the average computer user might encounter.

BANNER AD: An advertisement on a web page that links to a corresponding website when clicked.

BLOG: Short for 'web log' – an online personal journal that is frequently updated and intended to be read by the public. Blogs are kept by 'bloggers' and are commonly available as RSS feeds.

BROWSER: Typically refers to a 'web browser' program that allows a computer user to view web page content on their computer, eg Firefox, Internet Explorer or Safari.

CLICK-THROUGH: The number of times a web user 'clicks through' a paid advertisement link to the corresponding website.

CLOUD COMPUTING: The use of IT resources as an on-demand service across a network; through cloud computing, software, advanced computation and archived information can be accessed remotely, without the user needing local dedicated hardware.

COOKIE: A piece of information placed on a user's hard disk by a web server. Cookies contain data about the user's activity on a website, and are returned to the server whenever a browser makes further requests. They are important for remembering information such as login and registration details, 'shopping cart' data, user preferences etc, and are often set to expire after a fixed period.

DOMAIN: A set of words or letters, separated by dots, used to identify an internet server, eg www.whitakersalmanack.com, where 'www' denotes a web (http) server, 'whitakersalmanack' denotes the organisation name, 'co' denotes that the organisation is a company and 'uk' indicates United Kingdom.

FIREWALL: A protection system designed to prevent unauthorised access to or from a private network.

FTP: File Transfer Protocol – a set of network rules enabling a user to exchange files with a remote server.

HACKER: A person who attempts to break or 'hack' into websites. Motives typically involve the desire to procure personal information such as addresses, passwords or credit card details. Hackers may also delete code or incorporate traces of malicious code to damage the functionality of a website.

HIT: A single request from a web browser for a single item from a web server. In order for a web browser to display a page that contains three graphics, four 'hits' would occur at the server: one for the HTML page and one for each of the three graphics. Therefore the number of hits on a website is not synonymous with the number of visitors.

HTML: HyperText Mark-up Language – a programming language used to denote or mark up how an internet page should be presented to a user from an HTTP server via a web browser.

HTTP: HyperText Transfer Protocol – an internet protocol whereby a web server sends web pages, images and files to a web browser.

HYPERLINK: A piece of specially coded text that users can click on to navigate to the web page, or element of a web page, associated with that link's code. Links are typically distinguished through the use of bold, underlined or differently coloured text.

JAVA: A programming language used widely on the internet.

MALWARE: A combination of the words 'malicious' and 'software'. Malware is software designed with the intention of infiltrating a computer and damaging its system.

OPEN-SOURCE: Describes a computer program that has its source code (the instructions that make up a program) freely available for viewing and modification.

PAGERANK: A link analysis algorithm used by search engines that assigns a numerical value based on a website's relevance and reputation. In general, a site with a higher pagerank has more traffic than a site with a lower one.

PHISHING: The fraudulent practice of sending emails to acquire personal information by masquerading as a legitimate company.

PODCASTING: A form of audio and video broadcasting using the internet. Although the word is a portmanteau of 'iPod' and broadcasting, podcasting does not require the use of an iPod. A podcaster creates a list of files and makes it available in the RSS 2.0 format. The list can then be obtained using podcast 'retriever' software which makes the files available to digital devices (including iPods); users may then listen or watch at their convenience.

RSS FEED: Rich Site Summary or RDF Site Summary or Real Simple Syndication – a commonly used protocol for syndication and sharing of content, originally developed to facilitate the syndication of news articles, now widely used to share the content of blogs.

SEO: Search engine optimisation – the process of optimising the content of a web page to ensure that it is indexed by search engines.

SERVER: A node on a network that provides service to the terminals on the network. These computers have higher hardware specifications, ie more resources and greater speed, in order to handle large amounts of data.

SOCIAL NETWORKING: The practice of using a web-hosted service such as Facebook or Twitter to upload and share content and build friendship networks.

SPAM: A term used for unsolicited, generally junk, email.

TRAFFIC: The number of visitors to a website.

TWITTER: An online microblogging service that allows users to stay connected through the exchange of 140-character posts, known as 'tweets'.

URL: Uniform Resource Locator – address of a file accessible on the internet, eg http://www.whitakersalmanack.com

USER-GENERATED CONTENT (UGC): Refers to various media content produced or primarily influenced by end-users, as opposed to traditional media producers such as licensed broadcasters and production companies. These forms of media include digital video, blogging, podcasting, mobile phone photography and wikis.

WEB 2.0: Generally refers to a second generation of services available on the web that lets people collaborate and share information online. In contrast to the static web pages of the first generation, Web 2.0 gives users an experience closer to that of desktop applications.

WIKI: Software that allows users to freely create and edit web page content using any web browser.

THE ENVIRONMENT

The World Bank-commissioned report *Turn Down the Heat,* published on 18 November 2012, issued a stark warning that the world will witness a 4°C rise by the end of the 21st century. The report, reviewed by some of the world's foremost scientists, spells out that if nothing is done to limit global warming, the 22nd century will be marked by a rise in sea-levels, extreme heat-waves, decreasing food stocks, and the loss of ecosystems and diversity, particularly as a result of ocean acidification. If these devastating events occur, it is beyond doubt that the poorest and most vulnerable parts of the world would be hit hardest. The World Bank report highlighted that through greater efficiency and a more prudent approach to energy consumption and the management of natural resources, it should be possible to dramatically reduce the threat of global warming without scaling down efforts at poverty alleviation and financial growth. However, in this prolonged period of austerity, where climate change has unequivocally slipped down the list of priorities, it is hard to imagine governments looking beyond short-term economic recovery to address what could be a very bleak long-term picture.

CLIMATE CHANGE

The 2012 United Nations Climate Change Conference took place between 26 November and 8 December in Doha, Qatar, just a week after the publication of the World Bank's report.

One of the more promising advances at the conference was the unprecedented agreement in principle that the world's wealthier nations could be deemed financially responsible to other nations if they fail to reduce their carbon emissions. For the first time, 'loss' and 'damage from climate change' were enshrined in a legal document. However, the resultant agreement was a far cry from the original proposals calling for the creation of a new international body to collect funds and disseminate them to vulnerable developing countries; the USA, among other countries, was strongly opposed to the creation of a new body, suggesting that existing international institutions may be utilised for this purpose. The question of exactly how 'loss and damage' will be worked out and who will oversee it, will be one of the central questions at the 2013 conference, to be held in November in Warsaw.

At the conference the terms of the Durban Platform – agreed in principal at the 2011 conference – to develop a new legally binding international treaty on global warming by 2015, and to have this implemented by 2020, were reaffirmed. In the meantime the Kyoto Protocol has been extended until the end of 2020, although this agreement is rather limited in scope, as it currently only extends across Europe and Australia, which account for just 15 per cent of total world carbon emissions. Additionally, progress has been stifled by the absence of binding targets for developing countries, including the world's largest emitter, China, and the rapidly growing economies of Brazil and India. The USA refused to ratify the protocol, Canada withdrew in June 2012 and Russia, Japan and New Zealand have decided not to adhere to the new targets in the second commitment period.

CARBON DIOXIDE EMISSIONS

The UK's net emissions of carbon dioxide were provisionally estimated at 479.1 million tonnes in 2012 (4.5 per cent higher than the 2011 figure of 458.6 million tonnes). In 2012, all but one of the main sectors recorded rises in carbon dioxide emissions from 2011. The provisional estimates show increases of 5.5 per cent (9.9 million tonnes) from the energy supply sector, 11.8 per cent (7.8 million tonnes) from the residential sector, and 4.8 per cent (3.6 million tonnes) from the business sector. The Transport sector was the exception, with a reduction of 1.2 per cent (1.4 million tonnes) from 2011. The increase in carbon dioxide emissions between 2011 and 2012 can be mainly attributed to a greater use of coal for electricity generation at power stations, together with an increase in residential gas use.

UK CO_2 EMISSIONS BY FUEL
million tonnes

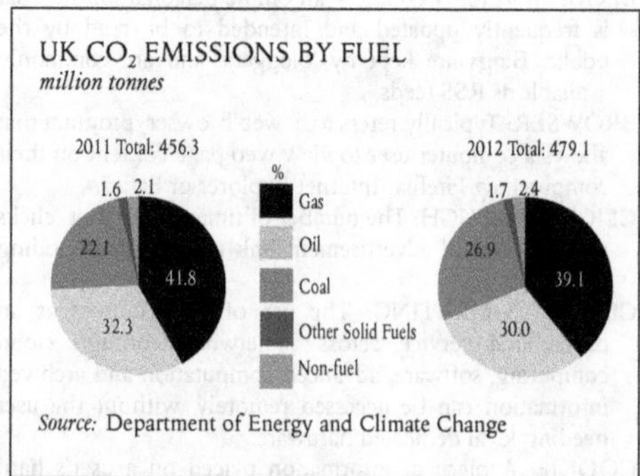

Source: Department of Energy and Climate Change

PLUG-IN CAR GRANT

Two measures the government has employed to reduce emissions further in the transport sector are the plug-in car grant, which was established in 2011, and the plug-in van grant, which commenced in March 2012. The plug-in car grant allows a contribution of 25 per cent (up to a maximum of £5,000) towards the cost of a car with exhaust pipe emissions of 75g CO_2/km or under, while the plug-in van grant provides purchasers with 20 per cent (up to a maximum of £8,000) towards the cost of a van with emissions of 75g CO_2/km or under. Potentially eligible cars include electric, plug-in hybrid and hydrogen-fuelled models. This fund was set-up to make qualifying cars a financially viable option compared with their diesel and petrol competitors. By the end of 2012, around 3,000 grants had been claimed through the scheme, more than double the number of grants claimed in 2011. As of 30 June 2013 4,553 claims had been made. More eligible cars are due to be launched before the end of the year, including the Tesla Model S, Ford Focus EV and BMW i3. The plug-in van grant has seen a modest uptake, with 310 claims as at 30 June 2013.

Plug-in car grants are currently eligible with 12 plug-in cars: the Chevrolet Volt, Citroen CZero, Mia, Mitsubishi i-MiEV, Nissan LEAF, Peugeot iOn, Renault Fluence ZE, Renault ZOE, Smart fortwo electric drive, Toyota Prius Plug-in Hybrid, Vauxhall Ampera and the Volvo V60. The vans eligible for the Plug-in van grant are: BD Otomotiv Veicoli eTrafic van, Daimler Mercedes-Benz Vito E-Cell,

Faam ECOMILE, Faam JOLLY 2000, Mia electric Mia U, Renault Kangoo Van ZE, and the Smith Electric Edison Van.

RENEWABLE ENERGY

According to the European Renewable Energy Council (EREC), the UK is not on track to meet its 2020 renewable energy targets. Preliminary figures published by the Renewable Energy Association (REA) revealed that the UK is the only EU member state which failed to achieve its first interim target by the end of 2011. However, the UK is not the only member state not expected to meet its targets. The EREC does not expect Belgium, Poland or Spain to come close to meeting their 2020 targets and admits to 'serious doubts' about the chances of Germany, Greece, Bulgaria and Portugal.

THE LONDON ARRAY

The London Array – the world's largest offshore wind farm – became fully operational in April 2013 in the Thames Estuary, approximately 20km off the Kent and Essex coast. Phase one of the project comprises 175 wind turbines generating a maximum output of 630MW – enough energy to power nearly 500,000 homes. Over 75 organisations helped to build the London Array with a combined workforce of around 6,700 people. Ownership of the farm is 50 per cent DONG energy (Denmark's largest energy company), 30 per cent E.ON UK Renewables and 20 per cent Masdar (a renewable energy company based in Abu Dhabi, UAE). Challenging financial conditions led DONG energy to approach the European Investment Bank in 2009 to secure a loan to help finance the project. A sum of £250m was agreed in June 2010, which was guaranteed by the Danish Export Credit Agency. A proposed extension to the wind farm would span an additional 40 sq. km along the eastern boundary of the existing phase one farm and would generate a further 370MW. However, progress is currently on hold following concerns voiced by the Royal Society for the Protection of Birds (RSPB) regarding the impact on the winter habitat of the red-throated diver.

FRACKING

In August 2013 the quiet village of Balcombe in Sussex became the unassuming centre of the global debate about hydraulic fracturing, or fracking after the oil and gas exploration company Cuadrilla Resources commenced test drilling at their site close to the village. Fracking is the fracturing of underground rock through the injection of a pressurised liquid – usually water mixed with various chemicals and sand – in order to extract gas and oil. While fracking has been carried out in North Sea oil fields for many years, it was only in 2007, that Cuadrilla was granted a licence to attempt shale gas extraction on the UK mainland. Cuadrilla began drilling near Blackpool in 2011, but voluntarily suspended their operations in June 2011 after fracking activity caused two minor earthquakes. However, Cuadrilla resumed their operations after a report published by the British Geological Survey in April 2012 deemed that fracking was a safe process and could be used nationwide.

Despite concern from environmental groups about dangerous contaminants entering water supplies and methane emissions from drill wells, the UK government expressed its support for the fracking industry, outlining that it has the capacity to reduce energy bills, reinvigorate regions of the UK and create more jobs. Prime minister David Cameron offered assurances that the industry is safe and would be properly regulated: 'Nothing is going to happen in this country unless its environmentally safe. There is no question of having earthquakes and fire coming out of taps and all the rest of it. There will be very clear environmental procedures and certificates you will have to get before you can frack'. In July 2013, the chancellor George Osborne announced significant tax breaks to encourage fracking companies, setting a 30 per cent tax rate for onshore gas production, compared with a top rate of 62 per cent on new North Sea oil operations. There is little doubt that fracking could increase the UK's energy security, but, it will further extend the UK's reliance on fossil fuels, rendering it increasingly difficult to reach carbon reduction targets to help mitigate climate change.

EUROPEAN UNION MEASURES

In June 2013, the European parliament agreed on a new Environment Action Programme (EAP) – the 7th EAP – which sets out key EU environment policy objectives through to 2020. The aim of this EAP is to lead Europe towards a resource-efficient, low-carbon and environmentally-friendly economy in which natural capital is both protected and improved, and the health and well-being of the citizens of member states are safeguarded. To help achieve this end, the EAP set out nine priorities:

- The limitation of landfilling to non-recyclable and non-recoverable waste by 2020
- The recognition of the need for a legally binding framework on climate change and energy policy beyond 2020 to enable member states and industry to make the necessary investments in emissions reduction, energy efficiency and renewable energy, taking into account the indicative milestones set out in the Low Carbon Economy Roadmap to 2050
- Agreement on the need to address EU soil quality issues including consideration of a binding legal framework
- Agreement on the establishment of a more coherent policy and legislative framework for sustainable consumption and production
- Agreement on the need to establish an EU-wide quantitative reduction headline target for marine litter
- Agreement that the combination effects of chemicals and safety concerns related to endocrine disruptors and nano-materials must be effectively addressed across all relevant EU legislation
- Agreement on the need to further develop inspection support capacity at EU level, in order to increase the efficiency and effectiveness of inspections. This will also contribute to a more level playing field within the EU
- Agreement on the need to phase-out environmentally harmful subsidies at member state and EU level
- The integration of environmental considerations including water protection and biodiversity conservation into land use planning decisions, with a view to making progress towards the objective of no net land take by 2050

EMISSIONS TRADING SCHEME

Commencing in 2005, the EU emissions trading system (EU ETS) is now in its third phase, which runs from 2013 to 2020. Following a major revision approved in 2009, the third phase is significantly different from phases one and two and incorporates the following key changes:

- A single EU-wide cap on emissions applies in place of the previous system of national caps
- Auctioning, not free allocation, is now the default method for allocating allowances. In 2013 more than 40 per cent of allowances will be auctioned, and this share will rise progressively each year

- For those allowances still given away for free, harmonised allocation rules apply which are based on EU-wide benchmarks of emissions performance
- Some more sectors and gases are included

GENETIC MODIFICATION

Genetic modification is a biotechnology that is being used to make new products, in particular new types of crop plant. Under EU legislation, genetically modified organisms (GMOs), including GM crops, can only be released from the environment if a science-based risk assessment shows that safety will not be compromised. GM normally involves the insertion of genes carrying a specific trait (eg pest resistance) from one organism into another, although other GM techniques are possible. The result is a GMO.

No GM crops are being grown commercially in the UK, but imported GM commodities, especially soya, are being used for animal feed, and to a lesser extent in some food products. Only one type of GM crop is currently authorised for cultivation in the EU: an insect-resistant maize (known as MON810). However, it is currently banned in seven EU countries (Austria, Germany, Greece, Hungary, Italy, Luxembourg and Poland). In 2012, five EU member states grew MON810 maize over 129,000 hectares. Spain was the top producer, followed by Portugal, the Czech Republic, Slovakia and Romania. Another GM crop had been granted approval by the EU in 2010 – a potato modified to produce more of a type of starch that is useful for papermaking and other industrial processes – but the crop's producer, German chemical firm BASF, announced it was halting development in February 2013.

CONTACTS

DEPARTMENT FOR ENVIRONMENT, FOOD AND RURAL AFFAIRS (DEFRA), Nobel House, 17 Smith Square, London SW1P 3JR **T** 0845-933 5577
W www.gov.uk/government/organisations/department-for-environment-food-rural-affairs

DEPARTMENT OF ENERGY AND CLIMATE CHANGE, 3 Whitehall Place, London SW1A 2AW **T** 0300-060 4000
W www.gov.uk/government/organisations/department-of-energy-climate-change

ENVIRONMENT AGENCY, National Customer Contact Centre, PO Box 544, Rotherham S60 1BY **T** 0370-850 6506
W www.environment-agency.gov.uk

EUROPEAN ENVIRONMENT AGENCY, Kongens Nytorv 6,1050 Copenhagen K, Denmark **T** +45 3336 7100
W www.eea.europa.eu

SCOTTISH GOVERNMENT, ENVIRONMENT AND FORESTRY DIRECTORATE, Victoria Quay, Edinburgh EH6 6QQ **T** 0845-774 1741 **W** www.scotland.gov.uk

WELSH GOVERNMENT ENVIRONMENT AND SUSTAINABLE DEVELOPMENT, Cathays Park, Cardiff CF10 3NQ **T** 0300-0603 300 **W** www.wales.gov.uk

CONSERVATION AND HERITAGE

NATIONAL PARKS

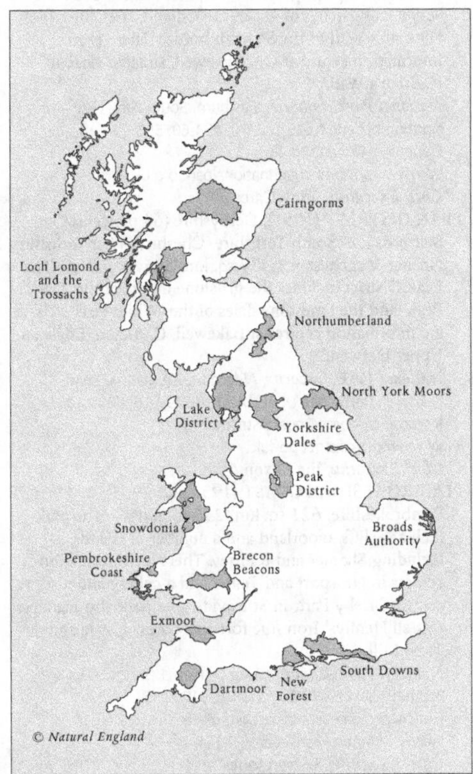

ENGLAND AND WALES

There are nine national parks in England, and three in Wales. In addition, the Norfolk and Suffolk Broads are considered to have equivalent status to a national park. Under the provisions of the National Parks and Access to the Countryside Act 1949, as clarified by the Natural Environment and Rural Communities Act 2006, the two purposes of the national parks are to conserve and enhance the parks' natural beauty, wildlife and cultural heritage, and to promote opportunities for the understanding and enjoyment of the special qualities of national parks by the public. If there is a conflict between the two purposes, then conservation takes precedence.

Natural England is the statutory body that has the power to designate national parks in England, and Natural Resources Wales (formerly Countryside Council for Wales) is responsible for national parks in Wales. Designations in England are confirmed by the Secretary of State for Environment, Food and Rural Affairs and those in Wales by the Welsh government. The designation of a national park does not affect the ownership of the land or remove the rights of the local community. The majority of the land in the national parks is owned by private landowners (around 75 per cent) or by bodies such as the National Trust and the Forestry Commission. The national park authorities own only a small percentage of the land themselves.

The Environment Act 1995 replaced the existing national park boards and committees with free-standing national park authorities (NPAs). NPAs are the sole local planning authorities for their areas and as such influence land use and development, and deal with planning applications. NPAs are responsible for carrying out the statutory purposes of national parks stated above.

In pursuing these purposes they have a statutory duty to seek to foster the economic and social well-being of the communities within national parks. The NPAs publish management plans setting out overarching policies for their area and appoint their own officers and staff.

The Broads Authority was established under the Norfolk and Suffolk Broads Act 1988 and meets the requirement for the authority to have a navigation function in addition to a regard for the needs of agriculture, forestry and the economic and social interests of those who live or work in the Broads.

MEMBERSHIP

Membership of English NPAs comprises local authority appointees, members directly appointed by the Secretary of State for Environment, Food and Rural Affairs and members appointed by the secretary after consultation with local parishes. Under the Natural Environment and Rural Communities Act 2006 every district, county or unitary authority with land in a national park is entitled to appoint at least one member unless it chooses to opt out. The total number of local authority and parish members must exceed the number of national members. Most of the English NPAs currently have 22 members, except the Peak District which has 30 and the South Downs which has 27 members.

The Broads Authority has 21 members: nine appointed by the constituent local authorities, two appointed by the Navigation Committee and ten appointed by the secretary of state. The secretary of state's appointees include at least three which are appointed after consultation with representatives of boating interests and at least two which are appointed after consultation with representatives of landowning and farming interests.

In Wales, two-thirds of NPA members are appointed by the constituent local authorities and one-third by the Welsh government, advised by Natural Resources Wales.

FUNDING

The English NPAs and the Broads Authority are funded by central government. In the financial year 2013–14 a core grant totalling £49.45m was allocated between the authorities.

In Wales, national parks are funded via a grant from the Welsh government. The grant for 2012–13 amounted to £11.42m. The three NPAs in Wales receive further funding via a local authority levy.

All NPAs and the Broads Authority can take advantage of grants from other bodies including lottery and European grants.

The national parks (with date that designation was confirmed) are:

BRECON BEACONS (1957), Powys (66 per cent)/ Carmarthenshire/Rhondda, Cynon and Taff/Merthyr Tydfil/Blaenau Gwent/Monmouthshire, 1,347 sq. km/ 520 sq. miles – The park is centred on the Brecon Beacons mountain range, which includes the three highest

mountains in southern Britain (Pen y Fan, Corn Du and Cribyn), but also includes the valley of the rivers Usk and Wye, the Black Mountains to the east and the Black Mountain to the west. There are information centres at the visitor centre at Libanus (near Brecon), Abergavenny and Llandovery, as well as the Waterfalls Centre in Pontneddfechan.
National Park Authority, Plas y Ffynnon, Cambrian Way, Brecon, Powys LD3 7HP T 01874-624437
W www.breconbeacons.org
Chief Executive, John Cook

BROADS (1989), Norfolk/Suffolk, 303 sq. km/117 sq. miles – The Broads are located between Norwich and Great Yarmouth on the flood plains of the six rivers flowing through the area to the sea. The area is one of fens, winding waterways, woodland and marsh. The 60 or so broads are man-made, and many are connected to the rivers by dykes, providing over 200km (125 miles) of navigable waterways. There are information centres at Hoveton, Whitlingham Country Park and Toad Hole Cottage at How Hill.
Broads Authority, Yare House, 62–64 Thorpe Road, Norwich NR1 1RY T 01603-610734 W www.broads-authority.gov.uk
Chief Executive, Dr John Packman

DARTMOOR (1951), Devon, 953 sq. km/368 sq. miles – The park consists of moorland and rocky granite tors, and is rich in prehistoric remains. There are visitor centres at Haytor, Princetown (main visitor centre) and Postbridge.
National Park Authority, Parke, Bovey Tracey, Devon TQ13 9JQ T 01626-832093 E hq@dartmoor-npa.gov.uk
W www.dartmoor-npa.gov.uk
Chief Executive, Kevin Bishop

EXMOOR (1954), Somerset (71 per cent)/Devon, 692 sq. km/267 sq. miles – Exmoor is a moorland plateau inhabited by wild Exmoor ponies and red deer. There are many ancient remains and burial mounds. There are national park centres at Dunster, Dulverton and Lynmouth.
National Park Authority, Exmoor House, Dulverton, Somerset TA22 9HL T 01398-323665 E info@exmoor-nationalpark.gov.uk
W www.exmoor-nationalpark.gov.uk
Chief Executive, Dr Nigel Stone

LAKE DISTRICT (1951), Cumbria, 2,292 sq. km/885 sq. miles – The Lake District includes England's highest mountains (Scafell Pike, Helvellyn and Skiddaw) but it is most famous for its glaciated lakes. There are national park information centres at Bowness-on-Windermere, Keswick, Ullswater and a visitor centre at Brockhole, Windermere.
National Park Authority, Murley Moss, Oxenholme Road, Kendal, Cumbria LA9 7RL T 01539-724555
E hq@lakedistrict.gov.uk W www.lakedistrict.gov.uk
Chief Executive, Richard Leafe

NEW FOREST (2005), Hampshire, 570 sq. km/220 sq. miles – The forest has been protected since 1079 when it was declared a royal hunting forest. The area consists of forest, ancient woodland, heathland, farmland, coastal saltmarsh and mudflats. Much of the forest is managed by the Forestry Commission, which provides several campsites. There is a visitor centre at Lyndhurst.
National Park Authority, Town Hall, Avenue Road, Lymington, Hants SO41 9ZG T 01590-646600
E enquiries@newforestnpa.gov.uk
W www.newforestnpa.gov.uk
Chief Executive, Alison Barnes

NORTH YORK MOORS (1952), North Yorkshire (96 per cent)/Redcar and Cleveland, 1,434 sq. km/554 sq. miles – The park consists of woodland and moorland, and includes the Hambleton Hills and the Cleveland Way. There are visitor centres at Danby and Sutton Bank.
National Park Authority, The Old Vicarage, Bondgate, Helmsley, York YO62 5BP T 01439-772700
E general@northyorkmoors.org.uk
W www.northyorkmoors.org.uk
Chief Executive, Andy Wilson

NORTHUMBERLAND (1956), Northumberland, 1,049 sq. km/405 sq. miles – The park is an area of hill country, comprising open moorland, blanket bogs and very small patches of ancient woodland, stretching from Hadrian's Wall to the Scottish border. There is an information centre at Once Brewed, situated close to Hadrian's Wall.
National Park Authority, Eastburn, South Park, Hexham, Northumberland NE46 1BS T 01434-605555
E enquiries@nnpa.org.uk
W www.northumberlandnationalpark.org.uk
Chief Executive, Tony Gates

PEAK DISTRICT (1951), Derbyshire (64 per cent)/Staffordshire/South Yorkshire/Cheshire/West Yorkshire/Greater Manchester, 1,437 sq. km/555 sq. miles – The Peak District includes the gritstone moors of the 'Dark Peak' and the limestone dales of the 'White Peak'. There are information centres at Bakewell, Castleton, Edale and Upper Derwent.
National Park Authority, Aldern House, Baslow Road, Bakewell, Derbyshire DE45 1AE T 01629-816200
E customer.service@peakdistrict.gov.uk
W www.peakdistrict.gov.uk
Chief Executive, Jim Dixon

PEMBROKESHIRE COAST (1952 and 1995), Pembrokeshire, 621 sq. km/236 sq. miles – The park includes cliffs, moorland and a number of islands, including Skomer and Ramsey. There are information centres in Newport and Tenby and a gallery and visitor centre, Oriel y Parc, in St Davids. The park also manages Castell Henllys' Iron Age fort and Carew Castle and Tidal Mill.
National Park Authority, Llanion Park, Pembroke Dock, Pembrokeshire SA72 6DY T 0845-345 7275
E info@pembrokeshirecoast.org.uk
W www.pembrokeshirecoast.org.uk
Chief Executive, Tegryn Jones

SNOWDONIA/ERYRI (1951), Gwynedd/Conwy, 2,132 sq. km/823 sq. miles – Snowdonia, which takes its name from Snowdon – the highest peak in England and Wales – is an area of deep valleys and rugged mountains. There are information centres at Aberdyfi, Beddgelert, Betws y Coed, Dolgellau and Harlech.
National Park Authority, Penrhyndeudraeth, Gwynedd LL48 6LF T 01766-770274 E parc@snowdonia-npa.gov.uk
W www.snowdonia-npa.gov.uk
Chief Executive, Aneurin Phillips

THE SOUTH DOWNS (2010), West Sussex/Hampshire, 1,648 sq. km/636 sq. miles – The South Downs contains a diversity of natural habitats, including flower-studded chalk grassland, ancient woodland, flood meadow, lowland heath and rare chalk heathland. There are visitor centres at Beachy Head, Queen Elizabeth Country Park in Hampshire and Seven Sisters Country Park in East Sussex.
National Park Authority, Hatton House, Bepton Road, Midhurst, W. Sussex GU29 9LU T 0300-303 1053
W www.southdowns.gov.uk
Chief Executive, Trevor Beattie

YORKSHIRE DALES (1954), North Yorkshire (88 per cent)/Cumbria, 1,762 sq. km/680 sq. miles – The Yorkshire Dales is composed primarily of limestone overlaid in places by millstone grit. The three peaks of Ingleborough, Whernside and Pen-y-ghent are within the

park. There are information centres at Grassington, Hawes, Aysgarth Falls, Malham and Reeth.
National Park Authority, Yoredale, Bainbridge, Leyburn, N. Yorks DL8 3EL T 0300-456 0030
E info@yorkshiredales.org.uk W www.yorkshiredales.org.uk
Chief Executive, David Butterworth

SCOTLAND

On 9 August 2000 the national parks (Scotland) bill received royal assent, giving parliament the ability to create national parks in Scotland. The first two Scottish national parks became operational in 2002 and 2003 respectively. The Act gives Scottish parks wider powers than in England and Wales, including statutory responsibilities for the local economy and rural communities. The board of each Scottish NPA consists of 25 members, of which five are directly elected by a postal ballot of the local electorate. The remaining 20 members, ten of which are nominated by the constituent local authorities, are chosen by the Scottish ministers. In Scotland, the national parks are central government bodies and are wholly funded by the Scottish government. Funding for 2013–14 totals £12.56m.

CAIRNGORMS (2003), North-East Scotland, 4,528 sq. km/1,748 sq. miles – The Cairngorms national park is the largest in the UK. It displays a vast collection of landforms, including five of the six highest mountains in the UK and contains 25 per cent of Britain's threatened species. The near natural woodlands contain remnants of the original ancient Caledonian pine forest. There are nine visitor centres within the park.
National Park Authority, 14 The Square, Grantown-on-Spey, Morayshire PH26 3HG T 01479-873535
E enquiries@cairngorms.co.uk W www.cairngorms.co.uk
Chief Executive, Grant Moir

LOCH LOMOND AND THE TROSSACHS (2002), Argyll and Bute/Perth and Kinross/Stirling/West Dunbartonshire, 1,865 sq. km/720 sq. miles – The park boundaries encompass lochs, rivers, forests, 21 mountains above 914m (3,000ft) including Ben More and a further 19 mountains between 762m (2,500ft) and 3,000ft. There is a national park centre in Balmaha and a visitor centre in Inveruglas. There are also nine visitor centres administered by VisitScotland.
National Park Authority, Carrochan, Carrochan Road, Balloch G83 8EG T 01389-722600 E info@lochlomond-trossachs.org
W www.lochlomond-trossachs.org
Chief Executive, Fiona Logan

NORTHERN IRELAND

There is a power to designate national parks in Northern Ireland under the Nature Conservation and Amenity Lands Order (Northern Ireland) 1985, but there are currently no national parks in Northern Ireland.

AREAS OF OUTSTANDING NATURAL BEAUTY

ENGLAND AND WALES

Under the National Parks and Access to the Countryside Act 1949, provision was made for the designation of areas of outstanding natural beauty (AONBs). Natural England is responsible for AONBs in England and Natural Resources Wales for the Welsh AONBs. Designations in England are confirmed by the Secretary of State for Environment, Food and Rural Affairs and those in Wales by the National Assembly for Wales. The Countryside and Rights of Way (CROW) Act 2000 placed greater responsibility on local authorities to protect AONBs and made it a statutory duty for relevant authorities to produce a management plan for their AONB area. The CROW Act also provided for the creation of conservation boards for larger and more complex AONBs. The first two conservation boards for the Cotswolds and Chilterns AONBs were established in July 2004.

The primary objective of the AONB designation is to conserve and enhance the natural beauty of the area. Where an AONB has a conservation board, it has the additional purpose of increasing public understanding and enjoyment of the special qualities of the area; the board has greater weight should there be a conflict of interests between the two. In addition, the board is also required to foster the economic and social well-being of the local communities but without incurring significant expenditure in doing so. Overall responsibility for AONBs lies with the relevant local authorities or conservation board. To coordinate planning and management responsibilities between local authorities in whose area they fall, AONBs are overseen by a joint advisory committee (or similar body) which includes representatives from the local authorities, landowners, farmers, residents and conservation and recreation groups. Core funding for AONBs is provided by central government through DEFRA and Natural Resources Wales.

The 38 AONBs (with date designation confirmed) are:

ARNSIDE AND SILVERDALE (1972), Cumbria/Lancashire, 75 sq. km/29 sq. miles
BLACKDOWN HILLS (1991), Devon/Somerset, 370 sq. km/143 sq. miles
CANNOCK CHASE (1958), Staffordshire, 70 sq. km/27 sq. miles
CHICHESTER HARBOUR (1964), Hampshire/West Sussex, 73 sq. km/28 sq. miles
CHILTERNS (1965; extended 1990), Bedfordshire/Buckinghamshire/Herefordshire/Oxfordshire, 839 sq. km/324 sq. miles
CLWYDIAN RANGE AND DEE VALLEY (1985; extended 2011), Denbighshire/Flintshire, 389 sq. km/150 sq. miles
CORNWALL (1959; Camel Estuary 1983), 963 sq. km/372 sq. miles
COTSWOLDS (1966; extended 1990), Gloucestershire/Oxfordshire/Warwickshire/Wiltshire/Worcestershire, 2,041 sq. km/788 sq. miles
CRANBORNE CHASE AND WEST WILTSHIRE DOWNS (1983), Dorset/Hampshire/Somerset/Wiltshire, 987 sq. km/381 sq. miles
DEDHAM VALE (1970; extended 1978, 1991), Essex/Suffolk, 90 sq. km/35 sq. miles
DORSET (1959), Dorset/Somerset, 1,129 sq. km/436 sq. miles
EAST DEVON (1963), 269 sq. km/104 sq. miles
FOREST OF BOWLAND (1964), Lancashire/North Yorkshire, 805 sq. km/311 sq. miles
GOWER (1956), Swansea, 188 sq. km/73 sq. miles
HIGH WEALD (1983), East Sussex/Kent/Surrey/West Sussex, 1,460 sq. km/564 sq. miles
HOWARDIAN HILLS (1987), North Yorkshire, 204 sq. km/79 sq. miles
ISLE OF WIGHT (1963), 192 sq. km/74 sq. miles
ISLES OF SCILLY (1976), 16 sq. km/6 sq. miles
KENT DOWNS (1968), 878 sq. km/339 sq. miles
LINCOLNSHIRE WOLDS (1973), 559 sq. km/216 sq. miles
LLYN (1957), Gwynedd, 161 sq. km/62 sq. miles
MALVERN HILLS (1959), Gloucestershire/Worcestershire, 105 sq. km/41 sq. miles
MENDIP HILLS (1972; extended 1989), Somerset, 199 sq. km/77 sq. miles

NIDDERDALE (1994), North Yorkshire, 601 sq. km/232 sq. miles
NORFOLK COAST (1968), 445 sq. km/172 sq. miles
NORTH DEVON (1960), 171 sq. km/66 sq. miles
NORTH PENNINES (1988), Cumbria/Durham/North Yorkshire/Northumberland, 1,983 sq. km/766 sq. miles
NORTH WESSEX DOWNS (1972), Hampshire/Oxfordshire/Wiltshire, 1,730 sq. km/668 sq. miles
NORTHUMBERLAND COAST (1958), 132 sq. km/51 sq. miles
QUANTOCK HILLS (1957), Somerset, 99 sq. km/38 sq. miles
SHROPSHIRE HILLS (1959), 808 sq. km/312 sq. miles
SOLWAY COAST (1964), Cumbria, 122 sq. km/47 sq. miles
SOUTH DEVON (1960), 339 sq. km/131 sq. miles
SUFFOLK COAST AND HEATHS (1970), 403 sq. km/156 sq. miles
SURREY HILLS (1958), 422 sq. km/163 sq. miles
TAMAR VALLEY (1995), Cornwall/Devon, 197 sq. km/76 sq. miles
WYE VALLEY (1971), Gloucestershire/Herefordshire/Monmouthshire, 326 sq. km/126 sq. miles
YNYS MON (ISLE OF ANGLESEY) (1967), 221 sq. km/85 sq. miles

NORTHERN IRELAND

The Department of the Environment for Northern Ireland, with advice from the Council for Nature Conservation and the Countryside, designates AONBs in Northern Ireland. At present there are eight and these cover a total area of 2,849 sq. km (1,100 sq. miles). Dates given are those of designation.

ANTRIM COAST AND GLENS (1988), Co. Antrim, 706 sq. km/272 sq. miles
BINEVENAGH (2006), Co. Londonderry, 166 sq. km/64 sq. miles
CAUSEWAY COAST (1989), Co. Antrim, 42 sq. km/16 sq. miles
LAGAN VALLEY (1965), Co. Down, 39 sq. km/15 sq. miles
MOURNE (1986), Co. Down, 570 sq. km/220 sq. miles
RING OF GULLION (1991), Co. Armagh, 154 sq. km/59 sq. miles
SPERRIN (1968; extended 2008), Co. Tyrone/Co. Londonderry, 1,182 sq. km/456 sq. miles
STRANGFORD LOUGH AND LECALE (2010)*, Co. Down, 528 sq. km/204 sq. miles

*Strangford Lough (1972) and Lecale Coast (1967) merged in 2010

NATIONAL SCENIC AREAS

In Scotland, national scenic areas have a broadly equivalent status to AONBs. Scottish Natural Heritage recognises areas of national scenic significance. At the beginning of July 2013 there were 40, covering a land area of 1,021,600 hectares (2,524,400 acres) and a marine area of 359,500 hectares (888,300 acres).

Development within national scenic areas is dealt with by local authorities, who are required to consult Scottish Natural Heritage concerning certain categories of development. Disagreements between Scottish Natural Heritage and local authorities are referred to the Scottish government. Land management uses can also be modified in the interest of scenic conservation.

ASSYNT-COIGACH, Highland, 90,200ha/222,884 acres
BEN NEVIS AND GLEN COE, Highland, 101,600ha/251,053 acres
CAIRNGORM MOUNTAINS, Highland/Aberdeenshire/Moray, 67,200ha/166,051 acres
CUILLIN HILLS, Highland, 21,900ha/54,115 acres
DEESIDE AND LOCHNAGAR, Aberdeenshire, 40,000ha/98,840 acres
DORNOCH FIRTH, Highland, 7,500ha/18,532 acres
EAST STEWARTRY COAST, Dumfries and Galloway, 4,500ha/11,119 acres
EILDON AND LEADERFOOT, Borders, 3,600ha/8,896 acres
FLEET VALLEY, Dumfries and Galloway, 5,300ha/13,096 acres
GLEN AFFRIC, Highland, 19,300ha/47,690 acres
GLEN STRATHFARRAR, Highland, 3,800ha/9,390 acres
HOY AND WEST MAINLAND, Orkney Islands, 14,800ha/36,571 acres
JURA, Argyll and Bute, 21,800ha/53,868 acres
KINTAIL, Highland, 15,500ha/38,300 acres
KNAPDALE, Argyll and Bute, 19,800ha/48,926 acres
KNOYDART, Highland, 39,500ha/97,604 acres
KYLE OF TONGUE, Highland, 18,500ha/45,713 acres
KYLES OF BUTE, Argyll and Bute, 4,400ha/10,872 acres
LOCH LOMOND, Argyll and Bute, 27,400ha/67,705 acres
LOCH NA KEAL, Mull, Argyll and Bute, 12,700ha/31,382 acres
LOCH RANNOCH AND GLEN LYON, Perthshire and Kinross, 48,400ha/119,596 acres
LOCH SHIEL, Highland, 13,400ha/33,111 acres
LOCH TUMMEL, Perthshire and Kinross, 9,200ha/22,733 acres
LYNN OF LORN, Argyll and Bute, 4,800ha/11,861 acres
MORAR, MOIDART AND ARDNAMURCHAN, Highland, 13,500ha/33,358 acres
NITH ESTUARY, Dumfries and Galloway, 9,300ha/22,980 acres
NORTH ARRAN, North Ayrshire, 23,800ha/58,810 acres
NORTH-WEST SUTHERLAND, Highland, 20,500ha/50,655 acres
RIVER EARN, Perthshire and Kinross, 3,000ha/7,413 acres
RIVER TAY, Perthshire and Kinross, 5,600ha/13,838 acres
ST KILDA, Eilean Siar (Western Isles), 900ha/2,224 acres
SCARBA, LUNGA AND THE GARVELLACHS, Argyll and Bute, 1,900ha/4,695 acres
SHETLAND, Shetland Isles, 11,600ha/28,664 acres
SMALL ISLANDS, Highland, 15,500ha/38,300 acres
SOUTH LEWIS, HARRIS AND NORTH UIST, Eilean Siar (Western Isles), 109,600ha/270,822 acres
SOUTH UIST MACHAIR, Eilean Siar (Western Isles), 6,100ha/15,073 acres
THE TROSSACHS, Stirling, 4,600ha/11,367 acres
TROTTERNISH, Highland, 5,000ha/12,355 acres
UPPER TWEEDDALE, Borders, 10,500ha/25,945 acres
WESTER ROSS, Highland, 145,300ha/359,036 acres

THE NATIONAL FOREST

The National Forest is being planted across 517 sq. km (200 sq. miles) of Derbyshire, Leicestershire and Staffordshire. Eight million trees, of mixed species but mainly broadleaved, covering over 6,230ha (15,394 acres) have been planted. The aim is to eventually cover about one-third of the designated area.

The project was developed in 1992–5 by the Countryside Commission and is now run by the National Forest Company, which was established in April 1995. The National Forest Company is responsible for the delivery of the government-approved National Forest Strategy and is sponsored by DEFRA.

NATIONAL FOREST COMPANY, Bath Yard, Moira, Swadlincote, Derbyshire DE12 6BA T 01283-551211
E enquiries@nationalforest.org W www.nationalforest.org
Chief Executive, Sophie Churchill, OBE

SITES OF SPECIAL SCIENTIFIC INTEREST

Site of Special Scientific Interest (SSSI) is a legal notification applied to land in England, Scotland or Wales which Natural England (NE), Scottish Natural Heritage (SNH) or the Natural Resources Wales (NRW) identifies as being of special interest because of its flora, fauna, geological, geomorphological or physiographical features. In some cases, SSSIs are managed as nature reserves.

NE, SNH and NRW must notify the designation of an SSSI to the local planning authority, every owner/occupier of the land, and the environment secretary, the Scottish ministers or the National Assembly for Wales. Forestry and agricultural departments and a number of other interested parties are also formally notified.

Objections to the notification of an SSSI can be made and ultimately considered at a full meeting of the Council of NE or NRW. In Scotland an objection will be dealt with by the main board of SNH or an appropriate subgroup, depending on the nature of the objection.

The protection of these sites depends on the cooperation of individual landowners and occupiers. Owner/occupiers must consult NE, SNH or NRW and gain written consent before they can undertake certain listed activities on the site. Funds are available through management agreements and grants to assist owners and occupiers in conserving sites' interests. Sites can also be protected by management schemes, management notices and other enforcement mechanisms. As a last resort a site can be purchased.

The number and area of SSSIs in Britain as at May 2013 was:

	Number	*Hectares*	*Acres*
England	4,124	1,077,555	2,662,696
Scotland	1,429	1,022,604	2,526,909
Wales	1,053	260,579	643,905

NORTHERN IRELAND

In Northern Ireland 360 areas of special scientific interest (ASSIs) have been declared by the Department of the Environment for Northern Ireland.

NATIONAL NATURE RESERVES

National Nature Reserves are defined in the National Parks and Access to the Countryside Act 1949 as modified by the Natural Environment and Rural Communities Act 2006. National Nature Reserves may be managed solely for the purpose of conservation, or for both the purposes of conservation and recreation, providing this does not compromise the conservation purpose.

NE, SNH or NRW can declare as a national nature reserve land which is held and managed as a nature reserve under an agreement; land held and managed by NE, SNH or NRW; or land held and managed as a nature reserve by an approved body. NE, SNH or NRW can make by-laws to protect reserves from undesirable activities; these are subject to confirmation by the Secretary of State for Environment, Food and Rural Affairs, the National Assembly for Wales or the Scottish ministers.

The number and area of national nature reserves in Britain as at May 2013 was:

	Number	*Hectares*	*Acres*
England	224	94,400	233,267
Scotland	52	128,286	317,002
Wales	72	25,616	63,299

NORTHERN IRELAND

Nature reserves are established and managed by the Department of the Environment for Northern Ireland, with advice from the Council for Nature Conservation and the Countryside. Nature reserves are declared under the Nature Conservation and Amenity Lands (Northern Ireland) Order 1985; to date, 49 nature reserves have been declared.

LOCAL NATURE RESERVES

Local Nature Reserves are defined in the National Parks and Access to the Countryside Act 1949 (as amended by the Natural Environment and Rural Communities Act 2006) as land designated for the study and preservation of flora and fauna, or of geological or physiographical features. Local Nature Reserves also have a statutory obligation to provide opportunities for the enjoyment of nature or open air recreation, providing this does not compromise the conservation purpose of the reserve. Local authorities in England, Scotland and Wales have the power to acquire, declare and manage reserves in consultation with NE, SNH and NRW. There is similar legislation in Northern Ireland, where the consulting organisation is the Environment Agency.

Any organisation, such as water companies, educational trusts, local amenity groups and charitable nature conservation bodies, such as wildlife trusts, may manage local nature reserves, provided that a local authority has a legal interest in the land. This means that the local authority must either own it, lease it or have a management agreement with the landowner.

The number and area of designated local nature reserves in Britain as at May 2013 was:

	Number	*Hectares*	*Acres*
England	1,513	38,967	96,287
Scotland	67	10,575	26,131
Wales	82	5,860	14,480

There are 17 local nature reserves in Northern Ireland.

FOREST RESERVES

The Forestry Commission is the government department responsible for forestry policy throughout Great Britain. Forestry is a devolved matter, with the separate Forestry Commissions for England, Scotland and Wales reporting directly to their appropriate minister. The equivalent body in Northern Ireland is the Forest Service, an agency of the Department of Agriculture and Rural Development for Northern Ireland. The Forestry Commission in each country is led by a director who is also a member of the GB Board of Commissioners. As at March 2013, UK woodland certified by the Forestry Commission (including Forestry Commission-managed woodland) amounted to around 1,362,000ha (3,365,574 acres): 355,000ha (877,224 acres) in England, 139,000ha (343,476 acres) in Wales, 803,000ha (1,984,256 acres) in Scotland and 65,000ha (160,618 acres) in Northern Ireland. For more information, *see* W www.forestry.gov.uk

There are 34 forest nature reserves in Northern Ireland, covering 1,512 hectares (3,736 acres), designated and administered by the Forest Service. There are also 16 national nature reserves on Forest Service-owned property.

MARINE NATURE RESERVES

Marine protected areas provide protection for marine flora and fauna, and geological and physiographical features on land covered by tidal waters or parts of the sea in or adjacent to the UK. These areas also provide opportunities for study and research.

The Marine and Coastal Access Act 2009 created a new kind of statutory protection for marine protected areas in England and Wales, marine conservation zones (MCZs), which are designed to increase the protection of species and habitats deemed to be of national importance. The Secretary of State for Environment, Food and Rural Affairs and the National Assembly for Wales have the power to designate MCZs. Individual MCZs can have varying levels of protection: some include specific activities that are appropriately managed, while others prohibit all damaging and disturbing activities. The act converted the waters around Lundy Island, a former marine protected area, to MCZ status.

In 2009, Natural England and the Joint Nature Conservation Committee (JNCC) gave sea-users and stakeholders the ability to recommend potential MCZs to the UK government by establishing four regional projects. In September 2011, these projects recommended 127 MCZs, which were reviewed by Natural England and the JNCC. Ministers are likely to make a decision on which sites to designate in late 2013.

Under the Marine (Scotland) Act 2010 the Scottish government is empowered to designate marine protected areas (MPAs) in the seas around Scotland; Scottish Natural Heritage and the JNCC developed 33 MPA proposals (with a further four awaiting assessment), which will be consulted on during late 2013.

In Northern Ireland, marine nature reserves may be established under the Nature Conservation and Amenity Lands Order (Northern Ireland) 1985.

Marine Conservation Zone:
LUNDY (2010), Bristol Channel

Marine Nature Reserve:
STRANGFORD LOUGH (1995), Northern Ireland

INTERNATIONAL CONVENTIONS

The UK is party to a number of international conventions.

BERN CONVENTION

The 1979 Bern Convention on the Conservation of European Wildlife and Natural Habitats came into force in the UK in June 1982. Currently there are 51 contracting parties and a number of other states attend meetings as observers.

The aims are to conserve wild flora and fauna and their natural habitats, especially where this requires the cooperation of several countries, and to promote such cooperation. The convention gives particular emphasis to endangered and vulnerable species.

All parties to the convention must promote national conservation policies and take account of the conservation of wild flora and fauna when setting planning and development policies. Reports on contracting parties' conservation policies must be submitted to the standing committee every four years.

SECRETARIAT OF THE BERN CONVENTION
STANDING COMMITTEE, Council of Europe, Avenue de L'Europe, 67075 Strasbourg-Cedex, France
T (+33) (3) 8841 2000 W www.coe.int

BIOLOGICAL DIVERSITY

The UK ratified the Convention on Biological Diversity in June 1994. As at July 2013 there were 193 parties to the convention.

There are seven programmes addressing agricultural biodiversity, marine and coastal biodiversity and the biodiversity of inland waters, dry and sub-humid lands, islands, mountains and forests. On 29 January 2000 the Conference of the Parties adopted a supplementary agreement to the convention known as the Cartagena Protocol on Biosafety. The protocol seeks to protect biological diversity from potential risks that may be posed by introducing modified living organisms, resulting from biotechnology, into the environment. As at July 2013, 166 countries were party to the protocol; the UK joined on 17 February 2004. The Nagoya–Kuala Lumpur supplementary protocol was adopted in October 2010. It provides international rules and procedure on liability and redress for damage to biodiversity resulting from living modified organisms. As at July 2013 51 countries have signed the protocol.

The UK Biodiversity Action Plan (UKBAP) is the UK government's response to the Convention on Biological Diversity and constitutes a record of UK biological resources and a detailed plan for their protection. The list of priority species and habitats under the UKBAP covers 1,150 species and 65 habitats. The UK Biodiversity Partnership Standing Committee guides and supports the UK Biodiversity Partnership in implementing UKBAP; it also coordinates between the four UK country groups which form the partnership and are responsible for implementing UKBAP at a national level. Information on UKBAP is available from the Joint Nature Conservation Committee (JNCC).

JNCC, Monkstone House, City Road, Peterborough PE1 1JY
T 01733-555948 W www.jncc.defra.gov.uk

BONN CONVENTION

The 1979 Convention on Conservation of Migratory Species of Wild Animals (also known as the CMS or Bonn Convention) came into force in the UK in October 1985. As at 1 July 2013, 119 countries were party to the convention.

It requires the protection of listed endangered migratory species and encourages international agreements covering these and other threatened species. International agreements can range from legally binding treaties to less formal memoranda of understanding.

Seven agreements have been concluded to date under the convention. They aim to conserve seals in the Wadden Sea; bat populations in Europe; small cetaceans of the Baltic, north-east Atlantic, Irish and North Seas; cetaceans of the Mediterranean Sea, Black Sea and contiguous Atlantic area; African-Eurasian migratory waterbirds; albatrosses and petrels; and gorillas and their habitats. A further 19 memorandums of understanding have been agreed for the Siberian crane, slender-billed curlew, marine turtles of the Atlantic coast of Africa, Indian Ocean and South-East Asia, the middle-European population of the great bustard, bukhara deer, aquatic warbler, West-African populations of the African elephant, saiga antelope, cetaceans of the Pacific Islands, dugongs (large marine mammals), eastern-Atlantic populations of the Mediterranean monk seals, ruddy-headed goose, grassland birds of southern South America, birds of prey of Africa and Eurasia, small cetaceans and manatees of West Africa, sharks, huemuls (Andean deer) and high Andean flamingoes.

UNEP/CMS SECRETARIAT, Hermann-Ehlers-Str. 10, 53113 Bonn, Germany T (+49) (228) 815 2401 E secretariat@cms.int
W www.cms.int

CITES

The 1973 Convention on International Trade in Endangered Species of Wild Fauna and Flora (CITES) is an agreement between governments to ensure that international trade in specimens of wild animals and plants does not threaten their survival. The convention came into force in the UK in October 1976 and there are currently 178 member countries. Countries party to the convention ban commercial international trade in an agreed list of endangered species and regulate and monitor trade in other species that might become endangered. The convention accords varying degrees of protection to more than 30,000 species of animals and plants whether they are traded as live specimens or as products derived from them, such as fur coats and dried herbs.

The Conference of the Parties to CITES meets every two to three years to review the convention's implementation. The Animal Health and Veterinary Laboratories Agency at the Department for Environment, Food and Rural Affairs carries out the government's responsibilities under CITES.

CITES is implemented in the EU through a series of EC regulations known as the Wildlife Trade Regulations.

CITES SECRETARIAT, International Environment House, 11 Chemin des Anémones, CH-1219 Châtelaine, Geneva, Switzerland **T** (+41) (22) 917 8139/8140 **E** info@cites.org **W** www.cites.org

INTERNATIONAL CONVENTION FOR THE REGULATION OF WHALING

The International Convention for the Regulation of Whaling was signed in Washington DC in 1946 and currently has 89 member countries.

The measures in the convention provide for the complete protection of certain species; designate specified areas as whale sanctuaries; set limits on the numbers and size of whales which may be taken; prescribe open and closed seasons and areas for whaling; and prohibit the capture of suckling calves and female whales accompanied by calves. The International Whaling Commission meets annually to review and revise these measures.

THE INTERNATIONAL WHALING COMMISSION, The Red House, 135 Station Road, Impington, Cambridge, Cambridgeshire CB24 9NP **T** 01223-233 971 **E** secretariat@iwcoffice.org **W** www.iwc.int

RAMSAR CONVENTION

The 1971 Convention on Wetlands of National Importance, called the Ramsar Convention, is an inter-governmental treaty that provides for the conservation and use of wetlands and their resources. The Convention entered into force in the UK in 1976.

Governments that are contracting parties to the convention must designate wetlands for inclusion in the List of Wetlands of International Importance (the 'Ramsar List') and include wetland conservation considerations in their land-use planning. As at July 2013, the Convention's 168 contracting parties had designated 2,131 wetland sites, covering 205,490,520 hectares. The UK currently has 169 designated sites covering 1,275,681 hectares.

The contracting parties meet every three years to assess the progress of the convention. The last meeting took place in Bucharest, Romania in July 2012.

The UK has set targets under the Ramsar Strategic Plan, 2009–15. Progress towards these is monitored by the UK Ramsar committee. The UK and the Republic of Ireland have established a formal protocol to ensure common monitoring standards for waterbirds in the two countries.

RAMSAR CONVENTION SECRETARIAT, Rue Mauverney 28, CH-1196 Gland, Switzerland **T** (+41) (22) 999 0170 **E** ramsar@ramsar.org **W** www.ramsar.org

UK LEGISLATION

The Wildlife and Countryside Act 1981 gives legal protection to a wide range of wild animals and plants. Every five years the statutory nature conservation agencies (Natural England, Natural Resources Wales and Scottish Natural Heritage), working jointly through the JNCC, are required to review schedules 5 (animals, other than birds) and 8 (plants) of the Wildlife and Countryside Act 1981. They make recommendations to the Secretary of State for Environment, Food and Rural Affairs, the National Assembly for Wales and the Scottish government for changes to these schedules. The most recent variations of schedules 5 and 8 for England came into effect on 1 October 2011, following the fifth quinquennial review. The sixth review is currently underway.

Under section 9 of the act it is an offence to kill, injure, take, possess or sell (whether alive or dead) any wild animal included in schedule 5 of the act and to disturb its place of shelter and protection or to destroy that place. However certain species listed on schedule 5 are protected against some, but not all, of these activities.

Under section 13 of the act it is illegal without a licence to pick, uproot, sell or destroy plants listed in schedule 8. Since January 2001, under the Countryside and Rights of Way Act 2000, persons found guilty of an offence under part 1 of the Wildlife and Countryside Act 1981 face a maximum penalty of up to £5,000 and/or up to a six-month custodial sentence per specimen.

BIRDS

The act lays down a close season for birds (listed on Schedule 2, part 1) from 1 February to 31 August inclusive, each year. Variations to these dates are made for:

Black grouse – 10 December to 20 August (10 December to 1 September for Somerset, Devon and New Forest)
Capercaillie – 1 February to 30 September (England and Wales only)
Grey partridge – 1 February to 1 September
Pheasant – 1 February to 1 October
Ptarmigan and Red grouse – 10 December to 12 August
Red-legged partridge – 1 February to 1 September
Snipe – 1 February to 11 August
Woodcock – 1 February to 30 September (England and Wales); 1 February to 31 August (Scotland)
Birds listed on schedule 2, part 1 (below high water mark) (*see* below) – 21 February to 31 August
Wild duck and wild geese, in or over any area below the high-water mark of ordinary spring tides – 21 February to 31 August
Sundays and Christmas Day in Scotland, and Sundays for any area of England or Wales prescribed by the Secretary of State.

Birds listed on schedule 2, part 1, which may be killed or taken outside the close season are: capercaillie (England and Wales only); coot; certain wild duck (gadwall, goldeneye, mallard, Northern pintail, common pochard, Northern shoveler, teal, tufted duck, Eurasian wigeon); certain wild geese (Canada, greylag, pink-footed, white-fronted (in England and Wales only); golden plover; moorhen; snipe; and woodcock.

Section 16 of the 1981 act allows licences to be issued on either an individual or general basis, to allow the killing, taking and sale of certain birds for specified reasons such as public health and safety. All other wild birds are fully protected by law throughout the year.

ANIMALS PROTECTED BY SCHEDULE 5
Adder *(Vipera berus)*
Anemone, Ivell's Sea *(Edwardsia ivelli)*
Anemone, Starlet Sea *(Nematosella vectensis)*
Bat, Horseshoe, all species *(Rhinolophidae)*
Bat, Typical, all species *(Vespertilionidae)*
Beetle *(Hypebaeus flavipes)*
Beetle, Bembridge Water *(Paracymus aeneus)*
Beetle, Lesser Silver Water *(Hydrochara caraboides)*
Beetle, Mire Pill *(Curimopsis nigrita)*
Beetle, Moccas *(Hypebaeus flavipes)*
Beetle, Rainbow Leaf *(Chrysolina ceredis)*
Beetle, Spangled Water *(Graphoderus zonatus)*
Beetle, Stag *(Lucanus cervus)*
Beetle, Violet Click *(Limoniscus violaceus)*
Beetle, Water *(Paracymus aeneus)*
Burbot *(Lota lota)*
Butterfly, Adonis Blue *(Lysandra bellargus)*
Butterfly, Black Hairstreak *(Strymonidia pruni)*
Butterfly, Brown Hairstreak *(Thecla betulae)*
Butterfly, Chalkhill Blue *(Lysandra coridon)*
Butterfly, Chequered Skipper *(Carterocephalus palaemon)*
Butterfly, Duke of Burgundy Fritillary *(Hamearis lucina)*
Butterfly, Glanville Fritillary *(Melitaea cinxia)*
Butterfly, Heath Fritillary *(Mellicta athalia* or *Melitaea athalia)*
Butterfly, High Brown Fritillary *(Argynnis adippe)*
Butterfly, Large Blue *(Maculinea arion)*
Butterfly, Large Copper *(Lycaena dispar)*
Butterfly, Large Heath *(Coenonympha tullia)*
Butterfly, Large Tortoiseshell *(Nymphalis polychloros)*
Butterfly, Lulworth Skipper *(Thymelicus acteon)*
Butterfly, Marsh Fritillary *(Eurodryas aurinia)*
Butterfly, Mountain Ringlet *(Erebia epiphron)*
Butterfly, Northern Brown Argus *(Aricia artaxerxes)*
Butterfly, Pearl-bordered Fritillary *(Boloria euphrosyne)*
Butterfly, Purple Emperor *(Apatura iris)*
Butterfly, Silver Spotted Skipper *(Hesperia comma)*
Butterfly, Silver-studded Blue *(Plebejus argus)*
Butterfly, Small Blue *(Cupido minimus)*
Butterfly, Swallowtail *(Papilio machaon)*
Butterfly, White Letter Hairstreak *(Stymonida w-album)*
Butterfly, Wood White *(Leptidea sinapis)*
Cat, Wild *(Felis silvestris)*
Cicada, New Forest *(Cicadetta montana)*
Crayfish, Atlantic Stream *(Austropotamobius pallipes)*
Cricket, Field *(Gryllus campestris)*
Cricket, Mole *(Gryllotalpa gryllotalpa)*
Cricket, Wart-biter *(Decticus verrucivorus)*
Damselfly, Southern *(Coenagrion mercuriale)*
Dolphin, all species *(Cetacea)*
Dormouse *(Muscardinus avellanarius)*
Dragonfly, Norfolk Aeshna *(Aeshna isosceles)*
Frog, Common *(Rana temporaria)*
Frog, Pool, Northern Clade *(Pelophylax lessonae)*
Goby, Couch's *(Gobius couchii)*
Goby, Giant *(Gobius cobitis)*
Hatchet Shell, Northern *(Thyasira gouldi)*
Hydroid, Marine *(Clavopsella navis)*
Lagoon Snail, De Folin's *(Caecum armoricum)*
Lagoon Worm, Tentacled *(Alkmaria romijni)*
Leech, Medicinal *(Hirudo medicinalis)*
Lizard, Sand *(Lacerta agilis)*
Lizard, Viviparous *(Lacerta vivipara)*
Marten, Pine *(Martes martes)*
Moth, Barberry Carpet *(Pareulype berberata)*
Moth, Black-veined *(Siona lineata* or *Idaea lineata)*
Moth, Fiery Clearwing *(Bembecia chrysidiformis)*
Moth, Fisher's Estuarine *(Gortyna borelii)*
Moth, New Forest Burnet *(Zygaena viciae)*
Moth, Reddish Buff *(Acosmetia caliginosa)*
Moth, Slender Scotch Burnet *(Zygaena loti)*
Moth, Sussex Emerald *(Thalera fimbrialis)*
Moth, Talisker Burnet *(Zygaena lonicerae)*
Mussel, Fan *(Atrina fragilis)*
Mussel, Freshwater Pearl *(Margaritifera margaritifera)*
Newt, Great Crested (or Warty) *(Triturus cristatus)*
Newt, Palmate *(Triturus helveticus)*
Newt, Smooth *(Triturus vulgaris)*
Otter, Common *(Lutra lutra)*
Porpoise, all species *(Cetacea)*
Sandworm, Lagoon *(Armandia cirrhosa)*
Sea Fan, Pink *(Eunicella verrucosa)*
Sea Slug, Lagoon *(Tenellia adspersa)*
Sea-mat, Trembling *(Victorella pavida)*
Seahorse, Short Snouted (England only) *(Hippocampus hippocampus)*
Seahorse, Spiny (England only) *(Hippocampus guttulatus)*
Shad, Allis *(Alosa alosa)*
Shad, Twaite *(Alosa fallax)*
Shark, Angel (England only) *(Squatina squatina)*
Shark, Basking *(Cetorhinus maximus)*
Shrimp, Fairy *(Chirocephalus diaphanus)*
Shrimp, Lagoon Sand *(Gammarus insensibilis)*
Shrimp, Tadpole (Apus) *(Triops cancriformis)*
Skate, White *(Rostroraja alba)*
Slow-worm *(Anguis fragilis)*
Snail, Glutinous *(Myxas glutinosa)*
Snail, Roman (England only) *(Helix pomatia)*
Snail, Sandbowl *(Catinella arenaria)*
Snake, Grass *(Natrix natrix* or *Natrix helvetica)*
Snake, Smooth *(Coronella austriaca)*
Spider, Fen Raft *(Dolomedes plantarius)*
Spider, Ladybird *(Eresus niger)*
Squirrel, Red *(Sciurus vulgaris)*
Sturgeon *(Acipenser sturio)*
Toad, Common *(Bufo bufo)*
Toad, Natterjack *(Bufo calamita)*
Turtle, Flatback *(Cheloniidae/Natator Depressus)*
Turtle, Green Sea *(Chelonia mydas)*
Turtle, Hawksbill *(Eretmochelys imbricate)*
Turtle, Kemp's Ridley Sea *(Lepidochelys kempii)*
Turtle, Leatherback Sea *(Dermochelys coriacea)*
Turtle, Loggerhead Sea *(Caretta caretta)*
Turtle, Olive Ridley *(Lepidochelys olivacea)*
Vendace *(Coregonus albula)*
Vole, Water *(Arvicola terrestris)*
Walrus *(Odobenus rosmarus)*
Whale, all species *(Cetacea)*
Whitefish *(Coregonus lavaretus)*

PLANTS PROTECTED BY SCHEDULE 8
Adder's Tongue, Least *(Ophioglossum lusitanicum)*
Alison, Small *(Alyssum alyssoides)*
Anomodon, Long-leaved *(Anomodon longifolius)*
Beech-lichen, New Forest *(Enterographa elaborata)*
Blackwort *(Southbya nigrella)*
Bluebell *(Hyacinthoides non-scripta)*
Bolete, Royal *(Boletus regius)*
Broomrape, Bedstraw *(Orobanche caryophyllacea)*
Broomrape, Oxtongue *(Orobanche loricata)*
Broomrape, Thistle *(Orobanche reticulata)*
Cabbage, Lundy *(Rhynchosinapis wrightii)*
Calamint, Wood *(Calamintha sylvatica)*
Caloplaca, Snow *(Caloplaca nivalis)*
Catapyrenium, Tree *(Catapyrenium psoromoides)*
Catchfly, Alpine *(Lychnis alpina)*
Catillaria, Laurer's *(Catellaria laureri)*

Centaury, Slender *(Centaurium tenuiflorum)*
Cinquefoil, Rock *(Potentilla rupestris)*
Cladonia, Convoluted *(Cladonia convoluta)*
Cladonia, Upright Mountain *(Cladonia stricta)*
Clary, Meadow *(Salvia pratensis)*
Club-rush, Triangular *(Scirpus triquetrus)*
Colt's-foot, Purple *(Homogyne alpina)*
Cotoneaster, Wild *(Cotoneaster integerrimus)*
Cottongrass, Slender *(Eriophorum gracile)*
Cow-wheat, Field *(Melampyrum arvense)*
Crocus, Sand *(Romulea columnae)*
Crystalwort, Lizard *(Riccia bifurca)*
Cudweed, Broad-leaved *(Filago pyramidata)*
Cudweed, Jersey *(Gnaphalium luteoalbum)*
Cudweed, Red-tipped *(Filago lutescens)*
Cut-grass *(Leersia oryzoides)*
Diapensia *(Diapensia lapponica)*
Dock, Shore *(Rumex rupestris)*
Earwort, Marsh *(Jamesoniella undulifolia)*
Eryngo, Field *(Eryngium campestre)*
Fern, Dickie's Bladder *(Cystopteris dickieana)*
Fern, Killarney *(Trichomanes speciosum)*
Flapwort, Norfolk *(Leiocolea rutheana)*
Fleabane, Alpine *(Erigeron borealis)*
Fleabane, Small *(Pulicaria vulgaris)*
Fleawort, South Stack *(Tephroseris integrifolia ssp maritima)*
Frostwort, Pointed *(Gymnomitrion apiculatum)*
Fungus, Hedgehog *(Hericium erinaceum)*
Galingale, Brown *(Cyperus fuscus)*
Gentian, Alpine *(Gentiana nivalis)*
Gentian, Dune *(Gentianella uliginosa)*
Gentian, Early *(Gentianella anglica)*
Gentian, Fringed *(Gentianella ciliata)*
Gentian, Spring *(Gentiana verna)*
Germander, Cut-leaved *(Teucrium botrys)*
Germander, Water *(Teucrium scordium)*
Gladiolus, Wild *(Gladiolus illyricus)*
Goblin Lights *(Catolechia wahlenbergii)*
Goosefoot, Stinking *(Chenopodium vulvaria)*
Grass-poly *(Lythrum hyssopifolia)*
Grimmia, Blunt-leaved *(Grimmia unicolor)*
Gyalecta, Elm *(Gyalecta ulmi)*
Hare's-ear, Sickle-leaved *(Bupleurum falcatum)*
Hare's-ear, Small *(Bupleurum baldense)*
Hawk's-beard, Stinking *(Crepis foetida)*
Hawkweed, Northroe *(Hieracium northroense)*
Hawkweed, Shetland *(Hieracium zetlandicum)*
Hawkweed, Weak-leaved *(Hieracium attenuatifolium)*
Heath, Blue *(Phyllodoce caerulea)*
Helleborine, Red *(Cephalanthera rubra)*
Horsetail, Branched *(Equisetum ramosissimum)*
Hound's-tongue, Green *(Cynoglossum germanicum)*
Knawel, Perennial *(Scleranthus perennis)*
Knotgrass, Sea *(Polygonum maritimum)*
Lady's-slipper *(Cypripedium calceolus)*
Lecanora, Tarn *(Lecanora archariana)*
Lecidea, Copper *(Lecidea inops)*
Leek, Round-headed *(Allium sphaerocephalon)*
Lettuce, Least *(Lactuca saligna)*
Lichen, Arctic Kidney *(Nephroma arcticum)*
Lichen, Ciliate Strap *(Heterodermia leucomelos)*
Lichen, Coralloid Rosette *(Heterodermia propagulifera)*
Lichen, Ear-lobed Dog *(Peltigera lepidophora)*
Lichen, Forked Hair *(Bryoria furcellata)*
Lichen, Golden Hair *(Teloschistes flavicans)*
Lichen, Orange-fruited Elm *(Caloplaca luteoalba)*
Lichen, River Jelly *(Collema dichotomum)*
Lichen, Scaly Breck *(Squamarina lentigera)*
Lichen, Starry Breck *(Buellia asterella)*
Lily, Snowdon *(Lloydia serotina)*
Liverwort, Lindenberg's Leafy *(Adelanthus lindenbergianus)*
Lungwort, Tree *(Lobaria pulmonaria)*
Marsh-mallow, Rough *(Althaea hirsuta)*
Marshwort, Creeping *(Apium repens)*
Milk-parsley, Cambridge *(Selinum carvifolia)*
Moss *(Drepanocladius vernicosus)*
Moss, Alpine Copper *(Mielichoferia mielichoferi)*
Moss, Baltic Bog *(Sphagnum balticum)*
Moss, Blue Dew *(Saelania glaucescens)*
Moss, Blunt-leaved Bristle *(Orthotrichum obtusifolium)*
Moss, Bright Green Cave *(Cyclodictyon laetevirens)*
Moss, Cordate Beard *(Barbula cordata)*
Moss, Cornish Path *(Ditrichum cornubicum)*
Moss, Derbyshire Feather *(Thamnobryum angustifolium)*
Moss, Flamingo *(Desmatodon cernuus)*
Moss, Glaucous Beard *(Barbula glauca)*
Moss, Green Shield *(Buxbaumia viridis)*
Moss, Hair Silk *(Plagiothecium piliferum)*
Moss, Knothole *(Zygodon forsteri)*
Moss, Large Yellow Feather *(Scorpidium turgescens)*
Moss, Millimetre *(Micromitrium tenerum)*
Moss, Multi-fruited River *(Cryphaea lamyana)*
Moss, Nowell's Limestone *(Zygodon gracilis)*
Moss, Polar Feather *(Hygrohypnum polare)*
Moss, Rigid Apple *(Bartramia stricta)*
Moss, Round-leaved Feather *(Rhyncostegium rotundifolium)*
Moss, Schleicher's Thread *(Bryum schleicheri)*
Moss, Slender Green Feather *(Drepanocladus vernicosus)*
Moss, Triangular Pygmy *(Acaulon triquetrum)*
Moss, Vaucher's Feather *(Hypnum vaucheri)*
Mudwort, Welsh *(Limosella austeralis)*
Naiad, Holly-leaved *(Najas marina)*
Naiad, Slender *(Najas flexilis)*
Nail, Rock *(Calicium corynellum)*
Orache, Stalked *(Halimione pedunculata)*
Orchid, Early Spider *(Ophrys sphegodes)*
Orchid, Fen *(Liparis loeselii)*
Orchid, Ghost *(Epipogium aphyllum)*
Orchid, Lapland Marsh *(Dactylorhiza lapponica)*
Orchid, Late Spider *(Ophrys fuciflora)*
Orchid, Lizard *(Himantoglossum hircinum)*
Orchid, Military *(Orchis militaris)*
Orchid, Monkey *(Orchis simia)*
Pannaria, Caledonia *(Panneria ignobilis)*
Parmelia, New Forest *(Parmelia minarum)*
Parmentaria, Oil Stain *(Parmentaria chilensis)*
Pear, Plymouth *(Pyrus cordata)*
Penny-cress, Perfoliate *(Thlaspi perfoliatum)*
Pennyroyal *(Mentha pulegium)*
Pertusaria, Alpine Moss *(Pertusaria bryontha)*
Petalwort *(Petallophyllum ralfsi)*
Physcia, Southern Grey *(Physcia tribacioides)*
Pigmyweed *(Crassula aquatica)*
Pine, Ground *(Ajuga chamaepitys)*
Pink, Cheddar *(Dianthus gratianopolitanus)*
Pink, Childing *(Petroraghia nanteuilii)*
Pink, Deptford (England and Wales only) *(Dianthus armeria)*
Polypore, Oak *(Buglossoporus pulvinus)*
Pseudocyphellaria, Ragged *(Pseudocyphellaria lacerata)*
Psora, Rusty Alpine *(Psora rubiformis)*
Puffball, Sandy Stilt *(Battarraea phalloides)*
Ragwort, Fen *(Senecio paludosus)*
Ramping-fumitory, Martin's *(Fumaria martinii)*
Rampion, Spiked *(Phyteuma spicatum)*
Restharrow, Small *(Ononis reclinata)*
Rock-cress, Alpine *(Arabis alpina)*
Rock-cress, Bristol *(Arabis stricta)*
Rustwort, Western *(Marsupella profunda)*

Sandwort, Norwegian *(Arenaria norvegica)*
Sandwort, Teesdale *(Minuartia stricta)*
Saxifrage, Drooping *(Saxifraga cernua)*
Saxifrage, Tufted *(Saxifraga cespitosa)*
Saxifrage, Yellow Marsh *(Saxifrage hirulus)*
Solenopsora, Serpentine *(Solenopsora liparina)*
Solomon's-seal, Whorled *(Polygonatum verticillatum)*
Sow-thistle, Alpine *(Cicerbita alpina)*
Spearwort, Adder's-tongue *(Ranunculus ophioglossifolius)*
Speedwell, Fingered *(Veronica triphyllos)*
Speedwell, Spiked *(Veronica spicata)*
Spike-rush, Dwarf *(Eleocharis parvula)*
Star-of-Bethlehem, Early *(Gagea bohemica)*
Starfruit *(Damasonium alisma)*
Stonewort, Bearded *(Chara canescens)*
Stonewort, Foxtail *(Lamprothamnium papulosum)*
Strapwort *(Corrigiola litoralis)*
Sulphur-tresses, Alpine *(Alectoria ochroleuca)*
Turpswort *(Geocalyx graveolens)*
Violet, Fen *(Viola persicifolia)*
Viper's-grass *(Scorzonera humilis)*
Water-plantain, Floating *(Luronium natans)*
Water-plantain, Ribbon-leaved *(Alisma gramineum)*
Wood-sedge, Starved *(Carex depauperata)*
Woodsia, Alpine *(Woodsia alpina)*
Woodsia, Oblong *(Woodsia ilvenis)*
Wormwood, Field *(Artemisia campestris)*
Woundwort, Downy *(Stachys germanica)*
Woundwort, Limestone *(Stachys alpina)*
Yellow-rattle, Greater *(Rhinanthus serotinus)*

WORLD HERITAGE SITES

The Convention Concerning the Protection of the World Cultural and Natural Heritage was adopted by the United Nations Educational, Scientific and Cultural Organization (UNESCO) in 1972 and ratified by the UK in 1984. As at July 2013, 190 states were party to the convention. The convention provides for the identification, protection and conservation of cultural and natural sites of outstanding universal value.

Cultural sites may be:
- an extraordinary exponent of human creative genius
- sites representing architectural and technological innovation or cultural interchange
- sites of artistic, historic, aesthetic, archaeological, scientific, ethnologic or anthropologic value
- 'cultural landscapes', ie sites whose characteristics are marked by significant interactions between human populations and their natural environment
- exceptional examples of a traditional settlement or land- or sea-use, especially those threatened by irreversible change
- unique or exceptional examples of a cultural tradition or a civilisation either still present or extinct

Natural sites may be:
- those displaying critical periods of earth's history
- superlative examples of on-going ecological and biological processes in the evolution of ecosystems
- those exhibiting remarkable natural beauty and aesthetic significance or those where extraordinary natural phenomena are witnessed
- the habitat of threatened species and plants

Governments which are party to the convention nominate sites in their country for inclusion in the World Heritage List. Nominations are considered by the World Heritage Committee, an inter-governmental committee composed of 21 representatives of the parties to the convention. The committee is advised by the International Council on Monuments and Sites (ICOMOS), the International Centre for the Study of the Preservation and Restoration of Cultural Property (ICCROM) and the International Union for the Conservation of Nature (IUCN). ICOMOS evaluates and reports on proposed cultural and mixed sites, ICCROM provides expert advice and training on how to conserve and restore cultural property and IUCN provides technical evaluations of natural heritage sites and reports on the state of conservation of listed sites. The Department for Culture, Media and Sport represents the UK government in matters relating to the convention.

A prerequisite for inclusion in the World Heritage List is the existence of an effective legal protection system in the country in which the site is situated and a detailed management plan to ensure the conservation of the site. Inclusion in the list does not confer any greater degree of protection on the site than that offered by the national protection framework.

If a site is considered to be in serious danger of decay or damage, the committee may add it to the World Heritage in Danger List. Sites on this list may benefit from particular attention or emergency measures to allay threats and allow them to retain their world heritage status, or in extreme cases of damage or neglect they may lose their world heritage status completely.

Financial support for the conservation of sites on the World Heritage List is provided by the World Heritage Fund, administered by the World Heritage Committee. The fund's income is derived from compulsory and voluntary contributions from the states party to the convention and from private donations.

WORLD HERITAGE CENTRE, UNESCO, 7 Place de Fontenoy, 75352 Paris 07 SP, France W http://whc.unesco.org

DESIGNATED SITES

As at 1 July 2013, following the 37th session of the World Heritage Committee, 981 sites were inscribed on the World Heritage List. Of these, 25 are in the UK and three in British overseas territories; 23 are listed for their cultural significance (†), four for their natural significance (*) and one for both cultural and natural significance. The year in which sites were designated appears in the first set of parentheses. In 2005 Hadrian's Wall, a World Heritage Site in its own right since 1987, was joined by the upper German-Raetian Limes to form the first section of a trans-national world heritage site, Frontiers of the Roman Empire; in 2008 the Antonine Wall was inscribed by UNESCO, becoming a further part of this site. The number in the second set of parentheses denotes the position of each site on the map.

UNITED KINGDOM

†Bath – the city (1987). (1)
†Blaenarvon industrial landscape, Wales (2000). (2)
†Blenheim Palace and Park, Oxfordshire (1987). (3)
†Canterbury Cathedral, St Augustine's Abbey, St Martin's Church, Kent (1988). (4)
†Castle and town walls of King Edward I, north Wales – Beaumaris, Caernarfon Castle, Conwy Castle, Harlech Castle (1986). (5)
†Cornwall and west Devon mining landscape (2006). (6)
†Derwent Valley Mills, Derbyshire (2001). (7)
*Dorset and east Devon coast (2001). (8)
†Durham Cathedral and Castle (1986). (9)
†Edinburgh old and new towns (1995). (10)
†Frontiers of the Roman Empire– Hadrian's Wall, northern England; Antonine Wall, central Scotland (1987, 2005, 2008). (11)

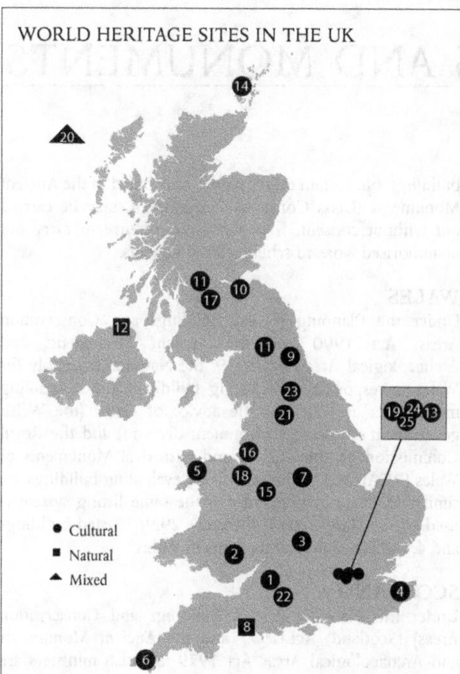

*Giant's Causeway and Causeway coast, Co. Antrim (1986). (12)
†Greenwich, London – maritime Greenwich, including the Royal Naval College, Old Royal Observatory, Queen's House, town centre (1997). (13)
†Heart of Neolithic Orkney (1999). (14)
†Ironbridge Gorge, Shropshire – the world's first iron bridge and other early industrial sites (1986). (15)
†Liverpool – six areas of the maritime mercantile city (2004). (16)
†New Lanark, South Lanarkshire, Scotland (2001). (17)
†Pontcysyllte Aqueduct and Canal, Wrexham, Wales (2009). (18)
†Royal Botanic Gardens, Kew (2003). (19)
†*St Kilda, Eilean Siar (Western Isles) (1986). (20)
†Saltaire, West Yorkshire (2001). (21)
†Stonehenge, Avebury and related megalithic sites, Wiltshire (1986). (22)
†Studley Royal Park, Fountains Abbey, St Mary's Church, N. Yorkshire (1986). (23)
†Tower of London (1988). (24)
†Westminster Abbey, Palace of Westminster, St Margaret's Church, London (1987). (25)

BRITISH OVERSEAS TERRITORIES
*Henderson Island, Pitcairn Islands, South Pacific Ocean (1988)
*Gough Island and Inaccessible Island (part of Tristan da Cunha), South Atlantic Ocean (1995)
†St George town and related fortifications, Bermuda (2000)

PROPOSED SITES

The list below has been submitted to UNESCO by the UK government for future consideration for designation:

Chatham Dockyard and its Defences
Creswell Crags
Darwin's Landscape Laboratory
England's Lake District
Flow Country
Forth Bridge
Gorham's Cave Complex
Island of St Helena
Jodrell Bank Observatory
Mousa, Old Scatness and Jarlshof: the Zenith of Iron Age Shetland
Slate Industry of North Wales
The Twin Monastery of Wearmouth Jarrow
Turks and Caicos Islands

HISTORIC BUILDINGS AND MONUMENTS

ENGLAND

Under the Planning (Listed Buildings and Conservation Areas) Act 1990, the Secretary of State for Culture, Media and Sport has a statutory duty to approve lists of buildings or groups of buildings in England which are of special architectural or historic interest. In November 2009 responsibility for compiling the list of buildings was passed to English Heritage. Under the Ancient Monuments and Archaeological Areas Act 1979 as amended by the National Heritage Act 1983, the secretary of state is also responsible for compiling a schedule of ancient monuments. Decisions are taken on the advice of English Heritage. On 1 April 2005 responsibility for the administration of the listing system was transferred from the secretary of state to English Heritage. On 4 April 2011, English Heritage launched the National Heritage List for England, a searchable database of all nationally designated heritage assets (W http://list.english-heritage.org.uk).

LISTED BUILDINGS

Listed buildings are classified into Grade I, Grade II* and Grade II. There are 375,762 listed buildings in England, of which approximately 92 per cent are Grade II listed. Almost all pre-1700 buildings are listed, as are most buildings of 1700 to 1840. English Heritage carries out thematic surveys of particular types of buildings with a view to making recommendations for listing. The main purpose of listing is to ensure that care is taken in deciding the future of a building. No changes which affect the architectural or historic character of a listed building can be made without listed building consent (in addition to planning permission where relevant). Applications for consent are normally dealt with by the local planning authority, although English Heritage is always consulted about proposals affecting Grade I and Grade II* properties. It is a criminal offence to demolish a listed building, or alter it in such a way as to affect its character, without consent.

Area	*No. of listed buildings*
1. Devon	20,814
2. Greater London	18,933
3. Kent	17,264
4. Somerset (incl Bath)	15,403
5. Hampshire (incl Isle of Wight)	13,523
6. Gloucestershire	12,900
7. Cornwall	12,561
8. North Yorkshire	12,216
9. Oxfordshire	12,155
10. Norfolk	10,576

* *Source:* National Heritage List for England

SCHEDULED MONUMENTS

There are 19,780 scheduled monuments in England. All monuments proposed for scheduling are considered to be of national importance. Where buildings are both scheduled and listed, ancient monuments legislation takes precedence. The main purpose of scheduling a monument is to preserve it for the future and to protect it from damage, destruction or any unnecessary interference. Once a monument has been scheduled, scheduled monument consent is required before any works can be carried out. The scope of the control is more extensive and more detailed than that applied to listed buildings, but certain minor works, as detailed in the Ancient Monuments (Class Consents) Order 1994, may be carried out without consent. It is a criminal offence to carry out unauthorised work to scheduled monuments.

WALES

Under the Planning (Listed Buildings and Conservation Areas) Act 1990 and the Ancient Monuments and Archaeological Areas Act 1979, the National Assembly for Wales is responsible for listing buildings and scheduling monuments in Wales on the advice of Cadw (the Welsh government's historic environment division) and the Royal Commission on the Ancient and Historical Monuments of Wales (RCAHMW). The criteria for evaluating buildings are similar to those in England and the same listing system is used. As at March 2013, there are 29,962 listed buildings and 4,180 scheduled monuments in Wales.

SCOTLAND

Under the Planning (Listed Buildings and Conservation Areas) (Scotland) Act 1997 and the Ancient Monuments and Archaeological Areas Act 1979, Scottish ministers are responsible for listing buildings and scheduling monuments in Scotland on the advice of Historic Scotland and the Royal Commission on the Ancient and Historical Monuments of Scotland (RCAHMS). The criteria for evaluating buildings are similar to those in England but an A, B, C(S) categorisation is used. As at March 2013 there were 47,647 listed buildings and 8,202 scheduled monuments in Scotland.

NORTHERN IRELAND

Under the Planning (Northern Ireland) Order 1991 and the Historic Monuments and Archaeological Objects (Northern Ireland) Order 1995, the Northern Ireland Environment Agency (part of the Department of the Environment Northern Ireland) is responsible for listing buildings and scheduling monuments. The Historic Buildings Council for Northern Ireland and the relevant district council must be consulted on listing proposals, and the Historic Monuments Council for Northern Ireland must be consulted on scheduling proposals. The criteria for evaluating buildings are similar to those in England but an A, B+, B1 and B2 categorisation is used. As at March 2013 there were around 8,600 listed buildings and 1,901 scheduled monuments in Northern Ireland.

ENGLAND

For more information on English Heritage properties, including those listed below, the official website is W www.english-heritage.org.uk

For more information on National Trust properties in England, including those listed below, the official website is W www.nationaltrust.org.uk

KEY

(EH) English Heritage property

(NT) National Trust property

* UNESCO World Heritage Site (*see also* World Heritage Sites)

A LA RONDE (NT), Exmouth, Devon EX8 5BD T 01395-265514
Unique 16-sided house completed *c.*1796

ALNWICK CASTLE, Alnwick, Northumberland NE66 1NQ
T 01665-510777 W www.alnwickcastle.com
Seat of the Dukes of Northumberland since 1309; Italian Renaissance-style interior; gardens with spectacular water features

ALTHORP, Northants NN7 4HQ T 01604-770107
W www.althorp.com
Spencer family seat; permanent Diana, Princess of Wales exhibition

ANGLESEY ABBEY (NT), Lode, Cambs CB25 9EJ
T 01223-810080
Jacobean house (*c.*1600) with gardens and a working watermill (Lode Mill) on the site of a 12th-century priory; fine furnishings and a unique clock collection

APSLEY HOUSE (EH), London W1J 7NT T 020-7499 5676
Built by Robert Adam 1771–8, home of the Dukes of Wellington since 1817 and known as 'No. 1 London'; collection of fine and decorative arts

ARUNDEL CASTLE, Arundel, W. Sussex BN18 9AB
T 01903-882173 W www.arundelcastle.org
Castle dating from the Norman Conquest; seat of the Dukes of Norfolk

AVEBURY (EH/NT), Wilts SN8 1RF T 01672-539250
Remains of stone circles constructed 4,000 years ago enclosing part of the later village of Avebury

BANQUETING HOUSE, Whitehall, London SW1A 2ER
T 0844-482 7777 W www.hrp.org.uk
Designed by Inigo Jones in 1619; ceiling paintings by Rubens; site of the execution of Charles I

BASILDON PARK (NT), Reading, Berks RG8 9NR
T 0118-984 3040
Palladian mansion built in 1776–83 by John Carr

BATTLE ABBEY (EH), Battle, E. Sussex TN33 0AD
T 01424-775705
Remains of the abbey founded by William the Conqueror on the site of the Battle of Hastings

BEESTON CASTLE (EH), Cheshire CW6 9TX
T 01829-260464
Built in the 13th century by Ranulf, sixth Earl of Chester on the site of an Iron Age hillfort

BELVOIR CASTLE, Grantham, Lincs NG32 1PE
T 01476-871002 W www.belvoircastle.com
Seat of the Dukes of Rutland; 19th-century Gothic-style castle; notable art collection

BERKELEY CASTLE, Glos GL13 9BQ T 01453-810332
W www.berkeley-castle.com
Completed late 12th century; site of the murder of Edward II (1327)

BIRDOSWALD FORT (EH), Brampton, Cumbria CA8 7DD
T 01697-747602
Stretch of Hadrian's Wall with Roman wall fort, turret and milecastle

*BLENHEIM PALACE, Woodstock, Oxon OX20 1PP
T 01993-810530 W www.blenheimpalace.com
Seat of the Dukes of Marlborough and Winston Churchill's birthplace; house designed by Vanbrugh; landscaped parkland by Capability Brown

BLICKLING ESTATE (NT), Blickling, Norfolk NR11 6NF
T 01263-738030
Jacobean house with state rooms; extensive gardens, temple and 18th-century orangery

BODIAM CASTLE (NT), Bodiam, E. Sussex TN32 5UA
T 01580-830196
Well-preserved medieval moated castle built in 1385

BOLSOVER CASTLE (EH), Bolsover, Derbys S44 6PR
T 01246-822844
17th-century castle on site of medieval fortress

BOSCOBEL HOUSE (EH), Bishops Wood, Staffs ST19 9AR
T 01902-850244
Timber-framed 17th-century hunting lodge; refuge of fugitive Charles II from parliamentary troops

BOUGHTON HOUSE, Kettering, Northants NN14 1BJ
T 01536-515731 W www.boughtonhouse.org.uk
17th-century house with French-style additions; home of the Dukes of Buccleuch and Queensbury

BOWOOD HOUSE, Calne, Wilts SN11 0LZ T 01249-812102
W www.bowood-house.co.uk
18th-century house in Capability Brown park, featuring Robert Adam orangery and renowned pinetum and arboretum

BUCKFAST ABBEY, Buckfastleigh, Devon TQ11 0EE
T 01364-645500 W www.buckfast.org.uk
Benedictine monastery on medieval foundations

BUCKINGHAM PALACE, London SW1A 1AA
T 020-7766 7300 W www.royalcollection.org.uk
Purchased by George III in 1761, and the Sovereign's official London residence since 1837; 19 state rooms, including the Throne Room, and Queen's Gallery

BUCKLAND ABBEY (NT), Yelverton, Devon PL20 6EY
T 01822-853607
13th-century Cistercian monastery; home of Sir Francis Drake

BURGHLEY HOUSE, Stamford, Lincs PE9 3JY T 01780-752451
W www.burghley.co.uk
Late Elizabethan house built by William Cecil, first Lord Burghley

CARISBROOKE CASTLE (EH), Newport, Isle of Wight PO30 1XY T 01983-522107
W www.carisbrookecastlemuseum.org.uk
Norman castle; museum; prison of Charles I 1647–8

CARLISLE CASTLE (EH), Carlisle, Cumbria CA3 8UR
T 01228-591922
Medieval castle; prison of Mary Queen of Scots

CASTLE ACRE PRIORY (EH), King's Lynn, Norfolk PE32 2XD
T 01760-755394
Remains include 12th-century church and prior's lodgings

CASTLE DROGO (NT), Drewsteignton, Devon EX6 6PB
T 01647-433306
Granite castle designed by Lutyens in 1911

CASTLE HOWARD, N. Yorks YO60 7DA T 01653-648333
W www.castlehoward.co.uk
Designed by Vanbrugh 1699–1726; mausoleum designed by Hawksmoor

CASTLE RISING CASTLE (EH), King's Lynn, Norfolk PE31 6AH T 01553-631330 W www.castlerising.co.uk
12th-century keep with gatehouse and bridge, surrounded by 20 acres of defensive earthworks

CHARLES DARWIN'S HOUSE (DOWN HOUSE) (EH), Downe, Kent BR6 7JT T 01689-859119
The family home where Darwin wrote *On the Origin of Species*

CHARTWELL (NT), Westerham, Kent TN16 1PS
T 01732-868381
Home and studio of Sir Winston Churchill

CHATSWORTH, Bakewell, Derbys DE45 1PP T 01246-565300
W www.chatsworth.org
Tudor mansion set in magnificent parkland; seat of the Dukes of Devonshire

CHESTERS ROMAN FORT (EH), Chollerford, Northumberland NE46 4EU T 01434-681379
Roman cavalry fort built to guard Hadrian's Wall

CHYSAUSTER ANCIENT VILLAGE (EH), Penzance, Cornwall TR20 8XA T 07831-757934
Remains of nearly 2,000-year-old Celtic settlement; eight stone-walled homesteads

CLANDON PARK (NT), West Clandon, Guildford, Surrey GU4 7RQ T 01483-222482 W www.clandonpark.co.uk

18th-century Palladian mansion and gardens, which contain a Maori meeting house, brought back from New Zealand in 1892

CLIFFORD'S TOWER (EH), York YO1 9SA T 01904-646940 W www.cliffordstower.com
13th-century keep built on a mound; remains of a castle built by William the Conqueror

CORBRIDGE ROMAN SITE (EH), Corbridge, Northumberland NE45 5NT T 01434-632349
Excavated central area of a Roman garrison town

CORFE CASTLE (NT), Wareham, Dorset BH20 5EZ T 01929-481294
Former royal castle dating from the 11th century and ruined during the English Civil War

CROFT CASTLE AND PARKLAND (NT), Yarpole, Herefordshire HR6 9PW T 01568-780120
17th-century quadrangular manor house with Georgian-Gothic interior; built close to ruin of pre-Conquest border castle

DEAL CASTLE (EH), Deal, Kent CT14 7BA T 01304-372762
Largest of the coastal defence forts built by Henry VIII; shaped like a rose with six inner and outer bastions

*DERWENT VALLEY MILLS, Belper, Derbyshire T 01629-536831
Series of 18th- and 19th-century cotton mills; birthplace of the modern factory

DOVER CASTLE (EH), Dover, Kent CT16 1HU T 01304-211067
Castle with Roman, Saxon and Norman features; tunnels used as wartime operations rooms

DR JOHNSON'S HOUSE, Gough Square, London EC4A 3DE T 020-7353 3745 W www.drjohnsonshouse.org
Home of Samuel Johnson 1748–59

DUNSTANBURGH CASTLE (EH/NT), Craster, nr Alnwick, Northumberland NE66 3TT T 01665-576231
14th-century castle ruins on a cliff with a substantial twin-towered gatehouse-keep

ELTHAM PALACE (EH), Eltham, London SE9 5QE T 020-8294 2548
Art Deco house next to remains of medieval palace once occupied by Henry VIII; moated gardens

FARLEIGH HUNGERFORD CASTLE (EH), Bath, Somerset BA2 7RS T 01225-754026
Late 14th-century castle with inner and outer courts; chapel with rare medieval wall paintings

FARNHAM CASTLE KEEP (EH), Farnham, Surrey GA9 0AG T 01252-721194 W www.farnhamcastle.com
Large 12th-century castle keep with motte and bailey wall

FISHBOURNE ROMAN PALACE, Fishbourne, Chichester, W. Sussex PO19 3QR T 01243-789829 W www.sussexpast.co.uk
Excavated Roman palace with largest collection of in-situ mosaics in Britain

*FOUNTAINS ABBEY (NT), nr Ripon, N. Yorks HG4 3DY T 01765-608888 W www.fountainsabbey.org.uk
Ruined Cistercian monastery and corn mill; site includes Studley Royal, a Georgian water garden and deer park

FRAMLINGHAM CASTLE (EH), Framlingham, Suffolk IP13 9BP T 01728-724189
Castle (*c.*1200) with high curtain walls enclosing an almshouse (1639); once the refuge of Mary Tudor

FURNESS ABBEY (EH), Barrow-in-Furness, Cumbria LA13 0PJ T 01229-823420
Remains of church and cloister buildings founded in 1123

GLASTONBURY ABBEY, Glastonbury, Somerset BA6 9EL T 01458-832267 W www.glastonburyabbey.com
12th-century abbey destroyed by fire in 1184 and later rebuilt; ruined in 1539 during dissolution of monasteries; site of an early Christian settlement

GOODRICH CASTLE (EH), Ross-on-Wye, Herefordshire HR9 6HY T 01600-890538
Remains of 12th- and 13th-century castle; contains a famous mortar that ruined the castle in 1646

GREENWICH, London SE10 9NF W www.visitgreenwich.org.uk
Former Royal Observatory (founded 1675) housing the time ball and zero meridian of longitude; the Queen's House, designed for Queen Anne, wife of James I, by Inigo Jones; Painted Hall and neoclassical Chapel (Old Royal Naval College)

GRIMES GRAVES (EH), Brandon, Norfolk IP26 5DE T 01842-810656
Neolithic flint mines; one shaft can be descended

GUILDHALL, London EC2V 7HH T 020-7606 3030 W www.guildhall.cityoflondon.gov.uk
Centre of civic government of the City built *c.*1441; facade built 1788–9

HADDON HALL, Bakewell, Derbys DE45 1LA T 01629-812855 W www.haddonhall.co.uk
Well-preserved 12th-century manor house

HAILES ABBEY (EH), Cheltenham, Glos GL54 5PB T 01242-602398
Ruins of a 13th-century Cistercian monastery

HAM HOUSE AND GARDEN (NT), Richmond-upon-Thames, Surrey TW10 7RS T 020-8940 1950
Stuart house with lavish interiors and formal gardens

HAMPTON COURT PALACE, East Molesey, Surrey KT8 9AU T 0844-482 7777 W www.hrp.org.uk
16th-century palace originally built for Cardinal Wolsey with 17th- and 18th-century additions by Wren; Royal Tennis Court and world-renowned maze

HARDWICK HALL (NT), Chesterfield, Derbys S44 5QJ T 01246-850430
Elizabethan house built for Bess of Hardwick

HARDY'S BIRTHPLACE (NT), Higher Bockhampton, Dorset DT2 8QJ T 01305-262366
Birthplace and home of Thomas Hardy

HAREWOOD HOUSE, Harewood, W. Yorks LS17 9LG T 0113-218 1010 W www.harewood.org
18th-century house designed by John Carr and Robert Adam; park by Capability Brown

HATFIELD HOUSE, Hatfield, Herts AL9 5NQ T 01707-287010 W www.hatfield-house.co.uk
Jacobean house built by Robert Cecil; features surviving wing of Royal Palace of Hatfield (*c.*1485), the childhood home of Elizabeth I

HELMSLEY CASTLE (EH), Helmsley, N. Yorks YO62 5AB T 01439-770442
12th-century keep and curtain wall with 16th-century buildings; spectacular earthwork defences

HEVER CASTLE, nr Edenbridge, Kent TN8 7NG T 01732-865224 W www.hevercastle.co.uk
13th-century double-moated castle; childhood home of Anne Boleyn

HIGH CROSS HOUSE (NT), nr Totnes, Devon TQ9 6ED T 01803-842382
Celebrated Modernist house containing original Bauhaus furniture

HOLKHAM HALL, Wells-next-the-Sea, Norfolk NR23 1AB T 01328-710227 W www.holkham.co.uk
Palladian mansion; notable fine art collection

HOUSESTEADS ROMAN FORT (EH), Hexham, Northumberland NE47 6NN T 01434-344363
Excavated Roman infantry fort on Hadrian's Wall with museum

*IRONBRIDGE GORGE, Ironbridge, Shropshire
Important Industrial Revolution site, featuring the world's first iron bridge

KEDLESTON HALL (NT), Derbys DE22 5JH T 01332-842191
Palladian mansion built 1759–65; complete Robert Adam interiors; museum of Asian artefacts

KELMSCOTT MANOR, nr Lechlade, Glos GL7 3HJ
T 01367-252486 W www.kelmscottmanor.org.uk
Built *c.*1600; summer home of William Morris, with products of Morris and Co.

KENILWORTH CASTLE (EH), Kenilworth, Warks CV8 1NE
T 01926-852078
Largest castle ruin in England; Norman keep with 13th-century outer walls

KENSINGTON PALACE, Kensington Gardens, London W8 4PX T 0870-482 7777 W www.hrp.org.uk
Built in 1605 and enlarged by Wren; birthplace of Queen Victoria; 'Victoria: love, duty and loss' exhibition

KENWOOD HOUSE (EH), Hampstead Lane, London NW3 7JR
T 020-8348 1286
Neoclassical villa housing the Iveagh bequest of paintings and furniture

KEW PALACE, Richmond-upon-Thames, Surrey TW9 3AB
T 0844-482 7777 W www.hrp.org.uk
Red-brick mansion (*c.*1631); includes Queen Charlotte's Cottage, used by King George III and family as a summerhouse

KINGSTON LACY (NT), Wimborne Minster, Dorset BH21 4EA
T 01202-883402
17th-century mansion with 19th-century alterations; important art collection

KNEBWORTH HOUSE, Knebworth, Herts SG3 6PY
T 01438-812661 W www.knebworthhouse.com
Tudor manor house concealed by 19th-century Gothic decoration; Lutyens gardens

KNOLE (NT), Sevenoaks, Kent TN15 0RP T 01732-462100
House built in 1456 set in 1,000-acre deer park; fine art and furniture collection; birthplace of Vita Sackville-West

LAMBETH PALACE, London SE1 7JU T 020-7898 1200
W www.archbishopofcanterbury.org
Official residence of the Archbishop of Canterbury since the 13th century

LANERCOST PRIORY (EH), Brampton, Cumbria CA8 2HQ
T 01697-73030 W www.lanercostpriory.org.uk
The nave of the Augustinian priory's church, *c.*1166, is still used; remains of other claustral buildings

LANHYDROCK (NT), Bodmin, Cornwall PL30 5AD
T 01208-265950
House dating from the 17th century; 50 rooms, including kitchen and nursery

LEEDS CASTLE, nr Maidstone, Kent ME17 1PL
T 01622-765400 W www.leeds-castle.com
Castle dating from the 12th century, situated on two islands in a lake; used as a royal palace by Henry VIII

LEVENS HALL, Kendal, Cumbria LA8 0PD T 01539-560321
W www.levenshall.co.uk
Elizabethan house with unique topiary garden (1694); steam engine collection

LINCOLN CASTLE, Lincoln, Lincs LN1 3AA T 01522-511068
W www.lincolnshire.gov.uk
Built by William the Conqueror in 1068 on a Roman site; one of only two double-motted castles in Britain

LINDISFARNE PRIORY (EH), Holy Island, Northumberland TD15 2RX T 01289-389200
Founded in AD 635; re-established in the 12th century as a Benedictine priory, now ruined

LITTLE MORETON HALL (NT), Congleton, Cheshire CW12 4SD T 01260-272018
Iconic timber-framed moated Tudor manor house with knot garden

LONGLEAT HOUSE, Warminster, Wilts BA12 7NW
T 01985-844400 W www.longleat.co.uk
Elizabethan house in Italian Renaissance style; Capability Brown parkland with lakes; safari park

LULLINGSTONE ROMAN VILLA (EH), Eynsford, Kent DA4 0JA T 01322-863467
Large villa occupied for much of the Roman period; fine mosaics and unique Christian paintings

MIDDLEHAM CASTLE (EH), Middleham, N. Yorks DL8 4QG
T 01969-623899
12th-century keep within later fortifications; childhood home of Richard III

MONTACUTE HOUSE (NT), Montacute, Somerset TA15 6XP
T 01935-823289
Elizabethan mansion with National Portrait Gallery collection of portraits from the period

MOUNT GRACE PRIORY (EH), Northallerton, N. Yorks DL6 3JG T 01609-883494
Carthusian priory with remains of monastic buildings

OLD SARUM (EH), Salisbury, Wilts SP1 3SD T 01722-335398
Iron Age hill fort enclosing remains of Norman castle and cathedral

ORFORD CASTLE (EH), Orford, Suffolk IP12 2ND
T 01394-450472
Polygonal tower keep of *c.*1170 and remains of coastal defence castle built by Henry II

OSBORNE HOUSE (EH), East Cowes, Isle of Wight PO32 6JX
T 01983-200022
Queen Victoria's seaside residence; built by Thomas Cubitt in Italian Renaissance style; summer house, Swiss Cottage and museum

OSTERLEY PARK (NT), Isleworth, Middx TW7 4RB
T 020-8232 5050 W www.osterleypark.org.uk
18th-century neoclassical mansion with Tudor stable block

PENDENNIS CASTLE (EH), Falmouth, Cornwall TR11 4LP
T 01326-316594
Well-preserved 16th-century coastal defence castle

PENSHURST PLACE, Penshurst, Kent TN11 8DG
T 01892-870307 W www.penshurstplace.com
Medieval house featuring Baron's Hall (1341) and gardens (1346); toy museum

PETWORTH HOUSE (NT), Petworth, W. Sussex GU28 0AE
T 01798-342207
Late 17th-century house set in Capability Brown landscaped deer park; fine art collection

PEVENSEY CASTLE (EH), Pevensey, E. Sussex BN24 5LE
T 01323-762604
Walls of a fourth-century Roman fort; remains of an 11th-century castle

PEVERIL CASTLE (EH), Castleton, Derbys S33 8WQ
T 01433-620613
Remains of a 12th-century castle defended on two sides by precipitous rocks

POLESDEN LACEY (NT), nr Dorking, Surrey RH5 6BD
T 01372-458203
Regency villa remodelled in the Edwardian era; fine paintings and furnishings; walled rose garden

PORTCHESTER CASTLE (EH), Portchester, Hants PO16 9QW
T 02392-378291
Walls of a late Roman fort enclosing a Norman keep and an Augustinian priory church

POWDERHAM CASTLE, Kenton, Devon EX6 8JQ
T 01626-890243 W www.powderham.co.uk
Medieval castle with 18th- and 19th-century alterations, including James Wyatt music room

RABY CASTLE, Staindrop, Co. Durham DL2 3AH
T 01833-660202 W www.rabycastle.com
14th-century castle with walled gardens

RAGLEY HALL, Alcester, Warks B49 5NJ T 01789-762090 W www.ragleyhall.com
17th-century Palladian house with gardens and lake

RICHBOROUGH ROMAN FORT (EH), Richborough, Kent CT13 9JW T 01304-612013
Remains of a Roman Saxon Shore fortress; landing-site of the Claudian invasion in AD 43

RICHMOND CASTLE (EH), Richmond, N. Yorks DL10 4QW T 01748-822493
12th-century keep with 11th-century curtain wall

RIEVAULX ABBEY (EH), nr Helmsley, N. Yorks YO62 5LB T 01439-798228
Remains of a Cistercian abbey founded *c.*1132

ROCHESTER CASTLE (EH), Rochester, Kent ME1 1SW T 01634-402276
11th-century castle partly on the Roman city wall, with a well-preserved square keep of *c.*1127

ROCKINGHAM CASTLE, Market Harborough, Leics LE16 8TH T 01536-770240 W www.rockinghamcastle.com
Built by William the Conqueror; formal gardens and 400-year-old 'elephant' hedge

ROMAN BATHS, Pump Room, Stall Street, Bath BA1 1LZ T 01225-477785 W www.romanbaths.co.uk
Extensive remains of a Roman temple and bathing complex which still flows with natural thermal water; museum

ROYAL PAVILION, Brighton BN1 1EE T 03000-290900 W www.brighton-hove-rpml.org.uk
Unique palace of George IV, in indo-gothic style with chinoiserie interiors and Regency gardens

ST AUGUSTINE'S ABBEY (EH), Canterbury, Kent CT1 1PF T 01227-378100
Remains of Benedictine monastery founded *c.*597

ST MAWES CASTLE (EH), St Mawes, Cornwall TR2 5DE T 01326-270526
Coastal defence castle built by Henry VIII

ST MICHAEL'S MOUNT (NT), Marazion, Cornwall TR17 0HT T 01736-710507 W www.stmichaelsmount.co.uk
12th-century church and castle with later additions, situated on an iconic rocky island

*SALTAIRE, nr Shipley, W. Yorks
Victorian industrial village founded by mill owner Titus Salt for his workers

SANDRINGHAM, Norfolk PE35 6EN T 01485-545408 W www.sandringhamestate.co.uk
The Queen's private residence; neo-Jacobean house built in 1870 with gardens and country park

SCARBOROUGH CASTLE (EH), Scarborough, N. Yorks YO11 1HY T 01723-372451
Remains of 12th-century keep and curtain walls

SHERBORNE CASTLE, Sherborne, Dorset DT9 5NR T 01935-812072 W www.sherbornecastle.com
16th-century castle built by Sir Walter Raleigh set in Capability Brown landscaped gardens

SHUGBOROUGH ESTATE (NT), Milford, Staffs ST17 0XB T 0845-459 8900 W www.shugborough.org.uk
Late 17th century house in 18th-century park with monuments, temples and pavilions in the Greek Revival style; seat of the Earls of Lichfield

SKIPTON CASTLE, Skipton, N. Yorks BD23 1AW T 01756-792442 W www.skiptoncastle.co.uk
Well-preserved D-shaped medieval castle with six round towers and inner courtyard

SMALLHYTHE PLACE (NT), Tenterden, Kent TN30 7NG T 01580-766111
Half-timbered 16th-century house

*STONEHENGE (EH), nr Amesbury, Wilts SP4 7DE T 01722-343830
World-famous prehistoric monument comprising concentric stone circles surrounded by a ditch and bank

STONOR PARK, Henley-on-Thames, Oxon RG9 6HF T 01491-638587 W www.stonor.com
Medieval house with Georgian facade; refuge for Catholic recusants after the Reformation

STOURHEAD (NT), Stourton, Wilts BA12 6QD T 01747-841152
18th-century Palladian mansion with world-renowned landscape gardens; King Alfred's Tower

STRATFIELD SAYE HOUSE, Hants RG7 2BT T 01256-882694 W www.stratfield-saye.co.uk
House built 1630–40; home of the Dukes of Wellington since 1817

STRATFORD-UPON-AVON, Warks T 01789-204016 W www.shakespeare.org.uk
Shakespeare's Birthplace Trust with Shakespeare Centre; Anne Hathaway's Cottage; Holy Trinity Church, where Shakespeare is buried

SUDELEY CASTLE, Winchcombe, Glos GL54 5JD T 01242-602308 W www.sudeleycastle.co.uk
Castle built in 1442; once owned by Richard III and former home to Catherine Parr, sixth wife of Henry VIII; restored in the 19th century

SULGRAVE MANOR, nr Banbury, Oxon OX17 2SD T 01295-760205 W www.sulgravemanor.org.uk
Home of George Washington's family

SUTTON HOUSE (NT), Hackney, London E9 6JQ T 020-8986 2264
Tudor house, built in 1535 by Sir Ralph Sadleir

SYON HOUSE, Brentford, Middx TW8 8JF T 020-8560 0882 W www.syonpark.co.uk
Built on the site of a former monastery; Robert Adam interior; Capability Brown park

TINTAGEL CASTLE (EH), Tintagel, Cornwall PL34 0HE T 01840-770328
13th-century cliff-top castle and 5th–6th-century Celtic settlement; linked with Arthurian legend

TOWER OF LONDON, London EC3N 4AB T 0844-482 7777 W www.hrp.org.uk
Royal palace and fortress begun by William the Conqueror in 1078; houses the Crown Jewels

TYNEMOUTH PRIORY AND CASTLE (EH), Tyne and Wear NE30 4BZ T 0191-257 1090
Remains of a Benedictine priory, founded *c.*1090, moated castle-towers, a gatehouse and keep on Saxon monastic site

UPPARK (NT), South Harting, W. Sussex GU31 5QR T 01730-825857
17th-century house, restored after fire; Fetherstonhaugh art collection; 18th-century dolls' house

WALMER CASTLE (EH), Walmer, Kent CT14 7LJ T 01304-364288
One of Henry VIII's coastal defence castles, now the residence of the Lord Warden of the Cinque Ports

WARKWORTH CASTLE (EH), Warkworth, Northumberland NE65 0UJ T 01665-711423
14th-century keep amid earlier ruins, with hermitage upstream

WHITBY ABBEY (EH), Whitby, N. Yorks YO22 4JT T 01947-603568
Remains of Norman church on the site of a monastery founded in AD 657

WILTON HOUSE, nr Salisbury, Wilts SP2 0BJ T 01722-746714 W www.wiltonhouse.com
17th-century house on the site of a Tudor house and ninth-century nunnery; Palladian bridge

WINDSOR CASTLE, Windsor, Berks SL4 1NJ T 020-7766 7304 W www.royalcollection.org.uk
Official residence of the Queen; oldest royal residence still in regular use; largest inhabited castle in the world. Also St George's Chapel; Queen Mary's Dolls' House

WOBURN ABBEY, Woburn, Beds MK17 9WA T 01525-290333 W www.woburn.co.uk
Built on the site of a Cistercian abbey; seat of the Dukes of Bedford; art collection; antiques centre
WROXETER ROMAN CITY (EH), nr Shrewsbury, Shropshire SY5 6PH T 01743-761330
Second-century public baths and part of the forum of the Roman town of *Viroconium*

WALES

For more information on Cadw properties, including those listed below, the official website is W www.cadw.wales.gov.uk
For more information on National Trust properties in Wales, including those listed below, the official website is W www.nationaltrust.org.uk
KEY
(C) Property of Cadw: Welsh Historic Monuments
(NT) National Trust property
* UNESCO World Heritage Site (*see also* World Heritage Sites)

*BEAUMARIS CASTLE (C), Anglesey LL58 8AP T 01248-810361
Concentrically planned 13th-century castle, still virtually intact
*BLAENAVON, Church Road, Blaenavon NP4 9AS T 01495-742333
18th- and 19th-century industrial landscape associated with coal and iron production
CAERLEON ROMAN BATHS AND AMPHITHEATRE (C), Newport NP18 1AE T 01633-422518
Rare example of a legionary bath-house and late first-century arena surrounded by bank for spectators
*CAERNARFON CASTLE (C), Gwynedd LL55 2AY T 01286-677617
Huge fortress with polygonal towers built between 1283 and 1330, initially for King Edward I of England; setting for the investiture of Prince Charles in 1969
CAERPHILLY CASTLE (C), Caerphilly CF83 1JD T 029-2088 3143
Concentrically planned castle (*c.*1270) notable for its scale and use of water defences
CARDIFF CASTLE, Cardiff CF10 3RB T 029-2087 8100 W www.cardiffcastle.com
Norman keep built on site of Roman fort; 'fairytale' gothic-revival mansion added in the 19th century
CASTELL COCH (C), Tongwynlais, Cardiff CF15 7JS T 029-2081 0101
'Fairytale'-style castle, rebuilt 1875–90 on medieval foundations
CHEPSTOW CASTLE (C), Monmouthshire NP16 5EY T 01291-624065
Rectangular keep amid extensive fortifications; developed throughout the Middle Ages
*CONWY CASTLE (C), Gwynedd LL32 8AY T 01492-592358
Built for Edward I in 1283–7 on narrow rocky outcrop; features eight towers and two barbicans
CRICCIETH CASTLE (C), Gwynedd LL52 0DP T 01766-522227
Native Welsh 13th-century castle, taken and altered by Edward I and Edward II
DENBIGH CASTLE (C), Denbighshire LL16 3NB T 01745-813385
Remains of the castle (begun 1282), including triple-towered gatehouses
DYFFRYN GARDENS (NT), St Nicholas, Cardiff CF5 6SU T 029-2059 3328
Edwardian gardens designed by Thomas Mawson, overlooked by a grand Edwardian mansion
*HARLECH CASTLE (C), Gwynedd LL46 2YH T 01766-780552
Well-preserved castle, constructed 1283–95, on an outcrop above the former shoreline; withstood seven-year siege 1461–8
PEMBROKE CASTLE, Pembrokeshire SA71 4LA T 01646-684585 W www.pembroke-castle.co.uk
Castle founded in 1093; Great Tower built in late 12th century; birthplace of King Henry VII
PENRHYN CASTLE (NT), Bangor, Gwynedd LL57 4HN T 01248-353084
Neo-Norman castle built in the 19th century; railway and dolls' museums; private art collection
*PONTCYSYLLTE AQUEDUCT AND CANAL, Trevor, Wrexham T 01978-292015
Longest and highest aqueduct in Great Britain; designed by Thomas Telford and finished in 1805
POWIS CASTLE (NT), Welshpool, Powys SY21 8RF T 01938-551944
Medieval castle with interior in variety of styles; 17th-century gardens; Clive of India museum
RAGLAN CASTLE (C), Monmouthshire NP15 2BT T 01291-690228
Remains of 15th-century castle with moated hexagonal keep
ST DAVIDS BISHOP'S PALACE (C), Pembrokeshire SA62 6PE T 01437-720517
Remains of residence of Bishops of St Davids built 1328–47
TINTERN ABBEY (C), nr Chepstow, Monmouthshire NP16 6SE T 01291-689251
Remains of 13th-century church and conventual buildings of a 12th-century Cistercian monastery
TRETOWER COURT AND CASTLE (C), nr Crickhowell, Powys NP8 1RF T 01874-730279
Medieval manor house rebuilt in the 15th century, with remains of 12th-century castle near by

SCOTLAND

For more information on Historic Scotland properties, including those listed below, the official website is W www.historic-scotland.gov.uk
For more information on National Trust for Scotland properties, including those listed below, the official website is W www.nts.org.uk
KEY
(HS) Historic Scotland property
(NTS) National Trust for Scotland property
* Part of the Heart of Neolithic Orkney UNESCO World Heritage Site

ABBOTSFORD HOUSE, Melrose, Roxburghshire TD6 9BQ T 01896-752043 W www.scottsabbotsford.co.uk
Home of Sir Walter Scott; features historic Scottish relics and formal gardens
BALMORAL CASTLE, Ballater, Aberdeenshire AB35 5TB T 01339-742534 W www.balmoralcastle.com
Baronial-style castle built for Victoria and Albert; the Queen's private residence
BLACKHOUSE, ARNOL (HS), Lewis, Western Isles HS2 9DB T 01851-710395
Traditional Lewis thatched house
BLAIR CASTLE, Blair Atholl, Perthshire PH18 5TL T 01796-481207 W www.blair-castle.co.uk
Mid-18th-century mansion with 13th-century tower; seat of the Dukes and Earls of Atholl

BOWHILL, Selkirk, Scottish Borders TD7 5ET T 01750-22204 W www.bowhill.org
Present house dates mainly from 1812; Seat of the Dukes of Buccleuch and Queensberry; fine collection of paintings

BROUGH OF BIRSAY (HS), Orkney KW17 2NH T 01856-841815
Remains of Norse and Pictish village on the tidal island of Birsay

CAERLAVEROCK CASTLE (HS), Glencaple, Dumfries and Galloway DG1 4RU T 01387-770244
Unique triangular 13th-century moated castle with classical Renaissance additions

CAIRNPAPPLE HILL (HS), Torphichen, West Lothian T 01506-634622
Neolithic ceremonial site and Bronze Age burial chambers

CALANAIS STANDING STONES (HS), Lewis, Western Isles HS2 9DY T 01851-621422
Standing stones in a cross-shaped setting, dating from between 2900 and 2600 BC

CATERTHUNS (BROWN AND WHITE) (HS), Menmuir, nr Brechin, Angus
Two large Iron Age hill forts

CAWDOR CASTLE, Nairn, Moray IV12 5RD T 01667-404401 W www.cawdorcastle.com
14th-century keep with 15th- and 17th-century additions

CLAVA CAIRNS (HS), nr Inverness, Inverness-shire T 01667-460232
Bronze Age cemetery complex of cairns and standing stones

CRATHES CASTLE (NTS), nr Banchory, Aberdeenshire AB31 5QJ T 08444-932166
16th-century baronial castle in woodland, fields and gardens

CULZEAN CASTLE (NTS), Maybole, Ayrshire KA19 8LE T 08444-932149 W www.culzeanexperience.org
18th-century Robert Adam castle with oval staircase and circular saloon

DRYBURGH ABBEY (HS), nr Melrose, Roxburghshire TD6 0RQ T 01835-822381
12th-century abbey containing the tomb of Sir Walter Scott

DUNVEGAN CASTLE, Skye IV55 8WF T 01470-521206 W www.dunvegancastle.com
13th-century castle with later additions; home of the chiefs of the Clan MacLeod

EDINBURGH CASTLE (HS), EH1 2NG T 0131-225 9846 W www.edinburghcastle.gov.uk
Fortress perched on extinct volcano; includes the Scottish Crown Jewels, Scottish National War Memorial, Scottish United Services Museum

EDZELL CASTLE (HS), nr Brechin, Angus DD9 7UE T 01356-648631
Ruined 16th-century tower house on medieval foundations; early 17th-century walled garden

EILEAN DONAN CASTLE, Dornie, Ross and Cromarty IV40 8DX T 01599-555202 W www.eileandonancastle.com
13th-century castle situated at the meeting point of three sea lochs; Jacobite relics

ELGIN CATHEDRAL (HS), Moray IV30 1HU T 01343-547171
13th-century cathedral and octagonal chapterhouse

FLOORS CASTLE, Kelso, Roxburghshire TD5 7SF T 01573-223333 W www.floorscastle.com
Largest inhabited castle in Scotland; seat of the Dukes of Roxburghe; built in the 1720s by William Adam

FORT GEORGE (HS), Ardersier, Inverness-shire IV2 7TD T 01667-460232
18th-century fort; still a working army barracks

GLAMIS CASTLE, Forfar, Angus DD8 1RJ T 01307-840393 W www.glamis-castle.co.uk
Seat of the Lyon family (later Earls of Strathmore and Kinghorne) since 1372; the setting for Shakepeare's *Macbeth*

GLASGOW CATHEDRAL (HS), Lanarkshire G4 0QZ T 0141-552 8198 W www.glasgowcathedral.org.uk
Late 12th-century cathedral with vaulted crypt

GLENELG BROCHS (HS), Glenelg, Ross and Cromarty T 01667-460232
Two broch towers (Dun Telve and Dun Troddan) with well-preserved structural features

HOPETOUN HOUSE, South Queensferry, West Lothian EH30 9SL T 0131-331 2451 W www.hopetoun.co.uk
Designed by Sir William Bruce in 1699 and enlarged by William Adam 1721–48

HUNTLY CASTLE (HS), Aberdeenshire AB54 4SH T 01466-793191
Ruin of a 16th- and 17th-century baronial residence

INVERARAY CASTLE, Argyll PA32 8XE T 01499-302203 W www.inveraray-castle.com
Gothic-style 18th-century castle designed by William Adam and Roger Morris; seat of the Dukes of Argyll

IONA ABBEY (HS), Iona, Inner Hebrides PA76 6SQ T 01681-700512
Monastery founded by St Columba in AD 563

JARLSHOF (HS), Sumburgh Head, Shetland ZE3 9JN T 01950-460112
Prehistoric settlement with later ninth-century Norse additions

JEDBURGH ABBEY (HS), Scottish Borders TD8 6JQ T 01835-863925
Ruined Augustinian abbey founded *c.*1138

KISIMUL CASTLE (HS), Castlebay, Barra, Western Isles HS9 5UZ T 01871-810313
Medieval island home of the Clan MacNeil

LINLITHGOW PALACE (HS), Kirkgate, Linlithgow, West Lothian EH49 7AL T 01506-842896
Ruined royal palace, founded in 1424, set in park; birthplace of James V and Mary, Queen of Scots

*MAESHOWE (HS), Stenness, Orkney KW16 3HA T 01856-761606
Neolithic chambered tomb with Viking runes

MEIGLE SCULPTURED STONES (HS), Meigle, Perthshire PH12 8SB T 01828-640612
Twenty-six carved Pictish stones dating from the late 8th to the late 10th centuries

MELROSE ABBEY (HS), Melrose, Roxburghshire TD6 9LG T 01896-822562
Ruin of Cistercian abbey founded *c.*1136 by David I; museum of medieval objects

MOUSA BROCH (HS), Island of Mousa, Shetland T 01856-841815
Finest surviving Iron Age broch tower

NEW ABBEY CORN MILL (HS), Dumfriesshire DG2 8BX T 01387-850260
Working water-powered mill built in the late 18th century

*NEW LANARK, South Lanarkshire, ML11 9DB T 01555-661 345
18th-century village built around a cotton mill

PALACE OF HOLYROODHOUSE, Edinburgh EH8 8DX T 0131-556 5100 W www.royalcollection.org.uk
The Queen's official Scottish residence; home to Mary, Queen of Scots; main part of the palace built 1671–9 close to ruined 12th-century Augustinian abbey

*RING O' BRODGAR (HS), Stenness, Orkney T 01856-841815
Neolithic circle of upright stones surrounded by circular ditch

ROSSLYN CHAPEL, Roslin, Midlothian EH25 9PU
T 0131-440 2159 W www.rosslynchapel.org.uk
Historic church built between 1446 and 1484 with unique stone carvings

ST ANDREWS CASTLE AND CATHEDRAL (HS), Fife KY16 9AR (castle); 9QL (cathedral) T 01334-477196 (castle); 01334-472563 (cathedral)
Ruins of 13th-century castle, the former residence of bishops of St Andrews, and remains of the largest cathedral in Scotland; museum

SCONE PALACE, Perth, Perthshire PH2 6BD
T 01738-552300
Georgian-Gothic house built 1802–12

*SKARA BRAE (HS), nr Stromness, Orkney KW16 3LR
T 01856-841815
Neolithic village with adjacent replica house

SMAILHOLM TOWER (HS), nr Kelso, Roxburghshire TD5 7PG
T 01573-460365
Well-preserved 15th-century tower-house

STIRLING CASTLE (HS), Stirlingshire FK8 1EJ
T 01786-450000 W www.stirlingcastle.gov.uk
Great Hall and gatehouse built for James IV *c.*1500; palace built for James V in 1538; site of coronations including Mary, Queen of Scots

*STONES OF STENNESS, Stenness, Orkney
T 01856 841815
Four surviving Neolithic standing stones and the uprights of a three-stone dolmen

TANTALLON CASTLE (HS), North Berwick, East Lothian EH39 5PN T 01620-892727
Ruined 14th-century curtain wall with towers

THREAVE CASTLE (HS), Castle Douglas, Kirkcudbrightshire DG7 1TJ T 07711-223101
Ruined late 14th-century tower on an island; accessible only by boat

URQUHART CASTLE (HS), Drumnadrochit, Inverness-shire IV63 6XJ T 01456-450551
13th-century castle remains on the banks of Loch Ness

NORTHERN IRELAND

For the Northern Ireland Environment Agency, the official website is W www.doeni.gov.uk/niea

For more information on National Trust properties in Northern Ireland, including those listed below, the official website is W www.nationaltrust.org.uk

KEY
(NIEA) Property in the care of the Northern Ireland Environment Agency
(NT) National Trust property

CARRICKFERGUS CASTLE (NIEA), Carrickfergus, Co. Antrim BT38 7BG T 028-9335 1273
Castle built in 1177 and taken by King John in 1210; garrisoned until 1928

CASTLE COOLE (NT), Enniskillen, Co. Fermanagh BT74 6JY
T 028-6632 2690
18th-century neoclassical mansion in parkland; designed by James Wyatt

CASTLE WARD (NT), Strangford, Co. Down BT30 7LS
T 028-4488 1204
18th-century house with Classical and Gothic facades

DEVENISH MONASTIC SITE (NIEA), nr Enniskillen, Co. Fermanagh T 028-6862 1588
Island monastery founded in the sixth century by St Molaise; church dating from 13th century

DOWNHILL DEMESNE AND HEZLETT HOUSE (NT), Castlerock, Co. Londonderry BT51 4RP T 028-7084 8728
Ruins of 18th-century mansion and a 17th century cottage in landscaped estate including Mussenden Temple

DUNLUCE CASTLE (NIEA), Bushmills, Co. Antrim BT57 8UY
T 028-2073 1938
Ruins of medieval stronghold of the McDonnells

FLORENCE COURT (NT), Enniskillen, Co. Fermanagh BT92 1DB T 028-6634 8249
Mid-18th-century house with Rococo decoration

GREY ABBEY (NIEA), Greyabbey, Co. Down BT22 2NQ
T 028-9181 1491
Substantial remains of a Cistercian abbey founded in 1193 set in landscaped parkland

MOUNT STEWART (NT), Newtownards, Co. Down BT22 2AD
T 028-4278 8387
18th-century house; octagonal Temple of the Winds

NENDRUM MONASTIC SITE (NIEA), Mahee Island, Co. Down T 028-9054 3037
Island monastery founded in the fifth century by St Machaoi

PATTERSON'S SPADE MILL (NT), Templepatrick, Co. Antrim BT39 0AP T 028-9443 3619
Last working water-driven spade mill in the UK

TULLY CASTLE (NIEA), Co. Fermanagh T 028-6862 1588
Fortified house and bawn built *c.*1619

MUSEUMS AND GALLERIES

There are approximately 2,500 museums and galleries in the UK. As at February 2013, 1,759 of these were fully accredited by Arts Council England. Accreditation indicates that the museum or gallery has an appropriate constitution, is soundly financed, has adequate collection management standards and public services and has access to professional curatorial advice. A further 60 museums and galleries have applied for, or are in the process of obtaining accreditation, and these applications are assessed by either Arts Council England; Museums, Archives and Libraries Wales (CyMAL); Museums Galleries Scotland or the Northern Ireland Museums Council.

The following is a selection of museums and art galleries in the UK. Opening hours and admission charges vary. Further information about museums and galleries in the UK is available from the Museums Association (W www.museumsassociation.org T 020-7566 7800).

W www.culture24.org includes a database of all the museums and galleries in the UK.

ENGLAND

* England's national museums and galleries, which receive funding from a government department, such as the DCMS or MoD. These institutions are deemed to have collections of national importance, and the government is able to call upon their staff for expert advice

ALTON

Jane Austen's House Museum, Chawton, Hants GU34 1SD T 01420-83262 W www.jane-austens-house-museum.org.uk
17th-century house which tells the author's story

BARNARD CASTLE

The Bowes Museum, Co. Durham DL12 8NP T 01833-690606 W www.bowesmuseum.org.uk
European art from the late medieval period to the 20th century; music and costume galleries; English period rooms from Elizabeth I to Victoria; local archaeology

BATH

American Museum, Claverton Manor BA2 7BD T 01225-460503 W www.americanmuseum.org
American decorative arts from the 17th to 20th centuries; American heritage exhibition

Fashion Museum, Bennett Street BA1 2QH T 01225-477789 W www.museumofcostume.co.uk
Fashion from the 17th century to the present day

Victoria Art Gallery, Bridge Street BA2 4AT T 01225-477233 W www.victoriagal.org.uk
European Old Masters and British art since the 15th century

BEAMISH

Beamish Museum, Co. Durham DH9 0RG T 0191-370 4000 W www.beamish.org.uk
Living working museum of a northern town during Georgian, Victorian and Edwardian times

BEAULIEU

National Motor Museum, Hants SO42 7ZN T 01590-612345 W www.beaulieu.co.uk
Displays of over 250 vehicles dating from 1880 to the present day

BIRMINGHAM

Aston Hall, Trinity Road B6 6JD T 0121-675 4722 W www.bmag.org.uk/aston-hall
Jacobean House containing paintings, furniture and tapestries from the 17th to 19th centuries

Barber Institute of Fine Arts, University of Birmingham, Edgbaston B15 2TS T 0121-414 7333 W www.barber.org.uk
Extensive coin collection; fine arts, including Old Masters

Birmingham Museum and Art Gallery, Chamberlain Square B3 3DH T 0121-303 1966 W www.bmag.org.uk
Includes notable collection of Pre-Raphaelite art

Museum of the Jewellery Quarter, Vyse Street, Hockley B18 6HA T 0121-554 3598 W www.bmag.org.uk/museum-of-the-jewellery-quarter
Preserved jewellery workshop

Thinktank, Curzon Street B4 7XG T 0121-202 2222 W www.thinktank.ac
Science museum featuring over 200 hands-on displays and a Planetarium

BOURNEMOUTH

Russell-Cotes Art Gallery and Museum, East Cliff Promenade BH1 3AA T 01202-451858 W www.russell-cotes.bournemouth.gov.uk
Seaside villa housing 19th- and 20th-century art and sculptures from around the world

BOVINGTON

Tank Museum, Dorset BH20 6JG T 01929-405096 W www.tankmuseum.org
Collection of 200 tanks from the earliest days of tank warfare to the present

BRADFORD

Bradford Industrial Museum, Moorside Mills, Moorside Road, Eccleshill BD2 3HP T 01274-435900 W www.bradfordmuseums.org
Engineering, textiles, transport and social history exhibits

Cartwright Hall Art Gallery, Lister Park BD9 4NS T 01274-431212 W www.bradfordmuseums.org
British 19th- and 20th-century fine art

**National Media Museum,* BD1 1NQ T 0844-856 3797 W www.nationalmediamuseum.org.uk
Photography, film and television interactive exhibits; features an IMAX cinema and the only permanent Cinerama screen in Europe

BRIGHTON

Booth Museum of Natural History, Dyke Road BN1 5AA T 03000-290900 W www.brighton-hove-rpml.org.uk/museums/boothmuseum
Zoology, botany and geology collections; British birds in recreated habitats

Brighton Museum and Art Gallery, Royal Pavilion Gardens BN1 1EE T 03000-290900 W www.brighton-hove-rpml.org.uk/museums/brightonmuseum
Includes fine art and design, fashion, world art; Brighton history

BRISTOL

Arnolfini, Narrow Quay BS1 4QA T 0117-917 2300 W www.arnolfini.org.uk
Contemporary visual arts, dance, performance, music, talks and workshops

Blaise Castle House Museum, Henbury Road BS10 7QS T 0117-903 9818 W www.bristol.gov.uk/node/2869
18th-century mansion; social history collections

Bristol Museum and Art Gallery, Queen's Road BS8 1RL T 0117-922 3571 W www.bristol.gov.uk/node/2904
Includes fine and decorative art, oriental art, ceramics and world culture; Bristol history

M Shed, Prince's Wharf BS1 4RN T 0117-352 6600 W www.mshed.org
The story of Bristol's heritage of engineering, transport, music and industry

CAMBRIDGE

Fitzwilliam Museum, Trumpington Street CB2 1RB T 01223-332900 W www.fitzmuseum.cam.ac.uk
Antiquities, fine and applied arts, clocks, ceramics, manuscripts, furniture, sculpture, coins and medals

**Imperial War Museum Duxford*, Duxford CB22 4QR T 01223-835000 W duxford.iwm.org.uk
Displays of military and civil aircraft, tanks and naval exhibits

Museum of Archaeology and Anthropology, Downing Street CB2 3DZ T 01223-333516 W www.maa.cam.ac.uk
Extensive global archaeological and anthropological collections

Sedgwick Museum of Earth Sciences, Downing Street CB2 3EQ T 01223-333456 W www.sedgwickmuseum.org
Extensive geological collection

University Museum of Zoology, Downing Street CB2 3EJ T 01223-336650 W www.museum.zoo.cam.ac.uk
Extensive zoological collection

Whipple Museum of the History of Science, Free School Lane CB2 3RH T 01223-330906 W www.hps.cam.ac.uk/whipple
Scientific instruments from the 14th century to the present

CARLISLE

Tullie House Museum and Art Gallery, Castle Street CA3 8TP T 01228-618718 W www.tulliehouse.co.uk
Prehistoric archaeology, Hadrian's Wall, Viking and medieval Cumbria, and the social history of Carlisle

CHATHAM

The Historic Dockyard, ME4 4TE T 01634-823800 W www.thedockyard.co.uk
Maritime attractions including HMS *Cavalier*, the UK's last Second World War destroyer

Royal Engineers Museum, Prince Arthur Road, Gillingham ME4 4UG T 01634-822839 W www.re-museum.co.uk
Regimental history, ethnography, decorative art and photography

CHELTENHAM

Art Gallery and Museum, Clarence Street GL50 3JT T 01242-237431 W www.cheltenhammuseum.org.uk
Re-opened in October 2013 after a £6m rennovation; paintings, arts and crafts

CHESTER

Grosvenor Museum, Grosvenor Street CH1 2DD T 01244-402033 W www.grosvenormuseum.co.uk
Roman collections, natural history, art, Chester silver, local history and costume

CHICHESTER

Weald and Downland Open Air Museum, Singleton PO18 0EU T 01243-811363 W www.wealddown.co.uk
Rebuilt vernacular buildings from south-east England; includes medieval houses, agricultural and rural craft buildings and a working watermill

COLCHESTER

Colchester Castle Museum, Castle Park CO1 1TJ T 01206-282939 W www.cimuseums.org.uk/castle
Due to re-open in spring 2014 following redevelopment; largest Norman keep in Europe standing on foundations of the Roman Temple of Claudius

COVENTRY

Coventry Transport Museum, Hales Street CV1 1JD T 024-7623 4270 W www.transport-museum.com
Extensive collection of motor vehicles and bicycles; land speed record-holding car

Herbert Art Gallery and Museum, Jordan Well CV1 5QP T 024-7683 2386 W www.theherbert.org
Local history, archaeology, industry and visual arts

DERBY

Derby Museum and Art Gallery, The Strand DE1 1BS T 01332-641901 W www.derbymuseums.org/museum-and-art-gallery-2
Includes paintings by Joseph Wright of Derby and Derby porcelain

Pickford's House Museum, Friar Gate DE1 1DA T 01332-715181 W www.derbymuseums.org/pickfords-house
Georgian town house designed by architect Joseph Pickford; museum of Georgian life and costume

DEVIZES

Wiltshire Heritage Museum, Long Street SN10 1NS T 01380-727369 W www.wiltshireheritage.org.uk
Natural and local history; art gallery; archaeological finds from prehistoric, Roman and Saxon sites

DORCHESTER

Dorset County Museum, High West Street DT1 1XA T 01305-262735 W www.dorsetcountymuseum.org
Includes a collection of Thomas Hardy's manuscripts, books, notebooks and drawings; local history, geology and Roman mosaics

DOVER

Dover Museum, Market Square CT16 1PB T 01304-201066 W www.dovermuseum.co.uk
Contains the Dover Bronze Age Boat Gallery and archaeological finds from Bronze Age, Roman and Saxon sites

EXETER

Royal Albert Memorial Museum and Art Gallery, Queen Street EX4 3RX T 01392-265858 W www.rammuseum.org.uk
Natural history; archaeology; worldwide fine and decorative art including Exeter silver

GATESHEAD

Baltic Centre for Contemporary Art, South Shore Road NE8 3BA T 0191-478 1810 W www.balticmill.com
Contemporary art exhibitions and events

Shipley Art Gallery, Prince Consort Road NE8 4JB T 0191-477 1495 W www.twmuseums.org.uk/shipley
Contemporary crafts

GAYDON

Heritage Motor Centre, Banbury Road, Warks CV35 0BJ T 01926-641188 W www.heritage-motor-centre.co.uk
The world's largest collection of British cars with nearly 300 vehicles spanning the classic, vintage and veteran eras

GLOUCESTER

Gloucester Waterways Museum, Gloucester Docks GL1 2EH T 01452-318200 W www.gloucesterwaterwaysmuseum.org.uk
200-year history of Britain's canals and inland waterways

GOSPORT

Royal Navy Submarine Museum, Haslar Jetty Road, Hants PO12 2AS T 023-9251 0354 W www.submarine-museum.co.uk
Underwater warfare exhibition, including submarines HMS *Alliance* and HMS *Holland 1* – the Royal Navy's first submarine

GRASMERE

Dove Cottage and the *Wordsworth Museum*, Cumbria LA22 9SH T 015394-35544 W www.wordsworth.org.uk
William Wordsworth's manuscripts, home and garden

HOVE

Hove Museum and Art Gallery, New Church Road BN3 4AB T 03000-290900 W www.brighton-hove-rpml.org.uk/museums/hovemuseum
Toys, cinema, local history and fine art collections

HULL

Ferens Art Gallery, Queen Victoria Square HU1 3RA
T 01482-300300 W www.hullcc.gov.uk
European Old Masters, Victorian, Edwardian and contemporary British art

Hull Maritime Museum, Queen Victoria Square HU1 3DX
T 01482-300300 W www.hullcc.gov.uk
Hull's maritime heritage including whaling, fishing, navigation and merchant trade

HUNTINGDON

The Cromwell Museum, Grammar School Walk PE29 3LF
T 01480-375830 W www.cambridgeshire.gov.uk/cromwell
Portraits and memorabilia relating to Oliver Cromwell

IPSWICH

Christchurch Mansion and *Wolsey Art Gallery,* Christchurch Park IP4 2BE T 01473-433554 W www.cimuseums.org.uk
Tudor house with paintings by Gainsborough, Constable and other Suffolk artists; furniture and 18th-century ceramics; temporary exhibitions

KEIGHLEY

The Brontë Parsonage Museum, Haworth, W. Yorks BD22 8DR
T 01535-642323 W www.bronte.org.uk
The former home of the literary Brontë sisters

KESWICK

Pencil Museum, Southey Works CA12 5NG T 01768-773626
W www.pencilmuseum.co.uk
500-year history of the pencil; demonstration events and workshops throughout the year

LEEDS

Armley Mills, Leeds Industrial Museum, Canal Road, Armley LS12 2QF T 0113-263 7861 W www.leeds.gov.uk/armleymills
Once the world's largest woollen mill, now a museum for textiles and Leeds' industrial heritage

Leeds Art Gallery, The Headrow LS1 3AA T 0113-247 8256
W www.leeds.gov.uk/artgallery
Includes English watercolours, sculpture, contemporary art and prints from the region's artists

**Royal Armouries Museum,* Armouries Drive LS10 1LT
T 0113-220 1999 W www.royalarmouries.org
National collection of over 8,500 items of arms and armour from BC to present over five galleries: War, Tournament, Oriental, Self Defence and Hunting

LEICESTER

Jewry Wall Museum, St Nicholas Circle LE1 4LB T 0116-225 4971
W www.leicester.gov.uk
Archaeology; Roman Jewry Wall and baths; mosaics

New Walk Museum and Art Gallery, 53 New Walk LE1 7EA
T 0116-255 4900 W www.leicester.gov.uk
Natural and cultural history; ancient Egypt gallery; European art and decorative arts

LINCOLN

The Collection, Danes Terrace LN2 1LP T 01522-782040
W www.thecollectionmuseum.com
Artefacts from the Stone Age to the Roman, Viking and Medieval eras; adjacent art gallery; collections of contemporary art and craft, sculpture, porcelain, clocks and watches

Museum of Lincolnshire Life, Burton Road LN1 3LY
T 01522-782040
W www.lincolnshire.gov.uk/museumoflincolnshirelife
Social history; agricultural, industrial and commercial exhibits

LIVERPOOL

**International Slavery Museum,* Albert Dock L3 4AX
T 0151-478 4499 W www.liverpoolmuseums.org.uk/ism
Explores historical and contemporary aspects of slavery

**Lady Lever Art Gallery,* Wirral CH62 5EQ T 0151-478 4136
W www.liverpoolmuseums.org.uk/ladylever
Paintings, furniture and porcelain

**Merseyside Maritime Museum,* Albert Dock L3 4AQ
T 0151-478 4499 W www.liverpoolmuseums.org.uk/maritime
Floating exhibits, working displays and craft demonstrations; incorporates the *UK Border Agency National Museum*

**Museum of Liverpool,* Pier Head L3 1DG
T 0151-478 4545 W www.liverpoolmuseums.org.uk/mol
Formerly the *Museum of Liverpool Life;* explores the significance of the city's geography, history and culture

* *Sudley House,* Mossley Hill Road L18 8BX T 0151-478 4016
W www.liverpoolmuseums.org.uk/sudley
Late 18th- and 19th-century paintings in former shipowner's home

**Tate Liverpool,* Albert Dock L3 4BB T 0151-702 7400
W www.tate.org.uk/liverpool
20th-century paintings and sculpture

**Walker Art Gallery,* William Brown Street L3 8EL
T 0151-478 4199 W www.liverpoolmuseums.org.uk/walker
Paintings from the 14th century to the present day

**World Museum Liverpool,* William Brown Street L3 8EN
T 0151-478 4393 W www.liverpoolmuseums.org.uk/wml
Includes Egyptian mummies, weapons and classical sculpture; planetarium, aquarium, vivarium and natural history centre

LONDON: GALLERIES

Barbican Art Gallery, Barbican Centre, Silk Street EC2Y 8DS
T 020-7638 4141 W www.barbican.org.uk
Art, music, theatre, dance and film exhibitions

Courtauld Institute of Art Gallery, Somerset House, Strand WC2R 0RN T 020-7848 2526 W www.courtauld.ac.uk
Impressionist and post-impressionist paintings

Dulwich Picture Gallery, Gallery Road SE21 7AD
T 020-8693 5254 W www.dulwichpicturegallery.org.uk
England's first public art gallery; designed by Sir John Soane to house 17th- and 18th-century paintings

Estorick Collection of Modern Italian Art, Canonbury Square N1 2AN T 020-7704 9522 W www.estorickcollection.com
Early 20th-century Italian drawings, paintings, sculptures and etchings, with an emphasis on Futurism

Hayward Gallery, Belvedere Road SE1 8XX T 020-7960 4200
W www.southbankcentre.co.uk
Temporary exhibitions

**National Gallery,* Trafalgar Square WC2N 5DN
T 020-7747 2885 W www.nationalgallery.org.uk
Western painting from the 13th to 19th centuries; early Renaissance collection in the Sainsbury Wing

**National Portrait Gallery,* St Martin's Place WC2H 0HE
T 020-7306 0055 W www.npg.org.uk
Portraits of eminent people in British history

Photographers' Gallery, Ramillies Street W1F 7LW
T 020-7087 9300 W www.thephotographersgallery.org.uk
Temporary exhibitions

The Queen's Gallery, Buckingham Palace SW1A 1AA
T 020-7766 7300 W www.royalcollection.org.uk
Art from the Royal Collection

Royal Academy of Arts, Burlington House, Piccadilly W1J 0BD
T 020-7300 8000 W www.royalacademy.org.uk
British art since 1750 and temporary exhibitions; annual Summer Exhibition

Saatchi Gallery, Duke of York's HQ, King's Road SW3 4RY
T 020-7823 2363 W www.saatchi-gallery.co.uk
Contemporary art including paintings, photographs, sculpture and installations

Serpentine Gallery, Kensington Gardens W2 3XA
T 020-7402 6075 W www.serpentinegallery.org
Temporary exhibitions of British and international contemporary art

**Tate Britain,* Millbank SW1P 4RG T 020-7887 8888
W www.tate.org.uk/britain

British art from the 16th century to the present; international modern art

**Tate Modern,* Bankside SE1 9TG T 020-7887 8888 W www.tate.org.uk/modern
International modern art from 1900 to the present

**Wallace Collection,* Manchester Square W1U 3BN T 020-7563 9500 W www.wallacecollection.org
Old Masters; French 18th-century paintings, furniture, armour, porcelain, clocks and sculpture

Whitechapel Art Gallery, Whitechapel High Street E1 7QX T 020-7522 7888 W www.whitechapelgallery.org
Temporary exhibitions of modern art

LONDON: MUSEUMS

Bank of England Museum, Threadneedle Street EC2R 8AH (entrance on Bartholomew Lane) T 020-7601 5545 W www.bankofengland.co.uk/museum
History of the Bank of England since 1694

**British Museum,* Great Russell Street WC1B 3DG T 020-7323 8299 W www.britishmuseum.org
Collection of art and antiquities spanning 2 million years of human history; temporary exhibitions; houses the Elgin Marbles from the Parthenon

Brunel Museum, Rotherhithe SE16 4LF T 020-7231 3840 W www.brunel-museum.org.uk
Explores the engineering achievements of Isambard Kingdom Brunel and his father, Marc Brunel

Cartoon Museum, Little Russell Street WC1A 2HH T 020-7580 8155 W www.cartoonmuseum.org
British cartoons, caricature and comic art from the 18th century to the present

Charles Dickens Museum, Doughty Street WC1N 2LX T 020-7405 2127 W www.dickensmuseum.com
Dickens's home from 1837–9; manuscripts, personal items and paintings

**Churchill War Rooms,* King Charles Street SW1A 2AQ T 020-7930 6961 W cwr.iwm.org.uk
Underground rooms used by Churchill and the government during the Second World War

Cutty Sark, King William Walk SE10 9HT T 020-8858 4422 W www.cuttysark.org.uk
The world's last remaining tea clipper; re-opened in April 2012 following extensive restoration

Design Museum, Shad Thames SE1 2YD T 020-7403 6933 W www.designmuseum.org
The development of design and the mass-production of consumer objects

Firepower, the Royal Artillery Museum, Royal Arsenal, Woolwich SE18 6ST T 020-8855 7755 W www.firepower.org.uk
The history and development of artillery over the last 700 years including the collections of the Royal Regiment of Artillery

Garden Museum, Lambeth Palace Road SE1 7LB T 020-7401 8865 W www.gardenmuseum.org.uk
History and development of gardens and gardening; temporary exhibitions, symposia and events

Geffrye Museum, Kingsland Road E2 8EA T 020-7739 9893 W www.geffrye-museum.org.uk
English urban domestic interiors from 1600 to the present day; also paintings, furniture, decorative arts, walled herb garden and period garden rooms

**HMS Belfast,* The Queen's Walk SE1 2JH T 020-7940 6300 W hmsbelfast.iwm.org.uk
Life and work on board a Second World War cruiser

**Horniman Museum,* London Road SE23 3PQ T 020-8699 1872 W www.horniman.ac.uk
Museum of anthropology, musical instruments and natural history; aquarium; reference library; gardens

**Imperial War Museum,* Lambeth Road SE1 6HZ T 020-7416 5320 W www.iwm.org.uk
All aspects of the two World Wars and other military operations involving Britain and the Commonwealth since 1914; partially closed for redevelopment until summer 2014

Jewish Museum, Albert Street NW1 7NB T 020-7284 7384 W www.jewishmuseum.org.uk
Jewish life, history, art and religion

London Metropolitan Archives, Northampton Road EC1R 0HB T 020-7332 3820 W www.cityoflondon.gov.uk/lma
Material on the history of London and its people dating from 1067 to the present day

London Transport Museum, Covent Garden Piazza WC2E 7BB T 020-7379 6344 W www.ltmuseum.co.uk
Vehicles, photographs and graphic art relating to the history of transport in London

MCC Museum, Lord's Cricket Ground, St John's Wood NW8 8QN T 020-7616 8595 W www.lords.org/mcc
Cricket exhibits including the Ashes, kits and paintings; guided tours by appointment

**Museum of Childhood (V&A),* Cambridge Heath Road E2 9PA T 020-8983 5200 W www.museumofchildhood.org.uk
Toys, games and exhibits relating to the social history of childhood from the 17th century to the present

**Museum of London,* London Wall EC2Y 5HN T 020-7001 9844 W www.museumoflondon.org.uk
History of London from prehistoric times to the present day; Galleries of Modern London

Museum of London Docklands, West India Quay, Canary Wharf E14 4AL T 020-7001 9844 W www.museumoflondon.org.uk/docklands
Explores the story of London's river, port and people over 2,000 years; includes the London Sugar Slavery Gallery

National Archives Museum, Kew TW9 4DU T 020-8876 3444 W www.nationalarchives.gov.uk/museum
Displays treasures from the archives, including the Domesday Book and Magna Carta

**National Army Museum,* Royal Hospital Road SW3 4HT T 020-7730 0717 W www.nam.ac.uk
Five-hundred-year history of the British soldier; exhibits include model of the Battle of Waterloo and recreated First World War trench

**National Maritime Museum,* Romney Road SE10 9NF T 020-8858 4422 W www.rmg.co.uk/national-maritime-museum
Maritime history of Britain; collections include globes, clocks, telescopes and paintings; comprises the main building, the Royal Observatory and the Queen's House

**Natural History Museum,* Cromwell Road SW7 5BD T 020-7942 5000 W www.nhm.ac.uk
Natural history collections and interactive Darwin Centre

Petrie Museum of Egyptian Archaeology, University College London, Malet Place WC1E 6BT T 020-7679 2884 W www.ucl.ac.uk/museums/petrie
Egyptian and Sudanese archaeology featuring around 80,000 objects

**Royal Air Force Museum,* Hendon NW9 5LL T 020-8205 2266 W www.rafmuseum.org.uk
Aviation from before the Wright brothers to the present

Royal Mews, Buckingham Palace SW1W 1QH T 020-7766 7302 W www.royalcollection.org.uk/visit/royalmews
State vehicles, including the Queen's gold state coach; home to the Queen's horses

**Science Museum,* Exhibition Road SW7 2DD T 0870 870 4868 W www.sciencemuseum.org.uk
Science, technology, industry and medicine exhibitions; children's interactive gallery; IMAX cinema

Shakespeare's Globe Exhibition, New Globe Walk, Bankside SE1 9DT T 020-7902 1400 W www.shakespearesglobe.com
Recreation of Elizabethan theatre using 16th-century techniques; includes a tour of the theatre

**Sir John Soane's Museum,* Lincoln's Inn Fields WC2A 3BP T 020-7405 2107 W www.soane.org
Art and antiquities collected by Soane throughout his lifetime; house designed by Soane

Tower Bridge Exhibition, SE1 2UP T 020-7403 3761 W www.towerbridge.org.uk
History of the bridge and display of Victorian steam machinery; panoramic views from walkways

**Victoria and Albert Museum,* Cromwell Road SW7 2RL T 020-7942 2000 W www.vam.ac.uk
Includes the National Art Library and the Gilbert Collection; fine and applied art and design; furniture, glass, textiles, theatre and dress collections; temporary exhibitions

Wellcome Collection, Euston Road NW1 2BE T 020-7611 2222 W www.wellcomecollection.org
Contemporary and historic exhibitions and collections including the Wellcome Library

Wimbledon Lawn Tennis Museum, Church Road SW19 5AE T 020-8944 1066 W www.wimbledon.com/museum
Tennis trophies, fashion and memorabilia; view of Centre Court

MALTON

Eden Camp, N. Yorks YO17 6RT T 01653-697777 W www.edencamp.co.uk
Restored POW camp and Second World War memorabilia

MANCHESTER

Gallery of Costume, Platt Hall, Rusholme M14 5LL T 0161-245 7245 W www.manchestergalleries.org
Exhibits from the 17th century to the present day

**Imperial War Museum North,* Trafford Wharf Road M17 1TZ T 0161-836 4000 W www.iwm.org.uk/north
History of war from the 20th century to the present

Manchester Art Gallery, Mosley Street M2 3JL T 0161-235 8888 W www.manchestergalleries.org
European fine and decorative art from the 17th to 20th centuries

Manchester Museum, Oxford Road M13 9PL T 0161-275 2648 W www.museum.manchester.ac.uk
Collections include decorative arts, natural history and zoology; three Ancient Worlds galleries

**Museum of Science and Industry,* Liverpool Road, Castlefield M3 4FP T 0161-832 2244 W www.mosi.org.uk
On site of world's oldest passenger railway station; galleries relating to space, energy, power, transport, aviation, textiles and social history

National Football Museum, Cathedral Gardens M4 3BG T 0161-605 8200 W www.nationalfootballmuseum.com
Home to the FIFA, FA and Football League collections including the 1966 World Cup final ball

People's History Museum, Left Bank, Spinningfields M3 3ER T 0161-838 9190 W www.phm.org.uk
History of British political and working life

Whitworth Art Gallery, Oxford Road M15 6ER T 0161-275 7450 W www.whitworth.manchester.ac.uk
Fine and modern art, wallpapers, prints, textiles and sculptures

MILTON KEYNES

Bletchley Park National Codes Centre, Bucks MK3 6EB T 01908-640404 W www.bletchleypark.org
Home of British codebreaking during the Second World War; Enigma machine; computer museum; wartime toys and memorabilia

MONKWEARMOUTH

Monkwearmouth Station Museum, North Bridge Street, Sunderland SR5 1AP T 0191-567 7075 W www.twmuseums.org.uk/monkwearmouth
Victorian train station; interactive galleries

NEWCASTLE UPON TYNE

Discovery Museum, Blandford Square NE1 4JA T 0191-232 6789 W www.twmuseums.org.uk/discovery
Science and industry, local history, fashion; Tyneside's maritime history; *Turbinia* (first steam-driven vessel) exhibition; digital jukebox of 2,000 film and TV titles from the BFI National Archive

Great North Museum: Hancock, Barras Bridge NE2 4PT T 0191-222 6765 W www.twmuseums.org.uk/greatnorthmuseum
Natural and ancient history; planetarium; Living Planet display incorporates live animal tanks and aquaria

Laing Art Gallery, New Bridge Street NE1 8AG T 0191-232 7734 W www.twmuseums.org.uk/laing
Historic, modern and contemporary art; gallery talks and artists' events

NEWMARKET

National Horseracing Museum, High Street CB8 8JH T 01638-667333 W www.nhrm.co.uk
The story of people and horses involved in racing; temporary exhibitions

NORTH SHIELDS

Stephenson Railway Museum, Middle Engine Lane NE29 8DX T 0191-200 7146 W www.twmuseums.org.uk/stephenson
Locomotive engines and rolling stock

NOTTINGHAM

Museum of Nottingham Life, Brewhouse Yard, Castle Boulevard NG7 1FB T 0115-876 1400 W www.nottinghamcity.gov.uk
Social history from the 17th to 20th centuries

Natural History Museum, Wollaton Hall, Wollaton NG8 2AE T 0115-876 3100 W www.nottinghamcity.gov.uk
Geology, botany and zoology specimens housed in an Elizabethan mansion

Nottingham Castle and Art Gallery, Lenton Road NG1 6EL T 0115-876 1400 W www.mynottingham.gov.uk/nottinghamcastle
Paintings, ceramics, silver, glass and jewellery; history of Nottingham

OXFORD

Ashmolean Museum, Beaumont Street OX1 2PH T 01865-278002 W www.ashmolean.org
European and Oriental fine and applied arts, archaeology, Egyptology and numismatics

Modern Art Oxford, Pembroke Street OX1 1BP T 01865-722733 W www.modernartoxford.org.uk
Temporary exhibitions

Museum of the History of Science, Broad Street OX1 3AZ T 01865-277280 W www.mhs.ox.ac.uk
Displays include early scientific instruments, chemical apparatus, clocks and watches

Oxford University Museum of Natural History, Parks Road OX1 3PW T 01865-272950 W www.oum.ox.ac.uk
Entomology, geology, mineralogy and petrology, and zoology

Pitt Rivers Museum, South Parks Road OX1 3PP T 01865-270927 W www.prm.ox.ac.uk
Anthropological and archaeological artefacts

PLYMOUTH

City Museum and Art Gallery, Drake Circus PL4 8AJ T 01752-304774 W www.plymouthmuseum.gov.uk
Local and natural history; ceramics; silver; Old Masters; world artefacts; temporary exhibitions

PORTSMOUTH

Charles Dickens Birthplace, Old Commercial Road PO1 4QL T 023-9282 1879 W www.charlesdickensbirthplace.co.uk
Dickens memorabilia

D-Day Museum, Clarence Esplanade, Southsea PO5 3NT T 023-9282 7261 W www.ddaymuseum.co.uk
Includes the Overlord embroidery

Portsmouth Historic Dockyard, HM Naval Base PO1 3LJ T 023-9283 9766 W www.historicdockyard.co.uk
Incorporates the **National Museum of the Royal Navy* (PO1 3NH T 023-9272 7574 W www.nmrn.org.uk), *HMS Victory* (PO1 3NH T 023-9283 9766 W www.hms-victory.com), *HMS Warrior* (PO1 3QX T 023-9277 8600 W www.hmswarrior.org), *Mary Rose* – new museum opened in May 2013 (PO1 3LX T 023-9281 2931 W www.maryrose.org) and *Action Stations* (PO1 3LJ T 023-9289 3338 W www.actionstations.org)
History of the Royal Navy and of the dockyard; warships and technology spanning 500 years

PRESTON

Harris Museum and Art Gallery, Market Square PR1 2PP T 01772-258248 W www.harrismuseum.org.uk
British art since the 18th century; ceramics, glass, costume and local history; contemporary exhibitions

ST ALBANS

Verulamium Museum, St Michael's Street AL3 4SW T 01727-751814 W www.stalbansmuseums.org.uk
Remains of Iron Age settlement and the third-largest city in Roman Britain; exhibits include Roman wall plasters, jewellery, mosaics and room reconstructions

ST IVES

**Tate St Ives,* Porthmeor Beach, Cornwall TR26 1TG T 01736-796226 W www.tate.org.uk/stives
Modern art, much by artists associated with St Ives; includes the Barbara Hepworth Museum and Sculpture Garden

SALISBURY

Salisbury & South Wiltshire Museum, The Close SP1 2EN T 01722-332151 W www.salisburymuseum.org.uk
Local history and archaeology

SHEFFIELD

Graves Gallery, Surrey Street S1 1XZ T 0114-278 2600 W www.museums-sheffield.org.uk
Twentieth-century British art; European art spanning four centuries

Millennium Galleries, Arundel Gate S1 2PP T 0114-278 2600 W www.museums-sheffield.org.uk
Incorporates four different galleries: the Special Exhibition Gallery, the Craft and Design Gallery, the Metalwork Gallery and the Ruskin Gallery, which houses John Ruskin's collection of paintings, drawings, books and medieval manuscripts

Weston Park Museum, Western Bank S10 2TP T 0114-278 2600 W www.museums-sheffield.org.uk
World history for families

SOUTHAMPTON

City Art Gallery, Commercial Road SO14 7LP T 023-8083 3007 W www.southampton.gov.uk/art
Western art from the Renaissance to the present

SeaCity Museum, Havelock Road SO14 7FY T 023-8083 3007 W www.seacitymuseum.co.uk
Opened in 2012, the museum tells the story of the city's maritime past and present

SOUTH SHIELDS

Arbeia Roman Fort, Baring Street NE33 2BB T 0191-456 1369 W www.twmuseums.org.uk/arbeia
Excavated ruins; reconstructions of original buildings

South Shields Museum and Art Gallery, Ocean Road NE33 2JA T 0191-456 8740 W www.twmuseums.org.uk/southshields
South Tyneside history; interactive art gallery

STOKE-ON-TRENT

Etruria Industrial Museum, Lower Bedford Street ST4 7AF T 01782-233144 W www.stokemuseums.org.uk/eim
Britain's sole surviving steam-powered potter's mill

Gladstone Pottery Museum, Uttoxeter Road, Longton ST3 1PQ T 01782-237777 W www.stokemuseums.org.uk/gpm
The last complete Victorian pottery factory in Britain

Potteries Museum and Art Gallery, Bethesda Street ST1 3DW T 01782-232323 W www.stokemuseums.org.uk/pmag
Pottery, china and porcelain collections and a Mark XVI Spitfire

The Wedgwood Museum, Barlaston ST12 9ER T 01782-371900 W www.wedgwoodmuseum.org.uk
The story of Josiah Wedgwood and the company he founded

SUNDERLAND

Sunderland Museum and Winter Gardens, Burdon Road SR1 1PP T 0191-553 2323 W www.twmuseums.org.uk/sunderland
Fine and decorative art, local history and gardens

TELFORD

Ironbridge Gorge Museums, TF8 7DQ T 01952-433424 W www.ironbridge.org.uk
Ten museums including the world's first cast iron bridge; Blists Hill (late Victorian working town); Broseley Pipeworks; Coalbrookdale Museum of Iron; Coalport China Museum; Jackfield Tile Museum; Tar Tunnel

WAKEFIELD

Hepworth Wakefield, Gallery Walk WF1 5AW T 01924-247360 W www.hepworthwakefield.org
Historic and modern art; temporary exhibitions of contemporary art

National Coal Mining Museum for England, New Road, Overton WF4 4RH T 01924-848806 W www.ncm.org.uk
Includes underground tours of one of Britain's oldest working mines

Yorkshire Sculpture Park, West Bretton WF4 4LG T 01924-832631 W www.ysp.co.uk
Open-air sculpture gallery including works by Henry Moore, Barbara Hepworth and others in 500 acres of parkland

WEYBRIDGE

Brooklands Museum, Brooklands Road KT13 0QN T 01932-857381 W www.brooklandsmuseum.com
Birthplace of British motorsport; world's first purpose-built motor racing circuit

WILMSLOW

Quarry Bank Mill and Styal Estate, Wilmslow SK9 4LA T 01625-527468 W www.quarrybankmill.org.uk
Europe's most powerful working waterwheel owned by the National Trust illustrating history of cotton industry; costumed guides at restored Apprentice House

WINCHESTER

INTECH, Telegraph Way, Hants SO21 1HZ T 01962-863791 W www.intech-uk.com
Interactive science centre and planetarium

WORCESTER

City Art Gallery and Museum, Foregate Street WR1 1DT T 01905-25371 W www.whub.org.uk/cms/museums-worcestershire/mag.aspx
Includes the Regimental museum, 19th-century chemist shop and changing art exhibitions

Museum of Worcester Porcelain, Severn Street WR1 2ND T 01905-21247 W www.worcesterporcelainmuseum.org.uk
Worcester porcelain from 1751 to the present day

YEOVIL
Fleet Air Arm Museum, RNAS Yeovilton, Somerset BA22 8HT
T 01935-840565 W www.fleetairarm.com
History of naval aviation; historic aircraft, including Concorde 002
YORK
Beningbrough Hall, Beningbrough YO30 1DD T 01904-472027
W www.nationaltrust.org.uk/beningbrough-hall
18th-century house with portraits from the National Portrait Gallery
JORVIK Viking Centre, Coppergate YO1 9WT T 01904-615505
W www.jorvik-viking-centre.co.uk
Reconstruction of Viking York based on archaeological evidence
**National Railway Museum,* Leeman Road YO26 4XJ
T 0844-815 3139 W www.nrm.org.uk
Includes locomotives, rolling stock and carriages
York Castle Museum, Eye of York YO1 9RY T 01904-687687
W www.yorkcastlemuseum.org.uk
Includes Kirkgate, a reconstructed Victorian street; costume and military collections
Yorkshire Museum, Museum Gardens YO1 7FR T 01904-687687
W www.yorkshiremuseum.org.uk
Yorkshire life from Roman to medieval times; geology and biology; York observatory

WALES

* Members of National Museum Wales, a public body that receives its funding through grant-in-aid from the Welsh Assembly

ABERYSTWYTH
Ceredigion Museum, Terrace Road SY23 2AQ T 01970-633088
W www.ceredigion.gov.uk
Local history, housed in a restored Edwardian theatre
Silver Mountain Experience, Ponterwyd SY23 3AB
T 01970-890620 W www.silvermountainexperience.co.uk
Tours of an 18th-century silver mine, exhibitions containing artefacts used therein
BLAENAFON
**Big Pit National Coal Museum,* Torfaen NP4 9XP
T 029-2057 3650 W www.museumwales.ac.uk/en/bigpit
Colliery with underground tour
BODELWYDDAN
Bodelwyddan Castle, Denbighshire LL18 5YA T 01745-584060
W www.bodelwyddan-castle.co.uk
Portraits from the National Portrait Gallery; furniture from the Victoria and Albert Museum; sculpture from the Royal Academy
CAERLEON
**National Roman Legion Museum,* NP18 1AE T 029-2057 3550
W www.museumwales.ac.uk/en/roman
Material from the sites of the Roman fortresses of Isca, Usk and their environs; Roman garden
CARDIFF
**National Museum Cardiff,* Cathays Park CF10 3NP
T 029-2039 7951 W www.museumwales.ac.uk/en/cardiff
Includes natural sciences, archaeology and Impressionist paintings
**St Fagans: National History Museum,* St Fagans CF5 6XB
T 029-2057 3500 W www.museumwales.ac.uk/en/stfagans
Open-air museum with re-erected buildings, agricultural equipment and costume
TECHNIQUEST, Stuart Street CF10 5BW T 029-2047 5475
W www.techniquest.org
Interactive science exhibits, planetarium and science theatre
CRICCIETH
Lloyd George Museum, Llanystumdwy LL52 0SH T 01766-522071
W www.gwynedd.gov.uk
Childhood home of David Lloyd George
DRE-FACH FELINDRE
**National Wool Museum,* Llandysul SA44 5UP T 029-2057 3070
W www.museumwales.ac.uk/en/wool
Exhibitions, a working woollen mill and craft workshops
LLANBERIS
**National Slate Museum,* Gwynedd LL55 4TY T 029-2057 3700
W www.museumwales.ac.uk/en/slate
Former slate quarry with original machinery and plant; slate crafts demonstrations; working waterwheel
LLANDRINDOD WELLS
National Cycle Collection, Automobile Palace, Temple Street
LD1 5DL T 01597-825531 W www.cyclemuseum.org.uk
Approximately 250 bicycles on display, from 1819 to the present
PRESTEIGNE
Judge's Lodging Museum, Broad Street LD8 2AD T 01544-260650
W www.judgeslodging.org.uk
Restored apartments, courtroom, cells and servants' quarters
SWANSEA
**National Waterfront Museum,* Oystermouth Road SA1 3RD
T 029-2057 3600 W www.museumwales.ac.uk/en/swansea
Wales during the Industrial Revolution
Swansea Museum, Victoria Road SA1 1SN T 01792-653763
W www.swansea.gov.uk/swanseamuseum
Archaeology, social history and Swansea pottery
TENBY
Tenby Museum and Art Gallery, Castle Hill SA70 7BP
T 01834-842809 W www.tenbymuseum.org.uk
Local archaeology, history, geology and art

SCOTLAND

* Members of National Museums of Scotland or National Galleries of Scotland, which are non-departmental public bodies funded by, and accountable to, the Scottish government

ABERDEEN
Aberdeen Art Gallery, Schoolhill AB10 1FQ T 01224-523700
W www.aagm.co.uk
Paintings, sculptures and graphics; temporary exhibitions
Aberdeen Maritime Museum, Shiprow AB11 5BY
T 01224-337700 W www.aagm.co.uk
Maritime history, including shipbuilding and North Sea oil
AYR
Robert Burns Birthplace Museum, Murdoch's Lone, Alloway
KA7 4PQ T 0844-493 2601 W www.burnsmuseum.org.uk
Comprises Burns Cottage, birthplace of the poet, gardens and a museum
EDINBURGH
Britannia, Leith EH6 6JJ T 0131-555 5566
W www.royalyachtbritannia.co.uk
Former royal yacht with royal barge and royal family picture gallery
City Art Centre, Market Street EH1 1DE T 0131-529 3993
W www.edinburghmuseums.org.uk
Scottish paintings, watercolours, sculpture and installation art from the 17th century to the present
Museum of Childhood, High Street EH1 1TG T 0131-529 4142
W www.edinburghmuseums.org.uk
Toys, games, clothes and exhibits relating to the social history of childhood
Museum of Edinburgh, Canongate, Royal Mile EH8 8DD
T 0131-529 4143 W www.edinburghmuseums.org.uk
Local history, silver, glass and Scottish pottery
**Museum of Flight,* East Fortune Airfield, East Lothian EH39 5LF
T 0300-123 6789 W www.nms.ac.uk/flight
Aviation from the early 20th century to the present

**National Museum of Scotland*, Chambers Street EH1 1JF
T 0300-123 6789 W www.nms.ac.uk/scotland
Scottish history; world cultures; natural world; art and design

**National War Museum of Scotland*, Edinburgh Castle EH1 2NG
T 0300-123 6789 W www.nms.ac.uk/war
Scotland's military history

**Scottish National Gallery*, The Mound EH2 2EL
T 0131-624 6200 W www.nationalgalleries.org
Fine art from the early Renaissance to the end of the 19th century

**Scottish National Gallery of Modern Art*, Belford Road EH4 3DR T 0131-624 6200 W www.nationalgalleries.org
Contemporary art housed in two buildings: Modern One and Modern Two; temporary exhibitions

**Scottish National Portrait Gallery*, Queen Street EH2 1JD T 0131-624 6200
W www.nationalgalleries.org/portraitgallery
Portraits of eminent people in Scottish history; Photography Gallery; Victorian Library

The Writers' Museum, Lady Stair's Close EH1 2PA
T 0131-529 4901 W www.edinburghmuseums.org.uk
Exhibitions relating to Robert Burns, Sir Walter Scott and Robert Louis Stevenson

FORT WILLIAM

West Highland Museum, Cameron Square PH33 6AJ
T 01397-702169 W www.westhighlandmuseum.org.uk
Highland life and exhibits relating to 1745 uprising

GLASGOW

Burrell Collection, Pollokshaws Road G43 1AT T 0141-287 2550
W www.glasgowlife.org.uk/museums
Paintings by major artists; medieval art, Chinese and Islamic art

Gallery of Modern Art, Royal Exchange Square G1 3AH
T 0141-287 3050 W www.glasgowlife.org.uk/museums
Collection of contemporary Scottish and world art

Hunterian, University of Glasgow G12 8QQ T 0141-330 4221
W www.gla.ac.uk/hunterian
Rennie Mackintosh and Whistler collections; Old Masters; Scottish paintings; archaeology; medicine; zoology

Kelvingrove Art Gallery & Museum, Argyle Street G3 8AG
T 0141-276 9599 W www.glasgowlife.org.uk/museums
Includes Old Masters; natural history; arms and armour

Museum of Piping, McPhater Street G4 0HW T 0141-353 0220
W www.thepipingcentre.co.uk
The history and origins of bagpiping

**Museum of Rural Life*, Philipshill Road, East Kilbride G76 9HR
T 0300-123 6789 W www.nms.ac.uk/rural
History of rural life and work

People's Palace and Winter Gardens, Glasgow Green G40 1AT
T 0141-276 0788 W www.glasgowlife.org.uk/museums
Social history of Glasgow since 1750

Riverside Museum, 100 Pointhouse Place G3 8RS
T 0141-287 2720 W www.glasgowlife.org.uk/museums
Scotland's museum of transport and travel; the Tall Ship *Glenlee*, a Clyde-built sailing ship, is berthed alongside

St Mungo Museum of Religious Art and Life, Castle Street G4 0RH T 0141-276 1625
W www.glasgowlife.org.uk/museums
Explores universal themes through objects from major world religions

NORTHERN IRELAND

* Members of National Museums Northern Ireland, a non-departmental public body of the Northern Ireland Office

ARMAGH

**Armagh County Museum*, The Mall East BT61 9BE
T 028-3752 3070 W www.nmni.com/acm
Local history; archaeology; crafts

BANGOR

North Down Museum, Town Hall BT20 4BT T 028-9127 1200
W www.northdownmuseum.com
Presents the history of North Down, including its early-Christian monastery

BELFAST

Titanic Belfast, Queen's Road, Titanic Quarter BT3 9EP
T 028-9076 6386 W www.titanicbelfast.com
Opened in 2012; the story of RMS *Titanic* from her conception to demise

**W5*, Odyssey, Queen's Quay BT3 9QQ T 028-9046 7700
W www.w5online.co.uk
Interactive science and technology centre

HOLYWOOD

**Ulster Folk and Transport Museum*, Cultra BT18 0EU
T 028-9042 8428 W www.nmni.com/uftm
Open-air museum with original buildings from Ulster town and rural life *c.*1900; indoor galleries including Irish rail and road transport

LONDONDERRY

The Tower Museum, Union Hall Place BT48 6LU T 028-7137 2411
W www.derrycity.gov.uk/museums/tower-museum
Tells the story of Ireland through the history of Londonderry

Workhouse Museum, Glendermott Road BT48 6BG
T 028-7131 8328
W www.derrycity.gov.uk/museums/workhouse-museum
Exhibitions on the Second World War, workhouse life, 19th-century poverty and the Famine

NEWTOWNARDS

The Somme Heritage Centre, Bangor Road BT23 7PH
T 028-9182 3202 W www.irishsoldier.org
Commemorates the part played by Irish forces in the First World War

OMAGH

**Ulster American Folk Park*, Castletown, Co. Tyrone BT78 5QU
T 028-8224 3292 W www.nmni.com/uafp
Open-air museum telling the story of Ulster's emigrants to America; restored or recreated dwellings and workshops; ship and dockside gallery

**Ulster Museum*, Botanic Gardens BT9 5AB T 028-9044 0000
W www.nmni.com/um
Irish antiquities; natural and local history; fine and applied arts

SIGHTS OF LONDON

For historic buildings, museums and galleries in London, *see* the Historic Buildings and Monuments, and Museums and Galleries sections.

BRIDGES

The bridges over the Thames in London, from east to west, are:

Queen Elizabeth II Bridge (2,872m/9,423ft), engineer: Cleveland Bridge, opened 1991

Tower Bridge (268m/880ft by 18m/60ft), architect: Horace Jones, engineer: John Wolfe Barry, opened 1894

London Bridge (262m/860ft by 32m/105ft), original 13th-century stone bridge rebuilt and opened 1831 (engineer: John Rennie), reconstructed in Arizona when current London Bridge opened 1973 (architect: Lord Holford, engineer: Mott, Hay and Anderson)

Cannon Street Railway Bridge (261m/855ft), engineers: John Hawkshaw and John Wolfe Barry, originally named the Alexandra Bridge, opened 1866; renovated 1979–82

Southwark Bridge (244m/800ft by 17m/56ft), engineer: John Rennie, opened 1819; rebuilt 1912–21 (architect: Ernest George, engineer: Mott, Hay and Anderson)

Millennium Bridge (325m/1,066ft by 4m/13ft), architect: Foster and Partners, engineer: Ove Arup and Partners, opened 2000; reopened after modification 2002

Blackfriars Railway Bridge (284m/933ft), engineers: John Wolfe Barry and Henri Marc Brunel, opened 1886

London, Chatham and Dover Railway Bridge (234m/933ft), engineer: Joseph Cubitt, opened in 1864; only the columns remain, the rest of the structure was removed in 1985

Blackfriars Bridge (294m/963ft by 32m/105ft), engineer: Robert Mylne, opened 1769; rebuilt 1869 (engineer: Joseph Cubitt); widened 1909

Waterloo Bridge (366m/1,200ft by 24m/80ft), engineer: John Rennie, opened 1817; rebuilt 1945 (architect: Sir Giles Gilbert Scott, engineer: Rendel, Palmer and Triton)

Golden Jubilee Bridges (325m/1,066ft by 4.7m/15ft), architect: Lifschutz Davidson, engineer: WSP Group, opened 2002; commonly known as the Hungerford Footbridges

Hungerford Railway Bridge (366m/1,200ft), engineer: Isambard Kingdom Brunel, suspension bridge opened 1845; present railway bridge opened 1864 (engineer: John Hawkshaw); widened in 1886

Westminster Bridge (228m/748ft by 26m/85ft), engineer: Charles Labelye, opened 1750; rebuilt 1862 (architect: Charles Barry, engineer: Thomas Page)

Lambeth Bridge (237m/776ft by 18m/60ft), engineer: Peter W. Barlow, original suspension bridge opened 1862; current structure opened 1932 (architect: Reginald Blomfield, engineer: George W. Humphreys)

Vauxhall Bridge (231m/759ft by 24m/80ft), engineer: James Walker, opened 1816; redesigned and opened 1906 (architect: William Edward Riley, engineers: Alexander Binnie and Maurice Fitzmaurice)

Grosvenor Railway Bridge (213m/699ft), engineer: John Fowler, opened 1860; rebuilt 1965; also known as the Victoria Railway Bridge

Chelsea Bridge (213m/699ft by 25m/83ft), original suspension bridge opened 1858 (engineer: Thomas Page); rebuilt 1937 (architects: George Topham Forrest and E. P. Wheeler, engineer: Rendel, Palmer and Triton)

Albert Bridge (216m/710ft by 12m/40ft), engineer: Rowland M. Ordish, opened 1873; restructured 1884 (engineer: Joseph Bazalgette); strengthened 1971–3

Battersea Bridge (204m/670ft by 17m/56ft), engineer: Henry Holland, opened 1771; rebuilt 1890 (engineer: Joseph Bazalgette)

Battersea Railway Bridge (204m/670ft), engineer: William Baker, opened 1863; also known as Cremorne Bridge

Wandsworth Bridge (189m/619ft by 18m/60ft), engineer: Julian Tolmé, opened 1873; rebuilt 1940 (architect: E. P. Wheeler, engineer: T. Pierson Frank)

Putney Railway Bridge (229m/750ft), engineers: W. H. Thomas and William Jacomb, opened 1889; also known as the Fulham Railway Bridge or the Iron Bridge – it has no official name

Putney Bridge (213m/699ft by 23m/74ft), architect: Jacob Ackworth, original wooden bridge opened 1729; current granite structure completed in 1886 (engineer: Joseph Bazalgette)

Hammersmith Bridge (210m/688ft by 10m/33ft), engineer: William Tierney Clarke; the first suspension bridge in London, originally built 1827; rebuilt 1887 (engineer: Joseph Bazalgette)

Barnes Railway Bridge (also footbridge, 110m/360ft), engineer: Joseph Locke, opened 1849; rebuilt 1895 (engineers: London and South Western Railway); the original structure stands unused

Chiswick Bridge (137m/450ft by 21m/70ft), architect: Herbert Baker, engineer: Alfred Dryland, opened 1933

Kew Railway Bridge (175m/575ft), engineer: W. R. Galbraith, opened 1869

Kew Bridge (110m/360ft by 17m/56ft), engineer: Robert Tunstall, original timber bridge built 1759; replaced by a Portland stone structure in 1789 (engineer: James Paine); current granite bridge renamed King Edward VII Bridge in 1903, but still known as Kew Bridge (engineers: John Wolfe Barry and Cuthbert Brereton)

Richmond Lock (91m/300ft by 11m/36ft), engineer: F. G. M. Stoney, lock and footbridge opened 1894

Twickenham Bridge (85m/280ft by 21m/70ft), architect: Maxwell Ayrton, engineer: Alfred Dryland, opened 1933

Richmond Railway Bridge (91m/300ft), engineer: Joseph Locke, opened 1848; rebuilt 1906–8 (engineer: J. W. Jacomb-Hood)

Richmond Bridge (85m/280ft by 10m/33ft), architect: James Paine, engineer: Kenton Couse, built 1777; widened 1939

Teddington Lock (198m/650ft), engineer: G. Pooley, two footbridges opened 1889; marks the end of the tidal reach of the Thames

Kingston Railway Bridge, architects: J. E. Errington and W. R. Galbraith, engineer: Thomas Brassey, opened 1863

Kingston Bridge (116m/382ft), engineer: Edward Lapidge, built 1825–8; widened 1911–14 (engineers: Basil Mott and David Hay) and 1999–2001

Hampton Court Bridge, engineers: Samuel Stevens and Benjamin Ludgator, built 1753; replaced by iron bridge 1865; present bridge opened 1933 (architect: Edwin Lutyens, engineer: W. P. Robinson)

CEMETERIES

In 1832, in response to the overcrowding of burial grounds in London, the government authorised the establishment of seven non-denominational cemeteries that would encircle the city. These large cemeteries, known as the 'magnificent seven', were seen by many Victorian families as places in which to demonstrate their wealth and stature, and as a result there are some highly ornate graves and tombs.

THE MAGNIFICENT SEVEN

Abney Park, Stoke Newington, N16 (13ha/32 acres), established 1840; tomb of William and Catherine Booth, founders of the Salvation Army, and memorials to many nonconformists and dissenters

Brompton, Old Brompton Road, SW10 (16.5ha/40 acres), established 1840; graves of Sir Henry Cole, Emmeline Pankhurst, John Wisden. Managed by the Royal Parks, it is the only Crown cemetery

Highgate, Swains Lane, N6 (15ha/38 acres), established 1839; graves of Douglas Adams, George Eliot, Michael Faraday, Radclyffe Hall, Karl Marx and Christina Rossetti; western side only accessible as part of a guided tour

Kensal Green, Harrow Road, W10 (29ha/72 acres), established 1832; tombs of Isambard Kingdom Brunel, Wilkie Collins, George Cruikshank, Tom Hood, Leigh Hunt, Charles Kemble, Harold Pinter, William Makepeace Thackeray and Anthony Trollope

Nunhead, Linden Grove, SE15 (21ha/52 acres), established 1840; closed in 1969, subsequently restored and opened for burials

Tower Hamlets, Southern Grove, E3 (11ha/27 acres), established 1841; bombed heavily during the Second World War and closed to burials in 1966; now a nature reserve

West Norwood Cemetery and Crematorium, Norwood High Street, SE27 (17ha/42 acres), established 1837; tombs of Sir Mrs Beeton, Henry Bessemer, Sir Henry Tate and Joseph Whitaker *(Whitaker's Almanack)*

OTHER CEMETERIES

Bunhill Fields, City Road, EC1 (1.6ha/4 acres), 17th-century nonconformist burial ground containing the graves of William Blake, John Bunyan and Daniel Defoe

City of London Cemetery and Crematorium, Aldersbrook Road, E12 (81ha/200 acres), established 1856; grave of Bobby Moore

Golders Green Crematorium, Hoop Lane, NW11 (5ha/12 acres), established 1902; retains the ashes of Kingsley Amis, Lionel Bart, Enid Blyton, Marc Bolan, Sigmund Freud, Keith Moon, Peter Sellers, Bram Stoker and H. G. Wells

Hampstead, Fortune Green Road, NW6 (10.5ha/26 acres), established 1876; graves of Alan Coren, Kate Greenaway, Joseph Lister and Marie Lloyd

MARKETS

Billingsgate, Trafalgar Way, E14 (fish), a market site for over 1,000 years, with the Lower Thames Street site dating from 1876; moved to the Isle of Dogs in 1982; owned and run by the City of London Corporation

Borough, Southwark Street, SE1 (vegetables, fruit, meat, dairy, bread), established on present site in 1756; privately owned and run

Brick Lane, E1 (jewellery, vintage clothes, bric-a-brac, food), open Sunday

Brixton, SW9 (African-Caribbean food, music, clothing), open Monday to Saturday

Broadway, E8 (food, fashion, crafts), re-established in 2004, open Saturday

Camden Lock, NW1 (second-hand clothing, jewellery, alternative fashion, crafts), established in 1973

Columbia Road, E2 (flowers), dates from 19th century; became dedicated flower market in the 20th century

Covent Garden, WC2 (antiques, handicrafts, jewellery, clothing, food), originally a fruit and vegetable market (*see* New Covent Garden market); it has been trading in its current form since 1980

Grays, Davies Street, W1K (antiques), indoor market in listed building, established 1977

Greenwich, SE10 (crafts, fashion, food), market revived in the 1980s

Leadenhall, Gracechurch Street, EC3V (meat, poultry, cheese, clothing), site of market since 14th century; present hall built 1881; owned and run by the City of London Corporation

New Covent Garden, SW8 (wholesale vegetables, fruit, flowers), established in 1670 under a charter of Charles II; relocated from central London in 1974

New Spitalfields, E10 (vegetables, fruit), established 1682, modernised 1928, moved out of the City to Leyton in 1991

Old Spitalfields, E1 (arts, crafts, books, clothes, organic food, antiques), continues to trade on the original Spitalfields site on Commercial Street

Petticoat Lane, Middlesex Street, E1, a market has existed on the site for over 500 years, now a Sunday morning market selling almost anything

Portobello Road, W11, originally for herbs and horse-trading from 1870; became famous for antiques after the closure of the Caledonian Market in 1948

Smithfield, EC1 (meat, poultry), built 1866–8, refurbished 1993–4; the site of St Bartholomew's Fair from 12th to 19th century; owned and run by the City of London Corporation

MONUMENTS

CENOTAPH

Whitehall, SW1. The Cenotaph (from the Greek meaning 'empty tomb') was built to commemorate 'The Glorious Dead' and is a memorial to all ranks of the sea, land and air forces who gave their lives in the service of the Empire during the First World War. Designed by Sir Edwin Lutyens and constructed in plaster as a temporary memorial in 1919, it was replaced by a permanent structure of Portland stone and unveiled by George V on 11 November 1920, Armistice Day. An additional inscription was made in 1946 to commemorate those who gave their lives in the Second World War

FOURTH PLINTH

Trafalgar Square, WC2. The fourth plinth (1841) was designed for an equestrian statue that was never built due to lack of funds. From 1999 temporary works have been displayed on the plinth including *Ecce Homo* (Mark Wallinger), *Monument* (Rachel Whiteread), *Alison Lapper Pregnant* (Marc Quinn), *One & Other* (Antony Gormley) and *Nelson's Ship in a Bottle* (Yinka Shonibare). *Powerless Structures, Fig. 101* (Michael Elmgreen and Ingar Dragset) occupied the plinth from February 2012 to June 2013. This was followed in July 2013 by *Hahn/Cock* (Katharina Fritsch)

LONDON MONUMENT

(Commonly called the Monument), Monument Street, EC3. Built to designs by Sir Christopher Wren and Robert Hooke between 1671 and 1677, the Monument commemorates the Great Fire of London, which broke out in Pudding Lane on 2 September 1666. The fluted Doric column is 36.6m (120ft) high, the moulded cylinder above the balcony supporting a flaming vase of gilt bronze is an additional 12.8m (42ft), and the column is based on a square plinth 12.2m (40ft) high (with fine carvings on the west face), making a total height of 61.6m (202ft) – the tallest isolated stone column in the world, with views of London from a gallery at the top (311 steps)

OTHER MONUMENTS
(sculptor's name in parentheses):
7 July Memorial (Carmody Groarke), Hyde Park
Viscount Alanbrooke (Roberts-Jones), Whitehall
Albert Memorial (Scott), Kensington Gore
Battle of Britain (Day), Victoria Embankment
Beatty (Wheeler), Trafalgar Square
Belgian Gratitude (setting by Blomfield, statue by Rousseau), Victoria Embankment
Boadicea (or Boudicca), *Queen of the Iceni* (Thornycroft), Westminster Bridge
Brunel (Marochetti), Victoria Embankment
Burghers of Calais (Rodin), Victoria Tower Gardens, Westminster
Burns (Steell), Embankment Gardens
Canada Memorial (Granche), Green Park
Carlyle (Boehm), Chelsea Embankment
Cavalry (Jones), Hyde Park
Edith Cavell (Frampton), St Martin's Place
Charles I (Le Sueur), Trafalgar Square
Charles II (Gibbons), Royal Hospital, Chelsea
Churchill (Roberts-Jones), Parliament Square
Cleopatra's Needle (20.9m/68.5ft high, *c.*1500 BC, erected in London in 1878; the sphinxes are Victorian), Thames Embankment
Clive (Tweed), King Charles Street
Captain Cook (Brock), The Mall
Oliver Cromwell (Thornycroft), outside Westminster Hall
Cunningham (Belsky), Trafalgar Square
Gen. Charles de Gaulle (Conner), Carlton Gardens
Diana, Princess of Wales Memorial Fountain (Gustafson Porter), Hyde Park
Disraeli, Earl of Beaconsfield (Raggi), Parliament Square
Lord Dowding (Winter), Strand
Duke of Cambridge (Jones), Whitehall
Duke of York (37.8m/124ft column, with statue by Westmacott), Carlton House Terrace
Edward VII (Mackennal), Waterloo Place
Elizabeth I (Kerwin, 1586, oldest outdoor statue in London; from Ludgate), Fleet Street
Eros (Shaftesbury Memorial) (Gilbert), Piccadilly Circus
Marechal/Marshall Foch (Mallisard, copy of one in Cassel, France), Grosvenor Gardens
Charles James Fox (Westmacott), Bloomsbury Square
Yuri Gagarin (Novikov, copy of Russian statue), The Mall
George III (Cotes Wyatt), Cockspur Street
George IV (Chantrey), Trafalgar Square
George V (Reid Dick and Scott), Old Palace Yard
George VI (McMillan), Carlton Gardens
Gladstone (Thornycroft), Strand
Guards' (Crimea; Bell), Waterloo Place
Guards Division (Ledward, figures, Bradshaw, cenotaph), Horse Guards' Parade
Haig (Hardiman), Whitehall
Sir Arthur (Bomber) Harris (Winter), Strand
Gen. Henry Havelock (Behnes), Trafalgar Square
International Brigades Memorial (Spanish Civil War) (Ian Walters), Jubilee Gardens, South Bank
Irving (Brock), north side of National Portrait Gallery
Isis (Gudgeon), Hyde Park
James II (Gibbons), Trafalgar Square
Jellicoe (McMillan), Trafalgar Square
Samuel Johnson (Fitzgerald), opposite St Clement Danes
Kitchener (Tweed), Horse Guards' Parade
Abraham Lincoln (Saint-Gaudens, copy of one in Chicago), Parliament Square
Mandela (Walters), Parliament Square
Milton (Montford), St Giles, Cripplegate
Mountbatten (Belsky), Foreign Office Green
Gen. Charles James Napier (Adams), Trafalgar Square
Nelson (Railton), Trafalgar Square, with Landseer's lions (cast from guns recovered from the wreck of the *Royal George*)
Florence Nightingale (Walker), Waterloo Place
Palmerston (Woolner), Parliament Square
Sir Keith Park (Johnson), Waterloo Place
Peel (Noble), Parliament Square
Pitt (Chantrey), Hanover Square
Portal (Nemon), Embankment Gardens
Prince Albert (Bacon), Holborn Circus
Queen Elizabeth Gate (Lund and Wynne), Hyde Park Corner
Queen Mother (Jackson), Carlton Gardens
Raleigh (McMillan), Greenwich
Richard I (Coeur de Lion) (Marochetti), Old Palace Yard
Roberts (Bates), Horse Guards' Parade
Franklin D. Roosevelt (Reid Dick), Grosvenor Square
Royal Air Force (Blomfield), Victoria Embankment
Royal Air Force Bomber Command Memorial (O'Connor), Green Park
Royal Artillery (Great War) (Jagger and Pearson), Hyde Park Corner
Royal Artillery (South Africa) (Colton), The Mall
Captain Scott (Lady Scott), Waterloo Place
Shackleton (Jagger), Kensington Gore
Shakespeare (Fontana, copy of one by Scheemakers in Westminster Abbey), Leicester Square
Smuts (Epstein), Parliament Square
Sullivan (Goscombe John), Victoria Embankment
Trenchard (McMillan), Victoria Embankment
Victoria Memorial (Webb and Brock), in front of Buckingham Palace
Raoul Wallenberg (Jackson), Great Cumberland Place
George Washington (Houdon copy), Trafalgar Square
Wellington (Boehm), Hyde Park Corner
Wellington (Chantrey), outside Royal Exchange
John Wesley (Adams Acton), City Road
Westminster School (Crimea) (Scott), Broad Sanctuary
William III (Bacon), St James's Square
Wolseley (Goscombe John), Horse Guards' Parade

PARKS, GARDENS AND OPEN SPACES

CITY OF LONDON CORPORATION OPEN SPACES
W www.cityoflondon.gov.uk
Ashtead Common (202ha/500 acres), Surrey
Burnham Beeches and *Fleet Wood* (220ha/540 acres), Bucks. Acquired by the City of London for the benefit of the public in 1880, Fleet Wood (26ha/65 acres) being presented in 1921
Coulsdon Common (51ha/127 acres), Surrey
Epping Forest (2,476ha/6,118 acres), Essex. Acquired by the City of London in 1878 and opened to the public in 1882. The Queen Elizabeth Hunting Lodge, built for Henry VIII in 1543, lies at the edge of the forest. The present forest is 19.3km (12 miles) long by around 3km (2 miles) wide, approximately one-tenth of its original area
**Epping Forest Buffer Land* (718ha/1,774 acres), Waltham Abbey/Epping
Farthing Downs and New Hill (95ha/235 acres), Surrey
Hampstead Heath (275ha/680 acres), NW3. Including Golders Hill (15ha/36 acres) and Parliament Hill (110ha/271 acres)

Highgate Wood (28ha/70 acres), N6/N10
Kenley Common (56ha/139 acres), Surrey
Queen's Park (12ha/30 acres), NW6
Riddlesdown (43ha/104 acres), Surrey
Spring Park (20ha/50 acres), Kent
Stoke Common (80ha/198 acres), Bucks. Ownership was transferred to the City of London in 2007
West Ham Park (31ha/77 acres), E15
West Wickham Common (10ha/26 acres), Kent
Also over 150 smaller open spaces within the City of London, including *Finsbury Circus* and *St Dunstan-in-the-East*
* Includes Copped Hall Park, Woodredon Estate and Warlies Park

OTHER PARKS AND GARDENS

CHELSEA PHYSIC GARDEN, 66 Royal Hospital Road SW3 4HS T 020-7352 5646 W www.chelseaphysicgarden.co.uk
A garden of general botanical research and education, maintaining a wide range of rare and unusual plants; established in 1673 by the Society of Apothecaries

HAMPTON COURT PARK AND GARDENS (304ha/750 acres), Surrey KT8 9AU T 0844-482 7777 W www.hrp.org.uk
Also known as Home Park, the park lies beyond the palace's formal gardens. It contains a herd of deer and a 750-year-old oak tree from the original park

HOLLAND PARK (22ha/54 acres), Ilchester Place W8 T 020-7361 3000 W www.rbkc.gov.uk The largest park in the Royal Borough of Kensington and Chelsea, includes the Kyoto Garden

KEW, ROYAL BOTANIC GARDENS (120ha/300 acres), Richmond, Surrey TW9 3AB T 020-8332 5655 W www.kew.org
Founded in 1759 and declared a UNESCO World Heritage Site in 2003

THAMES BARRIER PARK (9ha/22acres), North Woolwich Road E16 2HP T 020-7476 3741 Opened in 2000, landscaped gardens with spectacular views of the Thames Barrier

ROYAL PARKS

W www.royalparks.org.uk

Bushy Park (450ha/1,099 acres), Middx. Adjoins Hampton Court; contains an avenue of horse-chestnuts enclosed in a fourfold avenue of limes planted by William III

Green Park (19ha/47 acres), W1. Between Piccadilly and St James's Park, with Constitution Hill leading to Hyde Park Corner

Greenwich Park (74ha/183 acres), SE10. Enclosed by Humphrey, Duke of Gloucester, and laid out by Charles II from the designs of Le Nôtre. On a hill in Greenwich Park is the Royal Observatory (founded 1675). Its buildings are now managed by the National Maritime Museum (T 020-8858 4422 W www.rmg.co.uk) and the earliest building is named Flamsteed House, after John Flamsteed (1646–1719), the first astronomer royal

Hyde Park (142ha/350 acres), W1/W2. From Park Lane to Kensington Gardens and incorporating the Serpentine lake, Apsley House, the Achilles Statue, Rotten Row and the Ladies' Mile; fine gateway at Hyde Park Corner. To the north-east is Marble Arch, originally erected by George IV at the entrance to Buckingham Palace and re-erected in the present position in 1851

Kensington Gardens (111ha/275 acres), W2/W8. From the western boundary of Hyde Park to Kensington Palace; contains the Albert Memorial, Serpentine Gallery and Peter Pan statue

The Regent's Park and *Primrose Hill* (197ha/487 acres), NW1. From Marylebone Road to Primrose Hill surrounded by the Outer Circle; divided by the Broad Walk leading to the Zoological Gardens

Richmond Park (1,000ha/2,500 acres), Surrey. Designated a National Nature Reserve, a Site of Special Scientific Interest and a Special Area of Conservation

St James's Park (23ha/58 acres), SW1. From Whitehall to Buckingham Palace; ornamental lake of 4.9ha (12 acres); the Mall leads from Admiralty Arch to Buckingham Palace

PLACES OF HISTORICAL AND CULTURAL INTEREST

1 Canada Square
Canary Wharf E14 5AB T 020-7418 2000
W www.canarywharf.com
Also known as 'Canary Wharf', the steel and glass skyscraper is designed to sway 35cm in the strongest winds

30 St Mary Axe
EC3A 8EP W www.30stmaryaxe.com
Completed in 2004 and commonly known as the 'Gherkin', each of the floors rotates five degrees from the one below

Alexandra Palace
Alexandra Palace Way N22 7AY T 020-8365 2121
W www.alexandrapalace.com
The Victorian palace was severely damaged by fire in 1980 but was restored, and reopened in 1988. Alexandra Palace now provides modern facilities for exhibitions, conferences, banquets and leisure activities. There is a winter ice rink, a boating lake and a conservation area

Barbican Centre
Silk Street EC2Y 8DS T 020-7638 4141
W www.barbican.org.uk
Owned, funded and managed by the City of London Corporation, the Barbican Centre opened in 1982 and houses the Barbican Theatre, a studio theatre called The Pit and the Barbican Hall; it is also home to the London Symphony Orchestra. There are three cinemas, six conference rooms, two art galleries, a sculpture court, a lending library, trade and banqueting facilities and a conservatory

British Library
St Pancras, 96 Euston Road NW1 2DB T 0843-208 1144
W www.bl.uk
The largest building constructed in the UK in the 20th century with basements extending 24.5m underground. Holdings include the *Magna Carta,* the *Lindisfarne Gospels,* Shakespeare's First Folio, Beatles manuscripts and the first edition of *The Times* from 1788. Holds temporary exhibitions on a range of topics

Central Criminal Court
Old Bailey EC4M 7EH T 020-7248 3277
W www.cityoflondon.gov.uk
The highest criminal court in the UK, the 'Old Bailey' is located on the site of the old Newgate Prison. Trials held here have included those of Oscar Wilde, Dr Crippen and the Yorkshire Ripper. The courthouse has been rebuilt several times since 1674; Edward VII officially opened the current neo-baroque building in 1907

Charterhouse
Charterhouse Square EC1M 6AN T 020-7253 9503
W www.thecharterhouse.org
A Carthusian monastery from 1371 to 1538, purchased in 1611 by Thomas Sutton, who endowed it as a residence for aged men 'of gentle birth' and a school for poor scholars (removed to Godalming in 1872)

Downing Street
SW1 W www.number10.gov.uk
Number 10 Downing Street is the official town residence of the prime minister, number 11 of the Chancellor of the Exchequer and number 12 is the office of the government whips. The street was named after Sir George Downing,

Bt., soldier and diplomat, who was MP for Morpeth 1660–84

George Inn
The George Inn Yard SE1 1NH T 020-7407 2056
W www.nationaltrust.org.uk/george-inn
The last galleried inn in London, built in 1677. Now owned by the National Trust and run as an ordinary public house

Horse Guards
Whitehall SW1
Archway and offices built about 1753. The changing of the guard takes place daily at 11am (10am on Sundays) and the inspection at 4pm. Only those with the Queen's permission may drive through the gates and archway into *Horse Guards Parade*, where the colour is 'trooped' on the Queen's official birthday

HOUSES OF PARLIAMENT
House of Commons, Westminster SW1A 0AA T 020-7219 4272
W www.parliament.uk
House of Lords, Westminster SW1A 0PW T 020-7219 3107
W www.parliament.uk
The royal palace of Westminster, originally built by Edward the Confessor, was the normal meeting place of Parliament from about 1340. St Stephen's Chapel was used from about 1550 for the meetings of the House of Commons, which had previously been held in the Chapter House or Refectory of Westminster Abbey. The House of Lords met in an apartment of the royal palace. The fire of 1834 destroyed much of the palace, and the present Houses of Parliament were erected on the site from the designs of Sir Charles Barry and Augustus Welby Pugin between 1840 and 1867. The chamber of the House of Commons was destroyed by bombing in 1941, and a new chamber designed by Sir Giles Gilbert Scott was used for the first time in 1950. *Westminster Hall and the Crypt Chapel* was the only part of the old palace of Westminster to survive the fire of 1834. It was built by William II from 1097 to 1099 and altered by Richard II between 1394 and 1399. The hammerbeam roof of carved oak dates from 1396–8. The Hall was the scene of the trial of Charles I. *The Victoria Tower* of the House of Lords is 98.5m (323ft) high and *The Clock Tower* of the House of Commons is 96.3m (316ft) high and contains 'Big Ben', the hour bell said to be named after Sir Benjamin Hall, First Commissioner of Works when the original bell was cast in 1856. This bell, which weighed 16 tons 11 cwt, was found to be cracked in 1857. The present bell (13.5 tons) is a recasting of the original and was first brought into use in 1859. The dials of the clock are 7m (23ft) in diameter, the hands being 2.7m (9ft) and 4.3m (14ft) long (including balance piece).

During session, tours of the Houses of Parliament are only available to UK residents who have made advance arrangements through an MP or peer. Overseas visitors are no longer provided with permits to tour the Houses of Parliament during session, although they can tour on Saturdays and during the summer opening and attend debates for both houses in the Strangers' Galleries. During the summer recess, tickets for tours of the Houses of Parliament can be booked by telephone (T 0844-847 1672) or bought on site at the ticket office on Abingdon Green opposite Parliament and the Victoria Tower Gardens. The Strangers' Gallery of the House of Commons is open to the public when the house is sitting. To acquire tickets in advance, UK residents should write to their local MP and overseas visitors should apply to their embassy or high commission in the UK for a permit. If none of these arrangements has been made, visitors should join the public queue outside St Stephen's Entrance, where there is also a queue for entry to the House of Lords Gallery

INNS OF COURT
The Inns of Court are ancient unincorporated bodies of lawyers which for more than five centuries have had the power to call to the Bar those of their members who have qualified for the rank or degree of Barrister-at-Law. There are four Inns of Court as well as many lesser inns

Lincoln's Inn, WC2A 3TL T 020-7405 1393
W www.lincolnsinn.org.uk
The most ancient of the inns with records dating back to 1422. The hall and library buildings are from 1845, although the library is first mentioned in 1474; the old hall (late 15th century) and the chapel were rebuilt *c*.1619–23

Inner Temple, King's Bench Walk EC4Y 7HL
T 020-7797 8250 W www.innertemple.org.uk
Middle Temple, Middle Temple Lane EC4Y 9BT
T 020-7427 4800 W www.middletemple.org.uk
Records for the Middle and Inner Temple date back to the beginning of the 16th century. The site was originally occupied by the Order of Knights Templar *c*.1160–1312. The two inns have separate halls thought to have been formed *c*.1350. The division between the two societies was formalised in 1732 with Temple Church and the Masters House remaining in common. The Inner Temple Garden is normally open to the public on weekdays between 12.30pm and 3pm

Temple Church, EC4Y 7BB T 020-7353 8559
W www.templechurch.com
The nave forms one of five remaining round churches in England

Gray's Inn, South Square WC1R 5ET T 020-7458 7800
W www.graysinn.info
Founded early 14th century; hall 1556–8

No other 'Inns' are active, but there are remains of *Staple Inn*, a gabled front on Holborn (opposite Gray's Inn Road). *Clement's Inn* (near St Clement Danes Church), *Clifford's Inn*, Fleet Street, and *Thavies Inn*, Holborn Circus, are all rebuilt. *Serjeants' Inn*, Fleet Street, and another (demolished 1910) of the same name in Chancery Lane, were composed of Serjeants-at-Law, the last of whom died in 1922

Institute of Contemporary Arts
The Mall SW1Y 5AH T 020-7930 3647 W www.ica.org.uk
Exhibitions of modern art in the fields of film, theatre, new media and the visual arts

Lloyd's
Lime Street EC3M 7HA T 020-7327 1000 W www.lloyds.com
International insurance market which evolved during the 17th century from Lloyd's Coffee House. The present building was opened for business in May 1986, and houses the Lutine Bell. Underwriting is on three floors with a total area of 10,591 sq. m (114,000 sq. ft). The Lloyd's building is not open to the general public

London Central Mosque and the Islamic Cultural Centre
Park Road NW8 7RG T 020-7724 3363 W www.iccuk.org
The focus for London's Muslims; established in 1944 but not completed until 1977, the mosque can accommodate about 5,000 worshippers; guided tours are available

London Eye
South Bank SE1 7PB T 0870-990 8883 W www.londoneye.com
Opened in March 2000 as London's millennium landmark, this (137m/450ft) observation wheel is the tallest cantilevered observation wheel in the world. The wheel provides a 30-minute ride offering panoramic views of the capital

London Zoo
Regent's Park NW1 4RY T 0844-225 1826 W www.zsl.org

Madame Tussauds
Marylebone Road NW1 5LR **T** 0871-894 3000
W www.madametussauds.com
Waxwork exhibition

Mansion House
Cannon Street EC4N 8BH **T** 020-7626 2500
W www.cityoflondon.gov.uk
The official residence of the Lord Mayor. Built in the 18th century in the Palladian style. Open to groups by appointment only

Marlborough House
Pall Mall SW1Y 5HX **T** 020-7747 6500
W www.thecommonwealth.org
Built by Wren for the first Duke of Marlborough and completed in 1711, the house reverted to the Crown in 1835. In 1863 it became the London house of the Prince of Wales and was the London home of Queen Mary until her death in 1953. In 1959 Marlborough House was given by the Queen as the headquarters for the Commonwealth Secretariat and it was opened as such in 1965. The Queen's Chapel, Marlborough Gate, was begun in 1623 from the designs of Inigo Jones for the Infanta Maria of Spain, and completed for Queen Henrietta Maria. Marlborough House is not open to the public

Neasden Temple
BAPS Shri Swaminarayan Mandir, 105–119 Brentfield Road, Neasden NW10 8LD **T** 020-8965 2651 **W** www.mandir.org
The first and largest traditional Hindu Mandir outside of India; opened in 1995

Olympic Park
Stratford E20 **T** 0845-267 2012 **W** www.london2012.com
Built for the London 2012 Olympic Games, the park, which comprised nine sporting venues including the Olympic Stadium, Velodrome and Aquatics Centre in addition to the Olympic Village, is currently being redeveloped in line with the London 2012 legacy strategy

Port of London
Port of London Authority, Royal Pier Road, Kent DA12 2BG
T 01474-562200 **W** www.pla.co.uk
The Port of London covers the tidal section of the river Thames from Teddington to the seaward limit (the outer Tongue buoy and the Sunk light vessel), a distance of 150km (93 miles). The governing body is the Port of London Authority (PLA). Cargo is handled at privately operated riverside terminals between Fulham and Canvey Island, including the enclosed dock at Tilbury, 40km (25 miles) below London Bridge. Passenger vessels and cruise liners can be handled at moorings at Greenwich, Tower Bridge and Tilbury

Roman Remains
The city wall of Roman *Londinium* was largely rebuilt during the medieval period but sections may be seen near the White Tower in the Tower of London; at Tower Hill; at Coopers' Row; at All Hallows, London Wall, its vestry being built on the remains of a semi-circular Roman bastion; at St Alphage, London Wall, showing a succession of building repairs from the Roman until the late medieval period; and at St Giles, Cripplegate. Sections of the great forum and basilica, more than 165 sq. m (1,776 sq. ft), have been encountered during excavations in the area of Leadenhall, Gracechurch Street and Lombard Street. Traces of Roman activity along the river include a massive riverside wall built in the late Roman period, and a succession of Roman timber quays along Lower and Upper Thames Street. Finds from these sites can be seen at the Museum of London.

Other major buildings are the amphitheatre at Guildhall, remains of bath-buildings in Upper and Lower Thames Street, and the temple of Mithras in Walbrook

Royal Albert Hall
Kensington Gore SW7 2AP **T** 0845-401 5045
W www.royalalberthall.com
The elliptical hall, one of the largest in the world, was completed in 1871; since 1941 it has been the venue each summer for the Promenade Concerts founded in 1895 by Sir Henry Wood. Other events include pop and classical music concerts, dance, opera, sporting events, conferences and banquets

Royal Courts of Justice
Strand WC2A 2LL **T** 020-7947 7726 **W** www.justice.gov.uk
Victorian Gothic building that is home to the high court. Visitors are free to watch proceedings

Royal Hospital, Chelsea
Royal Hospital Road SW3 4SR **T** 020-7881 5200
W www.chelsea-pensioners.co.uk
Founded by Charles II in 1682, and built by Wren; opened in 1692 for old and disabled soldiers. The extensive grounds include the former Ranelagh Gardens and are the venue for the Chelsea Flower Show each May

Royal Naval College
Greenwich SE10 9NN **T** 020-8269 4747 **W** www.ornc.org
The building was the Greenwich Hospital until 1869. It was built by Charles II, largely from designs by John Webb, and by Queen Mary II and William III, from designs by Wren. It stands on the site of an ancient abbey, a royal house and Greenwich Palace, which was constructed by Henry VII. Henry VIII, Mary I and Elizabeth I were born in the royal palace and Edward VI died there

Royal Opera House
Covent Garden WC2E 9DD **T** 020-7240 1200
W www.roh.org.uk
Home of The Royal Ballet (1931) and The Royal Opera (1946). The Royal Opera House is the third theatre to be built on the site, opening 1858; the first was opened in 1732

St James's Palace
Pall Mall SW1A 1BQ **W** www.royal.gov.uk
Built by Henry VIII, only the Gatehouse and Presence Chamber remain; later alterations were made by Wren and Kent. Representatives of foreign powers are still accredited 'to the Court of St James's'. *Clarence House* (1825), the official London residence of the Prince of Wales and his sons, stands within the St James's Palace estate

St Paul's Cathedral
St Paul's Churchyard EC4M 8AD **T** 020-7246 8350
W www.stpauls.co.uk
Built 1675–1710. The cross on the dome is 111m (365ft) above ground level, the inner cupola 66.4m (218ft) above the floor. 'Great Paul' in the south-west tower weighs nearly 17 tons. The organ by Father Smith (enlarged by Willis and rebuilt by Mander) is in a case carved by Grinling Gibbons, who also carved the choir stalls

Shakespeare's Globe
New Globe Walk SE1 9DT **T** 020-7902 1400
W www.shakespearesglobe.com
Reconstructed in 1997, the open-air playhouse is a unique resource for the works of William Shakespeare through perfomance and education; a new indoor replica Jacobean theatre is scheduled to stage its first public performance in January 2014

Shard
London Bridge SE1 **T** 020-7493 5311 **W** www.the-shard.com
Completed in May 2012, the skyscraper stands at 310m (1,016ft) and possesses a unique facade of 11,000 glass panels and a 360° viewing gallery

Somerset House
Strand WC2R 1LA T 020-7845 4600
W www.somersethouse.org.uk
The river facade (183m/600ft long) was built in 1776–1801 from the designs of Sir William Chambers; the eastern extension, which houses part of King's College, was built by Smirke in 1829–35. Somerset House was the property of Lord Protector Somerset, at whose attainder in 1552 the palace passed to the Crown, and it was a royal residence until 1692. Somerset House has recently undergone extensive renovation and is home to the Embankment Galleries and the Courtauld Gallery. Open-air concerts and ice-skating (Dec–Jan) are held in the courtyard

SOUTH BANK, SE1
Arts complex on the south bank of the river Thames which consists of:
BFI Southbank T 020-7928 3232 W www.bfi.org.uk
Opened in 1952 and administered by the British Film Institute, has four auditoria of varying capacities. Venue for the annual London Film Festival
The *Royal Festival Hall* T 020-7960 4200
W www.southbankcentre.co.uk
Opened in 1951 for the Festival of Britain, adjacent are the *Queen Elizabeth Hall*, the *Purcell Room* and the *Hayward Gallery*
The *Royal National Theatre,* T 020-7452 3000
W www.nationaltheatre.org.uk
Opened in 1976; comprises the Olivier, the Lyttelton and Dorfman theatres. The Cottesloe Theatre closed in February 2013 and, following refurbishment, is due to re-open in spring 2014 as the Dorfman Theatre

Southwark Cathedral
London Bridge SE1 9DA T 020-7367 6700
W www.cathedral.southwark.anglican.org
Mainly 13th century, but the nave is largely rebuilt. The tomb of John Gower (1330–1408) is between the Bunyan and Chaucer memorial windows in the north aisle; Shakespeare's effigy, backed by a view of Southwark and the Globe Theatre, is in the south aisle; the tomb of Bishop Andrewes (*d.*1626) is near the screen. The Lady Chapel was the scene of the consistory courts of the reign of Mary (Gardiner and Bonner) and is still used as a consistory court. John Harvard, after whom Harvard University is named, was baptised here in 1607, and the chapel by the north choir aisle is his memorial chapel

Thames Embankments
Sir Joseph Bazalgette (1819–91) constructed the *Victoria Embankment,* on the north side from Westminster to Blackfriars for the Metropolitan Board of Works, 1864–70; (the seats, of which the supports of some are a kneeling camel, laden with spicery, and of others a winged sphinx, were presented by the Grocers' Company and by W. H. Smith, MP, in 1874); the *Albert Embankment,* on the south side from Westminster Bridge to Vauxhall, 1866–9, and the Chelsea Embankment, 1871–4. The total cost exceeded £2m. Bazalgette also inaugurated the London main drainage system, 1858–65. A medallion *(Flumini vincula posuit)* has been placed on a pier of the *Victoria Embankment* to commemorate the engineer

Thames Flood Barrier
W www.environment-agency.gov.uk
Officially opened in May 1984, though first used in February 1983, the barrier consists of ten rising sector gates which span approximately 520m from bank to bank of the Thames at Woolwich Reach. When not in use the gates lie horizontally, allowing shipping to navigate the river normally; when the barrier is closed, the gates turn through 90 degrees to stand vertically more than 50 feet above the river bed. The barrier took eight years to complete and can be raised within about 90 minutes

Trafalgar Tavern
Park Row, Greenwich SE10 9NW T 020-8858 2909
W www.trafalgartavern.co.uk
Regency-period riverside public house built in 1837. Charles Dickens and William Gladstone were patrons

Westminster Abbey
SW1P 3PA T 020-7222 5152 W www.westminster-abbey.org
Founded as a Benedictine monastery over 1,000 years ago, the church was rebuilt by Edward the Confessor in 1065 and again by Henry III in the 13th century. The abbey is the resting place for monarchs including Edward I, Henry III, Henry V, Henry VII, Elizabeth I, Mary I and Mary, Queen of Scots, and has been the setting of coronations since that of William the Conqueror in 1066. In Poets' Corner there are memorials to many literary figures, and many scientists and musicians are also remembered here. The grave of the Unknown Warrior is to be found in the nave

Westminster Cathedral
Francis Street SW1P 1QW T 020-7798 9055
W www.westminstercathedral.org.uk
Roman Catholic cathedral built 1895–1903 from the designs of John Francis Bentley. The campanile is 83m (273ft) high

HALLMARKS

Hallmarks are the symbols stamped on gold, silver, palladium or platinum articles to indicate that they have been tested at an official Assay Office and that they conform to one of the legal standards. The marking of gold and silver articles to identify the maker was instituted in England in 1363 under a statute of Edward III. In 1478 the Assay Office in Goldsmiths' Hall was established and all gold and silversmiths were required to bring their wares to be date-marked by the Hall, hence the term 'hallmarked'.

With certain exceptions, all gold, silver, palladium or platinum articles are required by law to be hallmarked before they are offered for sale. Current hallmarking requirements come under the UK Hallmarking Act 1973 and subsequent amendments. The act is built around the principle of description, where it is an offence for any person to apply to an unhallmarked article a description indicating that it is wholly or partly made of gold, silver, palladium or platinum. There is an exemption by weight: compulsory hallmarks are not needed on gold and palladium under 1g, silver under 7.78g and platinum under 0.5g. Also, some descriptions, such as rolled gold and gold plate, are permissible. The British Hallmarking Council is a statutory body created as a result of the Hallmarking Act. It ensures adequate provision for assaying and hallmarking, supervises the assay offices and ensures the enforcement of hallmarking legislation. The four assay offices at London, Birmingham, Sheffield and Edinburgh operate under the act.

BRITISH HALLMARKING COUNCIL Secretariat, 1 Colmore Square, Birmingham B4 6AA **T** 0800-763 1455
W www.bis.gov.uk/britishhallmarkingcouncil

COMPULSORY MARKS

Since January 1999 UK hallmarks have consisted of three compulsory symbols – the sponsor's mark, the millesimal fineness (purity) mark and the assay office mark. The distinction between UK and foreign articles has been removed, and more finenesses are now legal, reflecting the more common finenesses elsewhere in Europe.

SPONSOR'S MARK

Formerly known as the maker's mark, the sponsor's mark was instituted in England in 1363. Originally a device such as a bird or fleur-de-lis, now it consists of a combination of at least two initials (usually a shortened form of the manufacturer's name) and a shield design. The London Assay Office offers 45 standard shield designs but other designs are possible by arrangement.

MILLESIMAL FINENESS MARK

The millesimal fineness (purity) mark indicates the number of parts per thousand of pure metal in the alloy. The current finenesses allowed in the UK are:

Gold	999; 990; 916.6 (22 carat); 750 (18 carat); 585 (14 carat); 375 (9 carat)
Silver	999; 958.4 (Britannia); 925 (sterling); 800
Palladium	999; 950; 500
Platinum	999; 950; 900; 850

ASSAY OFFICE MARK

This mark identifies the particular assay office at which the article was tested and marked. The British assay offices are:

LONDON, Goldsmiths' Hall, Gutter Lane, London EC2V 8AQ **T** 020-7606 8971
W www.thegoldsmiths.co.uk

BIRMINGHAM, PO Box 151, Newhall Street, Birmingham B3 1SB **T** 0121-236 6951
W www.theassayoffice.co.uk

SHEFFIELD, Guardians' Hall, Beulah Road, Hillsborough, Sheffield S6 2AN **T** 0114-231 2121
W www.assayoffice.co.uk

EDINBURGH, Goldsmiths' Hall, 24 Broughton Street, Edinburgh EH1 3RH **T** 0131-556 1144
W www.edinburghassayoffice.co.uk

Assay offices formerly existed in other towns, eg Chester, Exeter, Glasgow, Newcastle, Norwich and York, each having its own distinguishing mark.

OPTIONAL MARKS

Since 1999 traditional pictorial marks such as a crown for gold, the Britannia for 958 silver, the lion passant for 925 silver (lion rampant in Scotland) and the orb for 950 platinum may be added voluntarily to the millesimal mark. In 2010 a pictorial mark for 950 palladium was introduced.

Gold – a crown

Sterling silver (Scotland)

Britannia silver

Platinum – an orb

Sterling silver (England)

Palladium – the Greek goddess Pallas Athene

OTHER MARKS

FOREIGN GOODS

Foreign goods imported into the UK are required to be hallmarked before sale, unless they already bear a convention mark (*see* below) or a hallmark struck by an independent assay office in the European Economic Area which is deemed to be equivalent to a UK hallmark.

The following are the assay office marks used for gold imported articles until the end of 1998. For silver and platinum the symbols remain the same but the shields differ in shape.

London

Sheffield

Birmingham

Edinburgh

CONVENTION HALLMARKS

The UK has been a signatory to the International Convention on Hallmarks since 1972. A convention hallmark struck by the UK assay offices is recognised by all member countries in the convention and, similarly, convention marks from member countries are legally recognised in the UK. There are currently 19 members of the hallmarking convention: Austria, Cyprus, Czech Republic, Denmark, Finland, Hungary, Ireland, Israel, Latvia, Lithuania, the

Netherlands, Norway, Poland, Portugal, Slovakia, Slovenia, Sweden, Switzerland, and the UK.

A convention hallmark comprises four marks: a sponsor's mark, a common control mark, a fineness mark, and an assay office mark.

Examples of common control marks (figures differ according to fineness, but the style of each mark remains the same for each article):

GOLD 375 SILVER 800 PALLADIUM 950 PLATINUM 850

COMMEMORATIVE MARKS

There are other marks to commemorate special events: the silver jubilee of King George V and Queen Mary in 1935, the coronation of Queen Elizabeth II in 1953, her silver jubilee in 1977, and her golden jubilee in 2002. During 1999 and 2000 there was a voluntary additional Millennium Mark. A mark to commemorate the Queen's diamond jubilee in 2012 was available from July 2011 to October 2012:

Diamond Jubilee Hallmark

DATE LETTER

The date letter shows the year in which an article was assayed and hallmarked. Each alphabetical cycle has a distinctive style of lettering or shape of shield. The date letters were different at the various assay offices and the particular office must be established from the assay office mark before reference is made to tables of date letters. Date letter marks became voluntary from 1 January 1999.

The table which follows shows one specimen shield and letter used by the London Assay Office on silver articles for each alphabetical cycle from 1498. The same letters are found on gold articles but the surrounding shield may differ. Until 1 January 1975 two calendar years are given for each specimen date letter as the letter changed annually in May on St Dunstan's Day (the patron saint of silversmiths). Since 1 January 1975, each date letter has indicated a calendar year from January to December and each office has used the same style of date letter and shield for all articles:

LONDON (GOLDSMITHS' HALL) DATE LETTERS FROM 1498

from	*to*
1498–9	1517–18
1518–19	1537–8
1538–9	1557–8
1558–9	1577–8
1578–9	1597–8
1598–9	1617–18
1618–19	1637–8
1638–9	1657–8
1658–9	1677–8
1678–9	1696–7
1697 (from March, 1697 only)	1715–16
1716–17	1735–6
1736–7	1738–9
1739–40	1755–6
1756–7	1775–6
1776–7	1795–6
1796–7	1815–16
1816–17	1835–6
1836–7	1855–6
1856–7	1875–6
1876–7	1895–6 (A to M square shield, N to Z as shown)
1896–7	1915–16
1916–17	1935–6
1936–7	1955–6
1956–7	1974
1975	1999
2000	

BRITISH CURRENCY

The unit of currency is the pound sterling (£) of 100 pence. The decimal system was introduced on 15 February 1971.

COIN

Gold Coins
One hundred pounds £100*
Fifty pounds £50*
Twenty-five pounds £25*
Ten pounds £10*
Five pounds £5
Two pounds £2
Sovereign £1
Half-sovereign 50p

Silver Coins
(Britannia coins)*
Two pounds £2
One pound £1
50 pence 50p
Twenty pence 20p

Maundy Money†
Fourpence 4p
Threepence 3p
Twopence 2p
Penny 1p

Bi-colour Coins‡
Two pounds £2

Nickel-Brass Coins
Two pounds £2 (pre-1997)§
One pound £1

Cupro-Nickel Coins
Crown £5 (since 1990)§
50 pence 50p
Crown 25p (pre-1990)§
20 pence 20p

*Nickel-plated Steel Coins*ℂ
10 pence 10p
5 pence 5p

Bronze Coins
2 pence 2p
1 penny 1p

*Copper-plated Steel Coins***
2 pence 2p
1 penny 1p

* Britannia coins: gold bullion introduced 1987; silver, 1997
† Ceremonial money given annually by the sovereign on Maundy Thursday to as many elderly men and women as there are years in the sovereign's age
‡ Cupro-nickel centre and nickel-brass outer ring
§ Commemorative coins; not intended for general circulation
ℂ Pre-2012 the 10p and 5p coins were struck in cupro-nickel
** Since September 1992, although in 1998 the 2p was struck in both copper-plated steel and bronze

GOLD COIN

Gold ceased to circulate during the First World War. Since then controls on buying, selling and holding gold coin have been imposed at various times but have subsequently been revoked. Under the Exchange Control (Gold Coins Exemption) Order 1979, gold coins may now be imported and exported without restriction, except gold coins which are more than 50 years old and valued at a sum in excess of £8,000; these cannot be exported without specific authorisation from the Department for Business, Innovation and Skills.

Value Added Taxation on the sale of gold coins was revoked in 2000.

SILVER COIN

Prior to 1920 silver coins were struck from sterling silver, an alloy of which 925 parts in 1,000 were silver. In 1920 the proportion of silver was reduced to 500 parts. Since 1947 all 'silver' coins, except Maundy money, have been struck from cupro-nickel, an alloy of 75 parts copper and 25 parts nickel, except for the 20p, composed of 84 parts copper, 16 parts nickel. Maundy coins continue to be struck from sterling silver.

BRONZE COIN

Bronze, introduced in 1860 to replace copper, is an alloy consisting mainly of copper with small amounts of zinc and tin. Bronze was replaced by copper-plated steel in September 1992 with the exception of 1998 when the 2p was made in both copper-plated steel and bronze.

LEGAL TENDER AND VALUE IN CIRCULATION

as at 31 March 2013

Denomination	*Legal up to*	*Face value (£m est)*
Gold*	any amount	–
£2	any amount	786
£1	any amount	1,528
50p	£10	460
20p	£10	541
10p	£5	160
5p	£5	191
2p	20p	132
1p	20p	113

* Dated 1838 onwards, if not below least current weight

£5 (Crown since 1990) and 25p (Crown pre-1990) up to £10 are also legal tender but are only redeemable at the Post Office.

The following coins have ceased to be legal tender:

Farthing	31 Dec 1960
Halfpenny (½d)	31 Jul 1969
Half-crown	31 Dec 1969
Threepence	31 Aug 1971
Penny (1d)	31 Aug 1971
Sixpence	30 Jun 1980
Halfpenny (½p)	31 Dec 1984
Old 5 pence	31 Dec 1990
Old 10 pence	30 Jun 1993
Old 50 pence	28 Feb 1998

The Channel Islands and the Isle of Man issue their own coinage, which is legal tender only in the island of issue.

COIN STANDARDS

	Metal	*Standard weight (g)*	*Standard diameter (mm)*
1p	bronze	3.56	20.3
1p	copper-plated steel	3.56	20.3
2p	bronze	7.13	25.9
2p	copper-plated steel	7.13	25.9
5p	nickel-plated steel	3.25	18.0
10p	nickel-plated steel	6.5	24.5
20p	cupro-nickel	5.0	21.4
25p Crown	cupro-nickel	28.28	38.6
50p	cupro-nickel	8.00	27.3
£1	nickel-brass	9.5	22.5
£2	nickel-brass	15.98	28.4
£2	cupro-nickel, nickel-brass	12.00	28.4
£5 Crown	cupro-nickel	28.28	38.6

The 'remedy' is the amount of variation from standard permitted in weight and fineness of coins when first issued from the Royal Mint.

THE TRIAL OF THE PYX

The Trial of the Pyx is the examination by a jury to ascertain that coins made by the Royal Mint, which have been set aside in the pyx (or box), are of the proper weight, diameter and composition required by law. The trial is held annually, presided over by the Queen's Remembrancer, with a jury of freemen of the Company of Goldsmiths.

BANKNOTES

Bank of England notes are issued in denominations of £5, £10, £20 and £50 for the amount of the fiduciary note issue, and are legal tender in England and Wales. No £1 notes have been issued since 1984 and in March 1998 the outstanding notes were written off in accordance with the provision of the Currency Act 1983.

The current E series of notes was introduced from June 1990, replacing the D series (*see* below). A new-style £20 note, the first in series F, was introduced in March 2007. A £50 note, the second in the F series, and the first banknote issued by the Bank of England to feature two portraits on the reverse, was issued in November 2011. The historical figures portrayed in these series are:

£5	May 2002–date	Elizabeth Fry
£5	Jun 1990–2003	George Stephenson*
£10	Nov 2000–date	Charles Darwin
£10	Apr 1992–2003	Charles Dickens*
£20	Mar 2007–date	Adam Smith
£20	Jun 1999–2010	Sir Edward Elgar*
£20	Jun 1991–2001	Michael Faraday*
£50	Nov 2011–date	Matthew Boulton and James Watt
£50	Apr 1994–date	Sir John Houblon

* These notes have been withdrawn from circulation

NOTE CIRCULATION

Note circulation is highest at the two peak spending periods of the year: around Christmas and during the summer holiday period.

The value of notes in circulation (£ million) at the end of February 2012 and 2013 was:

	2012	*2013*
£5	1,477	1,526
£10	6,841	7,234
£20	33,129	35,163
£50	9,899	10,323
Other notes*	3,575	3,776
Total	54,921	58,022

* Includes higher value notes used internally in the Bank of England, eg as cover for the note issues of banks in Scotland and Northern Ireland in excess of their permitted issue

LEGAL TENDER

Banknotes which are no longer legal tender are payable when presented at the head office of the Bank of England in London.

The white notes for £10, £20, £50, £100, £500 and £1,000, which were issued until April 1943, ceased to be legal tender in May 1945, and the white £5 note in March 1946.

The white £5 note issued between October 1945 and September 1956, the £5 notes issued between 1957 and 1963 (bearing a portrait of Britannia) and the first series to bear a portrait of the Queen, issued between 1963 and 1971, ceased to be legal tender in March 1961, June 1967 and September 1973 respectively.

The series of £1 notes issued during the years 1928 to 1960 and the 10 shilling notes issued from 1928 to 1961 (those without the royal portrait) ceased to be legal tender in May and October 1962 respectively. The £1 note first issued in March 1960 (bearing on the back a representation of Britannia) and the £10 note first issued in February 1964 (bearing a lion on the back), both bearing a portrait of the Queen on the front, ceased to be legal tender in June 1979. The £1 note first issued in 1978 ceased to be legal tender on 11 March 1988. The 10 shilling note was replaced by the 50p coin in October 1969, and ceased to be legal tender on 21 November 1970.

The D series of banknotes was introduced from 1970 and ceased to be legal tender from the dates shown below. The predominant identifying feature of each note was the portrayal on the back of a prominent figure from British history:

£1	Feb 1978–Mar 1988	Sir Isaac Newton
£5	Nov 1971–Nov 1991	Duke of Wellington
£10	Feb 1975–May 1994	Florence Nightingale
£20	Jul 1970–Mar 1993	William Shakespeare
£50	Mar 1981–Sep 1996	Sir Christopher Wren

The £1 coin was introduced on 21 April 1983 to replace the £1 note.

OTHER BANKNOTES

Scotland – Banknotes are issued by three Scottish banks. The Royal Bank of Scotland issues notes for £1, £5, £10, £20, £50 and £100. Bank of Scotland and the Clydesdale Bank issue notes for £5, £10, £20, £50 and £100. Scottish notes are not legal tender in the UK but they are an authorised currency.

Northern Ireland – Banknotes are issued by four banks in Northern Ireland. The Bank of Ireland and the Ulster Bank issue notes for £5, £10, £20, £50 and £100. The First Trust Bank and Danske Bank (formerly Northern Bank) issue notes for £10, £20, £50 and £100. Northern Ireland notes are not legal tender in the UK but in Northern Ireland they circulate widely and enjoy a status comparable to that of Bank of England notes.

Channel Islands – The States of Guernsey issues its own currency notes and coinage. The notes are for £1, £5, £10, £20 and £50, and the coins are for 1p, 2p, 5p, 10p, 20p, 50p, £1 and £2. The States of Jersey issues its own currency notes and coinage. The notes are for £1, £5, £10, £20, £50 and £100, and the coins are for 1p, 2p, 5p, 10p, 20p, 50p, £1 and £2.

The Isle of Man – The Isle of Man government issues notes for £1, £5, £10, £20 and £50. Although these notes are only legal tender in the Isle of Man, they are accepted at face value in branches of the clearing banks in the UK. The Isle of Man issues coins for 1p, 2p, 5p, 10p, 20p, 50p, £1, £2 and £5.

Although none of the series of notes specified above is legal tender in the UK, they are generally accepted by banks irrespective of their place of issue. At one time banks made a commission charge for handling Scottish and Irish notes but this was abolished some years ago.

BANKING AND PERSONAL FINANCE

There are two main types of deposit-taking institutions: banks and building societies, although National Savings and Investments also provides savings products. Banks and building societies are regulated by the Financial Services Authority (*see* Financial Services Regulation) and National Savings and Investments is accountable to HM Treasury.

The main institutions within the British banking system are the Bank of England (the central bank), retail banks, investment banks and overseas banks. In its role as the central bank, the Bank of England acts as banker to the government and as a note-issuing authority; it also oversees the efficient functioning of payment and settlement systems.

Since May 1997, the Bank of England has had operational responsibility for monetary policy. At monthly meetings of its monetary policy committee the Bank sets the interest rate at which it will lend to the money markets.

OFFICIAL INTEREST RATES 2005–13

4 August 2005	4.50%
3 August 2006	4.75%
9 November 2006	5.00%
11 January 2007	5.25%
10 May 2007	5.50%
5 July 2007	5.75%
6 December 2007	5.50%
7 February 2008	5.25%
10 April 2008	5.00%
8 October 2008	4.50%
6 November 2008	3.00%
4 December 2008	2.00%
8 January 2009	1.50%
5 February 2009	1.00%
5 March 2009	0.50%

RETAIL BANKING

Retail banks offer a wide variety of financial services to individuals and companies, including current and deposit accounts, loan and overdraft facilities, credit and debit cards, investment services, pensions, insurance and mortgages. All banks offer telephone and internet banking facilities in addition to traditional branch services.

The Financial Ombudsman Service provides independent and impartial arbitration in disputes between banks and their customers (*see* Financial Services Regulation).

PAYMENT CLEARINGS

The UK Payments Administration (UKPA) is a trade body that brings together the organisations responsible for delivering payment services. It also provides information on payment issues such as card fraud, cheques, plastic cards, electronic payments and cash. The Payments Council sets strategy for UK payments to ensure they meet the needs of users, payment service providers and the wider economy. Membership of the Payments Council is open to any member of a payment scheme that is widely used or significant in the UK. As at April 2013 the Payments Council had 32 members, comprising banks, financial services providers, one building society and the Post Office.

There are four organisations, overseen by UKPA, that manage the majority of payment clearings in the UK:

- BACS is responsible for the schemes behind the clearing and settlement of automated payments including direct debit and BACS direct credit (W www.bacs.co.uk)
- CHAPS Clearing Company provides electronic same-day clearing and real-time settlement services for sterling payments (W www.chapsco.co.uk)
- The Cheque and Credit Clearing Company manages the cheque clearing system (W www.chequeandcredit.co.uk)
- The Faster Payments Service allows customers to make faster electronic payments, usually by phone or online banking (W www.fasterpayments.org.uk)

PAYMENTS COUNCIL/UKPA, 2 Thomas More Square, London E1W 1YN
T 020-3217 8200 W www.ukpayments.org.uk

GLOSSARY OF FINANCIAL TERMS

AER (ANNUAL EQUIVALENT RATE) – A notional rate quoted on savings and investment products which demonstrates the return on interest, when compounded and paid annually.

APR (ANNUAL PERCENTAGE RATE) – Calculates the total amount of interest payable over the whole term of a product (such as investment or loan), allowing consumers to compare rival products on a like-for-like basis. Companies offering loans, credit cards, mortgages or overdrafts are required by law to provide the APR rate. Where typical APR is shown, it refers to the company's typical borrower and so is given as a best example; rate and costs may vary depending on individual circumstances.

MAJOR RETAIL BANKS' FINANCIAL RESULTS 2012

Bank group	*Profit/(loss) before taxation* £ *million*	*Profit/(loss) after taxation* £ *million*	*Total assets* £ *million*
Banco Santander Group*	7,117	1,858	1,068,874
Barclays	246	(236)	1,490,321
Cooperative Bank	(289)	(200)	49,573
HSBC*	13,378	9,934	1,744,418
Lloyds Banking Group	(570)	(1,343)	924,552
RBS Group	(3,412)	(3,776)	1,284,274

* Exchange rate as at April 2013 converting EUR and USD to GBP respectively

ANNUITY – A type of insurance policy that provides regular income in exchange for a lump sum. The annuity can be bought from a company other than the existing pension provider.

ASU – Accident, sickness and unemployment insurance taken out by a borrower to protect against being unable to work for these reasons. The policy will usually pay a percentage of the normal monthly mortgage repayment if the borrower is unable to work.

ATM (AUTOMATED TELLER MACHINES) – Commonly referred to as cash machines. Users can access their bank accounts using a card for simple transactions such as withdrawing money and viewing an account balance. Some banks and independent ATM deployers charge for transactions.

BANKER'S DRAFT – A cheque drawn on a bank against a cash deposit. Considered to be a secure way of receiving money in instances where a cheque could 'bounce' or where it is not desirable to receive cash.

BASE RATE – The interest rate set by the Bank of England at which it will lend to financial institutions. This acts as a benchmark for all other interest rates.

BASIS POINT – Unit of measure (usually one-hundredth of a percentage point) used to express movements in interest rates, foreign rates or bond yields.

BUY-TO-LET – The purchase of a residential property for the sole purpose of letting to a tenant. Not all lenders provide mortgage finance for this purpose. Buy-to-let lenders assess projected rental income (typical expectations are between 125 and 130 per cent of the monthly interest payment) in addition to, or instead of, the borrower's income. Buy-to-let mortgages are available as either interest only or repayment.

CAPITAL GAIN/LOSS – Increase/decrease in the value of a capital asset when it is sold or transferred compared to its initial worth.

CAPPED RATE MORTGAGE – The interest rate applied to a loan is guaranteed not to rise above a certain rate for a set period of time; the rate can therefore fall but will not rise above the capped rate. The level at which the cap is fixed is usually higher than for a fixed rate mortgage for a comparable period of time. The lender normally imposes early redemption penalties within the first few years.

CASH CARD – Issued by banks and building societies for withdrawing cash from ATMs.

CHARGE CARD – Charge cards, eg American Express and Diners Club, can be used in a similar way to credit cards but the debt must be settled in full each month.

CHIP AND PIN CARD – A credit/debit card which incorporates an embedded chip containing unique owner details. When used with a PIN, such cards offer greater security as they are less prone to fraud. Since 14 February 2006, most card transactions in the UK have required the use of a chip and pin card.

CREDIT CARD – Normally issued with a credit limit, credit cards can be used for purchases until the limit is reached. There is normally an interest-free period on the outstanding balance of up to 56 days. Charges can be avoided if the balance is paid off in full within the interest-free period. Alternatively part of the balance can be paid and in most cases there is a minimum amount set by the issuer (normally a percentage of the outstanding balance) which must be paid on a monthly basis. Some card issuers charge an annual fee and most issuers belong to at least one major credit card network, eg Mastercard or Visa.

CREDIT RATING – Overall credit worthiness of a borrower based on information from a credit reference agency, such as Experian or Equifax, which holds details of credit agreements, payment records, county court judgements etc for all adults in the UK. This information is supplied to lenders who use it in their credit scoring or underwriting systems to calculate the risk of granting a loan to an individual and the probability that it will be repaid. Each lender sets their own criteria for credit worthiness and may accept or reject a credit application based on an individual's credit rating.

CRITICAL ILLNESS COVER – Insurance that covers borrowers against critical illnesses such as stroke, heart attack or cancer and is designed to protect mortgage or other loan payments.

DEBIT CARD – Debit cards were introduced on a large scale in the UK in the mid-1980s, replacing cash and cheques to purchase goods and services. They can be used to withdraw cash from ATMs in the UK and abroad and may also function as a cheque guarantee card. Funds are automatically withdrawn from an individual's bank account after making a purchase and no interest is charged.

DIRECT DEBIT – An instruction from a customer to their bank, which authorises the payee to charge costs to the customer's bank account.

DISCOUNTED MORTGAGE – Discounted mortgages guarantee an interest rate set at a margin below the standard variable rate for a period of time. The discounted rate will move up or down with the standard variable rate, but the payment rate will retain the agreed differential below the standard variable rate. The lender normally imposes early redemption penalties within the first few years.

EARLY REDEMPTION PENALTY – *see* Redemption Penalty

ENDOWMENT MORTGAGE – Only the interest on a property loan is paid back to the lender each month as long as an endowment life insurance policy is taken out for an agreed amount of time, typically 25 years. When the policy matures the lender will take repayment of the money owed on the property loan and any surplus goes to the policyholder. If the endowment policy shows a shortfall on projected returns, the policy holder must make further provision to pay off the mortgage.

EQUITY – When applied to real estate, equity is the difference between the value of a property and the amount outstanding on any loan secured against it. Negative equity occurs when the loan is greater than the market value of the property.

FIXED RATE MORTGAGE – A repayment mortgage where the interest rate on the loan is fixed for a set amount of time, normally a period of between one and ten years. The interest rate does not vary with changes to the base rate resulting in the monthly mortgage payment remaining the same for the duration of the fixed period. The lender normally imposes early redemption penalties within the first few years.

ISA (INDIVIDUAL SAVINGS ACCOUNT) – A means by which investors can save (in a cash ISA) and invest (in a stocks and shares ISA) without paying any tax on the proceeds. There are limits on the amount that can be invested during any given tax year (*see* Taxation).

INTEREST ONLY MORTGAGE – Only interest is paid by the borrower and capital remains constant for the term of the loan. The onus is on the borrower to make provision to repay the capital at the end of the term. This is usually achieved through an investment vehicle such as an endowment policy or pension.

LOAN TO VALUE (LTV) – This is the ratio between the size of a mortgage loan sought and the mortgage lender's valuation. On a loan of £55,000, for example, on a property valued at £100,000 the loan to value is 55 per cent. This means that there is sufficient equity in the property for the lender to be reassured that if interest or capital repayments were stopped, it could sell the property and recoup the money owed. Fewer options are available to borrowers requiring high LTV.

LONDON INTERBANK OFFERED RATE (LIBOR) – Is the interest rate that London banks charge when lending to one another on the wholesale money market. LIBOR is set by supply and demand of money as banks lend to each other in order to balance their books on a daily basis.

MIG (MORTGAGE INDEMNITY GUARANTEE) – An insurance for the lender paid by the borrower on high LTV mortgages (typically more than 90 per cent). It is a policy designed to protect the lender against loss in the event of the borrower defaulting or ceasing to repay a mortgage and is usually paid as a one-off premium or can be added to the value of the loan. It offers no protection to the borrower. Not all lenders charge MIG premiums.

OVERDRAFT – An 'authorised' overdraft is an arrangement made between customer and bank allowing the balance of the customer's account to go below zero; interest is normally charged at an agreed rate and sometimes an arrangement fee is charged. If the negative balance exceeds the agreed terms or a prior arrangement for an overdraft facility has not been made (an 'unauthorised' overdraft) then additional penalty fees may be charged and higher interest rates may apply. Interest-free overdrafts are available for customers in certain circumstances, such as full-time higher education students and recent graduates.

PERSONAL PENSION PLAN (PPP) – Designed for the self-employed or those in non-pensionable employment. Contributions made to a PPP are exempt from tax and the retirement age may be selected at any time from age 50 to 75. Up to 25 per cent of the pension fund may be taken as a tax-free cash sum on retirement.

PHISHING – A fraudulent attempt to obtain bank account details and security codes through an email. The email purports to come from a *bona fide* bank or building society and attempts to steer the recipient, usually under the pretext that the banking institution is updating its security arrangements, to a website which requests personal details.

PIN (PERSONAL IDENTIFICATION NUMBER) – A PIN is issued alongside a cash card to allow the user to access a bank account via an ATM. PINs are also issued with smart, credit and debit cards and, since 14 February 2006, have been compulsory as a security measure in the majority of purchases.

PORTABLE MORTGAGE – A mortgage product that can be transferred to a different property in the event of a house move. Preferable where early redemption penalties are charged.

REDEMPTION PENALTY – A charge levied for paying off a loan, debt balance or mortgage before a date agreed with the lender.

REPAYMENT MORTGAGE – In contrast to the interest only mortgage, the monthly repayment includes an element of the capital sum borrowed in addition to the interest charged.

SELF-CERTIFICATION – Some lenders allow borrowers to self-certify their income. This type of scheme is useful to the self-employed who may not have accounts available or any other person who has difficulty proving their regular income.

SHARE – A share is a divided-up unit of the value of a company. If a company is worth £100m, and there are 50 million shares in issue, then each share is worth £2 (usually listed as pence). As the overall value of the company fluctuates so does the share price.

SMART CARD – *see* Chip and Pin Card

STANDING ORDER – An instruction made by the customer to their bank, which allows the transfer of a set amount to a payee at regular intervals.

TELEPHONE BANKING – Banking facilities which can be accessed via the telephone.

UNIT TRUST – A 'pooled' fund of assets, usually shares, owned by a number of individuals. Managed by professional, authorised fund-management groups, unit trusts have traditionally delivered better returns than average cash deposits, but do rise and fall in value as their underlying investment varies in value.

VARIABLE RATE MORTGAGE – Repayment mortgages where the interest rate set by the lender increases or decreases in relation to the base interest rate which can result in fluctuating monthly repayments.

WITH-PROFITS – Usually applies to pensions, endowments, savings schemes or bonds. The intention is to smooth out the rises and falls in the stock market for the benefit of the investor. Actuaries working for the insurance company, or fund managers, hold back some profits in good years in order to make up the difference in years when shares perform badly.

BANK FAMILY TREE

Includes the major retail banks operating in the UK as at April 2013. Financial results for these banks are given on page 487. Building societies are only included in instances where they demutualised to become a bank.

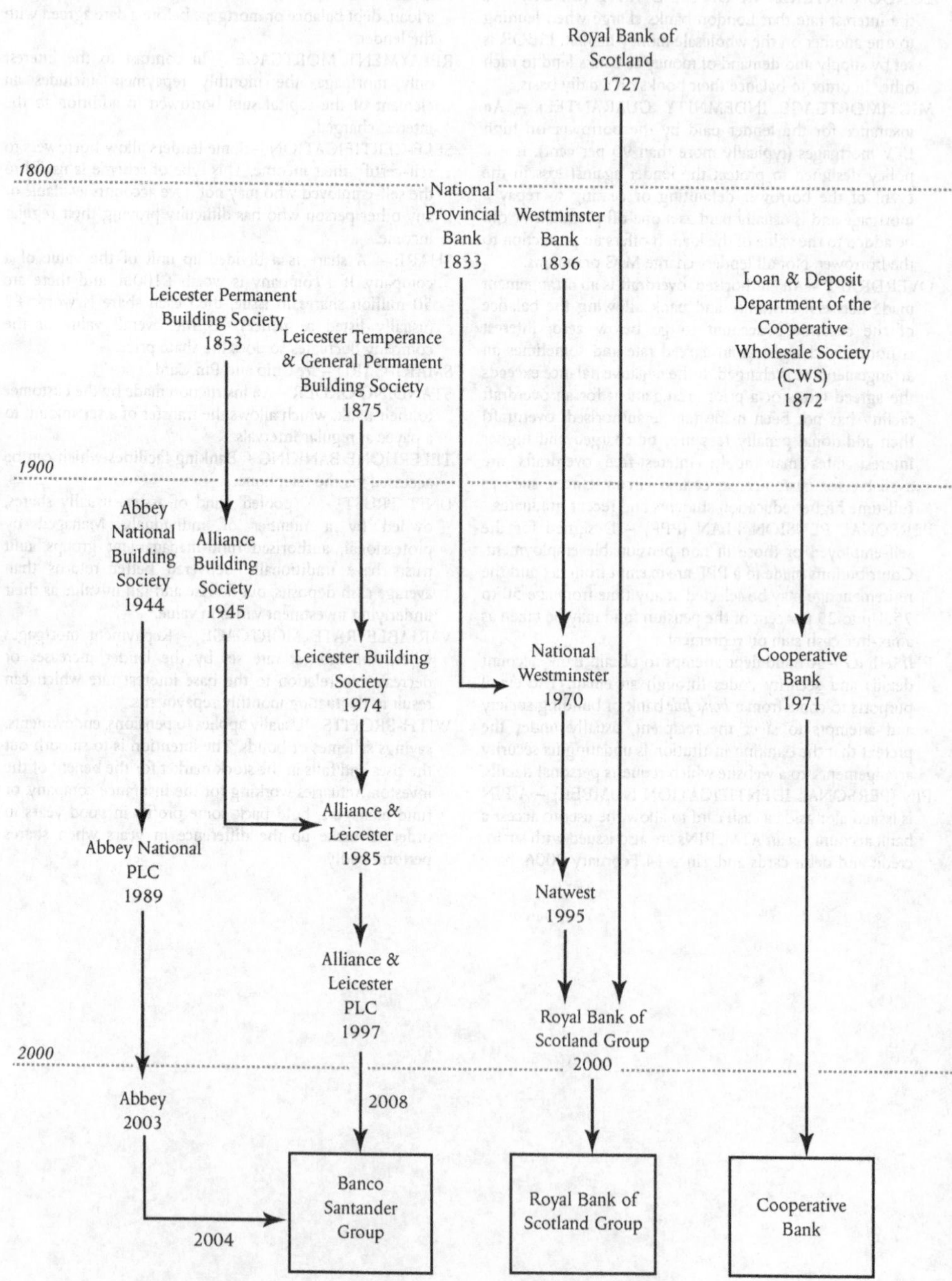

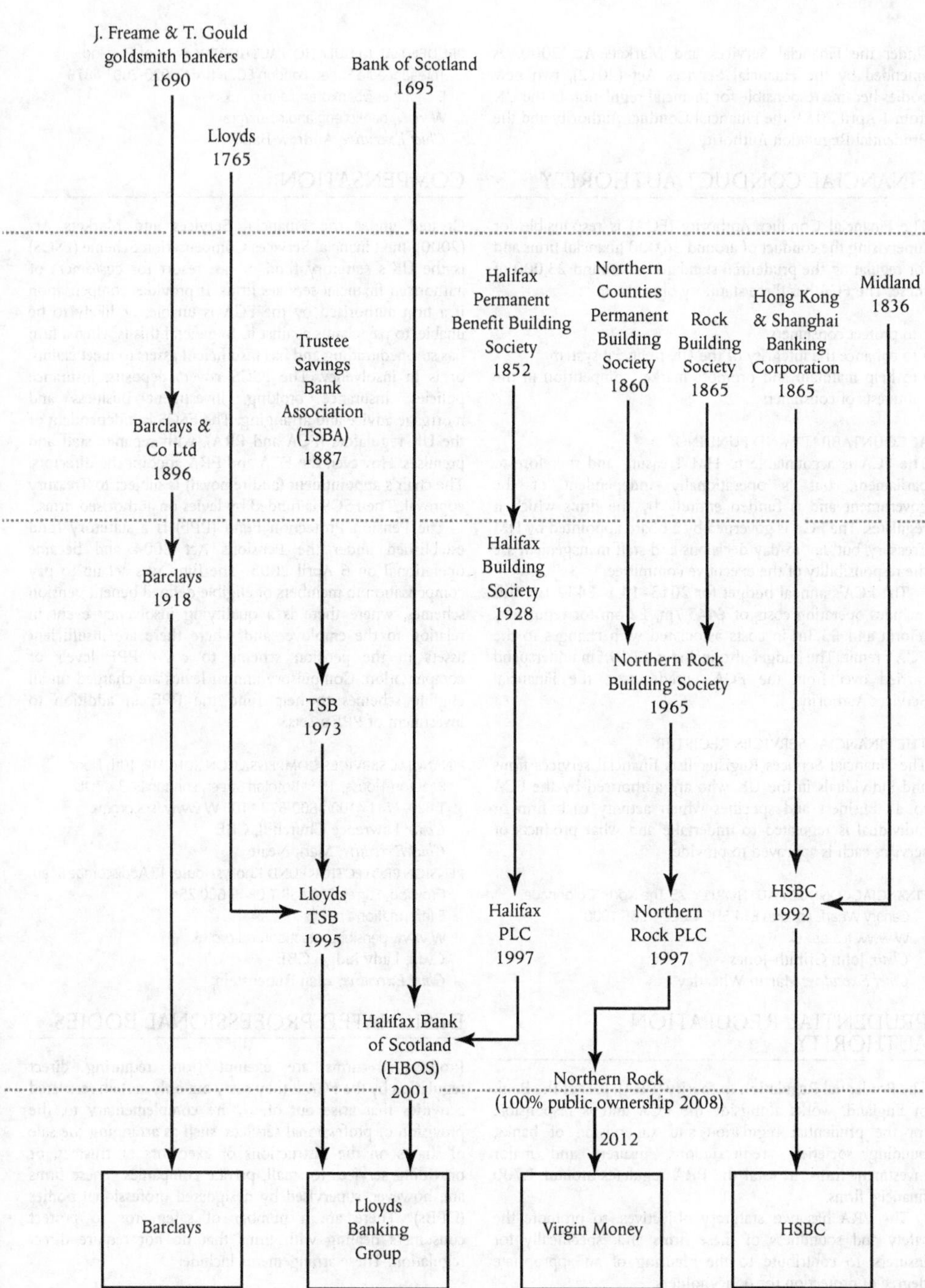
J. Freame & T. Gould goldsmith bankers 1690
Bank of Scotland 1695
Lloyds 1765
Halifax Permanent Benefit Building Society 1852
Northern Counties Permanent Building Society 1860
Rock Building Society 1865
Hong Kong & Shanghai Banking Corporation 1865
Midland 1836
Trustee Savings Bank Association (TSBA) 1887
Barclays & Co Ltd 1896
Halifax Building Society 1928
Barclays 1918
Northern Rock Building Society 1965
TSB 1973
Lloyds TSB 1995
Halifax PLC 1997
Northern Rock PLC 1997
HSBC 1992
Halifax Bank of Scotland (HBOS) 2001
Northern Rock (100% public ownership 2008)
2012
Barclays
Lloyds Banking Group
Virgin Money
HSBC

FINANCIAL SERVICES REGULATION

Under the Financial Services and Markets Act 2000, as amended by the Financial Services Act (2012), two new bodies became responsible for financial regulation in the UK from 1 April 2013: the Financial Conduct Authority and the Prudential Regulation Authority.

FINANCIAL CONDUCT AUTHORITY

The Financial Conduct Authority (FCA) is responsible for supervising the conduct of around 26,000 financial firms and for regulating the prudential standards of around 23,000 of these. The FCA has three statutory objectives:

- to protect consumers
- to enhance the integrity of the UK financial system
- to help maintain and promote market competition in the interests of consumers

ACCOUNTABILITY AND FUNDING

The FCA is accountable to HM Treasury and therefore to parliament, but is operationally independent of the government and is funded entirely by the firms which it regulates. The FCA is governed by a board appointed by HM Treasury, but day-to-day decisions and staff management are the responsibility of the executive committee.

The FCA's annual budget for 2013–14 is £432.1m; this includes operating costs of £445.7m, £2.6m for regulatory reform and £3.3m in costs associated with changes to the FCA's remit. The budget also includes a £19.5m underspend carried over from the FCA's predecessor, the Financial Services Authority.

THE FINANCIAL SERVICES REGISTER

The Financial Services Register lists financial services firms and individuals in the UK who are authorised by the FCA to do business and specifies which activity each firm or individual is regulated to undertake and what products or services each is approved to provide.

FINANCIAL CONDUCT AUTHORITY, 25 The North Colonnade, Canary Wharf, London E14 5HS **T** 020-7066 1000
W www.fca.org.uk
Chair, John Griffith-Jones
Chief Executive, Martin Wheatley

PRUDENTIAL REGULATION AUTHORITY

The Prudential Regulation Authority (PRA), part of the Bank of England, works alongside the FCA and is responsible for the prudential regulation and supervision of banks, building societies, credit unions, insurers and major investment firms. In total the PRA regulates around 1,700 financial firms.

The PRA has two statutory objectives: to promote the safety and soundness of these firms and, specifically for insurers, to contribute to the securing of an appropriate degree of protection for policyholders.

The PRA's board includes the Governor of the Bank of England, the Deputy Governor for Financial Stability and the Deputy Governor for Prudential Regulation (also the chief executive of the PRA) and is accountable to parliament.

PRUDENTIAL REGULATION AUTHORITY, Bank of England, Threadneedle Street, London EC2R 8AH **T** 020-7601 4878
E enquiries@bankofengland.co.uk
W www.bankofengland.co.uk/pra
Chief Executive, Andrew Bailey

COMPENSATION

Created under the Financial Services and Markets Act (2000), the Financial Services Compensation Scheme (FSCS) is the UK's statutory fund of last resort for customers of authorised financial services firms. It provides compensation if a firm authorised by the FCA is unable, or likely to be unable, to pay claims against it. In general this is when a firm has stopped trading and has insufficient assets to meet claims, or is in insolvency. The FSCS covers deposits, insurance policies, insurance broking, investment business and mortgage advice and arranging. The FSCS is independent of the UK regulators (FCA and PRA), with separate staff and premises. However, the FCA and PRA appoint the directors. The chair's appointment (and removal) is subject to Treasury approval. The FSCS is funded by levies on authorised firms.

The Pension Protection Fund (PPF) is a statutory fund established under the Pensions Act 2004 and became operational on 6 April 2005. The fund was set up to pay compensation to members of eligible defined benefit pension schemes, where there is a qualifying insolvency event in relation to the employer and where there are insufficient assets in the pension scheme to cover PPF levels of compensation. Compulsory annual levies are charged on all eligible schemes to help fund the PPF, in addition to investment of PPF assets.

FINANCIAL SERVICES COMPENSATION SCHEME, 10th Floor, Beaufort House, 15 St Botolph Street, London EC3A 7QU
T 020-7741 4100/0800-678 1100 **W** www.fscs.org.uk
Chair, Lawrence Churchill, CBE
Chief Executive, Mark Neale

PENSION PROTECTION FUND, Knollys House, 17 Addiscombe Road, Croydon, Surrey CR0 6SR **T** 0845-600 2541
E information@ppf.gsi.gov.uk
W www.pensionprotectionfund.org.uk
Chair, Lady Judge, CBE
Chief Executive, Alan Rubenstein

DESIGNATED PROFESSIONAL BODIES

Professional firms are exempt from requiring direct regulation by the FCA if they carry out only certain restricted activities that arise out of, or are complementary to, the provision of professional services, such as arranging the sale of shares on the instructions of executors or trustees, or providing services to small, private companies. These firms are, however, supervised by designated professional bodies (DPBs). There are a number of safeguards to protect consumers dealing with firms that do not require direct regulation. These arrangements include:

- the FCA's power to ban a specific firm from taking advantage of the exemption and to restrict the regulated activities permitted to the firms
- rules which require professional firms to ensure that their clients are aware that they are not authorised persons

- a requirement for the DPBs to supervise and regulate the firms and inform the FCA on how the professional firms carry on their regulated activities

See Professional Education section for contact details of the following DPBs:
Association of Chartered Certified Accountants
Council for Licensed Conveyancers
Institute and Faculty of Actuaries
Institute of Chartered Accountants in England and Wales
Institute of Chartered Accountants in Ireland
Institute of Chartered Accountants of Scotland
Law Society of England and Wales
Law Society of Northern Ireland
Law Society of Scotland
Royal Institution of Chartered Surveyors

RECOGNISED INVESTMENT EXCHANGES

The FCA currently supervises six recognised investment exchanges (RIEs) in the UK; recognition confers an exemption from the need to be authorised to carry out regulated activities in the UK. The RIEs are organised markets on which member firms can trade investments such as equities and derivatives. The RIEs are listed with their year of recognition in parentheses:

BATS TRADING (2013), 6th Floor 10 Lower Street, London EC3R 6AF **T** 020-7012 8900 **W** www.batstrading.co.uk

ICAP FUTURES EUROPE (2007), 2 Broadgate, London EC2M 7UR **T** 020-7050 7650 **W** www.isdx.com

ICE FUTURES EUROPE (2001), 5th Floor Milton Gate, 60 Chiswell Street, London EC1Y 4SA **T** 020-7065 7700 **W** www.theice.com

LIFFE ADMINISTRATION AND MANAGEMENT (2001), Cannon Bridge House, 1 Cousin Lane, London EC4R 3XX **T** 020-7623 0444 **W** www.nyx.com

LONDON METAL EXCHANGE (2001), 56 Leadenhall Street, London EC3A 2BJ **T** 020-7264 5555 **W** www.lme.co.uk

LONDON STOCK EXCHANGE (2001), 10 Paternoster Square, London EC4M 7LS **T** 020-7797 1000 **W** www.londonstockexchange.com

RECOGNISED CLEARING HOUSES

The FCA is also responsible for recognising and supervising recognised clearing houses (RCHs), which organise the settlement of transactions on recognised investment exchanges. There are currently five RCHs in the UK:

CME CLEARING EUROPE (2010), 1 New Change, London EC4M 9AF **T** 020-3379 3100 **W** www.cmeclearingeurope.co.uk

EUROCLEAR UK AND IRELAND (2001), Watling House, 33 Cannon Street, London EC4M 5SB **T** 020-7849 0000 **W** www.crestco.co.uk

EUROPEAN CENTRAL COUNTERPARTY (2008), Broadgate West, 1 Snowdon Street, London EC2A 2DQ **T** 020-7650 1401 **W** www.euroccp.co.uk

ICE CLEAR EUROPE (2008), 5th Floor, Milton Gate, 60 Chiswell Street, London EC1Y 4SA **T** 020-7265 3648 **W** www.theice.com/clear_europe

LCH (LONDON CLEARING HOUSE) CLEARNET (2001), Aldgate House, 33 Aldgate High Street, London EC3N 1EA **T** 020-7426 7000 **W** www.lchclearnet.com

OMBUDSMAN SCHEMES

The Financial Ombudsman Service was set up by the Financial Services and Markets Act 2000 to provide consumers with a free, independent service for resolving disputes with authorised financial firms. The Financial Ombudsman Service can consider complaints about most financial matters including: banking; credit cards and store cards; financial advice; hire purchase and pawnbroking; insurance; loans and credit; money transfer; mortgages; pensions; savings and investments; stocks, shares, unit trusts and bonds.

Complainants must first complain to the firm involved. They do not have to accept the ombudsman's decision and are free to go to court if they wish, but if a decision is accepted, it is binding for both the complainant and the firm.

The Pensions Ombudsman can investigate and decide complaints and disputes regarding the way occupational and personal pension schemes are administered and managed. The Pensions Ombudsman is also the Ombudsman for the Pension Protection Fund (PPF) and the Financial Assistance Scheme (which offers help to those who were a member of an under-funded defined benefit pension scheme that started to wind-up in specific financial circumstances between 1 January 1997 and 5 April 2005).

FINANCIAL OMBUDSMAN SERVICE, South Quay Plaza, 183 Marsh Wall, London E14 9SR **Helpline** 0800-023 4567 **T** 020-7964 1000 **E** complaint.info@financial-ombudsman.org.uk **W** www.financial-ombudsman.org.uk
Chief Executive and Chief Ombudsman, Natalie Ceeney, CBE
Deputy Chief Ombudsman, Tony Boorman

PENSIONS OMBUDSMAN, 11 Belgrave Road, London SW1V 1RB **T** 020-7630 2200 **E** enquiries@pensions-ombudsman.org.uk **W** www.pensions-ombudsman.org.uk
Pensions Ombudsman, Tony King
Deputy Pensions Ombudsman, Jane Irvine

PANEL ON TAKEOVERS AND MERGERS

The Panel on Takeovers and Mergers is an independent body, established in 1968, whose main functions are to issue and administer the City code and to ensure equality of treatment and opportunity for all shareholders in takeover bids and mergers. The panel's statutory functions are set out in the Companies Act 2006.

The panel comprises up to 35 members drawn from major financial and business institutions. The chair, deputy chair and up to 20 other members are nominated by the panel's own nomination committee. The remaining members are nominated by professional bodies representing the banking, insurance, investment, pension and accountancy industries and the CBI.

PANEL ON TAKEOVERS AND MERGERS, 10 Paternoster Square, London EC4M 7DY **T** 020-7382 9026 **W** www.thetakeoverpanel.org.uk
Chair, Sir Gordon Langley

NATIONAL SAVINGS AND INVESTMENTS

NS&I (National Savings and Investments) is an executive agency of HM Treasury and one of the UK's largest financial providers, with almost 25 million customers and over £100bn invested. NS&I offers savings and investment products to personal savers and investors and the money is used to manage the national debt. When people invest in NS&I they are lending money to the government which pays them interest or prizes in return. All products are financially secure because they are guaranteed by HM Treasury.

TAX-FREE PRODUCTS

SAVINGS CERTIFICATES

Index-linked Saving Certificates

Otherwise known as inflation-beating savings, index-linked saving certificates are fixed rate investments that pay tax-free returns guaranteed to be above inflation. They are sold in limited issues with a minimum and maximum investment.

Fixed Interest Saving Certificates

Fixed interest saving certificates are fixed rate investments that pay tax-free returns. They are sold in limited issues with a minimum and maximum investment.

PREMIUM BONDS

Introduced in 1956, premium bonds enable savers to enter a regular draw for tax-free prizes, while retaining the right to get their money back. A sum equivalent to interest on each bond is put into a prize fund and distributed by monthly prize draws. The prizes are drawn by ERNIE (electronic random number indicator equipment) and are free of all UK income tax and capital gains tax. A £1m jackpot is drawn each month in addition to other tax-free prizes ranging in value from £25 to £100,000.

Bonds are in units of £1, with a minimum purchase of £100, up to a maximum holding limit of £30,000 per person. Bonds become eligible for prizes once they have been held for one clear calendar month following the month of purchase. Each £1 unit can win only one prize per draw, but it will be awarded the highest for which it is drawn. Bonds remain eligible for prizes until they are repaid.

The scheme offers a facility to reinvest prize wins automatically. Upon completion of an automatic prize reinvestment mandate, holders receive new bonds which are immediately eligible for future prize draws. Bonds can only be held in the name of an individual and not by organisations.

As at April 2013, over 270 million prizes totalling more than £14bn had been distributed since the first prize draw in 1957.

CHILDREN'S BONDS

Children's bonus bonds were introduced in 1991. In September 2012 changes were made to the product; including a change in name to Children's Bonds, which reflects the way interest is paid. Any amount between £25 and £3,000 can be invested and interest is added at a fixed rate each year for five years. The minimum holding is £25 and the maximum holding is £3,000 per child per issue. They can be bought by parents, guardians and grandparents (including great grandparents) for any child under 16, but the investment must be managed by a parent or guardian. All returns are totally exempt from UK income tax.

OTHER PRODUCTS

GUARANTEED EQUITY BONDS

Guaranteed equity bonds are five-year investments where the returns are linked to the performance of the FTSE-100 index with a guarantee that the original capital invested will be returned even if the FTSE-100 index falls over the five years. They are sold in limited issues with a minimum investment of £1,000 and a maximum of £1m. The returns are subject to income tax on maturity, unless they are held in a self-invested pension plan (SIPP).

SAVINGS AND INVESTMENT ACCOUNTS

The direct saver account was launched in March 2010. Customers are able to invest between £1 and £2m per person. The account can be managed online or by telephone. Interest is paid without deduction of tax at source.

The investment account is a postal-only account which pays tiered rates of interest. It can be opened with a minimum balance of £20 and has a maximum limit of £1m. The interest is paid without deduction of tax at source.

Since April 1999 NS&I has offered cash individual savings accounts (ISAs). Its Direct ISA, launched in April 2006, can be opened and managed online and by telephone with a minimum investment of £100. Interest for the Direct ISA is calculated daily and is free of tax.

INCOME BONDS

NS&I income bonds were introduced in 1982. They are suitable for those who want to receive regular monthly payments of interest while preserving the full cash value of their capital. The minimum holding for each investment is £500 and the maximum £1m per person. A variable rate of interest is calculated on a day-to-day basis and paid monthly. Interest is taxable but is paid without deduction of tax at source.

GUARANTEED INCOME BONDS

Guaranteed income bonds were introduced in February 2008 and changes were made to the product in September 2012. They are designed for those who want to receive regular monthly payments of interest while preserving the full cash value of their capital. The minimum holding is £500 and the maximum £1m per person, per issue. Joint investors can now combine their allowance to invest up to £2m per issue. A fixed rate of interest is calculated on a day-to-day basis and paid monthly. Interest is taxable and tax is deducted at source. They are sold in limited issues.

GUARANTEED GROWTH BONDS

Guaranteed growth bonds were introduced in February 2008 and changes were made to the product in September 2012. As for Guaranteed income bonds, the minimum holding is £500 and the maximum £1m per person, per issue and joint investors can combine their allowance to invest up to £2m per issue. A fixed rate of interest is calculated on a day-to-day basis and is paid annually on the anniversary of the date of investment. Interest is taxable and tax is deducted at source. They are sold in limited issues.

FURTHER INFORMATION

Further information regarding products and their current availability can be obtained online (W www.nsandi.com) and by telephone (T 0500-007007).

THE NATIONAL DEBT

HISTORY

The early 1700s saw the meteoric rise of the banking and financial markets, with the emerging stock market revolving around government funds. The ability to raise money by means of creating debt through the issue of bills and bonds heralded the beginning of the National Debt.

The war years of 1914–18 saw an increase in the National Debt from £650m at the start of the war to £7,500m by 1919. The Treasury developed new expertise in foreign exchange, currency, credit and price control in order to manage the post-war economy. The slump of the 1930s necessitated the restructuring of the UK economy following the Second World War (the national debt stood at £21bn by its end) and the emphasis was placed on economic planning and financial relations.

The relatively high period of inflation in the 1970s and 1980s led to the rise of the national debt in nominal terms from £36bn in 1972 to £197bn in 1987 and then to £419bn in March 1998. Although in nominal terms the national debt has risen sharply in recent years, as a percentage of GDP, it has decreased dramatically from the end of the Second World War when it stood at 250 per cent of GDP (for current figures, *see* table below).

THE UK DEBT MANAGEMENT OFFICE

The decision in 1997 to transfer monetary policy to the Bank of England, while the Treasury retained control of fiscal policy, led to the creation of the UK Debt Management Office (DMO) as an executive agency of HM Treasury in April 1998. Initially the DMO was responsible only for the management of government marketable debt and for issuing gilts. In April 2000 responsibility for exchequer cash management and for issuing Treasury bills (short-dated securities with maturities of less than one year) was transferred from the Bank of England to the DMO. The national debt also includes the (non-marketable) liabilities of National Savings and Investments and other public sector and foreign currency debt.

In 2002 the operations of the long-standing statutory functions of the Public Works Loan Board, which lends capital to local authorities, and the Commissioners for the Reduction of the National Debt, which manages the investment portfolios of certain public funds, were integrated within the DMO (*see also* Government Departments).

UK PUBLIC SECTOR NET DEBT

	£ billion	*per cent of GDP*
2011–12 (outturn)	1,104	71.8
2011–12 (forecast)	1,189	75.9
2012–13 (forecast)	1,286	79.2

Source: HM Treasury: *Budget 2013* (Crown copyright)

THE LONDON STOCK EXCHANGE

The London Stock Exchange Group (LSEG) serves the needs of companies by providing facilities for raising capital. It also operates marketplaces for members to trade financial instruments including equities, bonds and derivatives, on behalf of investors and institutions such as pension funds and insurers.

LSEG's key subsidiary companies are London Stock Exchange, Borsa Italiana, Turquoise (a trading platform for European equities), FTSE (a global index provider), MillenniumIT (a provider of exchange technology) and MTS (an electronic platform for the trading of European government and corporate bonds).

HISTORY

The London Stock Exchange is one of the world's oldest stock exchanges, dating back more than 300 years when it began in the coffee houses of 17th-century London. It was formally established as a membership organisation in 1801.

RECENT DEVELOPMENTS

'BIG BANG'

In 1986 a package of reforms which are now known as 'Big Bang' transformed the London Stock Exchange and the City of London, liberalising the way in which banks and stock-broking firms operated and facilitating greater foreign investment. London Stock Exchange ceased granting voting rights to individual members and became a private company. Big Bang also saw the start of a move towards fully electronic trading and the closure of the trading floor.

INTRODUCTION OF SETS

In October 1997, the Exchange introduced SETS, its electronic order book. The system enhanced the efficiency and transparency of trading on the Exchange, allowing trades to be executed automatically and anonymously rather than negotiated by telephone.

DEMUTUALISATION AND LISTING

The London Stock Exchange demutualised in 2000 and listed on its own main market in 2001.

MERGER WITH BORSA ITALIANA

In October 2007 the London Stock Exchange merged with the Italian stock exchange, Borsa Italiana, creating London Stock Exchange Group (LSEG).

DIVERSIFICATION

Since 2009 LSEG has diversified its business beyond the listing and trading of UK and Italian equities:

- In 2009 LSEG purchased Sri Lankan technology company MillenniumIT which provides technology to stock exchanges, brokerages and regulators around the world. It also supplies the trading technology to LSEG's own markets
- In 2010 LSEG acquired a majority stake in Turquoise, a platform facilitating the trading of stocks listed in 19 European countries and the USA
- In 2011 LSEG became the owner of FTSE, the international business which creates and manages over 200,000 financial indices

UK EQUITY MARKETS

LSEG offers a range of listing options for companies, according to their size, history and requirements:

- The Main Market has the highest standards of regulation and disclosure obligations and is overseen by the UK Listing Authority (UKLA), a division of the Financial Conduct Authority (FCA). A Main Market listing enables established companies to raise capital, widen their investor base and have their shares traded alongside global peers. They are also eligible for inclusion in key indices, such as the FTSE 100 and the FTSE 250
- The Alternative Investment Market (AIM), established in June 1995, is specially designed to meet the needs of small and growing companies. It enables them to raise capital and broaden their investor base in a more flexible regulatory environment, while still being traded on an internationally recognised market. AIM companies retain an experienced Nominated Adviser (or 'Nomad') firm, which is responsible for ensuring the company's suitability for the market
- The Professional Securities Market (PSM), established in July 2005, allows companies to target professional investors only, on a market that offers greater flexibility in accounting standards
- The Specialist Fund Market (SFM), established in November 2007, is a market for highly specialised investment entities, such as hedge funds or private equity funds, that wish to target institutional investors only

As at April 2013 there were 2,465 companies quoted on LSEG's UK markets, with a combined value of £4.19 trillion: 1,318 on the UK Main Market, 1,092 on the AIM, 41 on the PSM and 14 entities on the SFM.

PLACEHOLDER

LONDON STOCK EXCHANGE, 10 Paternoster Square, London EC4M 7LS T 020-7797 1000
W www.londonstockexchangegroup.com
Chair, Chris Gibson-Smith, PHD
Chief Executive, Xavier Rolet

ECONOMIC STATISTICS

THE BUDGET (MARCH 2013)

GOVERNMENT EXPENDITURE

DEPARTMENTAL EXPENDITURE LIMITS *£ billion*

	Estimate 2012–13	*Projection 2013–14*	*Projection 2014–15*
Resource DEL			
Education	51.4	53.1	53.8
NHS (Health)	102.9	106.9	109.8
Transport	4.4	4.8	4.4
Business, Innovation and Skills	15.4	14.9	13.8
CLG Communities	1.4	2.0	1.3
CLG Local Government	24.0	23.9	21.7
Home Office	7.9	8.0	7.4
Justice	8.1	7.2	6.8
Law Officers' Departments	0.6	0.6	0.5
Defence	27.1	26.5	24.5
Foreign and Commonwealth Office	2.0	1.8	1.1
International Development	6.1	8.8	8.3
Energy and Climate Change	1.2	1.4	1.1
Environment, Food and Rural Affairs	1.9	1.9	1.7
Culture, Media and Sport	1.9	1.2	1.1
Work and Pensions	7.1	7.6	7.4
Scotland	25.0	25.3	25.3
Wales	13.3	13.5	13.5
Northern Ireland	9.5	9.5	9.5
Chancellor's departments	3.3	3.7	3.5
Cabinet Office	2.1	2.1	2.3
Independent bodies	1.4	1.5	1.4
Reserve	0.0	2.2	2.8
Special reserve	0.0	0.4	1.8
Green investment bank	0.0	1.0	0.0
Adjustment for budget exchange	0.0	(1.7)	(1.2)
Adjustment for DEL/AME switches*	0.0	(6.4)	(6.9)
Allowance for shortfall	(0.3)	(1.2)	(1.0)
TOTAL RESOURCE DEL	317.6	320.7	315.7
Capital DEL			
Education	4.5	4.0	4.6
NHS (Health)	3.7	4.4	4.6
Transport	7.8	8.7	8.9
Business, Innovation and Skills	1.1	1.8	2.1
CLG Communities	2.5	4.2	4.8
CLG Local Government	0.0	0.0	0.0
Home Office	0.4	0.4	0.5
Justice	0.3	0.3	0.3
Law Officers' Departments	0.0	0.0	0.0
Defence	7.4	9.8	9.0
Foreign and Commonwealth Office	0.1	0.1	0.1
International Development	1.7	1.9	2.0
Energy and Climate Change	2.1	2.2	2.2
Environment, Food and Rural Affairs	0.4	0.4	0.5
Culture, Media and Sport	0.3	0.2	0.3
Work and Pensions	0.4	0.4	0.2
Scotland	3.0	2.6	2.9
Wales	1.4	1.3	1.4
Northern Ireland	0.8	0.9	1.0
Chancellor's departments	0.2	0.2	0.1
Cabinet Office	0.3	0.4	0.4
Independent bodies	0.1	0.1	0.1
Reserve	0.0	0.9	1.1
Special reserve	0.0	0.1	0.3
Green investment bank	0.2	0.5	0.0
Adjustment for budget exchange	0.0	(1.1)	(0.4)
4G spectrum receipts	(2.3)	0.0	0.0
Allowance for shortfall	(0.3)	(2.3)	(2.0)
TOTAL CAPITAL DEL	36.1	42.2	44.9
TOTAL DEL	353.7	362.9	360.6

* The adjustment for changes to local government funding through the business rates retention scheme and council tax localisation

Source: HM Treasury – *Budget 2013* (Crown copyright)

TOTAL MANAGED EXPENDITURE *£ billion*

	Estimate 2012–13	*Projection 2013–14*	*Projection 2014–15*
Current Expenditure			
Resource Annually Managed Expenditure (AME)	317.4	334.1	345.1
Resource DELs	317.6	320.7	315.7
Ring-fenced depreciation	22.2	18.1	19.3
Capital Expenditure			
Capital AME	(20.0)	5.0	5.5
Capital DELs	36.1	42.2	44.9
TOTAL MANAGED EXPENDITURE	673.3	720.0	730.4
Total Managed Expenditure (% GDP)	43.6%	45.2%	44.0%

Source: HM Treasury – *Budget 2013* (Crown copyright)

GOVERNMENT RECEIPTS *£ billion*

	Outturn 2011–12	*Forecast 2012–13*	*Forecast 2013–14*
Income tax (gross of tax credits)[1]	152.7	150.5	154.7
Pay as you earn	132.0	130.7	133.7
Self assessment	20.3	20.6	20.3
Tax credits	(4.7)	(3.1)	(2.8)
National insurance contributions (NICs)	101.6	103.8	106.7
Value added tax	98.1	100.7	103.3
Corporation tax	43.1	40.3	39.3
Corporation tax credits	(0.9)	(1.0)	(1.0)
Petroleum revenue tax	2.0	1.7	2.1
Fuel duties	26.8	26.6	26.1
Business rates	24.9	25.7	26.7
Council tax	26.0	26.3	27.4
VAT refunds	14.0	14.0	14.6
Capital gains tax	4.3	3.9	5.1
Inheritance tax	2.9	3.1	3.3
Stamp duty land tax	6.1	6.9	7.7
Stamp taxes on shares	2.8	2.3	2.9
Tobacco duties	9.9	9.6	9.8
Spirits duties	2.9	2.9	2.9
Wine duties	3.4	3.5	3.6
Beer and cider duties	3.8	3.7	3.5

	Outturn 2011–12	Forecast 2012–13	Forecast 2013–14
Air passenger duty	2.6	2.8	2.9
Insurance premium tax	3.0	3.0	3.1
Climate change levy	0.7	0.7	1.5
Other HMRC taxes[2]	5.9	5.9	6.3
Vehicle excise duties	5.9	5.9	5.9
Bank levy	1.8	1.6	2.7
Licence fee receipts	3.1	3.1	3.1
Enviromental levies	0.5	2.0	2.3
Swiss capital tax	0.0	0.0	3.2
EU ETS Auction recipts	0.0	0.3	0.7
Other taxes	6.2	6.7	6.8
Total Taxes	549.5	553.7	574.3
Less own resources contribution to EU	(5.2)	(5.4)	(5.3)
Interest and dividends	5.7	14.8	18.9
Gross operating surplus	23.6	24.2	25.3
Other receipts	(1.0)	(0.6)	(0.9)
CURRENT RECEIPTS	572.6	586.8	612.4
UK oil and gas revenues[3]	11.3	6.5	6.8

[1] Income tax includes PAYE and Self Assessment receipts, and also includes tax on savings income and other income tax

[3] Consists of landfill tax, aggregates levy, betting and gaming duties, and customs duties and levies

[4] Consists of offshore corporation tax and petroleum revenue tax

Source: HM Treasury – *Budget 2013* (Crown copyright)

TRADE

TRADE IN GOODS *£ million*

	Exports	*Imports*	*Balance*
2006	242,899	319,741	(76,842)
2007	219,981	310,516	(90,535)
2008	251,565	345,826	(94,261)
2009	227,727	310,660	(82,933)
2010	265,243	363,828	(98,585)
2011	298,421	398,513	(100,092)
2012	299,457	407,350	(107,893)

Source: ONS (Crown copyright)

BALANCE OF PAYMENTS, 2012

Current Account	*£ million*
Trade in goods and services	
Trade in goods	(107,893)
Trade in services	73,992
Total trade in goods and services	(33,901)
Income	
Compensation of employees	(148)
Investment income	(2,106)
Total income	(2,254)
Total current transfers	(23,055)
TOTAL (CURRENT BALANCE)	(59,210)

Source: ONS (Crown copyright)

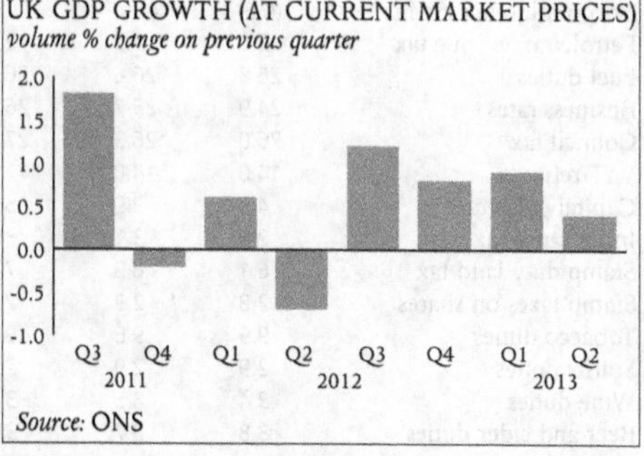

UK EMPLOYMENT

DISTRIBUTION OF THE WORKFORCE

	Dec 2011	*Dec 2012*
Workforce jobs	31,696,000	32,087,000
HM forces	190,000	179,000
Self-employment jobs	4,038,000	4,131,000
Employees jobs	27,446,000	27,757,000
Government-supported trainees	22,000	19,000

Source: ONS – *Labour Market Statistics 2013* (Crown copyright)

EMPLOYED AND UNEMPLOYED BY AGE AND GENDER *thousands*

	Apr–Jun 2012		*Apr–Jun 2013*	
Age	*Male*	*Female*	*Male*	*Female*
EMPLOYED				
16–17	164	188	142	176
18–24	1,723	1,615	1,676	1,589
25–34	3,701	2,960	3,807	3,111
35–49	5,689	5,011	5,595	4,983
50–64	3,996	3,506	4,072	3.617
65+	573	358	622	388
All aged 16+	15,838	13,637	15,914	13,863
UNEMPLOYED				
16–17	103	100	103	92
18–24	505	304	463	314
25–34	295	260	311	217
35–49	309	285	299	290
50–64	241	143	246	152
65+	12	–	22	–
All aged 16+	1,464	1,099	1,445	1,070

Source: ONS – *Labour Market Statistics 2013* (Crown copyright)

DURATION OF UNEMPLOYMENT, APR–JUN 2013 *thousands*

All unemployed	2,514
Duration of unemployment	
Less than 6 months	1,177
6 months–1 year	428
1 year +	909
1 year + *as percentage of total*	36.2

Source: ONS – *Labour Market Statistics 2013* (Crown copyright)

MEDIAN EARNINGS, 2012

	All	*Male*	*Female*
Median gross annual earnings *(£, thousands)*	26.5	28.7	23.1
Median gross weekly earnings *(£)*	405.00	497.60	319.00
Median hourly earnings, excluding overtime *(£)*	11.21	12.50	10.04

Source: ONS – *Annual Survey of Hours and Earnings 2012* (Crown copyright)

LABOUR STOPPAGES BY DURATION, 2012

Under 5 days	111
5–10 days	13
11–20 days	4
21–30 days	3
31–50 days	0
50+ days	0
All stoppages	131

Source: ONS (Crown copyright)

TRADE UNIONS

Year	*No. of unions*	*Total membership*
2008–9	193	7,627,693
2009–10	185	7,656,156
2010–11	176	7,328,905
2011–12	172	7,261,210
2012–13	166	7,197,415

Source: Annual Report of the Certification Officer 2012–13 (Crown copyright)

COST OF LIVING AND INFLATION RATES

The first cost of living index to be calculated took July 1914 as 100 and was based on the pattern of expenditure of working-class families in 1914. The cost of living index was superseded in 1947 by the general index of retail prices (RPI), although the older term is still popularly applied.

The Harmonised Index of Consumer Prices (HICP) was introduced in 1997 to enable comparisons within the European Union using an agreed methodology. In 2003 the National Statistician renamed the HICP as the Consumer Prices Index (CPI) to reflect its role as the main target measure of inflation for macroeconomic purposes. The RPI and indices based on it continue to be published alongside the CPI. Some pensions and index-linked gilts continue to be calculated with reference to RPI or its derivatives.

CPI AND RPI

The CPI and RPI measure the changes month by month in the average level of prices of goods and services purchased by households in the UK. The indices are compiled using a selection of around 700 goods and services, and the prices charged for these items are collected at regular intervals at about 150 locations throughout the country. The Office for National Statistics (ONS) reviews the components of the indices once every year to reflect changes in consumer preferences and the establishment of new products. The table below shows changes made by the ONS to the CPI 'shopping basket' in 2013.

CPI excludes a number of items that are included in RPI, mainly related to housing, such as council tax, and a range of owner-occupier housing costs, such as mortgage payments. The CPI covers all private households, whereas RPI excludes the top 4 per cent by income and pensioner households who derive at least three-quarters of their income from state benefits. The two indices use different methodologies to combine the prices of goods and services, which means that since 1996 the CPI inflation measure is less than the RPI inflation measure.

INFLATION RATE

The 12-monthly percentage change in the 'all items' index of the RPI or CPI is referred to as the rate of inflation. As the most familiar measure of inflation, RPI is often referred to as the 'headline rate of inflation'. CPI is the main measure of inflation for macroeconomic purposes and forms the basis for the government's inflation target, which is currently 2 per cent. The percentage change in prices between any two months/years can be obtained using this formula:

$$\frac{\text{Later date RPI/CPI} - \text{Earlier date RPI/CPI}}{\text{Earlier date RPI/CPI}} \times 100$$

eg to find the CPI rate of inflation for 2006, using the annual averages for 2005 and 2006:

$$\frac{102.3 - 100.0}{100.0} \times 100 = 2.3$$

From 14 February 2006 the reference year for CPI was re-based to 2005=100 to improve price comparison clarity across the EU. None of the underlying data, from which the re-referenced series was calculated, was revised. Historical rates of change (such as annual inflation figures), calculated from the re-based rounded index levels, were revised due to the effect of rounding. The CPI rate of inflation figure given in the table below may differ by plus or minus 0.1 percentage

CHANGES TO THE 'SHOPPING BASKET' OF GOODS AND SERVICES IN 2013

The table below shows changes to the CPI* basket of goods and services made by the ONS in 2013 in order to reflect changes in consumer preferences and the establishment of new products.

Goods and services group	*Removed items*	*New items*
Alcoholic beverages	–	white rum
Audio-visual equipment etc	freeview box	digital TV recorder/receiver
Books and newspapers	–	eBooks
Catering services	bottle of champagne; pub filled-roll/sandwich (cold); staff canteen desert/pudding	pub roll or sandwich (hot or cold)
Clothing	–	men's t-shirt
Food	butter (home produced); butter (imported); round lettuce	block butter; blueberries; continental deli-type meat; spreadable butter; vegetable stir fry
Furniture and Furnishings	–	kitchen wall unit
Maintenance of dwelling	pair of basin taps; gas service charge	–
Medical products etc	soft contact lenses (per pair)	daily disposable soft lenses pack (30 pairs)
Non-alcoholic beverages	–	hot chocolate drink
Recreational items etc	computer game with accessory; gas BBQ	BBQ charcoal (not disposable); electronic educational toy

* RPI goods and services are grouped together under different classifications

points from the figure calculated by the above equation. The change of reference period and revision due to rounding does not apply to the RPI which remains unchanged.

The RPI and CPI figures are published on either the second or third Tuesday of each month in an indices bulletin on the ONS website (W www.ons.gov.uk).

PURCHASING POWER OF THE POUND

Changes in the internal purchasing power of the pound may be defined as the 'inverse' of changes in the level of prices: when prices go up, the amount which can be purchased with a given sum of money goes down. To find the purchasing power of the pound in one month or year, given that it was 100p in a previous month or year, the calculation would be:

$$100\text{p} \times \frac{\text{Earlier month/year RPI}}{\text{Later month/year RPI}}$$

Thus, if the purchasing power of the pound is taken to be 100p in 1975, the comparable purchasing power in 2000 would be:

$$100\text{p} \times \frac{34.2}{170.3} = 20.1\text{p}$$

For longer term comparisons, it has been the practice to use an index which has been constructed by linking together the RPI for the period 1962 to date; an index derived from the consumers' expenditure deflator for the period from 1938 to 1962; and the pre-war 'cost of living' index for the period 1914 to 1938. This long-term index enables the internal purchasing power of the pound to be calculated for any year from 1914 onwards. It should be noted that these figures can only be approximate.

	Annual average RPI (1987=100)	*Purchasing power of £ (1998=1.00)*	*Annual average CPI (2005=100)**	*Rate of inflation (RPI/CPI)*
1914	2.8	58.18		
1915	3.5	46.54		
1920	7.0	23.27		
1925	5.0	32.58		
1930	4.5	36.20		
1935	4.0	40.72		
1938	4.4	37.02		
There are no official figures for 1939–45				
1946	7.4	22.01		
1950	9.0	18.10		
1955	11.2	14.54		
1960	12.6	12.93		
1965	14.8	11.00		
1970	18.5	8.80		
1975	34.2	4.76		
1980	66.8	2.44	18.0	
1985	94.6	1.72	6.1	
1990	126.1	1.29	71.5	9.5/7.0
1995	149.1	1.09	86.0	3.5/2.6
1998	162.9	1.00	91.1	3.4/1.6
2000	170.3	0.96	93.1	3.0/0.8
2005	192.0	0.85	100.0	2.8/2.1
2006	198.1	0.82	102.3	3.2/2.3
2007	206.6	0.79	104.7	4.3/2.3
2008	214.8	0.76	108.5	4.0/3.6
2009	213.7	0.76	110.8	–0.5/2.2
2010	223.6	0.73	114.5	4.6/3.3
2011	235.2	0.69	119.6	5.2/4.5
2012	242.7	0.67	123.0	3.2/2.8

* In accordance with an EU Commission regulation all published CPI figures were re-based to 2005=100 with effect from 14 February 2006, replacing the 1996=100 series

INSURANCE

AUTHORISATION AND REGULATION OF INSURANCE COMPANIES

Under the Financial Services and Markets Act 2000, the Financial Services Authority (FSA) was the authorising, enforcement, supervisory and rule-making body of insurers. Since 2005, this included insurance brokers and intermediaries.

The FSA's role was to ensure that firms to which it granted authorisation satisfied the necessary financial criteria, that the senior management of the company were 'fit and proper persons' and that unauthorised firms were not permitted to trade. In June 2010 the government announced its intention to replace the FSA with two successor bodies. In April 2013, under the Financial Services Act (2012), the prudential supervision of banks and insurers moved to a new operationally independent subsidiary of the Bank of England: the Prudential Regulation Authority (PRA). The FSA was renamed the Financial Conduct Authority (FCA) and now focuses on consumer protection and markets oversight. The government also established a new committee of the Bank of England with responsibility for delivering financial stability: the Financial Policy Committee (FPC). All life insurers, general insurers, reinsurers, insurance and reinsurance brokers, financial advisers and composite firms are statutorily regulated. *See also* Financial Services Regulation.

Firms wishing to effect or carry out contracts of insurance must apply to the PRA for authorisation to do so. The PRA assesses applicant insurers from a prudential perspective, using the same framework that is employed for supervision of existing insurers. The FCA assesses applicants from a conduct perspective. Although the PRA manages the authorisation process, an insurer will be granted authorisation only where both the FCA and the PRA are satisfied that an insurer meets the relevant requirements.

At the end of 2011 there were over 1,300 insurance organisations and friendly societies with authorisation from the FSA to transact one or more classes of insurance business in the UK. However, the single European insurance market, established in 1994, gave insurers authorised in any other European Union country automatic UK authorisation without further formality. This means a potential market of over 5,000 insurers.

COMPLAINTS

Disputes between consumers and financial businesses can be referred to the Financial Ombudsman Service (FOS). Consumers with a complaint about any form of money matter including insurance, mortgages, savings and credit must firstly take the matter to the highest level within the company. Thereafter, if it remains unresolved and it involves an amount below £150,000 (£100,000 for complaints received before 1 January 2012), they can refer, free of charge, to the FOS, which examines the facts of a complaint and delivers a decision binding on the provider (but not the consumer). Small businesses with a turnover of up to €2m (£1.7m) and fewer than ten employees also have access to the scheme. In 2011 the FOS handled around 1 million enquiries and around 250,000 complaints regarding financial services companies. *See also* Financial Services Regulation.

ASSOCIATION OF BRITISH INSURERS

Over 90 per cent of the domestic business of UK insurance companies is transacted by the 300 members of the Association of British Insurers (ABI). ABI is a trade association which protects and promotes the interests of all its insurance company members. Only insurers authorised in the EU are eligible for membership. Brokers, intermediaries, financial advisers and claims handlers may not join ABI but may have their own trade associations.

ASSOCIATION OF BRITISH INSURERS (ABI),
51 Gresham Street, London EC2V 7HQ
T 020-7600 3333 W www.abi.org.uk
Chair, Tidjane Thiam
Director-General, Otto Thoresen

BALANCE OF PAYMENTS

The financial services industry contributes 9.6 per cent to the UK's gross domestic product (GDP). In 2011 insurance sector net exports totalled £8.3bn, a 10 per cent decrease on 2010.

WORLDWIDE MARKET

The UK insurance industry is the largest in Europe and currently the third largest in the world behind the USA and Japan. China has the fastest growing insurance market and is expected to become the third largest market by 2015.

Market	*Premium Income ($bn)*	*Percentage of total*
USA	1,166	26.8
Japan	557	12.8
UK	310	7.1

TAKEOVERS AND MERGERS

Widespread concerns regarding global economies and uncertainty over regulatory and economic environments meant that the prolonged period of stagnation in insurance mergers and acquisitions continued during 2012 despite optimistic predictions in 2011. The small amount of activity recorded showed that there had been a 20 per cent decrease in the number of deals, with the majority of transactions involving investments in emerging markets and smaller acquisitions of additional distribution channels and niche business lines, rather than large takeovers.

The predicted sale of Direct Line Insurance by Royal Bank of Scotland did not materialise, although the expected sale of Groupama was finally completed in November 2012, when it was taken over by Ageas UK. Among the deals recorded was the merger by parent company Covéa (under the Covéa brand) of their three UK operations, Gateway, MMA and Provident Insurance, which was completed in October 2012.

INDUSTRY ISSUES

Since 2002 the European Commission (EC) has been formulating plans for Solvency II which aims to establish an EU-wide set of requirements for capital adequacy and management standards, modernising and consolidating a long list of EU directives known as Solvency I which was established in the 1970s. The Solvency II directive was originally scheduled to come into force in 2012, but it has been postponed several times. The latest suggested date is 2014, although this is far from certain, and a further delay to January 2015 or even 2016 has already been mooted. Implementation has also proved costly, with a survey by Ernst and Young suggesting that some insurers have already invested up to $250m on Solvency II compliance.

GENERAL INSURANCE

Damage caused by extremes of weather continued to cause problems for general insurers during 2012. The year began with a period of drought and fears of a recurrence of the subsidence problems of the late 1970s. This had markedly changed by June, the wettest on record, which saw £500m worth of storm and flood related claims in that one month alone. Further serious flooding followed in November.

Throughout the year negotiations continued between insurers and the government on the continuation of an agreement to offer flooding cover to every UK home. The proposed solution was for a flood insurance fund 'Flood Re', funded through a levy on insurers, to continue to offer cover at affordable rates. The existing arrangement, which began in 1953 and was due to expire at the end of June 2013, was extended for one month to allow more time for negotiations. On 27 June 2013 the government and the Association of British Insurers agreed a Memorandum of Understanding on Flood Re, following the necessary legislation, it is expected the scheme will be operational in 2015. In the meantime, insurers have agreed to continue voluntarily under the existing agreement.

The focus for motor insurers was split between reducing claims for whiplash and improving the accident record for young drivers. In 2011, 570,000 people claimed to have suffered a whiplash injury and the resulting insurance payouts amounted to £2bn. It is estimated that £90 of an average motor insurance premium is now used to pay whiplash claims. Claims for whiplash increased by 33 per cent at the same time as the number of reported accidents decreased by 16 per cent. In February 2012 the prime minister hosted a meeting at Downing Street to discuss ways in which this sort of claim could be reduced.

Historically, motor insurance prices for younger drivers have been very high. This is due to younger drivers being much more frequently involved in accidents, with 40 per cent of 17-year-olds having an accident within the first six months after passing their driving test. Insurers and the government are working together to improve the driving test and reduce the 5,419 deaths from motor accidents that involved at least one driver aged under 24.

Following a ruling by the European Court of Justice in March 2011, it has been illegal since 21 December 2012 for insurers to take a person's gender into account when calculating premiums and benefits. This has meant, for example, that younger women drivers have seen an increase in their premiums, despite the fact that they have a lower accident rate than their male peers.

Overall, most classes of general insurance business recorded small decreases in claims costs with the exception of weather damage related claims, which saw an increase of 70 per cent.

LONDON INSURANCE MARKET

The London Insurance Market is a unique wholesale marketplace and a distinct, separate sector of the UK insurance and reinsurance industry. It is the world's leading market for internationally traded insurance and reinsurance, its business comprising mainly overseas non-life large and high-exposure risks. It is the only place in the world where all 20 of the world's largest insurance companies have an office. The market is centred on the square mile of the City of London, which provides the required financial, banking, legal and other support services. Around 51 per cent of London market business is transacted at Lloyd's of London, the remainder through insurance companies and protection and indemnity clubs. In 2011 the market had a written gross premium income of over £45bn. Around 200 Lloyd's brokers service the market.

The trade association for the international insurers and reinsurers writing primarily non-marine insurance and all classes of reinsurance business in the London market is the International Underwriting Association (IUA).

INTERNATIONAL UNDERWRITING ASSOCIATION,
London Underwriting Centre, 3 Minster Court, Mincing Lane, London EC3R 7DD T 020-7617 4444 W www.iua.co.uk
Chair, Malcolm Newman
Chief Executive, Dave Matcham

BRITISH INSURANCE COMPANIES

The following insurance company figures refer to members and certain non-members of the ABI.

CLAIMS STATISTICS *(£m)*

	2008	*2009*	*2010*	*2011*	*2012*
Theft	531	555	530	603	540
Fire	1,273	1,205	1,073	1,156	977
Weather	904	662	706	618	1,046
Domestic subsidence	137	175	172	158	109
Business interruption	193	128	179	159	153
Total	3,038	2,725	2,660	2,694	2,825

WORLDWIDE GENERAL BUSINESS TRADING RESULTS *(£m)*

	2010	*2011*
Net written premiums	46,379	47,211
Underwriting results	(1,164)	797
Investment income	4,630	3,334
Overall trading profit	3,467	4,131
Profit as percentage of premium income	8.0	8.7

NET PREMIUM INCOME BY SECTOR 2011 *(£m)*

	UK	*Overseas*
Motor	11,658	5,025
Non-motor	19,325	8,176
Marine, aviation and transport	1,330	446
Reinsurance	882	287
Total general business	33,195	13,934
Ordinary long-term	117,157	27,091
TOTAL	150,352	41,025

LLOYD'S OF LONDON

Lloyd's of London is an international market for almost all types of general insurance. Lloyd's currently has a capacity to accept insurance premiums of around £23.7bn. Much of this business comes from outside the UK and makes a valuable contribution to the balance of payments.

A policy is underwritten at Lloyd's by a mixture of private and corporate members – the latter having been admitted for the first time in 1992. Specialist underwriters accept insurance risks at Lloyd's on behalf of members (referred to as 'Names') grouped in syndicates. There are currently 87 syndicates of varying sizes, each managed by one of the 52 underwriting agents approved by the Council of Lloyd's.

WORLDWIDE GENERAL BUSINESS UNDERWRITING RESULTS *(£m)*

	2010			*2011*		
	UK	*Overseas*	*Total*	*UK*	*Overseas*	*Total*
Motor						
Premiums	10,585	4,844	15,429	11,658	5,025	16,683
Profit (loss)	(1,825)	49	(1,776)	(425)	244	(181)
Percentage of premiums	17.2	1.0	11.5	3.6	4.9	1.1
Non-motor						
Premiums	18,919	8,715	27,634	19,325	8,176	27,501
Profit (loss)	283	207	490	810	(28)	782
Percentage of premiums	1.5	2.4	1.8	4.2	0.3	2.8

Members divide into three categories: corporate organisations, individuals who have no limit to their liability for losses, and those who have an agreed limit (known as NameCos).

Lloyd's is incorporated by an act of parliament (Lloyd's Acts 1871 onwards) and is governed by an 18-person council, made up of six working, six external and six nominated members. The structure immediately below this changed when, in 2002, Lloyd's members voted at an extraordinary general meeting to implement a new franchise system for the market with the aim of improving profitability. The first move was the introduction of a new governance structure, replacing the Lloyd's Market Board and the Lloyd's Regulatory Board with an 11-person Lloyd's Franchise Board. Four main committees report to this board.

The corporation is a non-profit making body chiefly financed by its members' subscriptions. It provides the premises, administrative staff and services enabling Lloyd's underwriting syndicates to conduct their business. It does not, however, assume corporate liability for the risks accepted by its members. Individual members are responsible to the full extent of their personal means for their underwriting affairs unless they have converted to limited liability companies.

Lloyd's syndicates have no direct contact with the public. All business is transacted through insurance brokers accredited by the Corporation of Lloyd's. In addition, non-Lloyd's brokers in the UK, when guaranteed by Lloyd's brokers, are able to deal directly with Lloyd's motor syndicates, a facility that has made the Lloyd's market more accessible to the insuring public.

The FSA has ultimate responsibility for the regulation of the Lloyd's market. However, in situations where Lloyd's internal regulatory and compensation arrangements are more far-reaching – as for example with the Lloyd's Central Fund which safeguards claim payments to policyholders – the regulatory role is delegated to the Council of Lloyd's.

Lloyd's also provides the most comprehensive shipping intelligence service in the world. The shipping and other information received from Lloyd's agents, shipowners, news agencies and other sources throughout the world is collated and distributed to the media as well as to the maritime and commercial sectors in general. *Lloyd's List* is London's oldest daily newspaper and contains news of general commercial interest as well as shipping information. It has been independent of Lloyd's since a management buy-out in 1992. *Lloyd's Shipping Index,* published weekly, lists some 23,000 ocean-going merchant vessels in alphabetical order and gives the latest known report of each.

DEVELOPMENTS IN 2012

After recording a loss of £513m in 2011, Lloyd's returned to profitability in 2012 with a profit of £2,771m. Total net claims fell from £12.9bn in 2011 to £10.1bn in 2012.

The most costly event of 2012 was Hurricane Sandy, which began in the western Carribean and made landfall on the east coast of Canada and the USA. At its height, the hurricane's winds spanned an area 1,000m wide and resulted in the deaths of around 250 people, mainly in Haiti. The resulting claims cost Lloyds £1.4bn. Nine out of ten of the largest insurance losses in 2012 occurred in the USA.

The only sector to record an overall loss was motor insurance (losing £42m) although the marine account saw a sharp fall in profit from £89m in 2011 to just £2m in 2012. By contrast, the property and reinsurance accounts both moved into profit.

LLOYD'S OF LONDON, One Lime Street, London EC3M 7HA
T 020-7327 1000 W www.lloyds.com
Chair, John Nelson
Chief Executive, Richard Ward

LLOYD'S MEMBERSHIP

	2011	*2012*
Individual	637	587
Corporate	1,529	1,576

LLOYD'S SEGMENTAL RESULTS 2012 *(£m)*

	Gross premiums written	*Net earned premium*	*Result*
Reinsurance	9,763	6,713	605
Casualty	4,543	3,469	152
Property	5,476	3,963	221
Marine	2,090	1,736	2
Motor	1,155	1,062	(42)
Energy	1,727	1,147	275
Aviation	669	526	170
Life	77	69	(1)
Total from syndicate operations	25,500	18,685	1,382

LIFE AND LONG-TERM INSURANCE AND PENSIONS

In 2012 a great deal of long-term and life insurer's time, money and resources was spent preparing for legal and regulatory changes at the end of the year and the spring of 2013. In addition to ongoing work on Solvency II (*see* Industry Issues), insurers also had to prepare for the introduction of the new regulatory structure which saw the FSA replaced in April 2013 by the Prudential Regulatory Authority, part of the Bank of England, and the Financial Conduct Authority.

One of the FSA's last initiatives was its Retail Distribution Review, which came into force on 31 December 2012. This introduced new standards for consumer advice and professionalism for intermediaries, and banned commission-based remuneration. Intermediaries are now designated as 'independent' (ie they are required to research the whole market for the contract which best suits the client's needs) or 'restricted' (they consider a range of investment products, but not all). All intermediaries are now required to declare their status and must hold a Chartered Insurance Institute diploma or an equivalent qualification.

The immediate effect of the new legislation was that many high street names cut back or withdrew their financial advice services, particularly those with less than £100,000 in investments.

Another major change began in October 2012 with the introduction of auto-enrolment into workplace pensions. Any worker aged 22 or over, working in the UK and earning £8,105 per annum, must be automatically enrolled into an occupational pension by their employer. Initially this legislation only applied to companies with over 120,000 employees, but this threshold will gradually reduce between 2012 and 2018, by which time all workers will be subject to the rule.

Preparations and new office systems were also required to comply with the European Court of Justice ruling banning the use of gender as an underwriting factor. The deadline for compliance was December 2012, and like their general insurance colleagues, life insurers had to change product rating and policy wordings.

Overall, the life and long-term insurance market continued to record disappointing new business figures with total new premium income increasing by 2.5 per cent in nominal terms between 2011 and 2012 – a real term decrease of 0.7 per cent. Single-premium pensions business in 2012 showed a small increase of 3 per cent to £32.1bn, while regular-premium pensions business decreased by 1.4 per cent to £4.3bn.

PAYMENTS TO POLICYHOLDERS *(£m)*

	2010	*2011*
Payments to UK policyholders	151,184	154,927
Payments to overseas policyholders	29,859	21,206
Total	181,043	176,133

WORLDWIDE LONG-TERM PREMIUM INCOME *(£m)*

	2007	*2008*	*2009*	*2010*	*2011*
UK Life Insurance					
Regular Premium	9,131	8,345	7,917	7,449	6,076
Single Premium	40,256	27,599	11,958	11,530	7,216
Total	49,387	35,944	19,875	18,979	13,292
Individual Pensions					
Regular Premium	8,714	9,648	9,629	10,644	10,979
Single Premium	24,368	18,721	15,820	19,414	17,936
Total	33,082	28,369	25,449	30,058	28,915
Other Pensions					
Regular Premium	5,670	5,901	5,695	4,454	3,851
Single Premium	93,020	57,013	63,388	52,449	55,217
Total	98,690	62,914	69,083	56,903	59,068
Other (eg income protection, annuities)	4,220	3,956	4,111	3,734	3,376
TOTAL UK PREMIUM INCOME	185,379	131,183	118,518	109,674	104,651
Overseas Premium Income					
Regular Premium	7,941	10,432	11,934	11,965	13,457
Single Premium	25,866	26,919	29,191	29,885	31,914
Total	33,807	37,351	41,125	41,850	45,371
TOTAL WORLDWIDE PREMIUM INCOME	219,186	168,534	159,643	151,524	150,022

PRIVATE MEDICAL INSURANCE

	2008	*2009*	*2010*	*2011*	*2012*
Number of people covered (thousand)	6,224	5,938	5,841	5,668	5,611
Corporate	4,571	4,384	4,305	4,232	4,210
Personal	1,653	1,554	1,536	1,436	1,401
Gross Earned Premiums (£m)	3,468	3,444	3,614	3,548	3,625
Corporate	1,831	1,838	1,982	1,929	2,010
Personal	1,637	1,606	1,632	1,619	1,615
Gross Claims Incurred (£m)	2,653	2,679	2,858	2,727	2,770

NEW BUSINESS *(£m)*

	2008	*2009*	*2010*	*2011*	*2012*
New regular premiums					
Investment and savings	75	77	57	35	27
Individual protection	858	883	805	762	759
Group protection	290	313	256	254	331
Individual pension	3,363	2,805	3,184	3,472	3,780
Group pension	989	962	910	986	614
Offshore business	19	21	37	32	18
TOTAL REGULAR	5,594	5,061	5,249	5,541	5,529
New single premiums					
Investments and savings	23,769	12,444	10,154	8,975	8,104
Individual protection	1,019	236	225	215	204
Individual pensions	18,389	14,811	15,155	16,047	16,359
Retirement income products	13,916	12,673	13,183	12,498	15,241
Occupational pensions	12,097	10,039	12,802	15,124	17,351
Offshore business	7,777	4,267	6,404	5,927	4,727
TOTAL SINGLE	76,967	54,470	57,923	58,786	61,986

TAXATION

The government raises money to pay for public services such as education, health and the social security system through tax. Each year the Chancellor of the Exchequer's budget sets out how much it will cost to provide these services and how much tax is therefore needed to pay for them. HM Revenue and Customs (HMRC) is the government department that collects it. There are several different types of tax. The varieties that individuals may have to pay include income tax payable on earnings, pensions, state benefits, savings and investments; capital gains tax (CGT) payable on the disposal of certain assets; inheritance tax (IHT) payable on estates upon death and certain lifetime gifts; stamp duty payable when purchasing property and shares; and value added tax (VAT) payable on goods and services, plus certain other duties such as fuel duty on petrol and excise duty on alcohol and tobacco. Government funds are also raised from companies and small businesses through corporation tax.

A feature of the 2013 Budget was the introduction of further measures to clamp down on various schemes and tactics used by individuals and companies to avoid tax, a strategy started in the 2012 Budget. Among these measures, it was announed that a General Anti-Avoidance Rule (GAAR) will be introduced in 2013 that will improve the government's ability to tackle tax avoidance without damaging the competitiveness of the UK as a place to do business.

Responding to an Office of Tax Simplification (OTS) report on small business taxation published in 2012, it was announced in the 2013 Budget that the government was bringing in a radically simpler way for small businesses to calculate their tax. Businesses with receipts of up to £77,000 will be able to work out their income on a cash basis and use simplified expenses rules, rather than always having to follow the rules for larger businesses.

In the drive to simplify the UK tax system, the government will be consulting on options to simplify the administrative process for collecting National Insurance contributions (NICs), including simplifying NICs for the self-employed.

Details of the OTS and its work can be found on the Treasury website (W www.hm-treasury.gov.uk/ots). The OTS welcomes views from individuals and can be contacted via email (E ots@ots.gsi.gov.uk).

HELP AND INFORMATION ON TAXATION

For detailed information on any aspect of taxation individuals may contact their local tax office or enquiry centre. The HMRC website (W www.hmrc.gov.uk) provides wide-ranging information online. All HMRC forms, leaflets and guides are listed on, and can be downloaded from, the website or ordered by telephone. A list of all HMRC telephone helplines and order lines is also on the website. Those most relevant to topics covered in this section on taxation are included at pertinent points throughout. Information on taxation is also available on the government's public information website for individuals and businesses (W www.gov.uk).

INCOME TAX

Income tax is levied on different sorts of income. Not all types of income are taxable, however, and individuals are only taxed on their 'taxable income' above a certain level. Reliefs and allowances can also reduce or, in some cases, cancel out an individual's income tax bill.

An individual's taxable income is assessed each tax year, starting on 6 April and ending on 5 April the following year. The information below relates specifically to the year of assessment 2013–14, ending on 5 April 2014, and has only limited application to earlier years. Changes due to come into operation at a later date are briefly mentioned where information is available. Types of income that are taxable include:

- earnings from employment or self-employment
- most pensions income including state, company and personal pensions
- interest on most savings
- income (dividends) from shares
- income from property
- income received from a trust
- certain state benefits
- an individual's share of any joint income

There are certain sorts of income on which individuals never pay tax. These are ignored altogether when working out how much income tax an individual may need to pay. Types of income that are not taxable include:

- certain state benefits and tax credits such as child benefit, working tax credit, child tax credit, pension credit, attendance allowance, disability living allowance, housing benefit and the first 28 weeks of incapacity benefit
- winter fuel payments
- income from National Savings and Investments savings certificates
- interest, dividends and other income from various tax-free investments, notably individual savings accounts (ISAs)
- premium bond and national lottery prizes

PERSONAL ALLOWANCE

Every individual resident in the UK for tax purposes has a 'personal allowance'. This is the amount of taxable income that an individual can earn or receive each year tax-free. This tax year (2013–14) the basic personal allowance or tax-free amount is £9,440, an increase of £1,335 from the 2012–13 figure of £8,105. Individuals may be entitled to a higher personal allowance if they were born before 5 April 1948. As previously announced, the cash value of these date-of-birth related allowances will now be frozen until they eventually align with the basic personal allowance. The government's goal is to have a single personal allowance for all taxpayers regardless of age.

Income tax is only due on an individual's taxable income that is above his or her tax-free allowance. Husbands and wives are taxed separately, with each entitled to his or her personal allowance. Each spouse may obtain other allowances and reliefs where the required conditions are satisfied.

Up to and including the tax year 2012–13, the amount of an individual's personal allowance depended on their age and income in the tax year. From 2013–14, the amount depends on their date of birth and their total income received from all taxable sources for the tax year. There are three date-of-birth related levels of personal allowance – *see* table below.

If an individual born before 5 April 1948 has an income over the £26,100 'income limit' for age-related allowances but not more than £100,000, their age-related allowance reduces by half the amount (£1 for every £2) he or she has over the £26,100 limit, until the basic rate allowance for those born after 5 April 1948 is reached.

Since April 2010 all three levels of personal allowance have been subject to a single income limit of £100,000, meaning that the personal allowance is reduced for individuals with an 'adjusted net income' (*see* below) over £100,000. Those individuals with an 'adjusted net income' below or equal to the £100,000 limit are entitled to the full amount of personal allowance. However, where an individual's adjusted net income is above the £100,000 limit, their personal allowance is reduced by half the amount (£1 for every £2) they have over that limit, irrespective of their age or date of birth, until their personal allowance is reduced to nil.

'Adjusted net income' is the measure of an individual's income that is used for the calculation of the existing income-related reductions to personal allowances for those born between 6 April 1938 and 5 April 1948 and for those born before 6 April 1938. It is calculated in a series of steps. The starting point is 'net income', which is the total of the individual's income subject to income tax less specified deductions such as payments made gross to pension schemes. This net income is then reduced by the grossed-up amount of the individual's Gift Aid contributions to charities and the grossed-up amount of the individual's pension contributions that have received tax relief at source. The final step is to add back any relief for payments to trade unions or police organisations deducted in arriving at the individual's net income. The result is the individual's adjusted net income.

It was announced in the 2013 Budget that the basic personal allowance for people born after 5 April 1948 will be increased to £10,000 in 2014–15. It will then increase in line with CPI (Consumer Prices Index) inflation in future years, starting from 2015–16.

LEVELS OF PERSONAL ALLOWANCE FOR 2013–14

Date of birth	*Personal allowance*	*Income limit*
After 5 April 1948	£9,440	£100,000
Between 6 April 1938 and 5 April 1948	£10,500	£26,100
Before 6 April 1938	£10,660	£26,100

BLIND PERSON'S ALLOWANCE

If an individual is registered blind or is unable to perform any work for which eyesight is essential, he or she can claim blind person's allowance, an extra amount of tax-free income added to the personal allowance. In 2013–14 the blind person's allowance is £2,160. It is the same for everyone who can claim it, whatever his or her age or level of income. If an individual is married or in a civil partnership and cannot use all of his or her blind person's allowance because of insufficient income, the unused part of the allowance can be passed to the spouse or civil partner.

Other deductible allowances and reliefs that have the effect of reducing an income tax bill are available to taxpayers in certain circumstances and will be explained in more detail later in this section.

CALCULATING INCOME TAX DUE

Individuals' liability to pay income tax is determined by establishing their level of taxable income for the year. For married couples and civil partners, income must be allocated between the couple by reference to the individual who is beneficially entitled to that income. Where income arises from jointly held assets, it is normally apportioned equally between the partners. If, however, the beneficial interests in jointly held assets are not equal, in most cases couples can make a special declaration to have income apportioned by reference to the actual interests in that income.

To work out an individual's liability for tax, his or her taxable income must be allocated between three different types: earned income (excluding income from savings and dividends); income from savings; and company dividends from shares and other equity-based investments.

After the tax-free personal allowance plus any deductible allowances and reliefs have been taken into account, the amount of tax an individual pays is calculated using different tax rates and a series of tax bands. The tax band applies to an individual's income after tax allowances and any reliefs have been taken into account. Individuals are not taxed on all of their income.

For the tax year 2013–14, the basic rate of income tax is 20 per cent (20 pence in the pound) and the higher rate is 40 per cent (40 pence in the pound). The additional rate, applied from 2010–11, was reduced from 6 April 2013 from 50 per cent (50 pence in the pound) to 45 per cent (45 pence in the pound).

A 10 per cent starting rate is available for savings income only, with a limit of £2,790 for 2013–14. If an individual's taxable non-savings income is above £2,790, the 10 per cent savings rate is not applicable.

The personal allowance for people born after 5 April 1948 increased by £1,335 to £9,440 for the 2013–14 tax year. The basic rate limit above which tax is payable at the higher rate of 40 per cent has simultaneously decreased by £2,360 to £32,010 in 2013–14 to focus the benefit on basic rate tax payers.

It was announced in the 2013 Budget that for 2014–15 and 2015–16 the increase in the higher rate threshold will be capped at 1 per cent.

The higher rate limit, above which tax is payable at the additional rate of 45 per cent, remains at £150,000 for 2013–14.

INCOME TAX RATES (PER CENT) AND TAX BANDS FOR 2013–14

Band	*Earned income*	*Band*	*Savings*	*Dividends*
£0–£32,010	20%	£0–£2,790*	10%	10%
£32,010+	40%	£2,790–£32,010	20%	10%
£150,000+	45%	£32,010+	40%	32.5%
		£150,000+	45%	37.5%

* If an individual's taxable non-savings income is above £2,790 the 20 per cent tax band applies to savings income from £0–£32,010

The first calculation is applied to earned income which includes income from employment or self-employment, most pension income and rental income plus the value of a wide range of employee fringe benefits such as company cars, living accommodation and private medical insurance (for more information on fringe benefits, *see* later section on payment of income tax). In working out the amount of an individual's net taxable earnings, all expenses incurred 'wholly, exclusively and necessarily' in the performance of his or her work duties, together with the cost of business travel, may be deducted. Fees and subscriptions to certain professional bodies may also be deducted. Redundancy payments and other sums paid on the termination of an employment are assessable income, but the first £30,000 is normally tax-free provided the payment is not linked with the recipient's retirement or performance.

The first £32,010 of taxable income remaining after the tax-free allowance plus any deductible allowances and reliefs have been taken into account, is taxed at the basic rate of 20 per cent. Taxable income between £32,010 and £150,000 is taxed at the higher rate of 40 per cent. Taxable income above £150,000 is taxed at the additional rate of 45 per cent.

Savings and dividends income is added to an individual's other taxable income and taxed last. This means that tax on such sorts of income is based on an individual's highest income tax band.

SAVINGS INCOME

The second calculation is applied to any income from savings received by an individual. The appropriate rate at which it must be taxed is determined by adding income from savings to an individual's other taxable income, excluding dividends.

There is a 10 per cent starting rate for savings income only, with a limit of £2,790. If an individual's taxable non-savings income exceeds this limit, the 10 per cent savings rate is not applicable. Savings income above £2,790 and below the £32,010 basic rate limit is taxable at 20 per cent. Savings income between £32,010 and £150,000 is taxable at 40 per cent. Savings income over £150,000 is taxed at 45 per cent. If savings income falls on both sides of a tax band, the relevant amounts are taxed at the rates for each tax band.

Most savings income, such as interest paid on bank and building society accounts, already has tax at a rate of 20 per cent deducted from it 'at source' – that is, before it is paid out to individuals. This is confirmed by the entry 'net interest' on bank and building society statements.

Higher rate taxpayers whose income is sufficient to pay 40 or 45 per cent tax on their savings income must let their tax office know what savings income they have received so that the extra tax they owe can be collected.

Non-taxpayers – ie individuals, including most children, whose taxable income is less than their tax allowances – can register to have their savings interest paid 'gross' without any tax being deducted from it at source. To do this, they must complete form R85, available at all banks and building societies. Parents or guardians need to fill in this form on behalf of those under 16. For individuals who are unsure whether they qualify as non-taxpayers and, therefore, whether they are able to register to have their savings interest paid gross, HMRC offers an 'R85 checker' on its website (W www.hmrc.gov.uk/calcs/r85/).

Non-taxpayers who have already had tax deducted from their savings interest can claim it back from HMRC by filling in form R40. For help or information about registering to get interest paid tax-free or to claim tax back on savings interest, individuals may visit W www.hmrc.gov.uk/taxon/bank.htm or call a dedicated savings helpline on T 0845-980 0645.

DIVIDEND INCOME

The third and final income tax calculation is on UK dividends, which means income from shares in UK companies and other share-based investments including unit trusts and open-ended investment companies (OEICs).

Dividend tax rates differ from those on savings income. The rate that an individual pays on his or her dividends depends on the amount of his or her overall taxable income (after allowances). Dividend income at or below the £32,010 basic rate tax limit is taxable at 10 per cent, between £32,010 and £150,000 at 32.5 per cent, and above £150,000 at 37.5 per cent.

When dividends are paid, a voucher is sent that shows the dividend paid and the amount of associated 'tax credit'. Companies pay dividends out of profits on which they have already paid or are due to pay tax. The tax credit takes account of this and is available to the shareholder to offset against any income tax that may be due on their dividend income. The dividend paid represents 90 per cent of their dividend income. The remaining 10 per cent is made up of the tax credit. In other words the tax credit represents 10 per cent of the dividend income.

Individuals who pay tax at the basic rate have no tax to pay on their dividend income because the tax liability is 10 per cent – the same amount as the tax credit. Higher rate taxpayers pay a total of 32.5 per cent tax on dividend income above the £32,010 basic rate income tax limit, but because the first 10 per cent of the tax due on their dividend income is already covered by the tax credit, in practice they owe only 22.5 per cent. For the same reason, additional rate taxpayers who pay a total of 37.5 per cent on dividend income above the £150,000 additional rate tax limit, owe only 27.5 per cent in practice.

Non-taxpayers cannot claim the 10 per cent tax credit. This is because income tax has not been deducted from the dividends paid to them. The view is that they have simply been given a 10 per cent credit against any income tax due.

If there is significant change to an individual's savings or other income, whatever his or her current tax bracket, it is the individual's responsibility to contact the relevant tax office immediately, even if he or she does not normally complete a tax return. This enables the tax office to work out whether extra or less tax should be paid.

INDIVIDUAL SAVINGS ACCOUNTS

There is a small selection of savings and investment products that are tax-free. This means that there is no tax to pay on any income generated in the form of interest or dividends, nor on any increase in the value of the capital invested. Their tax-efficient status has been granted by the government in order to give people an incentive to save more. For this reason there are usually limits and restrictions on the amount of money an individual may invest in such savings and investments. Individual savings accounts (ISAs) are the best known among tax-efficient savings and investments. They were introduced in 1999 to replace other similar schemes called PEPs and TESSAs. Individuals can use an ISA to save cash, or invest in stocks and shares.

Changes were made to the ISA rules which took effect from April 2008. These reforms removed the distinction between what were previously known as maxi and mini ISAs and simplified an individual's options.

For the 2013–14 tax year individuals may save up to £11,520 each tax year in an adult ISA and receive all profits free of tax provided that they are UK residents and are over 18 (over 16 for cash ISAs). An ISA must be in an individual's name and cannot be held jointly with another person.

Individuals may invest in two separate ISAs each tax year: a cash ISA and a stocks and shares ISA (an umbrella term covering investments in unit trusts, company shares, bonds, investment-type life insurance and so on). Up to £5,760 of an individual's ISA allowance may be saved in one cash ISA with one provider. The remainder of the £11,520 can be invested in one stocks and shares ISA with either the same or a different provider. Alternatively an individual may open a single stocks and shares ISA and invest the full £11,520 into it. Various non-cash assets can be held in a stocks and shares ISA including unit trusts, company shares, bonds, investment-type life insurance and investment trusts.

The government has announced that annually, over the course of this parliament, the ISA limits will increase in line with the retail prices index (RPI). Each September's RPI figure will be used to set the ISA limits for the following tax year. The limits will be rounded each year to the nearest multiple of £120 to enable savers to plan monthly savings more easily.

ISA savers have the option to transfer some or all of the money they have saved in previous tax years in cash ISAs to their stocks and shares ISA without affecting their annual ISA investment allowance. They may also choose to transfer all the money they have saved to date in a cash ISA in the current tax year to a stocks and shares ISA. However, the rules do not allow the reverse; that is, the transfer of monies saved in a stocks and shares ISA to a cash ISA.

Further details are available via HMRC's savings helpline (T 0845-604 1701).

DEDUCTIBLE ALLOWANCES AND RELIEF

Income taxpayers may be entitled to certain tax-deductible allowances and reliefs as well as their personal allowances. Examples include the married couple's allowance and maintenance payments relief, both of which are explained below. Unlike the tax-free allowances, these are not amounts of income that an individual can receive tax-free but amounts by which their tax bill can be reduced.

MARRIED COUPLE'S ALLOWANCE

A married couple's allowance (MCA) is available to taxpayers who are married or are in a civil partnership only where one or other partner was born before 6 April 1935. Eligible couples can start to claim the MCA from the year of marriage or civil partnership registration.

The MCA is restricted to give relief at a fixed rate of 10 per cent, which means that – unlike the personal allowance – it is not income that can be received without paying tax. Instead, it reduces an individual's tax bill by up to a fixed amount calculated as 10 per cent of the amount of the allowance to which they are entitled.

In 2013–14, the MCA is £7,915 at 10 per cent, worth up to £791.50 off a couple's tax bill. The MCA is made up of two parts. There is a minimum amount (£3,040 in 2013–14) which will always be due. The remaining amount (£4,875 in 2013–14) can be reduced if the husband's income exceeds certain limits.

The husband will normally receive the allowance, but the couple can jointly decide which of them will get the minimum amount of the allowance. Alternatively, they can decide to have the minimum amount of the allowance split equally between them. They must inform their tax office of their decision before the start of the new tax year in which they want the decision to take effect. Once this is done, the change will apply until the couple decides to alter it. The remaining part of the allowance must go to the husband unless he lacks sufficient income to use it.

If an individual does not have enough income to use all his or her share of the MCA, the tax office can transfer the unused part of it to his or her spouse or civil partner.

Like the personal allowance, the MCA can be gradually reduced at the rate of £1 of the allowance for every £2 of income above the income limit (£26,100 in 2013–14). The amount of MCA can only be affected by the husband's income, and it only starts to be affected if his personal allowance has already been reduced back to the basic level for people born after 5 April 1948. The wife's income never affects the amount of MCA. It does not matter whether all or part of the minimum amount of the allowance has been transferred to her. Whatever the level of the husband's income, the MCA can never be reduced below the minimum amount: in 2013–14 this is £3,040 at 10 per cent.

The same system of allowance allocation applies to civil partners based on the income of the highest earner.

MAINTENANCE PAYMENTS RELIEF

An allowance is available to reduce an individual's tax bill for maintenance payments he or she makes to his or her ex-spouse or former civil partner in certain circumstances. To be eligible one or other partner must have been born before 6 April 1935; the couple must be legally separated or divorced; the maintenance payments being made must be under a court order; and the payments must be for the maintenance of an ex spouse or former civil partner (provided he or she is not now remarried or in a new civil partnership) or for children who are under 21. For the tax year 2013–14, this allowance can reduce an individual's tax bill by:

- 10 per cent of £3,040 (maximum £304) – this applies where an individual makes maintenance payments of £3,040 or more a year
- 10 per cent of the amount the individual has actually paid – this applies where an individual makes maintenance payments of less than £3,040 a year

An individual cannot claim a tax reduction for any voluntary payments he or she makes for a child, ex-spouse or former civil partner. To claim maintenance payments relief, individuals should contact their tax office.

CHARITABLE DONATION

A number of charitable donations qualify for tax relief. Individuals can increase the value of regular or one-off charitable gifts of money, however small, by using the Gift Aid scheme that allows charities or community amateur sports clubs (CASCs) to reclaim 20 per cent basic rate tax relief on donations they receive.

The way the scheme works means that if a taxpayer gives £10 using Gift Aid, for example, the donation is worth £12.50 to the charity or CASC.

Individuals who pay 40 per cent higher rate income tax can claim back the difference between the 40 per cent and the 20 per cent basic rate of income tax on the total (gross) value of their donations. For example, a 40 per cent tax payer donates £100. The total value of this donation to the charity or CASC is £125, of which the individual can claim back 20 per cent (£25) for themselves. Similarly, those who pay 50 per cent additional rate income tax can claim back the difference between the 45 per cent and the 20 per cent basic rate on the total (gross) value of their donations. On a £100 donation, this means they can claim back £31.25.

In order to make a Gift Aid donation, individuals need to make a Gift Aid declaration. The charity or CASC will normally ask an individual to complete a simple form. One form can cover every gift made to the same charity or CASC for whatever period chosen, including both gifts made in the past and in the future. In April 2013 the government introduced a new scheme where charities are able to claim a Gift Aid-type tax refund on small, ad-hoc donations up to a total of £5,000 a year per charity, without the need for donors to fill in any forms at all. This means Gift Aid can be claimed on the contents of collecting tins, for example. If a charity collects the full £5,000, it will get £1,250 back.

Individuals can use Gift Aid provided the amount of income tax and/or capital gains tax they have paid in the tax year in which their donations are made is at least equal to the amount of basic rate tax the charity or CASC is reclaiming on their gifts. It is the responsibility of the individual to make sure this is the case. If an individual makes Gift Aid donations and has not paid sufficient tax, they may have to pay the shortfall to HMRC. The Gift Aid scheme is not suitable for non-taxpayers.

Individuals who complete a tax return and are due a tax refund can ask HMRC to treat all or part of it as a Gift Aid donation.

It was announced in the 2013 Budget that the government is looking at options to improve the take-up of Gift Aid on donations through digital channels. It is consulting on a range of options including enabling donors to complete a single Gift Aid declaration to cover all their donations through a specific channel. Any new measure will be introduced in 2014.

For employees or those in receipt of an occupational pension, a tax-efficient way of making regular donations to charities is to use the payroll giving scheme. It allows the donations to be paid from a salary or pension before income tax is deducted. This effectively reduces the cost of giving for donors, which may allow them to give more.

For example, it costs a basic-rate taxpayer only £8 in take-home pay to give £10 to charity from their pre-tax pay. Where a donor pays 40 per cent higher rate tax, that same £10 donation costs the taxpayer £6 and for donors who pay the additional 45 per cent rate tax, it costs £5.50.

Anyone who pays tax through the PAYE system can give to any charity of their choosing in this way, providing their employer or pension provider offers the payroll giving scheme. There is no limit to the amount individuals can donate.

A reduced rate of inheritance tax (IHT) applies where an individual, in their will, leaves 10 per cent or more of their net estate to charity. In such cases the current IHT 40 per cent rate is reduced to 36 per cent. The new rate applies where death occurs on or after 6 April 2012.

Details of tax-efficient charitable giving methods can be found at W www.hmrc.gov.uk/individuals/giving

TAX RELIEF ON PENSION CONTRIBUTIONS

Pensions are long-term investments designed to help ensure that people have enough income in retirement. The government encourages individuals to save towards a pension by offering tax relief on their contributions. Tax relief reduces an individual's tax bill or increases their pension fund.

The way tax relief is given on pension contributions depends on whether an individual pays into a company, public service or personal pension scheme.

For employees who pay into a company or public service pension scheme, most employers take the pension contributions from the employee's pay before deducting tax, which means that the individual – whether they pay income tax at the basic or higher rate – gets full tax relief straight away. Some employers, however, use the same method of paying pension contributions as that used by personal pension scheme payers described below.

Individuals who pay into a personal pension scheme make contributions from their net salary; that is, after tax has been deducted. For each pound that individuals contribute to their pension from net salary, the pension provider claims tax back from the government at the basic rate of 20 per cent and reinvests it on behalf of the individual into the scheme. In practice this means that for every £80 an individual pays into their pension, they receive £100 in their pension fund.

Higher rate taxpayers currently get 40 per cent tax relief on money they put into a pension. On contributions made from net salary, the first 20 per cent is claimed back from HMRC by the pension scheme in the same way as for a lower rate taxpayer. It is then up to individuals to claim back the other 20 per cent from their tax office, either when they fill in their annual tax return or by telephone or letter. In a similar fashion, individuals subject to the 45 per cent additional rate of income tax can get 45 per cent tax relief on their pension contributions.

Most providers of retirement annuities, which are a type of personal pension scheme set up before July 1988, do not offer a 'tax relief at source' scheme whereby they claim back tax at the basic rate, as is the case with more modern personal pensions. In such cases, contributing individuals need to claim the tax relief they are due through their tax return or by telephoning or writing to HMRC.

Non-taxpayers can still pay into a personal pension scheme and benefit from 20 per cent basic rate relief on the first £2,880 a year they contribute. In practice this means that the government tops up their £2,880 contribution to make it £3,600 which is the current universal pension allowance. Such pension contributions may be made on behalf of a non-taxpayer by another individual. An individual may, for example, contribute to a pension on behalf of a husband, wife, civil partner, child or grandchild. Tax relief will be added to their contribution at the basic rate, again on up to £2,880 a year benefiting the recipient, but their own tax bill will not be affected.

In any one tax year, individuals can get tax relief on pension contributions made into any number and type of registered pension schemes of 100 per cent of their annual earnings, irrespective of age, up to a maximum 'annual allowance'. For the tax year 2013–14 the annual allowance is £50,000. Individuals pay tax at 40 per cent on any contributions they make above the annual allowance. Everyone now also has a 'lifetime allowance' (£1.5m for 2013–14) which means taxpayers can save up to a total of £1.5m in their pension fund and still get tax relief at their highest income tax rate on all their contributions.

The government has announced that for the tax year 2014–15 onwards the annual allowance for pensions tax relieved savings will be reduced from £40,000 to £50,000 and the standard lifetime allowance will be reduced from £1.5m to £1.25m. A transitional 'fixed protection' regime will be introduced for those who believe they may be affected by the reduction in the lifetime allowance.

For information on pensions and tax relief visit W www.gov.uk/browse/working. Another useful source of information and advice is The Pensions Advisory Service (TPAS), an independent voluntary organisation grant-aided by the Department for Work and Pensions at W www.pensionsadvisoryservice.org.uk; its Pensions Helpline is on T 0845-601 2923.

PAYMENT OF INCOME TAX

Employees have their income tax deducted from their wages throughout the year by their employer who sends it on to HMRC. Those in receipt of a company pension have their due tax deducted in the same way by their pension provider. This system of collecting income tax is known as 'pay as you earn' (PAYE).

BENEFITS IN KIND

The PAYE system is also used to collect tax on certain fringe benefits or 'benefits in kind' that employees or directors receive from their employer, but are not included in their salary. These include company cars, private medical insurance paid for by the employer or cheap or free loans from the employer. Some fringe benefits are tax-free, including employer-paid contributions into an employee's pension fund, cheap or free canteen meals, works buses, in-house sports facilities, reasonable relocation expenses, provision of a mobile phone and workplace nursery places provided for the children of employees. For taxable fringe benefits, tax is paid on the 'taxable value' of the benefit.

Employers submit returns for individual employees earning at or above the £8,500 per annum threshold (including the value of expenses and benefits) to the tax office on the form P11D, with details of any fringe benefits they have been given. For those earning less than the £8,500 threshold (part-time employees) a P9D form is submitted. Employees should get a copy of this form by 6 July following the end of the tax year and must enter the value of the fringe benefits they have received on their tax return for the relevant year, even if tax has already been paid on them under PAYE. Fringe benefits may be taxed under PAYE by being offset against personal tax allowances in an individual's PAYE code. Otherwise tax will be collected after the end of the tax year by the issue of an assessment on the fringe benefits.

SELF-ASSESSMENT

Individuals who are not on PAYE, notably the self-employed, need to complete a self-assessment tax return each year, in paper form or online at the HMRC website (W www.hmrc.gov.uk), and pay any income tax owed in twice-yearly instalments. Some individuals with more complex tax affairs such as those who earn money from rents or investments above a certain level may also need to fill out a self-assessment return, even if they are on PAYE. HMRC uses the figures supplied on the tax return to work out the individual's tax bill, or they can choose to work it out themselves. It is called 'self-assessment' because individuals are responsible for making sure the details they provide are correct.

Tax returns are usually sent out in early April, following the end of the tax year to which they apply. They may also go out at other times, for example if an individual wants to claim an allowance or repayment or to register for self-assessment for the first time.

Individuals with simple tax affairs may receive a short four-page return. Those with more complex affairs must fill out a full return that has 12 core pages plus extra pages, depending on the sorts of income received.

Central to the self-assessment system is the requirement for individuals to contact their tax office if they do not receive a self-assessment return but think they should or if their financial circumstances change. Individuals have six months from when the tax year ends to report any new income, for example. If an individual becomes self-employed, they have three months after the calendar month in which they began self-employed work to let HMRC know. This can be done by telephoning the helpline number for the newly self-employed on T 0845-915 4515.

TAX RETURN FILING AND PAYMENT DEADLINES

There are also key deadlines for filing (sending in) completed tax returns and paying the tax due. Failure to do so can incur penalties, interest charges and surcharges.

KEY FILING DATES FOR SELF-ASSESSMENT RETURNS

Date	*Why the date is important*
31 Oct*	Deadline for filing paper returns* for tax year ending the previous 5 April
30 Dec	Deadline for online filing where the amount owed for tax year ending the previous 5 April is less than £3,000 and the taxpayer wants HMRC to collect any tax due through their PAYE tax code
31 Jan†	Deadline for online filing of returns for tax year ending the previous 5 April

* Or three months from the date the return was requested if this was after 31 July

† Or three months from the date the return was requested if this was after 31 October

KEY SELF-ASSESSMENT PAYMENT DATES

Date	*What payment is due?*
31 Jan	Deadline for paying the balance of any tax owed – the 'balancing payment' – for the tax year ending the previous 5 April. It is also the date by which a taxpayer must make any first 'payment on account' (advance payment) for the current tax year. For example, on 31 January 2014 a taxpayer may have to pay both the balancing payment for the year 2013–14 and the first payment on account for 2014–15.
31 Jul	Deadline for making a second payment on account for the current tax year

LATE FILING AND PAYMENT PENALTIES

Late filing of tax returns incurs an automatic £100 penalty although individuals may appeal against the penalty if they have a reasonable excuse. For late filing of 2012–13 tax returns the following penalties also apply:

- Over three months late – £10 each day, up to a maximum of £900, in addition to the penalty above
- Over six months late – an additional £300 or 5 per cent of the tax due, whichever is the higher, in addition to the penalty above
- Over 12 months late – a further £300 or 5 per cent of the tax due, whichever is the higher. In serious cases HMRC reserve the right to ask for 100 per cent of the tax due instead. In both instances this is in addition to the penalty above

Late payment of tax owing for 2012–13 incurs the following penalties:

- Over 30 days – 5 per cent of the tax unpaid at that date
- Over six months – an additional 5 per cent of the tax unpaid at that date
- Over 12 months – a further 5 per cent of the tax unpaid at that date

Interest is due on all outstanding amounts, including any unpaid penalties, until payment is received in full.

TAX CREDITS

Child tax credit and working tax credit are paid to qualifying individuals. Although the title of both credits incorporates the word 'tax', neither affects the amount of income tax payable or repayable. Both are forms of social security benefits. *See* Social Welfare.

CAPITAL GAINS TAX

Capital gains tax (CGT) is a tax on the gain or profit that an individual makes when they sell, give away or otherwise dispose of an asset – that is, something they own such as shares, land or buildings. An individual potentially has to pay CGT on gains they make from any disposal of assets during a tax year. There is, however, a tax-free allowance and some additional reliefs that may reduce an individual's CGT bill. The following information relates to the tax year 2013–14 ending on 5 April 2014.

CGT is paid by individuals who are either resident or ordinarily resident in the UK for the tax year, executors or administrators – 'personal representatives' – responsible for a deceased person's financial affairs and trustees of a settlement. Non-residents are not usually liable to CGT unless they carry on a business in the UK through a branch or agency. Special CGT rules may apply to individuals who used to live and work in the UK but have since left the country.

CAPITAL GAINS CHARGEABLE TO CGT

Typically, individuals have made a gain if they sell an asset for more than they paid for it. It is the gain that is taxed, not the amount the individual receives for the asset. For example, a man buys shares for £1,000 and later sells them for £3,000. He has made a gain of £2,000 (£3,000 less £1,000). If someone gives an asset away, the gain will be based on the difference between what the asset was worth when originally acquired compared with its worth at the time of disposal. The same is true when an asset is sold for less than its full worth in order to give away part of the value. For example, a woman buys a property for £120,000 and three years later, when the property's market value has risen to £180,000, she gives it to her son. The son may pay nothing for the property or pay less than its true worth, eg £100,000. Either way, she has made a gain of £60,000 (£180,000 less £120,000).

If an individual disposes of an asset he or she received as a gift, the gain is worked out according to the market value of the asset when it was received. For example, a man gives his sister a painting worth £8,000. She pays nothing for it. Later she sells the painting for £10,000. For CGT purposes, she is treated as making a gain of £2,000 (£10,000 less £8,000). If an individual inherits an asset, the estate of the person who died does not pay CGT at the time. If the inheritor later disposes of the asset, the gain is worked out by looking at the market value at the time of the death. For example, a woman acquires some shares for £5,000 and leaves them to her niece when she dies. No CGT is payable at the time of death when the shares are worth £8,000. Later the niece sells the shares for £10,000. She has made a gain of £2,000 (£10,000 less £8,000).

Individuals may also have to pay CGT if they dispose of part of an asset or exchange one asset for another. Similarly, CGT may be payable if an individual receives a capital sum of money from an asset without disposing of it, for example where he or she receives compensation when an asset is damaged.

Assets that may lead to a CGT charge when they are disposed of include:

- shares in a company
- units in a unit trust
- land and buildings (though not normally an individual's main home – *see* 'disposal of a home' section for details)
- higher value jewellery, paintings, antiques and other personal effects assets used in business such as goodwill

EXEMPT GAINS

Certain kinds of assets do not give rise to a chargeable gain when they are disposed of. Assets exempt from CGT include:

- an individual's private car
- an individual's main home, provided certain conditions are met
- tax-free investments such as assets held in an ISA
- UK government gilts or 'bonds'
- personal belongings including jewellery, paintings, antiques individually worth £6,000 or less
- cash in sterling or foreign currency held for an individual or his/her family's own personal use
- betting, lottery or pools winnings
- personal injury compensation

DISPOSAL OF A HOME: PRIVATE RESIDENCE RELIEF

Individuals do not have to pay CGT when they sell their main home if all the following conditions are met:

- they bought it and made any expenditure on it, primarily for use as their home rather than with a view to making a profit
- the property was their only home throughout the period they owned it (ignoring the last three years of ownership)
- the property was actually used as their home all the time that they owned it and, throughout the period, it was not used for any purpose other than as a home for the individual, his or her family and no more than one lodger
- the garden and area of grounds sold with the property does not exceed 5,000 sq. m (1.24 acres) including the site of the property

Even if all these conditions are not met, individuals may still be entitled to CGT relief when they sell the home. They may, for example, qualify for relief if they lived away from home temporarily while working abroad. Married couples or couples in a civil partnership may have relief from CGT on only one home. There is a special exception, however, where the spouse or partner each had a qualifying home before marriage or civil partnership and both live together in one of these homes after marriage or civil partnership and sell the other. Provided that it is sold within three years of marriage or the civil partnership, they may not have to pay any CGT (subject to the normal rules for this relief). If they sell it after more than three years it may qualify for partial relief. There are special rules on divorce and separation.

Certain other kinds of disposal similarly do not give rise to a chargeable gain. For example, individuals who are married or in a civil partnership and who live together may sell or give assets to their spouse or civil partner without having to pay CGT. Individuals may not, however, give or sell assets cheaply to their children without having to consider CGT. There is no CGT to pay on assets given to a registered charity.

CALCULATING CGT

CGT is worked out for each tax year and is charged on the total of an individual's taxable gains after taking into account certain costs and reliefs that can reduce or defer chargeable gains, allowable losses made on assets to which CGT normally applies and an annual exempt (tax-free) amount that applies to every individual. If the total of an individual's net gains in a tax year is less than the annual exempt amount (AEA), the individual will not have to pay CGT. For the tax year 2013–14 the AEA is £10,900. If an individual's net gains are more than the AEA, they pay CGT on the excess. Should any part of the exemption remain unused, this cannot be carried forward to a future year.

There are certain reliefs available that may eliminate, reduce or defer CGT. Some reliefs are available to many people while others are available only in special circumstances. Some reliefs are given automatically while others are given only if they are claimed. Some of the costs of buying, selling and improving assets may be deducted from total gains when working out an individual's chargeable gain.

RATES OF TAX

The net gains remaining, if any, calculated after subtracting the AEA, deducting costs and taking into account all CGT reliefs, incur liability to capital gains tax. Individuals pay CGT at a rate of 18 per cent on gains up to the unused amount of the basic rate income tax band (if any) and at 28 per cent on gains above that amount. The CGT rate charged to trustees and personal representatives is 28 per cent.

CGT for 2013–14 is due for payment in full on 31 January 2015. If payment is delayed, interest or surcharges may be imposed. A husband and wife or registered civil partners who live together are separately assessed to CGT. Each partner must independently calculate his or her gains and losses with each entitled to the AEA of £10,900 for 2013–14.

VALUATION OF ASSETS

The disposal proceeds – ie the amount received as consideration for the disposal of an asset – are the sum used to establish the gain or loss once certain allowable costs have been deducted. In most cases this is straightforward because the disposal proceeds are the amount actually received for disposing of the asset. This may include cash payable now or in the future and the value of any asset received in exchange for the asset disposed of. However, in certain circumstances, the disposal proceeds may not accurately reflect the value of the asset and the individual may be treated as disposing of an asset for an amount other than the actual amount (if any) that they received. This applies, in particular, where an asset is transferred as a gift or sold for a price known to be below market value. Disposal proceeds in such transactions are deemed to be equal to the market value of the asset at the time it was disposed of rather than the actual amount (if any) received for it.

Market value represents the price that an asset might reasonably be expected to fetch upon sale in the open market. In the case of unquoted shares or securities, it is to be assumed that the hypothetical purchaser in the open market would have available all the information that a prudent prospective purchaser of shares or securities might reasonably require if that person were proposing to purchase them from a willing vendor by private treaty and at arm's length. The market value of unquoted shares or securities will often be established following negotiations with the specialist HMRC Shares and Assets Valuation department. The valuation of land and interests in land in the UK is dealt with by the Valuation Office Agency. Special rules apply to determine the market value of shares quoted on the London Stock Exchange.

ALLOWABLE COSTS

When working out a chargeable gain, once the actual or notional disposal proceeds have been determined, certain allowable costs may be deducted. There is a general rule that no costs that could be taken into account when working out income or losses for income tax purposes may be deducted. Subject to this, allowable costs are:

- acquisition costs – the actual amount spent on acquiring the asset or, in certain circumstances, the equivalent market value
- incidental costs of acquiring the asset such as fees paid for professional advice, valuation costs, stamp duty and advertising costs to find a seller
- enhancement costs – incurred for the purpose of enhancing the value of the asset (not including normal maintenance and repair costs)
- expenditure on defending or establishing a person's rights over the asset
- incidental costs of disposing of the asset such as fees paid for professional advice, valuation costs, stamp duty and advertising costs to find a buyer

If an individual disposes of part of his or her interest in an asset, or part of a holding of shares of the same class in the same company, or part of a holding of units in the same unit trust, he or she can deduct part of the allowable costs of the asset or holding when working out the chargeable gain. Allowable costs may also be reduced by some reliefs.

ENTREPRENEURS' RELIEF

Entrepreneurs' Relief allows individuals in business and some trustees to claim relief on the first £10m of gains made on the disposal of any of the following: all or part of a business; the assets of a business after it has ceased; and shares in a company. The relief is available to taxpayers as individuals if they are in business, for example as a sole trader or as a partner in a trading business, or if they hold shares in their own personal trading company. This relief is not available for companies.

Depending on the type of disposal, certain qualifying conditions need to be met throughout a qualifying one-year period. For example, if an individual is selling all or part of their business, they must have owned the business during a one-year period that ends on the date of the disposal.

Where Entrepreneurs' Relief applies, qualifying gains liable to CGT are charged at 10 per cent. An individual can make claims for this relief on more than one occasion as long as the lifetime total of all their claims does not exceed £10m of gains qualifying for relief.

BUSINESS ASSET ROLL-OVER RELIEF

When certain types of business asset are sold or disposed of and the proceeds reinvested in new qualifying trading assets, business asset roll-over relief makes it possible to 'roll-over' or postpone the payment of any CGT that would normally be due. The gain is deducted from the base cost of the new asset and only becomes chargeable to CGT on the eventual disposal of that replacement asset unless a further roll-over situation then develops. Full relief is available if all the proceeds from the original asset are reinvested in the qualifying replacement asset.

For example, a trader sells a freehold office for £75,000 and makes a gain of £30,000. All of the proceeds are reinvested in a new freehold business premises costing £90,000. The trader can postpone the whole of the £30,000 gain made on the sale of the old office, as all of the proceeds have been reinvested. When the trader eventually sells the new business premises and the CGT bill becomes payable, the cost of the new premises will be treated as £60,000 (£90,000 less the £30,000 gain).

If only part of the proceeds from the disposal of an old asset is reinvested in a new one, it may still be possible to postpone paying tax on part of the gain until the eventual disposal of the new asset.

Relief is only available if the acquisition of the new asset takes place within a period between 12 months before, and 36 months after, the disposal of the old asset. However, HMRC may extend this time limit at their discretion where there is a clear intention to acquire a replacement asset. The most common types of business assets that qualify for roll-over relief are land, buildings occupied and used for the purposes of trade, and fixed plant and machinery. Assets used for the commercial letting of furnished holiday accommodation qualify if certain conditions are satisfied.

GIFTS HOLD-OVER RELIEF

The gift of an asset is treated as a disposal made for a consideration equal to market value, with a corresponding acquisition by the transferee at an identical value. In the case of gifts of business assets made by individuals and a limited range of trustees, a form of hold-over relief may be available. This relief, which must be claimed, in effect enables liability for CGT to be deferred and passed to the person to whom the gift is made. Relief is limited to the transfer of certain assets including the following:

- gifts of assets used for the purposes of a business carried on by the donor or his or her personal company

- gifts of shares in trading companies that are not listed on a stock exchange
- gifts of shares or securities in the donor's personal trading company
- gifts of agricultural land and buildings that would qualify for inheritance tax agricultural property relief
- gifts that are chargeable transfers for inheritance tax purposes
- certain types of gifts that are specifically exempt from inheritance tax

Hold-over relief is automatically due on certain sorts of gifts including gifts to charities and community amateur sports clubs, and gifts of works of art where certain undertakings have been given. There are certain rules to prevent gifts hold-over relief being used for tax-avoidance purposes. For example, restrictions may apply where an individual gifts assets to trustees administering a trust in which the individual retains an interest or the assets transferred comprise a dwelling-house. Subject to these exceptions, the effect of a valid claim for hold-over relief is similar to that following a claim for roll-over relief on the disposal of business assets.

OTHER CGT RELIEFS

There are certain other CGT reliefs available on the disposal of property, shares and business assets. For detailed information on all CGT reliefs and for more general guidance on CGT, see the capital gains tax pages on the HMRC website (W www.hmrc.gov.uk/cgt).

REPORTING AND PAYING CGT

Individuals are responsible for telling HMRC about capital gains on which they have to pay tax. Individuals who receive a self-assessment tax return may report capital gains by filling in the capital gains supplementary pages – the return explains how to obtain these pages if needed.

Individuals who do not normally complete a tax return but who need to report capital gains or losses should contact their local tax office.

There is a time limit for claiming capital losses. The deadline is four years from 31 January after the end of the tax year in which the loss was made.

INHERITANCE TAX

Inheritance tax (IHT) is a tax on the value of a person's estate on death and on certain gifts made by an individual during his or her lifetime, usually payable within six months of death. Broadly speaking, a person's estate is everything he or she owned at the time of death including property, possessions, money and investments, less his or her debts. Not everyone pays IHT. It only applies if the taxable value of an estate is above the current IHT threshold. If an estate, including any assets held in trust and gifts made within seven years of death, is less than the threshold, no IHT will be due.

The nil-rate band for 2013–14 is £325,000 and is frozen at this figure until 2017–18.

A claim can be made to transfer any unused IHT nil-rate band on a person's death to the estate of their surviving spouse or civil partner. This applies where the IHT nil-rate band of the first deceased spouse or civil partner was not fully used in calculating the IHT liability of their estate. When the surviving spouse or civil partner dies, the unused amount may be added to their own nil-rate band (*see* below for details).

IHT used to be something only very wealthy individuals needed to consider. This is no longer the case. The fact that the IHT threshold has not kept pace with house price inflation in recent years means that the estates of some 'ordinary' taxpayers, who would not consider themselves wealthy, are now liable for IHT purely because of the value of their home. However, there are a number of ways that individuals – while still alive – can legally reduce the IHT bill that will apply to their estates on death. Several valuable IHT exemptions are available (explained further below) which allow individuals to pass on assets during their lifetime or in their will without any IHT being due. Detailed information on IHT is available on the HMRC website (W www.hmrc.gov.uk/inheritancetax/index.htm). Further help is also available from the IHT and Probate Helpline (T 0845-302 0900).

DOMICILE

Liability to IHT depends on an individual's domicile at the time of any gift or on death. Domicile is a complex legal concept and what follows explains some of the main issues. An individual is domiciled in the country where he or she has a permanent home. Domicile is different from nationality or residence, and an individual can only have one domicile at any given time.

A 'domicile of origin' is normally acquired from the individual's father on birth, though this may not be the country in which he or she is born. For example, a child born in Germany while his or her father is working there, but whose permanent home is in the UK, will have the UK as his or her domicile of origin. Until a person legally changes his or her domicile, it will be the same as that of the person on whom they are legally dependent.

Individuals can legally acquire a new domicile – a 'domicile of choice' – from the age of 16 by leaving the current country of domicile and settling in another country and providing strong evidence of intention to live there permanently or indefinitely. Women who were married before 1974 acquired their husband's domicile and still retain it until they legally acquire a new domicile.

For IHT purposes, there is a concept of 'deemed domicile'. This means that even if a person is not domiciled in the UK under general law, he or she is treated as domiciled in the UK at the time of a transfer (ie at the time of a lifetime gift or on death) if he or she (a) was domiciled in the UK within the three years immediately before the transfer, or (b) was 'resident' in the UK in at least 17 of the 20 income tax years of assessment ending with the year in which a transfer is made. Where a person is domiciled, or treated as domiciled, in the UK at the time of a gift or on death, the location of assets is immaterial and full liability to IHT arises. A non-UK domiciled individual is also liable to IHT but only on chargeable property in the UK.

The assets of husband and wife and registered civil partners are not merged for IHT purposes, except that the IHT value of assets owned by one spouse or civil partner may be affected if the other also owns similar assets (eg shares in the same company or a share in their jointly owned house). Each spouse or partner is treated as a separate individual entitled to receive the benefit of his or her exemptions, reliefs and rates of tax.

IHT EXEMPTIONS

There are some important exemptions that allow individuals to legally pass assets on to others, both before and after their death – without being subject to IHT.

Exempt Beneficiaries

Assets can be given away to certain people and organisations without any IHT having to be paid. These gifts, which are exempt whether individuals make them during their lifetime or in their will, include gifts to:

- a husband, wife or civil partner, even if the couple is legally separated (but not if they are divorced or the civil partnership has dissolved). Note that gifts to an unmarried partner or a partner with whom the donor has not formed a civil partnership are not exempt

- a 'qualifying' charity established in the EU or another specified country
- some national institutions, including national museums, universities and the National Trust
- UK political parties

Annual Exemption

The first £3,000 of gifts made each tax year by each individual is exempt from IHT. If this exemption is not used, or not wholly used in any year, the balance may be carried forward to the following year only. A couple, therefore, may give away a total of £6,000 per tax year between them or £12,000 if they have not used their previous year's annual exemptions.

Wedding Gifts/Civil Partnership Ceremony Gifts

Some gifts are exempt from IHT because of the type of gift or reason for making it. Wedding or civil partnership ceremony gifts made to either of the couple are exempt from IHT up to certain amounts:

- gifts by a parent, £5,000
- gifts by a grandparent or other relative, £2,500
- gifts by anyone else, £1,000

The gift must be made on or shortly before the date of the wedding or civil partnership ceremony. If the ceremony is called off but the gift is made, this exemption will not apply.

Small Gifts

An individual can make small gifts, up to the value of £250, to any number of people in any one tax year without them being liable for IHT. However, a larger sum such as £500 cannot be given and exemption claimed for the first £250. In addition, this exemption cannot be used with any other exemption when giving to the same person. For example, a parent cannot combine a 'small gifts exemption' with a 'wedding/civil partnership ceremony gift exemption' to give a child £5,250 when he or she gets married or forms a civil partnership. Neither may an individual combine a 'small gifts exemption' with the 'annual exemption' to give someone £3,250. Note that it is possible to use the 'annual exemption' with any other exemption, such as the 'wedding/civil partnership ceremony gift exemption'. For example, if a child marries or forms a civil partnership, the parent can give him or her a total IHT-free gift of £8,000 by combining £5,000 under the wedding/civil partnership gift exemption and £3,000 under the annual exemption.

Normal Expenditure

Any gifts made out of individuals' after-tax income (not capital) are exempt from IHT if they are part of their normal expenditure and do not result in a fall in their standard of living. These can include regular payments to someone, such as an allowance or gifts for Christmas or a birthday and regular premiums paid on a life insurance policy for someone else.

Maintenance Gifts

An individual can make IHT-free maintenance payments to his or her spouse or registered civil partner, ex-spouse or former civil partner, relatives dependent because of old age or infirmity, and children (including adopted children and step-children) who are under 18 or in full-time education.

POTENTIALLY EXEMPT TRANSFERS

If an individual makes a gift to either another individual or certain types of trust and it is not covered by one of the above exemptions, it is known as a 'potentially exempt transfer' (PET). A PET is only free of IHT on two strict conditions: (a) the gift must be made at least seven years before the donor's death. If the donor does not survive seven years after making the gift, it will be liable for IHT and (b) the gift must be made as a true gift with no strings attached (technically known as a 'gift with reservation of benefit'). This means that the donor must give up all rights to the gift and stop benefiting from it in any way.

If a gift is made and the donor does retain some benefit from it then it will still count as part of his or her estate no matter how long he or she lives after making it. For example, a father could make a lifetime gift of his home to his child. However, HMRC would not accept this as a true gift if the father continued to live in the home (unless he paid his child a full commercial rent to do so) because he would be considered to still have a material interest in the gifted home. Its value, therefore, would still be liable for IHT.

In some circumstances a gift with strings attached might give rise to an income tax charge on the donor based on the value of the benefit he or she retains. In this case the donor can choose whether to pay the income tax or have the gift treated as a gift with reservation.

CHARGEABLE TRANSFERS

Any remaining lifetime gifts that are not (potentially or otherwise) exempt transfers are chargeable transfers or 'chargeable gifts', meaning that they incur liability to IHT. Chargeable transfers comprise mainly gifts to or from companies and gifts to particular types of trust. There is an immediate claim for IHT on chargeable gifts, and additional tax may be payable if the donor dies within seven years of making a chargeable gift.

DEATH

Immediately before the time of death an individual is deemed to make a transfer of value. This transfer will comprise the value of assets forming part of the deceased's estate after subtracting most liabilities. Any exempt transfers may be excluded such as transfers for the benefit of a surviving spouse or civil partner, and charities. Death may also trigger three additional liabilities:

- a PET made within the seven years before the death loses its potential status and becomes chargeable to IHT
- the value of gifts made with reservation may incur liability if any benefit was enjoyed within the seven years before the death
- additional tax may become payable for chargeable lifetime transfers made within the seven years before the death

The 'personal representative' (the person nominated to handle the affairs of the deceased person) arranges to value the estate and pay any IHT that is due. One or more personal representatives can be nominated in a person's will, in which case they are known as the 'executors'. If a person dies without leaving a will a court can nominate the personal representative, who is then known as the 'administrator'. Valuing the deceased person's estate is one of the first things his or her personal representative needs to do. The representative will not normally be able to take over management of the estate (called 'applying for probate') until all or some of any IHT that is due has been paid.

VALUATIONS

When valuing a deceased person's estate all assets (property, possessions and money) owned at the time of death and certain assets given away during the seven years before death must be included. The valuation must accurately reflect what those assets would reasonably fetch in the open market at the date of death. The value of all of the assets that the deceased owned should include:

- his or her share of any assets owned jointly with someone else, for example a house owned with a partner
- any assets that are held in a trust, from which the deceased had the right to benefit
- any assets given away, but in which he or she kept an interest (gifts with reservation)
- PETs given away within the last seven years

Most estate assets can be valued quite easily, for example money in bank accounts or stocks and shares. In other instances the help of a professional valuer may be needed. Advice on how to value different assets including joint or trust assets is available at W www.hmrc.gov.uk. When valuing an estate, special relief is made available for certain assets. The two main reliefs are business relief and agricultural property relief, outlined below. Once all assets have been valued, the next step is to deduct from the total assets everything that the deceased person owed such as unpaid bills, outstanding mortgages and other loans plus their funeral expenses.

The value of all of the assets, less the deductible debts, is their estate. IHT is only payable on any value above £325,000 for the tax year 2013–14 at the current rate of 40 per cent.

A new reduced rate of IHT was introduced at the beginning of the 2012–13 tax year to encourage individuals to pledge part of their estate to charity on death. Where 10 per cent or more of a deceased's net estate (after deducting IHT exemptions, reliefs and the nil-rate band) is left to charity, the 40 per cent rate is reduced to 36 per cent. This new rate applies where death has occurred on or after 6 April 2012.

RELIEF FOR SELECTED ASSETS

Agricultural Property

If an individual owns agricultural property and it is part of a working farm, it is possible to pass on some of this property free of IHT, either during that individual's lifetime or on their death. Agricultural property generally includes land or pasture used in the growing of crops or intensive rearing of animals for food consumption. It can also include farmhouses and farm cottages. The agricultural property can be owner-occupied or let. Relief is only due if the transferor has owned the property and it has been occupied for agricultural purposes for a minimum period.

The chargeable value transferred, either on a lifetime gift or on death, must be determined. This value may then be reduced by a percentage. Depending on the type of property, it will normally qualify for relief of 100 per cent. However, property rented out before 1 September 1995 usually only qualifies for relief of 50 per cent.

Business Relief

Business relief is available on transfers of certain types of business and of business assets if they qualify as relevant business property and the transferor has owned them for a minimum period. The relief can be claimed for transfers made during the person's lifetime or on their death. Where the chargeable value transferred is attributable to relevant business property, the business relief reduces that value by a percentage of either 50 or 100 per cent, depending on the type of asset. Business relief may be claimed on relevant business property including property and buildings or assets such as unlisted shares or machinery.

It is a general requirement that the property must have been retained for a period of two years before the transfer or death, and restrictions may be necessary if the property has not been used wholly for business purposes. The same property cannot obtain both business property relief and the relief available for agricultural property.

CALCULATION OF TAX PAYABLE

The calculation of IHT payable adopts the use of a cumulative or 'running' total. Looking back seven years from the death the chargeable value of gifts in that period is added to the total value of the estate at death. The gifts will use up all or part of the inheritance tax threshold (the 'nil-rate band' above which IHT becomes payable) first.

Lifetime Chargeable Transfers

The value transferred by lifetime chargeable transfers must be added to the seven-year running total to calculate whether any IHT is due. If the nil-rate band is exceeded, tax will be imposed on the excess at the rate of 20 per cent. However, if the donor dies within a period of seven years from the date of the chargeable lifetime transfer, additional tax may be due. This is calculated by applying tax at the full rate of 40 per cent in substitution for the rate of 20 per cent previously used. The amount of tax is then reduced to a percentage by applying tapering relief. This percentage is governed by the number of years from the date of the lifetime gift to the date of death, as follows:

PERIOD OF YEARS BEFORE DEATH

Not more than 3	100%
More than 3 but not more than 4	80%
More than 4 but not more than 5	60%
More than 5 but not more than 6	40%
More than 6 but not more than 7	20%

Should this exercise produce liability greater than that previously paid at the 20 per cent rate on the lifetime transfer, additional tax, representing the difference, must be paid. Where the calculation shows an amount falling below tax paid on the lifetime transfer, no additional liability can arise nor will the shortfall become repayable.

Tapering relief is, of course, only available if the calculation discloses a liability to IHT. There is no liability if the lifetime transfer falls within the nil-rate band.

Potentially Exempt Transfers

Where a PET loses immunity from liability to IHT because the donor dies within seven years of making the transfer, the value transferred enters into the running total. Any liability to IHT will be calculated by applying the full rate of 40 per cent, reduced to the percentage governed by tapering relief if the original transfer occurred more than three years before death. Again, liability to IHT can only arise if the nil-rate band is exceeded.

Death

On death, IHT is due on the value of the deceased's estate plus the running total of gifts made in the seven years before death if they come to more than the nil-rate band. IHT is then charged at the full rate of 40 per cent on the amount in excess of the nil-rate band.

Settled Property and Trusts

Trusts are special legal arrangements that can be used by individuals to control how their assets are distributed to their beneficiaries and minimise their IHT liability. Complex rules apply to establish IHT liability on settled property which includes property held in trust, and individuals are advised to take expert legal advice when setting up trusts.

RATES OF TAX

There are four rates:

- a nil-rate
- a lifetime rate of 20 per cent
- a full rate of 40 per cent
- a reduced rate of 36 per cent applicable to taxable estates where 10 per cent of the net estate has been left to charity (*see* above)

The nil-rate band has been frozen at £325,000 since 2009–10 and will remain frozen at this rate until 2017–18. Any excess over this level is taxable at 20 per cent, 40 per cent or 36 per cent as the case may be.

TRANSFER OF NIL-RATE BAND

Transfers of property between spouses or civil partners are generally exempt from IHT. This means that someone who dies leaving some or all of their property to their spouse or civil partner may not have fully used up their nil-rate band. Under rules introduced in autumn 2007, any nil-rate band unused on the first death can be used when the surviving spouse or civil partner dies. A transfer of unused nil-rate band from a deceased spouse or civil partner (no matter what the date of their death) may be made to the estate of their surviving spouse or civil partner.

Where a valid claim to transfer unused nil-rate band is made, the nil-rate band that is available when the surviving spouse or civil partner dies is increased by the proportion of the nil-rate band unused on the first death. For example, if on the first death the chargeable estate is £150,000 and the nil-rate band is £300,000, 50 per cent of the nil-rate band would be unused. If the nil-rate band when the survivor dies is £325,000, then that would be increased by 50 per cent to £487,500. The amount of the nil-rate band that can be transferred does not depend on the value of the first spouse or civil partner's estate. Whatever proportion of the nil-rate band is unused on the first death is available for transfer to the survivor.

The amount of additional nil-rate band that can be accumulated by any one surviving spouse or civil partner is limited to the value of the nil-rate band in force at the time of their death. This may be relevant, for example, where a person dies having survived more than one spouse or civil partner.

Where these rules have effect, personal representatives do not have to claim for the unused nil-rate band to be transferred at the time of the first death. Any claims for transfer of unused nil-rate band amounts are made by the personal representatives of the estate of the second spouse or civil partner to die when they make an IHT return.

Detailed guidance on how to transfer the nil-rate band can be found on the HMRC website (W www.hmrc.gov.uk).

PAYMENT OF TAX

IHT is normally due six months after the end of the month in which the death occurs or the chargeable transaction takes place. This is referred to as the 'due date'. Tax on some assets such as business property, certain shares and securities and land and buildings (including the deceased person's home) can be deferred and paid in equal instalments over ten years, though interest will be charged in most cases. If IHT is due on lifetime gifts and transfers, the person or transferee who received the gift or assets is normally liable to pay the IHT, though any IHT already paid at the time of a transfer into a trust or company will be taken into account. If tax owed is not paid by the due date, interest is charged on any unpaid IHT, no matter what caused the delay in payment.

CORPORATION TAX

Corporation tax is a tax on a company's profits, including all its income and gains. This tax is payable by UK resident companies and by non-resident companies carrying on a trade in the UK through a permanent establishment. The following comments are confined to companies resident in the UK. The word 'company' is also used to include:

- members' clubs, societies and associations
- trade associations
- housing associations
- groups of individuals carrying on a business but not as a partnership (for example, cooperatives)

A company's taxable income is charged by reference to income or gains arising in its 'accounting period', which is normally 12 months long. In some circumstances accounting periods can be shorter than 12 months, but never longer. The accounting period is also normally the period for which a company's accounts are drawn up, but the two periods do not have to coincide.

If a company is liable to pay corporation tax on its profits, several things must be done. HMRC must be informed that the company exists and is liable for tax. A self-assessment company tax return plus full accounts and calculation of tax liability must be filed by the statutory filing date, normally 12 months after the end of the accounting period. Companies have to work out their own tax liability and have to pay their tax without prior assessment by HMRC. Records of all company expenditure and income must be kept in order to work out the tax liability correctly. Companies are liable to penalties if they fail to carry out these obligations.

It was announced in the 2013 Budget that a radically simpler way for small businesses to calculate their tax was to be introduced with effect from the 2013–14 tax year. Businesses with receipts of up to £77,000 are now able to work out their income on a cash basis and use simplified expenses rules, rather than having to follow the rules for larger businesses.

Extensive corporation tax information is available on the HMRC website (W www.hmrc.gov.uk/businesses) and companies may file their company tax returns online (W www.hmrc.gov.uk/ct/ct-online/file-return/online.htm).

RATE OF TAX

The rate of corporation tax is fixed for a financial year starting on 1 April and ending on the following 31 March. If a company's accounting period does not coincide with the financial year, its profits must be apportioned between the financial years and the tax rates for each financial year applied to those profits. The corporation tax liability is the total tax for both financial years.

The main rate of corporation tax for 2013–14 is 23 per cent, a decrease from 24 per cent in 2012–13. For North Sea oil and gas ringfence activities, the main rate of corporation tax is 30 per cent. The main rate of corporation tax applies when profits (including ringfence profits) are at a rate exceeding £1.5m, or where there is no claim to another rate, or where another rate does not apply.

It was announced in the 2013 Budget that the main rate of corporation tax will be reduced to 21 per cent for the financial year commencing 1 April 2014, and again to 20 per cent for the financial year commencing 1 April 2015, at which time it will become unified with the small profits rate (*see* below).

SMALL PROFITS RATE

Where the profits of a company do not exceed stated limits, corporation tax becomes payable at the small profits rate (SPR).

The SPR for 2013–14 is 20 per cent and will remain at this rate for 2014–15 and 2015–16, at which it will become unified with the main corporation tax rate. For North Sea oil and gas ringfence activities, the small profits rate is 19 per cent.

A company can make profits of up to £300,000 without losing the benefit of the small profits rate. If, however, its profits exceed £300,000 but fall below £1.5m, then marginal SPR relief applies to ease the transition. The effect of marginal relief is that the average rate of corporation tax imposed on all profits steadily increases from the lower small companies' rate of 20 per cent to the main rate of 23 per cent, with tax being imposed on profits in the margin at an increased rate. HMRC has produced an easy-to-use corporation tax marginal relief rate calculator (W www.hmrc.gov.uk/calcs/mrr.htm).

Where a change in the rate of tax is introduced and the accounting period of a company overlaps 31 March, profits must be apportioned to establish the appropriate rate for each part of those profits.

The lower limit of £300,000 and the upper limit of £1.5m apply to a period of 12 months and must be proportionately reduced for shorter periods. Some restriction in the SPR and the marginal rate may be necessary if there are two or more associated companies, namely companies under common control.

CORPORATION TAX ON PROFITS

£ per year	*2012–13*	*2013–14*
£0–£300,000	20%	20%
£300,001–£1,500,000	Marginal relief	Marginal relief
£1,500,001 or more	24%	23%

CAPITAL ALLOWANCES

Businesses can claim tax allowances, called capital allowances, on certain purchases or investments. This means that a proportion of these costs can be deducted from a business' taxable profits and reduce its tax bill. Capital allowances are currently available on plant and machinery, buildings, and research and development. The amount of the allowance depends on what is being claimed for.

Detailed information on capital allowances is available from the Enhanced Capital Allowances website (W www.eca.gov.uk).

PAYMENT OF TAX

Corporation tax liabilities are normally due and payable in a single lump sum not later than nine months and one day after the end of the accounting period. For 'large' companies – those with profits over £1.5m which pay corporation tax at the main rate – there is a requirement to pay corporation tax in four quarterly instalments. Where a company is a member of a group, the profits of the entire group must be merged to establish whether the company is large.

HMRC runs a Business Payment Support Service (BPSS) which allows businesses facing temporary financial difficulties more time to pay their tax bills. Traders concerned about their ability to meet corporation tax, VAT or other payments owed to HMRC can call the Business Payment Support Line (T 0845-302 1435) seven days a week. This helpline is for new enquiries only, not for traders who have already been contacted by HMRC about an overdue payment. For details of the service visit W www.hmrc.gov.uk/payinghmrc/problems/bpps.htm

CAPITAL GAINS

Chargeable gains arising to a company are calculated in a manner similar to that used for individuals. However, companies are not entitled to the CGT annual exemption. Companies do not suffer CGT on chargeable gains but incur liability to corporation tax instead. Tax is due on the full chargeable gain of an accounting period after subtracting relief for any losses.

GROUPS OF COMPANIES

Each company within a group is separately charged to corporation tax on profits, gains and income. However, where one group member realises a loss for which special rules apply, other than a capital loss, a claim may be made to offset the deficiency against profits of some other member of the same group. The transfer of capital assets from one member of a group to a fellow member will usually incur no liability to tax on chargeable gains.

SPORTS CLUBS

Though corporation tax is payable by unincorporated associations including most clubs, a substantial exemption from liability to corporation tax, introduced in April 2002, is available to qualifying registered community amateur sports clubs (CASCs). Sports clubs that are registered as CASCs are exempt from liability to corporation tax on:

- profits from trading where the turnover of the trade is less than £30,000 in a 12-month period
- income from letting property where the gross rental income is less than £20,000 in a 12-month period
- bank and building society interest received
- chargeable gains

All of the exemptions depend upon the club having been a registered CASC for the whole of the relevant accounting period and the income or gains being used only for qualifying purposes. If the club has only been a registered CASC for part of an accounting period the exemption amounts of £30,000 (for trading) and £20,000 (for income from property) are reduced proportionately. Only interest and gains received after the club is registered are exempted.

Among other advantages available to registered clubs is that donations may be received under the Gift Aid arrangements. Charities are also generally exempt from corporation tax where they operate through a company structure.

VALUE ADDED TAX

Value added tax (VAT) is a tax on consumer expenditure charged when an individual buys goods and services in the European Union, including the UK. It is normally included in the sale price of goods and services and paid at the point of purchase. Each EU country has its own rate of VAT. From a business point of view, VAT is charged on most business transactions involving the supply of goods and services by a registered trader in the UK and Isle of Man. It is also charged on goods and some services imported from places outside the EU and on goods and some services coming into the UK from the other EU countries. VAT is administered by HMRC. A wide range of information on VAT, including VAT forms, is available online at W www.hmrc.gov.uk/vat/index.htm. HMRC also runs a VAT and Excise helpline (T 0845-010 9000).

RATES OF TAX

There are three rates of VAT in the UK. The standard rate, payable on most goods and services in the UK, has been 20 per cent since 4 January 2011 when it was increased from 17.5 per cent.

The reduced rate – currently 5 per cent – is payable on certain goods and services including, for example, domestic fuel and power, children's car seats, women's sanitary products, contraceptive products and the installation of energy-saving materials such as wall insulation and solar panels.

A zero, or nil, rate applies to certain items including, for example, children's clothes, books, newspapers, most food and drink, and drugs and aids for disabled people. There are numerous exceptions to the zero-rated categories, however. While most food and drink is zero-rated, items including ice creams, chocolates, sweets, potato crisps and alcoholic drinks are not. Neither are drinks or items sold for consumption in a restaurant or cafe. Takeaway cold items such as sandwiches are zero-rated, while takeaway hot foods like fish and chips are not.

REGISTRATION

All traders, including professional persons and companies, must register for VAT if they are making 'taxable supplies' of a value exceeding stated limits. All goods and services that are VAT-rated are defined as 'taxable supplies' including zero-rated items which must be included when calculating the total value of a trader's taxable supplies – his or her 'taxable turnover'. The limits that govern mandatory registration are amended periodically.

An unregistered trader must register for VAT if:

- at the end of any month the total value of his or her taxable turnover (not just profit) for the past 12 months or less is more than the current VAT threshold of £79,000 – *and*
- at any time he or she has reasonable grounds to expect that his or her taxable turnover will be more than the current registration threshold of £79,000 in the next 30 days alone

To register for VAT, one or more forms must be completed and sent to HMRC within 30 days of any of the above. Basic VAT registration can currently be completed online (W https://online.hmrc.gov.uk/registration/). Traders who do not register at the correct time can be fined. Traders must charge VAT on their taxable supplies from the date they first need to be registered. Traders who only supply zero-rated goods may not have to register for VAT even if their taxable turnover goes above the registration threshold. However, a trader in this position must inform HMRC first and apply to be 'exempt from registration'. A trader whose taxable turnover does not reach the mandatory registration limit may choose to register for VAT voluntarily if what he or she does counts as a business for VAT purposes. This step may be thought advisable to recover input tax (*see* below) or to compete with other registered traders. Registered traders may submit an application for deregistration if their taxable turnover subsequently falls. An application for deregistration can be made if the taxable turnover for the year beginning on the application date is not expected to exceed £77,000.

INPUT TAX

Registered traders suffer input tax when buying in goods or services for the purposes of their business. It is the VAT that traders pay out to their suppliers on goods and services coming *in* to their business. Relief can usually be obtained for input tax suffered, either by setting that tax against output tax due or by repayment. Most items of input tax can be relieved in this manner. Where a registered trader makes both exempt supplies and taxable supplies to his customers or clients, there may be some restriction in the amount of input tax that can be recovered.

OUTPUT TAX

When making a taxable supply of goods or services, registered traders must account for output tax, if any, on the value of that supply. Output tax is the term used to describe the VAT on the goods and services that they supply or sell – the VAT on supplies going *out* of the business and collected from customers on each sale made. Usually the price charged by the registered trader will be increased by adding VAT, but failure to make the required addition will not remove liability to account for output tax. The liability to account for output tax, and also relief for input tax, may be affected where a trader is using a special secondhand goods scheme.

EXEMPT SUPPLIES

VAT is not chargeable on certain goods and services because the law deems them 'exempt' from VAT. These include the provision of burial and cremation facilities, insurance, loans of money, certain types of education and training and some property transactions. The granting of a lease to occupy land or the sale of land will usually comprise an exempt supply, for example, but there are numerous exceptions. Exempt supplies do not enter into the calculation of taxable turnover that governs liability to mandatory registration (*see* above). Such supplies made by a registered trader may, however, limit the amount of input tax that can be relieved. It is for this reason that the exemption may be useful.

COLLECTION OF TAX

Registered traders submit VAT returns for accounting periods usually of three months in duration, but arrangements can be made to submit returns on a monthly basis. Very large traders must account for tax on a monthly basis, but this does not affect the three-monthly return. The return will show both the output tax due for supplies made by the trader in the accounting period and also the input tax for which relief is claimed. If the output tax exceeds input tax the balance must be remitted with the VAT return. Where input tax suffered exceeds the output tax due, the registered trader may claim the excess from HMRC.

This basis for collecting tax explains the structure of VAT. Where supplies are made between registered traders the supplier will account for an amount of tax that will usually be identical to the tax recovered by the person to whom the supply is made. However, where the supply is made to a person who is not a registered trader there can be no recovery of input tax and it is on this person that the final burden of VAT eventually falls. Where goods are acquired by a UK trader from a supplier within the EU, the trader must also account for the tax due on acquisition. There are a number of simplified arrangements to make VAT accounting easier for businesses, particularly small businesses, and there is advice on the HMRC website about how to choose the most appropriate scheme for a business:

Cash Accounting

This scheme allows businesses to only pay VAT on the basis of payments received from their customers rather than on invoice dates or time of supply. It can therefore be useful for businesses with cash flow problems that cannot pay their VAT as a result. Businesses may use the cash accounting scheme if taxable turnover is under £1.35m. There is no need to apply for the scheme – eligible businesses may start using it at the beginning of a new tax period. If a trader opts to use this scheme, he or she can do so until the taxable turnover reaches £1.6m.

Annual Accounting

If taxable turnover is under £1.35m a year, the trader may join the annual accounting scheme which allows them to make nine monthly or three quarterly instalments during the year based on an estimate of their total annual VAT bill. At the end of the year they submit a single return and any balance due. The advantages of this scheme for businesses are easier budgeting and cash flow planning because fixed payments are spread regularly throughout the year. Once a trader has joined the annual accounting scheme, membership may continue until the annual taxable turnover reaches £1.6m.

Flat Rate Scheme

This scheme allows small businesses with an annual taxable turnover of less than £150,000 to save on administration by paying VAT as a set flat percentage of their annual turnover instead of accounting internally for VAT on each individual 'in and out'. The percentage rate used is governed by the trade sector into which the business falls. The scheme can no longer be used once annual income exceeds £230,000.

Retail Schemes

There are special schemes that offer retailers an alternative if it is impractical for them to issue invoices for a large number of supplies direct to the public. These schemes include a provision to claim relief from VAT on bad debts where goods or services are supplied to a customer who does not pay for them.

VAT FACT SUMMARY
from 1 April 2013

Standard rate	20%
Reduced rate	5%
Registration (last 12 months or next 30 days)	£79,000
Deregistration (next 12 months under)	£77,000
Cash accounting scheme – up to	£1,350,000
Flat rate scheme – up to	£150,000
Annual accounting scheme – up to	£1,350,000

STAMP DUTY

For the majority of people, contact with stamp duty arises when they buy a property. Stamp duty is payable by the buyer as a way of raising revenue for the government based on the purchase price of a property, stocks and shares. This section aims to provide a broad overview of stamp duty as it may affect the average person.

STAMP DUTY LAND TAX

Stamp duty land tax was introduced on 1 December 2003 and covers the purchase of houses, flats and other land, buildings and certain leases in the UK.

Before 1 December 2003 property purchasers had to submit documents providing all details of the purchase to the Stamp Office for 'stamping'. The purchaser's solicitor or licensed conveyancer would then send the stamped documentation to the appropriate land registry to register ownership of the property. Under stamp duty land tax, purchasers do not have to send documents for stamping. Instead, a land transaction return form SDLT1, which contains all information regarding the purchase that is relevant to HMRC, is signed by the purchaser. Buyers of property are responsible for completing the land transaction return and payment of stamp duty, though the solicitor or licensed conveyancer acting for them in a land transaction will normally complete the relevant paperwork. Once HMRC has received the completed land transaction return and the payment of any stamp duty due, a certificate will be issued that enables a solicitor or licensed conveyancer to register the property in the new owner's name at the Land Registry.

The threshold for notification of residential property is currently £40,000. This means that taxpayers entering into a transaction involving residential or non-residential property where the chargeable consideration is less than £40,000 do not need to notify HMRC about the transaction.

RATES OF STAMP DUTY LAND TAX

Stamp duty is charged at different rates and has thresholds for different types of property and different values of transaction. The tax rate and payment threshold can vary according to whether the property is in residential or non-residential use and whether it is freehold or leasehold.

Below a certain threshold, currently £125,000, no stamp duty is payable on residential property purchases.

The following table shows the rates of stamp duty and payment thresholds that apply on residential property purchase prices during 2013–14:

Purchase price	*Rate of tax (% of purchase price)*
up to £125,000*	0%
over £125,000 to £250,000	1%
over £250,000 to £500,000	3%
over £500,000 to £1,000,000	4%
over £1,000,000 to £2,000,000	5%
over £2,000,000	7%

* Up to £150,000 for residential property transactions before 6 April 2013 in certain designated disadvantaged areas, a full list of which can be found at W www.hmrc.gov.uk

The disadvantaged areas relief was abolished for transactions with an effective date on or after 6 April 2013. Claims to relief for purchases of residential property where the effective date is before 6 April 2013 must be made on or before 5 May 2014.

When assessing how much stamp duty is payable, the entire purchase price must be taken into account so the relevant stamp duty rate is paid on the whole sum, not just on the amount over each tax threshold. For example, on a property bought for £250,000, 1 per cent (£2,500) is payable in stamp duty. On a property bought for £250,001, however, 3 per cent of the whole price (£7,500) is payable.

FIXTURES AND CHATTELS

As well as buying a property a purchaser may buy items inside the property. Some things inside a property are, in law, part of the land. These are called 'fixtures'. Examples are fitted kitchen units and bathroom suites. Because these fixtures are part of the land, any price paid for them must be taken into account for stamp duty purposes. Other things inside a property are not part of the land. These are called 'chattels'. Examples are free-standing cookers, curtains and fitted carpets. The purchase of chattels is not chargeable to stamp duty. However, where both a property and chattels are purchased, the amount shown on the land transaction return as the purchase price of the property must be a 'just and reasonable' apportionment of the total amount paid. As with other entries on the form, the purchaser is responsible for the accuracy of this information. HMRC pays especial attention to residential property purchases just below stamp duty thresholds to prevent arrangements between buyer and seller to hand over cash so that the purchase price on paper looks lower, or where the buyer has paid an unreasonably high amount to buy chattels.

STAMP DUTY RESERVE TAX

Stamp duty or stamp duty reserve tax (SDRT) is payable at the rate of 0.5 per cent when shares are purchased. Stamp duty is payable when the shares are transferred using a stock transfer form, whereas SDRT is payable on 'paperless' share transactions where the shares are transferred electronically without using a stock transfer form. Most share transactions nowadays are paperless and settled by stockbrokers through CREST (the electronic settlement and registration system). SDRT therefore now accounts for the majority of taxation collected on share transactions effected through the London Stock Exchange.

The flat rate of 0.5 per cent is based on the amount paid for the shares, not what they are worth. If, for example, shares are bought for £2,000, £10 SDRT is payable, whatever the value of the shares themselves. If shares are transferred for free, no SDRT is payable.

A higher rate of 1.5 per cent is payable where shares are transferred into a 'depositary receipt scheme' or a 'clearance service'. These are special arrangements where the shares are held by a third party.

CREST automatically deducts the SDRT and sends it to HMRC. A stockbroker will settle up with CREST for the cost of the shares and the SDRT and then bill the purchaser for these and the broker's fees. If shares are not purchased through CREST, the stamp duty must be paid by the purchaser to HMRC.

It was announced in the 2013 Budget that SDRT on share transactions in UK companies quoted on small company growth markets will be abolished from April 2014.

UK stamp duty or SDRT is not payable on the purchase of foreign shares, though there may be foreign taxes to pay. SDRT is already accounted for in the price paid for units in unit trusts or shares in open-ended investment companies.

HELP AND INFORMATION

Further information on stamp duty land tax is available via the stamp taxes helpline on T 0845-603 0135 or the HMRC website (W www.hmrc.gov.uk), where a stamp duty calculator for both shares and land and property can be found.

LEGAL NOTES

These notes outline certain aspects of the law as they might affect the average person. They are intended only as a broad guideline and are by no means definitive. The law is constantly changing so expert advice should always be taken. In some cases, sources of further information are given in these notes.

It is always advisable to consult a solicitor without delay. Anyone who does not have a solicitor can contact the following for assistance in finding one: Citizens Advice (W www.citizensadvice.org.uk), the Community Legal Service (W www.gov.uk) or the Law Society of England and Wales. For assistance in Scotland, contact Citizens Advice Scotland (W www.cas.org.uk) or the Law Society of Scotland.

Legal aid schemes exist to make the help of a lawyer available to those who would not otherwise be able to afford one. Entitlement for most types of legal aid depends on an individual's means but a solicitor or Citizens Advice will be able to advise on this.

LAW SOCIETY OF ENGLAND AND WALES, 113 Chancery Lane, London WC2A 1PL T 020-7242 1222 W www.lawsociety.org.uk

LAW SOCIETY OF SCOTLAND, 26 Drumsheugh Gardens, Edinburgh EH3 7YR T 0131-226 7411 W www.lawscot.org.uk

ABORTION

Abortion is governed by the Abortion Act 1967. Under its provisions, a legally induced abortion must be:

- performed by a registered medical practitioner
- carried out in an NHS hospital or other approved premises
- certified by two registered medical practitioners as justified on one or more of the following grounds:
  (a) that the pregnancy has not exceeded its 24th week and that the continuance of the pregnancy would involve risk, greater than if the pregnancy were terminated, of injury to the physical or mental health of the pregnant woman or any existing children of her family
  (b) that the termination is necessary to prevent grave permanent injury to the physical or mental health of the pregnant woman
  (c) that the continuance of the pregnancy would involve risk to the life of the pregnant woman, greater than if the pregnancy were terminated
  (d) that there is a substantial risk that if the child were born it would suffer from such physical or mental abnormalities as to be seriously handicapped.

In determining whether the continuance of a pregnancy would involve such risk of injury to health as is mentioned in grounds (a) or (b), account may be taken of the pregnant woman's actual or reasonably foreseeable environment.

The requirements relating to the opinion of two registered medical practitioners and to the performance of the abortion at an NHS hospital or other approved place cease to apply in circumstances where a registered medical practitioner is of the opinion, formed in good faith, that a termination is immediately necessary to save the life, or to prevent grave permanent injury to the physical or mental health, of the pregnant woman.

The Abortion Act 1967 does not apply to Northern Ireland, where abortion is not legal.

FAMILY PLANNING ASSOCIATION (UK), 50 Featherstone Street, London EC1Y 8QU T 020-7608 5240 W www.fpa.org.uk

BRITISH PREGNANCY ADVISORY SERVICE (BPAS), T 0845-730 4030 W www.bpas.org

ADOPTION OF CHILDREN

The Adoption and Children Act 2002 reformed the framework for domestic and intercountry adoption in England and Wales and some parts of it extend to Scotland and Northern Ireland. The Children and Adoption Act 2006 introduces further provisions for adoptions involving a foreign element.

WHO MAY APPLY FOR AN ADOPTION ORDER

A couple (whether married or two people living as partners in an enduring family relationship) may apply for an adoption order where both of them are over 21 or where one is only 18 but the natural parent and the other is 21. An adoption order may be made for one applicant where that person is 21 and: a) the court is satisfied that person is the partner of a parent of the person to be adopted; or b) they are not married and are not civil partners; or c) married or in a civil partnership but they are separated from their spouse or civil partner and living apart with the separation likely to be permanent; or d) their spouse/civil partner is either unable to be found, or their spouse/civil partner is incapable by reason of ill-health of making an application. There are certain qualifying conditions an applicant must meet eg residency in the British Isles.

ARRANGING AN ADOPTION

Adoptions may generally only be arranged by an adoption agency or by way of an order from the high court; breach of the restrictions on who may arrange an adoption would constitute a criminal offence. When deciding whether a child should be placed for adoption, the court or adoption agency must consider all the factors set out in the 'welfare checklist' – the paramount consideration being the child's welfare, throughout his or her life. These factors include the child's wishes, needs, age, sex, background and any harm which the child has suffered or is likely to suffer. At all times, the court or adoption agency must bear in mind that delay is likely to prejudice a child's welfare.

ADOPTION ORDER

Once an adoption has been arranged, a court order is necessary to make it legal; this may be obtained from the high court, county court or magistrates' court (including the family proceedings court). An adoption order may not be given unless the court is satisfied that the consent of the child's natural parents (or guardians) has been given correctly. Consent can be dispensed with on two grounds: where the parent or guardian cannot be found or is incapable of giving consent, or where the welfare of the child so demands.

An adoption order extinguishes the parental responsibility that a person other than the adopters (or adopter) has for the child. Where an order is made on the application of the partner of the parent, that parent keeps parental responsibility. Once adopted the child has the same status as a child born to the adoptive parents, but may lose rights to the estates of those losing their parental responsibility.

REGISTRATION AND CERTIFICATES

All adoption orders made in England and Wales are required to be registered in the Adopted Children Register which also contains particulars of children adopted under registrable foreign adoptions. The General Register Office keeps this register from which certificates may be obtained in a similar way to birth certificates. The General Register Office also has equivalents in Scotland and Northern Ireland.

TRACING NATURAL PARENTS OR CHILDREN WHO HAVE BEEN ADOPTED

An adult adopted person may apply to the Registrar-General to obtain a certified copy of his/her birth certificate. Adoption agencies and adoption support agencies should provide services to adopted persons to assist them in obtaining information about their adoption and facilitate contact with their relatives. There is an Adoption Contact Register which provides a safe and confidential way for birth parents and other relatives to assure an adopted person that contact would be welcome. The BAAF (*see* below) can provide addresses of organisations which offer advice, information and counselling to adopted people, adoptive parents and people who have had their children adopted.

BRITISH ASSOCIATION FOR ADOPTION AND FOSTERING (BAAF), Saffron House, 6–10 Kirkby Street, London EC1N 8TS
T 020-7421 2600 W www.baaf.org.uk

SCOTLAND

The relevant legislation is the Adoption and Children (Scotland) Act 2007 which came into force on 28 September 2009. In addition adoptions with a foreign element are governed by the Adoptions with a Foreign Element (Scotland) Regulations 2009. Pre-2009 adoptions are governed by Part IV of the Adoption (Scotland) Act 1978. The provisions of the 2007 act are similar to those described above. In Scotland, petitions for adoption are made to the sheriff court or the court of session.

BRITISH ASSOCIATION FOR ADOPTION AND FOSTERING (BAAF), BAAF Scottish Centre, 113 Rose Street, Edinburgh EH2 3DT T 0131-226 9270

BIRTHS (REGISTRATION)

It is the duty of the parents of a child born in England or Wales to register the birth within 42 days of the date of birth at the register office in the district in which the baby was born. If it is inconvenient to go to the district where the birth took place, the information for the registration may be given to a registrar in another district, who will send your details to the appropriate register office. Failure to register the birth within 42 days without reasonable cause may leave the parents liable to a penalty. If a birth has not been registered within 12 months of its occurrence it is possible for the late registration of the birth to be authorised by the Registrar-General, provided certain requirements can be met.

Births that take place in England may only be registered in English, but births that take place in Wales may be registered bilingually in Welsh and English. In order to do this, the details must be given in Welsh and the registrar must be able to understand and write in Welsh.

If the parents of the child were married to each other at the time of the birth (or conception), either the mother or the father may register the birth. If the parents were not married to each other at the time of the child's birth (or conception), the father's particulars may be entered in the register only where he attends the register office with the mother and they sign the birth register together. Where an unmarried parent is unable to attend the register office either parent may submit to the registrar a statutory declaration on Form 16 (or Form 16W for births which took place in Wales) acknowledging the father's paternity (this form may be obtained from any registrar in England or Wales or online at W www.gro.gov.uk); alternatively a parental responsibility agreement or appropriate court order may be produced to the registrar.

If the father's details are not included in the birth register, it may be possible to re-register the birth at a later date. If the parents do not register the birth of their child the following people may do so:

- the occupier of the house or hospital where the child was born
- a person who was present at the birth
- a person who is responsible for the child

Upon registration of the birth a short certificate is issued. It may be possible to register the birth while still at hospital. Hospitals will advise individually whether this is possible.

BIRTHS ABROAD

There are certain countries where birth registrations may be made for British citizens overseas (for more details on British citizenship *see* below). The British consul or high commission may register the births and issue certificates which are then sent to the General Register Office. If a birth is registered by the British consul or high commission, the registration would show the person's claim to British citizenship, British overseas territories citizenship or British overseas citizenship.

SCOTLAND

In Scotland the birth of a child must be registered within 21 days at the registration office of any registration district in Scotland.

If the child is born, either in or out of Scotland, on a ship, aircraft or land vehicle that ends its journey at any place in Scotland, the child, in most cases, will be registered as if born in that place.

CERTIFICATES OF BIRTHS, DEATHS OR MARRIAGES

Certificates of births, marriages and deaths that have taken place in England and Wales since 1837 can be obtained from the General Register Office (GRO).

Marriage or death certificates may also be obtained from the minister of the church in which the marriage or funeral took place. Any register office can advise about the best way to obtain certificates.

The fees for certificates are:

Online application:
- full certificate of birth, marriage, death or adoption, £9.25
- full certificate of birth, marriage, death or adoption with GRO reference supplied, £9.25

By postal/phone/fax application:
- full certificate of birth, marriage, death or adoption, £9.25
- full certificate of birth, marriage, death or adoption with GRO reference supplied, £9.25
- extra copies of the same birth, marriage or death certificate issued at the same time, £9.25

A priority service is available for an additional fee.

A complete set of the GRO indexes including births, deaths and marriages, civil partnerships, adoptions and provisional indexes for births and deaths from January 2011 to June 2012 are available at the British Library, City of Westminster Archives Centre, Manchester City Library, Newcastle City Library, Birmingham Central Library, Bridgend Reference and Information Library and Plymouth Central Library. Copies of GRO indexes may also be held at some libraries, family history societies, local records offices and The Church of Jesus Christ of Latter Day Saints family history centres. Some organisations may not hold a complete record of indexes and a small fee may be charged by some of them. GRO indexes are also available online.

The Society of Genealogists has many records of baptisms, marriages and deaths prior to 1837.

SCOTLAND

Certificates of births, deaths or marriages that have taken place in Scotland since 1855 can be obtained from the National Records of Scotland (formerly the General Register Office for Scotland) or from the appropriate local registrar.

Applicable fees – local registrar:

- each extract or abbreviated certificate of birth, death, marriage, civil partnership or adoption within a month of registration, £10.00
- each extract or abbreviated certificate of birth, death, marriage, civil partnership or adoption outwith a month of registration, £15.00

A priority service is available for an additional fee.

The National Records of Scotland also keeps the Register of Divorces (including decrees of declaration of nullity of marriage), and holds parish registers dating from before 1855.

Applicable fees – National Records of Scotland:

- personal application, or postal, telephone or fax order: £15.00

A priority service for a response within 24 hours is available for an additional fee of £15.00.

A search of birth, death and marriage records including records of Church of Scotland parishes and statutory records can be done at the ScotlandsPeople Centre. There are also indexes to some of the old parish registers death and burial records in the library at the centre and indexes and images of census records from 1841–1911 are available. The charges for such searches are as follows:

- full or part-day search pass, £15.00
- Quarterly search pass, £490.00
- annual search pass, £1,450.00

Online searching is also available. For more information, visit W www.scotlandspeople.gov.uk.

THE GENERAL REGISTER OFFICE, General Register Office, Certificate Services Section, PO Box 2, Southport PR8 2JD T 0845-603 7788 W www.gro.gov.uk/gro/content/certificates

THE NATIONAL RECORDS OF SCOTLAND, New Register House, 3 West Register Street, Edinburgh EH1 3YT T 0131-334 0380 W www.gro-scotland.gov.uk

SCOTLANDSPEOPLE CENTRE, General Register House, 2 Princes Street, Edinburgh EH1 3YY T 0131-314 4300 W www.scotlandspeoplehub.gov.uk

THE SOCIETY OF GENEALOGISTS, 14 Charterhouse Buildings, Goswell Road, London EC1M 7BA T 020-7251 8799 W www.sog.org.uk

BRITISH NATIONALITY

There are different types of British nationality status: British citizenship; British overseas citizenship; British national (overseas); British overseas territories citizenship; British protected persons; and British subjects. The most widely held of these is British citizenship. Everyone born in the UK before 1 January 1983 became a British citizen when the British Nationality Act 1981 came into force, with the exception of children born to certain diplomatic staff working in the UK at the time. Individuals born outside the UK before 1 January 1983 but who at that date were citizens of the UK and colonies and had a right of abode in the UK also became British citizens. British citizens have the right to live permanently in the UK and are free to leave and re-enter the UK at any time.

A person born on or after 1 January 1983 in the UK (including, for this purpose, the Channel Islands and the Isle of Man) is entitled to British citizenship if he/she falls into one of the following categories:

- he/she has a parent who is a British citizen
- he/she has a parent who is settled in the UK
- he/she is a newborn infant found abandoned in the UK
- his/her parents subsequently settle in the UK or become British citizens and an application is made before he/she is 18
- he/she lives in the UK for the first ten years of his/her life and is not absent for more than 90 days in each of those years
- he/she is adopted in the UK and one of the adopters is a British citizen
- the home secretary consents to his/her registration while he/she is a minor
- if he/she has always been stateless and lives in the UK for a period of five years before his/her 22nd birthday

A person born outside the UK may acquire British citizenship if he/she falls into one of the following categories:

- he/she has a parent who is a British citizen otherwise than by descent, eg a parent who was born in the UK
- he/she has a parent who is a British citizen serving the crown or a European community institution overseas and was recruited to that service in the UK (including qualifying territories for those born on or after 21 May 2002) or in the European Community (for services within an EU institution); or if the applicant himself/herself has at any time been in crown, or similar, service under the government of a British overseas territory
- the home secretary consents to his/her registration while he/she is a minor
- he/she is a British overseas territories citizen, a British overseas citizen, a British subject or a British protected person and has been lawfully resident in the UK for five years
- he/she is a British overseas territories citizen who acquired that citizenship from a connection with Gibraltar
- he/she is adopted or naturalised

Where parents are married, the status of either may confer citizenship on their child. Since July 2006, both parents are able to pass on nationality even if they are not married, provided that there is satisfactory evidence of paternity. For children born before July 2006, it must be shown that there is parental consent and that the child would have an automatic claim to citizenship or entitlement to registration had the parents been married. Where parents are not married, the status of the mother determines the child's citizenship.

Under the 1981 act, Commonwealth citizens and citizens of the Republic of Ireland were entitled to registration as British citizens before 1 January 1983. In 1983, citizens of the Falkland Islands were granted British citizenship.

Renunciation of British citizenship must be registered with the home secretary and will be revoked if no new citizenship or nationality is acquired within six months. If the renunciation was required in order to retain or acquire another citizenship or nationality, the citizenship may be reacquired only once. If the renunciation was for another reason, the home secretary may allow reacquisition more than once, depending on the circumstances. The secretary of state may deprive a person of a citizenship status if he or she is satisfied that the person has done anything seriously prejudicial to the vital interests of the UK, or a British overseas territory, unless making the order would have the effect of rendering such a person stateless. A person may also be deprived of a citizenship status which results from his registration or naturalisation if the secretary of state is satisfied that the registration or naturalisation was obtained by fraud, false representation or concealment of a material fact.

BRITISH DEPENDENT TERRITORIES CITIZENSHIP

Since 26 February 2002, this category of nationality no longer exists and has been replaced by British overseas territory citizenship.

If a person had this class of nationality only by reason of a connection to the territory of Hong Kong, they lost it automatically when Hong Kong was returned to the People's Republic of China. However, if after 30 June 1997, they had no other nationality and would have become stateless, or were born after 30 June 1997 and would have been born stateless (but had a parent who was a British national (overseas) or a British overseas citizen), they became a British overseas citizen.

BRITISH OVERSEAS CITIZENSHIP

Under the 1981 act, as amended by the British Overseas Territories Act 2002, this type of citizenship was conferred on any UK and colonies citizens who did not become either a British citizen or a British overseas territories citizen on 1 January 1983 and as such is now, for most purposes, only acquired by persons who would otherwise be stateless.

BRITISH OVERSEAS TERRITORIES CITIZENSHIP

This category of nationality replaced British dependent territories citizenship. Most commonly, this form of nationality is acquired where, after 31 December 1982, a person was a citizen of the UK and colonies and did not become a British citizen, and that person, and their parents or grandparents, were born, registered or naturalised in the specified British overseas territory. However, on 21 May 2002, people became British citizens if they had British overseas territories citizenship by connection with any British overseas territory except for the sovereign base areas of Akrotiri and Dhekelia in Cyprus.

RESIDUAL CATEGORIES

British subjects, British protected persons and British nationals (overseas) may be entitled to registration as British citizens on completion of five years' legal residence in the UK.

Citizens of the Republic of Ireland who were also British subjects before 1 January 1949 can retain that status if they fulfil certain conditions.

EUROPEAN UNION CITIZENSHIP

British citizens (including Gibraltarians who are registered for this purpose) are also EU citizens and are entitled to travel freely to other EU countries to work, study, reside and set up a business. EU citizens have the same rights with respect to the UK.

NATURALISATION

Naturalisation is granted at the discretion of the home secretary. The basic requirements are five years' residence (three years if the applicant is married to, or is the civil partner of a British citizen), good character, adequate knowledge of the English, Welsh or Scottish Gaelic language, passing the UK citizenship test (if the applicant is not married to, or is not the civil partner of a British citizen) and an intention to reside permanently in the UK.

STATUS OF ALIENS

Aliens, being persons without any of the above forms of British nationality, may not hold public office or vote in Britain and they may not own a British ship or aircraft. Citizens of the Republic of Ireland are not deemed to be aliens. Certain provisions of the Immigration and Asylum Act 1999 make provision about immigration and asylum and about procedures in connection with marriage by superintendent registrar's certificate.

CONSUMER LAW

SALE OF GOODS

A sale of goods contract is the most common type of contract. It is governed by the Sale of Goods Act 1979 (as amended by the Sale and Supply of Goods Act 1994). The act provides protection for buyers by implying terms into every sale of goods contract. These terms include:

- an implied term that the seller will pass good title to the buyer (unless it appears from the contract or is to be inferred from the circumstances that there is an intention that the seller should transfer only such title as he has)
- where the seller sells goods by reference to a description, an implied term that the goods will match that description and, where the sale is by sample and description, it will not be sufficient that the bulk of the goods correspond with the sample if the goods do not also correspond with the description
- where goods are sold by a business seller, an implied term that the goods will be of satisfactory quality ie they meet the standard that a reasonable person would regard as satisfactory, taking into account any description of the goods, the price, and all other relevant circumstances. The quality of the goods includes their state and condition, relevant aspects being whether they are fit for all the purposes for which such goods are commonly supplied, their appearance and finish, freedom from minor defects and their safety and durability. This term will not be implied, however, if a buyer has examined the goods (including in a sale by sample) and should have noticed the defect or if the seller specifically drew the buyer's attention to the defect
- where goods are sold by a business seller, an implied term that the goods are reasonably fit for any purpose made known to the seller by the buyer (either expressly or by implication), unless it is shown that the buyer does not rely on the seller's judgment, or it is not reasonable for him/her to do so
- where goods are sold by sample, implied terms that the bulk of the sample will correspond with the sample in quality, and that the goods are free from any defect rendering them unsatisfactory which would not have been apparent on a reasonable examination of the sample

Some of the above terms can be excluded from contracts by the seller. The seller's right to do this is, however, restricted by the Unfair Contract Terms Act 1977. The act offers more protection to a buyer who 'deals as a consumer' (that is where the seller is selling in the course of a business, the goods are of a type ordinarily bought for private use and the goods are bought by a buyer who is not a business buyer) and does not allow for the implied terms described above to be excluded. In a sale of secondhand goods by auction (at which individuals have the opportunity of attending the sale in person), a buyer does not deal as a consumer.

HIRE-PURCHASE AGREEMENTS

Terms similar to those implied in contracts of sales of goods are implied into contracts of hire-purchase, under the Supply of Goods (Implied Terms) Act 1973. The 1977 act limits the exclusion of these implied terms as before.

SUPPLY OF GOODS AND SERVICES

Under the Supply of Goods and Services Act 1982, similar terms are also implied in other types of contract under which ownership of goods passes, and contracts for the hire of goods (though not hire-purchase agreements). These types of contracts have additional implied terms:

- that the supplier will use reasonable care and skill in carrying out the service

- that the supplier will carry out the service in a reasonable time (unless the time has been agreed)
- that the supplier will make a reasonable charge (unless the charge has already been agreed)

The 1977 act limits the exclusion of these implied terms in a similar manner as before.

UNFAIR TERMS

The Unfair Terms in Consumer Contracts Regulations 1999 apply to contracts between business sellers (or suppliers of goods and services) and consumers. Where the terms have not been individually negotiated (ie where the terms were drafted in advance so that the consumer was unable to influence those terms), a term will be deemed unfair if it operates to the detriment of the consumer (ie causes a significant imbalance in the parties' rights and obligations arising under the contract). An unfair term does not bind the consumer but the contract may continue to bind the parties if it is capable of existing without the unfair term. The regulations contain a non-exhaustive list of terms that are regarded as potentially unfair. When a term does not fall into such a category, whether it will be regarded as fair or not will depend on many factors, including the nature of the goods or services, the surrounding circumstances (such as the bargaining strength of both parties) and the other terms in the contract.

CONSUMER PROTECTION

The Consumer Protection from Unfair Trading Regulations 2008 (CPRs) replaced much previous consumer protection regulation including the majority of the Trade Descriptions Act 1968. CPRs prohibit 31 specific practices, including pyramid schemes. In addition CPRs prohibit business sellers from making misleading actions and misleading omissions, which cause, or are likely to cause, the average consumer to take a different transactional decision. There is also a general duty not to trade unfairly.

Under the Consumer Protection Act 1987, producers of goods are liable for any injury, death or damage to any property exceeding £275 caused by a defect in their product (subject to certain defences).

Consumers are also afforded protection under the Consumer Protection (Distance Selling) Regulations 2000 and the Cancellation of Contracts made in a Consumer's Home or Place of Work etc Regulations 2008 in relation to cancellation rights.

CONSUMER CREDIT

In matters relating to the provision of credit (or the supply of goods on hire or hire-purchase), consumers are also protected by the Consumer Credit Act 1974 (as amended by the Consumer Credit Act 2006). Under this act, a licence, issued by the Office of Fair Trading, is required in order to conduct a consumer credit or consumer hire business or an ancillary credit business, subject to certain exemptions. Any 'fit' person as defined within the act may apply to the Office of Fair Trading for a licence. The provisions of the act only apply to 'regulated' agreements; there are a number of exemptions under which consumer credit agreements are not regulated by the act (such as first charge mortgages which are regulated instead by the FSA). Provisions include:

- in order for a creditor to enforce a regulated agreement, the agreement must comply with certain formalities and must be properly executed. An improperly executed regulated agreement is enforceable only on an order of the court. The debtor must also be given specified information by the creditor or his/her broker or agent during the negotiations which take place before the signing of the agreement. The agreement must also state certain information to ensure that the debtor or hirer is aware of the rights and duties conferred or imposed on him/her and the protection and remedies available to him/her under the act
- the right to withdraw from or cancel some contracts depending on the circumstances. For example, subject to certain exceptions, a borrower may withdraw from a regulated credit agreement within 14 days without giving any reason. The exceptions include agreements for credit exceeding £60,260 and agreements secured on land. The right to withdraw applies only to the credit agreement itself and not to goods or services purchased with it. The borrower must also repay the credit and any interest
- if the debtor is in breach of the agreement, the creditor must serve a default notice before taking any action such as repossessing the goods
- if the agreement is a hire-purchase or conditional sale agreement, the creditor cannot repossess the goods without a court order if the debtor has paid one third of the total price of the goods
- in agreements where the relationship between the creditor and the debtor is unfair to the debtor, the court may alter or set aside some of the terms of the agreement

Where a credit reference agency has been used to check the debtor's financial standing, the creditor may be required to give the agency's name to the debtor, who is entitled to see the agency's file on him. A fee of £2 is payable to the agency.

SCOTLAND

The legislation governing the sale and supply of goods applies to Scotland as follows:

- the Sale of Goods Act 1979 applies with some modifications and it has been amended by the Sale and Supply of Goods Act 1994
- the Supply of Goods (Implied Terms) Act 1973 applies
- the Supply of Goods and Services Act 1982 does not extend to Scotland but some of its provisions were introduced by the Sale and Supply of Goods Act 1994
- only Parts II and III of the Unfair Contract Terms Act 1977 apply
- the Trade Descriptions Act 1968 applies with minor modifications
- the Consumer Credit Act 1974 applies
- the Consumer Credit Act 2006 applies
- the Consumer Protection Act 1987 applies
- the General Product Safety Regulations 2005 apply
- the Unfair Terms in Consumer Contracts Regulations 1999 apply
- the Unfair Terms in Consumer Contracts (Amendment) Regulations 2001 apply
- the Consumer Protection (Distance Selling) Regulations 2000 apply
- the Sale and Supply of Goods to Consumers Regulations 2002 apply
- the Consumer Protection from Unfair Trading Regulations 2008 apply

PROCEEDINGS AGAINST THE CROWN

Until 1947, proceedings against the Crown were generally possible only by a procedure known as a petition of right, which put the private litigant at a considerable disadvantage. The Crown Proceedings Act 1947 placed the Crown (not the sovereign in his/her private capacity, but as the embodiment of the state) largely in the same position as a private individual and made proceedings in the high court involving the Crown subject to the same rules as any other case. The act did not, however, extinguish or limit the Crown's prerogative or statutory powers, and it continued the immunity of HM ships and aircraft. It also left certain Crown privileges unaffected. The act largely abolished the special procedures which previously applied to civil proceedings by and against the Crown. Civil proceedings may be initiated against the appropriate government department or, if there is doubt regarding which is the appropriate department, against the attorney-general.

In Scotland proceedings against the Crown founded on breach of contract could be taken before the 1947 act and no special procedures applied. The Crown could, however, claim certain special pleas. The 1947 act applies in part to Scotland and brings the practice of the two countries as closely together as the different legal systems permit. As a result of the Scotland Act 1998 actions against government departments should be raised against the Lord Advocate or the advocate-general. Actions should be raised against the Lord Advocate where the department involved administers a devolved matter. Devolved matters include agriculture, education, housing, local government, health and justice. Actions should be raised against the advocate-general where the department is dealing with a reserved matter. Reserved matters include defence, foreign affairs and social security.

DEATHS

WHEN A DEATH OCCURS

If the death (including stillbirth) was expected, the doctor who attended the deceased during their final illness should be contacted. If the death was sudden or unexpected, the family doctor (if known) and police should be contacted. If the cause of death is quite clear the doctor will provide:

- a medical certificate that shows the cause of death
- a formal notice that states that the doctor has signed the medical certificate and that explains how to get the death registered
- if the death was known to be caused by a natural illness but the doctor wishes to know more about the cause of death, he/she may ask the relatives for permission to carry out a post-mortem examination

In England and Wales a coroner is responsible for investigating deaths occurring:

- when there is no doctor who can issue a medical certificate of cause of death
- no doctor has treated the deceased during his or her last illness or when the doctor attending the patient did not see him or her within 14 days before death, or after death
- the death occurred during an operation or before recovery from the effect of an anaesthetic
- the death was sudden and unexplained or attended by suspicious circumstances
- the death might be due to an industrial injury or disease, or to accident, violence, neglect or abortion
- the death occurred in prison or in police custody

The doctor will write on the formal notice that the death has been referred to the coroner; if the post-mortem shows that death was due to natural causes, the coroner may issue a notification which gives the cause of death so that the death can be registered. If the cause of death was violent or unnatural, is still undetermined after a post-mortem, or took place in prison or police custody, the coroner must hold an inquest. The coroner must hold an inquest in these circumstances even if the death occurred abroad (and the body has been returned to England or Wales).

In Scotland the office of coroner does not exist. The local procurator fiscal inquires into sudden or suspicious deaths. A fatal accident inquiry will be held before the sheriff where the death has resulted from an accident during the course of the employment of the person who has died, or where the person who has died was in legal custody, or where the Lord Advocate deems it in the public interest that an inquiry be held.

REGISTERING A DEATH

In England and Wales the death must be registered by the registrar of births and deaths for the district in which it occurred. A death which occurs in Scotland can be registered in any registration district in Scotland. Information concerning a death can be given before any registrar of births and deaths in England and Wales. The registrar will pass the relevant details to the registrar for the district where the death occurred, who will then register the death.

In England and Wales the death must normally be registered within five days (unless the registrar says this period can be extended); in Scotland within eight days. If the death has been referred to the coroner/local procurator fiscal it cannot be registered until the registrar has received authority from the coroner/local procurator fiscal to do so. Failure to register a death involves a penalty in England and Wales and may lead to a court decree being granted by a sheriff in Scotland.

If the death occurred at a house or hospital, the death may be registered by:

- any relative of the deceased
- any person present at the death
- the occupier or any inmate of the house or hospital if he/she knew of the occurrence of the death
- any person making the funeral arrangements (but not the funeral director)
- an official from the hospital
- in Scotland, the deceased's executor or legal representative

For deaths that took place elsewhere, the death may be registered by:

- any relative of the deceased
- someone present at the death
- someone who found the body
- a person in charge of the body
- any person making the funeral arrangements

The majority of deaths are registered by a relative of the deceased. The registrar would normally allow one of the other listed persons to register the death only if there were no relatives available.

The person registering the death should take the medical certificate of the cause of death with them; it is also useful, though not essential, to take the deceased's birth and marriage/civil partnership certificates, NHS medical card, pension documentation and life assurance details. The details given to the registrar must be absolutely correct, otherwise it may be difficult to change them later. The person registering the death should check the entry carefully before it is signed. The registrar will issue a certificate for burial or cremation, and a certificate of registration of death (commonly known as a 'death certificate' which is issued for social security purposes if the deceased received a state pension or benefits) – both free of charge. A death certificate is a certified copy of the entry in the death register; copies can be provided on payment of a fee and may be required for the following purposes, in particular by the executor or administrator when sorting out the deceased's affairs:

- the will
- bank and building society accounts
- savings bank certificates and premium bonds
- insurance policies
- pension claims

If the death occurred abroad or on a foreign ship or aircraft, the death should be registered according to the local regulations of the relevant country and a death certificate should be obtained. In many countries the death can also be registered with the British consulate in that country and a record will be kept at the General Register Office. This avoids the expense of bringing the body back.

After 12 months (three months in Scotland) of death or the finding of a dead body, no death can be registered without the consent of the registrar-general.

BURIAL AND CREMATION

In most circumstances in England and Wales a certificate for burial or cremation must be obtained from the registrar before the burial or cremation can take place. If the death has been referred to the coroner, an order for burial or a certificate for cremation must be obtained. In Scotland a body may be buried (but not cremated) before the death is registered.

Funeral costs can normally be repaid out of the deceased's estate and will be given priority over any other claims. If the deceased has left a will it may contain directions concerning the funeral; however, these directions need not be followed by the executor.

The deceased's papers should also indicate whether a grave space had already been arranged. This information will be contained in a document known as a 'Deed of Grant'. Most town churchyards and many suburban churchyards are no longer open for burial because they are full. Most cemeteries are non-denominational and may be owned by local authorities or private companies; fees vary.

If the body is to be cremated, an application form, two cremation certificates (for which there is a charge) or a certificate for cremation if the death was referred to the coroner, and a certificate signed by the medical referee must be completed in addition to the certificate for burial or cremation (the form is not required if the coroner has issued a certificate for cremation). All the forms are available from the funeral director or crematorium. Most crematoria are run by local authorities; the fees usually include the medical referee's fee and the use of the chapel. Ashes may be scattered, buried in a churchyard or cemetery, or kept.

The registrar must be notified of the date, place and means of disposal of the body within 96 hours (England and Wales) or three days (Scotland).

If the death occurred abroad or on a foreign ship or aircraft, a local burial or cremation may be arranged. If the body is to be brought back to England or Wales, a death certificate from the relevant country or an authorisation for the removal of the body from the country of death from the coroner or relevant authority, together with a certificate of embalming will be required. The British consulate can help to arrange this documentation. To arrange a funeral in England or Wales, an authenticated translation of a foreign death certificate or a death certificate issued in Scotland or Northern Ireland which must show the cause of death, is needed, together with a certificate of no liability to register from the registrar in England and Wales in whose sub-district it is intended to bury or cremate the body. If it is intended to cremate the body, a cremation order will be required from the Home Office or a certificate for cremation. If the body is to be cremated in Scotland, an order from the Scottish government Health Department must be obtained.

THE GENERAL REGISTER OFFICE, General Register Office, PO Box 2, Southport PR8 2JD T 0845-603 7788 W www.gro.gov.uk/gro/content/certificates

THE NATIONAL RECORDS OF SCOTLAND, New Register House, 3 West Register Street, Edinburgh EH1 3YT T 0131-334 0380 W www.gro-scotland.gov.uk

DIVORCE, DISSOLUTION AND RELATED MATTERS

Divorce is a legal process carried out by the civil courts to end the marriage of an opposite sex couple, whilst dissolution is a similar process which ends a civil partnership. Divorce should be distinguished from judicial separation which is a court order confirming that the parties have separated but it does not legally dissolve the marriage/civil partnership. It is often applied for due to moral, religious or ethical grounds but it does allow for financial provision to be made as divorce does.

DIVORCE

The process for divorce begins with a petition and ends with what is known as a 'decree absolute' which dissolves the marriage.

The process begins with the lodging of a standard court form (known as an application for a matrimonial order) at any divorce county court or at the principal registry in London. This must be accompanied by a court form outlining the current and proposed arrangements for any children of the family under 16 or between 16 and 18 and in full-time education.

An application for a matrimonial order for divorce may only be presented to the court after one year of marriage and it must be based on matters which occurred within that time. The spouse who lodges this document is known as the 'petitioner' throughout the divorce proceedings and the other spouse is the 'respondent'.

The issue of where the petitioner normally lives or the connections the parties have abroad may have to be considered by the court to determine whether a court has authority to deal with a particular divorce (whether the court has jurisdiction). These matters concern the law relating to domicile and habitual residence and can be complex. As of 21 June 2012, European Union regulation allows spouses of differing nationalities or residencies to choose which participating member state to file for divorce in. However, the UK and Ireland have elected not to participate and currently continue to apply their own national laws.

There is only one ground for divorce, namely that the marriage has broken down irretrievably. This ground must be 'proved' by one of the following facts:

- the respondent has committed adultery and the petitioner finds it intolerable to live with him/her
- the respondent has behaved in such a way that the petitioner cannot reasonably be expected to live with him/her
- the respondent has deserted the petitioner for a continuous period of at least two years
- the two spouses have lived apart for at least two years and the respondent agrees to a divorce
- the two spouses have lived apart for at least five years

If the court is satisfied that the petitioner has proved one of those facts then it must grant a decree nisi (*see* below) unless it is satisfied that the marriage has not broken down.

The procedure is more complex if the divorce is defended, although this is very rare.

DECREE NISI

If the judge is satisfied that the petitioner has proved the contents of the divorce petition, a date will be set for the pronouncement of the decree nisi in open court. The decree nisi is a preliminary decree of divorce which must be obtained but the marriage will not be legally dissolved until the decree absolute. Neither party needs to attend and all the proceedings up to this point are usually carried out on paper.

DECREE ABSOLUTE

The final step in the divorce procedure is to obtain a decree absolute which formally ends the marriage. The petitioner can apply for this six weeks and one day after the date of the decree nisi. If the petitioner does not apply the respondent can apply, but only after three months from the earliest date on which the petitioner could have applied.

A decree absolute will not normally be granted until the parties have agreed, or the court has dealt with, the parties' financial situation (*see* below for details of financial provision).

DISSOLUTION OF CIVIL PARTNERSHIPS

The legal process for dissolution of a civil partnership follows a model closely based on divorce. Irretrievable breakdown of the partnership is the sole ground for dissolution. The facts to be proved to establish this are the same as for divorce, with the exception of adultery which, due to its legal definition, can only apply to opposite sex couples. Adultery can, however, be used as an example of unreasonable behaviour.

FINANCIAL RELIEF ANCILLARY TO DIVORCE, NULLITY AND JUDICIAL SEPARATION

Following a petition for divorce, nullity or judicial separation, it is open to either spouse or former spouse to make a claim for financial provision provided they have not remarried. It is common practice for such an application to be made at the same time, or shortly after, a divorce petition has been issued. The courts have wide powers to make financial provision where a marriage breaks down. Orders can be made for:

- spousal maintenance (periodical payments) which can be capitalised into a lump sum
- lump sum payments
- adjustment or transfer of interests in property
- adjustment of interests in trusts and settlements
- orders relating to pensions

EXERCISE OF THE COURT'S POWERS TO ORDER FINANCIAL PROVISION

The court must exercise its powers so as to achieve an outcome which is fair between the parties, although it has a wide discretion in determining what is a fair financial outcome. It will consider the worldwide assets of both parties, whether liquid or illiquid. In exercising its discretion, the court has to consider a range of statutory factors including:

- the income, earning capacity, property and other financial resources which either party has or is likely to have in the foreseeable future
- the financial needs, obligations and responsibilities which each of the parties to the marriage has or is likely to have in the foreseeable future
- the standard of living enjoyed by the family
- the age of each party and the duration of the marriage
- any physical or mental disability of either party
- the contribution which each of the parties has made or is likely to make in the foreseeable future to the welfare of the family, including any contribution by looking after the home or caring for the family
- the conduct of parties
- loss of benefits

When considering the above factors, however, the court must give paramount consideration to the welfare of any child of the family.

The court has a wide discretion in considering these factors in order to achieve an outcome it considers to be fair. However, the court has emphasised that a 50:50 division of assets is frequently the correct result unless there are compelling reasons to the contrary. It is important to bear in mind that the House of Lords (now the supreme court) in *White v White* said that if each spouse contributed equally in their different sphere it does not matter in principle which of them earned the money and built up the assets. The contributions of the 'breadwinner' and 'homemaker' are considered equal.

The Law Commission's Marital Property Agreements project began in October 2009 and a consultation paper was published on 11 January 2011. The project was extended on 6 February 2012 to cover two further issues of financial provision arising on divorce or the dissolution of a civil partnership, and a supplementary consultation paper was published in September 2012. The project is examining the status and enforceability of agreements made between spouses or civil partners (or those contemplating marriage or civil partnership) concerning their property or finances.

In October 2010, the supreme court gave judgement in *Radmacher v Granatino* and made it clear that a person now entering into a pre-nuptial agreement will be considered to have intended to be held to that agreement. However, the court will still be able to decide as to whether the agreement is fair and whether it should govern all the financial results of divorce. The supreme court did not give clear guidelines on when a pre-nuptial agreement would be considered 'fair' and it is likely to depend on the facts of an individual case.

In *Miller v Miller* and *MacFarlane v MacFarlane*, the House of Lords said that fairness required the court to consider three strands:

- the needs of the parties going forwards
- compensation for any economic disparity between the parties (such as where one party has sacrificed their career to become a full-time parent)
- sharing

The court also has a duty to consider making an order which will settle once and for all the parties' financial responsibilities towards each other, known as a 'clean break'.

FINANCIAL PROVISION ON DISSOLUTION OF A CIVIL PARTNERSHIP

The Civil Partnership Act 2004 makes provisions for financial relief for civil partners generally and extends the same rights and responsibilities invoked by marriage. Again the court must consider a number of factors when exercising its discretion and must take into account all of the circumstances of the case while giving first consideration to the welfare of any child of the family who is under 18. The list of statutory factors the court must consider resemble those for marriage and it is likely that the interpretation of these factors will be based on the courts' interpretation of the factors relating to marriage.

COHABITING COUPLES

Rights of unmarried couples are not the same as for married couples. Agreements, whether express or inferred by conduct, often determine interest in money and property. Reliance upon inferences is problematic, therefore it is advisable to consider entering into a contract, or 'cohabitation agreement', which establishes how money and property should be divided in the event of a relationship breakdown.

This area of law is still developing. In July 2007, the Law Commission published its report to parliament, recommending a scheme to provide remedies for eligible candidates. The cohabitation bill was subsequently introduced to parliament in December 2008 and the first day of the committee stage took place in April 2009. The next day of the committee stage is yet to be determined. On 6 September 2011, parliament announced that it had reviewed the Law Commission's report and would not be reforming cohabitation law in this term. In the meantime, cohabitation agreements continue to be governed by the general principles of contract law.

FINANCIAL PROVISION FOR CHILDREN

All parents are under a legal obligation to support their children financially and the parent who does not have day-to-day care of the child (the 'paying parent') pays child maintenance to the parent who does have main day-to-day care (the 'receiving parent'). In some cases, this person can be a grandparent or guardian.

Parents can arrange child maintenance themselves, ie a family-based arrangement, or through the Child Support Agency (CSA) or the Child Maintenance Service (CMS); together these organisations are known as the 'statutory child maintenance services'. When applying for the statutory maintenance service, the applicant will be told whether the CSA or CMS will manage their case, depending on the applicant's circumstances.

Statutory arrangements through the CSA or CMS include:

- 'Direct Pay' (known as 'Maintenance Direct' under a CSA arrangement) which enables parents to keep control of making and receiving payments. The statutory service works out the payment amounts for parents but will not be involved in other areas, such as collection and enforcement
- 'Collect and Pay' (known as the 'calculation and collection services' under a CSA arrangement) whereby the CSA or CMS calculates how much maintenance the paying parent owes. If payments aren't made on time, a range of enforcement actions can be taken

The CSA will only assess a maximum net weekly income of the paying parent of £2,000. If the paying parent's net weekly income exceeds £2,000, the receiving parent can apply to the court for extra top-up maintenance. The CMS currently only takes applications if the paying and receiving parents have four or more children together and the CMS assesses the paying parent's gross annual income.

Within 72 hours of a payment being missed, the CMS will contact the paying parent to seek continuing payments. Where there is persistent non-payment, the CMS is able to take money directly from the paying parent, either from their earnings or bank account, or to take court action.

Provision is also made under Schedule 1 of the Children Act 1989 for unmarried parents to apply to the court for lump sum and property adjustment orders and, in limited circumstances, orders for child maintenance.

SCOTLAND

Although some provisions are similar to those for England and Wales, there is separate legislation for Scotland covering nullity of marriage, judicial separation, divorce and ancillary matters. The principal legislation in relation to family law in Scotland is the Family Law (Scotland) Act 1985. The Family Law (Scotland) Act 2006 came in to force on 4 May 2006, and introduced reforms to various aspects of Scottish family law. The following is confined to major points on which the law in Scotland differs from that of England and Wales.

An action for judicial separation or divorce may be raised in the court of session; it may also be raised in the sheriff court if either party was resident in the sheriffdom for 40 days immediately before the date of the action or for 40 days ending not more than 40 days before the date of the action. The fee for starting a divorce petition in the sheriff court is £136.

The grounds for raising an action of divorce in Scotland have been subject to reform in terms of the 2006 act. The current grounds for divorce are:

- the defender has committed adultery. When adultery is cited as proof that the marriage has broken down irretrievably, it is not necessary in Scotland to prove that it is also intolerable for the pursuer to live with the defender
- the defender's behaviour is such that the pursuer cannot reasonably be expected to cohabit with the defender
- there has been no cohabitation between the parties for one year prior to the raising of the action for divorce, and the defender consents to the granting of decree of divorce
- there has been no cohabitation between the parties for two years prior to the raising of the action for divorce
- an interim gender recognition certificate under the Gender Recognition Act 2004 has, after the date of marriage, been issued to either party to the marriage

The previously available ground of desertion was abolished by the 2006 act.

A simplified procedure for 'do-it-yourself divorce' was introduced in 1983 for certain divorces. If the action is based on one or two years' separation and will not be opposed or because a gender recognition certificate has been issued; there are no children under 16; no financial claims; there is no sign that the applicant's spouse is unable to manage his or her affairs through mental illness or handicap; and there are no other court proceedings underway which might result in the end of the marriage, the applicant can write directly to the local sheriff court or to the court of session for the appropriate forms to enable him or her to proceed. The fee is £104 as at 1 April 2013, however the applicant may be exempt from paying the fee if they are in receipt of certain benefits; or if legal advice and assistance is being provided by a solicitor in terms of the Legal Aid (Scotland) Act 1986.

Where a divorce action has been raised, it may be put on hold for a variety of reasons. In all actions for divorce an extract decree, which brings the marriage to an end, will be made available 14 days after the divorce has been granted. Unlike in England, there is no decree nisi, only a final decree of divorce. Parties must ensure that all financial issues have been resolved prior to divorce, as it is not possible to seek further financial provision after divorce has been granted.

FINANCIAL PROVISION

In relation to financial provision on divorce, the first, and most important, principle is fair sharing of the matrimonial property. There is a presumption that fair share means an equal share of the matrimonial property, which can be departed from if justified by special circumstances. In terms of Scots law matrimonial property is defined as all property acquired by either spouse from the date of marriage up to the date of separation. Property acquired before the marriage is not deemed to be matrimonial unless it was acquired for use by the parties as a family home or as furniture for that home. Property acquired after the date of separation is not matrimonial property. Any property acquired by either of the parties by way of gift or inheritance during the marriage is excluded and does not form part of the matrimonial property.

When considering whether to make an award of financial provision a court shall also take account of any economic advantage derived by either party to the marriage as a result of contributions, financial or otherwise, by the other, and of any economic disadvantage suffered by either party for the benefit of the other party. The court must also ensure that the economic burden of caring for a child under the age of 16 is shared fairly between the parties.

A court can also consider making an order requiring one party to pay the other party a periodical allowance for a certain period of time following divorce. Such an order may be appropriate in cases where there is insufficient capital to effect a fair sharing of the matrimonial property. Orders for periodical allowance are uncommon, as courts will favour a 'clean break' where possible.

CHILDREN

The court has the power to award a residence order in respect of any children of the marriage or to make an order regulating the child's contact with the non-resident parent.

The court will only make such orders if it is deemed better for the child to do so than to make no order at all, and the welfare of the children is of paramount importance. The fact that a spouse has caused the breakdown of the marriage does not in itself preclude him/her from being awarded residence.

NULLITY

An action for 'declaration of nullity' can be brought if someone with a legitimate interest is able to show that the marriage is void or voidable. The action can only be brought in the court of session. Although the grounds on which a marriage may be void or voidable are similar to those on which a marriage can be declared invalid in England, there are some differences. Where a spouse is capable of sexual intercourse but refuses to consummate the marriage, this is not a ground for nullity in Scots law, though it could be a ground for divorce. Where a spouse was suffering from venereal disease at the time of marriage and the other spouse did not know, this is not a ground for nullity in Scots law, neither is the fact that a wife was pregnant by another man at the time of marriage without the knowledge of her husband.

COHABITING COUPLES

The law in Scotland now provides certain financial and property rights for cohabiting couples in terms of the Family Law (Scotland) Act 2006, or 'the 2006 Act'. The relevant 2006 act provisions do not place cohabitants in Scotland on an equal footing with married couples or civil partners, but provide some rights for cohabitants in the event that the relationship is terminated by separation or death. The provisions relate to couples who cease to cohabit after 4 May 2006.

The legislation provides for a presumption that any contents of the home shared by the cohabitants are owned in equal shares. A former cohabitant can also seek financial provision on termination of the relationship in the form of a capital payment if they can successfully demonstrate that they have been financially disadvantaged, and that conversely the other cohabitant has been financially advantaged, as a consequence of contributions made (financial or otherwise). An order can also be made in respect of the economic burden of caring for a child of whom the cohabitants are the parents. Such a claim must be made no later than one year after the day on which the cohabitants cease to cohabit.

The 2006 act also provides that a cohabitant may make a claim on their partner's estate in the event of that partner's death, providing that there is no will. A claim of this nature must be made no later than six months after the date of the partner's death.

THE PRINCIPAL REGISTRY, First Avenue House, 42–49 High Holborn, London WC1 6NP

THE COURT OF SESSION, Parliament House, Parliament Square, Edinburgh EH1 1RQ T 0131-225 2595 W www.scotcourts.gov.uk

THE CHILD SUPPORT AGENCY, T 08457-133133 W www.csa.gov.uk

EMPLOYMENT LAW

EMPLOYEES

A fundamental distinction in UK employment law is that drawn between an employee and someone who is self-employed. Further, there is an important, intermediate category introduced by legislation: 'workers' covers all employees but also catches others who do not have full employment status. An 'employee' is someone who has entered into or works under a contract of employment, while a 'worker' has entered into or works under a contract whereby he undertakes to do or perform personally any work or services for another party whose status is not that of a client or customer. Whether or not someone is an employee or a worker as opposed to being genuinely self-employed is an important and complex question, for it determines that person's statutory rights and protections. For certain purposes, such as protection against discrimination, protection extends to some genuinely self-employed people as well as workers and employees.

The greater the level of control that the employer has over the work carried out, the greater the depth of integration of the employee in the employer's business, and the closer the obligations to provide and perform work between the parties, the more likely it is that the parties will be employer and employee.

PAY AND CONDITIONS

The Employment Rights Act 1996 consolidated the statutory provisions relating to employees' rights. Employers must give each employee employed for one month or more a written statement containing the following information:

- names of employer and employee
- date when employment began and the date on which the employee's period of *continuous* employment began (taking into account any employment with a previous employer which counts towards that period)
- the scale, rate or other method of calculating remuneration and intervals at which it will be paid
- job title or description of job
- hours and the permitted place(s) of work and, where there are several such places, the address of the employer
- holiday entitlement and holiday pay
- provisions concerning incapacity for work due to sickness and injury, including provisions for sick pay
- details of pension scheme(s)
- length of notice the employee is obliged to give and entitled to receive in order to terminate the contract of employment
- length of notice period that employer and employee need to give to terminate employment
- if the employment is not intended to be permanent, the period for which it is expected to continue or, if it is for a fixed term, the end date of the contract
- details of any collective agreement (including the parties to the agreement) which directly affects the terms of employment
- details of disciplinary and grievance procedures (including the individual to whom a complaint should be made and the process of making that complaint)
- if the employee is to work outside the UK for more than one month, the period of such work and the currency in which payment is made and any additional remuneration or benefits payable to them
- a note stating whether a contracting-out certificate is in force

This must be given to the employee within two months of the start of their employment.

If the employer does not provide the written statement within two months (or a statement of any changes to these particulars within one month of the changes being made) then the employee can complain to an employment tribunal, which can specify the information that the employer should have given. When, in the context of an employee's successful tribunal claim, the employer is also found to have been in breach of the duty to provide the written statement at the time proceedings were commenced, the tribunal must award the employee two weeks' pay, and may award four weeks' pay, subject to the statutory cap, unless it would be unjust or inequitable to do so.

The Working Time Regulations 1998, the National Minimum Wage Act 1998, Employment Relations Act 1999, the Employment Act 2002 and the Employment Act 2008 now supplement the 1996 act.

FLEXIBLE WORKING
The Employment Act 2002 (and regulations made under it) gives employees who are responsible for the upbringing of a child, aged 17 or younger, the right to apply for flexible working for the purpose of caring for that child. The right has been extended to carers of adults. Whether an employee has this right depends on both the employee and the child/adult cared for meeting a number of criteria. If an application under the act is not dealt with in accordance with a prescribed procedure, or is rejected on other than specific grounds, the employee may complain to an employment tribunal.

SICK PAY
Employees absent from work through illness or injury are entitled to receive Statutory Sick Pay (SSP) from the employer from the fourth day of absence for a maximum period of 28 weeks in any three-year period.

MATERNITY AND PARENTAL RIGHTS
Under the Employment Relations Act 1999, the Employment Act 2002, the Maternity and Parental Leave Regulations 1999 (as amended in 2002 and 2006), the Paternity and Adoption Leave Regulations 2002 and 2003 and the Additional Paternity Leave Regulations 2010, both men and women are entitled to take leave when they become a parent (including by adoption). Women are protected from discrimination, detriment or dismissal by reason of their pregnancy or maternity, including discrimination by association and by perception. Men and adoptive parents are protected from suffering a detriment or dismissal for taking paternity, adoption or parental leave.

Any woman who needs to attend an antenatal appointment on the advice of a registered medical professional is entitled to paid leave from work to attend. All pregnant women are entitled to a maximum period of maternity leave of 52 weeks. This comprises 26 weeks' ordinary maternity leave, followed immediately by 26 weeks' additional maternity leave. A woman who takes ordinary maternity leave normally has the right to return to the job in which she was employed before her absence. If she takes additional maternity leave, she is entitled to return to the same job or, if that is not reasonably practicable, to another job that is suitable and appropriate for her to do. There is a two-week period of compulsory maternity leave, immediately following the birth of the child, wherein the employer is not permitted to allow the mother to work.

A woman will qualify for Statutory Maternity Pay (SMP), which is payable for up to 39 weeks, if she has been continuously employed for not less than 26 weeks prior to the 15th week before the expected week of childbirth. For further information *see* Social Welfare, Employer Payments.

Employees are entitled to adoption leave and adoption pay (at the same rates as SMP) subject to fulfilment of similar criteria to those in relation to maternity leave and pay, but note that there is a 26-week qualifying period for adoption leave. Where a couple is adopting a child, either one (but not both) of the parents may take adoption leave, and the other may take paternity leave.

Certain employees are entitled to paternity leave on the birth or adoption of a child. To be eligible, the employee must be the child's father, or the partner of the mother or adopter, and meet other conditions. These conditions are, firstly, that they must have been continuously employed for not less than 26 weeks prior to the 15th week before the expected week of childbirth (or, in the case of adoptions, 26 weeks ending with the week in which notification of the adoption match is given) and, secondly, that the employee must have or expect to have responsibility for the upbringing of the child. The employee may take either one week's leave, or two consecutive weeks' leave. This leave may be taken at any time between the date of the child's birth (or placement for adoption) and 56 days later. A statutory payment is available during this period.

For births and adoptions from 3 April 2011, an eligible employee has been able to take additional paternity leave at the end of the mother's or adopter's leave period provided the child is at least 20 weeks old or was placed for adoption at least 20 weeks previously. The maximum period of leave is 26 weeks and leave cannot extend beyond the child's first birthday.

For more information *see* Social Welfare, Employer Payments.

Any employee with one year's service who has, or expects to have, responsibility for a child may take parental leave to care for the child. Each parent is entitled to a total of 13 weeks parental leave for each of their children (or 18 weeks if the child is disabled). This leave must be taken (at the rate of no more than four weeks a year, and in blocks of whole weeks only) before the child's fifth birthday (18th birthday if the child is disabled) or before the fifth anniversary of the date of placement of an adopted child.

SUNDAY TRADING
The Sunday Trading Act 1994 allows shops to open on Sunday. The Employment Rights Act 1996 gives shop workers and betting workers the right not to be dismissed, selected for redundancy or to suffer any detriment (such as the denial of overtime, promotion or training) if they refuse to work on Sundays. This does not apply to those who, under their contracts, are employed to work on Sundays.

TERMINATION OF EMPLOYMENT
An employee may be dismissed without notice if guilty of gross misconduct but in other cases a period of notice must be given by the employer. The minimum periods of notice specified in the Employment Rights Act 1996 are:

- one week if the employee has been continuously employed for one month or more but for less than two years
- one week for each complete year of continuous employment, if the employee has been employed for two years or more, up to a maximum of 12 weeks' notice
- longer periods apply if these are specified in the contract of employment

If an employee is dismissed with less notice than he/she is entitled to by statute, or under their contract if longer, he/she will have a wrongful dismissal claim (unless the employer paid the employee in lieu of notice in accordance with a contractual provision entitling it to do so). This claim for wrongful dismissal can be brought by the employee either in the civil courts or the employment tribunal, but if brought in the tribunal the maximum amount that can be awarded is £25,000.

REDUNDANCY
An employee dismissed because of redundancy may be entitled to redundancy pay. This applies if:

- the employment commenced before 6 April 2012 and the employee has at least one year's continuous service or the employment commenced on or after 6 April 2012 and the employee has at least two years' continuous service
- the employee is dismissed by the employer (this can include cases of voluntary redundancy)

Redundancy can mean closure of the entire business, closure of a particular site of the business, or a reduction in the need for employees to carry out work of a particular kind.

An employee may not be entitled to a redundancy payment if offered a suitable alternative job by the same employer. The amount of statutory redundancy pay depends on the length of service, age, and their earnings, subject to a weekly maximum of (currently) £450. The maximum payment that can be awarded is £13,500. The redundancy payment is guaranteed by the government in cases where the employer becomes insolvent.

UNFAIR DISMISSAL

Complaints of unfair dismissal are dealt with by an employment tribunal. Any employee whose employment commenced before 6 April 2012 with at least one year's continuous service or any employee whose employment commenced on or after 6 April 2012 with at least two year's continuous service (subject to exceptions, including in relation to whistleblowers – *see* below) can make a complaint to the tribunal. At the tribunal, it is for the employee to show that the employer dismissed them either expressly or constructively and it is for the employer to prove that the dismissal was due to one or more potentially fair reasons: a statutory restriction preventing the continuation of the employee's contract; the employee's capability or qualifications for the job he/she was employed to do; the employee's conduct; redundancy; or some other substantial reason.

If the employer succeeds in showing this, the tribunal must then decide whether the employer acted reasonably in dismissing the employee for that reason. If the employee is found to have been unfairly dismissed, the tribunal can order that he/she be reinstated, re-engaged or compensated. Any person believing that they may have been unfairly dismissed should contact their local Citizens Advice bureau or seek legal advice. A claim must be brought within three months of the date of effective termination of employment.

The normal maximum compensatory award for unfair dismissal is £74,200 (as at 1 February 2013). If the dismissal occurred after 6 April 2009 and the employer unreasonably failed to follow the ACAS Code of Practice on Disciplinary and Grievance Procedures in carrying out the dismissal, the tribunal may increase the employee's compensation by up to 25 per cent.

WHISTLEBLOWING

Under the whistleblowing legislation (Public Interest Disclosure Act 1998, which inserted provisions into the Employment Rights Act 1996) dismissal of an employee is automatically unfair if the reason or principal reason for the dismissal is that the employee has made a protected disclosure. The legislation also makes it unlawful to subject workers (a broad category that includes employees and certain other individuals, such as agency workers) who have made a protected disclosure to any detriment on the ground that they have done so.

For a disclosure to qualify for protection, the claimant must show that he or she has disclosed information, which in his or her reasonable belief tends to show one or more of the following six categories of wrongdoing: criminal offences; breach of any legal obligation; miscarriages of justice; danger to the health and safety of any individual; damage to the environment; or the deliberate concealing of information about any of the other categories. The malpractices can be past, present, prospective or merely alleged.

A qualifying disclosure will only be protected if the manner of the disclosure fulfils certain conditions, which varies according to the type of disclosure. With effect from 25 June 2013, there is no requirement for the disclosure to have been made in 'good faith', although where it appears to the tribunal that the protected disclosure was not made in good faith, the tribunal may reduce any compensatory award it makes by up to 25 per cent if it considers that it is just and equitable to do so in all the circumstances.

Any whistleblower claim in the employment tribunal must normally be brought within three months of the date of dismissal or other act leading to a detriment.

An individual does not need to have been working with the employer for any particular period of time to be able to bring such a claim and compensation is uncapped (and can include an amount for injury to feelings).

DISCRIMINATION

Discrimination in employment on the grounds of sex (including gender reassignment), sexual orientation, being pregnant or on maternity leave, race, colour, nationality, ethnic or national origins, religion or belief, marital or civil partnership status, age or disability is unlawful. Discrimination legislation generally covers direct discrimination, indirect discrimination, harassment and victimisation. Only in limited circumstances can such discrimination be justified (rendering it lawful).

An individual does not need to be employed for any particular period of time to be able to claim discrimination (discrimination can be alleged at the recruitment phase), and discrimination compensation is uncapped (and can include an amount for injury to feelings). These features distinguish the discrimination laws from, for example, the unfair dismissal laws.

The Equality Act 2010 was passed on 8 April 2010 and the main provisions came into force on 1 October 2010. The Act unifies several pieces of discrimination legislation, providing one definition of direct discrimination, indirect discrimination, harassment and victimisation. The Equality Act applies to those employed in Great Britain but not to employees in Northern Ireland or (subject to EC exceptions) to those who work mainly abroad, and provides that:

- it is unlawful to discriminate on the grounds of sex, gender reassignment or marital/civil partner status, being pregnant or on maternity leave, including discrimination by association and by perception. This covers all aspects of employment (including advertising for jobs), but there are some limited exceptions, such as where the essential nature of the job requires it to be given to someone of a particular sex, or where decency and privacy requires it. The act entitles men and women to equality of remuneration for equivalent work or work of the same value
- individuals have the right not to be discriminated against on the grounds of race, colour, nationality, or ethnic or national origins and this applies to all aspects of employment. Employers may also take lawful positive action, including in relation to recruitment and promotion
- discrimination against a disabled person in all aspects of employment is unlawful. This includes protecting carers from discrimination by association with the disabled persons that they look after. In certain circumstances, the employer may show that the less favourable treatment is justified and so does not constitute discrimination. The act also imposes a duty on employers to make 'reasonable adjustments' to the arrangements and physical features of the workplace if these place disabled people at a substantial disadvantage compared with those who are not disabled. The definition of a 'disabled person' is wide and includes people diagnosed with HIV, cancer and multiple sclerosis
- discrimination against a person on the grounds of religion or belief (or lack of belief) including discrimination by

association and by perception, in all aspects of employment, is unlawful
- discrimination against an individual on the grounds of sexual orientation, including discrimination by association and by perception, in all aspects of employment, is unlawful
- age discrimination in the workplace is unlawful, and an employer may no longer dismiss an employee by reason of retirement once they have reached a certain age. However, it is lawful to discriminate because of age in relation to benefits based on length of service, redundancy pay, national minimum wage and insurance benefits.

The responsibility for monitoring equality in society rests with the Equality and Human Rights Commission.

In Northern Ireland similar provisions exist to those that were in force in Great Britain prior to the coming into force of the Equality Act but are contained in separate legislation (although the Disability Discrimination Act does extend to Northern Ireland).

In Northern Ireland there is one combined body working towards equality and eliminating discrimination, the Equality Commission for Northern Ireland.

WORKING TIME

The Working Time Regulations 1998 impose rules that limit working hours and provide for rest breaks and holidays. The regulations apply to workers and so cover not only employees but also other individuals who undertake to perform personally any work or services (eg freelancers). The regulations are complex and subject to various exceptions and qualifications but the basic provisions relating to adult day workers are as follows:

- No worker is permitted to work more than an average of 48 hours per week (unless they have made a genuine voluntary opt-out of this limit – it is not sufficient to make it a term of the contract that the worker opts out), and a worker is entitled to, but is not required to take, the following breaks:
- 11 consecutive hours' uninterrupted rest in every 24-hour period
- an uninterrupted rest period of 24 hours in each 7-day period or 48 hours in each fortnight (in addition to the daily rest period)
- 20 minutes' rest break provided that the working day is longer than 6 hours
- 5.6 weeks' paid annual leave (28 days full-time). This equates to 4 weeks plus public holidays

There are specific provisions relating to night work, young workers (ie those over school leaving age but under 18) and a variety of workers in specialised sectors (such as off-shore oil rig workers).

HUMAN RIGHTS

On 2 October 2000 the Human Rights Act 1998 came into force. This act incorporates the European Convention on Human Rights into the law of the UK. The main principles of the act are as follows:

- all legislation must be interpreted and given effect by the courts as compatible with the Convention so far as it is possible to do so. Before the second reading of a new bill the minister responsible for the bill must provide a statement regarding its compatibility with the Human Rights Act
- subordinate legislation (eg statutory instruments) which are incompatible with the Convention can be struck down by the courts
- primary legislation (eg an act of parliament) which is incompatible with the Convention cannot be struck down by a court, but the higher courts can make a declaration of incompatibility which is a signal to parliament to change the law
- all public authorities (including courts and tribunals) must not act in a way which is incompatible with the Convention
- individuals whose Convention rights have been infringed by a public authority may bring proceedings against that authority, but the act is not intended to create new rights as between individuals

The main human rights protected by the Convention are the right to life (article 2); protection from torture and inhuman or degrading treatment (article 3); protection from slavery or forced labour (article 4); the right to liberty and security of the person (article 5); the right to a fair trial (article 6); the right not to be subject to retrospective criminal offences (article 7); the right to respect for private and family life (article 8); freedom of thought, conscience and religion (article 9); freedom of expression (article 10); freedom of peaceful association and assembly (article 11); the right to marry and found a family (article 12); protection from discrimination (article 14); the right to property (article 1 protocol No.1); the right to education (article 2 protocol No.1); and the right to free elections (article 3 protocol No.1). Most of the Convention rights are subject to limitations which deem the breach of the right acceptable on the basis it is 'necessary in a democratic society'.

Human rights are also enshrined in the common law (of tort). Although this is of historical significance, the common law (for example the duty of confidentiality) remains especially important regarding violations of human rights that occur between private parties, where the Human Rights Act 1998 does not apply.

PARENTAL RESPONSIBILITY

The Children Act 1989 gives both the mother and father parental responsibility for the child if the parents are married to each other at the time of the child's birth. If the parents are not married, only the mother has parental responsibility. The father may acquire it in accordance with the provisions of section 4 of the Children Act 1989. He can do this in one of four ways: a) by being registered as the father on the child's birth certificate with the consent of the mother (only for fathers of children born after 1 December 2003, following changes to the Adoption and Children Act 2002); b) by applying to the court for a parental responsibility order; c) by entering into a parental responsibility agreement with the mother which must be in the prescribed form; or d) by obtaining a residence order from the court. Otherwise, a father can gain parental responsibility by marrying the mother of the child.

Where a child's parent, who has parental responsibility, marries or enters into a civil partnership with a person who is not the child's parent, the child's parent(s) with parental responsibility can agree for the step-parent to have parental responsibility, or the step-parent may acquire parental responsibility by order of the court (section 4A(1) Children Act 1989).

Where a child is adopted, parental responsibility will be given to the adopter of the child. However, before an order for adoption can be made, the court must be satisfied that every parent or guardian consents. The consent of a father without parental responsibility is not required, although adoption agencies and local authorities must be careful to establish, if possible, the identity of the father and satisfy themselves that any person claiming to be the father either has no intention to apply for parental responsibility or that if he did apply, the application would be likely to be refused.

In Scotland, the relevant legislation is the Children (Scotland) Act 1995, which gives the mother parental rights and responsibilities for her child whether or not she is married to the child's father. A father who is married to the mother, either at the time of the child's conception or subsequently, will also have automatic parental rights and responsibilities. Section 23 of the 2006 act provides that an unmarried father will obtain automatic parental responsibilities and rights if he is registered as the father on the child's birth certificate. For unmarried fathers who are not named on the birth certificate, or whose children were born before the 2006 act came into force, it is possible to acquire parental responsibilities and rights by applying to the court or by entering into a parental responsibilities and rights agreement with the mother. The father of any child, regardless of parental rights, has a duty to aliment that child until he/she is 18 (or under 25 if the child is still at an educational establishment or training for employment or for a trade, profession or vocation).

LEGITIMATION

Under the Legitimacy Act 1976, an illegitimate person automatically becomes legitimate when his/her parents marry. This applies even where one of the parents was married to a third person at the time of the birth. In such cases it is necessary to re-register the birth of the child. In Scotland, the status of illegitimacy has been abolished by section 21 of the 2006 act. The Law Reform Act 1987 reformed the law so as to remove so far as possible the legal disadvantages of illegitimacy.

JURY SERVICE

In England and Wales, the law concerning juries is largely consolidated in the Juries Act 1974. In England and Wales a person charged with a serious criminal offence is entitled to have their trial heard by a jury in a crown court, except in cases where there is a danger of jury tampering or where jury tampering has taken place.

In civil cases, there is a right to a jury in the Queen's Bench Division of the high court in cases where the person applying for a jury has been accused of fraud, as well as in cases of libel, slander, malicious prosecution or false imprisonment. The same applies to the county court. In all other cases in the Queen's Bench Division only the judge has discretion to order trial with a jury, though such an order is seldom made. In the chancery division of the high court a jury is never used. The same is true in the family division of the high court.

No right to a jury trial exists in Scotland, although more serious offences are heard before a jury. In England and Wales criminal cases and civil cases in the high court are generally heard by a jury of 12 members, but in the county court the jury is smaller, normally consisting of eight members. In the event that a juror is excused the trial can proceed so long as there are at least seven remaining jurors in the county court and nine in the case of the high court or crown court. At an inquest, there must be at least seven and no more than 11 members. In Scotland there are 12 members of a jury in a civil case in the court of session, and 15 in a criminal trial in the high court of justiciary. Jurors are normally asked to serve for ten working days, during which time they could sit on more than one case. Jurors selected for longer cases are expected to sit for the duration of the trial.

In England and Wales, every 'registered' parliamentary or local government elector between the ages of 18 and 70 who has lived in the UK (including, for this purpose, the Channel Islands and the Isle of Man) for any period of at least five years since reaching the age of 13 is qualified to serve on a jury unless he/she is 'mentally disordered' or disqualified. Those disqualified from jury service include:

- those who have at any time been sentenced by a court in the UK (including, for this purpose, the Channel Islands and the Isle of Man) to a term of imprisonment or youth custody of five years or more
- those who have been imprisoned for life, detained at Her Majesty's, or the Secretary of State's pleasure, detained for a period of at least five years, imprisoned or detained for public protection, or received an 'extended sentence' under the relevant provisions of the Criminal Justice Act 2003 or the Criminal Procedure (Scotland) Act 1995
- those who have within the previous ten years served any part of a sentence of imprisonment, youth custody or detention, been detained in a young offenders' institution, received a suspended sentence of imprisonment or order for detention, or received a community order
- those who are on bail in criminal proceedings

The court has the discretion to excuse a juror from service, or defer the date of service, if the juror can show there is good reason why he/she should be excused from attending or good reason why his attendance should be deferred. It is an offence (punishable by a fine) to fail to attend when summoned, to serve knowing that you are disqualified from service, or to make false representations in an attempt to evade service. If a juror fails to turn up for service, or attends but cannot serve due to being under the influence of drink or drugs, this is punishable as contempt of court. Any party can object to any juror if he/she can show cause to the trial judge.

It may be appropriate for a judge to excuse a juror from a particular case if he is personally concerned in the facts of the particular case, or closely connected with a party to the proceedings or with a prospective witness. The judge may also discharge any juror who, from a mental or physical incapacity, temporary or permanent, or alternatively due to linguistic difficulties, cannot pay proper attention to the evidence.

An individual juror (or the entire jury) can be discharged if it is shown that they or any of their number have, among other things, separated from the rest of the jury without the leave of the court; talked to any person out of court who is not a member of the jury; determined the verdict of the trial by drawing lots; come to a compromise on the verdict; been drunk, or otherwise incapacitated, while carrying out their duties as a juror; exerted improper pressure on the other members of the jury (eg harassment or bullying); declined to take part in the jury's functions; displayed actual or apparent bias (eg racism, sexism or other discriminatory or deliberate hostility); or inadvertently possessed knowledge of the bad character of a party to the proceedings which has not been adduced as evidence in the proceedings. The factual situations that arise are many, and include falling asleep during the trial, asking friends on Facebook for help in making a decision, consulting an ouija board in the course of deliberations, making telephone calls after retirement, and lunching with a barrister not connected with the proceedings.

In England and Wales, the jury's verdict need not be unanimous. In criminal proceedings, and civil proceedings in the high court, the agreement of 10 jurors will suffice when there are not fewer than 11 people on the jury (or 9 in a jury of 10). In civil proceedings in the county court the agreement of seven or eight jurors will suffice. Where a majority verdict is given, the court must be satisfied that the jury had reasonable time to consider its verdict based on the nature and complexity of the case. In criminal proceedings this must be no less than two hours and ten minutes (allowing time for the jury to settle after retiring).

A juror is immune from prosecution or civil claim in

respect of anything said or done by him or her in the discharge of their office. It is a contempt of court for a juror to disclose what happened in the jury room even after the trial is over. A juror may claim travelling expenses, a subsistence allowance and an allowance for other financial loss (eg loss of earnings or benefits, fees paid to carers or child-minders) up to a stated limit. For more information on jury service, visit W www.gov.uk/jury-service/overview

SCOTLAND

Qualification criteria for jury service in Scotland are similar to those in England and Wales, except that members of the judiciary are ineligible for ten years after ceasing to hold their post, and others concerned with the administration of justice are only eligible for service five years after ceasing to hold office. Certain persons have the right to apply to be excused – full-time members of the medical, dental, nursing, veterinary and pharmaceutical professions, full-time members of the armed forces, ministers of religion, persons who have served on a jury within the previous five years, members of the Scottish parliament, members of the Scottish government, junior Scottish ministers and those aged 71 years or over. Those who are incapable by reason of a mental disorder may also be excused. Such an application will be accepted if the application is made within 7 days of the person being notified that they may have to serve. For civil trials there is an age limit of 65 years. Those convicted of a crime and sentenced to a period of imprisonment of 5 years or more are automatically disqualified. The maximum fine for a person serving on a jury knowing himself/herself to be ineligible is £1,000. The maximum fine for failing to attend without good cause is also £1,000.

HER MAJESTY'S COURTS AND TRIBUNALS SERVICE, 102 Petty France, London SW1H 9AJ T 0845-456 8770

JURY CENTRAL SUMMONING BUREAU, T 0845-803 8003 E jurysummoning@hmcts.gsi.gov.uk

SCOTTISH COURTS SERVICE, Courts of Session, Parliament House, Parliament Square, Edinburgh EH1 1RQ T 0131-225 2595 W www.scotcourts.gov.uk

THE CLERK OF JUSTICIARY, High Court of Justiciary, Lawnmarket, Edinburgh EH2 2NS T 0131-240 6900

LANDLORD AND TENANT

RESIDENTIAL LETTINGS

The provisions outlined here apply only where the tenant lives in a separate dwelling from the landlord and where the dwelling is the tenant's only or main home. It does not apply to licensees such as lodgers, guests or service occupiers.

The 1996 Housing Act radically changed certain aspects of the legislation referred to below; in particular, the grant of assured and assured shorthold tenancies under the Housing Act 1988.

ASSURED SHORTHOLD TENANCIES

If a tenancy was granted on or after 15 January 1989 and before 28 February 1997, the tenant would have an assured tenancy unless the landlord served notice under section 20 in the prescribed form prior to the commencement of the tenancy, stating that the tenancy is to be an assured shorthold tenancy and the tenancy is for a minimum fixed term period of six months (*see* below). An assured tenancy gives that tenant greater security. The tenant could, for example, stay in possession of the dwelling for as long as the tenant observed the terms of the tenancy. The landlord cannot obtain possession from such a tenant unless the landlord can establish a specific ground for possession (set out in the Housing Act 1988) and obtains a court order. The rent payable is that agreed with the landlord at the start of the tenancy. The landlord has the right to increase the rent annually by serving a notice. If that happens the tenant can apply to have the rent fixed by the rent assessment committee of the local authority. The tenant or the landlord may request that the committee sets the rent in line with open market rents for that type of property.

Under the Housing Act 1996, all new lettings (below an annual rent threshold of £100,000 since October 2010) entered into on or after 28 February 1997 (for whatever term) will be assured shorthold tenancies unless the landlord serves a notice stating that the tenancy is not to be an assured shorthold tenancy. This means that the landlord is entitled to possession at the end of the tenancy provided he serves a notice under section 21 Housing Act 1988 and commences the proceedings in accordance with the correct procedure. The landlord must obtain a court order, however, to obtain possession if the tenant refuses to vacate at the end of the tenancy. If the tenancy is an assured shorthold tenancy, the court must grant the order. For both assured and assured shorthold tenancies, if the tenant is more than eight weeks in arrears, the landlord can serve notice and, if the tenant is still in arrears at the date of the hearing, the court must make an order for possession.

REGULATED TENANCIES

Before the Housing Act 1988 came into force on 15 January 1989 there were regulated tenancies; some are still in existence and are protected by the Rent Act 1977. Under this act it is possible for the landlord or the tenant to apply to the local rent officer to have a 'fair' rent registered. The fair rent is then the maximum rent payable.

SECURE TENANCIES

Secure tenancies are generally given to tenants of local authorities, housing associations (before 15 January 1989) and certain other bodies. This gives the tenant security of tenure unless the terms of the agreement are broken by the tenant and it is reasonable to make an order for possession. Those with secure tenancies may have the right to buy their property. In practice this right is generally only available to council tenants.

AGRICULTURAL PROPERTY

Tenancies in agricultural properties are governed by the Agricultural Holdings Act 1986, the Agricultural Tenancies Act 1995 (both amended by the Regulatory Reform (Agricultural Tenancies) (England and Wales) Order 2006), the Tribunals, Courts and Enforcement Act 2007, the Legal Services Act 2007 and the Rent (Agriculture) Act 1976, which give similar protections to those described above, eg security of tenure, right to compensation for disturbance, etc. Similar provisions are applied to Scotland by the Agricultural Holdings (Scotland) Act 2003 for those leases entered into on or after 27 November 2003. The Agricultural Holdings (Scotland) Act 1991 continues to apply to those leases in Scotland entered into prior to this date and in certain other circumstances outlined by the 2003 act. However, one distinction to note between the 1991 act and the 2003 act is that those leases governed by the former have full security of tenure, subject to certain exceptions, whereas leases under the 2003 act are fixed term arrangements of various durations.

EVICTION

The Protection from Eviction Act 1977 (as amended by the Housing Act 1988 and Nationality, Immigration and Asylum Act 2002) sets out the procedure a landlord must follow in order to obtain possession of property. It is unlawful for a landlord to evict a tenant otherwise than in accordance with the law. For common law tenancies and for Rent Act tenants a notice to quit in the prescribed form giving 28 days' notice is required. For secure and assured tenancies a notice seeking possession must be served. It is unlawful for the landlord to evict a person by putting their belongings on to the street, by changing the locks and so on. It is also unlawful for a landlord to harass a tenant in any way in order to persuade him/her to give up the tenancy. The tenant may be able to obtain an injunction to restrain the actions of the landlord and get back into the property and be awarded damages.

LANDLORD RESPONSIBILITIES

Under the Landlord and Tenant Act 1985, where the term of the lease is less than seven years, the landlord is responsible for maintaining the structure and exterior of the property, for sanitation, for heating and hot water, and all installations for the supply of water, gas and electricity.

While the responsibility of maintaining the premises remains intact, since July 2012 landlords are no longer permitted to enter the rental premises for the purpose of viewing their state and condition. This power of entry was revoked by the Protection of Freedoms Act 2012.

LEASEHOLDERS

Strictly speaking, leaseholders have bought a long lease rather than a property and in certain limited circumstances the landlord can end the tenancy. Under the Leasehold Reform Act 1967 (as amended by the Housing Acts 1969, 1974, 1980 and 1985), leaseholders of houses may have the right to buy the freehold or to take an extended lease for a term of 50 years. This applies to leases where the term of the lease is over 21 years, at a low rent, and where the leaseholder has occupied the house as his/her only or main residence for the last two years, or for a total of two years over the last ten. The tenant must give the landlord written notice of his desire to acquire the freehold or extend the leasehold.

The Leasehold Reform, Housing and Urban Development Act came into force in 1993 and allows the leaseholders of flats in certain circumstances to buy the freehold of the building in which they live.

Responsibility for maintenance of the structure, exterior and interior of the building should be set out in the lease. Usually the upkeep of the interior of his/her part of the property is the responsibility of the leaseholder, and responsibility for the structure, exterior and common interior areas is shared between the freeholder and the leaseholder(s).

If leaseholders are dissatisfied with charges made in respect of lease extensions, they are entitled to have their situation evaluated by the Leasehold Valuation Tribunal.

The Commonhold and Leasehold Reform Act 2002 makes provision for the freehold estate in land to be registered as commonhold land and for the legal interest in the land to be vested in a 'commonhold association' ie a private limited company.

BUSINESS LETTINGS

The Landlord and Tenant Acts 1927 and 1954 (as amended) give security of tenure to the tenants of most business premises. The landlord can only evict the tenant on one of the grounds laid down in the 1954 act, and in some cases where the landlord repossesses the property the tenant may be entitled to compensation.

SCOTLAND

In Scotland assured and short assured tenancies exist for lettings after 2 January 1989 and are similar to assured tenancies in England and Wales. The relevant legislation is the Housing (Scotland) Act 1988.

Most tenancies created before 2 January 1989 were regulated tenancies and the Rent (Scotland) Act 1984 still applies where these exist. The act defines, among other things, the circumstances in which a landlord can increase the rent when improvements are made to the property. The provisions of the Rent Act do not apply to tenancies where the landlord is the Crown, a local authority or a housing corporation.

The Housing (Scotland) Acts of 1987 and 2001 relate to local authority and registered social landlord responsibilities for housing, the right to buy, and local authority secured tenancies. The provisions are broadly similar to England and Wales. The Housing (Scotland) Act 2010 is now substantially in force. This reforms right-to-buy provisions, modernises social housing regulation, introduces the Scottish social housing charter and replaces the regulatory framework established by the 2001 act.

In Scotland, business premises are not controlled by statute to the same extent as in England and Wales, although the Tenancy of Shops (Scotland) Act 1949 gives some security to tenants of shops. Tenants of shops can apply to the sheriff, within 21 days of being served a notice to quit, for a renewal of tenancy if threatened with eviction. This application may be dismissed on various grounds including where the landlord has offered to sell the property to the tenant at an agreed price or, in the absence of agreement as to price, at a price fixed by a single arbiter appointed by the parties or the sheriff. The act extends to properties where the Crown or government departments are the landlords or the tenants.

Under the Leases Act 1449 the landlord's successors (either purchasers or creditors) are bound by the agreement made with any tenants so long as the following conditions are met:

- the lease, if for more than one year, must be in writing
- there must be a rent
- there must be a term of expiry
- the tenant must have entered into possession
- the subjects of the lease must be land
- the landlord, if owner, must be the proprietor with a recorded title, ie the title deeds recorded in the Register of Sasines or registered in the Land Register

The Antisocial Behaviour etc (Scotland) Act 2004 provides that all landlords letting property in Scotland must register with the local authority in which the let property is situated, unless the landlord is a local authority, or a registered social landlord. Exceptions also apply to holiday lets, owner-occupied accommodation and agricultural holdings. The act applies to partnerships, trusts and companies as well as to individuals.

LEGAL AID

The Access to Justice Act 1999 transformed what used to be known as the Legal Aid system. The Legal Aid Board was replaced by the Legal Services Commission, which is responsible for the development and administration of two legal funding schemes in England and Wales, namely the Criminal Defence Service and the Community Legal Service. The Criminal Defence Service assists people who are under police investigation or facing criminal charges. The Community Legal Service is designed to increase access to legal information and advice by involving a much wider network of funders and providers in giving publicly funded legal services. In Scotland, provision of legal aid is governed by the Legal Aid (Scotland) Act 1986 and the Legal Profession and Legal Aid (Scotland) Act 2007 and administered by the Scottish Legal Aid Board.

Under the Legal Aid, Sentencing and Punishment of Offenders Act 2012, which came into force on 12 April 2013, the Legal Services Commission was abolished and replaced by the newly created Legal Aid Agency. The act has also limited the areas of law that fall within the scope of legal aid funding, especially those related to civil legal services. However, the act does include provisions for funding in exceptional cases, such as where failure to provide legal aid would result in a violation of an individual's human rights or where providing legal aid would serve a wider public interest. Further, the act allows for areas of law to be added or omitted from the scope of legal aid independently, without subsequent legislation. The criminal legal services provisions are due to come into force some time in 2014.

LEGAL AID AGENCY, W www.justice.gov.uk/legal-aid

CIVIL LEGAL AID

From 1 January 2000, only organisations (such as solicitors or Citizens Advice) with a contract with the Legal Services Commission (now Legal Aid Agency) have been able to give initial help in any civil matter. Moreover, from that date decisions about funding were devolved from the Legal Services Commission to contracted organisations in relation to any level of publicly funded service in family and immigration cases. For other types of case, applications for public funding are made through a solicitor (or other contracted legal services providers) in much the same way as the former Legal Aid.

Under the civil funding scheme there are broadly six levels of service available:

- legal help
- help at court
- family help – either family help (lower) or family help (higher)
- legal representation – either investigative help or full representation
- family mediation
- such other services as authorised by specific orders

ELIGIBILITY

Eligibility for funding from the Community Legal Service depends broadly on five factors:

- the level of service sought (*see* above)
- whether the applicant qualifies financially
- the merits of the applicant's case
- a costs-benefits analysis (if the costs are likely to outweigh any benefit that might be gained from the proceedings, funding may be refused)
- whether there is any public interest in the case being litigated (ie whether the case has a wider public interest beyond that of the parties involved, eg a human rights case)

The limits on capital and income above which a person is not entitled to public funding vary with the type of service sought.

The Legal Aid, Sentencing and Punishment of Offenders Act 2012 which came into force on 1 April 2013 has abolished capital passporting, meaning that all applicants are subject to the same capital test regardless of whether or not they are receiving benefits. The 2012 act also amended the merits criteria so that legal aid may be refused where the case is suitable for alternative funding, such a Conditional Fee Agreement.

CONTRIBUTIONS

Some of those who qualify for Community Legal Service funding will have to contribute towards their legal costs. Contributions must be paid by anyone who has a disposable income or disposable capital exceeding a prescribed amount. The rules relating to applicable contributions are complex and detailed information can be obtained from the Legal Aid Agency.

STATUTORY CHARGE

A statutory charge is made if a person keeps or gains money or property in a case for which they have received legal aid. This means that the amount paid by the Community Legal Service fund on their behalf is deducted from the amount that the person receives. This does not apply if the court has ordered that the costs be paid by the other party (unless the amount paid by the other party does not cover all of the costs). In certain circumstances, the Legal Aid Agency may waive or postpone payment.

CONTINGENCY OR CONDITIONAL FEES

This system was introduced by the Courts and Legal Services Act 1990. It can offer legal representation on a 'no win, no fee' basis. It provides an alternative form of assistance, especially for those cases which are ineligible for funding by the Community Legal Service. The main area for such work is in the field of personal injuries.

Not all solicitors offer such a scheme and different solicitors may well have different terms. The effect of the agreement is that solicitors may not make any charges, or may waive some of their charges, until the case is concluded successfully. If a case is won then the losing party will usually have to pay towards costs, with the winning party contributing around one third.

SCOTLAND

Civil legal aid is available for cases in the following:

- the sheriff courts
- the court of session
- the Supreme Court
- the lands valuation appeal court
- the Scottish land court
- the Lands Tribunal for Scotland
- the Employment Appeal Tribunals
- the Proscribed Organisations Appeal Commissioner
- certain appeals before the Social Security Commissioners

Civil legal aid is not available for election petitions, small claims, simplified divorce procedures or petitions by a debtor for his own sequestration. In defamation actions additional criteria must be met in order for legal aid to be available.

Eligibility for civil legal aid is assessed in a similar way to that in England and Wales, though the financial limits differ in some respects. A person shall be eligible for civil legal aid if their disposable income does not exceed £26,239 a year. A person may be refused civil aid if their disposable capital exceeds £13,017 and it appears to the Legal Aid board that they can afford to pay without legal aid. Additionally:

- if disposable capital is between £7,853 and £13,017, the applicant will be required to pay a contribution which will be equal to the difference between £7,853 and their disposable capital
- if disposable income is between £3,522 and £11,540, a contribution of one third of the difference between £3,522 and the disposable income may be payable
- if disposable income is between £11,541 and £15,743, one third of the difference between £3,522 and £11,540 plus half the difference between £11,541 and the disposable income may be payable
- if disposable income is between £15,744 and £26,239, a contribution of the following: one third of the difference between £3,522 and £11,540, plus half the difference between £11,541 and £15,743, plus all the remaining disposable income between £15,744 and £26,239 – will be payable

CRIMINAL LEGAL AID

The Legal Aid Agency provides defendants facing criminal charges with free legal representation if they pass a merits test and a means test.

Criminal legal aid covers the cost of preparing a case and legal representation in criminal proceedings. It is also available for appeals against verdicts or sentences in magistrates' courts, the crown court or the court of appeal. It is not available for bringing a private prosecution in a criminal court.

If granted criminal legal aid, either the person may choose their own solicitor or the court will assign one. Contributions to the legal costs may be required. The rules relating to applicable contributions are complex and detailed information can be obtained from the Legal Aid Agency.

DUTY SOLICITORS

The Legal Aid Act 1988 also provides for free advice and assistance to anyone questioned by the police (whether under arrest or helping the police with their enquiries). No means test or contributions are required for this.

SCOTLAND

Legal advice and assistance operates in a similar way in Scotland. A person is eligible:

- if disposable income does not exceed £245 a week. If disposable income is between £105 and £245 a week, contributions are payable
- if disposable capital does not exceed £1,716 (if the person has dependent relatives, the savings allowance is higher)
- if receiving income support or income-related job seeker's allowance they qualify automatically provided their disposable capital is not over the limit

The procedure for application for criminal legal aid depends on the circumstances of each case. In solemn cases (more serious cases, such as murder) heard before a jury, a person is automatically entitled to criminal legal aid until they are given bail or placed in custody. Thereafter, it is for the court to decide whether to grant legal aid. The court will do this if the person accused cannot meet the expenses of the case without undue hardship on him or his dependants. In less serious cases the procedure depends on whether the person is in custody:

- anyone taken into custody has the right to free legal aid from the duty solicitor up to and including the first court appearance
- if the person is not in custody and wishes to plead guilty, they are not entitled to criminal legal aid but may be entitled to legal advice and assistance, including assistance by way of representation
- if the person is not in custody and wishes to plead not guilty, they can apply for criminal legal aid. This must be done within 14 days of the first court appearance at which they made the plea

The criteria used to assess whether or not criminal legal aid should be granted is similar to the criteria for England and Wales. When meeting with your solicitor, take evidence of your financial position such as details of savings, bank statements, pay slips, pension book or benefits book.

Once the relevant provisions of the Scottish Civil Justice Council and Criminal Legal Assistance Act 2013 comes into force (expected to be autumn 2013), a person in receipt of criminal legal aid or criminal assistance by way of representation, will be required, in most circumstances, to make contributions where their weekly disposable income is £82 or above if their disposable capital is £750 or more.

THE SCOTTISH LEGAL AID BOARD, 44 Drumsheugh Gardens, Edinburgh EH3 7SW T 0131-226 7061 W www.slab.org.uk

MARRIAGE

Any two persons may marry provided that:

- they are at least 16 years old on the day of the marriage (in England and Wales persons under the age of 18 must generally obtain the consent of their parents or guardian; if consent is refused an appeal may be made to the high court, the county court or a court of summary jurisdiction)
- they are not related to one another in a way which would prevent their marrying
- they are unmarried (a person who has already been married must produce documentary evidence that the previous marriage has been ended by death, divorce or annulment)
- they are capable of understanding the nature of a marriage ceremony and of consenting to marriage

It is now lawful for same sex couples to marry by way of civil or religious ceremony following the passing of the Marriage (Same Sex Couples) Act on 17 July 2013. In addition, an existing marriage will now be able to continue where one or both parties change their legal gender and both parties wish to remain married. The Act also makes provision for civil partners to convert their civil partnership into a marriage if they wish to do so.

The parties should check the marriage will be recognised as valid in their home country if either is not a British citizen.

DEGREES OF RELATIONSHIP

A marriage between persons within the prohibited degrees of consanguinity, affinity or adoption is void.

A man may not marry his mother, daughter, grandmother, granddaughter, sister, aunt, niece, adoptive mother, former adoptive mother, adopted daughter or former adopted daughter.

A woman may not marry her father, son, grandfather, grandson, brother, uncle, nephew, adoptive father, former adoptive father, adopted son or former adopted son. Under the Marriage (Prohibited Degrees of Relationship) Act 1986, some exceptions to the law permit a man or a woman to marry certain step-relatives or in-laws.

In addition to the above, a person may not marry a child of their former civil partner, a child of a former spouse, the former civil partner of a grandparent, the former civil partner of a parent, the former spouse of a grandparent, the former spouse of a parent, the grandchild of a former civil partner or the grandchild of a former spouse, unless the only reason they cannot marry is the affinity mentioned above and both persons are over 21 and the younger party has not at any time before attaining the age of 18 been a child of the family in relation to the other party. All references to brothers/sisters include half-brothers/sisters.

ENGLAND AND WALES

TYPES OF MARRIAGE CEREMONY

It is possible to marry by either religious or civil ceremony. A religious ceremony can take place at a church or chapel of the Church of England or the Church in Wales, or at any other place of worship which has been formally registered by the Registrar-General.

A civil ceremony can take place at a register office, a registered building or any other premises approved by the local authority.

An application for an approved premises licence must be made by the owners or trustees of the building concerned; it cannot be made by the prospective marriage couple. Approved premises must be regularly open to the public so that the marriage can be witnessed; the venue must be deemed to be a permanent and immovable structure. Open-air ceremonies are prohibited.

Non-Anglican marriages may also be solemnised following the issue of a Registrar-General's licence in unregistered premises where one of the parties is seriously ill, is not expected to recover, and cannot be moved to registered premises. Detained and housebound persons may be married at their place of residence.

MARRIAGE IN THE CHURCH OF ENGLAND OR THE CHURCH IN WALES

Marriage by banns

The marriage can take place in a parish in which one of the parties lives, or in a church in another parish if it is the usual place of worship of either or both of the parties. New regulations introduced in October 2008 also allow marriages to take place in a parish where one of the parties was baptised or prepared for confirmation (but not if combined rite); a parish where one of the parties lived or attended worship for six months or more; a parish where one of the parents of either of the parties lived for six months or more; a parish where one of the parents of either of the parties has attended public worship for six months or more in the child's lifetime; or a parish where the parents or grandparents of either of the parties were married. The banns (ie the announcement of the marriage ceremony) must be called in the parish in which the marriage is to take place on three Sundays before the day of the ceremony; if either or both of the parties lives in a different parish the banns must also be called there. After three months the banns are no longer valid. The minister will not perform the marriage unless satisfied that the banns have been properly called.

Marriage by common licence

The vicar who is to conduct the marriage will arrange for a common licence to be issued by the diocesan bishop; this dispenses with the necessity for banns. One of the parties must have lived in the parish for 15 days immediately before the issuing of the licence or must usually worship at the church. Eligibility requirements vary from diocese to diocese, but it is not normally required that the parties should have been baptised. The licence is valid for three months.

Marriage by special licence

A special licence is granted by the Archbishop of Canterbury in special circumstances for the marriage to take place at any place, with or without previous residence in the parish, or at any time. It is usually required that at least one of the parties has been baptised. The special licence will expire after three months. Application must be made to the registrar of the Faculty Office: 1 The Sanctuary, London SW1P 3JT T 020-7222 5381.

Marriage by certificate

The marriage can be conducted on the authority of the superintendent registrar's certificate, provided that the vicar's consent is obtained (the vicar is not obliged to accept the certificate). One of the parties must live in the parish or must usually worship at the church.

MARRIAGE BY OTHER RELIGIOUS CEREMONY

One of the parties must normally live in the registration district where the marriage is to take place. If the building where the parties wish to be married has not been registered, the couple can still have a religious ceremony there, but will also need to have a separate civil ceremony for the marriage to be valid. If the building is registered, in addition to giving notice to the superintendent registrar it may also be necessary to book a registrar, or authorised person to be present at the ceremony.

CIVIL MARRIAGE

A marriage may be solemnised at any register office, registered building or approved premises in England and Wales, without either of the parties being resident in the same district. The superintendent registrar of the district should be contacted, and, if the marriage is to take place at approved premises, the necessary arrangements at the venue must also be made.

NOTICE OF MARRIAGE

Unless it is to take place by banns or under common or special licence in the Church of England or the Church in Wales, a notice of the marriage must be given in person to the superintendent registrar. Notice of marriage may be given in the following ways:

- by certificate. Both parties must have lived in a registration district in England or Wales for at least seven days immediately before giving notice personally at the local register office. If they live in different registration districts, notice must be given in both districts by the respective party in person. The marriage can take place in any register office or other approved premises in England and Wales no sooner than 16 days after notice has been given, when the superintendent registrar issues a certificate
- by licence. One of the parties must have lived in a registration district in England or Wales for at least 15 days before giving notice at the register office; the other party need only be a resident of, or be physically in, England and Wales on the day notice is given

A notice of marriage is valid for 12 months, unless it is for the marriage of a detained or housebound person, when it will usually only be accepted within three months of publication. Notice for marriages taking place within the Church of England or Church of Wales are also only valid for three months following publication. It should be possible to make an advance (provisional) booking 12 months before the ceremony. In this case it is still necessary to give formal notice three months before the marriage. When giving notice of the marriage it is necessary to produce official proof, if relevant, that any previous marriage has ended in divorce or death by producing a decree absolute or death certificate; it is also necessary to provide proof of age, identity and nationality for each of the parties, for example, with a passport. If either party is under 18 years old, evidence of consent by their parent or guardian is required. There are special procedures for those wishing to get married in the UK that are subject to immigration control; the register office will be able to advise on these.

SOLEMNISATION OF THE MARRIAGE

On the day of the wedding there must be at least two other people present who are prepared to act as witnesses and sign the marriage register. A registrar of marriages must be present at a marriage in a register office or at approved premises, but an authorised person may act in the capacity of registrar in a registered building.

If the marriage takes place at approved premises, the room must be separate from any other activity on the premises at the time of the ceremony, and no food or drink can be sold or consumed in the room during the ceremony or for one hour beforehand.

The marriage must be solemnised with open doors. At some time during the ceremony the parties must make a declaration that they know of no legal impediment to the marriage and they must also say the contracting words; the declaratory and contracting words may vary according to the form of service. A civil marriage cannot contain any religious aspects, but it may be possible for non-religious music and/or readings to be included. It may also be possible to embellish the marriage vows taken by the couple.

CIVIL FEES

Notice and registration of Marriage at a Register Office

By superintendent registrar's certificate, £35 per person for the notice of the marriage (which is not refundable if the marriage does not in fact take place) and £45 for the registration of the marriage.

Marriage at a Register Office/Approved Premises

Fees for marriage at a register office are set by the local authority responsible. An additional fee will also be payable for the superintendent registrar's and registrar's attendance at the marriage on an approved premises. This is also set locally by the local authority responsible. A further charge is likely to be made by the owners of the building for the use of the premises. For marriages taking place in a religious building other than the Church of England or Church of Wales, an additional fee of £84 is payable for the registrar's attendance at the marriage unless an 'Authorised Person' appointed by the trustees of the building has agreed to register the marriage. Additional fees may be charged by the trustees of the building for the wedding and by the person who performs the ceremony.

ECCLESIASTICAL FEES

(Church of England and Church in Wales)

Marriage by banns

For publication of banns, £21*

For certificate of banns issued at time of publication, £13.00*

For marriage service, £381*

For marriage certificate at registration if required £4†

* These fees are revised from 1 January each calendar year. Some may not apply to the Church in Wales

† This fee is revised from 1 April each calendar year

SCOTLAND

REGULAR MARRIAGES

A regular marriage is one which is celebrated by a minister of religion or authorised registrar or other celebrant. Each of the parties must complete a marriage notice form and return it to the district registrar for the area in which they are to be married, irrespective of where they live, within the three month period prior to the date of the marriage and not later than 15 days prior to that date. The district registrar must then enter the date of receipt and certain details in a marriage book kept for this purpose, and must also enter the names of the parties and the proposed date of marriage in a list which is displayed in a conspicuous place at the registration office until the date of the marriage has passed. All persons wishing to enter into a regular marriage in Scotland must follow the same preliminary procedure regardless of whether they intend to have a religious or civil ceremony. Before the marriage ceremony takes place any person may submit an objection in writing to the district registrar.

A marriage schedule, which is prepared by the registrar, will be issued to one or both of the parties in person up to seven days before a religious marriage; for a civil marriage the schedule will be available at the ceremony. The schedule must be handed to the celebrant before the ceremony starts; it must be signed immediately after the wedding and the marriage must be registered within three days.

The authority to conduct a religious marriage is deemed to be vested in the authorised celebrant rather than the building in which it takes place; open-air religious ceremonies are therefore permissible in Scotland.

From 10 June 2002 it has been possible, under the Marriage (Scotland) Act 2002, for venues or couples to apply to the local council for a licence to allow a civil ceremony to take place at a venue other than a registration office. To obtain further information, a venue or couple should contact the district registrar in the area they wish to marry. A list of licensed venues is also available on the National Records of Scotland website.

MARRIAGE BY COHABITATION WITH HABIT AND REPUTE

Prior to the enactment of the Family Law (Scotland) Act 2006, if two people had lived together constantly as husband and wife and were generally held to be such by the neighbourhood and among their friends and relations, a presumption could arise from which marriage could be inferred. Before such a marriage could be registered, however, a decree of declarator of marriage had to be obtained from the court of session. Section 3 of the 2006 act provides that it will no longer be possible for a marriage to be constituted by cohabitation with habit and repute, but it will still be possible for couples whose period of cohabitation began before commencement of the 2006 act to seek a declarator under the old rule of law.

CIVIL FEES

The fee for submitting a notice of marriage to the district registrar is £30.00 a person. Solemnisation of a civil marriage costs £55.00, while the extract of the entry in the register of marriages attracts a fee of £10.00. The costs of religious marriage ceremonies can vary.

THE GENERAL REGISTER OFFICE, PO Box 2, Southport PR8 2JD T 0845-603 7788 W www.gro.gov.uk/gro/content/certificates

THE NATIONAL RECORDS OF SCOTLAND, New Register House, 3 West Register Street, Edinburgh EH1 3YT T 0131-314 4452 W www.gro-scotland.gov.uk

TOWN AND COUNTRY PLANNING

The planning system can help to protect the environment and assist individuals in assessing their land rights. There are a number of acts governing the development of land and buildings in England and Wales and advice should always be sought from Citizens Advice or the local planning authority before undertaking building works on any land or property. If development takes place which requires planning permission without permission being given, enforcement action may take place and the situation may need to be rectified. Planning law in Scotland is similar but certain Scotland-specific legislation applies so advice should always be sought.

PLANNING PERMISSION

Planning permission is needed if the work involves:

- making a material change in use, such as dividing off part of the house or garden so that it can be used as a separate home or dividing off part of the house for commercial use, eg for a workshop
- going against the terms of the original planning permission, eg there may be a restriction on fences in front gardens on an open-plan estate
- building, engineering or mining, except for the permitted developments below
- new or wider access to a main road
- additions or extensions to flats or maisonettes
- work which might obstruct the view of road users

Planning permission is not needed to carry out internal alterations or work which does not affect the external appearance of the building, and are not works for making good war damage or works begun after 5 December 1968 for the alteration of a building by providing additional space in it underground.

Under regulations which came into effect on 1 October 2008, there are certain types of development for which the

Secretary of State for the Environment, Food and Rural Affairs has granted general permissions (permitted development rights). These include house extensions and additions, outbuildings and garages, other ancillary garden buildings such as swimming pools or ponds, and laying patios, paths or driveways for domestic use. All developments are subject to a number of conditions.

Before carrying out any of the above permitted developments you should contact your local planning authority to find out whether the general permission has been modified in your area. For more information, visit W www.planningportal.gov.uk

OTHER RESTRICTIONS

It may be necessary to obtain other types of permissions before carrying out any development. These permissions are separate from planning permission and apply regardless of whether or not planning permission is needed, eg:

- building regulations will probably apply if a new building is to be erected, if an existing one is to be altered or extended, or if the work involves building over a drain or sewer. The building control department of the local authority will advise on this
- any alterations to a listed building or the grounds of a listed building must be approved by the local authority. Listing will include not only the main building but everything in the curtilage of the building
- local authority approval is necessary if a building (or, in some circumstances, gates, walls, fences or railings) in a conservation area is to be demolished; each local authority keeps a register of all local buildings that are in conservation areas
- a council order is required if your proposed development would obstruct a public path which crosses your property, and you should discuss any such proposals with the council at an early stage
- many trees are protected by tree preservation orders and must not be pruned or taken down without local authority consent
- bats and many other species are protected, and Natural England, Natural Resources Wales or Scottish Natural Heritage must be notified before any work is carried out that will affect the habitat of protected species, eg timber treatment, renovation or extensions of lofts
- developments in areas with special designations, such as National Parks, Areas of Outstanding Natural Beauty, National Scenic Areas or in the Norfolk or Suffolk Broads, are subject to greater restrictions. The local planning authority will advise or refer enquirers to the relevant authority

There may also be restrictions contained in the title to the property which require you to get someone else's agreement before carrying out certain developments, and which should be considered when works are planned.

VOTERS' QUALIFICATIONS

Those entitled to vote at parliamentary, and local government elections are those who, at the date of taking the poll, are:

- on the electoral roll
- aged 18 years or older
- British citizens, Commonwealth citizens or citizens of the Irish Republic who are resident in the UK
- those who suffer from no other legal bar to voting (eg prisoners). It should be noted that there is some uncertainty regarding the future of the legal bar on prisoners' voting following a decision taken by the European Court of Human Rights
- in Northern Ireland electors must have been resident in Northern Ireland during the whole of the three-month period prior to the relevant date
- citizens of any EU member state may vote in local elections if they meet the criteria listed above (save for the nationality requirements)

British citizens resident abroad are entitled to vote, provided they have been registered to vote in the UK within the last 15 years, as overseas electors in domestic parliamentary elections in the constituency in which they were last resident if they are on the electoral roll of the relevant constituency. Members of the armed forces and their spouses or civil partners, Crown servants and employees of the British Council who are overseas, along with their spouses and civil partners, are entitled to vote regardless of how long they have been abroad. British citizens who had never been registered as an elector in the UK are not eligible to register as an overseas voter unless they left the UK before they were 18, providing they left the country no more than 15 years ago. Overseas electors may opt to vote by proxy or by postal vote. Overseas voters may not vote in local government elections.

The main categories of people who are not entitled to vote at general elections are:

- sitting peers in the House of Lords
- convicted persons detained in pursuance of their sentences (though remand prisoners, unconvicted prisoners and civil prisoners can vote if on the electoral register). This is currently subject to review, as detailed above
- those convicted within the previous five years of corrupt or illegal election practices
- EU citizens (who may only vote in EU and local government elections)

Under the Representation of the Peoples Act 2000, several new groups of people are permitted to vote for the first time. These include: people who live on barges; people in mental health hospitals (other than those with criminal convictions) and homeless people who have made a 'declaration of local connection'.

REGISTERING TO VOTE

Voters must be entered on an electoral register. The Electoral Registration Officer (ERO) for each council area is responsible for preparing and publishing the register for his area by 1 December each year. Names may be added to the register to reflect changes in people's circumstances as they occur and each month during December to August, the ERO publishes a list of alterations to the published register.

A registration form is sent to all households in the autumn of each year and the householder or 'head of household' decides who to register. The householder is required to provide details of all occupants who are eligible to vote, including ones who will reach their 18th birthday in the year covered by the register. On 10 May 2012, the government introduced the electoral registration and administration bill, which received royal assent on 31 January 2013. The act replaced household registration with individual voter registration. Individuals will also be asked for identifying information such as date of birth and national insurance number. The act also introduced a number of changes relating to electoral administration and the conduct of elections. Anyone failing to supply information to the ERO when requested, or supplying false information, may be fined by up to £1,000. Application forms and more information are available from the Electoral Commission (W www.aboutmyvote.co.uk).

VOTING

Voting is not compulsory in the UK. Those who wish to vote do so in person at the allotted polling station. Postal votes are now available to anyone on request and you do not need to give a reason for using a postal vote.

A proxy (whereby the voter nominates someone to vote in person on their behalf) can be appointed to act in a specific election, for a specified period of time or indefinitely. For the appointment of an indefinite or long-term proxy, the voter needs to specify physical employment, study reasons or a disability to explain why they are making an application. With proxy votes where a particular election is specified, the voter needs to provide details of the circumstances by which they cannot reasonably be expected to go to the polling station. Applications for a proxy are normally available up to six working days before an election, but should the voter fall ill on election day, it is possible to appoint a proxy up until polling day.

Further information can be obtained from the local authority's ERO in England and Wales or the electoral registration office in Scotland, or the Chief Electoral Officer in Northern Ireland.

WILLS

A will is used to appoint executors (who will administer the estate), give directions as to the disposal of the body, appoint guardians for children, and determine how and to whom property is to be passed. A well-drafted will can operate to reduce the level of inheritance tax which the estate pays. It is best to have a will drawn up by a solicitor, but if a solicitor is not employed the following points must be taken into account:

- if possible the will must not be prepared on behalf of another person by someone who is to benefit from it or who is a close relative of a major beneficiary
- the language used must be clear and unambiguous and it is better to avoid the use of legal terms where the same thing can be expressed in plain language
- it is better to rewrite the whole document if a mistake is made. If necessary, alterations can be made by striking through the words with a pen, and the signature or initials of the testator and the witnesses must be put in the margin opposite the alteration. No alteration of any kind should be made after the will has been executed
- if the person later wishes to change the will or part of it, it is better to write a new will revoking the old. The use of codicils (documents written as supplements or containing modifications to the will) should be left to a solicitor
- the will should be typed or printed, or if handwritten be legible and preferably in ink

The form of a will varies to suit different cases – a solicitor will be able to advise as to wording, however, 'DIY' will-writing kits can be purchased from good stationery shops and many banks offer a will-writing service.

LAPSED LEGATEES

If a person who has been left property in a will dies before the person who made the will, the gift fails and will pass to the person entitled to everything not otherwise disposed of (the residuary estate).

If the person left the residuary estate dies before the person who made the will, their share will pass to the closest relative(s) of the testator under the intestacy rules. It is always better to draw up a new will if a beneficiary predeceases the person who made the will.

EXECUTORS

It is usual to appoint two executors, although one is sufficient. No more than four persons can deal with the estate of the person who has died. The name and address of each executor should be given in full (the addresses are not essential but including them adds clarity to the document). Executors should be 18 years of age or over. An executor may be a beneficiary of the will.

WITNESSES

A person who is a beneficiary of a will, or the spouse or civil partner of a beneficiary at the time the will is signed, must not act as a witness or else he/she will be unable to take his/her gift except in some limited circumstances. Husband and wife can both act as witnesses provided neither benefits from the will.

It is better that a person does not act as an executor and as a witness, as he/she can take no benefit under a will to which he/she is witness. The identity of the witnesses should be made as explicit as possible.

EXECUTION OF A WILL

The person making the will should sign his/her name in the presence of the two witnesses. It is advisable to sign at the foot of the document, so as to avoid uncertainty about the testator's intention. The witnesses must then sign their names while the person making the will looks on. If this procedure is not adhered to, the will may be considered invalid. There are certain exceptional circumstances where these rules are relaxed, eg where the person may be too ill to sign.

CAPACITY TO MAKE A WILL

Anyone aged 18 or over can make a will. However, if there is any suspicion that the person making the will is not, through reasons of infirmity or age, fully in command of his/her faculties, it is advisable to arrange for a medical practitioner to examine the person making the will at the time it is to be executed (to verify his/her mental capacity and to record that medical opinion in writing), and to ask the examining practitioner to act as a witness. If a person is not mentally able to make a will, the court may do this for him/her by virtue of the Mental Capacity Act 2005.

REVOCATION

A will may be revoked or cancelled in a number of ways:

- a later will revokes an earlier one if it says so; otherwise the earlier will is by implication revoked by the later one to the extent that it contradicts or repeats the earlier one
- a will is revoked if the physical document on which it is written is destroyed by the person whose will it is. There must be an intention to revoke the will and an act of destruction. It may not be sufficient to obliterate the will with a pen
- a will is revoked by the testator making a written declaration to this effect executed in the same way as a will
- a will is also revoked when the person marries or forms a civil partnership, unless it is clear from the will that the person intended the will to stand after that particular marriage or civil partnership
- where a marriage or civil partnership ends in divorce or dissolution or is annulled or declared void, gifts to the spouse or civil partner and the appointment of the spouse or civil partner as executor fail unless the will says that this is not to happen. A former spouse or civil partner is treated as having predeceased the testator. A separation does not change the effect of a married person or civil partner's will.

PROBATE AND LETTERS OF ADMINISTRATION

Probate is granted to the executors named in a will and once granted, the executors are obliged to carry out the instructions of the will. Letters of administration are granted where no executor is named in a will or is willing or able to act or where there is no will or no valid will; this gives a person, often the next of kin, similar powers and duties to those of an executor.

Applications for probate or for letters of administration can be made to the Principal Registry of the Family Division, to a district probate registry or to a probate sub-registry. Applicants will need the following documents: the Probate Application Form; the original will and codicils (if any); a certificate of death; oath for executors or administrators; and the appropriate tax form (an 'IHT 205' if no inheritance tax is owed; otherwise an 'IHT 400' and 'IHT 421'), in addition to a cheque for the relevant probate fee. Certain property, up to the value of £5,000, may be disposed of without a grant of probate or letters of administration, as can assets that do not pass under the will such as jointly owned assets which pass automatically on the death of one of the joint holders to the survivor.

WHERE TO FIND A PROVED WILL

Since 1858 wills which have been proved, that is wills on which probate or letters of administration have been granted, must have been proved at the Principal Registry of the Family Division or at a district probate registry. The Lord Chancellor has power to direct where the original documents are kept but most are filed where they were proved and may be inspected there and a copy obtained. The Principal Registry also holds copies of all wills proved at district probate registries and these may be inspected at First Avenue House, High Holborn, London. An index of all grants, both of probate and of letters of administration, is compiled by the Principal Registry and may be seen either at the Principal Registry or at a district probate registry.

It is also possible to discover when a grant of probate or letters of administration is issued by requesting a standing search. In response to a request and for a small fee, a district probate registry will supply the names and addresses of executors or administrators and the registry in which the grant was made, of any grant in the estate of a specified person made in the previous 12 months or following six months. This is useful for creditors of the deceased and for applicants who may be beneficiaries to a will but who have lost contact with the deceased.

INTESTACY

Intestacy occurs when someone dies without leaving a will or leaves a will which is invalid or which does not take effect for some reason. Intestacy can be partial, for instance, if there is a will which disposes of some but not all of the testator's property. In such cases the person's estate (property, possessions, other assets following the payment of debts) passes to certain members of the family. If a will has been written that disposes of only part of a person's property, these rules apply to the part which is undisposed of.

Some types of property do not follow the intestacy rules, for example, property held as joint tenants, insurance policies taken out for specified individuals or assigned into trust during the testator's lifetime and death benefits under a pension scheme.

If the person (intestate) leaves a spouse or a civil partner who survives for 28 days and children (legitimate, illegitimate and adopted children and other descendants), the estate is divided as follows:

- if the estate is worth more than £250,000, the spouse or civil partner takes the 'personal chattels' (household articles, including cars, but nothing used for business purposes), £250,000 and a life interest in half of the rest of the estate (which can be capitalised by the spouse or civil partner if he/she wishes)
- the rest of the estate goes to the children*

If the person leaves a spouse or civil partner who survives for 28 days but no children:

- if the estate is worth less than £450,000, the surviving spouse or civil partner takes it in its entirety
- if the estate is worth more than £450,000, the spouse or civil partner takes the personal chattels, £450,000 tax-free (interest payable as before) and full ownership of half of the rest of the estate
- the other half of the rest of the estate goes to the parents (equally, if both alive) or, if none, to the brothers and sisters of the whole blood*
- if there are no parents or brothers or sisters of the whole blood or their children, the spouse or civil partner takes the whole estate
- if the estate is worth less than £250,000, the surviving spouse or civil partner takes it in its entirety

If there is no surviving spouse or civil partner, the estate is distributed among those who survive the intestate as follows:

- to surviving children*, but if none to
- parents (equally, if both alive), but if none to
- brothers and sisters of the whole blood* (including issue of deceased ones), but if none to
- brothers and sisters of the half blood* (including issue of deceased ones), but if none to
- grandparents (equally, if more than one), but if none to
- aunts and uncles of the whole blood*, but if none to
- aunts and uncles of the half blood*, but if none to
- the Crown, Duchy of Lancaster or the Duke of Cornwall (*bona vacantia*)

* To inherit, a member of these groups must survive the intestate and attain the age of 18, or marry under that age. If they die under the age of 18 (unless married under that age), their share goes to others, if any, in the same group. If any member of these groups predeceases the intestate leaving children, their share is divided equally among their children.

In England and Wales the provisions of the Inheritance (Provision for Family and Dependants) Act 1975 may allow other people to claim provision from the deceased's assets. This act also applies to cases where a will has been made and allows a person to apply to the court if they feel that the will or rules of intestacy (or both) do not make adequate provision for them. The court can order payment from the deceased's assets or the transfer of property from them if the applicant's claim is accepted. The application must be made within six months of the grant of probate or letters of administration and the following people can make an application:

- the spouse or civil partner
- a former spouse or civil partner who has not remarried or formed a subsequent civil partnership
- a child of the deceased
- someone treated as a child of the deceased's family
- someone maintained by the deceased
- someone who has cohabited for two years before the death in the same household as the deceased and as the husband or wife or civil partner of the deceased

SCOTLAND

In Scotland any person over 12 and of sound mind can make a will. The person making the will can only freely dispose of the heritage and what is known as the 'dead's part' of the estate because:

- the spouse or civil partner has the right to inherit one-third of the moveable estate if there are children or other descendants, and one-half of it if there are not
- children are entitled to one-third of the moveable estate if there is a surviving spouse or civil partner, and one-half of it if there is not

The remaining portion of the moveable estate is the dead's part, and legacies and bequests are payable from this. Debts are payable out of the whole estate before any division.

From August 1995, wills no longer needed to be 'holographed' and it is now only necessary to have one witness. The person making the will still needs to sign each page. It is better that the will is not witnessed by a beneficiary although the attestation would still be sound and the beneficiary would not have to relinquish the gift.

Subsequent marriage or civil partnership does not revoke a will but the birth of a child who is not provided for may do so. A will may be revoked by a subsequent will, either expressly or by implication, but in so far as the two can be read together both have effect. If a subsequent will is revoked, the earlier will may be revived.

Wills may be registered in the sheriff court Books of the Sheriffdom in which the deceased lived or in the Books of Council and Session at the Registers of Scotland.

CONFIRMATION

Confirmation (the Scottish equivalent of probate) is obtained in the sheriff court of the sheriffdom in which the deceased was domiciled at the time of death. Executors are either 'nominate' (named by the deceased in the will) or 'dative' (appointed by the court in cases where no executor is named in a will or in cases of intestacy). Applicants for confirmation must first provide an inventory of the deceased's estate and a schedule of debts, with an affidavit. In estates under £36,000 gross, confirmation can be obtained under a simplified procedure at reduced fees, with no need for a solicitor. The local sheriff clerk's office can provide assistance.

PRINCIPAL REGISTRY (FAMILY DIVISION), First Avenue House, 42–49 High Holborn, London WC1 6NP
T 020-7947 6000

REGISTERS OF SCOTLAND, Meadowbank House, 153 London Road, Edinburgh EH8 7AU T 0845-607 0161

INTESTACY

The rules of distribution are contained in the Succession (Scotland) Act 1964 and are extended to include civil partners by the Civil Partnership Act 2004.

A surviving spouse or civil partner is entitled to 'prior rights'. This means that the spouse or civil partner has the right to inherit:

- the matrimonial or family home up to a value of £473,000, or one matrimonial or family home if there is more than one, or, in certain circumstances, the value of the home
- the furnishings and contents of that home, up to the value of £29,000
- a cash sum of £50,000 if the deceased left children or other descendants, or £89,000 if not

These figures are increased from time to time by regulations.

Once prior rights have been satisfied legal rights are settled. Legal rights are:

- *Jus relicti(ae) and rights under the section 131 of the Civil Partnership Act 2004* – the right of a surviving spouse or civil partner to one-half of the net moveable estate, after satisfaction of prior rights, if there are no surviving children; if there are surviving children, the spouse or civil partner is entitled to one-third of the net moveable estate
- *Legitim and rights under the section 131 of the Civil Partnership Act 2004* – the right of surviving children to one-half of the net moveable estate if there is no surviving spouse or civil partner; if there is a surviving spouse or civil partner, the children are entitled to one-third of the net moveable estate after the satisfaction of prior rights

Where there is no surviving spouse, civil partner or children, half of the estate is taken by the parents and half by the brothers and sisters. Failing that, the lines of succession, in general, are:

- to descendants
- if no descendants, then to collaterals (ie brothers and sisters) and parents
- surviving spouse or civil partner
- if no collaterals, parents, spouse or civil partner, then to ascendants collaterals (ie aunts and uncles), and so on in an ascending scale
- if all lines of succession fail, the estate passes to the Crown. Relatives of the whole blood are preferred to relatives of the half blood. The right of representation, ie the right of the issue of a person who would have succeeded if he/she had survived the intestate, also applies

INTELLECTUAL PROPERTY

Intellectual property is a broad term covering a number of legal rights provided by the government to help people protect their creative works and encourage further innovation. By using these legal rights people can own the things they create and control the way in which others use their innovations. Intellectual property owners can take legal action to stop others using their intellectual property, they can license their intellectual property to others or they can sell it on. Different types of intellectual property utilise different forms of protection including copyright, designs, patents and trade marks, which are all covered below in more detail.

INTELLECTUAL PROPERTY LAW IN 2013

- The Enterprise and Regulatory Reform Act 2013 limits the terms of protection for artistic works that are mass-produced; reduces the duration of copyright for existing works that are either not published, or which are published anonymously or pseudonymously; and allows the licensing of 'orphan works'
- A change to the Patent Act on 1 October 2013 allows pharmaceutical companies to trial new treatments using patented drugs without the fear of legal consequences
- The Intellectual Property bill makes changes to the law surrounding patents, designs and copyright and seeks to ensure that businesses comprehend better exactly what is protected under Intellectual Property law. At the time of going to press, the bill had undergone its third reading in the House of Lords.

COPYRIGHT

Copyright protects all original literary, dramatic, musical and artistic works, as well as sound and film recordings and broadcasts. Among the works covered by copyright are novels, computer programs, newspaper articles, sculptures, technical drawings, websites, maps and photographs. Under copyright the creators of these works can control the various ways in which their material may be exploited, the rights broadly covering copying, adapting, issuing (including renting and lending) copies to the public, performing in public, and broadcasting the material. The transfer of copyright works to formats accessible to visually impaired persons without infringement of copyright was enacted in 2002.

Copyright protection in the UK is automatic and there is no official registration system. The creator of a work can help to protect it by including the copyright symbol ©, the name of the copyright owner, and the year in which the work was created. In addition, steps can be taken by the work's creator to provide evidence that he/she had the work at a particular time (eg by depositing a copy with a bank or solicitor). The main legislation is the Copyright, Designs and Patents Act 1988 (as amended). As a result of an EU directive effective from January 1996, the term of copyright protection for literary, dramatic, musical (including song lyrics and musical compositions) and artistic works lasts for 70 years after the death of the creator. For film, copyright lasts for 70 years after the director, authors of the screenplay and dialogue, or the composer of any music specially created for the film have all died. Sound recordings are protected for 50 years after their publication (or their first performance if they are not published), and broadcasts for 50 years from the end of the year in which the broadcast/transmission was made. The typographical arrangement of published editions remains under copyright protection for 25 years from the end of the year in which the particular edition was published.

The main international treaties protecting copyright are the Berne Convention for the Protection of Literary and Artistic Works (administered by the World Intellectual Property Organisation (WIPO)), the Rome Convention for the Protection of Performers, Producers of Phonograms and Broadcasting Organisations (administered by UNESCO, the International Labour Organisation and WIPO), the Geneva Phonograms Convention (administered by WIPO), and the Universal Copyright Convention (developed by UNESCO); the UK is a signatory to these conventions. Copyright material created by UK nationals or residents is protected in the countries that have signed one of the above-named conventions by the national law of that country. A list of participating countries may be obtained from the UK Intellectual Property Office. The World Trade Organisation's Trade-Related Aspects of Intellectual Property Rights (TRIPS) agreement, signed in 1995, may also provide copyright protection abroad.

Two treaties which strengthen and update international standards of protection, particularly in relation to new technologies, were agreed in December 1996: the WIPO Copyright Treaty, and the WIPO Performances and Phonograms Treaty. In May 2001 the European Union passed a new directive (which in 2003 became law in the UK) aimed at harmonising copyright law throughout the EU to take account of the internet and other technologies. More information can be found online (W www.ipo.gov.uk).

LICENSING

Use of copyright material without seeking permission in each instance may be permitted under 'blanket' licences available from national copyright licensing agencies. The International Federation of Reproduction Rights Organisations facilitates agreements between its member licensing agencies and on behalf of its members with organisations such as WIPO, UNESCO, the European Union and the Council of Europe. More information can be found online (W www.ifrro.org).

DESIGN PROTECTION

Design protection covers the outward appearance of an article and in the UK takes two forms: registered design and design right, which are not mutually exclusive. Registered design protects the aesthetic appearance of an article, including shape, configuration, pattern or ornament, although artistic works such as sculptures are excluded, being generally protected by copyright. To achieve design protection the owner of the design must apply to the Intellectual Property Office. In order to qualify for protection, a design must be new and materially different from earlier UK published designs. Initial registration lasts for five years and can be extended in five-year increments to a maximum of 25 years. The current legislation is the Registered Designs Act 1949 which has been amended several times, most recently by the Regulatory Reform Order 2006.

UK applicants wishing to protect their designs in the EU can do so by applying for a Registered Community Design with the Office for Harmonisation in the Internal Market.

Outside the EU separate applications must be made in each country in which protection is sought.

Design right is an automatic right which applies to the shape or configuration of articles and does not require registration. Unlike registered design, two-dimensional designs do not qualify for protection but designs of electronic circuits are protected by design right. Designs must be original and non-commonplace. The term of design right is ten years from first marketing of the design, or 15 years after the creation of the design, whichever is earlier. This right is effective only in the UK. After five years anyone is entitled to apply for a licence of right, which allows others to make and sell products copying the design. The current legislation is Part 3 of the Copyright, Designs and Patents Act 1988, amended on 9 December 2001 to incorporate the European Designs Directive, and again in 2006.

PATENTS

A patent is a document issued by the UK Intellectual Property Office relating to an invention. It gives the proprietor the right for a limited period to stop others from making, using, importing or selling the invention without the inventor's permission. In return the patentee pays a fee to cover the costs of processing the patent and publicly discloses details of the invention.

To qualify for a patent an invention must be new, must be functional or technical, must exhibit an inventive step, and must be capable of industrial application. The patent is valid for a maximum of 20 years from the date on which the application was filed, subject to payment of annual fees from the end of the fifth year.

The UK Intellectual Property Office, established in 1852, is responsible for ensuring that all stages of an application comply with the Patents Act 1977, and that the invention meets the criteria for a patent.

WIPO is responsible for administering many of the international conventions on intellectual property. The Patent Cooperation Treaty allows inventors to file a single application for patent rights in some or all of the contracting states. This application is searched by an International Searching Authority to confirm the invention is novel and that the same concept has not already been made publicly available. The application and search report are then published by the International Bureau of WIPO. It may also be the subject of an (optional) international preliminary examination. Applicants must then deal directly with the patent offices in the countries where they are seeking patent rights. The European Patent Convention allows inventors to obtain patent rights in all the contracting states by filing a single application with the European Patent Office. More information can be found online (W www.ipo.gov.uk).

RESEARCH DISCLOSURES

Research disclosures are publicly disclosed details of inventions. Once published, an invention is considered no longer novel and becomes 'prior art'. Publishing a disclosure is significantly cheaper than applying for a patent; however, unlike a patent, it does not entitle the author to exclusive rights to use or license the invention. Instead, research disclosures are primarily published to ensure the inventor the freedom to use the invention. This works because publishing legally prevents other parties from patenting the disclosed innovation and in the UK, patent law dictates that by disclosing details of an invention, even the inventor relinquishes their right to a patent.

In theory, publishing details of an invention anywhere should be enough to constitute a research disclosure. However, to be effective, a research disclosure needs to be published in a location which patent examiners will include in their prior art searches. To ensure global legal precedent it must be included in a publication with a recognised date stamp and made publicly available throughout the world.

Research Disclosure, established in 1960 and operated by Questel Ireland Ltd, is the primary publisher of research disclosures. It is the only disclosure service recognised by the Patent Cooperation Treaty as a mandatory search resource which must be consulted by the international search authorities. More information can be found online (W www.researchdisclosure.com).

TRADE MARKS

Trade marks are a means of identification, which enable traders to make their goods and services readily distinguishable from those supplied by others. Trade marks can take the form of words, a logo or a combination of both. Registration prevents other traders using the same or similar trade marks for similar products or services for which the mark is registered.

In the UK trade marks are registered at the UK Intellectual Property Office. In order to qualify for registration a trade mark must be capable of distinguishing its proprietor's goods or services from those of other undertakings; it should be non-deceptive, should not describe the goods and services or any characteristics of them, should not be contrary to law or morality and should not be similar or identical to any earlier trade marks for the same or similar goods or services. The owner of a registered trade mark may include an fi symbol next to it, and must renew their registration every ten years to keep it in force. The relevant current legislation is the Trade Marks Act 1994 (as amended).

It is possible to obtain an international trade mark registration, effective in 81 countries, under the Madrid system for the international registration of marks, to which the UK is party. British companies can obtain international trade mark registration in those countries party to the system through a single application to WIPO.

EU trade mark regulation is administered by the Office for Harmonisation in the Internal Market (Trade Marks and Designs) in Alicante, Spain. The office registers Community trade marks, which are valid throughout the European Union. The registration of trade marks in individual member states continues in parallel with EU trade mark standards.

DOMAIN NAMES

An internet domain name (eg www.bloomsbury.com) has to be registered separately from a trade mark, and this can be done through a number of registrars which charge varying rates and compete for business. For each top-level domain name (eg .uk, .com), there is a central registry to store the unique internet names and addresses using that suffix. A list of accredited registrars can be found online (W www.icann.org).

CONTACTS

COPYRIGHT LICENSING AGENCY LTD, Saffron House, 6–10 Kirby Street, London EC1N 8TS T 020-7400 3100 W www.cla.co.uk

EUROPEAN PATENT OFFICE, 80298 Munich, Germany T (+49) 89 2399-0 W www.epo.org

INTELLECTUAL PROPERTY OFFICE, Concept House, Cardiff Road, Newport NP10 8QQ T 0300-300 2000 W www.ipo.gov.uk

WORLD INTELLECTUAL PROPERTY ORGANISATION, 34 chemin des Colombettes, CH-1211 Geneva 20, Switzerland T (+41) 22 338 9111 W www.wipo.int

THE MEDIA

CROSS-MEDIA OWNERSHIP

The rules surrounding cross-media ownership were overhauled as part of the 2003 Communications Act. The act simplified and relaxed existing rules to encourage dispersion of ownership and new market entry while preventing the most influential media in any community being controlled by too narrow a range of interests. However, transfers and mergers are not solely subject to examination on competition grounds by the competition authorities. The Secretary of State for Culture, Media and Sport has a broad remit to decide if a transaction is permissible and can intervene on public interest grounds (relating both to newspapers and cross-media criteria, if broadcasting interests are also involved). The Office of Communications (OFCOM) has an advisory role in this context. Government and parliamentary assurances were given that any intervention into local newspaper transfers would be rare and exceptional. Following a request from the Secretary of State for Culture, Media and Sport in June 2010 for a removal of all restrictions from the ownership of local media, OFCOM recommended the liberalisation of local cross-media regulations to enable a single owner to control newspapers, a TV licence and radio stations in one area.

REGULATION

OFCOM is the regulator for the communication industries in the UK and has responsibility for television, radio, telecommunications and wireless communications services. It replaced the Broadcasting Standards Commission, the Independent Television Commission, the Radio Authority, the Radio Communications Agency and OFTEL. OFCOM is required to report annually to parliament and exists to further the interests of consumers by balancing choice and competition with the duty to foster plurality; protect viewers and listeners and promote cultural diversity in the media; and to ensure full and fair competition between communications providers.

OFFICE OF COMMUNICATIONS (OFCOM)
Riverside House, 2A Southwark Bridge Road, London SE1 9HA
T 020-7981 3000 W www.ofcom.org.uk
Chief Executive, Ed Richards

COMPLAINTS

Under the Communications Act 2003 OFCOM's licensees are obliged to adhere to the provisions of its codes (including advertising, programme standards, fairness, privacy and sponsorship). Complainants should contact the broadcaster in the first instance (details can be found on OFCOM's website); however, if the complainant wishes the complaint to be considered by OFCOM, it will do so. Complaints should be made within a reasonable time, as broadcasters are only required to keep recordings for the following periods: radio, 42 days; television, 90 days; and cable and satellite, 60 days. OFCOM can fine a broadcaster, revoke a licence or take programmes off the air. Since November 2004 complaints relating to individual advertisements on TV or radio have been dealt with by the Advertising Standards Authority.

ADVERTISING STANDARDS AUTHORITY
Mid City Place, 71 High Holborn, London WC1V 6QT
T 020-7492 2222 W www.asa.org.uk
Chief Executive, Guy Parker

TELEVISION

There are six major television broadcasters operating in the UK. Four of these – the BBC, ITV, Channel 4 and Channel 5 – launched as free-to-air analogue terrestrial networks. BSkyB and Virgin Media Television provide satellite television services.

The BBC is the oldest broadcaster in the world. The corporation began a London-only television service from Alexandra Palace in 1936 and achieved nationwide coverage 15 years later. A second station, BBC Two, was launched in 1964. The BBC's other free-to-air channels available in the UK comprise BBC Three, BBC Four, BBC One HD, BBC Two HD, BBC News, BBC Parliament and the children's channels, CBeebies and CBBC. The services are funded by the licence fee. The corporation also has a commercial arm, BBC Worldwide, which was formed in 1994 and exists to maximise the value of the BBC's programme and publishing assets for the benefit of the licence payer. Its businesses include international programming distribution, magazines, other licensed products, live events and media monitoring.

The ITV (Independent Television) network began broadcasting in 1955 on Channel 3 in the London area, under the Television Act 1954 which made provision for commercial television in the UK. The ITV network originally comprised a number of independent licensees, the majority of which have now merged to form ITV plc. The network generates funds through broadcasting television advertisements. The ITV network channels now include ITV2, ITV3, ITV4 and CiTV, which all have an equivalent HD channel, with the exception of CiTV. ITV Network Centre is wholly owned by the ITV companies and undertakes commissioning and scheduling of programmes shown across the ITV network and, as with the other terrestrial channels, 25 per cent of programmes must come from independent producers.

Channel 4 and S4C (Sianel Pedwar Cymru – Channel Four Wales) were launched in 1982 to provide programmes with a distinctive character that appeal to interests not catered for by ITV. The broadcaster has a remit to be innovative, experimental and distinctive. Although publicly owned, Channel 4 receives no public funding and is financed predominantly through advertising, but unlike ITV, Channel 4 is not shareholder-owned. It has expanded to create the stations E4, More4, Film4, 4Music and, in July 2012, catchup channel 4seven. S4/C, the Welsh language public service broadcaster, receives annual funding from the Department for Culture, Media and Sport (DCMS). From 2013, the DCMS began to gradually reduce its grant by 94 per cent by 2015 as the BBC took over part-funding of S4/C, providing £76.3m from the licence fee in 2013–14.

Channel 5 began broadcasting in 1997. It was rebranded Five in 2002 but reverted to its original name, Channel 5, after the station was acquired by Northern & Shell in July 2010. Digital stations 5USA and 5* (formerly Five Life, then Fiver) were launched in October 2006.

BSkyB was formed after the merger in 1990 of Sky Television and British Sky Broadcasting. The company operates a satellite television service and has around 40 television channels, including Sky One and the Sky Sports and Sky Movies ranges. It is part-owned by Rupert Murdoch's News Corporation. Sky Digital was launched in 1998 and offers access to over 500 channels. With the 2005 acquisition of Easynet, an internet access provider and network operator, BSkyB now offers voice over IP (VoIP) telephony, video on demand and internet-based TV. With a free box, Sky+ and Sky+ HD customers are able to pause and rewind live TV and record up to 185 hours of regular programming and 60 hours of HD/3D television. As at July 2012, there were 4,343,000 Sky+ customers. In July 2010 BSkyB acquired Virgin Media Television, including its portfolio of channels such as Bravo and Challenge.

VIEWING FIGURES IN 2012

- Sport was the most watched genre on TV in 2012 due to the London 2012 Olympic Games and Euro 2012
- The viewing audiences for the Olympic opening and closing ceremonies peaked at around 27 million people for each ceremony
- The Diamond Jubilee concert attracted the largest non-sports programme audience with 15.3 million viewers
- BBC's *Strictly Come Dancing: Final* was the most watched entertainment programme, viewed by 13.4 million people

Source: OFCOM *Public Service Broadcasting Annual Report 2012*

THE TELEVISION LICENCE

In the UK and its dependencies, a television licence is required to receive any publicly broadcast television service, regardless of its source, including commercial, satellite and cable programming. A TV licence registered to a home address allows the viewer to watch television on laptops, tablets and mobile phones outside the place of residence. If a viewer only watches catch-up TV, not live TV, using services such as BBC iPlayer, and this is the only means by which the viewer watches broadcasts, a television licence is not required.

The TV licence is classified as a tax, therefore non-payment is a criminal offence. A fine of up to £1,000 can be imposed on those successfully prosecuted. The TV licence is issued on behalf of the BBC as the licensing authority under the Communications Act 2003. TV Licensing is the name of the agent contracted to collect the licence fee on behalf of the BBC. In 2012–13 income from licence fees totalled £3,243m, a decrease from £3,244m in 2011–12. In 2013 an annual colour television licence cost £145.50 and a black and white licence £49. Concessions are available for the elderly and people with disabilities. Further details can be found at W www.tvlicensing.co.uk/information

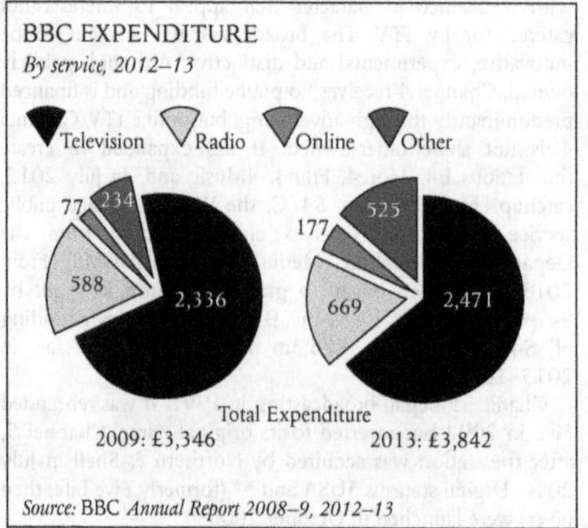

Source: BBC *Annual Report 2008–9, 2012–13*

DIGITAL TELEVISION

Digital broadcasting has dramatically increased the number and reception quality of television channels. Sound and pictures are converted into a digital format and compressed, using as few bits as possible to convey the information on a digital signal. This technique enables several television channels to be carried in the space used by the current analogue signals to carry one channel. Digital signals can be received by standard aerials using Freeview (*see* below), satellite dishes or cable. The signals are decoded and turned back into sound and pictures by either a set-top box or a decoder built into the television set (iDTV). A basic package of channels is available without charge and services are also offered by cable and satellite companies.

The Broadcasting Act 1996 provided for the licensing of 20 or more digital terrestrial television channels (on six frequency channels or 'multiplexes'). The first digital services went on air in autumn 1998.

In June 2002, following the collapse of ITV Digital, the digital terrestrial television licence was awarded to a consortium made up of the BBC, BSkyB and transmitter company Crown Castle by the Independent Television Commission. Freeview was launched on 30 October 2002: it offers around 50 digital channels and 24 radio stations and requires the purchase of a set-top box, but is subsequently free of charge. At the end of March 2013, 39 per cent of UK homes had Freeview on their main set. Freeview additionally offers the UK's top 4 channels in HD and the Freeview+ service which works in a similar fashion to Sky+.

As at March 2013, 97 per cent of British homes had access to digital TV. The digital channels combined have a greater share of viewing than any of the five main channels and continue to increase this lead.

The digital switchover which began in 2007 with a region-by-region switch off to convert analogue television to digital TV, was completed in October 2012 with analogue television sets able to be converted with the addition of a digital set-top box.

RECENT DEVELOPMENTS

The advent of digital television has coincided with the emergence of the internet as a viable alternative means of watching TV. Channel 4's 4oD (4 On Demand) service allows viewers to revisit and download programmes from the previous 30 days and access an archive of older footage using their PC or mobile device such as laptop, smart phone or tablet computer. The BBC launched its iPlayer service on Christmas Day 2007, enabling viewers to watch programmes broadcast over the previous seven days via the streaming option or download and store programmes for up to 30 days on their computer or mobile device. An integrated service, launched in June 2008, allows viewers to access BBC radio programmes in addition to televisual output. iPlayer also allows viewers to watch live TV. In 2009 iPlayer was extended to more than 20 devices, including mobile phones, televisions and games consoles. A high definition (HD) service was launched in the same year. ITV has a similar service called ITV Player, Channel 5's service is called Demand Five and S4/C provides a video-on-demand service called Clic. In July 2011, BSkyB launched Sky Go, allowing Sky TV customers to watch live TV on their PC or portable device. Online streaming of TV has been a major success, especially within a younger demographic. There were 272 million requests on BBC iPlayer in March 2013 and for the first time there were more requests on tablet devices than mobile phones.

HD TV provides more vibrant colours, greater detail and picture clarity than standard television, in addition to improved sound quality. While a standard television picture is made up of 576 lines of 720 pixels, an HD television screen uses 1,280 by 720 pixels up to 1,920 by 1,080 pixels. Sky Digital, ITV and the BBC all provide HD channels, with a growing number becoming available. To access HD channels, viewers need an 'HD ready' TV set and HD TV decoder, available through satellite services or a cable connection. Four HD channels (BBC One HD, BBC Two HD, ITV1 HD and Channel 4 HD) are available through Freeview HD with many new televisions incorporating built-in Freeview HD. In April 2010 Samsung released the first consumer 3D TV; in the same month Sky launched the UK's first dedicated 3D channel. Several sporting events have been broadcast in 3D including the Wimbledon Championships.

In June 2010 the BBC Trust gave permission for the BBC to participate in the development of Project Canvas, now known as YouView, a proposed standard for internet protocol television (IPTV) in partnership with ITV, BT, Channel 4, Channel 5, TalkTalk and Arqiva. With the launch of YouView in July 2012, viewers are able to watch programmes (including on-demand), pause and rewind live TV and listen to digital radio via a hybrid set-top box connected to a broadband connection with no subscription fee. Further content can be added to the YouView software allowing developers to place new apps and content on the service.

In February 2011, a new version of OFCOM's Broadcasting Code came into force, permitting product placement for the first time in UK-produced television programmes. A large 'P' logo designed by OFCOM and broadcasters is displayed at the beginning and end of each programme containing product placement. The first instance of product placement occurred on 28 February 2011.

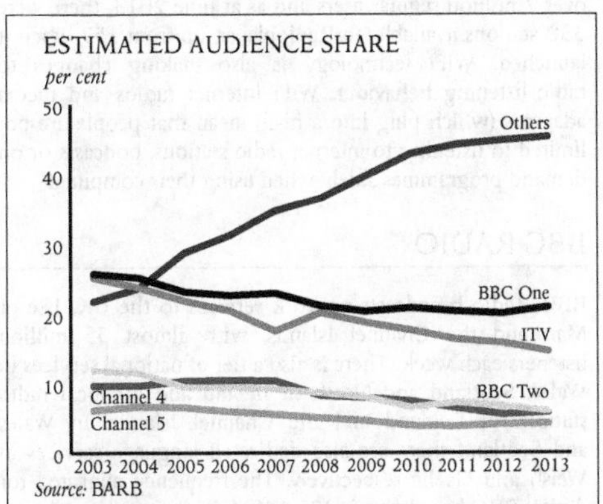

Source: BARB

CONTACTS

THE BRITISH BROADCASTING CORPORATION

BBC Broadcasting House Portland Place, London W1A 1AA
W www.bbc.co.uk

BBC North, Media City UK, Salford Quays, Manchester M50 2BH
Chair, Lord Patten of Barnes
Director-General, Tony Hall

BBC Worldwide, 201 Wood Lane, London W12 7TQ
W www.bbcworldwide.com

INDEPENDENT TELEVISION NETWORK

ITV Network Centre, 200 Gray's Inn Road, London WC1X 8HF
T 020-7156 6000 W www.itv.com
Chair, Archie Norman

INDEPENDENT TELEVISION NETWORK REGIONS AND COMPANIES

Anglia (eastern England), Anglia House, Norwich NR1 3JG
T 0844-881 6900 W www.itv.com/anglia
Border (Borders and the Isle of Man), Television House, The Watermark, Gateshead NE11 9SZ T 0844-881 51000 W www.itv.com/border
Calendar (Yorkshire), Kirkstall Road, Leeds LS3 1JS
T 0113-222 8885 W www.itv.com/calendar
Central (east, west and south Midlands), Gas Street, Birmingham B1 2JT T 0844-881 4000 W www.itv.com/central
Channel (Channel Islands), Television Centre, St Helier, Jersey JE1 3ZD T 01534-816816 W www.channelonline.tv
Granada (north-west England), Quay Street, Manchester M60 9EA T 0161-952 6018 W www.itv.com/granada
London, 200 Gray's Inn Road, London WC1X 8XZ
T 020-7430 4000 W www.itv.com/london
Meridian (south and south-east England), New Cut Road, Vinters Park, Maidstone, Kent ME14 5NZ T 0808-101 0095 W www.itv.com/meridian
STV (Scotland), Pacific Quay, Glasgow G51 1PQ
T 0141-300 3704 W www.stv.tv
Tyne Tees (north-east England), Television House, The Watermark, Gateshead, Tyne and Wear NE11 9SZ
T 0844-881 5153 W www.itv.com/tynetees
Ulster (Northern Ireland), Ormeau Road, Belfast BT7 1EB
T 028-9032 8122 W www.u.tv
Wales, Media Centre, Culverhouse Cross, Cardiff CF5 6XJ
T 0844-881 0100 W www.itv.com/wales
West, Television Centre, Bath Road, Bristol BS4 3HG
T 0808-101 0185 W www.itv.com/west

OTHER TELEVISION COMPANIES

Channel 4 Television, 124 Horseferry Road, London SW1P 2TX
T 020-7396 4444 W www.channel4.com
Channel 5 Broadcasting Ltd, 10 Lower Thames Street, London EC3R 6EN T 020-8612 7700 W www.channel5.com
Independent Television News (ITN), 200 Gray's Inn Road, London WC1X 8XZ T 020-7833 3000 W www.itn.co.uk
Provides news programming for ITV and Channel 4.
Sianel Pedwar Cymru (S4/C), Parc Ty Glas, Llanishen, Cardiff CF14 5DU T 0870-600 4141 W www.s4c.co.uk

DIRECT BROADCASTING BY SATELLITE TELEVISION

British Sky Broadcasting Group PLC, Grant Way, Isleworth, Isleworth TW7 5QD T 020-7705 3000 W www.sky.com
Chair, Nicholas Ferguson

RADIO

UK domestic radio services are broadcast across three wavebands: FM, medium wave and long wave (used by BBC Radio 4). In the UK the FM waveband extends in frequency from 87.5MHz to 108MHz and the medium waveband from 531kHz to 1602kHz. A number of radio stations are broadcast in both analogue and digital as well as a growing number in digital alone. As at June 2013, the BBC Radio network controlled around 54 per cent of the listening market (*see* BBC Radio section), and the independent sector (*see* Independent Radio section) just over 44 per cent.

ESTIMATED AUDIENCE SHARE

			Percentage
	Apr–Jun 2011	*Apr–Jun 2012*	*Apr–Jun 2013*
BBC Radio 1	8.5	8.3	6.8
BBC Radio 2	14.9	16.1	17.2
BBC Radio 3	1.2	1.1	1.2
BBC Radio 4	12.4	12.1	12.1
BBC Radio Five Live	4.6	4.5	4.1
Five Live Sports Extra	0.2	0.4	0.3
BBC 6 Music	0.9	1.1	1.5
BBC Asian Network UK	0.3	0.3	0.3
1Xtra	0.6	0.6	0.5
BBC Local/Regional	8.6	8.1	8.3
BBC World Service	0.9	0.6	0.6
All BBC	54.0	54.3	53.9
All independent	43.7	43.3	43.7
All national independent	12.2	12.7	13.3
All local independent	31.5	30.5	30.4
Other	2.3	2.5	2.4

Source: RAJAR

DIGITAL RADIO

DAB (digital audio broadcasting) allows more services to be broadcast to a higher technical quality and provides the data facility for text and pictures. It improves the robustness of high fidelity radio services, especially compared with current FM and AM radio transmissions. It was developed in a collaborative research project under the pan-European Eureka 147 initiative and has been adopted as a world standard by the International Telecommunication Union for new digital radio systems. The frequencies allocated for terrestrial digital radio in the UK are 174 to 239MHz. Additional spectrum (in the 'L-Band' range: 1452–1478MHz) was introduced in 2007.

Digital radio is available through digital radio sets, car radios, online, on games consoles, and on mobile devices such as phones and tablets. An alternative method is to listen to digital radio through television sets via Freeview, cable or satellite.

The listening share via all digital platforms at the end of June 2013 was 36.8 per cent, an increase from 31.5 per cent in June 2012. DAB accounts for 65 per cent of total digital listening, 16 per cent is online and 15 per cent on digital TV (DTV). In June 2009 the government published the white paper *Digital Britain*, which recommended that most services carried on the national and local DAB multiplexes should cease broadcasting on analogue radio by 2015. Ultra-local radio, consisting of small independent and community stations, would continue to broadcast on FM. There are two criteria that must be met for digital migration to occur:

- at least 50 per cent of radio listening is digital
- national DAB coverage is comparable to FM coverage, and local DAB reaches 90 per cent of the population and all major roads

LICENSING

The Broadcasting Act 1996 provided for the licensing of digital radio services (on multiplexes, where a number of stations share one frequency to transmit their services). To allocate the multiplexes, OFCOM advertises licences for which interested parties can bid. Once the licence has been awarded, the new owner seeks out services to broadcast on the multiplex. The BBC has a separate national multiplex for its services. There are local multiplexes around the country, each broadcasting an average of seven services, plus the local BBC station. There are also several regional multiplexes covering a wider area and broadcasting up to 11 services each.

INNOVATIONS

As with television, the opportunities offered by digital services and the internet have made important changes to radio. The internet offers a number of advantages compared to other digital platforms such as DAB including higher sound quality, a greater range of channel availability and flexibility in listening opportunity. Listeners can tune in to the majority of radio stations live on the internet or listen again online for seven days after broadcast. DAB radio does not allow the same interactivity: the data is only able to travel one-way from broadcaster to listener whereas the internet allows a two-way flow of information.

Since 2005 increasing numbers of radio stations offer all or part of their programmes as downloadable files, known as podcasts, to listen to on computers or mobile devices such as mp3 players or phones. Podcasting technology allows listeners to subscribe in order to receive automatically the latest episodes of regularly transmitted programmes as soon as they become available.

The relationship between radio stations and their audiences is also undergoing change. The quantity and availability of music on the internet has led to the creation of shows dedicated entirely to music sent in by listeners. Another new development in internet-based radio has been personalised radio stations, such as last.fm and Spotify. Last.fm 'recommends' songs based on the favourite artists and previous choices of the user. Spotify allows listeners access to the track, artist or genre of their choice, or to share and create playlists; either advertisements are played at set intervals or there is a subscription charge. Radioplayer (W www.radioplayer.co.uk), a joint-venture between the BBC and UK commercial radio allows audiences to listen to live and on demand radio from one place. The service attracts over 7 million regular users and as at June 2013, there were 330 stations available on Radioplayer, up from 157 when it launched. WiFi technology is also making changes to radio-listening behaviour. WiFi internet radios and media adaptors (which plug into a hi-fi) mean that people are not limited to listening to internet radio stations, podcasts or on demand programmes solely when using their computer.

BBC RADIO

BBC Radio broadcasts network services to the UK, Isle of Man and the Channel Islands, with almost 35 million listeners each week. There is also a tier of national services in Wales, Scotland and Northern Ireland and 40 local radio stations in England and the Channel Islands. In Wales and Scotland there are also dedicated language services in Welsh and Gaelic respectively. The frequency allocated for digital BBC broadcasts is 225.648MHz.

BBC Radio, Broadcasting House, Portland Place, London W1A 1AA W www.bbc.co.uk/radio

BBC NETWORK RADIO STATIONS

Radio 1 (contemporary pop music and entertainment news) – 24 hours a day, *Frequencies:* 97–99 FM and digital

Radio 2 (popular music, entertainment, comedy and the arts) – 24 hours a day, *Frequencies:* 88–91 FM and digital

Radio 3 (classical music, classic drama, documentaries and features) – 24 hours a day, *Frequencies:* 90–93 FM and digital

Radio 4 (news, documentaries, drama, entertainment and cricket on long wave in season) – 5.20am–1am daily, with

BBC World Service overnight, *Frequencies:* 92–95 FM/103–105 FM and 198 LW and digital
Radio Five Live (news and sport) – 24 hours a day, *Frequencies:* 909/693 MW and digital
Five Live Sports Extra (live sport) – schedule varies, digital only
6 Music (contemporary and classic pop and rock music) – 24 hours a day, digital only
Asian Network (news, music and sport) – 5am–1am, with Radio Five Live overnight, *Frequencies:* various MW frequencies in Midlands and digital
1Xtra (urban music: drum & bass, garage, hip hop, R&B) – 24 hours a day, digital only

BBC NATIONAL RADIO STATIONS

Radio Cymru (Welsh-language), *Frequencies:* 92–105 FM and digital
Radio Foyle, Frequencies: 93.1 FM and 792 MW and digital
Radio nan Gaidheal (Gaelic service), *Frequencies:* 103–105 FM and digital
Radio Scotland, Frequencies: 92–95 FM and 810 MW and digital. Local programmes for Orkney, Shetland and Highlands and Islands
Radio Ulster, Frequencies: 1341 MW and 92–95 FM and digital. Local programmes on Radio Foyle
Radio Wales, Frequencies: 657/882 MW and 93–104 FM and digital

BBC WORLD SERVICE

The BBC World Service broadcasts to an estimated weekly audience of 1.3 million people in the UK and 192 million worldwide, in 28 languages including English, and is now available in around 150 capital cities. It no longer broadcasts in Dutch, French for Europe, German, Hebrew, Italian, Japanese or Malay because it was found that most speakers of these languages preferred to listen to the English broadcasts. In 2006 services in ten languages (Bulgarian, Croatian, Czech, Greek, Hungarian, Kazakh, Polish, Slovak, Slovene and Thai) were terminated to provide funding for a new Arabic television channel, which was launched in March 2008. In August 2008 the BBC's Romanian World Service broadcasts were discontinued after 68 years. In January 2011 the BBC announced five more language services would be terminated: Albanian, Caribbean English, Macedonian, Portuguese for Africa and Serbian. The BBC World Service website offers interactive news services in 27 languages including English, Arabic, Chinese, Hindi, Persian, Portuguese for Brazil, Russian, Spanish and Urdu with audiostreaming available in all 27 languages.

LANGUAGES

Arabic, Azeri, Bangla, Burmese, Chinese, English, French, Hausa, Hindi, Indonesian, Kinyarwanda, Kirundi, Kyrgyz, Nepali, Pashto, Persian, Portuguese, Russian, Sinhala, Somali, Spanish, Swahili, Tamil, Turkish, Ukrainian, Urdu, Uzbek and Vietnamese.

UK frequencies: digital; overnight on BBC Radio 4.
BBC Learning English teaches English worldwide through radio, television and a wide range of published and online courses.
BBC Media Action is a registered charity established in 1999 by BBC World Service, known as the BBC World Service Trust until December 2011. It promotes development through the innovative use of the media in the developing world.
BBC Monitoring tracks the global media for the latest news reports emerging around the world.

BBC WORLD SERVICE, 1st Floor Brock House, 19 Langham Street, London W1A 1AA W www.bbc.co.uk/worldservice

INDEPENDENT RADIO

Until 1973, the BBC had a legal monopoly on radio broadcasting in the UK. During this time, the corporation's only competition came from pirate stations located abroad, such as Radio Luxembourg. Christopher Chataway, Minister for Post and Telecommunications in Edward Heath's government, changed this by creating the first licences for commercial radio stations. The Independent Broadcasting Authority (IBA) awarded the first of these licences to the London Broadcasting Company (LBC) to provide London's news and information service. LBC was followed by Capital Radio, to offer the city's entertainment service, Radio Clyde in Glasgow and BRMB in Birmingham.

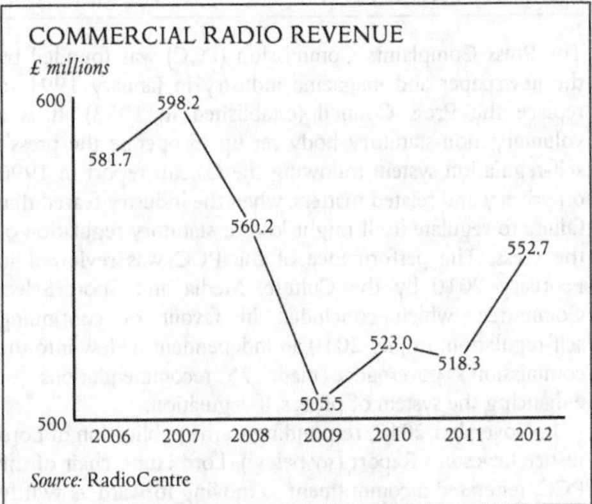

The IBA was dissolved when the Broadcasting Act of 1990 de-regulated broadcasting, to be succeeded by the less rigid Radio Authority (RA). The RA began advertising new licences for the development of independent radio in January 1991. It awarded national and local radio, satellite and cable services licences, and long-term restricted service licences for stations serving non-commercial establishments such as hospitals and universities. The first national commercial digital multiplex licence was awarded in October 1998 and a number of local digital multiplex licences followed.

At the end of 2003 the RA was replaced by OFCOM, which now carries out the licensing administration.

RadioCentre was formed in July 2006 as a result of the merger between the Radio Advertising Bureau (RAB) and the Commercial Radio Companies Association (CRCA), the former non-profit trade body for commercial radio companies in the UK, to operate essentially as a union for commercial radio stations. According to the 2011 Commercial Radio Audit, it is possible to listen to 95 per cent of independent radio stations online, while 150 commercial stations can be listened to on DAB radios. There are currently 296 licenced stations associated with RadioCentre.

RadioCentre, 6th Floor, 55 New Oxford Street, London WC1A 1BS T 020-7010 0600 W www.radiocentre.org
Chief Executive, Andrew Harrison

THE PRESS

The newspaper and periodical press in the UK is large and diverse, catering for a wide variety of views and interests. There is no state control or censorship of the press; however, it is subject to the laws on publication.

The press is not state-subsidised and receives few tax concessions. The income of most newspapers and periodicals is derived largely from sales and from advertising; the press remains one of the largest advertising mediums in the UK but continued to suffer a decline in advertising revenue following a 7.9 per cent decrease in advertising spend in the first quarter of 2013.

SELF-REGULATION

The Press Complaints Commission (PCC) was founded by the newspaper and magazine industry in January 1991 to replace the Press Council (established in 1953). It is a voluntary, non-statutory body set up to operate the press's self-regulation system following the Calcutt report in 1990 on privacy and related matters, when the industry feared that failure to regulate itself might lead to statutory regulation of the press. The performance of the PCC was reviewed in February 2010 by the Culture, Media and Sport Select Committee, which concluded in favour of continuing self-regulation. In July 2010 an independent review into the commission's governance made 75 recommendations for enhancing the system of press self-regulation.

In November 2012, responding to the publication of Lord Justice Leveson's Report (*see* below), Lord Hunt, chair of the PCC, reiterated a commitment to moving forward as swiftly as possible to a new regulatory body. As a result, the UK newspaper and magazine industry agreed to construct a new regulatory system, compliant with Lord Justice Leveson's recommendations. Lord Hunt began working with the industry to establish the new organisation in accordance with the agreed objectives.

LEVESON INQUIRY

The Leveson Inquiry, established under the Inquiries Act 2005, was announced by the prime minister on 13 July 2011 to investigate the role of press and police in the *News of the World* phone-hacking scandal. Lord Justice Leveson was appointed as chair of the inquiry. The hearings began on 14 November 2011 and ended on 24 July 2012 following the testimonies of 650 witnesses.

The Leveson Report was published in late November 2012 and featured several broad and complex recommendations as to how the press should be regulated. The report generally recommended that the press should continue to be self-regulated, with the government allowed no direct power over what is published, and that a new press standards body, with a new code of conduct, should be established by legislation in order to ensure regulation is independent and effective. Lord Justice Leveson concluded that this arrangement should give the public confidence that their complaints would be dealt with seriously and ensure the press would be protected from interference.

In March 2013, the three main political parties decided that an independent regulator with powers to demand prominent corrections and apologies from UK news publishers and the ability to impose fines of up to £1m would be established by royal charter. In response, the Newspaper Society, which represents national and local titles, announced it rejected 'state-sponsored' regulation and would apply for its own royal charter to establish a new system. At the time of going to press no further decisions on a new regulator had been reached.

NEWSPAPERS

Newspapers are mostly financially independent of any political party, though most adopt a political stance in their editorial comments, usually reflecting proprietorial influence. Ownership of the national and regional daily newspapers is concentrated in the hands of large corporations whose interests cover publishing and communications, although *The Guardian* and *The Observer* are owned by the Scott Trust, formed in 1936 to protect the financial and editorial independence of *The Guardian* in perpetuity. The rules on cross-media ownership, as amended by the Broadcasting Act 1996, which limited the extent to which newspaper organisations may become involved in broadcasting, have been relaxed by the Communications Act 2003: newspapers with over a 20 per cent share of national circulation may own national and/or local radio licences.

In October 2010, *The Independent* launched a concise newspaper, *i*, the first new daily newspaper since 1986. In July 2011, *News of the World* was closed by its parent company, News International, following accusations of phone-hacking. In February 2012 News International printed the first edition of *The Sun on Sunday*, a Sunday format of the daily tabloid paper *The Sun*. There are 14 daily and Sunday national papers and several hundred local papers that are published daily, weekly or twice-weekly. Scotland, Wales and Northern Ireland all have at least one daily and one Sunday national paper.

UK CIRCULATION

National Daily Newspapers	*June 2012*	*June 2013*
The Sun	2,583,552	2,243,903
Daily Mail	1,939,635	1,806,569
Daily Mirror	1,081,330	1,038,753
The Daily Telegraph	573,674	547,106
Daily Star	602,296	540,849
Daily Express	602,482	522,264
The Times	400,120	390,941
i	272,597	303,009
Financial Times	297,225	258,488
Daily Record	279,324	252,626
The Guardian	211,511	187,000
The Independent	90,001	73,060

National Sunday Newspapers	*June 2012*	*June 2013*
The Sun on Sunday	2,189,924	1,875,220
The Mail on Sunday	1,824,393	1,638,049
Sunday Mirror	1,088,499	1,037,542
The Sunday Times	915,969	840,201
Sunday Express	512,843	455,901
The Sunday Telegraph	450,276	422,590
The People	450,097	415,075
Daily Star Sunday	473,352	335,864
Sunday Mail	313,698	284,051
Sunday Post	279,120	244,257
The Observer	243,946	212,376
The Independent on Sunday	122,588	111,986

Source: Audit Bureau of Circulations Ltd

Newspapers are usually published in either broadsheet or smaller, tabloid format. The 'quality' daily papers – ie those providing detailed coverage of a wide range of public matters – have traditionally been broadsheets, the more populist newspapers tabloid. In 2004 this correlation between format and content was redefined when three traditionally broadsheet newspapers, *The Times, The Independent* and *The Scotsman,* switched to tabloid-sized editions, while *The Guardian* launched a 'Berliner' format in September 2005. In October 2005 *The Independent on Sunday* became the first Sunday broadsheet to be published in the tabloid (or 'compact') size, and *The Observer,* like its daily counterpart *The Guardian,* began publishing in the Berliner format in January 2006.

NEWSPAPERS ONLINE

The demand to read news instantly and while on the move has increased the popularity of newspaper websites. Most newspapers now operate their own websites in line with their print editions, often including the same material as seen in daily printed editions but can also include video and audio features. Many articles and columns additionally have the option of reader contributions and debate. Certain newspapers charge a subscription fee to access their websites but many are free to browse.

NATIONAL PRESS WEBSITE FIGURES FOR JUNE 2013

National Press Website	*Daily average browsers*	*Monthly total browsers*
MailOnline	8,111,988	120,829,031
guardian.co.uk	4,884,043	84,933,955
Telegraph	2,733,136	54,007,113
The Sun	1,814,963	29,603,055
Mirror Group Digital	1,440,082	29,354,671
The Independent	1,099,561	23,577,495

Source: Audit Bureau of Circulations Ltd

NATIONAL DAILY NEWSPAPERS

DAILY EXPRESS
Northern & Shell Building, 10 Lower Thames Street, London EC3R 6EN T 020-8612 7000 W www.express.co.uk
Editor, Hugh Whittow

DAILY MAIL
Northcliffe House, 2 Derry Street, London W8 5TT
T 020-7938 6000 W www.dailymail.co.uk
Editor, Paul Dacre

DAILY MIRROR
1 Canada Square, Canary Wharf, London E14 5AP
T 020-7293 3000 W www.mirror.co.uk
Editor, Lloyd Embley

DAILY RECORD
1 Central Quay, Glasgow G3 8DA T 0141-309 3000
W www.dailyrecord.co.uk
Editor, Allan Rennie

DAILY STAR
Northern & Shell Building, 10 Lower Thames Street, London EC3R 6EN T 020-8612 7000 W www.dailystar.co.uk
Editor, Dawn Neesom

THE DAILY TELEGRAPH
111 Buckingham Palace Road, London SW1W 0DT
T 020-7931 2000 W www.telegraph.co.uk
Editor, Tony Gallagher

FINANCIAL TIMES
1 Southwark Bridge, London SE1 9HL T 020-7873 3000
W www.ft.com
Editor, Lionel Barber

THE GUARDIAN
King's Place, 90 York Way, London N1 9GU T 020-3353 2000
W www.guardian.co.uk
Editor, Alan Rusbridger

THE HERALD
200 Renfield Street, Glasgow G2 3QB T 0141-302 7000
W www.heraldscotland.com
Editor, Magnus Llewellin

THE INDEPENDENT *AND* i
Northcliffe House, 2 Derry Street, London W8 5HF
T 020-7005 2000 W www.independent.co.uk
Editor, Amol Rajan and Oliver Duff

THE SCOTSMAN
Barclay House, 108 Holyrood Road, Edinburgh EH8 8AS
T 0131-620 8620 W www.scotsman.com
Editor, Ian Stewart

THE SUN
3 Thomas More Square, London E98 1XY T 020-7782 4000
W www.thesun.co.uk
Editor, David Dinsmore

THE TIMES
1 Pennington Street, London E98 1TT T 020-7782 5000
W www.thetimes.co.uk
Acting Editor, John Witherow

WEEKLY NEWSPAPERS

DAILY STAR SUNDAY
Northern and Shell Building, 10 Lower Thames Street, London EC3R 6EN T 020-8612 7424 W www.dailystar.co.uk/sunday
Editor, vacant

INDEPENDENT ON SUNDAY
Northcliffe House, 2 Derry Street, London W8 5TT
T 020-7005 2000 W www.independent.co.uk
Editor, Lisa Markwell

MAIL ON SUNDAY
2 Derry Street, London W8 HFT T 020-7938 6000
W www.mailonsunday.co.uk
Editor, Geordie Greig

THE OBSERVER
Kings Place, 90 York Way, London N1 9GU
T 020-3353 2000 W www.observer.co.uk
Editor, John Mulholland

THE PEOPLE
1 Canada Square, Canary Wharf, London E14 5AP
T 020-7293 3000 W www.people.co.uk
Editor, James Scott

SCOTLAND ON SUNDAY
Barclay House, 108 Holyrood Road, Edinburgh EH8 8AS
T 0131-620 8620 W www.scotlandonsunday.co.uk
Editor, Ian Stewart

THE SUN ON SUNDAY
3 Thomas More Square, London E98 1XY
T 020-7782 4000 W www.thesun.co.uk
Editor, David Dinsmore

SUNDAY EXPRESS
Northern & Shell Building, 10 Lower Thames Street, London EC4R 6EN T 020-8612 7000 W www.sundayexpress.co.uk
Editor, Martin Townsend

SUNDAY HERALD
200 Renfield Street, Glasgow G2 3QB T 0141-302 7000
W www.sundayherald.com
Editor, Richard Walker

SUNDAY MAIL
1 Central Quay, Glasgow G3 8DA T 0141-309 3000
W www.sundaymail.com
Editor, Allan Rennie

SUNDAY MIRROR
1 Canada Square, Canary Wharf, London E14 5AP
T 020-7293 3000 W www.sundaymirror.co.uk
Editor, Lloyd Embley

SUNDAY POST
144 Port Dundas Road, Glasgow G4 0HZ T 0141-332 9933
W www.sundaypost.com
Editor, Donald Martin

SUNDAY TELEGRAPH
111 Buckingham Palace Road, London SW1W 0DT
T 020-7931 2000 W www.telegraph.co.uk
Editor, Ian MacGregor

THE SUNDAY TIMES
3 Thomas More Square, London E98 1XY T 020-7782 5000
W www.thesundaytimes.co.uk
Acting Editor, Martin Ivens

REGIONAL DAILY NEWSPAPERS

EAST ANGLIA

CAMBRIDGE NEWS
Winship Road, Milton, Cambs. CB24 6PP T 01223-434434
W www.cambridge-news.co.uk
Editor, Paul Brackley

EAST ANGLIAN DAILY TIMES
Lower Brook Street, Ipswich IP4 1AN T 01473-230023
W www.eadt.co.uk
Editor, Terry Hunt

EASTERN DAILY PRESS
Prospect House, Rouen Road, Norwich NR1 1RE
T 01603-628311 W www.edp24.co.uk
Editor, Nigel Pickover

IPSWICH STAR
Lower Brook Street, Ipswich, Suffolk IP4 1AN
T 01473-230023 W www.ipswichstar.co.uk
Editor, Terry Hunt

NORWICH EVENING NEWS
Prospect House, Rouen Road, Norwich NR1 1RE
T 01603-628311 W www.eveningnews24.co.uk
Editor, Nigel Pickover

EAST MIDLANDS

BURTON MAIL
65–68 High Street, Burton upon Trent DE14 1LE
T 01283-512345 W www.burtonmail.co.uk
Editor, Kevin Booth

DERBY TELEGRAPH
Northcliffe House, Meadow Road, Derby DE1 2BH
T 01332-291111 W www.thisisderbyshire.co.uk
Editor, Neil White

THE LEICESTER MERCURY
St George Street, Leicester LE1 9FQ T 0116-251 2512
W www.leicestermercury.co.uk
Editor, Richard Bettsworth

LINCOLNSHIRE ECHO
Witham Wharf, Brayford Wharf East, Lincoln LN5 7HY
T 01522-820000 W www.thisislincolnshire.co.uk
Editor, Steven Fletcher

NORTHAMPTON CHRONICLE & ECHO
Upper Mounts, Northants NN1 3HR T 01604-467000
W www.northamptonchron.co.uk
Editor, David Summers

NOTTINGHAM POST
Castle Wharf House, Nottingham NG1 4AB
T 0115-948 2000 W www.thisisnottingham.co.uk
Editor, Mike Sassi

LONDON

EVENING STANDARD
Northcliffe House, 2 Derry Street, London W8 5TT
T 020-3367 7000 W www.standard.co.uk
Editor, Sarah Sands

METRO
Northcliffe House, 2 Derry Street, London W8 5TT
T 020-3615 0600 W www.metro.co.uk
Editor, Kenny Campbell

NORTH EAST

EVENING CHRONICLE
Groat Market, Newcastle upon Tyne NE1 1ED T 0191-201 6491
W www.chroniclelive.co.uk
Editor, Darren Thwaites

EVENING GAZETTE
Borough Road, Middlesbrough TS1 3AZ T 01642-245401
W www.gazettelive.co.uk
Editor, Chris Styles

HARTLEPOOL MAIL
New Clarence House, Wesley Square, Hartlepool TS24 8BX
T 01429-239333 W www.hartlepoolmail.co.uk
Editor, Joy Yates

THE JOURNAL
Groat Market, Newcastle upon Tyne NE1 1ED
T 0191-201 6491 W www.thejournal.co.uk
Editor, Brian Aitken

THE NORTHERN ECHO
PO Box 14, Priestgate, Darlington, Co. Durham DL1 1NF
T 01325-381313 W www.thenorthernecho.co.uk
Editor, Peter Barron

THE SHIELDS GAZETTE
Chapter Row, South Shields, Tyne & Wear NE33 1BL
T 0191-427 4800 W www.shieldsgazette.com
Editor, Joy Yates

THE SUNDAY SUN
Groat Market, Newcastle upon Tyne NE1 1ED
T 0191-201 6491 W www.sundaysun.co.uk
Editor, Colin Patterson

SUNDERLAND ECHO
Echo House, Pennywell, Sunderland SR4 9ER
T 0191-501 5800 W www.sunderlandecho.com
Editor, John Szymanski

NORTH WEST

THE BLACKPOOL GAZETTE
Avroe House, Avroe Crescent, Blackpool Business Park, Blackpool FY4 2DP T 01253-400888
W www.blackpoolgazette.co.uk
Editor, Gillian Gray

THE BOLTON NEWS
The Wellsprings, Victoria Square, Bolton BL1 1AR
T 01204-522345 W www.theboltonnews.co.uk
Editor, Ian Savage

CARLISLE NEWS AND STAR
Newspaper House, Dalston Road, Carlisle CA2 5UA
T 01228-612600 W www.newsandstar.co.uk
Editor, David Helliwell

LANCASHIRE EVENING POST
Oliver's Place, Preston PR2 9ZA T 01772-254841
W www.lep.co.uk
Editor, Gillian Gray

LANCASHIRE TELEGRAPH
1 High Street, Newspaper House, Blackburn, Lancs. BB1 1HT
T 01254 678678 W www.lancashiretelegraph.co.uk
Editor, Kevin Young

LIVERPOOL DAILY POST
PO Box 48, Old Hall Street, Liverpool L69 3EB
T 0151-227 2000 W www.liverpooldailypost.co.uk
Editor, Mark Thomas

LIVERPOOL ECHO
PO Box 48, Old Hall Street, Liverpool L69 3EB
T 0151-227 2000 W www.liverpoolecho.co.uk
Editor, Alastair Machray

MANCHESTER EVENING NEWS
Mitchell Henry House, Hollinwood Avenue, Chadderton OL9 8EF
T 0161-832 7200 W www.manchestereveningnews.co.uk
Editor, Rob Irvine

NORTH-WEST EVENING MAIL
Abbey Road, Barrow-in-Furness, Cumbria LA14 5QS
T 01229-840100 W www.nwemail.co.uk
Publishing Director, Jonathan Lee

OLDHAM EVENING CHRONICLE
PO Box 47, 172 Union Street, Oldham, Lancs. OL1 1EQ
T 0161-633 2121 W www.oldham-chronicle.co.uk
Editor, Dave Whaley

SOUTH EAST

THE ARGUS
Argus House, Crowhurst Road, Hollingbury, Brighton BN1 8AR
T 01273-544544 W www.theargus.co.uk
Editor, Michael Beard

ECHO
Newspaper House, Chester Hall Lane, Basildon, Essex SS14 3BL
T 01268-522792 W www.echo-news.co.uk
Editor, Martin McNeill

MEDWAY MESSENGER
Medway House, Ginsbury Close, Sir Thomas Longley Road, Medway City Estate, Strood, Kent ME2 4DU
T 01634-227800 W www.kentonline.co.uk
Editor, Bob Bounds

THE NEWS, PORTSMOUTH
1000 Lakeside, North Harbour, Portsmouth PO6 3EN
T 023-9266 4488 W www.portsmouth.co.uk
Editor, Mark Waldron

OXFORD MAIL
Osney Mead, Oxford OX2 0EJ T 01865-425262
W www.oxfordmail.co.uk
Editor, Simon O'Neill

READING EVENING POST
8 Tessa Road, Reading, Berks. RG1 8NS T 0118-918 3000
W www.getreading.co.uk
Editor, Andy Murrill

THE SOUTHERN DAILY ECHO
Newspaper House, Test Lane, Redbridge, Southampton SO16 9JX
T 023-8042 4777 W www.dailyecho.co.uk
Editor, Ian Murray

SOUTH WEST

BRISTOL POST
Temple Way, Bristol BS2 0BY T 0117-934 3000
W www.bristolpost.co.uk
Editor, Mike Norton

THE CITIZEN
6–8 The Oxebode, Gloucester GL1 2RZ T 01242-278000
W www.thisisgloucestershire.co.uk
Editor, Ian Mean

DAILY ECHO
Richmond Hill, Bournemouth BH2 6HH T 01202-554601
W www.bournemouthecho.co.uk
Editor, Toby Granville

DORSET ECHO
Fleet House, Hampshire Road, Weymouth, Dorset DT4 9XD
T 01305-830930 W www.dorsetecho.co.uk
Editor, Toby Granville

EXPRESS & ECHO
Heron Road, Sowton, Exeter EX2 7NF
T 01392-442211 W www.thisisexeter.co.uk
Editor, Paul Burton

GLOUCESTERSHIRE ECHO
St James's Square, Cheltenham GL50 3PR
T 01242-278000 W www.thisisgloucestershire.co.uk
Editor, Kevan Blackadder

THE HERALD
3rd Floor, Millbay Road, Plymouth PL1 3LF
T 01752-293000 W www.plymouthherald.co.uk
Editor, Ian Wood

HERALD EXPRESS
Barton Hill Road, Torquay, Devon TQ2 8JN T 01803-676000
W www.thisissouthdevon.co.uk
Editor, Jim Parker

SUNDAY INDEPENDENT
Sunday Independent Ltd, Tindle Suite, Webbs House, Cornwall PL14 6AH T 01579-342174 W www.sundayindependent.co.uk
Editor, John Noble

SWINDON ADVERTISER
100 Victoria Road, Old Town, Swindon SN1 3BE
T 01793-528144 W www.swindonadvertiser.co.uk
Editor, Gary Lawrence

WESTERN DAILY PRESS
Temple Way, Bristol BS99 7HD T 0117-934 3000
W www.westerndailypress.co.uk
Editor, Tim Dixon

THE WESTERN MORNING NEWS
3rd Floor, Millbay Road, Plymouth PL1 3LF T 01752-293000
W www.westernmorningnews.co.uk
Editor, Bill Martin

WEST MIDLANDS

BIRMINGHAM MAIL
6th Floor, Fort Dunlop, Fort Parkway, Birmingham B24 9FF
T 0121-234 5536 W www.birminghammail.co.uk
Editor, David Brookes

THE BIRMINGHAM POST
6th Floor, Fort Dunlop, Fort Parkway, Birmingham B24 9FF
T 0121-236 3366 W www.birminghampost.co.uk
Editor, Stacey Barnfield

COVENTRY TELEGRAPH
Corporation Street, Coventry CV1 1FP T 024-7663 3633
W www.coventrytelegraph.net
Editor, Alun Thorne

EXPRESS & STAR
51–53 Queen Street, Wolverhampton WV1 1ES
T 01902-313131 W www.expressandstar.com
Editor, Keith Harrison

THE SENTINEL
Sentinel House, Etruria, Stoke-on-Trent ST1 5SS
T 01782-602525 W www.stokesentinel.co.uk
Editor, Richard Bowyer

SHROPSHIRE STAR
Waterloo Road, Ketley, Telford TF1 5HU T 01952-242424
W www.shropshirestar.com
Editor, Martin Wright

WORCESTER NEWS
Berrows House, Hylton Road, Worcester WR2 5JX
T 01905-748200 W www.worcesternews.co.uk
Editor, Peter John

YORKSHIRE AND HUMBERSIDE

GRIMSBY TELEGRAPH
80 Cleethorpe Road, Grimsby, Lincs DN31 3EH
T 01472-360360 W www.thisisgrimsby.co.uk
Editor, Michelle Lalor

HALIFAX COURIER
Courier Buildings, King Cross Street, Halifax HX1 2SF
T 01422-260200 W www.halifaxcourier.co.uk
Editor, John Kenealy

THE HUDDERSFIELD DAILY EXAMINER
Pennine Business Park, Longbow Close, Bradley Road, Huddersfield HD2 1GQ T 01484-430000
W www.examiner.co.uk
Editor, Roy Wright

HULL DAILY MAIL
Blundell's Corner, Beverley Road, Hull HU3 1XS
T 01482-327111 W www.hulldailymail.co.uk
Editor, Neil Hodgkinson
THE PRESS
PO Box 29, 76–86 Walmgate, York YO1 9YN
T 01904-567131 W www.yorkpress.co.uk
Editor, Steve Hughes
SCARBOROUGH NEWS
17–23 Aberdeen Walk, Scarborough, N. Yorks YO11 1BB
T 01723-363636 W www.thescarboroughnews.co.uk
Editor, Ed Asquith
SHEFFIELD STAR
York Street, Sheffield S1 1PU T 0114-276 7676
W www.thestar.co.uk
Editor, Jeremy Clifford
TELEGRAPH & ARGUS
Hall Ings, Bradford BD1 1JR T 01274-729511
W www.telegraphandargus.co.uk
Editor, Perry Austin-Clarke
YORKSHIRE EVENING POST
26 Whitehall Road, Leeds LS12 1BE T 0113-243 2701
W www.yorkshireeveningpost.co.uk
Editor, Jeremy Clifford
YORKSHIRE POST
26 Whitehall Road, Leeds LS12 1BE T 0113-243 2701
W www.yorkshirepost.co.uk
Editor, Jeremy Clifford

SCOTLAND

THE COURIER
80 Kingsway East, Dundee DD4 8SL T 01382-223131
W www.thecourier.co.uk
Editor, Richard Neville
DUNDEE EVENING TELEGRAPH
80 Kingsway East, Dundee DD4 8SL T 01382-575320
W www.eveningtelegraph.co.uk
Editor, Richard Prest
EVENING EXPRESS
Aberdeen Journals Ltd, Lang Stracht, Mastrick, Aberdeen AB15 6DF T 01224-691212 W www.eveningexpress.co.uk
Editor, Alan McCabe
EVENING NEWS
Barclay House, 108 Holyrood Road, Edinburgh EH8 8AS
T 0131-620 8620 W www.edinburghnews.scotsman.com
Editor, Frank O'Donnell
GLASGOW EVENING TIMES
200 Renfield Street, Glasgow G2 3QB T 0141-302 7000
W www.eveningtimes.co.uk
Editor, Tony Carlin
INVERNESS COURIER
New Century House, Stadium Road, Inverness IV1 1FF
T 01463-233059 W www.inverness-courier.co.uk
Editor, Robert Taylor
PAISLEY DAILY EXPRESS
1 Central Quay, Glasgow G3 8DA T 0141-887 7911
W www.paisleydailyexpress.co.uk
Editor, John Hutcheson
THE PRESS AND JOURNAL
Lang Stracht, Aberdeen AB15 6DF T 01224-690222
W www.pressandjournal.co.uk
Editor, Damian Bates

WALES

THE LEADER
Mold Business Park, Mold, Flintshire CH7 1XY
T 01352-707707 W www.leaderlive.co.uk
Editor, Barrie Jones
SOUTH WALES ARGUS
Cardiff Road, Maesglas, Newport NP20 3QN
T 01633-810000 W www.southwalesargus.co.uk
Editor, Kevin Ward
SOUTH WALES ECHO
6 Park Street, Cardiff CF10 1XR T 029-2024 3630
W www.walesonline.co.uk
Editor, Tim Gordon
SOUTH WALES EVENING POST
Adelaide Street, Swansea SA1 1QT T 01792-510000
W www.southwales-eveningpost.co.uk
Editor, Jonathan Roberts
WESTERN MAIL
6 Park Street, Cardiff CF10 1XR T 029-2024 3630
W www.walesonline.co.uk
Editor, Alan Edmunds

NORTHERN IRELAND

BELFAST TELEGRAPH
124–144 Royal Avenue, Belfast BT1 1DN T 028-9026 4000
W www.belfasttelegraph.co.uk
Editor, Mike Gilson
IRISH NEWS
113–117 Donegall Street, Belfast BT1 2GE T 028-9032 2226
W www.irishnews.com
Editor, Noel Doran
NEWS LETTER
Ground Floor, Metro Building, 6–9 Donegall Sq. South, Belfast BT1 5JA T 028-9089 7700 W www.newsletter.co.uk
Editor, Rankin Armstrong
SUNDAY LIFE
124–144 Royal Avenue, Belfast BT1 1EB T 028-9026 4000
W www.sundaylife.co.uk
Editor, Martin Breen

CHANNEL ISLANDS

GUERNSEY PRESS AND STAR
PO Box 57, Braye Road, Vale, Guernsey GY1 3BW
T 01481-240240 W www.guernseypress.com
Editor, Richard Digard
JERSEY EVENING POST
Guiton House, Five Oaks, St Saviour, Jersey JE4 8XQ
T 01534-611611 W www.thisisjersey.com
Editor, Chris Bright

PERIODICALS

ART

AESTHETICA
PO Box 371, York YO23 1WL T 01904-629137
W www.aestheticamagazine.com
Editor, Cherie Federico
APOLLO
22 Old Queen Street, London SW1H 9HP
T 020-7961 0150 W www.apollo-magazine.com
Editor, Oscar Humphries
ART MONTHLY
28 Charing Cross Road, London WC2H 0DB
T 020-7240 0389 W www.artmonthly.co.uk
Editor, Patricia Bickers
ARTREVIEW
1 Honduras Street, London EC1Y 0TH T 020-7490 8138
W www.artreview.com
Editor, Mark Rappolt
TATE ETC.
Tate, Millbank, London SW1P 4RG T 020-7887 8724
W www.tate.org.uk
Editor, Simon Grant

BUSINESS AND FINANCE

THE ECONOMIST
25 St James's Street, London SW1A 1HG T 020-7830 7000
W www.economist.com
Editor, John Micklethwait

MANAGEMENT TODAY
Haymarket, Teddington Studios, Broom Road, Teddington TW11 9BE T 0845-155 7355
W www.managementtoday.co.uk
Editor, Matthew Gwyther

MARKETING WEEK
79 Wells Street, London W1T 3QN T 020-7970 4000
W www.marketingweek.co.uk
Editor, Ruth Mortimer

MONEYWEEK
8th Floor, Friars Bridge Court, 41-45 Blackfriars Road, London SE1 8NZ T 020-7633 3780 W www.moneyweek.com
Editor, Merryn Somerset Webb

PUBLIC FINANCE
17 Britton Street, London EC1M 5TP T 020-8950 9117
W www.publicfinance.co.uk
Editor, Mike Thatcher

CELEBRITY

CLOSER
Endeavour House, 189 Shaftesbury Avenue, London WC2H 8JG T 020-7437 9011 W www.closeronline.co.uk
Editor, Lisa Burrow

HEAT
Endeavour House, 189 Shaftesbury Avenue, London WC2H 8JG
T 020-7437 9011 W www.heatworld.com
Editor, Lucie Cave

HELLO!
Wellington House, 69–71 Upper Ground, London SE1 9PQ
T 020-7667 8901 W www.hellomagazine.com
Editor, Rosie Nixon

OK!
10 Lower Thames Street, London EC3R 6EN T 020-8612 7000
W www.ok.co.uk
Editor, Kirsty Tyler

CHILDREN'S AND FAMILY

THE BEANO
185 Fleet Street, London EC4A 2HS W www.beano.com
Editor, Mike Stirling

MOTHER & BABY
Endeavour House, 189 Shaftesbury Avenue, London WC2H 8JG T 020-7437 9011 W www.askamum.co.uk
Editor, Claire Irvin

PRACTICAL PARENTING & PREGNANCY
Vineyard House, 44 Brook Green, Hammersmith W6 7BT
T 0844-815 0049 W www.madeformums.com
Editor, Daniella Delaney

YOUR CAT
BPG Stamford Ltd, 1-6 Buckminster Yard, Main Street, Buckminster, Grantham, Lincs NG33 5SA
T 0844-848-8257 W www.yourcat.co.uk
Editor, Sue Parslow

YOUR DOG
BPG Stamford Ltd, 1-6 Buckminster Yard, Main Street, Buckminster, Grantham, Lincs NG33 5SA
T 0844-848 8257 W www.yourdog.co.uk
Editor, Sarah Wright

YOUR HORSE
Media House, Peterborough Business Park, Lynch Wood, Peterborough PE2 6EA T 01733-468000
W www.yourhorse.co.uk
Editor, Imogen Johnson

CLASSICAL AND OPERA MUSIC

BBC MUSIC
Immediate Media Company Bristol Ltd, Tower House, Fairfax Street, Bristol BS1 3BN T 0117-927 9009
W www.classical-music.com
Editor, Oliver Condy

CLASSICAL MUSIC
Rhinegold House, 20 Rugby Street, London WC1N 3QZ
T 020-7333 1729 W www.classicalmusicmagazine.org
Editor, Kimon Daltas

GRAMOPHONE
Haymarket, Teddington Studios, Broom Road, Teddington, Middlesex TW11 9BE T 020-8267 5000
W www.gramophone.co.uk
Editor, Martin Cullingford

OPERA
36 Black Lion Lane, London W6 9BE T 020-8563 8893
W www.opera.co.uk
Editor, John Allison

OPERA NOW
Rhinegold House, 20 Rugby Street, London WC1N 3QZ
T 020-7333 1729 W www.rhinegold.co.uk
Editor, Ashutosh Khandekar

COMPUTERS AND TECHNOLOGY

ANDROID
Imagine Publishing, Richmond House, 33 Richmond Hill, Bournemouth BH2 6EZ T 01202-586200
W www.littlegreenrobot.co.uk
Editor, Andy Betts

EDGE
Future Publishing Ltd, 30 Monmouth Street, Bath BA1 2BW
T 01225-442244 W www.edge-online.com
Editor, Tony Mott

MACFORMAT
Future Publishing Ltd, 30 Monmouth Street, Bath BA1 2BW
T 01225-442244 W www.macformat.techradar.com
Editor, Christopher Phin

PC PRO
Dennis Technology, 30 Cleveland Street, London W1T 4JD
T 0844-844 0083 W www.pcpro.co.uk
Editor, Barry Collins

STUFF
Haymarket, Teddington Studios, Broom Road, Teddington, Middlesex TW11 9BE T 020-8267 5036 W www.stuff.tv
Editor, Will Findlater

T3
Future Publishing, 10 Waterside Way, Northampton NN4 7XD
T 0844-848 2852 W www.t3.com
Editor, Luke Peters

WEB USER
Dennis Publishing, 30 Cleveland Street, London W1T 4JD
T 020-7907 6000 W www.webuser.co.uk
Editor, Daniel Booth

WIRED
Condé Nast, Vogue House, Hanover Square, London W1S 1JU
T 0844-848 5202 W www.wired.co.uk
Editor, Scott Dadich

CRAFT

CARDMAKING & PAPERCRAFT
Immediate Media, Tower House, Fairfax Street, Bristol BS1 3BN
T 0117-927 9009 W www.cardmakingandpapercraft.com
Editor, Kirstie Sleight

SIMPLY KNITTING
Future Publishing Ltd, 30 Monmouth Street, Bath BA1 2BW
T 0844-848 2852 W simplyknitting.themakingspot.com
Editor, Debora Bradley

THE WORLD OF CROSS STITCHING
Immediate Media, Tower House, Fairfax Street, Bristol BS1 3BN
T 0117-927 9009 W www.cross-stitching.com
Editor, Ruth Southorn

ENTERTAINMENT

EMPIRE
Endeavour House, 189 Shaftesbury Avenue, London WC2H 8JG
T 020-7437 9011 W www.empireonline.com
Editor, Mark Dinning

RADIO TIMES
Media Centre, 201 Wood Lane, London W12 7TQ
T 020-8433 3999 W www.radiotimes.com
Editor, Ben Preston

SIGHT & SOUND
PO Box 2068, Bournehall House, Bournehall Road, Bushey WD23 3ZF T 020-8955 7070 W www.bfi.org.uk/sightandsound
Editor, Nick James

TIME OUT
Universal House, 251 Tottenham Court Road, London W1T 7AB
T 020-7813 3000 W www.timeout.com
Editor, Tim Arthur

TOTAL FILM
2 Balcombe Street, London NW1 6NW T 020-7042 4000
W www.totalfilm.com
Editor, Jane Crowther

FASHION AND BEAUTY

COSMOPOLITAN
Hearst Magazines, 33 Broadwick Street, London W1F 0DQ
T 020-7439 5000 W www.cosmopolitan.co.uk
Editor, Louise Court

ELLE
Hearst Magazines, 72 Broadwick Street, London W1F 9EP
T 020-7150 7000 W www.elleuk.com
Editor, Lorraine Candy

GLAMOUR
Condé Nast, Vogue House, Hanover Square, London W1S 1JU
T 020-7499 9080 W www.glamourmagazine.co.uk
Editor, Natasha McNamara

GRAZIA
Endeavour House, 189 Shaftesbury Avenue, London WC2H 8JG
T 0845-601 1356 W www.graziadaily.co.uk
Editor, Angela Buttolph

HARPER'S BAZAAR
Hearst Magazines, 72 Broadwick Street, London W1F 9EP
T 0844-848 5203 W www.harpersbazaar.co.uk
Editor, Justine Picardie

MARIE CLAIRE
Blue Fin Building, 110 Southwark Street, London SE1 4SU
T 020-3148 7513 W www.marieclaire.co.uk
Editor, Trish Halpin

VOGUE
Condé Nast, Vogue House, Hanover Square, London W1S 1JU
T 0844-848 5202 W www.vogue.co.uk
Editor, Alexandra Shulman

FOOD AND DRINK

FOOD AND TRAVEL
Suite 51, The Business Centre, Ingate Place, London SW8 3NS
T 020-7501 0511 W www.foodandtravel.com
Editor, Guy Woodward

GOOD FOOD
201 Wood Lane, London W12 7TQ T 020-8433 1294
W www.bbcgoodfood.com
Editor, Gillian Carter

JAMIE
800 Guillat Avenue, Kent Science Park, Sittingbourne ME9 8GU
T 0844-249 0478 W www.jamieoliver.com/magazine
Editor, Andy Harris

OLIVE
BBC Worldwide, 201 Wood Lane, London W12 7TQ
T 020-8433 1402 W www.bbcgoodfood.com
Editor, Christine Hayes

WHISKY
St Faiths House, Mountergate, Norwich NR1 1PY
T 01603-633 808 W www.whiskymag.com
Editor, Rob Allanson

GENERAL INTEREST

BBC HISTORY
Tower House, Fairfax Street, Bristol BS1 3BN
T 0117-927 9009 W www.historyextra.com
Editor, Rob Attar

BOOKSELLER
Crowne House, 56-58 Southwark Street, London SE1 1UN
T 01604-251040 W www.thebookseller.com
Editor, Philip Jones

HISTORY TODAY
25 Bedford Avenue, London WC1B 3AT T 020-3219 7810
W www.historytoday.com
Editor, Paul Lay

LITERARY REVIEW
44 Lexington Street, London W1F OLW T 020-7437 9392
W www.literaryreview.co.uk
Editor, Nancy Sladek

NEW STATESMAN
John Carpenter House, 7 Carmelite Street, Blackfriars, London EC4Y 0AN T 020-7936 6400
W www.newstatesman.com
Editor, Jason Cowley

PRIVATE EYE
6 Carlisle Street, London W1D 3BN T 020-7437 4017
W www.private-eye.co.uk
Editor, Ian Hislop

PROSPECT
5th Floor, 23 Savile Row, London W1S 2ET T 020-7255 1281
W www.prospectmagazine.co.uk
Editor, Bronwen Maddox

RAILWAY
Mortons Media Ltd, Horncastle, Lincs LN9 6JR
T 01507-529529 W www.railwaymagazine.co.uk
Editor, Nick Pigott

READER'S DIGEST
9th Floor, 1 Eversholt Street, London NW1 2DN
T 0845-601 2711 W www.readersdigest.co.uk
Editor, Gill Hudson

SAGA
Saga Publishing Ltd, Enbrook Park, Folkestone, Kent CT20 3SE
T 01303-771111 W www.saga.co.uk
Editor, Katy Bravery

THE SPECTATOR
22 Old Queen Street, London SW1H 9HP T 020-7961 0200
W www.spectator.co.uk
Editor, Fraser Nelson

TLS (THE TIMES LITERARY SUPPLEMENT)
3 Thomas More Square, London E98 1BS T 020-7782 5000
W www.the-tls.co.uk
Editor, Peter Stothard

THE WEEK
30 Cleveland Street, London W1T 4JD T 020-7907 6000
W www.theweek.co.uk
Editor, Nigel Horne

WHO DO YOU THINK YOU ARE?
Tower House, Fairfax Street, Bristol BS1 3BN
T 0117-314 7400
W www.whodoyouthinkyouaremagazine.com
Editor, Sarah Williams

HEALTH AND FITNESS

HEALTH & FITNESS
30 Cleveland Street, London W1T 4JD T 020-7907 6000
W www.womensfitness.co.uk
Editor, Mary Comber

MEN'S FITNESS
Dennis Publishing, 30 Cleveland Street, London W1T 4JD
T 020-7907 6000 W www.mensfitness.co.uk
Editor, Jon Lipsey

MEN'S HEALTH
Hearst Magazines, 72 Broadwick Street, London W1F 9EP
T 01858-438851 W www.menshealth.co.uk
Editor, Toby Wiseman

RUNNER'S WORLD
72 Broadwick Street, London W1F 9EP T 020-7339 4409
W www.runnersworld.co.uk
Editor, Andy Dixon

WEIGHT WATCHERS
The River Group, 1 Neal Street, London WC2H 9QL
T 020-7420 7000 W www.weightwatchers.co.uk
Editor, Julie Lee

WOMEN'S FITNESS
30 Cleveland Street, London W1T 4JD T 020-7907 6000
W www.womensfitness.co.uk
Editor, Joanna Knight

YOGA & HEALTH
Yoga Today Ltd, PO Box 2130, Seaford, East Sussex BN25 9BF
T 01323-872466 W www.yogaandhealthmag.co.uk
Editor, Jane Sill

ZEST
Hearst Magazines, 72 Broadwick Street, London W1F 9EP
T 020-7439 5000 W www.zest.co.uk
Editor, Mandie Gower

HOBBIES AND GAMES

AIRFIX MODEL WORLD
Key Publishing Ltd, PO Box 100, Stamford PE9 1XQ
T 01780-755131 W www.airfixmodelworld.com
Editor, Glenn Sands

ANGLING TIMES
Bauer Consumer Media Ltd, 1 Lincoln Court, Lincoln Road, Peterborough PE1 2RF T 01733-395097
W www.gofishing.co.uk
Editor, Steve Fitzpatrick

BRITISH RAILWAY MODELLING
Warners Group Publications, The Maltings, West Street, Bourne, Lincs PE10 9PH T 01778-391000
W www.model-railways-live.co.uk
Editor, John Emerson

CHESS
Chess & Bridge Ltd, 44 Baker Street, London W1U 7RT
T 020-7486 7015 W www.chess.co.uk
Editor, John Saunders

COIN NEWS
Token Publishing Ltd, Orchard House, Duchy Road, Heathpark, Honiton, Devon EX14 1YD T 01404-46972
W www.tokenpublishing.com
Editor, John Mussell

HORNBY
Key Publishing Ltd, PO Box 100, Stamford PE9 1XQ
T 01780-755131 W www.hornbymagazine.com
Editor, Mike Wild

HOME AND GARDEN

GARDENERS' WORLD
Immediate Media, 5th Floor, Vineyard House, 44 Brook Green, London W6 7BT T 020-7150 5700
W www.gardenersworld.com
Editor, Lucy Hall

GOOD HOUSEKEEPING
Hearst Magazines, 72 Broadwick Street, London W1F 9EP
T 020-7439 5000 W www.goodhousekeeping.co.uk
Editor, Rosemary Ellis

LIVING ETC
IPC Media, Blue Fin Building, 110 Southwark Street, London SE1 0SU T 020-3148 7443
W www.housetohome.co.uk/livingetc
Editor, Suzanne Imre

STYLE AT HOME
IPC Media, Blue Fin Building, 110 Southwark Street, London SE1 0SU T 020-3148 6293 W www.housetohome.co.uk
Editor, Jennifer Morgan

MEN'S LIFESTYLE

ATTITUDE
Vitality Publishing Ltd, 3rd Floor, 207 Old Street, London EC1V 9NR T 020-7608 6300 W www.attitude.co.uk
Editor, Matthew Todd

ESQUIRE
Hearst Magazines, 72 Broadwick Street, London W1F 9EP
T 020-7439 5000 W www.esquire.co.uk
Editor, Alex Bilmes

FHM
Endeavour House, 189 Shaftesbury Avenue, London WC2H 8JG
T 020-7295 8534 W www.fhm.com
Editor, Joe Barnes

GAY TIMES
Millivres Prowler Group, Spectrum House, 32–34 Gordon House Road, London NW5 1LP
T 020-7424 7400 W www.gaytimes.co.uk
Editor, Darren Scott

GQ
Vogue House, 1 Hanover Square, London W1S 1JU
T 020-7499 9080 W www.gq-magazine.co.uk
Editor, Dylan Jones

LOADED
23 Lyon Road, Hersham, Surrey KT12 3PU T 020-8873 4440
W www.loaded.co.uk
Editor, Jamie Wallis

MOTORING

BIKE
Bauer Media, Media House, Lynchwood, Peterborough PE2 6EA
T 01733-468000 W www.bikemagazine.co.uk
Editor, Hugo Wilson

CARAVAN
Warners Group Publications, The Maltings, West Street, Bourne, Lincs PE10 9PH T 01778-391000
W www.outandaboutlive.co.uk
Editor, John Sootheran

F1 RACING
Haymarket, Teddington Studios, Broom Road, Teddington TW11 9BE T 020-8267 5806 W www.f1racing.co.uk
Editor, Anthony Rowlinson

OCTANE
Dennis Publishing Ltd, 30 Cleveland Street, London W1T 4JD
T 020-7907 6000 W www.classicandperformancecar.com
Editor, David Lillywhite

PRACTICAL CARAVAN
Haymarket, Teddington Studios, Teddington Lock, Broom Road, Teddington TW11 9BE T 020-8267 5629
W www.practicalcaravan.com
Editor, Nigel Donnelly

TOP GEAR
Energy Centre, Media Centre, 201 Wood Lane, London W12 7TQ
T 020-8433 3598 W www.topgear.com
Editor, Charlie Turner

PHOTOGRAPHY

AMATEUR PHOTOGRAPHER
Blue Fin Building, 110 Southwark Street, London SE1 0SU
T 020-3148 4138 W www.amateurphotographer.co.uk
Editor, Damien Demolder

DIGITAL PHOTOGRAPHER
Imagine Publishing, Richmond House, 33 Richmond Hill, Bournemouth BH2 6EZ T 01202-586200
W www.dphotographer.co.uk
Editor, April Madden

PHOTOGRAPHY MONTHLY
Archant House, Oriel Road, Cheltenham GL50 1BB
T 01242-211080 W www.photographymonthly.com
Editor, Jeff Meyer

PROFESSIONAL PHOTOGRAPHER
Archant House, Oriel Road, Cheltenham GL50 1BB
T 0844-848 5232 W www.photoanswers.co.uk
Editor, Adam Scorey

POPULAR MUSIC

CLASH
194 Hercules Road, London SE1 7LD T 020-7628 2312
W www.clashmusic.com
Editor, Simon Harper

CLASSIC ROCK
Future Publishing Ltd, Beauford Court, 30 Monmouth Street, Bath BA1 2BW T 01225-442244
W www.classicrockmagazine.com
Editor, Scott Rowley

GUITARIST
Future Publishing Ltd, Beauford Court, 30 Monmouth Street, Bath BA1 2BW T 01225-442244
W www.musicradar.com/guitarist
Editor, Mick Taylor

KERRANG!
Bauer Media, Media House, Lynchwood, Peterborough PE2 6EA
T 01733-468000 W www.kerrang.com
Editor, James McMahon

MOJO
Endeavour House, 189 Shaftesbury Avenue, London WC2H 8JG
T 020-7208 3443 W www.mojo4music.com
Editor, Phil Alexander

NME
9th Floor, Blue Fin Building, 110 Southwark Street, London SE1 0SU T 0845-676 7778 W www.nme.com
Editor, Mike Williams

Q
Endeavour House, 189 Shaftesbury Avenue, London WC2H 8JG
T 020-7295 5000 W www.qthemusic.com
Editor, Jane Johnson

UNCUT
Blue Fin Building, 110 Southwark Street, London SE1 0SU
T 020-3148 5000 W www.uncut.co.uk
Editor, Allan Jones

SCIENCE AND NATURE

BBC WILDLIFE
4th Floor, Tower House, Fairfax Street, Bristol BS1 3BN
T 0117-314 7366 W www.discoverwildlife.com
Editor, Sophie Stafford

BIRD WATCHING
Bauer Media, Media House, Lynch Wood, Peterborough PE2 6EA
T 01733-468000 W www.birdwatching.co.uk
Editor, Sheena Harvey

COUNTRYFILE
9th Floor, Tower House, Fairfax Street, Bristol BS1 3BN
T 0117-927 9009 W www.countryfile.com
Editor, Fergus Collins

FOCUS
Bristol Magazines Ltd, Tower House, Fairfax Street, Bristol BS1 3BN T 0117-314 7388
W www.sciencefocus.com
Editor, Graham Southorn

HOW IT WORKS
Imagine Publishing Ltd, Richmond House, 33 Richmond Hill, Bournemouth BH2 6EZ T 01202-586200
W www.howitworksdaily.com
Editor, Helen Porter

NEW SCIENTIST
Lacon House, 84 Theobalds Road, London WC1X 8NS
T 020-7611 1200 W www.newscientist.com
Editor, Sumit Paul-Choudhury

SKY AT NIGHT
Immediate Media Company Bristol Ltd, Tower House, Fairfax Street, Bristol BS1 3BN T 0844 844 0254
W www.skyatnightmagazine.com
Editor, Chris Bramley

SPORT

ALL OUT CRICKET
TriNorth Ltd, Unit 3.40 Canterbury Court, 1–3 Brixton Road, London SW9 6DE T 020-3176 0187 W www.alloutcricket.com
Editor, Phil Walker

BOXING MONTHLY
Topwave Ltd, 40 Morpeth Road, London E9 7LD
T 020-8986 4141 W www.boxing-monthly.co.uk
Editor, Glyn Leach

CLIMBER
Warners Group Publications Plc, West Street, Bourne, Lincs PE10 9PH T 01778-392004 W www.climber.co.uk
Editor, David Simmonite

COUNTRY WALKING
Bauer Media, Media House, Lynchwood, Peterborough PE2 6EA
T 01733-468000 W www.livefortheoutdoors.com
Editor, Vincent Crump

THE CRICKETER
The Cricketer Publishing Ltd, 2nd Floor, 123 Buckingham Palace Road, London SW1W 9SL T 020-7032 4911
W www.thecricketer.com
Editor, Andrew Miller

FOURFOURTWO
Haymarket, Teddington Studios, Broom Road, Teddington, Middlesex TW11 9BE T 020-8267 5661
W www.fourfourtwo.com
Editor, David Hall

GOLF MONTHLY
9th Floor, Blue Fin Building, 110 Southwark Street, London SE1 0SU T 020-3148 4527 W www.golf-monthly.co.uk
Editor, Michael Harris

HORSE & HOUND
Blue Fin Building, 110 Southwark Street, London SE1 0SU
T 020-3148 4562 W www.horseandhound.co.uk
Editor, Lucy Higginson

MATCH
Media House, Lynchwood, Peterborough PE2 6EA
T 01733-468008 W www.matchmag.co.uk
Editor, James Bandy

RUGBY WORLD
Blue Fin Building, 110 Southwark Street, London SE1 0SU
T 0844-848 0848 W www.rugbyworld.com
Editor, Owain Jones

SUPERBIKE
23 Lyon Road, Hersham, Surrey KT12 3PU
T 020-8873 4454 W www.superbike.co.uk
Editor, John Hogan

TENNISHEAD
Advantage Publishing (UK) Ltd, 30 Cleveland Street, London W1T 4JD T 020-7907 6387 W www.tennishead.net
Editor, Lee Goodall

WORLD SOCCER
Blue Fin Building, 110 Southwark Street, London SE1 0SU T 020-3148 6288 W www.worldsoccer.com
Editor, Gavin Hamilton

TRAVEL

CONDÉ NAST TRAVELLER
Vogue House, Hanover Square, London W1S 1JU T 0844-848 2851 W www.cntraveller.com
Editor, Melinda Stevens

FRANCE
Archant House, 3 Oriel Road, Cheltenham GL50 1BB T 01242-216050 W www.completefrance.com
Editor, Carolyn Boyd

LIVING FRANCE
Archant House, 3 Oriel Road, Cheltenham GL50 1BB T 01242-216050 W www.completefrance.com
Editor, Andy Duncan

LONELY PLANET
Media Centre (GH0S), 201 Wood Lane, London W12 7TQ T 020-8433 1333 W www.lonelyplanet.com
Editor, Peter Grunert

NATIONAL GEOGRAPHIC TRAVELLER
Absolute Publishing Ltd, 197–199 City Road, London EC1V 1JN T 020-7253 9906 W www.natgeotraveller.co.uk
Editor, Pat Riddell

BOOK PUBLISHER'S FAMILY TREE

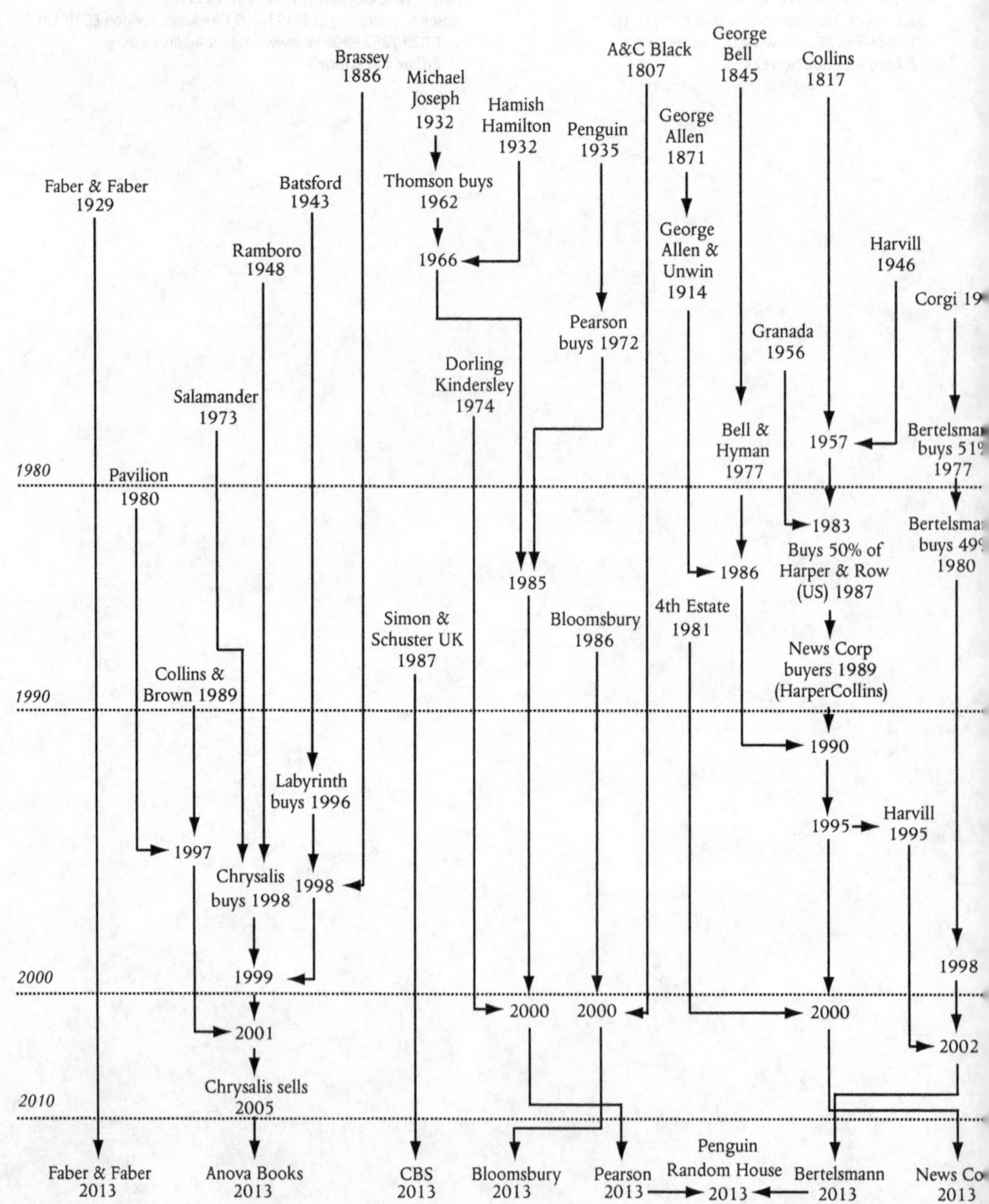

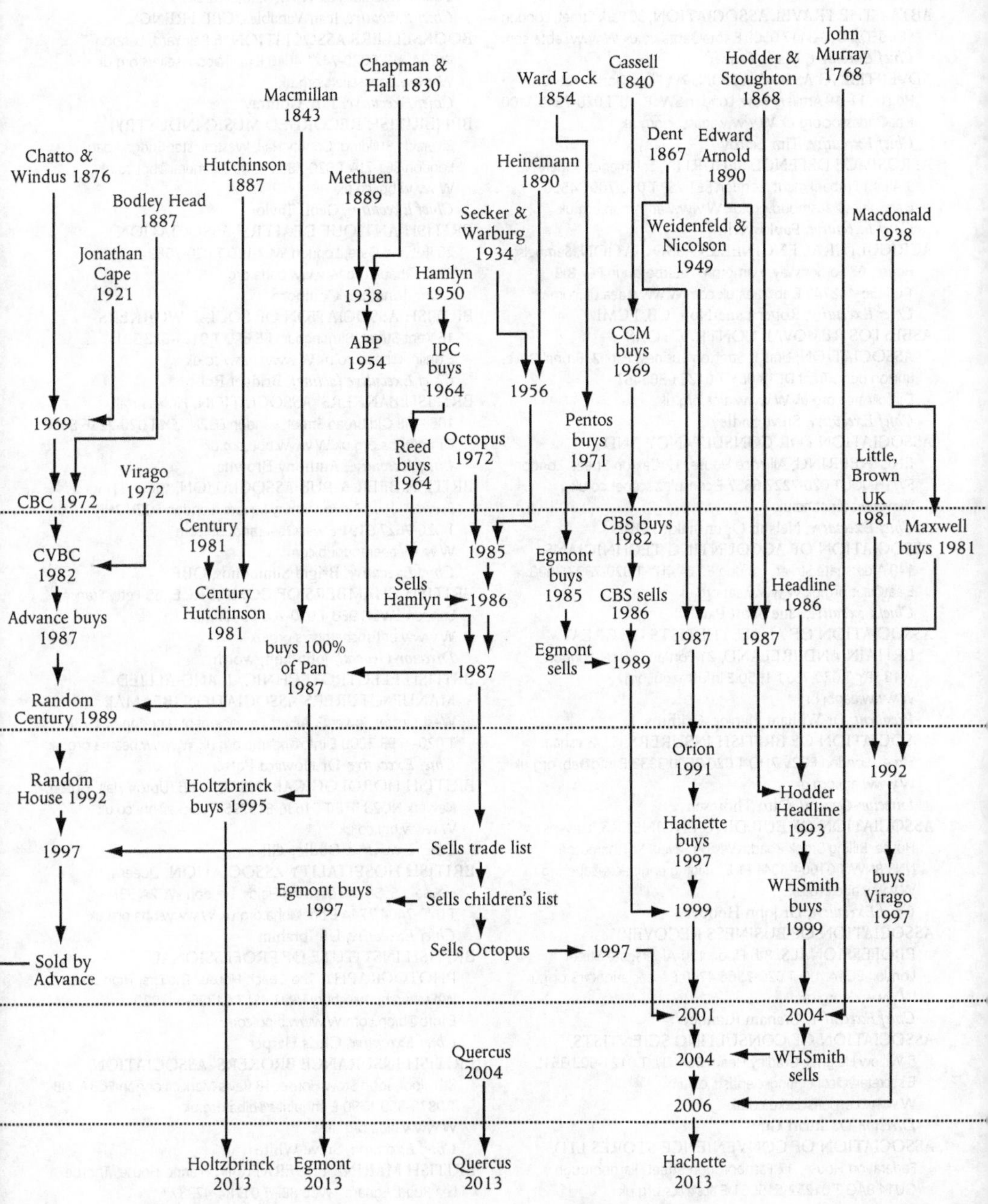

Chatto & Windus 1876
Bodley Head 1887
Jonathan Cape 1921
1969
Virago 1972
CBC 1972
CVBC 1982
Advance buys 1987
Random Century 1989
Random House 1992
1997
Sold by Advance
Macmillan 1843
Hutchinson 1887
Century 1981
Century Hutchinson 1981
buys 100% of Pan 1987
Holtzbrinck buys 1995
Egmont buys 1997
Holtzbrinck 2013
Egmont 2013
Chapman & Hall 1830
Methuen 1889
1938
ABP 1954
Hamlyn 1950
IPC buys 1964
Reed buys 1964
Octopus 1972
1985
Sells Hamlyn
1986
1987
Sells trade list
Sells children's list
Sells Octopus
Quercus 2004
Quercus 2013
Ward Lock 1854
Heinemann 1890
Secker & Warburg 1934
1956
Pentos buys 1971
Egmont buys 1985
Egmont sells
Cassell 1840
Dent 1867
Edward Arnold 1890
Weidenfeld & Nicolson 1949
CCM buys 1969
CBS buys 1982
CBS sells 1986
1989
1987
Orion 1991
Hachette buys 1997
1999
1997
2001
2004
2006
Hachette 2013
Hodder & Stoughton 1868
John Murray 1768
Macdonald 1938
Little, Brown UK 1981
Maxwell buys 1981
Headline 1986
1987
1992
Hodder Headline 1993
buys Virago 1997
WHSmith buys 1999
2004
WHSmith sells

TRADE AND PROFESSIONAL BODIES

The following is a list of employers' and trade associations and other professional bodies in the UK. It does not represent a comprehensive list. For further professional bodies *see* Professional Education.

ASSOCIATIONS

ABTA – THE TRAVEL ASSOCIATION, 30 Park Street, London SE1 9EQ **T** 020-3117 0500 **E** abta@abta.co.uk **W** www.abta.com
Chief Executive, Mark Tanzer

ADVERTISING ASSOCIATION, 7th Floor North, Artillery House, 11–19 Artillery Row, London SW1P 1RT **T** 020-7340 1100 **E** aa@adassoc.org.uk **W** www.adassoc.org.uk
Chief Executive, Tim Lefroy

AEROSPACE DEFENCE SECURITY, Salamanca Square, 9 Albert Embankment, London SE1 7SP **T** 020-7091 4500 **E** enquiries@adsgroup.org.uk **W** www.adsgroup.org.uk
Chief Executive, Paul Everitt

AGRICULTURAL ENGINEERS ASSOCIATION, Samuelson House, 62 Forder Way, Hampton, Peterborough PE7 8JB **T** 08456-448748 **E** ab@aea.uk.com **W** www.aea.uk.com
Chief Executive, Roger Lane-Nott, CB, FCMI

ASBESTOS REMOVAL CONTRACTORS ASSOCIATION, Unit 1, Stretton Business Park 2, Brunel Drive, Burton upon Trent DE13 0BY **T** 01283-566467 **E** info@arca.org.uk **W** www.arca.org.uk
Chief Executive, Steve Sadley

ASSOCIATION FOR CONSULTANCY AND ENGINEERING, Alliance House, 12 Caxton Street, London SW1H 0QL **T** 020-7222 6557 **E** consult@acenet.co.uk **W** www.acenet.co.uk
Chief Executive, Nelson Ogunshakin, OBE

ASSOCIATION OF ACCOUNTING TECHNICIANS, 140 Aldersgate Street, London EC1A 4HY **T** 020-7397 3000 **E** aat@aat.org.uk **W** www.aat.org.uk
Chief Executive, Jane Scott Paul

ASSOCIATION OF ANAESTHETISTS OF GREAT BRITAIN AND IRELAND, 21 Portland Place, London W1B 1PY **T** 020-7631 1650 **E** info@aagbi.org **W** www.aagbi.org
President, Dr William Harrop-Griffiths

ASSOCIATION OF BRITISH INSURERS, 51 Gresham Street, London EC2V 7HQ **T** 020-7600 3333 **E** info@abi.org.uk **W** www.abi.org.uk
Director-General, Otto Thoresen

ASSOCIATION OF BUILDING ENGINEERS, Lutyens House, Billing Brook Road, Weston Favell, Northampton NN3 8NW **T** 01604-404121 **E** building.engineers@abe.org.uk **W** www.abe.org.uk
Chief Executive, Dr John Hooper

ASSOCIATION OF BUSINESS RECOVERY PROFESSIONALS, 8th Floor, 120 Aldersgate Street, London EC1A 4JQ **T** 020-7566 4200 **E** association@r3.org.uk **W** www.r3.org.uk
Chief Executive, Graham Rumney

ASSOCIATION OF CONSULTING SCIENTISTS, 5 Willow Heights, Cradley Heath B64 7PL **T** 0121-602 3515 **E** secretary@consultingscientists.co.uk **W** www.consultsci.uku.co.uk
Director, Dr Stuart Guy

ASSOCIATION OF CONVENIENCE STORES LTD, Federation House, 17 Farnborough Street, Farnborough GU14 8AG **T** 01252-515001 **E** acs@acs.org.uk **W** www.acs.org.uk
Chief Executive, James Lowman

ASSOCIATION OF CORPORATE TREASURERS, 51 Moorgate, London EC2R 6BH **T** 020-7847 2540 **E** enquiries@treasurers.org **W** www.treasurers.org
Chief Executive, Colin Tyler

ASSOCIATION OF DRAINAGE AUTHORITIES, 6 Electric Parade, Surbiton KT6 5NT **T** 020-8399 7350 **E** admin@ada.org.uk **W** www.ada.org.uk
Chief Executive, Jean Venables, CBE FRENG

BOOKSELLERS ASSOCIATION, 6 Bell Yard, London WC2A 2JR **T** 020-7421 4640 **E** mail@booksellers.org.uk **W** www.booksellers.org.uk
Chief Executive, T. E. Godfray

BPI (BRITISH RECORDED MUSIC INDUSTRY), Riverside Building, County Hall, Westminster Bridge Road, London SE1 7JA **T** 020-7803 1300 **E** general@bpi.co.uk **W** www.bpi.co.uk
Chief Executive, Geoff Taylor

BRITISH ANTIQUE DEALERS' ASSOCIATION, 20 Rutland Gate, London SW7 1BD **T** 020-7589 4128 **E** info@bada.org **W** www.bada.org
Chair, Jonathan Coulborn

BRITISH ASSOCIATION OF SOCIAL WORKERS, 16 Kent Street, Birmingham B5 6RD **T** 0121-622 3911 **E** online@basw.co.uk **W** www.basw.co.uk
Chief Executive (acting), Bridget Robb

BRITISH BANKERS' ASSOCIATION, Pinners Hall, 105–108 Old Broad Street, London EC2N 1EX **T** 020-7216 8800 **E** info@bba.org.uk **W** www.bba.org.uk
Chief Executive, Anthony Browne

BRITISH BEER & PUB ASSOCIATION, Ground Floor, Brewers' Hall, Aldermanbury Square, London EC2V 7HR **T** 020-7627 9191 **E** web@beerandpub.com **W** www.beerandpub.com
Chief Executive, Brigid Simmonds, OBE

BRITISH CHAMBERS OF COMMERCE, 65 Petty France, London SW1H 9EU **T** 020-7654 5800 **W** www.britishchambers.org.uk
Director-General, John Longworth

BRITISH ELECTROTECHNICAL AND ALLIED MANUFACTURERS ASSOCIATION (BEAMA), Westminster Tower, 3 Albert Embankment, London SE1 7SL **T** 020-7793 3000 **E** info@beama.org.uk **W** www.beama.org.uk
Chief Executive, Dr Howard Porter

BRITISH HOROLOGICAL INSTITUTE, Upton Hall, Upton, Newark NG23 5TE **T** 01636-813795 **E** clocks@bhi.co.uk **W** www.bhi.co.uk
Chief Executive, Dudley Giles

BRITISH HOSPITALITY ASSOCIATION, Queens House, 55–56 Lincoln's Inn Fields, London WC2A 3BH **T** 020-7404 7744 **E** bha@bha.org.uk **W** www.bha.org.uk
Chief Executive, Ufi Ibrahim

BRITISH INSTITUTE OF PROFESSIONAL PHOTOGRAPHY, The Coach House, The Firs, High Street, Whitchurch, Aylesbury HP22 4SJ **T** 01296-642020 **E** info@bipp.com **W** www.bipp.com
Chief Executive, Chris Harper

BRITISH INSURANCE BROKERS' ASSOCIATION, 8th Floor, John Stow House, 18 Bevis Marks, London EC3A 7JB **T** 0870-950 1790 **E** enquiries@biba.org.uk **W** www.biba.org.uk
Chief Executive, Steve White

BRITISH MARINE FEDERATION, Marine House, Thorpe Lea Road, Egham TW20 8BF **T** 01784-473377 **E** info@britishmarine.co.uk **W** www.britishmarine.co.uk
Chief Executive, Howard Pridding

BRITISH MEDICAL ASSOCIATION, BMA House, Tavistock Square, London WC1H 9JP T 020-7387 4499 W www.bma.org.uk
Chief Executive, Tony Bourne

BRITISH OFFICE SUPPLIES AND SERVICES (BOSS) FEDERATION, c/o British Printing Industries Federation, 2 Villiers Court, Meriden Business Park, Copse Drive, Coventry CV5 9RN T 0845-450 1565 E info@bossfederation.co.uk W www.bossfederation.co.uk
Chief Executive, Michael Gardner

BRITISH PLASTICS FEDERATION, 5–6 Bath Place, Rivington Street, London EC2A 3JE T 020-7457 5000 E reception@bpf.co.uk W www.bpf.co.uk
Director-General, Peter Davis, OBE

BRITISH PORTS ASSOCIATION, 1st Floor, 30 Park Street, London SE1 9EQ T 020-7260 1780 E info@britishports.org.uk W www.britishports.org.uk
Director, David Whitehead

BRITISH PRINTING INDUSTRIES FEDERATION, 2 Villiers Court, Meriden Business Park, Copse Drive, Coventry CV5 9RN T 0845-250 7050 W www.britishprint.com
Chief Executive, Kathy Woodward

BRITISH PROPERTY FEDERATION, 5th Floor, St Albans House, 57–59 Haymarket, London SW1Y 4QX T 020-7828 0111 E info@bpf.org.uk W www.bpf.org.uk
Chief Executive, Liz Peace

BRITISH RETAIL CONSORTIUM, 21 Dartmouth Street, London SW1H 9BP T 020-7854 8900 E info@brc.org.uk W www.brc.org.uk
Director-General, Helen Dickinson

BRITISH TYRE MANUFACTURERS' ASSOCIATION LTD, 5 Berewyk Hall Court, White Colne, Colchester CO6 2QD T 01787-226995 E mail@btmauk.com W www.btmauk.com
Chief Executive, Graham Willson

BUILDING SOCIETIES ASSOCIATION, York House, 23 Kingsway, London WC2B 6UJ T 020-7520 5900 E simon.rex@bsa.org.uk W www.bsa.org.uk
Chief Executive, Robin Fieth

CHARTERED INSTITUTE OF ENVIRONMENTAL HEALTH, Chadwick Court, 15 Hatfields, London SE1 8DJ T 020-7928 6006 E information@cieh.org W www.cieh.org
Chief Executive, Graham Jukes

CHARTERED INSTITUTE OF JOURNALISTS, 2 Dock Offices, Surrey Quays Road, London SE16 2XU T 020-7252 1187 E memberservices@cioj.co.uk W www.cioj.co.uk
General Secretary, Dominic Cooper

CHARTERED INSTITUTE OF PURCHASING AND SUPPLY, Easton House, Church Street, Easton on the Hill, Stamford PE9 3NZ T 01780-756777 E info@cips.org W www.cips.org
Chief Executive, David Noble

CHARTERED INSTITUTE OF TAXATION, 1st Floor Artillery House, 11–19 Artillery Row, London SW1P 1RT T 020-7340 0550 E post@ciot.org.uk W www.tax.org.uk
Chief Executive, Peter Fanning

CHARTERED INSURANCE INSTITUTE, 42–48 High Road, South Woodford, London E18 2JP T 020-8989 8464 E customer.serv@cii.co.uk W www.cii.co.uk
Chief Executive, Dr Alexander Scott

CHARTERED MANAGEMENT INSTITUTE, Management House, Cottingham Road, Corby NN17 1TT T 01536-204222 E enquiries@managers.org.uk W www.managers.org.uk
Chief Executive, Anne Francke

CHARTERED QUALITY INSTITUTE, 2nd Floor North, Chancery Exchange, 10 Furnival Street, London EC4A 1AB T 020-7245 6722 E info@thecqi.org W www.thecqi.org
Chief Executive, Simon Feary

CHEMICAL INDUSTRIES ASSOCIATION, Kings Buildings, Smith Square, London SW1P 3JJ T 020-7834 3399 E enquiries@cia.org.uk W www.cia.org.uk
Chief Executive, Steve Elliott

CONFEDERATION OF PAPER INDUSTRIES, 1 Rivenhall Road, Swindon SN5 7BD T 01793-889600 E cpi@paper.org.uk W www.paper.org.uk
Director-General, David Workman

CONFEDERATION OF PASSENGER TRANSPORT UK, Drury House, 34–43 Russell Street, London WC2B 5HA T 020-7240 3131 W www.cpt-uk.org
Chief Executive, Simon Posner

CONSTRUCTION PRODUCTS ASSOCIATION, The Building Centre, 26 Store Street, London WC1E 7BT T 020-7323 3770 E enquiries@constructionproducts.org.uk W www.constructionproducts.org.uk
Chief Executive, Diana Montgomery

DAIRY UK, 93 Baker Street, London W1U 6QQ T 020-7486 7244 E info@dairyuk.org W www.dairyuk.org
Director-General, Jim Begg

EEF, THE MANUFACTURERS' ORGANISATION, Broadway House, Tothill Street, London SW1H 9NQ T 020-7222 7777 E enquiries@eef.org.uk W www.eef.org.uk
Chief Executive, Terry Scuoler

ENERGY UK, Charles House, 5–11 Regent Street, London SW1Y 4LR T 020-7930 9390 W www.energy-uk.org.uk
Chief Executive, Angela Knight, CBE

FEDERATION OF BAKERS, 6 Catherine Street, London WC2B 5JW T 020-7420 7190 E info@bakersfederation.org.uk W www.bakersfederation.org.uk
Director, Gordon Polson

FEDERATION OF MASTER BUILDERS, Gordon Fisher House, 14–15 Great James Street, London WC1N 3DP T 020-7242 7583 W www.fmb.org.uk
Chief Executive, Brian Berry

FEDERATION OF SPORTS AND PLAY ASSOCIATIONS, Federation House, Stoneleigh Park, Warks CV8 2RF T 024-7641 4999 E info@sportsandplay.com W www.sportsandplay.com
Managing Director, Jane Montgomery

FINANCE AND LEASING ASSOCIATION, 2nd Floor, Imperial House, 15–19 Kingsway, London WC2B 6UN T 020-7836 6511 E info@fla.org.uk W www.fla.org.uk
Director-General, Stephen Sklaroff

FOOD AND DRINK FEDERATION, 6 Catherine Street, London WC2B 5JJ T 020-7836 2460 E generalenquiries@fdf.org.uk W www.fdf.org.uk
Director-General, Melanie Leech

FREIGHT TRANSPORT ASSOCIATION LTD, Hermes House, St John's Road, Tunbridge Wells TN4 9UZ T 01892-526171 E enquiries@fta.co.uk W www.fta.co.uk
Chief Executive, Theo de Pencier

GLASGOW CHAMBER OF COMMERCE, 30 George Square, Glasgow G2 1EQ T 0141-204 2121 E chamber@glasgowchamberofcommerce.com W www.glasgowchamberofcommerce.com
Chief Executive, Stuart Patrick

INSTITUTE FOR ARCHAEOLOGISTS, School of Human and Environmental Science, Whiteknights, University of Reading, PO Box 227 RG6 6AB T 0118-378 6446 E admin@archaeologists.net W www.archaeologists.net
Hon. Chair, Jan Wills

INSTITUTE OF ADMINISTRATIVE MANAGEMENT, 6 Graphite Square, Vauxhall Walk, London SE11 5EE T 020-7091 2600 E info@instam.org W www.instam.org
Chair, David Holland

INSTITUTE OF BREWING & DISTILLING, 33 Clarges Street, London W1J 7EE T 020-7499 8144 E enquiries@ibd.org.uk W www.ibd.org.uk
Executive Director, Simon Jackson

INSTITUTE OF BRITISH ORGAN BUILDING, 13 Ryefields, Thurston, Bury St Edmunds IP31 3TD T 01359-233433 E administrator@ibo.co.uk W www.ibo.co.uk
President, Martin Goetze

INSTITUTE OF CHARTERED FORESTERS, 59 George Street, Edinburgh EH2 2JG T 0131-240 1425 E icf@charteredforesters.org W www.charteredforesters.org
Executive Director, Shireen Chambers, FRSA

INSTITUTE OF CHARTERED SECRETARIES AND ADMINISTRATORS, 16 Park Crescent, London W1B 1AH T 020-7580 4741 E info@icsaglobal.com W www.icsaglobal.com
Chief Executive, Simon Osborne

INSTITUTE OF CHARTERED SHIPBROKERS, 85 Gracechurch Street, London EC3V 0AA T 020-7623 1111 E enquiries@ics.org.uk W www.ics.org.uk
Director, Julie Lithgow

INSTITUTE OF DIRECTORS, 116 Pall Mall, London SW1Y 5ED T 020-7766 8866 E enquiries@iod.com W www.iod.com
Director-General, Simon Walker

INSTITUTE OF EXPORT, Export House, Minerva Business Park, Lynch Wood, Peterborough PE2 6FT T 01733-404400 E institute@export.org.uk W www.export.org.uk
Director General, Lesley Batchelor

INSTITUTE OF FINANCIAL ACCOUNTANTS, Burford House, 44 London Road, Sevenoaks TN13 1AS T 01732-458080 E mail@ifa.org.uk W www.ifa.org.uk
Chief Executive, David Woodgate

INSTITUTE OF HEALTHCARE MANAGEMENT, John Snow House, 59 Mansell Street, London E1 8AN T 020-7265 7321 E enquiries@ihm.org.uk W www.ihm.org.uk
Chief Executive, Shirley Cramer, CBE

INSTITUTE OF HOSPITALITY, Trinity Court, 34 West Street, Sutton, Surrey SM1 1SH T 020-8661 4900 E info@instituteofhospitality.org W www.instituteofhospitality.org
Chief Executive, Peter Ducker

INSTITUTE OF INTERNAL COMMUNICATION, Suite GA2, Oak House, Woodlands Business Park, Linford Wood MK14 6EY T 01908-313755 E enquiries@ioic.org.uk W www.ioic.org.uk
Chief Executive, Steve Doswell

INSTITUTE OF MANAGEMENT SERVICES, Brooke House, 24 Dam Street, Lichfield WS13 6AA T 01543-266909 E admin@ims-stowe.fsnet.co.uk W www.ims-productivity.com
Chair, Andrew Muir

INSTITUTE OF QUARRYING, McPherson House, 8A Regan Way, Chetwynd Business Park, Chilwell, Nottingham NG9 6RZ T 0115-972 9995 E mail@quarrying.org W www.quarrying.org
Executive Director, Phil James

INSTITUTE OF THE MOTOR INDUSTRY, Fanshaws, Brickendon, Hertford SG13 8PQ T 01992-511521 E comms@theimi.org.uk W www.theimi.org.uk
Chief Executive, Steve Nash

INSTITUTION OF OCCUPATIONAL SAFETY AND HEALTH, The Grange, Highfield Drive, Wigston LE18 1NN T 0116-257 3100 E techinfo@iosh.co.uk W www.iosh.co.uk
Chief Executive, Jan Chmiel

IP FEDERATION, 5th Floor, 63–66 Hatton Garden, London EC1N 8LE T 020-7242 3923 E admin@ipfederation.com W www.ipfederation.com
President, Dr Bobby Mukherjee

MAGISTRATES' ASSOCIATION, 28 Fitzroy Square, London W1T 6DD T 020-7387 2353 E information@magistrates-association.org.uk W www.magistrates-association.org.uk
Chief Executive, Chris Brace

MANAGEMENT CONSULTANCIES ASSOCIATION, 60 Trafalgar Square, London WC2N 5DS T 020-7321 3990 E info@mca.org.uk W www.mca.org.uk
Chief Executive, Alan Leaman, OBE

MASTER LOCKSMITHS ASSOCIATION, 5D Great Central Way, Wood Halse, Daventry, Northants NN11 3PZ T 01327-262 255 E enquiries@locksmiths.co.uk W www.locksmiths.co.uk
Director of Business Development, Steffan George

NATIONAL ASSOCIATION OF BRITISH MARKET AUTHORITIES, The Guildhall, Oswestry, Shrops SY11 1PZ T 01691-680713 E nabma@nabma.com W www.nabma.com
Chief Executive, Graham Wilson, OBE

NATIONAL ASSOCIATION OF ESTATE AGENTS, Arbon House, 6 Tournament Court, Edgehill Drive, Warwick CV34 6LG T 0844-387 0555 E info@nfopp.co.uk W www.naea.co.uk
Managing Director, Mark Hayward

NATIONAL CATTLE ASSOCIATION (DAIRY), Brick House, Risbury, Leominster HR6 0NQ T 01568-760632 E timbrigstocke@hotmail.com
Executive Secretary, Tim Brigstocke, MBE

NATIONAL FARMERS' UNION (NFU), Agriculture House, Stoneleigh Park, Stoneleigh CV8 2TZ T 024-7685 8500 W www.nfuonline.com
Director General, Andy Robertson

NATIONAL FEDERATION OF RETAIL NEWSAGENTS, Yeoman House, Sekforde Street, London EC1R 0HF T 020-7253 4225 E service@nfrnonline.com W www.nfrnonline.com
President, Alan Smith

NATIONAL LANDLORDS ASSOCIATION, 22–26 Albert Embankment, London SE1 7TJ T 020-7840 8900 E info@landlords.org.uk W www.landlords.org.uk
Chief Executive, Richard Lambert

NATIONAL MARKET TRADERS FEDERATION, Hampton House, Hawshaw Lane, Hoyland, Barnsley S74 0HA T 01226-749021 E genoffice@nmtf.co.uk W www.nmtf.co.uk
Chief Executive, Joe Harrison

NATIONAL PHARMACY ASSOCIATION, 38–42 St Peter's Street, St Albans, Herts AL1 3NP T 01727-832161 E npa@npa.co.uk W www.npa.co.uk
Chief Executive, Mike Holden

NEWSPAPER SOCIETY, St Andrew's House, 18–20 St Andrew Street, London EC4A 3AY T 020-7632 7400 E ns@newspapersoc.org.uk W www.newspapersoc.org.uk
Director, David Newell

OIL AND GAS UK, 6th Floor East, Portland House, Bressenden Place, London SW1E 5BH T 020-7802 2400 E info@oilandgasuk.co.uk W www.oilandgasuk.co.uk
Chief Executive, Malcolm Webb

PROPERTY CARE ASSOCIATION, Lakeview Court, Ermine Business Park, Huntingdon PE29 6XR T 0844-375 4301 E pca@property-care.org W www.property-care.org
Chief Executive, Stephen Hodgson

PUBLISHERS ASSOCIATION, 29B Montague Street, London WC1B 5BW T 020-7691 9191 E mail@publishers.org.uk W www.publishers.org.uk
Chief Executive, Richard Mollet

RADIOCENTRE, 6th Floor, 55 New Oxford Street, London WC1A 1BS T 020-7010 0600 E info@radiocentre.org W www.radiocentre.org
Chief Executive, Andrew Harrison

ROAD HAULAGE ASSOCIATION LTD, Roadway House, Bretton PE3 8DD T 01733-261131 E southern-eastern@rha.uk.net W www.rha.uk.net
Chief Executive, Geoff Dunning

ROYAL ASSOCIATION OF BRITISH DAIRY FARMERS, Dairy House, Unit 31, Abbey Park, Stareton, Kenilworth CV8 2LY T 0845-458 2711 E office@rabdf.co.uk W www.rabdf.co.uk
Chief Executive, Nick Everington

ROYAL FACULTY OF PROCURATORS IN GLASGOW, 12 Nelson Mandela Place, Glasgow G2 1BT T 0141-332 3593 E library@rfpg.org W www.rfpg.org
Chief Executive, John McKenzie

SHELLFISH ASSOCIATION OF GREAT BRITAIN, Fishmongers' Hall, London Bridge, London EC4R 9EL T 020-7283 8305 W www.shellfish.org.uk
Director, David Jarrad

SOCIETY OF LOCAL AUTHORITY CHIEF EXECUTIVES AND SENIOR MANAGERS (SOLACE), Hope House, 45 Great Peter Street, London SW1P 3LT T 0845-652 4010 E hope.house@solace.org.uk W www.solace.org.uk
Society Directors, Graham McDonald, Debbie Wood

SOCIETY OF MOTOR MANUFACTURERS AND TRADERS LTD, 71 Great Peter Street, London SW1P 2BN T 020-7235 7000 W www.smmt.co.uk
Chief Executive (acting), Mike Baunton, CBE

TIMBER TRADE FEDERATION, The Building Centre, 26 Store Street, London WC1E 7BT T 020-3205 0067 E ttf@ttf.co.uk W www.ttf.co.uk
Chief Executive, John White

TRADING STANDARDS INSTITUTE, 1 Sylvan Court, Sylvan Way, Southfields Business Park, Basildon SS15 6TH T 0845-608 9400 E institute@tsi.org.uk W www.tradingstandards.gov.uk
Chief Executive, Leon Livermore

UK CHAMBER OF SHIPPING, 30 Park Street, London SE1 9EQ T 020-7417 2800 E query@ukchamberofshipping.com W www.ukchamberofshipping.com
Chief Executive, Angus Frew

UK FASHION AND TEXTILE ASSOCIATION, 3 Queen Square, London WC1N 3AR T 020-7843 9460 E info@ukft.org W www.ukft.org
Chief Executive, John Miln

UK LEATHER FEDERATION, Leather Trade House, Kings Park Road, Moulton Park, Northampton NN3 6JD T 01604-679955 E info@uklf.org W www.ukleather.org
Director, Dr Kerry Senior

UK PETROLEUM INDUSTRY ASSOCIATION LTD, Quality House, Quality Court, Chancery Lane, London WC2A 1HP T 020-7269 7600 E info@ukpia.com W www.ukpia.com
Director-General, Chris Hunt

ULSTER FARMERS' UNION, 475 Antrim Road, Belfast BT15 3DA T 028-9037 0222 E info@ufuhq.com W www.ufuni.org
Chief Executive, Clarke Black

WINE AND SPIRIT TRADE ASSOCIATION, International Wine and Spirit Centre, 39–45 Bermondsey Street, London SE1 3XF T 020-7089 3877 E info@wsta.co.uk W www.wsta.co.uk
Chief Executive, Miles Beale

CBI

Centre Point, 103 New Oxford Street, London WC1A 1DU T 020-7379 7400 W www.cbi.org.uk

The CBI was founded in 1965 and is an independent non-party political body financed by industry and commerce. It works with the UK government, international legislators and policymakers to help UK businesses compete effectively. It is the recognised spokesman for the business viewpoint and is consulted as such by the government.

The CBI speaks for some 240,000 businesses that together employ approximately one-third of the private sector workforce. Member companies, which decide all policy positions, include 80 of the FTSE 100 index, some 200,000 small- and medium-size firms, more than 20,000 manufacturers and over 150 sectoral associations.

The CBI board meets four times a year in London under the chairmanship of the president. It is assisted by 16 expert standing committees which advise on the main aspects of policy. There are 13 regional councils and offices, covering the administrative regions of England, Wales, Scotland and Northern Ireland. There are also offices in Beijing, Brussels, Delhi and Washington DC.

Director-General, John Cridland

WALES: 2 Caspian Point, Caspian Way, Cardiff Bay, Cardiff CF10 4DQ T 029-2097 7600
Regional Director, Emma Watkins

SCOTLAND: 16 Robertson Street, Glasgow G2 8DS T 0141-222 2184
Regional Director, Iain McMillan

NORTHERN IRELAND: 2nd Floor, Hamilton House, 3 Joy Street, Belfast BT2 8LE T 028-9010 1100
Regional Director, Nigel Smyth

TRADE UNIONS

A trade union is an organisation of workers formed (historically) for the purpose of collective bargaining over pay and working conditions. Today, trade unions may also provide legal and financial advice, sickness benefits and education facilities to their members. Legally any employee has the right to join a trade union, but not all employers recognise all or any trade unions. Conversely an employee also has the right not to join a trade union, in particular since the practice of a 'closed shop' system, where all employees have to join the employer's preferred union, is no longer permitted. Below is a list of key dates in the development of the British trade unionist movement.

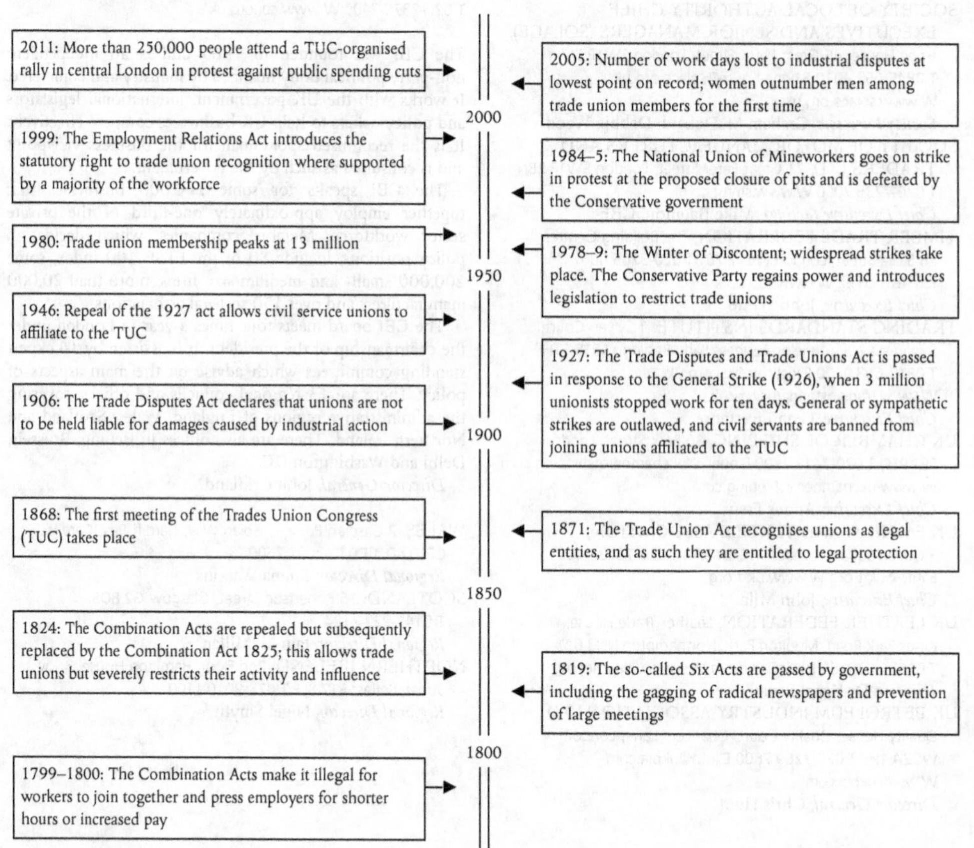

2011: More than 250,000 people attend a TUC-organised rally in central London in protest against public spending cuts
2005: Number of work days lost to industrial disputes at lowest point on record; women outnumber men among trade union members for the first time
2000
1999: The Employment Relations Act introduces the statutory right to trade union recognition where supported by a majority of the workforce
1984–5: The National Union of Mineworkers goes on strike in protest at the proposed closure of pits and is defeated by the Conservative government
1980: Trade union membership peaks at 13 million
1978–9: The Winter of Discontent; widespread strikes take place. The Conservative Party regains power and introduces legislation to restrict trade unions
1950
1946: Repeal of the 1927 act allows civil service unions to affiliate to the TUC
1927: The Trade Disputes and Trade Unions Act is passed in response to the General Strike (1926), when 3 million unionists stopped work for ten days. General or sympathetic strikes are outlawed, and civil servants are banned from joining unions affiliated to the TUC
1906: The Trade Disputes Act declares that unions are not to be held liable for damages caused by industrial action
1900
1868: The first meeting of the Trades Union Congress (TUC) takes place
1871: The Trade Union Act recognises unions as legal entities, and as such they are entitled to legal protection
1850
1824: The Combination Acts are repealed but subsequently replaced by the Combination Act 1825; this allows trade unions but severely restricts their activity and influence
1819: The so-called Six Acts are passed by government, including the gagging of radical newspapers and prevention of large meetings
1800
1799–1800: The Combination Acts make it illegal for workers to join together and press employers for shorter hours or increased pay

THE CENTRAL ARBITRATION COMMITTEE

22nd Floor, Euston Tower, 286 Euston Road, London NW1 3JJ
T 020-7904 2300 E enquiries@cac.gov.uk W www.cac.gov.uk

The Central Arbitration Committee's main role is concerned with requests for trade union recognition and de-recognition under the statutory procedures of Schedule A1 of the Employment Rights Act 1999. It also determines disclosure of information complaints under the Trade Union and Labour Relations (Consolidation) Act 1992, considers applications and complaints under the Information and Consultation Regulations 2004, and performs a similar role in relation to European works councils, companies, cooperative societies and cross-border mergers. It also provides voluntary arbitration in industrial disputes.

Chair, Sir Michael Burton
Chief Executive, Simon Gouldstone

TRADES UNION CONGRESS (TUC)

Congress House, 23–28 Great Russell Street, London WC1B 3LS
T 020-7636 4030
E info@tuc.org.uk W www.tuc.org.uk

The Trades Union Congress (TUC), founded in 1868, is an independent association of trade unions. The TUC promotes the rights and welfare of those in work and helps the unemployed. It helps its member unions promote membership in new areas and industries, and campaigns for rights at work for all employees, including part-time and temporary workers, whether union members or not. TUC representatives sit on many public bodies at national and international level such as government, political parties, employers and the European Union.

The governing body of the TUC is the annual congress. Between congresses, business is conducted by a general council, which meets five times a year, and an executive committee, which meets monthly. The full-time staff is headed by the general secretary who is elected by congress and is a permanent member of the general council.

There are 58 affiliated unions, with a total membership of around 6.4 million.

President (2012–13), Lesley Mercer
General Secretary, Frances O'Grady

SCOTTISH TRADES UNION CONGRESS (STUC)

333 Woodlands Road, Glasgow G3 6NG **T** 0141-337 8100
E info@stuc.org.uk **W** www.stuc.org.uk

The congress was formed in 1897 and acts as a national centre for the trade union movement in Scotland. The STUC promotes the rights to welfare of those in work and helps the unemployed. It helps its member unions to promote membership in new areas and industries, and campaigns for rights at work for all employees, including part-time and temporary workers, whether union members or not. It also makes representations to government and employers. In April 2012 it consisted of 37 affiliated unions, with a membership of more than 630,000, and 24 trades union councils.

The annual congress in April elects a 36-member general council on the basis of six sections.

President, Harry Frew
General Secretary, Grahame Smith

WALES TUC

1 Cathedral Road, Cardiff CF11 9SD **T** 029-2034 7010
E wtuc@tuc.org.uk
W www.tuc.org.uk/tuc/regions_info_wales.cfm

The Wales TUC was established in 1974 to ensure that the role of the TUC was effectively undertaken in Wales. Its structure reflects the four economic regions of Wales and matches the regional committee areas of the National Assembly of Wales. The regional committees oversee the implementation of Wales TUC policy and campaigns in the relevant regions, and liaise with local government, training organisations and regional economic development bodies. The Wales TUC seeks to reduce unemployment, increase the levels of skill and pay, and eliminate discrimination.

The governing body of Wales TUC is the conference, which meets annually in May and elects a general council (usually of around 50 people) that oversees the work of the TUC throughout the year.

There are over 50 affiliated unions, with a total membership of over 400,000.

President, David Evans
General Secretary, Martin Mansfield

TUC-AFFILIATED UNIONS

As at April 2013

ACCORD, Simmons House, 46 Old Bath Road, Charvil RG10 9QR **T** 0118-934 1808 **E** info@accordhq.org **W** www.accord-myunion.org
General Secretary, Ged Nichols *Membership:* 26,000

ADVANCE, 2nd Floor, 16–17 High Street, Tring HP23 5AH **T** 01442-891122 **E** info@advance-union.org **W** www.advance-union.org
General Secretary, Linda Rolph *Membership:* 8,250

AEGIS THE UNION, AEGON UK plc, Lochside Crescent, Edinburgh Park, Edinburgh EH12 9SE **T** 0131-549 5474 **E** members@aegistheunion.co.uk **W** www.aegistheunion.co.uk
General Secretary, Brian Linn *Membership:* 1,665

AEP (ASSOCIATION OF EDUCATIONAL PSYCHOLOGISTS), Unit 4, The Riverside Centre, Frankland Lane, Durham DH1 5TA **T** 0191-384 9512 **E** enquiries@aep.org.uk **W** www.aep.org.uk
General Secretary, Kate Fallon *Membership:* 3,263

ASLEF (ASSOCIATED SOCIETY OF LOCOMOTIVE ENGINEERS AND FIREMEN), 75–77 St John Street, Clerkenwell, London EC1M 4NN **T** 020-7324 2400 **E** info@aslef.org.uk **W** www.aslef.org.uk
General Secretary, Mick Whelan *Membership:* 18,000

ATL (ASSOCIATION OF TEACHERS AND LECTURERS), 7 Northumberland Street, London WC2N 5RD **T** 020-7930 6441 **E** info@atl.org.uk **W** www.atl.org.uk
General Secretary, Mary Bousted *Membership:* 170,000

BACM-TEAM (BRITISH ASSOCIATION OF COLLIERY MANAGEMENT – TECHNICAL, ENERGY AND ADMINISTRATIVE MANAGEMENT), Danum House, 6A South Parade, Doncaster DN1 2DY **T** 01302-815551 **E** enquiries@bacmteam.org.uk **W** www.bacmteam.org.uk
General Secretary, Patrick Carragher *Membership:* 2,218

BALPA (BRITISH AIRLINE PILOTS ASSOCIATION), BALPA House, 5 Heathrow Boulevard, 278 Bath Road, West Drayton UB7 0DQ **T** 020-8476 4000 **E** balpa@balpa.org **W** www.balpa.org
General Secretary, Jim McAuslan *Membership:* 10,000

BDA (BRITISH DIETETIC ASSOCIATION), 5th Floor, Charles House, 148–149 Great Charles Street, Birmingham B3 3HT **T** 0121-200 8080 **E** info@bda.uk.com **W** www.bda.uk.com
Chief Executive, Andy Burman *Membership:* 7,180

BECTU (BROADCASTING, ENTERTAINMENT, CINEMATOGRAPH AND THEATRE UNION), 373–377 Clapham Road, London SW9 9BT **T** 020-7346 0900 **E** info@bectu.org.uk **W** www.bectu.org.uk
General Secretary, Gerry Morrissey *Membership:* 23,779

BFAWU (BAKERS, FOOD AND ALLIED WORKERS' UNION), Stanborough House, Great North Road, Stanborough, Welwyn Garden City AL8 7TA **T** 01707-260150 **E** info@bfawu.org **W** www.bfawu.org
General Secretary, Ronnie Draper *Membership:* 20,816

BIOS (BRITISH AND IRISH ORTHOPTIC SOCIETY), 62 Wilson Street, London EC2A 2BU **T** 01353-665541 **E** bios@orthoptics.org.uk **W** www.orthoptics.org.uk
Employment Relations Officer, Lesley-Anne Baxter *Membership:* 1,500

BSU (BRITANNIA STAFF UNION), Court Lodge, Leonard Street, Leek ST13 5JP **T** 01538-399627 **E** staff.union@britannia.co.uk **W** www.britanniasu.org.uk
General Secretary, John Stoddard *Membership:* 2,802

COMMUNITY, 67–68 Long Acre, London WC2E 9FA **T** 020-7420 4000 **E** info@community-tu.org **W** www.community-tu.org
General Secretary, Michael J. Leahy, OBE *Membership:* 50,012

CSP (CHARTERED SOCIETY OF PHYSIOTHERAPY), 14 Bedford Row, London WC1R 4ED **T** 020-7306 6666 **E** enquiries@csp.org.uk **W** www.csp.org.uk
Chief Executive, Phil Gray *Membership:* 37,601

CWU (COMMUNICATION WORKERS UNION), 150 The Broadway, Wimbledon, London SW19 1RX **T** 020-8971 7200 **E** info@cwu.org **W** www.cwu.org
General Secretary, W. Hayes *Membership:* 203,651

EIS (EDUCATIONAL INSTITUTE OF SCOTLAND), 46 Moray Place, Edinburgh EH3 6BH **T** 0131-225 6244 **E** enquiries@eis.org.uk **W** www.eis.org.uk
General Secretary, Larry Flanagan *Membership:* 56,293

EQUITY, Guild House, Upper St Martin's Lane, London WC2H 9EG **T** 020-7379 6000 **E** info@equity.org.uk **W** www.equity.org.uk
General Secretary, Christine Payne *Membership:* 37,429

FBU (FIRE BRIGADES UNION), Bradley House, 68 Coombe Road, Kingston upon Thames KT2 7AE **T** 020-8541 1765 **E** office@fbu.org.uk **W** www.fbu.org.uk
General Secretary, Matt Wrack *Membership:* 47,148

FDA, 8 Leake Street, London SE1 7NN T 020-7401 5555 E info@fda.org.uk W www.fda.org.uk
General Secretary, Dave Penman *Membership:* 18,269

GMB, 22 Stephenson Way, London NW1 2HD T 020-7391 6700 E info@gmb.org.uk W www.gmb.org.uk
General Secretary, Paul Kenny *Membership:* 622,000

HCSA (HOSPITAL CONSULTANTS' AND SPECIALISTS' ASSOCIATION), 1 Kingsclere Road, Overton, Basingstoke RG25 3JA T 01256-771777 E conspec@hcsa.com W www.hcsa.com
Chief Executive, Eddie Saville *Membership:* 3,405

MU (MUSICIANS' UNION), 60–62 Clapham Road, London SW9 0JJ T 020-7582 5566 E info@theMU.org W www.theMU.org
General Secretary, John F. Smith *Membership:* 30,000

NACO (NATIONAL ASSOCIATION OF COOPERATIVE OFFICIALS), 6A Clarendon Place, Hyde SK14 2QZ T 0161-351 7900 E info@naco.coop W www.naco.coop
President, Mark Alexander *Membership:* 1,866

NACODS (NATIONAL ASSOCIATION OF COLLIERY OVERMEN, DEPUTIES AND SHOTFIRERS), Wadsworth House, 130–132 Doncaster Road, Barnsley S70 1TP T 01226-203743 E natnacods@googlemail.com W www.nacods.org.uk
General Secretary, Rowland Soar *Membership:* 323

NAPO (TRADE UNION AND PROFESSIONAL ASSOCIATION FOR FAMILY COURT AND PROBATION STAFF), 4 Chivalry Road, London SW11 1HT T 020-7223 4887 E info@napo.org.uk W www.napo.org.uk
General Secretary, Ian Lawrence *Membership:* 8,360

NASUWT (NATIONAL ASSOCIATION OF SCHOOLMASTERS/UNION OF WOMEN TEACHERS), Hillscourt Education Centre, Rose Hill, Rednal, Birmingham B45 8RS T 0121-453 6150 E nasuwt@mail.nasuwt.org.uk W www.nasuwt.org.uk
General Secretary, Ms Chris Keates
Membership: 294,172

NAUTILUS INTERNATIONAL, 1–2 The Shrubberies, George Lane, South Woodford, London E18 1BD T 020-8989 6677 E enquiries@nautilusint.org W www.nautilusint.org
General Secretary, Mark Dickinson *Membership:* 16,119

NGSU (NATIONWIDE GROUP STAFF UNION), Middleton Farmhouse, 37 Main Road, Middleton Cheney OX17 2QT T 01295-710767 E ngsu@ngsu.org.uk W www.ngsu.org.uk
General Secretary, Tim Poil *Membership:* 12,000

NUJ (NATIONAL UNION OF JOURNALISTS), Headland House, 308–312 Gray's Inn Road, London WC1X 8DP T 020-7843 3700 E info@nuj.org.uk W www.nuj.org.uk
General Secretary, Michelle Stanistreet *Membership:* 34,000

NUM (NATIONAL UNION OF MINEWORKERS), Miners' Offices, 2 Huddersfield Road, Barnsley S70 2LS T 01226-215555 E chris.kitchen@num.org.uk W www.num.org.uk
Secretary, C. Kitchen *Membership:* 1,855

NUT (NATIONAL UNION OF TEACHERS), Hamilton House, Mabledon Place, London WC1H 9BD T 020-7388 6191 E enquiries@nut.org.uk W www.teachers.org.uk
General Secretary, Christine Blower *Membership:* 326,930

PCS (PUBLIC AND COMMERCIAL SERVICES UNION), 160 Falcon Road, London SW11 2LN T 020-7924 2727 E editor@pcs.org.uk W www.pcs.org.uk
General Secretary, Mark Serwotka *Membership:* 270,000

PFA (PROFESSIONAL FOOTBALLERS' ASSOCIATION), 20 Oxford Court, Bishopsgate, Manchester M2 3WQ T 0161-236 0575 E info@thepfa.co.uk W www.thepfa.com
Chief Executive, Gordon Taylor, OBE
Membership: 4,300

POA (PROFESSIONAL TRADE UNION FOR PRISON, CORRECTIONAL AND SECURE PSYCHIATRIC WORKERS), Cronin House, 245 Church Street, London N9 9HW T 020-8803 0255 E general@poauk.org.uk W www.poauk.org.uk
General Secretary, Steve Gillan *Membership:* 33,079

PROSPECT, New Prospect House, 8 Leake Street, London SE1 7NN T 020-7902 6600 E enquiries@prospect.org.uk W www.prospect.org.uk
President, Alan Grey *Membership:* 118,048

RMT (NATIONAL UNION OF RAIL, MARITIME AND TRANSPORT WORKERS), Unity House, 39 Chalton Street, London NW1 1JD T 020-7387 4771 E info@rmt.org.uk W www.rmt.org.uk
General Secretary, Bob Crow *Membership:* 76,093

SCP (SOCIETY OF CHIROPODISTS AND PODIATRISTS), 1 Fellmonger's Path, Tower Bridge Road, London SE1 3LY T 0845-450 3720 E enq@scpod.org W www.feetforlife.org
General Secretary, Joanna Brown *Membership:* 9,101

SOR (SOCIETY OF RADIOGRAPHERS), 207 Providence Square, Mill Street, London SE1 2EW T 020-7740 7200 E info@sor.org W www.sor.org
Chief Executive, Richard Evans *Membership:* 21,958

TSSA (TRANSPORT SALARIED STAFFS' ASSOCIATION), Walkden House, 10 Melton Street, London NW1 2EJ T 020-7387 2101 E enquiries@tssa.org.uk W www.tssa.org.uk
General Secretary, Manuel Cortes *Membership:* 24,662

UCAC (UNDEB CENEDLAETHOL ATHRAWON CYMRU) (NATIONAL UNION OF THE TEACHERS OF WALES), Prif Swyddfa UCAC, Ffordd Penglais, Aberystwyth SY23 2EU T 01970-639950 E ucac@athrawon.com W www.athrawon.com
General Secretary, Elaine Edwards
Membership: 4,578

UCATT (UNION OF CONSTRUCTION, ALLIED TRADES AND TECHNICIANS), UCATT House, 177 Abbeville Road, London SW4 9RL T 020-7622 2442 E info@ucatt.org.uk W www.ucatt.org.uk
General Secretary, Steve Murphy
Membership: 83,760

UCU (UNIVERSITY AND COLLEGE UNION), Carlow Street, London NW1 7LH T 020-7756 2500 E hq@ucu.org.uk W www.ucu.org.uk
General Secretary, Sally Hunt *Membership:* 116,000

UNISON, 130 Euston Road, London NW1 2AY T 0845-355 0845 W www.unison.org.uk
General Secretary, Dave Prentis *Membership:* 1,300,000

UNITE, 128 Theobald's Road, London WC1X 8TN T 020-7611 2500 W www.unitetheunion.org
General Secretary, Len McCluskey
Membership: 1,407,399

UNITY, Hillcrest House, Garth Street, Hanley, Stoke-on-Trent ST1 2AB T 01782-272755 E harryhockaday@unitytheunion.org.uk W www.unitytheunion.org.uk
General Secretary, Harry Hockaday
Membership: 4,200

URTU (UNITED ROAD TRANSPORT UNION), Almond House, Oak Green, Stanley Green Business Park, Cheadle Hulme SK8 6QL T 0800-526639 E info@urtu.com W www.urtu.com
General Secretary, Robert Monks *Membership:* 14,000

USDAW (UNION OF SHOP, DISTRIBUTIVE AND ALLIED WORKERS), 188 Wilmslow Road, Manchester M14 6LJ T 0161-224 2804 E enquiries@usdaw.org.uk W www.usdaw.org.uk
General Secretary, John Hannett *Membership:* 427,236

WRITERS' GUILD OF GREAT BRITAIN (WGGB), 40 Rosebery Avenue, London EC1R 4RX T 020-7833 0777 E admin@writersguild.org.uk W www.writersguild.org.uk
General Secretary, Bernie Corbett *Membership:* 1,913

YORKSHIRE INDEPENDENT STAFF ASSOCIATION (YISA), c/o Yorkshire Building Society, Yorkshire House, Yorkshire Drive, Rooley Lane, Bradford BD5 8LJ T 01274-472629 E ahgrota@ybs.co.uk
General Secretary, Ania Grota *Membership:* 1,365

NON-AFFILIATED UNIONS

As at April 2013

ASCL (ASSOCIATION OF SCHOOL AND COLLEGE LEADERS), 130 Regent Road, Leicester LE1 7PG T 0116-299 1122 E info@ascl.org.uk W www.ascl.org.uk
General Secretary, Brian Lightman *Membership:* 17,229

BDA (BRITISH DENTAL ASSOCIATION), 64 Wimpole Street, London W1G 8YS T 020-7935 0875 E enquiries@bda.org W www.bda.org
Chief Executive, Peter Ward *Membership:* 22,433

CIOJ (CHARTERED INSTITUTE OF JOURNALISTS), 2 Dock Offices, Surrey Quays Road, London SE16 2XU T 020-7252 1187 E memberservices@cioj.co.uk W www.cioj.co.uk
General Secretary, Dominic Cooper *Membership:* 2,000

NAHT (NATIONAL ASSOCIATION OF HEAD TEACHERS), 1 Heath Square, Boltro Road, Haywards Heath RH16 1BL T 01444-472472 E info@naht.org.uk W www.naht.org.uk
General Secretary, Russell Hobby *Membership:* 39,622

NSEAD (NATIONAL SOCIETY FOR EDUCATION IN ART AND DESIGN), 3 Mason's Wharf, Potley Lane, Corsham SN13 9FY T 01225-810134 E info@nsead.org W www.nsead.org
General Secretary, Mrs Lesley Butterworth
Membership: 2,000

RCM (ROYAL COLLEGE OF MIDWIVES), 15 Mansfield Street, London W1G 9NH T 020-7312 3535 E info@rcm.org.uk W www.rcm.org.uk
General Secretary, Prof. Cathy Warwick, CBE
Membership: 41,653

SOCIETY OF AUTHORS, 84 Drayton Gardens, London SW10 9SB T 020-7373 6642 E info@societyofauthors.org W www.societyofauthors.org
Chief Executive, Nicola Solomon
Membership: 9,000

SSTA (SCOTTISH SECONDARY TEACHERS' ASSOCIATION), West End House, 14 West End Place, Edinburgh EH11 2ED T 0131-313 7300 E info@ssta.org.uk W www.ssta.org.uk
General Secretary (acting), Alan McKenzie
Membership: 8,500

CLUBS

Originally called gentlemen's clubs, these organisations are permanent institutions with a fixed clubhouse, which usually includes restaurants, bars, a library and overnight accommodation. Members are fee-paying and typically vetted for their suitability.

Gentlemen's clubs were created for males of the English upper class and grew out of the 17th-century fashion for coffee houses which enjoyed enormous popularity, despite opposition from Charles II, who believed they encouraged the spreading of royal disaffection. The first of the London clubs – White's – was founded in 1693 by Francesco Bianco in St James's Street, in the area that quickly became known as 'clubland'. Membership to the first of the clubs was a matter of hereditary privilege or special favour, a deliberately exclusionary measure which prompted an enormous growth in the number of clubs throughout the 19th century, fed by a burgeoning and aspirational middle class.

At the turn of the 20th century, there were more than 200 gentlemen's clubs in London alone, half of which had been founded since 1870. Inevitably, this level of competition could not be sustained, particularly given the number of men killed in two world wars. Financial restrictions necessitated greater provision for women and the relaxation of the social qualifications needed for membership. Nevertheless, waiting lists still exist for the leading clubs and a recommendation from at least one current member is almost always required to join.

ARMY AND NAVY CLUB (1837), 36 Pall Mall, London SW1Y 5JN T 020-7930 9721 E secretary@therag.co.uk W www.armynavyclub.co.uk
Chief Executive and Secretary, Cdr. R. W. W. Craig, RN
Former members: The Duke of Wellington

ARTS CLUB (1863), 40 Dover Street, London W1S 4NP T 020-7499 8581 E reservations@theartsclub.co.uk W www.theartsclub.co.uk
Secretary, Rémy Lysé
Former members: Charles Dickens, Algernon Charles Swinburne, Ivan Turgenev

ATHENAEUM (1824), 107 Pall Mall, London SW1Y 5ER T 020-7930 4843 E library@hellenist.org.uk W www.athenaeumclub.co.uk
Secretary, J. H. Ford
Former members: Matthew Arnold, Michael Faraday, Anthony Trollope

ATHENAEUM (1797), Church Alley, Liverpool L1 3DD T 0151-709 7770 E reception@theathenaeum.org.uk W www.theathenaeum.org.uk
Honorary Secretary, Anthony N. Richards, MBE
Former members: William H. Duncan, William Roscoe

AUTHORS' CLUB (1891), c/o Black's, 67 Dean Street, London W1D 4QH T 020-7287 3381 E mbarnard@authorsclub.co.uk W www.authorsclub.co.uk
Honorary Secretary, Margaret Barnard
Former members: Arthur Conan Doyle, Graham Greene, Thomas Hardy, HG Wells, Oscar Wilde

BATH & COUNTY CLUB (1858), Queen's Parade, Bath BA1 2NJ T 01225-423732 E secretary@bathandcountyclub.com W www.bathandcountyclub.com
Secretary, Jessica Bowen

*BEEFSTEAK CLUB (1876), 9 Irving Street, London WC2H 7AH T 020-7930 5722 E office@thebeefsteakclub.co.uk
Secretary, Maria Hibbert
Former members: John Betjeman, Rudyard Kipling, Harold Macmillan

*BOODLE'S (1762), 28 St James's Street, London SW1A 1HJ T 020-7930 7166 E secretary@boodles.org
Secretary, Andrew Phillips
Former members: Winston Churchill, Ian Fleming

*BROOKS'S (1764), St James's Street, London SW1A 1LN T 020-7493 4411 E secretary@brooksclub.org
Secretary, Graham Snell
Former members: Edward Gibbon, Roy Jenkins, William Pitt

*BUCK'S CLUB (1919), 18 Clifford Street, London W1S 3RF T 020-7734 2337 E secretary@bucksclub.co.uk
Secretary, Maj. Rupert Lendrum

CALEDONIAN CLUB (1891), 9 Halkin Street, London SW1X 7DR T 020-7235 5162 E admin@caledonianclub.com W www.caledonianclub.com
Secretary, Ian Campbell

CANNING CLUB (1910), 4 St James's Square, London SW1Y 4JU T 020-7827 5730 E canningclub@navalandmilitaryclub.co.uk
Secretary, Sarah Sinclair

CARLTON CLUB (1832), 69 St James's Street, London SW1A 1PJ T 020-7493 1164 E info@carltonclub.co.uk W www.carltonclub.co.uk
Secretary, Jonathan Orr Ewing
Former members: Stanley Baldwin, Benjamin Disraeli, Harold Macmillan, John Major, Margaret Thatcher

CAVALRY AND GUARDS CLUB (1890), 127 Piccadilly, London W1J 7PX T 020-7499 1261 E secretary@cavgds.co.uk W www.cavgds.co.uk
Secretary, David J Cowdery
Former members: Lawrence Oates

CHELSEA ARTS CLUB (1891), 143 Old Church Street, London SW3 6EB T 020-7376 3311 E secretary@chelseaartsclub.com W www.chelseaartsclub.com
Secretary, Geoffrey Matthews

CITY LIVERY CLUB (1914), Bell Wharf Lane, Upper Thames Street, London EC4R 3TB T 020-7248 0620 E clerk@cityliveryclub.com W www.cityliveryclub.com
Hon. Secretary, Dr Trevor Brignall

CITY OF LONDON CLUB (1832), 19 Old Broad Street, London EC2N 1DS T 020-7588 7991 E secretary@cityoflondonclub.com W www.cityoflondonclub.com
Secretary, Ian Faul
Former members: Robert Peel, Duke of Wellington

CITY UNIVERSITY CLUB (1895), 50 Cornhill, London EC3V 3PD T 020-7626 8571 E secretary@cityuniversityclub.co.uk W www.cityuniversityclub.co.uk
Secretary, Mrs MaryAnne Salisbury

*DISTRICT AND UNION CLUB (1849), Northwood, 1 West Park Road, Blackburn BB2 6DE T 01254-51474
Secretary, John Dean

*EAST INDIA CLUB (1849), 16 St James's Square, London SW1Y 4LH T 020-7930 1000 E secretary@eastindiaclub.co.uk W www.eastindiaclub.co.uk
Secretary, A. Bray

FARMERS CLUB (1842), 3 Whitehall Court, London SW1A 2EL T 020-7930 3557 E reception@thefarmersclub.com W www.thefarmersclub.com
Secretary, Air Cdre Stephen Skinner

FOX CLUB (2003), 46 Clarges Street, London W1J 7ER
T 020-7495 3656 E essi@foxclublondon.com
W www.foxclublondon.com
General Manager, Bethan Seaton

*GARRICK CLUB (1831), 15 Garrick Street, London WC2E 9AY T 020-7379 6478 E office@garrickclub.co.uk
W www.garrickclub.co.uk
Secretary, Olaf Born
Former members: Charles Dickens, Henry Irving, William Thackeray

GROUCHO CLUB (1985), 45 Dean Street, London W1D 4QB
T 020-7439 4685 E reception@thegrouchoclub.com
W www.thegrouchoclub.com
Manager, Bernie Katz

HURLINGHAM CLUB (1869), Ranelagh Gardens, London SW6 3PR T 020-7610 7400
E membership@hurlinghamclub.org.uk
W www.hurlinghamclub.org.uk
Chief Executive, Rear-Adm. Niall Kilgour, CB
Former members: King Edward VII

IN & OUT (NAVAL AND MILITARY CLUB) (1862), 4 St James's Square, London SW1Y 4JU T 020-7827 5757
E club@theinandout.co.uk W www.theinandout.co.uk
Secretary, Lt. Col. Christopher Hogan
Former members: Robert Falcon Scott

LANSDOWNE CLUB (1935), 9 Fitzmaurice Place, London W1J 5JD T 020-7629 7200
E secretary@LansdowneClub.com
W www.lansdowneclub.com
General Manager, Chris Pickup

LONDON PRESS CLUB (1882), 7–10 Adam Street, The Strand, London WC2N 6AA T 020-7520 9082
E info@londonpressclub.co.uk W www.londonpressclub.co.uk
Secretary, Peter Durrant
Former members: Lord Astor, Lord Rothermere, Edgar Wallace

NATIONAL CLUB (1845), c/o The Carlton Club, 69 St James's Street, London SW1A 1PJ T 01225-480606
E secretary@thenationalclub.org.uk
W www.thenationalclub.org.uk
Hon. Secretary, Revd R. J. R. Paice
Former members: Lord Coggan

NATIONAL LIBERAL CLUB (1882), Whitehall Place, London SW1A 2HE T 020-7930 9871 E secretary@nlc.org.uk
W www.nlc.org.uk
Secretary, S. J. Roberts
Former members: Winston Churchill, William Gladstone, Ramsay MacDonald, George Bernard Shaw, H. G. Wells

NEW CAVENDISH CLUB (1920), 44 Great Cumberland Place, London W1H 7BS T 020-7723 0391
E info@newcavendishclub.co.uk
W www.newcavendishclub.co.uk
Chair, Sue Ann Dowle
Former members: Lady Bonham-Carter

NEW CLUB (1874), 2 Montpellier Parade, Cheltenham GL50 1UD T 01242-541121 E secretary@thenewclub.co.uk
W www.thenewclub.co.uk
Hon. Secretary, Peter Walsh

NEW CLUB (1787), 86 Princes Street, Edinburgh EH2 2BB
T 0131-226 4881 E info@newclub.co.uk
W www.newclub.co.uk
Secretary, Col. A. P. W. Campbell
Former members: Alec Douglas-Home, Walter Scott

NORFOLK CLUB (1770), 17 Upper King Street, Norwich NR3 1RB T 01603-626767
E generalmanager@thenorfolkclub.co.uk
W www.thenorfolkclub.co.uk
General Manager, George A. Wortley

NORTHERN COUNTIES CLUB (1829), 11 Hood Street, Newcastle upon Tyne NE1 6LH T 0191-232 2744
E secretary@northerncountiesclub.co.uk
W www.northerncountiesclub.co.uk
General Manager, D. J. Devennie

ORIENTAL CLUB (1824), Stratford House, Stratford Place, London W1C 1ES T 020-7629 5126 E sec@orientalclub.org.uk
W www.orientalclub.org.uk
Secretary, M. Rivett
Former members: The Duke of Wellington (only president of the club)

OXFORD AND CAMBRIDGE CLUB (1830), 71 Pall Mall, London SW1Y 5HD T 020-7930 5151 E club@oandc.uk.com
W www.oxfordandcambridgeclub.co.uk
Secretary, Alistair E. Telfer
Former members: Clement Attlee, William Gladstone, Duke of Wellington

PORTLAND CLUB (1816), 69 Brook Street, London W1Y 4ER
T 020-7499 1523
Secretary, J. Burns, CBE

*PRATT'S CLUB (1841), 14 Park Place, London SW1A 1LP
T 020-7493 0397 E secretary@prattsclub.org
Secretary, Lt. Col. O. R. Breakwell
Former members: Winston Churchill

REFORM CLUB (1836), 104–105 Pall Mall, London SW1Y 5EW T 020-7930 9374 E generaloffice@reformclub.com
W www.reformclub.com
Secretary (acting), Ian Kenworthy
Former members: Isambard Kingdom Brunel, Guy Burgess, Arthur Conan Doyle, Henry James, David Lloyd George

ROYAL AIR FORCE CLUB (1918), 128 Piccadilly, London W1J 7PY T 020-7399 1000 E admin@rafclub.org.uk
W www.rafclub.org.uk
Secretary, P. N. Owen

ROYAL AUTOMOBILE CLUB (1897), 89 Pall Mall, London SW1Y 5HS T 020-7930 2345
E members@royalautomobileclub.co.uk
W www.royalautomobileclub.co.uk
Secretary, David Wilkinson
Former members: Winston Churchill, Rudyard Kipling, Charles Rolls

*ROYAL NORTHERN & UNIVERSITY CLUB (1854), 9 Albyn Place, Aberdeen AB10 1YE T 01224-583292
E secretary@rnuc.org.uk W www.rnuc.org.uk
Secretary, Sharon Findlater

ROYAL OVER-SEAS LEAGUE (1910), Over-Seas House, Park Place, St James's Street, London SW1A 1LR
T 020-7408 0214 E info@rosl.org.uk W www.rosl.org.uk
Director-General, Maj.-Gen. Roddy Porter, MBE

ST STEPHEN'S CLUB (1870), 34 Queen Anne's Gate, London SW1H 9AB T 020-7222 1382
E info@ststephensclub.co.uk W www.ststephensclub.co.uk
General Manager, Bernard Moray
Former members: Benjamin Disraeli

*SAVILE CLUB (1868), 69 Brook Street, London W1K 4ER
T 020-7629 5462 W www.savileclub.co.uk
Secretary, Julian Malone-Lee
Former members: Max Beerbohm, Thomas Hardy, Robert Louis Stevenson

SCOTTISH ARTS CLUB (1872), 24 Rutland Square, Edinburgh EH1 2BW T 0131-229 8157
E manager@scottishartsclub.co.uk
W www.scottishartsclub.co.uk
Secretary, Mhairi Kerr

SLOANE CLUB (1976), Lower Sloane Street, London SW1W 8BS T 020-7730 9131 E reservations@sloaneclub.co.uk
W www.sloaneclub.co.uk
Membership Secretary, Fran Bremner

*TRAVELLERS CLUB (1819), 106 Pall Mall, London SW1Y 5EP
T 020-7930 8688 E secretary@thetravellersclub.org.uk
W www.thetravellersclub.org.uk
Secretary, David Broadhead
Former members: Arthur Balfour, Alec Douglas-Home, Anthony Powell

TURF CLUB (1868), 5 Carlton House Terrace, London SW1Y 5AQ T 020-7930 8555 E mail@turfclub.co.uk
Secretary, Col. A. J. E. Malcolm, OBE

ULSTER REFORM CLUB (1885), 4 Royal Avenue, Belfast BT1 1DA T 028-9032 3411 E info@ulsterreformclub.com
W www.ulsterreformclub.com
Chief Executive, A. W. Graham

†UNIVERSITY WOMEN'S CLUB (1883), 2 Audley Square, London W1K 1DB T 020-7499 2268 E uwc@uwc-london.com
W www.universitywomensclub.com
Hon. Sec., Monica Sasso

*VINCENT'S (1863), 1A King Edward Street, Oxford OX1 4HS T 01865-722984 E bursar@vincents.org
W www.vincents.org
Bursar, Stephen Eeley
Former members: Roger Bannister, King Edward VIII

WESTERN CLUB (1825), 32 Royal Exchange Square, Glasgow G1 3AB T 0141-221 2016
E secretary@westernclub.co.uk W www.westernclub.co.uk
Secretary, Douglas H. Gifford

*WHITE'S (1693), 37–38 St James's Street, London SW1A 1JG
T 020-7493 6671
Secretary, D. A. Anderson
Former members: Beau Brummel, Evelyn Waugh

* Men only † Women only

TIME AND SPACE

ASTRONOMY

TIME MEASUREMENT AND CALENDARS

TIDES AND TIDAL PREDICTIONS

ASTRONOMY

The following pages give astronomical data for each month of the year 2014. There are four pages of data for each month. All data are given for 0h Greenwich Mean Time (GMT), ie at the midnight at the beginning of the day named. This applies also to data for the months when British Summer Time is in operation (for dates, *see* below).

The astronomical data are given in a form suitable for observation with the naked eye or with a small telescope. These data do not attempt to replace the *Astronomical Almanac* for professional astronomers.

A fuller explanation of how to use the astronomical data is given on pages 628–630.

CALENDAR FOR EACH MONTH

The calendar for each month comprises dates of general interest plus the dates of birth or death of well-known people. For key religious, civil and legal dates *see* page 7. For details of flag-flying days *see* page 19. For royal birthdays *see* pages 19 and 20–1. Public holidays are given in italics. *See* also pages 8 and 9.

Fuller explanations of the various calendars can be found under Time Measurement and Calendars.

The zodiacal signs through which the Sun is passing during each month are illustrated. The date of transition from one sign to the next, to the nearest hour, is given under Astronomical Phenomena.

JULIAN DATE

The Julian date on 2014 January 0.0 is 2456657.5. To find the Julian date for any other date in 2014 (at 0h GMT), add the day-of-the-year number on the extreme right of the calendar for each month to the Julian date for January 0.0.

BRITISH SUMMER TIME

British Summer Time is the legal time for general purposes during the period in which it is in operation (*see also* page 633). During this period, clocks are kept one hour ahead of Greenwich Mean Time. The hour of changeover is 01h Greenwich Mean Time. The duration of Summer Time in 2014 is from March 30 01h GMT to October 26 01h GMT.

SEASONS

The seasons are defined astronomically as follows:

Spring from the vernal equinox to the summer solstice
Summer from the summer solstice to the autumnal equinox
Autumn from the autumnal equinox to the winter solstice
Winter from the winter solstice to the vernal equinox

The time when seasons start in 2014 (to the nearest hour) are:

Northern Hemisphere

Vernal equinox	March 20d 17h GMT
Summer solstice	June 21d 11h GMT
Autumnal equinox	September 23d 02h GMT
Winter solstice	December 21d 23h GMT

Southern Hemisphere

Autumnal equinox	March 20d 17h GMT
Winter solstice	June 21d 11h GMT
Vernal equinox	September 23d 02h GMT
Summer solstice	December 21d 23h GMT

The longest day of the year, measured from sunrise to sunset, is at the summer solstice. The longest day in the UK will fall on 21 June in 2014.

The shortest day of the year is at the winter solstice. The shortest day in the UK will fall on 21 December in 2014.

The equinox is the point at which day and night are of equal length all over the world.

In popular parlance, the seasons in the northern hemisphere comprise the following months:

Spring	March, April, May
Summer	June, July, August
Autumn	September, October, November
Winter	December, January, February

JANUARY 2014

FIRST MONTH, 31 DAYS. *Janus*, god of the portal, facing two ways, past and future

1	*Wednesday*	The Act of Union legislative agreement forms the United Kingdom of Great Britain and Ireland 1801	day 1
2	*Thursday*	William Smyth, bishop given the deanery of Wimborne after the accession of King Henry VII *d.* 1514	2
3	*Friday*	Catherine of Valois, Queen Consort of England from 1420–1422 *d.* 1437	3
4	*Saturday*	The Rump Parliament votes to establish a High Court of Justice to try King Charles I for treason 1649	4
5	*Sunday*	King Edward the Confessor dies, shortly after naming Harold Godwinson as his successor 1066	5
6	*Monday*	King Richard II, who reigned from 1377–1399, House of Plantagenet *b.* 1367	week 1 day 6
7	*Tuesday*	Catherine of Aragon, first wife of King Henry VIII, divorced in 1533 *d.* 1536	7
8	*Wednesday*	Queen Elizabeth II christens the RMS *Queen Mary 2*, the largest ocean liner ever built 2004	8
9	*Thursday*	Peter Cook, British actor and comedian who played King Richard III in *Blackadder d.* 1995	9
10	*Friday*	William Laud, Archbishop of Canterbury and advisor to King Charles I, is beheaded for treason 1645	10
11	*Saturday*	Robert Devereux, Chief Commander of the Roundheads in the Civil War against King Charles I *b.* 1591	11
12	*Sunday*	The RMS *Queen Mary 2* sets sail on her maiden voyage from Southampton to Florida 2004	12
13	*Monday*	Henry Howard, Earl of Surrey and poet, is sentenced to death by King Henry VIII 1547	week 2 day 13
14	*Tuesday*	Prince Albert Victor, son of King Edward VII, whose younger brother became King George V *d.* 1892	14
15	*Wednesday*	Coronation of Queen Elizabeth I at Westminster Abbey 1559	15
16	*Thursday*	Philip II, married to Queen Mary I of England, becomes King of Spain 1556	16
17	*Friday*	The Long Parliament passes 'Vote of No Addresses' thus ending negotiations with King Charles I 1648	17
18	*Saturday*	King Henry VII marries Elizabeth of York at Westminster Abbey 1486	18
19	*Sunday*	The city of Rouen surrenders to King Henry V who annexes Normandy as part of England 1419	19
20	*Monday*	King George V, House of Windsor *d.* 1936	week 3 day 20
21	*Tuesday*	Anthony Ashley Cooper, 1st Earl of Shaftesbury, member of King Charles II's cabinet council *d.* 1683	21
22	*Wednesday*	Queen Victoria, who reigned from 1837–1901, House of Hanover *d.* 1901	22
23	*Thursday*	A disguised King Henry VIII jousts in Richmond and is applauded before revealing his identity 1510	23
24	*Friday*	King Edward III marries Philippa of Hainault at Yorkminster, aged 15 and 12 respectively 1328	24
25	*Saturday*	King Henry VIII marries Anne Boleyn with whom he has a daughter, Elizabeth 1533	25
26	*Sunday*	India becomes a republic, with the first president replacing King George VI as head of state 1950	26
27	*Monday*	The trial of Guy Fawkes and his conspirators begins after the attempt to kill King James I 1606	week 4 day 27
28	*Tuesday*	King Henry VII, who reigned from 1485–1509, House of Tudor *b.* 1457	28
29	*Wednesday*	King George III, House of Hanover *d.* 1820	29
30	*Thursday*	King Charles I is executed for treason outside the Banqueting House, Whitehall, London 1649	30
31	*Friday*	Conspirator Guy Fawkes jumps from the gallows, breaking his neck before his intended execution 1606	31

ASTRONOMICAL PHENOMENA

d	*h*	
1	15	Mercury in conjunction with Moon. Mercury 7°S.
1	19	Pluto in conjunction
2	11	Venus in conjunction with Moon. Venus 2°S.
4	11	Earth at perihelion (147 million km.)
5	21	Jupiter at opposition
7	22	Venus in conjunction with Mercury. Venus 6°N.
11	12	Venus in inferior conjunction
15	05	Jupiter in conjunction with Moon. Jupiter 5°N.
20	04	Sun's longitude 300° ♒
23	04	Mars in conjunction with Moon. Mars 4°N.
25	14	Saturn in conjunction with Moon. Saturn 0°.6 N.
29	03	Venus in conjunction with Moon. Venus 2°N.
30	00	Mercury at greatest elongation E. 18°
31	21	Venus at stationary point

MINIMA OF ALGOL

d	*h*	*d*	*h*	*d*	*h*
3	04.5	14	15.8	26	03.1
6	01.3	17	12.6	28	23.9
8	22.1	20	09.4	31	20.7
11	19.0	23	06.3		

CONSTELLATIONS

The following constellations are near the meridian at

	d	*h*		*d*	*h*
December	1	24	January	16	21
December	16	23	February	1	20
January	1	22	February	15	19

Draco (below the Pole), Ursa Minor (below the Pole), Camelopardalis, Perseus, Auriga, Taurus, Orion, Eridanus and Lepus

THE MOON

Phases, Apsides and Node	*d*	*h*	*m*
● New Moon	1	11	14
☽ First Quarter	8	03	39
○ Full Moon	16	04	52
☾ Last Quarter	24	05	19
● New Moon	30	21	38
Perigee (356,926km)	1	20	53
Apogee (406,533km)	16	01	35
Perigee (357,076km)	30	09	52

Mean longitude of ascending node on January 1, 214°

THE SUN

s.d. 16′.3

Day	Right Ascension			Dec. –		Equation of time		Rise 52°		Rise 56°		Transit		Set 52°		Set 56°		Sidereal time			Transit of first point of Aries		
	h	*m*	*s*	°	′	*m*	*s*	*h*	*m*	*h*	*m*	*h*	*m*	*h*	*m*	*h*	*m*	*h*	*m*	*s*	*h*	*m*	*s*
1	18	45	36	23	01	–3	18	8	08	8	31	12	04	15	59	15	36	6	42	17	17	14	53
2	18	50	00	22	56	–3	47	8	08	8	31	12	04	16	00	15	37	6	46	14	17	10	57
3	18	54	25	22	51	–4	15	8	08	8	31	12	04	16	01	15	39	6	50	10	17	07	01
4	18	58	49	22	45	–4	42	8	08	8	30	12	05	16	03	15	40	6	54	07	17	03	05
5	19	03	13	22	38	–5	10	8	07	8	30	12	05	16	04	15	41	6	58	03	16	59	09
6	19	07	36	22	32	–5	36	8	07	8	29	12	06	16	05	15	43	7	02	00	16	55	13
7	19	11	59	22	24	–6	03	8	06	8	28	12	06	16	06	15	44	7	05	56	16	51	17
8	19	16	21	22	17	–6	29	8	06	8	28	12	07	16	08	15	46	7	09	53	16	47	22
9	19	20	43	22	08	–6	54	8	05	8	27	12	07	16	09	15	48	7	13	49	16	43	26
10	19	25	05	22	00	–7	19	8	05	8	26	12	08	16	10	15	49	7	17	46	16	39	30
11	19	29	25	21	51	–7	43	8	04	8	25	12	08	16	12	15	51	7	21	43	16	35	34
12	19	33	45	21	41	–8	06	8	04	8	24	12	08	16	13	15	53	7	25	39	16	31	38
13	19	38	05	21	31	–8	29	8	03	8	23	12	09	16	15	15	54	7	29	36	16	27	42
14	19	42	24	21	21	–8	51	8	02	8	22	12	09	16	16	15	56	7	33	32	16	23	46
15	19	46	42	21	10	–9	13	8	01	8	21	12	09	16	18	15	58	7	37	29	16	19	50
16	19	50	59	20	59	–9	34	8	00	8	20	12	10	16	20	16	00	7	41	25	16	15	54
17	19	55	16	20	48	–9	54	7	59	8	19	12	10	16	21	16	02	7	45	22	16	11	58
18	19	59	32	20	36	–10	14	7	58	8	18	12	10	16	23	16	04	7	49	18	16	08	02
19	20	03	48	20	24	–10	33	7	57	8	16	12	11	16	25	16	06	7	53	15	16	04	07
20	20	08	02	20	11	–10	51	7	56	8	15	12	11	16	26	16	08	7	57	12	16	00	11
21	20	12	16	19	58	–11	08	7	55	8	14	12	11	16	28	16	10	8	01	08	15	56	15
22	20	16	30	19	44	–11	25	7	54	8	12	12	12	16	30	16	12	8	05	05	15	52	19
23	20	20	42	19	31	–11	41	7	53	8	11	12	12	16	31	16	14	8	09	01	15	48	23
24	20	24	54	19	16	–11	56	7	51	8	09	12	12	16	33	16	16	8	12	58	15	44	27
25	20	29	05	19	02	–12	10	7	50	8	07	12	12	16	35	16	18	8	16	54	15	40	31
26	20	33	15	18	47	–12	24	7	49	8	06	12	13	16	37	16	20	8	20	51	15	36	35
27	20	37	24	18	32	–12	37	7	48	8	04	12	13	16	39	16	22	8	24	48	15	32	39
28	20	41	33	18	16	–12	49	7	46	8	02	12	13	16	40	16	24	8	28	44	15	28	43
29	20	45	41	18	00	–13	00	7	45	8	01	12	13	16	42	16	26	8	32	41	15	24	47
30	20	49	48	17	44	–13	11	7	43	7	59	12	13	16	44	16	28	8	36	37	15	20	52
31	20	53	54	17	28	–13	20	7	42	7	57	12	13	16	46	16	31	8	40	34	15	16	56

DURATION OF TWILIGHT (in minutes)

Latitude	52°	56°	52°	56°	52°	56°	52°	56°
	1 January		*11 January*		*21 January*		*31 January*	
Civil	41	47	40	45	38	43	37	41
Nautical	84	96	82	93	80	90	78	87
Astronomical	125	141	123	138	120	134	117	130

THE NIGHT SKY

Mercury is not visible at first but as it reaches its greatest eastern elongation of 18 degrees on the 30th it becomes visible during the last 10 days of the month. It may be detected as an evening object for the last week of January, very low above the west-south-western horizon around the time of end of evening civil twilight, magnitude about –0.7.

Venus, is visible as a brilliant evening object very low in the south-western sky for the first week of the month, shortly after sunset, its magnitude fading slightly from –4.3 to –4.1. However, the planet passes through inferior conjunction on the 11th, when it is almost 6 degrees north of the ecliptic, and only 7 days after the Earth is at perihelion. Given exceptionally good conditions a few days later it might be detected very low in the south-eastern sky shortly before sunrise, until the end of the month. Its magnitude brightens from –4.1 to –4.5 during this period. The Moon, only one day old, will be only about one degree above Venus on the 2nd but is very unlikely to be detected with the naked eye.

Mars, magnitude +0.6, is a morning object, and by the end of the month should be visible low above the east-south-eastern horizon shortly after midnight. Mars is moving steadily retrograde in the constellation of Virgo, passing 5 degrees north of Spica on the 28th. The waning gibbous Moon passes about 5 degrees south of Mars on the night of the 22nd–23rd.

Jupiter, magnitude –2.7, reaches opposition on the 5th and is therefore visible throughout the hours of darkness. Jupiter is retrograding slowly in the constellation of Gemini. The gibbous Moon, almost Full, passes south of the planet on the evening of the 15th.

Saturn, magnitude +0.6, is visible low in the south-eastern sky in the early mornings before twilight inhibits observation. By the end of the month it may be seen shortly after 03h. Saturn remains in the constellation of Libra throughout the year. The waning crescent Moon passes south of Saturn on the 25th.

THE MOON

Day	R.A.		Dec.	Hor. Par.	Semi-diam.	Sun's Co-Long.	PA of Br. Limb	Ph.	Age	Rise				Transit		Set			
										52°		56°				52°		56°	
	h	m	°	′	′	°	°	%	d	h	m	h	m	h	m	h	m	h	m
1	18	16	−19.1	61.3	16.7	265	121	0	29.0	7	37	7	55	12	04	16	36	16	18
2	19	20	−17.3	61.4	16.7	278	230	1	0.6	8	24	8	39	13	06	17	55	17	41
3	20	22	−14.3	61.2	16.7	290	244	4	1.6	9	02	9	14	14	05	19	17	19	07
4	21	22	−10.3	60.7	16.5	302	245	10	2.6	9	34	9	42	15	01	20	38	20	33
5	22	18	−5.8	60.0	16.3	314	245	18	3.6	10	02	10	06	15	54	21	57	21	56
6	23	12	−1.2	59.1	16.1	326	245	27	4.6	10	28	10	27	16	44	23	13	23	16
7	0	05	+3.4	58.1	15.8	338	246	38	5.6	10	53	10	48	17	33	—		—	
8	0	56	+7.7	57.3	15.6	351	247	49	6.6	11	19	11	10	18	21	0	26	0	33
9	1	46	+11.5	56.4	15.4	3	249	59	7.6	11	46	11	35	19	09	1	36	1	47
10	2	36	+14.7	55.7	15.2	15	252	69	8.6	12	17	12	02	19	57	2	43	2	57
11	3	27	+17.1	55.2	15.0	27	255	77	9.6	12	52	12	35	20	46	3	46	4	03
12	4	18	+18.7	54.7	14.9	39	258	85	10.6	13	33	13	14	21	34	4	45	5	03
13	5	09	+19.4	54.4	14.8	51	260	91	11.6	14	20	14	01	22	22	5	37	5	56
14	5	59	+19.3	54.1	14.7	63	261	96	12.6	15	12	14	54	23	10	6	23	6	41
15	6	49	+18.3	54.0	14.7	76	256	99	13.6	16	09	15	53	23	57	7	02	7	19
16	7	38	+16.5	53.9	14.7	88	214	100	14.6	17	10	16	56	—		7	35	7	50
17	8	26	+14.1	54.0	14.7	100	133	99	15.6	18	12	18	02	0	42	8	04	8	16
18	9	13	+11.0	54.1	14.7	112	121	97	16.6	19	16	19	09	1	26	8	29	8	38
19	9	59	+7.5	54.3	14.8	124	118	93	17.6	20	20	20	17	2	10	8	53	8	58
20	10	45	+3.7	54.6	14.9	136	117	87	18.6	21	26	21	26	2	53	9	14	9	16
21	11	31	−0.3	55.1	15.0	148	116	80	19.6	22	32	22	36	3	36	9	36	9	34
22	12	18	−4.4	55.6	15.1	161	115	72	20.6	23	40	23	47	4	21	9	59	9	54
23	13	06	−8.4	56.3	15.3	173	113	63	21.6	—		—		5	07	10	24	10	15
24	13	56	−12.0	57.0	15.5	185	110	52	22.6	0	50	1	01	5	55	10	52	10	40
25	14	49	−15.2	57.9	15.8	197	107	42	23.6	2	00	2	15	6	47	11	27	11	11
26	15	46	−17.6	58.8	16.0	209	104	31	24.6	3	11	3	28	7	42	12	10	11	52
27	16	45	−19.1	59.7	16.3	221	100	21	25.6	4	18	4	37	8	41	13	03	12	44
28	17	47	−19.3	60.5	16.5	234	96	12	26.6	5	18	5	38	9	42	14	08	13	49
29	18	50	−18.2	61.1	16.6	246	94	6	27.6	6	10	6	28	10	44	15	22	15	06
30	19	53	−15.8	61.4	16.7	258	100	1	28.6	6	54	7	08	11	44	16	43	16	31
31	20	54	−12.3	61.3	16.7	270	180	0	0.1	7	30	7	40	12	43	18	06	17	58

MERCURY

Day	R.A.		Dec.	Diam.	Phase	Transit		5° high			
								52°		56°	
	h	m	°	″	%	h	m	h	m	h	m
1	18	53	−24.7	5	100	12	13	15	01	14	19
3	19	07	−24.5	5	100	12	19	15	10	14	29
5	19	22	−24.2	5	99	12	25	15	20	14	40
7	19	36	−23.7	5	99	12	32	15	30	14	53
9	19	50	−23.2	5	98	12	38	15	42	15	07
11	20	04	−22.5	5	97	12	44	15	54	15	21
13	20	18	−21.8	5	96	12	50	16	07	15	36
15	20	32	−20.9	5	94	12	56	16	20	15	51
17	20	46	−20.0	5	92	13	02	16	33	16	07
19	20	59	−18.9	5	90	13	08	16	47	16	22
21	21	12	−17.8	6	87	13	13	17	00	16	37
23	21	25	−16.6	6	82	13	17	17	13	16	52
25	21	37	−15.3	6	77	13	21	17	25	17	06
27	21	48	−14.1	6	71	13	24	17	36	17	19
29	21	57	−12.8	7	64	13	25	17	45	17	30
31	22	06	−11.5	7	56	13	25	17	52	17	38

VENUS

Day	R.A.		Dec.	Diam.	Phase	Transit		5° high			
								52°		56°	
	h	m	°	″	%	h	m	h	m	h	m
1	19	54	−18.2	60	4	13	08	9	28	9	51
6	19	43	−17.4	62	1	12	37	8	51	9	13
11	19	30	−16.7	63	0	12	05	8	14	8	35
16	19	17	−16.2	62	1	11	32	7	38	7	58
21	19	06	−15.9	59	4	11	02	7	06	7	26
26	18	59	−15.8	56	8	10	36	6	39	6	59
31	18	56	−15.8	52	12	10	14	6	17	6	37

MARS

Day	R.A.		Dec.	Diam.	Phase	Transit		5° high			
								52°		56°	
	h	m	°	″	%	h	m	h	m	h	m
1	12	46	−2.6	7	90	6	03	0	50	0	56
6	12	54	−3.4	7	90	5	52	0	43	0	49
11	13	02	−4.1	7	90	5	40	0	35	0	41
16	13	09	−4.8	8	91	5	27	0	26	0	33
21	13	16	−5.5	8	91	5	15	0	16	0	25
26	13	23	−6.0	8	91	5	01	0	06	0	15
31	13	28	−6.5	9	91	4	47	23	53	0	04

SUNRISE AND SUNSET

	London		*Bristol*		*Birmingham*		*Manchester*		*Newcastle*		*Glasgow*		*Belfast*	
	0° 05′	*51° 30′*	*2° 35′*	*51° 28′*	*1° 55′*	*52° 28′*	*2° 15′*	*53° 28′*	*1° 37′*	*54° 59′*	*4° 14′*	*55° 52′*	*5° 56′*	*54° 35′*
d	*h m*	*h m*	*h m*	*h m*	*h m*	*h m*	*h m*	*h m*	*h m*	*h m*	*h m*	*h m*	*h m*	*h m*
1	8 06	16 02	8 16	16 12	8 18	16 04	8 25	16 00	8 31	15 49	8 47	15 54	8 46	16 09
2	8 06	16 03	8 16	16 13	8 18	16 06	8 25	16 02	8 31	15 50	8 47	15 55	8 46	16 10
3	8 06	16 04	8 15	16 14	8 18	16 07	8 24	16 03	8 31	15 51	8 47	15 56	8 46	16 11
4	8 05	16 05	8 15	16 16	8 18	16 08	8 24	16 04	8 30	15 53	8 46	15 58	8 45	16 12
5	8 05	16 07	8 15	16 17	8 17	16 09	8 24	16 05	8 30	15 54	8 46	15 59	8 45	16 14
6	8 05	16 08	8 15	16 18	8 17	16 10	8 23	16 07	8 29	15 56	8 45	16 01	8 44	16 15
7	8 04	16 09	8 14	16 19	8 16	16 12	8 23	16 08	8 29	15 57	8 45	16 02	8 44	16 17
8	8 04	16 10	8 14	16 21	8 16	16 13	8 22	16 09	8 28	15 58	8 44	16 04	8 43	16 18
9	8 03	16 12	8 13	16 22	8 15	16 15	8 22	16 11	8 27	16 00	8 43	16 05	8 42	16 20
10	8 03	16 13	8 13	16 23	8 15	16 16	8 21	16 12	8 27	16 02	8 42	16 07	8 42	16 21
11	8 02	16 15	8 12	16 25	8 14	16 17	8 20	16 14	8 26	16 03	8 41	16 09	8 41	16 23
12	8 02	16 16	8 11	16 26	8 13	16 19	8 20	16 15	8 25	16 05	8 41	16 10	8 40	16 24
13	8 01	16 18	8 11	16 28	8 13	16 20	8 19	16 17	8 24	16 07	8 40	16 12	8 39	16 26
14	8 00	16 19	8 10	16 29	8 12	16 22	8 18	16 19	8 23	16 08	8 39	16 14	8 38	16 28
15	7 59	16 21	8 09	16 31	8 11	16 24	8 17	16 20	8 22	16 10	8 37	16 16	8 37	16 29
16	7 58	16 22	8 08	16 32	8 10	16 25	8 16	16 22	8 21	16 12	8 36	16 18	8 36	16 31
17	7 58	16 24	8 07	16 34	8 09	16 27	8 15	16 24	8 20	16 14	8 35	16 19	8 35	16 33
18	7 57	16 25	8 06	16 35	8 08	16 29	8 14	16 25	8 19	16 15	8 34	16 21	8 34	16 35
19	7 56	16 27	8 05	16 37	8 07	16 30	8 13	16 27	8 18	16 17	8 33	16 23	8 33	16 37
20	7 55	16 29	8 04	16 39	8 06	16 32	8 12	16 29	8 16	16 19	8 31	16 25	8 32	16 38
21	7 53	16 30	8 03	16 40	8 05	16 34	8 10	16 31	8 15	16 21	8 30	16 27	8 30	16 40
22	7 52	16 32	8 02	16 42	8 04	16 35	8 09	16 33	8 14	16 23	8 28	16 29	8 29	16 42
23	7 51	16 34	8 01	16 44	8 02	16 37	8 08	16 34	8 12	16 25	8 27	16 31	8 27	16 44
24	7 50	16 35	8 00	16 46	8 01	16 39	8 06	16 36	8 11	16 27	8 25	16 33	8 26	16 46
25	7 49	16 37	7 59	16 47	8 00	16 41	8 05	16 38	8 09	16 29	8 24	16 35	8 25	16 48
26	7 47	16 39	7 57	16 49	7 58	16 43	8 04	16 40	8 08	16 31	8 22	16 38	8 23	16 50
27	7 46	16 41	7 56	16 51	7 57	16 44	8 02	16 42	8 06	16 33	8 20	16 40	8 21	16 52
28	7 45	16 42	7 55	16 53	7 55	16 46	8 01	16 44	8 04	16 35	8 19	16 42	8 20	16 54
29	7 43	16 44	7 53	16 54	7 54	16 48	7 59	16 46	8 03	16 37	8 17	16 44	8 18	16 56
30	7 42	16 46	7 52	16 56	7 52	16 50	7 57	16 48	8 01	16 39	8 15	16 46	8 17	16 58
31	7 40	16 48	7 50	16 58	7 51	16 52	7 56	16 50	7 59	16 41	8 13	16 48	8 15	17 00

JUPITER

Day	*R.A.*		*Dec.*		*Transit*		*5° high*			
							52°		*56°*	
	h	*m*	°	′	*h*	*m*	*h*	*m*	*h*	*m*
1	7	10.0	+22	35	0	28	7	55	8	13
11	7	04.2	+22	46	23	38	7	11	7	29
21	6	58.6	+22	55	22	53	6	28	6	45
31	6	53.7	+23	03	22	09	5	44	6	02

Diameters – equatorial 47″ polar 44″

SATURN

Day	*R.A.*		*Dec.*		*Transit*		*5° high*			
							52°		*56°*	
	h	*m*	°	′	*h*	*m*	*h*	*m*	*h*	*m*
1	15	14.1	−15	44	8	31	4	33	4	53
11	15	17.5	−15	56	7	55	3	59	4	19
21	15	20.5	−16	06	7	18	3	23	3	43
31	15	22.8	−16	13	6	41	2	47	3	07

Diameters – equatorial 16″ polar 15″
Rings – major axis 37″ minor axis 14″

URANUS

Day	*R.A.*		*Dec.*		*Transit*		*10° high*			
							52°		*56°*	
	h	*m*	°	′	*h*	*m*	*h*	*m*	*h*	*m*
1	0	33.0	+2	49	17	48	22	56	22	52
11	0	33.6	+2	53	17	09	22	18	22	14
21	0	34.5	+2	59	16	31	21	40	21	36
31	0	35.6	+3	07	15	53	21	03	20	59

Diameter 4″

NEPTUNE

Day	*R.A.*		*Dec.*		*Transit*		*10° high*			
							52°		*56°*	
	h	*m*	°	′	*h*	*m*	*h*	*m*	*h*	*m*
1	22	21.6	−10	57	15	37	19	27	19	08
11	22	22.7	−10	51	14	59	18	49	18	31
21	22	23.9	−10	44	14	20	18	12	17	53
31	22	25.2	−10	36	13	42	17	35	17	16

Diameter 2″

FEBRUARY 2014

SECOND MONTH, 28 or 29 DAYS. *Februa*, Roman festival of Purification

1	*Saturday*	Coronation of King Edward III at Westminster Abbey 1327	day 32
2	*Sunday*	Coronation of King Charles I at Westminster Abbey 1626; Funeral of Queen Victoria 1901	33
3	*Monday*	Sweyn Forkbeard, first Danish King of England, who ruled briefly beginning in 1013 *d.* 1014	week 5 day 34
4	*Tuesday*	Experts confirm that a skeleton found beneath a Leicester car park is that of King Richard III 2013	35
5	*Wednesday*	George, Prince of Wales, begins a nine-year tenure as Prince Regent 1811	36
6	*Thursday*	Queen Anne, who reigned from 1702–1714, House of Stuart *b.* 1665; King George VI *d.* 1952	37
7	*Friday*	Edward of Caernarfon (King Edward II) becomes the first prince to use the title Prince of Wales 1301	38
8	*Saturday*	Mary, Queen of Scots, is executed after being implicated in a plot to kill Queen Elizabeth I 1587	39
9	*Sunday*	John Hooper, Bishop of Gloucester, is burned at the stake during the Marian persecutions 1555	40
10	*Monday*	Wedding of Queen Victoria and Prince Albert at St James's Palace 1840	week 6 day 41
11	*Tuesday*	King Henry VIII is recognised for the first time as supreme head of the Church of England 1531	42
12	*Wednesday*	Lady Jane Grey, nominal Queen of England for nine days, is beheaded for high treason 1554	43
13	*Thursday*	Catherine Howard, fifth wife of King Henry VIII, is executed at the Tower of London for adultery 1542	44
14	*Friday*	King Richard II dies after abdicating in favour of Henry of Bolingbroke (King Henry IV) 1400	45
15	*Saturday*	Funeral of King George VI at St George's Chapel, Windsor Castle 1952	46
16	*Sunday*	Funeral of King George III at St George's Chapel, Windsor Castle 1820	47
17	*Monday*	Denzil Holles, Parliamentarian who escaped arrest in 1642 as an opponent of King Charles I *b.* 1680	week 7 day 48
18	*Tuesday*	Queen Mary I, who reigned from 1553–1558, House of Tudor *b.* 1516	49
19	*Wednesday*	Derek Jarman, director of cult film *Jubilee* in which Queen Elizabeth I travels in time *d.* 1994	50
20	*Thursday*	Coronation of King Edward VI at Westminster Abbey 1547	51
21	*Friday*	King James I of Scotland is murdered at Friars Preachers Monastery in Perth 1437	52
22	*Saturday*	Henry, Duke of Cornwall, son of King Henry VIII and Catherine of Aragon, dies aged 52 days 1511	53
23	*Sunday*	Henry Grey, 1st Duke of Suffolk, father of Lady Jane Grey is beheaded for high treason 1554	54
24	*Monday*	Prince Adolphus Frederick, 1st Duke of Cambridge and 7th son of King George III *d.* 1774	week 8 day 55
25	*Tuesday*	Coronation of King Edward II at Westminster Abbey 1308	56
26	*Wednesday*	Margaret of England, daughter of King Henry III, who became Queen Consort of Scots in 1251 *d.* 1275	57
27	*Thursday*	John Evelyn, diarist who was commissioned to write by his companion King Charles II *d.* 1706	58
28	*Friday*	Henry, the Young King, who ruled England with his father King Henry II from 1170 to his death *b.* 1155	59

ASTRONOMICAL PHENOMENA

d	*h*	
1	05	Mercury in conjunction with Moon. Mercury 4°S.
6	22	Mercury at stationary point
11	05	Jupiter in conjunction with Moon. Jupiter 5°N.
15	05	Venus at greatest brilliancy
15	20	Mercury in inferior conjunction
18	18	Sun's longitude 330° ♓
19	22	Mars in conjunction with Moon. Mars 3°N.
21	22	Saturn in conjunction with Moon. Saturn 0°.3 N.
23	18	Neptune in conjunction
26	05	Venus in conjunction with Moon. Venus 0°.3 S.
27	20	Mercury in conjunction with Moon. Mercury 3°S.
28	14	Mercury at stationary point

MINIMA OF ALGOL

d	*h*	*d*	*h*	*d*	*h*
3	17.6	15	04.8	26	16.1
6	14.4	18	01.7		
9	11.2	20	22.5		
12	08.0	23	19.3		

CONSTELLATIONS

The following constellations are near the meridian at

	d	*h*		*d*	*h*
January	1	24	February	15	21
January	16	23	March	1	20
February	1	22	March	16	19

Draco (below the Pole), Camelopardalis, Auriga, Taurus, Gemini, Orion, Canis Minor, Monoceros, Lepus, Canis Major and Puppis

THE MOON

Phases, Apsides and Node	*d*	*h*	*m*
☽ First Quarter	6	19	22
○ Full Moon	14	23	53
☾ Last Quarter	22	17	15
Apogee (406,252km)	12	04	58
Perigee (360,428km)	27	19	44

Mean longitude of ascending node on February 1, 213°

THE SUN

s.d. 16′.2

Day	Right Ascension			Dec. –		Equation of time		Rise 52°		Rise 56°		Transit		Set 52°		Set 56°		Sidereal time			Transit of first point of Aries		
	h	m	s	°	′	m	s	h	m	h	m	h	m	h	m	h	m	h	m	s	h	m	s
1	20	58	00	17	11	−13	29	7	40	7	55	12	14	16	48	16	33	8	44	30	15	13	00
2	21	02	04	16	54	−13	37	7	39	7	53	12	14	16	50	16	35	8	48	27	15	09	04
3	21	06	08	16	36	−13	45	7	37	7	51	12	14	16	51	16	37	8	52	23	15	05	08
4	21	10	11	16	19	−13	51	7	35	7	49	12	14	16	53	16	39	8	56	20	15	01	12
5	21	14	13	16	01	−13	56	7	34	7	47	12	14	16	55	16	42	9	00	16	14	57	16
6	21	18	14	15	42	−14	01	7	32	7	45	12	14	16	57	16	44	9	04	13	14	53	20
7	21	22	15	15	24	−14	05	7	30	7	43	12	14	16	59	16	46	9	08	10	14	49	24
8	21	26	14	15	05	−14	08	7	28	7	41	12	14	17	01	16	48	9	12	06	14	45	28
9	21	30	13	14	46	−14	10	7	27	7	39	12	14	17	03	16	50	9	16	03	14	41	32
10	21	34	11	14	27	−14	12	7	25	7	37	12	14	17	04	16	53	9	19	59	14	37	37
11	21	38	08	14	07	−14	13	7	23	7	35	12	14	17	06	16	55	9	23	56	14	33	41
12	21	42	05	13	47	−14	12	7	21	7	32	12	14	17	08	16	57	9	27	52	14	29	45
13	21	46	00	13	27	−14	12	7	19	7	30	12	14	17	10	16	59	9	31	49	14	25	49
14	21	49	55	13	07	−14	10	7	17	7	28	12	14	17	12	17	01	9	35	45	14	21	53
15	21	53	50	12	47	−14	08	7	15	7	26	12	14	17	14	17	04	9	39	42	14	17	57
16	21	57	43	12	26	−14	04	7	13	7	23	12	14	17	16	17	06	9	43	39	14	14	01
17	22	01	36	12	05	−14	01	7	11	7	21	12	14	17	17	17	08	9	47	35	14	10	05
18	22	05	28	11	44	−13	56	7	09	7	19	12	14	17	19	17	10	9	51	32	14	06	09
19	22	09	19	11	23	−13	51	7	07	7	16	12	14	17	21	17	12	9	55	28	14	02	13
20	22	13	10	11	01	−13	45	7	05	7	14	12	14	17	23	17	14	9	59	25	13	58	17
21	22	17	00	10	40	−13	39	7	03	7	11	12	14	17	25	17	17	10	03	21	13	54	22
22	22	20	49	10	18	−13	31	7	01	7	09	12	13	17	27	17	19	10	07	18	13	50	26
23	22	24	38	9	56	−13	24	6	59	7	07	12	13	17	29	17	21	10	11	14	13	46	30
24	22	28	26	9	34	−13	15	6	57	7	04	12	13	17	30	17	23	10	15	11	13	42	34
25	22	32	14	9	12	−13	06	6	55	7	02	12	13	17	32	17	25	10	19	08	13	38	38
26	22	36	01	8	50	−12	57	6	53	6	59	12	13	17	34	17	27	10	23	04	13	34	42
27	22	39	48	8	27	−12	47	6	50	6	57	12	13	17	36	17	30	10	27	01	13	30	46
28	22	43	34	8	05	−12	36	6	48	6	54	12	13	17	38	17	32	10	30	57	13	26	50

DURATION OF TWILIGHT (in minutes)

Latitude	*52°*	*56°*	*52°*	*56°*	*52°*	*56°*	*52°*	*56°*
	1 February		*11 February*		*21 February*		*31 February*	
Civil	37	41	35	39	34	38	34	37
Nautical	77	86	75	83	74	81	73	80
Astronomical	117	130	114	126	113	124	112	124

THE NIGHT SKY

Mercury is visible as an evening object during the first week of the month, when it may be detected low above the west-south-western horizon around the time of end of evening civil twilight. Its magnitude fading noticeably from −0.4 to +1.4.

Venus, magnitude −4.6, reaches its greatest brilliancy on the 15th, low above the south-eastern horizon before sunrise, slowly rising earlier each day until by the end of the month it should be visible nearly two hours before sunrise. On the morning of the 26th the old crescent may be seen passing just north of the planet.

Mars continues to be visible low in the south-eastern sky before midnight, magnitude 0.0.

Jupiter, magnitude −2.5, is a conspicuous evening object in the southern skies. It is almost stationary below the twins, Castor and Pollux, in the western part of Gemini.

Saturn, magnitude +0.5, continues to be visible as a morning object in the south-eastern sky.

Zodiacal Light. The evening cone may be observed stretching up from the western horizon, along the ecliptic, after the end of twilight, from the 16th onwards. This faint phenomenon is only visible under good conditions and in the absence of both moonlight and artificial lighting.

THE MOON

Day	R.A.		Dec.	Hor. par.	Semi-diam.	Sun's Co-Long.	PA of Br. Limb	Ph.	Age	Rise 52°		Rise 56°		Transit		Set 52°		Set 56°	
	h	m	°	′	′	°	°	%	d	h	m	h	m	h	m	h	m	h	m
1	21	53	−8.0	61.0	16.6	282	234	2	1.1	8	01	8	07	13	39	19	29	19	25
2	22	50	−3.3	60.3	16.4	294	241	7	2.1	8	29	8	30	14	33	20	49	20	50
3	23	45	+1.5	59.5	16.2	307	244	14	3.1	8	55	8	53	15	24	22	06	22	11
4	0	38	+6.0	58.5	15.9	319	246	22	4.1	9	22	9	15	16	15	23	20	23	29
5	1	30	+10.1	57.5	15.7	331	248	32	5.1	9	50	9	40	17	04	—		—	
6	2	22	+13.6	56.6	15.4	343	251	42	6.1	10	20	10	07	17	53	0	30	0	43
7	3	13	+16.3	55.8	15.2	355	255	52	7.1	10	54	10	38	18	42	1	36	1	52
8	4	05	+18.1	55.1	15.0	8	258	62	8.1	11	33	11	15	19	31	2	37	2	55
9	4	56	+19.1	54.6	14.9	20	262	71	9.1	12	18	11	59	20	19	3	32	3	51
10	5	46	+19.2	54.3	14.8	32	266	79	10.1	13	08	12	49	21	07	4	20	4	39
11	6	36	+18.5	54.1	14.7	44	269	86	11.1	14	03	13	46	21	54	5	01	5	19
12	7	26	+17.0	54.0	14.7	56	271	92	12.1	15	02	14	47	22	40	5	37	5	52
13	8	14	+14.7	54.0	14.7	68	270	96	13.1	16	04	15	52	23	24	6	07	6	20
14	9	01	+11.9	54.1	14.8	80	263	99	14.1	17	07	16	59	—		6	34	6	43
15	9	48	+8.5	54.3	14.8	93	199	100	15.1	18	12	18	07	0	08	6	58	7	04
16	10	34	+4.7	54.6	14.9	105	131	99	16.1	19	17	19	16	0	52	7	21	7	24
17	11	20	+0.8	55.0	15.0	117	121	96	17.1	20	23	20	26	1	35	7	43	7	42
18	12	07	−3.3	55.4	15.1	129	117	92	18.1	21	31	21	37	2	20	8	06	8	02
19	12	55	−7.2	55.9	15.2	141	114	85	19.1	22	39	22	49	3	05	8	30	8	22
20	13	44	−11.0	56.4	15.4	153	111	77	20.1	23	48	—		3	52	8	57	8	46
21	14	36	−14.2	57.1	15.6	165	108	68	21.1	—		0	02	4	42	9	29	9	15
22	15	30	−16.8	57.8	15.7	178	104	58	22.1	0	57	1	13	5	35	10	07	9	50
23	16	26	−18.5	58.5	15.9	190	99	47	23.1	2	03	2	22	6	30	10	55	10	36
24	17	25	−19.2	59.2	16.1	202	95	36	24.1	3	04	3	23	7	28	11	52	11	33
25	18	26	−18.6	59.9	16.3	214	90	25	25.1	3	58	4	16	8	27	12	59	12	41
26	19	27	−16.8	60.4	16.5	226	86	16	26.1	4	44	5	00	9	26	14	14	14	00
27	20	27	−13.9	60.7	16.6	238	84	8	27.1	5	23	5	35	10	24	15	34	15	24
28	21	26	−10.1	60.8	16.6	251	86	3	28.1	5	57	6	04	11	21	16	56	16	50

MERCURY

Day	R.A.		Dec.	Diam.	Phase	Transit		5° high 52°		5° high 56°	
	h	m	°	″	%	h	m	h	m	h	m
1	22	09	−10.9	7	51	13	24	17	54	17	41
3	22	15	−9.9	8	42	13	21	17	57	17	45
5	22	18	−9.0	8	32	13	16	17	55	17	44
7	22	18	−8.4	9	23	13	07	17	50	17	39
9	22	16	−8.0	9	15	12	57	17	40	17	30
11	22	11	−8.0	10	8	12	43	17	26	17	16
13	22	04	−8.2	10	3	12	28	17	09	16	58
15	21	56	−8.7	10	1	12	12	16	49	16	38
17	21	47	−9.4	10	1	11	55	7	21	7	33
19	21	39	−10.2	10	3	11	39	7	10	7	22
21	21	31	−11.1	10	7	11	25	7	00	7	13
23	21	26	−11.9	10	12	11	12	6	51	7	06
25	21	22	−12.6	10	17	11	00	6	44	6	59
27	21	20	−13.2	10	22	10	51	6	38	6	54
29	21	20	−13.6	9	28	10	44	6	33	6	50
31	21	22	−14.0	9	33	10	38	6	29	6	47

VENUS

Day	R.A.		Dec.	Diam.	Phase	Transit		5° high 52°		5° high 56°	
	h	m	°	″	%	h	m	h	m	h	m
1	18	56	−15.8	51	13	10	10	6	13	6	33
6	18	58	−16.0	47	18	9	53	5	57	6	17
11	19	04	−16.3	43	22	9	39	5	45	6	06
16	19	13	−16.5	40	26	9	29	5	36	5	57
21	19	25	−16.6	37	30	9	22	5	30	5	51
26	19	40	−16.6	34	34	9	16	5	24	5	45
31	19	55	−16.5	32	38	9	12	5	20	5	41

MARS

Day	R.A.		Dec.	Diam.	Phase	Transit		5° high 52°		5° high 56°	
	h	m	°	″	%	h	m	h	m	h	m
1	13	29	−6.6	9	91	4	44	23	50	0	02
6	13	34	−7.1	9	92	4	30	23	38	23	47
11	13	39	−7.4	10	92	4	14	23	24	23	34
16	13	42	−7.7	10	93	3	58	23	09	23	19
21	13	45	−7.9	11	94	3	41	22	52	23	03
26	13	46	−8.0	11	94	3	22	22	34	22	45
31	13	46	−7.9	12	95	3	03	22	15	22	25

SUNRISE AND SUNSET

	London		*Bristol*		*Birmingham*		*Manchester*		*Newcastle*		*Glasgow*		*Belfast*	
	0° 05′	*51° 30′*	*2° 35′*	*51° 28′*	*1° 55′*	*52° 28′*	*2° 15′*	*53° 28′*	*1° 37′*	*54° 59′*	*4° 14′*	*55° 52′*	*5° 56′*	*54° 35′*
d	*h m*	*h m*	*h m*	*h m*	*h m*	*h m*	*h m*	*h m*	*h m*	*h m*	*h m*	*h m*	*h m*	*h m*
1	7 39	16 50	7 49	17 00	7 49	16 54	7 54	16 52	7 57	16 43	8 11	16 50	8 13	17 02
2	7 37	16 51	7 47	17 02	7 48	16 56	7 52	16 54	7 56	16 45	8 09	16 52	8 11	17 04
3	7 36	16 53	7 46	17 03	7 46	16 58	7 51	16 56	7 54	16 48	8 08	16 55	8 09	17 06
4	7 34	16 55	7 44	17 05	7 44	16 59	7 49	16 58	7 52	16 50	8 06	16 57	8 08	17 08
5	7 32	16 57	7 42	17 07	7 43	17 01	7 47	16 59	7 50	16 52	8 04	16 59	8 06	17 10
6	7 31	16 59	7 41	17 09	7 41	17 03	7 45	17 01	7 48	16 54	8 02	17 01	8 04	17 13
7	7 29	17 01	7 39	17 11	7 39	17 05	7 44	17 03	7 46	16 56	7 59	17 03	8 02	17 15
8	7 27	17 02	7 37	17 13	7 37	17 07	7 42	17 05	7 44	16 58	7 57	17 06	8 00	17 17
9	7 26	17 04	7 35	17 14	7 36	17 09	7 40	17 07	7 42	17 00	7 55	17 08	7 58	17 19
10	7 24	17 06	7 34	17 16	7 34	17 11	7 38	17 09	7 40	17 02	7 53	17 10	7 56	17 21
11	7 22	17 08	7 32	17 18	7 32	17 13	7 36	17 11	7 38	17 04	7 51	17 12	7 54	17 23
12	7 20	17 10	7 30	17 20	7 30	17 15	7 34	17 13	7 36	17 07	7 49	17 14	7 52	17 25
13	7 18	17 12	7 28	17 22	7 28	17 17	7 32	17 15	7 34	17 09	7 47	17 17	7 50	17 27
14	7 16	17 13	7 26	17 23	7 26	17 18	7 30	17 17	7 31	17 11	7 44	17 19	7 47	17 29
15	7 14	17 15	7 24	17 25	7 24	17 20	7 28	17 19	7 29	17 13	7 42	17 21	7 45	17 31
16	7 12	17 17	7 22	17 27	7 22	17 22	7 26	17 21	7 27	17 15	7 40	17 23	7 43	17 33
17	7 11	17 19	7 20	17 29	7 20	17 24	7 24	17 23	7 25	17 17	7 37	17 25	7 41	17 35
18	7 09	17 21	7 19	17 31	7 18	17 26	7 21	17 25	7 23	17 19	7 35	17 27	7 39	17 37
19	7 07	17 22	7 17	17 33	7 16	17 28	7 19	17 27	7 20	17 21	7 33	17 30	7 37	17 39
20	7 05	17 24	7 15	17 34	7 14	17 30	7 17	17 29	7 18	17 23	7 30	17 32	7 34	17 41
21	7 03	17 26	7 12	17 36	7 12	17 32	7 15	17 31	7 16	17 25	7 28	17 34	7 32	17 44
22	7 01	17 28	7 10	17 38	7 10	17 34	7 13	17 33	7 13	17 27	7 26	17 36	7 30	17 46
23	6 58	17 30	7 08	17 40	7 07	17 35	7 11	17 35	7 11	17 30	7 23	17 38	7 27	17 48
24	6 56	17 31	7 06	17 42	7 05	17 37	7 08	17 37	7 09	17 32	7 21	17 40	7 25	17 50
25	6 54	17 33	7 04	17 43	7 03	17 39	7 06	17 39	7 06	17 34	7 18	17 43	7 23	17 52
26	6 52	17 35	7 02	17 45	7 01	17 41	7 04	17 41	7 04	17 36	7 16	17 45	7 20	17 54
27	6 50	17 37	7 00	17 47	6 59	17 43	7 02	17 43	7 02	17 38	7 13	17 47	7 18	17 56
28	6 48	17 39	6 58	17 49	6 57	17 45	6 59	17 45	6 59	17 40	7 11	17 49	7 16	17 58

JUPITER

Day	*R.A.*		*Dec.*		*Transit*		*5° high*			
							52°		*56°*	
	h	*m*	°	′	*h*	*m*	*h*	*m*	*h*	*m*
1	6	53.2	+23	04	22	05	5	40	5	58
11	6	49.4	+23	10	21	22	4	57	5	15
21	6	46.8	+23	14	20	40	4	16	4	34
31	6	45.6	+23	16	20	00	3	36	3	54

Diameters – equatorial 44″ polar 41″

SATURN

Day	*R.A.*		*Dec.*		*Transit*		*5° high*			
							52°		*56°*	
	h	*m*	°	′	*h*	*m*	*h*	*m*	*h*	*m*
1	15	23.1	−16	14	6	38	2	43	3	04
11	15	24.8	−16	18	6	00	2	06	2	27
21	15	25.8	−16	20	5	22	1	28	1	49
31	15	26.2	−16	19	4	43	0	49	1	10

Diameters – equatorial 17″ polar 15″
Rings – major axis 38″ minor axis 15″

URANUS

Day	*R.A.*		*Dec.*		*Transit*		*10° high*			
							52°		*56°*	
	h	*m*	°	′	*h*	*m*	*h*	*m*	*h*	*m*
1	0	35.8	+3	08	15	49	20	59	20	55
11	0	37.2	+3	17	15	11	20	22	20	18
21	0	38.9	+3	28	14	33	19	45	19	41
31	0	40.7	+3	40	13	56	19	09	19	05

Diameter 4″

NEPTUNE

Day	*R.A.*		*Dec.*		*Transit*		*10° high*			
							52°		*56°*	
	h	*m*	°	′	*h*	*m*	*h*	*m*	*h*	*m*
1	22	25.3	−10	36	13	39	17	31	17	13
11	22	26.7	−10	28	13	01	16	54	16	36
21	22	28.1	−10	19	12	23	16	17	15	59
31	22	29.6	−10	11	11	45	15	40	15	22

Diameter 2″

♓ MARCH 2014 ♈

THIRD MONTH, 31 DAYS. *Mars,* Roman god of battle

1	*Saturday*	Caroline of Ansbach, Queen Consort of King George II *b.* 1683	day 60
2	*Sunday*	Disgruntled poet Roderick McLean attempts to assassinate Queen Victoria at Windsor train station 1882	61
3	*Monday*	Statute of Rhuddlan incorporates the Principality of Wales into England under King Edward I 1284	week 9 day 62
4	*Tuesday*	King Henry VI is deposed and imprisoned by his cousin Edward of York who becomes King Edward IV 1461	63
5	*Wednesday*	King Henry II, who reigned from 1154–1189, House of Plantagenet *b.* 1133	64
6	*Thursday*	John of Gaunt, 1st Duke of Lancaster who was the third surviving son of King Edward III *b.* 1340	65
7	*Friday*	William Longespée, 3rd Earl of Salisbury, military leader and illegitimate son of King Henry II *d.* 1226	66
8	*Saturday*	King William III, House of Orange *d.* 1702	67
9	*Sunday*	David Rizzio, Italian private secretary of Mary, Queen of Scots, is brutally murdered 1566	68
10	*Monday*	Prince Albert Edward (King Edward VII) marries Princess Alexandra at Windsor 1863	week 10 day 69
11	*Tuesday*	Queen Anne refuses the Scottish Militia Bill, the last time a monarch vetoes legislation 1708	70
12	*Wednesday*	Anne Hyde, first wife of King James II and mother of Queen Anne, Great Britain's first monarch *b.* 1637	71
13	*Thursday*	Richard Burbage, actor who was the first to perform the lead in Shakespeare's *Richard III d.*1619	72
14	*Friday*	Princess Louise of Prussia, who married Prince Arthur, the seventh child of Queen Victoria *d.* 1917	73
15	*Saturday*	The Royal Declaration of Indulgence is issued by King Charles II, suspending penal laws against Catholics 1672	74
16	*Sunday*	Prime minister Harold Wilson informs Queen Elizabeth II of his resignation 1976	75
17	*Monday*	Edward, the Black Prince, eldest son of King Edward III, becomes Duke of Cornwall 1337	week 11 day 76
18	*Tuesday*	Mary Tudor, fifth daughter of King Henry VII and wife of King Louis XII of France *b.* 1496	77
19	*Wednesday*	Alexander III, King of Scots, who became king aged 7 and whose death led to a succession crisis *d.* 1286	78
20	*Thursday*	King Henry IV, House of Lancaster *d.* 1413; Frederick, Prince of Wales, son of King George II *d.* 1751	79
21	*Friday*	Accession of King Henry V following the death of his father, King Henry IV 1413	80
22	*Saturday*	Thomas of Lancaster, brother of King Henry V, is killed in battle during the Hundred Years' War 1421	81
23	*Sunday*	Margaret of Anjou, wife of King Henry VI and a principal figure during the Wars of the Roses *b.* 1430	82
24	*Monday*	Queen Elizabeth I, who reigned from 1558–1603, House of Tudor *d.* 1603	week 12 day 83
25	*Tuesday*	King Richard I is wounded by a crossbow bolt in the neck, which leads to his death 1199	84
26	*Wednesday*	The Henley Regatta is first held in 1839; in 1851, Prince Albert becomes patron	85
27	*Thursday*	King James I, who reigned from 1603–1625, House of Stuart *d.* 1625	86
28	*Friday*	Dame Flora Robson, actress who twice portrayed Queen Elizabeth I in film *b.* 1902	87
29	*Saturday*	28,000 die at the Battle of Towton, after which Edward of York replaces King Henry VI as king 1461	88
30	*Sunday*	English forces of King Edward I sack Berwick during the First War of Scottish Independence 1296	89
31	*Monday*	Philippa of Lancaster, sister of King Henry IV, who married King John I of Portugal *b.* 1360	week 13 day 90

ASTRONOMICAL PHENOMENA

d	*h*	
1	16	Mars at stationary point
2	16	Saturn at stationary point
6	11	Jupiter at stationary point
10	11	Jupiter in conjunction with Moon. Jupiter 5°N.
14	06	Mercury at greatest elongation W. 28°
19	01	Mars in conjunction with Moon. Mars 3°N.
20	17	Sun's longitude 0° ♈
21	03	Saturn in conjunction with Moon. Saturn 0°.2 N.
22	20	Venus at greatest elongation W. 47°
27	08	Venus in conjunction with Moon. Venus 3°S.
29	00	Mercury in conjunction with Moon. Mercury 6°S.

MINIMA OF ALGOL

d	*h*	*d*	*h*	*d*	*h*
1	13.0	13	00.2	24	11.5
4	09.8	15	21.1	27	08.4
7	06.6	18	17.9	30	05.2
10	03.4	21	14.7		

CONSTELLATIONS

The following constellations are near the meridian at

	d	*h*		*d*	*h*
February	1	24	March	16	21
February	15	23	April	1	20
March	1	22	April	15	19

Cepheus (below the Pole), Camelopardalis, Lynx, Gemini, Cancer, Leo, Canis Minor, Hydra, Monoceros, Canis Major and Puppis

THE MOON

Phases, Apsides and Node	*d*	*h*	*m*
● New Moon	1	08	00
☽ First Quarter	8	13	27
○ Full Moon	16	17	08
☾ Last Quarter	24	01	46
● New Moon	30	18	45
Apogee (405,397km)	11	19	41
Perigee (365,682km)	27	18	26

Mean longitude of ascending node on March 1, 211°

THE SUN

s.d. 16′.1

Day	Right Ascension (h m s)	Dec. (° ′)	Equation of time (m s)	Rise 52° (h m)	Rise 56° (h m)	Transit (h m)	Set 52° (h m)	Set 56° (h m)	Sidereal time (h m s)	Transit of first point of Aries (h m s)
1	22 47 19	–7 42	–12 25	6 46	6 52	12 12	17 39	17 34	10 34 54	13 22 54
2	22 51 04	–7 19	–12 14	6 44	6 49	12 12	17 41	17 36	10 38 50	13 18 58
3	22 54 49	–6 56	–12 02	6 42	6 47	12 12	17 43	17 38	10 42 47	13 15 03
4	22 58 33	–6 33	–11 49	6 40	6 44	12 12	17 45	17 40	10 46 43	13 11 07
5	23 02 16	–6 10	–11 36	6 37	6 42	12 11	17 47	17 42	10 50 40	13 07 11
6	23 05 59	–5 47	–11 23	6 35	6 39	12 11	17 48	17 44	10 54 37	13 03 15
7	23 09 42	–5 24	–11 09	6 33	6 37	12 11	17 50	17 47	10 58 33	12 59 19
8	23 13 24	–5 00	–10 54	6 31	6 34	12 11	17 52	17 49	11 02 30	12 55 23
9	23 17 06	–4 37	–10 40	6 28	6 31	12 11	17 54	17 51	11 06 26	12 51 27
10	23 20 47	–4 13	–10 24	6 26	6 29	12 10	17 55	17 53	11 10 23	12 47 31
11	23 24 28	–3 50	–10 09	6 24	6 26	12 10	17 57	17 55	11 14 19	12 43 35
12	23 28 09	–3 26	–9 53	6 21	6 24	12 10	17 59	17 57	11 18 16	12 39 39
13	23 31 49	–3 03	–9 37	6 19	6 21	12 09	18 01	17 59	11 22 12	12 35 43
14	23 35 30	–2 39	–9 21	6 17	6 18	12 09	18 02	18 01	11 26 09	12 31 48
15	23 39 09	–2 15	–9 04	6 15	6 16	12 09	18 04	18 03	11 30 06	12 27 52
16	23 42 49	–1 52	–8 47	6 12	6 13	12 09	18 06	18 05	11 34 02	12 23 56
17	23 46 28	–1 28	–8 30	6 10	6 11	12 08	18 08	18 07	11 37 59	12 20 00
18	23 50 08	–1 04	–8 12	6 08	6 08	12 08	18 09	18 09	11 41 55	12 16 04
19	23 53 47	–0 40	–7 55	6 05	6 05	12 08	18 11	18 11	11 45 52	12 12 08
20	23 57 25	–0 17	–7 37	6 03	6 03	12 07	18 13	18 13	11 49 48	12 08 12
21	0 01 04	+0 07	–7 19	6 01	6 00	12 07	18 15	18 16	11 53 45	12 04 16
22	0 04 43	+0 31	–7 02	5 58	5 57	12 07	18 16	18 18	11 57 41	12 00 20
23	0 08 21	+0 54	–6 44	5 56	5 55	12 07	18 18	18 20	12 01 38	11 56 24
24	0 12 00	+1 18	–6 25	5 54	5 52	12 06	18 20	18 22	12 05 34	11 52 28
25	0 15 38	+1 42	–6 07	5 51	5 49	12 06	18 22	18 24	12 09 31	11 48 33
26	0 19 17	+2 05	–5 49	5 49	5 47	12 06	18 23	18 26	12 13 28	11 44 37
27	0 22 55	+2 29	–5 31	5 47	5 44	12 05	18 25	18 28	12 17 24	11 40 41
28	0 26 34	+2 52	–5 13	5 45	5 42	12 05	18 27	18 30	12 21 21	11 36 45
29	0 30 12	+3 16	–4 55	5 42	5 39	12 05	18 28	18 32	12 25 17	11 32 49
30	0 33 51	+3 39	–4 37	5 40	5 36	12 04	18 30	18 34	12 29 14	11 28 53
31	0 37 30	+4 02	–4 19	5 38	5 34	12 04	18 32	18 36	12 33 10	11 24 57

DURATION OF TWILIGHT (in minutes)

Latitude	52°	56°	52°	56°	52°	56°	52°	56°
	1 March		*11 March*		*21 March*		*31 March*	
Civil	34	37	34	37	34	37	34	38
Nautical	73	80	73	80	74	81	75	84
Astronomical	112	124	113	125	115	128	120	135

THE NIGHT SKY

Mercury is unsuitably placed for observation throughout the month.

Venus, magnitude –4.4, continues to be visible as a brilliant object in the morning skies, low above the east-south-eastern horizon but only for about an hour before sunrise. On the 22nd it reaches its greatest western elongation (47 degrees). On the morning of the 27th, the waning crescent Moon passes 3 degrees north of the planet.

Mars, its magnitude increasing notably during the month from –0.5 to –1.4, is visible in the mornings in the southern sky, its motion becoming retrograde early in March. The waning gibbous Moon passes 4 degrees south of the planet on the 18th–19th. On the last day of the month Mars passes 5 degrees north of Spica.

Jupiter, magnitude –2.3, continues to be visible as a conspicuous object in the south-western quadrant of the sky from shortly after sunset until well after midnight. Jupiter reaches its second stationary point on the 6th and then resumes its direct motion. On the 10th the waxing gibbous Moon passes 6 degrees south of the planet.

Saturn, magnitude +0.3, continues to be visible as a morning object and by the end of the month it is becoming visible low above the eastern horizon shortly after 23h. The waning gibbous Moon passes 1 degree south of the planet on the morning of the 21st.

Zodiacal Light. The evening cone may be observed stretching up from the western horizon, along the ecliptic, after the end of twilight, from the 18th onwards. This faint phenomenon is only visible under good conditions and in the absence of both moonlight and artificial lighting.

THE MOON

Day	*R.A.*		*Dec.*	*Hor. par.*	*Semi-diam.*	*Sun's Co-Long.*	*PA of Br. Limb*	*Ph.*	*Age*	*Rise*				*Transit*		*Set*			
										52°		*56°*				*52°*		*56°*	
	h	*m*	°	′	′	°	°	*%*	*d*	*h*	*m*	*h*	*m*	*h*	*m*	*h*	*m*	*h*	*m*
1	22	24	−5.6	60.6	16.5	263	110	0	29.1	6	26	6	30	12	16	18	18	18	16
2	23	20	−0.8	60.2	16.4	275	228	1	0.7	6	54	6	54	13	09	19	38	19	40
3	0	15	+3.9	59.5	16.2	287	242	4	1.7	7	21	7	17	14	02	20	55	21	02
4	1	09	+8.3	58.6	16.0	299	246	9	2.7	7	49	7	41	14	53	22	09	22	20
5	2	02	+12.1	57.7	15.7	312	250	17	3.7	8	19	8	08	15	44	23	19	23	33
6	2	55	+15.2	56.8	15.5	324	254	26	4.7	8	53	8	38	16	34	—			
7	3	48	+17.4	56.0	15.3	336	258	35	5.7	9	31	9	14	17	24	0	24	0	41
8	4	40	+18.7	55.3	15.1	348	263	45	6.7	10	14	9	56	18	14	1	22	1	41
9	5	31	+19.1	54.7	14.9	0	267	54	7.7	11	03	10	44	19	02	2	14	2	32
10	6	22	+18.6	54.3	14.8	13	271	64	8.7	11	56	11	39	19	49	2	58	3	16
11	7	11	+17.3	54.1	14.8	25	274	73	9.7	12	54	12	38	20	35	3	36	3	52
12	8	00	+15.3	54.1	14.7	37	278	80	10.7	13	54	13	42	21	20	4	08	4	22
13	8	47	+12.6	54.2	14.8	49	280	87	11.7	14	57	14	47	22	05	4	36	4	47
14	9	34	+9.4	54.4	14.8	61	281	93	12.7	16	01	15	55	22	49	5	02	5	09
15	10	21	+5.8	54.7	14.9	73	280	97	13.7	17	06	17	04	23	33	5	25	5	29
16	11	07	+1.9	55.1	15.0	86	270	99	14.7	18	13	18	14	—		5	48	5	48
17	11	55	−2.2	55.6	15.1	98	151	100	15.7	19	21	19	25	0	17	6	11	6	08
18	12	43	−6.2	56.0	15.3	110	119	98	16.7	20	30	20	38	1	03	6	35	6	29
19	13	32	−10.0	56.5	15.4	122	112	95	17.7	21	39	21	51	1	50	7	02	6	52
20	14	24	−13.4	57.0	15.5	134	108	89	18.7	22	48	23	04	2	39	7	32	7	19
21	15	18	−16.1	57.5	15.7	146	103	82	19.7	23	55	—		3	31	8	09	7	53
22	16	13	−18.0	58.0	15.8	159	99	72	20.7	—		0	13	4	25	8	53	8	35
23	17	11	−18.9	58.5	15.9	171	94	62	21.7	0	57	1	16	5	22	9	46	9	27
24	18	10	−18.7	59.0	16.1	183	89	51	22.7	1	52	2	10	6	19	10	48	10	30
25	19	09	−17.3	59.4	16.2	195	84	40	23.7	2	39	2	56	7	16	11	58	11	42
26	20	07	−14.9	59.7	16.3	207	80	29	24.7	3	20	3	33	8	12	13	13	13	01
27	21	05	−11.4	59.9	16.3	219	77	19	25.7	3	54	4	03	9	08	14	32	14	24
28	22	02	−7.3	60.0	16.3	232	76	10	26.7	4	24	4	30	10	02	15	51	15	47
29	22	57	−2.8	59.8	16.3	244	76	4	27.7	4	52	4	54	10	55	17	10	17	11
30	23	52	+1.9	59.5	16.2	256	80	1	28.7	5	19	5	17	11	47	18	28	18	33
31	0	46	+6.4	58.9	16.1	268	221	0	0.3	5	47	5	41	12	39	19	44	19	53

MERCURY

Day	*R.A.*		*Dec.*	*Diam.*	*Phase*	*Transit*		*5° high*			
								52°		*56°*	
	h	*m*	°	″	*%*	*h*	*m*	*h*	*m*	*h*	*m*
1	21	20	−13.6	9	28	10	44	6	33	6	50
3	21	22	−14.0	9	33	10	38	6	29	6	47
5	21	25	−14.2	9	38	10	34	6	26	6	44
7	21	30	−14.3	8	42	10	30	6	23	6	41
9	21	35	−14.2	8	46	10	28	6	21	6	38
11	21	42	−14.1	8	50	10	27	6	19	6	36
13	21	49	−13.8	7	53	10	27	6	16	6	33
15	21	57	−13.4	7	56	10	27	6	14	6	31
17	22	06	−13.0	7	59	10	28	6	12	6	28
19	22	15	−12.4	7	62	10	30	6	10	6	25
21	22	25	−11.7	7	64	10	32	6	08	6	22
23	22	35	−11.0	6	67	10	34	6	05	6	19
25	22	45	−10.1	6	69	10	36	6	03	6	15
27	22	56	−9.2	6	71	10	39	6	00	6	12
29	23	07	−8.2	6	74	10	42	5	58	6	08
31	23	18	−7.1	6	76	10	46	5	55	6	04

VENUS

Day	*R.A.*		*Dec.*	*Diam.*	*Phase*	*Transit*		*5° high*			
								52°		*56°*	
	h	*m*	°	″	*%*	*h*	*m*	*h*	*m*	*h*	*m*
1	19	49	−16.6	33	36	9	14	5	22	5	43
6	20	06	−16.4	30	40	9	11	5	17	5	38
11	20	24	−16.0	28	43	9	09	5	13	5	33
16	20	43	−15.4	27	46	9	09	5	09	5	28
21	21	02	−14.7	25	49	9	09	5	04	5	22
26	21	23	−13.7	24	51	9	09	4	58	5	15
31	21	43	−12.6	22	54	9	10	4	52	5	07

MARS

Day	*R.A.*		*Dec.*	*Diam.*	*Phase*	*Transit*		*5° high*			
								52°		*56°*	
	h	*m*	°	″	*%*	*h*	*m*	*h*	*m*	*h*	*m*
1	13	46	−8.0	12	95	3	11	22	23	22	33
6	13	46	−7.9	12	96	2	51	22	02	22	12
11	13	44	−7.7	13	97	2	30	21	40	21	50
16	13	42	−7.5	13	98	2	07	21	15	21	25
21	13	37	−7.1	14	98	1	43	20	49	20	59
26	13	32	−6.7	14	99	1	19	20	22	20	31
31	13	26	−6.1	15	100	0	53	19	53	20	02

SUNRISE AND SUNSET

	London				Bristol				Birmingham				Manchester				Newcastle				Glasgow				Belfast			
	0° 05′		51° 30′		2° 35′		51° 28′		1° 55′		52° 28′		2° 15′		53° 28′		1° 37′		54° 59′		4° 14′		55° 52′		5° 56′		54° 35′	
d	h	m	h	m	h	m	h	m	h	m	h	m	h	m	h	m	h	m	h	m	h	m	h	m	h	m	h	m
1	6	46	17	40	6	56	17	50	6	54	17	47	6	57	17	47	6	57	17	42	7	09	17	51	7	13	18	00
2	6	44	17	42	6	54	17	52	6	52	17	48	6	55	17	48	6	54	17	44	7	06	17	53	7	11	18	02
3	6	41	17	44	6	51	17	54	6	50	17	50	6	52	17	50	6	52	17	46	7	03	17	55	7	09	18	04
4	6	39	17	46	6	49	17	56	6	48	17	52	6	50	17	52	6	49	17	48	7	01	17	57	7	06	18	06
5	6	37	17	47	6	47	17	57	6	45	17	54	6	48	17	54	6	47	17	50	6	58	17	59	7	04	18	08
6	6	35	17	49	6	45	17	59	6	43	17	56	6	45	17	56	6	44	17	52	6	56	18	02	7	01	18	10
7	6	33	17	51	6	43	18	01	6	41	17	57	6	43	17	58	6	42	17	54	6	53	18	04	6	59	18	12
8	6	30	17	53	6	40	18	03	6	39	17	59	6	41	18	00	6	40	17	56	6	51	18	06	6	56	18	14
9	6	28	17	54	6	38	18	04	6	36	18	01	6	38	18	02	6	37	17	58	6	48	18	08	6	54	18	16
10	6	26	17	56	6	36	18	06	6	34	18	03	6	36	18	04	6	35	18	00	6	46	18	10	6	51	18	18
11	6	24	17	58	6	34	18	08	6	32	18	05	6	34	18	05	6	32	18	02	6	43	18	12	6	49	18	20
12	6	22	18	00	6	32	18	10	6	29	18	06	6	31	18	07	6	29	18	04	6	40	18	14	6	47	18	22
13	6	19	18	01	6	29	18	11	6	27	18	08	6	29	18	09	6	27	18	06	6	38	18	16	6	44	18	23
14	6	17	18	03	6	27	18	13	6	25	18	10	6	26	18	11	6	24	18	08	6	35	18	18	6	42	18	25
15	6	15	18	05	6	25	18	15	6	22	18	12	6	24	18	13	6	22	18	10	6	33	18	20	6	39	18	27
16	6	13	18	06	6	23	18	16	6	20	18	14	6	22	18	15	6	19	18	12	6	30	18	22	6	37	18	29
17	6	10	18	08	6	20	18	18	6	18	18	15	6	19	18	17	6	17	18	14	6	27	18	24	6	34	18	31
18	6	08	18	10	6	18	18	20	6	15	18	17	6	17	18	18	6	14	18	16	6	25	18	26	6	32	18	33
19	6	06	18	11	6	16	18	22	6	13	18	19	6	14	18	20	6	12	18	18	6	22	18	28	6	29	18	35
20	6	03	18	13	6	13	18	23	6	11	18	21	6	12	18	22	6	09	18	20	6	20	18	30	6	26	18	37
21	6	01	18	15	6	11	18	25	6	08	18	22	6	09	18	24	6	07	18	22	6	17	18	32	6	24	18	39
22	5	59	18	17	6	09	18	27	6	06	18	24	6	07	18	26	6	04	18	24	6	14	18	34	6	21	18	41
23	5	57	18	18	6	07	18	28	6	04	18	26	6	05	18	28	6	02	18	26	6	12	18	37	6	19	18	43
24	5	54	18	20	6	04	18	30	6	01	18	28	6	02	18	29	5	59	18	28	6	09	18	39	6	16	18	45
25	5	52	18	22	6	02	18	32	5	59	18	29	6	00	18	31	5	56	18	30	6	06	18	41	6	14	18	47
26	5	50	18	23	6	00	18	33	5	57	18	31	5	57	18	33	5	54	18	32	6	04	18	43	6	11	18	49
27	5	47	18	25	5	57	18	35	5	54	18	33	5	55	18	35	5	51	18	33	6	01	18	45	6	09	18	50
28	5	45	18	27	5	55	18	37	5	52	18	35	5	52	18	37	5	49	18	35	5	59	18	47	6	06	18	52
29	5	43	18	28	5	53	18	38	5	50	18	36	5	50	18	39	5	46	18	37	5	56	18	49	6	04	18	54
30	5	41	18	30	5	51	18	40	5	47	18	38	5	48	18	40	5	44	18	39	5	53	18	51	6	01	18	56
31	5	38	18	32	5	48	18	42	5	45	18	40	5	45	18	42	5	41	18	41	5	51	18	53	5	59	18	58

JUPITER

Day	R.A.		Dec.		Transit		5° high			
							52°		56°	
	h	m	°	′	h	m	h	m	h	m
1	6	45.7	+23	15	20	07	3	44	4	02
11	6	45.7	+23	16	19	28	3	04	3	22
21	6	47.0	+23	15	18	50	2	26	2	44
31	6	49.7	+23	13	18	14	1	49	2	07

Diameters – equatorial 40″ polar 38″

SATURN

Day	R.A.		Dec.		Transit		5° high			
							52°		56°	
	h	m	°	′	h	m	h	m	h	m
1	15	26.2	−16	19	4	50	0	57	1	18
11	15	26.0	−16	17	4	11	0	17	0	38
21	15	25.1	−16	12	3	31	23	32	23	53
31	15	23.6	−16	04	2	50	22	51	23	11

Diameters – equatorial 18″ polar 16″
Rings – major axis 40″ minor axis 15″

URANUS

Day	R.A.		Dec.		Transit		10° high			
							52°		56°	
	h	m	°	′	h	m	h	m	h	m
1	0	40.3	+3	38	14	03	19	16	19	12
11	0	42.3	+3	50	13	26	18	40	18	36
21	0	44.3	+4	03	12	49	18	04	18	00
31	0	46.4	+4	17	12	11	17	27	17	24

Diameter 4″

NEPTUNE

Day	R.A.		Dec.		Transit		10° high			
							52°		56°	
	h	m	°	′	h	m	h	m	h	m
1	22	29.3	−10	13	11	53	7	58	8	16
11	22	30.7	−10	05	11	15	7	19	7	37
21	22	32.1	−9	57	10	37	6	40	6	58
31	22	33.4	−9	49	9	59	6	01	6	19

Diameter 2″

APRIL 2014

FOURTH MONTH, 30 DAYS. *Aperire*, to open; Earth opens to receive seed.

1	*Tuesday*	Eleanor of Aquitaine, wife of King Henry II who encouraged her sons to rebel against him *d.* 1204	day 91
2	*Wednesday*	Arthur, Prince of Wales, the eldest son of King Henry VII who predeceased his father *d.* 1502	92
3	*Thursday*	King Henry IV, who reigned from 1399–1413, House of Lancaster *b.* 1366	93
4	*Friday*	Sir Francis Drake is knighted by Queen Elizabeth I after his circumnavigation of the world 1581	94
5	*Saturday*	Princess Victoria, granddaughter of Queen Victoria and maternal grandmother of the Duke of Edinburgh *b.* 1863	95
6	*Sunday*	King Richard I, House of Plantagenet *d.* 1199	96
7	*Monday*	William Wordsworth, who was appointed Poet Laureate by Queen Victoria in 1843 *b.* 1770	week 14 day 97
8	*Tuesday*	Prince George (King George IV) marries Princess Caroline of Brunswick to pay off his huge debts 1795	98
9	*Wednesday*	Coronation of King Henry V at Westminster Abbey 1413; King Edward IV, House of York *d.* 1483	99
10	*Thursday*	King James I forms the Charter of the Virginia Company of London to establish an American colony 1606	100
11	*Friday*	Coronation of William III and Mary II at Westminster Abbey 1689	101
12	*Saturday*	The Union Jack is adopted as the flag of Great Britain following the accession of King James VI 1606	102
13	*Sunday*	Guy Fawkes, whose effigy is burnt on 5 November due to his part in the failed Gunpowder Plot *b.* 1570 (presumed)	103
14	*Monday*	The Battle of Barnet, decisive in the Wars of the Roses, secures the throne for King Edward IV 1471	week 15 day 104
15	*Tuesday*	Prince William Augustus, known as 'Butcher' Cumberland for crushing the Jacobite Rising *b.* 1721	105
16	*Wednesday*	Jacobite army led by Bonnie Prince Charlie is defeated at the Battle of Culloden 1746	106
17	*Thursday*	David Bradley, actor who played King Henry VIII's court jester in the BBC series *The Tudors* *b.* 1942	107
18	*Friday*	John Leland, antiquary who was appointed by King Henry VIII to examine monastery libraries *d.* 1552	108
19	*Saturday*	Elizabeth Hamilton, mistress of King William III and lady-in-waiting to his wife Queen Mary II *d.* 1733	109
20	*Sunday*	Oliver Cromwell dissolves the Rump Parliament (established to try King Charles I for high treason) 1653	110
21	*Monday*	Queen Elizabeth II, reign 1952–present, House of Windsor *b.* 1926	week 16 day 111
22	*Tuesday*	Eleanor of Woodstock, daughter of King Edward II and younger sister of King Edward III *d.* 1355	112
23	*Wednesday*	Coronation of King Charles II 1661; Coronation of King James II 1685; Coronation of Queen Anne 1702	113
24	*Thursday*	Mary, Queen of Scots, marries the Dauphin Francis, briefly making her Queen Consort of France 1558	114
25	*Friday*	King Edward II, who reigned from 1307–1327, House of Plantagenet *b.* 1284	115
26	*Saturday*	Prince Albert (King George VI) marries Lady Elizabeth Bowes-Lyon at Westminster Abbey 1923	116
27	*Sunday*	The English forces of King Edward I defeat John Balliol, King of Scots, at the Battle of Dunbar 1296	117
28	*Monday*	King Edward IV, who reigned from 1461–1483, House of York *b.* 1442	week 17 day 118
29	*Tuesday*	Prince William marries Kate Middleton; bestowed the titles of the Duke and Duchess of Cambridge 2011	119
30	*Wednesday*	Queen Mary II, who reigned from 1689–1694, House of Stuart *b.* 1662	120

ASTRONOMICAL PHENOMENA

d	*h*	
2	07	Uranus in conjunction
6	22	Jupiter in conjunction with Moon. Jupiter 5°N.
8	21	Mars at opposition
14	16	Mars in conjunction with Moon. Mars 3°N.
15	00	Pluto at stationary point
15	08	Total eclipse of Moon (see page 628)
17	07	Saturn in conjunction with Moon. Saturn 0°.4 N.
20	04	Sun's longitude 30° ♉
25	20	Venus in conjuction with Moon. Venus 4°S.
26	03	Mercury in superior conjunction
29	07	Annual eclipse of Sun (see page 628)
29	14	Mercury in conjunction with Moon. Mercury 2°N.

MINIMA OF ALGOL

d	*h*	*d*	*h*	*d*	*h*
2	02.0	13	13.3	25	00.6
4	22.8	16	10.1	27	21.4
7	19.6	19	06.9	30	18.2
10	16.5	22	03.7		

CONSTELLATIONS

The following constellations are near the meridian at

	d	*h*		*d*	*h*
March	1	24	April	15	21
March	16	23	May	1	20
April	1	22	May	16	19

Cepheus (below the Pole), Cassiopeia (below the Pole), Ursa Major, Leo Minor, Leo., Sextans, Hydra and Crater

THE MOON

Phases, Apsides and Node	*d*	*h*	*m*
☽ First Quarter	7	08	31
○ Full Moon	15	07	42
☾ Last Quarter	22	07	52
● New Moon	29	06	14
Apogee (404,538km)	8	14	50
Perigee (369,729km)	23	00	20

Mean longitude of ascending node on April 1, 209°

THE SUN

s.d. 16′.0

Day	Right Ascension (h m s)	Dec. + (° ′)	Equation of time (m s)	Rise 52° (h m)	Rise 56° (h m)	Transit (h m)	Set 52° (h m)	Set 56° (h m)	Sidereal time (h m s)	Transit of first point of Aries (h m s)
1	0 41 08	4 26	−4 01	5 35	5 31	12 04	18 34	18 38	12 37 07	11 21 01
2	0 44 47	4 49	−3 44	5 33	5 28	12 04	18 35	18 40	12 41 03	11 17 05
3	0 48 26	5 12	−3 26	5 31	5 26	12 03	18 37	18 42	12 45 00	11 13 09
4	0 52 05	5 35	−3 09	5 28	5 23	12 03	18 39	18 44	12 48 57	11 09 14
5	0 55 44	5 58	−2 51	5 26	5 21	12 03	18 40	18 46	12 52 53	11 05 18
6	0 59 24	6 20	−2 34	5 24	5 18	12 02	18 42	18 48	12 56 50	11 01 22
7	1 03 03	6 43	−2 17	5 22	5 15	12 02	18 44	18 50	13 00 46	10 57 26
8	1 06 43	7 06	−2 00	5 19	5 13	12 02	18 46	18 52	13 04 43	10 53 30
9	1 10 23	7 28	−1 44	5 17	5 10	12 02	18 47	18 54	13 08 39	10 49 34
10	1 14 03	7 50	−1 27	5 15	5 08	12 01	18 49	18 56	13 12 36	10 45 38
11	1 17 44	8 12	−1 11	5 13	5 05	12 01	18 51	18 58	13 16 32	10 41 42
12	1 21 24	8 34	−0 55	5 10	5 03	12 01	18 52	19 00	13 20 29	10 37 46
13	1 25 05	8 56	−0 40	5 08	5 00	12 01	18 54	19 02	13 24 26	10 33 50
14	1 28 47	9 18	−0 25	5 06	4 57	12 00	18 56	19 04	13 28 22	10 29 54
15	1 32 28	9 40	−0 10	5 04	4 55	12 00	18 57	19 07	13 32 19	10 25 59
16	1 36 10	10 01	+0 05	5 02	4 52	12 00	18 59	19 09	13 36 15	10 22 03
17	1 39 53	10 22	+0 19	4 59	4 50	12 00	19 01	19 11	13 40 12	10 18 07
18	1 43 35	10 43	+0 33	4 57	4 47	11 59	19 03	19 13	13 44 08	10 14 11
19	1 47 19	11 04	+0 46	4 55	4 45	11 59	19 04	19 15	13 48 05	10 10 15
20	1 51 02	11 25	+0 59	4 53	4 42	11 59	19 06	19 17	13 52 01	10 06 19
21	1 54 46	11 45	+1 12	4 51	4 40	11 59	19 08	19 19	13 55 58	10 02 23
22	1 58 31	12 06	+1 24	4 49	4 38	11 59	19 09	19 21	13 59 54	9 58 27
23	2 02 15	12 26	+1 36	4 47	4 35	11 58	19 11	19 23	14 03 51	9 54 31
24	2 06 01	12 46	+1 47	4 45	4 33	11 58	19 13	19 25	14 07 48	9 50 35
25	2 09 47	13 05	+1 57	4 43	4 30	11 58	19 15	19 27	14 11 44	9 46 39
26	2 13 33	13 25	+2 08	4 40	4 28	11 58	19 16	19 29	14 15 41	9 42 44
27	2 17 20	13 44	+2 17	4 38	4 26	11 58	19 18	19 31	14 19 37	9 38 48
28	2 21 07	14 03	+2 26	4 36	4 23	11 57	19 20	19 33	14 23 34	9 34 52
29	2 24 55	14 22	+2 35	4 35	4 21	11 57	19 21	19 35	14 27 30	9 30 56
30	2 28 44	14 41	+2 43	4 33	4 19	11 57	19 23	19 37	14 31 27	9 27 00

DURATION OF TWILIGHT (in minutes)

Latitude	52°	56°	52°	56°	52°	56°	52°	56°
	1 April		*11 April*		*21 April*		*31 April*	
Civil	34	38	35	39	37	42	39	44
Nautical	76	84	79	89	83	96	89	106
Astronomical	120	136	127	147	137	165	152	204

THE NIGHT SKY

Mercury is unsuitably placed for observation throughout the month, as it passes through superior conjunction on the 26th.

Venus, magnitude −4.3, is still visible in the early mornings before dawn. However it will only be visible for a short while, low above the east-south-eastern horizon before sunrise. On the 25th the waning crescent Moon passes 3 degrees north of Venus.

Mars, magnitude −1.4, reaches opposition on the 8th and is therefore visible throughout the hours of darkness. On the 14th the Moon at last Quarter, passes 4 degrees south of the planet.

Jupiter is an evening object, magnitude −2.1, visible in the south-western sky until midnight. On the evening of the 6th the waxing crescent Moon passes 6 degrees south of the planet. The four Galilean satellites are readily observable with a small telescope or even a good pair of binoculars provided that they are held rigidly.

Saturn, magnitude +0.2, continues to be visible as a morning object and by the end of the month is visible after 21h, low in the south-eastern sky.

THE MOON

Day	*R.A.*		*Dec.*	*Hor. Par.*	*Semi-diam.*	*Sun's Co-Long.*	*PA of Br. Limb*	*Ph.*	*Age*	*Rise* 52°		56°		*Transit*		*Set* 52°		56°	
	h	*m*	°	′	′	°	°	%	*d*	*h*	*m*	*h*	*m*	*h*	*m*	*h*	*m*	*h*	*m*
1	1	40	+10.5	58.3	15.9	281	248	2	1.3	6	17	6	07	13	31	20	57	21	10
2	2	34	+13.9	57.5	15.7	293	254	6	2.3	6	49	6	36	14	23	22	06	22	21
3	3	27	+16.5	56.7	15.5	305	258	12	3.3	7	26	7	10	15	14	23	08	23	26
4	4	21	+18.2	56.0	15.3	317	263	20	4.3	8	08	7	50	16	05	—		—	
5	5	13	+18.9	55.3	15.1	329	267	28	5.3	8	55	8	36	16	54	0	04	0	23
6	6	05	+18.7	54.8	14.9	342	272	37	6.3	9	47	9	29	17	43	0	52	1	10
7	6	55	+17.7	54.4	14.8	354	276	47	7.3	10	43	10	27	18	29	1	33	1	49
8	7	44	+15.9	54.2	14.8	6	279	56	8.3	11	43	11	29	19	15	2	07	2	22
9	8	32	+13.5	54.2	14.8	18	283	65	9.3	12	44	12	34	19	59	2	37	2	49
10	9	19	+10.4	54.4	14.8	30	285	74	10.3	13	48	13	40	20	43	3	04	3	12
11	10	06	+7.0	54.7	14.9	43	287	82	11.3	14	52	14	48	21	27	3	28	3	33
12	10	52	+3.2	55.1	15.0	55	288	89	12.3	15	58	15	58	22	11	3	51	3	53
13	11	39	−0.9	55.6	15.1	67	288	94	13.3	17	06	17	09	22	57	4	13	4	12
14	12	27	−4.9	56.2	15.3	79	287	98	14.3	18	15	18	22	23	44	4	37	4	32
15	13	17	−8.8	56.8	15.5	91	282	100	15.3	19	26	19	37	—		5	03	4	55
16	14	09	−12.4	57.3	15.6	103	106	99	16.3	20	37	20	51	0	34	5	33	5	21
17	15	03	−15.4	57.8	15.8	116	102	97	17.3	21	46	22	03	1	26	6	08	5	53
18	15	59	−17.6	58.3	15.9	128	97	92	18.3	22	51	23	09	2	20	6	51	6	33
19	16	57	−18.8	58.7	16.0	140	93	85	19.3	23	49	—		3	17	7	42	7	23
20	17	56	−18.8	58.9	16.1	152	88	76	20.3	—		0	07	4	14	8	42	8	23
21	18	55	−17.7	59.1	16.1	164	83	65	21.3	0	38	0	55	5	11	9	49	9	33
22	19	54	−15.5	59.3	16.1	176	79	54	22.3	1	20	1	34	6	08	11	02	10	49
23	20	51	−12.3	59.3	16.2	189	75	42	23.3	1	56	2	06	7	02	12	18	12	09
24	21	46	−8.5	59.3	16.1	201	72	31	24.3	2	26	2	33	7	55	13	35	13	29
25	22	40	−4.1	59.1	16.1	213	71	21	25.3	2	54	2	57	8	47	14	52	14	50
26	23	34	+0.4	58.9	16.0	225	70	13	26.3	3	21	3	20	9	38	16	08	16	11
27	0	27	+4.9	58.5	16.0	238	70	6	27.3	3	47	3	43	10	29	17	23	17	30
28	1	20	+9.1	58.1	15.8	250	70	2	28.3	4	15	4	07	11	20	18	37	18	47
29	2	13	+12.7	57.5	15.7	262	59	0	29.3	4	46	4	34	12	11	19	47	20	01
30	3	07	+15.6	56.9	15.5	274	265	1	0.8	5	20	5	06	13	02	20	53	21	10

MERCURY

Day	*R.A.*		*Dec.*	*Diam.*	*Phase*	*Transit*		*5° high* 52°		56°	
	h	*m*	°	″	%	*h*	*m*	*h*	*m*	*h*	*m*
1	23	24	−6.5	6	77	10	48	5	53	6	02
3	23	36	−5.3	6	79	10	52	5	51	5	58
5	23	48	−4.0	6	81	10	56	5	48	5	54
7	0	00	−2.6	5	83	11	00	5	45	5	50
9	0	12	−1.2	5	86	11	05	5	42	5	46
11	0	25	+0.3	5	88	11	10	5	39	5	42
13	0	38	+1.9	5	90	11	15	5	36	5	38
15	0	52	+3.5	5	92	11	21	5	34	5	34
17	1	06	+5.2	5	94	11	27	5	31	5	30
19	1	20	+6.9	5	96	11	33	5	29	5	27
21	1	35	+8.6	5	98	11	40	5	27	5	23
23	1	50	+10.4	5	99	11	48	5	25	5	20
25	2	05	+12.1	5	100	11	56	5	24	5	17
27	2	22	+13.9	5	100	12	04	18	48	18	57
29	2	38	+15.5	5	99	12	13	19	06	19	16
31	2	55	+17.2	5	97	12	21	19	24	19	36

VENUS

Day	*R.A.*		*Dec.*	*Diam.*	*Phase*	*Transit*		*5° high* 52°		56°	
	h	*m*	°	″	%	*h*	*m*	*h*	*m*	*h*	*m*
1	21	47	−12.3	22	54	9	10	4	50	5	05
6	22	08	−10.9	21	57	9	12	4	43	4	57
11	22	29	−9.4	20	59	9	13	4	36	4	48
16	22	50	−7.8	19	61	9	14	4	28	4	38
21	23	11	−6.0	18	63	9	15	4	19	4	28
26	23	32	−4.1	18	65	9	17	4	10	4	17
31	23	53	−2.1	17	67	9	18	4	01	4	06

MARS

Day	*R.A.*		*Dec.*	*Diam.*	*Phase*	*Transit*		*5° high* 52°		56°	
	h	*m*	°	″	%	*h*	*m*	*h*	*m*	*h*	*m*
1	13	25	−6.0	15	100	0	48	5	42	5	34
6	13	18	−5.5	15	100	0	21	5	19	5	11
11	13	11	−4.9	15	100	23	49	4	55	4	47
16	13	03	−4.3	15	100	23	22	4	31	4	24
21	12	56	−3.8	15	99	22	55	4	07	4	00
26	12	50	−3.4	15	99	22	29	3	43	3	37
31	12	44	−3.0	15	98	22	05	3	20	3	14

SUNRISE AND SUNSET

	London				*Bristol*				*Birmingham*				*Manchester*				*Newcastle*				*Glasgow*				*Belfast*			
	0° 05′		*51° 30′*		*2° 35′*		*51° 28′*		*1° 55′*		*52° 28′*		*2° 15′*		*53° 28′*		*1° 37′*		*54° 59′*		*4° 14′*		*55° 52′*		*5° 56′*		*54° 35′*	
d	*h*	*m*	*h*	*m*	*h*	*m*	*h*	*m*	*h*	*m*	*h*	*m*	*h*	*m*	*h*	*m*	*h*	*m*	*h*	*m*	*h*	*m*	*h*	*m*	*h*	*m*	*h*	*m*
1	5	36	18	33	5	46	18	43	5	42	18	42	5	43	18	44	5	39	18	43	5	48	18	55	5	56	19	00
2	5	34	18	35	5	44	18	45	5	40	18	43	5	40	18	46	5	36	18	45	5	45	18	57	5	54	19	02
3	5	32	18	37	5	42	18	47	5	38	18	45	5	38	18	48	5	34	18	47	5	43	18	59	5	51	19	04
4	5	29	18	38	5	39	18	48	5	36	18	47	5	36	18	50	5	31	18	49	5	40	19	01	5	49	19	06
5	5	27	18	40	5	37	18	50	5	33	18	49	5	33	18	51	5	29	18	51	5	38	19	03	5	46	19	08
6	5	25	18	42	5	35	18	52	5	31	18	50	5	31	18	53	5	26	18	53	5	35	19	05	5	44	19	10
7	5	23	18	43	5	33	18	53	5	29	18	52	5	28	18	55	5	24	18	55	5	33	19	07	5	41	19	12
8	5	20	18	45	5	30	18	55	5	26	18	54	5	26	18	57	5	21	18	57	5	30	19	09	5	39	19	13
9	5	18	18	47	5	28	18	57	5	24	18	56	5	24	18	59	5	19	18	59	5	27	19	11	5	37	19	15
10	5	16	18	48	5	26	18	58	5	22	18	57	5	21	19	00	5	16	19	01	5	25	19	13	5	34	19	17
11	5	14	18	50	5	24	19	00	5	19	18	59	5	19	19	02	5	14	19	03	5	22	19	15	5	32	19	19
12	5	12	18	52	5	22	19	02	5	17	19	01	5	17	19	04	5	11	19	05	5	20	19	17	5	29	19	21
13	5	09	18	53	5	19	19	03	5	15	19	03	5	14	19	06	5	09	19	07	5	17	19	19	5	27	19	23
14	5	07	18	55	5	17	19	05	5	13	19	04	5	12	19	08	5	06	19	09	5	15	19	21	5	24	19	25
15	5	05	18	57	5	15	19	07	5	10	19	06	5	10	19	10	5	04	19	11	5	12	19	23	5	22	19	27
16	5	03	18	58	5	13	19	08	5	08	19	08	5	07	19	11	5	01	19	12	5	10	19	25	5	20	19	29
17	5	01	19	00	5	11	19	10	5	06	19	10	5	05	19	13	4	59	19	14	5	07	19	27	5	17	19	31
18	4	59	19	02	5	09	19	12	5	04	19	11	5	03	19	15	4	57	19	16	5	05	19	29	5	15	19	33
19	4	57	19	03	5	07	19	13	5	02	19	13	5	01	19	17	4	54	19	18	5	02	19	31	5	12	19	35
20	4	54	19	05	5	04	19	15	4	59	19	15	4	58	19	19	4	52	19	20	5	00	19	33	5	10	19	36
21	4	52	19	07	5	02	19	17	4	57	19	17	4	56	19	21	4	49	19	22	4	57	19	35	5	08	19	38
22	4	50	19	08	5	00	19	18	4	55	19	18	4	54	19	22	4	47	19	24	4	55	19	37	5	05	19	40
23	4	48	19	10	4	58	19	20	4	53	19	20	4	52	19	24	4	45	19	26	4	52	19	39	5	03	19	42
24	4	46	19	12	4	56	19	22	4	51	19	22	4	50	19	26	4	42	19	28	4	50	19	41	5	01	19	44
25	4	44	19	13	4	54	19	23	4	49	19	24	4	47	19	28	4	40	19	30	4	48	19	43	4	59	19	46
26	4	42	19	15	4	52	19	25	4	47	19	25	4	45	19	30	4	38	19	32	4	45	19	45	4	56	19	48
27	4	40	19	17	4	50	19	27	4	45	19	27	4	43	19	31	4	36	19	34	4	43	19	47	4	54	19	50
28	4	38	19	18	4	48	19	28	4	43	19	29	4	41	19	33	4	33	19	36	4	41	19	49	4	52	19	52
29	4	36	19	20	4	46	19	30	4	41	19	30	4	39	19	35	4	31	19	38	4	38	19	51	4	50	19	54
30	4	34	19	22	4	45	19	32	4	39	19	32	4	37	19	37	4	29	19	40	4	36	19	54	4	48	19	55

JUPITER

Day	*R.A.*		*Dec.*		*Transit*		*5° high*			
							52°		*56°*	
	h	*m*	°	′	*h*	*m*	*h*	*m*	*h*	*m*
1	6	50.0	+23	13	18	10	1	46	2	04
11	6	54.0	+23	08	17	35	1	10	1	28
21	6	59.1	+23	02	17	01	0	35	0	53
31	7	05.1	+22	54	16	27	0	01	0	18

Diameters – equatorial 37″ polar 34″

SATURN

Day	*R.A.*		*Dec.*		*Transit*		*5° high*			
							52°		*56°*	
	h	*m*	°	′	*h*	*m*	*h*	*m*	*h*	*m*
1	15	23.4	−16	03	2	46	22	47	23	07
11	15	21.3	−15	54	2	04	22	04	22	24
21	15	18.8	−15	44	1	23	21	21	21	41
31	15	16.0	−15	32	0	40	20	38	20	57

Diameters – equatorial 18″ polar 17″

Rings – major axis 42″ minor axis 16″

URANUS

Day	*R.A.*		*Dec.*		*Transit*		*10° high*			
							52°		*56°*	
	h	*m*	°	′	*h*	*m*	*h*	*m*	*h*	*m*
1	0	46.6	+4	18	12	08	6	51	6	55
11	0	48.7	+4	31	11	30	6	13	6	16
21	0	50.8	+4	44	10	53	5	35	5	37
31	0	52.8	+4	57	10	16	4	56	4	59

Diameter 4″

NEPTUNE

Day	*R.A.*		*Dec.*		*Transit*		*10° high*			
							52°		*56°*	
	h	*m*	°	′	*h*	*m*	*h*	*m*	*h*	*m*
1	22	33.5	−9	49	9	55	5	57	6	15
11	22	34.7	−9	42	9	17	5	19	5	36
21	22	35.7	−9	36	8	38	4	40	4	57
31	22	36.6	−9	31	8	00	4	01	4	18

Diameter 2″

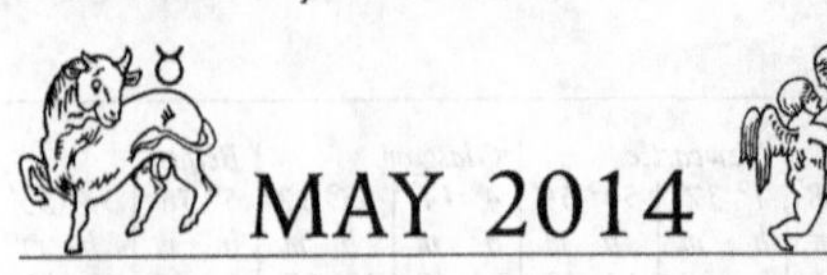

MAY 2014

FIFTH MONTH, 31 DAYS. *Maia*, goddess of growth and increase

1	*Thursday*	Queen Victoria opens the Great Exhibition at Hyde Park, celebrating the Industrial Revolution 1851	day 121
2	*Friday*	Mary, Queen of Scots, escapes from imprisonment in Lochleven Castle and raises an army of 6,000 1568	122
3	*Saturday*	King George VI declares the opening of the Festival of Britain 1951	123
4	*Sunday*	The House of York wins the Battle of Tewkesbury, a decisive clash during the Wars of the Roses 1471	124
5	*Monday*	The Short Parliament is dissolved by King Charles I three weeks after he summoned it 1640	week 18 day 125
6	*Tuesday*	King Edward VII, who reigned from 1901–1910, House of Saxe-Coburg and Gotha *d.* 1910	126
7	*Wednesday*	Mary of Modena, 2nd wife of King James II, exiled in France due to the Glorious Revolution *d.* 1718	127
8	*Thursday*	VE (Victory in Europe) Day radio broadcast by King George VI 1945	128
9	*Friday*	Thomas Blood's attempted theft of the crown jewels is rewarded by King Charles II 1671	129
10	*Saturday*	Journalist John Wilkes is imprisoned for writing an article attacking King George III 1768	130
11	*Sunday*	Gordon Brown resigns as prime minister after tendering his resignation to Queen Elizabeth II 2010	131
12	*Monday*	Coronation of King George VI at Westminster Abbey 1937	week 19 day 132
13	*Tuesday*	Mary, Queen of Scots, flees after her army is defeated at the Battle of Langside by the Earl of Moray 1568	133
14	*Wednesday*	Simon de Montfort captures King Henry III at the Battle of Lewes during the Barons' War 1264	134
15	*Thursday*	James Hadfield fires a pistol at King George III but misses in the Drury Lane Theatre 1800	135
16	*Friday*	Queen Elizabeth II becomes the first British monarch to address the United States Congress 1991	136
17	*Saturday*	Coronation of King Henry III at Westminster Abbey 1220	137
18	*Sunday*	King Henry II marries Eleanor of Aquitaine; he later imprisoned Eleanor for 15 years 1152	138
19	*Monday*	Irishman William Hamilton attempts to shoot Queen Victoria as her carriage passes 1849	week 20 day 139
20	*Tuesday*	Funeral of King Edward VII at St George's Chapel, Windsor Castle 1910	140
21	*Wednesday*	Charles VI of France and King Henry V sign the Treaty of Troyes 1420; King Henry VI *d.* 1471	141
22	*Thursday*	The Treaty of Le Goulet is signed by King John and King Philip II of France 1200	142
23	*Friday*	King Henry VIII's marriage to Catherine of Aragon is annulled, allowing him to marry Anne Boleyn 1533	143
24	*Saturday*	Queen Victoria, who reigned from 1837–1901, House of Hanover *b.* 1819	144
25	*Sunday*	Richard Cromwell, the third son of Oliver Cromwell, resigns as second Lord Protector of England 1659	145
26	*Monday*	The new Vauxhall Bridge is opened in London by the Prince of Wales (King George V) 1906	week 21 day 146
27	*Tuesday*	Coronation of King John at Westminster Abbey 1199	147
28	*Wednesday*	King George I, reign 1714–1727, House of Hanover *b.* 1660; King Edward VIII, House of Windsor *d.* 1972	148
29	*Thursday*	King Charles II, who reigned from 1660–1685, House of Stuart *b.* 1630	149
30	*Friday*	John Francis' second assassination attempt on Queen Victoria on The Mall, London 1842	150
31	*Saturday*	Margaret Beaufort, the mother of King Henry VII and descendent of King Edward III *b.* 1443	151

ASTRONOMICAL PHENOMENA

d	*h*	
4	13	Jupiter in conjunction with Moon. Jupiter 5°N.
10	18	Saturn at opposition
11	11	Mars in conjunction with Moon. Mars 3°N.
14	12	Saturn in conjunction with Moon. Saturn 0°.6 N.
20	02	Mars at stationary point
21	03	Sun's longitude 60° ♊
25	07	Mercury at greatest elongation E. 23°
25	14	Venus in conjunction with Moon. Venus 2°S.
30	16	Mercury in conjunction with Moon. Mercury 6°N.

MINIMA OF ALGOL

Algol is inconveniently situated for observation during May

CONSTELLATIONS

The following constellations are near the meridian at

	d	*h*		*d*	*h*
April	1	24	May	16	21
April	15	23	June	1	20
May	1	22	June	15	19

Cepheus (below the Pole), Cassiopeia (below the Pole), Ursa Minor, Ursa Major, Canes Venatici, Coma Berenices, Bootes, Leo, Virgo, Crater, Corvus and Hydra

THE MOON

Phases, Apsides and Node	*d*	*h*	*m*
☽ First Quarter	7	03	15
○ Full Moon	14	19	16
☾ Last Quarter	21	12	59
● New Moon	28	18	40
Apogee (404,357km)	6	10	24
Perigee (367,074km)	18	12	05

Mean longitude of ascending node on May 1, 208°

THE SUN

s.d. 15′.8

Day	Right Ascension h	m	s	Dec. + °	′	Equation of time m	s	Rise 52° h	m	Rise 56° h	m	Transit h	m	Set 52° h	m	Set 56° h	m	Sidereal time h	m	s	Transit of first point of Aries h	m	s
1	2	32	33	14	59	+2	51	4	31	4	16	11	57	19	25	19	39	14	35	23	9	23	04
2	2	36	22	15	17	+2	58	4	29	4	14	11	57	19	26	19	41	14	39	20	9	19	08
3	2	40	12	15	35	+3	04	4	27	4	12	11	57	19	28	19	43	14	43	17	9	15	12
4	2	44	03	15	53	+3	10	4	25	4	10	11	57	19	30	19	45	14	47	13	9	11	16
5	2	47	54	16	10	+3	16	4	23	4	08	11	57	19	31	19	47	14	51	10	9	07	20
6	2	51	46	16	27	+3	21	4	21	4	05	11	57	19	33	19	49	14	55	06	9	03	24
7	2	55	38	16	44	+3	25	4	20	4	03	11	57	19	35	19	51	14	59	03	8	59	29
8	2	59	30	17	00	+3	29	4	18	4	01	11	56	19	36	19	53	15	02	59	8	55	33
9	3	03	24	17	17	+3	32	4	16	3	59	11	56	19	38	19	55	15	06	56	8	51	37
10	3	07	17	17	33	+3	35	4	14	3	57	11	56	19	39	19	57	15	10	52	8	47	41
11	3	11	12	17	48	+3	37	4	13	3	55	11	56	19	41	19	59	15	14	49	8	43	45
12	3	15	07	18	03	+3	39	4	11	3	53	11	56	19	43	20	01	15	18	46	8	39	49
13	3	19	02	18	19	+3	40	4	09	3	51	11	56	19	44	20	03	15	22	42	8	35	53
14	3	22	58	18	33	+3	40	4	08	3	49	11	56	19	46	20	05	15	26	39	8	31	57
15	3	26	55	18	48	+3	40	4	06	3	47	11	56	19	47	20	06	15	30	35	8	28	01
16	3	30	52	19	02	+3	40	4	05	3	46	11	56	19	49	20	08	15	34	32	8	24	05
17	3	34	50	19	16	+3	38	4	03	3	44	11	56	19	50	20	10	15	38	28	8	20	09
18	3	38	48	19	29	+3	37	4	02	3	42	11	56	19	52	20	12	15	42	25	8	16	14
19	3	42	47	19	42	+3	34	4	01	3	40	11	56	19	53	20	14	15	46	21	8	12	18
20	3	46	47	19	55	+3	31	3	59	3	39	11	57	19	55	20	16	15	50	18	8	08	22
21	3	50	47	20	07	+3	28	3	58	3	37	11	57	19	56	20	17	15	54	15	8	04	26
22	3	54	47	20	19	+3	24	3	57	3	35	11	57	19	58	20	19	15	58	11	8	00	30
23	3	58	49	20	31	+3	19	3	55	3	34	11	57	19	59	20	21	16	02	08	7	56	34
24	4	02	50	20	43	+3	14	3	54	3	32	11	57	20	00	20	22	16	06	04	7	52	38
25	4	06	52	20	54	+3	08	3	53	3	31	11	57	20	02	20	24	16	10	01	7	48	42
26	4	10	55	21	04	+3	02	3	52	3	30	11	57	20	03	20	26	16	13	57	7	44	46
27	4	14	58	21	15	+2	56	3	51	3	28	11	57	20	04	20	27	16	17	54	7	40	50
28	4	19	02	21	25	+2	48	3	50	3	27	11	57	20	05	20	29	16	21	50	7	36	54
29	4	23	06	21	34	+2	41	3	49	3	26	11	57	20	07	20	30	16	25	47	7	32	59
30	4	27	11	21	43	+2	33	3	48	3	24	11	58	20	08	20	32	16	29	44	7	29	03
31	4	31	16	21	52	+2	24	3	47	3	23	11	58	20	09	20	33	16	33	40	7	25	07

DURATION OF TWILIGHT (in minutes)

Latitude	52°	56°	52°	56°	52°	56°	52°	56°
	1 May		*11 May*		*21 May*		*31 May*	
Civil	39	44	41	48	44	53	46	57
Nautical	89	106	97	120	106	141	115	187
Astronomical	152	204	176	TAN	TAN	TAN	TAN	TAN

THE NIGHT SKY

Mercury is an evening object after the first week of the month, visible in the evening sky, low above the north-western horizon after the end of civil twilight. During this period its magnitude fades noticeably from −1.1 to +1.3.

Venus, magnitude −4.0, is still a splendid object in the early mornings though still only visible for a short while low above the eastern horizon, for a short while before dawn.

Mars is still retrograding slowly in Virgo but reaches its second stationary point on the 20th and then resumes its direct motion. Its magnitude is −0.7. By the end of the month it will be lost to view over the western horizon well before midnight. The waxing gibbous Moon passes 4 degrees south of the planet on the 11th.

Jupiter, magnitude −1.9, is still visible as an evening object in the western sky in the early evenings until about 22h. The waxing crescent Moon passes 6 degrees south of Jupiter on the 4th.

Saturn, magnitude +0.2, reaches opposition on the 10th and is therefore visible throughout the hours of darkness, still in the constellation of Libra. Even in a small telescope the rings of Saturn are a beautiful sight. On the 14th of May the Full Moon passes 2 degrees south of the planet.

THE MOON

Day	R.A.		Dec.	Hor. Par.	Semi-diam.	Sun's Co-Long.	PA of Br. Limb	Ph.	Age	Rise				Transit		Set			
										52°		56°				52°		56°	
	h	m	°	′	′	°	°	%	d	h	m	h	m	h	m	h	m	h	m
1	4	01	+17.7	56.3	15.3	286	266	3	1.8	6	00	5	43	13	54	21	52	22	10
2	4	54	+18.8	55.7	15.2	299	269	8	2.8	6	45	6	27	14	45	22	44	23	03
3	5	47	+18.9	55.2	15.0	311	273	14	3.8	7	36	7	18	15	34	23	28	23	46
4	6	38	+18.2	54.7	14.9	323	277	22	4.8	8	31	8	14	16	22	—		—	
5	7	28	+16.6	54.4	14.8	335	281	30	5.8	9	30	9	15	17	09	0	06	0	21
6	8	16	+14.4	54.2	14.8	348	284	39	6.8	10	31	10	19	17	53	0	38	0	51
7	9	03	+11.5	54.3	14.8	360	287	49	7.8	11	33	11	25	18	37	1	05	1	15
8	9	50	+8.2	54.4	14.8	12	289	58	8.8	12	37	12	31	19	21	1	30	1	37
9	10	36	+4.5	54.8	14.9	24	290	68	9.8	13	42	13	40	20	04	1	53	1	57
10	11	22	+0.6	55.3	15.1	36	291	76	10.8	14	48	14	50	20	49	2	16	2	16
11	12	09	−3.4	55.9	15.2	49	291	84	11.8	15	56	16	02	21	35	2	39	2	36
12	12	58	−7.4	56.6	15.4	61	291	91	12.8	17	07	17	16	22	23	3	04	2	57
13	13	49	−11.2	57.4	15.6	73	291	96	13.8	18	18	18	31	23	15	3	32	3	21
14	14	43	−14.4	58.1	15.8	85	295	99	14.8	19	30	19	46	—		4	05	3	51
15	15	40	−17.0	58.7	16.0	97	59	100	15.8	20	38	20	57	0	10	4	44	4	28
16	16	39	−18.6	59.2	16.1	110	86	98	16.8	21	41	22	00	1	07	5	33	5	14
17	17	39	−19.0	59.5	16.2	122	84	94	17.8	22	35	22	53	2	06	6	31	6	12
18	18	40	−18.2	59.7	16.3	134	81	87	18.8	23	21	23	36	3	05	7	38	7	21
19	19	40	−16.2	59.7	16.3	146	77	78	19.8	23	59	—		4	03	8	51	8	37
20	20	38	−13.2	59.6	16.2	158	73	68	20.8	—		0	10	4	59	10	07	9	57
21	21	34	−9.5	59.3	16.2	170	71	56	21.8	0	31	0	39	5	52	11	24	11	17
22	22	28	−5.2	59.0	16.1	183	69	45	22.8	0	59	1	03	6	44	12	40	12	38
23	23	21	−0.7	58.6	16.0	195	68	34	23.8	1	25	1	26	7	34	13	56	13	57
24	0	13	+3.7	58.2	15.9	207	68	24	24.8	1	51	1	48	8	24	15	10	15	15
25	1	05	+7.9	57.7	15.7	219	68	15	25.8	2	18	2	11	9	14	16	22	16	32
26	1	57	+11.7	57.2	15.6	232	69	8	26.8	2	46	2	36	10	04	17	33	17	46
27	2	50	+14.8	56.7	15.5	244	69	3	27.8	3	19	3	05	10	54	18	40	18	55
28	3	43	+17.1	56.2	15.3	256	62	1	28.8	3	56	3	39	11	45	19	41	19	59
29	4	36	+18.5	55.7	15.2	268	315	0	0.3	4	38	4	20	12	36	20	36	20	55
30	5	29	+19.0	55.2	15.1	281	283	2	1.3	5	27	5	08	13	26	21	24	21	42
31	6	21	+18.6	54.8	14.9	293	282	5	2.3	6	20	6	02	14	15	22	05	22	21

MERCURY

Day	R.A.		Dec.	Diam.	Phase	Transit		5° high			
								52°		56°	
	h	m	°	″	%	h	m	h	m	h	m
1	2	55	+17.2	5	97	12	21	19	24	19	36
3	3	11	+18.7	5	94	12	30	19	41	19	55
5	3	28	+20.1	5	91	12	39	19	58	20	13
7	3	45	+21.3	6	86	12	48	20	13	20	30
9	4	01	+22.4	6	81	12	56	20	28	20	46
11	4	17	+23.3	6	75	13	04	20	41	21	00
13	4	32	+24.1	6	69	13	11	20	52	21	12
15	4	46	+24.7	6	63	13	17	21	02	21	22
17	5	00	+25.1	7	58	13	23	21	09	21	30
19	5	12	+25.4	7	52	13	27	21	15	21	36
21	5	24	+25.5	7	47	13	30	21	19	21	40
23	5	34	+25.5	8	42	13	33	21	21	21	42
25	5	44	+25.5	8	38	13	34	21	21	21	42
27	5	52	+25.3	8	33	13	34	21	19	21	40
29	5	59	+25.0	9	29	13	33	21	16	21	36
31	6	04	+24.7	9	25	13	30	21	11	21	30

VENUS

Day	R.A.		Dec.	Diam.	Phase	Transit		5° high			
								52°		56°	
	h	m	°	″	%	h	m	h	m	h	m
1	23	53	−2.1	17	67	9	18	4	01	4	06
6	0	15	0.0	16	69	9	20	3	52	3	55
11	0	36	+2.0	16	70	9	21	3	43	3	45
16	0	57	+4.1	15	72	9	23	3	34	3	34
21	1	19	+6.2	15	74	9	25	3	25	3	23
26	1	41	+8.3	14	75	9	27	3	17	3	13
31	2	03	+10.4	14	77	9	30	3	09	3	03

MARS

Day	R.A.		Dec.	Diam.	Phase	Transit		5° high			
								52°		56°	
	h	m	°	″	%	h	m	h	m	h	m
1	12	44	−3.0	15	98	22	05	3	20	3	14
6	12	40	−2.8	14	97	21	41	2	57	2	52
11	12	37	−2.7	14	96	21	18	2	35	2	29
16	12	35	−2.7	13	94	20	57	2	13	2	08
21	12	34	−2.9	13	93	20	37	1	52	1	46
26	12	35	−3.1	12	92	20	18	1	32	1	26
31	12	36	−3.5	12	92	20	00	1	12	1	05

SUNRISE AND SUNSET

	London		*Bristol*		*Birmingham*		*Manchester*		*Newcastle*		*Glasgow*		*Belfast*	
	0° 05′	*51° 30′*	*2° 35′*	*51° 28′*	*1° 55′*	*52° 28′*	*2° 15′*	*53° 28′*	*1° 37′*	*54° 59′*	*4° 14′*	*55° 52′*	*5° 56′*	*54° 35′*
d	*h m*	*h m*	*h m*	*h m*	*h m*	*h m*	*h m*	*h m*	*h m*	*h m*	*h m*	*h m*	*h m*	*h m*
1	4 33	19 23	4 43	19 33	4 37	19 34	4 35	19 39	4 27	19 42	4 34	19 56	4 46	19 57
2	4 31	19 25	4 41	19 35	4 35	19 36	4 33	19 40	4 25	19 43	4 32	19 58	4 43	19 59
3	4 29	19 27	4 39	19 37	4 33	19 37	4 31	19 42	4 23	19 45	4 29	20 00	4 41	20 01
4	4 27	19 28	4 37	19 38	4 31	19 39	4 29	19 44	4 20	19 47	4 27	20 02	4 39	20 03
5	4 25	19 30	4 35	19 40	4 29	19 41	4 27	19 46	4 18	19 49	4 25	20 03	4 37	20 05
6	4 23	19 32	4 34	19 41	4 27	19 42	4 25	19 47	4 16	19 51	4 23	20 05	4 35	20 07
7	4 22	19 33	4 32	19 43	4 26	19 44	4 23	19 49	4 14	19 53	4 21	20 07	4 33	20 09
8	4 20	19 35	4 30	19 45	4 24	19 46	4 21	19 51	4 12	19 55	4 19	20 09	4 31	20 10
9	4 18	19 36	4 28	19 46	4 22	19 47	4 19	19 53	4 10	19 57	4 17	20 11	4 29	20 12
10	4 17	19 38	4 27	19 48	4 20	19 49	4 18	19 54	4 08	19 59	4 15	20 13	4 27	20 14
11	4 15	19 39	4 25	19 49	4 19	19 51	4 16	19 56	4 06	20 00	4 13	20 15	4 26	20 16
12	4 13	19 41	4 24	19 51	4 17	19 52	4 14	19 58	4 05	20 02	4 11	20 17	4 24	20 18
13	4 12	19 42	4 22	19 52	4 15	19 54	4 12	19 59	4 03	20 04	4 09	20 19	4 22	20 19
14	4 10	19 44	4 20	19 54	4 14	19 55	4 11	20 01	4 01	20 06	4 07	20 21	4 20	20 21
15	4 09	19 46	4 19	19 55	4 12	19 57	4 09	20 03	3 59	20 08	4 05	20 23	4 18	20 23
16	4 07	19 47	4 17	19 57	4 11	19 59	4 07	20 04	3 57	20 09	4 03	20 25	4 17	20 25
17	4 06	19 48	4 16	19 58	4 09	20 00	4 06	20 06	3 56	20 11	4 01	20 26	4 15	20 26
18	4 04	19 50	4 15	20 00	4 08	20 02	4 04	20 08	3 54	20 13	4 00	20 28	4 13	20 28
19	4 03	19 51	4 13	20 01	4 06	20 03	4 03	20 09	3 52	20 15	3 58	20 30	4 12	20 30
20	4 02	19 53	4 12	20 03	4 05	20 05	4 01	20 11	3 51	20 16	3 56	20 32	4 10	20 31
21	4 00	19 54	4 11	20 04	4 03	20 06	4 00	20 12	3 49	20 18	3 55	20 33	4 09	20 33
22	3 59	19 56	4 09	20 05	4 02	20 07	3 58	20 14	3 48	20 19	3 53	20 35	4 07	20 35
23	3 58	19 57	4 08	20 07	4 01	20 09	3 57	20 15	3 46	20 21	3 52	20 37	4 06	20 36
24	3 57	19 58	4 07	20 08	4 00	20 10	3 56	20 17	3 45	20 23	3 50	20 38	4 04	20 38
25	3 56	20 00	4 06	20 09	3 58	20 12	3 55	20 18	3 44	20 24	3 49	20 40	4 03	20 39
26	3 55	20 01	4 05	20 11	3 57	20 13	3 53	20 20	3 42	20 26	3 47	20 42	4 02	20 41
27	3 54	20 02	4 04	20 12	3 56	20 14	3 52	20 21	3 41	20 27	3 46	20 43	4 01	20 42
28	3 53	20 03	4 03	20 13	3 55	20 16	3 51	20 22	3 40	20 29	3 45	20 45	3 59	20 43
29	3 52	20 05	4 02	20 14	3 54	20 17	3 50	20 24	3 39	20 30	3 43	20 46	3 58	20 45
30	3 51	20 06	4 01	20 16	3 53	20 18	3 49	20 25	3 37	20 31	3 42	20 48	3 57	20 46
31	3 50	20 07	4 00	20 17	3 52	20 19	3 48	20 26	3 36	20 33	3 41	20 49	3 56	20 48

JUPITER

Day	*R.A.*		*Dec.*		*Transit*		*5° high*			
							52°		*56°*	
	h	*m*	°	′	*h*	*m*	*h*	*m*	*h*	*m*
1	7	05.1	+22	54	16	27	0	01	0	18
11	7	12.0	+22	43	15	55	23	24	23	41
21	7	19.5	+22	30	15	23	22	51	23	08
31	7	27.5	+22	15	14	52	22	18	22	35

Diameters – equatorial 34″ polar 32″

SATURN

Day	*R.A.*		*Dec.*		*Transit*		*5° high*			
							52°		*56°*	
	h	*m*	°	′	*h*	*m*	*h*	*m*	*h*	*m*
1	15	16.0	–15	32	0	40	4	39	4	20
11	15	13.0	–15	21	23	54	3	58	3	39
21	15	10.0	–15	09	23	12	3	17	2	58
31	15	07.2	–14	59	22	30	2	36	2	17

Diameters – equatorial 19″ polar 17″
Rings – major axis 42″ minor axis 16″

URANUS

Day	*R.A.*		*Dec.*		*Transit*		*10° high*			
							52°		*56°*	
	h	*m*	°	′	*h*	*m*	*h*	*m*	*h*	*m*
1	0	52.8	+4	57	10	16	4	56	4	59
11	0	54.7	+5	09	9	38	4	18	4	20
21	0	56.4	+5	19	9	01	3	39	3	42
31	0	57.9	+5	29	8	23	3	01	3	03

Diameter 4″

NEPTUNE

Day	*R.A.*		*Dec.*		*Transit*		*10° high*			
							52°		*56°*	
	h	*m*	°	′	*h*	*m*	*h*	*m*	*h*	*m*
1	22	36.6	–9	31	8	00	4	01	4	18
11	22	37.3	–9	28	7	21	3	22	3	39
21	22	37.8	–9	25	6	42	2	43	2	59
31	22	38.1	–9	23	6	03	2	03	2	20

Diameter 2″

JUNE 2014

SIXTH MONTH, 30 DAYS. *Junius*, Roman *gens* (family)

1	*Sunday*	Anne Boleyn, mother of Elizabeth I, is crowned Queen Consort of England 1533	day 152
2	*Monday*	Coronation of Queen Elizabeth II at Westminster Abbey 1953	week 22 day 153
3	*Tuesday*	King George V, who reigned from 1910–1936, House of Windsor *b.* 1865	154
4	*Wednesday*	King George III, who reigned from 1760–1820, House of Hanover *b.* 1738	155
5	*Thursday*	Edmund 'Crouchback', named after the cross worn on the backs of Crusaders, son of King Henry III *d.* 1296	156
6	*Friday*	Southwark Bridge, crossing the Thames, is opened by King George V and Queen Consort Mary 1921	157
7	*Saturday*	Anne of Bohemia, first wife of King Richard II *d.* 1394	158
8	*Sunday*	King Richard I arrives at Acre in Palestine, beginning a siege during the Third Crusade 1191	159
9	*Monday*	A revamped Gatwick airport, costing £7.8m to build, is opened by Queen Elizabeth II 1958	week 23 day 160
10	*Tuesday*	18-year-old Edward Oxford attempts to assassinate Queen Victoria but both shots miss 1840	161
11	*Wednesday*	King Henry VIII marries his first wife, Catherine of Aragon 1509; King George I *d.* 1727	162
12	*Thursday*	Queen Elizabeth II opens Shakespeare's Globe, reconstructed home of Shakespearian theatre 1997	163
13	*Friday*	Kathy Burke, actor and comedian who played Queen Mary I in the 1998 film *Elizabeth* *b.* 1964	164
14	*Saturday*	The Parliamentarian New Model Army defeats the forces of King Charles I at the Battle of Naseby 1645	165
15	*Sunday*	King John seals the draft of the Magna Carta containing 63 clauses, at Runnymede 1215	166
16	*Monday*	The Battle of Stoke Field, the last battle of the Wars of the Roses, establishes Tudor dynasty 1487	week 24 day 167
17	*Tuesday*	King Edward I 'Longshanks', who reigned from 1272–1307, House of Plantagenet *b.* 1239	168
18	*Wednesday*	King Charles I is crowned King of Scots in Edinburgh 1633	169
19	*Thursday*	King John signs the Magna Carta at Runnymede 1215; King James I, who reigned from 1603–1625 *b.* 1566	170
20	*Friday*	King William IV, who reigned from 1830–1837, House of Hanover *d.* 1837	171
21	*Saturday*	King Edward III, who reigned from 1327–1377, House of Plantagenet *d.* 1377	172
22	*Sunday*	Diamond Jubilee of Queen Victoria 1897; Coronation of King George V at Westminster Abbey 1911	173
23	*Monday*	King Edward VIII, who reigned from January–December 1936, House of Windsor *b.* 1894	week 25 day 174
24	*Tuesday*	Coronation of King Henry VIII at Westminster Abbey 1509	175
25	*Wednesday*	Beatrice of England, daughter of King Henry III and sister of King Edward I *b.* 1242	176
26	*Thursday*	King George IV, who reigned from 1820–1830, House of Hanover *d.* 1830	177
27	*Friday*	Former British army officer Robert Pate injures Queen Victoria after hitting her with his cane 1850	178
28	*Saturday*	King Henry VIII, reign 1509–1547 *b.* 1491; Coronation of Queen Victoria at Westminster Abbey 1838	179
29	*Sunday*	Coronation of King Edward IV at Westminster Abbey 1461	180
30	*Monday*	Princess Henrietta, daughter of King Charles I, who fled to France at the age of 3 *d.* 1670	week 26 day 181

ASTRONOMICAL PHENOMENA

d	*h*	
1	07	Jupiter in conjunction with Moon. Jupiter 5°N.
7	12	Mercury at stationary point
8	00	Mars in conjunction with Moon. Mars 2°N.
9	20	Neptune at stationary point
10	19	Saturn in conjunction with Moon. Saturn 0°.6 N.
19	23	Mercury in inferior conjunction
21	11	Sun's longitude 90° ♋
24	13	Venus in conjunction with Moon. Venus 1°N.
26	12	Mercury in conjunction with Moon. Mercury 0°.3 S.
29	01	Jupiter in conjunction with Moon. Jupiter 5°N.

MINIMA OF ALGOL

Algol is inconveniently situated for observation during June

CONSTELLATIONS

The following constellations are near the meridian at

	d	*h*		*d*	*h*
May	1	24	June	15	21
May	16	23	July	1	20
June	1	22	July	16	19

Cassiopeia (below the Pole), Ursa Minor, Draco, Ursa Major, Canes Venatici, Bootes, Corona, Serpens, Virgo and Libra

THE MOON

Phases, Apsides and Node	*d*	*h*	*m*
☽ First Quarter	5	20	39
○ Full Moon	13	04	11
☾ Last Quarter	19	18	39
● New Moon	27	08	08
Apogee (404,988km)	3	04	30
Perigee (362,048km)	15	03	36
Apogee (405,953km)	30	19	19

Mean longitude of ascending node on June 1, 206°

THE SUN

s.d. 15′.8

Day	Right Ascension			Dec. +		Equation of time		Rise 52°		Rise 56°		Transit		Set 52°		Set 56°		Sidereal time			Transit of first point of Aries		
	h	*m*	*s*	°	′	*m*	*s*	*h*	*m*	*h*	*m*	*h*	*m*	*h*	*m*	*h*	*m*	*h*	*m*	*s*	*h*	*m*	*s*
1	4	35	21	22	01	+2	15	3	46	3	22	11	58	20	10	20	34	16	37	37	7	21	11
2	4	39	27	22	09	+2	06	3	45	3	21	11	58	20	11	20	36	16	41	33	7	17	15
3	4	43	33	22	16	+1	56	3	45	3	20	11	58	20	12	20	37	16	45	30	7	13	19
4	4	47	40	22	24	+1	46	3	44	3	19	11	58	20	13	20	38	16	49	26	7	09	23
5	4	51	47	22	31	+1	36	3	43	3	18	11	58	20	14	20	39	16	53	23	7	05	27
6	4	55	54	22	37	+1	25	3	43	3	18	11	59	20	15	20	40	16	57	19	7	01	31
7	5	00	02	22	43	+1	14	3	42	3	17	11	59	20	16	20	42	17	01	16	6	57	35
8	5	04	09	22	49	+1	03	3	42	3	16	11	59	20	17	20	43	17	05	13	6	53	39
9	5	08	17	22	54	+0	52	3	41	3	16	11	59	20	18	20	44	17	09	09	6	49	44
10	5	12	26	22	59	+0	40	3	41	3	15	11	59	20	19	20	44	17	13	06	6	45	48
11	5	16	34	23	04	+0	28	3	40	3	14	12	00	20	19	20	45	17	17	02	6	41	52
12	5	20	43	23	08	+0	16	3	40	3	14	12	00	20	20	20	46	17	20	59	6	37	56
13	5	24	52	23	11	+0	04	3	40	3	14	12	00	20	21	20	47	17	24	55	6	34	00
14	5	29	01	23	15	−0	09	3	40	3	13	12	00	20	21	20	47	17	28	52	6	30	04
15	5	33	10	23	18	−0	22	3	39	3	13	12	00	20	22	20	48	17	32	48	6	26	08
16	5	37	19	23	20	−0	34	3	39	3	13	12	01	20	22	20	49	17	36	45	6	22	12
17	5	41	29	23	22	−0	47	3	39	3	13	12	01	20	23	20	49	17	40	42	6	18	16
18	5	45	38	23	24	−1	00	3	39	3	13	12	01	20	23	20	50	17	44	38	6	14	20
19	5	49	48	23	25	−1	13	3	39	3	13	12	01	20	23	20	50	17	48	35	6	10	24
20	5	53	57	23	26	−1	26	3	40	3	13	12	02	20	24	20	50	17	52	31	6	06	29
21	5	58	07	23	26	−1	39	3	40	3	13	12	02	20	24	20	50	17	56	28	6	02	33
22	6	02	17	23	26	−1	52	3	40	3	13	12	02	20	24	20	51	18	00	24	5	58	37
23	6	06	26	23	26	−2	05	3	40	3	14	12	02	20	24	20	51	18	04	21	5	54	41
24	6	10	36	23	25	−2	18	3	41	3	14	12	02	20	24	20	51	18	08	17	5	50	45
25	6	14	45	23	23	−2	31	3	41	3	14	12	03	20	24	20	51	18	12	14	5	46	49
26	6	18	55	23	22	−2	44	3	41	3	15	12	03	20	24	20	51	18	16	11	5	42	53
27	6	23	04	23	20	−2	57	3	42	3	15	12	03	20	24	20	50	18	20	07	5	38	57
28	6	27	13	23	17	−3	09	3	42	3	16	12	03	20	24	20	50	18	24	04	5	35	01
29	6	31	22	23	14	−3	22	3	43	3	17	12	03	20	24	20	50	18	28	00	5	31	05
30	6	35	31	23	11	−3	34	3	44	3	17	12	04	20	23	20	49	18	31	57	5	27	09

DURATION OF TWILIGHT (in minutes)

Latitude	52°	56°	52°	56°	52°	56°	52°	56°
	1 June		*11 June*		*21 June*		*31 June*	
Civil	46	58	48	61	49	63	48	61
Nautical	116	TAN	124	TAN	127	TAN	124	TAN
Astronomical	TAN	TAN	TAN	TAN	TAN	TAN	TAN	TAN

THE NIGHT SKY

Mercury is unsuitably placed for observation during the month, as it passes through inferior conjunction on the 19th.

Venus, magnitude −3.9, continues to be visible as a splendid object in the early morning skies, low above the eastern horizon before dawn. Each morning it becomes visible for a little longer as the month progresses. This effect is the result of the planet's northward movement in declination which more than offsets the fact that it is slowly moving in towards the Sun. On the morning of the 24th the waning crescent Moon passes 2 degrees south of the planet.

Mars, magnitude −0.2, is still an evening object in the south-western sky, but no longer visible after 23h by the end of the month.

Jupiter, magnitude −1.8, is coming towards the end of its evening apparition and will be lost in the evening twilight by the end of the month. On the first day of the month the waxing crescent Moon passes 6 degrees south of Jupiter. On the 21st Jupiter, still in Gemini, passes 6 degrees south of Pollux.

Saturn, magnitude +0.3, continues to be visible as an evening object in the south-western sky. By the end of the month it will no longer be visible after midnight. On the evening of the 10th the waxing gibbous Moon passes about 1 degree south of the planet.

Twilight. Reference to the section above shows that astronomical twilight lasts all night for a period around the summer solstice (ie in June and July), even in southern England. Under these conditions the sky never gets completely dark as the Sun is always less than 18 degrees below the horizon.

THE MOON

Day	R.A.		Dec.	Hor. Par.	Semi-diam.	Sun's Co-Long.	PA. of Br. Limb	Ph.	Age	Rise				Transit		Set			
										52°		56°				52°		56°	
	h	m	°	′	′	°	°	%	d	h	m	h	m	h	m	h	m	h	m
1	7	12	+17.3	54.5	14.8	305	284	10	3.3	7	18	7	02	15	03	22	39	22	53
2	8	01	+15.3	54.2	14.8	317	286	17	4.3	8	18	8	05	15	48	23	08	23	19
3	8	48	+12.6	54.1	14.8	330	289	24	5.3	9	20	9	10	16	32	23	34	23	42
4	9	35	+9.5	54.2	14.8	342	290	33	6.3	10	23	10	16	17	16	23	57	—	
5	10	21	+5.9	54.4	14.8	354	292	42	7.3	11	26	11	23	17	58	—		0	02
6	11	06	+2.1	54.8	14.9	6	293	51	8.3	12	31	12	31	18	42	0	19	0	21
7	11	52	−1.8	55.3	15.1	18	293	61	9.3	13	37	13	41	19	26	0	42	0	40
8	12	40	−5.8	56.0	15.3	31	292	71	10.3	14	45	14	53	20	13	1	05	1	00
9	13	29	−9.6	56.8	15.5	43	291	80	11.3	15	56	16	07	21	02	1	31	1	22
10	14	21	−13.1	57.7	15.7	55	290	87	12.3	17	07	17	22	21	55	2	01	1	49
11	15	17	−16.0	58.6	16.0	67	289	94	13.3	18	18	18	36	22	51	2	37	2	21
12	16	15	−18.1	59.3	16.2	79	291	98	14.3	19	25	19	44	23	51	3	21	3	03
13	17	16	−19.0	60.0	16.3	92	334	100	15.3	20	25	20	44	—		4	15	3	56
14	18	18	−18.7	60.4	16.5	104	66	99	16.3	21	16	21	33	0	51	5	20	5	01
15	19	20	−17.1	60.6	16.5	116	72	95	17.3	21	58	22	12	1	52	6	33	6	17
16	20	21	−14.3	60.5	16.5	128	71	89	18.3	22	34	22	43	2	50	7	51	7	38
17	21	19	−10.7	60.2	16.4	140	69	80	19.3	23	04	23	10	3	47	9	10	9	02
18	22	15	−6.5	59.7	16.3	153	67	70	20.3	23	31	23	33	4	40	10	28	10	24
19	23	09	−2.0	59.1	16.1	165	67	59	21.3	23	57	23	55	5	32	11	45	11	45
20	0	02	+2.6	58.5	15.9	177	67	48	22.3	—		—		6	22	13	00	13	04
21	0	54	+6.9	57.8	15.8	189	68	37	23.3	0	23	0	18	7	12	14	13	14	21
22	1	46	+10.7	57.2	15.6	202	69	27	24.3	0	51	0	42	8	01	15	23	15	35
23	2	37	+14.0	56.6	15.4	214	71	18	25.3	1	21	1	09	8	51	16	30	16	45
24	3	30	+16.5	56.1	15.3	226	73	11	26.3	1	56	1	40	9	41	17	33	17	50
25	4	22	+18.2	55.6	15.1	238	74	5	27.3	2	36	2	18	10	31	18	30	18	49
26	5	14	+19.0	55.1	15.0	250	71	2	28.3	3	21	3	02	11	21	19	20	19	39
27	6	06	+18.8	54.7	14.9	263	40	0	29.3	4	12	3	54	12	10	20	03	20	21
28	6	57	+17.8	54.4	14.8	275	309	1	0.7	5	08	4	51	12	58	20	40	20	55
29	7	47	+16.1	54.2	14.8	287	295	3	1.7	6	08	5	53	13	44	21	11	21	24
30	8	35	+13.6	54.1	14.7	299	293	7	2.7	7	09	6	57	14	29	21	38	21	48

MERCURY

Day	R.A.		Dec.	Diam.	Phase	Transit		5° high			
								52°		56°	
	h	m	°	″	%	h	m	h	m	h	m
1	6	07	+24.5	10	23	13	28	21	07	21	27
3	6	10	+24.0	10	19	13	24	21	00	21	18
5	6	13	+23.5	10	15	13	18	20	50	21	08
7	6	14	+23.0	11	12	13	10	20	39	20	57
9	6	13	+22.5	11	9	13	02	20	27	20	44
11	6	12	+21.9	12	6	12	52	20	14	20	30
13	6	09	+21.4	12	4	12	41	20	00	20	15
15	6	05	+20.8	12	2	12	29	19	45	20	00
17	6	01	+20.3	12	1	12	17	19	29	19	44
19	5	56	+19.8	12	1	12	04	19	14	19	28
21	5	51	+19.4	12	1	11	52	4	44	4	30
23	5	47	+19.1	12	2	11	40	4	33	4	20
25	5	43	+18.9	12	3	11	28	4	23	4	10
27	5	40	+18.7	11	5	11	17	4	12	4	00
29	5	37	+18.7	11	8	11	07	4	03	3	50
31	5	36	+18.8	11	11	10	59	3	54	3	41

VENUS

Day	R.A.		Dec.	Diam.	Phase	Transit		5° high			
								52°		56°	
	h	m	°	″	%	h	m	h	m	h	m
1	2	08	+10.8	14	77	9	30	3	07	3	01
6	2	30	+12.7	13	79	9	33	3	00	2	53
11	2	53	+14.5	13	80	9	36	2	53	2	44
16	3	17	+16.2	13	82	9	40	2	48	2	37
21	3	41	+17.8	13	83	9	44	2	43	2	31
26	4	05	+19.2	12	84	9	49	2	40	2	26
31	4	30	+20.4	12	85	9	54	2	38	2	23

MARS

Day	R.A.		Dec.	Diam.	Phase	Transit		5° high			
								52°		56°	
	h	m	°	″	%	h	m	h	m	h	m
1	12	37	−3.6	12	91	19	56	1	08	1	01
6	12	40	−4.1	11	91	19	40	0	48	0	42
11	12	44	−4.7	11	90	19	24	0	30	0	22
16	12	48	−5.3	11	89	19	09	0	11	0	03
21	12	54	−6.0	10	89	18	55	23	49	23	41
26	13	00	−6.8	10	88	18	42	23	32	23	22
31	13	07	−7.6	9	88	18	29	23	14	23	04

SUNRISE AND SUNSET

	London				*Bristol*				*Birmingham*				*Manchester*				*Newcastle*				*Glasgow*				*Belfast*			
	0° 05′		*51° 30′*		*2° 35′*		*51° 28′*		*1° 55′*		*52° 28′*		*2° 15′*		*53° 28′*		*1° 37′*		*54° 59′*		*4° 14′*		*55° 52′*		*5° 56′*		*54° 35′*	
d	*h*	*m*	*h*	*m*	*h*	*m*	*h*	*m*	*h*	*m*	*h*	*m*	*h*	*m*	*h*	*m*	*h*	*m*	*h*	*m*	*h*	*m*	*h*	*m*	*h*	*m*	*h*	*m*
1	3	49	20	08	3	59	20	18	3	51	20	20	3	47	20	27	3	35	20	34	3	40	20	50	3	55	20	49
2	3	48	20	09	3	58	20	19	3	50	20	21	3	46	20	28	3	34	20	35	3	39	20	52	3	54	20	50
3	3	48	20	10	3	58	20	20	3	50	20	23	3	45	20	30	3	33	20	36	3	38	20	53	3	53	20	51
4	3	47	20	11	3	57	20	21	3	49	20	24	3	45	20	31	3	33	20	38	3	37	20	54	3	52	20	52
5	3	46	20	12	3	56	20	22	3	48	20	25	3	44	20	32	3	32	20	39	3	36	20	55	3	52	20	53
6	3	46	20	13	3	56	20	23	3	48	20	26	3	43	20	33	3	31	20	40	3	35	20	56	3	51	20	54
7	3	45	20	14	3	55	20	24	3	47	20	26	3	43	20	34	3	30	20	41	3	35	20	58	3	50	20	55
8	3	45	20	15	3	55	20	24	3	47	20	27	3	42	20	35	3	30	20	42	3	34	20	59	3	50	20	56
9	3	44	20	15	3	54	20	25	3	46	20	28	3	42	20	35	3	29	20	43	3	33	20	59	3	49	20	57
10	3	44	20	16	3	54	20	26	3	46	20	29	3	41	20	36	3	29	20	44	3	33	21	00	3	49	20	58
11	3	43	20	17	3	54	20	27	3	45	20	30	3	41	20	37	3	28	20	44	3	32	21	01	3	48	20	59
12	3	43	20	18	3	53	20	27	3	45	20	30	3	40	20	38	3	28	20	45	3	32	21	02	3	48	21	00
13	3	43	20	18	3	53	20	28	3	45	20	31	3	40	20	38	3	27	20	46	3	32	21	03	3	48	21	00
14	3	43	20	19	3	53	20	28	3	45	20	32	3	40	20	39	3	27	20	47	3	31	21	03	3	47	21	01
15	3	43	20	19	3	53	20	29	3	44	20	32	3	40	20	40	3	27	20	47	3	31	21	04	3	47	21	02
16	3	43	20	20	3	53	20	29	3	44	20	33	3	40	20	40	3	27	20	48	3	31	21	05	3	47	21	02
17	3	43	20	20	3	53	20	30	3	44	20	33	3	39	20	40	3	27	20	48	3	31	21	05	3	47	21	03
18	3	43	20	20	3	53	20	30	3	44	20	33	3	40	20	41	3	27	20	49	3	31	21	05	3	47	21	03
19	3	43	20	21	3	53	20	31	3	44	20	34	3	40	20	41	3	27	20	49	3	31	21	06	3	47	21	03
20	3	43	20	21	3	53	20	31	3	44	20	34	3	40	20	41	3	27	20	49	3	31	21	06	3	47	21	04
21	3	43	20	21	3	53	20	31	3	45	20	34	3	40	20	42	3	27	20	49	3	31	21	06	3	47	21	04
22	3	43	20	21	3	53	20	31	3	45	20	34	3	40	20	42	3	27	20	50	3	31	21	06	3	47	21	04
23	3	43	20	22	3	54	20	31	3	45	20	34	3	40	20	42	3	28	20	50	3	32	21	07	3	48	21	04
24	3	44	20	22	3	54	20	31	3	46	20	35	3	41	20	42	3	28	20	50	3	32	21	07	3	48	21	04
25	3	44	20	22	3	54	20	31	3	46	20	35	3	41	20	42	3	28	20	50	3	32	21	07	3	48	21	04
26	3	45	20	22	3	55	20	31	3	46	20	34	3	42	20	42	3	29	20	50	3	33	21	06	3	49	21	04
27	3	45	20	22	3	55	20	31	3	47	20	34	3	42	20	42	3	29	20	49	3	33	21	06	3	49	21	04
28	3	46	20	21	3	56	20	31	3	47	20	34	3	43	20	42	3	30	20	49	3	34	21	06	3	50	21	04
29	3	46	20	21	3	56	20	31	3	48	20	34	3	43	20	41	3	31	20	49	3	35	21	06	3	51	21	03
30	3	47	20	21	3	57	20	31	3	49	20	34	3	44	20	41	3	31	20	49	3	35	21	05	3	51	21	03

JUPITER

Day	*R.A.*		*Dec.*		*Transit*		*5° high*			
							52°		*56°*	
	h	*m*	°	′	*h*	*m*	*h*	*m*	*h*	*m*
1	7	28.3	+22	13	14	49	22	15	22	31
11	7	36.9	+21	55	14	18	21	42	21	58
21	7	45.7	+21	34	13	48	21	09	21	25
31	7	54.8	+21	11	13	17	20	37	20	52

Diameters – equatorial 32″ polar 30″

SATURN

Day	*R.A.*		*Dec.*		*Transit*		*5° high*			
							52°		*56°*	
	h	*m*	°	′	*h*	*m*	*h*	*m*	*h*	*m*
1	15	06.9	–14	58	22	25	2	32	2	13
11	15	04.4	–14	49	21	44	1	51	1	33
21	15	02.3	–14	43	21	02	1	10	0	52
31	15	00.7	–14	38	20	21	0	30	0	12

Diameters – equatorial 18″ polar 17″
Rings – major axis 41″ minor axis 15″

URANUS

Day	*R.A.*		*Dec.*		*Transit*		*10° high*			
							52°		*56°*	
	h	*m*	°	′	*h*	*m*	*h*	*m*	*h*	*m*
1	0	58.1	+5	29	8	19	2	57	2	59
11	0	59.4	+5	37	7	41	2	18	2	20
21	1	00.4	+5	44	7	03	1	39	1	41
31	1	01.2	+5	48	6	24	1	01	1	02

Diameter 4″

NEPTUNE

Day	*R.A.*		*Dec.*		*Transit*		*10° high*			
							52°		*56°*	
	h	*m*	°	′	*h*	*m*	*h*	*m*	*h*	*m*
1	22	38.1	–9	23	6	00	2	00	2	16
11	22	38.2	–9	23	5	20	1	20	1	37
21	22	38.1	–9	24	4	41	0	41	0	58
31	22	37.8	–9	26	4	01	0	02	0	18

Diameter 2″

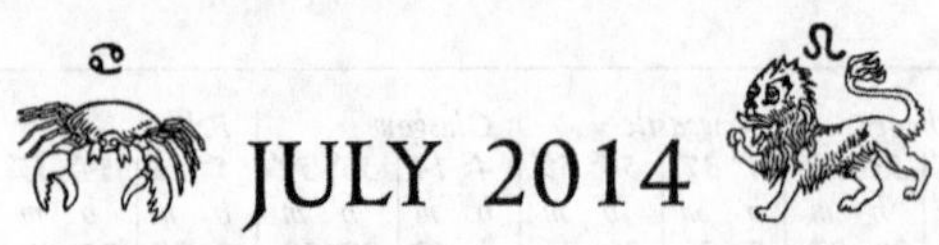

JULY 2014

SEVENTH MONTH, 31 DAYS. *Julius* Caesar, formerly *Quintilis*, fifth month of Roman pre-Julian calendar

1	*Tuesday*	Recently crowned William III (of Orange) defeats King James II at the Battle of the Boyne 1690	day 182
2	*Wednesday*	Parliamentarians defeat Royalists in the First English Civil War's Battle of Marston Moor 1644	183
3	*Thursday*	After being stolen in 1296, the Stone of Scone is returned to Scotland by the British government 1996	184
4	*Friday*	The Continental Congress issues the Declaration of Independence during King George III's reign 1776	185
5	*Saturday*	John Balliol, King of Scots, and King Philip IV of France form the Auld Alliance against King Edward I 1295	186
6	*Sunday*	King Henry II *d.* 1189; Coronation of King Richard III at Westminster Abbey 1483; King Edward VI *d.* 1553	187
7	*Monday*	King Edward I, who reigned from 1272–1307, House of Plantagenet *d.* 1307	week 27 day 188
8	*Tuesday*	Funeral of King William IV at St George's Chapel, Windsor 1837	189
9	*Wednesday*	Michael Fagan breaks into Buckingham Palace and spends ten minutes talking to Queen Elizabeth II 1982	190
10	*Thursday*	The Battle of Northampton, during the Wars of the Roses, is fought and King Henry VI is captured 1460	191
11	*Friday*	Pope Clement VII excommunicates King Henry VIII after his first marriage is annulled 1533	192
12	*Saturday*	Richard, Duke of Gloucester (King Richard III), marries Anne Neville at Westminster Abbey 1472	193
13	*Sunday*	The Royalists win the Battle of Roundway Down during the First English Civil War 1643	194
14	*Monday*	Louis VIII becomes King of France, seven years after being offered the English throne 1223	week 28 day 195
15	*Tuesday*	Funeral of King George IV at St George's Chapel, Windsor Castle 1830	196
16	*Wednesday*	Coronation of King Richard II 1377; Anne of Cleves, the fourth wife of King Henry VIII *d.* 1557	197
17	*Thursday*	King George V changes the name of the British royal house to the House of Windsor 1917	198
18	*Friday*	The Edict of Expulsion is issued by King Edward I, banishing all Jews from England 1290	199
19	*Saturday*	Coronation of King George IV at Westminster Abbey 1821	200
20	*Sunday*	The Warwolf, a large trebuchet, is used during the siege of Stirling Castle by King Edward I 1304	201
21	*Monday*	A rebellion led by Henry 'Hotspur' Percy is crushed by the army of King Henry IV 1403	week 29 day 202
22	*Tuesday*	Joan of England, the eldest legitimate daughter of King John and Queen Consort of Scotland *b.* 1210	203
23	*Wednesday*	Prince Andrew, Duke of York, marries Sarah Ferguson but they divorce ten years later 1986	204
24	*Thursday*	Mary, Queen of Scots, is forced to abdicate the throne to her infant son, who becomes King James VI 1567	205
25	*Friday*	Coronation of King James I at Westminster Abbey 1603	206
26	*Saturday*	Dame Helen Mirren, who won an Academy Award for her Queen Elizabeth II in *The Queen* *b.* 1945	207
27	*Sunday*	Queen Elizabeth II declares the London 2012 Olympic Games open, after acting with James Bond 2012	208
28	*Monday*	King Henry VIII marries his fifth wife, Catherine Howard 1540	week 30 day 209
29	*Tuesday*	James VI, King of Scots, is crowned in Stirling, 36 years before becoming King of England 1567	210
30	*Wednesday*	Prince Alfred Ernest Albert, fourth child of Queen Victoria and Prince Albert *d.* 1900	211
31	*Thursday*	William Courtenay, Archbishop, descendant of King Edward I and influence of King Richard II *d.* 1396	212

ASTRONOMICAL PHENOMENA

d	*h*	
1	13	Mercury at stationary point
4	00	Earth at aphelion (152 million km.)
4	08	Pluto at opposition
6	02	Mars in conjunction with Moon. Mars 0°.2 S.
8	02	Saturn in conjunction with Moon. Saturn 0°.4 N.
12	18	Mercury at greatest elongation W. 21°
20	21	Saturn at stationary point
22	03	Uranus at stationary point
22	22	Sun's longitude 120° ♌
24	18	Venus in conjunction with Moon. Venus 4°N.
24	21	Jupiter in conjunction
25	14	Mercury in conjunction with Moon. Mercury 5°N.
26	20	Jupiter in conjunction with Moon. Jupiter 5°N.

MINIMA OF ALGOL

d	*h*	*d*	*h*	*d*	*h*
2	20.1	14	07.4	25	18.6
5	16.9	17	04.2	28	15.4
8	13.8	20	01.0	31	12.2
11	10.6	22	21.8		

CONSTELLATIONS

The following constellations are near their meridian at

	d	*h*		*d*	*h*
June	1	24	July	16	21
June	15	23	August	1	20
July	1	22	August	16	19

Ursa Minor, Draco, Corona, Hercules, Lyra, Serpens, Ophiuchus, Libra, Scorpius and Sagittarius

THE MOON

Phases, Apsides and Node	*d*	*h*	*m*
☽ First Quarter	5	11	59
○ Full Moon	12	11	25
☾ Last Quarter	19	02	08
● New Moon	26	22	42
Perigee (358,252km)	13	08	33
Apogee (406,576km)	28	03	42

Mean longitude of ascending node on July 1, 205°

THE SUN

s.d. 15′.8

Day	Right Ascension			Dec. +		Equation of time		Rise 52°		Rise 56°		Transit		Set 52°		Set 56°		Sidereal time			Transit of first point of Aries		
	h	m	s	°	′	m	s	h	m	h	m	h	m	h	m	h	m	h	m	s	h	m	s
1	6	39	39	23	07	−3	46	3	44	3	18	12	04	20	23	20	49	18	35	53	5	23	14
2	6	43	47	23	03	−3	57	3	45	3	19	12	04	20	23	20	48	18	39	50	5	19	18
3	6	47	55	22	59	−4	09	3	46	3	20	12	04	20	22	20	48	18	43	47	5	15	22
4	6	52	03	22	54	−4	20	3	47	3	21	12	04	20	22	20	47	18	47	43	5	11	26
5	6	56	10	22	48	−4	31	3	47	3	22	12	05	20	21	20	47	18	51	40	5	07	30
6	7	00	17	22	43	−4	41	3	48	3	23	12	05	20	21	20	46	18	55	36	5	03	34
7	7	04	24	22	37	−4	51	3	49	3	24	12	05	20	20	20	45	18	59	33	4	59	38
8	7	08	30	22	30	−5	00	3	50	3	25	12	05	20	19	20	44	19	03	29	4	55	42
9	7	12	35	22	23	−5	10	3	51	3	27	12	05	20	19	20	43	19	07	26	4	51	46
10	7	16	41	22	16	−5	18	3	52	3	28	12	05	20	18	20	42	19	11	22	4	47	50
11	7	20	46	22	08	−5	27	3	53	3	29	12	06	20	17	20	41	19	15	19	4	43	54
12	7	24	50	22	00	−5	35	3	54	3	30	12	06	20	16	20	40	19	19	16	4	39	58
13	7	28	54	21	52	−5	42	3	55	3	32	12	06	20	15	20	39	19	23	12	4	36	03
14	7	32	58	21	43	−5	49	3	57	3	33	12	06	20	14	20	38	19	27	09	4	32	07
15	7	37	01	21	34	−5	55	3	58	3	35	12	06	20	13	20	36	19	31	05	4	28	11
16	7	41	03	21	24	−6	01	3	59	3	36	12	06	20	12	20	35	19	35	02	4	24	15
17	7	45	05	21	14	−6	07	4	00	3	38	12	06	20	11	20	34	19	38	58	4	20	19
18	7	49	07	21	04	−6	12	4	02	3	39	12	06	20	10	20	32	19	42	55	4	16	23
19	7	53	08	20	54	−6	16	4	03	3	41	12	06	20	09	20	31	19	46	51	4	12	27
20	7	57	08	20	43	−6	20	4	04	3	42	12	06	20	08	20	29	19	50	48	4	08	31
21	8	01	08	20	31	−6	23	4	05	3	44	12	06	20	06	20	28	19	54	45	4	04	35
22	8	05	07	20	20	−6	26	4	07	3	46	12	06	20	05	20	26	19	58	41	4	00	39
23	8	09	06	20	08	−6	29	4	08	3	47	12	07	20	04	20	24	20	02	38	3	56	43
24	8	13	05	19	55	−6	30	4	10	3	49	12	07	20	02	20	23	20	06	34	3	52	48
25	8	17	02	19	43	−6	32	4	11	3	51	12	07	20	01	20	21	20	10	31	3	48	52
26	8	20	59	19	30	−6	32	4	13	3	53	12	07	20	00	20	19	20	14	27	3	44	56
27	8	24	56	19	16	−6	32	4	14	3	54	12	07	19	58	20	17	20	18	24	3	41	00
28	8	28	52	19	03	−6	31	4	15	3	56	12	07	19	57	20	15	20	22	20	3	37	04
29	8	32	47	18	49	−6	30	4	17	3	58	12	06	19	55	20	14	20	26	17	3	33	08
30	8	36	42	18	34	−6	28	4	18	4	00	12	06	19	53	20	12	20	30	14	3	29	12
31	8	40	36	18	20	−6	26	4	20	4	02	12	06	19	52	20	10	20	34	10	3	25	16

DURATION OF TWILIGHT (in minutes)

Latitude	52°	56°	52°	56°	52°	56°	52°	56°
	1 July		*11 July*		*21 July*		*31 July*	
Civil	48	61	47	58	44	53	42	49
Nautical	124	TAN	117	TAN	107	146	98	123
Astronomical	TAN	TAN	TAN	TAN	TAN	TAN	182	TAN

THE NIGHT SKY

Mercury is unsuitably placed for observation at first but could possibly be seen, given good conditions, for a few days between the 18th and 21st as a difficult morning object low above the E.N.E. horizon at the beginning of civil twilight, magnitude −0.4. Observers as far north as Scotland are very unlikely to see it at all.

Venus, is still visible as a brilliant object in the east-north-eastern morning skies before sunrise, magnitude −3.9. The waning crescent Moon passes about 5 degrees south of the planet on the 24th. On the 2nd, Venus passes 4 degrees north of Aldebaran, in Taurus.

Mars, magnitude +0.4, is still an evening object, but by the end of the month it will not be visible for long after 21h. On the night of the 5th–6th the waxing gibbous Moon will be seen very close to Mars, which passes 1.4 degrees north of Spica (for the third time this year) on the 12th.

Jupiter passes through conjunction on the 24th and is therefore too close to the Sun for observation.

Saturn, magnitude +0.4, continues to be visible in the evenings, low above the western horizon although by the end of the month the long evening twilight severely restricts the time available for observation before the planet sets. The waxing gibbous Moon passes only about 1 degree south of the planet on the night of the 7th–8th.

THE MOON

Day	R.A.		Dec.	Hor. Par.	Semi-diam.	Sun's Co-Long.	PA. of Br. Limb	Ph.	Age	Rise				Transit		Set			
										52°		56°				52°		56°	
	h	m	°	′	′	°	°	%	d	h	m	h	m	h	m	h	m	h	m
1	9	22	+10.6	54.0	14.7	312	293	12	3.7	8	11	8	03	15	12	22	02	22	09
2	10	07	+7.2	54.1	14.7	324	294	19	4.7	9	14	9	09	15	55	22	25	22	28
3	10	53	+3.5	54.3	14.8	336	294	27	5.7	10	18	10	16	16	38	22	47	22	47
4	11	38	−0.4	54.7	14.9	348	294	36	6.7	11	22	11	24	17	21	23	09	23	06
5	12	24	−4.3	55.3	15.1	1	293	45	7.7	12	28	12	34	18	05	23	33	23	26
6	13	12	−8.1	56.0	15.2	13	292	55	8.7	13	36	13	45	18	52	—		23	50
7	14	02	−11.7	56.8	15.5	25	290	65	9.7	14	45	14	58	19	42	0	00	—	
8	14	54	−14.8	57.7	15.7	37	288	75	10.7	15	55	16	11	20	35	0	32	0	18
9	15	50	−17.2	58.7	16.0	50	285	84	11.7	17	04	17	22	21	32	1	11	0	54
10	16	50	−18.6	59.6	16.2	62	282	91	12.7	18	07	18	26	22	32	1	59	1	40
11	17	51	−18.9	60.4	16.4	74	283	97	13.7	19	04	19	22	23	34	2	58	2	39
12	18	54	−17.9	60.9	16.6	86	301	99	14.7	19	51	20	07	—		4	08	3	50
13	19	56	−15.7	61.2	16.7	98	45	99	15.7	20	31	20	43	0	35	5	25	5	10
14	20	57	−12.3	61.1	16.7	110	62	96	16.7	21	05	21	12	1	34	6	46	6	36
15	21	56	−8.2	60.8	16.6	123	64	90	17.7	21	34	21	38	2	31	8	08	8	02
16	22	53	−3.6	60.2	16.4	135	65	82	18.7	22	02	22	01	3	25	9	28	9	26
17	23	48	+1.1	59.5	16.2	147	65	73	19.7	22	29	22	24	4	17	10	46	10	48
18	0	41	+5.6	58.6	16.0	159	67	62	20.7	22	56	22	48	5	08	12	01	12	08
19	1	33	+9.6	57.8	15.7	172	69	51	21.7	23	26	23	14	5	59	13	13	13	24
20	2	26	+13.1	57.0	15.5	184	71	40	22.7	23	59	23	44	6	49	14	22	14	36
21	3	18	+15.8	56.3	15.3	196	74	31	23.7	—		—		7	38	15	26	15	43
22	4	10	+17.7	55.6	15.2	208	77	22	24.7	0	37	0	20	8	28	16	25	16	43
23	5	02	+18.7	55.1	15.0	220	80	14	25.7	1	20	1	01	9	18	17	17	17	36
24	5	54	+18.9	54.7	14.9	233	82	8	26.7	2	08	1	50	10	07	18	02	18	20
25	6	44	+18.1	54.4	14.8	245	82	4	27.7	3	02	2	45	10	55	18	41	18	57
26	7	34	+16.6	54.1	14.8	257	74	1	28.7	4	00	3	45	11	41	19	14	19	28
27	8	23	+14.4	54.0	14.7	269	7	0	0.1	5	00	4	48	12	27	19	43	19	53
28	9	10	+11.5	53.9	14.7	282	309	1	1.1	6	02	5	53	13	11	20	08	20	15
29	9	56	+8.3	54.0	14.7	294	300	4	2.1	7	05	6	59	13	54	20	31	20	35
30	10	41	+4.7	54.1	14.7	306	297	8	3.1	8	08	8	05	14	36	20	53	20	54
31	11	26	+0.9	54.4	14.8	318	296	14	4.1	9	12	9	12	15	19	21	15	21	13

MERCURY

Day	R.A.		Dec.	Diam.	Phase	Transit		5° high			
								52°		56°	
	h	m	°	″	%	h	m	h	m	h	m
1	5	36	+18.8	11	11	10	59	3	54	3	41
3	5	37	+18.9	10	14	10	51	3	45	3	32
5	5	38	+19.2	10	18	10	45	3	38	3	24
7	5	41	+19.5	9	23	10	41	3	31	3	17
9	5	46	+19.9	9	27	10	38	3	26	3	11
11	5	52	+20.3	8	32	10	36	3	21	3	07
13	5	59	+20.7	8	38	10	36	3	18	3	03
15	6	08	+21.1	7	43	10	37	3	17	3	01
17	6	18	+21.5	7	49	10	40	3	17	3	01
19	6	30	+21.9	7	56	10	44	3	18	3	02
21	6	42	+22.2	6	62	10	49	3	22	3	05
23	6	56	+22.3	6	69	10	55	3	27	3	10
25	7	12	+22.4	6	75	11	03	3	34	3	17
27	7	28	+22.3	6	81	11	11	3	43	3	26
29	7	44	+22.0	6	87	11	20	3	54	3	37
31	8	01	+21.5	5	92	11	30	4	06	3	50

VENUS

Day	R.A.		Dec.	Diam.	Phase	Transit		5° high			
								52°		56°	
	h	m	°	″	%	h	m	h	m	h	m
1	4	30	+20.4	12	85	9	54	2	38	2	23
6	4	55	+21.4	12	87	10	00	2	38	2	22
11	5	21	+22.1	12	88	10	06	2	39	2	22
16	5	46	+22.6	11	89	10	12	2	42	2	25
21	6	13	+22.8	11	90	10	18	2	47	2	30
26	6	39	+22.8	11	91	10	25	2	54	2	37
31	7	05	+22.5	11	92	10	32	3	03	2	46

MARS

Day	R.A.		Dec.	Diam.	Phase	Transit		5° high			
								52°		56°	
	h	m	°	″	%	h	m	h	m	h	m
1	13	07	−7.6	9	88	18	29	23	14	23	04
6	13	15	−8.5	9	87	18	17	22	57	22	46
11	13	23	−9.4	9	87	18	06	22	41	22	29
16	13	31	−10.4	9	87	17	55	22	24	22	11
21	13	40	−11.3	8	87	17	44	22	08	21	54
26	13	50	−12.3	8	87	17	34	21	52	21	37
31	14	00	−13.3	8	87	17	25	21	37	21	20

SUNRISE AND SUNSET

	London				Bristol				Birmingham				Manchester				Newcastle				Glasgow				Belfast			
	0° 05′		51° 30′		2° 35′		51° 28′		1° 55′		52° 28′		2° 15′		53° 28′		1° 37′		54° 59′		4° 14′		55° 52′		5° 56′		54° 35′	
d	h	m	h	m	h	m	h	m	h	m	h	m	h	m	h	m	h	m	h	m	h	m	h	m	h	m	h	m
1	3	47	20	21	3	58	20	30	3	49	20	33	3	45	20	41	3	32	20	48	3	36	21	05	3	52	21	03
2	3	48	20	20	3	58	20	30	3	50	20	33	3	45	20	40	3	33	20	48	3	37	21	04	3	53	21	02
3	3	49	20	20	3	59	20	30	3	51	20	33	3	46	20	40	3	34	20	47	3	38	21	04	3	54	21	02
4	3	50	20	19	4	00	20	29	3	52	20	32	3	47	20	39	3	35	20	47	3	39	21	03	3	55	21	01
5	3	50	20	19	4	01	20	29	3	52	20	32	3	48	20	39	3	36	20	46	3	40	21	03	3	56	21	01
6	3	51	20	18	4	01	20	28	3	53	20	31	3	49	20	38	3	37	20	45	3	41	21	02	3	57	21	00
7	3	52	20	18	4	02	20	28	3	54	20	30	3	50	20	37	3	38	20	44	3	42	21	01	3	58	20	59
8	3	53	20	17	4	03	20	27	3	55	20	30	3	51	20	37	3	39	20	44	3	43	21	00	3	59	20	58
9	3	54	20	16	4	04	20	26	3	56	20	29	3	52	20	36	3	40	20	43	3	44	20	59	4	00	20	57
10	3	55	20	16	4	05	20	26	3	57	20	28	3	53	20	35	3	41	20	42	3	46	20	58	4	01	20	57
11	3	56	20	15	4	06	20	25	3	58	20	27	3	54	20	34	3	42	20	41	3	47	20	57	4	02	20	56
12	3	57	20	14	4	07	20	24	3	59	20	26	3	55	20	33	3	44	20	40	3	48	20	56	4	03	20	55
13	3	58	20	13	4	08	20	23	4	01	20	25	3	56	20	32	3	45	20	39	3	50	20	55	4	05	20	53
14	3	59	20	12	4	10	20	22	4	02	20	24	3	58	20	31	3	46	20	38	3	51	20	54	4	06	20	52
15	4	01	20	11	4	11	20	21	4	03	20	23	3	59	20	30	3	48	20	36	3	52	20	52	4	07	20	51
16	4	02	20	10	4	12	20	20	4	04	20	22	4	00	20	29	3	49	20	35	3	54	20	51	4	09	20	50
17	4	03	20	09	4	13	20	19	4	06	20	21	4	02	20	28	3	50	20	34	3	55	20	50	4	10	20	49
18	4	04	20	08	4	14	20	18	4	07	20	20	4	03	20	27	3	52	20	32	3	57	20	48	4	12	20	47
19	4	06	20	07	4	16	20	17	4	08	20	19	4	04	20	25	3	53	20	31	3	59	20	47	4	13	20	46
20	4	07	20	06	4	17	20	16	4	10	20	18	4	06	20	24	3	55	20	30	4	00	20	45	4	15	20	45
21	4	08	20	05	4	18	20	14	4	11	20	16	4	07	20	23	3	57	20	28	4	02	20	44	4	16	20	43
22	4	09	20	03	4	20	20	13	4	12	20	15	4	09	20	21	3	58	20	27	4	04	20	42	4	18	20	42
23	4	11	20	02	4	21	20	12	4	14	20	14	4	10	20	20	4	00	20	25	4	05	20	41	4	19	20	40
24	4	12	20	01	4	22	20	10	4	15	20	12	4	12	20	18	4	01	20	23	4	07	20	39	4	21	20	39
25	4	14	19	59	4	24	20	09	4	17	20	11	4	13	20	17	4	03	20	22	4	09	20	37	4	22	20	37
26	4	15	19	58	4	25	20	08	4	18	20	09	4	15	20	15	4	05	20	20	4	10	20	35	4	24	20	35
27	4	16	19	56	4	27	20	06	4	20	20	08	4	16	20	14	4	06	20	18	4	12	20	34	4	26	20	34
28	4	18	19	55	4	28	20	05	4	21	20	06	4	18	20	12	4	08	20	17	4	14	20	32	4	27	20	32
29	4	19	19	53	4	30	20	03	4	23	20	05	4	20	20	10	4	10	20	15	4	16	20	30	4	29	20	30
30	4	21	19	52	4	31	20	02	4	24	20	03	4	21	20	09	4	12	20	13	4	18	20	28	4	31	20	28
31	4	22	19	50	4	32	20	00	4	26	20	01	4	23	20	07	4	13	20	11	4	19	20	26	4	33	20	27

JUPITER

Day	R.A.		Dec.		Transit		5° high			
							52°		56°	
	h	m	°	′	h	m	h	m	h	m
1	7	54.8	+21	11	13	17	20	37	20	52
11	8	04.0	+20	46	12	47	20	04	20	19
21	8	13.3	+20	19	12	17	19	31	19	46
31	8	22.5	+19	49	11	47	18	58	19	12

Diameters – equatorial 31″ polar 29″

SATURN

Day	R.A.		Dec.		Transit		5° high			
							52°		56°	
	h	m	°	′	h	m	h	m	h	m
1	15	00.7	–14	38	20	21	0	30	0	12
11	14	59.8	–14	37	19	41	23	46	23	28
21	14	59.4	–14	38	19	02	23	06	22	48
31	14	59.7	–14	42	18	23	22	27	22	08

Diameters – equatorial 17″ polar 16″
Rings – major axis 40″ minor axis 14″

URANUS

Day	R.A.		Dec.		Transit		10° high			
							52°		56°	
	h	m	°	′	h	m	h	m	h	m
1	1	01.2	+5	48	6	24	1	01	1	02
11	1	01.7	+5	51	5	45	0	21	0	23
21	1	01.9	+5	52	5	06	23	38	23	40
31	1	01.8	+5	51	4	27	22	59	23	01

Diameter 4″

NEPTUNE

Day	R.A.		Dec.		Transit		10° high			
							52°		56°	
	h	m	°	′	h	m	h	m	h	m
1	22	37.8	–9	26	4	01	0	02	0	18
11	22	37.3	–9	30	3	21	23	18	23	35
21	22	36.6	–9	34	2	41	22	39	22	56
31	22	35.8	–9	39	2	01	21	59	22	16

Diameter 2″

AUGUST 2014

EIGHTH MONTH, 31 DAYS. *Augustus*, formerly *Sextilis*, sixth month of Roman pre-Julian calendar

1	*Friday*	Queen Anne, House of Stuart *d.* 1714; King William IV opens the new London Bridge 1831	day 213
2	*Saturday*	King William II, House of Normandy *d.* 1100; Peter O'Toole, actor and King Henry II in *Becket b.* 1932	214
3	*Sunday*	Queen Elizabeth II officially opens the 11th Commonwealth Games in Edmonton Canada 1978	215
4	*Monday*	At the Battle of Evesham, Prince Edward (King Edward I) defeats Simon de Montfort 1265	week 31 day 216
5	*Tuesday*	Coronation of King Henry I at Westminster Abbey 1100	217
6	*Wednesday*	Prince Alfred Ernest Albert, fourth child of Queen Victoria and Prince Albert *b.* 1844	218
7	*Thursday*	Princess Amelia of the United Kingdom, the youngest of the 15 children of King George III *b.* 1783	219
8	*Friday*	Margaret Tudor marries James IV King of Scots, foreshadowing the Union of the Crowns 1503	220
9	*Saturday*	Coronation of King Edward VII at Westminster Abbey 1902	221
10	*Sunday*	The cornerstone of the Royal Observatory at Greenwich is laid, founded by King Charles II 1675	222
11	*Monday*	Mary of York, who died at the age of 14 before she could marry the King of Denmark *b.* 1467	week 32 day 223
12	*Tuesday*	King George IV, who reigned from 1820–1830, House of Hanover *b.* 1762	224
13	*Wednesday*	The Prince of Wales resigns as patron of Scotland's national museum 1991	225
14	*Thursday*	Katherine of York, daughter of King Edward IV and sister-in-law of King Henry VII *b.* 1479	226
15	*Friday*	VJ (Victory over Japan) Day broadcast by King George VI 1945	227
16	*Saturday*	King Henry VIII's troops defeat a French cavalry force at the 'Battle of the Spurs' 1513	228
17	*Sunday*	Richard, Duke of York, who with his brother Edward are known as the 'Princes in the Tower' *b.* 1473	229
18	*Monday*	Pope Paul IV, who rejected Queen Elizabeth I on the grounds of illegitimacy *d.* 1559	week 33 day 230
19	*Tuesday*	Coronation of King Edward I at Westminster Abbey 1274	231
20	*Wednesday*	During the Siege of Acre, King Richard I orders the execution of 2,700 Muslim prisoners 1191	232
21	*Thursday*	King William IV, who reigned from 1830–1837, House of Hanover *b.* 1765	233
22	*Friday*	King Richard III is killed during the Battle of Bosworth Field, ending the Wars of the Roses 1485	234
23	*Saturday*	King George III delivers his Proclamation of Rebellion, regarding agitation in American colonies 1775	235
24	*Sunday*	In Bordeaux, King John marries Isabella of Angouleme and they have five children 1200	236
25	*Monday*	Margaret of Anjou, wife of King Henry VI and principal figure during the Wars of the Roses *d.* 1482	week 34 day 237
26	*Tuesday*	The Battle of Crécy establishes the military supremacy of the English longbow in battle 1346	238
27	*Wednesday*	Lord Louis Mountbatten, cousin of Queen Elizabeth II, is killed by an IRA bomb on his boat in Ireland 1979	239
28	*Thursday*	At the Battle of Newburn, Scottish forces defeat the army of King Charles I 1640	240
29	*Friday*	The Treaty of Picquigny is signed by King Louis XI of France and King Edward IV, negotiating peace 1475	241
30	*Saturday*	King Louis XI of France, who signed the Treaty of Picquigny negotiating peace with England *d.* 1483	242
31	*Sunday*	King Henry V, who reigned from 1413–1422, House of Lancaster *d.* 1422	243

ASTRONOMICAL PHENOMENA

d	*h*	
2	20	Jupiter in conjunction with Mercury. Jupiter 0°.9 S.
3	12	Mars in conjunction with Moon. Mars 2°S.
4	10	Saturn in conjunction with Moon. Saturn 0°.04 N.
8	16	Mercury in superior conjunction
18	05	Jupiter in conjunction with Venus. Jupiter 0°.2 S.
23	05	Sun's longitude 150° ♍
23	14	Jupiter in conjunction with Moon. Jupiter 5°N.
24	02	Venus in conjunction with Moon. Venus 6°N.
25	19	Saturn in conjunction with Mars. Saturn 3°N.
27	02	Mercury in conjunction with Moon. Mercury 3°N.
29	15	Neptune at opposition
31	19	Saturn in conjunction with Moon. Saturn 0°.4 S.

MINIMA OF ALGOL

d	*h*	*d*	*h*	*d*	*h*
3	09.1	14	20.3	26	07.5
6	05.9	17	17.1	29	04.4
9	02.7	20	13.9		
11	23.5	23	10.7		

CONSTELLATIONS

The following constellations are near their meridian at

	d	*h*		*d*	*h*
July	1	24	August	16	21
July	16	23	September	1	20
August	1	22	September	15	19

Draco, Hercules, Lyra, Cygnus, Sagitta, Ophiuchus, Serpens, Aquila and Sagittarius

THE MOON

Phases, Apsides and Node	*d*	*h*	*m*
☽ First Quarter	4	00	50
○ Full Moon	10	18	09
☾ Last Quarter	17	12	26
● New Moon	25	14	13
Perigee (356,896km)	10	17	49
Apogee (406,514km)	24	06	24

Mean longitude of ascending node on August 1, 203°

THE SUN

s.d. 15′.8

Day	Right Ascension			Dec. +		Equation of time		Rise 52°		Rise 56°		Transit		Set 52°		Set 56°		Sidereal time			Transit of first point of Aries		
	h	m	s	°	′	m	s	h	m	h	m	h	m	h	m	h	m	h	m	s	h	m	s
1	8	44	29	18	05	−6	23	4	22	4	04	12	06	19	50	20	08	20	38	07	3	21	20
2	8	48	22	17	50	−6	19	4	23	4	06	12	06	19	48	20	06	20	42	03	3	17	24
3	8	52	14	17	34	−6	15	4	25	4	07	12	06	19	47	20	04	20	46	00	3	13	28
4	8	56	06	17	19	−6	10	4	26	4	09	12	06	19	45	20	02	20	49	56	3	09	33
5	8	59	57	17	03	−6	04	4	28	4	11	12	06	19	43	19	59	20	53	53	3	05	37
6	9	03	47	16	46	−5	58	4	29	4	13	12	06	19	41	19	57	20	57	49	3	01	41
7	9	07	37	16	30	−5	51	4	31	4	15	12	06	19	40	19	55	21	01	46	2	57	45
8	9	11	26	16	13	−5	44	4	33	4	17	12	06	19	38	19	53	21	05	43	2	53	49
9	9	15	15	15	56	−5	36	4	34	4	19	12	06	19	36	19	51	21	09	39	2	49	53
10	9	19	03	15	39	−5	27	4	36	4	21	12	05	19	34	19	49	21	13	36	2	45	57
11	9	22	50	15	21	−5	18	4	37	4	23	12	05	19	32	19	46	21	17	32	2	42	01
12	9	26	37	15	03	−5	08	4	39	4	25	12	05	19	30	19	44	21	21	29	2	38	05
13	9	30	23	14	45	−4	58	4	41	4	27	12	05	19	28	19	42	21	25	25	2	34	09
14	9	34	09	14	27	−4	47	4	42	4	29	12	05	19	26	19	39	21	29	22	2	30	13
15	9	37	54	14	08	−4	35	4	44	4	31	12	04	19	24	19	37	21	33	18	2	26	18
16	9	41	38	13	49	−4	24	4	45	4	33	12	04	19	22	19	35	21	37	15	2	22	22
17	9	45	23	13	30	−4	11	4	47	4	35	12	04	19	20	19	32	21	41	12	2	18	26
18	9	49	06	13	11	−3	58	4	49	4	36	12	04	19	18	19	30	21	45	08	2	14	30
19	9	52	49	12	52	−3	45	4	50	4	38	12	04	19	16	19	27	21	49	05	2	10	34
20	9	56	32	12	32	−3	31	4	52	4	40	12	03	19	14	19	25	21	53	01	2	06	38
21	10	00	14	12	12	−3	17	4	54	4	42	12	03	19	12	19	23	21	56	58	2	02	42
22	10	03	56	11	52	−3	02	4	55	4	44	12	03	19	10	19	20	22	00	54	1	58	46
23	10	07	37	11	32	−2	47	4	57	4	46	12	03	19	07	19	18	22	04	51	1	54	50
24	10	11	18	11	12	−2	31	4	58	4	48	12	02	19	05	19	15	22	08	47	1	50	54
25	10	14	59	10	51	−2	15	5	00	4	50	12	02	19	03	19	13	22	12	44	1	46	58
26	10	18	39	10	31	−1	58	5	02	4	52	12	02	19	01	19	10	22	16	40	1	43	03
27	10	22	18	10	10	−1	41	5	03	4	54	12	02	18	59	19	08	22	20	37	1	39	07
28	10	25	58	9	49	−1	24	5	05	4	56	12	01	18	56	19	05	22	24	34	1	35	11
29	10	29	37	9	27	−1	06	5	07	4	58	12	01	18	54	19	03	22	28	30	1	31	15
30	10	33	15	9	06	−0	48	5	08	5	00	12	01	18	52	19	00	22	32	27	1	27	19
31	10	36	53	8	45	−0	30	5	10	5	02	12	00	18	50	18	57	22	36	23	1	23	23

DURATION OF TWILIGHT (in minutes)

Latitude	52°	56°	52°	56°	52°	56°	52°	56°
	1 August		*11 August*		*21 August*		*31 August*	
Civil	41	49	39	45	37	42	35	40
Nautical	97	121	90	107	84	97	79	90
Astronomical	179	TAN	154	210	139	168	128	148

THE NIGHT SKY

Mercury passes through superior conjunction on the 8th and therefore remains unsuitably placed for observation throughout the month.

Venus, magnitude −3.9, continues to be visible as a splendid morning object, above the east-north-east horizon. However, it is no longer rising as early as it was in July. By the end of the month it will not be visible until well after 04h. On the 7th Venus passes 7 degrees south of Pollux, in Gemini, while on the morning of the 18th, around the time of beginning of civil twilight, Venus and Jupiter will be seen only a few tenths of a degree apart, very low in the east-north-eastern sky.

Mars is still visible in the south-western sky in the evenings as it moves from Virgo into Libra. Its magnitude is +0.6. The Moon, near first quarter, passes about 1 degree north of Mars on the 3rd. In the evening of the 25th, low in the south-western sky, Mars will be seen 3.4 degrees below Saturn, Mars being slightly brighter than Saturn.

Jupiter, after the first two weeks of the month, becomes visible as a morning object, low above the east-north-eastern horizon for a short while before sunrise, magnitude −1.8. Jupiter is in the constellation of Cancer. On the 23rd the waning crescent Moon passes 6 degrees south of the planet.

Saturn, magnitude +0.6, continues to be visible low above the south-western horizon for a short while in the evenings. On the 4th the Moon, at First Quarter, passes just south of the planet.

Neptune is at opposition on the 29th, in the constellation of Aquarius. It is not visible to the naked-eye since its magnitude is +7.9.

Meteors. The maximum of the famous Perseid meteor shower occurs on the 12th. In the early evening the waning crescent Moon will cause some interference as it rises in the east at about 20h, with the meteor shower radiant low in the north-north-east.

THE MOON

Day	R.A.		Dec.	Hor. Par.	Semi-diam.	Sun's Co-Long.	PA. of Br. Limb	Ph.	Age	Rise 52°		Rise 56°		Transit		Set 52°		Set 56°	
	h	m	°	′	′	°	°	%	d	h	m	h	m	h	m	h	m	h	m
1	12	12	−3.0	54.7	14.9	331	294	22	5.1	10	16	10	20	16	02	21	38	21	33
2	12	58	−6.8	55.2	15.1	343	293	30	6.1	11	22	11	30	16	47	22	03	21	55
3	13	47	−10.4	55.9	15.2	355	291	40	7.1	12	29	12	40	17	34	22	32	22	20
4	14	37	−13.6	56.7	15.4	7	288	50	8.1	13	37	13	51	18	25	23	07	22	52
5	15	30	−16.2	57.5	15.7	20	285	60	9.1	14	44	15	01	19	18	23	49	23	31
6	16	26	−18.0	58.5	15.9	32	281	71	10.1	15	48	16	07	20	15	—		—	
7	17	25	−18.8	59.4	16.2	44	277	80	11.1	16	47	17	06	21	14	0	41	0	22
8	18	27	−18.4	60.3	16.4	56	273	89	12.1	17	39	17	56	22	15	1	43	1	25
9	19	29	−16.8	60.9	16.6	68	272	95	13.1	18	23	18	36	23	15	2	56	2	40
10	20	30	−13.9	61.3	16.7	81	280	99	14.1	19	00	19	10	—		4	15	4	03
11	21	31	−10.1	61.4	16.7	93	20	100	15.1	19	33	19	38	0	14	5	38	5	30
12	22	30	−5.6	61.2	16.7	105	58	98	16.1	20	02	20	04	1	11	7	01	6	57
13	23	27	−0.9	60.6	16.5	117	63	92	17.1	20	31	20	28	2	06	8	22	8	23
14	0	22	+3.8	59.8	16.3	129	65	85	18.1	20	59	20	52	2	59	9	41	9	46
15	1	17	+8.1	58.9	16.1	141	68	76	19.1	21	29	21	19	3	52	10	57	11	06
16	2	11	+11.9	58.0	15.8	154	71	66	20.1	22	01	21	48	4	43	12	09	12	22
17	3	04	+14.9	57.1	15.5	166	74	56	21.1	22	38	22	22	5	34	13	17	13	32
18	3	57	+17.1	56.2	15.3	178	78	45	22.1	23	19	23	02	6	25	14	18	14	36
19	4	50	+18.4	55.5	15.1	190	82	35	23.1	—		23	48	7	15	15	13	15	31
20	5	41	+18.7	54.9	15.0	203	86	26	24.1	0	06	—		8	04	16	01	16	18
21	6	32	+18.3	54.5	14.9	215	89	18	25.1	0	58	0	40	8	52	16	41	16	58
22	7	22	+16.9	54.2	14.8	227	92	11	26.1	1	54	1	38	9	39	17	16	17	30
23	8	11	+14.9	54.0	14.7	239	93	6	27.1	2	54	2	40	10	25	17	46	17	58
24	8	58	+12.3	53.9	14.7	251	92	2	28.1	3	55	3	44	11	09	18	13	18	21
25	9	45	+9.1	54.0	14.7	264	76	0	29.1	4	57	4	50	11	53	18	37	18	42
26	10	30	+5.6	54.1	14.7	276	330	0	0.5	6	00	5	56	12	35	19	00	19	02
27	11	16	+1.9	54.3	14.8	288	303	2	1.5	7	04	7	03	13	18	19	22	19	21
28	12	01	−2.0	54.6	14.9	300	297	5	2.5	8	08	8	11	14	01	19	45	19	40
29	12	47	−5.8	54.9	15.0	313	294	10	3.5	9	13	9	19	14	46	20	09	20	01
30	13	35	−9.4	55.4	15.1	325	291	17	4.5	10	19	10	29	15	32	20	36	20	26
31	14	24	−12.6	56.0	15.2	337	288	25	5.5	11	25	11	38	16	20	21	08	20	54

MERCURY

Day	R.A.		Dec.	Diam.	Phase	Transit		5° high 52°		5° high 56°	
	h	m	°	″	%	h	m	h	m	h	m
1	8	10	+21.2	5	93	11	34	4	12	3	57
3	8	28	+20.5	5	97	11	44	4	26	4	12
5	8	45	+19.7	5	99	11	54	4	41	4	27
7	9	02	+18.6	5	100	12	03	19	07	19	19
9	9	19	+17.5	5	100	12	11	19	09	19	20
11	9	35	+16.2	5	99	12	20	19	10	19	20
13	9	51	+14.9	5	99	12	27	19	10	19	19
15	10	06	+13.5	5	97	12	34	19	09	19	17
17	10	20	+12.1	5	96	12	41	19	08	19	14
19	10	34	+10.6	5	94	12	46	19	06	19	11
21	10	47	+9.1	5	93	12	52	19	03	19	07
23	11	00	+7.6	5	91	12	57	19	00	19	03
25	11	13	+6.1	5	89	13	01	18	57	18	58
27	11	25	+4.5	5	87	13	05	18	53	18	53
29	11	36	+3.0	5	86	13	09	18	49	18	48
31	11	48	+1.6	5	84	13	12	18	45	18	43

VENUS

Day	R.A.		Dec.	Diam.	Phase	Transit		5° high 52°		5° high 56°	
	h	m	°	″	%	h	m	h	m	h	m
1	7	10	+22.4	11	92	10	33	3	05	2	48
6	7	36	+21.7	11	93	10	39	3	15	2	59
11	8	02	+20.8	11	94	10	45	3	27	3	12
16	8	28	+19.7	10	95	10	51	3	40	3	26
21	8	53	+18.3	10	95	10	57	3	53	3	41
26	9	18	+16.7	10	96	11	02	4	07	3	57
31	9	43	+14.9	10	97	11	07	4	22	4	13

MARS

Day	R.A.		Dec.	Diam.	Phase	Transit		5° high 52°		5° high 56°	
	h	m	°	″	%	h	m	h	m	h	m
1	14	02	−13.5	8	87	17	23	21	34	21	17
6	14	13	−14.5	8	87	17	14	21	18	21	00
11	14	24	−15.5	7	87	17	05	21	03	20	44
16	14	36	−16.5	7	87	16	57	20	49	20	28
21	14	47	−17.4	7	87	16	49	20	34	20	12
26	15	00	−18.4	7	87	16	42	20	21	19	56
31	15	13	−19.3	7	87	16	35	20	07	19	41

SUNRISE AND SUNSET

	London				Bristol				Birmingham				Manchester				Newcastle				Glasgow				Belfast			
	0° 05′		51° 30′		2° 35′		51° 28′		1° 55′		52° 28′		2° 15′		53° 28′		1° 37′		54° 59′		4° 14′		55° 52′		5° 56′		54° 35′	
d	h	m	h	m	h	m	h	m	h	m	h	m	h	m	h	m	h	m	h	m	h	m	h	m	h	m	h	m
1	4	24	19	49	4	34	19	58	4	27	20	00	4	24	20	05	4	15	20	09	4	21	20	24	4	34	20	25
2	4	25	19	47	4	35	19	57	4	29	19	58	4	26	20	03	4	17	20	07	4	23	20	22	4	36	20	23
3	4	27	19	45	4	37	19	55	4	30	19	56	4	28	20	01	4	19	20	05	4	25	20	20	4	38	20	21
4	4	28	19	43	4	38	19	53	4	32	19	54	4	29	20	00	4	20	20	03	4	27	20	18	4	39	20	19
5	4	30	19	42	4	40	19	52	4	34	19	53	4	31	19	58	4	22	20	01	4	29	20	16	4	41	20	17
6	4	31	19	40	4	42	19	50	4	35	19	51	4	33	19	56	4	24	19	59	4	31	20	14	4	43	20	15
7	4	33	19	38	4	43	19	48	4	37	19	49	4	35	19	54	4	26	19	57	4	33	20	12	4	45	20	13
8	4	35	19	36	4	45	19	46	4	39	19	47	4	36	19	52	4	28	19	55	4	35	20	09	4	47	20	11
9	4	36	19	35	4	46	19	44	4	40	19	45	4	38	19	50	4	30	19	53	4	36	20	07	4	48	20	09
10	4	38	19	33	4	48	19	43	4	42	19	43	4	40	19	48	4	31	19	51	4	38	20	05	4	50	20	07
11	4	39	19	31	4	49	19	41	4	43	19	41	4	41	19	46	4	33	19	49	4	40	20	03	4	52	20	05
12	4	41	19	29	4	51	19	39	4	45	19	39	4	43	19	44	4	35	19	47	4	42	20	00	4	54	20	02
13	4	42	19	27	4	53	19	37	4	47	19	37	4	45	19	42	4	37	19	44	4	44	19	58	4	56	20	00
14	4	44	19	25	4	54	19	35	4	48	19	35	4	47	19	40	4	39	19	42	4	46	19	56	4	58	19	58
15	4	46	19	23	4	56	19	33	4	50	19	33	4	48	19	38	4	41	19	40	4	48	19	53	4	59	19	56
16	4	47	19	21	4	57	19	31	4	52	19	31	4	50	19	35	4	43	19	38	4	50	19	51	5	01	19	54
17	4	49	19	19	4	59	19	29	4	53	19	29	4	52	19	33	4	44	19	35	4	52	19	49	5	03	19	51
18	4	50	19	17	5	00	19	27	4	55	19	27	4	53	19	31	4	46	19	33	4	54	19	46	5	05	19	49
19	4	52	19	15	5	02	19	25	4	57	19	25	4	55	19	29	4	48	19	31	4	56	19	44	5	07	19	47
20	4	54	19	13	5	04	19	23	4	58	19	23	4	57	19	27	4	50	19	28	4	58	19	42	5	09	19	44
21	4	55	19	11	5	05	19	21	5	00	19	20	4	59	19	24	4	52	19	26	5	00	19	39	5	10	19	42
22	4	57	19	09	5	07	19	19	5	02	19	18	5	00	19	22	4	54	19	24	5	02	19	37	5	12	19	40
23	4	58	19	07	5	08	19	16	5	03	19	16	5	02	19	20	4	56	19	21	5	04	19	34	5	14	19	37
24	5	00	19	04	5	10	19	14	5	05	19	14	5	04	19	18	4	58	19	19	5	06	19	32	5	16	19	35
25	5	01	19	02	5	12	19	12	5	07	19	12	5	06	19	15	4	59	19	16	5	08	19	29	5	18	19	33
26	5	03	19	00	5	13	19	10	5	08	19	09	5	07	19	13	5	01	19	14	5	09	19	27	5	20	19	30
27	5	05	18	58	5	15	19	08	5	10	19	07	5	09	19	11	5	03	19	12	5	11	19	24	5	21	19	28
28	5	06	18	56	5	16	19	06	5	12	19	05	5	11	19	08	5	05	19	09	5	13	19	22	5	23	19	26
29	5	08	18	54	5	18	19	04	5	13	19	03	5	13	19	06	5	07	19	07	5	15	19	19	5	25	19	23
30	5	09	18	51	5	20	19	01	5	15	19	00	5	14	19	04	5	09	19	04	5	17	19	17	5	27	19	21
31	5	11	18	49	5	21	18	59	5	17	18	58	5	16	19	01	5	11	19	02	5	19	19	14	5	29	19	18

JUPITER

Day	R.A.		Dec.		Transit		5° high			
							52°		56°	
	h	m	°	′	h	m	h	m	h	m
1	8	23.5	+19	46	11	44	4	33	4	19
11	8	32.6	+19	16	11	14	4	05	3	52
21	8	41.5	+18	44	10	43	3	38	3	25
31	8	50.1	+18	12	10	12	3	10	2	58

Diameters – equatorial 32″ polar 30″

SATURN

Day	R.A.		Dec.		Transit		5° high			
							52°		56°	
	h	m	°	′	h	m	h	m	h	m
1	14	59.7	−14	42	18	19	22	23	22	04
11	15	00.7	−14	49	17	40	21	44	21	25
21	15	02.3	−14	59	17	03	21	05	20	46
31	15	04.5	−15	10	16	26	20	27	20	08

Diameters – equatorial 17″ polar 15″
Rings – major axis 38″ minor axis 14″

URANUS

Day	R.A.		Dec.		Transit		10° high			
							52°		56°	
	h	m	°	′	h	m	h	m	h	m
1	1	01.8	+5	50	4	23	22	55	22	57
11	1	01.3	+5	48	3	43	22	15	22	17
21	1	00.6	+5	43	3	03	21	36	21	38
31	0	59.7	+5	37	2	23	20	56	20	58

Diameter 4″

NEPTUNE

Day	R.A.		Dec.		Transit		10° high			
							52°		56°	
	h	m	°	′	h	m	h	m	h	m
1	22	35.7	−9	39	1	57	21	55	22	12
11	22	34.8	−9	45	1	17	21	15	21	33
21	22	33.8	−9	51	0	37	20	36	20	53
31	22	32.8	−9	57	23	52	19	56	20	14

Diameter 2″

SEPTEMBER 2014

NINTH MONTH, 30 DAYS. *Septem* (seven), seventh month of Roman pre-Julian calendar

1	*Monday*	Anne Boleyn is named Marquess of Pembroke by King Henry VIII prior to their marriage 1532	week 35 day 244
2	*Tuesday*	George Augustus (King George II) marries Princess Caroline of Brandenburg-Ansbach 1705	245
3	*Wednesday*	King George VI broadcasts the start of war with Germany 1939	246
4	*Thursday*	Queen Elizabeth II opens the Forth Road Bridge, at the time, the fourth longest in the world 1964	247
5	*Friday*	Catherine Parr, the sixth and last wife of King Henry VIII, her third husband *d.* 1548	248
6	*Saturday*	The funeral of Diana, Princess of Wales, takes place, with a ceremony held at Westminster Abbey 1997	249
7	*Sunday*	Queen Elizabeth I, who reigned from 1558–1603, House of Tudor *b.* 1533	250
8	*Monday*	King Richard I, who reigned from 1189–1199, House of Plantagenet *b.* 1157	week 36 day 251
9	*Tuesday*	King William I, 'William the Conqueror', who reigned from 1066–1087, House of Normandy *d.* 1087	252
10	*Wednesday*	Colin Firth, actor who won an Oscar for his portrayal of King George VI in *The King's Speech b.* 1960	253
11	*Thursday*	The Siege of Drogheda ends with Oliver Cromwell's Roundheads massacring the defending Royalists 1649	254
12	*Friday*	Two bombs fall on Buckingham Palace, blowing out windows and destroying a chapel 1940	255
13	*Saturday*	King Philip II of Spain, who married Queen Mary I, becoming joint sovereign of England and Ireland *d.* 1598	256
14	*Sunday*	John of Lancaster, third son of King Henry IV and Regent of France on King Henry VI's behalf *d.* 1435	257
15	*Monday*	Sophia Dorothea, wife of King George I, imprisoned for 32 years for alleged infidelity *b.* 1666	week 37 day 258
16	*Tuesday*	King Henry V, reign 1413–1422, House of Lancaster *b.* 1387; King James II, House of Stuart *d.* 1701	259
17	*Wednesday*	'Charles the Simple', King of France, who married the daughter of English king Edward the Elder *b.* 879	260
18	*Thursday*	King George I sailed up the Thames to Greenwich, setting foot in England for the first time 1714	261
19	*Friday*	Jeremy Irons, actor who portrayed King Henry IV in the BBC series *The Hollow Crown b.* 1948	262
20	*Saturday*	Arthur Tudor, Prince of Wales, who predeceased his father King Henry VII in 1502 *b.* 1486	263
21	*Sunday*	King Edward II, who reigned from 1307–1327, House of Plantagenet *d.* 1327	264
22	*Monday*	Coronation of King George III at Westminster Abbey 1761	week 38 day 265
23	*Tuesday*	Yorkists win the Battle of Blore Heath, the first major conflict in the Wars of the Roses 1459	266
24	*Wednesday*	The Battle of Rowton Heath, during the English Civil War, ends with a Royalist defeat 1645	267
25	*Thursday*	Harold Hadrada, King of Norway, is killed by the English army at the Battle of Stamford Bridge 1066	268
26	*Friday*	Coronation of King William II at Westminster Abbey 1087	269
27	*Saturday*	Queen Elizabeth, wife of King George VI, launches RMS *Queen Elizabeth*, a liner named for her 1938	270
28	*Sunday*	William the Conqueror lands in England, establishing a camp near Hastings 1066	271
29	*Monday*	Margaret of England, daughter of King Henry III, who became Queen Consort of Scots in 1251 *b.* 1240	week 39 day 272
30	*Tuesday*	Henry IV is proclaimed king, becoming the tenth king of the House of Plantagenet 1399	273

ASTRONOMICAL PHENOMENA

d	*h*	
1	02	Mars in conjunction with Moon. Mars 4°S.
20	07	Jupiter in conjunction with Moon. Jupiter 5°N.
21	22	Mercury at greatest elongation E. 26°
23	01	Pluto at stationary point
23	02	Sun's longitude 180° ♎
23	12	Venus in conjunction with Moon. Venus 4°N.
26	13	Mercury in conjunction with Moon. Mercury 4°S.
28	05	Saturn in conjunction with Moon. Saturn 0°.7 S.
29	19	Mars in conjunction with Moon. Mars 6°S.

MINIMA OF ALGOL

d	*h*	*d*	*h*	*d*	*h*
1	01.2	12	12.4	23	23.7
3	22.0	15	09.2	26	20.5
6	18.8	18	06.0	29	17.3
9	15.6	21	02.8		

CONSTELLATIONS

The following constellations are near their meridian at

	d	*h*		*d*	*h*
August	1	24	September	15	21
August	16	23	October	1	20
September	1	22	October	16	19

Draco, Cepheus, Lyra, Cygnus, Vulpecula, Sagitta, Delphinus, Equuleus, Aquila, Aquarius and Capricornus

THE MOON

Phases, Apsides and Node	*d*	*h*	*m*
☽ First Quarter	2	11	11
○ Full Moon	9	01	38
☾ Last Quarter	16	02	05
● New Moon	24	06	14
Perigee (358,397km)	8	03	38
Apogee (405,819km)	20	14	30

Mean longitude of ascending node on September 1, 201°

THE SUN

s.d. 15′.9

Day	Right Ascension			Dec.		Equation of time		Rise 52°		Rise 56°		Transit		Set 52°		Set 56°		Sidereal time			Transit of first point of Aries		
	h	m	s	°	′	m	s	h	m	h	m	h	m	h	m	h	m	h	m	s	h	m	s
1	10	40	31	+8	23	−0	11	5	11	5	04	12	00	18	47	18	55	22	40	20	1	19	27
2	10	44	09	+8	01	+0	08	5	13	5	06	12	00	18	45	18	52	22	44	16	1	15	31
3	10	47	46	+7	39	+0	27	5	15	5	08	11	59	18	43	18	50	22	48	13	1	11	35
4	10	51	23	+7	17	+0	47	5	16	5	10	11	59	18	41	18	47	22	52	09	1	07	39
5	10	54	59	+6	55	+1	07	5	18	5	12	11	59	18	38	18	44	22	56	06	1	03	44
6	10	58	36	+6	33	+1	27	5	20	5	14	11	58	18	36	18	42	23	00	03	0	59	48
7	11	02	12	+6	10	+1	47	5	21	5	16	11	58	18	34	18	39	23	03	59	0	55	52
8	11	05	48	+5	48	+2	08	5	23	5	18	11	58	18	31	18	37	23	07	56	0	51	56
9	11	09	24	+5	25	+2	29	5	24	5	20	11	57	18	29	18	34	23	11	52	0	48	00
10	11	12	59	+5	03	+2	50	5	26	5	21	11	57	18	27	18	31	23	15	49	0	44	04
11	11	16	35	+4	40	+3	11	5	28	5	23	11	57	18	24	18	29	23	19	45	0	40	08
12	11	20	10	+4	17	+3	32	5	29	5	25	11	56	18	22	18	26	23	23	42	0	36	12
13	11	23	45	+3	54	+3	53	5	31	5	27	11	56	18	20	18	23	23	27	38	0	32	16
14	11	27	21	+3	31	+4	14	5	33	5	29	11	56	18	17	18	21	23	31	35	0	28	20
15	11	30	56	+3	08	+4	36	5	34	5	31	11	55	18	15	18	18	23	35	32	0	24	24
16	11	34	31	+2	45	+4	57	5	36	5	33	11	55	18	13	18	15	23	39	28	0	20	29
17	11	38	06	+2	22	+5	19	5	37	5	35	11	55	18	10	18	13	23	43	25	0	16	33
18	11	41	41	+1	59	+5	40	5	39	5	37	11	54	18	08	18	10	23	47	21	0	12	37
19	11	45	16	+1	36	+6	01	5	41	5	39	11	54	18	06	18	07	23	51	18	0	08	41
20	11	48	52	+1	12	+6	23	5	42	5	41	11	53	18	03	18	05	23	55	14	0	04	45
21	11	52	27	+0	49	+6	44	5	44	5	43	11	53	18	01	18	02	23	59	11	0	00	49
																					23	56	53
22	11	56	02	+0	26	+7	05	5	46	5	45	11	53	17	59	17	59	0	03	07	23	52	57
23	11	59	38	+0	02	+7	26	5	47	5	47	11	52	17	56	17	57	0	07	04	23	49	01
24	12	03	13	−0	21	+7	47	5	49	5	49	11	52	17	54	17	54	0	11	00	23	45	05
25	12	06	49	−0	44	+8	08	5	51	5	51	11	52	17	52	17	51	0	14	57	23	41	09
26	12	10	25	−1	08	+8	29	5	52	5	53	11	51	17	49	17	49	0	18	54	23	37	14
27	12	14	01	−1	31	+8	49	5	54	5	55	11	51	17	47	17	46	0	22	50	23	33	18
28	12	17	37	−1	54	+9	09	5	56	5	57	11	51	17	45	17	44	0	26	47	23	29	22
29	12	21	14	−2	18	+9	30	5	57	5	59	11	50	17	42	17	41	0	30	43	23	25	26
30	12	24	50	−2	41	+9	49	5	59	6	01	11	50	17	40	17	38	0	34	40	23	21	30

DURATION OF TWILIGHT (in minutes)

Latitude	52°	56°	52°	56°	52°	56°	52°	56°
	1 September		*11 September*		*21 September*		*31 September*	
Civil	35	39	34	38	34	37	34	37
Nautical	79	89	76	85	74	82	73	80
Astronomical	127	147	120	136	116	129	113	125

THE NIGHT SKY

Mercury is unsuitably placed for observation throughout the month.

Venus, magnitude −3.9, remains a brilliant object low above the eastern horizon before dawn, but gradually becomes more and more difficult to detect and becomes lost in the morning twilight during the last week of the month. However, on the 5th, Venus can be seen passing only 1 degree north of Regulus, in Leo.

Mars, magnitude +0.7, continues to be visible in the south-western skies in the evenings as it passes from Libra into Scorpius. By the end of the month it is on the borders of that constellation with Ophiuchus. On the first day of the month, and again on the 29th, the Moon, near first quarter, passes north of Mars. On the 27th, Mars passes 3 degrees north of Antares, in Scorpio.

Jupiter, magnitude −1.9, continues to be visible as a conspicuous morning object in the eastern sky, in Cancer. The crescent waning Moon passes 6 degrees south of the planet on the 20th.

Saturn, magnitude +0.6, may be seen low in the south-western sky in the early part of the evening but it is unlikely to be seen after the first three weeks of the month when it is lost in the gathering twilight.

Zodiacal Light. The morning cone may be observed stretching up from the eastern horizon, along the ecliptic, before the beginning of morning twilight, from the beginning of the month to the 7th, and again after the 22nd. This faint phenomenon is only visible under good conditions and in the absence of both moonlight and artificial lighting.

THE MOON

Day	R.A.		Dec.	Hor. Par.	Semi-diam.	Sun's Co-Long.	PA. of Br. Limb	Ph.	Age	Rise				Transit		Set			
										52°		56°				52°		56°	
	h	*m*	°	′	′	°	°	%	*d*	*h*	*m*	*h*	*m*	*h*	*m*	*h*	*m*	*h*	*m*
1	15	16	−15.3	56.6	15.4	349	284	35	6.5	12	31	12	47	17	11	21	46	21	30
2	16	10	−17.4	57.4	15.6	2	280	45	7.5	13	35	13	53	18	05	22	32	22	14
3	17	06	−18.5	58.2	15.9	14	276	56	8.5	14	34	14	53	19	01	23	28	23	10
4	18	04	−18.5	59.0	16.1	26	271	67	9.5	15	27	15	45	19	59	—		—	
5	19	04	−17.4	59.8	16.3	38	267	77	10.5	16	13	16	28	20	57	0	34	0	17
6	20	04	−15.2	60.5	16.5	50	263	86	11.5	16	53	17	05	21	55	1	47	1	33
7	21	04	−11.8	61.0	16.6	63	262	93	12.5	17	28	17	36	22	53	3	07	2	56
8	22	03	−7.7	61.2	16.7	75	264	98	13.5	17	59	18	03	23	49	4	29	4	23
9	23	01	−3.1	61.1	16.6	87	319	100	14.5	18	28	18	28	—		5	51	5	50
10	23	58	+1.7	60.6	16.5	99	59	99	15.5	18	57	18	53	0	44	7	13	7	16
11	0	54	+6.3	60.0	16.3	111	66	95	16.5	19	27	19	19	1	38	8	33	8	39
12	1	50	+10.4	59.1	16.1	123	70	88	17.5	20	00	19	48	2	32	9	49	9	59
13	2	45	+13.8	58.2	15.9	136	74	80	18.5	20	36	20	21	3	25	11	00	11	14
14	3	40	+16.3	57.2	15.6	148	78	71	19.5	21	17	21	00	4	17	12	06	12	23
15	4	34	+17.9	56.3	15.4	160	82	61	20.5	22	02	21	44	5	09	13	05	13	23
16	5	27	+18.6	55.6	15.1	172	87	51	21.5	22	53	22	35	5	59	13	56	14	14
17	6	18	+18.3	55.0	15.0	184	91	41	22.5	23	48	23	32	6	48	14	40	14	56
18	7	09	+17.2	54.5	14.9	197	95	32	23.5	—		—		7	36	15	17	15	32
19	7	58	+15.4	54.2	14.8	209	98	23	24.5	0	46	0	32	8	22	15	48	16	01
20	8	46	+12.9	54.1	14.7	221	101	16	25.5	1	47	1	35	9	07	16	16	16	26
21	9	32	+9.9	54.0	14.7	233	103	10	26.5	2	49	2	40	9	50	16	41	16	47
22	10	18	+6.6	54.1	14.8	245	103	5	27.5	3	51	3	46	10	33	17	04	17	08
23	11	04	+2.9	54.3	14.8	258	101	2	28.5	4	55	4	53	11	16	17	27	17	27
24	11	50	−1.0	54.6	14.9	270	80	0	29.5	5	59	6	01	12	00	17	50	17	47
25	12	36	−4.8	55.0	15.0	282	299	1	0.8	7	05	7	10	12	44	18	14	18	08
26	13	24	−8.5	55.4	15.1	294	291	3	1.8	8	11	8	20	13	30	18	41	18	31
27	14	13	−11.8	55.8	15.2	307	287	7	2.8	9	17	9	29	14	18	19	11	18	58
28	15	04	−14.7	56.3	15.4	319	283	13	3.8	10	23	10	38	15	08	19	47	19	32
29	15	57	−16.9	56.9	15.5	331	279	21	4.8	11	27	11	44	16	00	20	30	20	13
30	16	52	−18.2	57.5	15.7	343	275	31	5.8	12	27	12	45	16	54	21	22	21	03

MERCURY

Day	R.A.		Dec.	Diam.	Phase	Transit		5° high			
								52°		56°	
	h	*m*	°	″	%	*h*	*m*	*h*	*m*	*h*	*m*
1	11	53	+0.8	5	83	13	14	18	43	18	40
3	12	04	−0.6	5	81	13	16	18	38	18	34
5	12	14	−2.1	6	79	13	19	18	33	18	28
7	12	24	−3.4	6	77	13	21	18	28	18	21
9	12	34	−4.8	6	75	13	23	18	23	18	15
11	12	44	−6.1	6	73	13	24	18	17	18	08
13	12	53	−7.4	6	71	13	26	18	11	18	01
15	13	02	−8.6	6	68	13	26	18	05	17	54
17	13	10	−9.7	6	66	13	27	17	59	17	47
19	13	18	−10.8	7	63	13	27	17	53	17	39
21	13	26	−11.8	7	60	13	26	17	47	17	32
23	13	33	−12.7	7	57	13	25	17	40	17	24
25	13	39	−13.6	7	53	13	23	17	33	17	16
27	13	45	−14.3	8	49	13	21	17	26	17	09
29	13	49	−14.9	8	44	13	17	17	19	17	01
31	13	53	−15.3	8	39	13	13	17	12	16	53

VENUS

Day	R.A.		Dec.	Diam.	Phase	Transit		5° high			
								52°		56°	
	h	*m*	°	″	%	*h*	*m*	*h*	*m*	*h*	*m*
1	9	47	+14.5	10	97	11	08	4	25	4	16
6	10	11	+12.5	10	97	11	12	4	40	4	33
11	10	35	+10.3	10	98	11	16	4	56	4	50
16	10	58	+8.0	10	98	11	19	5	11	5	08
21	11	22	+5.7	10	99	11	23	5	27	5	25
26	11	45	+3.2	10	99	11	26	5	42	5	43
31	12	07	+0.7	10	99	11	29	5	58	6	01

MARS

Day	R.A.		Dec.	Diam.	Phase	Transit		5° high			
								52°		56°	
	h	*m*	°	″	%	*h*	*m*	*h*	*m*	*h*	*m*
1	15	15	−19.5	7	87	16	34	20	04	19	38
6	15	28	−20.3	7	88	16	27	19	52	19	23
11	15	42	−21.1	7	88	16	21	19	39	19	09
16	15	56	−21.8	6	88	16	16	19	28	18	56
21	16	10	−22.5	6	88	16	10	19	17	18	43
26	16	25	−23.1	6	88	16	05	19	06	18	30
31	16	40	−23.7	6	89	16	01	18	57	18	19

SUNRISE AND SUNSET

	London				*Bristol*				*Birmingham*				*Manchester*				*Newcastle*				*Glasgow*				*Belfast*			
	0° 05′		*51° 30′*		*2° 35′*		*51° 28′*		*1° 55′*		*52° 28′*		*2° 15′*		*53° 28′*		*1° 37′*		*54° 59′*		*4° 14′*		*55° 52′*		*5° 56′*		*54° 35′*	
d	*h*	*m*	*h*	*m*	*h*	*m*	*h*	*m*	*h*	*m*	*h*	*m*	*h*	*m*	*h*	*m*	*h*	*m*	*h*	*m*	*h*	*m*	*h*	*m*	*h*	*m*	*h*	*m*
1	5	13	18	47	5	23	18	57	5	18	18	56	5	18	18	59	5	12	18	59	5	21	19	11	5	31	19	16
2	5	14	18	45	5	24	18	55	5	20	18	54	5	20	18	57	5	14	18	57	5	23	19	09	5	32	19	13
3	5	16	18	43	5	26	18	52	5	22	18	51	5	21	18	54	5	16	18	54	5	25	19	06	5	34	19	11
4	5	17	18	40	5	27	18	50	5	23	18	49	5	23	18	52	5	18	18	52	5	27	19	04	5	36	19	08
5	5	19	18	38	5	29	18	48	5	25	18	47	5	25	18	49	5	20	18	49	5	29	19	01	5	38	19	06
6	5	21	18	36	5	31	18	46	5	27	18	44	5	27	18	47	5	22	18	47	5	31	18	58	5	40	19	03
7	5	22	18	33	5	32	18	43	5	28	18	42	5	28	18	45	5	24	18	44	5	33	18	56	5	42	19	01
8	5	24	18	31	5	34	18	41	5	30	18	40	5	30	18	42	5	25	18	42	5	35	18	53	5	43	18	58
9	5	25	18	29	5	35	18	39	5	32	18	37	5	32	18	40	5	27	18	39	5	37	18	51	5	45	18	56
10	5	27	18	27	5	37	18	37	5	33	18	35	5	34	18	37	5	29	18	36	5	39	18	48	5	47	18	53
11	5	29	18	24	5	39	18	34	5	35	18	33	5	35	18	35	5	31	18	34	5	41	18	45	5	49	18	51
12	5	30	18	22	5	40	18	32	5	37	18	30	5	37	18	32	5	33	18	31	5	42	18	43	5	51	18	48
13	5	32	18	20	5	42	18	30	5	38	18	28	5	39	18	30	5	35	18	29	5	44	18	40	5	52	18	46
14	5	33	18	17	5	43	18	27	5	40	18	25	5	40	18	28	5	37	18	26	5	46	18	37	5	54	18	43
15	5	35	18	15	5	45	18	25	5	42	18	23	5	42	18	25	5	38	18	24	5	48	18	35	5	56	18	41
16	5	36	18	13	5	47	18	23	5	43	18	21	5	44	18	23	5	40	18	21	5	50	18	32	5	58	18	38
17	5	38	18	11	5	48	18	21	5	45	18	18	5	46	18	20	5	42	18	19	5	52	18	30	6	00	18	36
18	5	40	18	08	5	50	18	18	5	47	18	16	5	47	18	18	5	44	18	16	5	54	18	27	6	02	18	33
19	5	41	18	06	5	51	18	16	5	48	18	14	5	49	18	15	5	46	18	13	5	56	18	24	6	03	18	30
20	5	43	18	04	5	53	18	14	5	50	18	11	5	51	18	13	5	48	18	11	5	58	18	22	6	05	18	28
21	5	45	18	01	5	55	18	11	5	52	18	09	5	53	18	10	5	50	18	08	6	00	18	19	6	07	18	25
22	5	46	17	59	5	56	18	09	5	53	18	07	5	54	18	08	5	52	18	06	6	02	18	16	6	09	18	23
23	5	48	17	57	5	58	18	07	5	55	18	04	5	56	18	06	5	53	18	03	6	04	18	14	6	11	18	20
24	5	49	17	54	5	59	18	04	5	57	18	02	5	58	18	03	5	55	18	01	6	06	18	11	6	13	18	18
25	5	51	17	52	6	01	18	02	5	58	17	59	6	00	18	01	5	57	17	58	6	08	18	08	6	14	18	15
26	5	53	17	50	6	03	18	00	6	00	17	57	6	01	17	58	5	59	17	55	6	10	18	06	6	16	18	13
27	5	54	17	48	6	04	17	58	6	02	17	55	6	03	17	56	6	01	17	53	6	12	18	03	6	18	18	10
28	5	56	17	45	6	06	17	55	6	03	17	52	6	05	17	53	6	03	17	50	6	14	18	00	6	20	18	08
29	5	57	17	43	6	07	17	53	6	05	17	50	6	07	17	51	6	05	17	48	6	16	17	58	6	22	18	05
30	5	59	17	41	6	09	17	51	6	07	17	48	6	09	17	48	6	07	17	45	6	18	17	55	6	24	18	03

JUPITER

Day	*R.A.*		*Dec.*		*Transit*		*5° high*			
							52°		*56°*	
	h	*m*	°	′	*h*	*m*	*h*	*m*	*h*	*m*
1	8	51.0	+18	08	10	09	3	08	2	55
11	8	59.2	+17	36	9	38	2	39	2	28
21	9	07.0	+17	04	9	07	2	11	2	00
31	9	14.2	+16	34	8	34	1	42	1	31

Diameters – equatorial 33″ polar 31″

SATURN

Day	*R.A.*		*Dec.*		*Transit*		*5° high*			
							52°		*56°*	
	h	*m*	°	′	*h*	*m*	*h*	*m*	*h*	*m*
1	15	04.8	−15	12	16	22	20	23	20	04
11	15	07.5	−15	25	15	45	19	45	19	26
21	15	10.8	−15	41	15	09	19	07	18	47
31	15	14.5	−15	57	14	34	18	30	18	10

Diameters – equatorial 16″ polar 14″

Rings – major axis 36″ minor axis 13″

URANUS

Day	*R.A.*		*Dec.*		*Transit*		*10° high*			
							52°		*56°*	
	h	*m*	°	′	*h*	*m*	*h*	*m*	*h*	*m*
1	0	59.6	+5	36	2	19	20	52	20	54
11	0	58.4	+5	28	1	38	20	12	20	14
21	0	57.0	+5	20	0	58	19	32	19	35
31	0	55.6	+5	11	0	17	18	52	18	55

Diameter 4″

NEPTUNE

Day	*R.A.*		*Dec.*		*Transit*		*10° high*			
							52°		*56°*	
	h	*m*	°	′	*h*	*m*	*h*	*m*	*h*	*m*
1	22	32.7	−9	58	23	48	3	49	3	31
11	22	31.7	−10	04	23	08	3	08	2	50
21	22	30.7	−10	10	22	28	2	27	2	09
31	22	29.8	−10	15	21	48	1	46	1	28

Diameter 2″

OCTOBER 2014

TENTH MONTH, 31 DAYS. *Octo* (eighth), eighth month of Roman pre-Julian calendar

1	*Wednesday*	King Henry III, reign 1216–1272, House of Plantagenet *b.* 1207; Coronation of Queen Mary I 1553	day 274
2	*Thursday*	King Richard III, who reigned from 1483–1485, House of York *b.* 1452	275
3	*Friday*	King Edward I orders Dafydd ap Gruffydd, Prince of Gwynedd, Wales, to be hung, drawn and quartered 1283	276
4	*Saturday*	Richard Cromwell, the third son of Oliver Cromwell and second Lord Protector of England *b.* 1626	277
5	*Sunday*	Guy Pearce, actor who portrayed King Edward VIII in the Oscar-winning film *The King's Speech b.* 1967	278
6	*Monday*	Kenneth Branagh's *Henry V* is released, earning him two Academy Award nominations 1989	week 40 day 279
7	*Tuesday*	King George III's Royal Proclamation of 1763 closes the North American frontier to expansion 1763	280
8	*Wednesday*	Margaret Douglas, whose son married Mary, Queen of Scots *b.* 1515	281
9	*Thursday*	Isabella of Angouleme, King John's wife, crowned Queen Consort of England at Westminster Abbey 1200	282
10	*Friday*	Mary of Waltham, daughter of King Edward III, who died soon after marrying John V of Brittany *b.* 1344	283
11	*Saturday*	King George II is crowned at Westminster Abbey, featuring four new anthems composed by Handel 1727	284
12	*Sunday*	King Edward VI, who reigned from 1547–1553, House of Tudor *b.* 1537	285
13	*Monday*	Coronation of King Henry IV at Westminster Abbey 1399	week 41 day 286
14	*Tuesday*	King Harold II is killed at the Battle of Hastings 1066; King James II, reign 1685–1688 *b.* 1633	287
15	*Wednesday*	Alfred, Prince of Saxe-Coburg and Gotha, grandson of Queen Victoria and Prince Albert *b.* 1874	288
16	*Thursday*	Queen's University in Canada is established in a Royal Charter issued by Queen Victoria 1841	289
17	*Friday*	While creating a diversion, the Scots fall to King Edward III at the Battle of Neville's Cross 1346	290
18	*Saturday*	Margaret Tudor, daughter of King Henry VII and great-grandmother of King James I *d.* 1541	291
19	*Sunday*	King John, who reigned from 1199–1216, House of Plantagenet *d.* 1216	292
20	*Monday*	Coronation of King George I at Westminster Abbey 1714	week 42 day 293
21	*Tuesday*	George Plantagenet, 1st Duke of Clarence, brother of two kings – Edward IV and Richard III *b.* 1449	294
22	*Wednesday*	Charles Stuart, son of King James II and the first person to be styled Duke of Cambridge *b.* 1660	295
23	*Thursday*	The Battle of Edgehill, the first pitched battle of the English Civil War ends inconclusively 1642	296
24	*Friday*	Jane Seymour, third wife of King Henry VIII and mother of Edward VI, dies soon after childbirth 1537	297
25	*Saturday*	King Stephen, House of Normandy *d.* 1154; King George II, House of Hanover *d.* 1760	298
26	*Sunday*	The Treaty of Ripon is signed between King Charles I and the Scottish Covenanters 1640	299
27	*Monday*	Catherine of Valois, Queen Consort of England from 1420–1422 *b.* 1401	week 43 day 300
28	*Tuesday*	Ted Hughes, Poet Laureate of Queen Elizabeth II following the refusal of Philip Larkin *d.* 1998	301
29	*Wednesday*	Sir Walter Raleigh is executed by order of King James I after defying the king during an expedition 1618	302
30	*Thursday*	Coronation of King Henry VII at Westminster Abbey 1485	303
31	*Friday*	Eleanor of England, daughter of King Henry II and Queen Consort of Castille *d.* 1214	304

ASTRONOMICAL PHENOMENA

d	*h*	
4	17	Mercury at stationary point
7	21	Uranus at opposition
8	11	Total eclipse of Moon (see page 628)
16	21	Mercury in inferior conjunction
17	18	Venus in conjunction with Mercury. Venus 2°N.
18	00	Jupiter in conjunction with Moon. Jupiter 5°N.
22	21	Mercury in conjunction with Moon. Mercury 0°.7 N.
23	12	Sun's longitude 210° ♏
23	21	Venus in conjunction with Moon. Venus 0°.05 N.
23	22	Partial eclipse of Sun (see page 628)
25	08	Venus in superior conjunction
25	16	Saturn in conjunction with Moon. Saturn 1°S.
25	19	Mercury at stationary point
28	13	Mars in conjunction with Moon. Mars 7°S.

MINIMA OF ALGOL

d	*h*	*d*	*h*	*d*	*h*
2	14.1	14	01.3	25	12.6
5	10.9	16	22.2	28	09.4
8	07.7	19	19.0	31	06.2
11	04.5	22	15.8		

CONSTELLATIONS

The following constellations are near their meridian at

	d	*h*		*d*	*h*
September	1	24	October	16	21
September	15	23	November	1	20
October	1	22	November	15	19

Ursa Major (below the Pole), Cepheus, Cassiopeia, Cygnus, Lacerta, Andromeda, Pegasus, Capricornus, Aquarius and Piscis Austrinus

THE MOON

Phases, Apsides and Node	*d*	*h*	*m*
☽ First Quarter	1	19	33
○ Full Moon	8	10	51
☾ Last Quarter	15	19	12
● New Moon	23	21	57
☽ First Quarter	31	02	48
Perigee (362,494km)	6	09	46
Apogee (404,862km)	18	06	10

Mean longitude of ascending node on October 1, 200°

THE SUN

s.d. 16′.1

Day	Right Ascension			Dec. –		Equation of time		Rise 52°		Rise 56°		Transit		Set 52°		Set 56°		Sidereal time			Transit of first point of Aries		
	h	*m*	*s*	°	′	*m*	*s*	*h*	*m*	*h*	*m*	*h*	*m*	*h*	*m*	*h*	*m*	*h*	*m*	*s*	*h*	*m*	*s*
1	12	28	27	3	04	+10	09	6	01	6	03	11	50	17	38	17	36	0	38	36	23	17	34
2	12	32	05	3	28	+10	28	6	02	6	05	11	49	17	36	17	33	0	42	33	23	13	38
3	12	35	42	3	51	+10	47	6	04	6	07	11	49	17	33	17	30	0	46	29	23	09	42
4	12	39	20	4	14	+11	06	6	06	6	09	11	49	17	31	17	28	0	50	26	23	05	46
5	12	42	58	4	37	+11	25	6	07	6	11	11	48	17	29	17	25	0	54	23	23	01	50
6	12	46	36	5	00	+11	43	6	09	6	13	11	48	17	26	17	23	0	58	19	22	57	55
7	12	50	15	5	23	+12	00	6	11	6	15	11	48	17	24	17	20	1	02	16	22	53	59
8	12	53	54	5	46	+12	18	6	12	6	17	11	48	17	22	17	17	1	06	12	22	50	03
9	12	57	34	6	09	+12	35	6	14	6	19	11	47	17	20	17	15	1	10	09	22	46	07
10	13	01	14	6	32	+12	51	6	16	6	21	11	47	17	17	17	12	1	14	05	22	42	11
11	13	04	55	6	54	+13	07	6	18	6	23	11	47	17	15	17	10	1	18	02	22	38	15
12	13	08	36	7	17	+13	23	6	19	6	25	11	47	17	13	17	07	1	21	58	22	34	19
13	13	12	17	7	40	+13	38	6	21	6	27	11	46	17	11	17	05	1	25	55	22	30	23
14	13	15	59	8	02	+13	52	6	23	6	29	11	46	17	08	17	02	1	29	52	22	26	27
15	13	19	42	8	24	+14	06	6	24	6	31	11	46	17	06	17	00	1	33	48	22	22	31
16	13	23	25	8	46	+14	19	6	26	6	33	11	46	17	04	16	57	1	37	45	22	18	35
17	13	27	09	9	08	+14	32	6	28	6	35	11	45	17	02	16	55	1	41	41	22	14	40
18	13	30	54	9	30	+14	44	6	30	6	37	11	45	17	00	16	52	1	45	38	22	10	44
19	13	34	39	9	52	+14	56	6	31	6	39	11	45	16	58	16	50	1	49	34	22	06	48
20	13	38	24	10	14	+15	07	6	33	6	41	11	45	16	56	16	47	1	53	31	22	02	52
21	13	42	10	10	35	+15	17	6	35	6	43	11	45	16	54	16	45	1	57	27	21	58	56
22	13	45	57	10	57	+15	27	6	37	6	45	11	44	16	51	16	43	2	01	24	21	55	00
23	13	49	45	11	18	+15	35	6	38	6	48	11	44	16	49	16	40	2	05	21	21	51	04
24	13	53	33	11	39	+15	44	6	40	6	50	11	44	16	47	16	38	2	09	17	21	47	08
25	13	57	22	12	00	+15	51	6	42	6	52	11	44	16	45	16	35	2	13	14	21	43	12
26	14	01	12	12	20	+15	58	6	44	6	54	11	44	16	43	16	33	2	17	10	21	39	16
27	14	05	03	12	41	+16	04	6	46	6	56	11	44	16	41	16	31	2	21	07	21	35	20
28	14	08	54	13	01	+16	09	6	47	6	58	11	44	16	39	16	29	2	25	03	21	31	25
29	14	12	46	13	21	+16	14	6	49	7	00	11	44	16	38	16	26	2	29	00	21	27	29
30	14	16	39	13	41	+16	18	6	51	7	02	11	44	16	36	16	24	2	32	56	21	23	33
31	14	20	32	14	00	+16	21	6	53	7	04	11	44	16	34	16	22	2	36	53	21	19	37

DURATION OF TWILIGHT (in minutes)

Latitude	52°	56°	52°	56°	52°	56°	52°	56°
	1 October		*11 October*		*21 October*		*31 October*	
Civil	34	37	34	37	34	38	35	39
Nautical	73	80	73	80	74	81	75	83
Astronomical	113	125	112	124	113	124	114	126

THE NIGHT SKY

Mercury becomes a morning object during the last week of the month, low above the east-south-eastern horizon before the beginning of civil twilight. During this time its magnitude brightens from +1.2 to −0.4.

Venus passes through superior conjunction on the 25th and therefore remains unsuitably placed for observation throughout the month.

Mars, continues its progress eastwards and ends the month in the constellation of Sagittarius. It is still visible low in the south-western sky in the early evenings. Its magnitude is +0.9. The waxing crescent Moon passes 6 degrees north of the planet on the 28th.

Jupiter, magnitude −2.0, continues to be visible as a brilliant morning object in the south-eastern sky and by the end of the month it becomes visible shortly after midnight. During October it passes into the constellation of Leo. The waning crescent Moon passes 6 degrees south of Jupiter on the 18th.

Saturn remains too close to the Sun for observation throughout October.

Uranus is at opposition on the 7th, in the constellation of Pisces. It is not visible to the naked eye, since its magnitude is +5.7.

THE MOON

Day	R.A.		Dec.	Hor. Par.	Semi-diam.	Sun's Co-Long.	PA. of Br. Limb	Ph.	Age	Rise				Transit		Set			
										52°		56°				52°		56°	
	h	m	°	′	′	°	°	%	d	h	m	h	m	h	m	h	m	h	m
1	17	49	−18.5	58.1	15.8	355	270	41	6.8	13	21	13	39	17	50	22	22	22	04
2	18	47	−17.8	58.7	16.0	8	266	52	7.8	14	08	14	24	18	46	23	30	23	15
3	19	45	−15.9	59.3	16.2	20	261	63	8.8	14	49	15	02	19	43	—		—	
4	20	43	−13.1	59.9	16.3	32	258	74	9.8	15	24	15	34	20	38	0	44	0	32
5	21	40	−9.3	60.3	16.4	44	255	84	10.8	15	56	16	01	21	33	2	03	1	54
6	22	37	−5.0	60.5	16.5	56	253	92	11.8	16	25	16	27	22	28	3	23	3	19
7	23	34	−0.4	60.4	16.5	68	253	97	12.8	16	54	16	52	23	22	4	43	4	44
8	0	30	+4.3	60.2	16.4	81	256	100	13.8	17	24	17	17	—		6	03	6	08
9	1	26	+8.6	59.7	16.3	93	71	100	14.8	17	55	17	45	0	16	7	22	7	30
10	2	22	+12.4	59.0	16.1	105	75	97	15.8	18	30	18	17	1	10	8	37	8	49
11	3	18	+15.3	58.1	15.8	117	79	92	16.8	19	10	18	54	2	04	9	47	10	03
12	4	13	+17.3	57.3	15.6	129	83	85	17.8	19	54	19	37	2	57	10	51	11	08
13	5	08	+18.4	56.4	15.4	141	88	77	18.8	20	44	20	26	3	50	11	47	12	05
14	6	01	+18.4	55.7	15.2	154	92	67	19.8	21	39	21	21	4	41	12	35	12	52
15	6	53	+17.6	55.0	15.0	166	96	58	20.8	22	36	22	21	5	30	13	15	13	31
16	7	43	+16.0	54.6	14.9	178	100	48	21.8	23	36	23	24	6	17	13	49	14	02
17	8	31	+13.7	54.3	14.8	190	103	39	22.8	—		—		7	02	14	18	14	29
18	9	18	+10.9	54.2	14.8	202	106	30	23.8	0	38	0	28	7	46	14	44	14	52
19	10	04	+7.6	54.2	14.8	215	108	22	24.8	1	40	1	34	8	30	15	08	15	12
20	10	50	+4.0	54.4	14.8	227	109	14	25.8	2	43	2	40	9	12	15	31	15	32
21	11	36	+0.2	54.7	14.9	239	110	8	26.8	3	48	3	48	9	56	15	53	15	51
22	12	22	−3.7	55.1	15.0	251	110	4	27.8	4	53	4	57	10	40	16	17	16	12
23	13	10	−7.4	55.5	15.1	263	112	1	28.8	5	59	6	07	11	26	16	43	16	35
24	13	59	−10.9	56.0	15.3	276	242	0	0.1	7	07	7	18	12	14	17	13	17	01
25	14	50	−14.0	56.6	15.4	288	277	1	1.1	8	14	8	28	13	04	17	47	17	33
26	15	44	−16.4	57.0	15.5	300	276	5	2.1	9	20	9	37	13	56	18	29	18	12
27	16	39	−18.0	57.5	15.7	312	273	10	3.1	10	22	10	40	14	51	19	18	19	00
28	17	36	−18.5	58.0	15.8	324	268	18	4.1	11	18	11	36	15	46	20	16	19	58
29	18	34	−18.0	58.4	15.9	337	264	27	5.1	12	07	12	24	16	42	21	21	21	05
30	19	31	−16.5	58.8	16.0	349	260	38	6.1	12	49	13	03	17	37	22	32	22	19
31	20	28	−13.9	59.1	16.1	1	256	49	7.1	13	25	13	36	18	32	23	47	23	38

MERCURY

Day	R.A.		Dec.	Diam.	Phase	Transit		5° high			
								52°		56°	
	h	m	°	″	%	h	m	h	m	h	m
1	13	53	−15.3	8	39	13	13	17	12	16	53
3	13	55	−15.6	8	34	13	06	17	05	16	45
5	13	55	−15.6	9	28	12	59	16	57	16	37
7	13	54	−15.4	9	22	12	49	16	49	16	30
9	13	51	−15.0	10	16	12	38	16	41	16	23
11	13	46	−14.2	10	10	12	25	16	33	16	16
13	13	40	−13.2	10	5	12	10	16	26	16	10
15	13	32	−11.8	10	1	11	54	7	32	7	46
17	13	24	−10.4	10	0	11	38	7	07	7	20
19	13	16	−8.9	10	2	11	23	6	43	6	54
21	13	10	−7.5	10	6	11	09	6	22	6	32
23	13	05	−6.4	9	13	10	58	6	04	6	13
25	13	04	−5.6	9	21	10	49	5	51	5	59
27	13	05	−5.2	8	31	10	42	5	43	5	51
29	13	08	−5.2	8	41	10	38	5	39	5	47
31	13	13	−5.6	7	50	10	36	5	39	5	47

VENUS

Day	R.A.		Dec.	Diam.	Phase	Transit		5° high			
								52°		56°	
	h	m	°	″	%	h	m	h	m	h	m
1	12	07	+0.7	10	99	11	29	5	58	6	01
6	12	30	−1.8	10	100	11	32	6	15	6	19
11	12	53	−4.3	10	100	11	36	6	31	6	38
16	13	16	−6.7	10	100	11	39	6	48	6	57
21	13	40	−9.1	10	100	11	43	7	05	7	17
26	14	03	−11.5	10	100	11	47	7	23	7	37
31	14	27	−13.7	10	100	11	51	7	40	7	57

MARS

Day	R.A.		Dec.	Diam.	Phase	Transit		5° high			
								52°		56°	
	h	m	°	″	%	h	m	h	m	h	m
1	16	40	−23.7	6	89	16	01	18	57	18	19
6	16	55	−24.1	6	89	15	56	18	49	18	09
11	17	11	−24.5	6	89	15	52	18	41	18	00
16	17	26	−24.7	6	90	15	48	18	35	17	53
21	17	42	−24.9	6	90	15	44	18	30	17	47
26	17	59	−25.0	6	90	15	41	18	26	17	43
31	18	15	−24.9	6	90	15	38	18	23	17	41

SUNRISE AND SUNSET

	London				*Bristol*				*Birmingham*				*Manchester*				*Newcastle*				*Glasgow*				*Belfast*			
	0° 05′		*51° 30′*		*2° 35′*		*51° 28′*		*1° 55′*		*52° 28′*		*2° 15′*		*53° 28′*		*1° 37′*		*54° 59′*		*4° 14′*		*55° 52′*		*5° 56′*		*54° 35′*	
d	*h*	*m*	*h*	*m*	*h*	*m*	*h*	*m*	*h*	*m*	*h*	*m*	*h*	*m*	*h*	*m*	*h*	*m*	*h*	*m*	*h*	*m*	*h*	*m*	*h*	*m*	*h*	*m*
1	6	01	17	38	6	11	17	48	6	08	17	45	6	10	17	46	6	09	17	43	6	19	17	53	6	26	18	00
2	6	02	17	36	6	12	17	46	6	10	17	43	6	12	17	44	6	10	17	40	6	21	17	50	6	27	17	58
3	6	04	17	34	6	14	17	44	6	12	17	41	6	14	17	41	6	12	17	38	6	23	17	47	6	29	17	55
4	6	06	17	32	6	16	17	42	6	14	17	38	6	16	17	39	6	14	17	35	6	25	17	45	6	31	17	53
5	6	07	17	29	6	17	17	39	6	15	17	36	6	17	17	36	6	16	17	33	6	27	17	42	6	33	17	50
6	6	09	17	27	6	19	17	37	6	17	17	34	6	19	17	34	6	18	17	30	6	29	17	40	6	35	17	48
7	6	11	17	25	6	21	17	35	6	19	17	31	6	21	17	32	6	20	17	28	6	31	17	37	6	37	17	45
8	6	12	17	23	6	22	17	33	6	21	17	29	6	23	17	29	6	22	17	25	6	33	17	35	6	39	17	43
9	6	14	17	20	6	24	17	30	6	22	17	27	6	25	17	27	6	24	17	23	6	35	17	32	6	41	17	40
10	6	16	17	18	6	26	17	28	6	24	17	24	6	27	17	25	6	26	17	20	6	37	17	29	6	43	17	38
11	6	17	17	16	6	27	17	26	6	26	17	22	6	28	17	22	6	28	17	18	6	40	17	27	6	45	17	35
12	6	19	17	14	6	29	17	24	6	27	17	20	6	30	17	20	6	30	17	15	6	42	17	24	6	46	17	33
13	6	21	17	12	6	31	17	22	6	29	17	18	6	32	17	18	6	32	17	13	6	44	17	22	6	48	17	31
14	6	22	17	10	6	32	17	20	6	31	17	15	6	34	17	15	6	34	17	10	6	46	17	19	6	50	17	28
15	6	24	17	07	6	34	17	17	6	33	17	13	6	36	17	13	6	36	17	08	6	48	17	17	6	52	17	26
16	6	26	17	05	6	36	17	15	6	35	17	11	6	38	17	11	6	38	17	06	6	50	17	14	6	54	17	24
17	6	27	17	03	6	37	17	13	6	36	17	09	6	39	17	08	6	40	17	03	6	52	17	12	6	56	17	21
18	6	29	17	01	6	39	17	11	6	38	17	07	6	41	17	06	6	42	17	01	6	54	17	09	6	58	17	19
19	6	31	16	59	6	41	17	09	6	40	17	05	6	43	17	04	6	44	16	58	6	56	17	07	7	00	17	16
20	6	33	16	57	6	43	17	07	6	42	17	02	6	45	17	02	6	46	16	56	6	58	17	05	7	02	17	14
21	6	34	16	55	6	44	17	05	6	43	17	00	6	47	17	00	6	48	16	54	7	00	17	02	7	04	17	12
22	6	36	16	53	6	46	17	03	6	45	16	58	6	49	16	57	6	50	16	51	7	02	17	00	7	06	17	10
23	6	38	16	51	6	48	17	01	6	47	16	56	6	51	16	55	6	52	16	49	7	04	16	57	7	08	17	07
24	6	40	16	49	6	49	16	59	6	49	16	54	6	53	16	53	6	54	16	47	7	06	16	55	7	10	17	05
25	6	41	16	47	6	51	16	57	6	51	16	52	6	54	16	51	6	56	16	45	7	08	16	53	7	12	17	03
26	6	43	16	45	6	53	16	55	6	53	16	50	6	56	16	49	6	58	16	42	7	11	16	50	7	14	17	01
27	6	45	16	43	6	55	16	53	6	54	16	48	6	58	16	47	7	00	16	40	7	13	16	48	7	16	16	59
28	6	46	16	41	6	56	16	51	6	56	16	46	7	00	16	45	7	02	16	38	7	15	16	46	7	18	16	56
29	6	48	16	39	6	58	16	49	6	58	16	44	7	02	16	43	7	04	16	36	7	17	16	44	7	20	16	54
30	6	50	16	37	7	00	16	47	7	00	16	42	7	04	16	41	7	06	16	34	7	19	16	41	7	22	16	52
31	6	52	16	35	7	02	16	45	7	02	16	40	7	06	16	39	7	08	16	32	7	21	16	39	7	24	16	50

JUPITER

Day	*R.A.*		*Dec.*		*Transit*		*5° high*			
							52°		*56°*	
	h	*m*	°	′	*h*	*m*	*h*	*m*	*h*	*m*
1	9	14.2	+16	34	8	34	1	42	1	31
11	9	20.8	+16	06	8	02	1	11	1	01
21	9	26.6	+15	40	7	28	0	40	0	30
31	9	31.6	+15	18	6	54	0	08	23	55

Diameters – equatorial 35″ polar 33″

SATURN

Day	*R.A.*		*Dec.*		*Transit*		*5° high*			
							52°		*56°*	
	h	*m*	°	′	*h*	*m*	*h*	*m*	*h*	*m*
1	15	14.5	−15	57	14	34	18	30	18	10
11	15	18.6	−16	14	13	59	17	52	17	32
21	15	22.9	−16	32	13	24	17	15	16	55
31	15	27.5	−16	50	12	49	16	39	16	17

Diameters – equatorial 15″ polar 14″

Rings – major axis 35″ minor axis 13″

URANUS

Day	*R.A.*		*Dec.*		*Transit*		*10° high*			
							52°		*56°*	
	h	*m*	°	′	*h*	*m*	*h*	*m*	*h*	*m*
1	0	55.6	+5	11	0	17	5	38	5	35
11	0	54.1	+5	02	23	32	4	56	4	53
21	0	52.6	+4	52	22	51	4	14	4	12
31	0	51.2	+4	44	22	11	3	33	3	30

Diameter 4″

NEPTUNE

Day	*R.A.*		*Dec.*		*Transit*		*10° high*			
							52°		*56°*	
	h	*m*	°	′	*h*	*m*	*h*	*m*	*h*	*m*
1	22	29.8	−10	15	21	48	1	46	1	28
11	22	29.0	−10	19	21	08	1	06	0	48
21	22	28.4	−10	23	20	28	0	25	0	07
31	22	28.0	−10	25	19	48	23	41	23	23

Diameter 2″

NOVEMBER 2014

ELEVENTH MONTH, 30 DAYS. *Novem* (nine), ninth month of Roman pre-Julian calendar

1	*Saturday*	William of Orange sets sail from the Netherlands to seize the throne from King James II 1688	day 305
2	*Sunday*	King Edward V, who reigned from April to June 1483, House of York *b.* 1470	306
3	*Monday*	Princess Sophia, the twelfth child and fifth daughter of King George III *b.* 1777	week 44 day 307
4	*Tuesday*	King William III, who reigned from 1689–1702, House of Orange *b.* 1650	308
5	*Wednesday*	Guy Fawkes is found guarding explosives beneath the House of Lords during the Gunpowder Plot 1605	309
6	*Thursday*	Coronation of King Henry VI at Westminster Abbey 1429	310
7	*Friday*	King Henry V buried at Westminster Abbey 1422	311
8	*Saturday*	Robert Catesby, the mastermind behind the Gunpowder Plot, is shot dead during a last stand 1605	312
9	*Sunday*	King Edward VII, who reigned from 1901–1910, House of Saxe-Coburg and Gotha *b.* 1841	313
10	*Monday*	King George II, who reigned from 1727–1760, House of Hanover *b.* 1683	week 45 day 314
11	*Tuesday*	Funeral of King George II at Westminster Abbey 1760; the Cenotaph is unveiled by King George V 1920	315
12	*Wednesday*	King Cnut (Canute), who ruled England from 1016–1035 and was also king of Denmark and Norway *d.* 1035	316
13	*Thursday*	King Edward III, who reigned from 1327–1377, House of Plantagenet *b.* 1312	317
14	*Friday*	Charles, Prince of Wales, eldest child and heir apparent of Queen Elizabeth II *b.* 1948	318
15	*Saturday*	Peter Phillips, the first royal baby to be born a commoner in over 500 years *b.* 1977	319
16	*Sunday*	Prince William and Kate Middleton announce their engagement a month after the prince proposed 2010	320
17	*Monday*	Queen Mary I, 'Bloody Mary', who reigned from 1553–1558, House of Tudor *d.* 1558	week 46 day 321
18	*Tuesday*	John II, Duke of Brittany, who in 1260 marries Beatrice of England, daughter of King Henry III *d.* 1305	322
19	*Wednesday*	King Charles I, who reigned from 1625–1649, House of Stuart *b.* 1600	323
20	*Thursday*	Wedding of Princess Elizabeth and Philip Mountbatten, Duke of Edinburgh 1947	324
21	*Friday*	King George V is taken seriously ill during an audience at Buckingham Palace 1928	325
22	*Saturday*	Laurence Olivier's film adaptation of William Shakespeare's *Henry V* is released 1944	326
23	*Sunday*	Perkin Warbeck, pretender to the throne who claimed to be the son of King Edward IV, is hanged 1499	327
24	*Monday*	Queen Elizabeth II outlines plans to abolish hereditary peerage in the House of Lords 1998	week 47 day 328
25	*Tuesday*	Elizabeth of York is crowned Queen Consort of England as wife of King Henry VII 1487	329
26	*Wednesday*	Princess Maud of Wales, youngest daughter of King Edward VII and Alexandra of Denmark *b.* 1869	330
27	*Thursday*	Princess Mary Adelaide of Cambridge, Duchess of Teck, great-grandmother of Queen Elizabeth II *b.* 1833	331
28	*Friday*	Margaret Tudor, daughter of King Henry VII and great-grandmother of King James I *b.* 1489	332
29	*Saturday*	Lionel of Antwerp, 1st Duke of Clarence, the second son of King Edward III to survive infancy *b.* 1338	333
30	*Sunday*	Edmund II 'Ironside', King of England in 1016 until agreeing to divide the kingdom with Cnut *d.* 1016	334

ASTRONOMICAL PHENOMENA

d	*h*	
1	15	Mercury at greatest elongation W. 19°
13	01	Saturn in conjunction with Venus. Saturn 2°N.
14	14	Jupiter in conjunction with Moon. Jupiter 5°N.
16	07	Neptune at stationary point
18	09	Saturn in conjunction
21	18	Mercury in conjunction with Moon. Mercury2°S.
22	06	Saturn in conjunction with Moon. Saturn 1°S.
22	10	Sun's longitude 240° ♐
23	02	Venus in conjunction with Moon. Venus 4°S.
26	03	Saturn in conjunction with Mercury. Saturn 2°N.
26	08	Mars in conjunction with Moon. Mars 7°S.

MINIMA OF ALGOL

d	*h*	*d*	*h*	*d*	*h*
3	03.0	14	14.3	26	01.6
5	23.9	17	11.1	28	22.4
8	20.7	20	07.9		
11	17.5	23	04.7		

CONSTELLATIONS

The following constellations are near their meridian at

	d	*h*		*d*	*h*
October	1	24	November	15	21
October	16	23	December	1	20
November	1	22	December	16	19

Ursa Major (below the Pole), Cepheus, Cassiopeia, Andromeda, Pegasus, Pisces, Aquarius and Cetus

THE MOON

Phases, Apsides and Node	*d*	*h*	*m*
○ Full Moon	6	22	23
☾ Last Quarter	14	15	15
● New Moon	22	12	32
☽ First Quarter	29	10	06
Perigee (367,908km)	3	00	37
Apogee (404,296km)	15	01	56
Perigee (369,862km)	27	23	05

Mean longitude of ascending node on November 1, 198°

THE SUN

s.d. 16′.2

Day	Right Ascension			Dec. –		Equation of time		Rise 52°		Rise 56°		Transit		Set 52°		Set 56°		Sidereal time			Transit of first point of Aries		
	h	m	s	°	′	m	s	h	m	h	m	h	m	h	m	h	m	h	m	s	h	m	s
1	14	24	26	14	20	+16	23	6	55	7	07	11	44	16	32	16	20	2	40	49	21	15	41
2	14	28	21	14	39	+16	25	6	56	7	09	11	44	16	30	16	18	2	44	46	21	11	45
3	14	32	17	14	58	+16	26	6	58	7	11	11	44	16	28	16	15	2	48	43	21	07	49
4	14	36	13	15	17	+16	26	7	00	7	13	11	44	16	26	16	13	2	52	39	21	03	53
5	14	40	11	15	35	+16	25	7	02	7	15	11	44	16	25	16	11	2	56	36	20	59	57
6	14	44	09	15	53	+16	23	7	04	7	17	11	44	16	23	16	09	3	00	32	20	56	01
7	14	48	08	16	11	+16	21	7	05	7	19	11	44	16	21	16	07	3	04	29	20	52	05
8	14	52	08	16	29	+16	18	7	07	7	22	11	44	16	20	16	05	3	08	25	20	48	10
9	14	56	08	16	46	+16	14	7	09	7	24	11	44	16	18	16	03	3	12	22	20	44	14
10	15	00	10	17	03	+16	09	7	11	7	26	11	44	16	16	16	01	3	16	18	20	40	18
11	15	04	12	17	20	+16	03	7	13	7	28	11	44	16	15	15	59	3	20	15	20	36	22
12	15	08	16	17	36	+15	56	7	14	7	30	11	44	16	13	15	58	3	24	12	20	32	26
13	15	12	20	17	53	+15	48	7	16	7	32	11	44	16	12	15	56	3	28	08	20	28	30
14	15	16	25	18	08	+15	40	7	18	7	34	11	44	16	10	15	54	3	32	05	20	24	34
15	15	20	31	18	24	+15	31	7	20	7	36	11	45	16	09	15	52	3	36	01	20	20	38
16	15	24	37	18	39	+15	21	7	21	7	38	11	45	16	08	15	51	3	39	58	20	16	42
17	15	28	45	18	54	+15	09	7	23	7	40	11	45	16	06	15	49	3	43	54	20	12	46
18	15	32	53	19	09	+14	58	7	25	7	42	11	45	16	05	15	47	3	47	51	20	08	50
19	15	37	03	19	23	+14	45	7	26	7	44	11	45	16	04	15	46	3	51	47	20	04	55
20	15	41	13	19	37	+14	31	7	28	7	46	11	46	16	03	15	44	3	55	44	20	00	59
21	15	45	24	19	50	+14	17	7	30	7	48	11	46	16	01	15	43	3	59	41	19	57	03
22	15	49	35	20	04	+14	02	7	31	7	50	11	46	16	00	15	41	4	03	37	19	53	07
23	15	53	48	20	16	+13	46	7	33	7	52	11	46	15	59	15	40	4	07	34	19	49	11
24	15	58	01	20	29	+13	29	7	35	7	54	11	47	15	58	15	39	4	11	30	19	45	15
25	16	02	15	20	41	+13	11	7	36	7	56	11	47	15	57	15	37	4	15	27	19	41	19
26	16	06	30	20	53	+12	53	7	38	7	58	11	47	15	56	15	36	4	19	23	19	37	23
27	16	10	46	21	04	+12	34	7	39	8	00	11	48	15	55	15	35	4	23	20	19	33	27
28	16	15	02	21	15	+12	14	7	41	8	01	11	48	15	54	15	34	4	27	16	19	29	31
29	16	19	19	21	25	+11	54	7	42	8	03	11	48	15	54	15	33	4	31	13	19	25	35
30	16	23	37	21	35	+11	33	7	44	8	05	11	49	15	53	15	32	4	35	10	19	21	40

DURATION OF TWILIGHT (in minutes)

Latitude	52°	56°	52°	56°	52°	56°	52°	56°
	1 November		*11 November*		*21 November*		*31 November*	
Civil	36	40	37	41	38	43	40	45
Nautical	75	84	78	87	80	90	82	93
Astronomical	115	127	117	130	120	134	123	138

THE NIGHT SKY

Mercury is visible in the mornings for the first two weeks of the month, low above the south-eastern horizon around the time of beginning of morning civil twilight. During this period its magnitude brightens slightly to –0.8 by mid-month.

Venus is on the far side of the Sun and will not be suitably placed for observation again until the end of the year.

Mars, magnitude +1.0, is still visible low in the south-western sky in the early evenings, in the constellation of Capricornus. The waxing crescent Moon passes 6 degrees north of the planet on the 26th.

Jupiter, magnitude –2.1, is still visible as a brilliant object in the morning skies. Observers will notice that it is approaching the bright star Regulus, in Leo. On the 14th the Moon, at last quarter, passes 6 degrees south of Jupiter.

Saturn passes through conjunction on the 18th and therefore is unsuitably placed for observation throughout the month.

THE MOON

Day	R.A.		Dec.	Hor. Par.	Semi-diam.	Sun's Co-Long.	PA. of Br. Limb	Ph.	Age	Rise				Transit		Set			
										52°		56°				52°		56°	
	h	m	°	′	′	°	°	%	d	h	m	h	m	h	m	h	m	h	m
1	21	24	−10.5	59.3	16.2	13	253	60	8.1	13	57	14	04	19	25	—		—	
2	22	20	−6.4	59.5	16.2	25	251	71	9.1	14	26	14	29	20	18	1	04	0	58
3	23	14	−2.0	59.6	16.2	37	249	81	10.1	14	54	14	53	21	10	2	22	2	20
4	0	09	+2.6	59.5	16.2	50	248	89	11.1	15	22	15	17	22	03	3	40	3	42
5	1	04	+7.0	59.3	16.2	62	248	95	12.1	15	51	15	43	22	56	4	57	5	04
6	1	59	+10.9	58.9	16.0	74	245	99	13.1	16	24	16	12	23	49	6	13	6	23
7	2	54	+14.2	58.4	15.9	86	143	100	14.1	17	01	16	47	—		7	26	7	40
8	3	50	+16.7	57.7	15.7	98	91	99	15.1	17	44	17	27	0	43	8	33	8	50
9	4	46	+18.1	57.0	15.5	110	91	95	16.1	18	32	18	14	1	37	9	34	9	52
10	5	41	+18.6	56.3	15.3	122	94	89	17.1	19	25	19	08	2	30	10	26	10	44
11	6	34	+18.1	55.6	15.2	135	98	82	18.1	20	23	20	07	3	20	11	11	11	27
12	7	25	+16.7	55.0	15.0	147	101	74	19.1	21	23	21	09	4	09	11	48	12	02
13	8	15	+14.6	54.6	14.9	159	104	65	20.1	22	24	22	14	4	56	12	19	12	31
14	9	03	+11.9	54.3	14.8	171	107	56	21.1	23	27	23	19	5	41	12	47	12	56
15	9	49	+8.8	54.2	14.8	183	109	47	22.1	—		—		6	24	13	11	13	17
16	10	35	+5.3	54.3	14.8	195	111	37	23.1	0	29	0	25	7	07	13	34	13	37
17	11	20	+1.6	54.5	14.9	208	112	28	24.1	1	33	1	32	7	50	13	56	13	56
18	12	06	−2.3	54.9	15.0	220	112	20	25.1	2	37	2	40	8	33	14	19	14	16
19	12	53	−6.1	55.5	15.1	232	112	13	26.1	3	43	3	49	9	18	14	44	14	37
20	13	42	−9.7	56.1	15.3	244	112	7	27.1	4	50	5	00	10	05	15	12	15	02
21	14	33	−13.0	56.7	15.5	256	114	3	28.1	5	59	6	12	10	55	15	45	15	31
22	15	26	−15.7	57.3	15.6	269	128	0	29.1	7	07	7	23	11	47	16	24	16	07
23	16	22	−17.6	57.9	15.8	281	247	0	0.5	8	12	8	30	12	42	17	11	16	53
24	17	20	−18.6	58.4	15.9	293	261	3	1.5	9	12	9	31	13	39	18	07	17	48
25	18	18	−18.4	58.8	16.0	305	260	8	2.5	10	05	10	23	14	36	19	11	18	54
26	19	17	−17.1	59.1	16.1	317	257	15	3.5	10	50	11	06	15	33	20	22	20	08
27	20	15	−14.7	59.2	16.1	330	254	24	4.5	11	29	11	41	16	28	21	36	21	26
28	21	12	−11.4	59.3	16.2	342	251	34	5.5	12	01	12	10	17	22	22	53	22	46
29	22	07	−7.5	59.2	16.1	354	249	45	6.5	12	31	12	35	18	14	—		—	
30	23	01	−3.2	59.1	16.1	6	248	57	7.5	12	58	12	59	19	06	0	09	0	06

MERCURY

Day	R.A.		Dec.	Diam.	Phase	Transit		5° high			
								52°		56°	
	h	m	°	″	%	h	m	h	m	h	m
1	13	17	−5.8	7	55	10	36	5	40	5	48
3	13	25	−6.6	7	63	10	36	5	44	5	53
5	13	34	−7.5	6	70	10	38	5	51	6	01
7	13	44	−8.5	6	76	10	40	5	59	6	10
9	13	55	−9.6	6	81	10	43	6	08	6	20
11	14	06	−10.8	6	85	10	47	6	18	6	32
13	14	18	−11.9	5	88	10	50	6	29	6	44
15	14	29	−13.1	5	91	10	54	6	40	6	57
17	14	41	−14.3	5	93	10	59	6	52	7	10
19	14	54	−15.5	5	95	11	03	7	04	7	23
21	15	06	−16.6	5	96	11	08	7	16	7	37
23	15	19	−17.6	5	97	11	12	7	28	7	51
25	15	31	−18.6	5	98	11	17	7	40	8	05
27	15	44	−19.6	5	99	11	22	7	52	8	19
29	15	57	−20.5	5	99	11	27	8	04	8	33
31	16	10	−21.3	5	99	11	32	8	16	8	47

VENUS

Day	R.A.		Dec.	Diam.	Phase	Transit		5° high			
								52°		56°	
	h	m	°	″	%	h	m	h	m	h	m
1	14	32	−14.1	10	100	11	52	15	59	15	41
6	14	57	−16.1	10	100	11	57	15	50	15	30
11	15	22	−18.0	10	100	12	02	15	43	15	19
16	15	47	−19.7	10	100	12	08	15	37	15	10
21	16	13	−21.1	10	99	12	15	15	32	15	02
26	16	40	−22.3	10	99	12	21	15	30	14	56
31	17	07	−23.2	10	99	12	29	15	29	14	53

MARS

Day	R.A.		Dec.	Diam.	Phase	Transit		5° high			
								52°		56°	
	h	m	°	″	%	h	m	h	m	h	m
1	18	18	−24.9	6	90	15	37	18	23	17	40
6	18	35	−24.7	5	91	15	34	18	22	17	40
11	18	51	−24.4	5	91	15	30	18	21	17	41
16	19	08	−24.0	5	91	15	27	18	22	17	44
21	19	24	−23.5	5	92	15	24	18	24	17	47
26	19	41	−22.9	5	92	15	21	18	26	17	52
31	19	57	−22.1	5	92	15	17	18	29	17	57

SUNRISE AND SUNSET

	London				*Bristol*				*Birmingham*				*Manchester*				*Newcastle*				*Glasgow*				*Belfast*			
	0° 05′		*51° 30′*		*2° 35′*		*51° 28′*		*1° 55′*		*52° 28′*		*2° 15′*		*53° 28′*		*1° 37′*		*54° 59′*		*4° 14′*		*55° 52′*		*5° 56′*		*54° 35′*	
d	*h*	*m*	*h*	*m*	*h*	*m*	*h*	*m*	*h*	*m*	*h*	*m*	*h*	*m*	*h*	*m*	*h*	*m*	*h*	*m*	*h*	*m*	*h*	*m*	*h*	*m*	*h*	*m*
1	6	54	16	34	7	04	16	44	7	04	16	38	7	08	16	37	7	10	16	30	7	23	16	37	7	26	16	48
2	6	55	16	32	7	05	16	42	7	05	16	36	7	10	16	35	7	12	16	27	7	25	16	35	7	28	16	46
3	6	57	16	30	7	07	16	40	7	07	16	35	7	12	16	33	7	14	16	25	7	27	16	33	7	30	16	44
4	6	59	16	28	7	09	16	38	7	09	16	33	7	13	16	31	7	16	16	23	7	29	16	31	7	32	16	42
5	7	01	16	27	7	11	16	37	7	11	16	31	7	15	16	29	7	18	16	21	7	32	16	29	7	34	16	40
6	7	02	16	25	7	12	16	35	7	13	16	29	7	17	16	27	7	20	16	19	7	34	16	27	7	36	16	38
7	7	04	16	23	7	14	16	33	7	15	16	27	7	19	16	25	7	22	16	18	7	36	16	25	7	38	16	36
8	7	06	16	22	7	16	16	32	7	16	16	26	7	21	16	24	7	24	16	16	7	38	16	23	7	40	16	34
9	7	08	16	20	7	18	16	30	7	18	16	24	7	23	16	22	7	26	16	14	7	40	16	21	7	42	16	33
10	7	09	16	18	7	19	16	29	7	20	16	23	7	25	16	20	7	28	16	12	7	42	16	19	7	44	16	31
11	7	11	16	17	7	21	16	27	7	22	16	21	7	27	16	19	7	30	16	10	7	44	16	17	7	46	16	29
12	7	13	16	15	7	23	16	26	7	24	16	19	7	29	16	17	7	32	16	08	7	46	16	15	7	48	16	27
13	7	15	16	14	7	25	16	24	7	25	16	18	7	31	16	15	7	34	16	07	7	48	16	13	7	50	16	26
14	7	16	16	13	7	26	16	23	7	27	16	16	7	32	16	14	7	36	16	05	7	50	16	12	7	52	16	24
15	7	18	16	11	7	28	16	21	7	29	16	15	7	34	16	12	7	38	16	03	7	53	16	10	7	54	16	22
16	7	20	16	10	7	30	16	20	7	31	16	13	7	36	16	11	7	40	16	02	7	55	16	08	7	56	16	21
17	7	21	16	09	7	31	16	19	7	33	16	12	7	38	16	09	7	42	16	00	7	57	16	07	7	57	16	19
18	7	23	16	07	7	33	16	17	7	34	16	11	7	40	16	08	7	44	15	59	7	59	16	05	7	59	16	18
19	7	25	16	06	7	35	16	16	7	36	16	10	7	42	16	07	7	46	15	57	8	01	16	03	8	01	16	16
20	7	26	16	05	7	36	16	15	7	38	16	08	7	43	16	05	7	48	15	56	8	03	16	02	8	03	16	15
21	7	28	16	04	7	38	16	14	7	39	16	07	7	45	16	04	7	50	15	54	8	05	16	00	8	05	16	14
22	7	30	16	03	7	40	16	13	7	41	16	06	7	47	16	03	7	52	15	53	8	06	15	59	8	07	16	12
23	7	31	16	02	7	41	16	12	7	43	16	05	7	49	16	02	7	53	15	52	8	08	15	58	8	09	16	11
24	7	33	16	01	7	43	16	11	7	44	16	04	7	50	16	01	7	55	15	51	8	10	15	56	8	10	16	10
25	7	34	16	00	7	44	16	10	7	46	16	03	7	52	15	59	7	57	15	49	8	12	15	55	8	12	16	09
26	7	36	15	59	7	46	16	09	7	48	16	02	7	54	15	58	7	59	15	48	8	14	15	54	8	14	16	08
27	7	38	15	58	7	47	16	08	7	49	16	01	7	55	15	57	8	00	15	47	8	16	15	53	8	16	16	07
28	7	39	15	57	7	49	16	07	7	51	16	00	7	57	15	57	8	02	15	46	8	18	15	52	8	17	16	06
29	7	41	15	56	7	50	16	06	7	52	15	59	7	58	15	56	8	04	15	45	8	19	15	51	8	19	16	05
30	7	42	15	56	7	52	16	06	7	54	15	58	8	00	15	55	8	05	15	44	8	21	15	50	8	21	16	04

JUPITER

Day	*R.A.*		*Dec.*		*Transit*		*5° high*			
							52°		*56°*	
	h	*m*	°	′	*h*	*m*	*h*	*m*	*h*	*m*
1	9	32.1	+15	16	6	50	0	04	23	52
11	9	36.0	+14	59	6	15	23	27	23	18
21	9	38.8	+14	48	5	38	22	52	22	42
31	9	40.5	+14	42	5	01	22	14	22	05

Diameters – equatorial 38″ polar 36″

SATURN

Day	*R.A.*		*Dec.*		*Transit*		*5° high*			
							52°		*56°*	
	h	*m*	°	′	*h*	*m*	*h*	*m*	*h*	*m*
1	15	28.0	−16	52	12	45	8	56	9	17
11	15	32.7	−17	10	12	11	8	23	8	45
21	15	37.6	−17	27	11	36	7	51	8	13
31	15	42.4	−17	43	11	02	7	18	7	41

Diameters – equatorial 15″ polar 14″
Rings – major axis 34″ minor axis 14″

URANUS

Day	*R.A.*		*Dec.*		*Transit*		*10° high*			
							52°		*56°*	
	h	*m*	°	′	*h*	*m*	*h*	*m*	*h*	*m*
1	0	51.1	+4	43	22	06	3	29	3	26
11	0	49.8	+4	35	21	26	2	48	2	45
21	0	48.8	+4	29	20	46	2	07	2	04
31	0	48.0	+4	25	20	06	1	26	1	23

Diameter 4″

NEPTUNE

Day	*R.A.*		*Dec.*		*Transit*		*10° high*			
							52°		*56°*	
	h	*m*	°	′	*h*	*m*	*h*	*m*	*h*	*m*
1	22	27.9	−10	25	19	44	23	37	23	19
11	22	27.7	−10	26	19	04	22	58	22	39
21	22	27.7	−10	26	18	25	22	18	22	00
31	22	27.9	−10	25	17	46	21	39	21	21

Diameter 2″

DECEMBER 2014

TWELFTH MONTH, 31 DAYS. *Decem* (ten), tenth month of Roman pre-Julian calendar

1	*Monday*	King Henry I, who reigned from 1100–1135, House of Normandy *d.* 1135	week 48 day 335
2	*Tuesday*	Adelaide of Saxe-Meiningen, Queen Consort through her marriage to King William IV *d.* 1849	336
3	*Wednesday*	Princess Victoria, the fourth child of King Edward VII and younger sister of King George V *d.* 1935	337
4	*Thursday*	Treaty of Paris, made by King Henry III and King Louis IX of France, ends 100 years of conflict 1259	338
5	*Friday*	John III, Duke of Brabant, the son of Margaret, daughter of King Edward I *d.* 1355	339
6	*Saturday*	King Henry VI, who reigned from 1422–1471, House of Lancaster *b.* 1421	340
7	*Sunday*	Henry Stuart, Lord Darnley, husband of Mary, Queen of Scots and father of King James I *b.* 1545	341
8	*Monday*	Mary Stuart is born at Linlithgow Palace and becomes Queen of Scots six days later 1542	week 49 day 342
9	*Tuesday*	Edward Hyde, 1st Earl of Clarendon, statesman, grandfather of two monarchs: Mary II and Anne *d.* 1674	343
10	*Wednesday*	King Edward VIII signs the Instrument of Abdication in order to marry Wallis Simpson 1936	344
11	*Thursday*	Llywelyn the Last, final prince of an independent Wales, is killed by the army of King Edward I 1282	345
12	*Friday*	Geoffrey Plantagenet, Archbishop of York, who was an illegitimate son of King Henry II *d.* 1212	346
13	*Saturday*	King George VI, who reigned from 1936–1952, House of Windsor *b.* 1895	347
14	*Sunday*	Prince Albert dies from a contemporary diagnosis of typhoid fever at Windsor Castle 1861	348
15	*Monday*	Prince George (King George IV) secretly marries Maria Fitzherbert in Mayfair 1785	week 50 day 349
16	*Tuesday*	At Notre Dame de Paris, 10-year-old King Henry VI of England is crowned King of France 1431	350
17	*Wednesday*	Pope Paul III excommunicates King Henry VIII from the Roman Catholic Church 1538	351
18	*Thursday*	Edith of Wessex, who married Edward the Confessor in 1045 *d.* 1075	352
19	*Friday*	Coronation of King Henry II at Westminster Abbey 1154	353
20	*Saturday*	King Richard I is captured by Leopold V, Duke of Austria, and held captive for two years 1192	354
21	*Sunday*	Benjamin Disraeli, Conservative prime minister and close friend of Queen Victoria *b.* 1804	355
22	*Monday*	Richard Plantagenet of Eastwell, a bricklayer who claimed to be King Richard III's son *d.* 1550	week 51 day 356
23	*Tuesday*	King James II flees from England to Paris and is helped by his cousin King Louis XIV 1688	357
24	*Wednesday*	King John, who reigned from 1199–1216, House of Plantagenet *b.* 1167	358
25	*Thursday*	Coronation of King William I at Westminster Abbey 1066	359
26	*Friday*	Coronation of King Stephen at Westminster Abbey 1135	360
27	*Saturday*	Anne de Mortimer, grandmother of two monarchs, Edward IV and Richard III *b.* 1390	361
28	*Sunday*	Queen Mary II, who reigned from 1689–1694, House of Stuart *d.* 1694	362
29	*Monday*	Thomas Becket, Archbishop of Canterbury, assassinated on behalf of King Henry II 1170	week 52 day 363
30	*Tuesday*	The House of Lancaster wins the Battle of Wakefield, a conflict during the Wars of the Roses 1460	364
31	*Wednesday*	King Louis XIV of France names King James II as Duke of Normandy 1360	365

ASTRONOMICAL PHENOMENA

d	*h*	
8	10	Mercury in superior conjunction
8	21	Jupiter at stationary point
12	00	Jupiter in conjunction with Moon. Jupiter 5°N.
19	21	Saturn in conjunction with Moon. Saturn 2°S.
21	23	Uranus at stationary point
21	23	Sun's longitude 270° ♑
22	16	Mercury in conjunction with Moon. Mercury 7°S.
23	03	Venus in conjunction with Moon. Venus 6°S.
25	05	Mars in conjunction with Moon. Mars 6°S.

MINIMA OF ALGOL

d	*h*	*d*	*h*	*d*	*h*
1	19.2	13	06.5	24	17.8
4	16.0	16	03.3	27	14.6
7	12.8	19	00.1	30	11.4
10	09.7	21	20.9		

CONSTELLATIONS

The following constellations are near their meridian at

	d	*h*		*d*	*h*
November	1	24	December	16	21
November	15	23	January	1	20
December	1	22	January	16	19

Ursa Major (below the Pole), Ursa Minor (below the Pole), Cassiopeia, Andromeda, Perseus, Triangulum, Aries, Taurus, Cetus and Eridanus

THE MOON

Phases, Apsides and Node	*d*	*h*	*m*
○ Full Moon	6	12	27
☾ Last Quarter	14	12	51
● New Moon	22	01	36
☽ First Quarter	28	18	31
Apogee (404,542km)	12	23	00
Perigee (364,819km)	24	16	34

Mean longitude of ascending node on December 1, 197°

THE SUN

s.d. 16′.3

Day	Right Ascension			Dec. –		Equation of time		Rise 52°		Rise 56°		Transit		Set 52°		Set 56°		Sidereal time			Transit of first point of Aries		
	h	m	s	°	′	m	s	h	m	h	m	h	m	h	m	h	m	h	m	s	h	m	s
1	16	27	55	21	45	+11	11	7	45	8	07	11	49	15	52	15	31	4	39	06	19	17	44
2	16	32	14	21	54	+10	49	7	47	8	08	11	49	15	52	15	30	4	43	03	19	13	48
3	16	36	34	22	03	+10	26	7	48	8	10	11	50	15	51	15	29	4	46	59	19	09	52
4	16	40	54	22	11	+10	02	7	49	8	11	11	50	15	51	15	29	4	50	56	19	05	56
5	16	45	14	22	19	+9	38	7	51	8	13	11	51	15	50	15	28	4	54	52	19	02	00
6	16	49	36	22	27	+9	13	7	52	8	14	11	51	15	50	15	27	4	58	49	18	58	04
7	16	53	57	22	34	+8	48	7	53	8	16	11	51	15	49	15	27	5	02	45	18	54	08
8	16	58	20	22	41	+8	22	7	54	8	17	11	52	15	49	15	26	5	06	42	18	50	12
9	17	02	43	22	47	+7	56	7	56	8	18	11	52	15	49	15	26	5	10	39	18	46	16
10	17	07	06	22	53	+7	29	7	57	8	20	11	53	15	49	15	26	5	14	35	18	42	20
11	17	11	30	22	58	+7	02	7	58	8	21	11	53	15	48	15	25	5	18	32	18	38	25
12	17	15	54	23	03	+6	35	7	59	8	22	11	54	15	48	15	25	5	22	28	18	34	29
13	17	20	18	23	07	+6	07	8	00	8	23	11	54	15	48	15	25	5	26	25	18	30	33
14	17	24	43	23	11	+5	38	8	01	8	24	11	55	15	48	15	25	5	30	21	18	26	37
15	17	29	08	23	15	+5	10	8	02	8	25	11	55	15	48	15	25	5	34	18	18	22	41
16	17	33	34	23	18	+4	41	8	02	8	26	11	56	15	49	15	25	5	38	15	18	18	45
17	17	37	59	23	20	+4	12	8	03	8	27	11	56	15	49	15	25	5	42	11	18	14	49
18	17	42	25	23	22	+3	42	8	04	8	28	11	57	15	49	15	25	5	46	08	18	10	53
19	17	46	51	23	24	+3	13	8	04	8	28	11	57	15	49	15	26	5	50	04	18	06	57
20	17	51	18	23	25	+2	43	8	05	8	29	11	58	15	50	15	26	5	54	01	18	03	01
21	17	55	44	23	26	+2	13	8	06	8	30	11	58	15	50	15	27	5	57	57	17	59	05
22	18	00	11	23	26	+1	43	8	06	8	30	11	59	15	51	15	27	6	01	54	17	55	10
23	18	04	37	23	26	+1	13	8	07	8	30	11	59	15	51	15	28	6	05	50	17	51	14
24	18	09	04	23	25	+0	43	8	07	8	31	12	00	15	52	15	28	6	09	47	17	47	18
25	18	13	30	23	24	+0	14	8	07	8	31	12	00	15	53	15	29	6	13	44	17	43	22
26	18	17	56	23	22	−0	16	8	08	8	31	12	01	15	53	15	30	6	17	40	17	39	26
27	18	22	23	23	20	−0	46	8	08	8	32	12	01	15	54	15	31	6	21	37	17	35	30
28	18	26	49	23	18	−1	16	8	08	8	32	12	01	15	55	15	32	6	25	33	17	31	34
29	18	31	15	23	14	−1	45	8	08	8	32	12	02	15	56	15	32	6	29	30	17	27	38
30	18	35	40	23	11	−2	14	8	08	8	32	12	02	15	57	15	34	6	33	26	17	23	42
31	18	40	06	23	07	−2	43	8	08	8	31	12	03	15	58	15	35	6	37	23	17	19	46

DURATION OF TWILIGHT (in minutes)

Latitude	52°	56°	52°	56°	52°	56°	52°	56°
	1 December		*11 December*		*21 December*		*31 December*	
Civil	40	45	41	47	41	47	41	47
Nautical	82	93	84	96	85	97	84	96
Astronomical	123	138	125	141	126	142	125	141

THE NIGHT SKY

Mercury is unsuitably placed for observation throughout the month, superior conjunction occurring on the 8th.

Venus remains unsuitably placed for observation until about the last 10 days of the month when it may be seen low above the south-western horizon for a very short while after sunset, magnitude −3.9.

Mars, magnitude +1.1, continues to be visible low in the south-western sky in the early evenings. It is still visible for a short while after darkness has fallen. The waxing crescent Moon passes 5 degrees north of Mars on the 25th.

Jupiter, magnitude −2.4, is still a prominent object in the southern sky, rising before midnight. On the 8th it reaches its first stationary point and thus begins its retrograde motion, several degrees short of Regulus. On the morning of the 12th the waning gibbous Moon will be seen about 6 degrees south of the planet.

Saturn is not visible at first but gradually becomes observable in the early mornings after about the first ten days of the month, low above the south-eastern horizon before the morning twilight inhibits observation. Its magnitude is +0.5. The waning crescent Moon can be observed only about 1 degree north of Saturn.

Meteors. The maximum of the well known Geminid meteor shower occurs on the night of the 13–14th. However the Moon, at last quarter, will cause some interference, as it will be rising at about 23h. By then the radiant is already high in the eastern sky, close to Castor, also in Gemini.

THE MOON

Day	R.A.		Dec.	Hor. Par.	Semi-diam.	Sun's Co-Long.	PA. of Br. Limb	Ph.	Age	Rise				Transit		Set			
										52°		56°				52°		56°	
	h	m	°	′	′	°	°	%	d	h	m	h	m	h	m	h	m	h	m
1	23	55	+1.2	58.9	16.1	18	247	68	8.5	13	25	13	22	19	56	1	25	1	26
2	0	48	+5.6	58.7	16.0	30	247	78	9.5	13	53	13	46	20	48	2	41	2	46
3	1	41	+9.7	58.4	15.9	42	248	86	10.5	14	23	14	13	21	40	3	55	4	04
4	2	36	+13.2	58.0	15.8	55	249	93	11.5	14	57	14	44	22	32	5	08	5	20
5	3	30	+15.9	57.5	15.7	67	247	97	12.5	15	36	15	20	23	25	6	17	6	32
6	4	25	+17.7	57.0	15.5	79	229	100	13.5	16	21	16	03	—		7	20	7	38
7	5	20	+18.6	56.4	15.4	91	124	100	14.5	17	12	16	54	0	18	8	16	8	35
8	6	14	+18.5	55.9	15.2	103	107	97	15.5	18	08	17	51	1	10	9	05	9	22
9	7	07	+17.4	55.3	15.1	115	106	94	16.5	19	08	18	53	2	00	9	46	10	01
10	7	58	+15.6	54.9	15.0	127	107	88	17.5	20	10	19	57	2	48	10	20	10	33
11	8	47	+13.1	54.5	14.9	140	109	81	18.5	21	12	21	03	3	34	10	49	10	59
12	9	34	+10.1	54.3	14.8	152	111	73	19.5	22	15	22	09	4	19	11	15	11	22
13	10	20	+6.7	54.2	14.8	164	112	64	20.5	23	17	23	15	5	02	11	38	11	42
14	11	05	+3.1	54.3	14.8	176	113	55	21.5	—		—		5	44	12	00	12	01
15	11	50	−0.7	54.6	14.9	188	113	46	22.5	0	21	0	21	6	27	12	23	12	20
16	12	36	−4.5	55.0	15.0	200	113	36	23.5	1	25	1	29	7	10	12	46	12	41
17	13	23	−8.2	55.6	15.1	212	112	27	24.5	2	31	2	38	7	56	13	12	13	03
18	14	12	−11.6	56.3	15.3	225	111	19	25.5	3	38	3	49	8	43	13	41	13	29
19	15	04	−14.6	57.1	15.6	237	109	11	26.5	4	46	5	00	9	34	14	17	14	02
20	15	59	−16.9	57.9	15.8	249	109	5	27.5	5	53	6	11	10	28	15	00	14	42
21	16	57	−18.3	58.7	16.0	261	113	2	28.5	6	58	7	16	11	25	15	52	15	33
22	17	56	−18.6	59.3	16.2	273	170	0	29.5	7	56	8	14	12	24	16	54	16	36
23	18	57	−17.7	59.8	16.3	286	243	1	1.0	8	46	9	02	13	23	18	05	17	49
24	19	57	−15.7	60.1	16.4	298	249	5	2.0	9	29	9	42	14	21	19	20	19	08
25	20	56	−12.6	60.1	16.4	310	249	12	3.0	10	05	10	14	15	17	20	39	20	30
26	21	54	−8.8	59.9	16.3	322	247	20	4.0	10	36	10	42	16	11	21	57	21	53
27	22	49	−4.5	59.6	16.2	334	247	30	5.0	11	04	11	06	17	03	23	14	23	14
28	23	43	0.0	59.2	16.1	346	246	41	6.0	11	31	11	30	17	54	—		—	
29	0	36	+4.4	58.7	16.0	359	247	53	7.0	11	58	11	53	18	45	0	30	0	34
30	1	29	+8.6	58.2	15.9	11	248	64	8.0	12	27	12	18	19	36	1	44	1	52
31	2	22	+12.2	57.7	15.7	23	250	74	9.0	12	59	12	47	20	27	2	56	3	08

MERCURY

Day	R.A.		Dec.	Diam.	Phase	Transit		5° high			
								52°		56°	
	h	m	°	″	%	h	m	h	m	h	m
1	16	10	−21.3	5	99	11	32	8	16	8	47
3	16	23	−22.1	5	100	11	38	8	27	9	00
5	16	37	−22.8	5	100	11	43	8	39	9	14
7	16	50	−23.4	5	100	11	49	8	50	9	27
9	17	04	−23.9	5	100	11	54	9	00	9	39
11	17	17	−24.4	5	100	12	00	14	50	14	09
13	17	31	−24.7	5	100	12	06	14	53	14	10
15	17	45	−25.0	5	99	12	12	14	56	14	13
17	17	59	−25.2	5	99	12	18	15	01	14	16
19	18	13	−25.3	5	99	12	24	15	06	14	21
21	18	27	−25.3	5	98	12	31	15	13	14	28
23	18	41	−25.2	5	97	12	37	15	21	14	36
25	18	55	−25.0	5	96	12	43	15	29	14	46
27	19	09	−24.7	5	95	12	49	15	39	14	57
29	19	23	−24.3	5	94	12	55	15	49	15	09
31	19	37	−23.8	5	92	13	01	16	00	15	22

VENUS

Day	R.A.		Dec.	Diam.	Phase	Transit		5° high			
								52°		56°	
	h	m	°	″	%	h	m	h	m	h	m
1	17	07	−23.2	10	99	12	29	15	29	14	53
6	17	34	−23.8	10	99	12	36	15	32	14	53
11	18	02	−24.2	10	98	12	44	15	37	14	57
16	18	29	−24.2	10	98	12	52	15	45	15	05
21	18	57	−23.9	10	97	13	00	15	56	15	18
26	19	24	−23.3	10	97	13	07	16	09	15	33
31	19	51	−22.4	10	96	13	14	16	24	15	52

MARS

Day	R.A.		Dec.	Diam.	Phase	Transit		5° high			
								52°		56°	
	h	m	°	″	%	h	m	h	m	h	m
1	19	57	−22.1	5	92	15	17	18	29	17	57
6	20	13	−21.3	5	93	15	14	18	33	18	03
11	20	29	−20.4	5	93	15	10	18	36	18	09
16	20	45	−19.4	5	93	15	07	18	40	18	15
21	21	01	−18.2	5	94	15	03	18	45	18	21
26	21	17	−17.1	5	94	14	59	18	49	18	27
31	21	32	−15.8	5	94	14	54	18	53	18	33

SUNRISE AND SUNSET

	London				*Bristol*				*Birmingham*				*Manchester*				*Newcastle*				*Glasgow*				*Belfast*			
	0° 05′		*51° 30′*		*2° 35′*		*51° 28′*		*1° 55′*		*52° 28′*		*2° 15′*		*53° 28′*		*1° 37′*		*54° 59′*		*4° 14′*		*55° 52′*		*5° 56′*		*54° 35′*	
d	*h*	*m*	*h*	*m*	*h*	*m*	*h*	*m*	*h*	*m*	*h*	*m*	*h*	*m*	*h*	*m*	*h*	*m*	*h*	*m*	*h*	*m*	*h*	*m*	*h*	*m*	*h*	*m*
1	7	43	15	55	7	53	16	05	7	55	15	58	8	02	15	54	8	07	15	43	8	23	15	49	8	22	16	03
2	7	45	15	54	7	55	16	04	7	57	15	57	8	03	15	53	8	09	15	43	8	24	15	48	8	24	16	02
3	7	46	15	54	7	56	16	04	7	58	15	56	8	04	15	53	8	10	15	42	8	26	15	47	8	25	16	01
4	7	47	15	53	7	57	16	03	7	59	15	56	8	06	15	52	8	12	15	41	8	27	15	46	8	27	16	01
5	7	49	15	53	7	59	16	03	8	01	15	55	8	07	15	52	8	13	15	41	8	29	15	46	8	28	16	00
6	7	50	15	52	8	00	16	03	8	02	15	55	8	09	15	51	8	15	15	40	8	30	15	45	8	30	16	00
7	7	51	15	52	8	01	16	02	8	03	15	55	8	10	15	51	8	16	15	40	8	32	15	45	8	31	15	59
8	7	52	15	52	8	02	16	02	8	04	15	54	8	11	15	50	8	17	15	39	8	33	15	44	8	32	15	59
9	7	53	15	52	8	03	16	02	8	06	15	54	8	12	15	50	8	18	15	39	8	34	15	44	8	33	15	58
10	7	55	15	51	8	04	16	02	8	07	15	54	8	13	15	50	8	20	15	38	8	36	15	43	8	35	15	58
11	7	56	15	51	8	05	16	01	8	08	15	54	8	15	15	50	8	21	15	38	8	37	15	43	8	36	15	58
12	7	57	15	51	8	06	16	01	8	09	15	54	8	16	15	50	8	22	15	38	8	38	15	43	8	37	15	58
13	7	58	15	51	8	07	16	01	8	10	15	54	8	17	15	49	8	23	15	38	8	39	15	43	8	38	15	58
14	7	58	15	51	8	08	16	01	8	11	15	54	8	18	15	49	8	24	15	38	8	40	15	43	8	39	15	58
15	7	59	15	51	8	09	16	02	8	12	15	54	8	18	15	50	8	25	15	38	8	41	15	43	8	40	15	58
16	8	00	15	52	8	10	16	02	8	12	15	54	8	19	15	50	8	26	15	38	8	42	15	43	8	41	15	58
17	8	01	15	52	8	11	16	02	8	13	15	54	8	20	15	50	8	27	15	38	8	43	15	43	8	41	15	58
18	8	02	15	52	8	11	16	02	8	14	15	54	8	21	15	50	8	27	15	39	8	44	15	43	8	42	15	58
19	8	02	15	52	8	12	16	03	8	15	15	55	8	22	15	50	8	28	15	39	8	44	15	44	8	43	15	59
20	8	03	15	53	8	13	16	03	8	15	15	55	8	22	15	51	8	29	15	39	8	45	15	44	8	44	15	59
21	8	03	15	53	8	13	16	03	8	16	15	56	8	23	15	51	8	29	15	40	8	46	15	44	8	44	15	59
22	8	04	15	54	8	14	16	04	8	16	15	56	8	23	15	52	8	30	15	40	8	46	15	45	8	45	16	00
23	8	04	15	54	8	14	16	05	8	17	15	57	8	24	15	52	8	30	15	41	8	47	15	45	8	45	16	01
24	8	05	15	55	8	15	16	05	8	17	15	57	8	24	15	53	8	31	15	41	8	47	15	46	8	45	16	01
25	8	05	15	56	8	15	16	06	8	18	15	58	8	24	15	54	8	31	15	42	8	47	15	47	8	46	16	02
26	8	05	15	56	8	15	16	07	8	18	15	59	8	25	15	54	8	31	15	43	8	47	15	48	8	46	16	03
27	8	06	15	57	8	15	16	07	8	18	15	59	8	25	15	55	8	31	15	44	8	48	15	48	8	46	16	03
28	8	06	15	58	8	16	16	08	8	18	16	00	8	25	15	56	8	31	15	45	8	48	15	49	8	46	16	04
29	8	06	15	59	8	16	16	09	8	18	16	01	8	25	15	57	8	32	15	46	8	48	15	50	8	46	16	05
30	8	06	16	00	8	16	16	10	8	18	16	02	8	25	15	58	8	31	15	47	8	48	15	51	8	46	16	06
31	8	06	16	01	8	16	16	11	8	18	16	03	8	25	15	59	8	31	15	48	8	47	15	52	8	46	16	07

JUPITER

Day	*R.A.*		*Dec.*		*Transit*		*5° high*			
							52°		*56°*	
	h	*m*	°	′	*h*	*m*	*h*	*m*	*h*	*m*
1	9	40.5	+14	42	5	01	22	14	22	05
11	9	40.9	+14	42	4	22	21	35	21	26
21	9	40.1	+14	49	3	42	20	54	20	45
31	9	37.9	+15	02	3	00	20	11	20	02

Diameters – equatorial 42″ polar 39″

SATURN

Day	*R.A.*		*Dec.*		*Transit*		*5° high*			
							52°		*56°*	
	h	*m*	°	′	*h*	*m*	*h*	*m*	*h*	*m*
1	15	42.4	−17	43	11	02	7	18	7	41
11	15	47.2	−17	59	10	27	6	45	7	08
21	15	51.8	−18	13	9	52	6	12	6	36
31	15	56.2	−18	25	9	17	5	39	6	03

Diameters – equatorial 15″ polar 14″

Rings – major axis 35″ minor axis 14″

URANUS

Day	*R.A.*		*Dec.*		*Transit*		*10° high*			
							52°		*56°*	
	h	*m*	°	′	*h*	*m*	*h*	*m*	*h*	*m*
1	0	48.0	+4	25	20	06	1	26	1	23
11	0	47.5	+4	22	19	26	0	46	0	43
21	0	47.3	+4	21	18	46	0	07	0	04
31	0	47.4	+4	22	18	07	23	24	23	21

Diameter 4″

NEPTUNE

Day	*R.A.*		*Dec.*		*Transit*		*10° high*			
							52°		*56°*	
	h	*m*	°	′	*h*	*m*	*h*	*m*	*h*	*m*
1	22	27.9	−10	25	17	46	21	39	21	21
11	22	28.3	−10	22	17	07	21	01	20	43
21	22	29.0	−10	19	16	28	20	23	20	05
31	22	29.8	−10	14	15	50	19	45	19	27

Diameter 2″

RISING AND SETTING TIMES

TABLE 1. SEMI-DIURNAL ARCS (HOUR ANGLES AT RISING/SETTING)

Dec.	*Latitude* 0°	10°	20°	30°	40°	45°	50°	52°	54°	56°	58°	60°	*Dec.*
	h m	*h m*	*h m*	*h m*	*h m*	*h m*	*h m*	*h m*	*h m*	*h m*	*h m*	*h m*	
0°	6 00	6 00	6 00	6 00	6 00	6 00	6 00	6 00	6 00	6 00	6 00	6 00	0°
1°	6 00	6 01	6 01	6 02	6 03	6 04	6 05	6 05	6 06	6 06	6 06	6 07	1°
2°	6 00	6 01	6 03	6 05	6 07	6 08	6 10	6 10	6 11	6 12	6 13	6 14	2°
3°	6 00	6 02	6 04	6 07	6 10	6 12	6 14	6 15	6 17	6 18	6 19	6 21	3°
4°	6 00	6 03	6 06	6 09	6 13	6 16	6 19	6 21	6 22	6 24	6 26	6 28	4°
5°	6 00	6 04	6 07	6 12	6 17	6 20	6 24	6 26	6 28	6 30	6 32	6 35	5°
6°	6 00	6 04	6 09	6 14	6 20	6 24	6 29	6 31	6 33	6 36	6 39	6 42	6°
7°	6 00	6 05	6 10	6 16	6 24	6 28	6 34	6 36	6 39	6 42	6 45	6 49	7°
8°	6 00	6 06	6 12	6 19	6 27	6 32	6 39	6 41	6 45	6 48	6 52	6 56	8°
9°	6 00	6 06	6 13	6 21	6 31	6 36	6 44	6 47	6 50	6 54	6 59	7 04	9°
10°	6 00	6 07	6 15	6 23	6 34	6 41	6 49	6 52	6 56	7 01	7 06	7 11	10°
11°	6 00	6 08	6 16	6 26	6 38	6 45	6 54	6 58	7 02	7 07	7 12	7 19	11°
12°	6 00	6 09	6 18	6 28	6 41	6 49	6 59	7 03	7 08	7 13	7 20	7 26	12°
13°	6 00	6 09	6 19	6 31	6 45	6 53	7 04	7 09	7 14	7 20	7 27	7 34	13°
14°	6 00	6 10	6 21	6 33	6 48	6 58	7 09	7 14	7 20	7 27	7 34	7 42	14°
15°	6 00	6 11	6 22	6 36	6 52	7 02	7 14	7 20	7 27	7 34	7 42	7 51	15°
16°	6 00	6 12	6 24	6 38	6 56	7 07	7 20	7 26	7 33	7 41	7 49	7 59	16°
17°	6 00	6 12	6 26	6 41	6 59	7 11	7 25	7 32	7 40	7 48	7 57	8 08	17°
18°	6 00	6 13	6 27	6 43	7 03	7 16	7 31	7 38	7 46	7 55	8 05	8 17	18°
19°	6 00	6 14	6 29	6 46	7 07	7 21	7 37	7 45	7 53	8 03	8 14	8 26	19°
20°	6 00	6 15	6 30	6 49	7 11	7 25	7 43	7 51	8 00	8 11	8 22	8 36	20°
21°	6 00	6 16	6 32	6 51	7 15	7 30	7 49	7 58	8 08	8 19	8 32	8 47	21°
22°	6 00	6 16	6 34	6 54	7 19	7 35	7 55	8 05	8 15	8 27	8 41	8 58	22°
23°	6 00	6 17	6 36	6 57	7 23	7 40	8 02	8 12	8 23	8 36	8 51	9 09	23°
24°	6 00	6 18	6 37	7 00	7 28	7 46	8 08	8 19	8 31	8 45	9 02	9 22	24°
25°	6 00	6 19	6 39	7 02	7 32	7 51	8 15	8 27	8 40	8 55	9 13	9 35	25°
26°	6 00	6 20	6 41	7 05	7 37	7 57	8 22	8 35	8 49	9 05	9 25	9 51	26°
27°	6 00	6 21	6 43	7 08	7 41	8 03	8 30	8 43	8 58	9 16	9 39	10 08	27°
28°	6 00	6 22	6 45	7 12	7 46	8 08	8 37	8 52	9 08	9 28	9 53	10 28	28°
29°	6 00	6 22	6 47	7 15	7 51	8 15	8 45	9 01	9 19	9 41	10 10	10 55	29°
30°	6 00	6 23	6 49	7 18	7 56	8 21	8 54	9 11	9 30	9 55	10 30	12 00	30°
35°	6 00	6 28	6 59	7 35	8 24	8 58	9 46	10 15	10 58	12 00	12 00	12 00	35°
40°	6 00	6 34	7 11	7 56	8 59	9 48	12 00	12 00	12 00	12 00	12 00	12 00	40°
45°	6 00	6 41	7 25	8 21	9 48	12 00	12 00	12 00	12 00	12 00	12 00	12 00	45°
50°	6 00	6 49	7 43	8 54	12 00	12 00	12 00	12 00	12 00	12 00	12 00	12 00	50°
55°	6 00	6 58	8 05	9 42	12 00	12 00	12 00	12 00	12 00	12 00	12 00	12 00	55°
60°	6 00	7 11	8 36	12 00	12 00	12 00	12 00	12 00	12 00	12 00	12 00	12 00	60°
65°	6 00	7 29	9 25	12 00	12 00	12 00	12 00	12 00	12 00	12 00	12 00	12 00	65°
70°	6 00	7 56	12 00	12 00	12 00	12 00	12 00	12 00	12 00	12 00	12 00	12 00	70°
75°	6 00	8 45	12 00	12 00	12 00	12 00	12 00	12 00	12 00	12 00	12 00	12 00	75°
80°	6 00	12 00	12 00	12 00	12 00	12 00	12 00	12 00	12 00	12 00	12 00	12 00	80°

Note: If latitude and declination are of the same sign, take out the respondent directly. If they are of opposite signs, subtract the respondent from 12h.

Table 1 gives the complete range of declinations in case any user wishes to calculate semi-diurnal arcs for bodies other than the Sun and Moon.

Example:

Lat.	Dec.	Semi-diurnal arc
+52°	+20°	7h 51m
+52°	−20°	4h 09m

TABLE 2. CORRECTION FOR REFRACTION AND SEMI-DIAMETER

	m	*m*	*m*	*m*	*m*	*m*	*m*	*m*	*m*	*m*	*m*	*m*	*m*
0°	3	3	4	4	4	5	5	5	6	6	6	7	0°
10°	3	3	4	4	4	5	5	6	6	6	7	7	10°
20°	4	4	4	4	5	5	6	7	7	8	8	9	20°
25°	4	4	4	4	5	6	7	8	8	9	11	13	25°
30°	4	4	4	5	6	7	8	9	11	14	21	—	30°

SUNRISE AND SUNSET

The local mean time of sunrise or sunset may be found by obtaining the hour angle from Table 1 and applying it to the time of transit. The hour angle is negative for sunrise and positive for sunset. A small correction to the hour angle, which always has the effect of increasing it numerically, is necessary to allow for the Sun's semi-diameter (16′) and for refraction (34′); it is obtained from Table 2. The resulting local mean time may be converted into the standard time of the country by taking the difference between the longitude of the standard meridian of the country and that of the place, adding it to the local mean time if the place is west of the standard meridian, and subtracting it if the place is east.

Example – Required the New Zealand Mean Time (12h fast on GMT) of sunset on May 23 at Auckland, latitude 36° 50′ S. (or minus), longitude 11h 39m E. Taking the declination as +20°.6 (page 595), we find

	h	*m*
New Zealand Standard Time	+ 12	00
Longitude	− 11	39
Longitudinal Correction	+ 0	21
Tabular entry for Lat. 30° and Dec. 20°, opposite signs	+ 5	11
Proportional part for 6° 50′ of Lat.	−	15
Proportional part for 0°.6 of Dec.	−	2
Correction (Table 2)	+	4
Hour angle	4	58
Sun transits (page 1095)	11	57
Longitudinal correction	+	21
New Zealand Mean Time	17	16

MOONRISE AND MOONSET

It is possible to calculate the times of moonrise and moonset using Table 1, though the method is more complicated because the apparent motion of the Moon is much more rapid and also more variable than that of the Sun.

TABLE 3. LONGITUDE CORRECTION

X / *A*	*40m*	*45m*	*50m*	*55m*	*60m*	*65m*	*70m*
h	*m*	*m*	*m*	*m*	*m*	*m*	*m*
1	2	2	2	3	3	3	3
2	3	4	4	5	5	5	6
3	5	6	6	7	8	8	9
4	7	8	8	9	10	11	12
5	8	9	10	11	13	14	15
6	10	11	13	14	15	16	18
7	12	13	15	16	18	19	20
8	13	15	17	18	20	22	23
9	15	17	19	21	23	24	26
10	17	19	21	23	25	27	29
11	18	21	23	25	28	30	32
12	20	23	25	28	30	33	35
13	22	24	27	30	33	35	38
14	23	26	29	32	35	38	41
15	25	28	31	34	38	41	44
16	27	30	33	37	40	43	47
17	28	32	35	39	43	46	50
18	30	34	38	41	45	49	53
19	32	36	40	44	48	51	55
20	33	38	42	46	50	54	58
21	35	39	44	48	53	57	61
22	37	41	46	50	55	60	64
23	38	43	48	53	58	62	67
24	40	45	50	55	60	65	70

The parallax of the Moon, about 57′, is near to the sum of the semi-diameter and refraction but has the opposite effect on these times. It is thus convenient to neglect all three quantities in the method outlined below.

Notation

ϕ = latitude of observer
λ = longitude of observer (measured positively towards the west)
T_{-1} = time of transit of Moon on previous day
T_0 = time of transit of Moon on day in question
T_1 = time of transit of Moon on following day
δ_0 = approximate declination of Moon
δ_R = declination of Moon at moonrise
δ_S = declination of Moon at moonset
h_0 = approximate hour angle of Moon
h_R = hour angle of Moon at moonrise
h_S = hour angle of Moon at moonset
t_R = time of moonrise
t_S = time of moonset

Method

1. With arguments ϕ, δ_0 enter Table 1 on page 626 to determine h_0 where h_0 is negative for moonrise and positive for moonset.

2. Form approximate times from
$t_R = T_0 + \lambda + h_0$
$t_S = T_0 + \lambda + h_0$

3. Determine δ_R, δ_S for times t_R, t_S respectively.

4. Re-enter Table 1 (as above) with
(*a*) arguments ϕ, δ_R to determine h_R
(*b*) arguments ϕ, δ_S to determine h_S

5. Form $t_R = T_0 + \lambda + h_R + AX$
$t_S = T_0 + \lambda + h_S + AX$

where $A = (\lambda + h)$

and $X = (T_0 - T_{-1})$ if $(\lambda + h)$ is negative
$X = (T_1 - T_0)$ if $(\lambda + h)$ is positive

AX is the respondent in Table 3.

Example – To find the times (GMT) of moonrise and moonset at Vancouver (ϕ = +49°, λ = +8h 12m) on 2014 December 22. The starting data (page 624) are

T_{-1} = 11h 25m
T_0 = 12h 24m
T_1 = 13h 23m
δ_0 = −18°

1. h_0 = 4h 32m
2. Approximate values
t_R = 22d 12h 24m + 8h 12m −4h 32m
= 22d 16h 04m
t_S = 22d 12h 24m + 8h 12m + 4h 32m
= 23d 01h 08m
3. δ_R = −18°.0
δ_S = −18°.4
4. h_R = −4h 32m
h_S = +4h 26m
5. t_R = 22d 12h 24m + 8h 12m + (−4h 32m) + 9m
= 22d 16h 13m
t_S = 22d 12h 24m + 8h 12m + (+4h 26m) + 32m
= 23d 01h 34m

To get the LMT of the phenomenon the longitude is subtracted from the GMT thus:

Moonrise = 22d 16h 13m – 8h 12m = 22d 08h 01m
Moonset = 23d 01h 34m – 8h 12m = 22d 17h 22m

ECLIPSES 2014

During 2014 there will be four eclipses, two of the Sun and two of the Moon. Penumbral eclipses of the Moon are not mentioned in this section as they are so difficult to observe.

1. A total eclipse of the Moon occurs on April 15 and is visible from Australia, the extreme eastern part of Asia, the Americas, Africa and western Europe. The partial phase begins at 05h 57m and ends at 09h 33m. Totality begins at 07h 06m and ends at 08h 25m.

2. An annular eclipse of the Sun occurs on April 29. The partial eclipse begins at 03h 53m in the Southern Ocean and ends at 08h 14m in Australia. The annular eclipse, only visible from Antarctica, begins at 05h 58m and ends at 06h 09m.

3. A total eclipse of the Moon occurs on October 8 and is visible from Australia, Asia, and the Americas. The partial phase begins at 09h 14m and ends at 12h 34m. Totality begins at 10h 24m and ends at 11h 24m.

4. A partial eclipse of the Sun occurs on October 23 and is visible from North America and the extreme eastern part of Russia. It begins at 19h 37m and ends at 23h 51m.

MEAN AND SIDEREAL TIME

The length of a sidereal day in mean time is 23h 56m 04s.09. Hence 1h MT = 1h+$9^{\mathrm{s}}.86$ ST and 1h ST = 1h − $9^{\mathrm{s}}.83$ MT.

Acceleration						Retardation					
h	*m*	*s*	*m*	*s*	*s*	*h*	*m*	*s*	*m*	*s*	*s*
1	0	10	0	00	0	1	0	10	0	00	0
2	0	20	3	02	1	2	0	20	3	03	1
3	0	30	9	07	2	3	0	29	9	09	2
4	0	39	15	13	3	4	0	39	15	15	3
5	0	49	21	18	4	5	0	49	21	21	4
6	0	59	27	23	5	6	0	59	27	28	5
7	1	09	33	28	6	7	1	09	33	34	6
8	1	19	39	34	7	8	1	19	39	40	7
9	1	29	45	39	8	9	1	28	45	46	8
10	1	39	51	44	9	10	1	38	51	53	9
11	1	48	57	49	10	11	1	48	57	59	10
12	1	58	60	00		12	1	58	60	00	
13	2	08				13	2	08			
14	2	18				14	2	18			
15	2	28				15	2	27			
16	2	38				16	2	37			
17	2	48				17	2	47			
18	2	57				18	2	57			
19	3	07				19	3	07			
20	3	17				20	3	17			
21	3	27				21	3	26			
22	3	37				22	3	36			
23	3	47				23	3	46			
24	3	57				24	3	56			

To convert an interval of mean time to the corresponding interval of sidereal time, enter the acceleration table with the given mean time (taking the hours and the minutes and seconds separately) and add the acceleration obtained to the given mean time. To convert an interval of sidereal time to the corresponding interval of mean time, take out the retardation for the given sidereal time and subtract.

The columns for the minutes and seconds of the argument are in the form known as critical tables. To use these tables, find in the appropriate left-hand column the two entries between which the given number of minutes and seconds lies; the quantity in the right-hand column between these two entries is the required acceleration or retardation. Thus the acceleration for 11m 26s (which lies between the entries 9m 07s and 15m 13s) is 2s. If the given number of minutes and seconds is a tabular entry, the required acceleration or retardation is the entry in the right-hand column above the given tabular entry, eg the retardation for 45m 46s is 7s.

Example – Convert 14h 27m 35s from ST to MT

	h	*m*	*s*
Given ST	14	27	35
Retardation for 14h		2	18
Retardation for 27m 35s			5
Corresponding MT	14	25	12

EXPLANATION OF ASTRONOMICAL DATA

Positions of the heavenly bodies are given only to the degree of accuracy required by amateur astronomers for setting telescopes, or for plotting on celestial globes or star atlases. Where intermediate positions are required, linear interpolation may be employed.

Definitions of the terms used cannot be given here. They must be sought in astronomical literature and textbooks.

A special feature has been made of the times when the various heavenly bodies are visible in the British Isles. Since two columns, calculated for latitudes 52° and 56°, are devoted to risings and settings, the range 50° to 58° can be covered by interpolation and extrapolation. The times given in these columns are Greenwich Mean Times for the meridian of Greenwich. An observer west of this meridian must add his/her longitude (in time) and vice versa.

In accordance with the usual convention in astronomy, + and − indicate respectively north and south latitudes or declinations.

All data are, unless otherwise stated, for 0h Greenwich Mean Time (GMT), ie at the midnight at the beginning of the day named. Allowance must be made for British Summer Time during the period that this is in operation.

PAGE ONE OF EACH MONTH

The calendar for each month is explained on page 577.

Under the heading Astronomical Phenomena will be found particulars of the more important conjunctions of the Sun, Moon and planets with each other, and also the dates of other astronomical phenomena of special interest.

Times of Minima of Algol are approximate times of the middle of the period of diminished light.

The Constellations listed each month are those that are near the meridian at the beginning of the month at 22h local mean time. Allowance must be made for British Summer Time if necessary. The fact that any star crosses the meridian 4m earlier each night or 2h earlier each month may be used, in conjunction with the lists given each month, to find what constellations are favourably placed at any moment. The table preceding the list of constellations may be extended indefinitely at the rate just quoted.

The principal phases of the Moon are the GMTs when the difference between the longitude of the Moon and that of the Sun is 0°, 90°, 180° or 270°. The times of perigee and apogee are those when the Moon is nearest to, and farthest from, the Earth, respectively. The nodes or points of intersection of the Moon's orbit and the ecliptic make a complete retrograde circuit of the ecliptic in about 19 years. From a knowledge of the longitude of the ascending node and the inclination, whose value does not vary much from 5°, the path of the Moon among the stars may be plotted on a celestial globe or star atlas.

PAGE TWO OF EACH MONTH

The Sun's semi-diameter, in arc, is given once a month.

The right ascension and declination (Dec.) is that of the true Sun. The right ascension of the mean Sun is obtained by applying the equation of time, with the sign given, to the right ascension of the true Sun, or, more easily, by applying 12h to the Sidereal Time. The direction in which the equation of time has to be applied in different problems is a frequent source of confusion and error. Apparent Solar Time is equal to the Mean Solar Time plus the Equation of Time. For example, at 12h GMT on August 8 the Equation of Time is –5m 44s and thus at 12h Mean Time on that day the Apparent Time is 12h – 5m 44s = 11h 54m 16s.

The Greenwich Sidereal Time at 0h and the Transit of the First Point of Aries (which is really the mean time when the sidereal time is 0h) are used for converting mean time to sidereal time and vice versa.

The GMT of transit of the Sun at Greenwich may also be taken as the local mean time (LMT) of transit in any longitude. It is independent of latitude. The GMT of transit in any longitude is obtained by adding the longitude to the time given if west, and vice versa.

LIGHTING-UP TIME

The legal importance of sunrise and sunset is that the Road Vehicles Lighting Regulations 1989 (SI 1989 No. 1796) as amended, make the use of front and rear position lamps on vehicles compulsory during the period between sunset and sunrise. Headlamps on vehicles are required to be used during the hours of darkness on unlit roads, on lit roads with a speed limit exceeding 30mph, or whenever visibility is seriously reduced. The hours of darkness are defined in these regulations as the period between half an hour after sunset and half an hour before sunrise.

In all laws and regulations 'sunset' refers to the local sunset, ie the time at which the Sun sets at the place in question. This common-sense interpretation has been upheld by legal tribunals.

SUNRISE AND SUNSET

The times of sunrise and sunset are those when the Sun's upper limb, as affected by refraction, is on the true horizon of an observer at sea-level. Assuming the mean refraction to be 34′, and the Sun's semi-diameter to be 16′, the time given is that when the true zenith distance of the Sun's centre is 90°+34′+16′ or 90° 50′, or, in other words, when the depression of the Sun's centre below the true horizon is 50′. The upper limb is then 34′ below the true horizon, but is brought there by refraction. An observer on a ship might see the Sun for a minute or so longer, because of the dip of the horizon, while another viewing the sunset over hills or mountains would record an earlier time. Nevertheless, the moment when the true zenith distance of the Sun's centre is 90° 50′ is a precise time dependent only on the latitude and longitude of the place, and independent of its altitude above sea-level, the contour of its horizon, the vagaries of refraction or the small seasonal change in the Sun's semi-diameter; this moment is suitable in every way as a definition of sunset (or sunrise) for all statutory purposes.

TWILIGHT

Light reaches us before sunrise and continues to reach us for some time after sunset. The interval between darkness and sunrise or sunset and darkness is called twilight. Astronomically speaking, twilight is considered to begin or end when the Sun's centre is 18° below the horizon, as no light from the Sun can then reach the observer. As thus defined twilight may last several hours; in high latitudes at the summer solstice the depression of 18° is not reached, and twilight lasts from sunset to sunrise.

The need for some sub-division of twilight is met by dividing the gathering darkness into four stages.

(1) *Sunrise or Sunset,* defined as above

(2) *Civil twilight,* which begins or ends when the Sun's centre is 6° below the horizon. This marks the time when operations requiring daylight may commence or must cease. In England it varies from about 30 to 60 minutes after sunset and the same interval before sunrise

(3) *Nautical twilight,* which begins or ends when the Sun's centre is 12° below the horizon. This marks the time when it is, to all intents and purposes, completely dark

(4) *Astronomical twilight,* which begins or ends when the Sun's centre is 18° below the horizon. This marks theoretical perfect darkness. It is of little practical importance, especially if nautical twilight is tabulated

To assist observers the durations of civil, nautical and astronomical twilights are given at intervals of ten days. The beginning of a particular twilight is found by subtracting the duration from the time of sunrise, while the end is found by adding the duration to the time of sunset. Thus the beginning of astronomical twilight in latitude 52°, on the Greenwich meridian, on March 11 is found as 06h 24m – 113m = 04h 31m and similarly the end of civil twilight as 17h 57m +34m = 18h 31m. The letters TAN (twilight all night) are printed when twilight lasts all night.

Under the heading The Night Sky will be found notes describing the position and visibility of the planets and other phenomena.

PAGE THREE OF EACH MONTH

The Moon moves so rapidly among the stars that its position is given only to the degree of accuracy that permits linear interpolation. The right ascension (RA) and declination (Dec.) are geocentric, ie for an imaginary observer at the centre of the Earth. To an observer on the surface of the Earth the position is always different, as the altitude is always less on account of parallax, which may reach 1°.

The lunar terminator is the line separating the bright from the dark part of the Moon's disk. Apart from irregularities of the lunar surface, the terminator is elliptical, because it is a circle seen in projection. It becomes the full circle forming the limb, or edge, of the Moon at New and Full Moon. The selenographic longitude of the terminator is measured from the mean centre of the visible disk, which may differ from the visible centre by as much as 8°, because of libration.

Instead of the longitude of the terminator the Sun's selenographic co-longitude (Sun's co-long.) is tabulated. It is numerically equal to the selenographic longitude of the morning terminator, measured eastwards from the mean centre of the disk. Thus its value is approximately 270° at New Moon, 360° at First Quarter, 90° at Full Moon and 180° at Last Quarter.

The Position Angle (PA) of the Bright Limb is the position angle of the midpoint of the illuminated limb, measured eastwards from the north point on the disk. The Phase column shows the percentage of the area of the Moon's disk illuminated; this is also the illuminated percentage of the diameter at right angles to the line of cusps. The terminator is a semi-ellipse whose major axis is the line of cusps, and whose semi-minor axis is determined by the tabulated percentage; from New Moon to Full Moon the east limb is dark, and vice versa.

The times given as moonrise and moonset are those when the upper limb of the Moon is on the horizon of an observer at sea-level. The Sun's horizontal parallax (Hor. par.) is about

9″, and is negligible when considering sunrise and sunset, but that of the Moon averages about 57′. Hence the computed time represents the moment when the true zenith distance of the Moon is 90° 50′ (as for the Sun) minus the horizontal parallax. The time required for the Sun or Moon to rise or set is about four minutes (except in high latitudes). *See also* page 627 and footnote below.

The GMT of transit of the Moon over the meridian of Greenwich is given; these times are independent of latitude but must be corrected for longitude. For places in the British Isles it suffices to add the longitude if west, and vice versa. For other places a further correction is necessary because of the rapid movement of the Moon relative to the stars. The entire correction is conveniently determined by first finding the west longitude λ of the place. If the place is in west longitude, λ is the ordinary west longitude; if the place is in east longitude λ is the complement to 24h (or 360°) of the longitude and will be greater than 12h (or 180°). The correction then consists of two positive portions, namely λ and the fraction λ/24 (or λ°/360) multiplied by the difference between consecutive transits. Thus for Christchurch, New Zealand, the longitude is 11h 31m east, so λ = 12h 29m and the fraction λ/24 is 0.52. The transit on the local date 20 March 2013 is found as follows:

		d	*h*	*m*
GMT of transit at Greenwich	January	7	17	33
λ			12	29
0.52 × (18h 21m – 17h 33m)				25
GMT of transit at Christchurch		8	06	27
Corr. to NZ Standard Time			12	00
Local standard time of transit	January	8	18	27

As is evident, for any given place the quantities λ and the correction to local standard time may be combined permanently, being here 24h 29m.

Positions of Mercury are given for every second day, and those of Venus and Mars for every fifth day; they may be interpolated linearly. The diameter (Diam.) is given in seconds of arc. The phase is the illuminated percentage of the disk. In the case of the inner planets this approaches 100 at superior conjunction and 0 at inferior conjunction. When the phase is less than 50 the planet is crescent-shaped or horned; for greater phases it is gibbous. In the case of the exterior planet Mars, the phase approaches 100 at conjunction and opposition, and is a minimum at the quadratures.

Since the planets cannot be seen when on the horizon, the actual times of rising and setting are not given; instead, the time when the planet has an apparent altitude of 5° has been tabulated. If the time of transit is between 00h and 12h the time refers to an altitude of 5° above the eastern horizon; if between 12h and 24h, to the western horizon. The phenomenon tabulated is the one that occurs between sunset and sunrise. The times given may be interpolated for latitude and corrected for longitude, as in the case of the Sun and Moon.

PAGE FOUR OF EACH MONTH

The GMTs of sunrise and sunset for seven cities, whose adopted positions in longitude (W.) and latitude (N.) are given immediately below the name, may be used not only for these phenomena, but also for lighting-up times (*see* page 1129 for a fuller explanation).

The particulars for the four outer planets resemble those for the planets on Page Three of each month, except that, under Uranus and Neptune, times when the planet is 10° high instead of 5° high are given; this is because of the inferior brightness of these planets. The diameters given for the rings of Saturn are those of the major axis (in the plane of the planet's equator) and the minor axis respectively. The former has a small seasonal change due to the slightly varying distance of the Earth from Saturn, but the latter varies from zero when the Earth passes through the ring plane every 15 years to its maximum opening half-way between these periods. The rings were last open at their widest extent (and Saturn at its brightest) in 2002; this will occur again in 2017. The Earth passed through the ring plane in 2009.

TIME

From the earliest ages, the natural division of time into recurring periods of day and night has provided the practical time-scale for the everyday activities of the human race. Indeed, if any alternative means of time measurement is adopted, it must be capable of adjustment so as to remain in general agreement with the natural time-scale defined by the diurnal rotation of the Earth on its axis. Ideally the rotation should be measured against a fixed frame of reference; in practice it must be measured against the background provided by the celestial bodies. If the Sun is chosen as the reference point, we obtain Apparent Solar Time, which is the time indicated by a sundial. It is not a uniform time but is subject to variations which amount to as much as a quarter of an hour in each direction. Such wide variations cannot be tolerated in a practical time-scale, and this has led to the concept of Mean Solar Time in which all the days are exactly the same length and equal to the average length of the Apparent Solar Day.

The positions of the stars in the sky are specified in relation to a fictitious reference point in the sky known as the First Point of Aries (or the Vernal Equinox). It is therefore convenient to adopt this same reference point when considering the rotation of the Earth against the background of the stars. The time-scale so obtained is known as Apparent Sidereal Time.

GREENWICH MEAN TIME

The daily rotation of the Earth on its axis causes the Sun and the other heavenly bodies to appear to cross the sky from east to west. It is convenient to represent this relative motion as if the Sun really performed a daily circuit around a fixed Earth. Noon in Apparent Solar Time may then be defined as the time at which the Sun transits across the observer's meridian. In Mean Solar Time, noon is similarly defined by the meridian transit of a fictitious Mean Sun moving uniformly in the sky with the same average speed as the true Sun. Mean Solar Time observed on the meridian of the transit circle telescope of the Royal Observatory at Greenwich is called

---

SUNRISE, SUNSET, MOONRISE AND MOONSET

The tables have been constructed for the meridian of Greenwich and for latitudes 52° and 56°. They give Greenwich Mean Time (GMT) throughout the year. To obtain the GMT of the phenomenon as seen from any other latitude and longitude in the British Isles, first interpolate or extrapolate for latitude by the usual rules of proportion. To the time thus found, the longitude (expressed in time) is to be added if west (as it usually is in Great Britain) or subtracted if east. If the longitude is expressed in degrees and minutes of arc, it must be converted to time at the rate of 1° = 4m and 15′ = 1m. A method of calculating rise and set time for other places in the world is given on page 627.

The GMT at which the planet transits the Greenwich meridian is also given. The times of transit are to be corrected to local meridians in the usual way, as already described.

Greenwich Mean Time (GMT). The mean solar day is divided into 24 hours and, for astronomical and other scientific purposes, these are numbered 0 to 23, commencing at midnight. Civil time is usually reckoned in two periods of 12 hours, designated am (*ante meridiem,* ie before noon) and pm (*post meridiem,* ie after noon), although the 24 hour clock is increasingly being used.

UNIVERSAL TIME

Before 1925 January 1, GMT was reckoned in 24 hours commencing at noon; since that date it has been reckoned from midnight. To avoid confusion in the use of the designation GMT before and after 1925, since 1928 astronomers have tended to use the term Universal Time (UT) or Weltzeit (WZ) to denote GMT measured from Greenwich Mean Midnight.

In precision work it is necessary to take account of small variations in Universal Time. These arise from small irregularities in the rotation of the Earth. Observed astronomical time is designated UT0. Observed time corrected for the effects of the motion of the poles (giving rise to a 'wandering' in longitude) is designated UT1. There is also a seasonal fluctuation in the rate of rotation of the Earth arising from meteorological causes, often called the annual fluctuation. UT1 corrected for this effect is designated UT2 and provides a time-scale free from short-period fluctuations. It is still subject to small secular and irregular changes.

APPARENT SOLAR TIME

As mentioned above, the time shown by a sundial is called Apparent Solar Time. It differs from Mean Solar Time by an amount known as the Equation of Time, which is the total effect of two causes which make the length of the apparent solar day non-uniform. One cause of variation is that the orbit of the Earth is not a circle but an ellipse, having the Sun at one focus. As a consequence, the angular speed of the Earth in its orbit is not constant; it is greatest at the beginning of January when the Earth is nearest the Sun.

The other cause is due to the obliquity of the ecliptic; the plane of the equator (which is at right angles to the axis of rotation of the Earth) does not coincide with the ecliptic (the plane defined by the apparent annual motion of the Sun around the celestial sphere) but is inclined to it at an angle of 23° 26′. As a result, the apparent solar day is shorter than average at the equinoxes and longer at the solstices. From the combined effects of the components due to obliquity and eccentricity, the equation of time reaches its maximum values in February (–14 minutes) and early November (+16 minutes). It has a zero value on four dates during the year, and it is only on these dates (approximately April 15, June 14, September 1 and December 25) that a sundial shows Mean Solar Time.

SIDEREAL TIME

A sidereal day is the duration of a complete rotation of the Earth with reference to the First Point of Aries. The term sidereal (or 'star') time is a little misleading since the time-scale so defined is not exactly the same as that which would be defined by successive transits of a selected star, as there is a small progressive motion between the stars and the First Point of Aries due to the precession of the Earth's axis. This makes the length of the sidereal day shorter than the true period of rotation by 0.008 seconds. Superimposed on this steady precessional motion are small oscillations (nutation), giving rise to fluctuations in apparent sidereal time amounting to as much as 1.2 seconds. It is therefore customary to employ Mean Sidereal Time, from which these fluctuations have been removed. The conversion of GMT to Greenwich sidereal time (GST) may be performed by adding the value of the GST at 0h on the day in question (page two of each month) to the GMT converted to sidereal time using the table on page 1102.

Example – To find the GST at August 8d 02h 41m 11s GMT

	h	*m*	*s*
GST at 0h	21	05	43
GMT	2	41	11
Acceleration for 2h			20
Acceleration for 41m 11s			7
Sum = GST =	23	47	21

If the observer is not on the Greenwich meridian then his/her longitude, measured positively westwards from Greenwich, must be subtracted from the GST to obtain Local Sidereal Time (LST). Thus, in the above example, an observer 5h east of Greenwich, or 19h west, would find the LST as 4h 49m 16s.

EPHEMERIS TIME

An analysis of observations of the positions of the Sun, Moon and planets taken over an extended period is used in preparing ephemerides. (An ephemeris is a table giving the apparent position of a heavenly body at regular intervals of time, eg one day or ten days, and may be used to compare current observations with tabulated positions.) Discrepancies between the positions of heavenly bodies observed over a 300-year period and their predicted positions arose because the time-scale to which the observations were related was based on the assumption that the rate of rotation of the Earth is uniform. It is now known that this rate of rotation is variable. A revised time-scale, Ephemeris Time (ET), was devised to bring the ephemerides into agreement with the observations.

The second of ET is defined in terms of the annual motion of the Earth in its orbit around the Sun (1/31556925.9747 of the tropical year for 1900 January 0d 12h ET). The precise determination of ET from astronomical observations is a lengthy process as the requisite standard of accuracy can only be achieved by averaging over a number of years.

In 1976 the International Astronomical Union adopted Terrestrial Dynamical Time (TDT), a new dynamical time-scale for general use whose scale unit is the SI second (*see* Atomic Time, below). TDT was renamed Terrestrial Time (TT) in 1991. ET is now of little more than historical interest.

TERRESTRIAL TIME

The uniform time system used in computing the ephemerides of the solar system is Terrestrial Time (TT), which has replaced ET for this purpose. Except for the most rigorous astronomical calculations, it may be assumed to be the same as ET. During 2014 the estimated difference TT – UT is about 67 seconds.

ATOMIC TIME

The fundamental standards of time and frequency must be defined in terms of a periodic motion adequately uniform, enduring and measurable. Progress has made it possible to use natural standards, such as atomic or molecular oscillations. Continuous oscillations are generated in an electrical circuit, the frequency of which is then compared or brought into coincidence with the frequency characteristic of the absorption or emission by the atoms or molecules when they change between two selected energy levels. Since the

13th General Conference on Weights and Measures in October 1967, the unit of time, the second, has been defined in the International System of units (SI) as 'the duration of 9 192 631 770 periods of the radiation corresponding to the transition between the two hyperfine levels of the ground state of the caesium-133 atom'.

In the UK, the national time scale is maintained by the National Physical Laboratory (NPL), using an ensemble of atomic clocks based on either caesium or hydrogen atoms. In addition the NPL (along with several other national laboratories) has constructed and operates a caesium fountain primary frequency standard, which utilises the cooling of caesium atoms by laser light to determine the duration of the SI second at the highest attainable level of accuracy. Caesium fountain primary standards typically achieve an accuracy of around 1 part in 1,000 000 000 000 000, which is equivalent to one second in 30 million years.

Timekeeping worldwide is based on two closely related atomic time scales that are established through international collaboration. International Atomic Time (TAI) is formed by combining the readings of more than 250 atomic clocks located in about 55 institutes and was set close to the astronomically based Universal Time (UT) near the beginning of 1958. It was formally recognised in 1971 and since 1988 January 1 has been maintained by the International Bureau of Weights and Measures (BIPM). Civil time in almost all countries is now based on Coordinated Universal Time (UTC), which differs from TAI by an integer number of seconds and was designed to make both atomic time and UT available with accuracy appropriate for most users. On 1 January 1972 UTC was set to be exactly 10 seconds behind TAI, and since then the UTC time-scale has been adjusted by the insertion (or, in principle, omission) of leap seconds in order to keep it within ±0.9 s of UT. These leap seconds are introduced, when necessary, at the same instant throughout the world, either at the end of December or at the end of June. The last leap second occurred immediately prior to 0h UTC on 2012 July 1 and was the 25th leap second. All leap seconds so far have been positive, with 61 seconds in the final minute of the UTC month. The time 23h 59m 60s UTC is followed one second later by 0h 0m 00s of the first day of the following month. Notices concerning the insertion of leap seconds are issued by the International Earth Rotation and Reference Systems Service (IERS).

The computation of UTC is carried out monthly by the BIPM and takes place in three stages. First, a weighted average known as Echelle Atomique Libre (EAL) is calculated from all of the contributing atomic clocks. In the second stage, TAI is generated by applying small corrections, derived from the results contributed by primary frequency standards, to the scale interval of EAL to maintain its value close to that of the SI second. Finally, UTC is formed from TAI by the addition of an integer number of seconds. The results are published monthly in the BIPM Circular T in the form of offsets at 5-day intervals between UTC and the time scales of contributing organisations.

RADIO TIME-SIGNALS

UTC is made generally available through time-signals and standard frequency broadcasts such as MSF in the UK, CHU in Canada and WWV and WWVH in the USA. These are based on national time-scales that are maintained in close agreement with UTC and provide traceability to the national time-scale and to UTC. The markers of seconds in the UTC scale coincide with those of TAI.

To disseminate the national time-scale in the UK, special signals (call-sign MSF) are broadcast by the National Physical Laboratory. From 2007 April 1 the MSF service, previously broadcast from British Telecom's radio station at Rugby, has been transmitted from Anthorn radio station in Cumbria. The signals are controlled from a caesium beam atomic frequency standard and consist of a precise frequency carrier of 60 kHz which is switched off, after being on for at least half a second, to mark every second. The first second of the minute begins with a period of 500 ms with the carrier switched off, to serve as a minute marker. In the other seconds the carrier is always off for at least one tenth of a second at the start and then it carries an on-off code giving the British clock time and date, together with information identifying the start of the next minute. Changes to and from summer time are made following government announcements. Leap seconds are inserted as announced by the IERS and information provided by them on the difference between UTC and UT is also signalled. Other broadcast signals in the UK include the BBC six pips signal, the BT Timeline ('speaking clock'), the NPL telephone and internet time services for computers, and a coded time-signal on the BBC 198 kHz transmitters which is used for timing in the electricity supply industry. From 1972 January 1 the six pips on the BBC have consisted of five short pips from second 55 to second 59 (six pips in the case of a leap second) followed by one lengthened pip, the start of which indicates the exact minute. From 1990 February 5 these signals have been controlled by the BBC with seconds markers referenced to the satellite-based US navigation system GPS (Global Positioning System) and time and day referenced to the MSF transmitter. Formerly they were generated by the Royal Greenwich Observatory. The NPL telephone and internet services are directly connected to the national time scale.

Accurate timing may also be obtained from the signals of international navigation systems such as the ground-based eLORAN, or the satellite-based American GPS or Russian GLONASS systems.

STANDARD TIME

Since 1880 the standard time in Britain has been Greenwich Mean Time (GMT); a statute that year enacted that the word 'time' when used in any legal document relating to Britain meant, unless otherwise specifically stated, the mean time of the Greenwich meridian. Greenwich was adopted as the universal meridian on 13 October 1884. A system of standard time by zones is used worldwide, standard time in each zone differing from that of the Greenwich meridian by an integral number of hours or, exceptionally, half-hours or quarter-hours, either fast or slow. The large territories of the USA and Canada are divided into zones approximately 7.5° on either side of central meridians.

Variations from the standard time of some countries occur during part of the year; they are decided annually and are usually referred to as Summer Time or Daylight Saving Time.

At the 180th meridian the time can be either 12 hours fast on Greenwich Mean Time or 12 hours slow, and a change of date occurs. The internationally recognised date or calendar line is a modification of the 180th meridian, drawn so as to include islands of any one group on the same side of the line, or for political reasons. The line is indicated by joining up the following coordinates:

Lat.	*Long.*	*Lat.*	*Long.*
90° S.	180°	48° N.	180°
51° S.	180°	53° N.	170° E.
45° S.	172.5° W.	65.5° N.	169° W.
15° S.	172.5° W.	68° N.	169° W.
5° S.	180°	90° N.	180°

Changes to the date line would require an international conference.

BRITISH SUMMER TIME

In 1916 an Act ordained that during a defined period of that year the legal time for general purposes in Great Britain should be one hour in advance of Greenwich Mean Time. The Summer Time Acts 1922 and 1925 defined the period during which Summer Time was to be in force, stabilising practice until the Second World War.

During the Second World War (1941–5) and in 1947 Double Summer Time (two hours in advance of Greenwich Mean Time) was used for the period in which ordinary Summer Time would have been in force. During these years clocks were also kept one hour in advance of Greenwich Mean Time in the winter. After the war, ordinary Summer Time was invoked each year from 1948–68.

Between 1968 October 27 and 1971 October 31 clocks were kept one hour ahead of Greenwich Mean Time throughout the year. This was known as British Standard Time.

The most recent legislation is the Summer Time Act 1972, which enacted that 'the period of summer time for the purposes of this Act is the period beginning at two o'clock, Greenwich Mean Time, in the morning of the day after the third Saturday in March or, if that day is Easter Day, the day after the second Saturday in March, and ending at two o'clock, Greenwich Mean Time, in the morning of the day after the fourth Saturday in October.'

The duration of Summer Time can be varied by Order in Council and in recent years alterations have been made to synchronise the period of Summer Time in Britain with that used in Europe. The rule for 1981–94 defined the period of Summer Time in the UK as from the last Sunday in March to the day following the fourth Saturday in October and the hour of changeover was altered to 01h Greenwich Mean Time.

There was no rule for the dates of Summer Time between 1995–7. Since 1998 the 9th European Parliament and Council Directive on Summer Time has harmonised the dates on which Summer Time begins and ends across member states as the last Sundays in March and October respectively. Under the directive Summer Time begins and ends at 01hr Greenwich Mean Time in each member state. Amendments to the Summer Time Act to implement the directive came into force in 2002.

The duration of Summer Time in 2014 is:
March 30 01h GMT to October 26 01h GMT

MEAN REFRACTION

Alt. ° ′	Ref. ′	Alt. ° ′	Ref. ′	Alt. ° ′	Ref. ′
1 20	21	3 12	13	7 54	6
1 30	20	3 34	12	9 27	5
1 41	19	4 00	11	11 39	4
1 52	18	4 30	10	15 00	3
2 05	17	5 06	9	20 42	2
2 19	16	5 50	8	32 20	1
2 35	15	6 44	7	62 17	0
2 52	14	7 54		90 00	
3 12					

The refraction table is in the form of a critical table (*see* page 1116).

ASTRONOMICAL CONSTANTS

Solar parallax	8″.794
Astronomical unit	149597870 km
Precession for the year 2013	50″.291
Precession in right ascension	3ˢ.075
Precession in declination	20″.043
Constant of nutation	9″.202
Constant of aberration	20″.496
Mean obliquity of ecliptic (2013)	23° 26′ 17″
Moon's equatorial hor. parallax	57′ 02″.70
Velocity of light in vacuo per second	299792.5 km
Solar motion per second	20.0 km
Equatorial radius of the Earth	6378.140 km
Polar radius of the Earth	6356.755 km
North galactic pole (IAU standard)	RA 12h 49m (1950.0). Dec.+27°.4 N.
Solar apex	RA 18h 06m Dec. + 30°
Length of year (in mean solar days)	
Tropical	365.24219
Sidereal	365.25636
Anomalistic (perihelion to perihelion)	365.25964
Eclipse	346.62003

Length of month (mean values)	*d*	*h*	*m*	*s*
New Moon to New	29	12	44	02.9
Sidereal	27	07	43	11.5
Anomalistic (perigee to perigee)	27	13	18	33.2

THE EARTH

The shape of the Earth is that of an oblate spheroid or solid of revolution whose meridian sections are ellipses not differing much from circles, while the sections at right angles are circles. The length of the equatorial axis is about 12,756 km, and that of the polar axis is 12,714 km. The mean density of the Earth is 5.5 times that of water, although that of the surface layer is less. The Earth and Moon revolve about their common centre of gravity in a lunar month; this centre in turn revolves round the Sun in a plane known as the ecliptic, that passes through the Sun's centre. The Earth's equator is inclined to this plane at an angle of 23.4°. This tilt is the cause of the seasons. In mid-latitudes, and when the Sun is high above the Equator, not only does the high noon altitude make the days longer, but the Sun's rays fall more directly on the Earth's surface; these effects combine to produce summer. In equatorial regions the noon altitude is large throughout the year, and there is little variation in the length of the day. In higher latitudes the noon altitude is lower, and the days in summer are appreciably longer than those in winter.

The average velocity of the Earth in its orbit is 30km a second. It makes a complete rotation on its axis in about 23h 56m of mean time, which is the sidereal day. Because of its annual revolution round the Sun, the rotation with respect to the Sun, or the solar day, is more than this by about four minutes. The extremity of the axis of rotation, or the North Pole of the Earth, is not rigidly fixed, but wanders over an area roughly 20 metres in diameter.

TERRESTRIAL MAGNETISM

The Earth's main magnetic field corresponds approximately to that of a very strong small bar magnet near the centre of the Earth, but with appreciable smooth spatial departures. The origin of the main field is generally ascribed to electric currents associated with fluid motions in the Earth's core. As a result not only does the main field vary in strength and direction from place to place, but also with time. Superimposed on the main field are local and regional anomalies whose magnitudes may in places approach that of the main field; these are due to the influence of mineral deposits in the Earth's crust. A small proportion of the field is of external origin, mostly associated with electric currents in the ionosphere. The configuration of the external field and the ionisation of the atmosphere depend on the incident particle and radiation flux from the Sun. There are, therefore, short-term and non-periodic as well as diurnal, 27-day, seasonal and 11-year periodic changes in the magnetic field, dependent upon the position of the Sun and the degree of solar activity.

A magnetic compass points along the horizontal component of a magnetic line of force. These lines of force converge on the 'magnetic dip-poles', the places where the Earth's magnetic field is vertical. These poles move with time, and their present approximate adopted mean positions are 85.9° N., 148.9° W. and 64.3° S., 136.9° E.

There is also a 'magnetic equator', at all points of which the vertical component of the Earth's magnetic field is zero and a magnetised needle remains horizontal. This line runs between 2° and 12° north of the geographical equator in Asia and Africa, turns sharply south off the west African coast, and crosses South America through Brazil, Bolivia and Peru; it re-crosses the geographical equator in mid-Pacific.

Reference has already been made to secular changes in the Earth's field. The following table indicates the changes in magnetic declination (or variation of the compass). Declination is the angle in the horizontal plane between the direction of true north and that in which a magnetic compass points. Similar, though much smaller, changes have occurred in 'dip' or magnetic inclination. Secular changes differ throughout the world. Although the London observations suggest a cycle with a period of several hundred years, an exact repetition is unlikely.

London		*Greenwich*	
1580	11° 15′ E.	1900	16° 29′ W.
1622	5° 56′ E.	1925	13° 10′ W.
1665	1° 22′ W.	1950	9° 07′ W.
1730	13° 00′ W.	1975	6° 39′ W.
1773	21° 09′ W.	1998	3° 32′ W.
1850	22° 24′ W.		

In order that up-to-date information on declination may be available, many governments publish magnetic charts on which there are lines (isogonic lines) passing through all places at which specified values of declination will be found at the date of the chart.

In the British Isles, isogonic lines now run approximately north-east to south-west. Though there are considerable local deviations due to geological causes, a rough value of magnetic declination may be obtained by assuming that at 50° N. on the meridian of Greenwich, the value in 2014 is 0° 38′ west and allowing an increase of 11′ for each degree of latitude northwards and one of 26′ for each degree of longitude westwards. For example, at 53° N., 5° W., declination will be about 0° 26′ + 33′ + 130′, ie 3° 09′ west. The average annual change at the present time is about 11′ decrease.

The number of magnetic observatories is about 180, irregularly distributed over the globe. There are three in Great Britain, run by the British Geological Survey: at Hartland, north Devon; at Eskdalemuir, Dumfries and Galloway; and at Lerwick, Shetland Islands. The following are some recent annual mean values of the magnetic elements for Hartland.

Year	*Declination West* ° ′	*Dip or inclination* ° ′	*Horizontal intensity nanoTesla (nT)*	*Vertical intensity nT*
1960	9 58.8	66 43.9	18707	43504
1965	9 30.1	66 34.0	18872	43540
1970	9 06.5	66 26.1	19033	43636
1975	8 32.3	66 17.0	19212	43733
1980	7 43.8	66 10.3	19330	43768
1985	6 56.1	66 07.9	19379	43796
1990	6 15.0	66 09.7	19539	43896
1995	5 33.2	66 07.3	19457	43951
2000	4 43.6	66 06.9	19508	44051
2005	3 56.4	66 06.0	19576	44177
2012	2 47.9	66 01.7	19691	44287

As well as navigation at sea, in the air and on land by compass the oil industry depends on the Earth's magnetic field as a directional reference. They use magnetic survey tools when drilling well-bores and require accurate estimates of the local magnetic field, taking into account the crustal and external fields.

MAGNETIC STORMS

Occasionally, sometimes with great suddenness, the Earth's magnetic field is subject for several hours to marked disturbance. During a severe storm in October 2003 the declination at Eskdalemuir changed by over 5° in six minutes. In many instances such disturbances are accompanied by widespread displays of aurorae, marked changes in the incidence of cosmic rays, an increase in the reception of 'noise' from the Sun at radio frequencies, and rapid changes in the ionosphere and induced electric currents within the Earth which adversely affect satellite operations, telecommunications and electric power transmission systems. The disturbances are caused by changes in the stream of ionised particles which emanates from the Sun and through which the Earth is continuously passing. Some of these changes are associated with visible eruptions on the Sun, usually in the region of sun-spots. There is a marked tendency for disturbances to recur after intervals of about 27 days, the apparent period of rotation of the Sun on its axis, which is consistent with the sources being located on particular areas of the Sun.

ELEMENTS OF THE SOLAR SYSTEM

Orb	*Mean distance from Sun* (Earth = 1)	km 10^6	*Sidereal period days*	*Synodic period days*	*Incl. of orbit to ecliptic* °	′	*Diameter km*	*Mass (Earth = 1)*	*Period of rotation on axis days*
Sun	—	—	—	—	—		1,392,000	332,981	25–35*
Mercury	0.39	58	88.0	116	7	00	4,879	0.0553	58.646
Venus	0.72	108	224.7	584	3	24	12,104	0.8150	243.019*r*
Earth	1.00	150	365.3	—	—		12,756*e*	1.0000	0.997
Mars	1.52	228	687.0	780	1	51	6,794*e*	0.1074	1.026
Jupiter	5.20	778	4,332.6	399	1	18	142,984*e* 133,708*p*	317.83	0.410*e*
Saturn	9.55	1429	10,759.2	378	2	29	120,536*e* 108,728*p*	95.16	0.426*e*
Uranus	19.22	2875	30,684.6	370	0	46	51,118*e*	14.54	0.718*r*
Neptune	30.11	4504	60,191.2	367	1	46	49,528*e*	17.15	0.671
Pluto †	39.80	5954	91,708.2	367	17	09	2,390	0.002	6.387

e equatorial, *p* polar, *r* retrograde, * depending on latitude, † reclassified as a dwarf planet since August 2006

THE SATELLITES

	Name	Star mag.	Mean distance from primary km	Sidereal period of revolution d
EARTH				
I	Moon	—	384,400	27.322
MARS				
I	Phobos	11	9,378	0.319
II	Deimos	12	23,459	1.262
JUPITER				
XVI	Metis	17	127,960	0.295
XV	Adrastea	19	128,980	0.298
V	Amalthea	14	181,300	0.498
XIV	Thebe	16	221,900	0.675
I	Io	5	421,600	1.769
II	Europa	5	670,900	3.551
III	Ganymede	5	1,070,000	7.155
IV	Callisto	6	1,883,000	16.689
XIII	Leda	20	11,165,000	240.92
VI	Himalia	15	11,460,000	250.57
X	Lysithea	18	11,717,000	259.22
VII	Elara	17	11,741,000	259.65
XII	Ananke	19	21,276,000	629.77*r*
XI	Carme	18	23,404,000	734.17*r*
VIII	Pasiphae	17	23,624,000	743.68*r*
IX	Sinope	18	23,939,000	758.90*r*
SATURN				
XVIII	Pan	20	133,583	0.575
XV	Atlas	18	137,640	0.602
XVI	Prometheus	16	139,353	0.613
XVII	Pandora	16	141,700	0.629
XI	Epimetheus	15	151,422	0.694
X	Janus	14	151,472	0.695
I	Mimas	13	185,520	0.942
II	Enceladus	12	238,020	1.370
III	Tethys	10	294,660	1.888
XIII	Telesto	19	294,660	1.888
XIV	Calypso	19	294,660	1.888
IV	Dione	10	377,400	2.737
XII	Helene	18	377,400	2.737
V	Rhea	10	527,040	4.518
VI	Titan	8	1,221,850	15.945

	Name	Star mag.	Mean distance from primary km	Sidereal period of revolution d
SATURN				
VII	Hyperion	14	1,481,000	21.277
VIII	Iapetus	11	3,561,300	79.330
IX	Phoebe	16	12,952,000	550.48*r*
URANUS				
VI	Cordelia	24	49,770	0.335
VII	Ophelia	24	53,790	0.376
VIII	Bianca	23	59,170	0.435
IX	Cressida	22	61,780	0.464
X	Desdemona	22	62,680	0.474
XI	Juliet	21	64,350	0.493
XII	Portia	21	66,090	0.513
XIII	Rosalind	22	66,940	0.558
XIV	Belinda	22	75,260	0.624
XV	Puck	20	86,010	0.762
V	Miranda	16	129,390	1.413
I	Ariel	14	191,020	2.520
II	Umbriel	15	266,300	4.144
III	Titania	14	435,910	8.706
IV	Oberon	14	583,520	13.463
XVI	Caliban	22	7,230,000	579.5*r*
XX	Stephano	24	8,002,000	676.5*r*
XVII	Sycorax	21	12,179,000	1,283.4*r*
XVIII	Prospero	23	16,418,000	1,992.8*r*
XIX	Setebos	23	17,459,000	2,202.2*r*
NEPTUNE				
III	Naiad	25	48,230	0.294
IV	Thalassa	24	50,080	0.311
V	Despina	23	52,530	0.335
VI	Galatea	22	61,950	0.429
VII	Larissa	22	73,550	0.555
VIII	Proteus	20	117,650	1.122
I	Triton	13	354,760	5.877
II	Nereid	19	5,513,400	360.136
PLUTO				
I	Charon	17	19,600	6.387

Currently the total number of satellites of the outer planets are: Jupiter 62, Saturn 60, Uranus 27, Neptune 13, Pluto 3.

TIME MEASUREMENT AND CALENDARS

MEASUREMENTS OF TIME

Measurements of time are based on the time taken by the earth to rotate on its axis (day); by the Moon to revolve around the earth (month); and by the earth to revolve around the sun (year). From these, which are not commensurable, certain average or mean intervals have been adopted for ordinary use.

THE DAY

The day begins at midnight and is divided into 24 hours of 60 minutes, each of 60 seconds. The hours are counted from midnight up to 12 noon (when the sun crosses the meridian), and these hours are designated am *(ante meridiem);* and again from noon up to 12 midnight, which hours are designated pm *(post meridiem),* except when the 24-hour reckoning is employed. The 24-hour reckoning ignores am and pm, numbering the hours 0 to 23 from midnight.

Colloquially the 24 hours are divided into day and night, day being the time while the sun is above the horizon (including the four stages of twilight defined in the Astronomy section). Day is subdivided into morning, ending at noon; afternoon, from noon to about 6pm; and evening, which may be said to extend from 6pm until midnight. Night begins at the close of astronomical twilight (*see* the Astronomy section) and extends beyond midnight to sunrise the next day.

The names of the days are derived from Old English translations or adaptations of the Roman titles.

Sunday	Sol	Sun
Monday	Luna	Moon
Tuesday	Tiw/Tyr (god of war)	Mars
Wednesday	Woden/Odin	Mercury
Thursday	Thor	Jupiter
Friday	Frigga/Freyja (goddess of love)	Venus
Saturday	Saeterne	Saturn

THE MONTH

The month in the ordinary calendar is approximately the twelfth part of a year, but the lengths of the different months vary from 28 (or 29) days to 31.

THE YEAR

The equinoctial or tropical year is the time that the earth takes to revolve around the sun from equinox to equinox, ie 365.24219 mean solar days, or 365 days 5 hours 48 minutes and 45 seconds.

The calendar year usually consists of 365 days but a year containing 366 days is called a bissextile (*see* Roman calendar) or leap year, one day being added to the month of February so that a date 'leaps over' a day of the week. In the Roman calendar the day that was repeated was the sixth day before the beginning of March, the equivalent of 24 February.

A year is a leap year if the date of the year is divisible by four without remainder, unless it is the last year of the century. The last year of a century is a leap year only if its number is divisible by 400 without remainder, eg the years 1800 and 1900 had only 365 days but the year 2000 had 366 days.

THE SOLSTICE

A solstice is the point in the tropical year at which the sun attains its greatest distance, north or south, from the Equator. In the northern hemisphere the furthest point north of the Equator marks the summer solstice and the furthest point south marks the winter solstice.

The date of the solstice varies according to locality. For example, if the summer solstice falls on 21 June late in the day by Greenwich time, that day will be the longest of the year at Greenwich, but it will fall on 22 June, local date, in Japan, and so 22 June will be the longest day there. The date of the solstice is also affected by the length of the tropical year, which is 365 days 6 hours less about 11 minutes 15 seconds. If a solstice happens late on 21 June in one year, it will be nearly 6 hours later in the next (unless the next year is a leap year), ie early on 22 June, and that will be the longest day.

This delay of the solstice does not continue because the extra day in a leap year brings it back a day in the calendar. However, because of the 11 minutes 15 seconds mentioned above, the additional day in a leap year brings the solstice back too far by 45 minutes, and the time of the solstice in the calendar is earlier, in a four-year pattern, as the century progresses. The last year of a century is in most cases not a leap year, and the omission of the extra day puts the date of the solstice later by about 6 hours. Compensation for this is made by the fourth centennial year being a leap year. The solstice has become earlier in date throughout the last century and, because the year 2000 was a leap year, the solstice will get earlier still throughout the 21st century. The date of the winter solstice, the shortest day of the year, is affected by the same factors as the longest day.

At Greenwich the sun sets at its earliest by the clock about ten days before the shortest day. The daily change in the time of sunset is due in the first place to the sun's movement southwards at this time of the year, which diminishes the interval between the sun's transit and its setting. However, the daily decrease of the Equation of Time causes the time of apparent noon to be continuously later day by day, which to some extent counteracts the first effect. The rates of the change of these two quantities are not equal or uniform; their combination causes the date of earliest sunset to be 12 or 13 December at Greenwich. In more southerly latitudes the effect of the movement of the sun is less, and the change in the time of sunset depends on that of the Equation of Time to a greater degree, and the date of earliest sunset is earlier than it is at Greenwich, eg on the Equator it is about 1 November.

THE EQUINOX

The equinox is the point at which the sun crosses the Equator and day and night are of equal length all over the world. This occurs in March and September.

DOG DAYS

The days about the heliacal rising of the Dog Star, noted from ancient times as the hottest period of the year in the northern hemisphere, are called the Dog Days. Their incidence has been variously calculated as depending on the Greater or Lesser Dog Star (Sirius or Procyon) and their duration has been reckoned as from 30 to 54 days. A generally accepted period is from 3 July to 15 August.

CHRISTIAN CALENDAR

In the Christian chronological system the years are distinguished by cardinal numbers before or after the birth of Christ, the period being denoted by the letters BC (Before Christ) or, more rarely, AC *(Ante Christum),* and AD *(Anno Domini* – In the Year of Our Lord). The correlative dates of the epoch are the fourth year of the 194th Olympiad, the

753rd year from the foundation of Rome, AM 3761 in Jewish chronology, and the 4,714th year of the Julian period.

The system was introduced into Italy in the sixth century. Though first used in France in the seventh century, it was not universally established there until about the eighth century. It has been said that the system was introduced into England by St Augustine (AD 596), but it was probably not generally used until some centuries later. It was ordered to be used by the bishops at the Council of Chelsea (AD 816).

THE JULIAN CALENDAR

In the Julian calendar (adopted by the Roman Empire in 45 BC) all the centennial years were leap years, and for this reason towards the close of the 16th century there was a difference of ten days between the tropical and calendar years; the equinox fell on 11 March of the calendar, whereas at the time of the Council of Nicaea (AD 325), it had fallen on 21 March. In 1582 Pope Gregory ordained that 5 October should be called 15 October and that of the end-century years only the fourth should be a leap year.

THE GREGORIAN CALENDAR

The Gregorian calendar was adopted by Italy, France, Spain and Portugal in 1582, by Prussia, the Roman Catholic German states, Switzerland, Holland and Flanders on 1 January 1583, by Poland in 1586, Hungary in 1587, the Protestant German and Netherland states and Denmark in 1700, and by Great Britain and its Dominions (including the North American colonies) in 1752, by the omission of 11 days (3 September being reckoned as 14 September). Sweden omitted the leap day in 1700 but observed leap days in 1704 and 1708, and reverted to the Julian calendar by having two leap days in 1712; the Gregorian calendar was adopted in 1753 by the omission of 11 days (18 February being reckoned as 1 March). Japan adopted the calendar in 1872, China in 1912, Bulgaria in 1916, Turkey and Soviet Russia in 1918, Yugoslavia and Romania in 1919, and Greece in 1923.

In the same year that the change was made in England from the Julian to the Gregorian calendar, the start of the new year was also changed from 25 March to 1 January.

THE ORTHODOX CHURCHES

Some Orthodox churches still use the Julian reckoning but the majority of Greek Orthodox churches and the Romanian Orthodox Church have adopted a modified 'New Calendar', observing the Gregorian calendar for fixed feasts and the Julian for movable feasts.

The Orthodox Church year begins on 1 September. There are four fast periods and, in addition to Pascha (Easter), twelve great feasts, as well as numerous commemorations of the saints of the Old and New Testaments throughout the year.

EASTER DAYS AND DOMINICAL LETTERS 1500 TO 2035

Dates up to and including 1752 are according to the Julian calendar. For dominical letters in leap years, *see* note below

		1500–1599	1600–1699	1700–1799	1800–1899	1900–1999	2000–2035
March							
d	22	1573	1668	1761	1818		
e	23	1505/16	1600	1788	1845/56	1913	2008
f	24		1611/95	1706/99		1940	
g	25	1543/54	1627/38/49	1722/33/44	1883/94	1951	2035
A	26	1559/70/81/92	1654/65/76	1749/58/69/80	1815/26/37	1967/78/89	
b	27	1502/13/24/97	1608/87/92	1785/96	1842/53/64	1910/21/32	2005/16
c	28	1529/35/40	1619/24/30	1703/14/25	1869/75/80	1937/48	2027/32
d	29	1551/62	1635/46/57	1719/30/41/52	1807/12/91	1959/64/70	
e	30	1567/78/89	1651/62/73/84	1746/55/66/77	1823/34	1902/75/86/97	
f	31	1510/21/32/83/94	1605/16/78/89	1700/71/82/93	1839/50/61/72	1907/18/29/91	2002/13/24
April							
g	1	1526/37/48	1621/32	1711/16	1804/66/77/88	1923/34/45/56	2018/29
A	2	1553/64	1643/48	1727/38	1809/20/93/99	1961/72	
b	3	1575/80/86	1659/70/81	1743/63/68/74	1825/31/36	1904/83/88/94	
c	4	1507/18/91	1602/13/75/86/97	1708/79/90	1847/58	1915/20/26/99	2010/21
d	5	1523/34/45/56	1607/18/29/40	1702/13/24/95	1801/63/74/85/96	1931/42/53	2015/26
e	6	1539/50/61/72	1634/45/56	1729/35/40/60	1806/17/28/90	1947/58/69/80	
f	7	1504/77/88	1667/72	1751/65/76	1822/33/44	1901/12/85/96	
g	8	1509/15/20/99	1604/10/83/94	1705/87/92/98	1849/55/60	1917/28	2007/12
A	9	1531/42	1615/26/37/99	1710/21/32	1871/82	1939/44/50	2023/34
b	10	1547/58/69	1631/42/53/64	1726/37/48/57	1803/14/87/98	1955/66/77	
c	11	1501/12/63/74/85/96	1658/69/80	1762/73/84	1819/30/41/52	1909/71/82/93	2004
d	12	1506/17/28	1601/12/91/96	1789	1846/57/68	1903/14/25/36/98	2009/20
e	13	1533/44	1623/28	1707/18	1800/73/79/84	1941/52	2031
f	14	1555/60/66	1639/50/61	1723/34/45/54	1805/11/16/95	1963/68/74	
g	15	1571/82/93	1655/66/77/88	1750/59/70/81	1827/38	1900/06/79/90	2001
A	16	1503/14/25/36/87/98	1609/20/82/93	1704/75/86/97	1843/54/65/76	1911/22/33/95	2006/17/28
b	17	1530/41/52	1625/36	1715/20	1808/70/81/92	1927/38/49/60	2022/33
c	18	1557/68	1647/52	1731/42/56	1802/13/24/97	1954/65/76	
d	19	1500/79/84/90	1663/74/85	1747/67/72/78	1829/35/40	1908/81/87/92	
e	20	1511/22/95	1606/17/79/90	1701/12/83/94	1851/62	1919/24/30	2003/14/25
f	21	1527/38/49	1622/33/44	1717/28	1867/78/89	1935/46/57	2019/30
g	22	1565/76	1660	1739/53/64	1810/21/32	1962/73/84	
A	23	1508	1671		1848	1905/16	2000
b	24	1519	1603/14/98	1709/91	1859		2011
c	25	1546	1641	1736	1886	1943	

No dominical letter is placed against the intercalary day 29 February, but since it is still counted as a weekday and given a name, the series of letters moves back one day every leap year after intercalation. Thus, a leap year beginning with the dominical letter C will change to a year with the dominical letter B on 1 March

MOVEABLE FEASTS TO THE YEAR 2035

Year	*Ash Wednesday*	*Easter*	*Ascension*	*Pentecost (Whit Sunday)*	*Advent Sunday*
2014	5 March	20 April	29 May	8 June	30 November
2015	18 February	5 April	14 May	24 May	29 November
2016	10 February	27 March	5 May	15 May	27 November
2017	1 March	16 April	25 May	4 June	3 December
2018	14 February	1 April	10 May	20 May	2 December
2019	6 March	21 April	30 May	9 June	1 December
2020	26 February	12 April	21 May	31 May	29 November
2021	17 February	4 April	13 May	23 May	28 November
2022	2 March	17 April	26 May	5 June	27 November
2023	22 February	9 April	18 May	28 May	3 December
2024	14 February	31 March	9 May	19 May	1 December
2025	5 March	20 April	29 May	8 June	30 November
2026	18 February	5 April	14 May	24 May	29 November
2027	10 February	28 March	6 May	16 May	28 November
2028	1 March	16 April	25 May	4 June	3 December
2029	14 February	1 April	10 May	20 May	2 December
2030	6 March	21 April	30 May	9 June	1 December
2031	26 February	13 April	22 May	1 June	30 November
2032	11 February	28 March	6 May	16 May	28 November
2033	2 March	17 April	26 May	5 June	27 November
2034	22 February	9 April	18 May	28 May	3 December
2035	7 February	25 March	3 May	13 May	2 December

NOTES

Ash Wednesday (first day in Lent) can fall at earliest on 4 February and at latest on 10 March

Mothering Sunday (fourth Sunday in Lent) can fall at earliest on 1 March and at latest on 4 April

Easter Day can fall at earliest on 22 March and at latest on 25 April

Ascension Day is forty days after Easter Day and can fall at earliest on 30 April and at latest on 3 June

Pentecost (Whit Sunday) is seven weeks after Easter and can fall at earliest on 10 May and at latest on 13 June

Trinity Sunday is the Sunday after Whit Sunday

Corpus Christi falls on the Thursday after Trinity Sunday

Sundays after Pentecost – there are not less than 18 and not more than 23

Advent Sunday is the Sunday nearest to 30 November

THE DOMINICAL LETTER

The dominical letter is one of the letters A–G which are used to denote the Sundays in successive years. If the first day of the year is a Sunday the letter is A; if the second, B; the third, C; and so on. A leap year requires two letters, the first for 1 January to 29 February, the second for 1 March to 31 December.

EPIPHANY

The feast of the Epiphany, commemorating the manifestation of Christ, later became associated with the offering of gifts by the Magi. The day was of great importance from the time of the Council of Nicaea (AD 325), as the primate of Alexandria was charged at every Epiphany feast with the announcement in a letter to the churches of the date of the forthcoming Easter. The day was also of importance in Britain as it influenced dates, ecclesiastical and lay, eg Plough Monday, when work was resumed in the fields, fell on the Monday in the first full week after Epiphany.

LENT

The Teutonic word *Lent,* which denotes the fast preceding Easter, originally meant no more than the spring season; but from Anglo-Saxon times, at least, it has been used as the equivalent of the more significant Latin term *Quadragesima,* meaning the 'forty days' or, more literally, the fortieth day. Ash Wednesday is the first day of Lent, which ends at midnight before Easter Day.

PALM SUNDAY

Palm Sunday, the Sunday before Easter and the beginning of Holy Week, commemorates the triumphal entry of Christ into Jerusalem.

MAUNDY THURSDAY

Maundy Thursday is the day before Good Friday, the name itself being a corruption of *dies mandati* (day of the mandate) when Christ washed the feet of the disciples and gave them the mandate to love one another.

EASTER DAY

Easter Day is the first Sunday after the full moon which happens on, or next after, the 21st day of March; if the full moon happens on a Sunday, Easter Day is the Sunday after.

This definition is contained in an Act of Parliament (24 Geo. II ch. 23) and explanation is given in the preamble to the Act that the day of full moon depends on certain tables that have been prepared. These tables are summarised in the early pages of the Book of Common Prayer. The moon referred to is not the real moon of the heavens, but a hypothetical moon on whose 'full' the date of Easter depends, and the lunations of this 'calendar' moon consist of 29 and 30 days alternately, with certain necessary modifications to make the date of its full agree as nearly as possible with that of the real moon, which is known as the Paschal Full Moon.

A FIXED EASTER

In 1928 the House of Commons agreed to a motion for the third reading of a bill proposing that Easter Day shall, in the calendar year next but one after the commencement of the Act and in all subsequent years, be the first Sunday after the second Saturday in April. Easter would thus fall on the second or third Sunday in April, ie between 9 and 15 April (inclusive). A clause in the bill provided that before it shall come into operation, regard shall be had to any opinion expressed officially by the various Christian churches. Efforts by the World Council of Churches to secure a unanimous choice of date for Easter by its member churches have so far been unsuccessful.

ROGATION DAYS

Rogation Days are the Monday, Tuesday and Wednesday preceding Ascension Day and from the fifth century were observed as public fasts with solemn processions and supplications. The processions were discontinued as religious observances at the Reformation, but survive in the ceremony known as 'beating the parish bounds'. Rogation Sunday is the Sunday before Ascension Day.

EMBER DAYS

The Ember days occur on the Wednesday, Friday and Saturday of the same week, four times a year. Used for the ordination of clergy, these days are set aside for fasting and prayer. The weeks in which they fall are: (a) after the third Sunday in Advent, (b) before the second Sunday in Lent, (c) before Trinity Sunday and (d) after Holy Cross day.

TRINITY SUNDAY

Trinity Sunday is eight weeks after Easter Day, on the Sunday following Pentecost (Whit Sunday). Subsequent Sundays are reckoned in the Book of Common Prayer calendar of the Church of England as 'after Trinity'.

Thomas Becket (1118–70) was consecrated Archbishop of Canterbury on the Sunday after Whit Sunday and his first act was to ordain that the day of his consecration should be held as a new festival in honour of the Holy Trinity.

HINDU CALENDAR

The Hindu calendar is a luni-solar calendar of 12 months, each containing 29 days, 12 hours. Each month is divided into a light fortnight (Shukla or Shuddha) and a dark fortnight (Krishna or Vadya) based on the waxing and waning of the Moon. In most parts of India the month starts with the light fortnight, ie the day after the new moon, although in some regions it begins with the dark fortnight, ie the day after the full moon.

The new year according to the civil calendar begins on the first day of the month of Chaitra (March/April) and ends in the month of Phalgun (March). The financial new year begins on the first day of Kartik (Diwali day). For most Hindus, the first day of Chaitra and the first day of Kartik are equally important.

The 12 months – Chaitra, Vaishakh, Jyeshtha, Ashadh, Shravan, Bhadrapad, Ashvin, Kartik, Margashirsh, Paush, Magh and Phalgun – have Sanskrit names derived from 12 asterisms (constellations). There are regional variations to the names of the months but the Sanskrit names are understood throughout India.

Every lunar month that has a solar transit is termed pure *(shuddha)*. The lunar month without a solar transit is impure *(mala)* and called an intercalary month. An intercalary month occurs approximately every 32 lunar months, whenever the difference between the Hindu year of 360 lunar days (354 days 8 hours solar time) and the 365 days 6 hours of the solar year reaches the length of one Hindu lunar month (29 days 12 hours).

The leap month may be added at any point in the Hindu year. The name given to the month varies according to when it occurs but is taken from the month immediately following it. There is no leap month in 2014.

The days of the week are called Raviwar (Sunday), Somawar (Monday), Mangalwar (Tuesday), Budhawar (Wednesday), Guruwar (Thursday), Shukrawar (Friday) and Shaniwar (Saturday). The names are derived from the Sanskrit names of the sun, the moon and five planets, Mars, Mercury, Jupiter, Venus and Saturn.

Most fasts and festivals are based on the lunar calendar but a few are determined by the apparent movement of the sun, eg Makar Sankranti and Pongal (in southern India), which are celebrated on 14/15 January to mark the start of the Sun's apparent journey northwards and a change of season.

Festivals celebrated throughout India are Chaitra (the New Year), Raksha-bandhan (the renewal of the kinship bond between brothers and sisters), Navaratri (a nine-night festival dedicated to the goddess Parvati), Dussehra (the victory of Rama over the demon army), Diwali (a festival of lights), Makar Sankranti, Shivaratri (dedicated to Shiva), and Holi (a spring festival). British Hindus commonly celebrate the festival of Diwali as the start of the financial new year.

Regional festivals are Durga-puja (dedicated to the goddess Durga (Parvati)), Sarasvati Puja (dedicated to the goddess Sarasvati), Ganesh Chaturthi (worship of Ganesh on the fourth day (Chaturthi) of the light half of Bhadrapad), Ram Navami (the birth festival of the god Rama) and Krishna Janmashtami (the birth festival of the god Krishna).

The main festivals celebrated in Britain are Navaratri, Dussehra, Durga-puja, Diwali, Holi, Sarasvati Puja, Ganesh Chaturthi, Raksha-bandhan, Ram Navami and Krishna Janmashtami. For dates of the main festivals in 2014, *see* page 7.

JEWISH CALENDAR

The story of the Flood in the Book of Genesis indicates the use of a calendar of some kind and that the writers recognised 30 days as the length of a lunation. However, after the diaspora, Jewish communities were left in considerable doubt as to the times of fasts and festivals. This led to the formation of the Jewish calendar as used today. It is said that this was done in AD 358 by Rabbi Hillel II, though some assert that it did not happen until much later.

The calendar is luni-solar, and is based on the lengths of the lunation and of the tropical year as found by Hipparchus (*c.*120 BC), which differ little from those adopted at the present day. The year AM 5774 (2013–14) is the 17th year of the 304th Metonic (Minor or Lunar) cycle of 19 years and the 6th year of the 207th Solar (or Major) cycle of 28 years since the Era of the Creation. Jews hold that the Creation occurred at the time of the autumnal equinox in the year known in the Christian calendar as 3760 BC (954 of the Julian period). The epoch or starting point of Jewish chronology corresponds to 7 October 3761 BC. At the beginning of each solar cycle, the Tekufah of Nisan (the vernal equinox) returns to the same day and hour.

The hour is divided into 1,080 minims, and the month between one new moon and the next is reckoned as 29 days 12 hours 793 minims. The normal calendar year, called a regular common year, consists of 12 months of 30 days and 29 days alternately. Since 12 months such as these comprise only 354 days, in order that each of them shall not diverge greatly from an average place in the solar year, a 13th month is occasionally added after the fifth month of the civil year (which commences on the first day of the month Tishri), or as the penultimate month of the ecclesiastical year (which commences on the first day of the month Nisan). The years when this happens are called Embolismic or leap years.

Of the 19 years that form a Metonic cycle, seven are leap years; they occur at places in the cycle indicated by the numbers 3, 6, 8, 11, 14, 17 and 19, these places being chosen so that the accumulated excesses of the solar years should be as small as possible.

A Jewish year is of one of the following six types:

minimal common	353 days
regular common	354 days
full common	355 days
minimal leap	383 days
regular leap	384 days
full leap	385 days

The regular year has alternate months of 30 and 29 days. In a full year, Marcheshvan, the second month of the civil year, has 30 days instead of 29; in minimal years Kislev, the third month, has 29 instead of 30. The additional month in leap years is called Adar Sheni (Adar II) and follows the month called Adar Rishon; the usual Adar festivals are observed in Adar Sheni. In a leap year Adar I has 30 days, in all other years it has 29. None of the variations mentioned are allowed to change the number of days in the other months, which still follow the alternation of the normal 12.

These are the main features of the Jewish calendar, which must be considered permanent because as a Jewish law it cannot be altered except by a Great Sanhedrin.

The Jewish day begins between sunset and nightfall. The time used is that of the meridian of Jerusalem, which is 2h 21m in advance of Greenwich Mean Time. Rules for the beginning of sabbaths and festivals were laid down for the latitude of London in the 18th century and hours for nightfall are fixed annually by the Chief Rabbi.

JEWISH CALENDAR 5774–75

AM 5774 is a full leap year of 13 months, 55 sabbaths and 385 days. AM 5775 is a regular common year of 12 months, 51 sabbaths and 354 days.

Month (length)	AM 5774	AM 5775
Tishri 1 (30)	5 September 2013	25 September 2014
Marcheshvan 1 (30/29)	5 October	25 October
Kislev 1 (29/30)	4 November	23 November
Tebet 1 (29)	4 December	23 December
Shebat 1 (30)	2 January 2014	21 January 2015
**Adar 1* (30)	1 February	
†*Adar Sheni 1* (29)	3 March	
Nisan 1 (30)	1 April	
Iyar 1 (29)	1 May	
Sivan 1 (30)	30 May	
Tammuz 1 (29)	29 June	
Ab 1 (30)	28 July	
Elul 1 (29)	27 August	

* Known as Adar Rishon in leap years (30 days)
† Additional month in leap years, known as Adar Sheni

JEWISH FASTS AND FESTIVALS

For dates of principal festivals in 2014, *see* page 7.

Tishri 1–2	Rosh Hashanah (New Year)
Tishri 3	*Fast of Gedaliah
Tishri 10	Yom Kippur (Day of Atonement)
Tishri 15–21	Succot (Feast of Tabernacles)
Tishri 21	Hoshana Rabba
Tishri 22	Shemini Atseret (Solemn Assembly)
Tishri 23	Simchat Torah (Rejoicing of the Law)
Kislev 25	Hanukkah (Dedication of the Temple) begins
Tebet 10	Fast of Tebet
†*Adar* 13	§Fast of Esther
†*Adar* 14	Purim
†*Adar* 15	Shushan Purim
Nisan 15–22	Pesach (Passover)
Sivan 6–7	Shavuot (Feast of Weeks)
Tammuz 17	*Fast of Tammuz
Ab 9	*Fast of Ab

* If these dates fall on the sabbath the fast is kept on the following day
† Adar Sheni in leap years
§ This fast is observed on Adar 11 (or Adar Sheni 11 in leap years) if Adar 13 falls on a sabbath

MUSLIM CALENDAR

The Muslim era is dated from the *Hijrah,* or flight of the Prophet Muhammad from Mecca to Medina, the corresponding date of which in the Julian calendar is 16 July AD 622. The lunar *hijri* calendar is used principally in Iran, Egypt, Malaysia, Pakistan, Mauritania, various Arab states and certain parts of India. Iran uses the solar hijri calendar as well as the lunar hijri calendar. The dating system was adopted about AD 639, commencing with the first day of the month Muharram.

The lunar calendar consists of 12 months of either 30 or 29 days, with the intercalation of one day at the end of the 12th month at stated intervals in each cycle of 30 years. The object of the intercalation is to reconcile the date of the first day of the month with the date of the actual new moon.

Some adherents still take the date of the evening of the first physical sighting of the crescent of the new moon as that of the first of the month. If cloud obscures the Moon the present month may be extended to 30 days, after which the new month will begin automatically regardless of whether the Moon has been seen. (Under religious law a month must have less than 31 days.) This means that the beginning of a new month and the date of religious festivals can vary from the published calendars.

In each cycle of 30 years, 19 years are common and contain 354 days, and 11 years are intercalary (leap years) of 355 days, the latter being called *kabisah.* The mean length of the Hijrah years is 354 days 8 hours 48 minutes and the period of mean lunation is 29 days 12 hours 44 minutes.

To ascertain if a year is common or kabisah, divide it by 30: the quotient gives the number of completed cycles and the remainder shows the place of the year in the current cycle. If the remainder is 2, 5, 7, 10, 13, 16, 18, 21, 24, 26 or 29, the year is kabisah and consists of 355 days.

MUSLIM CALENDAR 1435–36

Hijrah 1435 (remainder 25) is a common year and Hijrah 1436 (remainder 26) is a kabisah year. Calendar dates below are estimates based on calculations of moon phases.

Month (length)	1435 AH	1436 AH
Muharram 1 (30/29)	4 November 2013	25 October 2014
Safar 1 (29/30)	4 December	23 November
Rabi' I 1 (30/29)	2 January 2014	23 December
Rabi' II 1 (29/30)	1 February	21 January 2015
Jumada I 1 (30)	2 March	
Jumada II 1 (29)	1 April	
Rajab 1 (30)	30 April	
Sha'ban 1 (29)	30 May	
Ramadan 1 (30)	28 June	
Shawwal 1 (30)	28 July	
Dhu'l Qa'da 1 (29)	27 August	
Dhu'l Hijjah 1 (30)	25 September	

MUSLIM FESTIVALS

Ramadan is a month of fasting for all Muslims because it is the month in which the revelation of the *Qur'an* (Koran) began.

During Ramadan, Muslims abstain from food, drink and sexual pleasure from dawn until after sunset throughout the month.

The two major festivals are *Eid-ul-Fitr* and *Eid-ul-Adha*. Eid-ul-Fitr marks the end of the Ramadan fast and is celebrated on the day after the sighting of the new moon of the following month. Eid-ul-Adha, the festival of sacrifice (also known as the great festival), celebrates the submission of the Prophet Ibrahim (Abraham) to God. Eid-ul-Adha falls on the tenth day of Dhu'l-Hijjah, coinciding with the day when those on *hajj* (pilgrimage to Mecca) sacrifice animals.

Other days accorded special recognition are:

Muharram 1	New Year's Day
Muharram 10	Ashura (the day Prophet Noah left the Ark and Prophet Moses was saved from Pharaoh (Sunni), the death of the Prophet's grandson Husain (Shi'ite))
Rabi'u-l-Awwal (Rabi' I) 12	Mawlid ul-Nabi (birthday of the Prophet Muhammad)
Rajab 27	Laylat ul-Isra' wa'l-Mi'raj (The Night of Journey and Ascension)
*Ramadan**	Laylat ul-Qadr (Night of Power)

* Moveable feast

For dates of the major celebrations in 2013–14, *see* page 7.

SIKH CALENDAR

The Sikh calendar is a lunar calendar of 365 days divided into 12 months. The length of the months varies between 29 and 32 days.

There are no prescribed feast days and no fasting periods. The main celebrations are Baisakhi (the new year and the anniversary of the founding of the Khalsa), Diwali Mela (festival of light), Hola Mohalla Mela (a spring festival held in the Punjab), and the Gurpurbs (anniversaries associated with the ten Gurus).

For dates of the major celebrations in 2014, *see* page 7.

THAI CALENDAR

Thailand adopted the Suriyakati calendar, a modified version of the Gregorian calendar, during the reign of King Rama V in 1888, using 1 April as the first day of the year. In 1940 the date of the new year was changed to 1 January. The years are counted from the beginning of the Buddhist era (BE), which is calculated to have commenced upon the death of the Lord Buddha, taken to have occurred in 543 BC, so AD 2014 is BE 2557. The Chinese system of associating years with one of twelve animals is also in use in Thailand. The Chantarakati lunar calendar is used to determine religious holidays; the new year begins on the first day of the waxing moon in November or, if there is a leap month, in December.

CIVIL AND LEGAL CALENDAR

THE HISTORICAL YEAR

Before 1752, two calendar systems were used in England. The civil or legal year began on 25 March and the historical year on 1 January. Thus the civil or legal date 24 March 1658 was the same day as the historical date 24 March 1659; a date in that portion of the year is written as 24 March 1658/9, the earlier date showing the civil or legal year.

THE NEW YEAR

In England in the seventh century, and as late as the 13th, the year was reckoned from Christmas Day, but in the 12th century the Church in England began the year with the feast of the Annunciation of the Blessed Virgin ('Lady Day') on 25 March, and this practice was adopted generally in the 14th century. The civil or legal year in the British dominions (exclusive of Scotland) began with Lady Day until 1751. But in and since 1752 the civil year has begun with 1 January. New Year's Day in Scotland was changed from 25 March to 1 January in 1600.

Elsewhere in Europe, 1 January was adopted as the first day of the year by Venice in 1522, German states in 1544, Spain, Portugal and the Roman Catholic Netherlands in 1556, Prussia, Denmark and Sweden in 1559, France in 1564, Lorraine in 1579, the Protestant Netherlands in 1583, Russia in 1725, and Tuscany in 1751.

REGNAL YEARS

Regnal years are the years of a sovereign's reign and each begins on the anniversary of his or her accession, eg regnal year 63 of the present queen begins on 6 February 2014.

The system was used for dating Acts of Parliament until 1962. The Summer Time Act 1925, for example, is quoted as 15 and 16 Geo. V ch. 64, because it became law in the parliamentary session which extended over part of both of these regnal years. Acts of a parliamentary session during which a sovereign died were usually given two year numbers, the regnal year of the deceased sovereign and the regnal year of his or her successor, eg those passed in 1952 were dated 16 Geo. VI and 1 Elizabeth II. Since 1962 Acts of Parliament have been dated by the calendar year.

QUARTER AND TERM DAYS

Holy days and saints days were the usual means in early times for setting the dates of future and recurrent appointments. The quarter days in England and Wales are the feast of the Nativity (25 December), the feast of the Annunciation (25 March), the feast of St John the Baptist (24 June) and the feast of St Michael and All Angels (29 September).

The term days in Scotland are Candlemas (the feast of the Purification), Whitsunday, Lammas (Loaf Mass) and Martinmas (St Martin's Day). These fell on 2 February, 15 May, 1 August and 11 November respectively. However, by the Term and Quarter Days (Scotland) Act 1990, the dates of the term days were changed to 28 February (Candlemas), 28 May (Whitsunday), 28 August (Lammas) and 28 November (Martinmas).

RED-LETTER DAYS

Red-letter days were originally the holy days and saints days indicated in early ecclesiastical calendars by letters printed in red ink. The days to be distinguished in this way were approved at the Council of Nicaea in AD 325.

These days still have a legal significance, as judges of the Queen's Bench Division wear scarlet robes on red-letter days falling during the law sittings. The days designated as red-letter days for this purpose are:

Holy and saints days

The Conversion of St Paul, the Purification, Ash Wednesday, the Annunciation, the Ascension, the feasts of St Mark, SS Philip and James, St Matthias, St Barnabas, St John the Baptist, St Peter, St Thomas, St James, St Luke, SS Simon and Jude, All Saints, St Andrew.

Civil calendar (for dates, *see* page 7)

Includes the anniversaries of the Queen's accession, the Queen's birthday and the Queen's coronation, the Queen's official birthday, the birthday of the Duke of Edinburgh, the birthday of the Prince of Wales, St David's Day and Lord Mayor's Day.

PUBLIC HOLIDAYS

Public holidays are divided into two categories, common law and statutory. Common law holidays are holidays 'by habit and custom'; in England, Wales and Northern Ireland these are Good Friday and Christmas Day.

Statutory public holidays, known as bank holidays, were first established by the Bank Holidays Act 1871. They were, literally, days on which the banks (and other public institutions) were closed and financial obligations due on that day were payable the following day. The legislation currently governing public holidays in the UK, which is the Banking and Financial Dealings Act 1971, stipulates the days that are to be public holidays in England, Wales, Scotland and Northern Ireland.

If a public holiday falls on a Saturday or a Sunday then another day will be given in lieu, usually the following Monday. For dates of public holidays in 2014 and 2015, *see* pages 8–9.

CHRONOLOGICAL CYCLES AND ERAS

SOLAR (OR MAJOR) CYCLE

The solar cycle is a period of 28 years; in any corresponding year of each cycle the days of the week recur on the same day of the month.

METONIC (LUNAR, OR MINOR) CYCLE

In 432 BC, Meton, an Athenian astronomer, found that 235 lunations are very nearly, though not exactly, equal in duration to 19 solar years and so after 19 years the phases of the Moon recur approximately on the same days of the month. The dates of full moon in a cycle of 19 years were inscribed in figures of gold on public monuments in Athens, and the number showing the position of a year in the cycle is called the golden number of that year.

JULIAN PERIOD

The Julian period was proposed by Joseph Scaliger in 1582. The period is 7,980 Julian years, and its first year coincides with the year 4713 BC. The figure of 7,980 is the product of the number of years in the solar cycle, the Metonic cycle and the cycle of the Roman indiction (28 × 19 × 15).

ROMAN INDICTION

The Roman indiction is a period of 15 years, instituted for fiscal purposes about AD 300.

EPACT

The epact is the age of the calendar Moon, diminished by one day, on 1 January, in the ecclesiastical lunar calendar.

CHINESE CALENDAR

A lunar calendar was the sole calendar in use in China until 1911, when the government adopted the new (Gregorian) calendar for official and most business activities. The Chinese tend to follow both calendars, the lunar calendar playing an important part in personal life, eg birth celebrations, festivals, marriages; and in rural villages the lunar calendar dictates the cycle of activities, denoting the change of weather and farming activities.

The lunar calendar is used in Hong Kong, Singapore, Malaysia, Tibet and elsewhere in south-east Asia. The calendar has a cycle of 60 years. The new year begins at the first new moon after the sun enters the sign of Aquarius, ie the new year falls between 21 January and 19 February in the Gregorian calendar.

Each year in the Chinese calendar is associated with one of 12 animals: the rat, the ox, the tiger, the rabbit, the dragon, the snake, the horse, the sheep, the monkey, the chicken or rooster, the dog, and the pig.

The date of the Chinese new year and the astrological sign for the years 2014–17 are:

2014	31 January	Horse
2015	19 February	Goat or Sheep
2016	8 February	Monkey
2017	28 January	Rooster

COPTIC CALENDAR

In the Coptic calendar, which is used in parts of Egypt and Ethiopia, the year is made up of 12 months of 30 days each, followed, in general, by five complementary days. Every fourth year is an intercalary or leap year and in these years there are six complementary days. The intercalary year of the Coptic calendar immediately precedes the leap year of the Julian calendar. The era is that of Diocletian or the Martyrs, the origin of which is fixed at 29 August AD 284 (Julian date).

INDIAN ERAS

In addition to the Muslim reckoning, other eras are used in India. The Saka era of southern India, dating from 3 March AD 78, was declared the national calendar of the Republic of India with effect from 22 March 1957, to be used concurrently with the Gregorian calendar. As revised, the year of the new Saka era begins at the spring equinox, with five successive months of 31 days and seven of 30 days in ordinary years, and six months of each length in leap years. The year AD 2014 is 1936 of the revised Saka era.

The year AD 2014 corresponds to the following years in other eras:

Year 2071 of the Vikram Samvat era
Year 1421 of the Bengali San era
Year 1190 of the Kollam era
Year 5115 of the Kaliyuga era
Year 2557 of the Buddha Nirvana era

JAPANESE CALENDAR

The Japanese calendar is essentially the same as the Gregorian calendar, the years, months and weeks being of the same length and beginning on the same days as those of the Gregorian calendar. The numeration of the years is different, based on a system of epochs or periods, each of which begins at the accession of an emperor or other important occurrence. The method is not unlike the British system of regnal years, except that each year of a period closes on 31 December. The Japanese chronology begins about AD 650 and the three latest epochs are defined by the reigns of emperors, whose actual names are not necessarily used:

Epoch
Taisho – 1 August 1912 to 25 December 1926
Showa – 26 December 1926 to 7 January 1989
Heisei – 8 January 1989

The year Heisei 26 begins on 1 January 2014.

The months are known as First Month, Second Month, etc, First Month being equivalent to January. The days of the week are Nichiyobi (Sun-day), Getsuyobi (Moon-day), Kayobi (Fire-day), Suiyobi (Water-day), Mokuyobi (Wood-day), Kinyobi (Metal-day) and Doyobi (Earth-day).

THE MASONIC YEAR

Two dates are quoted in warrants, dispensations, etc, issued by the United Grand Lodge of England, those for the current year being expressed as *Anno Domini* 2014 – *Anno Lucis* 6014. This *Anno Lucis* (year of light) is based on the Book of Genesis 1:3, the 4,000-year difference being derived, in modified form, from *Ussher's Notation,* published in 1654, which places the Creation of the World in 4004 BC.

OLYMPIADS

Ancient Greek chronology was reckoned in Olympiads, cycles of four years corresponding with the Olympic Games held on the plain of Olympia, in Elis. The intervening years were the first, second, etc, of the Olympiad, which received the name of the victor at the Games. The first recorded Olympiad is that of Choroebus, 776 BC.

ZOROASTRIAN CALENDAR

Zoroastrians, followers of the Iranian prophet Zarathushtra (known to the Greeks as Zoroaster) are mostly to be found in Iran and in India, where they are known as Parsees.

The Zoroastrian era dates from the coronation of the last Zoroastrian Sasanian king in AD 631. The Zoroastrian calendar is divided into 12 months, each comprising 30 days, followed by five holy days of the Gathas at the end of each year to make the year consist of 365 days.

In order to synchronise the calendar with the solar year of 365 days, an extra month was intercalated once every 120 years. However, this intercalation ceased in the 12th century and the new year, which had fallen in the spring, slipped back to August. Because intercalation ceased at different times in Iran and India, there was one month's difference between the calendar followed in Iran (Kadmi calendar) and that followed by the Parsees (Shenshai calendar). In 1906 a group of Zoroastrians decided to bring the calendar back in line with the seasons again and restore the new year to 21 March each year (Fasli calendar).

The Shenshai calendar (new year in August) is mainly used by Parsees. The Fasli calendar (new year, 21 March) is mainly used by Zoroastrians living in Iran, in the Indian subcontinent, or elsewhere.

ROMAN CALENDAR

Roman historians adopted as an epoch the foundation of Rome, which is believed to have happened in the year 753 BC. The ordinal number of the years in Roman reckoning is followed by the letters AUC *(ab urbe condita)*, so that the year 2014 is 2767 AUC (MMDCCLXVII). The calendar that we know has developed from one said to have been established by Romulus using a year of 304 days divided into ten months, beginning with March. To this Numa added January and February, making the year consist of 12 months of 30 and 29 days alternately, with an additional day so that the total was 355. It is also said that Numa ordered an intercalary month of 22 or 23 days in alternate years, making 90 days in eight years, to be inserted after 23 February.

However, there is some doubt as to the origination and the details of the intercalation in the Roman calendar. In the year 46 BC Julius Caesar found that the calendar had been allowed to fall into some confusion. He sought the help of Egyptian astronomer Sosigenes, which led to the construction and adoption (45 BC) of the Julian calendar, and, by a slight alteration, to the Gregorian calendar now in use. The year 46 BC was made to consist of 445 days and is called the Year of Confusion.

In the Roman (Julian) calendar the days of the month were counted backwards from three fixed points, or days, and an intervening day was said to be so many days before the next coming point, the first and last being counted. These three points were the Kalends, the Nones and the Ides. Their positions in the months and the method of counting from them will be seen in the table below. The year containing 366 days was called *bissextilis annus*, as it had a doubled sixth day *(bissextus dies)* before the March Kalends on 24 February – *ante diem sextum Kalendas Martias*, or a.d. VI Kal. Mart.

Present days of the month	*March, May, July, October have thirty-one days*		*January, August, December have thirty-one days*		*April, June, September, November have thirty days*		*February has twenty-eight days, and in leap year twenty-nine*	
1	Kalendis		Kalendis		Kalendis		Kalendis	
2	VI		IV	ante	IV	ante	IV	ante
3	V	ante	III	Nonas	III	Nonas	III	Nonas
4	IV	Nonas	pridie Nonas		pridie Nonas		pridie Nonas	
5	III		Nonis		Nonis		Nonis	
6	pridie Nonas		VIII		VIII		VIII	
7	Nonis		VII		VII		VII	
8	VIII		VI	ante	VI	ante	VI	ante
9	VII		V	Idus	V	Idus	V	Idus
10	VI	ante	IV		IV		IV	
11	V	Idus	III		III		III	
12	IV		pridie Idus		pridie Idus		pridie Idus	
13	III		Idibus		Idibus		Idibus	
14	pridie Idus		XIX		XVIII		XVI	
15	Idibus		XVIII		XVII		XV	
16	XVII		XVII		XVI		XIV	
17	XVI		XVI		XV		XIII	
18	XV		XV		XIV		XII	
19	XIV		XIV		XIII		XI	
20	XIII		XIII		XII	ante Kalendas	X	ante Kalendas
21	XII		XII	ante Kalendas	XI	(of the month	IX	Martias
22	XI	ante Kalendas	XI	(of the month	X	following)	VIII	
23	X	(of the month	X	following)	IX		VII	
24	IX	following)	IX		VIII		*VI	
25	VIII		VIII		VII		V	
26	VII		VII		VI		IV	
27	VI		VI		V		III	
28	V		V		IV		pridie Kalendas	
29	IV		IV		III		Martias	
30	III		III		pridie Kalendas			
31	pridie Kalendas (Aprilis, Iunias, Sextilis, Novembris)		pridie Kalendas (Februarias, Septembris, Ianuarias)		(Maias, Quinctilis, Octobris, Decembris)			

* Repeated in leap year

CALENDAR FOR ANY YEAR 1780–2040

To select the correct calendar for any year between 1780 and 2040, consult the index below

*** leap year**

1780 N*	1813 K	1846 I	1879 G	1912 D*	1945 C	1978 A	2011 M
1781 C	1814 M	1847 K	1880 J*	1913 G	1946 E	1979 C	2012 B*
1782 E	1815 A	1848 N*	1881 M	1914 I	1947 G	1980 F*	2013 E
1783 G	1816 D*	1849 C	1882 A	1915 K	1948 J*	1981 I	2014 G
1784 J*	1817 G	1850 E	1883 C	1916 N*	1949 M	1982 K	2015 I
1785 M	1818 I	1851 G	1884 F*	1917 C	1950 A	1983 M	2016 L*
1786 A	1819 K	1852 J*	1885 I	1918 E	1951 C	1984 B*	2017 A
1787 C	1820 N*	1853 M	1886 K	1919 G	1952 F*	1985 E	2018 C
1788 F*	1821 C	1854 A	1887 M	1920 J*	1953 I	1986 G	2019 E
1789 I	1822 E	1855 C	1888 B*	1921 M	1954 K	1987 I	2020 H*
1790 K	1823 G	1856 F*	1889 E	1922 A	1955 M	1988 L*	2021 K
1791 M	1824 J*	1857 I	1890 G	1923 C	1956 B*	1989 A	2022 M
1792 B*	1825 M	1858 K	1891 I	1924 F*	1957 E	1990 C	2023 A
1793 E	1826 A	1859 M	1892 L*	1925 I	1958 G	1991 E	2024 D*
1794 G	1827 C	1860 B*	1893 A	1926 K	1959 I	1992 H*	2025 G
1795 I	1828 F*	1861 E	1894 C	1927 M	1960 L*	1993 K	2026 I
1796 L*	1829 I	1862 G	1895 E	1928 B*	1961 A	1994 M	2027 K
1797 A	1830 K	1863 I	1896 H*	1929 E	1962 C	1995 A	2028 N*
1798 C	1831 M	1864 L*	1897 K	1930 G	1963 E	1996 D*	2029 C
1799 E	1832 B*	1865 A	1898 M	1931 I	1964 H*	1997 G	2030 E
1800 G	1833 E	1866 C	1899 A	1932 L*	1965 K	1998 I	2031 G
1801 I	1834 G	1867 E	1900 C	1933 A	1966 M	1999 K	2032 J*
1802 K	1835 I	1868 H*	1901 E	1934 C	1967 A	2000 N*	2033 M
1803 M	1836 L*	1869 K	1902 G	1935 E	1968 D*	2001 C	2034 A
1804 B*	1837 A	1870 M	1903 I	1936 H*	1969 G	2002 E	2035 C
1805 E	1838 C	1871 A	1904 L*	1937 K	1970 I	2003 G	2036 F*
1806 G	1839 E	1872 D*	1905 A	1938 M	1971 K	2004 J*	2037 I
1807 I	1840 H*	1873 G	1906 C	1939 A	1972 N*	2005 M	2038 K
1808 L*	1841 K	1874 I	1907 E	1940 D*	1973 C	2006 A	2039 M
1809 A	1842 M	1875 K	1908 H*	1941 G	1974 E	2007 C	2040 B*
1810 C	1843 A	1876 N*	1909 K	1942 I	1975 G	2008 F*	
1811 E	1844 D*	1877 C	1910 M	1943 K	1976 J*	2009 I	
1812 H*	1845 G	1878 E	1911 A	1944 N*	1977 M	2010 K	

A

	January	*February*	*March*
Sun.	1 8 15 22 29	5 12 19 26	5 12 19 26
Mon.	2 9 16 23 30	6 13 20 27	6 13 20 27
Tue.	3 10 17 24 31	7 14 21 28	7 14 21 28
Wed.	4 11 18 25	1 8 15 22	1 8 15 22 29
Thur.	5 12 19 26	2 9 16 23	2 9 16 23 30
Fri.	6 13 20 27	3 10 17 24	3 10 17 24 31
Sat.	7 14 21 28	4 11 18 25	4 11 18 25

	April	*May*	*June*
Sun.	2 9 16 23 30	7 14 21 28	4 11 18 25
Mon.	3 10 17 24	1 8 15 22 29	5 12 19 26
Tue.	4 11 18 25	2 9 16 23 30	6 13 20 27
Wed.	5 12 19 26	3 10 17 24 31	7 14 21 28
Thur.	6 13 20 27	4 11 18 25	1 8 15 22 29
Fri.	7 14 21 28	5 12 19 26	2 9 16 23 30
Sat.	1 8 15 22 29	6 13 20 27	3 10 17 24

	July	*August*	*September*
Sun.	2 9 16 23 30	6 13 20 27	3 10 17 24
Mon.	3 10 17 24 31	7 14 21 28	4 11 18 25
Tue.	4 11 18 25	1 8 15 22 29	5 12 19 26
Wed.	5 12 19 26	2 9 16 23 30	6 13 20 27
Thur.	6 13 20 27	3 10 17 24 31	7 14 21 28
Fri.	7 14 21 28	4 11 18 25	1 8 15 22 29
Sat.	1 8 15 22 29	5 12 19 26	2 9 16 23 30

	October	*November*	*December*
Sun.	1 8 15 22 29	5 12 19 26	3 10 17 24 31
Mon.	2 9 16 23 30	6 13 20 27	4 11 18 25
Tue.	3 10 17 24 31	7 14 21 28	5 12 19 26
Wed.	4 11 18 25	1 8 15 22 29	6 13 20 27
Thur.	5 12 19 26	2 9 16 23 30	7 14 21 28
Fri.	6 13 20 27	3 10 17 24	1 8 15 22 29
Sat.	7 14 21 28	4 11 18 25	2 9 16 23 30

EASTER DAYS

March 26	1815, 1826, 1837, 1967, 1978, 1989
April 2	1809, 1893, 1899, 1961
April 9	1871, 1882, 1939, 1950, 2023, 2034
April 16	1786, 1797, 1843, 1854, 1865, 1911, 1922, 1933, 1995, 2006, 2017
April 23	1905

B (LEAP YEAR)

	January	*February*	*March*
Sun.	1 8 15 22 29	5 12 19 26	4 11 18 25
Mon.	2 9 16 23 30	6 13 20 27	5 12 19 26
Tue.	3 10 17 24 31	7 14 21 28	6 13 20 27
Wed.	4 11 18 25	1 8 15 22 29	7 14 21 28
Thur.	5 12 19 26	2 9 16 23	1 8 15 22 29
Fri.	6 13 20 27	3 10 17 24	2 9 16 23 30
Sat.	7 14 21 28	4 11 18 25	3 10 17 24 31

	April	*May*	*June*
Sun.	1 8 15 22 29	6 13 20 27	3 10 17 24
Mon.	2 9 16 23 30	7 14 21 28	4 11 18 25
Tue.	3 10 17 24	1 8 15 22 29	5 12 19 26
Wed.	4 11 18 25	2 9 16 23 30	6 13 20 27
Thur.	5 12 19 26	3 10 17 24 31	7 14 21 28
Fri.	6 13 20 27	4 11 18 25	1 8 15 22 29
Sat.	7 14 21 28	5 12 19 26	2 9 16 23 30

	July	*August*	*September*
Sun.	1 8 15 22 29	5 12 19 26	2 9 16 23 30
Mon.	2 9 16 23 30	6 13 20 27	3 10 17 24
Tue.	3 10 17 24 31	7 14 21 28	4 11 18 25
Wed.	4 11 18 25	1 8 15 22 29	5 12 19 26
Thur.	5 12 19 26	2 9 16 23 30	6 13 20 27
Fri.	6 13 20 27	3 10 17 24 31	7 14 21 28
Sat.	7 14 21 28	4 11 18 25	1 8 15 22 29

	October	*November*	*December*
Sun.	7 14 21 28	4 11 18 25	2 9 16 23 30
Mon.	1 8 15 22 29	5 12 19 26	3 10 17 24 31
Tue.	2 9 16 23 30	6 13 20 27	4 11 18 25
Wed.	3 10 17 24 31	7 14 21 28	5 12 19 26
Thur.	4 11 18 25	1 8 15 22 29	6 13 20 27
Fri.	5 12 19 26	2 9 16 23 30	7 14 21 28
Sat.	6 13 20 27	3 10 17 24	1 8 15 22 29

EASTER DAYS

April 1	1804, 1888, 1956, 2040
April 8	1792, 1860, 1928, 2012
April 22	1832, 1984

C

	January	*February*	*March*
Sun.	7 14 21 28	4 11 18 25	4 11 18 25
Mon.	1 8 15 22 29	5 12 19 26	5 12 19 26
Tue.	2 9 16 23 30	6 13 20 27	6 13 20 27
Wed.	3 10 17 24 31	7 14 21 28	7 14 21 28
Thur.	4 11 18 25	1 8 15 22	1 8 15 22 29
Fri.	5 12 19 26	2 9 16 23	2 9 16 23 30
Sat.	6 13 20 27	3 10 17 24	3 10 17 24 31

	April	*May*	*June*
Sun.	1 8 15 22 29	6 13 20 27	3 10 17 24
Mon.	2 9 16 23 30	7 14 21 28	4 11 18 25
Tue.	3 10 17 24	1 8 15 22 29	5 12 19 26
Wed.	4 11 18 25	2 9 16 23 30	6 13 20 27
Thur.	5 12 19 26	3 10 17 24 31	7 14 21 28
Fri.	6 13 20 27	4 11 18 25	1 8 15 22 29
Sat.	7 14 21 28	5 12 19 26	2 9 16 23 30

	July	*August*	*September*
Sun.	1 8 15 22 29	5 12 19 26	2 9 16 23 30
Mon.	2 9 16 23 30	6 13 20 27	3 10 17 24
Tue.	3 10 17 24 31	7 14 21 28	4 11 18 25
Wed.	4 11 18 25	1 8 15 22 29	5 12 19 26
Thur.	5 12 19 26	2 9 16 23 30	6 13 20 27
Fri.	6 13 20 27	3 10 17 24 31	7 14 21 28
Sat.	7 14 21 28	4 11 18 25	1 8 15 22 29

	October	*November*	*December*
Sun.	7 14 21 28	4 11 18 25	2 9 16 23 30
Mon.	1 8 15 22 29	5 12 19 26	3 10 17 24 31
Tue.	2 9 16 23 30	6 13 20 27	4 11 18 25
Wed.	3 10 17 24 31	7 14 21 28	5 12 19 26
Thur.	4 11 18 25	1 8 15 22 29	6 13 20 27
Fri.	5 12 19 26	2 9 16 23 30	7 14 21 28
Sat.	6 13 20 27	3 10 17 24	1 8 15 22 29

EASTER DAYS

March 25	1883, 1894, 1951, 2035
April 1	1866, 1877, 1923, 1934, 1945, 2018, 2029
April 8	1787, 1798, 1849, 1855, 1917, 2007
April 15	1781, 1827, 1838, 1900, 1906, 1979, 1990, 2001
April 22	1810, 1821, 1962, 1973

D (LEAP YEAR)

	January	*February*	*March*
Sun.	7 14 21 28	4 11 18 25	3 10 17 24 31
Mon.	1 8 15 22 29	5 12 19 26	4 11 18 25
Tue.	2 9 16 23 30	6 13 20 27	5 12 19 26
Wed.	3 10 17 24 31	7 14 21 28	6 13 20 27
Thur.	4 11 18 25	1 8 15 22 29	7 14 21 28
Fri.	5 12 19 26	2 9 16 23	1 8 15 22 29
Sat.	6 13 20 27	3 10 17 24	2 9 16 23 30

	April	*May*	*June*
Sun.	7 14 21 28	5 12 19 26	2 9 16 23 30
Mon.	1 8 15 22 29	6 13 20 27	3 10 17 24
Tue.	2 9 16 23 30	7 14 21 28	4 11 18 25
Wed.	3 10 17 24	1 8 15 22 29	5 12 19 26
Thur.	4 11 18 25	2 9 16 23 30	6 13 20 27
Fri.	5 12 19 26	3 10 17 24 31	7 14 21 28
Sat.	6 13 20 27	4 11 18 25	1 8 15 22 29

	July	*August*	*September*
Sun.	7 14 21 28	4 11 18 25	1 8 15 22 29
Mon.	1 8 15 22 29	5 12 19 26	2 9 16 23 30
Tue.	2 9 16 23 30	6 13 20 27	3 10 17 24
Wed.	3 10 17 24 31	7 14 21 28	4 11 18 25
Thur.	4 11 18 25	1 8 15 22 29	5 12 19 26
Fri.	5 12 19 26	2 9 16 23 30	6 13 20 27
Sat.	6 13 20 27	3 10 17 24 31	7 14 21 28

	October	*November*	*December*
Sun.	6 13 20 27	3 10 17 24	1 8 15 22 29
Mon.	7 14 21 28	4 11 18 25	2 9 16 23 30
Tue.	1 8 15 22 29	5 12 19 26	3 10 17 24 31
Wed.	2 9 16 23 30	6 13 20 27	4 11 18 25
Thur.	3 10 17 24 31	7 14 21 28	5 12 19 26
Fri.	4 11 18 25	1 8 15 22 29	6 13 20 27
Sat.	5 12 19 26	2 9 16 23 30	7 14 21 28

EASTER DAYS

March 24	1940
March 31	1872, 2024
April 7	1844, 1912, 1996
April 14	1816, 1968

E

	January	*February*	*March*
Sun.	6 13 20 27	3 10 17 24	3 10 17 24 31
Mon.	7 14 21 28	4 11 18 25	4 11 18 25
Tue.	1 8 15 22 29	5 12 19 26	5 12 19 26
Wed.	2 9 16 23 30	6 13 20 27	6 13 20 27
Thur.	3 10 17 24 31	7 14 21 28	7 14 21 28
Fri.	4 11 18 25	1 8 15 22	1 8 15 22 29
Sat.	5 12 19 26	2 9 16 23	2 9 16 23 30

	April	*May*	*June*
Sun.	7 14 21 28	5 12 19 26	2 9 16 23 30
Mon.	1 8 15 22 29	6 13 20 27	3 10 17 24
Tue.	2 9 16 23 30	7 14 21 28	4 11 18 25
Wed.	3 10 17 24	1 8 15 22 29	5 12 19 26
Thur.	4 11 18 25	2 9 16 23 30	6 13 20 27
Fri.	5 12 19 26	3 10 17 24 31	7 14 21 28
Sat.	6 13 20 27	4 11 18 25	1 8 15 22 29

	July	*August*	*September*
Sun.	7 14 21 28	4 11 18 25	1 8 15 22 29
Mon.	1 8 15 22 29	5 12 19 26	2 9 16 23 30
Tue.	2 9 16 23 30	6 13 20 27	3 10 17 24
Wed.	3 10 17 24 31	7 14 21 28	4 11 18 25
Thur.	4 11 18 25	1 8 15 22 29	5 12 19 26
Fri.	5 12 19 26	2 9 16 23 30	6 13 20 27
Sat.	6 13 20 27	3 10 17 24 31	7 14 21 28

	October	*November*	*December*
Sun.	6 13 20 27	3 10 17 24	1 8 15 22 29
Mon.	7 14 21 28	4 11 18 25	2 9 16 23 30
Tue.	1 8 15 22 29	5 12 19 26	3 10 17 24 31
Wed.	2 9 16 23 30	6 13 20 27	4 11 18 25
Thur.	3 10 17 24 31	7 14 21 28	5 12 19 26
Fri.	4 11 18 25	1 8 15 22 29	6 13 20 27
Sat.	5 12 19 26	2 9 16 23 30	7 14 21 28

EASTER DAYS

March 24	1799
March 31	1782, 1793, 1839, 1850, 1861, 1907, 1918, 1929, 1991, 2002, 2013
April 7	1822, 1833, 1901, 1985
April 14	1805, 1811, 1895, 1963, 1974
April 21	1867, 1878, 1889, 1935, 1946, 1957, 2019, 2030

F (LEAP YEAR)

	January	*February*	*March*
Sun.	6 13 20 27	3 10 17 24	2 9 16 23 30
Mon.	7 14 21 28	4 11 18 25	3 10 17 24 31
Tue.	1 8 15 22 29	5 12 19 26	4 11 18 25
Wed.	2 9 16 23 30	6 13 20 27	5 12 19 26
Thur.	3 10 17 24 31	7 14 21 28	6 13 20 27
Fri.	4 11 18 25	1 8 15 22 29	7 14 21 28
Sat.	5 12 19 26	2 9 16 23	1 8 15 22 29

	April	*May*	*June*
Sun.	6 13 20 27	4 11 18 25	1 8 15 22 29
Mon.	7 14 21 28	5 12 19 26	2 9 16 23 30
Tue.	1 8 15 22 29	6 13 20 27	3 10 17 24
Wed.	2 9 16 23 30	7 14 21 28	4 11 18 25
Thur.	3 10 17 24	1 8 15 22 29	5 12 19 26
Fri.	4 11 18 25	2 9 16 23 30	6 13 20 27
Sat.	5 12 19 26	3 10 17 24 31	7 14 21 28

	July	*August*	*September*
Sun.	6 13 20 27	3 10 17 24 31	7 14 21 28
Mon.	7 14 21 28	4 11 18 25	1 8 15 22 29
Tue.	1 8 15 22 29	5 12 19 26	2 9 16 23 30
Wed.	2 9 16 23 30	6 13 20 27	3 10 17 24
Thur.	3 10 17 24 31	7 14 21 28	4 11 18 25
Fri.	4 11 18 25	1 8 15 22 29	5 12 19 26
Sat.	5 12 19 26	2 9 16 23 30	6 13 20 27

	October	*November*	*December*
Sun.	5 12 19 26	2 9 16 23 30	7 14 21 28
Mon.	6 13 20 27	3 10 17 24	1 8 15 22 29
Tue.	7 14 21 28	4 11 18 25	2 9 16 23 30
Wed.	1 8 15 22 29	5 12 19 26	3 10 17 24 31
Thur.	2 9 16 23 30	6 13 20 27	4 11 18 25
Fri.	3 10 17 24 31	7 14 21 28	5 12 19 26
Sat.	4 11 18 25	1 8 15 22 29	6 13 20 27

EASTER DAYS

March 23	1788, 1856, 2008
April 6	1828, 1980
April 13	1884, 1952, 2036
April 20	1924

G

	January	*February*	*March*
Sun.	5 12 19 26	2 9 16 23	2 9 16 23 30
Mon.	6 13 20 27	3 10 17 24	3 10 17 24 31
Tue.	7 14 21 28	4 11 18 25	4 11 18 25
Wed.	1 8 15 22 29	5 12 19 26	5 12 19 26
Thur.	2 9 16 23 30	6 13 20 27	6 13 20 27
Fri.	3 10 17 24 31	7 14 21 28	7 14 21 28
Sat.	4 11 18 25	1 8 15 22	1 8 15 22 29

	April	*May*	*June*
Sun.	6 13 20 27	4 11 18 25	1 8 15 22 29
Mon.	7 14 21 28	5 12 19 26	2 9 16 23 30
Tue.	1 8 15 22 29	6 13 20 27	3 10 17 24
Wed.	2 9 16 23 30	7 14 21 28	4 11 18 25
Thur.	3 10 17 24	1 8 15 22 29	5 12 19 26
Fri.	4 11 18 25	2 9 16 23 30	6 13 20 27
Sat.	5 12 19 26	3 10 17 24 31	7 14 21 28

	July	*August*	*September*
Sun.	6 13 20 27	3 10 17 24 31	7 14 21 28
Mon.	7 14 21 28	4 11 18 25	1 8 15 22 29
Tue.	1 8 15 22 29	5 12 19 26	2 9 16 23 30
Wed.	2 9 16 23 30	6 13 20 27	3 10 17 24
Thur.	3 10 17 24 31	7 14 21 28	4 11 18 25
Fri.	4 11 18 25	1 8 15 22 29	5 12 19 26
Sat.	5 12 19 26	2 9 16 23 30	6 13 20 27

	October	*November*	*December*
Sun.	5 12 19 26	2 9 16 23 30	7 14 21 28
Mon.	6 13 20 27	3 10 17 24	1 8 15 22 29
Tue.	7 14 21 28	4 11 18 25	2 9 16 23 30
Wed.	1 8 15 22 29	5 12 19 26	3 10 17 24 31
Thur.	2 9 16 23 30	6 13 20 27	4 11 18 25
Fri.	3 10 17 24 31	7 14 21 28	5 12 19 26
Sat.	4 11 18 25	1 8 15 22 29	6 13 20 27

EASTER DAYS

March 23	1845, 1913
March 30	1823, 1834, 1902, 1975, 1986, 1997
April 6	1806, 1817, 1890, 1947, 1958, 1969
April 13	1800, 1873, 1879, 1941, 2031
April 20	1783, 1794, 1851, 1862, 1919, 1930, 2003, 2014, 2025

H (LEAP YEAR)

	January	*February*	*March*
Sun.	5 12 19 26	2 9 16 23	1 8 15 22 29
Mon.	6 13 20 27	3 10 17 24	2 9 16 23 30
Tue.	7 14 21 28	4 11 18 25	3 10 17 24 31
Wed.	1 8 15 22 29	5 12 19 26	4 11 18 25
Thur.	2 9 16 23 30	6 13 20 27	5 12 19 26
Fri.	3 10 17 24 31	7 14 21 28	6 13 20 27
Sat.	4 11 18 25	1 8 15 22 29	7 14 21 28

	April	*May*	*June*
Sun.	5 12 19 26	3 10 17 24 31	7 14 21 28
Mon.	6 13 20 27	4 11 18 25	1 8 15 22 29
Tue.	7 14 21 28	5 12 19 26	2 9 16 23 30
Wed.	1 8 15 22 29	6 13 20 27	3 10 17 24
Thur.	2 9 16 23 30	7 14 21 28	4 11 18 25
Fri.	3 10 17 24	1 8 15 22 29	5 12 19 26
Sat.	4 11 18 25	2 9 16 23 30	6 13 20 27

	July	*August*	*September*
Sun.	5 12 19 26	2 9 16 23 30	6 13 20 27
Mon.	6 13 20 27	3 10 17 24 31	7 14 21 28
Tue.	7 14 21 28	4 11 18 25	1 8 15 22 29
Wed.	1 8 15 22 29	5 12 19 26	2 9 16 23 30
Thur.	2 9 16 23 30	6 13 20 27	3 10 17 24
Fri.	3 10 17 24 31	7 14 21 28	4 11 18 25
Sat.	4 11 18 25	1 8 15 22 29	5 12 19 26

	October	*November*	*December*
Sun.	4 11 18 25	1 8 15 22 29	6 13 20 27
Mon.	5 12 19 26	2 9 16 23 30	7 14 21 28
Tue.	6 13 20 27	3 10 17 24	1 8 15 22 29
Wed.	7 14 21 28	4 11 18 25	2 9 16 23 30
Thur.	1 8 15 22 29	5 12 19 26	3 10 17 24 31
Fri.	2 9 16 23 30	6 13 20 27	4 11 18 25
Sat.	3 10 17 24 31	7 14 21 28	5 12 19 26

EASTER DAYS

March 29	1812, 1964
April 5	1896
April 12	1868, 1936, 2020
April 19	1840, 1908, 1992

I

	January	*February*	*March*
Sun.	4 11 18 25	1 8 15 22	1 8 15 22 29
Mon.	5 12 19 26	2 9 16 23	2 9 16 23 30
Tue.	6 13 20 27	3 10 17 24	3 10 17 24 31
Wed.	7 14 21 28	4 11 18 25	4 11 18 25
Thur.	1 8 15 22 29	5 12 19 26	5 12 19 26
Fri.	2 9 16 23 30	6 13 20 27	6 13 20 27
Sat.	3 10 17 24 31	7 14 21 28	7 14 21 28

	April	*May*	*June*
Sun.	5 12 19 26	3 10 17 24 31	7 14 21 28
Mon.	6 13 20 27	4 11 18 25	1 8 15 22 29
Tue.	7 14 21 28	5 12 19 26	2 9 16 23 30
Wed.	1 8 15 22 29	6 13 20 27	3 10 17 24
Thur.	2 9 16 23 30	7 14 21 28	4 11 18 25
Fri.	3 10 17 24	1 8 15 22 29	5 12 19 26
Sat.	4 11 18 25	2 9 16 23 30	6 13 20 27

	July	*August*	*September*
Sun.	5 12 19 26	2 9 16 23 30	6 13 20 27
Mon.	6 13 20 27	3 10 17 24 31	7 14 21 28
Tue.	7 14 21 28	4 11 18 25	1 8 15 22 29
Wed.	1 8 15 22 29	5 12 19 26	2 9 16 23 30
Thur.	2 9 16 23 30	6 13 20 27	3 10 17 24
Fri.	3 10 17 24 31	7 14 21 28	4 11 18 25
Sat.	4 11 18 25	1 8 15 22 29	5 12 19 26

	October	*November*	*December*
Sun.	4 11 18 25	1 8 15 22 29	6 13 20 27
Mon.	5 12 19 26	2 9 16 23 30	7 14 21 28
Tue.	6 13 20 27	3 10 17 24	1 8 15 22 29
Wed.	7 14 21 28	4 11 18 25	2 9 16 23 30
Thur.	1 8 15 22 29	5 12 19 26	3 10 17 24 31
Fri.	2 9 16 23 30	6 13 20 27	4 11 18 25
Sat.	3 10 17 24 31	7 14 21 28	5 12 19 26

EASTER DAYS

March 22	1818
March 29	1807, 1891, 1959, 1970
April 5	1795, 1801, 1863, 1874, 1885, 1931, 1942, 1953, 2015, 2026, 2037
April 12	1789, 1846, 1857, 1903, 1914, 1925, 1998, 2009
April 19	1829, 1835, 1981, 1987

J (LEAP YEAR)

	January	*February*	*March*
Sun.	4 11 18 25	1 8 15 22 29	7 14 21 28
Mon.	5 12 19 26	2 9 16 23	1 8 15 22 29
Tue.	6 13 20 27	3 10 17 24	2 9 16 23 30
Wed.	7 14 21 28	4 11 18 25	3 10 17 24 31
Thur.	1 8 15 22 29	5 12 19 26	4 11 18 25
Fri.	2 9 16 23 30	6 13 20 27	5 12 19 26
Sat.	3 10 17 24 31	7 14 21 28	6 13 20 27

	April	*May*	*June*
Sun.	4 11 18 25	2 9 16 23 30	6 13 20 27
Mon.	5 12 19 26	3 10 17 24 31	7 14 21 28
Tue.	6 13 20 27	4 11 18 25	1 8 15 22 29
Wed.	7 14 21 28	5 12 19 26	2 9 16 23 30
Thur.	1 8 15 22 29	6 13 20 27	3 10 17 24
Fri.	2 9 16 23 30	7 14 21 28	4 11 18 25
Sat.	3 10 17 24	1 8 15 22 29	5 12 19 26

	July	*August*	*September*
Sun.	4 11 18 25	1 8 15 22 29	5 12 19 26
Mon.	5 12 19 26	2 9 16 23 30	6 13 20 27
Tue.	6 13 20 27	3 10 17 24 31	7 14 21 28
Wed.	7 14 21 28	4 11 18 25	1 8 15 22 29
Thur.	1 8 15 22 29	5 12 19 26	2 9 16 23 30
Fri.	2 9 16 23 30	6 13 20 27	3 10 17 24
Sat.	3 10 17 24 31	7 14 21 28	4 11 18 25

	October	*November*	*December*
Sun.	3 10 17 24 31	7 14 21 28	5 12 19 26
Mon.	4 11 18 25	1 8 15 22 29	6 13 20 27
Tue.	5 12 19 26	2 9 16 23 30	7 14 21 28
Wed.	6 13 20 27	3 10 17 24	1 8 15 22 29
Thur.	7 14 21 28	4 11 18 25	2 9 16 23 30
Fri.	1 8 15 22 29	5 12 19 26	3 10 17 24 31
Sat.	2 9 16 23 30	6 13 20 27	4 11 18 25

EASTER DAYS

March 28	1880, 1948, 2032
April 4	1920
April 11	1784, 1852, 2004
April 18	1824, 1976

K

	January	*February*	*March*
Sun.	3 10 17 24 31	7 14 21 28	7 14 21 28
Mon.	4 11 18 25	1 8 15 22	1 8 15 22 29
Tue.	5 12 19 26	2 9 16 23	2 9 16 23 30
Wed.	6 13 20 27	3 10 17 24	3 10 17 24 31
Thur.	7 14 21 28	4 11 18 25	4 11 18 25
Fri.	1 8 15 22 29	5 12 19 26	5 12 19 26
Sat.	2 9 16 23 30	6 13 20 27	6 13 20 27

	April	*May*	*June*
Sun.	4 11 18 25	2 9 16 23 30	6 13 20 27
Mon.	5 12 19 26	3 10 17 24 31	7 14 21 28
Tue.	6 13 20 27	4 11 18 25	1 8 15 22 29
Wed.	7 14 21 28	5 12 19 26	2 9 16 23 30
Thur.	1 8 15 22 29	6 13 20 27	3 10 17 24
Fri.	2 9 16 23 30	7 14 21 28	4 11 18 25
Sat.	3 10 17 24	1 8 15 22 29	5 12 19 26

	July	*August*	*September*
Sun.	4 11 18 25	1 8 15 22 29	5 12 19 26
Mon.	5 12 19 26	2 9 16 23 30	6 13 20 27
Tue.	6 13 20 27	3 10 17 24 31	7 14 21 28
Wed.	7 14 21 28	4 11 18 25	1 8 15 22 29
Thur.	1 8 15 22 29	5 12 19 26	2 9 16 23 30
Fri.	2 9 16 23 30	6 13 20 27	3 10 17 24
Sat.	3 10 17 24 31	7 14 21 28	4 11 18 25

	October	*November*	*December*
Sun.	3 10 17 24 31	7 14 21 28	5 12 19 26
Mon.	4 11 18 25	1 8 15 22 29	6 13 20 27
Tue.	5 12 19 26	2 9 16 23 30	7 14 21 28
Wed.	6 13 20 27	3 10 17 24	1 8 15 22 29
Thur.	7 14 21 28	4 11 18 25	2 9 16 23 30
Fri.	1 8 15 22 29	5 12 19 26	3 10 17 24 31
Sat.	2 9 16 23 30	6 13 20 27	4 11 18 25

EASTER DAYS

March 28	1869, 1875, 1937, 2027
April 4	1790, 1847, 1858, 1915, 1926, 1999, 2010, 2021
April 11	1819, 1830, 1841, 1909, 1971, 1982, 1993
April 18	1802, 1813, 1897, 1954, 1965
April 25	1886, 1943, 2038

M

	January	*February*	*March*
Sun.	2 9 16 23 30	6 13 20 27	6 13 20 27
Mon.	3 10 17 24 31	7 14 21 28	7 14 21 28
Tue.	4 11 18 25	1 8 15 22	1 8 15 22 29
Wed.	5 12 19 26	2 9 16 23	2 9 16 23 30
Thur.	6 13 20 27	3 10 17 24	3 10 17 24 31
Fri.	7 14 21 28	4 11 18 25	4 11 18 25
Sat.	1 8 15 22 29	5 12 19 26	5 12 19 26

	April	*May*	*June*
Sun.	3 10 17 24	1 8 15 22 29	5 12 19 26
Mon.	4 11 18 25	2 9 16 23 30	6 13 20 27
Tue.	5 12 19 26	3 10 17 24 31	7 14 21 28
Wed.	6 13 20 27	4 11 18 25	1 8 15 22 29
Thur.	7 14 21 28	5 12 19 26	2 9 16 23 30
Fri.	1 8 15 22 29	6 13 20 27	3 10 17 24
Sat.	2 9 16 23 30	7 14 21 28	4 11 18 25

	July	*August*	*September*
Sun.	3 10 17 24 31	7 14 21 28	4 11 18 25
Mon.	4 11 18 25	1 8 15 22 29	5 12 19 26
Tue.	5 12 19 26	2 9 16 23 30	6 13 20 27
Wed.	6 13 20 27	3 10 17 24 31	7 14 21 28
Thur.	7 14 21 28	4 11 18 25	1 8 15 22 29
Fri.	1 8 15 22 29	5 12 19 26	2 9 16 23 30
Sat.	2 9 16 23 30	6 13 20 27	3 10 17 24

	October	*November*	*December*
Sun.	2 9 16 23 30	6 13 20 27	4 11 18 25
Mon.	3 10 17 24 31	7 14 21 28	5 12 19 26
Tue.	4 11 18 25	1 8 15 22 29	6 13 20 27
Wed.	5 12 19 26	2 9 16 23 30	7 14 21 28
Thur.	6 13 20 27	3 10 17 24	1 8 15 22 29
Fri.	7 14 21 28	4 11 18 25	2 9 16 23 30
Sat.	1 8 15 22 29	5 12 19 26	3 10 17 24 31

EASTER DAYS

March 27	1785, 1842, 1853, 1910, 1921, 2005
April 3	1825, 1831, 1983, 1994
April 10	1803, 1814, 1887, 1898, 1955, 1966, 1977, 2039
April 17	1870, 1881, 1927, 1938, 1949, 2022, 2033
April 24	1791, 1859, 2011

L (LEAP YEAR)

	January	*February*	*March*
Sun.	3 10 17 24 31	7 14 21 28	6 13 20 27
Mon.	4 11 18 25	1 8 15 22 29	7 14 21 28
Tue.	5 12 19 26	2 9 16 23	1 8 15 22 29
Wed.	6 13 20 27	3 10 17 24	2 9 16 23 30
Thur.	7 14 21 28	4 11 18 25	3 10 17 24 31
Fri.	1 8 15 22 29	5 12 19 26	4 11 18 25
Sat.	2 9 16 23 30	6 13 20 27	5 12 19 26

	April	*May*	*June*
Sun.	3 10 17 24	1 8 15 22 29	5 12 19 26
Mon.	4 11 18 25	2 9 16 23 30	6 13 20 27
Tue.	5 12 19 26	3 10 17 24 31	7 14 21 28
Wed.	6 13 20 27	4 11 18 25	1 8 15 22 29
Thur.	7 14 21 28	5 12 19 26	2 9 16 23 30
Fri.	1 8 15 22 29	6 13 20 27	3 10 17 24
Sat.	2 9 16 23 30	7 14 21 28	4 11 18 25

	July	*August*	*September*
Sun.	3 10 17 24 31	7 14 21 28	4 11 18 25
Mon.	4 11 18 25	1 8 15 22 29	5 12 19 26
Tue.	5 12 19 26	2 9 16 23 30	6 13 20 27
Wed.	6 13 20 27	3 10 17 24 31	7 14 21 28
Thur.	7 14 21 28	4 11 18 25	1 8 15 22 29
Fri.	1 8 15 22 29	5 12 19 26	2 9 16 23 30
Sat.	2 9 16 23 30	6 13 20 27	3 10 17 24

	October	*November*	*December*
Sun.	2 9 16 23 30	6 13 20 27	4 11 18 25
Mon.	3 10 17 24 31	7 14 21 28	5 12 19 26
Tue.	4 11 18 25	1 8 15 22 29	6 13 20 27
Wed.	5 12 19 26	2 9 16 23 30	7 14 21 28
Thur.	6 13 20 27	3 10 17 24	1 8 15 22 29
Fri.	7 14 21 28	4 11 18 25	2 9 16 23 30
Sat.	1 8 15 22 29	5 12 19 26	3 10 17 24 31

EASTER DAYS

March 27	1796, 1864, 1932, 2016
April 3	1836, 1904, 1988
April 17	1808, 1892, 1960

N (LEAP YEAR)

	January	*February*	*March*
Sun.	2 9 16 23 30	6 13 20 27	5 12 19 26
Mon.	3 10 17 24 31	7 14 21 28	6 13 20 27
Tue.	4 11 18 25	1 8 15 22 29	7 14 21 28
Wed.	5 12 19 26	2 9 16 23	1 8 15 22 29
Thur.	6 13 20 27	3 10 17 24	2 9 16 23 30
Fri.	7 14 21 28	4 11 18 25	3 10 17 24 31
Sat.	1 8 15 22 29	5 12 19 26	4 11 18 25

	April	*May*	*June*
Sun.	2 9 16 23 30	7 14 21 28	4 11 18 25
Mon.	3 10 17 24	1 8 15 22 29	5 12 19 26
Tue.	4 11 18 25	2 9 16 23 30	6 13 20 27
Wed.	5 12 19 26	3 10 17 24 31	7 14 21 28
Thur.	6 13 20 27	4 11 18 25	1 8 15 22 29
Fri.	7 14 21 28	5 12 19 26	2 9 16 23 30
Sat.	1 8 15 22 29	6 13 20 27	3 10 17 24

	July	*August*	*September*
Sun.	2 9 16 23 30	6 13 20 27	3 10 17 24
Mon.	3 10 17 24 31	7 14 21 28	4 11 18 25
Tue.	4 11 18 25	1 8 15 22 29	5 12 19 26
Wed.	5 12 19 26	2 9 16 23 30	6 13 20 27
Thur.	6 13 20 27	3 10 17 24 31	7 14 21 28
Fri.	7 14 21 28	4 11 18 25	1 8 15 22 29
Sat.	1 8 15 22 29	5 12 19 26	2 9 16 23 30

	October	*November*	*December*
Sun.	1 8 15 22 29	5 12 19 26	3 10 17 24 31
Mon.	2 9 16 23 30	6 13 20 27	4 11 18 25
Tue.	3 10 17 24 31	7 14 21 28	5 12 19 26
Wed.	4 11 18 25	1 8 15 22 29	6 13 20 27
Thur.	5 12 19 26	2 9 16 23 30	7 14 21 28
Fri.	6 13 20 27	3 10 17 24	1 8 15 22 29
Sat.	7 14 21 28	4 11 18 25	2 9 16 23 30

EASTER DAYS

March 26	1780
April 2	1820, 1972
April 9	1944
April 16	1876, 2028
April 23	1848, 1916, 2000

GEOLOGICAL TIME

Era	*Period*	*Epoch*	*Dates**	*Evolutionary Stages*
Cenozoic	Quaternary	Holocene	11,700 BP†–present	
		Pleistocene	2,588,000–11,700 BP	First humans
	Neogene	Pliocene	5.332–2.588 Mya ‡	Majority of still existing species
		Miocene	23.03–5.332 Mya	
	Palaeogene	Oligocene	33.9–23.03 Mya	
		Eocene	55.8–33.9 Mya	First modern mammals
		Palaeocene	65.5–55.8 Mya	
Mesozoic	Cretaceous		145.5–65.5 Mya	
	Jurassic		199.6–145.5 Mya	First birds
	Triassic		251–199.6 Mya	First mammals
Palaeozoic	Permian		299–251 Mya	First reptiles
	Carboniferous		359.2–299 Mya	First traces of land-living creatures
	Devonian		416–359.2 Mya	
	Silurian		443.7–416 Mya	
	Ordovician		488.3–443.7 Mya	First fish
	Cambrian		542–488.3 Mya	First invertebrates
Precambrian	Proterozoic		2,500–542 Mya	First primitive life forms, eg algae and bacteria
	Archaean		3,800–2,500 Mya	Earth uninhabited
	Hadean		4,600–3,800 Mya	

* approximate † BP = Before Present ‡ Mya = million years ago

PALAEOZOIC ('ANCIENT LIFE')

Cambrian – Mainly sandstones, slate and shales; limestones in Scotland. Shelled fossils and invertebrates, eg trilobites and brachiopods, and the earliest known vertebrates (jawless fish) appear

Ordovician – Mainly shales and mudstones, eg in north Wales; limestones in Scotland. First fish

Silurian – Shales, mudstones and some limestones, found mostly in Wales and southern Scotland

Devonian – Old red sandstone, shale, limestone and slate, eg in south Wales and the West Country

Carboniferous – Coal-bearing rocks, millstone grit, limestone and shale. First traces of land-living creatures

Permian – Marls, sandstones and clays. First reptile fossils

There were two great phases of mountain building in the Palaeozoic era: the Caledonian, characterised in Britain by NE–SW lines of hills and valleys; and the later Hercynian, widespread in west Germany and adjacent areas, and in Britain exemplified in E–W lines of hills and valleys.

The end of the Palaeozoic era was marked by the extensive glaciations of the Permian period in the southern continents and the decline of amphibians. It was succeeded by an era of warm conditions.

MESOZOIC ('MIDDLE FORMS OF LIFE')

Triassic – Mostly sandstone, eg in the W. Midlands; primitive mammals appear

Jurassic – Mainly limestones and clays, typically displayed in the Jura mountains, and in England in a NE–SW belt from Lincolnshire and the Wash to the Severn and the Dorset coast

Cretaceous – Mainly chalk, clay and sands, eg in Kent and Sussex

Giant reptiles were dominant during the Mesozoic era; marsupial mammals first appeared, as well as *Archaeopteryx lithographica,* the earliest known species of bird. Coniferous trees and flowering plants also developed during the era and, with the birds and the mammals, were the main species to survive into the Cenozoic era. The giant reptiles became extinct.

CENOZOIC ('RECENT LIFE')

Palaeocene, *Eocene* – The emergence of new forms of life, including existing species; primates appear

Oligocene – Fossils of a few still existing species

Miocene – Fossil remains show a balance of existing and extinct species

Pliocene, *Pleistocene* – Fossil remains show a majority of still existing species

Holocene – The present, post-glacial period. Existing species only, except for a few exterminated by humans

In the last 25 million years, from the Miocene through the Pliocene periods, the Alpine-Himalayan and the circum-Pacific phases of mountain building reached their climax. During the Pleistocene period ice-sheets locked up masses of water as land ice, lowering the sea-level by 100–200m. The glaciations and interglacials of the Ice Age are difficult to date and classify, but recent scientific opinion considers the Pleistocene period to have begun *c.*1.64 Mya. The last glacial retreat, merging into the Holocene period, was *c.*10,000 years ago.

HUMAN DEVELOPMENT

All members of the human race belong to one species of animal, *Homo sapiens,* the definition of a species being in biological terms that all its members can interbreed. As a species of mammal it is possible to group humans with other similar types, known as the primates. Amongst these is found a sub-group, the apes, which includes, in addition to humans, the chimpanzees, gorillas, orangutans and gibbons. All lack a tail, have shoulder blades at the back, and a Y-shaped chewing pattern on the surface of their molars, as well as showing the more general primate characteristics of four incisors, a thumb which is able to touch the fingers of the same hand, and finger and toe nails instead of claws. However, there once lived creatures, now extinct, which were closer to modern man than the chimpanzees and gorillas, and which shared with modern man the characteristics of having flat faces (ie the absence of a pronounced muzzle), being bipedal, and possessing large brains.

The debate surrounding evidence for the oldest human ancestors is ongoing. The earliest putative hominin for which there is significant fossil evidence is *Ardipithecus ramidus,* for which an almost complete skeleton, dating to at least 4.4 million years ago (Mya), was discovered in the Afar Rift, Ethiopia in 1992. Analysis of the *Ardipithecus ramidus* skeleton suggests the creature had characteristics of both humans and apes; able to climb trees and walk on two feet.

The subsequent Australopithecines have left more numerous remains in south and east Africa, among which sub-groups may be detected. Living between 4.2 and 1.5 Mya, they were relatives of modern humans in respect of the fact that they walked upright, did not have an extensive muzzle and had similar types of pre-molars. The first australopithecine remains were recognised at Taung in South Africa in 1924 and named *Australopithecus africanus,* dating between 3.3 and 2.3 Mya. The most impressive discovery was made at Hadar, Ethiopia, in 1974 when about half a skeleton of *Australopithecus afarensis,* known as 'Lucy', was found. Some 3.2 Mya, 'Lucy' (who is now considered to be male) certainly walked upright.

Also in east Africa, especially at Olduvai Gorge in Tanzania, between 2.5 and 1.8 Mya, lived a hominid group which not only walked upright, had a flat face, and a large brain case, but also made simple pebble and flake stone tools. Due to their distinctive characteristics, they have been grouped as a separate sub-species, now extinct, of the genus *Homo* and are known as *Homo habilis* or 'handy man'.

The use of fire, again a human characteristic, is associated with another group of extinct hominids whose remains, about a million years old, are found in south and east Africa, China, Indonesia, north Africa and Europe. The ability to make fire probably helped the colonisation of the colder northern areas and in this respect the site of Vertesszollos in Hungary is of particular importance. *Homo ergaster* in Africa and *Homo erectus* in Asia are the names given to this group of fossils and they relate to a number of famous individual discoveries, eg Solo Man, Heidelberg Man, and especially Peking Man who lived at the cave site at Choukoutien which has yielded evidence of fire and burnt bone.

The well-known group the Neanderthals, or *Homo neanderthalensis,* is an extinct form of human that lived between *c.*350,000 and *c.*24,000 years ago; spanning the last Ice Age and living alongside modern humans. The Neanderthals' ability to adapt to the cold climate on the edge of the ice-sheets is one of their characteristic features, with remains being found only in Europe, Asia and the Middle East. Complete Neanderthal skeletons were found during excavations at Tabun in Israel, together with evidence of tool-making and the use of fire. Distinguished by very large brains, it seems that Neanderthals were the first to develop recognisable social customs, especially deliberate burial rites. Why the Neanderthals became extinct is not clear but it may be connected with the climatic changes at the end of the Ice Ages, which would have seriously affected their food supplies; possibly they became too specialised for their own good.

The shin bone of Boxgrove Man found in 1993 – *Homo heidelbergensis* – and the Swanscombe skull are the best known early human fossil remains found in England. Some specialists prefer to group Swanscombe Man (or, more probably, woman) together with the Steinheim skull from Germany, seeing both as a separate sub-species. There is too little evidence as yet on which to form a final judgement.

Anatomically modern humans – *Homo sapiens sapiens* ('doubly wise man') – had evolved to our present physical condition and had colonised much of the world by about 40,000 years ago. There are many previously distinguished individual specimens, eg Cromagnon Man, the first early *Homo sapiens sapiens* of the European Upper Palaeolithic.

The discovery of the structure of DNA in 1953 has come to have a profound effect upon the study of human evolution. For example, it was claimed in 1987 that a common ancestor of all human beings was a person who lived in Africa some 200,000 years ago, thus encouraging the 'out of Africa' theory of hominid migration from east Africa to the Middle East and then throughout the world.

CULTURAL DEVELOPMENT

The Three Age system, whereby prehistory was divided into a Stone Age, a Bronze Age and an Iron Age, was devised by Christian Thomsen, curator of the National Museum of Denmark in the early 19th century, to facilitate the classification of the museum's collections. The adjectives referred to the materials from which the implements and weapons were made and came to be regarded as the dominant features of the societies to which they related. The Three Age system remains a generally accepted concept in the popular mind. However, it is now seen by archaeologists as an inadequate model for human development. Common sense suggests that there were no complete breaks between one so-called Age and another. Nor can the Three Age system be applied universally. In some areas it is necessary to insert a Copper Age, while in South Africa there would seem to be no Bronze Age at all; in Australia, Old Stone Age societies survived, while in South America, New Stone Age communities exist into modern times.

The concept of the 'Neolithic revolution', associated with the domestication of plants and animals, was a development of particular importance in the human cultural pattern. It reflected a gradual change from the hunter-gatherer economies to a more settled agricultural way of life and therefore, so the argument goes, made possible the development of urban civilisation. Though it appears that the cultivation of wheat and barley was first undertaken, together with the domestication of cattle and goats/sheep, around 10,000 years ago in the Fertile Crescent (the area bounded by the rivers Tigris and Euphrates), there is evidence that sorghum was first domesticated in Africa, rice was first deliberately planted and pigs domesticated in South East Asia, maize first cultivated in Central America and llamas first domesticated in South America. Cultural change took place independently in different parts of the world at different rates and different times.

The Neolithic period of cultural development has been difficult to date reliably because it took place long before writing was invented. With the development and refinement of radio-carbon dating and other scientific methods of producing absolute chronologies, it may eventually be possible to obtain a reliable chronological framework, in terms of years, against which the cultural development of any particular area may be set.

TIDES AND TIDAL PREDICTIONS

TIDES

Tides are the periodic rise and fall of the sea-level caused mainly by the gravitational pull of the Moon and the Sun. This generates the tide raising force (TRF), of which the Moon accounts for approximately 70 per cent and the Sun 30 per cent. When the Moon and the Sun are in line with the Earth they are said to be 'in conjunction' (or syzygy) and their combined TRFs are greatest. This produces the largest rise and fall of the tide, otherwise known as spring tides; they occur just after a full or new moon. The opposite effect, just after the Moon's first and last quarters, when the Sun and Moon form a right angle with the Earth, produces neap tides, with a relatively small tidal range between high water and low water.

A lunar day is about 24 hours and 50 minutes, giving two complete tidal cycles, with about 12 hours and 25 minutes between successive high waters. These are known as semi-diurnal tides and are applicable in the Atlantic Ocean and around the coasts of north-west Europe. Other parts of the world have diurnal tides, with only one high water and one low water each (lunar) day, or mixed tides which are partly diurnal and partly semi-diurnal.

Land and seabed conditions influence the tides locally. On the south coast of England, for example, double high waters occur between Swanage and Selsey Bill, and low water is much more sharply defined than high water. Tides can also be greatly affected by the Coriolis force, which is induced by the Earth's rotation and, in the northern hemisphere, tends to deflect any moving object to the right. Thus the easterly flood tidal stream in the English Channel is deflected towards the French coast causing higher high waters; on the ebb the opposite happens causing lower low waters. This, coupled with local geography, means that the mean spring range of the tide at St Malo is nearly 11m while the range on the English coast at Portland, 120 miles to the north, is a mere 2m.

Meteorological conditions also affect the tides. Prolonged strong winds and unusually high (or low) atmospheric pressure can significantly lower (or raise) the height of the tide; the wind alone can affect the predicted times of high and low water by as much as an hour. Variation of pressure by 34 millibars from the norm can cause a height difference of 0.3m. Intense minor depressions, line squalls, or other abrupt changes in the weather can cause wave oscillations known as seiches. The wave period of a seiche can vary from a few minutes to about 2 hours, with heights of up to a metre. Wick on the north-east coast of Scotland and Fishguard in south-west Wales are particularly prone to seiches.

TIDAL STREAMS

Tidal streams are the horizontal movements of water caused by the rise and fall of the tide. They normally change direction about every 6 hours. Tidal streams should not be confused with ocean currents, such as the Gulf Stream, which run indefinitely in the same direction. The rate, or set, of the stream at any particular place is proportional to the range of the tide. Thus, the rate during spring tides is greater than that at neaps. In the central English Channel the maximum spring rate is nearly 5 knots while the neap rate at the same position is just 3 knots. As with tidal heights, local geography plays a significant role in the rate of the tidal stream. For example, in the narrow waters of the Pentland Firth between mainland Scotland and the Orkney Islands, rates of 16 knots have been recorded.

The tidal stream does not necessarily turn at the same time as high or low water. In the English Channel the stream turns at approximately high and low water at Dover. However, high water at Dover is at about the same time as low water at Plymouth, and vice versa.

Around the UK, the main flood tidal stream sets eastward up the English Channel, north-east into the Bristol Channel, and north up the west coasts of Ireland and Scotland. However, the flood sets south-east through the North Channel and south into the Irish Sea, where it meets the northerly flood through St George's Channel at the Isle of Man. Off the east coasts of Scotland and England the stream sets south as far as the Thames Estuary before meeting the north-going stream from the eastern part of the Dover Strait.

DEFINITIONS

Highest Astronomical Tide (HAT) and **Lowest Astronomical Tide (LAT)** are the highest and lowest tide levels predicted to occur under average meteorological, and any combination of astronomical, conditions. For a given area, **Chart Datum (CD)** is the level, as close as possible to LAT, below which charted depths are given. It is also the reference for tidal predictions: the total depth at a given time being equal to the charted depth plus the height of the tide. **Ordnance Datum (OD)** at Newlyn is the datum level of land survey on mainland England, Scotland and Wales, from which heights on UK land maps are measured. CD depends on the tidal range and varies around the UK from about 5m above OD to about 6.5m below. The differences are noted in tide tables, allowing comparison of the tide levels along the coast and reference to Ordnance Survey data. **Duration** of the tide is the interval between low water and the next high water. It can be used to calculate the approximate time of low water when only the time of high water is known. **Mean Sea Level (MSL or ML)** is the average level of the sea's surface over a long period, normally observed over 18.6 years. The **Range** of the tide is the difference in height between successive high and low waters. It is greatest at spring tides, least at neaps. The range may be indicated by **Tidal Coefficients** which are proportional to, but not the same as, the range on a particular day. A coefficient of 95 indicates an average spring tide, while 45 is an average neap tide.

PREDICTIONS

The following data are daily predictions of the time and height of high water at London Bridge, Liverpool, Greenock and Leith. The time of the data is Greenwich Mean Time; this applies also to data for the months when British Summer Time is in operation and the hour's time difference should be added. The datum of predictions for each port shows the difference of height, in metres, of CD from Ordnance datum (Newlyn).

 The section was compiled with the assistance of Chris Stevens and Perrin Towler.

JANUARY 2014 *High Water* GMT

		LONDON BRIDGE Datum of Predictions 3.20m below				LIVERPOOL (Gladstone Dock) Datum of Predictions 4.93m below				GREENOCK Datum of Predictions 1.62m below				LEITH Datum of Predictions 2.90m below			
		hr	*ht m*	*hr*	*ht m*	*hr*	*ht m*	*hr*	*ht m*	*hr*	*ht m*	*hr*	*ht m*	*hr*	*ht m*	*hr*	*ht m*
W	1	01 04	6.9	13 29	7.3	10 37	9.6	23 04	9.6	12 07	3.7	—	—	01 56	5.7	14 13	5.8
TH	2	01 57	7.1	14 20	7.4	11 25	9.9	23 54	9.7	00 26	3.6	12 53	3.8	02 44	5.9	14 59	5.9
F	3	02 47	7.2	15 10	7.5	12 14	10.1	—	—	01 18	3.6	13 38	3.9	03 31	6.0	15 45	6.0
SA	4	03 34	7.2	15 59	7.5	00 43	9.7	13 02	10.0	02 08	3.6	14 24	3.9	04 19	5.9	16 32	6.0
SU	5	04 20	7.2	16 46	7.4	01 31	9.5	13 50	9.8	02 56	3.6	15 09	3.9	05 08	5.8	17 22	5.8
M	6	05 05	7.1	17 34	7.2	02 19	9.2	14 39	9.5	03 42	3.5	15 55	3.8	05 59	5.5	18 14	5.6
TU	7	05 50	6.9	18 23	6.9	03 08	8.8	15 30	9.0	04 27	3.4	16 43	3.6	06 54	5.2	19 12	5.3
W	8	06 40	6.7	19 16	6.6	04 01	8.3	16 26	8.5	05 13	3.3	17 34	3.4	07 53	5.0	20 16	5.0
TH	9	07 35	6.4	20 13	6.3	05 01	7.9	17 29	8.1	06 03	3.1	18 31	3.2	08 55	4.8	21 21	4.8
F	10	08 37	6.2	21 14	6.1	06 10	7.6	18 41	7.8	07 00	3.0	19 43	3.0	09 58	4.7	22 27	4.7
SA	11	09 43	6.1	22 22	6.0	07 25	7.7	19 52	7.8	08 15	3.0	21 09	3.0	11 04	4.7	23 35	4.7
SU	12	10 52	6.1	23 33	6.1	08 30	7.9	20 54	8.0	09 34	3.1	22 19	3.1	12 09	4.8	—	—
M	13	11 57	6.3	—	—	09 23	8.2	21 44	8.3	10 33	3.2	23 12	3.2	00 37	4.8	13 04	5.0
TU	14	00 29	6.4	12 49	6.5	10 06	8.6	22 26	8.5	11 20	3.4	23 58	3.2	01 28	4.9	13 49	5.1
W	15	01 15	6.5	13 33	6.7	10 43	8.8	23 02	8.7	11 59	3.5	—	—	02 10	5.1	14 27	5.3
TH	16	01 54	6.7	14 11	6.8	11 17	9.0	23 35	8.8	00 37	3.3	12 34	3.6	02 45	5.2	15 01	5.3
F	17	02 29	6.7	14 45	6.8	11 49	9.1	—	—	01 12	3.3	13 06	3.6	03 17	5.2	15 32	5.4
SA	18	03 00	6.8	15 16	6.9	00 07	8.9	12 21	9.1	01 45	3.3	13 38	3.7	03 49	5.3	16 04	5.4
SU	19	03 30	6.8	15 46	6.9	00 40	8.9	12 53	9.1	02 17	3.3	14 10	3.7	04 22	5.2	16 36	5.3
M	20	04 00	6.8	16 18	6.9	01 12	8.8	13 24	8.9	02 50	3.3	14 45	3.7	04 56	5.2	17 09	5.3
TU	21	04 31	6.8	16 51	6.8	01 44	8.6	13 55	8.8	03 24	3.3	15 22	3.7	05 32	5.1	17 43	5.1
W	22	05 05	6.6	17 27	6.6	02 19	8.4	14 30	8.5	03 59	3.2	16 01	3.6	06 11	5.0	18 21	5.0
TH	23	05 41	6.5	18 07	6.4	02 58	8.2	15 12	8.3	04 37	3.2	16 42	3.4	06 54	4.9	19 05	4.9
F	24	06 23	6.4	18 53	6.2	03 46	8.0	16 05	8.0	05 19	3.1	17 28	3.3	07 43	4.7	19 59	4.7
SA	25	07 14	6.2	19 52	6.0	04 48	7.7	17 16	7.8	06 09	2.9	18 25	3.1	08 43	4.6	21 11	4.6
SU	26	08 23	6.1	21 16	6.0	06 05	7.7	18 41	7.8	07 19	2.9	19 39	3.0	09 55	4.6	22 32	4.7
M	27	09 55	6.2	22 35	6.2	07 24	8.0	19 59	8.1	08 53	2.9	21 07	3.1	11 08	4.8	23 46	4.9
TU	28	11 10	6.5	23 46	6.5	08 33	8.5	21 06	8.6	10 08	3.1	22 23	3.2	12 13	5.1	—	—
W	29	12 16	6.9	—	—	09 32	9.1	22 03	9.1	11 04	3.4	23 24	3.3	00 49	5.3	13 09	5.4
TH	30	00 48	6.8	13 15	7.2	10 24	9.6	22 55	9.5	11 53	3.6	—	—	01 43	5.6	13 58	5.7
F	31	01 44	7.1	14 08	7.4	11 13	10.0	23 42	9.8	00 18	3.4	12 41	3.7	02 30	5.8	14 44	6.0

FEBRUARY 2014 *High Water* GMT

		LONDON BRIDGE				LIVERPOOL (Gladstone Dock)				GREENOCK				LEITH			
SA	1	02 33	7.3	14 57	7.5	12 00	10.2	—	—	01 09	3.5	13 26	3.8	03 16	6.0	15 29	6.1
SU	2	03 19	7.4	15 43	7.6	00 28	9.8	12 46	10.2	01 56	3.5	14 11	3.9	04 02	6.0	16 15	6.1
M	3	04 02	7.4	16 28	7.5	01 12	9.7	13 30	10.0	02 40	3.5	14 55	3.9	04 48	5.8	17 02	5.9
TU	4	04 44	7.4	17 11	7.2	01 55	9.4	14 13	9.6	03 21	3.5	15 37	3.8	05 35	5.6	17 51	5.7
W	5	05 25	7.1	17 53	6.9	02 37	8.9	14 57	9.1	04 00	3.4	16 19	3.6	06 24	5.3	18 43	5.3
TH	6	06 07	6.8	18 36	6.5	03 21	8.4	15 46	8.5	04 39	3.3	17 02	3.4	07 17	4.9	19 40	5.0
F	7	06 53	6.5	19 24	6.2	04 13	7.9	16 44	7.8	05 20	3.2	17 49	3.1	08 14	4.7	20 42	4.7
SA	8	07 49	6.2	20 21	5.9	05 19	7.4	17 56	7.4	06 07	3.0	18 45	2.9	09 15	4.5	21 48	4.4
SU	9	08 56	5.9	21 30	5.7	06 40	7.3	19 19	7.3	07 05	2.9	20 21	2.7	10 22	4.4	23 01	4.4
M	10	10 11	5.8	22 53	5.8	07 59	7.5	20 32	7.6	08 41	2.9	22 03	2.8	11 37	4.5	—	—
TU	11	11 27	6.1	—	—	09 00	7.9	21 26	8.0	10 08	3.0	22 57	3.0	00 16	4.5	12 43	4.7
W	12	00 00	6.1	12 26	6.4	09 45	8.3	22 08	8.3	10 59	3.2	23 40	3.1	01 12	4.7	13 30	5.0
TH	13	00 50	6.5	13 11	6.6	10 23	8.7	22 43	8.6	11 41	3.4	—	—	01 53	4.9	14 08	5.2
F	14	01 32	6.7	13 50	6.7	10 57	8.9	23 15	8.8	00 19	3.2	12 17	3.5	02 26	5.1	14 41	5.3
SA	15	02 08	6.8	14 24	6.8	11 29	9.1	23 46	9.0	00 54	3.2	12 48	3.5	02 56	5.2	15 12	5.4
SU	16	02 40	6.9	14 54	6.9	12 00	9.2	—	—	01 26	3.2	13 18	3.5	03 26	5.3	15 42	5.4
M	17	03 10	6.9	15 23	7.0	00 17	9.0	12 30	9.2	01 56	3.3	13 49	3.6	03 58	5.3	16 13	5.4
TU	18	03 39	7.0	15 55	7.0	00 48	9.0	13 00	9.1	02 25	3.3	14 23	3.6	04 30	5.3	16 45	5.4
W	19	04 10	7.0	16 28	6.9	01 19	8.9	13 31	9.0	02 56	3.3	14 59	3.6	05 05	5.3	17 18	5.3
TH	20	04 44	6.9	17 03	6.7	01 52	8.8	14 05	8.8	03 29	3.3	15 37	3.6	05 42	5.1	17 56	5.2
F	21	05 20	6.7	17 41	6.5	02 29	8.5	14 45	8.5	04 04	3.3	16 16	3.5	06 22	5.0	18 39	5.0
SA	22	06 00	6.6	18 25	6.3	03 14	8.2	15 35	8.1	04 41	3.2	17 00	3.3	07 09	4.8	19 32	4.8
SU	23	06 50	6.4	19 21	6.1	04 14	7.9	16 46	7.7	05 25	3.0	17 51	3.1	08 05	4.6	20 40	4.6
M	24	07 55	6.2	20 40	5.9	05 35	7.6	18 17	7.6	06 26	2.8	19 02	2.9	09 20	4.5	22 08	4.6
TU	25	09 28	6.2	22 09	6.1	07 01	7.8	19 44	7.9	08 16	2.8	20 49	2.9	10 42	4.6	23 28	4.8
W	26	10 50	6.4	23 28	6.4	08 16	8.3	20 55	8.5	09 49	3.0	22 16	3.1	11 54	4.9	—	—
TH	27	12 02	6.8	—	—	09 17	9.0	21 52	9.0	10 48	3.3	23 16	3.2	00 34	5.2	12 52	5.3
F	28	00 34	6.8	13 03	7.2	10 10	9.5	22 41	9.5	11 38	3.5	—	—	01 27	5.5	13 41	5.7

MARCH 2014 *High Water* GMT

		LONDON BRIDGE Datum of Predictions 3.20m below				LIVERPOOL (Gladstone Dock) Datum of Predictions 4.93m below				GREENOCK Datum of Predictions 1.62m below				LEITH Datum of Predictions 2.90m below			
		hr	*ht m*	*hr*	*ht m*	*hr*	*ht m*	*hr*	*ht m*	*hr*	*ht m*	*hr*	*ht m*	*hr*	*ht m*	*hr*	*ht m*
SA	1	01 28	7.1	13 54	7.4	10 57	9.9	23 26	9.8	00 06	3.4	12 25	3.7	02 13	5.8	14 26	5.9
SU	2	02 15	7.3	14 40	7.5	11 42	10.1	—	—	00 53	3.4	13 11	3.8	02 57	5.9	15 11	6.1
M	3	02 58	7.5	15 23	7.5	00 08	9.8	12 25	10.1	01 36	3.5	13 54	3.8	03 41	5.9	15 56	6.1
TU	4	03 39	7.5	16 03	7.4	00 49	9.7	13 06	9.9	02 16	3.5	14 36	3.8	04 25	5.8	16 41	5.9
W	5	04 18	7.5	16 42	7.2	01 28	9.4	13 46	9.5	02 53	3.5	15 16	3.7	05 09	5.5	17 27	5.6
TH	6	04 57	7.3	17 20	6.8	02 05	9.0	14 26	9.0	03 29	3.4	15 54	3.5	05 54	5.2	18 15	5.3
F	7	05 36	6.9	17 57	6.4	02 44	8.5	15 09	8.4	04 06	3.4	16 34	3.3	06 41	4.9	19 06	4.9
SA	8	06 16	6.5	18 37	6.1	03 30	7.9	16 01	7.7	04 45	3.2	17 17	3.0	07 33	4.6	20 03	4.6
SU	9	07 04	6.1	19 27	5.8	04 30	7.4	17 11	7.2	05 28	3.0	18 07	2.7	08 32	4.4	21 06	4.3
M	10	08 08	5.8	20 37	5.6	05 50	7.1	18 38	7.0	06 20	2.9	19 18	2.6	09 37	4.3	22 16	4.2
TU	11	09 28	5.7	22 04	5.6	07 17	7.2	19 59	7.3	07 33	2.8	21 35	2.6	10 52	4.3	23 40	4.3
W	12	10 48	5.9	23 22	6.0	08 26	7.6	20 58	7.7	09 28	2.9	22 31	2.8	12 08	4.5	—	—
TH	13	11 52	6.2	—	—	09 15	8.1	21 41	8.2	10 29	3.1	23 13	3.0	00 43	4.6	13 01	4.8
F	14	00 17	6.4	12 42	6.5	09 55	8.5	22 16	8.5	11 12	3.2	23 51	3.1	01 25	4.8	13 40	5.0
SA	15	01 02	6.6	13 22	6.7	10 30	8.8	22 48	8.8	11 49	3.3	—	—	01 58	5.0	14 14	5.2
SU	16	01 40	6.8	13 56	6.8	11 02	9.0	23 19	9.0	00 27	3.2	12 22	3.4	02 29	5.2	14 46	5.4
M	17	02 13	6.9	14 27	6.9	11 33	9.2	23 50	9.2	01 00	3.2	12 52	3.4	02 59	5.3	15 17	5.4
TU	18	02 44	7.0	14 58	7.0	12 04	9.2	—	—	01 30	3.3	13 24	3.5	03 31	5.4	15 48	5.5
W	19	03 15	7.1	15 31	7.0	00 22	9.2	12 36	9.2	01 58	3.3	14 00	3.5	04 04	5.4	16 21	5.5
TH	20	03 49	7.1	16 06	6.9	00 55	9.2	13 10	9.1	02 29	3.4	14 38	3.6	04 39	5.4	16 57	5.4
F	21	04 24	7.1	16 42	6.8	01 30	9.0	13 46	8.9	03 02	3.4	15 17	3.5	05 16	5.3	17 36	5.3
SA	22	05 02	6.9	17 20	6.5	02 09	8.8	14 29	8.6	03 37	3.4	15 57	3.4	05 58	5.1	18 22	5.1
SU	23	05 44	6.7	18 05	6.3	02 56	8.4	15 22	8.2	04 15	3.3	16 41	3.3	06 44	4.9	19 16	4.9
M	24	06 35	6.5	19 02	6.1	03 57	8.0	16 34	7.7	04 59	3.1	17 33	3.0	07 41	4.7	20 26	4.6
TU	25	07 43	6.2	20 21	5.9	05 18	7.7	18 05	7.6	05 59	2.9	18 43	2.8	08 57	4.5	21 52	4.6
W	26	09 13	6.2	21 51	6.1	06 43	7.9	19 30	7.9	07 50	2.8	20 42	2.8	10 22	4.6	23 12	4.8
TH	27	10 35	6.5	23 11	6.4	07 58	8.3	20 40	8.4	09 28	3.0	22 05	3.0	11 34	4.9	—	—
F	28	11 47	6.8	—	—	08 59	8.9	21 35	9.0	10 28	3.3	23 00	3.2	00 17	5.1	12 33	5.3
SA	29	00 17	6.8	12 47	7.1	09 51	9.4	22 22	9.4	11 19	3.5	23 48	3.3	01 09	5.4	13 22	5.6
SU	30	01 09	7.1	13 36	7.2	10 37	9.7	23 05	9.6	12 05	3.6	—	—	01 54	5.6	14 07	5.8
M	31	01 54	7.2	14 19	7.3	11 21	9.9	23 45	9.7	00 31	3.4	12 51	3.6	02 36	5.8	14 51	5.9

APRIL 2014 *High Water* GMT

		LONDON BRIDGE				LIVERPOOL (Gladstone Dock)				GREENOCK				LEITH			
TU	1	02 35	7.4	14 59	7.3	12 02	9.9	—	—	01 12	3.4	13 34	3.6	03 18	5.8	15 35	5.9
W	2	03 13	7.5	15 37	7.2	00 23	9.6	12 41	9.6	01 49	3.5	14 14	3.6	04 01	5.6	16 20	5.7
TH	3	03 52	7.5	16 13	7.1	01 00	9.3	13 19	9.3	02 24	3.5	14 53	3.5	04 43	5.5	17 04	5.5
F	4	04 30	7.2	16 48	6.8	01 36	9.0	13 57	8.8	02 59	3.5	15 30	3.4	05 25	5.2	17 49	5.2
SA	5	05 07	6.9	17 23	6.4	02 12	8.5	14 38	8.3	03 35	3.4	16 09	3.2	06 09	4.9	18 36	4.9
SU	6	05 46	6.5	18 00	6.1	02 55	8.0	15 26	7.7	04 14	3.3	16 51	3.0	06 56	4.7	19 27	4.5
M	7	06 28	6.1	18 44	5.8	03 48	7.5	16 28	7.2	04 56	3.1	17 40	2.7	07 50	4.4	20 24	4.3
TU	8	07 23	5.8	19 46	5.6	05 01	7.1	17 48	6.9	05 45	2.9	18 43	2.6	08 52	4.3	21 26	4.2
W	9	08 41	5.6	21 14	5.5	06 24	7.1	19 10	7.1	06 48	2.8	20 27	2.6	09 59	4.2	22 37	4.2
TH	10	10 00	5.7	22 33	5.8	07 37	7.4	20 15	7.5	08 20	2.8	21 47	2.7	11 13	4.4	23 50	4.4
F	11	11 07	6.1	23 35	6.2	08 33	7.8	21 02	8.0	09 42	2.9	22 35	2.9	12 15	4.6	—	—
SA	12	12 01	6.4	—	—	09 17	8.2	21 41	8.4	10 31	3.1	23 16	3.1	00 41	4.7	13 01	4.9
SU	13	00 23	6.5	12 45	6.6	09 55	8.6	22 15	8.7	11 11	3.2	23 54	3.2	01 20	5.0	13 39	5.1
M	14	01 05	6.8	13 22	6.8	10 29	8.9	22 48	9.0	11 46	3.3	—	—	01 55	5.2	14 14	5.3
TU	15	01 41	6.9	13 58	6.9	11 03	9.1	23 21	9.2	00 29	3.2	12 21	3.3	02 29	5.3	14 49	5.4
W	16	02 16	7.1	14 34	7.0	11 37	9.2	23 56	9.3	01 01	3.3	12 58	3.4	03 04	5.5	15 23	5.5
TH	17	02 52	7.2	15 11	7.0	12 14	9.3	—	—	01 31	3.4	13 38	3.5	03 39	5.5	16 00	5.5
F	18	03 30	7.2	15 48	6.9	00 33	9.3	12 53	9.2	02 04	3.5	14 19	3.5	04 16	5.5	16 39	5.5
SA	19	04 08	7.2	16 26	6.8	01 13	9.2	13 35	9.0	02 40	3.5	15 01	3.5	04 55	5.4	17 22	5.4
SU	20	04 49	7.0	17 08	6.5	01 57	8.9	14 22	8.7	03 18	3.5	15 44	3.4	05 39	5.2	18 11	5.2
M	21	05 35	6.8	17 55	6.3	02 48	8.6	15 19	8.2	03 59	3.4	16 31	3.2	06 28	5.0	19 08	4.9
TU	22	06 29	6.6	18 54	6.1	03 51	8.2	16 31	7.9	04 46	3.2	17 26	3.0	07 26	4.8	20 17	4.8
W	23	07 40	6.4	20 12	6.1	05 07	8.0	17 52	7.8	05 49	3.0	18 41	2.9	08 42	4.7	21 37	4.7
TH	24	09 02	6.4	21 35	6.2	06 24	8.1	19 11	8.0	07 31	2.9	20 27	2.8	10 03	4.7	22 51	4.9
F	25	10 17	6.6	22 50	6.5	07 35	8.4	20 18	8.4	09 02	3.0	21 43	3.0	11 12	5.0	23 55	5.1
SA	26	11 27	6.8	23 54	6.8	08 37	8.8	21 13	8.8	10 04	3.2	22 37	3.2	12 11	5.2	—	—
SU	27	12 26	7.0	—	—	09 29	9.1	22 00	9.1	10 56	3.4	23 24	3.3	00 47	5.3	13 02	5.4
M	28	00 47	7.0	13 15	7.0	10 16	9.4	22 42	9.3	11 44	3.5	—	—	01 33	5.5	13 48	5.6
TU	29	01 31	7.1	13 57	7.1	10 59	9.5	23 21	9.4	00 07	3.4	12 30	3.5	02 16	5.6	14 33	5.6
W	30	02 11	7.2	14 36	7.1	11 39	9.4	23 59	9.3	00 46	3.4	13 13	3.5	02 57	5.6	15 17	5.6

MAY 2014 *High Water* GMT

		LONDON BRIDGE				LIVERPOOL (Gladstone Dock)				GREENOCK				LEITH			
		Datum of Predictions 3.20m below				Datum of Predictions 4.93m below				Datum of Predictions 1.62m below				Datum of Predictions 2.90m below			
		hr	*ht m*	*hr*	*ht m*	*hr*	*ht m*	*hr*	*ht m*	*hr*	*ht m*	*hr*	*ht m*	*hr*	*ht m*	*hr*	*ht m*
TH	1	02 50	7.3	15 12	7.1	12 18	9.3	—	—	01 22	3.5	13 53	3.4	03 39	5.5	16 00	5.5
F	2	03 28	7.3	15 47	6.9	00 35	9.2	12 56	9.0	01 56	3.5	14 30	3.3	04 20	5.4	16 43	5.3
SA	3	04 05	7.2	16 21	6.7	01 10	8.9	13 33	8.6	02 32	3.5	15 08	3.2	05 00	5.2	17 25	5.1
SU	4	04 43	6.9	16 55	6.4	01 46	8.6	14 11	8.3	03 08	3.5	15 47	3.1	05 40	5.0	18 08	4.9
M	5	05 20	6.5	17 30	6.2	02 26	8.2	14 55	7.8	03 45	3.4	16 29	3.0	06 23	4.8	18 53	4.6
TU	6	05 59	6.2	18 10	6.0	03 14	7.8	15 49	7.4	04 26	3.2	17 17	2.8	07 12	4.6	19 44	4.4
W	7	06 45	5.9	19 00	5.7	04 14	7.4	16 55	7.1	05 12	3.0	18 14	2.7	08 07	4.4	20 39	4.3
TH	8	07 47	5.7	20 14	5.6	05 26	7.2	18 09	7.1	06 07	2.9	19 24	2.6	09 08	4.3	21 39	4.3
F	9	09 06	5.7	21 40	5.7	06 38	7.3	19 17	7.3	07 16	2.8	20 44	2.7	10 12	4.4	22 43	4.4
SA	10	10 13	6.0	22 45	6.0	07 40	7.6	20 12	7.7	08 33	2.9	21 46	2.9	11 16	4.5	23 43	4.6
SU	11	11 11	6.3	23 39	6.4	08 30	8.0	20 57	8.2	09 36	3.0	22 34	3.0	12 11	4.7	—	—
M	12	12 01	6.6	—	—	09 14	8.4	21 37	8.6	10 25	3.1	23 17	3.2	00 34	4.9	12 59	5.0
TU	13	00 25	6.7	12 47	6.8	09 54	8.7	22 15	9.0	11 07	3.2	23 55	3.2	01 19	5.1	13 41	5.2
W	14	01 08	6.9	13 30	6.9	10 33	9.0	22 54	9.2	11 50	3.3	—	—	01 59	5.3	14 21	5.4
TH	15	01 50	7.1	14 12	7.0	11 14	9.2	23 34	9.4	00 30	3.3	12 34	3.4	02 37	5.5	15 01	5.5
F	16	02 32	7.3	14 54	7.0	11 56	9.3	—	—	01 07	3.4	13 18	3.4	03 16	5.6	15 41	5.6
SA	17	03 14	7.3	15 36	7.0	00 16	9.5	12 40	9.3	01 44	3.5	14 04	3.4	03 56	5.6	16 25	5.6
SU	18	03 58	7.3	16 19	6.8	01 01	9.4	13 27	9.1	02 24	3.6	14 50	3.4	04 39	5.5	17 11	5.5
M	19	04 43	7.1	17 03	6.7	01 49	9.2	14 18	8.8	03 05	3.6	15 37	3.3	05 25	5.4	18 02	5.3
TU	20	05 32	7.0	17 53	6.5	02 42	8.9	15 16	8.5	03 49	3.5	16 27	3.2	06 16	5.2	18 59	5.1
W	21	06 28	6.7	18 51	6.4	03 43	8.6	16 21	8.1	04 40	3.3	17 25	3.1	07 16	5.0	20 06	4.9
TH	22	07 35	6.6	20 02	6.3	04 51	8.4	17 32	8.0	05 43	3.1	18 35	3.0	08 28	4.9	21 18	4.8
F	23	08 45	6.6	21 14	6.4	06 00	8.3	18 44	8.0	07 07	3.0	19 57	2.9	09 41	4.9	22 26	4.9
SA	24	09 53	6.6	22 23	6.5	07 09	8.4	19 51	8.2	08 31	3.1	21 10	3.0	10 48	5.0	23 29	5.0
SU	25	11 01	6.7	23 27	6.7	08 12	8.6	20 49	8.5	09 37	3.2	22 08	3.1	11 49	5.1	—	—
M	26	12 02	6.7	—	—	09 07	8.8	21 37	8.8	10 33	3.3	22 58	3.2	00 25	5.1	12 43	5.2
TU	27	00 23	6.8	12 54	6.8	09 55	8.9	22 21	9.0	11 23	3.3	23 42	3.3	01 14	5.3	13 32	5.3
W	28	01 10	6.9	13 37	6.8	10 39	9.0	23 00	9.1	12 09	3.3	—	—	01 58	5.4	14 18	5.4
TH	29	01 52	7.0	14 16	6.9	11 20	9.0	23 38	9.1	00 21	3.4	12 53	3.3	02 40	5.4	15 01	5.4
F	30	02 30	7.1	14 52	6.9	11 58	8.9	—	—	00 58	3.4	13 33	3.2	03 20	5.4	15 43	5.3
SA	31	03 08	7.1	15 26	6.8	00 13	9.0	12 35	8.8	01 32	3.5	14 10	3.2	04 00	5.3	16 23	5.2

JUNE 2014 *High Water* GMT

		LONDON BRIDGE				LIVERPOOL (Gladstone Dock)				GREENOCK				LEITH			
SU	1	03 45	7.0	16 00	6.7	00 49	8.9	13 11	8.6	02 07	3.5	14 47	3.1	04 37	5.2	17 01	5.1
M	2	04 21	6.8	16 33	6.5	01 24	8.7	13 48	8.4	02 43	3.5	15 25	3.1	05 15	5.1	17 40	4.9
TU	3	04 57	6.6	17 07	6.4	02 01	8.4	14 28	8.1	03 19	3.5	16 07	3.0	05 54	4.9	18 21	4.8
W	4	05 33	6.4	17 44	6.2	02 43	8.1	15 12	7.7	03 57	3.4	16 51	2.9	06 37	4.7	19 06	4.6
TH	5	06 13	6.2	18 26	6.0	03 30	7.8	16 04	7.5	04 40	3.2	17 40	2.8	07 24	4.6	19 55	4.5
F	6	07 00	6.0	19 18	5.8	04 28	7.5	17 05	7.3	05 29	3.1	18 35	2.8	08 18	4.5	20 51	4.4
SA	7	08 02	5.8	20 31	5.7	05 33	7.4	18 11	7.3	06 26	3.0	19 37	2.8	09 18	4.4	21 50	4.5
SU	8	09 17	5.9	21 50	5.9	06 38	7.5	19 14	7.6	07 31	2.9	20 45	2.8	10 21	4.5	22 51	4.6
M	9	10 22	6.1	22 52	6.3	07 38	7.8	20 10	8.0	08 38	3.0	21 46	3.0	11 22	4.7	23 50	4.8
TU	10	11 20	6.4	23 47	6.6	08 32	8.2	21 00	8.5	09 39	3.1	22 37	3.1	12 19	4.9	—	—
W	11	12 14	6.7	—	—	09 21	8.6	21 46	8.9	10 33	3.2	23 22	3.2	00 43	5.1	13 10	5.1
TH	12	00 38	6.9	13 05	6.9	10 08	8.9	22 31	9.3	11 23	3.3	—	—	01 30	5.3	13 57	5.4
F	13	01 28	7.1	13 54	7.0	10 55	9.2	23 16	9.5	00 04	3.4	12 13	3.3	02 14	5.5	14 41	5.6
SA	14	02 15	7.3	14 41	7.1	11 42	9.4	—	—	00 46	3.5	13 03	3.4	02 56	5.7	15 26	5.7
SU	15	03 03	7.4	15 27	7.1	00 02	9.7	12 30	9.4	01 29	3.6	13 52	3.4	03 40	5.7	16 12	5.8
M	16	03 50	7.4	16 13	7.0	00 51	9.7	13 20	9.3	02 12	3.7	14 42	3.4	04 25	5.7	17 00	5.7
TU	17	04 38	7.3	16 59	6.9	01 41	9.5	14 11	9.1	02 56	3.7	15 32	3.3	05 13	5.6	17 51	5.5
W	18	05 27	7.2	17 47	6.8	02 33	9.3	15 04	8.8	03 42	3.6	16 22	3.3	06 05	5.5	18 46	5.3
TH	19	06 20	7.0	18 41	6.7	03 28	9.0	16 02	8.4	04 32	3.5	17 15	3.2	07 02	5.3	19 48	5.1
F	20	07 19	6.8	19 42	6.6	04 27	8.7	17 05	8.1	05 29	3.3	18 12	3.1	08 08	5.1	20 53	4.9
SA	21	08 21	6.6	20 46	6.5	05 32	8.4	18 13	8.0	06 37	3.1	19 17	3.0	09 17	5.0	21 58	4.8
SU	22	09 24	6.5	21 51	6.5	06 39	8.2	19 21	8.0	07 54	3.0	20 27	3.0	10 23	4.9	23 01	4.9
M	23	10 30	6.4	22 57	6.5	07 46	8.2	20 24	8.2	09 09	3.1	21 35	3.0	11 26	4.9	—	—
TU	24	11 36	6.5	23 58	6.6	08 46	8.3	21 17	8.4	10 12	3.1	22 32	3.1	00 02	5.0	12 27	5.0
W	25	12 32	6.6	—	—	09 38	8.5	22 03	8.6	11 06	3.2	23 20	3.2	00 56	5.1	13 20	5.1
TH	26	00 50	6.7	13 19	6.7	10 23	8.6	22 43	8.8	11 54	3.2	—	—	01 43	5.2	14 06	5.1
F	27	01 36	6.9	14 00	6.7	11 04	8.7	23 20	8.9	00 02	3.3	12 39	3.2	02 26	5.3	14 48	5.2
SA	28	02 16	6.9	14 37	6.8	11 41	8.8	23 55	8.9	00 39	3.4	13 18	3.1	03 05	5.3	15 26	5.2
SU	29	02 54	7.0	15 11	6.8	12 16	8.7	—	—	01 13	3.5	13 53	3.1	03 41	5.3	16 02	5.2
M	30	03 29	6.9	15 43	6.7	00 29	8.9	12 51	8.7	01 46	3.5	14 27	3.1	04 16	5.3	16 37	5.1

JULY 2014 *High Water* GMT

	LONDON BRIDGE				LIVERPOOL				GREENOCK				LEITH			
	Datum of Predictions 3.20m below				(Gladstone Dock) Datum of Predictions 4.93m below				Datum of Predictions 1.62m below				Datum of Predictions 2.90m below			
	hr	*ht m*	*hr*	*ht m*	*hr*	*ht m*	*hr*	*ht m*	*hr*	*ht m*	*hr*	*ht m*	*hr*	*ht m*	*hr*	*ht m*
TU 1	04 02	6.8	16 14	6.7	01 03	8.8	13 25	8.5	02 20	3.5	15 03	3.1	04 51	5.2	17 13	5.1
W 2	04 35	6.7	16 46	6.6	01 38	8.7	14 01	8.3	02 54	3.5	15 41	3.1	05 27	5.1	17 51	5.0
TH 3	05 08	6.6	17 20	6.4	02 13	8.4	14 38	8.1	03 30	3.5	16 20	3.0	06 04	5.0	18 31	4.8
F 4	05 44	6.4	17 57	6.3	02 51	8.2	15 20	7.9	04 09	3.4	17 02	3.0	06 45	4.8	19 16	4.7
SA 5	06 23	6.2	18 39	6.1	03 35	7.9	16 09	7.6	04 53	3.2	17 48	2.9	07 31	4.7	20 05	4.6
SU 6	07 11	6.0	19 31	5.9	04 30	7.7	17 10	7.5	05 43	3.1	18 40	2.9	08 25	4.6	21 03	4.6
M 7	08 14	5.9	20 45	5.9	05 36	7.6	18 19	7.6	06 42	3.0	19 42	2.8	09 30	4.5	22 07	4.6
TU 8	09 34	6.0	22 07	6.1	06 47	7.7	19 27	7.9	07 51	2.9	20 53	2.9	10 39	4.6	23 11	4.8
W 9	10 42	6.3	23 13	6.5	07 55	8.0	20 28	8.4	09 01	3.0	22 00	3.0	11 44	4.8	—	—
TH 10	11 45	6.6	—	—	08 55	8.4	21 22	8.8	10 06	3.1	22 55	3.2	00 11	5.0	12 44	5.1
F 11	00 13	6.9	12 44	6.8	09 49	8.9	22 12	9.3	11 04	3.2	23 43	3.4	01 06	5.3	13 37	5.4
SA 12	01 08	7.2	13 37	7.0	10 40	9.2	23 01	9.7	11 58	3.3	—	—	01 54	5.5	14 24	5.7
SU 13	02 01	7.4	14 27	7.2	11 30	9.5	23 49	9.9	00 29	3.5	12 51	3.4	02 39	5.8	15 10	5.9
M 14	02 50	7.5	15 15	7.3	12 19	9.6	—	—	01 15	3.7	13 42	3.4	03 24	5.9	15 57	5.9
TU 15	03 39	7.6	16 01	7.3	00 38	10.0	13 07	9.6	02 00	3.7	14 32	3.4	04 10	6.0	16 44	5.9
W 16	04 26	7.5	16 45	7.3	01 26	9.9	13 55	9.4	02 46	3.8	15 20	3.4	04 58	5.9	17 34	5.7
TH 17	05 13	7.3	17 31	7.1	02 15	9.6	14 43	9.0	03 31	3.7	16 06	3.3	05 48	5.7	18 26	5.4
F 18	06 01	7.1	18 18	6.9	03 05	9.2	15 34	8.6	04 17	3.6	16 52	3.3	06 42	5.5	19 22	5.2
SA 19	06 53	6.8	19 12	6.7	03 58	8.8	16 30	8.2	05 06	3.4	17 39	3.1	07 43	5.2	20 24	4.9
SU 20	07 48	6.5	20 11	6.5	04 58	8.3	17 36	7.8	06 01	3.2	18 30	3.0	08 49	4.9	21 27	4.8
M 21	08 48	6.3	21 15	6.3	06 06	7.9	18 48	7.7	07 08	3.0	19 32	2.9	09 55	4.8	22 31	4.7
TU 22	09 53	6.1	22 23	6.3	07 19	7.8	19 59	7.8	08 38	2.9	20 55	2.9	11 03	4.7	23 38	4.8
W 23	11 06	6.2	23 33	6.4	08 27	7.9	20 59	8.1	09 56	2.9	22 07	3.0	12 10	4.8	—	—
TH 24	12 09	6.4	—	—	09 23	8.1	21 47	8.4	10 54	3.0	23 01	3.2	00 39	4.9	13 08	4.9
F 25	00 31	6.6	13 00	6.6	10 09	8.4	22 27	8.7	11 42	3.1	23 45	3.3	01 30	5.1	13 54	5.0
SA 26	01 19	6.8	13 43	6.7	10 48	8.6	23 03	8.9	12 24	3.1	—	—	02 11	5.2	14 33	5.1
SU 27	02 01	6.9	14 20	6.8	11 23	8.7	23 36	9.0	00 22	3.4	13 02	3.1	02 48	5.3	15 07	5.2
M 28	02 38	6.9	14 54	6.8	11 56	8.8	—	—	00 55	3.5	13 34	3.1	03 22	5.4	15 39	5.2
TU 29	03 11	6.9	15 24	6.9	00 09	9.0	12 28	8.8	01 25	3.5	14 05	3.1	03 54	5.4	16 11	5.2
W 30	03 40	6.9	15 53	6.9	00 41	9.0	13 00	8.8	01 56	3.5	14 37	3.1	04 26	5.3	16 45	5.2
TH 31	04 10	6.9	16 23	6.8	01 12	8.9	13 32	8.6	02 29	3.6	15 11	3.2	04 59	5.3	17 20	5.1

AUGUST 2014 *High Water* GMT

	LONDON BRIDGE				LIVERPOOL (Gladstone Dock)				GREENOCK				LEITH			
F 1	04 41	6.8	16 55	6.7	01 44	8.7	14 06	8.4	03 04	3.6	15 45	3.2	05 34	5.2	17 58	5.0
SA 2	05 15	6.6	17 29	6.5	02 16	8.5	14 42	8.2	03 42	3.5	16 23	3.1	06 11	5.0	18 39	4.9
SU 3	05 51	6.4	18 07	6.3	02 54	8.2	15 25	8.0	04 21	3.4	17 04	3.0	06 52	4.9	19 25	4.8
M 4	06 32	6.2	18 53	6.2	03 42	7.9	16 21	7.7	05 06	3.2	17 51	2.9	07 41	4.7	20 19	4.6
TU 5	07 25	6.0	19 54	6.0	04 45	7.7	17 33	7.6	06 00	3.0	18 50	2.9	08 45	4.6	21 25	4.6
W 6	08 43	5.9	21 24	6.1	06 06	7.6	18 52	7.8	07 08	2.9	20 07	2.9	10 02	4.6	22 37	4.7
TH 7	10 07	6.1	22 43	6.4	07 27	7.8	20 03	8.3	08 30	2.9	21 29	3.0	11 17	4.8	23 45	5.0
F 8	11 19	6.4	23 50	6.8	08 36	8.3	21 03	8.8	09 48	3.0	22 33	3.2	12 23	5.1	—	—
SA 9	12 23	6.8	—	—	09 35	8.9	21 57	9.4	10 52	3.2	23 26	3.4	00 44	5.3	13 19	5.4
SU 10	00 51	7.2	13 20	7.1	10 28	9.3	22 46	9.8	11 47	3.3	—	—	01 35	5.6	14 07	5.8
M 11	01 45	7.4	14 10	7.3	11 16	9.7	23 34	10.1	00 14	3.6	12 39	3.4	02 21	5.9	14 53	6.0
TU 12	02 35	7.6	14 57	7.4	12 03	9.8	—	—	01 01	3.7	13 28	3.4	03 05	6.1	15 38	6.0
W 13	03 22	7.6	15 41	7.5	00 20	10.2	12 48	9.8	01 46	3.8	14 15	3.4	03 51	6.1	16 24	6.0
TH 14	04 07	7.6	16 24	7.5	01 06	10.1	13 33	9.5	02 31	3.8	14 58	3.4	04 38	6.1	17 11	5.8
F 15	04 51	7.4	17 06	7.3	01 51	9.8	14 16	9.2	03 14	3.8	15 40	3.4	05 27	5.9	18 00	5.5
SA 16	05 35	7.0	17 50	7.1	02 36	9.3	15 02	8.7	03 56	3.6	16 20	3.3	06 18	5.5	18 53	5.2
SU 17	06 19	6.7	18 36	6.7	03 25	8.7	15 52	8.1	04 39	3.4	17 01	3.2	07 15	5.2	19 51	4.9
M 18	07 08	6.3	19 30	6.4	04 21	8.1	16 55	7.7	05 26	3.2	17 47	3.1	08 19	4.8	20 53	4.7
TU 19	08 04	6.0	20 34	6.1	05 31	7.6	18 13	7.4	06 21	2.9	18 40	2.9	09 25	4.6	21 58	4.6
W 20	09 10	5.8	21 47	6.0	06 52	7.4	19 32	7.6	07 53	2.7	19 58	2.9	10 36	4.5	23 10	4.6
TH 21	10 30	5.9	23 04	6.2	08 08	7.6	20 38	7.9	09 43	2.8	21 40	3.0	11 51	4.6	—	—
F 22	11 41	6.2	—	—	09 07	7.9	21 27	8.3	10 39	2.9	22 39	3.2	00 18	4.8	12 52	4.8
SA 23	00 08	6.5	12 35	6.5	09 52	8.3	22 07	8.7	11 24	3.1	23 24	3.3	01 10	5.0	13 37	5.0
SU 24	00 57	6.8	13 19	6.7	10 28	8.6	22 42	8.9	12 03	3.1	—	—	01 51	5.2	14 13	5.1
M 25	01 39	6.9	13 57	6.9	11 01	8.8	23 14	9.1	00 01	3.4	12 39	3.2	02 26	5.3	14 44	5.2
TU 26	02 15	6.9	14 30	6.9	11 32	8.9	23 45	9.2	00 33	3.5	13 10	3.2	02 58	5.4	15 13	5.3
W 27	02 46	6.9	15 00	7.0	12 02	9.0	—	—	01 02	3.5	13 39	3.2	03 29	5.5	15 44	5.4
TH 28	03 14	7.0	15 28	7.0	00 15	9.2	12 33	9.0	01 32	3.5	14 08	3.2	04 00	5.4	16 17	5.3
F 29	03 43	7.0	15 57	7.0	00 45	9.1	13 04	8.9	02 04	3.6	14 38	3.3	04 32	5.4	16 51	5.3
SA 30	04 14	6.9	16 29	6.9	01 15	8.9	13 36	8.7	02 40	3.6	15 11	3.3	05 05	5.3	17 27	5.2
SU 31	04 47	6.7	17 03	6.7	01 47	8.7	14 11	8.5	03 17	3.6	15 47	3.3	05 41	5.2	18 06	5.1

SEPTEMBER 2014 *High Water* GMT

		LONDON BRIDGE Datum of Predictions 3.20m below				LIVERPOOL (Gladstone Dock) Datum of Predictions 4.93m below				GREENOCK Datum of Predictions 1.62m below				LEITH Datum of Predictions 2.90m below			
		hr	*ht m*	*hr*	*ht m*	*hr*	*ht m*	*hr*	*ht m*	*hr*	*ht m*	*hr*	*ht m*	*hr*	*ht m*	*hr*	*ht m*
M	1	05 22	6.5	17 41	6.6	02 24	8.5	14 52	8.2	03 55	3.5	16 25	3.2	06 23	5.0	18 50	4.9
TU	2	06 02	6.3	18 26	6.4	03 10	8.1	15 46	7.9	04 37	3.3	17 09	3.1	07 12	4.8	19 43	4.7
W	3	06 52	6.0	19 24	6.2	04 13	7.7	17 01	7.7	05 26	3.1	18 06	2.9	08 14	4.7	20 50	4.6
TH	4	08 02	5.9	20 50	6.1	05 40	7.5	18 27	7.8	06 32	2.9	19 28	2.9	09 34	4.6	22 09	4.7
F	5	09 36	6.0	22 18	6.4	07 09	7.8	19 43	8.2	08 07	2.9	21 05	3.0	10 56	4.8	23 22	4.9
SA	6	10 55	6.3	23 31	6.8	08 23	8.3	20 47	8.9	09 39	3.0	22 15	3.3	12 05	5.1	—	—
SU	7	12 04	6.8	—	—	09 22	8.9	21 41	9.5	10 43	3.2	23 08	3.5	00 24	5.3	13 01	5.5
M	8	00 34	7.2	13 01	7.1	10 13	9.4	22 29	9.9	11 35	3.4	23 56	3.7	01 15	5.7	13 48	5.8
TU	9	01 28	7.4	13 50	7.3	10 59	9.8	23 15	10.2	12 22	3.4	—	—	02 00	6.0	14 32	6.0
W	10	02 15	7.6	14 35	7.5	11 43	9.9	23 59	10.3	00 43	3.8	13 08	3.5	02 45	6.2	15 16	6.0
TH	11	03 00	7.6	15 17	7.6	12 25	9.8	—	—	01 28	3.8	13 50	3.5	03 30	6.2	16 00	6.0
F	12	03 43	7.5	15 58	7.6	00 42	10.1	13 07	9.6	02 12	3.8	14 30	3.5	04 16	6.1	16 46	5.8
SA	13	04 24	7.3	16 38	7.4	01 25	9.7	13 47	9.2	02 53	3.7	15 08	3.5	05 04	5.8	17 33	5.5
SU	14	05 03	7.0	17 19	7.1	02 07	9.2	14 28	8.7	03 33	3.6	15 46	3.4	05 54	5.5	18 22	5.2
M	15	05 42	6.6	18 02	6.7	02 52	8.6	15 15	8.2	04 13	3.4	16 26	3.3	06 48	5.1	19 17	4.9
TU	16	06 23	6.2	18 49	6.3	03 44	7.9	16 14	7.6	04 56	3.1	17 11	3.2	07 47	4.7	20 17	4.6
W	17	07 13	5.9	19 51	5.9	04 52	7.3	17 31	7.3	05 47	2.8	18 02	3.0	08 51	4.5	21 22	4.5
TH	18	08 21	5.6	21 08	5.8	06 17	7.1	18 56	7.4	06 59	2.6	19 08	2.9	10 00	4.4	22 33	4.5
F	19	09 45	5.6	22 26	6.0	07 40	7.3	20 07	7.7	09 19	2.7	20 57	3.0	11 19	4.5	23 46	4.7
SA	20	11 03	6.0	23 35	6.3	08 41	7.8	20 59	8.2	10 15	2.9	22 07	3.2	12 25	4.7	—	—
SU	21	12 01	6.4	—	—	09 25	8.2	21 39	8.6	10 57	3.1	22 53	3.3	00 41	4.9	13 10	4.9
M	22	00 27	6.7	12 48	6.7	10 02	8.6	22 14	8.9	11 34	3.2	23 31	3.4	01 23	5.1	13 45	5.1
TU	23	01 09	6.8	13 27	6.8	10 34	8.9	22 46	9.1	12 09	3.3	—	—	01 58	5.3	14 15	5.3
W	24	01 45	6.9	14 01	6.9	11 04	9.0	23 17	9.2	00 04	3.5	12 41	3.3	02 30	5.4	14 44	5.4
TH	25	02 16	7.0	14 31	7.0	11 34	9.2	23 47	9.2	00 34	3.5	13 11	3.3	03 01	5.5	15 16	5.5
F	26	02 45	7.0	15 00	7.1	12 05	9.2	—	—	01 05	3.6	13 38	3.4	03 32	5.5	15 48	5.5
SA	27	03 15	7.0	15 32	7.1	00 18	9.2	12 37	9.1	01 40	3.6	14 08	3.4	04 05	5.5	16 22	5.4
SU	28	03 48	7.0	16 06	7.1	00 50	9.1	13 10	9.0	02 17	3.6	14 41	3.5	04 40	5.4	16 59	5.3
M	29	04 22	6.8	16 42	6.9	01 25	8.9	13 47	8.8	02 55	3.6	15 17	3.4	05 18	5.3	17 38	5.2
TU	30	04 58	6.6	17 21	6.7	02 04	8.6	14 31	8.4	03 35	3.5	15 56	3.4	06 01	5.1	18 23	5.0

OCTOBER 2014 *High Water* GMT

		LONDON BRIDGE				LIVERPOOL (Gladstone Dock)				GREENOCK				LEITH			
W	1	05 38	6.3	18 08	6.5	02 53	8.2	15 26	8.1	04 16	3.4	16 40	3.2	06 52	4.9	19 16	4.8
TH	2	06 29	6.1	19 06	6.3	03 58	7.8	16 42	7.8	05 05	3.2	17 35	3.1	07 55	4.7	20 23	4.7
F	3	07 37	5.9	20 31	6.2	05 26	7.6	18 08	7.9	06 10	3.0	19 00	3.0	09 16	4.7	21 46	4.7
SA	4	09 11	6.0	21 57	6.4	06 54	7.8	19 24	8.3	07 53	2.9	20 43	3.1	10 37	4.9	23 01	5.0
SU	5	10 33	6.3	23 11	6.8	08 07	8.4	20 28	8.9	09 29	3.1	21 54	3.3	11 45	5.2	—	—
M	6	11 42	6.7	—	—	09 05	8.9	21 22	9.5	10 29	3.3	22 47	3.6	00 02	5.3	12 41	5.5
TU	7	00 14	7.1	12 39	7.1	09 54	9.4	22 10	9.9	11 17	3.4	23 36	3.7	00 54	5.7	13 28	5.8
W	8	01 08	7.3	13 27	7.3	10 39	9.7	22 54	10.1	12 02	3.5	—	—	01 39	5.9	14 11	5.9
TH	9	01 54	7.4	14 11	7.4	11 21	9.8	23 37	10.1	00 23	3.8	12 44	3.6	02 24	6.1	14 53	6.0
F	10	02 36	7.4	14 52	7.6	12 01	9.8	—	—	01 08	3.8	13 24	3.6	03 09	6.1	15 37	5.9
SA	11	03 17	7.4	15 32	7.6	00 19	9.9	12 41	9.6	01 51	3.8	14 01	3.6	03 55	5.9	16 21	5.7
SU	12	03 55	7.2	16 12	7.4	01 00	9.5	13 19	9.2	02 31	3.7	14 38	3.6	04 42	5.7	17 06	5.4
M	13	04 33	6.9	16 51	7.1	01 40	9.0	13 57	8.8	03 10	3.5	15 16	3.6	05 30	5.4	17 52	5.2
TU	14	05 09	6.5	17 31	6.7	02 22	8.5	14 40	8.3	03 50	3.4	15 56	3.5	06 20	5.0	18 42	4.9
W	15	05 46	6.2	18 15	6.3	03 10	7.9	15 34	7.8	04 32	3.1	16 40	3.3	07 14	4.7	19 38	4.6
TH	16	06 28	5.9	19 08	5.9	04 12	7.3	16 45	7.4	05 22	2.9	17 29	3.1	08 12	4.5	20 41	4.5
F	17	07 27	5.6	20 22	5.7	05 31	7.1	18 07	7.3	06 26	2.7	18 30	3.0	09 15	4.3	21 46	4.4
SA	18	08 54	5.5	21 39	5.8	06 54	7.2	19 21	7.5	08 14	2.7	19 53	3.0	10 25	4.4	22 56	4.6
SU	19	10 14	5.7	22 48	6.1	08 01	7.6	20 19	8.0	09 33	2.9	21 18	3.1	11 36	4.6	23 58	4.8
M	20	11 18	6.1	23 45	6.4	08 49	8.0	21 03	8.4	10 19	3.1	22 12	3.3	12 28	4.8	—	—
TU	21	12 08	6.5	—	—	09 28	8.5	21 41	8.7	10 59	3.3	22 53	3.4	00 45	5.0	13 07	5.1
W	22	00 30	6.7	12 51	6.7	10 02	8.8	22 15	9.0	11 36	3.4	23 29	3.5	01 23	5.2	13 41	5.3
TH	23	01 09	6.8	13 27	6.9	10 34	9.1	22 48	9.2	12 10	3.4	—	—	01 58	5.4	14 14	5.4
F	24	01 43	6.9	14 00	7.0	11 06	9.2	23 21	9.3	00 03	3.5	12 42	3.5	02 32	5.5	14 47	5.5
SA	25	02 16	7.0	14 34	7.1	11 39	9.3	23 55	9.3	00 39	3.6	13 11	3.5	03 07	5.5	15 22	5.6
SU	26	02 51	7.0	15 09	7.2	12 14	9.3	—	—	01 17	3.6	13 43	3.6	03 42	5.6	15 57	5.6
M	27	03 27	7.0	15 46	7.2	00 31	9.2	12 51	9.2	01 57	3.6	14 19	3.6	04 19	5.5	16 35	5.5
TU	28	04 03	6.8	16 25	7.1	01 10	9.0	13 32	9.0	02 38	3.6	14 56	3.6	05 00	5.4	17 16	5.4
W	29	04 41	6.6	17 08	6.9	01 54	8.7	14 19	8.7	03 20	3.6	15 37	3.6	05 46	5.3	18 02	5.2
TH	30	05 24	6.4	17 57	6.6	02 47	8.3	15 17	8.4	04 04	3.4	16 23	3.4	06 39	5.1	18 56	5.0
F	31	06 16	6.2	18 58	6.4	03 52	8.0	16 29	8.1	04 55	3.2	17 19	3.3	07 42	4.9	20 04	4.8

NOVEMBER 2014 *High Water* GMT

		LONDON BRIDGE Datum of Predictions 3.20m below				LIVERPOOL (Gladstone Dock) Datum of Predictions 4.93m below				GREENOCK Datum of Predictions 1.62m below				LEITH Datum of Predictions 2.90m below			
		hr	*ht m*	*hr*	*ht m*	*hr*	*ht m*	*hr*	*ht m*	*hr*	*ht m*	*hr*	*ht m*	*hr*	*ht m*	*hr*	*ht m*
SA	1	07 23	6.0	20 18	6.3	05 13	7.8	17 48	8.1	06 00	3.0	18 40	3.1	09 00	4.8	21 25	4.9
SU	2	08 51	6.1	21 37	6.5	06 34	7.9	19 02	8.4	07 37	3.0	20 16	3.2	10 16	4.9	22 38	5.0
M	3	10 09	6.3	22 48	6.7	07 45	8.4	20 06	8.9	09 07	3.1	21 28	3.4	11 23	5.2	23 40	5.3
TU	4	11 18	6.7	23 52	7.0	08 44	8.8	21 01	9.3	10 07	3.3	22 25	3.6	12 18	5.4	—	—
W	5	12 16	6.9	—	—	09 34	9.2	21 50	9.6	10 55	3.5	23 15	3.7	00 33	5.6	13 07	5.6
TH	6	00 46	7.1	13 05	7.1	10 19	9.5	22 35	9.7	11 39	3.6	—	—	01 21	5.7	13 51	5.8
F	7	01 33	7.2	13 48	7.3	11 00	9.6	23 18	9.7	00 02	3.7	12 21	3.6	02 07	5.8	14 33	5.8
SA	8	02 14	7.2	14 29	7.4	11 40	9.6	23 59	9.6	00 48	3.7	12 59	3.7	02 52	5.8	15 16	5.8
SU	9	02 53	7.2	15 09	7.4	12 18	9.4	—	—	01 31	3.7	13 36	3.7	03 38	5.7	15 59	5.6
M	10	03 31	7.0	15 48	7.3	00 38	9.3	12 55	9.2	02 11	3.6	14 13	3.7	04 23	5.5	16 42	5.4
TU	11	04 07	6.8	16 27	7.0	01 17	8.9	13 32	8.8	02 50	3.5	14 51	3.7	05 07	5.3	17 25	5.2
W	12	04 41	6.5	17 05	6.6	01 57	8.5	14 12	8.4	03 29	3.3	15 30	3.6	05 53	5.0	18 10	5.0
TH	13	05 16	6.3	17 45	6.3	02 40	8.0	14 59	8.0	04 12	3.2	16 12	3.5	06 40	4.8	18 59	4.7
F	14	05 53	6.0	18 29	6.0	03 32	7.6	15 57	7.6	04 59	3.0	16 58	3.3	07 31	4.6	19 54	4.6
SA	15	06 38	5.8	19 25	5.8	04 37	7.2	17 09	7.4	05 55	2.9	17 52	3.2	08 26	4.4	20 55	4.5
SU	16	07 43	5.5	20 43	5.7	05 51	7.2	18 22	7.4	07 06	2.8	18 56	3.1	09 26	4.4	21 57	4.5
M	17	09 17	5.6	21 52	5.9	07 03	7.4	19 26	7.7	08 26	2.9	20 10	3.1	10 28	4.5	23 00	4.6
TU	18	10 25	5.9	22 52	6.2	08 01	7.8	20 19	8.0	09 30	3.1	21 17	3.2	11 28	4.7	23 56	4.8
W	19	11 22	6.2	23 45	6.5	08 47	8.2	21 03	8.4	10 19	3.3	22 08	3.3	12 20	4.9	—	—
TH	20	12 09	6.6	—	—	09 26	8.6	21 42	8.7	11 01	3.4	22 52	3.4	00 43	5.0	13 04	5.2
F	21	00 30	6.7	12 52	6.8	10 03	9.0	22 19	9.0	11 39	3.5	23 33	3.5	01 26	5.2	13 43	5.4
SA	22	01 12	6.9	13 31	7.0	10 39	9.2	22 57	9.2	12 14	3.6	—	—	02 05	5.4	14 21	5.5
SU	23	01 52	7.0	14 11	7.1	11 17	9.4	23 36	9.3	00 15	3.6	12 48	3.6	02 44	5.5	14 58	5.6
M	24	02 32	7.0	14 52	7.2	11 56	9.5	—	—	00 58	3.6	13 24	3.7	03 22	5.6	15 36	5.7
TU	25	03 13	7.0	15 33	7.3	00 17	9.3	12 38	9.5	01 42	3.6	14 02	3.8	04 03	5.6	16 16	5.6
W	26	03 53	6.9	16 16	7.2	01 01	9.2	13 23	9.3	02 26	3.6	14 43	3.8	04 47	5.6	17 00	5.5
TH	27	04 34	6.7	17 01	7.0	01 49	9.0	14 12	9.1	03 10	3.6	15 26	3.7	05 35	5.4	17 47	5.4
F	28	05 19	6.6	17 52	6.8	02 42	8.6	15 08	8.8	03 57	3.5	16 13	3.6	06 27	5.2	18 41	5.2
SA	29	06 10	6.4	18 52	6.6	03 43	8.3	16 13	8.5	04 49	3.3	17 08	3.4	07 28	5.0	19 45	5.0
SU	30	07 13	6.3	20 03	6.5	04 53	8.1	17 24	8.4	05 50	3.2	18 19	3.3	08 39	4.9	21 01	5.0

DECEMBER 2014 *High Water* GMT

		LONDON BRIDGE				LIVERPOOL (Gladstone Dock)				GREENOCK				LEITH			
M	1	08 30	6.2	21 14	6.5	06 07	8.0	18 34	8.4	07 10	3.1	19 44	3.3	09 51	4.9	22 13	5.0
TU	2	09 43	6.4	22 22	6.6	07 18	8.2	19 41	8.6	08 33	3.1	21 00	3.4	10 57	5.1	23 17	5.2
W	3	10 51	6.5	23 28	6.7	08 21	8.5	20 40	8.9	09 39	3.3	22 02	3.5	11 56	5.2	—	—
TH	4	11 52	6.7	—	—	09 14	8.9	21 32	9.1	10 32	3.4	22 56	3.5	00 14	5.3	12 48	5.4
F	5	00 26	6.8	12 45	6.9	10 01	9.1	22 19	9.2	11 19	3.5	23 46	3.6	01 06	5.4	13 35	5.5
SA	6	01 14	6.9	13 30	7.0	10 43	9.3	23 02	9.3	12 01	3.6	—	—	01 54	5.5	14 18	5.6
SU	7	01 57	6.9	14 12	7.1	11 23	9.3	23 43	9.2	00 33	3.6	12 40	3.7	02 40	5.6	15 01	5.6
M	8	02 36	6.9	14 52	7.2	12 00	9.3	—	—	01 16	3.5	13 17	3.7	03 23	5.5	15 42	5.5
TU	9	03 12	6.9	15 30	7.1	00 21	9.1	12 36	9.2	01 55	3.4	13 53	3.8	04 05	5.4	16 22	5.4
W	10	03 46	6.8	16 07	6.9	00 58	8.9	13 11	9.0	02 32	3.4	14 30	3.7	04 45	5.3	17 00	5.3
TH	11	04 20	6.6	16 43	6.7	01 34	8.6	13 48	8.7	03 10	3.3	15 07	3.7	05 25	5.1	17 39	5.1
F	12	04 52	6.4	17 18	6.5	02 13	8.3	14 28	8.4	03 51	3.2	15 46	3.6	06 06	4.9	18 21	4.9
SA	13	05 26	6.2	17 55	6.3	02 56	7.9	15 13	8.0	04 34	3.1	16 28	3.5	06 50	4.7	19 08	4.7
SU	14	06 04	6.1	18 38	6.0	03 45	7.6	16 08	7.7	05 22	3.0	17 14	3.3	07 38	4.6	20 00	4.6
M	15	06 49	5.8	19 30	5.9	04 44	7.3	17 12	7.5	06 16	2.9	18 07	3.2	08 32	4.5	20 59	4.5
TU	16	07 48	5.7	20 44	5.8	05 52	7.3	18 21	7.5	07 19	2.9	19 08	3.1	09 30	4.5	22 01	4.5
W	17	09 21	5.7	21 55	5.9	06 59	7.5	19 25	7.7	08 29	3.0	20 14	3.1	10 31	4.6	23 03	4.6
TH	18	10 29	6.0	22 56	6.2	07 58	7.9	20 20	8.0	09 33	3.1	21 20	3.2	11 31	4.8	—	—
F	19	11 26	6.3	23 52	6.5	08 48	8.3	21 09	8.4	10 26	3.3	22 17	3.3	00 02	4.8	12 27	5.0
SA	20	12 18	6.7	—	—	09 33	8.8	21 54	8.8	11 10	3.4	23 07	3.4	00 55	5.1	13 15	5.3
SU	21	00 43	6.8	13 06	7.0	10 16	9.2	22 38	9.1	11 50	3.5	23 55	3.5	01 41	5.3	13 58	5.5
M	22	01 31	6.9	13 53	7.2	10 58	9.5	23 22	9.4	12 29	3.7	—	—	02 24	5.5	14 39	5.7
TU	23	02 18	7.0	14 38	7.3	11 42	9.7	—	—	00 43	3.5	13 09	3.7	03 06	5.7	15 19	5.8
W	24	03 02	7.1	15 24	7.4	00 07	9.5	12 27	9.8	01 30	3.6	13 50	3.8	03 49	5.8	16 01	5.8
TH	25	03 46	7.1	16 10	7.4	00 53	9.5	13 14	9.7	02 16	3.6	14 33	3.9	04 34	5.8	16 46	5.8
F	26	04 30	7.0	16 56	7.2	01 41	9.3	14 03	9.5	03 03	3.6	15 18	3.8	05 21	5.6	17 34	5.7
SA	27	05 14	6.9	17 45	7.0	02 32	9.0	14 55	9.3	03 50	3.5	16 05	3.7	06 12	5.4	18 26	5.5
SU	28	06 01	6.7	18 39	6.8	03 26	8.6	15 51	8.9	04 38	3.4	16 56	3.6	07 09	5.2	19 25	5.2
M	29	06 57	6.6	19 41	6.6	04 26	8.3	16 54	8.6	05 31	3.3	17 55	3.4	08 13	5.0	20 35	5.1
TU	30	08 03	6.4	20 46	6.4	05 34	8.0	18 03	8.3	06 32	3.1	19 06	3.3	09 22	4.9	21 47	5.0
W	31	09 12	6.4	21 52	6.4	06 46	8.0	19 14	8.3	07 48	3.1	20 28	3.2	10 29	4.9	22 54	4.9

INDEX

N

Q

R